Visit classzone.com and get connected

Online resources for students and parents

ClassZone resources are linked together and provide instruction, practice, and learning support.

eEdition Plus ONLINE

This interactive version of the text encourages students to explore mathematics.

eWorkbook

Interactive practice, correlated to the text, provides support for key concepts and skills.

@HomeTutor

This interactive tutorial reinforces key skills and helps students prepare for tests.

Chapter–Based Support

State test practice, quizzes, vocabulary support, activities, and examples help students succeed.

McDougal Littell

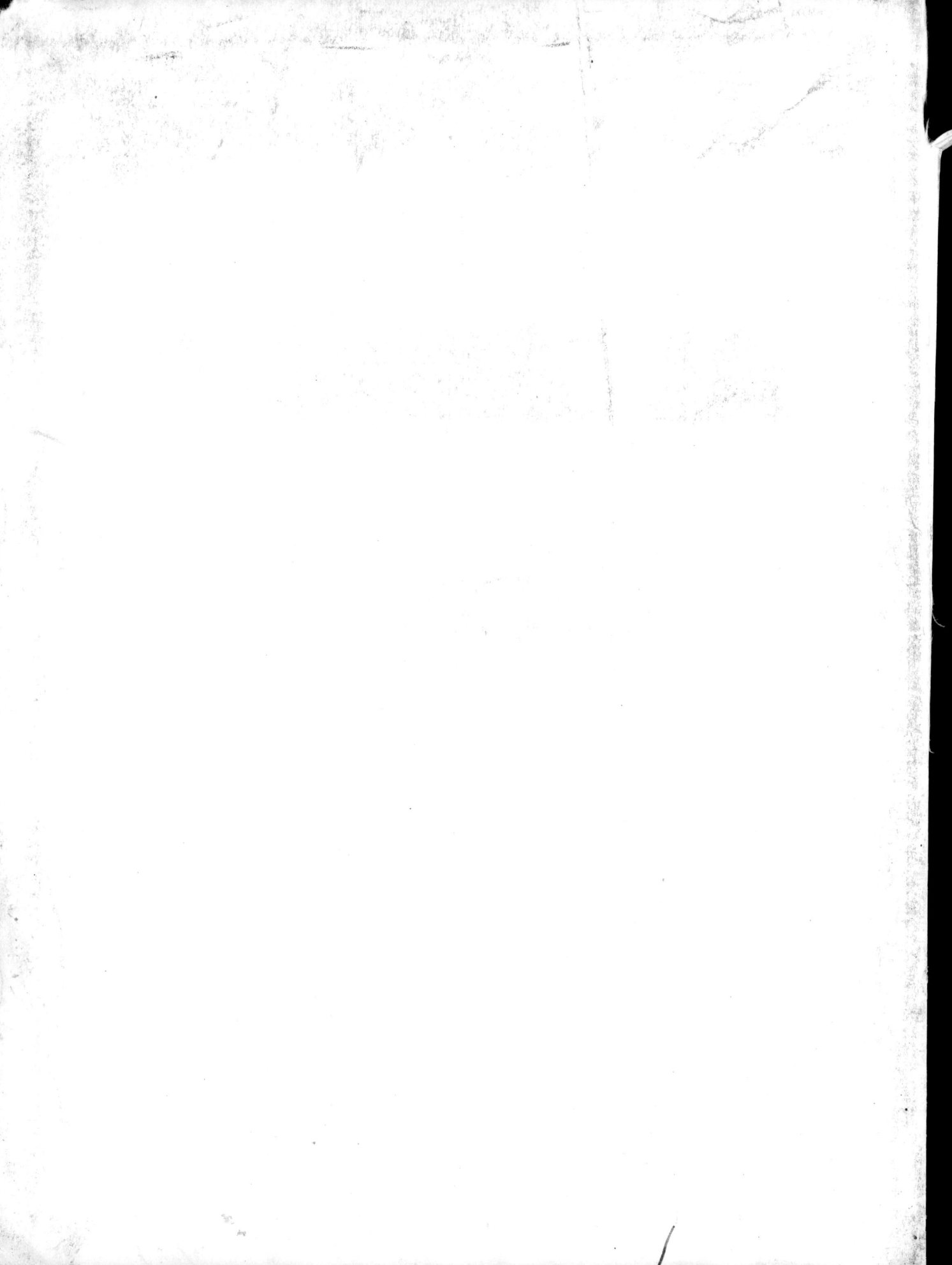

INDIANA

IN

ALGEBRA 1

Ron Larson
Laurie Boswell
Timothy D. Kanold
Lee Stiff

McDougal Littell
A DIVISION OF HOUGHTON MIFFLIN COMPANY

About *Algebra I*

The content of *Algebra 1* is organized around families of functions, with special emphasis on linear and quadratic functions. As you study each family of functions, you will learn to represent them in multiple ways—as verbal descriptions, equations, tables, and graphs. You will also learn to model real-world situations using functions in order to solve problems arising from those situations.

In addition to its algebra content, *Algebra 1* includes lessons on probability and data analysis as well as numerous examples and exercises involving geometry. These math topics often appear on standardized tests, so maintaining your familiarity with them is important. To help you prepare for standardized tests, *Algebra 1* provides instruction and practice on standardized test questions in a variety of formats—multiple choice, short response, extended response, and so on. Technology support for both learning algebra and preparing for standardized tests is available at classzone.com.

Printed in the United States of America

ISBN-13: 978-0-547-33081-5
ISBN-10: 0-547-33081-2

1 2 3 4 5 6 0914 13 12 11 10 09

About the Authors

Ron Larson is a professor of mathematics at Penn State University at Erie, where he has taught since receiving his Ph.D. in mathematics from the University of Colorado. Dr. Larson is well known as the author of a comprehensive program for mathematics that spans middle school, high school, and college courses. Dr. Larson's numerous professional activities keep him in constant touch with the needs of teachers and supervisors. He closely follows developments in mathematics standards and assessment.

Laurie Boswell is a mathematics teacher at The Riverside School in Lyndonville, Vermont, and has taught mathematics at all levels, elementary through college. A recipient of the Presidential Award for Excellence in Mathematics Teaching, she was also a Tandy Technology Scholar. She served on the NCTM Board of Directors (2002–2005), and she speaks frequently at regional and national conferences on topics related to instructional strategies and course content.

Timothy D. Kanold is the superintendent of Adlai E. Stevenson High School District 125 in Lincolnshire, Illinois. Dr. Kanold served as a teacher and director of mathematics for 17 years prior to becoming superintendent. He is the recipient of the Presidential Award for Excellence in Mathematics and Science Teaching, and a past president of the Council for Presidential Awardees in Mathematics. Dr. Kanold is a frequent speaker at national and international mathematics meetings.

Lee Stiff is a professor of mathematics education in the College of Education and Psychology of North Carolina State University at Raleigh and has taught mathematics at the high school and middle school levels. He served on the NCTM Board of Directors and was elected President of NCTM for the years 2000–2002. He is a recipient of the W. W. Rankin Award for Excellence in Mathematics Education presented by the North Carolina Council of Teachers of Mathematics.

Advisers and Reviewers

Curriculum Advisers and Reviewers

Leticia Alvarado
Mathematics Department Chair
Hornedo Middle School
El Paso, TX

Arlene Banks
Mathematics Teacher
Westridge Middle School
Overland Park, KS

Monette Bartel
Associate Adjunct Professor
College of the Canyons
Valencia, CA

Janice Beauchamp
Mathematics Teacher
Buchanan High School
Clovis, CA

Jan Berghaus
Mathematics Teacher
Shawnee Mission West High School
Overland Park, KS

Cindy Branson
Mathematics Teacher
Creekview High School
Carrollton, TX

Dennis Dickson
Mathematics Teacher
Leavenworth High School
Leavenworth, KS

Pauline Embree
Mathematics Department Chair
Rancho San Joaquin Middle School
Irvine, CA

Coleen Floberg
Mathematics Teacher
Highland Park High School
Topeka, KS

Rhonda Foote
Secondary Math Resource Specialist
North Kansas City School District
Kansas City, MO

Alberto Hernandez Galindo
Mathematics Department Chair
San Jose High Academy
San Jose, CA

Phillip Gegen
Mathematics Teacher
Oak Park High School
Kansas City, MO

Jason Godfrey
Mathematics Teacher
Grandview High School
Grandview, MO

Leticia Gonzales-Reynolds
Mathematics Teacher
Crockett High School
Austin, TX

Maria Gossett
Mathematics Department Chair
E.M. Daggett Middle School
Fort Worth, TX

Tom Griffith
Mathematics Department Chair
Scripps Ranch High School
San Diego, CA

Ruth Hadnot
Mathematics Department Chair
Chicago Military Academy-Bronzeville
Chicago, IL

Michael J. Klein
Educational Consultant
Macomb ISD
Clinton Township, MI

Debra Konvalin
Mathematics Teacher
Hiram W. Johnson High School
Sacramento, CA

Ronald J. Labrocca
Mathematics Chairperson
Stimson Middle School
Huntington Station, NY

William Lee Littles
Mathematics Teacher
Central High School
Beaumont, TX

Curriculum Advisers and Reviewers

Maria Magdalena Lucio
Mathematics Department Chair
Homer Hanna High School
Brownsville, TX

John McHugh
Mathematics Department Chair
Holbrook Middle School
Lowell, NC

Fizza Munaim
Mathematics Teacher
Eastwood High School
El Paso, TX

Alvin E. Nash, Jr.
Mathematics Teacher
Pasadena High School
Pasadena, CA

Anne Papakonstantinou
Director, School Mathematics Project
Rice University
Houston, TX

Richard Parr
Director of Education Technology, School Mathematics Project
Rice University
Houston, TX

Rebecca S. Poe
Mathematics Teacher
Winnsboro High School
Winnsboro, TX

Lori Rapp
Secondary Mathematics Specialist
Lewisville School District
The Colony, TX

Deborah Reilly
Mathematics Teacher
West Middle School
Leavenworth, KS

Jon Simon
Mathematics Teacher
Casa Grande High School
Petaluma, CA

Karen S. Skinner
Mathematics Teacher
New Mark Middle School
Kansas City, MO

Steve Snider
Mathematics Teacher
Spring Garden Middle School
St. Joseph, MO

Bertha Stimac
Instructional Specialist
Elsik 9th Grade Center
Houston, TX

Karen Stohlmann
Mathematics Teacher
Blue Valley Northwest High School
Overland Park, KS

Deborah Sylvester
Mathematics Teacher
Manhattan High School
Manhattan, KS

Tommie L. Walsh
Mathematics Teacher
Smylie Wilson Junior High School
Lubbock, TX

Mary Warner
Mathematics Teacher
Richard King High School
Corpus Christi, TX

Peggy S. Winfree White
Mathematics Teacher
Caprock High School
Amarillo, TX

Maureen Williams
Mathematics Department Chair
Southwest Junior High School
Lawrence, KS

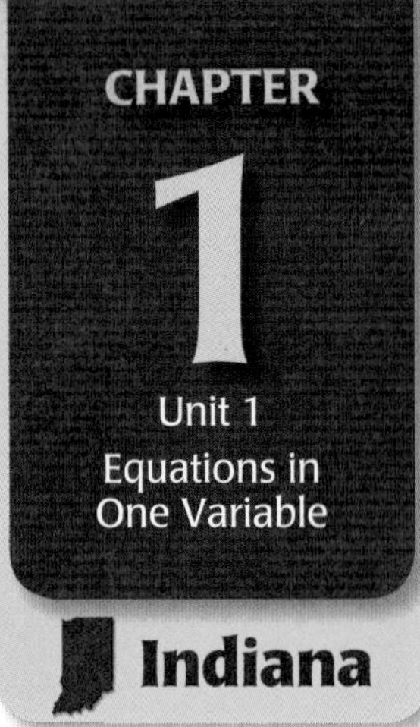

Indiana

Problem Solving, p. 29
$0.1s + 0.6 = 2$

Expressions, Equations, and Functions

Chapter 1 Highlights

PROBLEM SOLVING

- Mixed Review of Problem Solving, 27, 51
- Multiple Representations, 33, 39
- Multi-Step Problems, 6, 11, 19, 27, 40, 51
- Using Alternative Methods, 34
- Real-World Problem Solving Examples, 4, 10, 17, 23, 28, 30, 35, 37, 45

★ ASSESSMENT

- Standardized Test Practice Examples, 10, 30
- Multiple Choice, 5, 6, 11, 18, 24, 25, 31, 38, 46
- Short Response/Extended Response, 7, 12, 20, 26, 27, 32, 33, 40, 48, 51, 58
- Writing/Open-Ended, 5, 10, 12, 18, 19, 24, 25, 27, 31, 38, 39, 45, 46, 47, 51, 53

TECHNOLOGY

At classzone.com:

- Animated Algebra, 1, 7, 9, 14, 21, 29, 34, 37, 50
- @Home Tutor, xxii, 6, 11, 13, 19, 25, 32, 39, 41, 47, 53
- Online Quiz, 7, 12, 20, 26, 33, 40, 48
- Electronic Function Library, 52
- State Test Practice, 27, 51, 61

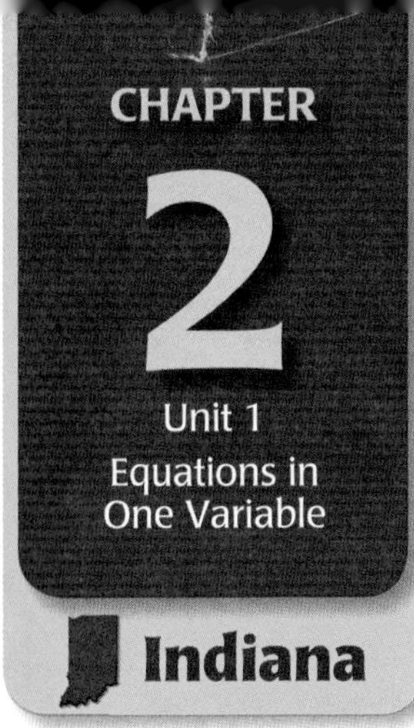

Multiplying Real Numbers, p. 90
Elevation = 6416 + (−0.12)(50)

Properties of Real Numbers

Chapter 2 Highlights

PROBLEM SOLVING

- **Mixed Review of Problem Solving,** 86, 119
- **Multiple Representations,** 83, 93, 116
- **Multi-Step Problems,** 69, 78, 86, 107, 115, 119
- **Using Alternative Methods,** 102
- **Real-World Problem Solving Examples,** 65, 76, 81, 90, 98, 104, 111

★ ASSESSMENT

- **Standardized Test Practice Examples,** 98
- **Multiple Choice,** 68, 69, 78, 82, 92, 99, 106, 107, 108, 114
- **Short Response/Extended Response,** 70, 79, 83, 86, 92, 93, 100, 101, 108, 115, 119, 126
- **Writing/Open-Ended,** 67, 77, 82, 83, 86, 91, 99, 106, 107, 113, 114, 119

TECHNOLOGY

At classzone.com:

- **Animated Algebra,** 63, 73, 80, 90, 93, 98
- **@Home Tutor,** 62, 69, 78, 83, 92, 100, 107, 115, 121
- **Online Quiz,** 70, 79, 84, 93, 101, 108, 116
- **State Test Practice,** 86, 119, 129

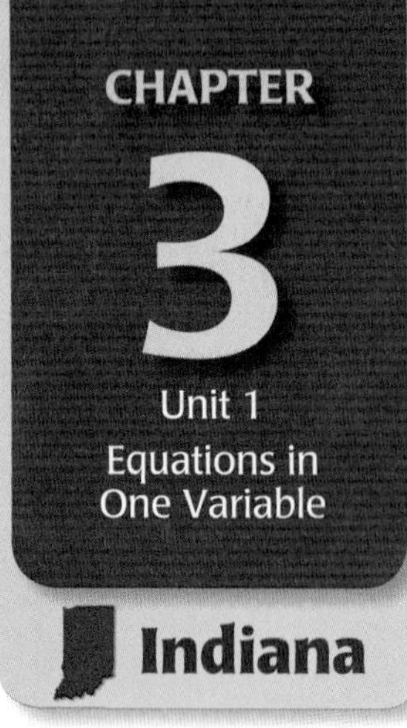

Indiana

Solving Equations, p. 143
$8517 = 2117 + 64d$

Solving Linear Equations

Chapter 3 Highlights

PROBLEM SOLVING

- **Mixed Review of Problem Solving,** 161, 190
- **Multiple Representations,** 139, 146, 147, 153, 159, 166, 172, 188
- **Multi-Step Problems,** 140, 146, 161, 167, 190
- **Using Alternative Methods,** 147
- **Real-World Problem Solving Examples,** 137, 143, 150, 155, 164, 170, 178, 186

★ ASSESSMENT

- **Standardized Test Practice Examples,** 149, 169
- **Multiple Choice,** 138, 144, 145, 151, 157, 165, 171, 179, 187, 198
- **Short Response/Extended Response,** 139, 140, 145, 146, 151, 152, 159, 161, 166, 167, 172, 173, 180, 181, 189, 190
- **Writing/Open-Ended,** 137, 139, 144, 150, 151, 157, 161, 165, 171, 179, 180, 181, 187, 188, 190

TECHNOLOGY

At classzone.com:

- **Animated Algebra,** 131, 133, 139, 154, 176, 185, 187
- **@Home Tutor,** 130, 139, 145, 152, 158, 160, 166, 172, 180, 188, 192
- **Online Quiz,** 140, 146, 153, 159, 167, 173, 181, 189
- **State Test Practice,** 161, 190, 201

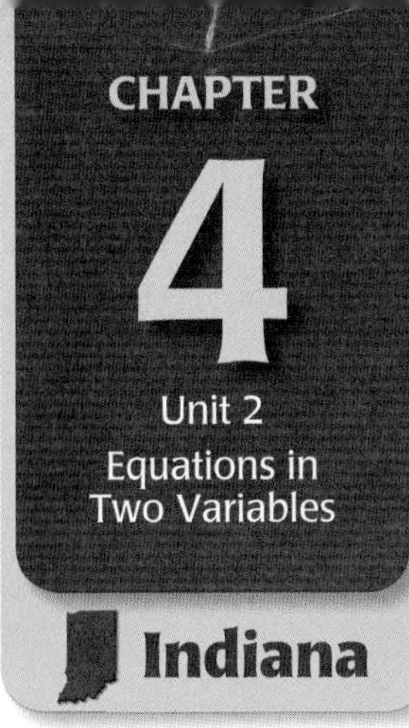

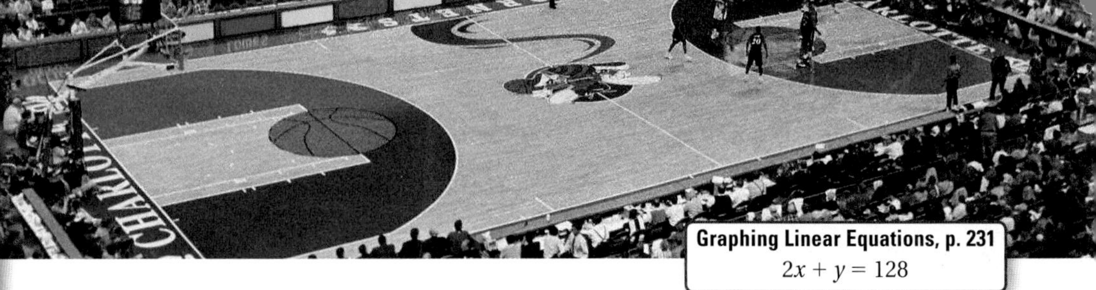

Graphing Linear Equations, p. 231
$2x + y = 128$

Graphing Linear Equations and Functions

Chapter 4 Highlights

PROBLEM SOLVING

- **Mixed Review of Problem Solving,** 233, 269
- **Multiple Representations,** 211, 221, 230, 259, 260
- **Multi-Step Problems,** 211, 220, 231, 233, 241, 269
- **Using Alternative Methods,** 260, 261
- **Real-World Problem Solving Examples,** 208, 218, 227, 228, 237, 238, 245, 246, 255, 256, 265

★ ASSESSMENT

- **Standardized Test Practice Examples,** 215, 262
- **Multiple Choice,** 209, 219, 220, 230, 239, 247, 257, 266, 276
- **Short Response/Extended Response,** 212, 221, 232, 233, 242, 249, 258, 259, 267, 268, 269
- **Writing/Open-Ended,** 209, 210, 214, 219, 229, 230, 233, 239, 241, 247, 248, 256, 257, 265, 266, 269, 271

TECHNOLOGY

At classzone.com:

- **Animated Algebra,** 205, 207, 216, 226, 238, 245, 254
- **@Home Tutor,** 204, 210, 211, 220, 222, 230, 241, 248, 249, 258, 267, 271
- **Online Quiz,** 212, 221, 232, 242, 250, 259, 268
- **Electronic Function Library,** 270
- **State Test Practice,** 233, 269, 279

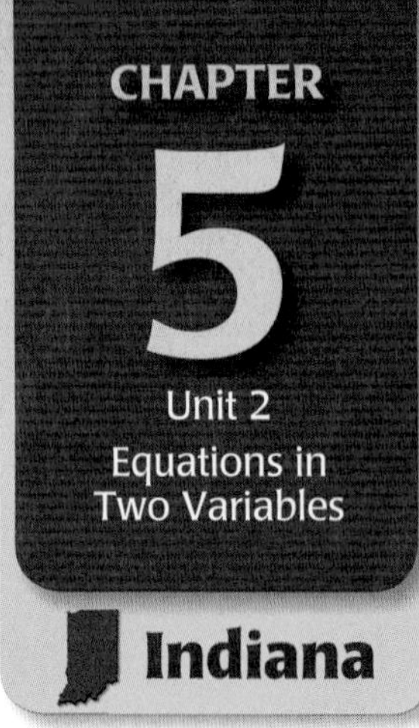

Slopes of Lines, p. 321
$12y = -7x + 42$

Indiana

Writing Linear Equations

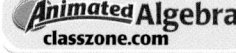

Chapter 5 Highlights

PROBLEM SOLVING

- **Mixed Review of Problem Solving,** 317, 343
- **Multiple Representations,** 288, 299, 315, 340
- **Multi-Step Problems,** 317, 343
- **Using Alternative Methods,** 300
- **Real-World Problem Solving Examples,** 285, 294, 295, 304, 313, 321, 326, 327, 337

★ ASSESSMENT

- **Standardized Test Practice Examples,** 293
- **Multiple Choice,** 286, 297, 305, 306, 314, 322, 323, 329, 339
- **Short Response/Extended Response,** 288, 289, 297, 298, 306, 307, 315, 317, 322, 323, 324, 329, 330, 340, 343, 350
- **Writing/Open-Ended,** 286, 287, 296, 297, 305, 314, 317, 322, 323, 328, 329, 338, 339, 343, 345

TECHNOLOGY

At *classzone.com*:

- **Animated Algebra,** 281, 283, 303, 307, 311, 327, 335
- **@Home Tutor,** 280, 288, 291, 298, 307, 315, 323, 330, 333, 339, 340, 342, 345
- **Online Quiz,** 289, 299, 308, 316, 324, 331, 341
- **State Test Practice,** 317, 343, 353

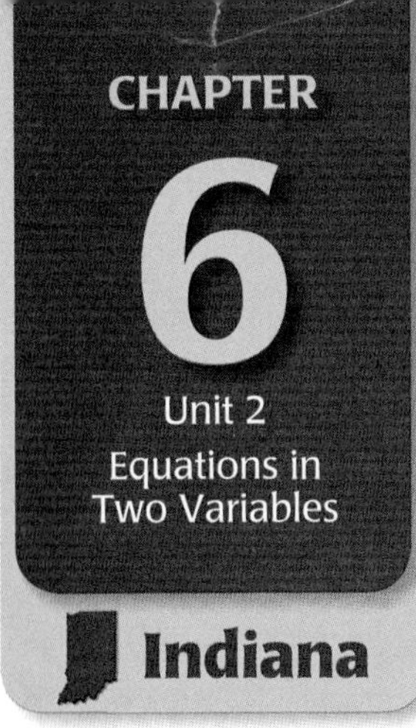

Graphing Inequalities, p. 356
$T \leq 134$

Solving and Graphing Linear Inequalities

Chapter 6 Highlights

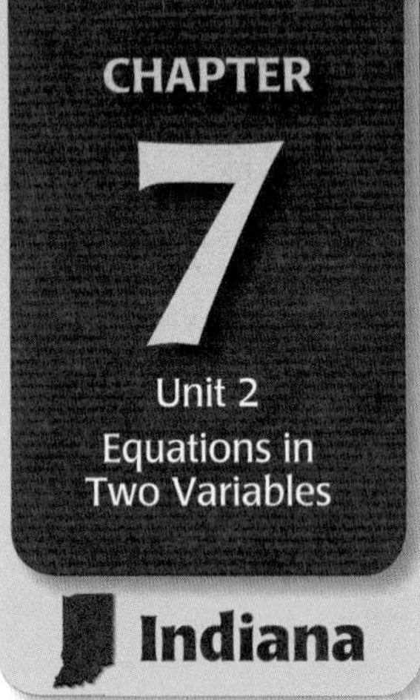

Solving Linear Systems, p. 446
$x - y = 4, x + y = 6$

Systems of Equations and Inequalities

Chapter 7 Highlights

PROBLEM SOLVING

- **Mixed Review of Problem Solving,** 458, 473
- **Multiple Representations,** 433, 442, 449, 456
- **Multi-Step Problems,** 440, 450, 458, 465, 473
- **Using Alternative Methods,** 442
- **Real-World Problem Solving Examples,** 430, 438, 446, 453, 461, 468

★ ASSESSMENT

- **Standardized Test Practice Examples,** 429, 453
- **Multiple Choice,** 431, 432, 439, 447, 455, 463, 469, 470, 480
- **Short Response/Extended Response,** 432, 440, 441, 448, 450, 456, 458, 465, 470, 471, 473
- **Writing/Open-Ended,** 430, 431, 439, 440, 447, 454, 455, 456, 458, 462, 464, 469, 473

TECHNOLOGY

At classzone.com:

- **Animated Algebra,** 425, 428, 435, 441, 446, 452, 459, 466
- **@Home Tutor,** 424, 432, 434, 440, 449, 456, 464, 471, 475
- **Online Quiz,** 433, 441, 450, 457, 465, 472
- **State Test Practice,** 458, 473, 483

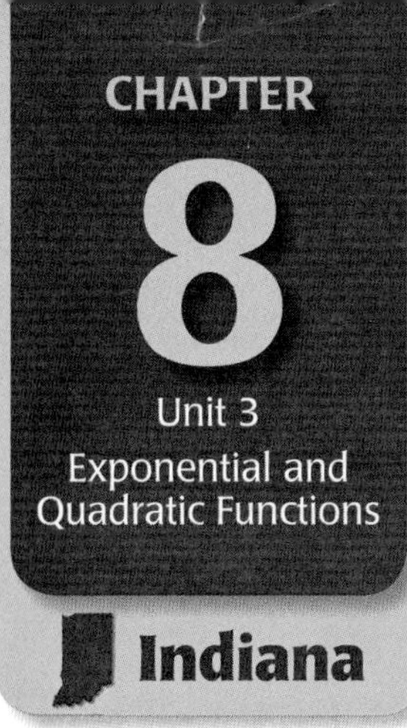

Scientific Notation, p. 516
9.065×10^9 miles

Exponents and Exponential Functions

Chapter 8 Highlights

PROBLEM SOLVING

- **Mixed Review of Problem Solving,** 511, 541
- **Multiple Representations,** 493, 500, 507, 517, 525, 528, 537
- **Multi-Step Problems,** 493, 511, 517, 525, 538, 541
- **Using Alternative Methods,** 528, 529
- **Real-World Problem Solving Examples,** 491, 498, 505, 514, 522, 523, 534

★ ASSESSMENT

- **Standardized Test Practice Examples,** 505, 523
- **Multiple Choice,** 492, 499, 506, 507, 515, 516, 524, 526, 535, 536, 548
- **Short Response/Extended Response,** 494, 501, 507, 508, 511, 516, 517, 526, 537, 541
- **Writing/Open-Ended,** 492, 493, 498, 499, 506, 511, 515, 516, 523, 524, 535, 536, 541, 543

TECHNOLOGY

At classzone.com:

- **Animated Algebra,** 487, 505, 512, 522, 534, 536
- **@Home Tutor,** 486, 493, 500, 507, 516, 519, 525, 537, 543
- **Online Quiz,** 494, 501, 508, 518, 527, 538
- **State Test Practice,** 511, 541, 551

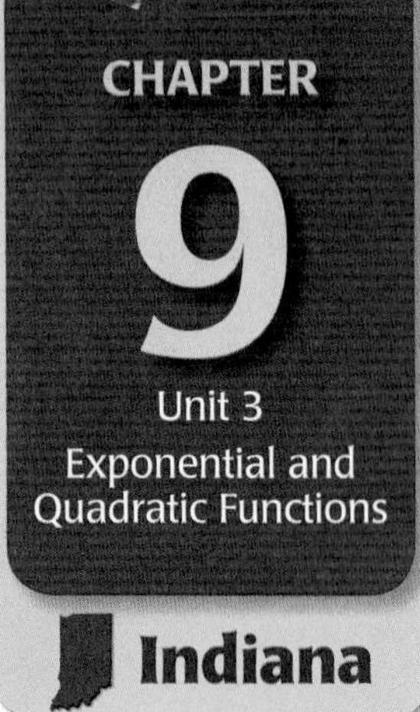

Subtracting Polynomials, p. 558
$B = -0.0262t^3 + 0.376t^2 - 0.574t + 9.67$

Indiana

Polynomials and Factoring

Chapter 9 Highlights

PROBLEM SOLVING

- **Mixed Review of Problem Solving,** 581, 614
- **Multiple Representations,** 573, 580, 589, 598
- **Multi-Step Problems,** 581, 614
- **Using Alternative Methods,** 590
- **Real-World Problem Solving Examples,** 556, 564, 571, 577, 585, 595, 602, 609

★ ASSESSMENT

- **Standardized Test Practice Examples,** 564, 596
- **Multiple Choice,** 557, 565, 566, 572, 578, 580, 586, 589, 596, 597, 603, 610
- **Short Response/Extended Response,** 558, 559, 567, 568, 573, 574, 579, 581, 587, 588, 597, 598, 604, 612, 614, 622
- **Writing/Open-Ended,** 557, 565, 572, 578, 581, 586, 596, 603, 610, 611, 614, 616

TECHNOLOGY

At classzone.com:

- **Animated Algebra,** 553, 555, 582, 592, 598, 601
- **@Home Tutor,** 552, 558, 560, 567, 573, 579, 588, 598, 604, 612, 616
- **Online Quiz,** 559, 568, 574, 580, 589, 599, 605, 613
- **State Test Practice,** 581, 614, 625

Solving Quadratic Equations, p. 648
$y = -0.04x^2 + 1.2x$

Indiana

Quadratic Equations and Functions

Chapter 10 Highlights

PROBLEM SOLVING

- **Mixed Review of Problem Solving,** 661, 694
- **Multiple Representations,** 658, 659, 667, 676, 690
- **Multi-Step Problems,** 658, 661, 668, 675, 683, 694
- **Using Alternative Methods,** 659
- **Real-World Problem Solving Examples,** 631, 637, 646, 654, 665, 672, 680, 687

★ ASSESSMENT

- **Standardized Test Practice Examples,** 631, 671
- **Multiple Choice,** 632, 633, 638, 647, 655, 657, 666, 674, 681, 688, 690
- **Short Response/Extended Response,** 634, 640, 648, 649, 656, 657, 661, 668, 676, 682, 690, 694
- **Writing/Open-Ended,** 632, 638, 639, 647, 655, 656, 661, 666, 667, 674, 681, 682, 688, 694

TECHNOLOGY

At classzone.com:

- **Animated Algebra,** 627, 634, 636, 642, 662, 668, 672, 684
- **@Home Tutor,** 626, 633, 639, 648, 651, 657, 667, 675, 682, 689, 690, 692, 696
- **Online Quiz,** 634, 640, 649, 658, 668, 676, 683, 691
- **Electronic Function Library,** 695
- **State Test Practice,** 661, 694, 705

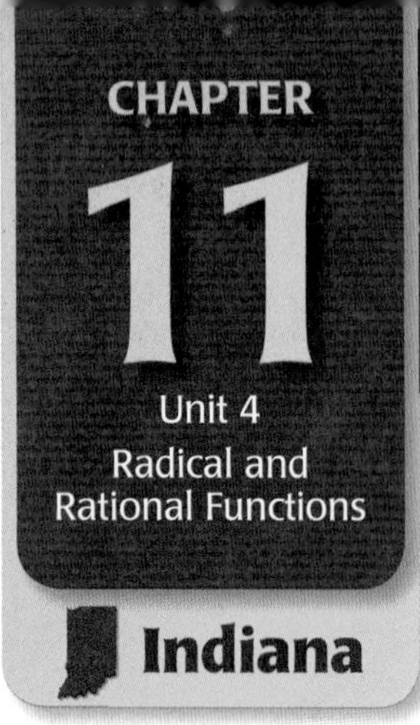

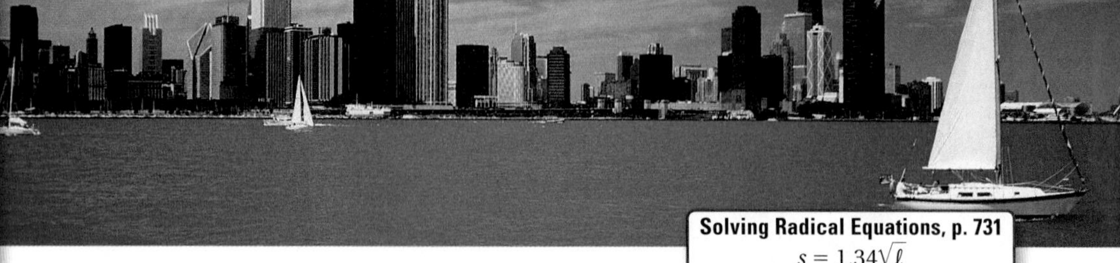

Solving Radical Equations, p. 731
$s = 1.34\sqrt{\ell}$

Radicals and Geometry Connections

Chapter 11 Highlights

PROBLEM SOLVING

- **Mixed Review of Problem Solving,** 735, 752
- **Multiple Representations,** 725
- **Multi-Step Problems,** 715, 725, 733, 735, 748, 752
- **Using Alternative Methods,** 751
- **Real-World Problem Solving Examples,** 713, 722, 731, 738, 739, 746

★ ASSESSMENT

- **Standardized Test Practice Examples,** 738, 746
- **Multiple Choice,** 713, 714, 723, 732, 740, 741, 747, 748
- **Short Response/Extended Response,** 716, 726, 734, 735, 742, 749, 752
- **Writing/Open-Ended,** 713, 723, 724, 732, 733, 735, 740, 741, 747, 748, 752

TECHNOLOGY

At classzone.com:

- **Animated Algebra,** 709, 711, 719, 722, 731, 737, 746
- **@Home Tutor,** 708, 715, 717, 725, 733, 741, 748, 749, 754, 755
- **Online Quiz,** 716, 726, 734, 742, 750
- **State Test Practice,** 735, 752, 761

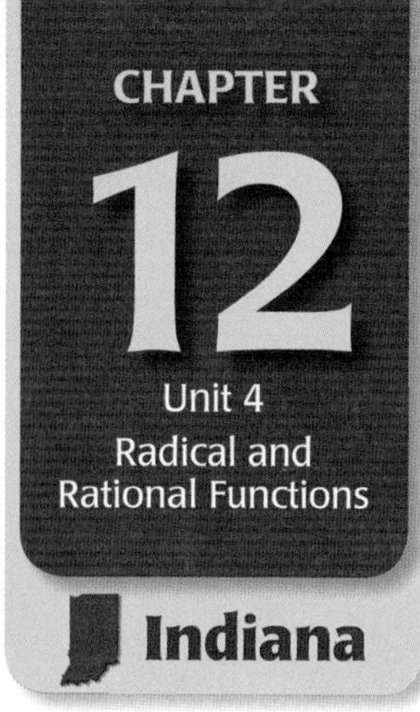

Dividing Rational Expressions, p. 807

$T = \frac{100 + 2.2x}{1 - 0.014x}$

Rational Equations and Functions

Chapter 12 Highlights

PROBLEM SOLVING

- **Mixed Review of Problem Solving,** 801, 829
- **Multiple Representations,** 771, 781, 790, 808
- **Multi-Step Problems,** 801, 818, 825, 829
- **Using Alternative Methods,** 827
- **Real-World Problem Solving Examples,** 768, 778, 787, 797, 805, 815, 822

★ ASSESSMENT

- **Multiple Choice,** 769, 777, 779, 788, 789, 791, 798, 806, 807, 817, 824, 836
- **Short Response/Extended Response,** 771, 772, 781, 790, 791, 800, 801, 808, 809, 818, 819, 825, 829
- **Writing/Open-Ended,** 769, 779, 780, 788, 789, 797, 798, 801, 806, 807, 816, 823, 829

TECHNOLOGY

At classzone.com:

- **Animated Algebra,** 763, 766, 777, 783, 791, 804, 814
- **@Home Tutor,** 762, 770, 780, 789, 793, 799, 807, 808, 817, 824, 831
- **Online Quiz,** 772, 782, 791, 800, 809, 819, 826
- **State Test Practice,** 801, 829, 839

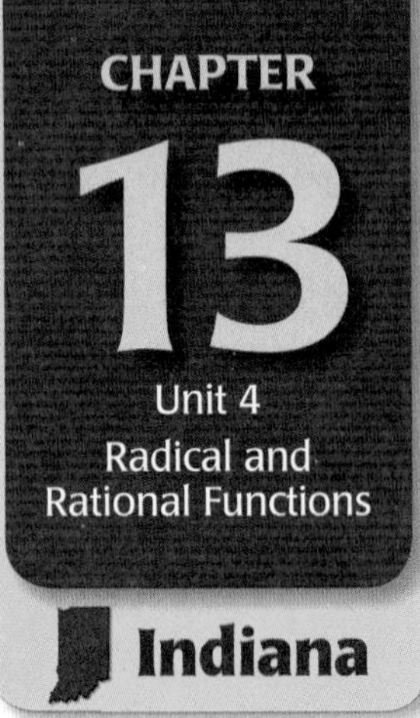

Using Permutations, p. 855

Probability $= \frac{{}_5P_5}{{}_7P_7}$

Indiana

Probability and Data Analysis

Chapter 13 Highlights

PROBLEM SOLVING

- **Mixed Review of Problem Solving,** 870, 894
- **Multiple Representations,** 854, 866
- **Multi-Step Problems,** 870, 894
- **Using Alternative Methods,** 868
- **Real-World Problem Solving Examples,** 844, 852, 853, 857, 863, 871, 872, 876, 882, 888, 889

★ ASSESSMENT

- **Standardized Test Practice Examples,** 845, 889
- **Multiple Choice,** 846, 847, 854, 858, 864, 865, 873, 877, 883, 890
- **Short Response/Extended Response,** 847, 848, 855, 858, 859, 866, 870, 874, 877, 878, 885, 891, 894
- **Writing/Open-Ended,** 846, 853, 858, 864, 865, 870, 873, 877, 883, 884, 889, 894, 896

TECHNOLOGY

At classzone.com:

- **Animated Algebra,** 841, 845, 848, 856, 875, 887
- **@Home Tutor,** 840, 847, 854, 859, 860, 866, 874, 877, 878, 884, 886, 890, 891, 893, 896
- **Online Quiz,** 848, 855, 859, 867, 874, 878, 885, 892
- **State Test Practice,** 870, 894, 905

Contents of Student Resources

Skills Review Handbook

INDIANA

Student Guide to the Standards

Indiana Algebra I Academic Standards

- The Indiana Algebra I Academic Standards are goals set by the state to ensure that you are being taught a thoughtful, complete curriculum.
- Teachers and other educators use the standards when developing courses and tests.
- Lessons in your book connect to a standard, which is listed next to the lesson in the table of contents beginning on IN6.

Covered bridge near Kokomo, Indiana © Corbis

Indiana Algebra I Academic Standards Decoder

Part 1 The math standards for Indiana are organized by core content area.

Part 2 Each core area is divided into standards.

Part 3 Each standard is broken down further into indicators. The information from the 3 parts will help you break the standard code!

Here is an example:

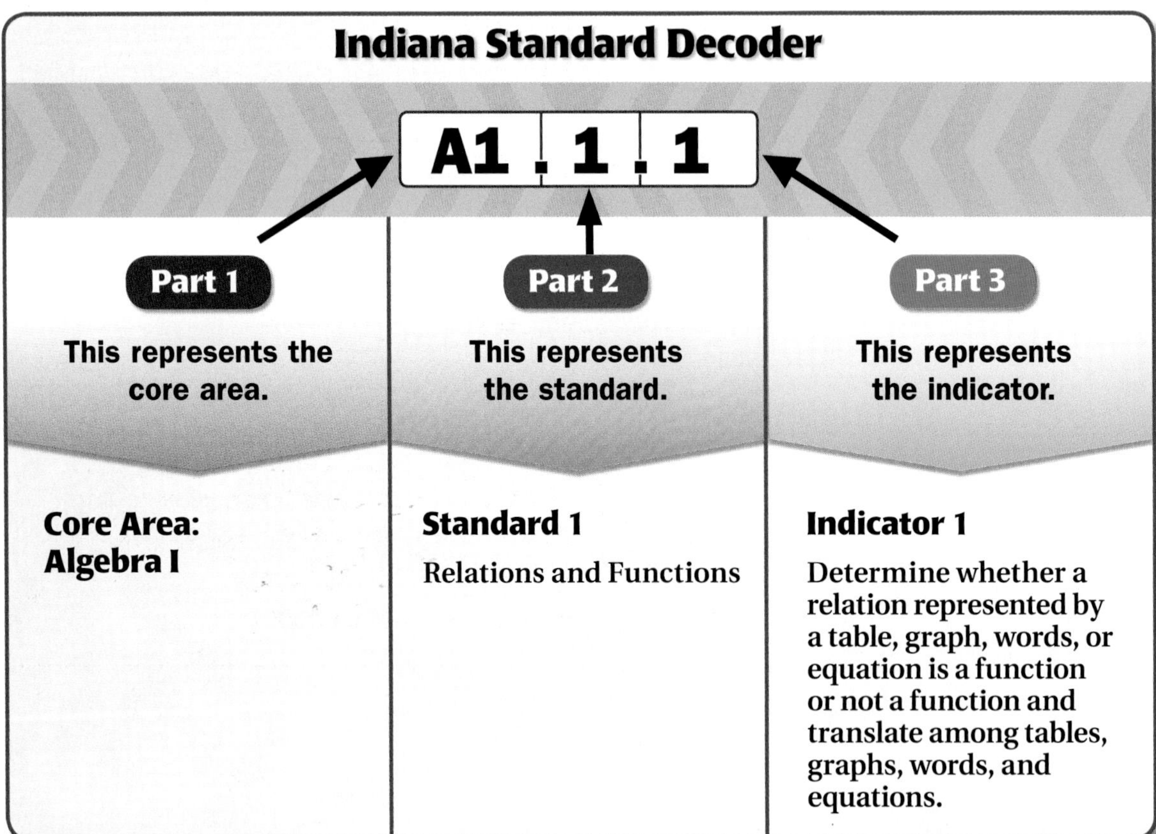

Indiana Standard Decoder
A1 . 1 . 1
Part 1
This represents the core area.
Part 2
This represents the standard.
Part 3
This represents the indicator.
Core Area: Algebra I
Standard 1
Relations and Functions
Indicator 1
Determine whether a relation represented by a table, graph, words, or equation is a function or not a function and translate among tables, graphs, words, and equations.

Indiana Algebra I Academic Standards

Standard 1: Relations and Functions

Indicators

A1.1.1 Determine whether a relation represented by a table, graph, words or equation is a function or not a function and translate among tables, graphs, words and equations.

A1.1.2 Identify the domain and range of relations represented by tables, graphs, words, and equations.

Here is what a question might look like on the Core 40 ECA:

A1.1.1 Determine whether a relation represented by a table, graph, words, or equation is a function or not a function and translate among tables, graphs, words, and equations.

Which expression can be used to find the values of $f(n)$ in the table below?

A. $2n$

B. $n + 1$

C. $n^2 + 1$

D. $n^3 + 1$

n	$f(n)$
1	2
2	5
3	10
4	17
5	26
6	37

Solution

Each time the value of n increases by 1, the value of $f(n)$ increases by an odd number. These odd number increments become larger as n increases:

$f(2) = 5 = f(1) + 3$

$f(3) = 10 = f(2) + 5$

$f(4) = 17 = f(3) + 7$

So, $f(n)$ is not a linear function.

By comparing $f(n)$ to the quadratic function n^2, however, you can see that for each value of n, the value of $f(n)$ is 1 more than n^2. So, an expression that can be used to find the values of $f(n)$ is $n^2 + 1$.

So, the correct answer is C.

STANDARDS

Standard 2: Linear Functions, Equations, and Inequalities

Indicators

A1.2.1 Translate among various representations of linear functions including tables, graphs, words and equations.

A1.2.2 Graph linear equations and show that they have constant rates of change.

A1.2.3 Determine the slope, x-intercept, and y-intercept of a line given its graph, its equation, or two points on the line and determine the equation of a line given sufficient information.

A1.2.4 Write, interpret, and translate among equivalent forms of equations for linear functions (slope-intercept, point-slope, and standard), recognizing that equivalent forms reveal more or less information about a given situation.

A1.2.5 Solve problems that can be modeled using linear equations and inequalities, interpret the solutions, and determine whether the solutions are reasonable.

A1.2.6 Graph a linear inequality in two variables.

Here is what a question might look like on the Core 40 ECA:

A1.2.3 Determine the slope, x-intercept, and y-intercept of a line given its graph, its equation, or two points on the line and determine the equation of a line given sufficient information.

What is the rate of change of the graph below?

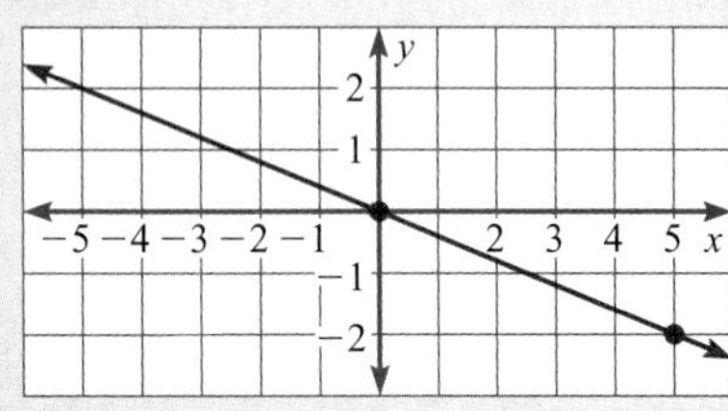

A. 0 B. −0.4

C. −1.4 D. −2.5

Solution

The rate of change is the slope. Choose two points on the graph, for example (0, 0) and (5, −2).

$m = \frac{y_2 - y_1}{x_2 - x_1}$ Equation for slope

$= \frac{-2 - 0}{5 - 0} = -0.4$ Substitute and simplify.

So, the correct answer is B.

Standard 3: Pairs of Linear Equations and Inequalities

Indicators

A1.3.1 Understand the relationship between a solution of a pair of linear equations in two variables and the graphs of the corresponding lines and solve pairs of linear equations in two variables by graphing, substitution or elimination.

A1.3.2 Graph the solution set for a pair of linear inequalities in two variables with and without technology and use the graph to find the solution set.

A1.3.3 Solve problems that can be modeled using pairs of linear equations in two variables, interpret the solutions, and determine whether the solutions are reasonable.

Here is what a question might look like on the Core 40 ECA:

A1.3.1 Understand the relationship between a solution of a pair of linear equations in two variables and the graphs of corresponding lines and solve pairs of linear equations in two variables by graphing, substitution, or elimination.

The Student Council charged $2 for students and $3 for adults to attend a soccer game. If 60 tickets were sold, then $140 was made. The graph below represents this situation.

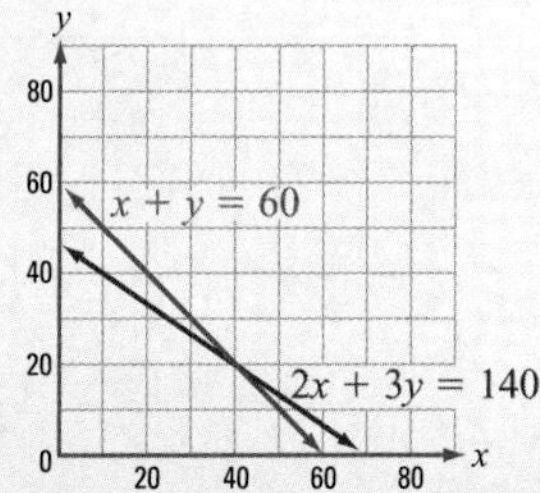

If x represents the number of student tickets sold, and y is the number of adult tickets sold, how many students and adult tickets were sold?

A. 40 students, 40 adults

B. 40 students, 20 adults

C. 20 students, 40 adults

D. 20 students, 20 adults

Solution

$x + y = 60$ Solve for x.

$x = 60 - y$

$2(60 - y) + 3y = 140$

$120 - 2y + 3y = 140$ Use substitution

$y = 20$

$x + 20 = 60$

$x = 40$

The correct answer is B.

Standard 4: Polynomials

Indicators

A1.4.1 Use the laws of exponents for variables with exponents and multiply, divide, and find powers of variables with exponents.

A1.4.2 Add, subtract and multiply polynomials and divide polynomials by monomials.

A.1.4.3 Factor common terms from polynomials and factor quadratic expressions.

Here is what questions might look like on the Core 40 ECA:

A1.4.2 Add, subtract, and multiply polynomials and divide polynomials by monomials.

Simplify the expression
$4(2x - 8) - 3(x + 5)$.

A. $5x - 3$

B. $5x - 17$

C. $5x - 27$

D. $5x - 47$

Solution for Question 1

$4(2x - 8) - 3(x + 5) = 8x - 32 - 3x - 15$

$= (8x - 3x) - (32 + 15)$

$= 5x - 47$

So, the correct answer is D.

Which expression is equivalent to
$-2(x - 6) + 5x(3x + 4)$?

A. $15x^2 + 18x + 12$

B. $15x^2 + 18x - 12$

C. $15x^2 - 2x + 32$

D. $15x^2 - 2x + 8$

Solution for Question 2

$-2(x - 6) + 5x(3x + 4) = -2x + 12 + 15x^2 + 20x$

$= 15x^2 + (-2x + 20x) + 12$

$= 15x^2 + 18 + 12$

So, the correct answer is A.

Standard 5: Quadratic Equations and Functions

Indicators

A1.5.1 Graph quadratic functions.

A1.5.2 Solve quadratic equations in the real number system with real number solutions by factoring, by completing the square, and by using the quadratic formula.

A1.5.3 Solve problems that can be modeled using quadratic equations, interpret the solutions, and determine whether the solutions are reasonable.

A1.5.4 Analyze and describe the relationships among the solutions of a quadratic equation, the zeros of a quadratic function, the *x*-intercepts of the graph of a quadratic function, and the factors of a quadratic expression.

A1.5.5 Sketch and interpret linear and non-linear graphs representing given situations and identify independent and dependent variables.

Here is what question might look like on the Core 40 ECA:

A1.5.2 Solve quadratic equations in the real number system with real number solutions by factoring, completing the square, and by using the quadratic formula.

Solve by factoring.
$3y^2 = -27y$

A. $y = 0$ or $y = -9$

B. $y = 3$ or $y = -9$

C. $y = 0$ or $y = 9$

D. $y = 3$ or $y = 9$

Solution

Write the original equation.
$3y^2 = -27y$

Add 27y to each side.
$3y^2 + 27y = 0$

Factor the left side.
$3y(y + 9) = 0$

Zero-product property
$3y = 0$ or $y + 9 = 0$

Solve for y.
$y = 0$ or $y = -9$

So, the correct answer is A.

STANDARDS

Standard 6: Rational and Radical Expressions and Equations

Indicators

A1.6.1 Add, subtract, multiply, divide, reduce, and evaluate rational expressions with polynomial denominators. Simplify rational expressions with linear and quadratic denominators, including denominators with negative exponents.

A1.6.2 Solve equations involving rational and common irrational expressions.

A1.6.3 Simplify radical expressions involving square roots.

A1.6.4 Solve equations that contain radical expressions on only one side of the equation and identify extraneous roots when they occur.

Here is what a question might look like on the Core 40 ECA:

A1.6.3 Simplify radical expressions involving square roots.

What is the simplified form of $\frac{7\sqrt{90}}{3\sqrt{98}}$?

A. $2\sqrt{5}$

B. 5

C. $\sqrt{5}$

D. $\sqrt{10}$

Solution

$\frac{7\sqrt{90}}{3\sqrt{98}} = \frac{7}{3} \cdot \frac{\sqrt{90}}{\sqrt{98}}$ Rewrite radical expression.

$= \frac{7}{3} \cdot \frac{\sqrt{2} \cdot \sqrt{5} \cdot \sqrt{9}}{\sqrt{2} \cdot \sqrt{49}}$ Product property of radicals.

$= \frac{7}{3} \cdot \frac{3\sqrt{5}}{7}$ Divide common factors.

$= \sqrt{5}$ Simplify.

The correct answer is C .

Standard 7: Data Analysis

Indicators

A1.7.1 Organize and display data using appropriate methods to detect patterns and departures from patterns. Summarize the data using measures of center (mean, median) and spread (range, percentiles, variance, standard deviation). Compare data sets using graphs and summary statistics.

A1.7.2 Distinguish between random and non-random sampling methods, identify possible sources of bias in sampling, describe how such bias can be controlled and reduced, evaluate the characteristics of a good survey and well-designed experiment, design simple experiments or investigations to collect data to answer questions of interest, and make inferences from sample results.

A1.7.3 Evaluate reports based on data published in the media by considering the source of the data, the design of the study, the way the data are analyzed and displayed and whether the report confuses correlation with causation.

Here is what a question might look like on the Core 40 ECA:

A1.7.1 Organize and display data using appropriate methods to detect patterns and departures from patterns. Summarize the data using measures of center (mean, median) and spread (range, percentiles, variance, standard deviation). Compare data sets using graphs and summary statistics.

Steven glanced at the graph below.

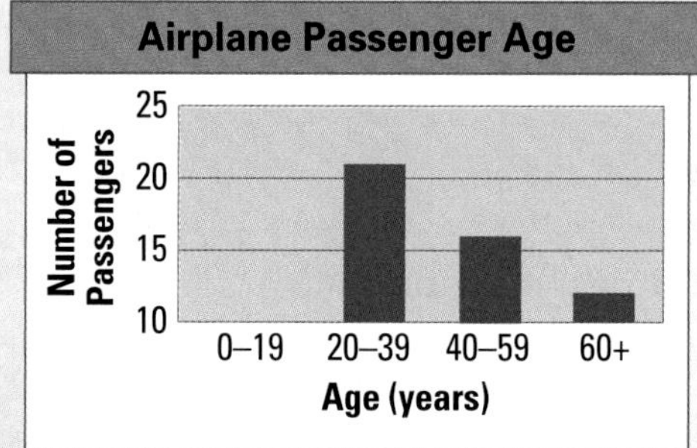

He concluded that there were no passengers under the age of 20 on the plane. Why might he be incorrect?

A. The bars of the graph fall between the numbers shown in the vertical scale.

B. The graph divides the passengers into too few age groups.

C. The vertical scale starts at 10.

D. The vertical scale ends too low.

Solution

The vertical scale of the graph starts at 10. So, if there are ten or fewer passengers in an age group this information will not appear on the graph.

It is possible that there are as many as 10 passengers in the 0- to 19-year-old range.

The most likely explanation of Steven's incorrect conclusion is that he failed to notice the vertical scale of the graph starts at 10. The correct answer is C.

1 Expressions, Equations, and Functions

Before

In previous courses, you learned the following skills, which you'll use in Chapter 1: using fractions and percents, and finding perimeter and area.

Prerequisite Skills

VOCABULARY CHECK

Copy and complete the statement.

1. In the fraction $\frac{2}{3}$, _?_ is the numerator and _?_ is the denominator.
2. Two fractions that represent the same number are called _?_ fractions.
3. The word *percent* (%) means "divided by _?_."

SKILLS CHECK

Perform the indicated operation. ***(Review pp. 914–915 for 1.1, 1.2.)***

4. $\frac{2}{3}+\frac{3}{5}$
5. $\frac{5}{6}-\frac{3}{4}$
6. $\frac{3}{5}\times\frac{2}{3}$
7. $\frac{1}{2}\div\frac{5}{8}$

Write the percent as a decimal. ***(Review p. 916 for 1.5.)***

8. 4%
9. 23%
10. 1.5%
11. 2.5%

12. Find the perimeter and area of the rectangle. ***(Review p. 924 for 1.5.)***

$4\frac{1}{2}$ in.

11 in.

@HomeTutor Prerequisite skills practice at classzone.com

Now

In Chapter 1, you will apply the big ideas listed below and reviewed in the Chapter Summary on page 52. You will also use the key vocabulary listed below.

Big Ideas

1. **Writing and evaluating algebraic expressions**
2. **Using expressions to write equations and inequalities**
3. **Representing functions as verbal rules, equations, tables, and graphs**

KEY VOCABULARY

- variable, *p. 2*
- algebraic expression, *p. 2*
- power, exponent, base, *p. 3*
- order of operations, *p. 8*
- verbal model, *p. 16*
- rate, unit rate, *p. 17*
- open sentence, *p. 21*
- equation, inequality, *p. 21*
- solution of an equation or inequality, *p. 22*
- formula, *p. 30*
- function, *p. 35*
- domain, range, *p. 35*
- independent variable, *p. 36*
- dependent variable, *p. 36*

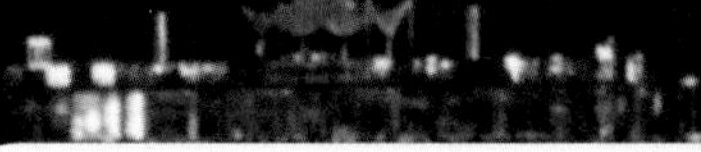

Why?

You can use multiple representations to describe a real-world situation. For example, you can solve an equation, make a table, or draw a diagram to determine a running route.

Animated Algebra

The animation illustrated below for Example 1 on page 28 helps you answer this question: How does the number of blocks you run affect the total distance?

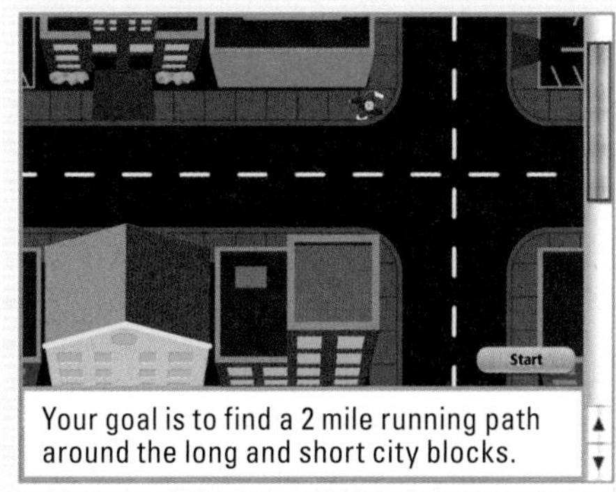

Start
Your goal is to find a 2 mile running path around the long and short city blocks.

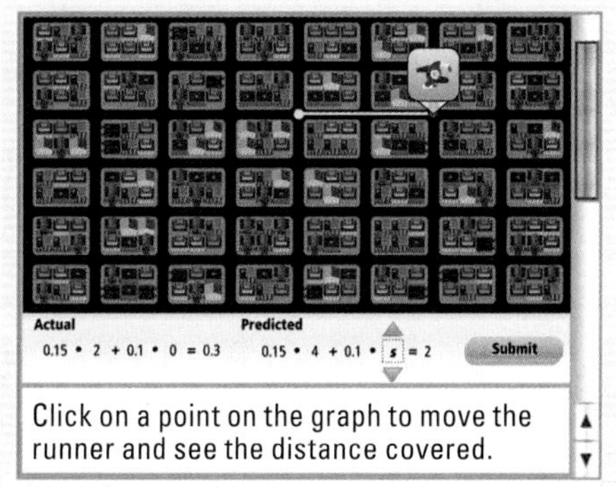

Click on a point on the graph to move the runner and see the distance covered.

Animated Algebra at classzone.com

Other animations for Chapter 1: pages 7, 9, 14, 21, 37, 50, and 52

1.1 Evaluate Expressions

Before	You used whole numbers, fractions, and decimals.
Now	You will evaluate algebraic expressions and use exponents.
Why	So you can calculate sports statistics, as in Ex. 50.

Key Vocabulary
- variable
- algebraic expression
- power
- base
- exponent

A **variable** is a letter used to represent one or more numbers. The numbers are the values of the variable. *Expressions* consist of numbers, variables, and operations. An **algebraic expression**, or *variable expression*, is an expression that includes at least one variable.

Algebraic expression			Meaning	Operation
$5(n)$	$5 \cdot n$	$5n$	5 times n	Multiplication
$\frac{14}{y}$	$14 \div y$		14 divided by y	Division
$6 + c$			6 plus c	Addition
$8 - x$			8 minus x	Subtraction

To **evaluate an algebraic expression**, substitute a number for each variable, perform the operation(s), and simplify the result, if necessary.

AVOID ERRORS
Use the multiplication symbol • instead of × in algebraic expressions to avoid confusing × with the variable *x*.

EXAMPLE 1 Evaluate algebraic expressions

Evaluate the expression when $n = 3$.

a. $13 \cdot n = 13 \cdot 3$ **Substitute 3 for *n*.**

$= 39$ **Multiply.**

b. $\frac{9}{n} = \frac{9}{3}$ **Substitute 3 for *n*.**

$= 3$ **Divide.**

c. $n - 1 = 3 - 1$ **Substitute 3 for *n*.**

$= 2$ **Subtract.**

d. $n + 8 = 3 + 8$ **Substitute 3 for *n*.**

$= 11$ **Add.**

GUIDED PRACTICE for Example 1

Evaluate the expression when $y = 2$.

1. $6y$ **2.** $\frac{8}{y}$ **3.** $y + 4$ **4.** $11 - y$

EXAMPLE 2 Evaluate an expression

MOVIES The total cost of seeing a movie at a theater can be represented by the expression $a + r$ where a is the cost (in dollars) of admission and r is the cost (in dollars) of refreshments. Suppose you pay $7.50 for admission and $7.25 for refreshments. Find the total cost.

Solution

Total cost $= a + r$	**Write expression.**
$= 7.50 + 7.25$	**Substitute 7.50 for a and 7.25 for r.**
$= 14.75$	**Add.**

▶ The total cost is $14.75.

EXPRESSIONS USING EXPONENTS A **power** is an expression that represents repeated multiplication of the same factor. For example, 81 is a power of 3 because $81 = 3 \cdot 3 \cdot 3 \cdot 3$. A power can be written in a form using two numbers, a **base** and an **exponent**. The exponent represents the number of times the base is used as a factor, so 81 can be written as 3^4.

base, exponent

$$3^4 = 3 \cdot 3 \cdot 3 \cdot 3$$

power, 4 factors of 3

EXAMPLE 3 Read and write powers

Write the power in words and as a product.

WRITE EXPONENTS
For a number raised to the first power, you usually do not write the exponent 1. For instance, you write 7^1 simply as 7.

Power	**Words**	**Product**
a. 7^1	seven to the first power	7
b. 5^2	five to the second power, or five *squared*	$5 \cdot 5$
c. $\left(\frac{1}{2}\right)^3$	one half to the third power, or one half *cubed*	$\frac{1}{2} \cdot \frac{1}{2} \cdot \frac{1}{2}$
d. z^5	z to the fifth power	$z \cdot z \cdot z \cdot z \cdot z$

✓ GUIDED PRACTICE for Examples 2 and 3

5. **WHAT IF?** In Example 2, suppose you go back to the theater with a friend to see an afternoon movie. You pay for both admissions. Your total cost (in dollars) can be represented by the expression $2a$. If each admission costs $4.75, what is your total cost?

Write the power in words and as a product.

6. 9^5 7. 2^8 8. n^4

EXAMPLE 4 Evaluate powers

Evaluate the expression.

a. x^4 when $x = 2$

b. n^3 when $n = 1.5$

Solution

a. $x^4 = 2^4$
$= 2 \cdot 2 \cdot 2 \cdot 2$
$= 16$

b. $n^3 = 1.5^3$
$= (1.5)(1.5)(1.5)$
$= 3.375$

✓ GUIDED PRACTICE for Example 4

Evaluate the expression.

9. x^3 when $x = 8$ **10.** k^2 when $k = 2.5$ **11.** d^4 when $d = \frac{1}{3}$

REVIEW AREA AND VOLUME
For help with area and volume, see pp. 924 and 927.

AREA AND VOLUME Exponents are used in the formulas for the area of a square and the volume of a cube. In fact, the words *squared* and *cubed* come from the formula for the area of a square and the formula for the volume of a cube.

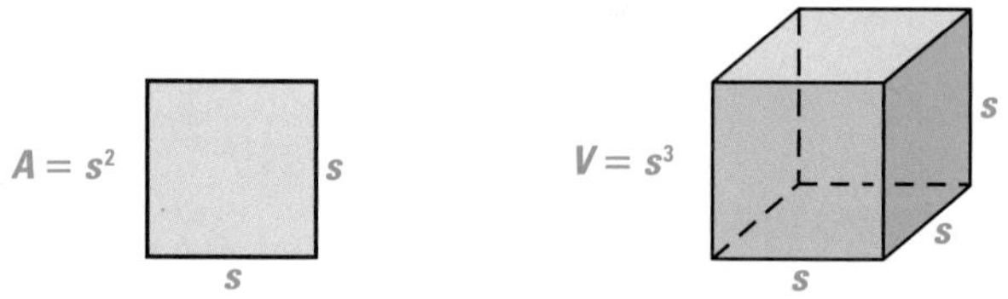

EXAMPLE 5 Evaluate a power

STORAGE CUBES Each edge of the medium-sized pop-up storage cube shown is 14 inches long. The storage cube is made so that it can be folded flat when not in use. Find the volume of the storage cube.

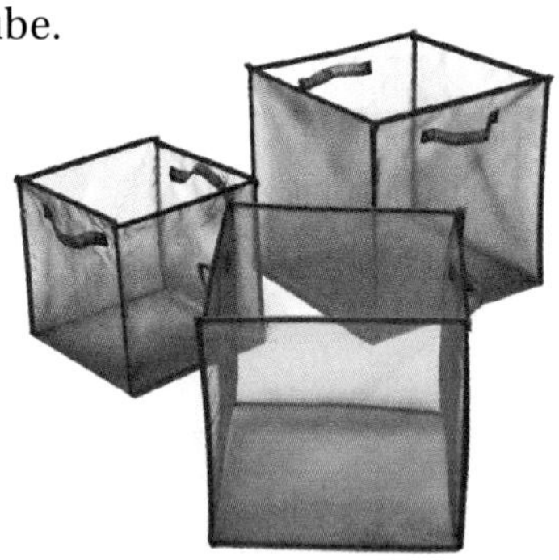

Solution

$V = s^3$ **Write formula for volume.**

$= 14^3$ **Substitute 14 for *s*.**

$= 2744$ **Evaluate power.**

▶ The volume of the storage cube is 2744 cubic inches.

✓ GUIDED PRACTICE for Example 5

12. WHAT IF? In Example 5, suppose the storage cube is folded flat to form a square. Find the area of the square.

1.1 EXERCISES

HOMEWORK KEY
○ = **WORKED-OUT SOLUTIONS** on p. WS1 for Exs. 19, 35, and 51
★ = **STANDARDIZED TEST PRACTICE** Exs. 2, 15, 44, 45, 52, and 54

SKILL PRACTICE

1. **VOCABULARY** Identify the exponent and the base in the expression 6^{12}.

2. ★ **WRITING** *Describe* the steps you would take to evaluate the expression n^5 when $n = 3$. Then evaluate the expression.

EXAMPLE 1 on p. 2 for Exs. 3–15

EVALUATING EXPRESSIONS **Evaluate the expression.**

3. $15x$ when $x = 4$
4. $0.4r$ when $r = 6$
5. $w - 8$ when $w = 20$
6. $1.6 - g$ when $g = 1.2$
7. $5 + m$ when $m = 7$
8. $0.8 + h$ when $h = 3.7$
9. $\frac{24}{f}$ when $f = 8$
10. $\frac{t}{5}$ when $t = 4.5$
11. $2.5m$ when $m = 4$
12. $\frac{1}{2}k$ when $k = \frac{2}{3}$
13. $y - \frac{1}{2}$ when $y = \frac{5}{6}$
14. $h + \frac{1}{3}$ when $h = 1\frac{1}{3}$

15. ★ **MULTIPLE CHOICE** What is the value of $2.5m$ when $m = 10$?

Ⓐ 0.25 Ⓑ 2.5 Ⓒ 12.5 Ⓓ 25

EXAMPLE 3 on p. 3 for Exs. 16–25

WRITING POWERS **Write the power in words and as a product.**

16. 12^5
17. 7^3
18. $(3.2)^2$
19. $(0.3)^4$
20. $\left(\frac{1}{2}\right)^8$
21. n^7
22. y^6
23. t^4

ERROR ANALYSIS ***Describe*** **and correct the error in evaluating the power.**

24. $(0.4)^2 = 2(0.4) = 0.8$ 

25. $5^4 = 4 \cdot 4 \cdot 4 \cdot 4 \cdot 4 = 1024$ 

EXAMPLE 4 on p. 4 for Exs. 26–37

EVALUATING POWERS **Evaluate the power.**

26. 3^2
27. 10^2
28. 1^5
29. 11^3
30. 5^3
31. 3^5
32. 2^6
33. 6^4
34. $\left(\frac{1}{4}\right)^2$
35. $\left(\frac{3}{5}\right)^3$
36. $\left(\frac{2}{3}\right)^4$
37. $\left(\frac{1}{6}\right)^3$

EVALUATING EXPRESSIONS **Evaluate the expression.**

38. x^2 when $x = \frac{3}{4}$
39. p^2 when $p = 1.1$
40. $x + y$ when $x = 11$ and $y = 6.4$
41. kn when $k = 9$ and $n = 4.5$
42. $w - z$ when $w = 9.5$ and $z = 2.8$
43. $\frac{b}{c}$ when $b = 24$ and $c = 2.5$

44. ★ **MULTIPLE CHOICE** Which expression has the greatest value when $x = 10$ and $y = 0.5$?

Ⓐ xy Ⓑ $x - y$ Ⓒ $\frac{x}{y}$ Ⓓ $\frac{y}{x}$

45. ★ **MULTIPLE CHOICE** Let b be the number of tokens you bought at an arcade, and let u be the number you have used. Which expression represents the number of tokens remaining?

Ⓐ $b + u$ Ⓑ $b - u$ Ⓒ bu Ⓓ $\frac{b}{u}$

46. **COMPARING POWERS** Let x and y be whole numbers greater than 0 with $y > x$. Which has the greater value, 3^x or 3^y? *Explain.*

47. **CHALLENGE** For which whole number value(s) of x greater than 0 is the value of x^2 greater than the value of 2^x? *Explain.*

PROBLEM SOLVING

EXAMPLE 2 on p. 3 for Exs. 48–50

48. **GEOMETRY** The perimeter of a square with a side length of s is given by the expression $4s$. What is the perimeter of the square shown?

7.5 m

@HomeTutor for problem solving help at classzone.com

49. **LEOPARD FROG** You can estimate the distance (in centimeters) that a leopard frog can jump using the expression 13ℓ where ℓ is the frog's length (in centimeters). What distance can a leopard frog that is 12.5 centimeters long jump?

@HomeTutor for problem solving help at classzone.com

50. **MULTI-STEP PROBLEM** Jen was the leading scorer on her soccer team. She scored 120 goals and had 20 assists in her high school career.

a. The number n of points awarded for goals is given by $2g$ where g is the number of goals scored. How many points did Jen earn for goals?

b. The point total is given by $n + a$ where a is the number of assists. Use your answer from part (a) to find Jen's point total.

EXAMPLE 5 on p. 4 for Exs. 51–52

51. **MULTI-STEP PROBLEM** You are buying a tank for three fish. You have a flame angel that is 3.5 inches long, a yellow sailfin tang that is 5.5 inches long, and a coral beauty that is 3 inches long. The area (in square inches) of water surface the fish need is given by the expression $12f$ where f is the sum of the lengths (in inches) of all the fish in the tank.

a. What is the total length of the three fish?

b. How many square inches of water surface do the fish need?

52. ★ **MULTIPLE CHOICE** For a snow sculpture contest, snow is packed into a cube-shaped box with an edge length of 8 feet. The box is frozen and removed, leaving a cube of snow. One cubic foot of the snow weighs about 30 pounds. You can estimate the weight (in pounds) of the cube using the expression $30V$ where V is the volume (in cubic feet) of the snow. About how much does the uncarved cube weigh?

Ⓐ 240 pounds Ⓑ 1920 pounds

Ⓒ 15,360 pounds Ⓓ 216,000 pounds

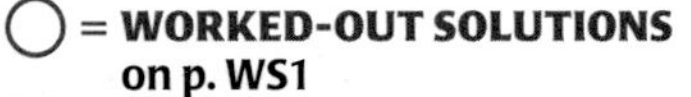

○ = **WORKED-OUT SOLUTIONS on p. WS1** ★ = **STANDARDIZED TEST PRACTICE**

53. FOOTBALL A football team's net score for the regular season is given by the expression $a - b$ where a is the total number of points the team scored and b is the total number of points scored against the team. The table shows the point totals for the 2003 National Football League Conference Champions. Which team's net score was greater?

Team	Points scored, a	Points scored against, b
New England Patriots	336	238
Carolina Panthers	325	304

54. ★ EXTENDED RESPONSE A manufacturer produces three different sizes of cube-shaped stacking bins with edge lengths as shown.

Bin A 6 in.

Bin B

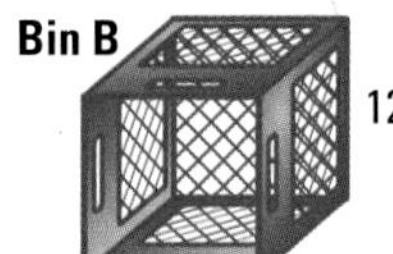

Bin C

a. **Evaluate** Find the volume of each bin.

b. **Compare** How many times greater is the edge length of bin B than the edge length of bin A? How many times greater is the volume of bin B than the volume of bin A?

c. **Compare** Answer the questions in part (b) for bin A and bin C.

d. **CHALLENGE** *Explain* how multiplying the edge length of a cube by a number n affects the volume of the cube. *Justify* your explanation.

at classzone.com

55. CHALLENGE You purchase a set of 100 cube-shaped miniature magnets, each with an edge length of $\frac{1}{8}$ inch. You arrange the cubes to form larger cubes, each one with a different edge length. How many cubes can you form? What is their total volume?

MIXED REVIEW

PREVIEW
Prepare for Lesson 1.2 in Exs. 56–59.

Perform the indicated operation.

56. $\frac{13}{16} - \frac{1}{8}$ *(p. 914)* **57.** $\frac{3}{4} + \frac{1}{3}$ *(p. 914)* **58.** $\frac{4}{7} \times \frac{7}{9}$ *(p. 915)* **59.** $\frac{3}{20} \div \frac{5}{8}$ *(p. 915)*

Write the percent as a decimal and as a fraction. *(p. 916)*

60. 37% **61.** 15% **62.** 125% **63.** 0.2%

Find the perimeter of the rectangle or square. *(p. 924)*

64. Rectangle: 9.1 m by 3.5 m

65. Square: 14 in. by 14 in.

1.2 Apply Order of Operations

Before You evaluated algebraic expressions and used exponents.

Now You will use the order of operations to evaluate expressions.

Why? So you can determine online music costs, as in Ex. 35.

Key Vocabulary
- **order of operations**

Mathematicians have established an **order of operations** to evaluate an expression involving more than one operation.

KEY CONCEPT *For Your Notebook*

Order of Operations

STEP 1 **Evaluate** expressions inside grouping symbols.

STEP 2 **Evaluate** powers.

STEP 3 **Multiply** and **divide** from left to right.

STEP 4 **Add** and **subtract** from left to right.

EXAMPLE 1 Evaluate expressions

Evaluate the expression $27 \div 3^2 \times 2 - 3$.

STEP 1 There are no grouping symbols, so go to Step 2.

STEP 2 **Evaluate** powers.

$27 \div 3^2 \times 2 - 3 = 27 \div 9 \times 2 - 3$ **Evaluate power.**

STEP 3 **Multiply** and **divide** from left to right.

$27 \div 9 \times 2 - 3 = 3 \times 2 - 3$ **Divide.**

$3 \times 2 - 3 = 6 - 3$ **Multiply.**

STEP 4 **Add** and **subtract** from left to right.

$6 - 3 = 3$ **Subtract.**

▶ The value of the expression $27 \div 3^2 \times 2 - 3$ is 3.

✓ **GUIDED PRACTICE** for Example 1

Evaluate the expression.

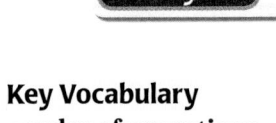

1. $20 - 4^2$ **2.** $2 \cdot 3^2 + 4$ **3.** $32 \div 2^3 + 6$ **4.** $15 + 6^2 - 4$

GROUPING SYMBOLS Grouping symbols such as parentheses ( ) and brackets [ ] indicate that operations inside the grouping symbols should be performed first. For example, to evaluate $2 \cdot 4 + 6$, you multiply first, then add. To evaluate $2(4 + 6)$, you add first, then multiply.

EXAMPLE 2 Evaluate expressions with grouping symbols

Evaluate the expression.

a. $7(\mathbf{13 - 8}) = 7(\mathbf{5})$ — **Subtract within parentheses.**

$= 35$ — **Multiply.**

b. $24 - (\mathbf{3^2} + 1) = 24 - (\mathbf{9} + 1)$ — **Evaluate power.**

$= 24 - 10$ — **Add within parentheses.**

$= 14$ — **Subtract.**

c. $2[30 - (\mathbf{8 + 13})] = 2[30 - \mathbf{21}]$ — **Add within parentheses.**

$= 2[9]$ — **Subtract within brackets.**

$= 18$ — **Multiply.**

AVOID ERRORS
When grouping symbols appear inside other grouping symbols, work from the innermost grouping symbols outward.

FRACTION BARS A fraction bar can act as a grouping symbol. Evaluate the numerator and denominator before you divide:

$$\frac{8 + 4}{5 - 2} = (8 + 4) \div (5 - 2) = 12 \div 3 = 4$$

EXAMPLE 3 Evaluate an algebraic expression

Evaluate the expression when $x = 4$.

$\frac{9x}{3(x + 2)} = \frac{9 \cdot 4}{3(4 + 2)}$ — **Substitute 4 for x.**

$= \frac{9 \cdot 4}{3 \cdot 6}$ — **Add within parentheses.**

$= \frac{36}{18}$ — **Multiply.**

$= 2$ — **Divide.**

Animated Algebra at classzone.com

✓ GUIDED PRACTICE for Examples 2 and 3

Evaluate the expression.

5. $4(3 + 9)$

6. $3(8 - 2^2)$

7. $2[(9 + 3) \div 4]$

Evaluate the expression when $y = 8$.

8. $y^2 - 3$

9. $12 - y - 1$

10. $\frac{10y + 1}{y + 1}$

EXAMPLE 4 Standardized Test Practice

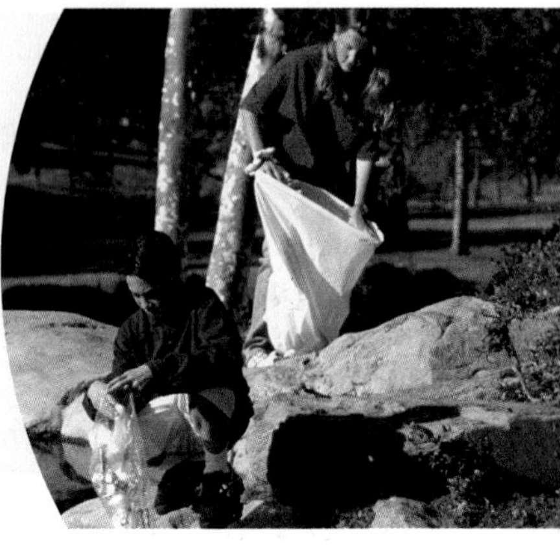

A group of 12 students volunteers to collect litter for one day. A sponsor provides 3 juice drinks and 2 sandwiches for each student and pays \$30 for trash bags. The sponsor's cost (in dollars) is given by the expression $12(3j + 2s) + 30$ where j is the cost of a juice drink and s is the cost of a sandwich. A juice drink costs \$1.25. A sandwich costs \$2. What is the sponsor's cost?

ELIMINATE CHOICES
You can eliminate choices A and D by estimating. When j is about 1 and s is 2, the value of the expression is about $12(3 + 4) + 30$, or \$114.

(A) \$79 (B) \$123 (C) \$129 (D) \$210

Solution

$12(3j + 2s) + 30 = 12(3 \cdot \mathbf{1.25} + 2 \cdot \mathbf{2}) + 30$	**Substitute 1.25 for j and 2 for s.**
$= 12(3.75 + 4) + 30$	**Multiply within parentheses.**
$= 12(7.75) + 30$	**Add within parentheses.**
$= 93 + 30$	**Multiply.**
$= 123$	**Add.**

▶ The sponsor's cost is \$123. The correct answer is B. (A) (B) (C) (D).

GUIDED PRACTICE for Example 4

11. **WHAT IF?** In Example 4, suppose the number of volunteers doubles. Does the sponsor's cost double as well? *Explain.*

1.2 EXERCISES

HOMEWORK KEY
○ = **WORKED-OUT SOLUTIONS on p. WS1 for Exs. 16 and 35**
★ = **STANDARDIZED TEST PRACTICE Exs. 2, 19, 31, 37, 39, and 40**

SKILL PRACTICE

1. **VOCABULARY** According to the order of operations, which operation would you perform first in simplifying $50 - 5 \times 4^2 \div 2$?

2. ★ **WRITING** *Describe* the steps you would use to evaluate the expression $2(3x + 1)^2$ when $x = 3$.

EXAMPLES 1 and 2 on pp. 8–9 for Exs. 3–21

EVALUATING EXPRESSIONS **Evaluate the expression.**

3. $13 - 8 + 3$
4. $8 - 2^2$
5. $3 \cdot 6 - 4$
6. $5 \cdot 2^3 + 7$
7. $48 \div 4^2 + \frac{3}{5}$
8. $1 + 5^2 \div 50$
9. $2^4 \cdot 4 - 2 \div 8$
10. $4^3 \div 8 + 8$
11. $(12 + 72) \div 4$
12. $24 + 4(3 + 1)$
13. $12(6 - 3.5)^2 - 1.5$
14. $24 \div (8 + 4^2)$
15. $\frac{1}{2}(21 + 2^2)$
16. $\frac{1}{6}(6 + 18) - 2^2$
17. $\frac{3}{4}[13 - (2 + 3)]^2$
18. $8[20 - (9 - 5)^2]$

19. ★ **MULTIPLE CHOICE** What is the value of $3[20 - (7 - 5)^2]$?

Ⓐ 48 Ⓑ 56 Ⓒ 192 Ⓓ 972

ERROR ANALYSIS ***Describe*** **and correct the error in evaluating the expression.**

20. $(1 + 13) \div 7 + 7 = 14 \div 7 + 7$
$= 14 \div 14$
$= 1$ ✗

21. $20 - \frac{1}{2} \cdot 6^2 = 20 - 3^2$
$= 20 - 9$
$= 11$ ✗

EXAMPLE 3 on p. 9 for Exs. 22–31

EVALUATING EXPRESSIONS **Evaluate the expression.**

22. $4n - 12$ when $n = 7$

23. $2 + 3x^2$ when $x = 3$

24. $6t^2 - 13$ when $t = 2$

25. $11 + r^3 - 2r$ when $r = 5$

26. $5(w - 4)$ when $w = 7$

27. $3(m^2 - 2)$ when $m = 1.5$

28. $\frac{9x + 4}{3x + 1}$ when $x = 7$

29. $\frac{k^2 - 1}{k + 3}$ when $k = 5$

30. $\frac{b^3 - 21}{5b + 9}$ when $b = 3$

31. ★ **MULTIPLE CHOICE** What is the value of $\frac{x^2}{25} + 3x$ when $x = 10$?

Ⓐ 26 Ⓑ 34 Ⓒ 43 Ⓓ 105

CHALLENGE **Insert grouping symbols in the expression so that the value of the expression is 14.**

32. $9 + 39 + 22 \div 11 - 9 + 3$

33. $2 \times 2 + 3^2 - 4 + 3 \times 5$

PROBLEM SOLVING

EXAMPLE 4 on p. 10 for Exs. 34–37

34. **SALES** Your school's booster club sells school T-shirts. Half the T-shirts come from one supplier at a cost of $5.95 each, and half from another supplier at a cost of $6.15 each. The average cost (in dollars) of a T-shirt is given by the expression $\frac{5.95 + 6.15}{2}$. Find the average cost.

@HomeTutor for problem solving help at classzone.com

35. **MULTI-STEP PROBLEM** You join an online music service. The total cost (in dollars) of downloading 3 singles at $.99 each and 2 albums at $9.95 each is given by the expression $3 \cdot 0.99 + 2 \cdot 9.95$.

a. Find the total cost.

b. You have $25 to spend. How much will you have left?

@HomeTutor for problem solving help at classzone.com

36. **PHYSIOLOGY** If you know how tall you were at the age of 2, you can estimate your adult height (in inches). Girls can use the expression $25 + 1.17h$ where h is the height (in inches) at the age of 2. Boys can use the expression $22.7 + 1.37h$. Estimate the adult height of each person to the nearest inch.

a. A girl who was 34 inches tall at age 2

b. A boy who was 33 inches tall at age 2

37. ★ **OPEN-ENDED** Write a numerical expression including parentheses that has the same value when you remove the parentheses.

38. **ONLINE SHOPPING** The regular shipping fee (in dollars) for an online computer store is given by the expression $0.5w + 4.49$ where w is the weight (in pounds) of the item. The fee (in dollars) for rush delivery is given by $0.99w + 6.49$. You purchase a 26.5 pound computer. How much do you save using regular shipping instead of rush delivery?

39. ★ **SHORT RESPONSE** You make and sell flags for $10 each. Each flag requires $4.50 worth of fabric. You pay $12.99 for a kit to punch holes to hang the flags. Your expenses (in dollars) are given by the expression $4.50m + 12.99$ where m is the number of flags you make. Your income is given by the expression $10s$ where s is the number of flags you sell. Your profit is equal to the difference of your income and your expenses.

    a. You make 50 flags and sell 38 of them. Find your income and your expenses. Then find your profit.

    b. *Explain* how you could use a single expression to determine your profit.

40. ★ **EXTENDED RESPONSE** Each year Heisman Trophy voters select the outstanding college football player. Each voter selects three players ranked first to third. A first place vote is worth 3 points, a second place vote is worth 2 points, and a third place vote is worth 1 point. Let f, s, and t be, respectively, the number of first place, second place, and third place votes a player gets. The table shows the votes for the winner and the runner-up in 2003.

Player	First place	Second place	Third place
Jason White	319	204	116
Larry Fitzgerald	253	233	128

    a. **Analyze** *Explain* why the expression $3f + 2s + t$ represents a player's point total.

    b. **Calculate** Use the expression in part (a) to determine how many more points Jason White got than Larry Fitzgerald got.

    c. **CHALLENGE** Can you rearrange the order of the votes for each player in such a way that Larry Fitzgerald would have won? *Explain*.

MIXED REVIEW

PREVIEW
Prepare for Lesson 1.3 in Exs. 41–48.

Copy and complete. *(p. 929)*

41. 360 in. = ? ft
42. 250 g = ? kg
43. $8 \text{ ft}^2 = \underline{?} \text{ in.}^2$
44. 80 L = ? mL

Find the value of the expression when $x = 5$. *(p. 2)*

45. $x + 4.7$
46. $19.3 - x$
47. $\frac{1}{2}x$
48. $x - \frac{3}{4}$

Evaluate the power. *(p. 2)*

49. 6^2
50. 10^4
51. $(0.2)^2$
52. $\left(\frac{2}{3}\right)^3$

EXTRA PRACTICE for Lesson 1.2, p. 938 **ONLINE QUIZ** at classzone.com

@HomeTutor
classzone.com
Keystrokes

1.2 Use Order of Operations

QUESTION How can you use a graphing calculator to evaluate an expression?

You can use a graphing calculator to evaluate an expression. When you enter the expression, it is important to use grouping symbols so that the calculator performs operations in the correct order.

EXAMPLE Evaluate an expression

Use a graphing calculator to evaluate an expression.

Lean body mass is the mass of the skeleton, muscles, and organs. Physicians use lean body mass to determine dosages of medicine.

Scientists have developed separate formulas for the lean body masses of men and women based on their mass m (in kilograms) and height h (in meters). Lean body mass in measured in units called BMI (Body Mass Index) units.

Men: $1.10m - \frac{128m^2}{10{,}000h^2}$ **Women:** $1.07m - \frac{148m^2}{10{,}000h^2}$

Find the lean body mass (in BMI units) of a man who is 1.8 meters tall and has a mass of 80 kilograms.

Solution

Enter the expression for men in the calculator. Substitute 80 for m and 1.8 for h. Because the fraction bar is a grouping symbol, enter the denominator using parentheses.

Use the following keystrokes.

1.10 [×] 80 [−] 128 [×] 80 [x²] [÷] [(] 10000 [×] 1.8 [x²] [)]

▶ The lean body mass of a man who is 1.8 meters tall and has a mass of 80 kilograms is about 62.7 BMI units.

PRACTICE

Use a calculator to evaluate the expression for $n = 4$. Round to the nearest thousandth.

1. $3 + 5 \cdot n \div 10$

2. $2 + \frac{3n^2}{4}$

3. $\frac{83}{3n^2} - 1.3$

4. $\frac{14.2n}{8 + n^3}$

5. $\frac{7 - n}{n^2}$

6. $5n^2 + \frac{4n^3 + 1}{3}$

7. Find the lean body mass (to the nearest tenth of a BMI unit) of a woman who is 1.6 meters tall and has a mass of 54 kilograms.

Investigating Algebra ACTIVITY *Use before Lesson 1.3*

Animated Algebra classzone.com

1.3 Patterns and Expressions

MATERIALS • graph paper

QUESTION **How can you use an algebraic expression to describe a pattern?**

EXPLORE **Create and describe a pattern**

STEP 1

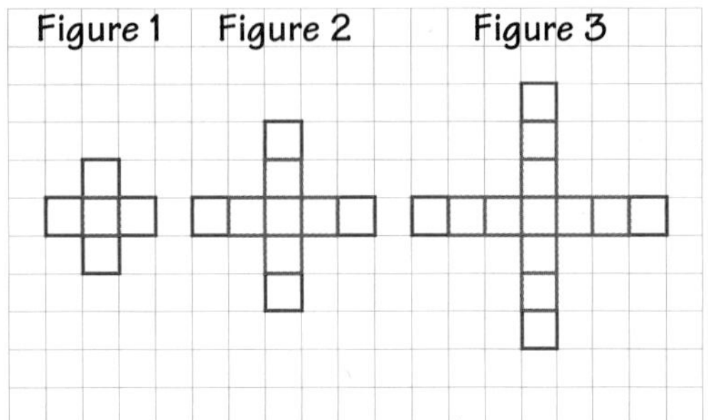

Draw a figure Draw a unit square on graph paper. Then draw a unit square against each side of the first square to form figure 1.

Copy figure 1 and draw a square on each "arm" to form figure 2. Use the same method to form figure 3.

STEP 2

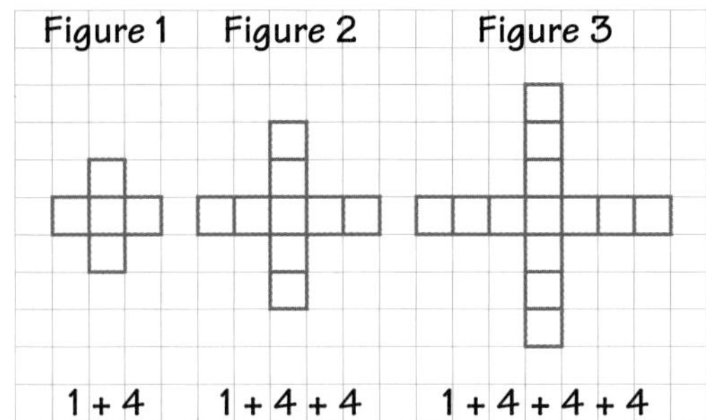

Write expressions For each figure, write a numerical expression that describes the number of squares in the figure.

DRAW CONCLUSIONS **Use your observations to complete these exercises**

In Exercises 1–3, use the pattern in Steps 1 and 2 above.

1. How is the figure number related to the number of times 4 is added in the numerical expression? Predict the number of squares in the fourth figure. Create figure 4 and check your prediction.
2. *Describe* how to calculate the number of squares in the nth figure.
3. Write an algebraic expression for the number of squares in the nth figure. (*Hint:* Remember that repeated addition can be written as multiplication.)
4. Write an algebraic expression for the number of squares in the nth figure of the pattern shown.

Figure 1 **Figure 2** **Figure 3** **Figure 4**

1.3 Write Expressions

Before You evaluated expressions.
Now You will translate verbal phrases into expressions.
Why? So you can find the time needed to do a job, as in Ex. 36.

Key Vocabulary
- **verbal model**
- **rate**
- **unit rate**

To translate verbal phrases into expressions, look for words that indicate mathematical operations.

KEY CONCEPT *For Your Notebook*

Translating Verbal Phrases

Operation	Verbal Phrase	Expression
Addition: sum, plus, total, more than, increased by	The sum of 2 and a number x	$2 + x$
	A number n plus 7	$n + 7$
Subtraction: difference, less than, minus, decreased by	The difference of a number n and 6	$n - 6$
	A number y minus 5	$y - 5$
Multiplication: times, product, multiplied by, of	12 times a number y	$12y$
	$\frac{1}{3}$ of a number x	$\frac{1}{3}x$
Division: quotient, divided by, divided into	The quotient of a number k and 2	$\frac{k}{2}$

Order is important when writing subtraction and division expressions. For instance, "the difference of a number n and 6" is written $n - 6$, *not* $6 - n$, and "the quotient of a number k and 2" is written $\frac{k}{2}$, *not* $\frac{2}{k}$.

AVOID ERRORS
When you translate verbal phrases, the words "the quantity" tell you what to group. In part (a), you write $6n - 4$, *not* $(6 - 4)n$.

EXAMPLE 1 Translate verbal phrases into expressions

Verbal Phrase	Expression
a. 4 less than the quantity 6 times a number n	$6n - 4$
b. 3 times the sum of 7 and a number y	$3(7 + y)$
c. The difference of 22 and the square of a number m	$22 - m^2$

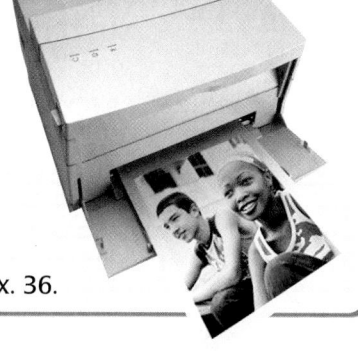

GUIDED PRACTICE for Example 1

1. Translate the phrase "the quotient when the quantity 10 plus a number x is divided by 2" into an expression.

EXAMPLE 2 Write an expression

CHOOSE A VARIABLE
To write an expression for a real-world problem, choose a letter that reminds you of the quantity represented, such as ℓ for length.

CUTTING A RIBBON A piece of ribbon ℓ feet long is cut from a ribbon 8 feet long. Write an expression for the length (in feet) of the remaining piece.

Solution

Draw a diagram and use a specific case to help you write the expression.

Suppose the piece cut is 2 feet long.

8 ft

(8 − 2) ft | 2 ft

The remaining piece is (8 − 2) feet long.

Suppose the piece cut is ℓ feet long.

8 ft

$(8 - \ell)$ ft | ℓ ft

The remaining piece is $(8 - \ell)$ feet long.

▸ The expression $8 - \ell$ represents the length (in feet) of the remaining piece.

VERBAL MODEL A **verbal model** describes a real-world situation using words as labels and using math symbols to relate the words. You can replace the words with numbers and variables to create a *mathematical model*, such as an expression, for the real-world situation.

EXAMPLE 3 Use a verbal model to write an expression

TIPS You work with 5 other people at an ice cream stand. All the workers put their tips into a jar and share the amount in the jar equally at the end of the day. Write an expression for each person's share (in dollars) of the tips.

Solution

AVOID ERRORS
Read the statement of the problem carefully. The number of people sharing tips is 6.

STEP 1 **Write** a verbal model.

STEP 2 **Translate** the verbal model into an algebraic expression. Let a represent the amount (in dollars) in the jar.

Amount in jar	÷	Number of people
a	÷	6

▸ An expression that represents each person's share (in dollars) is $\frac{a}{6}$.

✓ GUIDED PRACTICE for Examples 2 and 3

2. **WHAT IF?** In Example 2, suppose that you cut the original ribbon into p pieces of equal length. Write an expression that represents the length (in feet) of each piece.

3. **WHAT IF?** In Example 3, suppose that each of the 6 workers contributes an equal amount for an after-work celebration. Write an expression that represents the total amount (in dollars) contributed.

RATES A **rate** is a fraction that compares two quantities measured in different units. If the denominator of the fraction is 1 unit, the rate is called a **unit rate**.

EXAMPLE 4 Find a unit rate

READING
Per means "for each" or "for every" and can also be represented using the symbol /, as in mi/h.

A car travels 110 miles in 2 hours. Find the unit rate.

$$\frac{110 \text{ miles}}{2 \text{ hours}} = \frac{110 \text{ miles} \div 2}{2 \text{ hours} \div 2} = \frac{55 \text{ miles}}{1 \text{ hour}}$$

▶ The unit rate is 55 miles per hour, or 55 mi/h.

EXAMPLE 5 Solve a multi-step problem

CELL PHONES Your basic monthly charge for cell phone service is \$30, which includes 300 free minutes. You pay a fee for each extra minute you use. One month you paid \$3.75 for 15 extra minutes. Find your total bill if you use 22 extra minutes.

Solution

STEP 1 **Calculate** the unit rate.

$$\frac{3.75}{15} = \frac{0.25}{1} = \$.25 \text{ per minute}$$

STEP 2 **Write** a verbal model and then an expression. Let m be the number of extra minutes.

Basic charge (dollars)
+
Rate for extra minutes (dollars/minute)
•
Number of extra minutes (minutes)
30
+
0.25
•
m

USE UNIT ANALYSIS
You expect the answer, which is a cost, to be in dollars. You can use unit analysis to check that the expression produces an answer in dollars.

Use *unit analysis* to check that the expression $30 + 0.25m$ is reasonable.

$$\text{dollars} + \frac{\text{dollars}}{\cancel{\text{minute}}} \cdot \cancel{\text{minutes}} = \text{dollars} + \text{dollars} = \text{dollars}$$

Because the units are dollars, the expression is reasonable.

STEP 3 **Evaluate** the expression when $m = 22$.

$$30 + 0.25(22) = 35.5$$

▶ The total bill is \$35.50.

✓ GUIDED PRACTICE for Examples 4 and 5

4. Suppose your friends share cell phone service. They pay a basic charge of \$35 and \$8.80 for 40 extra minutes. Find their total bill if they use 35 extra minutes.

1.3 EXERCISES

HOMEWORK KEY
○ = **WORKED-OUT SOLUTIONS** on p. WS1 for Exs. 11, 21, and 33
★ = **STANDARDIZED TEST PRACTICE** Exs. 2, 13, 14, 34, and 37

SKILL PRACTICE

1. **VOCABULARY** Copy and complete: A(n) __?__ is a fraction that compares two quantities measured in different units.

2. ★ **WRITING** *Explain* how to write $\frac{20 \text{ miles}}{4 \text{ hours}}$ as a unit rate.

EXAMPLE 1 on p. 15 for Exs. 3–14

TRANSLATING PHRASES Translate the verbal phrase into an expression.

3. 8 more than a number x
4. The product of 6 and a number y
5. $\frac{1}{2}$ of a number m
6. 50 divided by a number h
7. The difference of 7 and a number n
8. The sum of 15 and a number x
9. The quotient of twice a number t and 12
10. 3 less than the square of a number p
11. 7 less than twice a number k
12. 5 more than 3 times a number w

13. ★ **MULTIPLE CHOICE** Which expression represents the phrase "the product of 15 and the quantity 12 more than a number x"?

Ⓐ $15 + 12 \cdot x$ Ⓑ $(15 + 12)x$ Ⓒ $15(x + 12)$ Ⓓ $15 \cdot 12 + x$

14. ★ **MULTIPLE CHOICE** Which expression represents the phrase "twice the quotient of 50 and the sum of a number y and 8"?

Ⓐ $\frac{2 \cdot 50}{y} + 8$ Ⓑ $2\left(\frac{50 + y}{8}\right)$ Ⓒ $2\left(\frac{50}{y + 8}\right)$ Ⓓ $\frac{2}{50} + (y + 8)$

EXAMPLES 2 and 3 on p. 16 for Exs. 15–21

WRITING EXPRESSIONS Write an expression for the situation.

15. Number of tokens needed for v video games if each game takes 4 tokens
16. Number of pages of a 5 page article left to read if you've read p pages
17. Each person's share if p people share 16 slices of pizza equally
18. Amount you spend if you buy a shirt for \$20 and jeans for j dollars
19. Number of days left in the week if d days have passed so far
20. Number of hours in m minutes
21. Number of months in y years

EXAMPLE 4 on p. 17 for Exs. 22–27

UNIT RATES Find the unit rate.

22. $\frac{32 \text{ students}}{4 \text{ groups}}$
23. $\frac{4.5 \text{ pints}}{3 \text{ servings}}$
24. $\frac{12 \text{ runs}}{5 \text{ innings}}$
25. $\frac{\$136}{20 \text{ shares}}$

ERROR ANALYSIS ***Describe*** **and correct the error in the units.**

26. $\frac{\$2}{\text{foot}} \cdot 24 \text{ feet} = \frac{\$48}{\text{ft}^2}$

27. $9 \text{ yards} \cdot \frac{3 \text{ feet}}{1 \text{ yard}} \cdot \frac{\$2}{\text{foot}} = \frac{\$54}{\text{ft}}$

COMPARING RATES **In Exercises 28 and 29, tell which rate is greater.**

28. $1\frac{1}{4}$ miles in 2 minutes and 4 seconds, or $1\frac{3}{16}$ miles in 1 minute and 55 seconds

29. $1.60 for 5 minutes, or $19.50 for 1 hour

30. **CHALLENGE** Look for a pattern in the expressions shown below. Use the pattern to write an expression for the sum of the whole numbers from 1 to n. Then find the sum of the whole numbers from 1 to 50.

$1 + 2 = \frac{2 \cdot 3}{2}$ $\quad$ $1 + 2 + 3 = \frac{3 \cdot 4}{2}$ $\quad$ $1 + 2 + 3 + 4 = \frac{4 \cdot 5}{2}$

PROBLEM SOLVING

EXAMPLE 5 on p. 17 for Exs. 31–34

31. **TICKET PRICES** Tickets to a science museum cost $19.95 each. There is a $3 charge for each order no matter how many tickets are ordered. Write an expression for the cost (in dollars) of ordering tickets. Then find the total cost if you order 5 tickets.

@HomeTutor for problem solving help at classzone.com

32. **FOSSIL FUELS** Fossil fuels are produced by the decay of organic material over millions of years. To make one gallon of gas, it takes about 98 tons of organic material, roughly the amount of wheat that could be harvested in a 40 acre field. Write an expression for the amount (in tons) of organic material it takes to make g gallons of gas. How many tons would it take to make enough gas to fill a car's 20 gallon gas tank?

@HomeTutor for problem solving help at classzone.com

33. **MULTI-STEP PROBLEM** A 48 ounce container of juice costs $2.64. A 64 ounce container of the same juice costs $3.84.

a. Find the cost per ounce of each container.

b. Which size container costs less per ounce?

c. You want to buy 192 ounces of juice. How much do you save using the container size from your answer to part (b)?

34. ★ **OPEN-ENDED** *Describe* a real-world situation that can be modeled by the rate $\frac{30}{x}$ where x is a period of time (in hours). Identify the units for 30. Choose a value for x and find the unit rate.

35. **WILDLIFE EDUCATION** A wildlife center presents a program about birds of prey. The center charges a basic fee of $325 and an additional fee for each bird exhibited. If 5 birds are exhibited, the additional fee is $125. What is the total cost if 7 birds are exhibited?

36. **DIGITAL PHOTOS** Your printer takes 36 seconds to print a small photo and 60 seconds to print a large one. Write an expression for the time (in seconds) your printer would take to print a batch including both small and large photos. Then find the time your printer would take to print 12 small photos and 5 large photos.

37. ★ **EXTENDED RESPONSE** A national survey determines the champion tree in a species. The champion is the tree with the greatest score, based on the tree's girth, its height, and its crown spread as shown.

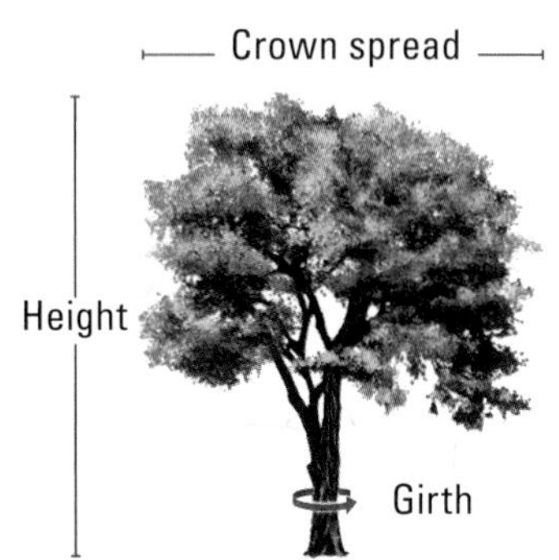

A tree's score is the sum of the girth in inches, the height in feet, and $\frac{1}{4}$ the crown spread in feet. The data for three champion trees are given. Note that the girth is given in feet.

Species	Girth (ft)	Height (ft)	Crown spread (ft)
Narrowleaf cottonwood	12	97	24
Green ash	21.5	95	95
Green buttonwood	14.5	51	68

a. **Write** Write an expression for a tree's score.

b. **Evaluate** Find the score for each tree in the table.

c. **CHALLENGE** Let n be any number greater than 0. Which change would have the greatest effect on a tree's score, an increase of n feet in the girth, in the height, or in the crown spread? *Explain* your reasoning.

MIXED REVIEW

Find the area of the rectangle. *(p. 924)*

38. 

39. 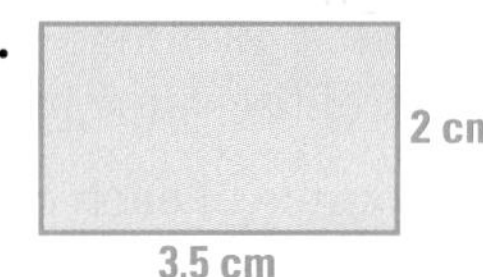

40. 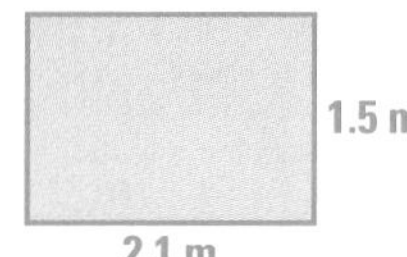

PREVIEW
Prepare for Lesson 1.4 in Exs. 41–46.

Evaluate the expression.

41. $18x$ when $x = 5$ *(p. 2)*
42. $y - 6$ when $y = 22$ *(p. 2)*
43. $5 + z$ when $z = 11$ *(p. 2)*
44. $\frac{g}{7} + 2$ when $g = 35$ *(p. 10)*
45. $5 - 2y^2$ when $y = 1$ *(p. 10)*
46. $\frac{a + 9}{2}$ when $a = 4$ *(p. 10)*

QUIZ *for Lessons 1.1–1.3*

Evaluate the expression.

1. $y + 10$ when $y = 43$ *(p. 2)*
2. $15 - b$ when $b = 9$ *(p. 2)*
3. t^2 when $t = 20$ *(p. 2)*
4. $3n - 5$ when $n = 8$ *(p. 8)*
5. $2y^2 - 1$ when $y = 5$ *(p. 8)*
6. $\frac{3x - 6}{8}$ when $x = 8$ *(p. 8)*

Translate the verbal phrase into an expression. *(p. 15)*

7. 7 less than a number y
8. 5 more than a number t
9. Twice a number k

10. **CAMPING** The rental cost for a campsite is \$25 plus \$2 per person. Write an expression for the total cost. Then find the total cost for 5 people. *(p. 15)*

1.4 Write Equations and Inequalities

Before You translated verbal phrases into expressions.

Now You will translate verbal sentences into equations or inequalities.

Why So you can calculate team competition statistics, as in Ex. 41.

Key Vocabulary
- equation
- inequality
- open sentence
- solution of an equation
- solution of an inequality

An **equation** is a mathematical sentence formed by placing the symbol = between two expressions. An **inequality** is a mathematical sentence formed by placing one of the symbols <, ≤, >, or ≥ between two expressions.

An **open sentence** is an equation or an inequality that contains an algebraic expression.

KEY CONCEPT *For Your Notebook*

Symbol	Meaning	Associated Words
=	is equal to	the same as
<	is less than	fewer than
≤	is less than or equal to	at most, no more than
>	is greater than	more than
≥	is greater than or equal to	at least, no less than

COMBINING INEQUALITIES Sometimes two inequalities are combined. For example, the inequalities $x > 4$ and $x < 9$ can be combined to form the inequality $4 < x < 9$, which is read "x is greater than 4 and less than 9."

EXAMPLE 1 Write equations and inequalities

	Verbal Sentence	Equation or Inequality
a.	The difference of twice a number k and 8 is 12.	$2k - 8 = 12$
b.	The product of 6 and a number n is at least 24.	$6n \geq 24$
c.	A number y is no less than 5 and no more than 13.	$5 \leq y \leq 13$

 Animated Algebra at classzone.com

✓ **GUIDED PRACTICE** for Example 1

1. Write an equation or an inequality: The quotient of a number p and 12 is at least 30.

SOLUTIONS When you substitute a number for the variable in an open sentence like $x + 2 = 5$ or $2y > 6$, the resulting statement is either true or false. If the statement is true, the number is a **solution of the equation** or a **solution of the inequality**.

EXAMPLE 2 Check possible solutions

Check whether 3 is a solution of the equation or inequality.

Equation/Inequality	Substitute	Conclusion
a. $8 - 2x = 2$	$8 - 2(3) \stackrel{?}{=} 2$	$2 = 2$ ✓ 3 is a solution.
b. $4x - 5 = 6$	$4(3) - 5 \stackrel{?}{=} 6$	$7 = 6$ ✗ 3 is *not* a solution.
c. $2z + 5 > 12$	$2(3) + 5 \stackrel{?}{>} 12$	$11 > 12$ ✗ 3 is *not* a solution.
d. $5 + 3n \le 20$	$5 + 3(3) \stackrel{?}{\le} 20$	$14 \le 20$ ✓ 3 is a solution.

READING
A question mark above a symbol indicates a question. For instance, $8 - 2(3) \stackrel{?}{=} 2$ means "Is $8 - 2(3)$ equal to 2?"

USING MENTAL MATH Some equations are simple enough to solve using mental math. Think of the equation as a question. Once you answer the question, check the solution.

EXAMPLE 3 Use mental math to solve an equation

Equation	Think	Solution	Check
a. $x + 4 = 10$	What number plus 4 equals 10?	6	$6 + 4 = 10$ ✓
b. $20 - y = 8$	20 minus what number equals 8?	12	$20 - 12 = 8$ ✓
c. $6n = 42$	6 times what number equals 42?	7	$6(7) = 42$ ✓
d. $\frac{a}{5} = 9$	What number divided by 5 equals 9?	45	$\frac{45}{5} = 9$ ✓

GUIDED PRACTICE for Examples 2 and 3

Check whether the given number is a solution of the equation or inequality.

2. $9 - x = 4$; 5

3. $b + 5 < 15$; 7

4. $2n + 3 \ge 21$; 9

Solve the equation using mental math.

5. $m + 6 = 11$

6. $5x = 40$

7. $\frac{r}{4} = 10$

EXAMPLE 4 Solve a multi-step problem

MOUNTAIN BIKING The last time you and 3 friends went to a mountain bike park, you had a coupon for \$10 off and paid \$17 for 4 tickets. What is the regular price of 4 tickets? If you pay the regular price this time and share it equally, how much does each person pay?

Solution

STEP 1 **Write** a verbal model. Let p be the regular price of 4 tickets. Write an equation.

Regular price	−	Amount of coupon	=	Amount paid
↓		↓		↓
p	−	10	=	17

STEP 2 **Use** mental math to solve the equation $p - 10 = 17$. Think: 10 less than what number is 17? Because $27 - 10 = 17$, the solution is 27.

▶ The regular price for 4 tickets is \$27.

STEP 3 **Find** the cost per person: $\frac{\$27}{4 \text{ people}} = \$6.75$ per person

▶ Each person pays \$6.75.

EXAMPLE 5 Write and check a solution of an inequality

BASKETBALL A basketball player scored 351 points last year. If the player plays 18 games this year, will an average of 20 points per game be enough to beat last year's total?

Solution

STEP 1 **Write** a verbal model. Let p be the average number of points per game. Write an inequality.

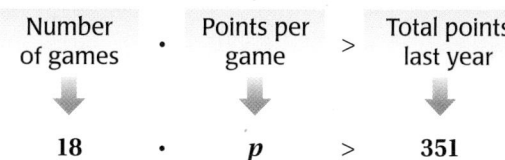

Number of games	•	Points per game	>	Total points last year
↓		↓		↓
18	•	p	>	351

USE UNIT ANALYSIS
Unit analysis shows that games $\cdot \frac{\text{points}}{\text{games}}$ = points, so the inequality is reasonable.

STEP 2 **Check** that 20 is a solution of the inequality $18p > 351$. Because $18(20) = 360$ and $360 > 351$, 20 is a solution. ✓

▶ An average of 20 points per game will be enough.

✓ GUIDED PRACTICE for Examples 4 and 5

8. **WHAT IF?** In Example 4, suppose that the price of 4 tickets with a half-off coupon is \$15. What is each person's share if you pay full price?

9. **WHAT IF?** In Example 5, suppose that the player plays 16 games. Would an average of 22 points per game be enough to beat last year's total?

1.4 EXERCISES

HOMEWORK KEY

○ = **WORKED-OUT SOLUTIONS** on p. WS1 for Exs. 7 and 41

★ = **STANDARDIZED TEST PRACTICE** Exs. 2, 16, 37, 44, 45, and 46

SKILL PRACTICE

1. **VOCABULARY** Give an example of an open sentence.

2. ★ **WRITING** *Describe* the difference between an expression and an equation.

EXAMPLE 1 on p. 21 for Exs. 3–16

WRITING OPEN SENTENCES **Write an equation or an inequality.**

3. The sum of 42 and a number n is equal to 51.
4. The difference of a number z and 11 is equal to 35.
5. The difference of 9 and the quotient of a number t and 6 is 5.
6. The sum of 12 and the quantity 8 times a number k is equal to 48.
7. The product of 9 and the quantity 5 more than a number t is less than 6.
8. The product of 4 and a number w is at most 51.
9. The sum of a number b and 3 is greater than 8 and less than 12.
10. The product of 8 and a number k is greater than 4 and no more than 16.
11. The difference of a number t and 7 is greater than 10 and less than 20.

STORE SALES **Write an inequality for the price p (in dollars) described.**

12. 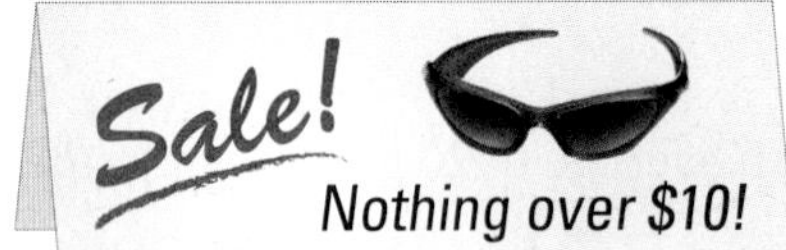
Sale!
Nothing over $10!

13. 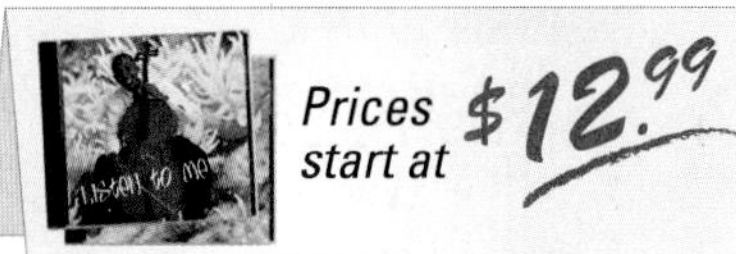
Prices start at
$12.99

ERROR ANALYSIS ***Describe*** **and correct the error in writing the verbal sentence as an equation or an inequality.**

14. The sum of a number n and 4 is no more than 13.

$n + 4 < 13$ ✗

15. The quotient of a number t and 4.2 is at most 15.

$\frac{t}{4.2} > 15$ ✗

16. ★ **MULTIPLE CHOICE** Which inequality corresponds to the sentence "The product of a number b and 3 is no less than 12"?

Ⓐ $3b < 12$ Ⓑ $3b \le 12$ Ⓒ $3b > 12$ Ⓓ $3b \ge 12$

EXAMPLE 2 on p. 22 for Exs. 17–28

CHECK POSSIBLE SOLUTIONS **Check whether the given number is a solution of the equation or inequality.**

17. $x + 9 = 17; 8$
18. $9 + 4y = 17; 1$
19. $6f - 7 = 29; 5$
20. $\frac{k}{5} + 9 = 11; 10$
21. $\frac{r}{3} - 4 = 4; 12$
22. $\frac{x - 5}{3} \ge 2.8; 11$
23. $15 - 4y > 6; 2$
24. $y - 3.5 < 6; 9$
25. $2 + 3x \le 8; 2$
26. $2p - 1 \ge 7; 3$
27. $4z - 5 < 3; 2$
28. $3z + 7 > 20; 4$

EXAMPLE 3 on p. 22 for Exs. 29–34

MENTAL MATH Solve the equation using mental math.

29. $x + 8 = 13$ **30.** $y + 16 = 25$ **31.** $z - 11 = 1$

32. $5w = 20$ **33.** $8b = 72$ **34.** $\frac{f}{6} = 4$

EQUATIONS AND INEQUALITIES In Exercises 35 and 36, write an open sentence. Then check whether $3\frac{1}{2}$ is a solution of the open sentence.

35. 2 less than the product of 3 and a number x is equal to the sum of x and 5.

36. 4 more than twice a number k is no greater than the sum of k and 11.

37. ★ **MULTIPLE CHOICE** Which equation has the same solution as $z - 9 = 3$?

Ⓐ $z - 4 = 16$ Ⓑ $\frac{1}{2}z = 7$ Ⓒ $z + 15 = 27$ Ⓓ $5z = 45$

38. CHALLENGE Use mental math to solve the equation $3x + 4 = 19$. *Explain* your thinking.

PROBLEM SOLVING

EXAMPLES 4 and 5 on p. 23 for Exs. 39–43

39. **CHARITY WALK** You are taking part in a charity walk, and you have walked 12.5 miles so far. Your goal is to walk 20 miles. How many more miles do you need to walk to meet your goal?

@HomeTutor for problem solving help at classzone.com

40. **COMPACT DISCS** You buy a storage rack that holds 40 CDs. You have 27 CDs. Write an inequality that describes how many more CDs you can buy and still have no more CDs than the rack can hold. You buy 15 CDs. Will they all still fit?

@HomeTutor for problem solving help at classzone.com

41. **ECO-CHALLENGE** Eco-Challenge Fiji was a competition that included jungle trekking, ocean swimming, mountain biking, and river kayaking. In 2002, the U.S. team finished second about 6 hours after the winning team from New Zealand. The U.S. team finished in about 173 hours. What was the winning team's time?

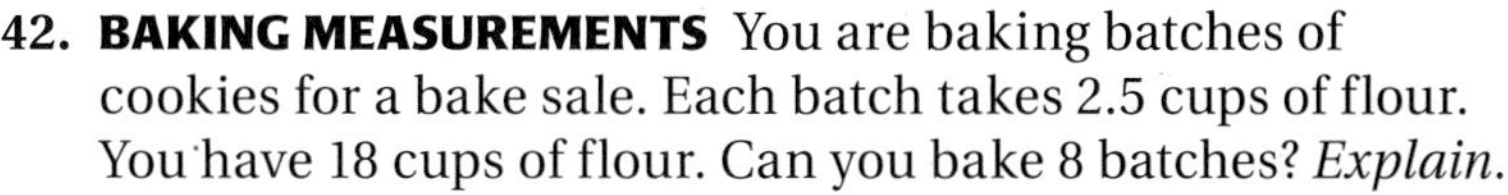

42. **BAKING MEASUREMENTS** You are baking batches of cookies for a bake sale. Each batch takes 2.5 cups of flour. You have 18 cups of flour. Can you bake 8 batches? *Explain.*

43. **EMPLOYMENT** Your friend takes a job cleaning up a neighbor's yard and mowing the grass, and asks you and two other friends to help. Your friend divides the amount the neighbor pays equally among all the members of the group. Each of you got \$25. How much did the neighbor pay?

44. ★ **OPEN-ENDED** Describe a real-world situation you could model using the equation $5x = 50$. Use mental math to solve the equation. *Explain* what the solution means in this situation.

45. ★ **SHORT RESPONSE** You have two part-time jobs. You earn \$6 per hour running errands and \$5 per hour walking dogs. You can work a total of 10 hours this weekend and hope to earn at least \$55. Let r be the number of hours you spend running errands.

a. Write an inequality that describes the situation. Your inequality should involve only one variable, r.

b. If you spend the same amount of time at each job, will you meet your goal? *Explain.*

c. Can you meet your goal by working all 10 hours at only one job? *Explain.*

46. ★ **EXTENDED RESPONSE** Your school's service club is sponsoring a dance in the school gym to raise money for a local charity. The expenses will be \$600. The club members will sell tickets for \$10. They hope to raise enough money to cover the expenses and have enough left to donate \$1000 to the charity.

a. How many tickets must they sell to cover their expenses?

b. How many tickets must they sell to cover their expenses and meet their goal?

c. The school allows no more than 200 students in the gymnasium for a dance. Can the club members sell enough tickets to exceed their goal? What is the greatest possible amount by which they can exceed their goal? *Explain* your reasoning.

47. **CHALLENGE** You and your friend are reading the same series of science fiction books. You tell your friend, "I've read 3 times as many books as you have." Your friend replies, "You've read only 4 more books than I have." How many books have each of you read?

48. **CHALLENGE** Each of the long sides of a rectangle has a length of x inches. Each of the other sides is 1 inch shorter than the long sides. The perimeter of the rectangle is 22 inches. Find the length and the width of the rectangle. *Justify* your answer.

MIXED REVIEW

PREVIEW
Prepare for Lesson 1.5 in Exs. 49–54.

Write the percent as a decimal. *(p. 916)*

49. 3%

50. 3.5%

51. 5.25%

Find the perimeter of the triangle or rectangle. *(p. 924)*

52.
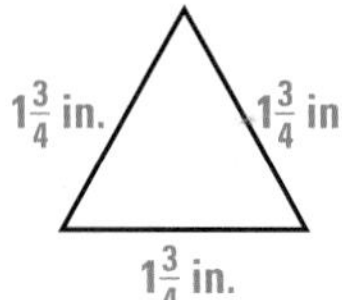

53.

54.
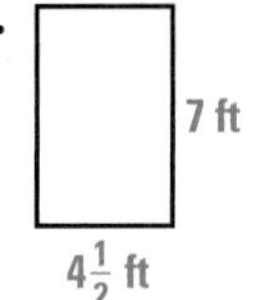

Evaluate the expression. *(p. 8)*

55. $9 \cdot 3^2 - 2$

56. $4 \div 2^2 + \frac{1}{7}$

57. $5 \div 0.25 \cdot 3$

MIXED REVIEW *of Problem Solving*

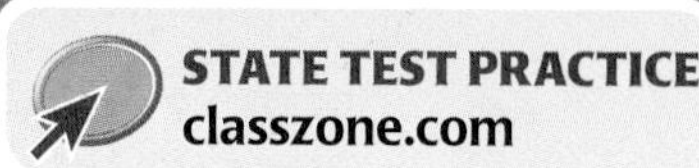

Lessons 1.1–1.4

1. **MULTI-STEP PROBLEM** You are making a photo quilt by transferring photos to squares of fabric. Each square should be big enough so that you can turn over an edge $\frac{5}{8}$ inch long on each side and have a finished square with a side length of $5\frac{3}{4}$ inches.

   a. What are the dimensions of each fabric square?

   b. How many square inches of fabric do you need if you want to include 48 squares?

   c. The fabric you buy is 36 inches wide. How long a piece of fabric do you need?

   d. You buy a piece of fabric that has the length you found in part (c). Once you've cut all the squares, how many square inches of fabric are left over?

2. **MULTI-STEP PROBLEM** A rule of thumb states that the ideal weight (in ounces) of a baseball bat for a high school baseball player is 5 ounces more than one third of the player's height (in inches).

   a. Write an expression that describes the ideal weight (in ounces) of a bat for a high school baseball player who is h inches tall.

   b. One player was 66 inches tall last year. This year the player is 69 inches tall. How much heavier should the player's new bat be than the bat used last year?

3. **SHORT RESPONSE** You collect miniature cars and display them on shelves that hold 20 cars each.

   a. Which expression would you evaluate to find the number of shelves you need for x cars: $20x$, $\frac{x}{20}$, or $\frac{20}{x}$? *Justify* your choice.

   b. Find the number of shelves you need to display 120 cars.

4. **OPEN-ENDED** *Describe* a real-world situation that you could model with the inequality $3x < 15$. *Explain* what a solution of the inequality means in this situation.

5. **SHORT RESPONSE** You pay $7.50 for 3 quarts of strawberries. You realize that you need more strawberries for your recipe. You return to the store with $4.50. Will you have enough money to buy 2 more quarts of strawberries? *Explain* your reasoning.

6. **EXTENDED RESPONSE** The number of calories in one serving of any food is the sum of the calories from fat, protein, and carbohydrate. The table shows the calories in 1 gram of each of the three food components.

Component	Calories in 1 gram
Fat	9
Protein	4
Carbohydrate	4

   a. Write an expression for the total number of calories in a serving of food that contains f grams of fat, p grams of protein, and c grams of carbohydrate.

   b. A serving of cheddar cheese contains 14 grams of fat, 11 grams of protein, and 1 gram of carbohydrate. How many calories are in a serving of cheddar cheese?

   c. A 100 pound teenager requires about 45 grams of protein per day. If the teenager tried to get all the required protein for one day from cheddar cheese, how many calories would the teenager consume? *Explain.*

7. **GRIDDED ANSWER** You are comparing two dorm-size refrigerators, both with cube-shaped interiors. One model has an interior edge length of 14 inches. Another model has an interior edge length of 16 inches. How many more cubic inches of storage space does the larger model have?

1.5 Use a Problem Solving Plan

Before You used problem solving strategies.

Now You will use a problem solving plan to solve problems.

Why? So you can determine a route, as in Example 1.

Key Vocabulary
- formula

KEY CONCEPT *For Your Notebook*

A Problem Solving Plan

STEP 1 **Read and Understand** Read the problem carefully. Identify what you know and what you want to find out.

STEP 2 **Make a Plan** Decide on an approach to solving the problem.

STEP 3 **Solve the Problem** Carry out your plan. Try a new approach if the first one isn't successful.

STEP 4 **Look Back** Once you obtain an answer, check that it is reasonable.

EXAMPLE 1 Read a problem and make a plan

RUNNING You run in a city where the short blocks on north-south streets are 0.1 mile long. The long blocks on east-west streets are 0.15 mile long. You will run 2 long blocks east, a number of short blocks south, 2 long blocks west, then back to your starting point. You want to run 2 miles. How many short blocks should you run?

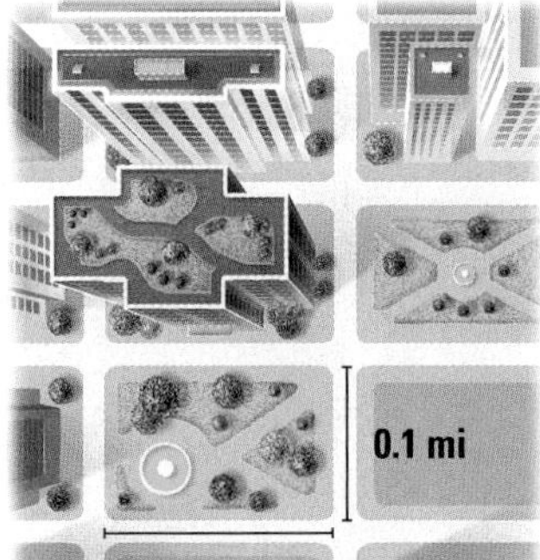

Solution

ANOTHER WAY For an alternative method for solving the problem in Example 1, turn to page 34 for the **Problem Solving Workshop**.

STEP 1 **Read and Understand**

What do you know?

You know the length of each size block, the number of long blocks you will run, and the total distance you want to run.

You can conclude that you must run an even number of short blocks because you run the same number of short blocks in each direction.

What do you want to find out?

You want to find out the number of short blocks you should run so that, along with the 4 long blocks, you run 2 miles.

STEP 2 **Make a Plan** Use what you know to write a verbal model that represents what you want to find out. Then write an equation and solve it, as in Example 2.

EXAMPLE 2 Solve a problem and look back

Solve the problem in Example 1 by carrying out the plan. Then check your answer.

Solution

STEP 3 **Solve the Problem** Write a verbal model. Then write an equation. Let s be the number of short blocks you run.

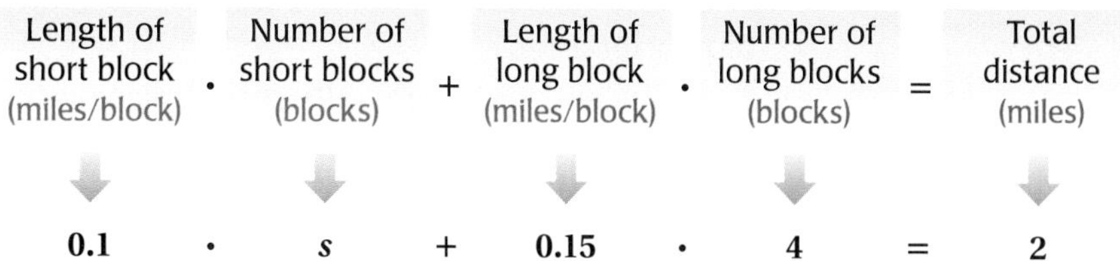

Length of short block (miles/block)
•
Number of short blocks (blocks)
+
Length of long block (miles/block)
•
Number of long blocks (blocks)
=
Total distance (miles)
0.1 • s + 0.15 • 4 = 2

REVIEW PROBLEM SOLVING
To review problem solving strategies, see p. 936.

The equation is $0.1s + 0.6 = 2$. One way to solve the equation is to use the strategy *guess, check, and revise.*

Guess an even number that is easily multiplied by 0.1. Try 20.

Check whether 20 is a solution.

$0.1s + 0.6 = 2$ **Write equation.**

$0.1(20) + 0.6 \stackrel{?}{=} 2$ **Substitute 20 for *s*.**

$2.6 = 2$ ✗ **Simplify; 20 does not check.**

Revise. Because $2.6 > 2$, try an even number less than 20. Try 14.

Check whether 14 is a solution.

$0.1s + 0.6 = 2$ **Write equation.**

$0.1(14) + 0.6 \stackrel{?}{=} 2$ **Substitute 14 for *s*.**

$2 = 2$ ✓ **Simplify.**

▶ To run 2 miles, you should run 14 short blocks along with the 4 long blocks you run.

STEP 4 **Look Back** Check your answer by making a table. You run 0.6 mile on long blocks. Each two short blocks add 0.2 mile.

Short blocks	0	2	4	6	8	10	12	14
Total distance	0.6	0.8	1.0	1.2	1.4	1.6	1.8	2.0

The total distance is 2 miles when you run 4 long blocks and 14 short blocks. The answer in Step 3 is correct.

at classzone.com

✓ **GUIDED PRACTICE** for Examples 1 and 2

1. **WHAT IF?** In Example 1, suppose that you want to run a total distance of 3 miles. How many short blocks should you run?

FORMULAS A **formula** is an equation that relates two or more quantities. You may find it helpful to use formulas in problem solving.

REVIEW FORMULAS
For additional formulas, see pp. 924–928 and the Table of Formulas on pp. 952–953.

KEY CONCEPT — *For Your Notebook*

Formulas

Temperature

$C = \frac{5}{9}(F - 32)$ where F = degrees Fahrenheit and C = degrees Celsius

Simple interest

$I = Prt$ where I = interest, P = principal, r = interest rate (as a decimal), and t = time

Distance traveled

$d = rt$ where d = distance traveled, r = rate (constant or average speed), and t = time

Profit

$P = I - E$ where P = profit, I = income, and E = expenses

EXAMPLE 3 Standardized Test Practice

You are making a leather book cover. You need a rectangular piece of leather as shown. Find the cost of the piece if leather costs \$.25 per square inch.

Ⓐ \$14.50 Ⓑ \$49.50

Ⓒ \$58.00 Ⓓ \$198.00

ELIMINATE CHOICES
You can eliminate choices A and D by estimating. The area of the piece of leather is about 200 square inches, and \$.25(200) is about \$50.

Solution

Use the formula for the area of a rectangle, $A = \ell w$, with $\ell = 18$ inches and $w = 11$ inches.

$A = \ell w$ **Write area formula.**

$= 18(11)$ **Substitute 18 for ℓ and 11 for w.**

$= 198$ **Simplify.**

The area is 198 square inches, so the total cost is \$.25(198) = \$49.50.

▶ The correct answer is B. Ⓐ Ⓑ Ⓒ Ⓓ

✓ GUIDED PRACTICE for Example 3

2. **GARDENING** A gardener determines the cost of planting daffodil bulbs to be \$2.40 per square foot. How much will it cost to plant daffodil bulbs in a rectangular garden that is 12 feet long and 5 feet wide?

Ⓐ \$40.80 Ⓑ \$60 Ⓒ \$81.60 Ⓓ \$144

1.5 EXERCISES

HOMEWORK KEY

○ = **WORKED-OUT SOLUTIONS** on p. WS2 for Exs. 5 and 17

★ = **STANDARDIZED TEST PRACTICE** Exs. 2, 11, 12, 20, and 22

◆ = **MULTIPLE REPRESENTATIONS** Ex. 21

SKILL PRACTICE

1. **VOCABULARY** Give an example of a formula.

2. ★ **WRITING** *Describe* how you can use a formula to solve the following problem: The inner edges of a cube-shaped pot have a length of 1.5 feet. How much does it cost to fill the planter if soil costs \$4 per cubic foot?

EXAMPLES 1 and 2 on pp. 28–29 for Exs. 3–5

READING AND UNDERSTANDING In Exercises 3–5, identify what you know and what you need to find out. You do *not* need to solve the problem.

3. **CRAFT SHOW** You make 35 dog collars and anticipate selling all of them at a craft show. You spent \$85 for materials and hope to make a profit of \$90. How much should you charge for each collar?

4. **DISTANCE RUNNING** A runner ran at a rate of 0.15 mile per minute for 40 minutes. The next day, the runner ran at a rate of 0.16 mile per minute for 50 minutes. How far did the runner run altogether?

5. **TEMPERATURE** One day, the temperature in Rome, Italy, was 30°C. The temperature in Dallas, Texas, was 83°F. Which temperature was higher?

ERROR ANALYSIS *Describe* and correct the error in solving the problem.

A town is fencing a rectangular field that is 200 feet long and 150 feet wide. At \$10 per foot, how much will it cost to fence the field?

6.
$P = 200 + 150 = 350$
$\$10(350) = \$3500$ ✗

7.
$A = (200)(150) = 30{,}000$
$\$10(30{,}000) = \$300{,}000$ ✗

EXAMPLE 3 on p. 30 for Exs. 8–12

CHOOSING A FORMULA In Exercises 8–10, state the formula that is needed to solve the problem. You do *not* need to solve the problem.

8. The temperature is 68°F. What is the temperature in degrees Celsius?

9. A store buys a baseball cap for \$5 and sells it for \$20. What is the profit?

10. Find the area of a triangle with a base of 25 feet and a height of 8 feet.

11. ★ **MULTIPLE CHOICE** What is the interest on \$1200 invested for 2 years in an account that earns simple interest at a rate of 5% per year?

(A) \$12 (B) \$60 (C) \$120 (D) \$240

12. ★ **MULTIPLE CHOICE** A car travels at an average speed of 55 miles per hour. How many miles does the car travel in 2.5 hours?

(A) 22 miles (B) 57.5 miles (C) 110 miles (D) 137.5 miles

13. **CHALLENGE** Write a formula for the length ℓ of a rectangle given its perimeter P and its width w. *Justify* your thinking.

PROBLEM SOLVING

EXAMPLES 1, 2, and 3 on pp. 28–30 for Exs. 14–18

14. **DVD STORAGE** A stackable storage rack holds 22 DVDs and costs \$21. How much would it cost to buy enough racks to hold 127 DVDs?

@HomeTutor for problem solving help at classzone.com

15. **FRAMING** For an art project, you make a square print with a side length of 8 inches. You make a frame using strips of wood $1\frac{1}{4}$ inches wide. What is the area of the frame?

@HomeTutor for problem solving help at classzone.com

16. **MOUNTAIN BOARDS** You have saved \$70 to buy a mountain board that costs \$250. You plan to save \$10 each week. How many weeks will it take to save for the mountain board?

17. **HIKING** You are hiking. The total weight of your backpack and its contents is $13\frac{3}{8}$ pounds. You want to carry no more than 15 pounds. How many extra water bottles can you add to your backpack if each bottle weighs $\frac{3}{4}$ pound?

18. **PIZZA** Thick crust pizza requires about 0.15 ounce of dough per square inch of surface area. You have two rectangular pans, one that is 16 inches long and 14 inches wide, and one that is 15.5 inches long and 10 inches wide. How much more dough do you need to make a thick crust pizza in the larger pan than in the smaller one?

19. **SONAR** A diver uses a sonar device to determine the distance to her diving partner. The device sends a sound wave and records the time it takes for the wave to reach the diving partner and return to the device. Suppose the wave travels at a rate of about 4800 feet per second.

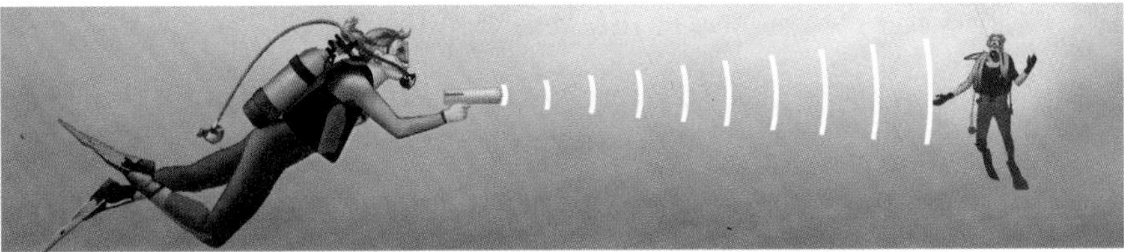

a. The wave returns 0.2 second after it was sent. How far did the wave travel?

b. How far away is the diving partner?

20. ★ **EXTENDED RESPONSE** A gardener is reseeding a city park that has the shape of a right triangle with a base of 150 feet and a height of 200 feet. The third side of the park is 250 feet long.

a. One bag of grass seed covers 3750 square feet and costs \$27.50. How many bags are needed? What is the total cost?

b. Wire fencing costs \$23.19 for each 50 foot roll. How much does it cost to buy fencing to enclose the area?

c. Fence posts cost \$3.19 each and should be placed every 5 feet. How many posts are needed, and how much will they cost altogether? *Explain.*

○ = WORKED-OUT SOLUTIONS on p. WS1

★ = STANDARDIZED TEST PRACTICE

= MULTIPLE REPRESENTATIONS

21. MULTIPLE REPRESENTATIONS Homeowners are building a square closet in a rectangular room that is 24 feet long and 18 feet wide. They want the remaining floor area to be at least 400 square feet. Because they don't want to cut any of the 1 foot by 1 foot square floor tiles, the side length of the closet floor should be a whole number of feet.

a. **Making a Table** Make a table showing possible side lengths of the closet floor and the remaining area for each side length.

b. **Writing an Inequality** Write an inequality to describe the situation. Use your table to find the greatest possible side length of the closet floor.

22. ★ **SHORT RESPONSE** A farmer plans to build a fence around a rectangular pen that is 16 feet long. The area of the pen is 80 square feet. Is 40 feet of fencing enough to fence in the pen? *Explain.*

23. CHALLENGE You and your friend live 12 miles apart. You leave home at the same time and travel toward each other. You walk at a rate of 4 miles per hour and your friend bicycles at a rate of 11 miles per hour.

a. How long after you leave home will you meet? How far from home will each of you be?

b. Suppose your friend bicycles at a rate of 12 miles per hour. How much sooner will you meet? How far from home will each of you be?

MIXED REVIEW

Write the decimal as a fraction and as a percent. *(p. 916)*

24. 0.85 25. 1.25 26. 0.245 27. 0.007

28. Find the surface area and volume of the rectangular prism. *(p. 927)*

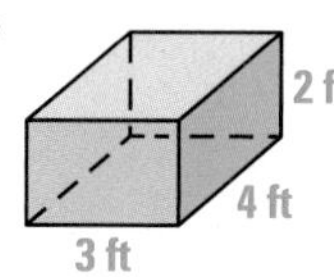

PREVIEW
Prepare for Lesson 1.6 in Exs. 29–32.

Translate the verbal phrase into an expression. *(p. 15)*

29. $\frac{1}{3}$ multiplied by a number v

30. 22 divided by a number h

31. 7 more than twice a number m

32. Twice the sum of a number y and 3

QUIZ for Lessons 1.4–1.5

Write an equation or an inequality. *(p. 21)*

1. 4 more than twice a number n is equal to 25.
2. The quotient of a number x and 2 is no more than 9.

Check whether the given number is a solution of the equation or inequality. *(p. 21)*

3. $13 - 2x = 5$; 4 4. $5d - 4 \geq 16$; 4 5. $4y + 3 \geq 15$; 3

6. **CAR TRAVEL** One car travels about 28.5 miles on each gallon of gas. Suppose the average price of gas is \$2 per gallon. About how much would the gas for a 978 mile trip cost? *(p. 28)*

Using ALTERNATIVE METHODS

Another Way to Solve Example 1, page 28

MULTIPLE REPRESENTATIONS In Example 1 on page 28, you saw how to solve a problem about running using an equation. You can also solve the problem by using the strategy *draw a diagram.*

PROBLEM

RUNNING You run in a city where the short blocks on north-south streets are 0.1 mile long. The long blocks on east-west streets are 0.15 mile long. You will run 2 long blocks east, a number of short blocks south, 2 long blocks west, then back to your starting point. You want to run a total of 2 miles. How many short blocks should you run?

METHOD

Drawing a Diagram You can draw a diagram to solve the problem.

STEP 1 **Read** the problem carefully. It tells you the lengths of a short block and a long block. You plan to run 4 long blocks and a distance of 2 miles.

STEP 2 **Draw** a pair of rectangles to represent running 1 short block in each direction. The total distance is $4(0.15) + 2(0.1) = 0.8$ mile. Continue adding pairs of rectangles until the total distance run is 2 miles.

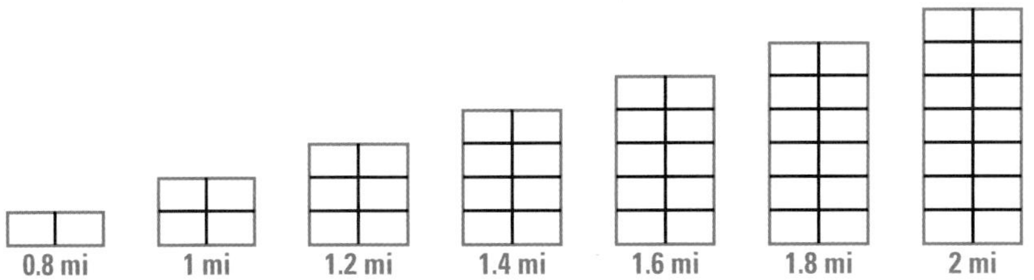

▶ You should run 14 short blocks.

Animated **Algebra** at classzone.com

PRACTICE

1. **BAKING** A cake pan is 9 inches wide and 11 inches long. How many 3 inch by 3 inch square pieces can you cut? Solve this problem using an equation. Then draw a diagram. *Explain* why a diagram is useful.

2. **SWIMMING** A 12 foot rope strung through 4 floats marks off the deep end of a pool. Each end of the rope is 3 feet from a float. The floats are equally spaced. How far apart are they? Solve this problem using two different methods.

3. **ERROR ANALYSIS** *Describe* and correct the error in solving Exercise 2.

$$4x + 6 = 12$$
$$4(1.5) + 6 = 12$$
The floats are 1.5 feet apart.

4. **GEOMETRY** The length of a rectangle is twice its width. The perimeter is 72 inches. What is its length? Solve this problem using two different methods.

1.6 Represent Functions as Rules and Tables

Before You wrote algebraic expressions and equations.

Now You will represent functions as rules and as tables.

Why? So you can describe consumer costs, as in Example 1.

Key Vocabulary
- **function**
- **domain**
- **range**
- **independent variable**
- **dependent variable**

When you pump gas, the total cost depends on the number of gallons pumped. The total cost is a *function* of the number of gallons pumped.

A **function** consists of:

- A set called the **domain** containing numbers called **inputs**, and a set called the **range** containing numbers called **outputs**.
- A pairing of inputs with outputs such that each input is paired with exactly one output.

EXAMPLE 1 Identify the domain and range of a function

The input-output table shows the cost of various amounts of regular unleaded gas from the same pump. Identify the domain and range of the function.

Input (gallons)	10	12	13	17
Output (dollars)	19.99	23.99	25.99	33.98

Solution

▶ The domain is the set of inputs: 10, 12, 13, and 17. The range is the set of outputs: 19.99, 23.99, 25.99, and 33.98.

✓ **GUIDED PRACTICE** for Example 1

1. Identify the domain and range of the function.

Input	0	1	2	4
Output	5	2	2	1

MAPPING DIAGRAMS A function may be represented by a *mapping diagram*. Notice that an output may be paired with more than one input, but no input is paired with more than one output.

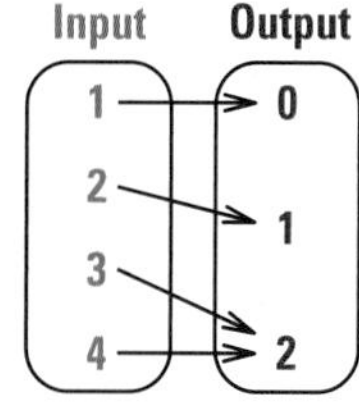

EXAMPLE 2 Identify a function

Tell whether the pairing is a function.

a.

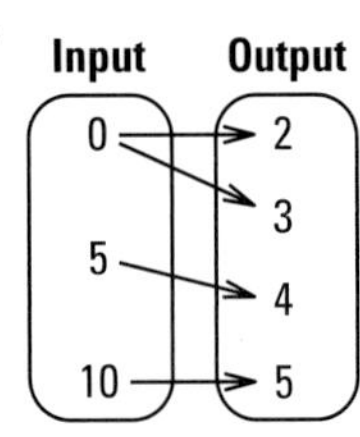

The pairing is *not* a function because the input 0 is paired with both 2 and 3.

b.

Input	Output
0	0
1	2
4	8
6	12

The pairing is a function because each input is paired with exactly one output.

✓ GUIDED PRACTICE for Example 2

Tell whether the pairing is a function.

2.

Input	3	6	9	12
Output	1	2	2	1

3.

Input	2	2	4	7
Output	0	1	2	3

FUNCTION RULES A function may be represented using a rule that relates one variable to another. The input variable is called the **independent variable.** The output variable is called the **dependent variable** because its value depends on the value of the input variable.

READING

Function rules typically give the dependent variable in terms of the independent variable. In an equation like $y = x + 3$, you know that y is the dependent variable.

KEY CONCEPT *For Your Notebook*

Functions

Verbal Rule

The output is 3 more than the input.

Equation

$y = x + 3$

Table

Input, x	0	1	2	3	4
Output, y	3	4	5	6	7

EXAMPLE 3 Make a table for a function

The domain of the function $y = 2x$ is 0, 2, 5, 7, and 8. Make a table for the function, then identify the range of the function.

Solution

x	0	2	5	7	8
$y = 2x$	$2(0) = 0$	$2(2) = 4$	$2(5) = 10$	$2(7) = 14$	$2(8) = 16$

The range of the function is 0, 4, 10, 14, and 16.

EXAMPLE 4 Write a function rule

Write a rule for the function.

Input	0	1	4	6	10
Output	2	3	6	8	12

Solution

Let x be the input, or independent variable, and let y be the output, or dependent variable. Notice that each output is 2 more than the corresponding input. So, a rule for the function is $y = x + 2$.

EXAMPLE 5 Write a function rule for a real-world situation

CONCERT TICKETS You are buying concert tickets that cost \$15 each. You can buy up to 6 tickets. Write the amount (in dollars) you spend as a function of the number of tickets you buy. Identify the independent and dependent variables. Then identify the domain and the range of the function.

Solution

CHOOSE A VARIABLE
To write a function rule for a real-world situation, choose letters for the variables that remind you of the quantities represented.

Write a verbal model. Then write a function rule. Let n represent the number of tickets purchased and A represent the amount spent (in dollars).

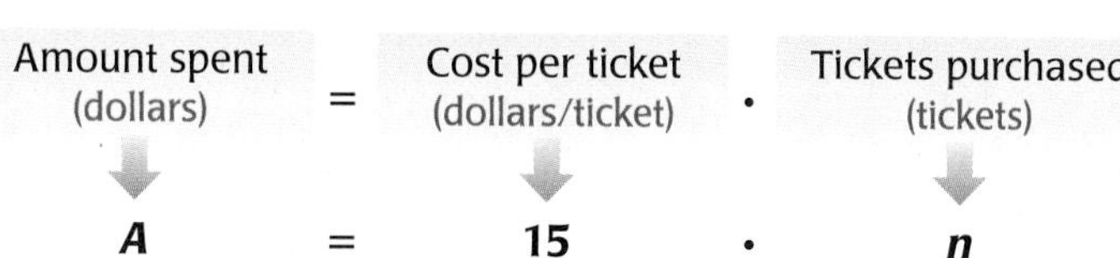

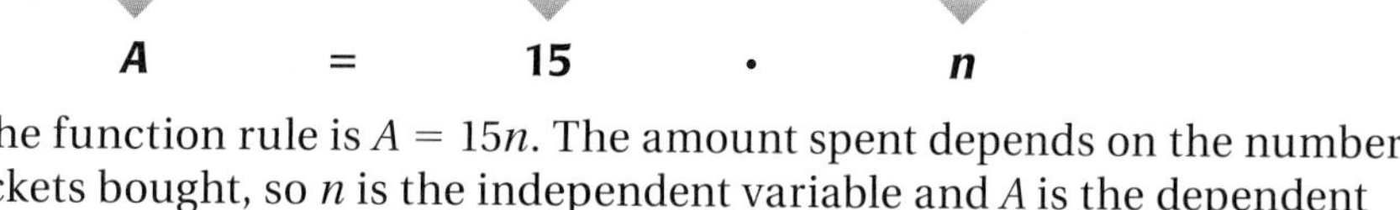

So, the function rule is $A = 15n$. The amount spent depends on the number of tickets bought, so n is the independent variable and A is the dependent variable.

Because you can buy up to 6 tickets, the domain of the function is 0, 1, 2, 3, 4, 5, and 6. Make a table to identify the range.

Number of tickets, n	0	1	2	3	4	5	6
Amount (dollars), A	0	15	30	45	60	75	90

The range of the function is 0, 15, 30, 45, 60, 75, and 90.

Animated Algebra at classzone.com

✓ GUIDED PRACTICE for Examples 3, 4, and 5

4. Make a table for the function $y = x - 5$ with domain 10, 12, 15, 18, and 29. Then identify the range of the function.

5. Write a rule for the function. Identify the domain and the range.

Time (hours)	1	2	3	4
Pay (dollars)	8	16	24	32

1.6 EXERCISES

HOMEWORK KEY

○ = **WORKED-OUT SOLUTIONS** on p. WS2 for Exs. 7 and 23

★ = **STANDARDIZED TEST PRACTICE** Exs. 2, 11, 12, 13, 26, and 27

◆ = **MULTIPLE REPRESENTATIONS** Exs. 23 and 24

SKILL PRACTICE

1. **VOCABULARY** Copy and complete: A(n) _?_ is a number in the domain of a function. A(n) _?_ is a number in the range of a function.

2. ★ **WRITING** In the equation $b = a - 2$, which variable is the independent variable and which is the dependent variable? *Explain.*

EXAMPLES 1 and 2 on pp. 35–36 for Exs. 3–11

DOMAIN AND RANGE **Identify the domain and range of the function.**

3.

Input	Output
0	5
1	7
2	15
3	44

4. 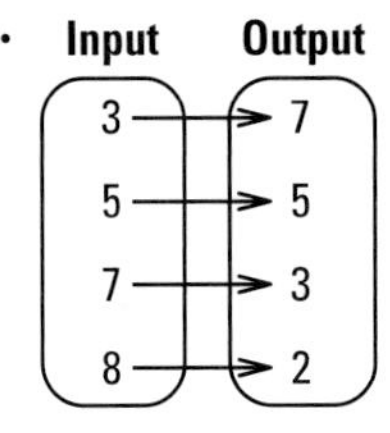

5.

Input	Output
6	5
12	7
21	10
42	17

IDENTIFYING FUNCTIONS **Tell whether the pairing is a function.**

6.

Input	Output
0	7.5
1	9.5
2	11.5
3	13.5

7. 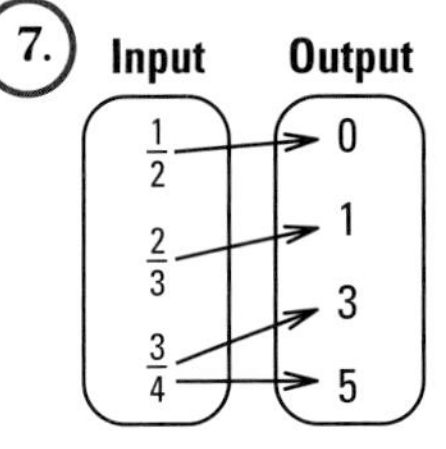

8.

Input	Output
7	13
11	8
21	13
35	20

ERROR ANALYSIS **In Exercises 9 and 10, describe and correct the error related to the function represented by the table.**

Input, *x*	1	2	3	4	5
Output, *y*	6	7	8	6	9

9. The pairing is not a function. One output is paired with two inputs. ✗

10. The pairing is a function. The range is 1, 2, 3, 4, and 5. 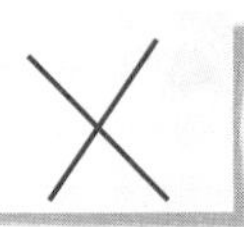

11. ★ **OPEN-ENDED** Draw a mapping diagram for a function with 6 inputs. Then make a table to represent the function.

EXAMPLES 3 and 4 on pp. 36–37 for Exs. 12–21

12. ★ **MULTIPLE CHOICE** The domain of the function $y = 5x - 1$ is 1, 3, 4, 5, and 6. Which number is in the range of the function?

Ⓐ 0 Ⓑ 4 Ⓒ 9 Ⓓ 15

13. ★ **MULTIPLE CHOICE** Each output of a function is 0.5 less than the corresponding input. Which equation is a rule for the function?

Ⓐ $y = x - 0.5$ Ⓑ $y = x + 0.5$ Ⓒ $y = 0.5 - x$ Ⓓ $y = 0.5x$

TABLES **Make a table for the function. Identify the range of the function.**

14. $y = x - 3$
Domain: 12, 15, 22, 30

15. $y = x + 3.5$
Domain: 4, 5, 7, 8, 12

16. $y = 3x + 4$
Domain: 0, 5, 7, 10

17. $y = \frac{1}{2}x + 3$
Domain: 4, 6, 9, 11

18. $y = \frac{2}{3}x + \frac{1}{3}$
Domain: 4, 6, 8, 12

19. $y = \frac{0.5x + 1}{2}$
Domain: 0, 2, 4, 6

FUNCTION RULES **Write a rule for the function.**

20.

Input, *x*	0	1	2	3
Output, *y*	2.2	3.2	4.2	5.2

21.

Input, *x*	15	20	21	30	42
Output, *y*	7	12	13	22	34

22. CHALLENGE Fill in the table in such a way that when t is the independent variable, the pairing is a function, and when t is the dependent variable, the pairing is not a function.

t	?	?	?	?
v	?	?	?	?

PROBLEM SOLVING

EXAMPLE 5
on p. 37
for Exs. 23–26

23. ◆ **MULTIPLE REPRESENTATIONS** You have 10 quarters that you can use for a parking meter.

a. **Describing in Words** Copy and complete: Each time you put 1 quarter in the meter, you have 1 less quarter, so _?_ is a function of _?_.

b. **Writing a Rule** Write a rule for the number y of quarters that you have left as a function of the number x of quarters you have used so far. Identify the domain of the function.

c. **Making a Table** Make a table and identify the range of the function.

@HomeTutor for problem solving help at classzone.com

24. ◆ **MULTIPLE REPRESENTATIONS** At a yard sale, you find 5 paperback books by your favorite author. Each book is priced at \$.75.

a. **Describing in Words** Copy and complete: For each book you buy, you spend \$.75, so _?_ is a function of _?_.

b. **Writing a Rule** Write a rule for the amount (in dollars) you spend as a function of the number of books you buy. Identify the domain of the function.

c. **Making a Table** Make a table and identify the range of the function.

@HomeTutor for problem solving help at classzone.com

25. SAVINGS You have \$100 saved and plan to save \$20 each month. Write a rule for the amount saved (in dollars) as a function of the number of months from now. Identify the independent and dependent variables, the domain, and the range. How much will you have saved altogether 12 months from now?

26. ★ **OPEN-ENDED** Write a function rule that models a real-world situation. Identify the independent variable and the dependent variable.

27. ★ **SHORT RESPONSE** Consider a pairing of the digits 2 through 9 on a telephone keypad with the associated letters.

   a. Make a table showing the pairing with the digits as inputs and the letters as outputs. Is the pairing a function? *Explain.*

   b. Make a table showing the pairing with the letters as inputs and the digits as outputs. Is the pairing a function? *Explain.*

28. **MULTI-STEP PROBLEM** The table shows the fuel efficiency of four compact cars from one manufacturer for model year 2004.

City fuel efficiency (mi/gal), c	24	26	27	28
Highway fuel efficiency (mi/gal), h	32	34	35	36

   a. **Write a Rule** Use the table to write a rule for the cars' highway fuel efficiency as a function of their city fuel efficiency.

   b. **Predict** Another of the manufacturer's compact cars has a city fuel efficiency of 30 miles per gallon. Predict the highway fuel efficiency.

   c. **Calculate** A study found that if gas costs \$2 per gallon, you can use the expression $\frac{11,550}{c} + \frac{9450}{h}$ to estimate a car's annual fuel cost (in dollars) for a typical driver. Evaluate the expression for the car in part (b).

29. **CHALLENGE** Each week you spend a total of 5 hours exercising. You swim part of the time and bike the rest.

300 calories per hour

440 calories per hour

   a. Write a rule for the total number of calories you burn for the whole 5 hours as a function of the time you spend swimming.

   b. One week you spend half the time swimming. How many calories do you burn during the whole 5 hours?

MIXED REVIEW

PREVIEW
Prepare for Lesson 1.7 in Exs. 30–33.

Plot the point in a coordinate plane. *(p. 921)*

30. $A(1, 3)$
31. $B(3, 1)$
32. $C(2, 4)$
33. $D(6, 2)$

Write an equation or an inequality. *(p. 21)*

34. The difference of 13 and a number w is 5.

35. The quotient of 21 and a number d is no less than 7.

36. **TRAVEL** On a 1375 mile flight, an airplane's average speed is 550 miles per hour. The flight is within a single time zone and leaves at 10 A.M. What time will the airplane arrive at its destination? *(p. 28)*

@HomeTutor
classzone.com
Keystrokes

1.6 Make a Table

QUESTION **How can you use a graphing calculator to create a table for a function?**

You can use a graphing calculator to create a table for a function when you want to display many pairs of input values and output values or when you want to find the input value that corresponds to a given output value.

In the example below, you will make a table to compare temperatures in degrees Celsius and temperatures in degrees Fahrenheit for temperatures at or above the temperature at which water freezes, 32°F.

EXAMPLE **Use a graphing calculator to make a table**

The formula $C = \frac{5}{9}(F - 32)$ gives the temperature in degrees Celsius as a function of the temperature in degrees Fahrenheit. Make a table for the function.

STEP 1 ***Enter equation***

Rewrite the function using x for F and y for C. Press Y= and enter $\frac{5}{9}(x - 32)$.

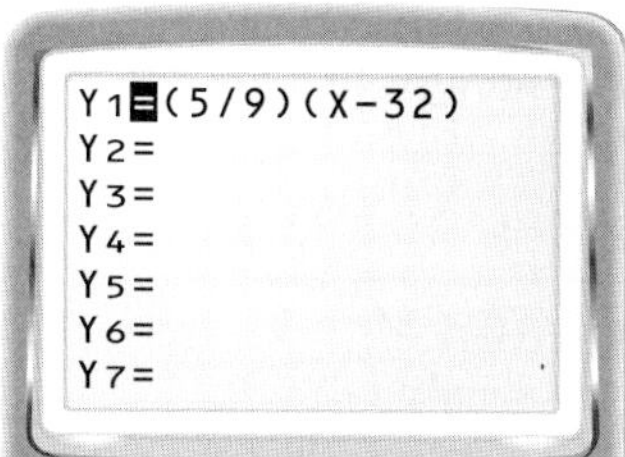

STEP 2 ***Set up table***

Go to the TABLE SETUP screen. Use a starting value (TblStart) of 32 and an increment (ΔTbl) of 1.

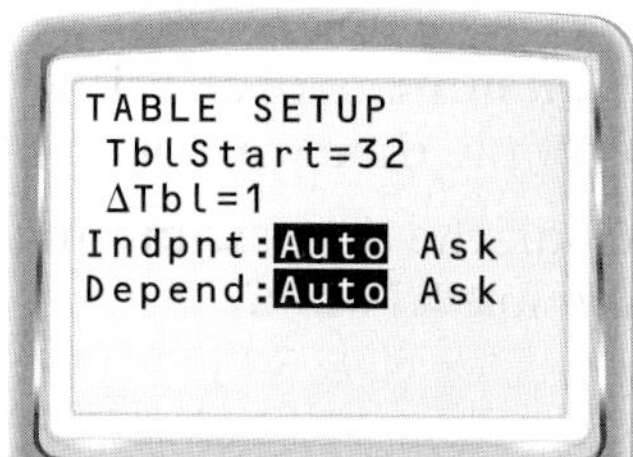

STEP 3 ***View table***

Display the table. Scroll down to see pairs of inputs and outputs.

X	Y1	Y2
32	0	
33	.55556	
34	1.1111	
35	1.6667	
36	2.2222	
37	2.7778	

PRACTICE

1. You see a sign that indicates that the outdoor temperature is 10°C. Find the temperature in degrees Fahrenheit. *Explain* how you found your answer.
2. Water boils at 100°C. What is the temperature in degrees Fahrenheit?

Make a table for the function. Use the given starting value and increment.

3. $y = \frac{3}{4}x + 5$
   TblStart = 0, ΔTbl = 1
4. $y = 4x + 2$
   TblStart = 0, ΔTbl = 0.5
5. $y = 7.5x - 0.5$
   TblStart = 1, ΔTbl = 1
6. $y = 0.5x + 6$
   TblStart = 3, ΔTbl = 3

1.7 Scatter Plots and Functions

MATERIALS • tape measure • graph paper

QUESTION **How can you tell whether a graph represents a function?**

A *scatter plot* is a type of display for paired data. Each data pair is plotted as a point. In this activity, you will work in a group to make a scatter plot. You will measure the height of each student in your group and the length of his or her forearm. The length of the forearm is the distance from the elbow to the wrist.

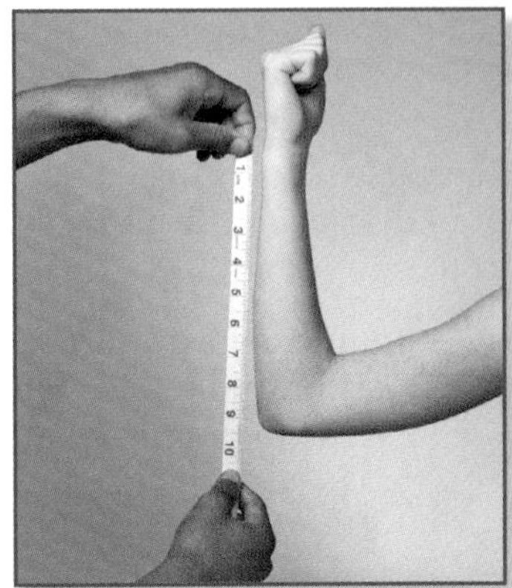

EXPLORE **Collect data and make a scatter plot**

STEP 1 ***Collect data*** Measure the height of each student in your group and the length of his or her forearm. Record the results for each student in one row of a table like the one shown.

Height (inches)	Forearm length (inches)
63	10
?	?

STEP 2 ***Make a scatter plot*** Use graph paper to draw axes labeled as shown. Then plot the data pairs (*height, forearm length*). For example, plot the point (63, 10) for a student with a height of 63 inches and a forearm length of 10 inches.

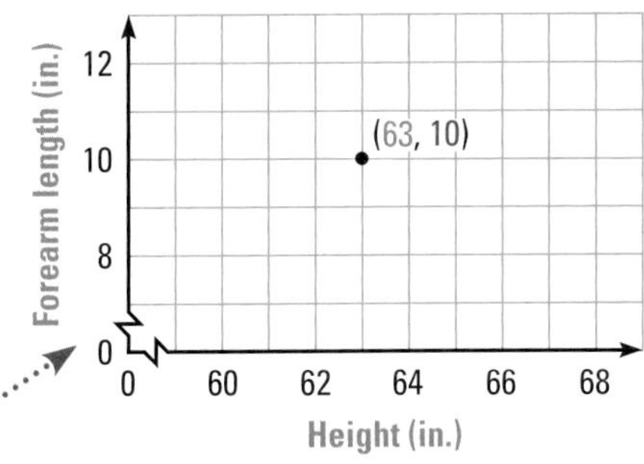

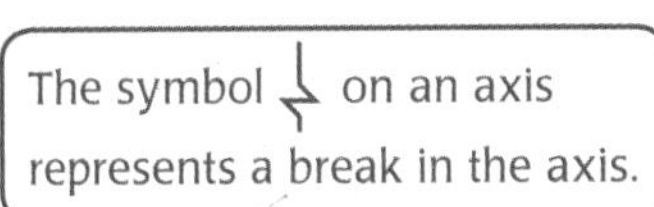

The symbol on an axis represents a break in the axis.

DRAW CONCLUSIONS **Use your observations to complete these exercises**

1. Examine your scatter plot. What does it suggest about the relationship between a person's height and the person's forearm length?
2. Compare your table with those of the other groups in your class. Determine which of the tables represent functions and which do not.
3. Is it possible to determine whether a table represents a function by looking at the corresponding scatter plot? *Explain.*

1.7 Represent Functions as Graphs

Before	You represented functions as rules and tables.
Now	You will represent functions as graphs.
Why?	So you can describe sales trends, as in Example 4.

Key Vocabulary
- **function,** *p. 35*
- **domain,** *p. 35*
- **range,** *p. 35*

REVIEW THE COORDINATE PLANE
For help with the coordinate plane, see p. 921.

You can use a graph to represent a function. Given a table that represents a function, each corresponding pair of input and output values forms an ordered pair of numbers that can be plotted as a point. The x-coordinate is the input. The y-coordinate is the output.

Table

Input, x	Output, y
1	2
2	3
4	5

Ordered Pairs

(input, output)
(1, 2)
(2, 3)
(4, 5)

Graph

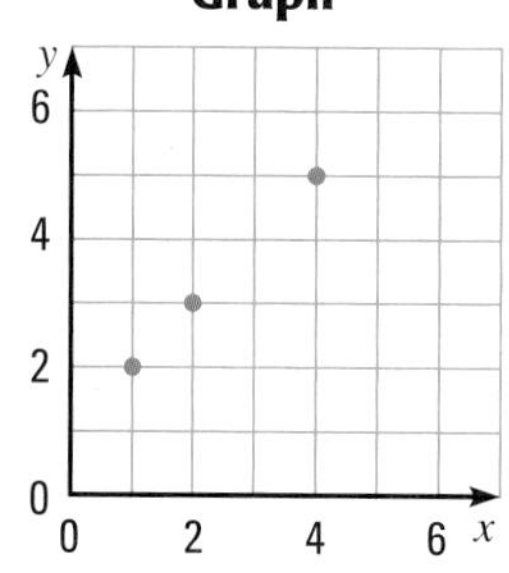

The horizontal axis of the graph is labeled with the input variable. The vertical axis is labeled with the output variable.

EXAMPLE 1 Graph a function

Graph the function $y = \frac{1}{2}x$ with domain 0, 2, 4, 6, and 8.

Solution

STEP 1 **Make** an input-output table.

x	0	2	4	6	8
y	0	1	2	3	4

STEP 2 **Plot** a point for each ordered pair (x, y).

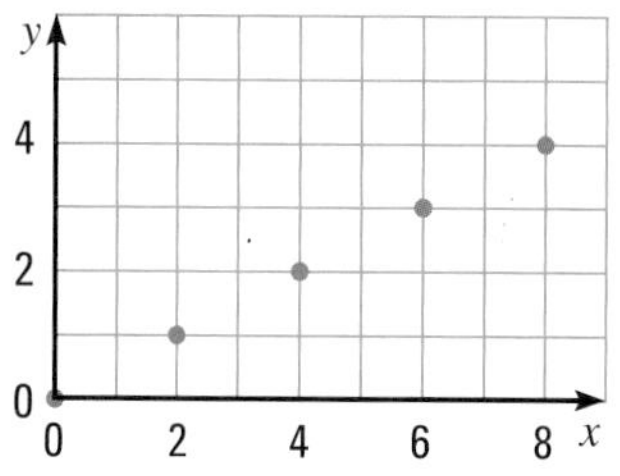

GUIDED PRACTICE for Example 1

1. Graph the function $y = 2x - 1$ with domain 1, 2, 3, 4, and 5.

EXAMPLE 2 Graph a function

SAT SCORES The table shows the average score s on the mathematics section of the Scholastic Aptitude Test (SAT) in the United States from 1997 to 2003 as a function of the time t in years since 1997. In the table, 0 corresponds to the year 1997, 1 corresponds to 1998, and so on. Graph the function.

Years since 1997, t	0	1	2	3	4	5	6
Average score, s	511	512	511	514	514	516	519

Solution

READING
The symbol ⌇ on the vertical number line represents a break in the axis.

STEP 1 **Choose** a scale. The scale should allow you to plot all the points on a graph that is a reasonable size.

- The t-values range from 0 to 6, so label the t-axis from 0 to 6 in increments of 1 unit.
- The s-values range from 511 to 519, so label the s-axis from 510 to 520 in increments of 2 units.

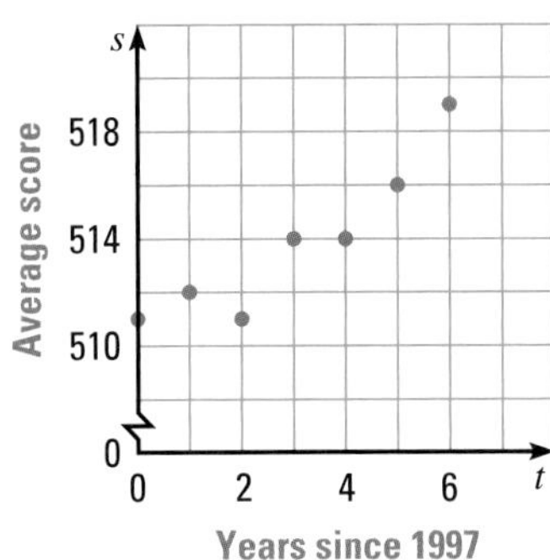

STEP 2 **Plot** the points.

✓ GUIDED PRACTICE for Example 2

2. **WHAT IF?** In Example 2, suppose that you use a scale on the s-axis from 0 to 520 in increments of 1 unit. *Describe* the appearance of the graph.

EXAMPLE 3 Write a function rule for a graph

Write a rule for the function represented by the graph. Identify the domain and the range of the function.

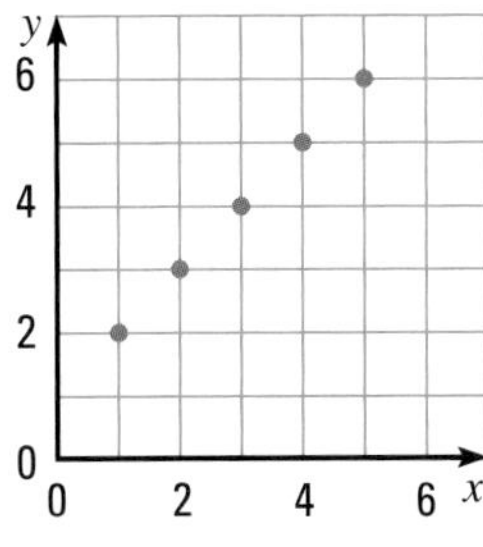

Solution

STEP 1 **Make** a table for the graph.

x	1	2	3	4	5
y	2	3	4	5	6

STEP 2 **Find** a relationship between the inputs and the outputs. Notice from the table that each output value is 1 more than the corresponding input value.

STEP 3 **Write** a function rule that describes the relationship: $y = x + 1$.

▶ A rule for the function is $y = x + 1$. The domain of the function is 1, 2, 3, 4, and 5. The range is 2, 3, 4, 5, and 6.

✓ **GUIDED PRACTICE** for Example 3

Write a rule for the function represented by the graph. Identify the domain and the range of the function.

3.

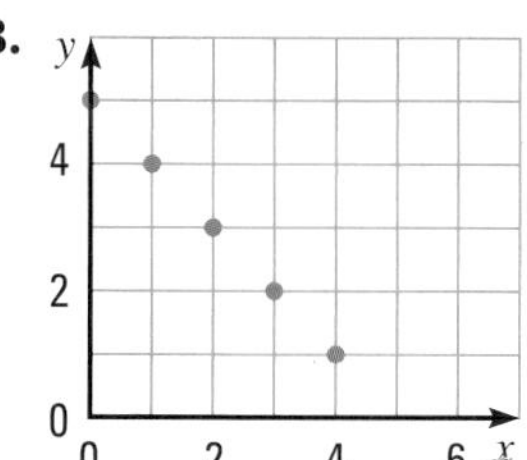

4.

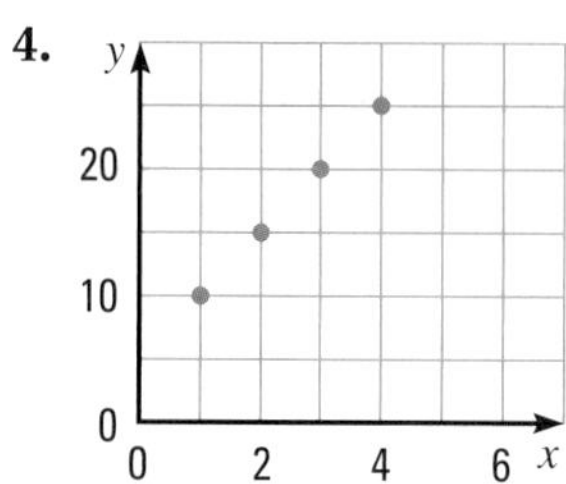

EXAMPLE 4 Analyze a graph

GUITAR SALES The graph shows guitar sales (in millions of dollars) for a chain of music stores for the period 1999–2005. Identify the independent variable and the dependent variable. Describe how sales changed over the period and how you would expect sales in 2006 to compare to sales in 2005.

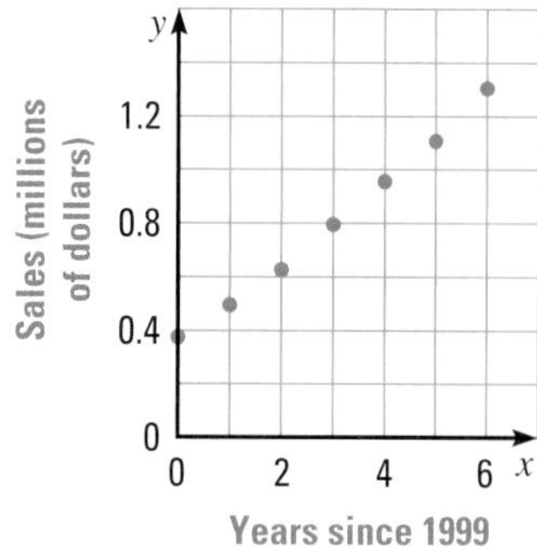

Solution

The independent variable is the number of years since 1999. The dependent variable is the sales (in millions of dollars). The graph shows that sales were increasing. If the trend continued, sales would be greater in 2006 than in 2005.

GUIDED PRACTICE for Example 4

5. **REASONING** Based on the graph in Example 4, is \$1.4 million a reasonable prediction of the chain's sales for 2006? *Explain.*

CONCEPT SUMMARY *For Your Notebook*

Ways to Represent a Function

You can use a verbal rule, an equation, a table, or a graph to represent a function.

Verbal Rule

The output is 1 less than twice the input.

Equation

$y = 2x - 1$

Table

x	y
1	1
2	3
3	5
4	7

Graph

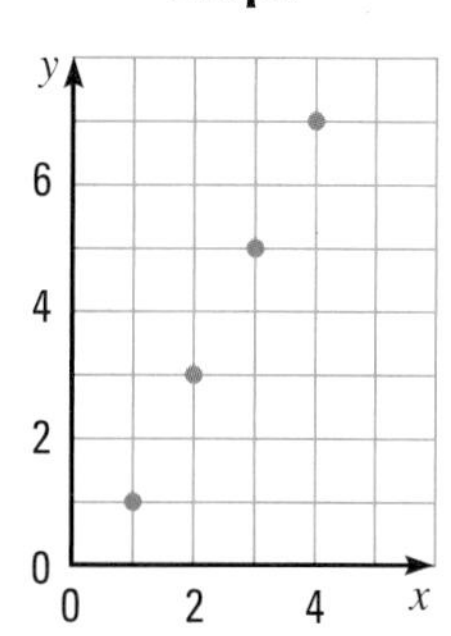

1.7 EXERCISES

HOMEWORK KEY

○ = **WORKED-OUT SOLUTIONS** on p. WS2 for Exs. 3 and 17

★ = **STANDARDIZED TEST PRACTICE** Exs. 2, 13, 18, 19, and 20

SKILL PRACTICE

1. **VOCABULARY** Copy and complete: Each point on the graph of a function corresponds to an ordered pair (x, y) where x is in the _?_ of the function and y is in the _?_ of the function.

2. ★ **WRITING** Given the graph of a function, describe how to write a rule for the function.

EXAMPLE 1 on p. 43 for Exs. 3–9

GRAPHING FUNCTIONS **Graph the function.**

3. $y = x + 3$; domain: 0, 1, 2, 3, 4, and 5
4. $y = \frac{1}{2}x + 1$; domain: 0, 1, 2, 3, 4, and 5
5. $y = 2x + 2$; domain: 0, 2, 5, 7, and 10
6. $y = 3x - 1$; domain: 1, 2, 3, 4, and 5
7. $y = x + 5$; domain: 0, 2, 4, 6, 8, and 10
8. $y = 2.5x$; domain: 0, 1, 2, 3, and 4

9. **ERROR ANALYSIS** *Describe* and correct the error in graphing the function $y = x - 1$ with domain 1, 2, 3, 4, and 5.

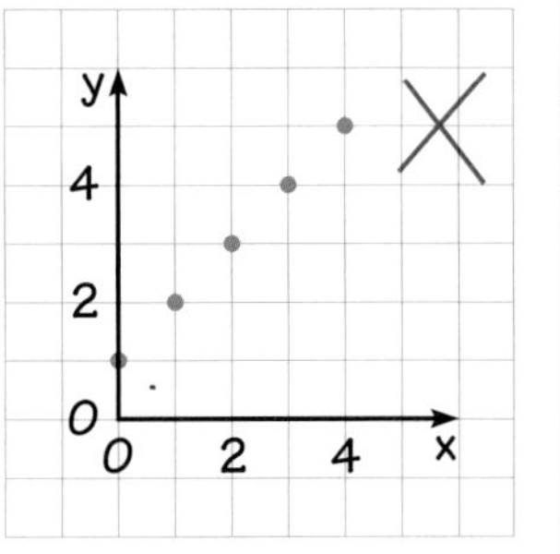

EXAMPLE 3 on p. 44 for Exs. 10–12

WRITING FUNCTION RULES **Write a rule for the function represented by the graph. Identify the domain and the range of the function.**

10.

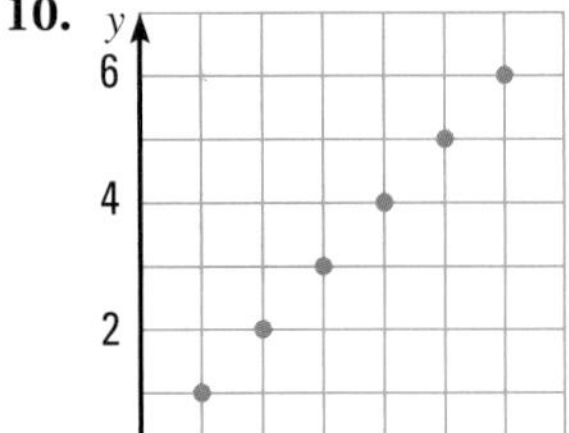

11.

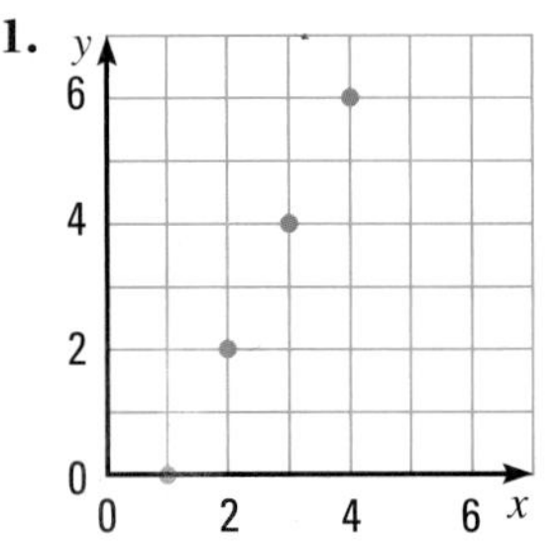

12.

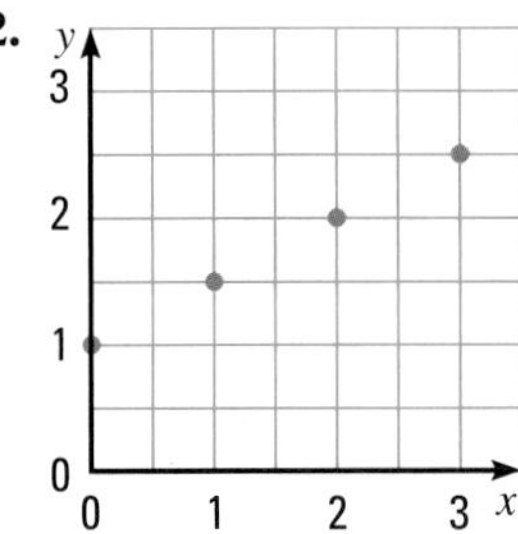

13. ★ **MULTIPLE CHOICE** The graph of which function is shown?

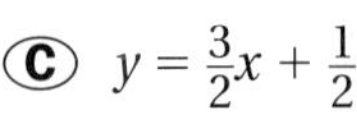

Ⓐ $y = \frac{1}{2}x + \frac{1}{2}$

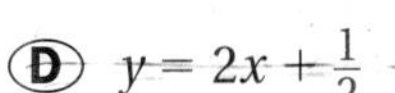

Ⓑ $y = x + \frac{1}{2}$

Ⓒ $y = \frac{3}{2}x + \frac{1}{2}$

Ⓓ $y = 2x + \frac{1}{2}$

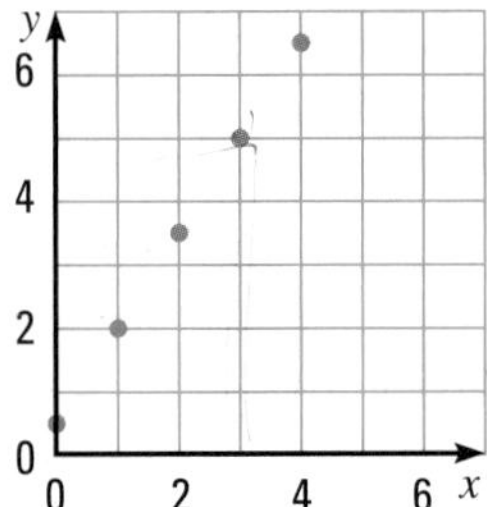

14. **CHALLENGE** The graph represents a function.

   a. Write a rule for the function.

   b. Find the value of y so that $(1.5, y)$ is on the graph of the function.

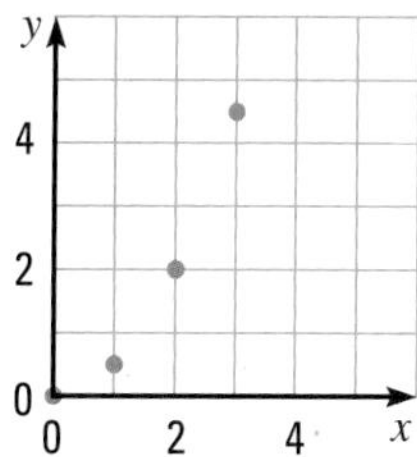

PROBLEM SOLVING

EXAMPLE 2 on p. 44 for Exs. 15–17

15. **ADVERTISING** The table shows the cost C (in millions of dollars) of a 30 second Super Bowl ad on TV as a function of the time t (in years) since 1997. Graph the function.

Years since 1997, t	0	1	2	3	4	5	6	7
Cost (millions of dollars), C	1.2	1.3	1.6	2.1	2.1	1.9	2.1	2.3

@HomeTutor for problem solving help at classzone.com

16. **CONGRESS** The table shows the number r of U.S. representatives for Texas as a function of the time t (in years) since 1930. Graph the function.

Years since 1930, t	0	10	20	30	40	50	60	70
Number of representatives, r	21	21	22	23	24	27	30	32

@HomeTutor for problem solving help at classzone.com

17. **ELECTIONS** The table shows the number v of voters in U.S. presidential elections as a function of the time t (in years) since 1984. First copy and complete the table. Round to the nearest million. Then graph the function represented by the first and third columns.

Years since 1984	Voters	Voters (millions)
0	92,652,680	?
4	91,594,693	?
8	104,405,155	?
12	96,456,345	?
16	105,586,274	?

EXAMPLE 4 on p. 45 for Exs. 18–19

18. ★ **WRITING** The graph shows the number of hours of daylight in Houston, Texas, on the fifteenth day of the month, with 1 representing January, and so on. Identify the independent variable and the dependent variable. *Describe* how the number of hours of daylight changes over a year.

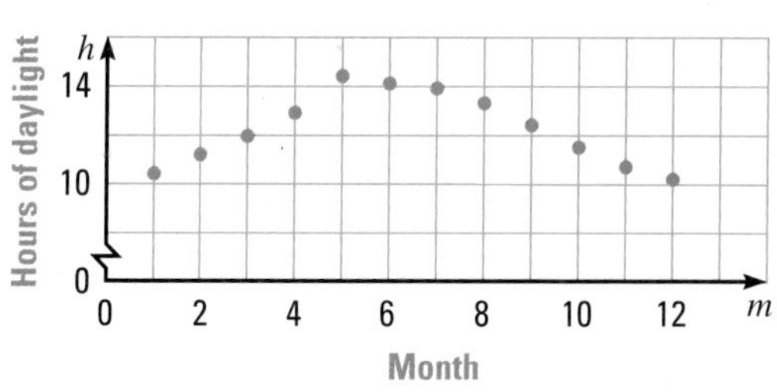

19. ★ **SHORT RESPONSE** A field biologist collected and measured alligator snapping turtle eggs. The graph shows the mass m (in grams) of an egg as a function of its length ℓ (in millimeters).

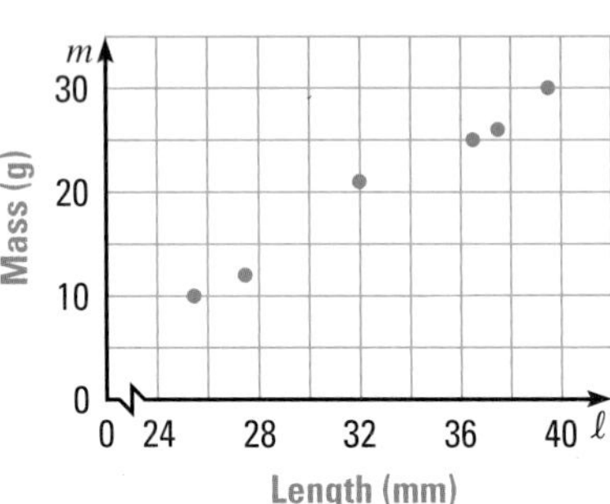

a. **Describe** As the lengths of the eggs increase, what happens to the masses of the eggs?

b. **Estimate** Is 27.5 g a reasonable estimate for the mass of an egg that is 38 mm long? *Explain.*

20. ★ **SHORT RESPONSE** Women first officially ran in the Boston Marathon in 1972. The graph shows the winning time t (in minutes) for both men and women as a function of the number n of years since 1972 for that year and every five years thereafter.

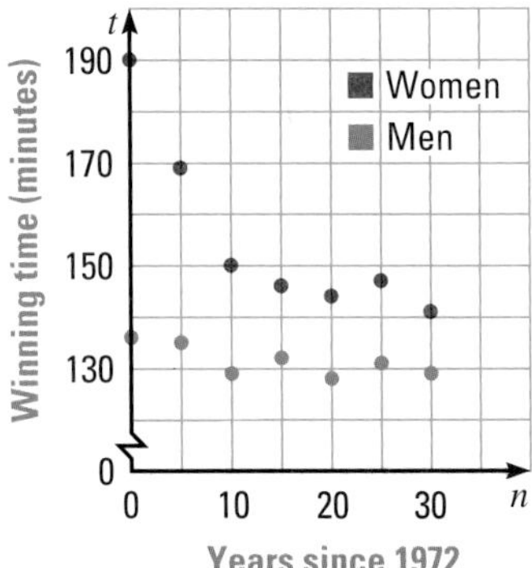

a. **CHALLENGE** *Explain* how you can estimate the difference in the men's and women's winning time for any year shown.

b. **CHALLENGE** *Compare* any trends you see in the graphs.

MIXED REVIEW

PREVIEW
Prepare for Lesson 2.1 in Exs. 21–24.

Copy and complete the statement using <, >, or =. *(p. 909)*

21. 0.53 _?_ 0.5
22. 3.9 _?_ 4.0
23. 1.64 _?_ 1.66
24. 0.80 _?_ 0.8

Solve the equation using mental math. *(p. 21)*

25. $x + 12 = 20$
26. $12z = 480$
27. $x - 8 = 5$
28. $\frac{n}{2} = 32$

Write a rule for the function. *(p. 35)*

29.

Input, x	2	3	7	10
Ouput, y	8	7	3	0

30.

Input, x	0	4	8	12
Ouput, y	5	7	9	11

QUIZ *for Lessons 1.6–1.7*

1. The domain of the function $y = 12 - 2x$ is 0, 2, 3, 4, and 5. Make a table for the function, then identify the range of the function. *(p. 35)*

Tell whether the pairing is a function. *(p. 35)*

2.

x	5	6	7	11
y	1	2	3	7

3.

x	4	6	9	15
y	1	3	6	3

Graph the function. *(p. 43)*

4. $y = 2x - 5$; domain: 5, 6, 7, 8, and 9
5. $y = 7 - x$; domain: 1, 2, 3, 4, and 5

EXTRA PRACTICE for Lesson 1.7, p. 938

ONLINE QUIZ at classzone.com

Extension

Use after Lesson 1.7

Determine Whether a Relation Is a Function

GOAL Determine whether a relation is a function when the relation is represented by a table or a graph.

Key Vocabulary
- **relation,** *p. 49*

A **relation** is any pairing of a set of inputs with a set of outputs. Every function is a relation, but not every relation is a function. A relation is a function if for every input there is exactly one output.

EXAMPLE 1 Determine whether a relation is a function

Determine whether the relation is a function.

a.

Input	4	4	5	6	7
Output	0	1	2	3	4

b.

Input	3	5	7	9
Output	1	2	3	2

Solution

a. The input 4 has two different outputs, 0 and 1. So, the relation is *not* a function.

b. Every input has exactly one output, so the relation is a function.

USING THE GRAPH OF A RELATION You can use the *vertical line test* to determine whether a relation represented by a graph is a function. When a relation is *not* a function, its graph contains at least two points with the same x-coordinate and different y-coordinates. Those points lie on a vertical line.

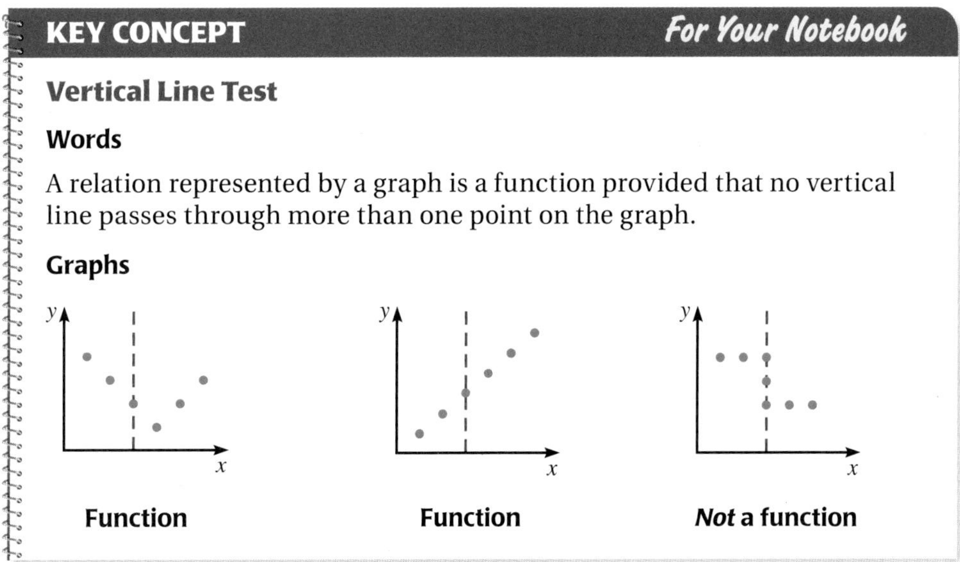

KEY CONCEPT
For Your Notebook
Vertical Line Test
Words
A relation represented by a graph is a function provided that no vertical line passes through more than one point on the graph.
Graphs
y
x
Function
y
x
Function
y
x
Not a function

EXAMPLE 2 Use the vertical line test

Determine whether the graph represents a function.

a.

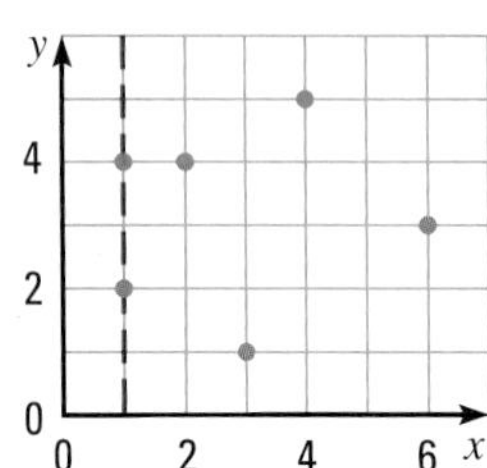

You can draw a vertical line through the points (1, 2) and (1, 4). The graph does *not* represent a function.

Animated Algebra at classzone.com

b.

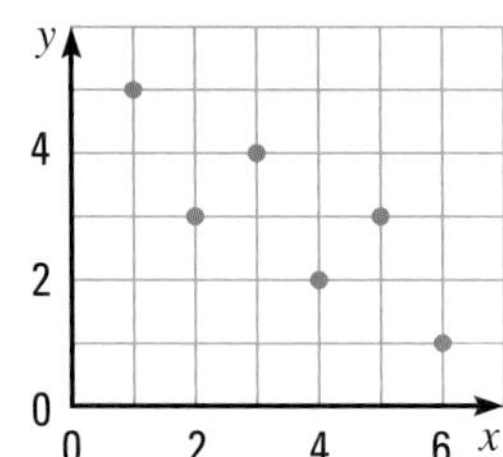

No vertical line can be drawn through more than one point. The graph represents a function.

PRACTICE

EXAMPLE 1 on p. 49 for Exs. 1–3

IDENTIFYING FUNCTIONS **Determine whether the relation is a function.**

1.

Input	Output
0	1
2	6
5	12
7	5
8	4

2.

Input	Output
3	7
4	8
4	9
5	10
6	11

3.

Input	Output
0.7	1.9
1.2	2.4
3.5	4.7
7.5	8.7
7.5	9.7

EXAMPLE 2 on p. 50 for Exs. 4–6

IDENTIFYING FUNCTIONS **Determine whether the graph represents a function.**

4.

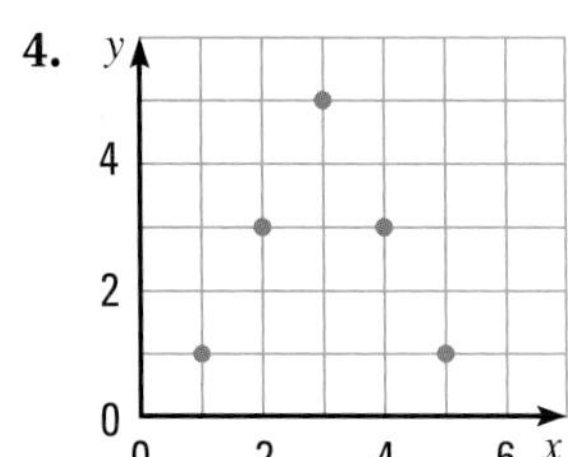

5.

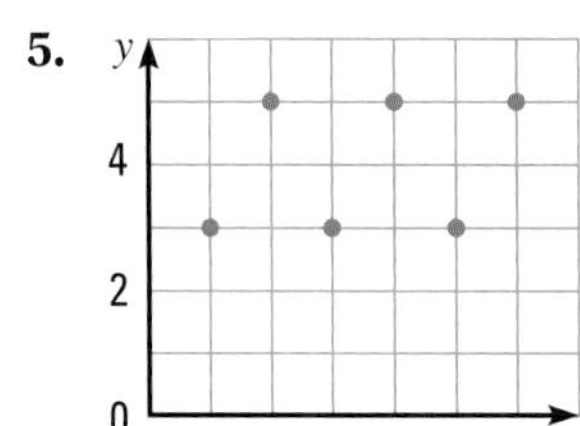

6.

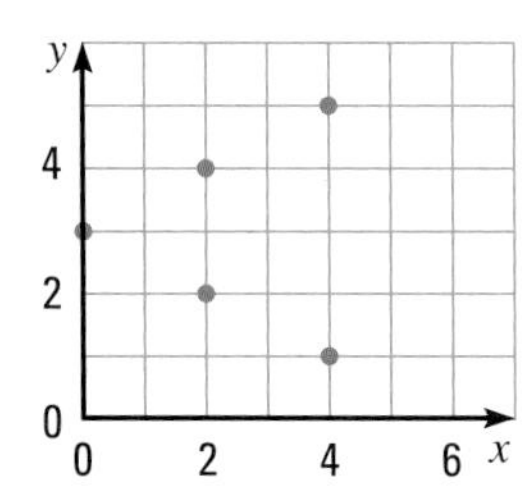

REASONING **Tell whether the pairing of x-values and y-values is necessarily a function. *Explain* your reasoning.**

7. A teacher makes a table that lists the number x of letters in the first name and the number y of letters in the last name of each student in the class.
8. Your doctor records your height x (in inches) and your weight y (in pounds) each time you have a medical exam.
9. You have a record of your age x (in years) and your height y (in inches) on each of your birthdays since you were born.

MIXED REVIEW of Problem Solving

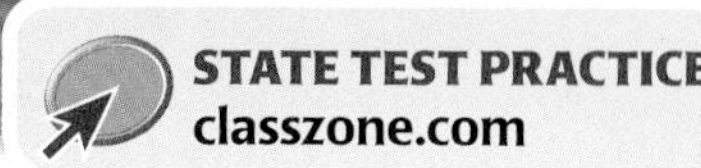

Lessons 1.5–1.7

1. **MULTI-STEP PROBLEM** A pizza shop charges \$7 for a large cheese pizza plus \$.95 for each topping.
   a. Use a verbal model to write an equation for the total cost C (in dollars) of a pizza with n toppings.
   b. The pizza shop offers 10 toppings. Write an input-output table for the total cost (in dollars) of a pizza as a function of the number n of toppings. *Explain* why the table represents a function and describe the domain and range of the function.
   c. You have \$15 to spend on a large pizza. What is the greatest number of toppings you can afford?

2. **SHORT RESPONSE** Your class is planning a car wash. You need \$75 worth of materials.

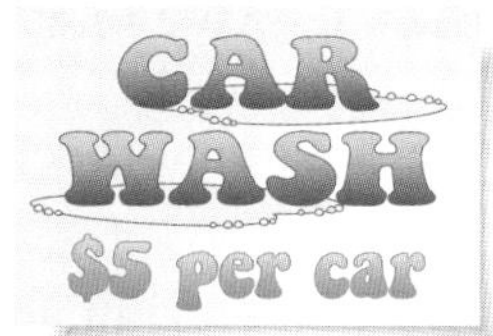

   a. Use a verbal model to write an equation that relates your profit to the number of cars you wash. Find your profit if you wash 120 cars.
   b. Does doubling the number of cars you wash double your profit? *Explain*.

3. **MULTI-STEP PROBLEM** You are painting a room in a community center. The room has four walls that are each 9 feet high and 25 feet long. There are two rectangular windows and two rectangular doors that do not need to be painted. Each window is 3.5 feet wide and 4 feet high. Each door is 3.5 feet wide and 7 feet high.
   a. Find the combined area of the windows and doors.
   b. Find the combined area of all four walls, excluding the windows and the doors.
   c. A gallon of paint covers about 400 square feet. How many one-gallon cans of paint will you need in order to give the room one coat of paint?
   d. The paint costs \$24.95 per gallon. How much will it cost for one coat of paint?

4. **GRIDDED ANSWER** You consider 68°F to be a comfortable room temperature. The temperature in a room is 18°C. How many degrees Celsius should you raise the temperature so that it will be 68°F?

5. **SHORT RESPONSE** Your family is driving from Charleston, South Carolina, to Jacksonville, Florida, a total distance of about 250 miles. You leave Charleston at 1:00 P.M. You travel at an average speed of 55 miles per hour without stopping. Will you get to Jacksonville before the 5:00 P.M. rush hour? *Explain*.

6. **GRIDDED ANSWER** A person invests \$1200 in an account earning 3% simple annual interest. How much will be in the account after 2 years?

7. **OPEN-ENDED** Write a problem that involves a real-world situation and that can be solved using the formula for distance traveled. Solve the problem and explain what the solution means in the situation.

8. **EXTENDED RESPONSE** You pay \$40 per hour for windsurfing lessons and rent equipment for \$20 per hour. The cost (in dollars) of lessons and the cost (in dollars) of rentals are both functions of the time (in hours).
   a. Write a rule for each function.
   b. Let the domains of the functions be the whole numbers from 0 to 6. Graph each function.
   c. You rent equipment for every lesson you take. What function gives your total cost? How would the graph of this function compare with the graphs in part (b)?

1 CHAPTER SUMMARY

Animated Algebra
classzone.com
Electronic Function Library

BIG IDEAS — For Your Notebook

Big Idea 1

Writing and Evaluating Algebraic Expressions

The cost of admission for one student at a planetarium is \$6. You can use a verbal model to write an expression for the total cost of admission for any number of students.

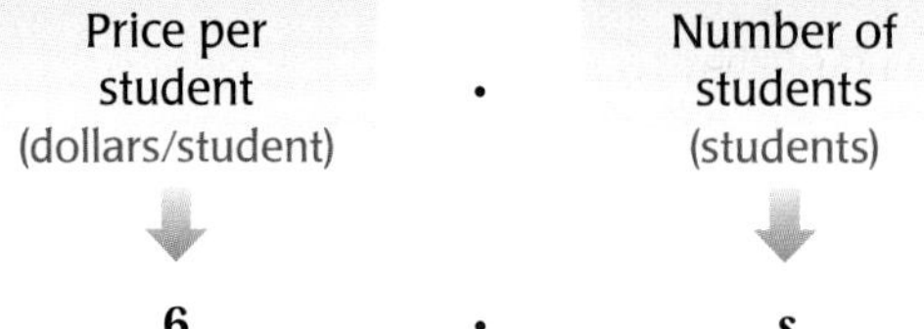

An expression is $6s$. Because $\frac{\text{dollars}}{\cancel{\text{student}}} \cdot \cancel{\text{students}} =$ dollars, the expression produces an answer in dollars. The expression is reasonable.

Big Idea 2

Using Expressions to Write Equations and Inequalities

You can use symbols to write an equation or inequality that compares the expression $6s$ to another expression.

The total cost of admission to the planetarium for s students at a rate of \$6 per student is \$150.

$6s = 150$ **Equation**

The total cost of admission to the planetarium for s students at a rate of \$6 per student is no more than \$150.

$6s \le 150$ **Inequality**

Big Idea 3

Representing Functions as Verbal Rules, Equations, Tables, and Graphs

You can use a verbal description, an equation, a table, or a graph to represent a function.

Words The total cost (in dollars) of admission to the planetarium is 6 times the number of students.

Equation

$C = 6s$

Table

Input, s	Output, C
0	0
1	6
2	12
3	18

Graph

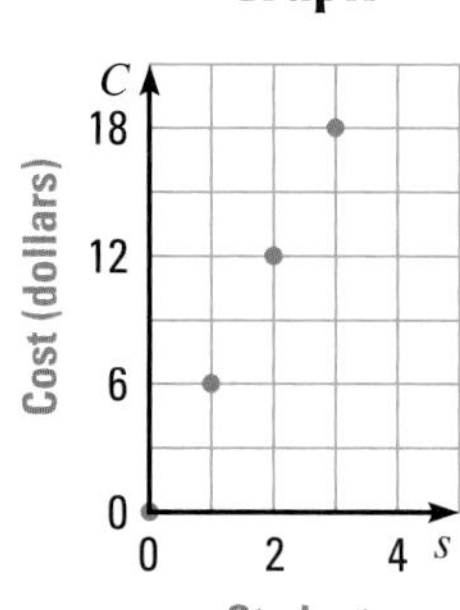

1 CHAPTER REVIEW

@HomeTutor
classzone.com
• Multi-Language Glossary
• Vocabulary practice

REVIEW KEY VOCABULARY

- variable, *p. 2*
- algebraic expression, *p. 2*
- evaluate an algebraic expression, *p. 2*
- power, exponent, base, *p. 3*
- order of operations, *p. 8*
- verbal model, *p. 16*
- rate, unit rate, *p. 17*
- equation, inequality, *p. 21*
- open sentence, *p. 21*
- solution of an equation or inequality, *p. 22*
- formula, *p. 30*
- function, *p. 35*
- input, output, *p. 35*
- domain, range, *p. 35*
- independent variable, *p. 36*
- dependent variable, *p. 36*

VOCABULARY EXERCISES

In Exercises 1–3, copy and complete the statement.

1. In the power 7^{12}, _?_ is the base and _?_ is the exponent.
2. A(n) _?_ is a statement that contains the symbol =.
3. A(n) _?_ is an expression that includes at least one variable.
4. **WRITING** *Describe* how you can tell by looking at the graph of a function which variable is the input variable and which is the output variable.

REVIEW EXAMPLES AND EXERCISES

Use the review examples and exercises below to check your understanding of the concepts you have learned in each lesson of Chapter 1.

1.1 Evaluate Expressions *pp. 2–7*

EXAMPLE

Evaluate $6 - n$ when $n = 4$.

$6 - n = 6 - 4$ **Substitute 4 for *n*.**

$= 2$ **Simplify.**

EXERCISES

EXAMPLES 1, 4, and 5 on pp. 2–4 for Exs. 5–12

Evaluate the expression.

5. $3 + x$ when $x = 13$
6. $y - 2$ when $y = 18$
7. $\frac{20}{k}$ when $k = 2$
8. $40w$ when $w = 0.5$
9. z^2 when $z = 20$
10. w^3 when $w = 0.1$
11. **DVD STORAGE** A DVD storage sleeve has the shape of a square with an edge length of 5 inches. What is the area of the front of the sleeve?
12. **NOTEPAPER** You store square notepaper in a cube-shaped box with an inside edge length of 3 inches. What is the volume of the box?

1 CHAPTER REVIEW

1.2 Apply Order of Operations

pp. 8–12

EXAMPLE

Evaluate $(5 + 3)^2 \div 2 \times 3$.

$(5 + 3)^2 \div 2 \times 3 = 8^2 \div 2 \times 3$	**Add within parentheses.**
$= 64 \div 2 \times 3$	**Evaluate power.**
$= 32 \times 3$	**Divide.**
$= 96$	**Multiply.**

EXERCISES

EXAMPLES 1, 2, and 3 on pp. 8–9 for Exs. 13–21

Evaluate the expression.

13. $12 - 6 \div 2$

14. $1 + 2 \cdot 9^2$

15. $3 + 2^3 - 6 \div 2$

16. $15 - (4 + 3^2)$

17. $\frac{20 - 12}{5^2 - 1}$

18. $50 - [7 + (3^2 \div 2)]$

Evaluate the expression when $x = 4$.

19. $15x - 8$

20. $3x^2 + 4$

21. $2(x - 1)^2$

1.3 Write Expressions

pp. 15–20

EXAMPLE

Write an expression for the entry fee in a jazz band competition if there is a base fee of $50 and a charge of $1 per member.

Write a verbal model. Then translate the verbal model into an algebraic expression. Let n represent the number of band members.

Base fee (dollars) + Cost per member (dollars/member) • Number of members (members)

$50 + 1 \cdot n$

▶ An expression for the entry fee (in dollars) is $50 + n$.

EXERCISES

EXAMPLES 1, 2, and 3 on pp. 15–16 for Exs. 22–27

Translate the verbal phrase into an expression.

22. The sum of a number k and 7

23. 5 less than a number z

24. The quotient of a number k and 12

25. 3 times the square of a number x

26. TOLL ROADS A toll road charges trucks a toll of $3 per axle. Write an expression for the total toll for a truck.

27. SCHOOL SUPPLIES You purchase some notebooks for $2.95 each and a package of pens for $2.19. Write an expression for the total amount (in dollars) that you spend.

1.4 Write Equations and Inequalities

pp. 21–26

EXAMPLE

Write an inequality for the sentence "The sum of 3 and twice a number k is no more than 15". Then check whether 4 is a solution of the inequality.

An inequality is $3 + 2k \le 15$.

To check whether 4 is a solution of the inequality, substitute 4 for k.

$3 + 2(4) \overset{?}{\le} 15$ **Substitute 4 for *k*.**

$11 \le 15$ ✓ **The solution checks. So, 4 is a solution.**

EXERCISES

EXAMPLES 1 and 2 on pp. 21–22 for Exs. 28–32

Write an equation or an inequality.

28. The product of a number z and 12 is 60.

29. The sum of 13 and a number t is at least 24.

Check whether the given number is a solution of the equation or inequality.

30. $3x - 4 = 10$; 5 **31.** $4y - 2 \ge 2$; 3 **32.** $2d + 4 < 9d - 7$; 3

1.5 Use a Problem Solving Plan

pp. 28–33

EXAMPLE

A rectangular banner is 12 feet long and has an area of 60 square feet. What is the perimeter of the banner?

STEP 1 **Read and Understand** You know the length of the rectangular banner and its area. You want to find the perimeter.

STEP 2 **Make a Plan** Use the area formula for a rectangle to find the width. Then use the perimeter formula for a rectangle.

STEP 3 **Solve the Problem** Substituting 12 for ℓ in the formula $A = \ell w$, $60 = 12w$. Because $12 \cdot 5 = 60$, $w = 5$. Then substituting 12 for ℓ and 5 for w in the formula $P = 2\ell + 2w$, $P = 2(12) + 2(5) = 34$ feet.

STEP 4 **Look Back** Use estimation. Since $\ell \approx 10$ and $A = 60$, $w \approx 6$. Then $P \approx 2(10) + 2(6) = 32$ feet, so your answer is reasonable.

EXERCISES

EXAMPLES 1, 2, and 3 on p. 28–30 for Exs. 33–34

33. U.S. HISTORY The flag that inspired the national anthem was a rectangle 30 feet wide and 42 feet long. Pieces of the flag have been lost. It is now 30 feet wide and 34 feet long. How many square feet have been lost?

34. PATTERNS A grocery clerk stacks three rows of cans of fruit for a display. Each of the top two rows has 2 fewer cans than the row beneath it. There are 30 cans altogether. How many cans are there in each row?

1 CHAPTER REVIEW

1.6 Represent Functions as Rules and Tables *pp. 35–40*

EXAMPLE

The domain of the function $y = 3x - 5$ is 2, 3, 4, and 5. Make a table for the function, then identify the range of the function.

x	2	3	4	5
$y = 3x - 5$	$3(2) - 5 = 1$	$3(3) - 5 = 4$	$3(4) - 5 = 7$	$3(5) - 5 = 10$

The range of the function is 1, 4, 7, and 10.

EXERCISES

EXAMPLES 1, 3, and 4 on p. 35–37 for Exs. 35–38

Make a table for the function. Identify the range of the function.

35. $y = x - 5$
Domain: 10, 12, 15, 20, 21

36. $y = 3x + 1$
Domain: 0, 2, 3, 5, 10

Write a rule for the function.

37.

Input, x	0	2	4	5
Output, y	4	6	8	9

38.

Input, x	0	3	4	6
Output, y	0	15	20	30

1.7 Represent Functions as Graphs *pp. 43–48*

EXAMPLE

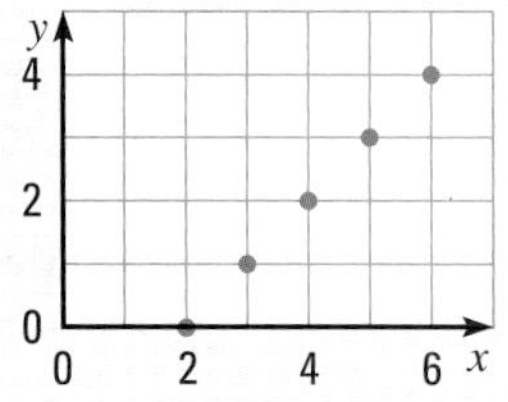

Write a rule for the function represented by the graph. Identify the domain and the range of the function.

Make a table for the graph.

x	2	3	4	5	6
y	0	1	2	3	4

Each y-value is 2 less than the corresponding x-value. A rule for the function is $y = x - 2$. The domain is 2, 3, 4, 5, and 6. The range is 0, 1, 2, 3, and 4.

EXERCISES

EXAMPLES 1, 3, and 4 on pp. 43–45 for Exs. 39–40

39. Graph the function $y = 4x - 3$ with domain 1, 2, 3, 4, and 5.

40. Write a rule for the function represented by the graph. Identify the domain and the range of the function.

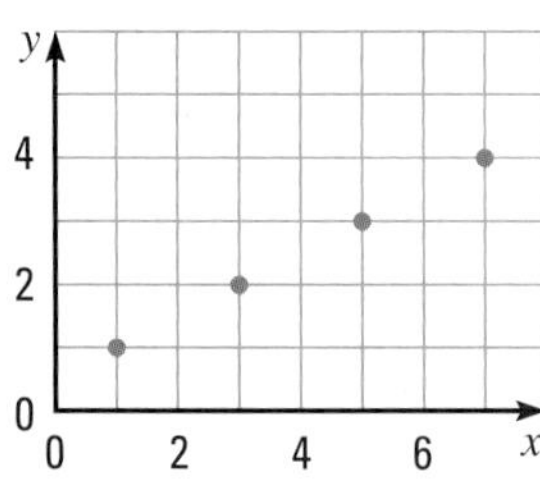

Now

In Chapter 2, you will apply the big ideas listed below and reviewed in the Chapter Summary on page 120. You will also use the key vocabulary listed below.

Big Ideas

1. **Performing operations with real numbers**
2. **Applying properties of real numbers**
3. **Classifying and reasoning with real numbers**

KEY VOCABULARY

- whole numbers, integers, *p. 64*
- rational number, *p. 64*
- opposites, absolute value, *p. 66*
- conditional statement, *p. 66*
- additive identity, *p. 76*
- additive inverse, *p. 76*
- multiplicative identity, *p. 89*
- equivalent expressions, *p. 96*
- distributive property, *p. 96*
- term, coefficient, constant term, like terms, *p. 97*
- multiplicative inverse, *p. 103*
- square root, radicand, *p. 110*
- perfect square, *p. 111*
- irrational number, *p. 111*
- real numbers, *p. 112*

Why?

You can use multiple representations to solve a problem about a real-world situation. For example, you can write an equation and make a table to find a skydiver's altitude over time.

Animated Algebra

The animation illustrated below for Exercise 54 on page 93 helps you answer this question: How does the time spent in free fall after a skydiver reaches terminal velocity affect the altitude of the skydiver?

A skydiver in freefall wants to open the parachute at an altitude of 2500 feet.

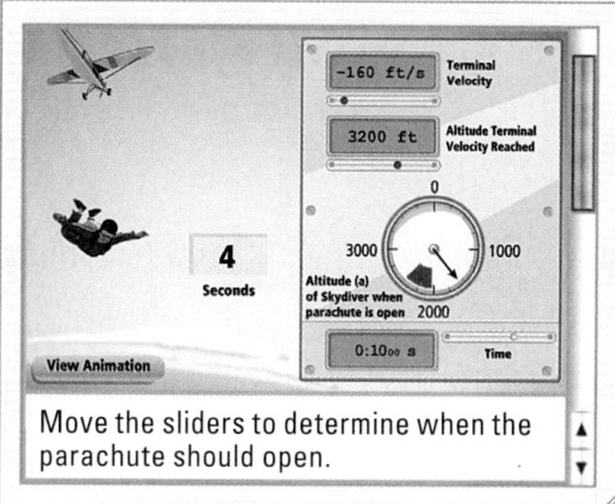

Move the sliders to determine when the parachute should open.

Animated Algebra at classzone.com

Other animations for Chapter 2: pages 73, 80, 90, and 98

2.1 Use Integers and Rational Numbers

Before You performed operations with whole numbers.

Now You will graph and compare positive and negative numbers.

Why? So you can compare temperatures, as in Ex. 58.

Key Vocabulary
- **whole numbers**
- **integers**
- **rational number**
- **opposites**
- **absolute value**
- **conditional statement**

Whole numbers are the numbers 0, 1, 2, 3, . . . and **integers** are the numbers . . . , −3, −2, −1, 0, 1, 2, 3, ... (The dots indicate that the numbers continue without end in both directions.) **Positive integers** are integers that are greater than 0. **Negative integers** are integers that are less than 0. The integer 0 is neither negative nor positive.

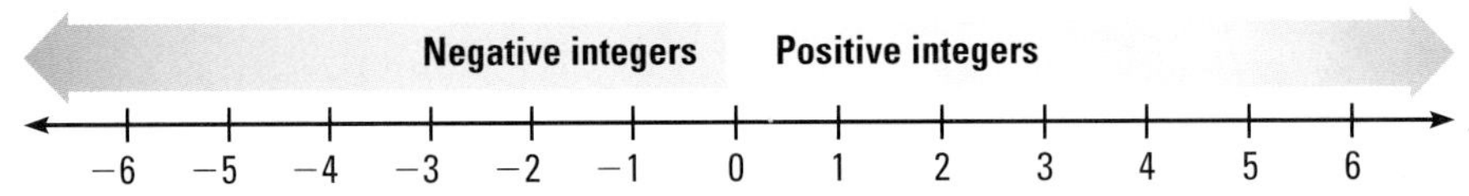

Zero is neither negative nor positive.

EXAMPLE 1 Graph and compare integers

Graph −3 and −4 on a number line. Then tell which number is greater.

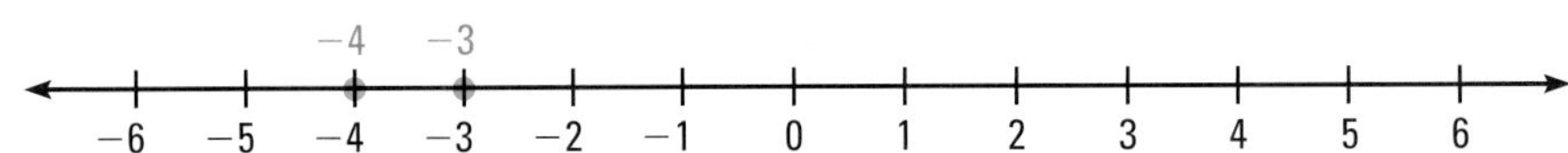

▶ On the number line, −3 is to the right of −4. So, $-3 > -4$.

RATIONAL NUMBERS The integers belong to the set of *rational numbers*. A **rational number** is a number $\frac{a}{b}$ where a and b are integers and $b \neq 0$. For example, $-\frac{1}{2}$ is a rational number because it can be written as $\frac{-1}{2}$ or $\frac{1}{-2}$. The rational numbers belong to the set of numbers called the *real numbers*.

READING Although you can write a negative fraction in different ways, you usually write it with the negative sign in front of the fraction.

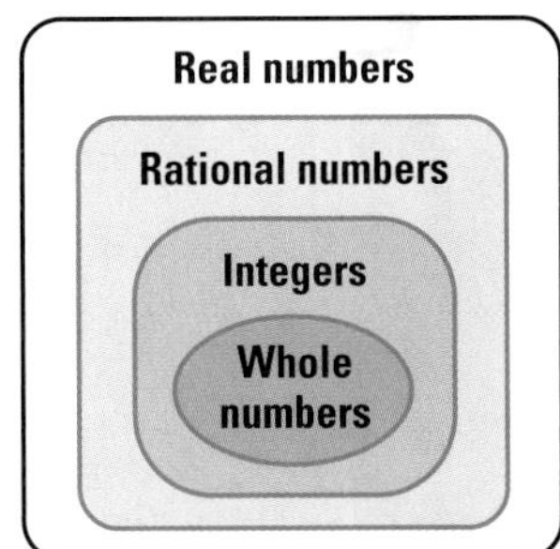

✓ GUIDED PRACTICE for Example 1

Graph the numbers on a number line. Then tell which number is greater.

1. 4 and 0 **2.** 2 and −5 **3.** −1 and −6

REVIEW FRACTIONS For help with writing fractions as decimals, see p. 916.

DECIMALS In decimal form, a rational number either terminates or repeats. For example, $\frac{3}{4} = 0.75$ is a *terminating decimal*, and $\frac{1}{3} = 0.333\ldots$ is a *repeating decimal*.

EXAMPLE 2 Classify numbers

Tell whether each of the following numbers is a whole number, an integer, or a rational number: 5, 0.6, $-2\frac{2}{3}$, and −24.

JUSTIFY AN ANSWER The number 0.6 is a rational number because it can be written as a quotient of two integers: $\frac{3}{5}$.

Number	Whole number?	Integer?	Rational number?
5	Yes	Yes	Yes
0.6	No	No	Yes
$-2\frac{2}{3}$	No	No	Yes
−24	No	Yes	Yes

EXAMPLE 3 Order rational numbers

ASTRONOMY A star's color index is a measure of the temperature of the star. The greater the color index, the cooler the star. Order the stars in the table from hottest to coolest.

Star	Rigel	Arneb	Denebola	Shaula
Color index	−0.03	0.21	0.09	−0.22

Solution

Begin by graphing the numbers on a number line.

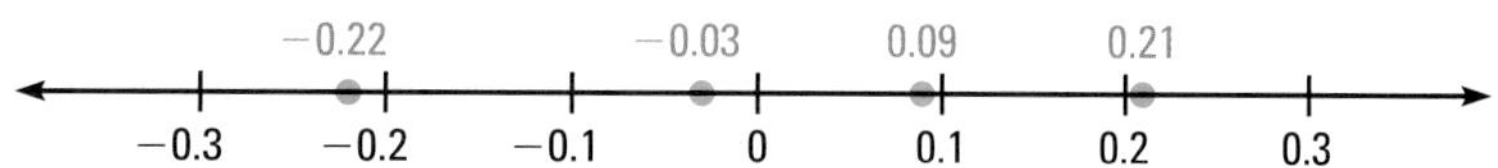

Read the numbers from left to right: −0.22, −0.03, 0.09, 0.21.

▶ From hottest to coolest, the stars are Shaula, Rigel, Denebola, and Arneb.

✓ GUIDED PRACTICE for Examples 2 and 3

Tell whether each number in the list is a whole number, an integer, or a rational number. Then order the numbers from least to greatest.

4. 3, −1.2, −2, 0

5. 4.5, $-\frac{3}{4}$, −2.1, 0.5

6. 3.6, −1.5, −0.31, −2.8

7. $\frac{1}{6}$, 1.75, $-\frac{2}{3}$, 0

OPPOSITES Two numbers that are the same distance from 0 on a number line but are on opposite sides of 0 are called **opposites**. For example, 4 and -4 are opposites because they are both 4 units from 0 but are on opposite sides of 0. The opposite of 0 is 0. You read the expression $-a$ as "the opposite of a."

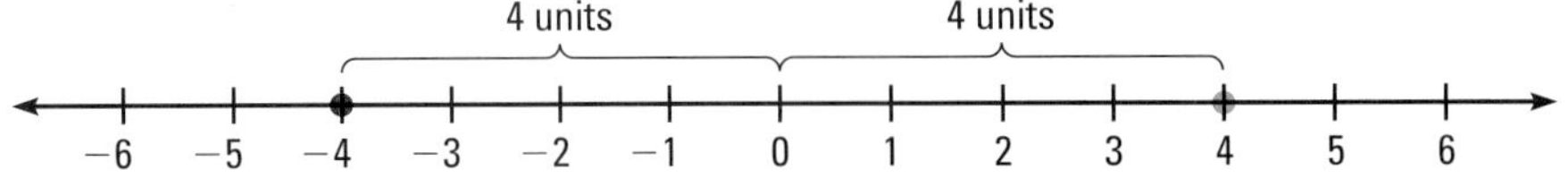

EXAMPLE 4 Find opposites of numbers

READING
Do not assume that $-a$ is a negative number. Notice that for $a = -2.5$, $-a = 2.5$.

a. If $a = -2.5$, then $-a = -(-2.5) = 2.5$.

b. If $a = \frac{3}{4}$, then $-a = -\frac{3}{4}$.

ABSOLUTE VALUE The **absolute value** of a number a is the distance between a and 0 on a number line. The symbol $|a|$ represents the absolute value of a.

KEY CONCEPT *For Your Notebook*

Absolute Value of a Number

Words If a is positive, then $|a| = a$. **Example** $|2| = 2$

Words If a is 0, then $|a| = 0$. **Example** $|0| = 0$

Words If a is negative, then $|a| = -a$. **Example** $|-2| = -(-2) = 2$

EXAMPLE 5 Find absolute values of numbers

AVOID ERRORS
The absolute value of a number is never negative. If a number a is negative, then its absolute value, $-a$, is positive.

a. If $a = -\frac{2}{3}$, then $|a| = \left|-\frac{2}{3}\right| = -\left(-\frac{2}{3}\right) = \frac{2}{3}$.

b. If $a = 3.2$, then $|a| = |3.2| = 3.2$.

CONDITIONAL STATEMENTS A **conditional statement** has a hypothesis and a conclusion. An **if-then statement** is a form of a conditional statement. The *if* part contains the hypothesis. The *then* part contains the conclusion.

conditional statement

If a is a positive number, then $|a| = a$.

hypothesis **conclusion**

In mathematics, if-then statements are either true or false. An if-then statement is true if the conclusion is always true when the hypothesis is satisfied. An if-then statement is false if for just one example, called a **counterexample**, the conclusion is false when the hypothesis is satisfied.

EXAMPLE 6 · Analyze a conditional statement

Identify the hypothesis and the conclusion of the statement "If a number is a rational number, then the number is an integer." Tell whether the statement is *true* or *false*. If it is false, give a counterexample.

Solution

Hypothesis: a number is a rational number

Conclusion: the number is an integer

The statement is false. The number 0.5 is a counterexample, because 0.5 is a rational number but not an integer.

✓ GUIDED PRACTICE for Examples 4, 5, and 6

For the given value of a, find $-a$ and $|a|$.

8. $a = 5.3$ **9.** $a = -7$ **10.** $a = -\frac{4}{9}$

Identify the hypothesis and the conclusion of the statement. Tell whether the statement is *true* or *false*. If it is false, give a counterexample.

11. If a number is a rational number, then the number is positive.

12. If the absolute value of a number is positive, then the number is positive.

2.1 EXERCISES

HOMEWORK KEY

○ = **WORKED-OUT SOLUTIONS on p. WS3 for Exs. 7, 29, and 53**

★ = **STANDARDIZED TEST PRACTICE Exs. 3, 4, 39, 50, 56, and 59**

SKILL PRACTICE

1. **VOCABULARY** Copy and complete: A number is a(n) _?_ if it can be written in the form $\frac{a}{b}$ where a and b are integers and $b \neq 0$.

2. **VOCABULARY** What is the opposite of −2?

3. ★ **WRITING** *Describe* the difference between whole numbers and positive integers.

4. ★ **WRITING** For a negative number x, is the absolute value of x a *positive number* or a *negative number*? *Explain.*

EXAMPLE 1 on p. 64 for Exs. 5–13

GRAPHING AND COMPARING INTEGERS Graph the numbers on a number line. Then tell which number is greater.

5. 0 and 7 **6.** 0 and −4 **(7.)** −5 and −6

8. −2 and −3 **9.** 5 and −2 **10.** −12 and 8

11. −1 and −5 **12.** 3 and −13 **13.** −20 and −2

EXAMPLES 2 and 3
on p. 65
for Exs. 14–22

CLASSIFYING AND ORDERING NUMBERS **Tell whether each number in the list is a whole number, an integer, or a rational number. Then order the numbers from least to greatest.**

14. 3, −5, −2.4, 1

15. 1.6, 1, −4, 0

16. 0.25, −0.5, 0.2, −2

17. $-\frac{2}{3}, -0.6, -1, \frac{1}{3}$

18. $-0.01, 0.1, 0, -\frac{1}{10}$

19. $16, -1.66, \frac{5}{3}, -1.6$

20. $-2.7, \frac{1}{2}, 0.3, -7$

21. $-4.99, 5, \frac{16}{3}, -5.1$

22. $-\frac{3}{5}, -0.4, -1, -0.5$

EXAMPLES 4 and 5
on p. 66
for Exs. 23–34

FINDING OPPOSITES AND ABSOLUTE VALUES **For the given value of a, find $-a$ and $|a|$.**

23. $a = 6$

24. $a = -3$

25. $a = -18$

26. $a = 0$

27. $a = 13.4$

28. $a = 2.7$

29. $a = -6.1$

30. $a = -7.9$

31. $a = -1\frac{1}{9}$

32. $a = -\frac{5}{6}$

33. $a = \frac{3}{4}$

34. $a = 1\frac{1}{3}$

EXAMPLE 6
on p. 67
for Exs. 35–38

ANALYZING CONDITIONAL STATEMENTS **Identify the hypothesis and the conclusion of the conditional statement. Tell whether the statement is *true* or *false*. If it is false, give a counterexample.**

35. If a number is a positive integer, then the number is a whole number.

36. If a number is negative, then its absolute value is negative.

37. If a number is positive, then its opposite is positive.

38. If a number is an integer, then the number is a rational number.

39. ★ **MULTIPLE CHOICE** Which number is a whole number?

Ⓐ $\left|-\frac{18}{9}\right|$ Ⓑ $-\frac{4}{3}$ Ⓒ 1.6 Ⓓ $-(-7.963)$

ERROR ANALYSIS ***Describe*** **and correct the error in the statement.**

40.

The numbers $-(-2)$, -4, $-|8|$, and -0.3 are negative numbers.

41.

The numbers $|-3.4|$, $-(-8)$, $-|-0.2|$, and 0.87 are positive numbers.

EVALUATING EXPRESSIONS **Evaluate the expression when $x = -0.75$.**

42. $-x$

43. $|x| + 0.25$

44. $|x| - 0.75$

45. $1 + |-x|$

46. $2 \cdot (-x)$

47. $(-x) \cdot 3$

48. $|x| + |x|$

49. $-x + |x|$

50. ★ **MULTIPLE CHOICE** Which number is a solution of $|x| + 1 = 1.3$?

Ⓐ −2.3 Ⓑ −0.3 Ⓒ 1.3 Ⓓ 2.3

51. **CHALLENGE** What can you conclude about the opposite of the opposite of a number? *Explain* your reasoning.

52. **CHALLENGE** For what values of a is the opposite of a greater than a? less than a? equal to a?

○ = WORKED-OUT SOLUTIONS on p. WS1

★ = STANDARDIZED TEST PRACTICE

PROBLEM SOLVING

EXAMPLE 3
on p. 65
for Exs. 53, 57

53. **GEOGRAPHY** The map shows various locations in Imperial County, California, and their elevations above or below sea level. Order the locations from lowest elevation to highest elevation.

Imperial County, CA

- Frink: −170 ft
- Fondo: −206 ft
- Alamorio: −135 ft
- Date City: 5 ft
- Calexico: 2 ft

@HomeTutor for problem solving help at classzone.com

54. **SPORTS** In golf, the goal is to have the least score among all the players. Which golf score, −8 or −12, is the better score?

@HomeTutor for problem solving help at classzone.com

EXAMPLE 5
on p. 66
for Exs. 55–56

55. **MUSIC** A guitar tuner is a device that tunes a guitar string to its exact pitch. Some tuners use the measure *cents* to indicate how far above or below the exact pitch, marked as 0 cents, the string tone is. Suppose that one string tone measures −3.4 cents, and a second string tone measures −3.8 cents. Which string tone is closer to the exact pitch? *Explain.*

56. ★ **MULTIPLE CHOICE** The change in value of a share of a stock was −\$.45 on Monday, −\$1.32 on Tuesday, \$.27 on Wednesday, and \$1.03 on Thursday. On which day was the absolute value of the change the greatest?

Ⓐ Monday Ⓑ Tuesday Ⓒ Wednesday Ⓓ Thursday

57. **MULTI-STEP PROBLEM** An equalizer on a stereo system is used to increase or decrease the intensity of sounds at different frequencies. The intensity is measured in decibels (dB), and the frequencies are measured in hertz (Hz). The table shows the intensity at different frequencies on a stereo system.

Frequency (Hz)	32	64	125	250	500	1000	2000	4000	8000
Intensity (dB)	8.8	7.1	5.8	1.5	−2.8	−1.5	2.7	2.8	2.9

a. Which frequency has the least sound intensity?

b. *Describe* the change in sound intensity as the frequency increases from 32 hertz to 8000 hertz.

58. **WEATHER** A wind chill index describes how much colder it feels outside when wind speed is considered with air temperature. The table shows the wind chill temperatures for given pairs of air temperature and wind speed.

Wind Chill Temperatures (°F)					
Wind speed (mi/h)	Air temperature (°F)				
	20	10	0	−10	−20
0	20	10	0	−10	−20
10	9	−4	−16	−28	−41
20	4	−9	−22	−35	−48
30	1	−12	−26	−39	−53

a. **Compare** Which feels colder, an air temperature of 0°F with a wind speed of 30 miles per hour, or an air temperature of −10°F with a wind speed of 10 miles per hour?

b. **Analyze** How does the wind chill temperature change under constant wind speed and decreasing air temperature? under constant air temperature and increasing wind speed?

59. ★ **EXTENDED RESPONSE** A star's apparent magnitude measures how bright the star appears to a person on Earth. A star's absolute magnitude measures its brightness if it were a distance of 33 light-years, or about 194 trillion miles, from Earth. The greater the magnitude, the dimmer the star.

Star	Arcturus	Achernar	Canopus	Capella	Sirius	Sun
Apparent magnitude	−0.04	0.46	−0.72	0.08	−1.46	−26.72
Absolute magnitude	0.2	−1.3	−2.5	0.4	1.4	4.8

Orion Constellation

a. **Order** Order the stars in the table from brightest to dimmest when viewed from Earth. Then order the stars from brightest to dimmest if they were 33 light-years from Earth.

b. **Compare** The star Rigel has an apparent magnitude of 0.12 and an absolute magnitude of −8.1. *Compare* its brightness with the Sun's brightness using both apparent magnitude and absolute magnitude.

c. **Analyze** Can you use the apparent magnitudes of two stars to predict which star is brighter in terms of absolute magnitude? *Explain* your answer using a comparison of the apparent and absolute magnitudes of two stars in the table.

60. **CHALLENGE** In an academic contest, the point values of the questions are given by the expression $50x$ where $x = 1, 2, 3$, and 4. You earn $50x$ points for a correct answer to a question and $-(50x)$ points for an incorrect answer. Order from least to greatest all the possible points you can earn when answering a question.

MIXED REVIEW

PREVIEW
Prepare for Lesson 2.2 in Exs. 61–66.

Add. *(p. 914)*

61. $\frac{1}{2} + \frac{1}{3}$

62. $\frac{5}{6} + \frac{1}{6}$

63. $2\frac{1}{2} + 1\frac{3}{4}$

Find the perimeter of the triangle or rectangle. *(p. 924)*

64.
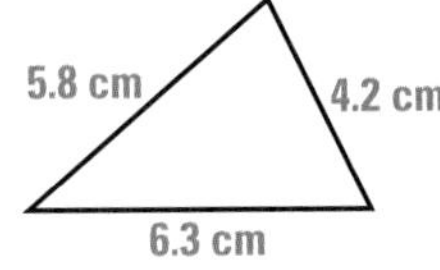

65.
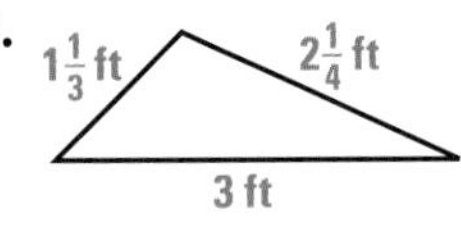

66.

Check whether the given number is a solution of the inequality. *(p. 21)*

67. $x + 2 < 3$; 2

68. $y - 8 < 6$; 13

69. $9 - 2z \leq 3$; 3

70. $2y + 3 \geq 14$; 5

71. $3 < 7x - 4$; 1

72. $2a \geq 15$; 7

Make a table for the function. Identify the range of the function. *(p. 43)*

73. $y = x - 3$
Domain: 5, 8, 14, 30

74. $y = 1.5x$
Domain: 0, 2, 6, 10

75. $y = 2x - 3$
Domain: 2, 4, 7, 11

Apply Sets to Numbers and Functions

GOAL Apply set theory to numbers and functions.

Key Vocabulary
- set
- element
- empty set
- universal set
- union
- intersection

A **set** is a collection of distinct objects. Each object in a set is called an **element** or *member* of the set. You can use *set notation* to write a set by enclosing the elements of the set in braces. For example, if A is the set of whole numbers less than 6, then $A = \{0, 1, 2, 3, 4, 5\}$.

Two special sets are the *empty set* and the *universal set.* The set with no elements is called the **empty set** and is written as $\emptyset$. The set of all elements under consideration is called the **universal set** and is written as U.

KEY CONCEPT — *For Your Notebook*

Union and Intersection of Two Sets

The **union** of two sets A and B is the set of all elements in *either* A or B and is written as $A \cup B$.

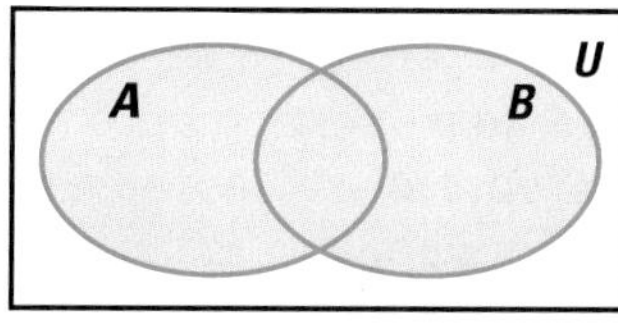

$A \cup B$

The **intersection** of two sets A and B is the set of all elements in *both* A and B and is written as $A \cap B$.

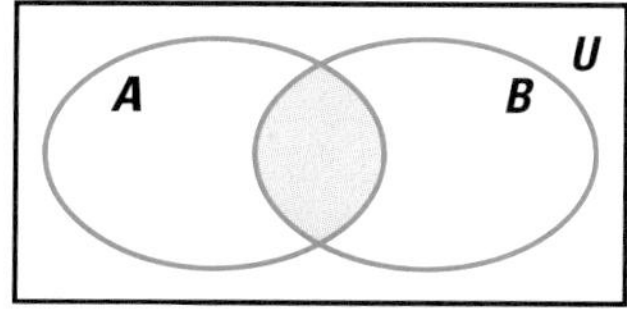

$A \cap B$

EXAMPLE 1 Find the union and intersection of two sets

Let U be the set of integers from 1 to 9. Let $A = \{2, 4, 6, 8\}$ and $B = \{2, 3, 5, 7\}$. Find (a) $A \cup B$ and (b) $A \cap B$.

Solution

a. The union of A and B consists of the elements that are in either set.

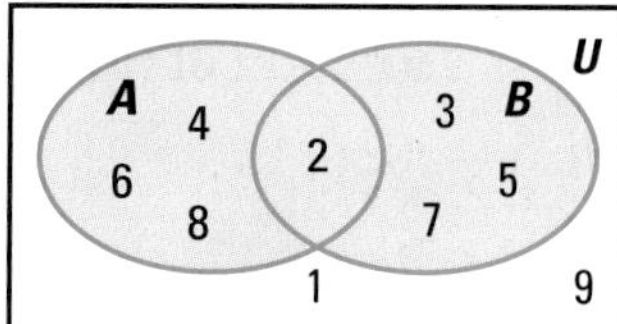

▸ $A \cup B = \{2, 3, 4, 5, 6, 7, 8\}$

b. The intersection of A and B consists of the elements that are in both sets.

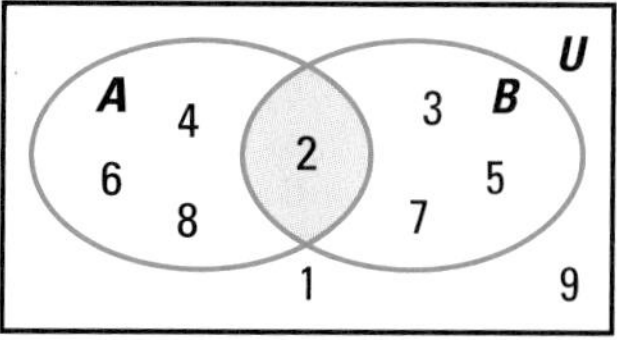

▸ $A \cap B = \{2\}$

FUNCTIONS AND SETS You can write the domain and range of a function as sets of input values and output values and the function as a set of ordered pairs, as illustrated for the mapping diagram below.

Domain
$D = \{1, 2, 3, 5\}$

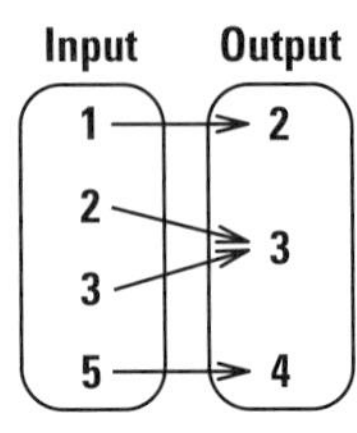

Range
$R = \{2, 3, 4\}$

$f = \{(1, 2), (2, 3), (3, 3), (5, 4)\}$

EXAMPLE 2 Write a function and its range as sets

Consider the function $y = x + 2$ with domain $D = \{0, 1, 2, 3\}$. Write the range and function using set notation.

Solution

x	0	1	2	3
y	$0 + 2 = 2$	$1 + 2 = 3$	$2 + 2 = 4$	$3 + 2 = 5$

▶ The range is $R = \{2, 3, 4, 5\}$.
The function is $f = \{(0, 2), (1, 3), (2, 4), (3, 5)\}$.

PRACTICE

EXAMPLE 1 on p. 71 for Exs. 1–4

Let U be the set of whole numbers from 0 to 10. Find $A \cup B$ and $A \cap B$ for the specified sets A and B.

1. $A = \{1, 3, 5, 7, 9\}$ and $B = \{3, 6, 9\}$
2. $A = \{1, 2, 3, 4, 5, 6\}$ and $B = \{4, 5, 6, 7, 8\}$
3. $A = \{0, 2, 4, 6, 8, 10\}$ and $B = \{1, 3, 5, 7, 9\}$
4. $A = \{0, 5, 10\}$ and $B = \{1, 4, 7, 10\}$

EXAMPLE 2 on p. 72 for Exs. 5–8

In Exercises 5–8, consider the specified function and domain. Write the range and function using set notation.

5. $y = 2x$ with domain $D = \{1, 2, 3, 4, 5\}$
6. $y = x - 1$ with domain $D = \{2, 4, 6, 8, 10\}$
7. $y = x + 3$ with domain $D = \{1, 5, 9, 13, 17\}$
8. $y = 3x + 2$ with domain $D = \{1, 2, 3, 4, 5\}$
9. Let A be the set of positive integers, and let B be the set of negative integers and 0. Find $A \cup B$ and $A \cap B$.
10. Let A be the set of integers, and let B be the set of rational numbers. Find $A \cup B$ and $A \cap B$.

Animated Algebra classzone.com

2.2 Addition of Integers

MATERIALS • algebra tiles

QUESTION **How can you use algebra tiles to find the sum of two integers?**

You can use algebra tiles to model addition of integers. Each + represents 1, and each − represents −1. Pairing a + with a − results in a sum of 0.

EXPLORE **Find the sum of two integers**

Find the sum −7 + 4.

STEP 1 Model −7 and 4 using algebra tiles.

− − − − − − −   + + + +

−7   4

STEP 2 Group pairs of positive and negative tiles. Count the remaining tiles.

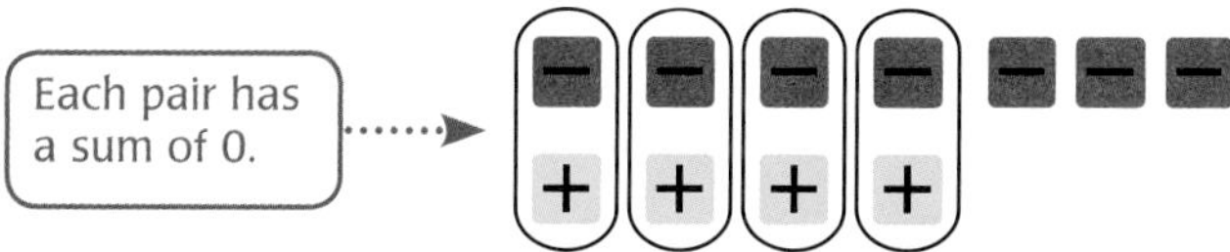

STEP 3 Copy and complete the statement: −7 + 4 = _?_.

DRAW CONCLUSIONS **Use your observations to complete these exercises**

Use algebra tiles to find the sum.

1. 3 + 8 **2.** 5 + (−1) **3.** −9 + 6 **4.** −2 + (−3)

5. −4 + 4 **6.** −7 + 5 **7.** 5 + (−7) **8.** −6 + 0

REASONING **In Exercises 9–13, answer the question and give an example from Exercises 1–8 to support your answer.**

9. Is the sum of two positive integers *positive* or *negative?*

10. Is the sum of two negative integers *positive* or *negative?*

11. Is the sum of a positive integer and a negative integer *always* positive?

12. What is the sum of an integer and its opposite?

13. What is the sum of an integer and 0?

14. In Exercises 6 and 7, the two integers being added are the same, but the order is reversed. What does this suggest about the sums $a + b$ and $b + a$ where a and b are integers?

2.2 Add Real Numbers

Before You added positive numbers.
Now You will add positive and negative numbers.
Why? So you can calculate a sports score, as in Ex. 57.

Key Vocabulary
- **additive identity**
- **additive inverse**

One way to add two real numbers is to use a number line. Start at the first number. Use the sign of the second number to decide whether to move left or right. Then use the absolute value of the second number to decide how many units to move. The number where you stop is the sum of the two numbers.

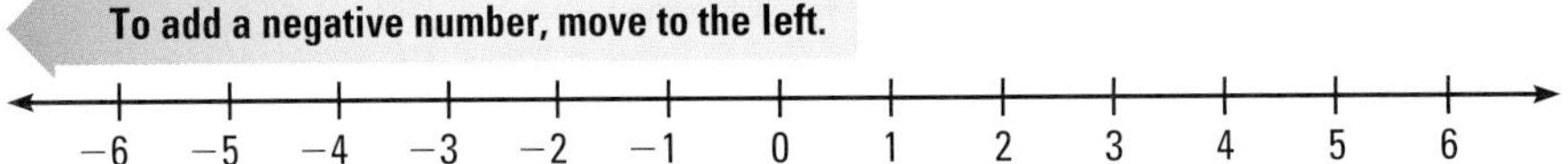
To add a positive number, move to the right.
To add a negative number, move to the left.
−6 −5 −4 −3 −2 −1 0 1 2 3 4 5 6

EXAMPLE 1 Add two integers using a number line

Use a number line to find the sum.

a. $-3 + 6$

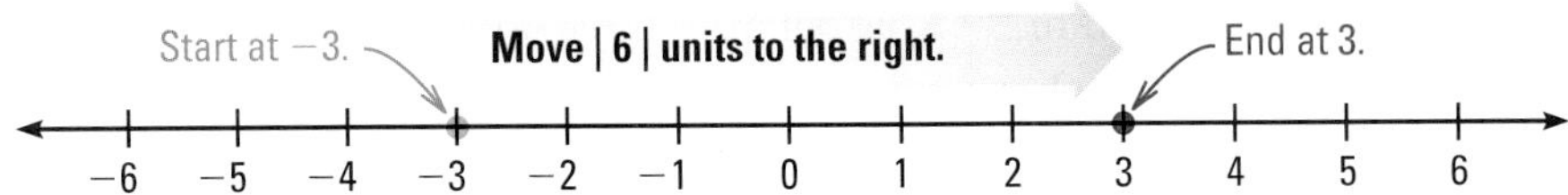
Start at −3.
Move | 6 | units to the right.
End at 3.
−6 −5 −4 −3 −2 −1 0 1 2 3 4 5 6

▸ The final position is 3. So, $-3 + 6 = 3$.

b. $-4 + (-5)$

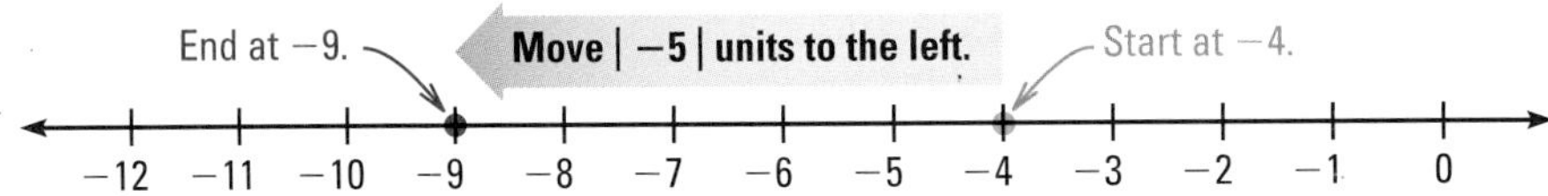
End at −9.
Move | −5 | units to the left.
Start at −4.
−12 −11 −10 −9 −8 −7 −6 −5 −4 −3 −2 −1 0

▸ The final position is −9. So, $-4 + (-5) = -9$.

✓ GUIDED PRACTICE for Example 1

Use a number line to find the sum.

1. $7 + (-2)$ **2.** $8 + (-11)$ **3.** $-8 + 4$ **4.** $-1 + (-4)$

KEY CONCEPT — *For Your Notebook*

Rules of Addition

Words To add two numbers with the *same* sign, add their absolute values. The sum has the same sign as the numbers added.

Examples $8 + 7 = 15$ $\quad -6 + (-10) = -16$

Words To add two numbers with *different* signs, subtract the lesser absolute value from the greater absolute value. The sum has the same sign as the number with the greater absolute value.

Examples $-12 + 7 = -5$ $\quad 18 + (-4) = 14$

EXAMPLE 2 Add real numbers

Find the sum.

a. $-5.3 + (-4.9) = -(|-5.3| + |-4.9|)$ **Rule of same signs**

$= -(5.3 + 4.9)$ **Take absolute values.**

$= -10.2$ **Add.**

b. $19.3 + (-12.2) = |19.3| - |-12.2|$ **Rule of different signs**

$= 19.3 - 12.2$ **Take absolute values.**

$= 7.1$ **Subtract.**

PROPERTIES OF ADDITION Notice that both $3 + (-2)$ and $-2 + 3$ have the same sum, 1. So, $3 + (-2) = -2 + 3$. This is an example of the *commutative property of addition.* The properties of addition are listed below.

KEY CONCEPT — *For Your Notebook*

Properties of Addition

COMMUTATIVE PROPERTY The order in which you add two numbers does not change the sum.

Algebra $a + b = b + a$ **Example** $3 + (-2) = -2 + 3$

ASSOCIATIVE PROPERTY The way you group three numbers in a sum does not change the sum.

Algebra $(a + b) + c = a + (b + c)$ **Example** $(-3 + 2) + 1 = -3 + (2 + 1)$

IDENTITY PROPERTY The sum of a number and 0 is the number.

Algebra $a + 0 = 0 + a = a$ **Example** $-5 + 0 = -5$

INVERSE PROPERTY The sum of a number and its opposite is 0.

Algebra $a + (-a) = -a + a = 0$ **Example** $-6 + 6 = 0$

The identity property states that the sum of a number a and 0 is a. The number 0 is the **additive identity**. The inverse property states that the sum of a number a and its opposite is 0. The opposite of a is its **additive inverse**.

EXAMPLE 3 Identify properties of addition

Statement	Property illustrated
a. $(x + 9) + 2 = x + (9 + 2)$	Associative property of addition
b. $8.3 + (-8.3) = 0$	Inverse property of addition
c. $-y + 0.7 = 0.7 + (-y)$	Commutative property of addition

EXAMPLE 4 Solve a multi-step problem

BUSINESS The table shows the annual profits of two piano manufacturers. Which manufacturer had the greater total profit for the three years?

Year	Profit (millions) for manufacturer A	Profit (millions) for manufacturer B
1	–\$5.8	–\$6.5
2	\$8.7	\$7.9
3	\$6.8	\$8.2

Solution

STEP 1 **Calculate** the total profit for each manufacturer.

ANOTHER WAY You can also find the sums by adding from left to right, as shown for manufacturer A: $-5.8 + 8.7 + 6.8 = 2.9 + 6.8 = 9.7$.

Manufacturer A:

$$\text{Total profit} = -5.8 + 8.7 + 6.8$$
$$= -5.8 + (8.7 + 6.8)$$
$$= -5.8 + 15.5$$
$$= 9.7$$

Manufacturer B:

$$\text{Total profit} = -6.5 + 7.9 + 8.2$$
$$= -6.5 + (7.9 + 8.2)$$
$$= -6.5 + 16.1$$
$$= 9.6$$

STEP 2 **Compare** the total profits: $9.7 > 9.6$.

▶ Manufacturer A had the greater total profit.

✓ GUIDED PRACTICE for Examples 2, 3, and 4

Find the sum.

5. $-0.6 + (-6.7)$ **6.** $10.1 + (-16.2)$ **7.** $-13.1 + 8.7$

Identify the property being illustrated.

8. $7 + (-7) = 0$ **9.** $-12 + 0 = -12$ **10.** $4 + 8 = 8 + 4$

11. WHAT IF? In Example 4, suppose that the profits for year 4 are $-\$1.7$ million for manufacturer A and $-\$2.1$ million for manufacturer B. Which manufacturer has the greater total profit for the four years?

2.2 EXERCISES

HOMEWORK KEY

○ = **WORKED-OUT SOLUTIONS** on p. WS3 for Exs. 13, 35, and 55

★ = **STANDARDIZED TEST PRACTICE** Exs. 2, 50, 56, 57, and 58

SKILL PRACTICE

1. **VOCABULARY** What number is called the additive identity?

2. ★ **WRITING** Without actually adding, how can you tell if the sum of two numbers will be zero?

EXAMPLE 1 on p. 74 for Exs. 3–11

USING A NUMBER LINE **Use a number line to find the sum.**

3. $-11 + 3$
4. $-1 + 6$
5. $13 + (-7)$
6. $5 + (-10)$
7. $-9 + (-4)$
8. $-8 + (-2)$
9. $-14 + 8$
10. $6 + (-12)$
11. $-11 + (-9)$

EXAMPLE 2 on p. 75 for Exs. 12–25

FINDING SUMS **Find the sum.**

12. $-2.4 + 3.9$
13. $-8.7 + 4.2$
14. $4.3 + (-10.2)$
15. $9.1 + (-2.5)$
16. $-6.5 + (-7.1)$
17. $-11.4 + (-3.8)$
18. $4\frac{1}{5} + \left(-9\frac{1}{2}\right)$
19. $8\frac{2}{3} + \left(-1\frac{3}{5}\right)$
20. $-12\frac{3}{4} + 6\frac{9}{10}$
21. $-\frac{4}{9} + 1\frac{4}{5}$
22. $-3\frac{3}{7} + \left(-14\frac{3}{4}\right)$
23. $-7\frac{1}{12} + \left(-13\frac{7}{8}\right)$

ERROR ANALYSIS ***Describe*** **and correct the error in finding the sum.**

24. $-13 + (-15) = 28$ ✗

25. $17 + (-31) = -48$ ✗

EXAMPLE 3 on p. 76 for Exs. 26–31

IDENTIFYING PROPERTIES **Identify the property being illustrated.**

26. $-3 + 3 = 0$
27. $(-6 + 1) + 7 = -6 + (1 + 7)$
28. $9 + (-1) = -1 + 9$
29. $-8 + 0 = -8$
30. $(x + 2) + 3 = x + (2 + 3)$
31. $y + (-4) = -4 + y$

EXAMPLE 4 on p. 76 for Exs. 32–37

FINDING SUMS **Find the sum.**

32. $-13 + 5 + (-7)$
33. $-18 + (-12) + (-19)$
34. $0.47 + (-1.8) + (-3.8)$
35. $-2.6 + (-3.4) + 7.6$
36. $-3\frac{1}{2} + \left(-7\frac{2}{5}\right) + \left(-9\frac{3}{10}\right)$
37. $8\frac{2}{3} + \left(-6\frac{3}{5}\right) + 3\frac{1}{4}$

EVALUATING EXPRESSIONS **Evaluate the expression for the given value of *x*.**

38. $3 + x + (-7);\ x = 6$
39. $x + (-5) + 5;\ x = -3$
40. $9.6 + (-x) + 2.3;\ x = -8.5$
41. $-1.7 + (-5.4) + (-x);\ x = 2.4$
42. $1\frac{1}{4} + |x| + \left(-3\frac{1}{2}\right);\ x = -8\frac{2}{5}$
43. $|x| + \left(-3\frac{1}{4}\right) + \left(7\frac{3}{10}\right);\ x = -3\frac{1}{3}$

FINDING SOLUTIONS Solve the equation using mental math.

44. $x + (-9) + 9 = 8$

45. $(-8) + x + (-2) = -10$

46. $x + (-2.8) + 9.2 = 0$

47. $-8.7 + x + 1.3 = 0$

TRANSLATING PHRASES In Exercises 48 and 49, translate the verbal phrase into an addition expression. Then find the sum.

48. The sum of the absolute value of -4 and the additive identity

49. The sum of the opposite of -18 and its additive inverse

50. ★ **MULTIPLE CHOICE** If $a + b$ is negative, which statement must be true?

Ⓐ $a < 0, b < 0$ Ⓑ $a < 0$ Ⓒ $a < 0, b > 0$ Ⓓ $a < -b$

51. **CHALLENGE** Consider the expression $|x| + (-x)$. Write a simplified expression for the sum if x is positive. Then write a simplified expression for the sum if x is negative. Give examples to support your answers.

52. **CHALLENGE** Evaluate $-50 + (-49) + (-48) + \cdots + 48 + 49 + 50$. *Explain* how you can use the properties of addition to obtain the sum.

PROBLEM SOLVING

EXAMPLE 1 on p. 74 for Ex. 53

53. **WEATHER** The temperature in your city at 6 A.M. was $-8°F$ and increased by $15°F$ by noon. What was the temperature at noon?

@HomeTutor for problem solving help at classzone.com

EXAMPLE 2 on p. 75 for Exs. 54–55

54. **PARKING GARAGES** The bottom level of a parking garage has an elevation of -45 feet. The top level of the garage is 100 feet higher. What is the elevation of the top level?

@HomeTutor for problem solving help at classzone.com

55. **MULTI-STEP PROBLEM** In optometry, the strength of an eyeglass lens is measured in diopters. Two lenses can be combined to create a new lens, and the sum of their strengths is the strength of the new lens.

   a. A lens of -4.75 diopters is combined with a lens of 6.25 diopters to form a new lens. What is the strength of the new lens?

   b. A lens of -2.5 diopters is combined with a lens of -1.25 diopters to form a new lens. What is the strength of the new lens?

   c. The greater the absolute value of the strength of a lens, the stronger the lens. Which new lens is stronger, the one in part (a) or in part (b)?

EXAMPLE 4 on p. 76 for Exs. 56–57

56. ★ **MULTIPLE CHOICE** The table shows the profits for a company from 1999 to 2004. Which three-year period had the greatest total profit?

Year	1999	2000	2001	2002	2003	2004
Profit (millions of dollars)	−13.76	54.91	38.54	−21.33	123.90	−14.82

Ⓐ 1999–2001 Ⓑ 2000–2002 Ⓒ 2001–2003 Ⓓ 2002–2004

◯ = WORKED-OUT SOLUTIONS on p. WS1

★ = STANDARDIZED TEST PRACTICE

57. ★ **SHORT RESPONSE** In golf, your score on a hole is the number of strokes above or below an expected number of strokes needed to hit a ball into the hole. As shown in the table, each score has a name. When you compare two scores, the lesser score is the better score.

Name	Double eagle	Eagle	Birdie	Par	Bogey	Double bogey
Score	−3	−2	−1	0	1	2

a. **Compare** For three holes, you score an eagle, a double bogey, and a birdie. Your friend scores a double eagle, a bogey, and a par. Who has the better total score?

b. **Explain** Your friend scores a double eagle and an eagle for the next two holes. Is it possible for you to have a better score on all five holes after your next two holes? *Explain* your reasoning.

58. ★ **EXTENDED RESPONSE** Atoms consist of protons, electrons, and neutrons. A group of x protons has a charge of x. A group of x electrons has a charge of $-x$. Neutrons have a charge of 0.

a. **Calculate** The total charge of an atom is the sum of the charges of its protons and electrons. Find the total charge of an atom that has 13 protons, 10 electrons, and 14 neutrons.

b. **Interpret** An atom is an ion only when it has a positive or a negative total charge. Is the atom in part (a) an ion?

c. **Explain** In an atom, only the number of electrons can change. Suppose an atom has a total charge of 5. For the atom not to be an ion, how should the number of electrons change? Your answer should include an algebraic equation that models the situation and an explanation of how you solved the equation.

59. **CHALLENGE** You sold three items in an Internet auction. The table shows the profit earned for each item. You now plan to sell a floor lamp. What is the least profit that you can earn on the lamp and have a positive total profit for the four items? *Explain* your answer.

Item	Profit (dollars)
Mantel clock	4.13
Framed mirror	−10.65
Metal lunch box	−5.87

MIXED REVIEW

PREVIEW
Prepare for Lesson 2.3 in Exs. 60–63.

Evaluate the expression.

60. $t - 7$ when $t = 21$ *(p. 2)*

61. $1.7 - y$ when $y = 0.8$ *(p. 2)*

62. $-a$ when $a = -13.5$ *(p. 64)*

63. $|c|$ when $c = -9.6$ *(p. 64)*

State the formula that is needed to solve the problem. Then solve the problem. *(p. 28)*

64. What is the interest on \$800 invested for 3 years in an account that earns simple interest at a rate of 1.5% per year?

65. Find the perimeter of a rectangle that is 28 feet wide and 40 feet long.

66. The temperature is 50°F. What is the temperature in degrees Celsius?

2.3 Subtract Real Numbers

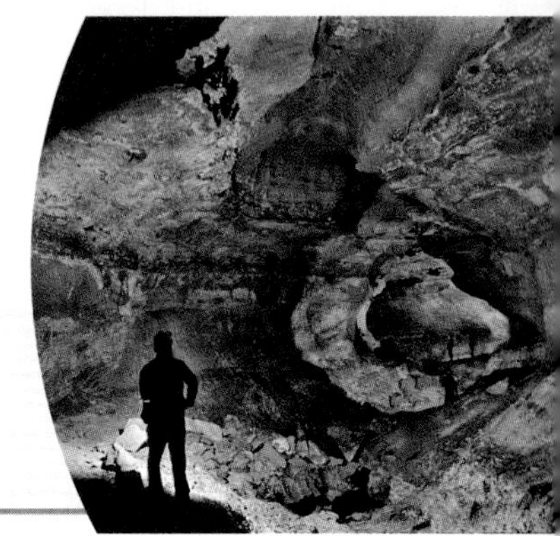

Before You added real numbers.

Now You will subtract real numbers.

Why? So you can find a change in temperature, as in Ex. 43.

Key Vocabulary
- **opposites,** *p. 66*

Because the expressions $12 - 3$ and $12 + (-3)$ have the same value, 9, you can conclude that $12 - 3 = 12 + (-3)$. Subtracting 3 from 12 is equivalent to adding the opposite of 3 to 12. This example illustrates the *subtraction rule.*

KEY CONCEPT *For Your Notebook*

Subtraction Rule

Words To subtract b from a, add the opposite of b to a.

Algebra $a - b = a + (-b)$ **Example** $14 - 8 = 14 + (-8)$

EXAMPLE 1 Subtract real numbers

Find the difference.

a. $-12 - 19 = -12 + (-19)$
$= -31$

b. $18 - (-7) = 18 + 7$
$= 25$

 Animated Algebra at classzone.com

✓ **GUIDED PRACTICE** for Example 1

Find the difference.

1. $-2 - 7$ **2.** $11.7 - (-5)$ **3.** $\frac{1}{3} - \frac{1}{2}$

EXAMPLE 2 Evaluate a variable expression

Evaluate the expression $y - x + 6.8$ when $x = -2$ and $y = 7.2$.

$y - x + 6.8 = 7.2 - (-2) + 6.8$ Substitute -2 for x and 7.2 for y.

$= 7.2 + 2 + 6.8$ Add the opposite of -2.

$= 16$ Add.

EVALUATING CHANGE You can use subtraction to find the change in a quantity, such as elevation or temperature. The change in a quantity is the difference of the new amount and the original amount. If the new amount is greater than the original amount, the change is positive. If the new amount is less than the original amount, the change is negative.

EXAMPLE 3 Evaluate change

TEMPERATURES One of the most extreme temperature changes in United States history occurred in Fairfield, Montana, on December 24, 1924. At noon, the temperature was 63°F. By midnight, the temperature fell to −21°F. What was the change in temperature?

Solution

The change C in temperature is the difference of the temperature m at midnight and the temperature n at noon.

STEP 1 **Write** a verbal model. Then write an equation.

Change in temperature	=	Temperature at midnight	−	Temperature at noon
C	=	m	−	n

AVOID ERRORS
When a quantity decreases, the change is negative. So, the change found in Example 3 should be a negative number.

STEP 2 **Find** the change in temperature.

$C = m - n$ **Write equation.**

$= -21 - 63$ **Substitute values.**

$= -21 + (-63)$ **Add the opposite of 63.**

$= -84$ **Add −21 and −63.**

▶ The change in temperature was −84°F.

USING A CALCULATOR To enter a negative number on a calculator, use the (−) key. To enter a subtraction sign, use the − key. You can use a calculator to check your answer in Example 3 using the following keystrokes.

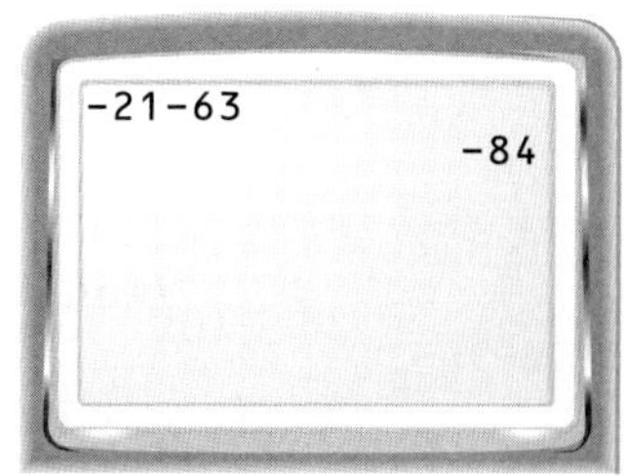

GUIDED PRACTICE for Examples 2 and 3

Evaluate the expression when $x = -3$ and $y = 5.2$.

4. $x - y + 8$

5. $y - (x - 2)$

6. $(y - 4) - x$

7. CAR VALUES A new car is valued at $15,000. One year later, the car is valued at $12,300. What is the change in the value of the car?

2.3 EXERCISES

HOMEWORK KEY

○ = **WORKED-OUT SOLUTIONS** on p. WS4 for Exs. 3, 21, and 43

★ = **STANDARDIZED TEST PRACTICE** Exs. 2, 38, 39, 40, and 46

◆ = **MULTIPLE REPRESENTATIONS** Ex. 45

SKILL PRACTICE

1. **VOCABULARY** Use the subtraction rule to rewrite the expression $-3 - 6$ as an addition expression.

2. ★ **WRITING** Without actually subtracting, how can you tell whether a change in a quantity will be negative?

EXAMPLE 1 on p. 80 for Exs. 3–14

FINDING DIFFERENCES **Find the difference.**

3. $13 - (-5)$
4. $16 - 32$
5. $-11 - (-3)$
6. $-15 - 29$
7. $-35.9 - (-50)$
8. $14.7 - (-2.3)$
9. $-3.6 - 22.2$
10. $-18.2 - (-15.4)$
11. $\frac{1}{2} - \frac{5}{6}$
12. $-\frac{5}{3} - \frac{8}{3}$
13. $\frac{1}{2} - \left(-\frac{1}{4}\right)$
14. $-\frac{7}{10} - \left(-\frac{2}{5}\right)$

EXAMPLE 2 on p. 80 for Exs. 15–25

ERROR ANALYSIS ***Describe*** **and correct the error in evaluating the expression when $x = 3$ and $y = -8$.**

15.
$$\begin{aligned} x - y + 2 &= 3 - 8 + 2 \\ &= 3 + (-8) + 2 \\ &= -5 + 2 \\ &= -3 \end{aligned}$$
✗

16.
$$\begin{aligned} x - (-4 + y) &= 3 - [-4 + (-8)] \\ &= 3 - (-12) \\ &= 3 - 12 \\ &= -9 \end{aligned}$$
✗

EVALUATING EXPRESSIONS **Evaluate the expression when $x = 7.1$ and $y = -2.5$.**

17. $x - (-y)$
18. $y - x - 12$
19. $x - (-6) + y$
20. $x - (y - 13)$
21. $-y - (1.9 - x)$
22. $-y - x$
23. $x - y - 2$
24. $5.3 - (y - x)$
25. $x + y - 2.8$

EXAMPLE 3 on p. 81 for Exs. 26–31

EVALUATING CHANGE **Find the change in temperature or elevation.**

26. From −5°C to −13°C
27. From −45°F to 62°F
28. From −300 feet to −100 feet
29. From 1200 meters to −80 meters
30. From 4.8°F to −12.6°F
31. From −90.7 miles to 36.4 miles

EVALUATING EXPRESSIONS **Evaluate the expression when $x = 3.6$, $y = 6.6$, and $z = -11$.**

32. $(x - y) - |z|$
33. $(x - |-y|) - z$
34. $x - |y - z|$
35. $(-x - y) - z - 5$
36. $x + y - z + 12.9$
37. $-z + y - x - (-2.4)$

38. ★ **MULTIPLE CHOICE** If the value of the expression $a - b$ is negative, which statement must be true?

Ⓐ $a > b$ Ⓑ $a = 0$ Ⓒ $a < b$ Ⓓ $b = 0$

39. ★ **OPEN-ENDED** Write a real-world problem that can be modeled by the expression $-23 - 14 - 8$. Then solve the problem.

40. ★ **WRITING** Tell whether the associative property and the commutative property hold for subtraction. Give examples to support your answers.

41. **CHALLENGE** Let a and b be negative numbers. Tell whether the value of the expression is positive or negative. *Explain* your reasoning.

 a. $|a + b|$ b. $-a - b$ c. $-|a| - |b|$ d. $a + b$

PROBLEM SOLVING

EXAMPLE 3 on p. 81 for Exs. 42–43

42. **VOLCANOES** Mahukona is a Hawaiian volcano whose summit has an elevation of −3600 feet. The summit once had an elevation of 800 feet. What was the change in elevation of the volcano's summit?

 @HomeTutor for problem solving help at classzone.com

43. **CAVES** The temperature inside Mammoth Cave in Kentucky is about 12.2°C year round. If the temperature outside the cave is −2.4°C, what is the change in temperature from outside to inside the cave?

 @HomeTutor for problem solving help at classzone.com

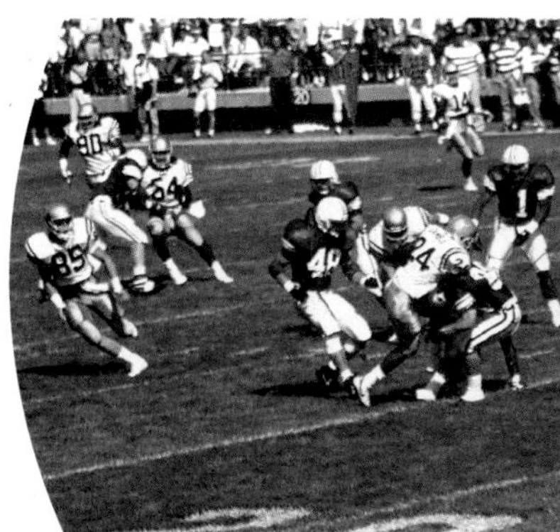

44. **FOOTBALL** In four plays a football team gains 3 yards, loses 7 yards, loses 2 yards, and gains 15 yards. How many yards did the team gain after four plays?

45. **MULTIPLE REPRESENTATIONS** In order to qualify for a girls' regional 1500 meter race, an athlete's personal best time for the season must be under the qualifying time of 5 minutes 42 seconds.

 a. **Writing an Equation** Write an equation that expresses d as the difference of the athlete's personal best time t (in seconds) and the qualifying time (in seconds).

 b. **Making a Table** Make a table that gives the values of d for $t = 341.7$, 343.8, 340.9, and 342.7. Which values of t in the table are under the qualifying time? How can you tell from the differences?

46. ★ **SHORT RESPONSE** A trade surplus or deficit is the difference of the value of all exports and the value of all imports. A positive difference is a surplus, and a negative difference is a deficit. The table shows the values of the United States' imports and exports for the period 2000–2003.

Year	2000	2001	2002	2003
Value of exports (trillions of dollars)	1.071	1.007	0.976	1.021
Value of imports (trillions of dollars)	1.449	1.369	1.398	1.517

 a. **Calculate** Find the trade surplus or deficit for each year.

 b. **Describe** *Describe* any trends in the surplus or deficit over the years.

47. **SNOWBOARDS** Snowboarders can rotate the shoe bindings on their snowboards. The binding setup shown below is written $+24°/-18°$. This means that the front angle is 24° counterclockwise from vertical, and the rear angle is 18° clockwise from vertical.

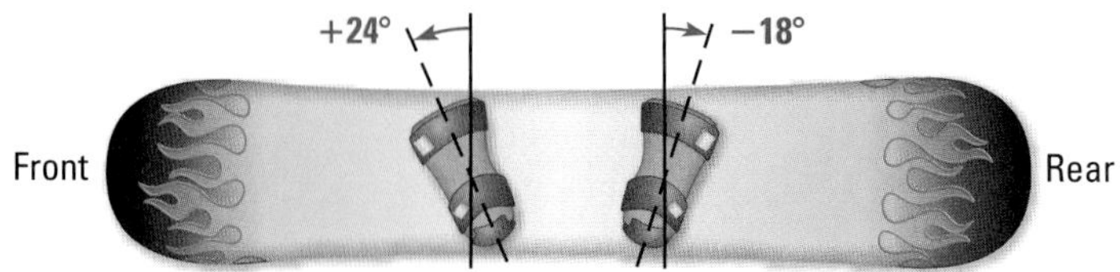

a. An instructor suggests a binding setup of $+30°/+15°$ for beginners. Your setup is initially $+24°/-4°$. Find the changes in angle measures needed to match the instructor's suggestion.

b. A mirror setup is a setup of $+n°/-n°$ where n is between 0 and 90. Your setup is initially $+13°/-6°$. You change the front angle measure by $-3°$. Find the change in the rear angle measure needed for a mirror setup.

48. **CHALLENGE** Greenwich Mean Time (GMT) is the time at the Royal Observatory in Greenwich, England. A location that is $+n$ hours from GMT is n hours ahead of GMT, and a location that is $-n$ hours from GMT is n hours behind GMT. Costa Rica is -6 hours from GMT, and India is $+5.5$ hours from GMT. If it is 7:45 A.M. in India, what time is it in Costa Rica?

MIXED REVIEW

Evaluate the expression.

49. $20x$ when $x = 15$ *(p. 2)*

50. $3x + 8$ when $x = 12$ *(p. 8)*

51. $15.5 + x$ when $x = -30.2$ *(p. 74)*

52. $-x + 19.4$ when $x = 8.2$ *(p. 74)*

PREVIEW
Prepare for Lesson 2.4 in Exs. 53–56.

Identify the property illustrated. *(p. 74)*

53. $1 + 7 = 7 + 1$

54. $-4.8 + 4.8 = 0$

55. $0 + (-9) = -9$

56. $(2 + 3) + 4 = 2 + (3 + 4)$

QUIZ *for Lessons 2.1–2.3*

1. Tell whether each of the following numbers is a whole number, an integer, or a rational number: $-\frac{5}{6}$, -8.2, 0, -9. Then order the numbers from least to greatest. *(p. 64)*

Find the sum or difference.

2. $5 + (-36)$ *(p. 74)*

3. $-8.2 + (-2.3)$ *(p. 74)*

4. $3\frac{1}{2} + (-2)$ *(p. 74)*

5. $-18 - (-9)$ *(p. 80)*

6. $-11.2 - 21.7$ *(p. 80)*

7. $4\frac{1}{2} - \left(-\frac{1}{5}\right)$ *(p. 80)*

Evaluate the expression when $x = 2.5$ and $y = -3.4$. *(p. 80)*

8. $x + y - 9$

9. $x - (y - 5.1)$

10. $12.1 - (y - x)$

EXTRA PRACTICE for Lesson 2.3, p. 939 **ONLINE QUIZ** at classzone.com

@HomeTutor
classzone.com
Keystrokes

2.3 Subtract Real Numbers

QUESTION **How can you use a spreadsheet to subtract the same number from various numbers?**

In a spreadsheet, the columns are identified by letters, and the rows are identified by numbers. Each cell has a name that is made up of a letter and a number. For example, B2 is the cell in column B and row 2. A cell can contain a label, a number, or a formula.

	A	B
1		
2		

EXAMPLE **Find the difference of two numbers**

A manufacturing company is making foam hand grips for bicycles and jump ropes. The ideal length of a hand grip is 5 inches. In a batch of ten hand grips, the actual lengths (in inches) are 4.878, 4.902, 5.115, 5.13, 4.877, 4.874, 4.799, 4.819, 4.879, and 5.124. Create a spreadsheet to find the difference of the actual length and the ideal length for each hand grip.

Solution

STEP 1 ***Enter data***
Enter the labels in the first row of the spreadsheet. Then enter the grip numbers and grip lengths in successive rows.

	A	B	C
1	Grip	Length (inches)	Difference
2	1	4.878	
3	2	4.902	

STEP 2 ***Calculate differences***
For each hand grip, enter the formula for the difference of the actual and ideal lengths in the appropriate cell in column C.

	A	B	C
1	Grip	Length (inches)	Difference
2	1	4.878	=B2−5
3	2	4.902	=B3−5

After you enter a formula, the cell should display the difference of the length of the grip and the ideal length. For example, C2 should display -0.122, and C3 should display -0.098.

DRAW CONCLUSIONS

1. The manufacturer will consider a hand grip acceptable if the absolute value of the difference of the actual length and the ideal length is at most 0.125 inch. How many hand grips from the batch are acceptable?
2. What are the least and greatest possible lengths that a hand grip can have and still be acceptable? *Explain* your reasoning.
3. For which of the ten hand grips is the length closest to the ideal length? How can you tell from the differences in column C?
4. In another batch of ten hand grips, the actual lengths (in inches) are 4.871, 5.019, 5.112, 4.987, 5.067, 4.899, 4.859, 5.132, 5.126, and 5.093. Create a spreadsheet to find the difference of the actual length and the ideal length for each hand grip.

MIXED REVIEW *of Problem Solving*

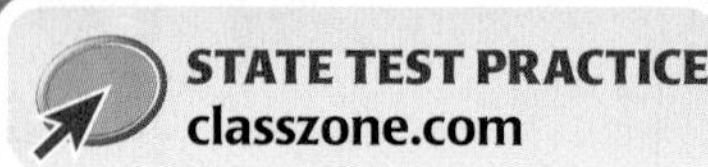

Lessons 2.1–2.3

1. **MULTI-STEP PROBLEM** The table shows the record low temperatures for several states in the United States.

State	Temperature (°F)
Alaska	−80
Arkansas	−29
California	−45
Hawaii	12
Kentucky	−37

   a. Order the temperatures from least to greatest.

   b. The record low temperature in Arizona is −40°F. Which states in the table have record low temperatures less than −40°F?

2. **MULTI-STEP PROBLEM** Your bank account incurs a \$35 fee for each withdrawal that either results in a negative balance or occurs while your account balance is negative. You have a balance of \$150. You withdraw \$165.

   a. What will the balance in your account be after the fee is charged?

   b. How much money do you need to deposit into the account so that the balance is \$0?

3. **GRIDDED ANSWER** At the close of trading on the New York Stock Exchange on Monday, the value of a share of a certain stock was \$10.65. Over the next three days, the change in value of a share was −\$.56, then −\$1.09, and then \$.89. What was the value of a share of the stock at the end of the three days?

4. **OPEN-ENDED** *Describe* a real-world situation that can be modeled by the expression −35.50 + (−12.43) + 50.43. Then find the value of the expression.

5. **SHORT RESPONSE** Net migration flow is the difference of the number of people migrating into a place and the number of people migrating out of a place. The table shows the number of people who migrated into and out of a certain city during the period 2001–2005.

Year	Number migrating into city	Number migrating out of city
2001	3302	3316
2002	3179	3623
2003	3053	3632
2004	3180	3695
2005	3174	3396

   Find the net migration flow for each year. Then describe any trends in the city's net migration flow during this period.

6. **EXTENDED RESPONSE** In meteorology, the lifted index measures the likelihood of a thunderstorm. The greater the lifted index, the less likely a storm will occur. The table shows the lifted index for two cities at various times during a day.

Time	Lifted index for city A	Lifted index for city B
12 A.M.	−5.6	−0.8
4 A.M.	−4.3	−1.8
8 A.M.	−3.8	−2.3
12 P.M.	−2.5	−2.6
4 P.M.	−3.0	−1.4
8 P.M.	−4.5	0.8

   a. At what time during that day is a storm least likely to occur in city A?

   b. Compare the likelihood of a storm between 12 A.M. and 8 P.M. for the two cities on that day.

   c. Would you expect a storm in city B but not in city A at 8 P.M. that day? *Explain.*

2.4 Multiplication by –1

MATERIALS • paper and pencil

QUESTION **What is the product of any integer *a* and –1?**

You can rewrite a multiplication expression as repeated addition. For example, $3 \cdot 8$ can be rewritten as $8 + 8 + 8$. Because the sum is 24, you can conclude that $3 \cdot 8 = 24$.

EXPLORE **Find the product of an integer and –1**

STEP 1 Copy and complete the table.

Multiplication Expression	Addition Expression	Sum
$5 \cdot (-1)$	$-1 + (-1) + (-1) + (-1) + (-1)$	-5
$4 \cdot (-1)$	?	?
$3 \cdot (-1)$	?	?
$2 \cdot (-1)$	?	?

STEP 2 Copy and complete the multiplication equations below.

$5 \cdot (-1) = \underline{?}$
$4 \cdot (-1) = \underline{?}$
$3 \cdot (-1) = \underline{?}$
$2 \cdot (-1) = \underline{?}$

Complete using the table from Step 1.

$1 \cdot (-1) = \underline{?}$
$0 \cdot (-1) = \underline{?}$
$-1 \cdot (-1) = \underline{?}$
$-2 \cdot (-1) = \underline{?}$
$-3 \cdot (-1) = \underline{?}$

Complete by extending the pattern in the first four products.

DRAW CONCLUSIONS **Use your observations to complete these exercises**

1. Copy and complete: For any integer a, $a \cdot (-1) = \underline{?}$.

Find the product.

2. $12 \cdot (-1)$
3. $10 \cdot (-1)$
4. $-23 \cdot (-1)$
5. $-47 \cdot (-1)$
6. $-18 \cdot (-1)$
7. $15 \cdot (-1)$

2.4 Multiply Real Numbers

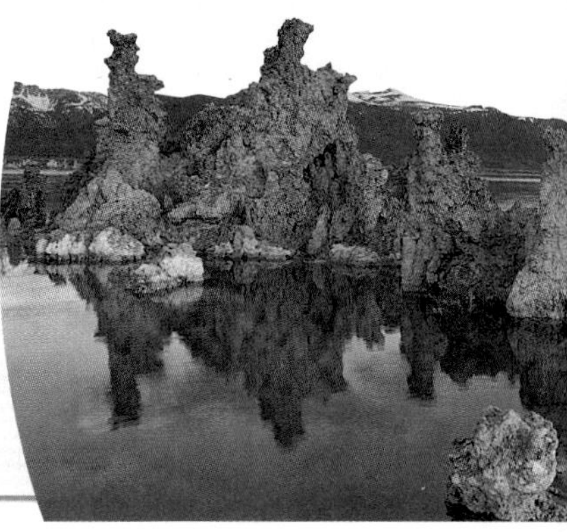

Before You added and subtracted real numbers.

Now You will multiply real numbers.

Why So you can calculate an elevation, as in Example 4.

Key Vocabulary
- **multiplicative identity**

In the activity on page 87, you saw that $a \cdot (-1) = -a$ for any integer a. This rule not only lets you write the product of a and -1 as $-a$, but it also lets you write $-a$ as $(-1)a$ and $a(-1)$. Using this rule, you can multiply any two real numbers. Here are two examples:

$$-2(3) = -1(2)(3) \qquad (-2)(-3) = -2(3)(-1)$$
$$= -1(6) \qquad = -6(-1)$$
$$= -6 \qquad = 6$$

KEY CONCEPT *For Your Notebook*

The Sign of a Product

Words The product of two real numbers with the *same* sign is positive.

Examples $3(4) = 12$ $\qquad -6(-3) = 18$

Words The product of two real numbers with *different* signs is negative.

Examples $2(-5) = -10$ $\qquad -7(2) = -14$

EXAMPLE 1 Multiply real numbers

MULTIPLY NEGATIVES
- A product is negative if it has an *odd* number of negative numbers.
- A product is positive if it has an *even* number of negative numbers.

Find the product.

a. $-3(6) = -18$ — **Different signs; product is negative.**

b. $2(-5)(-4) = (-10)(-4)$ — **Multiply 2 and −5.**

$= 40$ — **Same signs; product is positive.**

c. $-\frac{1}{2}(-4)(-3) = 2(-3)$ — **Multiply $-\frac{1}{2}$ and −4.**

$= -6$ — **Different signs; product is negative.**

 **GUIDED PRACTICE** for Example 1

Find the product.

1. $-2(-7)$ **2.** $-0.5(-4)(-9)$ **3.** $\frac{4}{3}(-3)(7)$

PROPERTIES OF MULTIPLICATION Notice that both $4(-5)$ and $-5(4)$ have a product of -20, so $4(-5) = -5(4)$. This equation is an example of the *commutative property of multiplication*. Properties of multiplication are listed below.

KEY CONCEPT *For Your Notebook*

Properties of Multiplication

COMMUTATIVE PROPERTY The order in which you multiply two numbers does not change the product.

Algebra $a \cdot b = b \cdot a$ **Example** $4 \cdot (-5) = -5 \cdot 4$

ASSOCIATIVE PROPERTY The way you group three numbers in a product does not change the product.

Algebra $(a \cdot b) \cdot c = a \cdot (b \cdot c)$ **Example** $(-2 \cdot 7) \cdot 4 = -2 \cdot (7 \cdot 4)$

IDENTITY PROPERTY The product of a number and 1 is that number.

Algebra $a \cdot 1 = 1 \cdot a = a$ **Example** $(-5) \cdot 1 = -5$

PROPERTY OF ZERO The product of a number and 0 is 0.

Algebra $a \cdot 0 = 0 \cdot a = 0$ **Example** $-3 \cdot 0 = 0$

PROPERTY OF −1 The product of a number and -1 is the opposite of the number.

Algebra $a \cdot (-1) = -1 \cdot a = -a$ **Example** $-2 \cdot (-1) = 2$

The identity property states that the product of a number a and 1 is a. The number 1 is called the **multiplicative identity**.

EXAMPLE 2 Identify properties of multiplication

	Statement	Property illustrated
a.	$(x \cdot 7) \cdot 0.5 = x \cdot (7 \cdot 0.5)$	Associative property of multiplication
b.	$8 \cdot 0 = 0$	Multiplicative property of zero
c.	$-6 \cdot y = y \cdot (-6)$	Commutative property of multiplication
d.	$9 \cdot (-1) = -9$	Multiplicative property of -1
e.	$1 \cdot v = v$	Identity property of multiplication

✓ **GUIDED PRACTICE** for Example 2

Identify the property illustrated.

4. $-1 \cdot 8 = -8$

5. $12 \cdot x = x \cdot 12$

6. $(y \cdot 4) \cdot 9 = y \cdot (4 \cdot 9)$

7. $0 \cdot (-41) = 0$

8. $-5 \cdot (-6) = -6 \cdot (-5)$

9. $-13 \cdot (-1) = 13$

EXAMPLE 3 Use properties of multiplication

JUSTIFY STEPS
To justify a step, you name the property used. Sometimes a step is a calculation, as when you multiply 0.25 and −4 in Example 3.

Find the product $(-4x) \cdot 0.25$. Justify your steps.

$(-4x) \cdot 0.25 = 0.25 \cdot (-4x)$	**Commutative property of multiplication**
$= [0.25 \cdot (-4)]x$	**Associative property of multiplication**
$= -1 \cdot x$	**Product of 0.25 and −4 is −1.**
$= -x$	**Multiplicative property of −1**

Animated Algebra at classzone.com

EXAMPLE 4 Solve a multi-step problem

READING
The average rate of change in elevation is the total change in elevation divided by the number of years that have passed.

LAKES In 1900 the elevation of Mono Lake in California was about 6416 feet. From 1900 to 1950, the average rate of change in elevation was about −0.12 foot per year. From 1950 to 2000, the average rate of change was about −0.526 foot per year. Approximate the elevation in 2000.

Solution

STEP 1 **Write** a verbal model.

New elevation (feet) = Original elevation (feet) + Average rate of change (feet/year) • Time passed (years)

STEP 2 **Calculate** the elevation in 1950. Use the elevation in 1900 as the original elevation. The time span is 1950 − 1900 = 50 years.

New elevation $= 6416 + (-0.12)(50)$	**Substitute values.**
$= 6416 + (-6)$	**Multiply −0.12 and 50.**
$= 6410$	**Add 6416 and −6.**

STEP 3 **Calculate** the elevation in 2000. Use the elevation in 1950 as the original elevation. The time span is 2000 − 1950 = 50 years.

New elevation $= 6410 + (-0.526)(50)$	**Substitute values.**
$= 6410 + (-26.3)$	**Multiply −0.526 and 50.**
$= 6383.7$	**Add 6410 and −26.3.**

▶ The elevation in 2000 was about 6383.7 feet above sea level.

GUIDED PRACTICE for Examples 3 and 4

Find the product. *Justify* your steps.

10. $\frac{3}{10}(5y)$ **11.** $0.8(-x)(-1)$ **12.** $(-y)(-0.5)(-6)$

13. Using the data in Example 4, approximate the elevation of Mono Lake in 1925 and in 1965.

2.4 EXERCISES

HOMEWORK KEY

○ = **WORKED-OUT SOLUTIONS** on p. WS4 for Exs. 11, 31, and 51

★ = **STANDARDIZED TEST PRACTICE** Exs. 2, 48, 52, 53, and 55

◆ = **MULTIPLE REPRESENTATIONS** Ex. 54

SKILL PRACTICE

1. VOCABULARY What number is called the multiplicative identity?

2. ★ WRITING *Describe* the difference between the identity property of multiplication and the multiplicative property of -1.

EXAMPLE 1 on p. 88 for Exs. 3–18

FINDING PRODUCTS **Find the product.**

3. $-4(7)$ **4.** $11(-2)$ **5.** $-9(-10)$ **6.** $-8(-11)$

7. $5(-7.2)$ **8.** $(-2.5)(-1.3)$ **9.** $-42\left(-\frac{1}{6}\right)$ **10.** $-\frac{1}{2}(-32)$

11. $-1.9(3.3)(7)$ **12.** $0.5(-20)(-3)$ **13.** $-\frac{5}{6}(-12)(-4)$ **14.** $-\frac{3}{4}(2)(-6)$

15. $-8(-4)(-2.5)$ **16.** $-1.6(-2)(-10)$ **17.** $18\left(-\frac{2}{3}\right)\left(-\frac{1}{5}\right)$ **18.** $-\frac{3}{4}\left(-\frac{1}{3}\right)\left(-\frac{8}{9}\right)$

EXAMPLE 2 on p. 89 for Exs. 19–27

IDENTIFYING PROPERTIES **Identify the property illustrated.**

19. $-\frac{2}{5} \cdot 0 = 0$ **20.** $0.3 \cdot (-3) = -3 \cdot 0.3$ **21.** $-143 \cdot 1 = -143$

22. $-1 \cdot (-6) = 6$ **23.** $(-2 \cdot 5) \cdot 4 = -2 \cdot (5 \cdot 4)$ **24.** $0 \cdot (-76.3) = 0$

25. $1 \cdot (ab) = ab$ **26.** $(3x)y = 3(xy)$ **27.** $s \cdot (-1) = -s$

EXAMPLE 3 on p. 90 for Exs. 28–36

USING PROPERTIES **Find the product. *Justify* your steps.**

28. $y(-2)(-8)$ **29.** $-18(-x)$ **30.** $\frac{3}{5}(-5q)$

31. $-2(-6)(-7z)$ **32.** $-5(-4)(-2.1)(-z)$ **33.** $-\frac{1}{5}(-10)(4)(-5c)$

34. $-5t(-t)$ **35.** $-6r(-2.8r)$ **36.** $\frac{1}{3}\left(-\frac{9}{10}\right)(-m)(-m)$

EVALUATING EXPRESSIONS **Evaluate the expression when $x = -2$ and $y = 3.6$.**

37. $2x + y$ **38.** $-x - 3y$ **39.** $xy - 5.4$

40. $|y| - 4x$ **41.** $1.5x - |-y|$ **42.** $x^2 - y^2$

ERROR ANALYSIS ***Describe*** **and correct the error in finding the product.**

43.

$$\begin{aligned} -1(7)(-3)(-2x) &= 7(-3)(-2x) \\ &= -21(-2x) \\ &= [-21 \cdot (-2)]x \\ &= 42x \end{aligned}$$

44.

$$\begin{aligned} (-5z)(-8)(z) &= (-8)(-5z)(z) \\ &= (-8)(-5)(z)(z) \\ &= -40(z \cdot z) \\ &= -40z^2 \end{aligned}$$

REASONING In Exercises 45–47, tell whether the statement is *true* or *false*. If it is false, give a counterexample.

45. If x is negative, then x^2 is positive.

46. If the product of three numbers is positive, then all three numbers are positive.

47. If the product of four numbers is 0, then at least one of the numbers is 0.

48. ★ **MULTIPLE CHOICE** Let a be a negative number. If the product abc is positive, which statement must be true?

Ⓐ $bc > 0$ Ⓑ $bc < 0$ Ⓒ $ac > 0$ Ⓓ $ab < 0$

49. **CHALLENGE** The product of n factors is negative. What is the greatest possible number of negative factors if n is even? if n is odd? Give several examples to support your answers.

PROBLEM SOLVING

EXAMPLE 4
on p. 90
for Exs. 50–53

50. **DEAD SEA** In 1940 the surface area of the Dead Sea was about 980 square kilometers. From 1940 to 2001, the average rate of change in surface area was about −5.7 square kilometers per year. Find the surface area of the Dead Sea in 2001.

@HomeTutor for problem solving help at classzone.com

51. **STOCKS** An investor purchases 50 shares of a stock at \$3.50 per share. The next day, the change in value of a share of the stock is −\$.25. What is the total value of the shares the next day?

@HomeTutor for problem solving help at classzone.com

52. ★ **SHORT RESPONSE** In 1913 the total volume of the glaciers on Mount Rainier was 5.62 cubic kilometers. The table shows the average rate of change in the volume for two periods of time.

Time period	Rate of change (km^3/yr)
1913–1971	−0.02241
1971–1994	−0.00565

a. Find the total volume of the glaciers in 1971 and in 1994.

b. About one third of the change in volume during the period 1913–1994 took place in the northeastern glaciers. Find the change in the volume of the northeastern glaciers. *Explain* your steps.

53. ★ **MULTIPLE CHOICE** The Rialto Bridge in Venice, Italy, is a footbridge built in the late 16th century. The maximum clearance between the water and the bridge is about 7.32 meters. Because of a rising sea level and a gradual sinking of the city, the clearance changes at an average rate of about −2 millimeters per year. Approximate the clearance after 15 years.

Ⓐ 5.32 meters Ⓑ 7.02 meters

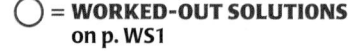

Ⓒ 7.29 meters Ⓓ 7.318 meters

54. MULTIPLE REPRESENTATIONS A skydiver in free fall will eventually reach a constant velocity, called terminal velocity. A skydiver reaches a terminal velocity of −160 feet per second at an altitude of 3200 feet.

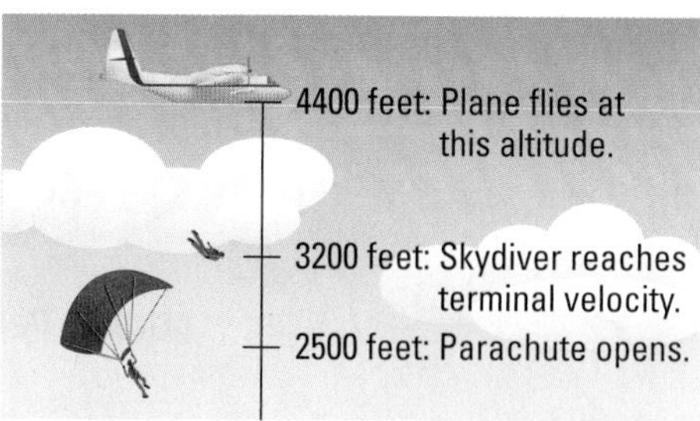

a. **Writing an Equation** Write an equation for the altitude a (in feet) of the skydiver as a function of the time t (in seconds) after reaching terminal velocity.

b. **Making a Table** Make a table of values for $t = 1, 2, 3, 4$, and 5 seconds. The skydiver wants to open the parachute after reaching an altitude of about 2500 feet. After how many seconds should the skydiver open the parachute?

at classzone.com

55. ★ **EXTENDED RESPONSE** The table shows the fuel capacities of two ferries in Puget Sound, Washington, and the average rates of change in tank fuel when the ferries are burning fuel.

Ferry	Fuel capacity (gal)	Rate of change (gal/h)
Rhododendron	11,250	−30
Spokane	135,000	−240

a. **Model** For each ferry, write an equation that gives the amount of tank fuel f (in gallons) as a function of the time t (in hours) that fuel is burned.

b. **Calculate** Both ferries start with a full tank. How many gallons of fuel will each ferry have left after 3 hours?

c. **Explain** If both ferries continue to burn fuel without refueling, which ferry will run out of fuel first? How many gallons will the other ferry have at that time? Your answer should include the following:

- the number of hours that each ferry will take to burn all of its fuel
- an explanation of how you used the equations in part (a)

56. CHALLENGE Due to soil erosion, the surface area of Dongting Lake in China is decreasing. Its surface area was about 2626.5 square kilometers in 1995. From 1950 to 1995, the average rate of change in surface area was about −38.3 square kilometers per year. From 1825 to 1950, the average rate of change was about −13.2 square kilometers per year. Approximate the surface area in 1825.

MIXED REVIEW

PREVIEW
Prepare for Lesson 2.5 in Exs. 57–60.

Evaluate the expression for the given value of the variable. *(p. 8)*

57. $1 + 9y^2$ when $y = 3$

58. $z^2 \cdot 2$ when $z = 6$

59. $2(x - 19)$ when $x = 24$

60. $9(17 + w)$ when $w = 8$

Find the sum or difference.

61. $-3 + (-6)$ *(p. 74)*

62. $7.8 + (-6.4) + (-9.4)$ *(p. 74)*

63. $-19.4 - (-6.4)$ *(p. 80)*

64. $-\frac{4}{7} - \frac{3}{14}$ *(p. 80)*

Perform Matrix Addition, Subtraction, Scalar Multiplication

GOAL Perform operations on matrices.

Key Vocabulary
- matrix
- dimensions of a matrix
- element
- scalar multiplication
- scalar

A **matrix** is a rectangular arrangement of numbers in rows and columns. If a matrix has m rows and n columns, the **dimensions of the matrix** are written as $m \times n$. For example, matrix A below has two rows and three columns. The dimensions of matrix A are 2×3 (read "2 by 3"). Each number in a matrix is called an **element**, or *entry*. In matrix A, the element in the first row and second column is 4.

$$A = \underbrace{\begin{bmatrix} 0 & 4 & -1 \\ -3 & 2 & 5 \end{bmatrix}}_{\text{3 columns}} \text{ 2 rows}$$

MATRIX ADDITION AND SUBTRACTION To add or subtract matrices (the plural of *matrix*), you add or subtract corresponding elements. You can add or subtract matrices only if they have the same dimensions.

EXAMPLE 1 Add or subtract two matrices

Perform the indicated operation, if possible.

a. $$\begin{bmatrix} 0 & 4 & -1 \\ -3 & 2 & 5 \end{bmatrix} + \begin{bmatrix} 2 & 1 & 3 \\ -2 & -6 & 4 \end{bmatrix} = \begin{bmatrix} 0+2 & 4+1 & -1+3 \\ -3+(-2) & 2+(-6) & 5+4 \end{bmatrix} = \begin{bmatrix} 2 & 5 & 2 \\ -5 & -4 & 9 \end{bmatrix}$$

b. $$\begin{bmatrix} -10 & 2 \\ -4 & 7 \\ 7 & -13 \end{bmatrix} - \begin{bmatrix} 9 & -2 \\ 4 & 8 \\ -5 & -11 \end{bmatrix} = \begin{bmatrix} -10-9 & 2-(-2) \\ -4-4 & 7-8 \\ 7-(-5) & -13-(-11) \end{bmatrix} = \begin{bmatrix} -10+(-9) & 2+2 \\ -4+(-4) & 7+(-8) \\ 7+5 & -13+11 \end{bmatrix} = \begin{bmatrix} -19 & 4 \\ -8 & -1 \\ 12 & -2 \end{bmatrix}$$

c. You can't perform the subtraction $\begin{bmatrix} 6 & -4 & -8 \end{bmatrix} - \begin{bmatrix} 1 \\ 12 \\ -6 \end{bmatrix}$ because the first matrix is a 1×3 matrix and the second matrix is a 3×1 matrix.

SCALAR MULTIPLICATION In **scalar multiplication**, every element in a matrix is multiplied by a real number called a **scalar**.

EXAMPLE 2 Perform scalar multiplication

Perform the indicated operation.

a. $6\begin{bmatrix} -7 & -\frac{1}{3} \\ \frac{1}{2} & 11 \end{bmatrix} = \begin{bmatrix} 6(-7) & 6\left(-\frac{1}{3}\right) \\ 6\left(\frac{1}{2}\right) & 6(11) \end{bmatrix}$

$= \begin{bmatrix} -42 & -2 \\ 3 & 66 \end{bmatrix}$

b. $-2\begin{bmatrix} 0.5 \\ -3.2 \\ 8.1 \end{bmatrix} = \begin{bmatrix} -2(0.5) \\ -2(-3.2) \\ -2(8.1) \end{bmatrix}$

$= \begin{bmatrix} -1 \\ 6.4 \\ -16.2 \end{bmatrix}$

PRACTICE

EXAMPLES 1 and 2 on pp. 94–95 for Exs. 1–10

Perform the indicated operation, if possible.

1. $\begin{bmatrix} 7 & 6 \\ 3 & 2 \end{bmatrix} + \begin{bmatrix} 9 & -2 \\ 5 & 10 \end{bmatrix}$

2. $\begin{bmatrix} -8 \\ -4 \\ 1 \end{bmatrix} + \begin{bmatrix} 11 \\ -9 \\ -6 \end{bmatrix}$

3. $\begin{bmatrix} -8 & -1 & -9 \\ -4 & -3 & 2 \end{bmatrix} - \begin{bmatrix} 7 & 3 & 0 \\ -2 & -5 & 7 \end{bmatrix}$

4. $\begin{bmatrix} 11 & -12 \\ 15 & -22 \end{bmatrix} - \begin{bmatrix} 7 \\ 8 \end{bmatrix}$

5. $\begin{bmatrix} -9.1 & 5.4 & 3.7 \end{bmatrix} + \begin{bmatrix} 1.3 & -6.7 \end{bmatrix}$

6. $\begin{bmatrix} \frac{3}{4} & -2 \\ 6 & -3 \end{bmatrix} - \begin{bmatrix} 8 & -2 \\ 6 & -\frac{5}{6} \end{bmatrix}$

7. $7\begin{bmatrix} -4 & -7 \\ \frac{1}{2} & \frac{4}{9} \end{bmatrix}$

8. $2\begin{bmatrix} 1.5 & -6 \\ -4.5 & 0 \end{bmatrix}$

9. $-6\begin{bmatrix} 12 \\ -3.4 \\ -0.7 \end{bmatrix}$

10. $-\frac{1}{2}\begin{bmatrix} 18 & -26 & \frac{7}{4} \\ -\frac{2}{3} & 20 & -2 \end{bmatrix}$

11. **NUTRITION** The matrix shows the amounts (in milligrams) of calcium and potassium in one ounce of different types of milk. Write a matrix for the amounts of calcium and potassium in 8 ounces of each type of milk.

	Calcium (mg)	Potassium (mg)
Lowfat milk	32.940	36.295
Reduced fat milk	33.855	42.700
Whole milk	30.805	40.565

CHALLENGE **Perform the indicated operations.**

12. $9\left(\begin{bmatrix} 1 & -12 & 8 \\ -7 & 10 & -4 \end{bmatrix} + \begin{bmatrix} 3 & -3 & -7 \\ -5 & -21 & -12 \end{bmatrix}\right)$

13. $\begin{bmatrix} -6 & -8 \\ 8 & 14 \end{bmatrix} - 7\begin{bmatrix} 5 & 13 \\ -10 & -11 \end{bmatrix}$

2.5 Apply the Distributive Property

Before You used properties to add and multiply real numbers.
Now You will apply the distributive property.
Why? So you can find calories burned, as in Example 5.

Key Vocabulary
- **equivalent expressions**
- **distributive property**
- **term**
- **coefficient**
- **constant term**
- **like terms**

The models below show two methods for finding the area of a rectangle that has a length of $(x + 2)$ units and a width of 3 units.

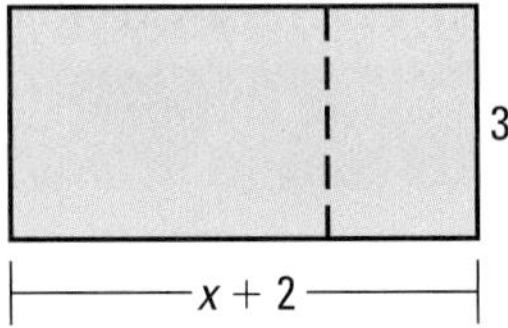

Area = 3(x + 2)

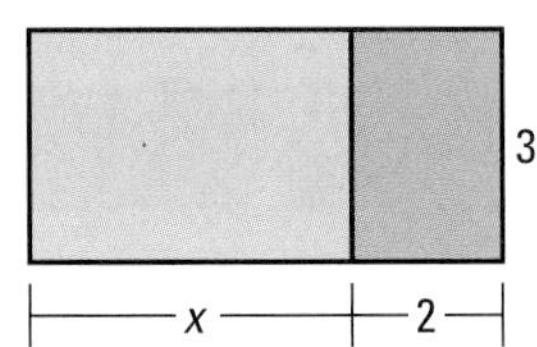

Area = 3(x) + 3(2)

The expressions $3(x + 2)$ and $3(x) + 3(2)$ are equivalent because they represent the same area. Two expressions that have the same value for all values of the variable are called **equivalent expressions**. The equation $3(x + 2) = 3(x) + 3(2)$ illustrates the **distributive property**, which can be used to find the product of a number and a sum or difference.

KEY CONCEPT *For Your Notebook*

The Distributive Property

Let a, b, and c be real numbers.

Words	Algebra	Examples
The product of a and $(b + c)$:	$a(b + c) = ab + ac$	$3(4 + 2) = 3(4) + 3(2)$
	$(b + c)a = ba + ca$	$(3 + 5)2 = 3(2) + 5(2)$
The product of a and $(b - c)$:	$a(b - c) = ab - ac$	$5(6 - 4) = 5(6) - 5(4)$
	$(b - c)a = ba - ca$	$(8 - 6)4 = 8(4) - 6(4)$

EXAMPLE 1 Apply the distributive property

AVOID ERRORS
Be sure to distribute the factor outside of the parentheses to *all* of the numbers inside the parentheses, not just to the first number.

Use the distributive property to write an equivalent expression.

a. $4(y + 3) = 4y + 12$

b. $(y + 7)y = y^2 + 7y$

c. $n(n - 9) = n^2 - 9n$

d. $(2 - n)8 = 16 - 8n$

EXAMPLE 2 Distribute a negative number

Use the distributive property to write an equivalent expression.

a. $-2(x + 7) = -2(x) + (-2)(7)$ — Distribute -2.

$= -2x - 14$ — Simplify.

b. $(5 - y)(-3y) = 5(-3y) - y(-3y)$ — Distribute $-3y$.

$= -15y + 3y^2$ — Simplify.

c. $-(2x - 11) = (-1)(2x - 11)$ — Multiplicative property of -1

$= (-1)(2x) - (-1)(11)$ — Distribute -1.

$= -2x + 11$ — Simplify.

TERMS AND COEFFICIENTS The parts of an expression that are added together are called **terms**. The number part of a term with a variable part is called the **coefficient** of the term.

READING
Note that $-x$ has a coefficient of -1 even though the 1 isn't written. Similarly, x has a coefficient of 1.

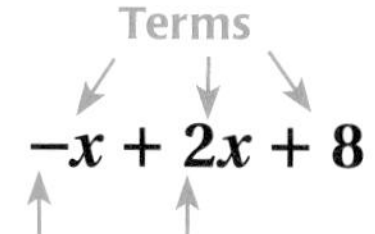

A **constant term** has a number part but no variable part, such as 8 in the expression above. **Like terms** are terms that have the same variable parts, such as $-x$ and $2x$ in the expression above. Constant terms are also like terms.

EXAMPLE 3 Identify parts of an expression

Identify the terms, like terms, coefficients, and constant terms of the expression $3x - 4 - 6x + 2$.

Solution

Write the expression as a sum: $3x + (-4) + (-6x) + 2$

Terms: $3x, -4, -6x, 2$

Like terms: $3x$ and $-6x$; -4 and 2

Coefficients: $3, -6$

Constant terms: $-4, 2$

GUIDED PRACTICE for Examples 1, 2, and 3

Use the distributive property to write an equivalent expression.

1. $2(x + 3)$
2. $-(4 - y)$
3. $(m - 5)(-3m)$
4. $(2n + 6)\left(\frac{1}{2}\right)$
5. Identify the terms, like terms, coefficients, and constant terms of the expression $-7y + 8 - 6y - 13$.

COMBINING LIKE TERMS The distributive property allows you to combine like terms that have variable parts. For example, $5x + 6x = (5 + 6)x = 11x$. A quick way to combine like terms with variable parts is to mentally add the coefficients and use the common variable part. An expression is *simplified* if it has no grouping symbols and if all of the like terms have been combined.

EXAMPLE 4 Standardized Test Practice

ANOTHER WAY
In Example 4, you can rewrite the expression $4(n + 9) - 3(2 + n)$ as $4(n + 9) + (-3)(2 + n)$ and then distribute -3 to the terms in $2 + n$.

Simplify the expression $4(n + 9) - 3(2 + n)$.

(A) $5n + 30$ (B) $n + 30$ (C) $5n + 3$ (D) $n + 3$

$4(n + 9) - 3(2 + n) = 4n + 36 - 6 - 3n$ **Distributive property**

$= n + 30$ **Combine like terms.**

▶ The correct answer is B. (A) (B) (C) (D)

EXAMPLE 5 Solve a multi-step problem

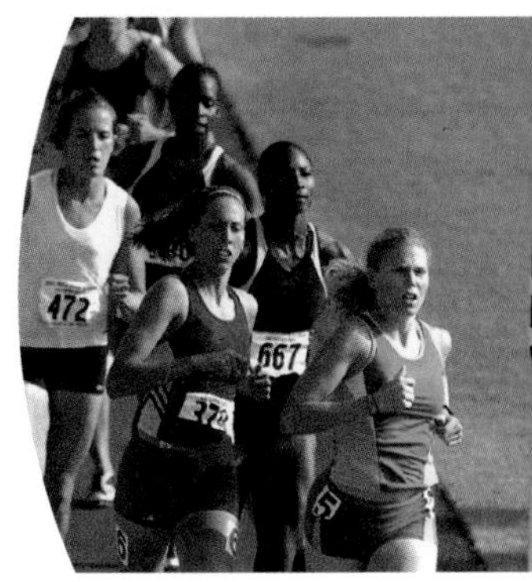

EXERCISING Your daily workout plan involves a total of 50 minutes of running and swimming. You burn 15 calories per minute when running and 9 calories per minute when swimming. Let r be the number of minutes that you run. Find the number of calories you burn in your 50 minute workout if you run for 20 minutes.

ANOTHER WAY
For an alternative method for solving the problem in Example 5, turn to page 102 for the **Problem Solving Workshop**.

Solution

The workout lasts 50 minutes, and your running time is r minutes. So, your swimming time is $(50 - r)$ minutes.

STEP 1 **Write** a verbal model. Then write an equation.

Amount burned (calories)	=	Burning rate when running (calories/minute)	·	Running time (minutes)	+	Burning rate when swimming (calories/minute)	·	Swimming time (minutes)
↓		↓		↓		↓		↓
C	=	**15**	·	r	+	**9**	·	**(50 − r)**

$C = 15r + 9(50 - r)$ **Write equation.**

$= 15r + 450 - 9r$ **Distributive property**

$= 6r + 450$ **Combine like terms.**

STEP 2 **Find** the value of C when $r = 20$.

$C = 6r + 450$ **Write equation.**

$= 6(\mathbf{20}) + 450 = 570$ **Substitute 20 for r. Then simplify.**

▶ You burn 570 calories in your 50 minute workout if you run for 20 minutes.

Animated Algebra at classzone.com

✓ GUIDED PRACTICE for Examples 4 and 5

6. Simplify the expression $5(6 + n) - 2(n - 2)$.

7. **WHAT IF?** In Example 5, suppose your workout lasts 45 minutes. How many calories do you burn if you run for 20 minutes? 30 minutes?

2.5 EXERCISES

HOMEWORK KEY

○ = **WORKED-OUT SOLUTIONS** on p. WS4 for Exs. 9, 23, and 51

★ = **STANDARDIZED TEST PRACTICE** Exs. 2, 27, 52, and 54

SKILL PRACTICE

1. **VOCABULARY** What are the coefficients of the expression $4x + 8 - 9x + 2$?

2. ★ **WRITING** Are the expressions $2(x + 1)$ and $2x + 1$ equivalent? *Explain.*

ERROR ANALYSIS ***Describe*** **and correct the error in simplifying the expression.**

3.
$$5y - (2y - 8) = 5y - 2y - 8$$
$$= 3y - 8$$

4.
$$8 + 2(4 + 3x) = 8 + 8 + 6x$$
$$= 22x$$

EXAMPLES 1 and 2 on pp. 96–97 for Exs. 5–20

USING THE DISTRIBUTIVE PROPERTY **Use the distributive property to write an equivalent expression.**

5. $4(x + 3)$
6. $8(y + 2)$
7. $(m + 5)5$
8. $(n + 6)3$
9. $(p - 3)(-8)$
10. $-4(q - 4)$
11. $2(2r - 3)$
12. $(s - 9)9$
13. $6v(v + 1)$
14. $-w(2w + 7)$
15. $-2x(3 - x)$
16. $3y(y - 6)$
17. $\frac{1}{2}\left(\frac{1}{2}m - 4\right)$
18. $-\frac{3}{4}(p - 1)$
19. $\frac{2}{3}(6n - 9)$
20. $\frac{5}{6}r(r - 1)$

EXAMPLE 3 on p. 97 for Exs. 21–26

IDENTIFYING PARTS OF AN EXPRESSION **Identify the terms, like terms, coefficients, and constant terms of the expression.**

21. $-7 + 13x + 2x + 8$
22. $9 + 7y - 2 - 5y$
23. $7x^2 - 10 - 2x^2 + 5$
24. $-3y^2 + 3y^2 - 7 + 9$
25. $2 + 3xy - 4xy + 6$
26. $6xy - 11xy + 2xy - 4xy + 7xy$

27. ★ **MULTIPLE CHOICE** Which two terms are like terms?

Ⓐ $-2, -5x$ Ⓑ $4x, -x$ Ⓒ $-2, -2y$ Ⓓ $5x, -3y$

EXAMPLE 4 on p. 98 for Exs. 28–39

SIMPLIFYING EXPRESSIONS **Simplify the expression.**

28. $7x + (-11x)$
29. $6y - y$
30. $5 + 2n + 2$
31. $(4a - 1)2 + a$
32. $3(2 - c) - c$
33. $6r + 2(r + 4)$
34. $15t - (t - 4)$
35. $3(m + 5) - 10$
36. $-6(v + 1) + v$
37. $7(w - 5) + 3w$
38. $6(5 - z) + 2z$
39. $(s - 3)(-2) + 17s$

GEOMETRY **Find the perimeter and area of the rectangle.**

40.
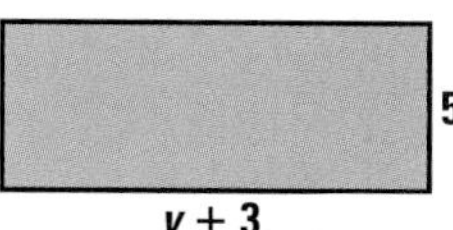

41.
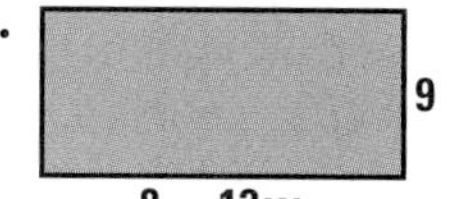

42.
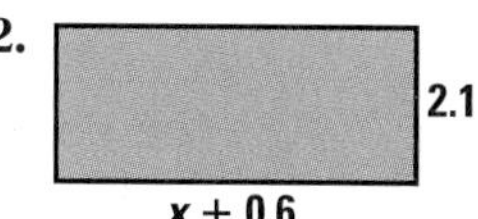

USING MENTAL MATH In Exercises 43–46, use the example below to find the total cost.

EXAMPLE Use the distributive property and mental math

Use the distributive property and mental math to find the total cost of 5 picture frames at $1.99 each.

Total cost $= 5(1.99)$	Write expression for total cost.
$= 5(2 - 0.01)$	Rewrite 1.99 as 2 – 0.01.
$= 5(2) - 5(0.01)$	Distributive property
$= 10 - 0.05$	Multiply using mental math.
$= 9.95$	Subtract. The total cost is $9.95.

43. 3 CDs at $12.99 each

44. 5 magazines at $3.99 each

45. 6 pairs of socks at $1.98 per pair

46. 25 baseballs at $2.98 each

TRANSLATING PHRASES In Exercises 47 and 48, translate the verbal phrase into an expression. Then simplify the expression.

47. Twice the sum of 6 and x, increased by 5 less than x

48. Three times the difference of x and 2, decreased by the sum of x and 10

49. **CHALLENGE** How can you use $a(b + c) = ab + ac$ to show that $(b + c)a = ba + ca$ is also true? *Justify* your steps.

PROBLEM SOLVING

EXAMPLE 5 on p. 98 for Exs. 50–52

50. **SPORTS** An archer shoots 6 arrows at a target. Some arrows hit the 9 point ring, and the rest hit the 10 point bull's-eye. Write an equation that gives the score s as a function of the number a of arrows that hit the 9 point ring. Then find the score if 2 arrows hit the 9 point ring.

@HomeTutor for problem solving help at classzone.com

51. **MOVIES** You have a coupon for $2 off the regular cost per movie rental. You rent 3 movies, and the regular cost of each rental is the same. Write an equation that gives the total cost C (in dollars) as a function of the regular cost r (in dollars) of a rental. Then find the total cost if a rental regularly costs $3.99.

@HomeTutor for problem solving help at classzone.com

52. ★ **SHORT RESPONSE** Each day you use your pay-as-you-go cell phone you pay $.25 per minute for the first 10 minutes and $.10 per minute for any time over 10 minutes. Write an equation that gives the daily cost C (in dollars) as a function of the time t (in minutes) when usage exceeds 10 minutes. Which costs more, using the phone for 10 minutes today and 15 minutes tomorrow, or using the phone for 25 minutes today? *Explain.*

53. **DIVING** In a diving competition, a diver's score is the product of the difficulty level d of a dive and the sum of the scores x, y, and z of 3 judges. Write a simplified expression that represents the diver's score.

54. ★ **EXTENDED RESPONSE** During the summer you give one hour saxophone lessons to 20 students each week. Use the information in the advertisement.

a. **Model** Write an equation that gives your weekly earnings y (in dollars) as a function of the number x of beginning students that you teach.

b. **Calculate** Find your weekly earnings if 15 of your 20 students are beginners.

c. **Explain** Suppose that you plan to teach for 10 weeks and want to earn $4000 for the summer. How many advanced students should you teach? Your answer should include the following:

- a table of values generated by the equation in part (a)
- an explanation of your method for answering the question

55. **CHALLENGE** A drama club plans to sell 100 tickets to a school musical. An adult ticket costs $6, and a student ticket costs $4. Students who attend the school get a $1 discount. The club expects two thirds of the student tickets to be discounted. Write an equation that gives the total revenue r (in dollars) as a function of the number a of adult tickets sold.

MIXED REVIEW

PREVIEW
Prepare for Lesson 2.6 in Exs. 56–61.

Multiply or divide. *(p. 915)*

56. $\frac{1}{2} \cdot \frac{2}{5}$ 57. $\frac{4}{7} \cdot \frac{1}{8}$ 58. $1\frac{2}{3} \cdot 2\frac{3}{10}$

59. $\frac{1}{5} \div \frac{3}{10}$ 60. $\frac{2}{3} \div \frac{4}{9}$ 61. $2\frac{3}{4} \div 1\frac{5}{8}$

Find the sum, difference, or product.

62. $-7 + (-4)$ *(p. 74)* 63. $8 + (-11)$ *(p. 74)* 64. $12 - 23$ *(p. 80)*

65. $-9 - 6$ *(p. 80)* 66. $(-11)(-2.1)$ *(p. 88)* 67. $15(3.5)$ *(p. 88)*

QUIZ *for Lessons 2.4–2.5*

Find the product. *(p. 88)*

1. $-5 \cdot (-5)$ 2. $18 \cdot \left(-\frac{7}{6}\right)$ 3. $8 \cdot \frac{4}{5} \cdot (-10)$ 4. $9 \cdot (-7) \cdot (-1.2)$

5. $(-3x) \cdot (-4)$ 6. $-\frac{2}{3}x \cdot 15$ 7. $x \cdot 1.5 \cdot (-6.4)$ 8. $(-2)(13x)$

Use the distributive property to write an equivalent expression. *(p. 96)*

9. $7(x + 14)$ 10. $-4(5x + 9)$ 11. $-5(2x - 6)$ 12. $(3 - x)6$

PROBLEM SOLVING WORKSHOP
LESSON 2.5

Using ALTERNATIVE METHODS

Another Way to Solve Example 5, page 98

MULTIPLE REPRESENTATIONS In Example 5 on page 98, you saw how to solve a problem about exercising using a verbal model and an equation. You can also solve the problem by breaking it into parts.

PROBLEM

EXERCISING Your daily workout plan involves a total of 50 minutes of running and swimming. You burn 15 calories per minute when running and 9 calories per minute when swimming. Find the number of calories you burn in your 50 minute workout if you run for 20 minutes.

METHOD

Breaking into Parts You can solve the problem by breaking it into parts.

STEP 1 **Find** the number of calories you burn when running.

15 calories per minute • 20 minutes = 300 calories

Your running time is 20 minutes, so your swimming time is 50 − 20 = 30 minutes.

STEP 2 **Find** the calories you burn when swimming.

9 calories per minute • 30 minutes = 270 calories

STEP 3 **Add** the calories you burn when doing each activity. You burn a total of 570 calories.

300 calories + 270 calories = 570 calories

PRACTICE

1. **VACATIONING** Your family is taking a vacation for 10 nights. You will spend some nights at a campground and the rest of the nights at a motel. A campground stay costs \$15 per night, and a motel stay costs \$60 per night. Find the total cost of lodging if you stay at a campground for 6 nights. Solve this problem using two different methods.

2. **WHAT IF?** In Exercise 1, suppose the vacation lasts 12 days. Find the total cost of lodging if you stay at the campground for 6 nights. Solve this problem using two different methods.

3. **FLORIST** During the summer, you work 35 hours per week at a florist shop. You get paid \$8 per hour for working at the register and \$9.50 per hour for making deliveries. Find the total amount you earn this week if you spend 5 hours making deliveries. Solve this problem using two different methods.

4. **ERROR ANALYSIS** *Describe* and correct the error in solving Exercise 3.

\$8 per hour • 5 hours = \$40

\$9.50 per hour • 30 hours = \$285

\$40 + \$285 = \$325

2.6 Divide Real Numbers

Before You multiplied real numbers.
Now You will divide real numbers.
Why? So you can calculate volleyball statistics, as in Ex. 57.

Key Vocabulary
- **multiplicative inverse**
- **reciprocal,** *p. 915*
- **mean,** *p. 918*

Reciprocals like $\frac{2}{3}$ and $\frac{3}{2}$ have the property that their product is 1:

$$\frac{2}{3} \cdot \frac{3}{2} = 1$$

The reciprocal of a nonzero number a, written $\frac{1}{a}$, is called the **multiplicative inverse** of a. Zero does not have a multiplicative inverse because there is no number a such that $0 \cdot a = 1$.

KEY CONCEPT *For Your Notebook*

Inverse Property of Multiplication

Words The product of a nonzero number and its multiplicative inverse is 1.

Algebra $a \cdot \frac{1}{a} = \frac{1}{a} \cdot a = 1, a \neq 0$ **Example** $8 \cdot \frac{1}{8} = 1$

EXAMPLE 1 **Find multiplicative inverses of numbers**

a. The multiplicative inverse of $-\frac{1}{5}$ is -5 because $-\frac{1}{5} \cdot (-5) = 1$.

b. The multiplicative inverse of $-\frac{6}{7}$ is $-\frac{7}{6}$ because $-\frac{6}{7} \cdot \left(-\frac{7}{6}\right) = 1$.

WRITE INVERSES
You can find the inverse of $-\frac{6}{7}$ as follows:

$$\frac{1}{-\frac{6}{7}} \cdot 1 = \frac{1}{-\frac{6}{7}} \cdot \frac{7}{7}$$
$$= -\frac{7}{6}$$

DIVISION Because the expressions $6 \div 3$ and $6 \cdot \frac{1}{3}$ have the same value, 2, you can conclude that $6 \div 3 = 6 \cdot \frac{1}{3}$. This example illustrates the *division rule.*

KEY CONCEPT *For Your Notebook*

Division Rule

Words To divide a number a by a nonzero number b, multiply a by the multiplicative inverse of b.

Algebra $a \div b = a \cdot \frac{1}{b}, b \neq 0$ **Example** $5 \div 2 = 5 \cdot \frac{1}{2}$

SIGN OF A QUOTIENT Because division can be expressed as multiplication, the sign rules for division are the same as the sign rules for multiplication.

AVOID ERRORS
You cannot divide a real number by 0, because 0 does not have a multiplicative inverse.

KEY CONCEPT *For Your Notebook*

The Sign of a Quotient

- The quotient of two real numbers with the *same* sign is positive.
- The quotient of two real numbers with *different* signs is negative.
- The quotient of 0 and any nonzero real number is 0.

EXAMPLE 2 Divide real numbers

Find the quotient.

a. $-16 \div 4 = -16 \cdot \frac{1}{4}$
$= -4$

b. $-20 \div \left(-\frac{5}{3}\right) = -20 \cdot \left(-\frac{3}{5}\right)$
$= 12$

✓ GUIDED PRACTICE for Examples 1 and 2

Find the multiplicative inverse of the number.

1. -27 **2.** -8 **3.** $-\frac{4}{7}$ **4.** $-\frac{1}{3}$

Find the quotient.

5. $-64 \div (-4)$ **6.** $-\frac{3}{8} \div \left(\frac{3}{10}\right)$ **7.** $18 \div \left(-\frac{2}{9}\right)$ **8.** $-\frac{2}{5} \div 18$

EXAMPLE 3 Find the mean

TEMPERATURES The table gives the daily minimum temperatures (in degrees Fahrenheit) in Barrow, Alaska, for the first 5 days of February 2004. Find the mean daily minimum temperature.

Day in February	1	2	3	4	5
Minimum temperature (°F)	−21	−29	−39	−39	−22

Point Barrow Observatory

Solution

To find the mean daily minimum temperature, find the sum of the minimum temperatures for the 5 days and then divide the sum by 5.

REVIEW MEAN
For help with finding a mean, see p. 918.

$$\text{Mean} = \frac{-21 + (-29) + (-39) + (-39) + (-22)}{5}$$

$$= -\frac{150}{5} = -30$$

▶ The mean daily minimum temperature was −30°F.

EXAMPLE 4 Simplify an expression

Simplify the expression $\frac{36x - 24}{6}$.

ANOTHER WAY
You can simplify the expression by first rewriting it as a difference of two fractions: $\frac{36x - 24}{6} = \frac{36x}{6} - \frac{24}{6} = 6x - 4$.

$\frac{36x - 24}{6} = (36x - 24) \div 6$ **Rewrite fraction as division.**

$= (36x - 24) \cdot \frac{1}{6}$ **Division rule**

$= 36x \cdot \frac{1}{6} - 24 \cdot \frac{1}{6}$ **Distributive property**

$= 6x - 4$ **Simplify.**

✓ GUIDED PRACTICE for Examples 3 and 4

9. Find the mean of the numbers -3, 4, 2.8, and -1.5.

10. TEMPERATURES Find the mean daily maximum temperature (in degrees Fahrenheit) in Barrow, Alaska, for the first 5 days of February 2004.

Day in February	1	2	3	4	5
Maximum temperature (°F)	−3	−20	−21	−22	−18

Simplify the expression.

11. $\frac{2x - 8}{-4}$ **12.** $\frac{-6y + 18}{3}$ **13.** $\frac{-10z - 20}{-5}$

OPERATIONS ON REAL NUMBERS In this chapter, you saw how to find the sum, difference, product, and quotient of two real numbers a and b. You can use the values of a and b to determine whether the result is positive, negative, or 0.

CONCEPT SUMMARY *For Your Notebook*

Rules for Addition, Subtraction, Multiplication, and Division

Let a and b be real numbers.

Expression	$a + b$	$a - b$	$a \cdot b$	$a \div b$
Positive if...	the number with the greater absolute value is positive.	$a > b$.	a and b have the same sign ($a \neq 0, b \neq 0$).	a and b have the same sign ($a \neq 0, b \neq 0$).
Negative if...	the number with the greater absolute value is negative.	$a < b$.	a and b have different signs ($a \neq 0, b \neq 0$).	a and b have different signs ($a \neq 0, b \neq 0$).
Zero if...	a and b are additive inverses.	$a = b$.	$a = 0$ or $b = 0$.	$a = 0$ and $b \neq 0$.

2.6 EXERCISES

HOMEWORK KEY ○ = **WORKED-OUT SOLUTIONS** on p. WS4 for Exs. 13, 35, and 53
★ = **STANDARDIZED TEST PRACTICE** Exs. 2, 23, 48, 49, 55, 56, and 57

SKILL PRACTICE

1. **VOCABULARY** Copy and complete: The product of a nonzero number and its _?_ is 1.

2. ★ **WRITING** How can you tell whether the mean of n numbers is negative without actually dividing the sum of the numbers by n? *Explain.*

EXAMPLE 1 on p. 103 for Exs. 3–10, 23

FINDING INVERSES **Find the multiplicative inverse of the number.**

3. -18
4. -9
5. -1
6. $-\frac{1}{2}$
7. $-\frac{3}{4}$
8. $-\frac{5}{9}$
9. $-4\frac{1}{3}$
10. $-2\frac{2}{5}$

EXAMPLE 2 on p. 104 for Exs. 11–22

FINDING QUOTIENTS **Find the quotient.**

11. $-21 \div 3$
12. $-18 \div (-6)$
13. $-1 \div \left(-\frac{7}{2}\right)$
14. $15 \div \left(-\frac{3}{4}\right)$
15. $13 \div \left(-4\frac{1}{3}\right)$
16. $-\frac{2}{3} \div 2$
17. $-\frac{1}{2} \div \frac{1}{5}$
18. $-\frac{1}{5} \div (-6)$
19. $-\frac{4}{7} \div (-2)$
20. $-1 \div \left(-\frac{6}{5}\right)$
21. $8 \div \left(-\frac{4}{11}\right)$
22. $-\frac{1}{3} \div \frac{5}{3}$

23. ★ **MULTIPLE CHOICE** If $-\frac{5}{7}x = 1$, what is the value of x?

Ⓐ $-1\frac{2}{5}$ Ⓑ $\frac{5}{7}$ Ⓒ 1 Ⓓ $\frac{12}{5}$

EXAMPLE 3 on p. 104 for Exs. 24–32

FINDING MEANS **Find the mean of the numbers.**

24. $-10, -8, 3$
25. $12, -8, -9$
26. $18, -9, 0, -5$
27. $-2, 9, -3, 5$
28. $-1, -4, -5, 10$
29. $7, -4, 1, -9, -6$
30. $-5.3, -2, 1.3$
31. $0.25, -4, -0.75, -1, 6$
32. $-0.6, 0.18, -2, 5, -0.5$

EXAMPLE 4 on p. 105 for Exs. 33–43

SIMPLIFYING EXPRESSIONS **Simplify the expression.**

33. $\frac{6x - 14}{2}$
34. $\frac{12y - 8}{-4}$
35. $\frac{9z - 6}{-3}$
36. $\frac{-6p + 15}{6}$
37. $\frac{5 - 25q}{10}$
38. $\frac{-18 - 21r}{-12}$
39. $\frac{-24a - 10}{-8}$
40. $\frac{-20b + 12}{-5}$
41. $\frac{36 - 27c}{9}$

ERROR ANALYSIS ***Describe*** **and correct the error in simplifying the expression.**

42.
$$\frac{12 - 18x}{6} = (12 - 18x) \cdot \left(-\frac{1}{6}\right)$$
$$= 12\left(-\frac{1}{6}\right) - 18x\left(-\frac{1}{6}\right)$$
$$= -2 + 3x$$

43.
$$\frac{-15x - 10}{-5} = (-15x - 10) \cdot \left(-\frac{1}{5}\right)$$
$$= -15x\left(-\frac{1}{5}\right) - 10\left(-\frac{1}{5}\right)$$
$$= 3x - 2$$

EVALUATING EXPRESSIONS **Evaluate the expression.**

44. $\frac{2y - x}{x}$ when $x = 1$ and $y = -4$

45. $\frac{4x}{3y + x}$ when $x = 6$ and $y = -8$

46. $\frac{-9x}{y^2 - 1}$ when $x = -3$ and $y = -2$

47. $\frac{y - x}{xy}$ when $x = -6$ and $y = -2$

48. ★ **WRITING** Tell whether division is commutative and associative. Give examples to support your answer.

49. ★ **MULTIPLE CHOICE** Let a and b be positive numbers, and let c and d be negative numbers. Which quotient has a value that is always negative?

Ⓐ $\frac{a}{b} \div \frac{c}{d}$ Ⓑ $\frac{a}{c} \div \frac{b}{d}$ Ⓒ $\frac{c^2}{a} \div \frac{b}{d}$ Ⓓ $\frac{a}{cd} \div b$

50. **CHALLENGE** Find the mean of the integers from −410 to 400. *Explain* how you got your answer.

51. **CHALLENGE** What is the mean of a number and three times its opposite? *Explain* your reasoning.

PROBLEM SOLVING

EXAMPLE 2 on p. 104 for Ex. 52

52. **SPORTS** Free diving means diving without the aid of breathing equipment. Suppose that an athlete free dives to an elevation of −42 meters in 60 seconds. Find the average rate of change in the diver's elevation.

@HomeTutor for problem solving help at classzone.com

EXAMPLE 3 on p. 104 for Exs. 53–54

53. **WEATHER** The daily mean temperature is the mean of the high and low temperatures for a given day. The high temperature for Boston, Massachusetts, on January 10, 2004, was −10.6°C. The low temperature was −18.9°C. Find the daily mean temperature for that day.

@HomeTutor for problem solving help at classzone.com

54. **MULTI-STEP PROBLEM** The table shows the changes in the values of one share of stock A and one share of stock B over 5 days.

Day of week	Monday	Tuesday	Wednesday	Thursday	Friday
Change in share value for stock A (dollars)	−0.45	−0.32	0.66	−1.12	1.53
Change in share value for stock B (dollars)	−0.37	0.14	0.59	−0.53	1.02

a. Find the average daily change in share value for each stock.

b. Which stock performed better over the 5 days? How much more money did the better performing stock earn, on average, per day?

c. Can you conclude that the stock that performed better over all 5 days also performed better over the first 4 days of the week? *Explain* your reasoning.

55. ★ **MULTIPLE CHOICE** In a trivia competition, your team earned 60, −100, 300, 120, and −80 points on 5 questions. The sixth question has a value of 300 points. By how many points will your team's mean score per question change if you answer the sixth question correctly?

Ⓐ 40 points Ⓑ 50 points Ⓒ 60 points Ⓓ 100 points

56. ★ **SHORT RESPONSE** The South Aral Sea in Russia was about 57 meters above sea level in 1965. Scientists once predicted that the elevation would be about 34 meters above sea level in 2002.

a. Estimate the average rate of change in elevation for the period 1965–2002 using the scientists' prediction. Round to the nearest hundredth of a meter per year.

b. More recent research suggests that the elevation decreased to about 30.5 meters above sea level in 2002. Use this information to predict the elevation in 2010. *Explain* the steps of your solution.

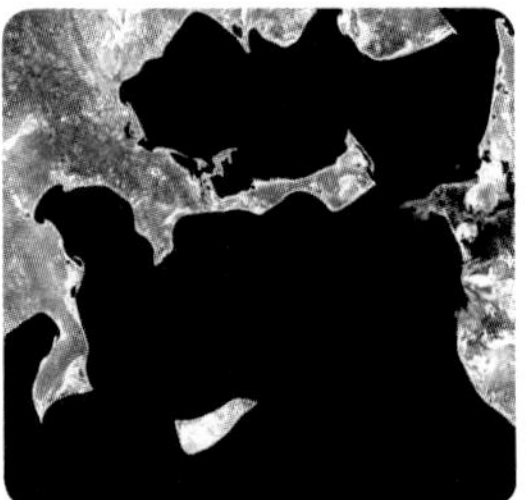
South Aral Sea, 1973

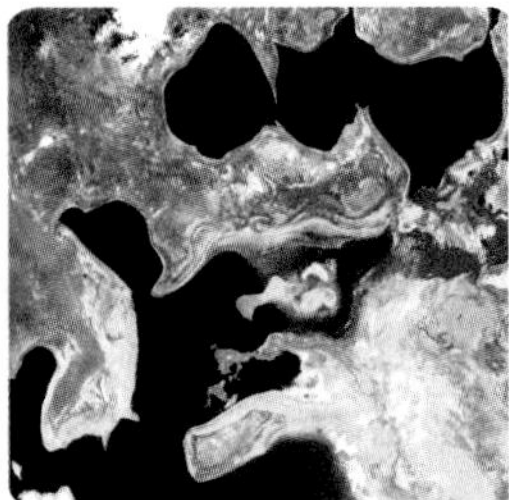
South Aral Sea, 2000

57. ★ **EXTENDED RESPONSE** In volleyball, an ace is a serve that the opponent doesn't hit. Ace efficiency is a measure of a player's ability to hit aces while minimizing service errors. The ace efficiency f is given by the formula $f = \frac{a - e}{s}$ where a is the number of aces, e is the number of service errors, and s is the total number of serves.

a. **Calculate** Find the ace efficiency for a player who has 108 aces and 125 service errors in 500 serves.

b. **Compare** If the player makes 30 more aces and 20 more service errors in the next 100 serves, will the ace efficiency improve? *Explain.*

c. **Justify** Under what conditions would a player's ace efficiency be 0? 1? −1? *Justify* your answers algebraically.

58. **CHALLENGE** The average daily balance of a checking account is the sum of the daily balances in a given period divided by the number of days in the period. Suppose that a period has 30 days. Find the average daily balance of an account that has a balance of \$110 for 18 days, −\$300 for 10 days, and \$100 for the rest of the period.

MIXED REVIEW

Evaluate the expression.

59. $6x$ when $x = 15$ (p. 2)

60. $4x + 2y$ when $x = 3$ and $y = 7$ (p. 8)

61. $x - y - 2$ when $x = 3$ and $y = -4$ (p. 80)

62. $-4xy$ when $x = -2$ and $y = -1.4$ (p. 88)

PREVIEW
Prepare for Lesson 2.7 in Exs. 63–64.

Identify the hypothesis and the conclusion of the statement. Tell whether the statement is *true* or *false*. If it is false, give a counterexample. (p. 64)

63. If a number is a whole number, then the number is a rational number.

64. If a number is a rational number, then the number is an integer.

Investigating Algebra ACTIVITY *Use before Lesson 2.7*

2.7 Writing Statements in If-Then Form

MATERIALS • paper and pencil

QUESTION **How can you write an *all* or *none* statement in if-then form?**

EXPLORE **Tell whether certain statements are true about a group**

STEP 1 ***Answer questions*** Copy the questions below and write your answers beside them.

1. Do you play an instrument?
2. Do you participate in a school sport?
3. Are you taking an art class?
4. Do you walk to school?

STEP 2 ***Write if-then statements*** Each of the *all* or *none* statements below can be written in if-then form. Copy each statement and complete its equivalent if-then form. The first one is done for you as an example.

1. All of the students in our group play an instrument.
   If a student is in our group, then the student plays an instrument.
2. None of the students in our group participates in a school sport.
   If _?_, then _?_.
3. None of the students in our group is taking an art class.
   If _?_, then _?_.
4. All of the students in our group walk to school.
   If _?_, then _?_.

STEP 3 ***Analyze statements*** Form a group with 2 or 3 classmates. Tell whether each if-then statement in Step 2 is *true* or *false* for your group. If the statement is false, give a counterexample.

DRAW CONCLUSIONS **Use your observations to complete these exercises**

1. *Describe* the similarity and difference in the if-then forms of the following statements:

   All of the students in our group listen to rock music.

   None of the students in our group listens to rock music.

Rewrite the given conditional statement in if-then form. Then tell whether the statement is *true* or *false*. If it is false, give a counterexample.

2. All of the positive numbers are integers.
3. All of the rational numbers can be written as fractions.
4. None of the negative numbers is a whole number.
5. None of the rational numbers has an opposite equal to itself.

2.7 Find Square Roots and Compare Real Numbers

Before You found squares of numbers and compared rational numbers.

Now You will find square roots and compare real numbers.

Why? So you can find side lengths of geometric shapes, as in Ex. 54.

Key Vocabulary
- **square root**
- **radicand**
- **perfect square**
- **irrational number**
- **real numbers**

Recall that the square of 4 is $4^2 = 16$ and the square of -4 is $(-4)^2 = 16$. The numbers 4 and -4 are called the *square roots* of 16. In this lesson, you will find the square roots of nonnegative numbers.

KEY CONCEPT *For Your Notebook*

Square Root of a Number

Words If $b^2 = a$, then b is a **square root** of a.

Example $3^2 = 9$ and $(-3)^2 = 9$, so 3 and -3 are square roots of 9.

All positive real numbers have two square roots, a positive square root (or *principal* square root) and a negative square root. A square root is written with the radical symbol $\sqrt{\ }$. The number or expression inside a radical symbol is the **radicand.**

radical symbol → $\sqrt{a}$ ← radicand

Zero has only one square root, 0. Negative real numbers do not have real square roots because the square of every real number is either positive or 0.

EXAMPLE 1 Find square roots

Evaluate the expression.

READING The symbol $\pm$ is read as "plus or minus" and refers to both the positive square root and the negative square root.

a. $\pm\sqrt{36} = \pm 6$ The positive and negative square roots of 36 are 6 and -6.

b. $\sqrt{49} = 7$ The positive square root of 49 is 7.

c. $-\sqrt{4} = -2$ The negative square root of 4 is -2.

✓ **GUIDED PRACTICE** for Example 1

Evaluate the expression.

1. $-\sqrt{9}$ **2.** $\sqrt{25}$ **3.** $\pm\sqrt{64}$ **4.** $-\sqrt{81}$

PERFECT SQUARES The square of an integer is called a **perfect square**. As shown in Example 1, the square root of a perfect square is an integer. As you will see in Example 2, you need to approximate a square root if the radicand is a whole number that is *not* a perfect square.

EXAMPLE 2 Approximate a square root

FURNITURE The top of a folding table is a square whose area is 945 square inches. Approximate the side length of the tabletop to the nearest inch.

Solution

You need to find the side length s of the tabletop such that $s^2 = 945$. This means that s is the positive square root of 945. You can use a table to determine whether 945 is a perfect square.

Number	28	29	30	31	32
Square of number	784	841	900	961	1024

As shown in the table, 945 is *not* a perfect square. The greatest perfect square less than 945 is 900. The least perfect square greater than 945 is 961.

$900 < 945 < 961$ **Write a compound inequality that compares 945 with both 900 and 961.**

$\sqrt{900} < \sqrt{945} < \sqrt{961}$ **Take positive square root of each number.**

$30 < \sqrt{945} < 31$ **Find square root of each perfect square.**

Because 945 is closer to 961 than to 900, $\sqrt{945}$ is closer to 31 than to 30.

▶ The side length of the tabletop is about 31 inches.

USING A CALCULATOR In Example 2, you can use a calculator to obtain a better approximation of the side length of the tabletop.

 945 

The side length is about 30.74 inches, which is closer to 31 than to 30.

GUIDED PRACTICE for Example 2

Approximate the square root to the nearest integer.

5. $\sqrt{32}$ **6.** $\sqrt{103}$ **7.** $-\sqrt{48}$ **8.** $-\sqrt{350}$

IRRATIONAL NUMBERS The square root of a whole number that is not a perfect square is an example of an *irrational number*. An **irrational number**, such as $\sqrt{945} = 30.74085\ldots$, is a number that cannot be written as a quotient of two integers. The decimal form of an irrational number neither terminates nor repeats.

REAL NUMBERS The set of **real numbers** is the set of all rational and irrational numbers, as illustrated in the Venn diagram below. Every point on the real number line represents a real number.

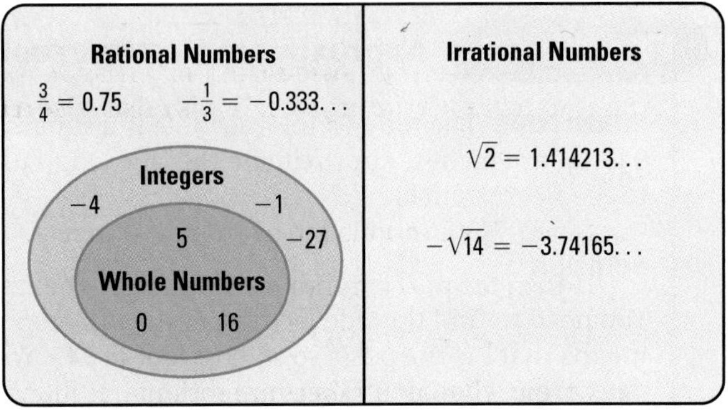

EXAMPLE 3 Classify numbers

Tell whether each of the following numbers is a real number, a rational number, an irrational number, an integer, or a whole number: $\sqrt{24}$, $\sqrt{100}$, $-\sqrt{81}$.

Number	Real number?	Rational number?	Irrational number?	Integer?	Whole number?
$\sqrt{24}$	Yes	No	Yes	No	No
$\sqrt{100}$	Yes	Yes	No	Yes	Yes
$-\sqrt{81}$	Yes	Yes	No	Yes	No

EXAMPLE 4 Graph and order real numbers

Order the numbers from least to greatest: $\frac{4}{3}$, $-\sqrt{5}$, $\sqrt{13}$, -2.5, $\sqrt{9}$.

Solution

Begin by graphing the numbers on a number line.

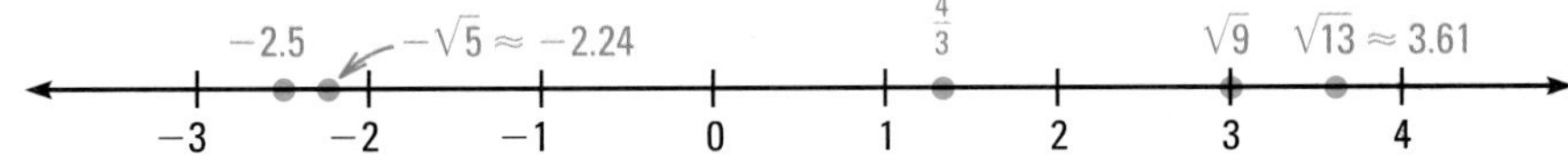

▸ Read the numbers from left to right: -2.5, $-\sqrt{5}$, $\frac{4}{3}$, $\sqrt{9}$, $\sqrt{13}$.

✓ GUIDED PRACTICE for Examples 3 and 4

9. Tell whether each of the following numbers is a real number, a rational number, an irrational number, an integer, or a whole number: $-\frac{9}{2}$, 5.2, 0, $\sqrt{7}$, 4.1, $-\sqrt{20}$. Then order the numbers from least to greatest.

CONDITIONAL STATEMENTS In the activity on page 109, you saw that a conditional statement not in if-then form can be written in that form.

EXAMPLE 5 Rewrite a conditional statement in if-then form

Rewrite the given conditional statement in if-then form. Then tell whether the statement is *true* or *false*. If it is false, give a counterexample.

Solution

a. Given: No fractions are irrational numbers.

If-then form: If a number is a fraction, then it is not an irrational number.

The statement is true.

b. Given: All real numbers are rational numbers.

If-then form: If a number is a real number, then it is a rational number.

The statement is false. For example, $\sqrt{2}$ is a real number but *not* a rational number.

GUIDED PRACTICE for Example 5

Rewrite the conditional statement in if-then form. Then tell whether the statement is *true* or *false*. If it is false, give a counterexample.

10. All square roots of perfect squares are rational numbers.
11. All repeating decimals are irrational numbers.
12. No integers are irrational numbers.

2.7 EXERCISES

HOMEWORK KEY

○ = **WORKED-OUT SOLUTIONS** on p. WS5 for Exs. 9, 19, and 49

★ = **STANDARDIZED TEST PRACTICE** Exs. 2, 23, 42, 43, 44, 50, and 53

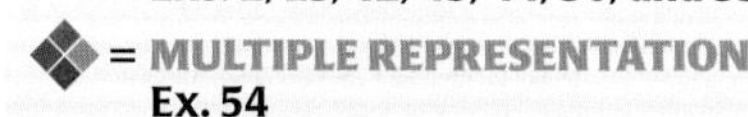

◆ = **MULTIPLE REPRESENTATIONS** Ex. 54

SKILL PRACTICE

1. **VOCABULARY** Copy and complete: The set of all rational and irrational numbers is called the set of _?_.

2. ★ **WRITING** Without calculating, how can you tell whether the square root of a whole number is rational or irrational?

EXAMPLE 1 on p. 110 for Exs. 3–14

EVALUATING SQUARE ROOTS **Evaluate the expression.**

3. $\sqrt{4}$
4. $-\sqrt{49}$
5. $-\sqrt{9}$
6. $\pm\sqrt{1}$
7. $\sqrt{196}$
8. $\pm\sqrt{121}$
9. $\pm\sqrt{2500}$
10. $-\sqrt{256}$
11. $-\sqrt{225}$
12. $\sqrt{361}$
13. $\pm\sqrt{169}$
14. $-\sqrt{1600}$

EXAMPLE 2 on p. 111 for Exs. 15–22

APPROXIMATING SQUARE ROOTS Approximate the square root to the nearest integer.

15. $\sqrt{10}$
16. $-\sqrt{18}$
17. $-\sqrt{3}$
18. $\sqrt{150}$
19. $-\sqrt{86}$
20. $\sqrt{40}$
21. $\sqrt{200}$
22. $-\sqrt{65}$

23. ★ **MULTIPLE CHOICE** Which number is between −30 and −25?

Ⓐ $-\sqrt{1610}$ Ⓑ $-\sqrt{680}$ Ⓒ $-\sqrt{410}$ Ⓓ $-\sqrt{27}$

EXAMPLES 3 and 4 on p. 112 for Exs. 24–29

CLASSIFYING AND ORDERING REAL NUMBERS Tell whether each number in the list is a real number, a rational number, an irrational number, an integer, or a whole number. Then order the numbers from least to greatest.

24. $\sqrt{49}$, 8, $-\sqrt{4}$, −3
25. $-\sqrt{12}$, −3.7, $\sqrt{9}$, 2.9
26. −11.5, $-\sqrt{121}$, −10, $\frac{25}{2}$, $\sqrt{144}$
27. $\sqrt{8}$, $-\frac{2}{5}$, −1, 0.6, $\sqrt{6}$
28. $-\frac{8}{3}$, $-\sqrt{5}$, 2.6, −1.5, $\sqrt{5}$
29. −8.3, $-\sqrt{80}$, $-\frac{17}{2}$, −8.25, $-\sqrt{100}$

EXAMPLE 5 on p. 113 for Exs. 30–33

ANALYZING CONDITIONAL STATEMENTS Rewrite the conditional statement in if-then form. Then tell whether the statement is *true* or *false*. If it is false, give a counterexample.

30. All whole numbers are real numbers.
31. All real numbers are irrational numbers.
32. No perfect squares are whole numbers.
33. No irrational numbers are whole numbers.

EVALUATING EXPRESSIONS Evaluate the expression for the given value of x.

34. $3 + \sqrt{x}$ when $x = 9$
35. $11 - \sqrt{x}$ when $x = 81$
36. $4 \cdot \sqrt{x}$ when $x = 49$
37. $-7 \cdot \sqrt{x}$ when $x = 36$
38. $-3 \cdot \sqrt{x} - 7$ when $x = 121$
39. $6 \cdot \sqrt{x} + 3$ when $x = 100$
40. $\frac{\sqrt{x}}{x}$ when $x = 4$
41. $\frac{\sqrt{x}}{5} - 17$ when $x = 25$

42. ★ **OPEN-ENDED** Without using a calculator, find three rational numbers between $-\sqrt{26}$ and $-\sqrt{15}$. *Explain* how you found the numbers.

43. ★ **MULTIPLE CHOICE** If $x = 36$, the value of which expression is a perfect square?

Ⓐ $\sqrt{x} + 17$ Ⓑ $87 - \sqrt{x}$ Ⓒ $5 \cdot \sqrt{x}$ Ⓓ $8 \cdot \sqrt{x} + 2$

44. ★ **WRITING** Simplify $(\sqrt{x})^2$ for $x \geq 0$ using the definition of square root. Then verify your answer using several values of x that are perfect squares.

45. **CHALLENGE** Find the first five perfect squares x such that $2 \cdot \sqrt{x}$ is also a perfect square. *Describe* your method.

46. **CHALLENGE** Let n be any whole number from 1 to 1000. For how many values of n is $\sqrt{n}$ a rational number? *Explain* your reasoning.

◯ = WORKED-OUT SOLUTIONS on p. WS1

★ = STANDARDIZED TEST PRACTICE

PROBLEM SOLVING

EXAMPLE 1 on p. 110 for Exs. 47, 49

47. **ART** The area of a square painting is 3600 square inches. Find the side length of the painting.

@HomeTutor for problem solving help at classzone.com

EXAMPLE 2 on p. 111 for Exs. 48, 50

48. **SOCCER** Some soccer drills are practiced in a square section of a field. If the section of a field for a soccer drill is 1620 square yards, find the side length of the section. Round your answer to the nearest yard.

@HomeTutor for problem solving help at classzone.com

49. **MAZES** The table shows the locations and areas of various life-size square mazes. Find the side lengths of the mazes. Then tell whether the side lengths are *rational* or *irrational* numbers.

Location of maze	Area (ft^2)
Dallas, Texas	1225
San Francisco, California	576
Corona, New York	2304
Waterville, Maine	900

Maze at Corona, New York

50. ★ **SHORT RESPONSE** You plan to use a square section of a park for a small outdoor concert. The section should have an area of 1450 square feet. You have 150 feet of rope to use to surround the section. Do you have enough rope? *Explain* your reasoning.

51. **MATH HISTORY** To calculate the value of the irrational number π, the Greek mathematician Archimedes first estimated the square root of a certain integer x. He found that $\sqrt{x}$ was between $\frac{265}{153}$ and $\frac{1351}{780}$. Find the value of x. *Explain* how you got your answer.

52. **MULTI-STEP PROBLEM** The Kelvin temperature scale was invented by Lord Kelvin in the 19th century and is often used for scientific measurements. To convert a temperature from degrees Celsius (°C) to kelvin (K), you add 273 to the temperature in degrees Celsius.
   - **a.** Convert 17°C to kelvin.
   - **b.** The speed s (in meters per second) of sound in air is given by the formula $s = 20.1 \cdot \sqrt{K}$ where K is the temperature in kelvin. Find the speed of sound in air at 17°C. Round your answer to the nearest meter per second.

53. ★ **SHORT RESPONSE** A homeowner is building a square patio and will cover the patio with square tiles. Each tile has an area of 256 square inches and costs \$3.45. The homeowner has \$500 to spend on tiles.
   - **a. Calculate** How many tiles can the homeowner buy?
   - **b. Explain** Find the side length (in feet) of the largest patio that the homeowner can build. *Explain* how you got your answer.

54. **MULTIPLE REPRESENTATIONS** The diagram shows the approximate areas (in square meters) of the square bases for the pyramids of Giza.

a. **Making a Table** Make a table that gives the following quotients (rounded to the nearest tenth) for each of the 3 pairs of pyramids:
   - (area of larger base) ÷ (area of smaller base)
   - (side length of larger base) ÷ (side length of smaller base)

   For each pair of pyramids, how are the two quotients related?

b. **Writing an Equation** Write an equation that gives the quotient q of the side lengths as a function of the quotient r of the areas.

55. **CHALLENGE** Write an equation that gives the edge length ℓ of a cube as a function of the surface area A of the cube.

MIXED REVIEW

Evaluate the expression. *(p. 8)*

56. $11 + 6 - 3$ 57. $18 - 3^2$ 58. $9 \cdot 2^2 - 1$ 59. $6(4^2 + 4)$

60. $12 \cdot 3 + 15$ 61. $6 \cdot 4 + 7 \cdot 5$ 62. $9(15 - 2 \cdot 4)$ 63. $5^2 - 2^3$

PREVIEW Prepare for Lesson 3.1 in Exs. 64–71.

Solve the equation using mental math. *(p. 21)*

64. $8 + x = 13$ 65. $x - 20 = 15$ 66. $4x = 32$ 67. $\frac{x}{7} = 5$

68. $x - 14 = 30$ 69. $x + 11 = 27$ 70. $\frac{x}{9} = 10$ 71. $6x = 48$

QUIZ *for Lessons 2.6–2.7*

Find the quotient. *(p. 103)*

1. $-20 \div (-5)$ 2. $-12 \div \frac{2}{3}$ 3. $\frac{4}{5} \div \left(-\frac{3}{10}\right)$ 4. $-18.2 \div (-3)$

5. Simplify the expression $\frac{15x - 6}{3}$. *(p. 103)*

6. Tell whether each of the following numbers is a real number, a rational number, an irrational number, an integer, or a whole number: -3, $-\sqrt{5}$, -3.7, $\sqrt{3}$. Then order the numbers from least to greatest. *(p. 110)*

7. Rewrite the following conditional statement in if-then form: "No irrational numbers are negative numbers." Tell whether the statement is *true* or *false*. If it is false, give a counterexample. *(p. 110)*

Use Logical Reasoning

GOAL Use inductive and deductive reasoning.

Key Vocabulary
- **inductive reasoning**
- **conjecture**
- **deductive reasoning**

When you make a conclusion based on several examples, you are using **inductive reasoning**. A conclusion reached using inductive reasoning is an example of a *conjecture*. A **conjecture** is a statement that is believed to be true but not yet shown to be true.

EXAMPLE 1 Use inductive reasoning

Your friend asks you to perform the following number trick: *Choose any number. Then double the number. Then add 8. Then multiply by 3. Then divide by 6. Then subtract 4.* Perform the number trick for three different numbers. Then make a conjecture based on the results.

Solution

Step 1: Choose any number.	Choose 5.	Choose 14.	Choose −6.
Step 2: Double the number.	10	28	−12
Step 3: Add 8.	18	36	−4
Step 4: Multiply by 3.	54	108	−12
Step 5: Divide by 6.	9	18	−2
Step 6: Subtract 4.	5	14	−6

Conjecture: The result in Step 6 is the same as the number in Step 1.

EXAMPLE 2 Show that a conjecture is true

Show that the conjecture made in Example 1 is true for all numbers x.

Solution

Step 1: Choose any number.	Choose x.
Step 2: Double the number.	$2x$
Step 3: Add 8.	$2x + 8$
Step 4: Multiply by 3.	$3(2x + 8) = 6x + 24$
Step 5: Divide by 6.	$\frac{6x + 24}{6} = x + 4$
Step 6: Subtract 4.	$(x + 4) - 4 = x$

The result in Step 6 is the same as the number chosen in Step 1. So, the conjecture made in Example 1 is true for all numbers x.

DEDUCTIVE REASONING In Example 2, you simplified the expression at each step. Had you not done this, you would have obtained the expression $\frac{3(2x + 8)}{6} - 4$. You can still show that $\frac{3(2x + 8)}{6} - 4 = x$ by applying *deductive reasoning*. When you make a conclusion based on statements that are assumed or shown to be true, you are using **deductive reasoning**.

EXAMPLE 3 Use deductive reasoning

Show that $\frac{3(2x + 8)}{6} - 4 = x$. Justify each step.

Solution

Step	Justification
$\frac{3(2x + 8)}{6} - 4 = \frac{6x + 24}{6} - 4$	Distributive property
$= (x + 4) - 4$	Divide $(6x + 24)$ by 6.
$= (x + 4) + (-4)$	Subtraction rule
$= x + [4 + (-4)]$	Associative property of addition
$= x + 0$	Inverse property of addition
$= x$	Identity property of addition

PRACTICE

EXAMPLES 1, 2, and 3 on pp. 117–118 for Exs. 1–3

In Exercises 1 and 2, perform the given number trick for three numbers. Make a conjecture based on the results. Then show that your conjecture is true for all numbers.

1. Choose any number. Then subtract 5. Then multiply by 6. Then divide by 3. Then add 10.

2. Choose any number. Then double it. Then add 12. Then multiply by 4. Then divide by 8. Then subtract the number you chose.

3. The steps below show that $\frac{4(3x + 5) - 20}{12} = x$. *Justify* each step.

$\frac{4(3x + 5) - 20}{12} = \frac{(12x + 20) - 20}{12}$ ___?___

$= \frac{(12x + 20) + (-20)}{12}$ ___?___

$= \frac{12x + [20 + (-20)]}{12}$ ___?___

$= \frac{12x + 0}{12}$ ___?___

$= \frac{12x}{12}$ ___?___

$= x$ ___?___

2.4 Multiply Real Numbers

pp. 88–90

EXAMPLE

Find the product.

a. $-4(12) = -48$ **Different signs; product is negative.**

b. $\frac{1}{2}(-6)(-3) = -3(-3)$ **Multiply $\frac{1}{2}$ and -6.**

$= 9$ **Same signs; product is positive.**

EXERCISES

EXAMPLES 1, 3, and 4 on pp. 88–90 for Exs. 29–35

Find the product.

29. $15(-4)$ **30.** $-7.5(-8)$ **31.** $-\frac{2}{5}(-5)(-9)$

Find the product. *Justify* your steps.

32. $-4(-y)(-7)$ **33.** $-\frac{1}{3}x \cdot (-18)$ **34.** $2.5(-4z)(-2)$

35. SWIMMING POOLS The water level of a swimming pool is 3.3 feet and changes at an average rate of -0.14 feet per day due to water evaporation. What will the water level of the pool be after 4 days?

2.5 Apply the Distributive Property

pp. 96–98

EXAMPLE

Use the distributive property to write an equivalent expression.

a. $5(x + 3) = 5(x) + 5(3)$ **Distribute 5.**

$= 5x + 15$ **Simplify.**

b. $(7 - y)(-2y) = 7(-2y) - y(-2y)$ **Distribute $-2y$.**

$= -14y + 2y^2$ **Simplify.**

EXERCISES

EXAMPLES 1, 2, 4, and 5 on pp. 96–98 for Exs. 36–42

Use the distributive property to write an equivalent expression.

36. $8(5 - x)$ **37.** $-3(y + 9)$ **38.** $(z - 4)(-z)$

Simplify the expression.

39. $3(x - 2) + 14$ **40.** $9.1 - 4(m + 3.2)$ **41.** $5n + \frac{1}{2}(8n - 7)$

42. PARTY COSTS You are buying 10 pizzas for a party. Cheese pizzas cost \$11 each, and single topping pizzas cost \$13 each. Write an equation that gives the total cost C (in dollars) as a function of the number p of cheese pizzas that you buy. Then find the total cost if you buy 4 cheese pizzas.

2 CHAPTER REVIEW

2.6 Divide Real Numbers

pp. 103–105

EXAMPLE

Find the quotient.

a. $196 \div (-7) = 196 \cdot \left(-\frac{1}{7}\right)$

$= -28$

b. $-\frac{14}{15} \div \left(-\frac{7}{3}\right) = -\frac{14}{15} \cdot \left(-\frac{3}{7}\right)$

$= \frac{2}{5}$

EXERCISES

EXAMPLES 2, 3, and 4 on pp. 104–105 for Exs. 43–49

Find the quotient.

43. $56 \div (-4)$

44. $-6 \div \frac{3}{13}$

45. $-\frac{4}{9} \div \left(-\frac{2}{3}\right)$

46. SCIENCE A scientist studies the diving abilities of three seals and records the elevations they reach before swimming back up to the surface. Find the mean of the following elevations (in meters) recorded: −380, −307, −354.

Simplify the expression.

47. $\frac{24x - 40}{8}$

48. $\frac{-36m + 18}{6}$

49. $\frac{-18n - 9}{-9}$

2.7 Find Square Roots and Compare Real Numbers

pp. 110–113

EXAMPLE

Order the following numbers from least to greatest: $\sqrt{25}, -\sqrt{18}, -4, 3.2$.

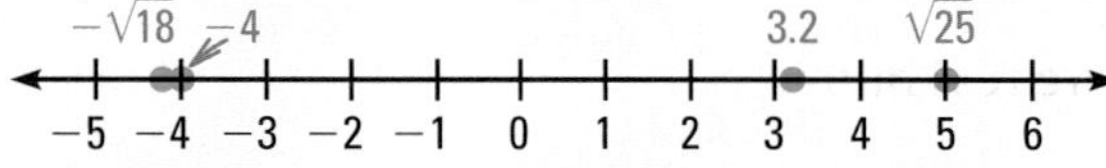

From least to greatest, the numbers are $-\sqrt{18}$, −4, 3.2, and $\sqrt{25}$.

EXERCISES

EXAMPLES 1, 2, 4, and 5 on pp. 110–113 for Exs. 50–60

Evaluate the expression.

50. $\sqrt{121}$

51. $-\sqrt{36}$

52. $\pm\sqrt{81}$

53. $\pm\sqrt{225}$

Approximate the square root to the nearest integer.

54. $\sqrt{97}$

55. $-\sqrt{48}$

56. $-\sqrt{142}$

57. $\sqrt{300}$

Order the numbers in the list from least to greatest.

58. $-\sqrt{49}, -6.8, 2, \sqrt{3}, 1.58$

59. $1.25, \sqrt{11}, -0.3, 0, -\sqrt{4}$

60. Rewrite the following conditional statement in if-then form: "All real numbers are irrational numbers." Tell whether the statement is *true* or *false*. If it is false, give a counterexample.

2 CHAPTER TEST

Tell whether the number is a real number, a rational number, an irrational number, an integer, or a whole number.

1. $-\frac{1}{4}$ **2.** $\sqrt{90}$ **3.** $-\sqrt{144}$ **4.** 8.95

Order the numbers in the list from least to greatest.

5. $-\frac{5}{3}, -2, 3, \frac{1}{2}, -1.07$ **6.** $\sqrt{15}, -4.3, 4.2, 0, -\sqrt{25}$

Find the sum, difference, product, or quotient.

7. $-5 + 2$ **8.** $1.3 + (-10.4)$ **9.** $-\frac{1}{3} + \frac{1}{6}$ **10.** $-\frac{2}{7} - \frac{5}{14}$

11. $-41 - 32$ **12.** $7.2 - (-11.6)$ **13.** $-11(-7)$ **14.** $-4.5(20)(2)$

15. $-\frac{1}{5}(-20)(-5)$ **16.** $-36 \div (-6)$ **17.** $-\frac{3}{5} \div 12$ **18.** $5 \div \left(-\frac{10}{11}\right)$

Evaluate the expression when $x = -6$ and $y = -10$.

19. $-x$ **20.** $|y|$ **21.** $8 - (x - y)$ **22.** $-4x + y$

Simplify the expression.

23. $-9(y - 7)$ **24.** $8(x - 4) - 10x$ **25.** $\frac{-7w - 21}{7}$ **26.** $\frac{-16v + 8}{-4}$

In Exercises 27 and 28, rewrite the conditional statement in if-then form. Then tell whether the statement is *true* or *false*. If it is false, give a counterexample.

27. No rational numbers are integers.

28. All irrational numbers are real numbers.

29. MUSIC The revenue from sales of digital pianos in the United States was \$152.4 million in 2001 and \$149.0 million in 2002. Find the change in revenue from 2001 to 2002.

30. ELEVATORS An elevator moves at a rate of −5.8 feet per second from a height of 300 feet above the ground. It takes 3 seconds for the elevator to make its first stop. How many feet above the ground is the elevator now?

31. SUMMER JOBS You plan to work a total of 25 hours per week at two summer jobs. You will earn \$8.75 per hour working at a cafe and \$10.50 per hour working at an auto shop. Write an equation that gives your weekly pay p (in dollars) as a function of the time t (in hours) spent working at the cafe. Then find your weekly pay if you work 10 hours at the cafe.

32. TEMPERATURES The low temperatures for Montreal, Quebec, in Canada on February 12 for each year during the period 2000–2004 are −6.7°F, −4.2°F, 4.1°F, −3.6°F, and 0.3°F. Find the mean of the temperatures.

2 ★ Standardized TEST PREPARATION

Scoring Rubric

Full Credit
- solution is complete and correct

Partial Credit
- solution is complete but errors are made, *or*
- solution is without error but incomplete

No Credit
- no solution is given, *or*
- solution makes no sense

EXTENDED RESPONSE QUESTIONS

PROBLEM

The *Alvin* is an HOV (human-operated vehicle) used to explore the ocean. A new HOV is being built that will carry explorers deeper and faster. The table shows the capabilities of the two vehicles.

Vehicle	Lowest elevation (m)	Velocity (m/sec)
Alvin	−4500	−30
New HOV	−6500	−44

a. For each vehicle, write an equation that gives the elevation e (in meters) to which the vehicle dives as a function of the elapsed time t (in seconds) of the dive.

b. If both vehicles begin diving from the surface of the ocean at the same time, what will their elevations be after 90 seconds?

c. If both vehicles continue diving, which vehicle will reach its lowest elevation first? *Explain* how you can use the equations you wrote in part (a) to find the answer.

Below are sample solutions to the problem. Read each solution and the comments in blue to see why the sample represents full credit, partial credit, or no credit.

Full credit solution

The correct equations are given.

a. Alvin: $e = -30t$ **New HOV:** $e = -44t$

b. Alvin: $e = -30t$ **New HOV:** $e = -44t$

$= -30(90)$ $= -44(90)$

$= -2700$ $= -3960$

The correct calculations are performed, and the correct elevations are given.

Alvin will be at an elevation of −2700 meters, and the new HOV will be at an elevation of −3960 meters.

c.

t (sec)	Elevation of Alvin (m)	Elevation of new HOV (m)
100	$e = -30(100) = -3000$	$e = -44(100) = -4400$
125	$e = -30(125) = -3750$	$e = -44(125) = -5500$
150	$e = -30(150) = -4500$	$e = -44(150) = -6600$

The reasoning is correct, and it includes use of the equations. The answer is correct.

After 150 seconds, Alvin reaches its lowest elevation, −4500 feet. Because $-6600 < -6500$, the new HOV has reached its lowest elevation in less than 150 seconds. So, the new HOV reaches its lowest elevation first.

Partial credit solution

The correct equations and elevations are given.

The answer is correct, but the reasoning is incorrect. The lowest elevations were not considered.

a. **Alvin:** $e = -30t$ **New HOV:** $e = -44t$

b. **Alvin:** $e = -30(90)$ **New HOV:** $e = -44(90)$

$= -2700$ $= -3960$

Alvin will be at an elevation of -2700 meters, and the new HOV will be at an elevation of -3960 meters.

c. The velocity of Alvin is -30 meters per second, and the velocity of the new HOV is -44 meters per second. So, each second the new HOV descends 14 meters more than Alvin. This means that the new HOV will reach its lowest elevation first.

No credit solution

The equations are incorrect and the elevations are incorrect.

The student's reasoning is incorrect and does not use the equations. The answer is incorrect.

a. **Alvin:** $e = \frac{-4500}{t}$ **New HOV:** $e = \frac{-6500}{t}$

b. **Alvin:** $e = \frac{-4500}{90} = -50$ **New HOV:** $e = \frac{-6500}{90} \approx -72$

Alvin will be at an elevation of -50 meters, and the new HOV will be at an elevation of about -72 meters.

c. Alvin has to travel only to -4500 meters, while the new HOV has to travel to -6500 meters. So, Alvin will reach its lowest elevation first.

PRACTICE Apply the Scoring Rubric

1. A student's solution to the problem on the previous page is given below. Score the solution as *full credit, partial credit,* or *no credit. Explain* your reasoning. If you choose *partial credit* or *no credit,* explain how you would change the solution so that it earns a score of full credit.

a. Alvin: $e = -30t$ New HOV: $e = -44t$

b. Alvin: $e = -30(90)$ New HOV: $e = -44(90)$

$= -2700$ meters $= -3960$ meters

c. The time it takes Alvin to reach its lowest elevation can be found by solving $-4500 = -30t$. Using mental math, I found that $t = 150$ seconds.

The time it takes the new HOV to reach its lowest elevation can be found by solving $-6500 = -44t$.

Try $t = 145$: $-44(145) = -6380$

Try $t = 150$: $-44(150) = -6600$

The new HOV reaches its lowest elevation, -6500 feet, after more than 145 seconds but less than 150 seconds. So, the new HOV will reach its lowest elevation first.

EXTENDED RESPONSE

1. Your friend owns a business designing and selling personalized greeting cards. The table shows the profits for the first five years of the business.

Year	1	2	3	4	5
Profit (dollars)	−680	−1259	−963	2795	1507

   a. Find the total profit for the five years. Then tell whether the profit was a *gain* or a *loss*.

   b. In which year did the business have the least profit? the greatest profit?

   c. Can you use the table to determine the year with the greatest expenses and the year with the greatest income? *Justify* your answer.

2. The area of the playing region of a checkerboard has 64 small squares of equal size arranged as shown.

   a. Write an equation that gives the side length s of the playing region as a function of the area A of the playing region.

   b. The area of the playing region of a certain checkerboard is 256 square inches. What is the side length of a small square on the checkerboard? *Explain* your answer.

   c. You want to make a checkerboard out of a rectangular piece of wood that measures 16 inches by 25 inches. Each small square will have a side length of 2.5 inches. Can you cut 64 whole small squares from the piece of wood? *Justify* your answer using a diagram.

3. The table shows the changes in elevation from one mile marker to the next mile marker on each of two trails. Trail A is 6 miles long, and trail B is 8 miles long.

Mile markers	0 to 1	1 to 2	2 to 3	3 to 4	4 to 5	5 to 6	6 to 7	7 to 8
Elevation change on trail A (ft)	420	−60	−16	425	470	345	—	—
Elevation change on trail B (ft)	−135	430	465	410	390	−40	−60	405

   a. Find the total change in elevation for each trail. Which trail has the greater total change in elevation?

   b. The average trail grade is the total elevation change (in feet) divided by the trail length (in feet). The lesser the average trail grade is, the easier it is to hike the trail. Which is easier to hike, *trail A* or *trail B*? *Explain.*

   c. If trail B is extended by 1 mile, is it possible for trail B to have the same average trail grade as trail A? Your answer should include the following:

   - a table of values that gives the average trail grade of trail B for various elevation changes from mile 8 to mile 9
   - an explanation of how you used the table to answer the question

MULTIPLE CHOICE

4. Which description does not apply to $-\sqrt{9}$?

Ⓐ Real number Ⓑ Whole number

Ⓒ Integer Ⓓ Rational number

5. Which list of numbers is in order from least to greatest?

Ⓐ $-\frac{10}{3}, -\sqrt{16}, -\sqrt{20}, -4.5$

Ⓑ $-4.5, -\frac{10}{3}, -\sqrt{16}, -\sqrt{20}$

Ⓒ $-4.5, -\sqrt{20}, -\sqrt{16}, -\frac{10}{3}$

Ⓓ $-\sqrt{20}, -4.5, -\sqrt{16}, -\frac{10}{3}$

6. Which statement illustrates the associative property of multiplication?

Ⓐ $(-5 \cdot 3) + 7 = 7 + (-5 \cdot 3)$

Ⓑ $8 + (9 + 10) = (8 + 9) + 10$

Ⓒ $4 \cdot (2 \cdot 12) = (2 \cdot 12) \cdot 4$

Ⓓ $11 \cdot (4 \cdot 7) = (11 \cdot 4) \cdot 7$

GRIDDED ANSWER

7. The table shows the change in the balance of your bank account when you withdraw money from an automated teller machine (ATM).

Change in Balance after Withdrawal of $x	
Your bank's ATM	**Another bank's ATM**
$-x$	$-x - 1.50$

You have $230 in your bank account. You make 8 ATM withdrawals of $20 each, 4 of which are made from your bank's ATM. What is the amount (in dollars) in your account now?

8. The table shows the scores earned by two teams in each of three rounds of an academic contest. What is the difference of the greater total score and the lesser total score?

Round	Team A's score	Team B's score
1	−125	100
2	300	−75
3	150	−50

SHORT RESPONSE

9. A homeowner is dividing a rectangular room into two rooms as shown. The homeowner plans to install carpet in the living room and wood flooring in the dining room. Carpet costs $2.50 per square foot, and wood flooring costs $4.25 per square foot.

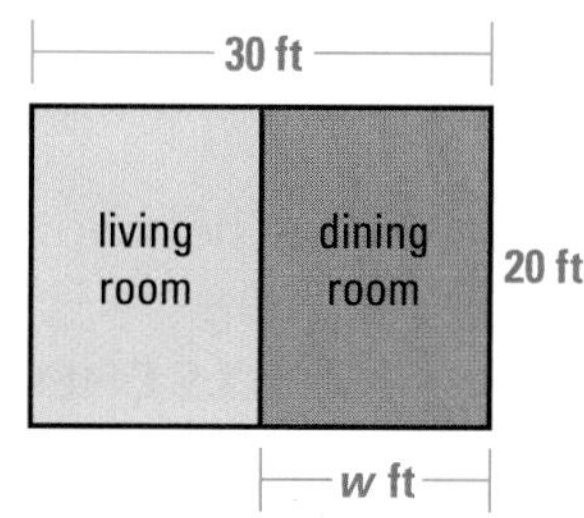

a. Write an equation that gives the total cost C (in dollars) of the project as a function of the width w (in feet) of the dining room.

b. How much money will the homeowner save by making the width of the dining room 12 feet instead of making the rooms the same size? *Explain* your answer.

10. A certain swimming pool contains 22,900 gallons of water when full. Due to evaporation, the amount of water in the pool changes at a rate of about −160 gallons per week.

a. If water is not added to the pool, find the approximate amount of water that will be left in the pool after 12 weeks.

b. A garden hose adds 2 gallons of water to the pool per minute. Estimate the time (in minutes) each day that the hose would need to add water in order to make up for the daily loss of water. *Explain* how you estimated the time.

3 Solving Linear Equations

Before

In previous courses and chapters, you learned the following skills, which you'll use in Chapter 3: simplifying expressions, writing percents as decimals, and using formulas.

Prerequisite Skills

VOCABULARY CHECK

Copy and complete the statement.

1. In the expression $3x + 7 + 7x$, ___?___ and ___?___ are like terms.
2. The reciprocal of $\frac{5}{8}$ is ___?___.

SKILLS CHECK

Simplify the expression. *(Review p. 96 for 3.2–3.6.)*

3. $5x - (6 - x)$
4. $3(x - 9) - 16$
5. $23 + 4(x + 2)$
6. $x(7 + x) + 9x^2$

Write the percent as a decimal. *(Review p. 916 for 3.7.)*

7. 54%
8. 99%
9. 12.5%
10. 150%

Find the perimeter of the rectangle. *(Review p. 924 for 3.8.)*

11. Rectangle: 16 ft by 7 ft
12. Rectangle: 20 cm by 14 cm
13. Rectangle: 11 in. by 4 in.

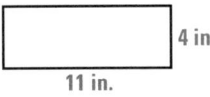

@HomeTutor Prerequisite skills practice at classzone.com

Now

In Chapter 3, you will apply the big ideas listed below and reviewed in the Chapter Summary on page 191. You will also use the key vocabulary listed below.

Big Ideas

1. **Solving equations in one variable**
2. **Solving proportion and percent problems**
3. **Rewriting equations in two or more variables**

KEY VOCABULARY

- inverse operations, *p. 134*
- equivalent equations, *p. 134*
- identity, *p. 156*
- ratio, *p. 162*
- proportion, *p. 163*
- cross product, *p. 168*
- scale drawing, *p. 170*
- scale model, *p. 170*
- scale, *p. 170*
- literal equation, *p. 184*

Why?

Knowing how to solve a linear equation can help you solve problems involving distance, rate, and time. For example, you can solve an equation to find the time it takes a jellyfish to travel a given distance at a given rate.

Animated Algebra

The animation illustrated below for Exercise 59 on page 139 helps you answer this question: How long does it take the jellyfish to travel 26 feet?

Start
You have to find the time it takes for the jellyfish to travel 26 feet.

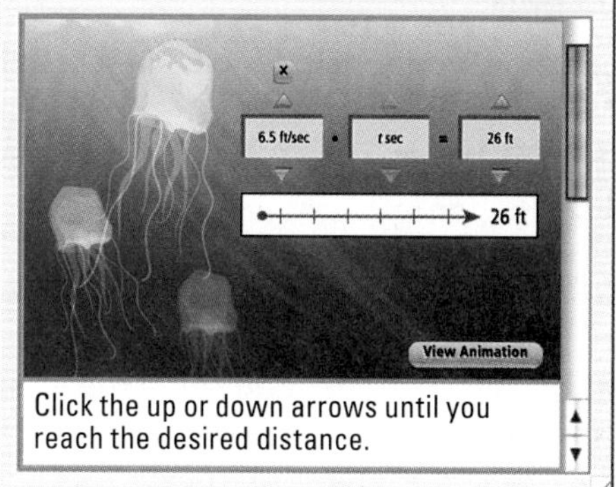
6.5 ft/sec
t sec
26 ft
26 ft
View Animation
Click the up or down arrows until you reach the desired distance.

Animated Algebra at classzone.com

Other animations for Chapter 3: pages 133, 154, 176, 185, and 187

Investigating Algebra ACTIVITY *Use before Lesson 3.1*

3.1 Modeling One-Step Equations

MATERIALS • algebra tiles

QUESTION **How can you use algebra tiles to solve one-step equations?**

You can model one-step equations using algebra tiles.

1-tile | **x-tile**

A 1-tile represents the number 1. An x-tile represents the variable x.

EXPLORE 1 **Solve an equation using subtraction**

Solve $x + 2 = 5$.

STEP 1 Model $x + 2 = 5$ using algebra tiles.

STEP 2 To find the value of x, isolate the x-tile on one side of the equation. You can do this by removing two 1-tiles from each side.

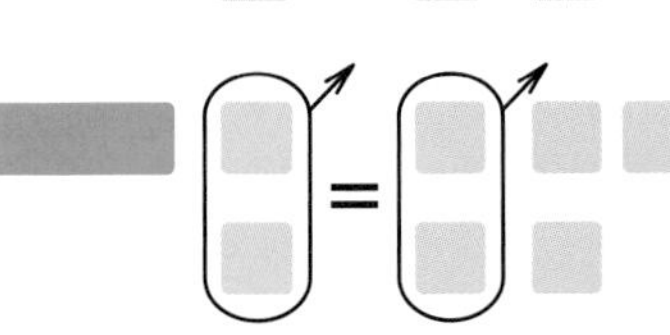

STEP 3 The x-tile is equal to three 1-tiles. So, the solution of $x + 2 = 5$ is 3.

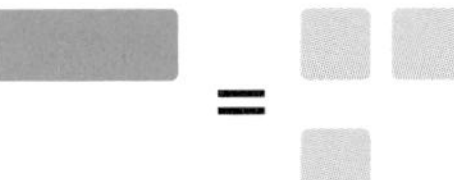

PRACTICE

Write the equation modeled by the algebra tiles.

1.

2.

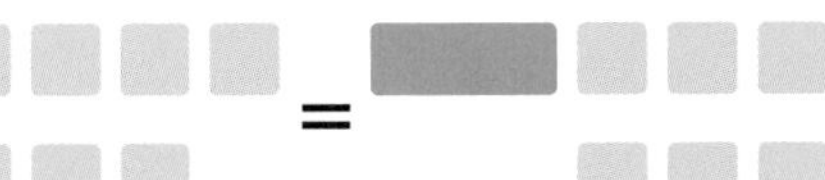

Use algebra tiles to model and solve the equation.

3. $x + 3 = 9$ **4.** $x + 2 = 7$ **5.** $x + 8 = 8$ **6.** $x + 3 = 7$

7. $x + 2 = 12$ **8.** $x + 7 = 12$ **9.** $15 = x + 5$ **10.** $13 = x + 10$

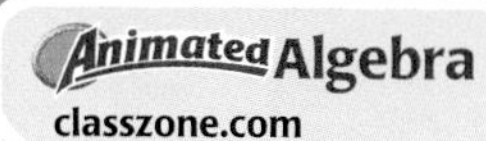

EXPLORE 2 Solve an equation using division

Solve $2x = 12$.

STEP 1 Model $2x = 12$ using algebra tiles.

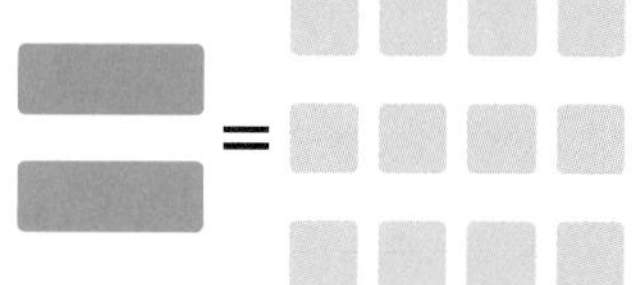

STEP 2 There are two x-tiles, so divide the x-tiles and 1-tiles into two equal groups.

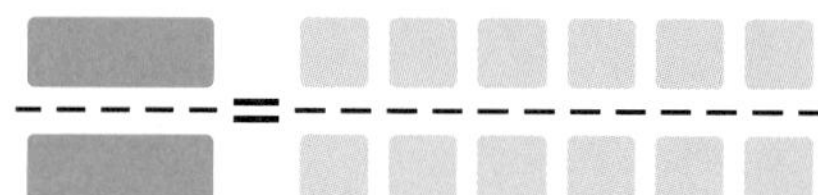

STEP 3 An x-tile is equal to six 1-tiles. So, the solution of $2x = 12$ is 6.

PRACTICE

Write the equation modeled by the algebra tiles.

11.

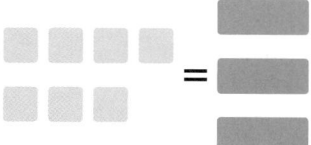

12.

Use algebra tiles to model and solve the equation.

13. $2x = 10$ **14.** $3x = 12$ **15.** $3x = 18$ **16.** $4x = 16$

17. $6 = 2x$ **18.** $12 = 4x$ **19.** $20 = 5x$ **20.** $21 = 7x$

DRAW CONCLUSIONS Use your observations to complete these exercises

21. An equation and explanation that correspond to each step in Explore 1 are shown below. Copy and complete the equations and explanations.

$x + 2 = 5$	**Original equation**
$x + 2 - \underline{\ ?\ } = 5 - \underline{\ ?\ }$	**Subtract _?_ from each side.**
$x = \underline{\ ?\ }$	**Simplify. Solution is _?_.**

22. Write an equation that corresponds to the algebra tile equation in each step of Explore 2. Based on your results, describe an algebraic method that you can use to solve $12x = 180$. Then use your method to find the solution.

3.1 Solve One-Step Equations

Before You solved equations using mental math.

Now You will solve one-step equations using algebra.

Why? So you can determine a weight limit, as in Ex. 56.

Key Vocabulary
- **inverse operations**
- **equivalent equations**
- **reciprocal,** *p. 915*

Inverse operations are two operations that undo each other, such as addition and subtraction. When you perform the same inverse operation on each side of an equation, you produce an *equivalent equation.* **Equivalent equations** are equations that have the same solution(s).

KEY CONCEPT *For Your Notebook*

Addition Property of Equality

Words Adding the same number to each side of an equation produces an equivalent equation.

Algebra If $x - a = b$, then $x - a + \mathbf{a} = b + \mathbf{a}$, or $x = b + a$.

Subtraction Property of Equality

Words Subtracting the same number from each side of an equation produces an equivalent equation.

Algebra If $x + a = b$, then $x + a - \mathbf{a} = b - \mathbf{a}$, or $x = b - a$.

EXAMPLE 1 Solve an equation using subtraction

Solve $x + 7 = 4$.

$x + 7 = 4$ **Write original equation.**

$x + 7 - 7 = 4 - 7$ **Use subtraction property of equality: Subtract 7 from each side.**

$x = -3$ **Simplify.**

▸ The solution is -3.

AVOID ERRORS
To obtain an equivalent equation, be sure to subtract the same number from each side.

CHECK Substitute -3 for x in the original equation.

$x + 7 = 4$ **Write original equation.**

$-3 + 7 \stackrel{?}{=} 4$ **Substitute −3 for *x*.**

$4 = 4$ ✓ **Simplify. Solution checks.**

EXAMPLE 2 Solve an equation using addition

USE HORIZONTAL FORMAT

In Example 2, both horizontal and vertical formats are used. In the rest of the book, equations will be solved using the horizontal format.

Solve $x - 12 = 3$.

Horizontal format		Vertical format
$x - 12 = 3$	Write original equation.	$x - 12 = \quad 3$
$x - 12 + 12 = 3 + 12$	Add 12 to each side.	$+12 \quad +12$
$x = 15$	Simplify.	$x \quad = \quad 15$

MULTIPLICATION AND DIVISION EQUATIONS Multiplication and division are inverse operations. So, the multiplication property of equality can be used to solve equations involving division, and the division property of equality can be used to solve equations involving multiplication.

KEY CONCEPT *For Your Notebook*

Multiplication Property of Equality

Words Multiplying each side of an equation by the same nonzero number produces an equivalent equation.

Algebra If $\frac{x}{a} = b$ and $a \neq 0$, then $a \cdot \frac{x}{a} = a \cdot b$, or $x = ab$.

Division Property of Equality

Words Dividing each side of an equation by the same nonzero number produces an equivalent equation.

Algebra If $ax = b$ and $a \neq 0$, then $\frac{ax}{a} = \frac{b}{a}$, or $x = \frac{b}{a}$.

EXAMPLE 3 Solve an equation using division

Solve $-6x = 48$.

$-6x = 48$ Write original equation.

$\frac{-6x}{-6} = \frac{48}{-6}$ Divide each side by -6.

$x = -8$ Simplify.

✓ GUIDED PRACTICE for Examples 1, 2, and 3

Solve the equation. Check your solution.

1. $y + 7 = 10$ **2.** $x - 5 = 3$ **3.** $q - 11 = -5$ **4.** $6 = t - 2$

5. $4x = 48$ **6.** $-65 = -5y$ **7.** $6w = -54$ **8.** $24 = -8n$

EXAMPLE 4 Solve an equation using multiplication

Solve $\frac{x}{4} = 5$.

Solution

$\frac{x}{4} = 5$ Write original equation.

$4 \cdot \frac{x}{4} = 4 \cdot 5$ Multiply each side by 4.

$x = 20$ Simplify.

✓ **GUIDED PRACTICE** for Example 4

Solve the equation. Check your solution.

9. $\frac{t}{-3} = 9$ **10.** $6 = \frac{c}{7}$ **11.** $13 = \frac{z}{-2}$ **12.** $\frac{a}{5} = -11$

USING RECIPROCALS Recall that the product of a number and its reciprocal is 1. You can isolate a variable with a fractional coefficient by multiplying each side of the equation by the reciprocal of the fraction.

EXAMPLE 5 Solve an equation by multiplying by a reciprocal

Solve $-\frac{2}{7}x = 4$.

REVIEW RECIPROCALS
For help with finding reciprocals, see p. 915.

Solution

The coefficient of x is $-\frac{2}{7}$. The reciprocal of $-\frac{2}{7}$ is $-\frac{7}{2}$.

$-\frac{2}{7}x = 4$ Write original equation.

$-\frac{7}{2}\left(-\frac{2}{7}x\right) = -\frac{7}{2}(4)$ Multiply each side by the reciprocal, $-\frac{7}{2}$.

$x = -14$ Simplify.

▶ The solution is −14. Check by substituting −14 for x in the original equation.

CHECK $-\frac{2}{7}x = 4$ Write original equation.

$-\frac{2}{7}(-14) \stackrel{?}{=} 4$ Substitute −14 for x.

$4 = 4$ ✓ Simplify. Solution checks.

GUIDED PRACTICE for Example 5

Solve the equation. Check your solution.

13. $\frac{5}{6}w = 10$ **14.** $\frac{2}{3}p = 14$ **15.** $9 = -\frac{3}{4}m$ **16.** $-8 = -\frac{4}{5}v$

EXAMPLE 6 Write and solve an equation

OLYMPICS In the 2004 Olympics, Shawn Crawford won the 200 meter dash. His winning time was 19.79 seconds. Find his average speed to the nearest tenth of a meter per second.

Solution

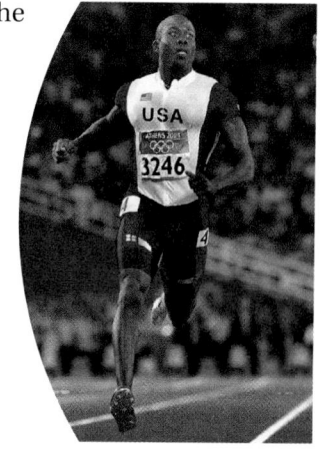

Let r represent Crawford's speed in meters per second. Write a verbal model. Then write and solve an equation.

Distance (meters)	=	Rate (meters/second)	·	Time (seconds)
↓		↓		↓
200	=	***r***	·	**19.79**

$$\frac{200}{19.79} = \frac{19.79r}{19.79}$$

$$10.1 \approx r$$

▶ Crawford's average speed was about 10.1 meters per second.

GUIDED PRACTICE for Example 6

17. **WHAT IF?** In Example 6, suppose Shawn Crawford ran 100 meters at the same average speed he ran the 200 meters. How long would it take him to run 100 meters? Round your answer to the nearest tenth of a second.

3.1 EXERCISES

HOMEWORK KEY

○ = **WORKED-OUT SOLUTIONS** on p. WS5 for Exs. 13 and 55

★ = **STANDARDIZED TEST PRACTICE** Exs. 2, 15, 16, 57, 58, and 61

◆ = **MULTIPLE REPRESENTATIONS** Ex. 59

SKILL PRACTICE

1. **VOCABULARY** Copy and complete: Two operations that undo each other are called __?__.

2. ★ **WRITING** Which property of equality would you use to solve the equation $14x = 35$? *Explain.*

EXAMPLES 1 and 2 on pp. 134–135 for Exs. 3–14

SOLVING ADDITION AND SUBTRACTION EQUATIONS **Solve the equation. Check your solution.**

3. $x + 5 = 8$
4. $m + 9 = 2$
5. $11 = f + 6$
6. $13 = 7 + z$
7. $6 = 9 + h$
8. $-3 = 5 + a$
9. $y - 4 = 3$
10. $t - 5 = 7$
11. $14 = k - 3$
12. $6 = w - 7$
13. $-2 = n - 6$
14. $-11 = b - 9$

EXAMPLES 1 and 2 on pp. 134–135 for Exs. 15, 16

15. ★ **MULTIPLE CHOICE** What is the solution of $-8 = d - 13$?

(A) -21 (B) -5 (C) 5 (D) 21

16. ★ **MULTIPLE CHOICE** What is the solution of $22 + v = -65$?

(A) -87 (B) -43 (C) 43 (D) 87

EXAMPLES 3 and 4 on pp. 135–136 for Exs. 17–30

SOLVING MULTIPLICATION AND DIVISION EQUATIONS **Solve the equation. Check your solution.**

17. $5g = 20$

18. $-4q = 52$

19. $48 = 8c$

20. $-108 = 9j$

21. $15 = -h$

22. $187 = -17r$

23. $\frac{y}{3} = 5$

24. $\frac{m}{2} = 14$

25. $8 = \frac{x}{6}$

26. $7 = \frac{t}{-7}$

27. $-11 = \frac{z}{-2}$

28. $-3 = \frac{d}{14}$

ERROR ANALYSIS ***Describe*** **and correct the error in solving the equation.**

29.

$x + 3.8 = 2.3$

$x + 3.8 - 3.8 = 2.3 + 3.8$

$x = 6.1$

30.

$\frac{x}{3} = 27$

$3 \cdot \frac{x}{3} = \frac{27}{3}$

$x = 9$

SOLVING EQUATIONS **Solve the equation. Check your solution.**

31. $b - 0.4 = 3.1$

32. $-3.2 + z = -7.4$

33. $-5.7 = w - 4.6$

34. $-6.1 = p + 2.2$

35. $8.2 = -4g$

36. $-3.3a = 19.8$

37. $\frac{3}{4} = \frac{1}{8} + v$

38. $\frac{n}{4.6} = -2.5$

39. $-0.12 = \frac{y}{-0.5}$

EXAMPLE 5 on p. 136 for Exs. 40–48

40. $\frac{1}{2}m = 21$

41. $\frac{1}{3}c = 32$

42. $-7 = \frac{1}{5}x$

43. $\frac{3}{2}k = 18$

44. $-21 = -\frac{3}{5}t$

45. $-\frac{2}{7}v = 16$

46. $\frac{8}{5}x = \frac{4}{15}$

47. $\frac{1}{3}y = \frac{1}{5}$

48. $-\frac{4}{3} = \frac{2}{3}z$

GEOMETRY **The rectangle or triangle has area A. Write and solve an equation to find the value of x.**

49. $A = 54 \text{ in.}^2$

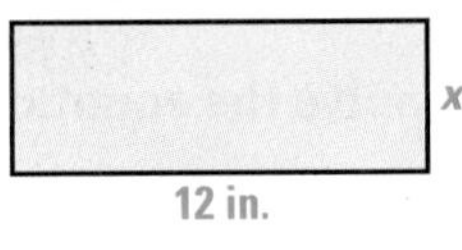

50. $A = 72 \text{ cm}^2$

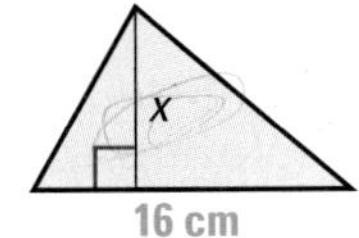

CHALLENGE **Find the value of b using the given information.**

51. $4a = 6$ and $b = a - 2$

52. $a - 6.7 = 3.1$ and $b = 5a$

○ = WORKED-OUT SOLUTIONS on p. WS1 ★ = STANDARDIZED TEST PRACTICE ◆ = MULTIPLE REPRESENTATIONS

PROBLEM SOLVING

EXAMPLE 6 on p. 137 for Exs. 53–57

53. **THE DEAD SEA** For the period 1999–2004, the maximum depth of the Dead Sea decreased by 9.9 feet. The maximum depth in 2004 was 1036.7 feet. What was the maximum depth in 1999?

@HomeTutor for problem solving help at classzone.com

54. **CRAFTS** You purchase a cane of polymer clay to make pendants for necklaces. The cane is 50 millimeters long. How thick should you make each pendant so that you will have 20 pendants of uniform thickness?

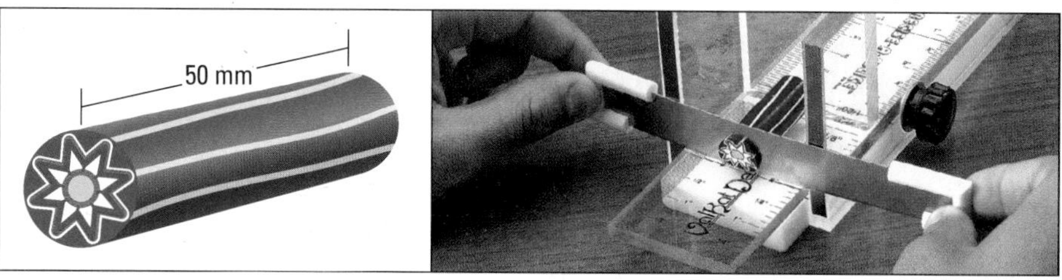

@HomeTutor for problem solving help at classzone.com

55. **TRAMPOLINES** A rectangular trampoline has an area of 187 square feet. The length of the trampoline is 17 feet. What is its width?

56. **WHEELCHAIRS** The van used to transport patients to and from a rehabilitation facility is equipped with a wheelchair lift. The maximum lifting capacity for the lift is 300 pounds. The wheelchairs used by the facility weigh 55 pounds each. What is the maximum weight of a wheelchair occupant who can use the lift?

57. ★ **SHORT RESPONSE** In Everglades National Park in Florida, there are 200 species of birds that migrate. This accounts for $\frac{4}{7}$ of all the species of birds sighted in the park.

   a. Write an equation to find the number of species of birds that have been sighted in Everglades National Park.

   b. There are 600 species of plants in Everglades National Park. Are there more species of birds or of plants in the park? *Explain.*

58. ★ **OPEN-ENDED** *Describe* a real-world situation that can be modeled by the equation $15x = 135$. Solve the equation and explain what the solution means in this situation.

59. **MULTIPLE REPRESENTATIONS** A box jellyfish can travel at a rate of 6.5 feet per second.

   a. **Making a Table** Make a table that shows the distance d the jellyfish can travel after 1, 2, 3, 4, and 5 seconds.

   b. **Drawing a Graph** Graph the ordered pairs from the table in a coordinate plane. How long does it take the jellyfish to travel 26 feet?

   c. **Writing an Equation** Write and solve an equation to find the time it takes the jellyfish to travel 26 feet.

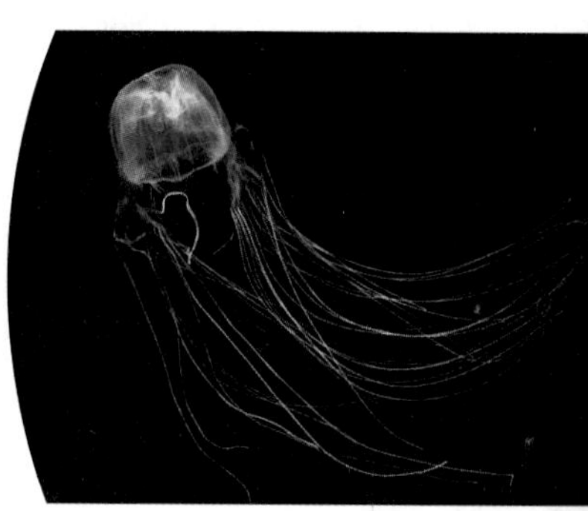

Animated Algebra at classzone.com

60. MULTI-STEP PROBLEM Tatami mats are a floor covering used in Japan. Tatami mats are equal in size, unless they are cut in half. The floor shown has an area of 81 square feet and is covered with 4.5 tatami mats.

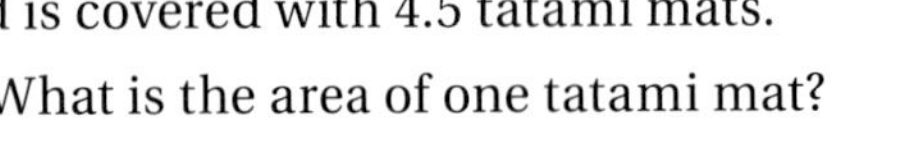

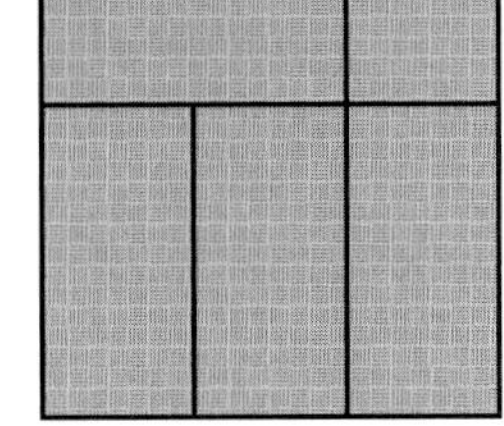

a. What is the area of one tatami mat?

b. What is the length of one tatami mat if it has a width of 3 feet?

61. ★ **EXTENDED RESPONSE** In baseball, a player's batting average is calculated by dividing the number of hits by the number of at bats.

a. **Calculate** Use the information in the table to find the number of hits Bill Mueller had in the 2003 Major League Baseball regular season. Round your answer to the nearest whole number.

Player	Team	Batting average	At bats
Bill Mueller	Boston Red Sox	0.326	524

b. **Calculate** The number of hits Bill Mueller had was 44 less than the number of hits Vernon Wells of the Toronto Blue Jays had in the 2003 regular season. How many hits did Vernon Wells have?

c. **Compare** In the 2003 regular season, Mueller had a higher batting average than Wells. Did Wells have fewer at bats than Mueller? *Explain* your reasoning.

62. **AMERICAN FLAGS** An American flag has a length that is 1.9 times its width. What is the area of a flag that has a length of 9.5 feet?

63. CHALLENGE At a farm where you can pick your own strawberries, the cost of picked strawberries is calculated using only the weight of the strawberries. The total weight of a container full of strawberries is 2.1 pounds. The cost of the strawberries is \$4.68. The weight of the container is 0.3 pound. What is the cost per pound for strawberries?

MIXED REVIEW

Translate the verbal phrase into an expression. *(p. 15)*

64. 4 more than a number k

65. The product of 8 and a number x

66. 40 divided by a number y

67. 10 less than twice a number w

PREVIEW
Prepare for Lesson 3.2 in Exs. 68–75.

A verbal description for a function and its domain are given. Write an equation for the function. Then describe the range. *(p. 35)*

68. The output is 9 more than the input.
Domain: −1, 0, 1, 2

69. The output is 3 times the input.
Domain: −4, −2, 0, 2

Simplify the expression. *(p. 103)*

70. $-9x + 15x$

71. $5x - 4x$

72. $12 + 3x - 3x$

73. $5x + 8 - x - 2$

74. $7.1x - 2.6x$

75. $-0.7x + 11.3x$

EXTRA PRACTICE for Lesson 3.1, p. 940

ONLINE QUIZ at classzone.com

3.2 Solve Two-Step Equations

Before You solved one-step equations.

Now You will solve two-step equations.

Why? So you can find a scuba diver's depth, as in Example 4.

Key Vocabulary
- **like terms,** *p. 97*
- **input,** *p. 35*
- **output,** *p. 35*

The equation $\frac{x}{2} + 5 = 11$ involves two operations performed on x: division by 2 and addition by 5. You typically solve such an equation by applying the inverse operations in the reverse order of the order of operations. This is shown in the table below.

Operations performed on x	Operations to isolate x
1. Divide by 2. 2. Add 5.	1. Subtract 5. 2. Multiply by 2.

EXAMPLE 1 Solve a two-step equation

Solve $\frac{x}{2} + 5 = 11$.

$\frac{x}{2} + 5 = 11$ Write original equation.

$\frac{x}{2} + 5 - 5 = 11 - 5$ Subtract 5 from each side.

$\frac{x}{2} = 6$ Simplify.

$2 \cdot \frac{x}{2} = 2 \cdot 6$ Multiply each side by 2.

$x = 12$ Simplify.

▶ The solution is 12. Check by substituting 12 for x in the original equation.

CHECK $\frac{x}{2} + 5 = 11$ Write original equation.

$\frac{12}{2} + 5 \stackrel{?}{=} 11$ Substitute 12 for x.

$11 = 11$ ✓ Simplify. Solution checks.

✓ GUIDED PRACTICE for Example 1

Solve the equation. Check your solution.

1. $5x + 9 = 24$ **2.** $4y - 4 = 16$ **3.** $-1 = \frac{z}{3} - 7$

EXAMPLE 2 Solve a two-step equation by combining like terms

REVIEW LIKE TERMS
For help with combining like terms, see p. 97.

Solve $7x - 4x = 21$.

$7x - 4x = 21$ Write original equation.

$3x = 21$ Combine like terms.

$\frac{3x}{3} = \frac{21}{3}$ Divide each side by 3.

$x = 7$ Simplify.

EXAMPLE 3 Find an input of a function

The output of a function is 3 less than 5 times the input. Find the input when the output is 17.

Solution

STEP 1 **Write** an equation for the function. Let x be the input and y be the output.

$y = 5x - 3$ y is 3 less than 5 times x.

STEP 2 **Solve** the equation for x when $y = 17$.

$y = 5x - 3$ Write original function.

$17 = 5x - 3$ Substitute 17 for y.

$17 + 3 = 5x - 3 + 3$ Add 3 to each side.

$20 = 5x$ Simplify.

$\frac{20}{5} = \frac{5x}{5}$ Divide each side by 5.

$4 = x$ Simplify.

▶ An input of 4 produces an output of 17.

CHECK $y = 5x - 3$ Write original function.

$17 \stackrel{?}{=} 5(4) - 3$ Substitute 17 for y and 4 for x.

$17 \stackrel{?}{=} 20 - 3$ Multiply 5 and 4.

$17 = 17$ ✓ Simplify. Solution checks.

✓ GUIDED PRACTICE for Examples 2 and 3

Solve the equation. Check your solution.

4. $4w + 2w = 24$
5. $8t - 3t = 35$
6. $-16 = 5d - 9d$
7. The output of a function is 5 more than -2 times the input. Find the input when the output is 11.
8. The output of a function is 4 less than 4 times the input. Find the input when the output is 3.

EXAMPLE 4 Solve a multi-step problem

SCUBA DIVING As a scuba diver descends into deeper water, the pressure of the water on the diver's body steadily increases.

The pressure at the surface of the water is 2117 pounds per square foot (lb/ft^2). The pressure increases at a rate of 64 pounds per square foot for each foot the diver descends. Find the depth at which a diver experiences a pressure of 8517 pounds per square foot.

ANOTHER WAY
For an alternative method for solving Example 4, turn to page 147 for the **Problem Solving Workshop**.

Solution

STEP 1 **Write** a verbal model. Then write an equation.

Pressure at given depth (lb/ft^2)	=	Pressure at surface (lb/ft^2)	+	Rate of change of pressure (lb/ft^2 per foot of depth)	·	Diver's depth (ft)
P	=	2117	+	64	·	d

STEP 2 **Find** the depth at which the pressure is 8517 pounds per square foot.

$P = 2117 + 64d$ — Write equation.

$8517 = 2117 + 64d$ — Substitute 8517 for P.

$8517 - 2117 = 2117 - 2117 + 64d$ — Subtract 2117 from each side.

$6400 = 64d$ — Simplify.

$\frac{6400}{64} = \frac{64d}{64}$ — Divide each side by 64.

$100 = d$ — Simplify.

▶ A diver experiences a pressure of 8517 pounds per square foot at a depth of 100 feet.

CHECK

$P = 2117 + 64d$ — Write original equation.

$8517 \stackrel{?}{=} 2117 + 64(100)$ — Substitute 8517 for P and 100 for d.

$8517 \stackrel{?}{=} 2117 + 6400$ — Multiply 64 and 100.

$8517 = 8517$ ✓ — Simplify. Solution checks.

✓ GUIDED PRACTICE for Example 4

9. **WHAT IF?** In Example 4, suppose the diver experiences a pressure of 5317 pounds per square foot. Find the diver's depth.

10. **JOBS** Kim has a job where she makes \$8 per hour plus tips. Yesterday, Kim made \$53 dollars, \$13 of which was from tips. How many hours did she work?

3.2 EXERCISES

HOMEWORK KEY

○ = **WORKED-OUT SOLUTIONS** on p. WS5 for Exs. 13, 19, and 39

★ = **STANDARDIZED TEST PRACTICE** Exs. 2, 21, 40, 41, and 44

◆ = **MULTIPLE REPRESENTATIONS** Ex. 43

SKILL PRACTICE

1. **VOCABULARY** Copy and complete: To solve the equation $2x + 3x = 20$, you would begin by combining $2x$ and $3x$ because they are _?_.

2. ★ **WRITING** *Describe* the steps you would use to solve the equation $4x + 7 = 15$.

EXAMPLE 1 on p. 141 for Exs. 3–14

SOLVING TWO-STEP EQUATIONS **Solve the equation. Check your solution.**

3. $3x + 7 = 19$
4. $5h + 4 = 19$
5. $7d - 1 = 13$
6. $2g - 13 = 3$
7. $10 = 7 - m$
8. $11 = 12 - q$
9. $\frac{a}{3} + 4 = 6$
10. $17 = \frac{w}{5} + 13$
11. $\frac{b}{2} - 9 = 11$
12. $-6 = \frac{z}{4} - 3$
13. $7 = \frac{5}{6}c - 8$
14. $10 = \frac{2}{7}n + 4$

EXAMPLE 2 on p. 142 for Exs. 15–23

COMBINING LIKE TERMS **Solve the equation. Check your solution.**

15. $8y + 3y = 44$
16. $2p + 7p = 54$
17. $11x - 9x = 18$
18. $36 = 9x - 3x$
19. $-32 = -5k + 13k$
20. $6 = -7f + 4f$

21. ★ **MULTIPLE CHOICE** What is the first step you can take to solve the equation $6 + \frac{x}{3} = -2$?

Ⓐ Subtract 2 from each side.

Ⓑ Add 6 to each side.

Ⓒ Divide each side by 3.

Ⓓ Subtract 6 from each side.

ERROR ANALYSIS ***Describe*** **and correct the error in solving the equation.**

22.

$$7 - 3x = 12$$
$$4x = 12$$
$$x = 3$$

23.

$$-2x + x = 10$$
$$\frac{-2x + x}{-2} = \frac{10}{-2}$$
$$x = -5$$

EXAMPLE 3 on p. 142 for Exs. 24–26

FINDING AN INPUT OF A FUNCTION **Write an equation for the function described. Then find the input.**

24. The output of a function is 7 more than 3 times the input. Find the input when the output is -8.

25. The output of a function is 4 more than 2 times the input. Find the input when the output is -10.

26. The output of a function is 9 less than 10 times the input. Find the input when the output is 11.

SOLVING EQUATIONS **Solve the equation. Check your solution.**

27. $5.6 = 1.1p + 1.2$

28. $7.2y + 4.7 = 62.3$

29. $1.2j - 4.3 = 1.7$

30. $16 - 2.4d = -8$

31. $14.4m - 5.1 = 2.1$

32. $-5.3 = 2.2v - 8.6$

33. $\frac{c}{5.3} + 8.3 = 11.3$

34. $3.2 + \frac{x}{2.5} = 4.6$

35. $-1.2 = \frac{z}{4.6} - 2.7$

36. **CHALLENGE** Solve the equations $3x + 2 = 5$, $3x + 2 = 8$, and $3x + 2 = 11$. Predict the solution of the equation $3x + 2 = 14$. *Explain.*

PROBLEM SOLVING

EXAMPLE 4 on p. 143 for Exs. 37–40

37. **DANCE CLASSES** A dance academy charges \$24 per class and a one-time registration fee of \$15. A student paid a total of \$687 to the academy. Find the number of classes the student took.

@HomeTutor for problem solving help at classzone.com

38. **CAR REPAIR** Tyler paid \$124 to get his car repaired. The total cost for the repairs was the sum of the amount paid for parts and the amount paid for labor. Tyler was charged \$76 for parts and \$32 per hour for labor. Find the amount of time it took to repair his car.

@HomeTutor for problem solving help at classzone.com

39. **ADVERTISING** A science museum wants to promote an upcoming exhibit by advertising on city buses for one month. The costs of the two types of advertisements being considered are shown. The museum has budgeted \$6000 for the advertisements. The museum decides to have 1 full bus wrap advertisement. How many half-side advertisements can the museum have?

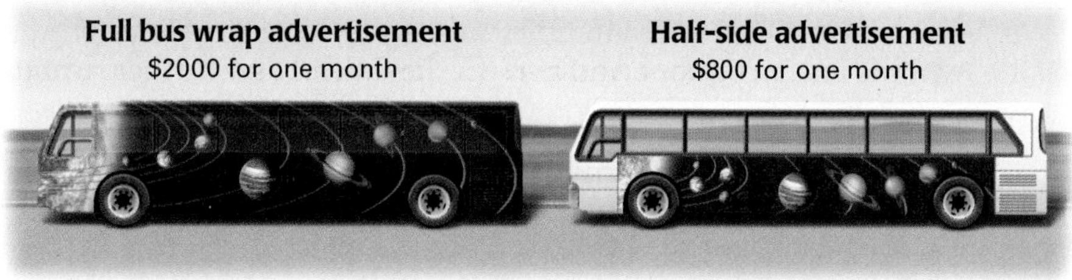

40. ★ **MULTIPLE CHOICE** A skateboarding park charges \$7 per session to skate and \$4 per session to rent safety equipment. Jared rents safety equipment every time he skates. During one year, he spends \$99 for skating charges and equipment rentals. Which equation can be used to find x, the number of sessions Jared attended?

Ⓐ $99 = 7x$ Ⓑ $99 = 7x + 4x$ Ⓒ $99 = 7x + 4$ Ⓓ $99 = 4x + 7$

41. ★ **SHORT RESPONSE** A guitar store offers a finance plan where you give a \$50 down payment on a guitar and pay the remaining balance in 6 equal monthly payments. You have \$50 and you can afford to pay up to \$90 per month for a guitar. Can you afford a guitar that costs \$542? *Explain.*

42. **MULTI-STEP PROBLEM** The capacity of a landfill is 4,756,505 tons. The landfill currently holds 2,896,112 tons. A cell is added to the landfill every day, and each cell averages 1600 tons.

a. Write an equation that gives the amount y (in tons) in the landfill as a function of the number x of days from now.

b. After how many days will the landfill reach capacity? Round your answer to the nearest day.

c. Use estimation to check your answer to part (b).

Trash is compacted into a pocket called a cell.
Cells are separated by layers of soil.

43. **MULTIPLE REPRESENTATIONS** Two computer technicians are upgrading the software on the 54 computers in a school. On average, Marissa upgrades 5 computers in 1 hour and Ryan upgrades 7 computers in 1 hour.

a. **Writing an Equation** Write an equation that gives the total number y of computers upgraded as a function of the number x of hours worked.

b. **Making a Table** Make a table that shows the number of computers upgraded by each technician and the total number of computers upgraded after 1, 2, 3, 4, and 5 hours.

c. **Drawing a Graph** Graph the ordered pairs that represent the total number y of computers upgraded after x hours. Use the graph to estimate the number of hours it took to upgrade all of the computers.

44. ★ **SHORT RESPONSE** At a restaurant, customers can dine inside the restaurant or pick up food at the take-out window. On an average day, 400 customers are served inside the restaurant, and 120 customers pick up food at the take-out window. After how many days will the restaurant have served 2600 customers? *Explain.*

45. **CHALLENGE** During a 1 mile race, one runner is running at a rate of 14.6 feet per second, and another runner is running at a rate of 11.3 feet per second. One lap around the track is 660 feet. After how many seconds will the faster runner be exactly one lap ahead of the other runner?

MIXED REVIEW

Find the sum, difference, or product.

46. $14 + (-6)$ *(p. 74)*
47. $-7 + (-13)$ *(p. 74)*
48. $16 - 21$ *(p. 80)*
49. $-9 - (-10)$ *(p. 80)*
50. $(3a)(-3a)(a)$ *(p. 88)*
51. $-2(-12)(2t)$ *(p. 88)*

Use the distributive property to write an equivalent expression. *(p. 96)*

52. $2(9z + 4)$
53. $-3(5b - 8)$
54. $(2k - 7)(-5)$

PREVIEW Prepare for Lesson 3.3 in Exs. 55–60.

Solve the equation. Check your solution. *(p. 134)*

55. $x + 9 = 2$
56. $m + 2 = 5$
57. $y - 18 = 12$
58. $-7r = 56$
59. $30s = 1200$
60. $-\frac{1}{9}c = -8$

PROBLEM SOLVING WORKSHOP
LESSON 3.2

Using ALTERNATIVE METHODS

Another Way to Solve Example 4, page 143

MULTIPLE REPRESENTATIONS In Example 4 on page 143, you saw how to solve a problem about scuba diving by using an equation. You can also solve the problem using a table.

PROBLEM

SCUBA DIVING As a scuba diver descends into deeper water, the pressure of the water on the diver's body steadily increases. The pressure at the surface of the water is 2117 pounds per square foot (lb/ft^2). The pressure increases at a rate of 64 pounds per square foot for each foot the diver descends. Find the depth at which a diver experiences a pressure of 8517 pounds per square foot.

METHOD

Making a Table An alternative approach is to make a table.

STEP 1 **Make** a table that shows the pressure as the depth increases. Because you are looking for a fairly high pressure, use larger increments in depth, such as 20 feet.

Every 1 ft of depth increases the pressure by 64 lb/ft^2.

Every 20 ft of depth increases the pressure by $64(20) = 1280$ lb/ft^2.

Depth (ft)	Pressure (lb/ft^2)
0	2117
1	2181
2	2245
20	3397
40	4677
60	5957
80	7237
100	8517

STEP 2 **Look** for the depth at which the pressure reaches 8517 pounds per square foot. This happens at a depth of 100 feet.

PRACTICE

1. **BASKETBALL** A sports club offers an organized basketball league. A team pays $600 to join the league. In addition to paying their share of the $600, team members who are not members of the sports club must pay a $25 fee to play. A team pays a total of $775. How many team members who are not club members are on the team? Solve this problem using two different methods.

2. **WHAT IF?** In Exercise 1, suppose you are on a team, but not a club member. The $600 cost is divided equally among the team members. How many players must there be on your team for you to pay $100 to play? Make a table to find the answer.

3. **FURNITURE** You have $370 to spend on a dining table and chairs. A table costs $220, and each chair costs $35. How many chairs can you buy in addition to the table? Solve this problem using two different methods.

3.3 Solve Multi-Step Equations

Before You solved one-step and two-step equations.

Now You will solve multi-step equations.

Why? So you can solve a problem about lifeguarding, as in Ex. 40.

Key Vocabulary
- **like terms,** *p. 97*
- **distributive property,** *p. 96*
- **reciprocal,** *p. 915*

Solving a linear equation may take more than two steps. Start by simplifying one or both sides of the equation, if possible. Then use inverse operations to isolate the variable.

EXAMPLE 1 Solve an equation by combining like terms

Solve $8x - 3x - 10 = 20$.

$8x - 3x - 10 = 20$	Write original equation.
$5x - 10 = 20$	Combine like terms.
$5x - 10 + 10 = 20 + 10$	Add 10 to each side.
$5x = 30$	Simplify.
$\frac{5x}{5} = \frac{30}{5}$	Divide each side by 5.
$x = 6$	Simplify.

EXAMPLE 2 Solve an equation using the distributive property

Solve $7x + 2(x + 6) = 39$.

Solution

When solving an equation, you may feel comfortable doing some steps mentally. Method 2 shows a solution where some steps are done mentally.

REVIEW PROPERTIES
For help with using the distributive property, see p. 96.

METHOD 1 Show All Steps

$$7x + 2(x + 6) = 39$$
$$7x + 2x + 12 = 39$$
$$9x + 12 = 39$$
$$9x + 12 - 12 = 39 - 12$$
$$9x = 27$$
$$\frac{9x}{9} = \frac{27}{9}$$
$$x = 3$$

METHOD 2 Do Some Steps Mentally

$$7x + 2(x + 6) = 39$$
$$7x + 2x + 12 = 39$$
$$9x + 12 = 39$$
$$9x = 27$$
$$x = 3$$

★ EXAMPLE 3 Standardized Test Practice

Which equation represents Step 2 in the solution process?

Step 1 $5x - 4(x - 3) = 17$

Step 2 $\boxed{}$

Step 3 $x + 12 = 17$

Step 4 $x = 5$

Ⓐ $5x - 4x - 12 = 17$ Ⓑ $5x - 4x - 3 = 17$

Ⓒ $5x - 4x + 3 = 17$ Ⓓ $5x - 4x + 12 = 17$

ELIMINATE CHOICES
You can eliminate choices B and C because −4 has not been distributed to *both* terms in the parentheses.

Solution

In Step 2, the distributive property is used to simplify the left side of the equation. Because $-4(x - 3) = -4x + 12$, Step 2 should be $5x - 4x + 12 = 17$.

▶ The correct answer is D. Ⓐ Ⓑ Ⓒ Ⓓ

GUIDED PRACTICE for Examples 1, 2, and 3

Solve the equation. Check your solution.

1. $9d - 2d + 4 = 32$ **2.** $2w + 3(w + 4) = 27$ **3.** $6x - 2(x - 5) = 46$

USING RECIPROCALS Although you can use the distributive property to solve an equation such as $\frac{3}{2}(3x + 5) = -24$, it is easier to multiply each side of the equation by the reciprocal of the fraction.

EXAMPLE 4 Multiply by a reciprocal to solve an equation

Solve $\frac{3}{2}(3x + 5) = -24$.

$\frac{3}{2}(3x + 5) = -24$	**Write original equation.**
$\frac{2}{3} \cdot \frac{3}{2}(3x + 5) = \frac{2}{3}(-24)$	**Multiply each side by $\frac{2}{3}$, the reciprocal of $\frac{3}{2}$.**
$3x + 5 = -16$	**Simplify.**
$3x = -21$	**Subtract 5 from each side.**
$x = -7$	**Divide each side by 3.**

GUIDED PRACTICE for Example 4

Solve the equation. Check your solution.

4. $\frac{3}{4}(z - 6) = 12$ **5.** $\frac{2}{5}(3r + 4) = 10$ **6.** $-\frac{4}{5}(4a - 1) = 28$

EXAMPLE 5 Write and solve an equation

BIRD MIGRATION A flock of cranes migrates from Canada to Texas. The cranes take 14 days (336 hours) to travel 2500 miles. The cranes fly at an average speed of 25 miles per hour. How many hours of the migration are the cranes *not* flying?

Solution

Let x be the amount of time the cranes are not flying. Then $336 - x$ is the amount of time the cranes are flying.

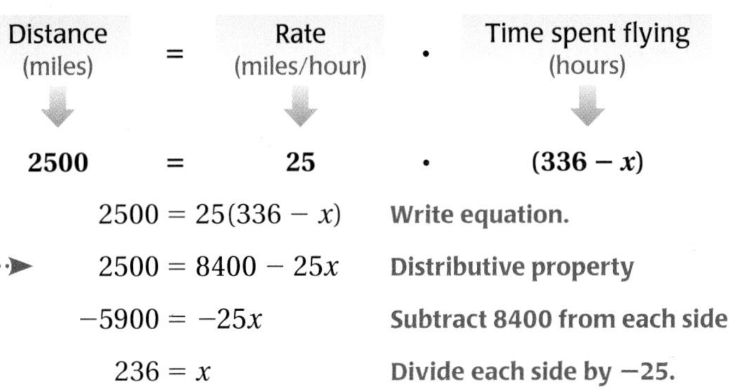

Distance (miles) = Rate (miles/hour) · Time spent flying (hours)
2500 = 25 · (336 − x)

$2500 = 25(336 - x)$ **Write equation.**

$2500 = 8400 - 25x$ **Distributive property**

$-5900 = -25x$ **Subtract 8400 from each side.**

$236 = x$ **Divide each side by −25.**

ANOTHER WAY You can also begin solving the equation by dividing each side of the equation by 25.

▸ The cranes were not flying for 236 hours of the migration.

GUIDED PRACTICE for Example 5

7. **WHAT IF?** Suppose the cranes take 12 days (288 hours) to travel the 2500 miles. How many hours of this migration are the cranes *not* flying?

3.3 EXERCISES

HOMEWORK KEY
○ = **WORKED-OUT SOLUTIONS** on p. WS6 for Exs. 17 and 39
★ = **STANDARDIZED TEST PRACTICE** Exs. 2, 18, 35, 36, and 41
◆ = **MULTIPLE REPRESENTATIONS** Ex. 42

SKILL PRACTICE

1. **VOCABULARY** What is the reciprocal of the fraction in the equation $\frac{3}{5}(2x + 8) = 18$?

2. ★ **WRITING** *Describe* the steps you would use to solve the equation $3(4y - 7) = 6$.

EXAMPLE 1 on p. 148 for Exs. 3–11

COMBINING LIKE TERMS **Solve the equation. Check your solution.**

3. $p + 2p - 3 = 6$
4. $12v + 14 + 10v = 80$
5. $11w - 9 - 7w = 15$
6. $5a + 3 - 3a = -7$
7. $6c - 8 - 2c = -16$
8. $9 = 7z - 13z - 21$
9. $-2 = 3y - 18 - 5y$
10. $23 = -4m + 2 + m$
11. $35 = -5 + 2x - 7x$

EXAMPLES 2 and 3
on pp. 148–149 for Exs. 12–18, 25

USING THE DISTRIBUTIVE PROPERTY **Solve the equation. Check your solution.**

12. $3 + 4(z + 5) = 31$

13. $14 + 2(4g - 3) = 40$

14. $5m + 2(m + 1) = 23$

15. $5h + 2(11 - h) = -5$

16. $27 = 3c - 3(6 - 2c)$

17. $-3 = 12y - 5(2y - 7)$

18. ★ **MULTIPLE CHOICE** What is the solution of $7v - (6 - 2v) = 12$?

Ⓐ -3.6　Ⓑ -2　Ⓒ 2　Ⓓ 3.6

EXAMPLE 4
on p. 149 for Exs. 19–24, 26

MULTIPLYING BY A RECIPROCAL **Solve the equation. Check your solution.**

19. $\frac{1}{3}(d + 3) = 5$

20. $\frac{3}{2}(x - 5) = -6$

21. $\frac{4}{3}(7 - n) = 12$

22. $4 = \frac{2}{9}(4y - 2)$

23. $-32 = \frac{8}{7}(3w - 1)$

24. $-14 = \frac{2}{5}(9 - 2b)$

ERROR ANALYSIS ***Describe*** **and correct the error in solving the equation.**

25.

$5x - 3(x - 6) = 2$
$5x - 3x - 18 = 2$
$2x - 18 = 2$
$2x = 20$
$x = 10$
✗

26.

$\frac{1}{2}(2x - 10) = 4$
$2x - 10 = 2$
$2x = 12$
$x = 6$
✗

SOLVING EQUATIONS **Solve the equation. Check your solution.**

27. $8.9 + 1.2(3a - 1) = 14.9$

28. $-11.2 + 4(2.1 + q) = -0.8$

29. $1.3t + 3(t + 8.2) = 37.5$

30. $1.6 = 7.6 - 5(k + 1.1)$

31. $0.5 = 4.1x - 2(1.3x - 4)$

32. $8.7 = 3.5m - 2.5(5.4 - 6m)$

GEOMETRY **Find the value of x for the triangle or rectangle.**

33. Perimeter = 24 feet

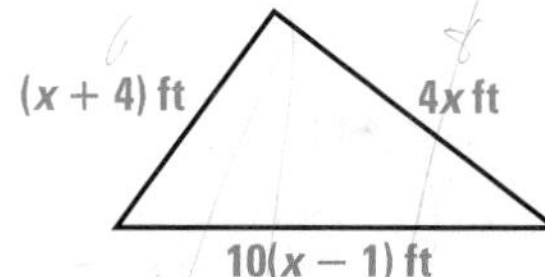

34. Perimeter = 26 meters

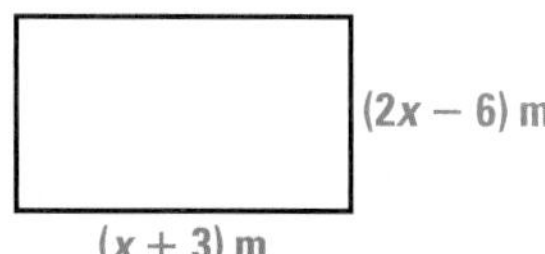

35. ★ **WRITING** The length of a rectangle is 3.5 inches more than its width. The perimeter of the rectangle is 31 inches. Find the length and the width of the rectangle. *Explain* your reasoning.

36. ★ **SHORT RESPONSE** Solve each equation by first dividing each side of the equation by the number outside the parentheses. When would you recommend using this method to solve an equation? *Explain.*

a. $9(x - 4) = 72$

b. $8(x + 5) = 60$

37. CHALLENGE An even integer can be represented by the expression $2n$. Find three consecutive even integers that have a sum of 54.

PROBLEM SOLVING

EXAMPLE 5 on p. 150 for Exs. 38–40

38. BASKETBALL A ticket agency sells tickets to a professional basketball game. The agency charges \$32.50 for each ticket, a convenience charge of \$3.30 for each ticket, and a processing fee of \$5.90 for the entire order. The total charge for an order is \$220.70. How many tickets were purchased?

@HomeTutor for problem solving help at classzone.com

39. HANGING POSTERS You want to hang 3 equally-sized travel posters on the wall in your room so that the posters on the ends are each 3 feet from the end of the wall. You want the spacing between posters to be equal. How much space should you leave between the posters?

@HomeTutor for problem solving help at classzone.com

40. LIFEGUARD TRAINING To qualify for a lifeguard training course, you have to swim continuously for 500 yards using either the front crawl or the breaststroke. You swim the front crawl at a rate of 45 yards per minute and the breaststroke at a rate of 35 yards per minute. You take 12 minutes to swim 500 yards. How much time did you spend swimming the front crawl? Use the verbal model below.

Distance = Rate for front crawl • Time for front crawl + Rate for breaststroke (Total time − Time for front crawl)

41. ★ EXTENDED RESPONSE The Busk-Ivanhoe Tunnel on the Colorado Midland Railway was built in the 1890s with separate work crews starting on opposite ends at different times. The crew working from Ivanhoe started 0.75 month later than the crew working from Busk.

Cutaway of Busk-Ivanhoe Tunnel

a. Starting at the time construction began on the Busk end, find the time it took to complete a total of 8473 feet of the tunnel. Round your answer to the nearest month.

b. After 8473 feet were completed, the work crews merged under the same supervision. The combined crew took 3 months to complete the remaining 921 feet of the tunnel. Find the rate at which the remainder of the tunnel was completed.

c. Was the tunnel being completed more rapidly before or after the work crews merged? *Explain* your reasoning.

42. **MULTIPLE REPRESENTATIONS** A roofing contractor gives estimates for shingling a roof in cost per square, where a square is a 10 foot by 10 foot section of roof. The contractor estimates $27.50 per square for materials, $17 per square for labor, $30 per square for overhead and profit, and a total of $750 for miscellaneous expenses.

a. **Writing an Equation** Write an equation that gives the estimate y (in dollars) as a function of the number x of squares of a roof. The contractor gives an estimate of $2314.50. About how many squares does the roof have?

b. **Making a Table** Make a table that shows the estimates for shingling a roof that has 5, 10, 15, 20, or 25 squares. Use your table to check your answer to part (a).

43. **CHALLENGE** A person has quarters and dimes that total $2.80. The number of dimes is 7 more than the number of quarters. How many of each coin does the person have?

MIXED REVIEW

Evaluate the expression for the given value(s) of the variable(s).

44. $x - y$ when $x = -7$ and $y = 2$ *(p. 80)*

45. $x - (-y)$ when $x = -4$ and $y = 5$ *(p. 80)*

46. $\frac{x-9}{4}$ when $x = 9$ *(p. 103)*

47. $\frac{4y+7}{3}$ when $y = 5$ *(p. 103)*

PREVIEW
Prepare for Lesson 3.4 in Exs. 48–56.

Solve the equation. Check your solution. *(p. 141)*

48. $5x + 1 = 26$

49. $-x + 4 = 13$

50. $3x - 5 = -14$

51. $3 - 2x = 19$

52. $\frac{x}{3} - 4 = 1$

53. $8 + \frac{x}{4} = -\frac{3}{4}$

54. $11x + 5x = 48$

55. $-4x + 11x = -28$

56. $\frac{2}{5}x - \frac{3}{5}x = -7$

QUIZ *for Lessons 3.1–3.3*

Solve the equation. Check your solution.

1. $x + 9 = 7$ *(p. 134)*

2. $y - 5 = -11$ *(p. 134)*

3. $-7b = -56$ *(p. 134)*

4. $\frac{z}{4} = 6$ *(p. 134)*

5. $-\frac{4}{3}t = -12$ *(p. 134)*

6. $9w - 4 = 14$ *(p. 141)*

7. $23 = 1 - d$ *(p. 141)*

8. $66 = 4m + 7m$ *(p. 141)*

9. $-104 = -5p - 3p$ *(p. 141)*

10. $2v + 5v - 8 = 13$ *(p. 148)*

11. $2a - 6(a - 4) = -4$ *(p. 148)*

12. $\frac{6}{5}(5 - 4g) = -18$ *(p. 148)*

13. **INTERNET SHOPPING** Dan purchases DVDs from a website. Each DVD costs $11, and the shipping and handling fees are $6.95. Dan is charged a total of $50.95. How many DVDs did he purchase? *(p. 141)*

3.4 Solve Equations with Variables on Both Sides

Before You solved equations with variables on one side.

Now You will solve equations with variables on both sides.

Why? So you can find the cost of a gym membership, as in Ex. 52.

Key Vocabulary
- **identity**

Some equations have variables on both sides. To solve such equations, you can collect the variable terms on one side of the equation and the constant terms on the other side of the equation.

EXAMPLE 1 Solve an equation with variables on both sides

Solve $7 - 8x = 4x - 17$.

$7 - 8x = 4x - 17$	Write original equation.
$7 - 8x + 8x = 4x - 17 + 8x$	Add $8x$ to each side.
$7 = 12x - 17$	Simplify each side.
$24 = 12x$	Add 17 to each side.
$2 = x$	Divide each side by 12.

ANOTHER WAY You could also begin solving the equation by subtracting $4x$ from each side to obtain $7 - 12x = -17$. When you solve this equation for x, you get the same solution, 2.

▶ The solution is 2. Check by substituting 2 for x in the original equation.

CHECK	$7 - 8x = 4x - 17$	Write original equation.
	$7 - 8(2) \stackrel{?}{=} 4(2) - 17$	Substitute 2 for x.
	$-9 \stackrel{?}{=} 4(2) - 17$	Simplify left side.
	$-9 = -9$ ✓	Simplify right side. Solution checks.

Animated Algebra at classzone.com

EXAMPLE 2 Solve an equation with grouping symbols

Solve $9x - 5 = \frac{1}{4}(16x + 60)$.

$9x - 5 = \frac{1}{4}(16x + 60)$	Write original equation.
$9x - 5 = 4x + 15$	Distributive property
$5x - 5 = 15$	Subtract $4x$ from each side.
$5x = 20$	Add 5 to each side.
$x = 4$	Divide each side by 5.

GUIDED PRACTICE for Examples 1 and 2

Solve the equation. Check your solution.

1. $24 - 3m = 5m$ **2.** $20 + c = 4c - 7$ **3.** $9 - 3k = 17 - 2k$

4. $5z - 2 = 2(3z - 4)$ **5.** $3 - 4a = 5(a - 3)$ **6.** $8y - 6 = \frac{2}{3}(6y + 15)$

EXAMPLE 3 Solve a real-world problem

CAR SALES A car dealership sold 78 new cars and 67 used cars this year. The number of new cars sold by the dealership has been increasing by 6 cars each year. The number of used cars sold by the dealership has been decreasing by 4 cars each year. If these trends continue, in how many years will the number of new cars sold be twice the number of used cars sold?

Solution

Let x represent the number of years from now. So, $6x$ represents the increase in the number of new cars sold over x years and $-4x$ represents the decrease in the number of used cars sold over x years. Write a verbal model.

New cars sold this year + Increase in new cars sold over x years = 2 (Used cars sold this year + Decrease in used cars sold over x years)

$$78 + 6x = 2(67 + (-4x))$$

$78 + 6x = 2(67 - 4x)$ **Write equation.**

$78 + 6x = 134 - 8x$ **Distributive property**

$78 + 14x = 134$ **Add $8x$ to each side.**

$14x = 56$ **Subtract 78 from each side.**

$x = 4$ **Divide each side by 14.**

▶ The number of new cars sold will be twice the number of used cars sold in 4 years.

CHECK You can use a table to check your answer.

Year	0	1	2	3	4
Used cars sold	67	63	59	55	51
New cars sold	78	84	90	96	102

The number of new cars sold is twice the number of used cars sold in 4 years.

GUIDED PRACTICE for Example 3

7. WHAT IF? In Example 3, suppose the car dealership sold 50 new cars this year instead of 78. In how many years will the number of new cars sold be twice the number of used cars sold?

NUMBER OF SOLUTIONS Equations do not always have one solution. An equation that is true for all values of the variable is an **identity**. So, the solution of an identity is all real numbers. Some equations have no solution.

EXAMPLE 4 Identify the number of solutions of an equation

Solve the equation, if possible.

a. $3x = 3(x + 4)$

b. $2x + 10 = 2(x + 5)$

Solution

a. $3x = 3(x + 4)$ Original equation

$3x = 3x + 12$ Distributive property

The equation $3x = 3x + 12$ is not true because the number $3x$ cannot be equal to 12 more than itself. So, the equation has no solution. This can be demonstrated by continuing to solve the equation.

$3x - 3x = 3x + 12 - 3x$ Subtract $3x$ from each side.

$0 = 12$ ✗ Simplify.

▶ The statement $0 = 12$ is not true, so the equation has no solution.

b. $2x + 10 = 2(x + 5)$ Original equation

$2x + 10 = 2x + 10$ Distributive property

▶ Notice that the statement $2x + 10 = 2x + 10$ is true for all values of x. So, the equation is an identity, and the solution is all real numbers.

GUIDED PRACTICE for Example 4

Solve the equation, if possible.

8. $9z + 12 = 9(z + 3)$

9. $7w + 1 = 8w + 1$

10. $3(2a + 2) = 2(3a + 3)$

SOLVING LINEAR EQUATIONS You have learned several ways to transform an equation to an equivalent equation. These methods are combined in the steps listed below.

CONCEPT SUMMARY *For Your Notebook*

Steps for Solving Linear Equations

STEP 1 **Use** the distributive property to remove any grouping symbols.

STEP 2 **Simplify** the expression on each side of the equation.

STEP 3 **Use** properties of equality to collect the variable terms on one side of the equation and the constant terms on the other side of the equation.

STEP 4 **Use** properties of equality to solve for the variable.

STEP 5 **Check** your solution in the original equation.

3.4 EXERCISES

HOMEWORK KEY

○ = **WORKED-OUT SOLUTIONS** on p. WS6 for Exs. 13 and 51

★ = **STANDARDIZED TEST PRACTICE** Exs. 2, 15, 16, 17, 29, and 53

◆ = **MULTIPLE REPRESENTATIONS** Ex. 52

SKILL PRACTICE

1. **VOCABULARY** Copy and complete: An equation that is true for all values of the variable is called a(n) _?_.

2. ★ **WRITING** *Explain* why the equation $4x + 3 = 4x + 1$ has no solution.

EXAMPLES 1 and 2 on p. 154 for Exs. 3–17

SOLVING EQUATIONS **Solve the equation. Check your solution.**

3. $8t + 5 = 6t + 1$
4. $k + 1 = 3k - 1$
5. $8c + 5 = 4c - 11$
6. $8 + 4m = 9m - 7$
7. $10b + 18 = 8b + 4$
8. $19 - 13p = -17p - 5$
9. $9a = 6(a + 4)$
10. $5h - 7 = 2(h + 1)$
11. $3(d + 12) = 8 - 4d$
12. $7(r + 7) = 5r + 59$
13. $40 + 14j = 2(-4j - 13)$
14. $5(n + 2) = \frac{3}{5}(5 + 10n)$

15. ★ **MULTIPLE CHOICE** What is the solution of the equation $8x + 2x = 15x - 10$?

(A) -2 (B) 0.4 (C) 2 (D) 5

16. ★ **MULTIPLE CHOICE** What is the solution of the equation $4y + y + 1 = 7(y - 1)$?

(A) -4 (B) -3 (C) 3 (D) 4

17. ★ **WRITING** *Describe* the steps you would use to solve the equation $3(2z - 5) = 2z + 13$.

EXAMPLE 4 on p. 156 for Exs. 18–28

SOLVING EQUATIONS **Solve the equation, if possible.**

18. $w + 3 = w + 6$
19. $16d = 22 + 5d$
20. $8z = 4(2z + 1)$
21. $12 + 5v = 2v - 9$
22. $22x + 70 = 17x - 95$
23. $2 - 15n = 5(-3n + 2)$
24. $12y + 6 = 6(2y + 1)$
25. $5(1 + 4m) = 2(3 + 10m)$
26. $2(3g + 2) = \frac{1}{2}(12g + 8)$

ERROR ANALYSIS ***Describe*** **and correct the error in solving the equation.**

27.

$3(x + 5) = 3x + 15$

$3x + 5 = 3x + 15$

$5 = 15$

The equation has no solution. ✗

28.

$6(2y + 6) = 4(9 + 3y)$

$12y + 36 = 36 + 12y$

$12y = 12y$

$0 = 0$

The solution is $y = 0$. ✗

29. ★ **OPEN-ENDED** Give an example of an equation that has no solution. *Explain* why your equation does not have a solution.

SOLVING EQUATIONS **Solve the equation, if possible.**

30. $8w - 8 - 6w = 4w - 7$

31. $3x - 4 = 2x + 8 - 5x$

32. $-15c + 7c + 1 = 3 - 8c$

33. $\frac{3}{2} + \frac{3}{4}a = \frac{1}{4}a - \frac{1}{2}$

34. $\frac{5}{8}m - \frac{3}{8} = \frac{1}{2}m + \frac{7}{8}$

35. $n - 10 = \frac{5}{6}n - 7 - \frac{1}{3}n$

36. $3.7b + 7 = 8.1b - 19.4$

37. $6.2h + 5 - 1.4h = 4.8h + 5$

38. $0.7z + 1.9 + 0.1z = 5.5 - 0.4z$

39. $5.4t + 14.6 - 10.1t = 12.8 - 3.5t - 0.6$

40. $\frac{1}{8}(5y + 64) = \frac{1}{4}(20 + 2y)$

41. $14 - \frac{1}{5}(j - 10) = \frac{2}{5}(25 + j)$

42. $5(1.2k + 6) = 7.1k + 34.4$

43. $-0.25(4v - 8) = 0.5(4 - 2v)$

GEOMETRY **Find the perimeter of the square.**

44.

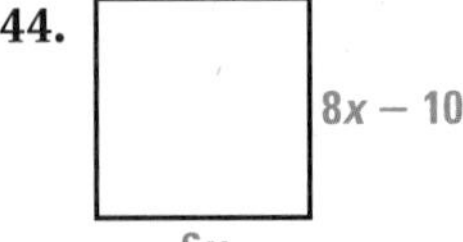

45.

5x

3x + 6

46.

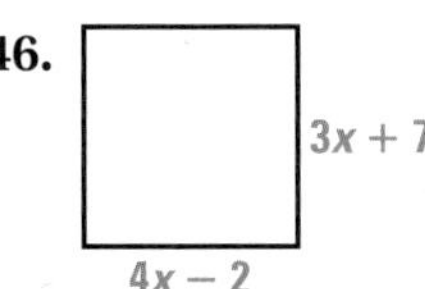

CHALLENGE **Find the value(s) of *a* for which the equation is an identity.**

47. $a(2x + 3) = 9x + 12 - x$

48. $10x - 35 + 3ax = 5ax - 7a$

PROBLEM SOLVING

EXAMPLE 3 on p. 155 for Exs. 49–51

49. CAMPING The membership fee for joining a camping association is \$45. A local campground charges members of the camping association \$35 per night for a campsite and nonmembers \$40 per night for a campsite. After how many nights of camping is the total cost for members, including the membership fee, the same as the total cost for nonmembers?

@HomeTutor for problem solving help at classzone.com

50. HIGH-SPEED INTERNET Dan and Sydney are getting high-speed Internet access at the same time. Dan's provider charges \$60 for installation and \$42.95 per month. Sydney's provider has free installation and charges \$57.95 per month. After how many months will Dan and Sydney have paid the same amount for high-speed Internet service?

@HomeTutor for problem solving help at classzone.com

51. LANGUAGES Information about students who take Spanish and students who take French at a high school is shown in the table. If the trends continue, in how many years will there be 3 times as many students taking Spanish as French?

Language	Students enrolled this year	Average rate of change
Spanish	555	33 more students each year
French	230	2 fewer students each year

52. **MULTIPLE REPRESENTATIONS** For $360, a rock-climbing gym offers a yearly membership where members can climb as many days as they want and pay $4 per day for equipment rental. Nonmembers pay $10 per day to use the gym and $6 per day for equipment rental.

a. **Writing an Equation** Write an equation to find the number of visits after which the total cost for a member and the total cost for a nonmember are the same. Then solve the equation.

b. **Making a Table** Make a table for the costs of members and nonmembers after 5, 10, 15, 20, 25, 30, and 35 visits. Use the table to check your answer to part (a).

53. ★ **EXTENDED RESPONSE** Flyball is a relay race for dogs. In each of the four legs of the relay, a dog jumps over hurdles, retrieves a ball from a flybox, and runs back over the hurdles. The last leg of a relay is shown below. The collie starts the course 0.3 second before the sheepdog.

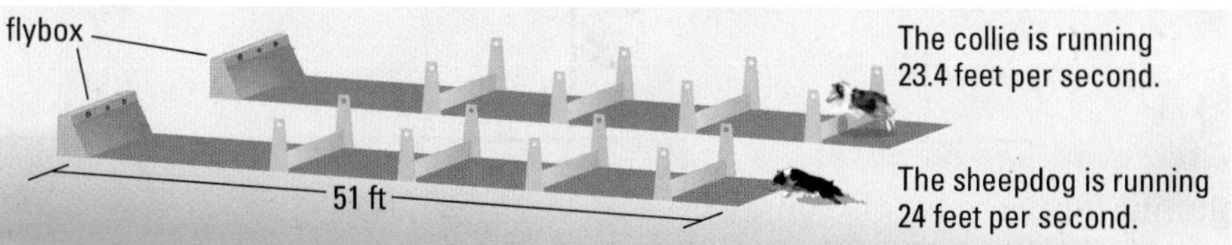
flybox
The collie is running 23.4 feet per second.
51 ft
The sheepdog is running 24 feet per second.

a. Let t represent the time (in seconds) it takes the collie to run the last leg. Write and solve an equation to find the number of seconds after which the sheepdog would catch up with the collie.

b. How long does it take the collie to run the last leg?

c. Use your answers from parts (a) and (b) to determine whether the sheepdog catches up and passes the collie during the last leg of the relay. *Explain* your reasoning.

CHALLENGE **Find the length and the width of the rectangle described.**

54. The length is 12 units more than the width. The perimeter is 7 times the width.

55. The length is 4 units less than 3 times the width. The perimeter is 22 units more than twice the width.

MIXED REVIEW

PREVIEW Prepare for Lesson 3.5 in Exs. 56–64.

Write the fraction in simplest form. *(p. 912)*

56. $\frac{5}{15}$ 57. $\frac{10}{12}$ 58. $\frac{4}{14}$ 59. $\frac{18}{48}$

Solve the equation. *(p. 134)*

60. $\frac{w}{3} = 6$ 61. $\frac{x}{18} = 2$ 62. $-11 = \frac{m}{4}$ 63. $12 = \frac{z}{-9}$

64. **FOOTBALL** The average rushing yards per game for a football player is found by dividing the total rushing yards for the season by the number of games played. How many total rushing yards did a player have if he played in 12 games and averaged 22 yards per game? *(p. 134)*

Spreadsheet ACTIVITY *Use after Lesson 3.4*

@HomeTutor
classzone.com
Keystrokes

3.4 Solve Equations Using Tables

QUESTION **How can you use a spreadsheet to solve an equation with variables on both sides?**

You can use a spreadsheet to solve an equation with variables on both sides by evaluating the left side of the equation and the right side of the equation using the same value of the variable. If the left side and right side are equal, then the value of the variable is a solution.

EXAMPLE **Solve an equation using a spreadsheet**

Solve $19(x - 1) - 72 = 6x$.

STEP 1 ***Enter data and formulas***

Label columns for possible solutions, left side, and right side in row 1. Enter the integers from 0 through 10 as possible solutions in column A. Then enter the formulas for the left side and the right side of the equation in columns B and C.

	A	B	C
1	Possible solutions	Left side	Right side
2	0	=19*(A2−1)−72	=6*A2
3	1	=19*(A3−1)−72	=6*A3
...	...	...	...
12	10	=19*(A12−1)−72	=6*A12

STEP 2 ***Compare columns***

Compare the values of the left side and the values of the right side. The left side and right side values are equal when $x = 7$. So, the solution is 7.

	A	B	C
1	Possible solutions	Left side	Right side
...	...	...	...
8	6	23	36
9	7	42	42
10	8	61	48

DRAW CONCLUSIONS **Use your observations to complete these exercises**

In Exercises 1–3, use a spreadsheet to solve the equation.

1. $15x + 6 = 6x + 24$ **2.** $8x - 17 = 5x + 70$ **3.** $18 - 2(x + 3) = x$

4. Not all equations have integer solutions. Consider the equation $4.9 + 4.8(7 - x) = 6.2x$.

a. Follow Step 1 above using $4.9 + 4.8(7 - x) = 6.2x$.

b. Add a fourth column that shows the difference of the value of the left side and the value of the right side. Find consecutive possible solutions between which the differences of the values of the left side and right side change sign.

c. Repeat Step 1. This time use the lesser of the two possible solutions from part (b) as the first possible solution, and increase each possible solution by 0.1. Can you identify a solution now? If so, what is it?

MIXED REVIEW *of Problem Solving*

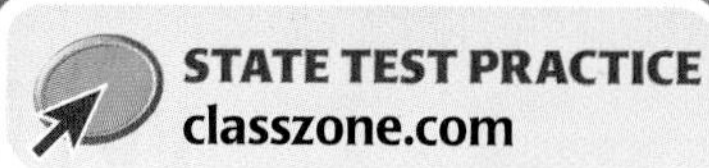

Lessons 3.1–3.4

1. **MULTI-STEP PROBLEM** A phone company charges \$.25 for the first minute of a long-distance call and \$.07 for each additional minute.
   a. Write an equation that gives the cost C of a long-distance call as a function of the length t (in minutes) of the call.
   b. Find the duration of a long-distance call that costs \$2.

2. **GRIDDED ANSWER** A veterinary assistant steps on a scale while holding a cat. The weight of the cat and assistant is 175 pounds. The assistant weighs 162 pounds. Find the weight (in pounds) of the cat.

3. **EXTENDED RESPONSE** A bowling alley charges \$1.50 for bowling shoes and \$3.75 for each game. Paul and Brandon each have \$15 to spend at the bowling alley.
   a. Paul brings his own bowling shoes. How many games can he bowl?
   b. Brandon needs to pay for bowling shoes. How many games can he bowl? Round your answer down to the nearest whole number.
   c. Both Paul and Brandon decide to bowl the number of games that Brandon can afford to bowl. Does Paul have enough money to buy a slice of pizza and a soda that cost a total of \$3.25? *Explain* your reasoning.

4. **GRIDDED ANSWER** The triangle has a perimeter of 82 inches. What is x?

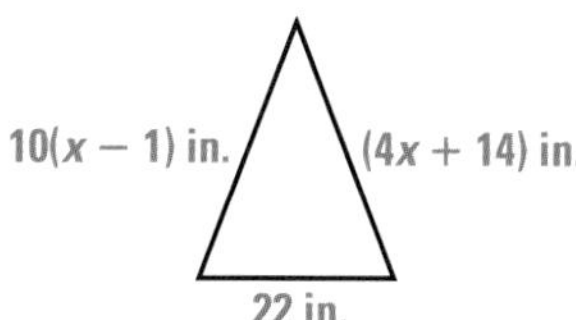

5. **SHORT RESPONSE** You are folding origami cranes that will be used as decorations at a wedding. If you make cranes for 1 hour without a break, you can make 40 cranes. During a 3 hour period, you make 100 cranes. How much time did you spend *not* making cranes? *Explain* your reasoning.

6. **SHORT RESPONSE** A ski resort offers a super-saver pass for \$90. The lift ticket rates with and without the super-saver pass are listed below.

Pass	Weekday lift ticket	Weekend/holiday lift ticket
With	\$22.50	\$36.00
Without	\$45.00	\$48.00

Suppose a skier skis only on weekdays. After how many visits to the ski resort will the cost for the super-saver pass and the lift tickets be equal to the cost of the lift tickets without the pass? *Explain* your reasoning.

7. **SHORT RESPONSE** The eruption of Mount St. Helens in 1980 decreased its elevation by 1313 feet. The current elevation is 8364 feet. What was the elevation of the volcano before the eruption? *Explain* your reasoning.

8. **EXTENDED RESPONSE** A garden supply store sells daffodil bulbs for \$.60 per bulb.
   a. Jen spends \$24 on daffodil bulbs. How many daffodil bulbs did she purchase?
   b. Jen decides to plant the daffodil bulbs along one side of her house that is 30 feet long. How many inches apart should she plant the bulbs so that they are equally spaced?
   c. Jen thinks that the daffodils will look better if the bulbs are planted 6 inches apart. How many more bulbs does she need? *Explain* your reasoning.

9. **OPEN-ENDED** *Describe* a real-world situation that can be modeled by the equation $4x + 15 = 47$. Then solve the equation and explain what your solution means in this situation.

3.5 Write Ratios and Proportions

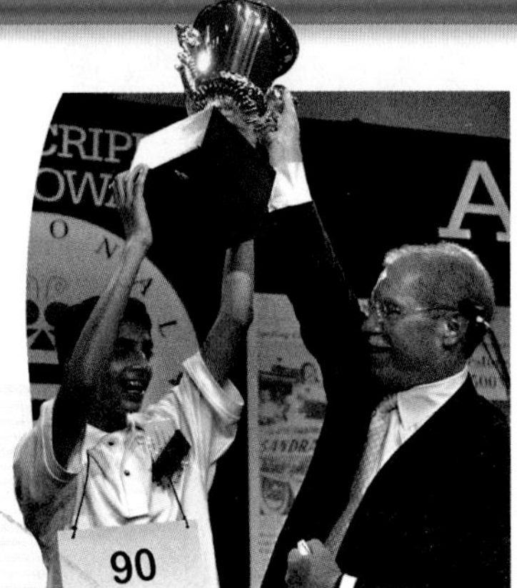

Before You solved equations involving division.

Now You will find ratios and write and solve proportions.

Why? So you can find a ratio involving a contest, as in Ex. 46.

Key Vocabulary
- **ratio**
- **proportion**
- **simplest form,** *p. 912*

Throughout this book you have been using rates, such as 50 miles per hour. A rate is a special type of *ratio.*

KEY CONCEPT *For Your Notebook*

Ratios

A **ratio** uses division to compare two quantities. You can write the ratio of two quantities a and b, where b is not equal to 0, in three ways.

a to b $\qquad a:b \qquad \frac{a}{b}$

Each ratio is read "the ratio of a to b." Ratios should be written in simplest form.

EXAMPLE 1 Write a ratio

VOLLEYBALL A volleyball team plays 14 home matches and 10 away matches.

a. Find the ratio of home matches to away matches.

b. Find the ratio of home matches to all matches.

Solution

a. $\frac{\text{home matches}}{\text{away matches}} = \frac{14}{10} = \frac{7}{5}$

b. $\frac{\text{home matches}}{\text{all matches}} = \frac{14}{14 + 10} = \frac{14}{24} = \frac{7}{12}$

GUIDED PRACTICE for Example 1

Derek and his brother decide to combine their CD collections. Derek has 44 CDs, and his brother has 52 CDs. Find the specified ratio.

1. The number of Derek's CDs to the number of his brother's CDs
2. The number of Derek's CDs to the number of CDs in the entire collection

PROPORTIONS A **proportion** is an equation that states that two ratios are equivalent. The general form of a proportion is given below.

> **READING**
> This proportion is read "*a* is to *b* as *c* is to *d*."

$$\frac{a}{b} = \frac{c}{d} \text{ where } b \neq 0, d \neq 0$$

If one of the numbers in a proportion is unknown, you can solve the proportion to find the unknown number. To solve a proportion with a variable in the numerator, you can use the same methods you used to solve equations.

EXAMPLE 2 Solve a proportion

Solve the proportion $\frac{11}{6} = \frac{x}{30}$.

$\frac{11}{6} = \frac{x}{30}$	**Write original proportion.**
$30 \cdot \frac{11}{6} = 30 \cdot \frac{x}{30}$	**Multiply each side by 30.**
$\frac{330}{6} = x$	**Simplify.**
$55 = x$	**Divide.**

✓ GUIDED PRACTICE for Example 2

Solve the proportion. Check your solution.

3. $\frac{w}{35} = \frac{4}{7}$ **4.** $\frac{9}{2} = \frac{m}{12}$ **5.** $\frac{z}{54} = \frac{5}{9}$

SETTING UP A PROPORTION There are different ways to set up a proportion. Consider the following problem.

A recipe for tomato salsa calls for 30 tomatoes to make 12 pints of salsa. How many tomatoes are needed to make 4 pints of salsa?

The tables below show two ways of arranging the information from the problem. In each table, x represents the number of tomatoes needed to make 4 pints of salsa. The proportions follow from the tables.

> **AVOID ERRORS**
> You cannot write a proportion that compares pints to tomatoes and tomatoes to pints.
> $\frac{\text{pints}}{\text{tomatoes}} \neq \frac{\text{tomatoes}}{\text{pints}}$

	Tomatoes	Pints
Smaller recipe	x	4
Normal recipe	30	12

Proportion: $\frac{x}{30} = \frac{4}{12}$

	Smaller recipe	Normal recipe
Tomatoes	x	30
Pints	4	12

Proportion: $\frac{x}{4} = \frac{30}{12}$

EXAMPLE 3 Solve a multi-step problem

ELEVATORS The elevator that takes passengers from the lobby of the John Hancock Center in Chicago to the observation level travels 150 feet in 5 seconds. The observation level is located on the 94th floor, at 1029 feet above the ground. Find the time it takes the elevator to travel from the lobby to the observation level.

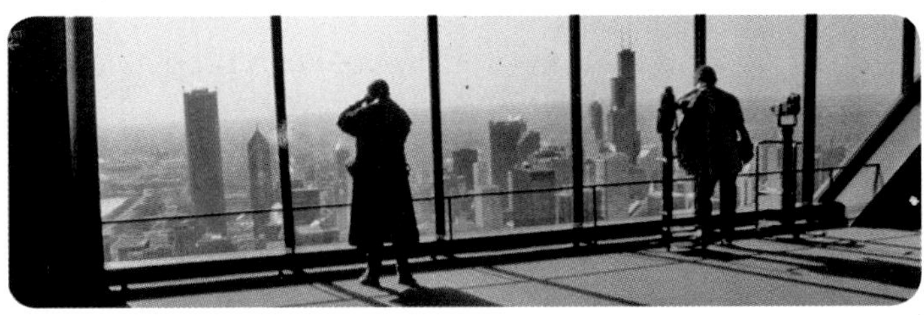

Solution

STEP 1 **Write** a proportion involving two ratios that compare the amount of time the elevator has ascended with the distance traveled.

$$\frac{5}{150} = \frac{x}{1029}$$ ← **seconds** ← **feet**

STEP 2 **Solve** the proportion.

$\frac{5}{150} = \frac{x}{1029}$ **Write proportion.**

$1029 \cdot \frac{5}{150} = 1029 \cdot \frac{x}{1029}$ **Multiply each side by 1029.**

$\frac{5145}{150} = x$ **Simplify.**

$34.3 = x$ **Use a calculator.**

▸ The elevator travels from the lobby to the observation level in 34.3 seconds.

CHECK You can use a table to check the reasonableness of your answer.

GENERATE TABLE As the amount of time increases by 5 seconds, the distance traveled increases by 150 feet.

Time (sec)	5	10	15	20	25	30	35
Distance traveled (ft)	150	300	450	600	750	900	1050

The solution, 34.3 seconds, is slightly less than 35 seconds, and 1029 feet is slightly less than 1050 feet. So, the solution is reasonable.

✓ GUIDED PRACTICE for Example 3

6. **WHAT IF?** In Example 3, suppose the elevator travels 125 feet in 5 seconds. Find the time it will take for the elevator to travel from the lobby to the observation level.

7. **ASTRONOMY** When two full moons appear in the same month, the second full moon is called a blue moon. On average, 2 blue moons occur every 5 years. Find the number of blue moons that are likely to occur in the next 25 years.

3.5 EXERCISES

HOMEWORK KEY

○ = **WORKED-OUT SOLUTIONS** on p. WS6 for Exs. 17 and 49

★ = **STANDARDIZED TEST PRACTICE** Exs. 2, 19, 20, 43, and 54

◆ = **MULTIPLE REPRESENTATIONS** Ex. 52

SKILL PRACTICE

1. **VOCABULARY** Copy and complete: A proportion is an equation that states that two __?__ are equivalent.

2. ★ **WRITING** Write a ratio of two quantities in three different ways.

SIMPLIFYING RATIOS **Tell whether the ratio is in simplest form. If not, write it in simplest form.**

3. 14 to 18
4. 5 : 13
5. $\frac{24}{25}$
6. 28 to 32

EXAMPLE 2 on p. 163 for Exs. 7–22

SOLVING PROPORTIONS **Solve the proportion. Check your solution.**

7. $\frac{2}{5} = \frac{x}{3}$
8. $\frac{4}{1} = \frac{z}{16}$
9. $\frac{c}{8} = \frac{11}{4}$
10. $\frac{36}{12} = \frac{x}{2}$
11. $\frac{16}{7} = \frac{m}{21}$
12. $\frac{k}{9} = \frac{10}{18}$
13. $\frac{5}{8} = \frac{t}{24}$
14. $\frac{d}{5} = \frac{80}{100}$
15. $\frac{v}{20} = \frac{8}{4}$
16. $\frac{r}{60} = \frac{40}{50}$
17. $\frac{16}{48} = \frac{n}{36}$
18. $\frac{49}{98} = \frac{s}{112}$

19. ★ **MULTIPLE CHOICE** What is the value of x in the proportion $\frac{8}{5} = \frac{x}{20}$?

Ⓐ 2 Ⓑ 23 Ⓒ 32 Ⓓ 40

20. ★ **MULTIPLE CHOICE** What is the value of z in the proportion $\frac{z}{15} = \frac{28}{35}$?

Ⓐ 8 Ⓑ 12 Ⓒ 18.75 Ⓓ 425

ERROR ANALYSIS ***Describe*** **and correct the error in solving the proportion.**

21.
$$\frac{3}{4} = \frac{x}{6}$$
$$\frac{1}{6} \cdot \frac{3}{4} = \frac{1}{6} \cdot \frac{x}{6}$$
$$\frac{1}{8} = x$$
✗

22.
$$\frac{m}{10} = \frac{50}{20}$$
$$10 \cdot \frac{m}{10} = 20 \cdot \frac{50}{20}$$
$$m = 50$$
✗

WRITING AND SOLVING PROPORTIONS **Write the sentence as a proportion. Then solve the proportion.**

23. 3 is to 8 as x is to 32.
24. 5 is to 7 as a is to 49.
25. x is to 4 as 8 is to 16.
26. y is to 20 as 9 is to 5.
27. b is to 10 as 7 is to 2.
28. 4 is to 12 as n is to 3.
29. 12 is to 18 as d is to 27.
30. t is to 21 as 40 is to 28.

SOLVING PROPORTIONS Solve the proportion. Check your solution.

31. $\frac{b}{0.5} = \frac{9}{2.5}$

32. $\frac{1.1}{1.2} = \frac{n}{3.6}$

33. $\frac{2.1}{7.7} = \frac{v}{8.8}$

34. $\frac{36}{54} = \frac{2x}{6}$

35. $\frac{3a}{4} = \frac{36}{12}$

36. $\frac{10h}{108} = \frac{5}{9}$

37. $\frac{6r}{10} = \frac{36}{15}$

38. $\frac{12}{42} = \frac{4w}{56}$

39. $\frac{m + 3}{8} = \frac{40}{64}$

40. $\frac{5}{13} = \frac{k - 4}{39}$

41. $\frac{7}{112} = \frac{c - 3}{8}$

42. $\frac{6 + n}{60} = \frac{15}{90}$

43. ★ **SHORT RESPONSE** Is it possible to write a proportion using the numbers 3, 4, 6, and 8? *Explain* your reasoning.

44. **CHALLENGE** If $\frac{a}{b} = \frac{c}{d}$ for nonzero numbers a, b, c, and d, is it also true that $\frac{a}{c} = \frac{b}{d}$? *Explain.*

PROBLEM SOLVING

EXAMPLE 1
on p. 162
for Exs. 45–49

45. **GOVERNMENT** There are 435 representatives in the U.S. House of Representatives. Of the 435 representatives, 6 are from Kentucky. Find the ratio of the number of representatives from Kentucky to the total number of representatives.

@HomeTutor for problem solving help at classzone.com

46. **CONTEST** Of the 30 champions of the National Spelling Bee from 1974 to 2003, 16 are boys. Find the ratio of the number of champions who are girls to the number who are boys.

@HomeTutor for problem solving help at classzone.com

PIZZA SALES The table shows the number of pizzas sold at a pizzeria during a week. Use the information to find the specified ratio.

Size	Small	Medium	Large
Pizzas	96	144	240

47. Small pizzas to large pizzas

48. Medium pizzas to large pizzas

(49.) Large pizzas to all pizzas

EXAMPLE 3
on p. 164
for Exs. 50–52

50. **READING** A student can read 7 pages of a book in 10 minutes. How many pages of the book can the student read in 30 minutes?

51. **SOCCER** In the first 4 games of the season, a soccer team scored a total of 10 goals. If this trend continues, how many goals will the team score in the 18 remaining games of the season?

52. **MULTIPLE REPRESENTATIONS** A movie is filmed so that the ratio of the length to the width of the image on the screen is 1.85 : 1.

   a. **Writing a Proportion** Write and solve a proportion to find the length of the image on the screen when the width of the image is 38 feet.

   b. **Making a Table** Make a table that shows the length of an image when the width of the image is 20, 25, 30, 35, and 40 feet. Use your table to check the reasonableness of your answer to part (a).

○ = WORKED-OUT SOLUTIONS on p. WS1

★ = STANDARDIZED TEST PRACTICE

= MULTIPLE REPRESENTATIONS

53. **MULTI-STEP PROBLEM** One day, the ratio of skiers to snowboarders on the mountain at a ski resort was 13 : 10. The resort sold a total of 253 lift tickets during the day.

a. Find the ratio of snowboarders on the mountain to all of the skiers and snowboarders on the mountain.

b. Use the ratio from part (a) to find the number of lift tickets sold to snowboarders during the day.

c. During the same day, the ratio of snowboarders who rented snowboards to snowboarders that have their own snowboards is 4 : 7. Find the number of snowboarders who rented a snowboard.

54. ★ **EXTENDED RESPONSE** You and a friend are waiting in separate lines to purchase concert tickets.

a. **Interpret** Every 10 minutes, the cashier at the head of your line helps 3 people. There are 11 people in line in front of you. Write a proportion that can be used to determine how long you will have to wait to purchase tickets.

b. **Interpret** Every 5 minutes, the cashier at the head of your friend's line helps 2 people. There are 14 people in line in front of your friend. Write a proportion that can be used to determine how long your friend will have to wait to purchase tickets.

c. **Compare** Will you or your friend be able to purchase concert tickets first? *Explain.*

55. **CHALLENGE** A car traveling 50 miles per hour goes 15 miles farther in the same amount of time as a car traveling 30 miles per hour. Find the distance that each car travels.

MIXED REVIEW

Tell whether the pairing is a function. *(p. 35)*

56.

Input	−4	−2	0	2	2
Output	2	2	0	−1	−2

57.

Input	−1	0	1	2	3
Output	5	5	5	5	5

Write a rule for the function represented by the graph. Identify the domain and range of the function. *(p. 43)*

58. 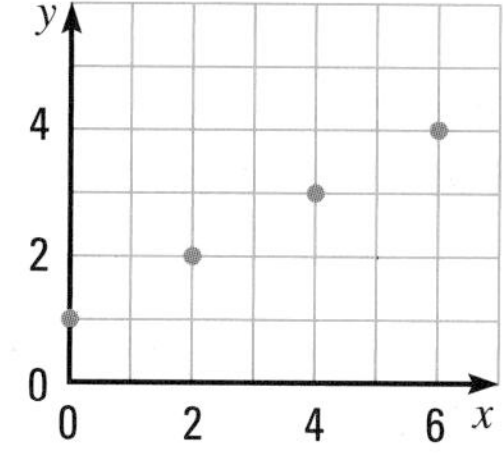

59. 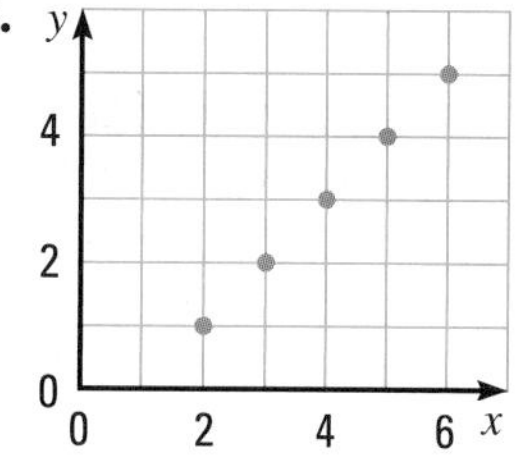

60. 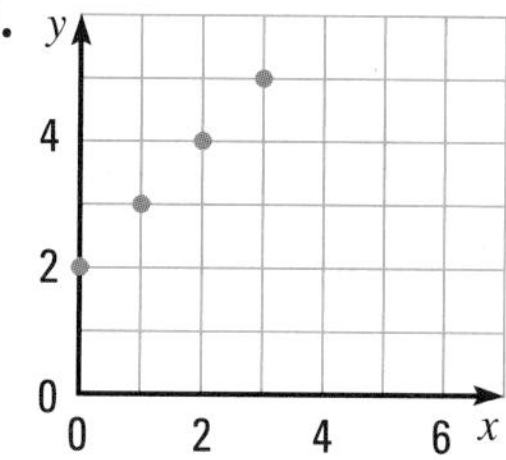

PREVIEW Prepare for Lesson 3.6 in Exs. 61–66.

Solve the equation. Check your solution.

61. $-2y = 18$ *(p. 134)*

62. $20x = 40$ *(p. 134)*

63. $56 = 7(z + 5)$ *(p. 148)*

64. $16(r + 3) = -48$ *(p. 148)*

65. $5(c - 12) = 2c$ *(p. 154)*

66. $b + 11 = 3(b - 1)$ *(p. 154)*

3.6 Solve Proportions Using Cross Products

Before You solved proportions using the multiplication property of equality.

Now You will solve proportions using cross products.

Why? So you can find the height of a scale model, as in Ex. 39.

Key Vocabulary
- **cross product**
- **scale drawing**
- **scale model**
- **scale**

In a proportion, a **cross product** is the product of the numerator of one ratio and the denominator of the other ratio. The following property involving cross products can be used to solve proportions.

KEY CONCEPT *For Your Notebook*

Cross Products Property

Words The cross products of a proportion are equal.

Example $\frac{3}{4} = \frac{6}{8}$ $\quad 4 \cdot 6 = 24$, $\quad 3 \cdot 8 = 24$

Algebra If $\frac{a}{b} = \frac{c}{d}$ where $b \neq 0$ and $d \neq 0$, then $ad = bc$.

The proportion $\frac{3}{4} = \frac{6}{8}$ can be written as $3:4 = 6:8$. In this form, 4 and 6 are called the *means* of the proportion, and 3 and 8 are called the *extremes* of the proportion. This is why the cross products property is also called the *means-extremes property.*

EXAMPLE 1 Use the cross products property

Solve the proportion $\frac{8}{x} = \frac{6}{15}$.

$\frac{8}{x} = \frac{6}{15}$	Write original proportion.
$8 \cdot 15 = x \cdot 6$	Cross products property
$120 = 6x$	Simplify.
$20 = x$	Divide each side by 6.

▸ The solution is 20. Check by substituting 20 for x in the original proportion.

CHECK $\frac{8}{20} \stackrel{?}{=} \frac{6}{15}$	Substitute 20 for x.
$8 \cdot 15 \stackrel{?}{=} 20 \cdot 6$	Cross products property
$120 = 120$ ✓	Simplify. Solution checks.

★ **EXAMPLE 2** **Standardized Test Practice**

What is the value of x in the proportion $\frac{4}{x} = \frac{8}{x-3}$?

Ⓐ -6 Ⓑ -3 Ⓒ 3 Ⓓ 6

Solution

ANOTHER WAY
Because 8 is twice 4, you can reason that $x - 3$ must be twice x:
$x - 3 = 2x$
$-3 = x$

$\frac{4}{x} = \frac{8}{x-3}$ Write original proportion.

$4(x - 3) = x \cdot 8$ Cross products property

$4x - 12 = 8x$ Simplify.

$-12 = 4x$ Subtract $4x$ from each side.

$-3 = x$ Divide each side by 4.

▶ The value of x is -3. The correct answer is B. Ⓐ Ⓑ Ⓒ Ⓓ

EXAMPLE 3 **Write and solve a proportion**

SEALS Each day, the seals at an aquarium are each fed 8 pounds of food for every 100 pounds of their body weight. A seal at the aquarium weighs 280 pounds. How much food should the seal be fed per day?

Solution

STEP 1 **Write** a proportion involving two ratios that compare the amount of food with the weight of the seal.

$\frac{8}{100} = \frac{x}{280}$ ← amount of food / ← weight of seal

STEP 2 **Solve** the proportion.

ANOTHER WAY
You can also solve the proportion by multiplying each side of the equation by 280.

$\frac{8}{100} = \frac{x}{280}$ Write proportion.

$8 \cdot 280 = 100 \cdot x$ Cross products property

$2240 = 100x$ Simplify.

$22.4 = x$ Divide each side by 100.

▶ A 280 pound seal should be fed 22.4 pounds of food per day.

GUIDED PRACTICE for Examples 1, 2, and 3

Solve the proportion. Check your solution.

1. $\frac{4}{a} = \frac{24}{30}$

2. $\frac{3}{x} = \frac{2}{x-6}$

3. $\frac{m}{5} = \frac{m-6}{4}$

4. **WHAT IF?** In Example 3, suppose the seal weighs 260 pounds. How much food should the seal be fed per day?

SCALE DRAWINGS AND SCALE MODELS The floor plan below is an example of a *scale drawing*. A **scale drawing** is a two-dimensional drawing of an object in which the dimensions of the drawing are in proportion to the dimensions of the object. A **scale model** is a three-dimensional model of an object in which the dimensions of the model are in proportion to the dimensions of the object.

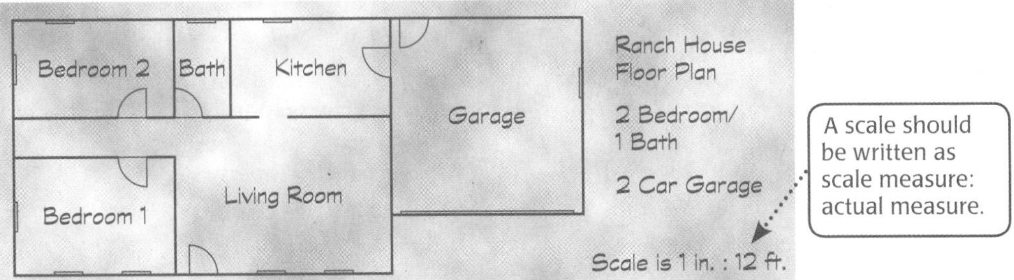

A scale should be written as scale measure: actual measure.

The **scale** of a scale drawing or scale model relates the drawing's or model's dimensions and the actual dimensions. For example, the scale 1 in. : 12 ft on the floor plan means that 1 inch in the floor plan represents an actual distance of 12 feet.

EXAMPLE 4 Use the scale on a map

MAPS Use a metric ruler and the map of Ohio to estimate the distance between Cleveland and Cincinnati.

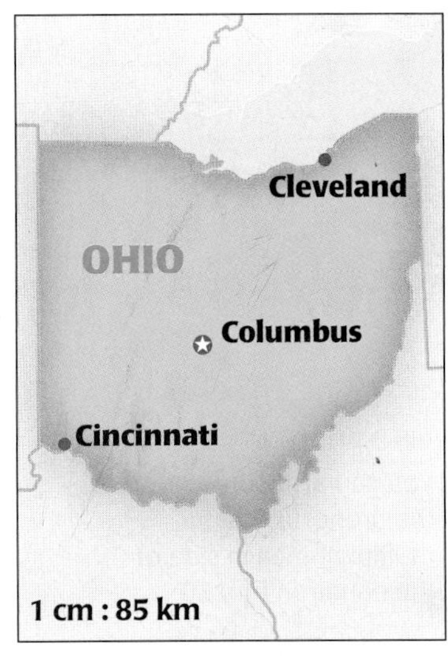

Solution

From the map's scale, 1 centimeter represents 85 kilometers. On the map, the distance between Cleveland and Cincinnati is about 4.2 centimeters.

Write and solve a proportion to find the distance d between the cities.

$$\frac{1}{85} = \frac{4.2}{d} \quad \begin{array}{l}\leftarrow \text{centimeters} \\ \leftarrow \text{kilometers}\end{array}$$

$1 \cdot d = 85 \cdot 4.2$ **Cross products property**

$d = 357$ **Simplify.**

▶ The actual distance between Cleveland and Cincinnati is about 357 kilometers.

GUIDED PRACTICE for Example 4

5. Use a metric ruler and the map in Example 4 to estimate the distance (in kilometers) between Columbus and Cleveland.

6. **MODEL SHIPS** The ship model kits sold at a hobby store have a scale of 1 ft : 600 ft. A completed model of the *Queen Elizabeth II* is 1.6 feet long. Estimate the actual length of the *Queen Elizabeth II*.

3.6 EXERCISES

HOMEWORK KEY

○ = **WORKED-OUT SOLUTIONS** on p. WS7 for Exs. 13 and 39

★ = **STANDARDIZED TEST PRACTICE** Exs. 2, 15, 16, 41, and 42

◆ = **MULTIPLE REPRESENTATIONS** Ex. 40

SKILL PRACTICE

1. **VOCABULARY** Copy and complete: In a proportion, a(n) __?__ is the product of the numerator of one ratio and the denominator of the other ratio.

2. ★ **WRITING** A scale drawing has a scale of 1 cm : 3 m. *Explain* how the scale can be used to find the actual distance between objects in the drawing.

EXAMPLES 1 and 2 on pp. 168–169 for Exs. 3–18

SOLVING PROPORTIONS **Solve the proportion. Check your solution.**

3. $\frac{2}{3} = \frac{4}{x}$
4. $\frac{3}{y} = \frac{15}{35}$
5. $\frac{13}{6} = \frac{52}{z}$
6. $\frac{10}{45} = \frac{v}{27}$
7. $\frac{5m}{6} = \frac{10}{12}$
8. $\frac{3k}{27} = \frac{2}{3}$
9. $\frac{-49}{7} = \frac{a+7}{6}$
10. $\frac{6}{t+4} = \frac{42}{77}$
11. $\frac{8}{12} = \frac{r}{r+1}$
12. $\frac{n}{n-12} = \frac{9}{5}$
13. $\frac{11}{w} = \frac{33}{w+24}$
14. $\frac{18}{d+13} = \frac{6}{d-13}$

15. ★ **MULTIPLE CHOICE** What is the value of h in the proportion $\frac{15}{-2h} = \frac{5}{12}$?

Ⓐ −36 Ⓑ −18 Ⓒ 18 Ⓓ 36

16. ★ **MULTIPLE CHOICE** What is the value of s in the proportion $\frac{7}{s-14} = \frac{21}{s+18}$?

Ⓐ −48 Ⓑ −16 Ⓒ 3 Ⓓ 30

ERROR ANALYSIS *Describe* and correct the error in solving the proportion.

17.

$$\frac{4}{3} = \frac{16}{x}$$
$$4 \cdot 16 = 4 \cdot x$$
$$64 = 4x$$
$$16 = x$$

18.

$$\frac{18}{14} = \frac{b+2}{b}$$
$$18b = 14b + 2$$
$$4b = 2$$
$$b = 0.5$$

SOLVING PROPORTIONS **Solve the proportion. Check your solution.**

19. $\frac{7}{3} = \frac{2x+5}{x}$
20. $\frac{a}{9a-2} = \frac{1}{8}$
21. $\frac{24}{5z+4} = \frac{4}{z-1}$
22. $\frac{c-8}{-2} = \frac{11-4c}{11}$
23. $\frac{k-8}{7+k} = \frac{-1}{5}$
24. $\frac{2}{-3} = \frac{4v+4}{2v+14}$
25. $\frac{m+1}{4} = \frac{3m+6}{7}$
26. $\frac{6}{4+2w} = \frac{-2}{w-10}$
27. $\frac{n+0.3}{n-3.2} = \frac{9}{2}$
28. $\frac{-3}{11} = \frac{5-h}{h+1.4}$
29. $\frac{4}{b-3.9} = \frac{2}{b+1}$
30. $\frac{16.5+3t}{3} = \frac{0.9-t}{-5}$

31. REASONING The statements below justify the cross products property. Copy and complete the justification.

$\frac{a}{b} = \frac{c}{d}$	**Given**
$bd \cdot \frac{a}{b} = bd \cdot \frac{c}{d}$	**a.** ___?___
$\frac{bd \cdot a}{b} = \frac{bd \cdot c}{d}$	**b.** ___?___
$ad = cb$	**c.** ___?___

32. CHALLENGE In the proportion $\frac{5}{h} = \frac{k}{14}$, what happens to the value of h as the value of k increases? *Explain.*

PROBLEM SOLVING

EXAMPLE 3 on p. 169 for Exs. 33–34

33. RECIPES A recipe that yields 12 buttermilk biscuits calls for 2 cups of flour. How much flour is needed to make 30 biscuits?

@HomeTutor for problem solving help at classzone.com

34. DIGITAL PHOTOGRAPHS It took 7.2 minutes to upload 8 digital photographs from your computer to a website. At this rate, how long will it take to upload 20 photographs?

@HomeTutor for problem solving help at classzone.com

EXAMPLE 4 on p. 170 for Exs. 35–39

MAPS A map has a scale of 1 cm : 15 km. Use the given map distance to find the actual distance.

35. 6 cm **36.** 3.2 cm **37.** 0.5 cm **38.** 4.7 cm

39. SCALE MODEL An exhibit at Tobu World Square in Japan includes a scale model of the Empire State Building. The model was built using a scale of 1 m : 25 m. The height of the actual Empire State Building is 443.2 meters. What is the height of the model?

40. ◆ MULTIPLE REPRESENTATIONS The diameter of the burst of a firework is proportional to the diameter of the shell of the firework.

a. **Writing a Proportion** Use the information in the diagram to find the burst diameter for a 4.75 inch shell.

b. **Making a Table** Make a table of burst diameters for 2, 3, 4, 5, and 6 inch shells. Use the table to check your answer to part (a).

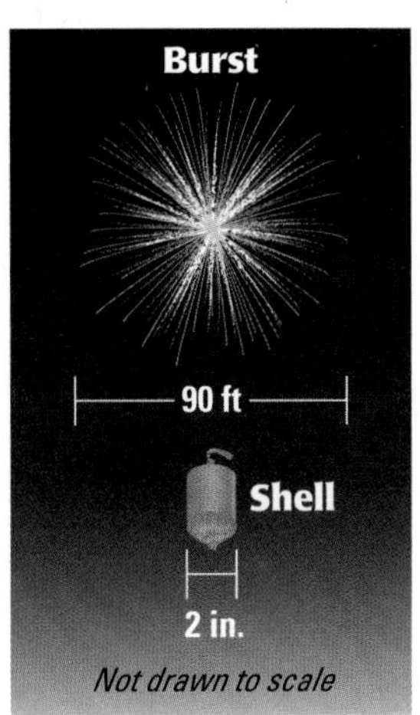

41. ★ SHORT RESPONSE The ratio of the length of a soccer field to the width of the field is 3 : 2. A scale drawing of a soccer field has a scale of 1 in. : 20 yd. The length of the field in the drawing is 6 inches. What is the actual width of the field? *Explain* your reasoning.

42. ★ **EXTENDED RESPONSE** A mole is a unit of measurement used in chemistry. The masses of one mole of three elements are in the table.

Element	Mass of 1 mole
Hydrogen	1.008 grams
Carbon	12.011 grams
Oxygen	15.999 grams

a. A 100 gram sample of ascorbic acid contains 4.58 grams of hydrogen. To the nearest tenth, find the number of moles of hydrogen.

b. A 100 gram sample of ascorbic acid contains 54.5 grams of oxygen. To the nearest tenth, find the number of moles of oxygen in the sample.

c. The ratio of moles of hydrogen to moles of carbon in ascorbic acid is 4:3. How does this ratio compare with the ratio of moles of hydrogen to moles of oxygen in ascorbic acid? *Explain.*

43. **CHALLENGE** At a typical National Football League game, the ratio of females to males in attendance is 2 : 3. Estimate the number of male and female spectators at a game that has 75,000 spectators.

MIXED REVIEW

Evaluate the expression for the given value of *x*. *(p. 110)*

44. $16 + \sqrt{x}$ when $x = 16$

45. $27 - \sqrt{x}$ when $x = 81$

46. $-3 \cdot \sqrt{x}$ when $x = 25$

47. $2 \cdot \sqrt{x} + 11$ when $x = 144$

PREVIEW Prepare for Lesson 3.7 in Exs. 48–55.

Solve the proportion. Check your solution. *(p. 162)*

48. $\frac{2}{3} = \frac{x}{21}$

49. $\frac{m}{6} = \frac{9}{2}$

50. $\frac{z}{11} = \frac{-10}{22}$

51. $\frac{12}{5} = \frac{b}{25}$

52. $\frac{12}{36} = \frac{2c}{6}$

53. $\frac{9}{-8} = \frac{3w}{24}$

54. $\frac{n-2}{50} = \frac{6}{30}$

55. $\frac{4}{13} = \frac{a+4}{39}$

QUIZ for Lessons 3.4–3.6

Solve the equation, if possible. *(p. 154)*

1. $y - 2 = y + 2$

2. $2x - 14 = -3x + 6$

3. $10z - 4 = 2(5z - 2)$

4. $6m + 5 - 3m = 7(m - 1)$

5. $2(7 - g) = 9g + 14 - 11g$

6. $13k + 3(k + 11) = 8k - 7$

7. $\frac{1}{4}(8j - 3) = 2j - 3$

8. $8 - 4w = \frac{1}{3}(6w - 12)$

9. $\frac{2}{5}(10t - 50) = 4(9 - 6t)$

Solve the proportion. Check your solution. *(pp. 162, 168)*

10. $\frac{24}{20} = \frac{x}{5}$

11. $\frac{6}{-7} = \frac{3z}{42}$

12. $\frac{14}{12} = \frac{w+11}{18}$

13. $\frac{18}{5a} = \frac{3}{-5}$

14. $\frac{10}{17} = \frac{k}{2k-3}$

15. $\frac{h-1}{3} = \frac{2h+1}{9}$

16. **GEOMETRY** The ratio of the length to the width of a rectangle is 5 : 4. The length of the rectangle is 60 inches. What is the width? *(p. 168)*

Extension

Use after Lesson 3.6

Apply Proportions to Similar Figures

GOAL Use similar figures to solve problems.

Key Vocabulary
- **congruent figures**
- **similar figures**
- **corresponding parts**

NAME SIMILAR FIGURES
When naming similar figures, list the letters of the corresponding vertices (corner points) in the same order.

Two figures are **congruent figures** if they have the same shape and size. The symbol $\cong$ indicates congruence. Of the triangles shown, $\triangle ABC \cong \triangle DEF$.

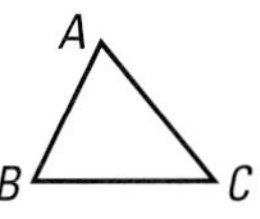

Two figures are **similar figures** if they have the same shape but not necessarily the same size. The symbol $\sim$ indicates that two figures are similar. All the triangles shown are similar; in particular, $\triangle ABC \sim \triangle JKL$.

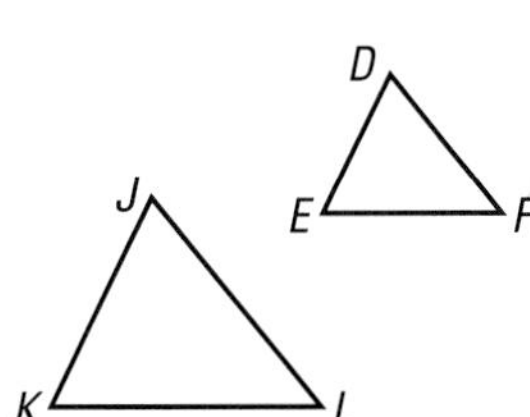

The sides or angles that have the same relative position within two figures are called **corresponding parts**.

KEY CONCEPT *For Your Notebook*

Properties of Similar Figures

In the diagram, $\triangle ABC \sim \triangle DEF$.

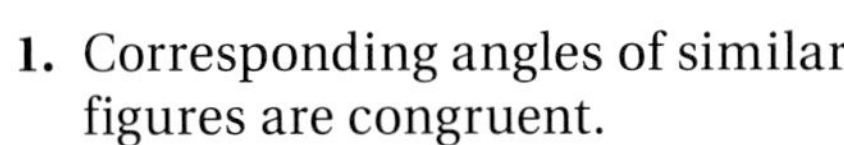

1. Corresponding angles of similar figures are congruent.
   $\angle A \cong \angle D$, $\angle B \cong \angle E$, $\angle C \cong \angle F$
2. The ratios of the lengths of corresponding sides of similar figures are equal.
   $\frac{AB}{DE} = \frac{BC}{EF} = \frac{AC}{DF} = \frac{1}{2}$

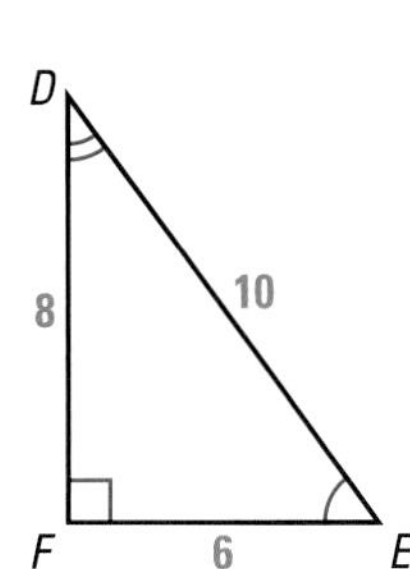

NAME LENGTHS OF SIDES
AB represents the length of the side whose endpoints are *A* and *B*.

EXAMPLE 1 Find an unknown side length

Given $\triangle JKL \sim \triangle QRS$, find *QR*.

Solution

Use the ratios of the lengths of corresponding sides to write a proportion.

$\frac{JK}{QR} = \frac{KL}{RS}$	Write proportion involving *QR*.
$\frac{18}{x} = \frac{8}{12}$	Substitute.
$216 = 8x$	Cross products property
$27 = x$	Divide each side by 8.

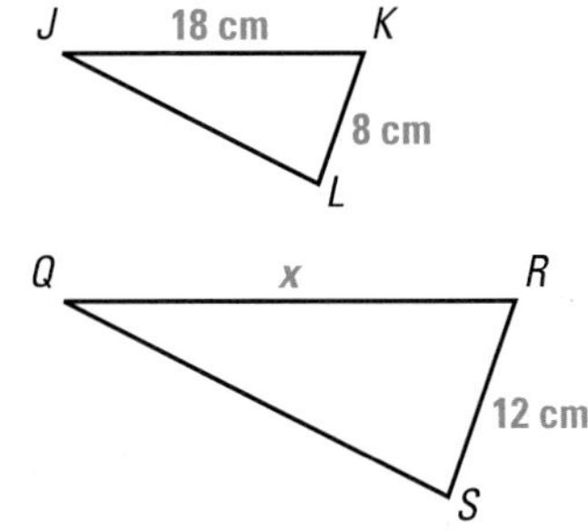

▸ *QR* is 27 centimeters.

INDIRECT MEASUREMENT You can use similar figures to find lengths that are difficult to measure directly.

EXAMPLE 2 Use similar figures to measure indirectly

CAPE HATTERAS LIGHTHOUSE A man stands next to the Cape Hatteras Lighthouse in North Carolina. The lighthouse and the man are perpendicular to the ground. The sun's rays strike the lighthouse and the man at the same angle, forming two similar triangles. Use indirect measurement to approximate the height of the lighthouse.

83.2 ft

5.8 ft

2.5 ft

Not drawn to scale

Solution

Write and solve a proportion to find the height h (in feet) of the lighthouse.

ANOTHER WAY
You can also use the proportion below to find the height of the lighthouse.

$\frac{5.8}{2.5} = \frac{h}{83.2}$

$$\begin{array}{l} \textbf{height} \longrightarrow \\ \textbf{height} \longrightarrow \end{array} \frac{5.8}{h} = \frac{2.5}{83.2} \begin{array}{l} \longleftarrow \textbf{length of shadow} \\ \longleftarrow \textbf{length of shadow} \end{array}$$

$2.5h = 5.8 \cdot 83.2$ **Cross products property**

$2.5h = 482.56$ **Multiply.**

$h = 193.024$ **Divide each side by 2.5.**

▶ The height of the lighthouse is about 193 feet.

PRACTICE

EXAMPLE 1
on p. 174
for Exs. 1–4

1. Given $\triangle JKL \sim \triangle MNP$, find JL.

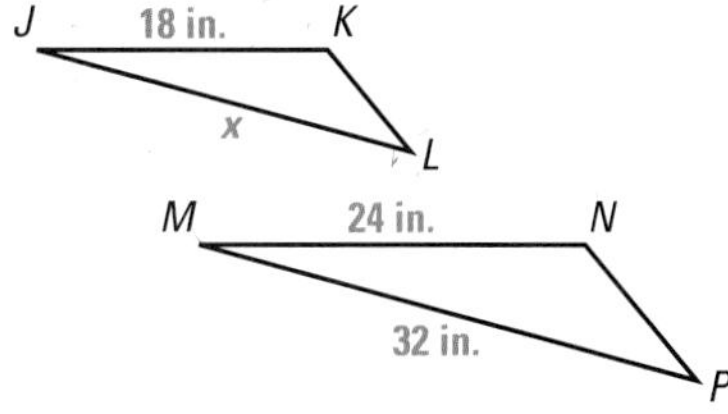

2. Given $\triangle EFG \sim \triangle UVW$, find UV.

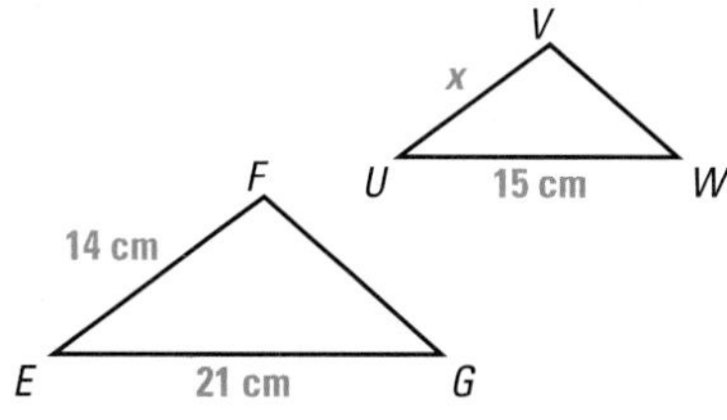

3. Given $ABCD \sim FGHJ$, find AD.

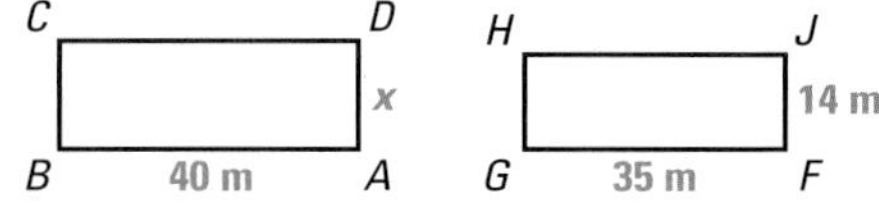

4. Given $JKLM \sim QRST$, find QT.

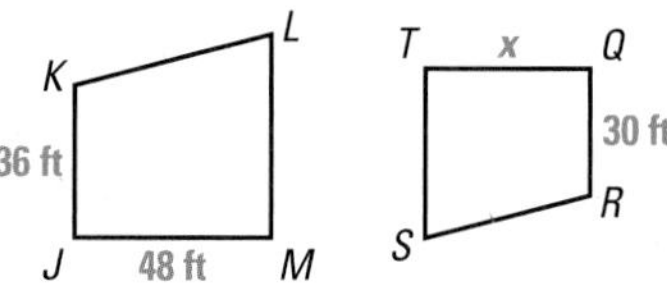

EXAMPLE 2
on p. 175
for Ex. 5

5. **FLAGPOLES** A 5 foot tall student stands near a flagpole. The flagpole and the student are perpendicular to the ground. The sun's rays strike the flagpole and the student at the same angle, forming two similar triangles. The flagpole casts a 15 foot shadow, and the student casts a 2 foot shadow. Use indirect measurement to find the height of the flagpole.

3.7 Solve Percent Problems

Before You solved proportions.

Now You will solve percent problems.

Why? So you can solve a problem about racing, as in Ex. 34.

Key Vocabulary
- **percent,** *p. 916*
- **proportion,** *p. 163*

Recall that *percent* means "divided by 100." For example $27\% = \frac{27}{100}$.

By writing a percent as a fraction, you can use a proportion to solve a percent problem.

KEY CONCEPT *For Your Notebook*

Solving Percent Problems Using Proportions

You can represent "a is p percent of b" using the proportion

$$\frac{a}{b} = \frac{p}{100}$$

where a is a part of the base b and $\frac{p}{100}$, or $p\%$, is the percent.

EXAMPLE 1 Find a percent using a proportion

What percent of 25 is 17?

Solution

Write a proportion where 25 is the base and 17 is a part of the base.

$\frac{a}{b} = \frac{p}{100}$ **Write proportion.**

$\frac{17}{25} = \frac{p}{100}$ **Substitute 17 for a and 25 for b.**

$1700 = 25p$ **Cross products property**

$68 = p$ **Divide each side by 25.**

▶ 17 is 68% of 25.

AVOID ERRORS
You can also solve for p by multiplying each side of the equation by 100.

 Animated Algebra at classzone.com

GUIDED PRACTICE for Example 1

Use a proportion to answer the question.

1. What percent of 20 is 15?

2. What number is 30% of 90?

THE PERCENT EQUATION In Example 1, the proportion $\frac{a}{b} = \frac{p}{100}$ is used to find a percent. When you write $\frac{p}{100}$ as $p\%$ and solve for a, you get the equation $a = p\% \cdot b$.

KEY CONCEPT *For Your Notebook*

The Percent Equation

You can represent "a is p percent of b" using the equation

$$a = p\% \cdot b$$

where a is a part of the base b and $p\%$ is the percent.

EXAMPLE 2 Find a percent using the percent equation

What percent of 136 is 51?

$a = p\% \cdot b$	Write percent equation.
$51 = p\% \cdot 136$	Substitute 51 for a and 136 for b.
$0.375 = p\%$	Divide each side by 136.
$37.5\% = p\%$	Write decimal as percent.

▶ 51 is 37.5% of 136.

DETERMINE THE BASE
When a problem talks about the percent *of* a number, the number is the base b, which is multiplied by the percent.

CHECK Substitute 0.375 for $p\%$ in the original equation.

$51 = p\% \cdot 136$	Write original equation.
$51 \stackrel{?}{=} 0.375 \cdot 136$	Substitute 0.375 for $p\%$.
$51 = 51$ ✓	Multiply. Solution checks.

EXAMPLE 3 Find a part of a base using the percent equation

What number is 15% of 88?

$a = p\% \cdot b$	Write percent equation.
$= 15\% \cdot 88$	Substitute 15 for p and 88 for b.
$= 0.15 \cdot 88$	Write percent as decimal.
$= 13.2$	Multiply.

▶ 13.2 is 15% of 88.

✓ **GUIDED PRACTICE** for Examples 2 and 3

Use the percent equation to answer the question.

3. What percent of 56 is 49?
4. What percent of 55 is 11?
5. What number is 45% of 92?
6. What number is 140% of 50?

EXAMPLE 4 Find a base using the percent equation

CHECK REASONABLENESS

Use 10%, or $\frac{1}{10}$, to check your answer:

$160 \cdot \frac{1}{10} = 16$

Because 16 is slightly less than 20, the solution is reasonable.

20 is 12.5% of what number?

$a = p\% \cdot b$	Write percent equation.
$20 = 12.5\% \cdot b$	Substitute 20 for *a* and 12.5 for *p*.
$20 = 0.125 \cdot b$	Write percent as decimal.
$160 = b$	Divide each side by 0.125.

▶ 20 is 12.5% of 160.

EXAMPLE 5 Solve a real-world percent problem

SURVEY A survey asked 220 students to name their favorite pasta dish. Find the percent of students who chose the given pasta dish.

a. macaroni and cheese

b. lasagna

Type of Pasta	Students
Spaghetti	83
Lasagna	40
Macaroni and cheese	33
Fettucine alfredo	22
Baked ziti	16
Pasta primavera	15
Other	11

Solution

a. The survey results show that 33 of the 220 students chose macaroni and cheese.

$a = p\% \cdot b$	Write percent equation.
$33 = p\% \cdot 220$	Substitute 33 for *a* and 220 for *b*.
$0.15 = p\%$	Divide each side by 220.
$15\% = p\%$	Write decimal as percent.

▶ 15% of the students chose macaroni and cheese as their favorite dish.

b. The survey results show that 40 of the 220 students chose lasagna.

$a = p\% \cdot b$	Write percent equation.
$40 = p\% \cdot 220$	Substitute 40 for *a* and 220 for *b*.
$0.18 \approx p\%$	Divide each side by 220.
$18\% \approx p\%$	Write decimal as percent.

▶ About 18% of the students chose lasagna as their favorite dish.

✓ GUIDED PRACTICE for Examples 4 and 5

In Exercises 7 and 8, use the percent equation to answer the question.

7. 65 is 62.5% of what number?

8. 50 is 125% of what number?

9. In Example 5, what percent of students chose fettucine alfredo?

CONCEPT SUMMARY — *For Your Notebook*

Types of Percent Problems

Percent problem	Example	Equation
Find a percent.	What percent of 136 is 51?	$51 = p\% \cdot 136$
Find part of a base.	What number is 15% of 88?	$a = 15\% \cdot 88$
Find a base.	20 is 12.5% of what number?	$20 = 12.5\% \cdot b$

3.7 EXERCISES

HOMEWORK KEY

○ = **WORKED-OUT SOLUTIONS on p. WS7 for Exs. 13 and 35**

★ = **STANDARDIZED TEST PRACTICE Exs. 2, 19, 30, 31, 38, and 39**

SKILL PRACTICE

1. **VOCABULARY** Identify the percent, the base, and the part of the base in the following statement: 54 is 15% of 360.

2. ★ **WRITING** Rewrite the statement "28 is 35% of 80" in the form $\frac{a}{b} = \frac{p}{100}$. *Explain* how you identified the values of a, b, and p.

EXAMPLE 1 on p. 176 for Exs. 3–8

USING PROPORTIONS **Use a proportion to answer the question.**

3. What percent of 75 is 27?
4. What percent of 120 is 66?
5. What number is 35% of 80?
6. What number is 60% of 85?
7. 81 is 54% of what number?
8. 42 is 200% of what number?

EXAMPLES 2, 3, and 4 on pp. 177–178 for Exs. 9–21

USING THE PERCENT EQUATION **Use the percent equation to answer the question.**

9. What percent of 80 is 56?
10. What percent of 225 is 99?
11. What percent of 153 is 9.18?
12. What number is 18% of 150?
13. What number is 115% of 60?
14. What number is 82% of 215?
15. 7 is 28% of what number?
16. 189 is 90% of what number?
17. 41.8 is 44% of what number?
18. 71.5 is 52% of what number?

19. ★ **MULTIPLE CHOICE** What number is 87.5% of 512?

(A) 5.85 (B) 448 (C) 585 (D) 4480

ERROR ANALYSIS ***Describe*** **and correct the error in answering the question.**

20. What percent of 95 is 19?

$95 = p\% \cdot 19$
$5 = p\%$
$500\% = p\%$
✗

21. 153 is 76.5% of what number?

$153 = 76.5\% \cdot b$
$153 = 76.5 \cdot b$
$2 = b$
✗

SOLVING PERCENT PROBLEMS **Answer the question when $n = 25$.**

22. What percent of 140 is $(n + 94)$?

23. What percent of $(4n)$ is 96?

24. What number is 52% of $(2n + 15)$?

25. 25.5 is $(n - 8)$% of what number?

SOLVING PERCENT PROBLEMS **Find the percent. Round your answer to the nearest whole percent, if necessary.**

26. \$3.00 tip for a \$18.70 taxi fare

27. \$1.44 tax on an item priced at \$24.00

28. 90 rock CDs out of 125 CDs

29. 241 freshmen out of 804 students

30. ★ **WRITING** Would you use a proportion or the percent equation to solve the following problem: What number is 25% of 600? *Explain.*

31. ★ **SHORT RESPONSE** The side length of a square is 40% of the side length of another square. Is the area of the smaller square 40% of the area of the larger square? *Explain.*

32. **CHALLENGE** Let y be 10% of a number. What is 50% of the number? Write your answer in terms of y.

PROBLEM SOLVING

EXAMPLE 5 on p. 178 for Exs. 33–36

33. **SCHOOL TRANSPORTATION** In a school transportation survey of 225 students, 18 of the students surveyed said that they walk to school. What percent of the students surveyed walk to school?

@HomeTutor for problem solving help at classzone.com

34. **DAYTONA 500** After completing 10 laps in the Daytona 500, a driver has completed 5% of the race. How many laps does the race have?

@HomeTutor for problem solving help at classzone.com

REVIEW CIRCLE GRAPHS For help with using a circle graph, see p. 935.

35. **MUSIC** The circle graph shows the results of a radio survey in which 250 listeners were asked to rate a song.

a. How many of the listeners who participated in the survey are "tired of" the song?

b. How many of the listeners who participated in the survey "love" the song?

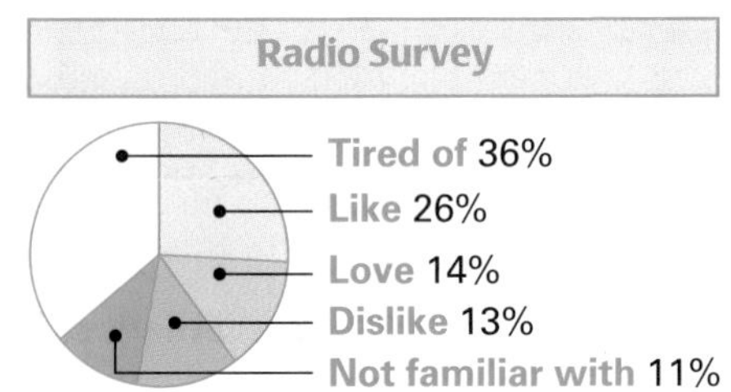

36. **HIKING** The table gives data about the number of people who started hiking the Appalachian Trail in Georgia and the number of those people who completed the trail in Maine. Copy and complete the table.

Year	Hikers who started	Hikers who completed	Percent completion
2001	2380	?	16.6%
2002	?	376	20%
2003	1750	352	?

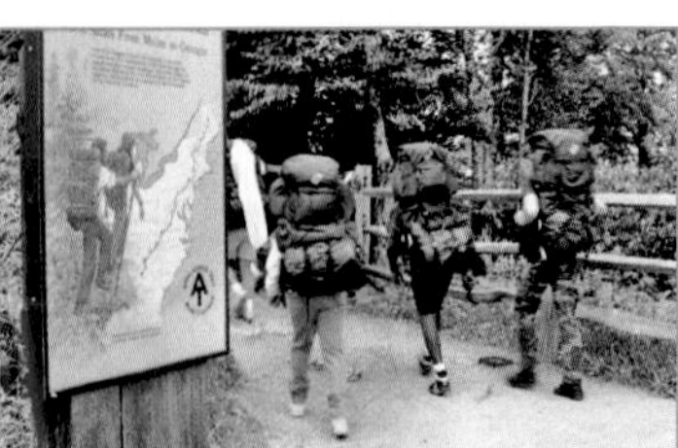

○ = **WORKED-OUT SOLUTIONS** on p. WS1

★ = **STANDARDIZED TEST PRACTICE**

37. **ART** The Louvre Museum, which is an art museum in France, has virtual tours of its exhibits on its website. The website can be viewed in four different languages. The table shows the number of hits received by each version of the website during one day. Find the percent of hits for each version of the website.

Version	English	French	Spanish	Japanese
Number of hits	4860	1350	1080	900

38. ★ **OPEN-ENDED** Write a real-world percent problem that can be solved using the proportion $\frac{x}{75} = \frac{15}{100}$. Then find the value of x and explain what the solution means in this situation.

39. ★ **EXTENDED RESPONSE** Two different stores are selling a bicycle that you want to buy.
    a. **Solve** At one store, the bicycle is on sale for 20% off the original price of $240. How much money will you save by purchasing the bicycle on sale at this store?
    b. **Solve** At the other store, the bicycle is on sale for 25% off the original price of $265. How much money will you save by purchasing the bicycle on sale at this store?
    c. **Compare** Which bicycle should you buy? *Explain.*

40. **CHALLENGE** Julia deposits 20% of her paycheck in her savings account. Then she deposits 60% of the remaining money in her checking account. She deposits $108.24 in her checking account. How much money did she deposit in her savings account?

MIXED REVIEW

PREVIEW
Prepare for Lesson 3.8 in Exs. 41–46.

Find the area of the triangle or rectangle. *(p. 924)*

41. 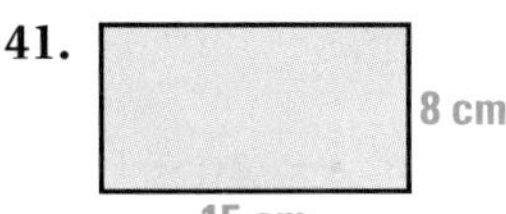

42. 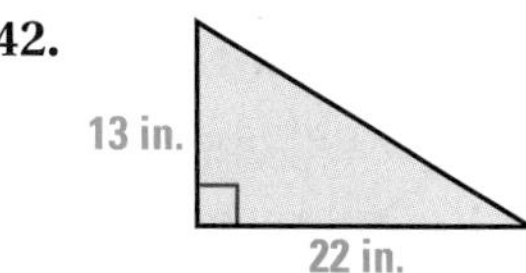

Make a table for the function. Identify the range of the function. *(p. 35)*

43. $y = x - 7$
Domain: $-5, -2, 1, 4$

44. $y = x + 4$
Domain: $-6, -4, -2, 0$

45. $y = 6x + 3$
Domain: $-1, 1, 3, 5$

46. $y = 5x - 5$
Domain: $-2, -1, 0, 1$

Find the sum or difference.

47. $-65 + (-27)$ *(p. 74)*

48. $33 + (-58)$ *(p. 74)*

49. $-43.9 + 89.4$ *(p. 74)*

50. $91.2 - (-20.3)$ *(p. 80)*

51. $-13 - 78$ *(p. 80)*

52. $28 - (-35)$ *(p. 80)*

Find Percent of Change

GOAL Solve percent of change problems.

Key Vocabulary
- **percent of change**
- **percent of increase**
- **percent of decrease**

A **percent of change** indicates how much a quantity increases or decreases with respect to the original amount. If the new amount is greater than the original amount, the percent of change is called a **percent of increase**. If the new amount is less than the original amount, the percent of change is called a **percent of decrease**.

KEY CONCEPT *For Your Notebook*

Percent of Change

The percent of change is the ratio of the amount of increase or decrease to the original amount.

$$\text{Percent of change, } p\% = \frac{\text{Amount of increase or decrease}}{\text{Original amount}}$$

The amount of increase is the new amount minus the original amount. The amount of decrease is the original amount minus the new amount.

EXAMPLE 1 Find a percent of change

Identify the percent of change as an *increase* or *decrease*. Then find the percent of change.

a. Original: 140
New: 189

b. Original: 70
New: 59.5

Solution

a. Because the new amount is greater than the original amount, the percent of change is an increase.

$$\begin{aligned} p\% &= \frac{\text{Amount of increase}}{\text{Original amount}} \\ &= \frac{189 - 140}{140} \\ &= \frac{49}{140} \\ &= 0.35 \\ &= 35\% \end{aligned}$$

▶ The percent of increase is 35%.

CHECK REASONABLENESS
Because 50 is one third (about 33%) of 150, it is reasonable that 49 is 35% of 140.

b. Because the new amount is less than the original amount, the percent of change is a decrease.

$$\begin{aligned} p\% &= \frac{\text{Amount of decrease}}{\text{Original amount}} \\ &= \frac{70 - 59.5}{70} \\ &= \frac{10.5}{70} \\ &= 0.15 \\ &= 15\% \end{aligned}$$

▶ The percent of decrease is 15%.

FINDING A NEW AMOUNT If you know the original amount and the percent of change, you can find the new amount.

- For a $p\%$ increase, multiply the original amount by $(100\% + p\%)$.
- For a $p\%$ decrease, multiply the original amount by $(100\% - p\%)$.

EXAMPLE 2 Find a new amount

SHOPPING Find the sale price of the pair of jeans described in the table.

Original price	$48.00
Discount	40%
Sale price	?

Solution

ANOTHER WAY
You can also find the sale price by first finding the change in price:
$0.4 \cdot 48 = 19.2.$
Then subtract the change in price from the original price:
$48.00 − $19.20 = $28.80.

The sale price is a decrease from the original price, so multiply the original price by $(100\% - p\%)$.

Sale price = **Original price** $\cdot$ $(100\% - p\%)$

$= \mathbf{48} \cdot (100\% - 40\%)$ **Substitute.**

$= 48 \cdot 0.6$ **Subtract percents. Then write as a decimal.**

$= 28.8$ **Multiply.**

▶ The sale price of the pair of jeans is $28.80.

PRACTICE

EXAMPLE 1
on p. 182
for Exs. 1–6

Identify the percent of change as an *increase* or *decrease*. Then find the percent of change.

1. Original: 16
New: 20
2. Original: 35
New: 49
3. Original: 80
New: 44
4. Original: 120
New: 78
5. Original: 360
New: 241.2
6. Original: 170
New: 283.9

EXAMPLE 2
on p. 183
for Exs. 7–14

Find the new amount.

7. Increase 14 by 45%.
8. Increase 78 by 80%.
9. Decrease 44 by 20%.
10. Decrease 108 by 90%.
11. **SUBWAY** The price for a token to ride a city's subway system is changing from $1.25 to $1.50. Find the percent of change.
12. **DVDS** The average price of a new DVD in 1998 was $24. In 2003, the average price was $21.12. Find the percent of change.
13. **POPULATION** In Arizona, the population increased by 48.6% from 1990 to 2002. Use the information in the table to find the population density in Arizona in 2002.
14. **DEPRECIATION** A new car is valued at $14,500. In one year, the car's value will depreciate, or decrease, by 15%. Find the value of the car after one year.

Year	Population density
1990	32.3 people per square mile
2002	?

3.8 Rewrite Equations and Formulas

Before You wrote functions and used formulas.

Now You will rewrite equations and formulas.

Why? So you can solve a problem about bowling, as in Ex. 33.

Key Vocabulary
- **literal equation**
- **formula,** *p. 30*

The equations $2x + 5 = 11$ and $6x + 3 = 15$ have the general form $ax + b = c$. The equation $ax + b = c$ is called a **literal equation** because the coefficients and constants have been replaced by letters. When you solve a literal equation, you can use the result to solve any equation that has the same form as the literal equation.

EXAMPLE 1 Solve a literal equation

Solve $ax + b = c$ for x. Then use the solution to solve $2x + 5 = 11$.

Solution

STEP 1 **Solve** $ax + b = c$ for x.

$ax + b = c$ — Write original equation.

$ax = c - b$ — Subtract b from each side.

$x = \frac{c - b}{a}$ — Assume $a \neq 0$. Divide each side by a.

STEP 2 **Use** the solution to solve $2x + 5 = 11$.

$x = \frac{c - b}{a}$ — Solution of literal equation

$= \frac{11 - 5}{2}$ — Substitute 2 for a, 5 for b, and 11 for c.

$= 3$ — Simplify.

▶ The solution of $2x + 5 = 11$ is 3.

VARIABLES IN DENOMINATORS In Example 1, you must assume that $a \neq 0$ in order to divide by a. In general, if you have to divide by a variable when solving a literal equation, you should assume that the variable does not equal 0.

GUIDED PRACTICE for Example 1

Solve the literal equation for x. Then use the solution to solve the specific equation.

1. $a - bx = c$; $12 - 5x = -3$

2. $ax = bx + c$; $11x = 6x + 20$

TWO OR MORE VARIABLES An equation in two variables, such as $3x + 2y = 8$, or a formula in two or more variables, such as $A = \frac{1}{2}bh$, can be rewritten so that one variable is a function of the other variable(s).

EXAMPLE 2 Rewrite an equation

Write $3x + 2y = 8$ so that y is a function of x.

$3x + 2y = 8$ — **Write original equation.**

$2y = 8 - 3x$ — **Subtract $3x$ from each side.**

$y = 4 - \frac{3}{2}x$ — **Divide each side by 2.**

EXAMPLE 3 Solve and use a geometric formula

The area A of a triangle is given by the formula $A = \frac{1}{2}bh$ where b is the base and h is the height.

a. Solve the formula for the height h.

b. Use the rewritten formula to find the height of the triangle shown, which has an area of 64.4 square meters.

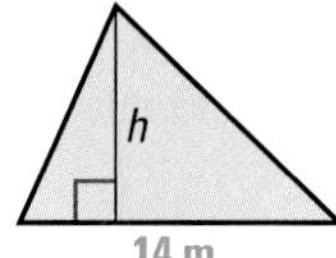

Solution

a. $A = \frac{1}{2}bh$ — **Write original formula.**

$2A = bh$ — **Multiply each side by 2.**

$\frac{2A}{b} = h$ — **Divide each side by b.**

b. Substitute 64.4 for A and 14 for b in the rewritten formula.

$h = \frac{2A}{b}$ — **Write rewritten formula.**

$= \frac{2(64.4)}{14}$ — **Substitute 64.4 for A and 14 for b.**

$= 9.2$ — **Simplify.**

▶ The height of the triangle is 9.2 meters.

USE UNIT ANALYSIS
When area is measured in square meters and the base is measured in meters, dividing twice the area by the base gives a result measured in meters.

Animated Algebra at classzone.com

✓ GUIDED PRACTICE for Examples 2 and 3

3. Write $5x + 4y = 20$ so that y is a function of x.

4. The perimeter P of a rectangle is given by the formula $P = 2\ell + 2w$ where ℓ is the length and w is the width.

a. Solve the formula for the width w.

b. Use the rewritten formula to find the width of the rectangle shown.

$P = 19.2$ ft

w

7.2 ft

EXAMPLE 4 Solve a multi-step problem

TEMPERATURE You are visiting Toronto, Canada, over the weekend. A website gives the forecast shown. Find the low temperatures for Saturday and Sunday in degrees Fahrenheit. Use the formula $C = \frac{5}{9}(F - 32)$ where C is the temperature in degrees Celsius and F is the temperature in degrees Fahrenheit.

3 Day Forecast for Toronto
Friday
Sunny
High 21°C
Low 13°C
Saturday
Sunny
High 22°C
Low 14°C
Sunday
Partly Cloudy
High 16°C
Low 10°C

REWRITE FORMULAS
When using a formula for multiple calculations, you may find it easier to rewrite the formula first.

Solution

STEP 1 **Rewrite** the formula. In the problem, degrees Celsius are given and degrees Fahrenheit need to be calculated. The calculations will be easier if the formula is written so that F is a function of C.

$C = \frac{5}{9}(F - 32)$ **Write original formula.**

$\frac{9}{5} \cdot C = \frac{9}{5} \cdot \frac{5}{9}(F - 32)$ **Multiply each side by $\frac{9}{5}$, the reciprocal of $\frac{5}{9}$.**

$\frac{9}{5}C = F - 32$ **Simplify.**

$\frac{9}{5}C + 32 = F$ **Add 32 to each side.**

▶ The rewritten formula is $F = \frac{9}{5}C + 32$.

STEP 2 **Find** the low temperatures for Saturday and Sunday in degrees Fahrenheit.

Saturday (low of 14°C)

$$F = \frac{9}{5}C + 32$$
$$= \frac{9}{5}(14) + 32$$
$$= 25.2 + 32$$
$$= 57.2$$

▶ The low for Saturday is 57.2°F.

Sunday (low of 10°C)

$$F = \frac{9}{5}C + 32$$
$$= \frac{9}{5}(10) + 32$$
$$= 18 + 32$$
$$= 50$$

▶ The low for Sunday is 50°F.

GUIDED PRACTICE for Example 4

5. Use the information in Example 4 to find the high temperatures for Saturday and Sunday in degrees Fahrenheit.

3.8 EXERCISES

HOMEWORK KEY

○ = **WORKED-OUT SOLUTIONS** on p. WS7 for Exs. 17 and 33

★ = **STANDARDIZED TEST PRACTICE** Exs. 2, 23, 29, 35, and 36

◆ = **MULTIPLE REPRESENTATIONS** Ex. 34

SKILL PRACTICE

1. **VOCABULARY** Copy and complete: When you write the equation $3x + 2 = 8$ as $ax + b = c$, the equation $ax + b = c$ is called a(n) __?__ because the coefficients and constants have been replaced by letters.

2. ★ **WRITING** *Describe* the steps you would take to solve $I = prt$ for t.

EXAMPLE 1 on p. 184 for Exs. 3–10

LITERAL EQUATIONS **Solve the literal equation for x. Then use the solution to solve the specific equation.**

3. $ax = bx - c$; $8x = 3x - 10$

4. $a(x + b) = c$; $2(x + 1) = 9$

5. $c = \frac{x + a}{b}$; $2 = \frac{x + 5}{7}$

6. $\frac{x}{a} = \frac{b}{c}$; $\frac{x}{8} = \frac{4.5}{12}$

7. $\frac{x}{a} + b = c$; $\frac{x}{4} + 6 = 13$

8. $ax + b = cx - d$; $2x + 9 = 7x - 1$

ERROR ANALYSIS ***Describe*** **and correct the error in solving the equation for x.**

9.
$$ax + b = 0$$
$$ax = b$$
$$x = \frac{b}{a}$$

10.
$$c = ax - bx$$
$$c = (a - b)x$$
$$c(a - b) = x$$

EXAMPLE 2 on p. 185 for Exs. 11–19

REWRITING EQUATIONS **Write the equation so that y is a function of x.**

11. $2x + y = 7$

12. $5x + 4y = 10$

13. $12 = 9x + 3y$

14. $18x - 2y = 26$

15. $14 = 7y - 6x$

16. $8x - 8y = 5$

17. $30 = 9x - 5y$

18. $3 + 6x = 11 - 4y$

19. $2 + 6y = 3x + 4$

EXAMPLE 3 on p. 185 for Exs. 20–23

REWRITING FORMULAS **Solve the formula for the indicated variable.**

20. Volume of a rectangular prism: $V = \ell wh$. Solve for w.

21. Surface area of a prism: $S = 2B + Ph$. Solve for h.

22. Length of movie projected at 24 frames per second: $\ell = 24f$. Solve for f.

Animated Algebra at classzone.com

23. ★ **MULTIPLE CHOICE** The formula for the area of a trapezoid is $A = \frac{1}{2}(b_1 + b_2)h$. Which equation is *not* equivalent to the formula?

(A) $h = \frac{2A}{b_1 + b_2}$ (B) $b_1 = \frac{2A}{h} - b_2$ (C) $b_2 = \frac{2A}{b_1} - h$ (D) $b_2 = \frac{2A}{h} - b_1$

REWRITING EQUATIONS **Write the equation so that y is a function of x.**

24. $4.2x - 2y = 16.8$

25. $9 - 0.5y = 2.5x$

26. $8x - 5x + 21 = 36 - 6y$

GEOMETRY Solve the formula for the indicated variable. Then evaluate the rewritten formula for the given values. (Use 3.14 for π.)

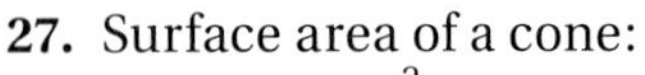

27. Surface area of a cone: $S = \pi r\ell + \pi r^2$. Solve for ℓ. Find ℓ when $S = 283$ cm^2 and $r = 5$ cm.

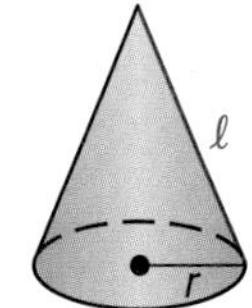

28. Area of a circular ring: $A = 4\pi pw$. Solve for p. Find p when $A = 905$ ft^2 and $w = 9$ ft.

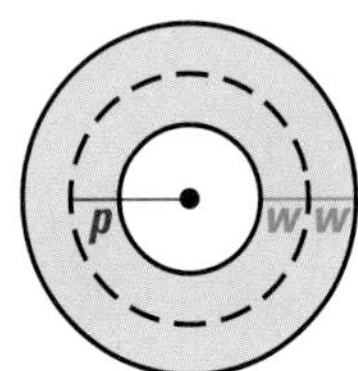

29. ★ **OPEN-ENDED** *Describe* a real-world situation where you would want to solve the distance traveled formula $d = rt$ for t.

CHALLENGE Solve the literal equation for a.

30. $x = \dfrac{a + b + c}{ab}$

31. $y = x\left(\dfrac{ab}{a - b}\right)$

PROBLEM SOLVING

EXAMPLE 4
on p. 186
for Exs. 32–34

32. **CARPENTRY** The penny size d of a nail is given by $d = 4n - 2$ where n is the length (in inches) of the nail.

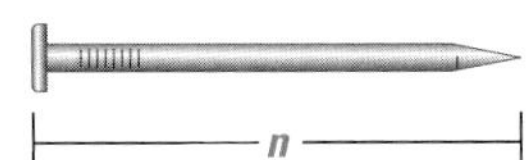

   a. Solve the formula for n.

   b. Use the new formula to find the lengths of nails with the following penny sizes: 5, 12, 16, and 20.

   @HomeTutor for problem solving help at classzone.com

33. **BOWLING** To participate in a bowling league, you pay a \$25 sign-up fee and \$12 for each league night that you bowl. So, the total cost C (in dollars) is given by the equation $C = 12x + 25$ where x is the number of league nights you bowled.

   a. Solve the equation for x.

   b. How many league nights have you bowled if you spent a total of \$145? \$181? \$205?

   @HomeTutor for problem solving help at classzone.com

34. **MULTIPLE REPRESENTATIONS** An athletic facility is building an indoor track like the one shown. The perimeter P (in feet) of the track is given by $P = 2\pi r + 2x$.

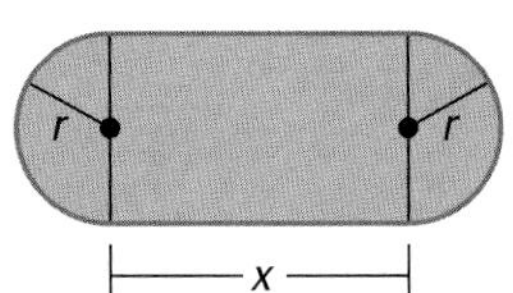

   a. **Writing an Equation** Solve the formula for x.

   b. **Making a Table** The perimeter of the track will be 660 feet. Use the rewritten formula to make a table that shows values of x to the nearest foot when r is 50 feet, 51 feet, 52 feet, and 53 feet. (Use 3.14 for π.)

   c. **Drawing a Graph** Plot the ordered pairs from your table. Look for a pattern in the points. Use the pattern to find x when r is 54 feet.

35. ★ **WRITING** You work as a server at a restaurant. During your shift, you keep track of the bills that you give the tables you serve and the tips you receive from the tables. You want to calculate the tip received from each table as a percent of the bill. *Explain* how to rewrite the percent equation to make it easier to calculate the percent tip from each table.

36. ★ **EXTENDED RESPONSE** One type of stone formation found in Carlsbad Caverns in New Mexico is called a column. This cylindrical stone formation is connected to the ceiling and the floor of a cave.

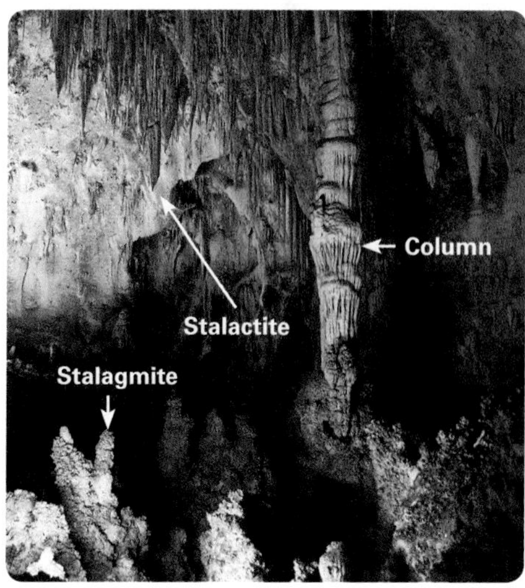

a. Rewrite the formula for the circumference of a circle, $C = 2\pi r$, so that you can easily calculate the radius of a column given its circumference.

b. What is the radius, to the nearest tenth of a foot, of a column that has a circumference of 7 feet? 8 feet? 9 feet? (Use 3.14 for π.)

c. *Explain* how you can find the *area* of a cross section of a column if you know its circumference.

37. **CHALLENGE** The distance d (in miles) traveled by a car is given by $d = 55t$ where t is the time (in hours) the car has traveled. The distance d (in miles) traveled is also given by $d = 20g$ where g is the number of gallons of gasoline used by the car. Write an equation that expresses g as a function of t.

MIXED REVIEW

PREVIEW
Prepare for Lesson 4.1 in Exs. 38–39.

Graph the function. *(p. 43)*

38. $y = x + 4$; domain: 0, 2, 4, 6, and 8

39. $y = 2x - 1$; domain: 1, 2, 3, 4, and 5

Use the distributive property to write an equivalent expression. *(p. 96)*

40. $3(2x + 3)$

41. $-2(x + 5)$

42. $(3x - 5)(-5)$

43. $(7x + 6)2$

Use the percent equation to answer the question. *(p. 176)*

44. What percent of 80 is 64?

45. What number is 95% of 120?

QUIZ *for Lessons 3.7–3.8*

Use the percent equation to answer the question. *(p. 176)*

1. What percent of 150 is 72?

2. What percent of 310 is 93?

3. 31 is 5% of what number?

4. What number is 46% of 55?

Write the equation so that *y* is a function of *x*. *(p. 184)*

5. $5x - 3y = 9$

6. $3x + 2y + 5x = 12$

7. $4(2x - y) = 6$

8. **GEOMETRY** The volume V of a cylinder is given by the formula $V = \pi r^2 h$ where r is the radius of the cylinder and h is the height of the cylinder. Solve the formula for h. *(p. 184)*

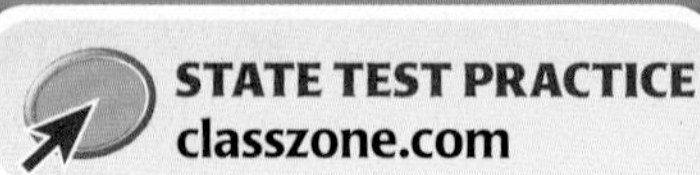

Lessons 3.5–3.8

1. **MULTI-STEP PROBLEM** The table below shows the results of a survey in which students at a school were asked to name their favorite sport to watch on TV.

Sport	Students
Baseball	7
Basketball	6
Football	10
Other	8

   a. There are 1209 students at the school. Write a proportion that you can use to predict the number of students at the school who would name baseball as their favorite sport to watch on TV.

   b. Solve the proportion.

2. **MULTI-STEP PROBLEM** The ratio of male students to female students in the freshman class at a high school is 4:5. There are 216 students in the freshman class.

   a. Find the ratio of female students to all students.

   b. Use the ratio to find the number of female students in the freshman class.

3. **SHORT RESPONSE** During a vacation, your family's car used 7 gallons of gasoline to travel 154 miles. Your family is planning another vacation in which you will travel 770 miles by car. If gasoline costs about \$2 per gallon, how much money should your family budget for gasoline for this vacation? *Explain* your reasoning.

4. **SHORT RESPONSE** In biology, the surface-area-to-volume quotient Q of a single spherical cell is given by the formula $Q = \frac{3}{r}$ where r is the radius of the cell. Suppose you need to calculate the diameters of cells given the surface-area-to-volume quotients of the cells. Given that $d = 2r$, explain how to write a formula for the diameter d of a cell given its surface-area-to-volume quotient.

5. **GRIDDED ANSWER** A basketball player made 60% of his free-throws during a season. The player made 84 free-throws. How many free-throw attempts did he have?

6. **EXTENDED RESPONSE** When a real estate agent sells a house, the agent receives 6% of the sale price as a commission. The agent lists the sale price for a house as \$208,000.

   a. How much of a commission should the agent expect to receive for selling this house at full price?

   b. The house actually sells for \$205,000. How much of a commission does the agent receive?

   c. The real estate agent gives 10% of her commission to her assistant. What percent of the selling price does the agent's assistant receive? *Explain* your reasoning.

7. **SHORT RESPONSE** The area A of a rhombus is given by the formula $A = \frac{1}{2}d_1d_2$ where d_1 and d_2 are the lengths of the diagonals.

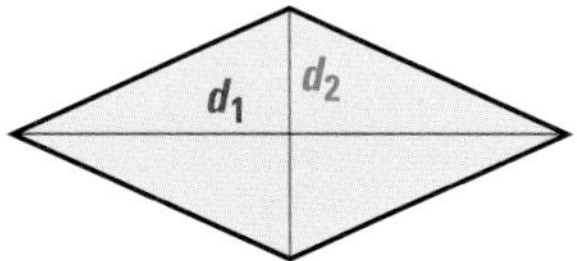

Suppose you need to find d_1 for different values of A and d_2. *Explain* how to rewrite the area formula to make it easier to find values for d_1.

8. **OPEN-ENDED** *Describe* how the dimensions of the rectangular garden below can be altered to increase the area of the garden by 25%.

3 CHAPTER SUMMARY

BIG IDEAS
For Your Notebook

Big Idea 1

Solving Equations in One Variable

You can solve equations in one variable by adding, subtracting, multiplying by, or dividing by the same number on each side.

Property	Words	Algebra
Addition Property of Equality	Add the same number to each side.	If $x - a = b$, then $x - a + a = b + a$, or $x = b + a$.
Subtraction Property of Equality	Subtract the same number from each side.	If $x + a = b$, then $x + a - a = b - a$, or $x = b - a$.
Multiplication Property of Equality	Multiply each side by the same nonzero number.	If $\frac{x}{a} = b$ and $a \neq 0$, then $a \cdot \frac{x}{a} = a \cdot b$, or $x = ab$.
Division Property of Equality	Divide each side by the same nonzero number.	If $ax = b$ and $a \neq 0$, then $\frac{ax}{a} = \frac{b}{a}$, or $x = \frac{b}{a}$.

Big Idea 2

Solving Proportion and Percent Problems

When solving a proportion, you can take the cross products, then use properties of equality.

$\frac{x - 3}{40} = \frac{4}{5}$ **Original proportion**

$5(x - 3) = 40 \cdot 4$ **Cross products property**

$5x - 15 = 160$ **Simplify.**

$5x = 175$ **Addition property of equality: Add 15 to each side.**

$x = 35$ **Division property of equality: Divide each side by 5.**

Big Idea 3

Rewriting Equations in Two or More Variables

If you have an equation in two or more variables, you can solve for one variable in terms of the others using properties of equality. For example, the formula for the perimeter P of a rectangle can be solved for the length ℓ.

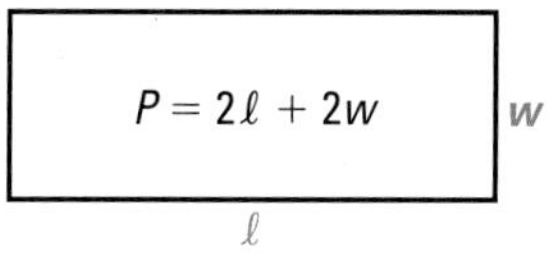

$P = 2\ell + 2w$ **Original formula**

$P - 2w = 2\ell$ **Subtraction property of equality: Subtract $2w$ from each side.**

$\frac{P - 2w}{2} = \ell$ **Division property of equality: Divide each side by 2.**

3 CHAPTER REVIEW

@HomeTutor
classzone.com
• Multi-Language Glossary
• Vocabulary practice

REVIEW KEY VOCABULARY

- inverse operations, *p. 134*
- equivalent equations, *p. 134*
- identity, *p. 156*
- ratio, *p. 162*
- proportion, *p. 163*
- cross product, *p. 168*
- scale drawing, *p. 170*
- scale model, *p. 170*
- scale, *p. 170*
- literal equation, *p. 184*

VOCABULARY EXERCISES

1. Copy and complete: A(n) __?__ is a two-dimensional drawing of an object in which the dimensions of the drawing are in proportion to the dimensions of the object.
2. Copy and complete: When you perform the same inverse operation on each side of an equation, you produce a(n) __?__ equation.
3. *Explain* why the equation $2x + 8x = 3x + 7x$ is an identity.
4. Copy and complete: In the proportion $\frac{7}{8} = \frac{28}{32}$, $7 \cdot 32$ and $8 \cdot 28$ are __?__.
5. *Describe* the steps you would take to write the equation $6x - 2y = 16$ in function form.

REVIEW EXAMPLES AND EXERCISES

Use the review examples and exercises below to check your understanding of the concepts you have learned in each lesson of Chapter 3.

3.1 Solve One-Step Equations *pp. 134–140*

EXAMPLE

Solve $\frac{x}{5} = 14$.

$\frac{x}{5} = 14$ **Write original equation.**

$5 \cdot \frac{x}{5} = 5 \cdot 14$ **Multiply each side by 5.**

$x = 70$ **Simplify.**

EXERCISES

EXAMPLES 1, 2, 3, 4 and 5 on pp. 134–136 for Exs. 6–12

Solve the equation. Check your solution.

6. $x - 4 = 3$
7. $-8 + a = 5$
8. $4m = -84$
9. $-5z = 75$
10. $11 = \frac{r}{6}$
11. $-27 = \frac{3}{4}w$
12. **PARKS** A rectangular city park has an area of 211,200 square feet. If the length of the park is 660 feet, what is the width of the park?

@HomeTutor
classzone.com
Chapter Review Practice

3.2 Solve Two-Step Equations

pp. 141–146

EXAMPLE

Solve $4x - 9 = 3$.

$4x - 9 = 3$ — Write original equation.

$4x - 9 + 9 = 3 + 9$ — Add 9 to each side.

$4x = 12$ — Simplify.

$\frac{4x}{4} = \frac{12}{4}$ — Divide each side by 4.

$x = 3$ — Simplify.

EXERCISES

EXAMPLES 1 and 2 on pp. 141–142 for Exs. 13–18

Solve the equation. Check your solution.

13. $9b + 5 = 23$ **14.** $11 = 5y - 4$ **15.** $\frac{n}{3} - 4 = 2$

16. $\frac{3}{2}v + 2 = 20$ **17.** $3t + 9t = 60$ **18.** $-110 = -4c - 6c$

3.3 Solve Multi-Step Equations

pp. 148–153

EXAMPLE

Solve $5x - 2(4x + 3) = 9$.

$5x - 2(4x + 3) = 9$ — Write original equation.

$5x - 8x - 6 = 9$ — Distributive property

$-3x - 6 = 9$ — Combine like terms.

$-3x = 15$ — Add 6 to each side.

$x = -5$ — Divide each side by -3.

EXERCISES

EXAMPLES 1, 2, 3 and 4 on pp. 148–149 for Exs. 19–28

Solve the equation. Check your solution.

19. $3w + 4w - 2 = 12$ **20.** $z + 5 - 4z = 8$ **21.** $c + 2c - 5 - 5c = 7$

22. $4y - (y - 4) = -20$ **23.** $8a - 3(2a + 5) = 13$ **24.** $16h - 4(5h - 7) = 4$

25. $\frac{3}{2}(b + 1) = 3$ **26.** $\frac{4}{3}(2x - 1) = -12$ **27.** $\frac{6}{5}(8k + 2) = -36$

28. FOOTBALL You purchase 5 tickets to a football game from an Internet ticket agency. In addition to the cost per ticket, the agency charges a convenience charge of $2.50 per ticket. You choose to pay for rush delivery, which costs $15. The total cost of your order is $352.50. What is the price per ticket not including the convenience charge?

3 CHAPTER REVIEW

3.4 Solve Equations with Variables on Both Sides

pp. 154–159

EXAMPLE

Solve the equation, if possible.

a. $-2(x - 5) = 7 - 2x$ **Original equation**

$-2x + 10 = 7 - 2x$ **Distributive property**

$-2x + 3 = -2x$ **Subtract 7 from each side.**

▶ The equation $-2x + 3 = -2x$ is not true because the number $-2x$ cannot be equal to 3 more than itself. So, the equation has no solution.

b. $5(3 - 2x) = -(10x - 15)$ **Original equation**

$15 - 10x = -10x + 15$ **Distributive property**

$15 - 10x = 15 - 10x$ **Rearrange terms.**

▶ The statement $15 - 10x = 15 - 10x$ is true for all values of x. So, the equation is an identity.

EXERCISES

EXAMPLES 1, 2, and 4 on pp. 154–156 for Exs. 29–37

Solve the equation, if possible.

29. $-3z - 1 = 8 - 3z$

30. $16 - 2m = 5m + 9$

31 $2.9w + 5 = 4.7w - 7.6$

32. $2y + 11.4 = 2.6 - 0.2y$

33. $4(x - 3) = -2(6 - 2x)$

34. $6(2a + 10) = 5(a + 5)$

35. $\frac{1}{12}(48 + 24b) = 2(17 - 4b)$

36. $1.5(n + 20) = 0.5(3n + 60)$

37. GEOMETRY Refer to the square shown.

a. Find the value of x.

b. Find the perimeter of the square.

$6x + 5$

$8x - 3$

3.5 Write Ratios and Proportions

pp. 162–167

EXAMPLE

You know that 5 pizzas will feed 20 people. How many pizzas do you need to order to feed 88 people?

$\frac{5}{20} = \frac{x}{88}$ ← number of pizzas / ← number of people

$88 \cdot \frac{5}{20} = 88 \cdot \frac{x}{88}$ **Multiply each side by 88.**

$22 = x$ **Simplify.**

▶ You need to order 22 pizzas.

@HomeTutor
classzone.com
Chapter Review Practice

EXERCISES

EXAMPLES 2 and 3 on pp. 163–164 for Exs. 38–44

Solve the proportion. Check your solution.

38. $\frac{56}{16} = \frac{x}{2}$ **39.** $\frac{y}{9} = \frac{25}{15}$ **40.** $\frac{2}{7} = \frac{m}{91}$

41. $\frac{5z}{3} = \frac{105}{6}$ **42.** $\frac{9}{4} = \frac{3a}{20}$ **43.** $\frac{c+2}{45} = \frac{8}{5}$

44. PAINTING The label on a can of paint states that one gallon of the paint will cover 560 square feet. How many gallons of that paint are needed to cover 1400 square feet?

3.6 Solve Proportions Using Cross Products

pp. 168–173

EXAMPLE

Solve the proportion $\frac{3}{10} = \frac{12}{x}$.

$\frac{3}{10} = \frac{12}{x}$	**Write original proportion.**
$3 \cdot x = 10 \cdot 12$	**Cross products property**
$3x = 120$	**Simplify.**
$x = 40$	**Divide each side by 3.**

EXAMPLE

A map has a scale of 1 cm : 15 km. The distance between two cities on the map is 7.2 centimeters. Estimate the actual distance between the cites.

$\frac{1}{15} = \frac{7.2}{d}$ ← **centimeters** / ← **kilometers**

$1 \cdot d = 15 \cdot 7.2$	**Cross products property**
$d = 108$	**Simplify.**

▸ The distance between the two cities is about 108 kilometers.

EXERCISES

EXAMPLES 1, 3, and 4 on pp. 168–170 for Exs. 45–52

Solve the proportion. Check your solution.

45. $\frac{5}{7} = \frac{20}{r}$ **46.** $\frac{6}{z} = \frac{12}{5}$ **47.** $\frac{126}{56} = \frac{9}{4b}$

48. $\frac{10}{3m} = \frac{-5}{6}$ **49.** $\frac{n+8}{5n-2} = \frac{3}{8}$ **50.** $\frac{5-c}{3} = \frac{2c+2}{-4}$

51. TYPING RATES A student can type 65 words in 2 minutes. How many words can the student type in 20 minutes?

52. MAPS A map has a scale of 1 cm : 12 km. The distance between two cities on the map is 6.8 centimeters. Estimate the actual distance between the cities.

3 CHAPTER REVIEW

3.7 Solve Percent Problems

pp. 176–181

EXAMPLE

42 is 40% of what number?

$a = p\% \cdot b$	Write percent equation.
$42 = 40\% \cdot b$	Substitute 42 for a and 40 for p.
$42 = 0.4 \cdot b$	Write percent as decimal.
$105 = b$	Divide each side by 0.4.

▶ 42 is 40% of 105.

EXERCISES

EXAMPLES 2, 3, 4, and 5 on pp. 177–179 for Exs. 53–57

Use the percent equation to answer the question.

53. What number is 30% of 55?

54. 117 is 78% of what number?

55. What percent of 56 is 21?

56. What percent of 60 is 18?

57. CONCERTS There were 7500 tickets sold for a concert, 20% of which were general admission tickets. How many general admission tickets were sold?

3.8 Rewrite Equations and Formulas

pp. 184–189

EXAMPLE

Write $5x + 4y - 7 = 5$ so that y is a function of x.

$5x + 4y - 7 = 5$	Write original equation.
$5x + 4y = 12$	Add 7 to each side.
$4y = 12 - 5x$	Subtract $5x$ from each side.
$y = 3 - \frac{5}{4}x$	Divide each side by 4.

EXERCISES

EXAMPLES 2 and 3 on p. 185 for Exs. 58–61

Write the equation so that y is a function of x.

58. $x + 7y = 0$

59. $3x = 2y - 18$

60. $4y - x = 20 - y$

61. AQUARIUMS A pet store sells aquariums that are rectangular prisms. The volume V of an aquarium is given by the formula $V = \ell wh$ where ℓ is the length, w is the width, and h is the height.

a. Solve the formula for h.

b. Use the rewritten formula to find the height of the aquarium shown, which has a volume of 5850 cubic inches.

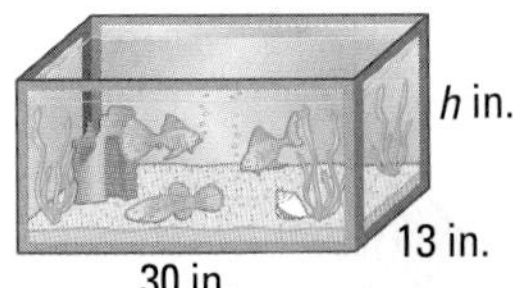

3 CHAPTER TEST

Solve the equation. Check your solution.

1. $5 + r = -19$

2. $z - 8 = -12$

3. $-11x = -77$

4. $\frac{a}{9} = 6$

5. $15q - 17 = 13$

6. $3y + 2 = 26$

7. $\frac{b}{4} + 5 = 14$

8. $\frac{m}{10} - 6 = 20$

9. $6j + 5j = 33$

10. $4k - 9k = 10$

11. $14c - 8c + 7 = 37$

12. $4w - 21 + 5w = 51$

13. $-19.4 - 15d + 22d = 4.4$

14. $-12h + 39 = -4h - 17$

15. $-5.7v - 44.2 = -8.3v$

16. $-6.5t + 15 = -9.7t + 43.8$

17. $3(3n + 4) = 54 + 6n$

18. $\frac{1}{3}(24p - 66) = 3p + 43$

Solve the proportion. Check your solution.

19. $\frac{3}{4} = \frac{z}{16}$

20. $\frac{72}{45} = \frac{8}{w}$

21. $\frac{k}{9} = \frac{63}{81}$

22. $\frac{-5n}{4} = \frac{15}{2}$

23. $\frac{34}{6} = \frac{2x + 1}{3}$

24. $\frac{-4a - 1}{-10a} = \frac{3}{8}$

Use the percent equation to answer the question.

25. What percent of 84 is 21?

26. What percent of 124 is 93?

27. What number is 15% of 64?

28. What number is 44% of 24.5?

29. 90 is what percent of 250?

30. 79.8 is what percent of 95?

Write the equation so that *y* is a function of *x*.

31. $8x + y = 14$

32. $-9x + 3y = 18$

33. $4x = -2y + 26$

34. MOVIES The ticket prices at a movie theater are shown in the table. A family purchases tickets for 2 adults and 3 children, and the family purchases 3 boxes of popcorn of the same size. The family spent a total of \$40.25. How much did each box of popcorn cost?

Ticket	Price
Adults	\$8.50
Children	\$5.50

35. ICE SKATING To become a member of an ice skating rink, you have to pay a \$30 membership fee. The cost of admission to the rink is \$5 for members and \$7 for nonmembers. After how many visits to the rink is the total cost for members, including the membership fee, the same as the total cost for nonmembers?

36. SCALE DRAWING You are making a scale drawing of your classroom using the scale 1 inch : 3 feet. The floor of your classroom is a rectangle with a length of 21 feet and a width of 18 feet. What should the length and width of the floor in your drawing be?

37. SURVEYS A survey asks high school seniors whether they would be willing to pay \$5 for their yearbook. Out of the 225 seniors surveyed, 198 said "yes." What percent of the seniors said "yes"?

3 ★ Standardized TEST PREPARATION

MULTIPLE CHOICE QUESTIONS

If you have difficulty solving a multiple choice problem directly, you may be able to use another approach to eliminate incorrect answer choices and obtain the correct answer.

PROBLEM 1

Sid's car gets 34 miles per gallon when driven on the highway and 26 miles per gallon when driven in the city. If Sid drove 414 miles on 13 gallons of gas, how many highway miles and how many city miles did Sid drive?

Ⓐ 91 highway miles, 323 city miles

Ⓑ 182 highway miles, 232 city miles

Ⓒ 232 highway miles, 182 city miles

Ⓓ 323 highway miles, 91 city miles

METHOD 1

SOLVE DIRECTLY Write and solve an equation for the situation.

STEP 1 **Write** an equation. Let x represent the amount of gas (in gallons) used for highway driving. Then $13 - x$ represents the amount of gas used for city driving.

$$414 = 34x + 26(13 - x)$$

STEP 2 **Solve** the equation.

$$414 = 34x + 338 - 26x$$

$$414 = 8x + 338$$

$$76 = 8x$$

$$9.5 = x$$

STEP 3 **Calculate** the number of highway miles driven.

$$34(9.5) = 323$$

STEP 4 **Calculate** the number of city miles driven.

$$26(13 - 9.5) = 91$$

Sid drove 323 highway miles and 91 city miles.

The correct answer is D. Ⓐ Ⓑ Ⓒ Ⓓ

METHOD 2

ELIMINATE CHOICES Another method is to consider the extremes to eliminate incorrect answer choices.

STEP 1 **Consider** driving all highway miles and all city miles.

All highway: $13 \text{ gal} \cdot \frac{34 \text{ mi}}{1 \text{ gal}} = 442 \text{ mi}$

All city: $13 \text{ gal} \cdot \frac{26 \text{ mi}}{1 \text{ gal}} = 338 \text{ mi}$

Because 414 is closer to 442 than to 338, you know that more highway miles were driven than city miles. So, you can eliminate choices A and B.

STEP 2 **Calculate** the gallons of gas that would be used for the remaining choices.

Choice C: $232 \text{ mi} \cdot \frac{1 \text{ gal}}{34 \text{ mi}} \approx 6.8 \text{ gal}$

$182 \text{ mi} \cdot \frac{1 \text{ gal}}{26 \text{ mi}} = 7 \text{ gal}$

Choice D: $323 \text{ mi} \cdot \frac{1 \text{ gal}}{34 \text{ mi}} = 9.5 \text{ gal}$

$91 \text{ mi} \cdot \frac{1 \text{ gal}}{26 \text{ mi}} = 3.5 \text{ gal}$

In choice D, the total number of gallons of gas is 13.

The correct answer is D. Ⓐ Ⓑ Ⓒ Ⓓ

PROBLEM 2

What is the value of x in the proportion $\frac{3}{2x - 10} = \frac{12}{x + 9}$?

Ⓐ 4 Ⓑ 6 Ⓒ 7 Ⓓ 8

METHOD 1

SOLVE DIRECTLY Find the value of x by using the cross products property to solve the proportion.

$$\frac{3}{2x - 10} = \frac{12}{x + 9}$$

$$3(x + 9) = (2x - 10) \cdot 12$$

$$3x + 27 = 24x - 120$$

$$147 = 21x$$

$$7 = x$$

The correct answer is C. Ⓐ Ⓑ Ⓒ Ⓓ

METHOD 2

ELIMINATE CHOICES Substitute each answer choice for x in the proportion and simplify.

Choice A: $\frac{3}{2(4) - 10} \stackrel{?}{=} \frac{12}{4 + 9}$

$\frac{3}{-2} = \frac{12}{13}$ ✗

Choice B: $\frac{3}{2(6) - 10} \stackrel{?}{=} \frac{12}{6 + 9}$

$\frac{3}{2} = \frac{4}{5}$ ✗

Choice C: $\frac{3}{2(7) - 10} \stackrel{?}{=} \frac{12}{7 + 9}$

$\frac{3}{4} = \frac{3}{4}$ ✓

The correct answer is C. Ⓐ Ⓑ Ⓒ Ⓓ

PRACTICE

Explain why you can eliminate the highlighted answer choice.

1. What is the solution of the equation $5(x + 13) = 8(4 + x)$?

   Ⓐ −11 Ⓑ −4 Ⓒ ✗ 0 Ⓓ 11

2. 45 is 80% of what number?

   Ⓐ ✗ 36 Ⓑ 56.25 Ⓒ 60 Ⓓ 64.5

3. A grocery store sells apples by the pound. A 3 pound bag of apples costs \$2.99. About how much does a 5 pound bag of apples cost?

   Ⓐ \$3.24 Ⓑ \$3.45 Ⓒ \$4.98 Ⓓ ✗ \$5.98

4. The surface area S of a cylinder is given by the formula $S = 2\pi rh + 2\pi r^2$ where r is the radius and h is the height of the cylinder. Which of the given formulas is *not* equivalent to the original formula?

   Ⓐ $S = 2\pi r(h + r)$ Ⓑ $h = 2\pi rS + 2\pi r^2$

   Ⓒ ✗ $h = \frac{S - 2\pi r^2}{2\pi r}$ Ⓓ $h = \frac{S}{2\pi r} - r$

3 ★ *Standardized* TEST PRACTICE

MULTIPLE CHOICE

1. How many solutions does the equation $3(x - 3) = 3x - 6$ have?

   (A) None (B) 1
   (C) 2 (D) Infinitely many

2. A karate studio offers a 6 week session for \$175. How much would you expect to pay for a 9 week session?

   (A) \$117 (B) \$200
   (C) \$229 (D) \$262.50

3. Andrew decides to get cable TV for \$43 per month. Doug buys a satellite dish for \$104 and pays \$30 per month for satellite TV. After how many months will Andrew and Doug have paid the same amount for their TV services?

   (A) 7 (B) 8
   (C) 9 (D) 10

4. The rates for using a swimming facility are given below. After how many visits will a family of 4 save money by having a membership rather than paying for all 4 family members for each visit?

Admission Prices	
One-day visit	\$3 per person
Family membership (unlimited visits)	\$150

   (A) 12 (B) 13
   (C) 38 (D) 50

5. The record for the longest distance and longest time ever flown by a model airplane was set in 2003 by Maynard Hill. The airplane flew 1888 miles from Canada to Ireland in 38 hours and 53 minutes. What was the plane's average speed?

   (A) About 36 mi/h (B) About 45 mi/h
   (C) About 49 mi/h (D) About 71,744 mi/h

6. The perimeter of the triangle shown is 16.5 inches. What is the length of the shortest side?

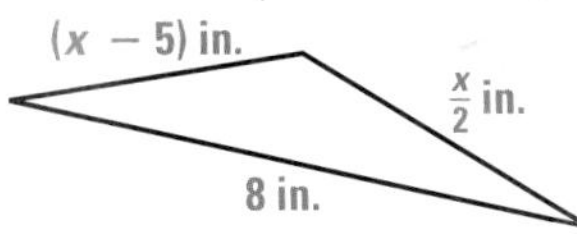

   (A) 3.5 in. (B) 4 in.
   (C) 4.5 in. (D) 9 in.

7. Jeanie completed a 27 mile duathlon (a race that is a combination of running and biking) in exactly 2 hours. She ran an average speed of 8.5 miles per hour and biked an average speed of 16 miles per hour. For how long did Jeanie bike during the race?

   (A) 1 hour 20 minutes
   (B) 1 hour 15 minutes
   (C) 45 minutes
   (D) 40 minutes

8. A model of the Gateway Arch in St. Louis, Missouri, was built using a scale of 1 ft : 500 ft. The model is 1.26 feet tall. What is the actual height of the Gateway Arch?

   (A) 75.6 ft (B) 396.8 ft
   (C) 630 ft (D) 7560 ft

9. A mountain biking park has a total of 48 trails, 37.5% of which are beginner trails. The rest are divided evenly between intermediate and expert trails. How many of each kind of trail is there?

   (A) 12 beginner, 18 intermediate, 18 expert
   (B) 18 beginner, 15 intermediate, 15 expert
   (C) 18 beginner, 12 intermediate, 18 expert
   (D) 30 beginner, 9 intermediate, 9 expert

10. What percent of 256 is 140.8?

   (A) 45% (B) 50%
   (C) 52.5% (D) 55%

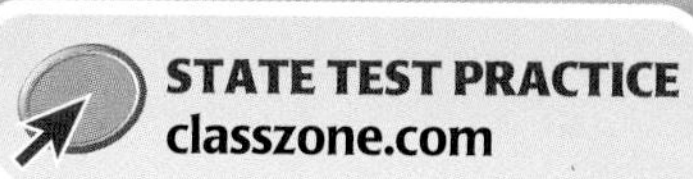

GRIDDED ANSWER

11. The circumference of a circle is 12 feet. What is the radius (in feet) of the circle? Round your answer to the nearest tenth.

12. What is the value of x in the equation $75 = 15x - 6(x + 7)$?

13. The perimeter of the rectangle shown is 41 centimeters. What is the value of x?

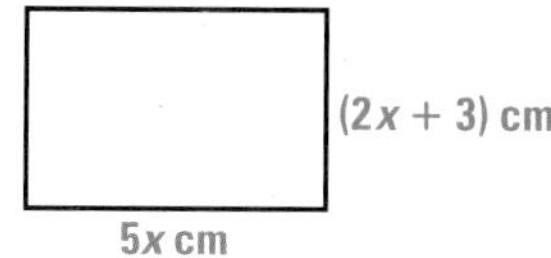

14. Chris pays $.29 for each digital photo he has printed. Debbie buys a photo printer for $180. It costs $.14 per photo for ink and paper to print a photo using the printer. After how many prints will Chris and Debbie have paid the same amount?

SHORT RESPONSE

15. Kendra is painting her dining room white and her living room blue. She spends a total of $132 on 5 cans of paint. The white paint costs $24 per can, and the blue paint costs $28 per can.

a. Write and solve an equation to find the number of cans of each color paint that Kendra bought.

b. How much would Kendra have saved by switching the colors of the dining room and living room? *Explain.*

16. Kim and Sandy are each knitting a scarf. Kim can knit 3 rows in 5 minutes. Sandy can knit 4 rows in 6 minutes. They start knitting at the same time and do not take any breaks. Kim wants her scarf to be 84 rows long. Sandy wants her scarf to be 88 rows long. Who will finish her scarf first? *Explain.*

EXTENDED RESPONSE

17. You are shopping for tools. You find two stores at which the regular prices of the tools are the same. Store A is currently offering $30 off any purchase of $100 or more. Store B is currently offering 12% off any purchase.

a. Compare the costs of buying $200 worth of tools from each store.

b. Compare the costs of buying $300 worth of tools from each store.

c. Let x be the regular price (in dollars) of your purchase, and assume that x is greater than 100. Write an equation you could use to find the value of x for which the costs of the tools after the discounts are the same. *Explain* how you wrote the equation.

d. Solve the equation from part (c). How can the solution help you to decide from which store you should buy the tools? *Explain.*

18. The circle graph shows the results of a survey that asked 225 randomly selected people how they get driving directions.

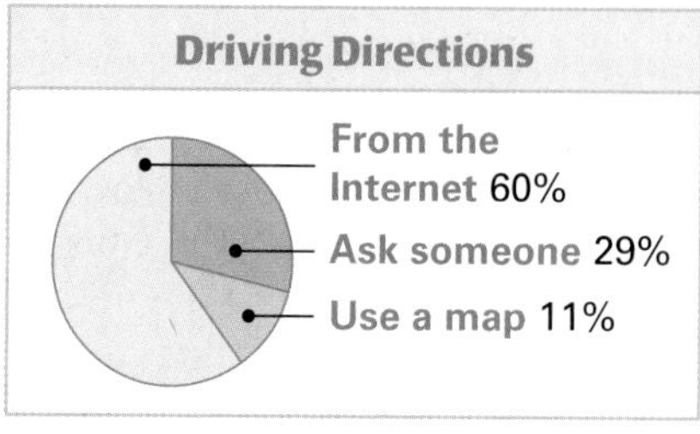

a. How many people said that they get directions from the Internet?

b. Suppose 15 more people were surveyed, and all 15 said that they get directions from the Internet. Calculate the new percent for the "From the Internet" category. *Explain* how you found your answer.

c. Instead of 15 more people, suppose x more people are surveyed and they all said that they get directions from the Internet. What value of x would make the percent for the "From the Internet" category be 70%? Your response should include a proportion and an explanation of how you used the proportion to find your answer.

3 CUMULATIVE REVIEW Chapters 1–3

Evaluate the expression. *(p. 8)*

1. $3 \cdot 4^2 - 21$
2. $4 + 4^2 \div 8$
3. $77 \div (11 - 4)$
4. $\frac{1}{2}(8 \cdot 6) - 4^2$
5. $3[50 - (13 - 7)^2]$
6. $\frac{3}{4}[(6 + 4)^2 - 40]$

Check whether the given number is a solution of the equation or inequality. *(p. 21)*

7. $7t - 11 = 52; 9$
8. $3b - 2 = 2b + 3; 4$
9. $8z - 11 > 21; 4$
10. $5a + 3 \leq 13; 2$
11. $5 - y \geq 5; 3$
12. $8x - 15 < 8; 7$

Find the sum or difference.

13. $-2\frac{1}{6} + \left(-4\frac{2}{3}\right)$ *(p. 74)*
14. $2.5 - (-2.05)$ *(p. 80)*
15. $-24.6 - (-5.5)$ *(p. 80)*

Find the product or quotient.

16. $\frac{5}{2}(-8)(-5)$ *(p. 88)*
17. $9 \div \left(-\frac{3}{7}\right)$ *(p. 103)*
18. $-\frac{7}{8} \div \frac{1}{2}$ *(p. 103)*

Evaluate the expression for the given value of the variable(s).

19. $\frac{32}{w} - 2$ when $w = 4$ *(p. 8)*
20. $7 + 3m^2 - 8m$ when $m = 5$ *(p. 8)*
21. $\frac{5y}{32 - y^3}$ when $y = 3$ *(p. 8)*
22. $5.15 + (-h) + 6.6$ when $h = 4.3$ *(p. 74)*
23. $17.4 - |-p|$ when $p = 3.5$ *(p. 80)*
24. $k^2 - 12.2k$ when $k = -1.6$ *(p. 88)*
25. $8.3x - (-y)$ when $x = 6$ and $y = 9$ *(p. 88)*
26. $\frac{y}{5x - y}$ when $x = 2$ and $y = 4$ *(p. 103)*

Solve the equation. Check your solution.

27. $m + 16 = 5$ *(p. 134)*
28. $-4 = \frac{w}{7}$ *(p. 134)*
29. $5 + 3x = 23$ *(p. 141)*
30. $\frac{a}{3} - 4 = 29$ *(p. 141)*
31. $-4 = -2b - 18 + 5b$ *(p. 148)*
32. $\frac{3}{8}(16n + 48) = 72$ *(p. 148)*
33. $-8z + 18 = 2(2z - 9)$ *(p. 154)*
34. $(15c + 30) = \frac{1}{3}(102 - 12c)$ *(p. 154)*

Solve the proportion. *(p. 168)*

35. $\frac{6}{d} = \frac{12}{17}$
36. $\frac{4}{7} = \frac{20}{m}$
37. $\frac{1}{9} = \frac{5}{3x}$
38. $\frac{3}{6h} = \frac{12}{72}$
39. $\frac{2}{11} = \frac{4}{t - 1}$
40. $\frac{12}{a + 1} = \frac{132}{35}$
41. $\frac{w + 2}{8} = \frac{w}{3}$
42. $\frac{4}{9} = \frac{z}{z + 10}$

43. **GARDENS** You want to put edging around a rectangular flower garden that is 15 feet long and 12 feet wide. The edging comes in 3 foot pieces, as shown. How many pieces of edging do you need to buy? *(p. 28)*

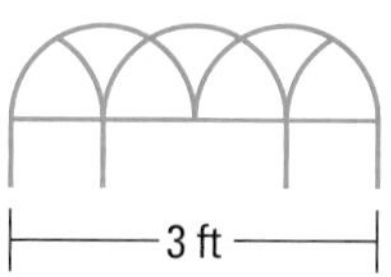

44. **MUSIC** The table shows the amount of time m (in hours per person per year) that adults listened to recorded music as a function of the time t (in years) since 1996. Graph the function. *(p. 43)*

Years since 1996, t	0	1	2	3	4	5
Hours listening to music, m	292	270	283	289	263	250

45. **STOCKS** The daily change in the price of a share of stock is the difference of the price of a share when trading closes and the price of a share when trading opened earlier that day. The table shows the prices of a share of stock during a 5 day period. Find the change in price for each day. *(p. 80)*

Day	1	2	3	4	5
Opening price (dollars)	39.16	38.82	38.37	38.12	39.14
Closing price (dollars)	38.82	38.37	38.12	39.14	39.22

46. **CRAFTS** You want to make a square mirror by applying silver leaf to a piece of glass. You have enough silver leaf to cover 854 square inches. Determine the side length of the square piece of glass you need to have cut for this project. Round your answer to the nearest inch. *(p. 110)*

47. **BANQUETS** The senior class at your high school has its prom at a banquet facility. The banquet facility charges $15.95 per person for a dinner buffet and $400 to rent the banquet hall for an evening. The class paid the banquet facility a total of $2633 for the dinner buffet and use of the banquet hall. How many people attended the prom? *(p. 141)*

48. **TELEVISIONS** The ratio of the length to the width of two different television screens is shown. The width of each screen is 16.2 inches. Find the length of each screen. *(p. 162)*

Standard

16 : 9
Wide screen

49. **BASKETBALL** The circle graph shows the positions of the 20 players on a basketball team. *(p. 176)*

a. How many players on the team play center?

b. How many players on the team play guard?

c. How many players on the team play forward?

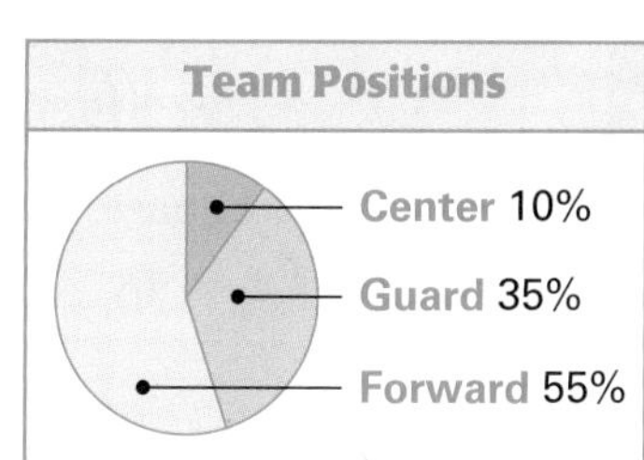

4 Graphing Linear Equations and Functions

Before

In previous chapters, you learned the following skills, which you'll use in Chapter 4: graphing functions and writing equations and functions.

Prerequisite Skills

VOCABULARY CHECK

Copy and complete the statement.

1. The set of inputs of a function is called the _?_ of the function. The set of outputs of a function is called the _?_ of the function.
2. A(n) _?_ uses division to compare two quantities.

SKILLS CHECK

Graph the function. *(Review p. 43 for 4.1–4.7.)*

3. $y = x + 6$; domain: 0, 2, 4, 6, and 8
4. $y = 2x + 1$; domain: 0, 1, 2, 3, and 4
5. $y = \frac{2}{3}x$; domain: 0, 3, 6, 9, and 12
6. $y = x - \frac{1}{2}$; domain: 1, 2, 3, 4, and 5
7. $y = x - 4$; 5, 6, 7, and 9
8. $y = \frac{1}{2}x + 1$; 2, 4, 6, and 8

Write the equation so that y is a function of x. *(Review p. 184 for 4.5.)*

9. $6x + 4y = 16$
10. $x + 2y = 5$
11. $-12x + 6y = -12$

@HomeTutor Prerequisite skills practice at classzone.com

Now

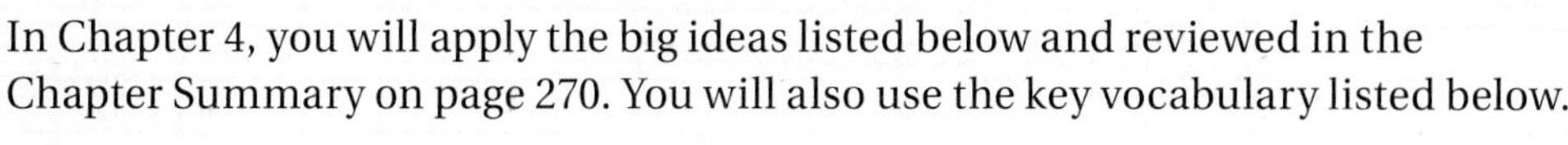

In Chapter 4, you will apply the big ideas listed below and reviewed in the Chapter Summary on page 270. You will also use the key vocabulary listed below.

Big Ideas

1. **Graphing linear equations and functions using a variety of methods**
2. **Recognizing how changes in linear equations and functions affect their graphs**
3. **Using graphs of linear equations and functions to solve real-world problems**

KEY VOCABULARY

- quadrant, *p. 206*
- standard form of a linear equation, *p. 216*
- linear function, *p. 217*
- *x*-intercept, *p. 225*
- *y*-intercept, *p. 225*
- slope, *p. 235*
- rate of change, *p. 237*
- slope-intercept form, *p. 244*
- parallel, *p. 246*
- direct variation, *p. 253*
- constant of variation, *p. 253*
- function notation, *p. 262*
- family of functions, *p. 263*
- parent linear function, *p. 263*

Why?

You can graph linear functions to solve problems involving distance. For example, you can graph a linear function to find the time it takes and in-line skater to travel a particular distance at a particular speed.

Animated Algebra

The animation illustrated below for Exercise 41 on page 267 helps you answer this question: How can you graph a function that models the distance an in-line skater travels over time?

Start
You want to graph a function that gives the distance traveled by an in-line skater.

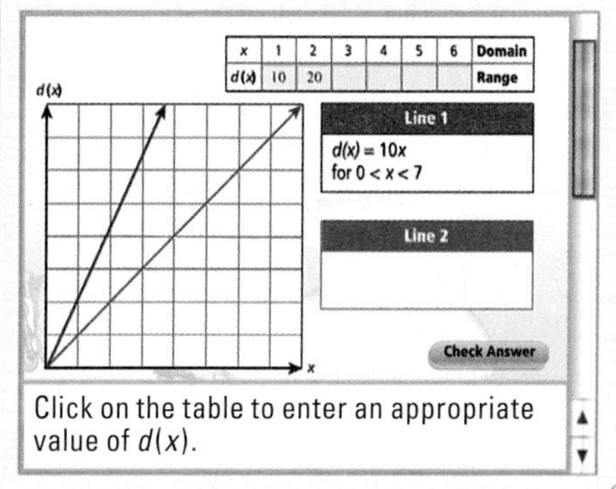

Check Answer
Click on the table to enter an appropriate value of d(x).

Animated Algebra at classzone.com

Other animations for Chapter 4: pages 207, 216, 226, 238, 245, and 254

4.1 Plot Points in a Coordinate Plane

Before You graphed numbers on a number line.

Now You will identify and plot points in a coordinate plane.

Why? So you can interpret photos of Earth taken from space, as in Ex. 36.

Key Vocabulary
- **quadrants**
- **coordinate plane,** *p. 921*
- **ordered pair,** *p. 921*

In Chapter 1, you used a coordinate plane to graph ordered pairs whose coordinates were nonnegative. If you extend the x-axis and y-axis to include negative values, you divide the coordinate plane into four regions called **quadrants**, labeled I, II, III, and IV as shown.

Points in Quadrant I have two positive coordinates. Points in the other three quadrants have at least one negative coordinate.

For example, point P is in Quadrant IV and has an x-coordinate of 3 and a y-coordinate of -2. A point on an axis, such as point Q, is not considered to be in any of the four quadrants.

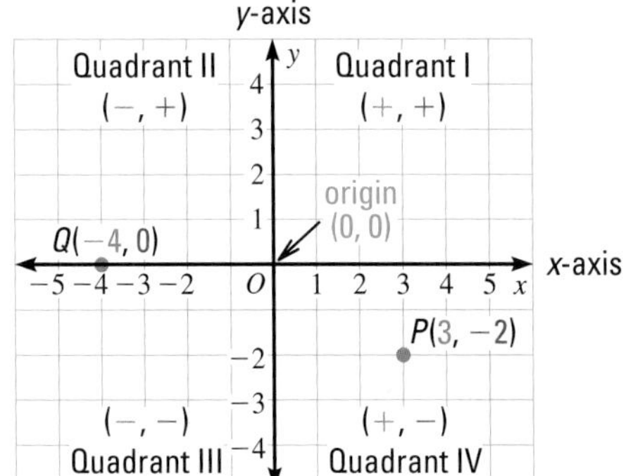

READING
The x-coordinate of a point is sometimes called the *abscissa*. The y-coordinate of a point is sometimes called the *ordinate*.

EXAMPLE 1 Name points in a coordinate plane

Give the coordinates of the point.

a. A **b.** B

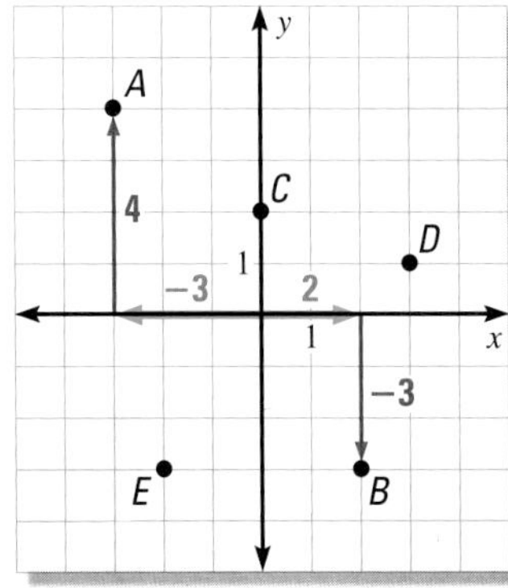

Solution

a. Point A is 3 units to the left of the origin and 4 units up. So, the x-coordinate is -3, and the y-coordinate is 4. The coordinates are $(-3, 4)$.

b. Point B is 2 units to the right of the origin and 3 units down. So, the x-coordinate is 2, and the y-coordinate is -3. The coordinates are $(2, -3)$.

✓ GUIDED PRACTICE for Example 1

1. Use the coordinate plane in Example 1 to give the coordinates of points C, D, and E.
2. What is the y-coordinate of any point on the x-axis?

EXAMPLE 2 Plot points in a coordinate plane

Plot the point in a coordinate plane. Describe the location of the point.

a. $A(-4, 4)$ **b.** $B(3, -2)$ **c.** $C(0, -4)$

Solution

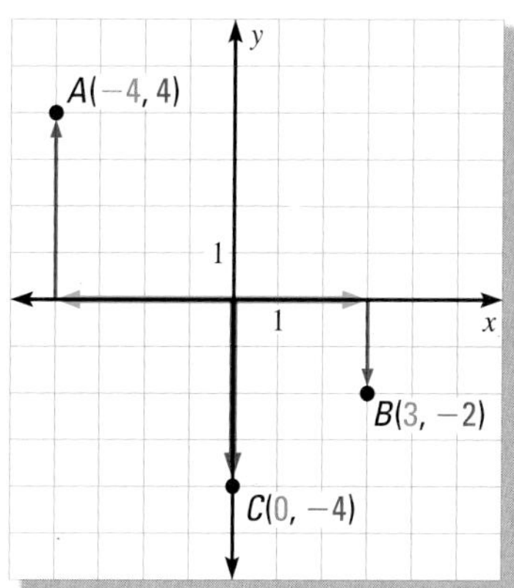

a. Begin at the origin. First move 4 units to the left, then 4 units up. Point A is in Quadrant II.

b. Begin at the origin. First move 3 units to the right, then 2 units down. Point B is in Quadrant IV.

c. Begin at the origin and move 4 units down. Point C is on the y-axis.

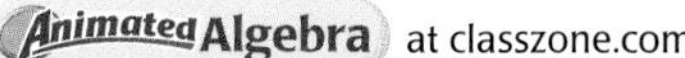
Animated Algebra at classzone.com

EXAMPLE 3 Graph a function

Graph the function $y = 2x - 1$ with domain −2, −1, 0, 1, and 2. Then identify the range of the function.

Solution

STEP 1 **Make** a table by substituting the domain values into the function.

x	$y = 2x - 1$
−2	$y = 2(-2) - 1 = -5$
−1	$y = 2(-1) - 1 = -3$
0	$y = 2(0) - 1 = -1$
1	$y = 2(1) - 1 = 1$
2	$y = 2(2) - 1 = 3$

STEP 2 **List** the ordered pairs: (−2, −5), (−1, −3), (0, −1), (1, 1), (2, 3). Then graph the function.

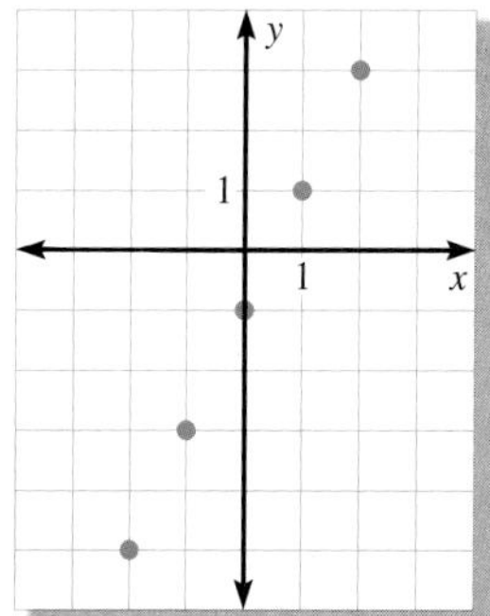

ANALYZE A FUNCTION

The function in Example 3 is called a *discrete* function. To learn about discrete functions, see p. 223.

STEP 3 **Identify** the range. The range consists of the y-values from the table: −5, −3, −1, 1, and 3.

✓ GUIDED PRACTICE for Examples 2 and 3

Plot the point in a coordinate plane. *Describe* the location of the point.

3. $A(2, 5)$ **4.** $B(-1, 0)$ **5.** $C(-2, -1)$ **6.** $D(-5, 3)$

7. Graph the function $y = -\frac{1}{3}x + 2$ with domain −6, −3, 0, 3, and 6. Then identify the range of the function.

EXAMPLE 4 Graph a function represented by a table

VOTING In 1920 the ratification of the 19th amendment to the United States Constitution gave women the right to vote. The table shows the number (to the nearest million) of votes cast in presidential elections both before and since women were able to vote.

REPUBLICAN CANDIDATES 1920

Presidential campaign button

−4 means 4 years before 1920, or 1916.

0 represents the year 1920.

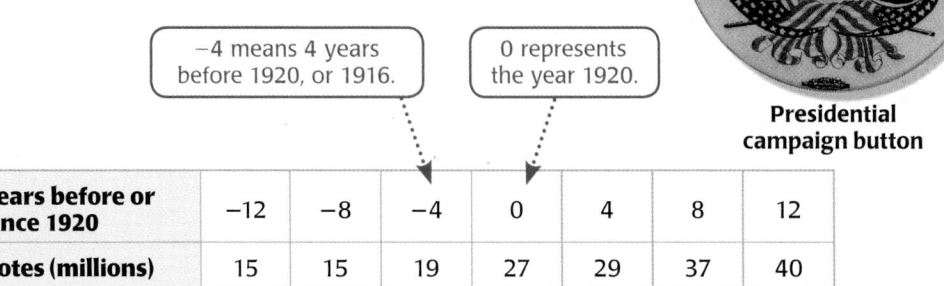

Years before or since 1920	−12	−8	−4	0	4	8	12
Votes (millions)	15	15	19	27	29	37	40

a. Explain how you know that the table represents a function.

b. Graph the function represented by the table.

c. Describe any trend in the number of votes cast.

Solution

a. The table represents a function because each input has exactly one output.

b. To graph the function, let x be the number of years before or since 1920. Let y be the number of votes cast (in millions).

The graph of the function is shown.

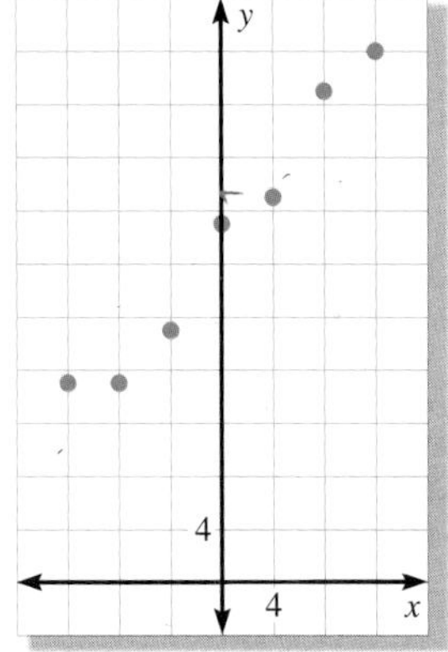

c. In the three election years before 1920, the number of votes cast was less than 20 million. In 1920, the number of votes cast was greater than 20 million. The number of votes cast continued to increase in the three election years since 1920.

✓ GUIDED PRACTICE for Example 4

8. VOTING The presidential election in 1972 was the first election in which 18-year-olds were allowed to vote. The table shows the number (to the nearest million) of votes cast in presidential elections both before and since 1972.

Years before or since 1972	−12	−8	−4	0	4	8	12
Votes (millions)	69	71	73	78	82	87	93

a. *Explain* how you know the graph represents a function.

b. Graph the function represented by the table.

c. *Describe* any trend in the number of votes cast.

4.1 EXERCISES

HOMEWORK KEY

○ = **WORKED-OUT SOLUTIONS** on p. WS7 for Exs. 15, 25, and 37

★ = **STANDARDIZED TEST PRACTICE** Exs. 2, 13, 23, 33, and 41

◆ = **MULTIPLE REPRESENTATIONS** Ex. 40

SKILL PRACTICE

1. VOCABULARY What is the x-coordinate of the point $(5, -3)$? What is the y-coordinate?

2. ★ WRITING One of the coordinates of a point is negative while the other is positive. Can you determine the quadrant in which the point lies? *Explain.*

EXAMPLE 1 on p. 206 for Exs. 3–13

NAMING POINTS Give the coordinates of the point.

3. A **4.** B

5. C **6.** D

7. E **8.** F

9. G **10.** H

11. J **12.** K

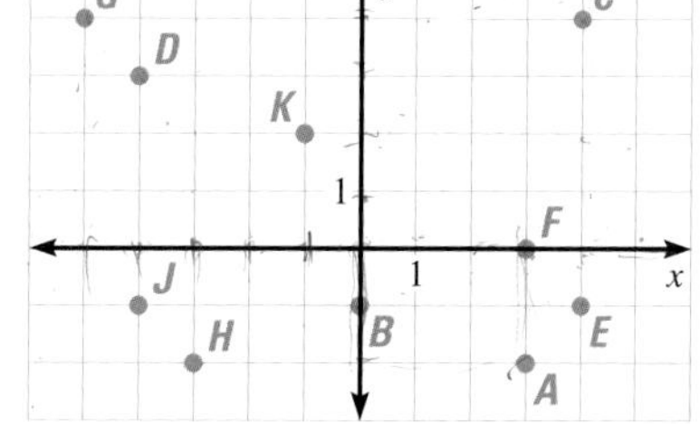

13. ★ MULTIPLE CHOICE A point is located 3 units to the left of the origin and 6 units up. What are the coordinates of the point?

Ⓐ $(3, 6)$ Ⓑ $(-3, 6)$ Ⓒ $(6, 3)$ Ⓓ $(6, -3)$

EXAMPLE 2 on p. 207 for Exs. 14–22

PLOTTING POINTS Plot the point in a coordinate plane. *Describe* the location of the point.

14. $P(5, 5)$ **(15.)** $Q(-1, 5)$ **16.** $R(-3, 0)$ **17.** $S(0, 0)$

18. $T(-3, -4)$ **19.** $U(0, 6)$ **20.** $V(1.5, 4)$ **21.** $W(3, -2.5)$

22. ERROR ANALYSIS *Describe* and correct the error in describing the location of the point $W(6, -6)$.

Point W(6, −6) is 6 units to the left of the origin and 6 units up.

EXAMPLE 3 on p. 207 for Exs. 23–27

23. ★ MULTIPLE CHOICE Which number is in the range of the function whose graph is shown?

Ⓐ -2 Ⓑ -1

Ⓒ 0 Ⓓ 2

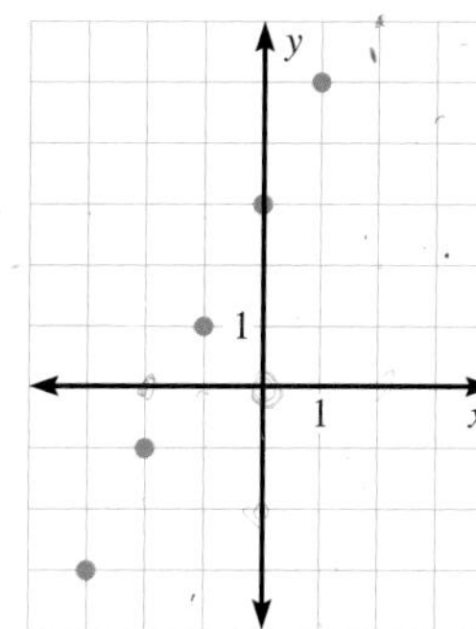

GRAPHING FUNCTIONS **Graph the function with the given domain. Then identify the range of the function.**

24. $y = -x + 1$; domain: $-2, -1, 0, 1, 2$

(25.) $y = 2x - 5$; domain: $-2, -1, 0, 1, 2$

26. $y = -\frac{2}{3}x - 1$; domain: $-6, -3, 0, 3, 6$

27. $y = \frac{1}{2}x + 1$; domain: $-6, -4, -2, 0, 2$

28. **GEOMETRY** Plot the points $W(-4, -2)$, $X(-4, 4)$, $Y(4, 4)$, and $Z(4, -2)$ in a coordinate plane. Connect the points in order. Connect point Z to point W. Identify the resulting figure. Find its perimeter and area.

REASONING **Without plotting the point, tell whether it is in Quadrant I, II, III, or IV. *Explain* your reasoning.**

29. $(4, -11)$

30. $(40, -40)$

31. $(-18, 15)$

32. $(-32, -22)$

33. ★ **WRITING** *Explain* how can you tell by looking at the coordinates of a point whether the point is on the x-axis or on the y-axis.

34. **REASONING** Plot the point $J(-4, 3)$ in a coordinate plane. Plot three additional points in the same coordinate plane so that each of the four points lies in a different quadrant and the figure formed by connecting the points is a square. *Explain* how you located the points.

35. **CHALLENGE** Suppose the point (a, b) lies in Quadrant IV. *Describe* the location of the following points: (b, a), $(2a, -2b)$, and $(-b, -a)$. *Explain* your reasoning.

PROBLEM SOLVING

36. **ASTRONAUT PHOTOGRAPHY** Astronauts use a coordinate system to describe the locations of objects they photograph from space. The x-axis is the equator, 0° latitude. The y-axis is the prime meridian, 0° longitude. The names and coordinates of some lakes photographed from space are given. Use the map to determine on which continent each lake is located.

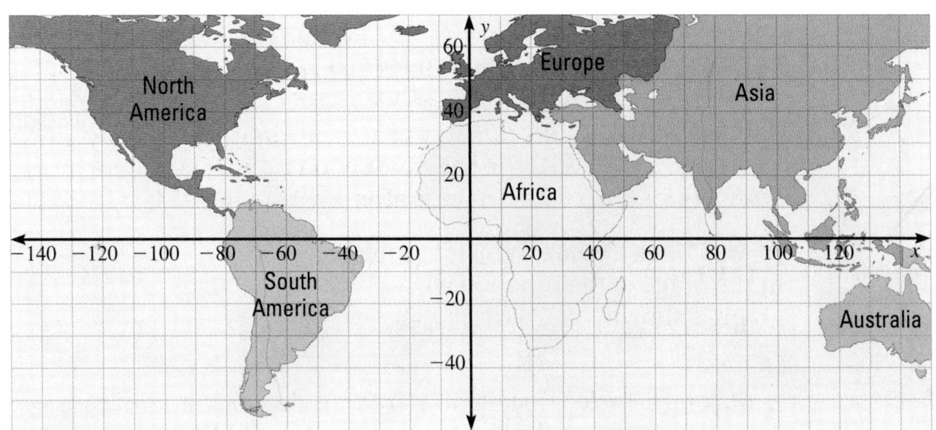

a. Lake Kulundinskoye: (80, 53)

b. Lake Champlain: (−73, 45)

c. Lake Van: (43, 39)

d. Lake Viedma: (−73, −50)

e. Lake Saint Clair: (−83, 43)

f. Starnberger Lake: (12, 48)

@HomeTutor for problem solving help at classzone.com

EXAMPLE 4
on p. 208
for Exs. 37–39

37. **RECORD TEMPERATURES** The table shows the record low temperatures (in degrees Fahrenheit) for Odessa, Texas, for each day in the first week of February. *Explain* how you know the table represents a function. Graph the data from the table.

Day in February	1	2	3	4	5	6	7
Record low (degrees Fahrenheit)	−8	−11	10	8	10	9	11

@HomeTutor for problem solving help at classzone.com

38. **STOCK VALUE** The table shows the change in value (in dollars) of a stock over five days.

Day	1	2	3	4	5
Change in value (dollars)	−0.30	0.10	0.15	0.35	0.11

a. *Explain* how you know the table represents a function. Graph the data from the table.

b. *Describe* any trend in the change in value of the stock.

39. **MULTI-STEP PROBLEM** The difference between what the federal government collects and what it spends during a fiscal year is called the federal surplus or deficit. The table shows the federal surplus or deficit (in billions of dollars) in the 1990s. (A negative number represents a deficit.)

Years since 1990	0	1	2	3	4	5	6	7	8	9
Surplus or deficit (billions)	−221	−269	−290	−255	−203	−164	−108	−22	69	126

a. Graph the function represented by the table.

b. What conclusions can you make from the graph?

40. **MULTIPLE REPRESENTATIONS** Low-density lipoproteins (LDL) transport cholesterol in the bloodstream throughout the body. A high LDL number is associated with an increased risk of cardiovascular disease. A patient's LDL number in 1999 was 189 milligrams per deciliter (mg/dL). To lower that number, the patient went on a diet. The annual LDL numbers for the patient in years after 1999 are 169, 154, 145, 139, and 136.

Years since 1999	1	2	?	?	?
Changes in LDL (mg/dL)	−20	−15	?	?	?

a. Making a Table Use the given information to copy and complete the table that shows the change in the patient's LDL number since 1999.

b. Drawing a Graph Graph the ordered pairs from the table.

c. Describing in Words Based on the graph, what can you conclude about the diet's effectiveness in lowering the patient's LDL number?

41. ★ **EXTENDED RESPONSE** In a scientific study, researchers asked men to report their heights and weights. Then the researchers measured the actual heights and weights of the men. The data for six men are shown in the table. One row of the table represents the data for one man.

Height (inches)			Weight (pounds)		
Reported	**Measured**	**Difference**	**Reported**	**Measured**	**Difference**
70	68	70 − 68 = 2	154	146	154 − 146 = 8
70	67.5	?	141	143	?
78.5	77.5	?	165	168	?
68	69	?	146	143	?
71	72	?	220	223	?
70	70	?	176	176	?

a. **Calculate** Copy and complete the table.

b. **Graph** For each participant, write an ordered pair (x, y) where x is the difference of the reported and measured heights and y is the difference of the reported and measured weights. Then plot the ordered pairs in a coordinate plane.

c. **CHALLENGE** What does the origin represent in this situation?

d. **CHALLENGE** Which quadrant has the greatest number of points? *Explain* what it means for a point to be in that quadrant.

MIXED REVIEW

Evaluate the expression.

42. $4 + 2x^2$ when $x = 6$ *(p. 2)*

43. $6 \cdot 2a^2$ when $a = 3$ *(p. 2)*

44. $4 + 2(-7) + 3$ *(p. 8)*

45. $3(35 - 18)$ *(p. 8)*

Use the distributive property to write an equivalent expression. *(p. 96)*

46. $6(x + 20)$

47. $3x(x + 9)$

48. $-(4 - 5y)$

49. **TRAVEL** You are traveling on the highway at an average speed of 55 miles per hour. How long will it take you to drive 66 miles? *(p. 168)*

PREVIEW Prepare for Lesson 4.2 in Exs. 50–54.

Write the equation so that y is a function of x. *(p. 184)*

50. $4x + y = 6$

51. $x + 7y = 14$

52. $4(y - 6x) = 12$

Tell whether the pairing is a function. *(p. 35)*

53.

Input	−5	−4	−3	−2
Output	−2	0	2	4

54.

Input	−1	0	1	2
Output	10	10	4	1

Perform Transformations

GOAL Perform and describe transformations in a coordinate plane.

Key Vocabulary
- **transformation**
- **translation**
- **vertical stretch or shrink**
- **reflection**

For a given set of points, a **transformation** produces an image by applying a rule to the coordinates of the points. Some types of transformations are *translations, vertical stretches, vertical shrinks,* and *reflections.*

A **translation** moves every point in a figure the same distance in the same direction either horizontally, vertically, or both. You can describe translations algebraically.

Horizontal translation: $(x, y) \rightarrow (x + h, y)$ **Vertical translation:** $(x, y) \rightarrow (x, y + k)$

EXAMPLE 1 Perform a translation

READ TRANSFORMATIONS
If a transformation is performed on a point *A*, the new location of point *A* is indicated by *A′* (read "*A* prime").

The transformation $(x, y) \rightarrow (x, y + 3)$ moves $\triangle ABC$ up 3 units.

Original		Image
$A(3, 0)$	$\rightarrow$	$A'(3, 3)$
$B(4, 2)$	$\rightarrow$	$B'(4, 5)$
$C(5, 0)$	$\rightarrow$	$C'(5, 3)$

The result of the transformation is $\triangle A'B'C'$.

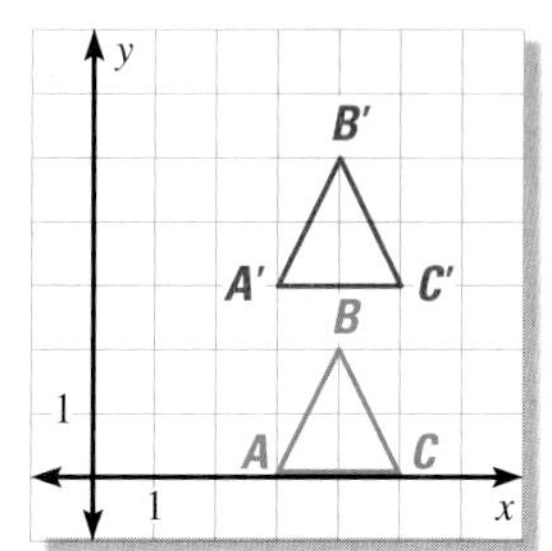

A **vertical stretch or shrink** moves every point in a figure away from the *x*-axis (a vertical stretch) or toward the *x*-axis (a vertical shrink), while points on the *x*-axis remain fixed. A **reflection** flips a figure in a line. You can describe vertical stretches and shrinks with or without reflection in the *x*-axis algebraically.

Vertical stretch:
$(x, y) \rightarrow (x, ay)$ where $a > 1$

Vertical shrink:
$(x, y) \rightarrow (x, ay)$ where $0 < a < 1$

Vertical stretch with reflection in the *x*-axis:
$(x, y) \rightarrow (x, ay)$ where $a < -1$

Vertical shrink with reflection in the *x*-axis:
$(x, y) \rightarrow (x, ay)$ where $-1 < a < 0$

EXAMPLE 2 Perform a vertical stretch with reflection

The transformation $(x, y) \rightarrow (x, -2y)$ vertically stretches $\triangle ABC$ and reflects it in the *x*-axis.

Original		Image
$A(3, 0)$	$\rightarrow$	$A'(3, 0)$
$B(4, 2)$	$\rightarrow$	$B'(4, -4)$
$C(5, 0)$	$\rightarrow$	$C'(5, 0)$

The result of the transformation is $\triangle A'B'C'$.

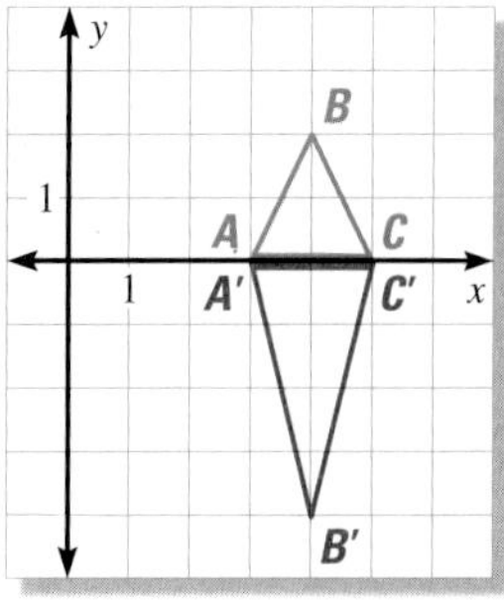

CONCPT SUMMARY *For Your Notebook*

Identifying Transformations

Translation		Vertical stretch or shrink	
Horizontal $(x, y) \to (x + h, y)$	**Vertical** $(x, y) \to (x, y + k)$	**Without reflection** $(x, y) \to (x, ay)$ where $a > 0$	**With reflection** $(x, y) \to (x, ay)$ where $a < 0$
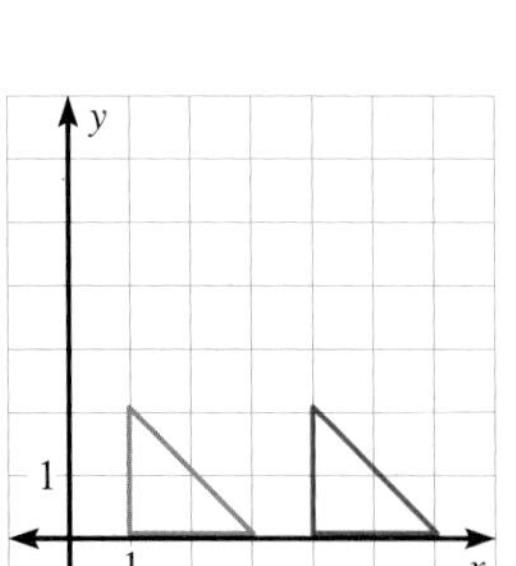	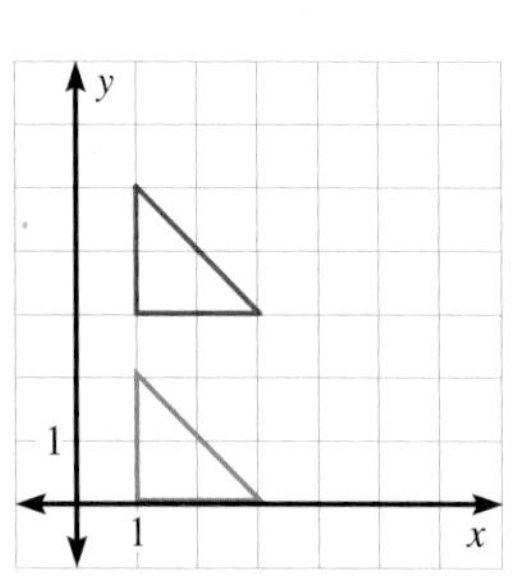	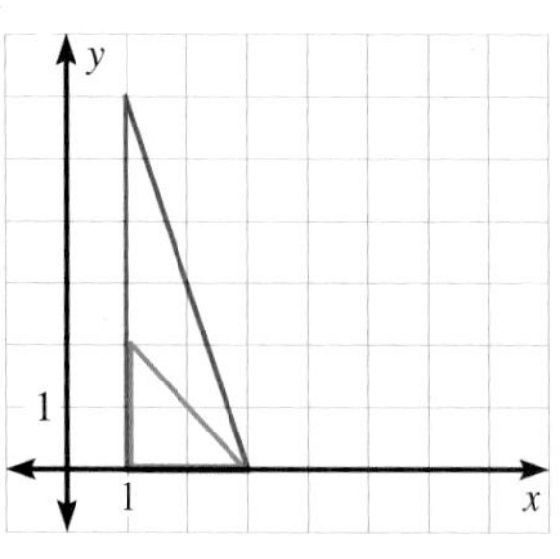	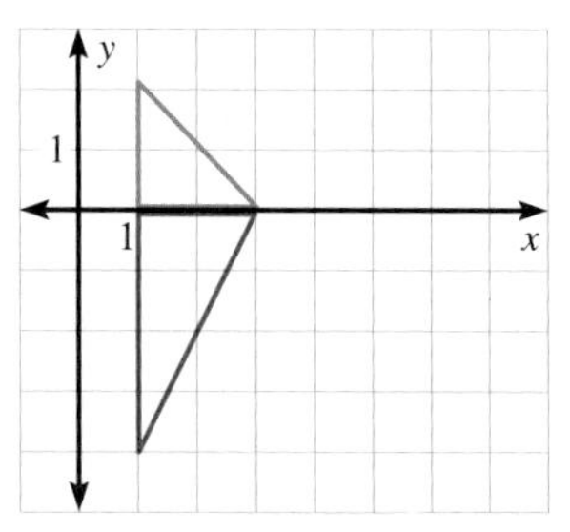

PRACTICE

1. **VOCABULARY** Does a translation or a vertical stretch always produce a figure that is the same size and shape as the original figure? *Explain.*

2. ★ **WRITING** *Describe* the vertical shrink $(x, y) \to (x, \frac{1}{2}y)$ in words.

EXAMPLES 1 and 2 on p. 213 for Exs. 3–14

DESCRIBING TRANSFORMATIONS **Use words to describe the transformation of the blue figure to the red figure.**

3. 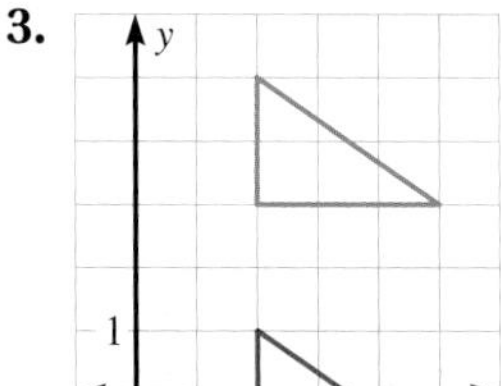

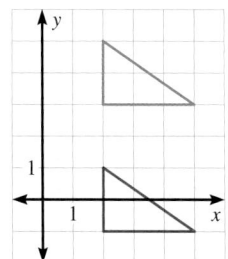

4. 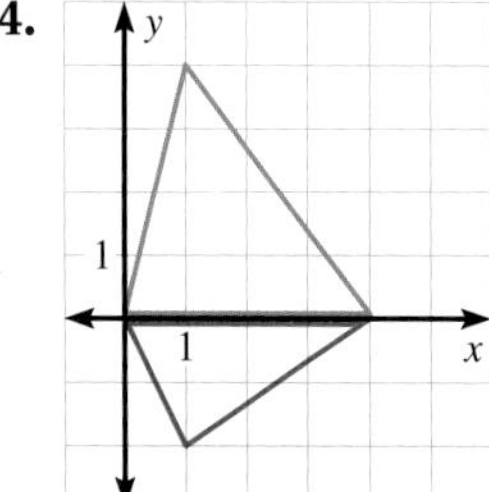

5. 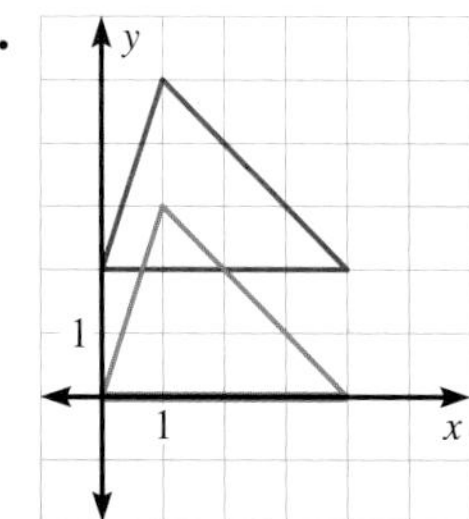

PERFORMING TRANSFORMATIONS **Square *ABCD* has vertices at (0, 0), (0, 2), (2, 2), and (2, 0). Perform the indicated transformation. Then give the coordinates of figure *A′B′C′D′*.**

6. $(x, y) \to (x, y - 5)$
7. $(x, y) \to (x, y + 1)$
8. $(x, y) \to (x, y - 7)$
9. $(x, y) \to (x, -y)$
10. $(x, y) \to (x, 4y)$
11. $(x, y) \to (x, -\frac{1}{2}y)$
12. $(x, y) \to (x + 2, y + 3)$
13. $(x, y) \to (x - 1, y + 4)$
14. $(x, y) \to (x + 3, y)$

15. ★ **WRITING** A square has vertices at (0, 0), (0, 3), (3, 3), and (3, 0). Tell how you could use a transformation to move the square so that it has new vertices at (0, 0), (0, −3), (3, −3), and (3, 0).

4.2 Graph Linear Equations

Before You plotted points in a coordinate plane.

Now You will graph linear equations in a coordinate plane.

Why? So you can find how meteorologists collect data, as in Ex. 40.

Key Vocabulary
- **standard form of a linear equation**
- **linear function**

An example of an equation in two variables is $2x + 5y = 8$. A **solution of an equation in two variables**, x and y, is an ordered pair (x, y) that produces a true statement when the values of x and y are substituted into the equation.

EXAMPLE 1 Standardized Test Practice

Which ordered pair is a solution of $3x - y = 7$?

Ⓐ (3, 4) Ⓑ (1, −4) Ⓒ (5, −3) Ⓓ (−1, −2)

Solution

Check whether each ordered pair is a solution of the equation.

Test (3, 4): $3x - y = 7$		Write original equation.
$3(3) - 4 \stackrel{?}{=} 7$		Substitute 3 for x and 4 for y.
$5 = 7$ ✗		Simplify.
Test (1, −4): $3x - y = 7$		Write original equation.
$3(1) - (-4) \stackrel{?}{=} 7$		Substitute 1 for x and −4 for y.
$7 = 7$ ✓		Simplify.

So, (3, 4) is *not* a solution, but (1, −4) is a solution of $3x - y = 7$.

▶ The correct answer is B. Ⓐ Ⓑ Ⓒ Ⓓ

GUIDED PRACTICE for Example 1

1. Tell whether $\left(4, -\frac{1}{2}\right)$ is a solution of $x + 2y = 5$.

GRAPHS The **graph of an equation in two variables** is the set of points in a coordinate plane that represent all solutions of the equation. If the variables in an equation represent real numbers, one way to graph the equation is to make a table of values, plot enough points to recognize a pattern, and then connect the points. When making a table of values, choose convenient values of x that include negative values, zero, and positive values.

EXAMPLE 2 Graph an equation

Graph the equation $-2x + y = -3$.

Solution

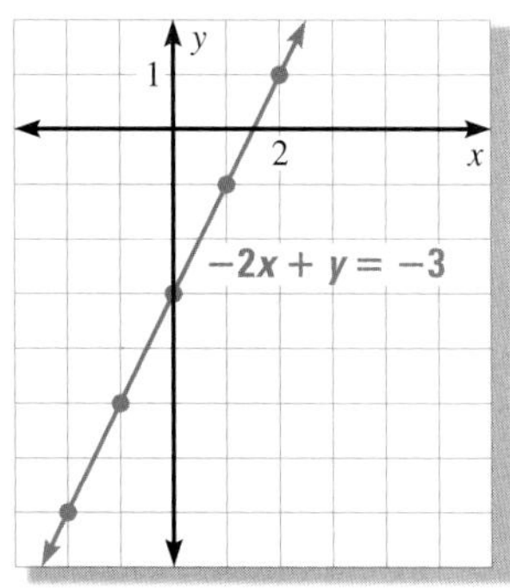

STEP 1 **Solve** the equation for y.

$$-2x + y = -3$$

$$y = 2x - 3$$

DRAW A GRAPH
If you continued to find solutions of the equation and plotted them, the line would fill in.

STEP 2 **Make** a table by choosing a few values for x and finding the values of y.

x	−2	−1	0	1	2
y	−7	−5	−3	−1	1

STEP 3 **Plot** the points. Notice that the points appear to lie on a line.

STEP 4 **Connect** the points by drawing a line through them. Use arrows to indicate that the graph goes on without end.

LINEAR EQUATIONS A **linear equation** is an equation whose graph is a line, such as the equation in Example 2. The **standard form** of a linear equation is

$$Ax + By = C$$

where A, B, and C are real numbers and A and B are not both zero.

Consider what happens when $A = 0$ or when $B = 0$. When $A = 0$, the equation becomes $By = C$, or $y = \frac{C}{B}$. Because $\frac{C}{B}$ is a constant, you can write $y = b$. Similarly, when $B = 0$, the equation becomes $Ax = C$, or $x = \frac{C}{A}$, and you can write $x = a$.

EXAMPLE 3 Graph $y = b$ and $x = a$

Graph (a) $y = 2$ and (b) $x = -1$.

Solution

FIND A SOLUTION
The equations $y = 2$ and $0x + 1y = 2$ are equivalent. For any value of x, the ordered pair $(x, 2)$ is a solution of $y = 2$.

a. For every value of x, the value of y is 2. The graph of the equation $y = 2$ is a horizontal line 2 units above the x-axis.

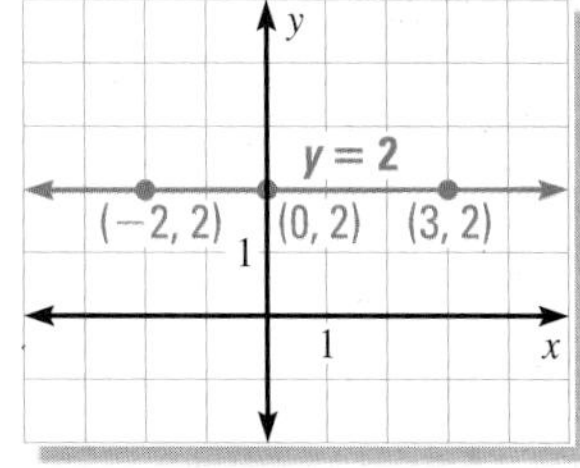

b. For every value of y, the value of x is −1. The graph of the equation $x = -1$ is a vertical line 1 unit to the left of the y-axis.

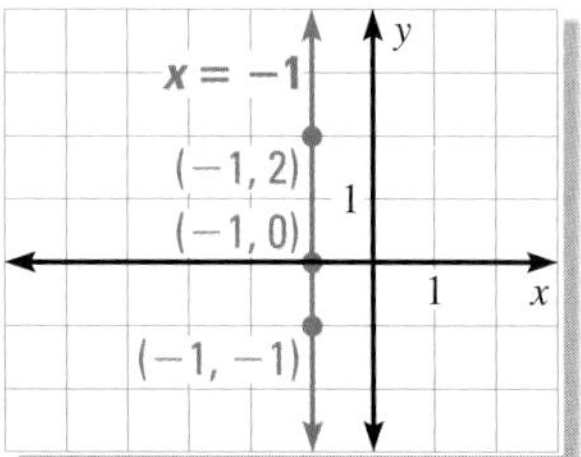

Animated Algebra at classzone.com

KEY CONCEPT — *For Your Notebook*

Equations of Horizontal and Vertical Lines

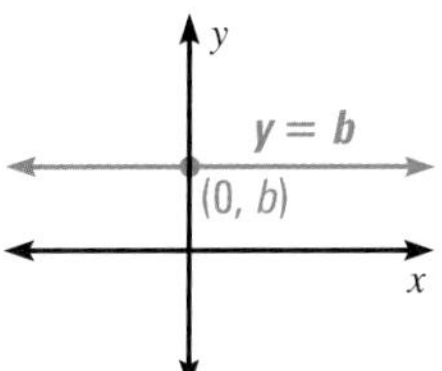

The graph of $y = b$ is a horizontal line. The line passes through the point $(0, b)$.

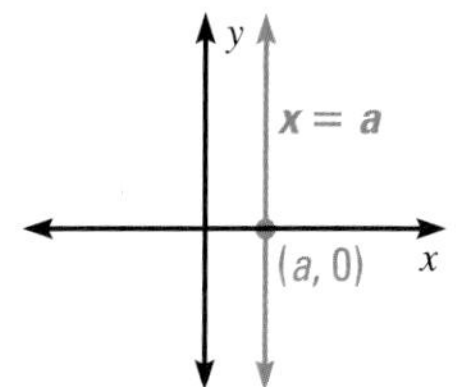

The graph of $x = a$ is a vertical line. The line passes through the point $(a, 0)$.

GUIDED PRACTICE for Examples 2 and 3

Graph the equation.

2. $y + 3x = -2$ **3.** $y = 2.5$ **4.** $x = -4$

LINEAR FUNCTIONS In Example 3, $y = 2$ is a function, while $x = -1$ is not a function. The equation $Ax + By = C$ represents a **linear function** provided $B \neq 0$ (that is, provided the graph of the equation is not a vertical line). If the domain of a linear function is not specified, it is understood to be all real numbers. The domain can be restricted, as shown in Example 4.

EXAMPLE 4 Graph a linear function

Graph the function $y = -\frac{1}{2}x + 4$ with domain $x \geq 0$. Then identify the range of the function.

Solution

ANALYZE A FUNCTION

The function in Example 4 is called a *continuous* function. To learn about continuous functions, see p. 223.

STEP 1 **Make** a table.

x	0	2	4	6	8
y	4	3	2	1	0

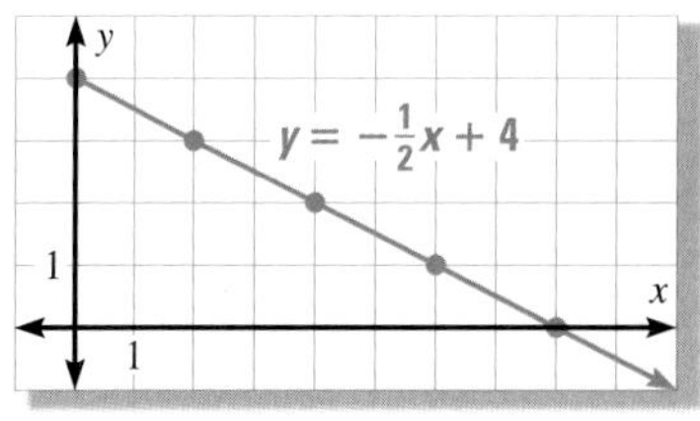

STEP 2 **Plot** the points.

STEP 3 **Connect** the points with a ray because the domain is restricted.

STEP 4 **Identify** the range. From the graph, you can see that all points have a y-coordinate of 4 or less, so the range of the function is $y \leq 4$.

GUIDED PRACTICE for Example 4

5. Graph the function $y = -3x + 1$ with domain $x \leq 0$. Then identify the range of the function.

EXAMPLE 5 Solve a multi-step problem

RUNNING The distance d (in miles) that a runner travels is given by the function $d = 6t$ where t is the time (in hours) spent running. The runner plans to go for a 1.5 hour run. Graph the function and identify its domain and range.

Solution

STEP 1 **Identify** whether the problem specifies the domain or the range. You know the amount of time the runner plans to spend running. Because time is the independent variable, the domain is specified in this problem. The domain of the function is $0 \le t \le 1.5$.

ANALYZE GRAPHS

In Example 2, the domain is unrestricted, and the graph is a *line*. In Example 4, the domain is restricted to $x \ge 0$, and the graph is a *ray*. Here, the domain is restricted to $0 \le t \le 1.5$, and the graph is a *line segment*.

STEP 2 **Graph** the function. Make a table of values. Then plot and connect the points.

t (hours)	0	0.5	1	1.5
d (miles)	0	3	6	9

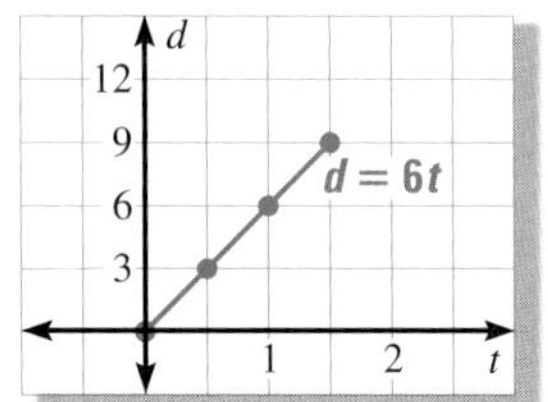

STEP 3 **Identify** the unspecified domain or range. From the table or graph, you can see that the range of the function is $0 \le d \le 9$.

EXAMPLE 6 Solve a related problem

WHAT IF? Suppose the runner in Example 5 instead plans to run 12 miles. Graph the function and identify its domain and range.

Solution

STEP 1 **Identify** whether the problem specifies the domain or the range. You are given the distance that the runner plans to travel. Because distance is the dependent variable, the range is specified in this problem. The range of the function is $0 \le d \le 12$.

STEP 2 **Graph** the function. To make a table, you can substitute d-values (be sure to include 0 and 12) into the function $d = 6t$ and solve for t.

SOLVE FOR t

To find the time it takes the runner to run 12 miles, solve the equation $6t = 12$ to get $t = 2$.

t (hours)	0	1	2
d (miles)	0	6	12

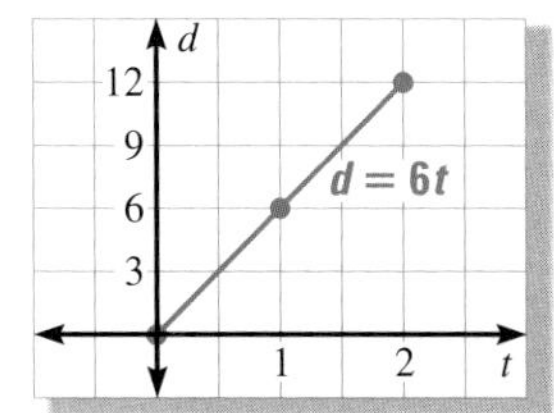

STEP 3 **Identify** the unspecified domain or range. From the table or graph, you can see that the domain of the function is $0 \le t \le 2$.

✓ GUIDED PRACTICE for Examples 5 and 6

6. **GAS COSTS** For gas that costs \$2 per gallon, the equation $C = 2g$ gives the cost C (in dollars) of pumping g gallons of gas. You plan to pump \$10 worth of gas. Graph the function and identify its domain and range.

4.2 EXERCISES

HOMEWORK KEY

○ = **WORKED-OUT SOLUTIONS** on p. WS8 for Exs. 3, 11, and 37

★ = **STANDARDIZED TEST PRACTICE** Exs. 2, 10, 32, 33, 39, and 41

◆ = **MULTIPLE REPRESENTATIONS** Ex. 40

SKILL PRACTICE

1. **VOCABULARY** The equation $Ax + By = C$ represents a(n) _?_ provided $B \neq 0$.

2. ★ **WRITING** Is the equation $y = 6x + 4$ in standard form? *Explain.*

EXAMPLE 1 on p. 215 for Exs. 3–10

CHECKING SOLUTIONS **Tell whether the ordered pair is a solution of the equation.**

3. $2y + x = 4$; $(-2, 3)$
4. $3x - 2y = -5$; $(-1, 1)$
5. $x = 9$; $(9, 6)$
6. $y = -7$; $(-7, 0)$
7. $-7x - 4y = 1$; $(-3, -5)$
8. $-5y - 6x = 0$; $(-6, 5)$

9. **ERROR ANALYSIS** *Describe* and correct the error in determining whether (8, 11) is a solution of $y - x = -3$.

$y - x = -3$

$8 - 11 = -3$

$-3 = -3$ (8, 11) is a solution.

10. ★ **MULTIPLE CHOICE** Which ordered pair is a solution of $6x + 3y = 18$?

Ⓐ $(-2, -10)$ Ⓑ $(-2, 10)$ Ⓒ $(2, 10)$ Ⓓ $(10, -2)$

EXAMPLES 2 and 3 on p. 216 for Exs. 11–25

GRAPHING EQUATIONS **Graph the equation.**

11. $y + x = 2$
12. $y - 2x = 5$
13. $y - 3x = 0$
14. $y + 4x = 1$
15. $2y - 6x = 10$
16. $3y + 4x = 12$
17. $x - 2y = 3$
18. $3x + 2y = 8$
19. $x = 0$
20. $y = 0$
21. $y = -4$
22. $x = 2$

MATCHING EQUATIONS WITH GRAPHS **Match the equation with its graph.**

23. $y - x = 0$
24. $x = -2$
25. $y = -1$

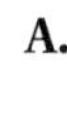

A.

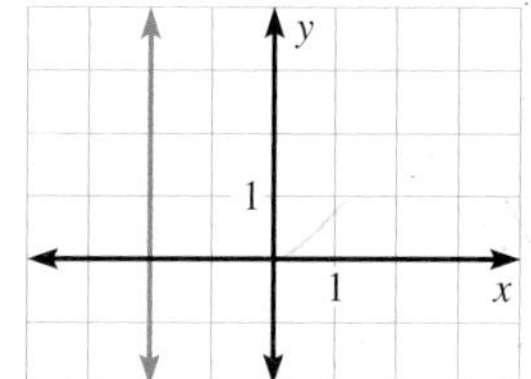

B.

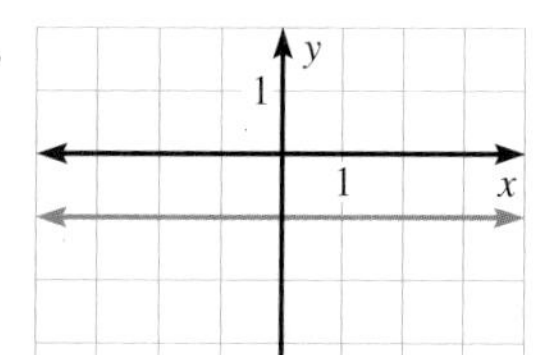

C.

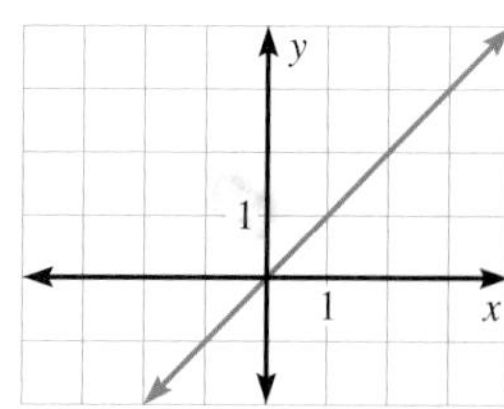

EXAMPLE 4 on p. 217 for Exs. 26–31

GRAPHING FUNCTIONS **Graph the function with the given domain. Then identify the range of the function.**

26. $y = 3x - 2$; domain: $x \geq 0$
27. $y = -5x + 3$; domain: $x \leq 0$
28. $y = 4$; domain: $x \leq 5$
29. $y = -6$; domain: $x \geq 5$
30. $y = 2x + 3$; domain: $-4 \leq x \leq 0$
31. $y = -x - 1$; domain: $-1 \leq x \leq 3$

32. ★ **OPEN-ENDED** Graph $x - y = 3$ and $2x - 2y = 6$. *Explain* why the equations look different but have the same graph. Find another equation that looks different from the two given equations but has the same graph.

33. ★ **MULTIPLE CHOICE** Which statement is true for the function whose graph is shown?

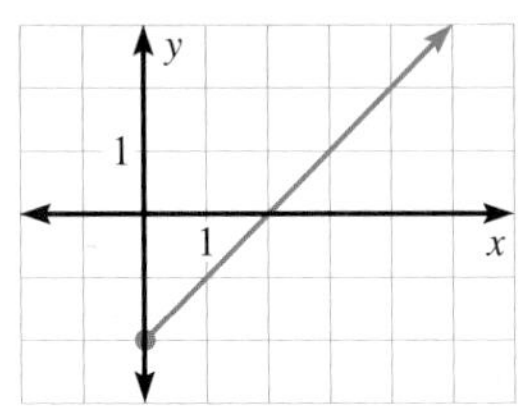

Ⓐ The domain is unrestricted.

Ⓑ The domain is $x \leq -2$.

Ⓒ The range is $y \leq -2$.

Ⓓ The range is $y \geq -2$.

34. **CHALLENGE** If $(3, n)$ is a solution of $Ax + 3y = 6$ and $(n, 5)$ is a solution of $5x + y = 20$, what is the value of A?

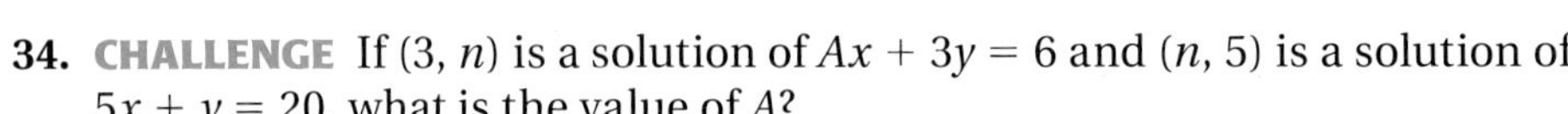

PROBLEM SOLVING

EXAMPLES 5 and 6 on p. 218 for Exs. 35–39

35. **BAKING** The weight w (in pounds) of a loaf of bread that a recipe yields is given by the function $w = \frac{1}{2}f$ where f is the number of cups of flour used. You have 4 cups of flour. Graph the function and identify its domain and range. What is the weight of the largest loaf of bread you can make?

@HomeTutor for problem solving help at classzone.com

36. **TRAVEL** After visiting relatives who live 200 miles away, your family drives home at an average speed of 50 miles per hour. Your distance d (in miles) from home is given by $d = 200 - 50t$ where t is the time (in hours) spent driving. Graph the function and identify its domain and range. What is your distance from home after driving for 1.5 hours?

@HomeTutor for problem solving help at classzone.com

37. **EARTH SCIENCE** The temperature T (in degrees Celsius) of Earth's crust can be modeled by the function $T = 20 + 25d$ where d is the distance (in kilometers) from the surface.

   a. A scientist studies organisms in the first 4 kilometers of Earth's crust. Graph the function and identify its domain and range. What is the temperature at the deepest part of the section of crust?

   b. Suppose the scientist studies organisms in a section of the crust where the temperature is between 20°C and 95°C. Graph the function and identify its domain and range. How many kilometers deep is the section of crust?

38. **MULTI-STEP PROBLEM** A fashion designer orders fabric that costs \$30 per yard. The designer wants the fabric to be dyed, which costs \$100. The total cost C (in dollars) of the fabric is given by the function

$$C = 30f + 100$$

where f is the number of yards of fabric.

   a. The designer orders 3 yards of fabric. How much does the fabric cost? *Explain.*

   b. Suppose the designer can spend \$500 on fabric. How many yards of fabric can the designer buy? *Explain.*

39. ★ **SHORT RESPONSE** An emergency cell phone charger requires you to turn a small crank in order to create the energy needed to recharge the phone's battery. If you turn the crank 120 times per minute, the total number r of revolutions that you turn the crank is given by

$$r = 120t$$

where t is the time (in minutes) spent turning the crank.

a. Graph the function and identify its domain and range.

b. Identify the domain and range if you stop turning the crank after 4 minutes. *Explain* how this affects the appearance of the graph.

40. ❖ **MULTIPLE REPRESENTATIONS** The National Weather Service releases weather balloons twice daily at over 90 locations in the United States in order to collect data for meteorologists. The height h (in feet) of a balloon is a function of the time t (in seconds) after the balloon is released, as shown.

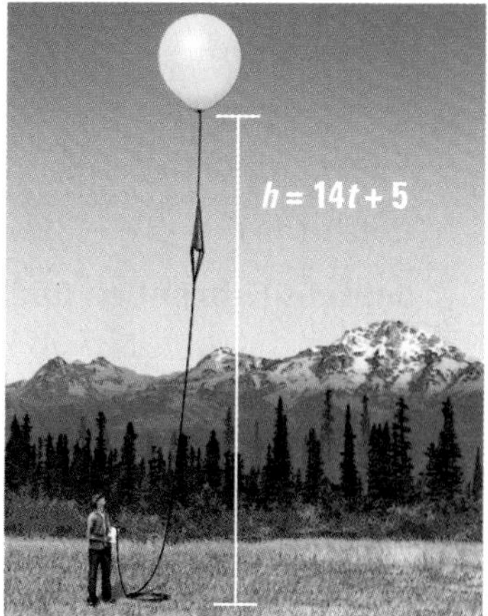

a. Making a Table Make a table showing the height of a balloon after t seconds for $t = 0$ through $t = 10$.

b. Drawing a Graph A balloon bursts after a flight of about 7200 seconds. Graph the function and identify the domain and range.

41. ★ **EXTENDED RESPONSE** Students can pay for lunch at a school in one of two ways. Students can either make a payment of \$30 per month or they can buy lunch daily for \$2.50 per lunch.

a. Graph Graph the function $y = 30$ to represent the monthly payment plan. Using the same coordinate plane, graph the function $y = 2.5x$ to represent the daily payment plan.

b. CHALLENGE What are the coordinates of the point that is a solution of both functions? What does that point mean in this situation?

c. CHALLENGE A student eats an average of 15 school lunches per month. How should the student pay, daily or monthly? *Explain*.

MIXED REVIEW

Solve the equation.

42. $12x = 144$ *(p. 134)*

43. $-4x = 30$ *(p. 134)*

44. $5.7x - 2x = 14.8$ *(p. 141)*

45. $x - 4(x + 13) = 26$ *(p. 148)*

46. $6x - 4x + 13 = 27 - 2x$ *(p. 154)*

47. $5x - \frac{1}{4}(24 + 8x) = 2x - 5$ *(p. 154)*

PREVIEW
Prepare for Lesson 4.3 in Exs. 48–55.

Plot the point in a coordinate plane. *Describe* the location of the point. *(p. 206)*

48. $(3, 5)$

49. $(-3, 2)$

50. $(0, -2)$

51. $(-5, 0)$

52. $(-2, -2)$

53. $\left(\frac{1}{3}, 0\right)$

54. $\left(-\frac{1}{2}, \frac{3}{4}\right)$

55. $(0, 6.2)$

Graphing Calculator ACTIVITY *Use after Lesson 4.2*

@HomeTutor
classzone.com
Keystrokes

4.2 Graphing Linear Equations

QUESTION How do you graph an equation on a graphing calculator?

EXAMPLE Use a graph to solve a problem

The formula to convert temperature from degrees Fahrenheit to degrees Celsius is $C = \frac{5}{9}(F - 32)$. Graph the equation. At what temperature are degrees Fahrenheit and degrees Celsius equal?

STEP 1 ***Rewrite and enter equation***

Rewrite the equation using x for F and y for C. Enter the equation into the Y= screen. Put parentheses around the fraction $\frac{5}{9}$.

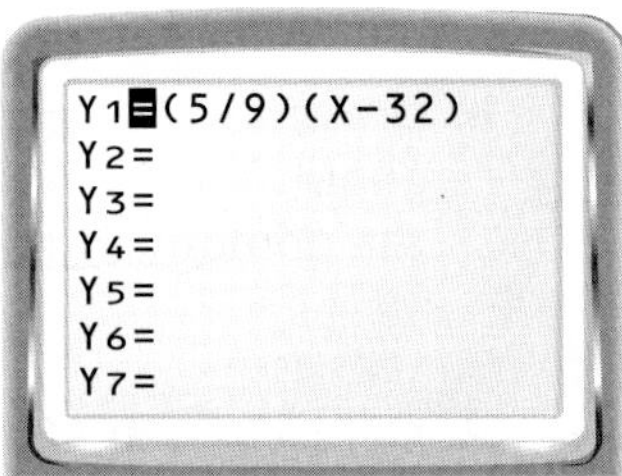

STEP 2 ***Set window***

The screen is a "window" that lets you look at part of a coordinate plane. Press WINDOW to set the borders of the graph. A friendly window for this equation is $-94 \le x \le 94$ and $-100 \le y \le 100$.

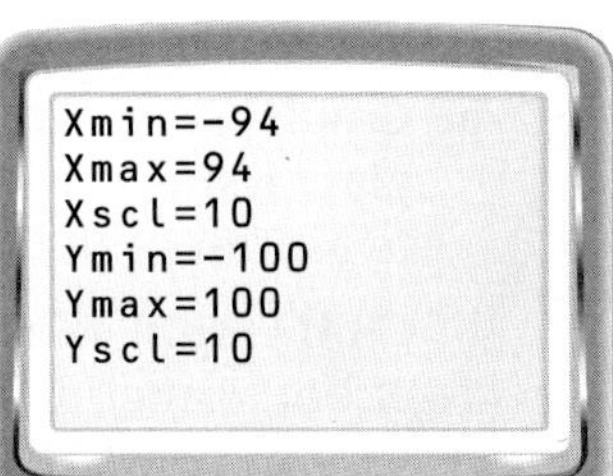

STEP 3 ***Graph and trace equation***

Press TRACE and use the left and right arrows to move the cursor along the graph until the x-coordinate and y-coordinate are equal. From the graph, you can see that degrees Fahrenheit and degrees Celsius are equal at -40.

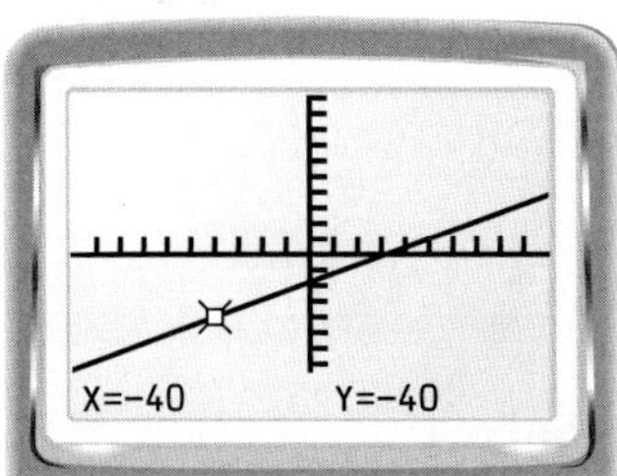

PRACTICE

Graph the equation. Find the unknown value in the ordered pair.

1. $y = 8 - x$; (2.4, ?) **2.** $y = 2x + 3$; (?, 0.8) **3.** $y = -4.5x + 1$; (1.4, ?)

4. SPEED OF SOUND The speed s (in meters per second) of sound in air can be modeled by $s = 331.1 + 0.61T$ where T is the air temperature in degrees Celsius. Graph the equation. Estimate the speed of sound when the temperature is 20°C.

Identify Discrete and Continuous Functions

GOAL Graph and classify discrete and continuous functions.

Key Vocabulary
- **discrete function**
- **continuous function**

The graph of a function can consist of individual points, as in the graph in Example 3 on page 207. The graph of a function can also be a line or a part of a line with no breaks, as in the graph in Example 4 on page 217.

KEY CONCEPT *For Your Notebook*

Identifying Discrete and Continuous Functions

A **discrete function** has a graph that consists of isolated points.

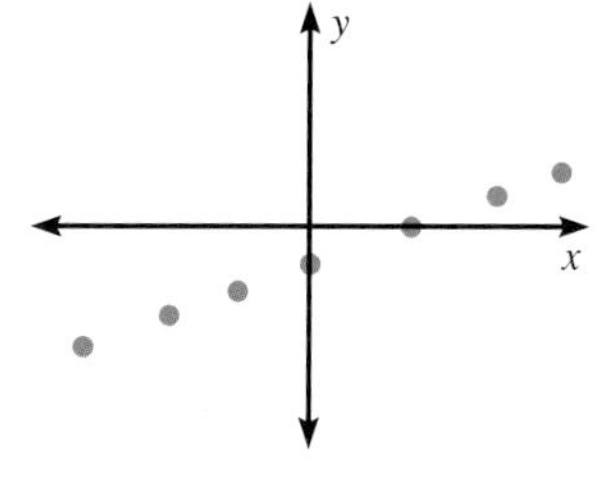

A **continuous function** has a graph that is unbroken.

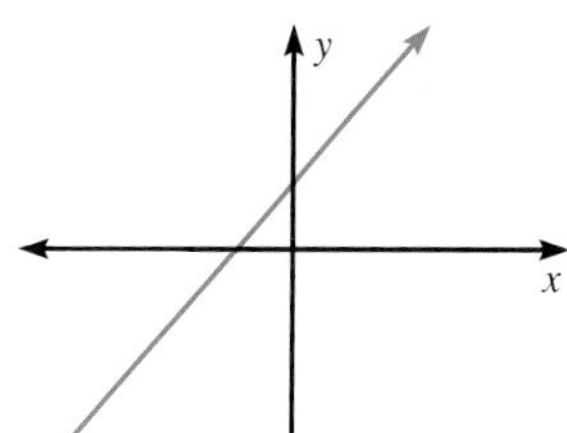

EXAMPLE 1 Graph and classify a function

Graph the function $y = 2x - 1$ with the given domain. Classify the function as discrete or continuous.

a. Domain: $x = 0, 1, 2, 3$

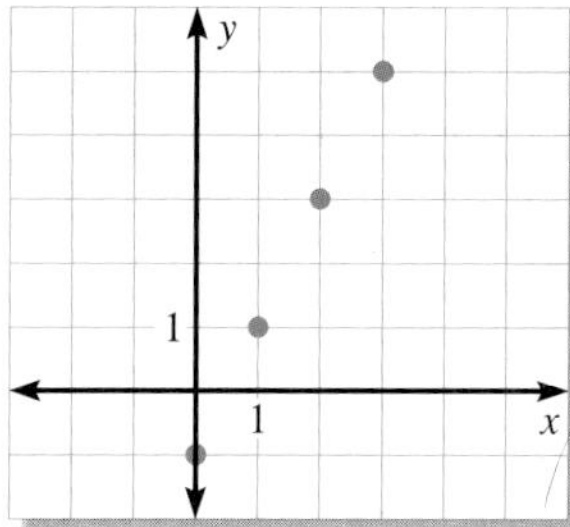

The graph consists of individual points, so the function is discrete.

b. Domain: $x \geq 0$

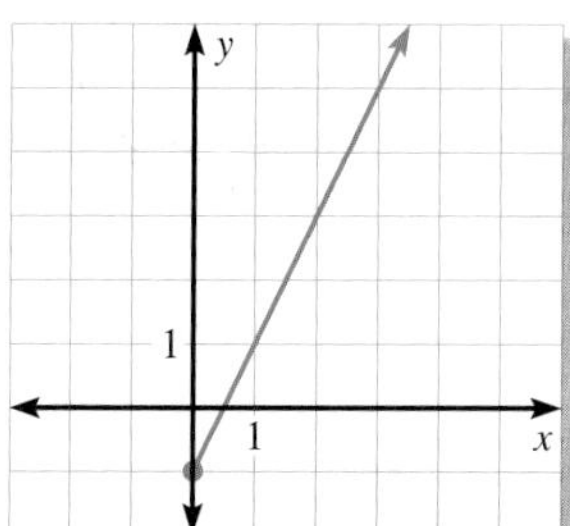

The graph is unbroken, so the function is continuous.

GRAPHS As a general rule, you can tell that a function is continuous if you do not have to lift your pencil from the paper to draw its graph, as in part (b) of Example 1.

EXAMPLE 2 Classify and graph a real-world function

Tell whether the function represented by the table is discrete or continuous. Explain. If continuous, graph the function and find the value of y when $x = 1.5$.

Duration of storm (hours), x	1	2	3
Amount of rain (inches), y	0.5	1	1.5

Solution

Although the table shows the amount of rain that has fallen after whole numbers of hours only, it makes sense to talk about the amount of rain after any amount of time during the storm. So, the table represents a continuous function.

The graph of the function is shown. To find the value of y when $x = 1.5$, start at 1.5 on the x-axis, move up to the graph, and move over to the y-axis. The y-value is about 0.75. So, about 0.75 inch of rain has fallen after 1.5 hours.

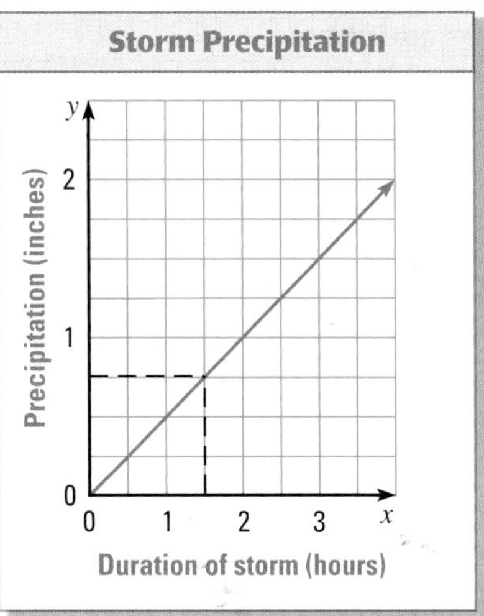

PRACTICE

EXAMPLE 1 on p. 223 for Exs. 1–6

Graph the function with the given domain. Classify the function as discrete or continuous.

1. $y = -2x + 3$; domain: $-2, -1, 0, 1, 2$
2. $y = x$; domain: all real numbers
3. $y = -\frac{1}{3}x + 1$; domain: $-12, -6, 0, 6, 12$
4. $y = 0.5x$; domain: $-2, -1, 0, 1, 2$
5. $y = 3x - 4$; domain: $x \leq 0$
6. $y = \frac{2}{3}x + \frac{1}{3}$; domain: $x \geq -2$

EXAMPLE 2 on p. 224 for Exs. 7–9

Tell whether the function represented by the table is discrete or continuous. *Explain.* If continuous, graph the function and find the value of y when $x = 3.5$. Round your answer to the nearest hundredth.

7.

Number of DVD rentals, x	1	2	3	4
Cost of rentals (dollars), y	4.50	9.00	13.50	18.00

8.

Hours since 12 P.M., x	2	4	6	8
Distance driven (miles), y	100	200	300	400

9.

Volume of water (cubic inches), x	3	6	9	12
Approximate weight of water (pounds), y	0.1	0.2	0.3	0.4

4.3 Graph Using Intercepts

Before You graphed a linear equation using a table of values.

Now You will graph a linear equation using intercepts.

Why So you can find a submersible's location, as in Example 5.

Key Vocabulary
- ***x*-intercept**
- ***y*-intercept**

You can use the fact that two points determine a line to graph a linear equation. Two convenient points are the points where the graph crosses the axes.

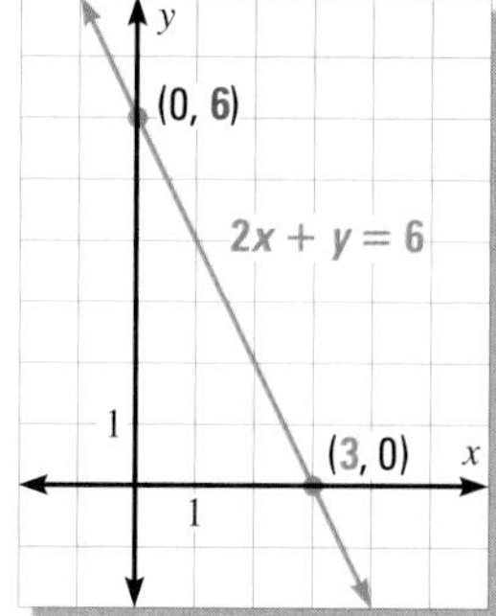

An ***x*-intercept** of a graph is the x-coordinate of a point where the graph crosses the x-axis. A ***y*-intercept** of a graph is the y-coordinate of a point where the graph crosses the y-axis.

To find the x-intercept of the graph of a linear equation, find the value of x when $y = 0$. To find the y-intercept of the graph, find the value of y when $x = 0$.

EXAMPLE 1 Find the intercepts of the graph of an equation

Find the x-intercept and the y-intercept of the graph of $2x + 7y = 28$.

Solution

To find the x-intercept, substitute 0 for y and solve for x.

$2x + 7y = 28$ **Write original equation.**

$2x + 7(0) = 28$ **Substitute 0 for y.**

$x = \frac{28}{2} = 14$ **Solve for x.**

To find the y-intercept, substitute 0 for x and solve for y.

$2x + 7y = 28$ **Write original equation.**

$2(0) + 7y = 28$ **Substitute 0 for x.**

$y = \frac{28}{7} = 4$ **Solve for y.**

▶ The x-intercept is 14. The y-intercept is 4.

✓ **GUIDED PRACTICE** for Example 1

Find the x-intercept and the y-intercept of the graph of the equation.

1. $3x + 2y = 6$ **2.** $4x - 2y = 10$ **3.** $-3x + 5y = -15$

EXAMPLE 2 Use intercepts to graph an equation

Graph the equation $x + 2y = 4$.

Solution

STEP 1 **Find** the intercepts.

$x + 2y = 4$	$x + 2y = 4$
$x + 2(0) = 4$	$0 + 2y = 4$
$x = 4 \leftarrow$ **x-intercept**	$y = 2 \leftarrow$ **y-intercept**

STEP 2 **Plot** points. The x-intercept is 4, so plot the point $(4, 0)$. The y-intercept is 2, so plot the point $(0, 2)$. Draw a line through the points.

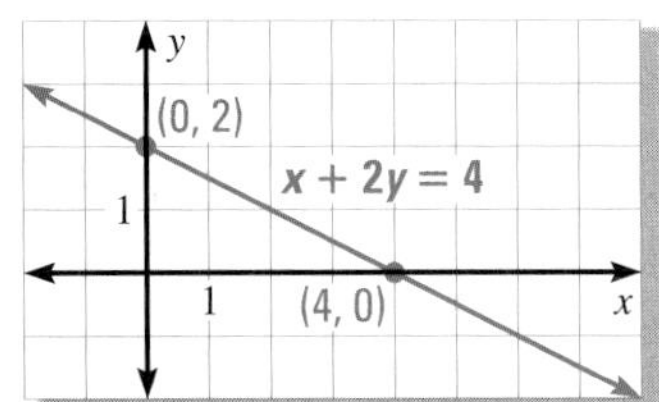

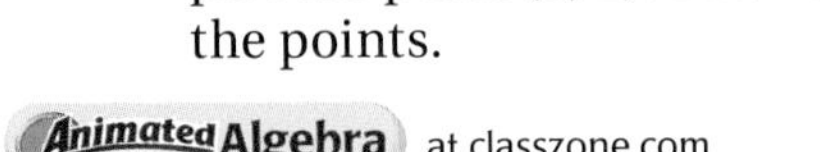

at classzone.com

CHECK A GRAPH
Be sure to check the graph by finding a third solution of the equation and checking to see that the corresponding point is on the graph.

EXAMPLE 3 Use a graph to find intercepts

The graph crosses the x-axis at $(2, 0)$. The x-intercept is 2. The graph crosses the y-axis at $(0, -1)$. The y-intercept is -1.

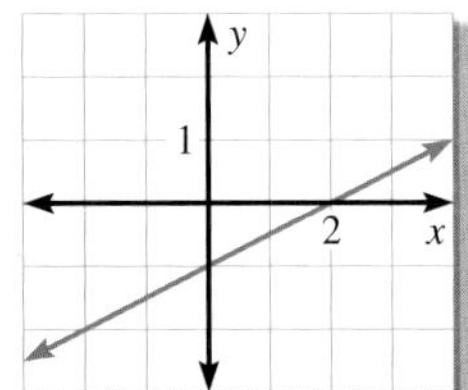

✓ GUIDED PRACTICE for Examples 2 and 3

4. Graph $6x + 7y = 42$. Label the points where the line crosses the axes.

5. Identify the x-intercept and the y-intercept of the graph shown at the right.

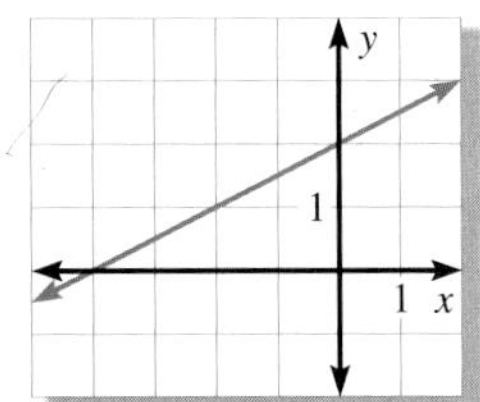

KEY CONCEPT *For Your Notebook*

Relating Intercepts, Points, and Graphs

Intercepts	**Points**
The x intercept of a graph is a.	The graph crosses the x-axis at $(a, 0)$.
The y-intercept of a graph is b.	The graph crosses the y-axis at $(0, b)$.

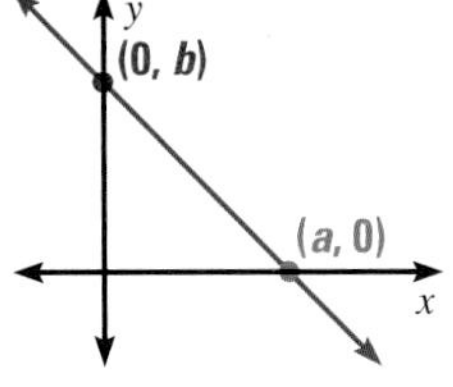

EXAMPLE 4 Solve a multi-step problem

EVENT PLANNING You are helping to plan an awards banquet for your school, and you need to rent tables to seat 180 people. Tables come in two sizes. Small tables seat 4 people, and large tables seat 6 people. This situation can be modeled by the equation

$$4x + 6y = 180$$

where x is the number of small tables and y is the number of large tables.

- Find the intercepts of the graph of the equation.
- Graph the equation.
- Give four possibilities for the number of each size table you could rent.

Solution

STEP 1 **Find** the intercepts.

$4x + 6y = 180$	$4x + 6y = 180$
$4x + 6(0) = 180$	$4(0) + 6y = 180$
$x = 45 \leftarrow$ **x-intercept**	$y = 30 \leftarrow$ **y-intercept**

DRAW A GRAPH
Although x and y represent whole numbers, it is convenient to draw an unbroken line segment that includes points whose coordinates are not whole numbers.

STEP 2 **Graph** the equation.

The x-intercept is 45, so plot the point (45, 0). The y-intercept is 30, so plot the point (0, 30).

Since x and y both represent numbers of tables, neither x nor y can be negative. So, instead of drawing a line, draw the part of the line that is in Quadrant I.

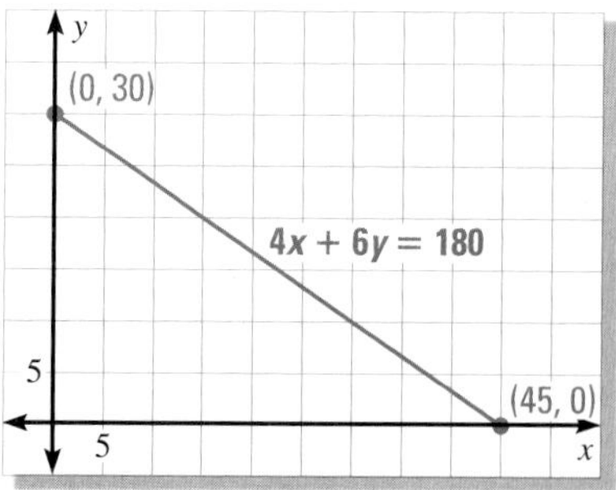

FIND SOLUTIONS
Other points, such as (12, 22), are also on the graph but are not as obvious as the points shown here because their coordinates are not multiples of 5.

STEP 3 **Find** the number of tables. For this problem, only whole-number values of x and y make sense. You can see that the line passes through the points **(0, 30)**, **(15, 20)**, **(30, 10)**, and **(45, 0)**.

So, four possible combinations of tables that will seat 180 people are: 0 small and 30 large, 15 small and 20 large, 30 small and 10 large, and 45 small and 0 large.

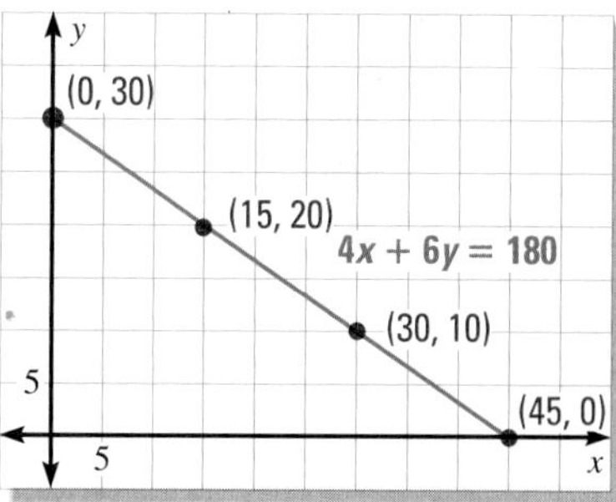

✓ GUIDED PRACTICE for Example 4

6. **WHAT IF?** In Example 4, suppose the small tables cost $9 to rent and the large tables cost $14. Of the four possible combinations of tables given in the example, which rental is the least expensive? *Explain.*

EXAMPLE 5 Use a linear model

SUBMERSIBLES A submersible designed to explore the ocean floor is at an elevation of −13,000 feet (13,000 feet below sea level). The submersible ascends to the surface at an average rate of 650 feet per minute. The elevation e (in feet) of the submersible is given by the function

$$e = 650t - 13,000$$

where t is the time (in minutes) since the submersible began to ascend.

- Find the intercepts of the graph of the function and state what the intercepts represent.
- Graph the function and identify its domain and range.

Solution

STEP 1 **Find** the intercepts.

$$0 = 650t - 13,000 \qquad e = 650(0) - 13,000$$

$$13,000 = 650t \qquad e = -13,000 \leftarrow \textbf{e-intercept}$$

$$20 = t \leftarrow \textbf{t-intercept}$$

NAME INTERCEPTS
Because t is the independent variable, the horizontal axis is the t-axis, and you refer to the "t-intercept" of the graph of the function. Similarly, the vertical axis is the e-axis, and you refer to the "e-intercept."

The t-intercept represents the number of minutes the submersible takes to reach an elevation of 0 feet (sea level). The e-intercept represents the elevation of the submersible after 0 minutes (the time the ascent begins).

STEP 2 **Graph** the function using the intercepts.

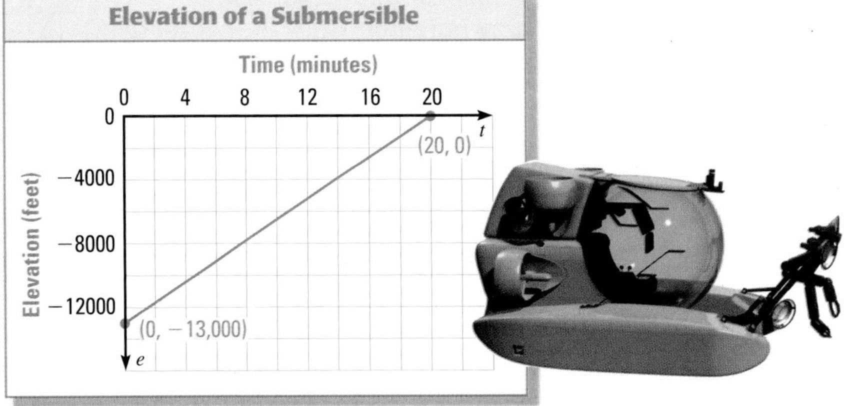

The submersible starts at an elevation of −13,000 feet and ascends to an elevation of 0 feet. So, the range of the function is $-13,000 \le e \le 0$. From the graph, you can see that the domain of the function is $0 \le t \le 20$.

✓ **GUIDED PRACTICE** for Example 5

7. **WHAT IF?** In Example 5, suppose the elevation of a second submersible is given by $e = 500t - 10,000$. Graph the function and identify its domain and range.

4.3 EXERCISES

HOMEWORK KEY

○ = **WORKED-OUT SOLUTIONS** on p. WS8 for Exs. 21 and 47

★ = **STANDARDIZED TEST PRACTICE** Exs. 2, 37, 41, 49, and 50

◆ = **MULTIPLE REPRESENTATIONS** Ex. 44

SKILL PRACTICE

1. **VOCABULARY** Copy and complete: The _?_ of the graph of an equation is the value of x when y is zero.

2. ★ **WRITING** What are the x-intercept and the y-intercept of the line passing through the points (0, 3) and (−4, 0)? *Explain*.

3. **ERROR ANALYSIS** *Describe* and correct the error in finding the intercepts of the line shown.

The x-intercept is 1, and the y-intercept is −2.

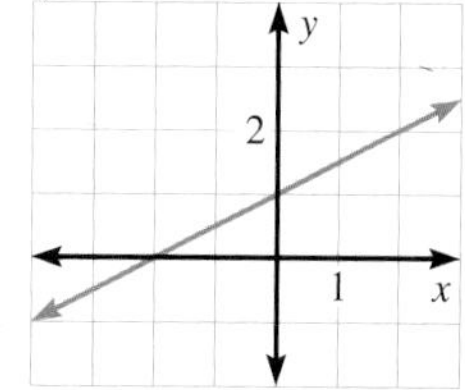

EXAMPLE 1
on p. 225
for Exs. 4–15

FINDING INTERCEPTS **Find the x-intercept and the y-intercept of the graph of the equation.**

4. $5x - y = 35$
5. $3x - 3y = 9$
6. $-3x + 9y = -18$
7. $4x + y = 4$
8. $2x + y = 10$
9. $2x - 8y = 24$
10. $3x + 0.5y = 6$
11. $0.2x + 3.2y = 12.8$
12. $y = 2x + 24$
13. $y = -14x + 7$
14. $y = -4.8x + 1.2$
15. $y = \frac{3}{5}x - 12$

EXAMPLE 2
on p. 226
for Exs. 16–27

GRAPHING LINES **Graph the equation. Label the points where the line crosses the axes.**

16. $y = x + 3$
17. $y = x - 2$
18. $y = 4x - 8$
19. $y = 5 + 10x$
20. $y = -2 + 8x$
21. $y = -4x + 3$
22. $3x + y = 15$
23. $x - 4y = 18$
24. $8x - 5y = 80$
25. $-2x + 5y = 15$
26. $0.5x + 3y = 9$
27. $y = \frac{1}{2}x + \frac{1}{4}$

EXAMPLE 3
on p. 226
for Exs. 28–30

USING GRAPHS TO FIND INTERCEPTS **Identify the x-intercept and the y-intercept of the graph.**

28.

29.

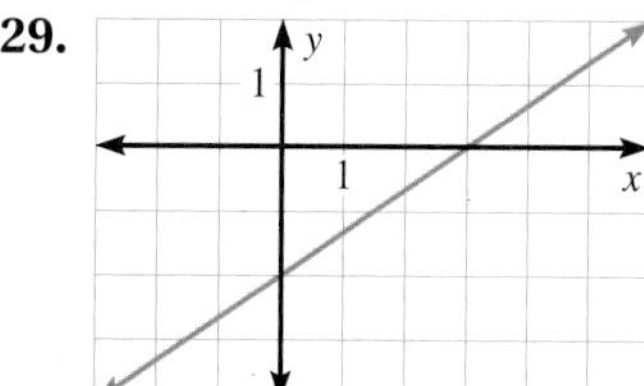

30.

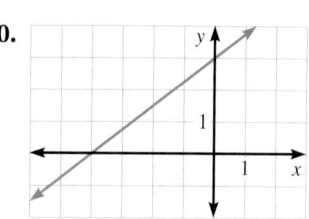

USING INTERCEPTS **Draw the line that has the given intercepts.**

31. x-intercept: 3
y-intercept: 5

32. x-intercept: -2
y-intercept: 4

33. x-intercept: -5
y-intercept: 6

34. x-intercept: 9
y-intercept: -1

35. x-intercept: -8
y-intercept: -11

36. x-intercept: -2
y-intercept: -6

37. ★ **MULTIPLE CHOICE** The x-intercept of the graph of $Ax + 5y = 20$ is 2. What is the value of A?

(A) 2 (B) 5 (C) 7.5 (D) 10

MATCHING EQUATIONS WITH GRAPHS **Match the equation with its graph.**

38. $2x - 6y = 6$

39. $2x - 6y = -6$

40. $2x - 6y = 12$

A.

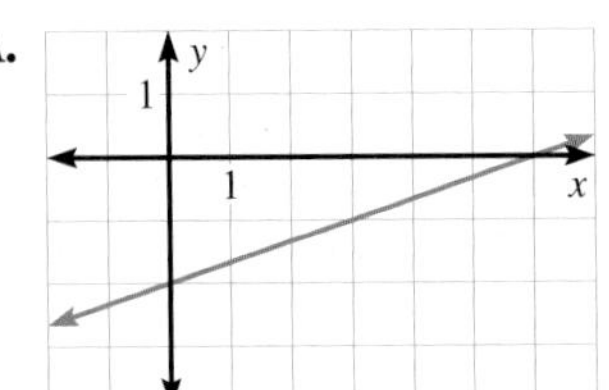

B.

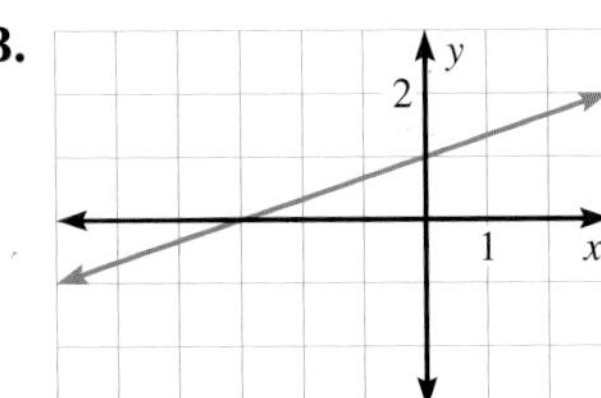

C.

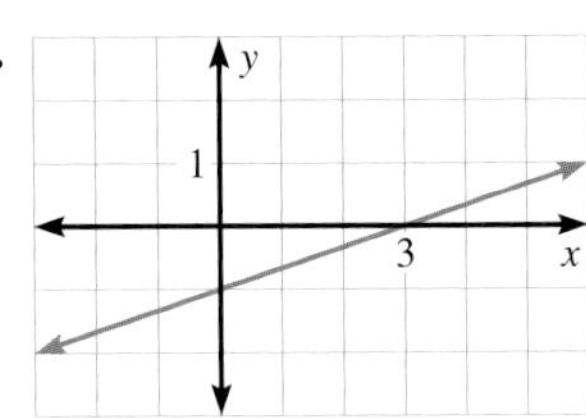

41. ★ **WRITING** Is it possible for a line *not* to have an x-intercept? Is it possible for a line *not* to have a y-intercept? *Explain.*

42. **REASONING** Consider the equation $3x + 5y = k$. What values could k have so that the x-intercept and the y-intercept of the equation's graph would both be integers? *Explain.*

43. **CHALLENGE** If $a \neq 0$, find the intercepts of the graph of $y = ax + b$ in terms of a and b.

PROBLEM SOLVING

EXAMPLES 4 and 5 on pp. 227–228 for Exs. 44–47

44. ◆ **MULTIPLE REPRESENTATIONS** The perimeter of a rectangular park is 72 feet. Let x be the park's width (in feet) and let y be its length (in feet).

   a. **Writing an Equation** Write an equation for the perimeter.

   b. **Drawing a Graph** Find the intercepts of the graph of the equation you wrote. Then graph the equation.

   @HomeTutor for problem solving help at classzone.com

45. **RECYCLING** In one state, small bottles have a refund value of \$.04 each, and large bottles have a refund value of \$.08 each. Your friend returns both small and large bottles and receives \$.56. This situation is given by $4x + 8y = 56$ where x is the number of small bottles and y is the number of large bottles.

   a. Find the intercepts of the graph of the equation. Graph the equation.

   b. Give three possibilities for the number of each size bottle your friend could have returned.

   @HomeTutor for problem solving help at classzone.com

46. **MULTI-STEP PROBLEM** Before 1979, there was no 3-point shot in professional basketball; players could score only 2-point field goals and 1-point free throws. In a game before 1979, a team scored a total of 128 points. This situation is given by the equation $2x + y = 128$ where x is the possible number of field goals and y is the possible number of free throws.

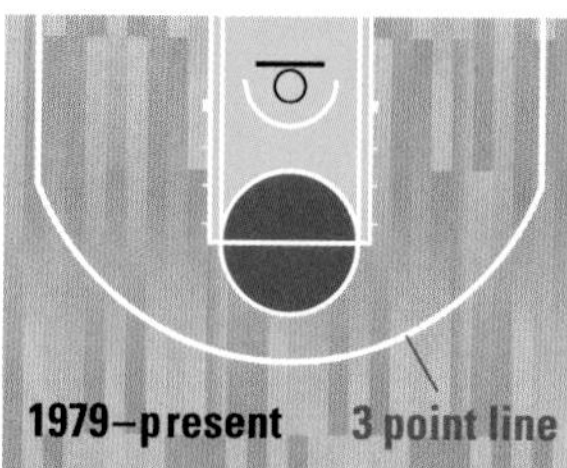

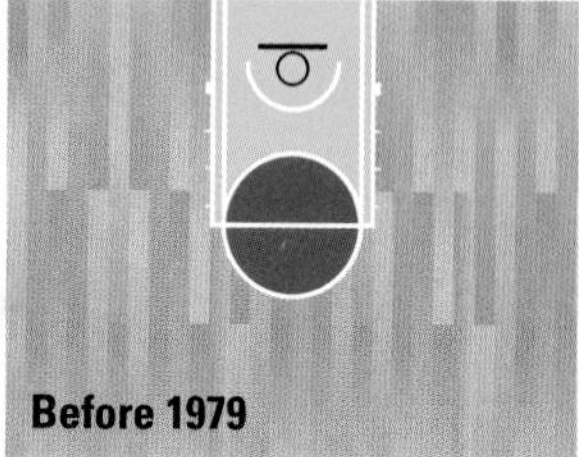

a. Find the intercepts of the graph of the equation. Graph the equation.

b. What do the intercepts mean in this situation?

c. What are three possible numbers of field goals and free throws the team could have scored?

d. If the team made 24 free throws, how many field goals were made?

47. **COMMUNITY GARDENS** A family has a plot in a community garden. The family is going to plant vegetables, flowers, or both. The diagram shows the area used by one vegetable plant and the area of the entire plot. The area f (in square feet) of the plot left for flowers is given by $f = 180 - 1.5v$ where v is the number of vegetable plants the family plants.

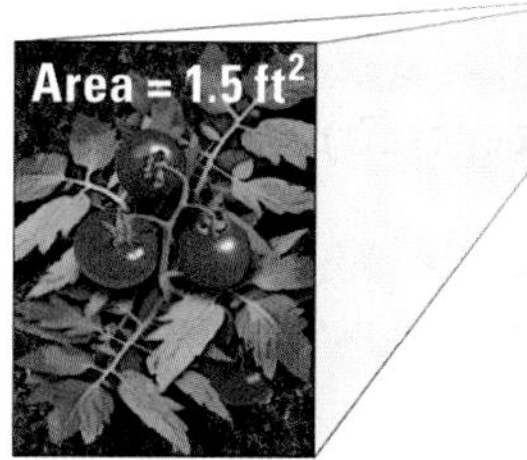

a. Find the intercepts of the graph of the function and state what the intercepts represent.

b. Graph the function and identify its domain and range.

c. The family decides to plant 80 vegetable plants. How many square feet are left to plant flowers?

48. **CAR SHARING** A member of a car-sharing program can use a car for \$6 per hour and \$.50 per mile. The member uses the car for one day and is charged \$44. This situation is given by

$$6t + 0.5d = 44$$

where t is the time (in hours) the car is used and d is the distance (in miles) the car is driven. Give three examples of the number of hours the member could have used the car and the number of miles the member could have driven the car.

49. ★ **SHORT RESPONSE** A humidifier is a device used to put moisture into the air by turning water to vapor. A humidifier has a tank that can hold 1.5 gallons of water. The humidifier can disperse the water at a rate of 0.12 gallon per hour. The amount of water w (in gallons) left in the humidifier after t hours of use is given by the function

$$w = 1.5 - 0.12t.$$

After how many hours of use will you have to refill the humidifier? *Explain* how you found your answer.

50. ★ **EXTENDED RESPONSE** You borrow \$180 from a friend who doesn't charge you interest. You work out a payment schedule in which you will make weekly payments to your friend. The balance B (in dollars) of the loan is given by the function $B = 180 - pn$ where p is the weekly payment and n is the number of weeks you make payments.

a. **Interpret** Without finding the intercepts, state what they represent.

b. **Graph** Graph the function if you make weekly payments of \$20.

c. **Identify** Find the domain and range of the function in part (b). How long will it take to pay back your friend?

d. **CHALLENGE** Suppose you make payments of \$20 for three weeks. Then you make payments of \$15 until you have paid your friend back. How does this affect the graph? How many payments do you make?

MIXED REVIEW

REVIEW GRAPHS

For help with line graphs, see p. 934.

In Exercises 51–53, use the line graph, which shows the number of points Alex scored in five basketball games. *(p. 934)*

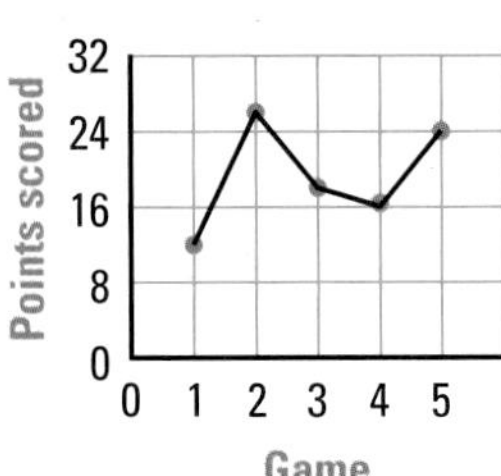

51. How many points did Alex score in game 4?

52. In which game did Alex score the most points?

53. How many more points did Alex score in game 5 than in game 1?

PREVIEW

Prepare for Lesson 4.4 in Exs. 54–56.

Solve the proportion. *(p. 168)*

54. $\frac{3}{5} = \frac{x}{30}$

55. $\frac{x}{x+6} = \frac{7}{6}$

56. $\frac{t-3}{12} = \frac{2t-2}{9}$

QUIZ *for Lessons 4.1–4.3*

Plot the point in a coordinate plane. *Describe* the location of the point. *(p. 206)*

1. $(-7, 2)$

2. $(0, -5)$

3. $(2, -6)$

Graph the equation. *(p. 215)*

4. $-4x - 2y = 12$

5. $y = -5$

6. $x = 6$

Find the x-intercept and the y-intercept of the graph of the equation. *(p. 225)*

7. $y = x + 7$

8. $y = x - 3$

9. $y = -5x + 2$

10. $x + 3y = 15$

11. $3x - 6y = 36$

12. $-2x - 5y = 22$

13. **SWIMMING POOLS** A public swimming pool that holds 45,000 gallons of water is going to be drained for maintenance at a rate of 100 gallons per minute. The amount of water w (in gallons) in the pool after t minutes is given by the function $w = 45{,}000 - 100t$. Graph the function. Identify its domain and range. How much water is in the pool after 60 minutes? How many minutes will it take to empty the pool? *(p. 225)*

MIXED REVIEW of Problem Solving

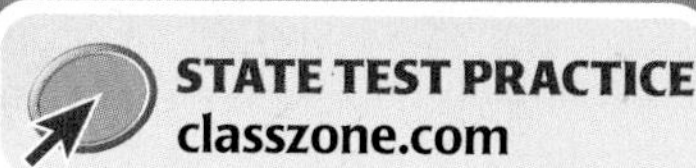

Lessons 4.1–4.3

1. **MULTI-STEP PROBLEM** An amusement park charges \$20 for an all-day pass and \$10 for a pass after 5 P.M. On Wednesday the amusement park collected \$1000 in pass sales. This situation can be modeled by the equation $1000 = 20x + 10y$ where x is the number of all-day passes sold and y is the number of passes sold after 5 P.M.

   a. Find the x-intercept of the graph of the equation. What does it represent?

   b. Find the y-intercept of the graph of the equation. What does it represent?

   c. Graph the equation using a scale of 10 on the x- and y-axes.

2. **MULTI-STEP PROBLEM** A violin player who plays every day received a violin with new strings. Players who play every day should replace the strings on their violins every 6 months. A particular brand of strings costs \$24 per pack. The table shows the total spent a (in dollars) on replacement strings with respect to time t (in months).

t (months)	a (dollars)
6	24
12	48
18	72
24	96
30	120

   a. *Explain* how you know the table represents a function.

   b. Graph the function.

3. **OPEN-ENDED** Create a table that shows the number of minutes you think you will spend watching TV next week. Let Monday be day 1, Tuesday be day 2, and so on. Graph the data. Does the graph represent a function? *Explain.*

4. **SHORT RESPONSE** You can hike at an average rate of 3 miles per hour. Your total hiking distance d (in miles) can be modeled by the function $d = 3t$ where t is the time (in hours) you hike. You plan on hiking for 10 hours this weekend.

   a. Is the domain or range specified in the problem? *Explain.*

   b. Graph the function and identify its domain and range. Use the graph to find how long it takes to hike 6 miles.

5. **EXTENDED RESPONSE** The table shows the departure d (in degrees Fahrenheit) from the normal monthly temperature in New England for the first six months of 2004. For example, in month 1, $d = -3$. So, the average temperature was 3 degrees below the normal temperature for January.

M (month)	1	2	3	4	5	6
d (°F)	−3	−1	2	2	4	−1

   a. *Explain* how you know the table represents a function.

   b. Graph the function and identify its domain and range.

   c. What does a point in Quadrant IV mean in terms of this situation?

6. **GRIDDED ANSWER** The graph shows the possible combinations of T-shirts and tank tops that you can buy with the amount of money you have. If you buy only T-shirts, how many can you buy?

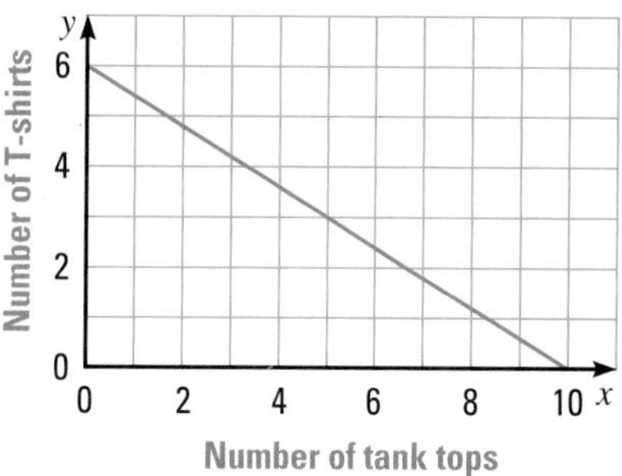

Investigating Algebra ACTIVITY *Use before Lesson 4.4*

4.4 Slopes of Lines

MATERIALS • several books • two rulers

QUESTION **How can you use algebra to describe the slope of a ramp?**

You can use the ratio of the vertical rise to the horizontal run to describe the *slope* of a ramp.

$$\textbf{slope} = \frac{\textbf{rise}}{\textbf{run}}$$

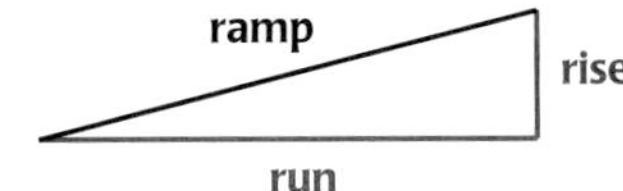

EXPLORE **Calculate the slopes of ramps**

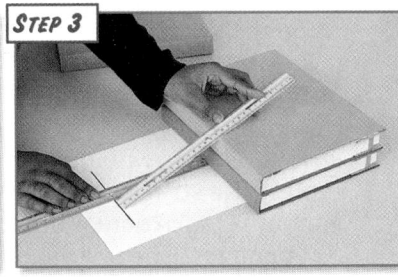

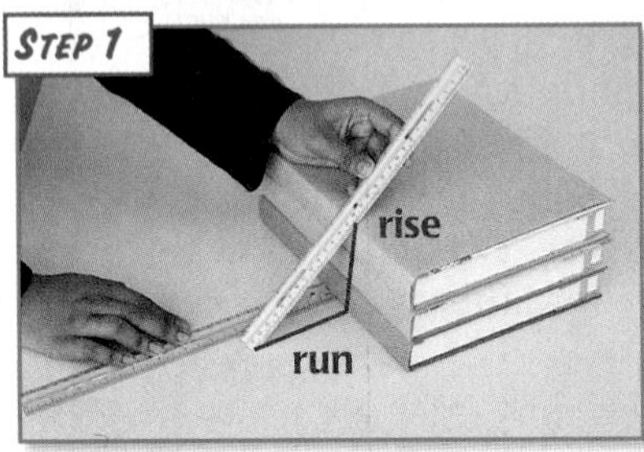

Make a ramp Make a stack of three books. Use a ruler as a ramp. Measure the rise and run of the ramp, and record them in a table. Calculate and record the slope of the ramp in your table.

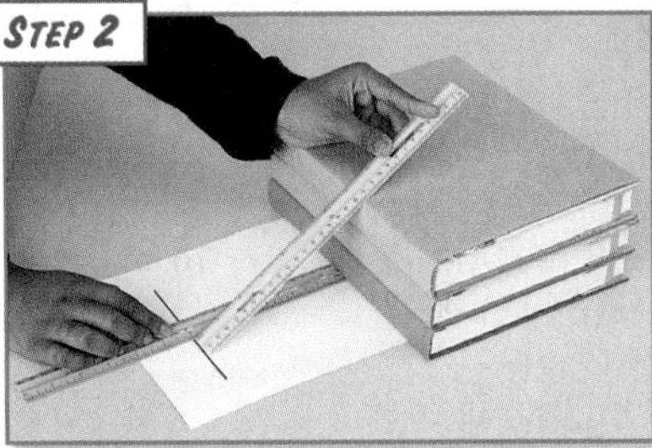

Change the run Without changing the rise, make three ramps with different runs by moving the lower end of the ruler. Measure and record the rise and run of each ramp. Calculate and record each slope.

STEP 3

Change the rise Without changing the run, make three ramps with different rises by adding or removing books. Measure and record the rise and run of each ramp. Calculate and record each slope.

DRAW CONCLUSIONS **Use your observations to complete these exercises**

Describe **how the slope of the ramp changes given the following conditions. Give three examples that support your answer.**

1. The run of the ramp increases, and the rise stays the same.
2. The rise of the ramp increases, and the run stays the same.

In Exercises 3–5, describe the relationship between the rise and the run of the ramp.

3. A ramp with a slope of 1
4. A ramp with a slope greater than 1
5. A ramp with a slope less than 1
6. Ramp A has a rise of 6 feet and a run of 2 feet. Ramp B has a rise of 10 feet and a run of 4 feet. Which ramp is steeper? How do you know?

4.4 Find Slope and Rate of Change

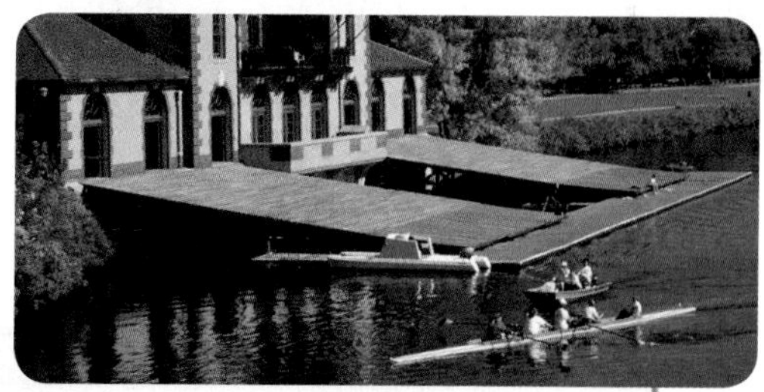

Before You graphed linear equations.

Now You will find the slope of a line and interpret slope as a rate of change.

Why? So you can find the slope of a boat ramp, as in Ex. 23.

Key Vocabulary
- **slope**
- **rate of change**

The **slope** of a nonvertical line is the ratio of the vertical change (the *rise*) to the horizontal change (the *run*) between any two points on the line. The slope of a line is represented by the letter m.

READING
Read x_1 as "x sub one." Think "x-coordinate of the first point." Read y_1 as "y sub one." Think "y-coordinate of the first point."

KEY CONCEPT *For Your Notebook*

Finding the Slope of a Line

Words

The slope m of the nonvertical line passing through the two points (x_1, y_1) and (x_2, y_2) is the ratio of the rise (change in y) to the run (change in x).

$$\text{slope} = \frac{\text{rise}}{\text{run}} = \frac{\text{change in } y}{\text{change in } x}$$

Symbols

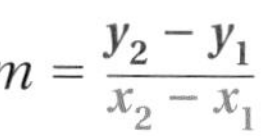

$$m = \frac{y_2 - y_1}{x_2 - x_1}$$

Graph

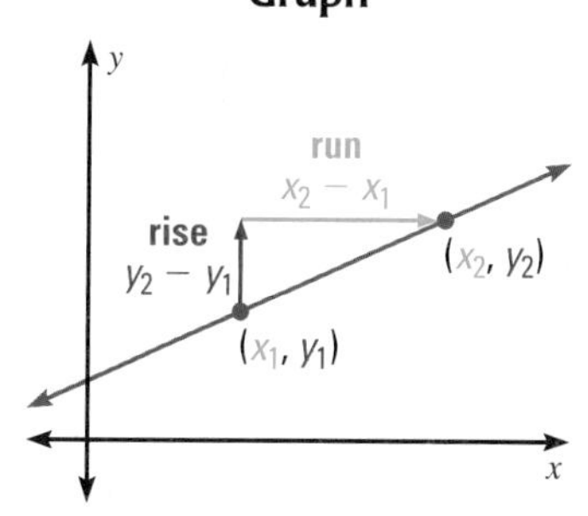

EXAMPLE 1 Find a positive slope

Find the slope of the line shown.

Let $(x_1, y_1) = (-4, 2)$ and $(x_2, y_2) = (2, 6)$.

$m = \frac{y_2 - y_1}{x_2 - x_1}$ **Write formula for slope.**

$= \frac{6 - 2}{2 - (-4)}$ **Substitute.**

$= \frac{4}{6} = \frac{2}{3}$ **Simplify.**

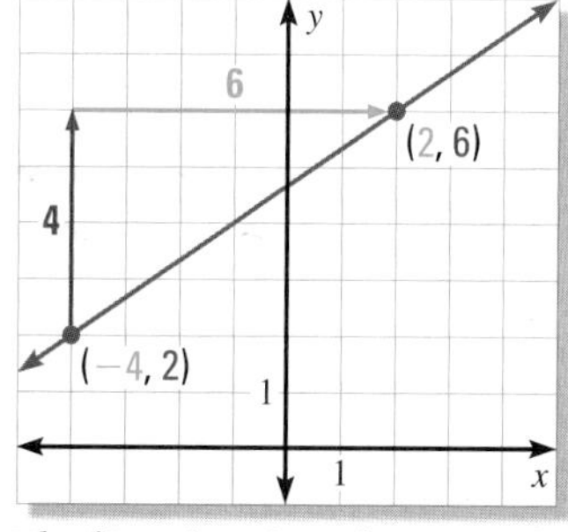

The line rises from left to right. The slope is positive.

AVOID ERRORS
Be sure to keep the x- and y-coordinates in the same order in both the numerator and denominator when calculating slope.

✓ **GUIDED PRACTICE** for Example 1

Find the slope of the line that passes through the points.

1. (5, 2) and (4, −1)

2. (−2, 3) and (4, 6)

3. $\left(\frac{9}{2}, 5\right)$ and $\left(\frac{1}{2}, -3\right)$

EXAMPLE 2 Find a negative slope

FIND SLOPE

In Example 2, if you used two other points on the line, such as (4, 3) and (5, 1), in the slope formula, the slope would still be −2.

Find the slope of the line shown.

Let $(x_1, y_1) = (3, 5)$ and $(x_2, y_2) = (6, -1)$.

$m = \frac{y_2 - y_1}{x_2 - x_1}$ **Write formula for slope.**

$= \frac{-1 - 5}{6 - 3}$ **Substitute.**

$= \frac{-6}{3} = -2$ **Simplify.**

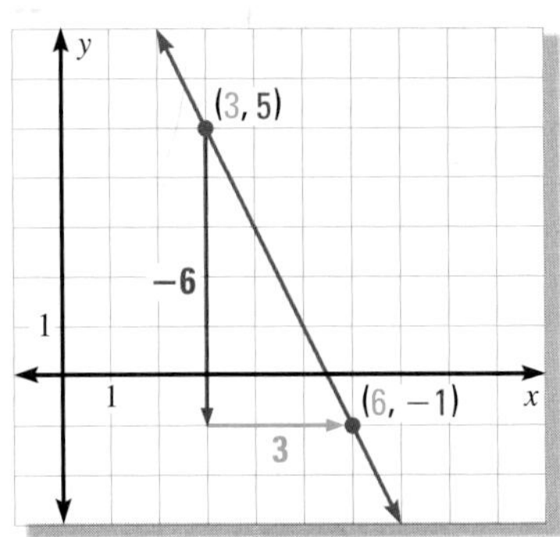

The line falls from left to right. The slope is negative.

EXAMPLE 3 Find the slope of a horizontal line

Find the slope of the line shown.

Let $(x_1, y_1) = (-2, 4)$ and $(x_2, y_2) = (4, 4)$.

$m = \frac{y_2 - y_1}{x_2 - x_1}$ **Write formula for slope.**

$= \frac{4 - 4}{4 - (-2)}$ **Substitute.**

$= \frac{0}{6} = 0$ **Simplify.**

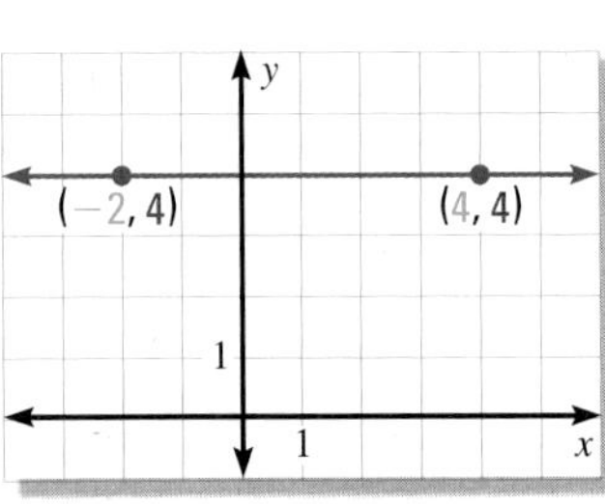

The line is horizontal. The slope is zero.

EXAMPLE 4 Find the slope of a vertical line

Find the slope of the line shown.

Let $(x_1, y_1) = (3, 5)$ and $(x_2, y_2) = (3, 1)$.

$m = \frac{y_2 - y_1}{x_2 - x_1}$ **Write formula for slope.**

$= \frac{1 - 5}{3 - 3}$ **Substitute.**

$= \cancel{\frac{-4}{0}}$ **Division by zero is undefined.**

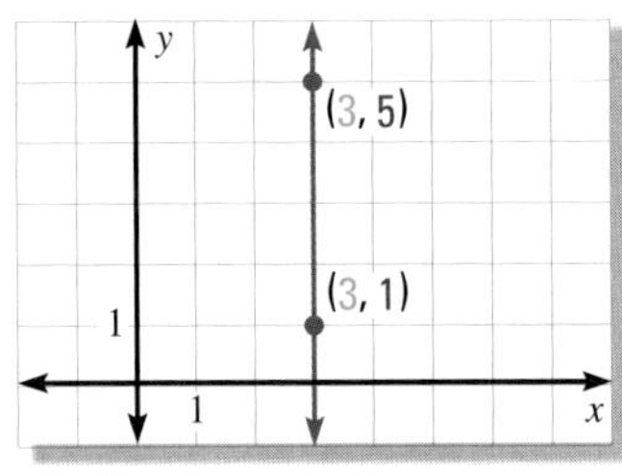

The line is vertical. The slope is undefined.

▶ Because division by zero is undefined, the slope of a vertical line is undefined.

✓ **GUIDED PRACTICE** for Examples 2, 3, and 4

Find the slope of the line that passes through the points.

4. (5, 2) and (5, −2) **5.** (0, 4) and (−3, 4) **6.** (0, 6) and (5, −4)

CONCEPT SUMMARY — *For Your Notebook*

Classification of Lines by Slope

A line with positive slope ($m > 0$) *rises* from left to right.

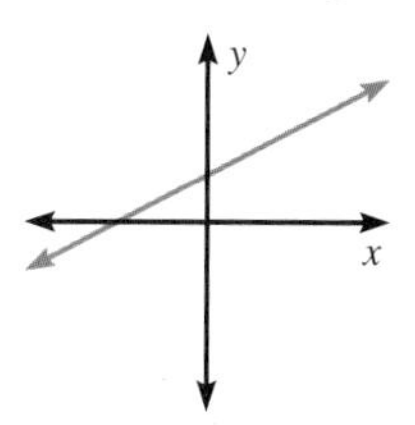

A line with negative slope ($m < 0$) *falls* from left to right.

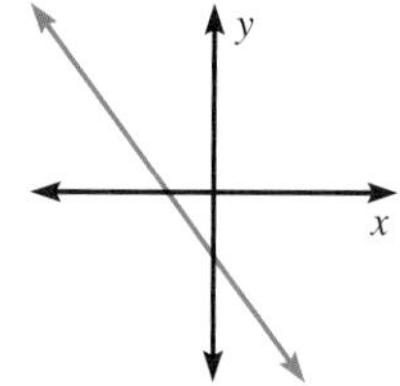

A line with zero slope ($m = 0$) is *horizontal.*

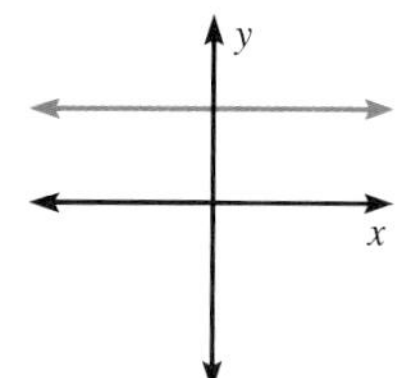

A line with undefined slope is *vertical.*

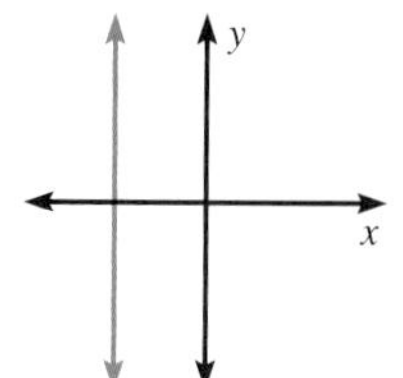

RATE OF CHANGE A **rate of change** compares a change in one quantity to a change in another quantity. For example, if you are paid \$60 for working 5 hours, then your hourly wage is \$12 per hour, a rate of change that describes how your pay increases with respect to time spent working.

EXAMPLE 5 Find a rate of change

INTERNET CAFE The table shows the cost of using a computer at an Internet cafe for a given amount of time. Find the rate of change in cost with respect to time.

Time (hours)	2	4	6
Cost (dollars)	7	14	21

Solution

$$\textbf{Rate of change} = \frac{\text{change in cost}}{\text{change in time}}$$

$$= \frac{14 - 7}{4 - 2} = \frac{7}{2} = 3.5$$

▶ The rate of change in cost is \$3.50 per hour.

ANALYZE UNITS
Because the cost is in dollars and time is in hours, the rate of change in cost with respect to time is expressed in dollars per hour.

✓ GUIDED PRACTICE for Example 5

7. **EXERCISE** The table shows the distance a person walks for exercise. Find the rate of change in distance with respect to time.

Time (minutes)	Distance (miles)
30	1.5
60	3
90	4.5

SLOPE AND RATE OF CHANGE You can interpret the slope of a line as a rate of change. When given graphs of real-world data, you can compare rates of change by comparing slopes of lines.

EXAMPLE 6 Use a graph to find and compare rates of change

COMMUNITY THEATER A community theater performed a play each Saturday evening for 10 consecutive weeks. The graph shows the attendance for the performances in weeks 1, 4, 6, and 10. Describe the rates of change in attendance with respect to time.

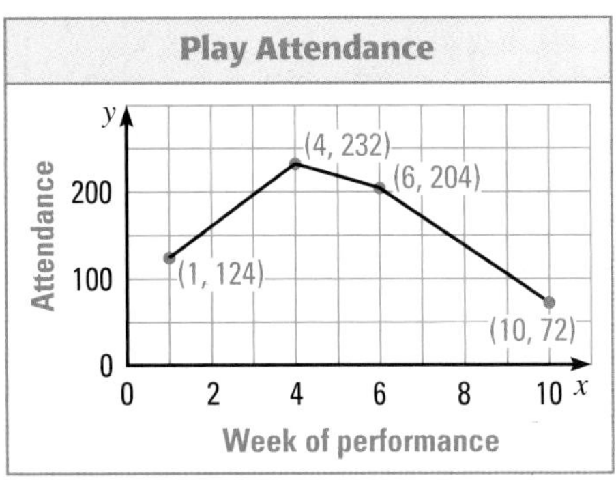

Solution

Find the rates of change using the slope formula.

Weeks 1–4: $\dfrac{232 - 124}{4 - 1} = \dfrac{108}{3} = 36$ people per week

Weeks 4–6: $\dfrac{204 - 232}{6 - 4} = \dfrac{-28}{2} = -14$ people per week

Weeks 6–10: $\dfrac{72 - 204}{10 - 6} = \dfrac{-132}{4} = -33$ people per week

INTERPRET RATE OF CHANGE
A negative rate of change indicates a decrease.

▶ Attendance increased during the early weeks of performing the play. Then attendance decreased, slowly at first, then more rapidly.

EXAMPLE 7 Interpret a graph

COMMUTING TO SCHOOL A student commutes from home to school by walking and by riding a bus. Describe the student's commute in words.

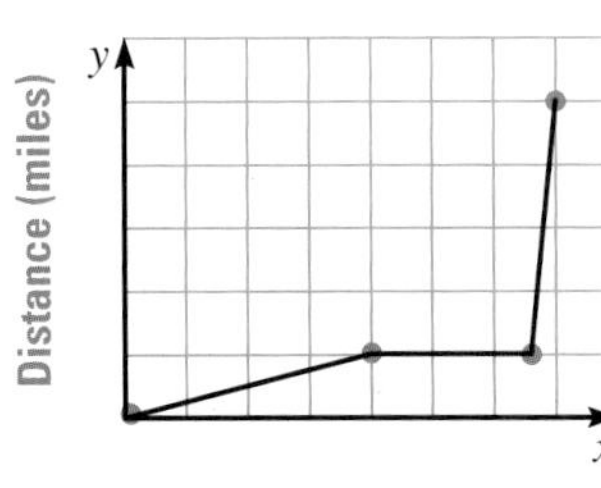

Solution

The first segment of the graph is not very steep, so the student is not traveling very far with respect to time. The student must be walking. The second segment has a zero slope, so the student must not be moving. He or she is waiting for the bus. The last segment is steep, so the student is traveling far with respect to time. The student must be riding the bus.

Animated Algebra at classzone.com

✓ GUIDED PRACTICE for Examples 6 and 7

8. **WHAT IF?** How would the answer to Example 6 change if you knew that attendance was 70 people in week 12?

9. **WHAT IF?** Using the graph in Example 7, draw a graph that represents the student's commute from school to home.

4.4 EXERCISES

HOMEWORK KEY

○ = **WORKED-OUT SOLUTIONS** on p. WS9 for Exs. 11 and 37

★ = **STANDARDIZED TEST PRACTICE** Exs. 2, 17, 18, 34, and 40

SKILL PRACTICE

1. **VOCABULARY** Copy and complete: The __?__ of a nonvertical line is the ratio of the vertical change to the horizontal change between any two points on the line.

2. ★ **WRITING** Without calculating the slope, how can you tell that the slope of the line that passes through the points (−5, −3) and (2, 4) is positive?

3. **ERROR ANALYSIS** *Describe* and correct the error in calculating the slope of the line passing through the points (5, 3) and (2, 6).

$$m = \frac{6-3}{5-2} = \frac{3}{3} = 1 \quad \times$$

EXAMPLES 1,2,3, and 4 on pp. 235–236 for Exs. 4–18

FINDING SLOPE **Tell whether the slope of the line is *positive, negative, zero,* or *undefined*. Then find the slope if it exists.**

4.

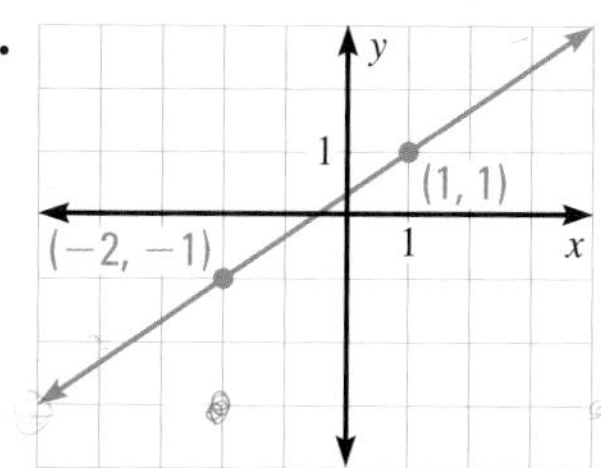

5.

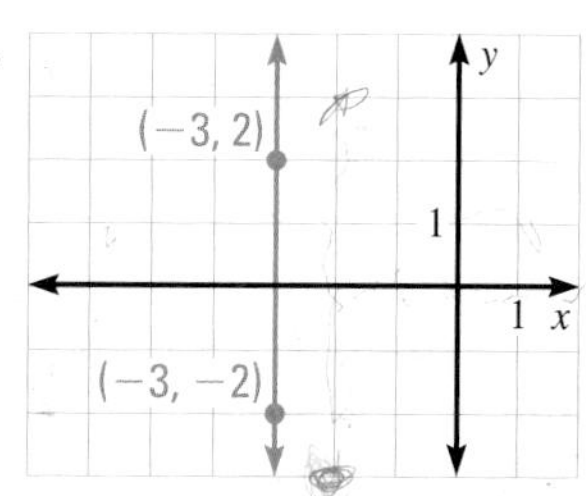

6.

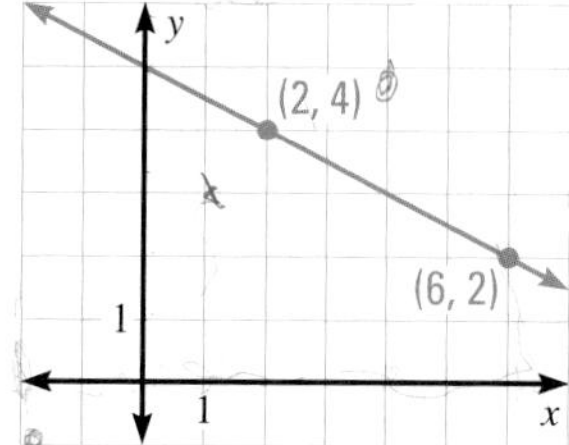

7. **ERROR ANALYSIS** *Describe* and correct the error in calculating the slope of the line shown.

$$m = \frac{12-6}{0-3} = \frac{6}{-3} = -2 \quad \times$$

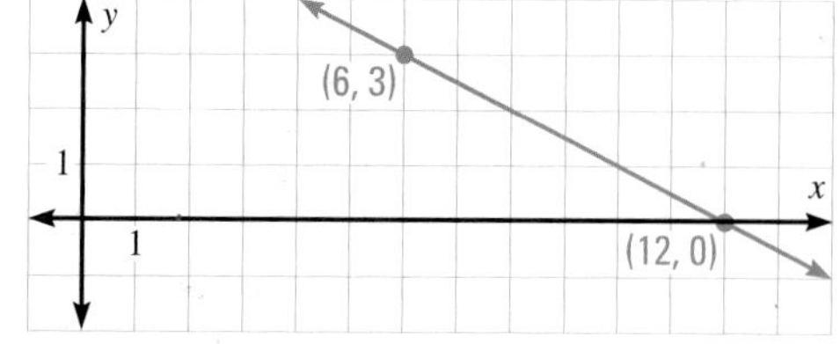

FINDING SLOPE **Find the slope of the line that passes through the points.**

8. (−2, −1) and (4, 5)
9. (−3, −2) and (−3, 6)
10. (5, −3) and (−5, −3)
11. (1, 3) and (3, −2)
12. (−3, 4) and (4, 1)
13. (1, −3) and (7, 3)
14. (0, 0) and (0, −6)
15. (−9, 1) and (1, 1)
16. (−10, −2) and (−8, 8)

17. ★ **MULTIPLE CHOICE** The slope of the line that passes through the points (−2, −3) and (8, −3) is __?__.

Ⓐ positive Ⓑ negative Ⓒ zero Ⓓ undefined

18. ★ **MULTIPLE CHOICE** What is the slope of the line that passes through the points (7, −9) and (−13, −6)?

Ⓐ $-\frac{3}{20}$ Ⓑ $\frac{3}{20}$ Ⓒ $\frac{3}{4}$ Ⓓ $\frac{5}{2}$

EXAMPLE 5 on p. 237 for Exs. 19–20

19. **MOVIE RENTALS** The table shows the number of days you keep a rented movie before returning it and the total cost of renting the movie. Find the rate of change in cost with respect to time and interpret its meaning.

Time (days)	4	5	6	7
Total cost (dollars)	6.00	8.25	10.50	12.75

20. **AMUSEMENT PARK** The table shows the amount of time spent at an amusement park and the admission fee the park charges. Find the rate of change in the fee with respect to time spent at the park and interpret its meaning.

Time (hours)	4	5	6
Admission fee (dollars)	34.99	34.99	34.99

FINDING SLOPE **Find the slope of the object. Round to the nearest tenth.**

21. Skateboard ramp

22. Pet ramp

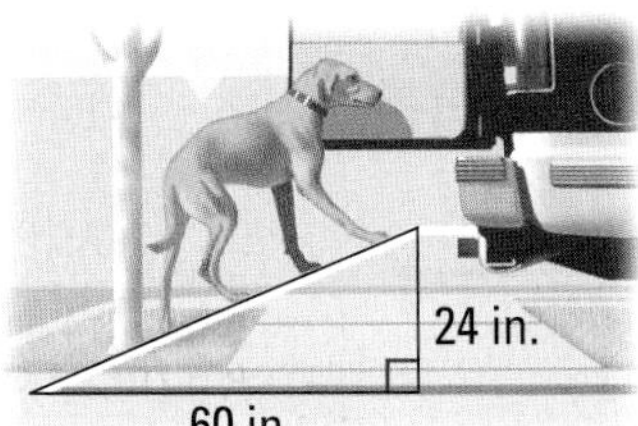

23. Boat ramp

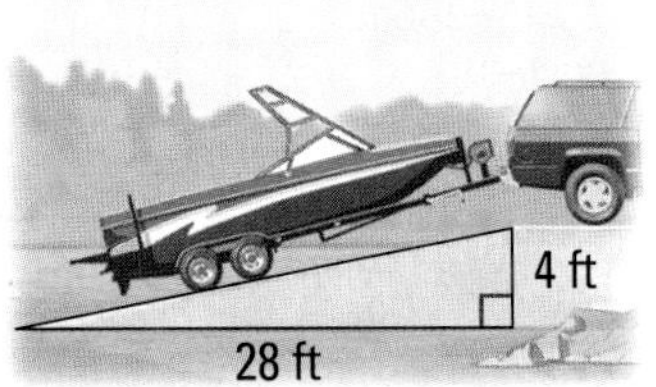

In Exercises 24–32, use the example below to find the value of x or y so that the line passing through the given points has the given slope.

EXAMPLE **Find a coordinate given the slope of a line**

Find the value of x so that the line that passes through the points $(2, 3)$ and $(x, 9)$ has a slope of $\frac{3}{2}$.

Solution

Let $(x_1, y_1) = (2, 3)$ and $(x_2, y_2) = (x, 9)$.

$m = \frac{y_2 - y_1}{x_2 - x_1}$ **Write formula for slope.**

$\frac{3}{2} = \frac{9 - 3}{x - 2}$ **Substitute values.**

$3(x - 2) = 2(9 - 3)$ **Cross products property**

$3x - 6 = 12$ **Simplify.**

$x = 6$ **Solve for x.**

24. $(x, 4), (6, -1); m = \frac{5}{6}$

25. $(0, y), (-2, 1); m = -8$

26. $(8, 1), (x, 7); m = -\frac{1}{2}$

27. $(5, 4), (-5, y); m = \frac{3}{5}$

28. $(-9, y), (0, -3); m = -\frac{7}{9}$

29. $(x, 9), (-1, 19); m = 5$

30. $(9, 3), (-6, 7y); m = 3$

31. $(-3, y + 1), (0, 4); m = 6$

32. $\left(\frac{x}{2}, 7\right), (-10, 15); m = 4$

○ = WORKED-OUT SOLUTIONS on p. WS1

★ = STANDARDIZED TEST PRACTICE

33. **REASONING** The point (−1, 8) is on a line that has a slope of −3. Is the point (4, −7) on the same line? *Explain* your reasoning.

34. ★ **WRITING** Is a line with undefined slope the graph of a function? *Explain.*

35. **CHALLENGE** Given two points (x_1, y_1) and (x_2, y_2) such that $x_1 \neq x_2$, show that $\frac{y_2 - y_1}{x_2 - x_1} = \frac{y_1 - y_2}{x_1 - x_2}$. What does this result tell you about calculating the slope of a line?

PROBLEM SOLVING

EXAMPLE 6 on p. 238 for Exs. 36–37

36. **OCEANOGRAPHY** Ocean water levels are measured hourly at a monitoring station. The table shows the water level (in meters) on one particular morning. *Describe* the rates of change in water levels throughout the morning.

Hours since 12:00 A.M.	1	3	8	10	12
Water level (meters)	2	1.4	0.5	1	1.8

@HomeTutor for problem solving help at classzone.com

37. **MULTI-STEP PROBLEM** Firing a piece of pottery in a kiln takes place at different temperatures for different amounts of time. The graph shows the temperatures in a kiln while firing a piece of pottery (after the kiln is preheated to 250°F).

a. Determine the time interval during which the temperature in the kiln showed the greatest rate of change.

b. Determine the time interval during which the temperature in the kiln showed the least rate of change.

@HomeTutor for problem solving help at classzone.com

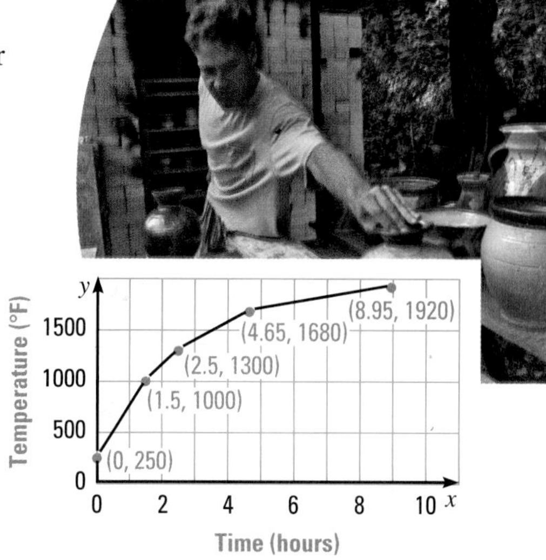

EXAMPLE 7 on p. 238 for Exs. 38–39

38. **FLYING** The graph shows the altitude of a plane during 4 hours of a flight. Give a verbal description of the flight.

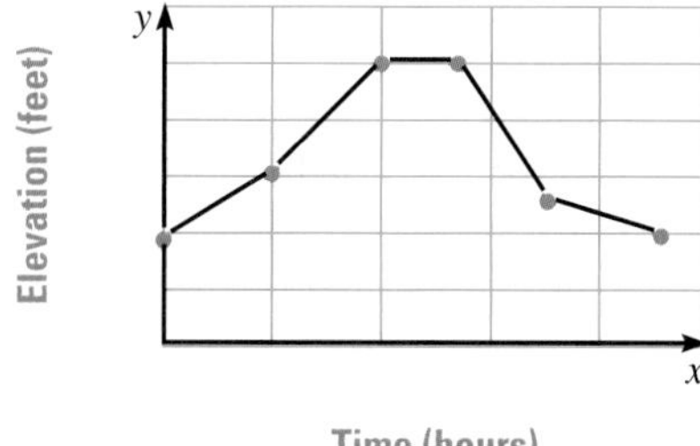

39. **HIKING** The graph shows the elevation of a hiker walking on a mountain trail. Give a verbal description of the hike.

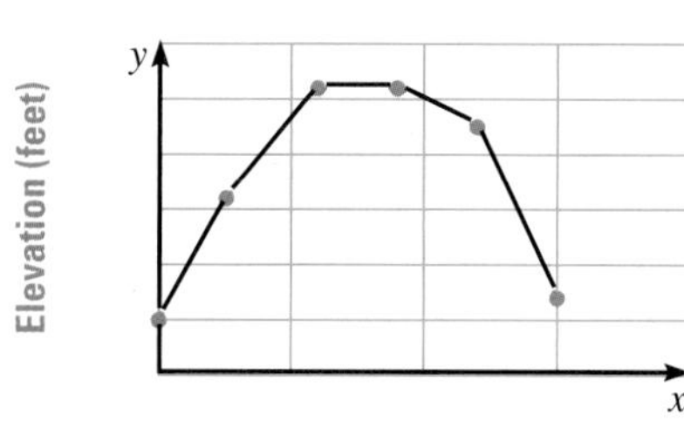

40. ★ **EXTENDED RESPONSE** The graph shows the number (in thousands) of undergraduate students who majored in biological science, engineering, or liberal arts in the United States from 1990 to 2000.

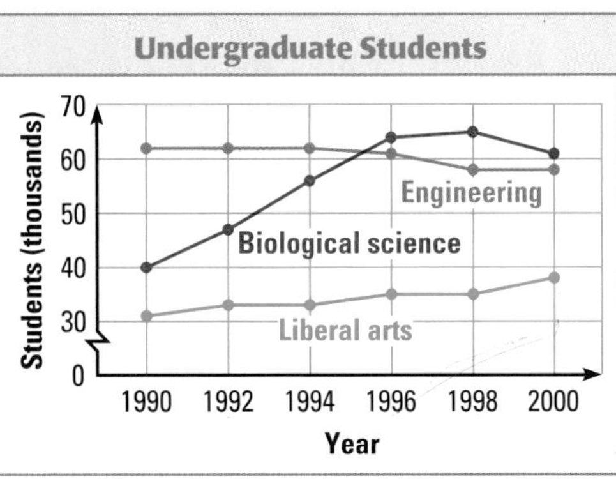

a. During which two-year period did the number of engineering students decrease the most? Estimate the rate of change for this time period.

b. During which two-year period did the number of liberal arts students increase the most? Estimate the rate of change for this time period.

c. How did the total number of students majoring in biological science, engineering, and liberal arts change in the 10 year period? *Explain* your thinking.

41. **CHALLENGE** Imagine the containers below being filled with water at a constant rate. Sketch a graph that shows the water level for each container during the time it takes to fill the container with water.

a. 

b. 

c. 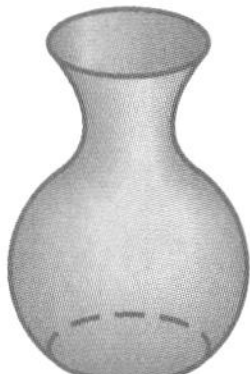

Mixed Review

Check whether the given number is a solution of the equation or inequality. *(p. 21)*

42. $4b - 7 = b + 11; 6$

43. $x - 8 = -2x - 14; -1$

44. $\frac{t}{4} + 9 = 13; 16$

45. $a + 9 > 20; 3$

46. $\frac{y + 3}{2} < 13; 23$

47. $2(p + 5) \leq 75; 4$

Evaluate the expression. Approximate the square root to the nearest integer, if necessary. *(p. 110)*

48. $\sqrt{16}$

49. $-\sqrt{9}$

50. $\pm\sqrt{45}$

51. $\sqrt{136}$

52. $\pm\sqrt{64}$

53. $-\sqrt{33}$

54. $\pm\sqrt{154}$

55. $\pm\sqrt{256}$

56. $\sqrt{4761}$

PREVIEW
Prepare for Lesson 4.5 in Exs. 57–62.

Find the x-intercept and the y-intercept of the graph of the equation. *(p. 225)*

57. $y = x + 7$

58. $y = -x - 1$

59. $y = 8 - 2x$

60. $y = 3x + 5$

61. $y = 4x - 10$

62. $y = -9 + 6x$

4.5 Slope and y-Intercept

QUESTION How can you use the equation of a line to find its slope and y-intercept?

EXPLORE Find the slopes and the y-intercepts of lines

STEP 1 *Find y when $x = 0$*
Copy the table below. Let $x_1 = 0$ and find y_1 for each equation. Use your answers to complete the second and fifth columns in the table.

STEP 2 *Find y when $x = 2$*
Let $x_2 = 2$ and find y_2 for each equation. Use your answers to complete the third column in the table.

STEP 3 *Compute the slope*
Use the slope formula and the ordered pairs you found in the second and third columns to complete the fourth column.

Line	$(0, y_1)$	$(2, y_2)$	Slope	y-intercept
$y = 4x + 3$	(0, 3)	(2, 11)	$\frac{11 - 3}{2 - 0} = 4$	3
$y = -2x + 3$	(0, ?)	(2, ?)	?	?
$y = \frac{1}{2}x + 4$	(0, ?)	(2, ?)	?	?
$y = -4x - 3$	(0, ?)	(2, ?)	?	?
$y = -\frac{1}{4}x - 3$	(0, ?)	(2, ?)	?	?

DRAW CONCLUSIONS Use your observations to complete these exercises

1. *Compare* the slope of each line with the equation of the line. What do you notice?
2. *Compare* the y-intercept of each line with the equation of the line. What do you notice?

Predict the slope and the y-intercept of the line with the given equation. Then check your predictions by finding the slope and y-intercept as you did in the table above.

3. $y = -5x + 1$
4. $y = \frac{3}{4}x + 2$
5. $y = -\frac{3}{2}x - 1$

6. **REASONING** Use the procedure you followed to complete the table above to show that the y-intercept of the graph of $y = mx + b$ is b and the slope of the graph is m.

4.5 Graph Using Slope-Intercept Form

Before You found slopes and graphed equations using intercepts.

Now You will graph linear equations using slope-intercept form.

Why? So you can model a worker's earnings, as in Ex. 43.

Key Vocabulary
- **slope-intercept form**
- **parallel**

In the activity on page 243, you saw how the slope and y-intercept of the graph of a linear equation in the form $y = mx + b$ are related to the equation.

KEY CONCEPT *For Your Notebook*

Finding the Slope and y-Intercept of a Line

Words

A linear equation of the form $y = mx + b$ is written in **slope-intercept form** where m is the slope and b is the y-intercept of the equation's graph.

Symbols

$y = mx + b$

slope y-intercept

$y = \frac{1}{3}x + 1$

Graph

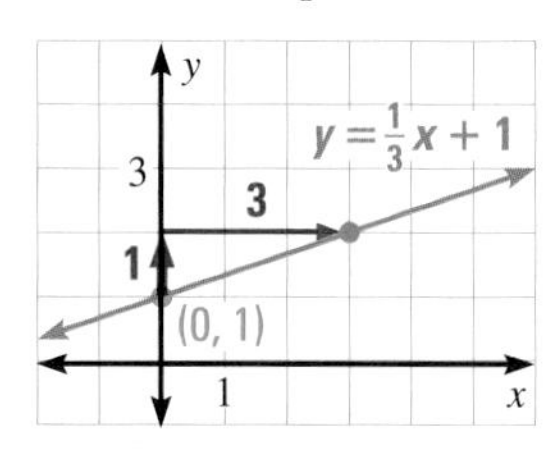

EXAMPLE 1 Identify slope and y-intercept

Identify the slope and y-intercept of the line with the given equation.

a. $y = 3x + 4$ **b.** $3x + y = 2$

Solution

a. The equation is in the form $y = mx + b$. So, the slope of the line is 3, and the y-intercept is 4.

b. Rewrite the equation in slope-intercept form by solving for y.

$3x + y = 2$	**Write original equation.**
$y = -3x + 2$	**Subtract $3x$ from each side.**

▶ The line has a slope of -3 and a y-intercept of 2.

REWRITE EQUATIONS
When you rewrite a linear equation in slope-intercept form, you are expressing y as a function of x.

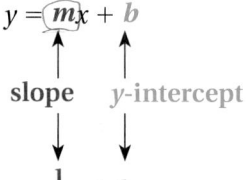

✓ **GUIDED PRACTICE** for Example 1

Identify the slope and y-intercept of the line with the given equation.

1. $y = 5x - 3$ **2.** $3x - 3y = 12$ **3.** $x + 4y = 6$

EXAMPLE 2 Graph an equation using slope-intercept form

Graph the equation $2x + y = 3$.

Solution

STEP 1 **Rewrite** the equation in slope-intercept form.

$y = -2x + 3$

STEP 2 **Identify** the slope and the y-intercept.

$m = -2$ and $b = 3$

STEP 3 **Plot** the point that corresponds to the y-intercept, $(0, 3)$.

STEP 4 **Use** the slope to locate a second point on the line. Draw a line through the two points.

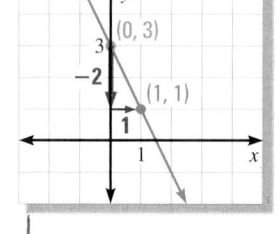

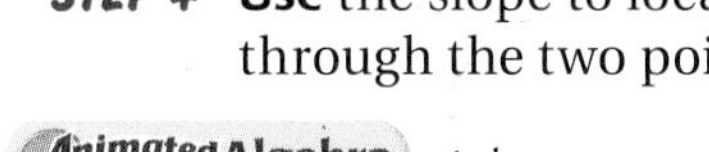

Animated Algebra at classzone.com

CHECK REASONABLENESS
To check the line drawn in Example 2, substitute the coordinates of the second point into the original equation. You should get a true statement.

MODELING In real-world problems that can be modeled by linear equations, the y-intercept is often an initial value, and the slope is a rate of change.

EXAMPLE 3 Change slopes of lines

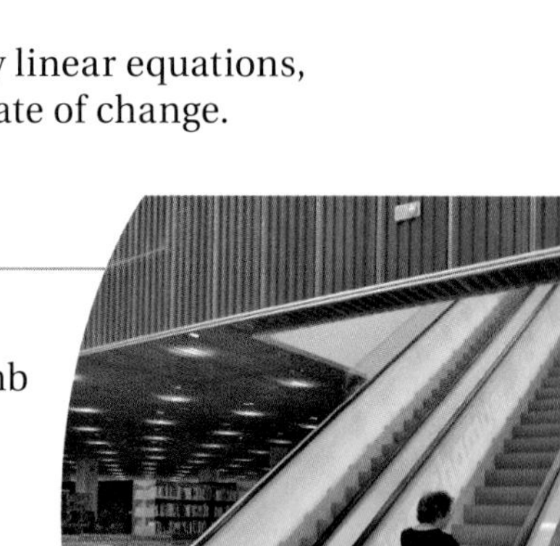

ESCALATORS To get from one floor to another at a library, you can take either the stairs or the escalator. You can climb stairs at a rate of 1.75 feet per second, and the escalator rises at a rate of 2 feet per second. You have to travel a vertical distance of 28 feet. The equations model the vertical distance d (in feet) you have left to travel after t seconds.

Stairs: $d = -1.75t + 28$ **Escalator:** $d = -2t + 28$

a. Graph the equations in the same coordinate plane.

b. How much time do you save by taking the escalator?

Solution

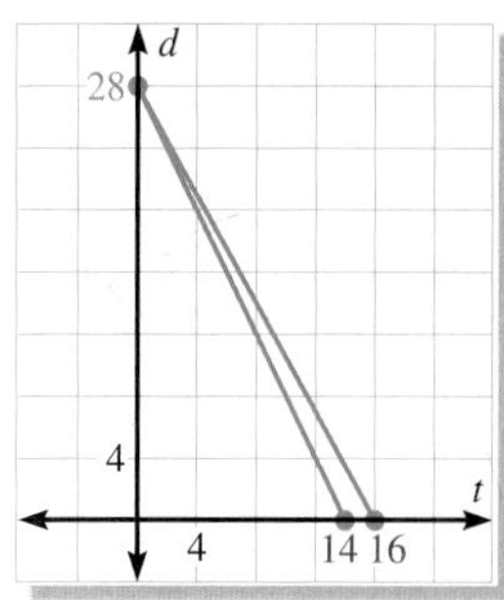

a. Draw the graph of $d = -1.75t + 28$ using the fact that the d-intercept is 28 and the slope is -1.75. Similarly, draw the graph of $d = -2t + 28$. The graphs make sense only in the first quadrant.

b. The equation $d = -1.75t + 28$ has a t-intercept of **16**. The equation $d = -2t + 28$ has a t-intercept of **14**. So, you save $16 - 14 = 2$ seconds by taking the escalator.

GUIDED PRACTICE for Examples 2 and 3

4. Graph the equation $y = -2x + 5$.

5. **WHAT IF?** In Example 3, suppose a person can climb stairs at a rate of 1.4 feet per second. How much time does taking the escalator save?

EXAMPLE 4 Change intercepts of lines

TELEVISION A company produced two 30 second commercials, one for \$300,000 and the second for \$400,000. Each airing of either commercial on a particular station costs \$150,000. The cost C (in thousands of dollars) to produce the first commercial and air it n times is given by $C = 150n + 300$. The cost to produce the second and air it n times is given by $C = 150n + 400$.

a. Graph both equations in the same coordinate plane.

b. Based on the graphs, what is the difference of the costs to produce each commercial and air it 2 times? 4 times? What do you notice about the differences of the costs?

Solution

a. The graphs of the equations are shown.

b. You can see that the vertical distance between the lines is \$100,000 when $n = 2$ and $n = 4$.

The difference of the costs is \$100,000 no matter how many times the commercials are aired.

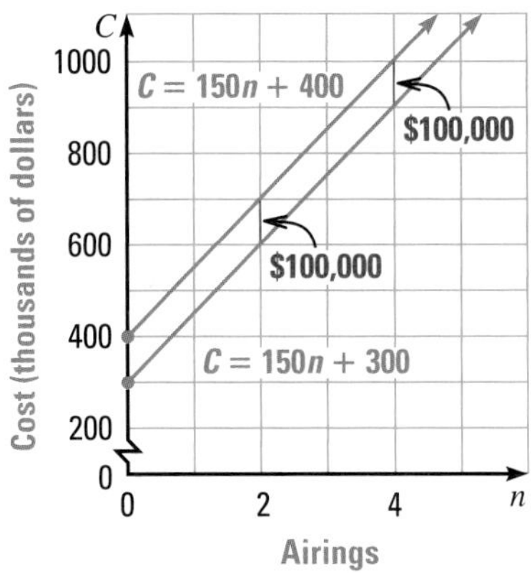

PARALLEL LINES Two lines in the same plane are **parallel** if they do not intersect. Because slope gives the rate at which a line rises or falls, two nonvertical lines with the same slope are parallel.

EXAMPLE 5 Identify parallel lines

Determine which of the lines are parallel.

Find the slope of each line.

Line *a*: $m = \frac{-1 - 0}{-1 - 2} = \frac{-1}{-3} = \frac{1}{3}$

Line *b*: $m = \frac{-3 - (-1)}{0 - 5} = \frac{-2}{-5} = \frac{2}{5}$

Line *c*: $m = \frac{-5 - (-3)}{-2 - 4} = \frac{-2}{-6} = \frac{1}{3}$

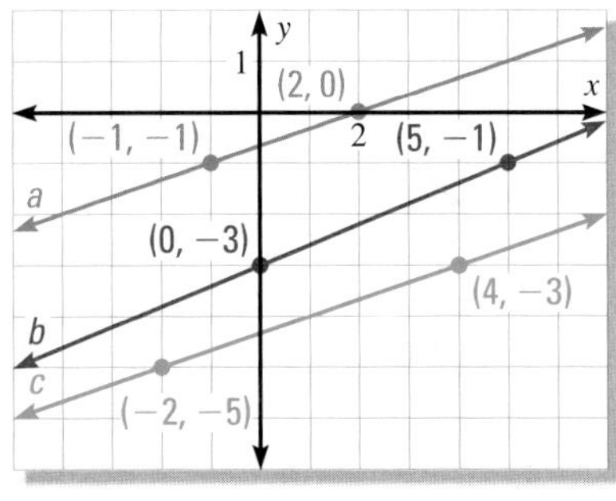

▸ Line a and line c have the same slope, so they are parallel.

✓ GUIDED PRACTICE for Examples 4 and 5

6. **WHAT IF?** In Example 4, suppose that the cost of producing and airing a third commercial is given by $C = 150n + 200$. Graph the equation. Find the difference of the costs of the second commercial and the third.

7. Determine which lines are parallel: line a through $(-1, 2)$ and $(3, 4)$; line b through $(2, 2)$ and $(5, 8)$; line c through $(-9, -2)$ and $(-3, 1)$.

4.5 EXERCISES

HOMEWORK KEY

○ = **WORKED-OUT SOLUTIONS** on p. WS9 for Exs. 11, 21, and 41

★ = **STANDARDIZED TEST PRACTICE** Exs. 2, 9, 10, 36, 42, and 44

SKILL PRACTICE

1. **VOCABULARY** Copy and complete: Two lines in the same plane are _?_ if they do not intersect.

2. ★ **WRITING** What is the slope-intercept form of a linear equation? *Explain* why this form is called slope-intercept form.

EXAMPLE 1 on p. 244 for Exs. 3–16

SLOPE AND *y*-INTERCEPT Identify the slope and *y*-intercept of the line with the given equation.

3. $y = 2x + 1$
4. $y = -x$
5. $y = 6 - 3x$
6. $y = -7 + 5x$
7. $y = \frac{2}{3}x - 1$
8. $y = -\frac{1}{4}x + 8$

9. ★ **MULTIPLE CHOICE** What is the slope of the line with the equation $y = -18x - 9$?

Ⓐ -18 Ⓑ -9 Ⓒ 9 Ⓓ 18

10. ★ **MULTIPLE CHOICE** What is the *y*-intercept of the line with the equation $x - 3y = -12$?

Ⓐ -12 Ⓑ -4 Ⓒ 4 Ⓓ 12

REWRITING EQUATIONS Rewrite the equation in slope-intercept form. Then identify the slope and the *y*-intercept of the line.

11. $4x + y = 1$
12. $x - y = 6$
13. $6x - 3y = -9$
14. $-12x - 4y = 2$
15. $2x + 5y = -10$
16. $-x - 10y = 20$

EXAMPLE 2 on p. 245 for Exs. 17–29

MATCHING EQUATIONS WITH GRAPHS Match the equation with its graph.

17. $2x + 3y = 6$
18. $2x + 3y = -6$
19. $2x - 3y = 6$

A.

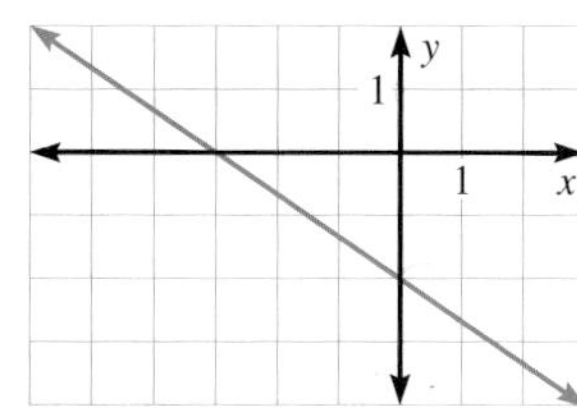

B.

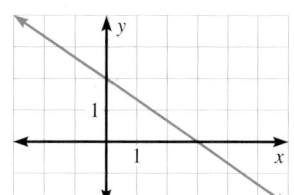

C.

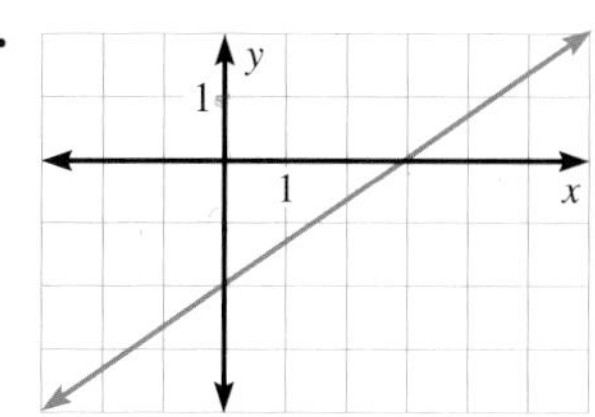

20. **ERROR ANALYSIS** *Describe* and correct the error in graphing the equation $y = 4x - 1$.

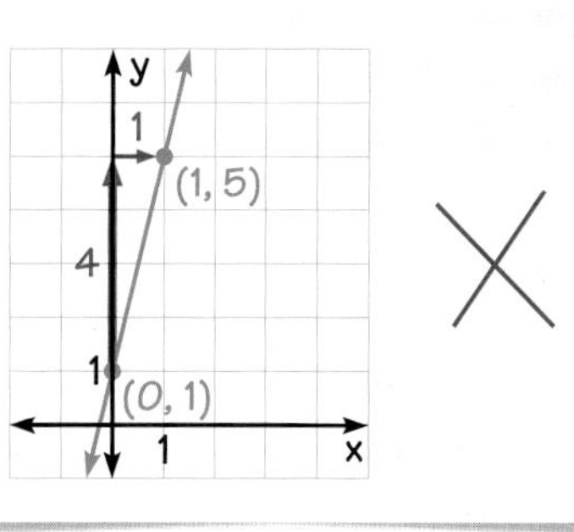

GRAPHING EQUATIONS Graph the equation.

21. $y = -6x + 1$
22. $y = 3x + 2$
23. $y = -x + 7$
24. $y = \frac{2}{3}x$
25. $y = \frac{1}{4}x - 5$
26. $y = -\frac{5}{2}x + 2$
27. $7x - 2y = -11$
28. $-8x - 2y = 32$
29. $-x - 0.5y = 2.5$

EXAMPLE 5 on p. 246 for Exs. 30–35

PARALLEL LINES Determine which lines are parallel.

30.

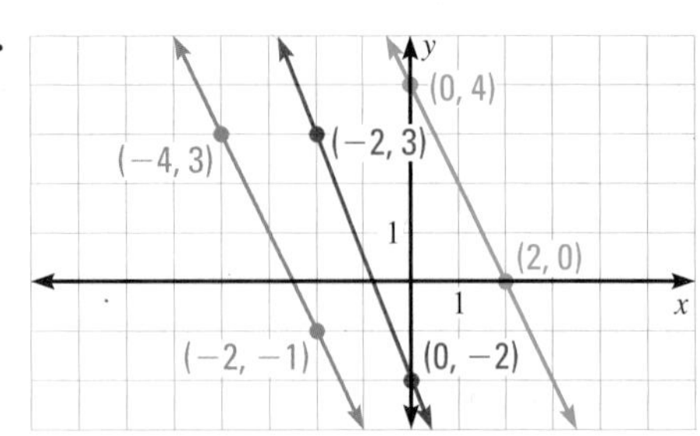

31.

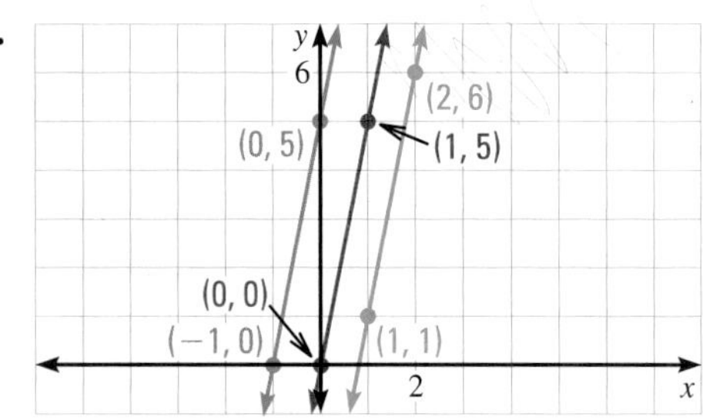

PARALLEL LINES Tell whether the graphs of the two equations are parallel lines. *Explain* your reasoning.

32. $y = 5x - 7$, $5x + y = 7$
33. $y = 3x + 2$, $-7 + 3x = y$
34. $y = -0.5x$, $x + 2y = 18$
35. $4x + y = 3$, $x + 4y = 3$

36. ★ **OPEN-ENDED** Write the equation of a line that is parallel to $6x + y = 24$. *Explain* your reasoning.

REASONING Find the value of *k* so that the lines through the given points are parallel.

37. Line 1: $(-4, -2)$ and $(0, 0)$
Line 2: $(2, 7)$ and $(k, 5)$

38. Line 1: $(-1, 9)$ and $(-6, -6)$
Line 2: $(-7, k)$ and $(0, -2)$

39. **CHALLENGE** Find the slope and y-intercept of the graph of the equation $Ax + By = C$ where $B \neq 0$. Use your results to find the slope and y-intercept of the graph of $3x + 2y = 18$.

PROBLEM SOLVING

EXAMPLES 3 and 4 on pp. 245–246 for Exs. 40–44

40. **HOCKEY** Your family spends \$60 on tickets to a hockey game and \$4 per hour for parking. The total cost C (in dollars) is given by $C = 60 + 4t$ where t is the time (in hours) your family's car is parked.

a. Graph the equation.

b. Suppose the parking fee is raised to \$5.50 per hour so that the total cost of tickets and parking for t hours is $C = 60 + 5.5t$. Graph the equation in the same coordinate plane as the equation in part (a).

c. How much more does it cost to go to a game for 4 hours after the parking fee is raised?

@HomeTutor for problem solving help at classzone.com

41. SPEED LIMITS In 1995 Pennsylvania changed its maximum speed limit on rural interstate highways, as shown below. The diagram also shows the distance d (in miles) a person could travel driving at the maximum speed limit for t hours both before and after 1995.

a. Graph both equations in the same coordinate plane.

b. Use the graphs to find the difference of the distances a person could drive in 3 hours before and after the speed limit was changed.

@HomeTutor for problem solving help at classzone.com

42. ★ SHORT RESPONSE A service station charges \$40 per hour for labor plus the cost of parts to repair a car. Parts can either be ordered from the car dealership for \$250 or from a warehouse for \$200. The equations below give the total repair cost C (in dollars) for a repair that takes t hours using parts from the dealership or from the warehouse.

Dealership: $C = 40t + 250$ **Warehouse:** $C = 40t + 200$

a. Graph both equations in the same coordinate plane.

b. Use the graphs to find the difference of the costs if the repair takes 3 hours. What if the repair takes 4 hours? What do you notice about the differences of the costs? *Explain.*

43. FACTORY SHIFTS Welders at a factory can work one of two shifts. Welders on the first shift earn \$12 per hour while workers on the second shift earn \$14 per hour. The total amount a (in dollars) a first-shift worker earns is given by $a = 12t$ where t is the time (in hours) worked. The total amount a second-shift worker earns is given by $a = 14t$.

a. Graph both equations in the same coordinate plane. What do the slopes and the a-intercepts of the graphs mean in this situation?

b. How much more money does a welder earn for a 40 hour week if he or she works the second shift rather than the first shift?

44. ★ EXTENDED RESPONSE An artist is renting a booth at an art show. A small booth costs \$350 to rent. The artist plans to sell framed pictures for \$50 each. The profit P (in dollars) the artist makes after selling p pictures is given by $P = 50p - 350$.

a. Graph the equation.

b. If the artist decides to rent a larger booth for \$500, the profit is given by $P = 50p - 500$. Graph this equation on the same coordinate plane you used in part (a).

c. The artist can display 80 pictures in the small booth and 120 in the larger booth. If the artist is able to sell all of the pictures, which booth should the artist rent? *Explain.*

45. **CHALLENGE** To use a rock climbing wall at a college, a person who does not attend the college has to pay a \$5 certification fee plus \$3 per visit. The total cost C (in dollars) for a person who does not attend the college is given by $C = 3v + 5$ where v is the number of visits to the rock climbing wall. A student at the college pays only an \$8 certification fee, so the total cost for a student is given by $C = 8$.

a. Graph both equations in the same coordinate plane. At what point do the lines intersect? What does the point of intersection represent?

b. When will a nonstudent pay more than a student? When will a student pay more than a nonstudent? *Explain.*

MIXED REVIEW

Simplify the expression. *(p. 96)*

46. $3(x + 24)$ **47.** $5(x - 5)$ **48.** $8(x - 6)$

Solve the equation.

49. $3x + x = 8$ *(p. 141)* **50.** $5(x - 3x) = 15$ *(p. 148)* **51.** $\frac{4}{3}(8x - 3) = 16$ *(p. 148)*

PREVIEW
Prepare for Lesson 4.6 in Exs. 52–57.

Find the slope of the line that passes through the points. *(p. 235)*

52. $(3, 4)$ and $(9, 5)$ **53.** $(4, -4)$ and $(-2, 2)$ **54.** $(-3, -7)$ and $(0, -7)$

Solve the proportion. Check your solution. *(p. 168)*

55. $\frac{4}{5} = \frac{x}{50}$ **56.** $\frac{2x}{x+4} = \frac{8}{9}$ **57.** $\frac{7t-2}{8} = \frac{3t-4}{5}$

QUIZ *for Lessons 4.4–4.5*

Find the slope of the line that passes through the points. *(p. 235)*

1. $(3, -11)$ and $(0, 4)$ **2.** $(2, 1)$ and $(8, 4)$ **3.** $(-4, -1)$ and $(-1, -1)$

Identify the slope and y-intercept of the line with the given equation. *(p. 244)*

4. $y = -x + 9$ **5.** $2x + 9y = -18$ **6.** $-x + 6y = 21$

Graph the equation. *(p. 244)*

7. $y = -2x + 11$ **8.** $y = \frac{5}{3}x - 8$ **9.** $-3x - 4y = -12$

10. **RED OAKS** Red oak trees grow at a rate of about 2 feet per year. You buy and plant two red oak trees, one that is 6 feet tall and one that is 8 feet tall. The height h (in feet) of the shorter tree can be modeled by $h = 2t + 6$ where t is the time (in years) since you planted the tree. The height of the taller tree can be modeled by $h = 2t + 8$. *(p. 244)*

a. Graph both equations in the same coordinate plane.

b. Use the graphs to find the difference of the heights of the trees 5 years after you plant them. What is the difference after 10 years? What do you notice about the difference of the heights of the two trees?

Extension

Use after Lesson 4.5

Solve Linear Equations by Graphing

GOAL Use graphs to solve linear equations.

In Chapter 3, you learned how to solve linear equations in one variable algebraically. You can also solve linear equations graphically.

KEY CONCEPT *For Your Notebook*

Steps for Solving Linear Equations Graphically

Use the following steps to solve a linear equation in one variable graphically.

STEP 1 **Write** the equation in the form $ax + b = 0$.

STEP 2 **Write** the related function $y = ax + b$.

STEP 3 **Graph** the equation $y = ax + b$.

The solution of $ax + b = 0$ is the x-intercept of the graph of $y = ax + b$.

EXAMPLE 1 Solve an equation graphically

Solve $\frac{5}{2}x + 2 = 3x$ graphically. Check your solution algebraically.

Solution

STEP 1 **Write** the equation in the form $ax + b = 0$.

$\frac{5}{2}x + 2 = 3x$ **Write original equation.**

$-\frac{1}{2}x + 2 = 0$ **Subtract 3x from each side.**

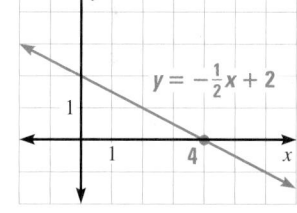

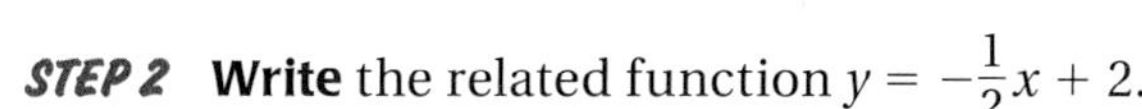

STEP 2 **Write** the related function $y = -\frac{1}{2}x + 2$.

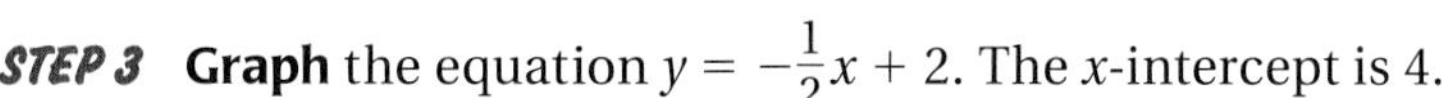

STEP 3 **Graph** the equation $y = -\frac{1}{2}x + 2$. The x-intercept is 4.

▶ The solution of $\frac{5}{2}x + 2 = 3x$ is 4.

CHECK Use substitution.

$\frac{5}{2}x + 2 = 3x$ **Write original equation.**

$\frac{5}{2}(4) + 2 \stackrel{?}{=} 3(4)$ **Substitute 4 for x.**

$10 + 2 = 12$ **Simplify.**

$12 = 12$ ✓ **Solution checks.**

EXAMPLE 2 Approximate a real-world solution

POPULATION The United States population P (in millions) can be modeled by the function $P = 2.683t + 213.1$ where t is the number of years since 1975. In approximately what year will the population be 350 million?

Solution

Substitute 350 for P in the linear model. You can answer the question by solving the resulting linear equation $350 = 2.683t + 213.1$.

STEP 1 **Write** the equation in the form $ax + b = 0$.

$350 = 2.683t + 213.1$	**Write equation.**
$0 = 2.683t - 136.9$	**Subtract 350 from each side.**
$0 = 2.683x - 136.9$	**Substitute *x* for *t*.**

STEP 2 **Write** the related function: $y = 2.683x - 136.9$.

SET THE WINDOW
Use the following viewing window for Example 2.
Xmin=−5
Xmax=60
Xscl=5
Ymin=−150
Ymax=10
Yscl=10

STEP 3 **Graph** the related function on a graphing calculator. Use the *trace* feature to approximate the x-intercept. You will know that you've crossed the x-axis when the y-values change from negative to positive. The x-intercept is about 51.

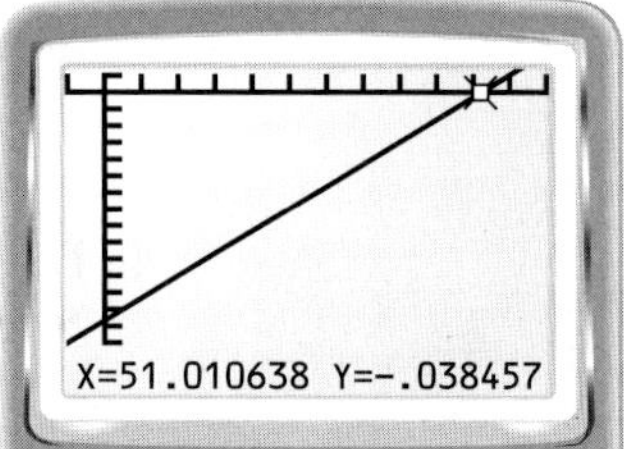

▶ Because x is the number of years since 1975, you can estimate that the population will be 350 million about 51 years after 1975, or in 2026.

PRACTICE

EXAMPLE 1
on p. 251
for Exs. 1–6

Solve the equation graphically. Then check your solution algebraically.

1. $6x + 5 = -7$
2. $-7x + 18 = -3$
3. $2x - 4 = 3x$
4. $\frac{1}{2}x - 3 = 2x$
5. $-4 + 9x = -3x + 2$
6. $10x - 18x = 4x - 6$

EXAMPLE 2
on p. 252
for Exs. 7–9

7. **CABLE TELEVISION** The number s (in millions) of cable television subscribers can be modeled by the function $s = 1.79t + 51.1$ where t is the number of years since 1990. Use a graphing calculator to approximate the year when the number of subscribers was 70 million.

8. **EDUCATION** The number b (in thousands) of bachelor's degrees in Spanish earned in the U.S. can be modeled by the function $b = 0.281t + 4.26$ where t is the number of years since 1990. Use a graphing calculator to approximate the year when the number of degrees will be 9000.

9. **TRAVEL** The number of miles m (in billions) traveled by vehicles in New York can be modeled by $m = 2.56t + 113$ where t is the number of years since 1994. Use a graphing calculator to approximate the year in which the number of vehicle miles of travel in New York was 130 billion.

4.6 Model Direct Variation

Before You wrote and graphed linear equations.
Now You will write and graph direct variation equations.
Why? So you can model distance traveled, as in Ex. 40.

Key Vocabulary
- **direct variation**
- **constant of variation**

Two variables x and y show **direct variation** provided $y = ax$ and $a \neq 0$. The nonzero number a is called the **constant of variation**, and y is said to *vary directly* with x.

The equation $y = 5x$ is an example of direct variation, and the constant of variation is 5. The equation $y = x + 5$ is *not* an example of direct variation.

EXAMPLE 1 Identify direct variation equations

Tell whether the equation represents direct variation. If so, identify the constant of variation.

a. $2x - 3y = 0$

b. $-x + y = 4$

Solution

To tell whether an equation represents direct variation, try to rewrite the equation in the form $y = ax$.

a. $2x - 3y = 0$ Write original equation.

$-3y = -2x$ Subtract $2x$ from each side.

$y = \frac{2}{3}x$ Simplify.

▶ Because the equation $2x - 3y = 0$ can be rewritten in the form $y = ax$, it represents direct variation. The constant of variation is $\frac{2}{3}$.

b. $-x + y = 4$ Write original equation.

$y = x + 4$ Add x to each side.

▶ Because the equation $-x + y = 4$ cannot be rewritten in the form $y = ax$, it does not represent direct variation.

✓ **GUIDED PRACTICE** for Example 1

Tell whether the equation represents direct variation. If so, identify the constant of variation.

1. $-x + y = 1$

2. $2x + y = 0$

3. $4x - 5y = 0$

DIRECT VARIATION GRAPHS Notice that a direct variation equation, $y = ax$, is a linear equation in slope-intercept form, $y = mx + b$, with $m = a$ and $b = 0$. The graph of a direct variation equation is a line with a slope of a and a y-intercept of 0. So, the line passes through the origin.

EXAMPLE 2 Graph direct variation equations

Graph the direct variation equation.

a. $y = \frac{2}{3}x$

b. $y = -3x$

Solution

a. Plot a point at the origin. The slope is equal to the constant of variation, or $\frac{2}{3}$. Find and plot a second point, then draw a line through the points.

b. Plot a point at the origin. The slope is equal to the constant of variation, or -3. Find and plot a second point, then draw a line through the points.

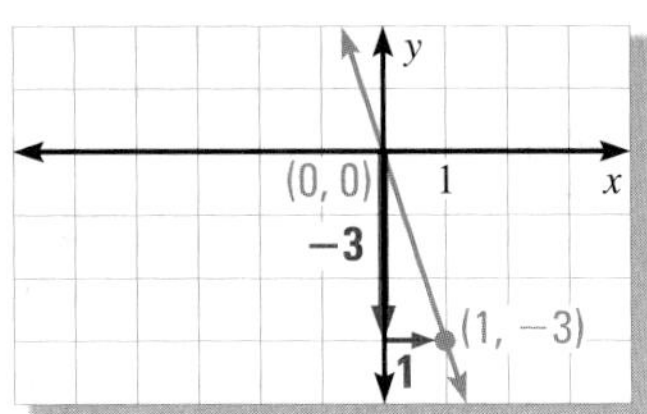

DRAW A GRAPH
If the constant of variation is positive, the graph of $y = ax$ passes through Quadrants I and III. If the constant of variation is negative, the graph of $y = ax$ passes through Quadrants II and IV.

Animated Algebra at classzone.com

EXAMPLE 3 Write and use a direct variation equation

The graph of a direct variation equation is shown.

a. Write the direct variation equation.

b. Find the value of y when $x = 30$.

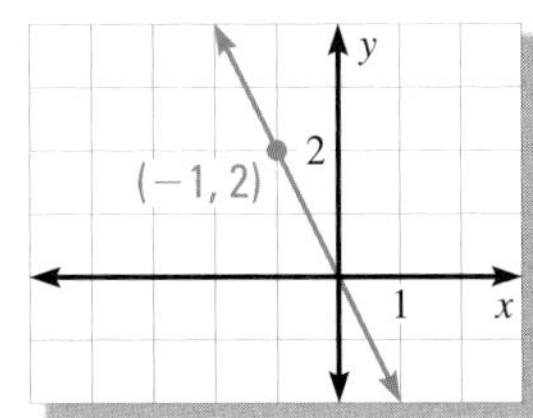

Solution

a. Because y varies directly with x, the equation has the form $y = ax$. Use the fact that $y = 2$ when $x = -1$ to find a.

$y = ax$ **Write direct variation equation.**

$2 = a(-1)$ **Substitute.**

$-2 = a$ **Solve for a.**

▶ A direct variation equation that relates x and y is $y = -2x$.

b. When $x = 30$, $y = -2(30) = -60$.

✓ **GUIDED PRACTICE** for Examples 2 and 3

4. Graph the direct variation equation $y = 2x$.

5. The graph of a direct variation equation passes through the point $(4, 6)$. Write the direct variation equation and find the value of y when $x = 24$.

KEY CONCEPT *For Your Notebook*

Properties of Graphs of Direct Variation Equations

- The graph of a direct variation equation is a line through the origin.
- The slope of the graph of $y = ax$ is a.

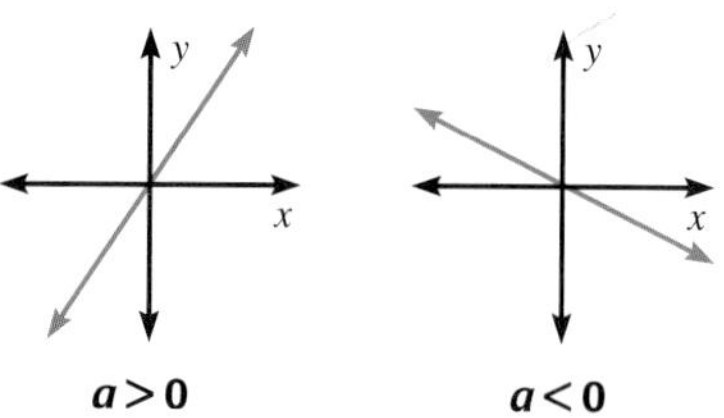

EXAMPLE 4 Solve a multi-step problem

ANOTHER WAY
For alternative methods for solving Example 4, turn to page 260 for the **Problem Solving Workshop**.

SALTWATER AQUARIUM The number s of tablespoons of sea salt needed in a saltwater fish tank varies directly with the number w of gallons of water in the tank. A pet shop owner recommends adding 100 tablespoons of sea salt to a 20 gallon tank.

- Write a direct variation equation that relates w and s.
- How many tablespoons of salt should be added to a 30 gallon saltwater fish tank?

Solution

STEP 1 **Write** a direct variation equation. Because s varies directly with w, you can use the equation $s = aw$. Also use the fact that $s = 100$ when $w = 20$.

$s = aw$ **Write direct variation equation.**

$100 = a(20)$ **Substitute.**

$5 = a$ **Solve for *a*.**

RECOGNIZE RATE OF CHANGE
The value of a in Example 4 is a rate of change: 5 tablespoons of sea salt per gallon of water.

▶ A direct variation equation that relates w and s is $s = 5w$.

STEP 2 **Find** the number of tablespoons of salt that should be added to a 30 gallon saltwater fish tank. Use your direct variation equation from Step 1.

$s = 5w$ **Write direct variation equation.**

$s = 5(30)$ **Substitute 30 for *w*.**

$s = 150$ **Simplify.**

▶ You should add 150 tablespoons of salt to a 30 gallon fish tank.

✓ **GUIDED PRACTICE** for Example 4

6. **WHAT IF?** In Example 4, suppose the fish tank is a 25 gallon tank. How many tablespoons of salt should be added to the tank?

RATIOS The direct variation equation $y = ax$ can be rewritten as $\frac{y}{x} = a$ for $x \neq 0$. So, in a direct variation, the ratio of y to x is constant for all nonzero data pairs (x, y).

EXAMPLE 5 Use a direct variation model

ONLINE MUSIC The table shows the cost C of downloading s songs at an Internet music site.

Number of songs, s	Cost, C (dollars)
3	2.97
5	4.95
7	6.93

a. Explain why C varies directly with s.

b. Write a direct variation equation that relates s and C.

CHECK RATIOS
For real-world data, the ratios may not be exactly equal. You may still be able to use a direct variation model when the ratios are approximately equal.

Solution

a. To explain why C varies directly with s, compare the ratios $\frac{C}{s}$ for all data pairs (s, C): $\frac{2.97}{3} = \frac{4.95}{5} = \frac{6.93}{7} = 0.99$.

Because the ratios all equal 0.99, C varies directly with s.

b. A direct variation equation is $C = 0.99s$.

GUIDED PRACTICE for Example 5

7. **WHAT IF?** In Example 5, suppose the website charges a total of \$1.99 for the first 5 songs you download and \$.99 for each song after the first 5. Is it reasonable to use a direct variation model for this situation? *Explain.*

4.6 EXERCISES

HOMEWORK KEY

○ = **WORKED-OUT SOLUTIONS** on p. WS9 for Exs. 7, 21, and 43

★ = **STANDARDIZED TEST PRACTICE** Exs. 2, 9, 28, 38, 43, 44, and 46

◆ = **MULTIPLE REPRESENTATIONS** Ex. 45

SKILL PRACTICE

1. **VOCABULARY** Copy and complete: Two variables x and y show __?__ provided $y = ax$ and $a \neq 0$.

2. ★ **WRITING** A line has a slope of -3 and a y-intercept of 4. Is the equation of the line a direct variation equation? *Explain.*

EXAMPLE 1 on p. 253 for Exs. 3–10

IDENTIFYING DIRECT VARIATION EQUATIONS Tell whether the equation represents direct variation. If so, identify the constant of variation.

3. $y = x$
4. $y = 5x - 1$
5. $2x + y = 3$
6. $x - 3y = 0$
7. $8x + 2y = 0$
8. $2.4x + 6 = 1.2y$

9. ★ **MULTIPLE CHOICE** Which equation is a direct variation equation?

Ⓐ $y = 7 - 3x$ Ⓑ $3x - 7y = 1$ Ⓒ $3x - 7y = 0$ Ⓓ $3y = 7x - 1$

10. **ERROR ANALYSIS** *Describe* and correct the error in identifying the constant of variation for the direct variation equation $-5x + 3y = 0$.

$-5x + 3y = 0$
$3y = 5x$
The constant of variation is 5.

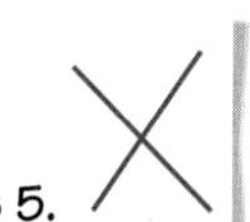

EXAMPLE 2 on p. 254 for Exs. 11–22

GRAPHING EQUATIONS **Graph the direct variation equation.**

11. $y = x$
12. $y = 3x$
13. $y = -4x$
14. $y = 5x$
15. $y = \frac{4}{3}x$
16. $y = \frac{1}{2}x$
17. $y = -\frac{1}{3}x$
18. $y = -\frac{3}{2}x$
19. $12y = -24x$
20. $10y = 25x$
21. $4x + y = 0$
22. $y - 1.25x = 0$

EXAMPLE 3 on p. 254 for Exs. 23–25

WRITING EQUATIONS **The graph of a direct variation equation is shown. Write the direct variation equation. Then find the value of y when $x = 8$.**

23.

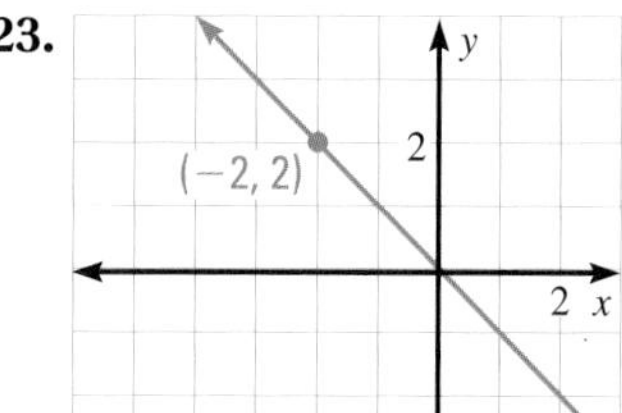

24.

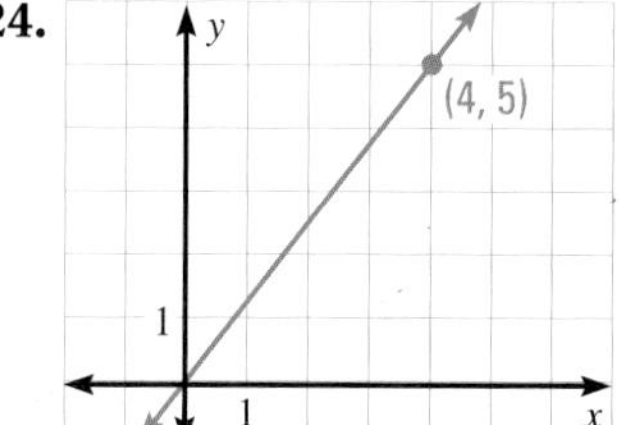

25.

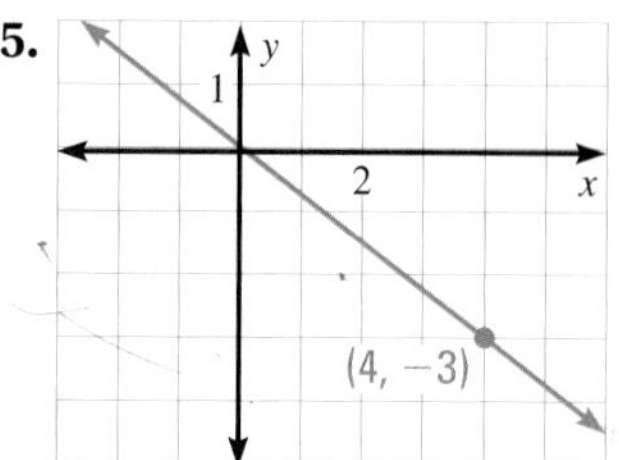

IDENTIFYING DIRECT VARIATION EQUATIONS **Tell whether the table represents direct variation. If so, write the direct variation equation.**

26.

x	1	2	3	4	6
y	5	10	15	20	30

27.

x	−3	−1	1	3	5
y	−2	0	2	4	6

28. ★ **WRITING** A student says that a direct variation equation can be used to model the data in the table. *Explain* why the student is mistaken.

x	2	4	8	16
y	1	2	4	6

WRITING EQUATIONS **Given that y varies directly with x, use the specified values to write a direct variation equation that relates x and y.**

29. $x = 3, y = 9$
30. $x = 2, y = 26$
31. $x = 14, y = 7$
32. $x = 15, y = -5$
33. $x = -2, y = -2$
34. $x = -18, y = -4$
35. $x = \frac{1}{4}, y = 1$
36. $x = -6, y = 15$
37. $x = -5.2, y = 1.4$

38. ★ **WRITING** If y varies directly with x, does x vary directly with y? If so, what is the relationship between the constants of variation? *Explain.*

39. **CHALLENGE** The slope of a line is $-\frac{1}{3}$, and the point $(-6, 2)$ lies on the line. Use the formula for the slope of a line to determine if the equation of the line is a direct variation equation.

PROBLEM SOLVING

EXAMPLE 4 on p. 255 for Exs. 40–42

40. BICYCLES The distance d (in meters) you travel on a bicycle varies directly with the number r of revolutions that the rear tire completes. You travel about 2 meters on a mountain bike for every revolution of the tire.

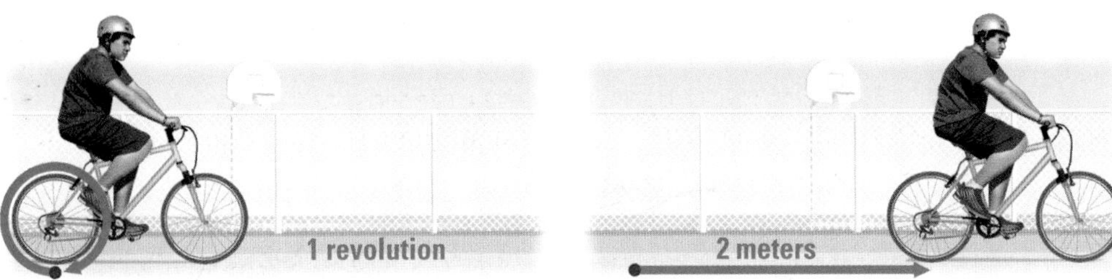

a. Write a direct variation equation that relates r and d.

b. How many meters do you travel in 1500 tire revolutions?

@HomeTutor for problem solving help at classzone.com

41. VACATION TIME At one company, the amount of vacation v (in hours) an employee earns varies directly with the amount of time t (in weeks) he or she works. An employee who works 2 weeks earns 3 hours of vacation.

a. Write a direct variation equation that relates t and v.

b. How many hours of vacation time does an employee earn in 8 weeks?

@HomeTutor for problem solving help at classzone.com

42. LANDSCAPING Landscapers plan to spread a layer of stone on a path. The number s of bags of stone needed depends on the depth d (in inches) of the layer. They need 10 bags to spread a layer of stone that is 2 inches deep. Write a direct variation equation that relates d and s. Then find the number of bags needed to spread a layer that is 3 inches deep.

EXAMPLE 5 on p. 256 for Exs. 43–44

43. ★ **SHORT RESPONSE** At a recycling center, computers and computer accessories can be recycled for a fee f based on weight w, as shown in the table.

Weight, w (pounds)	Fee, f (dollars)
10	2.50
15	3.75
30	7.50

a. *Explain* why f varies directly with w.

b. Write a direct variation equation that relates w and f. Find the total recycling fee for a computer that weighs 18 pounds and a printer that weighs 10 pounds.

44. ★ **SHORT RESPONSE** You can buy gold chain by the inch. The table shows the price of gold chain for various lengths.

Length, ℓ (inches)	7	9	16	18
Price, p (dollars)	8.75	11.25	20.00	22.50

a. *Explain* why p varies directly with ℓ.

b. Write a direct variation equation that relates ℓ and p. If you have $30, what is the longest chain that you can buy?

○ = WORKED-OUT SOLUTIONS on p. WS1

★ = STANDARDIZED TEST PRACTICE

 = MULTIPLE REPRESENTATIONS

45. **MULTIPLE REPRESENTATIONS** The total cost of riding the subway to and from school every day is \$1.50.

a. **Making a Table** Make a table that shows the number d of school days and the total cost C (in dollars) for trips to and from school for some values of d. Assume you travel to school once each school day and home from school once each school day.

b. **Drawing a Graph** Graph the ordered pairs from the table and draw a ray through them.

c. **Writing an Equation** Write an equation of the graph from part (b). Is it a direct variation equation? *Explain.* If there are 22 school days in one month, what will it cost to ride the subway to and from school for that month?

46. ★ **EXTENDED RESPONSE** The table shows the average number of field goals attempted t and the average number of field goals made m per game for all NCAA Division I women's basketball teams for 9 consecutive seasons.

Attempted field goals, t	61.8	61.9	61.8	60.8	59.5	59.0	58.9	59.2	58.4
Field goals made, m	25.7	25.6	25.6	25.2	24.5	24.6	24.5	24.3	24.0

a. **Write** Why is it reasonable to use a direct variation model for this situation? Write a direct variation equation that relates t and m. Find the constant of variation to the nearest tenth.

b. **Estimate** The highest average number of attempted field goals in one season was 66.2. Estimate the number of field goals made that season.

c. **Explain** If the average number of field goals made was increasing rather than decreasing and the number of attempted field goals continued to decrease, would the data show direct variation? *Explain.*

47. **CHALLENGE** In Exercise 40, you found an equation showing that the distance traveled on a bike varies directly with the number of revolutions that the rear tire completes. The number r of tire revolutions varies directly with the number p of pedal revolutions. In a particular gear, you travel about 1.3 meters for every 5 revolutions of the pedals. Show that distance traveled varies directly with pedal revolutions.

MIXED REVIEW

Graph the equation.

48. $y = -8$ *(p. 215)*
49. $x = 6$ *(p. 215)*
50. $2x + y = 4$ *(p. 225)*
51. $-2x + 5y = -30$ *(p. 225)*
52. $0.4x + 2y = 6$ *(p. 225)*
53. $y = 2x - 5$ *(p. 244)*
54. $y = \frac{1}{3}x$ *(p. 244)*
55. $y = -x + 3$ *(p. 244)*
56. $y = -\frac{3}{2}x + 2$ *(p. 244)*

PREVIEW
Prepare for Lesson 4.7 in Exs. 57–62.

Identify the slope and y-intercept of the line with the given equation. *(p. 244)*

57. $y = 3x + 5$
58. $y = -3x$
59. $y = 2x - 5$
60. $y = 4x - 11$
61. $y = \frac{4}{5}x - 3$
62. $y = \frac{5}{4}x + 3.1$

PROBLEM SOLVING WORKSHOP
LESSON 4.6

Using ALTERNATIVE METHODS

Another Way to Solve Example 4, page 255

MULTIPLE REPRESENTATIONS In Example 4 on page 255, you saw how to solve the problem about how much salt to add to a saltwater fish tank by writing and using a direct variation equation. You can also solve the problem using a graph or a proportion.

PROBLEM

SALTWATER AQUARIUM The number s of tablespoons of sea salt needed in a saltwater fish tank varies directly with the number w of gallons of water in the tank. A pet shop owner recommends adding 100 tablespoons of sea salt to a 20 gallon tank. How many tablespoons of salt should be added to a 30 gallon saltwater fish tank?

METHOD 1

Using a Graph An alternative approach is to use a graph.

STEP 1 **Read** the problem. It tells you an amount of salt for a certain size fish tank. You can also assume that if a fishtank has no water, then no salt needs to be added. Write ordered pairs for this information.

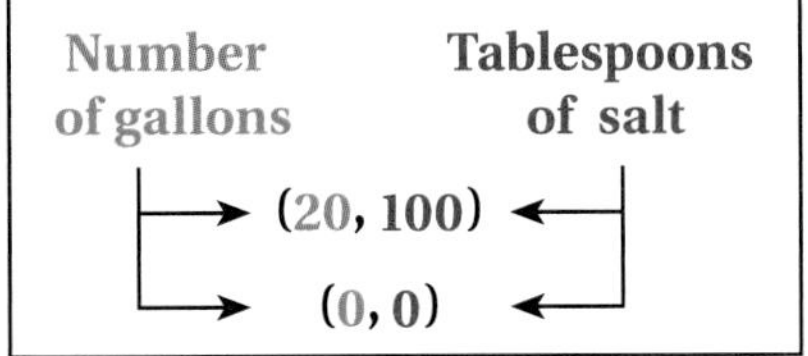

STEP 2 **Graph** the ordered pairs. Draw a line through the points.

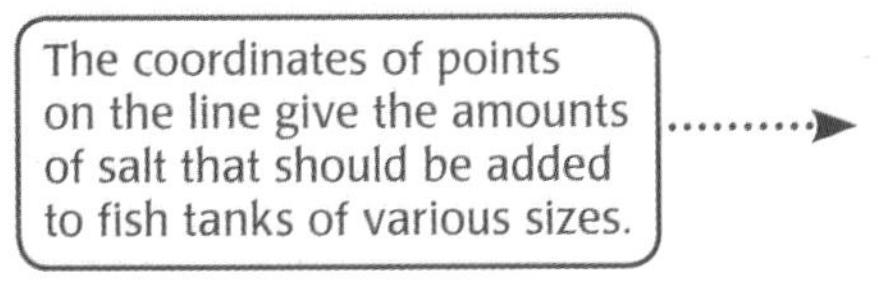

The coordinates of points on the line give the amounts of salt that should be added to fish tanks of various sizes.

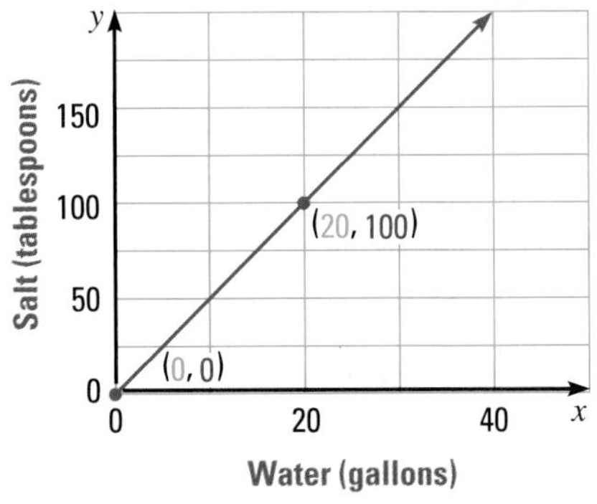

STEP 3 **Find** the point on the graph that has an x-coordinate of 30. The y-coordinate of this point is 150, so 150 tablespoons of salt should be added to a 30 gallon tank.

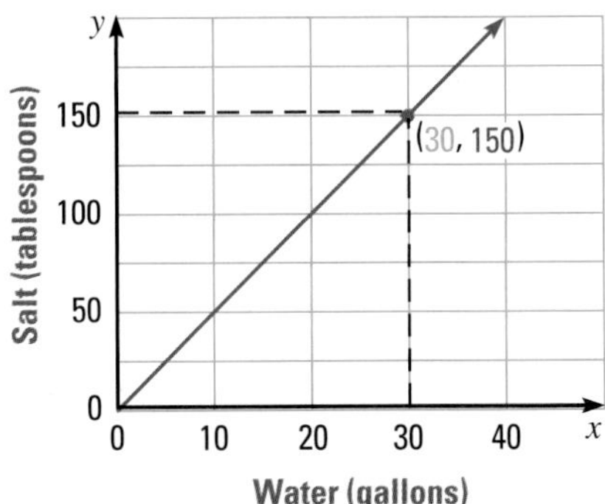

METHOD 2

Writing a Proportion Another alternative approach is to write and solve a proportion.

STEP 1 **Write** a proportion involving two ratios that each compare the amount of water (in gallons) to the amount of salt (in tablespoons).

$$\frac{20}{100} = \frac{30}{s}$$ ← amount of water (gallons) / ← amount of salt (tablespoons)

STEP 2 **Solve** the proportion.

$\frac{20}{100} = \frac{30}{s}$ — Write proportion.

$20s = 100 \cdot 30$ — Cross products property

$20s = 3000$ — Simplify.

$s = 150$ — Divide each side by 20.

▶ You should add 150 tablespoons of salt to a 30 gallon tank.

CHECK Check your answer by writing each ratio in simplest form.

$\frac{20}{100} = \frac{1}{5}$ and $\frac{30}{150} = \frac{1}{5}$

Because each ratio simplifies to $\frac{1}{5}$, the answer is correct.

PRACTICE

1. **WHAT IF?** Suppose the fish tank in the problem above is a 22 gallon tank. How many tablespoons of salt should be added to the tank? *Describe* which method you used to solve this problem.

2. **ADVERTISING** A local newspaper charges by the word for printing classified ads. A 14 word ad costs $5.88. How much would a 21 word ad cost? Solve this problem using two different methods.

3. **REASONING** In Exercise 2, how can you quickly determine the cost of a 7 word ad? *Explain* how you could use the cost of a 7 word ad to solve the problem.

4. **NUTRITION** A company sells fruit smoothies in two sizes of bottles: 6 fluid ounces and 10 fluid ounces. You know that a 6 ounce bottle contains 96 milligrams of sodium. How many milligrams of sodium does a 10 ounce bottle contain?

5. **ERROR ANALYSIS** A student solved the problem in Exercise 4 as shown. *Describe* and correct the error made.

   Let x = the number of milligrams of sodium in a 10 ounce bottle.

   $\frac{6}{x} = \frac{10}{96}$

   $576 = 10x$

   $57.6 = x$

   ✗

6. **SLEEPING** You find an online calculator that calculates the number of calories you burn while sleeping. The results for various sleeping times are shown. About how many more calories would you burn by sleeping for 9.5 hours than for 8 hours? Choose any method for solving the problem.

Hours of sleep	6.5	7	8.5	9
Calories burned	390	420	510	540

4.7 Graph Linear Functions

Before You graphed linear equations and functions.

Now You will use function notation.

Why? So you can model an animal population, as in Example 3.

Key Vocabulary
- **function notation**
- **family of functions**
- **parent linear function**

You have seen linear functions written in the form $y = mx + b$. By naming a function f, you can write it using **function notation**.

$$f(x) = mx + b \qquad \text{Function notation}$$

The symbol $f(x)$ is another name for y and is read as "the value of f at x," or simply as "f of x." It does *not* mean f times x. You can use letters other than f, such as g or h, to name functions.

EXAMPLE 1 Standardized Test Practice

What is the value of the function $f(x) = 3x - 15$ when $x = -3$?

Ⓐ -24 Ⓑ -6 Ⓒ -2 Ⓓ 8

Solution

$f(x) = 3x - 15$ Write original function.

$f(-3) = 3(-3) - 15$ Substitute -3 for x.

$= -24$ Simplify.

▶ The correct answer is A. Ⓐ Ⓑ Ⓒ Ⓓ

GUIDED PRACTICE for Example 1

1. Evaluate the function $h(x) = -7x$ when $x = 7$.

EXAMPLE 2 Find an *x*-value

For the function $f(x) = 2x - 10$, find the value of x so that $f(x) = 6$.

$f(x) = 2x - 10$ Write original function.

$6 = 2x - 10$ Substitute 6 for $f(x)$.

$8 = x$ Solve for x.

▶ When $x = 8$, $f(x) = 6$.

DOMAIN AND RANGE The domain of a function consists of the values of x for which the function is defined. The range consists of the values of $f(x)$ where x is in the domain of f. The graph of a function f is the set of all points $(x, f(x))$.

EXAMPLE 3 Graph a function

INTERPRET MODELS
The rate of change in the wolf population actually varied over time. The model simplifies the situation by assuming a steady rate of change.

GRAY WOLF The gray wolf population in central Idaho was monitored over several years for a project aimed at boosting the number of wolves. The number of wolves can be modeled by the function $f(x) = 37x + 7$ where x is the number of years since 1995. Graph the function and identify its domain and range.

Solution

To graph the function, make a table.

x	$f(x)$
0	$37(0) + 7 = 7$
1	$37(1) + 7 = 44$
2	$37(2) + 7 = 81$

The domain of the function is $x \geq 0$. From the graph or table, you can see that the range of the function is $f(x) \geq 7$.

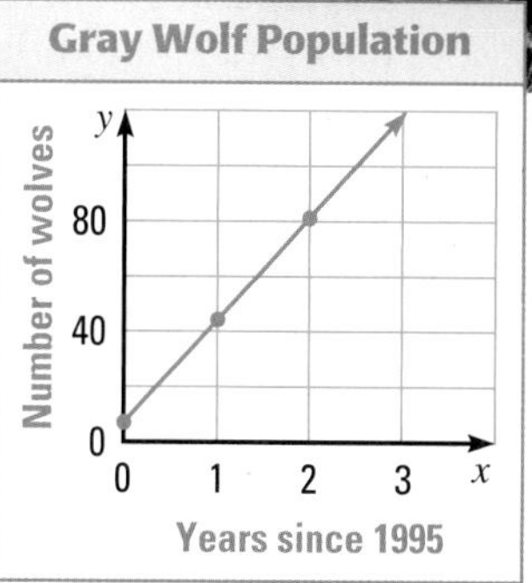

✓ **GUIDED PRACTICE** for Examples 2 and 3

2. **WOLF POPULATION** Use the model from Example 3 to find the value of x so that $f(x) = 155$. *Explain* what the solution means in this situation.

FAMILIES OF FUNCTIONS A **family of functions** is a group of functions with similar characteristics. For example, functions that have the form $f(x) = mx + b$ constitute the family of *linear* functions.

KEY CONCEPT *For Your Notebook*

Parent Function for Linear Functions

The most basic linear function in the family of all linear functions, called the **parent linear function**, is:

$$f(x) = x$$

The graph of the parent linear function is shown.

EXAMPLE 4 Compare graphs with the graph $f(x) = x$

Graph the function. Compare the graph with the graph of $f(x) = x$.

a. $g(x) = x + 3$

b. $h(x) = 2x$

Solution

a.

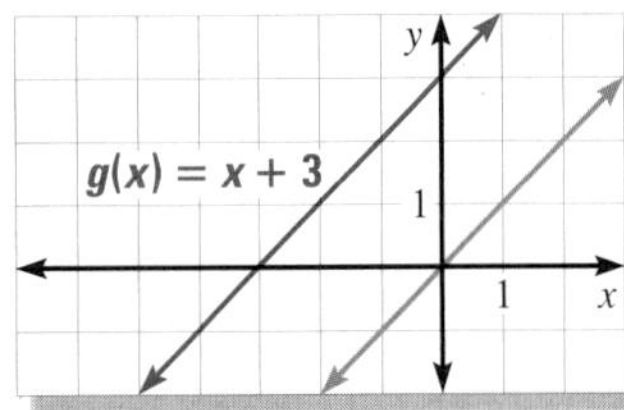

Because the graphs of g and f have the same slope, $m = 1$, the lines are parallel. Also, the y-intercept of the graph of g is 3 more than the y-intercept of the graph of f.

b.

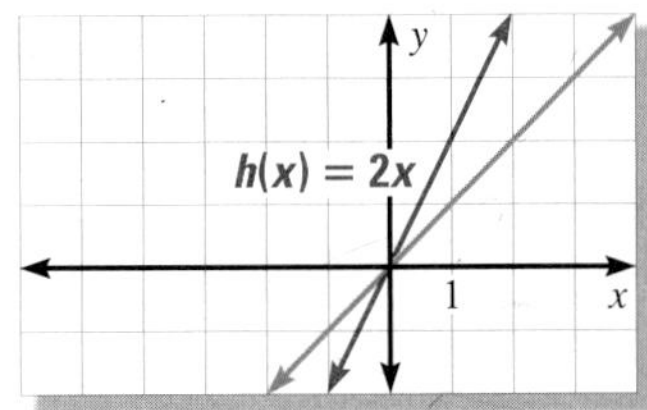

Because the slope of the graph of h is greater than the slope of the graph of f, the graph of h rises faster from left to right. The y-intercept for both graphs is 0, so both lines pass through the origin.

GUIDED PRACTICE for Example 4

3. Graph $h(x) = -3x$. Compare the graph with the graph of $f(x) = x$.

CONCEPT SUMMARY *For Your Notebook*

Comparing Graphs of Linear Functions with the Graph of $f(x) = x$

Changing m or b in the general linear function $g(x) = mx + b$ creates families of linear functions whose graphs are related to the graph of $f(x) = x$.

$g(x) = x + b$

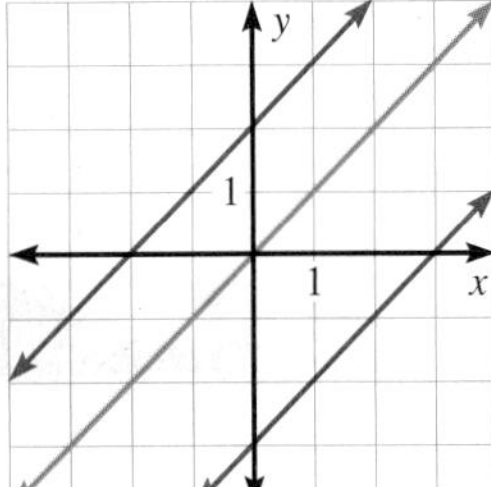

- The graphs have the same slope, but different y-intercepts.
- Graphs of this family are vertical translations of the graph of $f(x) = x$.

$g(x) = mx$ where $m > 0$

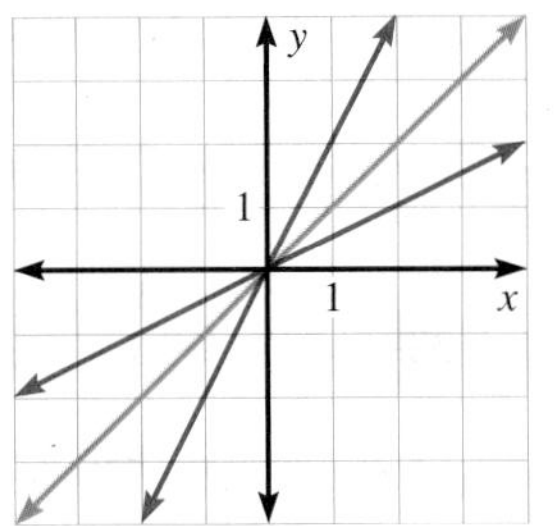

- The graphs have different (positive) slopes, but the same y-intercept.
- Graphs of this family are vertical stretches or shrinks of the graph of $f(x) = x$.

$g(x) = mx$ where $m < 0$

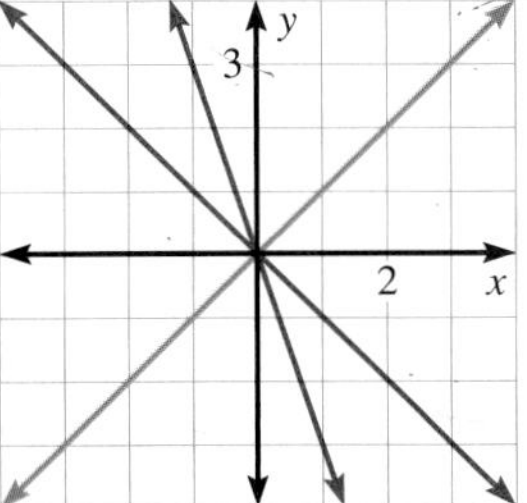

- The graphs have different (negative) slopes, but the same y-intercept.
- Graphs of this family are vertical stretches or shrinks with reflections in the x-axis of the graph of $f(x) = x$.

EXAMPLE 5 Graph real-world functions

CABLE A cable company charges new customers \$40 for installation and \$60 per month for its service. The cost to the customer is given by the function $f(x) = 60x + 40$ where x is the number of months of service. To attract new customers, the cable company reduces the installation fee to \$5. A function for the cost with the reduced installation fee is $g(x) = 60x + 5$. Graph both functions. How is the graph of g related to the graph of f?

Solution

The graphs of both functions are shown. Both functions have a slope of 60, so they are parallel. The y-intercept of the graph of g is 35 less than the graph of f. So, the graph of g is a vertical translation of the graph of f.

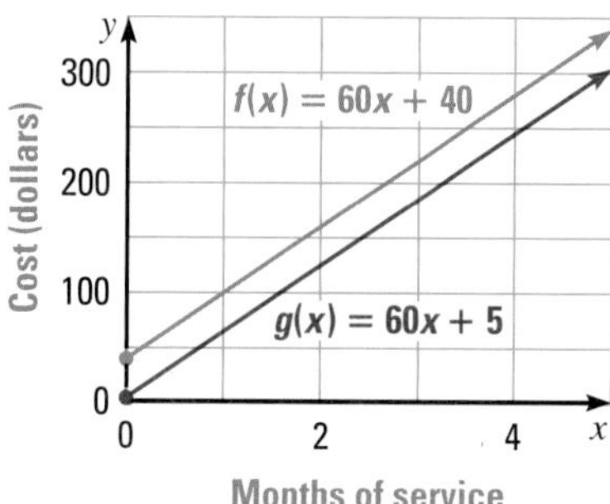

REVIEW TRANSFORMATIONS
For help with transformations, see pp. 922–923.

 **GUIDED PRACTICE** for Example 5

4. **WHAT IF?** In Example 5, suppose the monthly fee is \$70 so that the cost to the customer is given by $h(x) = 70x + 40$. Graph f and h in the same coordinate plane. How is the graph of h related to the graph of f?

4.7 EXERCISES

HOMEWORK KEY

○ = **WORKED-OUT SOLUTIONS on p. WS10 for Exs. 3, 17, and 39**

★ = **STANDARDIZED TEST PRACTICE Exs. 2, 13, 22, 35, 36, 44, and 45**

SKILL PRACTICE

1. **VOCABULARY** When you write the function $y = 3x + 12$ as $f(x) = 3x + 12$, you are using __?__.

2. ★ **WRITING** Would the functions $f(x) = -9x + 12$, $g(x) = -9x - 2$, and $h(x) = -9x$ be considered a family of functions? *Explain.*

EXAMPLE 1 on p. 262 for Exs. 3–13

EVALUATING FUNCTIONS **Evaluate the function when $x = -2$, 0, and 3.**

3. $f(x) = 12x + 1$
4. $g(x) = -3x + 5$
5. $p(x) = -8x - 2$
6. $h(x) = 2.25x$
7. $m(x) = -6.5x$
8. $f(x) = -0.75x - 1$
9. $s(x) = \frac{2}{5}x + 3$
10. $d(x) = -\frac{3}{2}x + 5$
11. $h(x) = \frac{3}{4}x - 6$

12. **ERROR ANALYSIS** *Describe* and correct the error in evaluating the function $g(x) = -5x + 3$ when $x = -3$.

$$g(-3) = -5(-3) + 3$$
$$-3g = 18$$
$$g = -6$$

13. ★ **MULTIPLE CHOICE** Given $f(x) = -6.8x + 5$, what is the value of $f(-2)$?

(A) -18.6 (B) -8.6 (C) 8.6 (D) 18.6

EXAMPLE 2 on p. 262 for Exs. 14–22

FINDING X-VALUES **Find the value of x so that the function has the given value.**

14. $f(x) = 6x + 9; 3$
15. $g(x) = -x + 5; 2$
16. $h(x) = -7x + 12; -9$
17. $j(x) = 4x + 11; -13$
18. $m(x) = 9x - 5; -2$
19. $n(x) = -2x - 21; -6$
20. $p(x) = -12x - 36; -3$
21. $q(x) = 8x - 32; -4$

22. ★ **MULTIPLE CHOICE** What value of x makes $f(x) = 5$ if $f(x) = -2x + 25$?

(A) -15 (B) -10 (C) 10 (D) 15

EXAMPLE 4 on p. 264 for Exs. 23–34

TRANSFORMATIONS OF LINEAR FUNCTIONS **Graph the function. Compare the graph with the graph of $f(x) = x$.**

23. $g(x) = x + 5$
24. $h(x) = 6 + x$
25. $q(x) = x - 1$
26. $m(x) = x - 6$
27. $d(x) = x + 7$
28. $t(x) = x - 3$
29. $r(x) = 4x$
30. $w(x) = 5x$
31. $h(x) = -3x$
32. $k(x) = -6x$
33. $g(x) = \frac{1}{3}x$
34. $m(x) = -\frac{7}{2}x$

35. ★ **MULTIPLE CHOICE** The graph of which function is shown?

(A) $f(x) = 3x + 8$

(B) $f(x) = 3x - 8$

(C) $f(x) = 8x + 3$

(D) $f(x) = 8x - 3$

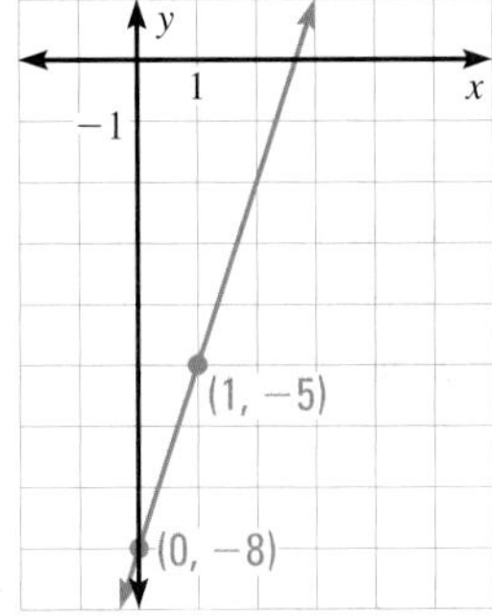

36. ★ **OPEN-ENDED** In this exercise you will compare the graphs of linear functions when their slopes and y-intercepts are changed.

a. Choose a linear function of the form $f(x) = mx + b$ where $m \neq 0$. Then graph the function.

b. Using the same m and b values as in part (a), graph the function $g(x) = 2mx + b$. How are the slope and y-intercept of the graph of g related to the slope and y-intercept of the graph of f?

c. Using the same m and b values as in part (a), graph the function $h(x) = mx + (b - 3)$. How are the slope and y-intercept of the graph of h related to the slope and y-intercept of the graph of f?

37. **REASONING** How is the graph of $g(x) = 1$ related to the graph of $h(x) = -1$?

38. **CHALLENGE** Suppose that $f(x) = 4x + 7$ and $g(x) = 2x$. What is a rule for $g(f(x))$? What is a rule for $f(g(x))$?

◯ = **WORKED-OUT SOLUTIONS on p. WS1**

★ = **STANDARDIZED TEST PRACTICE**

PROBLEM SOLVING

EXAMPLE 3 on p. 263 for Exs. 39–41

39. **MOVIE TICKETS** The average price of a movie ticket in the United States from 1980 to 2000 can be modeled by the function $f(x) = 0.10x + 2.75$ where x is the number of years since 1980.

    a. Graph the function and identify its domain and range.

    b. Find the value of x so that $f(x) = 4.55$. *Explain* what the solution means in this situation.

    @HomeTutor for problem solving help at classzone.com

40. **DVD PLAYERS** The number (in thousands) of DVD players sold in the United States from 1998 to 2003 can be modeled by $f(x) = 4250x + 330$ where x is the number of years since 1998.

    a. Graph the function and identify its domain and range.

    b. Find the value of x so that $f(x) = 13{,}080$. *Explain* what the solution means in this situation.

    @HomeTutor for problem solving help at classzone.com

41. **IN-LINE SKATING** An in-line skater's average speed is 10 miles per hour. The distance traveled after skating for x hours is given by the function $d(x) = 10x$. Graph the function and identify its domain and range. How long did it take the skater to travel 15 miles? *Explain*.

    Animated Algebra at classzone.com

EXAMPLE 5 on p. 265 for Exs. 42–43

42. **HOME SECURITY** A home security company charges new customers $155 for the installation of security equipment and a monthly fee of $40. To attract more customers, the company reduces its installation fee to $75. The functions below give the total cost for x months of service:

    Regular fee: $f(x) = 40x + 155$ **Reduced fee:** $g(x) = 40x + 75$

    Graph both functions. How is the graph of g related to the graph of f?

43. **THEATERS** A ticket for a play at a theater costs $16. The revenue (in dollars) generated from the sale of x tickets is given by $s(x) = 16x$. The theater managers raise the cost of tickets to $20. The revenue generated from the sale of x tickets at that price is given by $r(x) = 20x$. Graph both functions. How is the graph of r related to the graph of s?

44. ★ **EXTENDED RESPONSE** The cost of supplies, such as mustard and napkins, a pretzel vendor needs for one day is $75. Each pretzel costs the vendor $.50 to make. The total daily cost to the vendor is given by $C(x) = 0.5x + 75$ where x is the number of pretzels the vendor makes.

    a. **Graph** Graph the cost function.

    b. **Graph** The vendor sells each pretzel for $3. The revenue is given by $R(x) = 3x$ where x is the number of pretzels sold. Graph the function.

    c. **Explain** The vendor's profit is the difference of the revenue and the cost. *Explain* how you could use the graphs to find the vendor's profit for any given number of pretzels made and sold.

45. ★ **EXTENDED RESPONSE** The number of hours of daylight in Austin, Texas, during the month of March can be modeled by the function $\ell(x) = 0.03x + 11.5$ where x is the day of the month.

   a. **Graph** Graph the function and identify its domain and range.

   b. **Graph** The number of hours of darkness can be modeled by the function $d(x) = 24 - \ell(x)$. Graph the function on the same coordinate plane as you used in part (a). Identify its domain and range.

   c. **CHALLENGE** *Explain* how you could have obtained the graph of d from the graph of ℓ using translations and reflections.

   d. **CHALLENGE** What does the point where the graphs intersect mean in terms of the number of hours of daylight and darkness?

MIXED REVIEW

Solve the equation or proportion.

46. $y - 7 = -3$ *(p. 134)*
47. $4.5m = 49.5$ *(p. 134)*
48. $4z + 5z = -36$ *(p. 141)*
49. $5(x - 4) = 20$ *(p. 148)*
50. $3t + 4 + 5t = -4$ *(p. 148)*
51. $-5g = 3(g - 8)$ *(p. 154)*
52. $9n = 4(2n + 1)$ *(p. 154)*
53. $\frac{7}{6} = \frac{t}{42}$ *(p. 168)*
54. $\frac{5}{6} = \frac{p}{15}$ *(p. 168)*

PREVIEW
Prepare for Lesson 5.1 in Exs. 55–60.

Write the equation in slope-intercept form. Then graph the equation. *(p. 244)*

55. $x + 6y = 12$
56. $5x + y = -10$
57. $2x - 2y = 3$
58. $-2x - 3y = 21$
59. $-4x - 3y = -18$
60. $2x - y = 10$

QUIZ *for Lessons 4.6–4.7*

Given that *y* varies directly with *x*, use the specified values to write a direct variation equation that relates *x* and *y*. *(p. 253)*

1. $x = 5, y = 10$
2. $x = 4, y = 6$
3. $x = 2, y = -16$

Evaluate the function. *(p. 262)*

4. $g(x) = 6x - 5$ when $x = 4$
5. $h(x) = 14x + 7$ when $x = 2$
6. $j(x) = 0.2x + 12.2$ when $x = 244$
7. $k(x) = \frac{5}{6}x + \frac{1}{3}$ when $x = 4$

Graph the function. Compare the graph to the graph of $f(x) = x$. *(p. 262)*

8. $g(x) = -4x$
9. $h(x) = x - 2$

10. **HOURLY WAGE** The table shows the number of hours that you worked for each of three weeks and the amount that you were paid. What is your hourly wage? *(p. 253)*

Hours	12	16	14
Pay (dollars)	84	112	98

EXTRA PRACTICE for Lesson 4.7, p. 941

ONLINE QUIZ at classzone.com

Lessons 4.4–4.7

1. **MULTI-STEP PROBLEM** The amount of drink mix d (in tablespoons) that you need to add to w fluid ounces of water is given by $d = \frac{1}{4}w$.
   a. Graph the equation.
   b. Use the graph to find the amount of drink mix you need if you want to make enough drinks to serve 4 people. Assume 1 serving is 8 fluid ounces.

2. **MULTI-STEP PROBLEM** A water park charges \$25 per ticket for adults. Let s be the amount of money the park receives from adult ticket sales, and let t be the number of adult tickets sold.

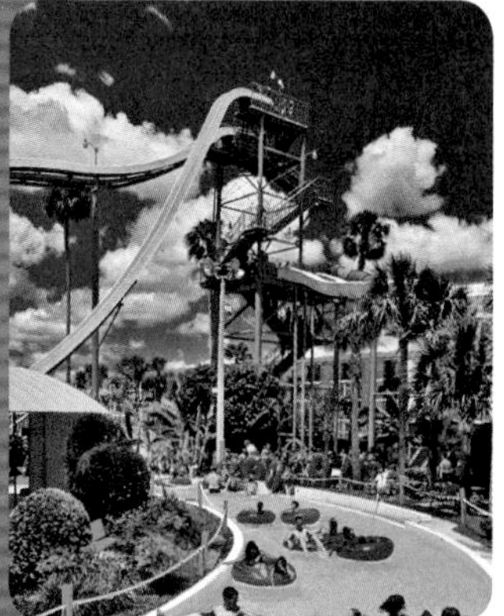

   a. Write a direct variation equation that relates t and s.
   b. How much money does the park earn when 90 adult tickets are sold?
   c. The park collected \$3325 in adult ticket sales in one day. How many tickets did the park sell?

3. **SHORT RESPONSE** You and your friend are each reading an essay that is 10 pages long. You read at a rate of 1 page per minute. Your friend reads at a rate of $\frac{2}{3}$ page per minute. The models below give the number p of pages you and your friend have left to read after reading for m minutes.

   You: $p = -m + 10$

   Your friend: $p = -\frac{2}{3}m + 10$

   Graph both equations in the same coordinate plane. *Explain* how you can use the graphs to find how many more minutes it took your friend to read the essay than it took you to read the essay.

4. **OPEN-ENDED** Draw a graph that represents going to a movie theater, watching a movie, and returning home from the theater. Let the x-axis represent time and the y-axis represent your distance from home.

5. **EXTENDED RESPONSE** A central observatory averages and then reports the number of sunspots recorded by various observatories. The table shows the average number of sunspots reported by the central observatory in years since 1995.

Years since 1995	Average number of sunspots
0	17.5
2	21.0
4	93.2
6	110.9

   a. Draw a line graph of the data.
   b. During which two-year period was the increase in sunspots the greatest? Find the rate of change for this time period.
   c. During which two-year period was the increase in sunspots the least? Find the rate of change for this time period.
   d. *Explain* how you could find the overall rate of change for the time period shown.

6. **GRIDDED ANSWER** To become a member at a gym, you have to pay a sign-up fee of \$125 and a monthly fee of \$40. To attract new customers, the gym lowers the sign-up fee to \$75. The function f gives the total cost with the regular sign-up fee. The function g gives the total cost with the reduced sign-up fee. The graphs of f and g are shown. The graph of g is a vertical translation of the graph of f by how many units down?

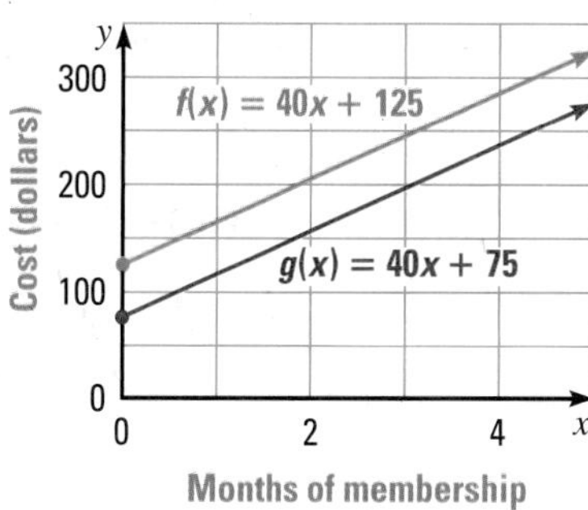

4 CHAPTER SUMMARY

Animated Algebra
classzone.com
Electronic Function Library

BIG IDEAS — For Your Notebook

Big Idea 1

Graphing Linear Equations and Functions Using a Variety of Methods

You can graph a linear equation or function by making a table, using intercepts, or using the slope and y-intercept.

A taxi company charges a \$2 fee to pick up a customer plus \$1 per mile to drive to the customer's destination. The total cost C (in dollars) that a customer pays to travel d miles is given by $C = d + 2$. Graph this function.

Method: Make a table.

d	C
0	2
1	3
2	4
3	5

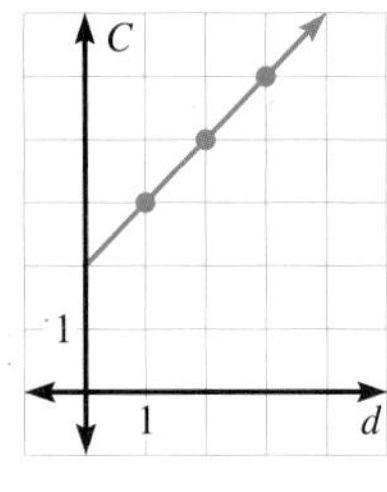

Method: Use slope and C-intercept.

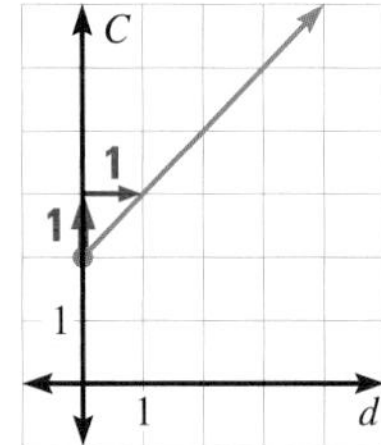

Big Idea 2

Recognizing How Changes in Linear Equations and Functions Affect Their Graphs

When you change the value of m or b in the equation $y = mx + b$, you produce an equation whose graph is related to the graph of the original equation.

Suppose the taxi company raises its rate to \$1.50 per mile. The total amount that a customer pays is given by $C = 1.5d + 2$. Graph the function.

You can see that the graphs have the same C-intercept, but different slopes.

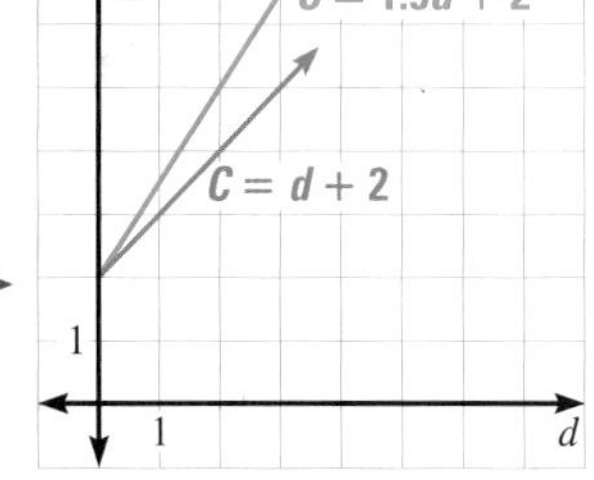

Big Idea 3

Using Graphs of Linear Equations and Functions to Solve Real-world Problems

You can use the graphs of $C = d + 2$ and $C = 1.5d + 2$ to find out how much more a customer pays to travel 4 miles at the new rate than at the old rate.

A customer pays \$2 more to travel 4 miles at the new rate.

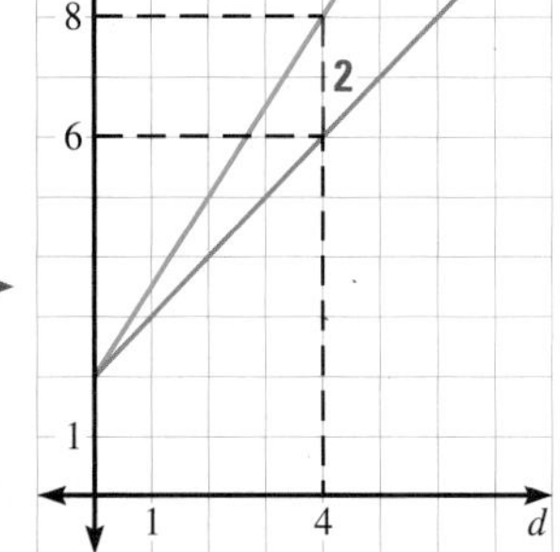

4 CHAPTER REVIEW

@HomeTutor
classzone.com
- Multi-Language Glossary
- Vocabulary practice

REVIEW KEY VOCABULARY

- quadrant, *p. 206*
- solution of an equation in two variables, *p. 215*
- graph of an equation in two variables, *p. 215*
- linear equation, *p. 216*
- standard form of a linear equation, *p. 216*
- linear function, *p. 217*
- *x*-intercept, *p. 225*
- *y*-intercept, *p. 225*
- slope, *p. 235*
- rate of change, *p. 237*
- slope-intercept form, *p. 244*
- parallel, *p. 246*
- direct variation, *p. 253*
- constant of variation, *p. 253*
- function notation, *p. 262*
- family of functions, *p. 263*
- parent linear function, *p. 263*

VOCABULARY EXERCISES

1. Copy and complete: The __?__ of a nonvertical line is the ratio of vertical change to horizontal change.
2. Copy and complete: When you write $y = 2x + 3$ as $f(x) = 2x + 3$, you use __?__.
3. **WRITING** *Describe* three different methods you could use to graph the equation $5x + 3y = 12$.
4. Tell whether the equation is written in slope-intercept form. If the equation is not in slope-intercept form, write it in slope-intercept form.

a. $3x + y = 6$ **b.** $y = 5x + 2$ **c.** $x = 4y - 1$ **d.** $y = -x + 6$

REVIEW EXAMPLES AND EXERCISES

Use the review examples and exercises below to check your understanding of the concepts you have learned in each lesson of Chapter 4.

4.1 Plot Points in a Coordinate Plane

pp. 206–212

EXAMPLE

Plot the points $A(-2, 3)$ and $B(0, -2)$ in a coordinate plane. Describe the location of the points.

Point $A(-2, 3)$: Begin at the origin and move 2 units to the left, then 3 units up. Point A is in Quadrant II.

Point $B(0, -2)$: Begin at the origin and move 2 units down. Point B is on the y-axis.

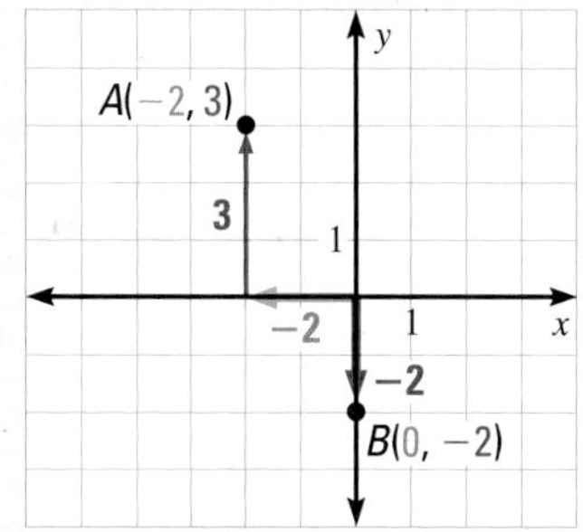

EXERCISES

EXAMPLE 2 on p. 207 for Exs. 5–7

Plot the point in a coordinate plane. *Describe* the location of the point.

5. $A(3, 4)$
6. $B(-5, 0)$
7. $C(-7, -2)$

4 CHAPTER REVIEW

4.2 Graph Linear Equations *pp. 215–221*

EXAMPLE

Graph the equation $y + 3x = 1$.

STEP 1 **Solve** the equation for y.

$$y + 3x = 1$$
$$y = -3x + 1$$

STEP 2 **Make** a table by choosing a few values for x and finding the values for y.

x	−1	0	1
y	4	1	−2

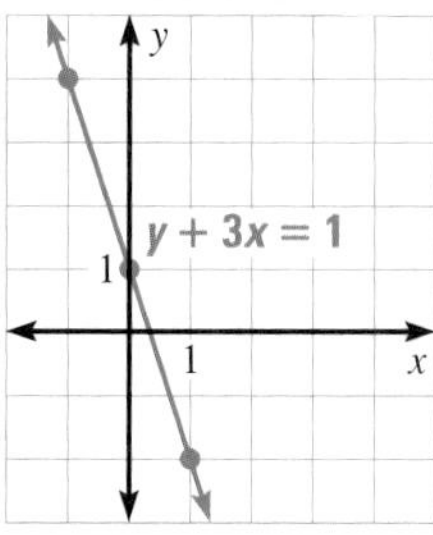

STEP 3 **Plot** the points.

STEP 4 **Connect** the points by drawing a line through them.

EXERCISES

EXAMPLE 2 on p. 216 for Exs. 8–10

Graph the equation.

8. $y + 5x = -5$ 9. $2x + 3y = 9$ 10. $2y - 14 = 4$

4.3 Graph Using Intercepts *pp. 225–232*

EXAMPLE

Graph the equation $-0.5x + 2y = 4$.

STEP 1 **Find** the intercepts.

$$-0.5x + 2y = 4 \qquad -0.5x + 2y = 4$$
$$-0.5x + 2(\mathbf{0}) = 4 \qquad -0.5(\mathbf{0}) + 2y = 4$$
$$x = -8 \leftarrow \textbf{x-intercept} \qquad y = 2 \leftarrow \textbf{y-intercept}$$

STEP 2 **Plot** the points that correspond to the intercepts: $(-8, 0)$ and $(0, 2)$.

STEP 3 **Connect** the points by drawing a line through them.

EXERCISES

EXAMPLES 2 and 4 on pp. 226–227 for Exs. 11–14

Graph the equation.

11. $-x + 5y = 15$ 12. $4x + 4y = -16$ 13. $2x - 6y = 18$

14. **CRAFT FAIR** You sell necklaces for \$10 and bracelets for \$5 at a craft fair. You want to earn \$50. This situation is modeled by the equation $10n + 5b = 50$ where n is the number of necklaces you sell and b is the number of bracelets you sell. Find the intercepts of the graph of the equation. Then graph the equation. Give three possibilities for the number of bracelets and necklaces that you could sell.

@HomeTutor
classzone.com
Chapter Review Practice

4.4 Find Slope and Rate of Change

pp. 235–242

EXAMPLE

Find the slope of the line shown.

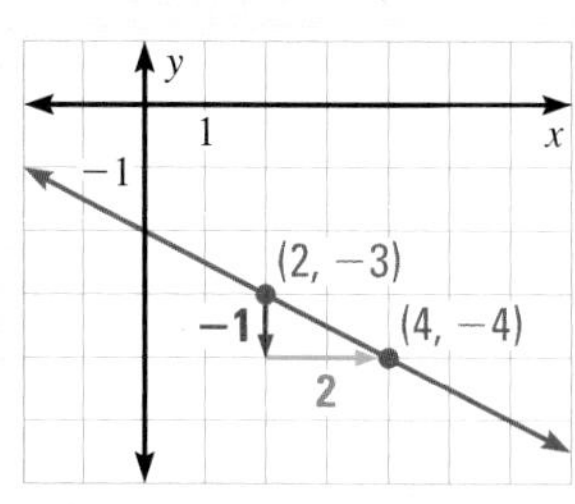

Let $(x_1, y_1) = (2, -3)$ and $(x_2, y_2) = (4, -4)$.

$$m = \frac{y_2 - y_1}{x_2 - x_1}$$ **Write formula for slope.**

$$= \frac{-4 - (-3)}{4 - 2}$$ **Substitute values.**

$$= -\frac{1}{2}$$ **Simplify.**

EXAMPLES 1,2,3, and 4 on pp. 235–236 for Exs. 15–17

EXERCISES

Find the slope of the line that passes through the points.

15. $(-1, 11)$ and $(2, 10)$ **16.** $(-2, 0)$ and $(4, 9)$ **17.** $(-5, 4)$ and $(1, -8)$

4.5 Graph Using Slope-Intercept Form

pp. 244–250

EXAMPLE

Graph the equation $2x + y = -1$.

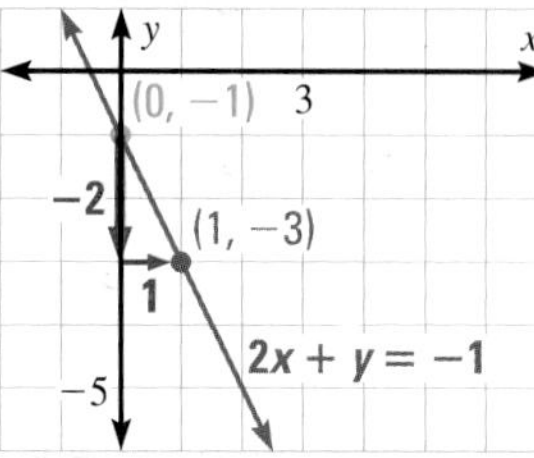

STEP 1 **Rewrite** the equation in slope-intercept form.

$2x + y = -1 \rightarrow y = -2x - 1$

STEP 2 **Identify** the slope and the y-intercept.

$m = -2$ and $b = -1$

STEP 3 **Plot** the point that corresponds to the y-intercept, $(0, -1)$.

STEP 4 **Use** the slope to locate a second point on the line. Draw a line through the two points.

EXAMPLES 2 and 3 on p. 245 for Exs. 18–21

EXERCISES

Graph the equation.

18. $4x - y = 3$ **19.** $3x - 6y = 9$ **20.** $-3x + 4y - 12 = 0$

21. RUNNING One athlete can run a 60 meter race at an average rate of 7 meters per second. A second athlete can run the race at an average rate of 6 meters per second. The distance d (in meters) the athletes have left to run after t seconds is given by the following equations:

Athlete 1: $d = -7t + 60$ **Athlete 2:** $d = -6t + 60$

Graph both models in the same coordinate plane. About how many seconds faster does the first athlete finish the race than the second athlete?

4 CHAPTER REVIEW

4.6 Model Direct Variation
pp. 253–259

EXAMPLE

Graph the direct variation equation $y = -\frac{2}{3}x$.

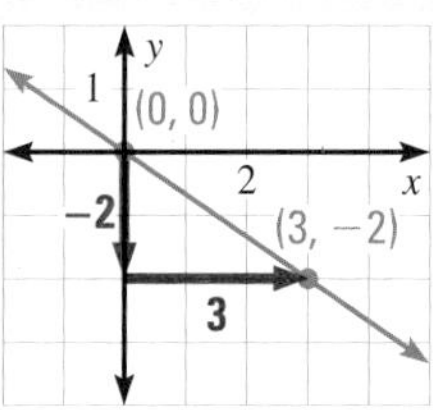

Plot a point at the origin. The slope is equal to the constant of variation, $-\frac{2}{3}$. Find and plot a second point, then draw a line through the points.

EXERCISES

EXAMPLES 1, 2, and 4 on pp. 253–255 for Exs. 22–28

Tell whether the equation represents direct variation. If so, identify the constant of variation.

22. $x - y = 3$ **23.** $x + 2y = 0$ **24.** $8x - 2y = 0$

Graph the direct variation equation.

25. $y = 4x$ **26.** $-5y = 3x$ **27.** $4x + 3y = 0$

28. SNOWSTORMS The amount s (in inches) of snow that fell during a snowstorm varied directly with the duration d (in hours) of the storm. In the first 2 hours of the storm 5 inches of snow fell. Write a direct variation equation that relates d and s. How many inches of snow fell in 6 hours?

4.7 Graph Linear Functions
pp. 262–268

EXAMPLE

Evaluate the function $f(x) = -6x + 5$ when $x = 3$.

$f(x) = -6x + 5$ **Write function.**

$f(3) = -6(3) + 5$ **Substitute 3 for x.**

$= -13$ **Simplify.**

EXERCISES

EXAMPLES 1 and 3 on pp. 262–263 for Exs. 29–34

Evaluate the function.

29. $g(x) = 2x - 3$ when $x = 7$ **30.** $h(x) = -\frac{1}{2}x - 7$ when $x = -6$

Graph the function. Compare the graph with the graph of $f(x) = x$.

31. $j(x) = x - 6$ **32.** $k(x) = -2.5x$ **33.** $t(x) = 2x + 1$

34. MOUNT EVEREST Mount Everest is rising at a rate of 2.4 inches per year. The number of inches that Mount Everest rises in x years is given by the function $f(x) = 2.4x$. Graph the function and identify its domain and range. Find the value of x so that $f(x) = 250$. *Explain* what the solution means in this situation.

4 CHAPTER TEST

Plot the point in a coordinate plane. *Describe* the location of the point.

1. $A(7, 1)$
2. $B(-4, 0)$
3. $C(3, -9)$

Draw the line that has the given intercepts.

4. x-intercept: 2
   y-intercept: -6
5. x-intercept: -1
   y-intercept: 8
6. x-intercept: -3
   y-intercept: -5

Find the slope of the line that passes through the points.

7. $(2, 1)$ and $(8, 4)$
8. $(-2, 7)$ and $(0, -1)$
9. $(3, 5)$ and $(3, 14)$

Identify the slope and y-intercept of the line with the given equation.

10. $y = -\frac{3}{2}x - 10$
11. $7x + 2y = -28$
12. $3x - 8y = 48$

Tell whether the equation represents direct variation. If so, identify the constant of variation.

13. $x + 4y = 4$
14. $-\frac{1}{3}x - y = 0$
15. $3x - 3y = 0$

Graph the equation.

16. $x = 3$
17. $y + x = 6$
18. $2x + 8y = -32$

Evaluate the function for the given value.

19. $f(x) = -4x$ when $x = 2.5$
20. $g(x) = \frac{5}{2}x - 6$ when $x = -2$

21. **BUSINESS** To start a dog washing business, you invest $300 in supplies. You charge $10 per hour for your services. Your profit P (in dollars) for working t hours is given by $P = 10t - 300$. Graph the equation. You will break even when your profit is $0. Use the graph to find the number of hours you must work in order to break even.

22. **PEDIATRICS** The dose d (in milligrams) of a particular medicine that a pediatrician prescribes for a patient varies directly with the patient's mass m (in kilograms). The pediatrician recommends a dose of 150 mg of medicine for a patient whose mass is 30 kg.

    a. Write a direct variation equation that relates m and d.

    b. What would the dose of medicine be for a patient whose mass is 50 kg?

23. **SCISSOR LIFT** The scissor lift is a device that can lower and raise a platform. The maximum and minimum heights of the platform of a particular scissor lift are shown. The scissor lift can raise the platform at a rate of 3.5 inches per second. The height of the platform after t seconds is given by $h(t) = 3.5t + 48$. Graph the function and identify its domain and range.

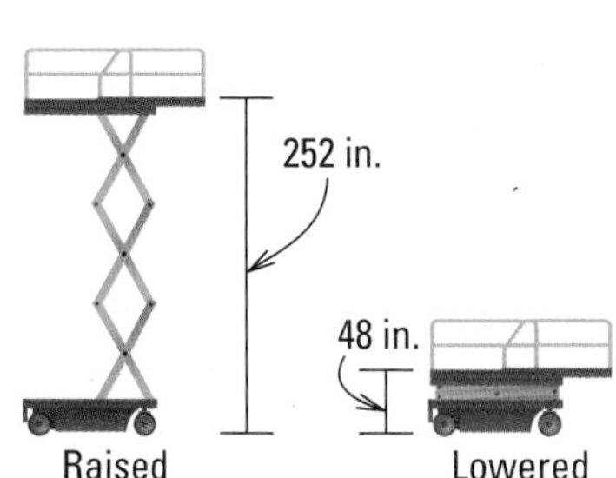

CONTEXT-BASED MULTIPLE CHOICE QUESTIONS

Some of the information you need to solve a context-based multiple choice question may appear in a table, a diagram, or a graph.

PROBLEM 1

A recipe from a box of pancake mix is shown. The number p of pancakes you can make varies directly with the number m of cups of mix you use. A full box of pancake mix contains 9 cups of mix. How many pancakes can you make when you use the full box?

(A) 63 (B) 65

(C) 126 (D) 131

2 cups pancake mix
1 cup milk
2 eggs
Combine ingredients. Pour batter on hot greased griddle. Flip when edges are dry. Makes 14 pancakes.

Plan

INTERPRET THE INFORMATION Use the number of pancakes and the number of cups of mix given in the recipe to write a direct variation equation. Then use the equation to find the number of pancakes that you can make when you use 9 cups of mix.

Solution

STEP 1 Use the values given in the recipe to find a direct variation equation.

Because the number p of pancakes you can make varies directly with the number m of cups of mix you use, you can write the equation $p = am$. From the recipe, you know that $p = 14$ when $m = 2$.

$p = am$ **Write direct variation equation.**

$14 = a(2)$ **Substitute.**

$7 = a$ **Solve for *a*.**

So, a direct variation equation that relates p and m is $p = 7m$.

STEP 2 Substitute 9 for m in the direct variation equation and solve for p.

Use the direct variation equation to find the number of pancakes you can make when you use a full box of mix.

$p = 7m$ **Write direct variation equation.**

$p = 7(9)$ **Substitute 9 for *m*.**

$p = 63$ **Simplify.**

You can make 63 pancakes when you use a full box of mix.

The correct answer is A. (A) (B) (C) (D)

PROBLEM 2

At a yard sale, Jack made $54 selling cassettes for $1 each and CDs for $3 each. This situation is modeled by the equation $x + 3y = 54$ where x is the number of cassettes and y is the number of CDs that Jack sold. The graph of the equation is shown. Which is a possible combination of cassettes and CDs that Jack sold?

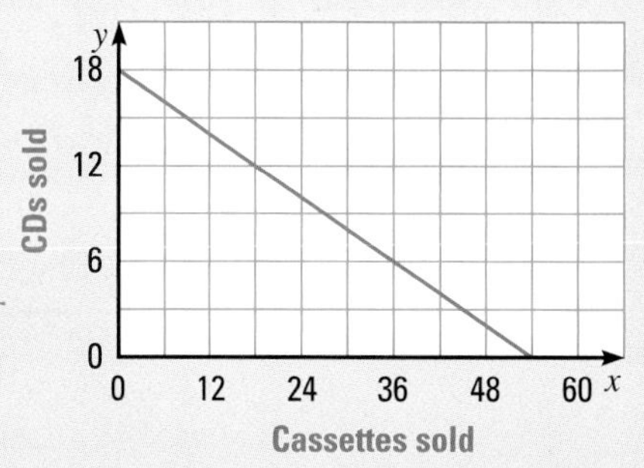

Ⓐ 12 cassettes, 4 CDs   Ⓑ 4 cassettes, 12 CDs

Ⓒ 18 cassettes, 12 CDs   Ⓓ 28.5 cassettes, 8.5 CDs

Plan

INTERPRET THE INFORMATION Each point on the line represents a solution of the equation. Identify the answer choice that describes a point on the graph shown and that makes sense in the context of the problem.

Solution

STEP 1 Write an ordered pair for each answer choice.

The answer choices correspond to the following ordered pairs.

Ⓐ (12, 4)   Ⓑ (4, 12)   Ⓒ (18, 12)   Ⓓ (28.5, 8.5)

STEP 2 Eliminate points not on the line and points that don't make sense. Check ordered pairs not eliminated to find the solution.

You can eliminate answer choices A and B because the points do not lie on the graph shown. You can also eliminate answer choice D because only whole number solutions make sense in this situation. Check that (18, 12) is a solution of the equation.

$x + 3y = 54$ **Write original equation.**

$18 + 3(12) = 54$ **Substitute.**

$54 = 54$ ✓   **Solution checks.**

The correct answer is C. Ⓐ Ⓑ Ⓒ Ⓓ

PRACTICE

1. In Problem 2, what is the greatest number of CDs Jack could have sold?

   Ⓐ 3   Ⓑ 18   Ⓒ 36   Ⓓ 54

2. The table shows the total cost for a certain number of people to ice skate at a particular rink. What is the cost per person?

   Ⓐ $.20   Ⓑ $1

   Ⓒ $5   Ⓓ $10

Number of people	Cost (dollars)
2	10
4	20
6	30

4 ★ Standardized TEST PRACTICE

MULTIPLE CHOICE

In Exercises 1 and 2, use the graph below.

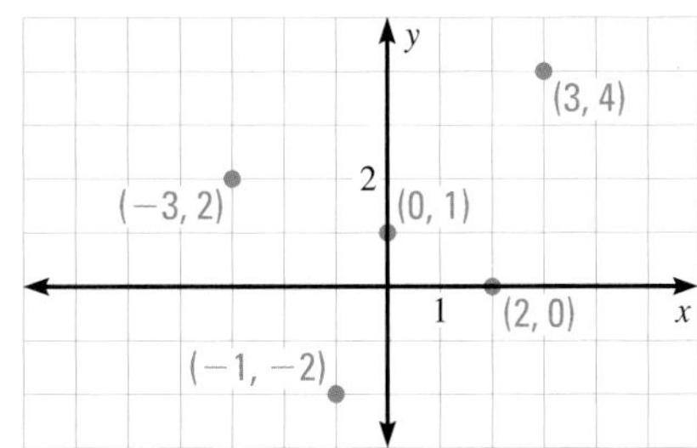

1. The graph represents a function. Which number is in the domain of the function?

   Ⓐ 22 Ⓑ −1

   Ⓒ 1 Ⓓ 4

2. The graph would no longer represent a function if which point were included?

   Ⓐ (−4, −2) Ⓑ (−2, 0)

   Ⓒ (1, 3) Ⓓ (3, −1)

In Exercises 3 and 4, use the graph below, which shows a traveler's movements through an airport to a terminal. The traveler has to walk and take a shuttle bus to get to the terminal.

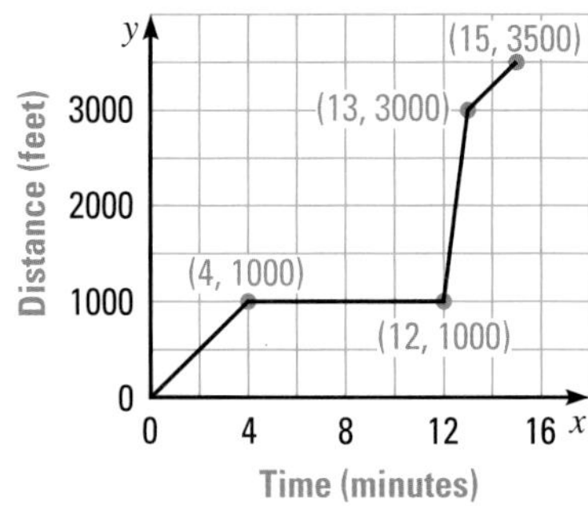

3. For how many minutes does the traveler wait for the shuttle bus?

   Ⓐ 1 min Ⓑ 2 min

   Ⓒ 4 min Ⓓ 8 min

4. For about what distance does the traveler ride on the shuttle bus?

   Ⓐ 100 ft Ⓑ 100 ft

   Ⓒ 2000 ft Ⓓ 3000 ft

In Exercises 5–7, use the following information.

At a yoga studio, new members pay a sign-up fee of \$50 plus a monthly fee of \$25. The total cost C (in dollars) of a new membership is given by $C = 25m + 50$ where m is the number of months of membership. The owner of the studio is considering changing the cost of a new membership. A graph of four different options for changing the cost is shown.

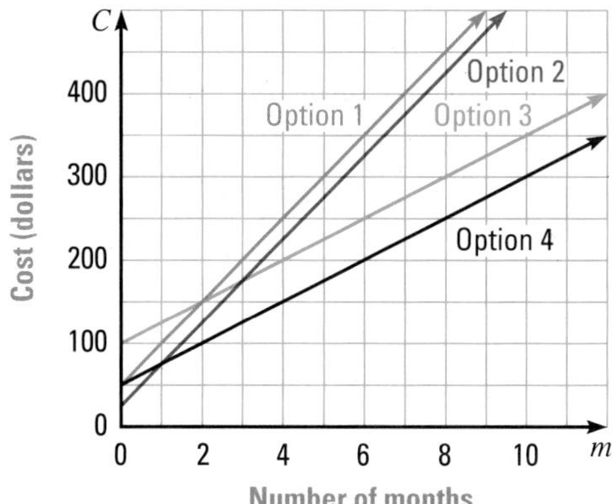

5. For which option are the sign-up fee and monthly fee kept the same?

   Ⓐ Option 1 Ⓑ Option 2

   Ⓒ Option 3 Ⓓ Option 4

6. For which option is the sign-up fee kept the same and the monthly fee raised?

   Ⓐ Option 1 Ⓑ Option 2

   Ⓒ Option 3 Ⓓ Option 4

7. For which option is the monthly fee kept the same and the sign-up fee raised?

   Ⓐ Option 1 Ⓑ Option 2

   Ⓒ Option 3 Ⓓ Option 4

8. The table shows the cost of a therapeutic massage for a given amount of time. What is the cost per minute?

Time (minutes)	30	45	60
Cost (dollars)	42.00	63.00	84.00

   Ⓐ \$.71 Ⓑ \$1.40

   Ⓒ \$2.80 Ⓓ \$14.00

GRIDDED ANSWER

9. What is the slope of the line shown?

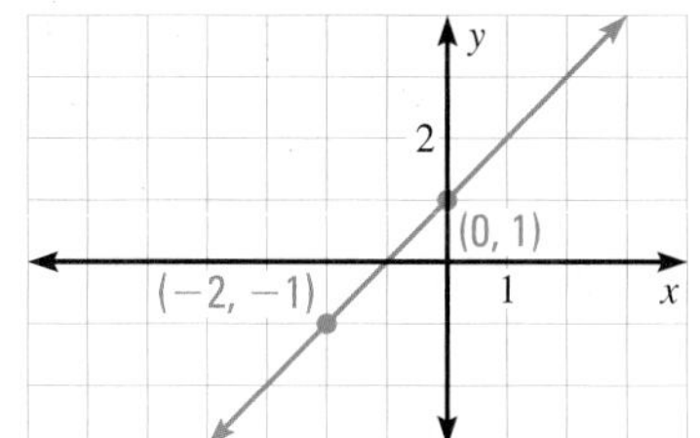

10. What is the y-intercept of the graph of the equation $4x + 8y = 16$?

11. What is the value of $f(x) = -1.8x - 9$ when $x = -5$?

12. The number w of cups of water varies directly with the number u of cups of uncooked rice. Use the table to find the value of the constant of variation a in the direct variation equation $w = au$.

Uncooked rice, u (cups)	$\frac{1}{2}$	1	$1\frac{1}{2}$
Water, w (cups)	$\frac{3}{4}$	$1\frac{1}{2}$	$2\frac{1}{4}$

SHORT RESPONSE

13. Patricia takes a bus to and from her job. She can either pay \$1.75 each way or get a monthly bus pass for \$58 and ride the bus an unlimited number of times. The functions below give the costs C (in dollars) of riding the bus n times in one month. The graphs of the functions are shown.

Monthly pass: $C = 58$

Pay per ride: $C = 1.75n$

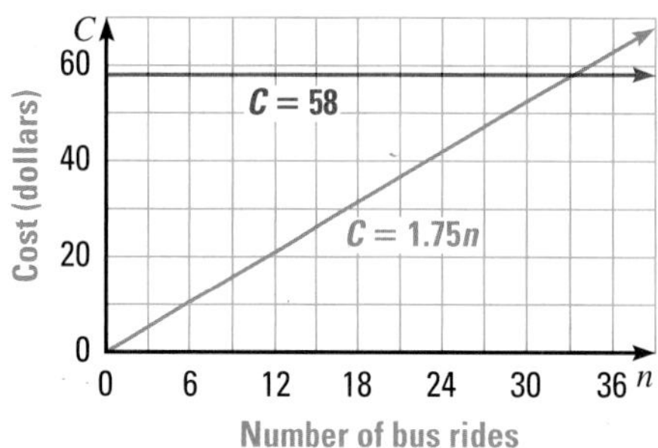

How many days in a month would Patricia need to take the bus to and from work to make buying a monthly pass worth the cost? *Explain.*

EXTENDED RESPONSE

14. A fog machine has a tank that holds 32 fluid ounces of fog fluid and has two settings: low and high. The low setting uses 0.2 fluid ounce of fluid per minute, and the high setting uses 0.25 fluid ounce per minute. The functions below give the amount f (in fluid ounces) of fluid left in the tank after t minutes when the machine starts with a full tank of fluid.

Low setting: $f = -0.2t + 32$ **High setting:** $f = -0.25t + 32$

a. Identify the slope and y-intercept of each function.

b. Graph each function in the same coordinate plane.

c. How much longer can the machine be run on the low setting than on the high setting? *Explain* how you found your answer.

15. At a pizzeria, a cheese pizza costs \$9. Toppings cost \$1.50 each.

a. The cost of a pizza is given by the function $f(x) = 1.5x + 9$ where x is the number of toppings. Graph the function.

b. You have \$14 and buy only a pizza. How many toppings can you get?

c. The pizzeria's owner decides to change the price of toppings to \$2 each. The new cost of a pizza is given by the function $g(x) = 2x + 9$. Graph the function in the same coordinate plane you used in part (a).

d. Can you get the same number of toppings at the new price as you did in part (b)? *Explain.*

5 Writing Linear Equations

Before

In previous chapters, you learned the following skills, which you'll use in Chapter 5: evaluating functions and finding the slopes and y-intercepts of lines.

Prerequisite Skills

VOCABULARY CHECK

Copy and complete the statement.

1. In the equation $y = mx + b$, the value of m is the _?_ of the graph of the equation.
2. In the equation $y = mx + b$, the value of b is the _?_ of the graph of the equation.
3. Two lines are _?_ if their slopes are equal.

SKILLS CHECK

Find the slope of the line that passes through the points.
(Review p. 235 for 5.1–5.6.)

4. (4, 5), (2, 3)
5. (0, −6), (8, 0)
6. (0, 0), (−1, 2)

Identify the slope and the y-intercept of the line with the equation.
(Review p. 244 for 5.1–5.6.)

7. $y = x + 1$
8. $y = \frac{3}{4}x - 6$
9. $y = -\frac{2}{5}x - 2$

Evaluate the function when $x = -2, 0,$ and 4. *(Review p. 262 for 5.7.)*

10. $f(x) = x - 10$
11. $f(x) = 2x + 4$
12. $f(x) = -5x - 7$

@HomeTutor Prerequisite skills practice at classzone.com

Now

In Chapter 5, you will apply the big ideas listed below and reviewed in the Chapter Summary on page 344. You will also use the key vocabulary listed below.

Big Ideas

1. **Writing linear equations in a variety of forms**
2. **Using linear models to solve problems**
3. **Modeling data with a line of fit**

KEY VOCABULARY

- point-slope form, *p. 302*
- converse, *p. 319*
- perpendicular, *p. 320*
- scatter plot, *p. 325*
- correlation, *p. 325*
- line of fit, *p. 326*
- best-fitting line, *p. 335*
- linear regression, *p. 335*
- interpolation, *p. 335*
- extrapolation, *p. 336*
- zero of a function, *p. 337*

Why?

You can use linear equations to solve problems involving a constant rate of change. For example, you can write an equation that models how traffic delays affected excess fuel consumption over time.

Animated Algebra

The animation illustrated below for Exercise 40 on p. 307 helps you to answer the question: In what year was a certain amount of excess fuel consumed?

Find the year in which the given amount of excess fuel was consumed.

Year	Excess Fuel
1992	30
1993	31.4
1992	
	34.2
	35.6
1995	37
	38.4
1997	39.8
	41.2
1999	
	44
2001	

35.6 gallons of annual excess fuel were consumed per person in the year______?

Continue

Click on the table in order to fill in the missing information.

Animated Algebra at classzone.com

Other animations for Chapter 5: pages 283, 303, 307, 311, 322, 327, and 335

5.1 Modeling Linear Relationships

MATERIALS • 8.5 inch by 11 inch piece of paper • inch ruler

QUESTION **How can you model a linear relationship?**

You know that the perimeter of a rectangle is given by the formula $P = 2\ell + 2w$. In this activity, you will find a linear relationship using that formula.

EXPLORE **Find perimeters of rectangles**

Width of fold (inches)	Perimeter of rectangle (inches)
0	39
1	?
2	?
3	?
4	?

STEP 1 ***Find perimeter***
Find the perimeter of a piece of paper that is 8.5 inches wide and 11 inches long. Record the result in a table like the one shown.

STEP 2 ***Change paper size***
Measure 1 inch from a short edge of the paper. Fold over 1 inch of the paper. You now have a rectangle with the same width and a different length than the original piece of paper. Find the perimeter of this new rectangle and record it in your table.

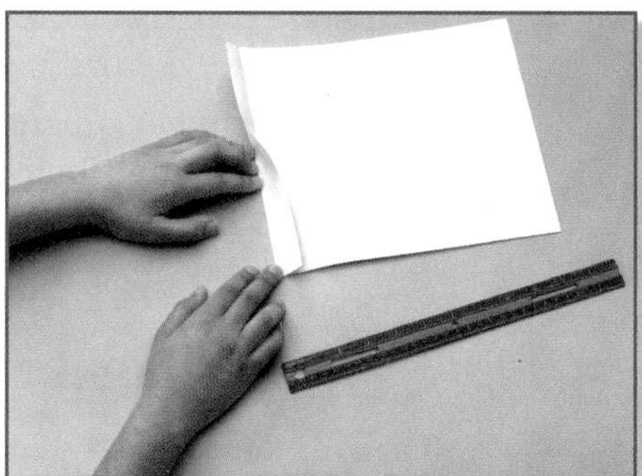

STEP 3 ***Find additional perimeters***
Unfold the paper and repeat Step 2, this time folding the paper 2 inches from a short edge. Find the perimeter of this rectangle and record the result in your table. Repeat with a fold of 3 inches and a fold of 4 inches.

DRAW CONCLUSIONS **Use your observations to complete these exercises**

1. What were the length and the width of the piece of paper before it was folded? By how much did these dimensions change with each fold?
2. What was the perimeter of the piece of paper before it was folded? By how much did the perimeter change with each fold?
3. Use the values from your table to predict the perimeter of the piece of paper after a fold of 5 inches. *Explain* your reasoning.
4. Write a rule you could use to find the perimeter of the piece of paper after a fold of n inches. Use the data in the table to show that this rule gives accurate results.

5.1 Write Linear Equations in Slope-Intercept Form

Before You graphed equations of lines.

Now You will write equations of lines.

Why? So you can model distances in sports, as in Ex. 52.

Key Vocabulary
- ***y*-intercept,** *p. 225*
- **slope,** *p. 235*
- **slope-intercept form,** *p. 244*

Recall that the graph of an equation in slope-intercept form, $y = mx + b$, is a line with a slope of m and a y-intercept of b. You can use this form to write an equation of a line if you know its slope and y-intercept.

EXAMPLE 1 Use slope and *y*-intercept to write an equation

Write an equation of the line with a slope of −2 and a *y*-intercept of 5.

$y = mx + b$ Write slope-intercept form.

$y = -2x + 5$ Substitute −2 for *m* and 5 for *b*.

EXAMPLE 2 Standardized Test Practice

Which equation represents the line shown?

Ⓐ $y = -\frac{2}{5}x + 3$ Ⓑ $y = -\frac{5}{2}x + 3$

Ⓒ $y = -\frac{2}{5}x + 1$ Ⓓ $y = 3x + \frac{2}{5}$

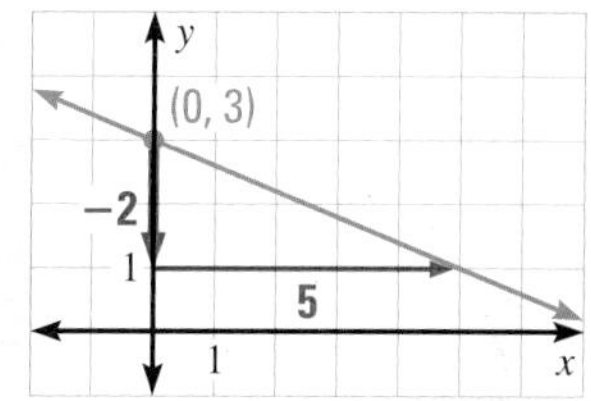

ELIMINATE CHOICES
In Example 2, you can eliminate choices C and D because the *y*-intercepts of the graphs of these equations are not 3.

The slope of the line is $\frac{\text{rise}}{\text{run}} = \frac{-2}{5} = -\frac{2}{5}$.

The line crosses the y-axis at (0, 3). So, the y-intercept is 3.

$y = mx + b$ Write slope-intercept form.

$y = -\frac{2}{5}x + 3$ Substitute $-\frac{2}{5}$ for *m* and 3 for *b*.

▶ The correct answer is A. Ⓐ Ⓑ Ⓒ Ⓓ

 at classzone.com

✓ GUIDED PRACTICE for Examples 1 and 2

Write an equation of the line with the given slope and *y*-intercept.

1. Slope is 8; y-intercept is −7.
2. Slope is $\frac{3}{4}$; y-intercept is −3.

USING TWO POINTS If you know the point where a line crosses the y-axis and any other point on the line, you can write an equation of the line.

EXAMPLE 3 Write an equation of a line given two points

Write an equation of the line shown.

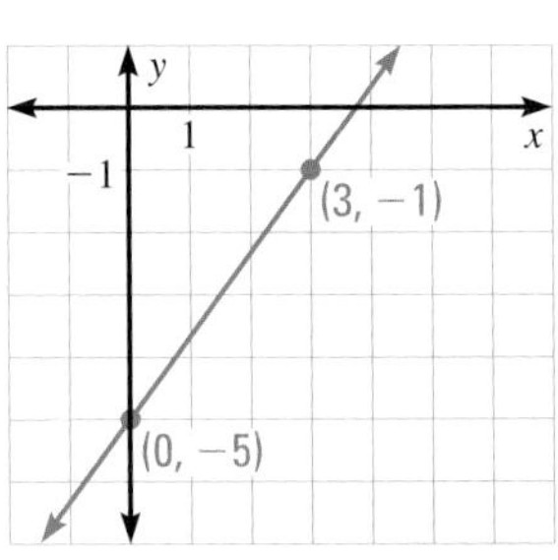

Solution

STEP 1 **Calculate** the slope.

$$m = \frac{y_2 - y_1}{x_2 - x_1} = \frac{-1 - (-5)}{3 - 0} = \frac{4}{3}$$

STEP 2 **Write** an equation of the line. The line crosses the y-axis at $(0, -5)$. So, the y-intercept is -5.

$y = mx + b$ **Write slope-intercept form.**

$y = \frac{4}{3}x - 5$ **Substitute $\frac{4}{3}$ for m and -5 for b.**

WRITING FUNCTIONS Recall that the graphs of linear functions are lines. You can use slope-intercept form to write a linear function.

EXAMPLE 4 Write a linear function

REVIEW FUNCTIONS
For help with using function notation, see p. 262.

Write an equation for the linear function f with the values $f(0) = 5$ and $f(4) = 17$.

Solution

STEP 1 **Write** $f(0) = 5$ as $(0, 5)$ and $f(4) = 17$ as $(4, 17)$.

STEP 2 **Calculate** the slope of the line that passes through $(0, 5)$ and $(4, 17)$.

$$m = \frac{y_2 - y_1}{x_2 - x_1} = \frac{17 - 5}{4 - 0} = \frac{12}{4} = 3$$

STEP 3 **Write** an equation of the line. The line crosses the y-axis at $(0, 5)$. So, the y-intercept is 5.

$y = mx + b$ **Write slope-intercept form.**

$y = 3x + 5$ **Substitute 3 for m and 5 for b.**

▶ The function is $f(x) = 3x + 5$.

✓ GUIDED PRACTICE for Examples 3 and 4

3. Write an equation of the line shown.

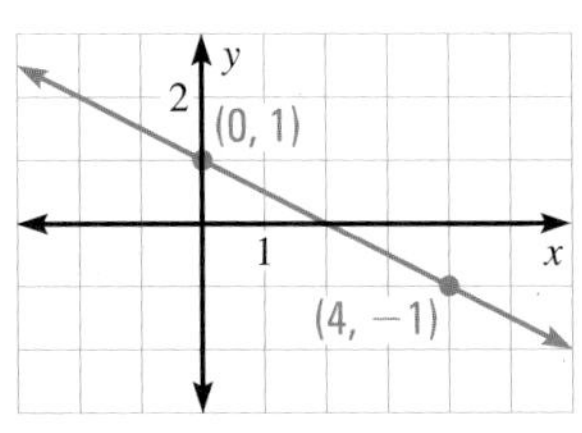

Write an equation for the linear function f with the given values.

4. $f(0) = -2, f(8) = 4$

5. $f(-3) = 6, f(0) = 5$

READING The value b is a starting value in a real-world situation modeled by $y = mx + b$, because when $x = 0$, the value of y is b.

MODELING REAL-WORLD SITUATIONS When a quantity y changes at a constant rate with respect to a quantity x, you can use the equation $y = mx + b$ to model the relationship. The value of m is the constant rate of change, and the value of b is an initial, or starting, value for y.

EXAMPLE 5 Solve a multi-step problem

RECORDING STUDIO A recording studio charges musicians an initial fee of \$50 to record an album. Studio time costs an additional \$35 per hour.

a. Write an equation that gives the total cost of an album as a function of studio time (in hours).

b. Find the total cost of recording an album that takes 10 hours of studio time.

Solution

a. The cost changes at a constant rate, so you can write an equation in slope-intercept form to model the total cost.

STEP 1 **Identify** the rate of change and the starting value.

Rate of change, *m*: cost per hour
Starting value, *b*: initial fee

STEP 2 **Write** a verbal model. Then write the equation.

Total cost (dollars)	=	Cost per hour (dollars per hour)	•	Studio time (hours)	+	Initial fee (dollars)
C	=	35	•	t	+	50

CHECK Use unit analysis to check the equation.

$$\text{dollars} = \frac{\text{dollars}}{\cancel{\text{hour}}} \cdot \cancel{\text{hours}} + \text{dollars} \checkmark$$

▸ The total cost C is given by the function $C = 35t + 50$ where t is the studio time (in hours).

b. Evaluate the function for $t = 10$.

$C = 35(10) + 50 = 400$ **Substitute 10 for *t* and simplify.**

▸ The total cost for 10 hours of studio time is \$400.

✓ GUIDED PRACTICE for Example 5

6. WHAT IF? In Example 5, suppose the recording studio raises its initial fee to \$75 and charges \$40 per hour for studio time.

a. Write an equation that gives the total cost of an album as a function of studio time (in hours).

b. Find the total cost of recording an album that takes 10 hours of studio time.

5.1 EXERCISES

HOMEWORK KEY

○ = **WORKED-OUT SOLUTIONS** on p. WS10 for Exs. 11, 19, and 47

★ = **STANDARDIZED TEST PRACTICE** Exs. 2, 9, 40, 43, 48, and 50

◆ = **MULTIPLE REPRESENTATIONS** Ex. 49

SKILL PRACTICE

1. **VOCABULARY** Copy and complete: The ratio of the rise to the run between any two points on a nonvertical line is called the _?_.

2. ★ **WRITING** *Explain* how you can use slope-intercept form to write an equation of a line given its slope and y-intercept.

EXAMPLE 1 on p. 283 for Exs. 3–9, 16

WRITING EQUATIONS **Write an equation of the line with the given slope and y-intercept.**

3. slope: 2; y-intercept: 9
4. slope: 1; y-intercept: 5
5. slope: -3; y-intercept: 0
6. slope: -7; y-intercept: 1
7. slope: $\frac{2}{3}$; y-intercept: -9
8. slope: $\frac{3}{4}$; y-intercept: -6

9. ★ **MULTIPLE CHOICE** Which equation represents the line with a slope of -1 and a y-intercept of 2?

Ⓐ $y = -x + 2$ Ⓑ $y = 2x - 1$ Ⓒ $y = x - 2$ Ⓓ $y = 2x + 1$

EXAMPLE 2 on p. 283 for Exs. 10–15

WRITING EQUATIONS **Write an equation of the line shown.**

10. 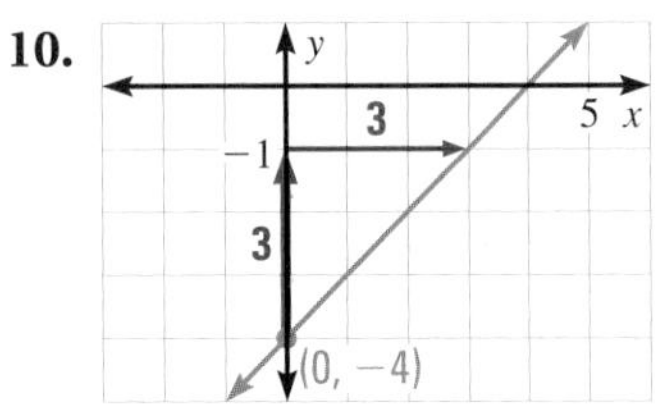

11. 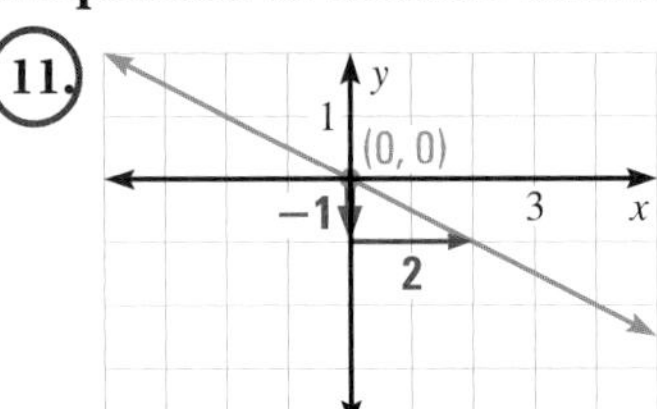

12. 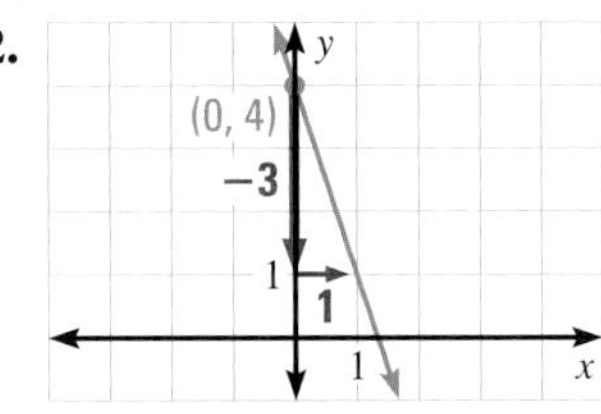

13. 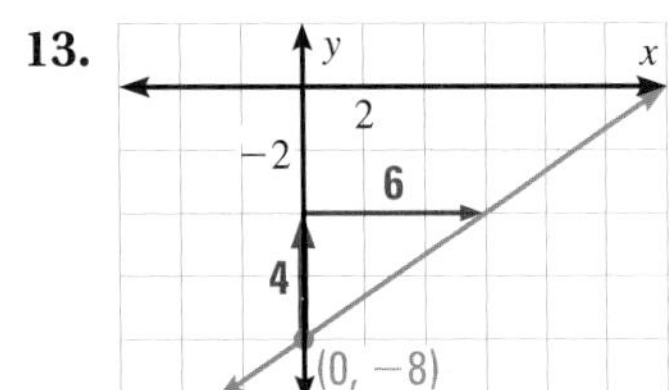

14. 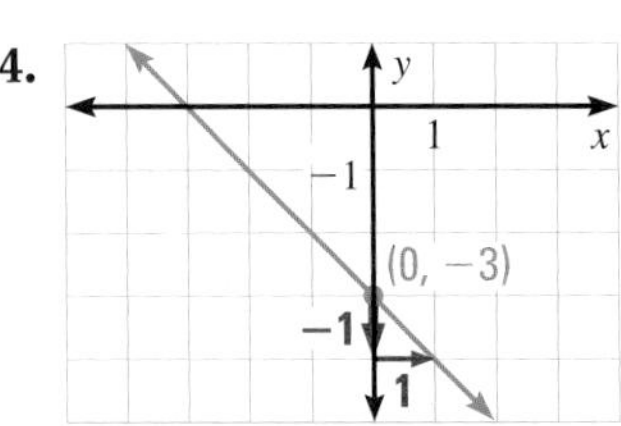

15. 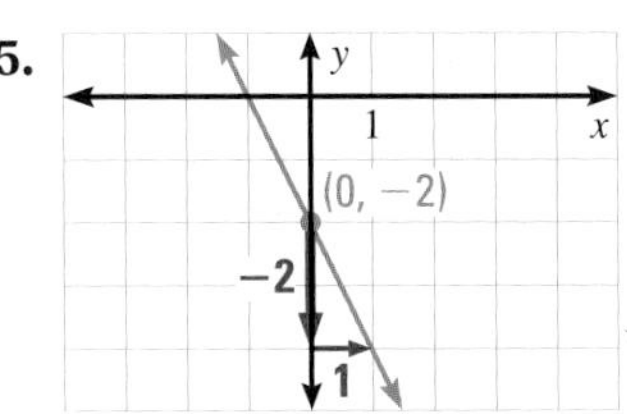

16. **ERROR ANALYSIS** *Describe* and correct the error in writing an equation of the line with a slope of 2 and a y-intercept of 7.

$y = 7x + 2$ ✗

EXAMPLE 3 on p. 284 for Exs. 17–29

17. **ERROR ANALYSIS** *Describe* and correct the error in writing an equation of the line shown.

$\text{slope} = \frac{0-4}{0-5} = \frac{-4}{-5} = \frac{4}{5}$

✗ $y = \frac{4}{5}x + 4$

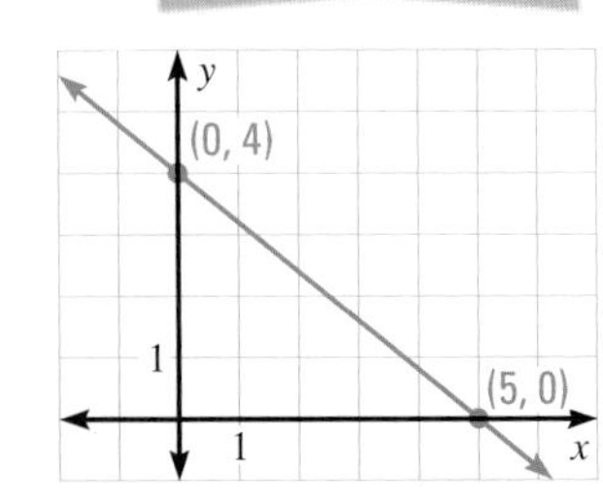

USING A GRAPH **Write an equation of the line shown.**

18.

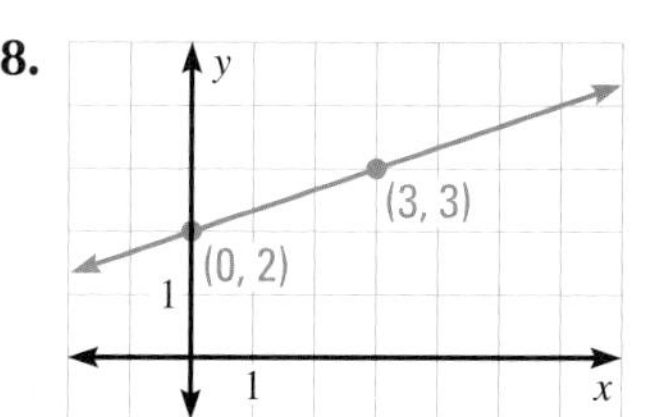

19.

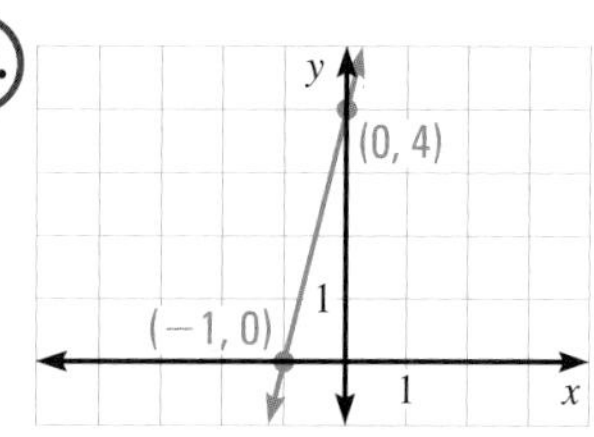

20.

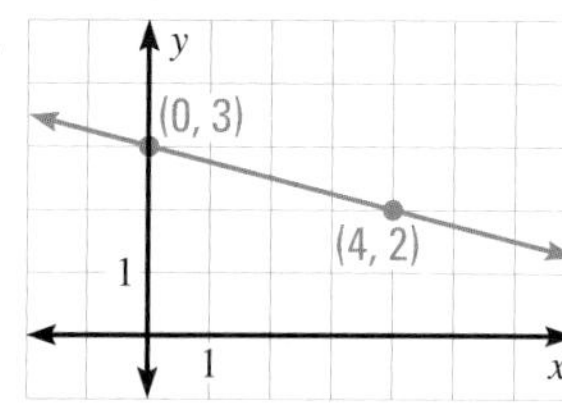

21.

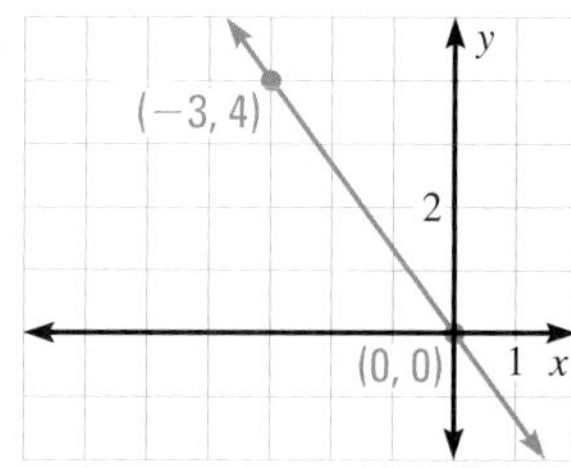

22.

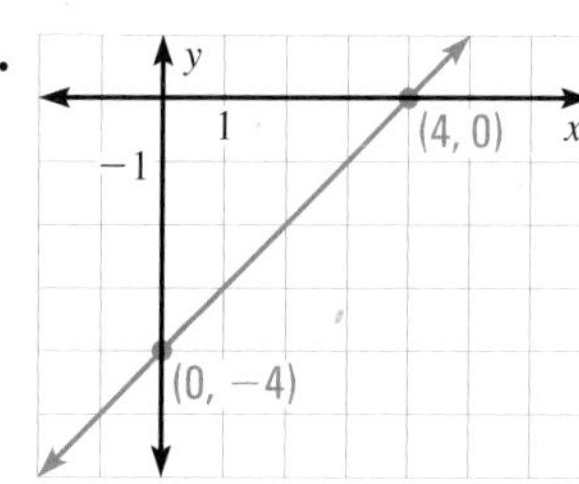

23.

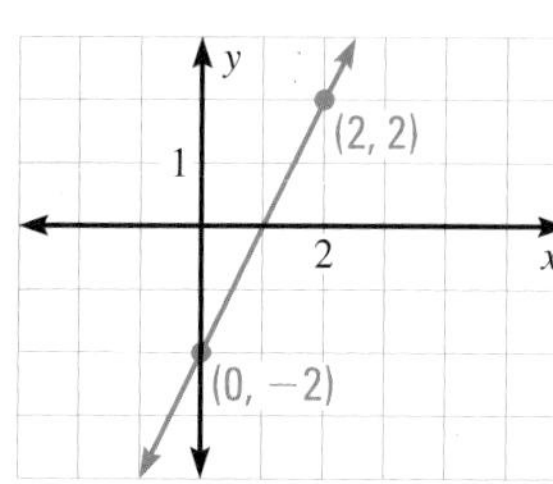

USING TWO POINTS **Write an equation of the line that passes through the given points.**

24. (−3, 1), (0, −8)

25. (2, −7), (0, −5)

26. (2, −4), (0, −4)

27. (0, 4), (8, 3.5)

28. (0, 5), (1.5, 1)

29. (−6, 0), (0, −24)

EXAMPLE 4
on p. 284
for Exs. 30–38

WRITING FUNCTIONS **Write an equation for the linear function *f* with the given values.**

30. $f(0) = 2, f(2) = 4$

31. $f(0) = 7, f(3) = 1$

32. $f(0) = -2, f(4) = -3$

33. $f(0) = -1, f(5) = -5$

34. $f(-2) = 6, f(0) = -4$

35. $f(-6) = -1, f(0) = 3$

36. $f(4) = 13, f(0) = 21$

37. $f(0) = 9, f(3) = 0$

38. $f(0.2) = 1, f(0) = 0.6$

39. **VISUAL THINKING** Write an equation of the line with a slope that is half the slope of the line shown and a *y*-intercept that is 2 less than the *y*-intercept of the line shown.

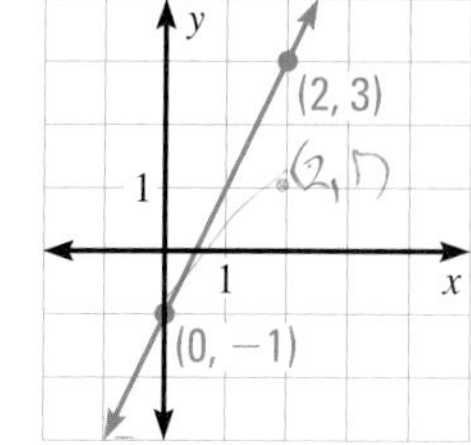

40. ★ **OPEN-ENDED** *Describe* a real-world situation that can be modeled by the function $y = 4x + 9$.

USING A DIAGRAM OR TABLE **Write an equation that represents the linear function shown in the mapping diagram or table.**

41.

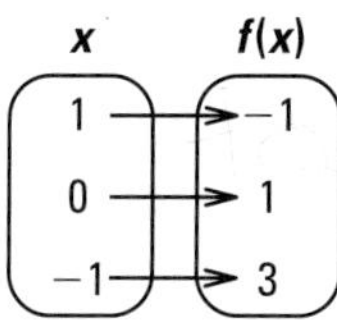

42.

x	$f(x)$
−4	−2
−2	−1
0	0

43. ★ **WRITING** A line passes through the points (3, 5) and (3, −7). Is it possible to write an equation of the line in slope-intercept form? *Justify* your answer.

44. **CHALLENGE** Show that the equation of the line that passes through the points $(0, b)$ and $(1, b + m)$ is $y = mx + b$. *Explain* how you can be sure that the point $(-1, b - m)$ also lies on the line.

PROBLEM SOLVING

EXAMPLE 5 on p. 285 for Exs. 45–49

45. **WEB SERVER** The initial fee to have a website set up using a server is \$48. It costs \$44 per month to maintain the website.

    a. Write an equation that gives the total cost of setting up and maintaining a website as a function of the number of months it is maintained.

    b. Find the total cost of setting up and maintaining the website for 6 months.

@HomeTutor for problem solving help at classzone.com

46. **PHOTOGRAPHS** A camera shop charges \$3.99 for an enlargement of a photograph. Enlargements can be delivered for a charge of \$1.49 per order. Write an equation that gives the total cost of an order with delivery as a function of the number of enlargements. Find the total cost of ordering 8 photograph enlargements with delivery.

@HomeTutor for problem solving help at classzone.com

47. **AQUARIUM** Your family spends \$30 for tickets to an aquarium and \$3 per hour for parking. Write an equation that gives the total cost of your family's visit to the aquarium as a function of the number of hours that you are there. Find the total cost of 4 hours at the aquarium.

48. ★ **SHORT RESPONSE** Scientists found that the number of ant species in Clark Canyon, Nevada, increases at a rate of 0.0037 species per meter of elevation. There are approximately 3 ant species at sea level.

    a. Write an equation that gives the number of ant species as a function of the elevation (in meters).

    b. Identify the dependent and independent variables in this situation.

    c. *Explain* how you can use the equation from part (a) to approximate the number of ant species at an elevation of 2 meters.

49. **MULTIPLE REPRESENTATIONS** The timeline shows the approximate total area of glaciers on Mount Kilimanjaro from 1970 to 2000.

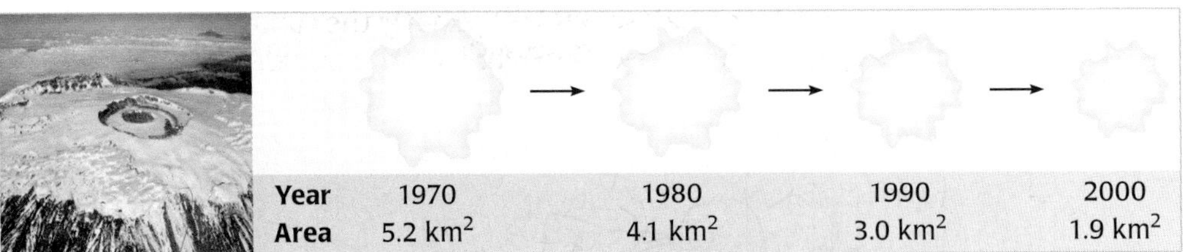

Year	1970	1980	1990	2000
Area	5.2 km^2	4.1 km^2	3.0 km^2	1.9 km^2

    a. **Making a Table** Make a table that shows the number of years x since 1970 and the area of the glaciers y (in square kilometers).

    b. **Drawing a Graph** Graph the data in the table. *Explain* how you know the area of glaciers changed at a constant rate.

    c. **Writing an Equation** Write an equation that models the area of glaciers as a function of the number of years since 1970. By how much did the area of the glaciers decrease each year from 1970 to 2000?

○ = WORKED-OUT SOLUTIONS on p. WS1 ★ = STANDARDIZED TEST PRACTICE ◆ = MULTIPLE REPRESENTATIONS

50. ★ **EXTENDED RESPONSE** The Harris Dam in Maine releases water into the Kennebec River. From 10:00 A.M. to 1:00 P.M. during each day of whitewater rafting season, water is released at a greater rate than usual.

Time interval	Release rate (gallons per hour)
12:00 A.M. to 10:00 A.M.	8.1 million
10:00 A.M. to 1:00 P.M.	130 million

a. On a day during rafting season, how much water is released by 10:00 A.M.?

b. Write an equation that gives, for a day during rafting season, the total amount of water (in gallons) released as a function of the number of hours since 10:00 A.M.

c. What is the domain of the function from part (b)? *Explain.*

51. **FIREFIGHTING** The diagram shows the time a firefighting aircraft takes to scoop water from a lake, fly to a fire, and drop the water on the fire.

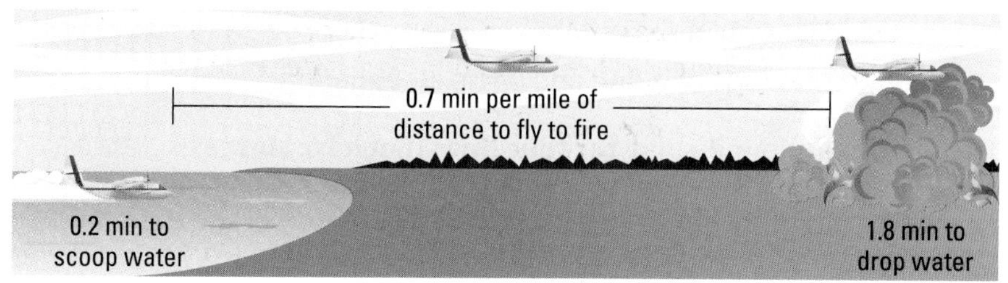

a. **Model** Write an equation that gives the total time (in minutes) that the aircraft takes to scoop, fly, and drop as a function of the distance (in miles) flown from the lake to the fire.

b. **Predict** Find the time the aircraft takes to scoop, fly, and drop if it travels 20 miles from the lake to the fire.

52. **CHALLENGE** The elevation at which a baseball game is played affects the distance a ball travels when hit. For every increase of 1000 feet in elevation, the ball travels about 7 feet farther. Suppose a baseball travels 400 feet when hit in a ball park at sea level.

a. **Model** Write an equation that gives the distance (in feet) the baseball travels as a function of the elevation of the ball park in which it is hit.

b. **Justify** *Justify* the equation from part (a) using unit analysis.

c. **Predict** If the ball were hit in exactly the same way at a park with an elevation of 3500 feet, how far would it travel?

MIXED REVIEW

Solve the equation. Check your solution.

53. $x + 11 = 6$ *(p. 134)*

54. $x - 7 = 13$ *(p. 134)*

55. $0.2x = -1$ *(p. 134)*

56. $3x + 9 = 21$ *(p. 141)*

57. $2x - 3 = 25$ *(p. 141)*

58. $4x - 8 = -10$ *(p. 141)*

PREVIEW
Prepare for Lesson 5.2 in Exs. 59–64.

Find the slope of the line that passes through the points. *(p. 235)*

59. $(-4, 6), (0, -2)$

60. $(-3, -2), (0, 1)$

61. $(5, 6), (-1, 3)$

62. $(-9, 3), (7, -1)$

63. $(3, -12), (5, -7)$

64. $(10, 4), (-8, 2)$

5.1 Investigate Families of Lines

QUESTION **How can you use a graphing calculator to find equations of lines using slopes and *y*-intercepts?**

Recall from Chapter 4 that you can create families of lines by varying the value of either m or b in $y = mx + b$. The constants m and b are called *parameters*. Given the value of one parameter, you can determine the value of the other parameter if you also have information that uniquely identifies one member of the family of lines.

EXAMPLE 1 **Find the slope of a line and write an equation**

In the same viewing window, display the four lines that have slopes of −1, −0.5, 0.5, and 1 and a *y*-intercept of 2. Then use the graphs to determine which line passes through the point (12, 8). Write an equation of the line.

STEP 1 ***Enter equations***

Press Y= and enter the four equations. Because the lines all have the same *y*-intercept, they constitute a family of lines and can be entered as shown.

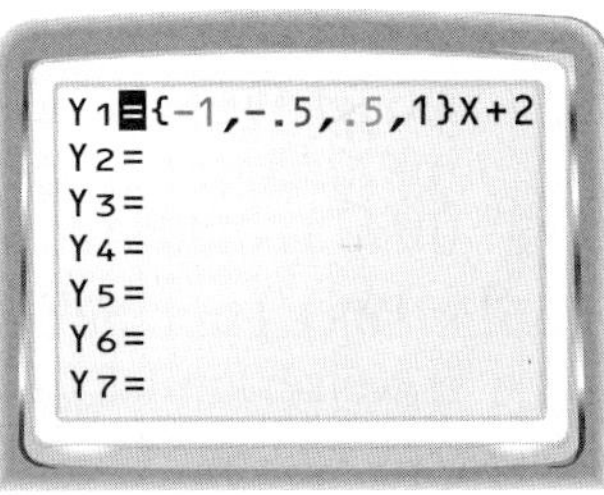

STEP 2 ***Display graphs***

Graph the equations in an appropriate viewing window. Press TRACE and use the left and right arrow keys to move along one of the lines until $x = 12$. Use the up and down arrow keys to see which line passes through (12, 8).

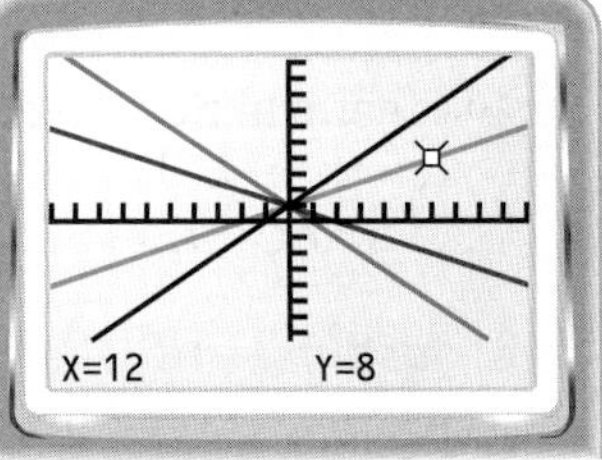

STEP 3 ***Find the line***

The line that passes through (12, 8) is the line with a slope of 0.5. So, an equation of the line is $y = 0.5x + 2$.

PRACTICE

Display the lines that have the same *y*-intercept but different slopes, as given, in the same viewing window. Determine which line passes through the given point. Write an equation of the line.

1. Slopes: −3, −2, 2, 3; *y*-intercept: 5; point: (−3, 11)
2. Slopes: 4, −2.5, 2.5, 4; *y*-intercept: −1; point: (4, −11)
3. Slopes: −2, −1, 1, 2; *y*-intercept: 1.5; point: (1, 3.5)

@HomeTutor
classzone.com
Keystrokes

EXAMPLE 2 Find the y-intercept of a line and write an equation

In the same viewing window, display the five lines that have a slope of 0.5 and y-intercepts of -2, -1, 0, 1, and 2. Then use the graphs to determine which line passes through the point $(-2, -2)$. Write an equation of the line.

STEP 1 Enter equations

Press Y= and enter the five equations. Because the lines all have the same slope, they constitute a family of lines and can be entered as shown below.

STEP 2 Display graphs

Graph the equations in an appropriate viewing window. Press TRACE and use the left and right arrow keys to move along one of the lines until $x = -2$. Use the up and down arrow keys to see which line passes through $(-2, -2)$.

STEP 3 Find the line

The line that passes through $(-2, -2)$ is the line with a y-intercept of -1. So, an equation of the line is $y = 0.5x - 1$.

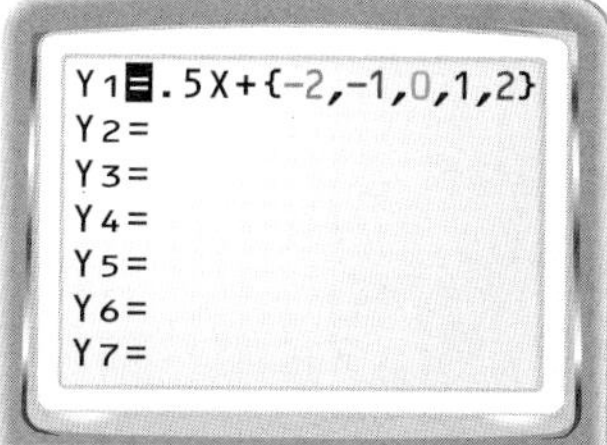

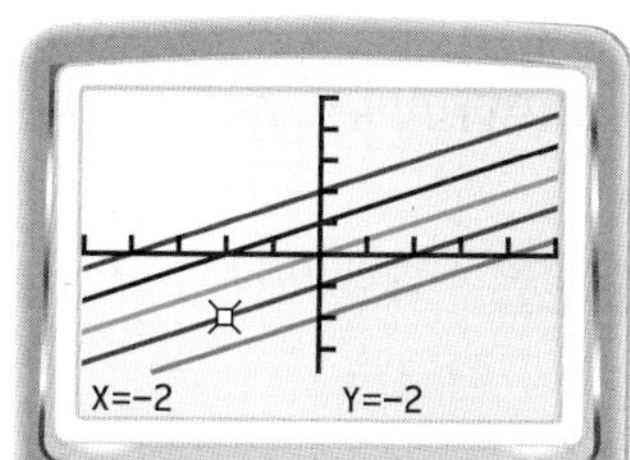

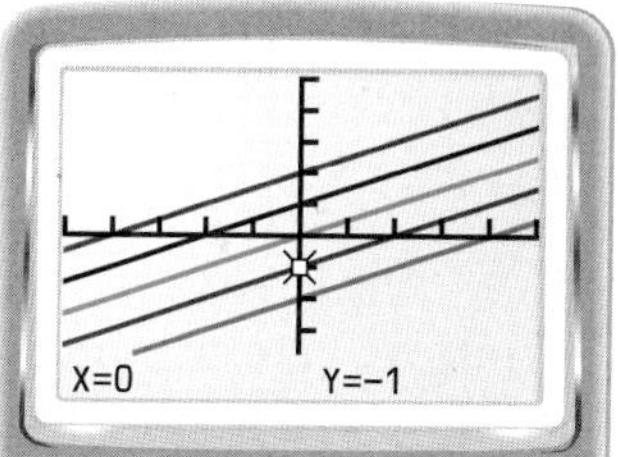

PRACTICE

Display the lines that have the same slope but different y-intercepts, as given, in the same viewing window. Determine which line passes through the given point. Write an equation of the line.

4. Slope: -3; y-intercepts: -2, -1, 0, 1, 2; point: $(4, -13)$
5. Slope: 1.5; y-intercepts: -2, -1, 0, 1, 2; point: $(-2, -1)$
6. Slope: -0.5; y-intercepts: -3, -1.5, 0, 1.5, 3; point: $(-4, 3.5)$
7. Slope: 4; y-intercepts: -3, -1, 0, 1, 3; point: $(2, 5)$
8. Slope: 2; y-intercepts: -6, -3, 0, 3, 6; point: $(-2, -7)$

DRAW CONCLUSIONS

9. Of all the lines having equations of the form $y = 0.5x + b$, which one passes through the point $(2, 2)$? *Explain* how you found your answer.
10. *Describe* a process you could use to find an equation of a line that has a slope of -0.25 and passes through the point $(8, -2)$.

5.2 Use Linear Equations in Slope-Intercept Form

Before You wrote an equation of a line using its slope and y-intercept.

Now You will write an equation of a line using points on the line.

Why So you can write a model for total cost, as in Example 5.

Key Vocabulary
- ***y*-intercept,** *p. 225*
- **slope,** *p. 235*
- **slope-intercept form,** *p. 244*

KEY CONCEPT *For Your Notebook*

Writing an Equation of a Line in Slope-Intercept Form

STEP 1 **Identify** the slope m. You can use the slope formula to calculate the slope if you know two points on the line.

STEP 2 **Find** the y-intercept. You can substitute the slope and the coordinates of a point (x, y) on the line in $y = mx + b$. Then solve for b.

STEP 3 **Write** an equation using $y = mx + b$.

EXAMPLE 1 **Write an equation given the slope and a point**

Write an equation of the line that passes through the point $(-1, 3)$ and has a slope of -4.

Solution

STEP 1 **Identify** the slope. The slope is -4.

STEP 2 **Find** the y-intercept. Substitute the slope and the coordinates of the given point in $y = mx + b$. Solve for b.

$y = mx + b$ Write slope-intercept form.

$3 = -4(-1) + b$ Substitute -4 for m, -1 for x, and 3 for y.

$-1 = b$ Solve for b.

AVOID ERRORS
When you substitute, be careful not to mix up the x- and y-values.

STEP 3 **Write** an equation of the line.

$y = mx + b$ Write slope-intercept form.

$y = -4x - 1$ Substitute -4 for m and -1 for b.

✓ **GUIDED PRACTICE** for Example 1

1. Write an equation of the line that passes through the point $(6, 3)$ and has a slope of 2.

EXAMPLE 2 Write an equation given two points

Write an equation of the line that passes through (−2, 5) and (2, −1).

Solution

STEP 1 **Calculate** the slope.

$$m = \frac{y_2 - y_1}{x_2 - x_1} = \frac{-1 - 5}{2 - (-2)} = \frac{-6}{4} = -\frac{3}{2}$$

ANOTHER WAY
You can also find the *y*-intercept using the coordinates of the other given point, (2, −1):
$y = mx + b$
$-1 = -\frac{3}{2}(2) + b$
$2 = b$

STEP 2 **Find** the *y*-intercept. Use the slope and the point (−2, 5).

$y = mx + b$ — **Write slope-intercept form.**

$5 = -\frac{3}{2}(-2) + b$ — **Substitute $-\frac{3}{2}$ for *m*, −2 for *x*, and 5 for *y*.**

$2 = b$ — **Solve for *b*.**

STEP 3 **Write** an equation of the line.

$y = mx + b$ — **Write slope-intercept form.**

$y = -\frac{3}{2}x + 2$ — **Substitute $-\frac{3}{2}$ for *m* and 2 for *b*.**

EXAMPLE 3 Standardized Test Practice

Which function has the values *f*(4) = 9 and *f*(−4) = −7?

Ⓐ $f(x) = 2x + 10$ Ⓑ $f(x) = 2x + 1$

Ⓒ $f(x) = 2x - 13$ Ⓓ $f(x) = 2x - 14$

ELIMINATE CHOICES
You can also evaluate each function when $x = 4$ and $x = -4$. Eliminate any choices for which $f(4) \neq 9$ or $f(-4) \neq -7$.

STEP 1 **Calculate** the slope. Write $f(4) = 9$ as (4, 9) and $f(-4) = -7$ as (−4, −7).

$$m = \frac{y_2 - y_1}{x_2 - x_1} = \frac{-7 - 9}{-4 - 4} = \frac{-16}{-8} = 2$$

STEP 2 **Find** the *y*-intercept. Use the slope and the point (4, 9).

$y = mx + b$ — **Write slope-intercept form.**

$9 = 2(4) + b$ — **Substitute 2 for *m*, 4 for *x*, and 9 for *y*.**

$1 = b$ — **Solve for *b*.**

STEP 3 **Write** an equation for the function. Use function notation.

$f(x) = 2x + 1$ — **Substitute 2 for *m* and 1 for *b*.**

▶ The answer is B. Ⓐ Ⓑ Ⓒ Ⓓ

GUIDED PRACTICE for Examples 2 and 3

2. Write an equation of the line that passes through (1, −2) and (−5, 4).

3. Write an equation for the linear function with the values $f(-2) = 10$ and $f(4) = -2$.

CONCEPT SUMMARY *For Your Notebook*

How to Write Equations in Slope-Intercept Form

Given slope m and y-intercept b	Given slope m and one point	Given two points
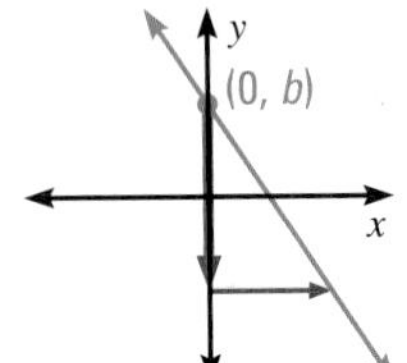	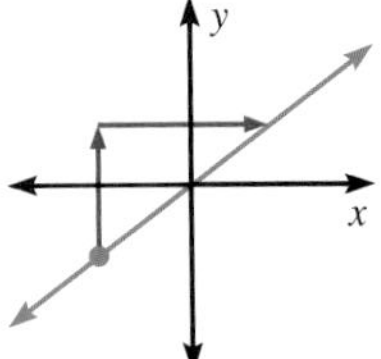	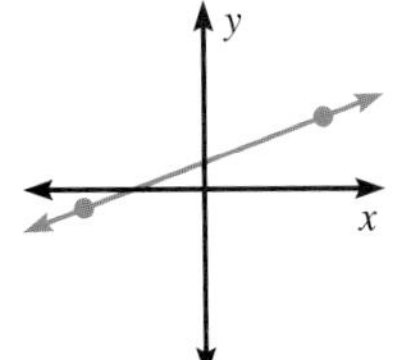
Substitute m and b in the equation $y = mx + b$.	Substitute m and the coordinates of the point in $y = mx + b$. Solve for b. Write the equation.	Use the points to find the slope m. Then follow the same steps described at the left.

MODELING REAL-WORLD SITUATIONS You can model a real-world situation that involves a constant rate of change with an equation in slope-intercept form.

EXAMPLE 4 Solve a multi-step problem

GYM MEMBERSHIP Your gym membership costs \$33 per month after an initial membership fee. You paid a total of \$228 after 6 months. Write an equation that gives the total cost as a function of the length of your gym membership (in months). Find the total cost after 9 months.

Solution

STEP 1 **Identify** the rate of change and starting value.

Rate of change, *m*: monthly cost, \$33 per month
Starting value, *b*: initial membership fee

STEP 2 **Write** a verbal model. Then write an equation.

Total cost	=	Monthly cost	•	Number of months	+	Membership fee
↓		↓		↓		↓
C	=	33	•	t	+	b

STEP 3 **Find** the starting value. Membership for 6 months costs \$228, so you can substitute 6 for t and 228 for C in the equation $C = 33t + b$.

$228 = 33(6) + b$ **Substitute 6 for *t* and 228 for *C*.**

$30 = b$ **Solve for *b*.**

STEP 4 **Write** an equation. Use the function from Step 2.

$C = 33t + 30$ **Substitute 30 for *b*.**

STEP 5 **Evaluate** the function when $t = 9$.

$C = 33(9) + 30 = 327$ **Substitute 9 for *t*. Simplify.**

▶ Your total cost after 9 months is \$327.

EXAMPLE 5 Solve a multi-step problem

BMX RACING In Bicycle Moto Cross (BMX) racing, racers purchase a one year membership to a track. They also pay an entry fee for each race at that track. One racer paid a total of \$125 after 5 races. A second racer paid a total of \$170 after 8 races. How much does the track membership cost? What is the entry fee per race?

ANOTHER WAY
For alternative methods for solving the problem in Example 5, turn to page 300 for the **Problem Solving Workshop**.

Solution

STEP 1 **Identify** the rate of change and starting value.

Rate of change, m: entry fee per race
Starting value, b: track membership cost

STEP 2 **Write** a verbal model. Then write an equation.

Total cost	=	Entry fee per race	•	Races entered	+	Membership cost
↓		↓		↓		↓
C	=	m	•	r	+	b

STEP 3 **Calculate** the rate of change. This is the entry fee per race. Use the slope formula. Racer 1 is represented by (5, 125). Racer 2 is represented by (8, 170).

$$m = \frac{y_2 - y_1}{x_2 - x_1} = \frac{170 - 125}{8 - 5} = \frac{45}{3} = 15$$

STEP 4 **Find** the track membership cost b. Use the data pair (5, 125) for racer 1 and the entry fee per race from Step 3.

$C = mr + b$ — Write the equation from Step 2.

$125 = 15(5) + b$ — Substitute 15 for m, 5 for r, and 125 for C.

$50 = b$ — Solve for b.

▶ The track membership cost is \$50. The entry fee per race is \$15.

✓ GUIDED PRACTICE for Examples 4 and 5

4. **GYM MEMBERSHIP** A gym charges \$35 per month after an initial membership fee. A member has paid a total of \$250 after 6 months. Write an equation that gives the total cost of a gym membership as a function of the length of membership (in months). Find the total cost of membership after 10 months.

5. **BMX RACING** A BMX race track charges a membership fee and an entry fee per race. One racer paid a total of \$76 after 3 races. Another racer paid a total of \$124 after 7 races.

   a. How much does the track membership cost?

   b. What is the entry fee per race?

   c. Write an equation that gives the total cost as a function of the number of races entered.

5.2 EXERCISES

HOMEWORK KEY

○ = **WORKED-OUT SOLUTIONS** on p. WS11 for Exs. 5, 11, and 49

★ = **STANDARDIZED TEST PRACTICE** Exs. 2, 29, 34–37, 41, and 49

◆ = **MULTIPLE REPRESENTATIONS** Ex. 53

SKILL PRACTICE

1. **VOCABULARY** What is the y-coordinate of a point where a graph crosses the y-axis called?

2. ★ **WRITING** If the equation $y = mx + b$ is used to model a quantity y as a function of the quantity x, why is b considered to be the starting value?

EXAMPLE 1 on p. 292 for Exs. 3–9

WRITING EQUATIONS **Write an equation of the line that passes through the given point and has the given slope m.**

3. $(1, 1)$; $m = 3$
4. $(5, 1)$; $m = 2$
5. $(-4, 7)$; $m = -5$
6. $(5, -5)$; $m = -2$
7. $(8, -4)$; $m = -\frac{3}{4}$
8. $(-3, -11)$; $m = \frac{1}{2}$

9. **ERROR ANALYSIS** *Describe* and correct the error in finding the y-intercept of the line that passes through the point $(6, -3)$ and has a slope of -2.

$y = mx + b$
$6 = -2(-3) + b$
$6 = 6 + b$
$0 = b$
✗

EXAMPLE 4 on p. 294 for Ex. 10

10. **ERROR ANALYSIS** An Internet service provider charges \$18 per month plus an initial set-up fee. One customer paid a total of \$81 after 2 months of service. *Describe* and correct the error in finding the set-up fee.

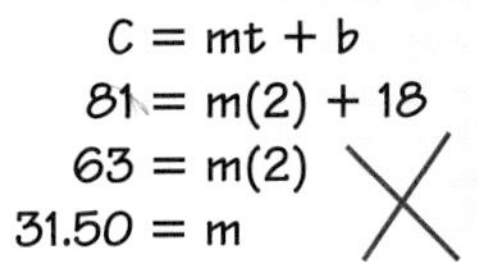
$C = mt + b$
$81 = m(2) + 18$
$63 = m(2)$
$31.50 = m$
✗

EXAMPLE 2 on p. 293 for Exs. 11–22

USING TWO POINTS **Write an equation of the line that passes through the given points.**

11. $(1, 4)$, $(2, 7)$
12. $(3, 2)$, $(4, 9)$
13. $(10, -5)$, $(-5, 1)$
14. $(-2, 8)$, $(-6, 0)$
15. $\left(\frac{9}{2}, 1\right)$, $\left(-\frac{7}{2}, 7\right)$
16. $\left(-5, \frac{3}{4}\right)$, $\left(-2, -\frac{3}{4}\right)$

USING A GRAPH **Write an equation of the line shown.**

17.
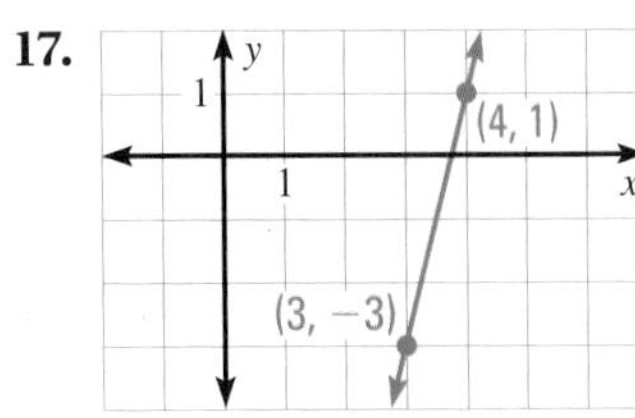

18.
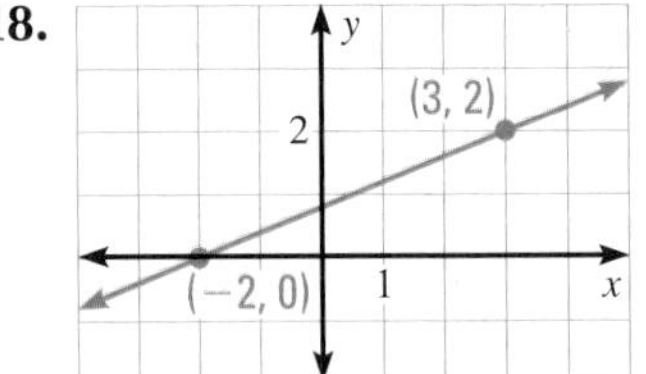

19.
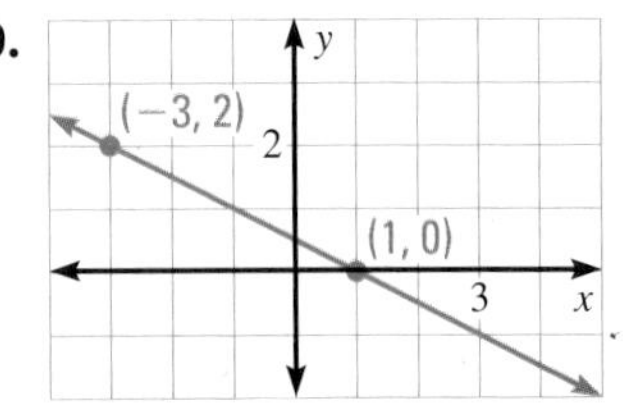

20. (−1, 3); (2, −0.5)

21.
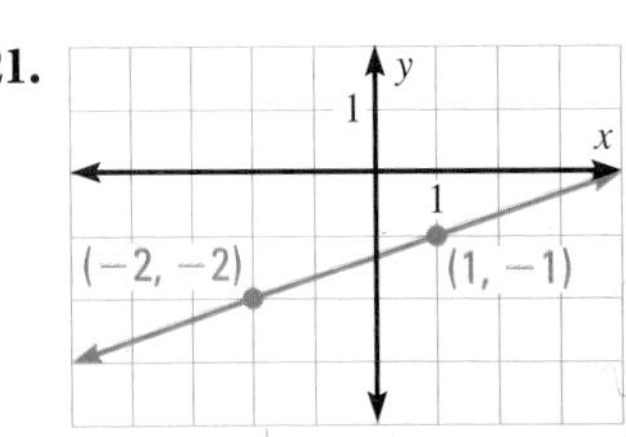

22.
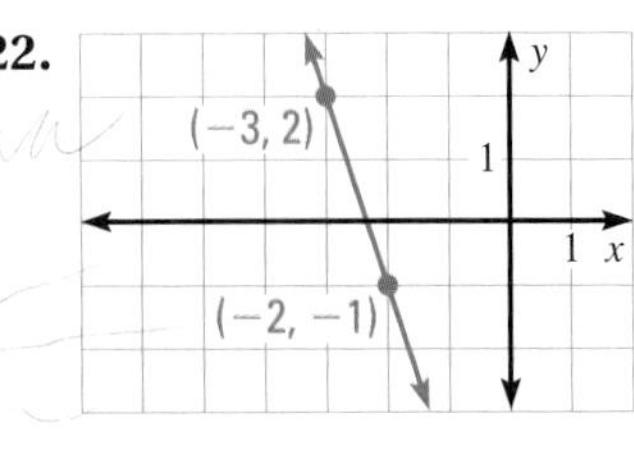

EXAMPLE 3 on p. 293 for Exs. 23–33

WRITING LINEAR FUNCTIONS **Write an equation for a linear function f that has the given values.**

23. $f(-2) = 15, f(1) = 9$

24. $f(-2) = -2, f(4) = -8$

25. $f(2) = 7, f(4) = 6$

26. $f(-4) = -8, f(-8) = -11$

27. $f(3) = 1, f(6) = 4$

28. $f(-5) = 9, f(11) = -39$

29. ★ **MULTIPLE CHOICE** Which function has the values $f(4) = -15$ and $f(7) = 57$?

Ⓐ $f(x) = 14x - 71$

Ⓑ $f(x) = 24x - 1361$

Ⓒ $f(x) = 24x + 360$

Ⓓ $f(x) = 24x - 111$

USING A TABLE OR DIAGRAM **Write an equation that represents the linear function shown in the table or mapping diagram.**

30.

x	$f(x)$
−4	6
4	4
8	3
12	2

31.

x	$f(x)$
−3	8
3	4
6	2
9	0

32.

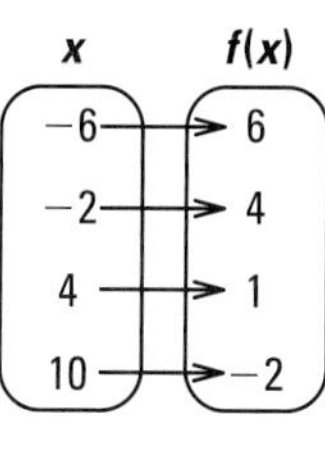

33.

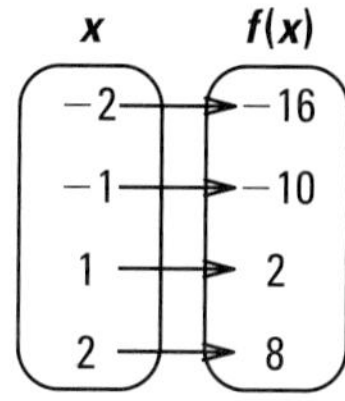

★ **SHORT RESPONSE** **Tell whether the given information is enough to write an equation of a line. *Justify* your answer.**

34. Two points on the line

35. The slope and a point on the line

36. The slope of the line

37. Both intercepts of the line

USING A GRAPH **In Exercises 38–41, use the graph at the right.**

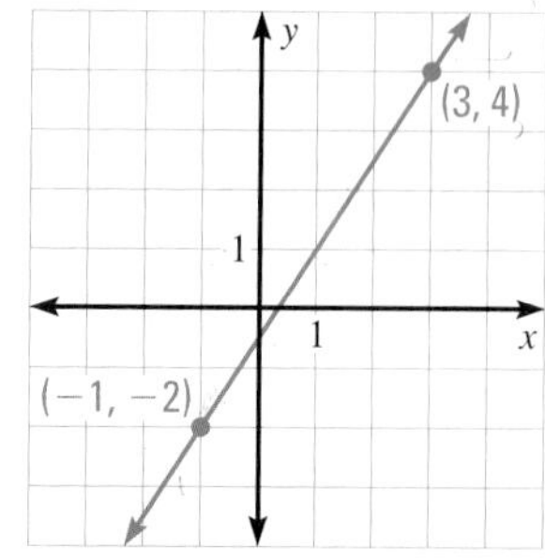

38. Write an equation of the line shown.

39. Write an equation of a line that has the same y-intercept as the line shown but has a slope that is 3 times the slope of the line shown.

40. Write an equation of a line that has the same slope as the line shown but has a y-intercept that is 6 more than the y-intercept of the line shown.

41. ★ **WRITING** Which of the lines from Exercises 38–40 intersect? Which of the lines never intersect? *Justify* your answers.

REASONING **Decide whether the three points lie on the same line. *Explain* how you know. If the points do lie on the same line, write an equation of the line that passes through all three points.**

42. $(-4, -2), (2, 2.5), (8, 7)$

43. $(2, 2), (-4, 5), (6, 1)$

44. $(-10, 4), (-3, 2.8), (-17, 6.8)$

45. $(-5.5, 3), (-7.5, 4), (-4, 5)$

46. **CHALLENGE** A line passes through the points $(-2, 3)$, $(2, 5)$, and $(6, k)$. Find the value of k. *Explain* your steps.

PROBLEM SOLVING

EXAMPLES 4 and 5 on pp. 294–295 for Exs. 47–50

47. **BIOLOGY** Four years after a hedge maple tree was planted, its height was 9 feet. Eight years after it was planted, the hedge maple tree's height was 12 feet. What is the growth rate of the hedge maple? What was its height when it was planted?

@HomeTutor for problem solving help at classzone.com

48. **TECHNOLOGY** You have a subscription to an online magazine that allows you to view 25 articles from the magazine's archives. You are charged an additional fee for each article after the first 25 articles viewed. After viewing 28 archived articles, you paid a total of \$34.80. After viewing 30 archived articles, you paid a total of \$40.70.

   a. What is the cost per archived article after the first 25 articles viewed?

   b. What is cost of the magazine subscription?

@HomeTutor for problem solving help at classzone.com

49. ★ **SHORT RESPONSE** You are cooking a roast beef until it is well-done. You must allow 30 minutes of cooking time for every pound of beef, plus some extra time. The last time you cooked a 2 pound roast, it was well-done after 1 hour and 25 minutes. How much time will it take to cook a 3 pound roast? *Explain* how you found your answer.

HINT In part (b), let *t* represent the number of years since 1981.

50. **TELEPHONE SERVICE** The annual household cost of telephone service in the United States increased at a relatively constant rate of \$27.80 per year from 1981 to 2001. In 2001 the annual household cost of telephone service was \$914.

   a. What was the annual household cost of telephone service in 1981?

   b. Write an equation that gives the annual household cost of telephone service as a function of the number of years since 1981.

   c. Find the household cost of telephone service in 2000.

51. **NEWSPAPERS** Use the information in the article about the circulation of Sunday newspapers.

   a. About how many Sunday newspapers were in circulation in 1970?

   b. Write an equation that gives the number of Sunday newspapers in circulation as a function of the number of years since 1970.

   c. About how many Sunday newspapers were in circulation in 2000?

Sunday Edition C9

SUNDAY PAPERS INCREASE

From 1970 to 2000, the number of Sunday newspapers in circulation increased at a relatively constant rate of 11.8 newspapers per year. In 1997 there were 903 Sunday newspapers in circulation.

52. **AIRPORTS** From 1990 to 2001, the number of airports in the United States increased at a relatively constant rate of 175 airports per year. There were 19,306 airports in the United States in 2001.

   a. How many U.S. airports were there in 1990?

   b. Write an equation that gives the number of U.S. airports as a function of the number of years since 1990.

   c. Find the year in which the number of U.S. airports reached 19,200.

○ = WORKED-OUT SOLUTIONS on p. WS1

★ = STANDARDIZED TEST PRACTICE

= MULTIPLE REPRESENTATIONS

53. **MULTIPLE REPRESENTATIONS** A hurricane is traveling at a constant speed on a straight path toward a coastal town, as shown below.

Hurricane position at 1:00 P.M.

216 mi
town

Hurricane position at 5:00 P.M.

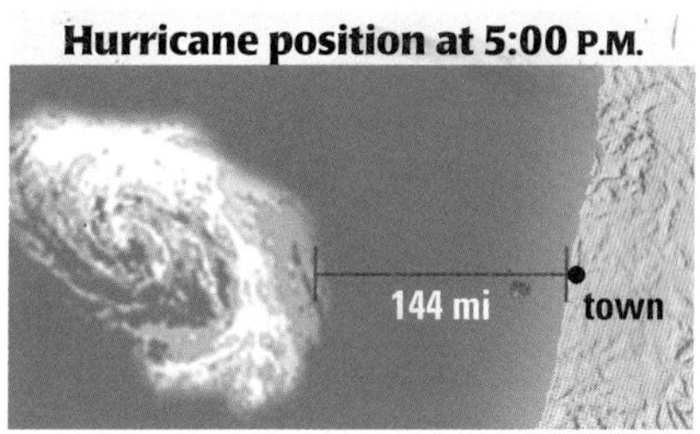

a. **Writing an Equation** Write an equation that gives the distance (in miles) of the hurricane from the town as a function of the number of hours since 12:00 P.M.

b. **Drawing a Graph** Graph the equation from part (a). *Explain* what the slope and the y-intercept of the graph mean in this situation.

c. **Describing in Words** Predict the time at which the hurricane will reach the town. Your answer should include the following information:
- an explanation of how you used your equation
- a description of the steps you followed to obtain your prediction

54. **CHALLENGE** An in-line skater practices at a race track. In two trials, the skater travels the same distance going from a standstill to his top racing speed. He then travels at his top racing speed for different distances.

Trial number	Time at top racing speed (seconds)	Total distance traveled (meters)
1	24	300
2	29	350

a. **Model** Write an equation that gives the total distance traveled (in meters) as a function of the time (in seconds) at top racing speed.

b. **Justify** What do the rate of change and initial value in your equation represent? *Explain* your answer using unit analysis.

c. **Predict** One lap around the race track is 200 meters. The skater starts at a standstill and completes 3 laps. Predict the number of seconds the skater travels at his top racing speed. *Explain* your method.

MIXED REVIEW

Solve the equation. Check your solution.

55. $3x + 2x - 3 = 12$ *(p. 148)*

56. $-2(q + 13) - 8 = 2$ *(p. 148)*

57. $-3a + 15 = 45 + 7a$ *(p. 154)*

58. $7c + 25 = -19 + 2c$ *(p. 154)*

PREVIEW
Prepare for Lesson 5.3 in Exs. 59–64.

Write an equation of the line that has the given characteristics. *(p. 283)*

59. Slope: -5; y-intercept: -2

60. Slope: $\frac{2}{7}$; y-intercept: -3

61. Slope: 1; passes through $(0, -4)$

62. Slope: 9; passes through $(0, 14)$

63. Passes through $(0, 6)$, $(5, 2)$

64. Passes through $(-12, 3)$, $(0, 2)$

PROBLEM SOLVING WORKSHOP
LESSON 5.2

Using ALTERNATIVE METHODS

Another Way to Solve Example 5, page 295

MULTIPLE REPRESENTATIONS In Example 5 on page 295, you saw how to solve a problem about BMX racing using an equation. You can also solve this problem using a graph or a table.

PROBLEM

BMX RACING In Bicycle Moto Cross (BMX) racing, racers purchase a one year membership to a track. They also pay an entry fee for each race at that track. One racer paid a total of \$125 after 5 races. A second racer paid a total of \$170 after 8 races. How much does the track membership cost? What is the entry fee per race?

METHOD 1

Using a Graph One alternative approach is to use a graph.

STEP 1 **Read** the problem. It tells you the number of races and amount paid for each racer. Write this information as ordered pairs.

Racer 1: (5, 125)

Racer 2: (8, 170)

STEP 2 **Graph** the ordered pairs. Draw a line through the points.

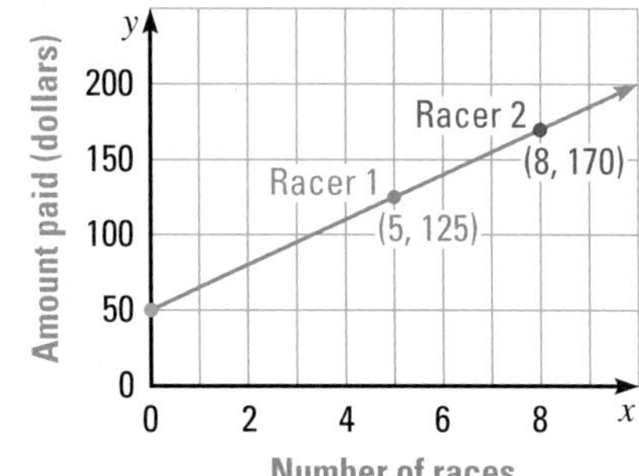

STEP 3 **Find** the slope of the line. This is the entry fee per race.

$$\text{Fee} = \frac{45 \text{ dollars}}{3 \text{ races}} = \$15 \text{ per race}$$

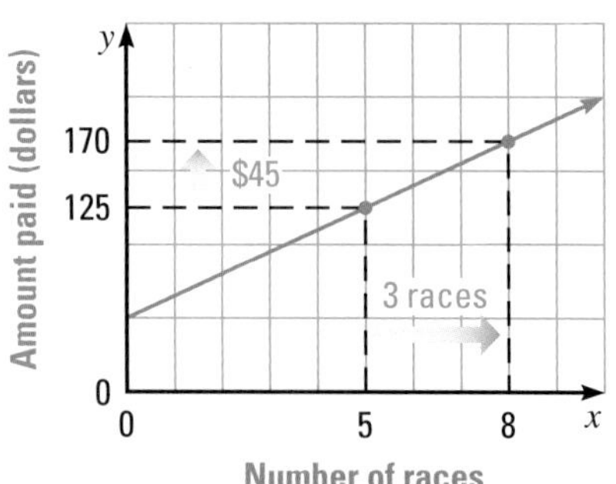

METHOD 2 **Using a Table** Another approach is to use a table showing the amount paid for various numbers of races.

STEP 1 **Calculate** the race entry fee.

Number of races	Amount paid
5	$125
6	?
7	?
8	$170

+ 3   + $45

The number of races increased by 3, and the amount paid increased by $45, so the race entry fee is $\$45 \div 3 = \$15$.

STEP 2 **Find** the membership cost.

Number of races	Amount paid
0	$50
1	$65
2	$80
3	$95
4	$110
5	$125

− $15 − $15 − $15 − $15 − $15

The membership cost is the cost with no races. Use the race entry fee and work backwards to fill in the table. The membership cost is $50.

PRACTICE

1. **CALENDARS** A company makes calendars from personal photos. You pay a delivery fee for each order plus a cost per calendar. The cost of 2 calendars plus delivery is $43. The cost of 4 calendars plus delivery is $81. What is the delivery fee? What is the cost per calendar? Solve this problem using two different methods.

2. **BOOKSHELVES** A furniture maker offers bookshelves that have the same width and depth but that differ in height and price, as shown in the table. Find the cost of a bookshelf that is 72 inches high. Solve this problem using two different methods.

Height (inches)	Price (dollars)
36	56.54
48	77.42
60	98.30

3. **WHAT IF?** In Exercise 2, suppose the price of the 60 inch bookshelf was $99.30. Can you still solve the problem? *Explain.*

4. **CONCERT TICKETS** All tickets for a concert are the same price. The ticket agency adds a fixed fee to every order. A person who orders 5 tickets pays $93. A person who orders 3 tickets pays $57. How much will 4 tickets cost? Solve this problem using two different methods.

5. **ERROR ANALYSIS** A student solved the problem in Exercise 4 as shown below. *Describe* and correct the error.

Let p = price paid for 4 tickets

$$\frac{57}{3} = \frac{p}{4}$$

$$228 = 3p$$

$$76 = p$$

✗

5.3 Write Linear Equations in Point-Slope Form

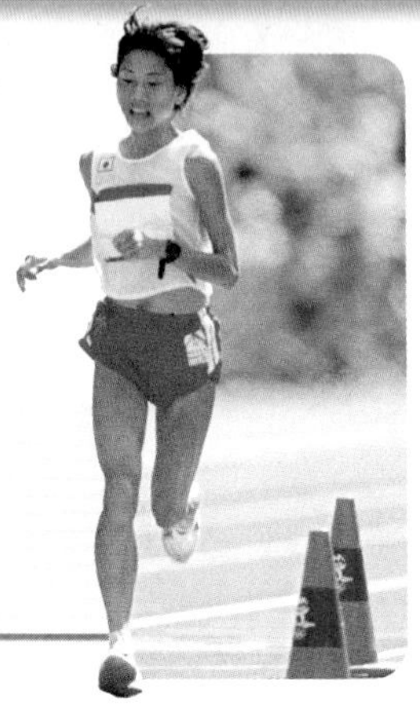

Before You wrote linear equations in slope-intercept form.

Now You will write linear equations in point-slope form.

Why? So you can model sports statistics, as in Ex. 43.

Key Vocabulary
- **point-slope form**

Consider the line that passes through the point (2, 3) with a slope of $\frac{1}{2}$. Let (x, y) where $x \neq 2$ be another point on the line. You can write an equation relating x and y using the slope formula, with $(x_1, y_1) = (2, 3)$ and $(x_2, y_2) = (x, y)$.

$m = \frac{y_2 - y_1}{x_2 - x_1}$ **Write slope formula.**

$\frac{1}{2} = \frac{y - 3}{x - 2}$ **Substitute $\frac{1}{2}$ for m, 3 for y_1, and 2 for x_1.**

$\frac{1}{2}(x - 2) = y - 3$ **Multiply each side by $(x - 2)$.**

The equation in *point-slope form* is $y - 3 = \frac{1}{2}(x - 2)$.

USE POINT-SLOPE FORM
When an equation is in point-slope form, you can read the x- and y-coordinates of a point on the line and the slope of the line.

KEY CONCEPT *For Your Notebook*

Point-Slope Form

The **point-slope form** of the equation of the nonvertical line through a given point (x_1, y_1) with a slope of m is $y - y_1 = m(x - x_1)$.

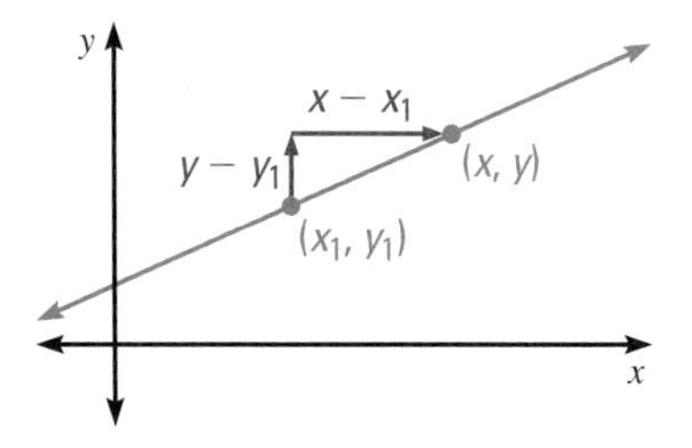

EXAMPLE 1 Write an equation in point-slope form

Write an equation in point-slope form of the line that passes through the point (4, −3) and has a slope of 2.

$y - y_1 = m(x - x_1)$ **Write point-slope form.**

$y + 3 = 2(x - 4)$ **Substitute 2 for m, 4 for x_1, and −3 for y_1.**

GUIDED PRACTICE for Example 1

1. Write an equation in point-slope form of the line that passes through the point (−1, 4) and has a slope of −2.

EXAMPLE 2 Graph an equation in point-slope form

Graph the equation $y + 2 = \frac{2}{3}(x - 3)$.

Solution

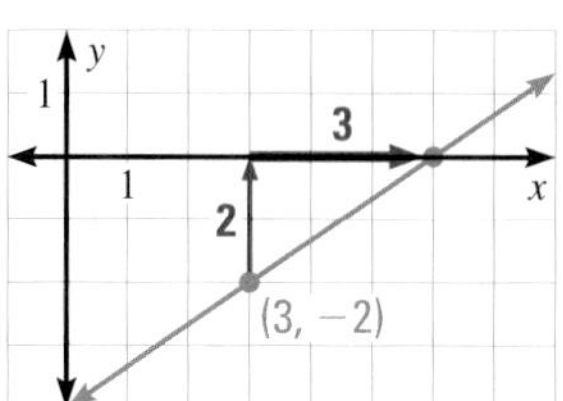

Because the equation is in point-slope form, you know that the line has a slope of $\frac{2}{3}$ and passes through the point (3, −2).

Plot the point (3, −2). Find a second point on the line using the slope. Draw a line through both points.

✓ GUIDED PRACTICE for Example 2

2. Graph the equation $y - 1 = -(x - 2)$.

EXAMPLE 3 Use point-slope form to write an equation

Write an equation in point-slope form of the line shown.

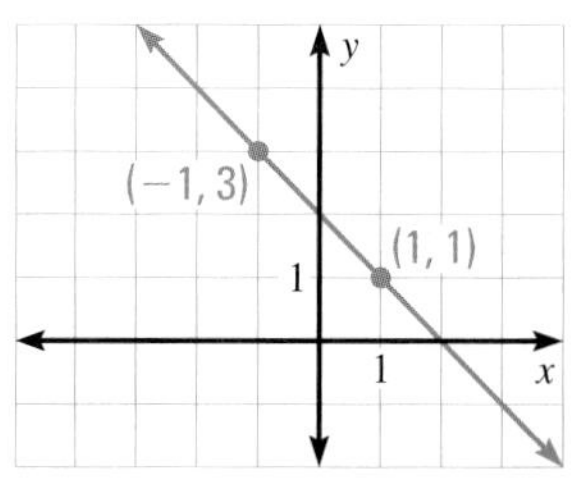

Solution

STEP 1 **Find** the slope of the line.

$$m = \frac{y_2 - y_1}{x_2 - x_1} = \frac{3 - 1}{-1 - 1} = \frac{2}{-2} = -1$$

STEP 2 **Write** the equation in point-slope form. You can use either given point.

Method 1 Use (−1, 3).	**Method 2** Use (1, 1).
$y - y_1 = m(x - x_1)$	$y - y_1 = m(x - x_1)$
$y - 3 = -(x + 1)$	$y - 1 = -(x - 1)$

CHECK Check that the equations are equivalent by writing them in slope-intercept form.

$y - 3 = -x - 1$	$y - 1 = -x + 1$
$y = -x + 2$	$y = -x + 2$

Animated Algebra activity at classzone.com

✓ GUIDED PRACTICE for Example 3

3. Write an equation in point-slope form of the line that passes through the points (2, 3) and (4, 4).

EXAMPLE 4 Solve a multi-step problem

STICKERS You are designing a sticker to advertise your band. A company charges \$225 for the first 1000 stickers and \$80 for each additional 1000 stickers. Write an equation that gives the total cost (in dollars) of stickers as a function of the number (in thousands) of stickers ordered. Find the cost of 9000 stickers.

Solution

STEP 1 **Identify** the rate of change and a data pair. Let C be the cost (in dollars) and s be the number of stickers (in thousands).

Rate of change, m: \$80 per 1 thousand stickers
Data pair (s_1, C_1): (1 thousand stickers, \$225)

STEP 2 **Write** an equation using point-slope form. Rewrite the equation in slope-intercept form so that cost is a function of the number of stickers.

$C - C_1 = m(s - s_1)$ **Write point-slope form.**

$C - 225 = 80(s - 1)$ **Substitute 80 for m, 1 for s_1, and 225 for C_1.**

$C = 80s + 145$ **Solve for C.**

AVOID ERRORS
Remember that s is given in thousands. To find the cost of 9000 stickers, substitute 9 for s.

STEP 3 **Find** the cost of 9000 stickers.

$C = 80(9) + 145 = 865$ **Substitute 9 for s. Simplify.**

▶ The cost of 9000 stickers is \$865.

EXAMPLE 5 Write a real-world linear model from a table

WORKING RANCH The table shows the cost of visiting a working ranch for one day and night for different numbers of people. Can the situation be modeled by a linear equation? *Explain.* If possible, write an equation that gives the cost as a function of the number of people in the group.

Number of people	4	6	8	10	12
Cost (dollars)	250	350	450	550	650

Solution

STEP 1 **Find** the rate of change for consecutive data pairs in the table.

$$\frac{350 - 250}{6 - 4} = 50, \quad \frac{450 - 350}{8 - 6} = 50, \quad \frac{550 - 450}{10 - 8} = 50, \quad \frac{650 - 550}{12 - 10} = 50$$

Because the cost increases at a constant rate of \$50 per person, the situation can be modeled by a linear equation.

STEP 2 **Use** point-slope form to write the equation. Let C be the cost (in dollars) and p be the number of people. Use the data pair (4, 250).

$C - C_1 = m(p - p_1)$ **Write point-slope form.**

$C - 250 = 50(p - 4)$ **Substitute 50 for m, 4 for p_1, and 250 for C_1.**

$C = 50p + 50$ **Solve for C.**

 **GUIDED PRACTICE** for Examples 4 and 5

4. **WHAT IF?** In Example 4, suppose a second company charges $250 for the first 1000 stickers. The cost of each additional 1000 stickers is $60.

   a. Write an equation that gives the total cost (in dollars) of the stickers as a function of the number (in thousands) of stickers ordered.

   b. Which company would charge you less for 9000 stickers?

5. **MAILING COSTS** The table shows the cost (in dollars) of sending a single piece of first class mail for different weights. Can the situation be modeled by a linear equation? *Explain.* If possible, write an equation that gives the cost of sending a piece of mail as a function of its weight (in ounces).

Weight (ounces)	1	4	5	10	12
Cost (dollars)	0.37	1.06	1.29	2.44	2.90

5.3 EXERCISES

HOMEWORK KEY

○ = **WORKED-OUT SOLUTIONS on p. WS11 for Exs. 3 and 39**

★ = **STANDARDIZED TEST PRACTICE Exs. 2, 12, 30–34, 38, and 41**

SKILL PRACTICE

1. **VOCABULARY** Identify the slope of the line given by the equation $y - 5 = -2(x + 5)$. Then identify one point on the line.

2. ★ **WRITING** *Describe* the steps you would take to write an equation in point-slope form of the line that passes through the points $(3, -2)$ and $(4, 5)$.

EXAMPLE 1 on p. 302 for Exs. 3–13

WRITING EQUATIONS **Write an equation in point-slope form of the line that passes through the given point and has the given slope *m*.**

3. $(2, 1), m = 2$
4. $(3, 5), m = -1$
5. $(7, -1), m = -6$
6. $(5, -1), m = -2$
7. $(-8, 2), m = 5$
8. $(-6, 6), m = \frac{3}{2}$
9. $(-11, -3), m = -9$
10. $(-3, -9), m = \frac{7}{3}$
11. $(5, -12), m = -\frac{2}{5}$

12. ★ **MULTIPLE CHOICE** Which equation represents the line that passes through the point $(-6, 2)$ and has a slope of -1?

    Ⓐ $y + 2 = -(x + 6)$
    Ⓑ $y + 2 = -(x - 6)$
    Ⓒ $y - 2 = -(x + 6)$
    Ⓓ $y + 1 = -2(x + 6)$

13. **ERROR ANALYSIS** *Describe* and correct the error in writing an equation of the line that passes through the point $(1, -5)$ and has a slope of -2.

    $y - 5 = -2(x - 1)$ ✗

EXAMPLE 2 on p. 303 for Exs. 14–19

GRAPHING EQUATIONS **Graph the equation.**

14. $y - 5 = 3(x - 1)$ **15.** $y + 3 = -2(x - 2)$ **16.** $y - 1 = 3(x + 6)$

17. $y + 8 = -(x + 4)$ **18.** $y - 1 = \frac{3}{4}(x + 1)$ **19.** $y + 4 = -\frac{5}{2}(x - 3)$

EXAMPLE 3 on p. 303 for Exs. 20–30

USING A GRAPH **Write an equation in point-slope form of the line shown.**

20.

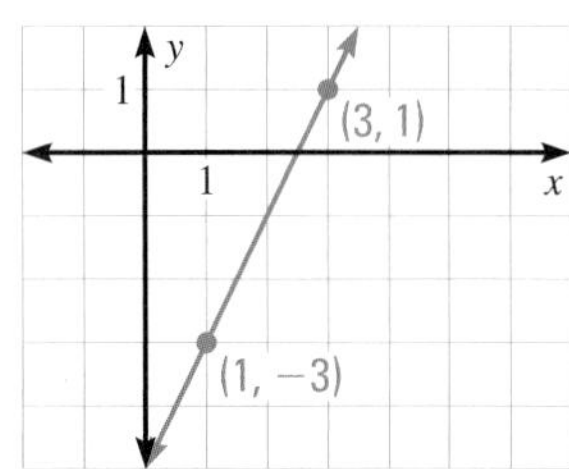

21.

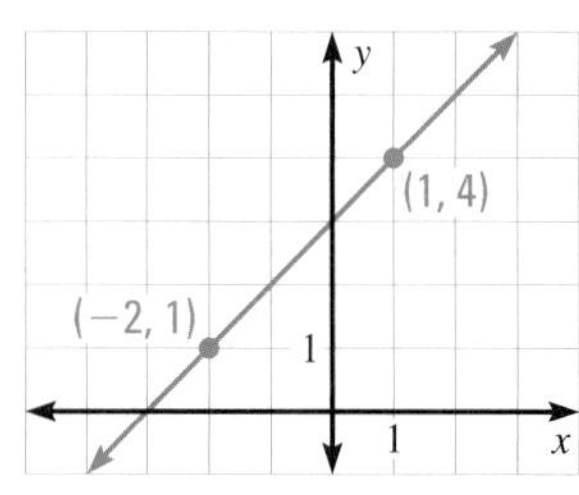

22.

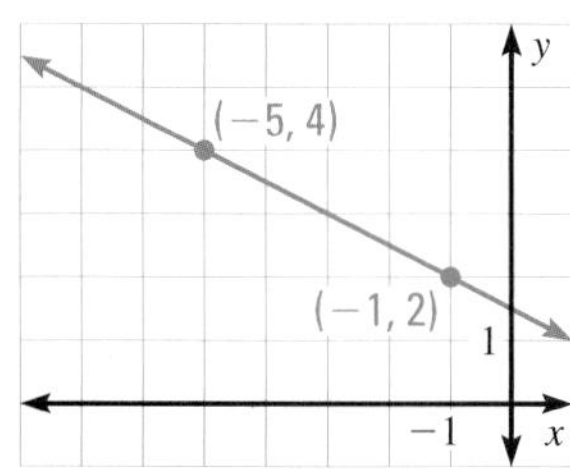

WRITING EQUATIONS **Write an equation in point-slope form of the line that passes through the given points.**

23. (7, 2), (2, 12) **24.** (6, −2), (12, 1) **25.** (−4, −1), (6, −7)

26. (4, 5), (−4, −5) **27.** (−3, −20), (4, 36) **28.** (−5, −19), (5, 13)

29. **ERROR ANALYSIS** *Describe* and correct the error in writing an equation of the line shown.

$m = \frac{4 - 2}{4 - 1} = \frac{2}{3}$ $y - 2 = \frac{2}{3}(x - 4)$

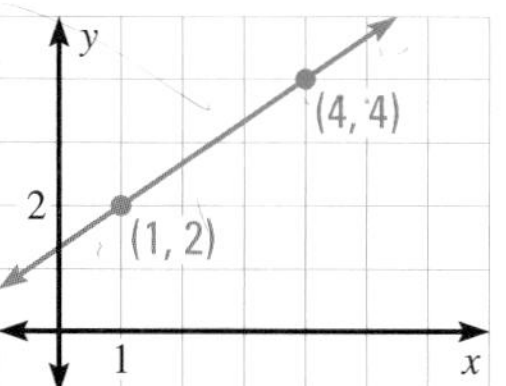

30. ★ **MULTIPLE CHOICE** The graph of which equation is shown?

Ⓐ $y + 4 = -3(x + 2)$ Ⓑ $y - 4 = -3(x - 2)$

Ⓒ $y - 4 = -3(x + 2)$ Ⓓ $y + 4 = -3(x - 2)$

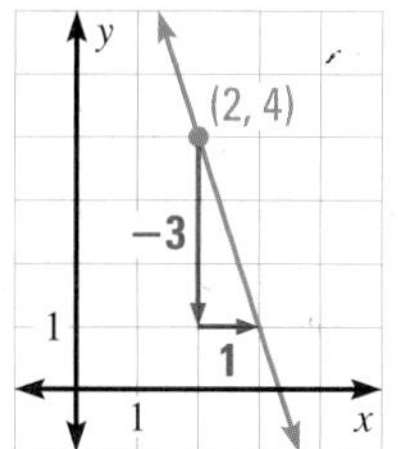

★ **SHORT RESPONSE** **Tell whether the data in the table can be modeled by a linear equation.** ***Explain.*** **If possible, write an equation in point-slope form that relates** y **and** x**.**

31.

x	2	4	6	8	10
y	−1	5	15	29	47

32.

x	1	2	3	5	7
y	1.2	1.4	1.6	2	2.4

33.

x	1	2	3	4	5
y	2	−3	4	−5	6

34.

x	−3	−1	1	3	5
y	16	10	4	−2	−8

CHALLENGE **Find the value of** k **so that the line passing through the given points has slope** m**. Write an equation of the line in point-slope form.**

35. $(k, 4k), (k + 2, 3k), m = -1$ **36.** $(-k + 1, 3), (3, k + 3), m = 3$

○ = WORKED-OUT SOLUTIONS on p. WS1 ★ = STANDARDIZED TEST PRACTICE

PROBLEM SOLVING

EXAMPLE 4 on p. 304 for Exs. 37, 39, 40

37. TELEVISION In order to use an excerpt from a movie in a new television show, the television producer must pay the director of the movie \$790 for the first 2 minutes of the excerpt and \$130 per minute after that.

a. Write an equation that gives the total cost (in dollars) of using the excerpt as a function of the length (in minutes) of the excerpt.

b. Find the total cost of using an excerpt that is 8 minutes long.

@HomeTutor for problem solving help at classzone.com

EXAMPLE 5 on p. 304 for Exs. 38, 41

38. ★ SHORT RESPONSE A school district pays an installation fee and a monthly fee for Internet service. The table shows the total cost of Internet service for the school district over different numbers of months. *Explain* why the situation can be modeled by a linear equation. What is the installation fee? What is the monthly service fee?

Months of service	2	4	6	8	10	12
Total cost (dollars)	9,378	12,806	16,234	19,662	23,090	26,518

@HomeTutor for problem solving help at classzone.com

39. COMPANY SALES During the period 1994–2004, the annual sales of a small company increased by \$10,000 per year. In 1997 the annual sales were \$97,000. Write an equation that gives the annual sales as a function of the number of years since 1994. Find the sales in 2000.

Animated Algebra at classzone.com

40. TRAFFIC DELAYS From 1990 to 2001 in Boston, Massachusetts, the annual excess fuel (in gallons per person) consumed due to traffic delays increased by about 1.4 gallons per person each year. In 1995 each person consumed about 37 gallons of excess fuel.

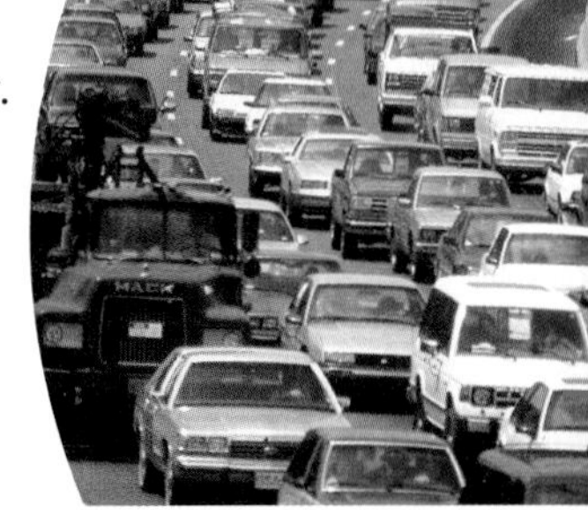

a. Write an equation that gives the annual excess fuel (in gallons per person) as a function of the number of years since 1990.

b. How much excess fuel was consumed per person in 2001?

Animated Algebra at classzone.com

41. ★ EXTENDED RESPONSE The table shows the cost of ordering sets of prints of digital photos from an online service. The cost per print is the same for the first 30 prints. There is also a shipping charge.

Number of prints	1	2	5	8
Total cost (dollars)	1.98	2.47	3.94	5.41

a. *Explain* why the situation can be modeled by a linear equation.

b. Write an equation in point-slope form that relates the total cost (in dollars) of a set of prints to the number of prints ordered.

c. Find the shipping charge for up to 10 prints.

d. The cost of 15 prints is \$9.14. The shipping charge increases after the first 10 prints. Find the shipping charge for 15 prints.

42. **AQUACULTURE** Aquaculture is the farming of fish and other aquatic animals. World aquaculture increased at a relatively constant rate from 1991 to 2002. In 1994 world aquaculture was about 20.8 million metric tons. In 2000 world aquaculture was about 35.5 million metric tons.

a. Write an equation that gives world aquaculture (in millions of metric tons) as a function of the number of years since 1991.

b. In 2001 China was responsible for 70.2% of world aquaculture. Approximate China's aquaculture in 2001.

43. **MARATHON** The diagram shows a marathon runner's speed at several outdoor temperatures.

a. Write an equation in point-slope form that relates running speed (in feet per second) to temperature (in degrees Fahrenheit).

b. Estimate the runner's speed when the temperature is 80°F.

44. CHALLENGE The number of cans recycled per pound of aluminum recycled in the U.S. increased at a relatively constant rate from 1972 to 2002. In 1977 about 23.5 cans per pound of aluminum were recycled. In 2000, about 33.1 cans per pound of aluminum were recycled.

a. Write an equation that gives the number of cans recycled per pound of aluminum recycled as a function of the number of years since 1972.

b. In 2002, there were 53.8 billion aluminum cans collected for recycling. Approximately how many pounds of aluminum were collected? *Explain* how you found your answer.

MIXED REVIEW

Evaluate the expression.

45. $|-3.2| - 2.8$ *(p. 80)*

46. $-6.1 - (-8.4)$ *(p. 80)*

47. $\sqrt{196}$ *(p. 110)*

Graph the equation.

48. $x = 0$ *(p. 215)*

49. $y = 8$ *(p. 215)*

50. $4x - 2y = 7$ *(p. 225)*

51. $-x + 5y = 1$ *(p. 225)*

52. $y = 2x - 7$ *(p. 244)*

53. $y = -\frac{3}{4}x + 2$ *(p. 244)*

PREVIEW
Prepare for Lesson 5.4 in Exs. 54–57.

Write an equation of the line that has the given characteristics.

54. Slope: −3; *y*-intercept: 5 *(p. 283)*

55. Slope: 8; passes through (2, 15) *(p. 292)*

56. Passes through (0, −3), (6, 1) *(p. 283)*

57. Passes through (3, 3), (6, −1) *(p. 292)*

Relate Arithmetic Sequences to Linear Functions

GOAL Identify, graph, and write the general form of arithmetic sequences.

Key Vocabulary
- **sequence**
- **arithmetic sequence**
- **common difference**

A **sequence** is an ordered list of numbers. The numbers in a sequence are called *terms*. In an **arithmetic sequence**, the difference between consecutive terms is constant. The constant difference is called the **common difference**.

An arithmetic sequence has the form $a_1, a_1 + d, a_1 + 2d, \ldots$ where a_1 is the first term and d is the common difference. For instance, if $a_1 = 2$ and $d = 6$, then the sequence $2, 2 + 6, 2 + 2(6), \ldots$ or $2, 8, 14, \ldots$ is arithmetic.

EXAMPLE 1 Identify an arithmetic sequence

Tell whether the sequence is arithmetic. If it is, find the next two terms.

a. $-4, 1, 6, 11, 16, \ldots$

b. $3, 5, 9, 15, 23, \ldots$

Solution

a. The first term is $a_1 = -4$. Find the differences of consecutive terms.

$a_2 - a_1 = 1 - (-4) = 5$ $\qquad a_3 - a_2 = 6 - 1 = 5$

$a_4 - a_3 = 11 - 6 = 5$ $\qquad a_5 - a_4 = 16 - 11 = 5$

▶ Because the terms have a common difference ($d = 5$), the sequence is arithmetic. The next two terms are $a_6 = 21$ and $a_7 = 26$.

b. The first term is $a_1 = 3$. Find the differences of consecutive terms.

$a_2 - a_1 = 5 - 3 = 2$ $\qquad a_3 - a_2 = 9 - 5 = 4$

$a_4 - a_3 = 15 - 9 = 6$ $\qquad a_5 - a_4 = 23 - 15 = 8$

▶ There is no common difference, so the sequence is not arithmetic.

GRAPHING A SEQUENCE To graph a sequence, let a term's position number in the sequence be the x-value. The term is the corresponding y-value.

EXAMPLE 2 Graph a sequence

Graph the sequence $-4, 1, 6, 11, 16, \ldots$.

Make a table pairing each term with its position number.

Position, x	1	2	3	4	5
Term, y	−4	1	6	11	16

Plot the pairs in the table as points in a coordinate plane.

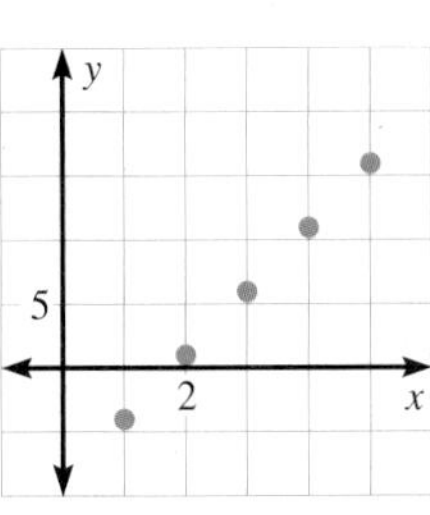

FUNCTIONS Notice that the points plotted in Example 2 appear to lie on a line. In fact, an arithmetic sequence is a linear function. You can think of the common difference d as the slope and $(1, a_1)$ as a point on the graph of the function. An equation in point-slope form for the function is $a_n - a_1 = d(n - 1)$. This equation can be rewritten as $a_n = a_1 + (n - 1)d$.

KEY CONCEPT *For Your Notebook*

Rule for an Arithmetic Sequence

The nth term of an arithmetic sequence with first term a_1 and common difference d is given by $a_n = a_1 + (n - 1)d$.

EXAMPLE 3 Write a rule for the nth term of a sequence

Write a rule for the nth term of the sequence $-4, 1, 6, 11, 16, \ldots$. Find a_{100}.

Solution

The first term of the sequence is $a_1 = -4$, and the common difference is $d = 5$.

$a_n = a_1 + (n - 1)d$ — Write general rule for an arithmetic sequence.

$a_n = -4 + (n - 1)5$ — Substitute -4 for a_1 and 5 for d.

Find a_{100} by substituting 100 for n.

$a_n = -4 + (n - 1)5$ — Write the rule for the sequence.

$a_{100} = -4 + (100 - 1)5$ — Substitute 100 for n.

$a_{100} = 491$ — Evaluate.

PRACTICE

EXAMPLE 1 on p. 309 for Exs. 1–3

Tell whether the sequence is arithmetic. If it is, find the next two terms. If it is not, explain why not.

1. $17, 14, 11, 8, 5, \ldots$ **2.** $1, 4, 16, 64, 256, \ldots$ **3.** $-8, -15, -22, -29, -36, \ldots$

EXAMPLE 2 on p. 309 for Exs. 4–9

Graph the sequence.

4. $1, 4, 7, 11, 14, \ldots$ **5.** $4, -3, -10, -17, -24, \ldots$ **6.** $5, -1, -7, -13, -19, \ldots$

7. $2, 3\frac{1}{2}, 5, 6\frac{1}{2}, 8, \ldots$ **8.** $0, 2, 4, 6, 8, \ldots$ **9.** $-3, -4, -5, -6, -7, \ldots$

EXAMPLE 3 on p. 310 for Exs. 10–15

Write a rule for the nth term of the sequence. Find a_{100}.

10. $-12, -5, 2, 9, 16, \ldots$ **11.** $51, 72, 93, 114, 135, \ldots$ **12.** $0.25, -0.75, -1.75, -2.75, \ldots$

13. $\frac{1}{4}, \frac{3}{8}, \frac{1}{2}, \frac{5}{8}, \frac{3}{4}, \ldots$ **14.** $0, -5, -10, -15, -20, \ldots$ **15.** $1, 1\frac{1}{3}, 1\frac{2}{3}, 2, 2\frac{1}{3}, \ldots$

16. **REASONING** For an arithmetic sequence with a first term of a_1 and a common difference of d, show that $a_{n+1} - a_n = d$.

5.4 Write Linear Equations in Standard Form

Before You wrote equations in point-slope form.

Now You will write equations in standard form.

Why? So you can find possible combinations of objects, as in Ex. 41.

Key Vocabulary
- **standard form,** *p. 215*

Recall that the linear equation $Ax + By = C$ is in standard form, where A, B, and C are real numbers and A and B are not both zero. All linear equations can be written in standard form.

EXAMPLE 1 Write equivalent equations in standard form

Write two equations in standard form that are equivalent to $2x - 6y = 4$.

Solution

To write one equivalent equation, multiply each side by 2.

$$4x - 12y = 8$$

To write another equivalent equation, multiply each side by 0.5.

$$x - 3y = 2$$

EXAMPLE 2 Write an equation from a graph

Write an equation in standard form of the line shown.

Solution

STEP 1 **Calculate** the slope.

$$m = \frac{1 - (-2)}{1 - 2} = \frac{3}{-1} = -3$$

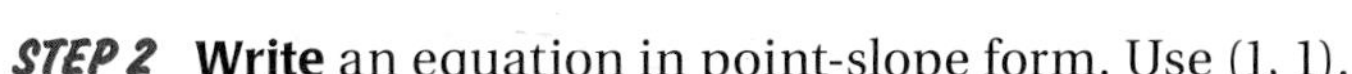

STEP 2 **Write** an equation in point-slope form. Use (1, 1).

$y - y_1 = m(x - x_1)$ **Write point-slope form.**

$y - 1 = -3(x - 1)$ **Substitute 1 for y_1, −3 for m, and 1 for x_1.**

STEP 3 **Rewrite** the equation in standard form.

$3x + y = 4$ **Simplify. Collect variable terms on one side, constants on the other.**

Animated Algebra at classzone.com

✓ GUIDED PRACTICE for Examples 1 and 2

1. Write two equations in standard form that are equivalent to $x - y = 3$.
2. Write an equation in standard form of the line through (3, −1) and (2, −3).

HORIZONTAL AND VERTICAL LINES Recall that equations of horizontal lines have the form $y = a$. Equations of vertical lines have the form $x = b$. You cannot write an equation for a vertical line in slope-intercept form or point-slope form, because a vertical line has no slope. However, you can write an equation for a vertical line in standard form.

EXAMPLE 3 Write an equation of a line

Write an equation of the specified line.

a. Blue line **b.** Red line

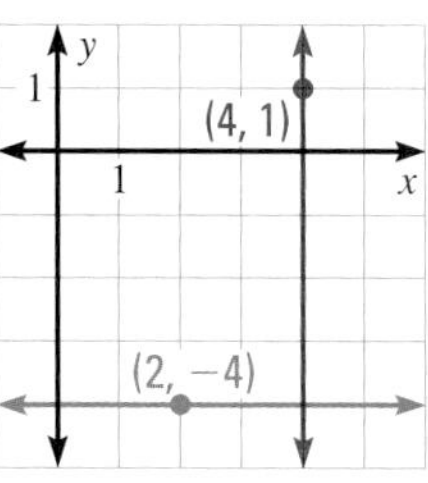

Solution

ANOTHER WAY
Using the slope-intercept form to find an equation of the horizontal line gives you $y = 0x - 4$, or $y = -4$.

a. The y-coordinate of the given point on the blue line is -4. This means that all points on the line have a y-coordinate of -4. An equation of the line is $y = -4$.

b. The x-coordinate of the given point on the red line is 4. This means that all points on the line have an x-coordinate of 4. An equation of the line is $x = 4$.

EXAMPLE 4 Complete an equation in standard form

Find the missing coefficient in the equation of the line shown. Write the completed equation.

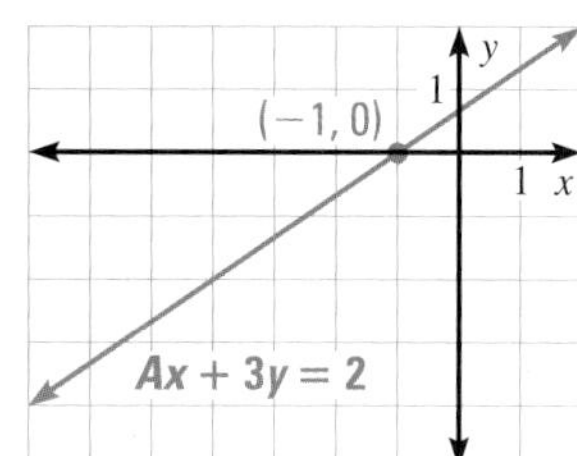

Solution

STEP 1 **Find** the value of A. Substitute the coordinates of the given point for x and y in the equation. Solve for A.

$Ax + 3y = 2$	Write equation.
$A(-1) + 3(0) = 2$	Substitute −1 for x and 0 for y.
$-A = 2$	Simplify.
$A = -2$	Divide by −1.

STEP 2 **Complete** the equation.

$-2x + 3y = 2$	Substitute −2 for A.

GUIDED PRACTICE for Examples 3 and 4

Write equations of the horizontal and vertical lines that pass through the given point.

3. $(-8, -9)$ **4.** $(13, -5)$

Find the missing coefficient in the equation of the line that passes through the given point. Write the completed equation.

5. $-4x + By = 7, (-1, 1)$ **6.** $Ax + y = -3, (2, 11)$

EXAMPLE 5 Solve a multi-step problem

LIBRARY Your class is taking a trip to the public library. You can travel in small and large vans. A small van holds 8 people and a large van holds 12 people. Your class could fill 15 small vans and 2 large vans.

a. Write an equation in standard form that models the possible combinations of small vans and large vans that your class could fill.

b. Graph the equation from part (a).

c. List several possible combinations.

Solution

a. Write a verbal model. Then write an equation.

Capacity of small van	·	Number of small vans	+	Capacity of large van	·	Number of large vans	=	People on trip
↓		↓		↓		↓		↓
8	·	s	+	12	·	ℓ	=	p

Because your class could fill 15 small vans and 2 large vans, use (15, 2) as the s- and ℓ-values to substitute in the equation $8s + 12\ell = p$ to find the value of p.

$8(15) + 12(2) = p$ **Substitute 15 for s and 2 for ℓ.**

$144 = p$ **Simplify.**

Substitute 144 for p in the equation $8s + 12\ell = p$.

▶ The equation $8s + 12\ell = 144$ models the possible combinations.

b. Find the intercepts of the graph.

Substitute 0 for s.	Substitute 0 for ℓ.
$8(0) + 12\ell = 144$	$8s + 12(0) = 144$
$\ell = 12$	$s = 18$

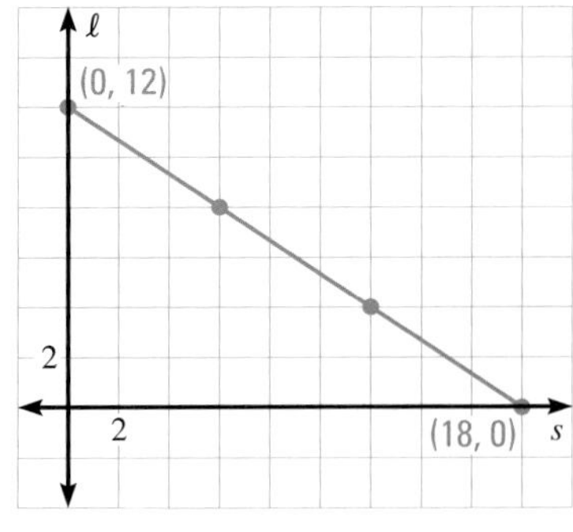

Plot the points (0, 12) and (18, 0). Connect them with a line segment. For this problem only nonnegative whole-number values of s and ℓ make sense.

LISTING COMBINATIONS
Other combinations of small and large vans are possible. Another way to find possible combinations is by substituting values for s or ℓ in the equation.

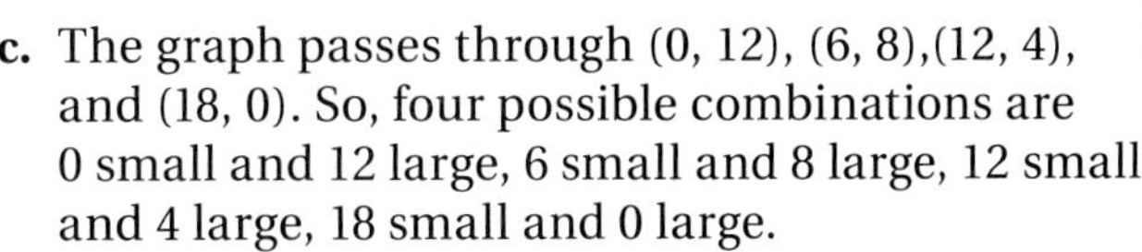

c. The graph passes through (0, 12), (6, 8),(12, 4), and (18, 0). So, four possible combinations are 0 small and 12 large, 6 small and 8 large, 12 small and 4 large, 18 small and 0 large.

GUIDED PRACTICE for Example 5

7. **WHAT IF?** In Example 5, suppose that 8 students decide not to go on the class trip. Write an equation that models the possible combinations of small and large vans that your class could fill. List several possible combinations.

5.4 EXERCISES

HOMEWORK KEY

○ = **WORKED-OUT SOLUTIONS** on p. WS11 for Exs. 17 and 39

★ = **STANDARDIZED TEST PRACTICE** Exs. 4, 30, 40, and 42

◆ = **MULTIPLE REPRESENTATIONS** Ex. 41

SKILL PRACTICE

VOCABULARY **Identify the form of the equation.**

1. $2x + 8y = -3$
2. $y = -5x + 8$
3. $y + 4 = 2(x - 6)$

4. ★ **WRITING** *Explain* how to write an equation of a line in standard form when two points on the line are given.

EXAMPLE 1 on p. 311 for Exs. 5–10

EQUIVALENT EQUATIONS **Write two equations in standard form that are equivalent to the given equation.**

5. $x + y = -10$
6. $5x + 10y = 15$
7. $-x + 2y = 9$
8. $-9x - 12y = 6$
9. $9x - 3y = -12$
10. $-2x + 4y = -5$

EXAMPLE 2 on p. 311 for Exs. 11–22

WRITING EQUATIONS **Write an equation in standard form of the line that passes through the given point and has the given slope *m* or that passes through the two given points.**

11. $(-3, 2)$, $m = 1$
12. $(4, -1)$, $m = 3$
13. $(0, 5)$, $m = -2$
14. $(-8, 0)$, $m = -4$
15. $(-4, -4)$, $m = -\frac{3}{2}$
16. $(-6, -10)$, $m = \frac{1}{6}$
17. $(-8, 4)$, $(4, -4)$
18. $(-5, 2)$, $(-4, 3)$
19. $(0, -1)$, $(-6, -9)$
20. $(3, 9)$, $(1, 1)$
21. $(10, 6)$, $(-12, -5)$
22. $(-6, -2)$, $(-1, -2)$

EXAMPLE 3 on p. 312 for Exs. 23–28

HORIZONTAL AND VERTICAL LINES **Write equations of the horizontal and vertical lines that pass through the given point.**

23. $(3, 2)$
24. $(-5, -3)$
25. $(-1, 3)$
26. $(5, 3)$
27. $(-1, 4)$
28. $(-6, -2)$

EXAMPLE 4 on p. 312 for Exs. 29–36

29. **ERROR ANALYSIS** *Describe* and correct the error in finding the value of A for the equation $Ax - 3y = 5$, if the graph of the equation passes through the point $(1, -4)$.

$$A(-4) - 3(1) = 5$$
$$A = -2$$

30. ★ **MULTIPLE CHOICE** The graph of the equation $Ax + 2y = -2$ is a line that passes through $(2, -2)$. What is the value of A?

Ⓐ -1 Ⓑ 1 Ⓒ 2 Ⓓ 3

COMPLETING EQUATIONS **Find the missing coefficient in the equation of the line that passes through the given point. Write the completed equation.**

31. $Ax + 3y = 5$, $(2, -1)$
32. $Ax - 4y = -1$, $(6, 1)$
33. $-x + By = 10$, $(-2, -2)$
34. $8x + By = 4$, $(-5, 4)$
35. $Ax - 3y = -5$, $(1, 0)$
36. $2x + By = -4$, $(-3, 7)$

37. **CHALLENGE** Write an equation in standard form of the line that passes through $(0, a)$ and $(b, 0)$ where $a \neq 0$ and $b \neq 0$.

PROBLEM SOLVING

EXAMPLE 5 on p. 313 for Exs. 38–41

38. **GARDENING** The diagram shows the prices of two types of ground cover plants. Write an equation in standard form that models the possible combinations of vinca and phlox plants a gardener can buy for $300. List three of these possible combinations.

@HomeTutor for problem solving help at classzone.com

39. **NUTRITION** A snack mix requires a total of 120 ounces of some corn cereal and some wheat cereal. Corn cereal comes in 12 ounce boxes.

   a. The last time you made this mix, you used 5 boxes of corn cereal and 4 boxes of wheat cereal. How many ounces are in a box of wheat cereal?

   b. Write an equation in standard form that models the possible combinations of boxes of wheat and corn cereal you can use.

   c. List all possible combinations of whole boxes of wheat and corn cereal you can use to make the snack mix.

@HomeTutor for problem solving help at classzone.com

40. ★ **SHORT RESPONSE** A dog kennel charges $20 per night to board your dog. You can also have a doggie treat delivered to your dog for $5. Write an equation that models the possible combinations of nights at the kennel and doggie treats that you can buy for $100. Graph the equation. *Explain* what the intercepts of the graph mean in this situation.

41. **MULTIPLE REPRESENTATIONS** As the student council treasurer, you prepare the budget for your class rafting trip. Each large raft costs $100 to rent, and each small raft costs $40 to rent. You have $1600 to spend.

   a. **Writing an Equation** Write an equation in standard form that models the possible combinations of small rafts and large rafts that you can rent.

   b. **Drawing a Graph** Graph the equation from part (a).

   c. **Making a Table** Make a table that shows several combinations of small and large rafts that you can rent.

42. ★ **SHORT RESPONSE** One bus ride costs $.75. One subway ride costs $1.00. A monthly pass can be used for unlimited subway and bus rides and costs the same as 36 subway rides plus 36 bus rides.

   a. Write an equation in standard form that models the possible combinations of bus and subway rides with the same value as the pass.

   b. You ride the bus 60 times in one month. How many times must you ride the subway in order for the cost of the rides to equal the value of the pass? *Explain* your answer.

43. **GEOMETRY** Write an equation in standard form that models the possible lengths and widths (in feet) of a rectangle having the same perimeter as a rectangle that is 10 feet wide and 20 feet long. Make a table that shows five possible lengths and widths of the rectangle.

44. **CHALLENGE** You are working in a chemistry lab. You have 1000 milliliters of pure acid. A dilution of acid is created by adding pure acid to water. A 40% dilution contains 40% acid and 60% water. You have been asked to make a 40% dilution and a 60% dilution of pure acid.

    a. Write an equation in standard form that models the possible quantities of each dilution you can prepare using all 1000 milliliters of pure acid.

    b. You prepare 700 milliliters of the 40% dilution. How much of the 60% dilution can you prepare?

    c. How much water do you need to prepare 700 milliliters of the 40% dilution?

MIXED REVIEW

PREVIEW
Prepare for Lesson 5.5 in Exs. 45–46.

Tell whether the graphs of the two equations are parallel lines. *Explain* your reasoning. *(p. 244)*

45. $1 - y = 4x,\ -6 = -4x - y$

46. $4x = 2y - 6,\ 4 + y = -2x$

Write an equation in point-slope form of the line that passes through the given point and has the given slope *m*. *(p. 302)*

47. $(3, -4),\ m = 1$

48. $(-6, 6),\ m = -2$

49. $(-8, -1),\ m = 5$

QUIZ *for Lessons 5.1–5.4*

Write an equation in slope-intercept form of the line that passes through the given point and has the given slope *m*.

1. $(2, 5),\ m = 3$ *(p. 292)*

2. $(-1, 4),\ m = -2$ *(p. 292)*

3. $(0, -7),\ m = 5$ *(p. 283)*

Write an equation in slope-intercept form of the line that passes through the given points.

4. $(0, 2), (9, 5)$ *(p. 283)*

5. $(5, 7), (19, 14)$ *(p. 292)*

6. $(4, 24), (-11, 19)$ *(p. 292)*

Write an equation in (a) point-slope form and (b) standard form of the line that passes through the given points. *(pp. 302, 311)*

7. $(-5, 2), (-4, 3)$

8. $(0, -1), (-6, -9)$

9. $(3, 9), (1, 1)$

10. **DVDS** The table shows the price per DVD for different quantities of DVDs. Write an equation that models the price per DVD as a function of the number of DVDs purchased. *(p. 302)*

Number of DVDs purchased	1	2	3	4	5	6
Price per DVD (dollars)	20	18	16	14	12	10

MIXED REVIEW of Problem Solving

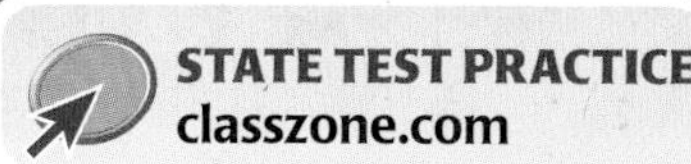

Lessons 5.1–5.4

1. **MULTI-STEP PROBLEM** A satellite radio company charges a monthly fee of $13 for service. To use the service, you must first buy equipment that costs $100.

   a. Identify the rate of change and starting value in this situation.

   b. Write an equation that gives the total cost of satellite radio as a function of the number of months of service.

   c. Find the total cost after 1 year of satellite radio service.

2. **MULTI-STEP PROBLEM** You hike 5 miles before taking a break. After your break, you continue to hike at an average speed of 3.5 miles per hour.

   a. Write an equation that gives the distance (in miles) that you hike as a function of the time (in hours) since your break.

   b. You hike for 4 hours after your break. Find the total distance you hike for the day.

3. **EXTENDED RESPONSE** The table shows the cost of a catered lunch buffet for different numbers of people.

Number of people	Cost (dollars)
12	192
18	288
24	384
30	480
36	576
42	672

   a. *Explain* why the situation can be modeled by a linear equation.

   b. Write an equation that gives the cost of the lunch buffet as a function of the number of people attending.

   c. What is the cost of a lunch buffet for 120 people?

4. **SHORT RESPONSE** You use a garden hose to fill a swimming pool at a constant rate. The pool is empty when you begin to fill it. The pool contains 15 gallons of water after 5 minutes. After 30 minutes, the pool contains 90 gallons of water. Write an equation that gives the volume (in gallons) of water in the pool as a function of the number of minutes since you began filling it. *Explain* how you can find the time it takes to put 150 gallons of water in the pool.

5. **EXTENDED RESPONSE** A city is paving a bike path. The same length of path is paved each day. After 4 days, there are 8 miles of path remaining to be paved. After 6 more days, there are 5 miles of path remaining to be paved.

   a. *Explain* how you know the situation can be modeled by a linear equation.

   b. Write an equation that gives the distance (in miles) remaining to be paved as a function of the number of days since the project began.

   c. In how many more days will the entire path be paved?

6. **OPEN-ENDED** Write an equation in standard form that models the possible combinations of nickels and dimes worth a certain amount of money (in dollars). List several of these possible combinations.

7. **GRIDDED ANSWER** You are saving money to buy a stereo system. You have saved $50 so far. You plan to save $20 each week for the next few months. How much money do you expect to have saved in 7 weeks?

8. **GRIDDED ANSWER** The cost of renting a moving van for a 26 mile trip is $62.50. The cost of renting the same van for a 38 mile trip is $65.50. The cost changes at a constant rate with respect to the length (in miles) of the trip. Find the total cost of renting the van for a 54 mile trip.

5.5 If–Then Statements and Their Converses

MATERIALS • index cards

QUESTION **Is the converse of a conditional statement true?**

In Lesson 2.1, you learned that an if-then statement is a form of a conditional statement where the *if* part contains the hypothesis and the *then* part contains the conclusion. The *converse* of an if-then statement interchanges the hypothesis and conclusion of the original statement.

EXPLORE **Write the converse**

STEP 1 ***Make cards***

Write each phrase below on a separate index card.

it swims	it is a tree	it flies	it needs water	it has wings
it is a duck	it grows	it is a bird	it is an airplane	it is a frog

STEP 2 ***Write the conditional statement***

Place the cards face down. Select a card at random to be the hypothesis. Select another card at random to be the conclusion. Write the statement and determine whether it is true or false. If it is false, give a counterexample.

Hypothesis: it is a duck   Conclusion: it has wings

Statement: If it is a duck, then it has wings.

The statement is true. All ducks have wings.

STEP 3 ***Write the converse***

Switch the order of the cards to create the converse statement. Determine whether the converse is true or false. If it is false, give a counterexample.

Hypothesis: it has wings   Conclusion: it is a duck

Statement: If it has wings, then it is a duck.

The statement is false. Airplanes have wings, but they are not ducks.

STEP 4 ***Repeat***

Repeat Steps 2 and 3 ten times. Keep a record of your conditional statements and their converses.

DRAW CONCLUSIONS **Use your observations to complete these exercises**

1. **REASONING** If a conditional statement is true, can you be sure that its converse is true? *Justify* your answer.
2. **REASONING** If the converse of a statement is true, can you be sure that the original statement is true? *Justify* your answer.

5.5 Write Equations of Parallel and Perpendicular Lines

Before You used slope to determine whether lines are parallel.

Now You will write equations of parallel and perpendicular lines.

Why? So you can analyze growth rates, as in Ex. 33.

Key Vocabulary
- **converse**
- **perpendicular lines**
- **conditional statement,** *p. 66*

The **converse** of a conditional statement interchanges the hypothesis and conclusion. The converse of a true statement is not necessarily true.

In Chapter 4, you learned that the statement "If two nonvertical lines have the same slope, then they are parallel" is true. Its converse is also true.

KEY CONCEPT *For Your Notebook*

Parallel Lines

- If two nonvertical lines in the same plane have the same slope, then they are parallel.
- If two nonvertical lines in the same plane are parallel, then they have the same slope.

EXAMPLE 1 Write an equation of a parallel line

Write an equation of the line that passes through $(-3, -5)$ and is parallel to the line $y = 3x - 1$.

Solution

STEP 1 **Identify** the slope. The graph of the given equation has a slope of 3. So, the parallel line through $(-3, -5)$ has a slope of 3.

STEP 2 **Find** the y-intercept. Use the slope and the given point.

$y = mx + b$ Write slope-intercept form.

$-5 = 3(-3) + b$ Substitute 3 for m, -3 for x, and -5 for y.

$4 = b$ Solve for b.

STEP 3 **Write** an equation. Use $y = mx + b$.

$y = 3x + 4$ Substitute 3 for m and 4 for b.

CHECK REASONABLENESS
You can check that your answer is reasonable by graphing both lines.

✓ **GUIDED PRACTICE** for Example 1

1. Write an equation of the line that passes through $(-2, 11)$ and is parallel to the line $y = -x + 5$.

PERPENDICULAR LINES Two lines in the same plane are **perpendicular** if they intersect to form a right angle. Horizontal and vertical lines are perpendicular to each other.

Compare the slopes of the perpendicular lines shown below.

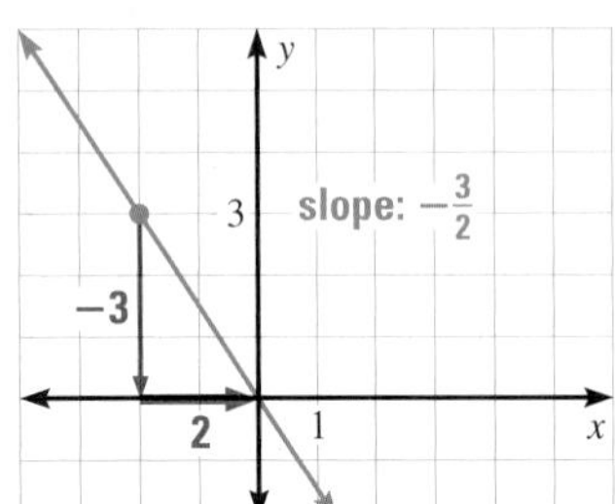

Rotate the line 90° in a clockwise direction about the origin to find a perpendicular line.

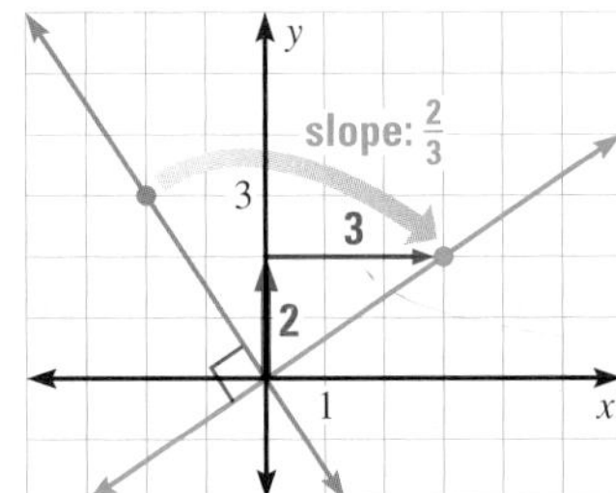

KEY CONCEPT *For Your Notebook*

USE FRACTIONS
The product of a nonzero number m and its negative reciprocal is -1:

$m\left(-\frac{1}{m}\right) = -1.$

Perpendicular Lines

- If two nonvertical lines in the same plane have slopes that are negative reciprocals, then the lines are perpendicular.
- If two nonvertical lines in the same plane are perpendicular, then their slopes are negative reciprocals.

EXAMPLE 2 Determine whether lines are parallel or perpendicular

Determine which lines, if any, are parallel or perpendicular.

Line *a*: $y = 5x - 3$ **Line *b*:** $x + 5y = 2$ **Line *c*:** $-10y - 2x = 0$

Solution

Find the slopes of the lines.

Line *a*: The equation is in slope-intercept form. The slope is 5.

Write the equations for lines b and c in slope-intercept form.

Line *b*: $x + 5y = 2$

$5y = -x + 2$

$y = -\frac{1}{5}x + \frac{2}{5}$

Line *c*: $-10y - 2x = 0$

$-10y = 2x$

$y = -\frac{1}{5}x$

▶ Lines b and c have slopes of $-\frac{1}{5}$, so they are parallel. Line a has a slope of 5, the negative reciprocal of $-\frac{1}{5}$, so it is perpendicular to lines b and c.

✓ **GUIDED PRACTICE** for Example 2

2. Determine which lines, if any, are parallel or perpendicular.

Line *a*: $2x + 6y = -3$ **Line *b*:** $y = 3x - 8$ **Line *c*:** $-1.5y + 4.5x = 6$

EXAMPLE 3 Determine whether lines are perpendicular

STATE FLAG The Arizona state flag is shown in a coordinate plane. Lines a and b appear to be perpendicular. Are they?

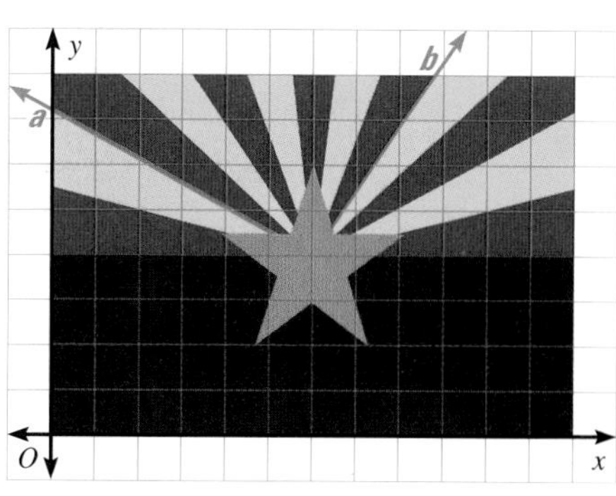

Line *a*: $12y = -7x + 42$

Line *b*: $11y = 16x - 52$

Solution

Find the slopes of the lines. Write the equations in slope-intercept form.

Line *a*: $12y = -7x + 42$ **Line *b*:** $11y = 16x - 52$

$$y = -\frac{7}{12}x + \frac{42}{12} \qquad y = \frac{16}{11}x - \frac{52}{11}$$

▶ The slope of line a is $-\frac{7}{12}$. The slope of line b is $\frac{16}{11}$. The two slopes are not negative reciprocals, so lines a and b are not perpendicular.

EXAMPLE 4 Write an equation of a perpendicular line

Write an equation of the line that passes through (4, −5) and is perpendicular to the line $y = 2x + 3$.

Solution

STEP 1 **Identify** the slope. The graph of the given equation has a slope of 2. Because the slopes of perpendicular lines are negative reciprocals, the slope of the perpendicular line through (4, −5) is $-\frac{1}{2}$.

STEP 2 **Find** the y-intercept. Use the slope and the given point.

$y = mx + b$ Write slope-intercept form.

$-5 = -\frac{1}{2}(4) + b$ Substitute $-\frac{1}{2}$ for m, 4 for x, and −5 for y.

$-3 = b$ Solve for b.

STEP 3 **Write** an equation.

$y = mx + b$ Write slope-intercept form.

$y = -\frac{1}{2}x - 3$ Substitute $-\frac{1}{2}$ for m and −3 for b.

✓ **GUIDED PRACTICE** for Examples 3 and 4

3. Is line a perpendicular to line b? *Justify* your answer using slopes.

Line *a*: $2y + x = -12$ **Line *b*:** $2y = 3x - 8$

4. Write an equation of the line that passes through (4, 3) and is perpendicular to the line $y = 4x - 7$.

5.5 EXERCISES

HOMEWORK KEY
○ = **WORKED-OUT SOLUTIONS** on p. WS12 for Exs. 19 and 33
★ = **STANDARDIZED TEST PRACTICE** Exs. 2, 16, 17, 28, 30, 34, and 36

SKILL PRACTICE

1. **VOCABULARY** Copy and complete: Two lines in a plane are __?__ if they intersect to form a right angle.

2. ★ **WRITING** *Explain* how you can tell whether two lines are perpendicular, given the equations of the lines.

EXAMPLE 1 on p. 319 for Exs. 3–11

PARALLEL LINES Write an equation of the line that passes through the given point and is parallel to the given line.

3. $(-1, 3)$, $y = 2x + 2$
4. $(6, 8)$, $y = -\frac{5}{2}x + 10$
5. $(5, -1)$, $y = -\frac{3}{5}x - 3$
6. $(-1, 2)$, $y = 5x + 4$
7. $(1, 7)$, $-6x + y = -1$
8. $(18, 2)$, $3y = x - 12$
9. $(-2, 5)$, $2y = 4x - 6$
10. $(9, 4)$, $y - x = 3$
11. $(-10, 0)$, $-y + 3x = 16$

EXAMPLE 2 on p. 320 for Exs. 12–16

PARALLEL OR PERPENDICULAR Determine which lines, if any, are parallel or perpendicular.

12. Line a: $y = 4x - 2$, Line b: $y = -\frac{1}{4}x$, Line c: $y = -4x + 1$

13. Line a: $y = \frac{3}{5}x + 1$, Line b: $5y = 3x - 2$, Line c: $10x - 6y = -4$

14. Line a: $y = 3x + 6$, Line b: $3x + y = 6$, Line c: $3y = 2x + 18$

15. Line a: $4x - 3y = 2$, Line b: $3x + 4y = -1$, Line c: $4y - 3x = 20$

16. ★ **MULTIPLE CHOICE** Which statement is true of the given lines?

Line a: $-2x + y = 4$ Line b: $2x + 5y = 2$ Line c: $x + 2y = 4$

Ⓐ Lines a and b are parallel.
Ⓑ Lines a and c are parallel.
Ⓒ Lines a and b are perpendicular.
Ⓓ Lines a and c are perpendicular.

17. ★ **SHORT RESPONSE** Determine which of the lines shown, if any, are parallel or perpendicular. *Justify* your answer using slopes.

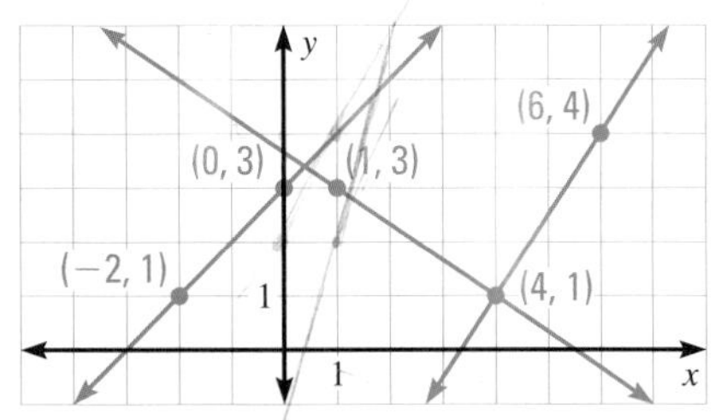

EXAMPLE 4 on p. 321 for Exs. 18–27

PERPENDICULAR LINES Write an equation of the line that passes through the given point and is perpendicular to the given line.

18. $(3, -3)$, $y = x + 5$
19. $(-9, 2)$, $y = 3x - 12$
20. $(5, 1)$, $y = 5x - 2$
21. $(7, 10)$, $y = 0.5x - 9$
22. $(-2, -4)$, $y = -\frac{2}{7}x + 1$
23. $(-4, -1)$, $y = \frac{4}{3}x + 6$
24. $(3, 3)$, $2y = 3x - 6$
25. $(-5, 2)$, $y + 3 = 2x$
26. $(8, -1)$, $4y + 2x = 12$

27. **ERROR ANALYSIS** *Describe* and correct the error in finding the y-intercept of the line that passes through (2, 1) and is perpendicular to the line $y = -\frac{1}{2}x + 3$.

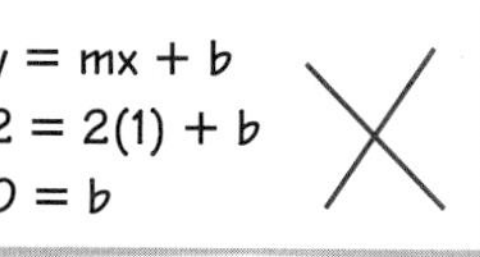

28. ★ **MULTIPLE CHOICE** Which equation represents the line that passes through (0, 0) and is parallel to the line passing through (2, 3) and (6, 1)?

Ⓐ $y = \frac{1}{2}x$ Ⓑ $y = -\frac{1}{2}x$ Ⓒ $y = -2x$ Ⓓ $y = 2x$

29. **REASONING** Is the line through (4, 3) and (3, −1) perpendicular to the line through (−3, 3) and (1, 2)? *Justify* your answer using slopes.

30. ★ **OPEN-ENDED** Write equations of two lines that are parallel. Then write an equation of a line that is perpendicular to those lines.

31. **CHALLENGE** Write a formula for the slope of a line that is perpendicular to the line through the points (x_1, y_1) and (x_2, y_2).

PROBLEM SOLVING

EXAMPLES 3 and 4 on p. 321 for Exs. 32, 34

32. **HOCKEY** A hockey puck leaves the blade of a hockey stick, bounces off a wall, and travels in a new direction, as shown.

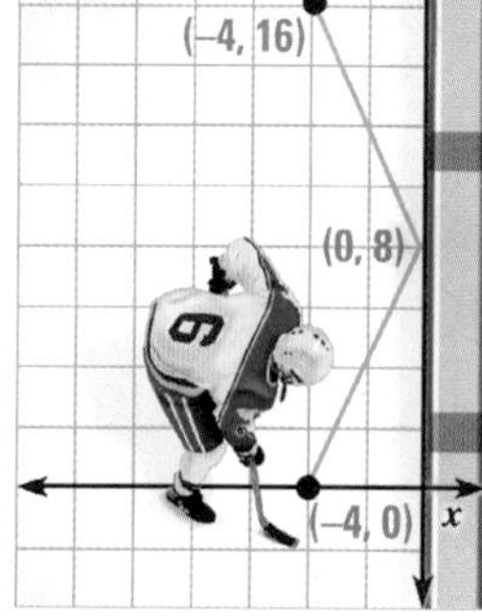

a. Write an equation that models the path of the puck from the blade of the hockey stick to the wall.

b. Write an equation that models the path of the puck after it bounces off the wall.

c. Does the path of the puck form a right angle? *Justify* your answer.

33. **BIOLOGY** While nursing, blue whale calves can gain weight at a rate of 200 pounds per day. Two particular calves weigh 6000 pounds and 6250 pounds at birth.

a. Write equations that model the weight of each calf as a function of the number of days since birth.

b. How much is each calf expected to weigh 30 days after birth?

c. How are the graphs of the equations from part (a) related? *Justify* your answer.

@HomeTutor for problem solving help at classzone.com

34. ★ **SHORT RESPONSE** The map shows several streets in a city. Determine which of the streets, if any, are parallel or perpendicular. *Justify* your answer using slopes.

Park: $3y - 2x = 12$ Main: $y = -6x + 44$

2nd St.: $3y = 2x - 13$ Sea: $2y = -3x + 37$

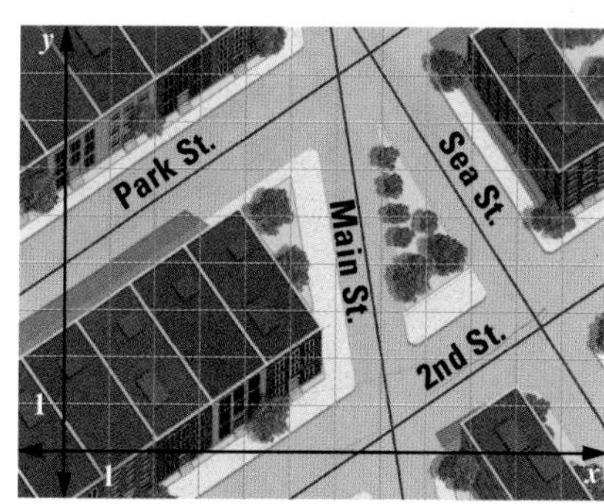

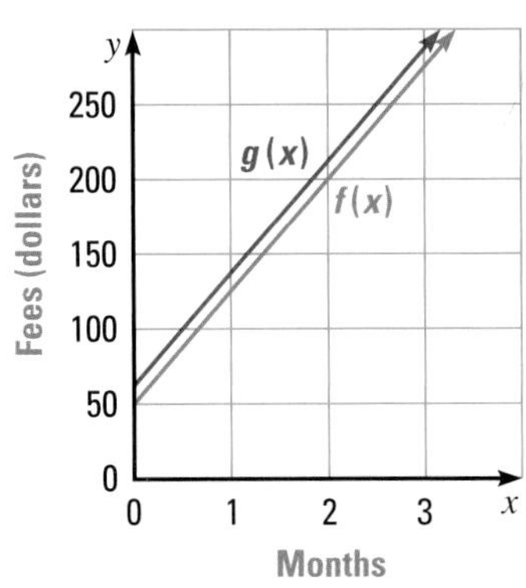

35. **SOFTBALL** A softball training academy charges students a monthly fee plus an initial registration fee. The total amounts paid by two students are given by the functions $f(x)$ and $g(x)$ where x is the numbers of months the students have been members of the academy. The graphs of f and g are parallel lines. Did the students pay different monthly fees or different registration fees? How do you know?

36. ★ **EXTENDED RESPONSE** If you are one of the first 100 people to join a new health club, you are charged a joining fee of \$49. Otherwise, you are charged a joining fee of \$149. The monthly membership cost is \$38.75.

    a. Write an equation that gives the total cost (in dollars) of membership as a function of the number of months of membership if you are one of the first 100 members to join.

    b. Write an equation that gives the total cost (in dollars) of membership as a function of the number of months of membership if you are *not* one of the first 100 members to join.

    c. How are the graphs of these functions related? How do you know?

    d. After 6 months, what is the difference in total cost for a person who paid \$149 to join and a person who paid \$49 to join? after 12 months?

37. **CHALLENGE** You and your friend have gift cards to a shopping mall. Your card has a value of \$50, and your friend's card has a value of \$30. If neither of you uses the cards, the value begins to decrease at a rate of \$2.50 per month after 6 months.

    a. Write two equations, one that gives the value of your card and another that gives the value of your friend's card as functions of the number of months after 6 months of nonuse.

    b. How are the graphs of these functions related? How do you know?

    c. What are the x-intercepts of the graphs of the functions, and what do they mean in this situation?

MIXED REVIEW

Solve the equation or proportion.

38. $5z + 6z = 77$ *(p. 141)*

39. $-8n = 4(3n + 5)$ *(p. 148)*

40. $\frac{3}{5} = \frac{t}{7}$ *(p. 162)*

PREVIEW
Prepare for Lesson 5.6 in Ex. 41.

41. **CAMPING** The table shows the cost C (in dollars) for one person to stay at a campground for n nights. *(p. 253)*

Number of nights, n	1	3	5	9
Cost, C (in dollars)	15	45	75	135

a. *Explain* why C varies directly with n.

b. Write a direct variation equation that relates C and n.

42. Write an equation in standard form of the line that passes through the points $(3, -9)$ and $(12, 9)$. *(p. 311)*

5.6 Fit a Line to Data

Before You modeled situations involving a constant rate of change.

Now You will make scatter plots and write equations to model data.

Why? So you can model scientific data, as in Ex. 19.

Key Vocabulary
- scatter plot
- correlation
- line of fit

A **scatter plot** is a graph used to determine whether there is a relationship between paired data. Scatter plots can show trends in the data.

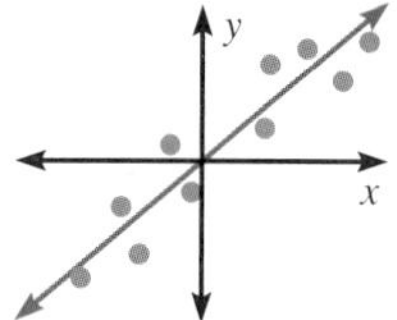

If y tends to increase as x increases, the paired data are said to have a **positive correlation**.

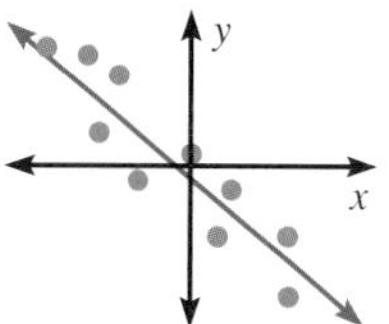

If y tends to decrease as x increases, the paired data are said to have a **negative correlation**.

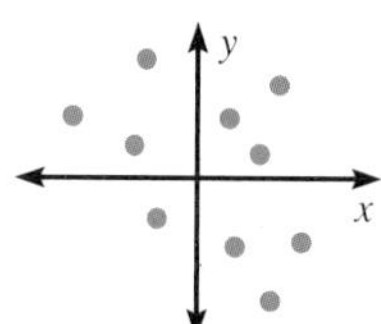

If x and y have no apparent relationship, the paired data are said to have **relatively no correlation**.

EXAMPLE 1 Describe the correlation of data

Describe **the correlation of the data graphed in the scatter plot.**

a.

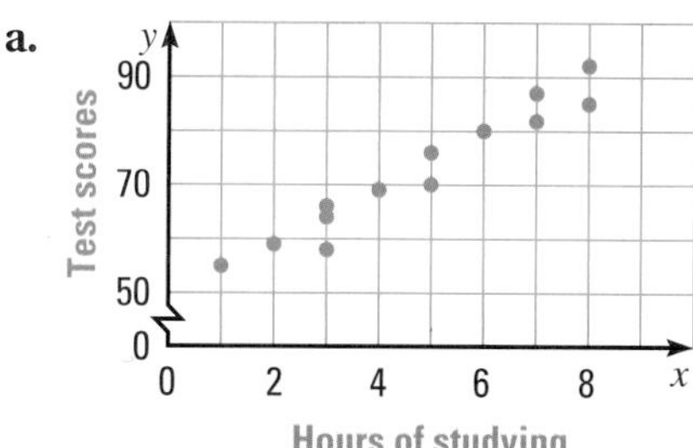

b.

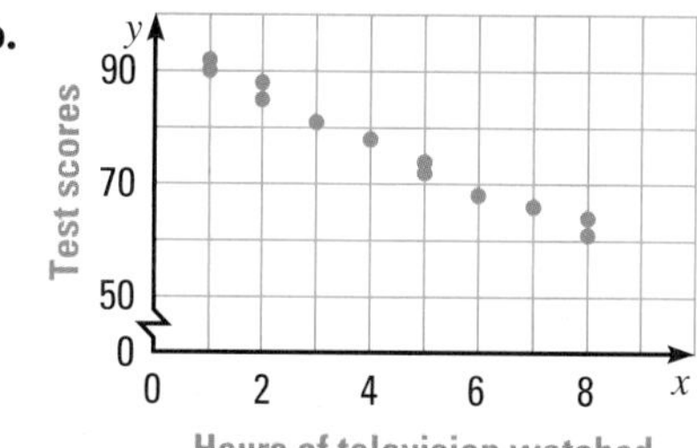

a. The scatter plot shows a positive correlation between hours of studying and test scores. This means that as the hours of studying increased, the test scores tended to increase.

b. The scatter plot shows a negative correlation between hours of television watched and test scores. This means that as the hours of television watched increased, the test scores tended to decrease.

✓ **GUIDED PRACTICE** for Example 1

1. Using the scatter plots in Example 1, predict a reasonable test score for 4.5 hours of studying and 4.5 hours of television watched.

EXAMPLE 2 Make a scatter plot

SWIMMING SPEEDS The table shows the lengths (in centimeters) and swimming speeds (in centimeters per second) of six fish.

Fish	Pike	Red gurnard	Black bass	Gurnard	Norway haddock
Length (cm)	37.8	19.2	21.3	26.2	26.8
Speed (cm/sec)	148	47	88	131	98

a. Make a scatter plot of the data.

b. *Describe* the correlation of the data.

Solution

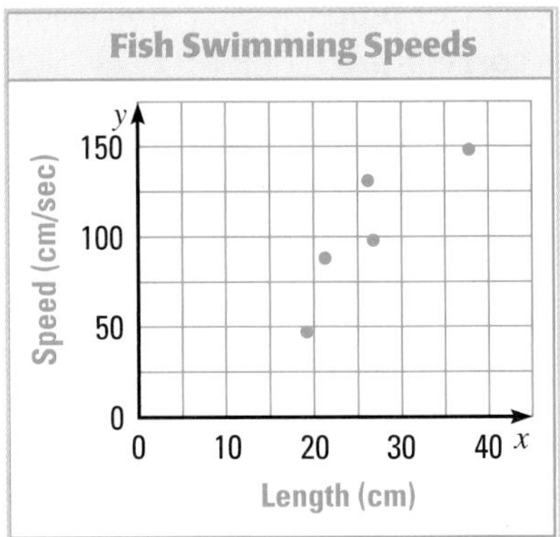

a. Treat the data as ordered pairs. Let x represent the fish length (in centimeters), and let y represent the speed (in centimeters per second). Plot the ordered pairs as points in a coordinate plane.

b. The scatter plot shows a positive correlation, which means that longer fish tend to swim faster.

✓ GUIDED PRACTICE for Example 2

2. Make a scatter plot of the data in the table. *Describe* the correlation of the data.

x	1	1	2	3	3	4	5	5	6
y	2	3	4	4	5	5	5	7	8

MODELING DATA When data show a positive or negative correlation, you can model the trend in the data using a **line of fit**.

KEY CONCEPT *For Your Notebook*

Using a Line of Fit to Model Data

STEP 1 **Make** a scatter plot of the data.

STEP 2 **Decide** whether the data can be modeled by a line.

STEP 3 **Draw** a line that appears to fit the data closely. There should be approximately as many points above the line as below it.

STEP 4 **Write** an equation using two points on the line. The points do not have to represent actual data pairs, but they must lie on the line of fit.

EXAMPLE 3 Write an equation to model data

BIRD POPULATIONS The table shows the number of active red-cockaded woodpecker clusters in a part of the De Soto National Forest in Mississippi. Write an equation that models the number of active clusters as a function of the number of years since 1990.

Year	1992	1993	1994	1995	1996	1997	1998	1999	2000
Active clusters	22	24	27	27	34	40	42	45	51

Solution

STEP 1 **Make** a scatter plot of the data. Let x represent the number of years since 1990. Let y represent the number of active clusters.

STEP 2 **Decide** whether the data can be modeled by a line. Because the scatter plot shows a positive correlation, you can fit a line to the data.

STEP 3 **Draw** a line that appears to fit the points in the scatter plot closely.

STEP 4 **Write** an equation using two points on the line. Use (2, 20) and (8, 42).

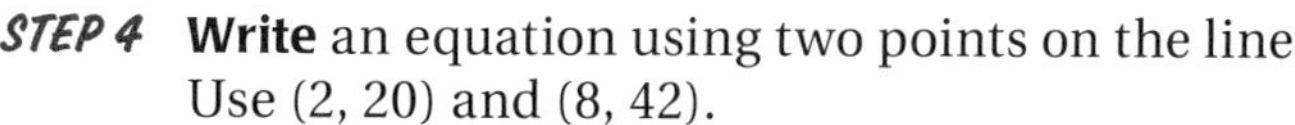

Find the slope of the line.

$$m = \frac{y_2 - y_1}{x_2 - x_1} = \frac{42 - 20}{8 - 2} = \frac{22}{6} = \frac{11}{3}$$

Find the y-intercept of the line. Use the point (2, 20).

$y = mx + b$ **Write slope-intercept form.**

$20 = \frac{11}{3}(2) + b$ **Substitute $\frac{11}{3}$ for m, 2 for x, and 20 for y.**

$\frac{38}{3} = b$ **Solve for b.**

An equation of the line of fit is $y = \frac{11}{3}x + \frac{38}{3}$.

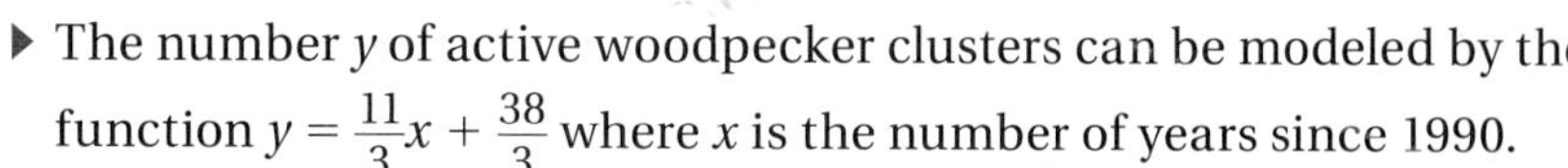

▶ The number y of active woodpecker clusters can be modeled by the function $y = \frac{11}{3}x + \frac{38}{3}$ where x is the number of years since 1990.

Animated **Algebra** at classzone.com

✓ GUIDED PRACTICE for Example 3

3. Use the data in the table to write an equation that models y as a function of x.

x	1	2	3	4	5	6	8
y	3	5	8	9	11	12	14

EXAMPLE 4 Interpret a model

Refer to the model for the number of woodpecker clusters in Example 3.

a. *Describe* the domain and range of the function.

b. At about what rate did the number of active woodpecker clusters change during the period 1992–2000?

Solution

a. The domain of the function is the the period from 1992 to 2000, or $2 \le x \le 10$. The range is the the number of active clusters given by the function for $2 \le x \le 10$, or $20 \le y \le 49.3$.

b. The number of active woodpecker clusters increased at a rate of $\frac{11}{3}$ or about 3.7 woodpecker clusters per year.

GUIDED PRACTICE for Example 4

4. In Guided Practice Exercise 2, at about what rate does y change with respect to x?

5.6 EXERCISES

HOMEWORK KEY

○ = **WORKED-OUT SOLUTIONS** on p. WS12 for Exs. 7 and 17

★ = **STANDARDIZED TEST PRACTICE** Exs. 2, 8, 11, 12, and 16

SKILL PRACTICE

1. **VOCABULARY** Copy and complete: When data have a positive correlation, the dependent variable tends to _?_ as the independent variable increases.

2. ★ **WRITING** *Describe* how paired data with a positive correlation, a negative correlation, and relatively no correlation differ.

DESCRIBING CORRELATIONS Tell whether x and y show a *positive correlation*, a *negative correlation*, or *relatively no correlation*.

EXAMPLE 1 on p. 325 for Exs. 3–5, 10, 11

3.

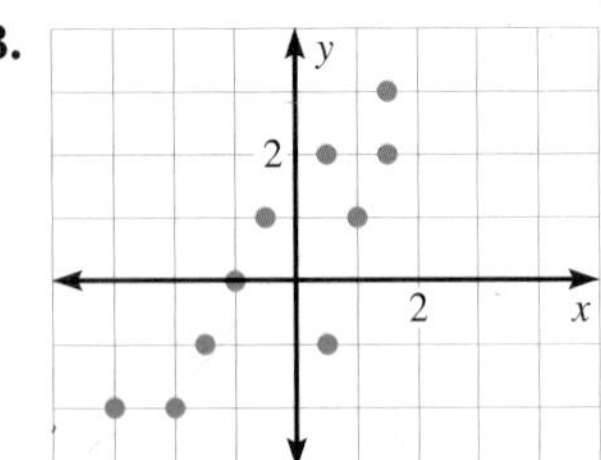

4.

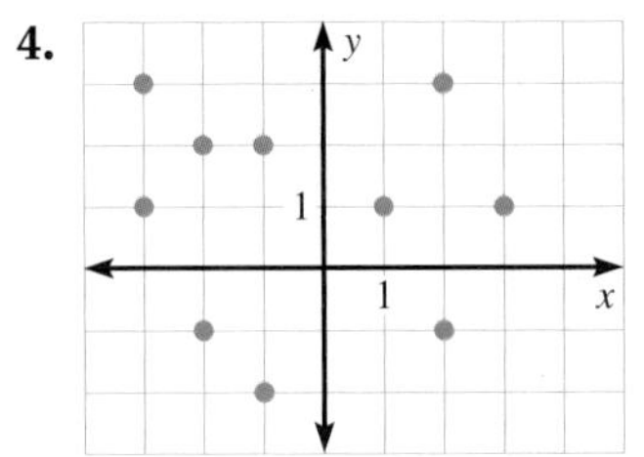

5.

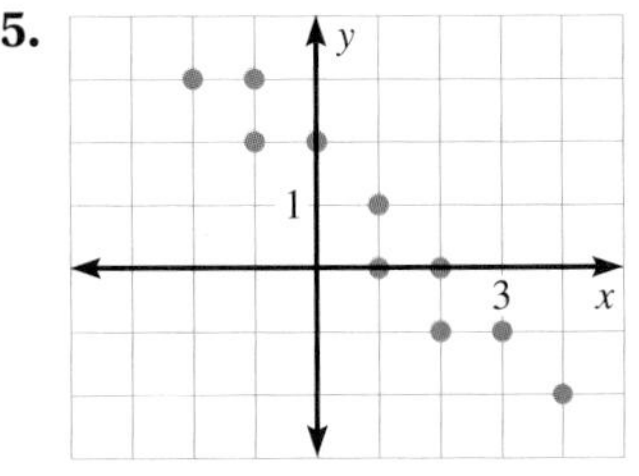

FITTING LINES TO DATA Make a scatter plot of the data in the table. Draw a line of fit. Write an equation of the line.

EXAMPLES 2 and 3 on pp. 326–327 for Exs. 6–9

6.

x	1	1	3	4	5	6	9
y	10	12	33	46	59	70	102

7.

x	1.2	1.8	2.3	3.0	4.4	5.2
y	10	7	5	−1	−4	−8

8. ★ **MULTIPLE CHOICE** Which equation best models the data in the scatter plot?

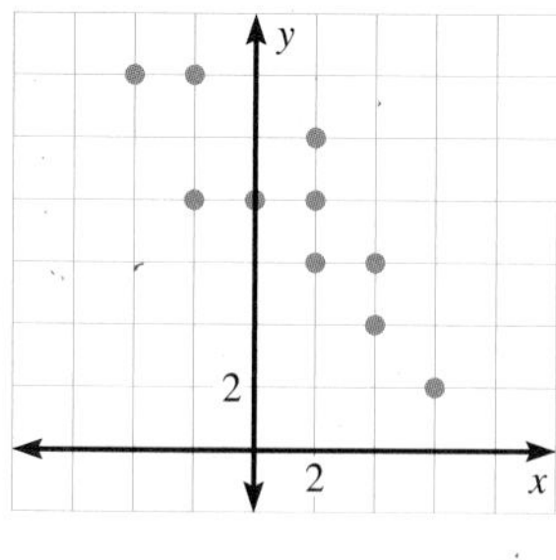

Ⓐ $y = -x - 6$ Ⓑ $y = x - 6$

Ⓒ $y = -x + 8$ Ⓓ $y = x + 8$

9. **ERROR ANALYSIS** *Describe* and correct the error in fitting the line to the data in the scatter plot.

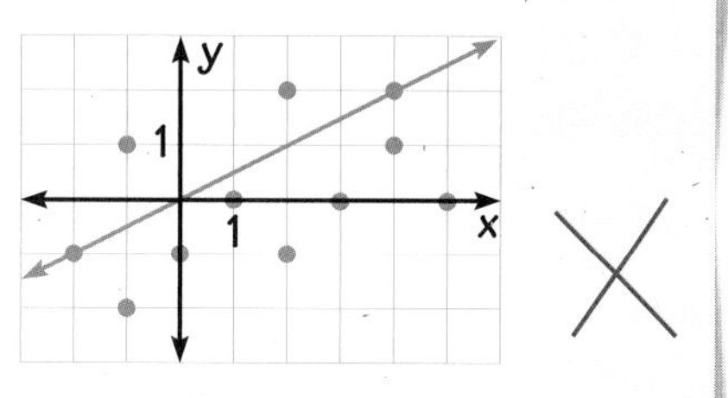

10. **ERROR ANALYSIS** *Describe* and correct the error in describing the correlation of the data in the scatter plot.

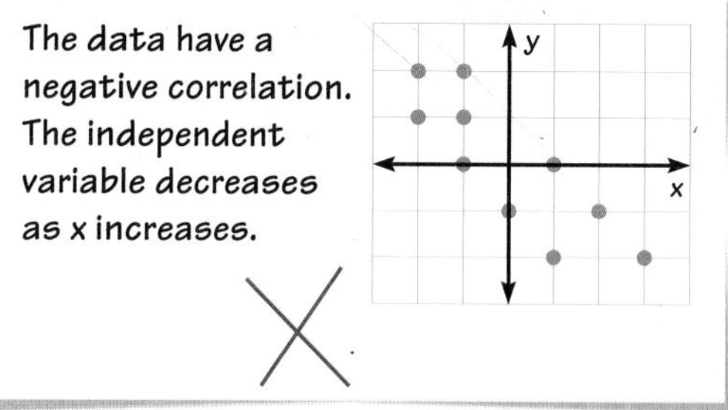

The data have a negative correlation. The independent variable decreases as x increases.

11. ★ **OPEN-ENDED** Give an example of a data set that shows a negative correlation.

12. ★ **SHORT RESPONSE** Make a scatter plot of the data. *Describe* the correlation of the data. Is it possible to fit a line to the data? If so, write an equation of the line. If not, explain why.

x	−12	−7	−4	−3	−1	2	5	6	7	9	15
y	150	50	15	10	1	5	22	37	52	90	226

MODELING DATA **Make a scatter plot of the data.** ***Describe*** **the correlation of the data. If possible, fit a line to the data and write an equation of the line.**

13.

x	10	12	15	20	30	45	60	99
y	−2	4	9	16	32	55	87	128

14.

x	−5	−3	−3	0	1	2	5	6
y	−4	12	10	−6	8	0	3	−9

15. **CHALLENGE** Which line shown is a better line of fit for the scatter plot? *Explain* your reasoning.

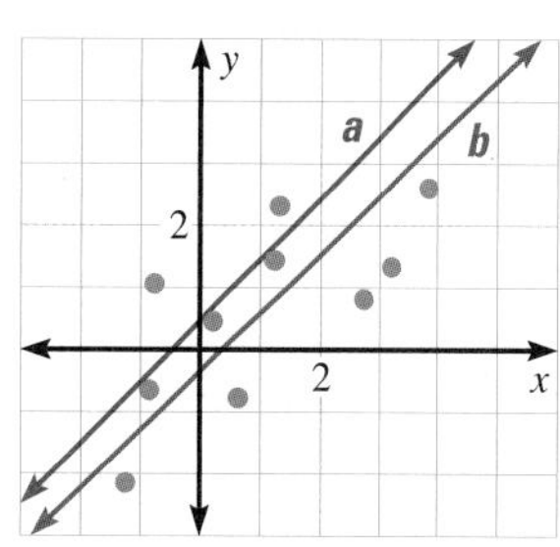

PROBLEM SOLVING

EXAMPLE 2 on p. 326 for Exs. 16

16. ★ **SHORT RESPONSE** The table shows the approximate home range size of big cats (members of the *Panthera* genus) in their natural habitat and the percent of time that the cats spend pacing in captivity.

Big cat (*Panthera* genus)	Lion	Jaguar	Leopard	Tiger
Home range size (km^2)	148	90	34	48
Pacing (percent of time)	48	21	11	16

a. Make a scatter plot of the data.

b. *Describe* the correlation of the data.

c. The snow leopard's home range size is about 39 square kilometers. It paces about 7% of its time in captivity. Does the snow leopard fit the pacing trend of cats in the *Panthera* genus? *Explain* your reasoning.

@HomeTutor for problem solving help at classzone.com

EXAMPLES 3 and 4 on pp. 327–328 for Exs. 17–18

17. **EARTH SCIENCE** The mesosphere is a layer of atmosphere that lies from about 50 kilometers above Earth's surface to about 90 kilometers above Earth's surface. The diagram shows the temperature at certain altitudes in the mesosphere.

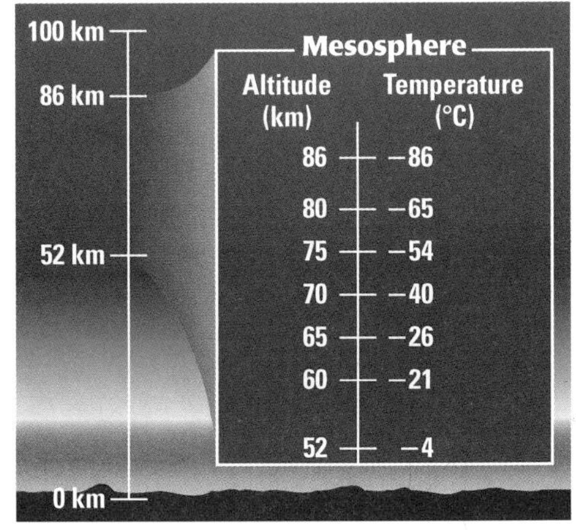

a. Make a scatter plot of the data.

b. Write an equation that models the temperature (in degrees Celsius) as a function of the altitude (in kilometers) above 50 kilometers.

c. At about what rate does the temperature change with increasing altitude in the mesosphere?

@HomeTutor for problem solving help at classzone.com

18. **ALLIGATORS** The table shows the weights of two alligators at various times during a feeding trial. Make two scatter plots, one for each alligator, where x is the number of weeks and y is the weight of the alligator. Draw lines of fit for both scatter plots. *Compare* the approximate growth rates.

Weeks	0	9	18	27	34	43	49
Alligator 1 weight (pounds)	6	8.6	10	13.6	15	17.2	19.8
Alligator 2 weight (pounds)	6	9.2	12.8	13.6	20.2	21.4	24.3

19. **GEOLOGY** The table shows the duration of several eruptions of the geyser Old Faithful and the interval between eruptions. Write an equation that models the interval as a function of an eruption's duration.

Duration (minutes)	1.5	2.0	2.5	3.0	3.5	4.0	4.5	5.0
Interval (minutes)	50	57	65	71	76	82	89	95

○ = WORKED-OUT SOLUTIONS on p. WS1 ★ = STANDARDIZED TEST PRACTICE

20. **DAYLIGHT** The table shows the number of hours and minutes of daylight in Baltimore, Maryland, for ten days in January.

Day in January	5	6	7	8	9	10	11	12	13	14
Daylight (hours and minutes)	9:30	9:31	9:32	9:34	9:35	9:36	9:37	9:38	9:40	9:41

a. Write an equation that models the hours of daylight (in minutes in excess of 9 hours) as a function of the number of days since January 5.

b. At what rate do the hours of daylight change over time in early January?

c. Do you expect the trend described by the equation to continue indefinitely? *Explain.*

21. **CHALLENGE** The table shows the estimated amount of time and the estimated amount of money the average person in the U.S. spent on the Internet each year from 1999 to 2005.

Year	1999	2000	2001	2002	2003	2004	2005
Internet time (hours)	88	107	136	154	169	182	193
Internet spending (dollars)	40.55	49.64	68.70	84.73	97.76	110.46	122.67

a. Write an equation that models the amount of time h (in hours) spent on the Internet as a function of the number of years y since 1999.

b. Write an equation that models the amount of money m spent on the Internet as a function of the time h (in hours) spent on the Internet.

c. Substitute the expression that is equal to h from part (a) in the function from part (b). What does the new function tell you?

d. Does the function from part (c) agree with the data given? *Explain.*

MIXED REVIEW

PREVIEW
Prepare for Lesson 5.7 in Exs. 22–24.

Evaluate the function when $x = -2, 5,$ and 0. *(p. 262)*

22. $f(x) = 5x - 8$

23. $g(x) = -10x$

24. $v(x) = 14 - 5x$

Write an equation of the line shown. *(p. 283)*

25. 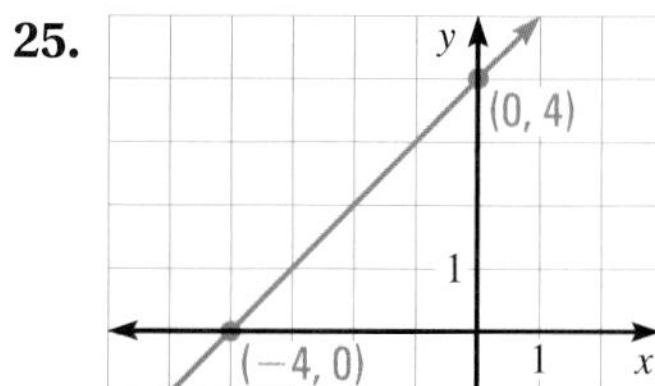

26. 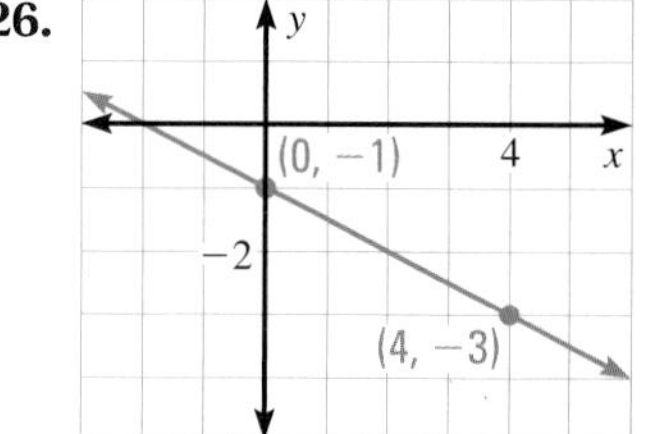

27. 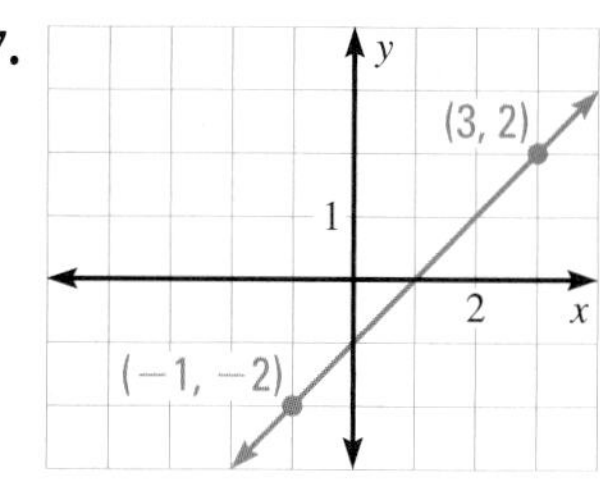

28. Determine which lines, if any, are parallel or perpendicular. *(p. 319)*

Line a: $y = 2x - 5$　　Line b: $2x + y = -5$　　Line c: $4x - 2y = 3$

5.6 Perform Linear Regression

QUESTION How can you model data with the best-fitting line?

The line that most closely follows a trend in data is the *best-fitting line*. The process of finding the best-fitting line to model a set of data is called *linear regression*. This process can be tedious to perform by hand, but you can use a graphing calculator to make a scatter plot and perform linear regression on a data set.

EXAMPLE 1 Create a scatter plot

The table shows the total sales from women's clothing stores in the United States from 1997 to 2002. Make a scatter plot of the data. *Describe* the correlation of the data.

Year	1997	1998	1999	2000	2001	2002
Sales (billions of dollars)	27.9	28.7	30.2	32.5	33.1	34.3

STEP 1 *Enter data*

Press STAT and select Edit. Enter years since 1997 (0, 1, 2, 3, 4, 5) into List 1 (L_1). These will be the x-values. Enter sales (in billions of dollars) into List 2 (L_2). These will be the y-values.

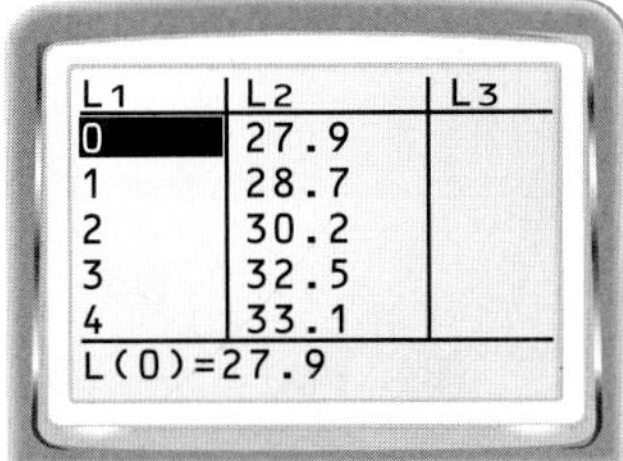

STEP 2 *Choose plot settings*

Press 2nd Y= and select Plot1. Turn Plot1 On. Select scatter plot as the type of display. Enter L_1 for the Xlist and L_2 for the Ylist.

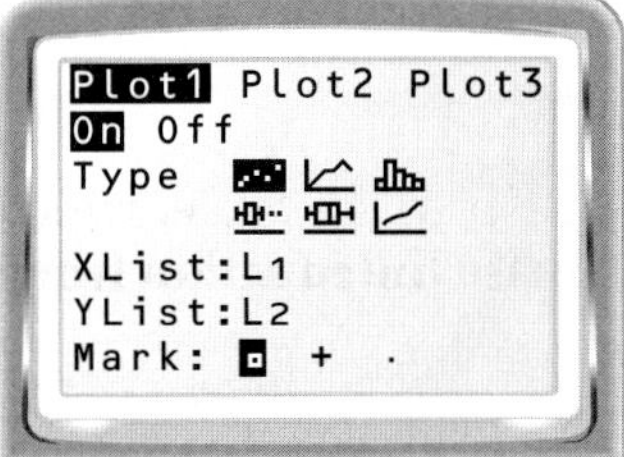

STEP 3 *Make a scatter plot*

Press ZOOM 9 to display the scatter plot so that the points for all data pairs are visible.

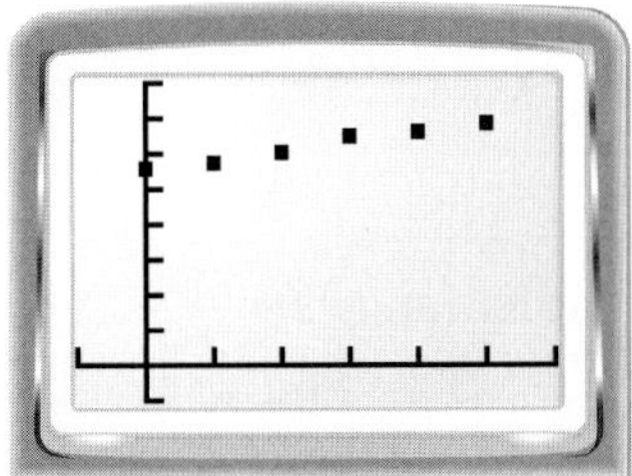

STEP 4 *Describe the correlation*

Describe the correlation of the data in the scatter plot.

The data have a positive correlation. This means that with each passing year, the sales of women's clothing tended to increase.

@HomeTutor classzone.com Keystrokes

MODELING DATA The *correlation coefficient r* for a set of paired data measures how well the best-fitting line fits the data. You can use a graphing calculator to find a value for r.

For r close to 1, the data have a strong positive correlation. For r close to -1, the data have a strong negative correlation. For r close to 0, the data have relatively no correlation.

EXAMPLE 2 Find the best-fitting line

Find an equation of the best-fitting line for the scatter plot from Example 1. Determine the correlation coefficient of the data. Graph the best-fitting line.

STEP 1 *Perform regression*

Press STAT. From the CALC menu, choose LinReg(ax+b). The a- and b-values given are for an equation of the form $y = ax + b$. Rounding these values gives the equation $y = 1.36x + 27.7$. Because r is close to 1, the data have a strong positive correlation.

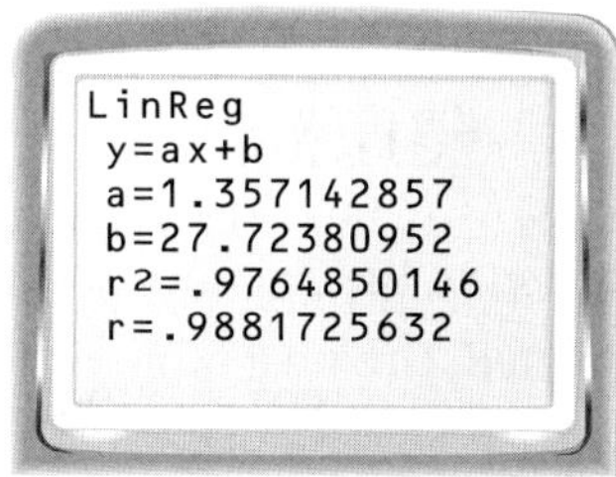

STEP 2 *Draw the best-fitting line*

Press Y= and enter $1.36x + 27.7$ for y_1. Press GRAPH.

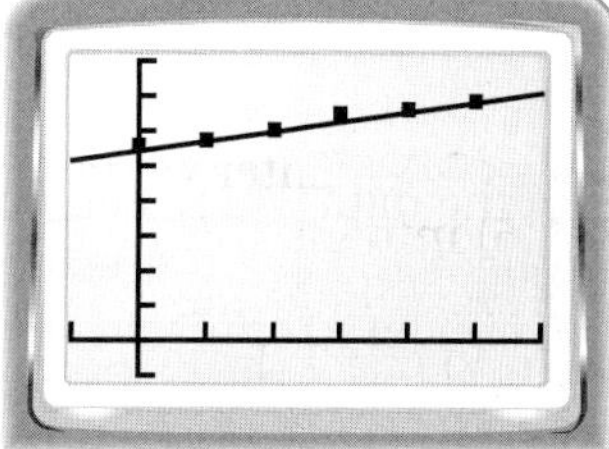

PRACTICE

In Exercises 1–5, refer to the table, which shows the total sales from men's clothing stores in the United States from 1997 to 2002.

Year	1997	1998	1999	2000	2001	2002
Sales (billions of dollars)	10.1	10.6	10.5	10.8	10.3	9.9

1. Make a scatter plot of the data. *Describe* the correlation.
2. Find the equation of the best-fitting line for the data.
3. Draw the best-fitting line for the data.

DRAW CONCLUSIONS

4. What does the value of r for the equation in Exercise 2 tell you about the correlation of the data?
5. **PREDICT** How could you use the best-fitting line to predict future sales of men's clothing? *Explain* your answer.

5.7 Collecting and Organizing Data

MATERIALS • metric ruler

QUESTION **How can you make a prediction using a line of fit?**

EXPLORE **Make a prediction using a line of fit**

A student in your class draws a rectangle with a short side that is 4 centimeters in length. Predict the length of the long side of the rectangle.

STEP 1 ***Collect data***

Ask each of 10 people to draw a rectangle. Do not let anyone drawing a rectangle see a rectangle drawn by someone else.

STEP 2 ***Organize data***

Measure the lengths (in centimeters) of the short and long sides of the rectangles you collected. Create a table like the one shown.

Short side (cm)	2.7	2.7	1.8	2.6	1.4	1.5	1.2	0.8	3.8
Long side (cm)	4.4	6.5	3.4	6	3.4	3	2.8	1.6	6.5

STEP 3 ***Graph data***

Make a scatter plot of the data where each point represents a rectangle that you collected. Let x represent the length of the short side of the rectangle, and let y represent the length of the long side.

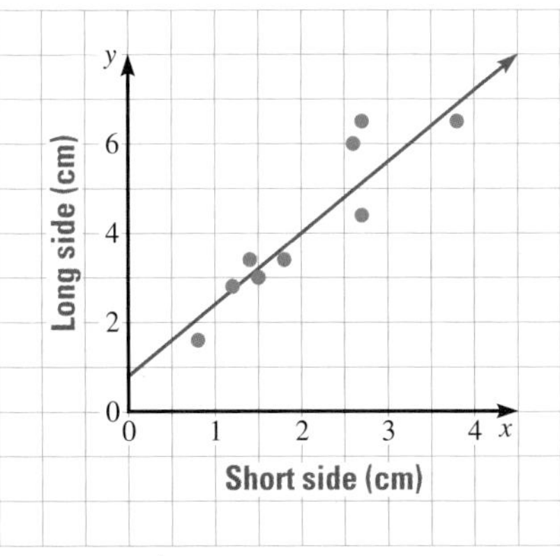

STEP 4 ***Model data***

Draw a line of fit.

STEP 5 ***Predict***

Use the line of fit to find the length of the long side that corresponds to a short side with a length of 4 centimeters. In this case, the long side length predicted by the line of fit has a length of about 7 centimeters.

DRAW CONCLUSIONS **Use your observations to complete these exercises**

1. **COMPARE** What is the slope of your line of fit? How does this slope compare with the slope of the line shown above?

2. **PREDICT** Suppose a student in your class draws a rectangle that has a long side with a length of 5 centimeters. Predict the length of the shorter side. *Explain* how you made your prediction.

3. **EXTEND** The *golden ratio* appears frequently in architectural structures, paintings, sculptures, and even in nature. This ratio of the long side of a rectangle to its short side is approximately 1.618. How does this ratio compare with the slopes of the lines you compared in Exercise 1?

5.7 Predict with Linear Models

Before	You made scatter plots and wrote equations of lines of fit.
Now	You will make predictions using best-fitting lines.
Why?	So you can model trends, as in Ex. 21.

Key Vocabulary
- **best-fitting line**
- **linear regression**
- **interpolation**
- **extrapolation**
- **zero of a function**

The line that most closely follows a trend in data is called the **best-fitting line**. The process of finding the best-fitting line to model a set of data is called **linear regression**. You can perform linear regression using technology. Using a line or its equation to approximate a value between two known values is called **linear interpolation**.

EXAMPLE 1 Interpolate using an equation

CD SINGLES The table shows the total number of CD singles shipped (in millions) by manufacturers for several years during the period 1993–1997.

Year	1993	1995	1996	1997
CD singles shipped (millions)	7.8	22	43	67

a. Make a scatter plot of the data.

b. Find an equation that models the number of CD singles shipped (in millions) as a function of the number of years since 1993.

c. Approximate the number of CD singles shipped in 1994.

REVIEW REGRESSION
For help with performing a linear regression to find the best-fitting line, see p. 332.

Solution

a. Enter the data into lists on a graphing calculator. Make a scatter plot, letting the number of years since 1993 be the x-values (0, 2, 3, 4) and the number of CD singles shipped be the y-values.

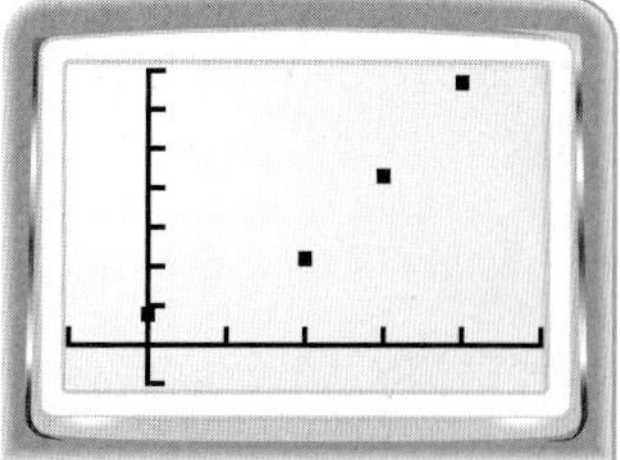

b. Perform linear regression using the paired data. The equation of the best-fitting line is approximately $y = 14x + 2.4$.

c. Graph the best-fitting line. Use the *trace* feature and the arrow keys to find the value of the equation when $x = 1$.

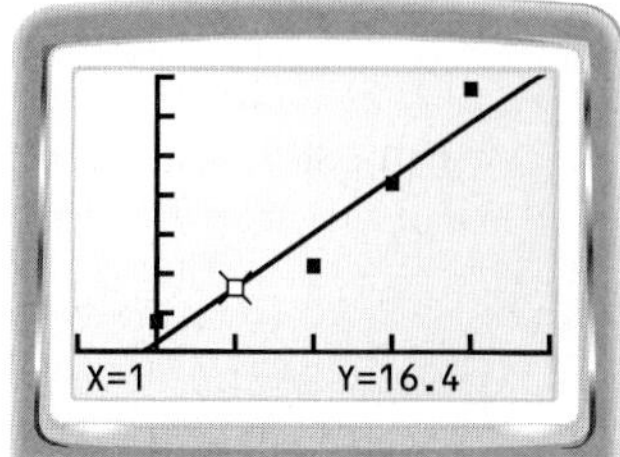

▶ About 16 million CD singles were shipped in 1994.

ANOTHER WAY
You can also estimate the number of CDs shipped in 1994 by evaluating $y = 14x + 2.4$ when $x = 1$.

 at classzone.com

EXTRAPOLATION Using a line or its equation to approximate a value outside the range of known values is called **linear extrapolation**.

EXAMPLE 2 Extrapolate using an equation

CD SINGLES Look back at Example 1.

a. Use the equation from Example 1 to approximate the number of CD singles shipped in 1998 and in 2000.

b. In 1998 there were actually 56 million CD singles shipped. In 2000 there were actually 34 million CD singles shipped. *Describe* the accuracy of the extrapolations made in part (a).

Solution

a. Evaluate the equation of the best-fitting line from Example 1 for $x = 5$ and $x = 7$.

```
Y1(5)
                72.4
Y1(7)
               100.4
```

The model predicts about 72 million CD singles shipped in 1998 and about 100 million CD singles shipped in 2000.

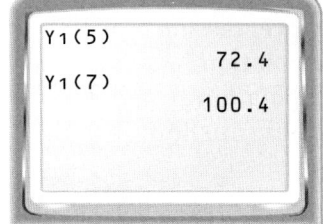

b. The differences between the predicted number of CD singles shipped and the actual number of CD singles shipped in 1998 and 2000 are 16 million CDs and 66 million CDs, respectively. The difference in the actual and predicted numbers increased from 1998 to 2000. So, the equation of the best-fitting line gives a less accurate prediction for the year that is farther from the given years.

ACCURACY As Example 2 illustrates, the farther removed an x-value is from the known x-values, the less confidence you can have in the accuracy of the predicted y-value. This is true in general but not in every case.

✓ GUIDED PRACTICE for Examples 1 and 2

1. **HOUSE SIZE** The table shows the median floor area of new single-family houses in the United States during the period 1995–1999.

Year	1995	1996	1997	1998	1999
Median floor area (square feet)	1920	1950	1975	2000	2028

a. Find an equation that models the floor area (in square feet) of a new single-family house as a function of the number of years since 1995.

b. Predict the median floor area of a new single-family house in 2000 and in 2001.

c. Which of the predictions from part (b) would you expect to be more accurate? *Explain* your reasoning.

EXAMPLE 3 Predict using an equation

SOFTBALL The table shows the number of participants in U.S. youth softball during the period 1997–2001. Predict the year in which the number of youth softball participants reaches 1.2 million.

Year	1997	1998	1999	2000	2001
Participants (millions)	1.44	1.4	1.411	1.37	1.355

Solution

STEP 1 Perform linear regression. Let x represent the number of years since 1997, and let y represent the number of youth softball participants (in millions). The equation for the best-fitting line is approximately $y = -0.02x + 1.435$.

STEP 2 Graph the equation of the best-fitting line. Trace the line until the cursor reaches $y = 1.2$. The corresponding x-value is shown at the bottom of the calculator screen.

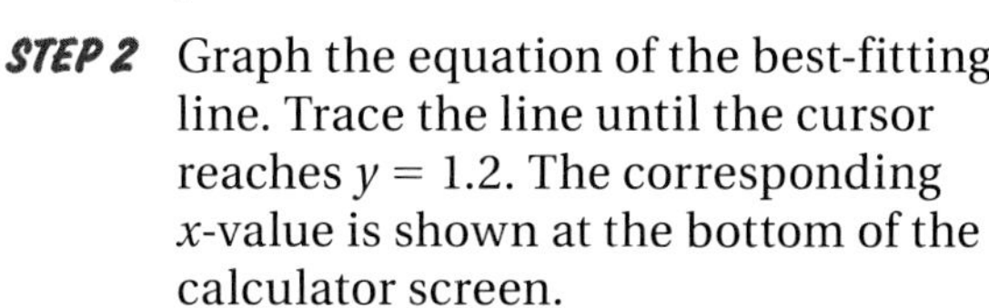

▶ There will be 1.2 million participants about 12 years after 1997, or in 2009.

ANOTHER WAY
You can also predict the year by substituting 1.2 for y in the equation and solving for x:

$y = 0.02x + 1.435$

$1.2 = -0.02x + 1.435$

$x = 11.75$

✓ GUIDED PRACTICE for Example 3

2. **SOFTBALL** In Example 3, in what year will there be 1.25 million youth softball participants in the U.S?

ZERO OF A FUNCTION A **zero of a function** $y = f(x)$ is an x-value for which $f(x) = 0$ (or $y = 0$). Because $y = 0$ along the x-axis of the coordinate plane, a zero of a function is an x-intercept of the function's graph.

KEY CONCEPT *For Your Notebook*

Relating Solutions of Equations, x-Intercepts of Graphs, and Zeros of Functions

In Chapter 3 you learned to solve an equation like $2x - 4 = 0$:

$$2x - 4 = 0$$
$$2x = 4$$
$$x = 2$$

The solution of $2x - 4 = 0$ is 2.

In Chapter 4 you found the x-intercept of the graph of a function like $y = 2x - 4$:

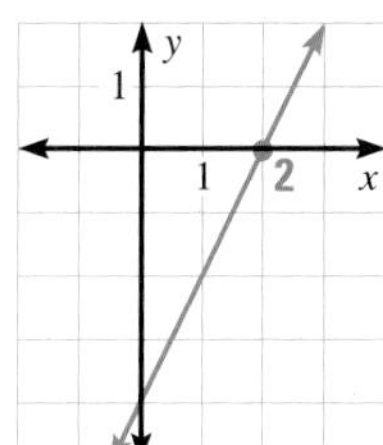

Now you are finding the zero of a function like $f(x) = 2x - 4$:

$$f(x) = 0$$
$$2x - 4 = 0$$
$$x = 2$$

The zero of $f(x) = 2x - 4$ is 2.

EXAMPLE 4 Find the zero of a function

SOFTBALL Look back at Example 3. Find the zero of the function. *Explain* what the zero means in this situation.

Solution

Substitute 0 for y in the equation of the best-fitting line and solve for x.

$y = -0.02x + 1.435$ **Write the equation.**

$0 = -0.02x + 1.435$ **Substitute 0 for *y*.**

$x \approx 72$ **Solve for *x*.**

▶ The zero of the function is about 72. The function has a negative slope, which means that the number of youth softball participants is decreasing. According to the model, there will be no youth softball participants 72 years after 1997, or in 2069.

GUIDED PRACTICE for Example 4

3. **JET BOATS** The number y (in thousands) of jet boats purchased in the U.S. can be modeled by the function $y = -1.23x + 14$ where x is the number of years since 1995. Find the zero of the function. *Explain* what the zero means in this situation.

5.7 EXERCISES

HOMEWORK KEY

○ = **WORKED-OUT SOLUTIONS** on p. WS13 for Exs. 3 and 19

★ = **STANDARDIZED TEST PRACTICE** Exs. 2, 14, 16, and 21

◆ = **MULTIPLE REPRESENTATIONS** Exs. 22

SKILL PRACTICE

1. **VOCABULARY** Copy and complete: Using a linear function to approximate a value within a range of known data values is called __?__.

2. ★ **WRITING** *Explain* how extrapolation differs from interpolation.

EXAMPLE 1 on p. 335 for Exs. 3–4

LINEAR INTERPOLATION **Make a scatter plot of the data. Find the equation of the best-fitting line. Approximate the value of y for $x = 5$.**

3.

x	0	2	4	6	7
y	2	7	14	17	20

4.

x	2	4	6	8	10
y	6.2	22.5	40.2	55.4	72.1

EXAMPLE 2 on p. 336 for Exs. 5–6

LINEAR EXTRAPOLATION **Make a scatter plot of the data. Find the equation of the best-fitting line. Approximate the value of y for $x = 10$.**

5.

x	0	1	2	3	4
y	20	32	39	53	63

6.

x	1	3	5	7	9
y	0.4	1.4	1.9	2.3	3.2

EXAMPLE 4
on p. 338
for Exs. 7–13

ZERO OF A FUNCTION **Find the zero of the function.**

7. $f(x) = 7.5x - 20$
8. $f(x) = -x + 7$
9. $f(x) = \frac{1}{8}x + 2$
10. $f(x) = 17x - 68$
11. $f(x) = -0.5x + 0.75$
12. $f(x) = 5x - 7$

13. **ERROR ANALYSIS** *Describe* and correct the error made in finding the zero of the function $y = 2.3x - 2$.

$y = 2.3(0) - 2$
$y = -2$

14. ★ **MULTIPLE CHOICE** Given the function $y = 12.6x + 3$, for what x-value does $y = 66$?

Ⓐ 0.2 Ⓑ 5 Ⓒ 5.5 Ⓓ 78.6

15. **ERROR ANALYSIS** *Describe* and correct the error in finding an equation of the best-fitting line using a graphing calculator.

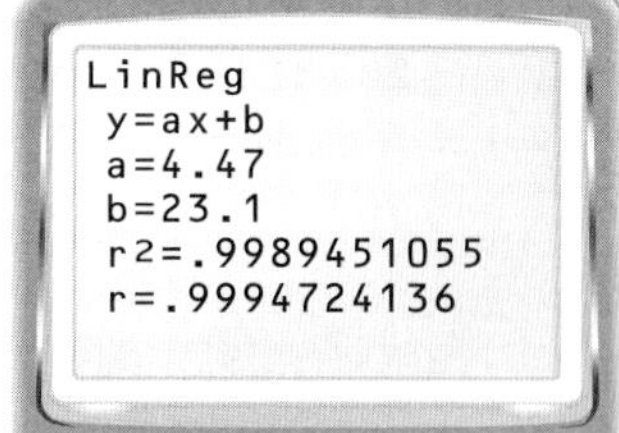

Equation of the best-fitting line is $y = 23.1x + 4.47$.

16. ★ **OPEN-ENDED** Give an example of a real-life situation in which you can use linear interpolation to find the zero of a function. *Explain* what the zero means in this situation.

17. **CHALLENGE** A quantity increases rapidly for 10 years. During the next 10 years, the quantity decreases rapidly.

a. Can you fit a line to the data? *Explain.*

b. How could you model the data using more than one line? *Explain* the steps you could take.

PROBLEM SOLVING

EXAMPLE 1
on p. 335
for Ex. 18

18. **SAILBOATS** Your school's sailing club wants to buy a sailboat. The table shows the lengths and costs of sailboats.

Length (feet)	11	12	14	14	16	22	23
Cost (dollars)	600	500	1900	1700	3500	6500	6000

a. Make a scatter plot of the data. Let x represent the length of the sailboat. Let y represent the cost of the sailboat.

b. Find an equation that models the cost (in dollars) of a sailboat as a function of its length (in feet).

c. Approximate the cost of a sailboat that is 20 feet long.

@HomeTutor for problem solving help at classzone.com

EXAMPLE 2
on p. 336
for Ex. 19

19. **FARMING** The table shows the living space recommended for pigs of certain weights.

Weight (pounds)	40	60	80	100	120	150	230
Area (square feet)	2.5	3	3.5	4	5	6	8

a. Make a scatter plot of the data.

b. Write an equation that models the recommended living space (in square feet) as a function of a pig's weight (in pounds).

c. About how much living space is recommended for a pig weighing 250 pounds?

@HomeTutor for problem solving help at classzone.com

EXAMPLE 3
on p. 338
for Ex. 20

20. **TELEVISION STATIONS** The table shows the number of UHF and VHF broadcast television stations each year from 1996 to 2002.

Year	1996	1997	1998	1999	2000	2001	2002
Television stations	1551	1563	1583	1616	1730	1686	1714

a. Find an equation that models the number of broadcast television stations as a function of the number of years since 1996.

b. At approximately what rate did the number of television stations change from 1996 to 2002?

c. Approximate the year in which there were 1790 television stations.

EXAMPLE 4
on p. 338
for Exs. 21–22

21. ★ **SHORT RESPONSE** The table shows the number of people who lived in high noise areas near U.S. airports for several years during the period 1985–2000.

a. Find an equation that models the number of people (in thousands) living in high noise areas as a function of the number of years since 1985.

b. Find the zero of the function from part (a). *Explain* what the zero means in this situation. Is this reasonable?

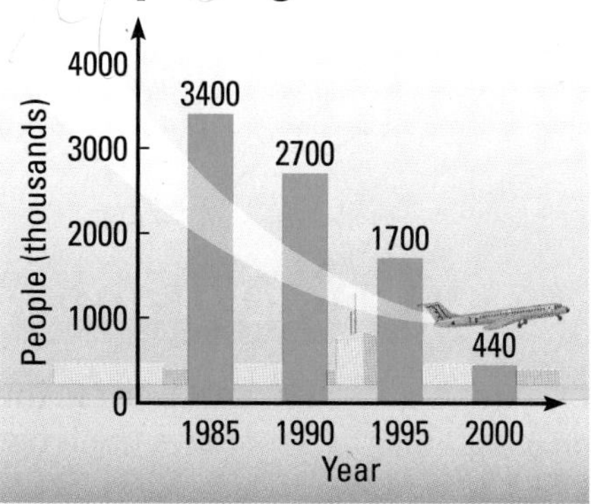

22. **MULTIPLE REPRESENTATIONS** The table shows the number of U.S. households with personal computers (PCs) from 1994 to 2002.

Year	1994	1995	1996	1997	1998	1999	2000	2001	2002
Households with PCs (millions)	32.0	33.6	38.8	44.0	51.2	61.1	66.0	69.1	72.7

a. Drawing a Graph Make a scatter plot of the data in the table.

b. Writing an Equation Find an equation that models the number of households with personal computers (in millions) as a function of the number of years since 1994.

c. Describing in Words Find the zero of the function from part (b). *Explain* what the zero means in this situation.

○ = **WORKED-OUT SOLUTIONS on p. WS1** ★ = **STANDARDIZED TEST PRACTICE**

= **MULTIPLE REPRESENTATIONS**

23. **CHALLENGE** The table shows the estimated populations of mallard ducks and all ducks in North America for several years during the period 1975–2000.

Year	1975	1980	1985	1990	1995	2000
Mallards (thousands)	7727	7707	4961	5452	8269	9470
All ducks (thousands)	37,790	36,220	25,640	25,080	35,870	41,840

a. Make two scatter plots where x is the number of years since 1975 and y is the number of mallards (in thousands) for one scatter plot, while y is the number of ducks (in thousands) for the other scatter plot. *Describe* the correlation of the data in each scatter plot.

b. Can you use the mallard duck population to predict the total duck population? *Explain.*

MIXED REVIEW

Find the sum, difference, product, or quotient.

24. $-19 + (-8)$ *(p. 74)*
25. $-7.3 + 5$ *(p. 74)*
26. $-4.03 + (-3.57)$ *(p. 74)*

27. $-2.8 - (-2.3)$ *(p. 80)*
28. $-4(5)(-5.5)$ *(p. 88)*
29. $-25 \div (-5)$ *(p. 103)*

PREVIEW
Prepare for Lesson 6.1 in Exs. 30–32.

Solve the equation. Check your solution.

30. $x - (-9) = 8$ *(p. 134)*
31. $3x - 4 = -4$ *(p. 141)*
32. $4x + 10x = 98$ *(p. 148)*

QUIZ *for Lessons 5.5–5.7*

1. PARALLEL LINES Write an equation of the line that passes through $(-6, 8)$ and is parallel to the line $y = 3x - 15$. *(p. 319)*

PERPENDICULAR LINES Write an equation of the line that passes through the given point and is perpendicular to the given line. *(p. 319)*

2. $(5, 5)$, $y = -x + 2$
3. $(10, -3)$, $y = 2x + 24$
4. $(2, 3)$, $x + 2y = -7$

5. CASSETTE TAPES The table shows the number of audio cassette tapes shipped for several years during the period 1994–2002. *(pp. 325, 335)*

Year	1994	1996	1998	2000	2002
Tapes shipped (millions)	345	225	159	76	31

a. Write an equation that models the number of tapes shipped (in millions) as a function of the number of years since 1994.

b. At about what rate did the number of tapes shipped change over time?

c. Approximate the year in which 125 million tapes were shipped.

d. Find the zero of the function from part (a). *Explain* what the zero means in this situation.

@HomeTutor
classzone.com
Keystrokes

5.7 Model Data from the Internet

QUESTION **How can you find reliable data on the Internet and use it to predict the total U.S voting-age population in 2010?**

EXAMPLE 1 **Collect and analyze data**

Find data for the total U.S. voting-age population over several years. Use an equation that models the data to predict the total U.S. voting-age population in 2010.

STEP 1 Find a data source

Reliable data about the U.S. population can be found in the online *Statistical Abstract*. Go to the address shown below. Click on a link to the most recent version of the *Statistical Abstract*.

Address http://www.census.gov

Voting-Age Population

Year	Total (mil.)
1980	157.1
1988	178.1
1990	182.1
1994	190.3
1996	193.7
1998	198.2

STEP 2 Find an appropriate data set

Choose the most recent "Elections" document. In this document, find the table of data entitled "Voting-Age Population."

STEP 3 Find a model

Use a graphing calculator to make a scatter plot. Let x represent the number of years since 1980. Let y represent the total U.S. voting-age population (in millions). Find an equation that models the total U.S. voting-age population (in millions) as a function of the number of years since 1980.

▶ $y = 2.23x + 159$

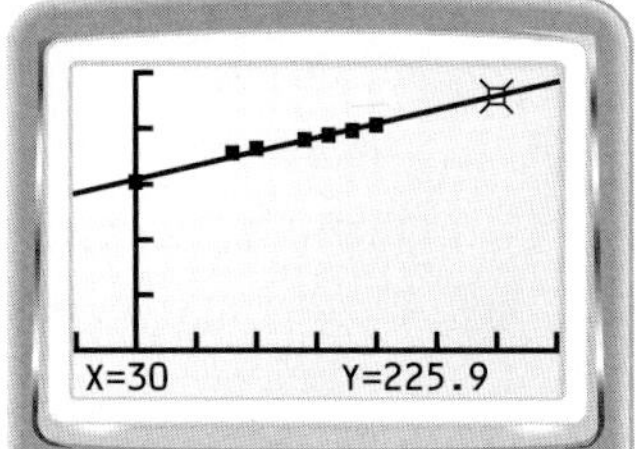

STEP 4 Predict

Use the model to predict the total voting-age population in 2010. You can either evaluate the equation for $x = 30$ or trace the graph of the equation, as shown.

▶ The total U.S. voting-age population will be about 225.9 million in 2010.

DRAW CONCLUSIONS

1. In the online *Statistical Abstract*, find data for the total value of agricultural imports over several years beginning with 1990.

2. Make a scatter plot of the data you found in Exercise 1. Find an equation that models the total value of agricultural imports (in millions of dollars) as a function of the number of years since 1990.

3. Predict the year in which the total value of agricultural imports will be \$45,000 million. *Describe* the method you used.

MIXED REVIEW of Problem Solving

STATE TEST PRACTICE
classzone.com

Lessons 5.5–5.7

1. **MULTI-STEP PROBLEM** The table shows the value of primary and secondary schools built in the U.S. each year from 1995 to 2000.

Year	Value (millions of dollars)
1995	1245
1996	1560
1997	2032
1998	2174
1999	2420
2000	2948

   a. Make a scatter plot of the data.

   b. Write an equation that models the value (in millions of dollars) of the schools built as a function of the number of years since 1995.

   c. At approximately what rate did the value change from 1995 to 2000?

   d. In what year would you predict the value of the schools built in the U.S. to be $3,600,000,000?

2. **GRIDDED ANSWER** A map of a city shows streets as lines on a coordinate grid. State Street has a slope of $-\frac{1}{2}$. Park Street runs perpendicular to State Street. What is the slope of Park Street on the map?

3. **OPEN-ENDED** The graph represents the cost for one kayak owner for storing a kayak at a marina over time. The total cost includes a standard initial fee and a monthly storage fee. Suppose a different kayak owner pays a lower initial fee during a special promotion. Write an equation that could give the total cost as a function of the number of months of storage for this kayak owner.

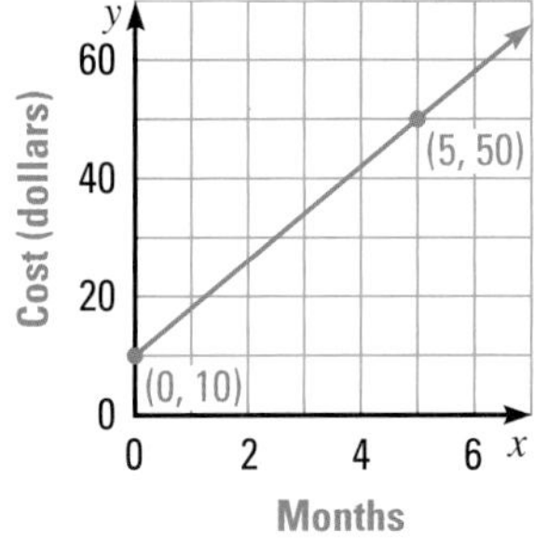

4. **SHORT RESPONSE** The table shows the heights and corresponding lengths of horses in a stable. Make a scatter plot of the data. *Describe* the correlation of the data.

Height (hands)	Length (inches)
17.0	76
16.0	72
16.2	74
15.3	71
15.1	69
16.3	75

5. **EXTENDED RESPONSE** The table shows the percent of revenue from U.S. music sales made through music clubs from 1998 through 2003.

Year	Percent of revenue
1998	9
1999	7.9
2000	7.6
2001	6.1
2002	4
2003	4.1

   a. Find an equation that models the percent of revenue from music clubs as a function of the number of years since 1998.

   b. At approximately what rate did the percent of revenue from music clubs change from 1998 to 2003?

   c. Find the zero of the function. *Explain* what the zero means in this situation.

6. **SHORT RESPONSE** The cost of bowling includes a $4.00 fee per game and a shoe rental fee. Shoes for adults cost $2.25. Shoes for children cost $1.75. Write equations that give the total cost of bowling for an adult and for a child as functions of the number of games bowled. How are the graphs of the equations related? *Explain.*

5 CHAPTER SUMMARY

BIG IDEAS

For Your Notebook

Big Idea 1

Writing Linear Equations in a Variety of Forms

Using given information about a line, you can write an equation of the line in three different forms.

Form	Equation	Important information
Slope-intercept form	$y = mx + b$	• The slope of the line is m. • The y-intercept of the line is b.
Point-slope form	$y - y_1 = m(x - x_1)$	• The slope of the line is m. • The line passes through (x_1, y_1).
Standard form	$Ax + By = C$	• A, B, and C are real numbers. • A and B are not both zero.

Big Idea 2

Using Linear Models to Solve Problems

You can write a linear equation that models a situation involving a constant rate of change. Analyzing given information helps you choose a linear model.

Choosing a Linear Model	
If this is what you know . . .	**. . . then use this equation form**
constant rate of change and initial value	slope-intercept form
constant rate of change and one data pair	slope-intercept form or point-slope form
two data pairs and the fact that the rate of change is constant	slope-intercept form or point-slope form
the sum of two variable quantities is constant	standard form

Big Idea 3

Modeling Data with a Line of Fit

You can use a line of fit to model data that have a positive or negative correlation. The line or an equation of the line can be used to make predictions.

Step 1 Make a scatter plot of the data.

Step 2 Decide whether the data can be modeled by a line.

Step 3 Draw a line that appears to follow the trend in data closely.

Step 4 Write an equation using two points on the line.

Step 5 Interpolate (between known values) or extrapolate (beyond known values) using the line or its equation.

5 CHAPTER REVIEW

@HomeTutor
classzone.com
- Multi-Language Glossary
- Vocabulary practice

REVIEW KEY VOCABULARY

- point-slope form, *p. 302*
- converse, *p. 319*
- perpendicular, *p. 320*
- scatter plot, *p. 325*
- positive correlation, negative correlation, relatively no correlation, *p. 325*
- line of fit, *p. 326*
- best-fitting line, *p. 335*
- linear regression, *p. 335*
- interpolation, *p. 335*
- extrapolation, *p. 336*
- zero of a function, *p. 337*

VOCABULARY EXERCISES

1. Copy and complete: If a best-fitting line falls from left to right, then the data have a(n) _?_ correlation.

2. Copy and complete: Using a linear function to approximate a value beyond a range of known values is called _?_.

3. **WRITING** What is the zero of a function, and how does it relate to the function's graph? *Explain.*

REVIEW EXAMPLES AND EXERCISES

Use the review examples and exercises below to check your understanding of the concepts you have learned in each lesson of Chapter 5.

5.1 Write Linear Equations in Slope-Intercept Form *pp. 283–289*

EXAMPLE

Write an equation of the line shown.

$y = mx + b$ **Write slope-intercept form.**

$y = -\frac{2}{3}x + 4$ **Substitute $-\frac{2}{3}$ for m and 4 for b.**

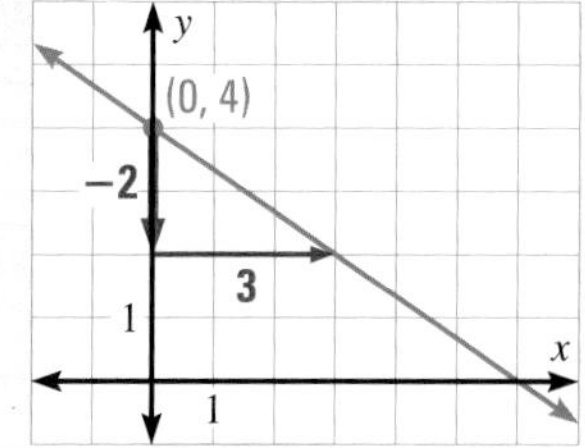

EXERCISES

EXAMPLES 1 and 5 on pp. 283, 285 for Exs. 4–7

Write an equation in slope-intercept form of the line with the given slope and y-intercept.

4. slope: 3
   y-intercept: −10

5. slope: $\frac{4}{9}$
   y-intercept: 5

6. slope: $-\frac{2}{11}$
   y-intercept: 7

7. **GIFT CARD** You have a \$25 gift card for a bagel shop. A bagel costs \$1.25. Write an equation that gives the amount (in dollars) that remains on the card as a function of the total number of bagels you have purchased so far. How much money is on the card after you buy 2 bagels?

5 CHAPTER REVIEW

5.2 Use Linear Equations in Slope-Intercept Form

pp. 292–299

EXAMPLE

Write an equation of the line that passes through the point (−2, −6) and has a slope of 2.

STEP 1 **Find** the y-intercept.

$y = mx + b$ **Write slope-intercept form.**

$-6 = 2(-2) + b$ **Substitute 2 for *m*, −2 for *x*, and −6 for *y*.**

$-2 = b$ **Solve for *b*.**

STEP 2 **Write** an equation of the line.

$y = mx + b$ **Write slope intercept form.**

$y = 2x - 2$ **Substitute 2 for *m* and −2 for *b*.**

EXERCISES

EXAMPLE 1 on p. 292 for Exs. 8–10

Write an equation in slope-intercept form of the line that passes through the given point and has the given slope *m*.

8. $(-3, -1)$; $m = 4$ **9.** $(-2, 1)$; $m = 1$ **10.** $(8, -4)$; $m = -3$

5.3 Write Linear Equations in Point-Slope Form

pp. 302–308

EXAMPLE

Write an equation in point-slope form of the line shown.

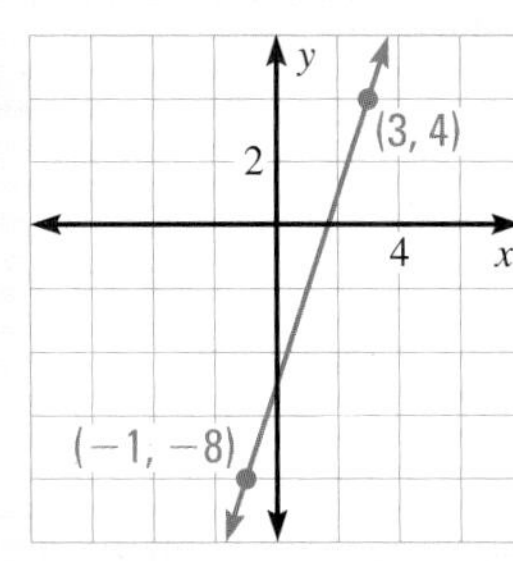

STEP 1 **Find** the slope of the line.

$$m = \frac{y_2 - y_1}{x_2 - x_1} = \frac{-8 - 4}{-1 - 3} = \frac{-12}{-4} = 3$$

STEP 2 **Write** an equation. Use (3, 4).

$y - y_1 = m(x - x_1)$ **Write point-slope form.**

$y - 4 = 3(x - 3)$ **Substitute 3 for *m*, 3 for x_1, and 4 for y_1.**

EXERCISES

EXAMPLES 3 and 5 on pp. 303, 304 for Exs. 11–14

Write an equation in point-slope form of the line that passes through the given points.

11. (4, 7), (5, 1) **12.** (9, −2), (−3, 2) **13.** (8, −8), (−3, −2)

14. BUS TRIP A bus leaves at 10 A.M. to take students on a field trip to a historic site. At 10:25 A.M., the bus is 100 miles from the site. At 11:15 A.M., the bus is 65 miles from the site. The bus travels at a constant speed. Write an equation in point-slope form that relates the distance (in miles) from the site and the time (in minutes) after 10:00 A.M. How far is the bus from the site at 11:30 A.M.?

5.4 Write Linear Equations in Standard Form *pp. 311–316*

EXAMPLE

Write an equation in standard form of the line shown.

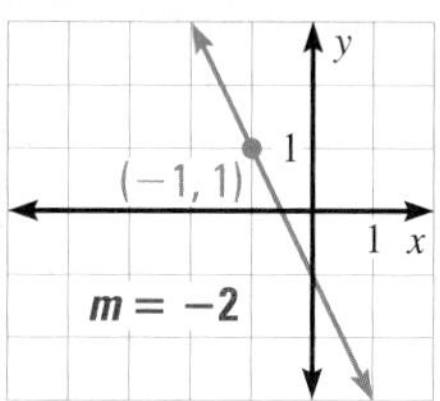

$y - y_1 = m(x - x_1)$	Write point-slope form.
$y - 1 = -2(x - (-1))$	Substitute 1 for y_1, −2 for *m*, and −1 for x_1.
$y - 1 = -2x - 2$	Distributive property
$2x + y = -1$	Collect variable terms on one side, constants on the other.

EXERCISES

EXAMPLES 2 and 5 on pp. 311, 313 for Exs. 15–17

Write an equation in standard form of the line that has the given characteristics.

15. Slope: −4; passes through (−2, 7)

16. Passes through (−1, −5) and (3, 7)

17. COSTUMES You are buying ribbon to make costumes for a school play. Organza ribbon costs \$.07 per yard. Satin ribbon costs \$.04 per yard. Write an equation to model the possible combinations of yards of organza ribbon and yards of satin ribbon you can buy for \$5. List several possible combinations.

5.5 Write Equations of Parallel and Perpendicular Lines *pp. 319–324*

EXAMPLE

Write an equation of the line that passes through (−4, −2) and is perpendicular to the line $y = 4x - 7$.

The slope of the line $y = 4x - 7$ is 4. The slope of the perpendicular line through (−4, −2) is $-\frac{1}{4}$. Find the *y*-intercept of the perpendicular line.

$y = mx + b$	Write slope-intercept form.
$-2 = -\frac{1}{4}(-4) + b$	Substitute $-\frac{1}{4}$ for *m*, −4 for *x*, and −2 for *y*.
$-3 = b$	Solve for *b*.

An equation of the perpendicular line through (−4, −2) is $y = -\frac{1}{4}x - 3$.

EXERCISES

EXAMPLES 1 and 4 on pp. 319, 321 for Exs. 18–20

Write an equation of the line that passes through the given point and is (a) parallel to the given line and (b) perpendicular to the given line.

18. (0, 2), $y = -4x + 6$

19. (2, −3), $y = -2x - 3$

20. (6, 0), $y = \frac{3}{4}x - \frac{1}{4}$

5 CHAPTER REVIEW

5.6 Fit a Line to Data

pp. 325–331

EXAMPLE

The table shows the time needed to roast turkeys of different weights. Make a scatter plot of the data. *Describe* the correlation of the data.

Weight (pounds)	6	8	12	14	18	20	24
Roast time (hours)	2.75	3.00	3.50	4.00	4.25	4.75	5.25

Treat the data as ordered pairs. Let x represent the turkey weight (in pounds), and let y represent the time (in hours) it takes to roast the turkey. Plot the ordered pairs as points in a coordinate plane.

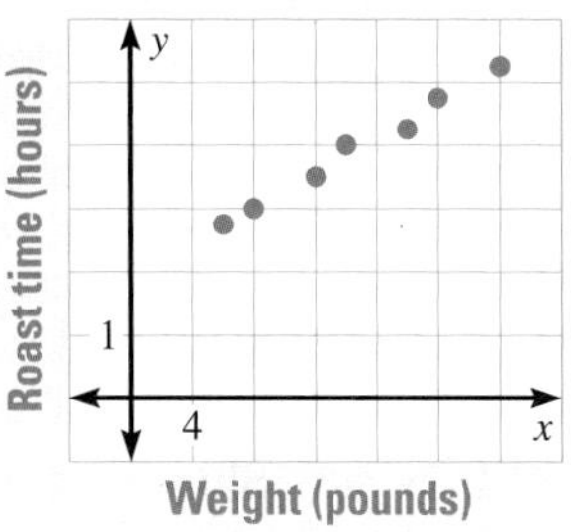

The scatter plot shows a positive correlation, which means that heavier turkeys tend to require more time to roast.

EXERCISES

EXAMPLE 2 on p. 326 for Ex. 21

21. **AIRPORTS** The table shows the number of airports in the Unites States for several years during the period 1990–2001. Make a scatter plot of the data. *Describe* the correlation of the data.

Years	1990	1995	1998	1999	2000	2001
Airports (thousands)	17.5	18.2	18.8	19.1	19.3	19.3

5.7 Predict with Linear Models

pp. 335–341

EXAMPLE

Use the scatter plot from the example for Lesson 5.6 above to estimate the time (in hours) it takes to roast a 10 pound turkey.

Draw a line that appears to fit the points in the scatter plot closely. There should be approximately as many points above the line as below it.

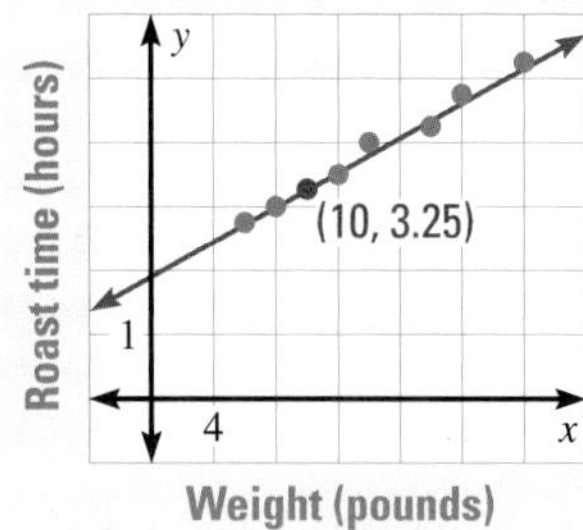

Find the point on the line whose x-coordinate is 10. At that point, you can see that the y-coordinate is about 3.25.

▸ It takes about 3.25 hours to roast a 10 pound turkey.

EXERCISES

EXAMPLE 2 on p. 336 for Ex. 22

22. **COOKING TIMES** Use the graph in the Example above to estimate the time (in hours) it takes to roast a turkey that weighs 30 pounds. *Explain* how you found your answer.

5 CHAPTER TEST

Write an equation in slope-intercept form of the line with the given slope and y-intercept.

1. slope: 5
   y-intercept: -7
2. slope: $\frac{2}{5}$
   y-intercept: -2
3. slope: $-\frac{4}{3}$
   y-intercept: 1

Write an equation in slope-intercept form of the line that passes through the given point and has the given slope m.

4. $(-2, -8)$; $m = 3$
5. $(1, 1)$; $m = -4$
6. $(-1, 3)$; $m = -6$

Write an equation in point-slope form of the line that passes through the given points.

7. $(4, 5)$, $(2, 9)$
8. $(-2, 2)$, $(8, -3)$
9. $(3, 4)$, $(1, -6)$

Write an equation in standard form of the line with the given characteristics.

10. Slope: 10; passes through $(6, 2)$
11. Passes through $(-3, 2)$ and $(6, -1)$

Write an equation of the line that passes through the given point and is (a) parallel to the given line and (b) perpendicular to the given line.

12. $(2, 0)$, $y = -5x + 3$
13. $(-1, 4)$, $y = -x - 4$
14. $(4, -9)$, $y = \frac{1}{4}x + 2$

Make a scatter plot of the data. Draw a line of fit. Write an equation of the line.

15.

x	0	1	2	3	4
y	15	35	53	74	94

16.

x	0	2	4	8	10
y	-2	6	15	38	50

17. **FIELD TRIP** Your science class is taking a field trip to an observatory. The cost of a presentation and a tour of the telescope is \$60 for the group plus an additional \$3 per person. Write an equation that gives the total cost C as a function of the number of people p in the group.

18. **GOLF FACILITIES** The table shows the number of golf facilities in the United States during the period 1997–2001.

    a. Make a scatter plot of the data where x is the number of years since 1997 and y is the number of golf facilities (in thousands).

    b. Write an equation that models the number of golf facilities (in thousands) as a function of the number of years since 1997.

    c. At about what rate did the number of golf facilities change during the period 1997–2001?

    d. Use the equation from part (b) to predict the number of golf facilities in 2004.

    e. Predict the year in which the number of golf facilities reached 16,000. *Explain* how you found your answer.

Year	Golf facilities (thousands)
1997	14.6
1998	14.9
1999	15.2
2000	15.5
2001	15.7

Scoring Rubric

Full Credit
- solution is complete and correct

Partial Credit
- solution is complete but has errors,

or
- solution is without error but incomplete

No Credit
- no solution is given,

or
- solution makes no sense

SHORT RESPONSE QUESTIONS

PROBLEM

The average monthly cost of basic cable increased by about \$1.47 each year from 1986 to 2003. In 1986 the average monthly cost of basic cable was \$10.67. Write an equation that gives the monthly cost (in dollars) of basic cable as a function of the number of years since 1986. In what year was the monthly cost of basic cable \$31.25? *Explain* your reasoning.

Below are sample solutions to the problem. Read each solution and the comments in blue to see why the sample represents full credit, partial credit, or no credit.

SAMPLE 1: Full credit solution

A verbal model shows how the equation is obtained.

Let y be the average monthly cost x years since 1986.

Monthly cost	=	Cost in 1986	+	Cost increase per year	•	Years since 1986
y	=	**10.67**	+	**1.47**	•	x

To find the year when the monthly cost was \$31.25, substitute 31.25 for y and solve for x.

Calculations are performed correctly.

$$y = 10.67 + 1.47x$$

$$31.25 = 10.67 + 1.47x$$

$$14 = x$$

The question is answered correctly.

The monthly cost was \$31.25 fourteen years after 1986, or in 2000.

SAMPLE 2: Partial credit solution

The equation is correct, and the student has explained what the variables represent.

Let y be the monthly cost. Let x be the number of years since 1986.

Monthly cost	=	Cost in 1986	+	Cost increase per year	•	Years since 1986
y	=	**10.67**	+	**1.47**	•	x

The answer is incorrect, because the student mistakenly substituted the cost for the variable that represents the years since 1986.

To find the year when the cost was \$31.25, substitute 31.25 for x.

$$y = 10.67 + 1.47x$$

$$= 10.67 + 1.47(31.25) \approx 56.61$$

The cost was \$31.25 about 57 years after 1986, or in 2042.

SAMPLE 3: Partial credit solution

The equation and answer are correct. There are no explanations to support the student's work.

$$y = 10.67 + 1.47x$$
$$31.25 = 10.67 + 1.47x$$
$$14 = x$$

The monthly cost was $31.25 fourteen years after 1986, or in 2000.

SAMPLE 4: No credit solution

The student's reasoning is incorrect, and the equation is incorrect. The answer is incorrect.

Year when cost is \$31.25 = \$31.25 ÷ 1.47

$$y = 31.25 \div 1.47 \approx 21.25$$

The year is about 21 years after 1986, or in 2007.

PRACTICE Apply the Scoring Rubric

Score the solution to the problem below as *full credit, partial credit,* or *no credit. Explain* your reasoning.

PROBLEM A hot air balloon is flying at an altitude of 870 feet. It descends at a rate of 15 feet per minute. Write an equation that gives the altitude (in feet) of the balloon as a function of the time (in minutes) since it began its descent. Find the time it takes the balloon to reach an altitude of 12 feet. *Explain* your reasoning.

1. Let y be the altitude (in feet) after x minutes.

Final altitude = Starting altitude + Decrease in altitude per minute • Minutes

$$y = 870 + (-15)x = 870 - 15(12) = 690$$

The balloon will take 690 minutes to reach an altitude of 12 feet.

2. Let y be the altitude (in feet) after x minutes.

Final altitude = Starting altitude + Decrease in altitude per minute • Minutes

$$y = 870 + (-15)x$$
$$12 = 870 - 15x$$
$$57.2 = x$$

The balloon will take about 57 minutes to reach an altitude of 12 feet.

3. $870 \div 15 = 58$

The balloon will take 58 minutes to reach an altitude of 12 feet.

5 ★ Standardized TEST PRACTICE

SHORT RESPONSE

1. You have $50 to spend on pretzels and juice drinks for a school dance. A box of pretzels costs $3.50, and a package of juice drinks costs $5.00. Write an equation in standard form that models the possible combinations of boxes of pretzels and packages of juice drinks that you can buy. What is the greatest number of boxes of pretzels you can buy? *Explain.*

2. You and your family are traveling home in a car at an average speed of 60 miles per hour. At noon you are 180 miles from home.
   a. Write an equation that gives your distance from home (in miles) as a function of the number of hours since noon.
   b. *Explain* why the graph of this equation is a line with a negative slope.

3. Robyn needs $2.20 to buy a bag of trail mix. Write an equation in standard form that models the possible combinations of nickels and dimes she could use to pay for the mix. How many nickels would she need if she used 14 dimes? *Explain* your reasoning.

4. On a street map, Main Street and Maple Street can be modeled by the equations $y = ax + 6$ and $x + 2y = 4$. For what value of a are the streets parallel? For what value of a are the streets perpendicular? *Justify* your answers.

5. The table shows the projected dollar amount spent per person in the U.S. on interactive television for several years during the period 1998–2006.

Year	Spending per person (dollars)
1998	0
2000	2.86
2002	6.63
2004	9.50
2006	12.85

   a. Make a scatter plot of the data.
   b. Predict the year in which spending per person in the U.S. on interactive television will reach $20. *Explain* how you found your answer.

6. You are mountain biking on a 10 mile trail. You biked 4 miles before stopping to take a break. After your break, you bike at a rate of 9 miles per hour.
   a. Write an equation that gives the length (in miles) of the trail you have completed as a function of the number of hours since your break ended.
   b. How much time (in minutes) after your break will it take you to complete the entire trail? *Explain.*

7. A guide gives dogsled tours during the winter months. The guide charges one amount for the first hour of a tour and a different amount for each hour after the first. You paid $55 for a 2 hour dogsled tour. Your friend paid $70 for a 3 hour tour.
   a. *Explain* why this situation can be modeled by a linear equation.
   b. Write an equation that gives the cost (in dollars) of a dogsled tour as a function of the number of hours after the first hour of the tour.

8. The scatter plot shows the total carbon dioxide emissions throughout the world for several years during the period 1950–1995.

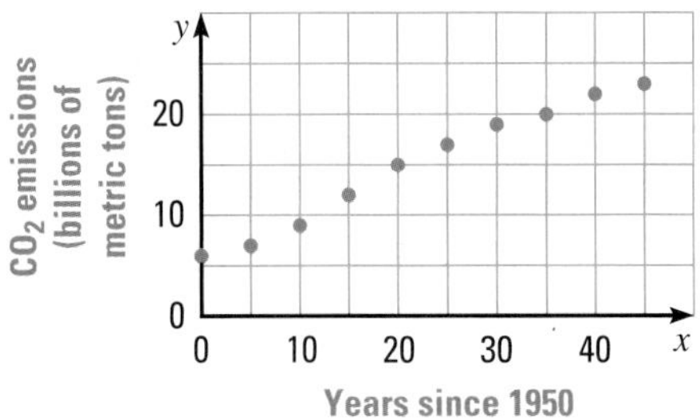

   a. Write an equation that models the carbon dioxide emissions (in billions of metric tons) as a function of the number of years since 1950.
   b. At about what rate did the amount of carbon dioxide emissions increase from 1950 to 1995? *Explain* how you found your answer.

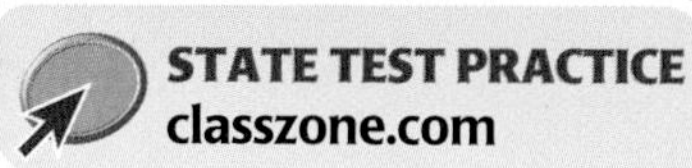

MULTIPLE CHOICE

9. Which equation represents the line that passes through (0, 8) and (2, 0)?

Ⓐ $y = 4x + 2$ Ⓑ $y = -4x + 2$

Ⓒ $y = 4x + 8$ Ⓓ $y = -4x + 8$

10. Which equation represents the line with a slope of 5 and a y-intercept of 2?

Ⓐ $y = 2x + 5$ Ⓑ $y = 2x - 5$

Ⓒ $y = 5x + 2$ Ⓓ $y = 5x - 2$

11. Which function has the values $f(1) = 8$ and $f(7) = -10$?

Ⓐ $f(x) = -3x + 11$ Ⓑ $f(x) = -2x + 10$

Ⓒ $f(x) = -3x + 25$ Ⓓ $f(x) = 3x - 24$

GRIDDED ANSWER

12. What is the slope of a line that is perpendicular to the line $y = -2x - 7$?

13. What is the y-intercept of the line that has a slope of $\frac{1}{2}$ and passes through (5, 4)?

14. What is the y-intercept of the line that is parallel to the line $y = 2x - 3$ and passes through the point (6, 11)?

15. What is the zero of the function $f(x) = -\frac{4}{5}x + 9$?

16. The graph of the equation $Ax + y = 2$ is a line that passes through (−2, 8). What is the value of A?

EXTENDED RESPONSE

17. The table shows the time several students spent studying for an exam and each student's grade on the exam.

Study time (hours)	1.5	0.5	0.5	1	1	3	2.5	3	0
Grade	90	60	70	72	80	88	89	94	58

a. Make a scatter plot of the data.

b. Write an equation that models a student's exam grade as a function of the time (in hours) the student spent studying for the exam.

c. How many hours would you need to study in order to earn a grade of 93 on the exam? *Justify* your answer using the data above.

18. The scatter plot shows the number of FM radio stations in the United States for several years during the period 1994–2000.

a. *Describe* the correlation of the data.

b. Write an equation that models the number of FM radio stations in the United States as a function of the number of years since 1994.

c. At about what rate did the number of radio stations change during the period 1994–2000?

d. Find the zero of the function from part (b). *Explain* what the zero means in this situation.

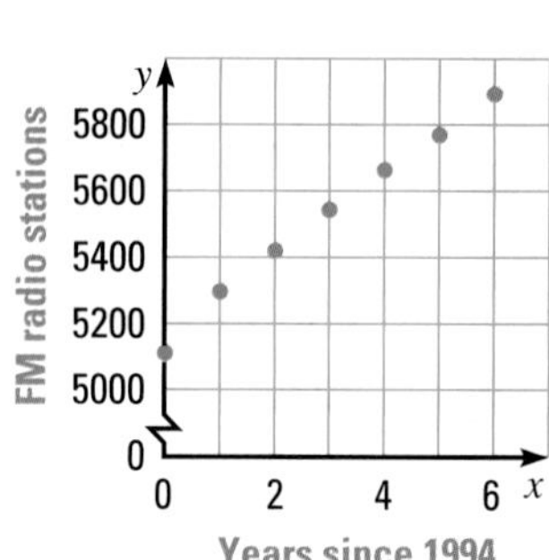

6 Solving and Graphing Linear Inequalities

Before

In previous chapters, you learned the following skills, which you'll use in Chapter 6: solving equations, graphing equations, and writing equations.

Prerequisite Skills

VOCABULARY CHECK

1. Identify one **ordered pair** that is a solution of $8x - 5y = -2$.
2. Are $7x - 4 = 10$ and $x = 3$ **equivalent equations**? *Explain.*
3. The **absolute value** of a number a is the distance between a and _?_ on a number line.

SKILLS CHECK

Check whether the given number is a solution of the equation or inequality. *(Review p. 21 for 6.1–6.6.)*

4. $x - 2 = 3; 5$ **5.** $s + 3 = 12; 9$ **6.** $6y > 20; 3$ **7.** $\frac{p-3}{5} \le 4; 23$

Solve the equation. Check your solution. *(Review pp. 134, 141, 148 for 6.1–6.6.)*

8. $m + 8 = -20$ **9.** $-7x = 35$ **10.** $-9r - 4 = 25$ **11.** $4t - 7t = 9$

For the given value of a, find $-a$ and $|a|$. *(Review p. 64 for 6.5–6.6.)*

12. $a = -3$ **13.** $a = -5.6$ **14.** $a = 14$ **15.** $a = 0$

Graph the equation. *(Review p. 215 for 6.7.)*

16. $y = -7x + 3$ **17.** $6x + 3y = -5$ **18.** $x = -8$ **19.** $y = 4$

@HomeTutor Prerequisite skills practice at classzone.com

Now

In Chapter 6, you will apply the big ideas listed below and reviewed in the Chapter Summary on page 414. You will also use the key vocabulary listed below.

Big Ideas

1. **Applying properties of inequality**
2. **Using statements with *and* or *or***
3. **Graphing inequalities**

KEY VOCABULARY

- graph of an inequality, *p. 356*
- equivalent inequalities, *p. 357*
- compound inequality, *p. 380*
- absolute value equation, *p. 390*
- absolute deviation, *p. 392*
- linear inequality in two variables, *p. 405*
- graph of an inequality in two variables, *p. 405*

Why?

You can use inequalities to solve problems in sound amplification. For example, you can solve an inequality to determine whether an amplifier provides enough amplification for a given number of people in an audience.

Animated Algebra

The animation illustrated below for Exercise 45 on page 387 helps you answer this question: Is a 2900 watt amplifier adequate for an audience of 350 people?

Start
You need to decide whether the amplifier is adequate for 350 people.

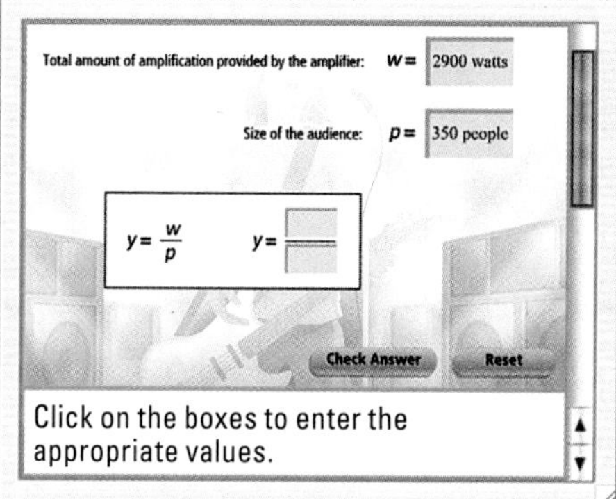

Animated Algebra at classzone.com

Other animations for Chapter 6: pages 358, 364, 382, 390, 391, 399, and 407

6.1 Solve Inequalities Using Addition and Subtraction

Before	You solved equations using addition and subtraction.
Now	You will solve inequalities using addition and subtraction.
Why	So you can describe desert temperatures, as in Example 1.

Key Vocabulary
- **graph of an inequality**
- **equivalent inequalities**
- **inequality,** *p. 21*
- **solution of an inequality,** *p. 22*

On a number line, the **graph of an inequality** in one variable is the set of points that represent all solutions of the inequality. To graph an inequality in one variable, use an open circle for < or > and a closed circle for ≤ or ≥. The graphs of $x < 3$ and $x \geq -1$ are shown below.

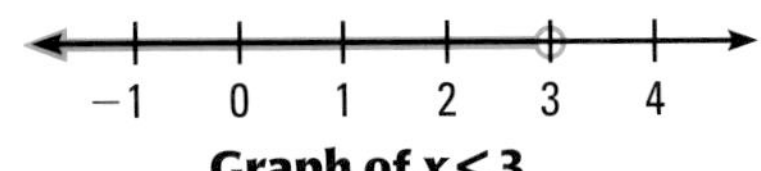

Graph of $x < 3$

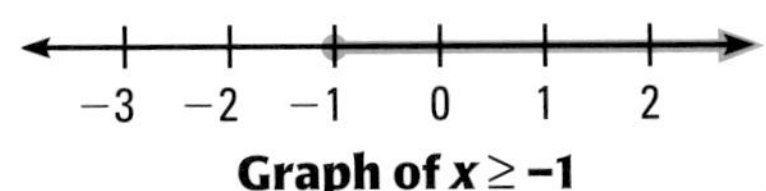

Graph of $x \geq -1$

EXAMPLE 1 Write and graph an inequality

DEATH VALLEY The highest temperature recorded in the United States was 134°F at Death Valley, California, in 1913. Use only this fact to write and graph an inequality that describes the temperatures in the United States.

Solution

Let T represent a temperature (in degrees Fahrenheit) in the United States. The value of T must be less than or equal to 134. So, an inequality is $T \leq 134$.

EXAMPLE 2 Write inequalities from graphs

Write an inequality represented by the graph.

a.

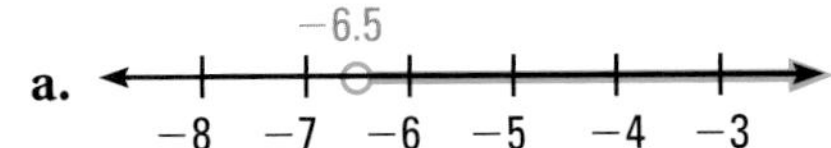

b.

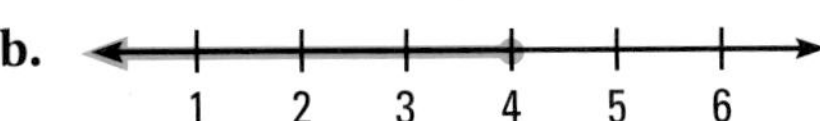

Solution

a. The open circle means that −6.5 is not a solution of the inequality. Because the arrow points to the right, all numbers greater than −6.5 are solutions.

▶ An inequality represented by the graph is $x > -6.5$.

b. The closed circle means that 4 is a solution of the inequality. Because the arrow points to the left, all numbers less than 4 are solutions.

▶ An inequality represented by the graph is $x \leq 4$.

✓ GUIDED PRACTICE for Examples 1 and 2

1. **ANTARCTICA** The lowest temperature recorded in Antarctica was −129°F at the Russian Vostok station in 1983. Use only this fact to write and graph an inequality that describes the temperatures in Antarctica.

Write an inequality represented by the graph.

2. 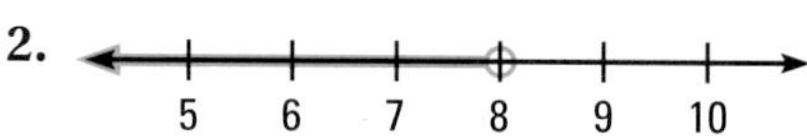

3. 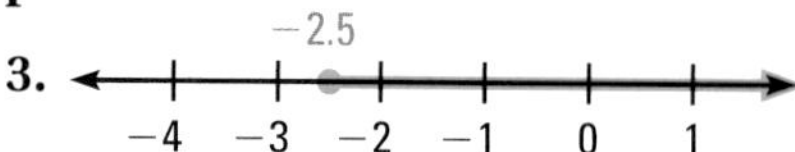

EQUIVALENT INEQUALITIES Just as you used properties of equality to produce equivalent equations, you can use properties of inequality to produce *equivalent inequalities.* **Equivalent inequalities** are inequalities that have the same solutions.

KEY CONCEPT *For Your Notebook*

Addition Property of Inequality

Words Adding the same number to each side of an inequality produces an equivalent inequality.

Algebra If $a > b$, then $a + c > b + c$. If $a \geq b$, then $a + c \geq b + c$.

If $a < b$, then $a + c < b + c$. If $a \leq b$, then $a + c \leq b + c$.

EXAMPLE 3 Solve an inequality using addition

Solve $x - 5 > -3.5$. Graph your solution.

$x - 5 > -3.5$ Write original inequality.

$x - 5 + 5 > -3.5 + 5$ Add 5 to each side.

$x > 1.5$ Simplify.

▶ The solutions are all real numbers greater than 1.5. Check by substituting a number greater than 1.5 for x in the original inequality.

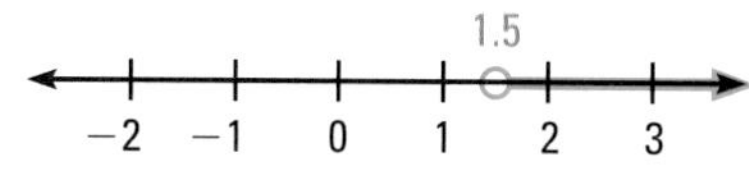

CHECK $x - 5 > -3.5$ Write original inequality.

$6 - 5 \overset{?}{>} -3.5$ Substitute 6 for x.

$1 > -3.5$  Solution checks.

✓ GUIDED PRACTICE for Example 3

Solve the inequality. Graph your solution.

4. $x - 9 \leq 3$

5. $p - 9.2 < -5$

6. $-1 \geq m - \frac{1}{2}$

KEY CONCEPT — *For Your Notebook*

Subtraction Property of Inequality

Words Subtracting the same number from each side of an inequality produces an equivalent inequality.

Algebra If $a > b$, then $a - c > b - c$. If $a \geq b$, then $a - c \geq b - c$.

If $a < b$, then $a - c < b - c$. If $a \leq b$, then $a - c \leq b - c$.

EXAMPLE 4 Solve an inequality using subtraction

Solve $9 \geq x + 7$. Graph your solution.

$9 \geq x + 7$	Write original inequality.
$9 - 7 \geq x + 7 - 7$	Subtract 7 from each side.
$2 \geq x$	Simplify.

▶ You can rewrite $2 \geq x$ as $x \leq 2$. The solutions are all real numbers less than or equal to 2.

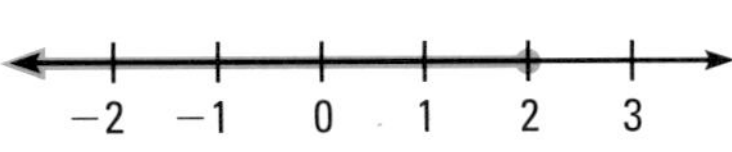

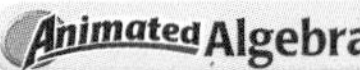

at classzone.com

EXAMPLE 5 Solve a real-world problem

READING The phrase "no more than" indicates that you use the ≤ symbol.

LUGGAGE WEIGHTS You are checking a bag at an airport. Bags can weigh no more than 50 pounds. Your bag weighs 16.8 pounds. Find the possible weights w (in pounds) that you can add to the bag.

Solution

Write a verbal model. Then write and solve an inequality.

Weight of bag	+	Weight you can add	≤	Weight limit
		↓		↓
16.8	+	w	≤	**50**

$16.8 + w \leq 50$	Write inequality.
$16.8 + w - \mathbf{16.8} \leq 50 - \mathbf{16.8}$	Subtract 16.8 from each side.
$w \leq 33.2$	Simplify.

▶ You can add no more than 33.2 pounds.

✓ GUIDED PRACTICE for Examples 4 and 5

7. Solve $y + 5.5 > 6$. Graph your solution.
8. **WHAT IF?** In Example 5, suppose your bag weighs 29.1 pounds. Find the possible weights (in pounds) that you can add to the bag.

6.1 EXERCISES

HOMEWORK KEY

○ = **WORKED-OUT SOLUTIONS** on p. WS13 for Exs. 7, 15, and 33

★ = **STANDARDIZED TEST PRACTICE** Exs. 2, 29, 34, 35, and 38

◆ = **MULTIPLE REPRESENTATIONS** Ex. 37

SKILL PRACTICE

1. **VOCABULARY** Copy and complete: To graph $x < -8$, you draw a(n) __?__ circle at -8, and you draw an arrow to the __?__.

2. ★ **WRITING** Are $x + 7 \geq 18$ and $x \geq 25$ equivalent inequalities? *Explain.*

EXAMPLE 1 on p. 356 for Exs. 3–5

WRITING AND GRAPHING INEQUALITIES Write and graph an inequality that describes the situation.

3. The speed limit on a highway is 60 miles per hour.
4. You must be at least 16 years old to go on a field trip.
5. A child must be taller than 48 inches to get on an amusement park ride.

EXAMPLE 2 on p. 356 for Exs. 6–9

WRITING INEQUALITIES Write an inequality represented by the graph.

6. 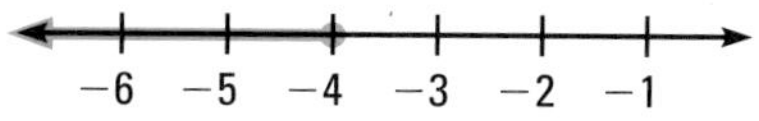

(7.) 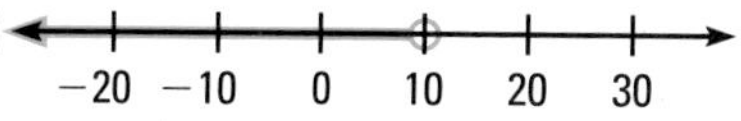

8. 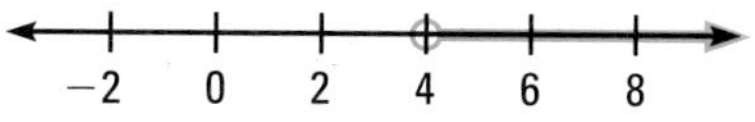

9. 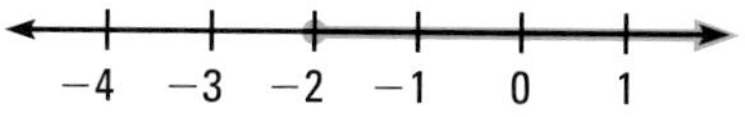

EXAMPLES 3 and 4 on pp. 357–358 for Exs. 10–23

SOLVING INEQUALITIES Solve the inequality. Graph your solution.

10. $x + 4 < 5$
11. $-8 \leq 8 + y$
12. $-1\frac{1}{4} \leq m + 3$
13. $n + 17 \leq 16\frac{4}{5}$
14. $8.2 + v > -7.6$
(15.) $w + 14.9 > -2.7$
16. $r - 4 < -5$
17. $1 \leq s - 8$
18. $-1\frac{1}{3} \leq p - 8\frac{1}{3}$
19. $q - 1\frac{1}{3} > -2\frac{1}{2}$
20. $2.1 \geq c - 6.7$
21. $d - 1.92 > -8.76$

ERROR ANALYSIS *Describe* and correct the error in solving the inequality or in graphing the solution.

22.

$x + 8 < -3$

$x + 8 - 8 < -3 + 8$

$x < 5$

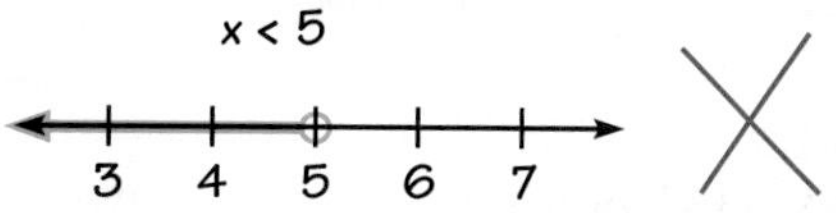

23.

$-17 \leq x - 14$

$-17 + 14 \leq x - 14 + 14$

$-3 \leq x$

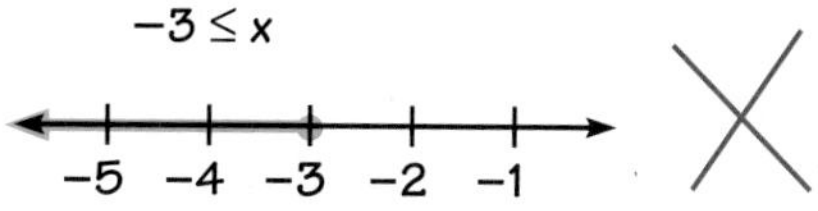

TRANSLATING SENTENCES Write the verbal sentence as an inequality. Then solve the inequality and graph your solution.

24. The sum of 11 and m is greater than -23.
25. The difference of n and 15 is less than or equal to 37.
26. The difference of c and 13 is less than -19.

GEOMETRY **Write and solve an inequality to find the possible values of x.**

27. Perimeter < 51.3 inches

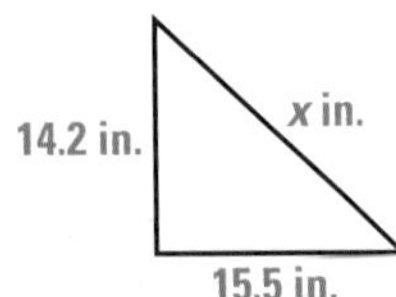

28. Perimeter ≤ 18.7 feet

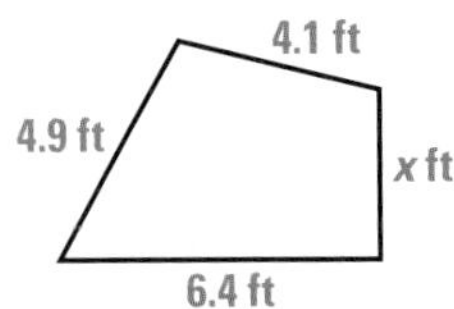

29. ★ **WRITING** Is it possible to check all the numbers that are solutions of an inequality? Does checking one solution guarantee that you have solved an inequality correctly? *Explain* your answers.

30. **CHALLENGE** Write and graph an inequality that represents the numbers that are *not* solutions of $x - 12 \geq 5.7$.

PROBLEM SOLVING

EXAMPLE 5
on p. 358
for Exs. 31–35

31. **INTERNET** You earn points from buying items at an Internet shopping site. You would like to redeem 2350 points to get an item for free, but you want to be sure to have more than 6000 points left over. What are the possible numbers of points you can have before making a redemption?

@HomeTutor for problem solving help at classzone.com

32. **SPORTS RECORDS** In 1982 Wayne Gretsky set a new record for the greatest number of hockey goals in one season with 92 goals. Suppose that a hockey player has 59 goals so far in a season. What are the possible numbers of additional goals that the player can make in order to match or break Wayne Gretsky's record?

@HomeTutor for problem solving help at classzone.com

33. **MULTI-STEP PROBLEM** In aerial ski competitions, athletes perform two acrobatic ski jumps, and the scores on both jumps are added together. The table shows your competitor's first and second scores and your first score.

Ski jump	Competitor's score	Your score
1	127.04	129.49
2	129.98	?

a. Write and solve an inequality to find the scores s that you can earn in your second jump in order to beat your competitor.

b. Will you beat your competitor if you earn 128.13 points? 126.78 points? 127.53 points? *Justify* your answers.

34. ★ **MULTIPLE CHOICE** You want to buy a jacket at a clothing store, and you can spend at most \$30. You have a coupon for \$3 off any item at the store. Which inequality can you use to find the original prices p of jackets that you can buy?

Ⓐ $3 + p \geq 30$ Ⓑ $30 + p \leq 3$ Ⓒ $p - 3 \leq 30$ Ⓓ $p - 30 \geq 3$

35. ★ **OPEN-ENDED** *Describe* a real-world situation that can be modeled by the inequality $x + 14 \geq 17$. *Explain* what the solution of the inequality means in this situation.

36. **VEHICLE WEIGHTS** According to a state law for vehicles traveling on state roads, the maximum total weight of the vehicle and its contents depends on the number of axles the vehicle has.

Maximum Total Weights

2 axles
34,000 lb

3 axles
54,000 lb

4 axles
69,000 lb

5 axles
80,000 lb

For each type of vehicle, write and solve an inequality to find the possible weights w (in pounds) of a vehicle when its contents weigh 14,200 pounds. Can a vehicle that has 2 axles and weighs 20,000 pounds hold 14,200 pounds of contents? *Explain.*

37. **MULTIPLE REPRESENTATIONS** Your friend is willing to spend no more than $17,000 for a new car. The car dealership offers $3000 cash back for the purchase of a new car.

a. **Making a Table** Make a table of values that gives the final price y of a car after the cash back offer is applied to the original price x. Use the following values for x: 19,459, 19,989, 20,549, 22,679, 23,999.

b. **Writing an Inequality** Write and solve an inequality to find the original prices of the cars that your friend will consider buying.

38. ★ **SHORT RESPONSE** A 4-member track team is trying to match or beat last year's winning time of 3 minutes 41.1 seconds for a 1600 meter relay race. The table shows the 400 meter times for the first three athletes.

Athlete	Time (sec)
1	53.34
2	56.38
3	57.46

a. **Calculate** What are the possible times that the last athlete can run 400 meters in order for the team to match or beat last year's time?

b. **Decide** So far this season the last athlete's fastest 400 meter time is 53.18 seconds, and his average 400 meter time is 53.92 seconds. In this race the last athlete expects to run faster than his slowest time this season. Is it possible for the team to fail to meet its goal? *Explain.*

39. **CHALLENGE** A public television station wants to raise at least $72,000 in a pledge drive. The station raised an average of $5953 per day for the first 3 days and an average of $6153 per day for the next 3 days. What are the possible additional amounts that the station can raise to meet its goal?

MIXED REVIEW

Find the sum, difference, product, or quotient.

40. $-18 + (-27)$ *(p. 74)*
41. $15 - (-23)$ *(p. 80)*
42. $7 \cdot (-9)$ *(p. 88)*
43. $-11 \cdot (-12)$ *(p. 88)*
44. $-27 \div (-3)$ *(p. 103)*
45. $-30 \div (-5)$ *(p. 103)*

PREVIEW
Prepare for Lesson 6.2 in Exs. 46–51.

Solve the equation. *(p. 134)*

46. $6x = 48$
47. $-5y = -35$
48. $400 = -48m$
49. $\frac{n}{5} = 10$
50. $\frac{r}{8} = -13$
51. $\frac{s}{-2} = -15$

6.2 Inequalities with Negative Coefficients

MATERIALS • index cards

QUESTION How do you solve an inequality with a negative coefficient?

EXPLORE Check solutions of inequalities

STEP 1 ***Write integers*** Write the integers from -5 to 5 on index cards. Place the cards face up as shown.

−5 −4 −3 −2 −1 0 1 2 3 4 5

STEP 2 ***Check solutions*** Determine whether each integer is a solution of $4x \geq 8$. If the integer is *not* a solution, turn over the card.

2 3 4 5

STEP 3 ***Check solutions*** Turn all the cards face up. Repeat Step 2 for $-4x \geq 8$.

−5 −4 −3 −2

DRAW CONCLUSIONS Use your observations to complete these exercises

1. State an operation that you can perform on both sides of $4x \geq 8$ to obtain the solutions found in Step 2. Then solve the inequality.

2. Copy and complete the steps below for solving $-4x \geq 8$.

$-4x \geq 8$	Write original inequality.
?	Add $4x$ to each side.
?	Subtract 8 from each side.
?	Divide each side by 4.
?	Rewrite inequality with x on the left side.

3. Does dividing both sides of $-4x \geq 8$ by -4 give the solution found in Exercise 2? If not, what else must you do to the inequality when you divide by -4?

4. Do you need to change the direction of the inequality symbol when you divide each side of an inequality by a positive number? by a negative number?

Solve the inequality.

5. $20x \geq 5$ **6.** $-9x \leq 45$ **7.** $-8x > 40$ **8.** $7x < 21$

6.2 Solve Inequalities Using Multiplication and Division

Before You solved inequalities using addition and subtraction.

Now You will solve inequalities using multiplication and division.

Why? So you can find possible distances traveled, as in Ex. 40.

Key Vocabulary
- **inequality,** *p. 21*
- **equivalent inequalities,** *p. 357*

Solving an inequality using multiplication is similar to solving an equation using multiplication, but it is different in an important way.

KEY CONCEPT *For Your Notebook*

Multiplication Property of Inequality

Words Multiplying each side of an inequality by a *positive* number produces an equivalent inequality.

Multiplying each side of an inequality by a *negative* number and *reversing the direction of the inequality symbol* produces an equivalent inequality.

Algebra If $a < b$ and $c > 0$, then $ac < bc$. If $a < b$ and $c < 0$, then $ac > bc$.

If $a > b$ and $c > 0$, then $ac > bc$. If $a > b$ and $c < 0$, then $ac < bc$.

This property is also true for inequalities involving $\leq$ and $\geq$.

EXAMPLE 1 **Solve an inequality using multiplication**

Solve $\frac{x}{4} < 5$. Graph your solution.

$\frac{x}{4} < 5$ Write original inequality.

$4 \cdot \frac{x}{4} < 4 \cdot 5$ Multiply each side by 4.

$x < 20$ Simplify.

▶ The solutions are all real numbers less than 20. Check by substituting a number less than 20 in the original inequality.

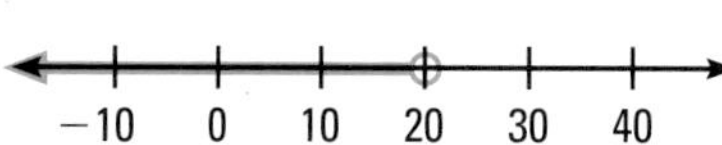

GUIDED PRACTICE for Example 1

Solve the inequality. Graph your solution.

1. $\frac{x}{3} > 8$

2. $\frac{m}{8} \leq -2$

3. $\frac{y}{2.5} \geq -4$

EXAMPLE 2 Solve an inequality using multiplication

Solve $\frac{x}{-6} < 7$. Graph your solution.

$\frac{x}{-6} < 7$	Write original inequality.
$-6 \cdot \frac{x}{-6} > -6 \cdot 7$	Multiply each side by −6. Reverse inequality symbol.
$x > -42$	Simplify.

AVOID ERRORS
Because you are multiplying by a negative number, be sure to reverse the inequality symbol.

▶ The solutions are all real numbers greater than −42. Check by substituting a number greater than −42 in the original inequality.

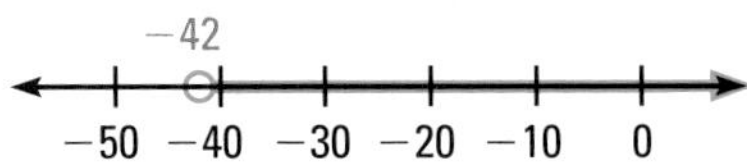

CHECK	$\frac{x}{-6} < 7$	Write original inequality.
	$\frac{0}{-6} \stackrel{?}{<} 7$	Substitute 0 for *x*.
	$0 < 7$ ✓	Solution checks.

USING DIVISION The rules for solving an inequality using division are similar to the rules for solving an inequality using multiplication.

KEY CONCEPT *For Your Notebook*

Division Property of Inequality

Words Dividing each side of an inequality by a *positive* number produces an equivalent inequality.

Dividing each side of an inequality by a *negative* number and *reversing the direction of the inequality symbol* produces an equivalent inequality.

Algebra If $a < b$ and $c > 0$, then $\frac{a}{c} < \frac{b}{c}$. If $a < b$ and $c < 0$, then $\frac{a}{c} > \frac{b}{c}$.

If $a > b$ and $c > 0$, then $\frac{a}{c} > \frac{b}{c}$. If $a > b$ and $c < 0$, then $\frac{a}{c} < \frac{b}{c}$.

This property is also true for inequalities involving ≤ and ≥.

EXAMPLE 3 Solve an inequality using division

Solve $-3x > 24$.

$-3x > 24$	Write original inequality.
$\frac{-3x}{-3} < \frac{24}{-3}$	Divide each side by −3. Reverse inequality symbol.
$x < -8$	Simplify.

Animated **Algebra** at classzone.com

GUIDED PRACTICE for Examples 2 and 3

Solve the inequality. Graph your solution.

4. $\frac{x}{-4} > 12$ **5.** $\frac{m}{-7} < 1.6$ **6.** $5v \geq 45$ **7.** $-6n < 24$

EXAMPLE 4 Standardized Test Practice

A student pilot plans to spend 80 hours on flight training to earn a private license. The student has saved $6000 for training. Which inequality can you use to find the possible hourly rates r that the student can afford to pay for training?

(A) $80r \geq 6000$ (B) $80r \leq 6000$ (C) $6000r \geq 80$ (D) $6000r \leq 80$

Solution

The total cost of training can be at most the amount of money that the student has saved. Write a verbal model for the situation. Then write an inequality.

ELIMINATE CHOICES
You need to multiply the hourly rate and the number of hours, which is 80, not 6000. So, you can eliminate choices C and D.

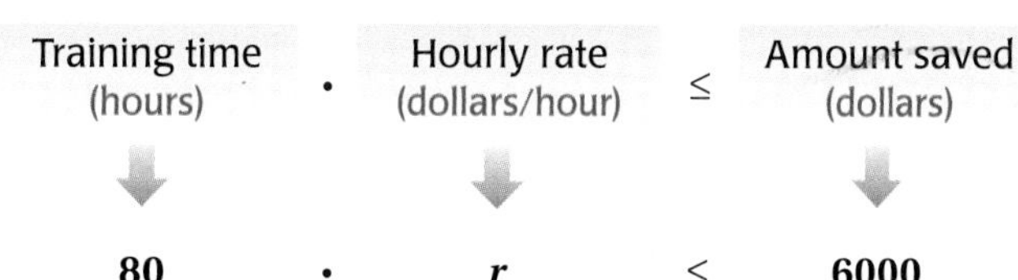

▶ The correct answer is B. (A) (B) (C) (D)

EXAMPLE 5 Solve a real-world problem

PILOTING In Example 4, what are the possible hourly rates that the student can afford to pay for training?

Solution

$80 \cdot r \leq 6000$ **Write inequality.**

$\frac{80r}{80} \leq \frac{6000}{80}$ **Divide each side by 80.**

$r \leq 75$ **Simplify.**

▶ The student can afford to pay at most $75 per hour for training.

GUIDED PRACTICE for Examples 4 and 5

8. **WHAT IF?** In Example 5, suppose the student plans to spend 90 hours on flight training and has saved $6300. Write and solve an inequality to find the possible hourly rates that the student can afford to pay for training.

6.2 EXERCISES

HOMEWORK KEY

◯ = **WORKED-OUT SOLUTIONS** on p. WS14 for Exs. 5, 9, and 39

★ = **STANDARDIZED TEST PRACTICE** Exs. 2, 27, 34, and 41

◆ = **MULTIPLE REPRESENTATIONS** Ex. 38

SKILL PRACTICE

1. **VOCABULARY** Which property are you using when you solve $5x \geq 30$ by dividing each side by 5?

2. ★ **WRITING** Are $\frac{x}{-4} < -9$ and $x < 36$ equivalent inequalities? *Explain* your answer.

EXAMPLES 1, 2, and 3 on pp. 363–364 for Exs. 3–29

SOLVING INEQUALITIES Solve the inequality. Graph your solution.

3. $2p \geq 14$
4. $\frac{x}{-3} < -10$
5. $-6y < -36$
6. $40 > \frac{w}{5}$
7. $\frac{q}{4} < 7$
8. $72 \leq 9r$
9. $\frac{g}{6} > -20$
10. $-11m \leq -22$
11. $-90 \geq 4t$
12. $\frac{n}{3} < -9$
13. $60 \leq -12s$
14. $\frac{v}{-4} \geq -8$
15. $-8.4f > 2.1$
16. $\frac{d}{-2} \leq 18.6$
17. $9.6 < -16c$
18. $0.07 \geq \frac{k}{7}$
19. $-1.5 \geq 6z$
20. $\frac{x}{-5} \leq -7.5$
21. $1.02 < -3j$
22. $\frac{y}{-4.5} \geq -10$
23. $\frac{r}{-30} < 1.8$
24. $1.9 \leq -5p$
25. $\frac{m}{0.6} > -40$
26. $-2t > -1.22$

27. ★ **WRITING** How is solving $ax > b$ where $a > 0$ similar to solving $ax > b$ where $a < 0$? How is it different?

ERROR ANALYSIS ***Describe*** **and correct the error in solving the inequality.**

28.

$$-15x > 45$$
$$\frac{-15x}{-15} > \frac{45}{-15}$$
$$x > -3$$

29.

$$\frac{x}{9} \leq -7$$
$$9 \cdot \frac{x}{9} \leq 9 \cdot (-7)$$
$$x \geq -63$$

TRANSLATING SENTENCES In Exercises 30–33, write the verbal sentence as an inequality. Then solve the inequality and graph your solution.

30. The product of 8 and x is greater than 50.
31. The product of -15 and y is less than or equal to 90.
32. The quotient of v and -9 is less than -18.
33. The quotient of w and 24 is greater than or equal to $-\frac{1}{6}$.

34. ★ **OPEN-ENDED** Write an inequality in the form $ax < b$ such that the solutions are all real numbers greater than 4.

35. **CHALLENGE** For the given values of a and b, tell whether the solution of $ax > b$ consists of *positive numbers, negative numbers,* or *both. Explain.*

a. $a < 0, b > 0$ **b.** $a > 0, b > 0$ **c.** $a > 0, b < 0$ **d.** $a < 0, b < 0$

PROBLEM SOLVING

EXAMPLES 4 and 5 on p. 365 for Exs. 36–39

36. **MUSIC** You have \$90 to buy CDs for your friend's party. The CDs cost \$18 each. What are the possible numbers of CDs that you can buy?

@HomeTutor for problem solving help at classzone.com

37. **JOB SKILLS** You apply for a job that requires the ability to type 40 words per minute. You practice typing on a keyboard for 5 minutes. The average number of words you type per minute must at least meet the job requirement. What are the possible numbers of words that you can type in 5 minutes in order to meet or exceed the job requirement?

@HomeTutor for problem solving help at classzone.com

38. **MULTIPLE REPRESENTATIONS** You are stacking books on a shelf that has a height of 66 centimeters. Each book has a thickness of 4 centimeters.

a. **Using a Model** Use a concrete model to find the possible numbers of books that you can stack as follows: Cut strips of paper 4 centimeters wide to represent the books. Then place the strips one above the other until they form a column no taller than 66 centimeters.

b. **Writing an Inequality** Write and solve an inequality to find the possible numbers of books that you can stack.

c. **Drawing a Graph** Write and graph an equation that gives the height y of stacked books as a function of the number x of books. Then graph $y = 66$ in the same coordinate plane. To find the possible numbers of books that you can stack, identify the integer x-coordinates of the points on the first graph that lie *on or below* the graph of $y = 66$.

d. **Choosing a Method** Suppose the shelf has a height of 100 centimeters. Which method would you use to find the possible numbers of books, *a concrete model, solving an inequality,* or *drawing a graph*? *Explain.*

39. **MANUFACTURING** A manufacturer of architectural moldings recommends that the length of a piece be no more than 15 times its minimum width w (in inches) in order to prevent cracking. For the piece shown, what could the values of w be?

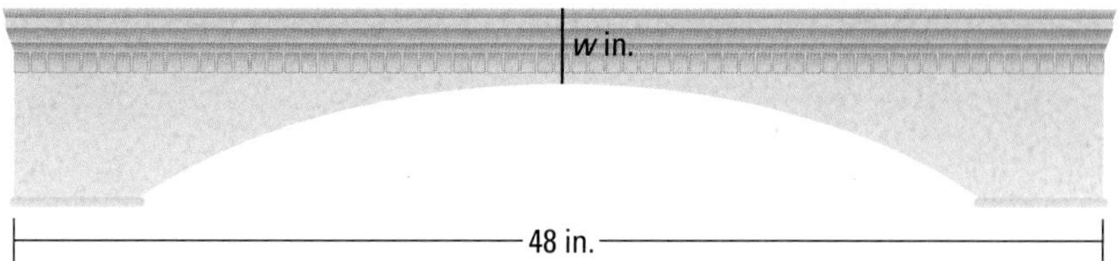

40. **RECREATION** A water-skiing instructor recommends that a boat pulling a beginning skier have a speed less than 18 miles per hour. Write and solve an inequality that you can use to find the possible distances d (in miles) that a beginner can travel in 45 minutes of practice time.

41. ★ **EXTENDED RESPONSE** A state agency that offers wild horses for adoption requires that a potential owner reserve 400 square feet of land per horse in a corral.

a. **Solve** A farmer has a rectangular corral whose length is 80 feet and whose width is 82 feet. Write and solve an inequality to find the possible numbers h of horses that the corral can hold.

b. **Explain** If the farmer increases the length and width of the corral by 20 feet each, will the corral be able to hold only 1 more horse? *Explain* your answer without calculating the new area of the corral.

c. **Calculate** The farmer decides to increase the length and width of the corral by 15 feet each. Find the possible numbers of horses that the corral can hold. Your answer should include the following:

- a calculation of the new area of the corral
- a description of your steps for solving the problem

42. **CHALLENGE** An electronics store is selling a laptop computer for \$1050. You can spend no more than \$900 for the laptop, so you wait for it to go on sale. Also, you plan to use a store coupon for 5% off the sale price. For which decreases in price will you consider buying the laptop?

MIXED REVIEW

Write an expression for the situation. *(p. 15)*

43. Total cost of t movie tickets if each ticket costs \$7.50

44. Distance left to travel on a 500 mile trip if you have traveled m miles

PREVIEW
Prepare for Lesson 6.3 in Exs. 45–50.

Solve the equation or inequality.

45. $9x + 6 = 7$ *(p. 141)*

46. $3y - 8 = 5y + 2y$ *(p. 154)*

47. $4(z + 1) = 6z$ *(p. 154)*

48. $p + 8 > 10$ *(p. 356)*

49. $q + 6 < -5$ *(p. 356)*

50. $r - 2 \geq -9$ *(p. 356)*

Write an equation in slope-intercept form of the line that has the given slope and y-intercept. *(p. 283)*

51. slope: -3; y-intercept: 4

52. slope: -8; y-intercept: $\frac{1}{4}$

53. slope: $\frac{1}{5}$; y-intercept: $-\frac{2}{3}$

QUIZ *for Lessons 6.1–6.2*

Solve the inequality. Graph your solution.

1. $x + 8 \geq -5$ *(p. 356)*

2. $y + 6 < 14$ *(p. 356)*

3. $-8 \leq v - 5$ *(p. 356)*

4. $w - 11 > 2$ *(p. 356)*

5. $-40 < -5r$ *(p. 363)*

6. $-93 < 3s$ *(p. 363)*

7. $-2m \geq 26$ *(p. 363)*

8. $\frac{n}{-4} > -7$ *(p. 363)*

9. $\frac{c}{6} \leq -8$ *(p. 363)*

10. **FOOD PREPARATION** You need to make at least 150 sandwiches for a charity event. You can make 3 sandwiches per minute. How long will it take you to make the number of sandwiches you need? *(p. 363)*

6.3 Solve Multi-Step Inequalities

Before You solved one-step inequalities.
Now You will solve multi-step inequalities.
Why? So you can compare animal habitats, as in Ex. 39.

Key Vocabulary
- **inequality,** *p. 21*

The steps for solving two-step and multi-step equations can be applied to linear inequalities. For inequalities, be sure to reverse the inequality symbol when multiplying or dividing by a negative number.

EXAMPLE 1 Solve a two-step inequality

Solve $3x - 7 < 8$. Graph your solution.

$3x - 7 < 8$ Write original inequality.

$3x < 15$ Add 7 to each side.

$x < 5$ Divide each side by 3.

▶ The solutions are all real numbers less than 5. Check by substituting a number less than 5 in the original inequality.

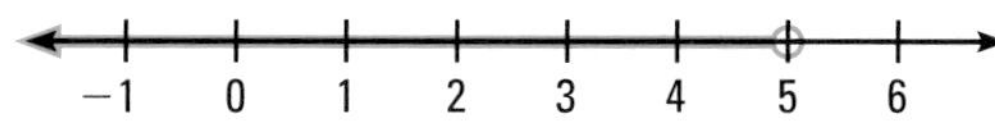

CHECK $3x - 7 < 8$ Write original inequality.

$3(0) - 7 \stackrel{?}{<} 8$ Substitute 0 for *x*.

$-7 < 8$ ✓ Solution checks.

EXAMPLE 2 Solve a multi-step inequality

Solve $-0.6(x - 5) \le 15$.

$-0.6(x - 5) \le 15$ Write original inequality.

$-0.6x + 3 \le 15$ Distributive property

$-0.6x \le 12$ Subtract 3 from each side.

$x \ge -20$ Divide each side by -0.6. Reverse inequality symbol.

GUIDED PRACTICE for Examples 1 and 2

Solve the inequality. Graph your solution.

1. $2x - 5 \le 23$

2. $-6y + 5 \le -16$

3. $-\frac{1}{4}(p - 12) > -2$

EXAMPLE 3 Solve a multi-step inequality

ANOTHER WAY

You can also solve the inequality by subtracting 17 and $6x$ from each side, as follows:

$6x - 7 > 2x + 17$

$6x - 24 > 2x$

$-24 > -4x$

$6 < x$

The inequality $6 < x$ is equivalent to $x > 6$.

Solve $6x - 7 > 2x + 17$. Graph your solution.

$6x - 7 > 2x + 17$	Write original inequality.
$6x > 2x + 24$	Add 7 to each side.
$4x > 24$	Subtract $2x$ from each side.
$x > 6$	Divide each side by 4.

▶ The solutions are all real numbers greater than 6.

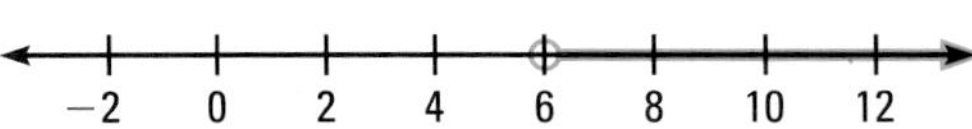

NUMBER OF SOLUTIONS If an inequality is equivalent to an inequality that is true, such as $-3 < 0$, then the solutions of the inequality are *all real numbers*. If an inequality is equivalent to an inequality that is false, such as $4 < -1$, then the inequality has *no solution*.

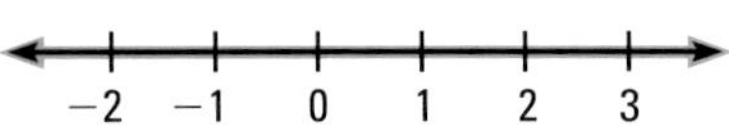

Graph of an inequality whose solutions are all real numbers

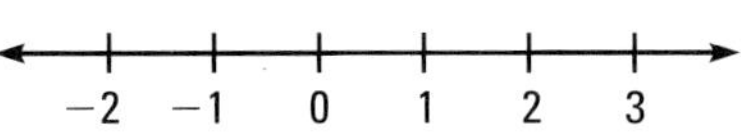

Graph of an inequality that has no solution

EXAMPLE 4 Identify the number of solutions of an inequality

Solve the inequality, if possible.

a. $14x + 5 < 7(2x - 3)$

b. $12x - 1 > 6(2x - 1)$

Solution

a. $14x + 5 < 7(2x - 3)$	Write original inequality.
$14x + 5 < 14x - 21$	Distributive property
$5 < -21$	Subtract $14x$ from each side.

▶ There are no solutions because $5 < -21$ is false.

b. $12x - 1 > 6(2x - 1)$	Write original inequality.
$12x - 1 > 12x - 6$	Distributive property
$-1 > -6$	Subtract $12x$ from each side.

▶ All real numbers are solutions because $-1 > -6$ is true.

✓ GUIDED PRACTICE for Examples 3 and 4

Solve the inequality, if possible. Graph your solution.

4. $5x - 12 \le 3x - 4$

5. $5(m + 5) < 5m + 17$

6. $1 - 8s \le -4(2s - 1)$

EXAMPLE 5 Solve a multi-step problem

CAR WASH Use the sign shown. A gas station charges \$.10 less per gallon of gasoline if a customer also gets a car wash. What are the possible amounts (in gallons) of gasoline that you can buy if you also get a car wash and can spend at most \$20?

ANOTHER WAY
For an alternative method for solving the problem in Example 5, turn to page 375 for the **Problem Solving Workshop**.

Solution

Because you are getting a car wash, you will pay \$2.09 − \$.10 = \$1.99 per gallon of gasoline. Let g be the amount (in gallons) of gasoline that you buy.

STEP 1 **Write** a verbal model. Then write an inequality.

Price of gasoline (dollars/gallon)	•	Amount of gasoline (gallons)	+	Price of car wash (dollars)	≤	Maximum amount (dollars)
1.99	•	g	+	**8**	≤	**20**

STEP 2 **Solve** the inequality.

$1.99g + 8 \leq 20$ **Write inequality.**

$1.99g \leq 12$ **Subtract 8 from each side.**

$g \leq 6.03015\ldots$ **Divide each side by 1.99.**

▶ You can buy up to slightly more than 6 gallons of gasoline.

CHECK You can use a table to check the reasonableness of your answer.

The table shows that you will pay \$19.94 for exactly 6 gallons of gasoline. Because \$19.94 is less than \$20, it is reasonable to conclude that you can buy slightly more than 6 gallons of gasoline.

Gasoline (gal)	Total amount spent (dollars)
0	8.00
1	9.99
2	11.98
3	13.97
4	15.96
5	17.95
6	19.94

✓ GUIDED PRACTICE for Example 5

7. **WHAT IF?** In Example 5, suppose that a car wash costs \$9 and gasoline regularly costs \$2.19 per gallon. What are the possible amounts (in gallons) of gasoline that you can buy?

8. **CAMP COSTS** You are saving money for a summer camp that costs \$1800. You have saved \$500 so far, and you have 14 more weeks to save the total amount. What are the possible average amounts of money that you can save per week in order to have a total of at least \$1800 saved?

6.3 EXERCISES

HOMEWORK KEY

○ = **WORKED-OUT SOLUTIONS** on p. WS14 for Exs. 5, 19, and 39

★ = **STANDARDIZED TEST PRACTICE** Exs. 2, 33, 39, 40, and 42

◆ = **MULTIPLE REPRESENTATIONS** Ex. 41

SKILL PRACTICE

1. **VOCABULARY** Copy and complete: The inequalities $3x - 1 < 11$, $3x < 12$, and $x < 4$ are called __?__.

2. ★ **WRITING** How do you know whether an inequality has no solutions? How do you know whether the solutions are all real numbers?

EXAMPLES 1, 2, and 3 on pp. 369–370 for Exs. 3–16

SOLVING INEQUALITIES **Solve the inequality. Graph your solution.**

3. $2x - 3 > 7$
4. $5y + 9 \leq 4$
5. $8v - 3 \geq -11$
6. $3(w + 12) < 0$
7. $7(r - 3) \geq -13$
8. $2(s + 4) \leq 16$
9. $4 - 2m > 7 - 3m$
10. $8n - 2 > 17n + 9$
11. $-10p > 6p - 8$
12. $4 - \frac{1}{2}q \leq 33 - q$
13. $-\frac{2}{3}d - 2 < \frac{1}{3}d + 8$
14. $8 - \frac{4}{5}f > -14 - 2f$

ERROR ANALYSIS ***Describe*** **and correct the error in solving the inequality.**

15.
$17 - 3x \geq 56$
$-3x \geq 39$
$x \geq -13$
✗

16.
$-4(2x - 3) < 28$
$-8x - 12 < 28$
$-8x < 40$
$x > -5$
✗

EXAMPLE 4 on p. 370 for Exs. 17–28

SOLVING INEQUALITIES **Solve the inequality, if possible.**

17. $3p - 5 > 2p + p - 7$
18. $5d - 8d - 4 \leq -4 + 3d$
19. $3(s - 4) \geq 2(s - 6)$
20. $2(t - 3) > 2t - 8$
21. $5(b + 9) \leq 5b + 45$
22. $2(4c - 7) \geq 8(c - 3)$
23. $6(x + 3) < 5x + 18 + x$
24. $4 + 9y - 3 \geq 3(3y + 2)$
25. $2.2h + 0.4 \leq 2(1.1h - 0.1)$
26. $9.5j - 6 + 5.5j \geq 3(5j - 2)$
27. $\frac{1}{5}(4m + 10) < \frac{4}{5}m + 2$
28. $\frac{3}{4}(8n - 4) < -3(1 - 2n)$

TRANSLATING PHRASES **Translate the verbal phrase into an inequality. Then solve the inequality and graph your solution.**

29. Four more than the product of 3 and x is less than 40.
30. Twice the sum of x and 8 is greater than or equal to -36.
31. The sum of $5x$ and $2x$ is greater than the difference of $9x$ and 4.
32. The product of 6 and the difference of $6x$ and 3 is less than or equal to the product of -2 and the sum of 4 and $8x$.

33. ★ **MULTIPLE CHOICE** For which values of a and b are all the solutions of $ax + b > 0$ positive?

   (A) $a > 0, b > 0$ (B) $a < 0, b < 0$ (C) $a > 0, b < 0$ (D) $a < 0, b = 0$

GEOMETRY **Write and solve an inequality to find the possible values of x.**

34. Area > 81 square feet

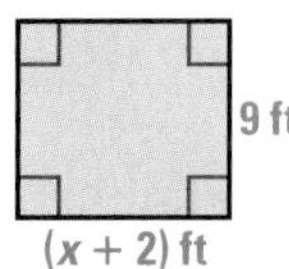

35. Area ≤ 44 square centimeters

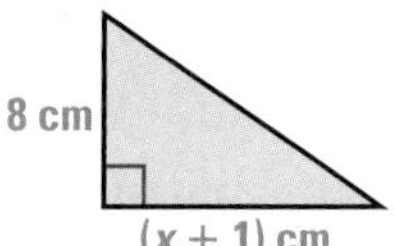

36. CHALLENGE For which value of a are all the solutions of $2(x - 5) \geq 3x + a$ less than or equal to 5?

PROBLEM SOLVING

EXAMPLE 5 on p. 371 for Exs. 37–40

37. CD BURNING A blank CD can hold 70 minutes of music. So far you have burned 25 minutes of music onto the CD. You estimate that each song lasts 4 minutes. What are the possible numbers of additional songs that you can burn onto the CD?

@HomeTutor for problem solving help at classzone.com

38. BUSINESS You spend \$46 on supplies to make wooden ornaments and plan to sell the ornaments for \$8.50 each. What are the possible numbers of ornaments that you can sell in order for your profit to be positive?

@HomeTutor for problem solving help at classzone.com

39. ★ **SHORT RESPONSE** A zookeeper is designing a rectangular habitat for swans, as shown. The zookeeper needs to reserve 500 square feet for the first 2 swans and 125 square feet for each additional swan.

20 ft

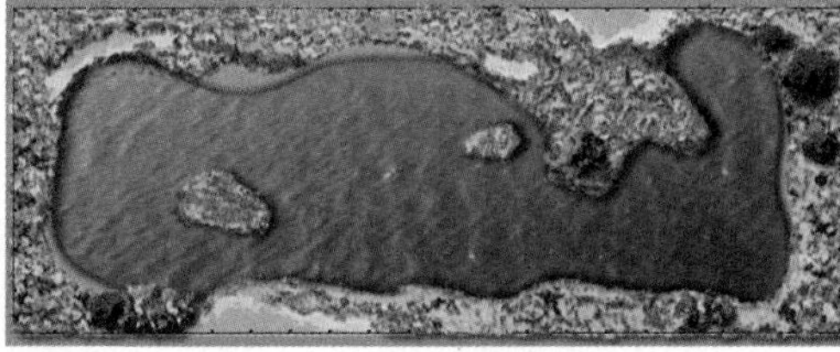

50 ft

a. **Calculate** What are the possible numbers of swans that the habitat can hold? *Explain* how you got your answer.

b. **Compare** Suppose that the zookeeper increases both the length and width of the habitat by 20 feet. What are the possible numbers of additional swans that the habitat can hold?

40. ★ **MULTIPLE CHOICE** A gym is offering a trial membership for 3 months by discounting the regular monthly rate by \$50. You will consider joining the gym if the total cost of the trial membership is less than \$100. Which inequality can you use to find the possible regular monthly rates that you are willing to pay?

(A) $3x - 50 < 100$ (B) $3x - 50 > 100$

(C) $3(x - 50) < 100$ (D) $3(x - 50) > 100$

41. **MULTIPLE REPRESENTATIONS** A baseball pitcher makes 53 pitches in the first four innings of a game and plans to pitch in the next 3 innings.

a. **Making a Table** Make a table that gives the total number t of pitches made if the pitcher makes an average of p pitches per inning in the next 3 innings. Use the following values for p: 15, 16, 17, 18, 19.

b. **Writing an Inequality** The baseball coach assigns a maximum of 105 pitches to the pitcher for the game. Write and solve an inequality to find the possible average numbers of pitches that the pitcher can make in each of the next three innings.

42. ★ **EXTENDED RESPONSE** A state imposes a sales tax on items of clothing that cost more than \$175. The tax applies only to the difference of the price of the item and \$175.

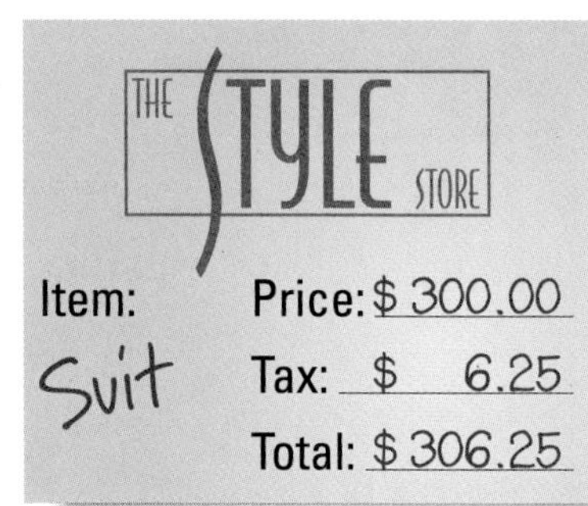

a. **Calculate** Use the receipt shown to find the tax rate (as a percent). *Explain* how you got your answer.

b. **Apply** A shopper has \$400 to spend on a winter coat. Write and solve an inequality to find the prices p of coats that the shopper can afford. Assume that $p \geq 175$.

c. **Compare** Another state imposes a 4% sales tax on the entire price of an item of clothing. For which prices would paying the 4% tax be cheaper than paying the tax described above? Your answer should include the following:

- writing and solving an inequality that describes the situation
- checking the reasonableness of your answer using one of the solutions of the inequality

43. **CHALLENGE** Your scores in four bowling league tournaments are 157, 161, 149, and 172. After the next game, you want your average score to be at least 167. What are the possible scores that you can earn in your next tournament in order to meet your goal?

MIXED REVIEW

44. Using the positive integers less than 10, draw a Venn diagram where set A consists of factors of 30 and set B consists of odd numbers. Then tell whether this statement is *true* or *false*: "If a positive integer less than 10 is odd, then it is a factor of 30." *Explain* your reasoning. *(p. 930)*

Simplify the expression.

45. $11(-y)(-y)$ *(p. 88)*

46. $\frac{3}{4} \cdot (-16y)$ *(p. 88)*

47. $-2(x + 1) - 7x$ *(p. 96)*

48. $5x + 4 - 3x$ *(p. 96)*

49. $8(x + 6) - 5$ *(p. 96)*

50. $\frac{-15x + 18}{-6}$ *(p. 103)*

PREVIEW
Prepare for Lesson 6.4 in Exs. 51–56.

Solve the inequality. Graph your solution.

51. $x + 7 < 8$ *(p. 356)*

52. $y - 4 \geq -2$ *(p. 356)*

53. $9 \leq z + 13$ *(p. 356)*

54. $4.8 > m - 7.4$ *(p. 356)*

55. $\frac{n}{4} < -1$ *(p. 363)*

56. $4p \geq 52$ *(p. 363)*

PROBLEM SOLVING WORKSHOP LESSON 6.3

Using ALTERNATIVE METHODS

Another Way to Solve Example 5, page 371

MULTIPLE REPRESENTATIONS In Example 5 on page 371, you saw how to solve a problem about buying gasoline using an inequality. You can also solve the problem by working backward or by using a graph.

PROBLEM

CAR WASH Use the sign shown. A gas station charges $.10 less per gallon of gasoline if a customer also gets a car wash. What are the possible amounts (in gallons) of gasoline that you can buy if you also get a car wash and can spend at most $20?

METHOD 1

Work backward One alternative approach is to work backward.

STEP 1 **Read** the problem. It gives you the following information:

- amount you can spend: up to $20
- price of a car wash: $8
- regular price per gallon of gasoline: $2.09
- discount per gallon of gasoline when you get a car wash: $.10

Because you are getting a car wash, gasoline costs $2.09 − $.10, or $1.99, per gallon.

STEP 2 **Work** backward.

- Start with the amount you have to spend: $20.
- Subtract the cost of a car wash: $20 − $8 = $12.
- Make a table of values showing the amount of money you have left after buying various amounts of gasoline.

Gasoline (gal)	Amount of money left	
0	$12.00	
1	$10.01	− $1.99
2	$8.02	− $1.99
3	$6.03	− $1.99
4	$4.04	− $1.99
5	$2.05	− $1.99
6	$.06	− $1.99

▶ You can buy up to slightly more than 6 gallons of gasoline.

METHOD 2 **Using a graph** Another alternative approach is to use a graph.

STEP 1 **Write** a verbal model. Then write an equation that gives the total amount of money y (in dollars) that you spend as a function of the amount x (in gallons) of gasoline that you buy.

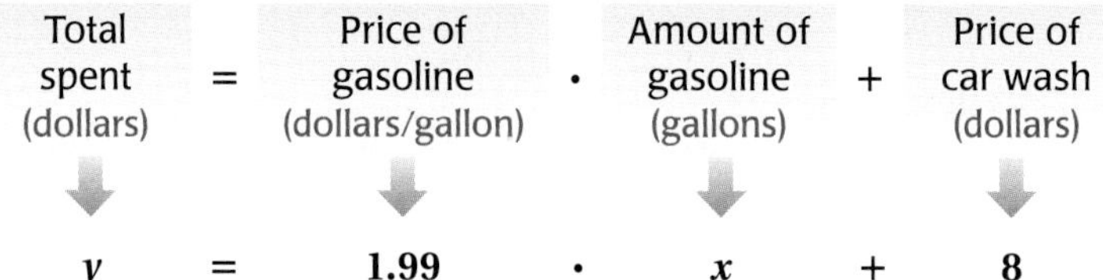

Total spent (dollars) = Price of gasoline (dollars/gallon) • Amount of gasoline (gallons) + Price of car wash (dollars)

$$y = 1.99 \cdot x + 8$$

STEP 2 **Graph** $y = 1.99x + 8$.

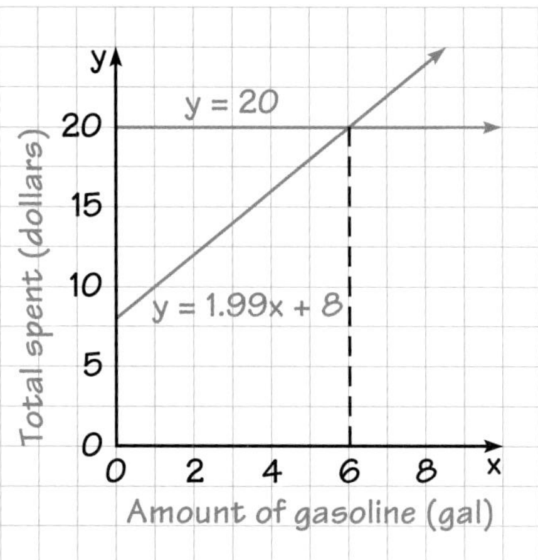

STEP 3 **Graph** $y = 20$ in the same coordinate plane. This equation gives the maximum amount of money that you can spend for gasoline and a car wash.

STEP 4 **Analyze** the graphs. The point of intersection shows that you can buy slightly more than 6 gallons of gasoline when you spend $20. Because you can spend *at most* $20, the solutions are the x-coordinates of the points on the graph of $y = 1.99x + 8$ that lie *on or below* the graph of $y = 20$.

▶ You can buy up to slightly more than 6 gallons of gasoline.

PRACTICE

1. **BAKING** You need to bake at least 100 cookies for a bake sale. You can bake 12 cookies per batch of dough. What are the possible numbers of batches that will allow you to bake enough cookies? Solve this problem using two different methods.

2. **VIDEO GAMES** A video game console costs $259, and games cost $29 each. You saved $400 to buy a console and games. What are the possible numbers of games that you can buy? Solve this problem using two different methods.

3. **WHAT IF?** In Exercise 2, suppose that you saved $500 and decide to buy a video game console that costs $299. What are the possible numbers of games that you can buy?

4. **MONEY** You need to have at least $100 in your checking account to avoid a low balance fee. You have $247 in your account, and you make withdrawals of $20 per week. What are the possible numbers of weeks that you can withdraw money and avoid paying the fee? Solve this problem using two different methods.

5. **RUNNING TIMES** You are running a 10 mile race. You run the first 3 miles in 24.7 minutes. Your goal is to finish the race in less than 1 hour 20 minutes. What should your average running time (in minutes per mile) be for the remaining miles?

Solve Linear Inequalities by Graphing

GOAL Use graphs to solve linear inequalities.

So far in Chapter 6 you have seen how to solve linear inequalities algebraically. You can also solve linear inequalities graphically.

KEY CONCEPT *For Your Notebook*

Solving Linear Inequalities Graphically

STEP 1 **Write** the inequality in one of the following forms: $ax + b < 0$, $ax + b \le 0$, $ax + b > 0$, or $ax + b \ge 0$.

STEP 2 **Write** the related equation $y = ax + b$.

STEP 3 **Graph** the equation $y = ax + b$.

- The solutions of $ax + b > 0$ are the x-coordinates of the points on the graph of $y = ax + b$ that lie above the x-axis.
- The solutions of $ax + b < 0$ are the x-coordinates of the points on the graph of $y = ax + b$ that lie below the x-axis.
- If the inequality symbol is $\le$ or $\ge$, then the x-intercept of the graph is also a solution.

EXAMPLE 1 Solve an inequality graphically

Solve $3x + 2 > 8$ graphically.

Solution

STEP 1 **Write** the inequality in the form $ax + b > 0$.

$3x + 2 > 8$ **Write original inequality.**

$3x - 6 > 0$ **Subtract 8 from each side.**

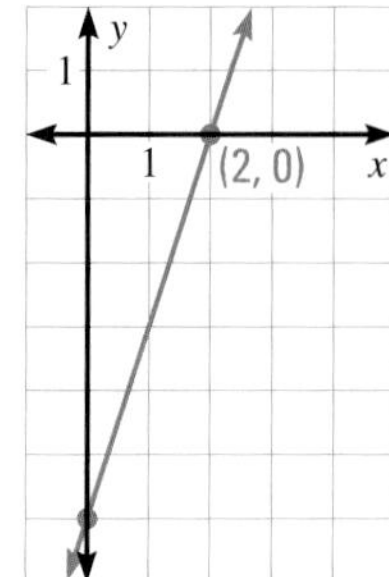

STEP 2 **Write** the related equation $y = 3x - 6$.

STEP 3 **Graph** the equation $y = 3x - 6$.

The inequality in Step 1 is in the form $ax + b > 0$, and the x-intercept of the graph in Step 3 is 2. So, $x > 2$.

▶ The solutions are all real numbers greater than 2. Check by substituting a number greater than 2 in the original inequality.

CHECK $3x + 2 > 8$ **Write original inequality.**

$3(4) + 2 \stackrel{?}{>} 8$ **Substitute 4 for *x*.**

$14 > 8$ ✓ **Solution checks.**

EXAMPLE 2 Approximate a real-world solution

CELL PHONES Your cell phone plan costs \$49.99 per month for a given number of minutes. Each additional minute or part of a minute costs \$.40. You budgeted \$55 per month for phone costs. What are the possible additional minutes x that you can afford each month?

Solution

STEP 1 **Write** a verbal model. Then write an inequality.

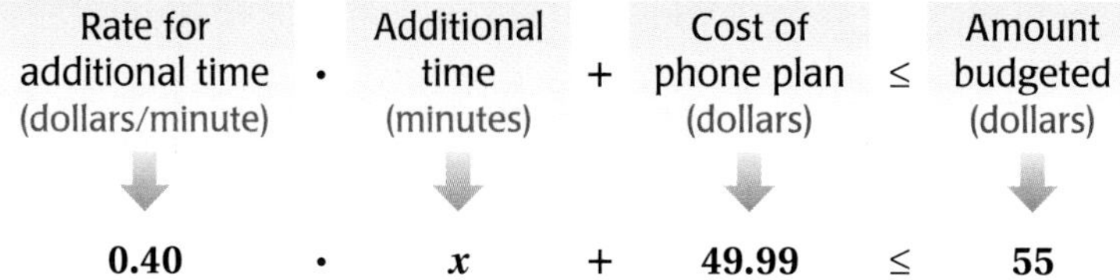

Rate for additional time (dollars/minute)
•
Additional time (minutes)
+
Cost of phone plan (dollars)
≤
Amount budgeted (dollars)
0.40
•
x
+
49.99
≤
55

Write the inequality in the form $ax + b \le 0$.

$0.40x + 49.99 \le 55$ **Write original inequality.**

$0.40x - 5.01 \le 0$ **Subtract 55 from each side.**

STEP 2 **Write** the related equation $y = 0.40x - 5.01$.

STEP 3 **Graph** the equation $y = 0.40x - 5.01$ on a graphing calculator.

Use the *trace* feature of the graphing calculator to find the x-intercept of the graph.

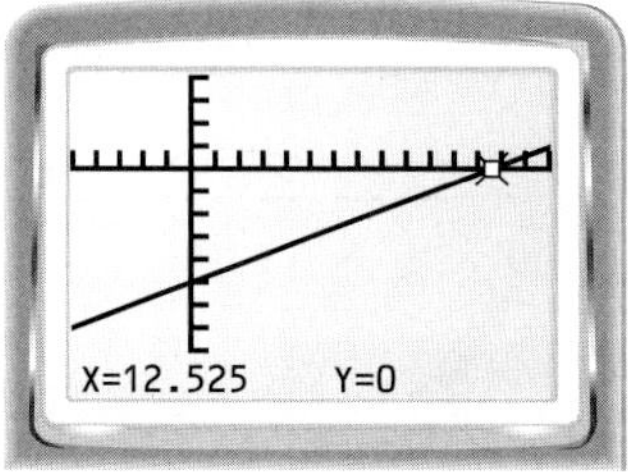

The inequality in Step 1 is in the form $ax + b \le 0$, and the x-intercept is about 12.5. Because a part of a minute costs \$.40, round 12.5 down to 12 to be sure that you stay within your budget.

▶ You can afford up to 12 additional minutes.

PRACTICE

EXAMPLES 1 and 2 on pp. 377–378 for Exs. 1–4

Solve the inequality graphically.

1. $2x + 5 > 11$

2. $\frac{1}{2}x + 6 \le 13$

3. $0.2x - 15.75 < 27$

4. CABLE COSTS Your family has a cable television package that costs \$40.99 per month. Pay-per-view movies cost \$3.95 each. Your family budgets \$55 per month for cable television costs. What are the possible numbers of pay-per-view movies that your family can afford each month?

6.4 Statements with *And* and *Or*

MATERIALS • paper and pencil

QUESTION **What is the difference between a statement with *and* and a statement with *or*?**

EXPLORE **Use a Venn diagram to answer questions about a group**

STEP 1 ***Answer questions*** Copy the questions below and write your answers beside them.

1. Are you taking an art class?
2. Are you taking a foreign language class?

STEP 2 ***Complete a Venn diagram*** Form a group with 3 or 4 classmates. Draw a Venn diagram, like the one shown below, where set A consists of students taking an art class, and set B consists of students taking a foreign language class. Then write the name of each student in the appropriate section of the diagram.

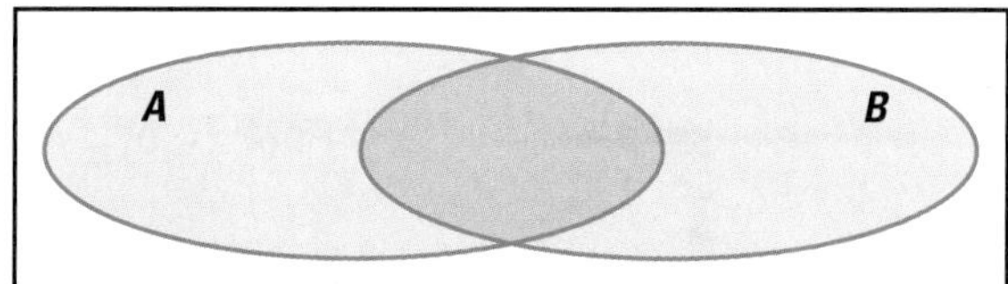

DRAW CONCLUSIONS **Use your observations to complete these exercises**

In Exercises 1–3, use your Venn diagram to list the students who belong in the given set.

1. Set A
2. Set B
3. Set A *and* set B
4. The students who belong in set A *or* set B are all of the students who belong only in set A, only in set B, or in set A *and* set B. List the students in your group who belong in set A *or* set B.
5. **OPEN-ENDED** Write a statement with *and* so that the statement is true for all students in your group.
6. **OPEN-ENDED** Write a statement with *or* so that the statement is true for all students in your group.

REASONING **Tell whether the statement is *true* or *false*.**

7. If a student belongs in set A *and* set B, then the student belongs in set A *or* set B.
8. If a student belongs in set A *or* set B, then the student belongs in set A *and* set B.

6.4 Solve Compound Inequalities

Before You solved one-step and multi-step inequalities.

Now You will solve compound inequalities.

Why? So you can describe possible heights, as in Example 2.

Key Vocabulary
- **compound inequality**

A **compound inequality** consists of two separate inequalities joined by *and* or *or*.

The graph of a compound inequality with *and* is the *intersection* of the graphs of the inequalities.

$x > -2$

$x \leq 1$

$-2 < x$ and $x \leq 1$
$-2 < x \leq 1$

The graph of a compound inequality with *or* is the *union* of the graphs of the inequalities.

$x \geq 0$

$x < -1$

$x < -1$ or $x \geq 0$

EXAMPLE 1 Write and graph compound inequalities

Translate the verbal phrase into an inequality. Then graph the inequality.

a. All real numbers that are greater than −2 *and* less than 3

Inequality: $-2 < x < 3$

Graph:

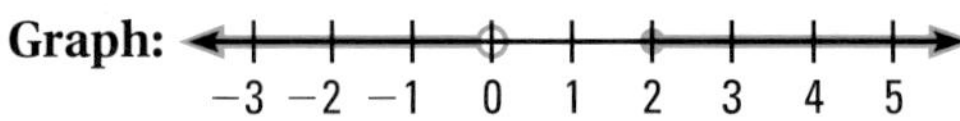

b. All real numbers that are less than 0 *or* greater than or equal to 2

Inequality: $x < 0$ *or* $x \geq 2$

Graph:

GUIDED PRACTICE for Example 1

Translate the verbal phrase into an inequality. Then graph the inequality.

1. All real numbers that are less than −1 *or* greater than or equal to 4
2. All real numbers that are greater than or equal to −3 *and* less than 5

EXAMPLE 2 Write and graph a real-world compound inequality

CAMERA CARS A crane sits on top of a camera car and faces toward the front. The crane's maximum height and minimum height above the ground are shown. Write and graph a compound inequality that describes the possible heights of the crane.

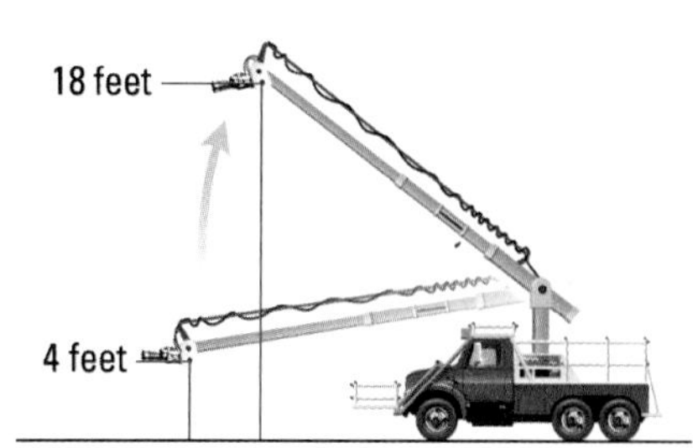

Solution

Let h represent the height (in feet) of the crane. All possible heights are greater than or equal to 4 feet *and* less than or equal to 18 feet. So, the inequality is $4 \le h \le 18$.

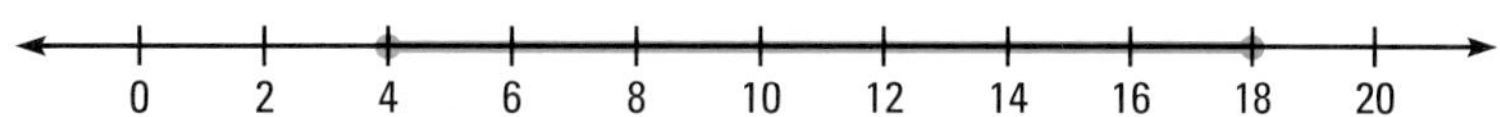

SOLVING COMPOUND INEQUALITIES A number is a solution of a compound inequality with *and* if the number is a solution of *both* inequalities. A number is a solution of a compound inequality with *or* if the number is a solution of *at least one* of the inequalities.

EXAMPLE 3 Solve a compound inequality with *and*

Solve $2 < x + 5 < 9$. Graph your solution.

Solution

Separate the compound inequality into two inequalities. Then solve each inequality separately.

$2 < x + 5$	*and*	$x + 5 < 9$	Write two inequalities.
$2 - 5 < x + 5 - 5$	*and*	$x + 5 - 5 < 9 - 5$	Subtract 5 from each side.
$-3 < x$	*and*	$x < 4$	Simplify.

The compound inequality can be written as $-3 < x < 4$.

▶ The solutions are all real numbers greater than -3 *and* less than 4.

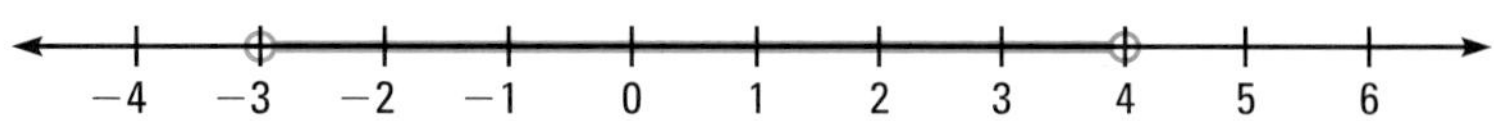

✓ **GUIDED PRACTICE** for Examples 2 and 3

3. **INVESTING** An investor buys shares of a stock and will sell them if the change c in value from the purchase price of a share is less than $-\$3.00$ or greater than \$4.50. Write and graph a compound inequality that describes the changes in value for which the shares will be sold.

Solve the inequality. Graph your solution.

4. $-7 < x - 5 < 4$
5. $10 \le 2y + 4 \le 24$
6. $-7 < -z - 1 < 3$

ANOTHER WAY In Example 3, you could solve $2 < x + 5 < 9$ by subtracting 5 from 2, $x + 5$, and 9 without first separating the compound inequality into two separate inequalities. To solve a compound inequality with *and*, you perform the same operation on each expression.

EXAMPLE 4 Solve a compound inequality with *and*

Solve $-5 \le -x - 3 \le 2$. Graph your solution.

$-5 \le -x - 3 \le 2$	**Write original inequality.**
$-5 + 3 \le -x - 3 + 3 \le 2 + 3$	**Add 3 to each expression.**
$-2 \le -x \le 5$	**Simplify.**
$-1(-2) \ge -1(-x) \ge -1(5)$	**Multiply each expression by −1 and reverse *both* inequality symbols.**
$2 \ge x \ge -5$	**Simplify.**
$-5 \le x \le 2$	**Rewrite in the form $a \le x \le b$.**

▶ The solutions are all real numbers greater than or equal to −5 *and* less than or equal to 2.

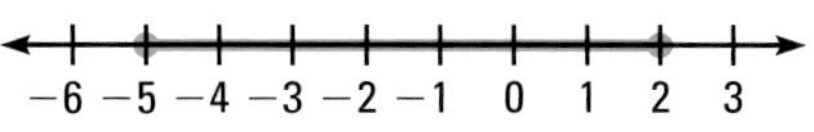

EXAMPLE 5 Solve a compound inequality with *or*

Solve $2x + 3 < 9$ *or* $3x - 6 > 12$. Graph your solution.

Solution

Solve the two inequalities separately.

$2x + 3 < 9$	*or*	$3x - 6 > 12$	**Write original inequality.**
$2x + 3 - 3 < 9 - 3$	*or*	$3x - 6 + 6 > 12 + 6$	**Addition or subtraction property of inequality**
$2x < 6$	*or*	$3x > 18$	**Simplify.**
$\frac{2x}{2} < \frac{6}{2}$	*or*	$\frac{3x}{3} > \frac{18}{3}$	**Division property of inequality**
$x < 3$	*or*	$x > 6$	**Simplify.**

▶ The solutions are all real numbers less than 3 *or* greater than 6.

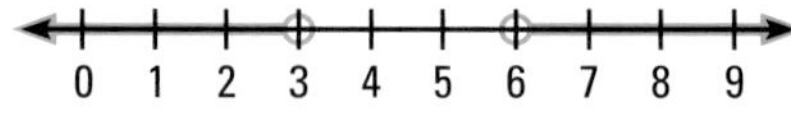

Animated Algebra at classzone.com

✓ GUIDED PRACTICE for Examples 4 and 5

Solve the inequality. Graph your solution.

7. $-14 < x - 8 < -1$

8. $-1 \le -5t + 2 \le 4$

9. $3h + 1 < -5$ *or* $2h - 5 > 7$

10. $4c + 1 \le -3$ *or* $5c - 3 > 17$

EXAMPLE 6 Solve a multi-step problem

ASTRONOMY The Mars Exploration Rovers *Opportunity* and *Spirit* are robots that were sent to Mars in 2003 in order to gather geological data about the planet. The temperature at the landing sites of the robots can range from −100°C to 0°C.

- Write a compound inequality that describes the possible temperatures (in degrees Fahrenheit) at a landing site.
- Solve the inequality. Then graph your solution.
- Identify three possible temperatures (in degrees Fahrenheit) at a landing site.

Solution

Let F represent the temperature in degrees Fahrenheit, and let C represent the temperature in degrees Celsius. Use the formula $C = \frac{5}{9}(F - 32)$.

STEP 1 **Write** a compound inequality. Because the temperature at a landing site ranges from −100°C to 0°C, the lowest possible temperature is −100°C, and the highest possible temperature is 0°C.

$-100 \le C \le 0$ **Write inequality using C.**

$-100 \le \frac{5}{9}(F - 32) \le 0$ **Substitute $\frac{5}{9}(F - 32)$ for C.**

STEP 2 **Solve** the inequality. Then graph your solution.

$-100 \le \frac{5}{9}(F - 32) \le 0$ **Write inequality from Step 1.**

$-180 \le F - 32 \le 0$ **Multiply each expression by $\frac{9}{5}$.**

$-148 \le F \le 32$ **Add 32 to each expression.**

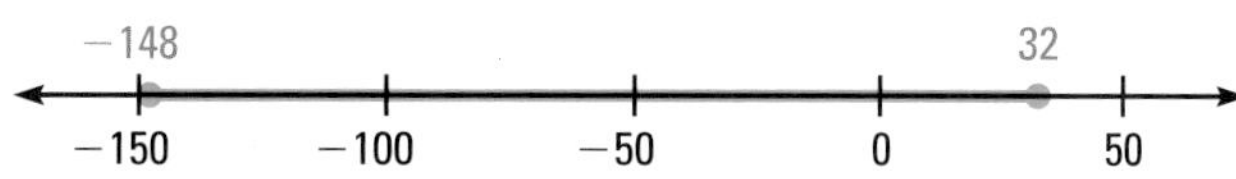

ANOTHER WAY

You can solve the compound inequality by multiplying through by 9:

$-100 \le \frac{5}{9}(F - 32) \le 0$

$-900 \le 5(F - 32) \le 0$

$-900 \le 5F - 160 \le 0$

$-740 \le 5F \le 160$

$-148 \le F \le 32$

STEP 3 **Identify** three possible temperatures.

The temperature at a landing site is greater than or equal to −148°F *and* less than or equal to 32°F. Three possible temperatures are −115°F, 15°F, and 32°F.

✓ GUIDED PRACTICE for Example 6

11. MARS Mars has a maximum temperature of 27°C at the equator and a minimum temperature of −133°C at the winter pole.

- Write and solve a compound inequality that describes the possible temperatures (in degrees Fahrenheit) on Mars.
- Graph your solution. Then identify three possible temperatures (in degrees Fahrenheit) on Mars.

6.4 EXERCISES

HOMEWORK KEY

○ = **WORKED-OUT SOLUTIONS** on p. WS14 for Exs. 7, 11, and 41

★ = **STANDARDIZED TEST PRACTICE** Exs. 2, 27, 39, and 45

◆ = **MULTIPLE REPRESENTATIONS** Ex. 43

SKILL PRACTICE

1. VOCABULARY Copy and complete: A(n) _?_ is an inequality that consists of two inequalities joined by *and* or *or*.

2. ★ WRITING *Describe* the difference between the graphs of $-6 \le x \le -4$ and $x \le -6$ *or* $x \ge -4$.

EXAMPLE 1 on p. 380 for Exs. 3–6

TRANSLATING VERBAL PHRASES Translate the verbal phrase into an inequality. Then graph the inequality.

3. All real numbers that are less than 6 *and* greater than 2

4. All real numbers that are less than or equal to -8 *or* greater than 12

5. All real numbers that are greater than or equal to -1.5 *and* less than 9.2

6. All real numbers that are greater than or equal to $-7\frac{1}{2}$ *or* less than or equal to -10

EXAMPLE 2 on p. 381 for Exs. 7–8

WRITING AND GRAPHING INEQUALITIES Write and graph an inequality that describes the situation.

7. The minimum speed on a highway is 40 miles per hour, and the maximum speed is 60 miles per hour.

8. The temperature inside a room is uncomfortable if the temperature is lower than 60°F or higher than 75°F.

EXAMPLES 3, 4, and 5 on pp. 381–382 for Exs. 9–22

SOLVING COMPOUND INEQUALITIES Solve the inequality. Graph your solution.

9. $6 < x + 5 \le 11$

10. $-7 > y - 8 \ge -12$

11. $-1 \le -4m \le 16$

12. $-6 < 3n + 9 < 21$

13. $-15 \le 5(3p - 2) < 20$

14. $7 > \frac{2}{3}(6q + 18) \ge -9$

15. $2r + 3 < 7$ *or* $-r + 9 \le 2$

16. $16 < -s - 6$ *or* $2s + 5 \ge 11$

17. $v + 13 < 8$ *or* $-8v < -40$

18. $-14 > w + 3$ *or* $5w - 13 > w + 7$

19. $9g - 6 > 12g + 1$ *or* $4 > -\frac{2}{5}g + 8$

20. $-2h - 7 > h + 5$ *or* $\frac{1}{4}(h + 8) \ge 9$

ERROR ANALYSIS ***Describe*** **and correct the error in solving the inequality or in graphing the solution.**

21.

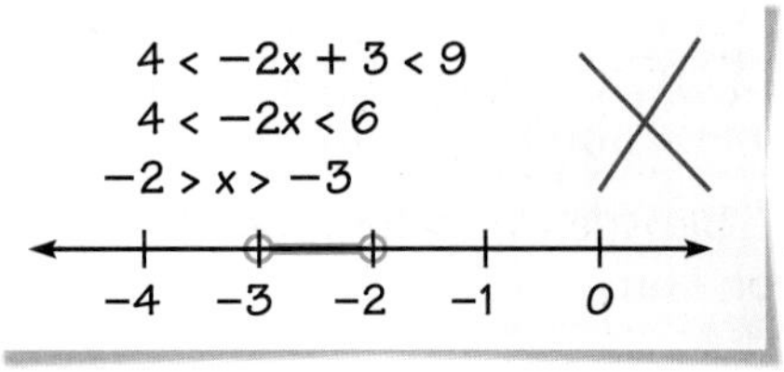
4 < −2x + 3 < 9
4 < −2x < 6
−2 > x > −3
−4
−3
−2
−1
0

22.

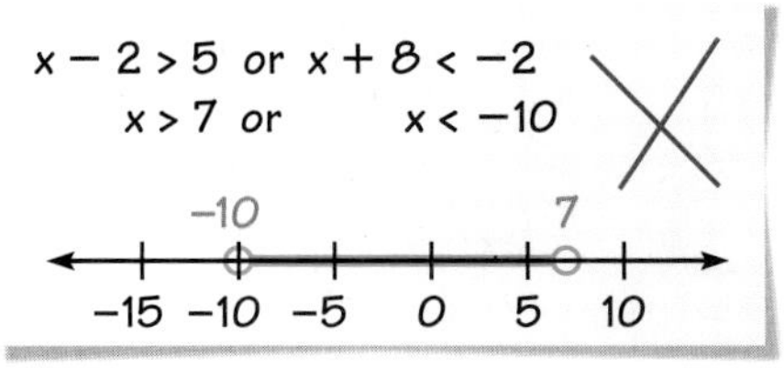
x − 2 > 5 or x + 8 < −2
x > 7 or x < −10
−10
7
−15
−10
−5
0
5
10

TRANSLATING SENTENCES Write the verbal sentence as an inequality. Then solve the inequality and graph your solution.

23. Five more than x is less than 8 *or* 3 less than x is greater than 5.

24. Three less than x is greater than -4 *and* less than -1.

25. Three times the difference of x and 4 is greater than or equal to -8 *and* less than or equal to 10.

26. The sum of $-2x$ and 8 is less than or equal to -5 *or* 6 is less than $-2x$.

27. ★ **MULTIPLE CHOICE** Consider the compound inequality $a > 3x + 8$ *or* $a > -4x - 1$. For which value of a does the solution consist of numbers greater than -6 *and* less than 5?

(A) 16 (B) 19 (C) 23 (D) 26

REASONING In Exercises 28 and 29, tell whether the statement is *true* or *false*. If it is false, give a counterexample.

28. If a is a solution of $x < 5$, then a is also a solution of $x < 5$ *and* $x \geq -4$.

29. If a is a solution of $x > 5$, then a is also a solution of $x > 5$ *or* $x \leq -4$.

30. Is the converse of the statement in Exercise 28 *true* or *false*? *Explain.*

31. Is the converse of the statement in Exercise 29 *true* or *false*? *Explain.*

32. **GEOMETRY** The sum of the lengths of any two sides of a triangle is greater than the length of the third side.

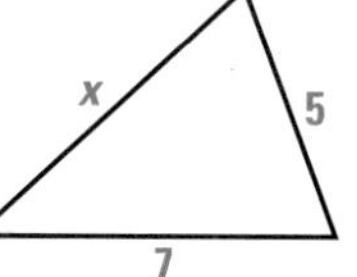

a. Write and solve three inequalities for the triangle shown.

b. Use the inequalities that you wrote in part (a) to write one inequality that describes all the possible values of x.

c. Give three possible lengths for the third side of the triangle.

CHALLENGE Solve the inequality, if possible. Graph your solution.

33. $-18 < x - 23$ *and* $x - 16 < -22$

34. $-3y + 7 \leq 11$ *and* $y + 4 > 11$

35. $2m - 1 \geq 5$ *or* $5m > -25$

36. $n + 19 \geq 10$ *or* $-5n + 3 > 33$

PROBLEM SOLVING

EXAMPLE 2 on p. 381 for Exs. 37, 39, 40

37. SLITSNAILS Slitsnails are large mollusks that live in deep waters. Slitsnails have been found at elevations from -2600 feet to -100 feet. Write and graph a compound inequality that represents the elevations at which slitsnails have been found.

@HomeTutor for problem solving help at classzone.com

EXAMPLE 6 on p. 383 for Exs. 38, 41–43

38. ICEBERGS The temperature inside an iceberg off the coast of Newfoundland, Canada, ranges from $-20°C$ to $-15°C$. Write and graph a compound inequality that describes the possible temperatures (in degrees Fahrenheit) of the iceberg's interior.

@HomeTutor for problem solving help at classzone.com

39. ★ **MULTIPLE CHOICE** The euro is the currency in several countries in Europe. In 2003, the dollar value of one euro ranged from \$1.0361 to \$1.2597. Which inequality represents the dollar values v that the euro was *not* worth during the year?

Ⓐ $1.0361 < v < 1.2597$

Ⓑ $v < 1.0361$ *or* $v > 1.2597$

Ⓒ $1.0361 \le v \le 1.2597$

Ⓓ $v \le 1.0361$ *or* $v \ge 1.2597$

40. **CURRENCY** On October 25, 1865, the steamship *S.S. Republic* sank along with a cargo of gold and silver coins. The list gives the prices of several recovered gold coins. Use the least price and greatest price to write a compound inequality that describes the prices p of the coins.

Prices of Recovered Gold Coins

\$9,098	\$20,995	\$9,798	\$33,592	\$12,597
\$16,796	\$9,798	\$10,498	\$5,319	\$73,486
\$11,897	\$32,895	\$7,349	\$6,578	\$29,395

41. **ANIMALS** A deer can eat 2% to 4% of its body weight in food per day. The percent p of the deer's body weight eaten in food is given by the equation $p = \frac{f}{d}$ where f is the amount (in pounds) of food eaten and d is the weight (in pounds) of the deer. Find the possible amounts of food that a 160 pound deer can eat per day.

42. **SKIS** A ski shop sells recreational skis with lengths ranging from 150 centimeters to 220 centimeters. The shop recommends that recreational skis be 1.16 times the skier's height (in centimeters). For which heights of skiers does the shop *not* provide recreational skis?

43. ◆ **MULTIPLE REPRESENTATIONS** Water can exist as either a solid, a liquid, or a gas. The table shows the temperatures (in degrees Celsius) at which water can exist in each state.

State of water	Solid	Liquid	Gas
Temperatures (°C)	Less than 0	0 to 100	Greater than 100

a. **Writing an Inequality** Write and solve a compound inequality to find the temperatures (in degrees Fahrenheit) at which water is *not* a liquid.

b. **Making a Table** Make a table that gives the temperature (in degrees Celsius) when the temperature (in degrees Fahrenheit) of water is 23°F, 86°F, 140°F, 194°F, and 239°F. For which temperatures in the table is water *not* a liquid?

44. **WEATHER** Wind chill temperature describes how much colder it feels when the speed of the wind is combined with air temperature. At a wind speed of 20 miles per hour, the wind chill temperature w (in degrees Fahrenheit) can be given by the model $w = -22 + 1.3a$ where a is the air temperature (in degrees Fahrenheit). What are the possible air temperatures if the wind chill temperature ranges from −9°F to −2.5°F at a wind speed of 20 miles per hour?

○ = WORKED-OUT SOLUTIONS on p. WS1 ★ = STANDARDIZED TEST PRACTICE ◆ = MULTIPLE REPRESENTATIONS

45. ★ **EXTENDED RESPONSE** Some musicians use audio amplifiers so that everyone in the audience can hear the performance. The amount y of amplification per person is given by the equation $y = \frac{w}{p}$ where w is the total amount (in watts) of amplification provided by the amplifier and p is the number of people in the audience.

a. **Solve** Each person requires 8 watts to 10 watts of amplification. Write and solve an inequality to find the possible total amounts of amplification that an amplifier would need to provide for 300 people.

b. **Decide** Will an amplifier that provides 2900 watts of amplification be strong enough for an audience of 350 people? 400 people? *Explain.*

c. **Justify** Your band usually performs before an audience of 500 to 600 people. What is the least amount of amplification that your amplifier should provide? *Justify* your answer.

Animated Algebra at classzone.com

46. **CHALLENGE** You and three friends are planning to eat at a restaurant, and all of you agree to divide the total cost of the meals and the 15% tip equally. Each person agrees to pay at least \$10 but no more than \$20. How much can you spend altogether on meals before the tip is applied?

MIXED REVIEW

Evaluate the expression.

47. $14x$ when $x = 3$ *(p. 2)*

48. $6d^3$ when $d = 4$ *(p. 8)*

49. $|m|$ when $m = -1$ *(p. 64)*

50. $-8t$ when $t = -5$ *(p. 88)*

PREVIEW
Prepare for Lesson 6.5 in Exs. 51–54.

Solve the equation.

51. $8x - 14 = -16$ *(p. 134)*

52. $2y + 8 + 5y = -1$ *(p. 141)*

53. $4(f - 3) = -28$ *(p. 148)*

54. $6r - 2 = 5r - 3$ *(p. 154)*

55. **MUSEUMS** You and some friends are taking a trip to a museum. Parking costs \$15, and the price of a ticket is \$14.50. Write an equation that gives the total cost C (in dollars) of the trip as a function of the number p of people who are going. *(p. 283)*

QUIZ *for Lessons 6.3–6.4*

Solve the inequality, if possible. Graph your solution.

1. $-\frac{1}{5}(x - 5) > x - 9$ *(p. 369)*

2. $\frac{1}{2}y - 8 \geq -2y + 3$ *(p. 369)*

3. $-4r + 7 \leq r + 10$ *(p. 369)*

4. $-2(s + 6) \leq -2s + 8$ *(p. 369)*

5. $a - 4 \geq -1$ *or* $3a < -24$ *(p. 380)*

6. $22 > -3c + 4 > 14$ *(p. 380)*

7. $-27 \leq 9m \leq -18$ *(p. 380)*

8. $5n + 2 > -18$ *or* $-3(n + 4) > 21$ *(p. 380)*

Graphing Calculator **ACTIVITY** *Use after Lesson 6.4*

@HomeTutor
classzone.com
Keystrokes

6.4 Solve Compound Inequalities

QUESTION How can you use a graphing calculator to display the solutions of a compound inequality?

EXAMPLE Display the solutions of a compound inequality on a graphing calculator

Display the solutions of $12 \le 3x \le 21$ on a graphing calculator.

STEP 1 *Rewrite inequality*

Rewrite $12 \le 3x \le 21$ as two separate inequalities joined by *and*.

$12 \le 3x \le 21$ Write original inequality.

$12 \le 3x$ *and* $3x \le 21$ Write as two inequalities joined by *and*.

STEP 2 *Enter inequalities*

Press Y= and enter the two inequalities, as shown. Inequality signs can be found in the TEST menu, and *and* and *or* can be found in the LOGIC menu.

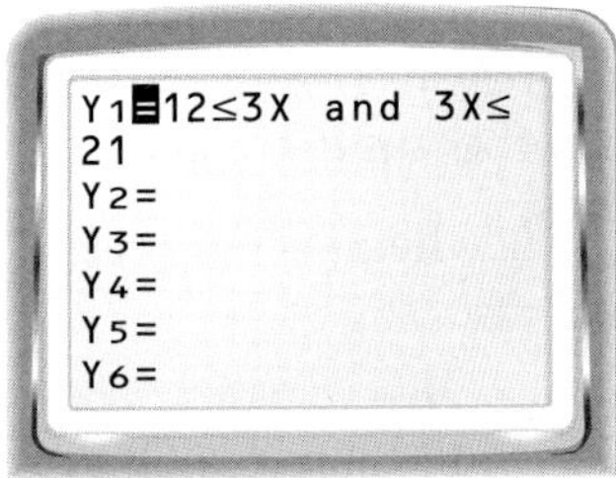

STEP 3 *Display solutions*

Press GRAPH to display the solutions of $12 \le 3x$ *and* $3x \le 21$. For each value of x that makes the inequality true, the calculator assigns a value of 1 to y and plots the point $(x, 1)$. For each value of x that makes the inequality false, the calculator assigns a value of 0 to y and plots the point $(x, 0)$.

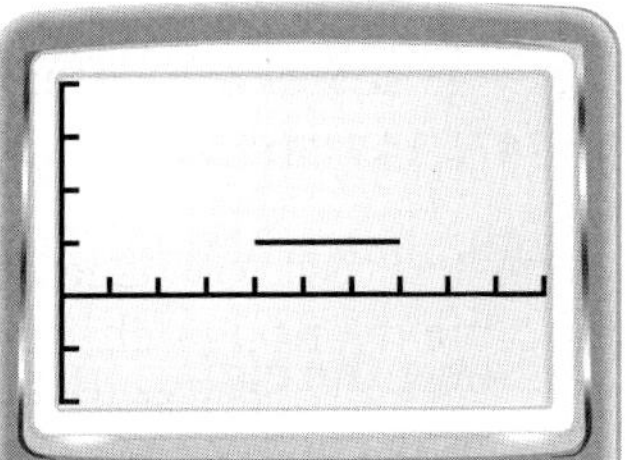

The screen in Step 3 shows the graph of $y = 1$ over the interval $4 \le x \le 7$. This suggests that the solutions are all real numbers greater than or equal to 4 *and* less than or equal to 7.

DRAW CONCLUSIONS

1. Display the solutions of $12 < 3x < 21$ on a graphing calculator. Then compare the graph of $12 < 3x < 21$ with the graph of $12 \le 3x \le 21$.
2. When displaying the solutions of an inequality on a graphing calculator, how do you know which inequality symbols you should use in your solution?

Display the solutions of the inequality on a graphing calculator.

3. $9 \le 3x \le 21$
4. $4 < 4x < 8$
5. $2 \le \frac{1}{4}x \le 12$
6. $-6x > 18$ *or* $9x > 45$
7. $4x \le 18$ *or* $5x \ge 25$
8. $8x \le 16$ *or* $3x \ge 30$

MIXED REVIEW of Problem Solving

Lessons 6.1–6.4

1. **MULTI-STEP PROBLEM** A nanotube thermometer is so tiny that it is invisible to the human eye. The thermometer can measure temperatures from 50°C to 500°C.
   a. Write and solve a compound inequality to find the temperatures (in degrees Fahrenheit) that the thermometer can measure.
   b. Graph your solution of the inequality.
   c. Can the thermometer measure a temperature of 1000°F? *Explain*.

2. **SHORT RESPONSE** You earned the following scores on five science tests: 75, 82, 90, 84, and 71. You want to have an average score of at least 80 after you take the sixth test.
   a. Write and solve an inequality to find the possible scores that you can earn on your sixth test in order to meet your goal.
   b. The greatest score that you can earn on a test is 100. Is it possible for you to have an average score of 90 after the sixth test? *Explain* your reasoning.

3. **GRIDDED ANSWER** You need at least 34 eggs to make enough chiffon cakes for a bake sale. Your grocery store sells cartons of eggs only by the dozen. Of all the possible numbers of cartons that you can buy, which is the least number?

4. **MULTI-STEP PROBLEM** You have a $300 gift card to use at a sporting goods store.
   a. You want to use your card to buy 2 pairs of shoes for $85 each and several pairs of socks. Write and solve an inequality to find the possible amounts of money that you can spend on socks using your card.
   b. Suppose that socks cost $4.75 per pair. Write and solve an inequality to find the possible numbers of socks that you can buy using the card.

5. **OPEN-ENDED** *Describe* a real-world situation that can be modeled by the inequality $17x \le 240$. *Explain* what the solution of the inequality means in this situation.

6. **SHORT RESPONSE** A rafting guide plans to take 6 adults on a rafting trip. The raft can hold up to 1520 pounds. The guide weighs 180 pounds and estimates that each adult will bring 10 pounds of baggage.

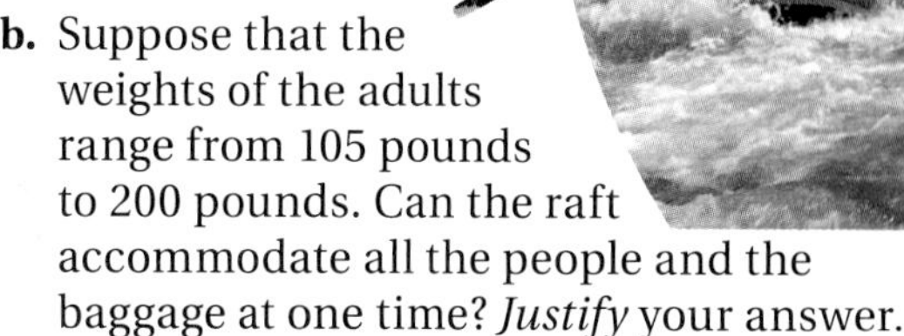

   a. Write and solve an inequality to find the possible average weights of an adult such that the raft will not exceed its maximum weight capacity.
   b. Suppose that the weights of the adults range from 105 pounds to 200 pounds. Can the raft accommodate all the people and the baggage at one time? *Justify* your answer.

7. **EXTENDED RESPONSE** In 1862 the United States imposed a tax on annual income in order to pay for the expenses of the Civil War. The table shows the tax rates for different incomes.

Annual income	Tax rate
$600 to $10,000	3% of income
Greater than $10,000	3% of the first $10,000 plus 5% of income over $10,000

   a. Write a compound inequality that represents the possible taxes paid by a person whose annual income was at least $600 but not greater than $10,000.
   b. For people whose taxes ranged from $400 to $750, tell whether their annual incomes were greater than $10,000 or less than $10,000. *Explain* how you know. Then find the possible annual incomes of those people.
   c. Suppose that the tax rate had been 4% of the total income for people whose annual incomes were greater than $10,000. For which incomes would paying the 4% rate have resulted in less taxes than paying the tax rate described above? *Explain*.

6.5 Solve Absolute Value Equations

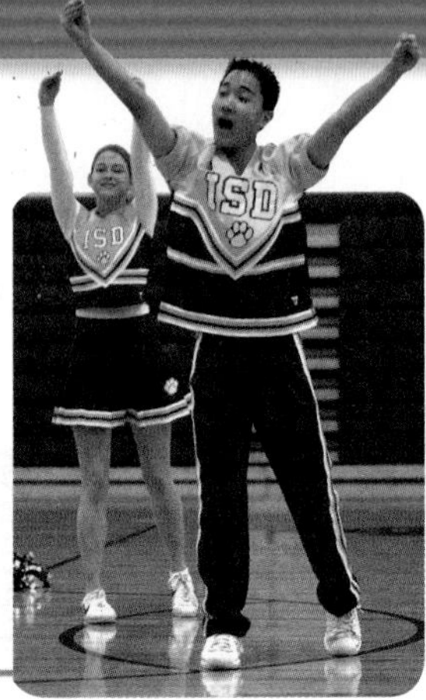

Before You solved linear equations.

Now You will solve absolute value equations.

Why? So you can analyze rules of a competition, as in Ex. 43.

Key Vocabulary
- **absolute value equation**
- **absolute deviation**
- **absolute value,** *p. 66*

The absolute value of a number a, written $|a|$, is the distance between a and 0 on a number line. An **absolute value equation**, such as $|x| = 4$, is an equation that contains an absolute value expression. The equation $|x| = 4$ means that the distance between x and 0 is 4. The solutions of the equation are 4 and -4, because they are the only numbers whose distance from 0 is 4.

EXAMPLE 1 Solve an absolute value equation

Solve $|x| = 7$.

Solution

The distance between x and 0 is 7. So, $x = 7$ *or* $x = -7$.

▸ The solutions are 7 and -7.

Animated Algebra at classzone.com

✓ **GUIDED PRACTICE** for Example 1

1. Solve **(a)** $|x| = 3$ and **(b)** $|x| = 15$.

SOLVING ABSOLUTE VALUE EQUATIONS In Example 1, notice that the expression inside the absolute value symbols equals 7 or the opposite of 7. This suggests the following rule for solving an absolute value equation.

KEY CONCEPT *For Your Notebook*

Solving an Absolute Value Equation

The equation $|ax + b| = c$ where $c \geq 0$ is equivalent to the statement $ax + b = c$ *or* $ax + b = -c$.

EXAMPLE 2 Solve an absolute value equation

Solve $|x - 3| = 8$.

Solution

Rewrite the absolute value equation as two equations. Then solve each equation separately.

AVOID ERRORS
You cannot solve the equation $|x - 3| = 8$ by adding 3 to each side because $|x - 3| + 3 \neq |x|$.

$|x - 3| = 8$ Write original equation.

$x - 3 = 8$ *or* $x - 3 = -8$ Rewrite as two equations.

$x = 11$ *or* $x = -5$ Add 3 to each side.

▶ The solutions are 11 and −5. Check your solutions.

CHECK

$\|x - 3\| = 8$	$\|x - 3\| = 8$	Write original inequality.
$\|11 - 3\| \stackrel{?}{=} 8$	$\|-5 - 3\| \stackrel{?}{=} 8$	Substitute for x.
$\|8\| \stackrel{?}{=} 8$	$\|-8\| \stackrel{?}{=} 8$	Subtract.
$8 = 8$ ✓	$8 = 8$ ✓	Simplify. The solution checks.

REWRITING EQUATIONS To solve an absolute value equation, you may first need to rewrite the equation in the form $|ax + b| = c$.

EXAMPLE 3 Rewrite an absolute value equation

Solve $3|2x - 7| - 5 = 4$.

Solution

First, rewrite the equation in the form $|ax + b| = c$.

$3|2x - 7| - 5 = 4$ Write original equation.

$3|2x - 7| = 9$ Add 5 to each side.

$|2x - 7| = 3$ Divide each side by 3.

Next, solve the absolute value equation.

$|2x - 7| = 3$ Write absolute value equation.

$2x - 7 = 3$ *or* $2x - 7 = -3$ Rewrite as two equations.

$2x = 10$ *or* $2x = 4$ Add 7 to each side.

$x = 5$ *or* $x = 2$ Divide each side by 2.

▶ The solutions are 5 and 2.

Animated Algebra at classzone.com

✓ **GUIDED PRACTICE** for Examples 2 and 3

Solve the equation.

2. $|r - 7| = 9$

3. $2|s| + 4.1 = 18.9$

4. $4|t + 9| - 5 = 19$

NO SOLUTIONS The absolute value of a number is never negative. So, when an absolute value expression equals a negative number, there are *no solutions.*

EXAMPLE 4 Decide if an equation has no solutions

Solve $|3x + 5| + 6 = -2$, if possible.

$|3x + 5| + 6 = -2$ Write original equation.

$|3x + 5| = -8$ Subtract 6 from each side.

▶ The absolute value of a number is never negative. So, there are no solutions.

ABSOLUTE DEVIATION The **absolute deviation** of a number x from a given value is the absolute value of the difference of x and the given value: absolute deviation $= |x - \text{given value}|$.

EXAMPLE 5 Use absolute deviation

BASKETBALLS Before the start of a professional basketball game, a basketball must be inflated to an air pressure of 8 pounds per square inch (psi) with an absolute error of 0.5 psi. (*Absolute error* is the absolute deviation of a measured value from an accepted value.) Find the minimum and maximum acceptable air pressures for the basketball.

Solution

Let p be the air pressure (in psi) of a basketball. Write a verbal model. Then write and solve an absolute value equation.

Absolute error	= |	Measured air pressure	−	Accepted air pressure	|
↓		↓		↓	
0.5	= |	p	−	**8**	|

$0.5 = |p - 8|$ Write original equation.

$0.5 = p - 8$ *or* $-0.5 = p - 8$ Rewrite as two equations.

$8.5 = p$ *or* $7.5 = p$ Add 8 to each side.

▶ The minimum and maximum acceptable pressures are 7.5 psi and 8.5 psi.

✓ GUIDED PRACTICE for Examples 4 and 5

Solve the equation, if possible.

5. $2|m - 5| + 4 = 2$

6. $-3|n + 2| - 7 = -10$

7. The absolute deviation of x from 7.6 is 5.2. What are the values of x that satisfy this requirement?

6.5 EXERCISES

HOMEWORK KEY

○ = **WORKED-OUT SOLUTIONS** on p. WS14 for Exs. 11, 23, and 45

★ = **STANDARDIZED TEST PRACTICE** Exs. 2, 32, 44, 48, and 49

SKILL PRACTICE

1. **VOCABULARY** Copy and complete: The equation $|x - 7| = 0.15$ is an example of a(n) _?_.

2. ★ **WRITING** Given $|x - 9| = 5$, describe the relationship between x, 9, and 5 using absolute deviation.

EXAMPLES 1, 2, and 3 on pp. 390–391 for Exs. 3–20

SOLVING EQUATIONS **Solve the equation.**

3. $|x| = 5$
4. $|y| = 36$
5. $|v| = 0.7$
6. $|w| = 9.2$
7. $|r| = \frac{1}{2}$
8. $|s| = \frac{7}{4}$
9. $|m + 3| = 7$
10. $|4n - 5| = 18$
11. $|3p + 7| = 4$
12. $|q + 8| = 2$
13. $|2d + 7| = 11$
14. $|f - 8| = 14$
15. $3|13 - 2t| = 15$
16. $4|b - 1| - 7 = 17$
17. $\frac{1}{3}|2c - 5| + 3 = 7$
18. $\frac{7}{4}|3j + 5| + 1 = 15$
19. $4|2k + 3| - 2 = 6$
20. $-3|5g + 1| - 6 = -9$

ERROR ANALYSIS ***Describe*** **and correct the error in solving the absolute value equation.**

21.
$|x + 4| = 13$
$x + 4 = 13$
$x = 9$

22.
$|x - 6| = -2$
$x - 6 = -2$ or $x - 6 = 2$
$x = 4$ or $x = 8$

EXAMPLE 4 on p. 392 for Exs. 23–31

SOLVING EQUATIONS **Solve the equation, if possible.**

23. $|x - 1| + 5 = 2$
24. $|y - 4| + 8 = 6$
25. $|m + 5| + 1.5 = 2$
26. $-4|8 - 5n| = 13$
27. $-3\left|1 - \frac{2}{3}v\right| = -9$
28. $-5\left|\frac{4}{5}w + 6\right| = -10$
29. $-10|14 - r| - 2 = -7$
30. $-2\left|\frac{1}{3}s - 5\right| + 3 = 8$
31. $-9|4p + 2| - 8 = -35$

32. ★ **MULTIPLE CHOICE** Which number is a solution of $|4x - 1| + 2 = 1$?
(A) $-\frac{1}{2}$ (B) 0 (C) 1 (D) There is no solution.

EXAMPLE 5 on p. 392 for Exs. 33–36

USING ABSOLUTE DEVIATION **Find the values of x that satisfy the definition of absolute deviation for the given value and the given absolute deviation.**

33. Given value: 5; absolute deviation: 8
34. Given value: 20; absolute deviation: 5
35. Given value: −9.1; absolute deviation: 1.6
36. Given value: −3.4; absolute deviation: 6.7

37. **SOLVING AN EQUATION** Interpreted geometrically, the equation $|x - a| = b$ means that the distance between x and a on a number line is b. Solve $|x - 3| = 7$ both geometrically and algebraically. *Compare* your solutions.

TRANSLATING SENTENCES In Exercises 38 and 39, write the verbal sentence as an absolute value equation. Then solve the equation.

38. Four more than the absolute deviation of x from 3 is 8.

39. Five times the absolute deviation of $2x$ from -9 is 15.

40. **REASONING** Is $a|x|$ equivalent to $|ax|$ when a is positive? when a is negative? when a is 0? Give examples to support your answers.

41. **CHALLENGE** How many solutions does the equation $a|x + b| + c = d$ have if $a > 0$ and $c = d$? if $a < 0$ and $c > d$?

PROBLEM SOLVING

EXAMPLE 5
on p. 392
for Exs. 42–46

42. **GUARDRAILS** A safety regulation requires that the height of a guardrail be 42 inches with an absolute deviation of 3 inches. Find the minimum and maximum heights of a guardrail.

@HomeTutor for problem solving help at classzone.com

43. **CHEERLEADING** A cheerleading team is preparing a dance program for a competition. The program must last 4 minutes with an absolute deviation of 5 seconds. Find the least and greatest possible times (in seconds) that the program can last.

@HomeTutor for problem solving help at classzone.com

44. ★ **MULTIPLE CHOICE** The diameter of a billiard ball must be 2.25 inches with an absolute error of 0.005 inch. What is the maximum possible diameter that a billiard ball can have?

Ⓐ 2.2 inches Ⓑ 2.245 inches Ⓒ 2.255 inches Ⓓ 2.3 inches

(45.) **SPORTS** In gymnastics meets last year, the mean of your friend's least and greatest scores was 54.675 points. The absolute deviation of his least and greatest scores from the mean was 2.213 points.

a. What were the least and greatest scores that he earned?

b. This year the mean of his least and greatest scores is 56.738 points, and the absolute deviation of the least and greatest scores from the mean is 0.45 point. How many points more than last year's greatest score is this year's greatest score?

46. **JEWELRY** A jewelry store advertisement states that a certain diamond bracelet weighs 12 carats, but the actual weight can vary by as much as 5% of the advertised weight. Find the minimum and maximum possible weights of the bracelet.

47. **CONTESTS** You currently have 450 points in an academic contest. You choose the value p of the question you want to answer. The value p represents the absolute deviation of your new score s from 450.

a. Write an absolute value equation that gives p in terms of s.

b. If you choose a question worth 150 points, what are the possible new scores that you can have after answering the question?

48. ★ **EXTENDED RESPONSE** The percent p of United States residents who were foreign born, or born outside of the United States, during the period 1910–2000 can be modeled by the equation $p = 0.165|t - 60| + 4.8$ where t is the number of years since 1910.

a. **Approximate** During the period 1910–2000, in approximately what year did foreign-born residents account for 13% of all residents?

b. **Predict** If the model holds for years after 2000, predict the year in which foreign-born residents will again account for 13% of all residents.

c. **Decide** According to the model, did foreign-born residents account for 4% of all residents at any time during the period 1910–2000? *Explain* your answer.

49. ★ **SHORT RESPONSE** A stock's average price p (in dollars) during the period February 2005 to October 2005 can be modeled by the equation $p = 2.3|m - 7| + 9.57$ where m is the number of months since February 2005.

a. **Approximate** In approximately what month and year was the average price \$16.15? If the model holds for months after October 2005, predict the month and year in which the average price will again be \$16.15.

b. **Justify** Is it possible to use the model to estimate the stock's lowest average price during this period? *Justify* your answer.

50. **CHALLENGE** In a recent Olympics, swimmers in a men's 200 meter butterfly event finished with times from 1 minute 54.04 seconds to 1 minute 57.48 seconds. Let t represent the slowest or fastest time (in seconds). Write an absolute value equation that describes the situation.

MIXED REVIEW

Write an equation of the line shown. *(p. 283)*

51.
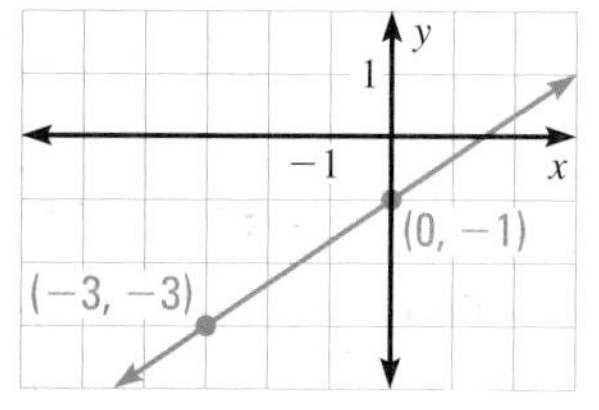

52.
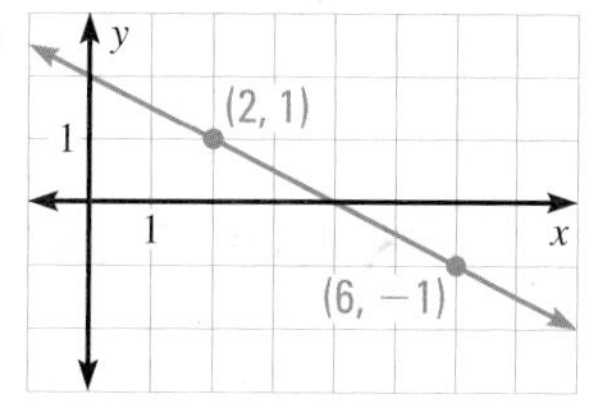

53.
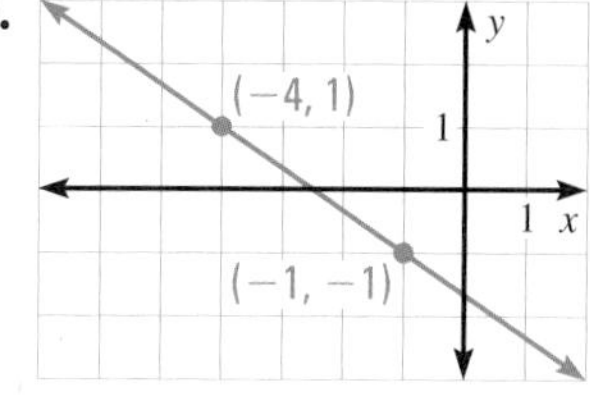

PREVIEW
Prepare for Lesson 6.6 in Exs. 54–59.

Solve the inequality. Graph your solution.

54. $r + 7 \geq 28$ *(p. 356)*

55. $-\frac{1}{2}s > -8$ *(p. 363)*

56. $-6t + 7 \leq 15$ *(p. 369)*

57. $-5(v - 2) < -16$ *(p. 369)*

58. $-14 < 1 - 5w < 12$ *(p. 380)*

59. $-3x > 9$ *or* $4x \geq 8$ *(p. 380)*

Extension Graph Absolute Value Functions

Use after Lesson 6.5

GOAL Graph absolute value functions.

Key Vocabulary
- **absolute value,** *p. 66*

The function $f(x) = |x|$ is an example of an *absolute value function* and is the parent function for all absolute value functions. You can graph absolute value functions by using a table of values, as shown below for $f(x) = |x|$.

KEY CONCEPT *For Your Notebook*

Graph of Parent Function for Absolute Value Functions

x	$f(x) = \|x\|$
−2	$\|-2\| = 2$
−1	$\|-1\| = 1$
0	$\|0\| = 0$
1	$\|1\| = 1$
2	$\|2\| = 2$

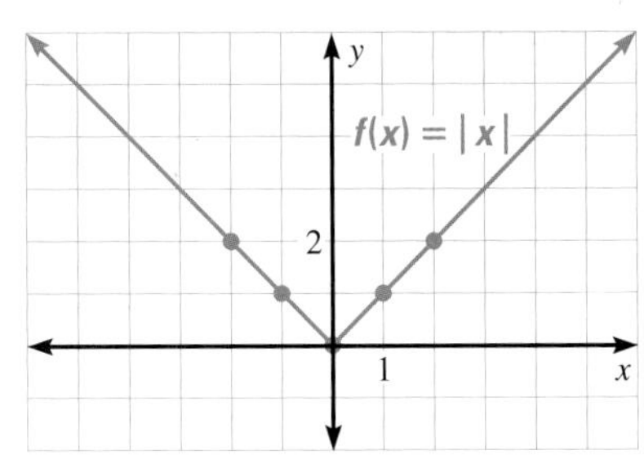

EXAMPLE 1 Graph $g(x) = |x - h|$ and $g(x) = |x| + k$

Graph each function. Compare the graph with the graph of $f(x) = |x|$.

a. $g(x) = |x - 2|$

STEP 1 **Make** a table of values.

x	0	1	2	3	4
$g(x)$	2	1	0	1	2

STEP 2 **Graph** the function.

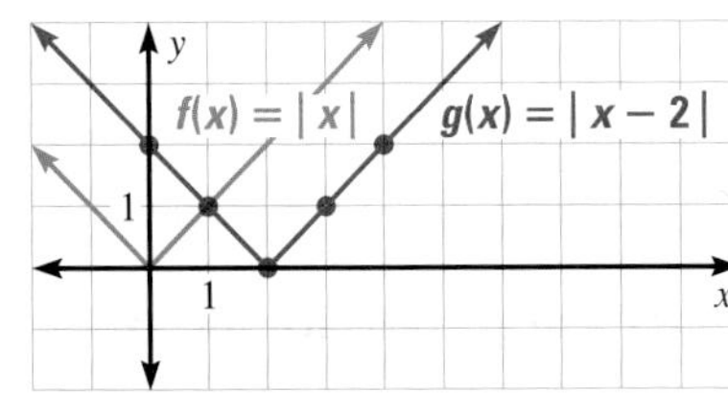

STEP 3 **Compare** the graphs of g and f. The graph of $g(x) = |x - 2|$ is 2 units to the right of the graph of $f(x) = |x|$.

b. $g(x) = |x| - 1$

STEP 1 **Make** a table of values.

x	−2	−1	0	1	2
$g(x)$	1	0	−1	0	1

STEP 2 **Graph** the function.

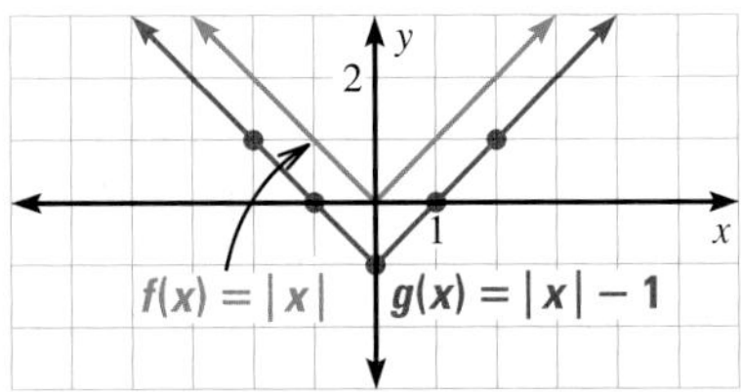

STEP 3 **Compare** the graphs of g and f. The graph of $g(x) = |x| - 1$ is 1 unit below the graph of $f(x) = |x|$.

APPLY TRANSFORMATIONS
The two graphs in Example 1 are translations of the graph of $f(x) = |x|$. The graph in part (a) is a horizontal translation. The graph in part (b) is a vertical translation.

EXAMPLE 2 Graph $g(x) = a|x|$

Graph each function. Compare the graph with the graph of $f(x) = |x|$.

a. $g(x) = 4|x|$

STEP 1 **Make** a table of values.

x	−2	−1	0	1	2
$g(x)$	8	4	0	4	8

STEP 2 **Graph** the function.

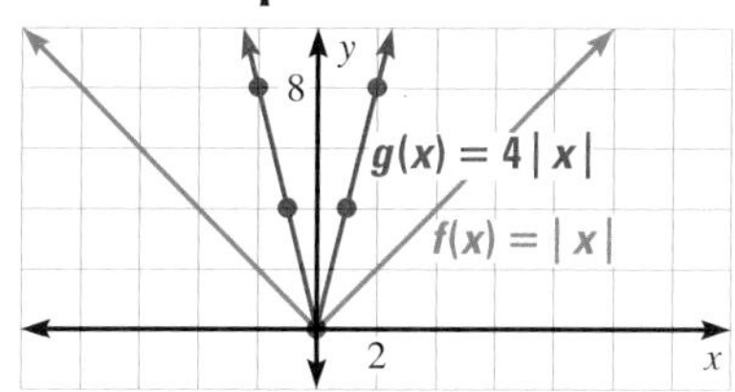

STEP 3 **Compare** the graphs of g and f. The graph of $g(x) = 4|x|$ opens up and is narrower than the graph of $f(x) = |x|$.

b. $g(x) = -0.5|x|$

STEP 1 **Make** a table of values.

x	−4	−2	0	2	4
$g(x)$	−2	−1	0	−1	−2

STEP 2 **Graph** the function.

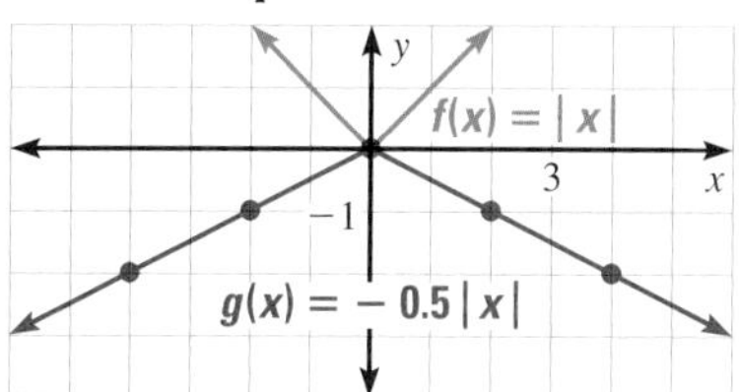

STEP 3 **Compare** the graphs of g and f. The graph of $g(x) = -0.5|x|$ opens down and is wider than the graph of $f(x) = |x|$.

APPLY TRANSFORMATIONS

The graph in part (a) of Example 2 is a vertical stretch of the graph of $f(x) = |x|$. The graph in part (b) is a vertical shrink with a reflection in the x-axis of the graph of $f(x) = |x|$.

KEY CONCEPT *For Your Notebook*

Comparing Graphs of Absolute Value Functions with the Graph of $f(x) = |x|$

$g(x) = |x - h|$

If $h > 0$, the graph of g is $|h|$ units to the right of the graph of $f(x) = |x|$.

If $h < 0$, the graph of g is $|h|$ units to the left of the graph of $f(x) = |x|$.

$g(x) = |x| + k$

If $k > 0$, the graph of g is $|k|$ units above the graph of $f(x) = |x|$.

If $k < 0$, the graph of g is $|k|$ units below the graph of $f(x) = |x|$.

$g(x) = a|x|$

If $|a| > 1$, the graph of g is narrower than the graph of $f(x) = |x|$. If $0 < |a| < 1$, the graph of g is wider.

If $a > 0$, the graph of g opens up. If $a < 0$, the graph opens down.

PRACTICE

EXAMPLES 1 and 2 on pp. 396–397 for Exs. 1–6

Graph the function. *Compare* the graph with the graph of $f(x) = |x|$.

1. $g(x) = |x + 3|$
2. $g(x) = |x| + 5$
3. $g(x) = |x| - 7$
4. $g(x) = 2|x|$
5. $g(x) = 0.6|x|$
6. $g(x) = -3|x|$

7. Make a table of values for $g(x) = 2|x - 3| + 4$. Use the following values for x: 1, 2, 3, 4, 5. Then graph the function and compare the graph with the graph of $f(x) = |x|$.

6.6 Solve Absolute Value Inequalities

Before You solved absolute value equations.

Now You will solve absolute value inequalities.

Why So you can analyze softball compression, as in Ex. 38.

Key Vocabulary
- **absolute value,** *p. 66*
- **equivalent inequalities,** *p. 357*
- **compound inequality,** *p. 380*
- **absolute deviation,** *p. 392*
- **mean,** *p. 918*

Recall that $|x| = 3$ means that the distance between x and 0 is 3. The inequality $|x| < 3$ means that the distance between x and 0 is *less than* 3, and $|x| > 3$ means that the distance between x and 0 is *greater than* 3. The graphs of $|x| < 3$ and $|x| > 3$ are shown below.

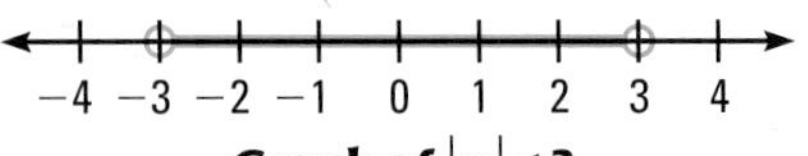

Graph of $|x| < 3$

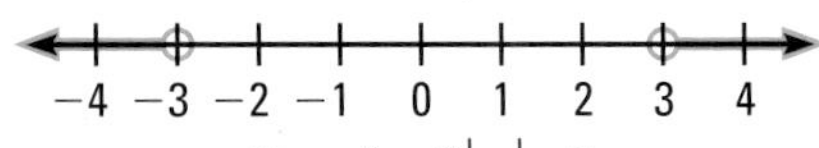

Graph of $|x| > 3$

EXAMPLE 1 Solve absolute value inequalities

Solve the inequality. Graph your solution.

a. $|x| \geq 6$ **b.** $|x| \leq 0.5$

Solution

a. The distance between x and 0 is greater than or equal to 6. So, $x \leq -6$ *or* $x \geq 6$.

▶ The solutions are all real numbers less than or equal to -6 *or* greater than or equal to 6.

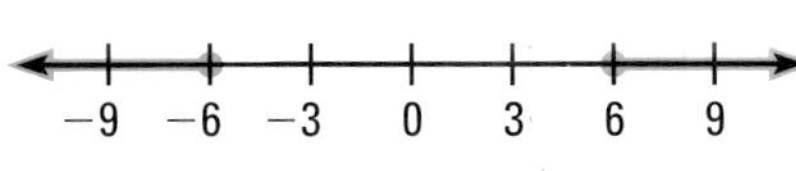

b. The distance between x and 0 is less than or equal to 0.5. So, $-0.5 \leq x \leq 0.5$.

▶ The solutions are all real numbers greater than or equal to -0.5 *and* less than or equal to 0.5.

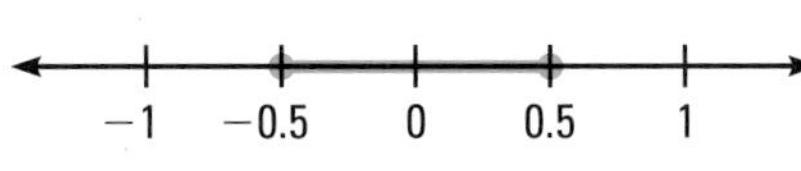

✓ **GUIDED PRACTICE** for Example 1

Solve the inequality. Graph your solution.

1. $|x| \leq 8$ **2.** $|u| < 3.5$ **3.** $|v| > \frac{2}{3}$

SOLVING ABSOLUTE VALUE INEQUALITIES In Example 1, the solutions of $|x| \geq 6$ and $|x| \leq 0.5$ suggest that you can rewrite an absolute value inequality as a compound inequality.

READING

You can use the words *between* and *beyond* to describe absolute value inequalites. For example, $|x| < 2$ means that x is between -2 *and* 2; $|x| > 2$ means that x is beyond -2 *or* beyond 2.

KEY CONCEPT *For Your Notebook*

Solving Absolute Value Inequalities

- The inequality $|ax + b| < c$ where $c > 0$ is equivalent to the compound inequality $-c < ax + b < c$.
- The inequality $|ax + b| > c$ where $c > 0$ is equivalent to the compound inequality $ax + b < -c$ *or* $ax + b > c$.

In the inequalities above, $<$ can be replaced by $\leq$ and $>$ can be replaced by $\geq$.

EXAMPLE 2 Solve an absolute value inequality

Solve $|x - 5| \geq 7$. Graph your solution.

$|x - 5| \geq 7$ Write original inequality.

$x - 5 \leq -7$ *or* $x - 5 \geq 7$ Rewrite as compound inequality.

$x \leq -2$ *or* $x \geq 12$ Add 5 to each side.

▶ The solutions are all real numbers less than or equal to -2 *or* greater than or equal to 12. Check several solutions in the original inequality.

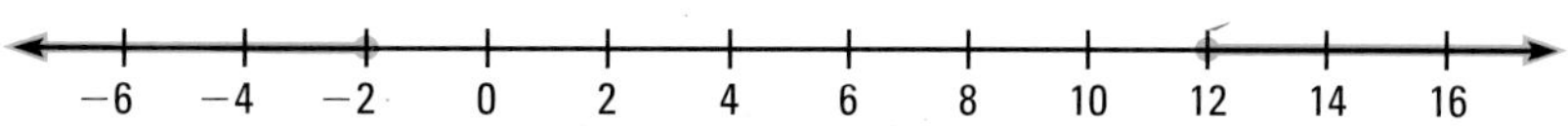

EXAMPLE 3 Solve an absolute value inequality

Solve $|-4x - 5| + 3 < 9$. Graph your solution.

$|-4x - 5| + 3 < 9$ Write original inequality.

$|-4x - 5| < 6$ Subtract 3 from each side.

$-6 < -4x - 5 < 6$ Rewrite as compound inequality.

$-1 < -4x < 11$ Add 5 to each expression.

$0.25 > x > -2.75$ Divide each expression by -4. Reverse inequality symbol.

$-2.75 < x < 0.25$ Rewrite in the form $a < x < b$.

▶ The solutions are all real numbers greater than -2.75 *and* less than 0.25.

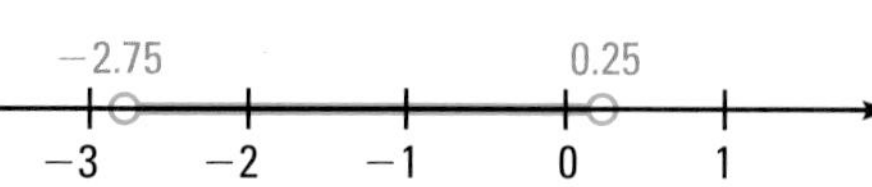

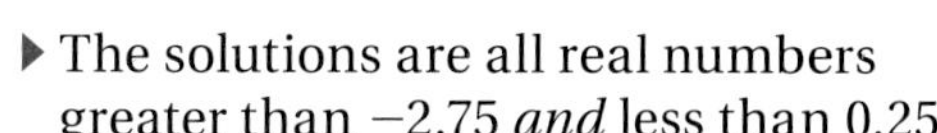

at classzone.com

✓ **GUIDED PRACTICE** for Examples 2 and 3

Solve the inequality. Graph your solution.

4. $|x + 3| > 8$ **5.** $|2w - 1| < 11$ **6.** $3|5m - 6| - 8 \leq 13$

EXAMPLE 4 Solve a multi-step problem

COMPUTERS You are buying a new computer and find 10 models in a store advertisement. The prices are \$890, \$750, \$650, \$370, \$660, \$670, \$450, \$650, \$725, and \$825.

- Find the mean of the computer prices.
- You are willing to pay the mean price with an absolute deviation of at most \$100. How many of the computer prices meet your condition?

Solution

STEP 1 **Find** the mean by dividing the sum of the prices by 10.

REVIEW MEAN
For help with finding a mean, see p. 918.

$$\text{Mean} = \frac{890 + 750 + 650 + 370 + 660 + 670 + 450 + 650 + 725 + 825}{10}$$

$$= \frac{6640}{10} = 664$$

STEP 2 **Write** and solve an inequality. An absolute deviation of at most \$100 from the mean, \$664, is given by the inequality $|x - 664| \le 100$.

$|x - 664| \le 100$ **Write absolute value inequality.**

$-100 \le x - 664 \le 100$ **Write as compound inequality.**

$564 \le x \le 764$ **Add 664 to each expression.**

▶ The prices you will consider must be at least \$564 and at most \$764. Six prices meet your condition: \$750, \$650, \$660, \$670, \$650, and \$725.

GUIDED PRACTICE for Example 4

7. **WHAT IF?** In Example 4, suppose that you are willing to pay the mean price with an absolute deviation of at most \$75. How many of the computer prices meet this condition?

CONCEPT SUMMARY *For Your Notebook*

Solving Inequalities

One-Step and Multi-Step Inequalities

- Follow the steps for solving an equation, but reverse the inequality symbol when multiplying or dividing by a negative number.

Compound Inequalities

- If necessary, rewrite the inequality as two separate inequalities. Then solve each inequality separately. Include *and* or *or* in the solution.

Absolute Value Inequalities

- If necessary, isolate the absolute value expression on one side of the inequality. Rewrite the absolute value inequality as a compound inequality. Then solve the compound inequality.

LINEAR INEQUALITIES IN ONE VARIABLE The steps for graphing a linear inequality in two variables can be used to graph a linear inequality in one variable in a coordinate plane.

The boundary line for an inequality in one variable is either vertical or horizontal. When testing a point to determine which half-plane to shade, do the following:

- If an inequality has only the variable x, substitute the x-coordinate of the test point into the inequality.
- If an inequality has only the variable y, substitute the y-coordinate of the test point into the inequality.

EXAMPLE 4 Graph a linear inequality in one variable

Graph the inequality $y \geq -3$.

Solution

STEP 1 **Graph** the equation $y = -3$.
The inequality is $\geq$, so use a solid line.

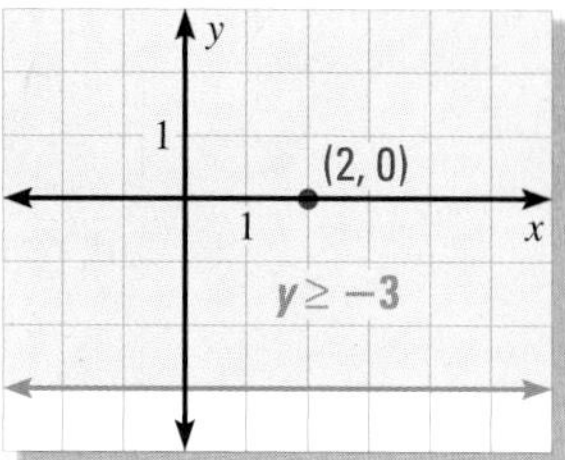

STEP 2 **Test** (2, 0) in $y \geq -3$. You substitute only the y-coordinate, because the inequality does not have the variable x.

$$0 \geq -3 \checkmark$$

STEP 3 **Shade** the half-plane that contains (2, 0), because (2, 0) is a solution of the inequality.

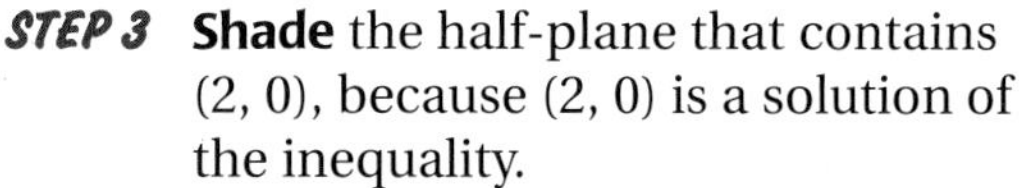

EXAMPLE 5 Graph a linear inequality in one variable

Graph the inequality $x < -1$.

Solution

STEP 1 **Graph** the equation $x = -1$.
The inequality is <, so use a dashed line.

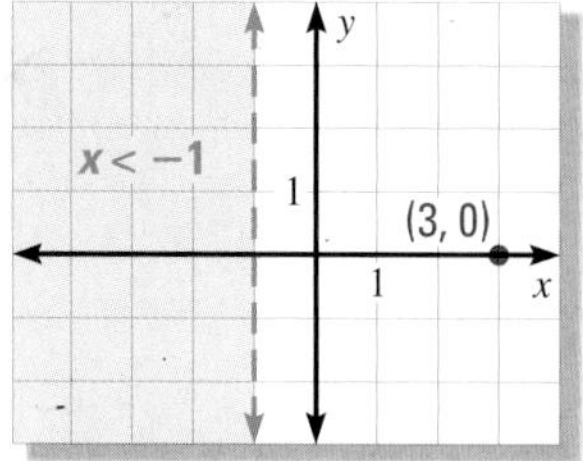

STEP 2 **Test** (3, 0) in $x < -1$. You substitute only the x-coordinate, because the inequality does not have the variable y.

$$3 < -1 \ \text{✗}$$

STEP 3 **Shade** the half-plane that does *not* contain (3, 0), because (3, 0) is not a solution of the inequality.

Animated Algebra at classzone.com

✓ **GUIDED PRACTICE** for Examples 4 and 5

Graph the inequality.

5. $y > 1$ **6.** $y \leq 3$ **7.** $x < -2$

EXAMPLE 6 Solve a multi-step problem

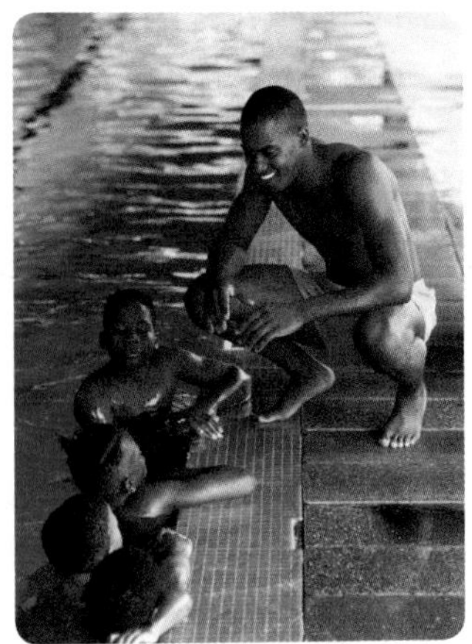

JOB EARNINGS You have two summer jobs at a youth center. You earn \$8 per hour teaching basketball and \$10 per hour teaching swimming. Let x represent the amount of time (in hours) you teach basketball each week, and let y represent the amount of time (in hours) you teach swimming each week. Your goal is to earn at least \$200 per week.

- Write an inequality that describes your goal in terms of x and y.
- Graph the inequality.
- Give three possible combinations of hours that will allow you to meet your goal.

Solution

STEP 1 **Write** a verbal model. Then write an inequality.

Basketball pay rate (dollars/hour)	•	Basketball time (hours)	+	Swimming pay rate (dollars/hour)	•	Swimming time (hours)	≥	Total earnings (dollars)
8	•	x	+	10	•	y	≥	200

STEP 2 **Graph** the inequality $8x + 10y \geq 200$.

First, graph the equation $8x + 10y = 200$ in Quadrant I. The inequality is ≥, so use a solid line.

Next, test (5, 5) in $8x + 10y \geq 200$:

$$8(5) + 10(5) \geq 200$$

$$90 \geq 200 \text{ ✗}$$

Swimming (hours)
$8x + 10y \geq 200$
(5, 5)
Basketball (hours)

Finally, shade the part of Quadrant I that does not contain (5, 5), because (5, 5) is not a solution of the inequality.

AVOID ERRORS
The variables can't represent negative numbers. So, the graph of the inequality does not include points in Quadrants II, III, or IV.

STEP 3 **Choose** three points on the graph, such as (13, 12), (14, 10), and (16, 9). The table shows the total earnings for each combination of hours.

Basketball time (hours)	13	14	16
Swimming time (hours)	12	10	9
Total earnings (dollars)	224	212	218

✓ GUIDED PRACTICE for Example 6

8. **WHAT IF?** In Example 6, suppose that next summer you earn \$9 per hour teaching basketball and \$12.50 per hour teaching swimming. Write and graph an inequality that describes your goal. Then give three possible combinations of hours that will help you meet your goal.

6.7 EXERCISES

HOMEWORK KEY

○ = **WORKED-OUT SOLUTIONS** on p. WS15 for Exs. 5, 19, and 57

★ = **STANDARDIZED TEST PRACTICE** Exs. 2, 15, 16, 39, 56, 59, and 60

◆ = **MULTIPLE REPRESENTATIONS** Ex. 55

SKILL PRACTICE

1. **VOCABULARY** Copy and complete: The ordered pair (2, −4) is a(n) __?__ of $3x - y > 7$.

2. ★ **WRITING** *Describe* the difference between graphing a linear inequality in two variables and graphing a linear equation in two variables.

EXAMPLE 1 on p. 405 for Exs. 3–15

CHECKING SOLUTIONS Tell whether the ordered pair is a solution of the inequality.

3. $x + y < -4$; (0, 0)
4. $x - y \leq 5$; (8, 3)
5. $y - x > -2$; (−1, −4)
6. $2x + 3y \geq 14$; (5, 2)
7. $4x - 7y > 28$; (−2, 4)
8. $-3y - 2x < 12$; (5, −6)
9. $2.8x + 4.1y \leq 1$; (0, 0)
10. $0.5y - 0.5x > 3.5$; (6, 2)
11. $x \geq -3$; (−4, 0)
12. $y \leq 8$; (−9, −7)
13. $\frac{3}{4}x - \frac{1}{3}y < 6$; (−8, 12)
14. $\frac{2}{5}x + y \geq 2$; (1, 2)

15. ★ **MULTIPLE CHOICE** Which ordered pair is *not* a solution of $x + 5y < 15$?

Ⓐ (−1, −3) Ⓑ (−1, 3) Ⓒ (1, 3) Ⓓ (3, 2)

EXAMPLES 2, 3, 4, and 5 on pp. 406–407 for Exs. 16–38

16. ★ **MULTIPLE CHOICE** The graph of which inequality is shown?

Ⓐ $x + y \leq -1$ Ⓑ $x + y \geq -1$

Ⓒ $x - y \leq -1$ Ⓓ $x - y \geq -1$

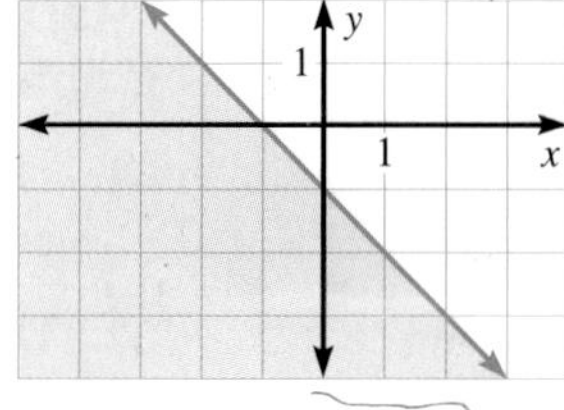

GRAPHING INEQUALITIES Graph the inequality.

17. $y > x + 3$
18. $y \leq x - 2$
19. $y < 3x + 5$
20. $y \geq -2x + 8$
21. $x + y < -8$
22. $x - y \leq -11$
23. $x + 8y > 16$
24. $5x - y \geq 1$
25. $2(x + 2) > 7y$
26. $y - 4 < x - 6$
27. $-4y \leq 16x$
28. $6(2x) \geq -24y$
29. $y < -3$
30. $x \geq 5$
31. $x > -2$
32. $y \leq 4$
33. $3(x - 2) > y + 8$
34. $x - 4 \leq -2(y + 6)$
35. $\frac{1}{2}(x + 2) + 3y < 8$
36. $2(x + 1) \geq \frac{1}{4}y - 1$

ERROR ANALYSIS *Describe* and correct the error in graphing the inequality.

37. $2y - x \geq 2$

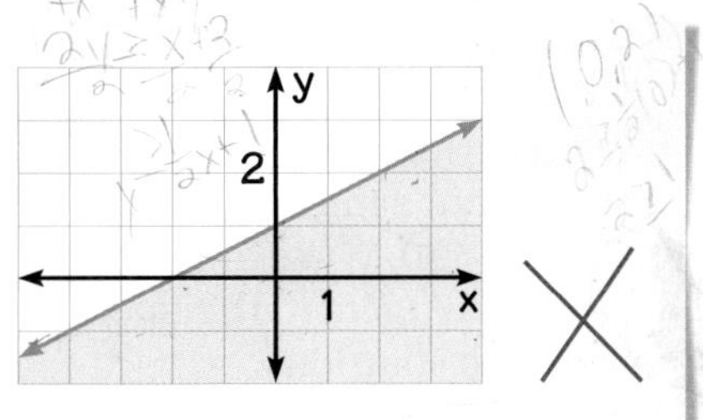

38. $x \leq -3$

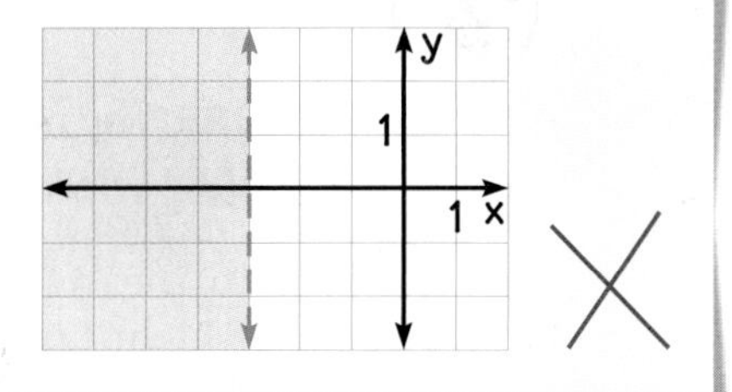

39. ★ **WRITING** Can you use (0, 0) as a test point when graphing $2x > -5y$? *Explain* your reasoning.

TRANSLATING SENTENCES **Write the verbal sentence as an inequality. Then graph the inequality.**

40. Four less than x is greater than or equal to y.
41. The product of -2 and y is less than or equal to the sum of x and 6.
42. The quotient of y and 2 is greater than the difference of 7 and x.
43. The sum of x and the product of 4 and y is less than -3.

USING A GRAPH **Write an inequality of the graph shown.**

44.

45.

46.

WRITING INEQUALITIES **Write an inequality whose graph contains only the points in the given quadrants.**

47. Quadrants I and II
48. Quadrants II and III
49. Quadrants III and IV
50. Quadrants I and IV

CHALLENGE **In Exercises 51 and 52, write and graph an inequality whose graph is described by the given information.**

51. The points (2, 5) and (−3, −5) lie on the boundary line. The points (6, 5) and (−2, −3) are solutions of the inequality.
52. The points (−7, −16) and (1, 8) lie on the boundary line. The points (−7, 0) and (3, 14) are *not* solutions of the inequality.

PROBLEM SOLVING

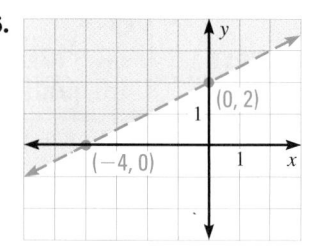

EXAMPLE 6 on p. 408 for Exs. 53–57

53. **BOBSLEDS** In a two-man bobsled competition, the sum of the weight x (in pounds) of the bobsled and the combined weight y (in pounds) of the athletes must not exceed 860 pounds. Write and graph an inequality that describes the possible weights of the bobsled and the athletes. Identify and interpret one of the solutions.

    @HomeTutor for problem solving help at classzone.com

54. **ELEVATORS** The number y of passengers riding an elevator can be no greater than the elevator's maximum weight capacity x (in pounds) divided by 150. Write and graph an inequality that relates the number of passengers to the maximum weight capacity. Identify and interpret one of the solutions.

    @HomeTutor for problem solving help at classzone.com

○ = **WORKED-OUT SOLUTIONS** on p. WS1 ★ = **STANDARDIZED TEST PRACTICE**

= **MULTIPLE REPRESENTATIONS**

55. **MULTIPLE REPRESENTATIONS** You tutor Spanish for \$15 per hour and French for \$10 per hour. You want to earn at least \$100 per week.

a. **Writing an Inequality** Write an inequality that describes your goal in terms of hours spent tutoring Spanish and hours spent tutoring French.

b. **Drawing a Graph** Graph the inequality. Then give three possible combinations of hours that meet your goal.

c. **Making a Table** Make a table that gives the amount of money that you will earn for each combination of hours given in part (b).

56. ★ **MULTIPLE CHOICE** To compete in a piano competition, you need to perform two musical pieces whose combined duration is no greater than 15 minutes. Which inequality describes the possible durations x and y (in minutes) of the pieces?

(A) $x + y < 15$ (B) $x + y \le 15$ (C) $x + y > 15$ (D) $x + y \ge 15$

57. **MULTI-STEP PROBLEM** You are making muffins and loaves of bread for a bake sale. You need $\frac{1}{6}$ batch of batter per muffin and $\frac{1}{2}$ batch of batter per loaf of bread. You have enough ingredients to make up to 12 batches of batter.

a. Write and graph an inequality that describes the possible combinations of muffins m and loaves ℓ of bread that you can make.

b. You make 4 loaves of bread. What are the possible numbers of muffins that you can make?

58. **NUTRITION** A nutritionist recommends that the fat calories y consumed per day should be at most 30% of the total calories x consumed per day.

a. Write and graph an inequality that relates the number of fat calories consumed to the total calories consumed.

b. Use the nutrition labels below. You normally consume 2000 calories per day. So far today you have eaten 6 crackers and 1 container of yogurt. What are the possible additional fat calories that you can consume today?

59. ★ **SHORT RESPONSE** You need to bring a duffel and a bedroll for a trip in the mountains. The sum of the weight x (in pounds) of the duffel and the weight y (in pounds) of the bedroll cannot exceed 30 pounds.

a. **Graph and Apply** Write and graph a linear inequality that describes the possible weights of the duffel and bedroll. Then give three possible combinations of weights of the duffel and bedroll.

b. **Interpret** Are (0, 30) and (30, 0) solutions of the inequality in part (a)? Do these ordered pairs make sense for this situation? *Explain.*

60. ★ **EXTENDED RESPONSE** A financial advisor suggests that if a person is an aggressive investor, the percent y of money that the person invests in stocks should be greater than the difference of 110 and the person's age x.

a. **Graph** Write and graph a linear inequality that relates the percent of money invested in stocks to an aggressive investor's age.

b. **Calculate** If an aggressive investor is 30 years old, what are the possible percents that the investor can invest in stocks? *Explain* your answer.

c. **Justify** Are there any ages for which none of the solutions of the inequality makes sense for this situation? *Justify* your answer.

61. **CHALLENGE** The formula $m = dV$ gives the mass m of an object in terms of the object's density d and its volume V. Water has a density of 1 gram per cubic centimeter. An object immersed in water will sink if its density is greater than the density of water. An object will float in water if its density is less than the density of water.

a. For an object that sinks, write and graph an inequality that relates its mass (in grams) to its volume (in cubic centimeters). For an object that floats, write and graph an inequality that relates its mass (in grams) to its volume (in cubic centimeters).

b. A cylindrical can has a radius of 5 centimeters, a height of 10 centimeters, and a mass of 2119.5 grams. Will the can sink or float in water? *Explain* your answer.

MIXED REVIEW

Solve the equation or inequality.

62. $-4a = 20$ *(p. 134)*

63. $3c + 8 = 17$ *(p. 141)*

64. $6m - 5 = -8m + 2$ *(p. 154)*

65. $\frac{n}{5} = \frac{n+1}{3}$ *(p. 168)*

66. $p - 9 \geq -15$ *(p. 356)*

67. $-2s + 3 < -4$ *(p. 369)*

68. $2x \geq 8$ *or* $5x < 10$ *(p. 380)*

69. $-2 < 9y - 2 \leq 5$ *(p. 380)*

70. $|g - 7| \geq 15$ *(p. 398)*

PREVIEW
Prepare for Lesson 7.1 in Exs. 71–76.

Graph the equation. *(p. 225)*

71. $x - y = 8$

72. $-6x + 2y = -12$

73. $12x + 3y = -9$

74. $y = -7x + 1$

75. $y = 5x + 2$

76. $y = 0.5x - 5$

QUIZ *for Lessons 6.5–6.7*

Solve the equation. *(p. 390)*

1. $|x| = 5$

2. $|c - 8| = 24$

3. $-2|r - 5| = -6$

Solve the inequality. Graph your solution. *(p. 398)*

4. $|y| > 4$

5. $|2t - 5| < 3$

6. $4|3s + 7| - 5 \geq 7$

Graph the inequality. *(p. 405)*

7. $x + y \geq 3$

8. $\frac{5}{7}x < 10$

9. $2y - x \leq 8$

EXTRA PRACTICE for Lesson 6.7, p. 943

ONLINE QUIZ at classzone.com

Lessons 6.5–6.7

1. **MULTI-STEP PROBLEM** You gathered 36 apples from your backyard apple tree in order to make apple pies and applesauce. You use 7 apples to make one apple pie and 5 apples to make one pint of applesauce.

   a. Write an inequality that describes the possible numbers of apple pies and pints of applesauce that you can make.

   b. Graph the inequality.

   c. Give three possible combinations of apple pies and pints of applesauce that you can make.

2. **SHORT RESPONSE** You are scooping ice cream as part of your training at an ice cream shop. The weight of a scoop must be 4 ounces with an absolute deviation of at most 0.5 ounce.

   a. Write an inequality to find the possible weights (in ounces) of each scoop.

   b. You make 10 scoops. You can start working at the shop if at least 80% of the scoops meet the weight requirement. The list shows the weights (in ounces) of your scoops.

   3.8, 4.2, 3.9, 4.5, 3.7, 4.6, 4.1, 3.3, 4.3, 4.2

   Can you start working at the shop? *Explain* your reasoning.

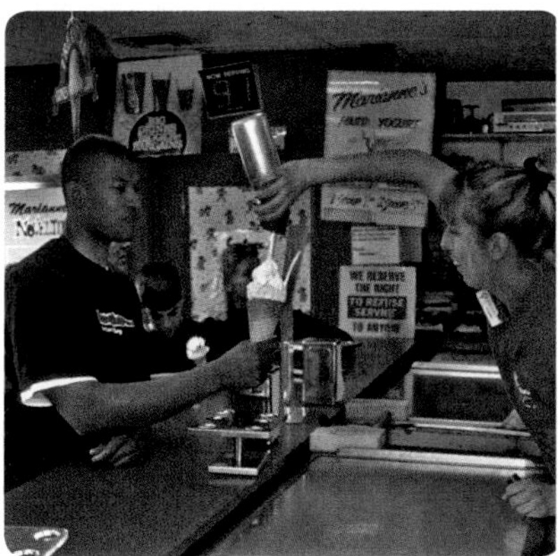

3. **GRIDDED ANSWER** You will be making a presentation in your history class. Your teacher gives you a time limit of 15 minutes with an absolute deviation of 1.5 minutes. What is the maximum possible duration (in minutes) of your presentation?

4. **OPEN-ENDED** *Describe* a real-world situation that can be modeled by the equation $|x - 50| = 10$. *Explain* what the solution of the equation means in this situation.

5. **EXTENDED RESPONSE** A tour operator recommends that a river rafter wear a protective suit under the temperature conditions described below.

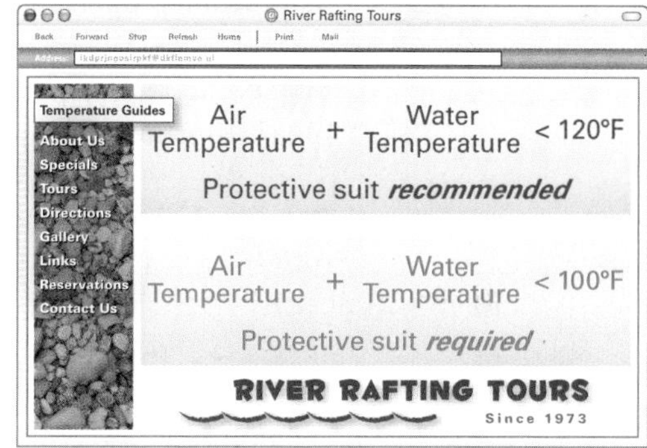

   a. Write and graph an inequality that describes the possible air temperatures and water temperatures for which a protective suit is recommended.

   b. If the water temperature is 40°F, for which air temperatures is a protective suit recommended?

   c. How would you change the graph in part (a) in order to describe the situations in which a protective suit is required? *Explain* your answer.

6. **MULTI-STEP PROBLEM** You are buying a new cell phone and see eight phones listed on a website. The prices of the phones are shown.

   \$139, \$249, \$229, \$199, \$179, \$359, \$199, \$209

   a. Find the mean price of the phones.

   b. You are willing to purchase a phone that has the mean price with an absolute deviation of at most \$50. Write and solve an inequality to find the prices of phones that you will consider.

   c. How many of the phones on the website will you consider buying?

6 CHAPTER SUMMARY

BIG IDEAS

For Your Notebook

Big Idea 1

Applying Properties of Inequality

You can apply the properties of inequality to solve inequalities. The properties listed below are also true for inequalities involving ≤ and ≥.

Property	If $a < b$, then ...	If $a > b$, then ...
Addition property of inequality	$a + c < b + c$.	$a + c > b + c$.
Subtraction property of inequality	$a - c < b - c$.	$a - c > b - c$.
Multiplication property of inequality	$ac < bc$ if $c > 0$. $ac > bc$ if $c < 0$.	$ac > bc$ if $c > 0$. $ac < bc$ if $c < 0$.
Division property of inequality	$\frac{a}{c} < \frac{b}{c}$ if $c > 0$. $\frac{a}{c} > \frac{b}{c}$ if $c < 0$.	$\frac{a}{c} > \frac{b}{c}$ if $c > 0$. $\frac{a}{c} < \frac{b}{c}$ if $c < 0$.

Big Idea 2

Using Statements with *And* or *Or*

An absolute value equation can be rewritten as two equations joined by *or*. An absolute value inequality can be rewritten as a compound inequality with *and* or *or*. In the statements below, < can be replaced by ≤, and > can be replaced by ≥.

Absolute value equation or inequality	Equivalent statement with *and* or *or*
$\lvert ax + b \rvert = c, c \geq 0$	$ax + b = c$ or $ax + b = -c$
$\lvert ax + b \rvert < c, c \geq 0$	$-c < ax + b < c$
$\lvert ax + b \rvert > c, c \geq 0$	$ax + b < -c$ or $ax + b > c$

Big Idea 3

Graphing Inequalities

You use a number line to graph an inequality in one variable. Similarly, you use a coordinate plane to graph a linear inequality in two variables (including cases where one of the variables has a coefficient of 0, such as $0x + y < 1$, or $y < 1$).

Graphing inequalities in one variable	Graphing linear inequalities in two variables
Graph simple inequalities: 1. Solve for the variable. 2. Draw an open circle for < or > and a closed circle for ≤ or ≥. Draw an arrow in the appropriate direction. Graph compound inequalities: 1. Solve the compound inequality. 2. Use the union of graphs of simple inequalities for *or*. Use the intersection for *and*.	1. Graph the boundary line. Use a solid line for ≤ or ≥ and a dashed line for < or >. 2. Test a point that does not lie on the boundary line. 3. Shade the half-plane containing the point if the ordered pair is a solution of the inequality. Shade the other half-plane if the ordered pair is *not* a solution.

@HomeTutor
classzone.com
- Multi-Language Glossary
- Vocabulary practice

REVIEW KEY VOCABULARY

- graph of an inequality, *p. 356*
- equivalent inequalities, *p. 357*
- compound inequality, *p. 380*
- absolute value equation, *p. 390*
- absolute deviation, *p. 392*
- linear inequality in two variables, *p. 405*
- solution of an inequality in two variables, *p. 405*
- graph of an inequality in two variables, half-plane, *p. 405*

VOCABULARY EXERCISES

1. Translate the verbal sentence into an absolute value equation: "The absolute deviation of x from 19 is 8."
2. Identify three ordered pairs that are solutions of $2x - 3y \geq -10$.
3. **WRITING** When you graph a linear inequality in two variables, how do you know whether the boundary line is a solid line or a dashed line? How do you know which half-plane to shade?

REVIEW EXAMPLES AND EXERCISES

Use the review examples and exercises below to check your understanding of the concepts you have learned in each lesson of Chapter 6.

6.1 Solve Inequalities Using Addition and Subtraction *pp. 356–361*

EXAMPLE

Solve $x - 2.1 \leq 1.4$. Graph your solution.

$x - 2.1 \leq 1.4$	**Write original inequality.**
$x - 2.1 + 2.1 \leq 1.4 + 2.1$	**Add 2.1 to each side.**
$x \leq 3.5$	**Simplify.**

▶ The solutions are all real numbers less than or equal to 3.5.

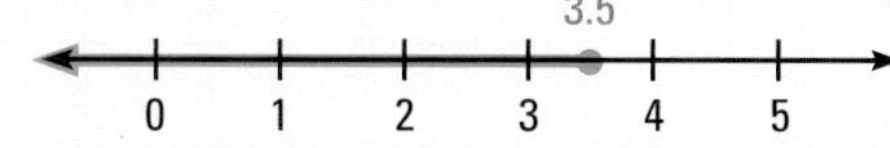

EXERCISES

EXAMPLES 1, 2, 3, and 4 on pp. 356–358 for Exs. 4–7

4. **GEOGRAPHY** The lowest elevation in Mexico is -10 meters at Laguna Salada. Write and graph an inequality that describes all elevations in Mexico that are greater than the lowest elevation.

Solve the inequality. Graph your solution.

5. $x + 5 > -13$
6. $m - 9 \geq -4$
7. $s + 3.7 < 1$

6 CHAPTER REVIEW

6.2 Solve Inequalities Using Multiplication and Division *pp. 363–368*

EXAMPLE

Solve $\frac{x}{-4} < 9$. Graph your solution.

$\frac{x}{-4} < 9$	**Write original inequality.**
$-4 \cdot \frac{x}{-4} > -4 \cdot 9$	**Multiply each side by −4. Reverse inequality symbol.**
$x > -36$	**Simplify.**

▶ The solutions are all real numbers greater than −36.

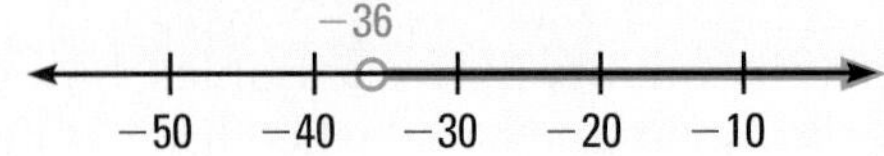

EXERCISES

EXAMPLES 1, 2, 3, 4, and 5 on pp. 363–365 for Exs. 8–12

Solve the inequality. Graph your solution.

8. $\frac{p}{2} \le 5$ **9.** $\frac{n}{-4.5} < -8$ **10.** $-3x > 27$ **11.** $2y \ge 18$

12. GYMNASTICS In men's gymnastics, an athlete competes in 6 events. Suppose that an athlete's average score per event is at most 9.7 points. Write and solve an inequality to find the possible total scores for the athlete.

6.3 Solve Multi-Step Inequalities *pp. 369–374*

EXAMPLE

Solve $-4x + 7 \ge -13$. Graph your solution.

$-4x + 7 \ge -13$	**Write original inequality.**
$-4x \ge -20$	**Subtract 7 from each side.**
$x \le 5$	**Divide each side by −4. Reverse inequality symbol.**

▶ The solutions are all real numbers less than or equal to 5.

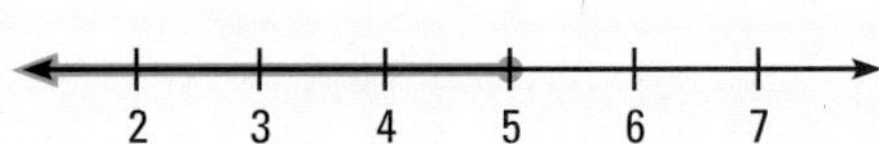

EXERCISES

EXAMPLES 1, 2, 3, and 4 on pp. 369–370 for Exs. 13–19

Solve the inequality, if possible. Graph your solution.

13. $2g + 11 < 25$ **14.** $\frac{2}{3}r - 4 \ge 1$ **15.** $1 - 3x \le -14 + 2x$

16. $3(q + 1) < 3q + 7$ **17.** $8(t - 1) > -8 + 8t$ **18.** $-3(2n - 1) \ge 1 - 8n$

19. TICKET PURCHASES You can order discount movie tickets from a website for $7 each. You must also pay a shipping fee of $4. You want to spend no more than $40 on movie tickets. Find the possible numbers of movie tickets that you can order.

@HomeTutor
classzone.com
Chapter Review Practice

6.4 Solve Compound Inequalities

pp. 380–387

EXAMPLE

Solve $-1 < -2x + 7 < 9$. Graph your solution.

$-1 < -2x + 7 < 9$ **Write original inequality.**

$-8 < -2x < 2$ **Subtract 7 from each expression.**

$4 > x > -1$ **Divide each expression by −2. Reverse both inequality symbols.**

$-1 < x < 4$ **Rewrite in the form $a < x < b$.**

▶ The solutions are all real numbers greater than −1 *and* less than 4.

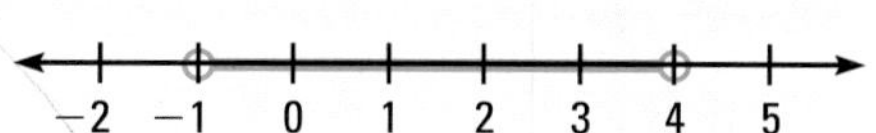

EXERCISES

EXAMPLES 3, 4, and 5 on pp. 381–382 for Exs. 20–23

Solve the inequality. Graph your solution.

20. $-6 \le 2t - 5 \le -3$

21. $-3 < -3x + 8 < 11$

22. $9s - 6 < 12$ *or* $3s + 1 > 13$

23. $-4w + 12 \ge 10$ *or* $5w - 14 > -4$

6.5 Solve Absolute Value Equations

pp. 390–395

EXAMPLE

Solve $4|5x - 3| + 6 = 30$.

First, rewrite the equation in the form $|ax + b| = c$.

$4|5x - 3| + 6 = 30$ **Write original equation.**

$4|5x - 3| = 24$ **Subtract 6 from each side.**

$|5x - 3| = 6$ **Divide each side by 4.**

Next, solve the absolute value equation.

$5x - 3 = 6$ *or* $5x - 3 = -6$ **Rewrite as two equations.**

$5x = 9$ *or* $5x = -3$ **Add 3 to each side.**

$x = 1.8$ *or* $x = -0.6$ **Divide each side by 5.**

▶ The solutions are −0.6 and 1.8.

EXERCISES

EXAMPLES 1, 2, 3, 4, and 5 on pp. 390–392 for Exs. 24–30

Solve the equation, if possible.

24. $|r| = 7$

25. $|a + 6| = 2$

26. $|2c + 5| = 21$

27. $2|x - 3| + 1 = 5$

28. $3|2q + 1| - 5 = 1$

29. $4|3p - 2| + 5 = 11$

30. BOWLING In tenpin bowling, the height of each bowling pin must be 15 inches with an absolute deviation of 0.03125 inch. Find the minimum and maximum possible heights of a bowling pin.

6 CHAPTER REVIEW

6.6 Solve Absolute Value Inequalities

pp. 398–403

EXAMPLE

Solve $3|2x + 11| + 2 \le 17$. Graph your solution.

$3|2x + 11| + 2 \le 17$	**Write original inequality.**
$3|2x + 11| \le 15$	**Subtract 2 from each side.**
$|2x + 11| \le 5$	**Divide each side by 3.**
$-5 \le 2x + 11 \le 5$	**Rewrite as compound inequality.**
$-16 \le 2x \le -6$	**Subtract 11 from each expression.**
$-8 \le x \le -3$	**Divide each expression by 2.**

▸ The solutions are all real numbers greater than or equal to -8 *and* less than or equal to -3.

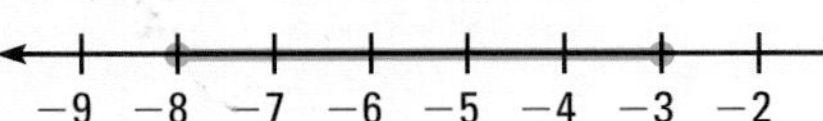

EXERCISES

EXAMPLES 1, 2, and 3 on pp. 398–399 for Exs. 31–36

Solve the inequality. Graph your solution.

31. $|m| \ge 8$ **32.** $|6k + 1| \ge 2$ **33.** $|3g - 2| < 5$

34. $6|3x + 5| \le 14$ **35.** $|2j - 9| - 2 > 10$ **36.** $5|d + 8| - 7 > 13$

6.7 Graph Linear Inequalities in Two Variables

pp. 405–412

EXAMPLE

Graph the inequality $y < 3x - 1$.

STEP 1 **Graph** the equation $y = 3x - 1$. The inequality is $<$, so use a dashed line.

STEP 2 **Test** (0, 0) in $y < 3x - 1$.

$$0 \stackrel{?}{<} 3(0) - 1$$

$$0 < -1 \text{ ✗}$$

STEP 3 **Shade** the half-plane that does not contain (0, 0), because (0, 0) is *not* a solution of the inequality.

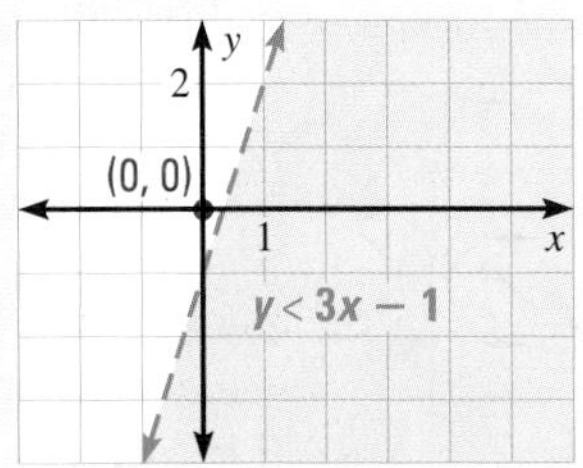

EXERCISES

EXAMPLES 1, 2, 3, 4, and 5 on pp. 405–407 for Exs. 37–44

Tell whether the ordered pair is a solution of $-3x + 2y \ge 16$.

37. (−2, 8) **38.** (−1, −1) **39.** (−2, 10) **40.** (9, −5)

Graph the inequality.

41. $y > 2x + 3$ **42.** $y \le \frac{1}{2}x - 1$ **43.** $3x - 2y < 12$ **44.** $y \ge 3$

6.4 Solve Compound Inequalities

pp. 380–387

EXAMPLE

Solve $-1 < -2x + 7 < 9$. Graph your solution.

$-1 < -2x + 7 < 9$	**Write original inequality.**
$-8 < -2x < 2$	**Subtract 7 from each expression.**
$4 > x > -1$	**Divide each expression by -2. Reverse both inequality symbols.**
$-1 < x < 4$	**Rewrite in the form $a < x < b$.**

▶ The solutions are all real numbers greater than -1 *and* less than 4.

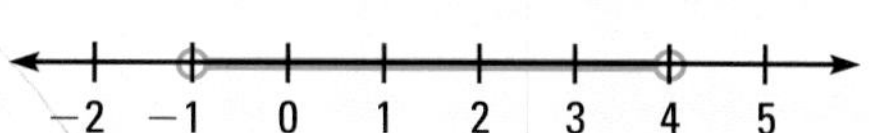

EXERCISES

EXAMPLES 3, 4, and 5 on pp. 381–382 for Exs. 20–23

Solve the inequality. Graph your solution.

20. $-6 \le 2t - 5 \le -3$

21. $-3 < -3x + 8 < 11$

22. $9s - 6 < 12$ *or* $3s + 1 > 13$

23. $-4w + 12 \ge 10$ *or* $5w - 14 > -4$

6.5 Solve Absolute Value Equations

pp. 390–395

EXAMPLE

Solve $4|5x - 3| + 6 = 30$.

First, rewrite the equation in the form $|ax + b| = c$.

$4|5x - 3| + 6 = 30$	**Write original equation.**
$4|5x - 3| = 24$	**Subtract 6 from each side.**
$|5x - 3| = 6$	**Divide each side by 4.**

Next, solve the absolute value equation.

$5x - 3 = 6$ *or* $5x - 3 = -6$	**Rewrite as two equations.**
$5x = 9$ *or* $5x = -3$	**Add 3 to each side.**
$x = 1.8$ *or* $x = -0.6$	**Divide each side by 5.**

▶ The solutions are -0.6 and 1.8.

EXERCISES

EXAMPLES 1, 2, 3, 4, and 5 on pp. 390–392 for Exs. 24–30

Solve the equation, if possible.

24. $|r| = 7$

25. $|a + 6| = 2$

26. $|2c + 5| = 21$

27. $2|x - 3| + 1 = 5$

28. $3|2q + 1| - 5 = 1$

29. $4|3p - 2| + 5 = 11$

30. BOWLING In tenpin bowling, the height of each bowling pin must be 15 inches with an absolute deviation of 0.03125 inch. Find the minimum and maximum possible heights of a bowling pin.

6 CHAPTER REVIEW

6.6 Solve Absolute Value Inequalities

pp. 398–403

EXAMPLE

Solve $3|2x + 11| + 2 \le 17$. Graph your solution.

$3|2x + 11| + 2 \le 17$	**Write original inequality.**
$3|2x + 11| \le 15$	**Subtract 2 from each side.**
$|2x + 11| \le 5$	**Divide each side by 3.**
$-5 \le 2x + 11 \le 5$	**Rewrite as compound inequality.**
$-16 \le 2x \le -6$	**Subtract 11 from each expression.**
$-8 \le x \le -3$	**Divide each expression by 2.**

▶ The solutions are all real numbers greater than or equal to -8 *and* less than or equal to -3.

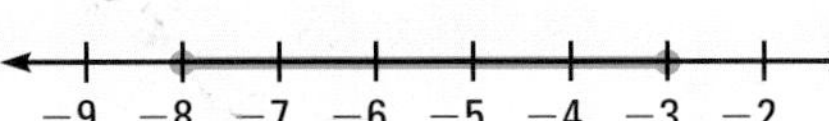

EXERCISES

EXAMPLES 1, 2, and 3 on pp. 398–399 for Exs. 31–36

Solve the inequality. Graph your solution.

31. $|m| \ge 8$ **32.** $|6k + 1| \ge 2$ **33.** $|3g - 2| < 5$

34. $6|3x + 5| \le 14$ **35.** $|2j - 9| - 2 > 10$ **36.** $5|d + 8| - 7 > 13$

6.7 Graph Linear Inequalities in Two Variables

pp. 405–412

EXAMPLE

Graph the inequality $y < 3x - 1$.

STEP 1 **Graph** the equation $y = 3x - 1$. The inequality is $<$, so use a dashed line.

STEP 2 **Test** (0, 0) in $y < 3x - 1$.

$$0 \overset{?}{<} 3(0) - 1$$

$$0 < -1 \text{ ✗}$$

STEP 3 **Shade** the half-plane that does not contain (0, 0), because (0, 0) is *not* a solution of the inequality.

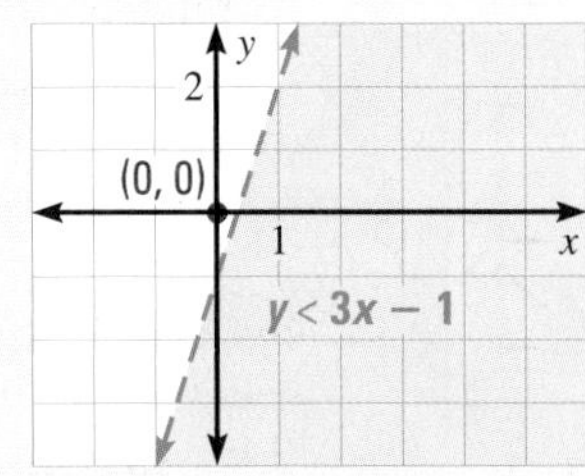

EXERCISES

EXAMPLES 1, 2, 3, 4, and 5 on pp. 405–407 for Exs. 37–44

Tell whether the ordered pair is a solution of $-3x + 2y \ge 16$.

37. $(-2, 8)$ **38.** $(-1, -1)$ **39.** $(-2, 10)$ **40.** $(9, -5)$

Graph the inequality.

41. $y > 2x + 3$ **42.** $y \le \frac{1}{2}x - 1$ **43.** $3x - 2y < 12$ **44.** $y \ge 3$

6 CHAPTER TEST

Translate the verbal phrase into an inequality. Then graph the inequality.

1. All real numbers that are less than 5
2. All real numbers that are greater than or equal to −1
3. All real numbers that are greater than −2 *and* less than or equal to 7
4. All real numbers that are greater than 8 *or* less than −4

Solve the inequality, if possible. Graph your solution.

5. $x - 9 \geq -5$
6. $-2 > 5 + y$
7. $-0.8 \leq z + 7.7$
8. $5m \geq 35$
9. $\frac{n}{6} < -1$
10. $\frac{r}{-3} \leq 4$
11. $-4s < 6s + 1$
12. $4t - 7 \leq 13$
13. $-8 > 5 - v$
14. $3(5w + 4) < 12w - 11$
15. $4p - 3 > 2(2p + 1)$
16. $9q - 12 \geq 3(3q - 4)$
17. $-2 \leq 4 - 3a \leq 13$
18. $-7 < 2c - 1 < 10\frac{1}{2}$
19. $-5 \leq 2 - h$ *or* $6h + 5 \geq 71$
20. $|2d + 8| > 3$
21. $2|3f - 7| + 5 < 11$
22. $|j - 7| - 1 \leq 3\frac{5}{6}$

Solve the equation, if possible.

23. $-\frac{3}{4}|x - 3| = \frac{1}{4}$
24. $|3y + 1| - 6 = -2$
25. $4|2z + 5| + 9 = 5$

Check whether the ordered pair is a solution of the inequality.

26. $2x - y < 4$; $(2, -1)$
27. $y + 3x \geq -5$; $(-3, -4)$
28. $y \leq -3$; $(4, -7)$

Graph the inequality.

29. $y < x + 4$
30. $y \geq 2x - 5$
31. $y \geq -6$

32. **BUSINESS** Your friend is starting a small business baking and decorating cakes and wants to make a profit of at least \$250 for the first month. The expenses for the first month are \$155. What are the possible revenues that your friend can earn in order to meet the profit goal?

33. **BICYCLES** A manufacturer of bicycle parts requires that a bicycle chain have a width of 0.3 inch with an absolute error of at most 0.0003 inch. Find the possible widths of bicycle chains that the manufacturer will accept.

34. **HORSES** You are planning to ride a horse to a campsite. The sum of your weight x (in pounds) and the combined weight y (in pounds) of your camping supplies can be at most 20% of the weight of the horse.

    a. Suppose that the horse weighs 1000 pounds. Write and graph an inequality that describes the possible combinations of your weight and the combined weight of the camping supplies.

    b. Identify and interpret one of the solutions of the inequality in part (a).

Scoring Rubric

Full Credit
- solution is complete and correct

Partial Credit
- solution is complete but errors are made, *or*
- solution is without error but incomplete

No Credit
- no solution is given, *or*
- solution makes no sense

EXTENDED RESPONSE QUESTIONS

PROBLEM

Your school chess club is selling chess sets for \$9 each to raise funds for a regional tournament. The club wants to sell at least 100 of them. The table shows the number of chess sets sold so far by each member of the club.

Member	1	2	3	4	5	6
Chess sets sold	17	16	12	13	16	10

a. Find the possible numbers a of additional chess sets that the club can sell in order to meet its goal.

b. If the club raises more than \$1000, it will donate the amount that exceeds \$1000 to a charity. Find the possible total numbers t of chess sets that the club can sell in order to donate at least \$100 to the charity.

c. Suppose the club has 61 chess sets left to sell. Write an inequality that describes the possible amounts that the club can donate to the charity. *Explain* your answer.

Below are sample solutions to the problem. Read each solution and the comments in blue to see why the sample represents full credit, partial credit, or no credit.

Sample 1: Full credit solution

The correct inequality is given. The solution is correct.

a. $17 + 16 + 12 + 13 + 16 + 10 + a \geq 100$

$$84 + a \geq 100$$

$$a \geq 16$$

The club will meet its goal if it sells at least 16 more chess sets.

The correct inequality is given. The student rounded correctly so that the answer makes sense.

b. $9t - 1000 \geq 100$

$$9t \geq 1100$$

$$t \geq 122.22\ldots$$

The club can donate only $\$9(122) - \$1000 = \$98$ if it sells 122 sets. So, the club can donate at least \$100 if it sells at least 123 sets.

The student's calculation of the least and greatest values is correct. The answer is correct.

c. If the club doesn't sell any more chess sets, it will have raised a total of $\$9(84) = \$756$. Because the club will not have raised at least \$1000, its donation to the charity would be \$0. If the club sells the remaining 61 chess sets, it will have raised a total of $\$756 + \$9(61) = \$1305$. So, the club's donation to the charity would be $\$1305 - \$1000 = \$305$. The inequality is $0 \leq d \leq 305$ where d is the donation in dollars.

Sample 2: Partial credit solution

The correct inequality is given. The solution is correct.

a. $84 + a \geq 100$

$a \geq 16$

The club must sell at least 16 chess sets.

The student solved the inequality correctly but gave the wrong answer.

b. $9t - 1000 \geq 100$

$9t \geq 1100$

$t \geq 122.22\ldots$

The club can donate at least \$100 if it sells at least 122 sets.

The reasoning doesn't make sense, and the inequality is incorrect.

c. If the club doesn't sell any more chess sets, it will raise \$0 more. So, the donation would be \$0. If the club sells the remaining 61 sets, it will raise $\$9(61) = \$549$ more. So, the donation would be at most \$549. The inequality is $0 \leq d \leq 549$ where d is the donation.

Sample 3: No credit solution

The inequalities in parts (a) and (b) are incorrect, and the answers are incorrect.

a. $84 + a \leq 100$

$a \leq 16$

The club will meet its goal if it sells up to 16 chess sets.

b. $9t \geq 1000$

$t \geq 111.11\ldots$

The club can donate at least \$100 if it sells at least 112 chess sets.

The student didn't consider the number of chess sets the club can sell.

c. The donation would be \$0 if the club raised up to \$1000. But the donation would be greater than \$0 if the club raised more than \$1000. The inequality is $d \geq 0$ where d is the donation.

PRACTICE Apply the Scoring Rubric

1. A student's solution to the problem on the previous page is given below. Score the solution as *full credit, partial credit,* or *no credit. Explain* your reasoning. If you choose *partial credit* or *no credit,* explain how you would change the solution so that it earns a score of full credit.

a. Because $a \geq 100 - 84$, the club must sell at least 16 sets to meet its goal.

b. The total amount raised is $9t$. In order to donate at least \$100, the club needs to raise a total of at least \$1100.

$9t \geq 1100$, so $t \geq 122.22\ldots$

c. If the club sells the remaining 61 sets, then it will have raised $\$9(61) = \$549$ more. The inequality is $d \leq 549$ where d is the donation.

EXTENDED RESPONSE

1. You plan to work a total of 20 hours per week at two part-time jobs. The table shows the hourly wage at each job.

Job	Working at a sandwich shop	After-school tutoring
Hourly wage (dollars)	5.50	7.00

   a. You want to earn from \$100 to \$120 per week. What are the possible numbers of hours that you can work at the sandwich shop so that you can meet your earnings goal?

   b. Suppose you need to reduce the total number of hours you work each week to 18 hours. Can you still meet your earnings goal? If so, what are the least and greatest numbers of hours that you can work at the sandwich shop? If not, explain why not.

   c. Show that it is not possible to earn more than \$150 after working 20 hours in one week by writing and solving an inequality that describes the situation and showing that the solutions do not make sense for the situation.

2. You plan to spend up to \$30 on flower bulbs for a garden. The table shows the prices of tulip bulbs and daffodil bulbs.

Flower bulb	Tulip	Daffodil
Price (dollars)	3	2

   a. Write and graph an inequality that describes the possible combinations of tulip bulbs and daffodil bulbs that you can buy.

   b. Give three possible combinations of tulip bulbs and daffodil bulbs that you can buy.

   c. Suppose you plan to spend up to \$40 on flower bulbs. How would you change the graph in part (a) in order to describe this situation? *Explain* your answer.

3. The average number of hits h per day that your website received during the period January 2001 to February 2004 can be modeled by the equation $h = -16|m - 30| + 500$ where m is the number of months since January 2001.

   a. In what month and year did your website receive an average of 100 hits per day? If the model holds for months after February 2004, predict the month and year in which your website will again receive an average of 100 hits per day.

   b. According to the model, did your website receive an average of 600 hits per day at any time during the period January 2001 to February 2004? *Explain* your answer.

   c. Can you use the model to find the month and year in which the average number of hits per day was the greatest? *Justify* your answer.

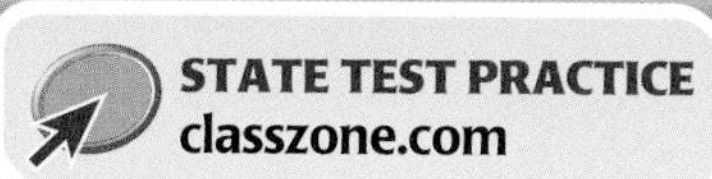

MULTIPLE CHOICE

4. In a piano competition, a pianist must perform a sonata that lasts no less than 8 minutes and no more than 10 minutes. Which inequality represents the durations d (in minutes) of sonatas that can be performed?

   (A) $8 < d < 10$ (B) $d \leq 8$ *or* $d \geq 10$

   (C) $8 \leq d \leq 10$ (D) $d < 8$ *or* $d > 10$

5. Which ordered pair is a solution of the inequality $4x - y \geq 3$?

   (A) (0, 0) (B) (−1, 2)

   (C) (1, 1) (D) (0, −2)

6. You are designing an obstacle course for a dog agility event. The course includes a tunnel that must have a height of 24 inches with an absolute deviation of 2 inches. Which equation can you use to find the minimum and maximum heights of the tunnel?

   (A) $|x + 24| = 2$ (B) $|x - 24| = 2$

   (C) $|x + 2| = 24$ (D) $|x - 2| = 24$

GRIDDED ANSWER

7. You scored the following points in four basketball games: 16, 24, 32, and 22. You want to score an average of more than 25 points per game after your fifth game. Of all the possible points you can score in your fifth game in order to meet your goal, which is the least?

8. In men's weightlifting, the bar that holds the weights must have a length of 2.2 meters with an absolute deviation of 1 millimeter. Of all the possible lengths that the bar can have, which is the greatest length (in millimeters)?

9. Of all the numbers that are solutions of the inequality $\left|-\frac{1}{3}x + 4\right| \leq 2$, which is the least number?

10. The perimeter of the rectangle shown is at least 47 inches and at most 52 inches. Find the greatest value of x that satisfies the condition.

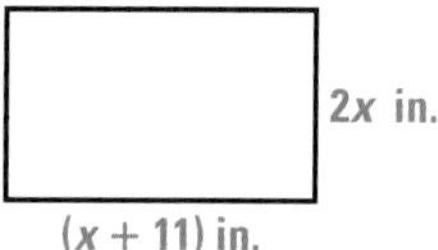

SHORT RESPONSE

11. You and 4 friends each order a three course dinner at a restaurant, and all of you agree to divide the total cost equally. The table shows the range of prices for each of the three courses.

Dinner course	Appetizer	Main course	Dessert
Price range (dollars)	2–4	12–20	3–6

   a. Find the least and greatest possible total costs C (in dollars). Then write an inequality that describes the possible total costs.

   b. Your share s (in dollars) of the total cost is given by $s = \frac{C}{5}$. You chose a \$3 appetizer, a \$15 main course, and a \$4 dessert. *Explain* why your share could be greater than or less than \$3 + \$15 + \$4 = \$22.

12. A family is planning a vacation and is willing to spend no more than \$2000 for 4 airplane tickets and 5 nights at a hotel. Write and graph an inequality that describes the combinations of prices x (in dollars) of an airplane ticket and prices y (in dollars) of a night at a hotel. If the family spends \$275 per airplane ticket, is the family willing to spend \$200 per night at a hotel? *Explain* your answer using the graph.

7 Systems of Equations and Inequalities

Before

In previous chapters, you learned the following skills, which you'll use in Chapter 7: graphing linear equations, solving equations, determining whether lines are parallel, and graphing linear inequalities in two variables.

Prerequisite Skills

VOCABULARY CHECK

Copy and complete the statement.

1. The least common multiple of 10 and 15 is __?__.
2. Two lines in the same plane are __?__ if they do not intersect.

SKILLS CHECK

Graph the equation. *(Review p. 225 for 7.1.)*

3. $x - y = 4$
4. $6x - y = -1$
5. $4x + 5y = 20$
6. $3x - 2y = -12$

Solve the equation. *(Review p. 148 for 7.2–7.4.)*

7. $5m + 4 - m = 20$
8. $10(z + 5) + z = 6$

Tell whether the graphs of the two equations are parallel lines. *Explain* your reasoning. *(Review p. 244 for 7.5.)*

9. $y = 2x - 3, y + 2x = -3$
10. $y - 5x = -1, y - 5x = 1$
11. $y = x + 10, x - y = -9$
12. $6x - y = 4, 4x - y = 6$

Graph the inequality. *(Review p. 405 for 7.6.)*

13. $y \leq -2x + 1$
14. $x - y < 5$
15. $x \geq -4$
16. $y > 3$

@HomeTutor Prerequisite skills practice at classzone.com

Now

In Chapter 7, you will apply the big ideas listed below and reviewed in the Chapter Summary on page 474. You will also use the key vocabulary listed below.

Big Ideas

1. **Solving linear systems by graphing**
2. **Solving linear systems using algebra**
3. **Solving systems of linear inequalities**

KEY VOCABULARY

- system of linear equations, *p. 427*
- solution of a system of linear equations, *p. 427*
- consistent independent system, *p. 427*
- inconsistent system, *p. 459*
- consistent dependent system, *p. 459*
- system of linear inequalities, *p. 466*
- solution of a system of linear inequalities, *p. 466*
- graph of a system of linear inequalities, *p. 466*

Why?

You can use a system of linear equations to solve problems about traveling with and against a current. For example, you can write and solve a system of linear equations to find the average speed of a kayak in still water.

Animated Algebra

The animation illustrated below for Example 4 on page 446 helps you answer this question: What is the average speed of the kayak in still water?

Start
You have to find the speed of the kayak in still water.

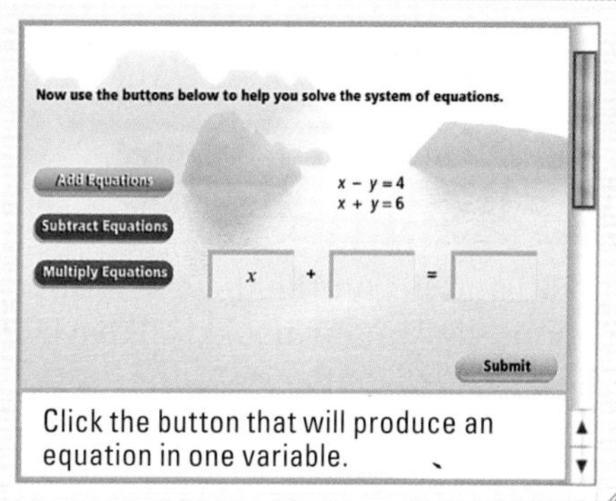
Now use the buttons below to help you solve the system of equations.
Add Equations
Subtract Equations
Multiply Equations
x − y = 4
x + y = 6
x
+
=
Submit
Click the button that will produce an equation in one variable.

Animated Algebra at classzone.com

Other animations for Chapter 7: pages 428, 435, 441, 446, 452, 459, and 466

7.1 Solving Linear Systems Using Tables

MATERIALS • pencil and paper

QUESTION How can you use a table to solve a linear system?

A *system of linear equations*, or *linear system*, consists of two or more linear equations in the same variables. A *solution of a linear system* is an ordered pair that satisfies each equation in the system. You can use a table to find a solution to a linear system.

EXPLORE Solve a linear system

Bill and his brother collect comic books. Bill currently has 15 books and adds 2 books to his collection every month. His brother currently has 7 books and adds 4 books to his collection every month. Use the equations below to find the number x of months after which Bill and his brother will have the same number y of comic books in their collections.

$y = 2x + 15$ Number of comic books in Bill's collection

$y = 4x + 7$ Number of comic books in his brother's collection

STEP 1 *Make a table*
Copy and complete the table of values shown.

x	$y = 2x + 15$	$y = 4x + 7$
0	15	7
1	?	?
2	?	?
3	?	?
4	?	?
5	?	?

STEP 2 *Find a solution*
Find an x-value that gives the same y-value for both equations.

STEP 3 *Interpret the solution*
Use your answer to Step 2 to find the number of months after which Bill and his brother have the same number of comic books.

DRAW CONCLUSIONS Use your observations to complete these exercises

1. When Bill and his brother have the same number of books in their collections, how many books will each of them have?

2. Graph the equations above on the same coordinate plane. What do you notice about the graphs and the solution you found above?

Use a table to solve the linear system.

3. $y = 2x + 3$
$y = -3x + 18$

4. $y = -x + 1$
$y = 2x - 5$

5. $y = -3x + 1$
$y = 5x - 31$

7.1 Solve Linear Systems by Graphing

Before You graphed linear equations.

Now You will graph and solve systems of linear equations.

Why? So you can analyze craft fair sales, as in Ex. 33.

Key Vocabulary
- **system of linear equations**
- **solution of a system of linear equations**
- **consistent independent system**

A **system of linear equations,** or simply a *linear system*, consists of two or more linear equations in the same variables. An example is shown below.

$x + 2y = 7$ **Equation 1**

$3x - 2y = 5$ **Equation 2**

A **solution of a system of linear equations** in two variables is an ordered pair that satisfies each equation in the system.

One way to find the solution of a linear system is by graphing. If the lines intersect in a single point, then the coordinates of the point are the solution of the linear system. A solution found using graphical methods should be checked algebraically.

EXAMPLE 1 Check the intersection point

Use the graph to solve the system. Then check your solution algebraically.

$x + 2y = 7$ **Equation 1**

$3x - 2y = 5$ **Equation 2**

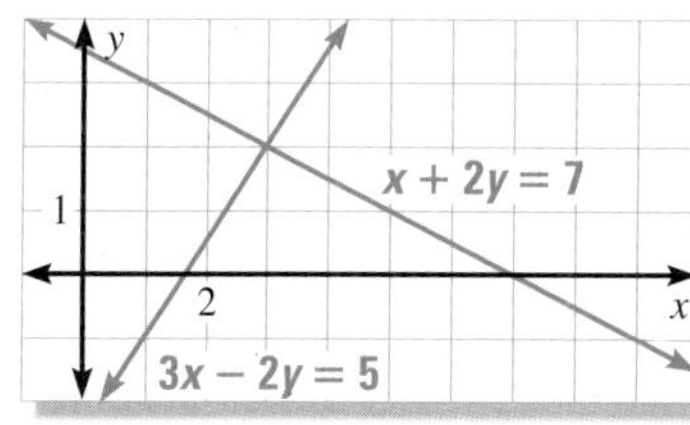

Solution

The lines appear to intersect at the point (3, 2).

CHECK Substitute 3 for x and 2 for y in each equation.

$x + 2y = 7$	$3x - 2y = 5$
$3 + 2(2) \stackrel{?}{=} 7$	$3(3) - 2(2) \stackrel{?}{=} 5$
$7 = 7$ ✓	$5 = 5$ ✓

▶ Because the ordered pair (3, 2) is a solution of each equation, it is a solution of the system.

TYPES OF LINEAR SYSTEMS In Example 1, the linear system has exactly one solution. A linear system that has exactly one solution is called a **consistent independent system** because the lines are distinct (are independent) and intersect (are consistent). You will solve consistent independent systems in Lessons 7.1–7.4. In Lesson 7.5 you will consider other types of systems.

KEY CONCEPT — *For Your Notebook*

Solving a Linear System Using the Graph-and-Check Method

STEP 1 **Graph** both equations in the same coordinate plane. For ease of graphing, you may want to write each equation in slope-intercept form.

STEP 2 **Estimate** the coordinates of the point of intersection.

STEP 3 **Check** the coordinates algebraically by substituting into each equation of the original linear system.

EXAMPLE 2 Use the graph-and-check method

Solve the linear system: $-x + y = -7$ Equation 1

$x + 4y = -8$ Equation 2

Solution

STEP 1 **Graph** both equations.

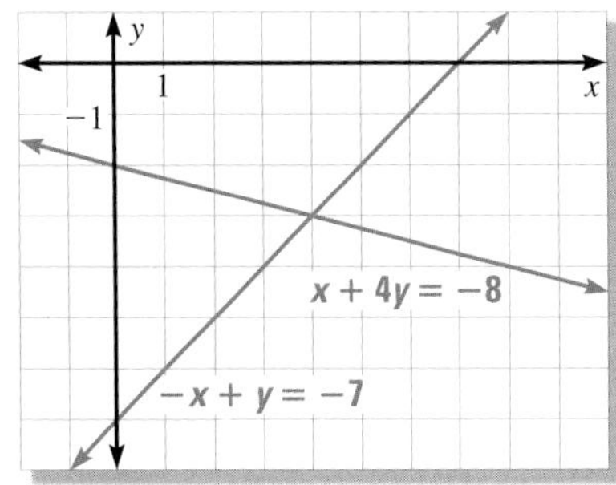

STEP 2 **Estimate** the point of intersection. The two lines appear to intersect at $(4, -3)$.

STEP 3 **Check** whether $(4, -3)$ is a solution by substituting 4 for x and -3 for y in each of the original equations.

Equation 1	**Equation 2**
$-x + y = -7$	$x + 4y = -8$
$-(4) + (-3) \stackrel{?}{=} -7$	$4 + 4(-3) \stackrel{?}{=} -8$
$-7 = -7$ ✓	$-8 = -8$ ✓

▶ Because $(4, -3)$ is a solution of each equation, it is a solution of the linear system.

 at classzone.com

✓ GUIDED PRACTICE for Examples 1 and 2

Solve the linear system by graphing. Check your solution.

1. $-5x + y = 0$
   $5x + y = 10$

2. $-x + 2y = 3$
   $2x + y = 4$

3. $x - y = 5$
   $3x + y = 3$

★ **EXAMPLE 3** **Standardized Test Practice**

The parks and recreation department in your town offers a season pass for \$90.

- As a season pass holder, you pay \$4 per session to use the town's tennis courts.
- Without the season pass, you pay \$13 per session to use the tennis courts.

Which system of equations can be used to find the number x of sessions of tennis after which the total cost y with a season pass, including the cost of the pass, is the same as the total cost without a season pass?

ELIMINATE CHOICES
You can eliminate choice A because neither of the equations include the cost of a season pass.

Ⓐ $y = 4x$
$y = 13x$

Ⓑ $y = 4x$
$y = 90 + 13x$

Ⓒ $y = 13x$
$y = 90 + 4x$

Ⓓ $y = 90 + 4x$
$y = 90 + 13x$

Solution

Write a system of equations where y is the total cost (in dollars) for x sessions.

EQUATION 1

Total cost (dollars)	=	Cost per session (dollars/session)	•	Number of sessions (sessions)
y	=	13	•	x

EQUATION 2

Total cost (dollars)	=	Cost for season pass (dollars)	+	Cost per session (dollars/session)	•	Number of sessions (sessions)
y	=	90	+	4	•	x

▶ The correct answer is C. Ⓐ Ⓑ Ⓒ Ⓓ

✓ **GUIDED PRACTICE** for Example 3

4. Solve the linear system in Example 3 to find the number of sessions after which the total cost with a season pass, including the cost of the pass, is the same as the total cost without a season pass.

5. WHAT IF? In Example 3, suppose a season pass costs \$135. After how many sessions is the total cost with a season pass, including the cost of the pass, the same as the total cost without a season pass?

EXAMPLE 4 Solve a multi-step problem

RENTAL BUSINESS A business rents in-line skates and bicycles. During one day, the business has a total of 25 rentals and collects $450 for the rentals. Find the number of pairs of skates rented and the number of bicycles rented.

Solution

STEP 1 **Write** a linear system. Let x be the number of pairs of skates rented, and let y be the number of bicycles rented.

$x + y = 25$ **Equation for number of rentals**

$15x + 30y = 450$ **Equation for money collected from rentals**

STEP 2 **Graph** both equations.

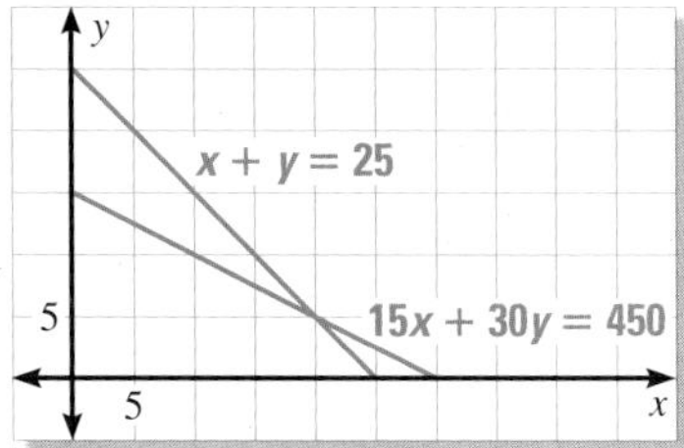

STEP 3 **Estimate** the point of intersection. The two lines appear to intersect at (20, 5).

STEP 4 **Check** whether (20, 5) is a solution.

$20 + 5 \stackrel{?}{=} 25$	$15(20) + 30(5) \stackrel{?}{=} 450$
$25 = 25$ ✓	$450 = 450$ ✓

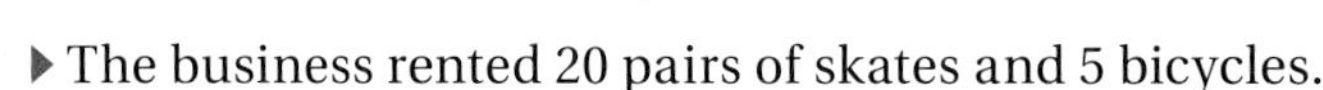

▶ The business rented 20 pairs of skates and 5 bicycles.

✓ **GUIDED PRACTICE** for Example 4

6. **WHAT IF?** In Example 4, suppose the business has a total of 20 rentals and collects $420. Find the number of bicycles rented.

7.1 EXERCISES

HOMEWORK KEY

○ = **WORKED-OUT SOLUTIONS** on p. WS16 for Exs. 15 and 31

★ = **STANDARDIZED TEST PRACTICE** Exs. 2, 6, 7, 27, 28, 29, and 32

◆ = **MULTIPLE REPRESENTATIONS** Ex. 35

SKILL PRACTICE

1. **VOCABULARY** Copy and complete: A(n) __?__ of a system of linear equations in two variables is an ordered pair that satisfies each equation in the system.

2. ★ **WRITING** *Explain* how to use the graph-and-check method to solve a linear system of two equations in two variables.

CHECKING SOLUTIONS Tell whether the ordered pair is a solution of the linear system.

3. $(-3, 1)$;
$x + y = -2$
$x + 5y = 2$

4. $(5, 2)$;
$2x - 3y = 4$
$2x + 8y = 11$

5. $(-2, 1)$;
$6x + 5y = -7$
$x - 2y = 0$

EXAMPLE 1
on p. 427
for Exs. 6–11

6. ★ **MULTIPLE CHOICE** Which ordered pair is a solution of the linear system $x + y = -2$ and $7x - 4y = 8$?

(A) $(-2, 0)$ (B) $(0, -2)$ (C) $(2, 0)$ (D) $(0, 2)$

7. ★ **MULTIPLE CHOICE** Which ordered pair is a solution of the linear system $2x + 3y = 12$ and $10x + 3y = -12$?

(A) $(-3, 3)$ (B) $(-3, 6)$ (C) $(3, 3)$ (D) $(3, 6)$

SOLVING SYSTEMS GRAPHICALLY **Use the graph to solve the linear system. Check your solution.**

8. $x - y = 4$
$4x + y = 1$

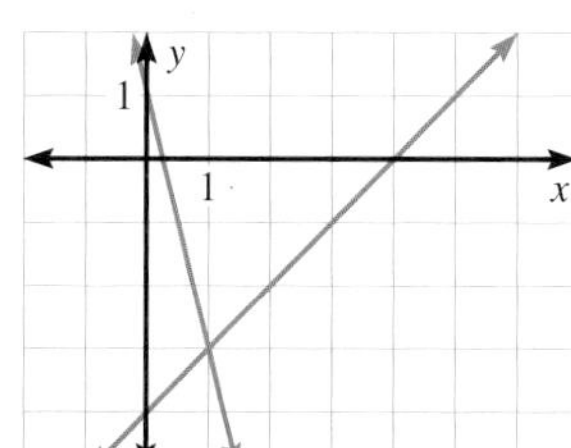

9. $-x + y = -2$
$2x - y = 6$

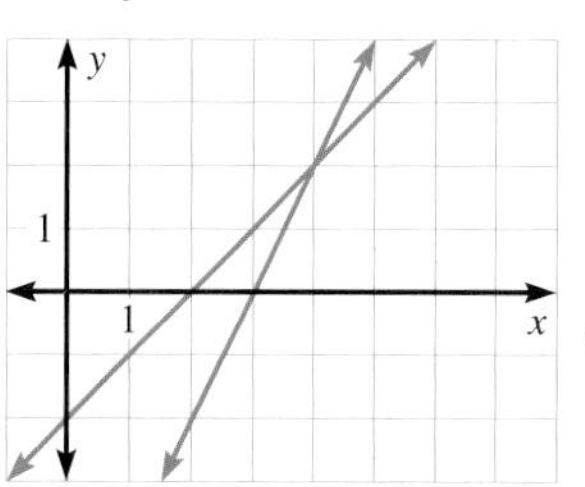

10. $x + y = 5$
$-2x + y = -4$

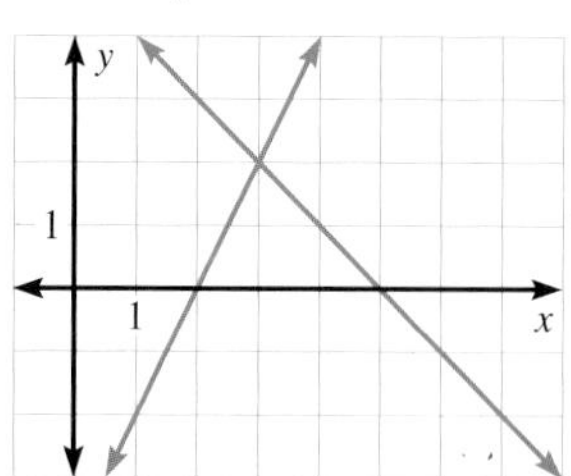

11. ERROR ANALYSIS *Describe* and correct the error in solving the linear system below.

$x - 3y = 6$ **Equation 1**
$2x - 3y = 3$ **Equation 2**

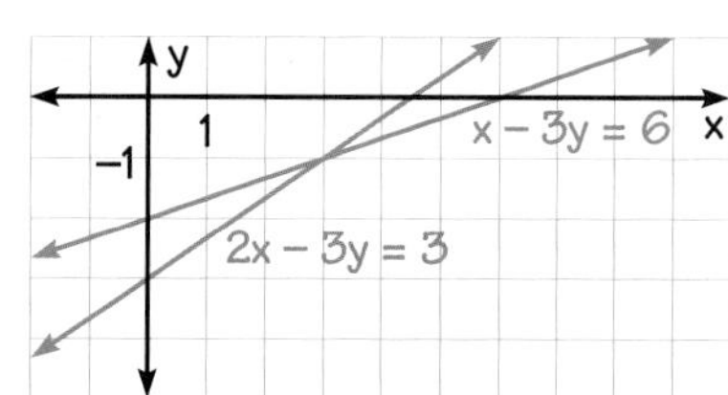

The solution is (3, −1).

EXAMPLE 2
on p. 428
for Exs. 12–26

GRAPH-AND-CHECK METHOD **Solve the linear system by graphing. Check your solution.**

12. $y = -x + 3$
$y = x + 1$

13. $y = -x + 4$
$y = 2x - 8$

14. $y = 2x + 2$
$y = 4x + 6$

15. $x - y = 2$
$x + y = -8$

16. $x + 2y = 1$
$-2x + y = -4$

17. $3x + y = 15$
$y = -15$

18. $2x - 3y = -1$
$5x + 2y = 26$

19. $6x + y = 37$
$4x + 2y = 18$

20. $7x + 5y = -3$
$-9x + y = -11$

21. $6x + 12y = -6$
$2x + 5y = 0$

22. $2x + y = 9$
$2x + 3y = 15$

23. $-5x + 3y = 3$
$4x + 3y = 30$

24. $\frac{3}{4}x + \frac{1}{4}y = \frac{13}{2}$
$x - \frac{3}{4}y = \frac{13}{2}$

25. $\frac{1}{5}x - \frac{2}{5}y = -\frac{8}{5}$
$-\frac{3}{4}x + y = 3$

26. $-1.6x - 3.2y = -24$
$2.6x + 2.6y = 26$

27. ★ **OPEN-ENDED** Find values for m and b so that the system $y = \frac{3}{5}x - 1$ and $y = mx + b$ has $(5, 2)$ as a solution.

28. ★ **WRITING** Solve the linear system shown by graphing. *Explain* why it is important to check your solution.

$y = 4x - 1.5$ **Equation 1**
$y = -2x + 1.5$ **Equation 2**

29. ★ **EXTENDED RESPONSE** Consider the equation $-\frac{1}{4}x + 6 = \frac{1}{2}x + 3$.

a. Solve the equation using algebra.

b. Solve the linear system below using a graph.

$y = -\frac{1}{4}x + 6$ **Equation 1**

$y = \frac{1}{2}x + 3$ **Equation 2**

c. How is the linear system in part (b) related to the original equation?

d. *Explain* how to use a graph to solve the equation $-\frac{2}{5}x + 5 = \frac{1}{5}x + 2$.

30. **CHALLENGE** The three lines given below form a triangle. Find the coordinates of the vertices of the triangle.

Line 1: $-3x + 2y = 1$ **Line 2:** $2x + y = 11$ **Line 3:** $x + 4y = 9$

PROBLEM SOLVING

EXAMPLES 3 and 4 on pp. 429–430 for Exs. 31–33

31. **TELEVISION** The graph shows a projection, from 1990 on, of the percent of eighth graders who watch 1 hour or less of television on a weekday and the percent of eighth graders who watch more than 1 hour of television on a weekday. Use the graph to predict the year when the percent of eighth graders who watch 1 hour or less will equal the percent who watch more than 1 hour.

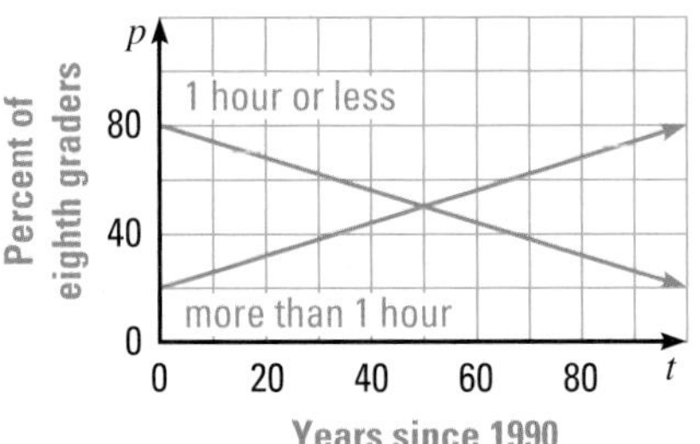

@HomeTutor for problem solving help at classzone.com

32. ★ **MULTIPLE CHOICE** A car dealership is offering interest-free car loans for one day only. During this day, a salesperson at the dealership sells two cars. One of his clients decides to pay off his $17,424 car in 36 monthly payments of $484. His other client decides to pay off his $15,840 car in 48 monthly payments of $330. Which system of equations can be used to determine the number x of months after which both clients will have the same loan balance y?

Ⓐ $y = -484x$
$y = -330x$

Ⓑ $y = -484x + 17{,}424$
$y = -330x + 15{,}840$

Ⓒ $y = -484x + 15{,}840$
$y = -330x + 17{,}424$

Ⓓ $y = 484x + 17{,}424$
$y = 330x + 15{,}840$

@HomeTutor for problem solving help at classzone.com

33. **CRAFTS** Kirigami is the Japanese art of making paper designs by folding and cutting paper. A student sells small and large greeting cards decorated with kirigami at a craft fair. The small cards cost $3 per card, and the large cards cost $5 per card. The student collects $95 for selling a total of 25 cards. How many of each type of card did the student sell?

34. **FITNESS** You want to burn 225 calories while exercising at a gym. The number of calories that you burn per minute on different machines at the gym is shown below.

Stair machine	*Elliptical trainer*	*Stationary bike*
You burn 5 Cal/min.	You burn 8 Cal/min.	You burn 6 Cal/min.

a. Suppose you have 40 minutes to exercise at the gym and you want to use the stair machine and stationary bike. How many minutes should you spend on each machine so that you burn 225 calories?

b. Suppose you have 30 minutes to exercise at the gym and you want to use the stair machine and the elliptical trainer. How many minutes should you spend on each machine so that you burn 225 calories?

35. **MULTIPLE REPRESENTATIONS** It costs \$15 for a yearly membership to a movie club at a movie theater. A movie ticket costs \$5 for club members and \$8 for nonmembers.

a. **Writing a System of Equations** Write a system of equations that you can use to find the number x of movies viewed after which the total cost y for a club member, including the membership fee, is the same as the cost for a nonmember.

b. **Making a Table** Make a table of values that shows the total cost for a club member and a nonmember after paying to see 1, 2, 3, 4, 5, and 6 movies.

c. **Drawing a Graph** Use the table to graph the system of equations. Under what circumstances does it make sense to become a movie club member? *Explain* your answer by using the graph.

36. **CHALLENGE** With a minimum purchase of \$25, you can open a credit account with a clothing store. The store is offering either \$25 or 20% off of your purchase if you open a credit account. You decide to open a credit account. Should you choose \$25 or 20% off of your purchase? *Explain.*

MIXED REVIEW

Solve the equation.

37. $x + 5 = -14$ *(p. 134)*

38. $-5x + 6 = 21$ *(p. 141)*

39. $3(x + 2) = -6$ *(p. 148)*

40. $11x + 9 = 13x - 3$ *(p. 154)*

41. $3x - 8 = 11x + 12$ *(p. 154)*

42. $4(x + 1) = -2x - 18$ *(p. 154)*

PREVIEW
Prepare for Lesson 7.2 in Exs. 43–48.

Write the equation so that y is a function of x. *(p. 184)*

43. $5y + 25 = 3x$

44. $7x = y + 9$

45. $4y + 11 = 3y + 4x$

46. $6x + 3y = 2x + 3$

47. $y + 2x + 6 = -1$

48. $4x - 12 = 5x + 2y$

@HomeTutor
classzone.com
Keystrokes

7.1 Solving Linear Systems by Graphing

QUESTION How can you use a graphing calculator to solve a linear system?

EXAMPLE Solve a linear system

Solve the linear system using a graphing calculator.

$5x + 2y = 6$ Equation 1

$x - 3y = -5$ Equation 2

STEP 1 *Rewrite equations*

Solve each equation for *y*.

Equation 1	Equation 2
$5x + 2y = 6$	$x - 3y = -5$
$2y = -5x + 6$	$-3y = -x - 5$
$y = -\frac{5}{2}x + 3$	$y = \frac{1}{3}x + \frac{5}{3}$

STEP 2 *Enter equations*

Press Y= and enter the equations.

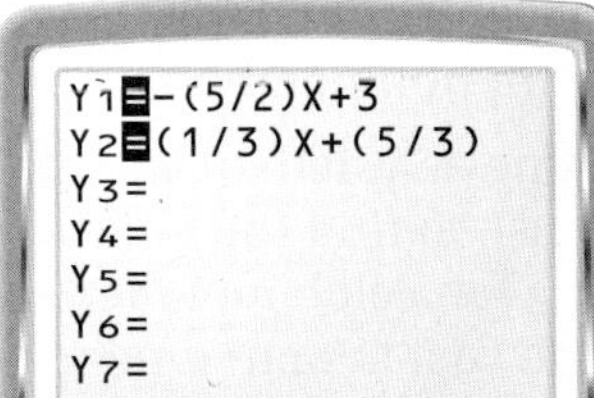

STEP 3 *Display graph*

Graph the equations using a standard viewing window.

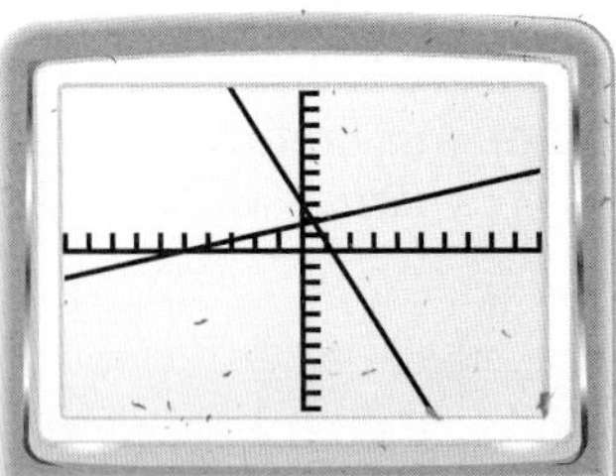

STEP 4 *Find point of intersection*

Use the *intersect* feature to find the point where the graphs intersect.

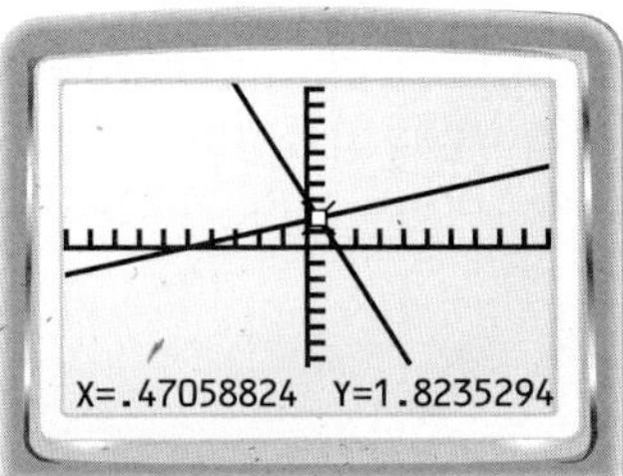

The solution is about (0.47, 1.8).

PRACTICE

Solve the linear system using a graphing calculator.

1. $y = x + 4$
   $y = -3x - 2$
2. $5x + y = -4$
   $x - y = -2$
3. $-0.45x - y = 1.35$
   $-1.8x + y = -1.8$
4. $-0.4x + 0.8y = -16$
   $1.2x + 0.4y = 1$

7.2 Solve Linear Systems by Substitution

Before You solved systems of linear equations by graphing.
Now You will solve systems of linear equations by substitution.
Why? So you can find tubing costs, as in Ex. 32.

Key Vocabulary
- **system of linear equations,** *p. 427*

KEY CONCEPT *For Your Notebook*

Solving a Linear System Using the Substitution Method

STEP 1 **Solve** one of the equations for one of its variables. When possible, solve for a variable that has a coefficient of 1 or −1.

STEP 2 **Substitute** the expression from Step 1 into the other equation and solve for the other variable.

STEP 3 **Substitute** the value from Step 2 into the revised equation from Step 1 and solve.

EXAMPLE 1 Use the substitution method

Solve the linear system: $y = 3x + 2$ Equation 1
$x + 2y = 11$ Equation 2

Solution

STEP 1 **Solve** for y. Equation 1 is already solved for y.

STEP 2 **Substitute** $3x + 2$ for y in Equation 2 and solve for x.

$x + 2y = 11$ Write Equation 2.

$x + 2(3x + 2) = 11$ Substitute $3x + 2$ for y.

$7x + 4 = 11$ Simplify.

$7x = 7$ Subtract 4 from each side.

$x = 1$ Divide each side by 7.

STEP 3 **Substitute** 1 for x in the original Equation 1 to find the value of y.

$y = 3x + 2 = 3(1) + 2 = 3 + 2 = 5$

▶ The solution is (1, 5).

CHECK Substitute 1 for x and 5 for y in each of the original equations.

$y = 3x + 2$	$x + 2y = 11$
$5 \stackrel{?}{=} 3(1) + 2$	$1 + 2(5) \stackrel{?}{=} 11$
$5 = 5$ ✓	$11 = 11$ ✓

Animated Algebra at classzone.com

EXAMPLE 2 Use the substitution method

Solve the linear system: $x - 2y = -6$ Equation 1
$4x + 6y = 4$ Equation 2

CHOOSE AN EQUATION
Equation 1 was chosen in Step 1 because x has a coefficient of 1. So, only one step is needed to solve Equation 1 for x.

Solution

STEP 1 **Solve** Equation 1 for x.

$x - 2y = -6$ Write original Equation 1.

$x = 2y - 6$ Revised Equation 1

STEP 2 **Substitute** $2y - 6$ for x in Equation 2 and solve for y.

$4x + 6y = 4$ Write Equation 2.

$4(2y - 6) + 6y = 4$ Substitute $2y - 6$ for x.

$8y - 24 + 6y = 4$ Distributive property

$14y - 24 = 4$ Simplify.

$14y = 28$ Add 24 to each side.

$y = 2$ Divide each side by 14.

STEP 3 **Substitute** 2 for y in the revised Equation 1 to find the value of x.

$x = 2y - 6$ Revised Equation 1

$x = 2(2) - 6$ Substitute 2 for y.

$x = -2$ Simplify.

▶ The solution is $(-2, 2)$.

CHECK Substitute -2 for x and 2 for y in each of the original equations.

Equation 1	Equation 2
$x - 2y = -6$	$4x + 6y = 4$
$-2 - 2(2) \stackrel{?}{=} -6$	$4(-2) + 6(2) \stackrel{?}{=} 4$
$-6 = -6$ ✓	$4 = 4$ ✓

CHECK REASONABLENESS When solving a linear system using the substitution method, you can use a graph to check the reasonableness of your solution. For example, the graph at the right verifies that $(-2, 2)$ is a solution of the linear system in Example 2.

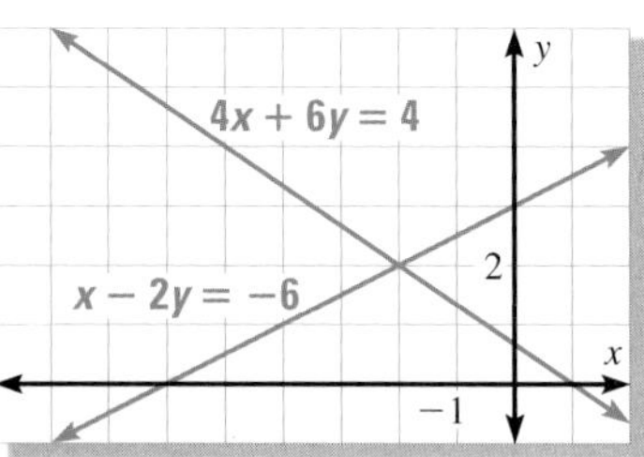

✓ GUIDED PRACTICE for Examples 1 and 2

Solve the linear system using the substitution method.

1. $y = 2x + 5$
$3x + y = 10$

2. $x - y = 3$
$x + 2y = -6$

3. $3x + y = -7$
$-2x + 4y = 0$

EXAMPLE 3 Solve a multi-step problem

ANOTHER WAY
For an alternative method for solving the problem in Example 3, turn to page 442 for the **Problem Solving Workshop**.

WEBSITES Many businesses pay website hosting companies to store and maintain the computer files that make up their websites. Internet service providers also offer website hosting. The costs for website hosting offered by a website hosting company and an Internet service provider are shown in the table. Find the number of months after which the total cost for website hosting will be the same for both companies.

Company	Set-up fee (dollars)	Cost per month (dollars)
Internet service provider	10	21.95
Website hosting company	None	22.45

Solution

STEP 1 **Write** a system of equations. Let y be the total cost after x months.

Equation 1: Internet service provider

Total cost	=	Set-up fee	+	Cost per month	·	Number of months
↓		↓		↓		↓
y	=	**10**	+	**21.95**	·	x

Equation 2: Website hosting company

Total cost	=	Cost per month	·	Number of months
↓		↓		↓
y	=	**22.45**	·	x

The system of equations is: $y = 10 + 21.95x$ **Equation 1**

$y = 22.45x$ **Equation 2**

STEP 2 **Substitute** $22.45x$ for y in Equation 1 and solve for x.

$y = 10 + 21.95x.$ **Write Equation 1.**

$22.45x = 10 + 21.95x$ **Substitute 22.45*x* for *y*.**

$0.5x = 10$ **Subtract 21.95*x* from each side.**

$x = 20$ **Divide each side by 0.5.**

▶ The total cost will be the same for both companies after 20 months.

✓ GUIDED PRACTICE for Example 3

4. In Example 3, what is the total cost for website hosting for each company after 20 months?

5. **WHAT IF?** In Example 3, suppose the Internet service provider offers \$5 off the set-up fee. After how many months will the total cost for website hosting be the same for both companies?

EXAMPLE 4 Solve a mixture problem

ANTIFREEZE For extremely cold temperatures, an automobile manufacturer recommends that a 70% antifreeze and 30% water mix be used in the cooling system of a car. How many quarts of pure (100%) antifreeze and a 50% antifreeze and 50% water mix should be combined to make 11 quarts of a 70% antifreeze and 30% water mix?

Solution

STEP 1 **Write** an equation for the total number of quarts and an equation for the number of quarts of antifreeze. Let x be the number of quarts of 100% antifreeze, and let y be the number of quarts of a 50% antifreeze and 50% water mix.

Equation 1: Total number of quarts

$x + y = 11$

Equation 2: Number of quarts of antifreeze

DRAW A DIAGRAM
Each bar shows the liquid in each mix. The green portion shows the percent of the mix that is antifreeze.

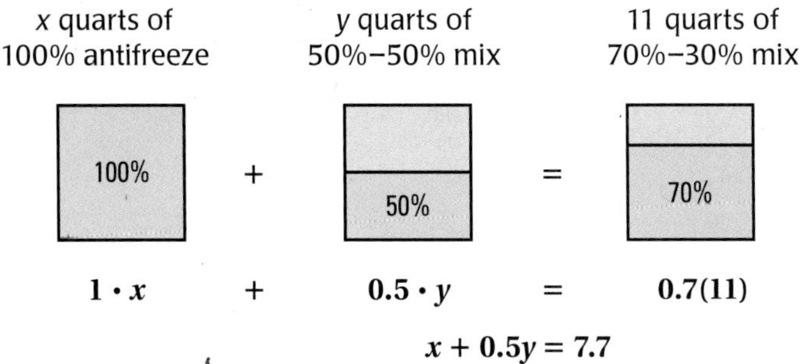

$$1 \cdot x + 0.5 \cdot y = 0.7(11)$$

$$x + 0.5y = 7.7$$

The system of equations is: $x + y = 11$ Equation 1

$x + 0.5y = 7.7$ Equation 2

STEP 2 **Solve** Equation 1 for x.

$x + y = 11$ Write Equation 1.

$x = 11 - y$ Revised Equation 1

STEP 3 **Substitute** $11 - y$ for x in Equation 2 and solve for y.

$x + 0.5y = 7.7$ Write Equation 2.

$(11 - y) + 0.5y = 7.7$ Substitute $11 - y$ for x.

$y = 6.6$ Solve for y.

STEP 4 **Substitute** 6.6 for y in the revised Equation 1 to find the value of x.

$x = 11 - y = 11 - 6.6 = 4.4$

▶ Mix 4.4 quarts of 100% antifreeze and 6.6 quarts of a 50% antifreeze and 50% water mix to get 11 quarts of a 70% antifreeze and 30% water mix.

✓ GUIDED PRACTICE for Example 4

6. **WHAT IF?** How many quarts of 100% antifreeze and a 50% antifreeze and 50% water mix should be combined to make 16 quarts of a 70% antifreeze and 30% water mix?

7.2 EXERCISES

HOMEWORK KEY

◯ = **WORKED-OUT SOLUTIONS** on p. WS16 for Exs. 13 and 33

★ = **STANDARDIZED TEST PRACTICE** Exs. 2, 18, 29, 33, and 37

SKILL PRACTICE

1. **VOCABULARY** Give an example of a system of linear equations.

2. ★ **WRITING** If you are solving the linear system shown using the substitution method, which equation would you solve for which variable? *Explain.*

   $2x - 3y = 24$ **Equation 1**

   $2x + y = 8$ **Equation 2**

EXAMPLE 1 on p. 435 for Exs. 3–8

SOLVING LINEAR SYSTEMS **Solve the linear system using substitution.**

3. $x = 17 - 4y$
   $y = x - 2$

4. $y = 2x - 1$
   $2x + y = 3$

5. $x = y + 3$
   $2x - y = 5$

6. $4x - 7y = 10$
   $y = x - 7$

7. $x = 16 - 4y$
   $3x + 4y = 8$

8. $-5x + 3y = 51$
   $y = 10x - 8$

EXAMPLE 2 on p. 436 for Exs. 9–19

9. $2x = 12$
   $x - 5y = -29$

10. $2x - y = 23$
    $x - 9 = -1$

11. $x + y = 0$
    $x - 2y = 6$

12. $2x + y = 9$
    $4x - y = -15$

13. $5x + 2y = 9$
    $x + y = -3$

14. $5x + 4y = 32$
    $9x - y = 33$

15. $11x - 7y = -14$
    $x - 2y = -4$

16. $20x - 30y = -50$
    $x + 2y = 1$

17. $6x + y = 4$
    $x - 4y = 19$

18. ★ **MULTIPLE CHOICE** Which ordered pair is a solution of the linear system $4x - y = 17$ and $-9x + 8y = 2$?

    (A) (6, 7) (B) (7, 6) (C) (7, 11) (D) (11, 7)

19. **ERROR ANALYSIS** *Describe* and correct the error in solving the linear system $4x + 2y = 6$ and $3x + y = 9$.

Step 1	Step 2	Step 3	The solution is (6, 1).
$3x + y = 9$	$4x + 2(9 - 3x) = 6$	$y = 9 - 3x$	
$y = 9 - 3x$	$4x + 18 - 6x = 6$	$6 = 9 - 3x$	
	$-2x = -12$	$-3 = -3x$	
	$x = 6$	$1 = x$	

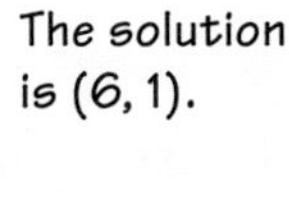

SOLVING LINEAR SYSTEMS **Solve the linear system using substitution.**

20. $4.5x + 1.5y = 24$
    $x - y = 4$

21. $35x + y = 20$
    $1.5x - 0.1y = 18$

22. $3x - 2y = 8$
    $0.5x + y = 17$

23. $0.5x + 0.6y = 5.7$
    $2x - y = -1$

24. $x - 9 = 0.5y$
    $2.2x - 3.1y = -0.2$

25. $0.2x + y = -1.8$
    $1.8y + 5.5x = 27.6$

26. $\frac{1}{2}x + \frac{1}{4}y = 5$
    $x - \frac{1}{2}y = 1$

27. $x + \frac{1}{3}y = -2$
    $-8x - \frac{2}{3}y = 4$

28. $\frac{3}{8}x + \frac{3}{4}y = 12$
    $\frac{2}{3}x + \frac{1}{2}y = 13$

29. ★ **WRITING** Suppose you solve a linear system using substitution. *Explain* how you can use a graph to check your solution.

30. **CHALLENGE** Find values of a and b so that the linear system shown has a solution of $(-9, 4)$.

$ax + by = -16$ **Equation 1**

$ax - by = -56$ **Equation 2**

PROBLEM SOLVING

EXAMPLE 3 on p. 437 for Exs. 31–33

31. **FUNDRAISING** During a football game, the parents of the football players sell pretzels and popcorn to raise money for new uniforms. They charge \$2.50 for a bag of popcorn and \$2 for a pretzel. The parents collect \$336 in sales during the game. They sell twice as many bags of popcorn as pretzels. How many bags of popcorn do they sell? How many pretzels do they sell?

@HomeTutor for problem solving help at classzone.com

32. **TUBING COSTS** A group of friends takes a day-long tubing trip down a river. The company that offers the tubing trip charges \$15 to rent a tube for a person to use and \$7.50 to rent a "cooler" tube, which is used to carry food and water in a cooler. The friends spend \$360 to rent a total of 26 tubes. How many of each type of tube do they rent?

@HomeTutor for problem solving help at classzone.com

33. ★ **SHORT RESPONSE** In the mobile shown, objects are attached to each end of a dowel. For the dowel to balance, the following must be true:

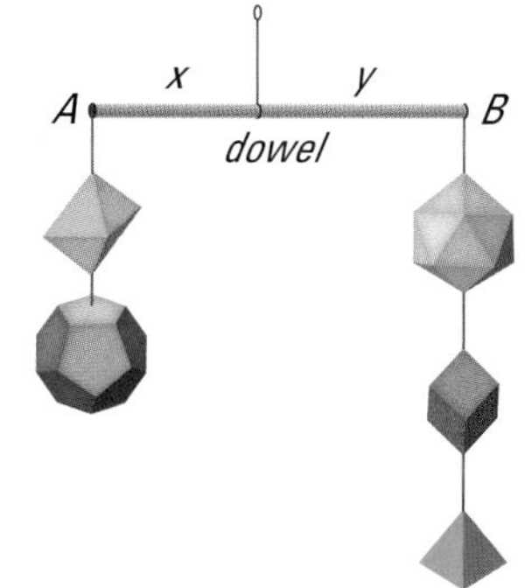

$x \cdot$ (Weight hanging from point A) $= y \cdot$ (Weight hanging from point B)

The weight of the objects hanging from point A is 1.5 pounds, and the weight of the objects hanging from point B is 1.2 pounds. The length of the dowel is 9 inches. How far from point A should the string be placed? *Explain.*

34. **MULTI-STEP PROBLEM** Two swimming teams are competing in a 400 meter medley relay. During the last leg of the race, the swimmer in lane 1 has a 1.2 second head start on the swimmer in lane 2, as shown.

a. Let t be the time since the swimmer in lane 2 started the last leg. After how many seconds into the leg will the swimmer in lane 2 catch up to the swimmer in lane 1?

b. Does the swimmer in lane 2 catch up to the swimmer in lane 1 before the race ends? *Explain.*

○ = **WORKED-OUT SOLUTIONS on p. WS1**

★ = **STANDARDIZED TEST PRACTICE**

EXAMPLE 4 on p. 438 for Ex. 35

35. **CHEMISTRY** In your chemistry lab, you have a bottle of 1% hydrochloric acid solution and a bottle of 5% hydrochloric acid solution. You need 100 milliliters of a 3% hydrochloric acid solution for an experiment. How many milliliters of each solution do you need to mix together?

36. **MONEY** Laura has $4.50 in dimes and quarters. She has 3 more dimes than quarters. How many quarters does she have?

37. ★ **SHORT RESPONSE** A gazelle can run 73 feet per second for several minutes. A cheetah can run 88 feet per second, but it can sustain this speed for only 20 seconds. A gazelle is 350 feet from a cheetah when both animals start running. Can the gazelle stay ahead of the cheetah? *Explain.*

Animated Algebra at classzone.com

38. **CHALLENGE** A gardener needs 6 bushels of a potting medium of 40% peat moss and 60% vermiculite. He decides to add 100% vermiculite to his current potting medium that is 50% peat moss and 50% vermiculite. The gardener has 5 bushels of the 50% peat moss and 50% vermiculite mix. Does he have enough of the 50% peat moss and 50% vermiculite mix to make 6 bushels of the 40% peat moss and 60% vermiculite mix? *Explain.*

MIXED REVIEW

Solve the proportion. Check your solution.

39. $\frac{3}{7} = \frac{x}{21}$ *(p. 162)*

40. $\frac{y}{30} = \frac{9}{10}$ *(p. 162)*

41. $\frac{12}{16} = \frac{3z}{4}$ *(p. 162)*

42. $\frac{35}{q} = \frac{5}{3}$ *(p. 168)*

43. $\frac{3}{2r} = \frac{-6}{16}$ *(p. 168)*

44. $\frac{4}{3} = \frac{s}{s-2}$ *(p. 168)*

PREVIEW Prepare for Lesson 7.3 in Exs. 45–50.

Write two equations in standard form that are equivalent to the given equation. *(p. 311)*

45. $x - 4y = 0$

46. $-3x + 9y = 6$

47. $-7x - y = 1$

48. $5x - 10y = 5$

49. $-2x - 12y = 8$

50. $6x + 15y = -3$

QUIZ *for Lessons 7.1–7.2*

Solve the linear system by graphing. Check your solution. *(p. 427)*

1. $x + y = -2$
   $-x + y = 6$

2. $x - y = 0$
   $5x + 2y = -7$

3. $x - 2y = 12$
   $-3x + y = -1$

Solve the linear system using substitution. *(p. 435)*

4. $y = x - 4$
   $-2x + y = 18$

5. $y = 4 - 3x$
   $5x - y = 22$

6. $x = y + 9$
   $5x - 3y = 7$

7. $2y + x = -4$
   $y - x = -5$

8. $5x - 4y = 27$
   $-2x + y = 3$

9. $3x - 5y = 13$
   $x + 4y = 10$

PROBLEM SOLVING WORKSHOP
LESSON 7.2

Using ALTERNATIVE METHODS

Another Way to Solve Example 3, page 437

MULTIPLE REPRESENTATIONS In Example 3 on page 437, you saw how to solve the problem about website hosting by solving a linear system algebraically. You can also solve the problem using a table.

PROBLEM

WEBSITES Many businesses pay website hosting companies to store and maintain the computer files that make up their websites. Internet service providers also offer website hosting. The costs for website hosting offered by a website hosting company and an Internet service provider are shown in the table. Find the number of months after which the total cost for website hosting will be the same for both companies.

Company	Set-up fee	Cost per month
Internet service provider	\$10	\$21.95
Website hosting company	None	\$22.45

METHOD

Making a Table An alternative approach is to make a table.

STEP 1 **Make** a table for the total cost of website hosting for both companies.

Include the set-up fee in the cost for the first month.

STEP 2 **Look** for the month in which the total cost of the service from the Internet service provider and the website hosting company is the same. This happens after 20 months.

Months	Internet service provider	Website hosting company
1	\$31.95	\$22.45
2	\$53.90	\$44.90
3	\$75.85	\$67.35
⋮	⋮	⋮
19	\$427.05	\$426.55
20	\$449.00	\$449.00
21	\$470.95	\$471.45

PRACTICE

1. **TAXIS** A taxi company charges \$2.80 for the first mile and \$1.60 for each additional mile. Another taxi company charges \$3.20 for the first mile and \$1.50 for each additional mile. After how many miles will each taxi cost the same? Use a table to solve the problem.

2. **SCHOOL PLAY** An adult ticket to a school play costs \$5 and a student ticket costs \$3. A total of \$460 was collected from the sale of 120 tickets. How many student tickets were purchased? Solve the problem using algebra. Then use a table to check your answer.

7.3 Linear Systems and Elimination

MATERIALS • algebra tiles

QUESTION How can you solve a linear system using algebra tiles?

You can use the following algebra tiles to model equations.

1-tiles **x-tiles** **y-tiles**

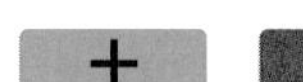

EXPLORE Solve a linear system using algebra tiles.

Solve the linear system: $3x - y = 5$ Equation 1
$x + y = 3$ Equation 2

STEP 1 ***Model equations***
Model each equation using algebra tiles. Arrange the algebra tiles so that one equation is directly below the other equation.

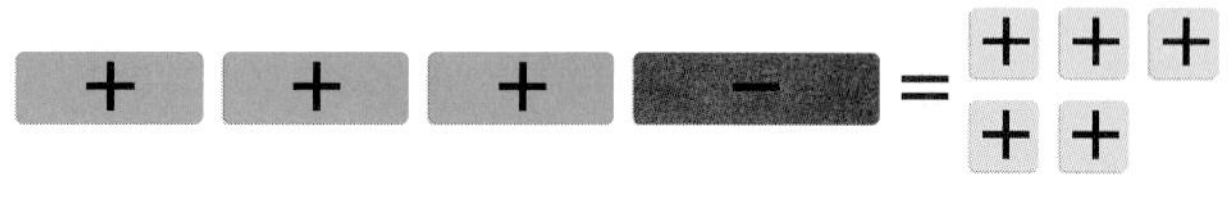

STEP 2 ***Add equations***
Combine the two equations to form one equation. Notice that the new equation has one positive y-tile and one negative y-tile. The y-tiles can be removed because the pair of y-tiles has a value of 0.

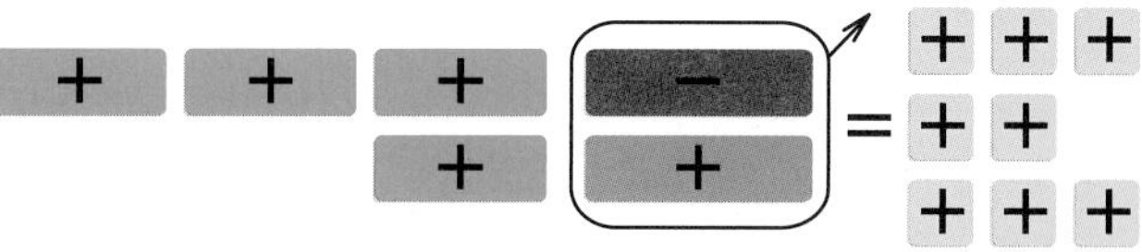

STEP 3 ***Solve for x***
Divide the remaining tiles into four equal groups. Each x-tile is equal to two 1-tiles. So, $x = 2$.

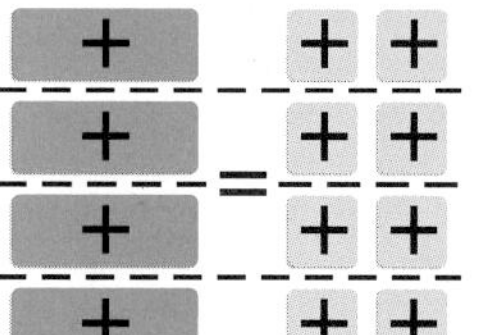

STEP 4 ***Solve for y***
To find the value of y, use the model for Equation 2. Because $x = 2$, you can replace the x-tile with two 1-tiles. Solve the new equation for y. So $y = 1$, and the solution of the system is (2, 1).

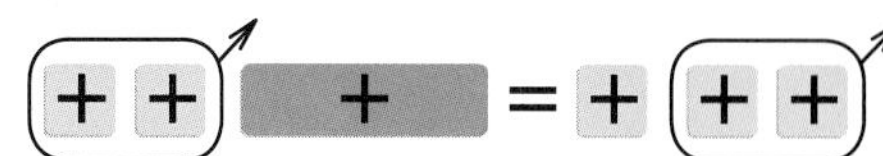

DRAW CONCLUSIONS Use your observations to complete these exercises

Use algebra tiles to model and solve the linear system.

1. $x + 3y = 8$
   $4x - 3y = 2$
2. $2x + y = 5$
   $-2x + 3y = 7$
3. $5x - 2y = -2$
   $x + 2y = 14$
4. $x + 2y = 3$
   $-x + 3y = 2$
5. **REASONING** Is it possible to solve the linear system $3x - 2y = 6$ and $2x + y = 11$ using the steps shown above? *Explain* your reasoning.

7.3 Solve Linear Systems by Adding or Subtracting

Before You solved linear systems by graphing and using substitution.

Now You will solve linear systems using elimination.

Why? So you can solve a problem about arranging flowers, as in Ex. 42.

Key Vocabulary
- **system of linear equations,** *p. 427*

When solving a linear system, you can sometimes add or subtract the equations to obtain a new equation in one variable. This method is called *elimination*.

KEY CONCEPT *For Your Notebook*

Solving a Linear System Using the Elimination Method

STEP 1 **Add or subtract** the equations to eliminate one variable.

STEP 2 **Solve** the resulting equation for the other variable.

STEP 3 **Substitute** in either original equation to find the value of the eliminated variable.

EXAMPLE 1 Use addition to eliminate a variable

Solve the linear system: $2x + 3y = 11$ **Equation 1**
$-2x + 5y = 13$ **Equation 2**

Solution

ADD EQUATIONS When the coefficients of one variable are opposites, add the equations to eliminate the variable.

STEP 1 **Add** the equations to eliminate one variable.

$$\begin{array}{r} 2x + 3y = 11 \\ -2x + 5y = 13 \\ \hline 8y = 24 \end{array}$$

STEP 2 **Solve** for y.

$$8y = 24$$
$$y = 3$$

STEP 3 **Substitute** 3 for y in either equation and solve for x.

$2x + 3y = 11$ **Write Equation 1.**

$2x + 3(3) = 11$ **Substitute 3 for y.**

$x = 1$ **Solve for x.**

▶ The solution is (1, 3).

CHECK Substitute 1 for x and 3 for y in each of the original equations.

$2x + 3y = 11$	$-2x + 5y = 13$
$2(1) + 3(3) \stackrel{?}{=} 11$	$-2(1) + 5(3) \stackrel{?}{=} 13$
$11 = 11$ ✓	$13 = 13$ ✓

EXAMPLE 2 Use subtraction to eliminate a variable

Solve the linear system: $4x + 3y = 2$ **Equation 1**
$5x + 3y = -2$ **Equation 2**

> **SUBTRACT EQUATIONS**
> When the coefficients of one variable are the same, subtract the equations to eliminate the variable.

Solution

STEP 1 **Subtract** the equations to eliminate one variable.

$$\begin{array}{r} 4x + 3y = 2 \\ 5x + 3y = -2 \\ \hline -x \qquad = 4 \end{array}$$

STEP 2 **Solve** for x.

$$x = -4$$

STEP 3 **Substitute** -4 for x in either equation and solve for y.

$4x + 3y = 2$ **Write Equation 1.**

$4(-4) + 3y = 2$ **Substitute −4 for *x*.**

$y = 6$ **Solve for *y*.**

▶ The solution is $(-4, 6)$.

EXAMPLE 3 Arrange like terms

Solve the linear system: $8x - 4y = -4$ **Equation 1**
$4y = 3x + 14$ **Equation 2**

> **AVOID ERRORS**
> Make sure that the equal signs are in the same column, just as the like terms are.

Solution

STEP 1 **Rewrite** Equation 2 so that the like terms are arranged in columns.

$$\begin{array}{r} 8x - 4y = -4 \\ 4y = 3x + 14 \end{array} \quad \longrightarrow \quad \begin{array}{r} 8x - 4y = -4 \\ -3x + 4y = 14 \\ \hline 5x \qquad = 10 \end{array}$$

STEP 2 **Add** the equations.

STEP 3 **Solve** for x.

$$x = 2$$

STEP 4 **Substitute** 2 for x in either equation and solve for y.

$4y = 3x + 14$ **Write Equation 2.**

$4y = 3(2) + 14$ **Substitute 2 for *x*.**

$y = 5$ **Solve for *y*.**

▶ The solution is $(2, 5)$.

GUIDED PRACTICE for Examples 1, 2, and 3

Solve the linear system.

1. $4x - 3y = 5$
   $-2x + 3y = -7$
2. $-5x - 6y = 8$
   $5x + 2y = 4$
3. $6x - 4y = 14$
   $-3x + 4y = 1$
4. $7x - 2y = 5$
   $7x - 3y = 4$
5. $3x + 4y = -6$
   $2y = 3x + 6$
6. $2x + 5y = 12$
   $5y = 4x + 6$

EXAMPLE 4 Write and solve a linear system

KAYAKING During a kayaking trip, a kayaker travels 12 miles upstream (against the current) and 12 miles downstream (with the current), as shown. The speed of the current remained constant during the trip. Find the average speed of the kayak in still water and the speed of the current.

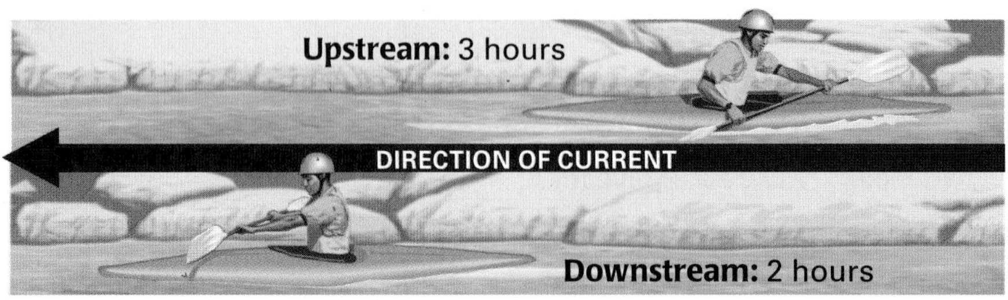

STEP 1 **Write** a system of equations. First find the speed of the kayak going upstream and the speed of the kayak going downstream.

Upstream: $d = rt$

$12 = r \cdot 3$

$4 = r$

Downstream: $d = rt$

$12 = r \cdot 2$

$6 = r$

Use the speeds to write a linear system. Let x be the average speed of the kayak in still water, and let y be the speed of the current.

COMBINE SPEEDS
When you go upstream, the speed at which you can travel in still water is decreased by the speed of the current. The opposite is true when you go downstream.

Equation 1: Going upstream

Speed of kayak in still water	−	Speed of current	=	Speed of kayak going upstream
x	−	y	=	4

Equation 2: Going downstream

Speed of kayak in still water	+	Speed of current	=	Speed of kayak going downstream
x	+	y	=	6

STEP 2 **Solve** the system of equations.

$x - y = 4$ **Write Equation 1.**

$x + y = 6$ **Write Equation 2.**

$2x = 10$ **Add equations.**

$x = 5$ **Solve for *x*.**

Substitute 5 for x in Equation 2 and solve for y.

$5 + y = 6$ **Substitute 5 for *x* in Equation 2.**

$y = 1$ **Subtract 5 from each side.**

▶ The average speed of the kayak in still water is 5 miles per hour, and the speed of the current is 1 mile per hour.

at classzone.com

 **GUIDED PRACTICE** for Example 4

7. WHAT IF? In Example 4, suppose it takes the kayaker 5 hours to travel 10 miles upstream and 2 hours to travel 10 miles downstream. The speed of the current remains constant during the trip. Find the average speed of the kayak in still water and the speed of the current.

7.3 EXERCISES

HOMEWORK KEY

○ = **WORKED-OUT SOLUTIONS** on p. WS16 for Exs. 17 and 41

★ = **STANDARDIZED TEST PRACTICE** Exs. 2, 15, 22, 36, and 44

◆ = **MULTIPLE REPRESENTATIONS** Ex. 42

SKILL PRACTICE

1. VOCABULARY Give an example of a linear system in two variables that can be solved by first adding the equations to eliminate one variable.

2. ★ **WRITING** *Explain* how to solve the linear system shown using the elimination method.

$2x - y = 2$ Equation 1

$2x + 3y = 22$ Equation 2

EXAMPLE 1 on p. 444 for Exs. 3–8

USING ADDITION **Solve the linear system using elimination.**

3. $x + 2y = 13$
 $-x + y = 5$

4. $9x + y = 2$
 $-4x - y = -17$

5. $-3x - y = 8$
 $7x + y = -12$

6. $3x - y = 30$
 $-3x + 7y = 6$

7. $-9x + 4y = -17$
 $9x - 6y = 3$

8. $-3x - 5y = -7$
 $-4x + 5y = 14$

EXAMPLE 2 on p. 445 for Exs. 9–15

USING SUBTRACTION **Solve the linear system using elimination.**

9. $x + y = 1$
 $-2x + y = 4$

10. $x - y = -4$
 $x + 3y = 4$

11. $2x - y = 7$
 $2x + 7y = 31$

12. $6x + y = -10$
 $5x + y = -10$

13. $5x + 6y = 50$
 $-x + 6y = 26$

14. $4x - 9y = -21$
 $4x + 3y = -9$

15. ★ **MULTIPLE CHOICE** Which ordered pair is a solution of the linear system $4x + 9y = -2$ and $11x + 9y = 26$?

(A) $(-2, 4)$ (B) $(2, -4)$ (C) $(4, -2)$ (D) $(4, 2)$

EXAMPLE 3 on p. 445 for Exs. 16–22

ARRANGING LIKE TERMS **Solve the linear system using elimination.**

16. $2x - y = 32$
 $y - 5x = 13$

17. $-8y + 6x = 36$
 $6x - y = 15$

18. $2x - y = -11$
 $y = -2x - 13$

19. $-x - y = 14$
 $x = 5y - 38$

20. $11y - 3x = 18$
 $-3x = -16y + 33$

21. $-5x + y = -23$
 $-y = 3x - 9$

22. ★ **MULTIPLE CHOICE** Which ordered pair is a solution of the linear system $2x + y = 10$ and $3y = 2x + 6$?

(A) $(-3, -4)$ (B) $(3, 4)$ (C) $(-4, 3)$ (D) $(4, 3)$

ERROR ANALYSIS ***Describe*** **and correct the error in finding the value of one of the variables in the given linear system.**

23. $5x - 7y = 16$
$-x - 7y = 8$

$5x - 7y = 16$
$-x - 7y = 8$
$4x \quad = 24$
$x = 6$
✗

24. $3x - 2y = -3$
$5y = 60 - 3x$

$3x - 2y = -3$
$-3x + 5y = 60$
$3y = 57$
$y = 19$
✗

SOLVING LINEAR SYSTEMS **Solve the linear system using elimination.**

25. $-x + \frac{1}{2}y = -19$
$x - y = 12$

26. $\frac{1}{4}x - \frac{2}{3}y = 7$
$\frac{1}{2}x + \frac{2}{3}y = -4$

27. $8x - \frac{1}{2}y = -38$
$\frac{1}{4}x - \frac{1}{2}y = -7$

28. $5.2x + 3.5y = 54$
$-3.6x + 3.5y = 10$

29. $1.3x - 3y = -17.6$
$-1.3x + 4.5y = 25.1$

30. $-2.6x - 3.2y = 4.8$
$1.9x - 3.2y = -4.2$

31. $\frac{4}{5}x + \frac{2}{5}y = 14$
$\frac{2}{5}y + \frac{1}{5}x = 11$

32. $2.7x + 1.5y = 36$
$3.5y = 2.7x - 6$

33. $4 - 4.8x = 1.7y$
$12.8 + 1.7y = -13.2x$

34. **WRITING AN EQUATION OF A LINE** Use the following steps to write an equation of the line that passes through the points (1, 2) and (−4, 12).

a. Write a system of linear equations by substituting 1 for x and 2 for y in $y = mx + b$ and −4 for x and 12 for y in $y = mx + b$.

b. Solve the system of linear equations from part (a). What is the slope of the line? What is the y-intercept?

c. Write an equation of the line that passes through (1, 2) and (−4, 12).

35. **GEOMETRY** The rectangle has a perimeter P of 14 feet, and twice its length ℓ is equal to 1 less than 4 times its width w. Write and solve a system of linear equations to find the length and the width of the rectangle.

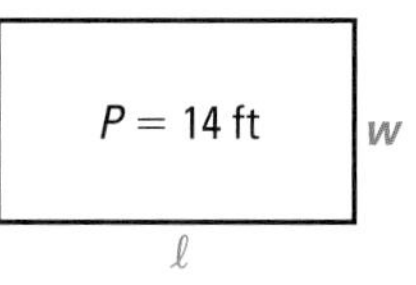

36. ★ **SHORT RESPONSE** Find the solution of the system of linear equations below. *Explain* your steps.

$x + 3y = 8$ **Equation 1**
$x - 6y = -19$ **Equation 2**
$5x - 3y = -14$ **Equation 3**

37. **CHALLENGE** For $a \neq 0$, what is the solution of the system $ax + 2y = 4$ and $ax - 3y = -6$?

38. **CHALLENGE** Solve for x, y, and z in the system of equations below. *Explain* your steps.

$x + 7y + 3z = 29$ **Equation 1**
$3z + x - 2y = -7$ **Equation 2**
$5y = 10 - 2x$ **Equation 3**

PROBLEM SOLVING

EXAMPLE 4 on p. 446 for Exs. 39–41

39. **ROWING** During a practice, a 4 person crew team rows a rowing shell upstream (against the current) and then rows the same distance downstream (with the current). The shell moves upstream at a speed of 4.3 meters per second and downstream at a speed of 4.9 meters per second. The speed of the current remains constant. Use the models below to write and solve a system of equations to find the average speed of the shell in still water and the speed of the current.

Upstream

Speed of shell in still water − Speed of current = Speed of shell

Downstream

Speed of shell in still water + Speed of current = Speed of shell

@HomeTutor for problem solving help at classzone.com

40. **OIL CHANGE** Two cars get an oil change at the same service center. Each customer is charged a fee x (in dollars) for the oil change plus y dollars per quart of oil used. The oil change for the car that requires 5 quarts of oil costs \$22.45. The oil change for the car that requires 7 quarts of oil costs \$25.45. Find the fee and the cost per quart of oil.

@HomeTutor for problem solving help at classzone.com

41. **PHONES** Cellular phone ring tones can be monophonic or polyphonic. Monophonic ring tones play one tone at a time, and polyphonic ring tones play multiple tones at a time. The table shows the ring tones downloaded from a website by two customers. Use the information to find the cost of a monophonic ring tone and a polyphonic ring tone, assuming that all monophonic ring tones cost the same and all polyphonic ring tones cost the same.

Customer	Monophonic ring tones	Polyphonic ring tones	Total cost (dollars)
Julie	3	2	12.85
Tate	1	2	8.95

42. **MULTIPLE REPRESENTATIONS** For a floral arrangement class, Alicia has to create an arrangement of twigs and flowers that has a total of 9 objects. She has to pay for the twigs and flowers that she uses in her arrangement. Each twig costs \$1, and each flower costs \$3.

    a. **Writing a System** Alicia spends \$15 on the twigs and flowers. Write and solve a linear system to find the number of twigs and the number of flowers she used.

    b. **Making a Table** Make a table showing the number of twigs in the arrangement and the total cost of the arrangement when the number of flowers purchased is 0, 1, 2, 3, 4, or 5. Use the table to check your answer to part (a).

43. **MULTI-STEP PROBLEM** On a typical day with light winds, the 1800 mile flight from Charlotte, North Carolina, to Phoenix, Arizona, takes longer than the return trip because the plane has to fly into the wind.

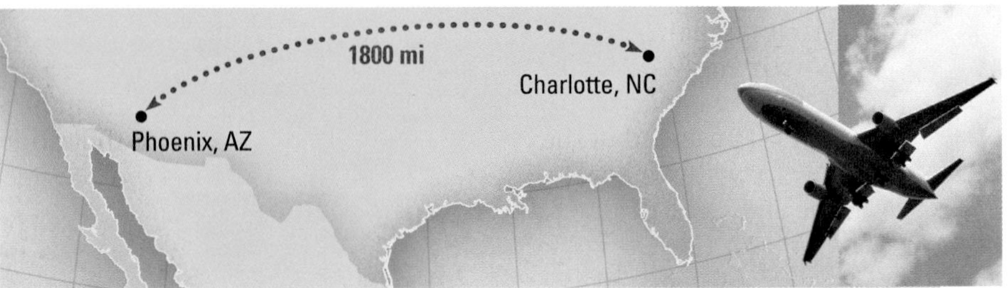

a. The flight from Charlotte to Phoenix is 4 hours 30 minutes long, and the flight from Phoenix to Charlotte is 4 hours long. Find the average speed (in miles per hour) of the airplane on the way to Phoenix and on the return trip to Charlotte.

b. Let s be the speed (in miles per hour) of the plane with no wind, and let w be the speed (in miles per hour) of the wind. Use your answer to part (a) to write and solve a system of equations to find the speed of the plane with no wind and the speed of the wind.

44. ★ **SHORT RESPONSE** The students in the graduating classes at the three high schools in a school district have to pay for their caps and gowns. A cap-and-gown set costs x dollars, and an extra tassel costs y dollars. At one high school, students pay \$3262 for 215 cap-and-gown sets and 72 extra tassels. At another high school, students pay \$3346 for 221 cap-and-gown sets and 72 extra tassels. How much will students at the third high school pay for 218 cap-and-gown sets and 56 extra tassels? *Explain.*

45. **CHALLENGE** A clothing manufacturer makes men's dress shirts. For the production process, an ideal sleeve length x (in centimeters) for each shirt size and an allowable deviation y (in centimeters) from the ideal length are established. The deviation is expressed as $\pm y$. For a specific shirt size, the minimum allowable sleeve length is 62.2 centimeters and the maximum allowable sleeve length is 64.8 centimeters. Find the ideal sleeve length and the allowable deviation.

MIXED REVIEW

Graph the equation.

46. $x - 5y = -12$ *(p. 225)*

47. $-2x + 3y = -15$ *(p. 225)*

48. $y + 9 = -(x + 2)$ *(p. 302)*

49. $y - 4 = \frac{2}{3}(x + 1)$ *(p. 302)*

Solve the linear system by graphing. Check your solution. *(p. 427)*

50. $y = x - 3$
$y = -x + 1$

51. $y = 2$
$2x - 3y = 6$

52. $2x + y = 6$
$6x - 2y = -12$

PREVIEW
Prepare for Lesson 7.4 in Exs. 53–55.

Find the least common multiple of the pair of numbers. *(p. 910)*

53. 9, 12

54. 18, 24

55. 15, 20

7.4 Solve Linear Systems by Multiplying First

Before You solved linear systems by adding or subtracting.

Now You will solve linear systems by multiplying first.

Why So you can solve a problem about preparing food, as in Ex. 39.

Key Vocabulary
- **least common multiple,** *p. 910*

In a linear system like the one below, neither variable can be eliminated by adding or subtracting the equations. For systems like these, you can multiply one or both of the equations by a constant so that adding or subtracting the equations will eliminate one variable.

$$\begin{array}{lcl} 5x + 2y = 16 & \xrightarrow{\times 2} & 10x + 4y = 32 \\ 3x - 4y = 20 & \longrightarrow & 3x - 4y = 20 \end{array}$$

The new system is equivalent to the original system.

EXAMPLE 1 Multiply one equation, then add

Solve the linear system: $6x + 5y = 19$ Equation 1
$2x + 3y = 5$ Equation 2

Solution

STEP 1 **Multiply** Equation 2 by -3 so that the coefficients of x are opposites.

$$\begin{array}{lcr} 6x + 5y = 19 & & 6x + 5y = 19 \\ 2x + 3y = 5 & \xrightarrow{\times(-3)} & -6x - 9y = -15 \\ \hline \end{array}$$

STEP 2 **Add** the equations. $-4y = 4$

STEP 3 **Solve** for y. $y = -1$

ANOTHER WAY You can also multiply Equation 2 by 3 and subtract the equations.

STEP 4 **Substitute** -1 for y in either of the original equations and solve for x.

$2x + 3y = 5$ Write Equation 2.

$2x + 3(-1) = 5$ Substitute -1 for y.

$2x + (-3) = 5$ Multiply.

$2x = 8$ Subtract -3 from each side.

$x = 4$ Divide each side by 2.

▶ The solution is $(4, -1)$.

CHECK Substitute 4 for x and -1 for y in each of the original equations.

Equation 1	Equation 2
$6x + 5y = 19$	$2x + 3y = 5$
$6(4) + 5(-1) \stackrel{?}{=} 19$	$2(4) + 3(-1) \stackrel{?}{=} 5$
$19 = 19$ ✓	$5 = 5$ ✓

MULTIPLYING BOTH EQUATIONS To eliminate one variable when adding or subtracting equations in a linear system, you may need to multiply both equations by constants. Use the least common multiple of the coefficients of one of the variables to determine the constants.

$2x - 9y = 1$ → × 4 → $8x - 36y = 4$

$7x - 12y = 23$ → × 3 → $21x - 36y = 69$

The least common multiple of −9 and −12 is −36.

EXAMPLE 2 Multiply both equations, then subtract

Solve the linear system: $4x + 5y = 35$ Equation 1
$2y = 3x - 9$ Equation 2

Solution

STEP 1 **Arrange** the equations so that like terms are in columns.

$4x + 5y = 35$ Write Equation 1.

$-3x + 2y = -9$ Rewrite Equation 2.

ANOTHER WAY
You can also multiply Equation 1 by 3 and Equation 2 by 4. Then add the revised equations to eliminate x.

STEP 2 **Multiply** Equation 1 by 2 and Equation 2 by 5 so that the coeffcient of y in each equation is the least common multiple of 5 and 2, or 10.

$4x + 5y = 35$ → × 2 → $8x + 10y = 70$

$-3x + 2y = -9$ → × 5 → $-15x + 10y = -45$

STEP 3 **Subtract** the equations. $23x = 115$

STEP 4 **Solve** for x. → $x = 5$

STEP 5 **Substitute** 5 for x in either of the original equations and solve for y.

$4x + 5y = 35$ Write Equation 1.

$4(5) + 5y = 35$ Substitute 5 for x.

$y = 3$ Solve for y.

▶ The solution is (5, 3).

CHECK Substitute 5 for x and 3 for y in each of the original equations.

Equation 1	Equation 2
$4x + 5y = 35$	$2y = 3x - 9$
$4(5) + 5(3) \stackrel{?}{=} 35$	$2(3) \stackrel{?}{=} 3(5) - 9$
$35 = 35$ ✓	$6 = 6$ ✓

Animated Algebra at classzone.com

✓ GUIDED PRACTICE for Examples 1 and 2

Solve the linear system using elimination.

1. $6x - 2y = 1$
$-2x + 3y = -5$

2. $2x + 5y = 3$
$3x + 10y = -3$

3. $3x - 7y = 5$
$9y = 5x + 5$

 **EXAMPLE 3** Standardized Test Practice

Darlene is making a quilt that has alternating stripes of regular quilting fabric and sateen fabric. She spends \$76 on a total of 16 yards of the two fabrics at a fabric store. Which system of equations can be used to find the amount x (in yards) of regular quilting fabric and the amount y (in yards) of sateen fabric she purchased?

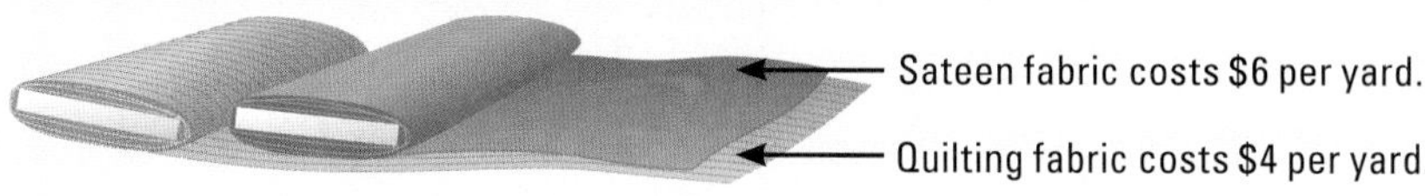
Sateen fabric costs $6 per yard.
Quilting fabric costs $4 per yard.

ELIMINATE CHOICES
You can eliminate choice A because $x + y$ cannot equal both 16 and 76.

Ⓐ $x + y = 16$
$x + y = 76$

Ⓑ $x + y = 16$
$4x + 6y = 76$

Ⓒ $x + y = 76$
$4x + 6y = 16$

Ⓓ $x + y = 16$
$6x + 4y = 76$

Solution

Write a system of equations where x is the number of yards of regular quilting fabric purchased and y is the number of yards of sateen fabric purchased.

Equation 1: Amount of fabric

Amount of quilting fabric	+	Amount of sateen fabric	=	Total yards of fabric
↓		↓		↓
x	+	y	=	16

Equation 2: Cost of fabric

Quilting fabric price (dollars/yd)	·	Amount of quilting fabric (yd)	+	Sateen fabric price (dollars/yd)	·	Amount of sateen fabric (yd)	=	Total cost (dollars)
↓		↓		↓		↓		↓
4	·	x	+	6	·	y	=	76

The system of equations is: $x + y = 16$ **Equation 1**
$4x + 6y = 76$ **Equation 2**

▶ The correct answer is B. Ⓐ Ⓑ Ⓒ Ⓓ

 **GUIDED PRACTICE** for Example 3

4. **SOCCER** A sports equipment store is having a sale on soccer balls. A soccer coach purchases 10 soccer balls and 2 soccer ball bags for \$155. Another soccer coach purchases 12 soccer balls and 3 soccer ball bags for \$189. Find the cost of a soccer ball and the cost of a soccer ball bag.

CONCEPT SUMMARY *For Your Notebook*

Methods for Solving Linear Systems

Method	Example	When to Use
Table (p. 426)	x: 0, 1, 2; $y = 2x$: 0, 2, 4; $y = 3x - 1$: −1, 2, 5	When x-values are integers, so that equal values can be seen in the table
Graphing (p. 427)	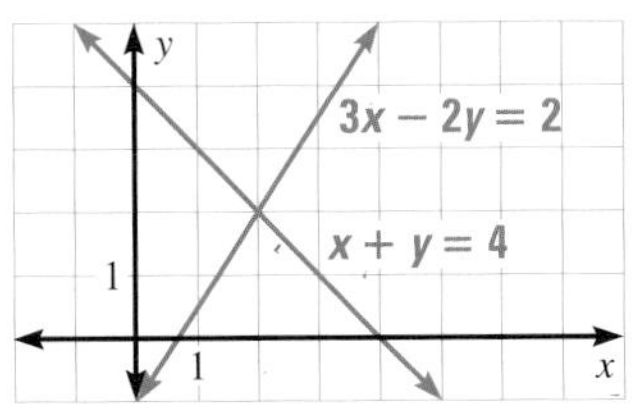	When you want to see the lines that the equations represent
Substitution (p. 435)	$\mathbf{y = 4 - 2x}$ $4x + 2y = 8$	When one equation is already solved for x or y
Addition (p. 444)	$4x + \mathbf{7y} = 15$ $6x - \mathbf{7y} = 5$	When the coefficients of one variable are opposites
Subtraction (p. 445)	$\mathbf{3x} + 5y = -13$ $\mathbf{3x} + y = -5$	When the coefficients of one variable are the same
Multiplication (p. 451)	$9x + 2y = 38$ $3x - 5y = 7$	When no corresponding coefficients are the same or opposites

Example table for Table method:

x	$y = 2x$	$y = 3x - 1$
0	0	−1
1	2	2
2	4	5

7.4 EXERCISES

HOMEWORK KEY

○ = **WORKED-OUT SOLUTIONS** on p. WS17 for Exs. 15 and 39

★ = **STANDARDIZED TEST PRACTICE** Exs. 2, 18, 34, 41, and 42

= **MULTIPLE REPRESENTATIONS** Ex. 40

SKILL PRACTICE

1. **VOCABULARY** What is the least common multiple of 12 and 18?

2. ★ **WRITING** *Explain* how to solve the linear system using the elimination method.

$2x - 3y = -4$ **Equation 1**

$7x + 9y = -5$ **Equation 2**

EXAMPLE 1 on p. 451 for Exs. 3–8

SOLVING LINEAR SYSTEMS **Solve the linear system using elimination.**

3. $x + y = 2$
   $2x + 7y = 9$

4. $3x - 2y = 3$
   $-x + y = 1$

5. $4x + 3y = 8$
   $x - 2y = 13$

6. $10x - 9y = 46$
   $-2x + 3y = 10$

7. $8x - 5y = 11$
   $4x - 3y = 5$

8. $11x - 20y = 28$
   $3x + 4y = 36$

EXAMPLE 2 on p. 452 for Exs. 9–20

SOLVING LINEAR SYSTEMS **Solve the linear system using elimination.**

9. $4x - 3y = 8$
   $5x - 2y = -11$

10. $-2x - 5y = 9$
    $3x + 11y = 4$

11. $7x - 6y = -1$
    $5x - 4y = 1$

12. $7x + 3y = -12$
    $2x + 5y = 38$

13. $9x - 8y = 4$
    $2x - 3y = -4$

14. $12x - 7y = -2$
    $-8x + 11y = 14$

15. $9x + 2y = 39$
    $6x + 13y = -9$

16. $-7x + 10y = 11$
    $-8x + 15y = 34$

17. $-14x + 15y = 15$
    $21x - 20y = -10$

18. ★ **MULTIPLE CHOICE** Which ordered pair is a solution of the linear system $15x + 8y = 6$ and $25x + 12y = 14$?

   (A) $(-3, -2)$ (B) $(-3, 2)$ (C) $(-2, -3)$ (D) $(2, -3)$

ERROR ANALYSIS ***Describe*** **and correct the error when solving the linear system.**

19.

$$\begin{array}{lll} 2x - 3y = -9 & \xrightarrow{\times 2} & 4x - 6y = -18 \\ 5x - 6y = -9 & & 5x - 6y = -9 \\ \hline & & 9x = -27 \\ & & x = -3 \end{array}$$

20.

$$\begin{array}{lll} 9x + 8y = 11 & \xrightarrow{\times 3} & 27x + 24y = 11 \\ 7x + 6y = 9 & \xrightarrow{\times 4} & 28x + 24y = 9 \\ \hline & & -x = 2 \\ & & x = -2 \end{array}$$

SOLVING LINEAR SYSTEMS **Solve the linear system using any algebraic method.**

21. $3x + 2y = 4$
    $2y = 8 - 5x$

22. $4x - 5y = 18$
    $3x = y + 11$

23. $8x - 9y = -15$
    $-4x = 19 + y$

24. $0.3x + 0.1y = -0.1$
    $-x + y = 3$

25. $4.4x - 3.6y = 7.6$
    $x - y = 1$

26. $3x - 2y = -20$
    $x + 1.2y = 6.4$

27. $0.2x - 1.5y = -1$
    $x - 4.5y = 1$

28. $1.5x - 3.5y = -5$
    $-1.2x + 2.5y = 1$

29. $4.9x + 2.4y = 7.4$
    $0.7x + 3.6y = -2.2$

30. $x + y = 0$
    $\frac{1}{2}x - \frac{1}{2}y = 2$

31. $3x + y = \frac{1}{3}$
    $2x - 3y = \frac{8}{3}$

32. $\frac{3}{5}x - \frac{3}{4}y = -3$
    $\frac{2}{5}x + \frac{1}{3}y = 8$

33. **GEOMETRY** A rectangle has a perimeter of 18 inches. A new rectangle is formed by doubling the width w and tripling the length ℓ, as shown. The new rectangle has a perimeter P of 46 inches.

   a. Write and solve a system of linear equations to find the length and width of the original rectangle.

   b. Find the length and width of the new rectangle.

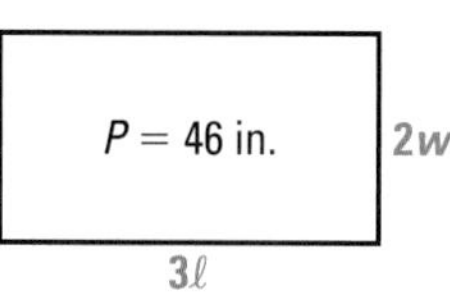

34. ★ **WRITING** For which values of a can you solve the linear system $ax + 3y = 2$ and $4x + 5y = 6$ without multiplying first? *Explain.*

CHALLENGE **Find the values of** ***a*** **and** ***b*** **so that the linear system has the given solution.**

$ax - by = 4$ **Equation 1**

$bx - ay = 10$ **Equation 2**

35. $(4, 2)$

36. $(2, 1)$

PROBLEM SOLVING

EXAMPLE 3 on p. 453 for Exs. 37–39

37. BOOK SALE A library is having a book sale to raise money. Hardcover books cost \$4 each and paperback books cost \$2 each. A person spends \$26 for 8 books. How many hardcover books did she purchase?

@HomeTutor for problem solving help at classzone.com

38. MUSIC A website allows users to download individual songs or an entire album. All individual songs cost the same to download, and all albums cost the same to download. Ryan pays \$14.94 to download 5 individual songs and 1 album. Seth pays \$22.95 to download 3 individual songs and 2 albums. How much does the website charge to download a song? an entire album?

@HomeTutor for problem solving help at classzone.com

39. FARM PRODUCTS The table shows the number of apples needed to make the apple pies and applesauce sold at a farm store. During a recent apple picking at the farm, 169 Granny Smith apples and 95 Golden Delicious apples were picked. How many apple pies and batches of applesauce can be made if every apple is used?

Type of apple	Granny Smith	Golden Delicious
Needed for a pie	5	3
Needed for a batch of applesauce	4	2

40. MULTIPLE REPRESENTATIONS Tickets for admission to a high school football game cost \$3 for students and \$5 for adults. During one game, \$2995 was collected from the sale of 729 tickets.

a. **Writing a System** Write and solve a system of linear equations to find the number of tickets sold to students and the number of tickets sold to adults.

b. **Drawing a Graph** Graph the system of linear equations. Use the graph to determine whether your answer to part (a) is reasonable.

41. ★ SHORT RESPONSE A dim sum restaurant offers two sizes of dishes: small and large. All small dishes cost the same and all large dishes cost the same. The bills show the cost of the food before the tip is included. What will 3 small and 2 large dishes cost before the tip is included? *Explain.*

42. ★ OPEN-ENDED *Describe* a real-world problem that can be solved using a system of linear equations. Then solve the problem and explain what the solution means in this situation.

43. **INVESTMENTS** Matt invested \$2000 in stocks and bonds. This year the bonds paid 8% interest, and the stocks paid 6% in dividends. Matt received a total of \$144 in interest and dividends. How much money did he invest in stocks? in bonds?

44. **CHALLENGE** You drive a car 45 miles at an average speed r (in miles per hour) to reach your destination. Due to traffic, your average speed on the return trip is $\frac{3}{4}r$. The round trip took a total of 1 hour 45 minutes. Find the average speed for each leg of your trip.

MIXED REVIEW

Graph the equation. *(pp. 215, 225, 244)*

45. $x - 8y = -10$

46. $-2x + 5y = -15$

47. $\frac{1}{4}x + \frac{1}{2}y = 8$

48. $y = \frac{2}{3}x - 1$

49. $y = -9x + 2$

50. $y - 1 = 2x - 7$

PREVIEW
Prepare for Lesson 7.5 in Exs. 51–52.

Determine which lines are parallel. *(p. 244)*

51.

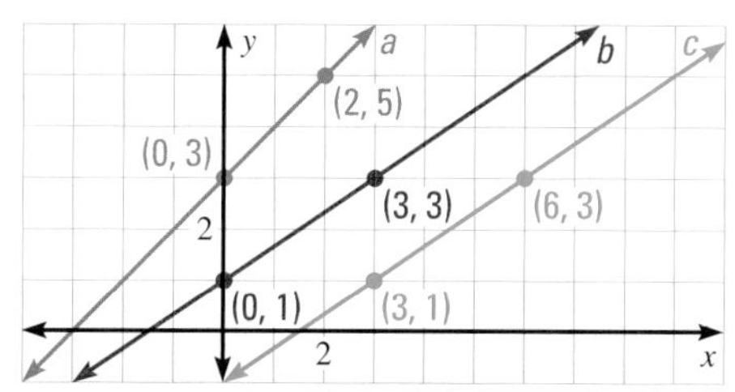

52.

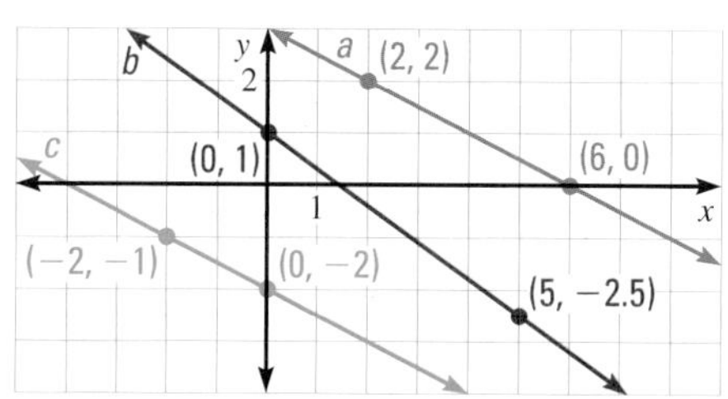

Solve the linear system using any method. *(pp. 427, 435, 444, 451)*

53. $y = 4x - 9$
$y = -8x + 15$

54. $y = -2x + 20$
$y = -6x + 40$

55. $x + 2y = 0$
$-x = y + 3$

56. $x + 2y = 2$
$-x + y = -11$

57. $7x - 8y = -15$
$5x + 8y = 3$

58. $8x + y = 5$
$-2x + y = 0$

QUIZ *for Lessons 7.3–7.4*

Solve the linear system using elimination. *(pp. 444, 451)*

1. $x + y = 4$
$-3x + y = -8$

2. $2x - y = 2$
$6x - y = -2$

3. $x + y = 5$
$-x + y = -3$

4. $x + 3y = -10$
$-x + 5y = -30$

5. $x + 3y = 10$
$3x - y = 13$

6. $x + 7y = 10$
$x + 2y = -8$

7. $4x - y = -2$
$3x + 2y = 7$

8. $x + 3y = 1$
$5x + 6y = 14$

9. $3x + y = 21$
$x + y = 1$

10. $2x - 3y = -5$
$5x + 2y = 16$

11. $7x + 2y = 13$
$4x + 3y = 13$

12. $\frac{1}{3}x + 5y = -3$
$-\frac{2}{3}x + 6y = -10$

MIXED REVIEW *of Problem Solving*

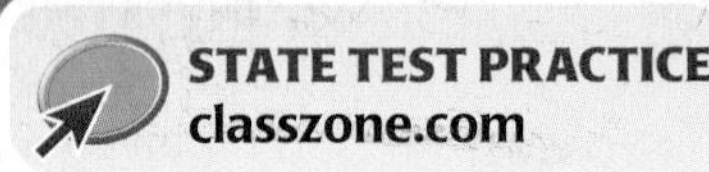

Lessons 7.1–7.4

1. **MULTI-STEP PROBLEM** Flying into the wind, a helicopter takes 15 minutes to travel 15 kilometers. The return flight takes 12 minutes. The wind speed remains constant during the trip.

   a. Find the helicopter's average speed (in kilometers per hour) for each leg of the trip.

   b. Write a system of linear equations that represents the situation.

   c. What is the helicopter's average speed in still air? What is the speed of the wind?

2. **SHORT RESPONSE** At a grocery store, a customer pays a total of \$9.70 for 1.8 pounds of potato salad and 1.4 pounds of coleslaw. Another customer pays a total of \$6.55 for 1 pound of potato salad and 1.2 pounds of coleslaw. How much do 2 pounds of potato salad and 2 pounds of coleslaw cost? *Explain.*

3. **GRIDDED ANSWER** During one day, two computers are sold at a computer store. The two customers each arrange payment plans with the salesperson. The graph shows the amount y of money (in dollars) paid for the computers after x months. After how many months will each customer have paid the same amount?

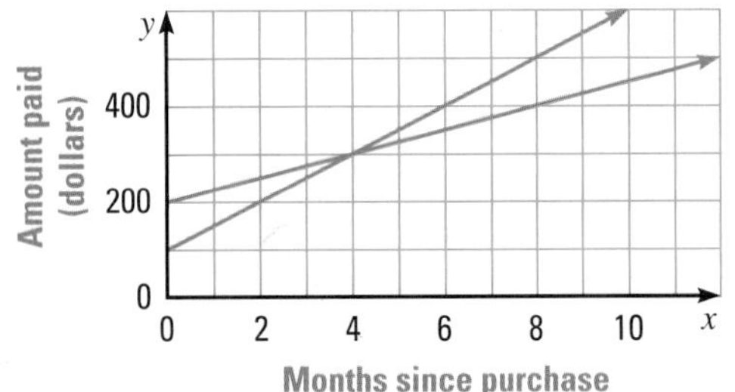

4. **OPEN-ENDED** *Describe* a real-world problem that can be modeled by a linear system. Then solve the system and interpret the solution in the context of the problem.

5. **SHORT RESPONSE** A hot air balloon is launched at Kirby Park, and it ascends at a rate of 7200 feet per hour. At the same time, a second hot air balloon is launched at Newman Park, and it ascends at a rate of 4000 feet per hour. Both of the balloons stop ascending after 30 minutes. The diagram shows the altitude of each park. Are the hot air balloons ever at the same height at the same time? *Explain.*

6. **EXTENDED RESPONSE** A chemist needs 500 milliliters of a 20% acid and 80% water mix for a chemistry experiment. The chemist combines x milliliters of a 10% acid and 90% water mix and y milliliters of a 30% acid and 70% water mix to make the 20% acid and 80% water mix.

   a. Write a linear system that represents the situation.

   b. How many milliliters of the 10% acid and 90% water mix and the 30% acid and 70% water mix are combined to make the 20% acid and 80% water mix?

   c. The chemist also needs 500 milliliters of a 15% acid and 85% water mix. Does the chemist need more of the 10% acid and 90% water mix than the 30% acid and 70% water mix to make this new mix? *Explain.*

7.5 Solve Special Types of Linear Systems

Before You found the solution of a linear system.

Now You will identify the number of solutions of a linear system.

Why? So you can compare distances traveled, as in Ex. 39.

Key Vocabulary
- **inconsistent system**
- **consistent dependent system**
- **system of linear equations,** *p. 427*
- **parallel,** *p. 244*

A linear system can have no solution or infinitely many solutions. A linear system has no solution when the graphs of the equations are parallel. A linear system with no solution is called an **inconsistent system.**

A linear system has infinitely many solutions when the graphs of the equations are the same line. A linear system with infinitely many solutions is called a **consistent dependent system.**

EXAMPLE 1 A linear system with no solution

Show that the linear system has no solution.

$3x + 2y = 10$ Equation 1
$3x + 2y = 2$ Equation 2

Solution

METHOD 1 Graphing

REVIEW GRAPHING
For help with graphing linear equations, see pp. 215, 225, and 244.

Graph the linear system.

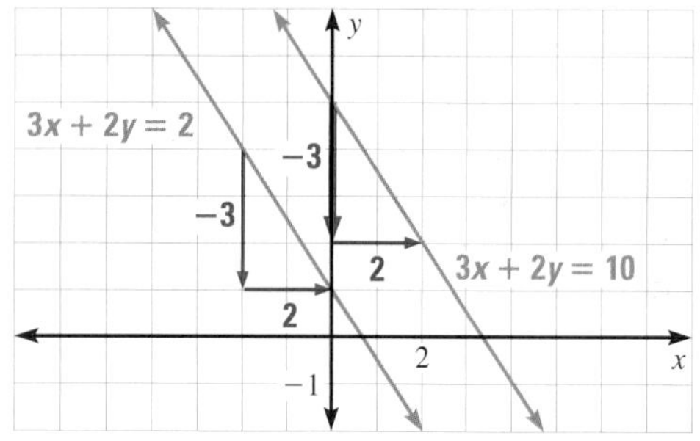

▶ The lines are parallel because they have the same slope but different y-intercepts. Parallel lines do not intersect, so the system has no solution.

METHOD 2 Elimination

Subtract the equations.

$$\begin{array}{r} 3x + 2y = 10 \\ \underline{3x + 2y = 2} \\ 0 = 8 \end{array}$$
← This is a false statement.

IDENTIFY TYPES OF SYSTEMS
The linear system in Example 1 is called an inconsistent system because the lines do not intersect (are not consistent).

▶ The variables are eliminated and you are left with a false statement regardless of the values of x and y. This tells you that the system has no solution.

Animated Algebra at classzone.com

EXAMPLE 2 A linear system with infinitely many solutions

Show that the linear system has infinitely many solutions.

$x - 2y = -4$ Equation 1

$y = \frac{1}{2}x + 2$ Equation 2

Solution

METHOD 1 Graphing

Graph the linear system.

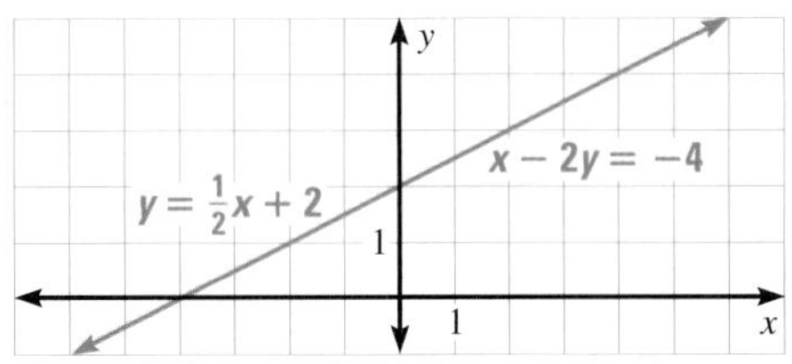

▶ The equations represent the same line, so any point on the line is a solution. So, the linear system has infinitely many solutions.

METHOD 2 Substitution

Substitute $\frac{1}{2}x + 2$ for y in Equation 1 and solve for x.

$x - 2y = -4$ Write Equation 1.

$x - 2\left(\frac{1}{2}x + 2\right) = -4$ Substitute $\frac{1}{2}x + 2$ for y.

$-4 = -4$ Simplify.

▶ The variables are eliminated and you are left with a statement that is true regardless of the values of x and y. This tells you that the system has infinitely many solutions.

IDENTIFY TYPES OF SYSTEMS

The linear system in Example 2 is called a consistent dependent system because the lines intersect (are consistent) and the equations are equivalent (are dependent).

GUIDED PRACTICE for Examples 1 and 2

Tell whether the linear system has *no solution* or *infinitely many solutions*. *Explain.*

1. $5x + 3y = 6$
$-5x - 3y = 3$

2. $y = 2x - 4$
$-6x + 3y = -12$

IDENTIFYING THE NUMBER OF SOLUTIONS When the equations of a linear system are written in slope-intercept form, you can identify the number of solutions of the system by looking at the slopes and y-intercepts of the lines.

Number of solutions	Slopes and *y*-intercepts
One solution	Different slopes
No solution	Same slope Different *y*-intercepts
Infinitely many solutions	Same slope Same *y*-intercept

EXAMPLE 3 Identify the number of solutions

Without solving the linear system, tell whether the linear system has *one solution*, *no solution*, or *infinitely many solutions*.

a. $5x + y = -2$ Equation 1
$-10x - 2y = 4$ Equation 2

b. $6x + 2y = 3$ Equation 1
$6x + 2y = -5$ Equation 2

Solution

a. $y = -5x - 2$ Write Equation 1 in slope-intercept form.

$y = -5x - 2$ Write Equation 2 in slope-intercept form.

▶ Because the lines have the same slope and the same y-intercept, the system has infinitely many solutions.

b. $y = -3x + \frac{3}{2}$ Write Equation 1 in slope-intercept form.

$y = -3x - \frac{5}{2}$ Write Equation 2 in slope-intercept form.

▶ Because the lines have the same slope but different y-intercepts, the system has no solution.

EXAMPLE 4 Write and solve a system of linear equations

ART An artist wants to sell prints of her paintings. She orders a set of prints for each of two of her paintings. Each set contains regular prints and glossy prints, as shown in the table. Find the cost of one glossy print.

Regular	Glossy	Cost
45	30	\$465
15	10	\$155

Solution

STEP 1 **Write** a linear system. Let x be the cost (in dollars) of a regular print, and let y be the cost (in dollars) of a glossy print.

$45x + 30y = 465$ Cost of prints for one painting
$15x + 10y = 155$ Cost of prints for other painting

STEP 2 **Solve** the linear system using elimination.

$$\begin{aligned} 45x + 30y &= 465 \\ 15x + 10y &= 155 \end{aligned} \quad \xrightarrow{\times(-3)} \quad \begin{aligned} 45x + 30y &= 465 \\ -45x - 30y &= -465 \\ \hline 0 &= 0 \end{aligned}$$

▶ There are infinitely many solutions, so you cannot determine the cost of one glossy print. You need more information.

✓ GUIDED PRACTICE for Examples 3 and 4

3. Without solving the linear system, tell whether it has *one solution*, *no solution*, or *infinitely many solutions*.

$x - 3y = -15$ Equation 1
$2x - 3y = -18$ Equation 2

4. **WHAT IF?** In Example 4, suppose a glossy print costs \$3 more than a regular print. Find the cost of a glossy print.

CONCEPT SUMMARY — *For Your Notebook*

Number of Solutions of a Linear System

One solution	No solution	Infinitely many solutions
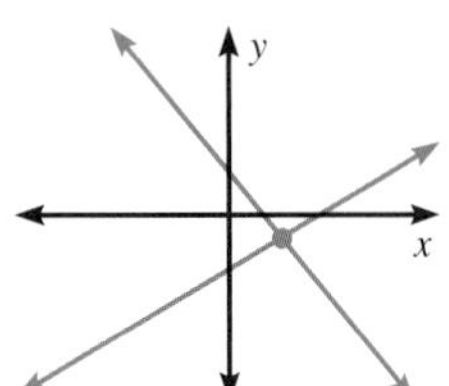	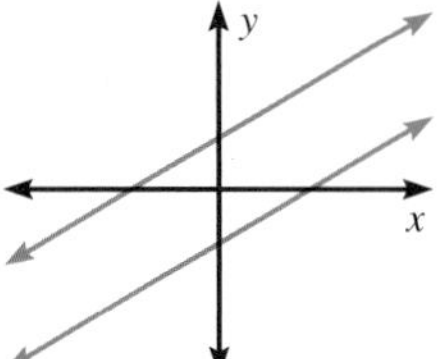	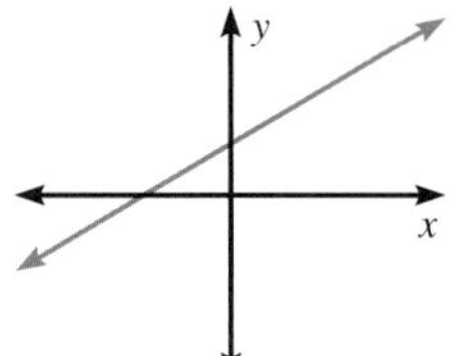
The lines intersect.	The lines are parallel.	The lines coincide.
The lines have different slopes.	The lines have the same slope and different *y*-intercepts.	The lines have the same slope and the same *y*-intercept.

7.5 EXERCISES

HOMEWORK KEY

○ = **WORKED-OUT SOLUTIONS on p. WS17 for Exs. 11 and 37**

★ = **STANDARDIZED TEST PRACTICE Exs. 3, 4, 24, 25, 32, 33, and 40**

SKILL PRACTICE

1. **VOCABULARY** Copy and complete: A linear system with no solution is called a(n) __?__ system.

2. **VOCABULARY** Copy and complete: A linear system with infinitely many solutions is called a(n) __?__ system.

3. ★ **WRITING** *Describe* the graph of a linear system that has no solution.

4. ★ **WRITING** *Describe* the graph of a linear system that has infinitely many solutions.

INTERPRETING GRAPHS Match the linear system with its graph. Then use the graph to tell whether the linear system has *one solution*, *no solution*, or *infinitely many solutions*.

5. $x - 3y = -9$
   $x - y = -1$

6. $x - y = -4$
   $-3x + 3y = 2$

7. $x + 3y = -1$
   $-2x - 6y = 2$

A. 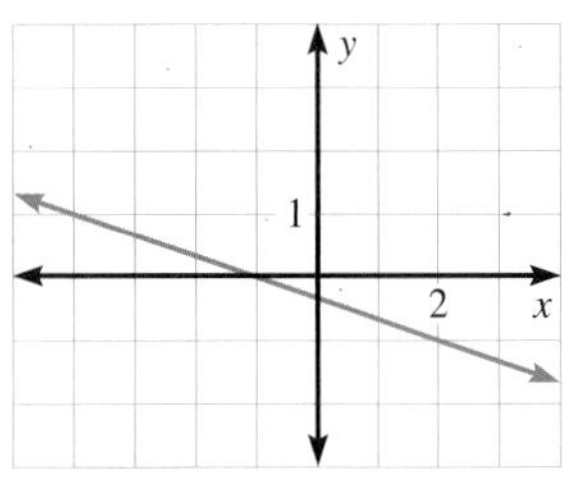

B. 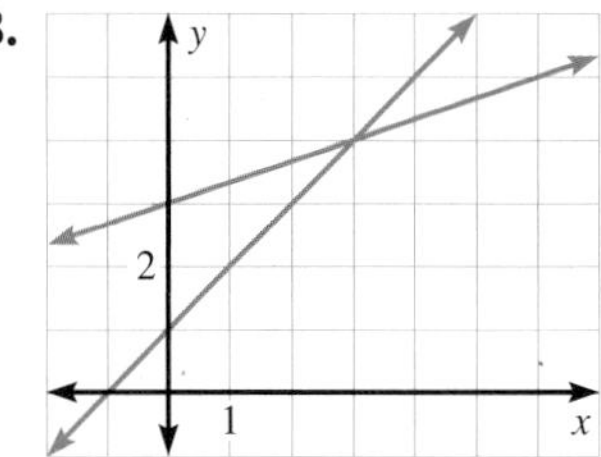

C. 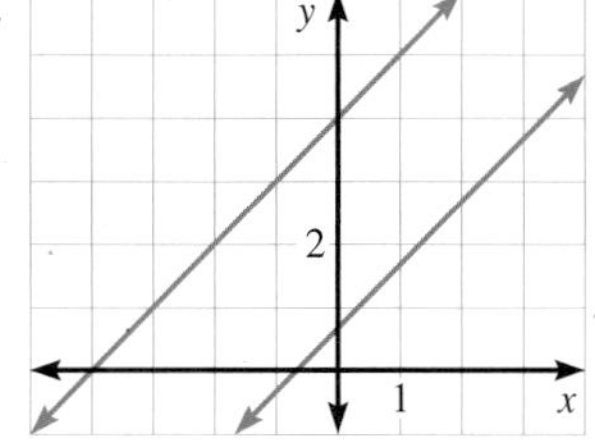

EXAMPLES 1 and 2 on pp. 459–460 for Exs. 8–25

INTERPRETING GRAPHS **Graph the linear system. Then use the graph to tell whether the linear system has *one solution, no solution,* or *infinitely many solutions.***

8. $x + y = -2$
$y = -x + 5$

9. $3x - 4y = 12$
$y = \frac{3}{4}x - 3$

10. $3x - y = -9$
$3x + 5y = -15$

11. $-2x + 2y = -16$
$3x - 6y = 30$

12. $-9x + 6y = 18$
$6x - 4y = -12$

13. $-3x + 4y = 12$
$-3x + 4y = 24$

14. ERROR ANALYSIS *Describe* and correct the error in solving the linear system below.

$6x + y = 36$
$5x - y = 8$

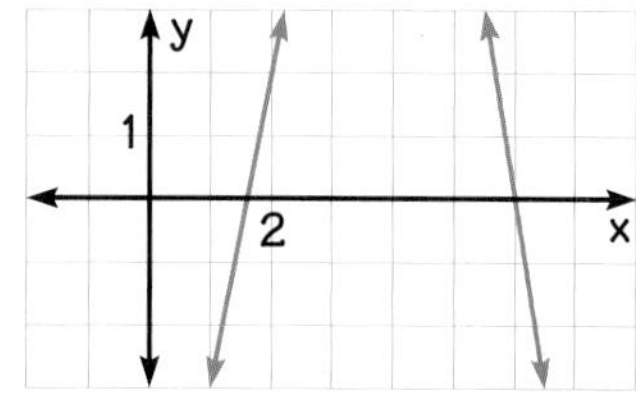

The lines do not intersect, so there is no solution.

SOLVING LINEAR SYSTEMS **Solve the linear system using substitution or elimination.**

15. $2x + 5y = 14$
$6x + 7y = 10$

16. $-16x + 2y = -2$
$y = 8x - 1$

17. $3x - 2y = -5$
$4x + 5y = 47$

18. $5x - 5y = -3$
$y = x + 0.6$

19. $x - y = 0$
$5x - 2y = 6$

20. $x - 2y = 7$
$-x + 2y = 7$

21. $-18x + 6y = 24$
$3x - y = -2$

22. $4y + 5x = 15$
$x = 8y + 3$

23. $6x + 3y = 9$
$2x + 9y = 27$

24. ★ **MULTIPLE CHOICE** Which of the linear systems has *exactly* one solution?

Ⓐ $-x + y = 9$
$x - y = 9$

Ⓑ $-x + y = 9$
$x - y = -9$

Ⓒ $-x + y = 9$
$-x - y = 9$

Ⓓ $x - y = -9$
$-x + y = -9$

25. ★ **MULTIPLE CHOICE** Which of the linear systems has infinitely many solutions?

Ⓐ $15x + 5y = 20$
$6x - 2y = 8$

Ⓑ $15x - 5y = 20$
$6x - 2y = -8$

Ⓒ $15x - 5y = -20$
$6x - 2y = 8$

Ⓓ $15x - 5y = 20$
$6x - 2y = 8$

EXAMPLE 3 on p. 461 for Exs. 26–31

IDENTIFYING THE NUMBER OF SOLUTIONS **Without solving the linear system, tell whether the linear system has *one solution, no solution,* or *infinitely many solutions.***

26. $y = -6x - 2$
$12x + 2y = -6$

27. $y = 7x + 13$
$-21x + 3y = 39$

28. $4x + 3y = 27$
$4x - 3y = -27$

29. $9x - 15y = 24$
$6x - 10y = 16$

30. $0.3x + 0.4y = 2.4$
$0.5x - 0.6y = 0.2$

31. $0.9x - 2.1y = 12.3$
$1.5x - 3.5y = 20.5$

32. ★ **OPEN-ENDED** Write a linear system so that it has infinitely many solutions, and one of the equations is $y = 3x + 2$.

33. ★ **OPEN-ENDED** Write a linear system so that it has no solution and one of the equations is $7x - 8y = -9$.

34. **REASONING** Give a counterexample for the following statement: If the graphs of the equations of a linear system have the same slope, then the linear system has no solution.

35. **CHALLENGE** Find values of p, q, and r that produce the solution(s).

    a. No solution

    b. Infinitely many solutions

    c. One solution of (4, 1)

$$px + qy = r \quad \text{Equation 1}$$
$$2x - 3y = 5 \quad \text{Equation 2}$$

PROBLEM SOLVING

EXAMPLE 4 on p. 461 for Exs. 36–38

36. **RECREATION** One admission to a roller skating rink costs x dollars and renting a pair of skates costs y dollars. A group pays $243 for admission for 36 people and 21 skate rentals. Another group pays $81 for admission for 12 people and 7 skate rentals. Is there enough information to determine the cost of one admission to the roller skating rink? *Explain.*

@HomeTutor for problem solving help at classzone.com

37. **TRANSPORTATION** A passenger train travels from New York City to Washington, D.C., then back to New York City. The table shows the number of coach tickets and business class tickets purchased for each leg of the trip. Is there enough information to determine the cost of one coach ticket? *Explain.*

Destination	Coach tickets	Business class tickets	Money collected (dollars)
Washington, D.C.	150	80	22,860
New York City	170	100	27,280

@HomeTutor for problem solving help at classzone.com

38. **PHOTOGRAPHY** In addition to taking pictures on your digital camera, you can record 30 second movies. All pictures use the same amount of memory, and all 30 second movies use the same amount of memory. The number of pictures and 30 second movies on 2 memory cards is shown.

    a. Is there enough information given to determine the amount of memory used by a 30 second movie? *Explain.*

    b. Given that a 30 second movie uses 50 times the amount of memory that a digital picture uses, can you determine the amount of memory used by a 30 second movie? *Explain.*

Size of card (megabytes)	64	256
Pictures	450	1800
Movies	7	28

39. **MULTI-STEP PROBLEM** Two people are training for a speed ice-climbing event. During a practice climb, one climber starts 15 seconds after the first climber. The rates that the climbers ascend are shown.

Climbs 10 feet every 30 seconds
Climbs 5 feet every 15 seconds

a. Let d be the distance (in feet) traveled by a climber t seconds after the first person starts climbing. Write a linear system that models the situation.

b. Graph the linear system from part (a). Does the second climber catch up to the first climber? *Explain.*

40. ★ **EXTENDED RESPONSE** Two employees at a banquet facility are given the task of folding napkins. One person starts folding napkins at a rate of 5 napkins per minute. The second person starts 10 minutes after the first person and folds napkins at a rate of 4 napkins per minute.

a. **Model** Let y be the number of napkins folded x minutes after the first person starts folding. Write a linear system that models the situation.

b. **Solve** Solve the linear system.

c. **Interpret** Does the solution of the linear system make sense in the context of the problem? *Explain.*

41. **CHALLENGE** An airplane has an average air speed of 160 miles per hour. The airplane takes 3 hours to travel with the wind from Salem to Lancaster. The airplane has to travel against the wind on the return trip. After 3 hours into the return trip, the airplane is 120 miles from Salem. Find the distance from Salem to Lancaster. If the problem cannot be solved with the information given, *explain* why.

MIXED REVIEW

Solve the equation, if possible. *(p. 154)*

42. $61 + 5c = 7 - 4c$

43. $3m - 2 = 7m - 50 + 8m$

44. $11z + 3 = 10(2z + 3)$

45. $-6(1 - w) = 14(w - 5)$

PREVIEW
Prepare for Lesson 7.6 in Exs. 46–61.

Solve the inequality. Then graph your solution.

46. $x + 15 < 23$ *(p. 356)*

47. $x - 1 \geq 10$ *(p. 356)*

48. $\frac{x}{4} > -2.5$ *(p. 363)*

49. $-7x \leq 84$ *(p. 363)*

50. $2 - 5x \geq 27$ *(p. 369)*

51. $3x - 9 > 3(x - 3)$ *(p. 369)*

52. $-2 < x + 3 \leq 11$ *(p. 380)*

53. $-7 \leq 5 - 2x \leq 7$ *(p. 380)*

54. $|x - 3| \geq 5$ *(p. 398)*

55. $2|2x - 1| - 9 \leq 1$ *(p. 398)*

Graph the inequality. *(p. 405)*

56. $x + y < -3$

57. $x - y \geq 1$

58. $2x - y < 5$

59. $-2x - 3y \leq 9$

60. $y \leq -4$

61. $x > 6.5$

7.6 Solve Systems of Linear Inequalities

Before You graphed linear inequalities in two variables.

Now You will solve systems of linear inequalities in two variables.

Why So you can find a marching band's competition score, as in Ex. 36.

Key Vocabulary
- **system of linear inequalities**
- **solution of a system of linear inequalities**
- **graph of a system of linear inequalities**

A **system of linear inequalities** in two variables, or simply a *system of inequalities*, consists of two or more linear inequalities in the same variables. An example is shown.

$x - y > 7$ **Inequality 1**
$2x + y < 8$ **Inequality 2**

A **solution of a system of linear inequalities** is an ordered pair that is a solution of each inequality in the system. For example, (6, −5) is a solution of the system above. The **graph of a system of linear inequalities** is the graph of all solutions of the system.

KEY CONCEPT *For Your Notebook*

Graphing a System of Linear Inequalities

STEP 1 **Graph** each inequality (as you learned to do in Lesson 6.7).

STEP 2 **Find** the intersection of the half-planes. The graph of the system is this intersection.

EXAMPLE 1 Graph a system of two linear inequalities

Graph the system of inequalities. $y > -x - 2$ **Inequality 1**
$y \leq 3x + 6$ **Inequality 2**

REVIEW GRAPHING INEQUALITIES
For help with graphing a linear inequality in two variables, see p. 405.

Solution

Graph both inequalities in the same coordinate plane. The graph of the system is the intersection of the two half-planes, which is shown as the darker shade of blue.

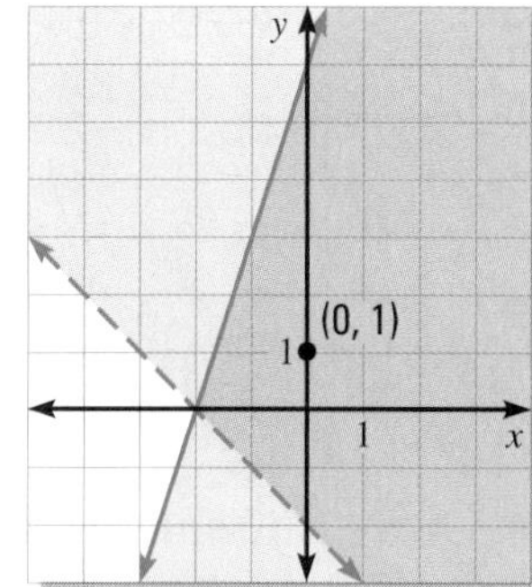

CHECK Choose a point in the dark blue region, such as (0, 1). To check this solution, substitute 0 for *x* and 1 for *y* into each inequality.

$1 \overset{?}{>} 0 - 2$ | $1 \overset{?}{\leq} 0 + 6$

$1 > -2$ ✓ | $1 \leq 6$ ✓

Animated **Algebra** at classzone.com

THE SOLUTION REGION In Example 1, the half-plane for each inequality is shaded, and the solution region is the intersection of the half-planes. From this point on, only the solution region will be shaded.

EXAMPLE 2 Graph a system of three linear inequalities

Graph the system of inequalities.

$y \geq -1$ **Inequality 1**
$x > -2$ **Inequality 2**
$x + 2y \leq 4$ **Inequality 3**

Solution

Graph all three inequalities in the same coordinate plane. The graph of the system is the triangular region shown.

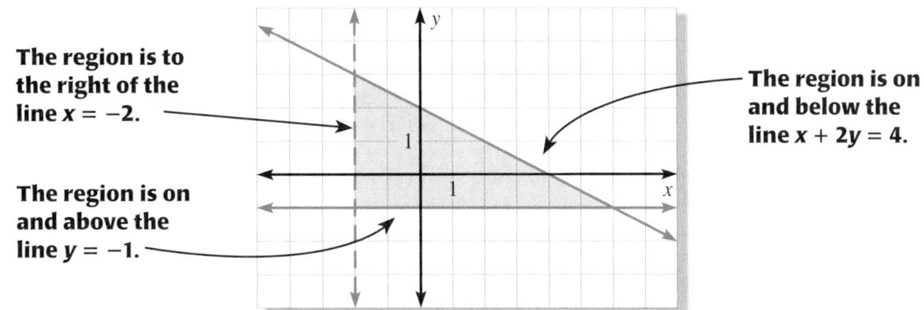
The region is to the right of the line $x = -2$.
The region is on and above the line $y = -1$.
The region is on and below the line $x + 2y = 4$.
y
x
1
1

GUIDED PRACTICE for Examples 1 and 2

Graph the system of linear inequalities.

1. $y < x - 4$
   $y \geq -x + 3$

2. $y \geq -x + 2$
   $y < 4$
   $x < 3$

3. $y > -x$
   $y \geq x - 4$
   $y < 5$

EXAMPLE 3 Write a system of linear inequalities

Write a system of inequalities for the shaded region.

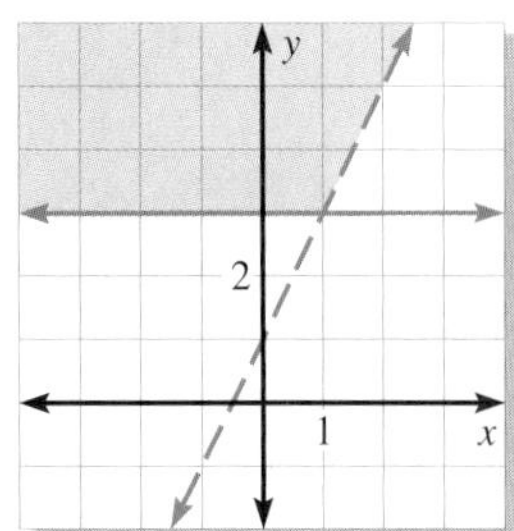
y
x
2
1

REVIEW EQUATIONS OF LINES
For help with writing an equation of a line, see pp. 283, 302, and 311.

Solution

INEQUALITY 1: One boundary line for the shaded region is $y = 3$. Because the shaded region is *above* the *solid* line, the inequality is $y \geq 3$.

INEQUALITY 2: Another boundary line for the shaded region has a slope of 2 and a y-intercept of 1. So, its equation is $y = 2x + 1$. Because the shaded region is *above* the *dashed* line, the inequality is $y > 2x + 1$.

▶ The system of inequalities for the shaded region is:

$y \geq 3$ **Inequality 1**
$y > 2x + 1$ **Inequality 2**

EXAMPLE 4 Write and solve a system of linear inequalities

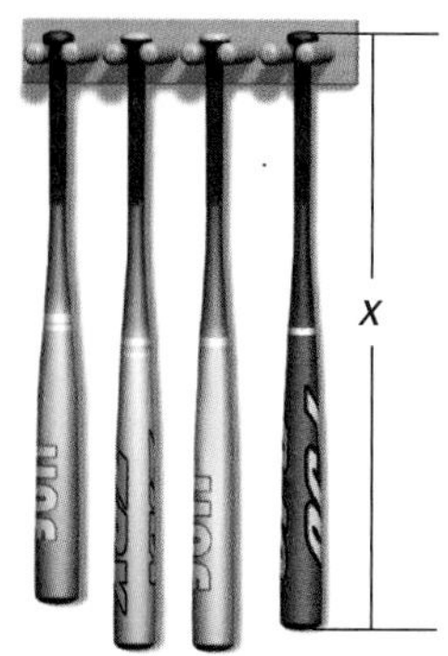

BASEBALL The National Collegiate Athletic Association (NCAA) regulates the lengths of aluminum baseball bats used by college baseball teams. The NCAA states that the length (in inches) of the bat minus the weight (in ounces) of the bat cannot exceed 3. Bats can be purchased at lengths from 26 to 34 inches.

a. Write and graph a system of linear inequalities that describes the information given above.

b. A sporting goods store sells an aluminum bat that is 31 inches long and weighs 25 ounces. Use the graph to determine if this bat can be used by a player on an NCAA team.

Solution

a. Let x be the length (in inches) of the bat, and let y be the weight (in ounces) of the bat. From the given information, you can write the following inequalities:

$x - y \leq 3$ **The difference of the bat's length and weight can be at most 3.**

$x \geq 26$ **The length of the bat must be at least 26 inches.**

$x \leq 34$ **The length of the bat can be at most 34 inches.**

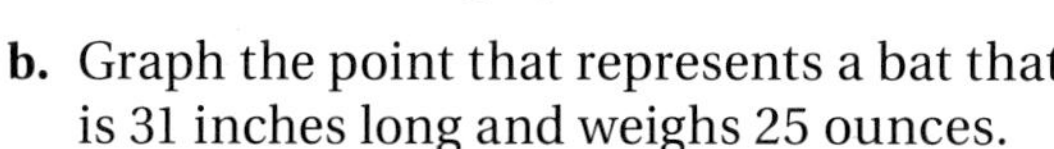

$y \geq 0$ **The weight of the bat cannot be a negative number.**

WRITING SYSTEMS OF INEQUALITIES
Consider the values of the variables when writing a system of inequalities. In many real-world problems, the values cannot be negative.

Graph each inequality in the system. Then identify the region that is common to all of the graphs of the inequalities. This region is shaded in the graph shown.

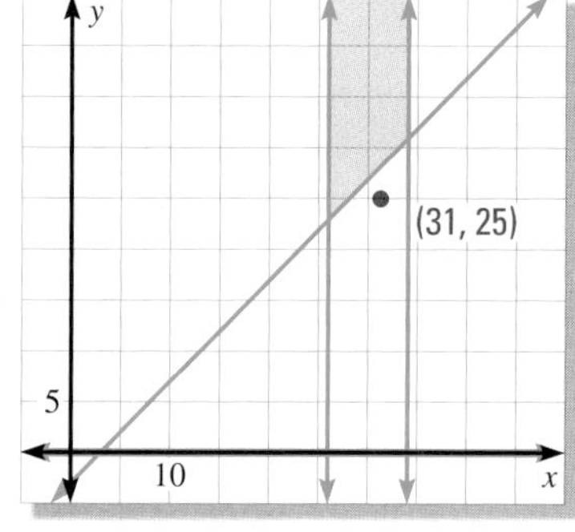

b. Graph the point that represents a bat that is 31 inches long and weighs 25 ounces.

▶ Because the point falls outside the solution region, the bat cannot be used by a player on an NCAA team.

✓ **GUIDED PRACTICE** for Examples 3 and 4

Write a system of inequalities that defines the shaded region.

4.

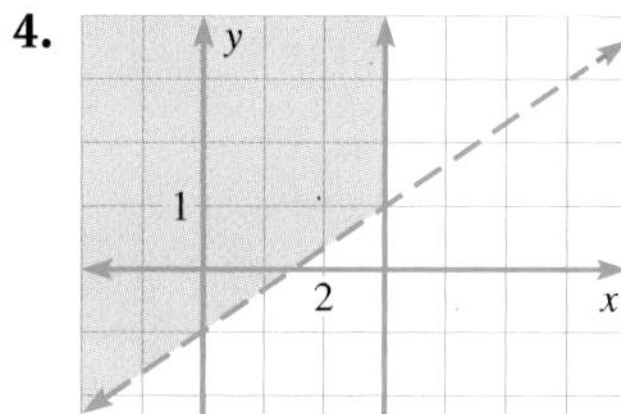

5.

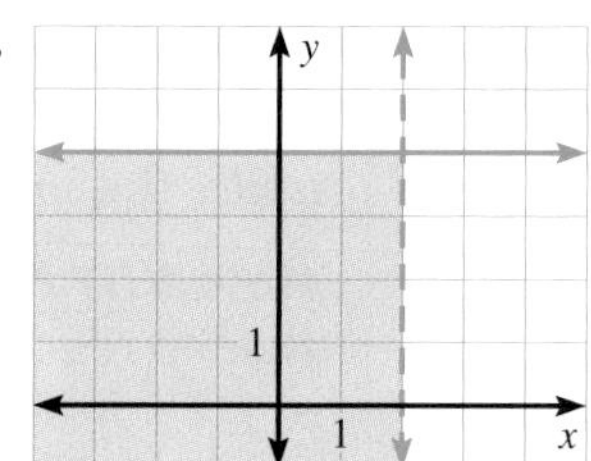

6. **WHAT IF?** In Example 4, suppose a Senior League (ages 10–14) player wants to buy the bat described in part (b). In Senior League, the length (in inches) of the bat minus the weight (in ounces) of the bat cannot exceed 8. Write and graph a system of inequalities to determine whether the described bat can be used by the Senior League player.

7.6 EXERCISES

HOMEWORK KEY

○ = **WORKED-OUT SOLUTIONS** on p. WS18 for Exs. 13 and 39

★ = **STANDARDIZED TEST PRACTICE** Exs. 2, 21, 22, 33, and 40

SKILL PRACTICE

1. **VOCABULARY** Copy and complete: A(n) __?__ of a system of linear inequalities is an ordered pair that is a solution of each inequality in the system.

2. ★ **WRITING** *Describe* the steps you would take to graph the system of inequalities shown.

   $x - y < 7$ **Inequality 1**
   $y \geq 3$ **Inequality 2**

CHECKING A SOLUTION **Tell whether the ordered pair is a solution of the system of inequalities.**

3. (1, 1)

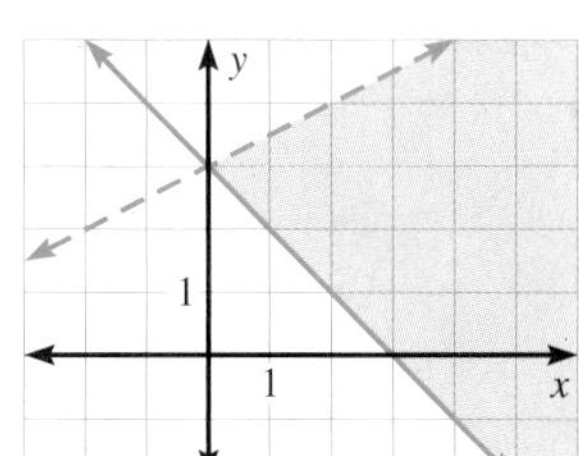

4. (0, 6)

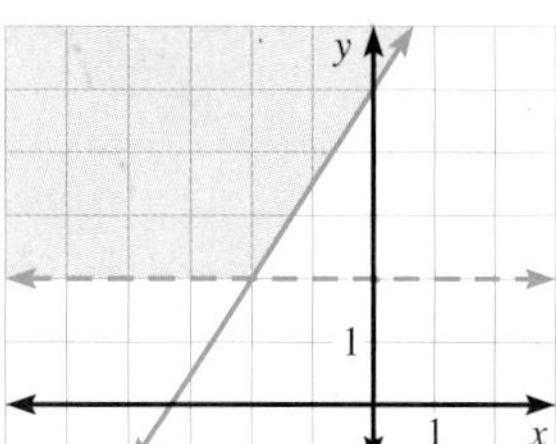

5. (3, −1)

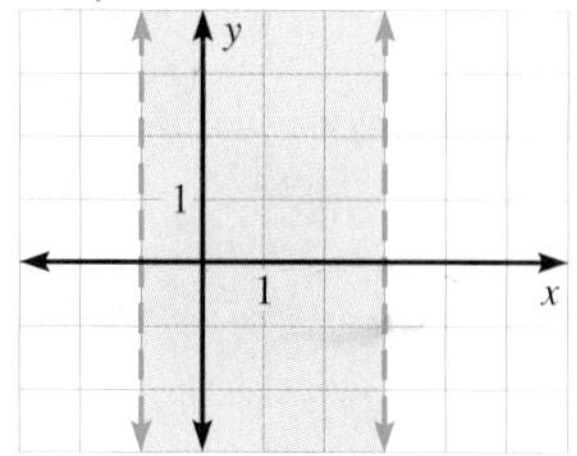

EXAMPLE 1 on p. 466 for Exs. 6–17

MATCHING SYSTEMS AND GRAPHS **Match the system of inequalities with its graph.**

6. $x - 4y > -8$
   $x \geq 2$

7. $x - 4y \geq -8$
   $x < 2$

8. $x - 4y > -8$
   $y \geq 2$

A.

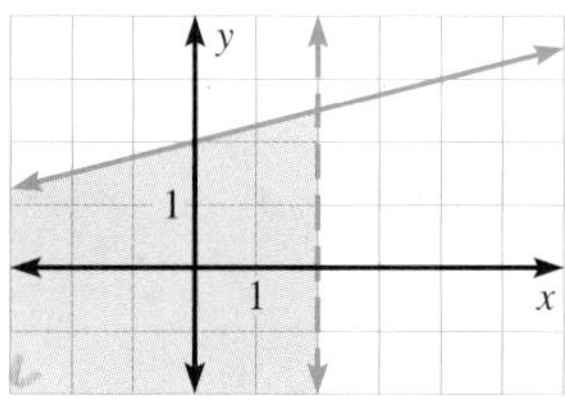

B.

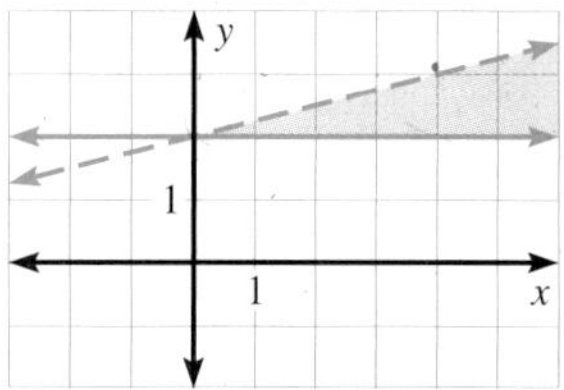

C.

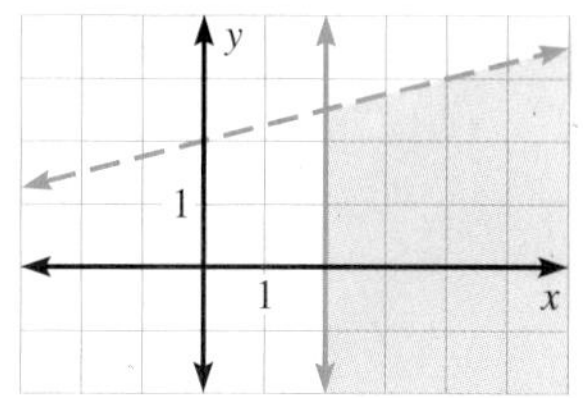

GRAPHING A SYSTEM **Graph the system of inequalities.**

9. $x > -5$
   $x < 2$

10. $y \leq 10$
    $y \geq 6$

11. $x > 3$
    $y > x$

12. $y < -2x + 3$
    $y \geq 4$

13. $y \geq 0$
    $y < 2.5x - 1$

14. $y \geq 2x + 1$
    $y < -x + 4$

15. $x < 8$
    $x - 4y \leq -8$

16. $y \geq -2$
    $2x + 3y > -6$

17. $y - 2x < 7$
    $y + 2x > -1$

EXAMPLE 2 on p. 467 for Exs. 18–21

18. $x < 4$
    $y > 1$
    $y \geq -x + 1$

19. $x \geq 0$
    $y \geq 0$
    $6x - y < 12$

20. $x + y \leq 10$
    $x - y \geq 2$
    $y \geq 2$

21. ★ **MULTIPLE CHOICE** Which ordered pair is a solution of the system $2x - y \leq 5$ and $x + 2y > 2$?

   Ⓐ (1, −1) Ⓑ (4, 1) Ⓒ (2, 0) Ⓓ (3, 2)

EXAMPLE 2
on p. 467
for Exs. 22–23

22. ★ **MULTIPLE CHOICE** The graph of which system of inequalities is shown?

Ⓐ $y < 2x$
$2x + 3y < 6$

Ⓑ $y < 2x$
$2x + 3y > 6$

Ⓒ $y > 2x$
$2x + 3y < 6$

Ⓓ $y > 2x$
$2x + 3y > 6$

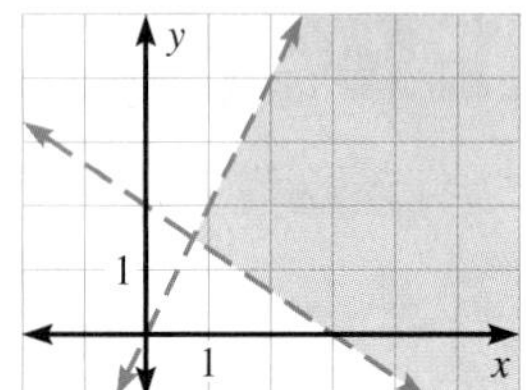

23. **ERROR ANALYSIS** *Describe* and correct the error in graphing this system of inequalities:

$x + y < 3$ **Inequality 1**
$x > -1$ **Inequality 2**
$x \leq 3$ **Inequality 3**

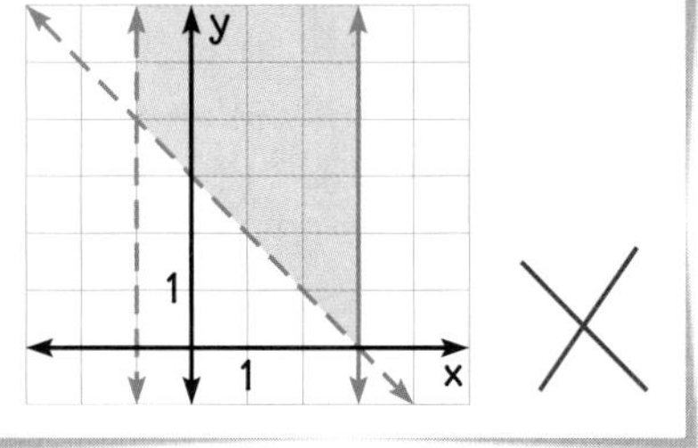

EXAMPLE 3
on p. 467
for Exs. 24–29

WRITING A SYSTEM **Write a system of inequalities for the shaded region.**

24.
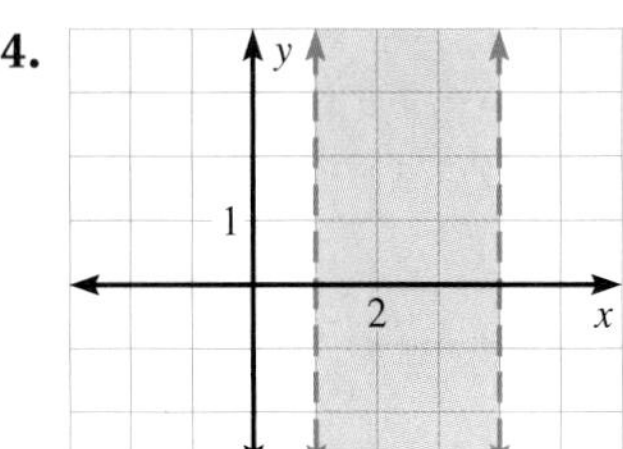

25.
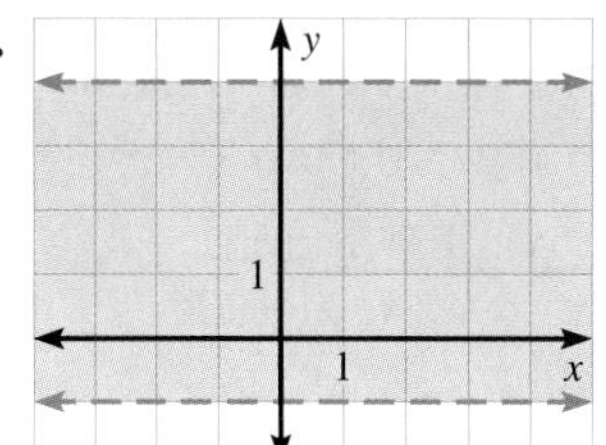

26.
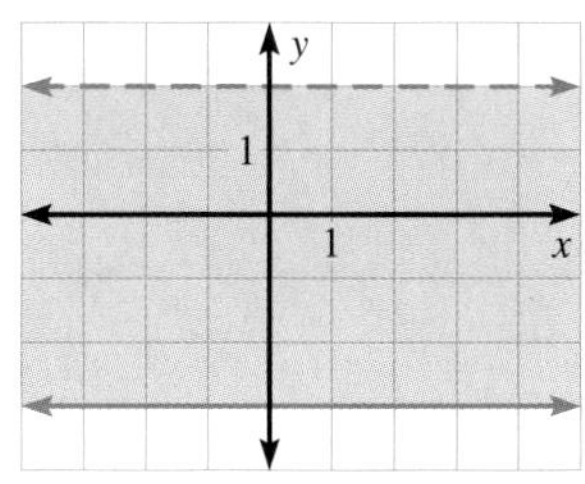

27.
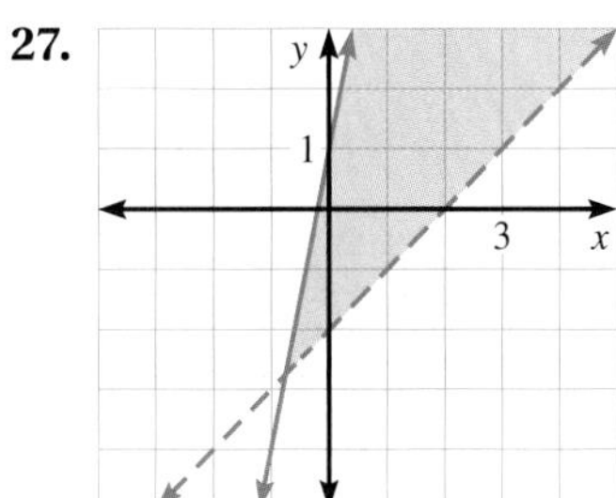

28.
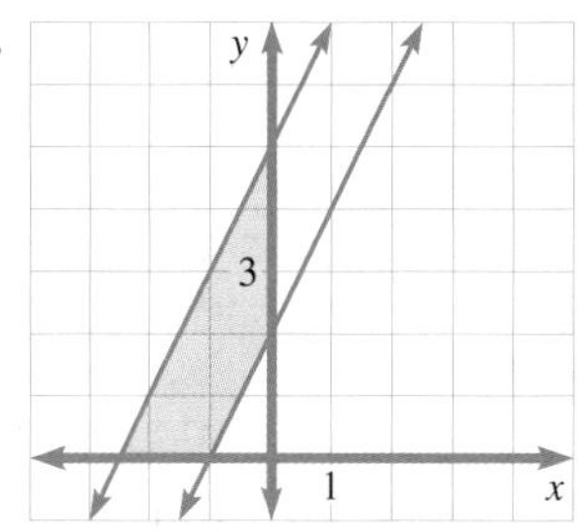

29.
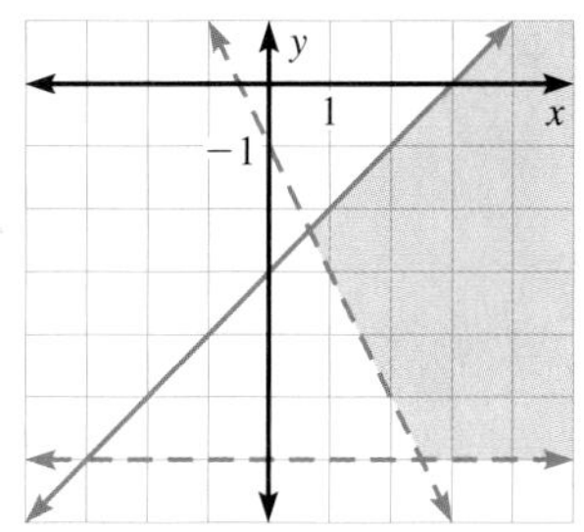

GRAPHING A SYSTEM **Graph the system of inequalities.**

30. $x > 4$
$x < 9$
$y \leq 2$
$y > -2$

31. $x + y < 4$
$x + y > -2$
$x - y \leq 3$
$x - y \geq -4$

32. $x \leq 10$
$3x + 2y \geq 9$
$x - 2y \leq 6$
$x + y \leq 5$

33. ★ **SHORT RESPONSE** Does the system of inequalities have any solutions? *Explain.*

$x - y > 5$ **Inequality 1**
$x - y < 1$ **Inequality 2**

CHALLENGE **Write a system of inequalities for the shaded region described.**

34. The shaded region is a rectangle with vertices at (2, 1), (2, 4), (6, 4), and (6, 1).

35. The shaded region is a triangle with vertices at (−3, 0), (3, 2), and (0, −2).

○ = **WORKED-OUT SOLUTIONS on p. WS1**

★ = **STANDARDIZED TEST PRACTICE**

PROBLEM SOLVING

EXAMPLE 4
on p. 468
for Exs. 36–38

36. COMPETITION SCORES In a marching band competition, scoring is based on a musical evaluation and a visual evaluation. The musical evaluation score cannot exceed 60 points, the visual evaluation score cannot exceed 40 points. Write and graph a system of inequalities for the scores that a marching band can receive.

@HomeTutor for problem solving help at classzone.com

37. NUTRITION For a hiking trip, you are making a mix of x ounces of peanuts and y ounces of chocolate pieces. You want the mix to have less than 70 grams of fat and weigh less than 8 ounces. An ounce of peanuts has 14 grams of fat, and an ounce of chocolate pieces has 7 grams of fat. Write and graph a system of inequalities that models the situation.

@HomeTutor for problem solving help at classzone.com

38. FISHING LIMITS You are fishing in a marina for surfperch and rockfish, which are two species of bottomfish. Gaming laws in the marina allow you to catch no more than 15 surfperch per day, no more than 10 rockfish per day, and no more than 15 total bottomfish per day.

a. Write and graph a system of inequalities that models the situation.

b. Use the graph to determine whether you can catch 11 surfperch and 9 rockfish in one day.

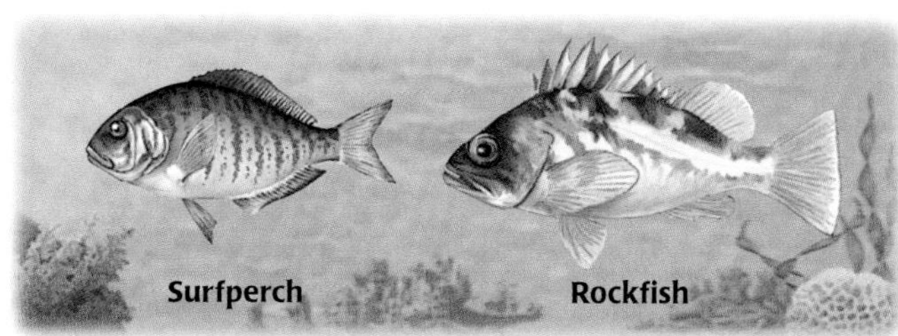

39. HEALTH A person's maximum heart rate (in beats per minute) is given by $220 - x$ where x is the person's age in years ($20 \le x \le 65$). When exercising, a person should aim for a heart rate that is at least 70% of the maximum heart rate and at most 85% of the maximum heart rate.

a. Write and graph a system of inequalities that models the situation.

b. A 40-year-old person's heart rate varies from 104 to 120 beats per minute while exercising. Does his heart rate stay in the suggested target range for his age? *Explain.*

40. ★ SHORT RESPONSE A photography shop has a self-service photo center that allows you to make prints of pictures. Each sheet of printed pictures costs \$8. The number of pictures that fit on each sheet is shown.

a. You want at least 16 pictures of any size, and you are willing to spend up to \$48. Write and graph a system of inequalities that models the situation.

b. Will you be able to purchase 12 pictures that are 3 inches by 5 inches and 6 pictures that are 4 inches by 6 inches? *Explain.*

Four 3 inch by 5 inch pictures fit on one sheet.

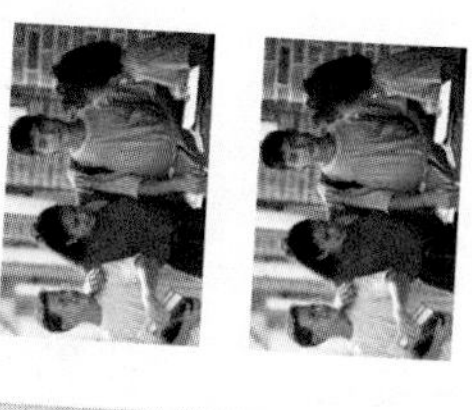

Two 4 inch by 6 inch pictures fit on one sheet.

41. CHALLENGE You make necklaces and keychains to sell at a craft fair. The table shows the time that it takes to make each necklace and keychain, the cost of materials for each necklace and keychain, and the time and money that you can devote to making necklaces and keychains.

	Necklace	Keychain	Available
Time to make (hours)	0.5	0.25	20
Cost to make (dollars)	2	3	120

a. Write and graph a system of inequalities for the number x of necklaces and the number y of keychains that you can make under the given constraints.

b. Find the vertices (corner points) of the graph.

c. You sell each necklace for \$10 and each keychain for \$8. The revenue R is given by the equation $R = 10x + 8y$. Find the revenue for each ordered pair in part (b). Which vertex results in the maximum revenue?

MIXED REVIEW

PREVIEW
Prepare for Lesson 8.1 in Exs. 42–47.

Evaluate the expression.

42. $13x^2$ when $x = 2$ *(p. 8)*

43. $64 \div z^3$ when $z = 2$ *(p. 8)*

44. $-|-c| - 3^2$ when $c = 8$ *(p. 64)*

45. $-8 + 3y - 16$ when $y = -6$ *(p. 88)*

46. $\frac{7 - 8w}{11w}$ when $w = 5$ *(p. 103)*

47. $21 + \sqrt{x}$ when $x = 144$ *(p. 110)*

Use any method to solve the linear system. *(pp. 427, 435, 444, 451)*

48. $y = 4x - 1$
$y = -8x + 23$

49. $y = -2x - 6$
$y = -5x - 12$

50. $x + 2y = -1$
$-x = y - 2$

51. $4x + y = 0$
$-x + y = 5$

52. $2x - y = -5$
$y = -x - 5$

53. $3x + 2y = 2$
$-3x + y = -11$

QUIZ *for Lessons 7.5–7.6*

Graph the linear system. Then use the graph to tell whether the linear system has *one solution, no solution,* or *infinitely many solutions.* *(p. 459)*

1. $x - y = 1$
$x - y = 6$

2. $6x + 2y = 16$
$2x - y = 2$

3. $3x - 3y = -2$
$-6x + 6y = 4$

Graph the system of linear inequalities. *(p. 466)*

4. $x > -3$
$x < 7$

5. $y \leq 2$
$y < 6x + 2$

6. $4x \geq y$
$-x + 4y < 4$

7. $x + y < 2$
$2x + y > -3$
$y \geq 0$

8. $y \geq 3x - 4$
$y \leq x$
$y \geq -5x - 15$

9. $x > -5$
$x < 0$
$y \leq 2x + 7$

EXTRA PRACTICE for Lesson 7.6, p. 944

ONLINE QUIZ at classzone.com

MIXED REVIEW of Problem Solving

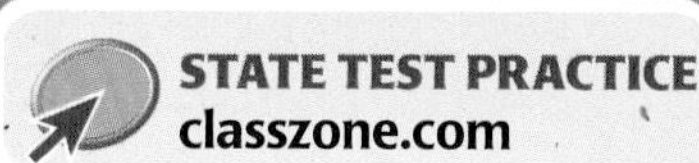

Lessons 7.5–7.6

1. **MULTI-STEP PROBLEM** A minimum of 600 bricks and 12 bags of sand are needed for a construction job. Each brick weighs 2 pounds, and each bag of sand weighs 50 pounds. The maximum weight that a delivery truck can carry is 3000 pounds.
   a. Let x be the number of bricks, and let y be the number of bags of sand. Write a system of linear inequalities that models the situation.
   b. Graph the system of inequalities.
   c. Use the graph to determine whether 700 bricks and 20 bags of sand can be delivered in one trip.

2. **MULTI-STEP PROBLEM** Dana decides to paint the ceiling and the walls of a room. She spends \$120 on 2 gallons of paint for the ceiling and 4 gallons of paint for the walls. Then she decides to paint the ceiling and the walls of another room using the same kinds of paint. She spends \$60 for 1 gallon of paint for the ceiling and 2 gallons of paint for the walls.

   a. Write a system of linear equations that models the situation.
   b. Is there enough information given to determine the cost of one gallon of each type of paint? *Explain.*
   c. A gallon of ceiling paint costs \$3 more than a gallon of wall paint. What is the cost of one gallon of each type of paint?

3. **SHORT RESPONSE** During a sale at a music and video store, all CDs are priced the same and all DVDs are priced the same. Karen buys 4 CDs and 2 DVDs for \$78. The next day, while the sale is still in progress, Karen goes back and buys 2 CDs and 1 DVD for \$39. Is there enough information to determine the cost of 1 CD? *Explain.*

4. **SHORT RESPONSE** Two airport shuttles, bus A and bus B, take passengers to the airport from the same bus stop. The graph shows the distance d (in miles) traveled by each bus t hours after bus A leaves the station. The distance from the bus stop to the airport is 25 miles. If bus A and bus B continue at the same rates, will bus B ever catch up to bus A? *Explain.*

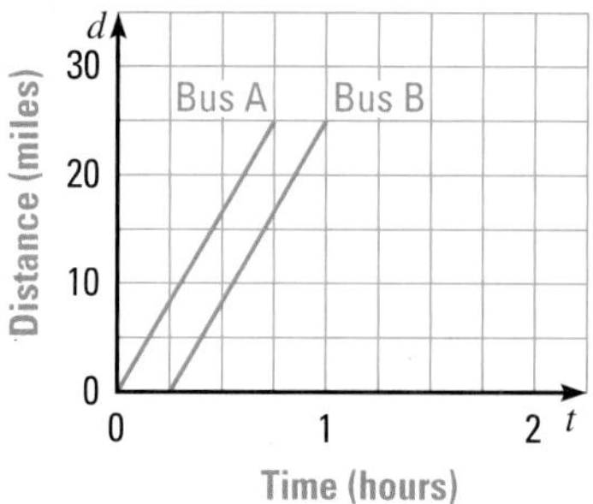

5. **EXTENDED RESPONSE** During the summer, you want to earn at least \$200 per week. You earn \$10 per hour working as a lifeguard, and you earn \$8 per hour working at a retail store. You can work at most 30 hours per week.
   a. Write and graph a system of linear inequalities that models the situation.
   b. If you work 5 hours per week as a lifeguard and 15 hours per week at the retail store, will you earn at least \$200 per week? *Explain.*
   c. You are scheduled to work 20 hours per week at the retail store. What is the range of hours you can work as a lifeguard to earn at least \$200 per week?

6. **OPEN-ENDED** *Describe* a real-world situation that can be modeled by a system of linear inequalities. Then write and graph the system of inequalities.

7. **GRIDDED ANSWER** What is the area (in square feet) of the triangular garden defined by the system of inequalities below?

$$y \geq 0$$
$$x \geq 0$$
$$4x + 5y \leq 60$$

7 CHAPTER SUMMARY

BIG IDEAS

For Your Notebook

Big Idea 1

Solving Linear Systems by Graphing

The graph of a system of two linear equations tells you how many solutions the system has.

One solution

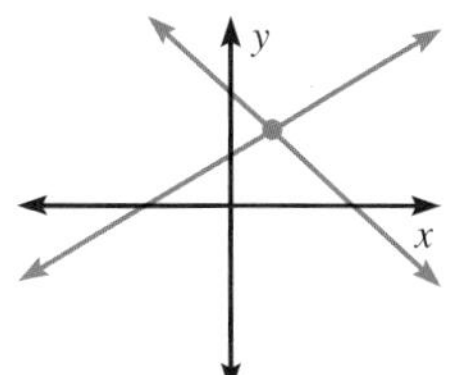

The lines intersect.

No solution

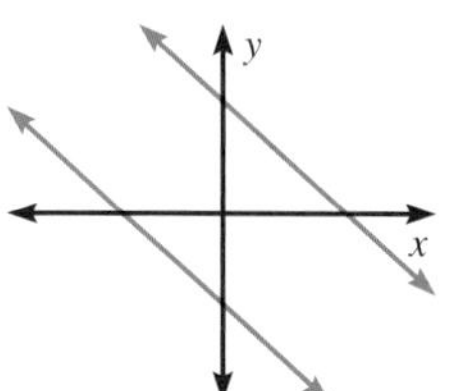

The lines are parallel.

Infinitely many solutions

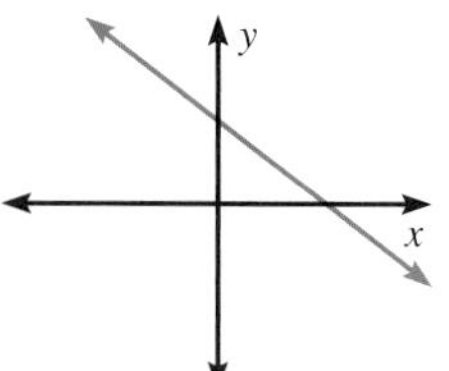

The lines coincide.

Big Idea 2

Solving Linear Systems Using Algebra

You can use any of the following algebraic methods to solve a system of linear equations. Sometimes it is easier to use one method instead of another.

Method	Procedure	When to use
Substitution	Solve one equation for x or y. Substitute the expression for x or y into the other equation.	When one equation is already solved for x or y
Addition	Add the equations to eliminate x or y.	When the coefficients of one variable are opposites
Subtraction	Subtract the equations to eliminate x or y.	When the coefficients of one variable are the same
Multiplication	Multiply one or both equations by a constant so that adding or subtracting the equations will eliminate x or y.	When no corresponding coefficients are the same or opposites

Big Idea 3

Solving Systems of Linear Inequalities

The graph of a system of linear inequalities is the intersection of the half-planes of each inequality in the system. For example, the graph of the system of inequalities below is the shaded region.

$x \le 6$ Inequality 1
$y < 2$ Inequality 2
$2x + 3y \ge 6$ Inequality 3

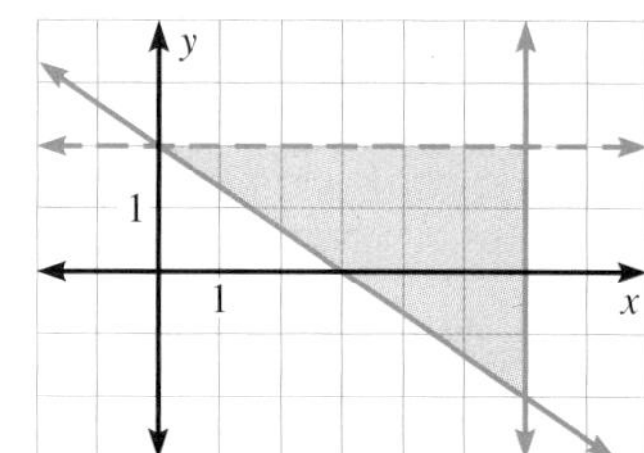

7 CHAPTER REVIEW

@HomeTutor
classzone.com
• Multi-Language Glossary
• Vocabulary practice

REVIEW KEY VOCABULARY

- system of linear equations, *p. 427*
- solution of a system of linear equations, *p. 427*
- consistent independent system, *p. 427*
- inconsistent system, *p. 459*
- consistent dependent system, *p. 459*
- system of linear inequalities, *p. 466*
- solution of a system of linear inequalities, *p. 466*
- graph of a system of linear inequalities, *p. 466*

VOCABULARY EXERCISES

1. Copy and complete: A(n) __?__ consists of two or more linear inequalities in the same variables.
2. Copy and complete: A(n) __?__ consists of two or more linear equations in the same variables.
3. *Describe* how you would graph a system of two linear inequalities.
4. Give an example of a consistent dependent system. *Explain* why the system is a consistent dependent system.

REVIEW EXAMPLES AND EXERCISES

Use the review examples and exercises below to check your understanding of the concepts you have learned in each lesson of Chapter 7.

7.1 Solve Linear Systems by Graphing pp. 427–433

EXAMPLE

Solve the linear system by graphing. Check your solution.

$y = x - 2$ **Equation 1**
$y = -3x + 2$ **Equation 2**

Graph both equations. The lines appear to intersect at $(1, -1)$. Check the solution by substituting **1** for x and **−1** for y in each equation.

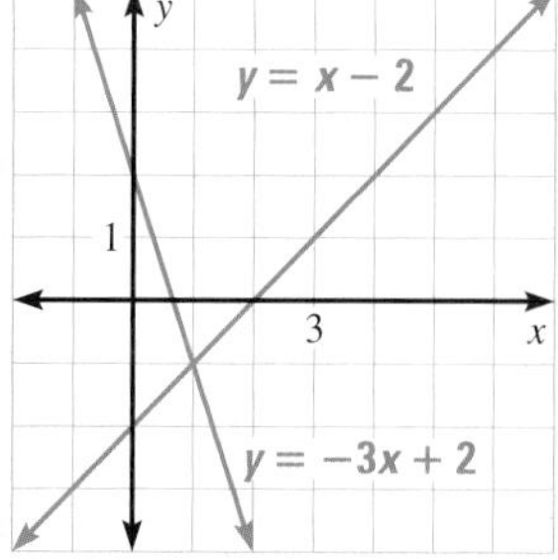

$y = x - 2$	$y = -3x + 2$
$-1 \stackrel{?}{=} 1 - 2$	$-1 \stackrel{?}{=} -3(1) + 2$
$-1 = -1$ ✓	$-1 = -1$ ✓

EXERCISES

EXAMPLES 1 and 2 on pp. 427–428 for Exs. 5–7

Solve the linear system by graphing. Check your solution.

5. $y = -3x + 1$
   $y = x - 7$
6. $y = 3x + 4$
   $y = -2x - 1$
7. $x + y = 3$
   $x - y = 5$

7 CHAPTER REVIEW

7.2 Solve Linear Systems by Substitution pp. 435–441

EXAMPLE

Solve the linear system: $3x + y = -9$ **Equation 1**
$y = 5x + 7$ **Equation 2**

STEP 1 **Substitute** $5x + 7$ for y in Equation 1 and solve for x.

$3x + y = -9$ **Write Equation 1.**

$3x + 5x + 7 = -9$ **Substitute 5x + 7 for y.**

$x = -2$ **Solve for x.**

STEP 2 **Substitute** -2 for x in Equation 2 to find the value of y.

$y = 5x + 7 = 5(-2) + 7 = -10 + 7 = -3$

▶ The solution is $(-2, -3)$. Check the solution by substituting -2 for x and -3 for y in each of the original equations.

EXERCISES

EXAMPLES 1, 2, and 3 on pp. 435–437 for Exs. 8–11

Solve the linear system using substitution.

8. $y = 2x - 7$
$x + 2y = 1$

9. $x + 4y = 9$
$x - y = 4$

10. $2x + y = -15$
$y - 5x = 6$

11. ART Kara spends \$16 on tubes of paint and disposable brushes for an art project. Each tube of paint costs \$3, and each disposable brush costs \$.50. Kara purchases twice as many brushes as tubes of paint. Find the number of brushes and the number of tubes of paint that she purchases.

7.3 Solve Linear Systems by Adding or Subtracting pp. 444–450

EXAMPLE

Solve the linear system: $5x - y = 8$ **Equation 1**
$-5x + 4y = -17$ **Equation 2**

STEP 1 **Add** the equations to eliminate one variable.

$$\begin{array}{r} 5x - y = 8 \\ -5x + 4y = -17 \\ \hline 3y = -9 \end{array}$$

STEP 2 **Solve** for y. $y = -3$

STEP 3 **Substitute** -3 for y in either equation and solve for x.

$5x - y = 8$ **Write Equation 1.**

$5x - (-3) = 8$ **Substitute −3 for y.**

$x = 1$ **Solve for x.**

▶ The solution is $(1, -3)$. Check the solution by substituting 1 for x and -3 for y in each of the original equations.

@HomeTutor
classzone.com
Chapter Review Practice

EXERCISES

EXAMPLES 1, 2, and 3 on pp. 444–445 for Exs. 12–17

Solve the linear system using elimination.

12. $x + 2y = 13$
$x - 2y = -7$

13. $4x - 5y = 14$
$-4x + y = -6$

14. $x + 7y = 12$
$-2x + 7y = 18$

15. $9x - 2y = 34$
$5x - 2y = 10$

16. $3x = y + 1$
$2x - y = 9$

17. $4y = 11 - 3x$
$3x + 2y = -5$

7.4 Solve Linear Systems by Multiplying First

pp. 451–457

EXAMPLE

Solve the linear system: $x - 2y = -7$ **Equation 1**
$3x - y = 4$ **Equation 2**

STEP 1 **Multiply** the first equation by -3.

$x - 2y = -7$ × (−3) → $-3x + 6y = 21$
$3x - y = 4$ → $3x - y = 4$

STEP 2 **Add** the equations. $5y = 25$

STEP 3 **Solve** for y. $y = 5$

STEP 4 **Substitute** 5 for y in either of the original equations and solve for x.

$x - 2y = -7$ **Write Equation 1.**

$x - 2(5) = -7$ **Substitute 5 for *y*.**

$x = 3$ **Solve for *x*.**

▸ The solution is (3, 5).

CHECK Substitute 3 for x and 5 for y in each of the original equations.

Equation 1	**Equation 2**
$x - 2y = -7$	$3x - y = 4$
$3 - 2(5) \stackrel{?}{=} -7$	$3(3) - 5 \stackrel{?}{=} 4$
$-7 = -7$ ✓	$4 = 4$ ✓

EXERCISES

EXAMPLES 1 and 2 on pp. 451–452 for Exs. 18–24

Solve the linear system using elimination.

18. $-x + y = -4$
$2x - 3y = 5$

19. $x + 6y = 28$
$2x - 3y = -19$

20. $3x - 5y = -7$
$-4x + 7y = 8$

21. $8x - 7y = -3$
$6x - 5y = -1$

22. $5x = 3y - 2$
$3x + 2y = 14$

23. $11x = 2y - 1$
$3y = 10 + 8x$

24. CAR MAINTENANCE You pay \$24.50 for 10 gallons of gasoline and 1 quart of oil at a gas station. Your friend pays \$22 for 8 gallons of the same gasoline and 2 quarts of the same oil. Find the cost of 1 quart of oil.

7 CHAPTER REVIEW

7.5 Solve Special Types of Linear Systems

pp. 459–465

EXAMPLE

Show that the linear system has no solution.

$-2x + y = -3$ **Equation 1**
$y = 2x + 1$ **Equation 2**

Graph the linear system.

The lines are parallel because they have the same slope but different y-intercepts. Parallel lines do not intersect, so the system has no solution.

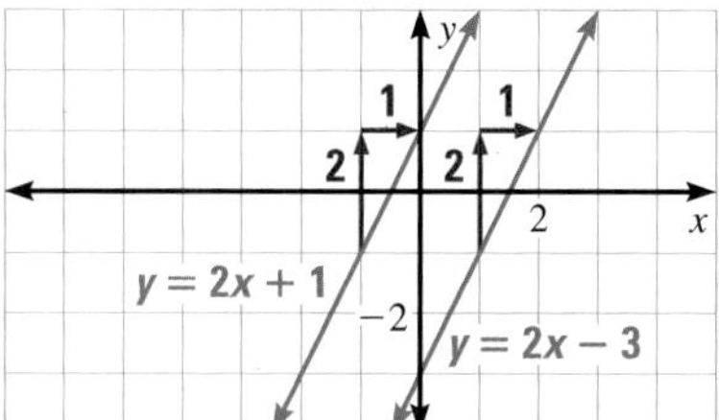

EXERCISES

EXAMPLES 1, 2, and 3 on pp. 459–461 for Exs. 25–27

Tell whether the linear system has *one solution*, *no solution*, or *infinitely many solutions*. *Explain.*

25. $x = 2y - 3$
$1.5x - 3y = 0$

26. $-x + y = 8$
$x + 8 = y$

27. $4x = 2y + 6$
$4x + 2y = 10$

7.6 Solve Systems of Linear Inequalities

pp. 466–472

EXAMPLE

Graph the system of linear inequalities.

$y < -2x + 3$ **Inequality 1**
$y \geq x - 3$ **Inequality 2**

The graph of $y < -2x + 3$ is the half-plane *below* the *dashed* line $y = -2x + 3$.

The graph of $y \geq x - 3$ is the half-plane *on and above* the *solid* line $y = x - 3$.

The graph of the system is the intersection of the two half-planes shown as the darker shade of blue.

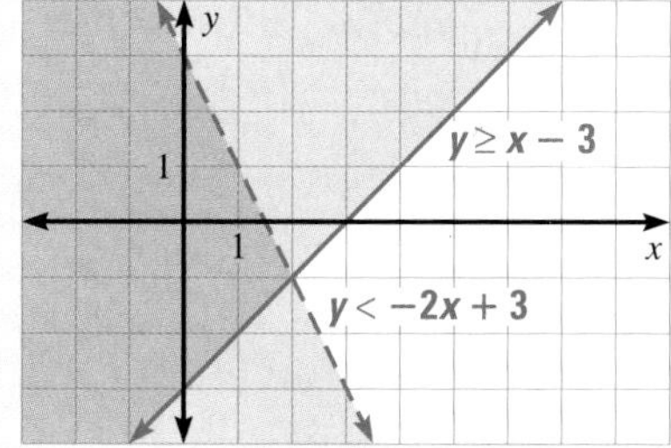

EXERCISES

EXAMPLES 1, 2, 3, and 4 on pp. 466–468 for Exs. 28–31

Graph the system of linear inequalities.

28. $y < x + 3$
$y > -3x - 2$

29. $y \leq -x - 2$
$y > 4x + 1$

30. $y \geq 0$
$x \leq 2$
$y < x + 4$

31. MOVIE COSTS You receive a \$40 gift card to a movie theater. A ticket to a matinee movie costs \$5, and a ticket to an evening movie costs \$8. Write and graph a system of inequalities for the number of tickets you can purchase using the gift card.

7 CHAPTER TEST

Solve the linear system by graphing. Check your solution.

1. $3x - y = -6$
$x + y = 2$

2. $-2x + y = 5$
$x + y = -1$

3. $y = 4x + 4$
$3x + 2y = 12$

4. $5x - 4y = 20$
$x + 2y = 4$

5. $x + 3y = 9$
$2x - y = 4$

6. $2x + 7y = 14$
$5x + 7y = -7$

Solve the linear system using substitution.

7. $y = 5x - 7$
$-4x + y = -1$

8. $x = y - 11$
$x - 3y = 1$

9. $3x + y = -19$
$x - y = 7$

10. $15x + y = 70$
$3x - 2y = -8$

11. $3y + x = 17$
$x + y = 8$

12. $0.5x + y = 9$
$1.6x + 0.2y = 13$

Solve the linear system using elimination.

13. $8x + 3y = -9$
$-8x + y = 29$

14. $x - 5y = -3$
$3x - 5y = 11$

15. $4x + y = 17$
$7y = 4x - 9$

16. $3x + 2y = -5$
$x - y = 10$

17. $3y = x + 5$
$-3x + 8y = 8$

18. $6x - 5y = 9$
$9x - 7y = 15$

Tell whether the linear system has *one solution, no solution,* or *infinitely many solutions.*

19. $15x - 3y = 12$
$y = 5x - 4$

20. $4x - y = -4$
$-8x + 2y = 2$

21. $-12x + 3y = 18$
$4x + y = -6$

22. $6x - 7y = 5$
$-12x + 14y = 10$

23. $3x - 4y = 24$
$3x + 4y = 24$

24. $10x - 2y = 14$
$15x - 3y = 21$

Graph the system of linear inequalities.

25. $y < 2x + 2$
$y \geq -x - 1$

26. $y \leq 3x - 2$
$y > x + 4$

27. $y \leq 3$
$x > -1$
$y > 3x - 3$

28. TRUCK RENTALS Carrie and Dave each rent the same size moving truck for one day. They pay a fee of x dollars for the truck and y dollars per mile they drive. Carrie drives 150 miles and pays \$215. Dave drives 120 miles and pays \$176. Find the amount of the fee and the cost per mile.

29. GEOMETRY The rectangle has a perimeter P of 58 inches. The length ℓ is one more than 3 times the width w. Write and solve a system of linear equations to find the length and width of the rectangle.

$P = 58$ in.
w
ℓ

30. COMMUNITY SERVICE A town committee has a budget of \$75 to spend on snacks for the volunteers participating in a clean-up day. The committee chairperson decides to purchase granola bars and at least 50 bottles of water. Granola bars cost \$.50 each, and bottles of water cost \$.75 each. Write and graph a system of linear inequalities for the number of bottles of water and the number of granola bars that can be purchased.

7 ★ Standardized TEST PREPARATION

MULTIPLE CHOICE QUESTIONS

If you have difficulty solving a multiple choice problem directly, you may be able to use another approach to eliminate incorrect answer choices and obtain the correct answer.

PROBLEM 1

Which ordered pair is the solution of the linear system $y = \frac{1}{2}x$ and $2x + 3y = -7$?

(A) (2, 1) (B) (1, −3) (C) (−2, −1) (D) (4, 2)

Method 1

SOLVE DIRECTLY Use substitution to solve the linear system.

STEP 1 **Substitute** $\frac{1}{2}x$ for y in the equation $2x + 3y = -7$ and solve for x.

$$2x + 3y = -7$$
$$2x + 3\left(\frac{1}{2}x\right) = -7$$
$$2x + \frac{3}{2}x = -7$$
$$\frac{7}{2}x = -7$$
$$x = -2$$

STEP 2 **Substitute** −2 for x in $y = \frac{1}{2}x$ to find the value of y.

$$y = \frac{1}{2}x$$
$$= \frac{1}{2}(-2)$$
$$= -1$$

The solution of the system is (−2, −1).

The correct answer is C. (A) (B) (C) (D)

Method 2

ELIMINATE CHOICES Substitute the values given in each answer choice for x and y in both equations.

Choice A: (2, 1)
Substitute 2 for x and 1 for y.

$$y = \frac{1}{2}x \qquad 2x + 3y = -7$$
$$1 \stackrel{?}{=} \frac{1}{2}(2) \qquad 2(2) + 3(1) \stackrel{?}{=} -7$$
$$1 = 1\ ✓ \qquad 7 = -7\ ✗$$

Choice B: (1, −3)
Substitute 1 for x and −3 for y.

$$y = \frac{1}{2}x$$
$$-3 \stackrel{?}{=} \frac{1}{2}(1)$$
$$-3 = \frac{1}{2}\ ✗$$

Choice C: (−2, −1)
Substitute −2 for x and −1 for y.

$$y = \frac{1}{2}x \qquad 2x + 3y = -7$$
$$-1 \stackrel{?}{=} \frac{1}{2}(-2) \qquad 2(-2) + 3(-1) \stackrel{?}{=} -7$$
$$-1 = -1\ ✓ \qquad -7 = -7\ ✓$$

The correct answer is C. (A) (B)  (C) (D)

PROBLEM 2

The sum of two numbers is -1, and the difference of the two numbers is 5. What are the numbers?

Ⓐ -5 and 4 Ⓑ 1 and 6 Ⓒ 2 and -3 Ⓓ -2 and 3

Method 1

SOLVE DIRECTLY Write and solve a system of equations for the numbers.

STEP 1 **Write** a system of equations. Let x and y be the numbers.

$x + y = -1$ Equation 1
$x - y = 5$ Equation 2

STEP 2 **Add** the equations to eliminate one variable. Then find the value of the other variable.

$$\begin{array}{l} x + y = -1 \\ \underline{x - y = 5} \\ \quad 2x = 4, \text{ so } x = 2 \end{array}$$

STEP 3 **Substitute** 2 for x in Equation 1 and solve for y.

$2 + y = -1$, so $y = -3$

The correct answer is C. Ⓐ Ⓑ Ⓒ Ⓓ

Method 2

ELIMINATE CHOICES Find the sum and difference of each pair of numbers. Because the difference is positive, be sure to subtract the lesser number from the greater number.

Choice A: -5 and 4

Sum: $-5 + 4 = -1$ ✓

Difference: $-5 - 4 = -9$ ✗

Choice B: 1 and 6

Sum: $1 + 6 = 7$ ✗

Choice C: 2 and -3

Sum: $2 + (-3) = -1$ ✓

Difference: $2 - (-3) = 5$ ✓

The correct answer is C. Ⓐ Ⓑ Ⓒ Ⓓ

PRACTICE

Explain why you can eliminate the highlighted answer choice.

1. The sum of two numbers is –27. One number is twice the other. What are the numbers?

   Ⓐ ✗ **9 and 18** Ⓑ -3 and 24 Ⓒ -18 and -9 Ⓓ -14 and -13

2. Which ordered pair is a solution of the linear system $5x + 2y = -11$ and $x = -\frac{1}{2}y - 4$?

   Ⓐ $\left(-\frac{7}{6}, -\frac{17}{3}\right)$ Ⓑ $\left(-\frac{23}{3}, \frac{1}{3}\right)$ Ⓒ $(-3, 2)$ Ⓓ ✗ $\mathbf{(-3, -13)}$

3. Long-sleeve and short-sleeve T-shirts can be purchased at a concert. A long-sleeve T-shirt costs \$25 and a short-sleeve T-shirt costs \$15. During a concert, the T-shirt vendor collects \$8415 from the sale of 441 T-shirts. How many short-sleeve T-shirts were sold?

   Ⓐ 100 Ⓑ ✗ **180** Ⓒ 261 Ⓓ 441

7 ★ Standardized TEST PRACTICE

MULTIPLE CHOICE

1. Which ordered pair is the solution of the linear system $y = \frac{1}{2}x + 1$ and $y = \frac{3}{2}x + 4$?

   Ⓐ $\left(3, \frac{5}{2}\right)$ Ⓑ $\left(-3, -\frac{1}{2}\right)$

   Ⓒ $\left(\frac{3}{2}, \frac{7}{4}\right)$ Ⓓ $(0, 1)$

2. How many solutions does the linear system $3x + 5y = 8$ and $3x + 5y = 1$ have?

   Ⓐ 0 Ⓑ 1

   Ⓒ 2 Ⓓ Infinitely many

3. The sum of two numbers is −3, and the difference of the two numbers is 11. What are the numbers?

   Ⓐ 4 and 7 Ⓑ −3 and 8

   Ⓒ 3 and 14 Ⓓ −7 and 4

4. Which ordered pair is the solution of the system of linear equations whose graph is shown?

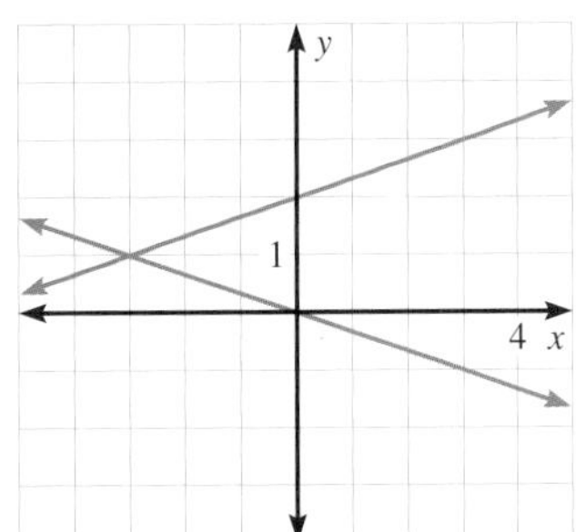

   Ⓐ $(3, -1)$ Ⓑ $(0, 0)$

   Ⓒ $(0, 2)$ Ⓓ $(-3, 1)$

5. Which ordered pair is the solution of the linear system $3x + y = -1$ and $y = -\frac{1}{2}x - \frac{7}{2}$?

   Ⓐ $\left(\frac{5}{2}, -\frac{17}{2}\right)$ Ⓑ $(1, -4)$

   Ⓒ $(-1, -3)$ Ⓓ $(0, -1)$

6. Which ordered pair is a solution of the system $x + 2y \leq -2$ and $y \leq -3x + 4$?

   Ⓐ $(0, 0)$ Ⓑ $(2, -2)$

   Ⓒ $(-2, 2)$ Ⓓ $(5, -4)$

7. How many solutions does the system of linear equations whose graph is shown have?

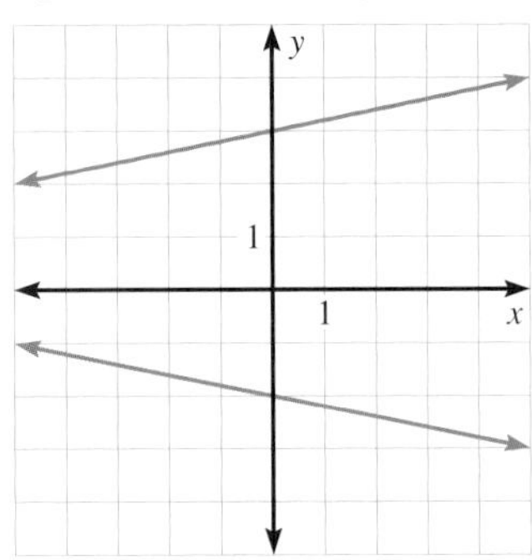

   Ⓐ 0 Ⓑ 1

   Ⓒ 2 Ⓓ Infinitely many

8. At a bakery, one customer pays \$5.67 for 3 bagels and 4 muffins. Another customer pays \$6.70 for 5 bagels and 3 muffins. Which system of equations can be used to determine the cost x (in dollars) of one bagel and the cost y (in dollars) of one muffin at the bakery?

   Ⓐ $x + y = 7$, $x + y = 8$ Ⓑ $y = 3x + 5.67$, $y = 5x + 6.7$

   Ⓒ $3x + 4y = 6.7$, $5x + 3y = 5.67$ Ⓓ $3x + 4y = 5.67$, $5x + 3y = 6.7$

9. The perimeter P (in feet) of each of the two rectangles below is given. What are the values of ℓ and w?

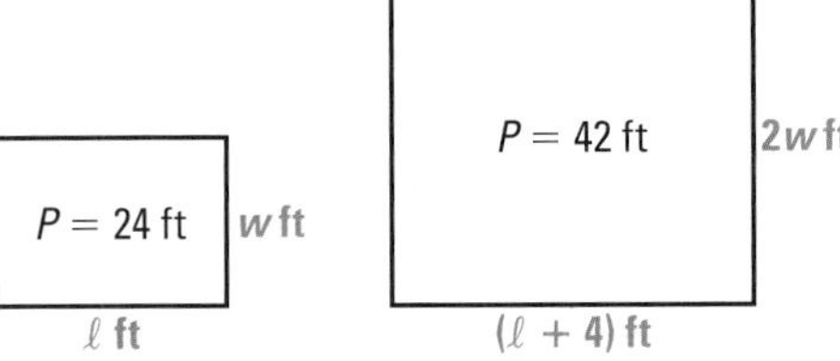

   Ⓐ $\ell = 7$ and $w = 5$

   Ⓑ $\ell = 8$ and $w = 4$

   Ⓒ $\ell = 11$ and $w = 10$

   Ⓓ $\ell = 12$ and $w = 9$

GRIDDED ANSWER

10. What is the x-coordinate of the solution of the system whose graph is shown?

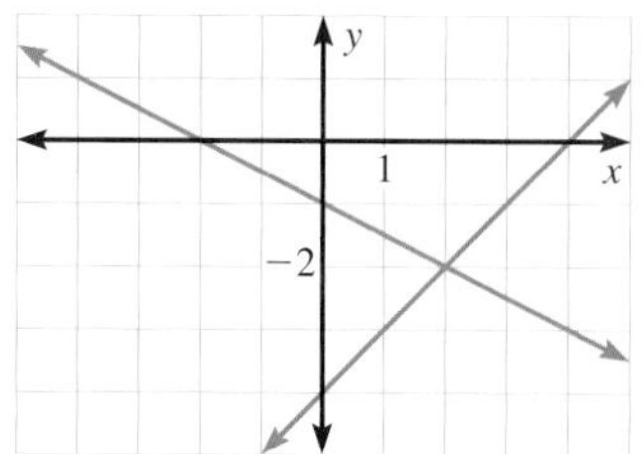

11. What is the x-coordinate of the solution of the system $y = \frac{1}{3}x + 8$ and $2x - y = 2$?

12. A science museum charges one amount for admission for an adult and a lesser amount for admission for a student. Admission to the museum for 28 students and 5 adults costs \$284. Admission for 40 students and 10 adults costs \$440. What is the admission cost (in dollars) for one student?

SHORT RESPONSE

13. Is it possible to find a value for c so that the linear system below has exactly one solution? *Explain.*

$5x + 3y = 21$ **Equation 1**

$y = -\frac{5}{3}x + c$ **Equation 2**

14. A rental car agency charges x dollars per day plus y dollars per mile to rent any of the mid-sized cars at the agency. The total costs for two customers are shown below.

Customer	Time (days)	Distance (miles)	Cost (dollars)
Jackson	3	150	217.50
Bree	2	112	148.00

How much will it cost to rent a mid-sized car for 5 days and drive 250 miles? *Explain.*

EXTENDED RESPONSE

15. A baseball player's batting average is the number of hits the player has divided by the number of at-bats. At the beginning of a game, a player has a batting average of .360. During the game, the player gets 3 hits during 5 at-bats, and his batting average changes to .375.

a. Write a system of linear equations that represents the situation.

b. How many at-bats has the player had so far this season?

c. Another player on the team has a batting average of .240 at the beginning of the same game. During the game, he gets 3 hits during 5 at-bats, and his batting average changes to .300. Has this player had more at-bats so far this season than the other player? *Explain.*

16. A gardener combines x fluid ounces of a 20% liquid fertilizer and 80% water mix with y fluid ounces of a 5% liquid fertilizer and 95% water mix to make 30 fluid ounces of a 10% liquid fertilizer and 90% water mix.

a. Write a system of linear equations that represents the situation.

b. Solve the system from part (a).

c. Suppose the gardener combines pure (100%) water and the 20% liquid fertilizer and 80% water mix to make the 30 fluid ounces of the 10% liquid fertilizer and 90% water mix. Is more of the 20% liquid fertilizer and 80% water mix used in this mix than in the original mix? *Explain.*

CUMULATIVE REVIEW Chapters 1–7

Evaluate the expression.

1. $2^5 \cdot 2 - 4 \div 2$ *(p. 8)*
2. $24 \div 6 + (9 - 6)$ *(p. 8)*
3. $5[(6 - 2)^2 - 5]$ *(p. 8)*
4. $\sqrt{144}$ *(p. 110)*
5. $-\sqrt{2500}$ *(p. 110)*
6. $\pm\sqrt{400}$ *(p. 110)*

Check whether the given number is a solution of the equation or inequality. *(p. 21)*

7. $7 + 3x = 16$; 3
8. $21y + 1 = 1$; 0
9. $20 - 12h = 12$; 1
10. $g - 3 > 2$; 5
11. $10 \geq 4 - x$; 0
12. $30 - 4p \geq 5$; 6

Simplify the expression.

13. $5(y - 1) + 4$ *(p. 96)*
14. $12w + (w - 2)3$ *(p. 96)*
15. $(g - 1)(-4) + 3g$ *(p. 96)*
16. $\frac{10h - 25}{5}$ *(p. 103)*
17. $\frac{21 - 4x}{-7}$ *(p. 103)*
18. $\frac{32 - 20m}{2}$ *(p. 103)*

Solve the equation.

19. $x - 8 = 21$ *(p. 134)*.
20. $-1 = x + 3$ *(p. 134)*
21. $6x = -42$ *(p. 134)*
22. $\frac{x}{3} = 8$ *(p. 134)*
23. $5 - 2x = 11$ *(p. 141)*
24. $\frac{2}{3}x - 3 = 17$ *(p. 141)*
25. $3(x - 2) = -15$ *(p. 148)*
26. $3(5x - 7) = 5x - 1$ *(p. 154)*
27. $-7(2x - 10) = 4x - 10$ *(p. 154)*

Graph the equation.

28. $x + 2y = -8$ *(p. 225)*
29. $-2x + 5y = -10$ *(p. 225)*
30. $3x - 4y = 12$ *(p. 225)*
31. $y = 3x - 7$ *(p. 244)*
32. $y = x + 6$ *(p. 244)*
33. $y = -\frac{1}{3}x$ *(p. 253)*

Write an equation of the line in slope-intercept form with the given slope and *y*-intercept. *(p. 283)*

34. slope: 5
    y-intercept: -1
35. slope: -1
    y-intercept: 3
36. slope: -7
    y-intercept: 0

Write an equation in point-slope form of the line that passes through the given points. *(p. 302)*

37. $(1, -10), (-5, 2)$
38. $(4, 7), (-4, 3)$
39. $(-9, -2), (-6, 8)$
40. $(-1, 1), (1, -3)$
41. $(2, 4), (8, 2)$
42. $(-6, 1), (3, -5)$

Solve the inequality. Then graph your solution.

43. $x - 9 < -13$ *(p. 356)*
44. $8 \leq x + 7$ *(p. 356)*
45. $8x \geq 56$ *(p. 363)*
46. $\frac{x}{-4} > 7$ *(p. 363)*
47. $1 - 2x < 11$ *(p. 369)*
48. $8 > -3x - 1$ *(p. 369)*
49. $4x - 10 \leq 7x + 8$ *(p. 369)*
50. $7x - 5 < 6x - 4$ *(p. 369)*
51. $-4 < 3x - 1 < 5$ *(p. 380)*
52. $3 \leq 9 - 2x \leq 15$ *(p. 380)*
53. $|3x| < 15$ *(p. 398)*
54. $|4x - 2| \geq 18$ *(p. 398)*

Solve the linear system using elimination. *(p. 451)*

55. $4x + y = 8$
$5x - 2y = -3$

56. $3x - 5y = 5$
$x - 5y = -4$

57. $12x + 7y = 3$
$8x + 5y = 1$

58. ART PROJECT You are making a tile mosaic on the rectangular tabletop shown. A bag of porcelain tiles costs $3.95 and covers 36 square inches. How much will it cost to buy enough tiles to cover the tabletop? *(p. 28)*

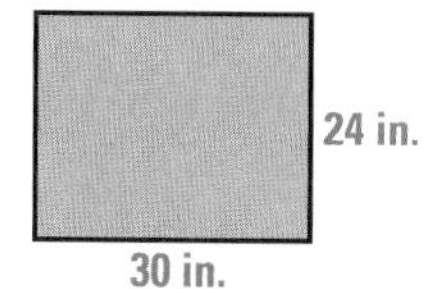

59. FOOD The table shows the changes in the price for a dozen grade A, large eggs over 4 years. Find the average yearly change to the nearest cent in the price for a dozen grade A, large eggs during the period 1999–2002. *(p. 103)*

Year	1999	2000	2001	2002
Change in price for a dozen grade A, large eggs (dollars)	−0.17	0.04	−0.03	0.25

60. HONEY PRODUCTION Honeybees visit about 2,000,000 flowers to make 16 ounces of honey. About how many flowers do honeybees visit to make 6 ounces of honey? *(p. 168)*

61. MUSIC The table shows the price p (in dollars) for various lengths of speaker cable. *(p. 253)*

Length, ℓ (feet)	3	5	12	15
Price, p (dollars)	7.50	12.50	30.00	37.50

a. *Explain* why p varies directly with ℓ.

b. Write a direct variation equation that relates ℓ and p.

62. CURRENCY The table shows the exchange rate between the currency of Bolivia (bolivianos) and U.S. dollars from 1998 to 2003. *(p. 335)*

Year	1998	1999	2000	2001	2002	2003
Bolivianos per U.S. dollar	5.51	5.81	6.18	6.61	7.17	7.66

a. Find an equation that models the bolivianos per U.S. dollar as a function of the number of years since 1998.

b. If the trend continues, predict the number of bolivianos per U.S. dollar in 2010.

63. BATTERIES A manufacturer of nickel-cadmium batteries recommends storing the batteries at temperatures ranging from −20°C to 45°C. Use an inequality to describe the temperatures (in degrees Fahrenheit) at which the batteries can be stored. *(p. 380)*

8 Exponents and Exponential Functions

Before

In previous chapters and courses, you learned the following skills, which you'll use in Chapter 8: evaluating expressions involving exponents, ordering numbers, writing percents as decimals, and writing function rules.

Prerequisite Skills

VOCABULARY CHECK

1. Identify the exponent and the base in the expression 13^8.
2. Copy and complete: An expression that represents repeated multiplication of the same factor is called a(n) _?_.

SKILLS CHECK

Evaluate the expression. *(Review p. 2 for 8.1–8.3.)*

3. x^2 when $x = 10$ **4.** a^3 when $a = 3$ **5.** r^2 when $r = \frac{5}{6}$ **6.** z^3 when $z = \frac{1}{2}$

Order the numbers from least to greatest. *(Review p. 909 for 8.4.)*

7. 6.12, 6.2, 6.01 **8.** 0.073, 0.101, 0.0098

Write the percent as a decimal. *(Review p. 916 for 8.5 and 8.6.)*

9. 4% **10.** 0.5% **11.** 13.8% **12.** 145%

13. Write a rule for the function. *(Review p. 35 for 8.5 and 8.6.)*

Input	0	1	4	6	10
Output	2	3	6	8	12

@HomeTutor Prerequisite skills practice at classzone.com

Now

In Chapter 8, you will apply the big ideas listed below and reviewed in the Chapter Summary on page 542. You will also use the key vocabulary listed below.

Big Ideas

1. **Applying properties of exponents to simplify expressions**
2. **Working with numbers in scientific notation**
3. **Writing and graphing exponential functions**

KEY VOCABULARY

- order of magnitude, *p. 491*
- scientific notation, *p. 512*
- exponential function, *p. 520*
- exponential growth, *p. 522*
- compound interest, *p. 523*
- exponential decay, *p. 533*

Why?

You can use exponents to explore exponential growth and decay. For example, you can write an exponential function to find the value of a collector car over time.

Animated Algebra

The animation illustrated below for Example 4 on page 522 helps you answer this question: If you know the growth rate of the value of a collector car over time, can you predict what the car will sell for at an auction?

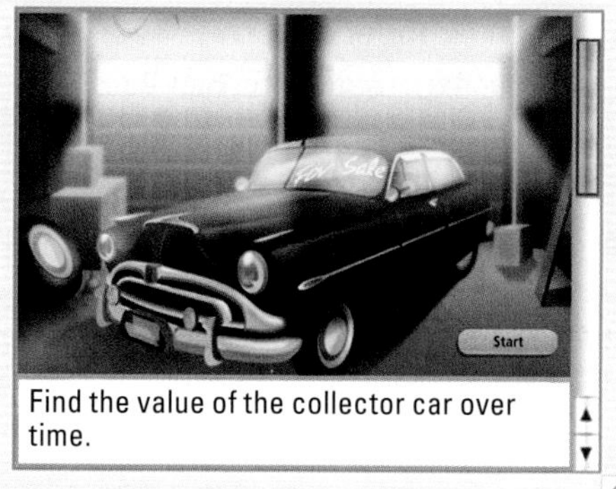

Find the value of the collector car over time.

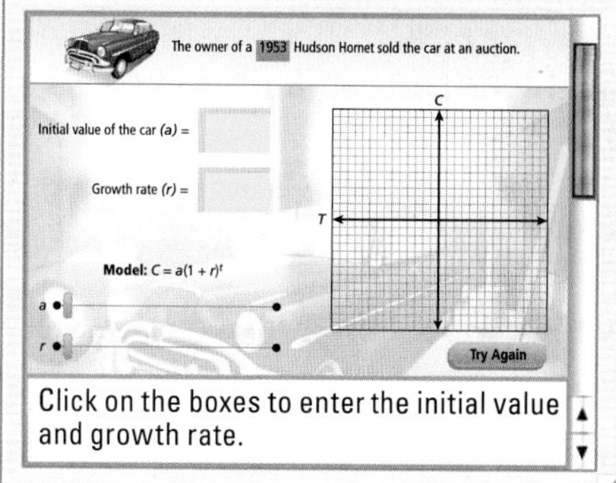

Click on the boxes to enter the initial value and growth rate.

Animated Algebra at classzone.com

Other animations for Chapter 8: pages 491, 505, 512, 534, and 536

8.1 Products and Powers

MATERIALS • paper and pencil

QUESTION **How can you find a product of powers and a power of a power?**

EXPLORE 1 **Find products of powers**

STEP 1 ***Copy and complete*** Copy and complete the table.

Expression	Expression as repeated multiplication	Number of factors	Simplified expression
$7^4 \cdot 7^5$	$(7 \cdot 7 \cdot 7 \cdot 7) \cdot (7 \cdot 7 \cdot 7 \cdot 7 \cdot 7)$	9	7^9
$(-4)^2 \cdot (-4)^3$	$[(-4) \cdot (-4)] \cdot [(-4) \cdot (-4) \cdot (-4)]$	?	?
$x^1 \cdot x^5$	?	?	?

STEP 2 ***Analyze results*** Find a pattern that relates the exponents of the factors in the first column and the exponent of the expression in the last column.

EXPLORE 2 **Find powers of powers**

STEP 1 ***Copy and complete*** Copy and complete the table.

Expression	Expanded expression	Expression as repeated multiplication	Number of factors	Simplified expression
$(5^3)^2$	$(5^3) \cdot (5^3)$	$(5 \cdot 5 \cdot 5) \cdot (5 \cdot 5 \cdot 5)$	6	5^6
$[(-6)^2]^4$	$[(-6)^2] \cdot [(-6)^2] \cdot [(-6)^2] \cdot [(-6)^2]$	?	?	?
$(a^3)^3$	?	?	?	?

STEP 2 ***Analyze results*** Find a pattern that relates the exponents of the expression in the first column and the exponent of the expression in the last column.

DRAW CONCLUSIONS **Use your observations to complete these exercises**

Simplify the expression. Write your answer using exponents.

1. $5^2 \cdot 5^3$ **2.** $(-6)^1 \cdot (-6)^4$ **3.** $m^6 \cdot m^4$

4. $(10^3)^3$ **5.** $[(-2)^3]^4$ **6.** $(c^2)^6$

In Exercises 7 and 8, copy and complete the statement.

7. If a is a real number and m and n are positive integers, then $a^m \cdot a^n = \underline{\ ?\ }$.

8. If a is a real number and m and n are positive integers, then $(a^m)^n = \underline{\ ?\ }$.

8.1 Apply Exponent Properties Involving Products

Before You evaluated exponential expressions.

Now You will use properties of exponents involving products.

Why? So you can evaluate agricultural data, as in Example 5.

Key Vocabulary
- **order of magnitude**
- **power,** *p. 3*
- **exponent,** *p. 3*
- **base,** *p. 3*

Notice what happens when you multiply two powers that have the same base.

$$a^2 \cdot a^3 = \overbrace{\underbrace{(a \cdot a)}_{\text{2 factors}} \cdot \underbrace{(a \cdot a \cdot a)}_{\text{3 factors}}}^{\text{5 factors}} = a^5 = a^{2+3}$$

The example above suggests the following property of exponents, known as the product of powers property.

KEY CONCEPT *For Your Notebook*

Product of Powers Property

Let a be a real number, and let m and n be positive integers.

Words To multiply powers having the same base, add the exponents.

Algebra $a^m \cdot a^n = a^{m+n}$ **Example** $5^6 \cdot 5^3 = 5^{6+3} = 5^9$

EXAMPLE 1 **Use the product of powers property**

SIMPLIFY EXPRESSIONS
When simplifying powers with numerical bases only, write your answers using exponents, as in parts (a), (b), and (c).

a. $7^3 \cdot 7^5 = 7^{3+5} = 7^8$

b. $9 \cdot 9^8 \cdot 9^2 = 9^1 \cdot 9^8 \cdot 9^2$
$= 9^{1+8+2}$
$= 9^{11}$

c. $(-5)(-5)^6 = (-5)^1 \cdot (-5)^6$
$= (-5)^{1+6}$
$= (-5)^7$

d. $x^4 \cdot x^3 = x^{4+3} = x^7$

✓ **GUIDED PRACTICE** for Example 1

Simplify the expression.

1. $3^2 \cdot 3^7$ **2.** $5 \cdot 5^9$ **3.** $(-7)^2(-7)$ **4.** $x^2 \cdot x^6 \cdot x$

POWER OF A POWER Notice what happens when you raise a power to a power.

$$(a^2)^3 = a^2 \cdot a^2 \cdot a^2 = (a \cdot a) \cdot (a \cdot a) \cdot (a \cdot a) = a^6 = a^{2 \cdot 3}$$

The example above suggests the following property of exponents, known as the power of a power property.

KEY CONCEPT *For Your Notebook*

Power of a Power Property

Let a be a real number, and let m and n be positive integers.

Words To find a power of a power, multiply exponents.

Algebra $(a^m)^n = a^{mn}$

Example $(3^4)^2 = 3^{4 \cdot 2} = 3^8$

EXAMPLE 2 Use the power of a power property

AVOID ERRORS
In part (d), notice that you can write $[(y + 2)^6]^2$ as $(y + 2)^{12}$, but you cannot write $(y + 2)^{12}$ as $y^{12} + 2^{12}$.

a. $(2^5)^3 = 2^{5 \cdot 3}$
$= 2^{15}$

b. $[(-6)^2]^5 = (-6)^{2 \cdot 5}$
$= (-6)^{10}$

c. $(x^2)^4 = x^{2 \cdot 4}$
$= x^8$

d. $[(y + 2)^6]^2 = (y + 2)^{6 \cdot 2}$
$= (y + 2)^{12}$

✓ **GUIDED PRACTICE** for Example 2

Simplify the expression.

5. $(4^2)^7$ **6.** $[(-2)^4]^5$ **7.** $(n^3)^6$ **8.** $[(m + 1)^5]^4$

POWER OF A PRODUCT Notice what happens when you raise a product to a power.

$$(ab)^3 = (ab) \cdot (ab) \cdot (ab) = (a \cdot a \cdot a) \cdot (b \cdot b \cdot b) = a^3b^3$$

The example above suggests the following property of exponents, known as the power of a product property.

KEY CONCEPT *For Your Notebook*

Power of a Product Property

Let a and b be real numbers, and let m be a positive integer.

Words To find a power of a product, find the power of each factor and multiply.

Algebra $(ab)^m = a^mb^m$

Example $(23 \cdot 17)^5 = 23^5 \cdot 17^5$

EXAMPLE 3 Use the power of a product property

SIMPLIFY EXPRESSIONS When simplifying powers with numerical *and* variable bases, be sure to evaluate the numerical power, as in parts (b), (c), and (d).

a. $(24 \cdot 13)^8 = 24^8 \cdot 13^8$

b. $(9xy)^2 = (9 \cdot x \cdot y)^2 = 9^2 \cdot x^2 \cdot y^2 = 81x^2y^2$

c. $(-4z)^2 = (-4 \cdot z)^2 = (-4)^2 \cdot z^2 = 16z^2$

d. $-(4z)^2 = -(4 \cdot z)^2 = -(4^2 \cdot z^2) = -16z^2$

EXAMPLE 4 Use all three properties

Simplify $(2x^3)^2 \cdot x^4$.

$(2x^3)^2 \cdot x^4 = 2^2 \cdot (x^3)^2 \cdot x^4$ Power of a product property

$= 4 \cdot x^6 \cdot x^4$ Power of a power property

$= 4x^{10}$ Product of powers property

Animated Algebra at classzone.com

ORDER OF MAGNITUDE The **order of magnitude** of a quantity can be defined as the power of 10 nearest the quantity. Order of magnitude can be used to estimate or perform rough calculations. For instance, there are about 91,000 species of insects in the United States. The power of 10 closest to 91,000 is 10^5, or 100,000. So, there are about 10^5 species of insects in the United States.

EXAMPLE 5 Solve a real-world problem

BEES In 2003 the U.S. Department of Agriculture (USDA) collected data on about 10^3 honeybee colonies. There are about 10^4 bees in an average colony during honey production season. About how many bees were in the USDA study?

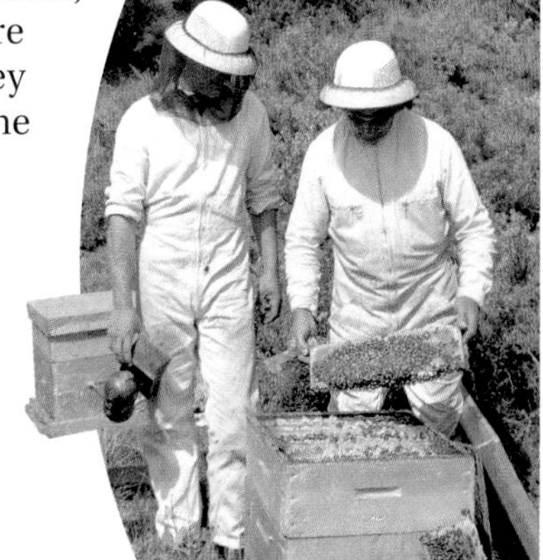

Solution

To find the total number of bees, find the product of the number of colonies, 10^3, and the number of bees per colony, 10^4.

$10^3 \cdot 10^4 = 10^{3+4} = 10^7$

▶ The USDA studied about 10^7, or 10,000,000, bees.

✓ GUIDED PRACTICE for Examples 3, 4, and 5

Simplify the expression.

9. $(42 \cdot 12)^2$ **10.** $(-3n)^2$ **11.** $(9m^3n)^4$ **12.** $5 \cdot (5x^2)^4$

13. WHAT IF? In Example 5, 10^2 honeybee colonies in the study were located in Idaho. About how many bees were studied in Idaho?

8.1 EXERCISES

HOMEWORK KEY

○ = **WORKED-OUT SOLUTIONS** on p. WS18 for Exs. 31 and 55

★ = **STANDARDIZED TEST PRACTICE** Exs. 2, 40, 41, 50, and 58

◆ = **MULTIPLE REPRESENTATIONS** Ex. 55

SKILL PRACTICE

1. **VOCABULARY** Copy and complete: The __?__ of the quantity 93,534,004 people is the power of 10 nearest the quantity, or 10^8 people.

2. ★ **WRITING** *Explain* when and how to use the product of powers property.

EXAMPLES 1,2,3, and 4 on pp. 489–491 for Exs. 3–41

SIMPLIFYING EXPRESSIONS **Simplify the expression. Write your answer using exponents.**

3. $4^2 \cdot 4^6$
4. $8^5 \cdot 8^2$
5. $3^3 \cdot 3$
6. $9 \cdot 9^5$
7. $(-7)^4(-7)^5$
8. $(-6)^6(-6)$
9. $2^4 \cdot 2^9 \cdot 2$
10. $(-3)^2(-3)^{11}(-3)$
11. $(3^5)^2$
12. $(7^4)^3$
13. $[(-5)^3]^4$
14. $[(-8)^9]^2$
15. $(15 \cdot 29)^3$
16. $(17 \cdot 16)^4$
17. $(132 \cdot 9)^6$
18. $((-14) \cdot 22)^5$

SIMPLIFYING EXPRESSIONS **Simplify the expression.**

19. $x^4 \cdot x^2$
20. $y^9 \cdot y$
21. $z^2 \cdot z \cdot z^3$
22. $a^4 \cdot a^3 \cdot a^{10}$
23. $(x^5)^2$
24. $(y^4)^6$
25. $[(b-2)^2]^6$
26. $[(d+9)^7]^3$
27. $(-5x)^2$
28. $-(5x)^2$
29. $(7xy)^2$
30. $(5pq)^3$
31. $(-10x^6)^2 \cdot x^2$
32. $(-8m^4)^2 \cdot m^3$
33. $6d^2 \cdot (2d^5)^4$
34. $(-20x^3)^2(-x^7)$
35. $-(2p^4)^3(-1.5p^7)$
36. $\left(\frac{1}{2}y^5\right)^3(2y^2)^4$
37. $(3x^5)^3(2x^7)^2$
38. $(-10n)^2(-4n^3)^3$

39. **ERROR ANALYSIS** *Describe* and correct the error in simplifying $c \cdot c^4 \cdot c^5$.

$$c \cdot c^4 \cdot c^5 = c^1 \cdot c^4 \cdot c^5$$
$$= c^{1 \cdot 4 \cdot 5}$$
$$= c^{20}$$

40. ★ **MULTIPLE CHOICE** Which expression is equivalent to $(-9)^6$?

Ⓐ $(-9)^2(-9)^3$ Ⓑ $(-9)(-9)^5$ Ⓒ $[(-9)^4]^2$ Ⓓ $[(-9)^3]^3$

41. ★ **MULTIPLE CHOICE** Which expression is equivalent to $36x^{12}$?

Ⓐ $(6x^3)^4$ Ⓑ $12x^4 \cdot 3x^3$ Ⓒ $3x^3 \cdot (4x^3)^3$ Ⓓ $(6x^5)^2 \cdot x^2$

SIMPLIFYING EXPRESSIONS **Find the missing exponent.**

42. $x^4 \cdot x^? = x^5$
43. $(y^8)^? = y^{16}$
44. $(2z^?)^3 = 8z^{15}$
45. $(3a^3)^? \cdot 2a^3 = 18a^9$

46. **POPULATION** The population of New York City in 2000 was 8,008,278. What was the order of magnitude of the population of New York City?

SIMPLIFYING EXPRESSIONS **Simplify the expression.**

47. $(-3x^2y)^3(11x^3y^5)^2$
48. $-(-xy^2z^3)^5(x^4yz)^2$
49. $(-2s)(-5r^3st)^3(-2r^4st^7)^2$

50. ★ **OPEN-ENDED** Write three expressions involving products of powers, powers of powers, or powers of products that are equivalent to $12x^8$.

51. **CHALLENGE** Show that when a and b are real numbers and n is a positive integer, $(ab)^n = a^n b^n$.

PROBLEM SOLVING

EXAMPLE 5 on p. 491 for Exs. 52–56

52. **ICE CREAM COMPOSITION** There are about 954,930 air bubbles in 1 cubic centimeter of ice cream. There are about 946 cubic centimeters in 1 quart. Use order of magnitude to find the approximate number of air bubbles in 1 quart of ice cream.

@HomeTutor for problem solving help at classzone.com

53. **ASTRONOMY** The order of magnitude of the radius of our solar system is 10^{13} meters. The order of magnitude of the radius of the visible universe is 10^{13} times as great. Find the approximate radius of the visible universe.

@HomeTutor for problem solving help at classzone.com

54. **COASTAL LANDSLIDE** There are about 1 billion grains of sand in 1 cubic foot of sand. In 1995 a stretch of beach at Sleeping Bear Dunes National Lakeshore in Michigan slid into Lake Michigan. Scientists believe that around 35 million cubic feet of sand fell into the lake. Use order of magnitude to find about how many grains of sand slid into the lake.

55. ◆ **MULTIPLE REPRESENTATIONS** There are about 10^{23} atoms of gold in 1 ounce of gold.

   a. **Making a Table** Copy and complete the table by finding the number of atoms of gold for the given amounts of gold (in ounces).

Gold (ounces)	10	100	1000	10,000	100,000
Number of atoms	?	?	?	?	?

   b. **Writing an Expression** A particular mine in California extracted about 96,000 ounces of gold in 1 year. Use order of magnitude to write an expression you can use to find the approximate number of atoms of gold extracted in the mine that year. Simplify the expression. Verify your answer using the table.

56. **MULTI-STEP PROBLEM** A microscope has two lenses, the objective lens and the eyepiece, that work together to magnify an object. The total magnification of the microscope is the product of the magnification of the objective lens and the magnification of the eyepiece.

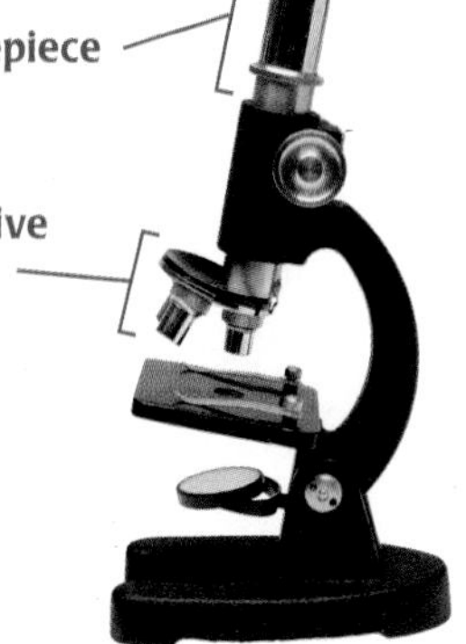

   a. Your microscope's objective lens magnifies an object 10^2 times, and the eyepiece magnifies an object 10 times. What is the total magnification of your microscope?

   b. You magnify an object that is 10^2 nanometers long. How long is the magnified image?

57. **VOLUME OF THE SUN** The radius of the sun is about 695,000,000 meters. The formula for the volume of a sphere, such as the sun, is $V = \frac{4}{3}\pi r^3$. Because the order of magnitude of $\frac{4}{3}\pi$ is 1, it does not contribute to the formula in a significant way. So, you can find the order of magnitude of the volume of the sun by cubing its radius. Find the order of magnitude of the volume of the sun.

58. ★ **EXTENDED RESPONSE** Rock salt can be mined from large deposits of salt called salt domes. A particular salt dome is roughly cylindrical in shape. The order of magnitude of the radius of the salt dome is 10^3 feet. The order of magnitude of the height of the salt dome is about 10 times that of its radius. The formula for the volume of a cylinder is $V = \pi r^2 h$.

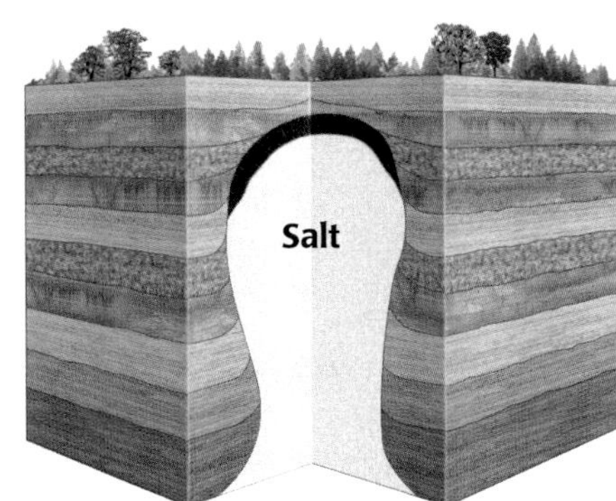

a. **Calculate** What is the order of magnitude of the height of the salt dome?

b. **Calculate** What is the order of magnitude of the volume of the salt dome?

c. **Explain** The order of magnitude of the radius of a salt dome can be 10 times the radius of the salt dome described in this exercise. What effect does multiplying the order of magnitude of the radius of the salt dome by 10 have on the volume of the salt dome? *Explain.*

59. **CHALLENGE** Your school is conducting a poll that has two parts, one part that has 13 questions and a second part that has 10 questions. Students can answer the questions in either part with "agree" or "disagree." What power of 2 represents the number of ways there are to answer the questions in the first part of the poll? What power of 2 represents the number of ways there are to answer the questions in the second part of the poll? What power of 2 represents the number of ways there are to answer all of the questions on the poll?

MIXED REVIEW

PREVIEW
Prepare for Lesson 8.2 in Exs. 60–65.

Find the product. *(p. 88)*

60. $\left(\frac{1}{2}\right)\left(-\frac{4}{5}\right)$ 61. $\left(-\frac{2}{3}\right)\left(\frac{7}{4}\right)$ 62. $\left(-\frac{6}{5}\right)\left(-\frac{3}{8}\right)$

Evaluate the expression for the given value of the variable. *(p. 2)*

63. x^4 when $x = 3$ 64. x^2 when $x = -2.2$ 65. x^3 when $x = \frac{3}{4}$

Graph the equation or inequality.

66. $y = -4$ *(p. 215)* 67. $3x - y = 15$ *(p. 225)* 68. $7x - 6y = 84$ *(p. 225)*

69. $y = -5x + 3$ *(p. 244)* 70. $y = \frac{1}{2}x - 5$ *(p. 244)* 71. $x \ge -3$ *(p. 405)*

72. $y < 1.5$ *(p. 405)* 73. $x + y \le 7$ *(p. 405)* 74. $2x - y < 3$ *(p. 405)*

EXTRA PRACTICE for Lesson 8.1, p. 945 **ONLINE QUIZ** at classzone.com

8.2 Apply Exponent Properties Involving Quotients

Before You used properties of exponents involving products.

Now You will use properties of exponents involving quotients.

Why? So you can compare magnitudes of earthquakes, as in Ex. 53.

Key Vocabulary
- **power,** *p. 3*
- **exponent,** *p. 3*
- **base,** *p. 3*

Notice what happens when you divide powers with the same base.

$$\frac{a^5}{a^3} = \frac{a \cdot a \cdot \cancel{a} \cdot \cancel{a} \cdot \cancel{a}}{\cancel{a} \cdot \cancel{a} \cdot \cancel{a}} = a \cdot a = a^2 = a^{5-3}$$

The example above suggests the following property of exponents, known as the quotient of powers property.

KEY CONCEPT — *For Your Notebook*

Quotient of Powers Property

Let a be a nonzero real number, and let m and n be positive integers such that $m > n$.

Words To divide powers having the same base, subtract exponents.

Algebra $\frac{a^m}{a^n} = a^{m-n}, a \neq 0$ **Example** $\frac{4^7}{4^2} = 4^{7-2} = 4^5$

EXAMPLE 1 Use the quotient of powers property

SIMPLIFY EXPRESSIONS
When simplifying powers with numerical bases only, write your answers using exponents, as in parts (a), (b), and (c).

a. $\frac{8^{10}}{8^4} = 8^{10-4}$

$= 8^6$

b. $\frac{(-3)^9}{(-3)^3} = (-3)^{9-3}$

$= (-3)^6$

c. $\frac{5^4 \cdot 5^8}{5^7} = \frac{5^{12}}{5^7}$

$= 5^{12-7}$

$= 5^5$

d. $\frac{1}{x^4} \cdot x^6 = \frac{x^6}{x^4}$

$= x^{6-4}$

$= x^2$

✓ GUIDED PRACTICE for Example 1

Simplify the expression.

1. $\frac{6^{11}}{6^5}$ **2.** $\frac{(-4)^9}{(-4)^2}$ **3.** $\frac{9^4 \cdot 9^3}{9^2}$ **4.** $\frac{1}{y^5} \cdot y^8$

POWER OF A QUOTIENT Notice what happens when you raise a quotient to a power.

$$\left(\frac{a}{b}\right)^4 = \frac{a}{b} \cdot \frac{a}{b} \cdot \frac{a}{b} \cdot \frac{a}{b} = \frac{a \cdot a \cdot a \cdot a}{b \cdot b \cdot b \cdot b} = \frac{a^4}{b^4}$$

The example above suggests the following property of exponents, known as the power of a quotient property.

KEY CONCEPT *For Your Notebook*

Power of a Quotient Property

Let a and b be real numbers with $b \neq 0$, and let m be a positive integer.

Words To find a power of a quotient, find the power of the numerator and the power of the denominator and divide.

Algebra $\left(\frac{a}{b}\right)^m = \frac{a^m}{b^m}, b \neq 0$

Example $\left(\frac{3}{2}\right)^7 = \frac{3^7}{2^7}$

EXAMPLE 2 Use the power of a quotient property

SIMPLIFY EXPRESSIONS
When simplifying powers with numerical *and* variable bases, evaluate the numerical power, as in part (b).

a. $\left(\frac{x}{y}\right)^3 = \frac{x^3}{y^3}$

b. $\left(-\frac{7}{x}\right)^2 = \left(\frac{-7}{x}\right)^2 = \frac{(-7)^2}{x^2} = \frac{49}{x^2}$

EXAMPLE 3 Use properties of exponents

a. $\left(\frac{4x^2}{5y}\right)^3 = \frac{(4x^2)^3}{(5y)^3}$ Power of a quotient property

$= \frac{4^3 \cdot (x^2)^3}{5^3y^3}$ Power of a product property

$= \frac{64x^6}{125y^3}$ Power of a power property

b. $\left(\frac{a^2}{b}\right)^5 \cdot \frac{1}{2a^2} = \frac{(a^2)^5}{b^5} \cdot \frac{1}{2a^2}$ Power of a quotient property

$= \frac{a^{10}}{b^5} \cdot \frac{1}{2a^2}$ Power of a power property

$= \frac{a^{10}}{2a^2b^5}$ Multiply fractions.

$= \frac{a^8}{2b^5}$ Quotient of powers property

GUIDED PRACTICE for Examples 2 and 3

Simplify the expression.

5. $\left(\frac{a}{b}\right)^2$ **6.** $\left(-\frac{5}{y}\right)^3$ **7.** $\left(\frac{x^2}{4y}\right)^2$ **8.** $\left(\frac{2s}{3t}\right)^3 \cdot \left(\frac{t^5}{16}\right)$

EXAMPLE 4 Solve a multi-step problem

FRACTAL TREE To construct what is known as a *fractal tree*, begin with a single segment (the trunk) that is 1 unit long, as in Step 0. Add three shorter segments that are $\frac{1}{2}$ unit long to form the first set of branches, as in Step 1. Then continue adding sets of successively shorter branches so that each new set of branches is half the length of the previous set, as in Steps 2 and 3.

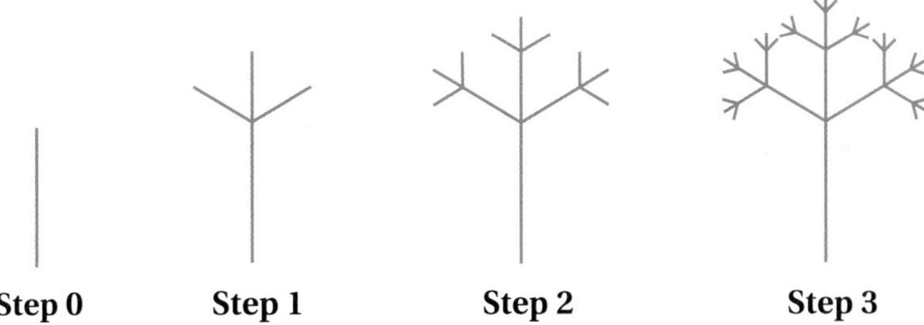

a. Make a table showing the number of new branches at each step for Steps 1–4. Write the number of new branches as a power of 3.

b. How many times greater is the number of new branches added at Step 5 than the number of new branches added at Step 2?

Solution

a.

Step	Number of new branches
1	$3 = 3^1$
2	$9 = 3^2$
3	$27 = 3^3$
4	$81 = 3^4$

b. The number of new branches added at Step 5 is 3^5. The number of new branches added at Step 2 is 3^2. So, the number of new branches added at Step 5 is $\frac{3^5}{3^2} = 3^3 = 27$ times the number of new branches added at Step 2.

GUIDED PRACTICE for Example 4

9. FRACTAL TREE In Example 4, add a column to the table for the length of the new branches at each step. Write the lengths of the new branches as powers of $\frac{1}{2}$. What is the length of a new branch added at Step 9?

EXAMPLE 5 Solve a real-world problem

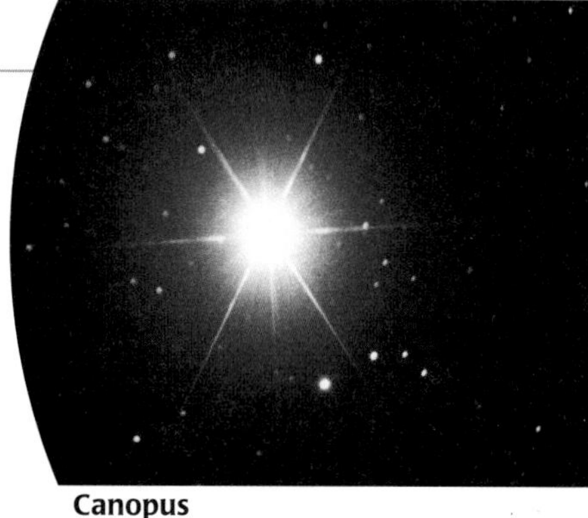
Canopus

ASTRONOMY The luminosity (in watts) of a star is the total amount of energy emitted from the star per unit of time. The order of magnitude of the luminosity of the sun is 10^{26} watts. The star Canopus is one of the brightest stars in the sky. The order of magnitude of the luminosity of Canopus is 10^{30} watts. How many times more luminous is Canopus than the sun?

Solution

$$\frac{\text{Luminosity of Canopus (watts)}}{\text{Luminosity of the sun (watts)}} = \frac{10^{30}}{10^{26}} = 10^{30-26} = 10^4$$

▶ Canopus is about 10^4 times as luminous as the sun.

GUIDED PRACTICE for Example 5

10. WHAT IF? Sirius is considered the brightest star in the sky. Sirius is less luminous than Canopus, but Sirius appears to be brighter because it is much closer to Earth. The order of magnitude of the luminosity of Sirius is 10^{28} watts. How many times more luminous is Canopus than Sirius?

8.2 EXERCISES

HOMEWORK KEY

○ = **WORKED-OUT SOLUTIONS** on p. WS18 for Exs. 33 and 51

★ = **STANDARDIZED TEST PRACTICE** Exs. 2, 19, 37, 46, and 54

◆ = **MULTIPLE REPRESENTATIONS** Ex. 49

SKILL PRACTICE

1. **VOCABULARY** Copy and complete: In the power 4^3, 4 is the __?__ and 3 is the __?__.

2. ★ **WRITING** *Explain* when and how to use the quotient of powers property.

EXAMPLES 1 and 2 on pp. 495–496 for Exs. 3–20

SIMPLIFYING EXPRESSIONS **Simplify the expression. Write your answer using exponents.**

3. $\frac{5^6}{5^2}$

4. $\frac{2^{11}}{2^6}$

5. $\frac{3^9}{3^5}$

6. $\frac{(-6)^8}{(-6)^5}$

7. $\frac{(-4)^7}{(-4)^4}$

8. $\frac{(-12)^9}{(-12)^3}$

9. $\frac{10^5 \cdot 10^5}{10^4}$

10. $\frac{6^7 \cdot 6^4}{6^6}$

11. $\left(\frac{1}{3}\right)^5$

12. $\left(\frac{3}{2}\right)^4$

13. $\left(-\frac{5}{4}\right)^4$

14. $\left(-\frac{2}{5}\right)^5$

15. $7^9 \cdot \frac{1}{7^2}$

16. $\frac{1}{9^5} \cdot 9^{11}$

17. $\left(\frac{1}{3}\right)^4 \cdot 3^{12}$

18. $4^9 \cdot \left(-\frac{1}{4}\right)^5$

19. ★ **MULTIPLE CHOICE** Which expression is equivalent to 16^6?

Ⓐ $\frac{16^4}{16^2}$ Ⓑ $\frac{16^{12}}{16^2}$ Ⓒ $\left(\frac{16^6}{16^3}\right)^2$ Ⓓ $\left(\frac{16^9}{16^6}\right)^3$

20. **ERROR ANALYSIS** *Describe* and correct the error in simplifying $\frac{9^5 \cdot 9^3}{9^4}$.

$\frac{9^5 \cdot 9^3}{9^4} = \frac{9^8}{9^4} = 9^{12}$ ✗

EXAMPLES 1, 2, and 3 on pp. 495–496 for Exs. 21–37

SIMPLIFYING EXPRESSIONS **Simplify the expression.**

21. $\frac{1}{y^8} \cdot y^{15}$ 22. $z^8 \cdot \frac{1}{z^7}$ 23. $\left(\frac{a}{y}\right)^9$ 24. $\left(\frac{j}{k}\right)^{11}$

25. $\left(\frac{p}{q}\right)^4$ 26. $\left(-\frac{1}{x}\right)^5$ 27. $\left(-\frac{4}{x}\right)^3$ 28. $\left(-\frac{a}{b}\right)^4$

29. $\left(\frac{4c}{d^2}\right)^3$ 30. $\left(\frac{a^7}{2b}\right)^5$ 31. $\left(\frac{x^2}{3y^3}\right)^2$ 32. $\left(\frac{3x^5}{7y^2}\right)^3$

33. $\left(\frac{3x^3}{2y}\right)^2 \cdot \frac{1}{x^2}$ 34. $\left(\frac{2x^3}{y}\right)^3 \cdot \frac{1}{6x^3}$ 35. $\frac{3}{8m^5} \cdot \left(\frac{m^4}{n^2}\right)^3$ 36. $\left(-\frac{5}{x}\right)^2 \cdot \left(\frac{2x^4}{y^3}\right)^2$

37. ★ **MULTIPLE CHOICE** Which expression is equivalent to $\left(\frac{7x^3}{2y^4}\right)^2$?

Ⓐ $\frac{7x^5}{2y^6}$ Ⓑ $\frac{7x^6}{2y^8}$ Ⓒ $\frac{49x^5}{4y^6}$ Ⓓ $\frac{49x^6}{4y^8}$

SIMPLIFYING EXPRESSIONS **Find the missing exponent.**

38. $\frac{(-8)^7}{(-8)^?} = (-8)^3$ 39. $\frac{7^? \cdot 7^2}{7^4} = 7^6$ 40. $\frac{1}{p^5} \cdot p^? = p^9$ 41. $\left(\frac{2c^3}{d^2}\right)^? = \frac{16c^{12}}{d^8}$

SIMPLIFYING EXPRESSIONS **Simplify the expression.**

42. $\left(\frac{2f^2g^3}{3fg}\right)^4$ 43. $\frac{2s^3t^3}{st^2} \cdot \frac{(3st)^3}{s^2t}$ 44. $\left(\frac{2m^5n}{4m^2}\right)^2 \cdot \left(\frac{mn^4}{5n}\right)^2$ 45. $\left(\frac{3x^3y}{x^2}\right)^3 \cdot \left(\frac{y^2x^4}{5y}\right)^2$

46. ★ **OPEN-ENDED** Write three expressions involving quotients that are equivalent to 14^7.

47. **REASONING** Name the definition or property that justifies each step to show that $\frac{a^m}{a^n} = \frac{1}{a^{n-m}}$ for $m < n$.

Let $m < n$. Given

$\frac{a^m}{a^n} = \frac{a^m}{a^n}\left(\frac{\frac{1}{a^m}}{\frac{1}{a^m}}\right)$?

$= \frac{1}{\frac{a^n}{a^m}}$?

$= \frac{1}{a^{n-m}}$?

48. **CHALLENGE** Find the values of x and y if you know that $\frac{b^x}{b^y} = b^9$ and $\frac{b^x \cdot b^2}{b^{3y}} = b^{13}$. *Explain* how you found your answer.

PROBLEM SOLVING

EXAMPLES 4 and 5 on pp. 497–498 for Exs. 49–51

49. ◆ **MULTIPLE REPRESENTATIONS** Draw a square with side lengths that are 1 unit long. Divide it into four new squares with side lengths that are one half the side length of the original square, as shown in Step 1. Keep dividing the squares into new squares, as shown in Steps 2 and 3.

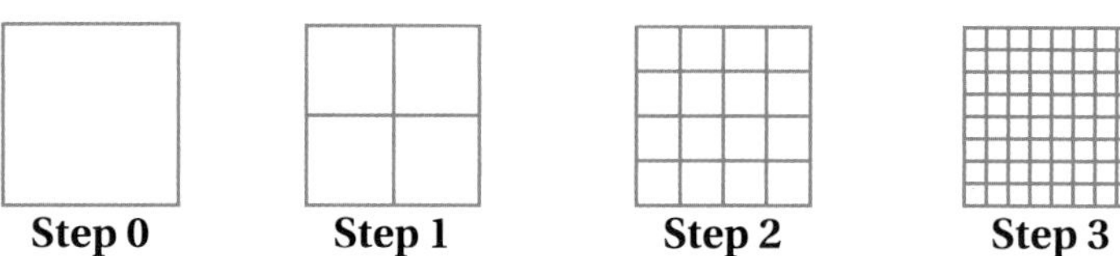

a. **Making a Table** Make a table showing the number of new squares and the side length of a new square at each step for Steps 1–4. Write the number of new squares as a power of 4. Write the side length of a new square as a power of $\frac{1}{2}$.

b. **Writing an Expression** Write and simplify an expression to find by how many times the number of new squares increased from Step 2 to Step 4.

@HomeTutor for problem solving help at classzone.com

50. **GROSS DOMESTIC PRODUCT** In 2003 the gross domestic product (GDP) for the United States was about 11 trillion dollars, and the order of magnitude of the population of the U.S. was 10^8. Use order of magnitude to find the approximate per capita (per person) GDP.

@HomeTutor for problem solving help at classzone.com

51. **SPACE TRAVEL** Alpha Centauri is the closest star system to Earth. Alpha Centauri is about 10^{13} kilometers away from Earth. A spacecraft leaves Earth and travels at an average speed of 10^4 meters per second. About how many years would it take the spacecraft to reach Alpha Centauri?

52. **ASTRONOMY** The brightness of one star relative to another star can be measured by comparing the magnitudes of the stars. For every increase in magnitude of 1, the relative brightness is diminished by a factor of 2.512. For instance, a star of magnitude 8 is 2.512 times less bright than a star of magnitude 7.

The constellation Ursa Minor (the Little Dipper) is shown. How many times less bright is Eta Ursae Minoris than Polaris?

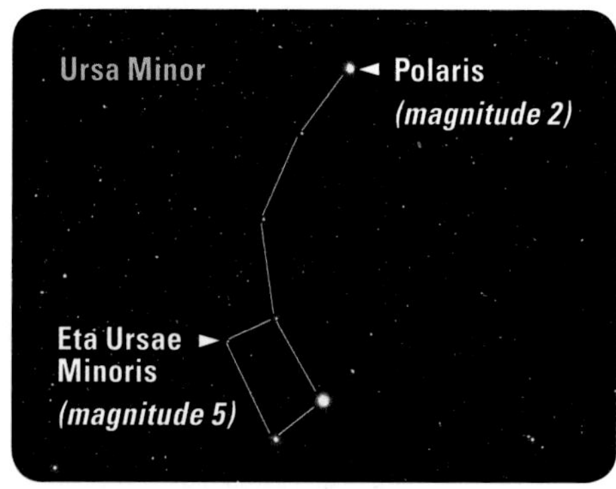

53. **EARTHQUAKES** The energy released by one earthquake relative to another earthquake can be measured by comparing the magnitudes (as determined by the Richter scale) of the earthquakes. For every increase of 1 in magnitude, the energy released is multiplied by a factor of about 31. How many times greater is the energy released by an earthquake of magnitude 7 than the energy released by an earthquake of magnitude 4?

○ = WORKED-OUT SOLUTIONS on p. WS1 ★ = STANDARDIZED TEST PRACTICE ◆ = MULTIPLE REPRESENTATIONS

54. ★ **EXTENDED RESPONSE** A byte is a unit used to measure computer memory. Other units are based on the number of bytes they represent. The table shows the number of bytes in certain units. For example, from the table you can calculate that 1 terabyte is equivalent to 2^{10} gigabytes.

a. **Calculate** How many kilobytes are there in 1 terabyte?

b. **Calculate** How many megabytes are there in 1 petabyte?

c. **CHALLENGE** Another unit used to measure computer memory is a bit. There are 8 bits in a byte. *Explain* how you can convert the number of bytes per unit given in the table to the number of bits per unit.

Unit	Number of bytes
Kilobyte	2^{10}
Megabyte	2^{20}
Gigabyte	2^{30}
Terabyte	2^{40}
Petabyte	2^{50}

MIXED REVIEW

PREVIEW
Prepare for Lesson 8.3 in Exs. 55–60.

Solve the equation. Check your solution. *(p. 134)*

55. $\frac{3}{4}k = 9$ 56. $\frac{2}{5}t = -4$ 57. $-\frac{2}{3}v = 14$

58. $-\frac{5}{2}y = -35$ 59. $-\frac{7}{5}z = \frac{14}{3}$ 60. $-\frac{3}{2}z = -\frac{3}{4}$

Write an equation of the line that passes through the given points. *(p. 292)*

61. $(-2, 1), (0, -5)$ 62. $(0, 3), (-4, 1)$ 63. $(0, -3), (7, -3)$

64. $(4, 3), (5, 6)$ 65. $(4, 1), (-2, 4)$ 66. $(-1, -3), (-3, 1)$

QUIZ *for Lessons 8.1–8.2*

Simplify the expression. Write your answer using exponents.

1. $3^2 \cdot 3^6$ *(p. 489)* 2. $(5^4)^3$ *(p. 489)* 3. $(32 \cdot 14)^7$ *(p. 489)*

4. $7^2 \cdot 7^6 \cdot 7$ *(p. 489)* 5. $(-4)(-4)^9$ *(p. 489)* 6. $\frac{7^{12}}{7^4}$ *(p. 495)*

7. $\frac{(-9)^9}{(-9)^7}$ *(p. 495)* 8. $\frac{3^7 \cdot 3^4}{3^6}$ *(p. 495)* 9. $\left(\frac{5}{4}\right)^4$ *(p. 495)*

Simplify the expression.

10. $x^2 \cdot x^5$ *(p. 489)* 11. $(3x^3)^2$ *(p. 489)* 12. $-(7x)^2$ *(p. 489)*

13. $(6x^5)^3 \cdot x$ *(p. 489)* 14. $(2x^5)^3(7x^7)^2$ *(p. 489)* 15. $\frac{1}{x^9} \cdot x^{21}$ *(p. 495)*

16. $\left(-\frac{4}{x}\right)^3$ *(p. 495)* 17. $\left(\frac{w}{v}\right)^6$ *(p. 495)* 18. $\left(\frac{x^3}{4}\right)^2$ *(p. 495)*

19. **AGRICULTURE** In 2004 the order of magnitude of the number of pounds of oranges produced in the United States was 10^{10}. The order of magnitude of the number of acres used for growing oranges was 10^6. About how many pounds of oranges per acre were produced in the United States in 2004? *(p. 495)*

8.3 Zero and Negative Exponents

MATERIALS • paper and pencil

QUESTION **How can you simplify expressions with zero or negative exponents?**

EXPLORE **Evaluate powers with zero and negative exponents**

STEP 1 ***Find a pattern***

Copy and complete the tables for the powers of 2 and 3.

Exponent, n	Value of 2^n
4	16
3	?
2	?
1	?

Exponent, n	Value of 3^n
4	81
3	?
2	?
1	?

As you read the tables from the *bottom up*, you see that each time the exponent is increased by 1, the value of the power is multiplied by the base. What can you say about the exponents and the values of the powers as you read the table from the *top down*?

STEP 2 ***Extend the pattern***

Copy and complete the tables using the pattern you observed in Step 1.

Exponent, n	Power, 2^n
3	8
2	?
1	?
0	?
−1	?
−2	?

Exponent, n	Power, 3^n
3	27
2	?
1	?
0	?
−1	?
−2	?

DRAW CONCLUSIONS **Use your observations to complete these exercises**

1. Find 2^n and 3^n for $n = -3, -4,$ and -5.
2. What appears to be the value of a^0 for any nonzero number a?
3. Write each power in the tables above as a power with a positive exponent. For example, you can write 3^{-1} as $\frac{1}{3^1}$.

8.3 Define and Use Zero and Negative Exponents

Before You used properties of exponents to simplify expressions.
Now You will use zero and negative exponents.
Why? So you can compare masses, as in Ex. 52.

Key Vocabulary
- **reciprocal,** *p. 915*

In the activity, you saw what happens when you raise a number to a zero or negative exponent. The activity suggests the following definitions.

KEY CONCEPT *For Your Notebook*

Definition of Zero and Negative Exponents

Words	Algebra	Example
a to the zero power is 1.	$a^0 = 1, a \neq 0$	$5^0 = 1$
a^{-n} is the reciprocal of a^n.	$a^{-n} = \frac{1}{a^n}, a \neq 0$	$2^{-1} = \frac{1}{2}$
a^n is the reciprocal of a^{-n}.	$a^n = \frac{1}{a^{-n}}, a \neq 0$	$2 = \frac{1}{2^{-1}}$

EXAMPLE 1 **Use definition of zero and negative exponents**

SIMPLIFY EXPRESSIONS
In this lesson, when simplifying powers with numerical bases, evaluate the numerical power.

a. $3^{-2} = \frac{1}{3^2}$ Definition of negative exponents

$= \frac{1}{9}$ Evaluate power.

b. $(-7)^0 = 1$ Definition of zero exponent

c. $\left(\frac{1}{5}\right)^{-2} = \frac{1}{\left(\frac{1}{5}\right)^2}$ Definition of negative exponents

$= \frac{1}{\frac{1}{25}}$ Evaluate power.

$= 25$ Simplify by multiplying numerator and denominator by 25.

d. $0^{-5} = \cancel{\frac{1}{0^5}}$ (Undefined) a^{-n} is defined only for a *nonzero* number a.

✓ **GUIDED PRACTICE** for Example 1

Evaluate the expression.

1. $\left(\frac{2}{3}\right)^0$
2. $(-8)^{-2}$
3. $\frac{1}{2^{-3}}$
4. $(-1)^0$

PROPERTIES OF EXPONENTS The properties of exponents you learned in Lessons 8.1 and 8.2 can be used with negative or zero exponents.

KEY CONCEPT *For Your Notebook*

Properties of Exponents

Let a and b be real numbers, and let m and n be integers.

$a^m \cdot a^n = a^{m+n}$	Product of powers property
$(a^m)^n = a^{mn}$	Power of a power property
$(ab)^m = a^m b^m$	Power of a product property
$\frac{a^m}{a^n} = a^{m-n}, a \neq 0$	Quotient of powers property
$\left(\frac{a}{b}\right)^m = \frac{a^m}{b^m}, b \neq 0$	Power of a quotient property

EXAMPLE 2 **Evaluate exponential expressions**

a. $6^{-4} \cdot 6^4 = 6^{-4+4}$ Product of powers property

$= 6^0$ Add exponents.

$= 1$ Definition of zero exponent

b. $(4^{-2})^2 = 4^{-2 \cdot 2}$ Power of a power property

$= 4^{-4}$ Multiply exponents.

$= \frac{1}{4^4}$ Definition of negative exponents

$= \frac{1}{256}$ Evaluate power.

c. $\frac{1}{3^{-4}} = 3^4$ Definition of negative exponents

$= 81$ Evaluate power.

d. $\frac{5^{-1}}{5^2} = 5^{-1-2}$ Quotient of powers property

$= 5^{-3}$ Subtract exponents.

$= \frac{1}{5^3}$ Definition of negative exponents

$= \frac{1}{125}$ Evaluate power.

✓ **GUIDED PRACTICE** for Example 2

Evaluate the expression.

5. $\frac{1}{4^{-3}}$ **6.** $(5^{-3})^{-1}$ **7.** $(-3)^5 \cdot (-3)^{-5}$ **8.** $\frac{6^{-2}}{6^2}$

EXAMPLE 3 Use properties of exponents

Simplify the expression. Write your answer using only positive exponents.

a. $(2xy^{-5})^3 = 2^3 \cdot x^3 \cdot (y^{-5})^3$ Power of a product property

$= 8 \cdot x^3 \cdot y^{-15}$ Power of a power property

$= \dfrac{8x^3}{y^{15}}$ Definition of negative exponents

b. $\dfrac{(2x)^{-2}y^5}{-4x^2y^2} = \dfrac{y^5}{(2x)^2(-4x^2y^2)}$ Definition of negative exponents

$= \dfrac{y^5}{(4x^2)(-4x^2y^2)}$ Power of a product property

$= \dfrac{y^5}{-16x^4y^2}$ Product of powers property

$= -\dfrac{y^3}{16x^4}$ Quotient of powers property

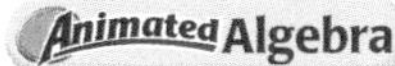 at classzone.com

EXAMPLE 4 Standardized Test Practice

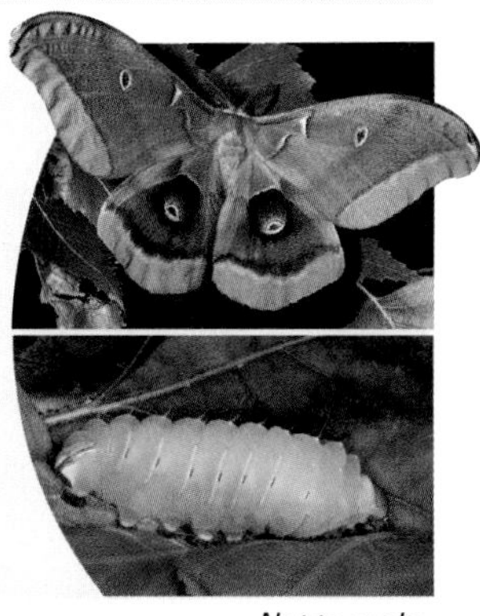

Not to scale

The order of magnitude of the mass of a polyphemus moth larva when it hatches is 10^{-3} gram. During the first 56 days of its life, the moth larva can eat about 10^5 times its own mass in food. About how many grams of food can the moth larva eat during its first 56 days?

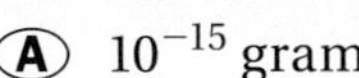

Ⓐ 10^{-15} gram Ⓑ 0.00000001 gram

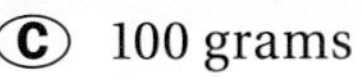

Ⓒ 100 grams Ⓓ 10,000,000 grams

Solution

To find the amount of food the moth larva can eat in the first 56 days of its life, multiply its original mass, 10^{-3}, by 10^5.

$10^5 \cdot 10^{-3} = 10^{5 + (-3)} = 10^2 = 100$

The moth larva can eat about 100 grams of food in the first 56 days of its life.

▶ The correct answer is C. Ⓐ Ⓑ Ⓒ Ⓓ

GUIDED PRACTICE for Examples 3 and 4

9. Simplify the expression $\dfrac{3xy^{-3}}{9x^3y}$. Write your answer using only positive exponents.

10. **SCIENCE** The order of magnitude of the mass of a proton is 10^4 times greater than the order of magnitude of the mass of an electron, which is 10^{-27} gram. Find the order of magnitude of the mass of a proton.

8.3 EXERCISES

HOMEWORK KEY

○ = **WORKED-OUT SOLUTIONS** on p. WS19 for Exs. 11 and 53

★ = **STANDARDIZED TEST PRACTICE** Exs. 2, 44, 45, 54, and 57

◆ = **MULTIPLE REPRESENTATIONS** Ex. 55

SKILL PRACTICE

1. **VOCABULARY** Which definitions or properties would you use to simplify the expression $3^5 \cdot 3^{-5}$? *Explain.*

2. ★ **WRITING** *Explain* why the expression 0^{-4} is undefined.

EXAMPLE 1 on p. 503 for Exs. 3–14

EVALUATING EXPRESSIONS **Evaluate the expression.**

3. 4^{-3}
4. 7^{-3}
5. $(-3)^{-1}$
6. $(-2)^{-6}$
7. 2^0
8. $(-4)^0$
9. $\left(\frac{3}{4}\right)^0$
10. $\left(\frac{-9}{16}\right)^0$
11. $\left(\frac{2}{7}\right)^{-2}$
12. $\left(\frac{4}{3}\right)^{-3}$
13. 0^{-3}
14. 0^{-2}

EXAMPLE 2 on p. 504 for Exs. 15–27

15. $2^{-2} \cdot 2^{-3}$
16. $7^{-6} \cdot 7^4$
17. $(2^{-1})^5$
18. $(3^{-2})^2$
19. $\frac{1}{3^{-3}}$
20. $\frac{1}{6^{-2}}$
21. $\frac{3^{-3}}{3^2}$
22. $\frac{6^{-3}}{6^{-5}}$
23. $4\left(\frac{3}{2}\right)^{-1}$
24. $16\left(\frac{2^{-3}}{2^2}\right)$
25. $6^0 \cdot \left(\frac{1}{4^{-2}}\right)$
26. $3^{-2} \cdot \left(\frac{5}{7^0}\right)$

27. **ERROR ANALYSIS** *Describe* and correct the error in evaluating the expression $-6 \cdot 3^0$.

$$-6 \cdot 3^0 = -6 \cdot 0$$
$$= 0$$

EXAMPLE 3 on p. 505 for Exs. 28–43

SIMPLIFYING EXPRESSIONS **Simplify the expression. Write your answer using only positive exponents.**

28. x^{-4}
29. $2y^{-3}$
30. $(4g)^{-3}$
31. $(-11h)^{-2}$
32. x^2y^{-3}
33. $5m^{-3}n^{-4}$
34. $(6x^{-2}y^3)^{-3}$
35. $(-15fg^2)^0$
36. $\frac{r^{-2}}{s^{-4}}$
37. $\frac{x^{-5}}{y^2}$
38. $\frac{1}{8x^{-2}y^{-6}}$
39. $\frac{1}{15x^{10}y^{-8}}$
40. $\frac{1}{(-2z)^{-2}}$
41. $\frac{9}{(3d)^{-3}}$
42. $\frac{(3x)^{-3}y^4}{-x^2y^{-6}}$
43. $\frac{12x^8y^{-7}}{(4x^{-2}y^{-6})^2}$

44. ★ **MULTIPLE CHOICE** Which expression simplifies to $2x^4$?

Ⓐ $2x^{-4}$ Ⓑ $\frac{32}{(2x)^{-4}}$ Ⓒ $\frac{1}{2x^{-4}}$ Ⓓ $\frac{8}{4x^{-4}}$

45. ★ **MULTIPLE CHOICE** Which expression is equivalent to $(-4 \cdot 2^0 \cdot 3)^{-2}$?

Ⓐ -12 Ⓑ $-\frac{1}{144}$ Ⓒ 0 Ⓓ $\frac{1}{144}$

CHALLENGE In Exercises 46–48, tell whether the statement is true for all nonzero values of a and b. If it is not true, give a counterexample.

46. $\frac{a^{-3}}{a^{-4}} = \frac{1}{a}$

47. $\frac{a^{-1}}{b^{-1}} = \frac{b}{a}$

48. $a^{-1} + b^{-1} = \frac{1}{a+b}$

49. REASONING For $n > 0$, what happens to the value of a^{-n} as n increases?

PROBLEM SOLVING

EXAMPLE 4 on p. 505 for Exs. 50–54

50. MASS The mass of a grain of salt is about 10^{-4} gram. About how many grains of salt are in a box containing 100 grams of salt?

@HomeTutor for problem solving help at classzone.com

51. MASS The mass of a grain of a certain type of rice is about 10^{-2} gram. About how many grains of rice are in a box containing 10^3 grams of rice?

@HomeTutor for problem solving help at classzone.com

52. BOTANY The average mass of the fruit of the wolffia angusta plant is about 10^{-4} gram. The largest pumpkin ever recorded had a mass of about 10^4 kilograms. About how many times greater is the mass of the largest pumpkin than the mass of the fruit of the wolffia angusta plant?

53. MEDICINE A doctor collected about 10^{-2} liter of blood from a patient to run some tests. The doctor determined that a drop of the patient's blood, or about 10^{-6} liter, contained about 10^7 red blood cells. How many red blood cells did the entire sample contain?

54. ★ SHORT RESPONSE One of the smallest plant seeds comes from an orchid, and one of the largest plant seeds comes from a giant fan palm. A seed from an orchid has a mass of 10^{-9} gram and is 10^{13} times less massive than a seed from a giant fan palm. A student says that the seed from the giant fan palm has a mass of about 1 kilogram. Is the student correct? *Explain.*

Orchid

Giant fan palm

55. MULTIPLE REPRESENTATIONS Consider folding a piece of paper in half a number of times.

a. Making a Table Each time the paper is folded, record the number of folds and the fraction of the original area in a table like the one shown.

Number of folds	0	1	2	3
Fraction of original area	?	?	?	?

b. Writing an Expression Write an exponential expression for the fraction of the original area of the paper using a base of $\frac{1}{2}$.

56. **SCIENCE** Diffusion is the movement of molecules from one location to another. The time t (in seconds) it takes molecules to diffuse a distance of x centimeters is given by $t = \frac{x^2}{2D}$ where D is the diffusion coefficient.

a. You can examine a cross section of a drop of ink in water to see how the ink diffuses. The diffusion coefficient for the molecules in the drop of ink is about 10^{-5} square centimeter per second. How long will it take the ink to diffuse 1 micrometer (10^{-4} centimeter)?

b. Check your answer to part (a) using unit analysis.

57. ★ **EXTENDED RESPONSE** The intensity of sound I (in watts per square meter) can be modeled by $I = 0.08Pd^{-2}$ where P is the power (in watts) of the sound's source and d is the distance (in meters) that you are from the source of the sound.

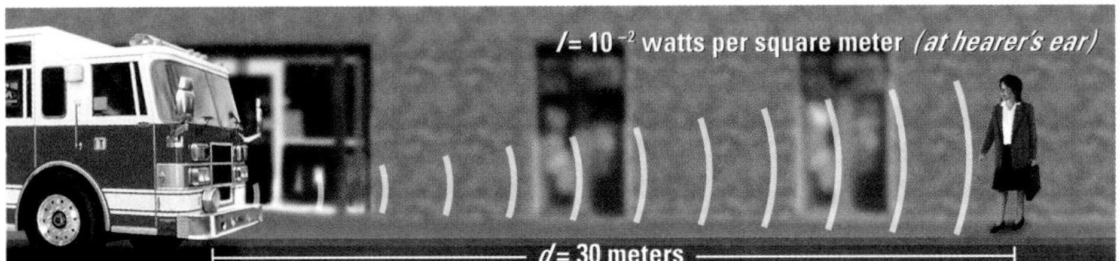

Not to scale

a. What is the power (in watts) of the siren of the firetruck shown in the diagram?

b. Using the power of the siren you found in part (a), simplify the formula for the intensity of sound from the siren.

c. *Explain* what happens to the intensity of the siren when you double your distance from it.

58. **CHALLENGE** Coal can be burned to generate energy. The heat energy in 1 pound of coal is about 10^4 BTU (British Thermal Units). Suppose you have a stereo. It takes about 10 pounds of coal to create the energy needed to power the stereo for 1 year.

a. About how many BTUs does your stereo use in 1 year?

b. Suppose the power plant that delivers energy to your home produces 10^{-1} pound of sulfur dioxide for each 10^6 BTU of energy that it creates. How much sulfur dioxide is added to the air by generating the energy needed to power your stereo for 1 year?

MIXED REVIEW

PREVIEW
Prepare for Lesson 8.4 in Exs. 59–62.

Evaluate the expression.

59. $10^3 \cdot 10^3$ *(p. 489)* 60. $10^2 \cdot 10^5$ *(p. 489)* 61. $\frac{10^9}{10^7}$ *(p. 495)* 62. $\frac{10^6}{10^3}$ *(p. 495)*

Solve the linear system. Then check your answer. *(pp. 427, 435, 444, 451)*

63. $y = 3x - 6$
$y = -7x - 1$

64. $y = -2x + 12$
$y = -5x + 24$

65. $5x + y = 40$
$-x + y = -8$

66. $-x - 2y = -6.5$
$3x - 6y = 16.5$

67. $3x + 4y = -5$
$x - 2y = 5$

68. $2x + 6y = 5$
$-2x - 3y = 2$

EXTRA PRACTICE for Lesson 8.3, p. 945 **ONLINE QUIZ** at classzone.com

Define and Use Fractional Exponents

GOAL Use fractional exponents.

Key Vocabulary
- cube root

In Lesson 2.7, you learned to write the square root of a number using a radical sign. You can also write a square root of a number using exponents.

For any $a \geq 0$, suppose you want to write $\sqrt{a}$ as a^k. Recall that a number b (in this case, a^k) is a square root of a number a provided $b^2 = a$. Use this definition to find a value for k as follows.

$$b^2 = a \qquad \text{Definition of square root}$$

$$(a^k)^2 = a \qquad \text{Substitute } a^k \text{ for } b.$$

$$a^{2k} = a^1 \qquad \text{Power of a power property}$$

Because the bases are the same in the equation $a^{2k} = a^1$, the exponents must be equal:

$$2k = 1 \qquad \text{Set exponents equal.}$$

$$k = \frac{1}{2} \qquad \text{Solve for } k.$$

So, for a nonnegative number a, $\sqrt{a} = a^{1/2}$.

You can work with exponents of $\frac{1}{2}$ and multiples of $\frac{1}{2}$ just as you work with integer exponents.

EXAMPLE 1 Evaluate expressions involving square roots

a. $16^{1/2} = \sqrt{16}$

$= 4$

b. $25^{-1/2} = \frac{1}{25^{1/2}}$

$= \frac{1}{\sqrt{25}}$

$= \frac{1}{5}$

c. $9^{5/2} = 9^{(1/2) \cdot 5}$

$= (9^{1/2})^5$

$= (\sqrt{9})^5$

$= 3^5$

$= 243$

d. $4^{-3/2} = 4^{(1/2) \cdot (-3)}$

$= (4^{1/2})^{-3}$

$= (\sqrt{4})^{-3}$

$= 2^{-3}$

$= \frac{1}{2^3}$

$= \frac{1}{8}$

FRACTIONAL EXPONENTS You can work with other fractional exponents just as you did with $\frac{1}{2}$.

CUBE ROOTS If $b^3 = a$, then b is the **cube root** of a. For example, $2^3 = 8$, so 2 is the cube root of 8. The cube root of a can be written as $\sqrt[3]{a}$ or $a^{1/3}$.

EXAMPLE 2 Evaluate expressions involving cube roots

a. $27^{1/3} = \sqrt[3]{27}$

$= \sqrt[3]{3^3}$

$= 3$

b. $8^{-1/3} = \frac{1}{8^{1/3}}$

$= \frac{1}{\sqrt[3]{8}}$

$= \frac{1}{2}$

c. $64^{4/3} = 64^{(1/3) \cdot 4}$

$= (64^{1/3})^4$

$= (\sqrt[3]{64})^4$

$= 4^4$

$= 256$

d. $125^{-2/3} = 125^{(1/3) \cdot (-2)}$

$= (125^{1/3})^{-2}$

$= (\sqrt[3]{125})^{-2}$

$= 5^{-2}$

$= \frac{1}{5^2}$

$= \frac{1}{25}$

PROPERTIES OF EXPONENTS The properties of exponents for integer exponents also apply to fractional exponents.

EXAMPLE 3 Use properties of exponents

a. $12^{-1/2} \cdot 12^{5/2} = 12^{(-1/2) + (5/2)}$

$= 12^{4/2}$

$= 12^2$

$= 144$

b. $\frac{6^{4/3} \cdot 6}{6^{1/3}} = \frac{6^{(4/3) + 1}}{6^{1/3}}$

$= \frac{6^{7/3}}{6^{1/3}}$

$= 6^{(7/3) - (1/3)}$

$= 6^2$

$= 36$

PRACTICE

EXAMPLES 1, 2, and 3 on pp. 509–510 for Exs. 1–12

Evaluate the expression.

1. $100^{3/2}$
2. $121^{-1/2}$
3. $81^{-3/2}$
4. $216^{2/3}$
5. $27^{-1/3}$
6. $343^{-2/3}$
7. $9^{7/2} \cdot 9^{-3/2}$
8. $\left(\frac{1}{16}\right)^{1/2}\left(\frac{1}{16}\right)^{-1/2}$
9. $36^{5/2} \cdot \frac{36^{-1/2}}{(36^{-1})^{-7/2}}$
10. $(27^{-1/3})^3$
11. $(-64)^{-5/3}(-64)^{4/3}$
12. $(-8)^{1/3}(-8)^{-2/3}(-8)^{1/3}$
13. **REASONING** Show that the cube root of a can be written as $a^{1/3}$ using an argument similar to the one given for square roots on the previous page.

MIXED REVIEW *of Problem Solving*

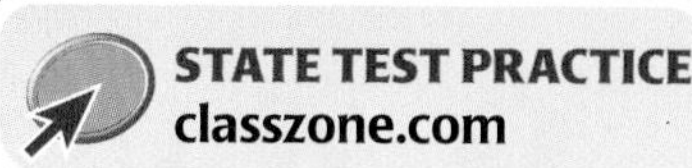

Lessons 8.1–8.3

1. **GRIDDED ANSWER** In 2004 the fastest computers could record about 10^9 bits per second. (A bit is the smallest unit of memory storage for computers.) Scientists believed that the speed limit at the time was about 10^{12} bits per second. About how many times more bits per second was the speed limit than the fastest computers?

2. **MULTI-STEP PROBLEM** An office supply store sells cubical containers that can be used to store paper clips, rubber bands, or other supplies.

   a. One of the containers has a side length of $4\frac{1}{2}$ inches. Find the container's volume by writing the side length as an improper fraction and substituting the length into the formula for the volume of a cube.

   b. Identify the property of exponents you used to find the volume in part (a).

3. **SHORT RESPONSE** Clouds contain millions of tiny spherical water droplets. The radius of one droplet is shown.

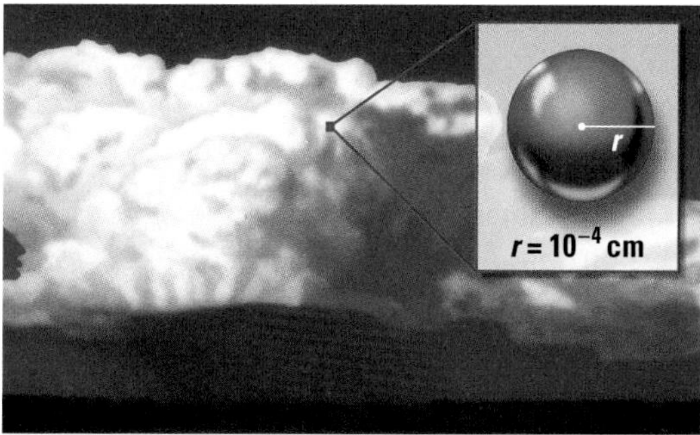

   a. Find the order of magnitude of the volume of the droplet.

   b. Droplets combine to form raindrops. The radius of a raindrop is about 10^2 times greater than the droplet's radius. Find the order of magnitude of the volume of the raindrop.

   c. *Explain* how you can find the number of droplets that combine to form the raindrop. Then find the number of droplets and identify any properties of exponents you used.

4. **GRIDDED ANSWER** The least intense sound that is audible to the human ear has an intensity of about 10^{-12} watt per square meter. The intensity of sound from a jet engine at a distance of 30 meters is about 10^{15} times greater than the least intense sound. Find the intensity of sound from the jet engine.

5. **EXTENDED RESPONSE** For an experiment, a scientist dropped a spoonful, or about 10^{-1} cubic inch, of biodegradable olive oil into a pond to see how the oil would spread out over the surface of the pond. The scientist found that the oil spread until it covered an area of about 10^5 square inches.

   a. About how thick was the layer of oil that spread out across the pond? Check your answer using unit analysis.

   b. The pond has a surface area of 10^7 square inches. If the oil spreads to the same thickness as in part (a), how many cubic inches of olive oil would be needed to cover the entire surface of the pond?

   c. *Explain* how you could find the amount of oil needed to cover a pond with a surface area of 10^x square inches.

6. **OPEN-ENDED** The table shows units of measurement of time and the durations of the units in seconds.

Name of unit	Duration (seconds)
Gigasecond	10^9
Megasecond	10^6
Millisecond	10^{-3}
Nanosecond	10^{-9}

   a. Use the table to write a conversion problem that can be solved by applying a property of exponents involving products.

   b. Use the table to write a conversion problem that can be solved by applying a property of exponents involving quotients.

8.4 Use Scientific Notation

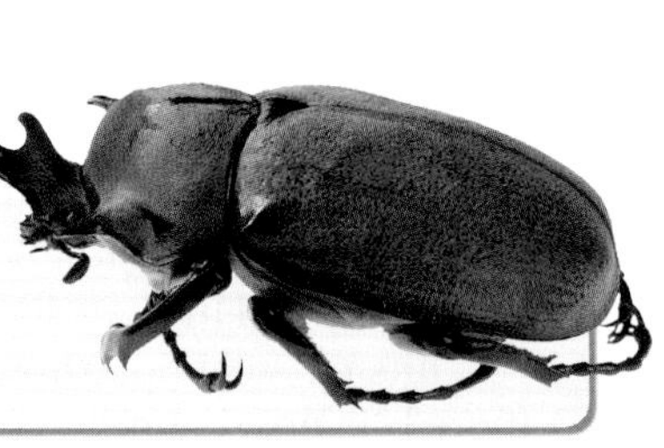

Before You used properties of exponents.
Now You will read and write numbers in scientific notation.
Why? So you can compare lengths of insects, as in Ex. 51.

Key Vocabulary
- **scientific notation**

Numbers such as 1,000,000, 153,000, and 0.0009 are written in *standard form*. Another way to write a number is to use *scientific notation.*

KEY CONCEPT *For Your Notebook*

Scientific Notation

A number is written in **scientific notation** when it is of the form $c \times 10^n$ where $1 \le c < 10$ and n is an integer.

Number	Standard form	Scientific notation
Two million	2,000,000	2×10^6
Five thousandths	0.005	5×10^{-3}

EXAMPLE 1 Write numbers in scientific notation

a. $42{,}590{,}000 = 4.259 \times 10^7$ Move decimal point 7 places to the left. Exponent is 7.

b. $0.0000574 = 5.74 \times 10^{-5}$ Move decimal point 5 places to the right. Exponent is −5.

EXAMPLE 2 Write numbers in standard form

READING A positive number in scientific notation is greater than 1 if the exponent is positive. A positive number in scientific notation is between 0 and 1 if the exponent is negative.

a. $2.0075 \times 10^6 = 2{,}007{,}500$ Exponent is 6. Move decimal point 6 places to the right.

b. $1.685 \times 10^{-4} = 0.0001685$ Exponent is −4. Move decimal point 4 places to the left.

Animated Algebra at classzone.com

✓ **GUIDED PRACTICE** for Examples 1 and 2

1. Write the number 539,000 in scientific notation. Then write the number 4.5×10^{-4} in standard form.

EXAMPLE 3 Order numbers in scientific notation

Order 103,400,000, 7.8×10^8, and 80,760,000 from least to greatest.

Solution

STEP 1 **Write** each number in scientific notation, if necessary.

$103{,}400{,}000 = 1.034 \times 10^8$ $\quad$ $80{,}760{,}000 = 8.076 \times 10^7$

STEP 2 **Order** the numbers. First order the numbers with different powers of 10. Then order the numbers with the same power of 10.

Because $\mathbf{10^7} < \mathbf{10^8}$, you know that $8.076 \times \mathbf{10^7}$ is less than both $1.034 \times \mathbf{10^8}$ and $7.8 \times \mathbf{10^8}$. Because $\mathbf{1.034} < \mathbf{7.8}$, you know that $\mathbf{1.034} \times 10^8$ is less than $\mathbf{7.8} \times 10^8$.

So, $8.076 \times 10^7 < 1.034 \times 10^8 < 7.8 \times 10^8$.

STEP 3 **Write** the original numbers in order from least to greatest.

80,760,000; 103,400,000; 7.8×10^8

EXAMPLE 4 Compute with numbers in scientific notation

Evaluate the expression. Write your answer in scientific notation.

a. $(8.5 \times 10^2)(1.7 \times 10^6)$

$= (8.5 \cdot 1.7) \times (10^2 \cdot 10^6)$ — Commutative property and associative property

$= 14.45 \times 10^8$ — Product of powers property

$= (1.445 \times 10^1) \times 10^8$ — Write 14.45 in scientific notation.

$= 1.445 \times (10^1 \times 10^8)$ — Associative property

$= 1.445 \times 10^9$ — Product of powers property

b. $(1.5 \times 10^{-3})^2 = 1.5^2 \times (10^{-3})^2$ — Power of a product property

$= 2.25 \times 10^{-6}$ — Power of a power property

c. $\dfrac{1.2 \times 10^4}{1.6 \times 10^{-3}} = \dfrac{1.2}{1.6} \times \dfrac{10^4}{10^{-3}}$ — Product rule for fractions

$= 0.75 \times 10^7$ — Quotient of powers property

$= (7.5 \times 10^{-1}) \times 10^7$ — Write 0.75 in scientific notation.

$= 7.5 \times (10^{-1} \times 10^7)$ — Associative property

$= 7.5 \times 10^6$ — Product of powers property

AVOID ERRORS

Notice that 14.45×10^8 is *not* written in scientific notation because $14.45 > 10$.

REVIEW FRACTIONS

For help with fractions, see p. 915.

✓ GUIDED PRACTICE for Examples 3 and 4

2. Order 2.7×10^5, 3.401×10^4, and 27,500 from least to greatest.

Evaluate the expression. Write your answer in scientific notation.

3. $(1.3 \times 10^{-5})^2$ $\qquad$ **4.** $\dfrac{4.5 \times 10^5}{1.5 \times 10^{-2}}$ $\qquad$ **5.** $(1.1 \times 10^7)(4.2 \times 10^2)$

EXAMPLE 5 Solve a multi-step problem

BLOOD VESSELS Blood flow is partially controlled by the cross-sectional area of the blood vessel through which the blood is traveling. Three types of blood vessels are venules, capillaries, and arterioles.

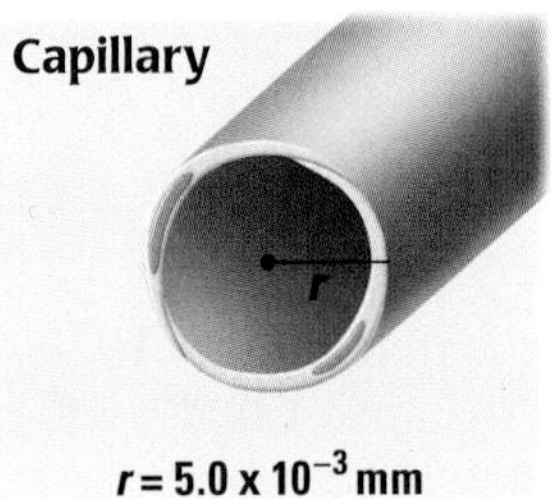

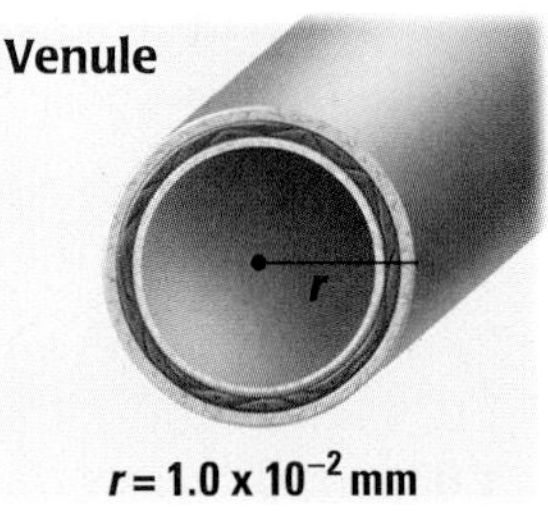

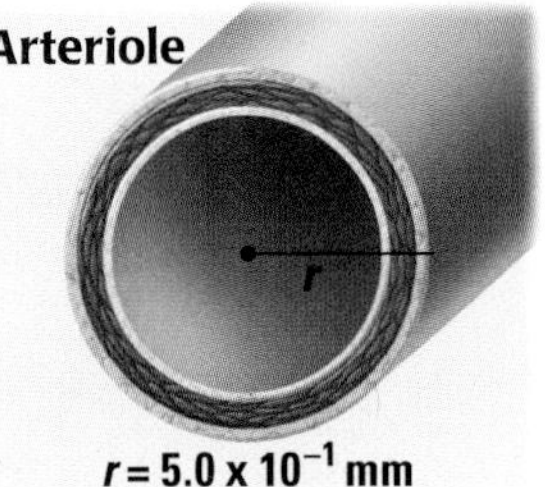

a. Let r_1 be the radius of a venule, and let r_2 be the radius of a capillary. Find the ratio of r_1 to r_2. What does the ratio tell you?

b. Let A_1 be the cross-sectional area of a venule, and let A_2 be the cross-sectional area of a capillary. Find the ratio of A_1 to A_2. What does the ratio tell you?

c. What is the relationship between the ratio of the radii of the blood vessels and the ratio of their cross-sectional areas?

Solution

a. From the diagram, you can see that the radius of the venule r_1 is 1.0×10^{-2} millimeter and the radius of the capillary r_2 is 5.0×10^{-3} millimeter.

$$\frac{r_1}{r_2} = \frac{1.0 \times 10^{-2}}{5.0 \times 10^{-3}} = \frac{1.0}{5.0} \times \frac{10^{-2}}{10^{-3}} = 0.2 \times 10^1 = 2$$

The ratio tells you that the radius of the venule is twice the radius of the capillary.

ANOTHER WAY You can also find the ratio of the cross-sectional areas by finding the areas using the values for r_1 and r_2, setting up a ratio, and then simplifying.

b. To find the cross-sectional areas, use the formula for the area of a circle.

$\frac{A_1}{A_2} = \frac{\pi r_1^2}{\pi r_2^2}$ **Write ratio.**

$= \frac{r_1^2}{r_2^2}$ **Divide numerator and denominator by π.**

$= \left(\frac{r_1}{r_2}\right)^2$ **Power of a quotient property**

$= 2^2 = 4$ **Substitute and simplify.**

The ratio tells you that the cross-sectional area of the venule is four times the cross-sectional area of the capillary.

c. The ratio of the cross-sectional areas of the blood vessels is the square of the ratio of the radii of the blood vessels.

✓ GUIDED PRACTICE for Example 5

6. **WHAT IF?** *Compare* the radius and cross-sectional area of an arteriole with the radius and cross-sectional area of a capillary.

8.4 EXERCISES

HOMEWORK KEY

○ = **WORKED-OUT SOLUTIONS** on p. WS19 for Exs. 3, 17, and 53

★ = **STANDARDIZED TEST PRACTICE** Exs. 2, 15, 48, 49, 54, and 59

◆ = **MULTIPLE REPRESENTATIONS** Ex. 58

SKILL PRACTICE

1. **VOCABULARY** Is 0.5×10^6 written in scientific notation? *Explain* why or why not.

2. ★ **WRITING** Is 7.89×10^6 between 0 and 1 or greater than 1? *Explain* how you know.

EXAMPLE 1 on p. 512 for Exs. 3–15

WRITING IN SCIENTIFIC NOTATION **Write the number in scientific notation.**

3. 8.5	**4.** 0.72	**5.** 82.4
6. 0.005	**7.** 72,000,000	**8.** 0.00406
9. 1,065,250	**10.** 0.000045	**11.** 1,060,000,000
12. 0.00000526	**13.** 900,000,000,000,000	**14.** 0.00000007008

15. ★ **MULTIPLE CHOICE** Which number represents 54,004,000,000 written in scientific notation?

(A) 54004×10^6 (B) 54.004×10^9

(C) 5.4004×10^{10} (D) 0.54004×10^{11}

EXAMPLE 2 on p. 512 for Exs. 16–28

WRITING IN STANDARD FORM **Write the number in standard form.**

16. 2.6×10^3	**17.** 7.5×10^7	**18.** 1.11×10^2
19. 3.03×10^4	**20.** 4.709×10^6	**21.** 1.544×10^{10}
22. 6.1×10^{-3}	**23.** 4.4×10^{-10}	**24.** 2.23×10^{-6}
25. 8.52×10^{-8}	**26.** 6.4111×10^{-10}	**27.** 1.2034×10^{-6}

28. **ERROR ANALYSIS** *Describe* and correct the error in writing 1.24×10^{-3} in standard form.

$1.24 \times 10^{-3} = 1240$

EXAMPLE 3 on p. 513 for Exs. 29–32

ORDERING NUMBERS **Order the numbers from least to greatest.**

29. 45,000; 6.7×10^3; 12,439; 2×10^4

30. 65,000,000; 6.2×10^6; 3.557×10^7; 55,004,000; 6.07×10^6

31. 0.0005; 9.8×10^{-6}; 5×10^{-3}; 0.00008; 0.04065; 8.2×10^{-3}

32. 0.0000395; 0.00010068; 2.4×10^{-5}; 5.08×10^{-6}; 0.000005

COMPARING NUMBERS **Copy and complete the statement using <, >, or =.**

33. 5.6×10^3 _?_ 56,000	**34.** 404,000.1 _?_ 4.04001×10^5
35. 9.86×10^{-3} _?_ 0.00986	**36.** 0.003309 _?_ 3.309×10^{-3}
37. 2.203×10^{-4} _?_ 0.0000203	**38.** 604,589,000 _?_ 6.04589×10^7

EXAMPLE 4
on p. 513
for Exs. 39–48

EVALUATING EXPRESSIONS **Evaluate the expression. Write your answer in scientific notation.**

39. $(4.4 \times 10^3)(1.5 \times 10^{-7})$

40. $(7.3 \times 10^{-5})(5.8 \times 10^2)$

41. $(8.1 \times 10^{-4})(9 \times 10^{-6})$

42. $\frac{6 \times 10^{-3}}{8 \times 10^{-6}}$

43. $\frac{5.4 \times 10^{-5}}{1.8 \times 10^{-2}}$

44. $\frac{4.1 \times 10^4}{8.2 \times 10^8}$

45. $(5 \times 10^{-8})^3$

46. $(7 \times 10^{-5})^4$

47. $(1.4 \times 10^3)^2$

48. ★ **MULTIPLE CHOICE** Which number is the value of $\frac{1.235 \times 10^4}{9.5 \times 10^7}$?

Ⓐ 0.13×10^{-4} Ⓑ 1.3×10^{-4} Ⓒ 1.3×10^{-3} Ⓓ 0.13×10^3

49. ★ **OPEN-ENDED** Write two numbers in scientific notation whose product is 2.8×10^4. Write two numbers in scientific notation whose quotient is 2.8×10^4.

50. **CHALLENGE** Add the numbers 3.6×10^5 and 6.7×10^4 *without* writing the numbers in standard form. Write your answer in scientific notation. *Describe* the steps you take.

PROBLEM SOLVING

EXAMPLE 3
on p. 513
for Exs. 51–52

51. **INSECT LENGTHS** The lengths of several insects are shown in the table.

a. List the lengths of the insects in order from least to greatest.

b. Which insects are longer than the fringed ant beetle?

Insect	Length (millimeters)
Fringed ant beetle	2.5×10^{-1}
Walking stick	555
Parasitic wasp	1.4×10^{-4}
Elephant beetle	1.67×10^2

@HomeTutor for problem solving help at classzone.com

52. **ASTRONOMY** The spacecrafts *Voyager 1* and *Voyager 2* were launched in 1977 to gather data about our solar system. As of March 12, 2004, *Voyager 1* had traveled a total distance of about 9,643,000,000 miles, and *Voyager 2* had traveled a total distance of about 9.065×10^9 miles. Which spacecraft had traveled the greater distance at that time?

@HomeTutor for problem solving help at classzone.com

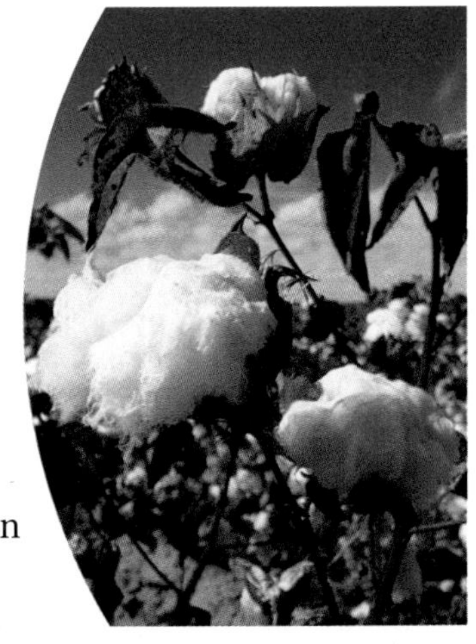

EXAMPLE 4
on p. 513
for Ex. 53

53. **AGRICULTURE** In 2002, about 9.7×10^8 pounds of cotton were produced in California. The cotton was planted on 6.9×10^5 acres of land. What was the average number of pounds of cotton produced per acre? Round your answer to the nearest whole number.

EXAMPLE 5
on p. 514
for Exs. 54–55

54. ★ **SHORT RESPONSE** The average flow rate of the Amazon River is about 7.6×10^6 cubic feet per second. The average flow rate of the Mississippi River is about 5.53×10^5 cubic feet per second. Find the ratio of the flow rate of the Amazon to the flow rate of the Mississippi. Round to the nearest whole number. What does the ratio tell you?

○ = WORKED-OUT SOLUTIONS on p. WS1 ★ = STANDARDIZED TEST PRACTICE  = MULTIPLE REPRESENTATIONS

55. **ASTRONOMY** The radius of Earth and the radius of the moon are shown.

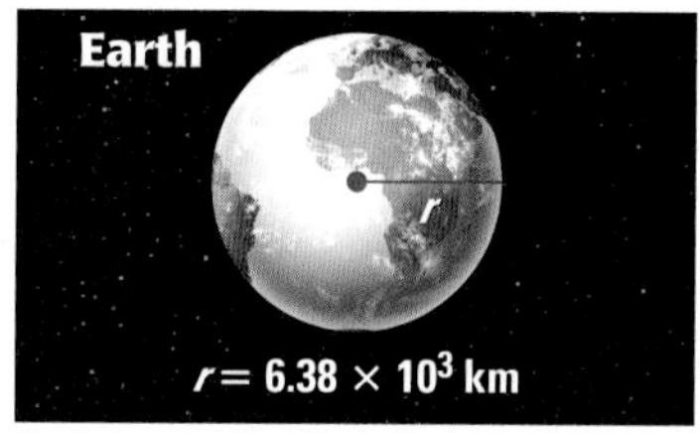

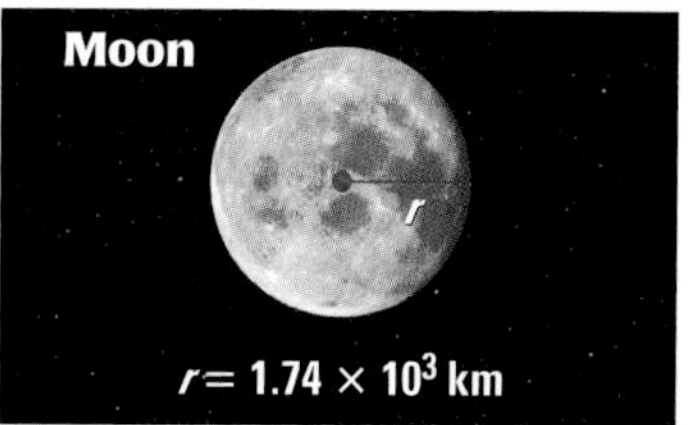

a. Find the ratio of the radius of Earth to the radius of the moon. Round to the nearest hundredth. What does the ratio tell you?

b. Assume Earth and the moon are spheres. Find the ratio of the volume of Earth to the volume of the moon. Round to the nearest hundredth. What does the ratio tell you?

c. What is the relationship between the ratios of the radii and the ratios of the volumes?

56. **MULTI-STEP PROBLEM** In 1954, 50 swarms of locusts were observed in Kenya. The largest swarm covered an area of 200 square kilometers. The average number of locusts in a swarm is about 5×10^7 locusts per square kilometer.

a. About how many locusts were in Kenya's largest swarm? Write your answer in scientific notation.

b. The average mass of a desert locust is 2 grams. What was the total mass (in kilograms) of Kenya's largest swarm? Write your answer in scientific notation.

57. **DIGITAL PHOTOGRAPHY** When a picture is taken with a digital camera, the resulting image is made up of square pixels (the smallest unit that can be displayed on a monitor). For one image, the side length of a pixel is 4×10^{-3} inch. A print of the image measures 1×10^3 pixels by 1.5×10^3 pixels. What are the dimensions of the print in inches?

58. ◆ **MULTIPLE REPRESENTATIONS** The speed of light is 1.863×10^5 miles per second.

a. **Writing an Expression** Assume 1 year is 365 days. Write an expression to convert the speed of light from miles per second to miles per year.

b. **Making a Table** Make a table that shows the distance light travels in 1, 10, 100, 1000, 10,000, and 100,000 years. Our galaxy has a diameter of about 5.875×10^{17} miles. Based on the table, about how long would it take for light to travel across our galaxy?

59. ★ **EXTENDED RESPONSE** When a person is at rest, approximately 7×10^{-2} liter of blood flows through the heart with each heartbeat. The human heart beats about 70 times per minute.

a. **Calculate** About how many liters of blood flow through the heart each minute when a person is at rest?

b. **Estimate** There are approximately 5.265×10^5 minutes in a year. Use your answer from part (a) to estimate the number of liters of blood that flow through the human heart in 1 year, in 10 years, and in 80 years. Write your answers in scientific notation.

c. **Explain** Are your answers to part (b) underestimates or overestimates? *Explain.*

60. **CHALLENGE** A solar flare is a sudden eruption of energy in the sun's atmosphere. Solar flares are classified according to their peak X-ray intensity (in watts per meter squared) and are denoted with a capital letter and a number, as shown in the table. For example, a C4 flare has a peak intensity of 4×10^{-6} watt per square meter.

Class	B*n*	C*n*	M*n*	X*n*
Peak intensity (w/m²)	$n \times 10^{-7}$	$n \times 10^{-6}$	$n \times 10^{-5}$	$n \times 10^{-4}$

a. In November 2003, a massive X45 solar flare was observed. In April 2004, a C9 flare was observed. How many times greater was the intensity of the X45 flare than that of the C9 flare?

b. A solar flare may be accompanied by a coronal mass ejection (CME), a bubble of mass ejected from the sun. A CME related to the X45 flare was estimated to be traveling at 8.2 million kilometers per hour. At that rate, how long would it take the CME to travel from the sun to Earth, a distance of about 1.5×10^{11} meters?

MIXED REVIEW

PREVIEW
Prepare for Lesson 8.5 in Exs. 61–68.

Write the percent as a decimal. *(p. 916)*

61. 33%
62. 62.7%
63. 0.9%
64. 0.04%
65. 3.95%
66. $\frac{1}{4}$%
67. $\frac{5}{2}$%
68. 133%

Graph the equation.

69. $x = -5$ *(p. 215)*
70. $y = 4$ *(p. 215)*
71. $3x - 7y = 42$ *(p. 225)*
72. $y - 2x = 12$ *(p. 225)*
73. $y = -2x + 6$ *(p. 244)*
74. $y = 1.5x - 9$ *(p. 244)*

QUIZ *for Lessons 8.3–8.4*

Simplify the expression. Write your answer using only positive exponents. *(p. 503)*

1. $(-4x)^4 \cdot (-4)^{-6}$
2. $(-3x^7y^{-2})^{-3}$
3. $\frac{1}{(5z)^{-3}}$
4. $\frac{(6x)^{-2}y^5}{-x^3y^{-7}}$

Write the number in standard form. *(p. 512)*

5. 6.02×10^6
6. 5.41×10^{11}
7. 8.007×10^{-5}
8. 9.253×10^{-7}

9. **DINOSAURS** The estimated masses of several dinosaurs are shown in the table. *(p. 512)*

a. List the masses of the dinosaurs in order from least to greatest.

b. Which dinosaurs are more massive than Brachiosaurus?

Dinosaur	Mass (kilograms)
Brachiosaurus	77,100
Diplodocus	1.06×10^4
Apatosaurus	29,900
Ultrasaurus	1.36×10^5

@HomeTutor classzone.com Keystrokes

8.4 Use Scientific Notation

QUESTION How can you use a graphing calculator to solve problems that involve numbers in scientific notation?

EXAMPLE Use numbers in scientific notation

Gold is one of many trace elements dissolved in seawater. There is about 1.1×10^{-8} gram of gold per kilogram of seawater. The mass of the oceans is about 1.4×10^{21} kilograms. About how much gold is present in the oceans?

STEP 1 *Write a verbal model*

Amount of gold present in oceans (grams)	=	Amount of gold in 1 kilogram of seawater (gram/kilogram)	•	Amount of seawater in oceans (kilograms)

STEP 2 *Find product* The product is $(1.1 \times 10^{-8}) \cdot (1.4 \times 10^{21})$.

(1.1 × 10 ^ (–) 8) (1.4 × 10 ^ 21) ENTER

STEP 3 *Read result*

The calculator indicates that a number is in scientific notation by using "E." You can read the calculator's result 1.54e13 as 1.54×10^{13}.

There are about 1.54×10^{13} grams of gold present in the oceans.

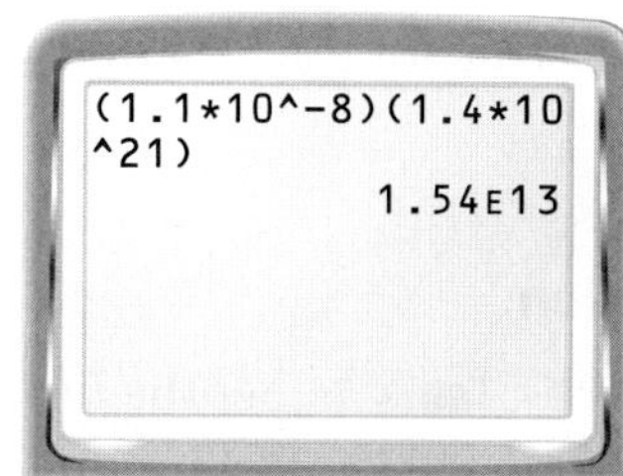

PRACTICE

Evaluate the expression. Write the result in scientific notation.

1. $(1.5 \times 10^4)(1.8 \times 10^9)$
2. $(2.6 \times 10^{-14})(1.4 \times 10^{20})$
3. $(7.0 \times 10^{25}) \div (2.8 \times 10^6)$
4. $(4.5 \times 10^{15}) \div (9.0 \times 10^{-2})$
5. **GASOLINE** A scientist estimates that it takes about 4.45×10^7 grams of carbon from ancient plant matter to produce 1 gallon of gasoline. In 2002 motor vehicles in the U.S. used about 1.37×10^{11} gallons of gasoline.
   a. If all of the gasoline used in 2002 by motor vehicles in the U.S. came from carbon from ancient plant matter, how many grams of carbon were used to produce the gasoline?
   b. There are about 5.0×10^{22} atoms of carbon in 1 gram of carbon. How many atoms of carbon were used?

8.5 Write and Graph Exponential Growth Functions

Before You wrote and graphed linear models.

Now You will write and graph exponential growth models.

Why? So you can find the value of a collector car, as in Example 4.

Key Vocabulary
- **exponential function**
- **exponential growth**
- **compound interest**

An **exponential function** is a function of the form $y = ab^x$ where $a \neq 0$, $b > 0$, and $b \neq 1$. Exponential functions are *nonlinear* functions. Observe how an exponential function compares with a linear function.

Linear function: $y = 3x + 2$

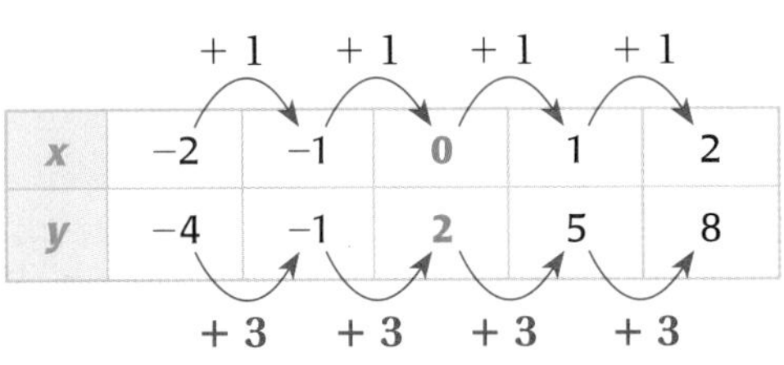

x	−2	−1	0	1	2
y	−4	−1	2	5	8

Exponential function: $y = 2 \cdot 3^x$

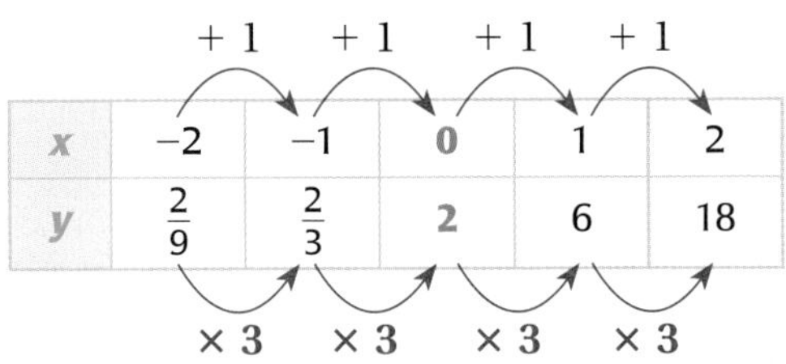

x	−2	−1	0	1	2
y	$\frac{2}{9}$	$\frac{2}{3}$	2	6	18

EXAMPLE 1 Write a function rule

Write a rule for the function.

x	−2	−1	0	1	2
y	2	4	8	16	32

Solution

STEP 1 **Tell** whether the function is exponential.

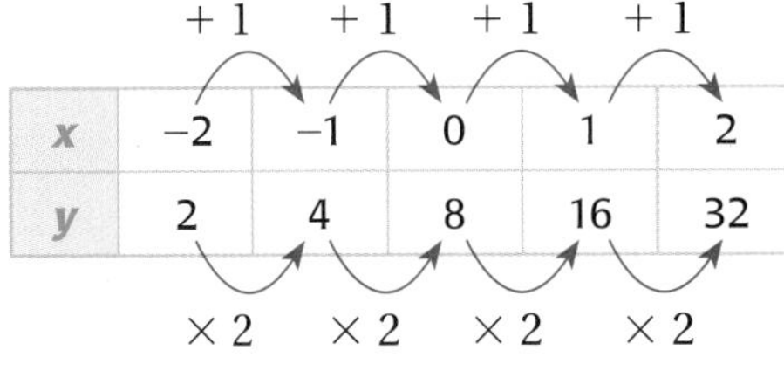

x	−2	−1	0	1	2
y	2	4	8	16	32

Here, the y-values are multiplied by 2 for each increase of 1 in x, so the table represents an exponential function of the form $y = ab^x$ where $b = 2$.

STEP 2 **Find** the value of a by finding the value of y when $x = 0$. When $x = 0$, $y = ab^0 = a \cdot 1 = a$. The value of y when $x = 0$ is 8, so $a = 8$.

STEP 3 **Write** the function rule. A rule for the function is $y = 8 \cdot 2^x$.

✓ GUIDED PRACTICE for Example 1

1. Write a rule for the function.

x	−2	−1	0	1	2
y	3	9	27	81	243

EXAMPLE 2 Graph an exponential function

Graph the function $y = 2^x$. Identify its domain and range.

Solution

READ A GRAPH
Notice that the graph has a *y*-intercept of 1 and that it gets closer to the negative *x*-axis as the *x*-values decrease.

STEP 1 **Make** a table by choosing a few values for x and finding the values of y. The domain is all real numbers.

x	−2	−1	0	1	2
y	$\frac{1}{4}$	$\frac{1}{2}$	1	2	4

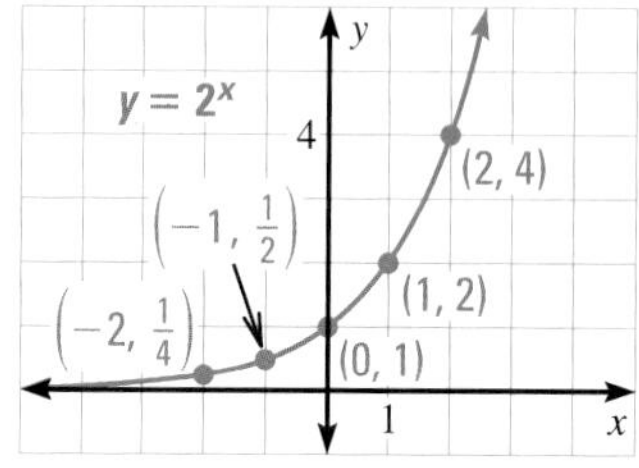

STEP 2 **Plot** the points.

STEP 3 **Draw** a smooth curve through the points. From either the table or the graph, you can see that the range is all positive real numbers.

EXAMPLE 3 Compare graphs of exponential functions

Graph the functions $y = 3 \cdot 2^x$ and $y = -3 \cdot 2^x$. Compare each graph with the graph of $y = 2^x$.

Solution

To graph each function, make a table of values, plot the points, and draw a smooth curve through the points.

x	$y = 2^x$	$y = 3 \cdot 2^x$	$y = -3 \cdot 2^x$
−2	$\frac{1}{4}$	$\frac{3}{4}$	$-\frac{3}{4}$
−1	$\frac{1}{2}$	$\frac{3}{2}$	$-\frac{3}{2}$
0	1	3	−3
1	2	6	−6
2	4	12	−12

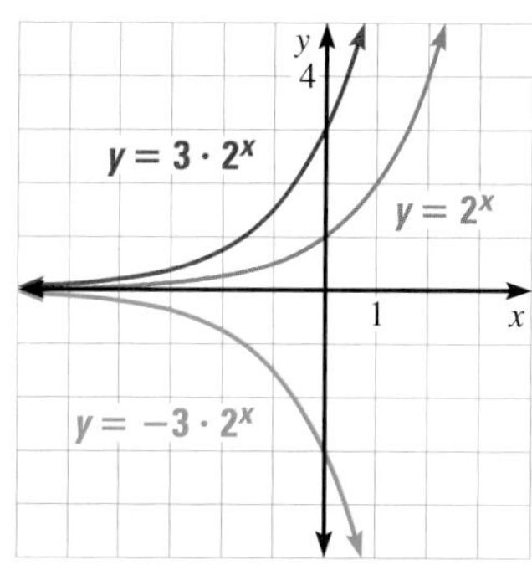

Because the *y*-values for $y = 3 \cdot 2^x$ are 3 times the corresponding *y*-values for $y = 2^x$, the graph of $y = 3 \cdot 2^x$ is a vertical stretch of the graph of $y = 2^x$.

Because the *y*-values for $y = -3 \cdot 2^x$ are −3 times the corresponding *y*-values for $y = 2^x$, the graph of $y = -3 \cdot 2^x$ is a vertical stretch with a reflection in the *x*-axis of the graph of $y = 2^x$.

✓ **GUIDED PRACTICE** for Examples 2 and 3

2. Graph $y = 5^x$ and identify its domain and range.

3. Graph $y = \frac{1}{3} \cdot 2^x$. Compare the graph with the graph of $y = 2^x$.

4. Graph $y = -\frac{1}{3} \cdot 2^x$. Compare the graph with the graph of $y = 2^x$.

EXPONENTIAL GROWTH When $a > 0$ and $b > 1$, the function $y = ab^x$ represents **exponential growth.** When a quantity grows exponentially, it increases by the same percent over equal time periods. To find the amount to which the quantity grows after t time periods, use the following model.

REWRITE EQUATIONS
Notice that you can rewrite $y = ab^x$ as $y = a(1 + r)^t$ by replacing b with $1 + r$ and x with t (for time).

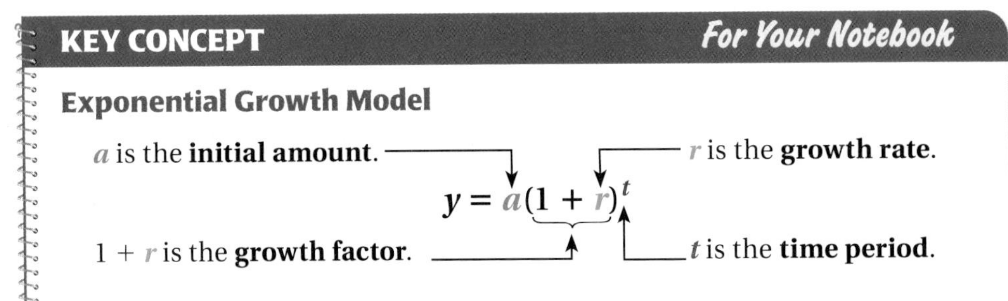

KEY CONCEPT
For Your Notebook
Exponential Growth Model
a is the initial amount.
r is the growth rate.
y = a(1 + r)^t
1 + r is the growth factor.
t is the time period.

Notice the relationship between the growth rate r and the growth factor $1 + r$. If the initial amount of a quantity is a units and the quantity is growing at a rate of r, then after one time period the new amount is:

$$\text{Initial amount} + \text{amount of increase} = a + r \cdot a = a(1 + r)$$

EXAMPLE 4 Solve a multi-step problem

ANOTHER WAY
For alternative methods for solving Example 4, turn to page 528 for the **Problem Solving Workshop**.

COLLECTOR CAR The owner of a 1953 Hudson Hornet convertible sold the car at an auction. The owner bought it in 1984 when its value was \$11,000. The value of the car increased at a rate of 6.9% per year.

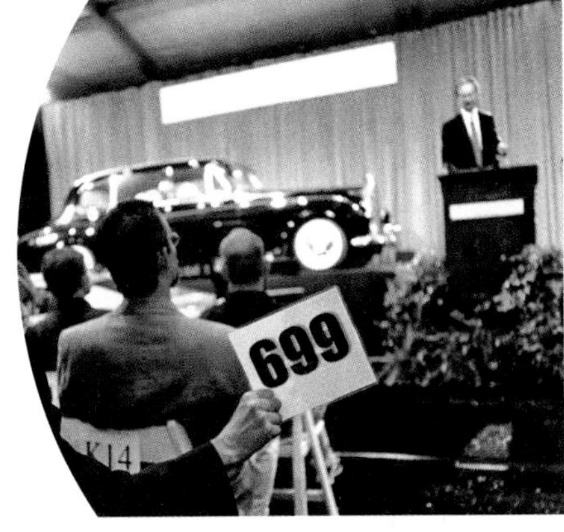

a. Write a function that models the value of the car over time.

b. The auction took place in 2004. What was the approximate value of the car at the time of the auction? Round your answer to the nearest dollar.

Solution

a. Let C be the value of the car (in dollars), and let t be the time (in years) since 1984. The initial value a is \$11,000, and the growth rate r is 0.069.

$C = a(1 + r)^t$ — **Write exponential growth model.**

$= 11{,}000(1 + 0.069)^t$ — **Substitute 11,000 for a and 0.069 for r.**

$= 11{,}000(1.069)^t$ — **Simplify.**

AVOID ERRORS
The growth rate in this example is 6.9%, or 0.069. So, the growth factor is 1 + 0.069, or 1.069, not 0.069.

b. To find the value of the car in 2004, 20 years after 1984, substitute 20 for t.

$C = 11{,}000(1.069)^{20}$ — **Substitute 20 for t.**

$\approx 41{,}778$ — **Use a calculator.**

▶ In 2004 the value of the car was about \$41,778.

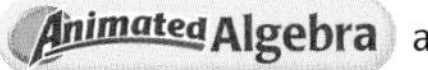 at classzone.com

COMPOUND INTEREST **Compound interest** is interest earned on both an initial investment and on previously earned interest. Compounding of interest can be modeled by exponential growth where a is the initial investment, r is the annual interest rate, and t is the number of years the money is invested.

EXAMPLE 5 Standardized Test Practice

You put \$250 in a savings account that earns 4% annual interest compounded yearly. You do not make any deposits or withdrawals. How much will your investment be worth in 5 years?

Ⓐ \$300 Ⓑ \$304.16 Ⓒ \$1344.56 Ⓓ \$781,250

ESTIMATE

You can use the simple interest formula, $I = prt$, to estimate the amount of interest earned: $(250)(0.04)(5) = 50$. Compounding interest will result in slightly more than \$50.

Solution

$y = a(1 + r)^t$ Write exponential growth model.

$= 250(1 + 0.04)^5$ Substitute 250 for a, 0.04 for r, and 5 for t.

$= 250(1.04)^5$ Simplify.

≈ 304.16 Use a calculator.

You will have \$304.16 in 5 years.

▶ The correct answer is B. Ⓐ Ⓑ Ⓒ Ⓓ

GUIDED PRACTICE for Examples 4 and 5

5. **WHAT IF?** In Example 4, suppose the owner of the car sold it in 1994. Find the value of the car to the nearest dollar.

6. **WHAT IF?** In Example 5, suppose the annual interest rate is 3.5%. How much will your investment be worth in 5 years?

8.5 EXERCISES

HOMEWORK KEY

○ = **WORKED-OUT SOLUTIONS** on p. WS19 for Exs. 13 and 41

★ = **STANDARDIZED TEST PRACTICE** Exs. 3, 8, 34, 35, 42, 43, 46, and 50

◆ = **MULTIPLE REPRESENTATIONS** Ex. 41

SKILL PRACTICE

1. **VOCABULARY** In the exponential growth model $y = a(1 + r)^t$, the quantity $1 + r$ is called the __?__.

2. **VOCABULARY** For what values of b does the exponential function $y = ab^x$ (where $a > 0$) represent exponential growth?

3. ★ **WRITING** How does the graph of $y = 2 \cdot 5^x$ compare with the graph of $y = 5^x$? *Explain.*

EXAMPLE 1 on p. 520 for Exs. 4–8

WRITING FUNCTIONS **Write a rule for the function.**

4.

x	−2	−1	0	1	2
y	1	2	4	8	16

5.

x	−2	−1	0	1	2
y	5	25	125	625	3125

6.

x	−2	−1	0	1	2
y	$\frac{1}{8}$	$\frac{1}{4}$	$\frac{1}{2}$	1	2

7.

x	−2	−1	0	1	2
y	$\frac{1}{81}$	$\frac{1}{27}$	$\frac{1}{9}$	$\frac{1}{3}$	1

8. ★ **WRITING** Given a table of values, describe how can you tell if the table represents a linear function or an exponential function.

EXAMPLE 2 on p. 521 for Exs. 9–21

GRAPHING FUNCTIONS **Graph the function and identify its domain and range.**

9. $y = 4^x$
10. $y = 7^x$
11. $y = 8^x$
12. $y = 9^x$
13. $y = (1.5)^x$
14. $y = (2.5)^x$
15. $y = (1.2)^x$
16. $y = (4.3)^x$
17. $y = \left(\frac{4}{3}\right)^x$
18. $y = \left(\frac{7}{2}\right)^x$
19. $y = \left(\frac{5}{3}\right)^x$
20. $y = \left(\frac{5}{4}\right)^x$

21. **ERROR ANALYSIS** The price P (in dollars) of a pound of flour was $.27 in 1999. The price has increased by about 2% each year. Let t be the number of years since 1999. *Describe* and correct the error in finding the price of a pound of flour in 2002.

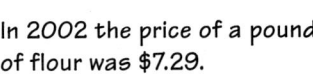

$P = a(1 + r)^t$

$= 0.27(1 + 2)^3 = 0.27(3)^3 = 7.29$

In 2002 the price of a pound of flour was $7.29.

EXAMPLE 3 on p. 521 for Exs. 22–34

COMPARING GRAPHS OF FUNCTIONS **Graph the function. Compare the graph with the graph of $y = 3^x$.**

22. $y = 2 \cdot 3^x$
23. $y = 4 \cdot 3^x$
24. $y = \frac{1}{4} \cdot 3^x$
25. $y = \frac{2}{3} \cdot 3^x$
26. $y = 0.5 \cdot 3^x$
27. $y = 2.5 \cdot 3^x$
28. $y = -2 \cdot 3^x$
29. $y = -4 \cdot 3^x$
30. $y = -\frac{1}{4} \cdot 3^x$
31. $y = -\frac{2}{3} \cdot 3^x$
32. $y = -0.5 \cdot 3^x$
33. $y = -2.5 \cdot 3^x$

34. ★ **MULTIPLE CHOICE** The graph of which function is shown?

Ⓐ $f(x) = 6^x$ Ⓑ $f(x) = \left(\frac{1}{3}\right)^x$

Ⓒ $f(x) = \frac{1}{3} \cdot 6^x$ Ⓓ $f(x) = 6 \cdot \left(\frac{1}{3}\right)^x$

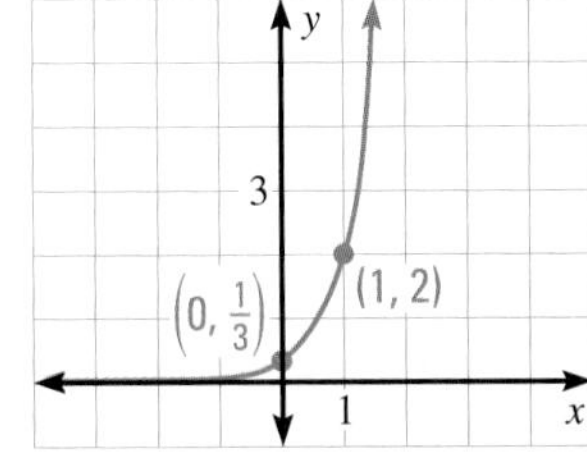

35. ★ **WRITING** If a population triples each year, what is the population's growth rate (as a percent)? *Explain.*

36. **CHALLENGE** Write a linear function and an exponential function whose graphs pass through the points (0, 2) and (1, 6).

37. **CHALLENGE** Compare the graph of the function $f(x) = 2^{x+2}$ with the graph of the function $g(x) = 4 \cdot 2^x$. Use properties of exponents to explain your observations.

○ = WORKED-OUT SOLUTIONS on p. WS1 ★ = STANDARDIZED TEST PRACTICE ◆ = MULTIPLE REPRESENTATIONS

PROBLEM SOLVING

GRAPHING CALCULATOR You may wish to use a graphing calculator to complete the following Problem Solving exercises.

EXAMPLES 4 and 5
on pp. 522–523 for Exs. 38–41

38. INVESTMENTS You deposit \$125 in a savings account that earns 5% annual interest compounded yearly. Find the balance in the account after the given amounts of time.

a. 1 year **b.** 2 years **c.** 5 years **d.** 20 years

@HomeTutor for problem solving help at classzone.com

39. MULTI-STEP PROBLEM One computer industry expert reported that there were about 600 million computers in use worldwide in 2001 and that the number was increasing at an annual rate of about 10%.

a. Write a function that models the number of computers in use over time.

b. Use the function to predict the number of computers that will be in use worldwide in 2009.

@HomeTutor for problem solving help at classzone.com

40. MULTI-STEP PROBLEM A research association reported that 3,173,000 gas grills were shipped by various manufacturers in the U.S. in 1985. Shipments increased by about 7% per year from 1985 to 2002.

a. Write a function that models the number of gas grills shipped over time.

b. About how many gas grills were shipped in 2002?

41. ◆ **MULTIPLE REPRESENTATIONS** A tree's cross-sectional area taken at a height of 4.5 feet from the ground is called its basal area and is measured in square inches. Tree growth can be measured by the growth of the tree's basal area. The initial basal area and annual growth rate for two particular trees are shown.

a. Writing a Model Write a function that models the basal area A of each tree over time.

b. Graphing a Function Use a graphing calculator to graph the functions from part (a) in the same coordinate plane. In about how many years will the trees have the same basal area?

42. ★ SHORT RESPONSE A company sells advertising blimps. The table shows the costs of advertising blimps of different lengths. Does the table represent an exponential function? *Explain.*

Length, ℓ (feet)	10	15	20	25
Cost, c (dollars)	400.00	700.00	1225.00	2143.75

43. ★ MULTIPLE CHOICE A weblog, or blog, refers to a website that contains a personal journal. According to one analyst, over one 18 month period, the number of blogs in existence doubled about every 6 months. The analyst estimated that there were about 600,000 blogs at the beginning of the period. How many blogs were there at the end of the period?

Ⓐ 660,000 Ⓑ 1,200,000 Ⓒ 4,800,000 Ⓓ 16,200,000

44. TELECOMMUNICATIONS For the period 1991–2001, the number y (in millions) of Internet users worldwide can be modeled by the function $y = 4.67(1.65)^x$ where x is the number of years since 1991.

a. Identify the initial amount, the growth factor, and the growth rate.

b. Graph the function. Identify its domain and range.

c. Use the graph to estimate the year in which the number of Internet users worldwide was about 21 million.

45. GRAPHING CALCULATOR The frequency (in hertz) of a note played on a piano is a function of the position of the key that creates the note. The position of some piano keys and the frequencies of the notes created by the keys are shown below. Use the exponential regression feature on a graphing calculator to find an exponential model for the frequency of piano notes. What is the frequency of the note created by the 30th key?

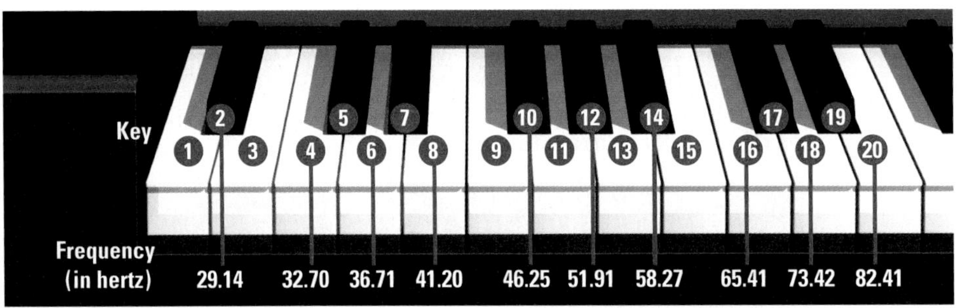

46. ★ EXTENDED RESPONSE In 1830, the population of the United States was 12,866,020. By 1890, the population was 62,947,714.

a. Model Assume the population growth from 1830 to 1890 was linear. Write a linear model for the U.S. population from 1830 to 1890. By about how much did the population grow per year from 1830 to 1890?

b. Model Assume the population growth from 1830 to 1890 was exponential. Write an exponential model for the U.S. population from 1830 to 1890. By approximately what percent did the population grow per year from 1830 to 1890?

c. Explain The U.S. population was 23,191,876 in 1850 and 38,558,371 in 1870. Which of the models in parts (a) and (b) is a better approximation of actual U.S. population for the time period 1850–1890? *Explain.*

★ = STANDARDIZED TEST PRACTICE

COMPOUND INTEREST **In Exercises 47–49, use the example below to find the balance of the account compounded with the given frequency.**

EXAMPLE **Use the general compound interest formula**

FINANCE You deposit $1000 in an account that pays 3% annual interest. Find the balance after 8 years if the interest is compounded monthly.

Solution

The general formula for compound interest is $A = P\left(1 + \frac{r}{n}\right)^{nt}$. In this formula, P is the initial amount, called principal, in an account that pays interest at an annual rate r and that is compounded n times per year. The amount A (in dollars) is the amount in the account after t years.

Here, the interest is compounded monthly. So, $n = 12$.

$A = P\left(1 + \frac{r}{n}\right)^{nt}$ — **Write compound interest formula.**

$= 1000\left(1 + \frac{0.03}{12}\right)^{12(8)}$ — **Substitute 1000 for *P*, 0.03 for *r*, 12 for *n*, and 8 for *t*.**

$= 1000(1.0025)^{96}$ — **Simplify.**

≈ 1270.868467 — **Use a calculator.**

▶ The account balance after 8 years will be about $1270.87.

47. Yearly **48.** Quarterly **49.** Daily ($n = 365$)

50. ★ **WRITING** Which compounding frequency yields the highest balance in the account in the example above: monthly, yearly, quarterly, or daily? *Explain* why this is so.

51. **CHALLENGE** You invest $500 in an account that earns interest compounded monthly. Use a table or graph to find the least annual interest rate (to the nearest tenth of a percent) that the account would have to earn if you want to have a balance of $600 in 4 years.

MIXED REVIEW

PREVIEW Prepare for Lesson 8.6 in Exs. 52–59.

Evaluate the expression.

52. $\left(\frac{1}{3}\right)^2$ *(p. 495)* **53.** $\left(\frac{1}{8}\right)^2$ *(p. 495)* **54.** $\left(\frac{1}{4}\right)^3$ *(p. 495)* **55.** $\left(\frac{1}{2}\right)^6$ *(p. 495)*

56. $\left(\frac{2}{3}\right)^{-2}$ *(p. 503)* **57.** $\left(\frac{7}{5}\right)^{-2}$ *(p. 503)* **58.** $\left(\frac{4}{3}\right)^{-3}$ *(p. 503)* **59.** $\left(\frac{3}{2}\right)^{-4}$ *(p. 503)*

Write an equation of the line shown. *(p. 283)*

60.

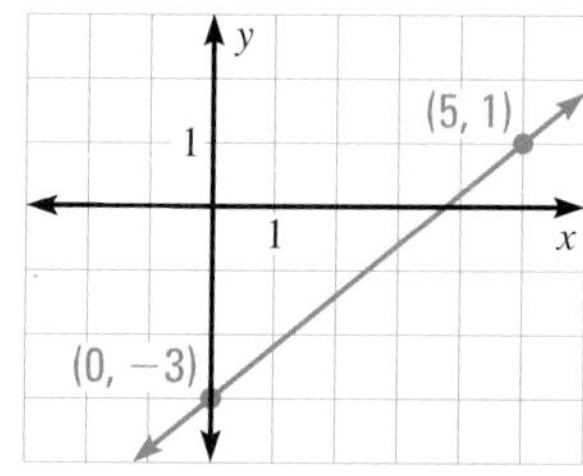

61.

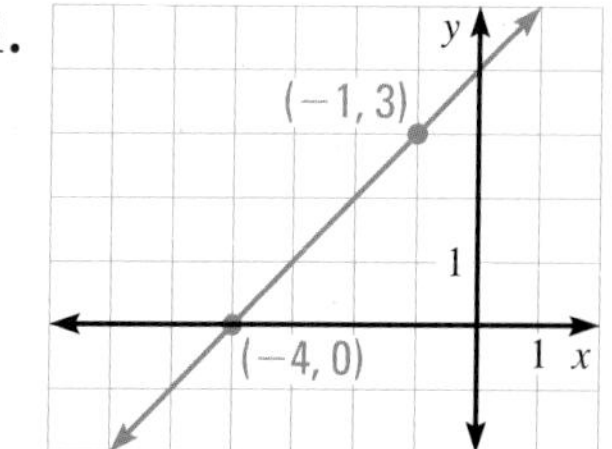

PROBLEM SOLVING WORKSHOP
LESSON 8.5

Using ALTERNATIVE METHODS

Another Way to Solve Example 4, page 522

MULTIPLE REPRESENTATIONS In Example 4 on page 522, you saw how to solve a problem about the value of a collector car over time by using an exponential model. You can also solve the problem by using a spreadsheet.

PROBLEM

COLLECTOR CAR The owner of a 1953 Hudson Hornet convertible sold the car at an auction. The owner bought it in 1984 when its value was \$11,000. The value of the car increased at a rate of 6.9% per year.

a. Write a function that models the value of the car over time.

b. The auction took place in 2004. What was the approximate value of the car at the time of the auction? Round your answer to the nearest dollar.

METHOD

Using a Spreadsheet An alternative approach is to use a spreadsheet.

a. The model for the value of the car over time is $C = 11{,}000(1.069)^t$, as shown in Example 4 on page 522.

b. You can find the value of the car in 2004 by creating a spreadsheet.

STEP 1 **Create** a table showing the years since 1984 and the value of the car. Enter the car's value in 1984. To find the value in any year after 1984, multiply the car's value in the preceding year by the growth factor, as shown in cell B3 below.

FORMAT A SPREADSHEET
Format the spreadsheet so that calculations are rounded to 2 decimal places.

	A	B
1	Years since 1984, *t*	Value, *C* (dollars)
2	0	11000
3	1	=B2*1.069

STEP 2 **Find** the value of the car in 2004 by using the *fill down* feature until you get to the desired cell.

	A	B
1	Years since 1984, *t*	Value, *C* (dollars)
2	0	11000
3	1	11759
...	...	...
21	19	39081.31
22	20	41777.92

▶ From the spreadsheet, you can see the value of the car was about \$41,778 in 2004.

PROBLEM

WHAT IF? Suppose the owner decided to sell the car when it was worth about \$28,000. In what year did the owner sell the car?

METHOD

Using a Spreadsheet To solve the equation algebraically, you need to substitute 28,000 for C and solve for t, but you have not yet learned how to solve this type of equation. An alternative to the algebraic approach is using a spreadsheet.

STEP 1 **Use** the same spreadsheet as on the previous page.

STEP 2 **Find** when the value of the car is about \$28,000.

	A	B
1	Years since 1984, *t*	Value, *C* (dollars)
2	0	11000
...	...	...
15	13	26188.03
16	14	27995.01

The value of the car is about \$28,000 when $t = 14$.

▶ The owner sold the car in 1998.

PRACTICE

1. **TRANSPORTATION** In 1997 the average intercity bus fare for a particular state was \$20. For the period 1997–2000, the bus fare increased at a rate of about 12% each year.
   a. Write a function that models the intercity bus fare for the period 1997–2000.
   b. Find the intercity bus fare in 1998. Use two different methods to solve the problem.
   c. In what year was the intercity bus fare \$28.10? *Explain* how you found your answer.

2. ERROR ANALYSIS *Describe* and correct the error in writing the function for part (a) of Exercise 1.

> Let b be the bus fare (in dollars) and t be the number of years since 1997.
> $b = 20(0.12)^t$ ✗

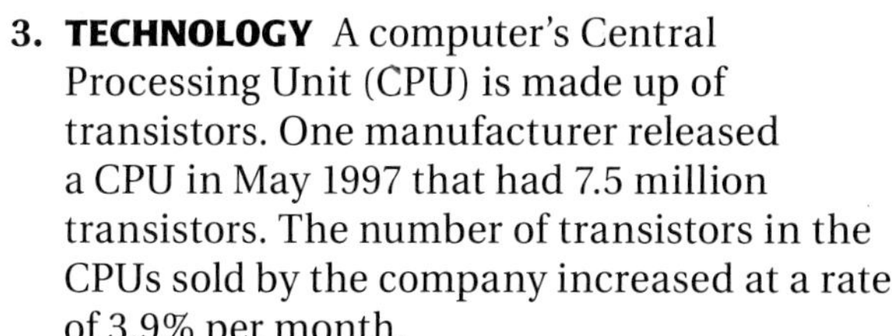

3. **TECHNOLOGY** A computer's Central Processing Unit (CPU) is made up of transistors. One manufacturer released a CPU in May 1997 that had 7.5 million transistors. The number of transistors in the CPUs sold by the company increased at a rate of 3.9% per month.
   a. Write a function that models the number T (in millions) of transistors in the company's CPUs t months after May 1997.
   b. Use a spreadsheet to find the number of transistors in a CPU released by the company in November 2000.

4. **HOUSING** The value of a home in 2002 was \$150,000. The value of the home increased at a rate of about 6.5% per year.
   a. Write a function that models the value of the home over time.
   b. Use a spreadsheet to find the year in which the value of the home was about \$200,000.

8.6 Exponential Models

MATERIALS • yarn • scissors

QUESTION **How can you model a situation using an exponential function?**

EXPLORE **Collect data so that you can write exponential models**

STEP 1 ***Fold and cut*** Take about 1 yard of yarn and consider it to be 1 unit long. Fold it in half and cut, as shown. You are left with two pieces of yarn, each half the length of the original piece of yarn.

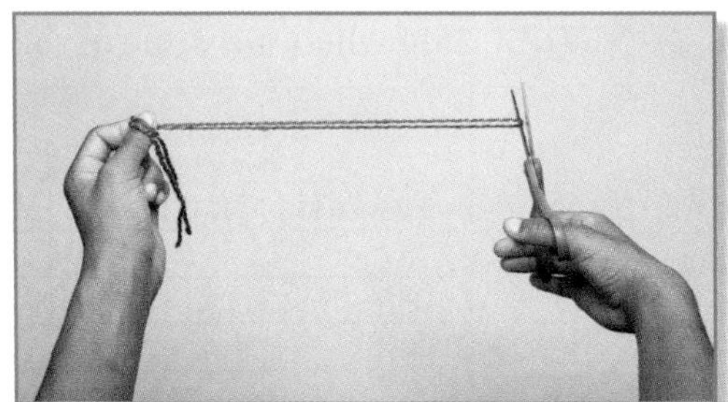

STEP 2 ***Copy and complete*** Copy the table. Notice that the row for stage 1 has the data from Step 1. For each successive stage, fold *all* the pieces of yarn in half and cut. Then record the number of new pieces and the length of each new piece until the table is complete.

Stage	Number of pieces	Length of each new piece
1	2	$\frac{1}{2}$
2	?	?
3	?	?
4	?	?
5	?	?

DRAW CONCLUSIONS **Use your observations to complete these exercises**

1. Use the data in the first and second columns of the table.
   a. Do the data represent an exponential function? *Explain* how you know.
   b. Write a function that models the number of pieces of yarn at stage x.
   c. Use the function to find the number of pieces of yarn at stage 10.
2. Use the data in the first and third columns of the table.
   a. Do the data represent an exponential function? *Explain* how you know.
   b. Write a function that models the length of each new piece of yarn at stage x.
   c. Use the function to find the length of each new piece of yarn at stage 10.

8.6 Write and Graph Exponential Decay Functions

Before You wrote and graphed exponential growth functions.

Now You will write and graph exponential decay functions.

Why? So you can use a graph to solve a sports problem, as in Ex. 50.

Key Vocabulary
- **exponential decay**

A table of values represents an exponential function $y = ab^x$ provided successive y-values are multiplied by b each time the x-values increase by 1.

EXAMPLE 1 Write a function rule

Tell whether the table represents an exponential function. If so, write a rule for the function.

a.

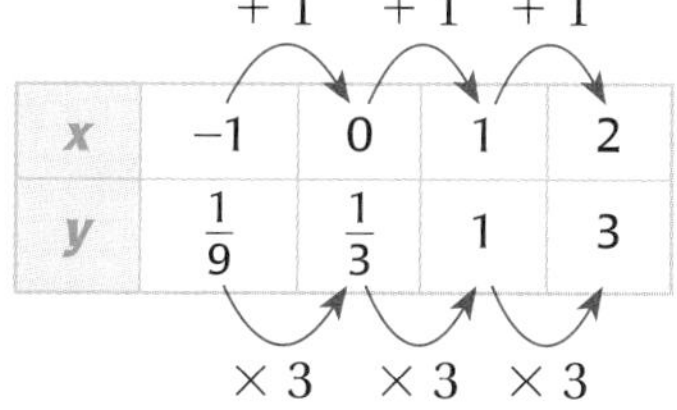

x	-1	0	1	2
y	$\frac{1}{9}$	$\frac{1}{3}$	1	3

The y-values are multiplied by 3 for each increase of 1 in x, so the table represents an exponential function of the form $y = ab^x$ with $b = 3$.

The value of y when $x = 0$ is $\frac{1}{3}$, so $a = \frac{1}{3}$.

The table represents the exponential function $y = \frac{1}{3} \cdot 3^x$.

b.

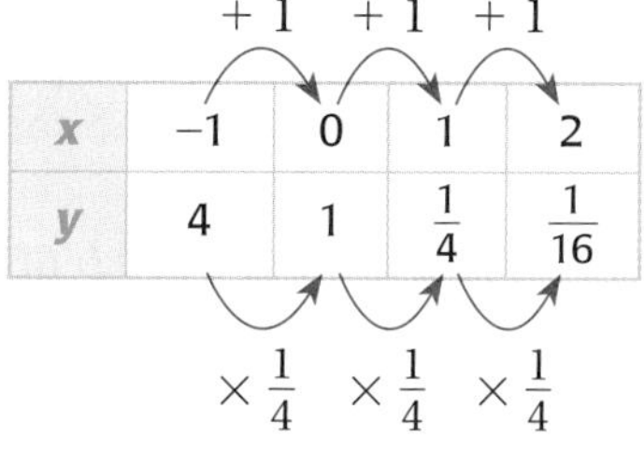

x	-1	0	1	2
y	4	1	$\frac{1}{4}$	$\frac{1}{16}$

The y-values are multiplied by $\frac{1}{4}$ for each increase of 1 in x, so the table represents an exponential function of the form $y = ab^x$ with $b = \frac{1}{4}$.

The value of y when $x = 0$ is 1, so $a = 1$.

The table represents the exponential function $y = \left(\frac{1}{4}\right)^x$.

✓ GUIDED PRACTICE for Example 1

1. Tell whether the table represents an exponential function. If so, write a rule for the function.

x	-1	0	1	2
y	5	1	$\frac{1}{5}$	$\frac{1}{25}$

EXAMPLE 2 Graph an exponential function

Graph the function $y = \left(\frac{1}{2}\right)^x$ and identify its domain and range.

Solution

READA GRAPH
Notice that the graph has a *y*-intercept of 1 and that it gets closer to the positive *x*-axis as the *x*-values increase.

STEP 1 **Make** a table of values. The domain is all real numbers.

x	-2	-1	0	1	2
y	4	2	1	$\frac{1}{2}$	$\frac{1}{4}$

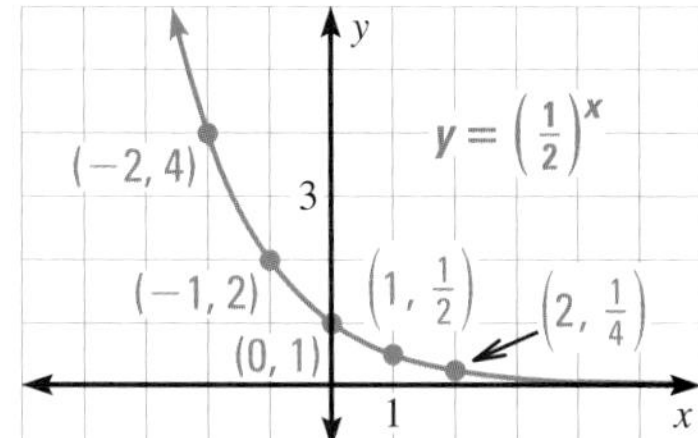

STEP 2 **Plot** the points.

STEP 3 **Draw** a smooth curve through the points. From either the table or the graph, you can see the range is all positive real numbers.

EXAMPLE 3 Compare graphs of exponential functions

Graph the functions $y = 3 \cdot \left(\frac{1}{2}\right)^x$ and $y = -\frac{1}{3} \cdot \left(\frac{1}{2}\right)^x$. Compare each graph with the graph of $y = \left(\frac{1}{2}\right)^x$.

Solution

x	$y = \left(\frac{1}{2}\right)^x$	$y = 3 \cdot \left(\frac{1}{2}\right)^x$	$y = -\frac{1}{3} \cdot \left(\frac{1}{2}\right)^x$
-2	4	12	$-\frac{4}{3}$
-1	2	6	$-\frac{2}{3}$
0	1	3	$-\frac{1}{3}$
1	$\frac{1}{2}$	$\frac{3}{2}$	$-\frac{1}{6}$
2	$\frac{1}{4}$	$\frac{3}{4}$	$-\frac{1}{12}$

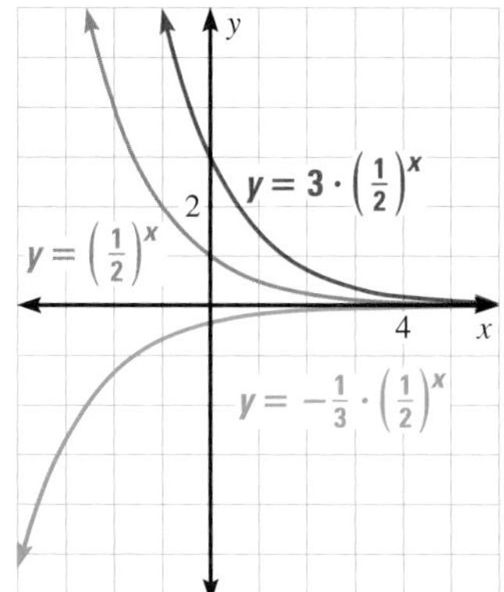

Because the *y*-values for $y = 3 \cdot \left(\frac{1}{2}\right)^x$ are 3 times the corresponding *y*-values for $y = \left(\frac{1}{2}\right)^x$, the graph of $y = 3 \cdot \left(\frac{1}{2}\right)^x$ is a vertical stretch of the graph of $y = \left(\frac{1}{2}\right)^x$.

Because the *y*-values for $y = -\frac{1}{3} \cdot \left(\frac{1}{2}\right)^x$ are $-\frac{1}{3}$ times the corresponding *y*-values for $y = \left(\frac{1}{2}\right)^x$, the graph of $y = -\frac{1}{3} \cdot \left(\frac{1}{2}\right)^x$ is a vertical shrink with reflection in the *x*-axis of the graph of $y = \left(\frac{1}{2}\right)^x$.

GUIDED PRACTICE for Examples 2 and 3

2. Graph $y = (0.4)^x$ and identify its domain and range.
3. Graph $y = 5 \cdot (0.4)^x$. Compare the graph with the graph of $y = (0.4)^x$.

COMPARE GRAPHS When $a > 0$ and $0 < b < 1$, the function $y = ab^x$ represents **exponential decay**. The graph of an exponential decay function falls from left to right. In comparison, the graph of an exponential growth function $y = ab^x$ where $a > 0$ and $b > 1$ rises from the left.

EXAMPLE 4 Classify and write rules for functions

Tell whether the graph represents *exponential growth* or *exponential decay*. Then write a rule for the function.

a.

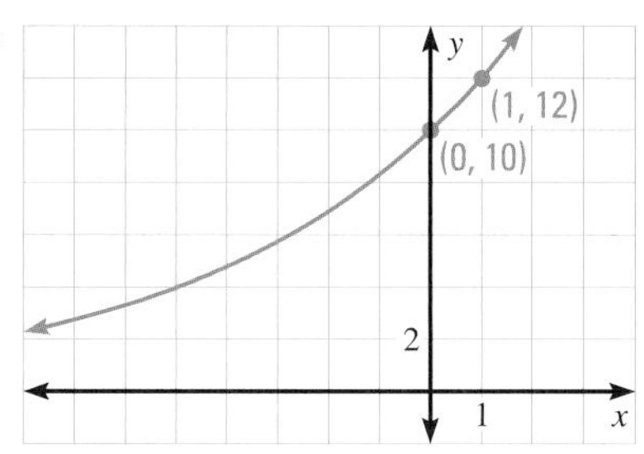

b.

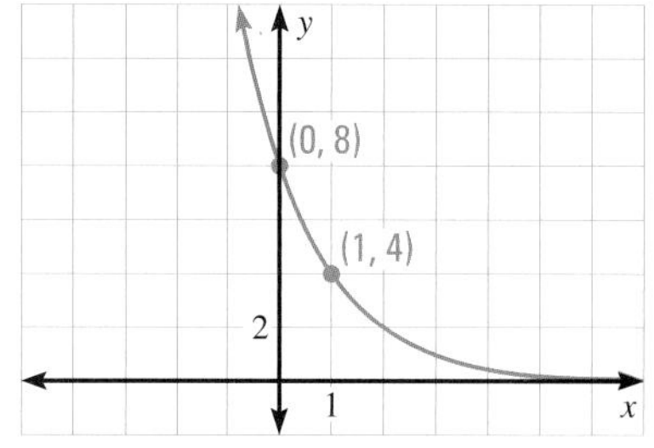

ANALYZE GRAPHS

For the function $y = ab^x$, where $x = 0$, the value of y is $y = ax^0 = a$. This means that the graph of $y = ab^x$ has a y-intercept of a.

Solution

a. The graph represents exponential growth ($y = ab^x$ where $b > 1$). The y-intercept is 10, so $a = 10$. Find the value of b by using the point (1, 12) and $a = 10$.

$y = ab^x$	**Write function.**
$12 = 10 \cdot b^1$	**Substitute.**
$1.2 = b$	**Solve.**

A function rule is $y = 10(1.2)^x$.

b. The graph represents exponential decay ($y = ab^x$ where $0 < b < 1$). The y-intercept is 8, so $a = 8$. Find the value of b by using the point (1, 4) and $a = 8$.

$y = ab^x$	**Write function.**
$4 = 8 \cdot b^1$	**Substitute.**
$0.5 = b$	**Solve.**

A function rule is $y = 8(0.5)^x$.

✓ **GUIDED PRACTICE** for Example 4

4. The graph of an exponential function passes through the points (0, 10) and (1, 8). Graph the function. Tell whether the graph represents *exponential growth* or *exponential decay*. Write a rule for the function.

CONCEPT SUMMARY *For Your Notebook*

Exponential Growth and Decay

Exponential Growth

$y = ab^x$, $a > 0$ and $b > 1$

(0, a)

Exponential Decay

$y = ab^x$, $a > 0$ and $0 < b < 1$

(0, a)

EXPONENTIAL DECAY When a quantity decays exponentially, it decreases by the same percent over equal time periods. To find the amount of the quantity left after t time periods, use the following model.

REWRITE EQUATIONS

Notice that you can rewrite $y = ab^x$ as $y = a(1 - r)^t$ by replacing b with $1 - r$ and x with t (for time).

KEY CONCEPT *For Your Notebook*

Exponential Decay Model

$$y = a(1 - r)^t$$

a is the **initial amount.**

r is the **decay rate.**

$1 - r$ is the **decay factor.**

t is the **time period.**

The relationship between the decay rate r and the decay factor $1 - r$ is similar to the relationship between the growth rate and growth factor in an exponential growth model. You will explore this relationship in Exercise 45.

EXAMPLE 5 Solve a multi-step problem

FORESTRY The number of acres of Ponderosa pine forests decreased in the western United States from 1963 to 2002 by 0.5% annually. In 1963 there were about 41 million acres of Ponderosa pine forests.

a. Write a function that models the number of acres of Ponderosa pine forests in the western United States over time.

b. To the nearest tenth, about how many million acres of Ponderosa pine forests were there in 2002?

Solution

a. Let P be the number of acres (in millions), and let t be the time (in years) since 1963. The initial value is 41, and the decay rate is 0.005.

$P = a(1 - r)^t$ **Write exponential decay model.**

$= 41(1 - 0.005)^t$ **Substitute 41 for *a* and 0.005 for *r*.**

$= 41(0.995)^t$ **Simplify.**

AVOID ERRORS

The decay rate in this example is 0.5%, or 0.005. So, the decay factor is 1 − 0.005, or 0.995, not 0.005.

b. To find the number of acres in 2002, 39 years after 1963, substitute 39 for t.

$P = 41(0.995)^{39} \approx 33.7$ **Substitute 39 for *t*. Use a calculator.**

▶ There were about 33.7 million acres of Ponderosa pine forests in 2002.

Animated **Algebra** at classzone.com

✓ **GUIDED PRACTICE** for Example 5

5. WHAT IF? In Example 5, suppose the decay rate of the forests remains the same beyond 2002. About how many acres will be left in 2010?

8.6 EXERCISES

HOMEWORK KEY

○ = **WORKED-OUT SOLUTIONS** on p. WS19 for Exs. 7 and 49

★ = **STANDARDIZED TEST PRACTICE** Exs. 2, 19, 36, 45, and 49

◆ = **MULTIPLE REPRESENTATIONS** Ex. 50

SKILL PRACTICE

1. **VOCABULARY** What is the decay factor in the exponential decay model $y = a(1 - r)^t$?

2. ★ **WRITING** *Explain* how you can tell if a graph represents *exponential growth* or *exponential decay.*

EXAMPLE 1 on p. 531 for Exs. 3–6

WRITING FUNCTIONS **Tell whether the table represents an exponential function. If so, write a rule for the function.**

3.

x	−1	0	1	2
y	2	8	32	128

4.

x	−1	0	1	2
y	50	10	2	0.4

5.

x	−1	0	1	2
y	6	2	$\frac{2}{3}$	$\frac{2}{9}$

6.

x	−1	0	1	2
y	−11	−7	−3	1

EXAMPLE 2 on p. 532 for Exs. 7–18

GRAPHING FUNCTIONS **Graph the function and identify its domain and range.**

7. $y = \left(\frac{1}{5}\right)^x$
8. $y = \left(\frac{1}{6}\right)^x$
9. $y = \left(\frac{2}{3}\right)^x$
10. $y = \left(\frac{3}{4}\right)^x$
11. $y = \left(\frac{4}{5}\right)^x$
12. $y = \left(\frac{3}{5}\right)^x$
13. $y = (0.3)^x$
14. $y = (0.5)^x$
15. $y = (0.1)^x$
16. $y = (0.9)^x$
17. $y = (0.7)^x$
18. $y = (0.25)^x$

EXAMPLE 3 on p. 532 for Exs. 19–31

19. ★ **MULTIPLE CHOICE** The graph of which function is shown?

Ⓐ $y = (0.25)^x$ Ⓑ $y = (0.5)^x$

Ⓒ $y = 0.25 \cdot (0.5)^x$ Ⓓ $y = 4 \cdot (0.5)^x$

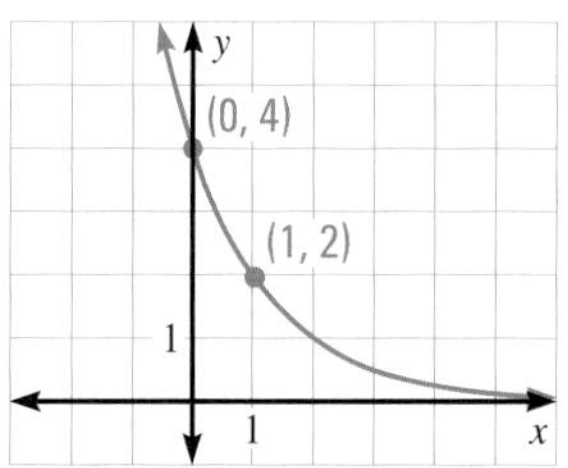

COMPARING FUNCTIONS **Graph the function. Compare the graph with the graph of $y = \left(\frac{1}{4}\right)^x$.**

20. $y = 5 \cdot \left(\frac{1}{4}\right)^x$
21. $y = 3 \cdot \left(\frac{1}{4}\right)^x$
22. $y = \frac{1}{2} \cdot \left(\frac{1}{4}\right)^x$
23. $y = \frac{1}{3} \cdot \left(\frac{1}{4}\right)^x$
24. $y = 0.2 \cdot \left(\frac{1}{4}\right)^x$
25. $y = 1.5 \cdot \left(\frac{1}{4}\right)^x$
26. $y = -5 \cdot \left(\frac{1}{4}\right)^x$
27. $y = -3 \cdot \left(\frac{1}{4}\right)^x$
28. $y = -\frac{1}{2} \cdot \left(\frac{1}{4}\right)^x$
29. $y = -\frac{1}{3} \cdot \left(\frac{1}{4}\right)^x$
30. $y = -0.2 \cdot \left(\frac{1}{4}\right)^x$
31. $y = -1.5 \cdot \left(\frac{1}{4}\right)^x$

MATCHING Match the function with its graph.

32. $y = (0.2)^x$

33. $y = 5(0.2)^x$

34. $y = \frac{1}{2}(0.2)^x$

A.

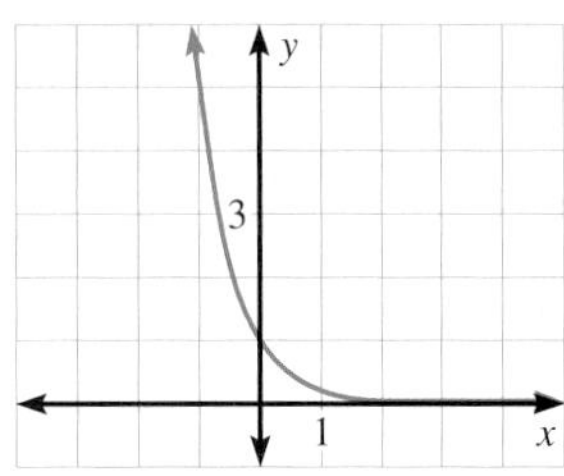

B.

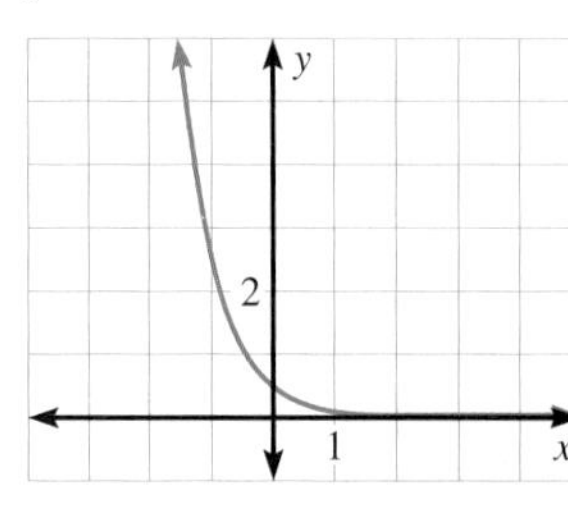

C.

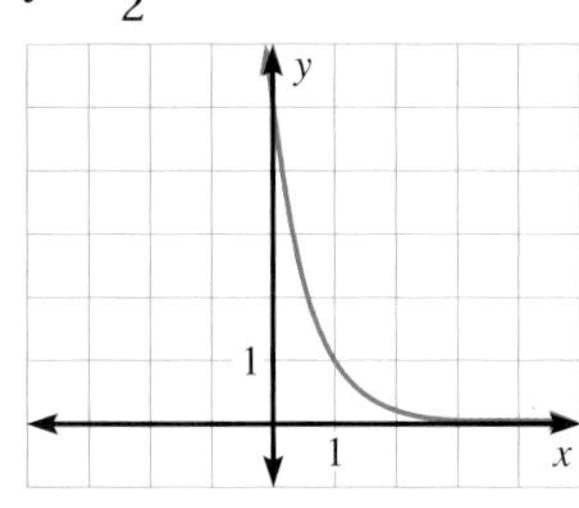

35. **POPULATION** A population of 90,000 decreases by 2.5% per year. Identify the initial amount, the decay factor, and the decay rate. Then write a function that models the population over time.

36. ★ **MULTIPLE CHOICE** What is the decay rate of the function $y = 4(0.97)^t$?

Ⓐ 4 Ⓑ 0.97 Ⓒ 0.3 Ⓓ 0.03

37. **ERROR ANALYSIS** In 2004 a person purchased a car for \$25,000. The value of the car decreased by 14% annually. *Describe* and correct the error in writing a function that models the value of the car since 2004.

$y = a(1 - r)^t$
$= 25{,}000(0.14)^t$

EXAMPLE 4 on p. 533 for Exs. 38–40

RECOGNIZING EXPONENTIAL MODELS Tell whether the graph represents *exponential growth* or *exponential decay*. Then write a rule for the function.

38.

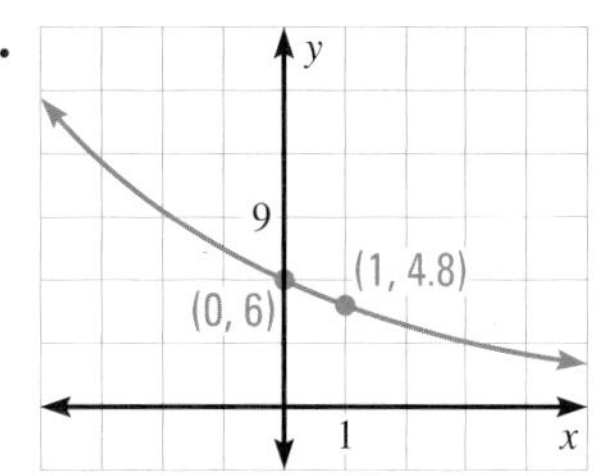

39.

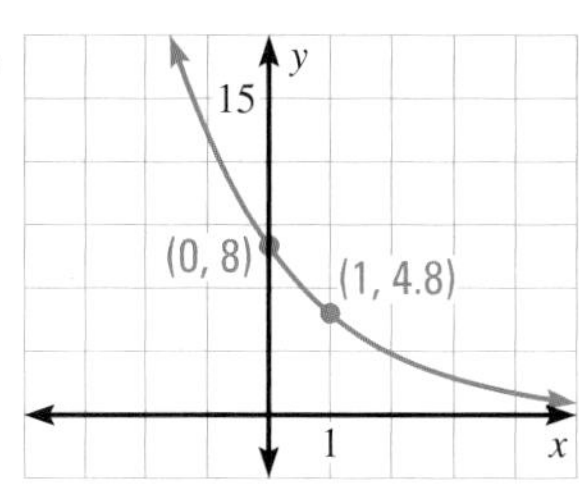

40.

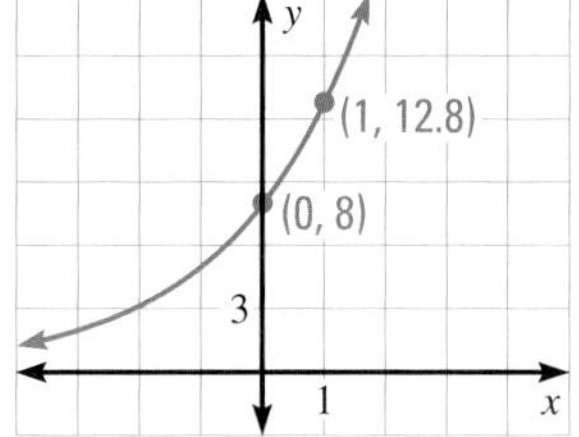

Animated Algebra at classzone.com

41. **REASONING** Without graphing, explain how the graphs of the given functions are related to the graph of $f(x) = (0.5)^x$.

a. $m(x) = \frac{1}{3} \cdot (0.5)^x$

b. $n(x) = -4 \cdot (0.5)^x$

c. $p(x) = (0.5)^x + 1$

CHALLENGE Write an exponential function of the form $y = ab^x$ whose graph passes through the given points.

42. $(0, 1), \left(2, \frac{1}{4}\right)$

43. $(1, 20), (2, 4)$

44. $\left(1, \frac{3}{2}\right), \left(2, \frac{3}{4}\right)$

45. ★ **WRITING** The initial amount of a quantity is a units and the quantity is decaying at a rate of r (a percent per time period). Show that the amount of the quantity after one time period is $a(1 - r)$. *Explain* how you found your answer.

46. **CHALLENGE** Compare the graph of the function $f(x) = 4^{x-2}$ with the graph of the function $g(x) = \frac{1}{16} \cdot 4^x$. Use properties of exponents to explain your observation.

PROBLEM SOLVING

GRAPHING CALCULATOR **You may wish to use a graphing calculator to complete the following Problem Solving exercises.**

EXAMPLE 5
on p. 534
for Exs. 47–50

47. **CELL PHONES** You purchase a cell phone for \$125. The value of the cell phone decreases by about 20% annually. Write a function that models the value of the cell phone over time. Then find the value of the cell phone after 3 years.

@HomeTutor for problem solving help at classzone.com

48. **ANIMAL POPULATION** Scientists studied the population of a species of bat in some caves in Missouri from 1983 to 2003. In 1983, there were 141,200 bats living in the caves. That number decreased by about 11% annually until 2003.

   a. Identify the initial amount, the decay factor, and the decay rate.

   b. Write a function that models the number of bats since 1983. Then find the number of bats in 2003.

@HomeTutor for problem solving help at classzone.com

49. ★ **SHORT RESPONSE** In 2003 a family bought a boat for \$4000. The boat depreciates (loses value) at a rate of 7% annually. In 2006 a person offers to buy the boat for \$3000. Should the family sell the boat? *Explain.*

50. **MULTIPLE REPRESENTATIONS** There are a total of 128 teams at the start of a citywide 3-on-3 basketball tournament. Half of the teams are eliminated after each round.

   a. **Writing a Model** Write a function for the number of teams left after x rounds.

   b. **Making a Table** Make a table for the function using $x = 0, 1, 2, \ldots, 7$.

   c. **Drawing a Graph** Use the table in part (b) to graph the function. After which round are there 4 teams left in the tournament?

51. **GUITARS** The frets on a guitar are the small metal bars that divide the fingerboard. The distance d (in inches) between the nut and the first fret or any two consecutive frets can be modeled by the function $d = 1.516(0.9439)^f$ where f is the number of the fret farthest from the nut.

   a. Identify the decay factor and the decay rate for the model.

   b. What is the distance between the nut and the first fret?

   c. The distance between the 12th and 13th frets is about half the distance between the nut and the first fret. Use this fact to find the distance between the 12th and 13th frets. Use the model to verify your answer.

52. **CHALLENGE** A college student finances a computer that costs \$1850. The financing plan states that as long as a minimum monthly payment of 2.25% of the remaining balance is made, the student does not have to pay interest for 24 months. The student makes only the minimum monthly payments until the last payment. What is the amount of the last payment if the student buys the computer without paying interest? Round your answer to the nearest cent.

53. **MULTI-STEP PROBLEM** Maximal oxygen consumption is the maximum volume of oxygen (in liters per minute) that the body uses during exercise. Maximal oxygen consumption varies from person to person and decreases with age by about 0.5% per year after age 25 for active adults.

  a. **Model** A 25-year-old female athlete has a maximal oxygen consumption of 4 liters per minute. Another 25-year-old female athlete has a maximal oxygen consumption of 3.5 liters per minute. Write a function for each athlete that models the maximal consumption each year after age 25.
  b. **Graph** Graph the models in the same coordinate plane.
  c. **Estimate** About how old will the first athlete be when her maximal oxygen consumption is equal to what the second athlete's maximal oxygen consumption is at age 25?

MIXED REVIEW

PREVIEW Prepare for Lesson 9.1 in Exs. 54–62.

Simplify the expression. *(p. 96)*

54. $-12x + (-3x)$
55. $8x - 3x$
56. $14 + x + 2x$
57. $7(2x + 1) - 5$
58. $13x + (x - 4)5$
59. $3x + 6(x + 9)$
60. $(5 - x) + x$
61. $(3x - 4)7 + 21$
62. $-(x - 1) - x^2$

Solve the equation.

63. $x + 14 = 8$ *(p. 134)*
64. $8x - 7 = 17$ *(p. 141)*
65. $4x + 2x - 6 = 18$ *(p. 148)*
66. $2x - 7(x + 5) = 20$ *(p. 148)*

QUIZ *for Lessons 8.5–8.6*

Graph the function.

1. $y = \left(\frac{5}{2}\right)^x$ *(p. 520)*
2. $y = 3 \cdot \left(\frac{1}{4}\right)^x$ *(p. 531)*
3. $y = \frac{1}{4} \cdot 3^x$ *(p. 520)*
4. $y = (0.1)^x$ *(p. 531)*
5. $y = 10 \cdot 5^x$ *(p. 520)*
6. $y = 7(0.4)^x$ *(p. 531)*

7. **COINS** You purchase a coin from a coin collector for \$25. Each year the value of the coin increases by 8%. Write a function that models the value of the coin over time. Then find the value of the coin after 10 years. Round to the nearest cent. *(p. 520)*

Extension
Use after Lesson 8.6

Relate Geometric Sequences to Exponential Functions

GOAL Identify, graph, and write geometric sequences.

Key Vocabulary
- **geometric sequence**
- **common ratio**

In a **geometric sequence**, the ratio of any term to the previous term is constant. This constant ratio is called the **common ratio** and is denoted by r.

A geometric sequence with first term a_1 and common ratio r has the form a_1, a_1r, a_1r^2, a_1r^3, ... For instance, if $a_1 = 5$ and $r = 2$, the sequence 5, $5 \cdot 2$, $5 \cdot 2^2$, $5 \cdot 2^3$, . . . , or 5, 10, 20, 40, . . . , is geometric.

EXAMPLE 1 Identify a geometric sequence

Tell whether the sequence is *arithmetic* or *geometric*. Then write the next term of the sequence.

a. 3, 6, 9, 12, 15, . . .

b. 128, 64, 32, 16, 8, . . .

Solution

a. The first term is $a_1 = 3$. Find the ratios of consecutive terms:

$$\frac{a_2}{a_1} = \frac{6}{3} = 2 \qquad \frac{a_3}{a_2} = \frac{9}{6} = 1\frac{1}{2} \qquad \frac{a_4}{a_3} = \frac{12}{9} = 1\frac{1}{3} \qquad \frac{a_5}{a_4} = \frac{15}{12} = 1\frac{1}{4}$$

Because the ratios are not constant, the sequence is not geometric. To see if the sequence is arithmetic, find the differences of consecutive terms.

$$a_2 - a_1 = 6 - 3 = 3 \qquad a_3 - a_2 = 9 - 6 = 3$$

$$a_4 - a_3 = 12 - 9 = 3 \qquad a_5 - a_4 = 15 - 12 = 3$$

The common difference is 3, so the sequence is arithmetic. The next term of the sequence is $a_6 = a_5 + 3 = 18$.

b. The first term is $a_1 = 128$. Find the ratios of consecutive terms:

$$\frac{a_2}{a_1} = \frac{64}{128} = \frac{1}{2} \qquad \frac{a_3}{a_2} = \frac{32}{64} = \frac{1}{2} \qquad \frac{a_4}{a_3} = \frac{16}{32} = \frac{1}{2} \qquad \frac{a_5}{a_4} = \frac{8}{16} = \frac{1}{2}$$

Because the ratios are constant, the sequence is geometric. The common ratio is $\frac{1}{2}$. The next term of the sequence is $a_6 = a_5 \cdot \frac{1}{2} = 4$.

REVIEW ARITHMETIC SEQUENCES
For help with identifying an arithmetic sequence and finding a common difference, see p. 309.

EXAMPLE 2 Graph a geometric sequence

ANALYZE A GRAPH
Notice that the graph in Example 2 appears to be exponential.

To graph the sequence from part (b) of Example 1, let each term's position number in the sequence be the x-value. The term is the corresponding y-value. Then make and plot the points.

Position, x	1	2	3	4	5
Term, y	128	64	32	16	8

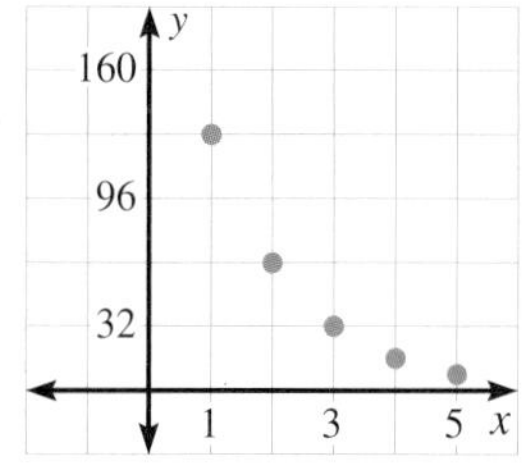

FUNCTIONS The table shows that a rule for finding the nth term of a geometric sequence is $a_n = a_1r^{n-1}$. Notice that the rule is an exponential function.

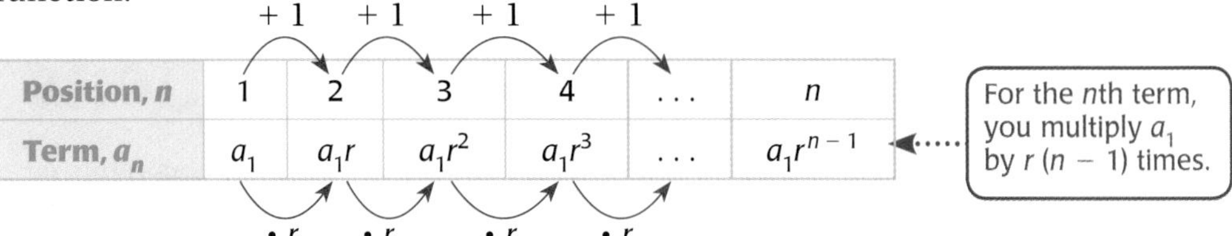

Position, n	1	2	3	4	. . .	n
Term, a_n	a_1	a_1r	a_1r^2	a_1r^3	. . .	a_1r^{n-1}

KEY CONCEPT *For Your Notebook*

General Rule for a Geometric Sequence

The nth term of a geometric sequence with first term a_1 and common ratio r is given by: $a_n = a_1r^{n-1}$.

EXAMPLE 3 Write a rule for a geometric sequence

Write a rule for the *n*th term of the geometric sequence in Example 1. Then find a_{10}.

Solution

To write a rule for the nth term of the sequence, substitute the values for a_1 and r in the general rule $a_n = a_1r^{n-1}$. Because $a_1 = 128$ and $r = \frac{1}{2}$, $a_n = 128 \cdot \left(\frac{1}{2}\right)^{n-1}$. The 10th term of the sequence is $a_{10} = 128 \cdot \left(\frac{1}{2}\right)^{10-1} = \frac{1}{4}$.

PRACTICE

EXAMPLES 1, 2, and 3 on pp. 539–540 for Exs. 1–10

Tell whether the sequence is *arithmetic* or *geometric*. Then graph the sequence.

1. 3, 12, 48, 192, . . .
2. 7, 16, 25, 34, . . .
3. 34, 28, 22, 16, . . .
4. 1024, 128, 16, 2, . . .
5. 9, −18, 36, −72, . . .
6. 29, 43, 57, 71, . . .

Write a rule for the *n*th term of the geometric sequence. Then find a_7.

7. 1, −5, 25, −125, . . .
8. 13, 26, 52, 104, . . .
9. 432, 72, 12, 2, . . .

10. **E-MAIL** A chain e-mail instructs the recipient to forward the e-mail to four more people. The table shows the number of rounds of sending the e-mail and the number of new e-mails generated. Write a rule for the nth term of the sequence. Then graph the first six terms of the sequence.

Number of rounds sending e-mail, n	1	2	3	4
Number of new e-mails generated, a_n	1	4	16	64

Lessons 8.4–8.6

1. **MULTI-STEP PROBLEM** The radius of the sun is about 96,600,000 kilometers. The radius of Earth is about 6370 kilometers.
   - **a.** Write each radius in scientific notation.
   - **b.** The surface area S of a sphere with radius r is given by $S = 4\pi r^2$. Assume the sun and Earth are perfect spheres. Find their surface areas. Write your answers in scientific notation.
   - **c.** What is the ratio of the surface area of the sun to the surface area of Earth? What does the ratio tell you?

2. **SHORT RESPONSE** The graph shows the value of a truck over time.

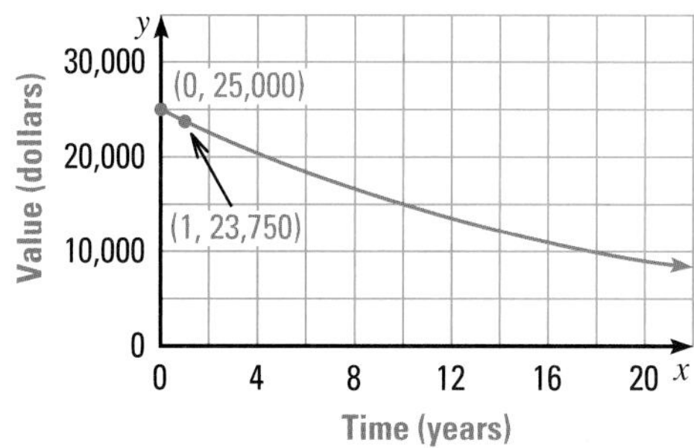

   - **a.** Write an equation for the function whose graph is shown.
   - **b.** At what rate is the truck losing value? *Explain.*

3. **GRIDDED ANSWER** A new laptop computer costs \$2000. The value of the computer decreases over time. The value V (in dollars) of the computer after t years is given by the function $V = 2000(0.82)^t$. What is the decay rate, written as a decimal, of the value of the computer?

4. **OPEN-ENDED** The value of a house in Iowa increased, on average, at a rate of about 4% per quarter from the first quarter in 2001 to the last quarter in 2004. Write a function that models the value of the house over time. Choose an initial value of the house and a quarter such that the value of the house is about \$275,000.

5. **EXTENDED RESPONSE** A musician is saving money to buy a new snare drum. The musician puts \$100 in a savings account that pays 3% annual interest compounded yearly.

   - **a.** Write a function that models the amount of money in the account over time.
   - **b.** Graph the function.
   - **c.** The musician wants a drum that costs \$149.95. Will there be enough in the account after 3 years? *Explain.*

6. **MULTI-STEP PROBLEM** The graph shows the value of a business over time.

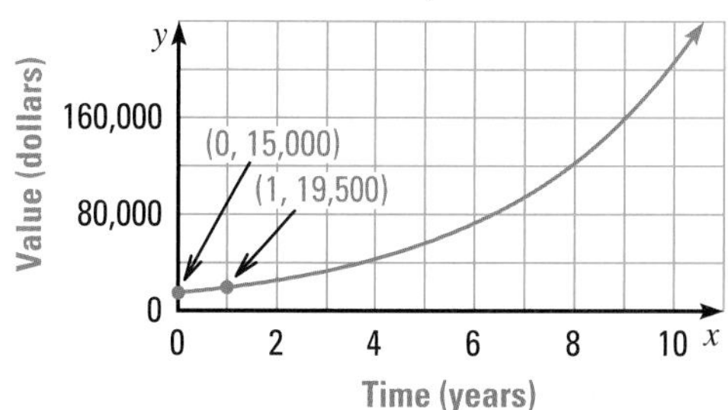

   - **a.** Does the graph represent *exponential growth* or *exponential decay*?
   - **b.** Write a function that models the value of the business over time.
   - **c.** How much is the business worth after 4 years?

7. **MULTI-STEP PROBLEM** The half-life of a medication is the time it takes for the medication to reduce to half of its original amount in a patient's bloodstream. A certain antibiotic has a half-life of about 8 hours.
   - **a.** A patient is administered 500 milligrams of the medication. Write a function that models the amount of the medication in the patient's bloodstream over time.
   - **b.** How much of the 500 milligram dose will be in the patient's bloodstream after 24 hours?

8 CHAPTER SUMMARY

BIG IDEAS

For Your Notebook

Big Idea 1

Applying Properties of Exponents to Simplify Expressions

You can use the properties of exponents to simplify expressions. For the properties listed below, *a* and *b* are real numbers, and *m* and *n* are integers.

Expression	Property
$a^m \cdot a^n = a^{m+n}$	**Product of powers property**
$(a^m)^n = a^{mn}$	**Power of a power property**
$(ab)^m = a^m b^m$	**Power of a product property**
$\frac{a^m}{a^n} = a^{m-n}, a \neq 0$	**Quotient of powers property**
$\left(\frac{a}{b}\right)^m = \frac{a^m}{b^m}, b \neq 0$	**Power of a quotient property**

Working with Numbers in Scientific Notation

You can write numbers in scientific notation.

Number	Standard form	Scientific notation
Four billion	4,000,000,000	4×10^9
Thirty-two thousandths	0.032	3.2×10^{-2}

You can also compute with numbers in scientific notation. For example:

$$(4 \times 10^9) \times (3.2 \times 10^{-2}) = 12.8 \times 10^7 = 1.28 \times 10^8, \text{ or } 128{,}000{,}000$$

Writing and Graphing Exponential Functions

You can write and graph exponential growth and decay functions. You can also model real-world situations involving exponential growth and exponential decay.

Exponential growth	Exponential decay
Function $y = ab^x, a > 0$ and $b > 1$	**Function** $y = ab^x, a > 0$ and $0 < b < 1$
Graph (0, *a*) *x* *y*	**Graph** (0, *a*) *x* *y*
Model $y = a(1 + r)^t$	**Model** $y = a(1 - r)^t$

8 CHAPTER REVIEW

@HomeTutor
classzone.com
- Multi-Language Glossary
- Vocabulary practice

REVIEW KEY VOCABULARY

- order of magnitude, *p. 491*
- zero exponent, *p. 503*
- negative exponent, *p. 503*
- scientific notation, *p. 512*
- exponential function, *p. 520*
- exponential growth, *p. 522*
- growth factor, growth rate, *p. 522*
- compound interest, *p. 523*
- exponential decay, *p. 533*
- decay factor, decay rate, *p. 534*

VOCABULARY EXERCISES

1. Copy and complete: The function $y = 1200(0.3)^t$ is an exponential _?_ function, and the base 0.3 is called the _?_.

2. WRITING *Explain* how you can tell whether a table represents a linear function or an exponential function.

Tell whether the function represents exponential growth or exponential decay. *Explain.*

3. $y = 3(0.85)^x$ **4.** $y = \frac{1}{2}(1.01)^x$ **5.** $y = 2(2.1)^x$

REVIEW EXAMPLES AND EXERCISES

Use the review examples and exercises below to check your understanding of the concepts you have learned in each lesson of Chapter 8.

8.1 Apply Exponent Properties Involving Products *pp. 489–494*

EXAMPLE

Simplify $(3y^3)^4 \cdot y^5$.

$(3y^3)^4 \cdot y^5 = 3^4 \cdot (y^3)^4 \cdot y^5$ **Power of a product property**

$= 81 \cdot y^{12} \cdot y^5$ **Power of a power property**

$= 81y^{17}$ **Product of powers property**

EXERCISES

EXAMPLES 1, 2, 3, 4, and 5 on pp. 489–491 for Exs. 6–15

Simplify the expression.

6. $4^4 \cdot 4^3$ **7.** $(-3)^7(-3)$ **8.** $z^3 \cdot z^5 \cdot z^5$

9. $(y^4)^5$ **10.** $[(-7)^4]^4$ **11.** $[(b + 2)^8]^3$

12. $(6^4 \cdot 31)^5$ **13.** $-(8xy)^2$ **14.** $(2x^2)^4 \cdot x^5$

15. **EARTH SCIENCE** The order of magnitude of the mass of Earth's atmosphere is 10^{18} kilograms. The order of magnitude of the mass of Earth's oceans is 10^3 times greater. What is the order of magnitude of the mass of Earth's oceans?

8 CHAPTER REVIEW

8.2 Apply Exponent Properties Involving Quotients — pp. 495–501

EXAMPLE

Simplify $\left(\frac{x^3}{y}\right)^4 \cdot \frac{2}{x^5}$.

$\left(\frac{x^3}{y}\right)^4 \cdot \frac{2}{x^5} = \frac{(x^3)^4}{y^4} \cdot \frac{2}{x^5}$ Power of a quotient property

$= \frac{x^{12}}{y^4} \cdot \frac{2}{x^5}$ Power of a power property

$= \frac{2x^{12}}{y^4x^5}$ Multiply fractions.

$= \frac{2x^7}{y^4}$ Quotient of powers property

EXERCISES

EXAMPLES 1, 2, and 3 on pp. 495–496 for Exs. 16–24

Simplify the expression.

16. $\frac{(-3)^7}{(-3)^3}$ 17. $\frac{5^2 \cdot 5^4}{5^3}$ 18. $\left(\frac{m}{n}\right)^3$ 19. $\frac{17^{12}}{17^8}$

20. $\left(-\frac{1}{x}\right)^4$ 21. $\left(\frac{7x^5}{y^2}\right)^2$ 22. $\frac{1}{p^2} \cdot p^6$ 23. $\frac{6}{7r^{10}} \cdot \left(\frac{r^5}{s}\right)^5$

24. **PER CAPITA INCOME** The order of magnitude of the population of Montana in 2003 was 10^6 people. The order of magnitude of the total personal income (in dollars) for Montana in 2003 was 10^{10}. What was the order of magnitude of the mean personal income in Montana in 2003?

8.3 Define and Use Zero and Negative Exponents — pp. 503–508

EXAMPLE

Evaluate $(2x^0y^{-5})^3$.

$(2x^0y^{-5})^3 = 2^3 \cdot x^0 \cdot y^{-15}$ Power of a power property

$= 8 \cdot 1 \cdot y^{-15}$ Definition of zero exponent

$= \frac{8}{y^{15}}$ Definition of negative exponents

EXERCISES

EXAMPLES 1, 2, and 4 on pp. 503–505 for Exs. 25–29

Evaluate the expression.

25. 14^0 26. 3^{-4} 27. $\left(\frac{2}{3}\right)^{-3}$ 28. $7^{-5} \cdot 7^5$

29. **UNITS OF MEASURE** Use the fact that 1 femtogram $= 10^{-18}$ kilogram and 1 nanogram $= 10^{-12}$ kilogram to complete the following statement: 1 nanogram = __?__ femtogram(s).

@HomeTutor
classzone.com
Chapter Review Practice

8.4 Use Scientific Notation

pp. 512–518

EXAMPLE

Write the number in scientific notation.

a. $2097 = 2.097 \times 10^3$ — Move decimal point left 3 places. Exponent is 3.

b. $0.00032 = 3.2 \times 10^{-4}$ — Move decimal point right 4 places. Exponent is −4.

Write the number in standard form.

a. $4.3201 \times 10^2 = 432.01$ — Exponent is 2. Move decimal point right 2 places.

b. $2.068 \times 10^{-3} = 0.002068$ — Exponent is −3. Move decimal point left 3 places.

EXERCISES

EXAMPLES 1, 2, 4, and 5 on pp. 512–514 for Exs. 30–34

30. Write 78,120 in scientific notation.

31. Write 7.5×10^{-5} in standard form.

Evaluate the expression. Write your answer in scientific notation.

32. $(6.3 \times 10^3)(1.9 \times 10^{-5})$

33. $\frac{6.5 \times 10^9}{1.6 \times 10^{-4}}$

34. MASS The mass m_1 of a gate of the Thames Barrier in London is about 1.5×10^6 kilograms. The mass m_2 of the Great Pyramid of Giza is about 6×10^9 kilograms. Find the ratio of m_1 to m_2. What does the ratio tell you?

8.5 Write and Graph Exponential Growth Functions

pp. 520–527

EXAMPLE

Graph the function $y = 4^x$ and identify its domain and range.

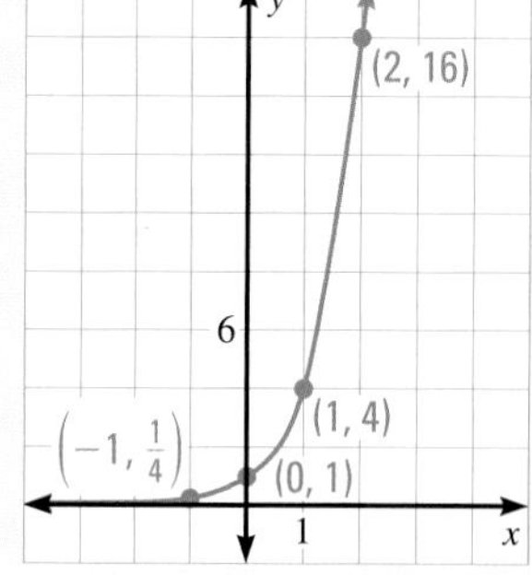

STEP 1 **Make** a table. The domain is all real numbers.

x	−1	0	1	2
y	$\frac{1}{4}$	1	4	16

STEP 2 **Plot** the points.

STEP 3 **Draw** a smooth curve through the points.

STEP 4 **Identify** the range. As you can see from the graph, the range is all positive real numbers.

EXERCISES

EXAMPLES 2 and 3 on p. 521 for Exs. 35–39

Graph the function and identify its domain and range.

35. $y = 6^x$

36. $y = (1.1)^x$

37. $y = (3.5)^x$

38. $y = \left(\frac{5}{2}\right)^x$

39. Graph the function $y = -5 \cdot 2^x$. Compare the graph with the graph of $y = 2^x$.

8 CHAPTER REVIEW

8.6 Write and Graph Exponential Decay Functions

pp. 531–538

EXAMPLE 1

Tell whether the graph represents *exponential growth* or *exponential decay.* Then write a rule for the function.

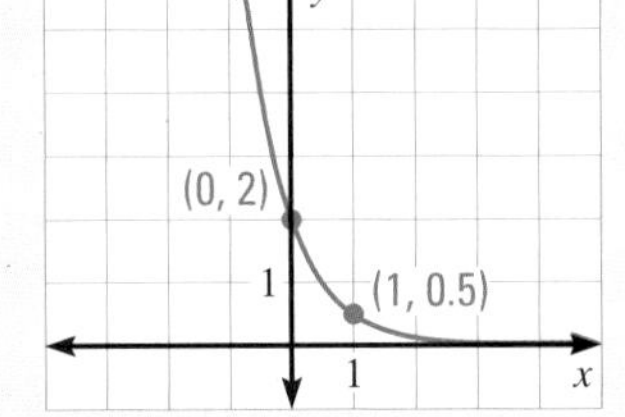

The graph represents exponential decay ($y = ab^x$ where $0 < b < 1$). The y-intercept is 2, so $a = 2$. Find the value of b by using the point (1, 0.5) and $a = 2$.

$y = ab^x$ **Write function.**

$0.5 = 2 \cdot b^1$ **Substitute.**

$0.25 = b$ **Solve for *b*.**

A function rule is $y = 2(0.25)^x$.

EXAMPLE 2

CAR VALUE A family purchases a car for \$11,000. The car depreciates (loses value) at a rate of about 16% annually. Write a function that models the value of the car over time. Find the approximate value of the car in 4 years.

Let V represent the value (in dollars) of the car, and let t represent the time (in years since the car was purchased). The initial value is 11,000, and the decay rate is 0.16.

$V = a(1 - r)^t$ **Write exponential decay model.**

$= 11{,}000(1 - 0.16)^t$ **Substitute 11,000 for *a* and 0.16 for *r*.**

$= 11{,}000(0.84)^t$ **Simplify.**

To find the approximate value of the car in 4 years, substitute 4 for t.

$V = 11{,}000(0.84)^t = 11{,}000(0.84)^4 \approx \$5477$

The approximate value of the car in 4 years is \$5477.

EXERCISES

EXAMPLES 4 and 5 on pp. 533–534 for Exs. 40–42

Tell whether the graph represents *exponential growth* or *exponential decay.* Then write a rule for the function.

40.

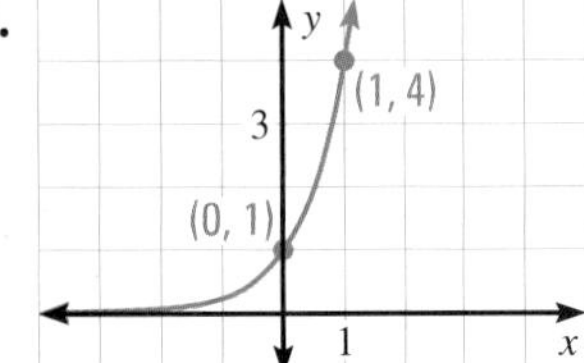

41.

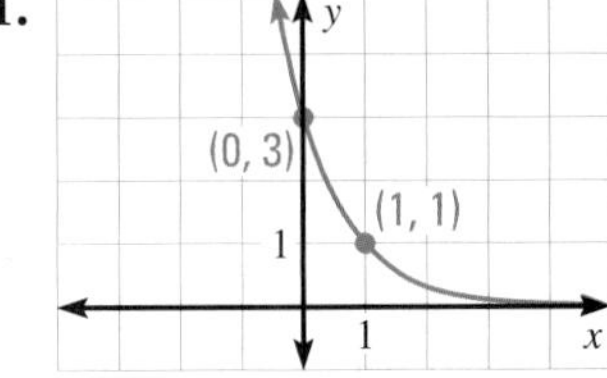

42. CAR VALUE The value of a car is \$13,000. The car depreciates (loses value) at a rate of about 15% annually. Write an exponential decay model for the value of the car. Find the approximate value of the car in 4 years.

8 CHAPTER TEST

Simplify the expression. Write your answer using exponents.

1. $(62 \cdot 17)^4$
2. $(-3)(-3)^6$
3. $\frac{8^4 \cdot 8^5}{8^3}$
4. $(8^4)^3$
5. $\frac{2^{15}}{2^8}$
6. $5^3 \cdot 5^0 \cdot 5^5$
7. $[(-4)^3]^2$
8. $\frac{(-5)^{10}}{(-5)^3}$

Simplify the expression.

9. $t^2 \cdot t^6$
10. $\left(\frac{s}{t}\right)^6$
11. $\frac{1}{9^{-2}}$
12. $-(6p)^2$
13. $(5xy)^2$
14. $\frac{1}{z^7} \cdot z^9$
15. $(x^5)^3$
16. $\left(-\frac{4}{c}\right)^2$

Simplify the expression. Write your answer using only positive exponents.

17. $\left(\frac{a^{-3}}{3b}\right)^4$
18. $\frac{3}{4d} \cdot \frac{(2d)^4}{c^3}$
19. $y^0 \cdot (8x^6y^{-3})^{-2}$
20. $(5r^5)^3 \cdot r^{-2}$

Write the number in scientific notation.

21. 423.6
22. 7,194,548
23. 500.32
24. 71.23884
25. 0.562
26. 0.0348
27. 0.000123
28. 0.5603002

Write the number in standard form.

29. 4.02×10^5
30. 5.3121×10^4
31. 9.354×10^8
32. 1.307×10^{19}
33. 1.3×10^{-3}
34. 3.32×10^{-4}
35. 7.506×10^{-5}
36. 9.3119×10^{-7}
37. Graph the function $y = 4^x$. Identify its domain and range.
38. Graph the function $y = \frac{1}{2} \cdot 4^x$. Compare the graph with the graph of $y = 4^x$.
39. **ANIMATION** About 1.2×10^7 bytes of data make up a single frame of an animated film. There are 24 frames in 1 second of a film. About how many bytes of data are there in 1 hour of an animated film?
40. **SALARY** A recent college graduate accepts a job at a law firm. The job has a salary of \$32,000 per year. The law firm guarantees an annual pay increase of 3% of the employee's salary.
    a. Write a function that models the employee's salary over time. Assume that the employee receives only the guaranteed pay increase.
    b. Use the function to find the employee's salary after 5 years.
41. **SCIENCE** At sea level, Earth's atmosphere exerts a pressure of 1 atmosphere. Atmospheric pressure P (in atmospheres) decreases with altitude and can be modeled by $P = (0.99987)^a$ where a is the altitude (in meters).
    a. Identify the initial amount, decay factor, and decay rate.
    b. Use a graphing calculator to graph the function.
    c. Estimate the altitude at which the atmospheric pressure is about half of what it is at sea level.

8 ★ *Standardized* TEST PREPARATION

CONTEXT-BASED MULTIPLE CHOICE QUESTIONS

Some of the information you need to solve a context-based multiple choice question may appear in a table, a diagram, or a graph.

PROBLEM 1

A scientist monitors bacteria cell growth in an experiment. The scientist records the number of bacteria cells in a petri dish every 20 minutes, as shown in the table.

Number of 20 minute time periods, t	0	1	2	3	4
Number of bacteria cells, c	15	30	60	120	240

How many bacteria cells will there be after 3 hours?

Ⓐ 7.69×10^{10} Ⓑ 7680 Ⓒ 270 Ⓓ 120

Plan

INTERPRET THE TABLE Determine whether the table represents a linear or an exponential function. Use the information in the table to write a function. Then use the function to find the number of bacteria cells after 3 hours.

Solution

STEP 1 Determine whether the function is exponential.

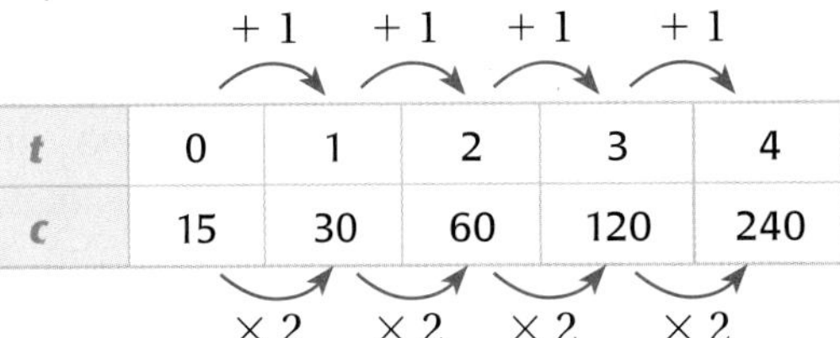

+1 +1 +1 +1

t	0	1	2	3	4
c	15	30	60	120	240

×2 ×2 ×2 ×2

Because the c-values are multiplied by 2 for each increase of 1 in t, the table represents an exponential function of the form $c = ab^t$ where $b = 2$.

STEP 2 Write the function rule.

The value of c when $t = 0$ is 15, as shown in the table, so $a = 15$. Substitute the values of a and b in the function $c = ab^t$.

A function rule is $c = 15 \cdot 2^t$.

STEP 3 Find the number of cells after 3 hours.

There are 180 minutes in 3 hours. So there are nine 20 minute periods in 3 hours. Substitute 9 for t in the function rule you wrote in Step 2.

$$c = 15 \cdot 2^t$$
$$= 15 \cdot 2^9$$
$$= 7680$$

There are 7680 bacteria cells in the petri dish after 3 hours.

The correct answer is B. Ⓐ Ⓑ Ⓒ Ⓓ

PROBLEM 2

A fish tank is a rectangular prism and is partially filled with sand, as shown. The dimensions of the fish tank are given. The order of magnitude of the number of grains of sand in 1 cubic inch is 10^3. Find the order of magnitude of the total number of grains of sand in the fish tank.

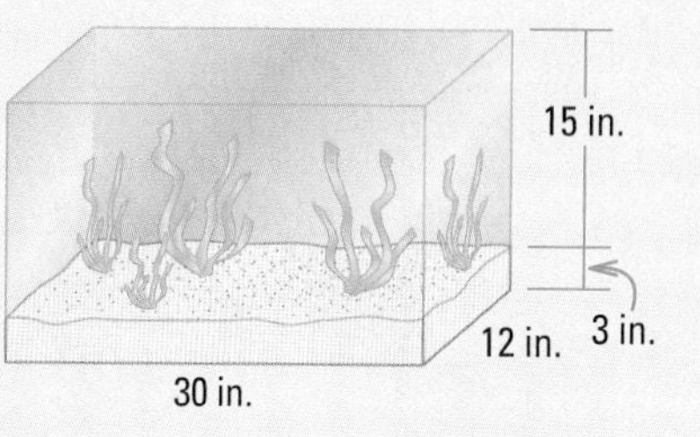

Ⓐ 10^2 grains Ⓑ 10^3 grains Ⓒ 10^5 grains Ⓓ 10^6 grains

Plan

INTERPRET THE DIAGRAM Use the information in the diagram to find the order of magnitude of the volume of sand in the fish tank. Multiply the volume by the order of magnitude of the number of grains of sand in 1 cubic inch.

Solution

STEP 1 Find the order of magnitude of the volume of sand in the fish tank.

Use the formula for the volume of a rectangular prism.

$V = lwh$ **Write formula for volume of rectangular prism.**

$= 30 \cdot 12 \cdot 3$ **Substitute given values.**

$= 1080$ **Multiply.**

The order of magnitude of the volume of sand is 10^3 cubic inches.

STEP 2 Find the order of magnitude of the number of grains of sand in the fish tank.

Multiply the order of magnitude of the volume of sand in the fish tank by the order of magnitude of the grains of sand in 1 cubic inch.

$10^3 \cdot 10^3 = 10^{3+3} = 10^6$

The order of magnitude of the total number of grains of sand in the fish tank is 10^6.

The correct answer is D. Ⓐ Ⓑ Ⓒ Ⓓ

PRACTICE

1. In Problem 2, consider the section of the fish tank occupied by water only. The order of magnitude of the weight of water per cubic inch is 10^{-2} pound. The tank is filled to the top. What is the order of magnitude of the weight of the water in the fish tank?

   Ⓐ 10^{-8} pound Ⓑ 10^{-6} pound Ⓒ 10^2 pounds Ⓓ 10^6 pounds

2. What is the volume of the cylinder shown?

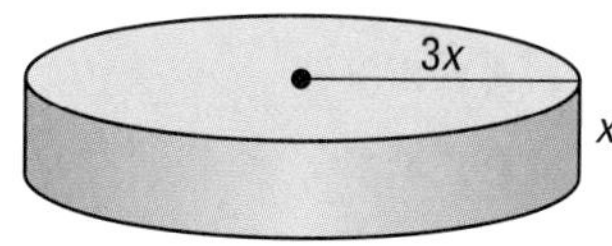

   Ⓐ $9\pi x^3$ Ⓑ $3\pi x^3$

   Ⓒ $9\pi x^2$ Ⓓ $3\pi x^2$

8 ★ Standardized TEST PRACTICE

MULTIPLE CHOICE

1. The table represents which function?

x	−2	−1	0	1	2
y	$\frac{1}{75}$	$\frac{1}{15}$	$\frac{1}{3}$	$\frac{5}{3}$	$\frac{25}{3}$

Ⓐ $y = \frac{1}{3} \cdot 5^x$ Ⓑ $y = -\frac{1}{3} \cdot 5^x$

Ⓒ $y = 3 \cdot 5^x$ Ⓓ $y = -3 \cdot 5^x$

2. What is the volume of the cube?

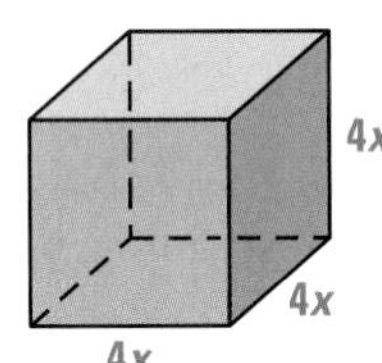

Ⓐ $4x^3$ Ⓑ $12x^3$

Ⓒ $16x^2$ Ⓓ $64x^3$

In Exercises 3 and 4, use the table below.

3. List the elements in order from least concentration to greatest concentration.

Element in Seawater	Concentration (parts per million)
Sulfur	904
Chloride	1.95×10^4
Magnesium	1.29×10^3
Sodium	10,770

Ⓐ Sulfur, sodium, magnesium, chloride

Ⓑ Chloride, sodium, magnesium, sulfur

Ⓒ Sulfur, chloride, magnesium, sodium

Ⓓ Sulfur, magnesium, sodium, chloride

4. About how many times greater is the concentration of chloride than the concentration of magnesium?

Ⓐ 0.066 Ⓑ 0.66

Ⓒ 1.5 Ⓓ 15

In Exercises 5–7, use the table below.

Unit	Number of meters
Kilometer	10^3
Centimeter	10^{-2}
Millimeter	10^{-3}
Nanometer	10^{-9}

5. How many millimeters are in 1 kilometer?

Ⓐ 1 Ⓑ 10

Ⓒ 10^3 Ⓓ 10^6

6. How many nanometers are in a centimeter?

Ⓐ 10^{-11} Ⓑ 10^{-7}

Ⓒ 10^7 Ⓓ 10^{18}

7. A micrometer is 10^3 times greater than a nanometer. How many meters are in a micrometer?

Ⓐ 10^{-27} Ⓑ 10^{-12}

Ⓒ 10^{-6} Ⓓ 10^6

In Exercises 8 and 9, use the graph below.

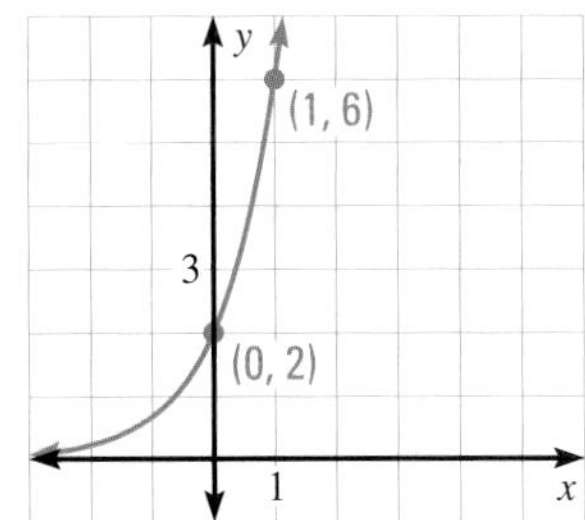

8. The graph of which exponential function is shown?

Ⓐ $y = 3^x$ Ⓑ $y = -3^x$

Ⓒ $y = -2 \cdot 3^x$ Ⓓ $y = 2 \cdot 3^x$

9. How does the graph compare with the graph of $y = 3^x$?

Ⓐ It is a vertical stretch.

Ⓑ It is a vertical shrink.

Ⓒ It is a reflection in the x-axis.

Ⓓ It is the same graph.

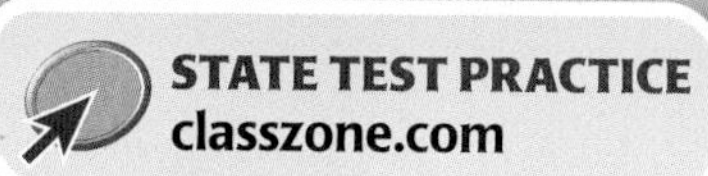

GRIDDED ANSWER

10. If $\left(\frac{x^{-6}}{x^{-5}}\right)^{-3} = x^n$ and $x \neq 0$, what is the value of n?

11. Write the number 7.8×10^{-1} in standard form.

12. What power of 10 is used when you write 12,560,000 in scientific notation?

13. The table shows the values for an exponential function.

x	−2	−1	0	1	2
y	$\frac{3}{25}$	$\frac{3}{5}$	3	15	?

What is the missing value in the table?

14. An initial investment of $200 is losing value at a rate of 1.5% per year. What is the value of the investment (in dollars) after 3 years? Round your answer to the nearest cent.

15. What is the value of $(2x)^3 \cdot x^2$ when $x = \frac{1}{2}$? Write your answer as a fraction.

SHORT RESPONSE

16. A female sockeye salmon lays about 10^3 eggs in one season.

a. About how many eggs will 10^4 female sockeyes lay?

b. Suppose about 10^6 of the eggs survive to become young salmon. What percent of eggs survive? *Explain* how you found your answer.

17. You deposit $75 in a bank account that pays 3% annual interest compounded yearly. If you do not make any deposits or withdrawals, how much will your investment be worth in 3 years? *Explain.*

18. Membership in an after-school athletic club declined at a rate of 5% per year for the period 2000–2005. There were 54 members in 2000.

a. Identify the initial amount, the decay rate, and the decay factor.

b. In what year did the club have 44 members? *Explain.*

EXTENDED RESPONSE

19. Europa, one of Jupiter's moons, is roughly spherical. The equatorial radius of Europa is 1.569×10^6 meters.

a. Find the volume of Europa. Write your answer in scientific notation.

b. Find the average density d (in kilograms per cubic meters) of Europa by using the formula $d = \frac{m}{V}$ where m is the mass of Europa (about 4.8×10^{22} kilograms) and V is the volume you calculated in part (a).

c. *Explain* how you could have used order of magnitude to approximate the density of Europa. How would the approximation compare with the density you calculated in part (b)?

20. A gardener is growing a water lily plant. The plant starts out with 4 lily pads and the number of lily pads increases at a rate of about 6.5% per day for the first 20 days.

a. Write a function that models the number of lily pads the plant has over the first 20 days.

b. Graph the model and identify its domain and range.

c. On about what day did the plant have 10 lily pads? *Explain* how you found your answer.

9 Polynomials and Factoring

Before

In previous chapters, you learned the following skills, which you'll use in Chapter 9: using the distributive property, combining like terms, and using the properties of exponents.

Prerequisite Skills

VOCABULARY CHECK

Copy and complete the statement.

1. Terms that have the same variable part are called __?__.
2. For a function $f(x)$, a(n) __?__ is an x-value for which $f(x) = 0$.

SKILLS CHECK

Find the greatest common factor of the pair of numbers. *(Review p. 910 for 9.4.)*

3. 121, 77
4. 96, 32
5. 81, 42
6. 12, 56

Simplify the expression. *(Review p. 96 for 9.1–9.8.)*

7. $3x + (-6x)$
8. $5 + 4x + 2$
9. $4(2x - 1) + x$
10. $-(x + 4) - 6x$

Simplify the expression. *(Review p. 489 for 9.2–9.8.)*

11. $(3xy)^3$
12. $xy^2 \cdot xy^3$
13. $(x^5)^3$
14. $(-x)^3$

@HomeTutor Prerequisite skills practice at classzone.com

Now

In Chapter 9, you will apply the big ideas listed below and reviewed in the Chapter Summary on page 615. You will also use the key vocabulary listed below.

Big Ideas

1. **Adding, subtracting, and multiplying polynomials**
2. **Factoring polynomials**
3. **Writing and solving polynomial equations to solve problems**

KEY VOCABULARY

- monomial, *p. 554*
- degree, *p. 554*
- polynomial, *p. 554*
- leading coefficient, *p. 554*
- binomial, *p. 555*
- trinomial, *p. 555*
- roots, *p. 575*
- vertical motion model, *p. 577*
- perfect square trinomial, *p. 601*
- factor by grouping, *p. 606*
- factor completely, *p. 607*

Why?

You can use a polynomial function to model vertical motion. For example, you can use a polynomial function to model the height of a jumping animal as a function of time.

Animated Algebra

The animation illustrated below for Exercise 62 on page 598 helps you to answer this question: How does changing the initial vertical velocity of a serval, an African cat, affect its jumping height?

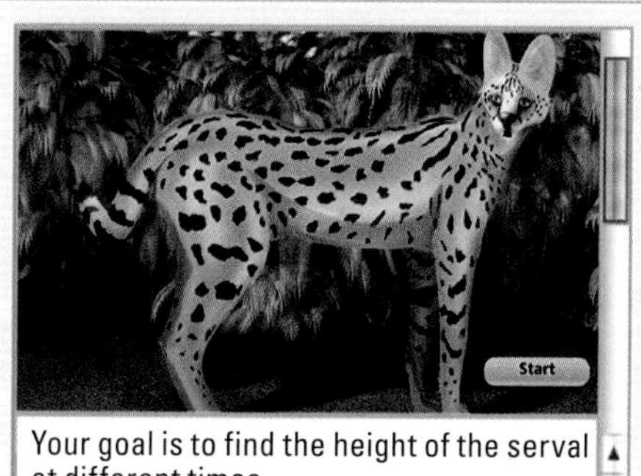

Your goal is to find the height of the serval at different times.

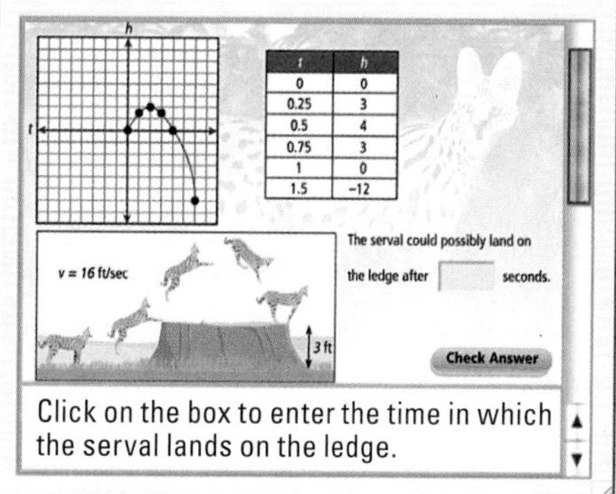

Click on the box to enter the time in which the serval lands on the ledge.

Animated Algebra at classzone.com

Other animations for Chapter 9: pages 555, 582, 592, and 601

9.1 Add and Subtract Polynomials

Before You added and subtracted integers.

Now You will add and subtract polynomials.

Why? So you can model trends in recreation, as in Ex. 37.

Key Vocabulary
- monomial
- degree
- polynomial
- leading coefficient
- binomial
- trinomial

A **monomial** is a number, a variable, or the product of a number and one or more variables with whole number exponents. The **degree of a monomial** is the sum of the exponents of the variables in the monomial. The degree of a nonzero constant term is 0. The constant 0 does not have a degree.

Monomial	Degree
10	0
$3x$	1
$\frac{1}{2}ab^2$	$1 + 2 = 3$
$-1.8m^5$	5

Not a monomial	Reason
$5 + x$	A sum is not a monomial.
$\frac{2}{n}$	A monomial cannot have a variable in the denominator.
4^a	A monomial cannot have a variable exponent.
x^{-1}	The variable must have a whole number exponent.

A **polynomial** is a monomial or a sum of monomials, each called a *term* of the polynomial. The **degree of a polynomial** is the greatest degree of its terms.

When a polynomial is written so that the exponents of a variable decrease from left to right, the coefficient of the first term is called the **leading coefficient**.

leading coefficient → 2; degree → 3; constant term → 12

$$2x^3 + x^2 - 5x + 12$$

EXAMPLE 1 Rewrite a polynomial

Write $15x - x^3 + 3$ so that the exponents decrease from left to right. Identify the degree and leading coefficient of the polynomial.

Solution

Consider the degree of each of the polynomial's terms.

Degree is 1. Degree is 3. Degree is 0.

$$15x - x^3 + 3$$

The polynomial can be written as $-x^3 + 15x + 3$. The greatest degree is 3, so the degree of the polynomial is 3, and the leading coefficient is -1.

BINOMIALS AND TRINOMIALS A polynomial with two terms is called a **binomial**. A polynomial with three terms is called a **trinomial**.

EXAMPLE 2 Identify and classify polynomials

Tell whether the expression is a polynomial. If it is a polynomial, find its degree and classify it by the number of its terms. Otherwise, tell why it is not a polynomial.

	Expression	Is it a polynomial?	Classify by degree and number of terms
a.	9	Yes	0 degree monomial
b.	$2x^2 + x - 5$	Yes	2nd degree trinomial
c.	$6n^4 - 8^n$	No; variable exponent	
d.	$n^{-2} - 3$	No; negative exponent	
e.	$7bc^3 + 4b^4c$	Yes	5th degree binomial

ADDING POLYNOMIALS To add polynomials, add like terms. You can use a vertical or a horizontal format.

EXAMPLE 3 Add polynomials

Find the sum.

a. $(2x^3 - 5x^2 + x) + (2x^2 + x^3 - 1)$ **b.** $(3x^2 + x - 6) + (x^2 + 4x + 10)$

Solution

ALIGN TERMS
If a particular power of the variable appears in one polynomial but not the other, leave a space in that column, or write the term with a coefficient of 0.

a. Vertical format: Align like terms in vertical columns.

$$\begin{array}{r} 2x^3 - 5x^2 + x \phantom{{}-1} \\ +\ \ x^3 + 2x^2 \phantom{{}+x} - 1 \\ \hline 3x^3 - 3x^2 + x - 1 \end{array}$$

b. Horizontal format: Group like terms and simplify.

$$(3x^2 + x - 6) + (x^2 + 4x + 10) = (3x^2 + x^2) + (x + 4x) + (-6 + 10)$$
$$= 4x^2 + 5x + 4$$

Animated Algebra at classzone.com

✓ GUIDED PRACTICE for Examples 1, 2, and 3

1. Write $5y - 2y^2 + 9$ so that the exponents decrease from left to right. Identify the degree and leading coefficient of the polynomial.
2. Tell whether $y^3 - 4y + 3$ is a polynomial. If it is a polynomial, find its degree and classify it by the number of its terms. Otherwise, tell why it is not a polynomial.
3. Find the sum $(5x^3 + 4x - 2x) + (4x^2 + 3x^3 - 6)$.

SUBTRACTING POLYNOMIALS To subtract a polynomial, add its opposite. To find the opposite of a polynomial, multiply each of its terms by -1.

EXAMPLE 4 Subtract polynomials

Find the difference.

a. $(4n^2 + 5) - (-2n^2 + 2n - 4)$ **b.** $(4x^2 - 3x + 5) - (3x^2 - x - 8)$

Solution

a.
$$\begin{array}{r} (4n^2 \quad\quad + 5) \\ -(-2n^2 + 2n - 4) \\ \hline \end{array} \quad \longrightarrow \quad \begin{array}{r} 4n^2 \quad\quad + 5 \\ + 2n^2 - 2n + 4 \\ \hline 6n^2 - 2n + 9 \end{array}$$

AVOID ERRORS
Remember to multiply *each* term in the polynomial by -1 when you write the subtraction as addition.

b. $(4x^2 - 3x + 5) - (\mathbf{3x^2 - x - 8}) = 4x^2 - 3x + 5 \mathbf{- 3x^2 + x + 8}$

$= (4x^2 \mathbf{- 3x^2}) + (-3x \mathbf{+ x}) + (5 \mathbf{+ 8})$

$= x^2 - 2x + 13$

EXAMPLE 5 Solve a multi-step problem

BASEBALL ATTENDANCE Major League Baseball teams are divided into two leagues. During the period 1995–2001, the attendance N and A (in thousands) at National and American League baseball games, respectively, can be modeled by

$N = -488t^2 + 5430t + 24{,}700$ and

$A = -318t^2 + 3040t + 25{,}600$

where t is the number of years since 1995. About how many people attended Major League Baseball games in 2001?

Solution

STEP 1 **Add** the models for the attendance in each league to find a model for M, the total attendance (in thousands).

$M = (-488t^2 + 5430t + 24{,}700) + (\mathbf{-318t^2 + 3040t + 25{,}600})$

$= (-488t^2 \mathbf{- 318t^2}) + (5430t \mathbf{+ 3040t}) + (24{,}700 \mathbf{+ 25{,}600})$

$= -806t^2 + 8470t + 50{,}300$

AVOID ERRORS
Because a value of M represents *thousands* of people, $M \approx 72{,}100$ represents 72,100,000 people.

STEP 2 **Substitute** 6 for t in the model, because 2001 is 6 years after 1995.

$M = -806(6)^2 + 8470(6) + 50{,}300 \approx 72{,}100$

▶ About 72,100,000 people attended Major League Baseball games in 2001.

GUIDED PRACTICE for Examples 4 and 5

4. Find the difference $(4x^2 - 7x) - (5x^2 + 4x - 9)$.

5. **BASEBALL ATTENDANCE** Look back at Example 5. Find the difference in attendance at National and American League baseball games in 2001.

9.1 EXERCISES

HOMEWORK KEY

○ = **WORKED-OUT SOLUTIONS** on p. WS20 for Exs. 21 and 39

★ = **STANDARDIZED TEST PRACTICE** Exs. 2, 9, 10, 39, and 41

SKILL PRACTICE

1. **VOCABULARY** Copy and complete: A number, a variable, or the product of one or more variables is called a(n) _?_.

2. ★ **WRITING** Is 6 a polynomial? *Explain* why or why not.

EXAMPLE 1 on p. 554 for Exs. 3–9

REWRITING POLYNOMIALS **Write the polynomial so that the exponents decrease from left to right. Identify the degree and leading coefficient of the polynomial.**

3. $9m^5$
4. $2 - 6y$
5. $2x^2y^2 - 8xy$
6. $5n^3 + 2n - 7$
7. $5z + 2z^3 - z^2 + 3z^4$
8. $-2h^2 + 2h^4 - h^6$

9. ★ **MULTIPLE CHOICE** What is the degree of $-4x^3 + 6x^4 - 1$?

Ⓐ -4 Ⓑ 3 Ⓒ 4 Ⓓ 6

EXAMPLE 2 on p. 555 for Exs. 10–16

10. ★ **MULTIPLE CHOICE** Which expression is *not* a monomial?

Ⓐ $-5x^2$ Ⓑ $0.2y^4$ Ⓒ $3mn$ Ⓓ $3s^{-2}$

IDENTIFYING AND CLASSIFYING POLYNOMIALS **Tell whether the expression is a polynomial. If it is a polynomial, find its degree and classify it by the number of its terms. Otherwise, tell why it is not a polynomial.**

11. -4^x
12. $w^{-3} + 1$
13. $3x - 5$
14. $\frac{4}{5}f^2 - \frac{1}{2}f + \frac{2}{3}$
15. $6 - n^2 + 5n^3$
16. $10y^4 - 3y^2 + 11$

EXAMPLES 3 and 4 on pp. 555–556 for Exs. 17–28

ADDING AND SUBTRACTING POLYNOMIALS **Find the sum or difference.**

17. $(5a^2 - 3) + (8a^2 - 1)$
18. $(h^2 + 4h - 4) + (5h^2 - 8h + 2)$
19. $(4m^2 - m + 2) + (-3m^2 + 10m + 7)$
20. $(7k^2 + 2k - 6) + (3k^2 - 11k - 8)$
21. $(6c^2 + 3c + 9) - (3c - 5)$
22. $(3x^2 - 8) - (4x^3 + x^2 - 15x + 1)$
23. $(-n^2 + 2n) - (2n^3 - n^2 + n + 12)$
24. $(9b^3 - 13b^2 + b) - (-13b^2 - 5b + 14)$
25. $(4d - 6d^3 + 3d^2) - (9d^3 + 7d - 2)$
26. $(9p^2 - 6p^3 + 3 - 11p) + (7p^3 - 3p^2 + 4)$

ERROR ANALYSIS ***Describe*** **and correct the error in finding the sum or difference of the polynomials.**

27.

$$\begin{array}{r} x^3 - 4x^2 + 3 \\ + \ -3x^3 + 8x - 2 \\ \hline -2x^3 + 4x^2 + 1 \end{array}$$

28.

$(6x^2 - 5x) - (2x^2 + 3x - 2)$

$= (6x^2 - 2x^2) + (-5x + 3x) - 2$

$= 4x^2 - 2x - 2$

29. **POLYNOMIAL FUNCTIONS** Find the sum $f(x) + g(x)$ and the difference $f(x) - g(x)$ for the functions $f(x) = 3x^2 + x - 7$ and $g(x) = -x^2 + 5x - 2$.

GEOMETRY **Write a polynomial that represents the perimeter of the figure.**

30.

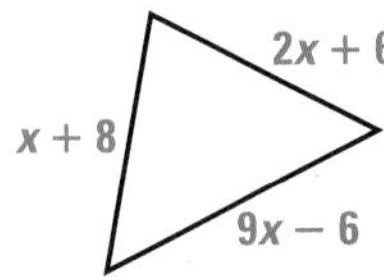

31.

3x − 2
2x
2x + 1
5x − 2

ADDING AND SUBTRACTING POLYNOMIALS **Find the sum or difference.**

32. $(3r^2s + 5rs + 3) + (-8rs^2 - 9rs - 12)$

33. $(x^2 + 11xy - 3y^2) + (-2x^2 - xy + 4y^2)$

34. $(5mn + 3m - 9n) - (13mn + 2m)$

35. $(8a^2b - 6a) - (2a^2b - 4b + 19)$

36. **CHALLENGE** Consider any integer x. The next consecutive integer can be represented by the binomial $(x + 1)$.

a. Write a polynomial for the sum of any two consecutive integers.

b. *Explain* how you can be sure that the sum of two consecutive integers is always odd. Use the polynomial from part (a) in your explanation.

PROBLEM SOLVING

EXAMPLE 5 on p. 556 for Exs. 37–39

37. **BACKPACKING AND CAMPING** During the period 1992–2002, the participation B (in millions of people) in backpacking and the participation C (in millions of people) in camping can be modeled by

$$B = -0.0262t^3 + 0.376t^2 - 0.574t + 9.67 \text{ and}$$
$$C = -0.0182t^3 + 0.522t^2 - 2.59t + 47$$

where t is the number of years since 1992. About how many more people camped than backpacked in 2002?

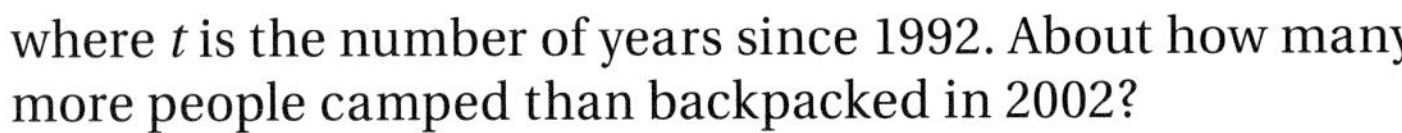

@HomeTutor for problem solving help at classzone.com

38. **CAR COSTS** During the period 1990–2002, the average costs D (in dollars) for a new domestic car and the average costs I (in dollars) for a new imported car can be modeled by

$$D = 442.14t + 14{,}433 \quad \text{and} \quad I = -137.63t^2 + 2705.2t + 15{,}111$$

where t is the number of years since 1990. Find the difference in average costs (in dollars) for a new imported car and a new domestic car in 2002.

@HomeTutor for problem solving help at classzone.com

39. ★ **SHORT RESPONSE** During the period 1998–2002, the number A (in millions) of books for adults and the number J (in millions) of books for juveniles sold can be modeled by

$$A = 9.5t^3 - 58t^2 + 66t + 500 \quad \text{and} \quad J = -15t^2 + 64t + 360$$

where t is the number of years since 1998.

a. Write an equation that gives the total number (in millions) of books for adults and for juveniles sold as a function of the number of years since 1998.

b. Were more books sold in 1998 or in 2002? *Explain* your answer.

40. **SCHOOL ENROLLMENT** During the period 1985–2012, the projected enrollment B (in thousands of students) in public schools and the projected enrollment R (in thousands of students) in private schools can be modeled by

$$B = -18.53t^2 + 975.8t + 48{,}140 \quad \text{and} \quad R = 80.8t + 8049$$

where t is the number of years since 1985. Write an equation that models the total school enrollment (in thousands of students) as a function of the number of years since 1985. What percent of all students is expected to be enrolled in public schools in 2012?

41. ★ **EXTENDED RESPONSE** The award for the best pitchers in baseball is named after the pitcher Cy Young. During the period 1890–1911, the total number of Cy Young's wins W and losses L can be modeled by

$$W = -0.44t^2 + 34t + 4.7 \quad \text{and} \quad L = 15t + 15$$

where t is the number of years since 1890.

a. A game credited to a pitcher as a win or a loss is called a decision. Write an equation that models the number of decisions for Cy Young as a function of the number of years since 1890.

b. Cy Young's career in Major League Baseball lasted from 1890 to 1911. Approximately how many total decisions did Cy Young have during his career?

c. About what percent of the decisions in Cy Young's career were wins? *Explain* how you found your answer.

Cy Young Award

42. **CHALLENGE** In 1970 the United States produced 63.5 quadrillion BTU (British Thermal Units) of energy and consumed 67.86 quadrillion BTU. From 1970 through 2001, the total U.S. energy production increased by about 0.2813 quadrillion BTU per year, and the total U.S. energy consumption increased by about 0.912 quadrillion BTU per year.

a. Write two equations that model the total U.S. energy production and consumption (in quadrillion BTU) as functions of the number of years since 1970.

b. How much more energy was consumed than produced in the U.S. in 1970 and in 2001? What was the change in the amount of energy consumed from 1970 to 2001?

MIXED REVIEW

PREVIEW
Prepare for Lesson 9.2 in Exs. 43–48.

Simplify the expression.

43. $0.6(3 - x)$ *(p. 96)*
44. $4(y + 6)$ *(p. 96)*
45. $4(1 - b) - 5b$ *(p. 96)*
46. $-4(16c - 8)$ *(p. 96)*
47. $(6t^7)^2$ *(p. 489)*
48. $n(2m^2n)$ *(p. 489)*

Graph the equation or inequality.

49. $y = -8$ *(p. 215)*
50. $x - 3y = 15$ *(p. 215)*
51. $y = -5x - 14$ *(p. 215)*
52. $x \geq -3$ *(p. 405)*
53. $x + y \leq 9$ *(p. 405)*
54. $2x - y < 7$ *(p. 405)*

@HomeTutor
classzone.com
Keystrokes

9.1 Graph Polynomial Functions

QUESTION How can you use a graph to check your work with polynomials?

EXAMPLE Check a sum or difference of polynomials

Tell whether the sum or difference is correct.

a. $(x^2 - 2x + 3) + (2x^2 + 4x - 5) \stackrel{?}{=} 3x^2 + 2x - 2$

b. $(x^3 + x + 1) - (5x^3 - 2x + 7) \stackrel{?}{=} -4x^3 - x - 6$

***STEP 1* Enter expressions**

Let y_1 equal the original expression.
Let y_2 equal the sum.

a.

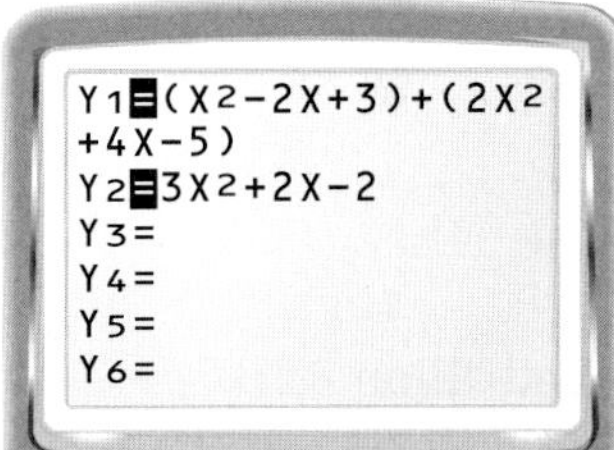

b.

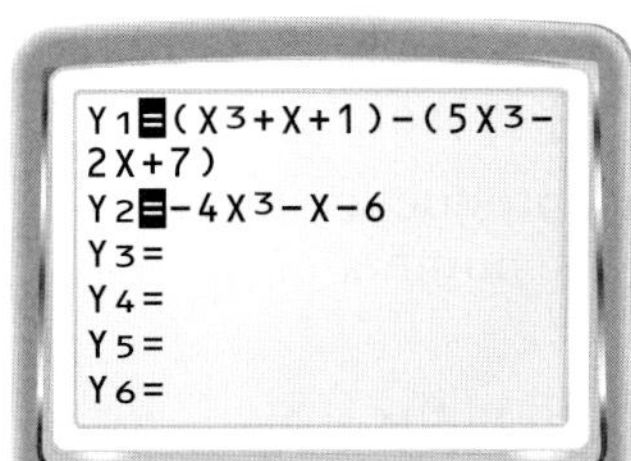

***STEP 2* Graph expressions**

For y_1, choose a normal graph style.
For y_2, choose a thicker graph style.

a.

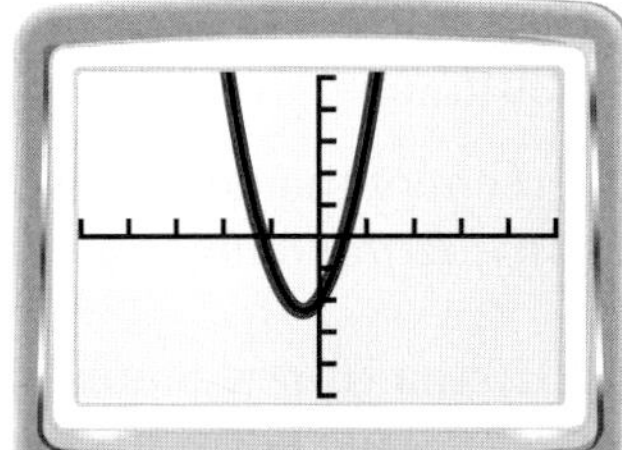

b.

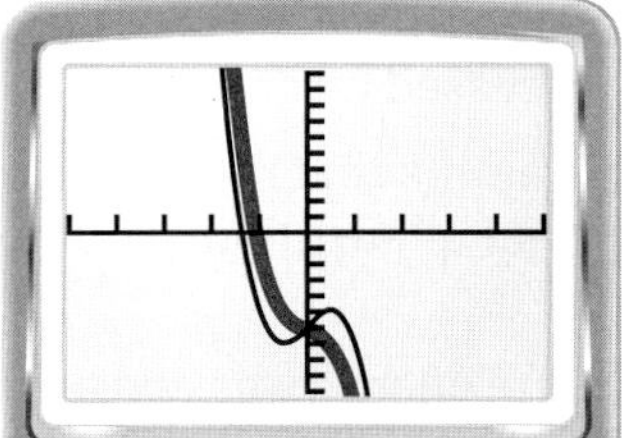

***STEP 3* Analyze graphs**

a. The thick curve coincides with the thin curve, so the sum is correct.

b. The thick curve deviates from the thin curve, so the difference is incorrect.

PRACTICE

Find the sum or difference. Use a graphing calculator to check your answer.

1. $(6x^2 + 4x - 1) + (x^2 - 2x + 2)$

2. $(3x^2 - 2x + 1) - (4x^2 - 5x + 1)$

Tell whether the sum or difference is correct. Correct any incorrect answers.

3. $(3x^2 - 2x + 4) + (-x^2 + 3x + 2) \stackrel{?}{=} 2x^2 + x + 6$

4. $(-4x^2 - 5x - 1) - (-5x^2 + 6x + 3) \stackrel{?}{=} -9x^2 + x + 2$

9.2 Multiplication with Algebra Tiles

MATERIALS • algebra tiles

QUESTION **How can you multiply binomials using algebra tiles?**

You can use the following algebra tiles to model polynomials. Notice that the value of each tile is the same as its area.

1-tile **x-tile**

x^2-tile

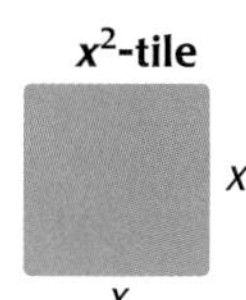

EXPLORE **Multiply binomials**

Find the product $(x + 3)(2x + 1)$.

STEP 1 ***Model the rectangle's dimensions***

Model each binomial with algebra tiles. Arrange the first binomial vertically and the second horizontally, as shown. These polynomials model the length and width of a rectangle.

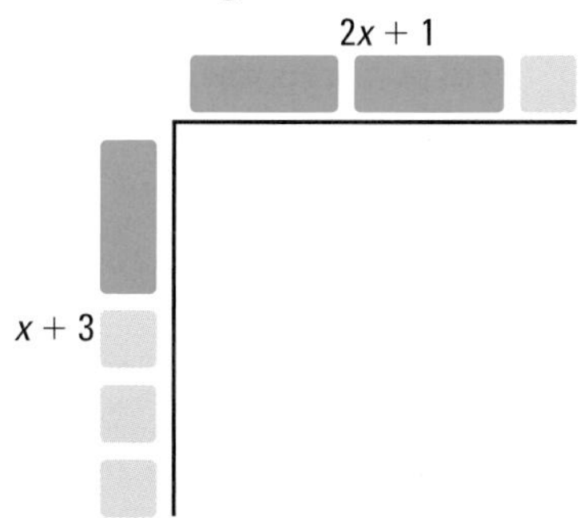

STEP 2 ***Fill in the area***

Fill in the rectangle with the appropriate algebra tiles.

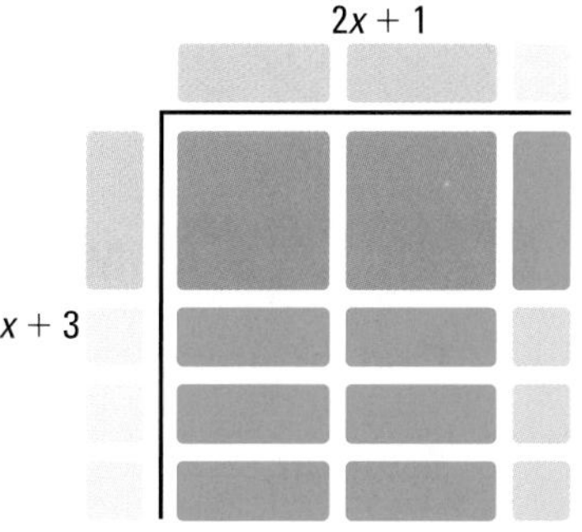

STEP 3 ***Find the product***

The rectangle you created represents the polynomial $2x^2 + 7x + 3$. So, $(x + 3)(2x + 1) = 2x^2 + 7x + 3$.

DRAW CONCLUSIONS **Use your observations to complete these exercises**

Use algebra tiles to find the product. Include a drawing of your model.

1. $(x + 1)(x + 3)$
2. $(x + 5)(x + 4)$
3. $(2x + 1)(x + 2)$
4. $(3x + 2)(x + 1)$
5. $(3x + 2)(2x + 1)$
6. $(4x + 1)(2x + 3)$
7. **REASONING** Find the product $x(2x + 1)$ and the product $3(2x + 1)$. What is the sum of these two products? What do your answers suggest you can do to find the product $(x + 3)(2x + 1)$?

9.2 Multiply Polynomials

Before You added and subtracted polynomials.

Now You will multiply polynomials.

Why? So you can determine areas, as in Example 7.

Key Vocabulary
- **polynomial,** *p. 554*
- **binomial,** *p. 555*

The diagram shows that a rectangle with width x and length $2x + 3$ has an area of $2x^2 + 3x$. You can also find this product by using the distributive property.

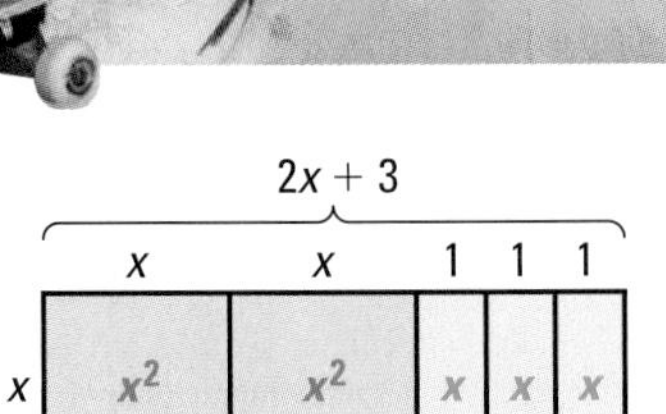

$$x(2x + 3) = x(2x) + x(3) = 2x^2 + 3x$$

In this lesson, you will learn several methods for multiplying polynomials. Each method is based on the distributive property.

EXAMPLE 1 Multiply a monomial and a polynomial

REVIEW PROPERTIES OF EXPONENTS
For help with using the properties of exponents, see p. 489.

Find the product $2x^3(x^3 + 3x^2 - 2x + 5)$.

$2x^3(x^3 + 3x^2 - 2x + 5)$ — **Write product.**

$= 2x^3(x^3) + 2x^3(3x^2) - 2x^3(2x) + 2x^3(5)$ — **Distributive property**

$= 2x^6 + 6x^5 - 4x^4 + 10x^3$ — **Product of powers property**

EXAMPLE 2 Multiply polynomials using a table

Find the product $(x - 4)(3x + 2)$.

Solution

STEP 1 **Write** subtraction as addition in each polynomial.

$$(x - 4)(3x + 2) = [x + (-4)](3x + 2)$$

STEP 2 **Make** a table of products.

	$3x$	2
x	$3x^2$	
-4		

→

	$3x$	2
x	$3x^2$	$2x$
-4	$-12x$	-8

▶ The product is $3x^2 + 2x - 12x - 8$, or $3x^2 - 10x - 8$.

✓ GUIDED PRACTICE for Examples 1 and 2

Find the product.

1. $x(7x^2 + 4)$
2. $(a + 3)(2a + 1)$
3. $(4n - 1)(n + 5)$

EXAMPLE 3 Multiply polynomials vertically

Find the product $(b^2 + 6b - 7)(3b - 4)$.

Solution

AVOID ERRORS

Remember that the terms of $(3b - 4)$ are $3b$ and -4. They are *not* $3b$ and 4.

STEP 1 Multiply by -4.

$$\begin{array}{r} b^2 + 6b - 7 \\ \times \qquad 3b - 4 \\ \hline -4b^2 - 24b + 28 \end{array}$$

STEP 2 Multiply by $3b$.

$$\begin{array}{r} b^2 + 6b - 7 \\ \times \qquad 3b - 4 \\ \hline -4b^2 - 24b + 28 \\ 3b^3 + 18b^2 - 21b \qquad \end{array}$$

STEP 3 Add products.

$$\begin{array}{r} b^2 + 6b - 7 \\ \times \qquad 3b - 4 \\ \hline -4b^2 - 24b + 28 \\ 3b^3 + 18b^2 - 21b \qquad \\ \hline 3b^3 + 14b^2 - 45b + 28 \end{array}$$

EXAMPLE 4 Multiply polynomials horizontally

Find the product $(2x^2 + 5x - 1)(4x - 3)$.

$(2x^2 + 5x - 1)(4x - 3)$	Write product.
$= 2x^2(4x - 3) + 5x(4x - 3) - 1(4x - 3)$	Distributive property
$= 8x^3 - 6x^2 + 20x^2 - 15x - 4x + 3$	Distributive property
$= 8x^3 + 14x^2 - 19x + 3$	Combine like terms.

FOIL PATTERN The letters of the word FOIL can help you to remember how to use the distributive property to multiply binomials. The letters should remind you of the words **F**irst, **O**uter, **I**nner, and **L**ast.

First Outer Inner Last

$$(2x + 3)(4x + 1) = 8x^2 + 2x + 12x + 3$$

EXAMPLE 5 Multiply binomials using the FOIL pattern

Find the product $(3a + 4)(a - 2)$.

$(3a + 4)(a - 2)$	
$= (3a)(a) + (3a)(-2) + (4)(a) + (4)(-2)$	Write products of terms.
$= 3a^2 + (-6a) + 4a + (-8)$	Multiply.
$= 3a^2 - 2a - 8$	Combine like terms.

✓ **GUIDED PRACTICE** for Examples 3, 4, and 5

Find the product.

4. $(x^2 + 2x + 1)(x + 2)$ **5.** $(3y^2 - y + 5)(2y - 3)$ **6.** $(4b - 5)(b - 2)$

EXAMPLE 6 Standardized Test Practice

The dimensions of a rectangle are $x + 3$ and $x + 2$. Which expression represents the area of the rectangle?

ELIMINATE CHOICES

When you multiply $x + 3$ and $x + 2$, the product will have a constant term of $3 \cdot 2 = 6$. So, you can eliminate choice D.

Ⓐ $x^2 + 6$ Ⓑ $x^2 + 5x + 6$ Ⓒ $x^2 + 6x + 6$ Ⓓ $x^2 + 6x$

Solution

Area = length • width	**Formula for area of a rectangle**
$= (x + 3)(x + 2)$	**Substitute for length and width.**
$= x^2 + 2x + 3x + 6$	**Multiply binomials.**
$= x^2 + 5x + 6$	**Combine like terms.**

▶ The correct answer is B. Ⓐ Ⓑ Ⓒ Ⓓ

CHECK You can use a graph to check your answer. Use a graphing calculator to display the graphs of $y_1 = (x + 3)(x + 2)$ and $y_2 = x^2 + 5x + 6$ in the same viewing window. Because the graphs coincide, you know that the product of $x + 3$ and $x + 2$ is $x^2 + 5x + 6$.

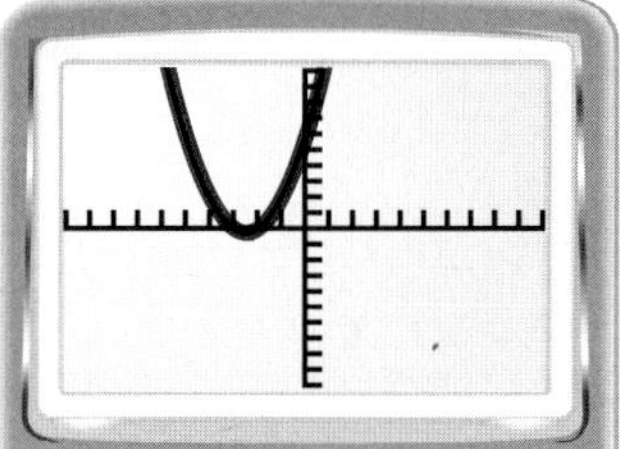

EXAMPLE 7 Solve a multi-step problem

SKATEBOARDING You are designing a rectangular skateboard park on a lot that is on the corner of a city block. The park will have a walkway along two sides. The dimensions of the lot and the walkway are shown in the diagram.

- Write a polynomial that represents the area of the skateboard park.
- What is the area of the park if the walkway is 3 feet wide?

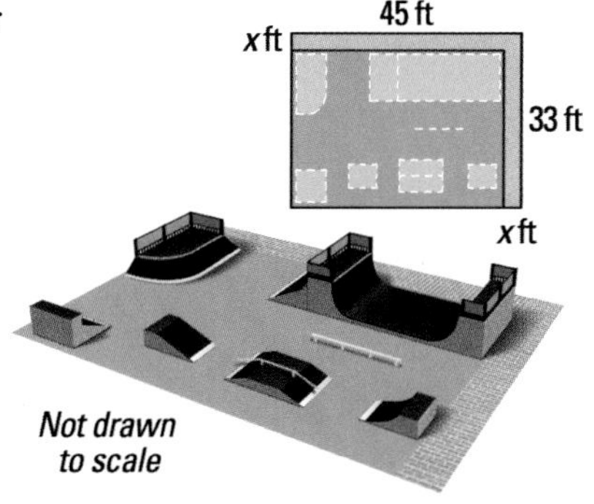

Solution

STEP 1 **Write** a polynomial using the formula for the area of a rectangle. The length is $45 - x$. The width is $33 - x$.

Area = length • width	**Formula for area of a rectangle**
$= (45 - x)(33 - x)$	**Substitute for length and width.**
$= 1485 - 45x - 33x + x^2$	**Multiply binomials.**
$= 1485 - 78x + x^2$	**Combine like terms.**

STEP 2 **Substitute** 3 for x and evaluate.

Area $= 1485 - 78(3) + (3)^2 = 1260$

▶ The area of the park is 1260 square feet.

 **GUIDED PRACTICE** for Examples 6 and 7

7. The dimensions of a rectangle are $x + 5$ and $x + 9$. Which expression represents the area of the rectangle?

   (A) $x^2 + 45x$ (B) $x^2 + 45$

   (C) $x^2 + 14x + 45$ (D) $x^2 + 45x + 45$

8. **GARDEN DESIGN** You are planning to build a walkway that surrounds a rectangular garden, as shown. The width of the walkway around the garden is the same on every side.

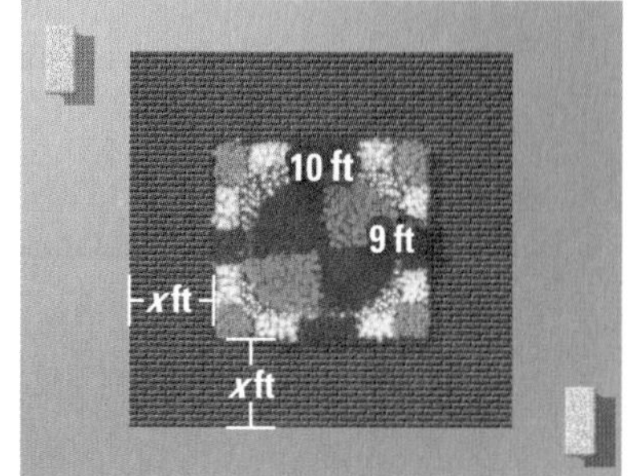

   a. Write a polynomial that represents the combined area of the garden and the walkway.

   b. Find the combined area when the width of the walkway is 4 feet.

9.2 EXERCISES

HOMEWORK KEY

○ = **WORKED-OUT SOLUTIONS** on p. WS20 for Exs. 23 and 51

★ = **STANDARDIZED TEST PRACTICE** Exs. 2, 26, 44, 52, and 53

SKILL PRACTICE

1. **VOCABULARY** Copy and complete: The FOIL pattern can be used to multiply any two __?__.

2. ★ **WRITING** *Explain* how the letters of the word FOIL can help you multiply polynomials.

EXAMPLE 1 on p. 562 for Exs. 3–8

MULTIPLYING POLYNOMIALS **Find the product.**

3. $x(2x^2 - 3x + 9)$
4. $4y(-y^3 - 2y - 1)$
5. $z^2(4z^4 + z^3 - 11z^2 - 6)$
6. $3c^3(8c^4 - c^2 - 3c + 5)$
7. $-a^5(-9a^2 + 5a + 13)$
8. $-5b^3(4b^5 - 2b^3 + b - 11)$

EXAMPLE 2 on p. 562 for Exs. 9–15

USING TABLES **Use a table to find the product.**

9. $(x + 2)(x - 3)$
10. $(y - 5)(2y + 3)$
11. $(4b - 3)(b - 7)$
12. $(5s + 2)(s + 8)$
13. $(3k - 1)(4k + 9)$
14. $(8n - 5)(3n - 6)$

EXAMPLES 3 and 4 on p. 563 for Exs. 16–26

ERROR ANALYSIS ***Describe*** **and correct the error in finding the product of the polynomials.**

15.

$(x - 5)(3x + 1)$

	3x	1
x	$3x^2$	x
5	15x	5

$(x - 5)(3x + 1) = 3x^2 + 16x + 5$ ✗

16.

$$\begin{array}{r} 2x^2 - 3x - 4 \\ \times \qquad x + 7 \\ \hline 14x^2 - 21x - 28 \\ 2x^3 - 3x^2 - 4x \qquad \\ \hline 2x^3 + 11x^4 - 25x^2 - 28 \end{array}$$

✗

MULTIPLYING POLYNOMIALS Use a vertical or a horizontal format to find the product.

17. $(y + 6)(y - 5)$
18. $(5x - 8)(2x - 5)$
19. $(7w + 5)(11w - 3)$
20. $(b - 2)(b^2 - b + 1)$
21. $(s + 4)(s^2 + 6s - 5)$
22. $(-r + 7)(2r^2 - r - 9)$
23. $(5x + 2)(-3x^2 + 4x - 1)$
24. $(y^2 + 8y - 6)(4y - 3)$
25. $(6z^2 + z - 1)(9z - 5)$

26. ★ **MULTIPLE CHOICE** What is the product of $2x - 9$ and $4x + 1$?

(A) $8x^2 - 38x - 9$ (B) $8x^2 - 34x - 9$

(C) $8x^2 + 34x - 9$ (D) $8x^2 + 38x - 9$

EXAMPLE 5 on p. 563 for Exs. 27–32

USING THE FOIL PATTERN Use the FOIL pattern to find the product.

27. $(2r - 1)(5r + 3)$
28. $(7a - 2)(3a - 4)$
29. $(4m + 9)(2m + 7)$
30. $(8t + 11)(6t - 1)$
31. $(4x - 5)(12x - 7)$
32. $(8z + 3)(5z + 4)$

SIMPLIFYING EXPRESSIONS Simplify the expression.

33. $p(2p - 3) + (p - 3)(p + 3)$
34. $x^2(7x + 5) - (2x + 6)(x - 1)$
35. $-3c^2(c + 11) - (4c - 5)(3c - 2)$
36. $2w^3(2w^3 - 7w - 1) + w(5w^2 + 2w)$

EXAMPLES 6 and 7 on p. 564 for Exs. 37–42

GEOMETRY Write a polynomial that represents the area of the shaded region.

37.
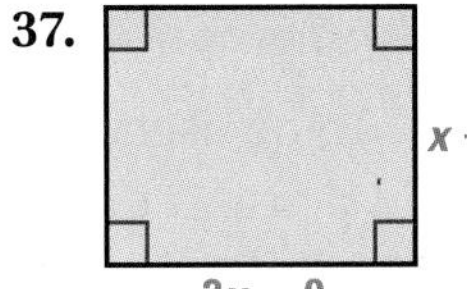

38.
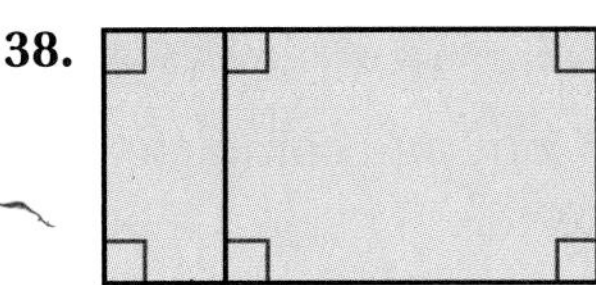

39.
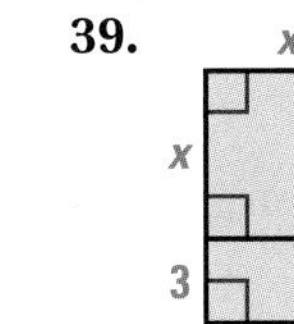

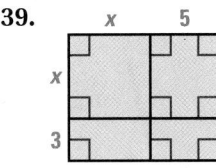

40.
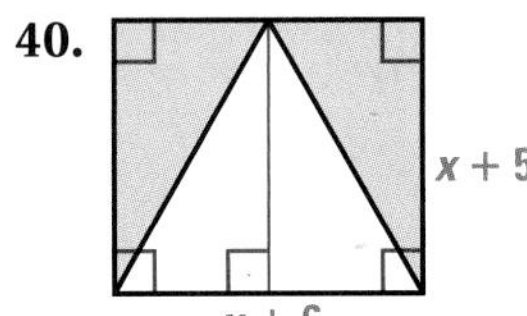

41.
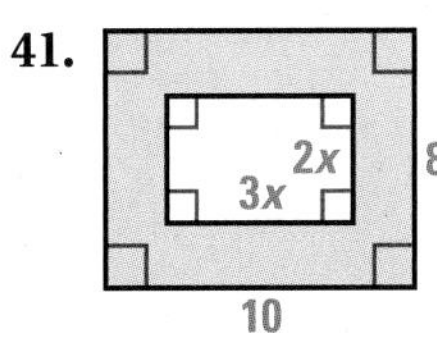

42.
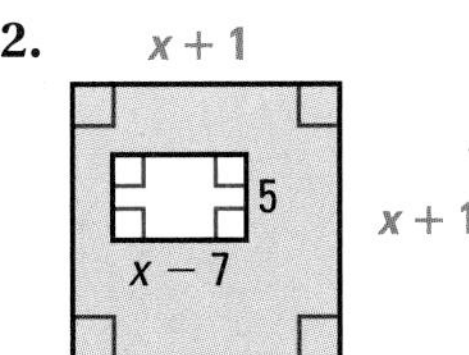

43. **POLYNOMIAL FUNCTIONS** Find the product $f(x) \cdot g(x)$ for the functions $f(x) = x - 11$ and $g(x) = 2x + 12$.

44. ★ **MULTIPLE CHOICE** Which polynomial represents $f(x) \cdot g(x)$ if $f(x) = -2x^2$ and $g(x) = x^3 - 5x^2 + 2x - 1$?

(A) $-2x^5 - 10x^4 + 4x^3 - 2x^2$ (B) $-2x^5 + 10x^4 - 4x^3 - 2x^2$

(C) $-2x^5 + 10x^4 - 4x^3 + 2x^2$ (D) $2x^5 - 10x^4 + 4x^3 - 2x^2$

45. **REASONING** Find the product $(x^2 - 7x)(2x^2 + 3x + 1)$. Show that the product is correct by using a graphing calculator. *Explain* your reasoning.

CHALLENGE Find the product.

46. $(x - y)(3x + 4y)$
47. $(x^2y + 9y)(2x + 3y)$
48. $(x^2 - 5xy + y^2)(4xy)$

PROBLEM SOLVING

EXAMPLE 7 on p. 564 for Exs. 49–50

49. **PICTURE FRAME** You are designing a frame to surround a rectangular picture. The width of the frame around the picture is the same on every side, as shown.

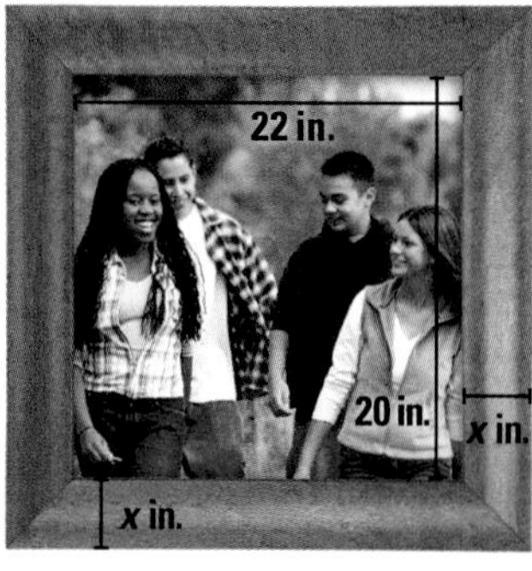

a. Write a polynomial that represents the total area of the picture and the frame.

b. Find the combined area of the picture and the frame when the width of the frame is 4 inches.

@HomeTutor for problem solving help at classzone.com

50. **SWIMMING POOL** A rectangular swimming pool is bordered on one side by a deck. A contractor is hired to build a walkway along the remaining three sides of the pool. The width of the walkway is the same on every side, as shown.

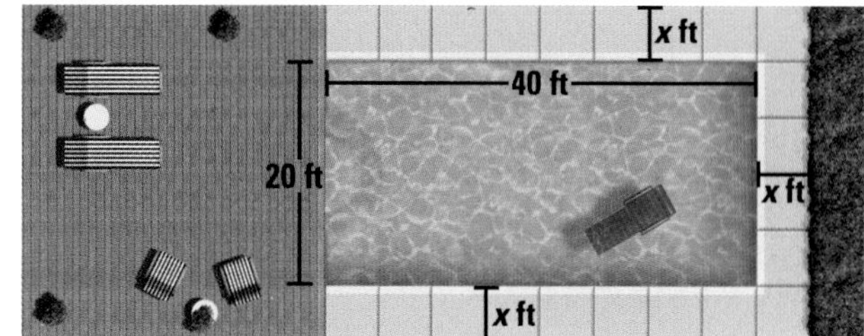

a. Write a polynomial that represents the total area of the pool and the walkway.

b. Find the combined area of the pool and the walkway when the width of the walkway is 5 feet.

@HomeTutor for problem solving help at classzone.com

51. **SOUND RECORDINGS** During the period 1997–2002, the amount of money R (in millions of dollars) spent on sound recordings in the U.S. and the percent P (in decimal form) of this amount spent by people who are between 15 and 19 years old can be modeled by

$$R = -336t^2 + 1730t + 12{,}300 \text{ and } P = 0.00351t^2 - 0.0249t + 0.171$$

where t is the number of years since 1997.

a. Find the values of R and P for $t = 0$. What does the product $R \cdot P$ mean for $t = 0$ in this situation?

b. Write an equation that models the amount spent on sound recordings by people who are between 15 and 19 years old as a function of the number of years since 1997.

c. How much money did people between 15 and 19 years old spend on sound recordings in 2002?

52. ★ **SHORT RESPONSE** During the period 1980–2002, the number H (in thousands) of housing units in the U.S. and the percent P (in decimal form) of housing units that were vacant can be modeled by

$$H = 1570t + 89{,}000 \quad \text{and} \quad P = 0.0013t + 0.094$$

where t is the number of years since 1980.

a. Write an equation that models the number (in thousands) of vacant housing units as a function of the number of years since 1980. *Explain* how you found this equation.

b. How many housing units were vacant in 2002?

53. ★ **EXTENDED RESPONSE** The bar graph shows the number of households with a television for various years during the period 1990–2001.

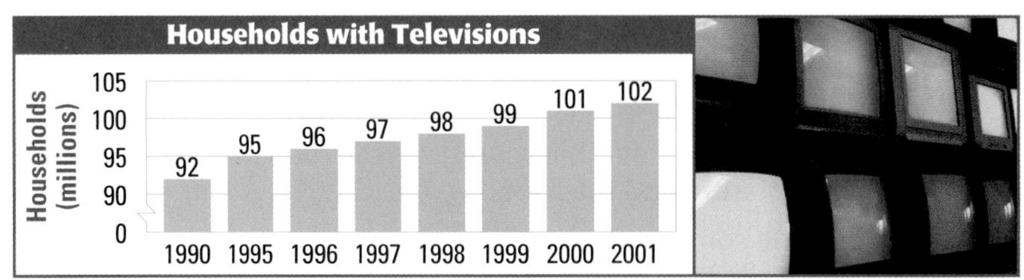

a. Find a linear equation that models the number of households T (in millions) with a television as a function of the number of years since 1990. *Explain* how you found your model.

b. During the period 1990–2001, the percent P (in decimal form) of television households that also have a VCR can be modeled by

$$P = -0.0015t^2 + 0.032t + 0.069$$

where t is the number of years since 1990. Write an equation that models the number of households V (in millions) with a VCR and a television as a function of the number of years since 1990.

c. Use the equation from part (b) to predict the number of households that had a VCR and a television in 2002 and in 2005.

54. **CHALLENGE** For the period 1990–2001, the total United States energy consumption C (in quadrillion British Thermal Units, or BTU) and the percent P of the total energy that was consumed in the United States for industrial purposes can be modeled by

$$C = 1.5t + 84$$
$$P = -0.05t^2 + 0.25t + 38$$

where t is the number of years since 1990.

a. Find the percent of total energy that was consumed in the United States for industrial purposes in 2000.

b. Write an equation that gives the total energy (in quadrillion BTU) consumed in the United States for industrial purposes as a function of the number of years since 1990. To write the equation, you may need to rewrite one of the given equations.

MIXED REVIEW

PREVIEW
Prepare for Lesson 9.3 in Exs. 55–60.

Simplify the expression. *(p. 96)*

55. $5(2x - 7) + 5x$
56. $2x + 3(4x - 1)$
57. $15x - 7(x + 3)$
58. $-2x(x + 1) + 2x$
59. $x(x - 4) - 9x$
60. $11x + (x - 1)(8x)$

Solve the system.

61. $2x + y = -5$, $y = -3x + 2$ *(p. 435)*
62. $x - 2y = -7$, $x + 2y = 13$ *(p. 444)*
63. $-2x + 4y = -2$, $x - 2y = -1$ *(p. 451)*
64. $-6x + 4y = 40$, $-3x + 2y = 20$ *(p. 451)*
65. $x \geq -3$, $y < 5$ *(p. 466)*
66. $y \leq 2x - 5$, $y > -3x + 1$ *(p. 466)*

9.3 Find Special Products of Polynomials

Before You multiplied polynomials.

Now You will use special product patterns to multiply polynomials.

Why? So you can make a scientific prediction, as in Example 4.

Key Vocabulary
- **binomial,** *p. 555*
- **trinomial,** *p. 555*

The diagram shows a square with a side length of $(a + b)$ units. You can see that the area of the square is

$$(a + b)^2 = a^2 + 2ab + b^2.$$

	a	b
a	a^2	ab
b	ab	b^2

This is one version of a pattern called the square of a binomial. To find another version of this pattern, use algebra: replace b with $-b$.

$(a + (-b))^2 = a^2 + 2a(-b) + (-b)^2$ **Replace b with $-b$ in the pattern above.**

$(a - b)^2 = a^2 - 2ab + b^2$ **Simplify.**

KEY CONCEPT *For Your Notebook*

Square of a Binomial Pattern

Algebra	**Example**
$(a + b)^2 = a^2 + 2ab + b^2$	$(x + 5)^2 = x^2 + 10x + 25$
$(a - b)^2 = a^2 - 2ab + b^2$	$(2x - 3)^2 = 4x^2 - 12x + 9$

EXAMPLE 1 Use the square of a binomial pattern

USE PATTERNS
When you use special product patterns, remember that a and b can be numbers, variables, or variable expressions.

Find the product.

a. $(3x + 4)^2 = (3x)^2 + 2(3x)(4) + 4^2$ **Square of a binomial pattern**

$= 9x^2 + 24x + 16$ **Simplify.**

b. $(5x - 2y)^2 = (5x)^2 - 2(5x)(2y) + (2y)^2$ **Square of a binomial pattern**

$= 25x^2 - 20xy + 4y^2$ **Simplify.**

✓ **GUIDED PRACTICE** for Example 1

Find the product.

1. $(x + 3)^2$ **2.** $(2x + 1)^2$ **3.** $(4x - y)^2$ **4.** $(3m + n)^2$

SUM AND DIFFERENCE PATTERN To find the product $(x + 2)(x - 2)$, you can multiply the two binomials using the FOIL pattern.

$(x + 2)(x - 2) = x^2 - 2x + 2x - 4$ **Use FOIL pattern.**

$= x^2 - 4$ **Combine like terms.**

This suggests a pattern for the product of the sum and difference of two terms.

KEY CONCEPT ***For Your Notebook***

Sum and Difference Pattern

Algebra	**Example**
$(a + b)(a - b) = a^2 - b^2$	$(x + 3)(x - 3) = x^2 - 9$

EXAMPLE 2 Use the sum and difference pattern

Find the product.

a. $(t + 5)(t - 5) = t^2 - 5^2$ **Sum and difference pattern**

$= t^2 - 25$ **Simplify.**

b. $(3x + y)(3x - y) = (3x)^2 - y^2$ **Sum and difference pattern**

$= 9x^2 - y^2$ **Simplify.**

✓ **GUIDED PRACTICE** for Example 2

Find the product.

5. $(x + 10)(x - 10)$ **6.** $(2x + 1)(2x - 1)$ **7.** $(x + 3y)(x - 3y)$

SPECIAL PRODUCTS AND MENTAL MATH The special product patterns can help you use mental math to find certain products of numbers.

EXAMPLE 3 Use special products and mental math

Use special products to find the product 26 • 34.

Solution

Notice that 26 is 4 less than 30 while 34 is 4 more than 30.

$26 \cdot 34 = (30 - 4)(30 + 4)$ **Write as product of difference and sum.**

$= 30^2 - 4^2$ **Sum and difference pattern**

$= 900 - 16$ **Evaluate powers.**

$= 884$ **Simplify.**

EXAMPLE 4 Solve a multi-step problem

BORDER COLLIES The color of the dark patches of a border collie's coat is determined by a combination of two genes. An offspring inherits one patch color gene from each parent. Each parent has two color genes, and the offspring has an equal chance of inheriting either one.

The gene B is for black patches, and the gene r is for red patches. Any gene combination with a B results in black patches. Suppose each parent has the same gene combination Br. The Punnett square shows the possible gene combinations of the offspring and the resulting patch color.

- What percent of the possible gene combinations of the offspring result in black patches?
- Show how you could use a polynomial to model the possible gene combinations of the offspring.

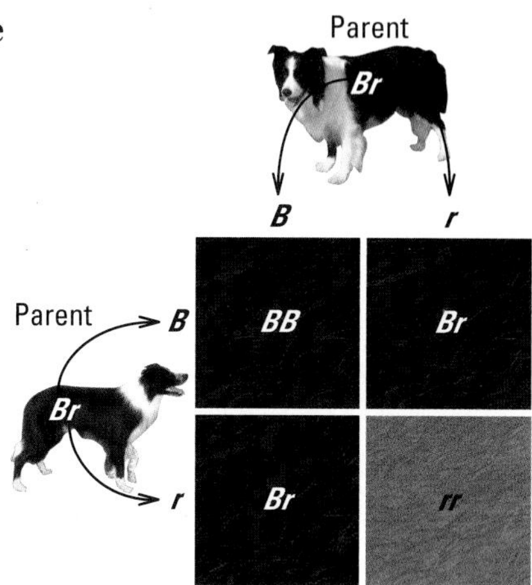

Solution

STEP 1 **Notice** that the Punnett square shows 4 possible gene combinations of the offspring. Of these combinations, 3 result in black patches.

▶ 75% of the possible gene combinations result in black patches.

STEP 2 **Model** the gene from each parent with $0.5B + 0.5r$. There is an equal chance that the collie inherits a black or red gene from each parent.

The possible genes of the offspring can be modeled by $(0.5B + 0.5r)^2$. Notice that this product also represents the area of the Punnett square.

Expand the product to find the possible patch colors of the offspring.

$$(0.5B + 0.5r)^2 = (0.5B)^2 + 2(0.5B)(0.5r) + (0.5r)^2$$
$$= 0.25B^2 + 0.5Br + 0.25r^2$$

Consider the coefficients in the polynomial.

$$0.25B^2 + 0.5Br + 0.25r^2$$

25% *BB*, black patches — 50% *Br*, black patches — 25% *rr*, red patches

The coefficients show that 25% + 50% = 75% of the possible gene combinations will result in black patches.

✓ GUIDED PRACTICE for Examples 3 and 4

8. *Describe* how you can use special products to find 21^2.

9. BORDER COLLIES Look back at Example 4. What percent of the possible gene combinations of the offspring result in red patches?

9.3 EXERCISES

HOMEWORK KEY

○ = **WORKED-OUT SOLUTIONS** on p. WS21 for Exs. 11 and 41

★ = **STANDARDIZED TEST PRACTICE** Exs. 2, 17, 18, 42, and 44

◆ = **MULTIPLE REPRESENTATIONS** Ex. 41

SKILL PRACTICE

1. VOCABULARY Give an example of two binomials whose product you can find using the sum and difference pattern.

2. ★ WRITING *Explain* how to use the square of a binomial pattern.

EXAMPLE 1 on p. 569 for Exs. 3–10, 18

SQUARE OF A BINOMIAL **Find the product.**

3. $(x + 8)^2$ **4.** $(a + 6)^2$ **5.** $(2y + 5)^2$

6. $(t - 7)^2$ **7.** $(n - 11)^2$ **8.** $(6b - 1)^2$

ERROR ANALYSIS ***Describe*** **and correct the error in multiplying.**

9. $(s - 3)^2 = s^2 + 9$ ✗

10. $(2d - 10)^2 = 4d^2 - 20d + 100$

EXAMPLE 2 on p. 570 for Exs. 11–17

SUM AND DIFFERENCE PATTERN **Find the product.**

11. $(t + 4)(t - 4)$ **12.** $(m - 6)(m + 6)$ **13.** $(2x + 1)(2x - 1)$

14. $(3x - 1)(3x + 1)$ **15.** $(7 + w)(7 - w)$ **16.** $(3s - 8)(3s + 8)$

17. ★ MULTIPLE CHOICE Find the product $(7x + 3)(7x - 3)$.

Ⓐ $7x^2 - 9$ Ⓑ $49x^2 - 9$ Ⓒ $49x^2 - 21x - 9$ Ⓓ $49x^2 - 42x - 9$

18. ★ MULTIPLE CHOICE Find the product $(5n - 3)^2$.

Ⓐ $5n^2 - 9$ Ⓑ $25n^2 - 9$ Ⓒ $25n^2 - 15n + 9$ Ⓓ $25n^2 - 30n + 9$

EXAMPLE 3 on p. 570 for Exs. 19–22

MENTAL MATH ***Describe*** **how you can use mental math to find the product.**

19. $16 \cdot 24$ **20.** $28 \cdot 32$ **21.** 17^2 **22.** 44^2

SPECIAL PRODUCT PATTERNS **Find the product.**

23. $(r + 9s)^2$ **24.** $(6x + 5)^2$ **25.** $(3m + 11n)(3m - 11n)$

26. $(7a + 8b)(7a - 8b)$ **27.** $(3m - 7n)^2$ **28.** $(13 - 2x)^2$

29. $(3f - 9)(3f + 9)$ **30.** $(9 - 4t)(9 + 4t)$ **31.** $(3x + 8y)^2$

32. $(-x - 2y)^2$ **33.** $(2a - 5b)(2a + 5b)$ **34.** $(6x + y)(6x - y)$

MULTIPLYING FUNCTIONS **Perform the indicated operation using the functions $f(x) = 3x + 0.5$ and $g(x) = 3x - 0.5$.**

35. $f(x) \cdot g(x)$ **36.** $(f(x))^2$ **37.** $(g(x))^2$

38. CHALLENGE Write two binomials that have the product $x^2 - 121$. *Explain.*

39. CHALLENGE Write a pattern for the cube of a binomial $(a + b)^3$.

PROBLEM SOLVING

EXAMPLE 4 on p. 571 for Exs. 40–42

40. **PEA PLANTS** In pea plants, the gene G is for green pods, and the gene y is for yellow pods. Any gene combination with a G results in a green pod. Suppose two pea plants have the same gene combination Gy. The Punnett square shows the possible gene combinations of an offspring pea plant and the resulting pod color.

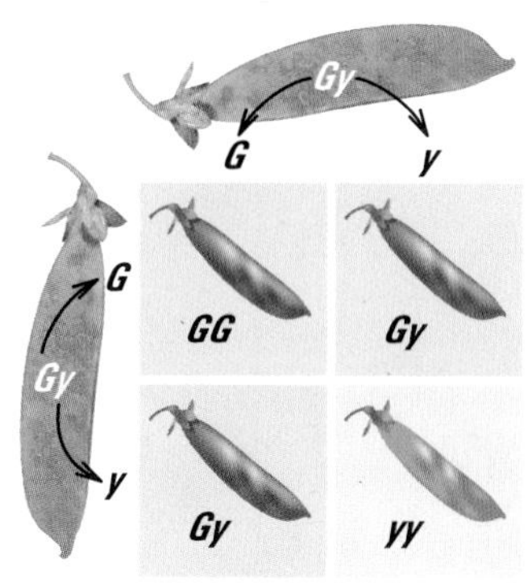

   a. What percent of possible gene combinations of the offspring plant result in a yellow pod?

   b. Show how you could use a polynomial to model the possible gene combinations of the offspring.

   @HomeTutor for problem solving help at classzone.com

41. ◆ **MULTIPLE REPRESENTATIONS** In humans, the gene s is for straight thumbs, and the gene C is for curved thumbs. Any gene combination with a C results in a curved thumb. Suppose each parent has the same gene combination Cs.

   a. **Making a Diagram** Make a Punnett square that shows the possible gene combinations inherited by a child.

   b. **Writing a Model** Write a polynomial that models the possible gene combinations of the child.

   c. **Interpreting a Model** What percent of the possible gene combinations of the child result in a curved thumb?

   @HomeTutor for problem solving help at classzone.com

42. ★ **SHORT RESPONSE** In ball pythons, the gene N is for normal coloring, and the gene a is for no coloring, or albino. Any gene combination with an N results in normal coloring. Suppose one parent python has the gene combination Na and the other parent python has the gene combination aa. What percent of the possible gene combinations of the offspring result in an albino python? *Explain* how you found your answer.

43. **FOOTBALL STATISTICS** During the 2004 regular season, the San Diego Chargers' quarterback Drew Brees completed 65.5% of the passes he attempted. The area model shows the possible outcomes of two attempted passes.

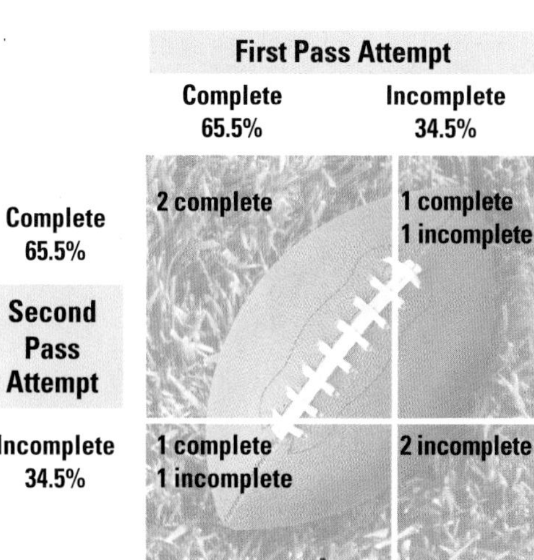

   a. What percent of the possible outcomes of two attempted passes results in Drew Brees's throwing at least one complete pass? *Explain* how you found your answer using the area model.

   b. Show how you could use a polynomial to model the possible results of two attempted passes.

44. ★ **EXTENDED RESPONSE** The iris of an eye surrounds the pupil. It regulates the amount of light entering the eye by opening and closing the pupil. For parts (a)–(c) below, leave your answers in terms of π.

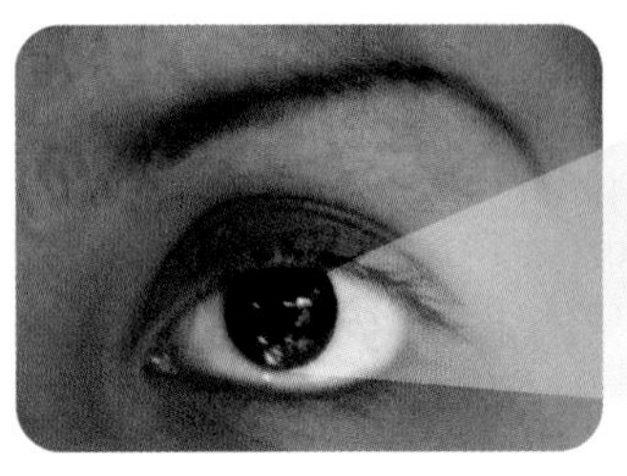

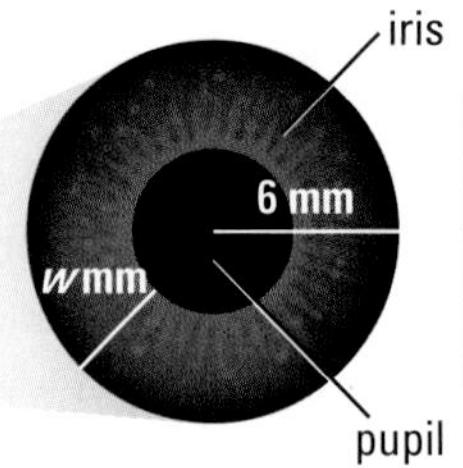

The iris of a human eye has a width w that varies from 0.5 millimeter to 4 millimeters.

a. Write a polynomial that represents the pupil's radius.

b. Write a polynomial that represents the pupil's area.

c. What is the least possible area and the greatest possible area of the pupil? *Explain* how you found your answers.

45. **CHALLENGE** You use 100 feet of fencing to form a square with a side length of 25 feet. You want to change the dimensions of the enclosed region. For every 1 foot you increase the width, you must decrease the length by 1 foot. Write a polynomial that gives the area of the rectangle after you increase the width by x feet and decrease the length by x feet. *Explain* why *any* change in dimensions results in an area less than that of the original square.

MIXED REVIEW

PREVIEW
Prepare for Lesson 9.4 in Exs. 46–53.

Find the greatest common factor of the pair of numbers. *(p. 910)*

46. 25, 30	**47.** 36, 54	**48.** 14, 21	**49.** 36, 50
50. 65, 39	**51.** 13, 20	**52.** 77, 143	**53.** 24, 162

Solve the equation. Check your solution.

54. $x + 11 = 6$ *(p. 134)*

55. $11x + 8 = -14$ *(p. 141)*

56. $2x - 5(x - 13) = 35$ *(p. 148)*

57. $9x + 4 - 4x = 6x + 7$ *(p. 154)*

QUIZ *for Lessons 9.1–9.3*

Find the sum, difference, or product.

1. $(x^2 - 3x + 5) + (-2x^2 + 11x + 1)$ *(p. 554)*
2. $(8y^3 - 7y^2 + y) - (9y^2 - 5y + 7)$ *(p. 554)*
3. $(2r + 11)(r - 6)$ *(p. 562)*
4. $(m + 3)(-2m^2 + 5m - 1)$ *(p. 562)*
5. $(2 + 8p)(2 - 10p)$ *(p. 562)*
6. $(15 - 2s)^2$ *(p. 569)*
7. $(5w + 9z)^2$ *(p. 569)*
8. $(5x - 4y)(5x + 4y)$ *(p. 569)*
9. **AREA** The length of a rectangular rug is 2 times its width. The rug is centered in a rectangular room. Each edge is 3 feet from the nearest wall. Write a polynomial that represents the area of the room. *(p. 564)*

9.4 Solve Polynomial Equations in Factored Form

Before You solved linear equations.

Now You will solve polynomial equations.

Why So you can analyze vertical motion, as in Ex. 55.

Key Vocabulary
- **roots**
- **vertical motion model**

In Lesson 2.4, you learned the property of zero: For any real number a, $a \cdot 0 = 0$. This is equivalent to saying:

For real numbers a and b, if $a = 0$ or $b = 0$, then $ab = 0$.

The converse of this statement is also true (as shown in Exercise 49), and it is called the zero-product property.

KEY CONCEPT *For Your Notebook*

Zero-Product Property

Let a and b be real numbers. If $ab = 0$, then $a = 0$ or $b = 0$.

The zero-product property is used to solve an equation when one side is zero and the other side is a product of polynomial factors. The solutions of such an equation are also called **roots**.

EXAMPLE 1 Use the zero-product property

Solve $(x - 4)(x + 2) = 0$.

$(x - 4)(x + 2) = 0$	Write original equation.
$x - 4 = 0$ *or* $x + 2 = 0$	Zero-product property
$x = 4$ *or* $x = -2$	Solve for x.

▶ The solutions of the equation are 4 and −2.

CHECK Substitute each solution into the original equation to check.

$(4 - 4)(4 + 2) \stackrel{?}{=} 0$	$(-2 - 4)(-2 + 2) \stackrel{?}{=} 0$
$0 \cdot 6 \stackrel{?}{=} 0$	$-6 \cdot 0 \stackrel{?}{=} 0$
$0 = 0$ ✓	$0 = 0$ ✓

 **GUIDED PRACTICE** for Example 1

1. Solve the equation $(x - 5)(x - 1) = 0$.

REVIEW GCF
For help with finding the GCF, see p. 910.

FACTORING To solve a polynomial equation using the zero-product property, you may need to *factor* the polynomial, or write it as a product of other polynomials. Look for the *greatest common factor* (GCF) of the polynomial's terms. This is a monomial with an integer coefficient that divides evenly into each term.

EXAMPLE 2 Find the greatest common monomial factor

Factor out the greatest common monomial factor.

a. $12x + 42y$

b. $4x^4 + 24x^3$

Solution

a. The GCF of 12 and 42 is 6. The variables x and y have no common factor. So, the greatest common monomial factor of the terms is 6.

▶ $12x + 42y = 6(2x + 7y)$

b. The GCF of 4 and 24 is 4. The GCF of x^4 and x^3 is x^3. So, the greatest common monomial factor of the terms is $4x^3$.

▶ $4x^4 + 24x^3 = 4x^3(x + 6)$

✓ **GUIDED PRACTICE** for Example 2

2. Factor out the greatest common monomial factor from $14m + 35n$.

EXAMPLE 3 Solve an equation by factoring

Solve $2x^2 + 8x = 0$.

$2x^2 + 8x = 0$	Write original equation.
$2x(x + 4) = 0$	Factor left side.
$2x = 0$ *or* $x + 4 = 0$	Zero-product property
$x = 0$ *or* $x = -4$	Solve for x.

▶ The solutions of the equation are 0 and -4.

EXAMPLE 4 Solve an equation by factoring

Solve $6n^2 = 15n$.

AVOID ERRORS
To use the zero-product property, you must write the equation so that one side is 0. For this reason, $15n$ must be subtracted from each side.

$6n^2 - 15n = 0$	Subtract $15n$ from each side.
$3n(2n - 5) = 0$	Factor left side.
$3n = 0$ *or* $2n - 5 = 0$	Zero-product property
$n = 0$ *or* $n = \frac{5}{2}$	Solve for n.

▶ The solutions of the equation are 0 and $\frac{5}{2}$.

GUIDED PRACTICE for Examples 3 and 4

Solve the equation.

3. $a^2 + 5a = 0$ **4.** $3s^2 - 9s = 0$ **5.** $4x^2 = 2x$

VERTICAL MOTION A *projectile* is an object that is propelled into the air but has no power to keep itself in the air. A thrown ball is a projectile, but an airplane is not. The height of a projectile can be described by the **vertical motion model**.

UNDERSTAND THE MODEL
The vertical motion model takes into account the effect of gravity but ignores other, less significant, factors such as air resistance.

KEY CONCEPT *For Your Notebook*

Vertical Motion Model

The height h (in feet) of a projectile can be modeled by

$$h = -16t^2 + vt + s$$

where t is the time (in seconds) the object has been in the air, v is the initial vertical velocity (in feet per second), and s is the initial height (in feet).

EXAMPLE 5 Solve a multi-step problem

ARMADILLO A startled armadillo jumps straight into the air with an initial vertical velocity of 14 feet per second. After how many seconds does it land on the ground?

Solution

STEP 1 **Write** a model for the armadillo's height above the ground.

$h = -16t^2 + vt + s$ Vertical motion model

$h = -16t^2 + 14t + 0$ Substitute 14 for v and 0 for s.

$h = -16t^2 + 14t$ Simplify.

STEP 2 **Substitute** 0 for h. When the armadillo lands, its height above the ground is 0 feet. Solve for t.

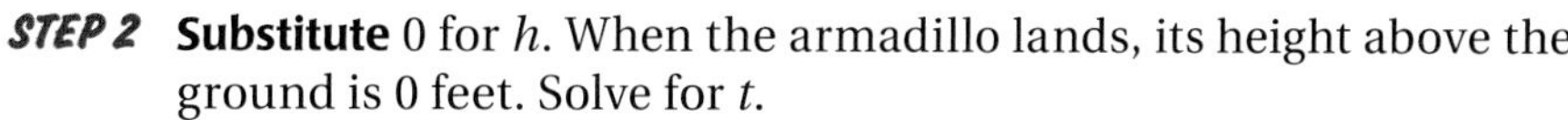

$0 = -16t^2 + 14t$ Substitute 0 for h.

$0 = 2t(-8t + 7)$ Factor right side.

$2t = 0$ *or* $-8t + 7 = 0$ Zero-product property

$t = 0$ *or* $t = 0.875$ Solve for t.

▶ The armadillo lands on the ground 0.875 second after the armadillo jumps.

AVOID ERRORS
The solution $t = 0$ means that before the armadillo jumps, its height above the ground is 0 feet.

GUIDED PRACTICE for Example 5

6. WHAT IF? In Example 5, suppose the initial vertical velocity is 12 feet per second. After how many seconds does the armadillo land on the ground?

9.4 EXERCISES

HOMEWORK KEY

○ = **WORKED-OUT SOLUTIONS** on p. WS21 for Exs. 3 and 55

★ = **STANDARDIZED TEST PRACTICE** Exs. 2, 15, 39, 53, and 56

◆ = **MULTIPLE REPRESENTATIONS** Ex. 58

SKILL PRACTICE

1. **VOCABULARY** What is the vertical motion model and what does each variable in the model represent?

2. ★ **WRITING** *Explain* how to use the zero-product property to find the solutions of the equation $3x(x - 7) = 0$.

EXAMPLE 1 on p. 575 for Exs. 3–16

ZERO-PRODUCT PROPERTY **Solve the equation.**

3. $(x - 5)(x + 3) = 0$
4. $(y + 9)(y - 1) = 0$
5. $(z - 13)(z - 14) = 0$
6. $(c + 6)(c + 8) = 0$
7. $(d - 7)\left(d + \frac{4}{3}\right) = 0$
8. $\left(g - \frac{1}{8}\right)(g + 18) = 0$
9. $(m - 3)(4m + 12) = 0$
10. $(2n - 14)(3n + 9) = 0$
11. $(3n + 11)(n + 1) = 0$
12. $(3x + 1)(x + 6) = 0$
13. $(2y + 5)(7y - 5) = 0$
14. $(8z - 6)(12z + 14) = 0$

15. ★ **MULTIPLE CHOICE** What are the roots of the equation $(y - 12)(y + 6) = 0$?

Ⓐ −12 and −6 Ⓑ −12 and 6 Ⓒ −6 and 12 Ⓓ 6 and 12

16. **ERROR ANALYSIS** *Describe* and correct the error in solving $(z - 15)(z + 21) = 0$.

$(z - 15)(z + 21) = 0$

$z = -15$ or $z = 21$

EXAMPLE 2 on p. 576 for Exs. 17–26

FACTORING EXPRESSIONS **Factor out the greatest common monomial factor.**

17. $2x + 2y$
18. $6x^2 - 15y$
19. $3s^4 + 16s$
20. $5d^6 + 2d^5$
21. $7w^5 - 35w^2$
22. $9m^7 - 3m^2$
23. $15n^3 + 25n$
24. $12a^5 + 8a$
25. $\frac{5}{2}x^6 - \frac{1}{2}x^4$

26. **ERROR ANALYSIS** *Describe* and correct the error in factoring out the greatest common monomial factor of $18x^8 - 9x^4 - 6x^3$.

$18x^8 - 9x^4 - 6x^3 = 3x(6x^7 - 3x^3 - 2x^2)$

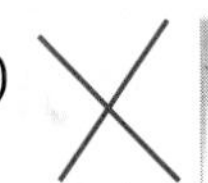

EXAMPLES 3 and 4 on p. 576 for Exs. 27–39

SOLVING EQUATIONS **Solve the equation.**

27. $b^2 + 6b = 0$
28. $5w^2 - 5w = 0$
29. $-10n^2 + 35n = 0$
30. $2x^2 + 15x = 0$
31. $18c^2 + 6c = 0$
32. $-32y^2 - 24y = 0$
33. $3k^2 = 6k$
34. $6h^2 = 3h$
35. $4s^2 = 10s$
36. $-42z^2 = 14z$
37. $28m^2 = -8m$
38. $-12p^2 = -30p$

39. ★ **MULTIPLE CHOICE** What are the solutions of $4x^2 = x$?

Ⓐ −4 and 0 Ⓑ $-\frac{1}{4}$ and 0 Ⓒ 0 and $\frac{1}{4}$ Ⓓ 0 and 4

FACTORING EXPRESSIONS Factor out the greatest common monomial factor.

40. $20x^2y^2 - 4xy$

41. $8a^2b - 6ab^2$

42. $18s^2t^5 - 2s^3t$

43. $v^3 - 5v^2 + 9v$

44. $-2g^4 + 14g^2 + 6g$

45. $6q^5 - 21q^4 - 15q^2$

HINT
For help with finding zeros of functions, see p. 335.

FINDING ZEROS OF FUNCTIONS Find the zeros of the function.

46. $f(x) = x^2 - 15x$

47. $f(x) = -2x^2 + x$

48. $f(x) = 3x^2 - 27x$

49. **CHALLENGE** Consider the equation $ab = 0$. Assume that $a \neq 0$ and solve the equation for b. Then assume that $b \neq 0$ and solve the equation for a. What conclusion can you draw about the values of a and b?

50. **CHALLENGE** Consider the equation $z = x^2 - xy$. For what values of x and y does $z = 0$?

PROBLEM SOLVING

EXAMPLE 5
on p. 577 for Exs. 51–53

51. **MOTION** A cat leaps from the ground into the air with an initial vertical velocity of 11 feet per second. After how many seconds does the cat land on the ground?

@HomeTutor for problem solving help at classzone.com

52. **SPITTLEBUG** A spittlebug jumps into the air with an initial vertical velocity of 10 feet per second.

a. Write an equation that gives the height of the spittlebug as a function of the time (in seconds) since it left the ground.

b. The spittlebug reaches its maximum height after 0.3125 second. How high can it jump?

@HomeTutor for problem solving help at classzone.com

53. ★ **SHORT RESPONSE** A penguin jumps out of the water while swimming. This action is called porpoising. The height h (in feet) of the porpoising penguin can be modeled by $h = -16t^2 + 4.5t$ where t is the time (in seconds) since the penguin jumped out of the water. Find the zeros of the function. *Explain* what the zeros mean in this situation.

VERTICAL MOTION In Exercises 54 and 55, use the information below.

The height h (in meters) of a projectile can be modeled by $h = -4.9t^2 + vt + s$ where t is the time (in seconds) the object has been in the air, v is the initial vertical velocity (in meters per second), and s is the initial height (in meters).

54. **SOCCER** A soccer ball is kicked upward from the ground with an initial vertical velocity of 3.6 meters per second. After how many seconds does it land?

55. **RABBIT HIGH JUMP** A rabbit in a high jump competition leaves the ground with an initial vertical velocity of 4.9 meters per second.

a. Write an equation that gives the height of the rabbit as a function of the time (in seconds) since it left the ground.

b. What is a reasonable domain for the function? *Explain* your answer.

56. ★ **MULTIPLE CHOICE** Two rectangular rooms in a building's floor plan have different dimensions but the same area. The dimensions (in meters) are shown. What is the value of w?

Ⓐ 3 m Ⓑ 4 m Ⓒ 6 m Ⓓ 8 m

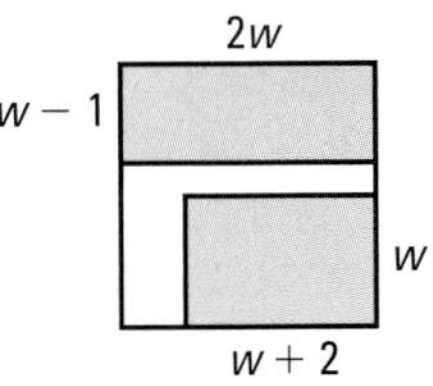

57. **TABLETOP AREAS** A display in your school library sits on top of two rectangular tables arranged in an L shape, as shown. The tabletops have the same area.

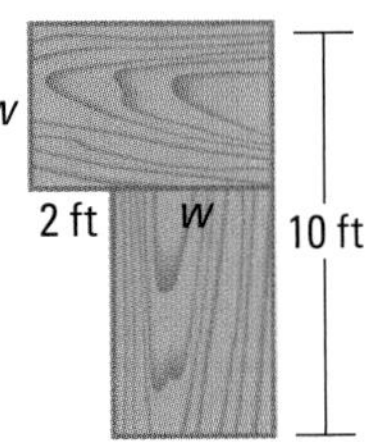

a. Write an equation that relates the areas of the tabletops.

b. Find the value of w.

c. What is the combined area of the tabletops?

58. **MULTIPLE REPRESENTATIONS** An arch frames the entrance to a garden. The shape of the arch is modeled by the graph of the equation $y = -2x^2 + 8x$ where x and y are measured in feet. On a coordinate plane, the ground is represented by the x-axis.

a. Making a Table Make a table of values that shows the height of the arch for $x = 0, 1, 2, 3,$ and 4 feet.

b. Drawing a Graph Plot the ordered pairs in the table as points in a coordinate plane. Connect the points with a smooth curve that represents the arch.

c. Interpreting a Graph How wide is the base of the arch?

59. **CHALLENGE** The shape of an arched doorway is modeled by the graph of the function $y = -0.5x(x - 8)$ where x and y are measured in feet. On a coordinate plane, the floor is represented by the x-axis.

a. How wide is the doorway at its base? *Justify* your answer using the zeros of the function.

b. The doorway's highest point occurs above the center of its base. How high is the highest point of the arched doorway? *Explain* how you found your answer.

MIXED REVIEW

PREVIEW
Prepare for Lesson 9.5 in Exs. 60–71.

Find the product.

60. $45(-x)(-x)$ *(p. 88)*
61. $-9a(-6a)(-a)$ *(p. 88)*
62. $-7(8n)(-4)$ *(p. 88)*
63. $(y - 1)(y + 7)$ *(p. 562)*
64. $(m - 5)(m - 13)$ *(p. 562)*
65. $(2b + 5)(b + 3)$ *(p. 562)*
66. $(3p + 8)(4p - 1)$ *(p. 562)*
67. $(5z - 2)(5z - 4)$ *(p. 562)*
68. $(9t + 7)(4t + 5)$ *(p. 562)*
69. $(2c + 7)^2$ *(p. 569)*
70. $(9 - 5w)^2$ *(p. 569)*
71. $(3g - 4h)^2$ *(p. 569)*

Graph the system of linear inequalities. *(p. 466)*

72. $x > -3$
$x \leq 3$

73. $x \geq 0$
$-3x + y < -1$
$y \geq 0$

74. $x < 6$
$y > -4$
$y < 2$
$y \leq x$

Lessons 9.1–9.4

1. **MULTI-STEP PROBLEM** You are making a blanket with a fringe border of equal width on each edge, as shown.

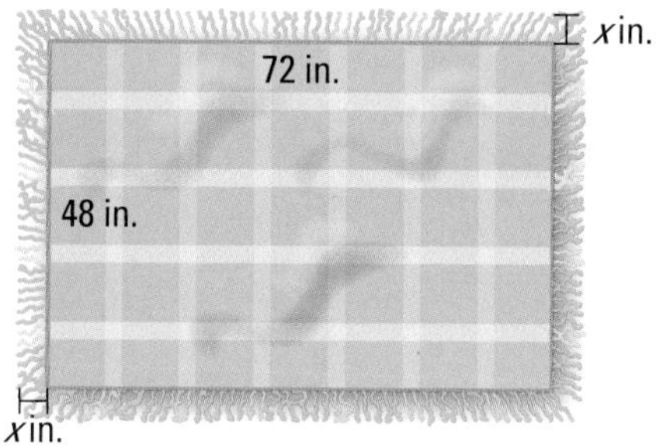

   a. Write a polynomial that represents the total area of the blanket with the fringe.

   b. Find the total area of the blanket with fringe when the width of the fringe is 4 inches.

2. **OPEN-ENDED** A horse with pinto coloring has white fur with patches of color. The gene P is for pinto coloring, and the gene s is for solid coloring. Any gene combination with a P results in pinto coloring.

   a. Suppose a male horse has the gene combination Ps. Choose a color gene combination for a female horse. Create a Punnett square to show the possible gene combinations of the two horses' offspring.

   b. What percent of the possible gene combinations of the offspring result in pinto coloring?

   c. Show how you could use a polynomial to model the possible color gene combinations of the offspring.

3. **SHORT RESPONSE** One football is kicked into the air with an initial vertical velocity of 44 feet per second. Another football is kicked into the air with an initial vertical velocity of 40 feet per second.

   a. Which football is in the air for more time?

   b. *Justify* your answer to part (a).

4. **GRIDDED ANSWER** During the period 1996–2000, the total value T (in millions of dollars) of toys imported to the United States can be modeled by

$$T = 82.9t^3 - 848t^2 + 3030t + 9610$$

where t is the number of years since 1996. What is the degree of the polynomial that represents T?

5. **EXTENDED RESPONSE** During the period 1992–2000, the number C (in millions) of people participating in cross-country skiing and the number S (in millions) of people participating in snowboarding can be modeled by

$$C = 0.067t^3 - 0.107t^2 + 0.27t + 3.5$$

$$S = 0.416t + 1.24$$

where t is the number of years since 1992.

   a. Write an equation that models the total number of people T (in millions) participating in cross-country skiing and snowboarding as a function of the number of years since 1992.

   b. Find the total participation in these activities in 1992 and 2000.

   c. What was the average rate of change in total participation from 1992 to 2000? *Explain* how you found this rate.

6. **SHORT RESPONSE** A circular rug has an interior circle and two rings around the circle, as shown.

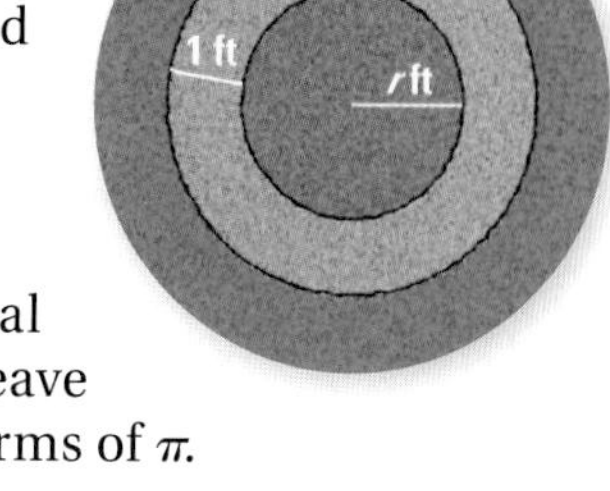

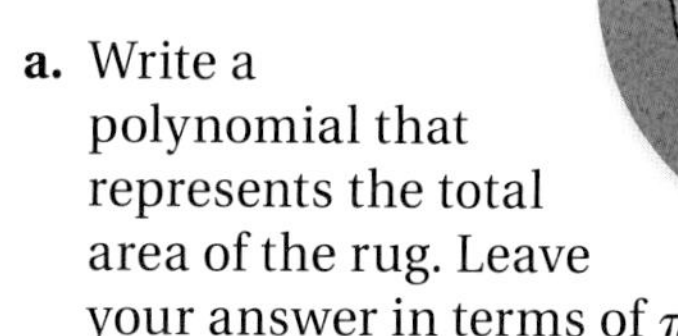

   a. Write a polynomial that represents the total area of the rug. Leave your answer in terms of π.

   b. The interior circle of the rug has a diameter of 3 feet. What is the area of the rug? Leave your answer in terms of π. *Explain* how you found your answer.

Animated Algebra
classzone.com

9.5 Factorization with Algebra Tiles

MATERIALS • algebra tiles

QUESTION **How can you factor a trinomial using algebra tiles?**

You have seen that algebra tiles can be used to model polynomials and to multiply binomials. Now, you will use algebra tiles to factor trinomials.

EXPLORE **Factor the trinomial $x^2 + 6x + 8$**

STEP 1 ***Make a rectangle***
Model the trinomial with algebra tiles. You will need one x^2-tile, six x-tiles, and eight 1-tiles. Arrange all of the tiles to form a rectangle. There can be no gaps or leftover tiles. The area of the rectangle represents the trinomial.

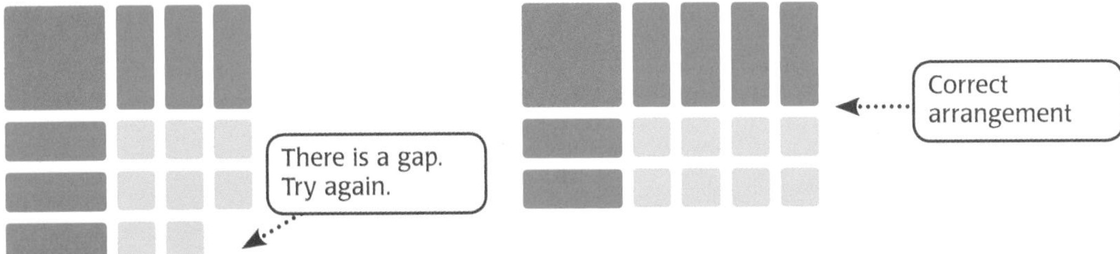

STEP 2 ***Find the side lengths***
The side lengths of the rectangle represent the polynomials $x + 2$ and $x + 4$. So, $x^2 + 6x + 8 = (x + 2)(x + 4)$.

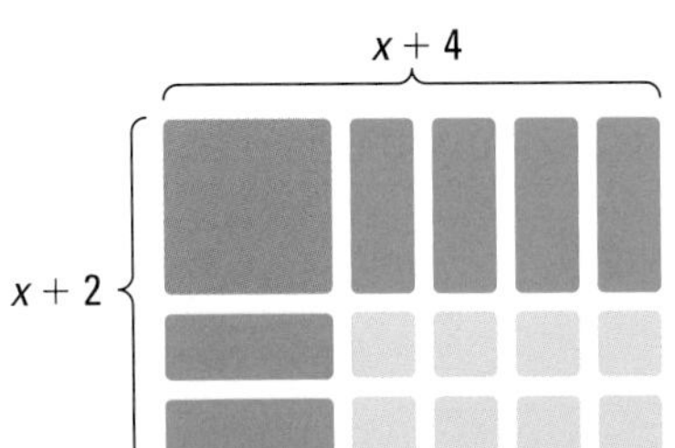

DRAW CONCLUSIONS **Use your observations to complete these exercises**

1. Use multiplication to show that $x + 4$ and $x + 2$ are factors of the polynomial $x^2 + 6x + 8$.

Use algebra tiles to factor the trinomial. Include a drawing of your model.

2. $x^2 + 6x + 5$
3. $x^2 + 9x + 14$
4. $x^2 + 5x + 6$
5. $x^2 + 8x + 16$
6. $x^2 + 5x + 4$
7. $x^2 + 8x + 12$
8. **REASONING** The factors of the trinomial $x^2 + 6x + 8$ have the form $x + p$ and $x + q$, as shown above. How are p and q related to 6 and 8?

9.5 Factor $x^2 + bx + c$

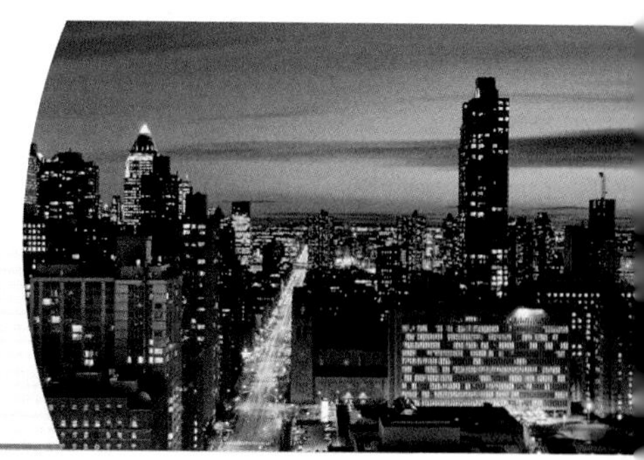

Before You factored out the greatest common monomial factor.

Now You will factor trinomials of the form $x^2 + bx + c$.

Why So you can find the dimensions of figures, as in Ex. 61.

Key Vocabulary
- **zero of a function,** *p. 337*

From Lesson 9.2, you know that

$$(x + 3)(x + 4) = x^2 + (4 + 3)x + 4 \cdot 3 = x^2 + 7x + 12.$$

You will reverse this process to factor trinomials of the form $x^2 + bx + c$.

KEY CONCEPT *For Your Notebook*

Factoring $x^2 + bx + c$

Algebra $x^2 + bx + c = (x + p)(x + q)$ provided $p + q = b$ and $pq = c$.

Example $x^2 + 5x + 6 = (x + 3)(x + 2)$ because $3 + 2 = 5$ and $3 \cdot 2 = 6$.

EXAMPLE 1 Factor when *b* and *c* are positive

Factor $x^2 + 11x + 18$.

Solution

Find two positive factors of 18 whose sum is 11. Make an organized list.

Factors of 18	Sum of factors	
18, 1	18 + 1 = 19	✗
9, 2	9 + 2 = **11**	← Correct sum
6, 3	6 + 3 = 9	✗

The factors 9 and 2 have a sum of 11, so they are the correct values of p and q.

▶ $x^2 + 11x + 18 = (x + 9)(x + 2)$

CHECK $(x + 9)(x + 2) = x^2 + 2x + 9x + 18$ **Multiply binomials.**

$= x^2 + 11x + 18$ ✓ **Simplify.**

GUIDED PRACTICE for Example 1

Factor the trinomial.

1. $x^2 + 3x + 2$ **2.** $a^2 + 7a + 10$ **3.** $t^2 + 9t + 14$

FACTORING When factoring a trinomial, first consider the signs of p and q.

$(x + p)(x + q)$	$x^2 + bx + c$	Signs of b and c
$(x + 2)(x + 3)$	$x^2 + 5x + 6$	b is positive; c is positive.
$(x + 2)(x + (-3))$	$x^2 - x - 6$	b is negative; c is negative.
$(x + (-2))(x + 3)$	$x^2 + x - 6$	b is positive; c is negative.
$(x + (-2))(x + (-3))$	$x^2 - 5x + 6$	b is negative; c is positive.

By observing the signs of b and c in the table, you can see that:

- b and c are positive when both p and q are positive.
- b is negative and c is positive when both p and q are negative.
- c is negative when p and q have different signs.

EXAMPLE 2 Factor when b is negative and c is positive

Factor $n^2 - 6n + 8$.

Because b is negative and c is positive, p and q must both be negative.

Factors of 8	Sum of factors	
−8, −1	$-8 + (-1) = -9$	✗
−4, −2	$-4 + (-2) = -6$	← Correct sum

▸ $n^2 - 6n + 8 = (n - 4)(n - 2)$

EXAMPLE 3 Factor when b is positive and c is negative

Factor $y^2 + 2y - 15$.

Because c is negative, p and q must have different signs.

Factors of −15	Sum of factors	
−15, 1	$-15 + 1 = -14$	✗
15, −1	$15 + (-1) = 14$	✗
−5, 3	$-5 + 3 = -2$	✗
5, −3	$5 + (-3) = 2$	← Correct sum

▸ $y^2 + 2y - 15 = (y + 5)(y - 3)$

✓ GUIDED PRACTICE for Examples 2 and 3

Factor the trinomial.

4. $x^2 - 4x + 3$ **5.** $t^2 - 8t + 12$ **6.** $m^2 + m - 20$ **7.** $w^2 + 6w - 16$

EXAMPLE 4 Solve a polynomial equation

Solve the equation $x^2 + 3x = 18$.

$x^2 + 3x = 18$	**Write original equation.**
$x^2 + 3x - 18 = 0$	**Subtract 18 from each side.**
$(x + 6)(x - 3) = 0$	**Factor left side.**
$x + 6 = 0$ *or* $x - 3 = 0$	**Zero-product property**
$x = -6$ *or* $x = 3$	**Solve for *x*.**

▶ The solutions of the equation are −6 and 3.

GUIDED PRACTICE for Example 4

8. Solve the equation $s^2 - 2s = 24$.

EXAMPLE 5 Solve a multi-step problem

BANNER DIMENSIONS You are making banners to hang during school spirit week. Each banner requires 16.5 square feet of felt and will be cut as shown. Find the width of one banner.

ANOTHER WAY
For alternative methods for solving Example 5, turn to page 590 for the **Problem Solving Workshop**.

Solution

STEP 1 **Draw** a diagram of two banners together.

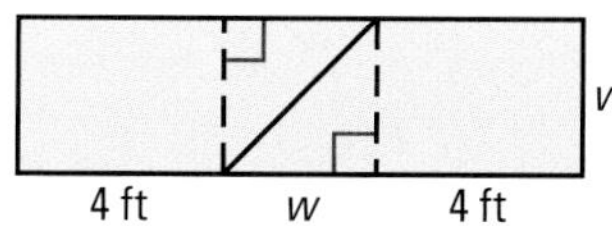

STEP 2 **Write** an equation using the fact that the area of 2 banners is $2(16.5) = 33$ square feet. Solve the equation for w.

$A = \ell \cdot w$	**Formula for area of a rectangle**
$33 = (4 + w + 4) \cdot w$	**Substitute 33 for *A* and $(4 + w + 4)$ for ℓ.**
$0 = w^2 + 8w - 33$	**Simplify and subtract 33 from each side.**
$0 = (w + 11)(w - 3)$	**Factor right side.**
$w + 11 = 0$ *or* $w - 3 = 0$	**Zero-product property**
$w = -11$ *or* $w = 3$	**Solve for *w*.**

▶ The banner cannot have a negative width, so the width is 3 feet.

GUIDED PRACTICE for Example 5

9. **WHAT IF?** In Example 5, suppose the area of a banner is to be 10 square feet. What is the width of one banner?

9.5 EXERCISES

HOMEWORK KEY

○ = **WORKED-OUT SOLUTIONS** on p. WS21 for Exs. 7 and 61

★ = **STANDARDIZED TEST PRACTICE** Exs. 2, 29, 42, 61, 62, and 63

◆ = **MULTIPLE REPRESENTATIONS** Ex. 64

SKILL PRACTICE

1. **VOCABULARY** Copy and complete: The _?_ of $t^2 + 3t + 2$ are $t + 2$ and $t + 1$.

2. ★ **WRITING** If $x^2 - 8x + 12 = (x + p)(x + q)$, what are the signs of p and q? *Justify* your answer.

EXAMPLES 1, 2, and 3 on pp. 583–584 for Exs. 3–19

FACTORING TRINOMIALS **Factor the trinomial.**

3. $x^2 + 4x + 3$
4. $a^2 + 6a + 8$
5. $b^2 - 17b + 72$
6. $s^2 - 10s + 16$
7. $z^2 + 8z - 48$
8. $w^2 + 18w + 56$
9. $y^2 - 7y - 18$
10. $n^2 - 9n + 14$
11. $x^2 + 3x - 70$
12. $f^2 + 4f - 32$
13. $m^2 - 7m - 120$
14. $d^2 - 20d + 99$
15. $p^2 + 20p + 64$
16. $x^2 + 6x - 72$
17. $c^2 + 15c + 44$

ERROR ANALYSIS ***Describe*** **and correct the error in factoring the trinomial.**

18. $s^2 - 17s - 60 = (s - 5)(s - 12)$

19. $m^2 - 10m + 24 = (m - 12)(m + 2)$

EXAMPLE 4 on p. 585 for Exs. 20–29

SOLVING EQUATIONS **Solve the equation.**

20. $x^2 - 10x + 21 = 0$
21. $n^2 - 7n - 30 = 0$
22. $w^2 - 15w + 44 = 0$
23. $a^2 + 5a = 50$
24. $r^2 + 2r = 24$
25. $t^2 + 9t = -20$
26. $y^2 - 2y - 8 = 7$
27. $m^2 + 22 = -23m$
28. $b^2 + 5 = 8b - 10$

29. ★ **MULTIPLE CHOICE** What are the solutions of the equation $x^2 - 8x = 240$?

(A) −20 and −12 (B) −20 and 12

(C) 20 and −12 (D) 12 and 20

FINDING ZEROS OF FUNCTIONS **Find the zeros of the polynomial function.**

30. $f(x) = x^2 + 11x + 18$
31. $g(x) = x^2 + 5x + 6$
32. $h(x) = x^2 - 18x + 32$
33. $f(x) = x^2 - 14x + 45$
34. $h(x) = x^2 - 5x - 24$
35. $g(x) = x^2 - 14x - 51$
36. $g(x) = x^2 + 10x - 39$
37. $f(x) = -x^2 + 16x - 28$
38. $f(x) = -x^2 + 24x + 180$

SOLVING EQUATIONS **Solve the equation.**

39. $s(s + 1) = 72$
40. $x^2 - 10(x - 1) = -11$
41. $q(q + 19) = -34$

42. ★ **SHORT RESPONSE** Write an equation of the form $x^2 + bx + c = 0$ that has the solutions -4 and 6. *Explain* how you found your answer.

GEOMETRY Find the dimensions of the rectangle or triangle that has the given area.

43. Area: 100 square inches

$(x - 15)$ in.

x in.

44. Area: 34 square meters

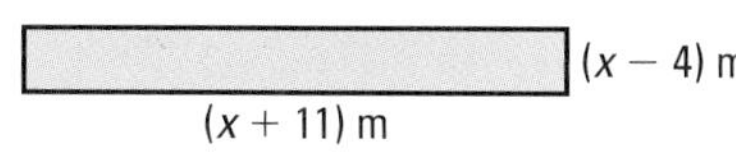

45. Area: 78 square yards

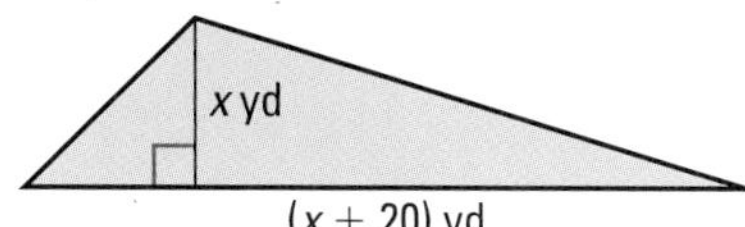

46. Area: 119 square feet

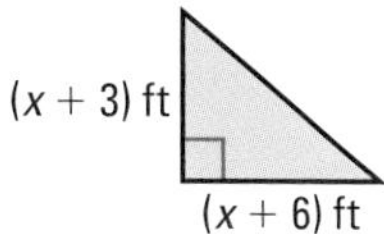

FACTORING TRINOMIALS In Exercises 47–55, use the example below to factor the trinomial.

EXAMPLE **Factor a trinomial in two variables**

Factor $x^2 + 9xy + 14y^2$.

Solution

To factor the trinomial, you must find factors of the form $x + py$ and $x + qy$.

First, consider the signs of the factors needed. In this example, b is 9, and c is 14. Because both b and c are positive, you must find two positive factors of 14 that have a sum of 9.

Factors of 14	Sum of factors	
14, 1	14 + 1 = 15	✗
7, 2	7 + 2 = 9	← Correct sum

The factors 7 and 2 have a sum of 9, so 7 and 2 are the correct values of p and q.

▸ $x^2 + 9xy + 14y^2 = (x + 7y)(x + 2y)$

47. $x^2 - 4xy + 4y^2$

48. $y^2 - 6yz + 5z^2$

49. $c^2 + 13cd + 36d^2$

50. $r^2 + 15rs + 50s^2$

51. $a^2 + 2ab - 15b^2$

52. $x^2 + 8xy - 65y^2$

53. $m^2 - mn - 42n^2$

54. $u^2 - 3uv - 108v^2$

55. $g^2 + 4gh - 60h^2$

CHALLENGE Find all integer values of b for which the trinomial has factors of the form $x + p$ and $x + q$ where p and q are integers.

56. $x^2 + bx + 15$

57. $x^2 - bx + 21$

58. $x^2 + bx - 42$

PROBLEM SOLVING

EXAMPLE 5 on p. 585 for Exs. 59–61

59. CARD DESIGN You are designing a gift card that has a border along one side, as shown. The area of the white part of the card is 30 square centimeters. What is the area of the border?

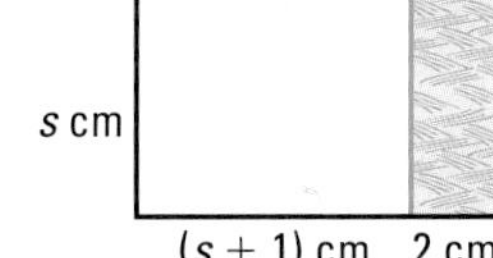

@HomeTutor for problem solving help at classzone.com

60. CONSTRUCTION A contractor is building a porch along two sides of a house. The house is rectangular with a width of 32 feet and a length of 50 feet. The porch will have the same width on each side of the house.

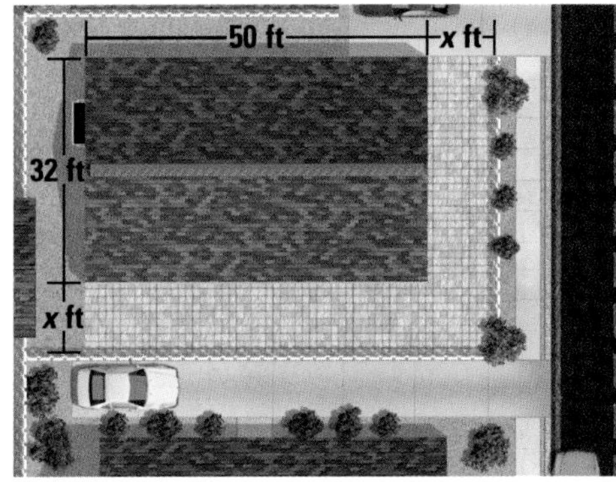

a. Write a polynomial that represents the combined area of the first floor of the house and the porch.

b. The owners want the combined area of the first floor and the porch to be 2320 square feet. How wide should the contractor build the porch?

@HomeTutor for problem solving help at classzone.com

61. ★ **SHORT RESPONSE** You trimmed a large square picture so that you could fit it into a frame. You trimmed 6 inches from the length and 5 inches from the width. The area of the resulting picture is 20 square inches. What was the perimeter of the original large square picture? *Explain* how you found your answer.

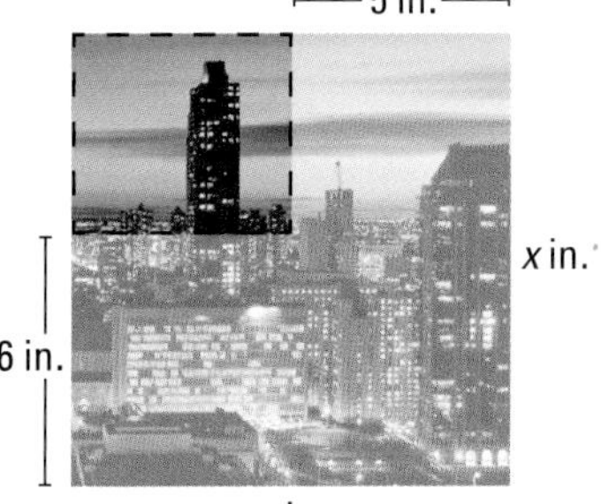

62. ★ **EXTENDED RESPONSE** A town has a rectangular park. The parks department is planning to install two brick paths that will intersect at right angles. One path will be 130 feet long, and the other path will be 500 feet long. The paths will have the same width.

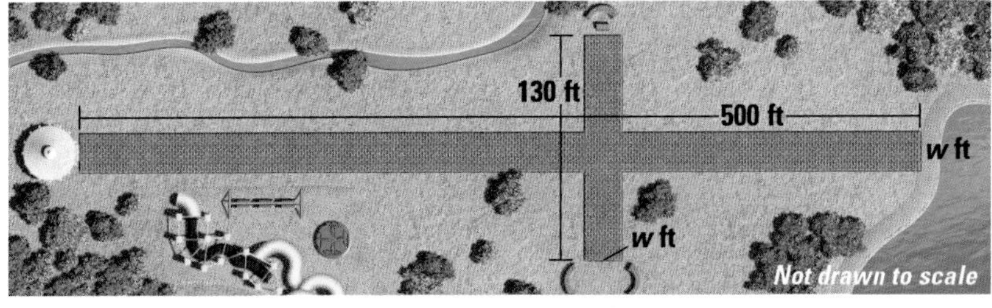

HINT Add the path areas, but subtract the overlap, so that it is not counted twice.

a. Write a polynomial that represents the combined area of the two paths.

b. The parks department can afford brick for 3125 square feet of path. Write and solve an equation to find the width of the paths.

c. In part (b) you used one solution of the equation to find your answer. *Explain* how you chose which solution to use.

○ = **WORKED-OUT SOLUTIONS** on p. WS1 ★ = **STANDARDIZED TEST PRACTICE** ◆ = **MULTIPLE REPRESENTATIONS**

63. ★ **MULTIPLE CHOICE** A square quilt has a border that is 1 foot wide on each side. The quilt has an area of 25 square feet. What is the side length of the quilt without the border?

(A) 2 feet (B) 3 feet (C) 4 feet (D) 5 feet

64. **MULTIPLE REPRESENTATIONS** You toss a set of keys to a friend who is standing at a window 20 feet above the ground in a building that is 5 feet away from where you are standing. The path of the keys can be modeled by the graph of the equation $y = -x^2 + 8x + 5$ where x and y are measured in feet. On a coordinate plane, the ground is represented by the x-axis, and you are standing at the origin.

a. **Making a Table** Make a table of values that shows the height of the keys for $x = 2, 4, 6$, and 8 feet.

b. **Drawing a Graph** Plot the ordered pairs in the table as points in a coordinate plane. Connect the points with a smooth curve.

c. **Interpreting a Graph** Based on your graph, do you expect the keys to reach your friend? *Explain* your answer.

d. **Using an Equation** Find the value of x when $y = 20$. (You may need to factor out a -1 in order to factor the trinomial.) What do you notice? *Explain* how the x-value justifies your answer from part (c).

65. **CHALLENGE** A rectangular stage is positioned in the center of a rectangular room, as shown. The area of the stage is 120 square feet.

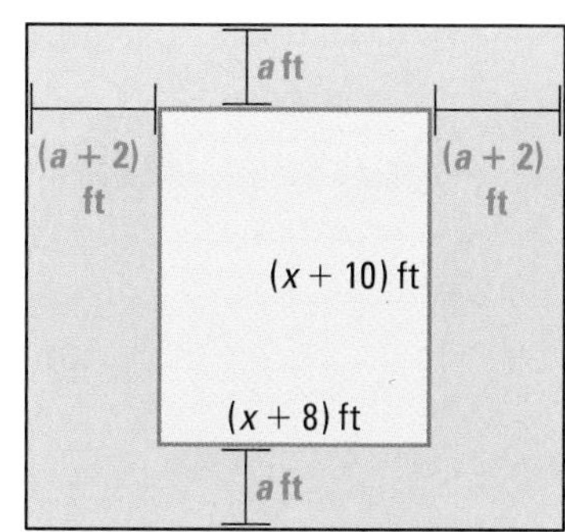

a. Use the dimensions given in the diagram to find the length and width of the stage.

b. The combined area of the stage and the surrounding floor is 360 square feet. Find the length and width of the room.

MIXED REVIEW

Solve the equation.

66. $x + 12 = 4$ *(p. 134)*

67. $5y - 2 = 13$ *(p. 141)*

68. $6n + 4 = -14$ *(p. 141)*

69. $3a - 5a + 12 = -6$ *(p. 148)*

70. $3 - 2(w + 7) = -1$ *(p. 148)*

71. $-6 + 2(d - 9) = 8d$ *(p. 154)*

72. $(x - 8)(x + 3) = 0$ *(p. 575)*

73. $(3t + 5)(t + 2) = 0$ *(p. 575)*

PREVIEW
Prepare for Lesson 9.6 in Exs. 74–81.

Find the product.

74. $(3x + 7)(x - 5)$ *(p. 562)*

75. $(3a - 4)(2a - 9)$ *(p. 562)*

76. $(c + 2)(c^2 + c - 4)$ *(p. 562)*

77. $(7 + 3y)(7 - 5y)$ *(p. 562)*

78. $(2k - 8)(2k + 8)$ *(p. 569)*

79. $(14 - 2n)^2$ *(p. 569)*

80. $(5x + 16y)^2$ *(p. 569)*

81. $(3x - 6y)(3x + 6y)$ *(p. 569)*

PROBLEM SOLVING WORKSHOP
LESSON 9.5

Using ALTERNATIVE METHODS

Another Way to Solve Example 5, page 585

MULTIPLE REPRESENTATIONS In Example 5 on page 585, you saw how to solve the problem about a school banner by solving an equation. You can also solve the problem using a table or a graph.

PROBLEM

BANNER DIMENSIONS You are making banners to hang during school spirit week. Each banner requires 16.5 square feet of felt and will be cut as shown. Find the width of one banner.

METHOD 1

Using a Table Consider the separate geometric figures that form one banner and find their areas in terms of w. Then find the total area of the banner for different values of w until you find a value that gives a total area of 16.5 square feet. Use a table to organize your work.

STEP 1 **Write** equations for the area of the pieces and the total area.

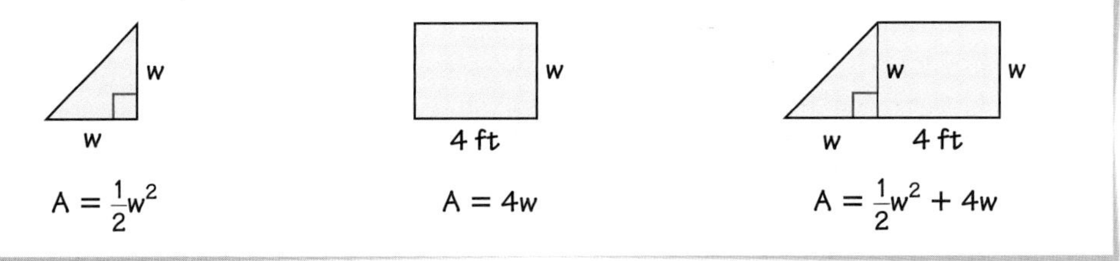

STEP 2 **Organize** your work in a table.

w	Triangle's area $\left(\frac{1}{2}w^2\right)$	Rectangle's area $(4w)$	Total area $\left(\frac{1}{2}w^2 + 4w\right)$	
1	0.5	4	4.5	← $4.5 < 16.5$, so try a greater value of w.
2	2	8	10	← $10 < 16.5$, so try a greater value of w.
3	4.5	12	16.5	← Correct area

▶ The width of the banner is 3 feet.

METHOD 2 **Using a Graph** Another approach is to use a graph.

STEP 1 **Write** an equation for the area of the banner. The area of the banner can be thought of as the area of a triangle plus the area of a rectangle.

Area of banner = Area of triangle + Area of rectangle

$$A = \frac{1}{2}w^2 + 4w$$

STEP 2 **Graph** the equation for the area of the banner using a graphing calculator. Graph $y_1 = 0.5x^2 + 4x$. Because you are looking for the value of x that gives an area of 16.5 square feet, you should display the graph of $y_2 = 16.5$ in the same viewing window.

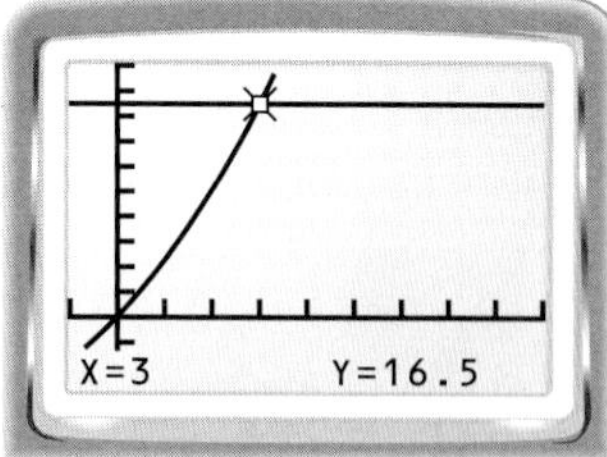

STEP 3 **Find** the intersection of the graphs by using the *intersect* feature on your calculator. The graphs intersect at (3, 16.5).

▶ The width of the banner is 3 feet.

PRACTICE

1. **COUNTER DESIGN** A contractor is building a counter in a kitchen using the diagram shown. The countertop will have an area of 12 square feet. How wide should it be? Solve this problem using two different methods.

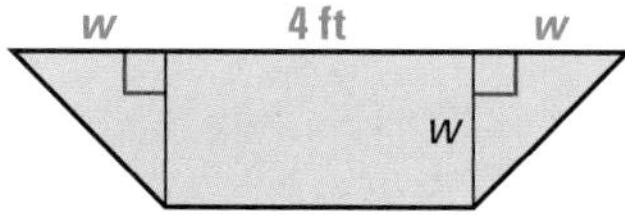

2. **ERROR ANALYSIS** *Describe* and correct the error in using an equation to solve the problem in Exercise 1.

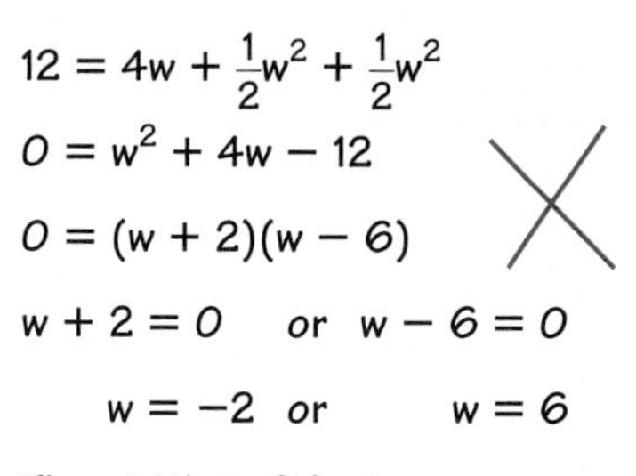

$12 = 4w + \frac{1}{2}w^2 + \frac{1}{2}w^2$

$0 = w^2 + 4w - 12$

$0 = (w + 2)(w - 6)$

$w + 2 = 0$ or $w - 6 = 0$

$w = -2$ or $w = 6$

The width is 6 feet.

3. **FOUNTAIN DESIGN** A square fountain in a city plaza is surrounded by brick patios as shown. The combined area of the fountain and brick patios is 205 square feet. What is the side length of the fountain? Solve this problem using two different methods.

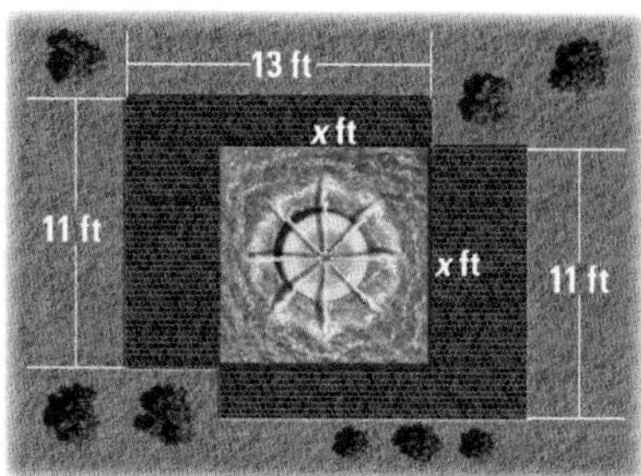

4. **WHAT IF?** You want to make a larger banner using the same pattern shown in the problem on page 585. The new banner will have an area of 24 square feet. Find the width of the new banner. *Describe* the method you used to find your answer.

Animated Algebra classzone.com

9.6 More Factorization with Algebra Tiles

MATERIALS • algebra tiles

QUESTION How can you factor a trinomial using algebra tiles?

EXPLORE Factor the trinomial $2x^2 + 7x + 3$

STEP 1 *Make a rectangle*

Model the trinomial with algebra tiles. Arrange all of the tiles to form a rectangle. You may have to try a few arrangements to make the rectangle. There can be no gaps or leftover tiles.

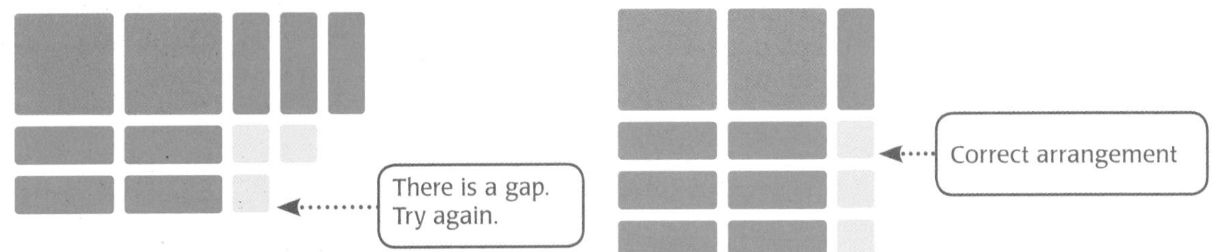

STEP 2 *Find the side lengths*

The side lengths of the rectangle represent the polynomials $x + 3$ and $2x + 1$. So $2x^2 + 7x + 3 = (x + 3)(2x + 1)$.

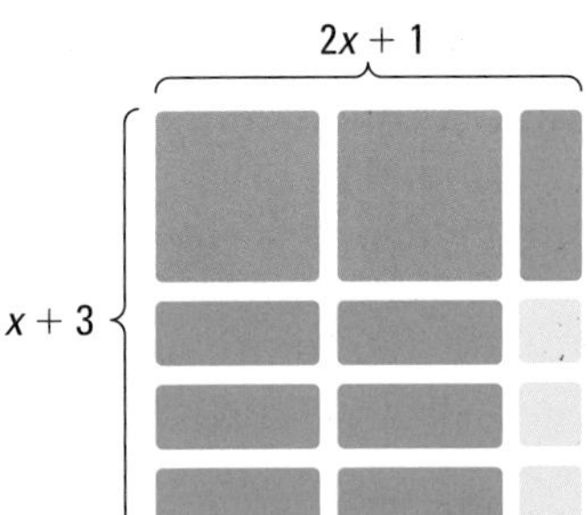

DRAW CONCLUSIONS Use your observations to complete these exercises

1. Use multiplication to show that $x + 3$ and $2x + 1$ are factors of the polynomial $2x^2 + 7x + 3$.

Use algebra tiles to factor the trinomial. Include a drawing of your model.

2. $2x^2 + 5x + 3$
3. $3x^2 + 5x + 2$
4. $4x^2 + 9x + 2$
5. $3x^2 + 13x + 4$
6. $4x^2 + 11x + 6$
7. $4x^2 + 8x + 3$
8. **REASONING** Factor the trinomial $2x^2 + 11x + 5$ into two binomials. How is the leading coefficient of the trinomial related to the leading coefficients of its binomial factors?

9.6 Factor $ax^2 + bx + c$

Before You factored trinomials of the form $x^2 + bx + c$.

Now You will factor trinomials of the form $ax^2 + bx + c$.

Why? So you can find the dimensions of a building, as in Ex. 61.

Key Vocabulary
- **trinomial,** *p. 555*

When factoring a trinomial of the form $ax^2 + bx + c$, first consider the signs of b and c, as in Lesson 9.5. This approach works when a is positive.

EXAMPLE 1 Factor when b is negative and c is positive

Factor $2x^2 - 7x + 3$.

Solution

REVIEW FACTORING
For help with determining the signs of the factors of a trinomial, see p. 584.

Because b is negative and c is positive, both factors of c must be negative. Make a table to organize your work.

You must consider the order of the factors of 3, because the x-terms of the possible factorizations are different.

Factors of 2	Factors of 3	Possible factorization	Middle term when multiplied	
1, 2	−1, −3	$(x - 1)(2x - 3)$	$-3x - 2x = -5x$	✗
1, 2	−3, −1	$(x - 3)(2x - 1)$	$-x - 6x = -7x$	← Correct

▸ $2x^2 - 7x + 3 = (x - 3)(2x - 1)$

EXAMPLE 2 Factor when b is positive and c is negative

Factor $3n^2 + 14n - 5$.

Solution

Because b is positive and c is negative, the factors of c have different signs.

Factors of 3	Factors of −5	Possible factorization	Middle term when multiplied	
1, 3	1, −5	$(n + 1)(3n - 5)$	$-5n + 3n = -2n$	✗
1, 3	−1, 5	$(n - 1)(3n + 5)$	$5n - 3n = 2n$	✗
1, 3	5, −1	$(n + 5)(3n - 1)$	$-n + 15n = 14n$	← Correct
1, 3	−5, 1	$(n - 5)(3n + 1)$	$n - 15n = -14n$	✗

▸ $3n^2 + 14n - 5 = (n + 5)(3n - 1)$

✓ GUIDED PRACTICE for Examples 1 and 2

Factor the trinomial.

1. $3t^2 + 8t + 4$ **2.** $4s^2 - 9s + 5$ **3.** $2h^2 + 13h - 7$

FACTORING WHEN *a* IS NEGATIVE To factor a trinomial of the form $ax^2 + bx + c$ when a is negative, first factor -1 from each term of the trinomial. Then factor the resulting trinomial as in the previous examples.

EXAMPLE 3 Factor when *a* is negative

Factor $-4x^2 + 12x + 7$.

Solution

STEP 1 **Factor** -1 from each term of the trinomial.

$$-4x^2 + 12x + 7 = -(4x^2 - 12x - 7)$$

STEP 2 **Factor** the trinomial $4x^2 - 12x - 7$. Because b and c are both negative, the factors of c must have different signs. As in the previous examples, use a table to organize information about the factors of a and c.

Factors of 4	Factors of −7	Possible factorization	Middle term when multiplied	
1, 4	1, −7	$(x + 1)(4x - 7)$	$-7x + 4x = -3x$	✗
1, 4	7, −1	$(x + 7)(4x - 1)$	$-x + 28x = 27x$	✗
1, 4	−1, 7	$(x - 1)(4x + 7)$	$7x - 4x = 3x$	✗
1, 4	−7, 1	$(x - 7)(4x + 1)$	$x - 28x = -27x$	✗
2, 2	1, −7	$(2x + 1)(2x - 7)$	$-14x + 2x = -12x$	← Correct
2, 2	−1, 7	$(2x - 1)(2x + 7)$	$14x - 2x = 12x$	✗

AVOID ERRORS
Remember to include the −1 that you factored out in Step 1.

▶ $-4x^2 + 12x + 7 = -(2x + 1)(2x - 7)$

CHECK You can check your factorization using a graphing calculator. Graph $y_1 = -4x^2 + 12x + 7$ and $y_2 = -(2x + 1)(2x - 7)$. Because the graphs coincide, you know that your factorization is correct.

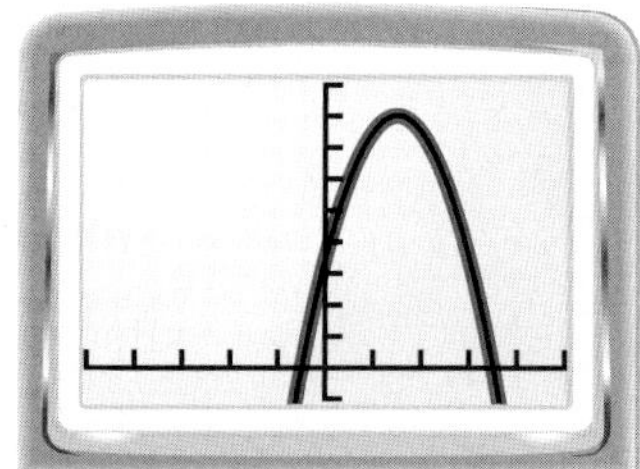

✓ GUIDED PRACTICE for Example 3

Factor the trinomial.

4. $-2y^2 - 5y - 3$ **5.** $-5m^2 + 6m - 1$ **6.** $-3x^2 - x + 2$

FINDING A COMMON FACTOR In Lesson 9.4, you learned to factor out the greatest common monomial factor from the terms of a polynomial. Sometimes you may need to do this before finding two binomial factors of a trinomial.

EXAMPLE 4 Write and solve a polynomial equation

DISCUS An athlete throws a discus from an initial height of 6 feet and with an initial vertical velocity of 46 feet per second.

a. Write an equation that gives the height (in feet) of the discus as a function of the time (in seconds) since it left the athlete's hand.

b. After how many seconds does the discus hit the ground?

Solution

USE VERTICAL MOTION MODEL
For help with using the vertical motion model, see p. 577.

a. Use the vertical motion model to write an equation for the height h (in feet) of the discus. In this case, $v = 46$ and $s = 6$.

$h = -16t^2 + vt + s$ — Vertical motion model

$h = -16t^2 + 46t + 6$ — Substitute 46 for v and 6 for s.

b. To find the number of seconds that pass before the discus lands, find the value of t for which the height of the discus is 0. Substitute 0 for h and solve the equation for t.

$0 = -16t^2 + 46t + 6$ — Substitute 0 for h.

$0 = -2(8t^2 - 23t - 3)$ — Factor out -2.

$0 = -2(8t + 1)(t - 3)$ — Factor the trinomial. Find factors of 8 and -3 that produce a middle term with a coefficient of -23.

$8t + 1 = 0$ *or* $t - 3 = 0$ — Zero-product property

$t = -\frac{1}{8}$ *or* $t = 3$ — Solve for t.

The solutions of the equation are $-\frac{1}{8}$ and 3. A negative solution does not make sense in this situation, so disregard $-\frac{1}{8}$.

▶ The discus hits the ground after 3 seconds.

✓ GUIDED PRACTICE for Example 4

7. **WHAT IF?** In Example 4, suppose another athlete throws the discus with an initial vertical velocity of 38 feet per second and releases it from a height of 5 feet. After how many seconds does the discus hit the ground?

8. **SHOT PUT** In a shot put event, an athlete throws the shot put from an initial height of 6 feet and with an initial vertical velocity of 29 feet per second. After how many seconds does the shot put hit the ground?

★ EXAMPLE 5 Standardized Test Practice

A rectangle's length is 13 meters more than 3 times its width. The area is 10 square meters. What is the width?

Ⓐ $\frac{2}{3}$ m Ⓑ 3 m Ⓒ 5 m Ⓓ 10 m

$w(3w + 13) = 10$	Write an equation to model area.
$3w^2 + 13w - 10 = 0$	Simplify and subtract 10 from each side.
$(w + 5)(3w - 2) = 0$	Factor left side.
$w + 5 = 0$ *or* $3w - 2 = 0$	Zero-product property
$w = -5$ *or* $w = \frac{2}{3}$	Solve for *w*.

Reject the negative width.

▸ The correct answer is A. Ⓐ Ⓑ Ⓒ Ⓓ

✓ GUIDED PRACTICE for Example 5

9. A rectangle's length is 1 inch more than twice its width. The area is 6 square inches. What is the width?

Ⓐ $\frac{1}{2}$ in. Ⓑ $\frac{3}{2}$ in. Ⓒ 2 in. Ⓓ $\frac{5}{2}$ in.

9.6 EXERCISES

HOMEWORK KEY

 = **WORKED-OUT SOLUTIONS** on p. WS22 for Exs. 5, 25, and 61

★ = **STANDARDIZED TEST PRACTICE** Exs. 2, 3, 22, 41, 51, and 60

◆ = **MULTIPLE REPRESENTATIONS** Ex. 62

SKILL PRACTICE

1. **VOCABULARY** What is another word for the solutions of $x^2 + 2x + 1 = 0$?

2. ★ **WRITING** *Explain* how you can use a graph to check a factorization.

3. ★ **WRITING** *Compare* factoring $6x^2 - x - 2$ with factoring $x^2 - x - 2$.

EXAMPLES 1, 2, and 3 on pp. 593–594 for Exs. 4–22

FACTORING TRINOMIALS **Factor the trinomial.**

4. $-x^2 + x + 20$
5. $-y^2 + 2y + 8$
6. $-a^2 + 12a - 27$
7. $5w^2 - 6w + 1$
8. $-3p^2 - 10p - 3$
9. $6s^2 - s - 5$
10. $2t^2 + 5t - 63$
11. $2c^2 - 7c + 3$
12. $3n^2 - 17n + 10$
13. $-2h^2 + 5h + 3$
14. $-6k^2 - 13k - 6$
15. $10x^2 - 3x - 27$
16. $4m^2 + 9m + 5$
17. $3z^2 + z - 14$
18. $4a^2 + 9a - 9$
19. $4n^2 + 16n + 15$
20. $-5b^2 + 7b - 2$
21. $6y^2 - 5y - 4$

22. ★ **MULTIPLE CHOICE** What is the correct factorization of $8x^2 - 10x + 3$?

Ⓐ $(2x - 3)(4x - 1)$ Ⓑ $(2x - 1)(4x - 3)$

Ⓒ $(4x + 1)(2x - 3)$ Ⓓ $(8x - 3)(x - 1)$

EXAMPLES 4 and 5 on pp. 595–596 for Exs. 23–39

SOLVING EQUATIONS Solve the equation.

23. $2x^2 - 3x - 35 = 0$
24. $3w^2 + 22w + 7 = 0$
25. $4s^2 + 11s - 3 = 0$
26. $7a^2 + 2a = 5$
27. $8t^2 - 2t = 3$
28. $6m^2 - 5m = 14$
29. $b(20b - 3) - 2 = 0$
30. $4(3y^2 - 7y + 4) = 1$
31. $p(3p + 14) = 5$
32. $4n^2 - 2n - 90 = 0$
33. $10c^2 - 14c + 4 = 0$
34. $-16k^2 + 8k + 24 = 0$
35. $6r^2 - 15r = 99$
36. $56z^2 + 2 = 22z$
37. $30x^2 + 25x = 20$

ERROR ANALYSIS *Describe* and correct the error in solving the equation.

38.

$5x^2 + x = 4$

$x(5x + 1) = 4$

$x = 4$ or $5x + 1 = 4$

$x = 4$ or $x = \frac{3}{5}$

39.

$12x^2 + 5x - 2 = 0$

$(3x - 1)(4x + 2) = 0$

$3x - 1 = 0$ or $4x + 2 = 0$

$x = \frac{1}{3}$ or $x = -\frac{1}{2}$

40. **GEOMETRY** The length of a rectangle is 7 inches more than 5 times its width. The area of the rectangle is 6 square inches. What is the width?

41. ★ **SHORT RESPONSE** The length of a rectangle is 1 inch more than 4 times its width. The area of the rectangle is 3 square inches. What is the perimeter of the rectangle? *Explain* how you found your answer.

FINDING ZEROS OF FUNCTIONS Find the zeros of the polynomial function.

42. $g(x) = 2x^2 + x - 1$
43. $f(x) = -x^2 + 12x - 35$
44. $h(x) = -3x^2 + 2x + 5$
45. $f(x) = 3x^2 + x - 14$
46. $g(x) = 8x^2 - 6x - 14$
47. $f(x) = 12x^2 - 24x - 63$

SOLVING EQUATIONS Multiply each side of the equation by an appropriate power of 10 to obtain integer coefficients. Then solve the equation.

48. $0.3x^2 - 0.7x - 4.0 = 0$
49. $0.8x^2 - 1.8x - 0.5 = 0$
50. $0.4x^2 - 0.4x = 9.9$

51. ★ **MULTIPLE CHOICE** What are the solutions of the equation $0.4x^2 - 1.1x = 2$?

Ⓐ -12.5 and 40 Ⓑ -4 and 1.25 Ⓒ -1.25 and 4 Ⓓ -0.125 and 0.4

WRITING EQUATIONS Write a polynomial equation that has the given solutions. The equation must have integer coefficients. *Explain* your reasoning.

52. -3 and 2
53. $-\frac{1}{2}$ and 5
54. $-\frac{3}{4}$ and $-\frac{1}{3}$

CHALLENGE Factor the trinomial.

55. $2x^2 - 11xy + 5y^2$
56. $3x^2 + 2xy - 8y^2$
57. $6x^3 - 10x^2y - 56xy^2$

PROBLEM SOLVING

EXAMPLE 4 on p. 595 for Exs. 58, 60

58. DIVING A diver dives from a cliff when her center of gravity is 46 feet above the surface of the water. Her initial vertical velocity leaving the cliff is 9 feet per second. After how many seconds does her center of gravity enter the water?

@HomeTutor for problem solving help at classzone.com

EXAMPLE 5 on p. 596 for Exs. 59, 61

59. SCRAPBOOK DESIGN You plan to make a scrapbook. On the cover, you want to show three pictures with space between them, as shown. Each of the pictures is twice as long as it is wide.

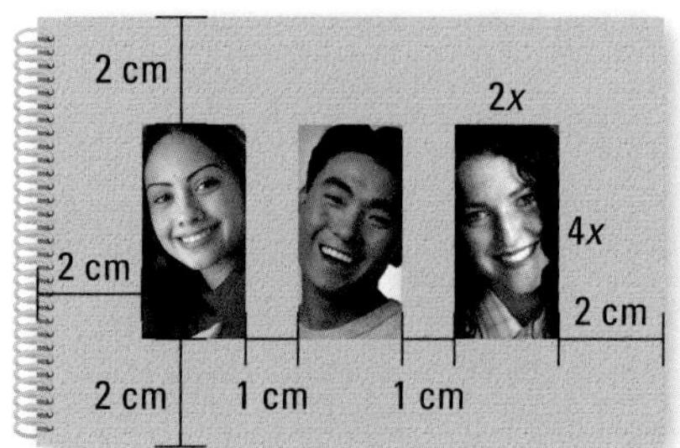

a. Write a polynomial that represents the area of the scrapbook cover.

b. The area of the cover will be 96 square centimeters. Find the length and width of the pictures you will use.

@HomeTutor for problem solving help at classzone.com

60. ★ SHORT RESPONSE You throw a ball into the air with an initial vertical velocity of 31 feet per second. The ball leaves your hand when it is 6 feet above the ground. You catch the ball when it reaches a height of 4 feet. After how many seconds do you catch the ball? *Explain* how you can use the solutions of an equation to find your answer.

61. PARTHENON The Parthenon in Athens, Greece, is an ancient structure that has a rectangular base. The length of the Parthenon's base is 8 meters more than twice its width. The area of the base is about 2170 square meters. Find the length and width of the Parthenon's base.

62. MULTIPLE REPRESENTATIONS An African cat called a serval leaps from the ground in an attempt to catch a bird. The serval's initial vertical velocity is 24 feet per second.

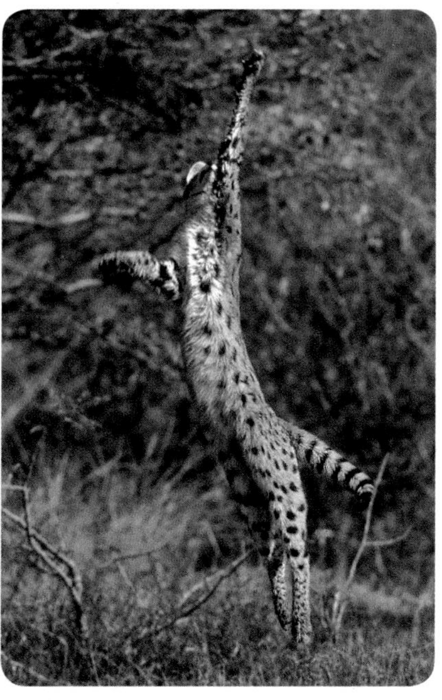

a. **Writing an Equation** Write an equation that gives the serval's height (in feet) as a function of the time (in seconds) since it left the ground.

b. **Making a Table** Use the equation from part (a) to make a table that shows the height of the serval for $t = 0, 0.3, 0.6, 0.9, 1.2,$ and 1.5 seconds.

c. **Drawing a Graph** Plot the ordered pairs in the table as points in a coordinate plane. Connect the points with a smooth curve. After how many seconds does the serval reach a height of 9 feet? *Justify* your answer using the equation from part (a).

Animated Algebra at classzone.com

63. **CHALLENGE** A bush cricket jumps from the ground into the air with an initial vertical velocity of 4 feet per second.

a. Write an equation that gives the cricket's height (in feet) as a function of the time (in seconds) since it left the ground.

b. After how many seconds is the cricket 3 inches off the ground?

c. Does the cricket jump higher than 3 inches? *Explain* your reasoning using your answer from part (b).

MIXED REVIEW

Check whether the given number is a solution of the equation or inequality.

64. $b - 9 = 18$; 3 *(p. 21)*
65. $8 - 3h = 2$; 2 *(p. 21)*
66. $\frac{28 - 2x}{x} < 5$; 4 *(p. 21)*
67. $6t + 18 = 0$; -3 *(p. 21)*
68. $6c = 3c$; 2 *(p. 21)*
69. $|x + 3| = 2$; -5 *(p. 64)*
70. $|y - 2| + 6 = 5$; 1 *(p. 64)*
71. $|3n - 11| < 1$; 2 *(p. 64)*
72. $4|3a - 8| > 2$; 3 *(p. 64)*

PREVIEW
Prepare for Lesson 9.7 in Exs. 73–81.

Find the product. *(p. 569)*

73. $(a - 9)^2$
74. $(k + 12)^2$
75. $(3x - 2)^2$
76. $(m + 4)(m - 4)$
77. $(2c + 1)(2c - 1)$
78. $(5n - 3)(5n + 3)$
79. $(8 - 3y)^2$
80. $(2s - 5t)^2$
81. $(x + 2y)(x - 2y)$

QUIZ *for Lessons 9.4–9.6*

Factor out the greatest common monomial factor. *(p. 575)*

1. $16a^2 - 40b$
2. $9xy^2 + 6x^2y$
3. $4n^4 - 22n^3 - 8n^2$
4. $3x^2 + 6xy - 3y^2$
5. $12abc^2 - 6a^2c$
6. $-36s^3 + 18s^2 - 54s$

Factor the trinomial.

7. $r^2 + 15r + 56$ *(p. 583)*
8. $s^2 - 6s + 5$ *(p. 583)*
9. $w^2 + 6w - 40$ *(p. 583)*
10. $-a^2 + 9a + 22$ *(p. 593)*
11. $2x^2 - 9x + 4$ *(p. 593)*
12. $5m^2 + m - 6$ *(p. 593)*
13. $6h^2 - 19h + 3$ *(p. 593)*
14. $-7y^2 - 23y - 6$ *(p. 593)*
15. $18c^2 + 12c - 6$ *(p. 593)*

Solve the equation.

16. $(4p - 7)(p + 5) = 0$ *(p. 575)*
17. $-8u^2 + 28u = 0$ *(p. 575)*
18. $51x^2 = -17x$ *(p. 575)*
19. $b^2 - 11b = -24$ *(p. 583)*
20. $m^2 + 12m = -35$ *(p. 583)*
21. $q^2 + 19 = -20q$ *(p. 583)*
22. $3t^2 - 11t + 10 = 0$ *(p. 593)*
23. $4y^2 + 31y = 8$ *(p. 593)*
24. $14s^2 + 12s = 2$ *(p. 593)*

25. **BASEBALL** A baseball player hits a baseball into the air with an initial vertical velocity of 72 feet per second. The player hits the ball from a height of 3 feet. *(p. 593)*

a. Write an equation that gives the baseball's height as a function of the time (in seconds) after it is hit.

b. After how many seconds is the baseball 84 feet above the ground?

9.7 Factor Special Products

Before You factored polynomials of the form $ax^2 + bx + c$.

Now You will factor special products.

Why? So you can use a scientific model, as in Ex. 48.

Key Vocabulary
- **perfect square trinomial**

You can use the special product patterns you studied in Lesson 9.3 to factor polynomials, such as the difference of two squares.

KEY CONCEPT *For Your Notebook*

Difference of Two Squares Pattern

Algebra	Example
$a^2 - b^2 = (a + b)(a - b)$	$4x^2 - 9 = (2x)^2 - 3^2 = (2x + 3)(2x - 3)$

EXAMPLE 1 Factor the difference of two squares

Factor the polynomial.

a. $y^2 - 16 = y^2 - 4^2$ — Write as $a^2 - b^2$.

$= (y + 4)(y - 4)$ — Difference of two squares pattern

b. $25m^2 - 36 = (5m)^2 - 6^2$ — Write as $a^2 - b^2$.

$= (5m + 6)(5m - 6)$ — Difference of two squares pattern

c. $x^2 - 49y^2 = x^2 - (7y)^2$ — Write as $a^2 - b^2$.

$= (x + 7y)(x - 7y)$ — Difference of two squares pattern

EXAMPLE 2 Factor the difference of two squares

Factor the polynomial $8 - 18n^2$.

$8 - 18n^2 = 2(4 - 9n^2)$ — Factor out common factor.

$= 2[2^2 - (3n)^2]$ — Write $4 - 9n^2$ as $a^2 - b^2$.

$= 2(2 + 3n)(2 - 3n)$ — Difference of two squares pattern

GUIDED PRACTICE for Examples 1 and 2

1. Factor the polynomial $4y^2 - 64$.

PERFECT SQUARE TRINOMIALS The pattern for finding the square of a binomial gives you the pattern for factoring trinomials of the form $a^2 + 2ab + b^2$ and $a^2 - 2ab + b^2$. These are called **perfect square trinomials**.

KEY CONCEPT *For Your Notebook*

Perfect Square Trinomial Pattern

Algebra	Example
$a^2 + 2ab + b^2 = (a + b)^2$	$x^2 + 6x + 9 = x^2 + 2(x \cdot 3) + 3^2 = (x + 3)^2$
$a^2 - 2ab + b^2 = (a - b)^2$	$x^2 - 10x + 25 = x^2 - 2(x \cdot 5) + 5^2 = (x - 5)^2$

EXAMPLE 3 Factor perfect square trinomials

Factor the polynomial.

a. $n^2 - 12n + 36 = n^2 - 2(n \cdot 6) + 6^2$ — Write as $a^2 - 2ab + b^2$.

$= (n - 6)^2$ — Perfect square trinomial pattern

b. $9x^2 - 12x + 4 = (3x)^2 - 2(3x \cdot 2) + 2^2$ — Write as $a^2 - 2ab + b^2$.

$= (3x - 2)^2$ — Perfect square trinomial pattern

c. $4s^2 + 4st + t^2 = (2s)^2 + 2(2s \cdot t) + t^2$ — Write as $a^2 + 2ab + b^2$.

$= (2s + t)^2$ — Perfect square trinomial pattern

Animated Algebra at classzone.com

EXAMPLE 4 Factor a perfect square trinomial

Factor the polynomial $-3y^2 + 36y - 108$.

$-3y^2 + 36y - 108 = -3(y^2 - 12y + 36)$ — Factor out -3.

$= -3[y^2 - 2(y \cdot 6) + 6^2]$ — Write $y^2 - 12y + 36$ as $a^2 - 2ab + b^2$.

$= -3(y - 6)^2$ — Perfect square trinomial pattern

CHECK Check your factorization using a graphing calculator. Graph $y_1 = -3x^2 + 36x - 108$ and $y_2 = -3(x - 6)^2$. Because the graphs coincide, you know that your factorization is correct.

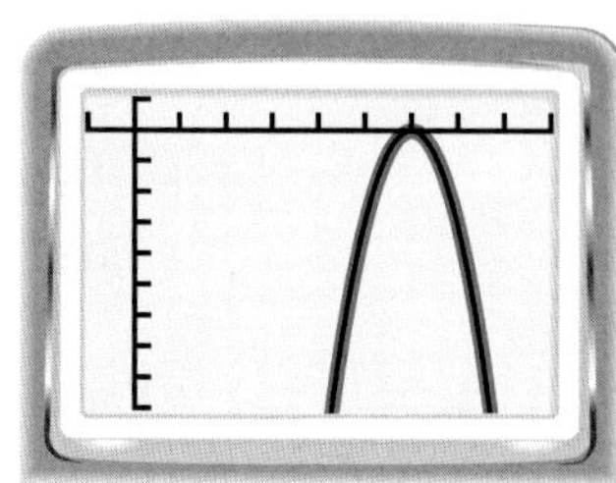

GUIDED PRACTICE for Examples 3 and 4

Factor the polynomial.

2. $h^2 + 4h + 4$

3. $2y^2 - 20y + 50$

4. $3x^2 + 6xy + 3y^2$

EXAMPLE 5 Solve a polynomial equation

Solve the equation $x^2 + \frac{2}{3}x + \frac{1}{9} = 0$.

$x^2 + \frac{2}{3}x + \frac{1}{9} = 0$	Write original equation.
$9x^2 + 6x + 1 = 0$	Multiply each side by 9.
$(3x)^2 + 2(3x \cdot 1) + (1)^2 = 0$	Write left side as $a^2 + 2ab + b^2$.
$(3x + 1)^2 = 0$	Perfect square trinomial pattern
$3x + 1 = 0$	Zero-product property
$x = -\frac{1}{3}$	Solve for x.

FIND SOLUTIONS
This equation has two identical solutions, because it has two identical factors.

▶ The solution of the equation is $-\frac{1}{3}$.

EXAMPLE 6 Solve a vertical motion problem

FALLING OBJECT A window washer drops a wet sponge from a height of 64 feet. After how many seconds does the sponge land on the ground?

Solution

Use the vertical motion model to write an equation for the height h (in feet) of the sponge as a function of the time t (in seconds) after it is dropped.

The sponge was dropped, so it has no initial vertical velocity. Find the value of t for which the height is 0.

$h = -16t^2 + vt + s$	Vertical motion model
$0 = -16t^2 + (0)t + 64$	Substitute 0 for h, 0 for v, and 64 for s.
$0 = -16(t^2 - 4)$	Factor out −16.
$0 = -16(t - 2)(t + 2)$	Difference of two squares pattern
$t - 2 = 0$ *or* $t + 2 = 0$	Zero-product property
$t = 2$ *or* $t = -2$	Solve for t.

Disregard the negative solution of the equation.

▶ The sponge lands on the ground 2 seconds after it is dropped.

GUIDED PRACTICE for Examples 5 and 6

Solve the equation.

5. $a^2 + 6a + 9 = 0$ **6.** $w^2 - 14w + 49 = 0$ **7.** $n^2 - 81 = 0$

8. **WHAT IF?** In Example 6, suppose the sponge is dropped from a height of 16 feet. After how many seconds does it land on the ground?

9.7 EXERCISES

HOMEWORK KEY

○ = **WORKED-OUT SOLUTIONS** on p. WS22 for Exs. 11 and 49

★ = **STANDARDIZED TEST PRACTICE** Exs. 2, 23, 24, 49, and 50

SKILL PRACTICE

1. VOCABULARY Copy and complete: The polynomial $9n^2 + 6n + 1$ is called a(n) _?_ trinomial.

2. ★ **WRITING** *Explain* how to factor the difference of two squares.

EXAMPLES 1 and 2 on p. 600 for Exs. 3–8

DIFFERENCE OF TWO SQUARES **Factor the polynomial.**

3. $x^2 - 25$ **4.** $n^2 - 64$ **5.** $81c^2 - 4$

6. $49 - 121p^2$ **7.** $-3m^2 + 48n^2$ **8.** $225x^2 - 144y^2$

EXAMPLES 3 and 4 on p. 601 for Exs. 9–14

PERFECT SQUARE TRINOMIALS **Factor the polynomial.**

9. $x^2 - 4x + 4$ **10.** $y^2 - 10y + 25$ **11.** $49a^2 + 14a + 1$

12. $9t^2 - 12t + 4$ **13.** $m^2 + m + \frac{1}{4}$ **14.** $2x^2 + 12xy + 18y^2$

EXAMPLES 1, 2, 3, and 4 on pp. 600–601 for Exs. 15–24

FACTORING POLYNOMIALS **Factor the polynomial.**

15. $4c^2 - 400$ **16.** $4f^2 - 36f + 81$ **17.** $-9r^2 + 4s^2$

18. $z^2 + 12z + 36$ **19.** $72 - 32y^2$ **20.** $45r^2 - 120rs + 80s^2$

ERROR ANALYSIS ***Describe*** **and correct the error in factoring.**

21.

$$36x^2 - 81 = 9(4x^2 - 9) = 9((2x)^2 - 3^2) = 9(2x - 3)^2$$

22.

$$y^2 - 6y + 9 = y^2 - 2(y \cdot 3) + 3^2 = (y - 3)(y + 3)$$

23. ★ **MULTIPLE CHOICE** Which is the correct factorization of $-45x^2 + 20y^2$?

Ⓐ $-5(3x + 2y)^2$ Ⓑ $5(3x - 2y)^2$

Ⓒ $-5(3x + 2y)(3x - 2y)$ Ⓓ $5(3x + 2y)(3x - 2y)$

24. ★ **MULTIPLE CHOICE** Which is the correct factorization of $16m^2 - 8mn + n^2$?

Ⓐ $(4m - n)^2$ Ⓑ $(4m + n)^2$

Ⓒ $(8m - n)^2$ Ⓓ $(4m - n)(4m + n)$

EXAMPLE 5 on p. 602 for Exs. 25–39

SOLVING EQUATIONS **Solve the equation.**

25. $x^2 + 8x + 16 = 0$ **26.** $16a^2 - 8a + 1 = 0$ **27.** $4w^2 - 36 = 0$

28. $32 - 18m^2 = 0$ **29.** $27c^2 + 108c + 108 = 0$ **30.** $-2h^2 - 28h - 98 = 0$

31. $6p^2 = 864$ **32.** $-3t^2 = -108$ **33.** $8k^2 = 98$

34. $-\frac{4}{3}x + \frac{4}{9} = -x^2$ **35.** $y^2 - \frac{5}{3}y = -\frac{25}{36}$ **36.** $\frac{2}{9} = 8n^2$

37. $-9c^2 = -16$ **38.** $-20s - 3 = 25s^2 + 1$ **39.** $y^4 - 2y^3 + y^2 = 0$

CHALLENGE Determine the value(s) of k for which the expression is a perfect square trinomial.

40. $x^2 + kx + 36$

41. $4x^2 + kx + 9$

42. $16x^2 + kx + 4$

43. $25x^2 + 10x + k$

44. $49x^2 - 84x + k$

45. $4x^2 - 48x + k$

PROBLEM SOLVING

EXAMPLE 6 on p. 602 for Exs. 46–48

46. FALLING BRUSH While standing on a ladder, you drop a paintbrush from a height of 25 feet. After how many seconds does the paintbrush land on the ground?

@HomeTutor for problem solving help at classzone.com

47. FALLING OBJECT A hickory nut falls from a branch that is 100 feet above the ground. After how many seconds does the hickory nut land on the ground?

@HomeTutor for problem solving help at classzone.com

48. GRASSHOPPER A grasshopper jumps straight up from the ground with an initial vertical velocity of 8 feet per second.

a. Write an equation that gives the height (in feet) of the grasshopper as a function of the time (in seconds) since it leaves the ground.

b. After how many seconds is the grasshopper 1 foot off the ground?

49. ★ **SHORT RESPONSE** A ball is thrown up into the air from a height of 5 feet with an initial vertical velocity of 56 feet per second. How many times does the ball reach a height of 54 feet? *Explain* your answer.

50. ★ **EXTENDED RESPONSE** An arch of balloons decorates the stage at a high school graduation. The balloons are tied to a frame. The shape of the frame can be modeled by the graph of the equation $y = -\frac{1}{4}x^2 + 3x$ where x and y are measured in feet.

a. Make a table of values that shows the height of the balloon arch for $x = 0, 2, 5, 8,$ and 11 feet.

b. For what additional values of x does the equation make sense? *Explain.*

c. At approximately what distance from the left end does the arch reach a height of 9 feet? Check your answer algebraically.

○ = WORKED-OUT SOLUTIONS on p. WS1

★ = STANDARDIZED TEST PRACTICE

51. FRAMING A square mirror is framed with stained glass as shown. Each corner of the frame began as a square with a side length of d inches before it was cut to fit the mirror. The mirror has a side length of 3 inches. The area of the stained glass frame is 91 square inches.

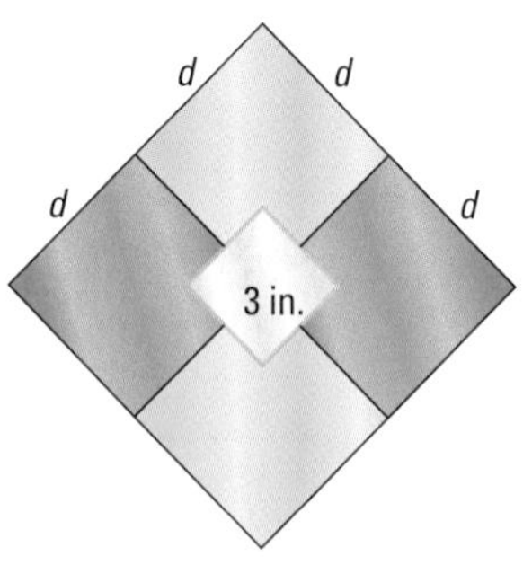

a. Write a polynomial that represents the area of the stained glass frame.

b. What is the side length of the frame?

52. CHALLENGE You have 120 folding chairs to set up in a park for an outdoor play. You want each row to have an odd number of chairs. You also want each row after the first to have 2 more chairs than the row in front of it. The first row will have 15 chairs.

a. Copy and complete the table below.

n	nth odd integer	Sum of first n odd integers	Sum as a power
1	1	1	1^2
2	3	$1 + 3 = 4$	2^2
3	5	$1 + 3 + 5 = 9$	?
4	7	?	?
5	9	?	?

b. *Describe* the relationship between n and the sum of the first n odd integers. Then find the sum of the first 10 odd integers.

c. *Explain* how to find the sum of the odd integers from 11 to 21.

d. How many rows of chairs will you need for the outdoor play? *Explain* your thinking.

MIXED REVIEW

PREVIEW
Prepare for Lesson 9.8 in Exs. 53–61.

Solve the equation.

53. $a + 6 = 3$ *(p. 134)* **54.** $5y - 2 = -32$ *(p. 141)* **55.** $8m + 4 = 20$ *(p. 141)*

56. $5b - 3b + 6 = 4$ *(p. 148)* **57.** $(x - 9)(x + 1) = 0$ *(p. 575)* **58.** $x^2 + 17x = -66$ *(p. 583)*

59. $x^2 = -12x + 45$ *(p. 583)* **60.** $2y^2 + y = 15$ *(p. 593)* **61.** $22z - 35 = 3z^2$ *(p. 593)*

Graph the linear equation.

62. $y = -6$ *(p. 215)* **63.** $x = 14$ *(p. 215)* **64.** $2x + y = 8$ *(p. 225)*

65. $-4x + 5y = -20$ *(p. 225)* **66.** $0.6x + 0.2y = 3.6$ *(p. 225)* **67.** $y = -\frac{3}{2}x - 9$ *(p. 225)*

68. $y = \frac{5}{2}x$ *(p. 244)* **69.** $y = -12x + 3$ *(p. 244)* **70.** $y = \frac{4}{3}x + 2$ *(p. 244)*

Find the product.

71. $(2a - 3)(5a - 2)$ *(p. 562)* **72.** $(2x^2 + x + 3)(x - 1)$ *(p. 562)* **73.** $(c + 3)(c + 5)$ *(p. 562)*

74. $(3x - 4)(2x - 7)$ *(p. 562)* **75.** $(2k - 11)(2k + 11)$ *(p. 569)* **76.** $(y - 7)^2$ *(p. 569)*

9.8 Factor Polynomials Completely

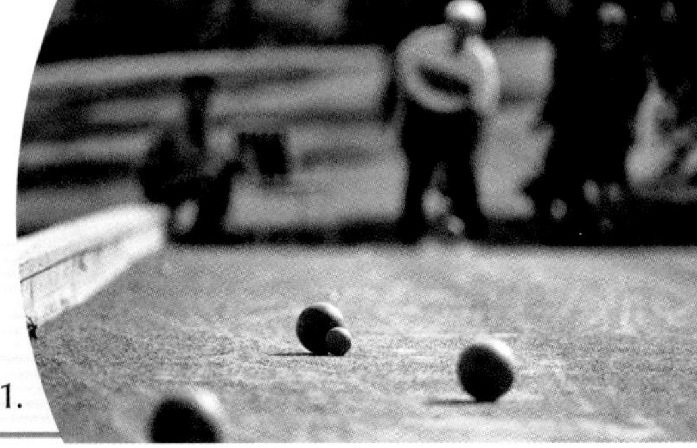

Before	You factored polynomials.
Now	You will factor polynomials completely.
Why?	So you can model the height of a projectile, as in Ex. 71.

Key Vocabulary
- **factor by grouping**
- **factor completely**

You have used the distributive property to factor a greatest common monomial from a polynomial. Sometimes, you can factor out a common binomial.

EXAMPLE 1 Factor out a common binomial

Factor the expression.

a. $2x(x + 4) - 3(x + 4)$

b. $3y^2(y - 2) + 5(2 - y)$

Solution

a. $2x(x + 4) - 3(x + 4) = (x + 4)(2x - 3)$

b. The binomials $y - 2$ and $2 - y$ are opposites. Factor -1 from $2 - y$ to obtain a common binomial factor.

$3y^2(y - 2) + 5(2 - y) = 3y^2(y - 2) - 5(y - 2)$ **Factor −1 from (2 − y).**

$= (y - 2)(3y^2 - 5)$ **Distributive property**

GROUPING You may be able to use the distributive property to factor polynomials with four terms. Factor a common monomial from pairs of terms, then look for a common binomial factor. This is called **factor by grouping**.

EXAMPLE 2 Factor by grouping

Factor the polynomial.

a. $x^3 + 3x^2 + 5x + 15$

b. $y^2 + y + yx + x$

Solution

CHECK WORK
Remember that you can check a factorization by multiplying the factors.

a. $x^3 + 3x^2 + 5x + 15 = (x^3 + 3x^2) + (5x + 15)$ **Group terms.**

$= x^2(x + 3) + 5(x + 3)$ **Factor each group.**

$= (x + 3)(x^2 + 5)$ **Distributive property**

b. $y^2 + y + yx + x = (y^2 + y) + (yx + x)$ **Group terms.**

$= y(y + 1) + x(y + 1)$ **Factor each group.**

$= (y + 1)(y + x)$ **Distributive property**

EXAMPLE 3 Factor by grouping

Factor $x^3 - 6 + 2x - 3x^2$.

Solution

The terms x^3 and -6 have no common factor. Use the commutative property to rearrange the terms so that you can group terms with a common factor.

$x^3 - 6 + 2x - 3x^2 = x^3 - 3x^2 + 2x - 6$	Rearrange terms.
$= (x^3 - 3x^2) + (2x - 6)$	Group terms.
$= x^2(x - 3) + 2(x - 3)$	Factor each group.
$= (x - 3)(x^2 + 2)$	Distributive property

CHECK Check your factorization using a graphing calculator. Graph $y_1 = x^3 - 6 + 2x - 3x^2$ and $y_2 = (x - 3)(x^2 + 2)$. Because the graphs coincide, you know that your factorization is correct.

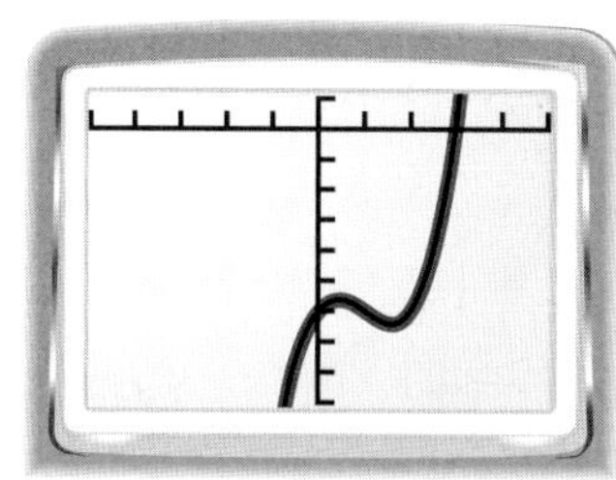

GUIDED PRACTICE for Examples 1, 2, and 3

Factor the expression.

1. $x(x - 2) + (x - 2)$
2. $a^3 + 3a^2 + a + 3$
3. $y^2 + 2x + yx + 2y$

READING
If a polynomial has two or more terms and is unfactorable, it is called a *prime polynomial*.

FACTORING COMPLETELY You have seen that the polynomial $x^2 - 1$ can be factored as $(x + 1)(x - 1)$. This polynomial is factorable. Notice that the polynomial $x^2 + 1$ cannot be written as the product of polynomials with integer coefficients. This polynomial is unfactorable. A factorable polynomial with integer coefficients is **factored completely** if it is written as a product of unfactorable polynomials with integer coefficients.

CONCEPT SUMMARY *For Your Notebook*

Guidelines for Factoring Polynomials Completely

To factor a polynomial completely, you should try each of these steps.

1. Factor out the greatest common monomial factor. *(Lesson 9.4)*	$3x^2 + 6x = 3x(x + 2)$
2. Look for a difference of two squares or a perfect square trinomial. *(Lesson 9.7)*	$x^2 + 4x + 4 = (x + 2)^2$
3. Factor a trinomial of the form $ax^2 + bx + c$ into a product of binomial factors. *(Lessons 9.5 and 9.6)*	$3x^2 - 5x - 2 = (3x + 1)(x - 2)$
4. Factor a polynomial with four terms by grouping. *(Lesson 9.8)*	$x^3 + x - 4x^2 - 4 = (x^2 + 1)(x - 4)$

EXAMPLE 4 Factor completely

Factor the polynomial completely.

a. $n^2 + 2n - 1$ **b.** $4x^3 - 44x^2 + 96x$ **c.** $50h^4 - 2h^2$

Solution

a. The terms of the polynomial have no common monomial factor. Also, there are no factors of -1 that have a sum of 2. This polynomial cannot be factored.

b. $4x^3 - 44x^2 + 96x = 4x(x^2 - 11x + 24)$ Factor out $4x$.

$= 4x(x - 3)(x - 8)$ Find two negative factors of 24 that have a sum of -11.

c. $50h^4 - 2h^2 = 2h^2(25h^2 - 1)$ Factor out $2h^2$.

$= 2h^2(5h - 1)(5h + 1)$ Difference of two squares pattern

✓ **GUIDED PRACTICE** for Example 4

Factor the polynomial completely.

4. $3x^3 - 12x$ **5.** $2y^3 - 12y^2 + 18y$ **6.** $m^3 - 2m^2 - 8m$

EXAMPLE 5 Solve a polynomial equation

Solve $3x^3 + 18x^2 = -24x$.

$3x^3 + 18x^2 = -24x$ Write original equation.

$3x^3 + 18x^2 + 24x = 0$ Add $24x$ to each side.

$3x(x^2 + 6x + 8) = 0$ Factor out $3x$.

$3x(x + 2)(x + 4) = 0$ Factor trinomial.

$3x = 0$ *or* $x + 2 = 0$ *or* $x + 4 = 0$ Zero-product property

$x = 0$ $x = -2$ $x = -4$ Solve for x.

▸ The solutions of the equation are 0, -2, and -4.

CHECK Check each solution by substituting it for x in the equation. One check is shown here.

$$3(-2)^3 + 18(-2)^2 \stackrel{?}{=} -24(-2)$$

$$-24 + 72 \stackrel{?}{=} 48$$

$$48 = 48 \checkmark$$

GUIDED PRACTICE for Example 5

Solve the equation.

7. $w^3 - 8w^2 + 16w = 0$ **8.** $x^3 - 25x = 0$ **9.** $c^3 - 7c^2 + 12c = 0$

EXAMPLE 6 Solve a multi-step problem

TERRARIUM A terrarium in the shape of a rectangular prism has a volume of 4608 cubic inches. Its length is more than 10 inches. The dimensions of the terrarium are shown. Find the length, width, and height of the terrarium.

Solution

STEP 1 **Write** a verbal model. Then write an equation.

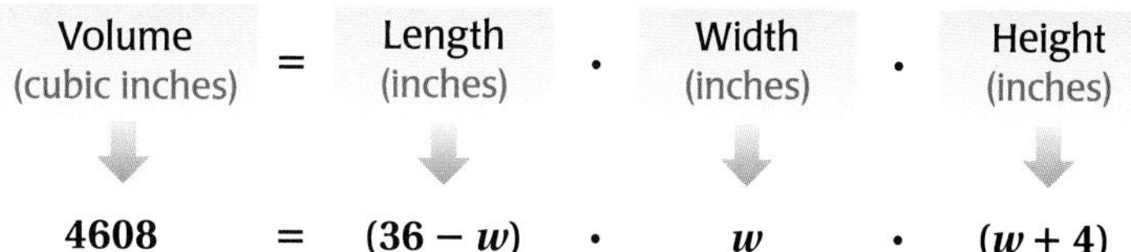

Volume (cubic inches) = Length (inches) · Width (inches) · Height (inches)

$$4608 = (36 - w) \cdot w \cdot (w + 4)$$

STEP 2 **Solve** the equation for w.

$4608 = (36 - w)(w)(w + 4)$ — Write equation.

$0 = 32w^2 + 144w - w^3 - 4608$ — Multiply. Subtract 4608 from each side.

$0 = (-w^3 + 32w^2) + (144w - 4608)$ — Group terms.

$0 = -w^2(w - 32) + 144(w - 32)$ — Factor each group.

$0 = (w - 32)(-w^2 + 144)$ — Distributive property

$0 = -1(w - 32)(w^2 - 144)$ — Factor -1 from $-w^2 + 144$.

$0 = -1(w - 32)(w - 12)(w + 12)$ — Difference of two squares pattern

$w - 32 = 0$ *or* $w - 12 = 0$ *or* $w + 12 = 0$ — Zero-product property

$w = 32$ $\quad w = 12$ $\quad w = -12$ — Solve for w.

STEP 3 **Choose** the solution of the equation that is the correct value of w. Disregard $w = -12$, because the width cannot be negative.

You know that the length is more than 10 inches. Test the solutions 12 and 32 in the expression for the length.

Length $= 36 - 12 = 24$ ✓ *or* Length $= 36 - 32 = 4$ ✗

The solution 12 gives a length of 24 inches, so 12 is the correct value of w.

STEP 4 **Find** the height.

Height $= w + 4 = 12 + 4 = 16$

▶ The width is 12 inches, the length is 24 inches, and the height is 16 inches.

✓ **GUIDED PRACTICE** for Example 6

10. DIMENSIONS OF A BOX A box in the shape of a rectangular prism has a volume of 72 cubic feet. The box has a length of x feet, a width of $(x - 1)$ feet, and a height of $(x + 9)$ feet. Find the dimensions of the box.

9.8 EXERCISES

HOMEWORK KEY
○ = **WORKED-OUT SOLUTIONS** on p. WS23 for Exs. 13, 23, and 71
★ = **STANDARDIZED TEST PRACTICE** Exs. 2, 12, 41, 55, 71, and 73

SKILL PRACTICE

1. **VOCABULARY** What does it mean for a polynomial to be factored completely?

2. ★ **WRITING** *Explain* how you know if a polynomial is unfactorable.

EXAMPLE 1 on p. 606 for Exs. 3–12

BINOMIAL FACTORS **Factor the expression.**

3. $x(x-8)+(x-8)$
4. $5y(y+3)-2(y+3)$
5. $6z(z-4)-7(z-4)$
6. $10(a-6)-3a(a-6)$
7. $b^2(b+5)-3(b+5)$
8. $7c^2(c+9)+2(c+9)$
9. $x(13+x)-(x+13)$
10. $y^2(y-4)+5(4-y)$
11. $12(z-1)-5z^2(1-z)$

12. ★ **MULTIPLE CHOICE** Which is the correct factorization of $x^2(x-8)+5(8-x)$?

Ⓐ $(x^2+5)(x-8)$ Ⓑ $(x^2+5)(8-x)$
Ⓒ $(x^2-5)(x-8)$ Ⓓ $(x^2-5)(8-x)$

EXAMPLES 2 and 3 on pp. 606–607 for Exs. 13–22

FACTORING BY GROUPING **Factor the polynomial.**

13. x^3+x^2+2x+2
14. y^3-9y^2+y-9
15. $z^3-4z^2+3z-12$
16. $c^3+7c^2+5c+35$
17. $a^3+13a^2-5a-65$
18. $2s^3-3s^2+18s-27$
19. $5n^3-4n^2+25n-20$
20. $x^2+8x-xy-8y$
21. $y^2+y+5xy+5x$

22. **ERROR ANALYSIS** *Describe* and correct the error in factoring.

$$a^3+8a^2-6a-48 = a^2(a+8)+6(a+8)$$
$$= (a+8)(a^2+6)$$

EXAMPLE 4 on p. 608 for Exs. 23–42

FACTORING COMPLETELY **Factor the polynomial completely.**

23. x^4-x^2
24. $36a^4-4a^2$
25. $3n^5-48n^3$
26. $4y^6-16y^4$
27. $75c^9-3c^7$
28. $72p-2p^3$
29. $32s^4-8s^2$
30. $80z^8-45z^6$
31. $m^2-5m-35$
32. $6g^3-24g^2+24g$
33. $3w^4+24w^3+48w^2$
34. $3r^5+3r^4-90r^3$
35. $b^3-5b^2-4b+20$
36. $h^3+4h^2-25h-100$
37. $9t^3+18t-t^2-2$
38. $2x^5y-162x^3y$
39. $7a^3b^3-63ab^3$
40. $-4s^3t^3+24s^2t^2-36st$

41. ★ **MULTIPLE CHOICE** What is the completely factored form of $3x^6-75x^4$?

Ⓐ $3x^4(x^2-25)$ Ⓑ $3x^4(x-5)^2$ Ⓒ $3x^4(x+5)^2$ Ⓓ $3x^4(x-5)(x+5)$

42. **ERROR ANALYSIS** *Describe* and correct the error in factoring the polynomial completely.

$$x^3-6x^2-9x+54 = x^2(x-6)-9(x-6)$$
$$= (x-6)(x^2-9)$$

✗

EXAMPLE 5
on p. 608
for Exs. 43–54

SOLVING EQUATIONS **Solve the equation.**

43. $x^3 + x^2 - 4x - 4 = 0$

44. $a^3 - 11a^2 - 9a + 99 = 0$

45. $4y^3 - 7y^2 - 16y + 28 = 0$

46. $5n^3 - 30n^2 + 40n = 0$

47. $3b^3 + 24b^2 + 45b = 0$

48. $2t^5 + 2t^4 - 144t^3 = 0$

49. $z^3 - 81z = 0$

50. $c^4 - 100c^2 = 0$

51. $12s - 3s^3 = 0$

52. $2x^3 - 10x^2 + 40 = 8x$

53. $3p + 1 = p^2 + 3p^3$

54. $m^3 - 3m^2 = 4m - 12$

55. ★ **WRITING** Is it possible to find three solutions of the equation $x^3 + 2x^2 + 3x + 6 = 0$? *Explain* why or why not.

GEOMETRY **Find the length, width, and height of the rectangular prism with the given volume.**

56. Volume = 12 cubic inches

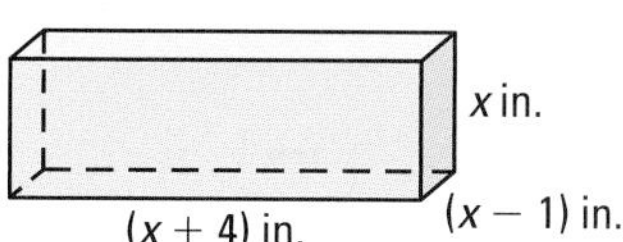

57. Volume = 96 cubic feet

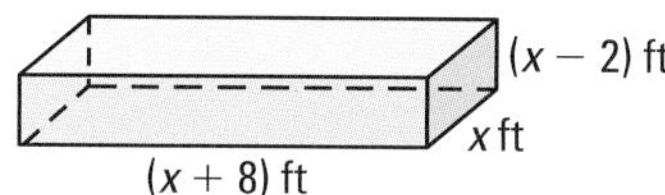

FACTORING COMPLETELY **Factor the polynomial completely.**

58. $x^3 + 2x^2y - x - 2y$

59. $8b^3 - 4b^2a - 18b + 9a$

60. $4s^2 - s + 12st - 3t$

FACTOR BY GROUPING **In Exercises 61–66, use the example below to factor the trinomial by grouping.**

EXAMPLE **Factor a trinomial by grouping**

Factor $8x^2 + 10x - 3$ by grouping.

Solution

Notice that the polynomial is in the form $ax^2 + bx + c$.

STEP 1 **Write** the product ac as the product of two factors that have a sum of b. In this case, the product ac is $8(-3) = -24$. Find two factors of -24 that have a sum of 10.

$-24 = 12 \cdot (-2)$ and $12 + (-2) = 10$

STEP 2 **Rewrite** the middle term as two terms with coefficients 12 and -2.

$8x^2 + \mathbf{10x} - 3 = 8x^2 + \mathbf{12x} - \mathbf{2x} - 3$

STEP 3 **Factor** by grouping.

$8x^2 + 12x - 2x - 3 = (8x^2 + 12x) + (-2x - 3)$ Group terms.

$= 4x(2x + 3) - (2x + 3)$ Factor each group.

$= (2x + 3)(4x - 1)$ Distributive property

61. $6x^2 + 5x - 4$

62. $10s^2 + 19s + 6$

63. $12n^2 - 13n + 3$

64. $16a^2 + 14a + 3$

65. $21w^2 + 8w - 4$

66. $15y^2 - 31y + 10$

67. **CHALLENGE** Use factoring by grouping to show that a trinomial of the form $a^2 + 2ab + b^2$ can be factored as $(a + b)^2$. *Justify* your steps.

PROBLEM SOLVING

EXAMPLE 6 on p. 609 for Exs. 68–70

68. CYLINDRICAL VASE A vase in the shape of a cylinder has a height of 6 inches and a volume of 24π cubic inches. What is the radius of the vase?

@HomeTutor for problem solving help at classzone.com

69. CARPENTRY You are building a birdhouse that will have a volume of 128 cubic inches. The birdhouse will have the dimensions shown.

a. Write a polynomial that represents the volume of the birdhouse.

b. What are the dimensions of the birdhouse?

@HomeTutor for problem solving help at classzone.com

70. BAG SIZE A gift bag is shaped like a rectangular prism and has a volume of 1152 cubic inches. The dimensions of the gift bag are shown. The height is greater than the width. What are the dimensions of the gift bag?

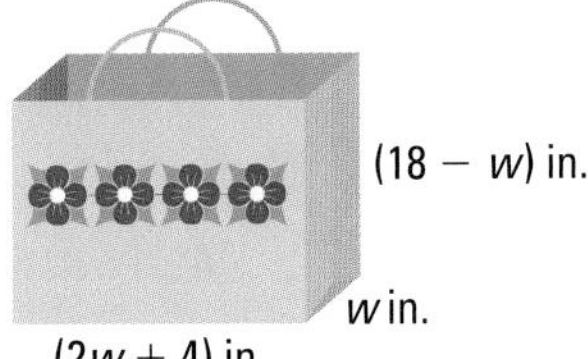

71. ★ **SHORT RESPONSE** A pallino is the small target ball that is tossed in the air at the beginning of a game of bocce. The height h (in meters) of the pallino after you throw it can be modeled by $h = -4.9t^2 + 3.9t + 1$ where t is the time (in seconds) since you released it.

a. Find the zeros of the function.

b. Do the zeros of the function have any meaning in this situation? *Explain* your reasoning.

72. JUMPING ROBOT The path of a jumping robot can be modeled by the graph of the equation $y = -10x^2 + 30x$ where x and y are both measured in feet. On a coordinate plane, the ground is represented by the x-axis, and the robot's starting position is the origin.

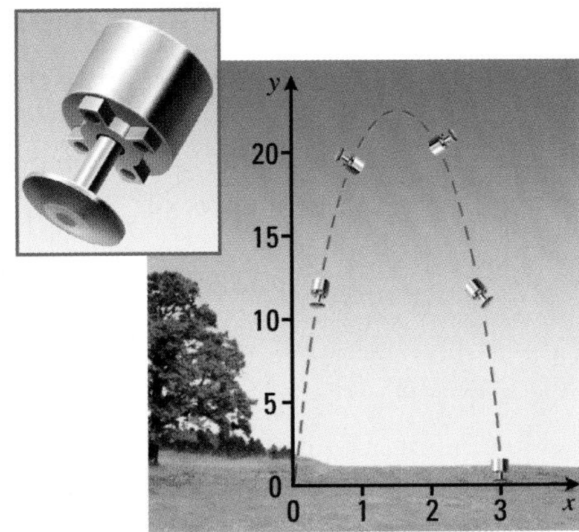

a. The robot's maximum height is 22.5 feet. What is the robot's horizontal distance from its starting point when its height is 22.5 feet?

b. How far has the robot traveled horizontally when it lands on the ground? *Explain* your answer.

73. ★ **EXTENDED RESPONSE** The width of a box is 4 inches more than the height h. The length is the difference of 9 inches and the height.

a. Write a polynomial that represents the volume of the box.

b. The volume of the box is 180 cubic inches. What are all the possible dimensions of the box?

c. Which dimensions result in a box with the smallest possible surface area? *Explain* your reasoning.

74. **CHALLENGE** A plastic cube is used to display an autographed baseball. The cube has an outer surface area of 54 square inches.

a. What is the length of an outer edge of the cube?

b. What is the greatest volume the cube can possibly have? *Explain* why the actual volume inside of the cube may be less than the greatest possible volume.

MIXED REVIEW

PREVIEW
Prepare for Lesson 10.1 in Exs. 75–86.

Graph the equation. *(p. 244)*

75. $y - 2x = 0$
76. $y + 2x = 3$
77. $y + 5x = 2$
78. $2y - 6x = 6$
79. $-3y + 4x = 12$
80. $-4x + 2y = 8$
81. $x - 4y = 2$
82. $x - 2y = -10$
83. $y = 5$
84. $y = 0$
85. $x = -4$
86. $x = 2$

Write an equation of the line shown.

87.
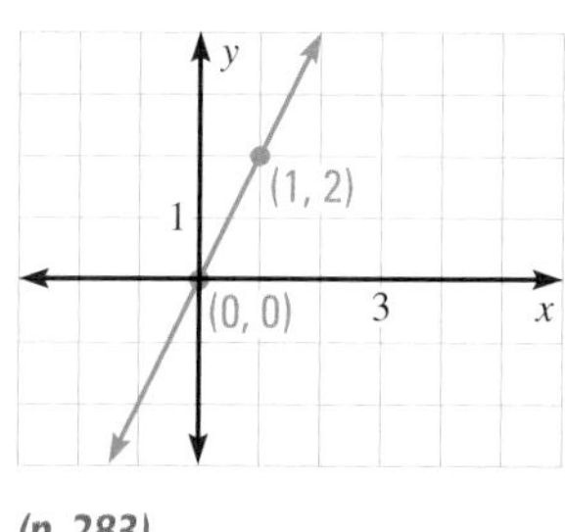

(p. 283)

88.
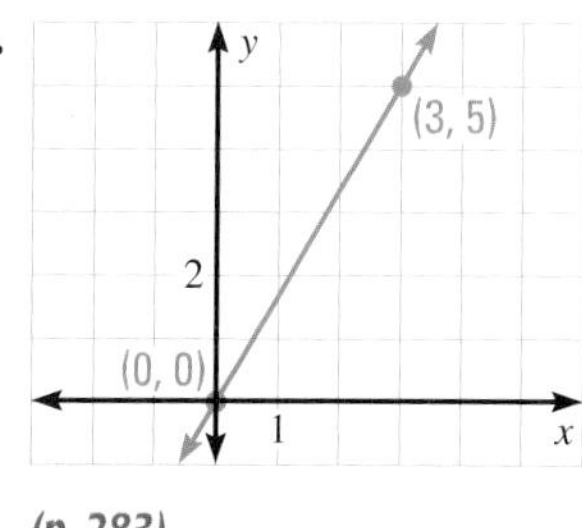

(p. 283)

89.
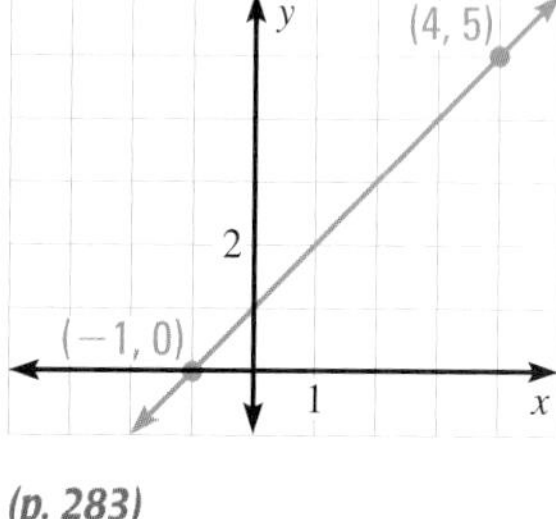

(p. 283)

QUIZ *for Lessons 9.7–9.8*

Factor the polynomial. *(p. 600)*

1. $x^2 - 400$
2. $18 - 32z^2$
3. $169x^2 - 25y^2$
4. $n^2 - 6n + 9$
5. $100a^2 + 20a + 1$
6. $8r^2 - 40rs + 50s^2$

Factor the polynomial completely. *(p. 606)*

7. $3x^5 - 75x^3$
8. $72s^4 - 8s^2$
9. $3x^4y - 300x^2y$
10. $a^3 - 4a^2 - 21a$
11. $2h^4 + 28h^3 + 98h^2$
12. $z^3 - 4z^2 - 16z + 64$

Solve the equation.

13. $x^2 + 10x + 25 = 0$ *(p. 600)*
14. $48 - 27m^2 = 0$ *(p. 600)*
15. $w^3 - w^2 - 4w + 4 = 0$ *(p. 606)*
16. $4x^3 - 28x^2 + 40x = 0$ *(p. 606)*
17. $3x^5 - 6x^4 - 45x^3 = 0$ *(p. 606)*
18. $x^3 - 121x = 0$ *(p. 606)*

19. **VOLUME** The cylinder shown has a volume of 72π cubic inches. *(p. 600)*

a. Write a polynomial that represents the volume of the cylinder. Leave your answer in terms of π.

b. Find the radius of the cylinder.

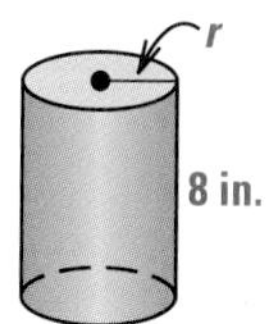

MIXED REVIEW *of Problem Solving*

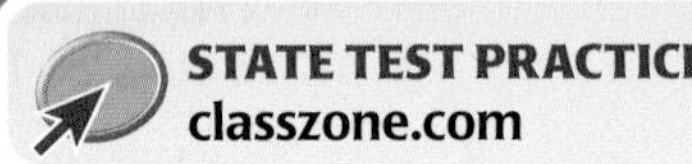

Lessons 9.5–9.8

1. **MULTI-STEP PROBLEM** A rectangular room has the dimensions shown.

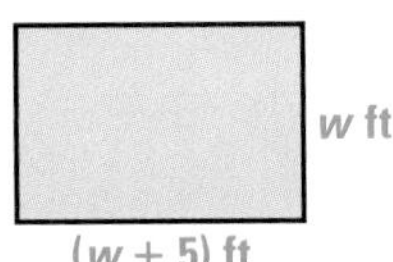

   a. Write a polynomial that represents the area of the room.

   b. The room has an area of 150 square feet. What are the length and width of the room?

2. **MULTI-STEP PROBLEM** A block of clay has the dimensions shown.

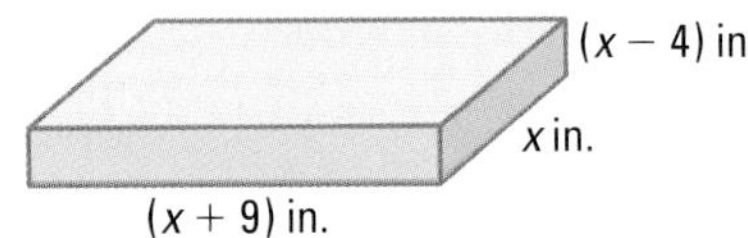

   a. Write a polynomial that represents the volume of the clay.

   b. The clay has a volume of 180 cubic inches. What are the length, width, and height of the block?

3. **MULTI-STEP PROBLEM** You are making a wooden game board. You cut a square piece of wood, as shown.

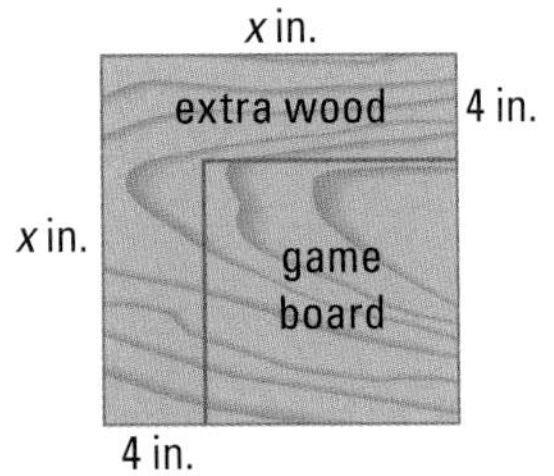

   a. Write a polynomial that represents the area of the game board.

   b. The area of the game board is 100 square inches. What was the area of the original piece of wood? *Explain* how you found your answer.

4. **OPEN-ENDED** *Describe* a situation that can be modeled using the vertical motion model $h = -16t^2 + 48t$. Then find the value of t when $h = 0$. *Explain* what this value of t means in this situation.

5. **EXTENDED RESPONSE** You hit a baseball straight up into the air. The baseball is hit with an initial vertical velocity of 80 feet per second when it is 3 feet off the ground.

   a. Write an equation that gives the height (in feet) of the baseball as a function of the time (in seconds) since it was hit.

   b. After how many seconds does the ball reach a height of 99 feet?

   c. Does the ball reach a height of 99 feet more than once? *Justify* your answer.

6. **EXTENDED RESPONSE** The length of a box is 25 inches more than its height. The width of the box is 1 inch less than its height.

   a. Draw a diagram of the box. Label its dimensions in terms of the height h.

   b. Write a polynomial that represents the volume of the box.

   c. The box has a volume of 600 cubic inches. What is the area of its top? *Explain*.

7. **SHORT RESPONSE** A tennis player hits a ball with an initial vertical velocity of 63 feet per second. Can you find the number of seconds the tennis ball is in the air? *Explain* why not or find the number of seconds.

8. **GRIDDED ANSWER** During an experiment in physics class, you drop a ball from a height of 144 feet. After how many seconds does the ball hit the ground?

9. **SHORT RESPONSE** A football is kicked toward a goal post that is 10 feet high. The path of the football is modeled by the graph of $y = -0.005x^2 + 0.6x$ where x and y are measured in feet. On a coordinate plane, the x-axis represents the ground, and the ball leaves the ground at the origin. The ball hits the goal post on the way down. How far from the goal post is the kicker? *Explain*.

9 CHAPTER SUMMARY

BIG IDEAS

For Your Notebook

Big Idea 1

Adding, Subtracting, and Multiplying Polynomials

You can perform operations with polynomials using the steps below.

Operation	Steps
Add	Group like terms and add.
Subtract	First, rewrite subtraction as addition. Second, group like terms and add.
Multiply	First, multiply terms using the distributive property. Second, combine like terms.

Big Idea 2

Factoring Polynomials

When factoring a polynomial, you should use the following checklist so that you can be sure you have factored the polynomial completely.

STEP 1 **Factor** out the greatest common monomial factor.

STEP 2 **Look** for special products to factor.

STEP 3 **Factor** a trinomial into a pair of binomials, if possible.

STEP 4 **Factor** a polynomial with four terms by grouping, if possible.

Big Idea 3

Writing and Solving Polynomial Equations to Solve Problems

You can write polynomials that model real-world situations in order to solve problems. For example, you can use the vertical motion model.

Height (in feet) of a projectile: $h = -16t^2 + vt + s$ where t is the time (in seconds) the object has been in the air, v is the initial vertical velocity (in feet per second), and s is the initial height (in feet).

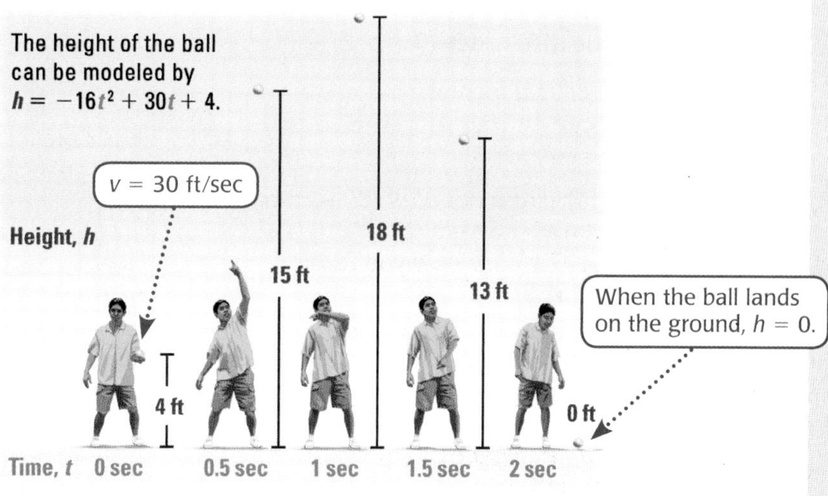

9 CHAPTER REVIEW

@HomeTutor
classzone.com
- Multi-Language Glossary
- Vocabulary practice

REVIEW KEY VOCABULARY

- monomial, *p. 554*
- degree of a monomial, *p. 554*
- polynomial, *p. 554*
- degree of a polynomial, *p. 554*
- leading coefficient, *p. 554*
- binomial, *p. 555*
- trinomial, *p. 555*
- roots, *p. 575*
- vertical motion model, *p. 577*
- perfect square trinomial, *p. 601*
- factor by grouping, *p. 606*
- factor completely, *p. 607*

VOCABULARY EXERCISES

1. Copy and complete: The greatest degree of the terms in a polynomial is called the _?_.

2. **WRITING** Is $2x^{-1}$ a monomial? *Explain* why or why not.

3. **WRITING** What does it mean for a polynomial to be factored completely? Give an example of a polynomial that has been factored completely.

In Exercises 4–6, match the polynomial with its classification.

4. $5x - 22$
5. $-11x^3$
6. $x^2 + x + 1$

A. Monomial
B. Binomial
C. Trinomial

REVIEW EXAMPLES AND EXERCISES

Use the review examples and exercises below to check your understanding of the concepts you have learned in each lesson of Chapter 9.

9.1 Add and Subtract Polynomials *pp. 554–559*

EXAMPLE

Find the difference $(3x^2 + 2) - (4x^2 - x - 9)$.

Use a vertical format.

$$\begin{array}{r} 3x^2 \quad\quad + 2 \\ - \quad (4x^2 - x - 9) \\ \hline \end{array} \quad \rightarrow \quad \begin{array}{r} 3x^2 \quad\quad + 2 \\ + \quad -4x^2 + x + 9 \\ \hline -x^2 + x + 11 \end{array}$$

EXERCISES

EXAMPLES 3 and 4 on pp. 555–556 for Exs. 7–12

Find the sum or difference.

7. $(9x + 6x^3 - 8x^2) + (-5x^3 + 6x)$
8. $(7a^3 - 4a^2 - 2a + 1) + (a^3 - 1)$
9. $(11y^5 + 3y^2 - 4) + (y^2 - y + 1)$
10. $(3n^2 - 4n + 1) - (8n^2 - 4n + 17)$
11. $(2s^3 + 8) - (-3s^3 + 7s - 5)$
12. $(-k^2 + 7k + 5) - (2k^4 - 3k^3 - 6)$

@HomeTutor
classzone.com
Chapter Review Practice

9.2 Multiply Polynomials

pp. 562–568

EXAMPLE

Find the product.

a. $(x^2 + 4x - 5)(2x - 1)$

b. $(5y + 6)(y - 3)$

Solution

a. Use a horizontal format.

$(x^2 + 4x - 5)(2x - 1)$	Write product.
$= x^2(2x - 1) + 4x(2x - 1) - 5(2x - 1)$	Distributive property
$= 2x^3 - x^2 + 8x^2 - 4x - 10x + 5$	Distributive property
$= 2x^3 + 7x^2 - 14x + 5$	Combine like terms.

b. Use a vertical format.

STEP 1 **Multiply** by -3.

$$\begin{array}{r} 5y + 6 \\ \times \quad y - 3 \\ \hline -15y - 18 \end{array}$$

STEP 2 **Multiply** by y.

$$\begin{array}{r} 5y + 6 \\ \times \quad y - 3 \\ \hline -15y - 18 \\ 5y^2 + 6y \quad\quad \end{array}$$

STEP 3 **Add** products.

$$\begin{array}{r} 5y + 6 \\ \times \quad y - 3 \\ \hline -15y - 18 \\ 5y^2 + 6y \quad\quad \\ \hline 5y^2 - 9y - 18 \end{array}$$

EXERCISES

EXAMPLES 1, 2, 3, and 4 on pp. 562–563 for Exs. 13–21

Find the product.

13. $(x^2 - 2x + 1)(x - 3)$

14. $(y^2 + 5y + 4)(3y + 2)$

15. $(x - 4)(x + 2)$

16. $(5b^2 - b - 7)(b + 6)$

17. $(z + 8)(z - 11)$

18. $(2a - 1)(a - 3)$

19. $(6n + 7)(3n + 1)$

20. $(4n - 5)(7n - 3)$

21. $(3x - 2)(x + 4)$

9.3 Find Special Products of Polynomials

pp. 569–574

EXAMPLE

Find the product $(3x + 2)(3x - 2)$.

$(3x + 2)(3x - 2) = (3x)^2 - 2^2$	Sum and difference pattern
$= 9x^2 - 4$	Simplify.

EXERCISES

EXAMPLES 1 and 2 on pp. 569–570 for Exs. 22–27

Find the product.

22. $(x + 11)^2$

23. $(6y + 1)^2$

24. $(2x - y)^2$

25. $(4a - 3)^2$

26. $(k + 7)(k - 7)$

27. $(3s + 5)(3s - 5)$

CHAPTER REVIEW

9.4 Solve Polynomial Equations in Factored Form

pp. 575–580

EXAMPLE

Solve $6x^2 + 42x = 0$.

$6x^2 + 42x = 0$	Write original equation.
$6x(x + 7) = 0$	Factor left side.
$6x = 0$ *or* $x + 7 = 0$	Zero-product property
$x = 0$ *or* $x = -7$	Solve for x.

▶ The solutions of the equation are 0 and −7.

EXERCISES

EXAMPLES 3 and 4 on p. 576 for Exs. 28–33

Solve the equation.

28. $2a^2 + 26a = 0$ **29.** $3t^2 - 33t = 0$ **30.** $8x^2 - 4x = 0$

31. $m^2 = 9m$ **32.** $5y^2 = -50y$ **33.** $21h^2 = 7h$

9.5 Factor $x^2 + bx + c$

pp. 583–589

EXAMPLE

Factor $x^2 + 2x - 63$.

Find two factors of −63 whose sum is 2. One factor will be positive, and the other will be negative. Make an organized list of factors.

Factors of −63	Sum of factors	
1, −63	1 + (−63) = −62	✗
−1, 63	−1 + 63 = 62	✗
3, −21	3 + (−21) = −18	✗
−3, 21	−3 + 21 = 18	✗
9, −7	9 + (−7) = 2	⟵ Correct sum
−9, 7	−9 + 7 = −2	✗

▶ $x^2 + 2x - 63 = (x + 9)(x - 7)$

EXERCISES

EXAMPLES 1,2 and 3 on pp. 583–584 for Exs. 34–42

Factor the trinomial.

34. $n^2 + 15n + 26$ **35.** $s^2 + 10s - 11$ **36.** $b^2 - 5b - 14$

37. $a^2 + 5a - 84$ **38.** $t^2 - 24t + 135$ **39.** $x^2 + 4x - 32$

40. $p^2 + 9p + 14$ **41.** $c^2 + 8c + 15$ **42.** $y^2 - 10y + 21$

@HomeTutor
classzone.com
Chapter Review Practice

9.6 Factor $ax^2 + bx + c$

pp. 593–599

EXAMPLE

THROWN BALL You throw a ball up into the air. At 4 feet above the ground, the ball leaves your hand with an initial vertical velocity of 30 feet per second.

a. Write an equation that gives the height (in feet) of the ball as a function of the time (in seconds) since it left your hand.

b. After how many seconds does the ball land on the ground?

Solution

a. Use the vertical motion model $h = -16t^2 + vt + s$ to write an equation for the height h (in feet) of the ball as a function of the time t (in seconds). In this case, $v = 30$ and $s = 4$.

$h = -16t^2 + vt + s$ **Vertical motion model**

$h = -16t^2 + 30t + 4$ **Substitute 30 for *v* and 4 for *s*.**

b. When the ball lands on the ground, its height is 0 feet. Substitute 0 for h and solve the equation for t.

$0 = -16t^2 + 30t + 4$ **Substitute 0 for *h*.**

$0 = -2(8t^2 - 15t - 2)$ **Factor out −2.**

$0 = -2(8t + 1)(t - 2)$ **Factor the trinomial. Find factors of 8 and −2 that produce a middle term with a coefficient of −15.**

$8t + 1 = 0$ *or* $t - 2 = 0$ **Zero-product property**

$t = -\frac{1}{8}$ *or* $t = 2$ **Solve for *t*.**

The solutions of the equation are $-\frac{1}{8}$ and 2. A negative solution does not make sense in this situation, so disregard $-\frac{1}{8}$.

▶ The ball lands on the ground after 2 seconds.

EXERCISES

EXAMPLES 1, 2, 3, and 4 on pp. 593–595 for Exs. 43–50

Solve the equation.

43. $7x^2 - 8x = -1$ **44.** $4n^2 + 3 = 7n$ **45.** $3s^2 + 4s + 4 = 8$

46. $6z^2 + 13z = 5$ **47.** $-4r^2 = 18r + 18$ **48.** $9a^2 = 6a + 24$

49. THROWN BALL You throw a ball up into the air with an initial vertical velocity of 46 feet per second. The ball leaves your hand when it is 6 feet above the ground. After how many seconds does the ball land on the ground?

50. GEOMETRY The length of a rectangle is 1 inch less than twice the width. The area of the rectangle is 21 square inches. What is the length of the rectangle?

9 CHAPTER REVIEW

9.7 Factor Special Products

pp. 600–605

EXAMPLE

Factor the polynomial.

a. $100x^2 - y^2$

b. $4x^2 - 36x + 81$

Solution

a. $100x^2 - y^2 = (10x)^2 - y^2$ — Write as $a^2 - b^2$.

$= (10x + y)(10x - y)$ — Difference of two squares pattern

b. $4x^2 - 36x + 81 = (2x)^2 - 2(2x \cdot 9) + 9^2$ — Write as $a^2 - 2ab + b^2$.

$= (2x - 9)^2$ — Perfect square trinomial pattern

EXERCISES

EXAMPLES 1, 2, 3, 4, and 6 on pp. 600–602 for Exs. 51–57

Factor the polynomial.

51. $z^2 - 225$

52. $a^2 - 16y^2$

53. $12 - 48n^2$

54. $x^2 + 20x + 100$

55. $16p^2 - 8p + 1$

56. $-2y^2 + 32y - 128$

57. DROPPED OBJECT You drop a penny from a height of 16 feet. After how many seconds does the penny land on the ground?

9.8 Factor Polynomials Completely

pp. 606–613

EXAMPLE

Factor the polynomial completely.

a. $y^3 - 4y^2 + 8y - 32$

b. $5x^3 - 40x^2 + 80x$

Solution

a. $y^3 - 4y^2 + 8y - 32 = (y^3 - 4y^2) + (8y - 32)$ — Group terms.

$= y^2(y - 4) + 8(y - 4)$ — Factor each group.

$= (y - 4)(y^2 + 8)$ — Distributive property

b. $5x^3 - 40x^2 + 80x = 5x(x^2 - 8x + 16)$ — Factor out 5x.

$= 5x(x - 4)^2$ — Perfect square trinomial pattern

EXERCISES

EXAMPLE 4 on p. 608 for Exs. 58–66

Factor the polynomial completely.

58. $a^3 + 6a - 5a^2 - 30$

59. $y^2 + 3y + yx + 3x$

60. $x^3 - 11x^2 - x + 11$

61. $5s^4 - 125s^2$

62. $147n^5 - 3n^3$

63. $2z^3 + 2z^2 - 60z$

64. $x^3 + 5x^2 - x - 5$

65. $2b^3 + 3b^2 - 8b - 12$

66. $x^3 + x^2 - 6x - 6$

9 CHAPTER TEST

Find the sum or difference.

1. $(a^2 - 4a + 6) + (-3a^2 + 13a + 1)$
2. $(5x^2 - 2) + (8x^3 + 2x^2 - x + 9)$
3. $(15n^2 + 7n - 1) - (4n^2 - 3n - 8)$
4. $(9c^3 - 11c^2 + 2c) - (-6c^2 - 3c + 11)$

Find the product.

5. $(2z + 9)(z - 7)$
6. $(5m - 8)(5m - 7)$
7. $(b + 2)(-b^2 + 4b - 3)$
8. $(5 + 7y)(1 - 9y)$
9. $(2x^2 - 3x + 5)(x - 4)$
10. $(5p - 6)(5p + 6)$
11. $(12 - 3g)^2$
12. $(2s + 9t)^2$
13. $(11a - 4b)(11a + 4b)$

Factor the polynomial.

14. $x^2 + 8x + 7$
15. $2n^2 - 11n + 15$
16. $-12r^2 + 5r + 3$
17. $t^2 - 10t + 25$
18. $-3n^2 + 75$
19. $3x^2 + 29x - 44$
20. $x^2 - 49$
21. $2a^4 + 21a^3 + 49a^2$
22. $y^3 + 2y^2 - 81y - 162$

Solve the equation.

23. $25a = 10a^2$
24. $21z^2 + 85z - 26 = 0$
25. $x^2 - 22x = -121$
26. $a^2 - 11a + 24 = 0$
27. $t^2 + 7t = 60$
28. $4x^2 = 22x + 42$
29. $56b^2 + b = 1$
30. $n^3 - 121n = 0$
31. $a^3 + a^2 = 64a + 64$

32. **VERTICAL MOTION** A cricket jumps off the ground with an initial vertical velocity of 4 feet per second.
    a. Write an equation that gives the height (in feet) of the cricket as a function of the time (in seconds) since it jumps.
    b. After how many seconds does the cricket land on the ground?

33. **POSTER AREA** Two posters have the lengths and widths shown. The posters have the same area.
    a. Write an equation that relates the areas of the two posters.
    b. Find the length and width of each poster.

34. **CONSTRUCTION** A construction worker is working on the roof of a building. A drop of paint falls from a rafter that is 225 feet above the ground. After how many seconds does the paint hit the ground?

35. **BOX DIMENSIONS** A cardboard box that is a rectangular prism has the dimensions shown.
    a. Write a polynomial that represents the volume of the box.
    b. The volume of the box is 60 cubic inches. What are the length, width, and height of the box?

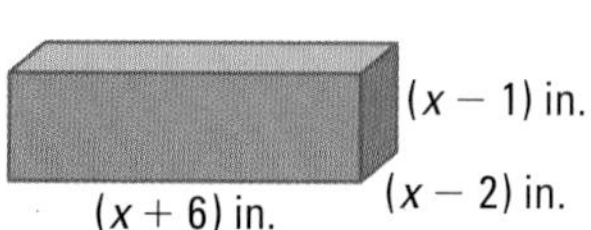

Scoring Rubric

Full Credit
- solution is complete and correct

Partial Credit
- solution is complete but errors are made,

or
- solution is without error but incomplete

No Credit
- no solution is given,

or
- solution makes no sense

SHORT RESPONSE QUESTIONS

PROBLEM

A rectangular photo has an area of 24 square inches. You trim the photo so that it fits into a square frame. You trim 3 inches from the length and 1 inch from the width of the photo. Write and solve an equation to find the side length of the resulting square photo. *Explain* how you chose one solution of the equation to find the side length.

Below are sample solutions to the problem. Read each solution and the comments in blue to see why the sample represents full credit, partial credit, or no credit.

SAMPLE 1: Full credit solution

A diagram shows how the equation is obtained.

Draw a diagram. Use the formula for the area of a rectangle.

$A = \ell \cdot w$

$= (x + 3)(x + 1)$

$= x^2 + 4x + 3$

The correct calculations are performed.

Substitute 24 for A and solve.

$24 = x^2 + 4x + 3$

$0 = x^2 + 4x - 21$

$0 = (x - 3)(x + 7)$

$0 = x - 3$ *or* $0 = x + 7$

$x = 3$ *or* $x = -7$

The question is answered correctly and includes an explanation.

A solution represents the side length of the square photo. A negative side length does not make sense, so choose $x = 3$. The side length is 3 inches.

SAMPLE 2: Partial credit solution

The length of the rectangular photo is $x + 3$. The width is $x + 1$.

The equation is correct, and the student has explained how it was obtained.

$A = (x + 3)(x + 1)$

$24 = x^2 + 4x + 3$

$0 = x^2 + 4x - 21$

$0 = (x - 3)(x + 7)$

The question is answered correctly but does not include an explanation.

$x = 3$ *or* $x = -7$

The side length of the square photo is 3 inches.

SAMPLE 3: Partial credit solution

The equation and its solutions are correct, but the student found the length and width of the original photo instead of the trimmed photo.

$24 = (x + 3)(x + 1)$

$0 = x^2 + 4x - 21$

$0 = (x - 3)(x + 7)$

$x = 3 \quad or \quad x = -7$

A negative solution does not make sense in the situation. The length is $3 + 3 = 6$ inches, and the width is $3 + 1 = 4$ inches.

SAMPLE 4: No credit solution

The student's reasoning is incorrect, and the equation is incorrect. The answer is incorrect.

$(x - 3)(x - 1) = 24$

$x^2 - 4x - 21 = 0$

$(x - 3)(x + 7) = 0$

$x = -3$ or 7, so the side length of the square is 7 inches.

PRACTICE Apply the Scoring Rubric

Score the solution to the problem below as *full credit, partial credit,* or *no credit. Explain* your reasoning.

PROBLEM You are making a banner for a surprise birthday party. The banner will have the dimensions shown in the diagram. Its area will be 6 square feet. Write and solve an equation to find the length and width of the banner. *Explain* your reasoning.

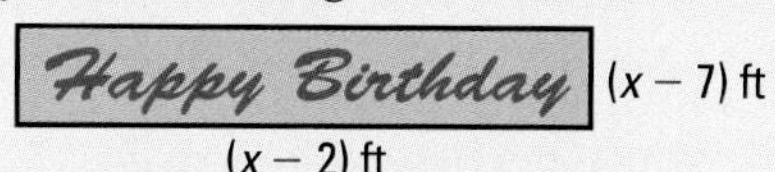

1. $6 = (x - 2)(x - 7)$

$6 = x^2 - 9x + 14$

$0 = x^2 - 9x + 8$

$0 = (x - 8)(x - 1)$

$x = 8$ or $x = 1$

In this problem, the solutions of the equation are 8 and 1. If $x = 1$, then the width of the banner is $x - 7 = -6$. A width cannot be negative, so disregard the solution $x = 1$.

The length of the banner is $8 - 2 = 6$ feet, and the width is $8 - 7 = 1$ foot.

2. $6 = (x - 2)(x - 7)$

$6 = x^2 - 2x - 7x + 14$

$0 = x^2 - 9x + 20$

$0 = (x - 5)(x - 4)$

$x = 5$ or $x = 4$

The equation has two solutions. They are 5 and 4. So, the width of the banner is 5 feet, and the length of the banner is 4 feet.

9 ★ Standardized TEST PRACTICE

SHORT RESPONSE

1. A cat jumps straight up from the ground with an initial vertical velocity of 10 feet per second.
   a. Write an equation that gives the height of the cat (in feet) as a function of the time (in seconds) since it left the ground.
   b. Find the zeros of the function from part (a). *Explain* what the zeros mean in this situation.

2. A fish tank is shaped like a rectangular prism with a volume of 576 cubic inches. Its length is greater than 10 inches. The dimensions of the tank are shown in the diagram.

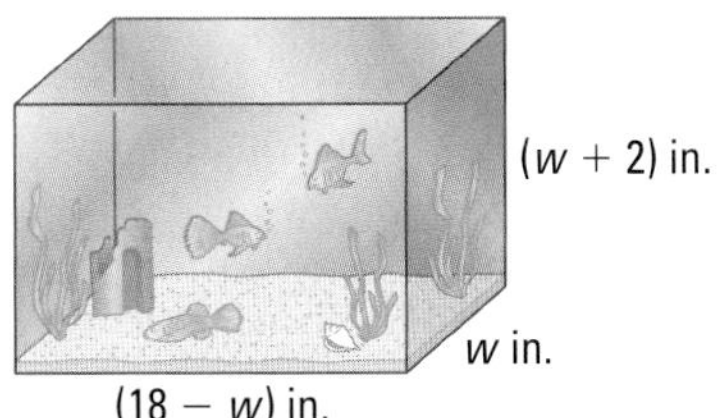

   a. Write a polynomial that represents the volume of the fish tank.
   b. Find the length, width, and height of the fish tank. *Explain* your reasoning using the solutions of the equation from part (a).

3. You throw a ball from an initial height of 5 feet and with an initial vertical velocity of 36 feet per second.
   a. Write an equation that gives the height of the ball (in feet) as a function of the time (in seconds) since it left your hand.
   b. How many times does the ball reach a height of 25 feet? *Explain* your reasoning using the function from part (a).

4. A pencil falls off a shelf with a height of 4 feet.
   a. What is the initial vertical velocity of the pencil? *Explain* your answer.
   b. After how many seconds does the pencil hit the ground?

5. During the period 1985–2000, the number S (in thousands) of students enrolled in public school in the United States and the percent p (in decimal form) of the students enrolled in public school who are also enrolled in a foreign language class can be modeled by

$$S = 27.5x^2 - 336x + 12{,}400 \text{ and}$$
$$p = 0.008x + 0.336$$

   where x is the number of years since 1985.
   a. Write an equation that models the number (in thousands) of public school students in the United States enrolled in a foreign language class as a function of the number of years since 1985. *Explain* how you found this equation.
   b. How many public school students in the United States were enrolled in a foreign language class in 2000?

6. Students in an environmental club are planning a garden with four rectangular plots of land separated by stone paths, as shown. The stone paths will have the same width.

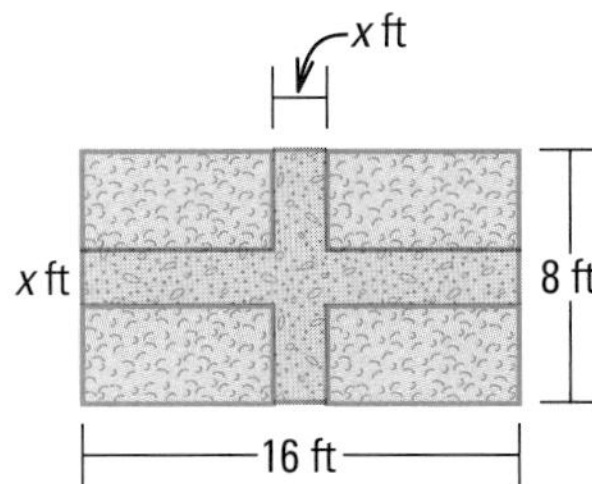

   a. The students plan to cover 80 square feet of path with stone. Write and solve an equation to find the width of the paths.
   b. In part (a) you used one solution of an equation to find your answer. *Explain* how you chose which solution to use.

7. The shape of an entrance to a tunnel can be modeled by the graph of the equation $y = -0.2x(x - 20)$ where x and y are measured in feet. On a coordinate plane, the ground is represented by the x-axis. How wide is the tunnel at its base? *Explain* how you found your answer.

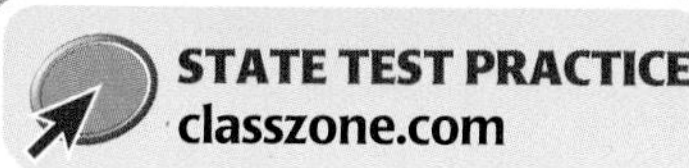

MULTIPLE CHOICE

8. Which is the correct factorization of $25x^2 - 144$?

Ⓐ $(5x + 9)(5x - 16)$

Ⓑ $(5x - 12)^2$

Ⓒ $(5x + 18)(5x - 8)$

Ⓓ $(5x - 12)(5x + 12)$

9. What are the solutions of the equation $(x + 4)(x - 12) = 0$?

Ⓐ 4 and −12 Ⓑ 4 and 12

Ⓒ −4 and −12 Ⓓ −4 and 12

10. What are the solutions of the equation $x^2 - 26 = 11x$?

Ⓐ −2 and 13 Ⓑ 2 and 13

Ⓒ −2 and −13 Ⓓ 2 and −13

GRIDDED ANSWER

11. The equation $x^2 - 20x + 100 = 0$ has two identical solutions. What is the solution of the equation?

12. The square of the binomial $x + 3$ has the form $x^2 + bx + 9$. What is the value of b?

13. What is the degree of the polynomial $6x^4 - 3x^2 + 10x$?

14. The function $f(x) = 4x^2 - 36$ has two zeros. What is the greater of the two zeros?

15. The area of a rectangle is 28 square inches. The length of the rectangle is 3 inches more than its width. What is the width (in inches) of the rectangle?

16. A pine cone falls from a tree branch that is 144 feet above the ground. After how many seconds does the pine cone land on the ground?

EXTENDED RESPONSE

17. The shape of a stone arch in a park can be modeled by the graph of the equation $y = -x^2 + 6x$ where x and y are measured in feet. On a coordinate plane, the ground is represented by the x-axis.

a. Make a table of values that shows the height of the stone arch for $x = 0, 1, 2, 3, 4$, and 5 feet.

b. Plot the ordered pairs in the table from part (a) as points in a coordinate plane. Connect the points with a smooth curve.

c. How wide is the base of the arch? *Justify* your answer using the zeros of the given function.

d. At how many points does the arch reach a height of 9 feet? *Justify* your answer algebraically.

18. A box is a rectangular prism with a volume of 768 cubic inches. The length of the box is 4 inches more than its height. Its width is the difference of 16 and its height.

a. Draw a diagram of the box and label its dimensions in terms of its height.

b. Write a polynomial that represents the volume of the box.

c. Use the polynomial from part (b) to find two sets of possible dimensions of the box.

d. Which set of dimensions results in a box with the least possible surface area? *Explain* your reasoning.

10 Quadratic Equations and Functions

Before

In previous chapters, you learned the following skills, which you'll use in Chapter 10: reflecting points in a line and finding square roots.

Prerequisite Skills

VOCABULARY CHECK

Copy and complete the statement.

1. The x-coordinate of a point where a graph crosses the x-axis is a(n) __?__.
2. A(n) __?__ is a function of the form $y = a \cdot b^x$ where $a \neq 0$, $b > 0$, and $b \neq 1$.

SKILLS CHECK

Draw the blue figure. Then draw its image after a reflection in the red line. *(Review p. 922 for 10.1–10.3.)*

3.

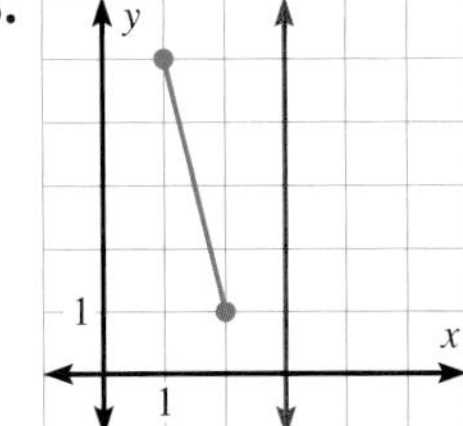

4.

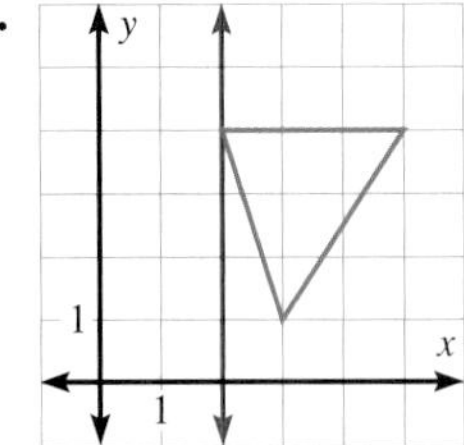

5.

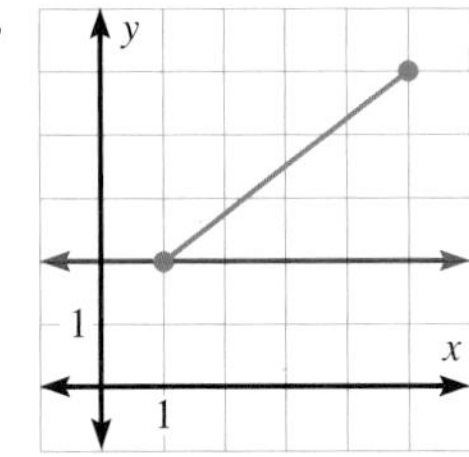

Evaluate the expression. *(Review p. 110 for 10.4–10.6.)*

6. $\sqrt{81}$ **7.** $-\sqrt{25}$ **8.** $\sqrt{1}$ **9.** $\pm\sqrt{64}$

@HomeTutor Prerequisite skills practice at classzone.com

Now

In Chapter 10, you will apply the big ideas listed below and reviewed in the Chapter Summary on page 695. You will also use the key vocabulary listed below.

Big Ideas

1. **Graphing quadratic functions**
2. **Solving quadratic equations**
3. **Comparing linear, exponential, and quadratic models**

KEY VOCABULARY

- quadratic function, *p. 628*
- parabola, *p. 628*
- parent quadratic function, *p. 628*
- vertex, *p. 628*
- axis of symmetry, *p. 628*
- minimum value, *p. 636*
- maximum value, *p. 636*
- quadratic equation, *p. 643*
- completing the square, *p. 663*
- quadratic formula, *p. 671*
- discriminant, *p. 678*

Why?

You can use a quadratic model for real-world situations involving vertical motion. For example, you can write and solve a quadratic equation to find the time a snowboarder is in the air during a jump.

Animated Algebra

The animation illustrated below for Exercise 50 on page 668 helps you answer this question: How many seconds is the snowboarder in the air during a jump?

Start
You need to find the time that the snowboarder is in the air.

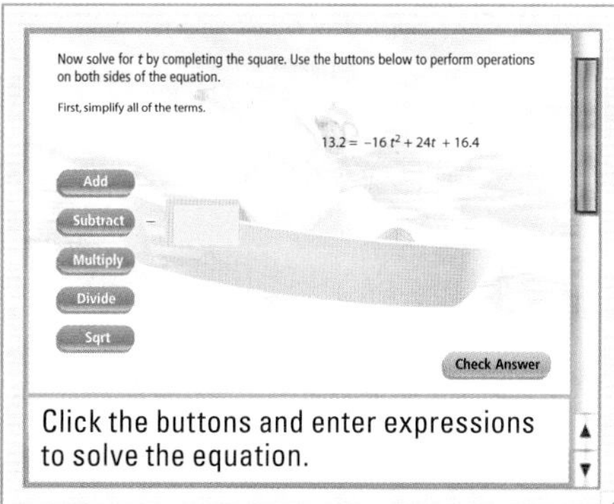
Now solve for t by completing the square. Use the buttons below to perform operations on both sides of the equation.
First, simplify all of the terms.
$13.2 = -16t^2 + 24t + 16.4$
Add
Subtract
Multiply
Divide
Sqrt
Check Answer
Click the buttons and enter expressions to solve the equation.

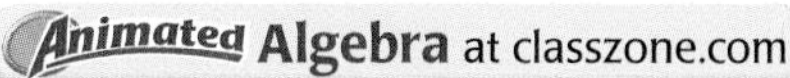
Animated Algebra at classzone.com

Other animations for Chapter 10: pages 634, 636, 642, 662, 668, 672, 684, and 695

10.1 Graph $y = ax^2 + c$

Before You graphed linear and exponential functions.

Now You will graph simple quadratic functions.

Why? So you can solve a problem involving an antenna, as in Ex. 40.

Key Vocabulary
- **quadratic function**
- **parabola**
- **parent quadratic function**
- **vertex**
- **axis of symmetry**

A **quadratic function** is a nonlinear function that can be written in the **standard form** $y = ax^2 + bx + c$ where $a \neq 0$. Every quadratic function has a U-shaped graph called a **parabola**. In this lesson, you will graph quadratic functions where $b = 0$.

KEY CONCEPT *For Your Notebook*

Parent Quadratic Function

The most basic quadratic function in the family of quadratic functions, called the **parent quadratic function**, is $y = x^2$. The graph of $y = x^2$ is shown below.

The lowest or highest point on a parabola is the **vertex**. The vertex of the graph of $y = x^2$ is (0, 0).

$y = x^2$; (0, 0); 1; 1; x; y

The line that passes through the vertex and divides the parabola into two symmetric parts is called the **axis of symmetry**. The axis of symmetry for the graph of $y = x^2$ is the y-axis, $x = 0$.

EXAMPLE 1 Graph $y = ax^2$ where $|a| > 1$

STEP 1 **Make** a table of values for $y = 3x^2$.

x	−2	−1	0	1	2
y	12	3	0	3	12

STEP 2 **Plot** the points from the table.

STEP 3 **Draw** a smooth curve through the points.

STEP 4 **Compare** the graphs of $y = 3x^2$ and $y = x^2$. Both graphs open up and have the same vertex, (0, 0), and axis of symmetry, $x = 0$. The graph of $y = 3x^2$ is narrower than the graph of $y = x^2$ because the graph of $y = 3x^2$ is a vertical stretch (by a factor of 3) of the graph of $y = x^2$.

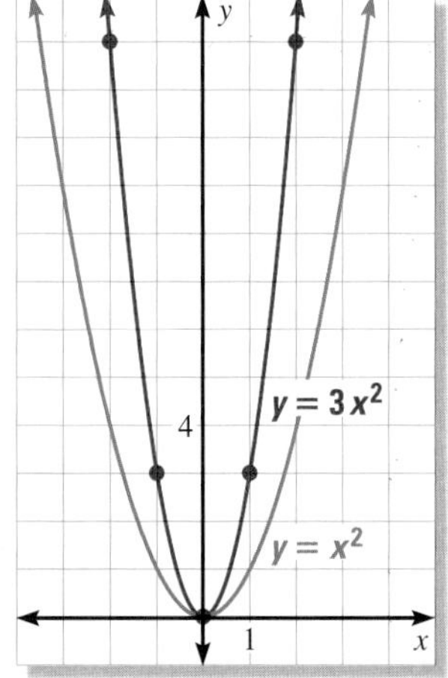

PLOT ADDITIONAL POINTS

If you are having difficulty seeing the shape of the parabola, plot additional points.

EXAMPLE 2 Graph $y = ax^2$ where $|a| < 1$

Graph $y = -\frac{1}{4}x^2$. Compare the graph with the graph of $y = x^2$.

MAKE A TABLE
To make the calculations easier, choose values of x that are multiples of 2.

STEP 1 **Make** a table of values for $y = -\frac{1}{4}x^2$.

x	−4	−2	0	2	4
y	−4	−1	0	−1	−4

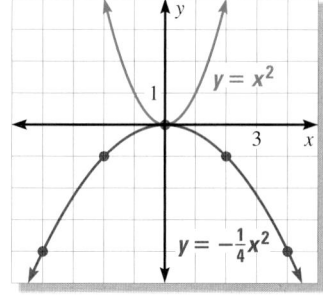

STEP 2 **Plot** the points from the table.

STEP 3 **Draw** a smooth curve through the points.

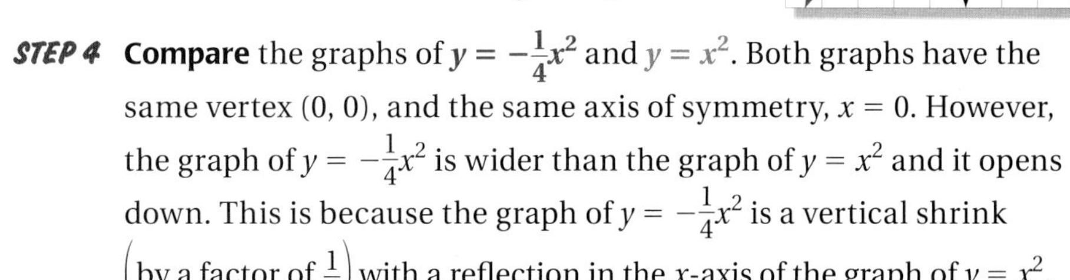

STEP 4 **Compare** the graphs of $y = -\frac{1}{4}x^2$ and $y = x^2$. Both graphs have the same vertex (0, 0), and the same axis of symmetry, $x = 0$. However, the graph of $y = -\frac{1}{4}x^2$ is wider than the graph of $y = x^2$ and it opens down. This is because the graph of $y = -\frac{1}{4}x^2$ is a vertical shrink $\left(\text{by a factor of } \frac{1}{4}\right)$ with a reflection in the x-axis of the graph of $y = x^2$.

GRAPHING QUADRATIC FUNCTIONS Examples 1 and 2 suggest the following general result: a parabola opens up when the coefficient of x^2 is positive and opens down when the coefficient of x^2 is negative.

EXAMPLE 3 Graph $y = x^2 + c$

Graph $y = x^2 + 5$. Compare the graph with the graph of $y = x^2$.

STEP 1 **Make** a table of values for $y = x^2 + 5$.

x	−2	−1	0	1	2
y	9	6	5	6	9

STEP 2 **Plot** the points from the table.

STEP 3 **Draw** a smooth curve through the points.

STEP 4 **Compare** the graphs of $y = x^2 + 5$ and $y = x^2$. Both graphs open up and have the same axis of symmetry, $x = 0$. However, the vertex of the graph of $y = x^2 + 5$, (0, 5), is different than the vertex of the graph of $y = x^2$, (0, 0), because the graph of $y = x^2 + 5$ is a vertical translation (of 5 units up) of the graph of $y = x^2$.

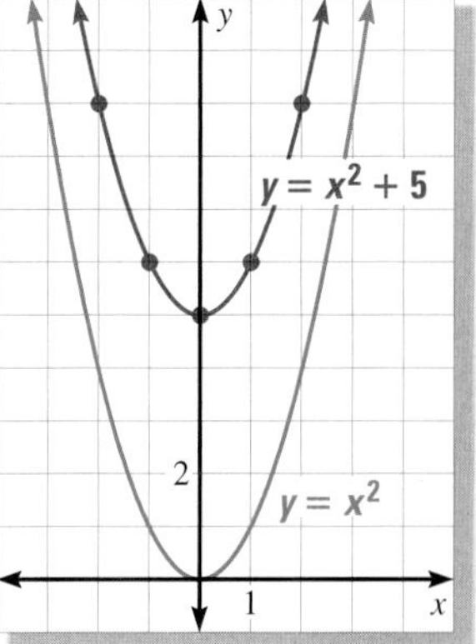

✓ GUIDED PRACTICE for Examples 1, 2, and 3

Graph the function. Compare the graph with the graph of $y = x^2$.

1. $y = -4x^2$

2. $y = \frac{1}{3}x^2$

3. $y = x^2 + 2$

EXAMPLE 4 Graph $y = ax^2 + c$

Graph $y = \frac{1}{2}x^2 - 4$. Compare the graph with the graph of $y = x^2$.

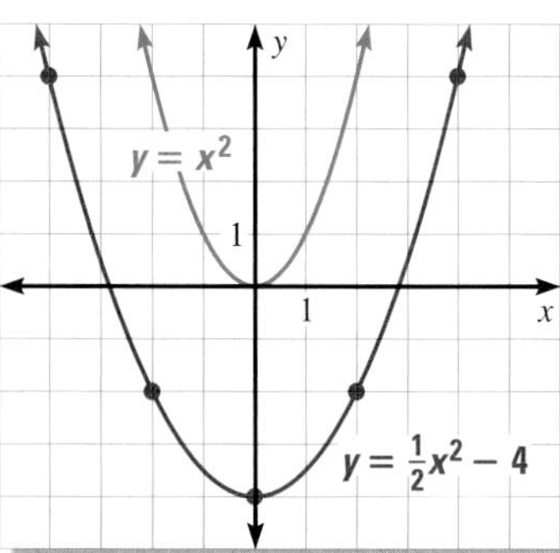

STEP 1 **Make** a table of values for $y = \frac{1}{2}x^2 - 4$.

x	−4	−2	0	2	4
y	4	−2	−4	−2	4

STEP 2 **Plot** the points from the table.

STEP 3 **Draw** a smooth curve through the points.

STEP 4 **Compare** the graphs of $y = \frac{1}{2}x^2 - 4$ and $y = x^2$. Both graphs open up and have the same axis of symmetry, $x = 0$. However, the graph of $y = \frac{1}{2}x^2 - 4$ is wider and has a lower vertex than the graph of $y = x^2$ because the graph of $y = \frac{1}{2}x^2 - 4$ is a vertical shrink and a vertical translation of the graph of $y = x^2$.

✓ GUIDED PRACTICE for Example 4

Graph the function. Compare the graph with the graph of $y = x^2$.

4. $y = 3x^2 - 6$ **5.** $y = -5x^2 + 1$ **6.** $y = \frac{3}{4}x^2 - 2$

KEY CONCEPT *For Your Notebook*

$y = ax^2, a > 0$

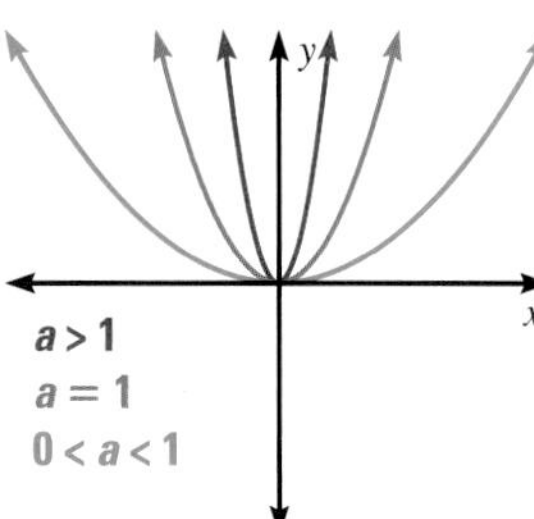

Compared with the graph of $y = x^2$, the graph of $y = ax^2$ is:

- a vertical stretch if $a > 1$,
- a vertical shrink if $0 < a < 1$.

$y = ax^2, a < 0$

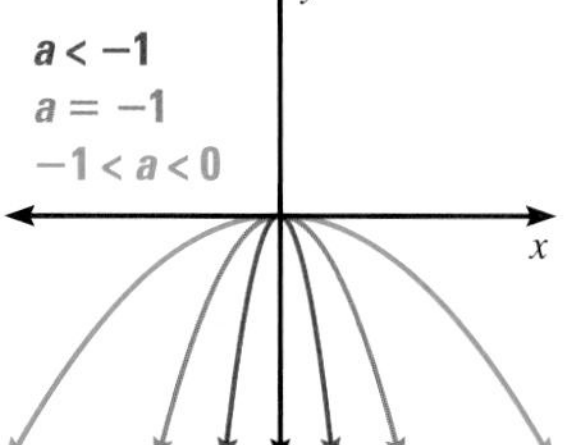

Compared with the graph of $y = x^2$, the graph of $y = ax^2$ is:

- a vertical stretch with a reflection in the x-axis if $a < -1$,
- a vertical shrink with a reflection in the x-axis if $-1 < a < 0$.

$y = x^2 + c$

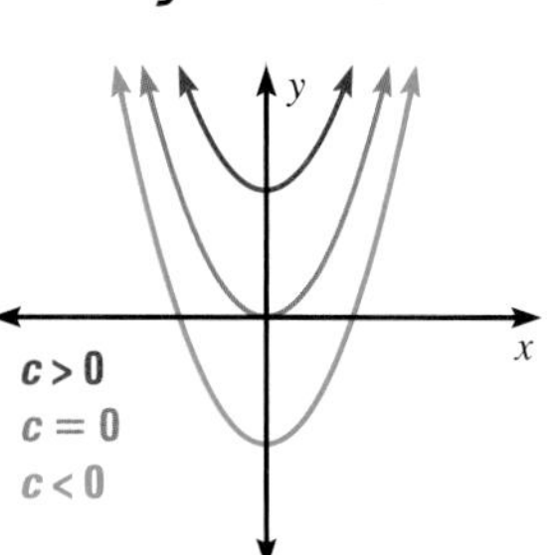

Compared with the graph of $y = x^2$, the graph of $y = x^2 + c$ is:

- an upward vertical translation if $c > 0$,
- a downward vertical translation if $c < 0$.

EXAMPLE 5 Standardized Test Practice

How would the graph of the function $y = x^2 + 6$ be affected if the function were changed to $y = x^2 + 2$?

(A) The graph would shift 2 units up.

(B) The graph would shift 4 units up.

(C) The graph would shift 4 units down.

(D) The graph would shift 4 units to the left.

ELIMINATE CHOICES
You can eliminate choice D because changing the value of c in a function of the form $y = x^2 + c$ translates the graph up or down.

Solution

The vertex of the graph of $y = x^2 + 6$ is 6 units above the origin, or (0, 6). The vertex of the graph of $y = x^2 + 2$ is 2 units above the origin, or (0, 2). Moving the vertex from (0, 6) to (0, 2) translates the graph 4 units down.

▶ The correct answer is C. (A) (B) (C) (D)

EXAMPLE 6 Use a graph

SOLAR ENERGY A solar trough has a reflective parabolic surface that is used to collect solar energy. The sun's rays are reflected from the surface toward a pipe that carries water. The heated water produces steam that is used to produce electricity.

The graph of the function $y = 0.09x^2$ models the cross section of the reflective surface where x and y are measured in meters. Use the graph to find the domain and range of the function in this situation.

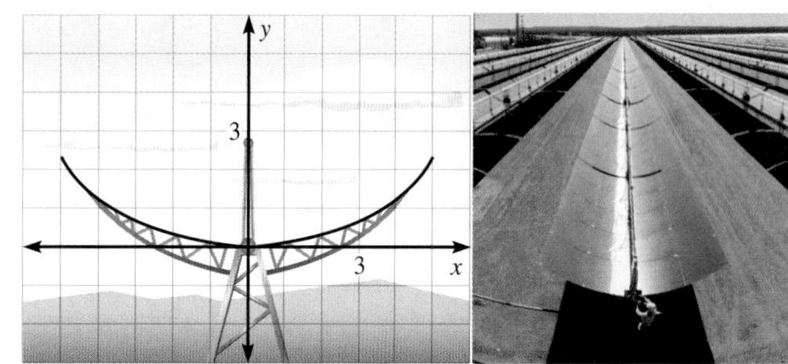

Solution

STEP 1 **Find** the domain. In the graph, the reflective surface extends 5 meters on either side of the origin. So, the domain is $-5 \le x \le 5$.

STEP 2 **Find** the range using the fact that the lowest point on the reflective surface is (0, 0) and the highest point, 5, occurs at each end.

$y = 0.09(5)^2 = 2.25$ **Substitute 5 for x. Then simplify.**

The range is $0 \le y \le 2.25$.

✓ GUIDED PRACTICE for Examples 5 and 6

7. *Describe* how the graph of the function $y = x^2 + 2$ would be affected if the function were changed to $y = x^2 - 2$.

8. **WHAT IF?** In Example 6, suppose the reflective surface extends just 4 meters on either side of the origin. Find the domain and range of the function in this situation.

10.1 EXERCISES

HOMEWORK KEY

○ = **WORKED-OUT SOLUTIONS** on p. WS23 for Exs. 7 and 41

★ = **STANDARDIZED TEST PRACTICE** Exs. 2, 22, 33, 43, and 44

SKILL PRACTICE

1. **VOCABULARY** Copy and complete: Every quadratic function has a U-shaped graph called a(n) __?__.

2. ★ **WRITING** *Explain* how you can tell whether the graph of a quadratic function opens up or down.

MATCHING **Match the quadratic function with its graph.**

3. $y = \frac{1}{2}x^2 - 4$

4. $y = \frac{1}{2}x^2 - 2$

5. $y = -\frac{1}{2}x^2 + 2$

A.

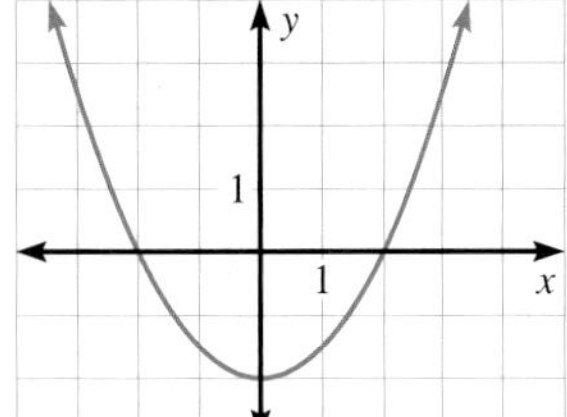

B.

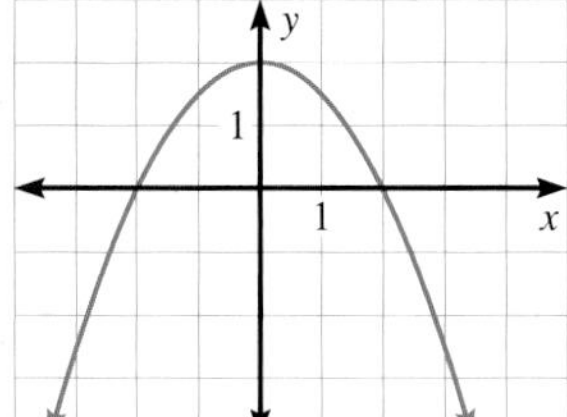

C.

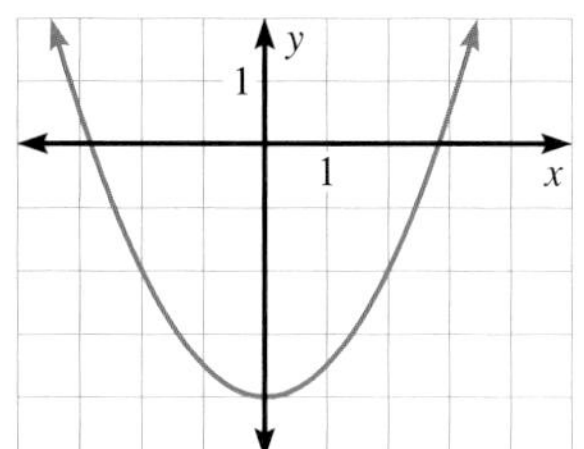

EXAMPLES 1, 2, and 3 on pp. 628–629 for Exs. 6–23

GRAPHING QUADRATIC FUNCTIONS **Graph the function. Compare the graph with the graph of $y = x^2$.**

6. $y = 8x^2$

7. $y = -2x^2$

8. $y = -3x^2$

9. $y = 5x^2$

10. $y = \frac{11}{2}x^2$

11. $y = \frac{2}{3}x^2$

12. $y = -\frac{3}{4}x^2$

13. $y = -\frac{1}{9}x^2$

14. $y = \frac{3}{8}x^2$

15. $y = -\frac{1}{5}x^2$

16. $y = x^2 - 7$

17. $y = x^2 + 9$

18. $y = x^2 + 6$

19. $y = x^2 - 4$

20. $y = x^2 - 1$

21. $y = x^2 + \frac{7}{4}$

22. ★ **MULTIPLE CHOICE** What is the vertex of the graph of the function $y = -\frac{3}{4}x^2 + 7$?

Ⓐ $(-7, 0)$ Ⓑ $(0, -7)$ Ⓒ $(0, 7)$ Ⓓ $(7, 0)$

23. **ERROR ANALYSIS** *Describe* and correct the error in drawing and comparing the graphs of $y = x^2$ and $y = x^2 - 2$.

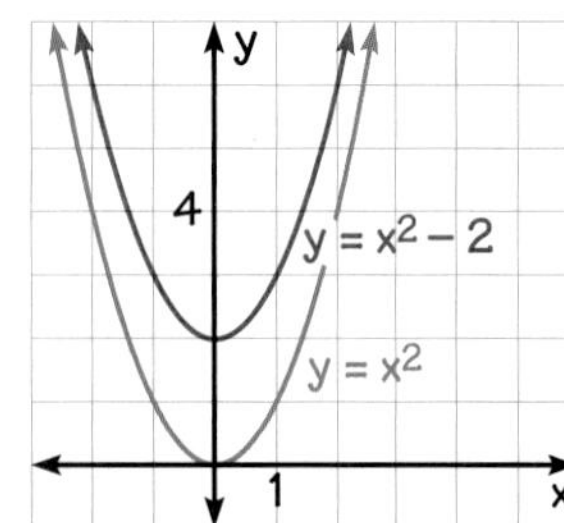

Both graphs open up and have the same axis of symmetry. However, the vertex of the graph of $y = x^2 - 2$, (0, 2), is 2 units above the vertex of the graph of $y = x^2$, (0, 0).

EXAMPLE 4
on p. 630
for Exs. 24–32

GRAPHING QUADRATIC FUNCTIONS **Graph the function. Compare the graph with the graph of $y = x^2$.**

24. $y = 7x^2 + 7$ **25.** $y = -x^2 + 5$ **26.** $y = 2x^2 - 12$

27. $y = -2x^2 - 1$ **28.** $y = -3x^2 - 2$ **29.** $y = \frac{3}{4}x^2 - 3$

30. $y = \frac{1}{5}x^2 + 10$ **31.** $y = \frac{1}{2}x^2 - 5$ **32.** $y = -\frac{2}{3}x^2 + 9$

EXAMPLE 5
on p. 631
for Exs. 33–36

33. ★ **MULTIPLE CHOICE** How would the graph of the function $y = x^2 + 3$ be affected if the function were changed to $y = x^2 + 9$?

Ⓐ The graph would shift 9 units to the right.

Ⓑ The graph would shift 6 units up.

Ⓒ The graph would shift 9 units up.

Ⓓ The graph would shift 6 units down.

COMPARING GRAPHS **Tell how you can obtain the graph of *g* from the graph of *f* using transformations.**

34. $f(x) = x^2 - 5$
$g(x) = x^2 + 8$

35. $f(x) = 3x^2 - 11$
$g(x) = 3x^2 - 16$

36. $f(x) = 4x^2$
$g(x) = 2x^2$

CHALLENGE **Write a function of the form $y = ax^2 + c$ whose graph passes through the two given points.**

37. $(-1, 9), (0, 3)$ **38.** $(2, 1), (5, -20)$ **39.** $(-2, -16.5), (1, 4.5)$

PROBLEM SOLVING

GRAPHING CALCULATOR **You may wish to use a graphing calculator to complete the following Problem Solving exercises.**

EXAMPLE 6
on p. 631
for Exs. 40–41

40. ASTRONOMY A cross section of the parabolic surface of the antenna shown can be modeled by the graph of the function $y = 0.012x^2$ where x and y are measured in meters.

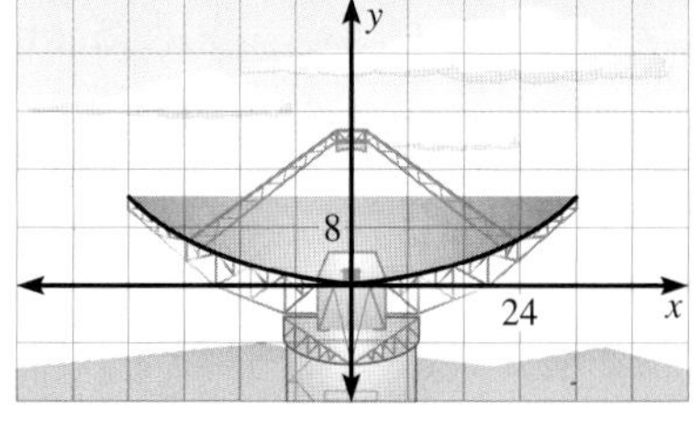

a. Find the domain of the function in this situation.

b. Find the range of the function in this situation.

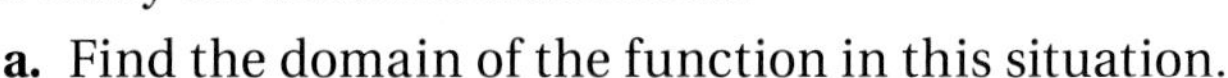
@HomeTutor for problem solving help at classzone.com

41. SAILING Sailors need to consider the speed of the wind when adjusting the sails on their boat. The force F (in pounds per square foot) on a sail when the wind is blowing perpendicular to the sail can be modeled by the function $F = 0.004v^2$ where v is the wind speed (in knots).

a. Graph the function for wind speeds from 0 knots to 50 knots.

b. Use the graph to estimate the wind speed that will produce a force of 1 pound per square foot on a sail.

c. Estimate the wind speed that will produce a force of 5 pounds per square foot on a sail.

@HomeTutor for problem solving help at classzone.com

REVIEW VERTICAL MOTION
For help with the vertical motion model, see p. 575.

42. **FALLING OBJECTS** Two acorns drop from an oak tree. One falls 45 feet, while the other falls 32 feet.

   a. For each acorn, write an equation that gives the height h (in feet) of the acorn as a function of the time t (in seconds) it has fallen.

   b. *Describe* how the graphs of the two equations are related.

43. ★ **SHORT RESPONSE** The breaking strength w (in pounds) of a manila rope can be modeled by the function $w = 8900d^2$ where d is the diameter (in inches) of the rope.

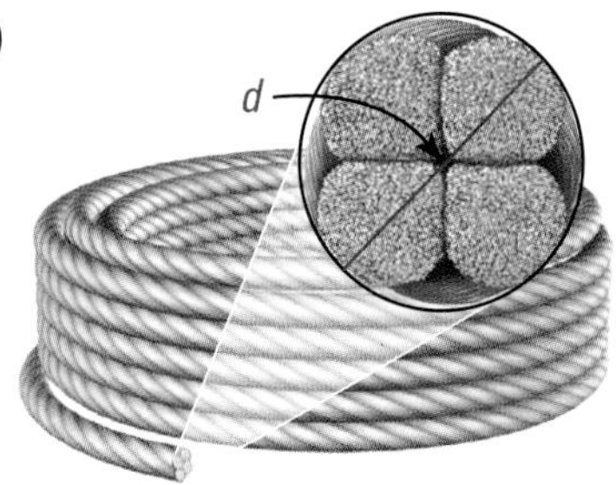

   a. Graph the function.

   b. If a manila rope has 4 times the breaking strength of another manila rope, does the rope have 4 times the diameter of the other rope? *Explain.*

44. ★ **EXTENDED RESPONSE** For an engineering contest, you have to create a container for an egg so that the container can be dropped from a height of 30 feet without breaking the egg.

   a. The distance y (in feet) that the container falls is given by the function $y = 16t^2$ where t is the time (in seconds) the container has fallen. Graph the function.

   b. The height y (in feet) of the dropped container is given by the function $y = -16t^2 + 30$ where t is the time (in seconds) since the container is dropped. Graph the function.

   c. How are the graphs from part (a) and part (b) related? *Explain* how you can use each graph to find the number of seconds after which the container has fallen 10 feet.

   Animated Algebra at classzone.com

45. **CHALLENGE** The kinetic energy E (in joules) of an object in motion is given by $E = \frac{1}{2}mv^2$ where m is the object's mass (in kilograms) and v is the object's velocity (in meters per second). Suppose a baseball has 918.75 joules of energy when traveling 35 meters per second. Use this information to write and graph an equation that gives the energy E of the baseball as a function of its velocity v.

MIXED REVIEW

PREVIEW
Prepare for Lesson 10.2 in Exs. 46–51.

Evaluate the expression. *(p. 8)*

46. $x^2 + 5$ when $x = 2$
47. $4y^2 + 1$ when $y = 0$
48. $16 + 3m^2$ when $m = 5$
49. $5b^2 + 11$ when $b = 10$
50. $20 - 8w^2$ when $w = 1$
51. $7z^2 - 22$ when $z = 3$

Solve the linear system using substitution. *(p. 435)*

52. $x = 20 - 3y$
    $2x - y = -4$
53. $y = 2x - 10$
    $11 = 3x - 2y$
54. $x = 11y + 4$
    $2x - 17y = 13$

Use the FOIL pattern to find the product. *(p. 562)*

55. $(2p + 3)(p + 2)$
56. $(7x + 5)(3x - 1)$
57. $(5n - 10)(5n - 9)$

10.2 Graph $y = ax^2 + bx + c$

Before You graphed simple quadratic functions.

Now You will graph general quadratic functions.

Why? So you can investigate a cable's height, as in Example 4.

Key Vocabulary
- **minimum value**
- **maximum value**

You can use the properties below to graph any quadratic function. You will justify the formula for the axis of symmetry in Exercise 38 on page 639.

KEY CONCEPT *For Your Notebook*

Properties of the Graph of a Quadratic Function

The graph of $y = ax^2 + bx + c$ is a parabola that:

- opens up if $a > 0$ and opens down if $a < 0$.
- is narrower than the graph of $y = x^2$ if $|a| > 1$ and wider if $|a| < 1$.
- has an axis of symmetry of $x = -\frac{b}{2a}$.
- has a vertex with an x-coordinate of $-\frac{b}{2a}$.
- has a y-intercept of c. So, the point $(0, c)$ is on the parabola.

$y = ax^2 + bx + c, a > 0$

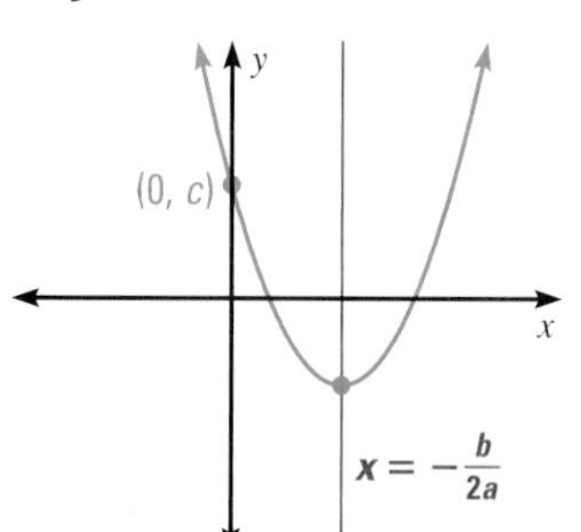

EXAMPLE 1 Find the axis of symmetry and the vertex

Consider the function $y = -2x^2 + 12x - 7$.

a. Find the axis of symmetry of the graph of the function.

b. Find the vertex of the graph of the function.

Solution

a. For the function $y = -2x^2 + 12x - 7$, $a = -2$ and $b = 12$.

$$x = -\frac{b}{2a} = -\frac{12}{2(-2)} = 3$$ **Substitute −2 for *a* and 12 for *b*. Then simplify.**

IDENTIFY THE VERTEX
Because the vertex lies on the axis of symmetry, $x = 3$, the x-coordinate of the vertex is 3.

b. The x-coordinate of the vertex is $-\frac{b}{2a}$, or 3.

To find the y-coordinate, substitute 3 for x in the function and find y.

$$y = -2(3)^2 + 12(3) - 7 = 11$$ **Substitute 3 for *x*. Then simplify.**

▶ The vertex is (3, 11).

EXAMPLE 2 Graph $y = ax^2 + bx + c$

Graph $y = 3x^2 - 6x + 2$.

STEP 1 **Determine** whether the parabola opens up or down. Because $a > 0$, the parabola opens up.

AVOID ERRORS
Be sure to include the negative sign before the fraction when calculating the axis of symmetry.

STEP 2 **Find** and draw the axis of symmetry: $x = -\frac{b}{2a} = -\frac{-6}{2(3)} = 1$.

STEP 3 **Find** and plot the vertex.

The x-coordinate of the vertex is $-\frac{b}{2a}$, or 1.

To find the y-coordinate, substitute 1 for x in the function and simplify.

$y = 3(\mathbf{1})^2 - 6(\mathbf{1}) + 2 = -1$

So, the vertex is $(1, -1)$.

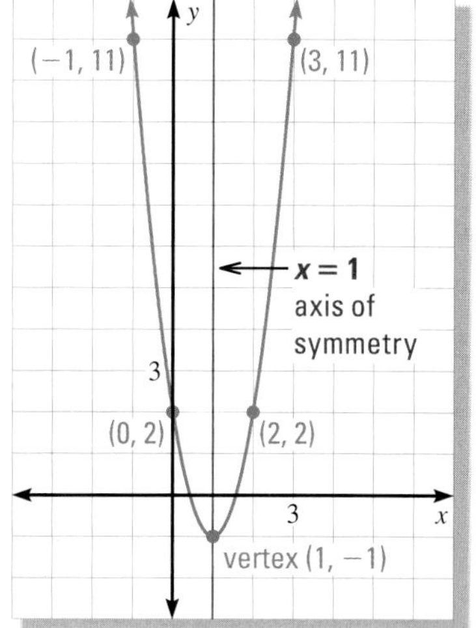

STEP 4 **Plot** two points. Choose two x-values less than the x-coordinate of the vertex. Then find the corresponding y-values.

x	0	−1
y	2	11

REVIEW REFLECTIONS
For help with reflections, see p. 922.

STEP 5 **Reflect** the points plotted in Step 4 in the axis of symmetry.

STEP 6 **Draw** a parabola through the plotted points.

Animated Algebra at classzone.com

✓ GUIDED PRACTICE for Examples 1 and 2

1. Find the axis of symmetry and the vertex of the graph of the function $y = x^2 - 2x - 3$.
2. Graph the function $y = 3x^2 + 12x - 1$. Label the vertex and axis of symmetry.

KEY CONCEPT *For Your Notebook*

Minimum and Maximum Values

For $y = ax^2 + bx + c$, the y-coordinate of the vertex is the **minimum value** of the function if $a > 0$ or the **maximum value** of the function if $a < 0$.

$y = ax^2 + bx + c, a > 0$

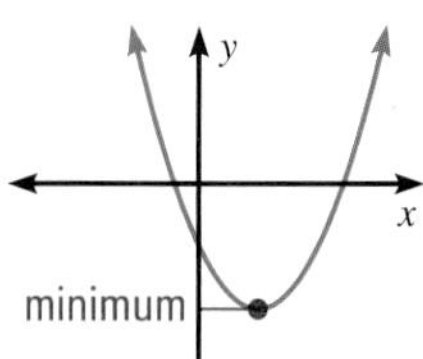

$y = ax^2 + bx + c, a < 0$

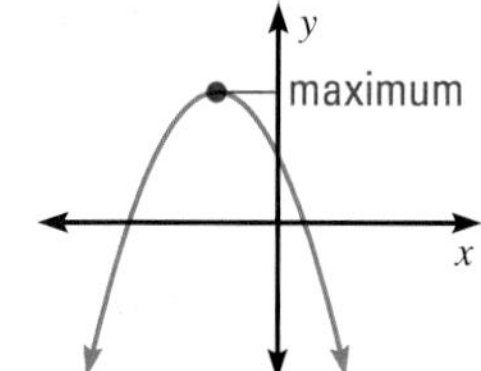

EXAMPLE 3 Find the minimum or maximum value

Tell whether the function $f(x) = -3x^2 - 12x + 10$ has a *minimum value* or a *maximum value*. Then find the minimum or maximum value.

Solution

Because $a = -3$ and $-3 < 0$, the parabola opens down and the function has a maximum value. To find the maximum value, find the vertex.

$x = -\frac{b}{2a} = -\frac{-12}{2(-3)} = -2$ **The x-coordinate is $-\frac{b}{2a}$.**

$f(-2) = -3(-2)^2 - 12(-2) + 10 = 22$ **Substitute −2 for x. Then simplify.**

▶ The maximum value of the function is $f(-2) = 22$.

EXAMPLE 4 Find the minimum value of a function

SUSPENSION BRIDGES The suspension cables between the two towers of the Mackinac Bridge in Michigan form a parabola that can be modeled by the graph of $y = 0.000097x^2 - 0.37x + 549$ where x and y are measured in feet. What is the height of the cable above the water at its lowest point?

Solution

The lowest point of the cable is at the vertex of the parabola. Find the x-coordinate of the vertex. Use $a = 0.000097$ and $b = -0.37$.

$x = -\frac{b}{2a} = -\frac{-0.37}{2(0.000097)} \approx 1910$ **Use a calculator.**

Substitute 1910 for x in the equation to find the y-coordinate of the vertex.

$y \approx 0.000097(1910)^2 - 0.37(1910) + 549 \approx 196$

▶ The cable is about 196 feet above the water at its lowest point.

✓ **GUIDED PRACTICE** for Examples 3 and 4

3. Tell whether the function $f(x) = 6x^2 + 18x + 13$ has a *minimum value* or a *maximum value*. Then find the minimum or maximum value.

4. **SUSPENSION BRIDGES** The cables between the two towers of the Takoma Narrows Bridge form a parabola that can be modeled by the graph of the equation $y = 0.00014x^2 - 0.4x + 507$ where x and y are measured in feet. What is the height of the cable above the water at its lowest point? Round your answer to the nearest foot.

10.2 EXERCISES

HOMEWORK KEY
○ = **WORKED-OUT SOLUTIONS** on p. WS23 for Exs. 9 and 41
★ = **STANDARDIZED TEST PRACTICE** Exs. 2, 12, 27, 37, 42, and 44

SKILL PRACTICE

1. **VOCABULARY** *Explain* how you can tell whether a quadratic function has a maximum value or minimum value without graphing the function.

2. ★ **WRITING** *Describe* the steps you would take to graph a quadratic function in standard form.

EXAMPLE 1 on p. 635 for Exs. 3–14

FINDING AXIS OF SYMMETRY AND VERTEX **Find the axis of symmetry and the vertex of the graph of the function.**

3. $y = 2x^2 - 8x + 6$
4. $y = x^2 - 6x + 11$
5. $y = -3x^2 + 24x - 22$
6. $y = -x^2 - 10x$
7. $y = 6x^2 + 6x$
8. $y = 4x^2 + 7$
9. $y = -\frac{2}{3}x^2 - 1$
10. $y = \frac{1}{2}x^2 + 8x - 9$
11. $y = -\frac{1}{4}x^2 + 3x - 2$

12. ★ **MULTIPLE CHOICE** What is the vertex of the graph of the function $y = -3x^2 + 18x - 13$?

Ⓐ $(-3, -94)$ Ⓑ $(-3, -14)$ Ⓒ $(3, -13)$ Ⓓ $(3, 14)$

ERROR ANALYSIS ***Describe*** **and correct the error in finding the axis of symmetry of the graph of the given function.**

13. $y = 2x^2 + 16x - 1$

$x = \frac{b}{2a} = \frac{16}{2(2)} = 4$

The axis of symmetry is x = 4.

14. $y = -\frac{3}{2}x^2 + 18x - 5$

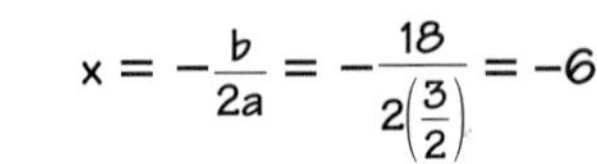

The axis of symmetry is x = −6.

EXAMPLE 2 on p. 636 for Exs. 15–27

GRAPHING QUADRATIC FUNCTIONS **Graph the function. Label the vertex and axis of symmetry.**

15. $y = x^2 + 6x + 2$
16. $y = x^2 + 4x + 8$
17. $y = 2x^2 + 7x + 21$
18. $y = 5x^2 + 10x - 3$
19. $y = 4x^2 + x - 32$
20. $y = -4x^2 + 4x + 8$
21. $y = -3x^2 - 2x - 5$
22. $y = -8x^2 - 12x + 1$
23. $y = -x^2 + \frac{1}{4}x + \frac{1}{2}$
24. $y = \frac{1}{3}x^2 + 6x - 9$
25. $y = -\frac{1}{2}x^2 + 6x + 3$
26. $y = -\frac{1}{4}x^2 - x + 1$

27. ★ **MULTIPLE CHOICE** Which function has the graph shown?

Ⓐ $y = -2x^2 + 8x + 3$

Ⓑ $y = -\frac{1}{2}x^2 + 2x + 3$

Ⓒ $y = \frac{1}{2}x^2 + 2x + 3$

Ⓓ $y = 2x^2 + 8x + 3$

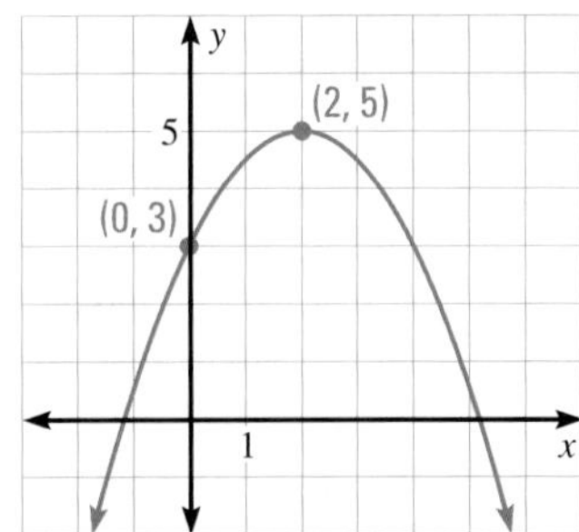

EXAMPLE 3
on p. 637
for Exs. 28–36

MAXIMUM AND MINIMUM VALUES **Tell whether the function has a *minimum value* or a *maximum value*. Then find the minimum or maximum value.**

28. $f(x) = x^2 - 6$

29. $f(x) = -5x^2 + 7$

30. $f(x) = 4x^2 + 32x$

31. $f(x) = -3x^2 + 12x - 20$

32. $f(x) = x^2 + 7x + 8$

33. $f(x) = -2x^2 - x + 10$

34. $f(x) = \frac{1}{2}x^2 - 2x + 5$

35. $f(x) = -\frac{3}{8}x^2 + 9x$

36. $f(x) = \frac{1}{4}x^2 + 7x + 11$

37. ★ **WRITING** Compare the graph of $y = x^2 + 4x + 1$ with the graph of $y = x^2 - 4x + 1$.

38. REASONING Follow the steps below to justify the equation for the axis of symmetry for the graph of $y = ax^2 + bx + c$. Because the graph of $y = ax^2 + bx + c$ is a vertical translation of the graph of $y = ax^2 + bx$, the two graphs have the same axis of symmetry. Use the function $y = ax^2 + bx$ in place of $y = ax^2 + bx + c$.

a. Find the x-intercepts of the graph of $y = ax^2 + bx$. (You can do this by finding the zeros of the function $y = ax^2 + bx$ using factoring.)

b. Because a parabola is symmetric about its axis of symmetry, the axis of symmetry passes through a point halfway between the x-intercepts of the parabola. Find the x-coordinate of this point. What is an equation of the vertical line through this point?

39. CHALLENGE Write a function of the form $y = ax^2 + bx$ whose graph contains the points (1, 6) and (3, 6).

PROBLEM SOLVING

GRAPHING CALCULATOR **You may wish to use a graphing calculator to complete the following Problem Solving exercises.**

EXAMPLE 4
on p. 637
for Exs. 40–42

40. SPIDERS Fishing spiders can propel themselves across water and leap vertically from the surface of the water. During a vertical jump, the height of the body of the spider can be modeled by the function $y = -4500x^2 + 820x + 43$ where x is the duration (in seconds) of the jump and y is the height (in millimeters) of the spider above the surface of the water. After how many seconds does the spider's body reach its maximum height? What is the maximum height?

@HomeTutor for problem solving help at classzone.com

41. ARCHITECTURE The parabolic arches that support the roof of the Dallas Convention Center can be modeled by the graph of the equation $y = -0.0019x^2 + 0.71x$ where x and y are measured in feet. What is the height h at the highest point of the arch as shown in the diagram?

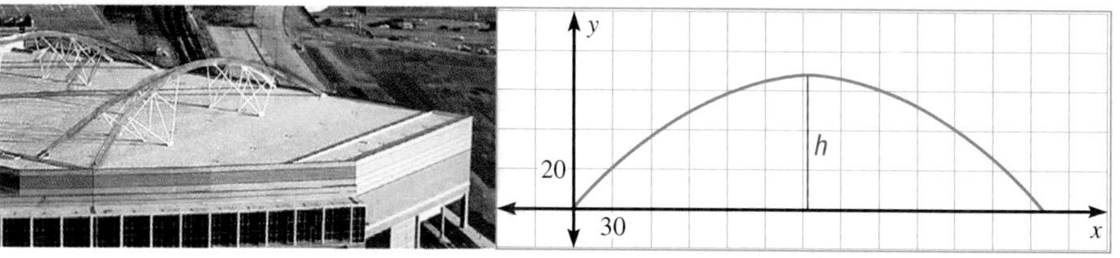

@HomeTutor for problem solving help at classzone.com

42. ★ **EXTENDED RESPONSE** Students are selling packages of flower bulbs to raise money for a class trip. Last year, when the students charged \$5 per package, they sold 150 packages. The students want to increase the cost per package. They estimate that they will lose 10 sales for each \$1 increase in the cost per package. The sales revenue R (in dollars) generated by selling the packages is given by the function $R = (5 + n)(150 - 10n)$ where n is the number of \$1 increases.

a. Write the function in standard form.

b. Find the maximum value of the function.

c. At what price should the packages be sold to generate the most sales revenue? *Explain* your reasoning.

43. **AIRCRAFT** An aircraft hangar is a large building where planes are stored. The opening of one airport hangar is a parabolic arch that can be modeled by the graph of the equation $y = -0.007x^2 + 1.7x$ where x and y are measured in feet. Graph the function. Use the graph to determine how wide the hangar is at its base.

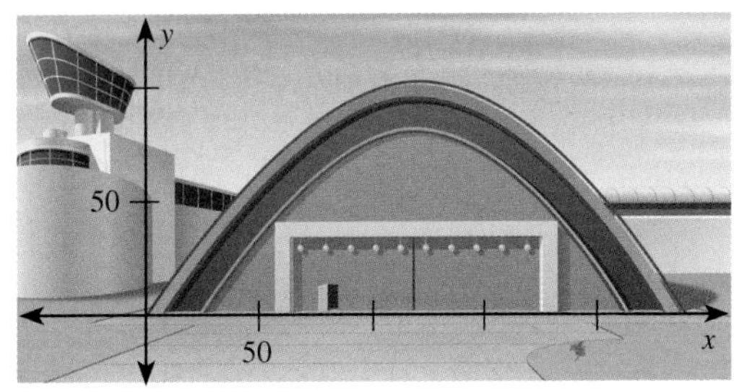

44. ★ **SHORT RESPONSE** The casts of some Broadway shows go on tour, performing their shows in cities across the United States. For the period 1990–2001, the number of tickets sold S (in millions) for Broadway road tours can be modeled by the function $S = 332 + 132t - 10.4t^2$ where t is the number of years since 1990. Was the greatest number of tickets for Broadway road tours sold in 1995? *Explain.*

45. **CHALLENGE** During an archery competition, an archer shoots an arrow from 1.5 meters off of the ground. The arrow follows the parabolic path shown and hits the ground in front of the target 90 meters away. Use the y-intercept and the points on the graph to write an equation for the graph that models the path of the arrow.

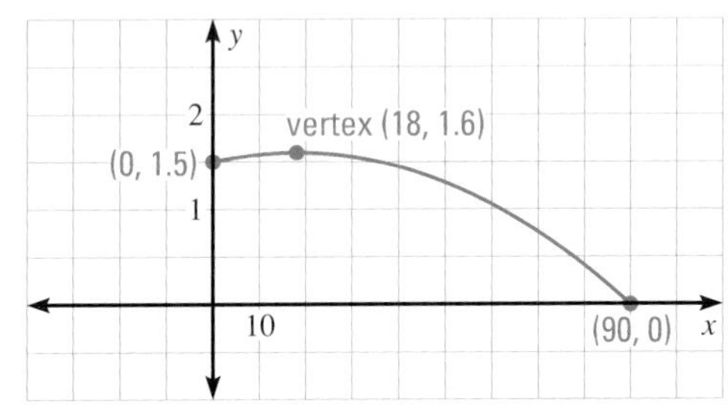

MIXED REVIEW

Graph the equation. *(pp. 215, 225, 244)*

46. $y = 3$

47. $x - 5y = 15$

48. $y = -\frac{2}{3}x - 6$

Simplify.

49. $-3(4 - 2x) - 9$ *(p. 96)*

50. $2(1 - a) - 5a$ *(p. 96)*

51. $\frac{12y - 4}{-4}$ *(p. 103)*

52. $(-2mn)^4$ *(p. 489)*

53. $5 \cdot (7w^7)^2$ *(p. 489)*

54. $\frac{6u^3}{v} \cdot \frac{uv^2}{36}$ *(p. 495)*

PREVIEW
Prepare for Lesson 10.3 in Exs. 55–58.

Find the zeros of the polynomial function.

55. $f(x) = x^2 - 4x - 21$ *(p. 583)*

56. $f(x) = x^2 + 10x + 24$ *(p. 583)*

57. $f(x) = 5x^2 + 18x + 9$ *(p. 593)*

58. $f(x) = 2x^2 + 4x - 6$ *(p. 593)*

Graph Quadratic Functions in Intercept Form

GOAL Graph quadratic functions in intercept form.

Key Vocabulary
- **intercept form**

In Lesson 10.2 you graphed quadratic functions written in standard form. Quadratic functions can also be written in **intercept form**, $y = a(x - p)(x - q)$ where $a \neq 0$. In this form, the x-intercepts of the graph can easily be determined.

KEY CONCEPT *For Your Notebook*

Graph of Intercept Form $y = a(x - p)(x - q)$

Characteristics of the graph of $y = a(x - p)(x - q)$:

- The x-intercepts are p and q.
- The axis of symmetry is halfway between $(p, 0)$ and $(q, 0)$. So, the axis of symmetry is $x = \frac{p + q}{2}$.
- The parabola opens up if $a > 0$ and opens down if $a < 0$.

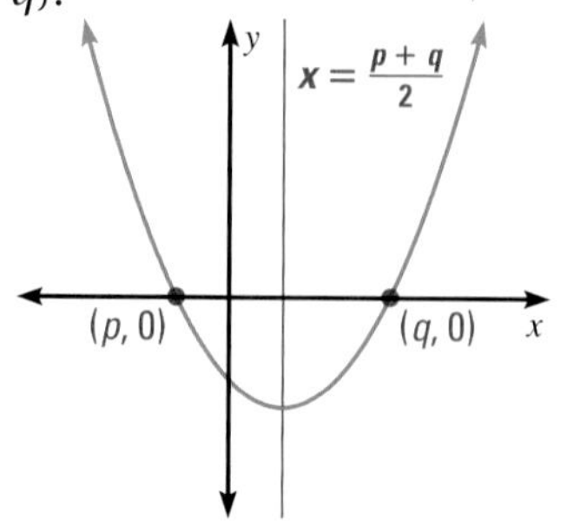

EXAMPLE 1 Graph a quadratic function in intercept form

Graph $y = -(x + 1)(x - 5)$.

Solution

FIND ZEROS OF A FUNCTION
Notice that the x-intercepts of the graph are also the zeros of the function:
$0 = -(x + 1)(x - 5)$
$x + 1 = 0$ *or* $x - 5 = 0$
$x = -1$ *or* $x = 5$

STEP 1 **Identify** and plot the x-intercepts. Because $p = -1$ and $q = 5$, the x-intercepts occur at the points $(-1, 0)$ and $(5, 0)$.

STEP 2 **Find** and draw the axis of symmetry.

$$x = \frac{p + q}{2} = \frac{-1 + 5}{2} = 2$$

STEP 3 **Find** and plot the vertex.

The x-coordinate of the vertex is 2.

To find the y-coordinate of the vertex, substitute 2 for x and simplify.

$$y = -(2 + 1)(2 - 5) = 9$$

So, the vertex is $(2, 9)$.

STEP 4 **Draw** a parabola through the vertex and the points where the x-intercepts occur.

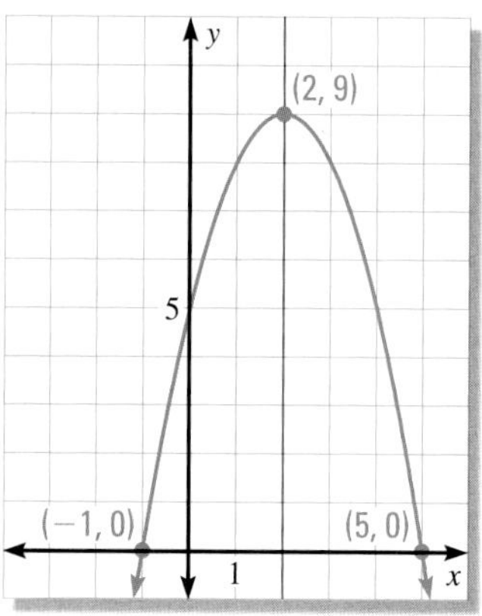

EXAMPLE 2 Graph a quadratic function

Graph $y = 2x^2 - 8$.

Solution

STEP 1 **Rewrite** the quadratic function in intercept form.

$y = 2x^2 - 8$ — Write original function.

$= 2(x^2 - 4)$ — Factor out common factor.

$= 2(x + 2)(x - 2)$ — Difference of two squares pattern

STEP 2 **Identify** and plot the x-intercepts. Because $p = -2$ and $q = 2$, the x-intercepts occur at the points $(-2, 0)$ and $(2, 0)$.

STEP 3 **Find** and draw the axis of symmetry.

$$x = \frac{p + q}{2} = \frac{-2 + 2}{2} = 0$$

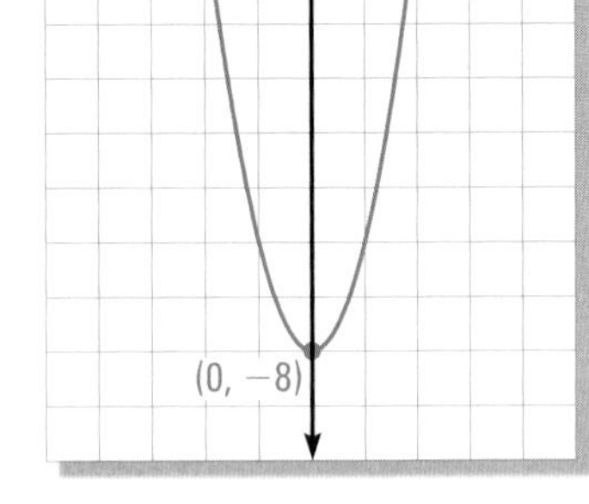

STEP 4 **Find** and plot the vertex.

The x-coordinate of the vertex is 0.

The y-coordinate of the vertex is:

$y = 2(0)^2 - 8 = -8$

So, the vertex is $(0, -8)$.

STEP 5 **Draw** a parabola through the vertex and the points where the x-intercepts occur.

 at classzone.com

PRACTICE

EXAMPLE 1 on p. 641 for Exs. 1–9

Graph the quadratic function. Label the vertex, axis of symmetry, and x-intercepts.

1. $y = (x + 2)(x - 3)$ **2.** $y = (x + 5)(x + 2)$ **3.** $y = (x + 9)^2$

4. $y = -2(x - 5)(x + 1)$ **5.** $y = -5(x + 7)(x + 2)$ **6.** $y = 3(x - 6)(x - 3)$

7. $y = -\frac{1}{2}(x + 4)(x - 2)$ **8.** $y = (x - 7)(2x - 3)$ **9.** $y = 2(x + 10)(x - 3)$

EXAMPLE 2 on p. 642 for Exs. 10–15

10. $y = -x^2 + 8x - 16$ **11.** $y = -x^2 - 9x - 18$ **12.** $y = 12x^2 - 48$

13. $y = -6x^2 + 294$ **14.** $y = 3x^2 - 24x + 36$ **15.** $y = 20x^2 - 6x - 2$

16. Follow the steps below to write an equation of the parabola shown.

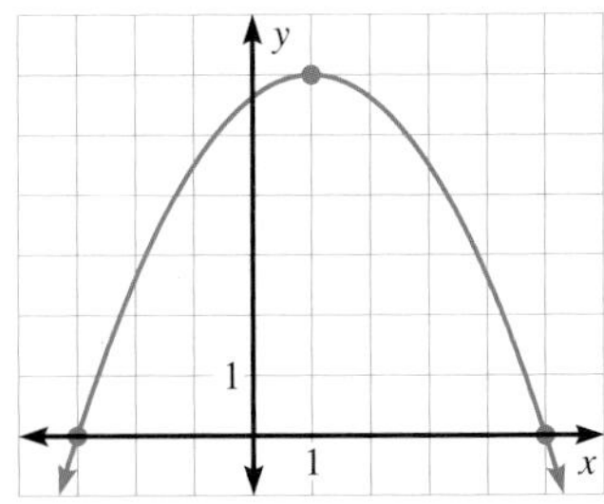

a. Find the x-intercepts.

b. Use the values of p and q and the coordinates of the vertex to find the value of a in the equation $y = a(x - p)(x - q)$.

c. Write a quadratic equation in intercept form.

10.3 Solve Quadratic Equations by Graphing

Before You solved quadratic equations by factoring.

Now You will solve quadratic equations by graphing.

Why? So you can solve a problem about sports, as in Example 6.

Key Vocabulary
- **quadratic equation**
- ***x*-intercept,** *p. 225*
- **roots,** *p. 575*
- **zero of a function,** *p. 337*

A **quadratic equation** is an equation that can be written in the **standard form** $ax^2 + bx + c = 0$ where $a \neq 0$.

In Chapter 9, you used factoring to solve a quadratic equation. You can also use graphing to solve a quadratic equation. Notice that the solutions of the equation $ax^2 + bx + c = 0$ are the x-intercepts of the graph of the related function $y = ax^2 + bx + c$.

Solve by Factoring

$$x^2 - 6x + 5 = 0$$

$$(x - 1)(x - 5) = 0$$

$$x = 1 \quad or \quad x = 5$$

Solve by Graphing

To solve $x^2 - 6x + 5 = 0$, graph $y = x^2 - 6x + 5$. From the graph you can see that the x-intercepts are 1 and 5.

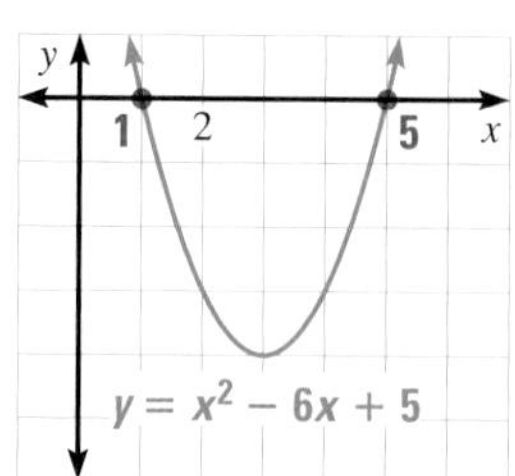

READING
In this course, *solutions* refers to real-number solutions.

To solve a quadratic equation by graphing, first write the equation in standard form, $ax^2 + bx + c = 0$. Then graph the related function $y = ax^2 + bx + c$. The x-intercepts of the graph are the solutions, or roots, of $ax^2 + bx + c = 0$.

EXAMPLE 1 Solve a quadratic equation having two solutions

Solve $x^2 - 2x = 3$ by graphing.

Solution

STEP 1 **Write** the equation in standard form.

$x^2 - 2x = 3$ — Write original equation.

$x^2 - 2x - 3 = 0$ — Subtract 3 from each side.

STEP 2 **Graph** the function $y = x^2 - 2x - 3$. The x-intercepts are -1 and 3.

▶ The solutions of the equation $x^2 - 2x = 3$ are -1 and 3.

CHECK You can check -1 and 3 in the original equation.

$x^2 - 2x = 3$	$x^2 - 2x = 3$	Write original equation.
$(-1)^2 - 2(-1) \stackrel{?}{=} 3$	$(3)^2 - 2(3) \stackrel{?}{=} 3$	Substitute for *x*.
$3 = 3$ ✓	$3 = 3$ ✓	Simplify. Each solution checks.

EXAMPLE 2 Solve a quadratic equation having one solution

Solve $-x^2 + 2x = 1$ by graphing.

Solution

STEP 1 **Write** the equation in standard form.

$-x^2 + 2x = 1$ Write original equation.

$-x^2 + 2x - 1 = 0$ Subtract 1 from each side.

STEP 2 **Graph** the function $y = -x^2 + 2x - 1$. The x-intercept is 1.

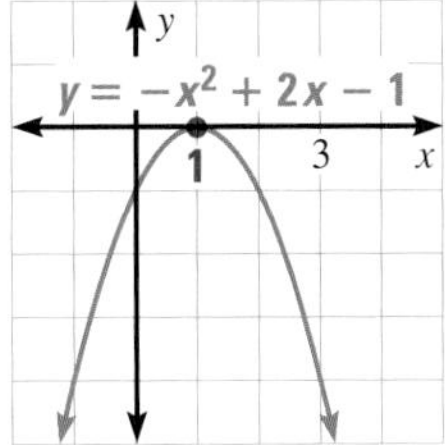

▸ The solution of the equation $-x^2 + 2x = 1$ is 1.

EXAMPLE 3 Solve a quadratic equation having no solution

Solve $x^2 + 7 = 4x$ by graphing.

Solution

STEP 1 **Write** the equation in standard form.

$x^2 + 7 = 4x$ Write original equation.

$x^2 - 4x + 7 = 0$ Subtract $4x$ from each side.

STEP 2 **Graph** the function $y = x^2 - 4x + 7$. The graph has no x-intercepts.

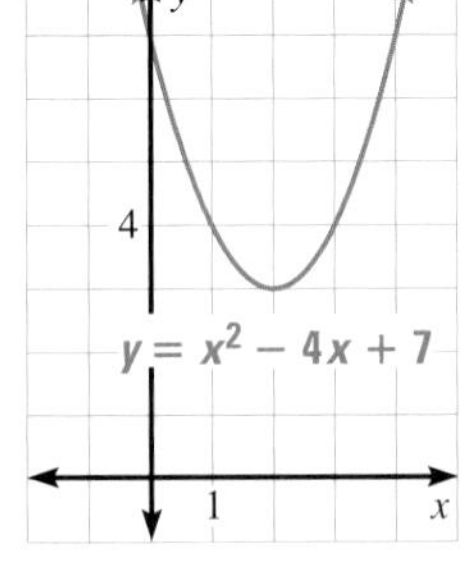

▸ The equation $x^2 + 7 = 4x$ has no solution.

AVOID ERRORS

Do not confuse y-intercepts and x-intercepts. Although the graph has a y-intercept, it does not have any x-intercepts.

✓ GUIDED PRACTICE for Examples 1, 2, and 3

Solve the equation by graphing.

1. $x^2 - 6x + 8 = 0$ **2.** $x^2 + x = -1$ **3.** $-x^2 + 6x = 9$

KEY CONCEPT *For Your Notebook*

Number of Solutions of a Quadratic Equation

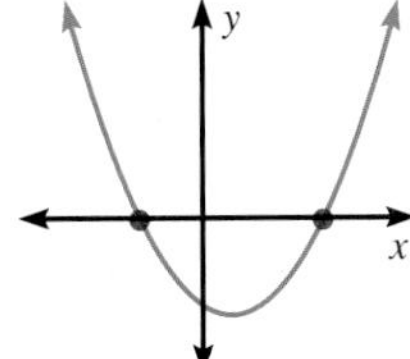

A quadratic equation has **two solutions** if the graph of its related function has **two x-intercepts.**

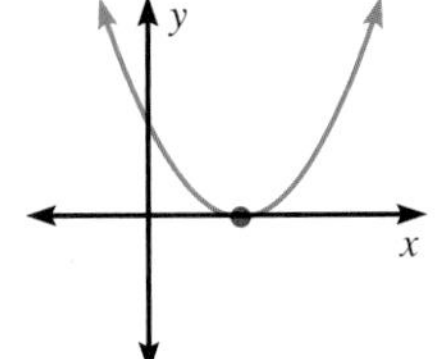

A quadratic equation has **one solution** if the graph of its related function has **one x-intercept.**

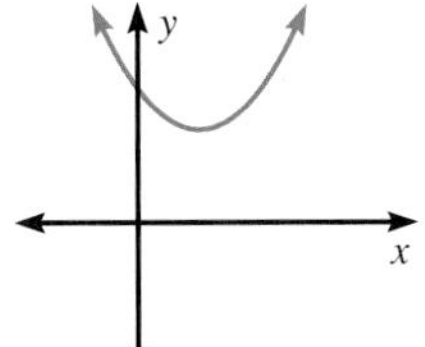

A quadratic equation has **no real solution** if the graph of its related function has **no x-intercepts.**

FINDING ZEROS Because a zero of a function is an x-intercept of the function's graph, you can use the function's graph to find the zeros of a function.

EXAMPLE 4 Find the zeros of a quadratic function

Find the zeros of $f(x) = x^2 + 6x - 7$.

ANOTHER WAY
You can find the zeros of a function by factoring:
$f(x) = x^2 + 6x - 7$
$0 = x^2 + 6x - 7$
$0 = (x + 7)(x - 1)$
$x = -7$ *or* $x = 1$

Solution

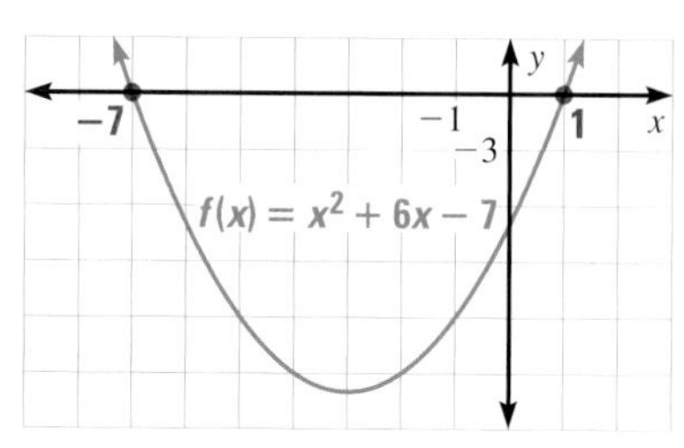

Graph the function $f(x) = x^2 + 6x - 7$.
The x-intercepts are -7 and 1.

▶ The zeros of the function are -7 and 1.

CHECK Substitute -7 and 1 in the original function.

$f(-7) = (-7)^2 + 6(-7) - 7 = 0$ ✓

$f(1) = (1)^2 + 6(1) - 7 = 0$ ✓

APPROXIMATING ZEROS The zeros of a function are not necessarily integers. To approximate zeros, look at the signs of the function values. If two function values have opposite signs, then a zero falls between the x-values that correspond to the function values.

EXAMPLE 5 Approximate the zeros of a quadratic function

Approximate the zeros of $f(x) = x^2 + 4x + 1$ to the nearest tenth.

Solution

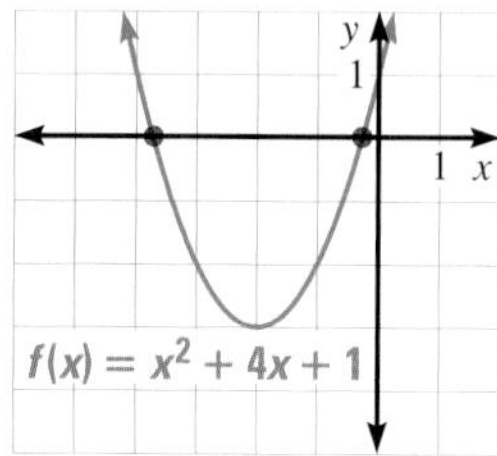

STEP 1 **Graph** the function $f(x) = x^2 + 4x + 1$. There are two x-intercepts: one between -4 and -3 and another between -1 and 0.

STEP 2 **Make** a table of values for x-values between -4 and -3 and between -1 and 0 using an increment of 0.1. Look for a change in the signs of the function values.

INTERPRET FUNCTION VALUES
The function value that is closest to 0 indicates the x-value that best approximates a zero of the function.

x	−3.9	−3.8	**−3.7**	−3.6	−3.5	−3.4	−3.3	−3.2	−3.1
$f(x)$	0.61	0.24	**−0.11**	−0.44	−0.75	−1.04	−1.31	−1.56	−1.79

x	−0.9	−0.8	−0.7	−0.6	−0.5	−0.4	**−0.3**	−0.2	−0.1
$f(x)$	−1.79	−1.56	−1.31	−1.04	−0.75	−0.44	**−0.11**	0.24	0.61

▶ In each table, the function value closest to 0 is -0.11. So, the zeros of $f(x) = x^2 + 4x + 1$ are about -3.7 and about -0.3.

✓ GUIDED PRACTICE for Examples 4 and 5

4. Find the zeros of $f(x) = x^2 + x - 6$.

5. Approximate the zeros of $f(x) = -x^2 + 2x + 2$ to the nearest tenth.

EXAMPLE 6 Solve a multi-step problem

SPORTS An athlete throws a shot put with an initial vertical velocity of 40 feet per second as shown.

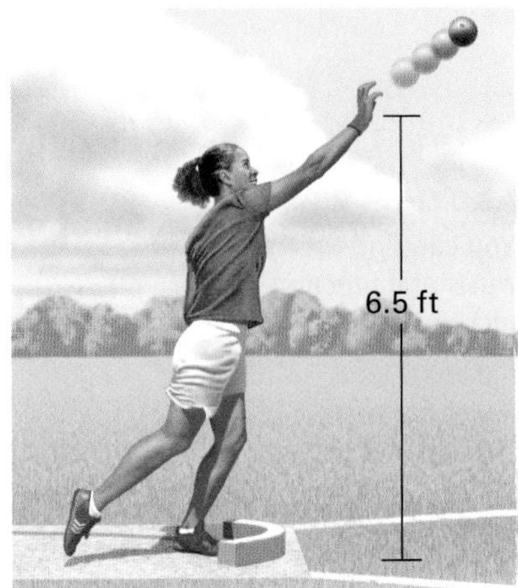

a. Write an equation that models the height h (in feet) of the shot put as a function of the time t (in seconds) after it is thrown.

b. Use the equation to find the time that the shot put is in the air.

Solution

a. Use the initial vertical velocity and the release height to write a vertical motion model.

$h = -16t^2 + vt + s$ **Vertical motion model**

$h = -16t^2 + 40t + 6.5$ **Substitute 40 for *v* and 6.5 for *s*.**

b. The shot put lands when $h = 0$. To find the time t when $h = 0$, solve $0 = -16t^2 + 40t + 6.5$ for t.

To solve the equation, graph the related function $h = -16t^2 + 40t + 6.5$ on a graphing calculator. Use the *trace* feature to find the t-intercepts.

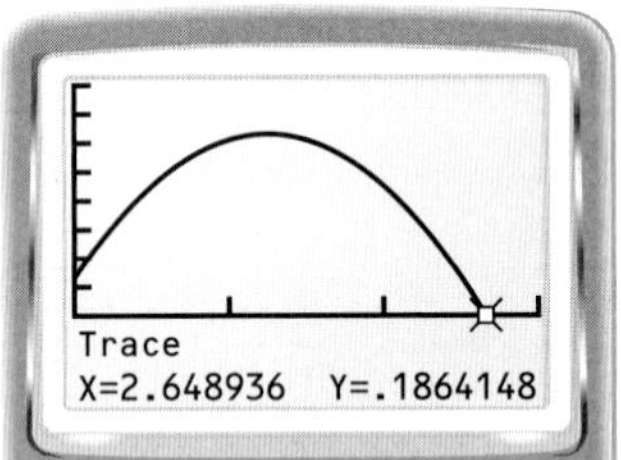

▶ There is only one positive t-intercept. The shot put is in the air for about 2.6 seconds.

USE A GRAPHING CALCULATOR

When entering $h = -16t^2 + 40t + 6.5$ in a graphing calculator, use y instead of h and x instead of t.

GUIDED PRACTICE for Example 6

6. **WHAT IF?** In Example 6, suppose the initial vertical velocity is 30 feet per second. Find the time that the shot put is in the air.

CONCEPT SUMMARY *For Your Notebook*

Relating Solutions of Equations, x-Intercepts of Graphs, and Zeros of Functions

Solutions of an Equation
The solutions of the equation $\boldsymbol{-x^2 + 8x - 12 = 0}$ are 2 and 6.

x-Intercepts of a Graph
The x-intercepts of the graph of $\boldsymbol{y = -x^2 + 8x - 12}$ occur where $\boldsymbol{y = 0}$, so the x-intercepts are 2 and 6, as shown.

Zeros of a Function
The zeros of the function $\boldsymbol{f(x) = -x^2 + 8x - 12}$ are the values of x for which $\boldsymbol{f(x) = 0}$, so the zeros are 2 and 6.

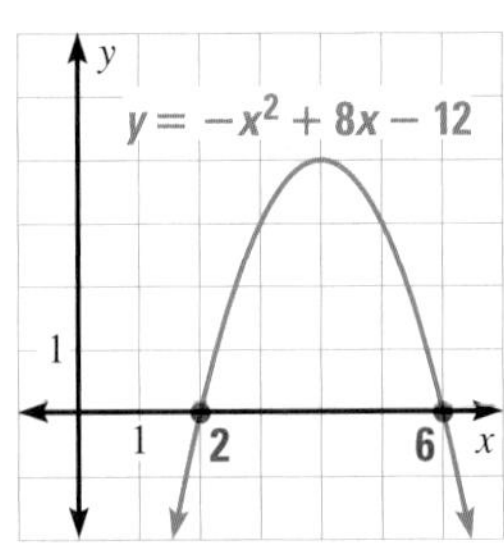

10.3 EXERCISES

HOMEWORK KEY

○ = **WORKED-OUT SOLUTIONS** on p. WS24 for Exs. 5 and 51

★ = **STANDARDIZED TEST PRACTICE** Exs. 2, 46, 53, and 54

SKILL PRACTICE

1. **VOCABULARY** Write $2x^2 + 11 = 9x$ in standard form.

2. ★ **WRITING** Is $3x^2 - 2 = 0$ a quadratic equation? *Explain.*

EXAMPLES 1, 2, and 3 on pp. 643–644 for Exs. 3–21

SOLVING EQUATIONS **Solve the equation by graphing.**

3. $x^2 - 5x + 4 = 0$
4. $x^2 + 5x + 6 = 0$
5. $x^2 + 6x = -8$
6. $x^2 - 4x = 5$
7. $x^2 - 16 = 6x$
8. $x^2 - 12x = -35$
9. $x^2 - 6x + 9 = 0$
10. $x^2 + 8x + 16 = 0$
11. $x^2 + 10x = -25$
12. $x^2 + 81 = 18x$
13. $-x^2 - 14x = 49$
14. $-x^2 + 16x = 64$
15. $x^2 - 5x + 7 = 0$
16. $x^2 - 2x + 3 = 0$
17. $x^2 + x = -2$
18. $\frac{1}{5}x^2 - 5 = 0$
19. $\frac{1}{2}x^2 + 2x = 6$
20. $-\frac{1}{4}x^2 - 8 = x$

21. **ERROR ANALYSIS** The graph of the function related to the equation $0 = x^2 - 4x + 4$ is shown. *Describe* and correct the error in solving the equation.

The only solution of the equation $0 = x^2 - 4x + 4$ is 4.

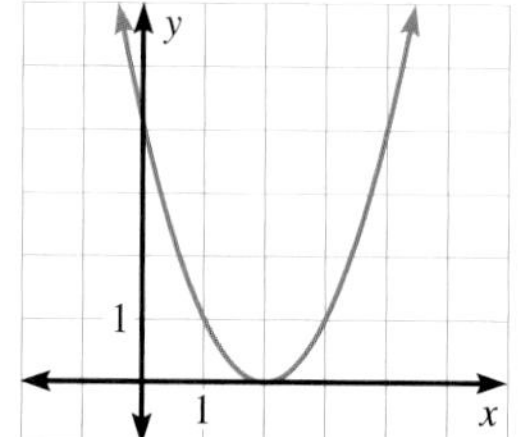

EXAMPLE 4 on p. 645 for Exs. 22–30

FINDING ZEROS **Find the zeros of the function.**

22. $f(x) = x^2 + 4x - 5$
23. $f(x) = x^2 - x - 12$
24. $f(x) = x^2 - 5x - 6$
25. $f(x) = x^2 + 3x - 10$
26. $f(x) = -x^2 + 8x + 9$
27. $f(x) = x^2 + x - 20$
28. $f(x) = -x^2 - 7x + 8$
29. $f(x) = x^2 - 12x + 11$
30. $f(x) = -x^2 + 4x + 12$

SOLVING EQUATIONS **Solve the equation by graphing.**

31. $2x^2 + x = 3$
32. $4x^2 - 5 = 8x$
33. $4x^2 - 4x + 1 = 0$
34. $x^2 + x = -\frac{1}{4}$
35. $3x^2 + 1 = 2x$
36. $5x^2 + x + 3 = 0$

EXAMPLE 5 on p. 645 for Exs. 37–46

APPROXIMATING ZEROS **Approximate the zeros of the function to the nearest tenth.**

37. $f(x) = x^2 + 4x + 2$
38. $f(x) = x^2 - 5x + 3$
39. $f(x) = x^2 - 2x - 5$
40. $f(x) = -x^2 - 3x + 3$
41. $f(x) = -x^2 + 7x - 5$
42. $f(x) = -x^2 - 5x - 2$
43. $f(x) = 2x^2 + x - 2$
44. $f(x) = -3x^2 + 8x - 2$
45. $f(x) = 5x^2 + 30x + 30$

46. ★ **MULTIPLE CHOICE** Which function has a zero between −3 and −2?

    (A) $f(x) = -3x^2 + 4x + 11$
    (B) $f(x) = 4x^2 - 3x - 11$
    (C) $f(x) = 3x^2 + 4x - 11$
    (D) $f(x) = 3x^2 + 11$

CHALLENGE Use the given surface area S of the cylinder to find the radius r to the nearest tenth. (Use 3.14 for π.)

47. $S = 251\ \text{ft}^2$

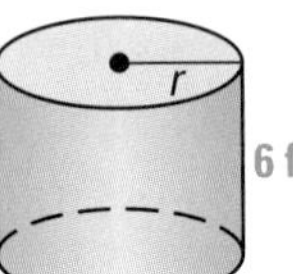

48. $S = 716\ \text{m}^2$

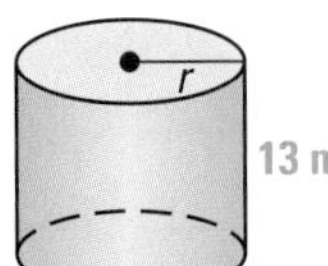

49. $S = 1074\ \text{cm}^2$

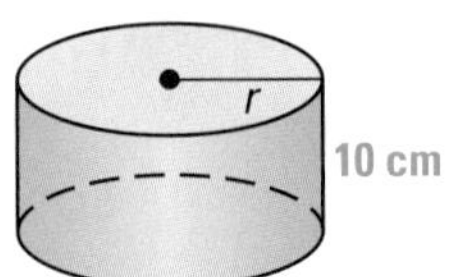

PROBLEM SOLVING

GRAPHING CALCULATOR You may wish to use a graphing calculator to complete the following Problem Solving exercises.

EXAMPLE 6 on p. 646 for Exs. 50–52

50. **SOCCER** The height y (in feet) of a soccer ball after it is kicked can be modeled by the graph of the equation $y = -0.04x^2 + 1.2x$ where x is the horizontal distance (in feet) that the ball travels. The ball is not touched, and it lands on the ground. Find the distance that the ball was kicked.

@HomeTutor for problem solving help at classzone.com

51. **SURVEYING** To keep water off a road, the road's surface is shaped like a parabola as in the cross section below. The surface of the road can be modeled by the graph of $y = -0.0017x^2 + 0.041x$ where x and y are measured in feet. Find the width of the road to the nearest tenth of a foot.

@HomeTutor for problem solving help at classzone.com

52. **DIVING** During a cliff diving competition, a diver begins a dive with his center of gravity 70 feet above the water. The initial vertical velocity of his dive is 8 feet per second.

 a. Write an equation that models the height h (in feet) of the diver's center of gravity as a function of time t (in seconds).

 b. How long after the diver begins his dive does his center of gravity reach the water?

53. ★ **SHORT RESPONSE** An arc of water sprayed from the nozzle of a fountain can be modeled by the graph of $y = -0.75x^2 + 6x$ where x is the horizontal distance (in feet) from the nozzle and y is the vertical distance (in feet). The diameter of the circle formed by the arcs on the surface of the water is called the display diameter. Find the display diameter of the fountain. *Explain* your reasoning.

54. ★ **EXTENDED RESPONSE** Two softball players are practicing catching fly balls. One player throws a ball to the other. She throws the ball upward from a height of 5.5 feet with an initial vertical velocity of 40 feet per second for her teammate to catch.

a. Write an equation that models the height h (in feet) of the ball as a function of time t (in seconds) after it is thrown.

b. If her teammate misses the ball and it lands on the ground, how long was the ball in the air?

c. If her teammate catches the ball at a height of 5.5 feet, how long was the ball in the air? *Explain* your reasoning.

55. **CHALLENGE** A stream of water from a fire hose can be modeled by the graph of $y = -0.003x^2 + 0.58x + 3$ where x and y are measured in feet. A firefighter is holding the hose 3 feet above the ground, 137 feet from a building. Will the stream of water pass through a window if the top of the window is 26 feet above the ground? *Explain.*

MIXED REVIEW

PREVIEW
Prepare for Lesson 10.4 in Exs. 56–58.

Evaluate the expression. *(p. 110)*

56. $-\sqrt{25}$ **57.** $\sqrt{400}$ **58.** $\pm\sqrt{625}$

Simplify the expression. *(p. 495)*

59. $\frac{(-8)^{10}}{(-8)^7}$ **60.** $\frac{9^2 \cdot 9^6}{9^4}$ **61.** $\left(-\frac{1}{2}\right)^3$

Write the number in standard form. *(p. 512)*

62. 4.4×10^{-6} **63.** 1.7×10^5 **64.** 6.804×10^8

QUIZ *for Lessons 10.1–10.3*

Graph the function. Compare the graph with the graph of $y = x^2$. *(p. 628)*

1. $y = -\frac{1}{2}x^2$ **2.** $y = 2x^2 - 5$ **3.** $y = -x^2 + 3$

Graph the function. Label the vertex and axis of symmetry.

4. $y = x^2 + 5$ *(p. 628)* **5.** $y = -5x^2 + 1$ *(p. 628)*

6. $y = x^2 + 4x - 2$ *(p. 635)* **7.** $y = 2x^2 - 12x + 5$ *(p. 635)*

8. $y = -\frac{1}{2}x^2 + 2x - 5$ *(p. 635)* **9.** $y = -4x^2 - 10x + 2$ *(p. 635)*

Solve the equation by graphing. *(p. 643)*

10. $x^2 - 7x = 8$ **11.** $x^2 + 6x + 9 = 0$ **12.** $x^2 + 10x = 11$

13. $x^2 - 7 = -6x$ **14.** $-x^2 + x - 1 = 0$ **15.** $x^2 - 4x + 9 = 0$

Find the zeros of the function. *(p. 643)*

16. $f(x) = x^2 + 3x - 10$ **17.** $f(x) = x^2 - 8x + 12$ **18.** $f(x) = -x^2 + 5x + 14$

10.3 Find Minimum and Maximum Values and Zeros

QUESTION How can you find the minumum or maximum value and the zeros of a quadratic function using a graphing calculator?

EXAMPLE 1 Find the maximum value of a function

Find the maximum value of the function $y = -2x^2 - 6x + 7$.

STEP 1 ***Enter the function***

Press Y= and enter the function $y = -2x^2 - 6x + 7$.

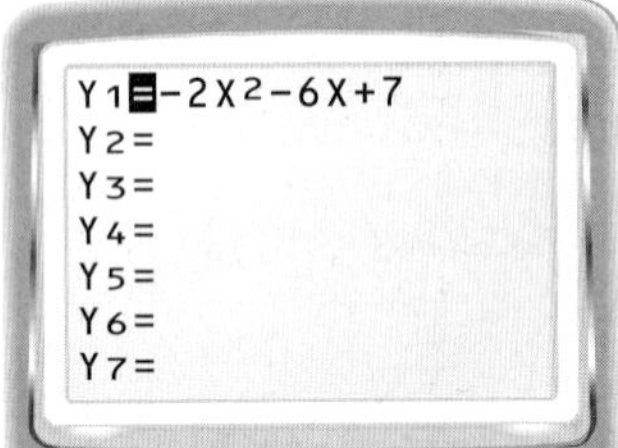

STEP 2 ***Adjust the window***

Display the graph. Adjust the viewing window as needed so that the vertex of the parabola is visible.

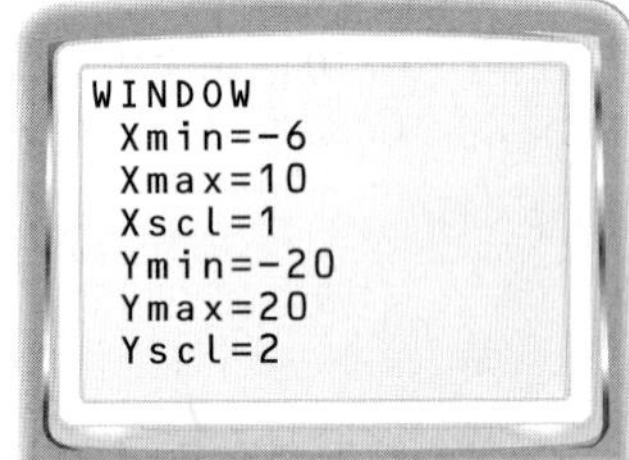

STEP 3 ***Use the maximum feature***

The *maximum* feature is located under the CALCULATE menu.

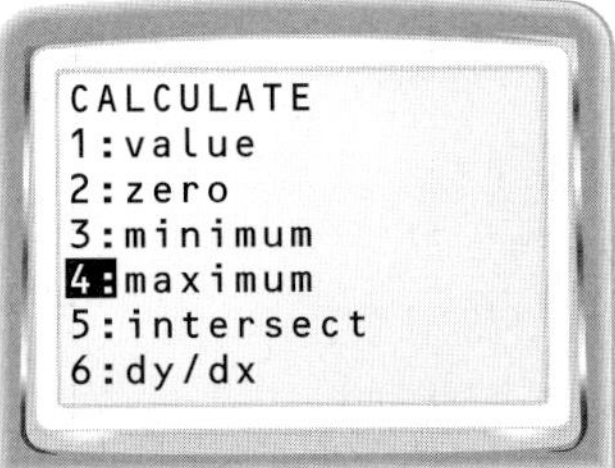

STEP 4 ***Find the maximum value***

Follow the graphing calculator's procedure to find the maximum of the function.

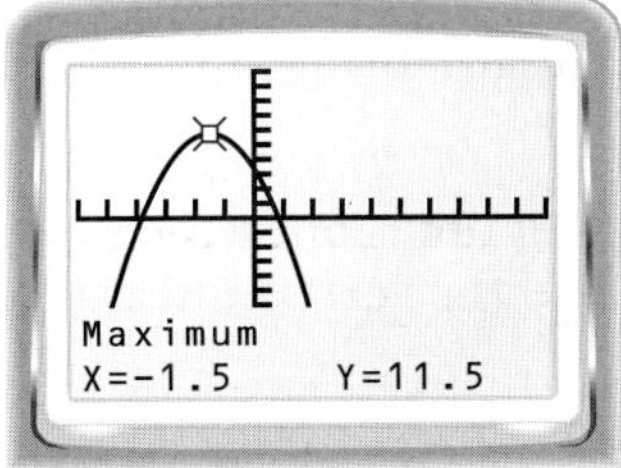

▶ The maximum value of the function $y = -2x^2 - 6x + 7$ is 11.5.

PRACTICE

Find the maximum or minimum value of the function.

1. $y = 3x^2 - 8x + 7$

2. $y = -x^2 + 3x + 10$

3. $y = -4x^2 - 6x - 6$

4. $y = 5x^2 + 10x - 8$

5. $y = -1.4x^2 + 3.8x - 6.1$

6. $y = 2.57x^2 - 8.45x - 5.04$

@HomeTutor
classzone.com
Keystrokes

EXAMPLE 2 **Approximate the zeros of a function**

Approximate the zeros of the function $y = 3x^2 + 2x - 4$.

STEP 1 ***Enter the function***

Press [Y=] and enter the function $y = 3x^2 + 2x - 4$.

Y1=3X2+2X-4
Y2=
Y3=
Y4=
Y5=
Y6=
Y7=

STEP 2 ***Adjust the window***

Display the graph. Adjust the viewing window as needed so that the x-intercepts of the parabola are visible.

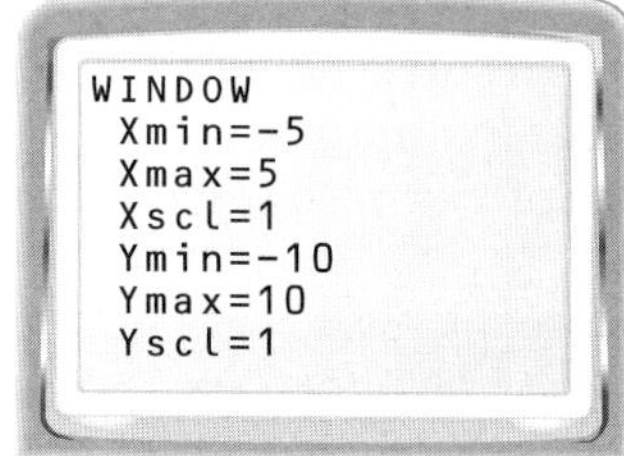

STEP 3 ***Use the zero feature***

The *zero* feature is under the CALCULATE menu.

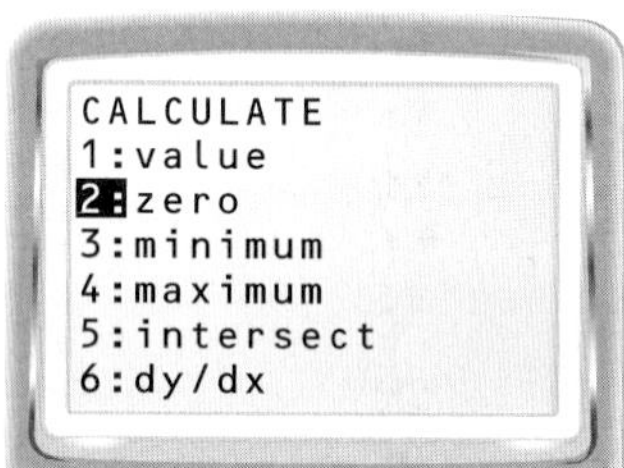

STEP 4 ***Find the zeros***

Follow the graphing calculator's procedure to find a zero of the function. Then repeat the process to find the other zero.

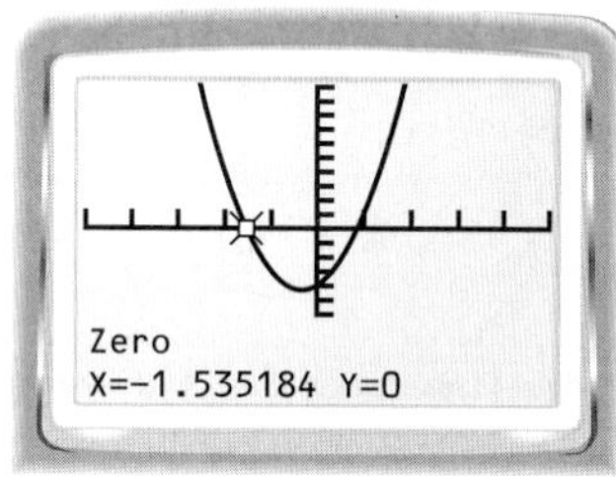

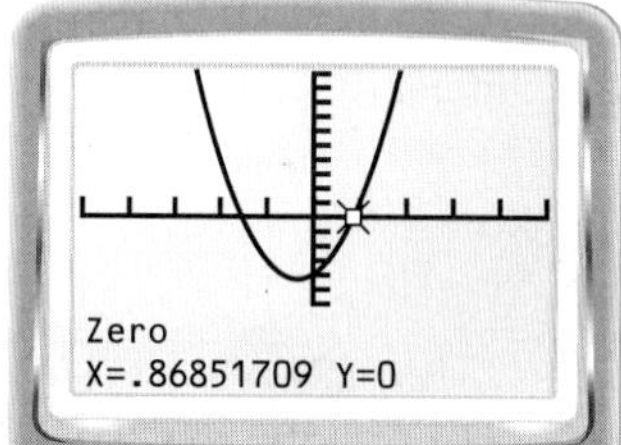

▶ The zeros are about −1.54 and about 0.87.

PRACTICE

Approximate the zeros of the quadratic function to the nearest hundredth.

7. $y = 2x^2 - 5x - 8$

8. $y = -3x^2 + 6x - 2$

9. $y = -x^2 + 4x + 9$

10. $y = 4x^2 - 7x + 1$

11. $y = -2.5x^2 + 7.7x - 4.9$

12. $y = 1.56x^2 - 5.19x - 2.25$

13. $y = -0.82x^2 - 4x + 12.4$

14. $y = 5.36x^2 + 17x + 2.67$

DRAW CONCLUSIONS

15. If a quadratic function has only one zero, what is the maximum or minimum value of the function? *Explain.*

16. If a quadratic function has a maximum value that is greater than 0, how many zeros does the function have? *Explain.*

10.4 Use Square Roots to Solve Quadratic Equations

Before You solved a quadratic equation by graphing.

Now You will solve a quadratic equation by finding square roots.

Why? So you can solve a problem about a falling object, as in Example 5.

Key Vocabulary
- **square root,** *p. 110*
- **perfect square,** *p. 111*

To use square roots to solve a quadratic equation of the form $ax^2 + c = 0$, first isolate x^2 on one side to obtain $x^2 = d$. Then use the following information about the solutions of $x^2 = d$ to solve the equation.

KEY CONCEPT *For Your Notebook*

Solving $x^2 = d$ by Taking Square Roots

- If $d > 0$, then $x^2 = d$ has two solutions: $x = \pm\sqrt{d}$.
- If $d = 0$, then $x^2 = d$ has one solution: $x = 0$.
- If $d < 0$, then $x^2 = d$ has no solution.

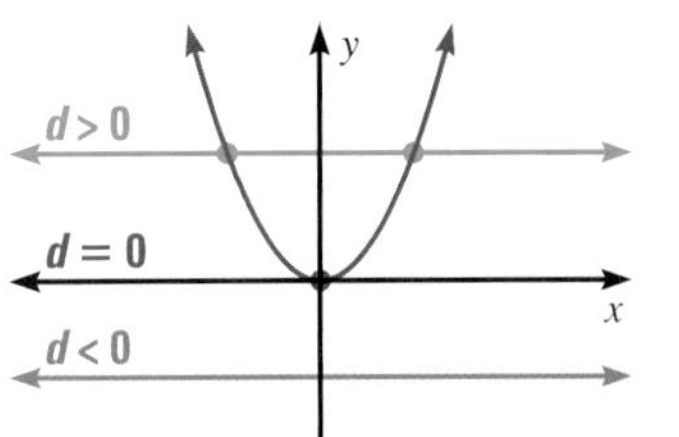

READING Recall that in this course, *solutions* refers to real-number solutions.

EXAMPLE 1 Solve quadratic equations

Solve the equation.

a. $2x^2 = 8$ **b.** $m^2 - 18 = -18$ **c.** $b^2 + 12 = 5$

Solution

a. $2x^2 = 8$ Write original equation.

$x^2 = 4$ Divide each side by 2.

$x = \pm\sqrt{4} = \pm 2$ Take square roots of each side. Simplify.

▶ The solutions are −2 and 2.

ANOTHER WAY You can also use factoring to solve $2x^2 - 8 = 0$:

$2x^2 - 8 = 0$

$2(x^2 - 4) = 0$

$2(x - 2)(x + 2) = 0$

$x = 2$ *or* $x = -2$

b. $m^2 - 18 = -18$ Write original equation.

$m^2 = 0$ Add 18 to each side.

$m = 0$ The square root of 0 is 0.

▶ The solution is 0.

c. $b^2 + 12 = 5$ Write original equation.

$b^2 = -7$ Subtract 12 from each side.

▶ Negative real numbers do not have real square roots. So, there is no solution.

SIMPLIFYING SQUARE ROOTS In cases where you need to take the square root of a fraction whose numerator and denominator are perfect squares, the radical can be written as a fraction. For example, $\sqrt{\frac{16}{25}}$ can be written as $\frac{4}{5}$ because $\left(\frac{4}{5}\right)^2 = \frac{16}{25}$.

EXAMPLE 2 Take square roots of a fraction

Solve $4z^2 = 9$.

Solution

$4z^2 = 9$ Write original equation.

$z^2 = \frac{9}{4}$ Divide each side by 4.

$z = \pm\sqrt{\frac{9}{4}}$ Take square roots of each side.

$z = \pm\frac{3}{2}$ Simplify.

▸ The solutions are $-\frac{3}{2}$ and $\frac{3}{2}$.

APPROXIMATING SQUARE ROOTS In cases where d in the equation $x^2 = d$ is not a perfect square or a fraction whose numerator and denominator are not perfect squares, you need to approximate the square root. A calculator can be used to find an approximation.

EXAMPLE 3 Approximate solutions of a quadratic equation

Solve $3x^2 - 11 = 7$. Round the solutions to the nearest hundredth.

Solution

$3x^2 - 11 = 7$ Write original equation.

$3x^2 = 18$ Add 11 to each side.

$x^2 = 6$ Divide each side by 3.

$x = \pm\sqrt{6}$ Take square roots of each side.

$x \approx \pm 2.45$ Use a calculator. Round to the nearest hundredth.

▸ The solutions are about −2.45 and about 2.45.

✓ GUIDED PRACTICE for Examples 1, 2, and 3

Solve the equation.

1. $c^2 - 25 = 0$
2. $5w^2 + 12 = -8$
3. $2x^2 + 11 = 11$
4. $25x^2 = 16$
5. $9m^2 = 100$
6. $49b^2 + 64 = 0$

Solve the equation. Round the solutions to the nearest hundredth.

7. $x^2 + 4 = 14$
8. $3k^2 - 1 = 0$
9. $2p^2 - 7 = 2$

EXAMPLE 4 Solve a quadratic equation

Solve $6(x-4)^2 = 42$. Round the solutions to the nearest hundredth.

$6(x-4)^2 = 42$	Write original equation.
$(x-4)^2 = 7$	Divide each side by 6.
$x - 4 = \pm\sqrt{7}$	Take square roots of each side.
$x = 4 \pm \sqrt{7}$	Add 4 to each side.

▶ The solutions are $4 + \sqrt{7} \approx 6.65$ and $4 - \sqrt{7} \approx 1.35$.

CHECK To check the solutions, first write the equation so that 0 is on one side as follows: $6(x-4)^2 - 42 = 0$. Then graph the related function $y = 6(x-4)^2 - 42$. The x-intercepts appear to be about 6.6 and about 1.3. So, each solution checks.

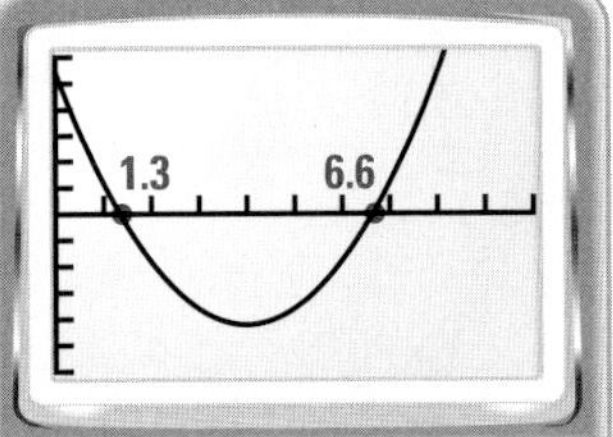

EXAMPLE 5 Solve a multi-step problem

ANOTHER WAY
For alternative methods for solving the problem in Example 5, turn to page 659 for the **Problem Solving Workshop**.

SPORTS EVENT During an ice hockey game, a remote-controlled blimp flies above the crowd and drops a numbered table-tennis ball. The number on the ball corresponds to a prize. Use the information in the diagram to find the amount of time that the ball is in the air.

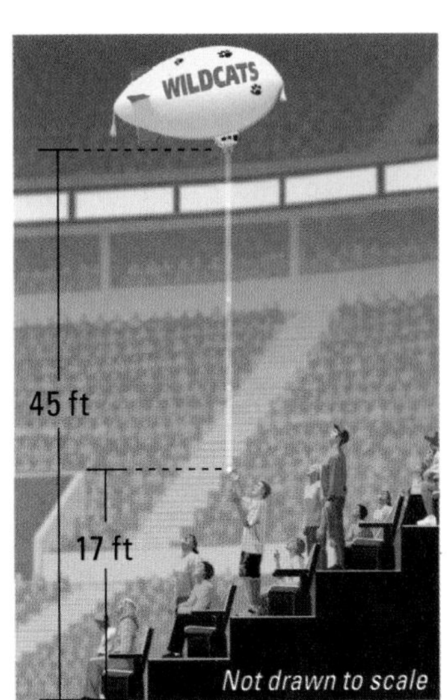

Solution

STEP 1 **Use** the vertical motion model to write an equation for the height h (in feet) of the ball as a function of time t (in seconds).

$h = -16t^2 + vt + s$	Vertical motion model
$h = -16t^2 + 0t + 45$	Substitute for v and s.

DETERMINE VELOCITY
When an object is dropped, it has an initial vertical velocity of 0 feet per second.

STEP 2 **Find** the amount of time the ball is in the air by substituting 17 for h and solving for t.

$h = -16t^2 + 45$	Write model.
$17 = -16t^2 + 45$	Substitute 17 for h.
$-28 = -16t^2$	Subtract 45 from each side.
$\frac{28}{16} = t^2$	Divide each side by -16.
$\sqrt{\frac{28}{16}} = t$	Take positive square root.
$1.32 \approx t$	Use a calculator.

INTERPRET SOLUTION
Because the time cannot be a negative number, ignore the negative square root.

▶ The ball is in the air for about 1.32 seconds.

✓ GUIDED PRACTICE for Examples 4 and 5

Solve the equation. Round the solutions to the nearest hundredth, if necessary.

10. $2(x - 2)^2 = 18$ **11.** $4(q - 3)^2 = 28$ **12.** $3(t + 5)^2 = 24$

13. WHAT IF? In Example 5, suppose the table-tennis ball is released 58 feet above the ground and is caught 12 feet above the ground. Find the amount of time that the ball is in the air. Round your answer to the nearest hundredth of a second.

10.4 EXERCISES

HOMEWORK KEY

○ = **WORKED-OUT SOLUTIONS** on p. WS24 for Exs. 25 and 59

★ = **STANDARDIZED TEST PRACTICE** Exs. 2, 15, 16, 29, 51, 52, 57, and 60

◆ = **MULTIPLE REPRESENTATIONS** Ex. 62

SKILL PRACTICE

1. VOCABULARY Copy and complete: If $b^2 = a$, then b is a(n) _?_ of a.

2. ★ **WRITING** *Describe* two methods for solving a quadratic equation of the form $ax^2 + c = 0$.

EXAMPLES 1 and 2 on pp. 652–653 for Exs. 3–16

SOLVING EQUATIONS **Solve the equation.**

3. $3x^2 - 3 = 0$ **4.** $2x^2 - 32 = 0$ **5.** $4x^2 - 400 = 0$

6. $2m^2 - 42 = 8$ **7.** $15d^2 = 0$ **8.** $a^2 + 8 = 3$

9. $4g^2 + 10 = 11$ **10.** $2w^2 + 13 = 11$ **11.** $9q^2 - 35 = 14$

12. $25b^2 + 11 = 15$ **13.** $3z^2 - 18 = -18$ **14.** $5n^2 - 17 = -19$

15. ★ **MULTIPLE CHOICE** Which of the following is a solution of the equation $61 - 3n^2 = -14$?

Ⓐ 5 Ⓑ 10 Ⓒ 25 Ⓓ 625

16. ★ **MULTIPLE CHOICE** Which of the following is a solution of the equation $13 - 36x^2 = -12$?

Ⓐ $-\frac{6}{5}$ Ⓑ $\frac{1}{6}$ Ⓒ $\frac{5}{6}$ Ⓓ 5

EXAMPLE 3 on p. 653 for Exs. 17–29

APPROXIMATING SQUARE ROOTS **Solve the equation. Round the solutions to the nearest hundredth.**

17. $x^2 + 6 = 13$ **18.** $x^2 + 11 = 24$ **19.** $14 - x^2 = 17$

20. $2a^2 - 9 = 11$ **21.** $4 - k^2 = 4$ **22.** $5 + 3p^2 = 38$

23. $53 = 8 + 9m^2$ **24.** $-21 = 15 - 2z^2$ **(25.)** $7c^2 = 100$

26. $5d^2 + 2 = 6$ **27.** $4b^2 - 5 = 2$ **28.** $9n^2 - 14 = -3$

29. ★ **MULTIPLE CHOICE** The equation $17 - \frac{1}{4}x^2 = 12$ has a solution between which two integers?

Ⓐ 1 and 2 Ⓑ 2 and 3 Ⓒ 3 and 4 Ⓓ 4 and 5

ERROR ANALYSIS ***Describe* and correct the error in solving the equation.**

30. $2x^2 - 54 = 18$

$2x^2 - 54 = 18$

$2x^2 = 72$

$x^2 = 36$

$x = \sqrt{36}$

$x = 6$

The solution is 6.

31. $7d^2 - 6 = -17$

$7d^2 - 6 = -17$

$7d^2 = -11$

$d^2 = -\frac{11}{7}$

$d \approx \pm 1.25$

The solutions are about -1.25 and about 1.25.

EXAMPLE 4
on p. 654
for Exs. 32–40

SOLVING EQUATIONS **Solve the equation. Round the solutions to the nearest hundredth.**

32. $(x - 7)^2 = 6$ **33.** $7(x - 3)^2 = 35$ **34.** $6(x + 4)^2 = 18$

35. $20 = 2(m + 5)^2$ **36.** $5(a - 2)^2 = 70$ **37.** $21 = 3(z + 14)^2$

38. $\frac{1}{2}(c - 8)^2 = 3$ **39.** $\frac{3}{2}(n + 1)^2 = 33$ **40.** $\frac{4}{3}(k - 6)^2 = 20$

SOLVING EQUATIONS **Solve the equation. Round the solutions to the nearest hundredth, if necessary.**

41. $3x^2 - 35 = 45 - 2x^2$ **42.** $42 = 3(x^2 + 5)$ **43.** $11x^2 + 3 = 5(4x^2 - 3)$

44. $\left(\frac{t - 5}{3}\right)^2 = 49$ **45.** $11\left(\frac{w - 7}{2}\right)^2 - 20 = 101$ **46.** $(4m^2 - 6)^2 = 81$

GEOMETRY **Use the given area A of the circle to find the radius r or the diameter d to the nearest hundredth.**

47. $A = 144\pi \text{ in.}^2$

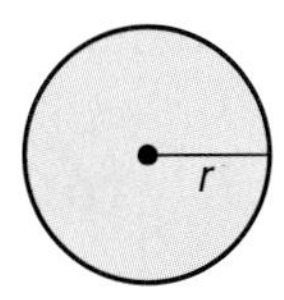

48. $A = 21\pi \text{ m}^2$

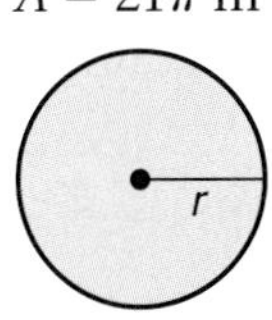

49. $A = 34\pi \text{ ft}^2$

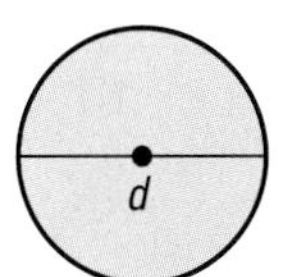

50. REASONING An equation of the graph shown is $y = \frac{1}{2}(x - 2)^2 + 1$. Two points on the parabola have y-coordinates of 9. Find the x-coordinates of these points.

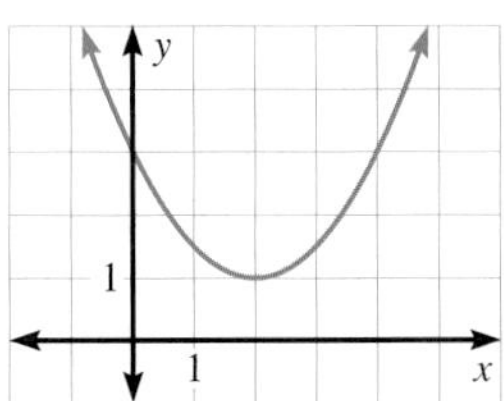

51. ★ SHORT RESPONSE Solve $x^2 = 1.44$ without using a calculator. *Explain* your reasoning.

52. ★ OPEN-ENDED Give values for a and c so that $ax^2 + c = 0$ has (a) two solutions, (b) one solution, and (c) no solution.

CHALLENGE **Solve the equation without graphing.**

53. $x^2 - 12x + 36 = 64$ **54.** $x^2 + 14x + 49 = 16$ **55.** $x^2 + 18x + 81 = 25$

○ = WORKED-OUT SOLUTIONS on p. WS1 ★ = STANDARDIZED TEST PRACTICE

PROBLEM SOLVING

EXAMPLE 5 on p. 654 for Exs. 56–57

56. **FALLING OBJECT** Fenway Park is a Major League Baseball park in Boston, Massachusetts. The park offers seats on top of the left field wall. A person sitting in one of these seats accidentally drops his sunglasses on the field. The height h (in feet) of the sunglasses can be modeled by the function $h = -16t^2 + 38$ where t is the time (in seconds) since the sunglasses were dropped. Find the time it takes for the sunglasses to reach the field. Round your answer to the nearest hundredth of a second.

@HomeTutor for problem solving help at classzone.com

57. ★ **MULTIPLE CHOICE** Which equation can be used to find the time it takes for an object to hit the ground after it was dropped from a height of 68 feet?

Ⓐ $-16t^2 = 0$ Ⓑ $-16t^2 - 68 = 0$ Ⓒ $-16t^2 + 68 = 0$ Ⓓ $-16t^2 = 68$

@HomeTutor for problem solving help at classzone.com

58. **INTERNET USAGE** For the period 1995–2001, the number y (in thousands) of Internet users worldwide can be modeled by the function $y = 12{,}697x^2 + 55{,}722$ where x is the number of years since 1995. Between which two years did the number of Internet users worldwide reach 100,000,000?

59. **GEMOLOGY** To find the weight w (in carats) of round faceted gems, gemologists use the formula $w = 0.0018D^2ds$ where D is the diameter (in millimeters) of the gem, d is the depth (in millimeters) of the gem, and s is the specific gravity of the gem. Find the diameter to the nearest tenth of a millimeter of each round faceted gem in the table.

	Gem	Weight (carats)	Depth (mm)	Specific gravity	Diameter (mm)
a.	Amethyst	1	4.5	2.65	?
b.	Diamond	1	4.5	3.52	?
c.	Ruby	1	4.5	4.00	?

60. ★ **SHORT RESPONSE** In deep water, the speed s (in meters per second) of a series of waves and the wavelength L (in meters) of the waves are related by the equation $2\pi s^2 = 9.8L$.

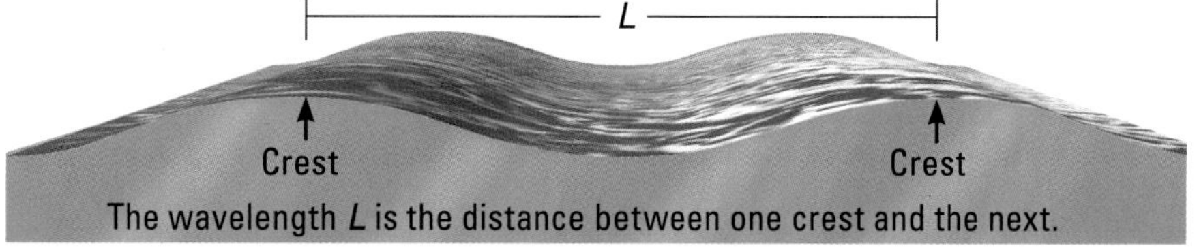

The wavelength L is the distance between one crest and the next.

a. Find the speed to the nearest hundredth of a meter per second of a series of waves with the following wavelengths: 6 meters, 10 meters, and 25 meters. (Use 3.14 for π.)

b. Does the speed of a series of waves increase or decrease as the wavelength of the waves increases? *Explain.*

61. **MULTI-STEP PROBLEM** The Doyle log rule is a formula used to estimate the amount of lumber that can be sawn from logs of various sizes. The amount of lumber V (in board feet) is given by $V = \frac{L(D - 4)^2}{16}$ where L is the length (in feet) of a log and D is the small-end diameter (in inches) of the log.

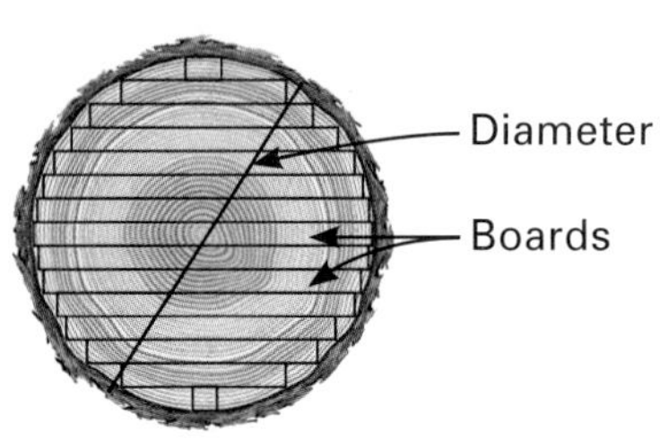

a. Solve the formula for D.

b. Use the rewritten formula to find the diameters, to the nearest tenth of a foot, of logs that will yield 50 board feet and have the following lengths: 16 feet, 18 feet, 20 feet, and 22 feet.

62. **MULTIPLE REPRESENTATIONS** A ride at an amusement park lifts seated riders 250 feet above the ground. Then the riders are dropped. They experience free fall until the brakes are activated at 105 feet above the ground.

a. **Writing an Equation** Use the vertical motion model to write an equation for the height h (in feet) of the riders as a function of the time t (in seconds) into the free fall.

b. **Making a Table** Make a table that shows the height of the riders after 0, 1, 2, 3, and 4 seconds according to the model. Use the table to estimate the amount of time the riders experience free fall.

c. **Solving an Equation** Use the equation to find the amount of time, to the nearest tenth of a second, that the riders experience free fall.

63. **CHALLENGE** The height h (in feet) of a dropped object on any planet can be modeled by $h = -\frac{g}{2}t^2 + s$ where g is the acceleration (in feet per second per second) due to the planet's gravity, t is the time (in seconds) after the object is dropped, and s is the initial height (in feet) of the object. Suppose the same object is dropped from the same height on Earth and Mars. Given that g is 32 feet per second per second on Earth and 12 feet per second per second on Mars, on which planet will the object hit the ground first? *Explain.*

MIXED REVIEW

PREVIEW Prepare for Lesson 10.5 in Exs. 64–67.

Evaluate the power. *(p. 2)*

64. $\left(\frac{5}{2}\right)^2$ 65. $\left(\frac{9}{5}\right)^2$ 66. $\left(\frac{3}{4}\right)^2$ 67. $\left(\frac{7}{2}\right)^2$

Write an equation of the line with the given slope and y-intercept. *(p. 283)*

68. slope: -9
y-intercept: 11

69. slope: 7
y-intercept: -7

70. slope: 3
y-intercept: -2

Write an equation of the line that passes through the given point and is perpendicular to the given line. *(p. 319)*

71. $(1, -1), y = 2x$ 72. $(0, 8), y = 4x + 1$ 73. $(-9, -4), y = -3x + 6$

PROBLEM SOLVING WORKSHOP
LESSON 10.4

Using ALTERNATIVE METHODS

Another Way to Solve Example 5, page 654

MULTIPLE REPRESENTATIONS In Example 5 on page 654, you saw how to solve a problem about a dropped table-tennis ball by using a square root. You can also solve the problem by using factoring or by using a table.

PROBLEM

SPORTS EVENT During an ice hockey game, a remote-controlled blimp flies above the crowd and drops a numbered table-tennis ball. The number on the ball corresponds to a prize. Use the information in the diagram to find the amount of time that the ball is in the air.

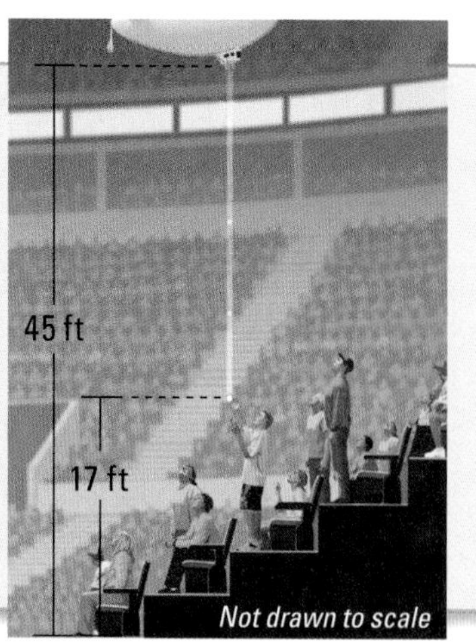

METHOD 1

Using Factoring One alternative approach is to use factoring.

STEP 1 **Write** an equation for the height h (in feet) of the ball as a function of time t (in seconds) after it is dropped using the vertical motion model.

$h = -16t^2 + vt + s$ — **Vertical motion model**

$h = -16t^2 + 0t + 45$ — **Substitute 0 for *v* and 45 for *s*.**

STEP 2 **Substitute** 17 for h to find the time it takes the ball to reach a height of 17 feet. Then write the equation so that 0 is on one side.

$17 = -16t^2 + 45$ — **Substitute 17 for *h*.**

$0 = -16t^2 + 28$ — **Subtract 17 from each side.**

STEP 3 **Solve** the equation by factoring. Replace 28 with the closest perfect square, 25, so that the right side of the equation is factorable as a difference of two squares.

USE AN APPROXIMATION
By replacing 28 with 25, you will obtain an answer that is an approximation of the amount of time that the ball is in the air.

$0 = -16t^2 + 25$ — **Use 25 as an approximation for 28.**

$0 = -(16t^2 - 25)$ — **Factor out −1.**

$0 = -(4t - 5)(4t + 5)$ — **Difference of two squares pattern**

$4t - 5 = 0$ *or* $4t + 5 = 0$ — **Zero-product property**

$t = \frac{5}{4}$ *or* $t = -\frac{5}{4}$ — **Solve for *t*.**

▶ The ball is in the air about $\frac{5}{4}$, or 1.25, seconds.

METHOD 2 **Using a Table** Another approach is to make and use a table.

STEP 1 **Make** a table that shows the height h (in feet) of the ball by substituting values for time t (in seconds) in the function $h = -16t^2 + 45$. Use increments of 1 second.

Time t (seconds)	Height h (feet)
0	45
1	29
2	−19

STEP 2 **Identify** the time interval in which the height of the ball is 17 feet. This happens between 1 and 2 seconds.

STEP 3 **Make** a second table using increments of 0.1 second to get a closer approximation.

Time t (seconds)	Height h (feet)
1.0	29.00
1.1	25.64
1.2	21.96
1.3	**17.96**
1.4	13.64

▶ The ball is in the air about 1.3 seconds.

PRACTICE

1. **WHAT IF?** In the problem on page 659, suppose the ball is caught at a height of 10 feet. For how many seconds is the ball in the air? Solve this problem using two different methods.

2. **OPEN-ENDED** *Describe* a problem about a dropped object. Then solve the problem and explain what your solution means in this situation.

3. **GEOMETRY** The box below is a rectangular prism with the dimensions shown.

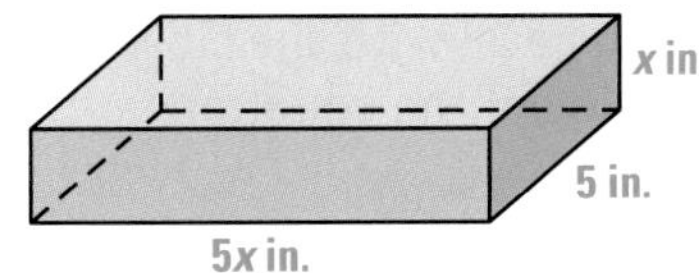

   a. Write an equation that gives the volume V (in cubic inches) of the box as a function of x.

   b. The volume of the box is 83 cubic inches. Find the dimensions of the box. Use factoring to solve the problem.

   c. Make a table to check your answer from part (b).

4. **TRAPEZE** You are learning how to perform on a trapeze. While hanging from a still trapeze bar, your shoe comes loose and falls to a safety net that is 6 feet off the ground. If your shoe falls from a height of 54 feet, how long does it take your shoe to hit the net? Choose any method for solving the problem. Show your steps.

5. **ERROR ANALYSIS** A student solved the problem in Exercise 4 as shown below. *Describe* and correct the error.

Let t be the time (in seconds) that the shoe is in the air.

$6 = -16t^2 + 54$

$0 = -16t^2 + 60$

Replace 60 with the closest perfect square, 64.

$0 = -16t^2 + 64$

$0 = -16(t - 2)(t + 2)$

$t = 2$ or $t = -2$

It takes about 2 seconds.

MIXED REVIEW *of Problem Solving*

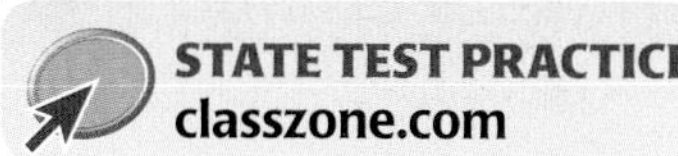

Lessons 10.1–10.4

1. **MULTI-STEP PROBLEM** A company's yearly profits from 1996 to 2006 can be modeled by the function $y = x^2 - 8x + 80$ where y is the profit (in thousands of dollars) and x is the number of years since 1996.

   a. In what year did the company experience its lowest yearly profit?

   b. What was the lowest yearly profit?

2. **MULTI-STEP PROBLEM** Use the rectangle below.

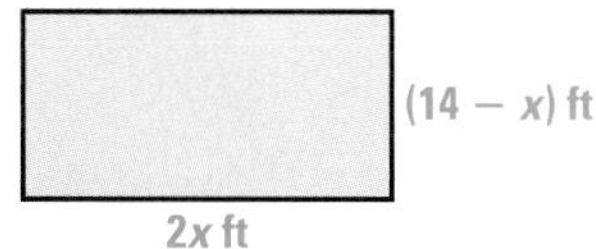

   a. Find the value of x that gives the greatest possible area of the rectangle.

   b. What is the greatest possible area of the rectangle?

3. **EXTENDED RESPONSE** You throw a lacrosse ball twice using a lacrosse stick.

   a. For your first throw, the ball is released 8 feet above the ground with an initial vertical velocity of 35 feet per second. Use the vertical motion model to write an equation for the height h (in feet) of the ball as a function of time t (in seconds).

   b. For your second throw, the ball is released 7 feet above the ground with an initial vertical velocity of 45 feet per second. Use the vertical motion model to write an equation for the height h (in feet) of the ball as a function of time t (in seconds).

   c. If no one catches either throw, for which throw is the ball in the air longer? *Explain.*

4. **OPEN-ENDED** Describe a real-world situation of an object being dropped. Then write an equation that models the height of the object as a function of time. Use the equation to determine the time it takes the object to hit the ground.

5. **SHORT RESPONSE** A football player is attempting a field goal. The path of the kicked football can be modeled by the graph of $y = -0.03x^2 + 1.8x$ where x is the horizontal distance (in yards) traveled by the football and y is the corresponding height (in feet) of the football. Will the football pass over the goal post that is 10 feet above the ground and 45 yards away? *Explain.*

6. **GRIDDED ANSWER** The force F (in newtons) a rider feels while a train goes around a curve is given by $F = \frac{mv^2}{r}$ where m is the mass (in kilograms) of the rider, v is the velocity (in meters per second) of the train, and r is the radius (in meters) of the curve. A rider with a mass of 75 kilograms experiences a force of 18,150 newtons, while going around a curve that has a radius of 8 meters. Find the velocity (in meters per second) the train travels around the curve.

7. **SHORT RESPONSE** The opening of the tunnel shown can be modeled by the graph of the equation $y = -0.18x^2 + 4.4x - 12$ where x and y are measured in feet.

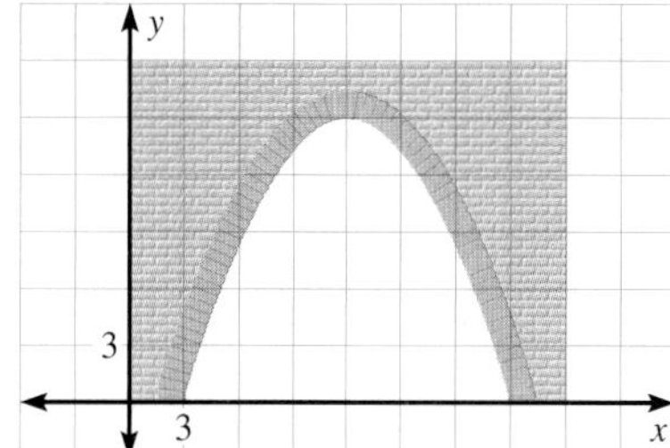

   a. Find the maximum height of the tunnel.

   b. A semi trailer is 7.5 feet wide, and the top of the trailer is 10.5 feet above the ground. Given that traffic travels one way on one lane through the center of the tunnel, will the semi trailer fit through the opening of the tunnel? *Explain.*

Animated Algebra classzone.com

10.5 Completing the Square Using Algebra Tiles

MATERIALS • algebra tiles

QUESTION How can you use algebra tiles to complete the square?

For an expression of the form $x^2 + bx$, you can add a constant c to the expression so that the expression $x^2 + bx + c$ is a perfect square trinomial. This process is called *completing the square.*

EXPLORE Complete the square

Find the value of c that makes $x^2 + 4x + c$ a perfect square trinomial.

STEP 1 ***Model expression***

Use algebra tiles to model the expression $x^2 + 4x$. You will need one x^2-tile and four x-tiles for this expression.

STEP 2 ***Rearrange tiles***

Arrange the tiles to form a square. The arrangement will be incomplete in one of the corners.

STEP 3 ***Complete the square***

Determine the number of 1-tiles needed to complete the square. The number of 1-tiles is the value of c. So, the perfect square trinomial is $x^2 + 4x + 4$ or $(x + 2)^2$.

DRAW CONCLUSIONS Use your observations to complete these exercises

1. Copy and complete the table using algebra tiles.

Expression	Number of 1-tiles needed to complete the square	Expression written as a square
$x^2 + 4x$	4	$x^2 + 4x + 4 = (x + 2)^2$
$x^2 + 6x$	?	?
$x^2 + 8x$	?	?
$x^2 + 10x$	?	?

2. In the statement $x^2 + bx + c = (x + d)^2$, how are b and d related? How are c and d related?

3. Use your answer to Exercise 2 to predict the number of 1-tiles you would need to add to complete the square for the expression $x^2 + 18x$.

10.5 Solve Quadratic Equations by Completing the Square

Before You solved quadratic equations by finding square roots.

Now You will solve quadratic equations by completing the square.

Why? So you can solve a problem about snowboarding, as in Ex. 50.

Key Vocabulary
- **completing the square**
- **perfect square trinomial,** *p. 601*

For an expression of the form $x^2 + bx$, you can add a constant c to the expression so that the expression $x^2 + bx + c$ is a perfect square trinomial. This process is called **completing the square**.

KEY CONCEPT *For Your Notebook*

Completing the Square

Words To complete the square for the expression $x^2 + bx$, add the square of half the coefficient of the term bx.

Algebra $x^2 + bx + \left(\frac{b}{2}\right)^2 = \left(x + \frac{b}{2}\right)^2$

EXAMPLE 1 Complete the square

Find the value of c that makes the expression $x^2 + 5x + c$ a perfect square trinomial. Then write the expression as the square of a binomial.

STEP 1 **Find** the value of c. For the expression to be a perfect square trinomial, c needs to be the square of half the coefficient of bx.

$c = \left(\frac{5}{2}\right)^2 = \frac{25}{4}$ Find the square of half the coefficient of bx.

STEP 2 **Write** the expression as a perfect square trinomial. Then write the expression as the square of a binomial.

$x^2 + 5x + c = x^2 + 5x + \frac{25}{4}$ Substitute $\frac{25}{4}$ for c.

$= \left(x + \frac{5}{2}\right)^2$ Square of a binomial

GUIDED PRACTICE for Example 1

Find the value of c that makes the expression a perfect square trinomial. Then write the expression as the square of a binomial.

1. $x^2 + 8x + c$
2. $x^2 - 12x + c$
3. $x^2 + 3x + c$

SOLVING EQUATIONS The method of completing the square can be used to solve any quadratic equation. To use completing the square to solve a quadratic equation, you must write the equation in the form $x^2 + bx = d$.

EXAMPLE 2 Solve a quadratic equation

Solve $x^2 - 16x = -15$ by completing the square.

Solution

$x^2 - 16x = -15$	Write original equation.
$x^2 - 16x + (-8)^2 = -15 + (-8)^2$	Add $\left(\frac{-16}{2}\right)^2$, or $(-8)^2$, to each side.
$(x - 8)^2 = -15 + (-8)^2$	Write left side as the square of a binomial.
$(x - 8)^2 = 49$	Simplify the right side.
$x - 8 = \pm 7$	Take square roots of each side.
$x = 8 \pm 7$	Add 8 to each side.

▶ The solutions of the equation are $8 + 7 = 15$ and $8 - 7 = 1$.

CHECK You can check the solutions in the original equation.

If $x = 15$:	**If $x = 1$:**
$(15)^2 - 16(15) \stackrel{?}{=} -15$	$(1)^2 - 16(1) \stackrel{?}{=} -15$
$-15 = -15$ ✓	$-15 = -15$ ✓

AVOID ERRORS
When completing the square to solve an equation, be sure you add the term $\left(\frac{b}{2}\right)^2$ to both sides of the equation.

EXAMPLE 3 Solve a quadratic equation in standard form

Solve $2x^2 + 20x - 8 = 0$ by completing the square.

Solution

$2x^2 + 20x - 8 = 0$	Write original equation.
$2x^2 + 20x = 8$	Add 8 to each side.
$x^2 + 10x = 4$	Divide each side by 2.
$x^2 + 10x + 5^2 = 4 + 5^2$	Add $\left(\frac{10}{2}\right)^2$, or 5^2, to each side.
$(x + 5)^2 = 29$	Write left side as the square of a binomial.
$x + 5 = \pm\sqrt{29}$	Take square roots of each side.
$x = -5 \pm \sqrt{29}$	Subtract 5 from each side.

▶ The solutions are $-5 + \sqrt{29} \approx 0.39$ and $-5 - \sqrt{29} \approx -10.39$.

AVOID ERRORS
Be sure that the coefficient of x^2 is 1 before you complete the square.

GUIDED PRACTICE for Examples 2 and 3

Solve the equation by completing the square. Round your solutions to the nearest hundredth, if necessary.

4. $x^2 - 2x = 3$ **5.** $m^2 + 10m = -8$ **6.** $3g^2 - 24g + 27 = 0$

EXAMPLE 4 Solve a multi-step problem

CRAFTS You decide to use chalkboard paint to create a chalkboard on a door. You want the chalkboard to have a uniform border as shown. You have enough chalkboard paint to cover 6 square feet. Find the width of the border to the nearest inch.

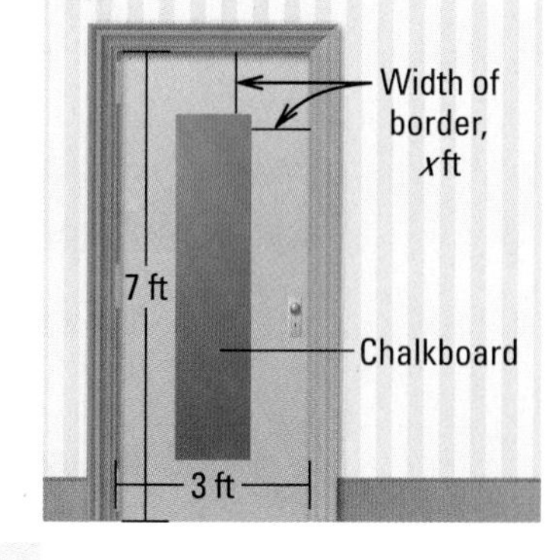

Solution

STEP 1 **Write** a verbal model. Then write an equation. Let x be the width (in feet) of the border.

Area of chalkboard (square feet)	=	Length of chalkboard (feet)	•	Width of chalkboard (feet)
6	=	**(7 − 2x)**	•	**(3 − 2x)**

WRITE EQUATION
The width of the border is subtracted twice because it is at the top and the bottom of the door, as well as at the left and the right.

STEP 2 **Solve** the equation.

$$6 = (7 - 2x)(3 - 2x)$$ **Write equation.**

$$6 = 21 - 20x + 4x^2$$ **Multiply binomials.**

$$-15 = 4x^2 - 20x$$ **Subtract 21 from each side.**

$$-\frac{15}{4} = x^2 - 5x$$ **Divide each side by 4.**

$$-\frac{15}{4} + \frac{25}{4} = x^2 - 5x + \frac{25}{4}$$ **Add $\left(-\frac{5}{2}\right)^2$, or $\frac{25}{4}$, to each side.**

$$-\frac{15}{4} + \frac{25}{4} = \left(x - \frac{5}{2}\right)^2$$ **Write right side as the square of a binomial.**

$$\frac{5}{2} = \left(x - \frac{5}{2}\right)^2$$ **Simplify left side.**

$$\pm\sqrt{\frac{5}{2}} = x - \frac{5}{2}$$ **Take square roots of each side.**

$$\frac{5}{2} \pm \sqrt{\frac{5}{2}} = x$$ **Add $\frac{5}{2}$ to each side.**

The solutions of the equation are $\frac{5}{2} + \sqrt{\frac{5}{2}} \approx 4.08$ and $\frac{5}{2} - \sqrt{\frac{5}{2}} \approx 0.92$.

It is not possible for the width of the border to be 4.08 feet because the width of the door is 3 feet. So, the width of the border is 0.92 foot. Convert 0.92 foot to inches.

$$0.92 \text{ ft} \cdot \frac{12 \text{ in.}}{1 \text{ ft}} = 11.04 \text{ in.}$$ **Multiply by conversion factor.**

▶ The width of the border should be about 11 inches.

✓ **GUIDED PRACTICE** for Example 4

7. **WHAT IF?** In Example 4, suppose you have enough chalkboard paint to cover 4 square feet. Find the width of the border to the nearest inch.

10.5 EXERCISES

HOMEWORK KEY

○ = **WORKED-OUT SOLUTIONS** on p. WS24 for Exs. 19 and 47

★ = **STANDARDIZED TEST PRACTICE** Exs. 2, 24, 25, 42, and 49

◆ = **MULTIPLE REPRESENTATIONS** Ex. 47

SKILL PRACTICE

1. **VOCABULARY** Copy and complete: The process of writing an expression of the form $x^2 + bx$ as a perfect square trinomial is called __?__.

2. ★ **WRITING** Give an example of an expression that is a perfect square trinomial. *Explain* why the expression is a perfect square trinomial.

EXAMPLE 1 on p. 663 for Exs. 3–11

COMPLETING THE SQUARE Find the value of c that makes the expression a perfect square trinomial. Then write the expression as the square of a binomial.

3. $x^2 + 6x + c$
4. $x^2 + 12x + c$
5. $x^2 - 4x + c$
6. $x^2 - 8x + c$
7. $x^2 - 3x + c$
8. $x^2 + 5x + c$
9. $x^2 + 2.4x + c$
10. $x^2 - \frac{1}{2}x + c$
11. $x^2 - \frac{4}{3}x + c$

EXAMPLES 2 and 3 on p. 664 for Exs. 12–27

SOLVING EQUATIONS Solve the equation by completing the square. Round your solutions to the nearest hundredth, if necessary.

12. $x^2 + 2x = 3$
13. $x^2 + 10x = 24$
14. $c^2 - 14c = 15$
15. $n^2 - 6n = 72$
16. $a^2 - 8a + 15 = 0$
17. $y^2 + 4y - 21 = 0$
18. $w^2 - 5w = \frac{11}{4}$
19. $z^2 + 11z = -\frac{21}{4}$
20. $g^2 - \frac{2}{3}g = 7$
21. $k^2 - 8k - 7 = 0$
22. $v^2 - 7v + 1 = 0$
23. $m^2 + 3m + \frac{5}{4} = 0$

24. ★ **MULTIPLE CHOICE** What are the solutions of $4x^2 + 16x = 9$?

(A) $-\frac{1}{2}, -\frac{9}{2}$ (B) $-\frac{1}{2}, \frac{9}{2}$ (C) $\frac{1}{2}, -\frac{9}{2}$ (D) $\frac{1}{2}, \frac{9}{2}$

25. ★ **MULTIPLE CHOICE** What are the solutions of $x^2 + 12x + 10 = 0$?

(A) $-6 \pm \sqrt{46}$ (B) $-6 \pm \sqrt{26}$ (C) $6 \pm \sqrt{26}$ (D) $6 \pm \sqrt{46}$

ERROR ANALYSIS *Describe* and correct the error in solving the given equation.

26. $x^2 - 14x = 11$

$$x^2 - 14x = 11$$
$$x^2 - 14x + 49 = 11$$
$$(x - 7)^2 = 11$$
$$x - 7 = \pm\sqrt{11}$$
$$x = 7 \pm \sqrt{11}$$

27. $x^2 - 2x - 4 = 0$

$$x^2 - 2x - 4 = 0$$
$$x^2 - 2x = 4$$
$$x^2 - 2x + 1 = 4 + 1$$
$$(x + 1)^2 = 5$$
$$x + 1 = \pm\sqrt{5}$$
$$x = 1 \pm \sqrt{5}$$

SOLVING EQUATIONS Solve the equation by completing the square. Round your solutions to the nearest hundredth, if necessary.

28. $2x^2 - 8x - 14 = 0$ **29.** $2x^2 + 24x + 10 = 0$ **30.** $3x^2 - 48x + 39 = 0$

31. $4y^2 + 4y - 7 = 0$ **32.** $9n^2 + 36n + 11 = 0$ **33.** $3w^2 - 18w - 20 = 0$

34. $3p^2 - 30p - 11 = 6p$ **35.** $3a^2 - 12a + 3 = -a^2 - 4$ **36.** $15c^2 - 51c - 30 = 9c + 15$

37. $7m^2 + 24m - 2 = m^2 - 9$ **38.** $g^2 + 2g + 0.4 = 0.9g^2 + g$ **39.** $11z^2 - 10z - 3 = -9z^2 + \frac{3}{4}$

GEOMETRY Find the value of x. Round your answer to the nearest hundredth, if necessary.

40. Area of triangle = 108 m^2

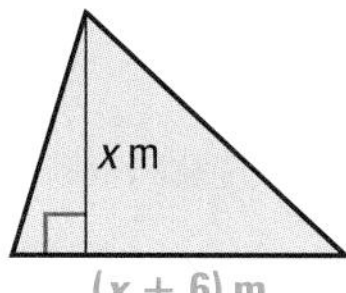

41. Area of rectangle = 288 $in.^2$

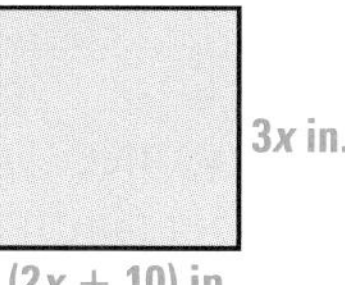

42. ★ **WRITING** How many solutions does $x^2 + bx = c$ have if $c < -\left(\frac{b}{2}\right)^2$? *Explain.*

43. **CHALLENGE** The product of two consecutive negative integers is 210. Find the integers.

44. **CHALLENGE** The product of two consecutive positive even integers is 288. Find the integers.

PROBLEM SOLVING

EXAMPLE 4 on p. 665 for Exs. 45–46

45. **LANDSCAPING** You are building a rectangular brick patio surrounded by crushed stone in a rectangular courtyard as shown. The crushed stone border has a uniform width x (in feet). You have enough money in your budget to purchase patio bricks to cover 140 square feet. Solve the equation $140 = (20 - 2x)(16 - 2x)$ to find the width of the border.

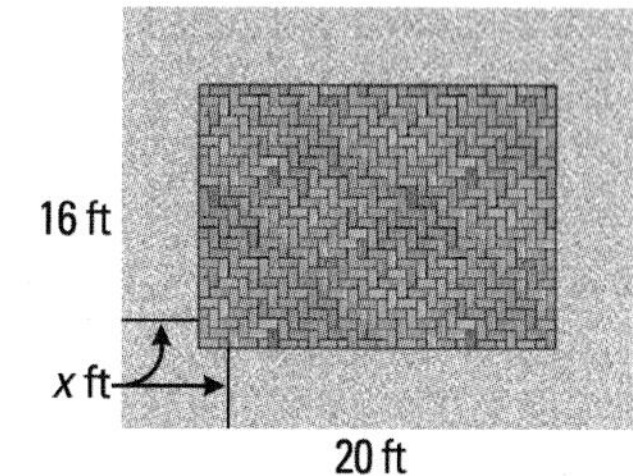

@HomeTutor for problem solving help at classzone.com

46. **TRAFFIC ENGINEERING** The distance d (in feet) that it takes a car to come to a complete stop on dry asphalt can be modeled by $d = 0.05s^2 + 1.1s$ where s is the speed of the car (in miles per hour). A car has 78 feet to come to a complete stop. Find the maximum speed at which the car can travel.

@HomeTutor for problem solving help at classzone.com

47. ◆ **MULTIPLE REPRESENTATIONS** For the period 1985–2001, the average salary y (in thousands of dollars) per season of a Major League Baseball player can be modeled by $y = 7x^2 - 4x + 392$ where x is the number of years since 1985.

a. **Solving an Equation** Write and solve an equation to find the year when the average salary was \$1,904,000.

b. **Drawing a Graph** Use a graph to check your solution to part (a).

48. **MULTI-STEP PROBLEM** You have 80 feet of fencing to make a rectangular horse pasture that covers 750 square feet. A barn will be used as one side of the pasture as shown.

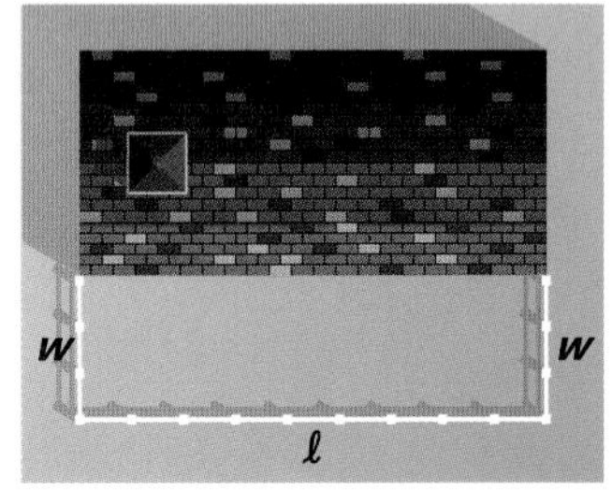

a. Write equations for the perimeter and area of the pasture.

b. Use substitution to solve the system of equations from part (a). What are the possible dimensions of the pasture?

49. ★ **SHORT RESPONSE** You purchase stock for \$16 per share, and you sell the stock 30 days later for \$23.50 per share. The price y (in dollars) of a share during the 30 day period can be modeled by $y = -0.025x^2 + x + 16$ where x is the number of days after the stock is purchased. Could you have sold the stock earlier for \$23.50 per share? *Explain.*

50. **SNOWBOARDING** During a "big air" competition, snowboarders launch themselves from a half pipe, perform tricks in the air, and land back in the half pipe.

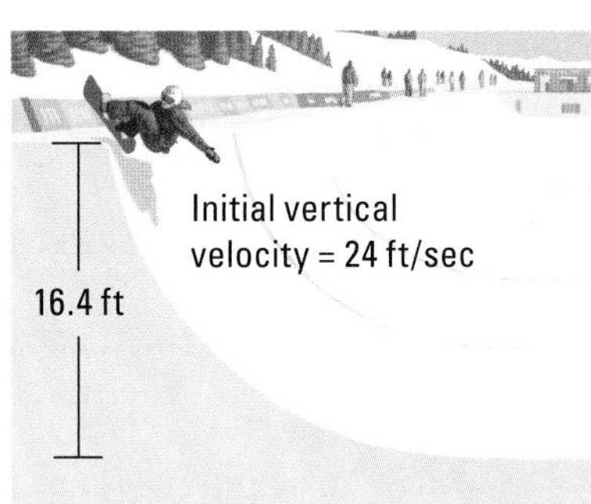

Cross section of a half pipe

a. **Model** Use the vertical motion model to write an equation that models the height h (in feet) of a snowboarder as a function of the time t (in seconds) she is in the air.

b. **Apply** How long is the snowboarder in the air if she lands 13.2 feet above the base of the half pipe? Round your answer to the nearest tenth of a second.

Animated **Algebra** at classzone.com

51. **CHALLENGE** You are knitting a rectangular scarf. The pattern you have created will result in a scarf that has a length of 60 inches and a width of 4 inches. However, you happen to have enough yarn to cover an area of 480 square inches. You decide to increase the dimensions of the scarf so that all of your yarn will be used. If the increase in the length is 10 times the increase in the width, what will the dimensions of the scarf be?

MIXED REVIEW

PREVIEW
Prepare for Lesson 10.6 in Exs. 52–57.

Evaluate the expression for the given value of x. *(p. 74)*

52. $3 + x - 6;\ x = 8$

53. $11 - (-x) + 15;\ x = -1$

54. $-x + 18 - 20;\ x = -10$

55. $32 - x - 5;\ x = 5$

56. $x + 14.7 - 16.2;\ x = 2.3$

57. $-9.2 - (-11.4) - x;\ x = -4.5$

Solve the proportion. *(p. 168)*

58. $\frac{8}{m-3} = \frac{4}{3}$

59. $\frac{3}{a} = \frac{5}{a+5}$

60. $\frac{c+2}{6} = \frac{2c-3}{5}$

Solve the equation.

61. $(x - 4)(x + 9) = 0$ *(p. 575)*

62. $x^2 - 15x + 26 = 0$ *(p. 583)*

63. $3x^2 + 10x + 7 = 0$ *(p. 593)*

64. $4x^2 - 20x + 25 = 0$ *(p. 600)*

EXTRA PRACTICE for Lesson 10.5, p. 947 **ONLINE QUIZ** at classzone.com

Extension

Use after Lesson 10.5

Graph Quadratic Functions in Vertex Form

GOAL Graph quadratic functions in vertex form.

Key Vocabulary
- **vertex form**

In Lesson 10.2, you graphed quadratic functions in standard form. Quadratic functions can also be written in **vertex form**, $y = a(x - h)^2 + k$ where $a \neq 0$. In this form, the vertex of the graph can be easily determined.

KEY CONCEPT *For Your Notebook*

Graph of Vertex Form $y = a(x - h)^2 + k$

The graph of $y = a(x - h)^2 + k$ is the graph of $y = ax^2$ translated h units horizontally and k units vertically.

Characteristics of the graph of $y = a(x - h)^2 + k$:

- The vertex is (h, k).
- The axis of symmetry is $x = h$.
- The graph opens up if $a > 0$, and the graph opens down if $a < 0$.

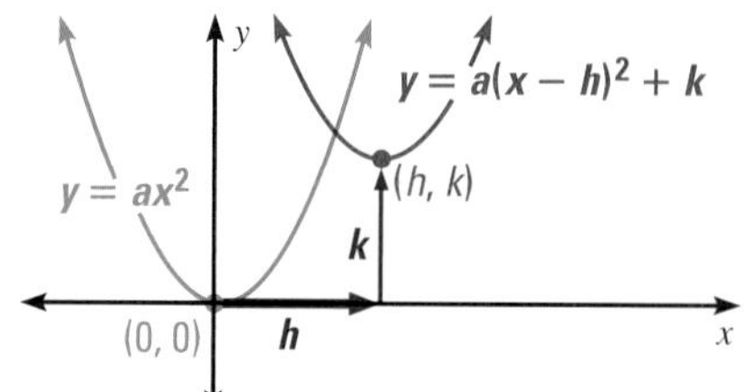

EXAMPLE 1 **Graph a quadratic function in vertex form**

Graph $y = -(x + 2)^2 + 3$.

Solution

STEP 1 **Identify** the values of a, h, and k: $a = -1$, $h = -2$, and $k = 3$. Because $a < 0$, the parabola opens down.

STEP 2 **Draw** the axis of symmetry, $x = -2$.

STEP 3 **Plot** the vertex $(h, k) = (-2, 3)$.

STEP 4 **Plot** four points. Evaluate the function for two x-values less than the x-coordinate of the vertex.

$\boldsymbol{x = -3}$: $y = -(-3 + 2)^2 + 3 = 2$

$\boldsymbol{x = -5}$: $y = -(-5 + 2)^2 + 3 = -6$

Plot the points $(-3, 2)$ and $(-5, -6)$ and their reflections, $(-1, 2)$ and $(1, -6)$, in the axis of symmetry.

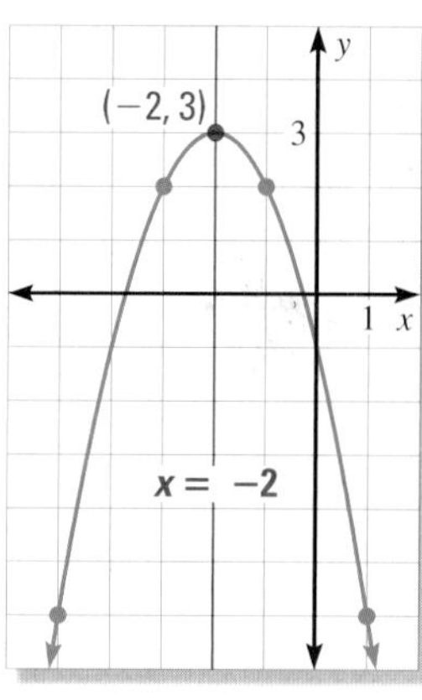

STEP 5 **Draw** a parabola through the plotted points.

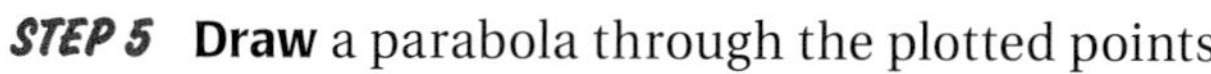

EXAMPLE 2 Graph a quadratic function

Graph $y = x^2 - 8x + 11$.

Solution

STEP 1 **Write** the function in vertex form by completing the square.

$y = x^2 - 8x + 11$	Write original function.
$y + \square = (x^2 - 8x + \square) + 11$	Prepare to complete the square.
$y + 16 = (x^2 - 8x + 16) + 11$	Add $\left(\frac{-8}{2}\right)^2 = (-4)^2 = 16$ to each side.
$y + 16 = (x - 4)^2 + 11$	Write $x^2 - 8x + 16$ as a square of a binomial.
$y = (x - 4)^2 - 5$	Subtract 16 from each side.

STEP 2 **Identify** the values of a, h, and k: $a = 1$, $h = 4$, and $k = -5$. Because $a > 0$, the parabola opens up.

STEP 3 **Draw** the axis of symmetry, $x = 4$.

STEP 4 **Plot** the vertex $(h, k) = (4, -5)$.

STEP 5 **Plot** four more points. Evaluate the function for two x-values less than the x-coordinate of the vertex.

$x = 3$: $y = (3 - 4)^2 - 5 = -4$
$x = 1$: $y = (1 - 4)^2 - 5 = 4$

Plot the points $(3, -4)$ and $(1, 4)$ and their reflections, $(5, -4)$ and $(7, 4)$, in the axis of symmetry.

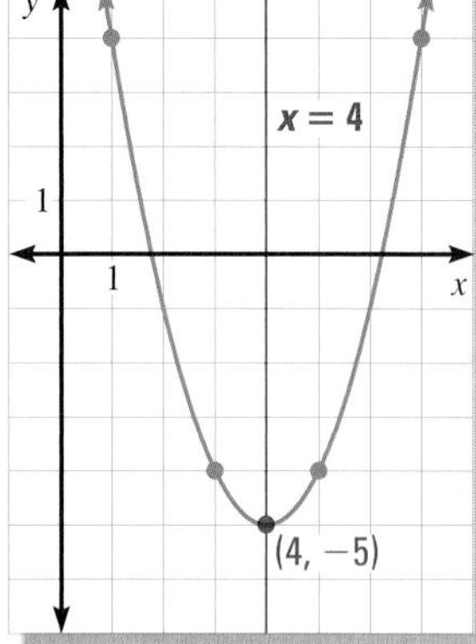

STEP 6 **Draw** a parabola through the plotted points.

PRACTICE

EXAMPLE 1
on p. 669
for Exs. 1–6

Graph the quadratic function. Label the vertex and axis of symmetry.

1. $y = (x + 2)^2 - 5$ **2.** $y = -(x - 4)^2 + 1$ **3.** $y = x^2 + 3$

4. $y = 3(x - 1)^2 - 2$ **5.** $y = -2(x + 5)^2 - 2$ **6.** $y = -\frac{1}{2}(x + 4)^2 + 4$

EXAMPLE 2
on p. 670
for Exs. 7–12

Write the function in vertex form, then graph the function. Label the vertex and axis of symmetry.

7. $y = x^2 - 12x + 36$ **8.** $y = x^2 + 8x + 15$ **9.** $y = -x^2 + 10x - 21$

10. $y = 2x^2 - 12x + 19$ **11.** $y = -3x^2 - 6x - 1$ **12.** $y = -\frac{1}{2}x^2 - 6x - 21$

13. Write an equation in vertex form of the parabola shown. Use the coordinates of the vertex and the coordinates of a point on the graph to write the equation.

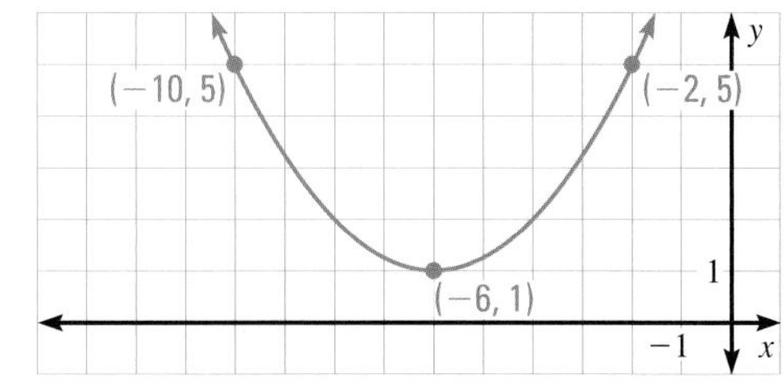

10.6 Solve Quadratic Equations by the Quadratic Formula

Before	You solved quadratic equations by completing the square.
Now	You will solve quadratic equations using the quadratic formula.
Why?	So you can solve a problem about film production, as in Example 3.

Key Vocabulary
- **quadratic formula**

By completing the square for the quadratic equation $ax^2 + bx + c = 0$, you can develop a formula that gives the solutions of any quadratic equation in standard form. This formula is called the **quadratic formula**. (The quadratic formula is developed on page 727.)

KEY CONCEPT *For Your Notebook*

The Quadratic Formula

The solutions of the quadratic equation $ax^2 + bx + c = 0$ are

$x = \dfrac{-b \pm \sqrt{b^2 - 4ac}}{2a}$ where $a \neq 0$ and $b^2 - 4ac \geq 0$.

★ EXAMPLE 1 Standardized Test Practice

What are the solutions of $3x^2 + 5x = 8$?

Ⓐ -1 and $-\frac{8}{3}$ Ⓑ -1 and $\frac{8}{3}$ Ⓒ 1 and $-\frac{8}{3}$ Ⓓ 1 and $\frac{8}{3}$

ANOTHER WAY
Instead of solving the equation, you can check the answer choices in the equation.

Solution

$3x^2 + 5x = 8$ **Write original equation.**

$3x^2 + 5x - 8 = 0$ **Write in standard form.**

$x = \dfrac{-b \pm \sqrt{b^2 - 4ac}}{2a}$ **Quadratic formula**

$x = \dfrac{-5 \pm \sqrt{5^2 - 4(3)(-8)}}{2(3)}$ **Substitute values in the quadratic formula: $a = 3$, $b = 5$, and $c = -8$.**

$= \dfrac{-5 \pm \sqrt{121}}{6}$ **Simplify.**

$= \dfrac{-5 \pm 11}{6}$ **Simplify the square root.**

The solutions of the equation are $\frac{-5 + 11}{6} = 1$ and $\frac{-5 - 11}{6} = -\frac{8}{3}$.

▶ The correct answer is C. Ⓐ Ⓑ Ⓒ Ⓓ

EXAMPLE 2 Solve a quadratic equation

Solve $2x^2 - 7 = x$.

$2x^2 - 7 = x$ — Write original equation.

$2x^2 - x - 7 = 0$ — Write in standard form.

$x = \frac{-b \pm \sqrt{b^2 - 4ac}}{2a}$ — Quadratic formula

$= \frac{-(-1) \pm \sqrt{(-1)^2 - 4(2)(-7)}}{2(2)}$ — Substitute values in the quadratic formula: $a = 2$, $b = -1$, and $c = -7$.

$= \frac{1 \pm \sqrt{57}}{4}$ — Simplify.

▶ The solutions are $\frac{1 + \sqrt{57}}{4} \approx 2.14$ and $\frac{1 - \sqrt{57}}{4} \approx -1.64$.

Animated Algebra at classzone.com

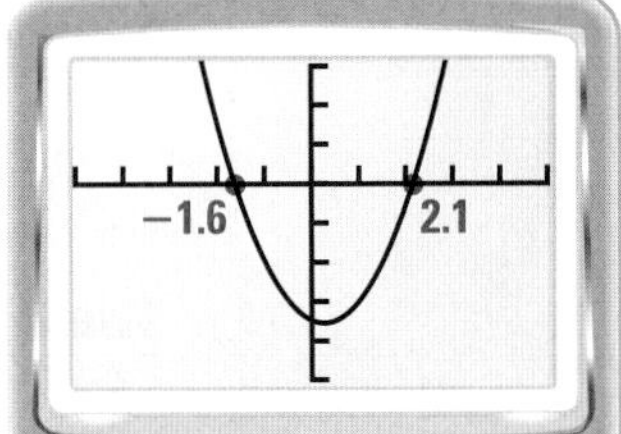

CHECK Write the equation in standard form, $2x^2 - x - 7 = 0$. Then graph the related function $y = 2x^2 - x - 7$. The x-intercepts are about -1.6 and 2.1. So, each solution checks.

✓ GUIDED PRACTICE for Examples 1 and 2

Use the quadratic formula to solve the equation. Round your solutions to the nearest hundredth, if necessary.

1. $x^2 - 8x + 16 = 0$ **2.** $3n^2 - 5n = -1$ **3.** $4z^2 = 7z + 2$

EXAMPLE 3 Use the quadratic formula

FILM PRODUCTION For the period 1971–2001, the number y of films produced in the world can be modeled by the function $y = 10x^2 - 94x + 3900$ where x is the number of years since 1971. In what year were 4200 films produced?

Solution

$y = 10x^2 - 94x + 3900$ — Write function.

$4200 = 10x^2 - 94x + 3900$ — Substitute 4200 for y.

$0 = 10x^2 - 94x - 300$ — Write in standard form.

$x = \frac{-(-94) \pm \sqrt{(-94)^2 - 4(10)(-300)}}{2(10)}$ — Substitute values in the quadratic formula: $a = 10$, $b = -94$, and $c = -300$.

$= \frac{94 \pm \sqrt{20{,}836}}{20}$ — Simplify.

The solutions of the equation are $\frac{94 + \sqrt{20{,}836}}{20} \approx 12$ and $\frac{94 - \sqrt{20{,}836}}{20} \approx -3$.

▶ There were 4200 films produced about 12 years after 1971, or in 1983.

INTERPRET SOLUTIONS
The solution -3 can be ignored because -3 represents the year 1968, which is not in the given time period.

GUIDED PRACTICE for Example 3

4. **WHAT IF?** In Example 3, find the year when 4750 films were produced.

CONCEPT SUMMARY *For Your Notebook*

Methods for Solving Quadratic Equations

Method	Lesson(s)	When to Use
Factoring	9.4–9.8	Use when a quadratic equation can be factored easily.
Graphing	10.3	Use when approximate solutions are adequate.
Finding square roots	10.4	Use when solving an equation that can be written in the form $x^2 = d$.
Completing the square	10.5	Can be used for *any* quadratic equation $ax^2 + bx + c = 0$ but is simplest to apply when $a = 1$ and b is an even number.
Quadratic formula	10.6	Can be used for *any* quadratic equation.

EXAMPLE 4 Choose a solution method

Tell what method you would use to solve the quadratic equation. ***Explain*** **your choice(s).**

a. $10x^2 - 7 = 0$ **b.** $x^2 + 4x = 0$ **c.** $5x^2 + 9x - 4 = 0$

Solution

a. The quadratic equation can be solved using square roots because the equation can be written in the form $x^2 = d$.

b. The equation can be solved by factoring because the expression $x^2 + 4x$ can be factored easily. Also, the equation can be solved by completing the square because the equation is of the form $ax^2 + bx + c = 0$ where $a = 1$ and b is an even number.

c. The quadratic equation cannot be factored easily, and completing the square will result in many fractions. So, the equation can be solved using the quadratic formula.

GUIDED PRACTICE for Example 4

Tell what method you would use to solve the quadratic equation. ***Explain*** **your choice(s).**

5. $x^2 + x - 6 = 0$ **6.** $x^2 - 9 = 0$ **7.** $x^2 + 6x = 5$

10.6 EXERCISES

HOMEWORK KEY

○ = **WORKED-OUT SOLUTIONS** on p. WS25 for Exs. 19 and 47

★ = **STANDARDIZED TEST PRACTICE** Exs. 2, 12, 25, and 50

◆ = **MULTIPLE REPRESENTATIONS** Ex. 49

SKILL PRACTICE

1. **VOCABULARY** What formula can be used to solve any quadratic equation?

2. ★ **WRITING** What method(s) would you use to solve $-x^2 + 8x = 1$? *Explain* your choice(s).

EXAMPLES 1 and 2 on pp. 671–672 for Exs. 3–27

SOLVING QUADRATIC EQUATIONS **Use the quadratic formula to find the roots of the equation. Round your solutions to the nearest hundredth, if necessary.**

3. $x^2 + 5x - 104 = 0$
4. $4x^2 - x - 18 = 0$
5. $6x^2 - 2x - 28 = 0$
6. $m^2 + 3m + 1 = 0$
7. $-z^2 + z + 14 = 0$
8. $-2n^2 - 5n + 16 = 0$
9. $4w^2 + 20w + 25 = 0$
10. $2t^2 + 3t - 11 = 0$
11. $-6g^2 + 9g + 8 = 0$

12. ★ **MULTIPLE CHOICE** What are the solutions of $10x^2 - 3x - 1 = 0$?

Ⓐ $-\frac{1}{5}$ and $-\frac{1}{2}$ Ⓑ $-\frac{1}{5}$ and $\frac{1}{2}$ Ⓒ $\frac{1}{5}$ and $-\frac{1}{2}$ Ⓓ $\frac{1}{5}$ and $\frac{1}{2}$

SOLVING QUADRATIC EQUATIONS **Use the quadratic formula to solve the equation. Round your solutions to the nearest hundredth, if necessary.**

13. $x^2 - 5x = 14$
14. $3x^2 - 4 = 11x$
15. $9 = 7x^2 - 2x$
16. $2m^2 + 9m + 7 = 3$
17. $-10 = r^2 - 10r + 12$
18. $3g^2 - 6g - 14 = 3g$
19. $6z^2 = 2z^2 + 7z + 5$
20. $8h^2 + 8 = 6 - 9h$
21. $4t^2 - 3t = 5 - 3t^2$
22. $-4y^2 - 3y + 3 = 2y + 4$
23. $7n + 5 = -3n^2 + 2$
24. $5w^2 + 4 = w + 6$

25. ★ **MULTIPLE CHOICE** What are the solutions of $x^2 + 14x = 2x - 11$?

Ⓐ -2 and -22 Ⓑ -1 and -11 Ⓒ 1 and 11 Ⓓ 2 and 22

ERROR ANALYSIS ***Describe*** **and correct the error in solving the equation.**

26. $7x^2 - 5x - 1 = 0$

$$x = \frac{-5 \pm \sqrt{(-5)^2 - 4(7)(-1)}}{2(7)}$$
$$= \frac{-5 \pm \sqrt{53}}{14}$$
$$x \approx -0.88 \text{ and } x \approx 0.16$$

27. $-2x^2 + 3x = 1$

$$x = \frac{-3 \pm \sqrt{3^2 - 4(-2)(1)}}{2(-2)}$$
$$= \frac{-3 \pm \sqrt{17}}{-4}$$
$$x \approx -0.28 \text{ and } x \approx 1.78$$

EXAMPLE 4 on p. 673 for Exs. 28–33

CHOOSING A METHOD **Tell what method(s) you would use to solve the quadratic equation.** ***Explain*** **your choice(s).**

28. $3x^2 - 27 = 0$
29. $5x^2 = 25$
30. $2x^2 - 12x = 0$
31. $m^2 + 5m + 6 = 0$
32. $z^2 - 4z + 1 = 0$
33. $-10g^2 + 13g = 4$

SOLVING QUADRATIC EQUATIONS Solve the quadratic equation using any method. Round your solutions to the nearest hundredth, if necessary.

34. $-2x^2 = -32$

35. $x^2 - 8x = -16$

36. $x^2 + 2x - 6 = 0$

37. $x^2 = 12x - 36$

38. $x^2 + 4x = 9$

39. $-4x^2 + x = -17$

40. $11x^2 - 1 = 6x^2 + 2$

41. $-2x^2 + 5 = 3x^2 - 10x$

42. $(x + 13)^2 = 25$

GEOMETRY Use the given area A of the rectangle to find the value of x. Then give the dimensions of the rectangle.

43. $A = 91 \text{ m}^2$

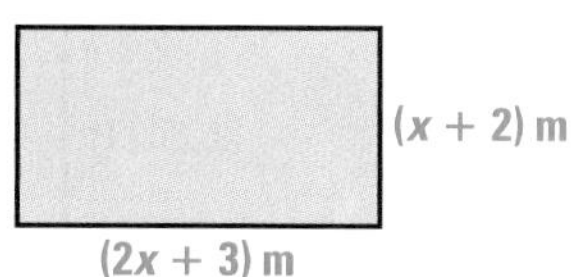

44. $A = 209 \text{ ft}^2$

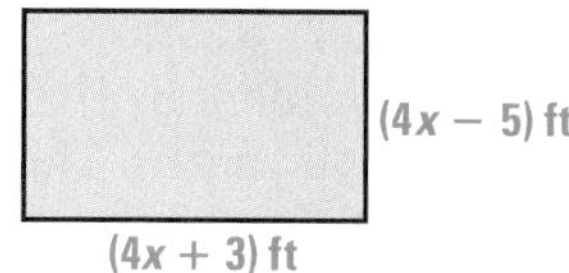

45. **CHALLENGE** The solutions of the quadratic equation $ax^2 + bx + c = 0$ are $x = \frac{-b + \sqrt{b^2 - 4ac}}{2a}$ and $x = \frac{-b - \sqrt{b^2 - 4ac}}{2a}$. Find the mean of the solutions. How is the mean of the solutions related to the graph of $y = ax^2 + bx + c$? *Explain.*

PROBLEM SOLVING

EXAMPLE 3 on p. 672 for Exs. 46–47

46. **ADVERTISING** For the period 1990–2000, the amount of money y (in billions of dollars) spent on advertising in the U.S. can be modeled by the function $y = 0.93x^2 + 2.2x + 130$ where x is the number of years since 1990. In what year was 164 billion dollars spent on advertising?

@HomeTutor for problem solving help at classzone.com

47. **CELL PHONES** For the period 1985–2001, the number y (in millions) of cell phone service subscribers in the U.S. can be modeled by the function $y = 0.7x^2 - 4.3x + 5.5$ where x is the number of years since 1985. In what year were there 16,000,000 cell phone service subscribers?

@HomeTutor for problem solving help at classzone.com

48. **MULTI-STEP PROBLEM** A football is punted from a height of 2.5 feet above the ground and with an initial vertical velocity of 45 feet per second.

a. Use the vertical motion model to write an equation that gives the height h (in feet) of the football as a function of the time t (in seconds) after it has been punted.

b. The football is caught 5.5 feet above the ground as shown in the diagram. Find the amount of time that the football is in the air.

49. **MULTIPLE REPRESENTATIONS** For the period 1997–2002, the number y (in thousands) of 16- and 17-year-olds employed in the United States can be modeled by the function $y = -46.7x^2 + 169x + 2650$ where x is the number of years since 1997.

a. **Solving an Equation** Write and solve an equation to find the year during which 2,500,000 16- and 17-year-olds were employed.

b. **Drawing a Graph** Graph the function on a graphing calculator. Use the *trace* feature to find the year when 2,500,000 16- and 17-year-olds were employed. Use the graph to check your answer from part (a).

50. ★ **SHORT RESPONSE** NASA creates a weightless environment by flying a plane in a series of parabolic paths. The height h (in feet) of a plane after t seconds in a parabolic flight path can be modeled by the graph of $h = -11t^2 + 700t + 21{,}000$. The passengers experience a weightless environment when the height of the plane is greater than or equal to 30,800 feet. Find the period of weightlessness on such a flight. *Explain.*

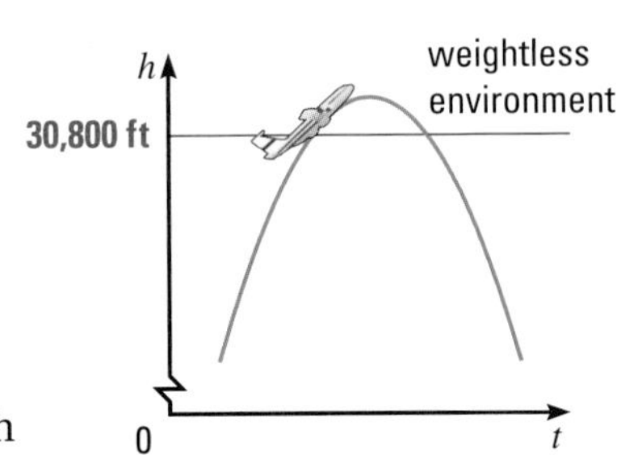

51. **CHALLENGE** Mineral deposits have formed a uniform coating that is 4 millimeters thick on the inside of a water pipe. The cross-sectional area of the pipe has decreased by 10%. What was the original diameter of the pipe (to the nearest tenth of a millimeter)?

MIXED REVIEW

PREVIEW Prepare for Lesson 10.7 in Exs. 52–55.

Evaluate the expression.

52. $9x^2$ when $x = 2$ *(p. 8)*

53. $\frac{6 - 5w}{2w}$ when $w = 10$ *(p. 103)*

54. $2 + \sqrt{x}$ when $x = 121$ *(p. 110)*

55. $8 - \sqrt{x}$ when $x = 49$ *(p. 110)*

Graph the equation.

56. $x = 8$ *(p. 215)*

57. $3x - y = 2$ *(p. 225)*

58. $y = -\frac{2}{5}x - 6$ *(p. 244)*

59. $y = -7x^2$ *(p. 628)*

60. $y = 8x^2 - 2$ *(p. 628)*

61. $y = -x^2 - 6x + 5$ *(p. 635)*

QUIZ *for Lessons 10.4–10.6*

Solve the equation using square roots. *(p. 652)*

1. $3x^2 - 48 = 0$

2. $-6x^2 = -24$

3. $x^2 + 5 = 16$

Solve the equation by completing the square. *(p. 663)*

4. $x^2 + 2x + 6 = 0$

5. $x^2 + 10x - 12 = 0$

6. $x^2 - 8x = -6$

7. $x^2 - 12x = 30$

8. $x^2 - 5x = -\frac{9}{4}$

9. $x^2 + x = -7.75$

Solve the equation using the quadratic formula. *(p. 671)*

10. $x^2 + 4x + 1 = 0$

11. $-3x^2 + 3x = -1$

12. $4x^2 - 11x = 3$

EXTRA PRACTICE for Lesson 10.6, p. 947 **ONLINE QUIZ** at classzone.com

10.7 The Discriminant

QUESTION **How can you determine the number of solutions of a quadratic equation?**

In the quadratic formula, $x = \frac{-b \pm \sqrt{b^2 - 4ac}}{2a}$, the expression $b^2 - 4ac$ is called the *discriminant.*

EXPLORE **Determine how the discriminant is related to the number of solutions of a quadratic equation**

STEP 1 ***Find the number of solutions***

Find the number of solutions of the equations below by finding the number of x-intercepts of the graphs of the related functions.

$0 = x^2 - 6x - 7$

$0 = x^2 - 6x + 9$

$0 = x^2 - 6x + 12$

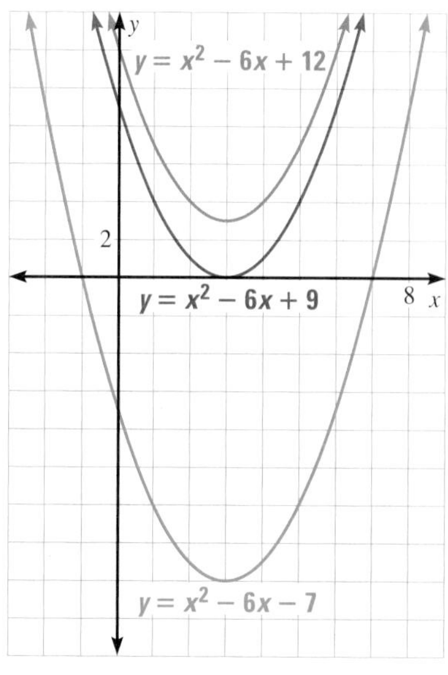

STEP 2 ***Find the value of*** $b^2 - 4ac$

For each equation in Step 1, determine whether the value of $b^2 - 4ac$ is positive, negative, or zero.

STEP 3 ***Make a table***

Organize your results from Steps 1 and 2 in a table as shown.

Equation	Number of solutions	Value of $b^2 - 4ac$
$0 = x^2 - 6x - 7$	?	?
$0 = x^2 - 6x + 9$	?	?
$0 = x^2 - 6x + 12$	?	?

STEP 4 ***Make a conjecture***

Make a generalization about the value of the discriminant and the number of solutions of a quadratic equation.

DRAW CONCLUSIONS **Use your observations to complete these exercises**

1. Repeat Steps 1–3 using the following equations: $x^2 + 4x - 5 = 0$, $x^2 + 4x + 4 = 0$, and $x^2 + 4x + 6 = 0$. Is your conjecture still true?
2. Notice that the expression $b^2 - 4ac$ is under the radical sign in the quadratic formula. Use this observation to explain why the value of $b^2 - 4ac$ determines the number of solutions of a quadratic equation.

10.7 Interpret the Discriminant

Before	You used the quadratic formula.
Now	You will use the value of the discriminant.
Why?	So you can solve a problem about gymnastics, as in Ex. 49.

Key Vocabulary
- **discriminant**

In the quadratic formula, the expression $b^2 - 4ac$ is called the **discriminant** of the associated equation $ax^2 + bx + c = 0$.

$$x = \frac{-b \pm \sqrt{b^2 - 4ac}}{2a} \longleftarrow \text{discriminant}$$

Because the discriminant is under the radical symbol, the value of the discriminant can be used to determine the number of solutions of a quadratic equation and the number of x-intercepts of the graph of the related function.

READING Recall that in this course, *solutions* refers to real-number solutions.

KEY CONCEPT *For Your Notebook*

Using the Discriminant of $ax^2 + bx + c = 0$

Value of the discriminant	$b^2 - 4ac > 0$	$b^2 - 4ac = 0$	$b^2 - 4ac < 0$
Number of solutions	Two solutions	One solution	No solution
Graph of $y = ax^2 + bx + c$	Two x-intercepts	One x-intercept	No x-intercept

EXAMPLE 1 **Use the discriminant**

	Equation $ax^2 + bx + c = 0$	Discriminant $b^2 - 4ac$	Number of solutions
a.	$2x^2 + 6x + 5 = 0$	$6^2 - 4(2)(5) = -4$	No solution
b.	$x^2 - 7 = 0$	$0^2 - 4(1)(-7) = 28$	Two solutions
c.	$4x^2 - 12x + 9 = 0$	$(-12)^2 - 4(4)(9) = 0$	One solution

EXAMPLE 2 Find the number of solutions

Tell whether the equation $3x^2 - 7 = 2x$ has *two solutions, one solution,* or *no solution.*

Solution

STEP 1 **Write** the equation in standard form.

$3x^2 - 7 = 2x$ Write equation.

$3x^2 - 2x - 7 = 0$ Subtract $2x$ from each side.

STEP 2 **Find** the value of the discriminant.

$b^2 - 4ac = (-2)^2 - 4(3)(-7)$ Substitute 3 for a, −2 for b, and −7 for c.

$= 88$ Simplify.

▶ The discriminant is positive, so the equation has two solutions.

✓ GUIDED PRACTICE for Examples 1 and 2

Tell whether the equation has *two solutions, one solution,* or *no solution.*

1. $x^2 + 4x + 3 = 0$
2. $2x^2 - 5x + 6 = 0$
3. $-x^2 + 2x = 1$

EXAMPLE 3 Find the number of x-intercepts

Find the number of x-intercepts of the graph of $y = x^2 + 5x + 8$.

Solution

Find the number of solutions of the equation $0 = x^2 + 5x + 8$.

$b^2 - 4ac = (5)^2 - 4(1)(8)$ Substitute 1 for a, 5 for b, and 8 for c.

$= -7$ Simplify.

▶ The discriminant is negative, so the equation has no solution. This means that the graph of $y = x^2 + 5x + 8$ has no x-intercepts.

CHECK You can use a graphing calculator to check the answer. Notice that the graph of $y = x^2 + 5x + 8$ has no x-intercepts.

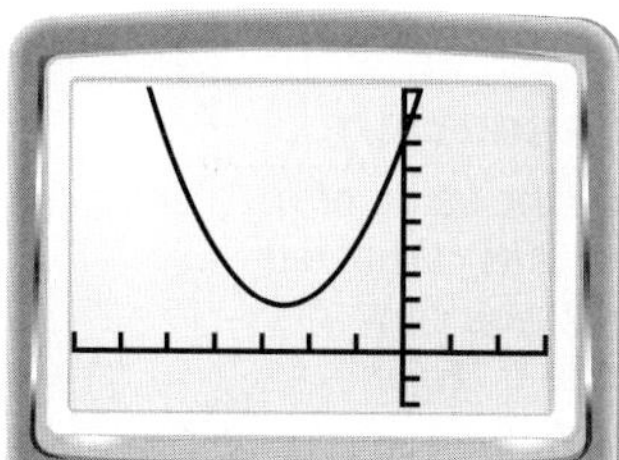

✓ GUIDED PRACTICE for Example 3

Find the number of x-intercepts of the graph of the function.

4. $y = x^2 + 10x + 25$
5. $y = x^2 - 9x$
6. $y = -x^2 + 2x - 4$

EXAMPLE 4 Solve a multi-step problem

FOUNTAINS The Centennial Fountain in Chicago shoots a water arc that can be modeled by the graph of the equation $y = -0.006x^2 + 1.2x + 10$ where x is the horizontal distance (in feet) from the river's north shore and y is the height (in feet) above the river. Does the water arc reach a height of 50 feet? If so, about how far from the north shore is the water arc 50 feet above the water?

Solution

STEP 1 **Write** a quadratic equation. You want to know whether the water arc reaches a height of 50 feet, so let $y = 50$. Then write the quadratic equation in standard form.

$y = -0.006x^2 + 1.2x + 10$ **Write given equation.**

$50 = -0.006x^2 + 1.2x + 10$ **Substitute 50 for *y*.**

$0 = -0.006x^2 + 1.2x - 40$ **Subtract 50 from each side.**

STEP 2 **Find** the value of the discriminant of $0 = -0.006x^2 + 1.2x - 40$.

$b^2 - 4ac = (1.2)^2 - 4(-0.006)(-40)$ $a = -0.006, b = 1.2, c = -40$

$= 0.48$ **Simplify.**

STEP 3 **Interpret** the discriminant. Because the discriminant is positive, the equation has two solutions. So, the water arc reaches a height of 50 feet at two points on the water arc.

STEP 4 **Solve** the equation $0 = -0.006x^2 + 1.2x - 40$ to find the distance from the north shore where the water arc is 50 feet above the water.

$x = \frac{-b \pm \sqrt{b^2 - 4ac}}{2a}$ **Quadratic formula**

$= \frac{-1.2 \pm \sqrt{0.48}}{2(-0.006)}$ **Substitute values in the quadratic formula.**

$x \approx 42$ *or* $x \approx 158$ **Use a calculator.**

▶ The water arc is 50 feet above the water about 42 feet from the north shore and about 158 feet from the north shore.

USE A SHORTCUT
Because the value of $b^2 - 4ac$ was calculated in Step 2, you can substitute 0.48 for $b^2 - 4ac$.

✓ GUIDED PRACTICE for Example 4

7. **WHAT IF?** In Example 4, does the water arc reach a height of 70 feet? If so, about how far from the north shore is the water arc 70 feet above the water?

10.7 EXERCISES

HOMEWORK KEY

○ = **WORKED-OUT SOLUTIONS** on p. WS25 for Exs. 9 and 47

★ = **STANDARDIZED TEST PRACTICE** Exs. 2, 18, 19, 40, 41, and 47

SKILL PRACTICE

1. **VOCABULARY** Write the quadratic formula and circle the expression that represents the discriminant.

2. ★ **WRITING** *Explain* how the discriminant of $ax^2 + bx + c = 0$ is related to the graph of $y = ax^2 + bx + c$.

EXAMPLES 1 and 2 on pp. 678–679 for Exs. 3–21

USING THE DISCRIMINANT **Tell whether the equation has *two solutions, one solution,* or *no solution.***

3. $x^2 + x + 1 = 0$
4. $2x^2 - 5x - 6 = 0$
5. $-2x^2 + 8x - 4 = 0$
6. $3m^2 - 6m + 7 = 0$
7. $9v^2 - 6v + 1 = 0$
8. $-3q^2 + 8 = 0$
9. $25p^2 - 16p = 0$
10. $2h^2 + 3 = 4h$
11. $10 = x^2 - 5x$
12. $\frac{1}{4}z^2 + 2 = z$
13. $-3g^2 - 4g = \frac{4}{3}$
14. $8r^2 + 10r - 1 = 4r$
15. $3n^2 + 3 = 10n - 3n^2$
16. $8x^2 + 9 = 4x^2 - 4x + 8$
17. $w^2 - 7w + 29 = 4 - 7w$

18. ★ **MULTIPLE CHOICE** What is the value of the discriminant of the equation $5x^2 - 7x - 2 = 0$?

Ⓐ -9 Ⓑ 9 Ⓒ 59 Ⓓ 89

19. ★ **MULTIPLE CHOICE** How many solutions does $-x^2 + 4x = 8$ have?

Ⓐ None Ⓑ One Ⓒ Two Ⓓ Three

ERROR ANALYSIS ***Describe*** **and correct the error in finding the number of solutions of the equation.**

20. $4x^2 + 12x + 9 = 0$

$$b^2 - 4ac = 12^2 - 4(4)(9)$$
$$= 144 - 144$$
$$= 0$$

The equation has two solutions.

21. $3x^2 - 7x - 4 = -9$

$$b^2 - 4ac = (-7)^2 - 4(3)(-4)$$
$$= 49 - (-48)$$
$$= 97$$

The equation has two solutions.

EXAMPLE 3 on p. 679 for Exs. 22–30

FINDING THE NUMBER OF x-INTERCEPTS **Find the number of x-intercepts of the graph of the function.**

22. $y = x^2 - 2x - 4$
23. $y = 2x^2 - x - 1$
24. $y = 4x^2 + 4x + 1$
25. $y = 2x^2 - 5x + 5$
26. $y = x^2 - 6x + 9$
27. $y = 6x^2 + x + 2$
28. $y = -13x^2 + 2x + 6$
29. $y = \frac{1}{4}x^2 - 3x + 9$
30. $y = \frac{2}{3}x^2 - 5x + 12$

REASONING **Give a value of c for which the equation has (a) two solutions, (b) one solution, and (c) no solution.**

31. $x^2 - 2x + c = 0$
32. $x^2 - 8x + c = 0$
33. $4x^2 + 12x + c = 0$

USING THE DISCRIMINANT Tell whether the vertex of the graph of the function lies above, below, or on the x-axis. *Explain* your reasoning.

34. $y = x^2 - 3x + 2$

35. $y = 3x^2 - 6x + 3$

36. $y = 6x^2 - 2x + 4$

37. $y = -15x^2 + 10x - 25$

38. $y = -3x^2 - 4x + 8$

39. $y = 9x^2 - 24x + 16$

40. ★ **OPEN-ENDED** Write a function of the form $y = ax^2 + bx + c$ whose graph has one x-intercept.

41. ★ **EXTENDED RESPONSE** Use the rectangular prism shown.

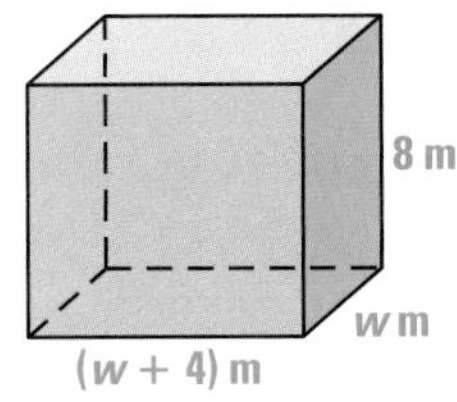

a. The surface area of the prism is 314 square meters. Write an equation that you can solve to find the value of w.

b. Use the discriminant to determine the number of values of w in the equation from part (a).

c. Solve the equation. Do the value(s) of w make sense in the context of the problem? *Explain.*

CHALLENGE Find all values of k for which the equation has (a) two solutions, (b) one solution, and (c) no solution.

42. $2x^2 + x + 3k = 0$

43. $x^2 - 4kx + 36 = 0$

44. $kx^2 + 5x - 16 = 0$

PROBLEM SOLVING

EXAMPLE 4 on p. 680 for Exs. 45–46

45. BIOLOGY The amount y (in milliliters per gram of body mass per hour) of oxygen consumed by a parakeet during flight can be modeled by the function $y = 0.06x^2 - 4x + 87$ where x is the speed (in kilometers per hour) of the parakeet.

a. Use the discriminant to show that it is possible for a parakeet to consume 25 milliliters of oxygen per gram of body mass per hour.

b. Find the speed(s) at which the parakeet consumes 25 milliliters of oxygen per gram of body mass per hour. Round your solution(s) to the nearest tenth.

@HomeTutor for problem solving help at classzone.com

46. FOOD For the period 1950–1999, the average amount y (in pounds per person per year) of butter consumed in the United States can be modeled by $y = 0.0051x^2 - 0.37x + 11$ where x is the number of years since 1950. According to the model, did the butter consumption in the United States ever reach 5 pounds per person per year? If so, in what year(s)?

@HomeTutor for problem solving help at classzone.com

47. ★ **SHORT RESPONSE** The frame of the tent shown is defined by a rectangular base and two parabolic arches that connect the opposite corners of the base. The graph of $y = -0.18x^2 + 1.6x$ models the height y (in feet) of one of the arches x feet along the diagonal of the base. Can a child that is 4 feet tall walk under one of the arches without having to bend over? *Explain.*

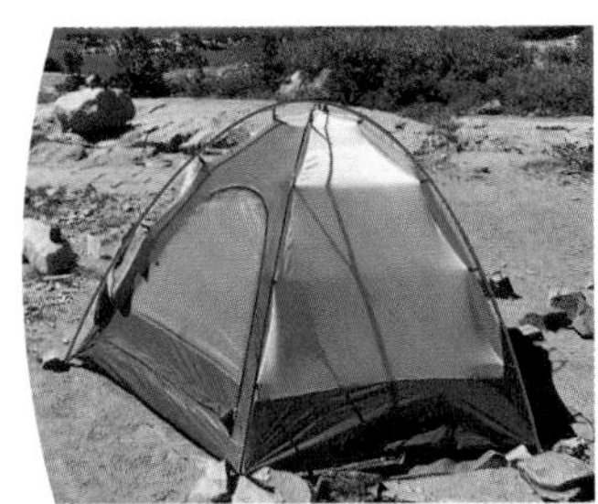

○ = WORKED-OUT SOLUTIONS on p. WS1 ★ = STANDARDIZED TEST PRACTICE

48. **SCIENCE** Between the months of April and September, the number y of hours of daylight per day in Seattle, Washington, can be modeled by $y = -0.00046x^2 + 0.076x + 13$ where x is the number of days since April 1.

a. Do any of the days between April and September in Seattle have 17 hours of daylight? If so, how many?

b. Do any of the days between April and September in Seattle have 14 hours of daylight? If so, how many?

49. **MULTI-STEP PROBLEM** During a trampoline competition, a trampolinist leaves the mat when her center of gravity is 6 feet above the ground. She has an initial vertical velocity of 32 feet per second.

a. Use the vertical motion model to write an equation that models the height h (in feet) of the center of gravity of the trampolinist as a function of the time t (in seconds) into her jump.

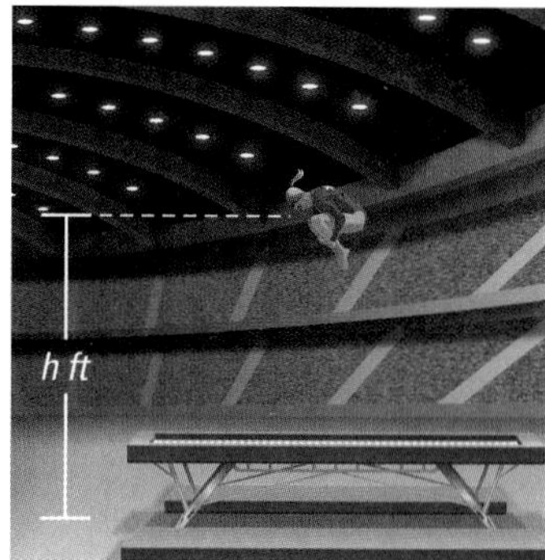

b. Does her center of gravity reach a height of 24 feet during the jump? If so, at what time(s)?

c. On another jump, the trampolinist leaves the mat when her center of gravity is 6 feet above the ground and with an initial vertical velocity of 35 feet per second. Does her center of gravity reach a height of 24 feet on this jump? If so, at what time(s)?

50. **CHALLENGE** Last year, a manufacturer sold backpacks for \$24 each. At this price, the manufacturer sold about 1000 backpacks per week. A marketing analyst predicts that for every \$1 reduction in the price of the backpack, the manufacturer will sell 100 more backpacks per week.

a. Write a function that models the weekly revenue R (in dollars) that the manufacturer will receive for x reductions of \$1 in the price of the backpack.

b. Is it possible for the manufacturer to receive a weekly revenue of \$28,000? \$30,000? What is the maximum weekly revenue that the manufacturer can receive? *Explain* your answers using the discriminants of quadratic equations.

MIXED REVIEW

PREVIEW
Prepare for Lesson 10.8 in Exs. 51–56.

Graph the function.

51. $y = 5x - 10$ *(p. 225)*

52. $y = \frac{1}{4}x$ *(p. 244)*

53. $y = \frac{3}{4}x - 5$ *(p. 244)*

54. $y = 5^x$ *(p. 520)*

55. $y = (0.2)^x$ *(p. 531)*

56. $y = 6x^2 - 3$ *(p. 628)*

Solve the equation.

57. $a + 5 = 2$ *(p. 134)*

58. $f - 6 = 13$ *(p. 134)*

59. $4z - 3 = -7$ *(p. 141)*

60. $9w + 4 = -41$ *(p. 141)*

61. $2b - b - 6 = 8$ *(p. 148)*

62. $5 + 2(x - 4) = 9$ *(p. 148)*

Solve the equation by factoring. *(p. 593)*

63. $2x^2 - 3x - 5 = 0$

64. $4n^2 + 2n - 6 = 0$

65. $5a^2 + 21a + 4 = 0$

10.8 Compare Linear, Exponential, and Quadratic Models

Before You graphed linear, exponential, and quadratic functions.

Now You will compare linear, exponential, and quadratic models.

Why? So you can solve a problem about biology, as in Ex. 23.

Key Vocabulary
- **linear function,** *p. 217*
- **exponential function,** *p. 520*
- **quadratic function,** *p. 628*

So far you have studied linear functions, exponential functions, and quadratic functions. You can use these functions to model data.

KEY CONCEPT *For Your Notebook*

Linear, Exponential, and Quadratic Functions

Linear Function	Exponential Function	Quadratic Function
$y = mx + b$	$y = ab^x$	$y = ax^2 + bx + c$

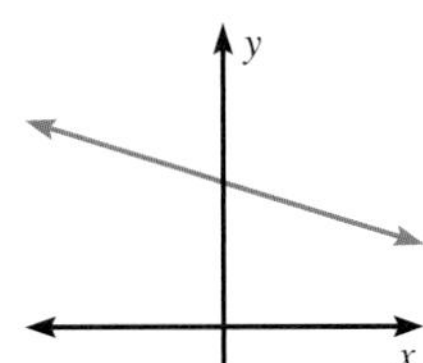

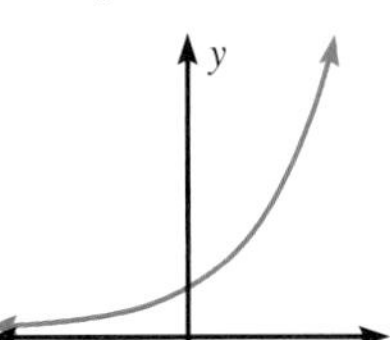

EXAMPLE 1 Choose functions using sets of ordered pairs

Use a graph to tell whether the ordered pairs represent a *linear function*, an *exponential function*, or a *quadratic function*.

a. $\left(-4, \frac{1}{32}\right), \left(-2, \frac{1}{8}\right), \left(0, \frac{1}{2}\right), (2, 2), (4, 8)$

b. $(-4, 1), (-2, 2), (0, 3), (2, 4), (4, 5)$

c. $(-4, 5), (-2, 2), (0, 1), (2, 2), (4, 5)$

Solution

a. Exponential function

b.

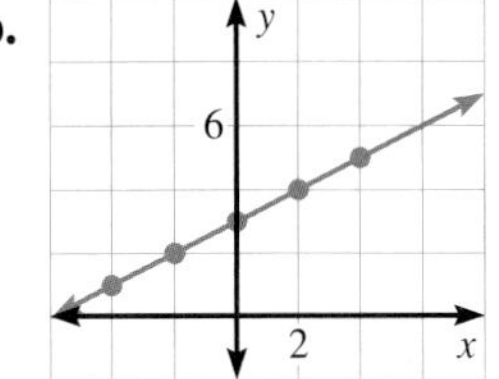

Linear function

c.

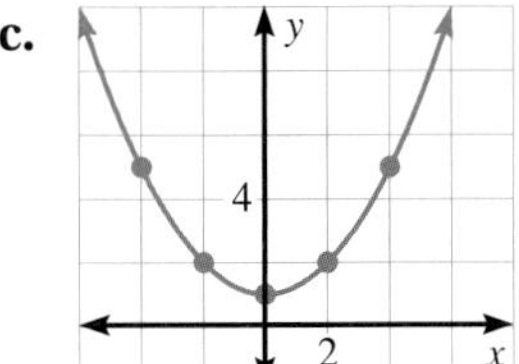

Quadratic function

Animated Algebra at classzone.com

DIFFERENCES AND RATIOS A table of values represents a linear function if the *differences* of successive y-values are all equal. A table of values represents an exponential function if the *ratios* of successive y-values are all equal. In both cases, the increments between successive x-values need to be equal.

Linear function: $y = 3x + 5$

x	−1	0	1	2
y	2	5	8	11

Differences: $5 - 2 = 3$ 3 3

Exponential function: $y = 0.5(2)^x$

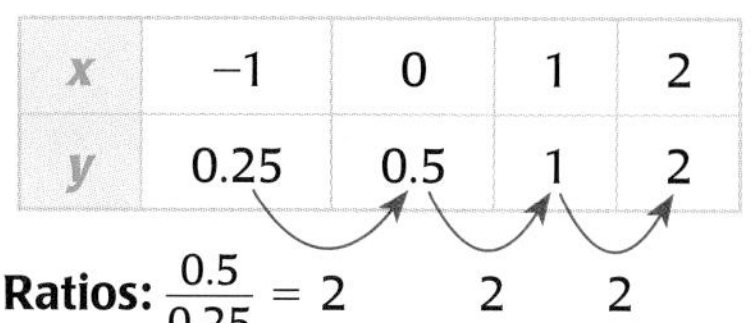

x	−1	0	1	2
y	0.25	0.5	1	2

Ratios: $\frac{0.5}{0.25} = 2$ 2 2

You can use differences to tell whether a table of values represents a quadratic function, as shown.

CHECK VALUES OF x
When deciding what function is represented by a table of values, be sure that the values of x are increasing by the same amount.

Quadratic function: $y = x^2 - 2x + 2$

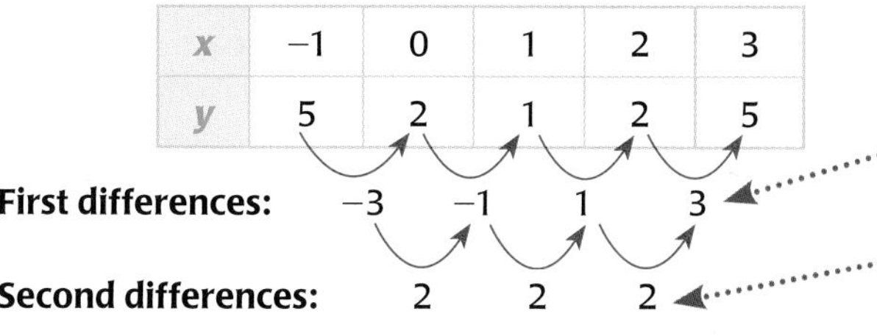

x	−1	0	1	2	3
y	5	2	1	2	5

First differences: −3 −1 1 3 ← First find the differences of successive y-values, or *first differences*.

Second differences: 2 2 2 ← Then find the differences of successive first differences, or *second differences*.

The table of values represents a quadratic function if the second differences are all equal.

EXAMPLE 2 Identify functions using differences or ratios

Use differences or ratios to tell whether the table of values represents a *linear function*, an *exponential function*, or a *quadratic function*.

a.

x	−2	−1	0	1	2
y	−6	−6	−4	0	6

First differences: 0 2 4 6

Second differences: 2 2 2

▶ The table of values represents a quadratic function.

b.

x	−2	−1	0	1	2
y	−2	1	4	7	10

Differences: 3 3 3 3

▶ The table of values represents a linear function.

✓ GUIDED PRACTICE for Examples 1 and 2

1. Tell whether the ordered pairs represent a *linear function*, an *exponential function*, or a *quadratic function*: (0, −1.5), (1, −0.5), (2, 2.5), (3, 7.5).

2. Tell whether the table of values represents a *linear function*, an *exponential function*, or a *quadratic function*.

x	−2	−1	0	1
y	0.08	0.4	2	10

WRITING AN EQUATION When you decide that a set of ordered pairs represents a linear, an exponential, or a quadratic function, you can write an equation for the function. In this lesson, when you write an equation for a quadratic function, the equation will have the form $y = ax^2$.

EXAMPLE 3 Write an equation for a function

Tell whether the table of values represents a *linear function*, an *exponential function*, or a *quadratic function*. Then write an equation for the function.

x	−2	−1	0	1	2
y	2	0.5	0	0.5	2

Solution

STEP 1 **Determine** which type of function the table of values represents.

x	−2	−1	0	1	2
y	2	0.5	0	0.5	2

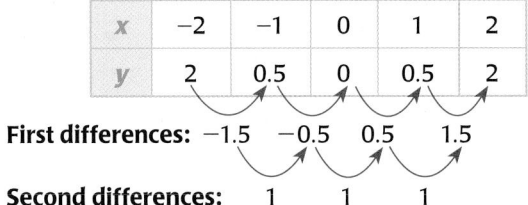

First differences: −1.5 −0.5 0.5 1.5

Second differences: 1 1 1

The table of values represents a quadratic function because the second differences are equal.

STEP 2 **Write** an equation for the quadratic function. The equation has the form $y = ax^2$. Find the value of a by using the coordinates of a point that lies on the graph, such as (1, 0.5).

$y = ax^2$ **Write equation for quadratic function.**

$0.5 = a(1)^2$ **Substitute 1 for *x* and 0.5 for *y*.**

$0.5 = a$ **Solve for *a*.**

AVOID ERRORS
In Example 3, do not use (0, 0) to find the value of *a*, even though (0, 0) lies on the graph of $y = ax^2$. If you do, you will obtain an undefined value for *a*.

▶ The equation is $y = 0.5x^2$.

CHECK Plot the ordered pairs from the table. Then graph $y = 0.5x^2$ to see that the graph passes through the plotted points.

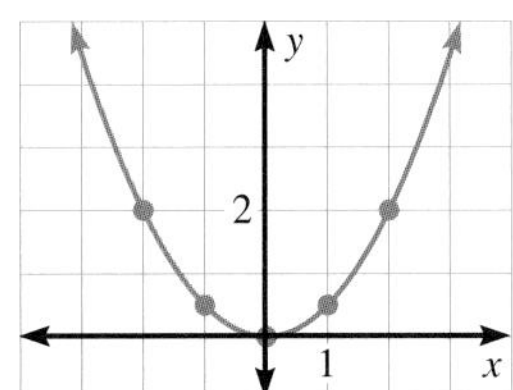

✓ GUIDED PRACTICE for Example 3

Tell whether the table of values represents a *linear function*, an *exponential function*, or a *quadratic function*. Then write an equation for the function.

3.

x	−3	−2	−1	0	1
y	−7	−5	−3	−1	1

4.

x	−2	−1	0	1	2
y	8	2	0	2	8

EXAMPLE 4 Solve a multi-step problem

CYCLING The table shows the breathing rates y (in liters of air per minute) of a cyclist traveling at different speeds x (in miles per hour). Tell whether the data can be modeled by a *linear function*, an *exponential function*, or a *quadratic function*. Then write an equation for the function.

Speed of cyclist, x (mi/h)	20	21	22	23	24	25
Breathing rate, y (L/min)	51.4	57.1	63.3	70.3	78.0	86.6

Solution

STEP 1 **Graph** the data. The graph has a slight curve. So, a linear function does not appear to model the data.

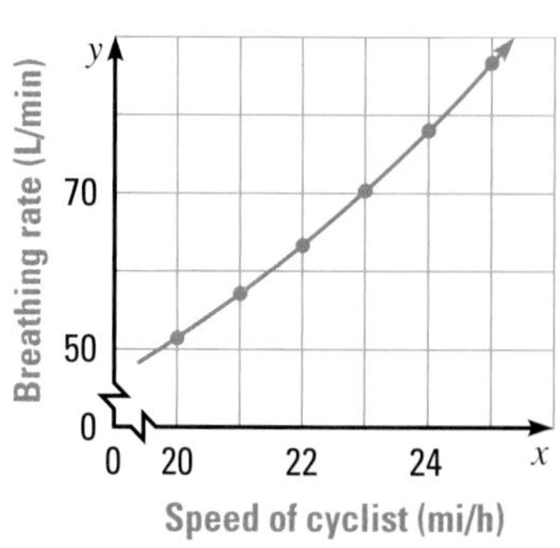

STEP 2 **Decide** which function models the data.

In the table below, notice that $\frac{57.1}{51.4} \approx 1.11$, $\frac{63.3}{57.1} \approx 1.11$, $\frac{70.3}{63.3} \approx 1.11$, $\frac{78.0}{70.3} \approx 1.11$, and $\frac{86.6}{78.0} \approx 1.11$. So, the ratios are all approximately equal. An exponential function models the data.

Speed of cyclist, x (mi/h)	20	21	22	23	24	25
Breathing rate, y (L/min)	51.4	57.1	63.3	70.3	78.0	86.6

Ratios: 1.11 1.11 1.11 1.11 1.11

STEP 3 **Write** an equation for the exponential function. The breathing rate increases by a factor of 1.11 liters per minute, so $b = 1.11$. Find the value of a by using one of the data pairs, such as (20, 51.4).

REVIEW EXPONENTIAL FUNCTIONS
For help with writing an equation for an exponential function, see p. 520.

$y = ab^x$ **Write equation for exponential function.**

$51.4 = a(1.11)^{20}$ **Substitute 1.11 for *b*, 20 for *x*, and 51.4 for *y*.**

$\frac{51.4}{(1.11)^{20}} = a$ **Solve for *a*.**

$6.38 \approx a$ **Use a calculator.**

▶ The equation is $y = 6.38(1.11)^x$.

GUIDED PRACTICE for Example 4

5. In Example 4, suppose the cyclist is traveling at 15 miles per hour. Find the breathing rate of the cyclist at this speed.

10.8 EXERCISES

HOMEWORK KEY

○ = **WORKED-OUT SOLUTIONS** on p. WS25 for Exs. 7, 13, and 25

★ = **STANDARDIZED TEST PRACTICE** Exs. 2, 18, 26, and 27

◆ = **MULTIPLE REPRESENTATIONS** Ex. 25

SKILL PRACTICE

1. **VOCABULARY** Copy and complete: A function that is of the form $y = ab^x$ is a(n) _?_.

2. ★ **WRITING** *Describe* how you can tell whether a table of values represents a quadratic function.

EXAMPLE 1 on p. 684 for Exs. 3–11

MATCHING Match the function with the graph that the function represents.

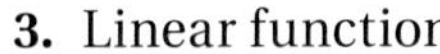

3. Linear function　　4. Exponential function　　5. Quadratic function

A. 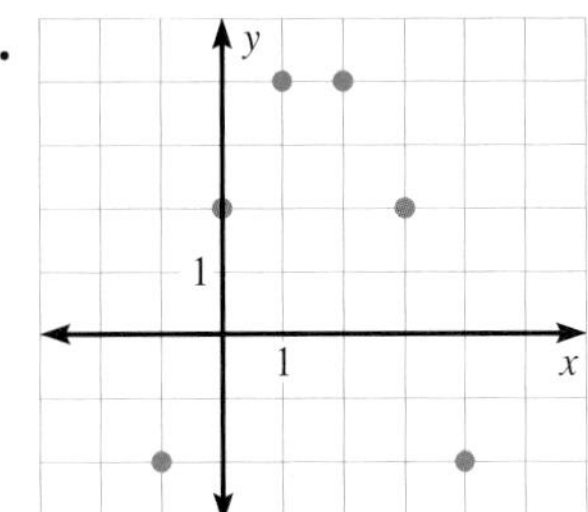

B. 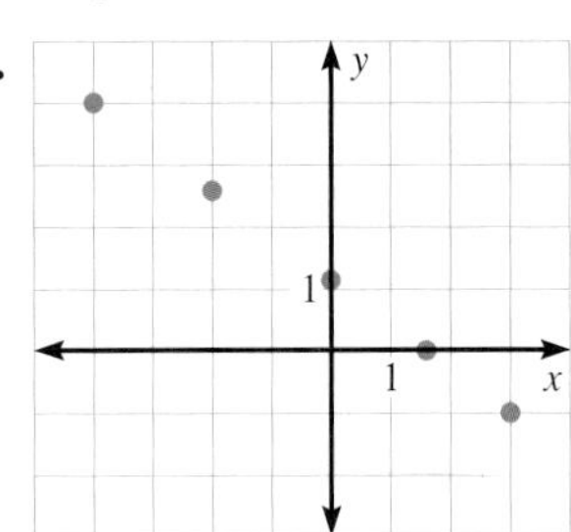

C. 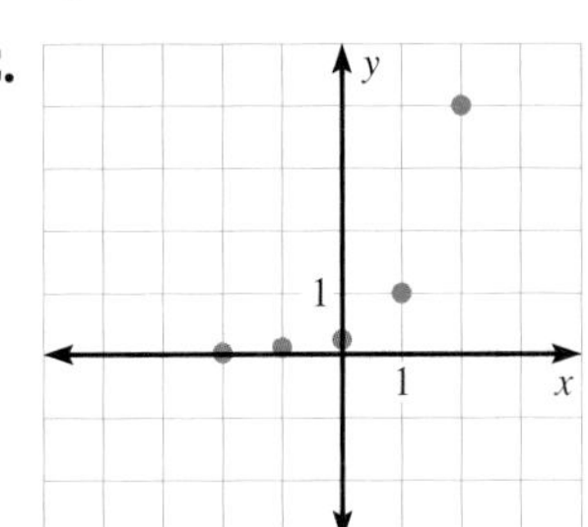

USING A GRAPH Use a graph to tell whether the ordered pairs represent a *linear function*, an *exponential function*, or a *quadratic function*.

6. $(-4, -7), (-2, -1), (0, 1), (2, -1), (4, -7)$

7. $(-5, -1), (-3, 0), (-1, 1), (1, 2), (3, 3)$

8. $\left(-1, \frac{1}{16}\right), \left(0, \frac{1}{4}\right), (1, 1), (2, 4), (3, 16)$

9. $(-1, 8), (1, 2), \left(3, \frac{1}{2}\right), \left(5, \frac{1}{8}\right), \left(7, \frac{1}{32}\right)$

10. $(-4, -4), (-2, -3.5), (0, -3), (2, -2.5)$

11. $(-1, 0.5), (0, -0.5), (1, 0.5), (2, 3.5)$

EXAMPLES 2 and 3 on p. 685–686 for Exs. 12–19

USING DIFFERENCES AND RATIOS Tell whether the table of values represents a *linear function*, an *exponential function*, or a *quadratic function*. Then write an equation for the function.

12.

x	0	1	2	3	4
y	1	0	−1	−2	−3

13. 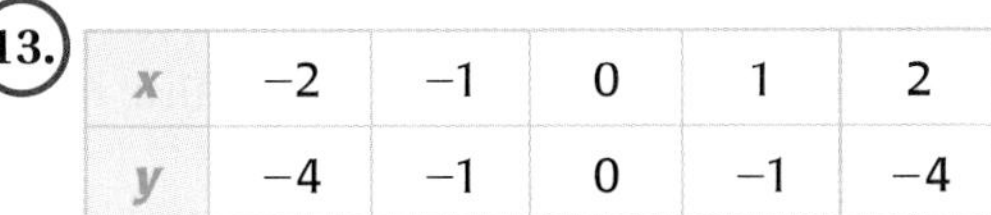

x	−2	−1	0	1	2
y	−4	−1	0	−1	−4

14.

x	−3	−2	−1	0	1
y	13.5	6	1.5	0	1.5

15.

x	−2	−1	0	1	2
y	−5	−2	1	4	7

16. 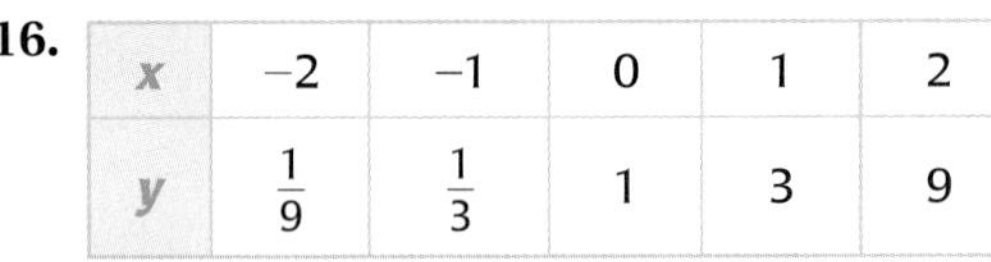

x	−2	−1	0	1	2
y	$\frac{1}{9}$	$\frac{1}{3}$	1	3	9

17. 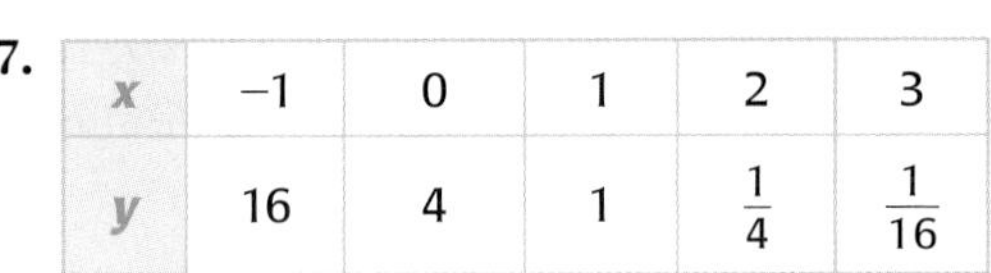

x	−1	0	1	2	3
y	16	4	1	$\frac{1}{4}$	$\frac{1}{16}$

18. ★ **MULTIPLE CHOICE** Which function is represented by the following ordered pairs: $(-1, 4), (0, 0), (1, 4), (2, 16), (3, 36)$?

Ⓐ $y = 0.25x^2$　　Ⓑ $y = 4^x$　　Ⓒ $y = 4x^2$　　Ⓓ $y = 4x$

19. **ERROR ANALYSIS** *Describe* and correct the error in writing an equation for the function represented by the ordered pairs.

(0, 0), (1, 2.5), (2, 10), (3, 22.5), (4, 40)

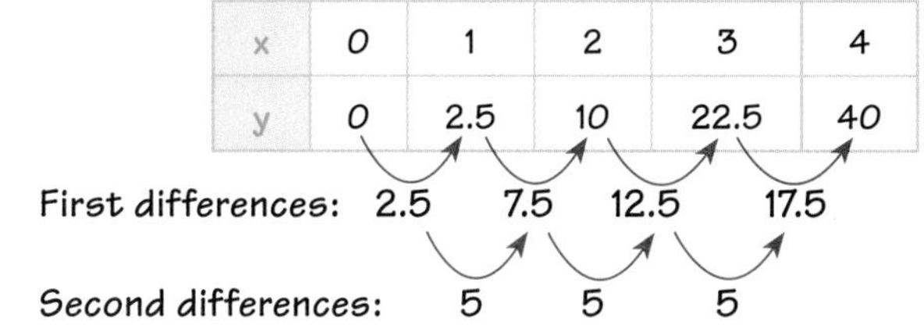

x 0 1 2 3 4
y 0 2.5 10 22.5 40
First differences: 2.5 7.5 12.5 17.5
Second differences: 5 5 5

The ordered pairs represent a quadratic function.

$y = ax^2$

$2 = a(10)^2$

$0.02 = a$

So, the equation is $y = 0.02x^2$.

20. **REASONING** Use the graph shown.

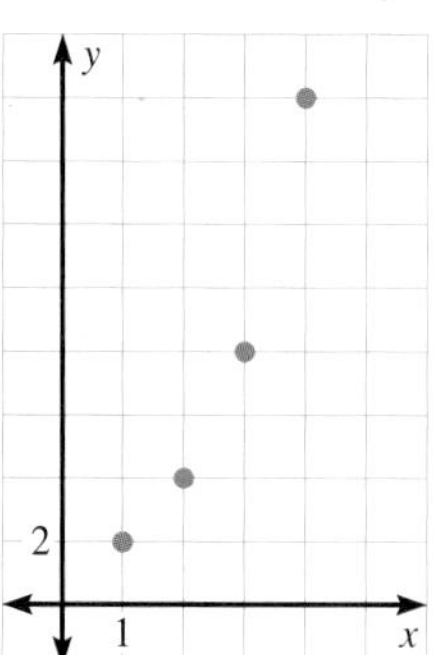

a. Tell whether the graph represents an *exponential function* or a *quadratic function* by looking at the graph.

b. Make a table of values for the points on the graph. Then use differences or ratios to check your answer in part (a).

c. Write an equation for the function that the table of values from part (b) represents.

21. **GEOMETRY** The table shows the area A (in square centimeters) of an equilateral triangle for various side lengths s (in centimeters). Write an equation for the function that the table of values represents. Then find the area of an equilateral triangle that has a side length of 10 centimeters.

Side length, s (cm)	1	2	3	4	5
Area, A (cm^2)	$0.25\sqrt{3}$	$\sqrt{3}$	$2.25\sqrt{3}$	$4\sqrt{3}$	$6.25\sqrt{3}$

22. **CHALLENGE** In the ordered pairs below, the y-values are given in terms of m. Tell whether the ordered pairs represent a *linear function*, an *exponential function*, or a *quadratic function*.

$(1, 3m - 1), (2, 10m + 2), (3, 26m), (4, 51m - 7), (5, 85m - 19)$

PROBLEM SOLVING

EXAMPLE 4
on p. 687
for Exs. 23–25

23. **LIZARDS** The table shows the body temperature B (in degrees Celsius) of a desert spiny lizard at various air temperatures A (in degrees Celsius). Tell whether the data can be modeled by a *linear function*, an *exponential function*, or a *quadratic function*. Then write an equation for the function.

Air temperature, A (°C)	26	27	28	29	30
Body temperature, B (°C)	33.44	33.78	34.12	34.46	34.80

@HomeTutor for problem solving help at classzone.com

24. **NAUTILUS** A chambered nautilus is a marine animal that lives in the outermost chamber of its shell. When the nautilus outgrows a chamber, it adds a new, larger chamber to its shell. The table shows the volumes (in cubic centimeters) of consecutive chambers of a nautilus. Tell whether the data can be modeled by a *linear function*, an *exponential function*, or a *quadratic function*. Then write an equation for the function.

Chamber	1	2	3	4	5	6
Volume (cm^3)	0.836	0.889	0.945	1.005	1.068	1.135

@HomeTutor for problem solving help at classzone.com

(25.) ◆ **MULTIPLE REPRESENTATIONS** Fold a rectangular piece of paper in half. Open the paper and record the number of folds and the number of sections created. Repeat by increasing the number of folds by 1 fold each time.

a. Making a Table Copy and complete the table.

Folds	1	2	3	4	5
Sections	?	?	?	?	?

b. Drawing a Graph Graph the data in part (a). Use the graph and the table to tell whether the data can be modeled by a *linear function*, an *exponential function*, or a *quadratic function*.

c. Writing a Model Write an equation for the function that models the data. Then find the number of sections that are created by 7 folds.

26. ★ **MULTIPLE CHOICE** The table shows the cost of a custom circular rug for various diameters (in feet). What is the approximate cost of a custom circular rug that has a diameter of 8 feet?

Diameter (ft)	2	3	4	5	6
Cost (dollars)	28.40	63.90	113.60	177.50	255.60

Ⓐ \$333.70 Ⓑ \$411.80 Ⓒ \$454.40 Ⓓ \$908.80

27. ★ **EXTENDED RESPONSE** The time it takes for a clock's pendulum to swing from one side to the other and back again, as shown in the back view of the clock, is called the pendulum's period. The table shows the period t (in seconds) of a pendulum of length ℓ (in feet).

Period, t (sec)	1	2	3	4	5
Length, ℓ (ft)	0.82	3.28	7.38	13.12	20.5

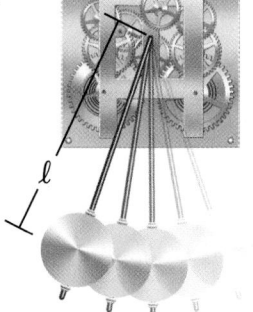

a. Model Tell whether the data can be modeled by a *linear function*, an *exponential function*, or a *quadratic function*. Then write an equation for the function.

b. Apply Find the length of a pendulum that has a period of 0.5 second.

c. Analyze How does decreasing the length of the pendulum by 50% change the period? *Justify* your answer using several examples.

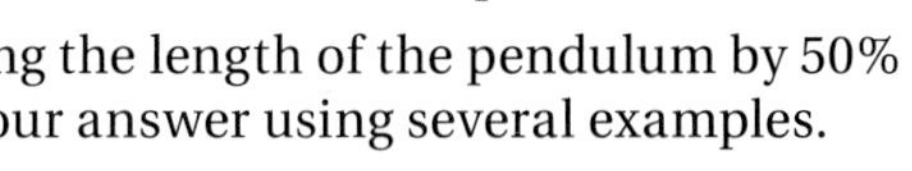

28. CHALLENGE The table shows the height h (in feet) that a pole vaulter's center of gravity reaches for various running speeds s (in feet per second) at the moment the pole vaulter launches himself into the air.

Running speed, s (ft/sec)	30	31	32	33	34
Height of center of gravity, h (ft)	$14\frac{1}{16}$	$15\frac{1}{64}$	16	$17\frac{1}{64}$	$18\frac{1}{16}$

a. A pole vaulter is running at $31\frac{1}{2}$ feet per second when he launches himself into the air. Find the height that the pole vaulter's center of gravity reaches.

b. Find the speed at which the pole vaulter needs to be running when he launches himself into the air in order for his center of gravity to reach a height of 19 feet. Round your answer to the nearest foot per second.

MIXED REVIEW

PREVIEW
Prepare for Lesson 11.1 in Exs. 29–43.

Approximate the square root to the nearest integer. *(p. 110)*

29. $\sqrt{32}$ **30.** $\sqrt{45}$ **31.** $-\sqrt{10}$

32. $-\sqrt{60}$ **33.** $-\sqrt{79}$ **34.** $\sqrt{57}$

Graph the function. Compare the graph with the graph of $f(x) = x$. *(p. 262)*

35. $g(x) = x - 4$ **36.** $g(x) = x + 1$ **37.** $g(x) = 8x$

38. $g(x) = -x$ **39.** $g(x) = \frac{1}{4}x$ **40.** $g(x) = -\frac{1}{2}x$

Graph the function. Compare the graph with the graph of $y = x^2$. *(p. 628)*

41. $y = 7x^2$ **42.** $y = -\frac{1}{5}x^2$ **43.** $y = 2x^2 + 3$

QUIZ *for Lessons 10.7–10.8*

Tell whether the equation has *two solutions*, *one solution*, or *no solution*. *(p. 678)*

1. $x^2 + x + 5 = 0$ **2.** $5x^2 + 4x - 1 = 0$

Find the number of x-intercepts of the graph of the function. *(p. 678)*

3. $y = -3x^2 + 4x - 2$ **4.** $y = \frac{4}{9}x^2 + 4x + 9$

Tell whether the table of values represents a *linear function*, an *exponential function*, or a *quadratic function*. Then write an equation for the function. *(p. 684)*

5.

x	−6	−3	0	3	6
y	−9	−2.25	0	−2.25	−9

6.

x	1	2	3	4	5
y	5	1	$\frac{1}{5}$	$\frac{1}{25}$	$\frac{1}{125}$

10.8 Perform Regressions

QUESTION How can you use a graphing calculator to find models for data?

On page 335, you used a graphing calculator to perform linear regression on data to find a linear model for the data. A graphing calculator can also be used to perform exponential regression and quadratic regression.

EXAMPLE 1 Use exponential regression to find a model

The table shows the sales (in millions of dollars) of organic milk, organic half and half, and organic cream in the U.S. each year for the period 1996–2000. Find an exponential model for the data.

Year	1996	1997	1998	1999	2000
Sales (millions of dollars)	15.8	30.7	46	75.7	104

STEP 1 *Enter data*

Enter the data into two lists. Let $x = 0$ represent 1996.

L1	L2	L3
0	15.8	
1	30.7	
2	46	
3	75.7	
4	104	

L2(4)=104

STEP 2 *Make scatter plot*

Make a scatter plot of the data. Notice that the points show an exponential trend.

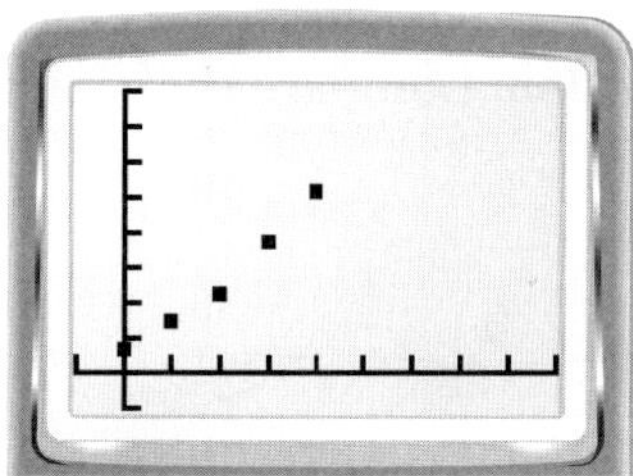

STEP 3 *Perform regression*

Use the exponential regression feature to obtain the model $y = 17.5(1.6)^x$.

STEP 4 *Check model*

Check how well the model fits the data by graphing the model and the data.

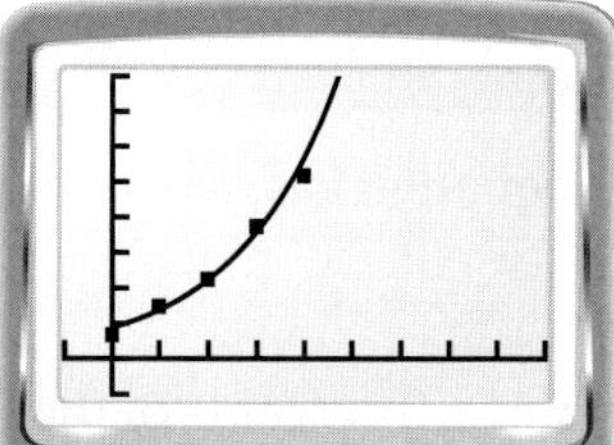

PRACTICE

1. The table shows the value (in dollars) of a car over time. Find an exponential model for the data in the table.

Age of car (years)	0	1	2	3	4	5
Value (dollars)	15,600	13,510	11,700	10,132	8774	7598

@HomeTutor
classzone.com
Keystrokes

EXAMPLE 2 Use quadratic regression to find a model

In September 2001, the first U.S. digital satellite radio station was launched. The table shows the number of subscribers of the service for various months after its launch. Find a quadratic model for the data.

Months after launch	0	3	6	9	12	15
Subscribers	500	31,000	76,000	135,500	201,500	360,000

STEP 1 Make scatter plot

Enter the data into two lists and make a scatter plot of the data. Notice that the points show a quadratic trend.

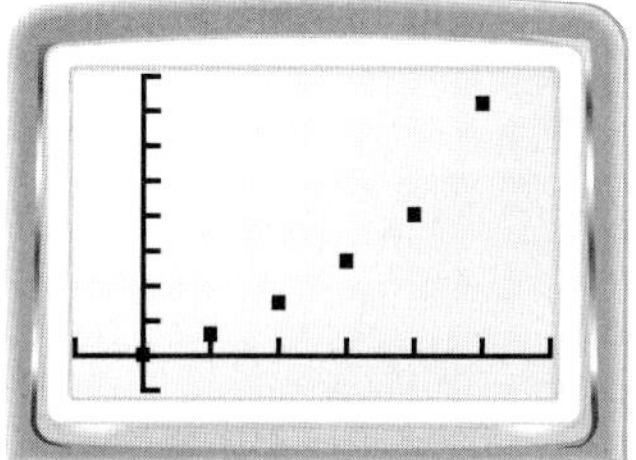

STEP 2 Perform regression

Use the quadratic regression feature to obtain the model $y = 1440x^2 + 1010x + 8000$.

STEP 3 Check model

Check how well the model fits the data by graphing the model and the data.

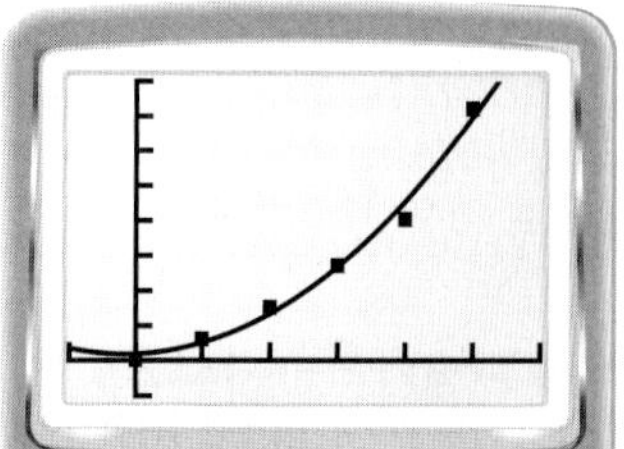

PRACTICE

2. The table shows the maximum weight (in pounds) that can be supported by a 16 foot floor beam of different depths. Find a quadratic model for the data.

Depth (inches)	6	7.5	9	10.5	12	13.5
Weight (pounds)	68	137	242	389	586	838

DRAW CONCLUSIONS

3. The table shows the temperature (in degrees Fahrenheit) of a cup of hot chocolate over time. Find an exponential model and a quadratic model for the data. Make a scatter plot of the data and graph both models. Which model fits the data better? *Explain.*

Time (minutes)	0	10	20	30	40	50	60
Temperature (°F)	200	157	128	109	99	92	90

MIXED REVIEW of Problem Solving

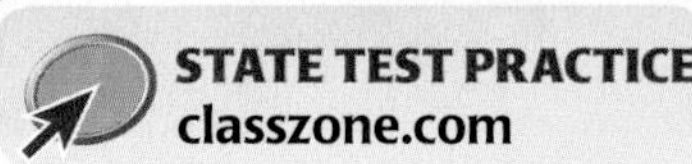

Lessons 10.5–10.8

1. **MULTI-STEP PROBLEM** Different masses (in kilograms) are hung from a spring. The distances (in centimeters) that the spring stretches are shown in the table.

Mass (kilograms)	Distance (centimeters)
1	2.6
2	5.2
3	7.8
4	10.4
5	13.0

   a. Tell whether the data can be modeled by a *linear function*, an *exponential function*, or a *quadratic function*.

   b. Write an equation for the function.

2. **MULTI-STEP PROBLEM** In slow-pitch softball, the ball is pitched in an underhand motion. A batter in a softball game is pitched a ball that has an initial height of 2 feet above the ground and an initial vertical velocity of 35 feet per second.

   a. Write an equation for the height h (in feet) of the ball as a function of the time t (in seconds) after it is pitched.

   b. The batter hits the ball when it is 2.5 feet above the ground. How long after the ball is pitched is the ball hit? Round your answer to the nearest tenth of a second.

3. **SHORT RESPONSE** Part of a cheerleading routine involves throwing a flyer straight up into the air and catching her on the way down. The flyer begins this stunt with her center of gravity 4.5 feet above the ground, and she is thrown with an initial vertical velocity of 30 feet per second. Will her center of gravity reach a height of 20 feet? *Explain.*

4. **OPEN-ENDED** In Exercise 3, suppose the flyer wants to have her center of gravity reach a height of at least 25 feet above the ground. Give an initial vertical velocity that will accomplish this. Use the discriminant to show that your answer is correct.

5. **SHORT RESPONSE** For the period 1990–2000, the sales y (in billions of dollars) of computers, computer accessories, and computer software can be modeled by the function $y = -0.05x^2 + 2.2x + 7$ where x is the number of years since 1990.

   a. Use the discriminant to determine the number of values of x that correspond to $y = 24$.

   b. Were there any years during the period 1990–2000 in which the sales reached 24 billion dollars? *Explain.*

6. **GRIDDED ANSWER** The trapezoid below has an area of 54 square inches. What is the value of x?

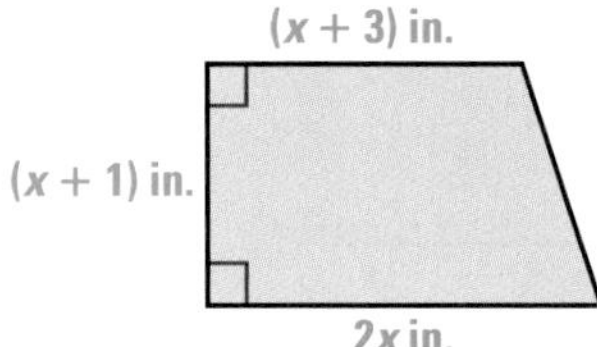

7. **SHORT RESPONSE** You have 24 feet of fencing that you are using to make a rectangular dog pen. You want the dog pen to enclose 150 square feet. Is it possible for the 24 feet of fencing to enclose a rectangular area of 150 square feet? *Explain.*

8. **EXTENDED RESPONSE** You are making a tiled tabletop with a uniform mosaic tile border as shown.

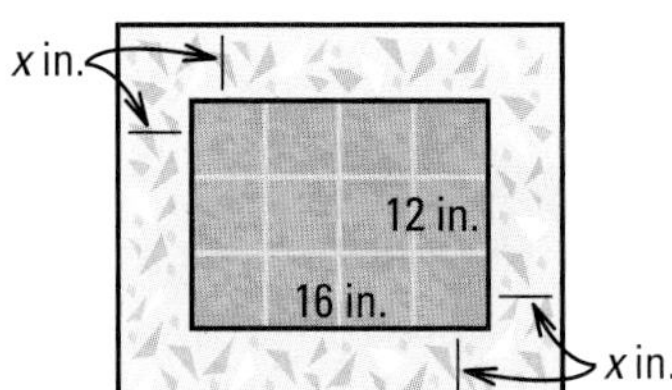

   a. Write an equation for the area A (in square inches) of the border.

   b. You have enough mosaic tiles to cover 130 square inches. What should the width of the border be? Round your answer to the nearest inch.

   c. *Explain* why you could ignore one of the values of x in part (b).

10 CHAPTER SUMMARY

Animated Algebra
classzone.com
Electronic Function Library

BIG IDEAS

For Your Notebook

Big Idea 1

Graphing Quadratic Functions

You can use the properties below to graph any quadratic function.

The graph of $y = ax^2 + bx + c$ is a parabola that:

- opens up if $a > 0$ and opens down if $a < 0$.
- is narrower than the graph of $y = x^2$ if $|a| > 1$ and wider if $|a| < 1$.
- has an axis of symmetry of $x = -\frac{b}{2a}$.
- has a vertex with an x-coordinate of $-\frac{b}{2a}$.
- has a y-intercept of c. So, the point $(0, c)$ is on the parabola.

$y = ax^2 + bx + c, a > 0$

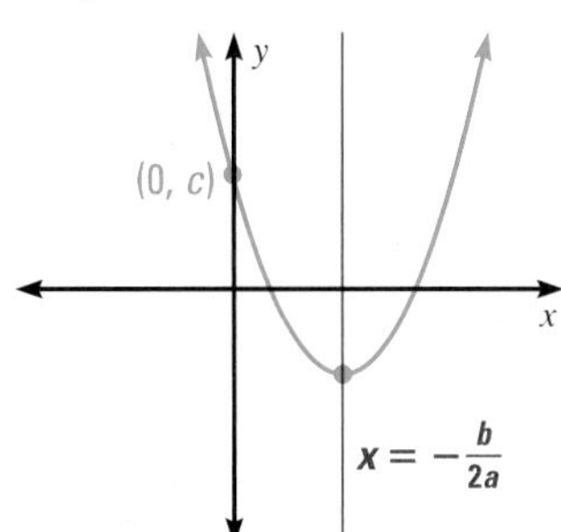

Big Idea 2

Solving Quadratic Equations

You can use the following methods to solve a quadratic equation. Sometimes it is easier to use one method instead of another.

Method	Lesson	When to use
Graphing	10.3	Use when approximate solutions are adequate.
Finding square roots	10.4	Use when solving an equation that can be written in the form $x^2 = d$.
Completing the square	10.5	Can be used for *any* quadratic equation $y = ax^2 + bx + c$ but is simplest to apply when $a = 1$ and b is an even number.
Quadratic formula	10.6	Can be used for *any* quadratic equation

Big Idea 3

Comparing Linear, Exponential, and Quadratic Models

You can use linear, exponential, and quadratic functions to model data.

Function	Example	x- and y-values
Linear	$y = 5x + 1$	If the increments between successive x-values are equal, the differences of successive y-values are all equal.
Exponential	$y = 3(2)^x$	If the increments between successive x-values are equal, the ratios of successive y-values are all equal.
Quadratic	$y = x^2 - 4x + 6$	If the increments between successive x-values are equal, the differences of successive first differences of y-values are all equal.

10 CHAPTER REVIEW

@HomeTutor
classzone.com
• Multi-Language Glossary
• Vocabulary practice

REVIEW KEY VOCABULARY

- quadratic function, *p. 628*
- standard form of a quadratic function, *p. 628*
- parabola, *p. 628*
- parent quadratic function, *p. 628*
- vertex of a parabola, *p. 628*
- axis of symmetry, *p. 628*
- minimum value, *p. 636*
- maximum value, *p. 636*
- intercept form of a quadratic function, *p. 641*
- quadratic equation, *p. 643*
- standard form of a quadratic equation, *p. 643*
- completing the square, *p. 663*
- vertex form of a quadratic function, *p. 669*
- quadratic formula, *p. 671*
- discriminant, *p. 678*

VOCABULARY EXERCISES

1. Copy and complete: The line that passes through the vertex and divides a parabola into two symmetric parts is called the __?__.

Tell whether the function has a *minimum value* or a *maximum value*.

2. $f(x) = 5x^2 - 4x$
3. $f(x) = -x^2 + 6x + 2$
4. $f(x) = 0.3x^2 - 7.7x + 1.8$

REVIEW EXAMPLES AND EXERCISES

Use the review examples and exercises below to check your understanding of the concepts you have learned in each lesson of Chapter 10.

10.1 Graph $y = ax^2 + c$

pp. 628–634

EXAMPLE

Graph $y = -x^2 + 3$. Compare the graph with the graph of $y = x^2$.

Make a table of values for $y = -x^2 + 3$. Then plot the points from the table and draw a smooth curve through the points.

x	−2	−1	0	1	2
y	−1	2	3	2	−1

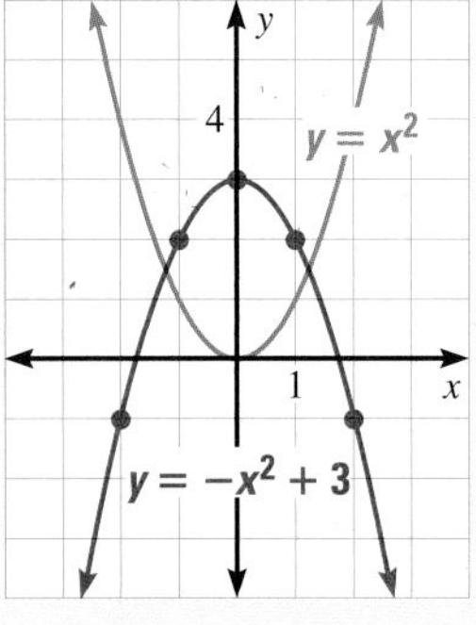

Both graphs have the same axis of symmetry, $x = 0$. However, the graph of $y = -x^2 + 3$ has a different vertex than the graph of $y = x^2$, and it opens down. This is because the graph of $y = -x^2 + 3$ is a vertical translation (of 3 units up) and a reflection in the x-axis of the graph of $y = x^2$.

EXAMPLES 1, 2, and 4 on pp. 628–630 for Exs. 5–7

EXERCISES

Graph the function. Compare the graph with the graph of $y = x^2$.

5. $y = -4x^2$
6. $y = \frac{1}{3}x^2$
7. $y = 2x^2 - 1$

10.2 Graph $y = ax^2 + bx + c$ — pp. 635–640

EXAMPLE

Graph $y = -x^2 + 2x + 1$.

STEP 1 **Determine** whether the parabola opens up or down. Because $a < 0$, the parabola opens down.

STEP 2 **Find** and draw the axis of symmetry:

$$x = -\frac{b}{2a} = -\frac{2}{2(-1)} = 1$$

STEP 3 **Find** and plot the vertex. The x-coordinate of the vertex is $-\frac{b}{2a}$, or 1. The y-coordinate of the vertex is $y = -(1)^2 + 2(1) + 1 = 2$.

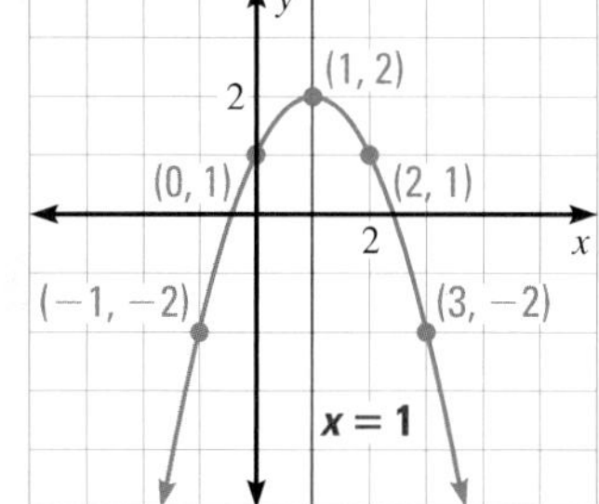

STEP 4 **Plot** four more points. Evaluating the function for $x = 0$ and $x = -1$ gives the points (0, 1) and (−1, −2). Plot these points and their reflections in the axis of symmetry.

STEP 5 **Draw** a parabola through the plotted points.

EXAMPLE 2 on p. 636 for Exs. 8–10

EXERCISES

Graph the function. Label the vertex and axis of symmetry.

8. $y = x^2 + 4x + 1$ **9.** $y = 2x^2 - 4x - 3$ **10.** $y = -2x^2 + 8x + 5$

10.3 Solve Quadratic Equations by Graphing — pp. 643–649

EXAMPLE

Solve $x^2 - 7x = -12$ by graphing.

STEP 1 **Write** the equation in standard form.

$x^2 - 7x = -12$ **Write original equation.**

$x^2 - 7x + 12 = 0$ **Add 12 to each side.**

STEP 2 **Graph** the related function $y = x^2 - 7x + 12$. The x-intercepts of the graph are 3 and 4.

▶ The solutions of the equation $x^2 - 7x + 12 = 0$ are 3 and 4.

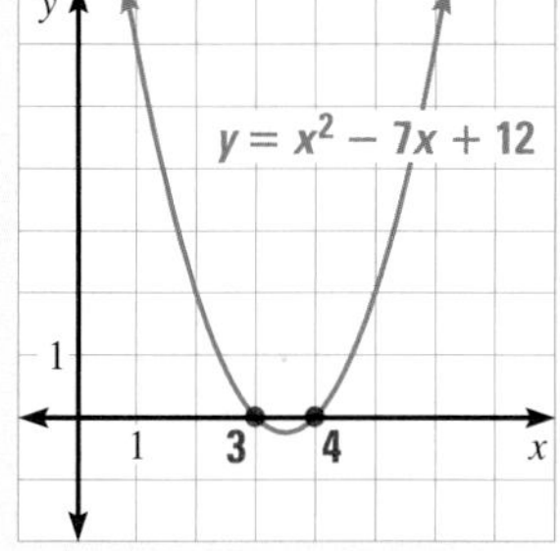

EXAMPLES 1, 2, and 3 on pp. 643–644 for Exs. 11–13

EXERCISES

Solve the equation by graphing.

11. $4x^2 + x + 3 = 0$ **12.** $x^2 + 2x = -1$ **13.** $-x^2 + 8 = 7x$

10 CHAPTER REVIEW

10.4 Use Square Roots to Solve Quadratic Equations *pp. 652–658*

EXAMPLE

Solve $5(x-6)^2 = 30$. Round the solutions to the nearest hundredth.

$5(x-6)^2 = 30$ — Write original equation.

$(x-6)^2 = 6$ — Divide each side by 5.

$x - 6 = \pm\sqrt{6}$ — Take square roots of each side.

$x = 6 \pm \sqrt{6}$ — Add 6 to each side.

▶ The solutions of the equation are $6 + \sqrt{6} \approx 8.45$ and $6 - \sqrt{6} \approx 3.55$.

CHECK To check the solutions, first rewrite the equation so that 0 is on the one side as follows: $5(x-6)^2 - 30 = 0$. Then graph the related function $y = 5(x-6)^2 - 30$. The x-intercepts are about 8.4 and about 3.5. So, each solution checks.

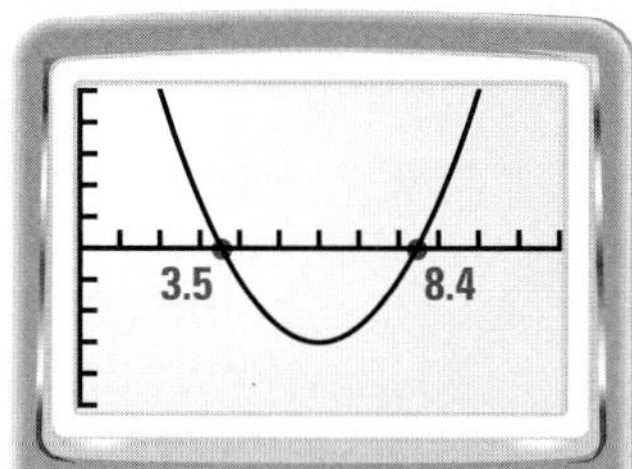

EXERCISES

Solve the equation. Round your solutions to the nearest hundredth, if necessary.

EXAMPLES 1–4 on p. 652–654 for Exs. 14–19

14. $6x^2 - 54 = 0$ **15.** $3x^2 + 7 = 4$ **16.** $g^2 + 11 = 24$

17. $7n^2 + 5 = 9$ **18.** $2(a+7)^2 = 34$ **19.** $3(w-4)^2 = 5$

10.5 Solve Quadratic Equations by Completing the Square *pp. 663–668*

EXAMPLE

Solve $3x^2 + 12x = 18$ by completing the square.

$3x^2 + 12x = 18$ — Write original equation.

$x^2 + 4x = 6$ — Divide each side by 3.

$x^2 + 4x + 2^2 = 6 + 2^2$ — Add $\left(\frac{4}{2}\right)^2$, or 2^2, to each side.

$(x+2)^2 = 10$ — Write left side as the square of a binomial.

$x + 2 = \pm\sqrt{10}$ — Take square roots of each side.

$x = -2 \pm \sqrt{10}$ — Subtract 2 from each side.

▶ The solutions of the equation are $-2 + \sqrt{10} \approx 1.16$ and $-2 - \sqrt{10} \approx -5.16$.

@HomeTutor
classzone.com
Chapter Review Practice

EXERCISES

EXAMPLES 2 and 3 on p. 664 for Exs. 20–23

Solve the equation by completing the square. Round your solutions to the nearest hundredth, if necessary.

20. $x^2 - 14x = 51$

21. $2a^2 + 12a - 4 = 0$

22. $2n^2 + 4n + 1 = 10n + 9$

23. $5g^2 - 3g + 6 = 2g^2 + 9$

10.6 Solve Quadratic Equations by the Quadratic Formula *pp. 671–676*

EXAMPLE

Solve $4x^2 + 3x = 1$.

$4x^2 + 3x = 1$ — **Write original equation.**

$4x^2 + 3x - 1 = 0$ — **Write in standard form.**

$x = \frac{-b \pm \sqrt{b^2 - 4ac}}{2a}$ — **Quadratic formula**

$= \frac{-3 \pm \sqrt{3^2 - 4(4)(-1)}}{2(4)}$ — **Substitute values in the quadratic formula: $a = 4$, $b = 3$, and $c = -1$.**

$= \frac{-3 \pm \sqrt{25}}{8}$ — **Simplify.**

$= \frac{-3 \pm 5}{8}$ — **Simplify the square root.**

▶ The solutions of the equation are $\frac{-3+5}{8} = \frac{1}{4}$ and $\frac{-3-5}{8} = -1$.

CHECK You can check the solutions in the original equation.

If $x = \frac{1}{4}$:

$4x^2 + 3x = 1$

$4\left(\frac{1}{4}\right)^2 + 3\left(\frac{1}{4}\right) \stackrel{?}{=} 1$

$1 = 1$ ✓

If $x = -1$:

$4x^2 + 3x = 1$

$4(-1)^2 + 3(-1) \stackrel{?}{=} 1$

$1 = 1$ ✓

EXERCISES

EXAMPLES 1, 2, and 3 on p. 671–672 for Exs. 24–30

Use the quadratic formula to solve the equation. Round your solutions to the nearest hundredth, if necessary.

24. $x^2 - 2x - 15 = 0$

25. $2m^2 + 7m - 3 = 0$

26. $-w^2 + 5w = 3$

27. $5n^2 - 7n = -1$

28. $t^2 - 4 = 6t + 8$

29. $2h - 1 = 10 - 9h^2$

30. The area A of the rectangle shown is 500 square meters. Find the value of x. Then give the dimensions of the rectangle.

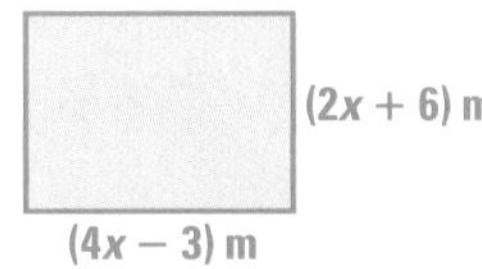

10 CHAPTER REVIEW

10.7 Interpret the Discriminant

pp. 678–683

EXAMPLE

	Equation $ax^2 + bx + c = 0$	**Discriminant** $b^2 - 4ac$	**Number of solutions**
a.	$-16x^2 + 8x - 1 = 0$	$8^2 - 4(-16)(-1) = 0$	One solution
b.	$4x^2 - 5x + 2 = 0$	$(-5)^2 - 4(4)(2) = -7$	No solution
c.	$x^2 + 3x = 0$	$3^2 - 4(1)(0) = 9$	Two solutions

EXERCISES

EXAMPLES 1 and 2 on pp. 678–679 for Exs. 31–36

Tell whether the equation has *two solutions*, *one solution*, or *no solution*.

31. $x^2 - 2x + 2 = 0$

32. $4g^2 + 12g + 9 = 0$

33. $5w^2 - 4w - 1 = 0$

34. $\frac{1}{8}v^2 - 6 = 0$

35. $n^2 - 3n = 4 - 2n^2$

36. $2q^2 + 1 = 3q - 5$

10.8 Compare Linear, Exponential, and Quadratic Models

pp. 684–691

EXAMPLE

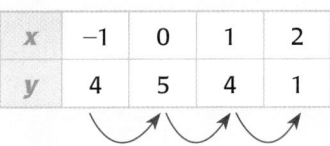

Use differences or ratios to tell whether the table of values represents a *linear function*, an *exponential function*, or a *quadratic function*.

a.

x	−1	0	1	2
y	5	3	1	−1

Differences: −2 −2 −2

▸ The table of values represents a linear function.

b.

x	−1	0	1	2
y	4	5	4	1

First differences: 1 −1 −3

Second differences: −2 −2

▸ The table of values represents a quadratic function.

EXERCISES

EXAMPLE 2 on pp. 685 for Exs. 37–38

Tell whether the table of values represents a *linear function*, an *exponential function*, or a *quadratic function*.

37.

x	1	2	3	4	5	6
y	1	2	4	8	16	32

38.

x	−2	−1	0	1	2	3
y	0	3	6	9	12	15

10 CHAPTER TEST

Match the quadratic function with its graph.

1. $y = x^2 - 2$ **2.** $y = x^2 + 2$ **3.** $y = -2x^2$

A.

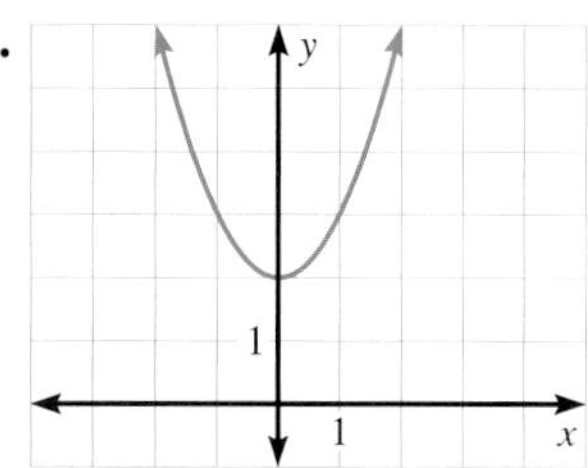

B.

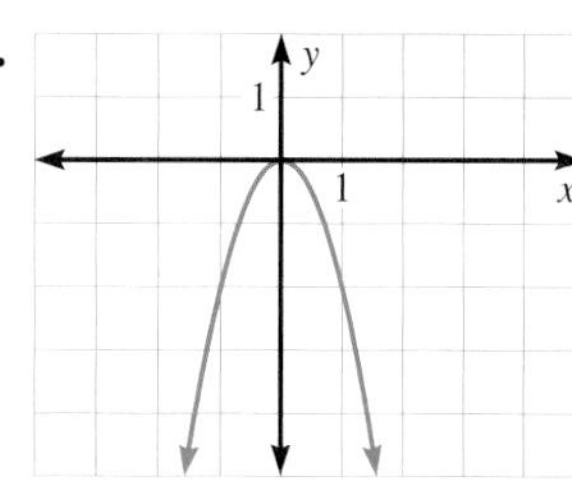

C.

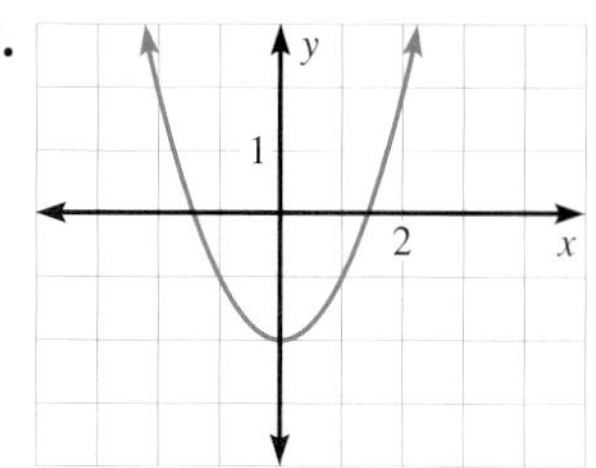

Graph the function. Label the vertex and axis of symmetry.

4. $y = 2x^2 + 6x - 5$ **5.** $y = -4x^2 - 8x + 25$ **6.** $y = \frac{1}{4}x^2 - x - 7$

Approximate the zeros of the function to the nearest tenth.

7. $f(x) = x^2 + 5x + 1$ **8.** $f(x) = x^2 - 8x + 3$ **9.** $f(x) = -3x^2 - 2x + 5$

Solve the equation. Round your solutions to the nearest hundredth, if necessary.

10. $3x^2 = 108$ **11.** $-5w^2 + 51 = 6$ **12.** $-p^2 + 2p + 3 = 0$

13. $-2t^2 + 6t + 9 = 0$ **14.** $5m^2 - m = 5$ **15.** $2x^2 - 12x - 1 = -7x + 6$

Tell whether the equation has *two solutions*, *one solution*, or *no solution*.

16. $3x^2 - 4x + 9 = 0$ **17.** $4g^2 - 12g + 11 = 0$ **18.** $-2n^2 + 7n - 1 = 0$

19. $-m^2 - 17m = 0$ **20.** $-6x^2 - x - 5 = 0$ **21.** $10x^2 - 13 = 0$

Tell whether the table of values represents a *linear function*, an *exponential function*, or a *quadratic function*. Then write an equation for the function.

22.

x	−3	−2	−1	0	1	2
y	18	8	2	0	2	8

23.

x	−4	0	4	8	12	16
y	1	2	3	4	5	6

24. TENNIS You are playing tennis with a friend. The path of the tennis ball after you hit the ball can be modeled by the graph of the equation $y = -0.005x^2 + 0.17x + 3$ where x is the horizontal distance (in feet) from where you hit the ball and y is the height of the ball (in feet) above the court.

a. What is the maximum height reached by the tennis ball? Round your answer to the nearest tenth of a foot.

b. Suppose you are standing 30 feet from the net, which has a height of 3 feet. Will the ball clear the net? *Explain* your reasoning.

c. If your friend does not hit the ball back to you, how far from you does the ball strike the ground?

Scoring Rubric

Full Credit
- solution is complete and correct

Partial Credit
- solution is complete but errors are made, *or*
- solution is without error but is incomplete

No Credit
- no solution is given, *or*
- solution makes no sense

EXTENDED RESPONSE QUESTIONS

PROBLEM

A skateboarder in a half pipe launches himself from the half pipe, performs a trick in the air, and lands back in the half pipe. The top of the half pipe is 12 feet above the base of the half pipe as shown.

a. During his first run, the skateboarder leaves the half pipe with an initial vertical velocity of 17 feet per second. Write an equation that models the height h (in feet) of a skateboarder as a function of the time t (in seconds) after leaving the half pipe.

b. How long is the skateboarder in the air if he lands 5 feet above the base of the half pipe? Round your answer to the nearest hundredth of a second.

c. During his second run, the skateboarder leaves the half pipe with an initial vertical velocity that is greater than his initial vertical velocity during his first run. He again lands 5 feet above the base of the half pipe. During which run is his time spent in the air greater? *Explain.*

Below are sample solutions to the problem. Read each solution and the comments in blue to see why the sample represents full credit, partial credit, or no credit.

SAMPLE 1: Full credit solution

The correct equation is given.

a. $h = -16t^2 + 17t + 12$

b. $5 = -16t^2 + 17t + 12$

$0 = -16t^2 + 17t + 7$

$$t = \frac{-17 \pm \sqrt{17^2 - 4(-16)(7)}}{2(-16)} \approx -0.32 \text{ or } 1.38$$

The correct equation is given, and the answer that makes sense is given.

The skateboarder is in the air for about 1.38 seconds.

c. $5 = -16t^2 + 18t + 12$ $\qquad$ $5 = -16t^2 + 20t + 12$

$0 = -16t^2 + 18t + 7$ $\qquad$ $0 = -16t^2 + 20t + 7$

$$t = \frac{-18 \pm \sqrt{18^2 - 4(-16)(7)}}{2(-16)} \qquad t = \frac{-20 \pm \sqrt{20^2 - 4(-16)(7)}}{2(-16)}$$

$t \approx -0.31$ (crossed out) or $t \approx 1.43$ $\qquad$ $t \approx -0.29$ (crossed out) or $t \approx 1.54$

The answer is correct, and it includes an explanation.

The examples above show that the time the skateboarder spends in the air increases as the initial vertical velocity increases and the landing height remains constant. So, the skateboarder spends more time in the air during his second run.

SAMPLE 2: Partial credit solution

The correct equation is given.

In parts (b) and (c), the reasoning is correct but errors are made in calculating the values of t. So, the answers are incorrect.

a. $h = -16t^2 + 17t + 12$

b. $0 = -16t^2 + 17t + 7$

$$t = \frac{-17 \pm \sqrt{17^2 - 4(-16)(7)}}{2(-16)} \approx -1.38 \text{ or } 0.32$$

The skateboarder is in the air for about 0.32 second.

c. $0 = -16t^2 + 19t + 7$

$$t = \frac{-19 \pm \sqrt{19^2 - 4(-16)(7)}}{2(-16)} \approx -1.48 \text{ or } 0.3$$

With an initial vertical velocity of 19 feet per second, the skateboarder is in the air for about 0.3 second, which is less than 0.32 second. So, the skateboarder spends more time in the air during his first run.

SAMPLE 3: No credit solution

The equation is incorrect.

In parts (b) and (c), the incorrect equations are solved, and no answers are given.

a. $h = -16t^2 + 12t + 17$

b. $0 = -16t^2 + 12t + 17$

$$t = \frac{-12 \pm \sqrt{12^2 - 4(-16)(17)}}{2(-16)} \approx -0.72 \text{ or } 1.47$$

c. $0 = -16t^2 + 15t + 17$

$$t = \frac{-15 \pm \sqrt{15^2 - 4(-16)(17)}}{2(-16)} \approx -0.66 \text{ or } 1.6$$

PRACTICE Apply Scoring Rubric

1. A student's solution to the problem on the previous page is given below. Score the solution as *full credit, partial credit,* or *no credit. Explain* your reasoning. If you choose *partial credit* or *no credit,* explain how you would change the solution so that it earns a score of full credit.

a. $h = -16t^2 + 17t + 12$

b. $0 = -16t^2 + 17t + 7$

$$t = \frac{-17 \pm \sqrt{17^2 - 4(-16)(7)}}{2(-16)} \approx 0.32$$

The skateboarder is in the air for about 0.32 second.

c. A greater initial vertical velocity means that the skateboarder will go higher. This means that he will be in the air longer. So, the skateboarder will be in the air longer during his second run.

EXTENDED RESPONSE

1. A community garden is being planned in the town-owned field behind the housing development where you live. The rectangular garden will border the development and extend into the field. Each household that joins the project will have a rectangular plot that is 20 feet wide. The town has already permitted the plots to extend 10 feet into the field, and promised another foot for every household that reserves a plot.

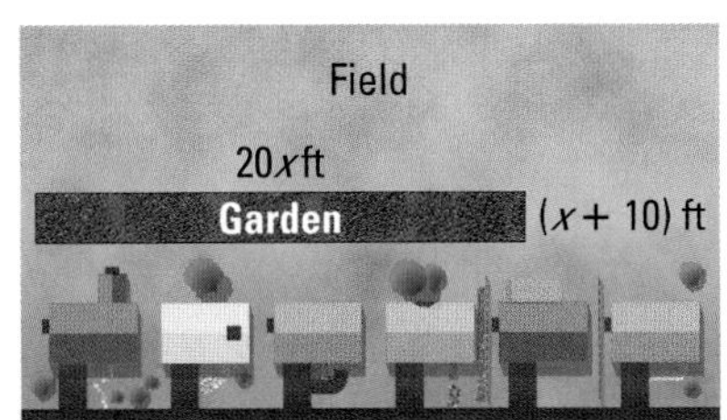

   a. Write an equation that gives the area A (in square feet) of the community garden as a function of the number x of households that reserve a plot.

   b. The housing association decides that the entire area of the garden cannot exceed 4000 square feet. What is the maximum number of plots there can be? *Explain.*

   c. The maximum number of plots is used. One of the residents decides to plant a uniform border of wildflowers around all four sides of her plot. She has enough wildflower seeds to cover 111 square feet. How wide should the border be? *Explain.*

2. During a water-polo practice, a player positioned directly in front of the goal throws the ball at the goal. The ball follows a parabolic path that can be modeled by the graph of the equation $y = -0.018x^2 + 0.25x + 0.7$ where y is the height (in feet) of the ball above the surface of the water x feet from the player.

   a. What is the maximum height of the ball to the nearest tenth of a foot?

   b. The ball goes into the goal. The goal is bounded by the surface of the water and a crossbar that is 3 feet high above the surface of the water. Give a possible distance that the player is from the goal. *Explain.*

   c. Describe all possible distances that the player can be from the goal in order for the ball to go into the goal. *Explain.*

3. A farm machine called a planter plants multiple rows of seeds while being pulled by a tractor. Planters can be purchased in various sizes. The operation costs of a 6 row, 8 row, 12 row, 16 row, and 24 row planter are analyzed. The operation cost y (in dollars per acre) for a planter that plants x rows at once for two different sizes of fields is shown in the table.

Acres planted	Operation cost (dollars per acre), y
400	$y = 0.071x^2 - 1.1x + 17$
800	$y = 0.062x^2 - 1.6x + 20$

   a. Which planter costs the least per acre to operate for planting 400 acres?

   b. Which planter costs the least per acre to operate for planting 800 acres?

   c. A farmer who is planting 800 acres uses the planter that costs the least per acre to operate. The operation cost function takes into account that a tractor operator is paid \$.82 per acre to drive the tractor pulling the planter. The farmer drives the tractor, so he doesn't have to pay for labor. Does his planter still cost the least per acre to operate? *Explain.*

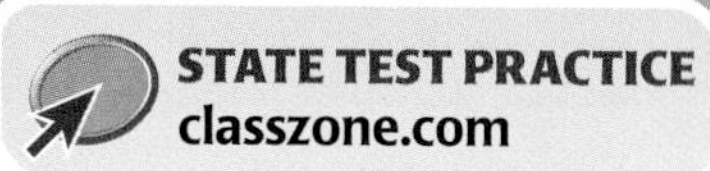

MULTIPLE CHOICE

4. How would the graph of the function $y = -3x^2 + 6$ be affected if the function were changed to $y = -3x^2 - 1$?

   (A) The graph would shift 5 units up.

   (B) The graph would shift 5 units down.

   (C) The graph would shift 7 units up.

   (D) The graph would shift 7 units down.

5. A volleyball player serves the ball from a height of 6.5 feet above the ground with an initial vertical velocity of 21 feet per second. Which function models the height h (in feet) of the ball t seconds after it is served?

   (A) $h = 21t - t^2 + 6.5$

   (B) $h = -16t^2 + 6.5$

   (C) $h = 16t^2 + 21t + 6.5$

   (D) $h = 6.5 + 21t - 16t^2$

GRIDDED ANSWER

6. The value of the discriminant of the equation $7x^2 - 8x + c = 6$ is -20. What is the value of c?

7. The area of the rectangle below is 170 square meters. What is the value of x?

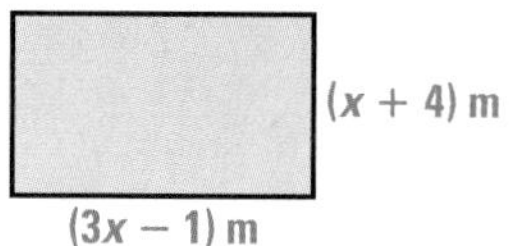

8. A cross section of the glass lamp shade below can be modeled by the graph of the equation $y = -0.625x^2 + 5x$ where x and y are measured in inches. How tall (in inches) is the shade?

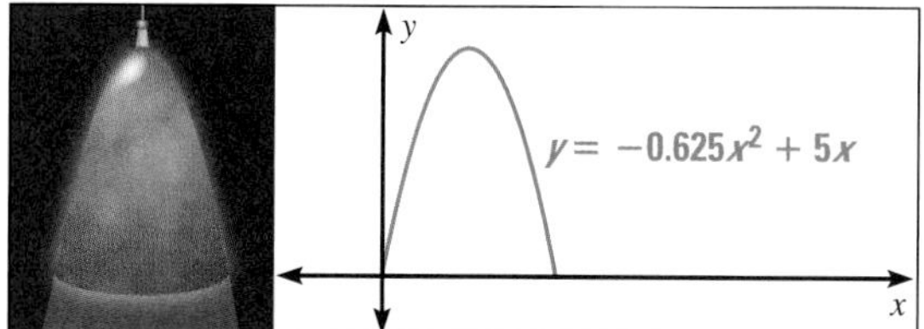

SHORT RESPONSE

9. From January to May in 2003, the monthly snowfall y (in inches) recorded at the observatory at Mount Washington in New Hampshire can be modeled by the function $y = -5.34x^2 + 17.4x + 21.2$ where x is the number of months since January. Did the greatest monthly snowfall during the given time period occur in January? *Explain.*

10. You throw a tennis ball upward from a height of 4 feet with an initial vertical velocity of 36 feet per second.

    a. Write an equation that models the height h (in feet) of the tennis ball as a function of the time t (in seconds) after it is thrown.

    b. Does the ball reach a height of 30 feet? *Explain.*

11. A band wants to have customized stickers printed. The table shows the cost y (in dollars) for x customized stickers.

Stickers, *x*	1000	2000	3000	4000
Cost (dollars), *y*	199	239	279	319

    a. Tell whether the data can be modeled by a *linear function*, an *exponential function*, or a *quadratic function*. Then write an equation for the function.

    b. If the number of stickers printed is doubled, does the price double? *Explain.*

CUMULATIVE REVIEW Chapters 1–10

Evaluate the expression for the given value of x. *(p. 64)*

1. $-|x| + 9$ when $x = -6$
2. $|-x| + 2.6$ when $x = 2$
3. $0.7 - |x|$ when $x = -0.5$

Solve the equation.

4. $5 - 2a = 13$ *(p. 141)*
5. $13y + 16 - y = 4$ *(p. 148)*
6. $-(w + 1) = w + 3$ *(p. 154)*

Graph the equation. *(pp. 215, 225, 244, 253)*

7. $x = -6$
8. $y = -3x$
9. $y = 6.5x$
10. $y = \frac{4}{3}x - 8$
11. $y = -3x + 9$
12. $y + x = 8$
13. $2y - x = 2$
14. $2x + 5y = -40$

Write an equation of the line that passes through the given point and is perpendicular to the given line. *(p. 319)*

15. $(0, 3), y = -5x + 2$
16. $(2, 2), y = -x - 7$
17. $(8, 3), y = \frac{1}{2}x + 2$

Solve the inequality. Then graph the solution.

18. $m - 8 < -15$ *(p. 356)*
19. $\frac{x}{-3} > 12$ *(p. 363)*
20. $1 - 4n < -11$ *(p. 369)*
21. $5b - 7 \le 7b - 5$ *(p. 369)*
22. $12 < z + 9 \le 16$ *(p. 380)*
23. $4 \le 2c + 7 \le 21$ *(p. 380)*

Solve the linear system. *(pp. 427, 435, 444, 451, 459)*

24. $y = 5x - 4$
    $-4x + y = -2$
25. $x - 4y = -44$
    $-3x + 12y = 132$
26. $-4x + 7y = -33$
    $-3x + 2y = -15$

Simplify the expression.

27. $(-9r)^3$ *(p. 489)*
28. $(2p^4)^3 \cdot p^7$ *(p. 489)*
29. $\frac{(3x)^4y}{xy^3}$ *(p. 495)*

Graph the function.

30. $y = (2.5)^x$ *(p. 520)*
31. $y = (0.8)^x$ *(p. 531)*
32. $y = \frac{1}{2} \cdot \left(\frac{1}{4}\right)^x$ *(p. 531)*

Find the sum or difference. *(p. 554)*

33. $(x^2 - 3x + 8) + (-2x^2 + 15x + 4)$
34. $(5m^2 - 6) - (8m^3 + m^2 - 2m + 11)$

Find the product.

35. $(z + 9)(2z - 7)$ *(p. 562)*
36. $(5b - 2)(8b - 7)$ *(p. 562)*
37. $(q + 2)(-3q^2 + 6q - 1)$ *(p. 562)*
38. $(7 + y)^2$ *(p. 569)*
39. $(2k - 11)^2$ *(p. 569)*
40. $(12w - 5)(12w + 5)$ *(p. 569)*

Factor the expression.

41. $x^2 + 6x - 72$ *(p. 583)*
42. $2m^2 - 5mn - 3n^2$ *(p. 593)*
43. $25d^2 + 60d + 36$ *(p. 600)*
44. $-2a^2 + 50b^2$ *(p. 600)*
45. $z^2(z - 6) + 4(6 - z)$ *(p. 606)*
46. $y^3 + 8y^2 - 9y - 72$ *(p. 606)*

Graph the function. Label the vertex and axis of symmetry. *(p. 635)*

47. $y = x^2 - 4x + 1$ **48.** $y = 3x^2 + 6x + 4$ **49.** $y = -x^2 - 4x + 10$

Solve the equation. Round your solutions to the nearest hundredth, if necessary. *(pp. 643, 652, 663, 671)*

50. $5x^2 = 720$ **51.** $-x^2 + 12 = 1$ **52.** $x^2 + 6x - 13 = 0$

53. $-2x^2 + 7x - 3 = 0$ **54.** $4x^2 - 9x = 9$ **55.** $-7x^2 + 7x + 3 = 4x - 1$

56. SPORTS The Pan American Games is a sports event that is held every four years. Athletes from countries in North America, Central America, and South America compete in the games. The table shows the number c of countries that participated in each Pan American Games as a function of the time t (in years) since 1951. Graph the function. *(p. 43)*

Years since 1951, t	0	4	8	12	16	20	24	28	32
Countries, c	21	22	25	22	29	32	33	34	36

57. INCOME A salesperson earns a 5% commission on the sales of computers. If the salesperson's computer sales total \$9500, how much is the commission? *(p. 176)*

58. CUSTOM PRINTING You create a design for a T-shirt. The table shows the cost for printing your design on T-shirts at a printing company. The printing company requires that your design be printed on a minimum of 6 T-shirts. *(p. 302)*

T-shirts	6	7	8	9	10
Cost (dollars)	78	81	84	87	90

a. *Explain* why the situation can be modeled by a linear equation.

b. Write an equation in point-slope form that gives the cost of the T-shirts as a function of the number of T-shirts printed.

59. GEOMETRY A rectangle has a perimeter of 54 inches. Its length is 3 more than twice its width. Find the dimensions of the rectangle. *(p. 435)*

60. SCHOOL ENROLLMENT In 1990, 5000 students were enrolled at a school. The number of students enrolled at the school increased by about 2% per year from 1990 to 2005. Write a model for the number of students enrolled at the school over time. According to the model, how many students were enrolled at the school in 2005? *(p. 520)*

61. LANDSCAPING An arc of water sprayed from a lawn sprinkler can be modeled by the graph of the equation $y = -0.05x^2 + 0.9x$ where x is the distance (in feet) from the sprinkler and y is the height (in feet) of the arc.

a. Graph the function. Label the vertex and axis of symmetry. *(p. 635)*

b. How far from the sprinkler does the water hit the ground? *(p. 643)*

11 Radicals and Geometry Connections

Before

In previous chapters, you learned the following skills, which you'll use in Chapter 11: comparing the graphs of functions with the graphs of parent functions, evaluating square roots, using the distributive property, factoring trinomials, and evaluating expressions.

Prerequisite Skills

VOCABULARY CHECK

Copy and complete the statement.

1. The number or expression inside a radical symbol is called the __?__ .
2. If $b^2 = a$, then b is a(n) __?__ of a.

SKILLS CHECK

3. Graph $y = 3 \cdot 2^x$. Compare the graph with the graph of $y = 2^x$. *(Review p. 520 for 11.1.)*

Evaluate the expression. *(Review p. 110 for 11.2.)*

4. $\sqrt{81}$
5. $-\sqrt{64}$
6. $\pm\sqrt{100}$
7. $-\sqrt{121}$

Use the distributive property to write an equivalent expression. *(Review p. 96 for 11.2.)*

8. $4(y - 3)$
9. $2(x - 2)$
10. $-x(x + 11)$
11. $4x(x - 9)$

Factor the trinomial. *(Review p. 583 for 11.3.)*

12. $x^2 + 4x + 4$
13. $m^2 + 9m + 8$
14. $r^2 + 8r + 7$
15. $b^2 + 10b + 16$
16. Evaluate a^2 when $a = 7$. *(Review p. 2 for 11.4–11.5.)*

@HomeTutor Prerequisite skills practice at classzone.com

Now

In Chapter 11, you will apply the big ideas listed below and reviewed in the Chapter Summary on page 753. You will also use the key vocabulary listed below.

Big Ideas

1. Graphing square root functions
2. Using properties of radicals in expressions and equations
3. Working with radicals in geometry

KEY VOCABULARY

- radical expression, *p. 710*
- radical function, *p. 710*
- square root function, *p. 710*
- parent square root function, *p. 710*
- simplest form of a radical expression, *p. 719*
- rationalizing the denominator, *p. 721*
- radical equation, *p. 729*
- extraneous solution, *p. 730*
- hypotenuse, *p. 737*
- legs of a right triangle, *p. 737*
- Pythagorean theorem, *p. 737*
- distance formula, *p. 744*
- midpoint, *p. 745*
- midpoint formula, *p. 745*

Why?

You can use radical equations to solve real-world problems. For example, you can find the length of a sailboat's waterline given the hull speed of the sailboat.

Animated Algebra

The animation illustrated below for Example 5 on page 731 helps you answer this question: What is the length of a sailboat's waterline if the sailboat has a hull speed of 8 nautical miles per hour?

Start
You need to find the length of the sailboat's waterline.

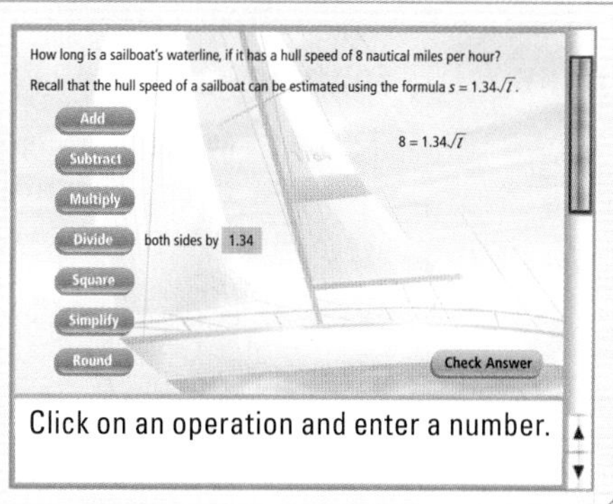

Animated Algebra at classzone.com

Other animations for Chapter 11: pages 711, 719, 722, 737, 746, and 753

11.1 Graph Square Root Functions

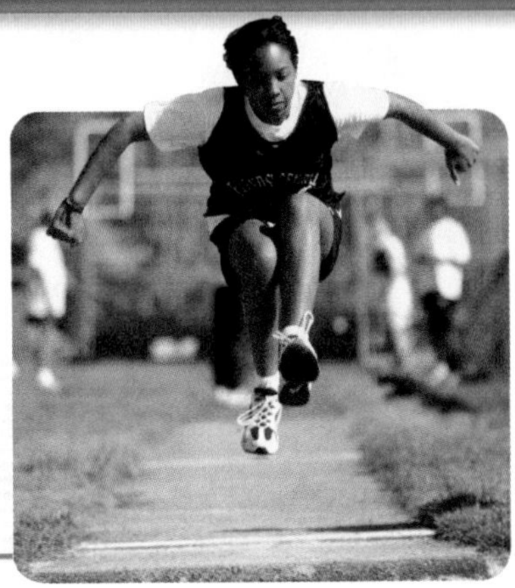

Before You graphed linear, exponential, and quadratic functions.

Now You will graph square root functions.

Why? So you can analyze the speed of an athlete, as in Ex. 45.

Key Vocabulary
- radical expression
- radical function
- square root function
- parent square root function

A **radical expression** is an expression that contains a radical, such as a square root, cube root, or other root. A **radical function** contains a radical expression with the independent variable in the radicand. For example, $y = \sqrt[3]{2x}$ and $y = \sqrt{x + 2}$ are radical functions. If the radical is a square root, then the function is called a **square root function**.

KEY CONCEPT — *For Your Notebook*

Parent Function for Square Root Functions

The most basic square root function in the family of all square root functions, called the **parent square root function**, is:

$$y = \sqrt{x}$$

The graph of the parent square root function is shown.

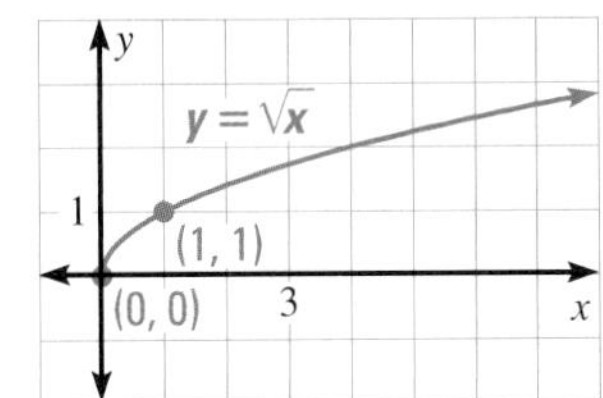

EXAMPLE 1 Graph a function of the form $y = a\sqrt{x}$

Graph the function $y = 3\sqrt{x}$ and identify its domain and range. Compare the graph with the graph of $y = \sqrt{x}$.

REVIEW SQUARE ROOTS
For help with square roots, see p. 110.

Solution

STEP 1 **Make** a table. Because the square root of a negative number is undefined, x must be nonnegative. So, the domain is $x \geq 0$.

x	0	1	2	3	4
y	0	3	4.2	5.2	6

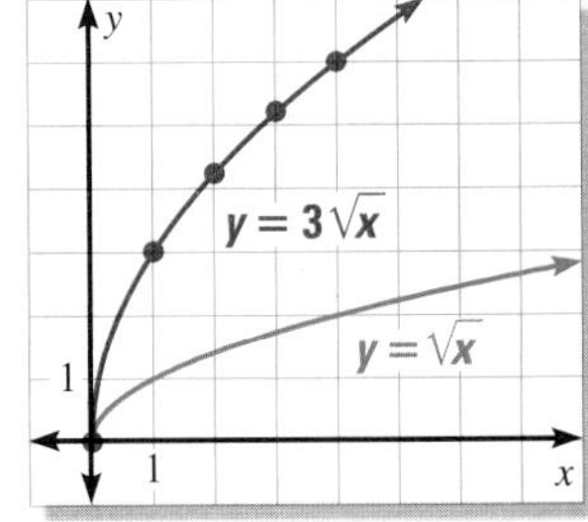

STEP 2 **Plot** the points.

STEP 3 **Draw** a smooth curve through the points. From either the table or the graph, you can see the range of the function is $y \geq 0$.

STEP 4 **Compare** the graph with the graph of $y = \sqrt{x}$. The graph of $y = 3\sqrt{x}$ is a vertical stretch (by a factor of 3) of the graph of $y = \sqrt{x}$.

EXAMPLE 2 Graph a function of the form $y = a\sqrt{x}$

Graph the function $y = -0.5\sqrt{x}$ and identify its domain and range. Compare the graph with the graph of $y = \sqrt{x}$.

Solution

To graph the function, make a table, plot the points, and draw a smooth curve through the points. The domain is $x \geq 0$.

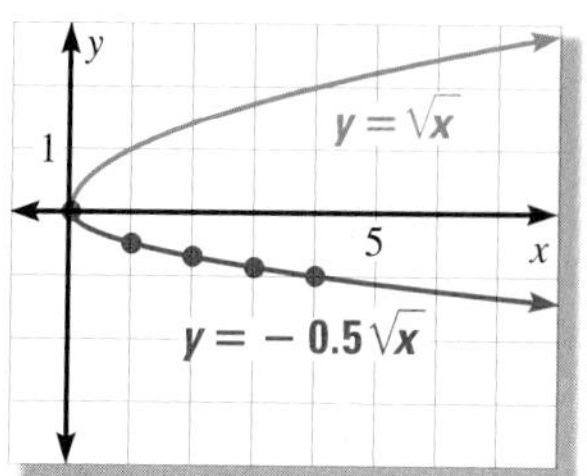

x	0	1	2	3	4
y	0	−0.5	−0.7	−0.9	−1

The range is $y \leq 0$. The graph of $y = -0.5\sqrt{x}$ is a vertical shrink (by a factor of 0.5) with a reflection in the x-axis of the graph of $y = \sqrt{x}$.

GRAPHS OF SQUARE ROOT FUNCTIONS Examples 1 and 2 illustrate the following:

- When $|a| > 1$, the graph of $y = a\sqrt{x}$ is a vertical stretch of the graph of $y = \sqrt{x}$. When $0 < |a| < 1$, the graph of $y = a\sqrt{x}$ is a vertical shrink of the graph of $y = \sqrt{x}$.
- When $a < 0$, the graph of $y = a\sqrt{x}$ is the reflection in the x-axis of the graph of $y = |a|\sqrt{x}$.

EXAMPLE 3 Graph a function of the form $y = \sqrt{x} + k$

Graph the function $y = \sqrt{x} + 2$ and identify its domain and range. Compare the graph with the graph of $y = \sqrt{x}$.

Solution

To graph the function, make a table, then plot and connect the points. The domain is $x \geq 0$.

x	0	1	2	3	4
y	2	3	3.4	3.7	4

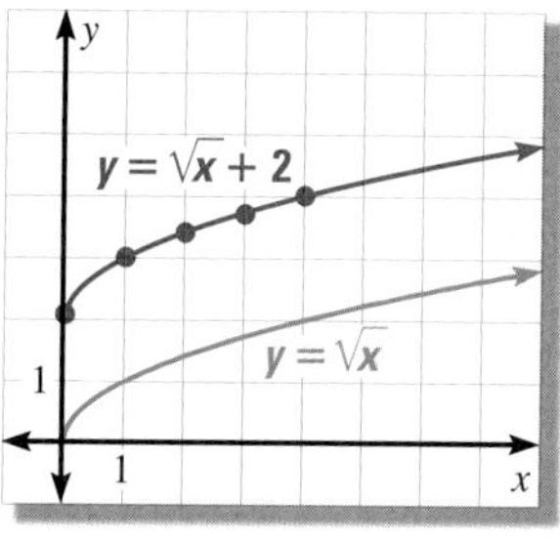

The range is $y \geq 2$. The graph of $y = \sqrt{x} + 2$ is a vertical translation (of 2 units up) of the graph of $y = \sqrt{x}$.

Animated Algebra at classzone.com

✓ GUIDED PRACTICE for Examples 1, 2, and 3

Graph the function and identify its domain and range. Compare the graph with the graph of $y = \sqrt{x}$.

1. $y = 2\sqrt{x}$ **2.** $y = -2\sqrt{x}$ **3.** $y = \sqrt{x} - 1$ **4.** $y = \sqrt{x} + 3$

EXAMPLE 4 Graph a function of the form $y = \sqrt{x - h}$

Graph the function $y = \sqrt{x - 4}$ and identify its domain and range. Compare the graph with the graph of $y = \sqrt{x}$.

Solution

To graph the function, make a table, then plot and connect the points. To find the domain, find the values of x for which the radicand, $x - 4$, is nonnegative. The domain is $x \geq 4$.

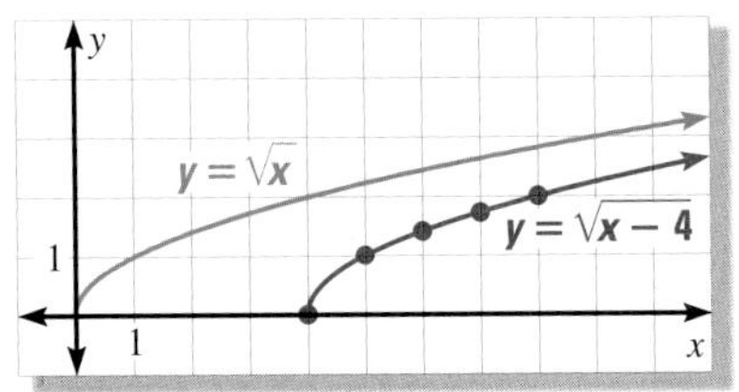

x	4	5	6	7	8
y	0	1	1.4	1.7	2

The range is $y \geq 0$. The graph of $y = \sqrt{x - 4}$ is a horizontal translation (of 4 units to the right) of the graph of $y = \sqrt{x}$.

KEY CONCEPT — For Your Notebook

Graphs of Square Root Functions

To graph a function of the form $y = a\sqrt{x - h} + k$, you can follow these steps.

STEP 1 **Sketch** the graph of $y = a\sqrt{x}$. The graph of $y = a\sqrt{x}$ starts at the origin and passes through the point $(1, a)$.

STEP 2 **Shift** the graph $|h|$ units horizontally (to the right if h is positive and to the left if h is negative) and $|k|$ units vertically (up if k is positive and down if k is negative).

EXAMPLE 5 Graph a function of the form $y = a\sqrt{x - h} + k$

Graph the function $y = 2\sqrt{x + 4} - 1$.

STEP 1 **Sketch** the graph of $y = 2\sqrt{x}$.

STEP 2 **Shift** the graph $|h|$ units horizontally and $|k|$ units vertically. Notice that

$$y = 2\sqrt{x + 4} - 1 = 2\sqrt{x - (-4)} + (-1).$$

So, $h = -4$ and $k = -1$. Shift the graph left 4 units and down 1 unit.

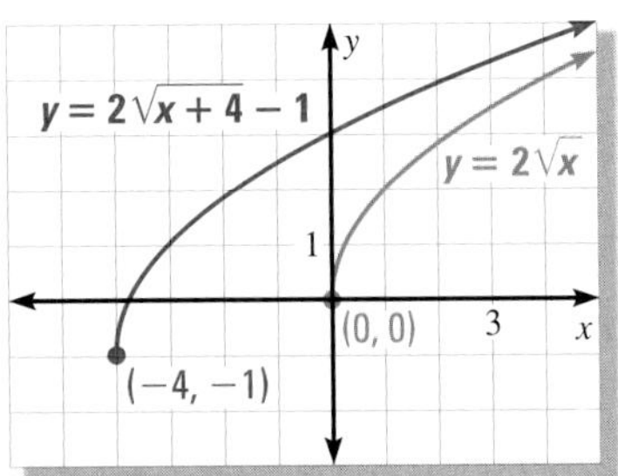

✓ GUIDED PRACTICE for Examples 4 and 5

5. Graph the function $y = \sqrt{x + 3}$ and identify its domain and range. Compare the graph with the graph of $y = \sqrt{x}$.

6. Identify the domain and range of the function in Example 5.

EXAMPLE 6 Solve a real-world problem

MICROPHONE SALES For the period 1988–2002, the amount of sales y (in millions of dollars) of microphones in the United States can be modeled by the function $y = 93\sqrt{x + 2.2}$ where x is the number of years since 1988. Graph the function on a graphing calculator. In what year were microphone sales about \$325 million?

ANOTHER WAY
You can graph $y = 93\sqrt{x + 2.2}$ and $y = 325$. The x-coordinate of the point where the graphs intersect represents the year in which sales were about \$325 million.

Solution

The graph of the function is shown.

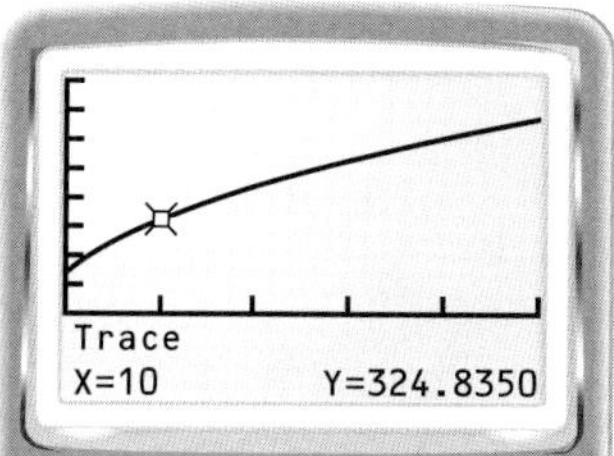

Using the *trace* feature, you can see that $y \approx 325$ when $x = 10$. So, microphone sales were about \$325 million 10 years after 1988, or in 1998.

✓ GUIDED PRACTICE for Example 6

7. **MICROPHONE SALES** Use the function in Example 6 to find the year in which microphone sales were about \$250 million.

11.1 EXERCISES

HOMEWORK KEY
○ = **WORKED-OUT SOLUTIONS** on p. WS26 for Exs. 7, 23, and 45
★ = **STANDARDIZED TEST PRACTICE** Exs. 2, 15, 16, 29, 39, 41, and 48

SKILL PRACTICE

1. **VOCABULARY** Copy and complete: A function containing a radical expression with the independent variable in the radicand is called a(n) _?_.

2. ★ **WRITING** Is the graph of $y = 1.25\sqrt{x}$ a vertical stretch or a vertical shrink of the graph of $y = \sqrt{x}$? *Explain* your answer.

EXAMPLES 1 and 2 on pp. 710–711 for Exs. 3–16

GRAPHING FUNCTIONS **Graph the function and identify its domain and range. Compare the graph with the graph of $y = \sqrt{x}$.**

3. $y = 4\sqrt{x}$
4. $y = 5\sqrt{x}$
5. $y = 0.5\sqrt{x}$
6. $y = 0.25\sqrt{x}$
7. $y = \frac{3}{2}\sqrt{x}$
8. $y = \frac{1}{3}\sqrt{x}$
9. $y = -3\sqrt{x}$
10. $y = -6\sqrt{x}$
11. $y = -0.8\sqrt{x}$
12. $y = -0.75\sqrt{x}$
13. $y = -\frac{1}{4}\sqrt{x}$
14. $y = -\frac{5}{2}\sqrt{x}$

15. ★ **MULTIPLE CHOICE** The graph of which function is a vertical shrink of the graph of $y = \sqrt{x}$?

    Ⓐ $y = -5\sqrt{x}$ Ⓑ $y = -\sqrt{x}$ Ⓒ $y = \frac{1}{2}\sqrt{x}$ Ⓓ $y = 8\sqrt{x}$

16. ★ **WRITING** The range of the function $y = a\sqrt{x}$ is $y \le 0$. What can you conclude about the value of a? How do you know?

EXAMPLES 3 and 4
on pp. 711–712
for Exs. 17–29

GRAPHING FUNCTIONS Graph the function and identify its domain and range. Compare the graph with the graph of $y = \sqrt{x}$.

17. $y = \sqrt{x} + 1$
18. $y = \sqrt{x} + 5$
19. $y = \sqrt{x} - 3$
20. $y = \sqrt{x} - 4$
21. $y = \sqrt{x} + \frac{3}{4}$
22. $y = \sqrt{x} - 4.5$
23. $y = \sqrt{x - 1}$
24. $y = \sqrt{x - 6}$
25. $y = \sqrt{x + 2}$
26. $y = \sqrt{x + 4}$
27. $y = \sqrt{x + 1.5}$
28. $y = \sqrt{x - \frac{1}{2}}$

29. ★ **MULTIPLE CHOICE** The graph of which function is a horizontal translation of 3 units to the right of the graph of $y = \sqrt{x}$?

(A) $y = \sqrt{x} + 3$
(B) $y = \sqrt{x} - 3$
(C) $y = \sqrt{x + 3}$
(D) $y = \sqrt{x - 3}$

EXAMPLE 5
on p. 712
for Exs. 30–39

GRAPHING FUNCTIONS Graph the function.

30. $y = \sqrt{x + 3} - 2$
31. $y = \sqrt{x - 2} + 5$
32. $y = 2\sqrt{x} + 1$
33. $y = -\sqrt{x + 1} + 2$
34. $y = -3\sqrt{x + 2} - 6$
35. $y = 4\sqrt{x + 4} - 4$
36. $y = \frac{1}{2}\sqrt{x - 5} - 3$
37. $y = -\frac{3}{2}\sqrt{x - 1} - 5$
38. $y = -\frac{3}{4}\sqrt{x + 8} - 3$

39. ★ **MULTIPLE CHOICE** The graph of which function is shown?

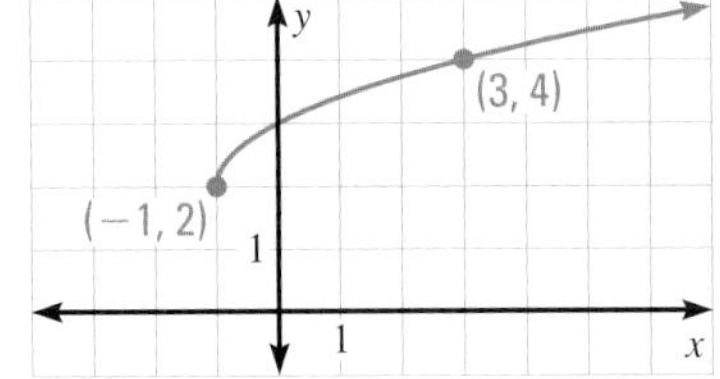

(A) $y = \sqrt{x + 1} + 2$
(B) $y = \sqrt{x - 1} + 2$
(C) $y = \sqrt{x + 1} - 2$
(D) $y = \sqrt{x - 1} - 2$

40. **ERROR ANALYSIS** *Describe* and correct the error in explaining how to graph the function $y = -5\sqrt{x - 9} - 10$.

> To graph $y = -5\sqrt{x - 9} - 10$, sketch the graph of $y = -5\sqrt{x}$. Then shift the graph 9 units to the left and 10 units down.

41. ★ **MULTIPLE CHOICE** How is the graph of $g(x) = 4\sqrt{x} - 3$ related to the graph of $h(x) = 4\sqrt{x} + 3$?

(A) It is a vertical stretch by a factor of 3 of the graph of h.
(B) It is a vertical translation of 3 units down of the graph of h.
(C) It is a vertical translation of 6 units down of the graph of h.
(D) It is a horizontal translation of 6 units to the left of the graph of h.

42. **CHALLENGE** Write a rule for a radical function that has a domain of all real numbers greater than or equal to −5 and a range of all real numbers less than or equal to 3.

PROBLEM SOLVING

EXAMPLE 6 on p. 713 for Exs. 43–45

GRAPHING CALCULATOR **You may wish to use a graphing calculator to complete the following Problem Solving exercises.**

43. **SUSPENSION BRIDGE** The time t (in seconds) it takes an object dropped from a height h (in feet) to reach the ground is given by the function $t = \frac{1}{4}\sqrt{h}$.

   a. Graph the function and identify its domain and range.

   b. The Royal Gorge Bridge in Colorado is the world's highest suspension bridge. It takes about 8 seconds for a stone dropped from the bridge to reach the gorge below. About how high is the bridge?

   @HomeTutor for problem solving help at classzone.com

44. **OCEANOGRAPHY** Ocean waves can be shallow water, intermediate depth, or deep water waves. The speed s (in meters per second) of a shallow water wave can be modeled by the function $s = 3.13\sqrt{d}$ where d is the depth (in meters) of the water over which the wave is traveling.

   a. Graph the function and identify its domain and range.

   b. A tsunami is a type of shallow water wave. Suppose a tsunami has a speed of 200 meters per second. Over approximately what depth of water is the tsunami traveling?

   @HomeTutor for problem solving help at classzone.com

45. **LONG JUMP** A function for the speed at which a long jumper is running before jumping is $s = 10.9\sqrt{h}$ where s and h are defined in the diagram. Graph the function and identify its domain and range. To the nearest tenth, approximate the maximum height reached when the long jumper's speed before jumping is 10.25 meters per second.

46. **MULTI-STEP PROBLEM** The reading age of written materials is the age at which an average person can read and understand the materials. A function that is sometimes used to identify the reading age r (in years) of written materials is $r = \sqrt{w} + 8$ where w is the average number of words with 3 or more syllables in samples taken from the written materials.

   a. Graph the function and identify its domain and range.

   b. What is the average number of words with 3 or more syllables in samples taken from material that can be read and understood by a 10-year-old?

47. **BIOLOGY** Biologists studied two types of duck in the northern Great Plains of the United States from 1987 to 1990. The biologists found functions, given below, that model the number y of breeding pairs of each type of duck in wetlands with area x (in hectares).

a. Graph the functions in the same coordinate plane. Identify the domain and range of each function.

b. Find the area (to the nearest hectare) for 1 breeding pair of each type of duck.

48. ★ **EXTENDED RESPONSE** The amount of mozzarella cheese y (in pounds per person) consumed in the United States for the period 1980–2001 can be modeled by $y = 2\sqrt{x + 1}$ where x is the number of years since 1980.

a. **Graph** Graph the function and identify its domain and range.

b. **Apply** In what year was the amount of mozzarella cheese consumed equal to 2 pounds per person?

c. **Explain** In what year was the amount of mozzarella cheese consumed per person double the amount consumed per person in 1980? *Explain.*

49. **CHALLENGE** The flow rate r (in gallons per minute) of water through a high-pressure water hose is given by $r = 29.7d^2\sqrt{p}$ where d is the nozzle diameter (in inches) and p is the nozzle pressure (in pounds per square inch). For what value of d would the graph of the function be identical to the graph of the parent square root function? For what values of d would the graph be a vertical stretch? a vertical shrink?

MIXED REVIEW

Write the prime factorization of the number if it is not a prime number. If the number is prime, write *prime*. *(p. 910)*

50. 7	**51.** 14	**52.** 18	**53.** 9
54. 24	**55.** 13	**56.** 53	**57.** 72

PREVIEW
Prepare for Lesson 11.2 in Exs. 58–61.

Evaluate the expression. *(p. 110)*

58. $\sqrt{16}$	**59.** $\sqrt{64}$	**60.** $\sqrt{144}$	**61.** $\sqrt{900}$

Factor the expression.

62. $x^2 - 31x + 58$ *(p. 583)*

63. $2x^2 - 7x + 6$ *(p. 593)*

64. $7x^2 + 9x + 2$ *(p. 593)*

65. $6x^2 - 11x - 35$ *(p. 593)*

66. $400x^2 - 9y^2$ *(p. 600)*

67. $25x^2 + 20xy + 4y^2$ *(p. 600)*

EXTRA PRACTICE for Lesson 11.1, p. 948 **ONLINE QUIZ** at classzone.com

@HomeTutor classzone.com Keystrokes

11.1 Graph Square Root Functions

QUESTION How can you use a graphing calculator to graph square root functions?

EXAMPLE Graph the function $y = \sqrt{2x + 3}$ and describe its domain and range

***STEP 1* Enter the function**

Enter the function into a graphing calculator. Use parentheses around the radicand.

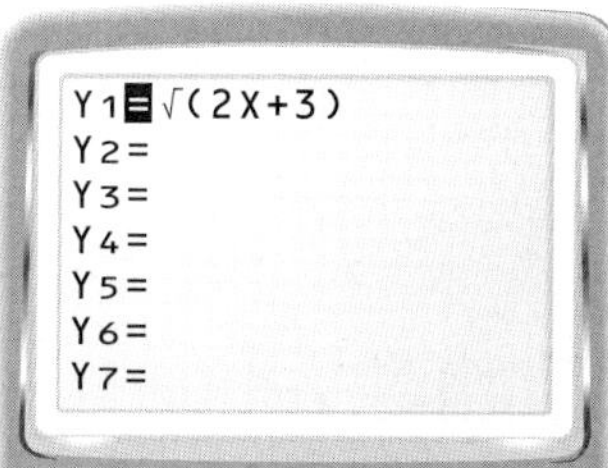

***STEP 2* Graph the function**

Graph the function. Adjust the viewing window if necessary.

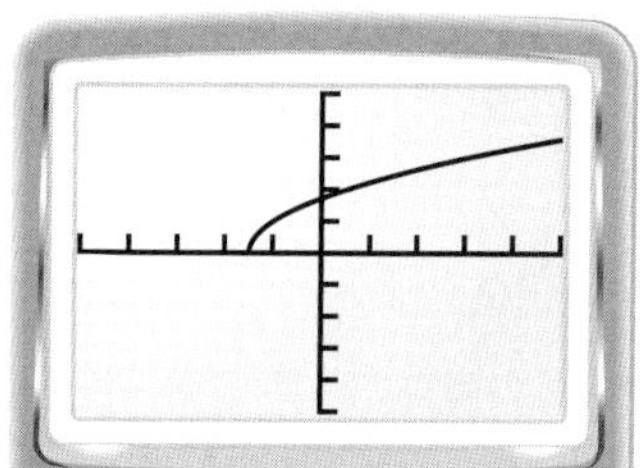

***STEP 3* Describe the domain and range**

From the graph, you can see that the domain is all real numbers greater than or equal to -1.5, or $x \geq -1.5$. The range is all nonnegative numbers, or $y \geq 0$.

PRACTICE

Graph the function using a graphing calculator. Then describe the domain and range of the function.

1. $y = \sqrt{4x}$
2. $y = \sqrt{9x}$
3. $y = \sqrt{7x}$
4. $y = -\sqrt{10x}$
5. $y = -3\sqrt{x}$
6. $y = 1.5\sqrt{3x}$
7. $y = 4.4\sqrt{8x}$
8. $y = \sqrt{2x + 8}$
9. $y = \sqrt{3x + 4}$
10. $y = -\sqrt{2x - 5}$
11. $y = -\sqrt{4x - 6}$
12. $y = \frac{1}{2}\sqrt{6 - 5x}$
13. **ROLLER COASTER** If friction is ignored, the velocity v (in meters per second) of a roller coaster when it reaches the bottom of a hill can be calculated using the formula $v = \sqrt{19.6h}$ where h (in meters) is the height of the hill.
    a. Graph the function and describe its domain and range.
    b. Use the graph to find the height of a hill if the velocity of the roller coaster at the bottom of the hill is 55 meters per second.

11.2 Properties of Radicals

MATERIALS • calculator

QUESTION How can you simplify products and quotients of square roots?

EXPLORE Simplify products and quotients of square roots

STEP 1 *Find products of square roots*

Copy and complete the table without using a calculator. Compare the values in the second and third columns.

Values of a and b	Value of $\sqrt{a} \cdot \sqrt{b}$	Value of $\sqrt{ab}$
$a = 4, b = 9$	?	?
$a = 9, b = 16$	?	?
$a = 25, b = 4$	?	?
$a = 16, b = 36$	?	?

STEP 2 *Find products of square roots*

Use a calculator to copy and complete the table. Compare the values in the second and third columns.

Values of a and b	Value of $\sqrt{a} \cdot \sqrt{b}$	Value of $\sqrt{ab}$
$a = 2, b = 3$	?	?
$a = 10, b = 5$	?	?
$a = 7, b = 11$	?	?
$a = 13, b = 6$	?	?

STEP 3 *Find quotients of square roots*

Copy and complete the table without using a calculator. Compare the values in the second and third columns.

Values of a and b	Value of $\frac{\sqrt{a}}{\sqrt{b}}$	Value of $\sqrt{\frac{a}{b}}$
$a = 4, b = 16$	?	?
$a = 9, b = 25$	?	?
$a = 36, b = 4$	?	?
$a = 4, b = 49$	?	?

STEP 4 *Find quotients of square roots*

Use a calculator to copy and complete the table. Compare the values in the second and third columns.

Values of a and b	Value of $\frac{\sqrt{a}}{\sqrt{b}}$	Value of $\sqrt{\frac{a}{b}}$
$a = 1, b = 2$	?	?
$a = 3, b = 8$	?	?
$a = 12, b = 7$	?	?
$a = 6, b = 11$	?	?

DRAW CONCLUSIONS Use your observations to complete these exercises

In Exercises 1 and 2, copy and complete the statement.

1. The product of two square roots is equal to __?__.
2. The quotient of a square root and a nonzero square root is equal to __?__.
3. **REASONING** Do you think that $\sqrt{a} + \sqrt{b} = \sqrt{a + b}$ for any $a \geq 0$ and any $b \geq 0$? *Justify* your answer.

11.2 Simplify Radical Expressions

Before You found square roots.

Now You will simplify radical expressions.

Why? So you can find the distance to the horizon, as in Ex. 68.

Key Vocabulary
- **simplest form of a radical expression**
- **rationalizing the denominator**

A radical expression is in **simplest form** if the following conditions are true:

- No perfect square factors other than 1 are in the radicand.
- No fractions are in the radicand.
- No radicals appear in the denominator of a fraction.

You can use the following property to simplify radical expressions.

KEY CONCEPT *For Your Notebook*

Product Property of Radicals

Words The square root of a product equals the product of the square roots of the factors.

Algebra $\sqrt{ab} = \sqrt{a} \cdot \sqrt{b}$ where $a \ge 0$ and $b \ge 0$

Example $\sqrt{4x} = \sqrt{4} \cdot \sqrt{x} = 2\sqrt{x}$

You can also use the fact that $\sqrt{a^2} = a$, where $a \ge 0$, to simplify radical expressions. In this lesson, whenever a variable appears in the radicand *assume that it has only nonnegative values.*

REVIEW SQUARE ROOTS
For help finding square roots of perfect squares, see p. 110.

EXAMPLE 1 Use the product property of radicals

a. $\sqrt{32} = \sqrt{16 \cdot 2}$ — Factor using perfect square factor.

$= \sqrt{16} \cdot \sqrt{2}$ — Product property of radicals

$= 4\sqrt{2}$ — Simplify.

b. $\sqrt{9x^3} = \sqrt{9 \cdot x^2 \cdot x}$ — Factor using perfect square factors.

$= \sqrt{9} \cdot \sqrt{x^2} \cdot \sqrt{x}$ — Product property of radicals

$= 3x\sqrt{x}$ — Simplify.

Animated Algebra at classzone.com

GUIDED PRACTICE for Example 1

1. Simplify (**a**) $\sqrt{24}$ and (**b**) $\sqrt{25x^2}$.

EXAMPLE 2 Multiply radicals

a. $\sqrt{6} \cdot \sqrt{6} = \sqrt{6 \cdot 6}$ **Product property of radicals**

$= \sqrt{36}$ **Multiply.**

$= 6$ **Simplify.**

b. $\sqrt{3x} \cdot 4\sqrt{x} = 4\sqrt{3x \cdot x}$ **Product property of radicals**

$= 4\sqrt{3x^2}$ **Multiply.**

$= 4 \cdot \sqrt{3} \cdot \sqrt{x^2}$ **Product property of radicals**

$= 4x\sqrt{3}$ **Simplify.**

WRITE RADICALS
When writing a product involving a radical, write the radical last to avoid confusion. For instance, if you write the product of x and $\sqrt{2}$ as $\sqrt{2}x$, it might be read as $\sqrt{2x}$.

c. $\sqrt{7xy^2} \cdot 3\sqrt{x} = 3\sqrt{7xy^2 \cdot x}$ **Product property of radicals**

$= 3\sqrt{7x^2y^2}$ **Multiply.**

$= 3 \cdot \sqrt{7} \cdot \sqrt{x^2} \cdot \sqrt{y^2}$ **Product property of radicals**

$= 3xy\sqrt{7}$ **Simplify.**

KEY CONCEPT *For Your Notebook*

Quotient Property of Radicals

Words The square root of a quotient equals the quotient of the square roots of the numerator and denominator.

Algebra $\sqrt{\frac{a}{b}} = \frac{\sqrt{a}}{\sqrt{b}}$ where $a \ge 0$ and $b > 0$

Example $\sqrt{\frac{16}{25}} = \frac{\sqrt{16}}{\sqrt{25}} = \frac{4}{5}$

EXAMPLE 3 Use the quotient property of radicals

a. $\sqrt{\frac{13}{100}} = \frac{\sqrt{13}}{\sqrt{100}}$ **Quotient property of radicals**

$= \frac{\sqrt{13}}{10}$ **Simplify.**

b. $\sqrt{\frac{7}{x^2}} = \frac{\sqrt{7}}{\sqrt{x^2}}$ **Quotient property of radicals**

$= \frac{\sqrt{7}}{x}$ **Simplify.**

✓ GUIDED PRACTICE for Examples 2 and 3

2. Simplify (**a**) $\sqrt{2x^3} \cdot \sqrt{x}$ and (**b**) $\sqrt{\frac{1}{y^2}}$.

RATIONALIZING THE DENOMINATOR Example 4 shows how to eliminate a radical from the denominator of a radical expression by multiplying the expression by an appropriate form of 1. The process of eliminating a radical from an expression's denominator is called **rationalizing the denominator.**

EXAMPLE 4 Rationalize the denominator

MULTIPLY BY 1
In part (a), notice that $\frac{\sqrt{7}}{\sqrt{7}}$ is equal to 1, so multiplying by it does not change the value of the expression.

a. $\frac{5}{\sqrt{7}} = \frac{5}{\sqrt{7}} \cdot \frac{\sqrt{7}}{\sqrt{7}}$ Multiply by $\frac{\sqrt{7}}{\sqrt{7}}$.

$= \frac{5\sqrt{7}}{\sqrt{49}}$ Product property of radicals

$= \frac{5\sqrt{7}}{7}$ Simplify.

b. $\frac{\sqrt{2}}{\sqrt{3b}} = \frac{\sqrt{2}}{\sqrt{3b}} \cdot \frac{\sqrt{3b}}{\sqrt{3b}}$ Multiply by $\frac{\sqrt{3b}}{\sqrt{3b}}$.

$= \frac{\sqrt{6b}}{\sqrt{9b^2}}$ Product property of radicals

$= \frac{\sqrt{6b}}{\sqrt{9} \cdot \sqrt{b^2}}$ Product property of radicals

$= \frac{\sqrt{6b}}{3b}$ Simplify.

SUMS AND DIFFERENCES You can use the distributive property to simplify sums and differences of radical expressions when the expressions have the same radicand.

EXAMPLE 5 Add and subtract radicals

a. $4\sqrt{10} + \sqrt{13} - 9\sqrt{10} = 4\sqrt{10} - 9\sqrt{10} + \sqrt{13}$ Commutative property

$= (4 - 9)\sqrt{10} + \sqrt{13}$ Distributive property

$= -5\sqrt{10} + \sqrt{13}$ Simplify.

b. $5\sqrt{3} + \sqrt{48} = 5\sqrt{3} + \sqrt{16 \cdot 3}$ Factor using perfect square factor.

$= 5\sqrt{3} + \sqrt{16} \cdot \sqrt{3}$ Product property of radicals

$= 5\sqrt{3} + 4\sqrt{3}$ Simplify.

$= (5 + 4)\sqrt{3}$ Distributive property

$= 9\sqrt{3}$ Simplify.

✓ **GUIDED PRACTICE** for Examples 4 and 5

Simplify the expression.

3. $\frac{1}{\sqrt{3}}$ **4.** $\frac{1}{\sqrt{x}}$ **5.** $\frac{3}{\sqrt{2x}}$ **6.** $2\sqrt{7} + 3\sqrt{63}$

EXAMPLE 6 Multiply radical expressions

a. $\sqrt{5}(4 - \sqrt{20}) = 4\sqrt{5} - \sqrt{5} \cdot \sqrt{20}$ **Distributive property**

$= 4\sqrt{5} - \sqrt{100}$ **Product property of radicals**

$= 4\sqrt{5} - 10$ **Simplify.**

b. $(\sqrt{7} + \sqrt{2})(\sqrt{7} - 3\sqrt{2})$

$= (\sqrt{7})^2 + \sqrt{7}(-3\sqrt{2}) + \sqrt{2} \cdot \sqrt{7} + \sqrt{2}(-3\sqrt{2})$ **Multiply.**

$= 7 - 3\sqrt{7 \cdot 2} + \sqrt{7 \cdot 2} - 3(\sqrt{2})^2$ **Product property of radicals**

$= 7 - 3\sqrt{14} + \sqrt{14} - 6$ **Simplify.**

$= 1 - 2\sqrt{14}$ **Simplify.**

REVIEW FOIL METHOD
For help with the FOIL method, see p. 562.

Animated **Algebra** at classzone.com

EXAMPLE 7 Solve a real-world problem

ASTRONOMY The orbital period of a planet is the time that it takes the planet to travel around the sun. You can find the orbital period P (in Earth years) using the formula $P = \sqrt{d^3}$ where d is the average distance (in astronomical units, abbreviated AU) of the planet from the sun.

a. Simplify the formula.

b. Jupiter's average distance from the sun is shown in the diagram. What is Jupiter's orbital period?

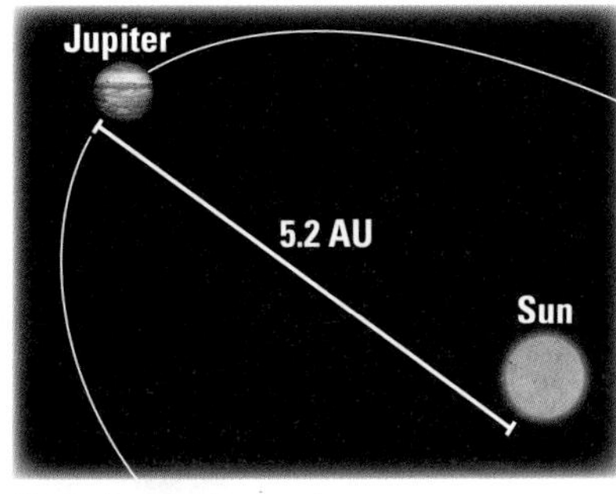

Not drawn to scale

Solution

a. $P = \sqrt{d^3}$ **Write formula.**

$= \sqrt{d^2 \cdot d}$ **Factor using perfect square factor.**

$= \sqrt{d^2} \cdot \sqrt{d}$ **Product property of radicals**

$= d\sqrt{d}$ **Simplify.**

b. Substitute 5.2 for d in the simplified formula.

$P = d\sqrt{d} = 5.2\sqrt{5.2}$

▶ The orbital period of Jupiter is $5.2\sqrt{5.2}$, or about 11.9, Earth years.

✓ GUIDED PRACTICE for Examples 6 and 7

7. Simplify the expression $(4 - \sqrt{5})(1 - \sqrt{5})$.

8. **ASTRONOMY** Neptune's average distance from the sun is about 6 times Jupiter's average distance from the sun. Is the orbital period of Neptune 6 times the orbital period of Jupiter? *Explain.*

11.2 EXERCISES

HOMEWORK KEY

○ = **WORKED-OUT SOLUTIONS** on p. WS26 for Exs. 9, 37, and 69

★ = **STANDARDIZED TEST PRACTICE** Exs. 2, 23, 25, 64, and 71

◆ = **MULTIPLE REPRESENTATIONS** Ex. 70

SKILL PRACTICE

1. **VOCABULARY** Copy and complete: The process of eliminating a radical from the denominator of a radical expression is called _?_.

2. ★ **WRITING** Is the expression $\sqrt{\frac{2x}{9}}$ written in simplest form? *Explain* why or why not.

EXAMPLES 1, 2, and 3 on pp. 719–720 for Exs. 3–25

USING PRODUCT AND QUOTIENT PROPERTIES Simplify the expression.

3. $\sqrt{20}$ 4. $\sqrt{48}$ 5. $\sqrt{96}$ 6. $\sqrt{72}$

7. $\sqrt{125b}$ 8. $\sqrt{4x^2}$ 9. $\sqrt{81m^3}$ 10. $\sqrt{32m^5}$

11. $\sqrt{5} \cdot \sqrt{30}$ 12. $\sqrt{50} \cdot \sqrt{18}$ 13. $\sqrt{14x} \cdot \sqrt{2x}$ 14. $\sqrt{3b^3} \cdot \sqrt{18b}$

15. $2\sqrt{a^4b^5}$ 16. $\sqrt{64s^4t^3}$ 17. $\sqrt{m^2n} \cdot \sqrt{n}$ 18. $\sqrt{75xy} \cdot \sqrt{2x^3}$

19. $\sqrt{\frac{4}{49}}$ 20. $\sqrt{\frac{7}{81}}$ 21. $\sqrt{\frac{a^3}{121}}$ 22. $\sqrt{\frac{100}{4x^2}}$

23. ★ **MULTIPLE CHOICE** Which expression is equivalent to $\sqrt{\frac{9x}{16}}$?

(A) $\frac{\sqrt{3x}}{4}$ (B) $\frac{3\sqrt{x}}{4}$ (C) $\frac{3\sqrt{x}}{16}$ (D) $\frac{3x}{4}$

24. **ERROR ANALYSIS** *Describe* and correct the error in simplifying the expression $\sqrt{72}$.

$$\sqrt{72} = \sqrt{4} \cdot \sqrt{18} = 2\sqrt{18}$$

25. ★ **WRITING** *Describe* two different sequences of steps you could take to simplify the expression $\sqrt{45} \cdot \sqrt{5}$.

EXAMPLE 4 on p. 721 for Exs. 26–33

RATIONALIZING THE DENOMINATOR Simplify the expression.

26. $\frac{2}{\sqrt{2}}$ 27. $\frac{4}{\sqrt{3}}$ 28. $\sqrt{\frac{5}{48}}$ 29. $\sqrt{\frac{4}{52}}$

30. $\frac{3}{\sqrt{a}}$ 31. $\frac{1}{\sqrt{2x}}$ 32. $\sqrt{\frac{2x^2}{5}}$ 33. $\sqrt{\frac{8}{3n^3}}$

EXAMPLES 5 and 6 on pp. 721–722 for Exs. 34–45

PERFORMING OPERATIONS ON RADICALS Simplify the expression.

34. $2\sqrt{2} + 6\sqrt{2}$ 35. $\sqrt{5} - 6\sqrt{5}$ 36. $2\sqrt{6} - 5\sqrt{54}$

37. $9\sqrt{32} + \sqrt{2}$ 38. $\sqrt{12} + 6\sqrt{3} + 2\sqrt{6}$ 39. $3\sqrt{7} - 5\sqrt{14} + 2\sqrt{28}$

40. $\sqrt{5}(5 - \sqrt{5})$ 41. $\sqrt{6}(7\sqrt{3} + 6)$ 42. $\sqrt{3}(6\sqrt{2} - 4\sqrt{3})$

43. $(4 - \sqrt{2})(5 + \sqrt{2})$ 44. $(2\sqrt{5} + 7)^2$ 45. $(\sqrt{7} + \sqrt{3})(6 + \sqrt{8})$

SIMPLIFYING RADICAL EXPRESSIONS **Simplify the expression.**

46. $\sqrt{75m^2np^4}$

47. $\sqrt{512rs^6} \cdot \sqrt{t^3}$

48. $\sqrt{\frac{600a}{4b^3}}$

49. $\sqrt{\frac{50gh^2}{125f^3}}$

50. $\frac{4}{\sqrt{3}} + \frac{7}{\sqrt{12}}$

51. $\frac{2\sqrt{6}}{\sqrt{30}} - \frac{3}{\sqrt{20}}$

52. $\frac{7}{\sqrt{x}} + \frac{3}{2\sqrt{x}}$

53. $\frac{3}{\sqrt{x^3}} + \frac{4}{\sqrt{x}}$

54. $\frac{6m}{\sqrt{m^3}} - \frac{8}{\sqrt{m}}$

CONJUGATES **In Exercises 55–62, use the example to simplify the expression.**

EXAMPLE **Rationalize the denominator using conjugates**

Simplify $\frac{9}{2 - \sqrt{3}}$.

Solution

The binomials $a\sqrt{b} + c\sqrt{d}$ and $a\sqrt{b} - c\sqrt{d}$ are called *conjugates*. They differ only by the sign of one term. The product of two conjugates $a\sqrt{b} + c\sqrt{d}$ and $a\sqrt{b} - c\sqrt{d}$ does not contain a radical: $(2 + \sqrt{3})(2 - \sqrt{3}) = 2^2 - (\sqrt{3})^2 = 4 - 3 = 1$. You can use conjugates to simplify the expression.

$\frac{9}{2 - \sqrt{3}} = \frac{9}{2 - \sqrt{3}} \cdot \frac{2 + \sqrt{3}}{2 + \sqrt{3}}$ Multiply the numerator and denominator by the conjugate of the denominator.

$= \frac{9(2 + \sqrt{3})}{(2 - \sqrt{3})(2 + \sqrt{3})}$ Multiply fractions.

$= \frac{18 + 9\sqrt{3}}{4 - 3}$ Simplify numerator and denominator.

$= 18 + 9\sqrt{3}$ Simplify.

55. $\frac{1}{\sqrt{7} + 1}$

56. $\frac{2}{5 - \sqrt{3}}$

57. $\frac{\sqrt{10}}{7 - \sqrt{2}}$

58. $\frac{\sqrt{5}}{6 + \sqrt{5}}$

59. $\frac{3}{\sqrt{7} + \sqrt{6}}$

60. $\frac{11}{\sqrt{11} - \sqrt{7}}$

61. $\frac{\sqrt{6}}{\sqrt{2} - \sqrt{3}}$

62. $\frac{\sqrt{7} + 1}{\sqrt{7} + \sqrt{2}}$

63. **REASONING** Multiply the binomials $a\sqrt{b} + c\sqrt{d}$ and $a\sqrt{b} - c\sqrt{d}$ to show that the product does not contain a radical.

64. ★ **WRITING** According to the definition of square root, a number b is a square root of a number a if $b^2 = a$. How can you use the definition to show that $\sqrt{x^2} = x$? *Explain.*

65. **MULTIPLYING FUNCTIONS** Let $f(x) = \sqrt{x} - \sqrt{4x}$, and let $g(x) = \sqrt{x}$. Find $h(x) = f(x) \cdot g(x)$.

66. **CHALLENGE** Consider the expression $\sqrt{2^m}$. Assume m is a positive integer. For what values of m will the expression contain a radical when simplified? For what values of m will the expression contain no radical when simplified? *Explain.*

○ = WORKED-OUT SOLUTIONS on p. WS1 ★ = STANDARDIZED TEST PRACTICE ◆ = MULTIPLE REPRESENTATIONS

PROBLEM SOLVING

EXAMPLE 7 on p. 722 for Exs. 67, 68

67. **FINANCE** You invest \$225 in a savings account for two years. The account has an annual interest rate that changes from year to year. You can find the average annual interest rate r that the account earned over two years using the formula $r = \sqrt{\frac{V_2}{V_0}} - 1$ where V_0 is the initial investment and V_2 is the amount in the account after two years. At the end of two years, you have \$270 in the account. What was the average annual interest rate (written as a percent) the account earned over two years?

@HomeTutor for problem solving help at classzone.com

68. **DISTANCE TO THE HORIZON** The distance d (in miles) that a person can see to the horizon is given by the formula $d = \sqrt{\frac{3h}{2}}$ where h is the person's eye level (in feet) above the water. To the nearest mile, find the distance that the person shown can see to the horizon.

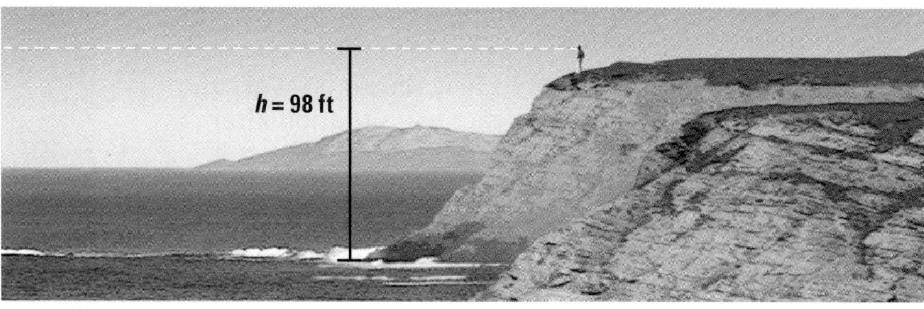

@HomeTutor for problem solving help at classzone.com

69. **MULTI-STEP PROBLEM** You are making a cube-shaped footrest. You want to cover the footrest with fabric. At a fabric store, you choose fabric that costs \$6 per square yard.

a. You have \$30 to spend on fabric. How much fabric can you buy?

b. The edge length s (in yards) of the largest footrest you can cover can be found using the formula $s = \sqrt{\frac{S}{6}}$ where S is the surface area of the footrest (in square yards). Use unit analysis to check the units in the formula.

c. Find the edge length of the largest footrest you can cover to the nearest tenth of a yard.

70. ◆ **MULTIPLE REPRESENTATIONS** The velocity v (in feet per second) of an object that has been dropped can be found using the equation $v = \sqrt{64d}$ where d is the distance the object falls (in feet) before hitting the ground.

a. **Writing an Equation** Write the equation in simplified form.

b. **Drawing a Graph** Graph the equation. For what value of d is the velocity about 16 feet per second?

c. **Solving an Equation** Use the equation from part (a) to find the exact value of d when the velocity is 16 feet per second.

71. ★ **SHORT RESPONSE** Physicians can calculate the body surface area S (in square meters) of an adult using the formula $S = \sqrt{\frac{hw}{3600}}$ where h is the adult's height (in centimeters) and w is the adult's mass (in kilograms).

a. Simplify the formula.

b. Does an adult who is 1.7 meters tall and has a mass of 70 kilograms have a greater body surface area than an adult who is 1.5 meters tall and has a mass of 70 kilograms? *Explain* what effect height has on surface area if two people have the same mass.

72. **CHALLENGE** The speed s (in miles per hour) at which a vehicle is traveling before an accident is given by $s = \sqrt{30df}$ where d is the length of the skid mark (in feet) and f is the coefficient of friction. The coefficient of friction varies depending on the type of road surface and on the road conditions.

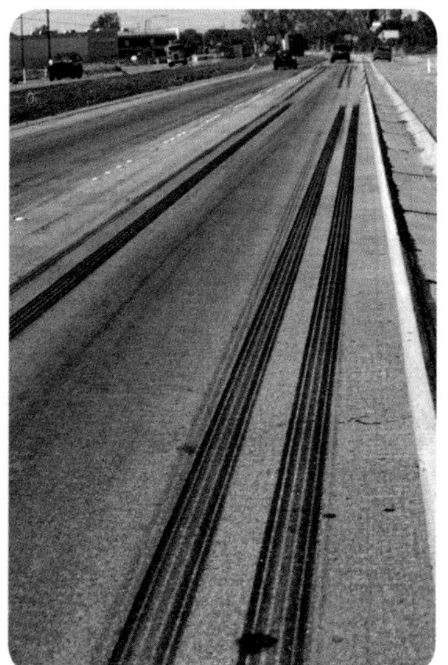

a. A driver is traveling on a newly paved road with a coefficient of friction of 0.80. The driver sees a hazard in the road and is forced to brake. The car skids to a halt leaving a skid mark that is 100 feet long. At what speed was the car traveling when the driver applied the brakes?

b. A perception-reaction time is the amount of time it takes for a person to react to a situation after perceiving it, such as applying the brakes after seeing a hazard in the road. The driver in part (a) has a perception-reaction time of 1.5 seconds. How many feet does the car travel before the driver applies the brakes? *Explain* how you found your answer.

c. What is the total distance (in feet) traveled from the time the driver in part (a) sees the hazard until the time the car skids to a halt?

MIXED REVIEW

Graph the function and identify its domain and range.

73. $y = -6$ for $x \ge 0$ *(p. 215)*

74. $y = -\frac{1}{3}x$ *(p. 215)*

75. $5x + y = 3$ *(p. 244)*

76. $y = 0.4x - 7$ *(p. 244)*

77. $y = 4^x$ *(p. 520)*

78. $y = (0.4)^x$ *(p. 531)*

79. $y = -7x^2$ *(p. 628)*

80. $y = 5x^2 + 2$ *(p. 628)*

81. $y = 3x^2 - 10x - 8$ *(p. 635)*

82. Write the equation of the line that passes through (1, 2) and is perpendicular to the line $y = \frac{1}{2}x + 3$. *(p. 319)*

PREVIEW Prepare for Lesson 11.3 in Exs. 83–94.

Solve the equation. *(pp. 575, 583, 593, and 600)*

83. $(a - 3)(a + 8) = 0$

84. $(2y + 3)(2y + 5) = 0$

85. $-12m^2 + 48 = 0$

86. $x^2 - 8x + 16 = 0$

87. $d^2 + 8d = -2$

88. $x^2 - 2x = 24$

89. $10z - 21 = -2z^2$

90. $5x^2 + 13x + 6 = 0$

91. $4x^2 - 11x - 3 = 0$

92. $8x^2 - 64 = 0$

93. $4z^2 = 36$

94. $b^2 + 12b + 36 = 0$

Derive the Quadratic Formula

GOAL Solve quadratic equations and check solutions.

In Lesson 10.6, you learned how to find solutions of quadratic equations using the quadratic formula. You can use the method of completing the square and the quotient property of radicals to derive the quadratic formula.

$ax^2 + bx + c = 0$	**Write standard form of a quadratic equation.**
$ax^2 + bx = -c$	**Subtract c from each side.**
$x^2 + \frac{b}{a}x = -\frac{c}{a}$	**Divide each side by a, $a \neq 0$.**
$x^2 + \frac{b}{a}x + \left(\frac{b}{2a}\right)^2 = -\frac{c}{a} + \left(\frac{b}{2a}\right)^2$	**Add $\left(\frac{b}{2a}\right)^2$ to each side to complete the square.**
$\left(x + \frac{b}{2a}\right)^2 = -\frac{c}{a} + \frac{b^2}{4a^2}$	**Write left side as the square of a binomial.**
$\left(x + \frac{b}{2a}\right)^2 = \frac{b^2 - 4ac}{4a^2}$	**Simplify right side.**
$x + \frac{b}{2a} = \pm\sqrt{\frac{b^2 - 4ac}{4a^2}}$	**Take square roots of each side.**
$x + \frac{b}{2a} = \frac{\pm\sqrt{b^2 - 4ac}}{2a}$	**Quotient property of radicals**
$x = \frac{-b \pm \sqrt{b^2 - 4ac}}{2a}$	**Subtract $\frac{b}{2a}$ from each side.**

SOLVING QUADRATIC EQUATIONS You can use the quadratic formula and properties of radicals to solve quadratic equations.

EXAMPLE 1 Solve an equation

Solve $x^2 - 6x + 3 = 0$.

Solution

$x^2 - 6x + 3 = 0$	**Identify $a = 1$, $b = -6$, and $c = 3$.**
$x = \frac{-(-6) \pm \sqrt{(-6)^2 - 4(1)(3)}}{2(1)}$	**Substitute values in the quadratic formula.**
$= \frac{6 \pm \sqrt{24}}{2}$	**Simplify.**
$= \frac{6 \pm \sqrt{4 \cdot 6}}{2}$	**Product property of radicals**
$= \frac{6 \pm 2\sqrt{6}}{2} = 3 \pm \sqrt{6}$	**Simplify.**

▶ The solutions of the equation are $3 + \sqrt{6}$ and $3 - \sqrt{6}$.

EXAMPLE 2 Check the solutions of an equation

Check the solutions of the equation from Example 1.

Solution

The solutions of $x^2 - 6x + 3 = 0$ are $3 + \sqrt{6}$ and $3 - \sqrt{6}$. You can check each solution by substituting it into the original equation.

Check $x = 3 + \sqrt{6}$:

$$x^2 - 6x + 3 = 0$$ Write original equation.

$$(3 + \sqrt{6})^2 - 6(3 + \sqrt{6}) + 3 \stackrel{?}{=} 0$$ Substitute $3 + \sqrt{6}$ for x.

$$9 + 6\sqrt{6} + 6 - 18 - 6\sqrt{6} + 3 \stackrel{?}{=} 0$$ Multiply.

$$0 = 0 \checkmark$$ Solution checks.

Check $x = 3 - \sqrt{6}$:

$$x^2 - 6x + 3 = 0$$ Write original equation.

$$(3 - \sqrt{6})^2 - 6(3 - \sqrt{6}) + 3 \stackrel{?}{=} 0$$ Substitute $3 - \sqrt{6}$ for x.

$$9 - 6\sqrt{6} + 6 - 18 + 6\sqrt{6} + 3 \stackrel{?}{=} 0$$ Multiply.

$$0 = 0 \checkmark$$ Solution checks.

PRACTICE

EXAMPLES 1 and 2 on pp. 727–728 for Exs. 1–18

Solve the equation using the quadratic formula. Check the solution.

1. $x^2 + 4x + 2 = 0$
2. $x^2 + 6x - 1 = 0$
3. $x^2 + 8x + 8 = 0$
4. $x^2 - 7x + 1 = 0$
5. $3x^2 + 6x - 1 = 0$
6. $2x^2 - 4x - 3 = 0$
7. $5x^2 - 2x - 2 = 0$
8. $4x^2 + 10x + 3 = 0$
9. $x^2 - x - 3 = 0$
10. $x^2 - 2x - 8 = 0$
11. $-x^2 + 7x + 3 = 0$
12. $x^2 + 3x - 9 = 0$
13. $-\frac{5}{2}x^2 + 10x - 5 = 0$
14. $\frac{1}{2}x^2 + 3x - 9 = 0$
15. $3x^2 - 2 = 0$
16. $-2x^2 - 7x = 0$
17. $3x^2 + x = 6$
18. $x^2 - 4x = -2$
19. Show that $\frac{-b + \sqrt{b^2 - 4ac}}{2a}$ and $\frac{-b - \sqrt{b^2 - 4ac}}{2a}$ are solutions of $ax^2 + bx + c = 0$ by substituting.
20. Derive a formula to find solutions of equations that have the form $ax^2 + x + c = 0$. Use your formula to find solutions of $-2x^2 + x + 8 = 0$.
21. Find the sum and product of $\frac{-b + \sqrt{b^2 - 4ac}}{2a}$ and $\frac{-b - \sqrt{b^2 - 4ac}}{2a}$. Write a quadratic expression whose solutions have a sum of 2 and a product of $\frac{1}{2}$.
22. What values can a have in the equation $ax^2 + 12x + 3 = 0$ in order for the equation to have one or two real solutions? *Explain.*

11.3 Solve Radical Equations

Before You solved linear, quadratic, and exponential equations.

Now You will solve radical equations.

Why? So you can use scientific formulas to study animals, as in Ex. 39.

Key Vocabulary
- **radical equation**
- **extraneous solution**

An equation that contains a radical expression with a variable in the radicand is a **radical equation.** To solve a radical equation, you need to isolate the radical on one side and then square both sides of the equation.

KEY CONCEPT *For Your Notebook*

Squaring Both Sides of an Equation

Words If two expressions are equal, then their squares are equal.

Algebra If $a = b$, then $a^2 = b^2$. **Example** If $\sqrt{x} = 3$, then $(\sqrt{x})^2 = 3^2$.

EXAMPLE 1 Solve a radical equation

Solve $2\sqrt{x} - 8 = 0$.

Solution

$2\sqrt{x} - 8 = 0$	Write original equation.
$2\sqrt{x} = 8$	Add 8 to each side.
$\sqrt{x} = 4$	Divide each side by 2.
$(\sqrt{x})^2 = 4^2$	Square each side.
$x = 16$	Simplify.

▶ The solution is 16.

CHECK Check the solution by substituting it in the original equation.

$2\sqrt{x} - 8 = 0$	Write original equation.
$2\sqrt{16} - 8 \stackrel{?}{=} 0$	Substitute 16 for *x*.
$2 \cdot 4 - 8 \stackrel{?}{=} 0$	Simplify.
$0 = 0$ ✓	Solution checks.

GUIDED PRACTICE for Example 1

1. Solve (**a**) $\sqrt{x} - 7 = 0$ and (**b**) $12\sqrt{x} - 3 = 0$.

EXAMPLE 2 Solve a radical equation

Solve $4\sqrt{x-7} + 12 = 28$.

Solution

$4\sqrt{x-7} + 12 = 28$	Write original equation.
$4\sqrt{x-7} = 16$	Subtract 12 from each side.
$\sqrt{x-7} = 4$	Divide each side by 4.
$(\sqrt{x-7})^2 = 4^2$	Square each side.
$x - 7 = 16$	Simplify.
$x = 23$	Add 7 to each side.

▶ The solution is 23.

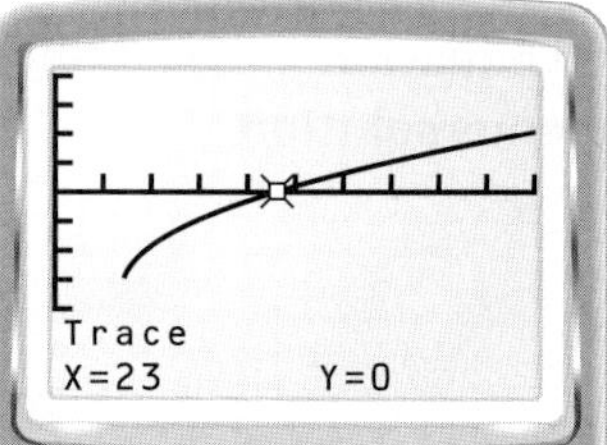

CHECK To check the solution using a graphing calculator, first rewrite the equation so that one side is 0: $4\sqrt{x-7} - 16 = 0$. Then graph the related equation $y = 4\sqrt{x-7} - 16$. You can see that the graph crosses the x-axis at $x = 23$.

EXAMPLE 3 Solve an equation with radicals on both sides

Solve $\sqrt{3x-17} = \sqrt{x+21}$.

SOLVE EQUATIONS
To solve a radical equation that contains two radical expressions, be sure that each side of the equation has only one radical expression before squaring each side.

Solution

$\sqrt{3x-17} = \sqrt{x+21}$	Write original equation.
$(\sqrt{3x-17})^2 = (\sqrt{x+21})^2$	Square each side.
$3x - 17 = x + 21$	Simplify.
$2x - 17 = 21$	Subtract x from each side.
$2x = 38$	Add 17 to each side.
$x = 19$	Divide each side by 2.

▶ The solution is 19. Check the solution.

GUIDED PRACTICE for Examples 2 and 3

Solve the equation.

2. $\sqrt{x-5} + 7 = 12$ **3.** $\sqrt{x+4} = \sqrt{2x-1}$ **4.** $\sqrt{4x-3} - \sqrt{x} = 0$

EXTRANEOUS SOLUTIONS Squaring both sides of the equation $a = b$ can result in a solution of $a^2 = b^2$ that is *not* a solution of the original equation. Such a solution is called an **extraneous solution.** When you square both sides of an equation, check each solution in the original equation to be sure there are no extraneous solutions.

EXAMPLE 4 Solve an equation with an extraneous solution

Solve $\sqrt{6 - x} = x$.

$\sqrt{6 - x} = x$	Write original equation.
$(\sqrt{6 - x})^2 = x^2$	Square each side.
$6 - x = x^2$	Simplify.
$0 = x^2 + x - 6$	Write in standard form.
$0 = (x - 2)(x + 3)$	Factor.
$x - 2 = 0$ *or* $x + 3 = 0$	Zero-product property
$x = 2$ *or* $x = -3$	Solve for *x*.

REVIEW FACTORING
For help with factoring, see pp. 583, 593, 600, and 606.

CHECK Check 2 and -3 in the original equation.

If $x = 2$: $\sqrt{6 - 2} \stackrel{?}{=} 2$ **If $x = -3$:** $\sqrt{6 - (-3)} \stackrel{?}{=} -3$

$2 = 2$ ✓ $3 = -3$ ✗

▶ Because -3 does not check in the original equation, it is an extraneous solution. The only solution of the equation is 2.

at classzone.com

EXAMPLE 5 Solve a real-world problem

SAILING The hull speed *s* (in nautical miles per hour) of a sailboat can be estimated using the formula $s = 1.34\sqrt{\ell}$ where ℓ is the length (in feet) of the sailboat's waterline, as shown. Find the length (to the nearest foot) of the sailboat's waterline if it has a hull speed of 8 nautical miles per hour.

Solution

$s = 1.34\sqrt{\ell}$	Write original equation.
$8 = 1.34\sqrt{\ell}$	Substitute 8 for *s*.
$\frac{8}{1.34} = \sqrt{\ell}$	Divide each side by 1.34.
$\left(\frac{8}{1.34}\right)^2 = (\sqrt{\ell})^2$	Square each side.
$35.6 \approx \ell$	Simplify.

▶ The sailboat has a waterline length of about 36 feet.

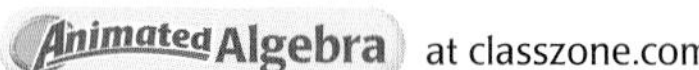

GUIDED PRACTICE for Examples 4 and 5

5. Solve $\sqrt{3x + 4} = x$.

6. **WHAT IF?** In Example 5, suppose the sailboat's hull speed is 6.5 nautical miles per hour. Find the sailboat's waterline length to the nearest foot.

11.3 EXERCISES

HOMEWORK KEY

○ = **WORKED-OUT SOLUTIONS** on p. WS27 for Exs. 11 and 37

★ = **STANDARDIZED TEST PRACTICE** Exs. 2, 21, 34, and 40

SKILL PRACTICE

1. **VOCABULARY** Copy and complete: To find the solution of $\sqrt{12 - x} = x$, you square both sides of the equation and solve. The solutions of $(\sqrt{12 - x})^2 = x^2$ are -4 and 3, but -4 is a(n) __?__ of $\sqrt{12 - x} = x$.

2. ★ **WRITING** Is $x + x\sqrt{2} = 4$ a radical equation? *Explain* why or why not.

EXAMPLES 1, 2, and 3 on pp. 729–730 for Exs. 3–21, 28

SOLVING EQUATIONS **Solve the equation. Check for extraneous solutions.**

3. $3\sqrt{x} - 6 = 0$
4. $2\sqrt{x} - 9 = 0$
5. $\sqrt{3x} + 4 = 16$
6. $\sqrt{5x} + 5 = 0$
7. $\sqrt{x + 7} + 5 = 11$
8. $\sqrt{x - 8} - 4 = -2$
9. $2\sqrt{x - 4} - 2 = 2$
10. $3\sqrt{x - 1} - 5 = 5$
11. $\sqrt{6 - 2x} + 12 = 21$
12. $5\sqrt{x - 3} + 4 = 14$
13. $2\sqrt{x - 11} - 8 = 4$
14. $\sqrt{3x - 2} = \sqrt{x}$
15. $\sqrt{7 - 2x} = \sqrt{9 - x}$
16. $\sqrt{3x + 8} = \sqrt{x + 4}$
17. $\sqrt{9x - 30} = \sqrt{4x + 5}$
18. $\sqrt{21 - x} - \sqrt{1 - x} = 0$
19. $\sqrt{x - 12} - \sqrt{x - 8} = 0$
20. $\sqrt{\frac{1}{2}x - 2} - \sqrt{x - 8} = 0$

21. ★ **MULTIPLE CHOICE** Which is the solution of the equation $10\sqrt{x + 3} + 3 = 18$?

Ⓐ $-\frac{3}{2}$ Ⓑ $-\frac{3}{4}$ Ⓒ $\frac{3}{4}$ Ⓓ $\frac{3}{2}$

EXAMPLE 4 on p. 731 for Exs. 22–27, 29

SOLVING EQUATIONS **Solve the equation. Check for extraneous solutions.**

22. $x = \sqrt{42 - x}$
23. $\sqrt{4 - 3x} = x$
24. $\sqrt{11x - 24} = x$
25. $\sqrt{14x - 3} = 4x$
26. $2x = \sqrt{1 - 3x}$
27. $\sqrt{2 - x} = x + 4$

ERROR ANALYSIS ***Describe*** **and correct the error in solving the equation.**

28.

$\sqrt{3x} + 9 = 0$

$\sqrt{3x} = -9$

$3x = 81$

$x = 27$ ✗

29.

$x = \sqrt{18 - 7x}$

$x^2 = 18 - 7x$

$x^2 + 7x - 18 = 0$

$(x - 2)(x + 9) = 0$

$x - 2 = 0$ or $x + 9 = 0$

$x = 2$ or $x = -9$ ✗

30. **GEOMETRY** The formula for the slant height s (in inches) of a cone is $s = \sqrt{h^2 + r^2}$ where h is the height of the cone (in inches) and r is the radius of its base (in inches), as shown. Find the height of the cone if you know the slant height is 4 inches and the radius is 2 inches.

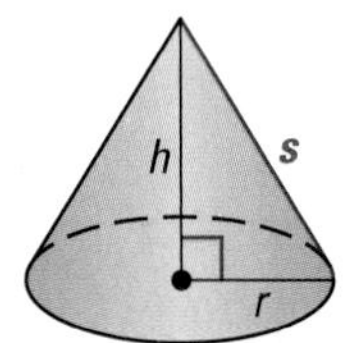

SOLVING EQUATIONS **Solve the equation. Check for extraneous solutions.**

31. $\sqrt{x} + 2 = \sqrt{x - 1}$

32. $2 - \sqrt{x + 1} = \sqrt{x + 3}$

33. $\sqrt{5x + 9} + \sqrt{5x} = 9$

34. ★ **WRITING** A student solves the equation $\sqrt{x + 2} = x$ and finds that $x = 2$ or $x = -1$. Without checking by substituting into the equation, which is the extraneous solution, 2 or -1? How do you know?

35. **CHALLENGE** Write a radical equation that has 3 and 4 as solutions.

PROBLEM SOLVING

EXAMPLE 5 on p. 731 for Exs. 36–38

36. **FORESTS** The dark green areas on the image shown represent regions with heavy foliage. In Texas, the area of land y (in millions of acres) that was covered by forest during the period 1907–2002 can be modeled by the function $y = 2.5\sqrt{143 - x}$ where x is the number of years since 1907. In what year were about 20 million acres of land covered by forest in Texas?

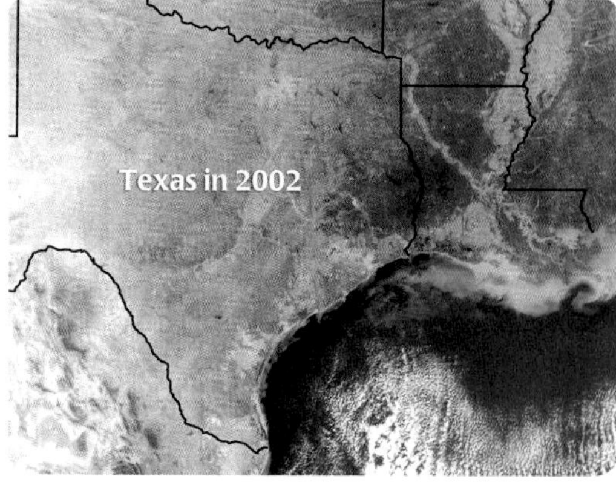

@HomeTutor for problem solving help at classzone.com

37. **PER CAPITA CONSUMPTION** The annual banana consumption y (in pounds per person) in the United States for the period 1970–2000 can be modeled by the function $y = \sqrt{18x + 272}$ where x is the number of years since 1970. In what year were about 20 pounds of bananas consumed per person?

@HomeTutor for problem solving help at classzone.com

38. **MULTI-STEP PROBLEM** The velocity v (in meters per second) at which a trapeze performer swings can be modeled by the function $v = \sqrt{19.6d}$ where d is the difference (in meters) between the highest and lowest position of the performer's center of gravity during the swing.

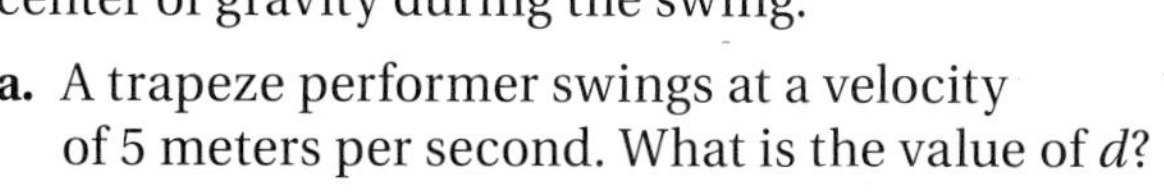

a. A trapeze performer swings at a velocity of 5 meters per second. What is the value of d?

b. Suppose the performer jumps straight up off the starting board, increasing the velocity of the swing by 0.4 meter per second. By how many meters does the value of d increase?

39. **BIOLOGY** A bushbaby is a small animal that can perform standing jumps of over 2 meters. Scientists found that the time t (in seconds) in which a bushbaby must extend its legs in order to jump to a height h (in meters) is given by the function $t = 0.45\ell\sqrt{\frac{1}{h}}$ where ℓ is the length of the bushbaby's legs (in meters). A particular bushbaby has a leg length of 0.16 meter. The bushbaby can extend its legs in 0.05 second. About how high does the bushbaby jump? Round your answer to the nearest tenth of a meter.

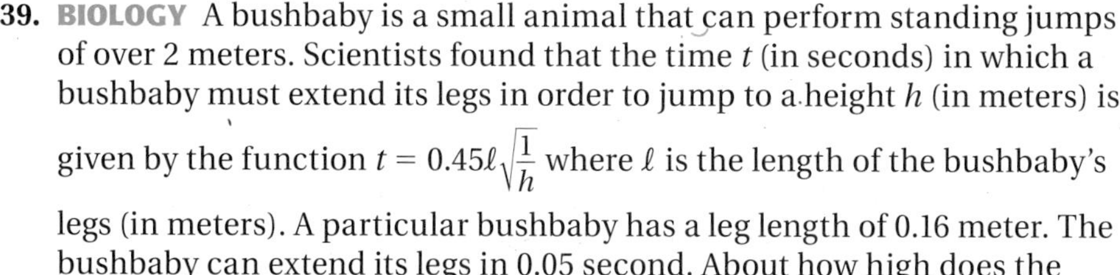

40. ★ **SHORT RESPONSE** The amount of time t (in seconds) it takes a simple pendulum to complete one full swing is called the period of the pendulum and is given by $t = 2\pi\sqrt{\frac{\ell}{32}}$ where ℓ is the length of the pendulum (in feet).

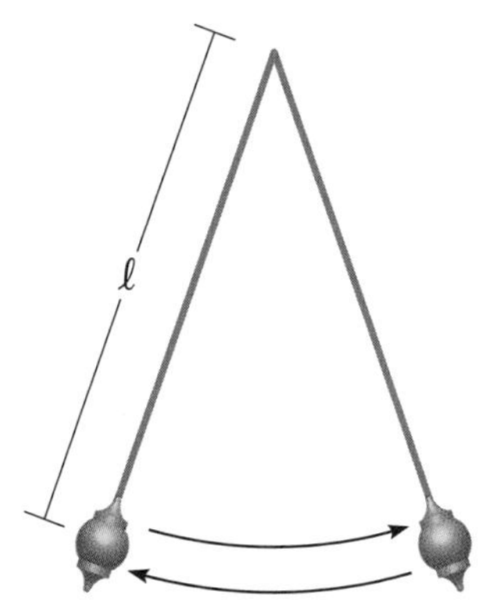

a. **Apply** A visitor at a museum notices that a pendulum on display has a period of about 11 seconds. About how long is the pendulum? Use 3.14 for π and round your answer to the nearest foot.

b. **Explain** Does increasing the length of a pendulum increase or decrease its period? *Explain.*

41. **CHALLENGE** The frequency f (in cycles per second) of a string of an electric guitar is given by the equation $f = \frac{1}{2\ell}\sqrt{\frac{T}{m}}$ where ℓ is the length of the string (in meters), T is the string's tension (in newtons), and m is the string's mass per unit length (in kilograms per meter). The high E string of a particular electric guitar is 0.64 meter long with a mass per unit length of 0.000401 kilogram per meter. How much tension is required to produce a frequency of about 330 cycles per second? Would you need more or less tension if you want to create the same frequency on a string with greater mass per unit length? *Explain.*

MIXED REVIEW

Make a scatter plot of the data. *Describe* the correlation of the data. If possible, fit a line to the data and write an equation for the line. *(p. 325)*

42.

x	0	1	2	3	4
y	−5	−2	2	4	7

43.

x	2	4	6	8	10
y	0	11	24	31	44

PREVIEW
Prepare for Lesson 11.4 in Exs. 44–49.

Solve the equation.

44. $x^2 + 21x + 20 = 0$ *(p. 583)*
45. $x^2 - 21x + 38 = 0$ *(p. 583)*
46. $x^2 - 8x - 9 = 0$ *(p. 583)*
47. $11x^2 - 11 = 0$ *(p. 600)*
48. $5x^2 - 125 = 0$ *(p. 600)*
49. $8x^2 - 32 = 0$ *(p. 600)*

QUIZ *for Lessons 11.1–11.3*

1. Graph the function $y = \sqrt{x - 3}$ and identify its domain and range. Compare the graph with the graph of $y = \sqrt{x}$. *(p. 710)*

Simplify the expression. *(p. 719)*

2. $\sqrt{150}$
3. $\sqrt{2c^2} \cdot \sqrt{8c}$
4. $(7 + \sqrt{5})(2 - \sqrt{5})$
5. $\frac{14}{\sqrt{2}}$
6. $\sqrt{\frac{98}{x^6}}$
7. $\sqrt{\frac{80x^3}{5y}}$

Solve the equation. Check for extraneous solutions. *(p. 729)*

8. $\sqrt{x} - 15 = 0$
9. $\sqrt{4x - 7} = \sqrt{2x + 19}$
10. $\sqrt{6x - 5} = x$

MIXED REVIEW of Problem Solving

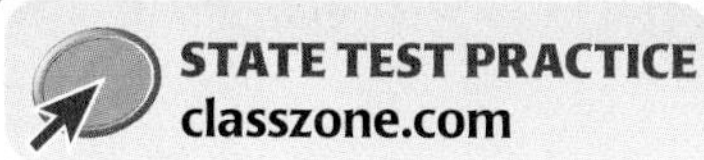

Lessons 11.1–11.3

1. **OPEN-ENDED** The velocity v (in meters per second) of a car moving in a circular path that has radius r (in meters) is given by $v = \sqrt{\frac{Fr}{m}}$ where F is the force (in newtons) pulling the car toward the center of the circular path and m is the mass of the car (in kilograms).

A 1200 kilogram car is traveling at a constant velocity of 20 meters per second in a circular path of radius r meters where $r \geq 100$. Choose two different values of r to show how the force, F, acting on the car changes as the radius increases.

2. **MULTI-STEP PROBLEM** The number y of companies listed on the New York Stock Exchange for the period 1999–2002 can be modeled by the function $y = 3018 - 146\sqrt{x}$ where x is the number of years since 1999.

   a. Graph the function.

   b. How many companies were listed on the New York Stock Exchange in 1999?

   c. In what year were there about 220 companies fewer than the number of companies listed on the New York Stock Exchange in 1999?

3. **GRIDDED ANSWER** The voltage V (in volts) of an amplifier is given by the function $V = \sqrt{PR}$ where P is the power (in watts) and R is the resistance (in ohms). A particular amplifier produces 10 volts and has a resistance of 4 ohms. How many watts are produced by the amplifier?

4. **MULTI-STEP PROBLEM** For the period 1994–2001, the annual consumption of corn products y (in pounds per person) in the United States can be modeled by the function $y = 6.1\sqrt{x + 15.8}$ where x is the number of years since 1994.

   a. Graph the function.

   b. In what year were about 25 pounds of corn products consumed per person?

5. **EXTENDED RESPONSE** Competitors in a ski mountaineering race must climb a mountain and ski down it as quickly as possible. The race begins with the firing of a starting gun. Near Earth's surface, the speed of sound s (in meters per second) through air is given by $s = 20\sqrt{T + 273}$ where T is the air temperature (in degrees Celsius).

   a. A typical temperature at the start of a race is $-5°C$. What is the speed of sound at this temperature?

   b. The person firing the starting gun is standing 50 meters away from the racers. How long will it take for the racers to hear the starting gun?

   c. What happens to the time it takes for the racers to hear the starting gun if the temperature at the start of the race is lower? *Explain.*

6. **SHORT RESPONSE** A person's maximum running speed s (in meters per second) can be approximated by the function $s = \pi\sqrt{\frac{9.8\ell}{6}}$ where ℓ is the person's leg length (in meters).

   a. To the nearest tenth of a meter, what is the leg length of a person whose maximum running speed is about 3.8 meters per second?

   b. What happens to running speed as leg length increases? *Explain.*

11.4 The Pythagorean Theorem

MATERIALS • graph paper • scissors

QUESTION **How are the lengths of the sides of a right triangle related to each other?**

EXPLORE **Examine the relationship among the lengths of the sides of a right triangle**

STEP 1 ***Make right triangles***
Cut a right triangle out of graph paper. Make three copies of it.

STEP 2 ***Arrange as a square***
Arrange the right triangles to form a square within a square, as shown.

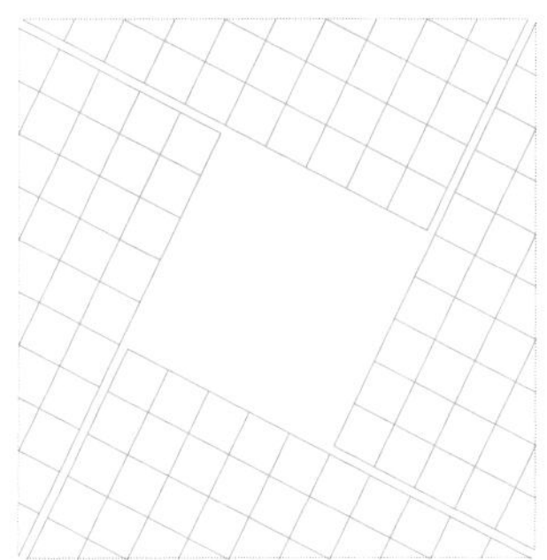

DRAW CONCLUSIONS **Use your observations to complete these exercises**

1. How are the areas of the triangles and inner square related to the area of the outer square?

In Exercises 2–4, let *a*, *b*, and *c* be the lengths of the sides of a right triangle with $a < b < c$, as shown. Write an expression for the area of the figure described below.

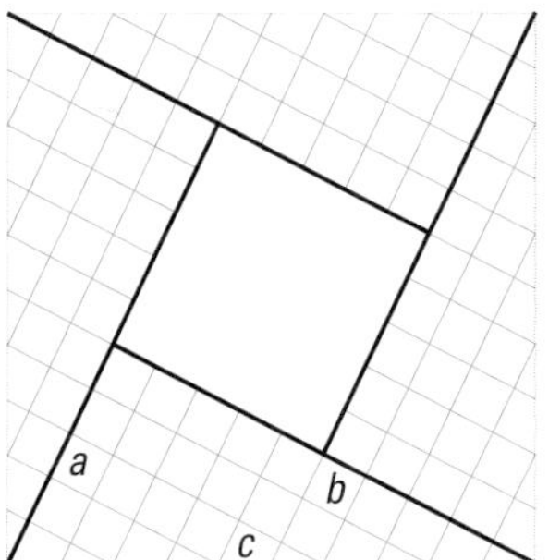

2. One of the right triangles in terms of a and b
3. The outer square in terms of c
4. The inner square in terms of a and b
5. Use the relationship you determined in Exercise 1 and your results from Exercises 2–4 to write an equation that relates a, b, and c. Simplify the equation.
6. **REASONING** The triangle shown is a right triangle. Find the value of x. *Explain* how you found your answer.

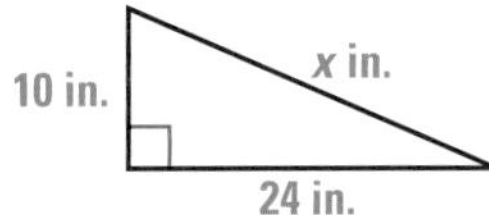

11.4 Apply the Pythagorean Theorem and Its Converse

Before You solved radical equations.

Now You will use the Pythagorean theorem and its converse.

Why? So you can examine angles in architecture, as in Ex. 35.

Key Vocabulary
- **hypotenuse**
- **legs of a right triangle**
- **Pythagorean theorem**

The **hypotenuse** of a right triangle is the side opposite the right angle. It is the longest side of a right triangle. The **legs** are the two sides that form the right angle.

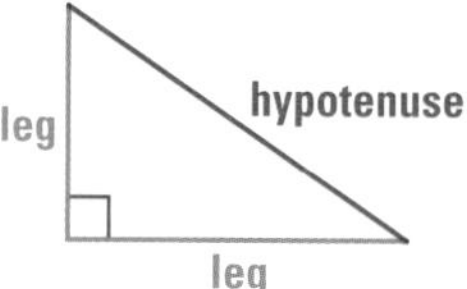

A *theorem* is a statement that can be proved true. The **Pythagorean theorem** states the relationship among the lengths of the sides of a right triangle.

KEY CONCEPT *For Your Notebook*

The Pythagorean Theorem

Words If a triangle is a right triangle, then the sum of the squares of the lengths of the legs equals the square of the length of the hypotenuse.

Algebra $a^2 + b^2 = c^2$

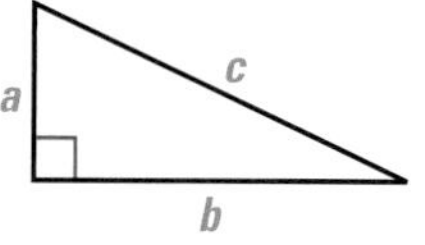

EXAMPLE 1 Use the Pythagorean theorem

Find the unknown length for the triangle shown.

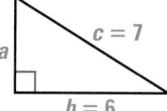

a
$c = 7$
$b = 6$

Solution

$a^2 + b^2 = c^2$	Pythagorean theorem
$a^2 + 6^2 = 7^2$	Substitute 6 for b and 7 for c.
$a^2 + 36 = 49$	Simplify.
$a^2 = 13$	Subtract 36 from each side.
$a = \sqrt{13}$	Take positive square root of each side.

▶ The side length a is $\sqrt{13}$.

REVIEW QUADRATIC EQUATIONS
For help with solving quadratic equations by using square roots, see p. 652.

Animated Algebra at classzone.com

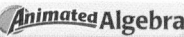

✓ **GUIDED PRACTICE** for Example 1

1. The lengths of the legs of a right triangle are $a = 5$ and $b = 12$. Find c.

EXAMPLE 2 Use the Pythagorean theorem

A right triangle has one leg that is 2 inches longer than the other leg. The length of the hypotenuse is $\sqrt{10}$ inches. Find the unknown lengths.

Solution

Sketch a right triangle and label the sides with their lengths. Let x be the length of the shorter leg.

$a^2 + b^2 = c^2$	Pythagorean theorem
$x^2 + (x + 2)^2 = (\sqrt{10})^2$	Substitute.
$x^2 + x^2 + 4x + 4 = 10$	Simplify.
$2x^2 + 4x - 6 = 0$	Write in standard form.
$2(x - 1)(x + 3) = 0$	Factor.
$x - 1 = 0$ *or* $x + 3 = 0$	Zero-product property
$x = 1$ *or* $x = -3$	Solve for x.

▶ Because length is nonnegative, the solution $x = -3$ does not make sense. The legs have lengths of 1 inch and $1 + 2 = 3$ inches.

EXAMPLE 3 Standardized Test Practice

A soccer player makes a corner kick to another player, as shown. To the nearest yard, how far does the player kick the ball?

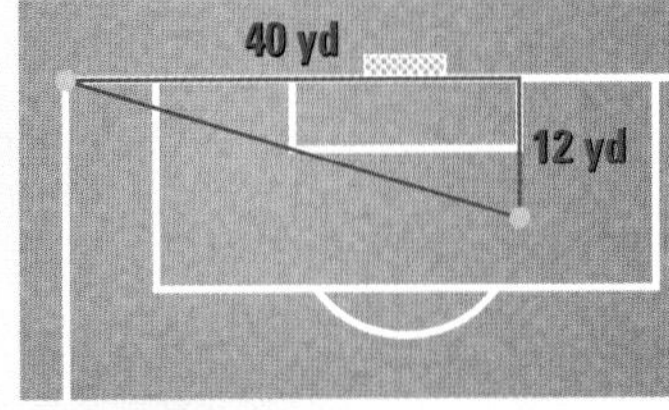

ELIMINATE CHOICES
The hypotenuse is the longest side of the triangle, so the length must be greater than 40 yards. Eliminate choices A and B.

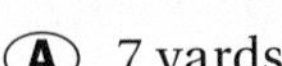

Ⓐ 7 yards Ⓑ 38 yards

Ⓒ 42 yards Ⓓ 52 yards

Solution

The path of the kicked ball is the hypotenuse of a right triangle. The length of one leg is 12 yards, and the length of the other leg is 40 yards.

$c^2 = a^2 + b^2$	Pythagorean theorem
$c^2 = 12^2 + 40^2$	Substitute 12 for a and 40 for b.
$c^2 = 1744$	Simplify.
$c = \sqrt{1744} \approx 42$	Take positive square root of each side.

▶ The correct answer is C. Ⓐ Ⓑ Ⓒ Ⓓ

GUIDED PRACTICE for Examples 2 and 3

2. A right triangle has one leg that is 3 inches longer than the other leg. The length of the hypotenuse is 15 inches. Find the unknown lengths.

3. **SWIMMING** A rectangular pool is 30 feet wide and 60 feet long. You swim diagonally across the pool. To the nearest foot, how far do you swim?

REVIEW REASONING For help with if-then statements and converses, see pp. 64, 110, and 319.

CONVERSE OF THE PYTHAGOREAN THEOREM Recall that when you reverse the hypothesis and conclusion of an if-then statement, the new statement is called the converse. Although not all converses of true statements are true, the converse of the Pythagorean theorem is true.

KEY CONCEPT *For Your Notebook*

Converse of the Pythagorean Theorem

If a triangle has side lengths a, b, and c such that $a^2 + b^2 = c^2$, then the triangle is a right triangle.

EXAMPLE 4 Determine right triangles

Tell whether the triangle with the given side lengths is a right triangle.

a. 8, 15, 17

$8^2 + 15^2 \stackrel{?}{=} 17^2$

$64 + 225 \stackrel{?}{=} 289$

$289 = 289$ ✓

▶ The triangle is a right triangle.

b. 5, 8, 9

$5^2 + 8^2 \stackrel{?}{=} 9^2$

$25 + 64 \stackrel{?}{=} 81$

$89 = 81$ ✗

▶ The triangle is *not* a right triangle.

EXAMPLE 5 Use the converse of the Pythagorean theorem

CONSTRUCTION A construction worker is making sure one corner of the foundation of a house is a right angle. To do this, the worker makes a mark 8 feet from the corner along one wall and another mark 6 feet from the same corner along the other wall. The worker then measures the distance between the two marks and finds the distance to be 10 feet. Is the corner a right angle?

Solution

$8^2 + 6^2 \stackrel{?}{=} 10^2$	Check to see if $a^2 + b^2 = c^2$ when $a = 8$, $b = 6$, and $c = 10$.
$64 + 36 \stackrel{?}{=} 100$	Simplify.
$100 = 100$ ✓	Add.

▶ Because the sides that the construction worker measured form a right triangle, the corner of the foundation is a right angle.

GUIDED PRACTICE for Examples 4 and 5

Tell whether the triangle with the given side lengths is a right triangle.

4. 7, 11, 13

5. 15, 36, 39

6. 15, 112, 113

7. WINDOW DESIGN A window has the shape of a triangle with side lengths of 120 centimeters, 120 centimeters, and 180 centimeters. Is the window a right triangle? *Explain.*

11.4 EXERCISES

HOMEWORK KEY

○ = **WORKED-OUT SOLUTIONS** on p. WS27 for Exs. 9, 23, and 35

★ = **STANDARDIZED TEST PRACTICE** Exs. 2, 15, 29, 30, and 37

SKILL PRACTICE

1. **VOCABULARY** Copy and complete: In a right triangle, the side opposite the right angle is called the __?__.

2. ★ **WRITING** *Explain* how you can tell whether a triangle with side lengths of 9, 12, and 15 is a right triangle.

EXAMPLE 1 on p. 737 for Exs. 3–16

USING THE PYTHAGOREAN THEOREM **Let a and b represent the lengths of the legs of a right triangle, and let c represent the length of the hypotenuse. Find the unknown length.**

3. $a = 3, c = 5$	4. $b = 3, c = 7$	5. $a = 5, b = 6$
6. $b = 5, c = 10$	7. $a = 8, b = 8$	8. $a = 5, b = 12$
(9.) $a = 8, b = 12$	10. $a = 7, c = 25$	11. $b = 15, c = 17$
12. $a = 9, c = 41$	13. $b = 3, c = 3.4$	14. $a = 1.2, c = 3.7$

15. ★ **MULTIPLE CHOICE** A tennis court is 36 feet by 78 feet. What is the length of a diagonal? Round your answer to the nearest tenth of a foot.

   Ⓐ 42.0 feet   Ⓑ 69.2 feet   Ⓒ 85.9 feet   Ⓓ 114.0 feet

16. **ERROR ANALYSIS** *Describe* and correct the error in finding the unknown length.

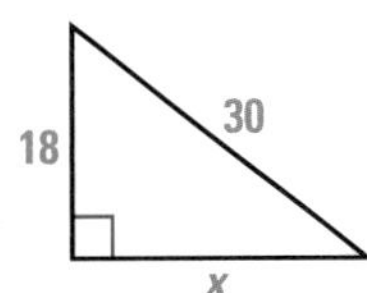

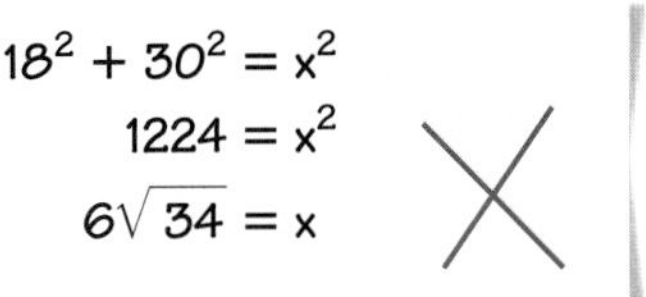

EXAMPLE 2 on p. 738 for Exs. 17–22

USING THE PYTHAGOREAN THEOREM **Find the unknown lengths.**

17. $x + 1$, $2\sqrt{5}$, $x + 3$

18.

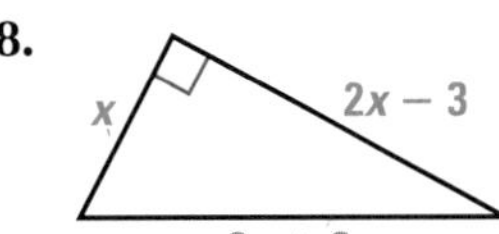

19.

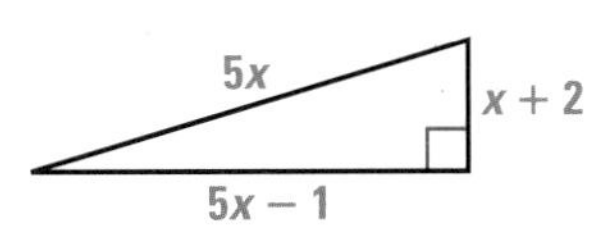

20. A right triangle has one leg that is 2 inches longer than the other leg. The length of the hypotenuse is $\sqrt{130}$ inches. Find the lengths of the legs.

21. A right triangle has one leg that is 3 times as long as the other leg. The length of the hypotenuse is $\sqrt{40}$ inches. Find the lengths of the legs.

22. A right triangle has one leg that is $\frac{1}{2}$ of the length of the other leg. The length of the hypotenuse is $6\sqrt{5}$ inches. Find the lengths of the legs.

EXAMPLE 4 on p. 739 for Exs. 23–28

DETERMINING RIGHT TRIANGLES **Tell whether the triangle with the given side lengths is a right triangle.**

(23.) 2, 3, 4	24. 9, 12, 15	25. 8, 16, 18
26. 9, 21, 24	27. 11, 60, 61	28. 24, 143, 145

29. ★ **MULTIPLE CHOICE** What is the area of the largest square in the coordinate plane shown?

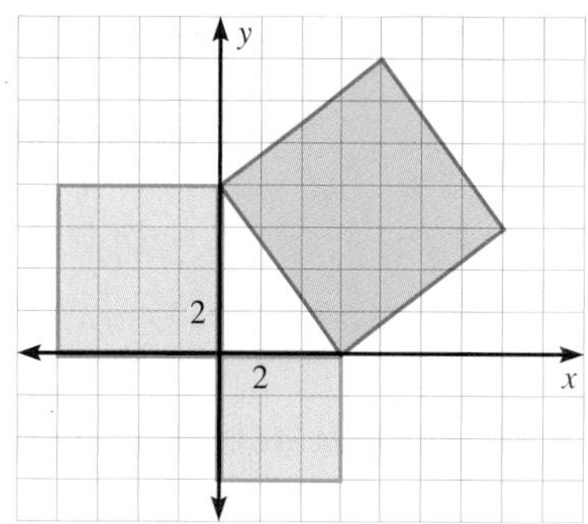

Ⓐ 100 square units

Ⓑ 64 square units

Ⓒ 36 square units

Ⓓ 25 square units

30. ★ **WRITING** Given that two side lengths of a right triangle are 11 inches and 6 inches, is it possible to find the length of the third side? *Explain.*

31. **REASONING** A *Pythagorean triple* is a group of integers a, b, and c that represent the side lengths of a right triangle. For example, the integers 3, 4, and 5 form a Pythagorean triple. Choose any two positive integers m and n such that $m < n$. Then find a, b, and c as follows: $a = n^2 - m^2$, $b = 2mn$, and $c = n^2 + m^2$. Show that the numbers you generated form a Pythagorean triple. Then use the converse of the Pythagorean theorem to show that the equations for a, b, and c always generate Pythagorean triples.

32. **CHALLENGE** The edge length of the cube is 7 inches.

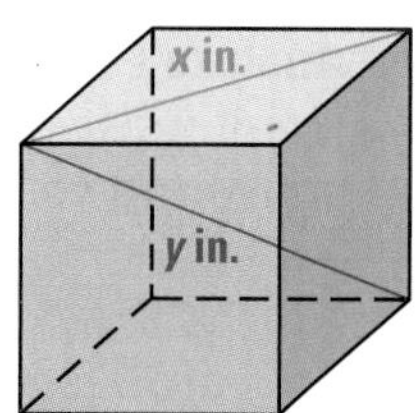

a. Find the value of x.

b. Find the value of y.

PROBLEM SOLVING

EXAMPLES 3 and 5 on pp. 738–739 for Exs. 33–35

33. **ARCHITECTURE** An earthquake-resistant building has dampers built into its structure to help minimize damage caused by an earthquake. A section of the structural frame of such a building is shown. What is the length of the damper? Round your answer to the nearest foot.

@HomeTutor for problem solving help at classzone.com

34. **SAILS** A sail has the shape of a triangle. The side lengths are 146 inches, 131 inches, and 84 inches. Is the sail a right triangle? *Explain.*

@HomeTutor for problem solving help at classzone.com

35. **FLATIRON BUILDING** A top view of the Flatiron Building in New York City is shown. The triangle indicates the basic shape of the building's roof. Is the triangle a right triangle? *Explain.*

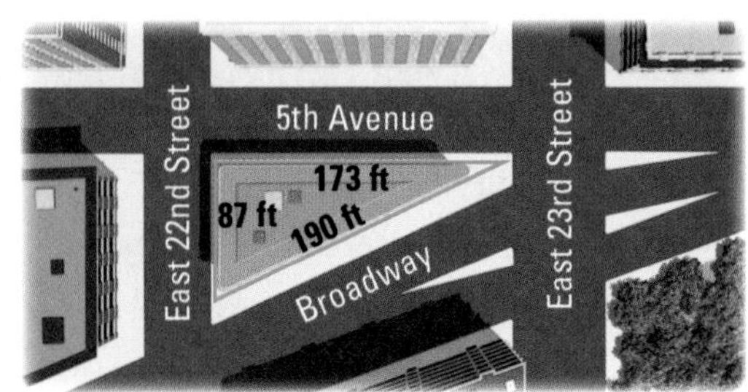

36. **SCREEN SIZES** The size of a television is indicated by the length of a diagonal of the television screen. The aspect ratio of a television screen is the ratio of the length of the screen to the width of the screen. The size of a particular television is 30 inches, and its aspect ratio is 4 : 3. What are the width and the length of the television screen?

37. ★ **EXTENDED RESPONSE** The *Wheel of Theodorus* is a figure formed by a chain of right triangles with consecutive triangles sharing a common side. The hypotenuse of one triangle becomes a leg of the next, as shown.

a. **Calculate** What is the length of the longest hypotenuse in the diagram?

b. **Extend** Extend the diagram to include two more triangles. What is the length of the longest hypotenuse in the new diagram?

c. **Analyze** Find a formula for the length of the hypotenuse of the nth triangle. *Explain* how you found your answer.

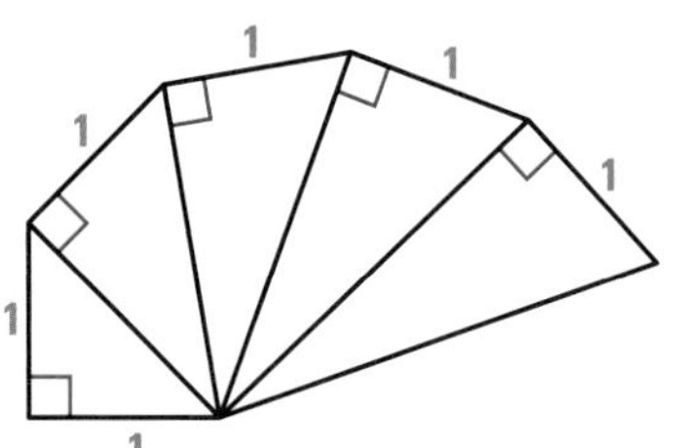

38. **CHALLENGE** A baseball diamond has the shape of a square with side lengths of 90 feet. A catcher wants to get a player running from first base to second base out, so the catcher must throw the ball to second base before the runner reaches second base.

a. The catcher is 5 feet behind home plate. How far does the catcher have to throw the ball to reach second base? Round your answer to the nearest foot.

b. The catcher throws the ball at a rate of 90 feet per second when the player is 30 feet away from second base. Will the catcher get the player out if the player is running at a rate of 22 feet per second? *Explain.*

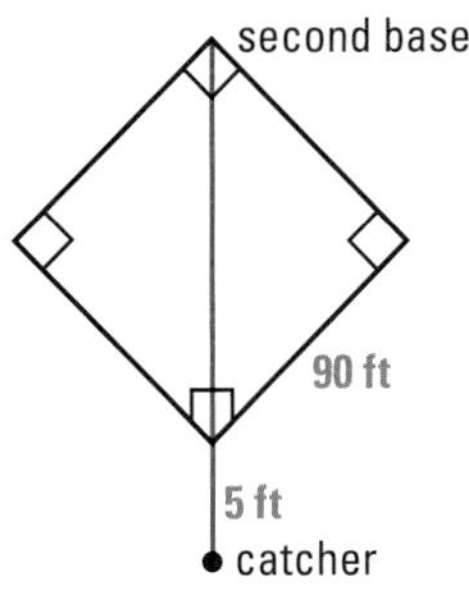

Not drawn to scale

MIXED REVIEW

PREVIEW Prepare for Lesson 11.5 in Exs. 39–46.

Plot the point in a coordinate plane. *Describe* the location of the point. *(p. 206)*

39. (5, 4)	**40.** (−2, 6)	**41.** (−1, −3)	**42.** (0, 5)
43. (0, 0)	**44.** (−8, −2)	**45.** (−1.5, 0)	**46.** (3.25, −2.5)

Evaluate the expression.

47. $5x^2$ when $x = 3$ *(p. 8)*

48. $-|x| - 8$ when $x = -2$ *(p. 64)*

49. $\sqrt{x - y}$ when $x = 9, y = -7$ *(p. 110)*

50. $\sqrt{xy}$ when $x = 27, y = 3$ *(p. 110)*

Investigating Algebra ACTIVITY *Use before Lesson 11.5*

11.5 Distance in The Coordinate Plane

MATERIALS • graph paper

QUESTION **How can you find the distance between two points?**

EXPLORE **Find the distance between points $A(-3, -2)$ and $B(4, -2)$**

STEP 1 ***Plot points***

Plot the points $A(-3, -2)$ and $B(4, -2)$ in the same coordinate plane.

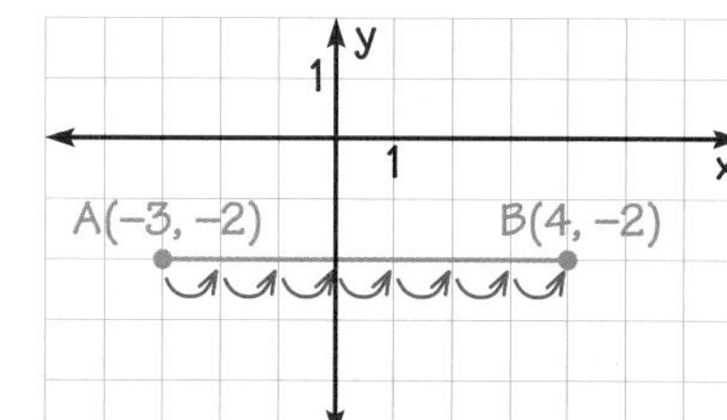

STEP 2 ***Find distance***

Find the distance between the points by counting the grid spaces between them.

STEP 3 ***Find distance***

Find the distance by subtracting the x-coordinate of point A from the x-coordinate of point B.

STEP 4 ***Compare results***

How does your result from Step 2 compare with your result from Step 3?

DRAW CONCLUSIONS **Use your observations to complete these exercises**

1. Subtract the x-coordinate of point B from the x-coordinate of point A. How is the value different from the values found in Steps 2 and 3 above? How could you make them the same?
2. Assume points $C(x_1, y_1)$ and $D(x_2, y_2)$ lie on the same horizontal line. Write an expression that can be used to find the distance between the points.
3. Assume points $C(x_1, y_1)$ and $D(x_2, y_2)$ lie on the same vertical line. Write an expression that can be used to find the distance between the points. Check your expression using $(-2, 4)$ and $(-2, -3)$.

In Exercises 4–12, find the distance between the two points.

4. $(2, 3), (-5, 3)$
5. $(0, -4), (7, -4)$
6. $(-1, 5), (2, 5)$
7. $(4, -6), (6, -6)$
8. $(-5, -4), (-2, -4)$
9. $(2, 8), (2, 3)$
10. $(5, -6), (5, -2)$
11. $(0, -4), (0, 2)$
12. $(-3, 0), (-3, 6)$

13. **REASONING** Plot the points $A(6, 5)$, $B(2, 5)$, and $C(6, 2)$. Find the distance between points A and B. Find the distance between points A and C. Use the distances and the Pythagorean theorem to find the distance between points B and C.

11.5 Apply the Distance and Midpoint Formulas

Before You used the Pythagorean theorem and its converse.

Now You will use the distance and midpoint formulas.

Why? So you can calculate distances traveled, as in Ex. 47.

Key Vocabulary
- **distance formula**
- **midpoint**
- **midpoint formula**

To find the distance between the points $A(-2, -1)$ and $B(3, 2)$, draw a right triangle, as shown. The lengths of the legs of the right triangle are as follows.

$$AC = |3 - (-2)| = 5$$

$$BC = |-1 - 2| = 3$$

You can use the Pythagorean theorem to find AB, the length of the hypotenuse of the right triangle.

$(AB)^2 = (AC)^2 + (BC)^2$ **Pythagorean theorem**

$AB = \sqrt{(AC)^2 + (BC)^2}$ **Take positive square root of each side.**

$AB = \sqrt{5^2 + 3^2} = \sqrt{34}$ **Substitute 5 for *AC* and 3 for *BC* and simplify.**

This example suggests that you can find the distance between two points in a coordinate plane using the following formula, called the **distance formula**.

KEY CONCEPT *For Your Notebook*

The Distance Formula

The distance d between any two points (x_1, y_1) and (x_2, y_2) is

$$d = \sqrt{(x_2 - x_1)^2 + (y_2 - y_1)^2}.$$

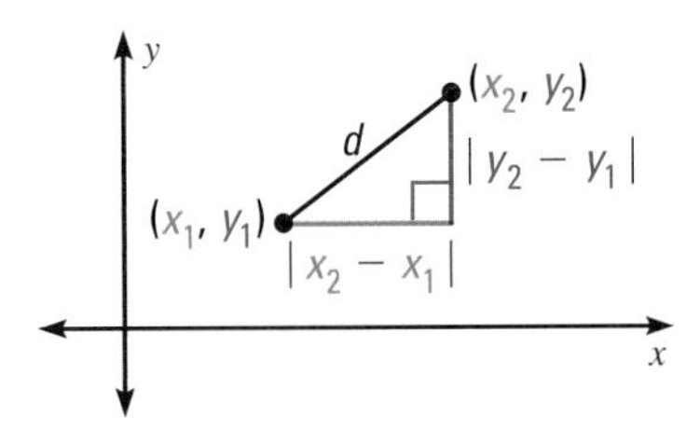

EXAMPLE 1 Find the distance between two points

Find the distance between (−1, 3) and (5, 2).

Let $(x_1, y_1) = (-1, 3)$ and $(x_2, y_2) = (5, 2)$.

$d = \sqrt{(x_2 - x_1)^2 + (y_2 - y_1)^2}$ **Distance formula**

$= \sqrt{(5 - (-1))^2 + (2 - 3)^2}$ **Substitute.**

$= \sqrt{6^2 + (-1)^2} = \sqrt{37}$ **Simplify.**

▶ The distance between the points is $\sqrt{37}$ units.

EXAMPLE 2 Find a missing coordinate

The distance between (3, −5) and (7, b) is 5 units. Find the value of b.

Solution

Use the distance formula with $d = 5$. Let $(x_1, y_1) = (3, -5)$ and $(x_2, y_2) = (7, b)$. Then solve for b.

$d = \sqrt{(x_2 - x_1)^2 + (y_2 - y_1)^2}$ — Distance formula

$5 = \sqrt{(7 - 3)^2 + (b - (-5))^2}$ — Substitute.

$5 = \sqrt{16 + b^2 + 10b + 25}$ — Multiply.

$5 = \sqrt{b^2 + 10b + 41}$ — Simplify.

$25 = b^2 + 10b + 41$ — Square each side.

$0 = b^2 + 10b + 16$ — Write in standard form.

$0 = (b + 2)(b + 8)$ — Factor.

$b + 2 = 0$ *or* $b + 8 = 0$ — Zero-product property

$b = -2$ *or* $b = -8$ — Solve for b.

▶ The value of b is −2 or −8.

INTERPRET GEOMETRICALLY
The point (7, b) lies on the line $x = 7$. If you let the point (3, −5) be the center of a circle with radius 5, you will see that the circle crosses the line at (7, −2) and (7, −8).

✓ **GUIDED PRACTICE** for Examples 1 and 2

Find the distance between the points.

1. (3, 0), (3, 6)
2. (−2, 1), (2, 5)
3. (6, −2), (−4, 7)
4. The distance between (1, a) and (4, 2) is 3 units. Find the value of a.

MIDPOINT The **midpoint** of a line segment is the point on the segment that is equidistant from the endpoints. You can find the coordinates of the midpoint of a line segment using the following formula, called the **midpoint formula**.

KEY CONCEPT *For Your Notebook*

The Midpoint Formula

The midpoint M of the line segment with endpoints $A(x_1, y_1)$ and $B(x_2, y_2)$ is

$$M\left(\frac{x_1 + x_2}{2}, \frac{y_1 + y_2}{2}\right).$$

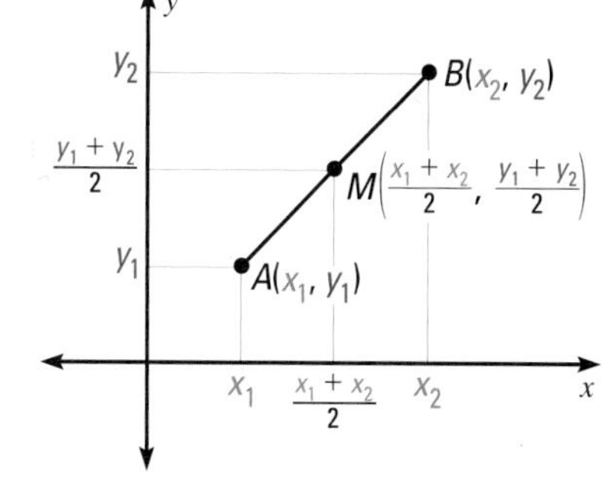

★ EXAMPLE 3 Standardized Test Practice

What is the midpoint of the line segment with endpoints (−1, −2) and (3, −4)?

Ⓐ (2, −1) Ⓑ (1, −3) Ⓒ (−2, 1) Ⓓ (−3, 1)

ELIMINATE CHOICES

The *y*-coordinate of the midpoint has to be negative because it is an average of the *y*-coordinates of the endpoints of the line segment. Eliminate choices C and D.

Solution

Let $(x_1, y_1) = (-1, -2)$ and $(x_2, y_2) = (3, -4)$.

$$\left(\frac{x_1 + x_2}{2}, \frac{y_1 + y_2}{2}\right) = \left(\frac{-1 + 3}{2}, \frac{-2 + (-4)}{2}\right) \quad \textbf{Substitute.}$$

$$= (1, -3) \quad \textbf{Simplify.}$$

▶ The correct answer is B. Ⓐ Ⓑ Ⓒ Ⓓ

Animated Algebra at classzone.com

EXAMPLE 4 Solve a real-world problem

ANOTHER WAY

For alternative methods for solving Example 4, turn to page 751 for the **Problem Solving Workshop**.

SIGHTSEEING You and a friend are sightseeing in Washington, D.C. You are at the National Gallery of Art, and your friend is at the Washington Monument, as shown on the map. You want to meet at the landmark that is closest to the midpoint of your locations. At which landmark should you meet?

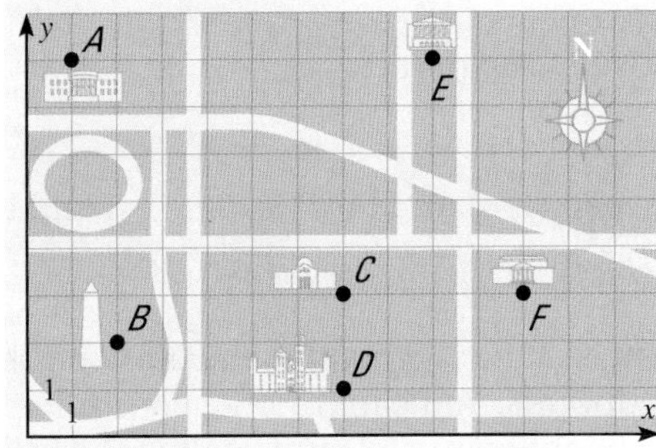

SIGHTS IN WASHINGTON, D.C.

A) White House
B) Washington Monument
C) Natural History Museum
D) Smithsonian Institution
E) National Portrait Gallery
F) National Gallery of Art

Solution

Your coordinates are (11, 3), and your friend's coordinates are (2, 2). First, find the midpoint of your locations, which is

$$\left(\frac{x_1 + x_2}{2}, \frac{y_1 + y_2}{2}\right) = \left(\frac{11 + 2}{2}, \frac{3 + 2}{2}\right) = (6.5, 2.5).$$

Next, find the distance from the midpoint to the Smithsonian Institution, located at (7, 1), and to the Natural History Museum, located at (7, 3).

Distance to Smithsonian Institution: $d = \sqrt{(6.5 - 7)^2 + (2.5 - 1)^2} \approx 1.58$ units

Distance to Natural History Museum: $d = \sqrt{(6.5 - 7)^2 + (2.5 - 3)^2} \approx 0.71$ unit

▶ You should meet at the Natural History Museum.

✓ **GUIDED PRACTICE** for Examples 3 and 4

5. Find the midpoint of the line segment with endpoints (4, 3) and (2, 5).

6. **WHAT IF?** In Example 4, suppose you are at the Smithsonian and your friend is at the National Portrait Gallery. Which landmark on the map is closest to the midpoint of your locations?

11.5 EXERCISES

HOMEWORK KEY
○ = **WORKED-OUT SOLUTIONS** on p. WS27 for Exs. 7, 23, and 49
★ = **STANDARDIZED TEST PRACTICE** Exs. 2, 15, 34, 37, 45, and 50

SKILL PRACTICE

1. **VOCABULARY** Copy and complete: The point on a line segment that is equidistant from its endpoints is called the _?_ of the line segment.

2. ★ **WRITING** You want to know the distance between the points (3, 2) and (6, 8). Does it matter which point represents (x_1, y_1) and which point represents (x_2, y_2)? *Explain.*

EXAMPLE 1 on p. 744 for Exs. 3–15

FINDING DISTANCE Find the distance between the two points.

3. (4, 8), (4, 7)
4. (5, −9), (8, −9)
5. (2, −2), (6, 1)
6. (5, 1), (0, 3)
7. (−4, 1), (3, −1)
8. (2, 4), (−5, 0)
9. (−6, 7), (2, 9)
10. (−10, 8), (2, −3)
11. (7, 5), (−12, −1)
12. (4, 2.5), (2.5, −3)
13. $\left(5, -\frac{1}{2}\right), \left(-3, \frac{5}{2}\right)$
14. $\left(-\frac{3}{4}, \frac{7}{2}\right), \left(\frac{5}{4}, \frac{1}{4}\right)$

15. ★ **MULTIPLE CHOICE** What is the distance between (4.5, 1) and (−2.5, −5)?

(A) $\sqrt{13}$ (B) $\sqrt{24}$ (C) $\sqrt{68.5}$ (D) $\sqrt{85}$

EXAMPLE 2 on p. 745 for Exs. 16–21

FINDING MISSING COORDINATES The distance *d* between two points is given. Find the value of *b*.

16. (0, *b*), (3, 1); $d = 5$
17. (13, −3), (*b*, 2); $d = 13$
18. (−9, −2), (*b*, 5); $d = 7$
19. (*b*, −6), (−5, 2); $d = 10$
20. (−6, 8), (−1, *b*); $d = \sqrt{29}$
21. (*b*, −4), (4, 7); $d = 11\sqrt{2}$

EXAMPLE 3 on p. 746 for Exs. 22–34

FINDING THE MIDPOINT Find the midpoint of the line segment with the given endpoints.

22. (0, 1), (8, 3)
23. (6, −3), (4, −7)
24. (−5, 0), (1, 14)
25. (11, −4), (−9, −4)
26. (−6, 6), (4, −4)
27. (−17, −8), (−5, −4)
28. (2, 7), (5, 3)
29. (−2, 3), (−2, −3)
30. (12, −5), (−12, 4)
31. (−15, −8), (−1, −1)
32. (18, −17), (12, −7)
33. (−50, −75), (8, 9)

34. ★ **MULTIPLE CHOICE** What is the midpoint of the line segment with endpoints (2, 1) and (4, 7)?

(A) (1, 3) (B) (1.5, 5.5) (C) (3, 4) (D) (4, 3)

ERROR ANALYSIS ***Describe* and correct the error in finding the distance between (−17, −2) and (3, 8), and the midpoint of the line segment with endpoints (−17, −2) and (3, 8).**

35.

Distance:

$d = \sqrt{(3 - (-17))^2 - (8 - (-2))^2}$

$= \sqrt{400 - 100}$

$= \sqrt{300} = 10\sqrt{3}$

36.

Midpoint:

$\left(\frac{3 - (-17)}{2}, \frac{8 - (-2)}{2}\right) = \left(\frac{20}{2}, \frac{10}{2}\right)$

$= (10, 5)$

37. ★ **MULTIPLE CHOICE** What is the distance between point *A* and the midpoint of the line segment that joins points *A* and *B*?

Ⓐ $\sqrt{17}$ units　Ⓑ $3\sqrt{5}$ units

Ⓒ $2\sqrt{17}$ units　Ⓓ $\sqrt{117}$ units

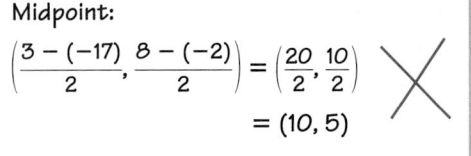

FINDING ENDPOINTS **The midpoint and an endpoint of a line segment are given. Find the other endpoint.**

38. endpoint: (1, 2)
midpoint: (−6, 4)

39. endpoint: (−2, −4)
midpoint: (3, −3)

40. endpoint: (7, 5)
midpoint: (1, 0.5)

RIGHT TRIANGLES **Use the distance formula and the converse of the Pythagorean theorem to determine whether the points are vertices of a right triangle.**

41. (3, 5), (3, −1), (−2, −1)

42. (3, −1), (1, 4), (−3, 0)

43. (−5, −2), (0, −4), (−2, 3)

44. (−2, 1), (−4, 3), (−8, −1)

45. ★ **WRITING** *Explain* how you can use the distance formula to verify that the midpoint of a line segment is equidistant from its endpoints.

46. **CHALLENGE** The midpoint of a line segment is (0, 0). The line segment has a length of 2 units. Give three possible sets of endpoints for the line segment. *Explain* how you found your answer.

PROBLEM SOLVING

EXAMPLE 4
on p. 746
for Exs. 47–50

47. **MULTI-STEP PROBLEM** A rescue helicopter and an ambulance are both traveling from the dispatch center to the scene of an accident. The distance between consecutive grid lines represents 1 mile.

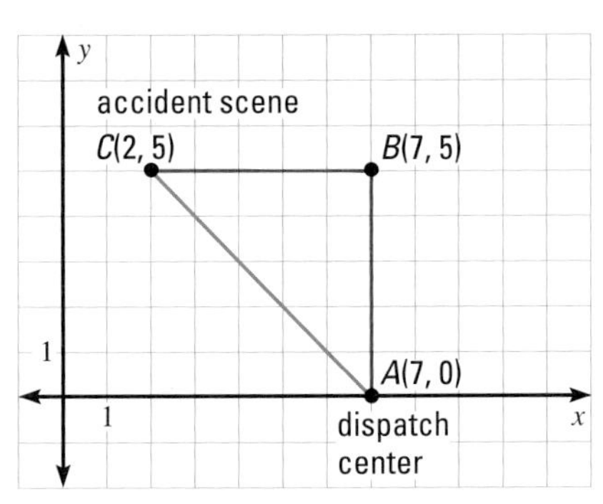

a. Find the distance that the ambulance traveled (red route).

b. How many times greater is the distance that the ambulance traveled than the distance that the helicopter traveled (blue route)?

@HomeTutor for problem solving help at classzone.com

48. SUBWAY A student is taking the subway to the public library. The student can get off the subway at one of two stops, as shown in the map. The distance between consecutive grid lines represents 0.25 mile. Which stop is closer to the library?

@HomeTutor for problem solving help at classzone.com

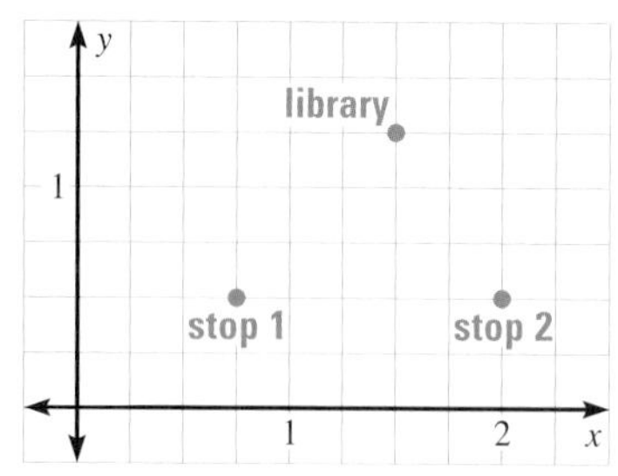

49. ARCHAEOLOGY Underwater archaeologists sometimes lay survey grids of the site they are studying. A sample survey grid is shown. The distance between consecutive grid lines represents 50 feet.

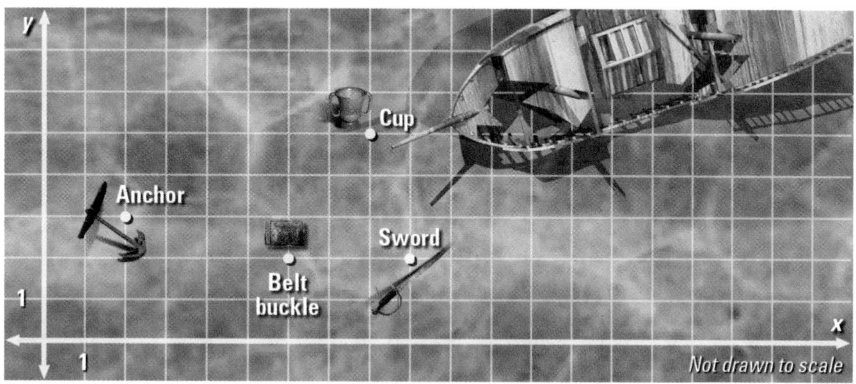

a. Which is shorter, the distance between the anchor and the sword or the distance between the anchor and the cup?

b. Which two objects are closest together? Which two objects are farthest apart?

50. ★ SHORT RESPONSE The point of no return in aviation is the farthest point to which a plane can fly and still have enough fuel to return to its starting place or to fly to an alternative landing destination. After a plane passes the point of no return, it must fly to its planned destination. The distance between consecutive grid lines represents 50 nautical miles.

a. The flight path of a plane is from airport A to airport B. The plane is currently at the midpoint of the flight path. How far away is the plane from airport A? Round your answer to the nearest nautical mile.

b. The plane's point of no return is calculated to be 200 nautical miles. Has the plane reached its point of no return? *Explain.*

y
airport B
(4, 7)
airport A
(1, 1)
1
1
x

REVIEW GEOMETRY
For help with classifying quadrilaterals, see p. 919.

51. ROAD SIGN Describe the quadrilateral formed by the sides of the road sign shown by answering the following questions.

- Are opposite sides parallel?
- Do the sides form right angles?
- Which sides, if any, are congruent?

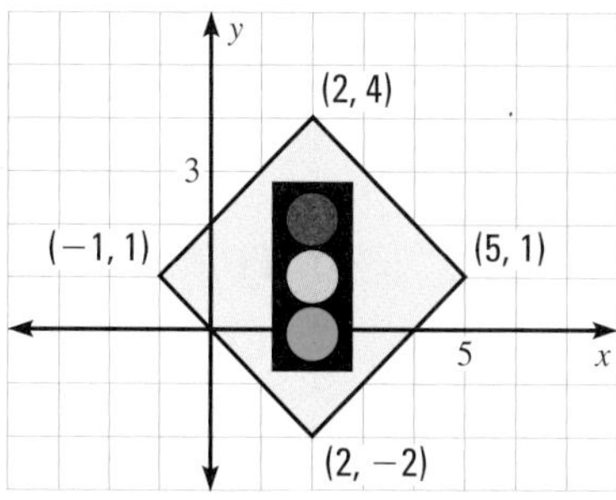

52. **CHALLENGE** A computer programmer is creating a baseball player's strike zone for a video game, as shown. The strike zone is a rectangular region over home plate through which a ball must pass to be called a strike. In the animation, $\overline{AB}$ is the top of the strike zone and lies on a horizontal line that passes through the midpoint of $\overline{XY}$. The distance between grid lines represents 1 foot.

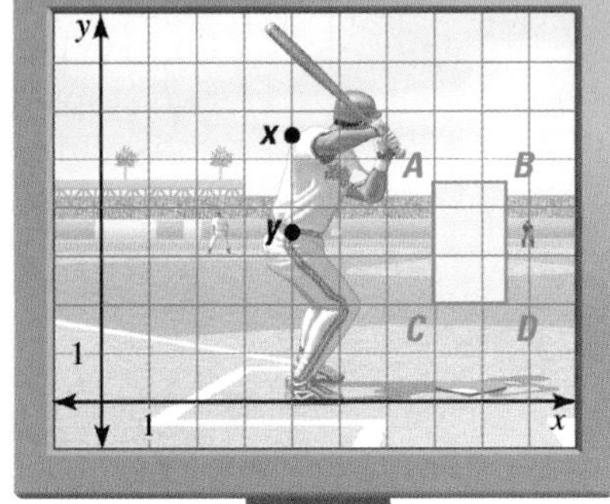

a. If the coordinates of X are (4, 5.5) and the coordinates of Y are (4, 3.5), what is the midpoint of $\overline{XY}$?

b. The coordinates of C are (7, 2) and the coordinates of D are (8.5, 2). Find the coordinates of point A and point B.

c. What is the area of the strike zone in the animation?

MIXED REVIEW

PREVIEW Prepare for Lesson 12.1 in Exs. 53–58.

Given that y varies directly with x, use the specified values to write a direct variation equation that relates x and y. *(p. 253)*

53. $x = 10, y = 30$
54. $x = 81, y = 27$
55. $x = -6, y = -9$
56. $x = 12, y = -1.5$
57. $x = -11, y = -11$
58. $x = \frac{2}{3}, y = 6$

Graph the function.

59. $y = 4^x$ *(p. 520)*
60. $y = 3 \cdot 4^x$ *(p. 520)*
61. $y = (0.5)^x$ *(p. 531)*
62. $y = 2 \cdot (0.5)^x$ *(p. 531)*
63. $y = x^2 - 6$ *(p. 628)*
64. $y = 2x^2 - x + 8$ *(p. 635)*

QUIZ for Lessons 11.4–11.5

Let a and b represent the lengths of the legs of a right triangle, and let c represent the length of the hypotenuse. Find the unknown length. *(p. 737)*

1. $a = 6, c = 10$
2. $b = 2, c = 6$
3. $a = 4, b = 7$

Find the unknown lengths. *(p. 737)*

4. 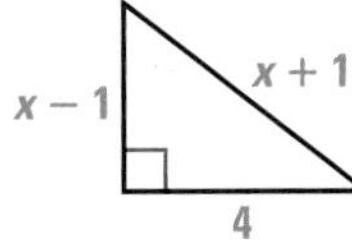

5. 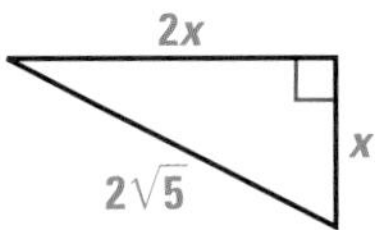

6. 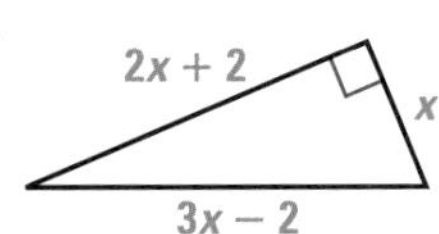

Find the distance between the two points. *(p. 744)*

7. (7, 2), (7, 5)
8. (−1, −3), (4, −3)
9. (0, 0), (−6, 9)

Find the midpoint of the line segment with the given endpoints. *(p. 744)*

10. (0, 5), (−6, 3)
11. (8, −1), (2, −7)
12. (−5, −3), (5, −3)
13. (0, 6), (1.5, 4)
14. (2.5, −3), (0.5, 6)
15. $\left(-\frac{1}{4}, \frac{3}{4}\right), \left(\frac{1}{4}, \frac{5}{4}\right)$

PROBLEM SOLVING WORKSHOP
LESSON 11.5

Using ALTERNATIVE METHODS

Another Way to Solve Example 4, page 746

MULTIPLE REPRESENTATIONS In Example 4 on page 746, you saw how to solve a problem about finding a meeting place by using the midpoint and distance formulas. You can also solve the problem by folding a map and using a compass.

PROBLEM

SIGHTSEEING You and a friend are sightseeing in Washington, D.C. You are at the National Gallery of Art, and your friend is at the Washington Monument, as shown on the map. You want to meet at the landmark that is closest to the midpoint of your locations. At which landmark should you meet?

METHOD 1

Folding a map and using a compass An alternative approach is to fold a map and use a compass. First, draw a line connecting your location to your friend's location. Then fold the map so that your locations coincide. The point where the line connecting your locations is folded represents the midpoint. Place the point of your compass at the midpoint. Adjust the opening of the compass to match the distance between the midpoint and the apparent closest landmark. Swing the compass to see if the other landmark is closer.

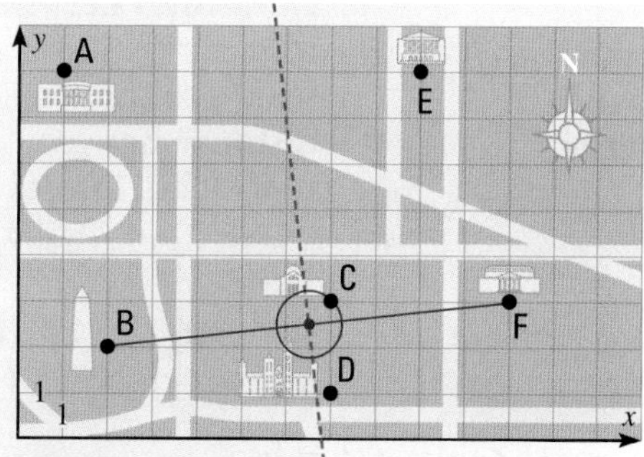

SIGHTS IN WASHINGTON, D.C.

A) White House
B) Washington Monument
C) Natural History Museum
D) Smithsonian Institution
E) National Portrait Gallery
F) National Gallery of Art

▶ Because the Smithsonian lies outside the circle, the Natural History Museum is closer to the midpoint of your locations.

PRACTICE

1. **WHAT IF?** In the problem above, suppose your friend is at the White House.
   a. At which landmark should you meet?
   b. Suppose you can walk directly to the landmark in part (a). If the distance between consecutive grid lines represents 0.06 mile, how far do you have to walk?

2. **MAPS** A student makes a map of a town in which the student's house is located at (1, 2) and a friend's house is located at (8, 5). A grocery store is located at (5, 3), and a shoe store is located at (3, 4). The student and the friend want to meet at the store that is closer to the midpoint between their houses. At which store should they meet? Solve this problem using two methods.

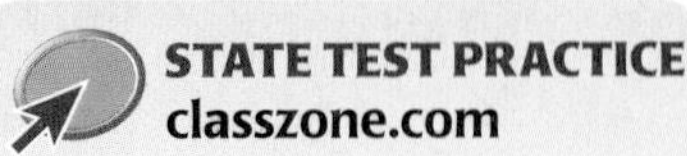

Lessons 11.4–11.5

1. **SHORT RESPONSE** Construction workers are building a staircase for a house. Use the drawing of the staircase to answer the following questions. Round each answer to the nearest inch.

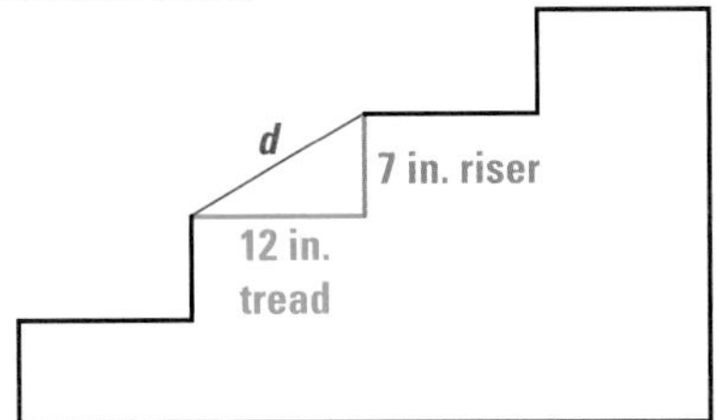

   a. Find the distance d between the edges of two consecutive steps.

   b. Suppose the workers install a handrail that is as long as the distance between the front edge of the bottom step and the front edge of the top step. How long is the handrail? *Explain.*

2. **MULTI-STEP PROBLEM** At the start of a football game, the kicker on one team must kick the ball to the opposing team. To position himself for the starting kick, the kicker places a football on a tee, walks 8 yards behind the tee, then 6 yards to his left.

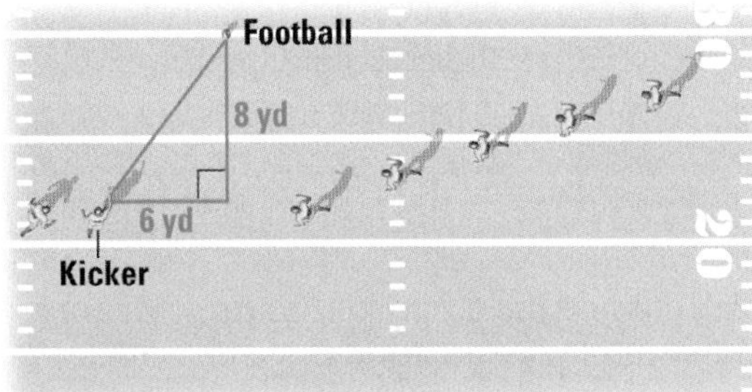

   a. What is the kicker's distance (in yards) from the football?

   b. The kicker takes 11 strides to kick the ball. What is his average stride length? Round your answer to the nearest tenth of a foot.

3. **GRIDDED ANSWER** You go on a hiking trip. You walk 2 miles directly east and then 4 miles directly north. If you could walk in a straight path back to your starting point, how far would you have to walk? Round your answer to the nearest tenth of a mile.

4. **SHORT RESPONSE** A map of a town is shown. A student is at the school. The student's friend is at the stadium. They want to meet at the place that is closest to the midpoint of their locations. At which location should they meet? *Explain* how you found your answer.

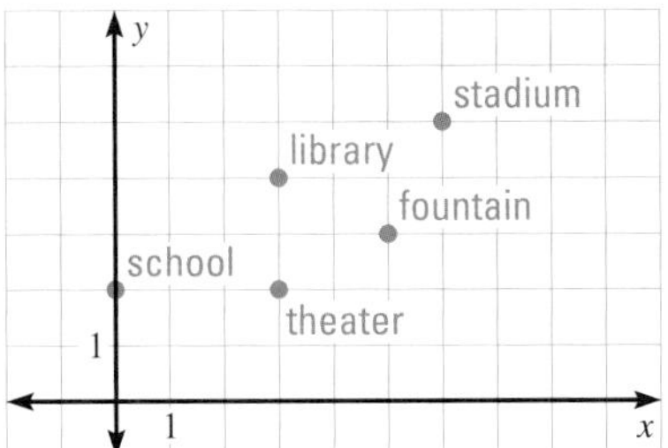

5. **OPEN-ENDED** City planners want to build a rectangular park. They want the park to have a straight path that is 2500 feet long and connects opposite corners of the park. What are three possibilities for the length and width of the park?

6. **EXTENDED RESPONSE** One ferry makes round trips shown in red. A second ferry makes round trips shown in blue. The distance between consecutive grid lines represents 1 mile.

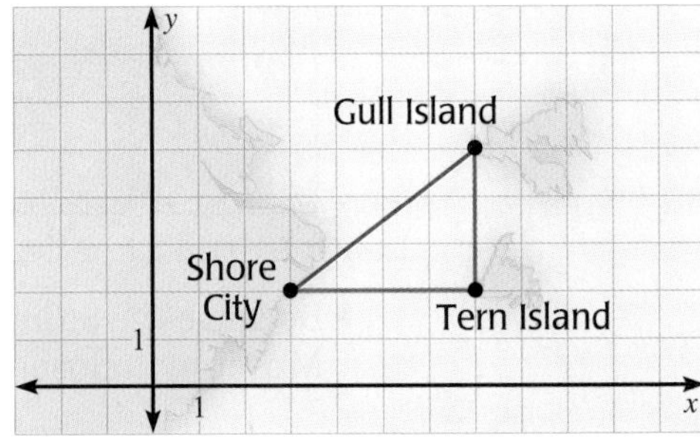

   a. Find the distance (in miles) of a round trip for the first ferry.

   b. Find the distance (in miles) of a round trip for the second ferry.

   c. Each stop the ferries make takes 10 minutes. The first ferry travels at 20 miles per hour, and the second ferry travels at 16 miles per hour. The ferries leave Shore City at the same time each day. When will they be back at the city at the same time? *Explain.*

BIG IDEAS

For Your Notebook

Big Idea 1

Graphing Square Root Functions

You can graph a square root function $y = a\sqrt{x - h} + k$ and compare its graph with the graph of the parent function, $y = \sqrt{x}$, based on the constants a, h, and k.

Constant	Comparison of graphs
a	• When $a > 0$, the graph is a vertical stretch or shrink of the parent graph. • When $a < 0$, the graph is a vertical stretch or shrink with a reflection in the x-axis of the parent graph.
h	The graph is a horizontal translation of the parent graph.
k	The graph is a vertical translation of the parent graph.

Big Idea 2

Using Properties of Radicals in Expressions and Equations

You can use the properties of radicals to simplify radical expressions and to solve radical equations.

Product property of radicals	$\sqrt{ab} = \sqrt{a} \cdot \sqrt{b}$ where $a \geq 0$ and $b \geq 0$
Quotient property of radicals	$\sqrt{\frac{a}{b}} = \frac{\sqrt{a}}{\sqrt{b}}$ where $a \geq 0$ and $b > 0$

Big Idea 3

Working with Radicals in Geometry

You can use radicals to solve problems involving the following geometric theorems and formulas.

Pythagorean theorem	If a triangle is a right triangle, then the sum of the squares of the lengths of the legs, a and b, equals the square of the length of the hypotenuse c. $a^2 + b^2 = c^2$
Converse of Pythagorean theorem	If a triangle has side lengths a, b, and c such that $a^2 + b^2 = c^2$, then the triangle is a right triangle.
Distance formula	$d = \sqrt{(x_2 - x_1)^2 + (y_2 - y_1)^2}$
Midpoint formula	$M\left(\frac{x_1 + x_2}{2}, \frac{y_1 + y_2}{2}\right)$

11 CHAPTER REVIEW

@HomeTutor
classzone.com
- Multi-Language Glossary
- Vocabulary practice

REVIEW KEY VOCABULARY

- radical expression, *p. 710*
- radical function, *p. 710*
- square root function, *p. 710*
- parent square root function, *p. 710*
- simplest form of a radical expression, *p. 719*
- rationalizing the denominator, *p. 721*
- radical equation, *p. 729*
- extraneous solution, *p. 730*
- hypotenuse, legs of a right triangle, *p. 737*
- Pythagorean theorem, *p. 737*
- distance formula, *p. 744*
- midpoint, midpoint formula, *p. 745*

VOCABULARY EXERCISES

1. *Describe* how the graph of the function $y = 3\sqrt{x}$ compares with the graph of the parent square root function.
2. *Describe* the steps you would take to rationalize the denominator of a radical expression.

Tell which theorem or formula you would use to complete the exercise.

3. Tell whether a triangle with side lengths 2, 4, and 6 is a right triangle.
4. The point $(b, 4)$ is 10 units away from the point $(5, 10)$. Find b.

REVIEW EXAMPLES AND EXERCISES

Use the review examples and exercises below to check your understanding of the concepts you have learned in each lesson of Chapter 11.

11.1 Graph Square Root Functions *pp. 710–716*

EXAMPLE

Graph the function $y = \sqrt{x - 3}$ and identify its domain and range. Compare the graph with the graph of $y = \sqrt{x}$.

To graph the function, make a table, plot the points, and draw a smooth curve through the points. The domain is $x \geq 3$.

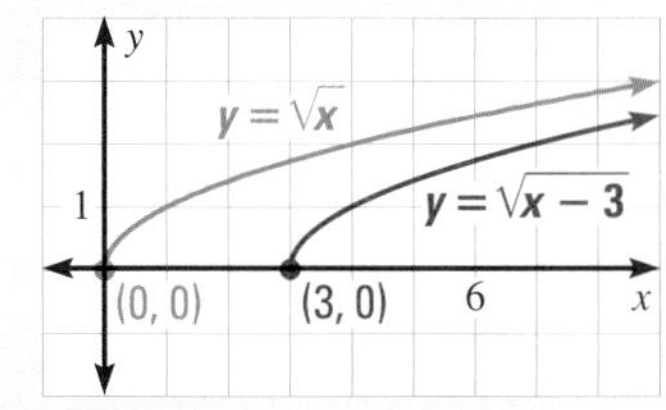

x	3	4	5	6
y	0	1	1.4	1.7

The range is $y \geq 0$. The graph of $y = \sqrt{x - 3}$ is a horizontal translation (of 3 units to the right) of the graph of $y = \sqrt{x}$.

EXERCISES

EXAMPLES 2, 3, and 4 on pp. 711–712 for Exs. 5–7

Graph the function and identify its domain and range. Compare the graph with the graph of $y = \sqrt{x}$.

5. $y = -2\sqrt{x}$
6. $y = \sqrt{x} + 7$
7. $y = \sqrt{x + 7}$

@HomeTutor
classzone.com
Chapter Review Practice

11.2 Simplify Radical Expressions

pp. 719–726

EXAMPLE

Simplify $7\sqrt{5} - \sqrt{45}$.

$$7\sqrt{5} - \sqrt{45} = 7\sqrt{5} - \sqrt{9 \cdot 5}$$ Factor using perfect square factor.

$$= 7\sqrt{5} - \sqrt{9} \cdot \sqrt{5}$$ Product property of radicals

$$= 7\sqrt{5} - 3\sqrt{5}$$ Simplify.

$$= (7 - 3)\sqrt{5}$$ Distributive property

$$= 4\sqrt{5}$$ Simplify.

EXERCISES

EXAMPLES 1–7 on pp. 719–722 for Exs. 8–16

Simplify the expression.

8. $\sqrt{98}$
9. $\sqrt{121x^3}$
10. $\sqrt{7} \cdot \sqrt{21}$
11. $\sqrt{7x} \cdot 7\sqrt{x}$
12. $\sqrt{\frac{5}{x^2}}$
13. $\frac{2}{\sqrt{5}}$
14. $3\sqrt{2} - \sqrt{128}$
15. $\sqrt{2}(7 - \sqrt{6})$

16. **GEOMETRY** The lateral surface area L of a square pyramid with height h and base length ℓ is given by $L = 2\ell\sqrt{0.25\ell^2 + h^2}$. Find L (in square feet) for a square pyramid that has a height of 4 feet and a base length of 4 feet.

11.3 Solve Radical Equations

pp. 729–734

EXAMPLE

Solve $\sqrt{x + 90} = x$.

$$\sqrt{x + 90} = x$$ Write original equation.

$$\left(\sqrt{x + 90}\right)^2 = x^2$$ Square each side.

$$x + 90 = x^2$$ Simplify.

$$0 = x^2 - x - 90$$ Write in standard form.

$$0 = (x - 10)(x + 9)$$ Factor.

$$x - 10 = 0 \quad \textit{or} \quad x + 9 = 0$$ Zero-product property

$$x = 10 \quad \textit{or} \quad x = -9$$ Solve for x.

▸ Checking 10 and -9 in the original equation shows that -9 is an extraneous solution. The only solution of the equation is 10.

EXERCISES

EXAMPLES 1, 2, 3, and 4 on pp. 729–731 for Exs. 17–22

Solve the equation. Check for extraneous solutions.

17. $\sqrt{x} - 28 = 0$
18. $8\sqrt{x - 5} + 34 = 58$
19. $\sqrt{5x - 3} = \sqrt{x + 17}$
20. $\sqrt{5x} + 6 = 5$
21. $\sqrt{x} + 36 = 0$
22. $x = \sqrt{2 - x}$

11 CHAPTER REVIEW

11.4 Apply the Pythagorean Theorem and Its Converse pp. 737–742

EXAMPLE

Find the unknown length for the triangle shown.

a = 6, c = 11, b

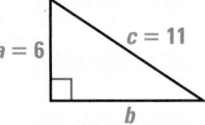

$a^2 + b^2 = c^2$	Pythagorean theorem
$6^2 + b^2 = 11^2$	Substitute 6 for *a* and 11 for *c*.
$36 + b^2 = 121$	Simplify.
$b^2 = 85$	Subtract 36 from each side.
$b = \sqrt{85}$	Take positive square root of each side.

EXERCISES

EXAMPLES 1 and 4 on pp. 737, 739 for Exs. 23–29

Let *a* and *b* represent the lengths of the legs of a right triangle, and let *c* represent the length of the hypotenuse. Find the unknown length.

23. $a = 7, b = 13$ **24.** $a = 10, c = 21$ **25.** $a = 8, c = 11$

26. $a = 9, b = 17$ **27.** $b = 4, c = 15$ **28.** $b = 6, c = 6.5$

29. REFLECTING POOL The Reflecting Pool in front of the Lincoln Memorial in Washington, D.C., is rectangular with a length of 2029 feet and a width of 167 feet. To the nearest foot, what is the length of a diagonal of the Reflecting Pool?

11.5 Apply the Distance and Midpoint Formulas pp. 744–750

EXAMPLE

Find the distance between (−3, 8) and (5, −12).

Let $(x_1, y_1) = (-3, 8)$ and $(x_2, y_2) = (5, -12)$.

$d = \sqrt{(x_2 - x_1)^2 + (y_2 - y_1)^2}$	Distance formula
$= \sqrt{(5 - (-3))^2 + (-12 - 8)^2}$	Substitute.
$= \sqrt{464} = 4\sqrt{29}$	Simplify.

EXERCISES

EXAMPLES 1, 3, and 4 on pp. 744, 746 for Exs. 30–36

Find the distance between the two points.

30. (−1, −3), (9, −13) **31.** (−8, −4), (0, 2) **32.** (7, 1), (4, −0.25)

Find the midpoint of the line segment with the given endpoints.

33. (−2, −4), (9, −4) **34.** (−8, 0), (−8, 2) **35.** (6, 1), (4, −5)

36. ISLANDS On a coordinate grid, an island is located at (1, 6). Another island is located at (4, 9). What is the distance between the islands if the distance between consecutive grid lines represents 2 miles?

11 CHAPTER TEST

Graph the function and identify its domain and range. Compare the graph with the graph of $y = \sqrt{x}$.

1. $y = 3\sqrt{x}$
2. $y = -\sqrt{x}$
3. $y = \sqrt{x - 5}$
4. $y = -\sqrt{x - 1} + 4$

Simplify the expression.

5. $\sqrt{72m^6}$
6. $\sqrt{8z^3} \cdot \sqrt{6z^3}$
7. $\sqrt{\frac{20}{3n^3}}$
8. $7\sqrt{6} - 2\sqrt{12} + \sqrt{24}$
9. $\sqrt{3}(7 - \sqrt{15})$
10. $(8 - \sqrt{7})(1 + \sqrt{7})$

Solve the equation. Check for extraneous solutions.

11. $\sqrt{x} = 8$
12. $\sqrt{x + 5} - 6 = -2$
13. $-4\sqrt{3x} - 6 = 30$
14. $\sqrt{5x - 11} = \sqrt{x}$
15. $\sqrt{x + 7} = \sqrt{2x - 3}$
16. $x = \sqrt{12 - x}$

Find the unknown lengths.

17. 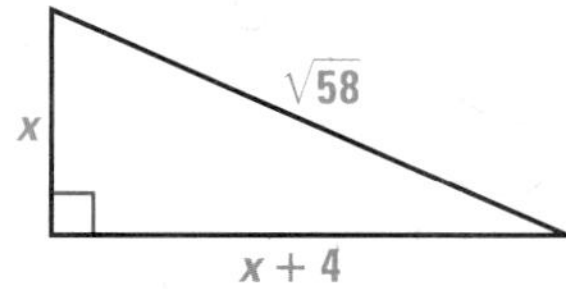

18. 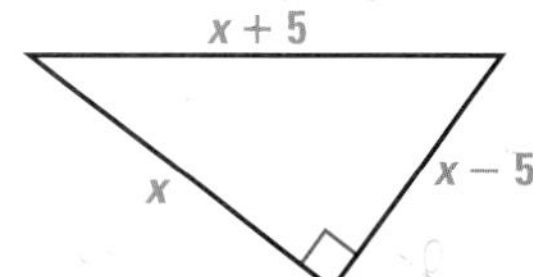

19. 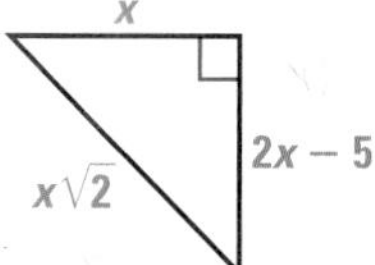

Tell whether the triangle with the given side lengths is a right triangle.

20. 8, 16, 20
21. 11, 60, 61
22. 7.5, 10, 12.5

Find the distance between the given points. Then find the midpoint of the line segment whose endpoints are the given points.

23. (6, 6), (9, 10)
24. (−8, 7), (4, 3)
25. $\left(5, -\frac{3}{2}\right), \left(-2, \frac{9}{2}\right)$

26. **LADDERS** A ladder that is 25 feet long is placed against a house. The bottom of the ladder is 10 feet from the base of the house. How far up the house does the ladder reach? Round your answer to the nearest tenth of a foot.

27. **BIRD HOUSES** The front view of a bird house is shown. Find the height of the house to the nearest tenth of a foot.

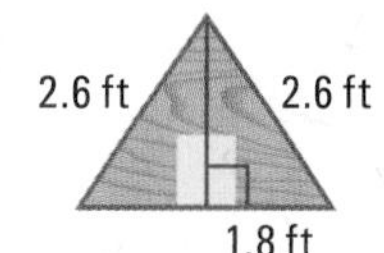

28. **LACROSSE** Two lacrosse players are playing on a field, as shown. The distance between consecutive grid lines represents 2 meters.

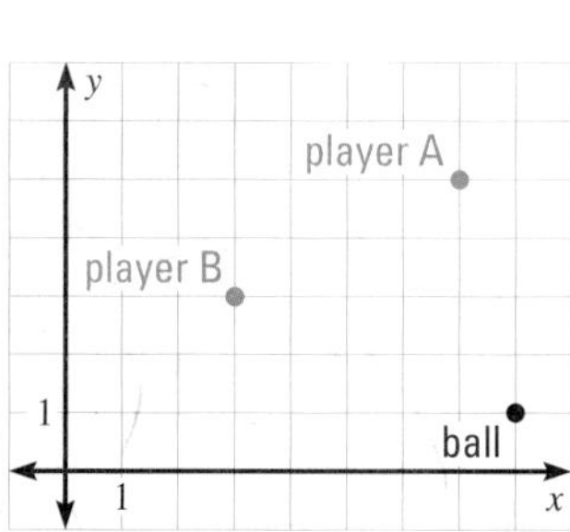

   a. How far is each player from the ball? Round your answer to the nearest tenth of a meter.
   b. Both players start running toward the ball. Player A can run at a rate of 6 meters per second. Player B can run at a rate of 7 meters per second. Who will reach the ball first?

MULTIPLE CHOICE QUESTIONS

If you have difficulty solving a multiple choice problem directly, you may be able to use another approach to eliminate incorrect answer choices and obtain the correct answer.

PROBLEM 1

What is the solution of the equation $\sqrt{3 - x} = 2x$?

Ⓐ $1, -\frac{3}{4}$ Ⓑ $-1, \frac{3}{4}$ Ⓒ -1 Ⓓ $\frac{3}{4}$

METHOD 1

SOLVE DIRECTLY Solve the radical equation and check for extraneous solutions.

STEP 1 **Solve** the radical equation.

$$\sqrt{3 - x} = 2x$$
$$3 - x = 4x^2$$
$$0 = 4x^2 + x - 3$$
$$0 = (4x - 3)(x + 1)$$
$$4x - 3 = 0 \text{ or } x + 1 = 0$$
$$x = \frac{3}{4} \text{ or } \quad x = -1$$

STEP 2 **Check** $\frac{3}{4}$ and -1 in the original equation.

Check $\frac{3}{4}$: $\sqrt{3 - \frac{3}{4}} \stackrel{?}{=} 2\left(\frac{3}{4}\right)$

$$\frac{3}{2} = \frac{3}{2} \checkmark$$

Solution checks.

Check -1: $\sqrt{3 - (-1)} \stackrel{?}{=} 2(-1)$

$$2 = -2 \text{ ✗}$$

Solution does not check.

The only solution is $\frac{3}{4}$.

The correct answer is D. Ⓐ Ⓑ Ⓒ Ⓓ

METHOD 2

ELIMINATE CHOICES Substitute the values given in each answer choice for x in the equation.

Choice A: $1, -\frac{3}{4}$

$\sqrt{3 - 1} \stackrel{?}{=} 2(1)$ | $\sqrt{3 - \left(-\frac{3}{4}\right)} \stackrel{?}{=} -\frac{3}{4}$

$\sqrt{2} = 2$ ✗ | $\frac{\sqrt{15}}{2} = -\frac{3}{4}$ ✗

The values do not check, so choice A can be eliminated.

Choice B: $-1, \frac{3}{4}$

$\sqrt{3 - (-1)} \stackrel{?}{=} 2(-1)$ | $\sqrt{3 - \frac{3}{4}} \stackrel{?}{=} 2\left(\frac{3}{4}\right)$

$2 = -2$ ✗ | $\frac{3}{2} = \frac{3}{2}$ ✓

Because -1 does not check, both choice B and choice C can be eliminated.

Choice D: $\frac{3}{4}$

You know that $\frac{3}{4}$ is a solution from checking the values in choice B.

The only solution is $\frac{3}{4}$.

The correct answer is D. Ⓐ Ⓑ Ⓒ Ⓓ

PROBLEM 2

A carpenter is building a wooden bench and wants to be sure that the back and the seat make a right angle. The back is 24 inches tall, and the seat is 18 inches deep. What should the distance from the front of the seat to the top of the back be?

Ⓐ 6 inches Ⓑ 15.9 inches Ⓒ 30 inches Ⓓ 42 inches

METHOD 1

SOLVE DIRECTLY Use the Pythagorean theorem to find the unknown distance.

STEP 1 **Identify** the known values by drawing a diagram.

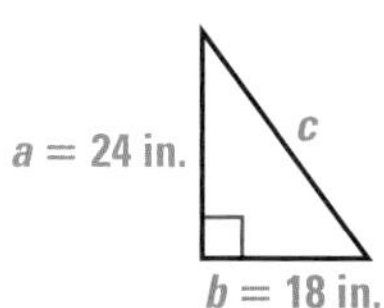

STEP 2 **Substitute** the values of a and b and solve for c.

$$a^2 + b^2 = c^2$$
$$18^2 + 24^2 = c^2$$
$$900 = c^2$$
$$\sqrt{900} = c$$
$$30 = c$$

The distance from the front of the seat to the top of the back should be 30 inches.

The correct answer is C. Ⓐ Ⓑ Ⓒ Ⓓ

METHOD 2

ELIMINATE CHOICES You can eliminate choices either by using the fact that the hypotenuse is the longest side of a right triangle or by using the converse of the Pythagorean theorem. Check to see if the value given in each answer choice could represent the length of the hypotenuse of a right triangle with leg lengths of 18 and 24 inches.

Choice A: 6 inches

$6 < 18$ ✗

Choice B: 15.9 inches

$15.9 < 18$ ✗

Choice C: 30 inches

$30 > 24$, so use the converse of the Pythagorean theorem.

$$18^2 + 24^2 \stackrel{?}{=} 30^2$$
$$900 = 900 \checkmark$$

The correct answer is C. Ⓐ Ⓑ Ⓒ Ⓓ

PRACTICE

Explain why you can eliminate the highlighted answer choice.

1. What is the solution of the equation $\sqrt{20 - x} = x$?

   Ⓐ 4, −5 Ⓑ −4, 5 Ⓒ ✗−5 Ⓓ 4

2. Which of the following represents the side lengths of a right triangle?

   Ⓐ 1, 2, 3 Ⓑ ✗6, 8, 14 Ⓒ 12, 13, 15 Ⓓ 8, 15, 17

3. A side view of a wheelchair ramp can be represented by the hypotenuse of a right triangle. The triangle has a length of 24 feet and a height of 2 feet. To the nearest tenth, how long is the ramp?

   Ⓐ ✗22 feet Ⓑ 23.9 feet Ⓒ 24.1 feet Ⓓ 26 feet

11 ★ Standardized TEST PRACTICE

MULTIPLE CHOICE

1. What is the solution of the equation $\sqrt{2x + 8} = x$?

   (A) $-2, 4$ (B) $24, 2$

   (C) -2 (D) 4

2. Which expression is equivalent to $\sqrt{4x^2 y} \cdot \sqrt{y}$?

   (A) $4xy$ (B) $2xy$

   (C) $2x\sqrt{y}$ (D) $4x\sqrt{y}$

3. The graph of which function is shown?

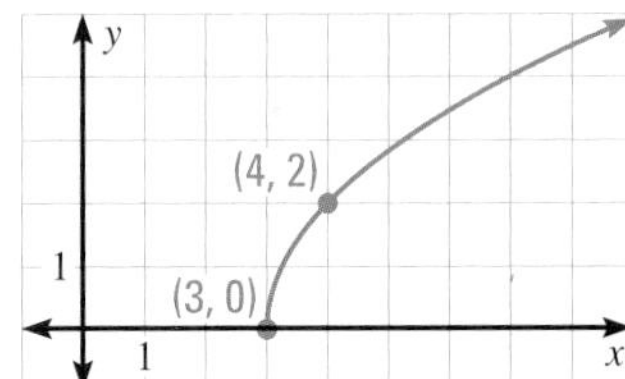

   (A) $y = \sqrt{x - 3}$ (B) $y = 2\sqrt{x - 3}$

   (C) $y = 2\sqrt{x + 3}$ (D) $y = 2\sqrt{x} - 3$

4. How does the graph of $y = \sqrt{x} + 3$ compare with the graph of $y = \sqrt{x}$?

   (A) It is a vertical stretch by a factor of 3 of the graph of $y = \sqrt{x}$.

   (B) It is a vertical translation of 3 units up of the graph of $y = \sqrt{x}$.

   (C) It is a vertical translation of 3 units down of the graph of $y = \sqrt{x}$.

   (D) It is a horizontal translation of 3 units to the right of the graph of $y = \sqrt{x}$.

5. Which expression represents the length of a diagonal of the rectangle?

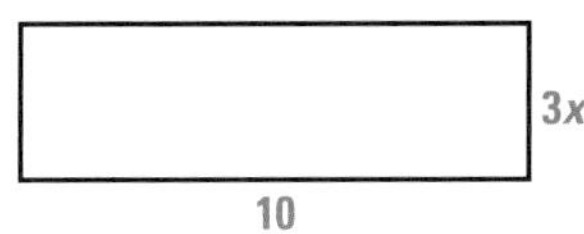

   (A) $3x^2 + 100$

   (B) $9x^2 + 100$

   (C) $\sqrt{9x^2 + 100}$

   (D) $\sqrt{3x^2 + 100}$

6. What is the solution of the equation $\sqrt{x + 3} = x - 9$?

   (A) $-13, -6$ (B) $13, 6$

   (C) 13 (D) 6

7. The table below represents which function?

x	4	5	8	13
y	5	8	11	14

   (A) $y = 3\sqrt{x - 4} + 5$

   (B) $y = 3\sqrt{x - 3} + 8$

   (C) $y = 3\sqrt{x - 4} + 8$

   (D) $y = 3\sqrt{x - 3} + 5$

In Exercises 8 and 9, use the map of the college campus shown.

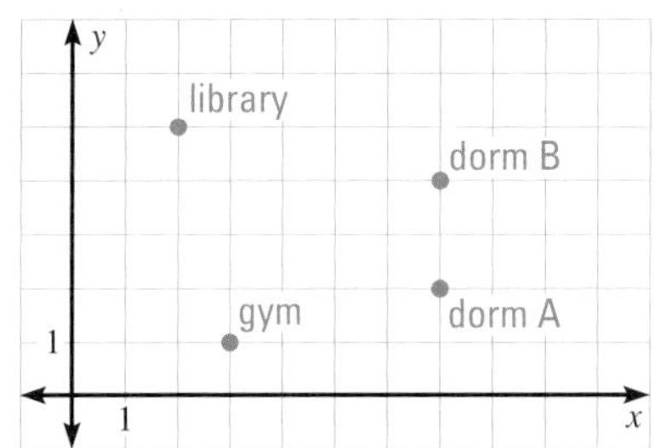

8. Which of the following pairs of buildings are closest together?

   (A) Dorm A and the library

   (B) Dorm B and the gym

   (C) The gym and the library

   (D) Dorm B and the library

9. A student who lives in dorm A forgets a book at the library. The student jogs at a rate of 6 miles per hour from the dorm straight to the library and back. The distance between consecutive grid lines represents 0.1 mile. To the nearest tenth of an hour, how long does it take the student to jog to the library and back?

   (A) 0.1 hour (B) 0.2 hour

   (C) 0.3 hour (D) 0.4 hour

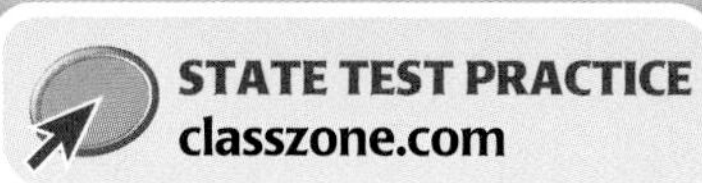

GRIDDED ANSWER

10. A line segment has endpoints (8, 0) and (14, 8). What is the distance from either endpoint to the midpoint?

11. A right triangle has a hypotenuse of 18 centimeters. The length of one leg is 8 centimeters. To the nearest tenth of a centimeter, how long is the other leg?

12. The leg lengths of a triangle are shown.

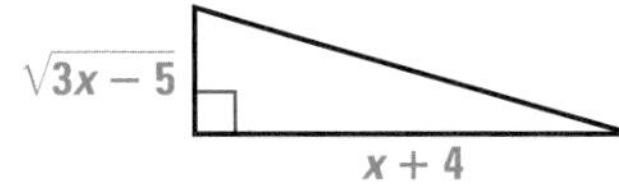

To the nearest tenth, what is the length of the hypotenuse when $x = 3$?

13. A rectangular table is 7 feet long and 3.5 feet wide. To the nearest tenth of a foot, what is the length of a diagonal of the table?

14. What is the solution of the equation $2\sqrt{x} = 3\sqrt{8} - \sqrt{2}$? Write your answer as a decimal.

SHORT RESPONSE

15. A person lives in Glenville. The person's friend lives in Newport.

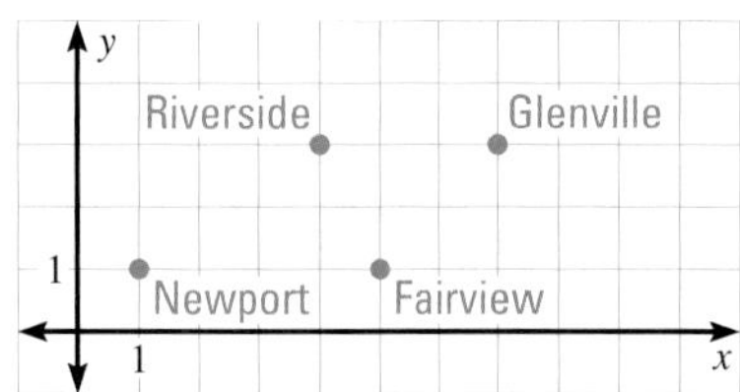

The friends decide to meet at the city that is closer to the midpoint of their locations. In which city should they meet? *Explain.*

16. The front view of a shed is shown. Roofers are going to replace the tin roof of the shed.

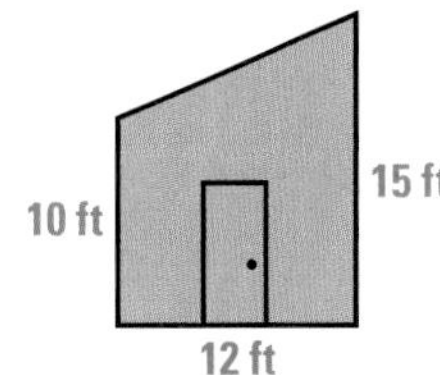

If the depth of the shed is 20 feet, how many square feet of tin will the roofers need? *Explain.*

EXTENDED RESPONSE

17. For the period 1900–2000, the life expectancy at birth e (in years) for people born in the United States can be modeled by the function $e = 3.66\sqrt{t} + 40.6$ where t is the number of years since 1900.

a. Graph the function and identify its domain and range.

b. In what year was the life expectancy at birth about 75 years? *Explain.*

c. During which decade (1900–1909, 1910–1919, and so on) did life expectancy increase the most? *Explain.*

18. A planet's mean radius r (in meters) is given by $r = \sqrt{\frac{(6.67 \times 10^{-11})M}{a}}$ where a is the planet's acceleration due to gravity (in meters per second squared) and M is the planet's mass (in kilograms).

a. For Earth, the value of a is about 9.8 meters per second squared, and the value of M is about 5.98×10^{24} kilograms. Find the value of r.

b. For Jupiter, the value of a is about 24.8 meters per second squared, and the value of M is about 1.9×10^{27} kilograms. Find the value of r.

c. Jupiter's mass is abouut 300 times Earth's mass, and Jupiter's acceleration due to gravity is about 2.5 times that of Earth's. If you multiply M by 300 and a by 2.5, what happens to the value of r? *Compare* your answer with your results from parts (a) and (b).

12 Rational Equations and Functions

Before

In previous chapters and courses, you learned the following skills, which you'll use in Chapter 12: performing operations on numerical fractions, solving equations, and factoring polynomials.

Prerequisite Skills

VOCABULARY CHECK

1. What is the **least common denominator** of $\frac{3}{8}$ and $\frac{7}{10}$?
2. Which equation is a **direct variation** equation, $\frac{y}{5} = x$ or $\frac{5}{y} = x$?
3. What is the **degree** of the polynomial $4x - 2 + 5x^2$?
4. Identify the **extraneous solution** when solving $\sqrt{x + 2} = x$.

SKILLS CHECK

Factor the polynomial. *(Review pp. 583, 600, 606 for 12.4–12.6.)*

5. $x^2 - 2x - 15$
6. $2x^2 - 8x + 6$
7. $9x^2 - 25$
8. $3x^3 - 48x$

Add, subtract, multiply, or divide. *(Review pp. 914, 915 for 12.5–12.6.)*

9. $\frac{1}{3} + \frac{3}{4}$
10. $\frac{7}{8} - \frac{2}{5}$
11. $\frac{5}{9} \times \frac{3}{5}$
12. $\frac{3}{10} \div \frac{6}{25}$

Solve the equation or proportion. *(Review pp. 134, 162, 583, 729 for 12.7.)*

13. $4x = 9$
14. $\frac{x}{10} = \frac{3}{5}$
15. $x^2 + x = 6$
16. $\sqrt{x - 9} = 2$

@HomeTutor Prerequisite skills practice at classzone.com

Now

In Chapter 12, you will apply the big ideas listed below and reviewed in the Chapter Summary on page 830. You will also use the key vocabulary listed below.

Big Ideas

1. **Graphing rational functions**
2. **Performing operations on rational expressions**
3. **Solving rational equations**

KEY VOCABULARY

- inverse variation, *p. 765*
- constant of variation, *p. 765*
- hyperbola, *p. 767*
- branches, asymptotes of a hyperbola, *p. 767*
- rational function, *p. 775*
- rational expression, *p. 794*
- excluded value, *p. 794*
- simplest form of a rational expression, *p. 795*
- least common denominator (LCD) of rational expressions, *p. 813*
- rational equation, *p. 820*

Why?

You can use rational functions to solve problems in biology. For example, you can graph a rational function to describe how a microorganism's efficiency at performing metabolic tasks changes as its dimensions change.

Animated Algebra

The animation illustrated below for Exercise 49 on page 791 helps you answer this question: How does changing one dimension of a cylindrical microorganism change the ratio of the cylinder's surface area to its volume?

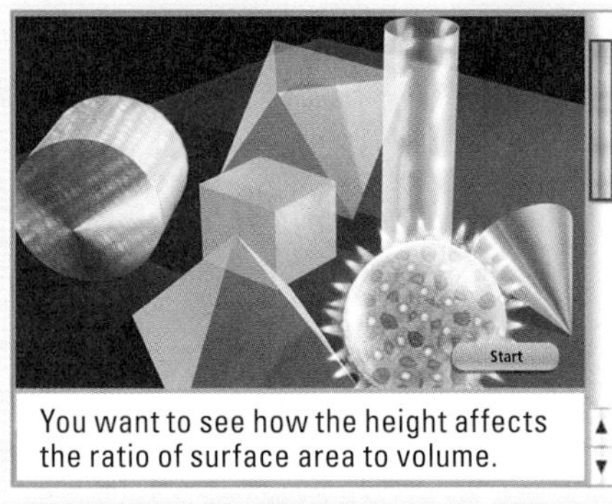

You want to see how the height affects the ratio of surface area to volume.

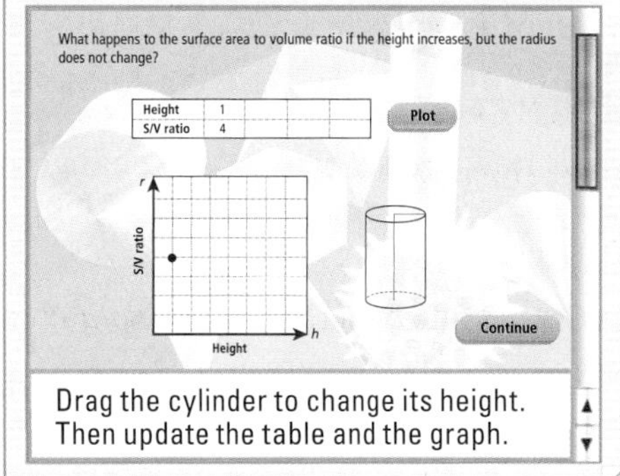

Drag the cylinder to change its height. Then update the table and the graph.

Animated **Algebra** at classzone.com

Other animations for Chapter 12: pages 766, 777, 783, 804, 814, and 830

12.1 Relationships Between Dimensions of a Rectangle

MATERIALS • 12 square tiles

QUESTION **Given a rectangle with a fixed area, how is one dimension related to the other?**

EXPLORE **Graph the relationship between the dimensions of a rectangle**

STEP 1 ***Form rectangle***

Draw the x- and y-axes on a sheet of paper as shown. Use all of the tiles to form a rectangle in Quadrant I with the lower left vertex on the origin. Then label the upper right vertex with the coordinates (x, y) where x is the horizontal length of the rectangle and y is the vertical length.

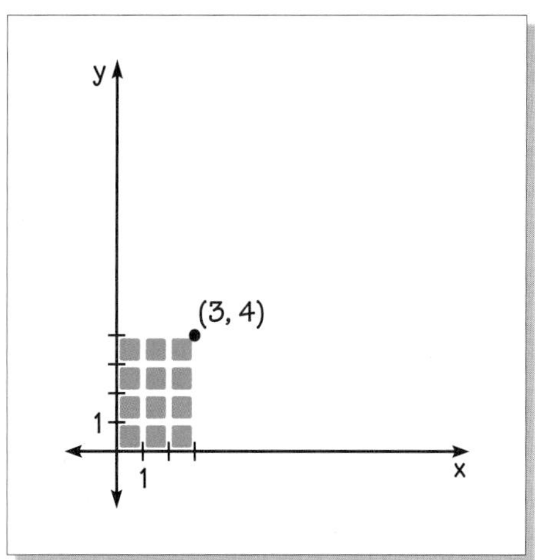

STEP 2 ***Draw curve***

Repeat Step 1 for all possible rectangles that can be formed with the tiles. Then connect the points by drawing a smooth curve through them.

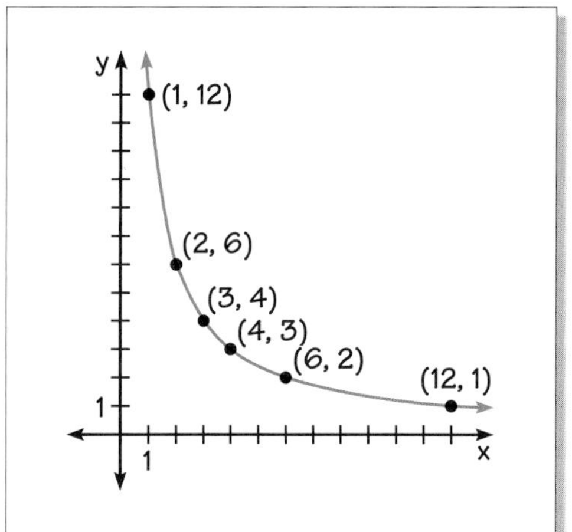

DRAW CONCLUSIONS **Use your observations to complete these exercises**

1. *Describe* how the vertical length changes as the horizontal length increases. *Describe* how the vertical length changes as the horizontal length decreases.
2. Does the graph cross the axes? *Explain* your reasoning.
3. Write an equation that gives the vertical length y as a function of the horizontal length x.
4. Let A represent the area of a rectangle. For $A = 40$, write an equation that gives y as a function of x. Then graph the equation.
5. *Compare* the graph of the equation that you wrote in Exercise 4 with the graph of the equation that you wrote in Exercise 3.

12.1 Model Inverse Variation

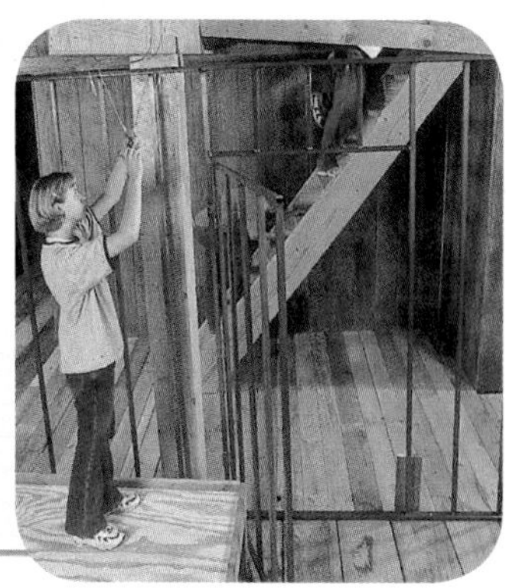

Before You wrote and graphed direct variation equations.

Now You will write and graph inverse variation equations.

Why? So you can find a person's work time, as in Example 6.

Key Vocabulary
- **inverse variation**
- **constant of variation**
- **hyperbola**
- **branches of a hyperbola**
- **asymptotes of a hyperbola**

Recall that two variables x and y show direct variation if $y = ax$ and $a \neq 0$. The variables x and y show **inverse variation** if $y = \frac{a}{x}$ and $a \neq 0$. The nonzero number a is the **constant of variation**, and y is said to *vary inversely* with x.

EXAMPLE 1 Identify direct and inverse variation

Tell whether the equation represents *direct variation, inverse variation,* or *neither.*

a. $xy = 4$ **b.** $\frac{y}{2} = x$ **c.** $y = 2x + 3$

Solution

a. $xy = 4$ Write original equation.

$y = \frac{4}{x}$ Divide each side by x.

Because $xy = 4$ can be written in the form $y = \frac{a}{x}$, $xy = 4$ represents inverse variation. The constant of variation is 4.

b. $\frac{y}{2} = x$ Write original equation.

$y = 2x$ Multiply each side by 2.

Because $\frac{y}{2} = x$ can be written in the form $y = ax$, $\frac{y}{2} = x$ represents direct variation.

c. Because $y = 2x + 3$ cannot be written in the form $y = \frac{a}{x}$ or $y = ax$, $y = 2x + 3$ does not represent either direct variation or inverse variation.

✓ GUIDED PRACTICE for Example 1

Tell whether the equation represents *direct variation, inverse variation,* or *neither.*

1. $y = \frac{2}{x}$ **2.** $4y = 3x$ **3.** $5x - y = 3$ **4.** $xy = \frac{1}{2}$

EXAMPLE 2 Graph an inverse variation equation

Graph $y = \frac{4}{x}$.

Solution

STEP 1 **Make** a table by choosing several integer values of x and finding the values of y. Then plot the points. To see how the function behaves for values of x very close to 0 and very far from 0, make a second table for such values and plot the points.

AVOID ERRORS
Note that y is undefined when $x = 0$. There is no point $(0, y)$ on the graph of $y = \frac{4}{x}$.

x	y
−4	−1
−2	−2
−1	−4
0	undefined
1	4
2	2
4	1

x	y
−10	−0.4
−5	−0.8
−0.5	−8
−0.4	−10
0.4	10
0.5	8
5	0.8
10	0.4

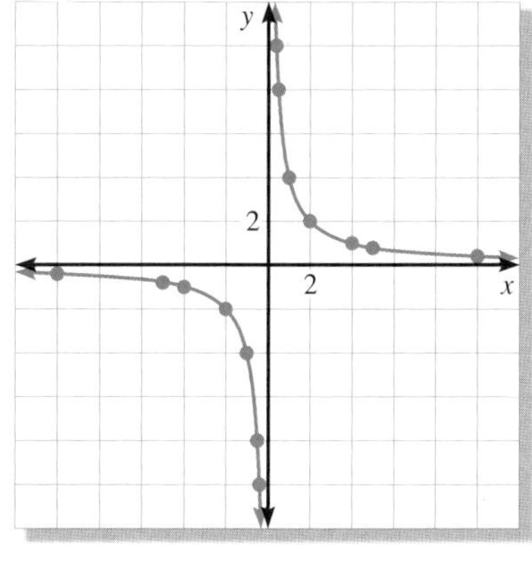

STEP 2 **Connect** the points in Quadrant I by drawing a smooth curve through them. Repeat for the points in Quadrant III.

GRAPHS OF INVERSE VARIATION As shown in Example 2, as you move away from the origin along the x-axis, the graph of an inverse variation equation approaches the x-axis without crossing it. As you move away from the origin along the y-axis, the graph approaches the y-axis without crossing it.

EXAMPLE 3 Graph an inverse variation equation

Graph $y = \frac{-4}{x}$.

Solution

COMPARE GRAPHS
The graph of an inverse variation equation lies in Quadrants I and III if $a > 0$, and the graph lies in Quadrants II and IV if $a < 0$.

Notice that $y = \frac{-4}{x} = -1 \cdot \frac{4}{x}$. So, for every nonzero value of x, the value of y in $y = \frac{-4}{x}$ is the opposite of the value of y in $y = \frac{4}{x}$. You can graph $y = \frac{-4}{x}$ by reflecting the graph of $y = \frac{4}{x}$ (see Example 2) in the x-axis.

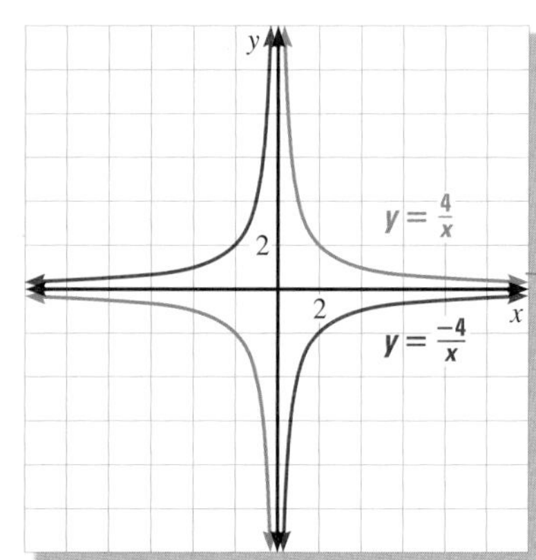

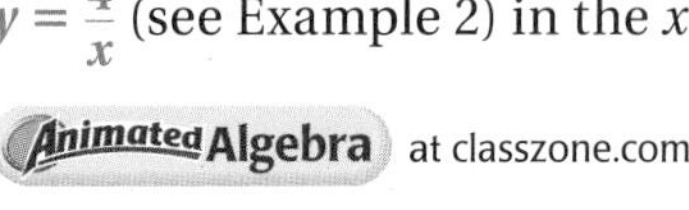

at classzone.com

CONCEPT SUMMARY *For Your Notebook*

Graphs of Direct Variation and Inverse Variation Equations

Direct variation

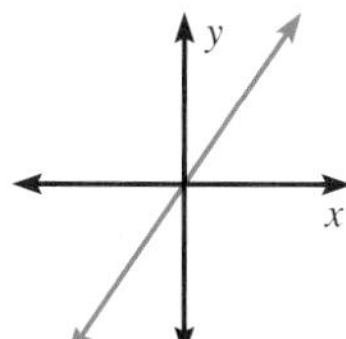

$y = ax, a > 0$

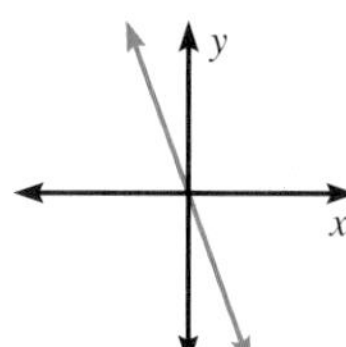

$y = ax, a < 0$

Inverse variation

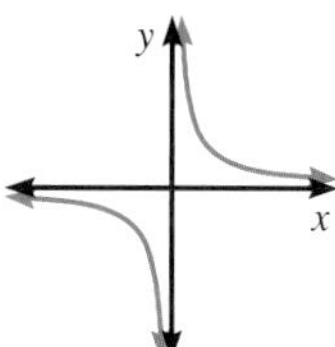

$y = \frac{a}{x}, a > 0$

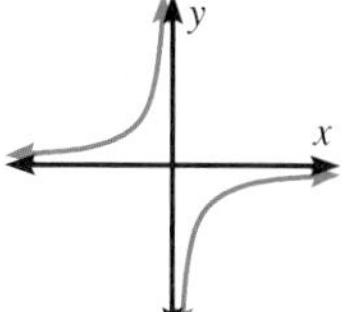

$y = \frac{a}{x}, a < 0$

HYPERBOLAS The graph of the inverse variation equation $y = \frac{a}{x}$ $(a \neq 0)$ is a **hyperbola**. The two symmetrical parts of a hyperbola are called the **branches of the hyperbola**. The lines that the hyperbola approaches but doesn't intersect are called the **asymptotes of the hyperbola**. The asymptotes of the graph of $y = \frac{a}{x}$ are the x-axis and the y-axis.

EXAMPLE 4 Use an inverse variation equation

The variables x and y vary inversely, and $y = 6$ when $x = -3$.

a. Write an inverse variation equation that relates x and y.

b. Find the value of y when $x = 4$.

Solution

a. Because y varies inversely with x, the equation has the form $y = \frac{a}{x}$.

Use the fact that $x = -3$ and $y = 6$ to find the value of a.

$y = \frac{a}{x}$ **Write inverse variation equation.**

$6 = \frac{a}{-3}$ **Substitute −3 for x and 6 for y.**

$-18 = a$ **Multiply each side by −3.**

An equation that relates x and y is $y = \frac{-18}{x}$.

b. When $x = 4$, $y = \frac{-18}{4} = -\frac{9}{2}$.

✓ **GUIDED PRACTICE** for Examples 2, 3, and 4

5. Graph **(a)** $y = \frac{3}{x}$ and **(b)** $y = \frac{-3}{x}$.

6. The variables x and y vary inversely, and $y = -2$ when $x = 12$. Write an inverse variation equation that relates x and y. Then find the value of y when $x = -3$.

PRODUCTS By multiplying both sides of $y = \frac{a}{x}$ by x, you can write the equation as $xy = a$. This means that a set of ordered pairs (x, y) shows inverse variation if all the products xy are constant.

EXAMPLE 5 Write an inverse variation equation

Tell whether the table represents inverse variation. If so, write the inverse variation equation.

x	−5	−3	4	8	24
y	2.4	4	−3	−1.5	−0.5

Solution

Find the products xy for all pairs (x, y):

$-5(2.4) = -12 \quad -3(4) = -12 \quad 4(-3) = -12 \quad 8(-1.5) = -12 \quad 24(-0.5) = -12$

The products are equal to the same number, −12. So, y varies inversely with x.

▶ The inverse variation equation is $xy = -12$, or $y = \frac{-12}{x}$.

EXAMPLE 6 Solve a multi-step problem

THEATER A theater company plans to hire people to build a stage set. The work time t (in hours per person) varies inversely with the number p of people hired. The company estimates that 25 people working for 300 hours each can complete the job. Find the work time per person if the company hires 30 people.

Solution

STEP 1 **Write** the inverse variation equation that relates p and t.

$t = \frac{a}{p}$ **Write inverse variation equation.**

$300 = \frac{a}{25}$ **Substitute 25 for p and 300 for t.**

$7500 = a$ **Multiply each side by 25.**

The inverse variation equation is $t = \frac{7500}{p}$.

STEP 2 **Find** t when $p = 30$: $t = \frac{7500}{p} = \frac{7500}{30} = 250$.

▶ If 30 people are hired, the work time per person is 250 hours.

✓ **GUIDED PRACTICE** for Examples 5 and 6

7. Tell whether the ordered pairs $(-5, 2)$, $(-4, 2.5)$, $(8, -1.25)$, and $(20, -0.5)$ represent inverse variation. If so, write the inverse variation equation.

8. **WHAT IF?** In Example 6, suppose the theater company estimates that 20 people working for 270 hours each can complete the job. Find the work time per person if the company hires 30 people.

12.1 EXERCISES

HOMEWORK KEY

○ = **WORKED-OUT SOLUTIONS** on p. WS28 for Exs. 17, 33, and 57

★ = **STANDARDIZED TEST PRACTICE** Exs. 2, 43, 59, and 60

◆ = **MULTIPLE REPRESENTATIONS** Ex. 58

SKILL PRACTICE

1. **VOCABULARY** Identify the constant of variation in the equation $y = \frac{-3}{x}$.

2. ★ **WRITING** *Describe* the difference between a direct variation equation and an inverse variation equation.

EXAMPLE 1 on p. 765 for Exs. 3–14, 43

DESCRIBING EQUATIONS **Tell whether the equation represents *direct variation, inverse variation,* or *neither.***

3. $y = -2x$ **4.** $xy = 1$ **5.** $y = x + 5$ **6.** $x = \frac{-1}{y}$

7. $xy = 5$ **8.** $\frac{y}{x} = 4$ **9.** $x = 7y$ **10.** $2x + y = 6$

11. $2x = \frac{8}{y}$ **12.** $x = -7$ **13.** $3x - 3y = 0$ **14.** $3xy = 20$

EXAMPLES 2 and 3 on p. 766 for Exs. 15–26

GRAPHING EQUATIONS **Graph the inverse variation equation.**

15. $y = \frac{2}{x}$ **16.** $y = \frac{-1}{x}$ **(17.)** $y = \frac{-7}{x}$ **18.** $y = \frac{10}{x}$

19. $y = \frac{-5}{x}$ **20.** $y = \frac{18}{x}$ **21.** $y = \frac{9}{x}$ **22.** $y = \frac{-2}{x}$

23. $y = \frac{15}{x}$ **24.** $y = \frac{6}{x}$ **25.** $y = \frac{-12}{x}$ **26.** $y = \frac{-8}{x}$

EXAMPLE 4 on p. 767 for Exs. 27–42

27. **ERROR ANALYSIS** The variables x and y vary inversely, and $y = 8$ when $x = 2$. *Describe* and correct the error in writing an inverse variation equation that relates x and y.

y = ax
8 = a(2)
4 = a
So, y = 4x.

USE INVERSE VARIATION **Given that y varies inversely with x, use the specified values to write an inverse variation equation that relates x and y. Then find the value of y when $x = 2$.**

28. $x = 5, y = 2$ **29.** $x = 3, y = 7$ **30.** $x = -5, y = 4$

31. $x = 13, y = -1$ **32.** $x = -15, y = -15$ **(33.)** $x = -22, y = -6$

34. $x = 8, y = 3$ **35.** $x = 9, y = -2$ **36.** $x = 3, y = 3$

37. $x = -2, y = -10$ **38.** $x = -3, y = 40$ **39.** $x = -7, y = -10$

40. $x = -17, y = 8$ **41.** $x = 6, y = 11$ **42.** $x = -12, y = -13$

43. ★ **MULTIPLE CHOICE** The variables x and y vary inversely, and $y = 6$ when $x = 4$. What is the constant of variation?

Ⓐ 1.5 Ⓑ 4 Ⓒ 6 Ⓓ 24

EXAMPLE 5
on p. 768
for Exs. 44–47

WRITING EQUATIONS Tell whether the table represents inverse variation. If so, write the inverse variation equation.

44.

x	4	8	12	16	20
y	1	2	3	4	5

45.

x	−20	−5	14	32	50
y	−80	−20	56	128	200

46.

x	−10	−5	15	20	40
y	−30	−60	20	15	7.5

47.

x	−12	−10	−8	−5	−4
y	2	2.4	3	4.8	6

48. **REASONING** The variables x and y vary inversely. How does the value of y change if the value of x is doubled? tripled? Give examples.

GEOMETRY Translate the verbal sentence into an equation using the appropriate geometric formula. Then tell whether the equation represents *direct variation, inverse variation,* or *neither.*

49. The circumference of a circle with radius r units is C units.

50. The perimeter of a rectangle with length ℓ units and width w units is 27 units.

51. The volume of a rectangular prism with base B square units and height h units is 400 cubic units.

52. **CHALLENGE** The variables x and y vary inversely with constant of variation a. The variables y and z vary inversely with constant of variation b. Write an equation that gives z as a function of x. Then tell whether x and z vary *directly* or *inversely.*

53. **CHALLENGE** The points $(3, a^2 - 7a + 10)$ and $(3a + 1, a + 2)$ lie on the graph of an inverse variation equation. Find the coordinates of the points.

PROBLEM SOLVING

EXAMPLE 5
on p. 768
for Exs. 54, 57

54. **BICYCLES** The table shows the bicycle speed s (in miles per hour) for various pedaling speeds p (in pedal rotations per mile). Tell whether the table represents inverse variation. If so, write the inverse variation equation that relates p and s.

Pedaling speed, p (pedal rotations/mi)	831	612	420	305
Bicycle speed, s (mi/h)	4.33	5.88	8.57	11.8

@HomeTutor for problem solving help at classzone.com

EXAMPLE 6
on p. 768
for Exs. 55–56, 58

55. **ECONOMICS** The owner of an electronics store determines that the monthly demand d (in units) for a computer varies inversely with the price p (in dollars) of the computer. When the price is \$700, the monthly demand is 250 units. Write the inverse variation equation that relates p and d. Then find the monthly demand when the price is \$500.

@HomeTutor for problem solving help at classzone.com

○ = WORKED-OUT SOLUTIONS on p. WS1 ★ = STANDARDIZED TEST PRACTICE ◆ = MULTIPLE REPRESENTATIONS

56. **SPORTS** An athlete is running a 200 meter dash. Write and graph an equation that relates the athlete's average running speed r (in meters per second) and the time t (in seconds) that the athlete will take to finish the race. Is the equation an inverse variation equation? *Explain.*

57. **MULTI-STEP PROBLEM** The table shows the vibration frequencies f (in hertz) for various lengths ℓ (in centimeters) of strings on a stringed instrument.

Length of string, ℓ (cm)	42.1	37.5	33.4	31.5
Frequency, f (Hz)	523	587	659	698

a. **Decide** Tell whether an inverse variation equation can be used to model the data. If so, write and graph the inverse variation equation.

b. **Calculate** Find the frequency of a string with a length of 29.4 centimeters.

c. **Describe** *Describe* the change in the frequency as the length of the string decreases. Does your answer in part (b) support your description?

58. **MULTIPLE REPRESENTATIONS** You plan to save the same amount of money each month to pay for a summer sports camp that costs $1200.

a. **Making a Table** Let a represent the amount (in dollars) that you plan to save each month. Make a table that shows the number m of months that you need to save money for the following values of a: 75, 100, 120, 150, 200, and 240. *Describe* how the number of months changes as the amount of money that you save each month increases.

b. **Drawing a Graph** Use the values in the table to draw a graph of the situation. Does the graph suggest a situation that represents *direct variation* or *inverse variation*? *Explain* your choice.

c. **Writing an Equation** Write the equation that relates a and m.

59. ★ **SHORT RESPONSE** As shown in the diagram, the focal length of a camera lens is the distance between the lens and the point at which light rays meet after passing through the aperture, or opening, in the lens. The f-stop s is the ratio of the focal length f (in millimeters) to the diameter a (in millimeters) of the aperture.

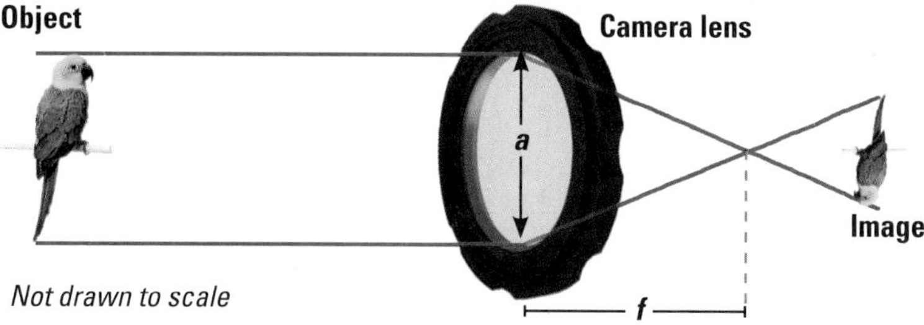

a. **Model** A photographer has a camera with a focal length of 35 millimeters. Write and graph an equation that relates a and s. Tell whether the equation represents inverse variation.

b. **Compare** The greater the diameter of the aperture, the more light that passes through the aperture. For the camera in part (a), does more light pass through the aperture when the f-stop is 4 or when the f-stop is 8? *Explain.*

60. ★ **EXTENDED RESPONSE** The photo below shows a replica of an airplane designed by Orville and Wilbur Wright, who were aviation pioneers in the early 20th century. The aspect ratio r of a wing from similar airplanes is given by the formula $r = \frac{s^2}{A}$ where s is the span, or the distance (in feet) between the wing tips, and A is the area (in square feet) of the wing.

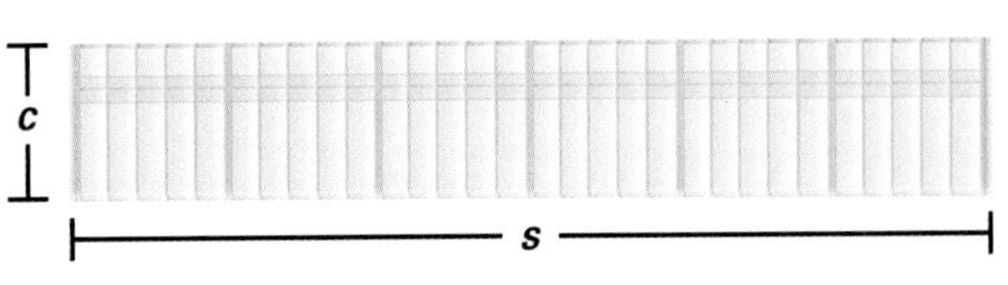

a. **Model** The length c of the chord of a wing is the distance (in feet) between the front and the back of the wing. For the rectangular wing shown, rewrite the formula for r in terms of c and s.

b. **Analyze** How does the value of r change when s is constant and c increases? when c is constant and s increases?

c. **Interpret** The greater the aspect ratio, the easier it is for an airplane to glide. Orville and Wilbur Wright designed an airplane with two rectangular wings that each had an aspect ratio of $\frac{20}{3}$ and a span of 40 feet. For what values of c would the airplane have glided more easily? *Explain.*

61. **CHALLENGE** A fulcrum is placed under the center of a board. In order for two objects to balance on the board, the distance (in feet) of each object from the center of the board must vary inversely with its weight (in pounds). In the diagram shown, what is the distance of each animal from the center of the board?

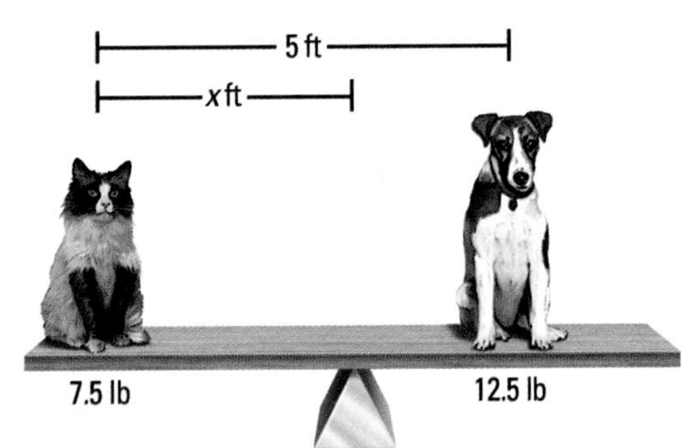

MIXED REVIEW

62. **MOVIES** You buy discount movie tickets from a website. Tickets cost \$3.60 each. You pay a shipping fee of \$3 per order. Write an equation that gives the total cost C (in dollars) of the tickets as a function of the number t of tickets bought. Then find the total cost of 8 tickets. *(p. 283)*

PREVIEW
Prepare for Lesson 12.2 in Exs. 63–68.

Graph the function. Identify its domain and range.

63. $y = 5^x$ *(p. 520)*
64. $y = 0.4^x$ *(p. 531)*
65. $y = x^2 + 5$ *(p. 628)*
66. $y = x^2 + 6x - 20$ *(p. 635)*
67. $y = -\sqrt{x}$ *(p. 710)*
68. $y = 2\sqrt{x - 1} + 1$ *(p. 710)*

Solve the equation. Check for extraneous solutions. *(p. 729)*

69. $\sqrt{x} = 10$
70. $\sqrt{x + 6} - 4 = 8$
71. $\sqrt{x - 2} = -10$
72. $2\sqrt{x} - 5 = 23$
73. $\sqrt{4x - 3} = \sqrt{2x + 7}$
74. $x = \sqrt{x + 30}$

12.2 Graphing $y = \frac{a}{x - h} + k$

MATERIALS • graph paper • graphing calculator

QUESTION What characteristics does the graph of $y = \frac{a}{x - h} + k$ have?

EXPLORE 1 Use tables to graph a function

Graph $y = \frac{2}{x - 3} + 4$ using a table.

STEP 1 *Use a table*

Make a table of values for $y = \frac{2}{x - 3} + 4$ by choosing several integer values of x. Round the values of y, if necessary. Then plot the points.

x	0	1	2	3	4	5	6
y	3.3	3	2	undefined	6	5	4.7

STEP 2 *Check close to and far from 3*

To see how the function behaves for values of x closer to 3 and farther from 3, make tables for such values and plot the points.

x	2.2	2.4	2.6	2.8	3.2	3.4	3.6
y	1.5	0.7	−1	−6	14	9	7.3

x	−4	−3	−2	−1	7	8	9
y	3.71	3.66	3.6	3.5	4.5	4.4	4.3

STEP 3 *Draw a graph*

Draw a smooth curve through the points (x, y) where $x > 3$. Repeat for the points (x, y) where $x < 3$.

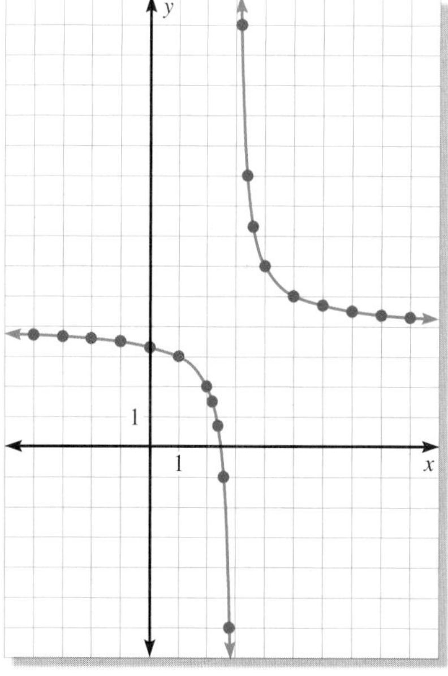

PRACTICE

1. *Describe* how the values of y change as the values of x get close to 3. What is the equation of the vertical asymptote?
2. *Describe* how the values of y change as the values of x get far from 3. What is the equation of the horizontal asymptote?

Graph the function using a table.

3. $y = \frac{5}{x - 4} - 6$
4. $y = \frac{-10}{x + 3} - 1$
5. $y = \frac{-11}{x + 13} + 9$

EXPLORE 2 **Use a graphing calculator to graph a function**

Graph $y = \frac{-3.4}{x + 1.7} - 2.8$ using a graphing calculator.

Enter $y_1 = \frac{-3.4}{x + 1.7} - 2.8$ into your graphing calculator. Press MODE and select either connected mode or dot mode. Then graph the function.

Connected mode

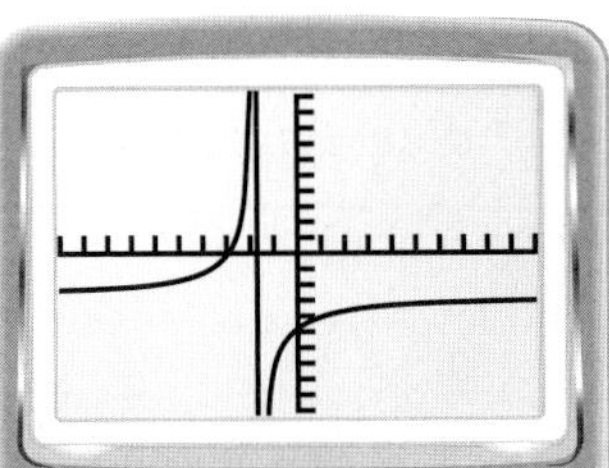

Dot mode

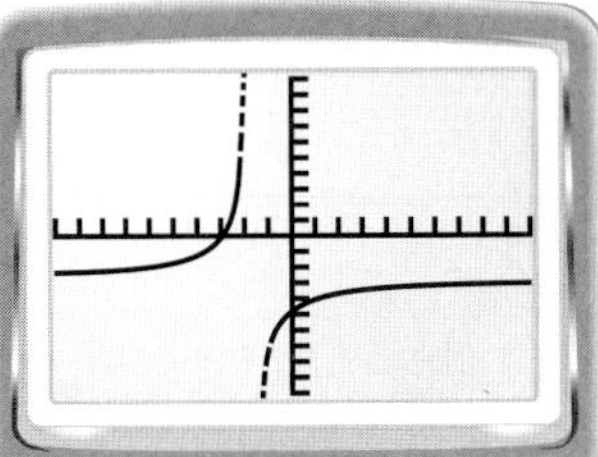

In connected mode, the screen appears to show the line $x = -1.7$. This line is *not* part of the graph. The calculator is instead connecting the two branches of the hyperbola. In dot mode, the screen does not show the line, but the points that are plotted are not connected by a smooth curve.

PRACTICE

6. *Describe* how the value of y changes as the value of x gets closer to -1.7. Use the *trace* feature of the graphing calculator to find the equation of the vertical asymptote.

7. *Describe* how the value of y changes as the value of x gets farther from -1.7. Use the *trace* feature of the graphing calculator to find the equation of the horizontal asymptote.

Graph the function using a graphing calculator.

8. $y = \frac{5.3}{x - 4.6} - 1.2$

9. $y = \frac{-7.1}{x - 3.2} + 4.5$

10. $y = \frac{-10.2}{x + 12.4} + 9.8$

DRAW CONCLUSIONS **Use your observations to complete these exercises**

11. How are the constants in the equations of the asymptotes in Exercises 1 and 2 related to the constants in the function $y = \frac{2}{x - 3} + 4$?

12. How are the constants in the equations of the asymptotes in Exercises 6 and 7 related to the constants in the function $y = \frac{-3.4}{x + 1.7} - 2.8$?

13. **CONJECTURE** Copy and complete: The graph of $y = \frac{a}{x - h} + k$ has a vertical asymptote of $x = \underline{\ ?\ }$ and a horizontal asymptote of $y = \underline{\ ?\ }$.

12.2 Graph Rational Functions

Before You graphed inverse variation equations.

Now You will graph rational functions.

Why? So you can find the cost of a group trip, as in Ex. 39.

Key Vocabulary
- **rational function**
- **hyperbola,** *p. 767*
- **branches of a hyperbola,** *p. 767*
- **asymptotes of a hyperbola,** *p. 767*

The inverse variation equation $y = \frac{a}{x}$ $(a \neq 0)$ is a type of *rational function.*

A **rational function** has a rule given by a fraction whose numerator and denominator are polynomials and whose denominator is not 0.

KEY CONCEPT *For Your Notebook*

Parent Rational Function

The function $y = \frac{1}{x}$ is the parent function for any rational function whose numerator has degree 0 or 1 and whose denominator has degree 1. The function and its graph have the following characteristics:

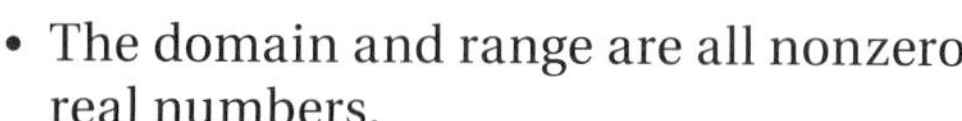

- The domain and range are all nonzero real numbers.

- The horizontal asymptote is the x-axis. The vertical asymptote is the y-axis.

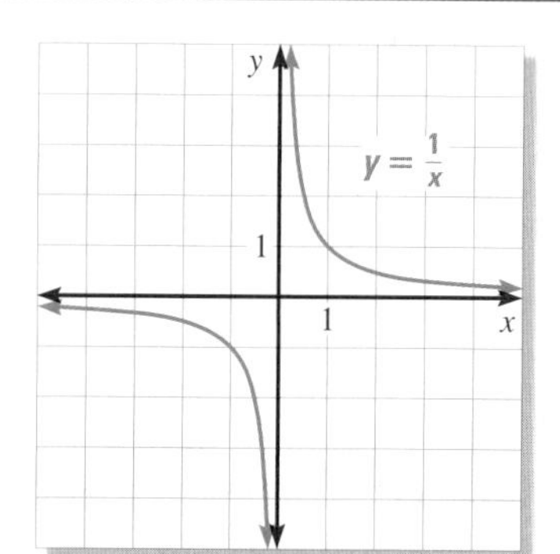

EXAMPLE 1 **Compare graph of $y = \frac{a}{x}$ with graph of $y = \frac{1}{x}$**

REWRITE FUNCTION

In the function $y = \frac{1}{3x}$, the value of a is $\frac{1}{3}$ as shown:

$y = \frac{1}{3x} = \frac{1}{3} \cdot \frac{1}{x}$

$= \frac{\frac{1}{3}}{x}$

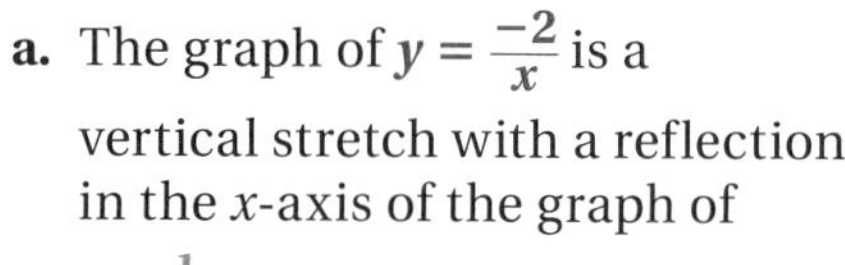

a. The graph of $y = \frac{-2}{x}$ is a vertical stretch with a reflection in the x-axis of the graph of $y = \frac{1}{x}$.

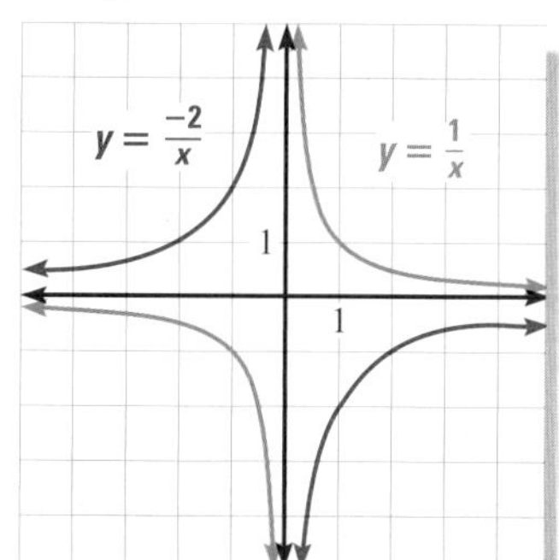

b. The graph of $y = \frac{1}{3x}$ is a vertical shrink of the graph of $y = \frac{1}{x}$.

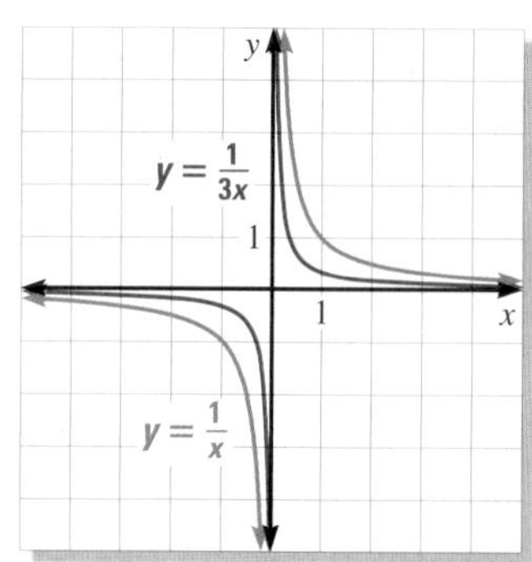

EXAMPLE 2 Graph $y = \frac{1}{x} + k$

Graph $y = \frac{1}{x} + 3$ and identify its domain and range. Compare the graph with the graph of $y = \frac{1}{x}$.

Solution

Graph the function using a table of values.

The domain is all real numbers except 0. The range is all real numbers except 3.

The graph of $y = \frac{1}{x} + 3$ is a vertical translation (of 3 units up) of the graph of $y = \frac{1}{x}$.

x	y
−2	2.5
−1	2
−0.5	1
0	undefined
0.5	5
1	4
2	3.5

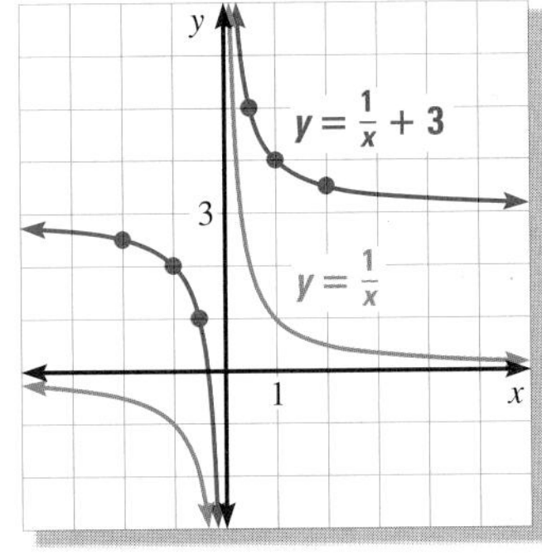

EXAMPLE 3 Graph $y = \frac{1}{x - h}$

Graph $y = \frac{1}{x - 2}$ and identify its domain and range. Compare the graph with the graph of $y = \frac{1}{x}$.

Solution

Graph the function using a table of values.

The domain is all real numbers except 2. The range is all real numbers except 0.

The graph of $y = \frac{1}{x - 2}$ is a horizontal translation (of 2 units to the right) of the graph of $y = \frac{1}{x}$.

x	y
0	−0.5
1	−1
1.5	−2
2	undefined
2.5	2
3	1
4	0.5

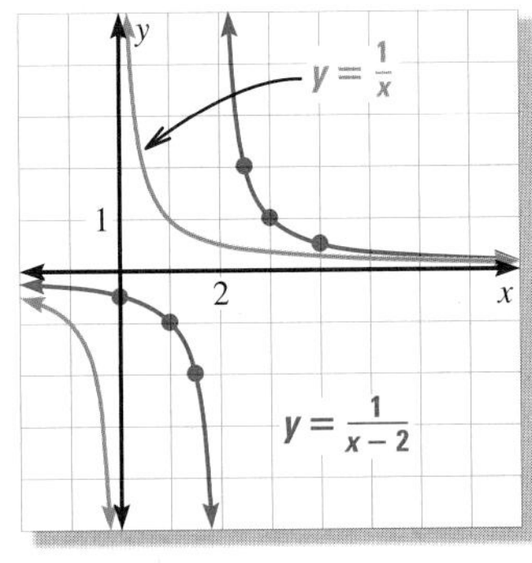

✓ GUIDED PRACTICE for Examples 1, 2, and 3

Graph the function and identify its domain and range. ***Compare*** **the graph with the graph of $y = \frac{1}{x}$.**

1. $y = \frac{-4}{x}$

2. $y = \frac{1}{x} - 4$

3. $y = \frac{1}{x + 5}$

4. *Describe* how the graph of $y = \frac{1}{x + 3}$ is related to the graph of $y = \frac{1}{x}$.

GRAPHING RATIONAL FUNCTIONS You can graph a rational function of the form $y = \frac{a}{x-h} + k$ $(a \neq 0)$ by using the values of a, k, and h.

KEY CONCEPT *For Your Notebook*

Graph of $y = \frac{a}{x-h} + k$

The graph of $y = \frac{a}{x-h} + k$ is a hyperbola that has the following characteristics:

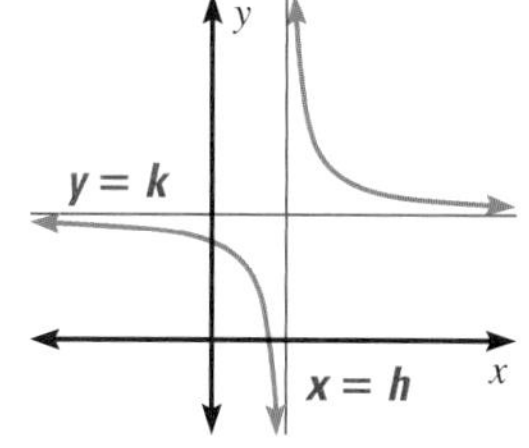

- If $|a| > 1$, the graph is a vertical stretch of the graph of $y = \frac{1}{x}$. If $0 < |a| < 1$, the graph is a vertical shrink of the graph of $y = \frac{1}{x}$. If $a < 0$, the graph is a reflection in the x-axis of the graph of $y = \frac{1}{x}$.
- The horizontal asymptote is $y = k$. The vertical asymptote is $x = h$.

The domain of the function is all real numbers except $x = h$. The range is all real numbers except $y = k$.

EXAMPLE 4 Graph $y = \frac{a}{x-h} + k$

Graph $y = \frac{2}{x+1} - 3$.

Solution

AVOID ERRORS

The asymptotes are used to help you draw a hyperbola. They are *not* part of the hyperbola.

STEP 1 **Identify** the asymptotes of the graph. The vertical asymptote is $x = -1$. The horizontal asymptote is $y = -3$.

STEP 2 **Plot** several points on each side of the vertical asymptote.

STEP 3 **Graph** two branches that pass through the plotted points and approach the asymptotes.

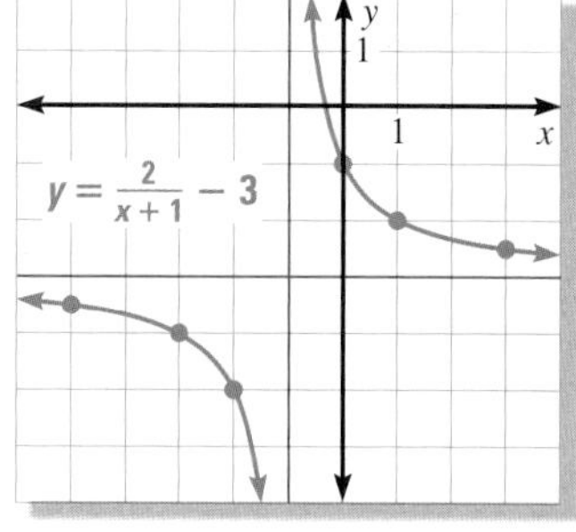

Animated Algebra at classzone.com

✓ **GUIDED PRACTICE** for Example 4

5. Graph $y = \frac{4}{x-5} + 6$.

6. For which function is the domain all real numbers except -3 and the range all real numbers except 7?

Ⓐ $y = \frac{2}{x-3} + 7$ Ⓑ $y = \frac{2}{x-3} - 7$ Ⓒ $y = \frac{2}{x+3} + 7$ Ⓓ $y = \frac{2}{x+3} - 7$

EXAMPLE 5 Solve a multi-step problem

TRIP EXPENSES Your art club is planning a bus trip to an art museum. The cost for renting a bus is \$495, and the cost will be divided equally among the people who are going on the trip. A museum ticket costs \$12.50 per person.

- Write an equation that gives the cost C (in dollars per person) of the trip as a function of the number p of people going on the trip.
- Graph the equation. *Describe* the change in the cost as the number of people increases.
- Use the graph to approximate the number of people who need to go on the trip so that the cost is about \$25 per person.

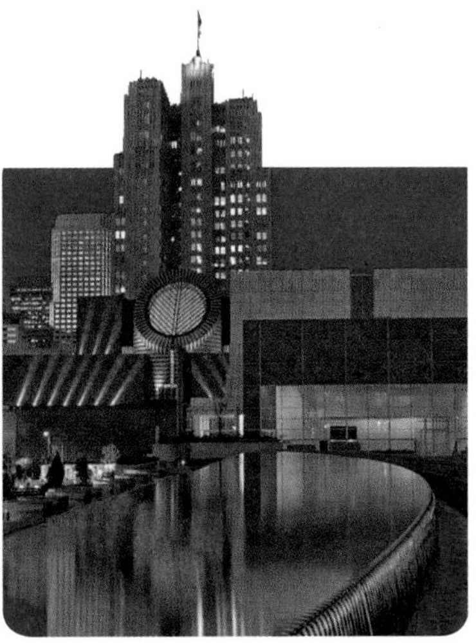

San Francisco Art Museum

Solution

STEP 1 **Write** a verbal model. Then write an equation.

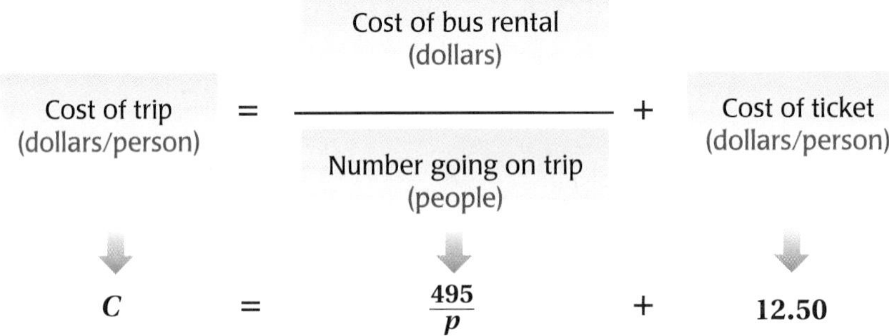

STEP 2 **Graph** $C = \frac{495}{p} + 12.50$ on a graphing calculator. The vertical asymptote is $p = 0$. The horizontal asymptote is $C = 12.5$. As the number of people increases, the cost decreases.

STEP 3 **Approximate** the number of people needed in order for the cost to be about \$25. When $C \approx 25$, the value of p is about 40. So, if about 40 people go on the trip, each person will pay about \$25.

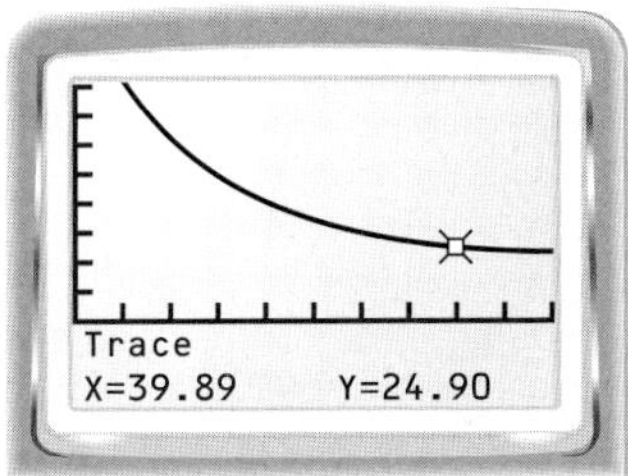

GUIDED PRACTICE for Example 5

7. **WHAT IF?** In Example 5, suppose the club rents a larger bus for \$610. Write and graph an equation that gives the cost C (in dollars per person) of the trip as a function of the number p of people going on the trip. Then approximate the number of people who need to go on the trip so that the cost is about \$25 per person.

12.2 EXERCISES

HOMEWORK KEY

○ = **WORKED-OUT SOLUTIONS** on p. WS28 for Exs. 7, 21, and 41

★ = **STANDARDIZED TEST PRACTICE** Exs. 2, 18, 28, 29, 36, 42, and 44

◆ = **MULTIPLE REPRESENTATIONS** Ex. 41

SKILL PRACTICE

1. **VOCABULARY** Identify the vertical asymptote and horizontal asymptote of the graph of $y = \frac{1}{x-3} - 6$.

2. ★ **WRITING** *Describe* the difference between the graph of $y = \frac{1}{x+2}$ and the graph of $y = \frac{1}{x}$.

EXAMPLES 1, 2, and 3 on pp. 775–776 for Exs. 3–17

GRAPHING FUNCTIONS **Graph the function and identify its domain and range. *Compare* the graph with the graph of $y = \frac{1}{x}$.**

3. $y = \frac{3}{x}$
4. $y = \frac{1}{2x}$
5. $y = \frac{-3}{x}$
6. $y = \frac{-2}{3x}$
7. $y = \frac{-1}{4x}$
8. $y = \frac{1}{x} + 7$
9. $y = \frac{1}{x} - 5$
10. $y = \frac{1}{x} + 4$
11. $y = \frac{1}{x} + 8$
12. $y = \frac{1}{x} - 6$
13. $y = \frac{1}{x+3}$
14. $y = \frac{1}{x-7}$
15. $y = \frac{1}{x+8}$
16. $y = \frac{1}{x-1}$
17. $y = \frac{1}{x-6}$

EXAMPLE 4 on p. 777 for Exs. 18–31

18. ★ **MULTIPLE CHOICE** For which function is the domain all real numbers except -5 and the range all real numbers except 0?

    (A) $y = \frac{5}{x}$ (B) $y = \frac{5}{x-5}$ (C) $y = \frac{5}{x+5}$ (D) $y = \frac{-5}{x-5}$

GRAPHING FUNCTIONS **Graph the function.**

19. $y = \frac{1}{x-2} - 8$
20. $y = \frac{2}{x-6} + 3$
21. $y = \frac{4}{x+7} + 5$
22. $y = \frac{-3}{x+3} - 4$
23. $y = \frac{-1}{x+5} + 6$
24. $y = \frac{2}{x-1} + 2$
25. $y = \frac{1}{x-4} + 2$
26. $y = \frac{4}{x-3} - 1$
27. $y = \frac{-5}{x-1} - 4$

28. ★ **MULTIPLE CHOICE** The graph of which function has the same horizontal asymptote as the graph of $y = \frac{1}{x}$?

    (A) $y = \frac{2}{x} + 3$ (B) $y = \frac{1}{x} - 1$ (C) $y = \frac{-10}{x}$ (D) $y = \frac{-10}{x-1} + 1$

29. ★ **OPEN-ENDED** Write an equation whose graph is a hyperbola that has the following characteristics:
    - The vertical asymptote is $x = -1$.
    - The horizontal asymptote is $y = 2$.

ERROR ANALYSIS ***Describe*** **and correct the error in identifying the asymptotes of the graph of the given rational function.**

30. $y = \frac{3}{x + 1} - 4$

Vertical asymptote: x = 1

Horizontal asymptote: y = −4

31. $y = \frac{-2}{x - 6} + 7$

Vertical asymptote: x = 6

Horizontal asymptote: y = −7

WRITING EQUATIONS **Write an equation whose graph is a hyperbola that has the given asymptotes and passes through the given point.**

32. $x = 7, y = 8; (-6, 0)$

33. $x = -2, y = 5; (0, -9)$

34. $x = 3, y = -2; (5, -1)$

35. $x = -4, y = -4; (-8, 3)$

36. ★ **WRITING** Let f be a function of the form $f(x) = \frac{a}{x - h} + k$. Can you graph f if you know only two points on the graph? *Explain.*

37. **GEOMETRY** The height h of a trapezoid is given by the formula

$$h = \frac{2A}{b_1 + b_2}$$

where A is the area and b_1 and b_2 are the bases.

a. Let $A = 50$ and $b_1 = 4$. Write h as a function of b_2. Then graph the function and identify its domain and range.

b. Use the graph to approximate the value of b_2 when $h = 6$.

38. **CHALLENGE** *Describe* how to find the asymptotes of the graph of $g(x) = \frac{3}{2x - 4} + 8$. Then graph the function.

PROBLEM SOLVING

GRAPHING CALCULATOR **You may wish to use a graphing calculator to complete the following Problem Solving exercises.**

EXAMPLE 5
on p. 778
for Exs. 39–42

39. **TEAM SPORTS** A figure skating troupe is planning an out-of-town trip. The expenses for the trip are shown in the flyer. Write an equation that gives the cost C (in dollars per person) as a function of the number p of people going on the trip. Then graph the equation.

@HomeTutor for problem solving help at classzone.com

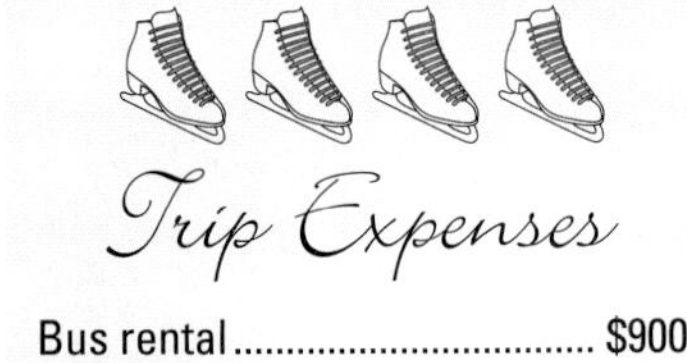

Bus rental $900

Food and lodging (per person) $400

40. **CHARITY EVENTS** A committee of 5 people is responsible for making 500 sandwiches for a charity picnic. The committee hopes to recruit extra people for the task. Write an equation that gives the average number s of sandwiches made per person as a function of the number p of extra people recruited for the task. Then graph the equation.

@HomeTutor for problem solving help at classzone.com

41. **MULTIPLE REPRESENTATIONS** Your movie rental membership lets you rent any number of movies for \$22 per month. You rent at least 2 movies per month.

a. **Writing an Equation** Write an equation that gives the average cost C (in dollars per rental) as a function of the number r of additional rentals beyond 2 rentals.

b. **Drawing a Graph** Graph the equation from part (a). Then use the graph to approximate the number of additional rentals needed per month so that the average cost is \$1.50 per rental.

42. ★ **SHORT RESPONSE** The Mount Washington Auto Road in New Hampshire is a 7.6 mile uphill road that leads to the mountain's 6288 foot peak. The year's fastest time t (in seconds) for driving up the road during the period 1904–1998 can be modeled by

$$t = \frac{56{,}000}{x + 40}$$

where x is the number of years since 1904. Graph the function. *Describe* how the fastest times changed during the period. Was the *change* in the fastest time from year to year *increasing* or *decreasing*? *Explain.*

43. **DIVING DEPTHS** The percent p (in decimal form) of time that an elephant seal spends gliding through the water while diving can be modeled by

$$p = \frac{-28.2}{d} + 0.859$$

where d is the depth (in meters) of the dive. Graph the equation and identify its domain and range. *Describe* how the percent of time gliding changes as the depth increases.

44. ★ **EXTENDED RESPONSE** Oxygen cost is a measure of a person's walking efficiency. The models below give the oxygen cost c (in millimeters per kilogram of body mass per meter) as a function of the walking speed v (in meters per minute) for various age groups.

Ages 6–12 | **Ages 13–19** | **Ages 20–59**

$c = \frac{2.61}{v} + 0.188$ | $c = \frac{1.68}{v} + 0.147$ | $c = \frac{2.60}{v} + 0.129$

a. **Graph** Normal walking speeds range from 40 meters per minute to 100 meters per minute. Graph the models in the same coordinate plane. Use the domain $40 \le v \le 100$.

b. **Interpret** The greater the oxygen cost, the less efficient the person is while walking. Use the graphs to tell whether a person is *more efficient* or *less efficient* while walking as the person's speed increases.

c. **Compare** Which age group has the least efficient walkers at the speeds given in part (a)? *Justify* your choice.

45. **CHALLENGE** To decide whether a person qualifies for a loan to buy a house, a lender uses the ratio r of the person's expected monthly housing expenses to monthly income. Suppose the person has a monthly income of \$4150 and expects to pay \$1200 per month in housing expenses. The person also expects to receive a raise of x dollars this month.

a. Write and graph an equation that gives r as a function of x.

b. The person will qualify for a loan if the ratio is 0.28. What must the amount of the raise be in order for the person to qualify for a loan?

MIXED REVIEW

PREVIEW
Prepare for Lesson 12.3 in Exs. 46–51.

Write the mixed number as an improper fraction, or write the improper fraction as a mixed number. *(p. 913)*

46. $1\frac{4}{7}$ **47.** $2\frac{3}{8}$ **48.** $5\frac{1}{9}$

49. $\frac{8}{5}$ **50.** $\frac{13}{6}$ **51.** $\frac{15}{4}$

Find the surface area and volume of the solid. For spheres and cylinders, give your answers in terms of π and as decimals rounded to the nearest tenth. *(p. 927)*

52.

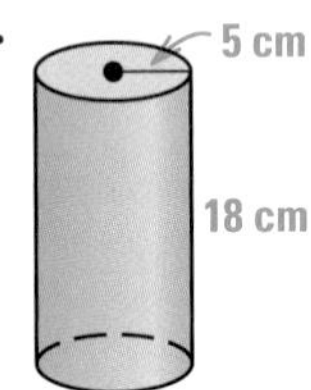

53.

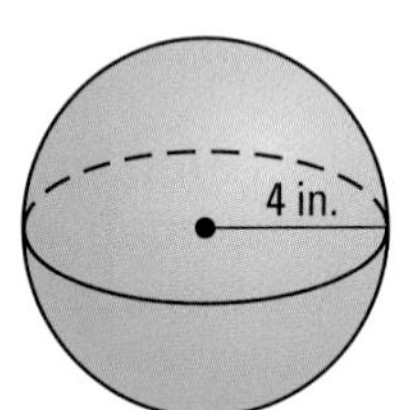

54.

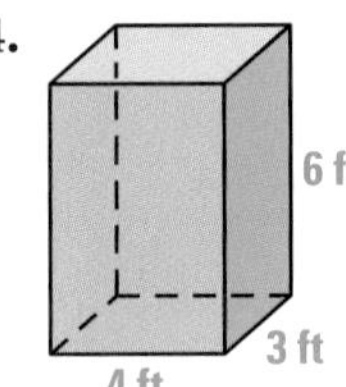

Simplify the expression.

55. $5x + 7 - 14x - 8$ *(p. 96)* **56.** $15x - (7 - 2x)$ *(p. 96)* **57.** $\frac{12x - 4}{2}$ *(p. 103)*

58. $\frac{-32x + 4}{-8}$ *(p. 103)* **59.** $\sqrt{81x^2}$ *(p. 719)* **60.** $\sqrt{100x^3y^2}$ *(p. 719)*

QUIZ *for Lessons 12.1–12.2*

Tell whether the equation represents *direct variation, inverse variation,* or *neither.* *(p. 765)*

1. $\frac{1}{5}xy = 1$ **2.** $y = -9x$ **3.** $5x + y = 3$

Given that y varies inversely with x, use the specified values to write an inverse variation equation that relates x and y. Then find the value of y when $x = 3$. *(p. 765)*

4. $x = 6, y = 4$ **5.** $x = -3, y = 7$ **6.** $x = \frac{5}{2}, y = 2$

Graph the function. Identify its domain and range. *(p. 775)*

7. $y = \frac{4}{x}$ **8.** $y = \frac{-2}{x - 6}$ **9.** $y = \frac{3}{x + 2} - 5$

 EXTRA PRACTICE for Lesson 12.2, p. 949 **ONLINE QUIZ** at classzone.com

Animated Algebra classzone.com

12.3 Dividing Polynomials Using Algebra Tiles

MATERIALS • algebra tiles

QUESTION How can you divide polynomials using algebra tiles?

In the equation $36 \div 5 = 7\frac{1}{5}$, the dividend is 36, the divisor is 5, the quotient is 7, and the remainder is 1. This equation illustrates the following rule:

$$\text{Dividend} \div \text{Divisor} = \text{Quotient} + \frac{\text{Remainder}}{\text{Divisor}}$$

This rule can also be applied when dividing polynomials.

EXPLORE Divide polynomials

Divide $2x^2 + 3x + 5$ by $x + 1$.

STEP 1 *Model using algebra tiles*

Think of $2x^2 + 3x + 5$ as the area of a figure. Try to arrange the tiles to form a rectangle with $x + 1$ as one of the side lengths.

Notice that the other side length is $2x + 1$, but there are four 1-tiles remaining.

STEP 2 *Write equation*

The divisor is $x + 1$, the quotient is $2x + 1$, and the remainder is 4.
So, $(2x^2 + 3x + 5) \div (x + 1) = 2x + 1 + \frac{4}{x + 1}$.

DRAW CONCLUSIONS Use your observations to complete these exercises

1. To check that $36 \div 5 = 7\frac{1}{5}$, you can evaluate $5 \cdot 7 + 1$ to obtain 36. Use this method to check the division equation in Step 2 above.

Use algebra tiles to divide the polynomials. Include a drawing of your model.

2. $(2x^2 + 7x + 6) \div (x + 2)$
3. $(2x^2 + 9x + 10) \div (x + 3)$
4. $(4x^2 + 4x + 5) \div (2x + 1)$
5. $(2x^2 + 5x + 7) \div (2x + 3)$
6. $(3x^2 + 7x + 3) \div (x + 2)$
7. $(4x^2 + 6x + 5) \div (x + 1)$
8. **REASONING** For which of the division problems in Exercises 2–7 is the divisor a factor of the dividend? How do you know?

12.3 Divide Polynomials

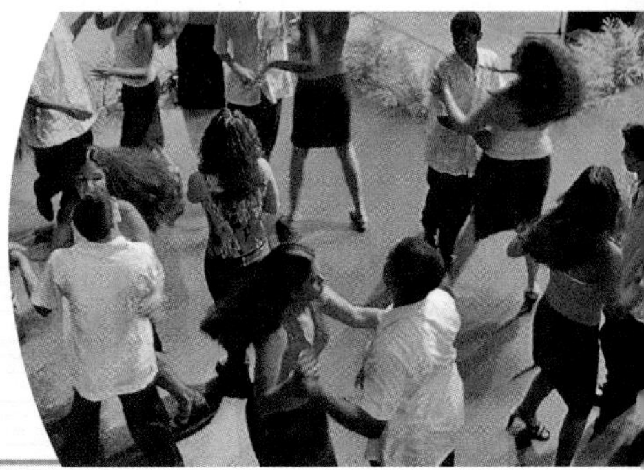

Before You multiplied polynomials.

Now You will divide polynomials.

Why? So you can describe an average cost, as in Ex. 43.

Key Vocabulary
- **monomial,** *p. 554*
- **polynomial,** *p. 554*
- **binomial,** *p. 555*
- **rational function,** *p. 775*

Just as you can find the product of two polynomials, you can divide the product by one of the polynomials to obtain the other polynomial. For example, $x^2 + 5x + 6 = (x + 2)(x + 3)$ is equivalent to $\frac{x^2 + 5x + 6}{x + 2} = x + 3$.

EXAMPLE 1 Divide a polynomial by a monomial

Divide $4x^3 + 8x^2 + 10x$ by $2x$.

Solution

Method 1: Write the division as a fraction.

$$(4x^3 + 8x^2 + 10x) \div 2x = \frac{4x^3 + 8x^2 + 10x}{2x}$$ Write as fraction.

$$= \frac{4x^3}{2x} + \frac{8x^2}{2x} + \frac{10x}{2x}$$ Divide each term by $2x$.

$$= 2x^2 + 4x + 5$$ Simplify.

Method 2: Use long division.

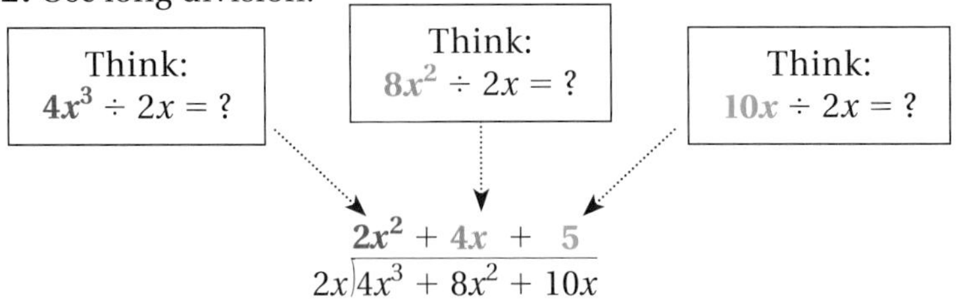

Think: $4x^3 \div 2x = ?$
Think: $8x^2 \div 2x = ?$
Think: $10x \div 2x = ?$
$2x^2 + 4x + 5$
$2x\overline{)4x^3 + 8x^2 + 10x}$

▸ $(4x^3 + 8x^2 + 10x) \div 2x = 2x^2 + 4x + 5$

CHECK $2x(2x^2 + 4x + 5) \stackrel{?}{=} 4x^3 + 8x^2 + 10x$

$2x(2x^2) + 2x(4x) + 2x(5) \stackrel{?}{=} 4x^3 + 8x^2 + 10x$

$4x^3 + 8x^2 + 10x = 4x^3 + 8x^2 + 10x$ ✓

✓ GUIDED PRACTICE for Example 1

Divide.

1. $(6x^3 + 3x^2 - 12x) \div 3x$

2. $(12y^4 - 16y^3 + 20y^2) \div 4y$

DIVIDING BY A BINOMIAL As shown in Example 1, you can use two methods when dividing a polynomial by a monomial. To divide a polynomial by a binomial, use long division.

EXAMPLE 2 Divide a polynomial by a binomial

Divide $x^2 + 2x - 3$ by $x - 1$.

Solution

STEP 1 **Divide** the first term of $x^2 + 2x - 3$ by the first term of $x - 1$.

$$\begin{array}{r} x \\ x - 1 \overline{) x^2 + 2x - 3} \\ \underline{x^2 - x} \\ 3x \end{array}$$

Think: $x^2 \div x = ?$

Multiply x and $x - 1$.

Subtract $x^2 - x$ from $x^2 + 2x$.

AVOID ERRORS
Be sure to *subtract* $x^2 - x$ from $x^2 + 2x$ in order to obtain $3x$. Do *not* add the expressions.

STEP 2 **Bring** down -3. Then divide the first term of $3x - 3$ by the first term of $x - 1$.

$$\begin{array}{r} x + 3 \\ x - 1 \overline{) x^2 + 2x - 3} \\ \underline{x^2 - x} \\ 3x - 3 \\ \underline{3x - 3} \\ 0 \end{array}$$

Think: $3x \div x = ?$

Multiply 3 and $x - 1$.

Subtract $3x - 3$ from $3x - 3$.

▶ $(x^2 + 2x - 3) \div (x - 1) = x + 3$

NONZERO REMAINDERS In Example 2, if the dividend had been $x^2 + 2x - 2$, the remainder would have been 1. When you obtain a nonzero remainder, you can apply the following rule: Dividend $\div$ Divisor $=$ Quotient $+ \frac{\text{Remainder}}{\text{Divisor}}$.

EXAMPLE 3 Divide a polynomial by a binomial

Divide $2x^2 + 11x - 9$ by $2x - 3$.

$$\begin{array}{r} x + 7 \\ 2x - 3 \overline{) 2x^2 + 11x - 9} \\ \underline{2x^2 - 3x} \\ 14x - 9 \\ \underline{14x - 21} \\ 12 \end{array}$$

Multiply x and $2x - 3$.

Subtract $2x^2 - 3x$. Bring down -9.

Multiply 7 and $2x - 3$.

Subtract $14x - 21$.

CHECK DIVISION
To check your answer, multiply the quotient by the divisor, then add the remainder to the product.

▶ $(2x^2 + 11x - 9) \div (2x - 3) = x + 7 + \frac{12}{2x - 3}$

GUIDED PRACTICE for Examples 2 and 3

3. Divide: $(a^2 + 3a - 4) \div (a + 1)$

4. Divide: $(9b^2 + 6b + 8) \div (3b - 4)$

REWRITING POLYNOMIALS When dividing polynomials, you may first need to rewrite the polynomials so that the exponents decrease from left to right. When rewriting polynomials, insert any missing terms using zero coefficients. For example, $8 + 3x^2$ should be rewritten as $3x^2 + 0x + 8$.

EXAMPLE 4 Rewrite polynomials

Divide $5y + y^2 + 4$ by $2 + y$.

REVIEW POLYNOMIALS
For help with rewriting a polynomial, see p. 554.

$y + 3$	
$y + 2\overline{)y^2 + 5y + 4}$	Rewrite polynomials.
$y^2 + 2y$	Multiply y and $y + 2$.
$3y + 4$	Subtract $y^2 + 2y$. Bring down 4.
$3y + 6$	Multiply 3 and $y + 2$.
-2	Subtract $3y + 6$.

▶ $(5y + y^2 + 4) \div (2 + y) = y + 3 + \frac{-2}{y + 2}$

EXAMPLE 5 Insert missing terms

Divide $13 + 4m^2$ by $-1 + 2m$.

$2m + 1$	
$2m - 1\overline{)4m^2 + 0m + 13}$	Rewrite polynomials. Insert missing term.
$4m^2 - 2m$	Multiply $2m$ and $2m - 1$.
$2m + 13$	Subtract $4m^2 - 2m$. Bring down 13.
$2m - 1$	Multiply 1 and $2m - 1$.
14	Subtract $2m - 1$.

▶ $(13 + 4m^2) \div (-1 + 2m) = 2m + 1 + \frac{14}{2m - 1}$

EXAMPLE 6 Rewrite and graph a rational function

Graph $y = \frac{2x - 1}{x - 2}$.

Solution

USE ASYMPTOTES
Use the graphing technique in Lesson 12.2 to graph the function. For instance, the lines $x = 2$ and $y = 2$ are asymptotes of the graph.

STEP 1 **Rewrite** the rational function in the form $y = \frac{a}{x - h} + k$.

$$\begin{array}{r} 2 \\ x - 2\overline{)2x - 1} \\ \underline{2x - 4} \\ 3 \end{array}$$

So, $y = \frac{3}{x - 2} + 2$.

STEP 2 **Graph** the function.

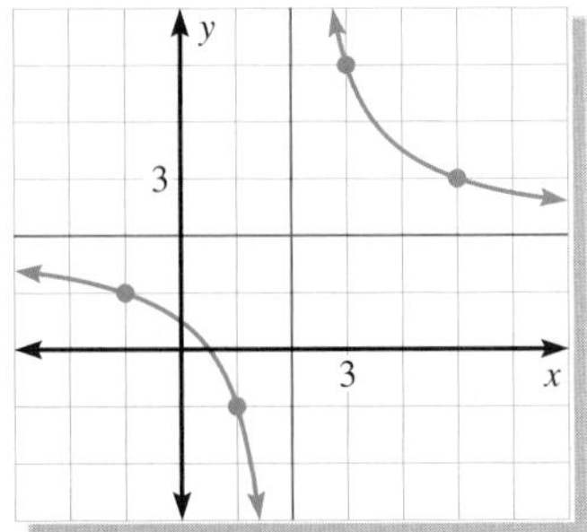

✓ **GUIDED PRACTICE** for Examples 4, 5, and 6

5. Divide: $(8m - 7 + 4m^2) \div (5 + 2m)$

6. Divide: $(n^2 - 6) \div (-3 + n)$

7. Graph $y = \frac{3x + 1}{x + 1}$.

EXAMPLE 7 Solve a multi-step problem

PRINTING COSTS You are creating brochures that promote your school's sports events. You pay \$20 for computer time. The cost of printing a brochure is \$.60. Write and graph an equation that gives the average cost C (in dollars per brochure) as a function of the number b of brochures printed.

Solution

STEP 1 **Write** a verbal model. Then write an equation.

$$\underset{\text{(dollars/brochure)}}{\text{Average cost}} = \frac{\underset{\text{time (dollars)}}{\text{Cost of computer}} + \underset{\text{(dollars/brochure)}}{\text{Printing cost}} \cdot \underset{\text{(brochures)}}{\text{Number printed}}}{\underset{\text{(brochures)}}{\text{Number printed}}}$$

$$C = \frac{20 + 0.6b}{b}$$

STEP 2 **Rewrite** the rational function.

$$C = \frac{20 + 0.6b}{b}$$

$$= \frac{20}{b} + \frac{0.6b}{b}$$

$$= \frac{20}{b} + 0.6$$

STEP 3 **Graph** the function.

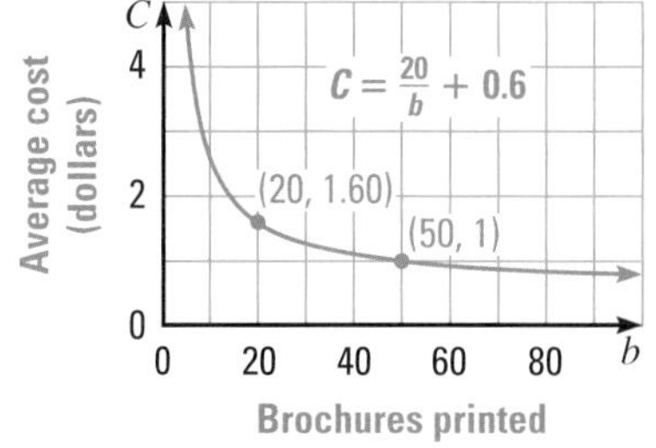

 **GUIDED PRACTICE** for Example 7

8. **WHAT IF?** In Example 7, suppose the cost of printing a brochure is \$.80. Write and graph an equation that gives the average cost C (in dollars per brochure) as a function of the number b of brochures printed.

9. **INTERNET COSTS** A cable Internet service provider charges an installation fee of \$100 and a monthly service charge of \$45. Write and graph an equation that gives the average cost C (in dollars per month) as a function of the number m of months of Internet service.

12.3 EXERCISES

HOMEWORK KEY

○ = **WORKED-OUT SOLUTIONS** on p. WS29 for Exs. 7, 25, and 45

★ = **STANDARDIZED TEST PRACTICE** Exs. 2, 19, 33, 34, 38, 47, 48, and 49

◆ = **MULTIPLE REPRESENTATIONS** Ex. 46

SKILL PRACTICE

1. **VOCABULARY** Copy and complete: To divide a polynomial by a(n) __?__, you can either write the division as a fraction or use long division.

2. ★ **WRITING** *Describe* the steps you would take in graphing the rational function $f(x) = \frac{3x - 2}{x + 6}$.

EXAMPLES 1, 2, 3, 4, and 5 on pp. 784–786 for Exs. 3–21

DIVIDING POLYNOMIALS Divide.

3. $(8x^3 - 12x^2 + 16x) \div 4x$
4. $(10y^3 + 20y^2 + 55y) \div 5y$
5. $(12r^4 - 30r^2 - 72r) \div (-6r)$
6. $(21s^4 + 49s^3 - 35s^2) \div (-7s)$
7. $(3v^2 - v - 10) \div (v - 2)$
8. $(7w^2 + 3w - 4) \div (w + 1)$
9. $(2m^2 - 5m - 12) \div (2m + 3)$
10. $(6n^2 + 7n - 3) \div (3n - 1)$
11. $(a^2 - 5a + 3) \div (a - 1)$
12. $(c^2 - 2c - 4) \div (c + 4)$
13. $(-21 - 4p + 3p^2) \div (3 + p)$
14. $(8q + q^2 + 7) \div (7 + q)$
15. $(9x + x^2 + 6) \div (6 + x)$
16. $(4y^2 - 5) \div (2y + 5)$
17. $(5 - t^2) \div (t - 3)$
18. $(7 - 8x^2) \div (3 + 2x)$

19. ★ **MULTIPLE CHOICE** What is the remainder when you divide $x^2 + 4x + 9$ by $x - 4$?

Ⓐ $x - 4$ Ⓑ 41 Ⓒ $x + 8$ Ⓓ $\frac{41}{x - 4}$

ERROR ANALYSIS ***Describe*** **and correct the error in dividing the polynomials.**

20. $(5x + 6) \div (x + 2)$

$$\begin{array}{r} 5 \\ x + 2\overline{)5x + 6} \\ \underline{5x + 10} \\ -4 \end{array}$$

$$(5x + 6) \div (x + 2) = 5 + \frac{-4}{5x + 6}$$

21. $(8x - 9) \div (x - 3)$

$$\begin{array}{r} 8 \\ x - 3\overline{)8x - 9} \\ \underline{8x - 24} \\ -33 \end{array}$$

$$(8x - 9) \div (x - 3) = 8 + \frac{-33}{x - 3}$$

EXAMPLE 6 on p. 786 for Exs. 22–30

GRAPHING FUNCTIONS Graph the function.

22. $y = \frac{x + 10}{x}$
23. $y = \frac{2x - 7}{x}$
24. $y = \frac{x + 4}{x - 3}$
25. $y = \frac{2x - 4}{x - 1}$
26. $y = \frac{5x + 2}{x + 3}$
27. $y = \frac{6x - 4}{x + 5}$
28. $y = \frac{2 - x}{x + 9}$
29. $y = \frac{2 + 4x}{x - 3}$
30. $y = \frac{7 - 10x}{x + 7}$

GEOMETRY **Divide the surface area of the rectangular prism by its volume.**

31. 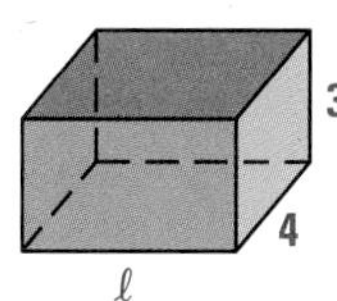

32. 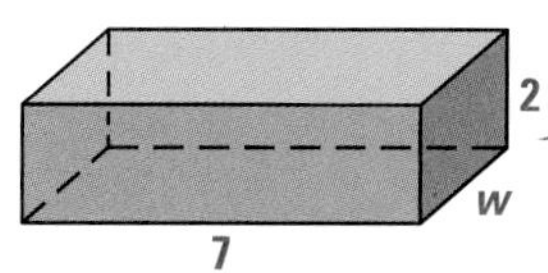

33. ★ **MULTIPLE CHOICE** What is the horizontal asymptote of the graph of $y = \frac{bx + c}{x - d}$?

Ⓐ $y = b$ Ⓑ $y = c$ Ⓒ $y = d$ Ⓓ $y = 0$

34. ★ **MULTIPLE CHOICE** The graph of which function is shown?

Ⓐ $y = \frac{2x + 5}{x - 3}$ Ⓑ $y = \frac{2x + 5}{x + 3}$

Ⓒ $y = \frac{2x - 5}{x - 3}$ Ⓓ $y = \frac{2x - 5}{x + 3}$

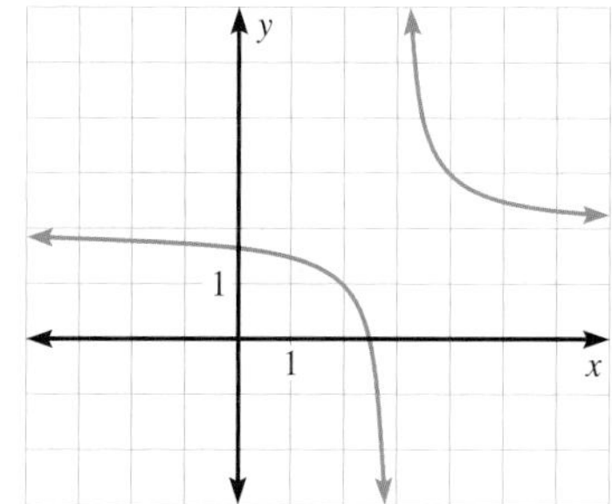

REASONING **In Exercises 35–37, find the value of *k* using the given information.**

35. When $8x^2 + 26x + k$ is divided by $x + 3$, the remainder is 4.

36. When $100x^2 + k$ is divided by $5x + 2$, the remainder is 0.

37. The graph of $y = \frac{kx + 4}{x - 6}$ has $y = -5$ as its horizontal asymptote.

38. ★ **OPEN-ENDED** Write a function of the form $f(x) = \frac{bx + c}{x - h}$ such that the graph of the function has $x = 4$ and $y = 6$ as its asymptotes.

CHALLENGE **Graph the function.**

39. $y = \frac{6x + 10}{3x + 6}$

40. $y = \frac{12x - 7}{4x - 8}$

41. $y = \frac{10x + 3}{2x - 6}$

PROBLEM SOLVING

EXAMPLE 7 on p. 787 for Exs. 42–45

42. **MOVIE RENTALS** You order movie rental coupons from a website for \$3 each. The total cost of your order includes a \$4 shipping fee. Write an equation that gives the average cost *C* (in dollars per coupon) as a function of the number *r* of coupons ordered. Then graph the function.

@HomeTutor for problem solving help at classzone.com

43. **MEMBERSHIP FEES** You pay \$80 for an annual membership to a dance club and pay \$3 per dance class. Write an equation that gives the average cost *C* (in dollars per class) as a function of the number *d* of dance classes that you take. Then graph the function.

@HomeTutor for problem solving help at classzone.com

44. **INVESTING** An investor plans to purchase shares of a stock through a brokerage company. Each share costs \$10, and the company charges a transaction fee of \$20.

a. **Model** Write and graph an equation that gives the average cost C (in dollars per share) as a function of the number s of shares that the investor purchases.

b. **Approximate** Use the graph to approximate the number of shares purchased if the average cost is \$12 per share.

(45.) **CELL PHONE PLAN** You are thinking about subscribing to the cell phone plan described in the advertisement below.

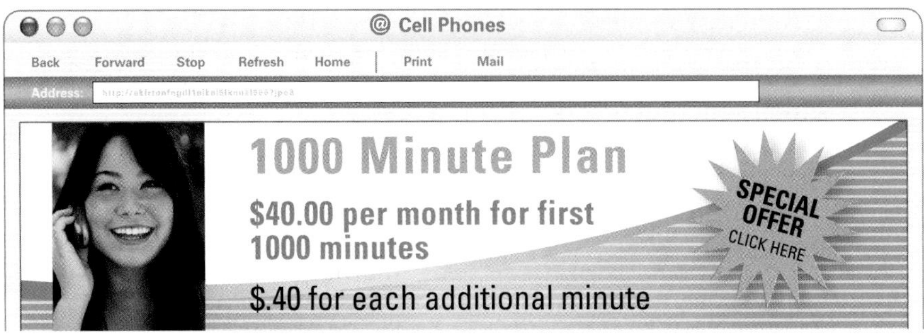

a. **Model** Write an equation that gives the average cost C (in dollars per minute) as a function of the time t (in minutes) of cell phone use for 1000 or more minutes.

b. **Describe** Graph the function. *Describe* how the average cost per minute changes as time increases.

c. **Approximate** Use the graph to approximate the number of minutes used if the average cost is \$.05 per minute.

46. ◆ **MULTIPLE REPRESENTATIONS** The table shows several restaurant bills and their corresponding tips.

Bill, b (dollars)	15.42	26.75	42.18	58.66	63.48	75.89	97.14
Tip, t (dollars)	3.00	5.00	7.50	10.00	10.15	11.50	13.60

a. **Writing an Equation** Make a scatter plot of the data. Then write a linear equation that models the tip t as a function of the bill b.

b. **Writing an Equation** Write an equation that gives the percent tip p (in decimal form) as a function of the bill b.

c. **Drawing Graphs** Draw the graphs of both equations in the same coordinate plane. *Compare* how the tip changes with how the percent tip changes as the bill increases.

47. ★ **SHORT RESPONSE** The number y (in millions) of households that owned VCRs during the period 1984–2000 can be modeled by

$$y = \frac{60 + 120x}{7 + x}$$

where x is the number of years since 1984.

a. **Describe** Graph the model. *Describe* how the number of households that owned VCRs changed during this period.

b. **Justify** Do you expect that the number of households that own VCRs will ever exceed 150 million? *Justify* your answer.

○ = **WORKED-OUT SOLUTIONS on p. WS1**   ★ = **STANDARDIZED TEST PRACTICE**   ◆ = **MULTIPLE REPRESENTATIONS**

48. ★ **MULTIPLE CHOICE** A building's ratio y of surface area to volume is a measure of how well the building minimizes heat loss. A company plans to build a store in the shape of a rectangular prism. The store will have a length of 500 feet and a width of 300 feet, but the company hasn't decided on a height h (in feet). Which equation gives the ratio y as a function of the height h?

Ⓐ $y = \frac{4}{375} + \frac{2}{h}$

Ⓑ $y = 1600 + \frac{1}{150{,}000h}$

Ⓒ $y = 1600 + \frac{2}{h}$

Ⓓ $y = 300 + \frac{500}{h}$

49. ★ **EXTENDED RESPONSE** The ratio of a microorganism's surface area to its volume is a measure of how efficiently the microorganism can perform certain metabolic tasks. Suppose a microorganism is shaped approximately like a cylinder and grows by increasing its length but not its radius.

a. **Model and Graph** Write an equation that gives the ratio y of surface area to volume in terms of the length ℓ (in micrometers) and the radius r (in micrometers). Then graph the equation for a microorganism whose radius is 50 micrometers.

b. **Interpret** The greater the ratio, the less efficiently a microorganism performs metabolic tasks. As the microorganism's length increases, is the microorganism *more efficient* or *less efficient* at performing metabolic tasks? *Explain* your choice.

c. **Explain** How would the microorganism's efficiency change if the length remained constant but the radius increased? *Explain.*

Animated Algebra at classzone.com

50. **CHALLENGE** The effective tax rate is the percent of total income that a worker pays in taxes. Suppose that a worker doesn't pay taxes on income up to $10,000 and pays taxes of 6% on total income that exceeds $10,000. Will the effective tax rate be 6% for any amount of total income? *Justify* your answer graphically.

MIXED REVIEW

Write the fraction in simplest form. *(p. 912)*

51. $\frac{8}{12}$ 52. $\frac{9}{45}$ 53. $\frac{18}{30}$

Simplify the expression.

54. $4x^4 \cdot (2x^3)^4$ *(p. 489)* 55. $z^6 \cdot \frac{1}{z^2}$ *(p. 495)* 56. $\frac{4a^3}{b^4} \cdot \left(\frac{b}{a^2}\right)^{-3}$ *(p. 495)*

57. $\sqrt{150}$ *(p. 719)* 58. $\frac{4}{\sqrt{3}}$ *(p. 719)* 59. $\frac{3}{\sqrt{15}}$ *(p. 719)*

PREVIEW
Prepare for Lesson 12.4 in Exs. 60–65.

Factor the polynomial.

60. $14x - 8x^2$ *(p. 575)* 61. $x^2 - 13x + 40$ *(p. 583)* 62. $-x^2 + 11x - 28$ *(p. 593)*

63. $12x^2 - 13x + 1$ *(p. 593)* 64. $-2x^2 - 3x + 20$ *(p. 593)* 65. $5x^4 - 5x^2$ *(p. 600)*

Graphing Calculator ACTIVITY *Use after Lesson 12.3*

12.3 Find Asymptotes of Graphs

QUESTION How can you find the asymptotes of the graph of a rational function?

EXAMPLE 1 Graph a rational function

Graph $y = \dfrac{2x + 1}{3x^2 - 4x + 5}$ using a graphing calculator. Identify any vertical or horizontal asymptotes.

STEP 1 ***Enter function***

Press Y= and enter the function as shown.

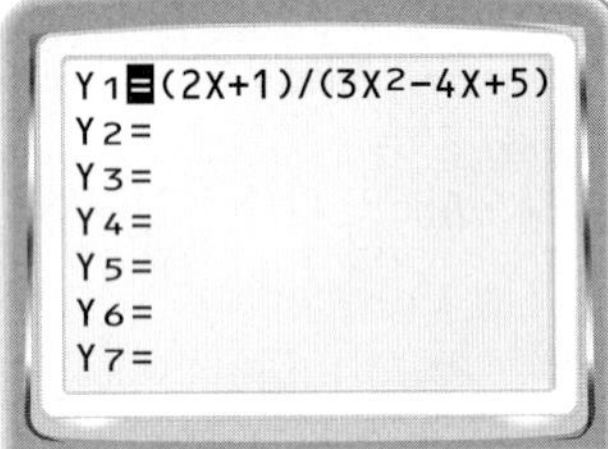

STEP 2 ***Identify asymptotes***

Graph the function. Use the *trace* feature to identify the asymptotes.

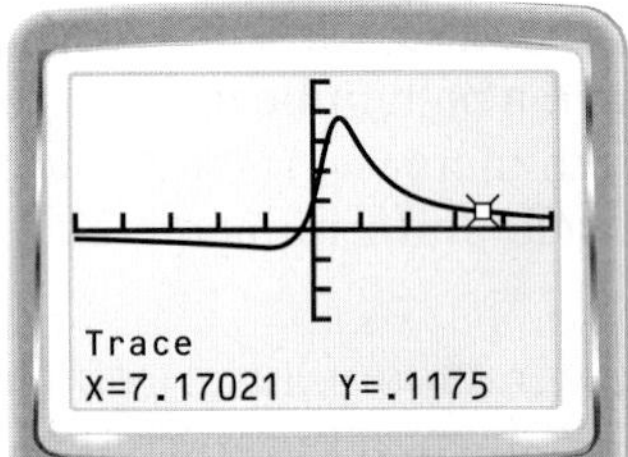

The graph doesn't approach a vertical line. So, the graph doesn't have a vertical asymptote. The graph approaches the x-axis. So, $y = 0$ is a horizontal asymptote.

PRACTICE

Graph the function using a graphing calculator. Identify any vertical or horizontal asymptotes.

1. $y = \dfrac{8}{x - 2}$

2. $y = \dfrac{4}{6x - 7}$

3. $y = \dfrac{x - 9}{x^2 + 1}$

4. $y = \dfrac{x + 5}{x^2 + 4x + 4}$

5. $y = \dfrac{x + 1}{4x^2 - 36}$

6. $y = \dfrac{5}{10x^2 + 9}$

7. Make a table that shows the following information for each function in Exercises 1–6:

- vertical asymptotes, if any
- values, if any, of x that make the function undefined
- horizontal asymptotes, if any
- degree of numerator
- degree of denominator

@HomeTutor
classzone.com
Keystrokes

EXAMPLE 2 Graph a rational function

Graph $y = \frac{2x^2 + 1}{x^2 - 9}$ using a graphing calculator. Identify any vertical or horizontal asymptotes.

STEP 1 *Enter function*

Press Y= and enter the function as shown.

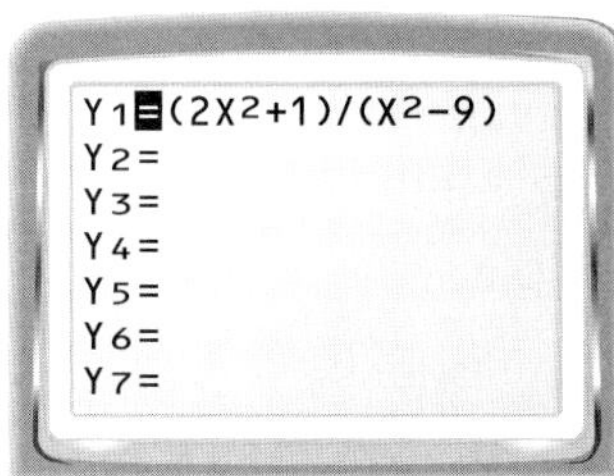

STEP 2 *Identify asymptotes*

Graph the function. Use the *trace* feature to identify the asymptotes.

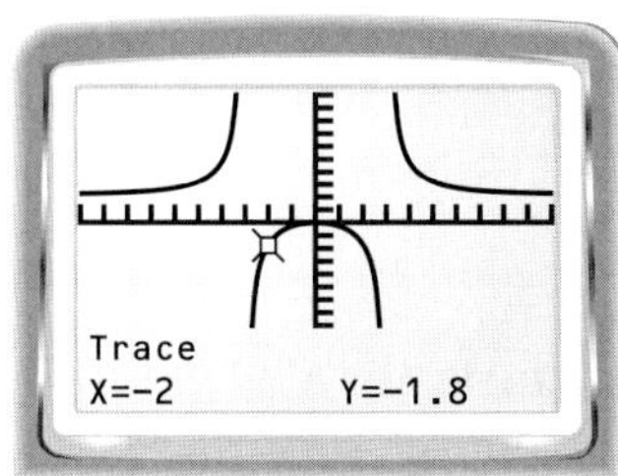

The graph approaches one of two vertical lines, $x = -3$ and $x = 3$. So, $x = -3$ and $x = 3$ are vertical asymptotes. The graph also approaches the line $y = 2$. So, $y = 2$ is a horizontal asymptote.

PRACTICE

Graph the function using a graphing calculator. Identify any vertical or horizontal asymptotes.

8. $y = \frac{-6x}{x + 9}$ **9.** $y = \frac{5x - 12}{x - 1}$ **10.** $y = \frac{10x}{2x - 9}$

11. $y = \frac{12x^2 - 7}{4x^2 + 2}$ **12.** $y = \frac{27x^2 - x}{9x^2 - 16}$ **13.** $y = \frac{18x^2 - 1}{6x^2 - 6}$

14. Repeat Exercise 7 for the functions in Exercises 8–13. For each function, include in your table the quotient of the leading coefficient of the numerator and the leading coefficient of the denominator.

DRAW CONCLUSIONS

15. What vertical asymptotes, if any, does the graph of a rational function whose numerator and denominator do not have any common factors have?

16. If the degree of the numerator of a rational function is less than the degree of the denominator, what is a horizontal asymptote of the graph?

17. If the degree of the numerator of a rational function equals the degree of the denominator, what is a horizontal asymptote of the graph?

18. CONJECTURE Suppose the degree of the numerator of a rational function is greater than the degree of the denominator. Does the graph of the function have a horizontal asymptote? Give examples.

12.4 Simplify Rational Expressions

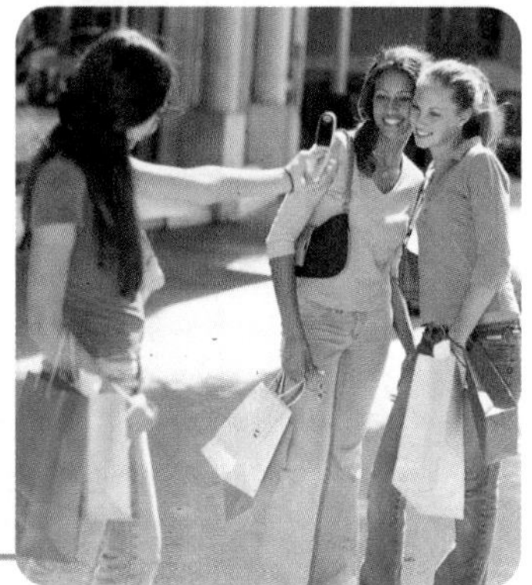

Before You simplified polynomials.
Now You will simplify rational expressions.
Why So you can model a cost over time, as in Example 5.

Key Vocabulary
- **rational expression**
- **excluded value**
- **simplest form of a rational expression**

A **rational expression** is an expression that can be written as a ratio of two polynomials where the denominator is not 0. A rational expression is undefined when the denominator is 0. A number that makes a rational expression undefined is called an **excluded value**. For example, $\frac{2}{x-3}$ is undefined when $x = 3$. So, 3 is an excluded value.

EXAMPLE 1 Find excluded values

Find the excluded values, if any, of the expression.

a. $\frac{x+8}{10x}$ **b.** $\frac{5}{2y+14}$ **c.** $\frac{4v}{v^2-9}$ **d.** $\frac{7w+2}{8w^2+w+5}$

Solution

a. The expression $\frac{x+8}{10x}$ is undefined when $10x = 0$, or $x = 0$.

▶ The excluded value is 0.

b. The expression $\frac{5}{2y+14}$ is undefined when $2y + 14 = 0$, or $x = -7$.

▶ The excluded value is -7.

c. The expression $\frac{4v}{v^2-9}$ is undefined when $v^2 - 9 = 0$, or $(v + 3)(v - 3) = 0$. The solutions of the equation are -3 and 3.

▶ The excluded values are -3 and 3.

REVIEW DISCRIMINANT
For help with finding the discriminant of a quadratic equation, see p. 678.

d. The expression $\frac{7w+2}{8w^2+w+5}$ is undefined when $8w^2 + w + 5 = 0$. The discriminant is $b^2 - 4ac = 1^2 - 4(8)(5) < 0$. So, the quadratic equation has no real roots.

▶ There are no excluded values.

GUIDED PRACTICE for Example 1

Find the excluded values, if any, of the expression.

1. $\frac{x+2}{3x-5}$ **2.** $\frac{2}{5y^2+2y+3}$ **3.** $\frac{n-6}{2n^2-5n-12}$ **4.** $\frac{2m}{m^2-4}$

SIMPLIFYING A RATIONAL EXPRESSION To simplify a rational expression, you factor the numerator and denominator and then divide out any common factors. A rational expression is in **simplest form** if the numerator and denominator have no factors in common other than 1.

KEY CONCEPT *For Your Notebook*

Simplifying Rational Expressions

Let a, b, and c be polynomials where $b \neq 0$ and $c \neq 0$.

Algebra $\frac{ac}{bc} = \frac{a \cdot \cancel{c}}{b \cdot \cancel{c}} = \frac{a}{b}$ **Example** $\frac{2x + 4}{3x + 6} = \frac{2\cancel{(x + 2)}}{3\cancel{(x + 2)}} = \frac{2}{3}$

EXAMPLE 2 Simplify expressions by dividing out monomials

Simplify the rational expression, if possible. State the excluded values.

a. $\frac{r}{2r}$ **b.** $\frac{5x}{5(x + 2)}$ **c.** $\frac{6m^3 - 12m^2}{18m^2}$ **d.** $\frac{y}{7 - y}$

Solution

AVOID ERRORS
When finding excluded values, be sure to use the original expression, not the simplified expression.

a. $\frac{r}{2r} = \frac{\cancel{r}}{2\cancel{r}}$ Divide out common factor.

$= \frac{1}{2}$ Simplify.

▶ The excluded value is 0.

b. $\frac{5x}{5(x + 2)} = \frac{\cancel{5} \cdot x}{\cancel{5} \cdot (x + 2)}$ Divide out common factor.

$= \frac{x}{x + 2}$ Simplify.

▶ The excluded value is −2.

c. $\frac{6m^3 - 12m^2}{18m^2} = \frac{6m^2(m - 2)}{6 \cdot 3 \cdot m^2}$ Factor numerator and denominator.

$= \frac{\cancel{6m^2}(m - 2)}{\cancel{6} \cdot 3 \cdot \cancel{m^2}}$ Divide out common factors.

$= \frac{m - 2}{3}$ Simplify.

▶ The excluded value is 0.

d. The expression $\frac{y}{7 - y}$ is already in simplest form.

▶ The excluded value is 7.

GUIDED PRACTICE for Example 2

Simplify the rational expression, if possible. State the excluded values.

5. $\frac{4a^3}{22a^6}$ **6.** $\frac{2c}{c + 5}$ **7.** $\frac{2s^2 + 8s}{3s + 12}$ **8.** $\frac{8x}{8x^3 + 16x^2}$

EXAMPLE 3 Simplify an expression by dividing out binomials

Simplify $\frac{x^2 - 3x - 10}{x^2 + 6x + 8}$. State the excluded values.

$$\frac{x^2 - 3x - 10}{x^2 + 6x + 8} = \frac{(x - 5)(x + 2)}{(x + 4)(x + 2)}$$ **Factor numerator and denominator.**

$$= \frac{(x - 5)\cancel{(x + 2)}}{(x + 4)\cancel{(x + 2)}}$$ **Divide out common factor.**

$$= \frac{x - 5}{x + 4}$$ **Simplify.**

▶ The excluded values are −4 and −2.

CHECK In the graphing calculator activity on page 560, you saw how to use a graph to check a sum or difference of polynomials.

Check your simplification using a graphing calculator.

Graph $y_1 = \frac{x^2 - 3x - 10}{x^2 + 6x + 8}$ and $y_2 = \frac{x - 5}{x + 4}$.

The graphs coincide. So, the expressions are equivalent for all values of x other than the excluded values (−4 and −2).

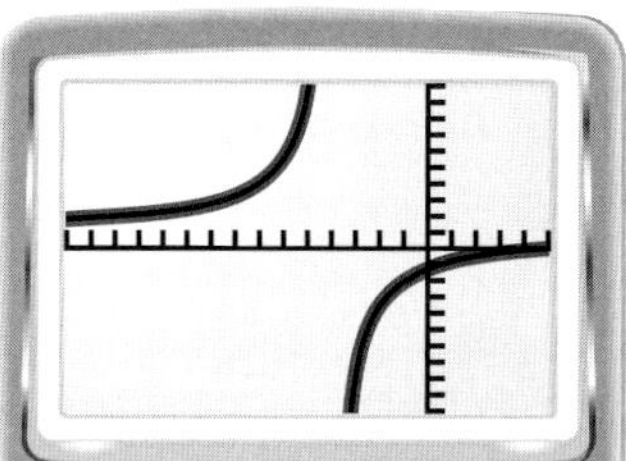

INTERPRET THE GRAPH

Although the graphs of y_1 and y_2 appear to pass through (−2, −3.5), the point is not on either graph because −2 is an excluded value of both y_1 and y_2.

OPPOSITES When simplifying a rational expression, look for factors that are opposites of each other. For example, $x - 1$ and $1 - x$ are opposites, because $x - 1 = -(1 - x)$.

EXAMPLE 4 Recognize opposites

Simplify $\frac{x^2 - 7x + 12}{16 - x^2}$. State the excluded values.

$$\frac{x^2 - 7x + 12}{16 - x^2} = \frac{(x - 3)(x - 4)}{(4 - x)(4 + x)}$$ **Factor numerator and denominator.**

$$= \frac{(x - 3)(x - 4)}{-(x - 4)(4 + x)}$$ **Rewrite $4 - x$ as $-(x - 4)$.**

$$= \frac{(x - 3)\cancel{(x - 4)}}{-\cancel{(x - 4)}(4 + x)}$$ **Divide out common factor.**

$$= \frac{x - 3}{-(4 + x)} = -\frac{x - 3}{x + 4}$$ **Simplify.**

▶ The excluded values are −4 and 4.

GUIDED PRACTICE for Examples 3 and 4

Simplify the rational expression. State the excluded values.

9. $\frac{x^2 + 3x + 2}{x^2 + 7x + 10}$

10. $\frac{y^2 - 64}{y^2 - 16y + 64}$

11. $\frac{5 + 4z - z^2}{z^2 - 3z - 10}$

EXAMPLE 5 Simplify a rational model

CELL PHONE COSTS The average cost C (in dollars per minute) for cell phone service in the United States during the period 1991–2000 can be modeled by

$$C = \frac{46 - 2.2x}{100 - 18x + 2.2x^2}$$

where x is the number of years since 1991. Rewrite the model so that it has only whole number coefficients. Then simplify the model.

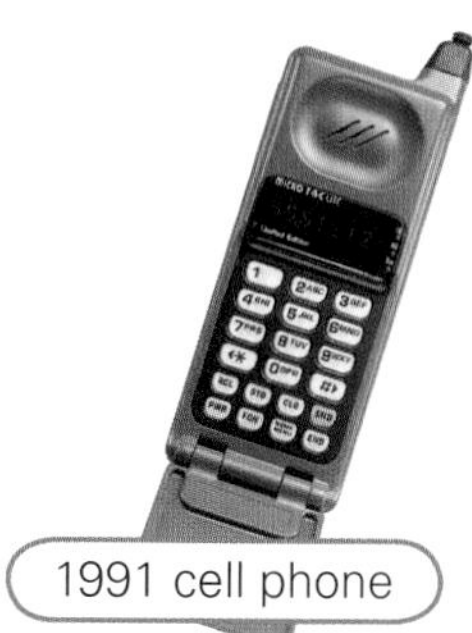

1991 cell phone

Solution

$$C = \frac{46 - 2.2x}{100 - 18x + 2.2x^2}$$ **Write model.**

$$= \frac{460 - 22x}{1000 - 180x + 22x^2}$$ **Multiply numerator and denominator by 10.**

$$= \frac{2(230 - 11x)}{2(500 - 90x + 11x^2)}$$ **Factor numerator and denominator.**

$$= \frac{\cancel{2}(230 - 11x)}{\cancel{2}(500 - 90x + 11x^2)}$$ **Divide out common factor.**

$$= \frac{230 - 11x}{500 - 90x + 11x^2}$$ **Simplify.**

 **GUIDED PRACTICE** for Example 5

12. In Example 5, approximate the average cost per minute in 2000.

12.4 EXERCISES

HOMEWORK KEY

○ = **WORKED-OUT SOLUTIONS** on p. WS29 for Exs. 9, 23, and 43

★ = **STANDARDIZED TEST PRACTICE** Exs. 2, 33, 34, 35, and 45

SKILL PRACTICE

1. **VOCABULARY** Copy and complete: A value that makes a rational expression undefined is called a(n) _?_.

2. ★ **WRITING** Is $\frac{(x + 3)(x - 6)}{(x - 3)(6 - x)}$ in simplest form? *Explain.*

EXAMPLE 1 on p. 794 for Exs. 3–10

FINDING EXCLUDED VALUES **Find the excluded values, if any, of the expression.**

3. $\frac{4x}{20}$
4. $\frac{13}{2y}$
5. $\frac{5}{r + 1}$
6. $\frac{-s}{3s + 4}$
7. $\frac{-m}{4m^2 - 3m + 9}$
8. $\frac{n + 2}{n^2 - 64}$
9. $\frac{-3}{2p^2 - p}$
10. $\frac{5q}{q^2 - 6q + 9}$

EXAMPLES 2, 3, and 4 on pp. 795–796 for Exs. 11–33

ERROR ANALYSIS ***Describe*** **and correct the error in simplifying the rational expression or in stating the excluded values.**

11. $\dfrac{2x^2 - x - 3}{2x^2 - 11x + 12}$

$$\frac{2x^2 - x - 3}{2x^2 - 11x + 12} = \frac{(x + 1)(2x - 3)}{(2x - 3)(x - 4)}$$
$$= \frac{(x + 1)\cancel{(2x - 3)}}{\cancel{(2x - 3)}(x - 4)}$$
$$= \frac{x + 1}{x - 4}$$

The excluded value is 4. ✗

12. $\dfrac{2(x - 5)}{(x - 5)(x + 2)}$

$$\frac{2(x - 5)}{(x - 5)(x + 2)} = \frac{2\cancel{(x - 5)}}{\cancel{(x - 5)}(x + 2)}$$
$$= \frac{2}{x + 2}$$
$$= \frac{\cancel{2}}{x + \cancel{2}}$$
$$= \frac{1}{x + 1}$$

The excluded values are −2 and 5. ✗

SIMPLIFYING EXPRESSIONS **Simplify the rational expression, if possible. State the excluded values.**

13. $\dfrac{10x}{25}$ **14.** $\dfrac{63}{18y}$ **15.** $\dfrac{-48a^2}{16a}$ **16.** $\dfrac{27b^2}{30b^5}$

17. $\dfrac{3c + 33}{c + 11}$ **18.** $\dfrac{d + 8}{d - 8}$ **19.** $\dfrac{2u - 6}{3 - u}$ **20.** $\dfrac{v + 2}{v^2 - 4}$

21. $\dfrac{2}{f^2 - 9}$ **22.** $\dfrac{g + 4}{g^2 - 16}$ **(23.)** $\dfrac{h + 3}{h^2 - h - 12}$ **24.** $\dfrac{j - 2}{j^2 - 6j + 8}$

25. $\dfrac{-48w}{16w^2 - 40w}$ **26.** $\dfrac{12y^4}{12y^2 + 18y}$ **27.** $\dfrac{6z^2 - 24z}{2z^2 - 8z}$ **28.** $\dfrac{14x^2 + 21x}{2x^2 + x - 3}$

29. $\dfrac{s^2 + 16s + 64}{s^2 + 7s - 8}$ **30.** $\dfrac{t^2 - 4t - 45}{2t^2 - 21t + 27}$ **31.** $\dfrac{m + 5}{m^3 + 10m^2 + 25m}$ **32.** $\dfrac{-n^2 - 3n + 28}{3n^3 + 9n^2 - 84n}$

33. ★ **WRITING** Are the rational expressions $\dfrac{x^2 + x}{x^2 - 1}$ and $\dfrac{x^2}{x^2 - x}$ equivalent? *Explain* how you know. What are the excluded values, if any, of the rational expressions?

34. ★ **OPEN-ENDED** Write a rational expression whose excluded values are −3 and −5.

35. ★ **MULTIPLE CHOICE** The expression $\dfrac{a}{x^2 + 5x - 6}$ simplifies to $\dfrac{2x + 5}{x + 6}$. What is a?

Ⓐ $2x^2 + 7x + 5$ Ⓑ $2x^2 + 5x - 1$ Ⓒ $2x^2 + 3x - 5$ Ⓓ $2x^2 + 7x - 5$

GEOMETRY **Write and simplify a rational expression for the ratio of the perimeter of the given figure to its area.**

36. Square

5x

37. Rectangle

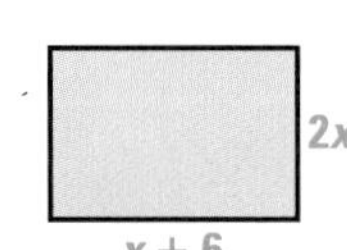

38. Triangle

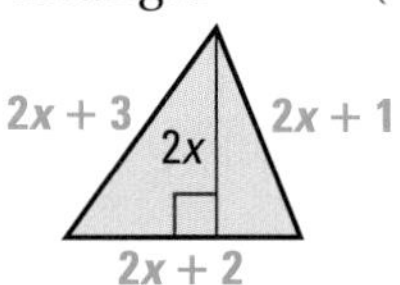

39. **CHALLENGE** Find two polynomials whose ratio simplifies to $\dfrac{3x - 1}{2x + 1}$ and whose sum is $5x^2 + 20x$. *Describe* your steps.

○ = **WORKED-OUT SOLUTIONS on p. WS1** ★ = **STANDARDIZED TEST PRACTICE**

PROBLEM SOLVING

EXAMPLE 5 on p. 797 for Exs. 40–43

40. **CREDIT CARD FEES** The average late payment fee F (in dollars) on a credit card account during the period 1994–2003 can be modeled by

$$F = \frac{12 + 1.6x^2}{1 + 0.04x^2}$$

where x is the number of years since 1994. Rewrite the model so that it has only whole number coefficients. Then simplify the model and approximate the average late payment fee in 2003.

@HomeTutor for problem solving help at classzone.com

41. **TELEVISION** For the period 1980–2003, the percent p (in decimal form) of non-network television commercials in the United States that lasted 15 seconds can be modeled by

$$p = \frac{0.12x^2 - 0.48}{0.88x^2 + 100}$$

where x is the number of years since 1980. Rewrite the model so that it has only whole number coefficients. Then simplify the model and approximate the percent of non-network television commercials in 2003 that lasted 15 seconds.

@HomeTutor for problem solving help at classzone.com

42. **CAR RADIOS** A company forecasts that the number R (in thousands) of digital car radios sold annually and the sales S (in millions of dollars) of digital car radios during the period 2004–2007 can be modeled by

$$R = 190x^2 + 55x + 140 \quad \text{and} \quad S = 170x + 60$$

where x is the number of years since 2004. Write and simplify a model that gives the average price P (in thousands of dollars) of a digital car radio as a function of x. Then predict the average price in 2007.

43. **HOUSES** The total number H of new single-family houses and the number W of new single-family wood houses in the United States during the period 1990–2002 can be modeled by

$$H = 34{,}500x + 913{,}000$$
$$\text{and } W = -20{,}200x + 366{,}000$$

where x is the number of years since 1990. Write and simplify a model that gives the percent p (in decimal form) of the houses that were wood houses as a function of x. *Describe* how the percent that were wood houses changed during the period 1990–2002.

44. **AIRPORTS** The total number A of airports and the number P of private airports in the United States during the period 1989–2002 can be modeled by

$$A = 0.18x^3 + 140x + 17{,}000 \quad \text{and} \quad P = 0.16x^3 + 120x + 12{,}000$$

where x is the number of years since 1989. Using only whole number coefficients, write a model that gives the percent p (in decimal form) of all airports that were private airports. Simplify the model and approximate the percent of airports in 2002 that were private airports.

45. ★ **EXTENDED RESPONSE** The revenue R (in millions of dollars) from sales of printed music in the United States during the period 1988–2002 can be modeled by

$$R = \frac{300 + 20x}{1 + 0.008x}$$

where x is the number of years since 1988.

a. **Model and Calculate** Rewrite the model so that it has only whole number coefficients. Then simplify the model and approximate the revenue from sales of printed music in 2002.

b. **Graph** Graph the model. *Describe* how revenue changed during the period.

c. **Decide** Can you use the model to conclude that the number of copies of printed music sold increased over time? *Explain.*

46. **CHALLENGE** The average annual expenses E (in dollars) of a middle income family and the average annual amount T (in dollars) spent on telephone service during the period 1992–2001 can be modeled by

$$E = 1240x + 24{,}800 \qquad \text{and} \qquad T = 31x + 620$$

where x is the number of years since 1992. Write and simplify a model to show that the average annual amount spent on telephone service was 2.5% of the average annual expenses during the period.

MIXED REVIEW

PREVIEW Prepare for Lesson 12.5 in Exs. 47–54.

Multiply or divide. *(p. 915)*

47. $\frac{1}{3} \times \frac{1}{3}$ 48. $\frac{2}{7} \times \frac{4}{5}$ 49. $\frac{8}{5} \times \frac{1}{4}$ 50. $\frac{5}{9} \times \frac{9}{10}$

51. $\frac{1}{4} \div \frac{1}{4}$ 52. $\frac{2}{5} \div \frac{4}{11}$ 53. $\frac{4}{9} \div \frac{4}{3}$ 54. $\frac{14}{27} \div \frac{7}{4}$

Simplify the expression.

55. $5x - (-4x + 3)$ *(p. 96)* 56. $(-2x^2)^4$ *(p. 489)* 57. $8x^3 \cdot (3x^4)^3$ *(p. 489)*

58. $\frac{y^6}{8} \cdot \frac{2}{y^2}$ *(p. 495)* 59. $\frac{12m^4}{n^4} \cdot \left(\frac{n}{m^0}\right)^6$ *(p. 495)* 60. $\frac{x^2}{y^4} \cdot \left(\frac{y^6}{x^{-5}}\right)^{-1}$ *(p. 495)*

QUIZ *for Lessons 12.3–12.4*

Divide. *(p. 784)*

1. $(y^2 - 5y + 6) \div (y - 3)$ 2. $(x^2 + 3x - 28) \div (x - 6)$

Graph the function. *(p. 784)*

3. $y = \frac{x + 3}{x - 4}$ 4. $y = \frac{2x - 1}{x + 3}$

Simplify the rational expression, if possible. State the excluded values. *(p. 794)*

5. $\frac{w + 10}{w^2 - 100}$ 6. $\frac{250x^3}{14x}$ 7. $\frac{y + 7}{y - 7}$ 8. $\frac{z^2 - 4z - 45}{3z^2 + 25z + 50}$

EXTRA PRACTICE for Lesson 12.4, p. 949 **ONLINE QUIZ** at classzone.com

MIXED REVIEW *of Problem Solving*

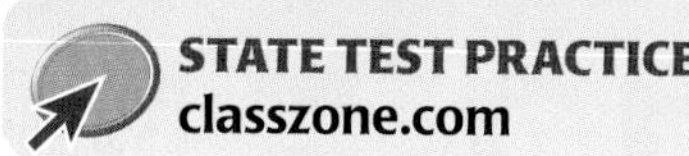

Lessons 12.1–12.4

1. **MULTI-STEP PROBLEM** A bookseller uses shipping cartons in the shape of rectangular prisms. The cartons have the same size base but vary in height.

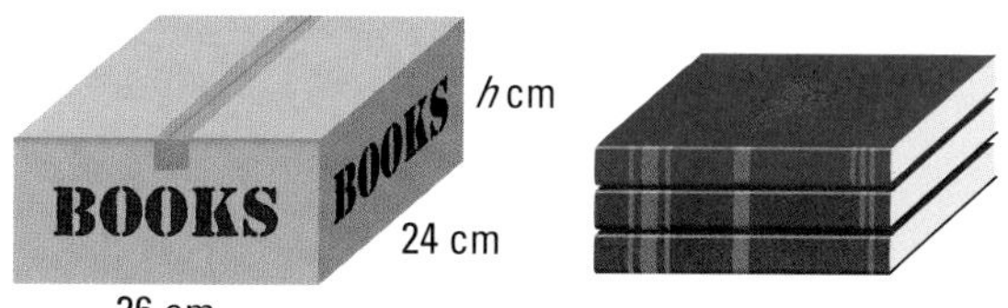

   a. Write an equation that gives the ratio r of surface area to volume as a function of the height h. Then graph the equation.

   b. The lesser the ratio, the more efficient the carton is. *Describe* how the efficiency of the carton changes as the height increases.

2. **GRIDDED ANSWER** You and some friends are taking a car trip to an amusement park. Admission costs \$50 per person, and everyone will share the combined cost of gas and parking, which is \$30. How much more (in dollars) will one person pay if 4 people go on the trip than if 5 people go?

3. **OPEN-ENDED** A city's population density (in people per square mile) is the ratio of the population of the city to the area (in square miles) of the city. Suppose that a city has a population of 150,000 people and an area of 40 square miles. *Describe* two ways that the population density can decrease to 3125 people per square mile.

4. **MULTI-STEP PROBLEM** The average amount A (in pounds per person) of fish and shellfish consumed in the United States during the period 1992–2001 can be modeled by

$$A = \frac{52x + 3800}{3.2x + 260}$$

   where x is the number of years since 1992.

   a. Rewrite the model so that it has only whole number coefficients. Then simplify the model.

   b. Approximate the average amount of fish and shellfish consumed per person in 2001.

5. **EXTENDED RESPONSE** A professional baseball team may pay a luxury tax if the team's combined annual salary exceeds a certain amount. In 2003, a team whose combined annual salary exceeded \$117 million paid a luxury tax of 17.5% on the amount over \$117 million.

   a. Write an equation that gives the percent p (in decimal form) of the salary paid in luxury tax as a function of the salary s (in millions of dollars) for $s > 117$.

   b. Graph the function. *Describe* how the percent changed as the salary increased.

   c. Was it possible for a team to pay 17.5% of its salary in luxury tax? *Explain.*

6. **SHORT RESPONSE** You plan to hike a mountain trail that is 15 miles long and stop halfway to camp overnight for 10 hours.

   a. Write an equation that gives the combined time t (in hours) for hiking and camping as a function of the average rate r (in miles per hour) at which you hike. Then graph the equation.

   b. *Explain* how the graph would change if you camped for 12 hours instead of 10 hours.

7. **SHORT RESPONSE** The table shows the relationship between the volume V (in liters) and the pressure P (in kilopascals) of a gas in a cylindrical container.

Volume, V (L)	Pressure, P (kPa)
20	1
5	4
2.5	8
1.6	12.5
0.4	50

   a. *Explain* why the volume and pressure are inversely related. Then write an equation that relates the volume and the pressure.

   b. Suppose that only the height of the container can be changed. *Describe* how the pressure changes as the height increases.

12.5 Multiply and Divide Rational Expressions

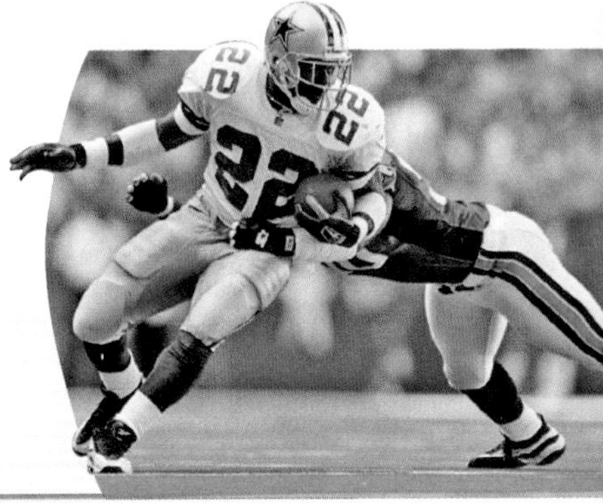

Before You multiplied and divided polynomials.
Now You will multiply and divide rational expressions.
Why? So you can describe football data, as in Ex. 35.

Key Vocabulary
- **multiplicative inverse,** *p. 103*
- **polynomial,** *p. 554*
- **rational expression,** *p. 794*

Multiplying and dividing rational expressions is similar to multiplying and dividing numerical fractions.

KEY CONCEPT *For Your Notebook*

Multiplying and Dividing Rational Expressions

Let a, b, c, and d be polynomials.

Algebra $\frac{a}{b} \cdot \frac{c}{d} = \frac{ac}{bd}$ where $b \neq 0$ and $d \neq 0$

$\frac{a}{b} \div \frac{c}{d} = \frac{a}{b} \cdot \frac{d}{c} = \frac{ad}{bc}$ where $b \neq 0$, $c \neq 0$, and $d \neq 0$

Examples $\frac{x+2}{x} \cdot \frac{3}{x^2} = \frac{3(x+2)}{x^3}$ $\qquad \frac{x}{x-1} \div \frac{4}{x} = \frac{x}{x-1} \cdot \frac{x}{4} = \frac{x^2}{4(x-1)}$

EXAMPLE 1 Multiply rational expressions involving monomials

Find the product $\frac{2x^2}{3x} \cdot \frac{6x^2}{12x^3}$.

$\frac{2x^2}{3x} \cdot \frac{6x^2}{12x^3} = \frac{(2x^2)(6x^2)}{(3x)(12x^3)}$ **Multiply numerators and denominators.**

$= \frac{12x^4}{36x^4}$ **Product of powers property**

$= \frac{\cancel{12} \cdot \cancel{x^4}}{3 \cdot \cancel{12} \cdot \cancel{x^4}}$ **Factor and divide out common factors.**

$= \frac{1}{3}$ **Simplify.**

APPLY EXCLUDED VALUES
When performing operations with rational expressions, remember that the answer may have excluded values. In Example 1, the excluded value is 0.

GUIDED PRACTICE for Example 1

Find the product.

1. $\frac{2y^3}{5y} \cdot \frac{15y^3}{8y^5}$

2. $\frac{7z^2}{4z^3} \cdot \frac{z^3}{14z}$

EXAMPLE 2 Multiply rational expressions involving polynomials

Find the product $\frac{3x^2 + 3x}{4x^2 - 24x + 36} \cdot \frac{x^2 - 4x + 3}{x^2 - x}$.

$$\frac{3x^2 + 3x}{4x^2 - 24x + 36} \cdot \frac{x^2 - 4x + 3}{x^2 - x}$$

$$= \frac{(3x^2 + 3x)(x^2 - 4x + 3)}{(4x^2 - 24x + 36)(x^2 - x)}$$ **Multiply numerators and denominators.**

$$= \frac{3\cancel{x}(x + 1)\cancel{(x - 3)}\cancel{(x - 1)}}{4\cancel{x}\cancel{(x - 3)}(x - 3)\cancel{(x - 1)}}$$ **Factor and divide out common factors.**

$$= \frac{3(x + 1)}{4(x - 3)}$$ **Simplify.**

CHECK Check your simplification using a graphing calculator.

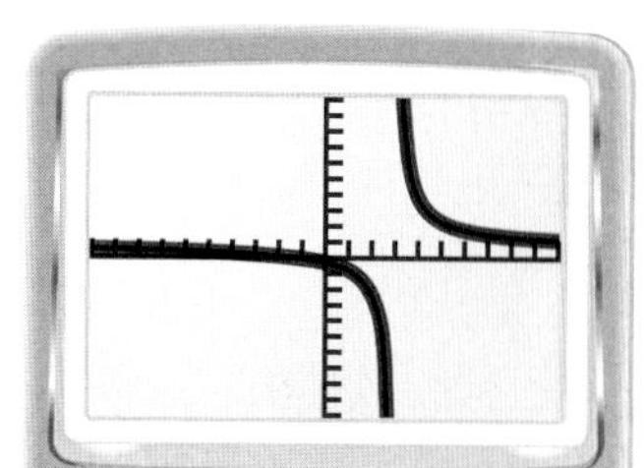

Graph $y_1 = \frac{3x^2 + 3x}{4x^2 - 24x + 36} \cdot \frac{x^2 - 4x + 3}{x^2 - x}$

and $y_2 = \frac{3(x + 1)}{4(x - 3)}$.

The graphs coincide. So, the expressions are equivalent for all values of x other than the excluded values (0, 1, and 3).

MULTIPLYING BY A POLYNOMIAL When you multiply a rational expression by a polynomial, first write the polynomial as a fraction with a denominator of 1.

EXAMPLE 3 Multiply a rational expression by a polynomial

Find the product $\frac{5x}{x^2 + 5x + 6} \cdot (x + 3)$.

$$\frac{5x}{x^2 + 5x + 6} \cdot (x + 3)$$

$$= \frac{5x}{x^2 + 5x + 6} \cdot \frac{x + 3}{1}$$ **Rewrite polynomial as a fraction.**

$$= \frac{5x(x + 3)}{x^2 + 5x + 6}$$ **Multiply numerators and denominators.**

$$= \frac{5x\cancel{(x + 3)}}{(x + 2)\cancel{(x + 3)}}$$ **Factor and divide out common factor.**

$$= \frac{5x}{x + 2}$$ **Simplify.**

✓ GUIDED PRACTICE for Examples 2 and 3

Find the product.

3. $\frac{x^2 + x - 2}{x^2 + 2x} \cdot \frac{2x^2 + 2x}{5x^2 - 15x + 10}$

4. $\frac{2w^2}{w^2 - 7w + 12} \cdot (w - 4)$

DIVIDING RATIONAL EXPRESSIONS To divide by a rational expression, multiply by its multiplicative inverse.

EXAMPLE 4 Divide rational expressions involving polynomials

Find the quotient $\frac{7x^2 - 7x}{x^2 + 2x - 3} \div \frac{x + 1}{x^2 - 7x - 8}$.

$$\frac{7x^2 - 7x}{x^2 + 2x - 3} \div \frac{x + 1}{x^2 - 7x - 8}$$

REVIEW INVERSES
For help with finding the multiplicative inverse of a number, see p. 103.

$$= \frac{7x^2 - 7x}{x^2 + 2x - 3} \cdot \frac{x^2 - 7x - 8}{x + 1}$$ Multiply by multiplicative inverse.

$$= \frac{(7x^2 - 7x)(x^2 - 7x - 8)}{(x^2 + 2x - 3)(x + 1)}$$ Multiply numerators and denominators.

$$= \frac{7x\cancel{(x - 1)}(x - 8)\cancel{(x + 1)}}{(x + 3)\cancel{(x - 1)}\cancel{(x + 1)}}$$ Factor and divide out common factors.

$$= \frac{7x(x - 8)}{x + 3}$$ Simplify.

DIVIDING BY A POLYNOMIAL When you divide a rational expression by a polynomial, first write the polynomial as a fraction with a denominator of 1. Then multiply by the multiplicative inverse of the polynomial.

EXAMPLE 5 Divide a rational expression by a polynomial

Find the quotient $\frac{2x^2 + 16x + 24}{3x^2} \div (x + 6)$.

$$\frac{2x^2 + 16x + 24}{3x^2} \div (x + 6)$$

$$= \frac{2x^2 + 16x + 24}{3x^2} \div \frac{x + 6}{1}$$ Rewrite polynomial as fraction.

$$= \frac{2x^2 + 16x + 24}{3x^2} \cdot \frac{1}{x + 6}$$ Multiply by multiplicative inverse.

$$= \frac{2x^2 + 16x + 24}{3x^2(x + 6)}$$ Multiply numerators and denominators.

$$= \frac{2(x + 2)\cancel{(x + 6)}}{3x^2\cancel{(x + 6)}}$$ Factor and divide out common factor.

$$= \frac{2(x + 2)}{3x^2}$$ Simplify.

Animated Algebra at classzone.com

✓ GUIDED PRACTICE for Examples 4 and 5

Find the quotient.

5. $\frac{m^2 - 4}{2m^2 + 4m} \div \frac{6m - 3m^2}{4m + 44}$

6. $\frac{n^2 - 6n + 9}{12n} \div (n - 3)$

EXAMPLE 6 Solve a multi-step problem

ADVERTISING The amount A (in millions of dollars) spent on all advertising and the amount T (in millions of dollars) spent on television advertising in the United States during the period 1970–2003 can be modeled by

$$A = \frac{13{,}000 + 3700x}{1 - 0.015x} \quad \text{and} \quad T = \frac{1800 + 860x}{1 - 0.016x}$$

where x is the number of years since 1970. Write a model that gives the percent p (in decimal form) of the amount spent on all advertising that was spent on television advertising. Then approximate the percent spent on television advertising in 2003.

Solution

STEP 1 **Write** a verbal model. Then write an equation.

Percent spent on television advertising	=	Amount spent on television advertising	÷	Amount spent on all advertising
p	=	T	÷	A

STEP 2 **Find** the quotient.

$$p = T \div A \qquad \textbf{Write equation.}$$

$$= \frac{1800 + 860x}{1 - 0.016x} \div \frac{13{,}000 + 3700x}{1 - 0.015x} \qquad \textbf{Substitute for } T \textbf{ and for } A.$$

$$= \frac{1800 + 860x}{1 - 0.016x} \cdot \frac{1 - 0.015x}{13{,}000 + 3700x} \qquad \textbf{Multiply by multiplicative inverse.}$$

$$= \frac{(1800 + 860x)(1 - 0.015x)}{(1 - 0.016x)(13{,}000 + 3700x)} \qquad \textbf{Multiply numerators and denominators.}$$

$$= \frac{\cancel{20}(90 + 43x)(1 - 0.015x)}{(1 - 0.016x)(\cancel{20})(650 + 185x)} \qquad \textbf{Factor and divide out common factor.}$$

$$= \frac{(90 + 43x)(1 - 0.015x)}{(1 - 0.016x)(650 + 185x)} \qquad \textbf{Simplify.}$$

STEP 3 **Approximate** the percent spent on television advertising in 2003. Because $2003 - 1970 = 33$, $x = 33$. Substitute 33 for x in the model and use a calculator to evaluate.

$$p = \frac{(90 + 43 \cdot 33)(1 - 0.015 \cdot 33)}{(1 - 0.016 \cdot 33)(650 + 185 \cdot 33)} \approx 0.239$$

▶ About 24% of the amount spent on all advertising was spent on television advertising in 2003.

✓ GUIDED PRACTICE for Example 6

7. In Example 6, find the values of T and of A separately when $x = 33$. Then divide the value of T by the value of A. *Compare* your answer with the answer in Step 3 above.

12.5 EXERCISES

HOMEWORK KEY

○ = **WORKED-OUT SOLUTIONS** on p. WS30 for Exs. 5, 15, and 35

★ = **STANDARDIZED TEST PRACTICE** Exs. 2, 21, 26, 27, 28, 36, and 37

◆ = **MULTIPLE REPRESENTATIONS** Ex. 35

SKILL PRACTICE

1. **VOCABULARY** Copy and complete: To divide by a rational expression, multiply by its _?_.

2. ★ **WRITING** *Describe* how to multiply a rational expression by a polynomial.

EXAMPLES 1, 2, and 3 on pp. 802–803 for Exs. 3–10, 12

MULTIPLYING EXPRESSIONS Find the product.

3. $\frac{9p^2}{7} \cdot \frac{5}{6p^4}$

4. $\frac{5}{8q^6} \cdot \frac{4q^5}{3}$

5. $\frac{v^2 + v - 12}{5v + 10} \cdot \frac{-v - 2}{v^2 + 5v + 4}$

6. $\frac{y - 2}{-2y^2 - 10y} \cdot \frac{4y^2 + 20y}{y^2 - 4}$

7. $\frac{5x}{2x^3 - 17x^2 - 9x} \cdot \frac{4x^2 - 20x - 144}{20}$

8. $\frac{r^5}{7r^3 + 56r} \cdot (r^2 + 8)$

9. $\frac{-3m}{m^2 - 7m + 10} \cdot (m - 5)$

10. $\frac{2n - 6}{3n^2 - 7n - 6} \cdot (3n^2 + 14n + 8)$

EXAMPLES 4 and 5 on p. 804 for Exs. 11, 13–21

ERROR ANALYSIS ***Describe*** **and correct the error in finding the product or quotient.**

11. $\frac{x^3}{5} \div \frac{15x^3}{2}$

$$\frac{x^3}{5} \div \frac{15x^3}{2} = \frac{5}{x^3} \cdot \frac{15x^3}{2} = \frac{75\cancel{x^3}}{2\cancel{x^3}} = \frac{75}{2}$$

12. $\frac{x - 2}{x + 5} \cdot \frac{x}{2 - x}$

$$\frac{x - 2}{x + 5} \cdot \frac{x}{2 - x} = \frac{(x - 2)x}{(x + 5)(2 - x)} = \frac{\cancel{(x - 2)}x}{(x + 5)\cancel{(2 - x)}} = \frac{x}{x + 5}$$

DIVIDING EXPRESSIONS Find the quotient.

13. $\frac{16r^2}{3} \div \frac{12}{5r}$

14. $\frac{25s^{12}}{18} \div \frac{5s^6}{2}$

15. $\frac{2w^2 + 5w}{w^2 - 81} \div \frac{w^2}{w + 9}$

16. $\frac{c^2 + c}{c^2 + c - 30} \div \frac{c - 6}{c^2 - 11c + 30}$

17. $\frac{a^2 + 3a - 10}{a^2 + 6a - 7} \div \frac{9a^3 - 18a^2}{3a^2 + 18a - 21}$

18. $\frac{2x^2 - 9x + 9}{35x + 14} \div \frac{-3x^2 + 13x - 12}{15x^2 - 14x - 8}$

19. $\frac{4k^2 + 4k - 15}{2k - 3} \div (2k + 5)$

20. $\frac{t^2 - 9t - 22}{5t - 1} \div (5t^2 + 9t - 2)$

21. ★ **MULTIPLE CHOICE** What common factor do you divide out when finding the quotient $\frac{x^2 - 3x + 2}{x^2 - 2x - 3} \div \frac{x^2 + 4x + 3}{x^2 - 7x + 12}$?

Ⓐ $x - 1$ Ⓑ $x - 3$ Ⓒ $x + 1$ Ⓓ $x + 3$

TRANSLATING PHRASES Translate the verbal phrase into a product or quotient of rational expressions. Then find the product or quotient.

22. The product of $x + 3$ and the ratio of $x + 5$ to $x^2 - 9$

23. The product of $8x^2$ and the multiplicative inverse of $2x^3$

24. The quotient of $x^2 + 3x - 18$ and the ratio of $x + 6$ to 2

25. The quotient of the multiplicative inverse of $x^2 - 3x - 4$ and twice the multiplicative inverse of $x^2 - 1$

26. ★ **MULTIPLE CHOICE** What is the quotient $\frac{x^2 - 1}{-(x + 1)} \div (x - 1)$?

Ⓐ -1 Ⓑ 0 Ⓒ 1 Ⓓ $x^2 - 1$

★ **OPEN-ENDED Let a, b, c, and d be different polynomials. Find two rational expressions $\frac{a}{b}$ and $\frac{c}{d}$ that satisfy the given conditions.**

27. The product of the rational expressions is $\frac{x - 3}{x + 2}$, and the excluded values are -2, -1, 4, and 5.

28. The quotient of the rational expressions is $\frac{x - 6}{x + 4}$, and the excluded values are -4, -2, 3, and 6.

GEOMETRY Write an expression for the area of the figure. Find a value of x less than 5 for which the given dimensions and the area are positive.

29. Rectangle

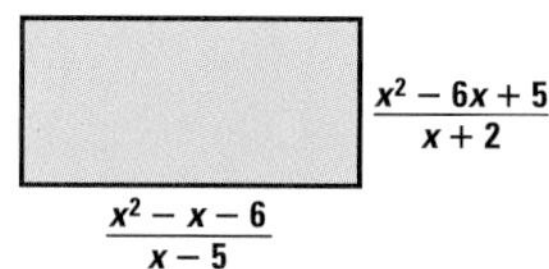

30. Triangle

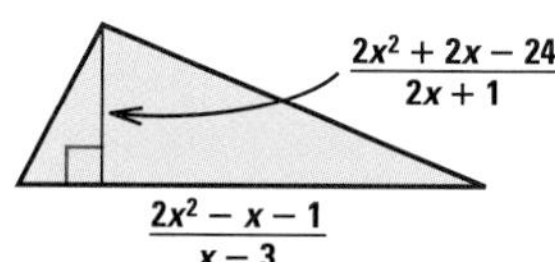

CHALLENGE Let a be a polynomial in the given equation. Find a.

31. $\frac{a}{x + 2} \cdot \frac{3x^2 + 5x - 2}{x - 4} = 6x^2 + 7x - 3$

32. $\frac{8x^2 - 2x - 3}{x - 5} \div \frac{2x + 1}{a} = 12x^2 - x - 6$

PROBLEM SOLVING

EXAMPLE 6 on p. 805 for Exs. 33–35

33. **VEHICLES** The total distance M (in billions of miles) traveled by all motor vehicles and the distance T (in billions of miles) traveled by trucks in the United States during the period 1980–2002 can be modeled by

$$M = 1500 + 63x \qquad \text{and} \qquad T = \frac{100 + 2.2x}{1 - 0.014x}$$

where x is the number of years since 1980. Write a model that gives the percent p (in decimal form) of the total motor vehicle distance that was traveled by trucks as a function of x. Then approximate the percent traveled by trucks in 2002.

@HomeTutor for problem solving help at classzone.com

34. **CONSUMER SPENDING** The average annual amount T (in dollars) spent on reading and entertainment and the average annual amount E (in dollars) spent on entertainment by consumers in the United States during the period 1985–2002 can be modeled by

$$T = \frac{1300 + 84x}{1 + 0.015x} \quad \text{and} \quad E = \frac{1100 + 64x}{1 + 0.0062x}$$

where x is the number of years since 1985. Write a model that gives the percent p (in decimal form) of the amount spent on reading and entertainment that was spent on entertainment as a function of x. Then approximate the percent spent on entertainment in 2000.

@HomeTutor for problem solving help at classzone.com

35. ◆ **MULTIPLE REPRESENTATIONS** Football player Emmitt Smith's career number Y of rushing yards gained and his career number A of rushing attempts from 1990 (when he started playing professional football) through the 2002 football season can be modeled by

$$Y = \frac{860 + 1800x}{1 + 0.024x} \quad \text{and} \quad A = \frac{230 + 380x}{1 + 0.014x}$$

where x is the number of years since 1990.

a. **Writing an Equation** A football player's rushing average is the number of rushing yards gained divided by the number of rushing attempts. Write a model that gives Smith's career rushing average R as a function of x for the period 1990–2002.

b. **Making a Table** Make a table that shows Smith's approximate career rushing average (rounded to the nearest hundredth) for each year during the period. *Describe* how the career rushing average changed over time.

36. ★ **SHORT RESPONSE** Baseball player Hank Aaron's career number B of times at bat and career number H of hits during the period 1954–1976 can be modeled by

$$B = \frac{300 + 700x}{1 + 0.01x} \quad \text{and} \quad H = \frac{62 + 240x}{1 + 0.017x}$$

where x is the number of years since 1954.

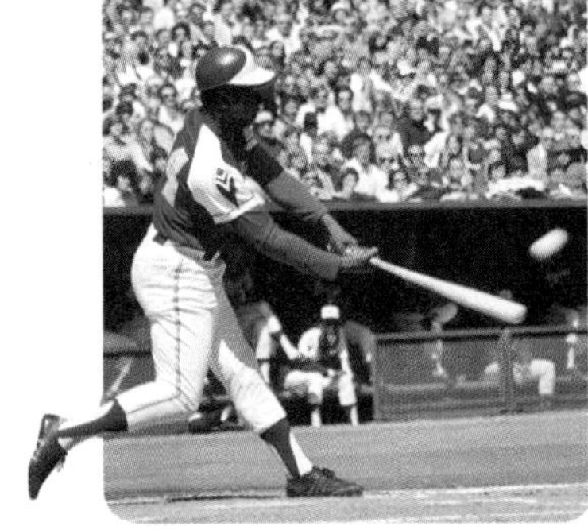

a. **Model** A baseball player's batting average is the number of hits divided by the number of times at bat. Write a model that gives Hank Aaron's career batting average A as a function of x.

b. **Decide** The table shows Aaron's actual career number of times at bat and actual career number of hits for three different years. For which year does the model give the best approximation of A? *Explain* your choice.

Year	1954	1959	1976
Career times at bat	468	3524	12,364
Career hits	131	1137	3771

○ = WORKED-OUT SOLUTIONS on p. WS1 ★ = STANDARDIZED TEST PRACTICE ◆ = MULTIPLE REPRESENTATIONS

37. ★ **EXTENDED RESPONSE** The gross revenue R (in millions of dollars) from movie tickets sold and the average movie ticket price P (in dollars) in the United States during the period 1991–2002 can be modeled by

$$R = \frac{4700 - 74x}{1 - 0.053x} \quad \text{and} \quad P = 0.015x^2 + 4.1$$

where x is the number of years since 1991.

a. **Model** Write a model that gives the number T of movie tickets sold (in millions) as a function of x.

b. **Describe** Graph the model on a graphing calculator and describe how the number of tickets sold changed over time. Can you use the graph to describe how the gross revenue and ticket prices changed over time? *Explain* your reasoning.

c. **Compare** The table shows the actual number of tickets sold for each year during the period. Make a scatter plot of the data on the same screen as the graph of the model in part (b). *Compare* the scatter plot with the graph of the model.

Year	1991	1992	1993	1994	1995	1996
Tickets (millions)	1141	1173	1244	1292	1263	1339

Year	1997	1998	1999	2000	2001	2002
Tickets (millions)	1388	1481	1465	1421	1487	1639

38. **CHALLENGE** The total amount F (in billions of dollars) spent on food other than groceries and the amount E (in billions of dollars) spent at restaurants in the U.S. during the period 1977–2003 can be modeled by

$$F = \frac{88 + 9.2x}{1 - 0.0097x} \quad \text{and} \quad E = \frac{54 + 6.5x}{1 - 0.012x}$$

where x is the number of years since 1977. Write a model that gives the percent p (in decimal form) of the amount spent on food other than groceries that was spent at restaurants as a function of x. Approximate the percent that was spent at locations other than restaurants in 2002.

MIXED REVIEW

PREVIEW
Prepare for Lesson 12.6 in Exs. 39–52.

Add or subtract. *(p. 914)*

39. $\frac{2}{5} + \frac{2}{3}$
40. $\frac{3}{8} + \frac{5}{12}$
41. $\frac{1}{4} + \frac{5}{6}$
42. $\frac{7}{9} + \frac{8}{21}$
43. $\frac{7}{8} - \frac{7}{10}$
44. $\frac{7}{15} - \frac{1}{4}$
45. $\frac{9}{14} - \frac{5}{21}$
46. $\frac{5}{17} - \frac{2}{51}$

Find the sum, difference, or product.

47. $(25x^2 - 6x) + (4x^2 - 5)$ *(p. 554)*
48. $(7x^2 + 5x + 1) + (-6x^2 + 13x)$ *(p. 554)*
49. $(2x^2 - x + 12) - (3x + 8)$ *(p. 554)*
50. $(7x^2 + 16) - (8x^3 + 3x^2 - 7)$ *(p. 554)*
51. $(5x - 6)(4x - 5)$ *(p. 562)*
52. $(2x + 9)(3x - 7)$ *(p. 562)*

Simplify Complex Fractions

Use after Lesson 12.5

GOAL Simplify complex fractions.

Key Vocabulary
- **complex fraction**

A **complex fraction** is a fraction that contains a fraction in its numerator, denominator, or both. To simplify a complex fraction, divide its numerator by its denominator.

READING
The widest fraction bar separates the numerator of a complex fraction from the denominator.

KEY CONCEPT *For Your Notebook*

Simplifying a Complex Fraction

Let a, b, c, and d be polynomials where $b \neq 0$, $c \neq 0$, and $d \neq 0$.

Algebra $\dfrac{\frac{a}{b}}{\frac{c}{d}} = \dfrac{a}{b} \div \dfrac{c}{d} = \dfrac{a}{b} \cdot \dfrac{d}{c}$

Example $\dfrac{\frac{x}{2}}{\frac{x}{3}} = \dfrac{x}{2} \div \dfrac{x}{3} = \dfrac{x}{2} \cdot \dfrac{3}{x} = \dfrac{3x}{2x} = \dfrac{3}{2}$

EXAMPLE 1 Simplify a complex fraction

Simplify the complex fraction.

a. $\dfrac{\frac{3x}{2}}{-6x^3} = \dfrac{3x}{2} \div (-6x^3)$ **Write fraction as quotient.**

$= \dfrac{3x}{2} \cdot \dfrac{1}{-6x^3}$ **Multiply by multiplicative inverse.**

$= \dfrac{3x}{-12x^3}$ **Multiply numerators and denominators.**

$= -\dfrac{1}{4x^2}$ **Simplify.**

b. $\dfrac{x^2 - 1}{\frac{x+1}{x-1}} = (x^2 - 1) \div \dfrac{x+1}{x-1}$ **Write fraction as quotient.**

$= (x^2 - 1) \cdot \dfrac{x-1}{x+1}$ **Multiply by multiplicative inverse.**

$= \dfrac{(x^2 - 1)(x - 1)}{x + 1}$ **Multiply numerators and denominators.**

$= \dfrac{\cancel{(x+1)}(x - 1)(x - 1)}{\cancel{x+1}}$ **Factor and divide out common factor.**

$= (x - 1)^2$ **Simplify.**

EXAMPLE 2 Simplify a complex fraction

Simplify $\dfrac{\frac{2x^2 - 8x}{x^2 + 4x + 4}}{\frac{x^3 - 16x}{x + 2}}$.

$$\frac{\frac{2x^2 - 8x}{x^2 + 4x + 4}}{\frac{x^3 - 16x}{x + 2}} = \frac{2x^2 - 8x}{x^2 + 4x + 4} \div \frac{x^3 - 16x}{x + 2}$$ **Write fraction as quotient.**

$$= \frac{2x^2 - 8x}{x^2 + 4x + 4} \cdot \frac{x + 2}{x^3 - 16x}$$ **Multiply by multiplicative inverse.**

$$= \frac{(2x^2 - 8x)(x + 2)}{(x^2 + 4x + 4)(x^3 - 16x)}$$ **Multiply numerators and denominators.**

$$= \frac{2\cancel{x}\cancel{(x - 4)}\cancel{(x + 2)}}{\cancel{(x + 2)}(x + 2)\cancel{x}(x + 4)\cancel{(x - 4)}}$$ **Factor and divide out common factors.**

$$= \frac{2}{(x + 2)(x + 4)}$$ **Simplify.**

PRACTICE

EXAMPLES 1 and 2 on pp. 810–811 for Exs. 1–9

Simplify the complex fraction.

1. $\dfrac{\frac{-9x^5}{7}}{-12x^2}$

2. $\dfrac{\frac{-2}{11x^4}}{18x^4}$

3. $\dfrac{\frac{x^2 + 7x}{2x - 6}}{x^2 - 49}$

4. $\dfrac{-24x^4}{\frac{8x^2}{-4x^3}}$

5. $\dfrac{x^2 + 4x}{\frac{x + 4}{x^2 - x}}$

6. $\dfrac{2x^2 + 5x - 3}{\frac{x^2 + 4x + 3}{15x}}$

7. $\dfrac{\frac{x^2 - x - 20}{4}}{\frac{x - 5}{10}}$

8. $\dfrac{\frac{x^2 - 2x - 8}{6x - 3x^2}}{\frac{x^3 + 4x^2}{x^2 - 4}}$

9. $\dfrac{\frac{2x^2 + 5x - 3}{3x^2 + 4x + 1}}{\frac{10x^2 - 5x}{2x^3 - 2x}}$

GEOMETRY Write a rational expression for the ratio of the surface area S of the given solid to its volume V.

10. Sphere

11. Cone

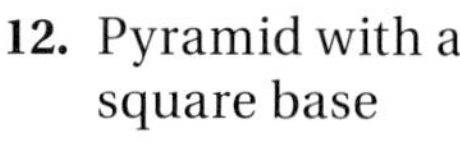

12. Pyramid with a square base

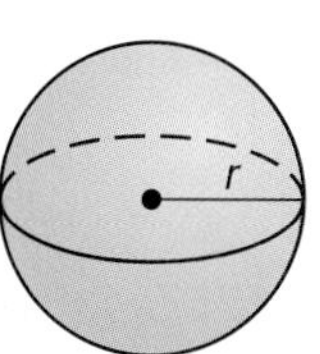

$S = 4\pi r^2$

$V = \dfrac{4\pi r^3}{3}$

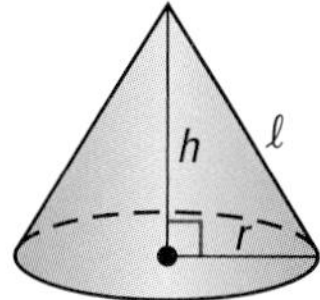

$S = \pi r^2 + \pi r\ell$

$V = \dfrac{\pi r^2 h}{3}$

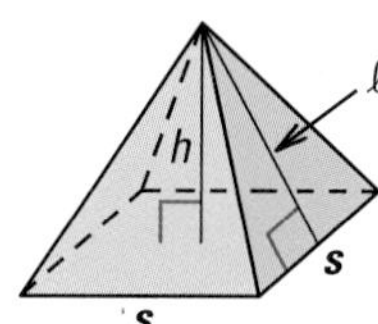

$S = s^2 + 2s\ell$

$V = \dfrac{s^2 h}{3}$

13. Are the complex fractions $\dfrac{\frac{a}{b}}{c}$ and $\dfrac{a}{\frac{b}{c}}$ equivalent? *Explain* your answer.

12.6 Add and Subtract Rational Expressions

Before You multiplied and divided rational expressions.

Now You will add and subtract rational expressions.

Why? So you can solve work problems, as in Ex. 49.

Key Vocabulary
- **least common denominator (LCD) of rational expressions**

Adding and subtracting rational expressions with the same denominator is similar to adding and subtracting numerical fractions with the same denominator.

KEY CONCEPT *For Your Notebook*

Adding and Subtracting Rational Expressions with the Same Denominator

Let a, b, and c be polynomials where $c \neq 0$.

Algebra $\frac{a}{c} + \frac{b}{c} = \frac{a+b}{c}$ $\qquad$ $\frac{a}{c} - \frac{b}{c} = \frac{a-b}{c}$

Examples $\frac{2}{x} + \frac{3}{x} = \frac{2+3}{x} = \frac{5}{x}$ $\qquad$ $\frac{5}{4x} - \frac{2}{4x} = \frac{5-2}{4x} = \frac{3}{4x}$

EXAMPLE 1 **Add and subtract with the same denominator**

a. $\frac{5}{3x} + \frac{7}{3x} = \frac{12}{3x}$ **Add numerators.**

$= \frac{\cancel{3} \cdot 4}{\cancel{3} \cdot x}$ **Factor and divide out common factor.**

$= \frac{4}{x}$ **Simplify.**

b. $\frac{3x}{x-1} - \frac{x+5}{x-1} = \frac{3x-(x+5)}{x-1}$ **Subtract numerators.**

$= \frac{2x-5}{x-1}$ **Simplify.**

CHECK Check your simplification using a graphing calculator. For part (b), graph $y_1 = \frac{3x}{x-1} - \frac{x+5}{x-1}$ and $y_2 = \frac{2x-5}{x-1}$. The graphs coincide. So, the expressions are equivalent for all values of x other than the excluded value of 1.

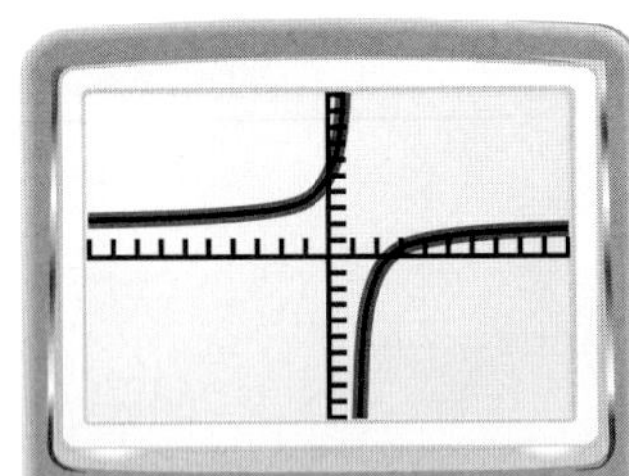

✓ GUIDED PRACTICE for Example 1

Find the sum or difference.

1. $\frac{2}{y} + \frac{y+1}{y}$

2. $\frac{4x+1}{2x-1} - \frac{2x-3}{2x-1}$

LEAST COMMON DENOMINATOR The **least common denominator (LCD)** of two or more rational expressions is the product of the factors of the denominators of the rational expressions with each common factor used only once.

EXAMPLE 2 Find the LCD of rational expressions

Find the LCD of the rational expressions.

a. $\frac{1}{4r}, \frac{r+3}{10r^2}$ **b.** $\frac{5}{(x-3)^2}, \frac{3x+4}{x^2-x-6}$ **c.** $\frac{3}{c-2}, \frac{c+8}{2c+7}$

Solution

a. Find the least common multiple (LCM) of $4r$ and $10r^2$.

$4r = 2 \cdot 2 \cdot r$ ← **The common factors are circled.**

$10r^2 = 2 \cdot 5 \cdot r \cdot r$

$\text{LCM} = 2 \cdot r \cdot 2 \cdot 5 \cdot r = 20r^2$

AVOID ERRORS
When finding the LCD, be sure to use the common factors only once.

▶ The LCD of $\frac{1}{4r}$ and $\frac{r+3}{10r^2}$ is $20r^2$.

b. Find the least common multiple (LCM) of $(x-3)^2$ and $x^2 - x - 6$.

$(x-3)^2 = (x-3) \cdot (x-3)$

$x^2 - x - 6 = (x-3) \cdot (x+2)$

$\text{LCM} = (x-3) \cdot (x-3) \cdot (x+2) = (x-3)^2(x+2)$

▶ The LCD of $\frac{5}{(x-3)^2}$ and $\frac{3x+4}{x^2-x-6}$ is $(x-3)^2(x+2)$.

c. Find the least common multiple of $c - 2$ and $2c + 7$.

Because $c - 2$ and $2c + 7$ cannot be factored, they don't have any factors in common. The least common multiple is their product, $(c-2)(2c+7)$.

▶ The LCD of $\frac{3}{c-2}$ and $\frac{c+8}{2c+7}$ is $(c-2)(2c+7)$.

✓ GUIDED PRACTICE for Example 2

Find the LCD of the rational expressions.

3. $\frac{1}{28m}, \frac{m+1}{7m^3}$

4. $\frac{2}{x^2+4x-5}, \frac{x^2+2}{x^2+7x+10}$

5. $\frac{5a}{a+3}, \frac{a+6}{a-4}$

DIFFERENT DENOMINATORS To add or subtract rational expressions that have different denominators, use the LCD to write equivalent rational expressions that have the same denominator just as you would for numerical fractions.

EXAMPLE 3 Add expressions with different denominators

Find the sum $\frac{9}{8x^2} + \frac{5}{12x^3}$.

$$\frac{9}{8x^2} + \frac{5}{12x^3} = \frac{9 \cdot 3x}{8x^2 \cdot 3x} + \frac{5 \cdot 2}{12x^3 \cdot 2}$$ Rewrite fractions using LCD, $24x^3$.

$$= \frac{27x}{24x^3} + \frac{10}{24x^3}$$ Simplify numerators and denominators.

$$= \frac{27x + 10}{24x^3}$$ Add fractions.

EXAMPLE 4 Subtract expressions with different denominators

Find the difference $\frac{10}{3x} - \frac{7x}{x + 2}$.

$$\frac{10}{3x} - \frac{7x}{x+2} = \frac{10(x+2)}{3x(x+2)} - \frac{7x(3x)}{(x+2)(3x)}$$ Rewrite fractions using LCD, $3x(x + 2)$.

$$= \frac{10(x+2) - 7x(3x)}{3x(x+2)}$$ Subtract fractions.

$$= \frac{-21x^2 + 10x + 20}{3x(x+2)}$$ Simplify numerator.

EXAMPLE 5 Subtract expressions with different denominators

Find the difference $\frac{x + 4}{x^2 + 3x - 10} - \frac{x - 1}{x^2 + 2x - 8}$.

$$\frac{x+4}{x^2 + 3x - 10} - \frac{x-1}{x^2 + 2x - 8}$$

$$= \frac{x+4}{(x-2)(x+5)} - \frac{x-1}{(x+4)(x-2)}$$ Factor denominators.

$$= \frac{(x+4)(x+4)}{(x-2)(x+5)(x+4)} - \frac{(x-1)(x+5)}{(x+4)(x-2)(x+5)}$$ Rewrite fractions using LCD, $(x - 2)(x + 5)(x + 4)$.

$$= \frac{(x+4)(x+4) - (x-1)(x+5)}{(x-2)(x+5)(x+4)}$$ Subtract fractions.

$$= \frac{x^2 + 8x + 16 - (x^2 + 4x - 5)}{(x-2)(x+5)(x+4)}$$ Find products in numerator.

$$= \frac{4x + 21}{(x-2)(x+5)(x+4)}$$ Simplify.

AVOID ERRORS

Because you are subtracting $x^2 + 4x - 5$ in the numerator, you need to add the opposite of *every* term in $x^2 + 4x - 5$.

Animated Algebra at classzone.com

✓ GUIDED PRACTICE for Examples 3, 4, and 5

Find the sum or difference.

6. $\frac{3}{2x} + \frac{7}{5x^4}$

7. $\frac{y}{y+1} + \frac{3}{y+2}$

8. $\frac{2z-1}{z^2 + 2z - 8} - \frac{z+1}{z^2 - 4}$

EXAMPLE 6 Solve a multi-step problem

BOAT TRAVEL A boat travels 24 kilometers upstream (against the current) and 24 kilometers downstream (with the current) as shown in the diagram. Write an equation that gives the total travel time t (in hours) as a function of the boat's average speed r (in kilometers per hour) in still water. Find the total travel time if the boat's average speed in still water is 10 kilometers per hour.

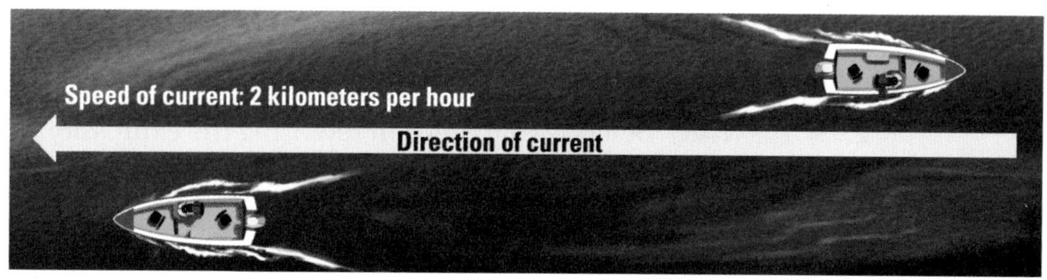

Solution

STEP 1 **Write** a verbal model. Then write an equation.

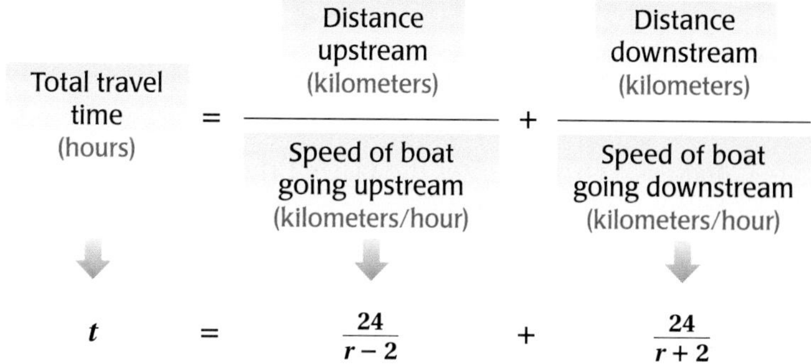

$$t = \frac{24}{r-2} + \frac{24}{r+2}$$

COMBINE SPEEDS When you go upstream, you subtract the speed of the current from the speed at which you travel in still water. When you go downstream, you add the speeds.

STEP 2 **Find** the sum of the expressions on the right side of the equation.

$$t = \frac{24}{r-2} + \frac{24}{r+2}$$ **Write equation.**

$$= \frac{24(r+2)}{(r-2)(r+2)} + \frac{24(r-2)}{(r+2)(r-2)}$$ **Rewrite fractions using LCD, $(r-2)(r+2)$.**

$$= \frac{24(r+2) + 24(r-2)}{(r-2)(r+2)}$$ **Add fractions.**

$$= \frac{48r}{(r-2)(r+2)}$$ **Simplify.**

STEP 3 **Calculate** the value of t when $r = 10$.

$$t = \frac{48(10)}{(10-2)(10+2)} = \frac{480}{(8)(12)} = \frac{480}{96} = 5$$

▶ The total travel time is 5 hours.

✓ GUIDED PRACTICE for Example 6

9. **WHAT IF?** In Example 6, suppose the speed of the current is 3 kilometers per hour. Find the total travel time.

12.6 EXERCISES

HOMEWORK KEY

○ = **WORKED-OUT SOLUTIONS** on p. WS30 for Exs. 7, 29, and 45

★ = **STANDARDIZED TEST PRACTICE** Exs. 2, 32, 44, and 48

SKILL PRACTICE

1. **VOCABULARY** Copy and complete: The _?_ of two rational expressions is the product of the factors of their denominators with each common factor used only once.

2. ★ **WRITING** *Describe* your steps in rewriting the expressions $\frac{1}{x+2}$ and $\frac{2x}{x^2-4}$ so that they have the same denominator.

EXAMPLE 1 on p. 812 for Exs. 3–11

ADDING AND SUBTRACTING EXPRESSIONS **Find the sum or difference.**

3. $\frac{2}{5x}+\frac{3}{5x}$

4. $\frac{y+1}{2y}+\frac{5}{2y}$

5. $\frac{6z}{z^2}-\frac{2z}{z^2}$

6. $\frac{7}{a+2}-\frac{3a}{a+2}$

7. $\frac{b}{b-3}+\frac{b+1}{b-3}$

8. $\frac{c+2}{c-9}+\frac{c+5}{c-9}$

9. $\frac{7}{m^2+1}-\frac{8}{m^2+1}$

10. $\frac{2n+1}{n^2-16}-\frac{n}{n^2-16}$

11. $\frac{3r}{r^2+r-7}+\frac{1}{r^2+r-7}$

EXAMPLE 2 on p. 813 for Exs. 12–17, 32

FINDING THE LCD **Find the LCD of the rational expressions.**

12. $\frac{1}{24x}, \frac{x+2}{6x^3}$

13. $\frac{3}{15v^2}, \frac{v^2-4}{20v^3}$

14. $\frac{4w}{w+5}, \frac{w+3}{w-2}$

15. $\frac{s-1}{s+2}, \frac{s+2}{s-1}$

16. $\frac{1}{t^2-4t}, \frac{6}{t^2-2t-8}$

17. $\frac{u+9}{u^2+8u+7}, \frac{-3}{u^2-2u-3}$

EXAMPLES 3, 4, and 5 on p. 814 for Exs. 18–31

ERROR ANALYSIS ***Describe*** **and correct the error in finding the sum or difference.**

18. $\frac{8}{2x+3}-\frac{4x}{x+2}$

$$\frac{8}{2x+3}-\frac{4x}{x+2}=\frac{8-4x}{2x+3-(x+2)}$$
$$=\frac{8-4x}{2x+3-x-2}$$
$$=\frac{8-4x}{x+1}$$

✗

19. $\frac{5x}{x-4}+\frac{2}{x+3}$

$$\frac{5x}{x-4}+\frac{2}{x+3}=\frac{5x(x-4)+2(x+3)}{(x-4)(x+3)}$$
$$=\frac{5x^2-20x+2x+6}{(x-4)(x+3)}$$
$$=\frac{5x^2-18x+6}{(x-4)(x+3)}$$

✗

ADDING AND SUBTRACTING EXPRESSIONS **Find the sum or difference.**

20. $\frac{5x}{4}+\frac{2}{5x}$

21. $\frac{13}{3y}+\frac{2}{11y}$

22. $\frac{7}{2z}-\frac{2}{3z^2}$

23. $\frac{7r}{r-2}-\frac{2r}{r-3}$

24. $\frac{s}{5s-2}-\frac{1}{4s+1}$

25. $\frac{c+3}{c-6}+\frac{c}{3c+10}$

26. $\frac{d-5}{d+7}+\frac{d-5}{4d}$

27. $\frac{f+3}{7f}-\frac{3f}{f+4}$

28. $\frac{1}{g^2+5g+6}-\frac{1}{g^2-4}$

29. $\frac{2j}{j^2-1}+\frac{j-1}{j^2-7j+6}$

30. $\frac{k+7}{k^2+6k+9}+\frac{k-5}{k^2-5k-24}$

31. $\frac{v+2}{2v^2-v-15}-\frac{v-2}{v^2+2v-15}$

32. ★ **MULTIPLE CHOICE** Which is a factor of the LCD of $\frac{3}{x^2 - 4x}$ and $\frac{4x}{x+2}$?

Ⓐ 3 Ⓑ $x - 4$ Ⓒ $4x$ Ⓓ $x - 2$

33. **GEOMETRY** The height h of a rectangular prism is given by

$$h = \frac{S}{2(\ell + w)} - \frac{\ell w}{\ell + w}$$

where S is the surface area, ℓ is the length, and w is the width. Find the difference of the expressions on the right side of the equation.

USING ORDER OF OPERATIONS Use the order of operations to write the expression as a single rational expression.

34. $2\left(\frac{x}{x+1}\right) - 3\left(\frac{x-4}{x+2}\right)$

35. $5\left(\frac{3x}{x-2} + \frac{4}{x^2 + 6x - 16}\right)$

36. $\frac{x-3}{x^2 + 9x + 20} + \frac{5x}{x+2} \cdot \frac{12}{x+4}$

37. $\frac{x+5}{x-9} - \frac{3x^2 + 2x - 1}{x+4} \div \frac{x^2 - 3x - 4}{x^2 - 16}$

WRITING EQUATIONS For the given hyperbola, write an equation of the form $y = \frac{a}{b}$ where a and b are first-degree polynomials.

38.

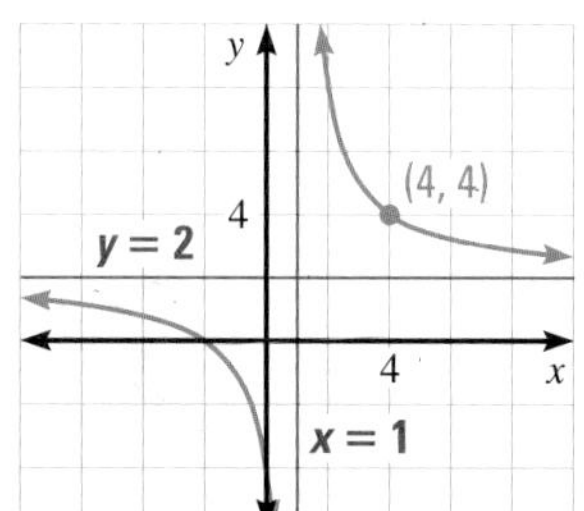

39.

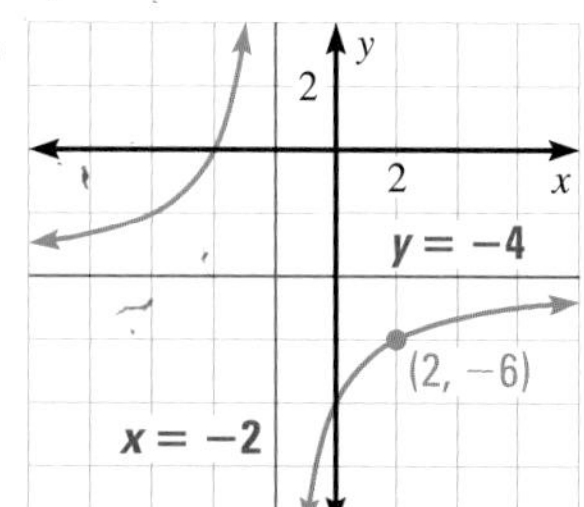

40.

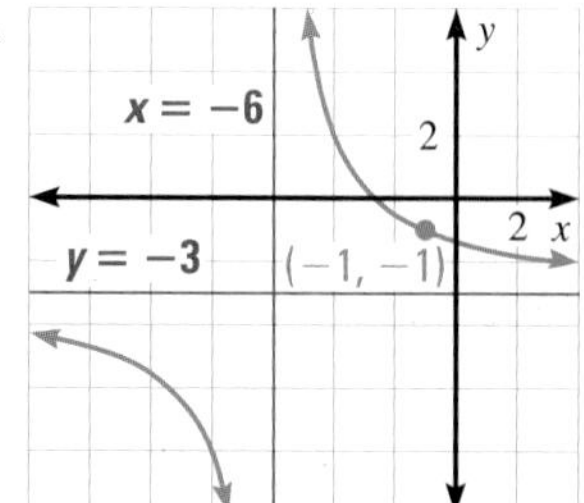

41. **CHALLENGE** Let a, b, c, and d be first-degree polynomials. Find two rational expressions $\frac{a}{b}$ and $\frac{c}{d}$ such that $\frac{a}{b} - \frac{c}{d} = \frac{5x + 7}{(x+2)(x+3)}$.

PROBLEM SOLVING

EXAMPLE 6 on p. 815 for Exs. 42–46

42. **CANOEING** A canoeist travels 16 miles upstream (against the current) and 16 miles downstream (with the current). The speed of the current is 1 mile per hour. Write an equation that gives the total travel time t (in hours) as a function of the canoeist's average speed r (in miles per hour) in still water. Then find the total travel time if the canoeist's average speed in still water is 6 miles per hour.

@HomeTutor for problem solving help at classzone.com

43. **DRIVING** Matt drives 200 miles to another city. On the drive back home, his average speed decreases by 5 miles per hour. Write an equation that gives the total driving time t (in hours) as a function of his average speed r (in miles per hour) when driving to the city. Then find the total driving time if he drives to the city at an average speed of 50 miles per hour.

@HomeTutor for problem solving help at classzone.com

44. ★ **SHORT RESPONSE** An airplane makes a round trip between two destinations as shown in the diagram. The airplane flies against the wind when traveling west and flies with the wind when traveling east. Assume that the speed of the wind remains constant during each flight.

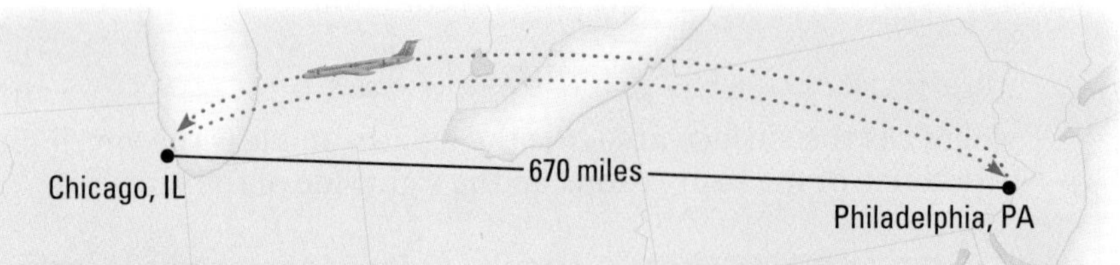

a. **Model** Write an equation that gives the total flying time t (in hours) as a function of the speed w (in miles per hour) of the wind. Then find the total flying time if the speed of the wind is 15 miles per hour.

b. **Decide** For what value of w does the flying time one way take half as long as the total flying time? *Explain* your reasoning.

45. **ELEVATORS** According to the law in one state, the minimum weight W (in pounds) that a passenger elevator must hold is given by

$$W = \frac{2A^2}{3} + \frac{200A}{3} \text{ if } A \le 50 \qquad \text{and} \qquad W = \frac{7A^2}{150} + (125A - 1367) \text{ if } A > 50$$

where A represents the area (in square feet) of the elevator platform.

a. Write the right side of each equation as a single rational expression.

b. What is the minimum weight that an elevator must hold if the area of the platform is 30 square feet? 60 square feet?

46. **MULTI-STEP PROBLEM** A parallel electric circuit consists of a power source and several parallel resistors through which electricity can flow. For a parallel circuit with two resistors, let r_1 represent the resistance (in ohms) of one resistor, and let r_2 represent the resistance (in ohms) of the other resistor.

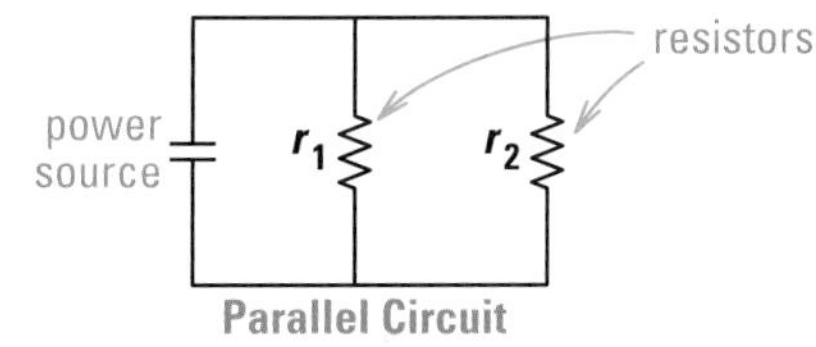

Parallel Circuit

a. **Model** The total resistance r_T is equal to the multiplicative inverse of $\frac{1}{r_1} + \frac{1}{r_2}$. Write $\frac{1}{r_1} + \frac{1}{r_2}$ as a single rational expression. Then write an equation that gives r_T in terms of r_1 and r_2.

b. **Calculate** Find the total resistance when one resistor has a resistance of 2 ohms and the other resistor has a resistance of 6 ohms.

47. **RADIO STATIONS** Radio stations use either amplitude modulation (AM) broadcasting or frequency modulation (FM) broadcasting. The percent a (in decimal form) of commercial radio stations that used AM broadcasting during the period 1990–2003 can be modeled by

$$a = \frac{2.8 + 0.085x}{5.3 + 0.30x}$$

where x is the number of years since 1990. Write a model that gives the percent f (in decimal form) of commercial radio stations that used FM broadcasting as a function of x. Then approximate the value of f in 2003.

○ = **WORKED-OUT SOLUTIONS on p. WS1**   ★ = **STANDARDIZED TEST PRACTICE**

48. ★ **EXTENDED RESPONSE** The axle load for a tow vehicle is the weight (in pounds) that an axle on the vehicle supports. The rear axle load R and the front axle load F are given by the formulas

$$R = \frac{t(w + h)}{w} \qquad \text{and} \qquad F = \frac{th}{w}$$

where t represents the weight (in pounds) that presses down on the hitch by a trailer and w and h represent the distances (in feet) shown.

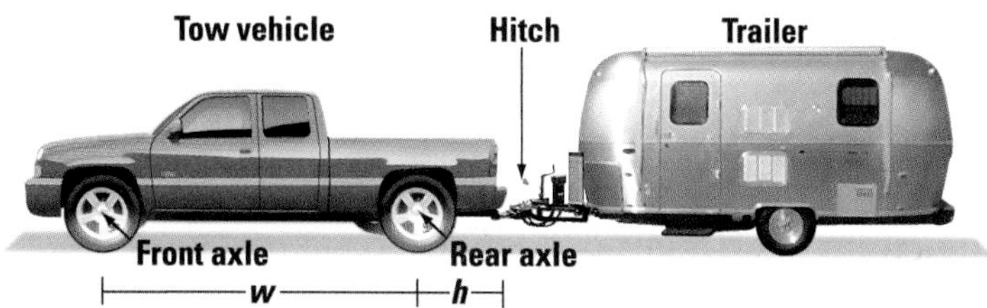

a. **Calculate** For a certain tow vehicle, $t = 300$, $w = 9$, and $h = 3.5$. Find the rear axle load and the front axle load.

b. **Compare** Find the difference of the rear axle load and the front axle load found in part (a). *Compare* your answer with the given value of t.

c. **Model** Write an equation that gives t in terms of R and F. *Justify* your answer algebraically.

49. **CHALLENGE** You and your friend plan to spend 10 minutes mowing your family's lawn together. You can mow the entire lawn alone in 30 minutes.

a. Write an equation that gives the fraction y of the lawn that you and your friend can mow in 10 minutes as a function of the time t (in minutes) in which your friend can mow the entire lawn alone.

b. Suppose your friend can mow the entire lawn alone in 20 minutes. Can the entire lawn be mowed if you and your friend work together for 10 minutes? *Explain.*

MIXED REVIEW

PREVIEW
Prepare for Lesson 12.7 in Exs. 50–57.

Solve the equation or proportion.

50. $-4(f - 5) = -16$ *(p. 148)*

51. $2x + 11 + 3x = 21$ *(p. 148)*

52. $5g - 18 = 4g - 3$ *(p. 154)*

53. $7.5k = 5(2k + 1)$ *(p. 154)*

54. $\frac{7}{3} = \frac{m}{6}$ *(p. 168)*

55. $\frac{14}{10} = \frac{v}{15}$ *(p. 168)*

56. $x^2 - 9x + 14 = 0$ *(p. 583)*

57. $-7m^2 + 56 = 0$ *(p. 653)*

58. **SPORTS** An athlete kicks a football upward from the ground with an initial vertical velocity of 64 feet per second. After how many seconds does the football land on the ground? *(p. 575)*

Factor the expression.

59. $12x^2 - 24x$ *(p. 575)*

60. $x^2 - 9x - 22$ *(p. 583)*

61. $x^2 + 15x + 56$ *(p. 583)*

62. $100 - 9x^2$ *(p. 600)*

12.7 Solve Rational Equations

Before	You simplified rational expressions.
Now	You will solve rational equations.
Why?	So you can calculate a hockey statistic, as in Ex. 31.

Key Vocabulary
- **rational equation**
- **cross product,** *p. 168*
- **extraneous solution,** *p. 730*
- **least common denominator (LCD) of rational expressions,** *p. 813*

A **rational equation** is an equation that contains one or more rational expressions. One method for solving a rational equation is to use the cross products property. You can use this method when both sides of the equation are single rational expressions.

EXAMPLE 1 Use the cross products property

Solve $\frac{6}{x+4} = \frac{x}{2}$. Check your solution.

$\frac{6}{x+4} = \frac{x}{2}$	Write original equation.
$12 = x^2 + 4x$	Cross products property
$0 = x^2 + 4x - 12$	Subtract 12 from each side.
$0 = (x + 6)(x - 2)$	Factor polynomial.
$x + 6 = 0$ *or* $x - 2 = 0$	Zero-product property
$x = -6$ *or* $x = 2$	Solve for *x*.

▶ The solutions are −6 and 2.

REVIEW CROSS PRODUCTS
For help with using the cross products property, see p. 168.

CHECK **If $x = -6$:** $\frac{6}{-6+4} \stackrel{?}{=} \frac{-6}{2}$, $-3 = -3$ ✓ **If $x = 2$:** $\frac{6}{2+4} \stackrel{?}{=} \frac{2}{2}$, $1 = 1$ ✓

GUIDED PRACTICE for Example 1

Solve the equation. Check your solution.

1. $\frac{5}{y-2} = \frac{y}{3}$

2. $\frac{2}{z+5} = \frac{z}{7}$

USING THE LCD Given an equation with fractional coefficients such as $\frac{2}{3}x + \frac{1}{6} = \frac{3}{4}$, you can multiply each side by the least common denominator (LCD), 12. The equation becomes $8x + 2 = 9$, which you may find easier to solve than the original equation. You can use this method to solve a rational equation.

EXAMPLE 2 Multiply by the LCD

Solve $\frac{x}{x-2} + \frac{1}{5} = \frac{2}{x-2}$. Check your solution.

$$\frac{x}{x-2} + \frac{1}{5} = \frac{2}{x-2}$$ Write original equation.

$$\frac{x}{x-2} \cdot 5(x-2) + \frac{1}{5} \cdot 5(x-2) = \frac{2}{x-2} \cdot 5(x-2)$$ Multiply by LCD, $5(x-2)$.

$$\frac{x \cdot 5\cancel{(x-2)}}{\cancel{x-2}} + \frac{\cancel{5}(x-2)}{\cancel{5}} = \frac{2 \cdot 5\cancel{(x-2)}}{\cancel{x-2}}$$ Multiply and divide out common factors.

$$5x + x - 2 = 10$$ Simplify.

$$6x - 2 = 10$$ Combine like terms.

$$6x = 12$$ Add 2 to each side.

$$x = 2$$ Divide each side by 6.

AVOID ERRORS
Be sure to identify the excluded values for the rational expressions in the original equation.

The solution appears to be 2, but the expressions $\frac{x}{x-2}$ and $\frac{2}{x-2}$ are undefined when $x = 2$. So, 2 is an extraneous solution.

▶ There is no solution.

EXAMPLE 3 Factor to find the LCD

Solve $\frac{3}{x-7} + 1 = \frac{8}{x^2 - 9x + 14}$. Check your solution.

Solution

Write each denominator in factored form. The LCD is $(x-2)(x-7)$.

$$\frac{3}{x-7} + 1 = \frac{8}{(x-2)(x-7)}$$

$$\frac{3}{x-7} \cdot (x-2)(x-7) + 1 \cdot (x-2)(x-7) = \frac{8}{(x-2)(x-7)} \cdot (x-2)(x-7)$$

$$\frac{3(x-2)\cancel{(x-7)}}{\cancel{x-7}} + (x-2)(x-7) = \frac{8\cancel{(x-2)}\cancel{(x-7)}}{\cancel{(x-2)}\cancel{(x-7)}}$$

$$3(x-2) + (x^2 - 9x + 14) = 8$$

$$x^2 - 6x + 8 = 8$$

$$x^2 - 6x = 0$$

$$x(x-6) = 0$$

$$x = 0 \text{ or } x - 6 = 0$$

$$x = 0 \text{ or } \quad x = 6$$

▶ The solutions are 0 and 6.

CHECK **If $x = 0$:**

$$\frac{3}{0-7} + 1 \stackrel{?}{=} \frac{8}{0^2 - 9 \cdot 0 + 14}$$

$$\frac{4}{7} = \frac{4}{7} \checkmark$$

If $x = 6$:

$$\frac{3}{6-7} + 1 \stackrel{?}{=} \frac{8}{6^2 - 9 \cdot 6 + 14}$$

$$-2 = -2 \checkmark$$

EXAMPLE 4 Solve a multi-step problem

PAINT MIXING You have an 8 pint mixture of paint that is made up of equal amounts of yellow paint and blue paint. To create a certain shade of green, you need a paint mixture that is 80% yellow. How many pints of yellow paint do you need to add to the mixture?

ANOTHER WAY
For an alternative method for solving the problem in Example 4, turn to page 827 for the **Problem Solving Workshop.**

Solution

Because the amount of yellow paint equals the amount of blue paint, the mixture has 4 pints of yellow paint. Let p represent the number of pints of yellow paint that you need to add.

STEP 1 **Write** a verbal model. Then write an equation.

$$\frac{\text{Pints of yellow paint in mixture} + \text{Pints of yellow paint needed}}{\text{Pints of paint in mixture} + \text{Pints of yellow paint needed}} = \text{Desired percent yellow in mixture}$$

$$\frac{4+p}{8+p} = 0.8$$

STEP 2 **Solve** the equation.

$\dfrac{4+p}{8+p} = 0.8$ — Write equation.

$4 + p = 0.8(8 + p)$ — Cross products property

$4 + p = 6.4 + 0.8p$ — Distributive property

$0.2p = 2.4$ — Rewrite equation.

$p = 12$ — Solve for p.

▶ You need to add 12 pints of yellow paint.

CHECK $\dfrac{4+p}{8+p} = 0.8$ — Write original equation.

$\dfrac{4+12}{8+12} \stackrel{?}{=} 0.8$ — Substitute 12 for p.

$\dfrac{16}{20} \stackrel{?}{=} 0.8$ — Simplify numerator and denominator.

$0.8 = 0.8$ ✓ — Write fraction as decimal. Solution checks.

✓ **GUIDED PRACTICE** for Examples 2, 3, and 4

Solve the equation. Check your solution.

3. $\dfrac{a}{a+4} + \dfrac{1}{3} = \dfrac{-12}{a+4}$

4. $\dfrac{n}{n-11} - 1 = \dfrac{22}{n^2 - 5n - 66}$

5. **WHAT IF?** In Example 4, suppose you need a paint mixture that is 75% yellow. How many pints of yellow paint do you need to add to the mixture?

12.7 EXERCISES

HOMEWORK KEY

○ = **WORKED-OUT SOLUTIONS** on p. WS31 for Exs. 7, 15, and 33

★ = **STANDARDIZED TEST PRACTICE** Exs. 2, 24, 28, and 35

SKILL PRACTICE

1. **VOCABULARY** The equation $\frac{3}{x-1} = \frac{7}{x} + 4$ is an example of a(n) __?__.

2. ★ **WRITING** *Describe* two methods for solving a rational equation. Which method can you use to solve any kind of rational equation? *Explain.*

EXAMPLE 1 on p. 820 for Exs. 3–13, 24

SOLVING EQUATIONS Solve the equation. Check your solution.

3. $\frac{5}{r} = \frac{r}{20}$

4. $\frac{3}{s-13} = \frac{s}{10}$

5. $\frac{2}{t} = \frac{10}{t-6}$

6. $\frac{2}{c+3} = \frac{-5}{c-1}$

7. $\frac{2m}{m+4} = \frac{3}{m-1}$

8. $\frac{n-3}{n-6} = \frac{n+1}{n+5}$

9. $\frac{w}{2} = \frac{15}{w+1}$

10. $\frac{2x}{4-x} = \frac{x}{x-4}$

11. $\frac{2y}{y-3} = \frac{24}{y}$

ERROR ANALYSIS ***Describe*** **and correct the error in solving the equation.**

12. $\frac{x+1}{2x+2} = \frac{3}{2x}$

$$\frac{x+1}{2x+2} = \frac{3}{2x}$$
$$(x+1)2x = 3(2x+2)$$
$$2x^2 + 2x = 6x + 6$$
$$2x^2 - 4x - 6 = 0$$
$$2(x-3)(x+1) = 0$$
$$x - 3 = 0 \quad \text{or} \quad x + 1 = 0$$
$$x = 3 \quad \text{or} \quad x = -1$$

The solutions are 3 and −1.

13. $\frac{4x+1}{8x-1} = \frac{3}{5}$

$$\frac{4x+1}{8x-1} = \frac{3}{5}$$
$$5(4x+1) = 3(8x-1)$$
$$20x + 1 = 24x - 3$$
$$1 = 4x - 3$$
$$4 = 4x$$
$$1 = x$$

The solution is 1.

EXAMPLES 2 and 3 on p. 821 for Exs. 14–23

SOLVING EQUATIONS Solve the equation. Check your solution.

14. $\frac{6x}{x-11} + 1 = \frac{3}{x-11}$

15. $\frac{z}{z+7} - 3 = \frac{-1}{z+7}$

16. $\frac{a+7}{a+4} - 1 = \frac{a+10}{2a+8}$

17. $\frac{1}{b+3} + 2 = \frac{b^2-3}{b^2+12b+27}$

18. $\frac{m}{m-2} - \frac{3m}{m-4} = \frac{-2m+2}{m^2-6m+8}$

19. $\frac{3n}{n+1} = \frac{12}{n^2-1} + \frac{n+4}{n-1}$

20. $\frac{3}{p-1} - \frac{2}{p-1} = \frac{-6}{p^2-3p+2}$

21. $\frac{5}{q+4} = \frac{q}{q-3} + \frac{2q-27}{q^2+q-12}$

22. $\frac{r+2}{r^2+6r-7} = \frac{8}{r^2+3r-4}$

23. $\frac{9}{s^2-4} = \frac{4-5s}{s-2}$

24. ★ **OPEN-ENDED** Write a rational equation that can be solved using the cross products property. Then solve the equation.

25. **REASONING** Consider the equation $\frac{2}{x-a} = \frac{x}{x-a}$ where a is a real number. For what value(s) of a does the equation have exactly one solution? no solution? *Explain* your answers.

26. **USING ANOTHER METHOD** Another way to solve a rational equation is to write each side of the equation as a single rational expression and then use the cross products property. Use this method to solve the equation $\frac{x}{x+1} + \frac{x-2}{2} = \frac{2x-1}{4}$.

27. **SOLVING SYSTEMS OF EQUATIONS** Consider the following system:

$$y = 3x + 1$$

$$y = \frac{-5}{x-3} - 6$$

a. Solve the system algebraically.

b. Check your solution by graphing the equations.

28. ★ **MULTIPLE CHOICE** Let a be a real number. How many solutions does the equation $\frac{2}{x-a} = \frac{1}{x+a} + \frac{2a}{x^2-a^2}$ have?

Ⓐ Zero Ⓑ One Ⓒ Two Ⓓ Infinitely many

29. **REASONING** Is the expression $\frac{x+a}{x+1+a}$ ever equivalent to $\frac{x}{x+1}$ for some nonzero value of a? *Justify* your answer algebraically.

30. **CHALLENGE** Let a and b be real numbers. The solutions of the equation $ax + b = \frac{30}{x+2} - 1$ are -8 and 8. What are the values of a and b? *Explain* your answer.

PROBLEM SOLVING

EXAMPLE 4 on p. 822 for Exs. 31–34

31. **ICE HOCKEY** In ice hockey, a goalie's save percentage (in decimal form) is the number of shots blocked by a goalie divided by the number of shots made by an opposing team. Suppose a goalie has blocked 160 out of 200 shots. How many consecutive shots does the goalie need to block in order to raise the save percentage to 0.840?

@HomeTutor for problem solving help at classzone.com

32. **RUNNING TIMES** You are running a 6000 meter charity race. Your average speed in the first half of the race is 50 meters per minute faster than your average speed in the second half. You finish the race in 27 minutes. What is your average speed in the second half of the race?

@HomeTutor for problem solving help at classzone.com

○ = WORKED-OUT SOLUTIONS on p. WS1

★ = STANDARDIZED TEST PRACTICE

33. **CLEANING SOLUTIONS** You have a cleaning solution that consists of 2 cups of vinegar and 7 cups of water. You need a cleaning solution that consists of 5 parts water and 1 part vinegar in order to clean windows. How many cups of water do you need to add to your cleaning solution so that you can use it to clean windows?

34. **MULTI-STEP PROBLEM** Working together, a painter and an assistant can paint a certain room in 2 hours. The painter can paint the room alone in half the time it takes the assistant to paint the room alone. Let t represent the time (in hours) that the painter can paint the room alone.

a. Copy and complete the table.

Person	Fraction of room painted each hour	Time (hours)	Fraction of room painted
Painter	$\frac{1}{t}$	2	?
Assistant	?	2	?

b. *Explain* why the sum of the expressions in the fourth column of the table must be 1.

c. Write a rational equation that you can use to find the time that the painter takes to paint the room alone. Then solve the equation.

d. How long does the assistant take to paint the room alone?

35. ★ **EXTENDED RESPONSE** You and your sister can rake a neighbor's front lawn together in 30 minutes. Your sister takes 1.5 times as long as you to rake the lawn by herself.

a. **Solve** Write an equation that you can use to find the time t (in minutes) you take to rake the lawn by yourself. Then solve the equation.

b. **Compare** With more experience, both of you can now rake the lawn together in 20 minutes, and your sister can rake the lawn alone in the same amount of time as you. Tell how you would change the equation in part (a) in order to describe this situation. Then solve the equation.

c. **Explain** *Explain* why your solution of the equation in part (b) makes sense. Then justify your explanation algebraically for any given amount of time that both of you rake the lawn together.

36. **TELEVISION** The average time t (in minutes) that a person in the United States watched television per day during the period 1950–2000 can be modeled by

$$t = \frac{265 + 8.85x}{1 + 0.0114x}$$

where x is the number of years since 1950.

a. Approximate the year in which a person watched television for an average of 6 hours per day.

b. About how many years had passed when the average time a person spent watching television per day increased from 5 hours to 7 hours?

37. **SCIENCE** Atmospheric pressure, measured in pounds per square inch (psi), is the pressure exerted on an object by the weight of the atmosphere above the object. The atmospheric pressure p (in psi) can be modeled by

$$p = \frac{14.55(56{,}267 - a)}{55{,}545 + a}$$

where a is the altitude (in feet). Is the change in altitude greater when the atmospheric pressure changes from 10 psi to 9 psi or from 8 psi to 7 psi? *Explain* your answer.

38. **CHALLENGE** Butterfat makes up about 1% of the volume of milk in 1% milk. Butterfat can make up no more than 0.2% of the volume of milk in skim milk. A container holds 15 fluid ounces of 1% milk. How many fluid ounces of butterfat must be removed in order for the milk to be considered skim milk? Round your answer to the nearest hundredth.

MIXED REVIEW

PREVIEW
Prepare for Lesson 13.1 in Exs. 39–44.

Write the fraction as a decimal and as a percent. Round decimals to the nearest thousandth. Round percents to the nearest tenth of a percent. *(p. 916)*

39. $\frac{1}{4}$ 40. $\frac{1}{8}$ 41. $\frac{7}{10}$

42. $\frac{24}{25}$ 43. $\frac{25}{30}$ 44. $\frac{7}{2}$

Evaluate the expression.

45. $(9^2 - 7) \div 2$ *(p. 8)* 46. $6[4 - (16 - 14)^2]$ *(p. 8)* 47. $\sqrt{289}$ *(p. 110)*

48. $\pm\sqrt{1600}$ *(p. 110)* 49. $\frac{3^2}{3^{-7}}$ *(p. 495)* 50. $\frac{4^2}{4^5}$ *(p. 495)*

51. $\left(-\frac{1}{8}\right)^3$ *(p. 495)* 52. $\frac{1.61 \times 10^{-7}}{2.3 \times 10^{-3}}$ *(p. 512)* 53. $(1.2 \times 10^6)^2$ *(p. 512)*

QUIZ *for Lessons 12.5–12.7*

Find the product or quotient. *(p. 802)*

1. $\frac{5}{8x^2} \cdot \frac{4x^3}{15}$ 2. $\frac{3y^2 + 6y}{y^2 - 16} \div \frac{y^2}{y - 4}$

Find the sum or difference. *(p. 812)*

3. $\frac{8a}{a + 11} - \frac{5a - 1}{a + 11}$ 4. $\frac{6n}{n + 3} + \frac{n - 1}{n^2 + 5n + 6}$

Solve the equation. Check your solution. *(p. 820)*

5. $\frac{2z}{z + 5} = \frac{z}{z - 3}$ 6. $\frac{2x}{x} + \frac{3 - x}{x + 1} = \frac{-4}{x^2 + x}$

7. **BATTING AVERAGES** A softball player's batting average is the number of hits divided by the number of times at bat. A softball player has a batting average of .200 after 90 times at bat. How many consecutive hits does the player need in order to raise the batting average to .250? *(p. 820)*

PROBLEM SOLVING WORKSHOP
LESSON 12.7

Using ALTERNATIVE METHODS

Another Way to Solve Example 4, page 822

MULTIPLE REPRESENTATIONS In Example 4 on page 822, you saw how to solve a problem about mixing paint by using a rational equation. You can also solve the problem by using a table or by reinterpreting the problem.

PROBLEM

PAINT MIXING You have an 8 pint mixture of paint that is made up of equal amounts of yellow paint and blue paint. To create a certain shade of green, you need a paint mixture that is 80% yellow. How many pints of yellow paint do you need to add to the mixture?

METHOD 1

Use a Table One alternative approach is to use a table.

The mixture has 8 pints of paint. Because the mixture has an equal amount of yellow paint and blue paint, the mixture has $8 \div 2 = 4$ pints of yellow paint.

STEP 1 **Make** a table that shows the percent of the mixture that is yellow paint after you add various amounts of yellow paint.

Yellow paint (pints)	Paint in mixture (pints)	Percent of mixture that is yellow paint
4	8	$\frac{4}{8} = 50\%$
6	10	$\frac{6}{10} = 60\%$
8	12	$\frac{8}{12} \approx 67\%$
10	14	$\frac{10}{14} \approx 71\%$
12	16	$\frac{12}{16} = 75\%$
14	18	$\frac{14}{18} \approx 78\%$
15	19	$\frac{15}{19} \approx 79\%$
16	20	$\frac{16}{20} = 80\%$

A mixture with 6 pints of yellow paint is the result of adding 2 pints of yellow paint to the mixture.

This amount of yellow paint gives you the percent yellow you want.

STEP 2 **Find** the number of pints of yellow paint needed. Subtract the number of pints of yellow paint already in the mixture from the total number of pints of yellow paint you have: $16 - 4 = 12$.

▶ You need to add 12 pints of yellow paint.

METHOD 2

Reinterpret Problem Another alternative approach is to reinterpret the problem.

STEP 1 **Reinterpret** the problem. A mixture with 80% yellow paint means that $\frac{4}{5}$ of the mixture is yellow and $\frac{1}{5}$ of the mixture is blue. So, the ratio of yellow paint to blue paint needs to be 4 : 1. You need 4 times as many pints of yellow paint as pints of blue paint.

STEP 2 **Write** a verbal model. Then write an equation. Let p represent the number of pints of yellow paint that you need to add.

Pints of yellow paint already in mixture	+	Pints of yellow paint you need to add	= 4 ·	Pints of blue paint in mixture
↓		↓		↓
4	+	p	= 4 ·	4

STEP 3 **Solve** the equation.

$4 + p = 4 \cdot 4$ **Write equation.**

$4 + p = 16$ **Multiply.**

$p = 12$ **Subtract 4 from each side.**

▶ You need to add 12 pints of yellow paint to the mixture.

PRACTICE

1. **INVESTING** Jill has $10,000 in various investments, including $1000 in a mutual fund. Jill wants the amount in the mutual fund to make up 20% of the amount in all of her investments. How much money should she add to the mutual fund? Solve this problem using two different methods.

2. **ERROR ANALYSIS** *Describe* and correct the error in solving Exercise 1.

Amount in mutual fund	Amount in all investments	Percent in mutual fund
1000	10,000	10%
1400	10,400	About 13%
1800	10,800	About 17%
2250	11,250	20%

Jill needs to add $2250 to her mutual fund. ✗

3. **BASKETBALL** A basketball player has made 40% of 30 free throw attempts so far. How many consecutive free throws must the player make in order to increase the percent of free throw attempts made to 50%? Solve this problem using two different methods.

4. **WHAT IF?** In Exercise 3, suppose the basketball player instead wants to increase the percent of free throw attempts made to 60%. How many consecutive free throws must the player make?

5. **SNOW SHOVELING** You and your friend are shoveling snow out of a driveway. You can shovel the snow alone in 50 minutes. Both of you can shovel the snow in 30 minutes when working together. How many minutes will your friend take to shovel the snow alone? Solve this problem using two different methods.

MIXED REVIEW of Problem Solving

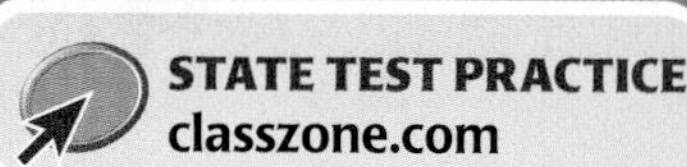

Lessons 12.5–12.7

1. **MULTI-STEP PROBLEM** For the period 1991–2002, the average total revenue T (in dollars per admission) that a movie theater earned and the average revenue C (in dollars per admission) from concessions in the United States can be modeled by

$$T = \frac{0.018x^2 + 5.4}{1 - 0.0011x^2} \text{ and } C = \frac{0.013x^2 + 1.1}{0.0011x^2 + 1}$$

where x is the number of years since 1991.

   a. Write a model that gives the percent p (in decimal form) of the average total revenue per admission that came from concessions as a function of x.

   b. About what percent of the average total revenue came from concessions in 2001?

2. **SHORT RESPONSE** The diagram of the truck shows the distance between the first axle and the last axle for each of two groups of consecutive axles.

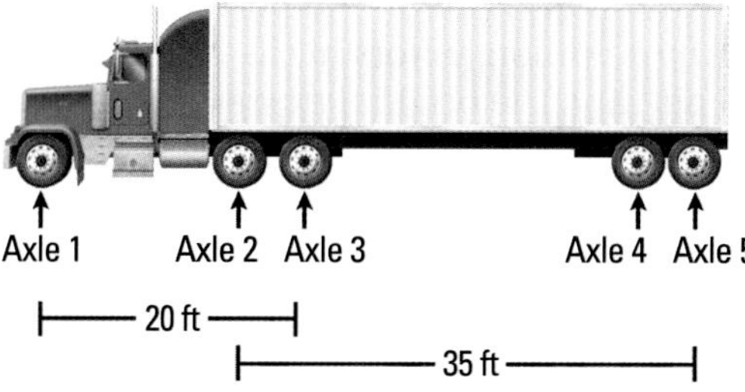

The maximum weight W (to the nearest 500 pounds) that a truck on a highway can carry on a group of consecutive axles is given by the formula

$$W = 500\left(\frac{d}{n - 1} + 12n + 36\right)$$

where d is the distance (in feet) between the first axle and the last axle of the group and n is the number of axles in the group.

   a. Rewrite the expression on the right side of the equation as a single rational expression. Then find the maximum weight that the truck shown can carry on axles 1–3.

   b. Can the truck carry 65,500 pounds on axles 2–5? *Explain* your answer.

3. **MULTI-STEP PROBLEM** A rower travels 5 miles upstream (against the current) and 5 miles downstream (with the current). The speed of the current is 1 mile per hour.

   a. Write an equation that gives the total travel time t (in hours) as a function of the rower's average speed r (in miles per hour) in still water.

   b. Find the total travel time if the rower's average speed in still water is 7 miles per hour.

4. **GRIDDED ANSWER** You take 7 minutes to fill your washing machine tub using only the cold water valve. You take 4 minutes to fill the tub using both the cold water valve and the hot water valve. How many minutes will you take to fill the tub using only the hot water valve?

5. **OPEN-ENDED** *Describe* a real-world situation that can be modeled by the equation $\frac{115 + x}{170 + x} = 0.75$. *Explain* what the solution of the equation means in this situation.

6. **EXTENDED RESPONSE** The number D (in thousands) of all college degrees earned and the number M (in thousands) of master's degrees earned in the United States during the period 1984–2001 can be modeled by

$$D = \frac{1800 + 17x^2}{1 + 0.0062x^2} \text{ and } M = \frac{280 + 2.5x^2}{1 + 0.0040x^2}$$

where x is the number of years since 1984.

   a. Write a model that gives the percent p (in decimal form) of all college degrees earned that were master's degrees.

   b. Approximate the percent of all college degrees earned that were master's degrees in 2000.

   c. Graph the equation in part (a) on a graphing calculator. *Describe* how the percent of college degrees that were master's degrees changed during the period. Can you use the graph to describe how the *number* of master's degrees changed during the period? *Explain.*

12 CHAPTER SUMMARY

Animated Algebra
classzone.com
Electronic Function Library

BIG IDEAS

For Your Notebook

Big Idea 1

Graphing Rational Functions

The graphs of $y = \frac{a}{x}$ $(a \neq 0)$ and $y = \frac{a}{x - h} + k$ $(a \neq 0)$ are hyperbolas that have two symmetrical branches. The characteristics of the functions and their graphs are given below. To graph a rational function whose numerator and denominator are first-degree polynomials, you can first use long division to rewrite the function so that it has the form $y = \frac{a}{x - h} + k$.

Function	Vertical asymptote	Horizontal asymptote	Domain	Range
$y = \frac{a}{x}$	$x = 0$	$y = 0$	All real numbers except $x = 0$	All real numbers except $y = 0$
$y = \frac{a}{x - h} + k$	$x = h$	$y = k$	All real numbers except $x = h$	All real numbers except $y = k$

Performing Operations on Rational Expressions

Performing operations on rational expressions is similar to performing operations on numerical fractions. Any common factors in the numerator and denominator should be divided out, and the original expression should be used when finding excluded values.

Operation	Rule
Multiplication	$\frac{a}{b} \cdot \frac{c}{d} = \frac{ac}{bd}$ where $b \neq 0$ and $d \neq 0$
Division	$\frac{a}{b} \div \frac{c}{d} = \frac{a}{b} \cdot \frac{d}{c}$ where $b \neq 0$, $c \neq 0$, and $d \neq 0$
Addition	Same denominator: $\frac{a}{c} + \frac{b}{c} = \frac{a + b}{c}$ where $c \neq 0$ Different denominators: Use LCD of rational expressions.
Subtraction	Same denominator: $\frac{a}{c} - \frac{b}{c} = \frac{a - b}{c}$ where $c \neq 0$ Different denominators: Use LCD of rational expressions.

Big Idea 3

Solving Rational Equations

You can use the following steps to solve a rational equation.

1. Rewrite the rational equation by using the cross products property or by multiplying each side by the least common denominator (LCD) of the rational expressions in the equation.
2. Solve the rewritten equation.
3. Check for extraneous solutions.

12 CHAPTER REVIEW

@HomeTutor
classzone.com
- Multi-Language Glossary
- Vocabulary practice

REVIEW KEY VOCABULARY

- inverse variation, *p. 765*
- constant of variation, *p. 765*
- hyperbola, branches of a hyperbola, asymptotes of a hyperbola, *p. 767*
- rational function, *p. 775*
- rational expression, *p. 794*
- excluded value, *p. 794*
- simplest form of a rational expression, *p. 795*
- least common denominator (LCD) of rational expressions, *p. 813*
- rational equation, *p. 820*

VOCABULARY EXERCISES

1. Copy and complete: A(n) _?_ of a hyperbola is a line that the hyperbola approaches but doesn't intersect.
2. **WRITING** *Explain* how you can use an LCD to solve a rational equation.
3. Identify the vertical asymptote and horizontal asymptote of the graph of $y = \frac{-5}{x+2} - 4$.

REVIEW EXAMPLES AND EXERCISES

Use the review examples and exercises below to check your understanding of the concepts you have learned in each lesson of Chapter 12.

12.1 Model Inverse Variation *pp. 765–772*

EXAMPLE

The variables x and y vary inversely, and $y = 14$ when $x = 4$. Write the inverse variation equation that relates x and y. Then find the value of y when $x = 7$.

$y = \frac{a}{x}$ **Write inverse variation equation.**

$14 = \frac{a}{4}$ **Substitute 4 for x and 14 for y.**

$56 = a$ **Simplify.**

▶ The inverse variation equation is $y = \frac{56}{x}$. When $x = 7$, $y = \frac{56}{7} = 8$.

EXERCISES

EXAMPLES 4 and 5 on pp. 767–768 for Exs. 4–7

Given that y varies inversely with x, use the specified values to write an inverse variation equation that relates x and y. Then find y when $x = 5$.

4. $x = 9, y = 2$
5. $x = 3, y = 21$
6. $x = -6, y = 6$
7. Tell whether the ordered pairs $(-10, 0.8)$, $(-4, 2)$, $(5, -1.6)$, and $(16, -0.5)$ represent inverse variation. If so, write the inverse variation equation.

12 CHAPTER REVIEW

12.2 Graph Rational Functions

pp. 775–782

EXAMPLE

Graph $y = \frac{-1}{x-2} - 3$.

STEP 1 **Identify** the asymptotes of the graph. The vertical asymptote is $x = 2$, and the horizontal asymptote is $y = -3$.

STEP 2 **Plot** several points on each side of the vertical asymptote.

STEP 3 **Graph** two branches that pass through the plotted points and approach the asymptotes.

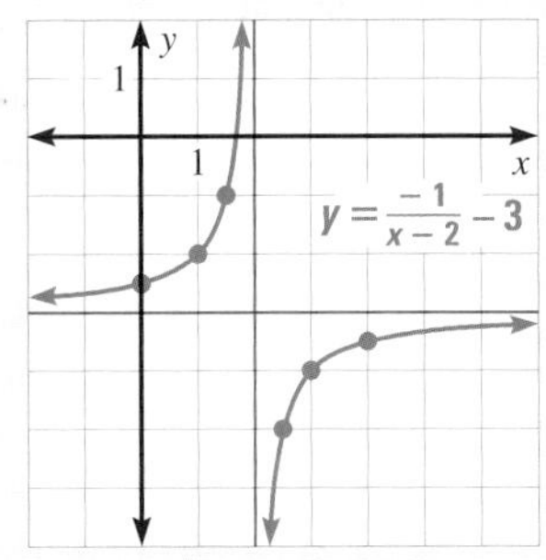

EXERCISES

EXAMPLES 2, 3, and 4 on pp. 776–777 for Exs. 8–10

Graph the function.

8. $y = \frac{4}{x} + 1$

9. $y = \frac{1}{x-6}$

10. $y = \frac{2}{x+1} + 1$

12.3 Divide Polynomials

pp. 784–791

EXAMPLE

Divide $x^2 + 7x - 2$ by $x - 2$.

$$\begin{array}{r l}
x + 9 & \\
x - 2 \overline{)\, x^2 + 7x - 2} & \\
\underline{x^2 - 2x} & \text{Multiply } x \text{ and } x - 2. \\
9x - 2 & \text{Subtract } x^2 - 2x. \text{ Bring down } -2. \\
\underline{9x - 18} & \text{Multiply 9 and } x - 2. \\
16 & \text{Subtract } 9x - 18.
\end{array}$$

▶ $(x^2 + 7x - 2) \div (x - 2) = x + 9 + \frac{16}{x-2}$

EXERCISES

EXAMPLES 2, 3, 4, 5, and 7 on pp. 785–787 for Exs. 11–15

Divide.

11. $(x^2 + 12x + 35) \div (x + 7)$

12. $(y^2 - 5y - 8) \div (y - 3)$

13. $(4z + z^2 - 1) \div (5 + z)$

14. $(3a^2 - 2) \div (3 + 3a)$

15. CHARITY DONATIONS Sean intends to collect \$500 in individual donations for a charity. His company will contribute \$2 for every donation collected. Write and graph an equation that gives the average amount a (including the company contribution) that the charity will receive per individual donation as a function of the number d of donations.

@HomeTutor
classzone.com
Chapter Review Practice

12.4 Simplify Rational Expressions

pp. 794–800

EXAMPLE

Simplify $\frac{x^2 - 3x - 18}{x^2 + 11x + 24}$. State the excluded values.

$$\frac{x^2 - 3x - 18}{x^2 + 11x + 24} = \frac{(x + 3)(x - 6)}{(x + 3)(x + 8)}$$ Factor numerator and denominator.

$$= \frac{\cancel{(x + 3)}(x - 6)}{\cancel{(x + 3)}(x + 8)}$$ Divide out common factor.

$$= \frac{x - 6}{x + 8}$$ Simplify.

▸ The excluded values are −8 and −3.

EXERCISES

EXAMPLES 1, 2, 3, and 4 on pp. 794–796 for Exs. 16–21

Find the excluded values, if any, of the expression.

16. $\frac{x + 3}{2x - 4}$

17. $\frac{3}{y^2 - 4y - 12}$

18. $\frac{8z}{9z^2 - 1}$

Simplify the expression, if possible. State the excluded values.

19. $\frac{5m^3 - 15m^2}{20m^2}$

20. $\frac{3n^2 - n - 2}{2n^2 - 3n + 1}$

21. $\frac{4 - r^2}{r^2 - r - 2}$

12.5 Multiply and Divide Rational Expressions

pp. 802–809

EXAMPLE

Find the quotient $\frac{5x^2 + 3x - 2}{4x} \div (5x - 2)$.

$$\frac{5x^2 + 3x - 2}{4x} \div (5x - 2) = \frac{5x^2 + 3x - 2}{4x} \div \frac{5x - 2}{1}$$ Rewrite polynomial as fraction.

$$= \frac{5x^2 + 3x - 2}{4x} \cdot \frac{1}{5x - 2}$$ Multiply by multiplicative inverse.

$$= \frac{5x^2 + 3x - 2}{4x(5x - 2)}$$ Multiply numerators and denominators.

$$= \frac{\cancel{(5x - 2)}(x + 1)}{4x\cancel{(5x - 2)}}$$ Factor and divide out common factor.

$$= \frac{x + 1}{4x}$$ Simplify.

EXERCISES

EXAMPLES 3 and 4 on pp. 803–804 for Exs. 22–24

Find the product or quotient.

22. $\frac{-x^3}{x^2 + 5x - 14} \cdot (2 - x)$

23. $\frac{6v^8}{2v^5} \div \frac{8v}{14v^5}$

24. $\frac{w^2 - 9}{2w + 1} \div \frac{w + 3}{4w^2 - 1}$

12 CHAPTER REVIEW

12.6 Add and Subtract Rational Expressions

pp. 812–819

EXAMPLE

Find the difference $\frac{x}{x-4} - \frac{5}{x+3}$.

$$\frac{x}{x-4} - \frac{5}{x+3} = \frac{x(x+3)}{(x-4)(x+3)} - \frac{5(x-4)}{(x+3)(x-4)}$$ Rewrite fractions using LCD, $(x-4)(x+3)$.

$$= \frac{x(x+3) - 5(x-4)}{(x-4)(x+3)}$$ Subtract fractions.

$$= \frac{x^2 - 2x + 20}{(x-4)(x+3)}$$ Simplify numerator.

EXERCISES

EXAMPLES 1, 3, 5, and 6 on pp. 812–815 for Exs. 25–28

Find the sum or difference.

25. $\frac{x+13}{5x-3} - \frac{9x-20}{5x-3}$

26. $\frac{5}{6a} + \frac{1}{9a^3}$

27. $\frac{6}{c+1} - \frac{c}{c^2-2c-8}$

28. BICYCLING You ride your bike to a beach that is 15 miles away. Your average speed on the way home is 5 miles per hour less than your average speed on the way to the beach. Write an equation that gives the total travel time t (in hours) as a function of your average speed r (in miles per hour) on the way to the beach. Then find the total travel time if you biked to the beach at an average speed of 15 miles per hour.

12.7 Solve Rational Equations

pp. 820–826

EXAMPLE

Solve $\frac{2x}{x-1} + \frac{2}{3} = \frac{10}{x-1}$.

$$\frac{2x}{x-1} + \frac{2}{3} = \frac{10}{x-1}$$ Write original equation.

$$\frac{2x}{x-1} \cdot 3(x-1) + \frac{2}{3} \cdot 3(x-1) = \frac{10}{x-1} \cdot 3(x-1)$$ Multiply each expression by LCD, $3(x-1)$.

$$\frac{2x \cdot 3\cancel{(x-1)}}{\cancel{(x-1)}} + \frac{2 \cdot \cancel{3}(x-1)}{\cancel{3}} = \frac{10 \cdot 3\cancel{(x-1)}}{\cancel{(x-1)}}$$ Divide out common factors.

$$6x + 2x - 2 = 30$$ Simplify.

$$8x - 2 = 30$$ Combine like terms.

$$x = 4$$ Solve for x.

EXERCISES

EXAMPLES 1, 2, and 3 on pp. 820–821 for Exs. 29–31

Solve the equation. Check your solution.

29. $\frac{18}{x-3} = \frac{x}{3}$

30. $\frac{4}{y+6} - 2 = \frac{20}{y^2+3y-18}$

31. $\frac{1}{z+3} - \frac{5}{6} = \frac{2}{z+3}$

12 CHAPTER TEST

Given that y varies inversely with x, use the specified values to write an inverse variation equation that relates x and y. Then find y when $x = 3$.

1. $x = 2, y = 5$

2. $x = 9, y = 9$

3. $x = \frac{9}{2}, y = 4$

4. Tell whether the table represents inverse variation. If so, write the inverse variation equation.

x	-10	-2	4	5	20
y	0.5	2.5	-1.25	-1	-0.25

Graph the function.

5. $y = \frac{-6}{x}$

6. $y = \frac{2}{x - 5} + 2$

7. $y = \frac{3x - 1}{x + 4}$

Divide.

8. $(v^2 - 16v + 49) \div (v - 8)$

9. $(8w - 2w^2 - 6) \div (w - 1)$

10. $(6x^2 + x) \div (2x + 1)$

Simplify the expression, if possible. State the excluded values.

11. $\frac{42x^4}{3x^2}$

12. $\frac{2y - 8}{4 - y}$

13. $\frac{z^2 - 4z - 77}{z^2 - 13z + 22}$

Find the sum, difference, product, or quotient.

14. $\frac{r^2 - 9r + 18}{r^2 + 11r + 30} \cdot \frac{r + 5}{r^2 - 36}$

15. $\frac{s^2 + 3s - 10}{s^2 - 9} \div \frac{s - 2}{s + 3}$

16. $\frac{x^2 - 9x}{x + 3} \div (x^2 - 6x - 27)$

17. $\frac{4}{m + 2} - \frac{3m}{m - 3}$

18. $\frac{2n + 7}{n - 1} - \frac{8n}{n + 5}$

19. $\frac{p + 1}{p^2 - 49} + \frac{p - 1}{p^2 + 10p + 21}$

Solve the equation. Check your solution.

20. $\frac{7}{u + 1} = \frac{4}{u + 4}$

21. $\frac{t + 11}{t - 11} = \frac{11t + 121}{t^2 - 6t - 55}$

22. $\frac{8}{x + 4} = \frac{5x}{x^2 - 2x - 24} - 1$

23. GOLF Your local golf club offers two payment options to anyone who wants to use its course. For the first option, you pay a one-time fee of $750 to join for the season plus $25 each time you use the golf course. For the second option, you instead pay $45 each time you use the golf course.

a. Using the first option, write an equation that gives your average cost C (in dollars) per use of the golf course as a function of the number g of times you use the golf course. Then graph the equation.

b. Use the graph to approximate the number of times you need to use the golf course before the average cost is less than $45.

24. CLEANING You and your brother start a house cleaning business for the summer. Your brother needs twice the time you need to clean a certain room. Working together, the two of you need 60 minutes to clean the room.

a. Write an equation that you can use to find the time t (in minutes) you need to clean the room by yourself. Then solve the equation.

b. How long will each of you need to clean the room individually?

CONTEXT-BASED MULTIPLE CHOICE QUESTIONS

Some of the information you need to solve a context-based multiple choice question may appear in a table, a diagram, or a graph.

PROBLEM 1

Gary competes in the triathlon described in the flyer. His average biking speed is 8 times his average swimming speed. His average running speed is 4 times his average swimming speed. He takes 0.75 minute to transition from swimming to biking and 0.25 minute to transition from biking to running. He finishes the triathlon in 2 hours 25 minutes. What is his average swimming speed?

OAK CITY TRIATHLON

July 29, 8 A.M.

Swim: 1.5 kilometers
Bike: 40 kilometers
Run: 10 kilometers

(A) 0.0625 kilometer per minute (B) 0.125 kilometer per minute

(C) 0.25 kilometer per minute (D) 0.5 kilometer per minute

Plan

INTERPRET THE INFORMATION Use the distance for each stage of the triathlon and Gary's average speed for each stage to write a rational equation that describes the situation. Then solve the equation to find his average swimming speed.

Solution

STEP 1 Use the information in the problem to write an equation that describes the situation.

The time that Gary takes to complete each stage of the triathlon is the distance of the stage divided by the average speed for that stage. The sum of the times of each stage and the transition times equals 2 hours 25 minutes, or 145 minutes. Let x represent Gary's average swimming speed (in kilometers per minute).

$$\frac{1.5}{x} + \frac{40}{8x} + \frac{10}{4x} + 0.75 + 0.25 = 145$$

STEP 2 Solve the equation to find Gary's average swimming speed.

$$\frac{1.5}{x} \cdot \mathbf{8x} + \frac{40}{8x} \cdot \mathbf{8x} + \frac{10}{4x} \cdot \mathbf{8x} + 0.75 \cdot \mathbf{8x} + 0.25 \cdot \mathbf{8x} = 145 \cdot \mathbf{8x}$$

$$\frac{1.5 \cdot 8\cancel{x}}{\cancel{x}} + \frac{40 \cdot \cancel{8x}}{\cancel{8x}} + \frac{10 \cdot 8\cancel{x}}{4\cancel{x}} + 0.75 \cdot 8x + 0.25 \cdot 8x = 145 \cdot 8x$$

$$12 + 40 + 20 + 6x + 2x = 1160x$$

$$72 + 8x = 1160x$$

$$0.0625 = x$$

Gary's average swimming speed is 0.0625 kilometer per minute.

The correct answer is A. (A) (B) (C) (D)

PROBLEM 2

The graph of which function is shown?

Ⓐ $y = \frac{2}{x - 3} + 4$ Ⓑ $y = \frac{2}{x + 3} + 4$

Ⓒ $y = \frac{1}{x + 3} + 4$ Ⓓ $y = \frac{1}{x + 4} - 3$

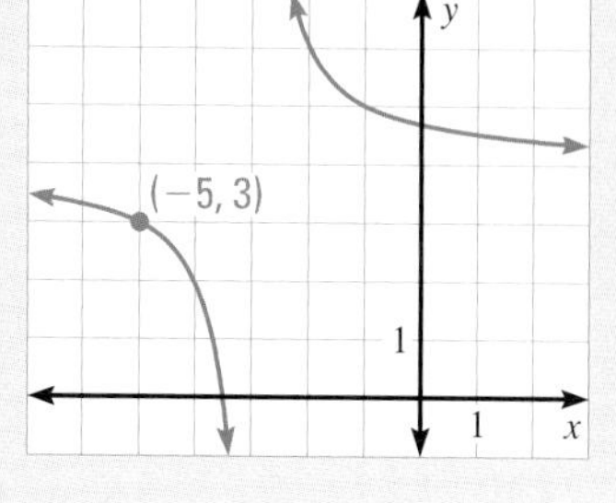

Plan

INTERPRET THE GRAPH The graph is a hyperbola that represents a rational function of the form $y = \frac{a}{x - h} + k$. Use the asymptotes and the fact that $(-5, 3)$ lies on the graph to find the function.

Solution

STEP 1 Find the values of h and k.

The hyperbola has a vertical asymptote of $x = -3$ and a horizontal asymptote of $y = 4$. So, the function has the form $y = \frac{a}{x - (-3)} + 4$, or $y = \frac{a}{x + 3} + 4$.

STEP 2 Find the value of a.

To find the value of a, substitute the coordinates of $(-5, 3)$ into the function.

$3 = \frac{a}{-5 + 3} + 4$ **Substitute −5 for *x* and 3 for *y*.**

$2 = a$ **Solve for *a*.**

The function is $y = \frac{2}{x + 3} + 4$. The correct answer is B. Ⓐ Ⓑ Ⓒ Ⓓ

PRACTICE

1. A community service club is recruiting volunteers to work at a charity event. The table shows the number of hours that each volunteer needs to work for various numbers of volunteers that the club recruits. If the club recruits 50 volunteers, how many hours does each volunteer need to work?

Volunteers	Work time (hours/person)
20	4
25	3.2
32	2.5

Ⓐ 1 hour Ⓑ 1.6 hours Ⓒ 2 hours Ⓓ 2.8 hours

2. What is the area of the right triangle shown?

Ⓐ $\frac{x^2 - 12x + 35}{2}$ Ⓑ $\frac{x^2 + 12x - 35}{2}$

Ⓒ $\frac{x^2 + 12x - 35}{4}$ Ⓓ $x^2 - 12x + 35$

$\frac{x^2 - 2x - 35}{x + 9}$

$\frac{x^2 + 4x - 45}{x + 5}$

12 ★ Standardized TEST PRACTICE

MULTIPLE CHOICE

In Exercises 1–3, use the following information. The length of a string on a stringed instrument varies inversely with the frequency of vibration. The table gives several notes and their approximate frequencies (in hertz).

Note	Frequency (Hz)
C	65.4
D	73.4
E	82.4
F	87.3
G	98.0

1. The string corresponding to which note has the shortest length?

Ⓐ C note　Ⓑ D note
Ⓒ E note　Ⓓ G note

2. If the string that produces the C note has a length of 42 centimeters, what is the approximate length of the string that produces the F note?

Ⓐ 28 cm　Ⓑ 31 cm
Ⓒ 35 cm　Ⓓ 46 cm

3. If the string that produces the D note has a length of 56 centimeters, what is the approximate length of the string that produces the G note?

Ⓐ 31 cm　Ⓑ 35 cm
Ⓒ 42 cm　Ⓓ 65 cm

4. Which equation gives the ratio r of the surface area of the rectangular prism to its volume as a function of the height h?

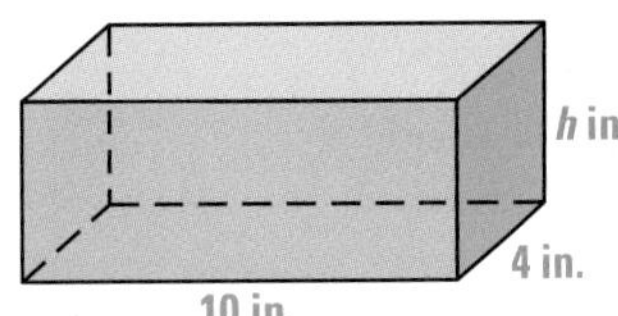

Ⓐ $r = \frac{2}{h} + 0.7$　Ⓑ $r = \frac{1}{20h} + 0.7$
Ⓒ $r = \frac{1}{20h} + 28$　Ⓓ $r = \frac{2}{h} + 0.05$

5. Which point lies on the hyperbola shown?

Ⓐ $(-7, 2.5)$　Ⓑ $(-9, 2.6)$
Ⓒ $(9, 3.4)$　Ⓓ $(11, 3.2)$

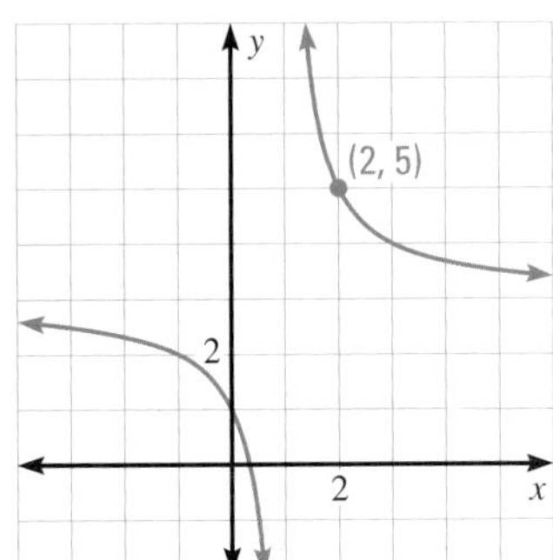

In Exercises 6–8, use the following information.

Jan is hiking a trail and plans to rest for 2 hours along the way. The hyperbola shown is the graph of her combined time t (in hours) for hiking and resting as a function of her average hiking speed r (in miles per hour).

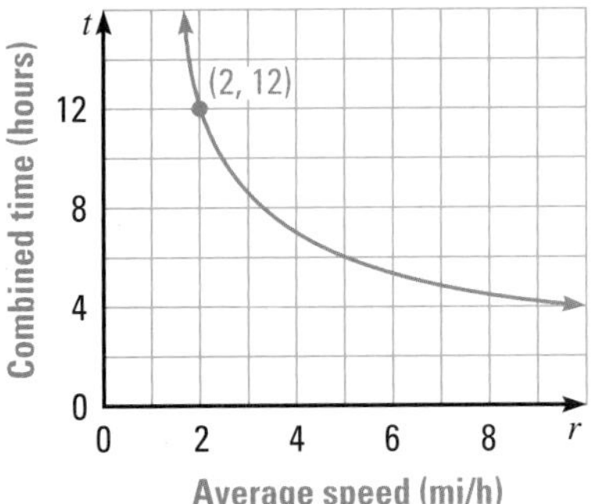

6. If $r = 5$, what is the value of t?

Ⓐ 5　Ⓑ 6
Ⓒ 7　Ⓓ 10

7. What is the length of the trail?

Ⓐ 10 miles　Ⓑ 20 miles
Ⓒ 30 miles　Ⓓ 40 miles

8. Suppose Jan's combined time for hiking and resting is 8 hours 15 minutes. What is her average hiking speed?

Ⓐ 3 mi/h　Ⓑ 3.2 mi/h
Ⓒ 3.4 mi/h　Ⓓ 3.6 mi/h

STATE TEST PRACTICE
classzone.com

GRIDDED ANSWER

9. The variables x and y vary inversely, and $y = 15$ when $x = 2$. What is the value of y when $x = 5$?

10. You and your friend wash cars to raise money for your school club. Both of you can wash a certain car in 10 minutes when working together. Your friend can wash the car alone in twice the time that you can wash the car alone. How many minutes do you take to wash the car alone?

11. What is the remainder when you divide $2x^2 - 5x + 10$ by $2x + 1$?

12. What is the excluded value of the rational expression $\frac{6x^2 + 19x - 7}{x^2 - 8x + 16}$?

13. You and several friends are planning a ski trip. Your plane ticket costs \$180. A ski lodge costs \$2000 to rent. Everyone will share the cost of renting the ski lodge equally. How much more money (in dollars) would you spend if 8 people go on the trip than if 10 people go?

SHORT RESPONSE

14. A town's two street sweepers can clean the streets together in 20 hours. The older sweeper takes 4 times as long as the newer sweeper to clean the streets by itself.

a. Write an equation that you can use to find the time t (in hours) that the newer sweeper takes to clean the streets by itself. Then solve the equation.

b. Suppose that the older sweeper takes only twice as long as the newer sweeper to clean the streets by itself. Will the two sweepers take 10 hours to clean the streets together? *Explain.*

15. Your cousin is driving 500 miles to your house. On her way, she takes a 45 minute lunch break. Write and graph an equation that gives the total time t (in hours) of your cousin's trip as a function of her average driving speed r (in miles per hour). How would the graph change if she took a 60 minute lunch break? *Explain* your answer.

EXTENDED RESPONSE

16. The table shows the taxes paid for various incomes.

Income (dollars)	Taxes paid (dollars)
10,000	420
15,000	720
20,000	1020
25,000	1320

a. Write a linear equation that gives the taxes paid t (in dollars) as a function of the income i (in dollars).

b. Write a rational equation that gives the percent p (in decimal form) of income that is paid in taxes as a function of the income i (in dollars). Use the equation to find the income of a person who pays 4.5% of income in taxes.

c. Does the function in part (b) make sense for incomes less than \$3000? *Justify* your answer algebraically.

17. A greeting card company offers you the opportunity to sell its cards, but you must first pay the company a one-time fee of \$300 plus \$2 for each card that you sell.

a. Write and graph an equation that gives the average cost C per card (including the fee) as a function of the number of cards s that you sell.

b. You want to sell enough cards so that the average cost per card (including the fee) drops to \$3. Write and solve an equation to find the number of cards that you need to sell.

c. Is it possible for you to sell enough cards so that the average cost per card drops to \$1.75? *Explain* your answer.

13 Probability and Data Analysis

Before

In previous courses, you learned the following skills, which you'll use in Chapter 13: finding the mean, median, and mode(s) of data and using a display to analyze data.

Prerequisite Skills

VOCABULARY CHECK

1. Copy and complete: The _?_ of a numerical data set is the middle number when the values are written in numerical order.

SKILLS CHECK

Find the mean, median, and mode(s) of the data. *(Review p. 918 for 13.6.)*

2. 0.2, 1.3, 0.9, 1.5, 2.1, 1.8, 0.6

3. 103, 121, 111, 194, 99, 160, 134, 160

In Exercises 4 and 5, use the bar graph, which shows the numbers of adults who participate in leisure activities, according to the results of a survey. *(Review p. 933 for 13.7.)*

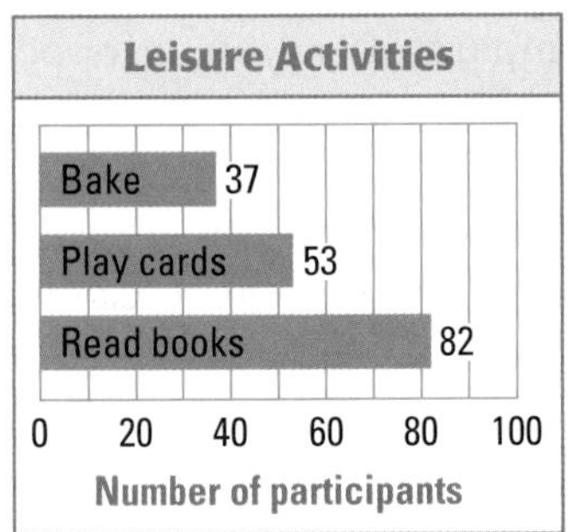

4. Which activities have fewer than 60 participants?

5. Of those surveyed, how many more read books than play cards?

@HomeTutor Prerequisite skills practice at classzone.com

Now

In Chapter 13, you will apply the big ideas listed below and reviewed in the Chapter Summary on page 895. You will also use the key vocabulary listed below.

Big Ideas

1. **Finding probabilities of simple and compound events**
2. **Analyzing sets of data**
3. **Making and interpreting data displays**

KEY VOCABULARY

- outcome, *p. 843*
- event, *p. 843*
- probability, *p. 843*
- odds, *p. 845*
- permutation, *p. 851*
- combination, *p. 856*
- compound event, *p. 861*
- survey, *p. 871*
- sample, *p. 871*
- measure of dispersion, *p. 876*
- range, *p. 876*
- stem-and-leaf plot, *p. 881*
- frequency, *p. 882*
- histogram, *p. 882*
- box-and-whisker plot, *p. 887*
- interquartile range, *p. 888*
- outlier, *p. 889*

Why?

You can use probability and data analysis to make predictions. For example, you can use data about a kicker's past successes in football games to find the chance of his success in the future.

Animated Algebra

The animation illustrated below for Exercise 22 on page 848 helps you to answer this question: What is the probability that the kicker makes an attempted field goal?

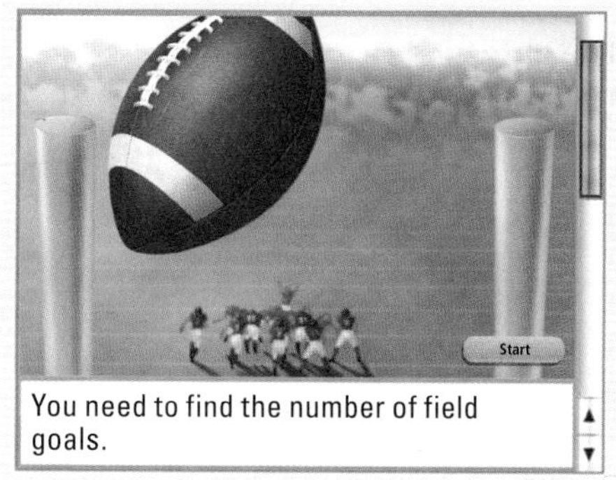

Start
You need to find the number of field goals.

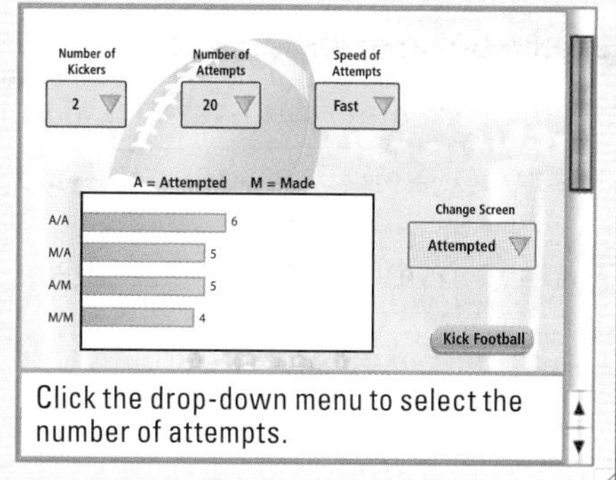

Animated Algebra at classzone.com

Other animations for Chapter 13: pages 845, 856, 875, and 887

13.1 Find a Probability

MATERIALS • paper bag

QUESTION **What is the chance that you would select the initials of a student in your class from a bag of letters?**

You can perform an experiment and record the results to approximate the likelihood of selecting the initials of a student in your class.

EXPLORE Perform an experiment

STEP 1 ***Select letters***

Write each of the 26 letters of the alphabet on separate pieces of paper. Put all of the letters into a bag. Select a letter at random (without looking into the bag). Replace the letter and select a second letter at random.

STEP 2 ***Record the results***

Record the results of the selections in a table like the one shown.

- If the first letter is the first initial of any student in your class, put a tally mark in the "first initial" column.
- If the second letter is the last initial of any student in your class, put a tally mark in the "last initial" column.
- If the two letters are the first and last initials of any student in your class, put a tally mark in the "both initials" column, but do not put a tally mark in the other columns.

Perform this experiment 30 times.

	First initial	Last initial	Both initials
Tally	卌	卌 II	I
Frequency	?	?	?

STEP 3 ***Record the frequencies***

Record the *frequency*, the total number of tally marks, of each possible result.

DRAW CONCLUSIONS Use your observations to complete these excercises

1. For what fraction of the times that you performed the experiment did you select the first initial of a student in your class? the last initial? both?
2. Which of these results do you think is least likely to happen if you repeat the experiment 30 more times? *Explain* your choice.
3. **REASONING** You perform the experiment 90 times. How many times do you expect to select both the first and last initials of a student in your class? *Explain* how you made your prediction.

13.1 Find Probabilities and Odds

Before You made organized lists and tree diagrams.

Now You will find sample spaces and probabilities.

Why? So you can find the likelihood of an event, as in Example 2.

Key Vocabulary
- outcome
- event
- sample space
- probability
- odds

A possible result of an experiment is an **outcome**. For instance, when you roll a number cube there are 6 possible outcomes: a 1, 2, 3, 4, 5, or 6. An **event** is an outcome or a collection of outcomes, such as rolling an odd number. The set of all possible outcomes is called a **sample space**.

EXAMPLE 1 Find a sample space

You flip a coin and roll a number cube. How many possible outcomes are in the sample space? List the possible outcomes.

REVIEW TREE DIAGRAMS
For help with tree diagrams, see p. 931.

Solution

Use a tree diagram to find the outcomes in the sample space.

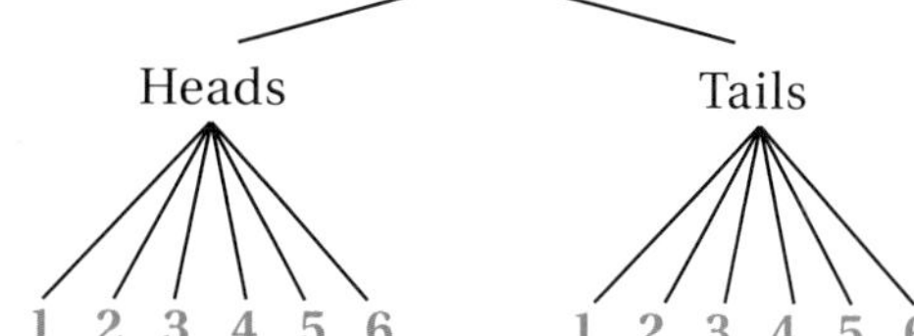

Coin flip Heads Tails

Number cube roll 1 2 3 4 5 6 1 2 3 4 5 6

The sample space has 12 possible outcomes. They are listed below.

Heads, 1	Heads, 2	Heads, 3	Heads, 4	Heads, 5	Heads, 6
Tails, 1	Tails, 2	Tails, 3	Tails, 4	Tails, 5	Tails, 6

✓ GUIDED PRACTICE for Example 1

1. You flip 2 coins and roll a number cube. How many possible outcomes are in the sample space? List the possible outcomes.

PROBABILITY The **probability of an event** is a measure of the likelihood, or chance, that the event will occur. Probability is a number from 0 to 1 and can be expressed as a decimal, fraction, or percent.

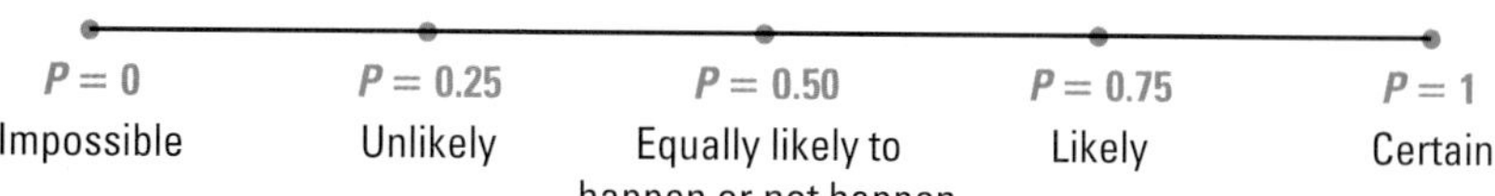

$P = 0$	$P = 0.25$	$P = 0.50$	$P = 0.75$	$P = 1$
Impossible	Unlikely	Equally likely to happen or not happen	Likely	Certain

THEORETICAL PROBABILITY The outcomes for a specified event are called *favorable outcomes.* When all outcomes are equally likely, the **theoretical probability** of the event can be found using the following:

$$\textbf{Theoretical probability} = \frac{\textbf{Number of favorable outcomes}}{\textbf{Total number of outcomes}}$$

The probability of event A is written as $P(A)$.

EXAMPLE 2 Find a theoretical probability

T-SHIRTS You and your friends designed T-shirts with silk screened emblems, and you are selling the T-shirts to raise money. The table below shows the number of T-shirts you have in each design. A student chooses a T-shirt at random. What is the probability that the student chooses a red T-shirt?

	Gold emblem	Silver emblem
Green T-shirt	10	8
Red T-shirt	6	6

Solution

You and your friends have a total of $10 + 6 + 8 + 6 = 30$ T-shirts. So, there are 30 possible outcomes. Of all the T-shirts, 12 T-shirts are red. There are 12 favorable outcomes.

$$P(\text{red T-shirt}) = \frac{\text{Number of favorable outcomes}}{\text{Total number of outcomes}}$$

$$= \frac{\text{Number of red T-shirts}}{\text{Total number of T-shirts}}$$

$$= \frac{12}{30}$$

$$= \frac{2}{5}$$

GUIDED PRACTICE for Example 2

2. **T-SHIRTS** In Example 2, what is the probability that the student chooses a T-shirt with a gold emblem?
3. You toss a coin and roll a number cube. What is the probability that the coin shows tails and the number cube shows 4?

EXPERIMENTAL PROBABILITY An **experimental probability** is based on repeated *trials* of an experiment. The number of trials is the number of times the experiment is performed. Each trial in which a favorable outcome occurs is called a *success.*

$$\textbf{Experimental probability} = \frac{\textbf{Number of successes}}{\textbf{Number of trials}}$$

★ EXAMPLE 3 Standardized Test Practice

Each section of the spinner shown has the same area. The spinner was spun 20 times. The table shows the results. For which color is the experimental probability of stopping on the color the same as the theoretical probability?

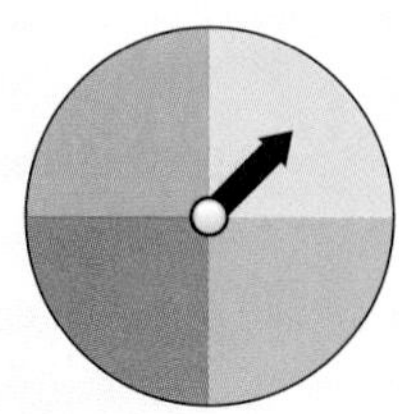

Spinner Results			
Red	Green	Blue	Yellow
5	9	3	3

Ⓐ Red Ⓑ Green Ⓒ Blue Ⓓ Yellow

Solution

The theoretical probability of stopping on each of the four colors is $\frac{1}{4}$. Use the outcomes in the table to find the experimental probabilities.

$P(\text{red}) = \frac{5}{20} = \frac{1}{4}$ $P(\text{green}) = \frac{9}{20}$ $P(\text{blue}) = \frac{3}{20}$ $P(\text{yellow}) = \frac{3}{20}$

▶ The correct answer is A. Ⓐ Ⓑ Ⓒ Ⓓ

Animated Algebra at classzone.com

ODDS The odds of an event compare the number of favorable and unfavorable outcomes when all outcomes are equally likely.

$$\textbf{Odds in favor} = \frac{\textbf{Number of favorable outcomes}}{\textbf{Number of unfavorable outcomes}}$$

$$\textbf{Odds against} = \frac{\textbf{Number of unfavorable outcomes}}{\textbf{Number of favorable outcomes}}$$

EXAMPLE 4 Find the odds

READING
Odds are read as the ratio of one number to another. For instance, the odds $\frac{3}{1}$ are read as "three to one." Odds are usually written as $a : b$.

SPINNER In Example 3, find the odds against stopping on green.

Solution

The 4 possible outcomes are all equally likely. Green is the 1 favorable outcome. The other 3 colors are unfavorable outcomes.

$$\text{Odds against green} = \frac{\text{Number of unfavorable outcomes}}{\text{Number of favorable outcomes}} = \frac{3}{1} \text{ or } 3 : 1.$$

✓ GUIDED PRACTICE for Examples 3 and 4

4. In Example 3, for which color is the experimental probability of stopping on the color greater than the theoretical probability?
5. In Example 3, what are the odds in favor of stopping on blue?

13.1 EXERCISES

HOMEWORK KEY

○ = **WORKED-OUT SOLUTIONS** on p. WS31 for Exs. 3 and 21

★ = **STANDARDIZED TEST PRACTICE** Exs. 2, 14–16, 21, and 22

SKILL PRACTICE

1. **VOCABULARY** Copy and complete: A number that describes the likelihood of an event is the _?_ of the event.

2. ★ **WRITING** *Explain* how the probability of an event differs from the odds in favor of the event when all outcomes are equally likely.

EXAMPLE 1 on p. 843 for Exs. 3–6

SAMPLE SPACE In Exercises 3–6, find the number of possible outcomes in the sample space. Then list the possible outcomes.

3. A bag contains 4 red cards numbered 1–4, 4 white cards numbered 1–4, and 4 black cards numbered 1–4. You choose a card at random.

4. You toss two coins.

5. You roll a number cube and toss three coins.

6. You roll two number cubes.

EXAMPLE 2 on p. 844 for Exs. 7–8

PROBABILITY AND ODDS In Exercises 7–13, refer to the spinner shown. The spinner is divided into sections with the same area.

7. What is the probability that the spinner stops on a multiple of 3?

8. **ERROR ANALYSIS** *Describe* and correct the error in finding the probability of stopping on a multiple of 9.

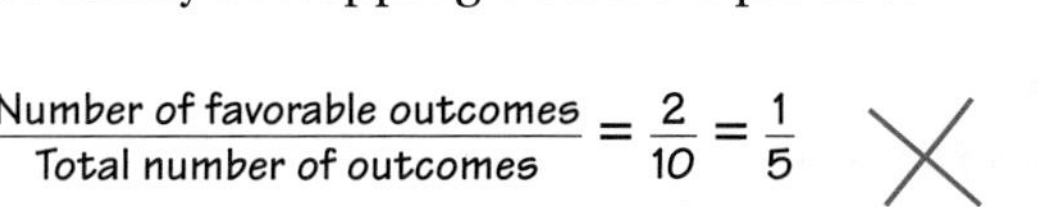

Number of favorable outcomes / Total number of outcomes = 2/10 = 1/5

EXAMPLE 3 on p. 845 for Exs. 9–10

9. You spin the spinner 30 times. It stops on 12 three times. What is the experimental probability of stopping on 12?

10. You spin the spinner 10 times. It stops on an even number 6 times. What is the experimental probability of stopping on an even number?

EXAMPLE 4 on p. 845 for Exs. 11–14

11. What are the odds in favor of stopping on a multiple of 4?

12. What are the odds against stopping on a number less than 12?

13. **ERROR ANALYSIS** *Describe* and correct the error in finding the odds in favor of stopping on a multiple of 3.

Odds in favor of a multiple of 3 = $\frac{\text{Number of favorable outcomes}}{\text{Total number of outcomes}} = \frac{9}{10}$ or 9 : 10

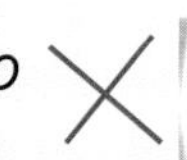

14. ★ **MULTIPLE CHOICE** The odds in favor of an event are 5 : 8. What are the odds against the event?

Ⓐ 3 : 8 Ⓑ 8 : 3 Ⓒ 5 : 8 Ⓓ 8 : 5

15. ★ **OPEN-ENDED** *Describe* a real-world event whose probability is 0. *Describe* another real-world event whose probability is 1.

16. ★ **MULTIPLE CHOICE** According to a meteorologist, there is a 40% chance that it will rain today. What are the odds in favor of rain?

(A) 2 : 5 (B) 2 : 3 (C) 3 : 2 (D) 4 : 1

17. **NUMBER CUBES** Make a table showing all of the possible sums that result from rolling two number cubes. (Columns represent the possible outcomes of the first number cube. Rows represent the possible outcomes of the second number cube. The cells of the table represent the sums of the two outcomes.) Then find the probability of rolling each sum.

18. **CHALLENGE** A bag holds red, white, and blue marbles. You randomly draw a marble from the bag. The odds against drawing a white marble are 47 : 3.

   a. There are fewer than 100 marbles in the bag. How many marbles are in the bag? *Justify* your answer.

   b. The probability of drawing a red marble is 0.5. What is the probability of drawing a blue marble? *Explain* how you found your answer.

PROBLEM SOLVING

EXAMPLE 2 on p. 844 for Exs. 19–20

19. **MUSIC PROGRAM** You have created a playlist of 7 songs on your MP3 player. You play these songs in a random shuffle, where each song has an equally likely chance of being played. What is the probability that the second song on the list will be played first?

@HomeTutor for problem solving help at classzone.com

20. **SURVEY** A survey asked a total of 600 students (100 male students and 100 female students who were 11, 13, and 15 years old) about their exercise habits. The table shows the numbers of students who said they exercise 2 hours or more each week.

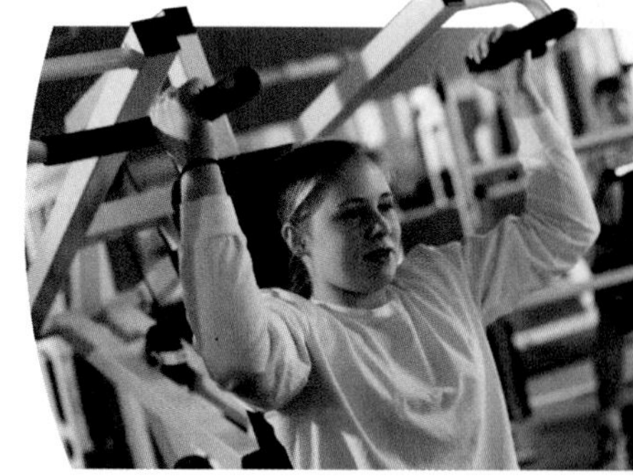

	11 years	13 years	15 years
Female	53	57	51
Male	65	68	67

   a. What is the probability that a randomly selected female student who participated in this survey exercises 2 hours or more each week?

   b. What is the probability that a randomly selected 15-year-old student who participated in this survey exercises 2 hours or more each week?

   c. What is the probability that a randomly selected student who participated in this survey exercises 2 hours or more each week?

@HomeTutor for problem solving help at classzone.com

EXAMPLES 2 and 4 on pp. 844–845 for Ex. 21

21. ★ **SHORT RESPONSE** Suppose there are 15 girls and 12 boys in your homeroom. The teacher chooses one student representative at random. What is the probability that a boy is chosen? What are the odds in favor of choosing a boy? *Explain* how the probablity and odds are related.

22. ★ **EXTENDED RESPONSE** The table shows the 2003 regular season field goal statistics for kicker Adam Vinatieri.

	Point difference at end of game		
	0–7 points	8–14 points	≥ 15 points
Field goals attempted	20	11	3
Field goals made	16	7	2

a. During the 2003 regular season, what was the probability that Adam Vinatieri would make an attempted field goal, regardless of the point difference?

b. Find the probabilities that Vinatieri made an attempted field goal when the point difference at the end of the game was 0–7 points, 8–14 points, and at least 15 points.

c. During what kinds of games was Adam Vinatieri most likely to make attempted field goals? *Justify* your answer.

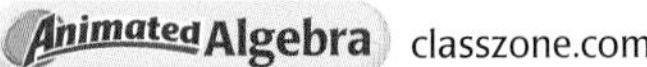

classzone.com

23. **CHALLENGE** The table shows the results of Congressional elections that involved incumbent candidates (representatives or senators who ran for re-election) during the period 1980–2000.

	Incumbent representatives		Incumbent senators	
	Ran	Re-elected	Ran	Re-elected
Presidential election year	2373	2235	163	130
Midterm election year	1984	1873	145	130

a. Did a representative or a senator have a better chance of being re-elected? *Justify* your answer using the data in the table.

b. Did a member of Congress have a better chance of being re-elected during a presidential election year than during a midterm election year? *Justify* your answer.

MIXED REVIEW

PREVIEW
Prepare for Lesson 13.2 in Exs. 24–26.

Use the indicated counting method to answer the question. *(p. 931)*

24. You have 3 posters to hang beside each other on a wall. In how many different ways can you hang the posters? (Make a list.)

25. Members of a credit union choose a personal identification number (PIN) for their debit card. The PIN consists of 4 digits from 0 to 9. Digits cannot be repeated. How many PINs are possible? (Use the counting principle.)

26. Weekly pottery classes are offered on Monday, Wednesday, and Thursday. On each of those days there is a class at 5:00 and a class at 7:00. How many classes are offered? (Make a tree diagram.)

Perform Simulations

GOAL Perform simulations to make predictions.

Key Vocabulary
- **simulation**

A **simulation** is an experiment that you can perform to make predictions about real-world situations.

EXAMPLE 1 Perform a simulation

CONCESSION PRIZES Each time you buy an item from the concession stand at a baseball stadium, you receive a prize coupon, chosen at random. There is an equal chance of winning each prize from the following list: hot dog, popcorn, peanuts, pretzel, ice cream, and small drink. About how many times must you buy an item from the concession stand before you win each prize at least once?

Solution

You can perform a simulation to answer the question.

STEP 1 **Write** each prize on a separate piece of paper. Put the pieces of paper in a container.

STEP 2 **Draw** a piece of paper from the container at random. Record the result in a table like the one shown. Put the piece of paper back in the container. Repeat until you put a tally mark in the last empty cell of the table.

Prize	Hot dog	Popcorn	Peanuts	Pretzel	Ice cream	Small drink
Tally	I	IIII	II	𝍸	𝍸 I	II

The sum of all of the tally marks is the number of times you must buy an item from the concession stand before you win each prize at least once.

▶ In this simulation, you must buy an item from the concession stand 20 times.

USING A GRAPHING CALCULATOR You can also use the random integer generator on a graphing calculator to perform simulations.

The random integer generator is found by pressing the MATH key and selecting the PRB menu. It is the fifth item on the list and is displayed as randInt(.

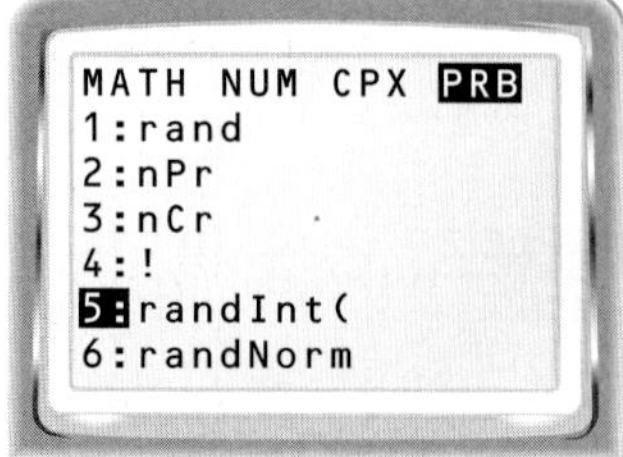

EXAMPLE 2 Perform a simulation using technology

GAME CARDS You receive a game card with every purchase at a sandwich shop. Each card has two circles to scratch. One circle reveals a prize, and the other says "Not a Winner." You cannot claim a prize if you scratch both circles. There is a $\frac{1}{6}$ chance that a card is for a CD, a $\frac{1}{2}$ chance that it is for a drink, and a $\frac{1}{3}$ chance that it is for a sandwich. About how many game cards must you scratch before you win a CD?

Solution

STEP 1 **Use** List 1 to show whether you scratch the circle with the prize. Generate a list of 50 random 1s and 0s. Each 1 means that you scratch the circle with the prize, and each 0 means that you scratch "Not a Winner."

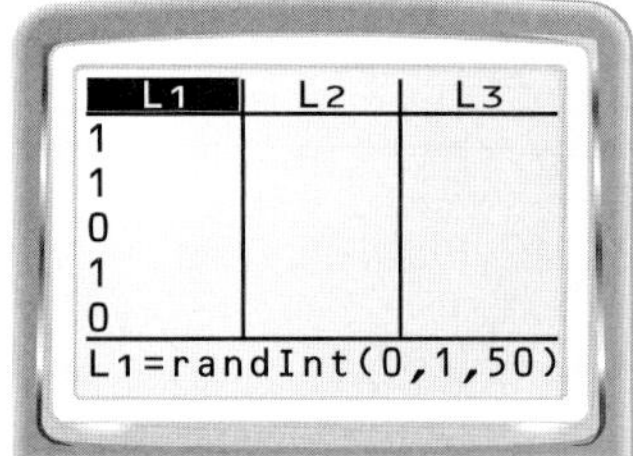

Press STAT and select Edit. Highlight L_1. Enter randInt(0,1,50).

STEP 2 **Use** List 2 to show whether your game card contains the CD as the prize. Generate a list of 50 random integers from 1 to 6. Each 1 represents a prize card with a CD.

Highlight L_2. Enter randInt(1,6,50).

STEP 3 **Compare** the results of your two lists using List 3. Multiply the numbers from List 1 and List 2. Each 0 in List 3 means that you chose the wrong circle, so the prize does not matter. Because $1 \cdot 1 = 1$, you chose the correct circle *and* your card contains the CD prize when you see a 1 in L_3.

L1	L2	L3
1	3	3
1	2	2
0	1	0
1	1	1
0	2	0

L3=L1∗L2

Highlight L_3. Enter L_1*L_2.

STEP 4 **Find** the first occurrence of a 1 in List 3. In this simulation, you can see that the first occurrence of a 1 in List 3 happens after 4 trials.

▶ For this simulation, you must scratch 4 game cards before you win a CD.

PRACTICE

EXAMPLE 1
on p. 849
for Exs. 1–3

1. In Example 1, suppose you can receive a prize coupon for nachos in addition to the items listed in the example. About how many times must you buy an item from the concession stand before you win each prize at least once? *Explain* how you found your answer.

EXAMPLE 2
on p. 850
for Exs. 2–3

2. In Example 2, about how many game cards must you scratch before you win one of each prize? *Explain* how you found your answer.

3. In Example 2, there are 3 prizes. *Explain* why the results of the simulation would be inaccurate if you generated random integers from 1 to 3.

13.2 Find Probabilities Using Permutations

Before You used the counting principle.

Now You will use the formula for the number of permutations.

Why? So you can find the number of possible arrangements, as in Ex. 38.

Key Vocabulary
- **permutation**
- ***n* factorial**

A **permutation** is an arrangement of objects in which order is important. For instance, the 6 possible permutations of the letters A, B, and C are shown.

ABC ACB BAC BCA CAB CBA

EXAMPLE 1 Count permutations

Consider the number of permutations of the letters in the word JULY.

a. In how many ways can you arrange all of the letters?

b. In how many ways can you arrange 2 of the letters?

Solution

REVIEW COUNTING PRINCIPLE
For help with using the counting principle, see p. 931.

a. Use the counting principle to find the number of permutations of the letters in the word JULY.

$$\text{Number of permutations} = \text{Choices for 1st letter} \cdot \text{Choices for 2nd letter} \cdot \text{Choices for 3rd letter} \cdot \text{Choices for 4th letter}$$

$$= 4 \cdot 3 \cdot 2 \cdot 1$$

$$= 24$$

▶ There are 24 ways you can arrange all of the letters in the word JULY.

b. When arranging 2 letters of the word JULY, you have 4 choices for the first letter and 3 choices for the second letter.

$$\text{Number of permutations} = \text{Choices for 1st letter} \cdot \text{Choices for 2nd letter}$$

$$= 4 \cdot 3$$

$$= 12$$

▶ There are 12 ways you can arrange 2 of the letters in the word JULY.

✓ GUIDED PRACTICE for Example 1

1. In how many ways can you arrange the letters in the word MOUSE?
2. In how many ways can you arrange 3 of the letters in the word ORANGE?

FACTORIAL In Example 1, you evaluated the expression $4 \cdot 3 \cdot 2 \cdot 1$. This expression can be written as 4! and is read "4 *factorial*." For any positive integer n, the product of the integers from 1 to n is called ***n* factorial** and is written as $n!$. The value of 0! is defined to be 1.

$$n! = n \cdot (n-1) \cdot (n-2) \cdot \ldots \cdot 3 \cdot 2 \cdot 1 \text{ and } 0! = 1$$

In Example 1, you also found the permutations of four objects taken two at a time. You can find the number of permutations using the formulas below.

KEY CONCEPT *For Your Notebook*

Permutations

Formulas	Examples
The number of permutations of n objects is given by: $_nP_n = n!$	The number of permutations of 4 objects is: $_4P_4 = 4! = 4 \cdot 3 \cdot 2 \cdot 1 = 24$
The number of permutations of n objects taken r at a time, where $r \le n$, is given by: $_nP_r = \frac{n!}{(n-r)!}$	The number of permutations of 4 objects taken 2 at a time is: $_4P_2 = \frac{4!}{(4-2)!} = \frac{4 \cdot 3 \cdot \cancel{2!}}{\cancel{2!}} = 12$

EXAMPLE 2 Use a permutations formula

CD RECORDING Your band has written 12 songs and plans to record 9 of them for a CD. In how many ways can you arrange the songs on the CD?

Solution

To find the number of permutations of 9 songs chosen from 12, find $_{12}P_9$.

$_{12}P_9 = \frac{12!}{(12-9)!}$ — Permutations formula

$= \frac{12!}{3!}$ — Subtract.

$= \frac{12 \cdot 11 \cdot 10 \cdot 9 \cdot 8 \cdot 7 \cdot 6 \cdot 5 \cdot 4 \cdot \cancel{3!}}{\cancel{3!}}$ — Expand factorials. Divide out common factor, 3!.

$= 79{,}833{,}600$ — Multiply.

▶ There are 79,833,600 ways to arrange 9 songs out of 12.

DIVIDE COMMON FACTORS
When you divide out common factors, remember that 3! is a factor of 12!.

✓ **GUIDED PRACTICE** for Example 2

3. **WHAT IF?** In Example 2, suppose your band has written 15 songs. You will record 9 of them for a CD. In how many ways can you arrange the songs on the CD?

EXAMPLE 3 Find a probability using permutations

PARADE For a town parade, you will ride on a float with your soccer team. There are 12 floats in the parade, and their order is chosen at random. Find the probability that your float is first and the float with the school chorus is second.

Solution

STEP 1 **Write** the number of possible outcomes as the number of permutations of the 12 floats in the parade. This is ${}_{12}P_{12} = 12!$.

STEP 2 **Write** the number of favorable outcomes as the number of permutations of the other floats, given that the soccer team is first and the chorus is second. This is ${}_{10}P_{10} = 10!$.

STEP 3 **Calculate** the probability.

$$P\begin{pmatrix}\text{soccer team is first} \\ \text{chorus is second}\end{pmatrix} = \frac{10!}{12!}$$ **Form a ratio of favorable to possible outcomes.**

$$= \frac{\cancel{10!}}{12 \cdot 11 \cdot \cancel{10!}}$$ **Expand factorials. Divide out common factor, 10!.**

$$= \frac{1}{132}$$ **Simplify.**

GUIDED PRACTICE for Example 3

4. **WHAT IF?** In Example 3, suppose there are 14 floats in the parade. Find the probability that the soccer team is first and the chorus is second.

13.2 EXERCISES

HOMEWORK KEY

○ = **WORKED-OUT SOLUTIONS** on p. WS32 for Exs. 21 and 35

★ = **STANDARDIZED TEST PRACTICE** Exs. 2, 11, 30, 33, and 35

◆ = **MULTIPLE REPRESENTATIONS** Ex. 34

SKILL PRACTICE

1. **VOCABULARY** Copy and complete: An arrangement of objects in which order is important is called a(n) __?__.

2. ★ **WRITING** *Explain* what the notation ${}_9P_2$ means. What is the value of this expression?

EXAMPLES 1 and 2 on pp. 851–852 for Exs. 3–11

COUNTING PERMUTATIONS **Find the number of ways you can arrange (a) all of the letters in the given word and (b) 2 of the letters in the word.**

3. AT	4. TRY	5. GAME	6. CAT
7. WATER	8. ROCK	9. APRIL	10. FAMILY

11. ★ **OPEN-ENDED** *Describe* a real-world situation where the number of possibilities is given by ${}_5P_2$.

EXAMPLE 2
on p. 852
for Exs. 12–30

FACTORIALS AND PERMUTATIONS **Evaluate the expression.**

12. 1! **13.** 3! **14.** 0! **15.** 5!

16. 8! **17.** 10! **18.** 12! **19.** 13!

20. ${}_5P_2$ **(21.)** ${}_7P_3$ **22.** ${}_9P_1$ **23.** ${}_6P_5$

24. ${}_8P_8$ **25.** ${}_{12}P_0$ **26.** ${}_{30}P_2$ **27.** ${}_{25}P_5$

ERROR ANALYSIS ***Describe*** **and correct the error in evaluating the expression.**

28. $${}_{11}P_7 = \frac{11!}{(11-7)} = \frac{11!}{4} = 9{,}979{,}200 \quad \times$$

29. $${}_5P_3 = \frac{5!}{3!} = \frac{5 \cdot 4 \cdot \cancel{3!}}{\cancel{3!}} = 20 \quad \times$$

30. ★ **MULTIPLE CHOICE** The judges in an art contest award prizes for first, second, and third place out of 11 entries. Which expression gives the number of ways the judges can award first, second, and third place?

Ⓐ $\frac{3!}{11!}$ Ⓑ $\frac{8!}{11!}$ Ⓒ $\frac{11!}{8!}$ Ⓓ $\frac{11!}{3!}$

31. **CHALLENGE** Consider a set of 4 objects and a set of n objects.

a. Are there more permutations of all 4 of the objects or of 3 of the 4 objects? *Justify* your answer using an organized list.

b. In general, are there more permutations of n objects taken n at a time or of n objects taken $n - 1$ at a time? *Justify* your answer using the formula for the number of permutations.

PROBLEM SOLVING

EXAMPLE 2
on p. 852
for Exs. 32–33

32. **MOVIES** Six friends go to a movie theater. In how many different ways can they sit together in a row of 6 empty seats?

@HomeTutor for problem solving help at classzone.com

33. ★ **MULTIPLE CHOICE** You plan to visit 4 stores during a shopping trip. In how many orders can you visit these stores?

Ⓐ 4 Ⓑ 16 Ⓒ 24 Ⓓ 256

@HomeTutor for problem solving help at classzone.com

EXAMPLE 3
on p. 853
for Exs. 34–38

34. ◆ **MULTIPLE REPRESENTATIONS** You and your friend are two of 4 servers working a shift in a restaurant. The host assigns tables of new diners to the servers in a particular order. This order remains the same, so that all servers are likely to wait on the same number of tables by the end of the shift.

a. Making a List List all the possible orders in which the host can assign tables to the servers.

b. Using a Formula Use the formula for permutations to find the number of ways in which the host can assign tables to the servers.

c. Describe in Words What is the likelihood that you and your friend are assigned the first 2 tables? *Explain* your answer using probability.

35. ★ **SHORT RESPONSE** Every student in your history class is required to present a project in front of the class. Each day, 4 students make their presentations in an order chosen at random by the teacher. You make your presentation on the first day.

a. What is the probability that you are chosen to be the first or second presenter on the first day? *Explain* how you found your answer.

b. What is the probability that you are chosen to be the second or third presenter on the first day? *Compare* your answer with that in part (a).

36. **HISTORY EXAM** On an exam, you are asked to list 5 historical events in the order in which they occurred. You guess the order of the events at random. What is the probability that you choose the correct order?

37. **SPIRIT** You make 6 posters to hold up at a basketball game. Each poster has a letter of the word TIGERS. You and 5 friends sit next to each other in a row. The posters are distributed at random. What is the probability that TIGERS is spelled correctly when you hold up the posters?

38. **BAND COMPETITION** Seven marching bands will perform at a competition. The order of the performances is determined at random. What is the probability that your school band will perform first, followed by the band from the one other high school in your town?

39. **CHALLENGE** You are one of 10 students performing in a school talent show. The order of the performances is determined at random. The first five performers go on stage before the intermission, while the remaining five performers go on stage after the intermission.

a. What is the probability that you are the last performer before the intermission and your rival performs immediately before you?

b. What is the probability that you are *not* the first performer?

MIXED REVIEW

PREVIEW
Prepare for Lesson 13.3 in Exs. 40–43.

40. You are randomly assigned a day of the week to work an extra shift at your part-time job. Find the probability that you are assigned to work on Saturday. *(p. 843)*

41. You choose a letter at random out of a bag that contains one of each letter of the alphabet. Find the probability that you choose the letter K. *(p. 843)*

42. You roll a number cube. Find the probability that you roll an even number. *(p. 843)*

43. You toss a coin twice. Find the probability that the coin shows tails twice. *(p. 843)*

13.3 Find Probabilities Using Combinations

Before You used permutations to count possibilities.

Now You will use combinations to count possibilities.

Why? So you can find the probability of an event, as in Example 3.

Key Vocabulary
- **combination**

A **combination** is a selection of objects in which order is *not* important. For instance, in a drawing for 3 identical prizes, you would use combinations, because the order of the winners would not matter. If the prizes were different, you would use permutations, because the order would matter.

EXAMPLE 1 Count combinations

Count the combinations of two letters from the list A, B, C, D.

Solution

List all of the permutations of two letters in the list A, B, C, D. Because order is not important in a combination, cross out any duplicate pairs.

AB	AC	AD	~~BA~~	BC	BD
~~CA~~	~~CB~~	CD	~~DA~~	~~DB~~	~~DC~~

BD and DB are the same pair.

▶ There are 6 possible combinations of 2 letters from the list A, B, C, D.

 Animated Algebra at classzone.com

✓ GUIDED PRACTICE for Example 1

1. Count the combinations of 3 letters from the list A, B, C, D, E.

COMBINATIONS In Example 1, you found the number of combinations of objects by making an organized list. You can also find the number of combinations using the following formula.

KEY CONCEPT *For Your Notebook*

Combinations

Formula

The number of combinations of n objects taken r at a time, where $r \leq n$, is given by:

$${}_nC_r = \frac{n!}{(n-r)! \cdot r!}$$

Example

The number of combinations of 4 objects taken 2 at a time is:

$${}_4C_2 = \frac{4!}{(4-2)! \cdot 2!} = \frac{4 \cdot 3 \cdot \cancel{2!}}{\cancel{2!} \cdot (2 \cdot 1)} = 6$$

EXAMPLE 2 Use the combinations formula

LUNCH MENU You order a sandwich at a restaurant. You can choose 2 side dishes from a list of 8. How many combinations of side dishes are possible?

Solution

The order in which you choose the side dishes is not important. So, to find the number of combinations of 8 side dishes taken 2 at a time, find ${}_8C_2$.

$${}_8C_2 = \frac{8!}{(8-2)! \cdot 2!}$$ Combinations formula

$$= \frac{8!}{6! \cdot 2!}$$ Subtract.

$$= \frac{8 \cdot 7 \cdot \cancel{6!}}{\cancel{6!} \cdot (2 \cdot 1)}$$ Expand factorials. Divide out common factor, 6!.

$$= 28$$ Simplify.

▶ There are 28 different combinations of side dishes you can order.

EXAMPLE 3 Find a probability using combinations

PHOTOGRAPHY A yearbook editor has selected 14 photos, including one of you and one of your friend, to use in a collage for the yearbook. The photos are placed at random. There is room for 2 photos at the top of the page. What is the probability that your photo and your friend's photo are the two placed at the top of the page?

Solution

STEP 1 **Write** the number of possible outcomes as the number of combinations of 14 photos taken 2 at a time, or ${}_{14}C_2$, because the order in which the photos are chosen is not important.

$${}_{14}C_2 = \frac{14!}{(14-2)! \cdot 2!} = \frac{14!}{12! \cdot 2!} = \frac{14 \cdot 13 \cdot \cancel{12!}}{\cancel{12!} \cdot (2 \cdot 1)} = 91$$

STEP 2 **Find** the number of favorable outcomes. Only one of the possible combinations includes your photo and your friend's photo.

STEP 3 **Calculate** the probability.

$P(\text{your photo and your friend's photos are chosen}) = \frac{1}{91}$

GUIDED PRACTICE for Examples 2 and 3

2. **WHAT IF?** In Example 2, suppose you can choose 3 side dishes out of the list of 8 side dishes. How many combinations are possible?

3. **WHAT IF?** In Example 3, suppose there are 20 photos in the collage. Find the probability that your photo and your friend's photo are the two placed at the top of the page.

13.3 EXERCISES

HOMEWORK KEY

◯ = **WORKED-OUT SOLUTIONS** on p. WS32 for Exs. 7 and 25

★ = **STANDARDIZED TEST PRACTICE** Exs. 2, 14–20, and 25

SKILL PRACTICE

1. **VOCABULARY** Copy and complete: A(n) __?__ is a selection of objects in which order is not important.

2. ★ **WRITING** *Explain* how a combination differs from a permutation.

EXAMPLE 1 on p. 856 for Exs. 3, 4

3. **COMBINATIONS** How many combinations of 3 letters from the list A, B, C, D, E, F are possible?

4. **ERROR ANALYSIS** *Describe* and correct the error in listing all of the possible combinations of 2 letters from the list A, B, C.

AB	BA	CA
AC	BC	CB

EXAMPLE 2 on p. 857 for Exs. 5–15

5. **ERROR ANALYSIS** *Describe* and correct the error in evaluating ${}_9C_4$.

$${}_9C_4 = \frac{9!}{(9-4)!} = \frac{9!}{5!} = 3024$$

COMBINATIONS Evaluate the expression.

6. ${}_5C_1$ 7. ${}_8C_5$ 8. ${}_9C_9$ 9. ${}_8C_6$

10. ${}_{12}C_3$ 11. ${}_{11}C_4$ 12. ${}_{15}C_8$ 13. ${}_{20}C_5$

14. ★ **MULTIPLE CHOICE** What is the value of ${}_{10}C_6$?

Ⓐ 7 Ⓑ 60 Ⓒ 210 Ⓓ 151,200

15. ★ **MULTIPLE CHOICE** You have the first season of your favorite television show on a set of DVDs. The set contains 13 episodes. You have time to watch 3 episodes. How many combinations of 3 episodes can you watch?

Ⓐ 286 Ⓑ 572 Ⓒ 1716 Ⓓ 589,680

★ **SHORT RESPONSE In Exercises 16–19, tell whether the question can be answered using *combinations* or *permutations*. *Explain* your choice, then answer the question.**

16. Four students from your class of 120 students will be selected to organize a fundraiser. How many groups of 4 students are possible?

17. Ten students are auditioning for 3 different roles in a play. In how many ways can the 3 roles be filled?

18. To complete an exam, you must answer 8 questions from a list of 10 questions. In how many ways can you complete the exam?

19. In how many ways can 5 people sit in a car that holds 5 passengers?

20. ★ **WRITING** Which is greater, ${}_6P_r$ or ${}_6C_r$? *Justify* your answer.

21. **REASONING** Write an equation that relates ${}_nP_r$ and ${}_nC_r$. *Explain* your reasoning.

22. **CHALLENGE** Prove that ${}_nC_r = {}_nC_{n-r}$. *Explain* why this makes sense.

PROBLEM SOLVING

EXAMPLE 2
on p. 857
for Ex. 23

23. **RESTAURANT** You are ordering a burrito with 2 main ingredients and 3 toppings. The menu below shows the possible choices. How many different burritos are possible?

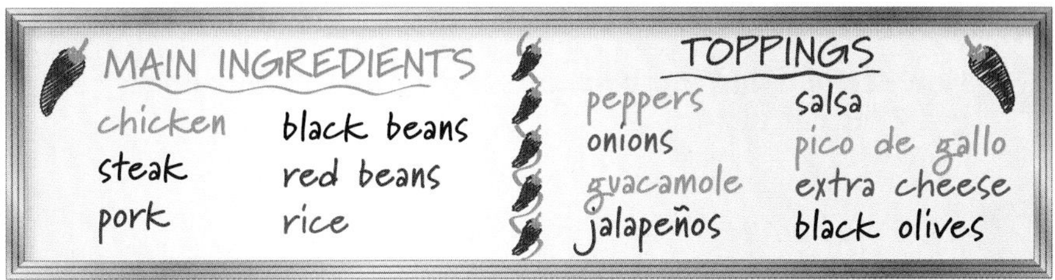

MAIN INGREDIENTS
chicken
black beans
steak
red beans
pork
rice
TOPPINGS
peppers
salsa
onions
pico de gallo
guacamole
extra cheese
jalapeños
black olives

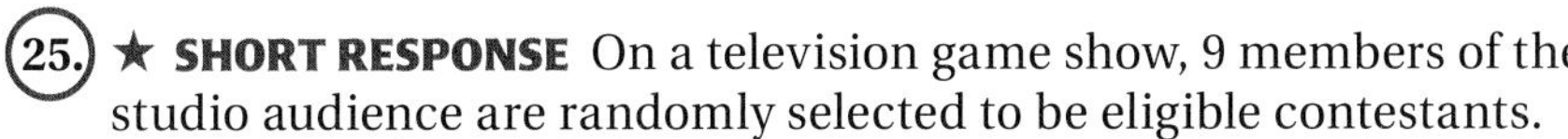
@HomeTutor for problem solving help at classzone.com

EXAMPLE 3
on p. 857
for Exs. 24–26

24. **WORK SCHEDULE** You work 3 evenings each week at a bookstore. Your supervisor assigns you 3 evenings at random from the 7 possibilities. What is the probability that your schedule this week includes working on Friday?

@HomeTutor for problem solving help at classzone.com

25. ★ **SHORT RESPONSE** On a television game show, 9 members of the studio audience are randomly selected to be eligible contestants.

 a. Six of the 9 eligible contestants are randomly chosen to play a game on the stage. How many combinations of 6 players from the group of eligible contestants are possible?

 b. You and your two friends are part of the group of 9 eligible contestants. What is the probability that all three of you are chosen to play the game on stage? *Explain* how you found your answer.

26. **REPRESENTATIVES** Your teacher chooses 2 students at random to represent your homeroom. The homeroom has a total of 30 students, including your best friend. What is the probability that you and your best friend are chosen? What is the probability that you are chosen first and your best friend is chosen second? Which event is more likely to occur?

27. **CHALLENGE** There are 30 students in your class. Your science teacher will choose 5 students at random to complete a group project. Find the probability that you and your 2 best friends in the science class are chosen to work in the group. *Explain* how you found your answer.

MIXED REVIEW

PREVIEW
Prepare for Lesson 13.4 in Exs. 28–32.

Find the product. *(p. 915)*

28. $\frac{1}{6} \cdot \frac{4}{5}$

29. $\frac{4}{25} \cdot \frac{7}{24}$

30. $\frac{13}{30} \cdot \frac{5}{26}$

31. $\frac{7}{24} \cdot \frac{4}{51}$

32. You roll a number cube. What is the probability that you roll a multiple of 3? *(p. 843)*

33. In how many ways can you arrange 3 letters from the list P, Q, R, S, T, L? *Explain* how you found your answer. *(p. 851)*

@HomeTutor
classzone.com
Keystrokes

13.3 Find Permutations and Combinations

QUESTION How can you find combinations and permutations using a graphing calculator?

EXAMPLE 1 Find the number of combinations

STARTERS There are 15 players on your softball team, but only 9 of them can be the starting players in one game. How many combinations of starting players are possible?

Solution

You are finding ${}_nC_r$ where $n = 15$ and $r = 9$. Enter 15 for n.
Press MATH. Go to the PRB menu and select ${}_nC_r$.
Then enter 9 for r.

▶ There are 5005 possible combinations of starting players.

EXAMPLE 2 Find the number of permutations

BATTING ORDER Before each softball game, your coach announces the batting order of the 9 starting players. This is the order in which the starting players will bat. How many batting orders can be formed using 9 players on your team of 15 players?

Solution

You are finding ${}_nP_r$ where $n = 15$ and $r = 9$. Enter 15 for n.
Press MATH. Go to the PRB menu and select ${}_nP_r$.
Then enter 9 for r.

▶ There are 1,816,214,400 possible batting orders.

PRACTICE

Evaluate the expression.

1. ${}_7C_4$
2. ${}_6C_6$
3. ${}_{10}C_3$
4. ${}_{16}C_8$
5. ${}_9P_5$
6. ${}_7P_6$
7. ${}_{11}P_8$
8. ${}_{12}P_5$
9. **GROUP PROJECT** Your teacher selects 3 students from a class of 28 students to work on a project in a group. Within the group, one member must be the writer, one must be the researcher, and one must be the presenter.
   a. How many different groups of 3 can your teacher select?
   b. After the group is formed, in how many ways can the roles in the group be assigned?

13.4 Find Probabilities of Compound Events

Before You found the probability of a simple event.

Now You will find the probability of a compound event.

Why? So you can analyze scientific data, as in Ex. 23.

Key Vocabulary
- **compound event**
- **mutually exclusive events**
- **overlapping events**
- **independent events**
- **dependent events**

A **compound event** combines two or more events, using the word *and* or the word *or*. To find the probability that either event *A* or event *B* occurs, determine how the events are related. **Mutually exclusive events** have no common outcomes. **Overlapping events** have at least one common outcome.

REVIEW VENN DIAGRAMS
For help with using Venn diagrams, see p. 930.

For instance, suppose you roll a number cube.

Mutually Exclusive Events

Event *A*: Roll a 3.

Event *B*: Roll an even number.

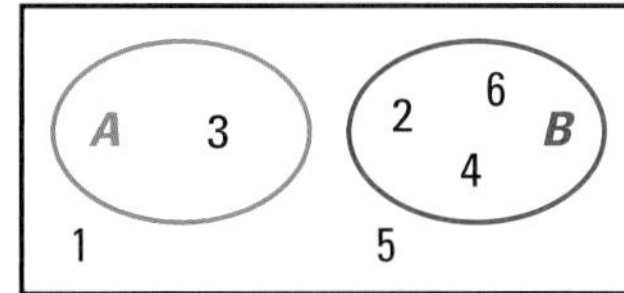

Set *A* has 1 number, and set *B* has 3 numbers.

$P(3 \text{ or even}) = \frac{1}{6} + \frac{3}{6}$

$\mathbf{P(A \text{ or } B) = P(A) + P(B)}$

Overlapping Events

Event *A*: Roll an odd number.

Event *B*: Roll a prime number.

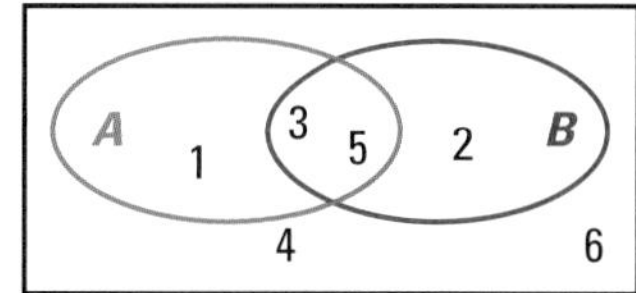

Set *A* has 3 numbers, and set *B* has 3 numbers. There are 2 numbers in both sets.

$P(\text{odd or prime}) = \frac{3}{6} + \frac{3}{6} - \frac{2}{6}$

$\mathbf{P(A \text{ or } B) = P(A) + P(B) - P(A \text{ and } B)}$

EXAMPLE 1 Find the probability of *A* or *B*

You roll a number cube. Find the probability that you roll a 2 or an odd number.

Solution

Because 2 is an even number, rolling a 2 and rolling an odd number are mutually exclusive events.

$$P(2 \text{ or odd}) = P(2) + P(\text{odd})$$
$$= \frac{1}{6} + \frac{3}{6}$$
$$= \frac{4}{6}$$
$$= \frac{2}{3}$$

EXAMPLE 2 Find the probability of *A* or *B*

You roll a number cube. Find the probability that you roll an even number or a prime number.

Solution

Because 2 is both an even number and a prime number, rolling an even number and rolling a prime number are overlapping events. There are 3 even numbers, 3 prime numbers, and 1 number that is both.

$$P(\text{even or prime}) = P(\text{even}) + P(\text{prime}) - P(\text{even and prime})$$

$$= \frac{3}{6} + \frac{3}{6} - \frac{1}{6}$$

$$= \frac{5}{6}$$

GUIDED PRACTICE for Examples 1 and 2

1. You roll a number cube. Find the probability that you roll a 2 or a 5.
2. You roll a number cube. Find the probability that you roll a number less than 4 or an odd number.

INDEPENDENT AND DEPENDENT EVENTS To find the probability that event A and event B both occur, determine how the events are related. Two events are **independent events** if the occurrence of one event has no effect on the occurrence of the other. Two events are **dependent events** if the occurrence of one event affects the occurrence of the other.

For instance, consider the probability of choosing a green marble and then a blue marble from the bag shown. If you choose one marble and replace it before choosing the second, then the events are independent. If you do not replace the first marble, then the sample space has changed, and the events are dependent.

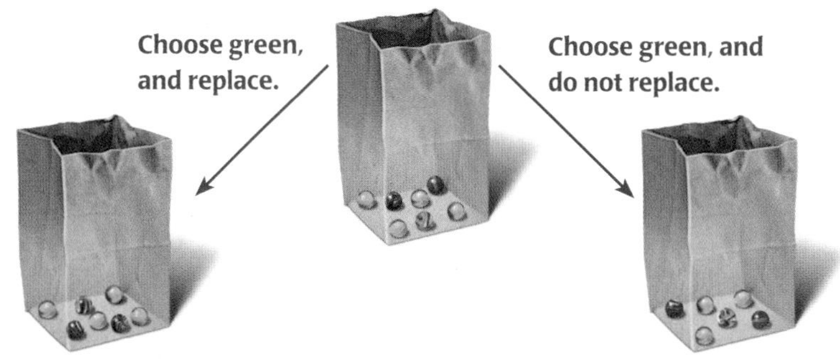
Choose green, and replace.
Choose green, and do not replace.

Independent Events

With replacement:

$P(\text{green and blue}) = \frac{4}{7} \cdot \frac{1}{7} = \frac{4}{49}$

$\mathbf{P(A \text{ and } B) = P(A) \cdot P(B)}$

Dependent Events

Without replacement:

$P(\text{green and blue}) = \frac{4}{7} \cdot \frac{1}{6} = \frac{2}{21}$

$\mathbf{P(A \text{ and } B) = P(A) \cdot P(B \text{ given } A)}$

EXAMPLE 3 Find the probability of *A* and *B*

BUS SCHEDULE You take a city bus from your neighborhood to a location within walking distance of your school. The express bus arrives at your neighborhood between 7:30 and 7:36. The local bus arrives at your neighborhood between 7:30 and 7:40. You arrive at the bus stop at 7:33. Find the probability that you have missed both the express bus and the local bus.

ANOTHER WAY
For alternative methods for solving the problem in Example 3, turn to page 868 for the **Problem Solving Workshop**.

Solution

The events are independent. The arrival of one bus does not affect the arrival of the other bus.

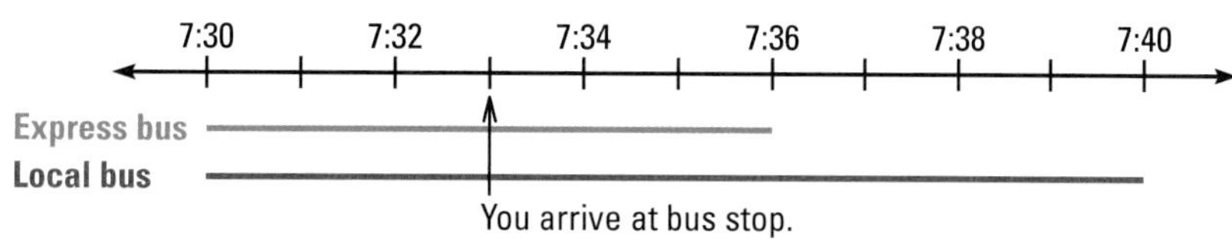

There are 6 minutes when the express bus can arrive. You are not at the bus stop for 3 of those minutes.

$P(\text{you miss express bus}) = \frac{3}{6} = \frac{1}{2}$

There are 10 minutes when the local bus can arrive. You are not at the bus stop for 3 of those minutes.

$P(\text{you miss local bus}) = \frac{3}{10}$

Multiply the probabilities of the two events:

$$P(\text{you miss both buses}) = \frac{1}{2} \cdot \frac{3}{10} = \frac{3}{20}$$

▶ The probability that you miss the express bus and the local bus is $\frac{3}{20}$.

EXAMPLE 4 Find the probability of *A* and *B*

PEN COLORS A box contains 3 blue pens and 5 black pens. You choose one pen at random, do not replace it, then choose a second pen at random. What is the probability that both pens are blue?

Solution

Because you do not replace the first pen, the events are dependent. Before you choose a pen, there are 8 pens, and 3 of them are blue. After you choose a blue pen, there are 7 pens left and 2 of them are blue.

$$P(\text{blue and then blue}) = P(\text{blue}) \cdot P(\text{blue given blue})$$

$$= \frac{3}{8} \cdot \frac{2}{7} = \frac{6}{56} = \frac{3}{28}$$

GUIDED PRACTICE for Examples 3 and 4

3. **MARBLES** A bag contains 4 red, 5 green, and 2 blue marbles. You randomly draw 2 marbles, one at a time. Find the probabililty that both are red if:

   a. you replace the first marble.

   b. you do not replace the first marble.

13.4 EXERCISES

HOMEWORK KEY

○ = **WORKED-OUT SOLUTIONS** on p. WS32 for Exs. 5 and 23

★ = **STANDARDIZED TEST PRACTICE** Exs. 2, 8, 13, 20, and 24

◆ = **MULTIPLE REPRESENTATIONS** Ex. 25

SKILL PRACTICE

1. **VOCABULARY** Copy and complete: The probability of _?_ events is found using the formula $P(A \text{ and } B) = P(A) \cdot P(B \text{ given } A)$.

2. ★ **WRITING** *Explain* how overlapping events differ from mutually exclusive events.

EXAMPLES 1 and 2 on pp. 861–862 for Exs. 3–8

PROBABILITY OF A OR B **In Exercises 3–6, you roll a number cube. Tell whether the events *A* and *B* are *mutually exclusive* or *overlapping*. Then find *P*(*A* or *B*).**

3. **Event *A*:** Roll a 6.
Event *B*: Roll a prime number.

4. **Event *A*:** Roll an even number.
Event *B*: Roll a 5.

5. **Event *A*:** Roll an odd number.
Event *B*: Roll a number less than 5.

6. **Event *A*:** Roll a multiple of 3.
Event *B*: Roll an even number.

7. **ERROR ANALYSIS** A bag contains 7 yellow marbles, 4 red marbles, and 5 blue marbles. *Describe* and correct the error in finding the probability that you randomly draw a yellow or blue marble.

$$P(\text{yellow or blue}) = P(\text{yellow}) \cdot P(\text{blue})$$
$$= \frac{7}{16} \cdot \frac{5}{16} = \frac{35}{256}$$

8. ★ **MULTIPLE CHOICE** A bag contains tiles with the numbers 1–10 on them. You randomly choose a tile from the bag. What is the probability that you choose an even number or a number less than 5?

Ⓐ 0.7 Ⓑ 0.8 Ⓒ 0.9 Ⓓ 1

EXAMPLES 3 and 4 on p. 863 for Exs. 9–12

PROBABILITY OF A AND B **In Exercises 9–12, tell whether the events *A* and *B* are *dependent* or *independent*. Then find *P*(*A* and *B*).**

9. You roll two number cubes.
Event *A*: You roll a 2 first.
Event *B*: You roll a 5 second.

10. You write each of the letters of the word BIOLOGY on pieces of paper and place them in a bag. You randomly draw one letter, do not replace it, then randomly draw a second letter.
Event *A*: The first letter is O.
Event *B*: The second letter is B.

11. You flip a coin and roll a number cube.
Event *A*: The coin shows heads.
Event *B*: The number cube shows 2.

12. A box contains 3 milk chocolates, 3 white chocolates, and 4 dark chocolates. You choose a chocolate at random, eat it, then choose a second chocolate at random.
Event *A*: You choose a dark chocolate.
Event *B*: You choose a dark chocolate.

13. ★ **MULTIPLE CHOICE** A vase holds 7 red roses and 5 pink roses. You randomly choose a rose, place it in a different vase, then randomly choose another rose. What is the approximate probability that both the first and second roses are red?

Ⓐ 0.29 Ⓑ 0.32 Ⓒ 0.34 Ⓓ 0.37

CHESS PIECES In Exercises 14–17, consider a bag that contains all of the chess pieces in a set, as shown in the diagram.

	King	Queen	Bishop	Rook	Knight	Pawn
Black	1	1	2	2	2	8
White	1	1	2	2	2	8

14. You choose one piece at random. Find the probability that you choose a black piece or a queen.

15. You choose one piece at random, replace it, then choose a second piece at random. Find the probability that you choose a rook, then a bishop.

16. You choose one piece at random, do not replace it, then choose a second piece at random. Find the probability that you choose a king, then a pawn.

17. **ERROR ANALYSIS** *Describe* and correct the error in finding the probability that you randomly choose a pawn and a second pawn, without replacement.

$$P(\text{pawn and pawn}) = P(\text{pawn}) \cdot P(\text{pawn})$$
$$= \frac{16}{32} \cdot \frac{16}{32} = \frac{1}{4}$$

✗

In Exercises 18 and 19, use the following information. Two mutually exclusive events for which one or the other must occur are called *complementary* events. If events A and B are complementary events, then $P(A) + P(B) = 1$.

18. **WEATHER** A local meteorologist reports that there is a 70% chance of rain tomorrow. What is the probability that it will *not* rain tomorrow?

19. **BASKETBALL** You make 31% of your attempted 3-point shots. What is the probability that you miss your next attempted 3-point shot?

20. ★ **WRITING** You write the letters of the word WISDOM on pieces of paper and place them in a bag. You randomly choose 2 letters from the bag at the same time. *Explain* whether these events are independent or dependent. What is the probability that you choose the letters S and D?

21. **CHALLENGE** The sections of the spinner shown all have the same area. You spin the spinner.

   a. Find the probability that the spinner stops on red *or* a prime number *or* a multiple of 3. You may want to draw a Venn diagram to find the answer.

   b. Write a general formula for $P(A \text{ or } B \text{ or } C)$ where A, B, and C are overlapping events. *Explain* your reasoning.

Problem Solving

EXAMPLES 3 and 4 on p. 863 for Exs. 22–23

22. **CONTEST** You can win concert tickets from a radio station if you are the first person to call when the song of the day is played, or if you are the first person to correctly answer the trivia question. The song of the day is played between 5:00 and 5:30 P.M. The trivia question is asked between 5:15 and 5:45 P.M. You begin listening to the radio station at 5:20. Find the probability that you miss the song of the day and the trivia question.

@HomeTutor for problem solving help at classzone.com

(23.) **WALRUS** When a walrus forages for food, it waves its flipper to move sediment 70% of the time. When using the flipper wave technique, a walrus uses its right flipper 89% of the time. Find the probability that a walrus foraging for food uses a flipper and it is the right flipper.

@HomeTutor for problem solving help at classzone.com

EXAMPLES 1, 2, 3, and 4 on pp. 861–863 for Ex. 24

24. ★ **SHORT RESPONSE** A survey of 887,403 households found that 270,658 households have a dog, 326,591 have a cat, and 81,641 have both.

    a. What is the probability that one of the households surveyed, chosen at random, has a dog and a cat?

    b. What is the probability that one of the households surveyed, chosen at random, has a dog or a cat?

    c. *Explain* how your answers to parts (a) and (b) are related.

EXAMPLES 1 and 2 on pp. 861–862 for Ex. 25

25. ◆ **MULTIPLE REPRESENTATIONS** You have student government meetings on Monday and Wednesday. You tutor in the morning on Monday, Thursday, Friday, and Saturday.

    a. **Making a Table** Make a table that shows your schedule for the week.

    b. **Drawing a Diagram** Make a Venn diagram that shows the days of the week that you participate in each activity.

    c. **Using a Formula** Your class is taking a field trip that could be scheduled for any day of the week. Find the probability that it is scheduled for a day when you tutor or have a student government meeting.

26. **EARTH SCIENCE** The table shows the ranges of annual mean temperature and precipitation for 57 cities in the U.S. Find the probability that a city in this study has an annual mean temperature in the range 39°F–52°F or an annual precipitation in the range 0–24 inches.

Precipitation (inches)	Temperature (degrees Fahrenheit)	
	39–52	**53–66**
0–24	7	7
25–49	21	22

○ = WORKED-OUT SOLUTIONS on p. WS1 ★ = STANDARDIZED TEST PRACTICE ◆ = MULTIPLE REPRESENTATIONS

27. **CHALLENGE** You have 5 tickets to a play. You invite 4 friends to see the play. You hand out the tickets at random. One ticket is for an aisle seat, and the other tickets are for the next 4 seats in the row.

a. What is the probability that you will get the aisle seat?

b. What is the probability that you will get the aisle seat and your best friend will get the ticket for the seat next to you?

c. *Explain* how you could solve the problem in part (b) using permutations.

MIXED REVIEW

PREVIEW
Prepare for Lesson 13.5 in Exs. 28–29.

In Exercises 28 and 29, the spinner shown has sections with equal area. *(p. 843)*

28. You flip a coin and spin the spinner. How many possible outcomes are in the sample space? List the possible outcomes.

29. You roll a number cube and spin the spinner. How many possible outcomes are in the sample space? List the possible outcomes.

Evaluate the expression.

30. ${}_5P_3$ *(p. 851)*

31. ${}_{15}P_0$ *(p. 851)*

32. ${}_{15}C_0$ *(p. 856)*

33. ${}_5C_3$ *(p. 856)*

34. **ELECTIVES** Your school offers 10 elective courses each semester. You have time in your schedule for 2 of these courses. How many combinations of 2 elective courses can you choose? *(p. 856)*

QUIZ *for Lessons 13.1–13.4*

1. **MARBLES** A bag contains 16 red marbles and 8 white marbles. You select a marble at random. *(p. 843)*

a. What is the probability that you select a red marble?

b. What are the odds in favor of selecting a red marble?

2. **PASSWORD** The password for an e-mail account is the word FISH followed by a 3-digit number. The 3-digit number contains the digits 1, 2, and 3. How many different passwords are possible? *(p. 851)*

3. **SHUFFLE** A CD plays on random shuffle. The CD has 12 songs on it. Your CD player selects a song at random, plays it, then selects a second song at random. No song is repeated until every song has been played. What is the probability that song 3 is played first and song 1 is played second? *(p. 851)*

Evaluate the expression.

4. ${}_5P_4$ *(p. 851)*

5. ${}_8P_5$ *(p. 851)*

6. ${}_5C_2$ *(p. 856)*

7. ${}_8C_5$ *(p. 856)*

8. **NUMBER TILES** Tiles numbered 1–30 are placed in a bag. You select a tile at random. Find the probability that you select an odd number or a prime number. Are the events mutually exclusive or overlapping? *Explain.* *(p. 861)*

PROBLEM SOLVING WORKSHOP LESSON 13.4

Using ALTERNATIVE METHODS

Another Way to Solve Example 3, page 863

MULTIPLE REPRESENTATIONS In Example 3 on page 863, you saw how to solve the problem about a bus schedule by using a number line and a formula. You can also solve the problem by performing a simulation or using geometry.

PROBLEM

BUS SCHEDULE You take a city bus from your neighborhood to a location within walking distance of your school. The express bus arrives at your neighborhood between 7:30 and 7:36. The local bus arrives at your neighborhood between 7:30 and 7:40. You arrive at the bus stop at 7:33. Find the probability that you have missed both the express bus and the local bus.

METHOD 1

Performing a Simulation One alternative approach is to perform a simulation.

STEP 1 **Read** the problem. Notice that there is a 6 minute interval when the express bus could arrive and a 10 minute interval when the local bus could arrive. Let 1 represent the first minute, from 7:30 to 7:31, that a bus could arrive. Let 2 represent the second minute, from 7:31 to 7:32, that a bus could arrive. Continue to number the minutes when a bus could arrive.

STEP 2 **Generate** random integers. Use a graphing calculator to generate a random integer from 1 to 6. This number represents the minute that the express bus arrives. Then generate a random integer from 1 to 10. This number represents the minute that the local bus arrives. Perform this simulation 10 times.

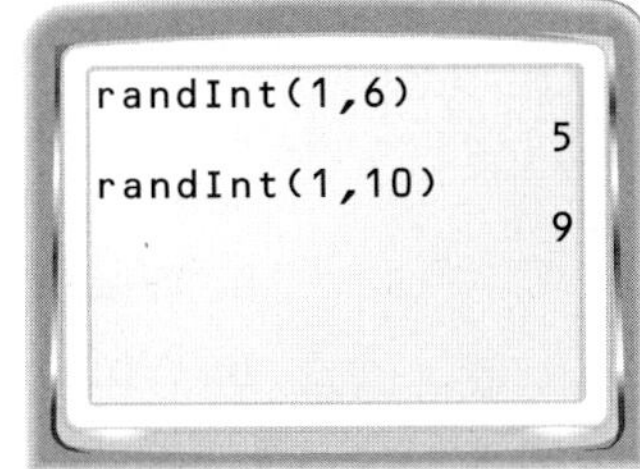

You are not at the bus stop until the fourth minute, so if both numbers that you generate are less than 4, then you miss both buses.

First number	5	4	2	5	2	1	2	3	3	1
Second number	9	1	1	8	4	7	9	10	6	2
Miss both buses?	No	No	Yes	No	No	No	No	No	No	Yes

STEP 3 **Find** the experimental probability that you miss both buses.

$$P(\text{miss both buses}) = \frac{2}{10} = \frac{1}{5}$$

METHOD 2

Using Geometry Another approach is to use geometry. Use the formula for the area of a rectangle to find the number of possible outcomes and the number of favorable outcomes.

STEP 1 **Draw** a rectangle whose side lengths represent the number of minutes that each bus could arrive.

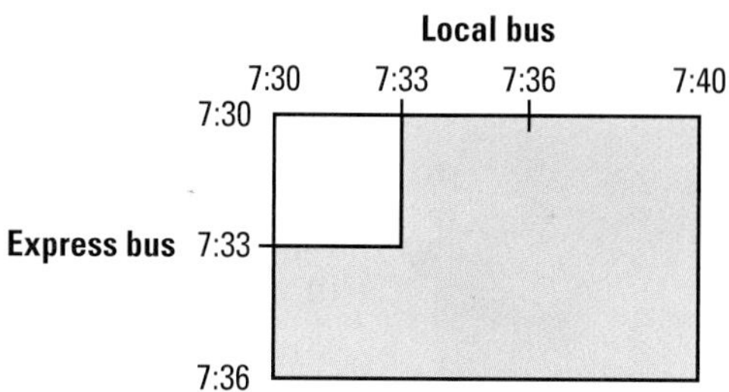

STEP 2 **Draw** a square within the rectangle to represent the number of minutes that you are *not* at the bus stop.

STEP 3 **Calculate** the area of the rectangle that represents the time a bus could arrive. Also calculate the area of the square that represents the time that you are *not* at the bus stop.

Time a bus could arrive:
$A = 6 \cdot 10 = 60$

Time you are *not* at bus stop:
$A = 3 \cdot 3 = 9$

STEP 4 **Find** the probability that you miss both buses by forming the ratio of the areas from step 2.

$P(\text{miss both buses}) = \frac{9}{60} = \frac{3}{20}$

PRACTICE

1. **WHAT IF?** In the problem on page 868, suppose you arrive at 7:34. What is the probability that you miss both buses?

2. **VISITING FRIENDS** Two friends are planning to visit you this evening. You expect one friend to arrive at your house between 7:00 and 7:30 P.M. You expect the other friend to arrive between 7:10 and 7:20 P.M. You have to run an errand from 7:00 until 7:15 P.M. What is the probability that you are home when both friends arrive? Solve this problem using two different methods.

3. **WHAT IF?** In Exercise 2, suppose a third friend plans to visit you this evening. This friend plans to arrive at your house between 7:00 and 7:20 P.M. What is the probability that you are home when all three of your friends arrive? *Explain* how you found your answer.

4. **RAFFLE** You enter two different raffles during your neighborhood's street fair. The winner of the first raffle will be announced between 6:00 and 6:30 P.M. The winner of the second raffle will be announced between 6:15 and 6:45 P.M. You leave the fair at 5:00 P.M. and return at 6:20 P.M. What is the probability that you hear the winner of each raffle announced? Solve this problem using two different methods.

5. **ERROR ANALYSIS** A student solved the problem in Exercise 4 as shown. *Describe* and correct the error.

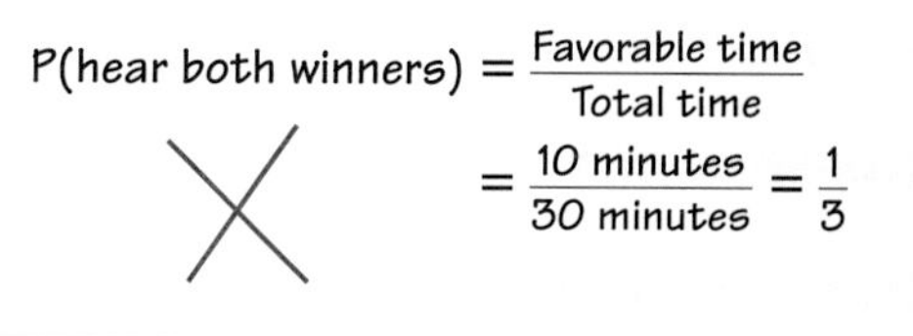

P(hear both winners) = Favorable time / Total time
= 10 minutes / 30 minutes = 1/3

Lessons 13.1–13.4

1. **MULTI-STEP PROBLEM** There are 5743 known amphibian species in the world. Of these, 1856 species are judged to be at risk of extinction, and another 113 species may already be extinct.

   a. Find the probability that an amphibian species chosen at random is at risk of extinction or may already be extinct.

   b. Find the probability that two different amphibian species, each chosen at random, are at risk of extinction.

The Puerto Rican crested toad is at risk of extinction.

2. **MULTI-STEP PROBLEM** You are ordering an omelet with two ingredients. You can choose from the following list: cheese, mushrooms, onions, tomatoes, peppers, sausage, ham, and steak.

   a. Make an organized list of all the possible omelets that you can order.

   b. Use a permutation or combination formula to find the number of possible omelets.

3. **MULTI-STEP PROBLEM** In NCAA women's basketball tournaments from 1982 to 2003, teams seeded, or ranked, number one have won 283 games and lost 71 games in the tournament. Suppose a team is chosen at random from all those that have been seeded number one.

   a. What is the probability that the team won a game in the tournament?

   b. What are the odds in favor of the team's having won a game in the tournament?

4. **SHORT RESPONSE** A meteorologist reports that there is a 15% chance of snow tomorrow. What are the odds in favor of snow tomorrow? *Explain* how you found your answer.

5. **OPEN-ENDED** *Describe* a real-world situation in which the number of possible arrangements is given by ${}_{10}P_2$.

6. **SHORT RESPONSE** In the United States there are 21 states (not including Washington, D.C.) with teams in the National Football League and 17 states with Major League Baseball teams. There are 15 states that have both types of teams. Suppose a state is chosen at random.

   a. Find the probability that the state has either a National Football League team or a Major League Baseball team.

   b. There are 21 states that have a team in the National Basketball Association. What additional information would you need in order to find the probability that the state chosen at random has either a team in the National Basketball Association or a Major League Baseball team? *Explain* your reasoning.

7. **EXTENDED RESPONSE** A survey asked a total of 400 students, 100 male students and 100 female students who were 13 and 15 years old, about their eating habits. The table shows the numbers of students who said that they eat fruit every day.

	13 years old	15 years old
Male	60	53
Female	61	58

   a. Find the probability that a female student, chosen at random from the students surveyed, eats fruit every day.

   b. Find the probability that a 15-year-old student, chosen at random from the students surveyed, eats fruit every day.

   c. You select a student at random from the students surveyed. Find the odds against the student's eating fruit every day. *Explain* your reasoning.

8. **GRIDDED ANSWER** A music club gives you 6 free CDs for joining. You would like to own 11 of the free CDs that are offered. How many combinations of 6 CDs from the 11 CDs can you choose?

13.5 Analyze Surveys and Samples

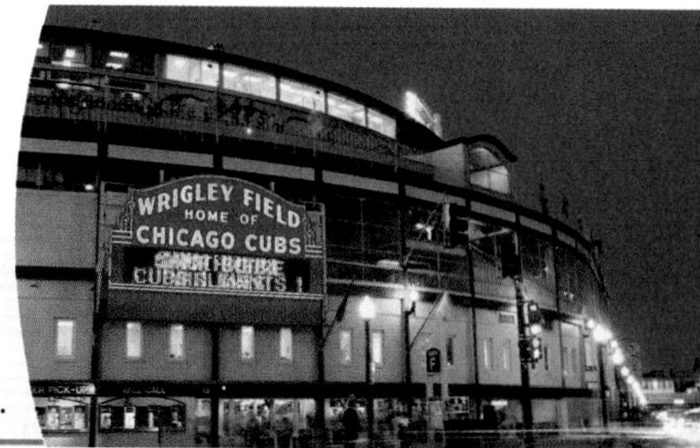

Before You found experimental probabilities.

Now You will identify populations and sampling methods.

Why? So you can analyze surveys of sports fans, as in Ex. 15.

Key Vocabulary
- **survey**
- **population**
- **sample**
- **biased sample**
- **biased question**

A **survey** is a study of one or more characteristics of a group. The entire group you want information about is called a **population**. You may find it difficult to survey an entire population. Instead, you can survey a **sample**, which is a part of the population. Five types of samples are listed below.

KEY CONCEPT *For Your Notebook*

Sampling Methods

In a **random sample**, every member of the population has an equal chance of being selected.

In a **stratified random sample**, the population is divided into distinct groups. Members are selected at random from each group.

In a **systematic sample**, a rule is used to select members of the population.

In a **convenience sample**, only members of the population who are easily accessible are selected.

In a **self-selected sample**, members of the population select themselves by volunteering.

EXAMPLE 1 Classify a sampling method

EMPLOYEE SAFETY The owners of a company with several factories conduct a survey to determine whether employees are informed about safety regulations. At each factory, 50 employees are chosen at random to complete the survey. Identify the population and classify the sampling method.

Solution

The population is all company employees. Because the population is divided into distinct groups (individual factories), with employees chosen at random from each group, the sample is a stratified random sample.

GUIDED PRACTICE for Example 1

1. WHAT IF? In Example 1, suppose the owners survey each employee whose last name begins with M. Classify the sampling method.

BIASED SAMPLES A sample chosen for a survey should be representative of the population. A **biased sample** is a sample that is not representative. In a biased sample, parts of the population may be over-represented or under-represented.

Random samples and stratified random samples (as in Example 1) are the most likely types of samples to be representative. A systematic sample may be representative if the rule used to choose individuals is not biased.

EXAMPLE 2 Identify a potentially biased sample

In Example 1, suppose the owners question 50 workers chosen at random from one factory. Is the method likely to result in a biased sample?

Solution

Workers at other factories may hold significantly different opinions, so the method may result in a biased sample.

BIASED QUESTIONS A question that encourages a particular response is a **biased question**. Survey questions should be worded to avoid bias.

EXAMPLE 3 Identify potentially biased questions

Tell whether the question is potentially biased. Explain your answer. If the question is potentially biased, rewrite it so that it is not.

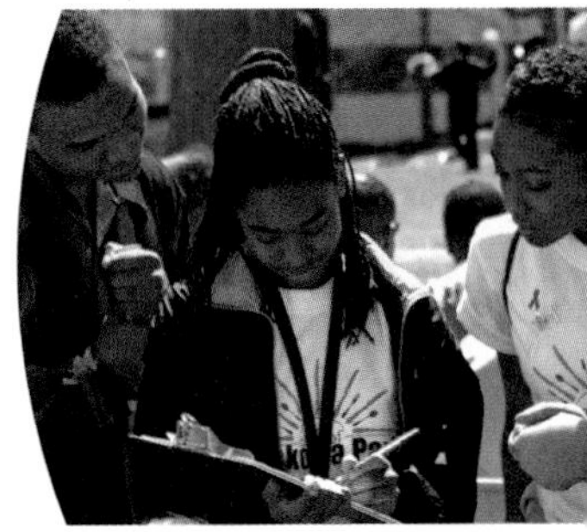

a. Don't you agree that the voting age should be lowered to 16 because many 16-year-olds are responsible and informed?

b. Do you think the city should risk an increase in pollution by allowing expansion of the Northern Industrial Park?

Solution

a. This question is biased because it suggests that lowering the voting age is a good thing to do. An unbiased question is "Do you think the voting age should be lowered to 16?"

b. This question is biased because it suggests that the proposed expansion will be bad for the environment. An unbiased question is "Do you think the city should allow expansion of the Northern Industrial Park?"

GUIDED PRACTICE for Examples 2 and 3

2. **SOCCER** In a survey about Americans' interest in soccer, the first 25 people admitted to a high school soccer game were asked, "How interested are you in the world's most popular sport, soccer?"

   a. Is the sampling method likely to result in a biased sample? *Explain.*

   b. Is the question potentially biased? *Explain* your answer. If the question is potentially biased, rewrite it so that it is not.

13.5 EXERCISES

HOMEWORK KEY

○ = **WORKED-OUT SOLUTIONS** on p. WS33 for Exs. 3 and 15

★ = **STANDARDIZED TEST PRACTICE** Exs. 2, 6, and 17

SKILL PRACTICE

1. **VOCABULARY** Copy and complete: In a(n) __?__ sample, participants are chosen using a rule.

2. ★ **WRITING** *Explain* how a sample is related to a population.

POPULATIONS AND SAMPLES In Exercises 3–5, identify the population and classify the sampling method.

EXAMPLE 1 on p. 871 for Exs. 3–6

3. **RESTAURANT SERVICE** A restaurant manager wants to evaluate the restaurant's quality of service. Diners are given mail-in comment cards.

4. **EXTRACURRICULAR ACTIVITIES** Your school wants to know if students are satisfied with the school's extracurricular activities. In each grade, every tenth student on an alphabetized list is surveyed.

5. **CUSTOMER SATISFACTION** An airline wants to gather information on passenger satisfaction during a flight. A computer randomly selects 30 passengers to complete a survey.

6. ★ **MULTIPLE CHOICE** Scientists wanted to gather information about the birds in a particular region. They chose observation sites and asked bird watchers at those sites to record the number and types of birds they saw in 3 minutes. What population was being studied?

   (A) Birds (B) Sites (C) Scientists (D) Bird watchers

EXAMPLE 2 on p. 872 for Exs. 7–8

BIASED SAMPLES Tell whether the sampling method used is likely to result in a biased sample. *Explain.*

7. **NEIGHBORHOOD WATCH** A family wants to gather information from other residents on their street about forming a neighborhood watch. They survey every third house on both sides of the street.

8. **NURSE SURVEY** The American Nurses Association wanted to gather information about the working environment for nurses in hospitals. A survey for nurses was posted on the association's website.

EXAMPLE 3 on p. 872 for Exs. 9–11

BIASED QUESTIONS In Exercises 9 and 10, tell whether the question is potentially biased. *Explain* your answer.

9. Do you support the incumbent's tax plan or the challenger's tax plan?

10. Do you prefer the ease of shopping online or the fun of going to a mall?

11. **ERROR ANALYSIS** *Describe* and correct the error in revising the survey question "Don't you think the minimum driving age should be lower?" so that it is not biased.

Not biased:
Is the minimum driving age too high or too low?

12. **CHALLENGE** Two toothpaste manufacturers each claim that 4 out of every 5 dentists use their brand exclusively. Both manufacturers can support their claims with survey results. *Explain* how this is possible.

PROBLEM SOLVING

EXAMPLES 2 and 3 on p. 872 for Exs. 13–16

In Exercises 13 and 14, explain why the question is biased. Then rewrite it so that it is not.

13. Don't you agree that the school needs a new athletic field more than a new science lab?

@HomeTutor for problem solving help at classzone.com

14. Would you pay even higher concert ticket prices to finance a new arena?

@HomeTutor for problem solving help at classzone.com

15. **BASEBALL** Every Major League Baseball (MLB) season, players are chosen to represent the two leagues in an All-Star game. At each MLB park, fans are given ballots to vote for their favorite players. Are the ballots collected at the Chicago Cubs' park, Wrigley Field, necessarily representative of the opinions of all Chicago Cubs fans? *Explain.*

16. **WATER SAMPLING** Scientists designed a project in which students performed tests on local water sources each day. Students from 18 countries participated in the project. The results of the survey were used to assess the quality of the world's fresh water. Is the sample likely to be biased? *Explain.*

17. ★ **SHORT RESPONSE** You plan to report on the academic performance of students in your school for your school newspaper.
    a. *Describe* how you could choose a representative sample.
    b. Write an unbiased question you could use to collect information on how many hours per night a student studies. *Explain* why your question is unbiased.

18. **CHALLENGE** A systematic sample of a population is used for a survey containing unbiased questions. *Explain* how it is possible for the survey to be biased. *Describe* a situation in which this might occur.

MIXED REVIEW

PREVIEW Prepare for Lesson 13.6 in Exs. 19–23.

Order the numbers from least to greatest. *(p. 909)*

19. 0.02, 0.015, 0.021, 0.012
20. 6.51, 6.15, 6.02, 6.23
21. 12.3, 11.9, 11.09, 12.08

Find the mean, median, and mode(s) of the data. *(p. 918)*

22. Cost (in dollars) of computer monitors: 296, 215, 426, 390, 351, 215, 289
23. Size (in megabytes) of files to be downloaded: 10.9, 12.1, 6.4, 2.8, 5.1, 7.6

Evaluate the expression.

24. ${}_5P_3$ *(p. 851)*
25. ${}_{10}P_4$ *(p. 851)*
26. ${}_8C_4$ *(p. 856)*
27. ${}_7C_2$ *(p. 856)*

13.6 Use Measures of Central Tendency and Dispersion

Before You analyzed surveys and samples.
Now You will compare measures of central tendency and dispersion.
Why? So you can analyze and compare data, as in Example 1.

Key Vocabulary
- **measure of dispersion**
- **range**
- **mean absolute deviation**

KEY CONCEPT *For Your Notebook*

Measures of Central Tendency

The **mean**, or *average*, of a numerical data set is denoted by $\overline{x}$, which is read as "x-bar." For the data set $x_1, x_2, \dots, x_n$, the mean is $\overline{x} = \frac{x_1 + x_2 + \dots + x_n}{n}$.

The **median** of a numerical data set is the middle number when the values are written in numerical order. If the data set has an even number of values, the median is the mean of the two middle values.

The **mode** of a data set is the value that occurs most frequently. There may be one mode, no mode, or more than one mode.

EXAMPLE 1 Compare measures of central tendency

The heights (in feet) of 8 waterfalls in the state of Washington are listed below. Which measure of central tendency best represents the data?

1000, 1000, 1181, 1191, 1200, 1268, 1328, 2584

Solution

$$\overline{x} = \frac{1000 + 1000 + 1181 + 1191 + 1200 + 1268 + 1328 + 2584}{8} = \frac{10{,}752}{8} = 1344$$

The median is the mean of the two middle values, 1191 and 1200, or 1195.5.

The mode is 1000.

▶ The median best represents the data. The mode is significantly less than most of the data, and the mean is significantly greater than most of the data.

Animated Algebra at classzone.com

✓ **GUIDED PRACTICE** for Example 1

1. **WHAT IF?** In Example 1, suppose you eliminate the greatest data value, 2584. Which measure of central tendency best represents the remaining data? *Explain* your reasoning.

MEASURES OF DISPERSION A **measure of dispersion** describes the dispersion, or spread, of data. Two such measures are the *range*, which gives the length of the interval containing the data, and the *mean absolute deviation*, which gives the average variation of the data from the mean.

KEY CONCEPT *For Your Notebook*

Measures of Dispersion

The **range** of a numerical data set is the difference of the greatest value and the least value.

The **mean absolute deviation** of the data set $x_1, x_2, \ldots, x_n$ is given by:

$$\text{Mean absolute deviation} = \frac{|x_1 - \bar{x}| + |x_2 - \bar{x}| + \ldots + |x_n - \bar{x}|}{n}$$

REVIEW ABSOLUTE VALUE
For help with absolute value, see p. 66.

EXAMPLE 2 Compare measures of dispersion

RUNNING The top 10 finishing times (in seconds) for runners in two men's races are given. The times in a 100 meter dash are in set *A*, and the times in a 200 meter dash are in set *B*. Compare the spread of the data for the two sets using (**a**) the range and (**b**) the mean absolute deviation.

A: 10.62, 10.94, 10.94, 10.98, 11.05, 11.13, 11.15, 11.28, 11.29, 11.32

B: 21.37, 21.40, 22.23, 22.23, 22.34, 22.34, 22.36, 22.60, 22.66, 22.73

Solution

a. *A*: $11.32 - 10.62 = 0.7$ *B*: $22.73 - 21.37 = 1.36$

▶ The range of set *B* is greater than the range of set *A*. So, the data in *B* cover a wider interval than the data in *A*.

b. The mean of set *A* is 11.07, so the mean absolute deviation is:

$$\frac{|10.62 - 11.07| + |10.94 - 11.07| + \ldots + |11.32 - 11.07|}{10} = 0.164$$

The mean of set *B* is 22.226, so the mean absolute deviation is:

$$\frac{|21.37 - 22.226| + |21.40 - 22.226| + \ldots + |22.73 - 22.226|}{10} = 0.3364$$

▶ The mean absolute deviation of set *B* is greater, so the average variation from the mean is greater for the data in *B* than for the data in *A*.

REVIEW NEGATIVE NUMBERS
When using the formula for mean absolute deviation, you will encounter negative numbers. For help with negative numbers, see p. 64.

GUIDED PRACTICE for Example 2

2. **RUNNING** The top 10 finishing times (in seconds) for runners in a men's 400 meter dash are 46.89, 47.65, 48.15, 49.05, 49.19, 49.50, 49.68, 51.09, 53.31, and 53.68. *Compare* the spread of the data with that of set *A* in Example 2 using (**a**) the range and (**b**) the mean absolute deviation.

13.6 EXERCISES

HOMEWORK KEY

○ = **WORKED-OUT SOLUTIONS** on p. WS33 for Exs. 7 and 19

★ = **STANDARDIZED TEST PRACTICE** Exs. 2, 9, 17, 19, and 22

SKILL PRACTICE

1. **VOCABULARY** Copy and complete: The value that occurs most frequently in a data set is called the _?_ of the data.

2. ★ **WRITING** How are measures of central tendency and measures of dispersion used to compare data?

EXAMPLE 1 on p. 875 for Exs. 3–10

MEASURES OF CENTRAL TENDENCY Find the mean, median, and mode(s) of the data.

3. 1, 1, 1, 2, 3, 3, 5, 5, 6
4. 9, 10, 12, 15, 16
5. 13, 16, 19, 20, 22, 25, 30, 31
6. 14, 15, 15, 14, 14, 16, 18, 15
7. 5.52, 5.44, 3.60, 5.76, 3.80, 7.22
8. 300, 320, 341, 348, 360, 333

9. ★ **MULTIPLE CHOICE** What is the median of the data set?

0.7, 0.3, 0.7, 0.8, 0.9, 0.4, 1.0, 1.6, 1.2

Ⓐ 0.7 Ⓑ 0.8 Ⓒ 0.9 Ⓓ 1.0

10. **ERROR ANALYSIS** *Describe* and correct the error in finding the median of the data set.

7 4 6 2 4 6 8 8 3

The median is 4.

EXAMPLE 2 on p. 876 for Exs. 11–16

MEASURES OF DISPERSION Find the range and mean absolute deviation of the data. Round to the nearest hundredth, if necessary.

11. 30, 35, 20, 85, 60
12. 111, 135, 115, 120, 145, 130
13. 30, 45, 52, 48, 100, 45, 42, 45
14. 505, 510, 480, 550, 495, 500
15. 1.25, 1.50, 1.70, 0.85, 1.00, 1.25
16. 38.2, 80.1, 2.6, 84.2, 2.5, 5.5

17. ★ **WRITING** *Explain* why the mean absolute deviation of a data set is generally a better measure of dispersion than the range.

18. **CHALLENGE** Write a data set that has a mean of 10, a median of 10, and modes of 5 and 8.

PROBLEM SOLVING

EXAMPLE 1 on p. 875 for Exs. 19–20

19. ★ **SHORT RESPONSE** The weights (in pounds) of ten pumpkins are 22, 21, 24, 24, 5, 24, 5, 23, 24, and 24.
    a. What is the range of the pumpkin weights?
    b. Find the mean, median, and mode(s) of the pumpkin weights.
    c. Which measure of central tendency best represents the data? *Explain.*

@HomeTutor for problem solving help at classzone.com

20. **POPULATION** The population densities (in people per square mile) for each of the 10 most densely populated states in 2003 were 719.0, 418.5, 315.6, 563.6, 820.6, 1164.6, 406.5, 279.3, 275.9, and 1029.9.

a. Find the mean, median, and mode(s) of the data set.

b. Which measure of central tendency best represents the data? *Explain.*

@HomeTutor for problem solving help at classzone.com

EXAMPLE 2 on p. 876 for Ex. 21

21. **BOWLING** The average scores of the bowlers on two different bowling teams are given. *Compare* the spreads of the data sets using (**a**) the range and (**b**) the mean absolute deviation.

Team 1: 162, 150, 173, 202 **Team 2:** 140, 153, 187, 196

22. ★ **EXTENDED RESPONSE** The Mississippi River discharges an average of 230 million tons of sediment per year. The average sediment discharges (in millions of tons per year) of the seven U.S. rivers with the greatest discharges are 230, 80, 65, 40, 25, 15, and 11. For parts (a)–(c) below, round your answers to the nearest whole number, if necessary.

a. Find the mean and median of the data. Which measure represents the data better? *Explain.*

b. Find the mean of the data for the other six rivers, excluding the Mississippi River. Does this mean represent the data better than the mean you found in part (a)? *Explain.*

c. Find the range and mean absolute deviation of the data for all seven rivers. *Describe* what the measures tell you about the dispersion of the data.

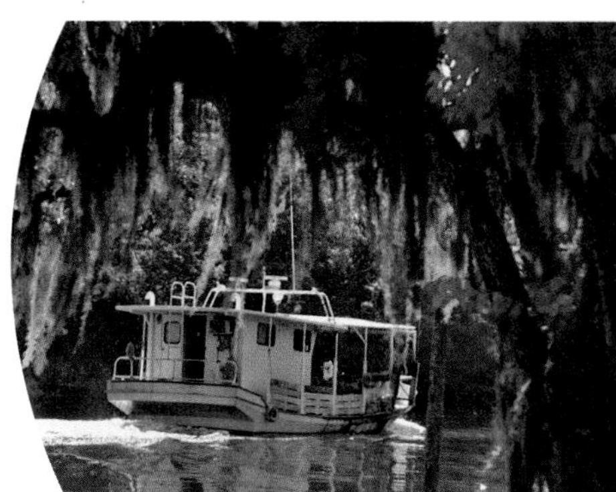

Fishing boat on the Mississippi River

23. **CHALLENGE** So far, you have scored 84, 92, 76, 88, and 76 on five of the six tests you will take in a particular class. Your goal is to finish the year with a test average of 85 or greater.

a. Let x represent your last test score. Write an expression for the mean of your test scores. Then write and solve an inequality to find the possible scores you can achieve in order to meet your goal.

b. After the last test, your teacher tells you that the median of your six test scores is 86. Can you tell whether you met your goal? *Explain.*

MIXED REVIEW

PREVIEW Prepare for Lesson 13.7 in Ex. 24.

24. **POPULATION** The bar graph shows the populations of Alabama, Kentucky, Mississippi, and Tennessee (the East South Central states) according to the U.S. Census of 2000. *(p. 933)*

a. What was the total population of the four states?

b. How much greater was the population of Tennessee than the population of Kentucky?

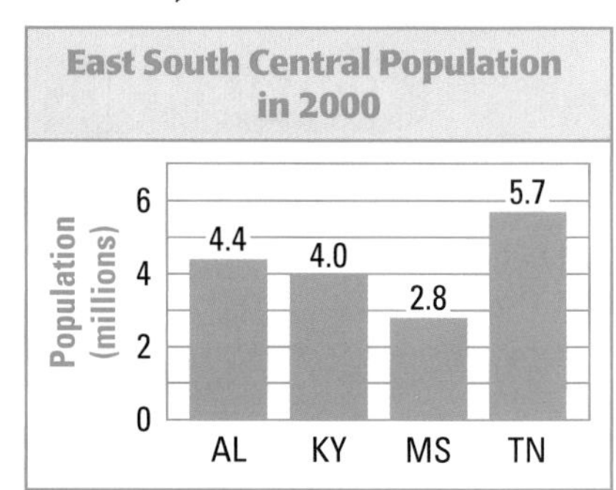

Extension

Use after Lesson 13.6

Calculate Variance and Standard Deviation

GOAL Find the variance and standard deviation of a data set.

Key Vocabulary
- **variance**
- **standard deviation**

In addition to range and mean absolute deviation, *variance* and *standard deviation* are also measures of dispersion that can be used to describe the spread of a set of data.

KEY CONCEPT *For Your Notebook*

Variance and Standard Deviation

The **variance** of a numerical data set is denoted by σ^2, which is read as "sigma squared." For the data set $x_1, x_2, \ldots, x_n$, the variance is given by:

$$\sigma^2 = \frac{(x_1 - \overline{x})^2 + (x_2 - \overline{x})^2 + \ldots + (x_n - \overline{x})^2}{n}$$

The **standard deviation** of a numerical data set is denoted by σ, which is read as "sigma." For the data set $x_1, x_2, \ldots, x_n$, the standard deviation is the square root of the variance and is given by:

$$\sigma = \sqrt{\frac{(x_1 - \overline{x})^2 + (x_2 - \overline{x})^2 + \ldots + (x_n - \overline{x})^2}{n}}$$

EXAMPLE 1 Find variance and standard deviation

E-MAIL SIZES The sizes of e-mails (in kilobytes) in your inbox are 1, 2, 2, 7, 4, 1, 10, 3, and 6. Find the variance and standard deviation of the data.

Solution

STEP 1 **Find** the mean.

$$\overline{x} = \frac{1 + 2 + 2 + 7 + 4 + 1 + 10 + 3 + 6}{9} = \frac{36}{9} = 4$$

STEP 2 **Find** the variance.

$$\sigma^2 = \frac{(1 - 4)^2 + (2 - 4)^2 + \ldots + (6 - 4)^2}{9} = \frac{76}{9} = 8.444\ldots$$

STEP 3 **Find** the standard deviation.

$$\sigma = \sqrt{\sigma^2} = \sqrt{8.444\ldots} \approx 2.9$$

▶ The variance is about 8.4, and the standard deviation is about 2.9.

IMPROVE ACCURACY
The more accurate the value of σ^2 you use to calculate σ, the more accurate the value of σ you obtain. In the final answer, both results are rounded.

USING A CALCULATOR You can use a graphing calculator to find the standard deviation of a data set.

EXAMPLE 2 Find standard deviation

HOUSEHOLDS In 2000 the numbers (in thousands) of households in the 13 states with Atlantic Ocean coastline are given. Find the standard deviation of the data.

299 6338 3006 518 1981 2444 475 3065
7057 3132 408 1534 2699

Solution

STEP 1 **Enter** the data into a graphing calculator. Press STAT and select Edit. Enter the data into List 1 (L_1).

STEP 2 **Calculate** the standard deviation. Press STAT. From the CALC menu select 1-Var Stats.

On this screen, σ_x stands for standard deviation.

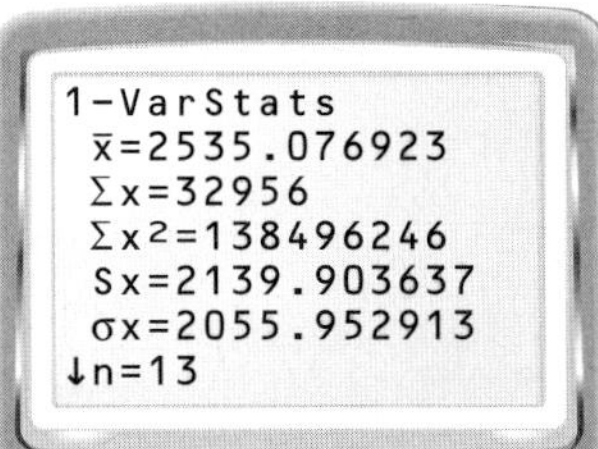

▶ The standard deviation of the data is about 2056.

PRACTICE

EXAMPLE 1 on p. 879 for Exs. 1–3

Use the formulas for variance and standard deviation to find the variance and standard deviation of the data. Round to the nearest tenth, if necessary.

1. 4, 5, 3, 2, 4, 7, 8, 9, 4, 6, 7, 8, 9, 1
2. 14, 16, 19, 20, 28, 7, 24, 15, 16, 30, 33, 24
3. 110, 205, 322, 608, 1100, 240, 185, 552, 418, 300

EXAMPLE 2 on p. 880 for Exs. 4–7

In Exercises 4–6, use a graphing calculator to find the standard deviation of the data. Round to the nearest tenth, if necessary.

4. 3.5, 3.8, 4.1, 3.0, 3.8, 3.6, 3.3, 4.0, 3.8, 3.9, 3.2, 3.0, 3.3, 4.2, 3.0
5. 66, 43, 9, 28, 7, 5, 90, 9, 78, 6, 69, 55, 28, 43, 10, 54, 13, 88, 21, 4
6. 1002, 1540, 480, 290, 2663, 3800, 690, 1301, 1750, 2222, 4040, 800
7. **REASONING** The heights (in feet) of 9 pecan trees are 72, 84, 81, 78, 80, 86, 70, 80, and 88. For parts (a)–(c) below, round your answers to the nearest tenth.
   a. Find the standard deviation of the data.
   b. Suppose you include a pecan tree with a height of 136 feet. *Predict* the effect of the additional data on the standard deviation of the data set.
   c. Find the standard deviation of the new data set in part (b). *Compare* the results to your prediction in part (b).

13.7 Interpret Stem-and-Leaf Plots and Histograms

Before You found measures of central tendency and dispersion.
Now You will make stem-and-leaf plots and histograms.
Why? So you can analyze historical data, as in Ex. 20.

Key Vocabulary
- **stem-and-leaf plot**
- **frequency**
- **frequency table**
- **histogram**

A **stem-and-leaf plot** is a data display that organizes data based on their digits. Each value is separated into a *stem* (the leading digit(s)) and a *leaf* (the last digit). A stem-and-leaf plot has a key that tells you how to read the data. A stem-and-leaf plot shows how the data are distributed.

EXAMPLE 1 Make a stem-and-leaf plot

BASEBALL The number of home runs hit by the 20 baseball players with the best single-season batting averages in Major League Baseball since 1900 are listed below. Make a stem-and-leaf plot of the data.

14, 25, 8, 8, 7, 7, 19, 37, 39, 18, 42, 23, 4, 32, 14, 21, 3, 12, 19, 41

Solution

STEP 1 **Separate** the data into stems and leaves.

Home Runs

Stem	Leaves
0	8 8 7 7 4 3
1	4 9 8 4 2 9
2	5 3 1
3	7 9 2
4	2 1

Key: 1 | 4 = 14 home runs

STEP 2 **Write** the leaves in increasing order.

Home Runs

Stem	Leaves
0	3 4 7 7 8 8
1	2 4 4 8 9 9
2	1 3 5
3	2 7 9
4	1 2

Key: 1 | 4 = 14 home runs

INTERPRET INTERVALS
Each stem in a stem-and-leaf plot defines an interval. For instance, the stem 2 represents the interval 20–29. The data values in this interval are 21, 23, and 25.

✓ GUIDED PRACTICE for Example 1

1. **U.S. HISTORY** The years in which each of the first 20 states were admitted to the Union are listed below. Make a stem-and-leaf plot of the years.

   1788, 1787, 1788, 1816, 1792, 1812, 1788, 1788, 1817, 1788,
   1787, 1788, 1789, 1803, 1787, 1790, 1788, 1796, 1791, 1788

2. **REASONING** In Example 1, describe the distribution of the data on the intervals represented by the stems. Are the data clustered together in a noticeable way? *Explain.*

EXAMPLE 2 Interpret a stem-and-leaf plot

GYMNASTICS The back-to-back stem-and-leaf plot shows the ages of members of the U.S men's and women's 2004 Olympic gymnastics teams. Compare the ages of the gymnasts on the two teams.

2004 Olympic Gymnast Ages

Men		Women
	1	6 6 8 8
7 4 3 1 1	2	5 6
0	3	

Key: 1 | 2 | 5 = 21, 25

Solution

Consider the distribution of the data. The interval for 10–19 years old contains more than half of the female gymnasts. The interval for 20–29 years old contains more than half of the male gymnasts. The clustering of the data shows that the men's team was generally older than the women's team.

FREQUENCY The **frequency** of an interval is the number of data values in that interval. A stem-and-leaf plot shows the frequencies of intervals determined by the stems. A **frequency table** is also used to group data values into equal intervals, with no gaps between intervals and no intervals overlapping.

A **histogram** is a bar graph that displays data from a frequency table. Each bar represents an interval. Because intervals have equal size, the bars have equal width. A bar's length indicates the frequency. There is no space between bars.

EXAMPLE 3 Make a histogram

SANDWICH PRICES The prices (in dollars) of sandwiches at a restaurant are listed below. Make a histogram of the data.

4.00, 4.00, 4.25, 4.50, 4.75, 4.25, 5.95, 5.50, 5.50, 5.75

Solution

CHOOSE AN INTERVAL SIZE
To choose the interval size for a frequency table, divide the range of the data by the number of intervals you want the table to have. Use the quotient as an approximate interval size.

STEP 1 **Choose** intervals of equal size that cover all of the data values. Organize the data using a frequency table.

Prices	Sandwiches
\$4.00–4.49	IIII
\$4.50–4.99	II
\$5.00–5.49	
\$5.50–5.99	IIII

STEP 2 **Draw** the bars of the histogram using the intervals from the frequency table.

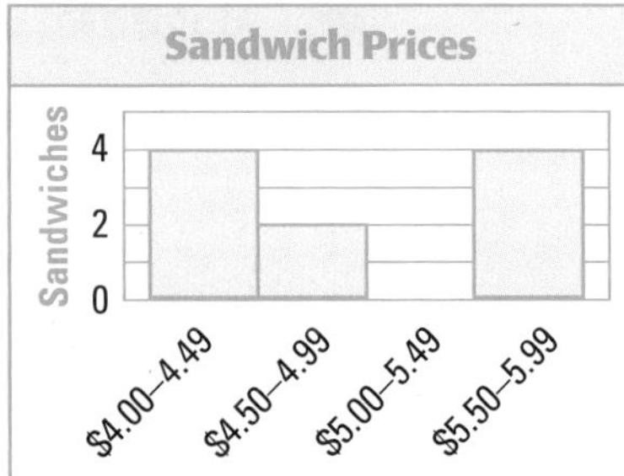

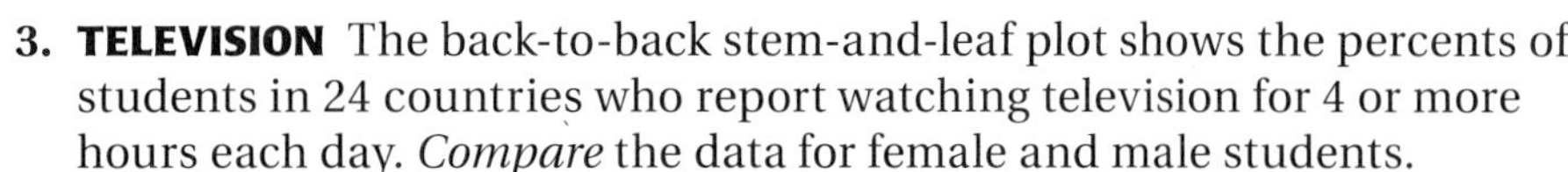

GUIDED PRACTICE for Examples 2 and 3

3. **TELEVISION** The back-to-back stem-and-leaf plot shows the percents of students in 24 countries who report watching television for 4 or more hours each day. *Compare* the data for female and male students.

Female		Male
9 9 9 8 8 8 6 6 5 4	1	7 8 9
6 6 5 4 3 3 0 0	2	0 1 2 2 4 5 5 6 6 7 7 8
8 3 2 2 1	3	4 6 6 8 8 9
1	4	0 6 6

Key: 4 | 1 | 7 = 14%, 17%

4. **PRECIPITATION** The average number of days each month with precipitation of 0.01 inch or more in Buffalo, New York, are 20, 17, 16, 14, 13, 11, 10, 10, 11, 12, 16, and 19. Make a histogram of the data.

13.7 EXERCISES

HOMEWORK KEY

○ = **WORKED-OUT SOLUTIONS** on p. WS33 for Exs. 3 and 19

★ = **STANDARDIZED TEST PRACTICE** Exs. 2, 8, 9, 15, and 20

SKILL PRACTICE

1. **VOCABULARY** Copy and complete: The number of data values in an interval is the __?__ of that interval.

2. ★ **WRITING** *Explain* how a histogram differs from a bar graph.

EXAMPLE 1 on p. 881 for Exs. 3–7

STEM-AND-LEAF PLOTS **Make a stem-and-leaf plot of the data.**

3. 17, 31, 42, 33, 38, 20, 24, 30, 39, 38, 35, 20, 55

4. 2, 8, 17, 7, 14, 20, 32, 5, 33, 6, 6, 8, 11, 9

5. 121, 124, 133, 111, 109, 182, 105, 127, 156, 179, 142

6. 1.23, 1.05, 1.11, 1.29, 1.31, 1.19, 1.45, 1.22, 1.19, 1.35

7. **ERROR ANALYSIS** *Describe* and correct the error in making a stem-and-leaf plot of the following data: 18, 19, 18, 19, 20, 20, 21, 22, 18, 19, 20, 21, 23, 21.

1	888999
2	00011123

✗

STEM-AND-LEAF PLOT **In Exercises 8 and 9, consider the back-to-back stem-and-leaf plot that shows data sets *A* and *B*.**

Set *A*		Set *B*
1 1 1	2	
4 3 3 2	3	1 2 2
2 0	4	1 1 3 4
	5	0 1

Key: 2 | 3 | 1 = 32, 31

8. ★ **MULTIPLE CHOICE** What is the median of data set *A*?

Ⓐ 21 Ⓑ 32 Ⓒ 33 Ⓓ 34

9. ★ **MULTIPLE CHOICE** What is the range of data set *B*?

Ⓐ 18 Ⓑ 19 Ⓒ 20 Ⓓ 21

EXAMPLE 3 on p. 882 for Exs. 10–14

10. ERROR ANALYSIS *Describe* and correct the error in creating a histogram using the frequency table below.

Ages	0–9	10–19	20–29	30–39
Frequency	III	~~IIII~~ I		IIII

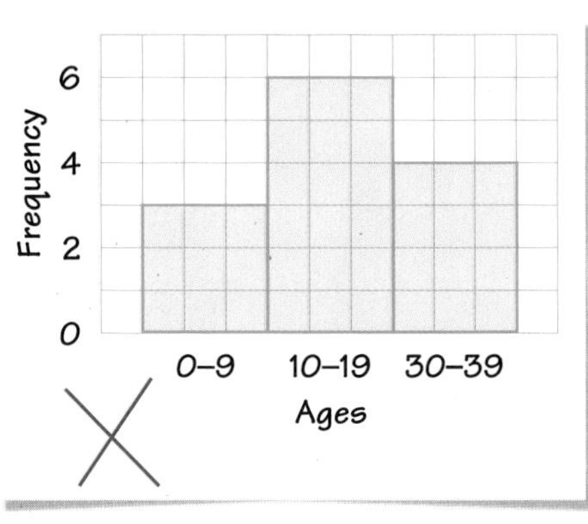

HISTOGRAMS **Make a histogram of the data.**

11. 55, 82, 94, 75, 61, 69, 77, 98, 81, 83, 75, 90, 51

12. 12, 0, 22, 31, 14, 7, 7, 45, 31, 28, 21, 25, 25, 18

13. 0.01, 0.13, 0.09, 1.10, 1.33, 0.99, 0.50, 0.95, 1.05, 1.50, 0.75, 1.01

14. 111, 109, 224, 657, 284, 120, 119, 415, 180, 105, 208, 108

15. ★ **WRITING** *Explain* why a histogram can show the distribution of the data below better than a stem-and-leaf plot.

15, 21, 18, 10, 12, 11, 17, 18, 16, 12, 20, 12, 17, 16

16. CHALLENGE Create a stem-and-leaf plot that has the same distribution of data as the histogram shown. *Explain* the steps you took to create the stem-and-leaf plot.

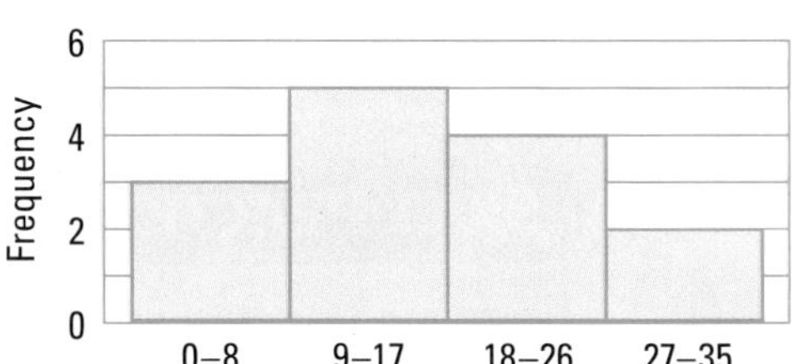

PROBLEM SOLVING

EXAMPLE 1 on p. 881 for Ex. 17

17. **HEIGHTS** The heights (in inches) of players on a boys' basketball team are as follows: 80, 76, 81, 69, 81, 78, 74, 68, 78, 74, 81, 72, 69, 81, 70. Make a stem-and-leaf plot of the heights.

@HomeTutor for problem solving help at classzone.com

EXAMPLE 3 on p. 882 for Exs. 18–19

18. **SURVEY** A survey asked people how many 8 ounce glasses of water they drink in one day. The results are below. Make a histogram of the data.

3, 0, 9, 1, 4, 2, 11, 5, 3, 6, 0, 5, 7, 8, 5, 2, 9, 6, 10, 2, 4

@HomeTutor for problem solving help at classzone.com

19. **MEMORY** A survey asked people how many phone numbers they have memorized. The results are shown in the table.

Phone numbers	1–5	6–10	11–15	16–20	21–25
Frequency	88	85	50	28	14

a. Make a histogram of the data.

b. What is the probability that a person surveyed, chosen at random, has 11–25 phone numbers memorized?

○ = **WORKED-OUT SOLUTIONS on p. WS1** ★ = **STANDARDIZED TEST PRACTICE**

EXAMPLE 2
on p. 882
for Ex. 20

20. ★ **EXTENDED RESPONSE** The back-to-back stem-and-leaf plot shows the numbers of days the House of Representatives and the Senate spent in session each year from 1996 to 2004.

a. What was the median number of days the House of Representatives spent in session? the Senate?

b. What is the range of the number of days the House of Representatives spent in session? the Senate?

c. *Compare* the data for the House of Representatives and the Senate. What does the distribution of the data tell you?

Days in Session

House		Senate
9 0	11	
3 2	12	
7 5 3 2	13	2 3
2	14	1 3 9
	15	3
	16	2 7
	17	3

Key: 2 | 14 | 1 = 142, 141

21. MAYFLOWER The known ages (in years) of adult male passengers on the *Mayflower* at the time of its departure are listed below.

21, 34, 29, 38, 30, 54, 39, 20, 35, 64, 37, 45, 21, 25, 55, 45, 40, 38, 38, 21, 21, 20, 34, 38, 50, 41, 48, 18, 32, 21, 32, 49, 30, 42, 30, 25, 38, 25, 20

a. Make a stem-and-leaf plot of the ages.

b. Find the median age and range of the ages.

c. According to one source, the age of passenger Thomas English was unknown at the time of the *Mayflower's* departure. What is the probability that he was 18–29 years old? *Explain* your reasoning.

Replica of the *Mayflower*

22. CHALLENGE Refer to the histogram shown.

a. Find the midpoint of each interval. Multiply each midpoint by the frequency of its interval. Add these products. Divide the sum by the sum of all the frequencies.

b. Does the your final result in part (a) best approximate the mean, the median, or the mode of the data? *Explain* your answer.

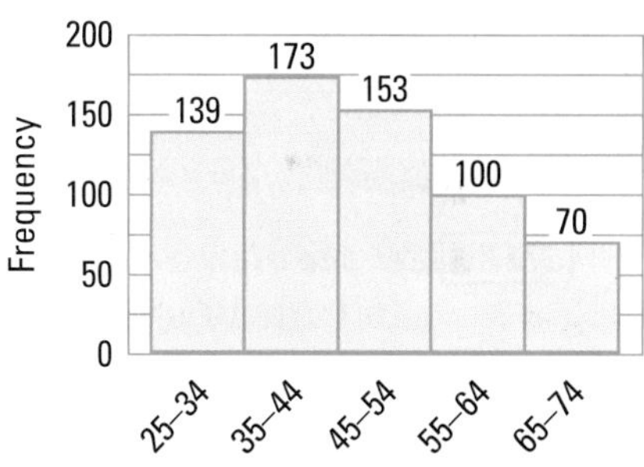

MIXED REVIEW

PREVIEW
Prepare for Lesson 13.8 in Exs. 23–25.

Find the mean, median, and mode(s) of the data. *(p. 918)*

23. Ages of family members (in years): 62, 35, 51, 28, 22, 25, 16, 58, 30, 14

24. Minutes of exercise each day: 35, 20, 25, 20, 0, 30, 45, 40, 20, 30, 35, 0

25. Hours worked per week: 10, 9, 11, 12, 8, 15, 20, 9, 16, 14, 15, 12

Tell whether the question is potentially biased. *Explain* your answer. If the question is biased, rewrite it so that it is not. *(p. 871)*

26. Don't you agree that science fiction movies are boring?

27. Is your ideal vacation a trip to Florida or a trip to Alaska?

Graphing Calculator ACTIVITY *Use after Lesson 13.7*

@HomeTutor
classzone.com
Keystrokes

13.7 Draw Histograms

QUESTION How can you use a graphing calculator to make a histogram?

EXAMPLE Make a histogram

POPULATION The populations (in thousands) of metropolitan areas in the states with the greatest metropolitan populations in the United States in 2000 are listed below. Make a histogram of the data.

4527 32,750 14,837 5667 10,542 4390 4911 6101 8169 3795 8414
17,473 5437 9214 10,392 3862 17,692 5528 4899 3640

STEP 1 *Enter the data*

Go to the STAT menu and choose Edit. Enter the data into List 1.

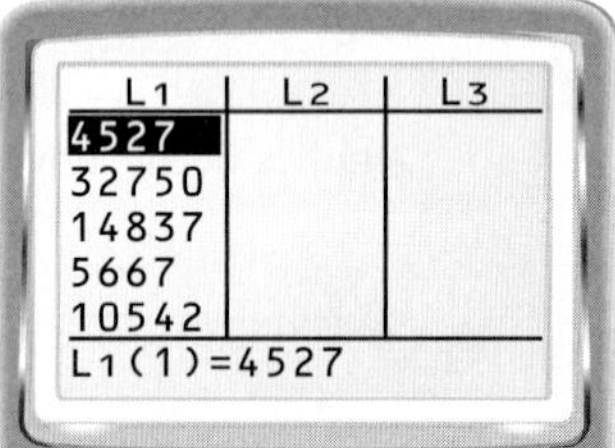

STEP 2 *Select histogram*

Go to the STAT PLOT screen. Select Plot 1. Use the settings shown below.

STEP 3 *Set the viewing window*

Go to the WINDOW screen. Use the settings shown below.

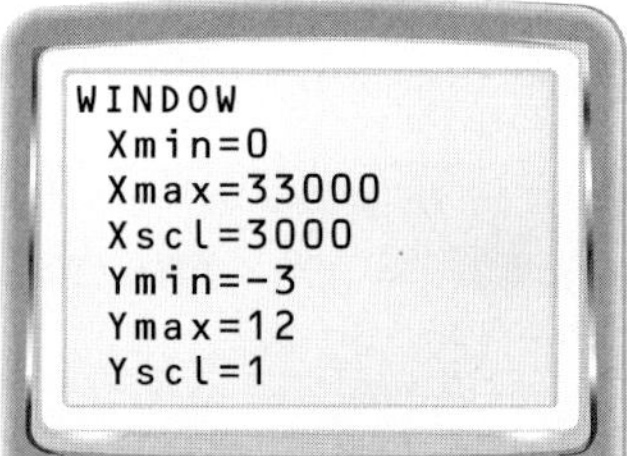

STEP 4 *Graph*

Press GRAPH. Use the *trace* feature to move from bar to bar.

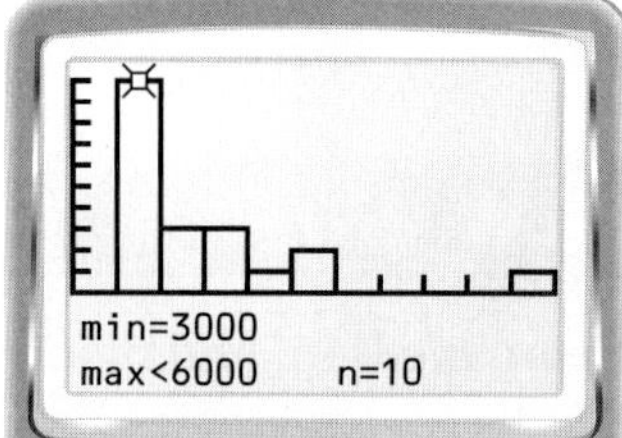

DRAW CONCLUSIONS

1. *Describe* the distribution of the population data in the example above.

2. **BOWLING** Use a graphing calculator to make a histogram of the following bowling scores: 200, 210, 105, 300, 180, 175, 162, 110, 140, 300, 152, 165, 175, 115, 250, 270, 145, 182, 164, 122, 141, 135, 189, 170, 151, 158.

13.8 Interpret Box-and-Whisker Plots

Before You made stem-and-leaf plots and histograms.

Now You will make and interpret box-and-whisker plots.

Why? So you can compare sets of scientific data, as in Ex. 19.

Key Vocabulary
- box-and-whisker plot
- quartile
- interquartile range
- outlier

A **box-and-whisker plot** organizes data values into four groups. Ordered data are divided into lower and upper halves by the median. The median of the lower half is the **lower quartile**. The median of the upper half is the **upper quartile**.

EXAMPLE 1 Make a box-and-whisker plot

SONG LENGTHS The lengths of songs (in seconds) on a CD are listed below. Make a box-and-whisker plot of the song lengths.

173, 206, 179, 257, 198, 251, 239, 246, 295, 181, 261

Solution

STEP 1 **Order** the data. Then find the median and the quartiles.

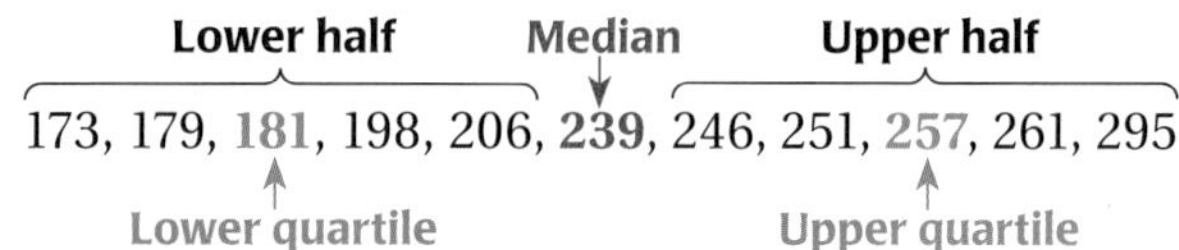

STEP 2 **Plot** the median, the quartiles, the maximum value, and the minimum value below a number line.

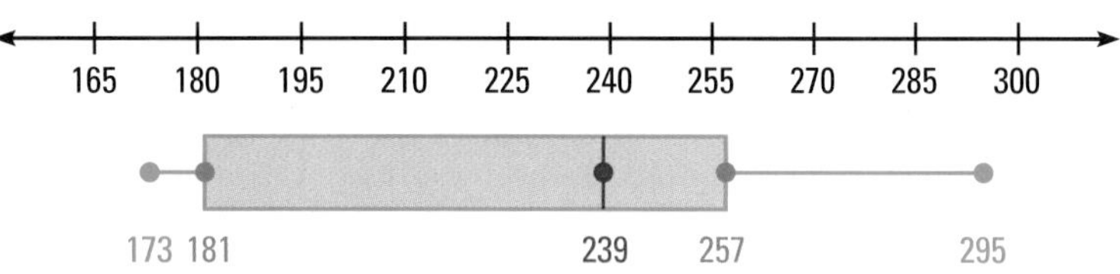

STEP 3 **Draw** a box from the lower quartile to the upper quartile. Draw a vertical line through the median. Draw a line segment (a "whisker") from the box to the maximum and another from the box to the minimum.

at classzone.com

GUIDED PRACTICE for Example 1

1. Make a box-and-whisker plot of the ages of eight family members: 60, 15, 25, 20, 55, 70, 40, 30.

INTERPRET A BOX-AND-WHISKER PLOT A box-and-whisker plot separates data into four groups: the two parts of the box and the two whiskers. Each part contains approximately the same number of data values.

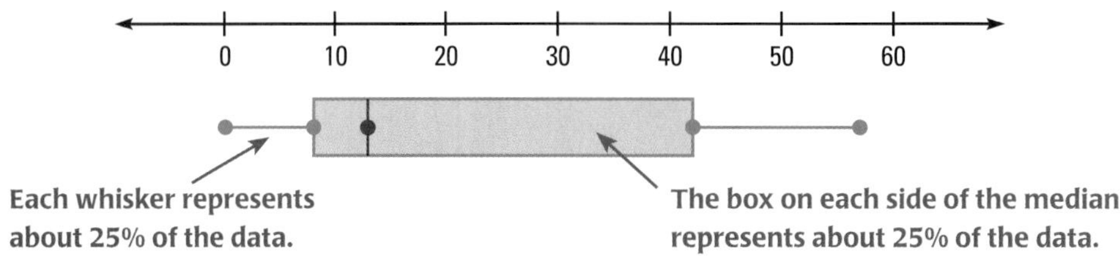

INTERPRET VARIATION

The interquartile range measures the variation in the middle half of the data and ignores the extreme values, whose variation may not be representative of the data.

You know that the range of a data set is the difference of the maximum value and the minimum value. The **interquartile range** of a data set is the difference of the upper quartile and the lower quartile.

EXAMPLE 2 Interpret a box-and-whisker plot

PRECIPITATION The box-and-whisker plots below show the normal precipitation (in inches) each month in Dallas and in Houston, Texas.

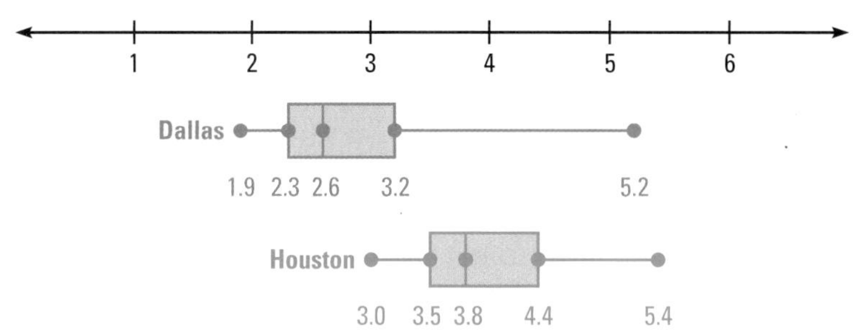

a. For how many months is Houston's precipitation less than 3.5 inches?

b. Compare the precipitation in Dallas with the precipitation in Houston.

Solution

a. For Houston, the lower quartile is 3.5. A whisker represents 25% of the data, so for 25% of 12 months, or 3 months, Houston has less than 3.5 inches of precipitation.

b. The median precipitation for a month in Dallas is 2.6 inches. The median for Houston is 3.8 inches. In general, Houston has more precipitation.

For Dallas, the interquartile range is $3.2 - 2.3$, or 0.9 inch. For Houston, the interquartile range is $4.4 - 3.5 = 0.9$ inch. So, the cities have the same variation in the middle 50% of the data. The range for Dallas is greater than the range for Houson. When all the data are considered, Dallas has more variation in precipitation.

INTERPRET QUARTILES

When the number of data values is a multiple of 4, the median and quartiles will divide the data into four groups of *exactly* the same size.

✓ **GUIDED PRACTICE** for Example 2

2. PRECIPITATION In Example 2, for how many months was the precipitation in Dallas more than 2.6 inches?

OUTLIERS A value that is widely separated from the rest of the data in a data set is called an **outlier**. Typically, a data value is considered to be an outlier if it is greater than the upper quartile by more than 1.5 times the interquartile range or if it is less than the lower quartile by more than 1.5 times the interquartile range.

EXAMPLE 3 Standardized Test Practice

The normal monthly amounts of precipitation (in inches) in Dallas are: 1.9, 2.4, 3.1, 3.2, 5.2, 3.2, 2.1, 2.0, 2.4, 4.1, 2.6, 2.6. These data were used to create the box-and-whisker plot in Example 2. Which value, if any, is an outlier?

Ⓐ 1.9 Ⓑ 5.2 Ⓒ 1.9 and 5.2 Ⓓ No outlier

Solution

From Example 2, you know the interquartile range of the data is 0.9 inch. Find 1.5 times the interquartile range: $1.5(0.9) = 1.35$.

From Example 2, you also know that the lower quartile is 2.3 and the upper quartile is 3.2. A value less than $2.3 - 1.35 = 0.95$ is an outlier. A value greater than $3.2 + 1.35 = 4.55$, is an outlier. Notice that $5.2 > 4.55$.

▶ The correct answer is B. Ⓐ Ⓑ Ⓒ Ⓓ

✓ GUIDED PRACTICE for Example 3

3. Which value, if any, is an outlier in the data set?

3.7, 3.0, 3.4, 3.6, 5.2, 5.4, 3.2, 3.8, 4.3, 4.5, 4.2, 3.7

Ⓐ 3.0 Ⓑ 5.4 Ⓒ 3.0 and 5.4 Ⓓ No outlier

13.8 EXERCISES

HOMEWORK KEY
○ = **WORKED-OUT SOLUTIONS** on p. WS33 for Exs. 3 and 17
★ = **STANDARDIZED TEST PRACTICE** Exs. 2, 8, 9, 18, and 19

SKILL PRACTICE

1. **VOCABULARY** What is the interquartile range of a data set?

2. ★ **WRITING** *Explain* how you can identify an outlier in a data set.

EXAMPLE 1 on p. 887 for Exs. 3–7

BOX-AND-WHISKER PLOTS **Make a box-and-whisker plot of the data.**

3. 1, 7, 0, 7, 2, 6, 3, 6, 0, 7, 8
4. 10, 1, 7, 5, 1, 8, 5, 4, 6, 5, 9, 12
5. 52, 20, 24, 45, 35, 32, 39, 42, 23, 64
6. 0.8, 0.4, 0.3, 0.6, 0.7, 0.2, 0.7, 0.9

7. **ERROR ANALYSIS** *Describe* and correct the error in creating a box-and-whisker plot of the data 0, 2, 4, 0, 6, 10, 8, 12, 5.

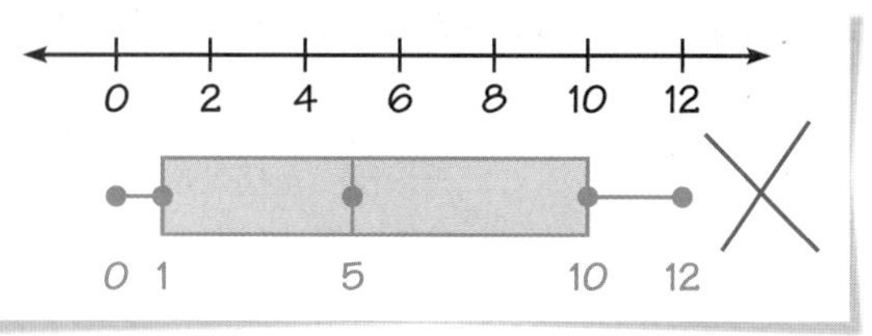

BOX-AND-WHISKER PLOT In Exercises 8–10, use the box-and-whisker plot.

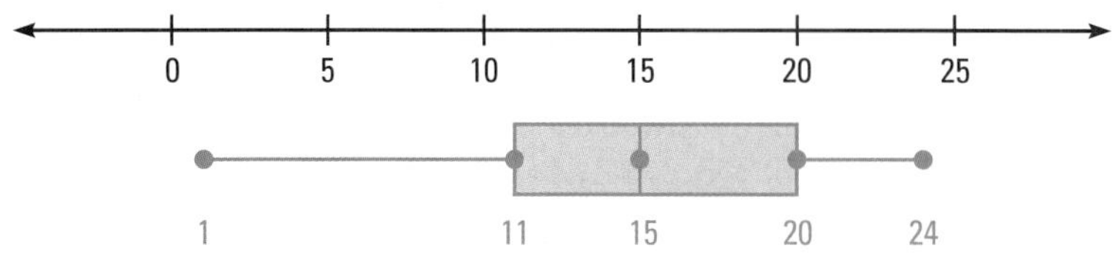

EXAMPLE 2
on p. 888
for Exs. 8–10

8. ★ **MULTIPLE CHOICE** About what percent of the data are greater than 20?

   (A) 25% (B) 50% (C) 75% (D) 100%

9. ★ **MULTIPLE CHOICE** About what percent of the data are less than 15?

   (A) 25% (B) 50% (C) 75% (D) 100%

10. **ERROR ANALYSIS** *Describe* and correct the error in interpreting the box-and-whisker plot.

About 25% of the data values lie between 11 and 20.

EXAMPLES 1 and 3
on pp. 887, 889
for Exs. 11–13

OUTLIERS Make a box-and-whisker plot of the data. Identify any outliers.

11. Hours worked per week: 15, 15, 10, 12, 22, 10, 8, 14, 18, 22, 18, 15, 12, 11, 10
12. Prices of MP3 players: \$124, \$95, \$105, \$110, \$95, \$124, \$300, \$190, \$114
13. Annual salaries: \$30,000, \$35,000, \$48,000, \$68,500, \$32,000, \$38,000

14. **CHALLENGE** Two data sets have the same mean, the same interquartile range, and the same range. Is it possible for the box-and-whisker plots of such data sets to be different? *Justify* your answer by creating data sets that fit the situation.

PROBLEM SOLVING

EXAMPLE 1
on p. 887
for Exs. 15–16

15. **SEAWAY** The average sailing times to the Atlantic Ocean from several ports on the St. Lawrence Seaway are shown on the map. Make a box-and-whisker plot of the sailing times.

@HomeTutor for problem solving help at classzone.com

16. **BASEBALL STATISTICS** In 2004, Ichiro Suzuki scored 101 runs. The numbers of runs he scored against different opposing teams are listed below. Make a box-and-whisker plot of the numbers of runs scored.

Runs scored: 18, 8, 4, 8, 2, 8, 0, 9, 0, 4, 2, 5, 9, 1, 2, 1, 2, 11, 7

@HomeTutor for problem solving help at classzone.com

EXAMPLES 1 and 3 on pp. 887, 889 for Exs. 17–18

17. **RETAIL SALES** The retail sales (in billions of dollars) of the nine U.S. states with the highest retail sales in 2002 are listed below.

California: \$153.1	Florida: \$118.2	Georgia: \$38.4
Illinois: \$52.4	New Jersey: \$35.8	New York: \$54.7
Ohio: \$50.7	Pennsylvania: \$49.9	Texas: \$107.0

a. Make a box-and-whisker plot of the retail sales.

b. Which states, if any, had retail sales in 2002 that can be considered outliers?

18. ★ **SHORT RESPONSE** The stem-and-leaf plot shows the ages of the first 43 presidents of the United States when they first took the oath of office.

Stem	Leaves
4	2 3 6 6 7 8 9 9
5	0 0 1 1 1 1 2 2 4 4 4 4 4 5 5 5 5 6 6 6 7 7 7 7 8
6	0 1 1 1 2 4 4 5 8 9

Key: 4 | 2 = 42 years

a. Make a box-and-whisker plot of the ages.

b. Ronald Reagan was the oldest United States president, and Theodore Roosevelt was the youngest. Can either of these presidents' ages be considered outliers? *Explain* why or why not.

EXAMPLE 2 on p. 888 for Ex. 19

19. ★ **EXTENDED RESPONSE** The box-and-whisker plots show the diameters (in kilometers) of craters on Jupiter's moons Callisto and Ganymede.

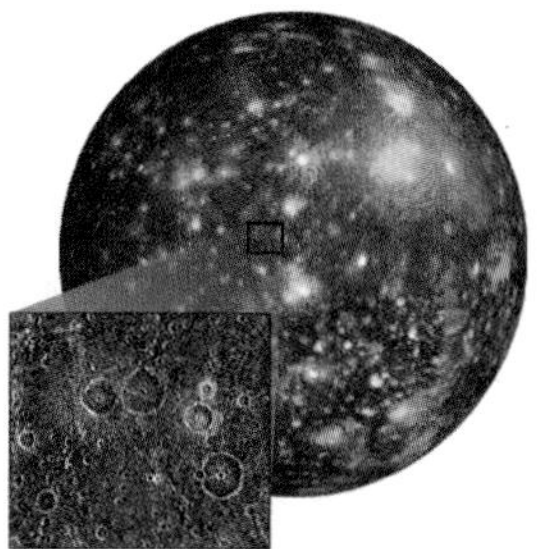

Callisto

a. *Compare* the diameters of craters on Callisto with the diameters of craters on Ganymede.

b. The largest crater in the United States is the Chesapeake Bay in Virginia, with a diameter of 90 kilometers. *Compare* the diameter of the Chesapeake Bay with diameters of craters on Callisto and Ganymede.

c. The largest crater on Earth is Vredefort in South Africa, with a diameter of 300 kilometers. *Compare* the diameter of Vredefort with the diameter of craters on Callisto and Ganymede.

20. **CHALLENGE** The box-and-whisker plots show the heights (in inches) of singers in a chorus, according to their voice parts. A soprano part has the highest pitch, followed by alto, tenor, and bass, respectively. Draw a conclusion about voice parts and heights. *Justify* your conclusion.

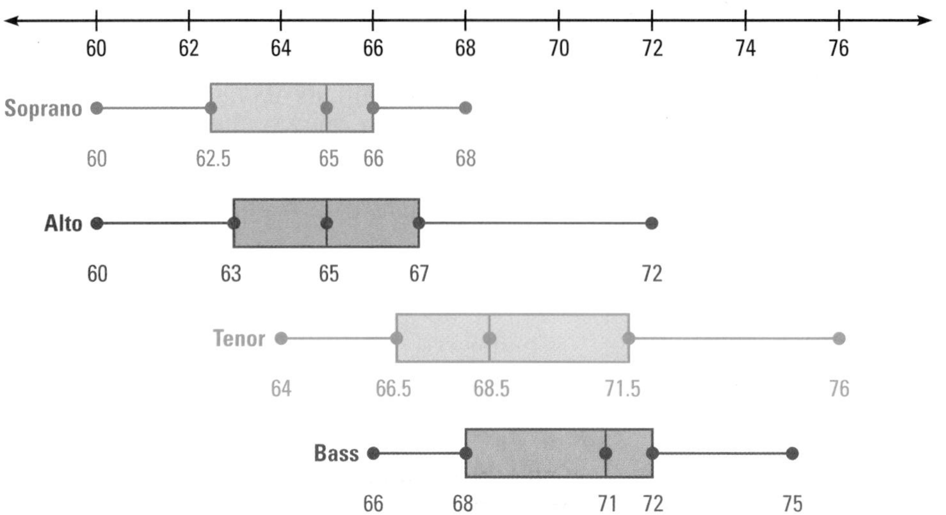

MIXED REVIEW

Make a stem-and-leaf plot of the data. *(p. 881)*

21. 56, 55, 54, 57, 28, 28, 53, 52, 56, 28, 25, 23, 17, 51, 54, 23, 20, 10

22. 71, 60, 39, 43, 81, 32, 33, 41, 37, 34, 51, 41, 32, 34, 48, 35, 36, 58

Make a histogram of the data. *(p. 881)*

23. 1.24, 2.45, 1.11, 2.09, 2.19, 1.99, 1.75, 1.65, 2.10, 2.30

24. 1.5, 5.12, 7.5, 7.1, 7.14, 9.7, 10.24, 1.3, 1.6, 1.6, 3.3, 3.12

QUIZ *for Lessons 13.5–13.8*

1. **HOTEL SURVEY** A hotel manager leaves guest comment cards in each room. Identify the population and classify the sampling method. *(p. 871)*

In Exercises 2 and 3, find the range and mean absolute deviation of the data. Round to the nearest hundredth, if necessary. *(p. 875)*

2. 62, 63, 70, 40, 50, 60

3. 14, 18, 22, 14, 14, 6, 17

4. Make a histogram of the data: 44, 52, 60, 47, 65, 40, 49, 45, 32, 68, 39. *(p. 881)*

5. Make a stem-and-leaf plot of the data: 1.8, 2.2, 1.2, 2.8, 3.6, 3.3, 1.8, 2.2. *(p. 881)*

6. **TEST SCORES** The scores on a math exam are given below. Make a box-and-whisker plot of the data. Identify any outliers. *(p. 887)*

   76, 55, 88, 92, 79, 85, 90, 88, 85, 92, 100, 91, 90, 86, 88

 EXTRA PRACTICE for Lesson 13.8, p. 950 **ONLINE QUIZ** at classzone.com

Graphing Calculator ACTIVITY *Use after Lesson 13.8*

@HomeTutor
classzone.com
Keystrokes

13.8 Draw Box-and-Whisker Plots

QUESTION How can you use a graphing calculator to make a box-and-whisker plot?

EXAMPLE Make a box-and-whisker plot

REPTILE SPECIES The number of known reptile species per 10,000 square kilometers in the countries of Asia (excluding the Middle East) and of Central America, South America, and the Caribbean are listed below. Make box-and-whisker plots of the numbers of species.

Asia: 36, 26, 49, 11, 32, 35, 27, 58, 91, 26, 8, 8, 12, 12, 23, 110, 4, 51, 41, 41, 62, 350, 77, 18, 81, 23, 18, 59

Central America, South America, and the Caribbean: 81, 125, 47, 69, 57, 107, 77, 73, 35, 123, 69, 116, 87, 37, 45, 53, 20, 124, 126, 35, 73, 60, 64

STEP 1 Enter the data

Enter the data for Asia into List 1. Enter the data for Central America, South America, and the Caribbean into List 2.

STEP 2 Select box-and-whisker plot

Go to the STAT PLOT screen and select the box-and-whisker plot for both Plot 1 and Plot 2. The Xlist for Plot 1 should be L_1, so that it displays the data from List 1. The Xlist for Plot 2 should be L_2, so that it displays the data from List 2. Make sure both plots are on.

STEP 3 Set the viewing window

Press ZOOM 9 to set the window so that it shows all of the data.

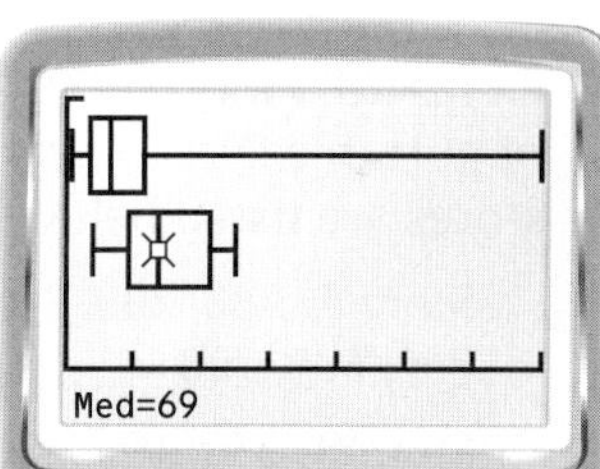

STEP 4 Graph

Press GRAPH. Use the trace feature to examine the box-and-whisker plots more closely. Notice that the graphing calculator refers to the lower quartile as Q_1 and the upper quartile as Q_3.

DRAW CONCLUSIONS

1. **REPTILE SPECIES** *Compare* the number of reptile species per 10,000 square kilometers in the countries of Central America, South America, and the Caribbean with the number in Asia.
2. **BIRD SPECIES** The number of threatened bird species per 10,000 square kilometers in the countries of two regions are listed below. Make box-and-whisker plots of the data and compare the data for the two regions.

   Middle East and Northern Africa: 13, 8, 11, 14, 12, 8, 4, 3, 5, 2, 11, 5, 11, 7, 6, 14, 4, 13

   North and South America: 5, 50, 41, 27, 103, 18, 64, 53, 3, 26, 64, 2, 11, 22

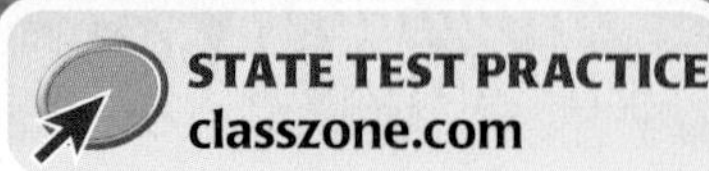

Lessons 13.5–13.8

1. **MULTI-STEP PROBLEM** The ages of people who attended an opening reception for a theater production are listed below.

   54, 25, 28, 64, 30, 42, 33, 50, 27, 35, 40, 39, 41, 52, 49, 48, 56, 60, 58, 37, 56, 45, 57, 62

   a. Make a frequency table of the data.

   b. Make a histogram of the data.

2. **MULTI-STEP PROBLEM** A doctor would like to extend her office hours to better accommodate her patients. She asks each patient who visits her office on Tuesday which day the patient thinks the hours should be extended.

   a. Identify the population and classify the sampling method.

   b. Tell whether the survey method used is likely to result in a biased sample.

3. **GRIDDED ANSWER** The average lengths (in hours) of several morning commutes are listed below. How many minutes is the mean commute?

   0.25, 0.20, 0.50, 0.50, 0.50, 0.05, 0.65, 1.00, 1.50, 0.75, 0.50, 1.10, 0.60, 0.80, 1.00, 0.10

4. **EXTENDED RESPONSE** The prices (in dollars) of portable DVD players at two different stores are listed below.

   Store A: 280, 200, 260, 230, 200, 150, 300, 260, 500, 190

   Store B: 350, 190, 230, 250, 400, 200, 200, 220, 185, 150

   a. Find the mean, median, and mode(s) of each data set. Which measure of central tendency best represents each data set? *Explain* your reasoning.

   b. Find the range and mean absolute deviation of each data set. Which store's prices are more spread out? *Explain.*

   c. Can any of the prices of the portable DVD players be considered outliers? *Explain* your reasoning.

5. **OPEN-ENDED** A clothing store sells several different styles of jeans. The mean price of the jeans is \$27. The median price of the jeans is \$27.50. The mode of the prices is \$20. Make a list of prices of jeans that has these measures of central tendency.

6. **SHORT RESPONSE** The back-to-back stem-and-leaf plot below shows the lengths (in meters) of the eight best men's and women's final long jump results from the 2004 Olympics. *Compare* the lengths of the jumps by men with those by women.

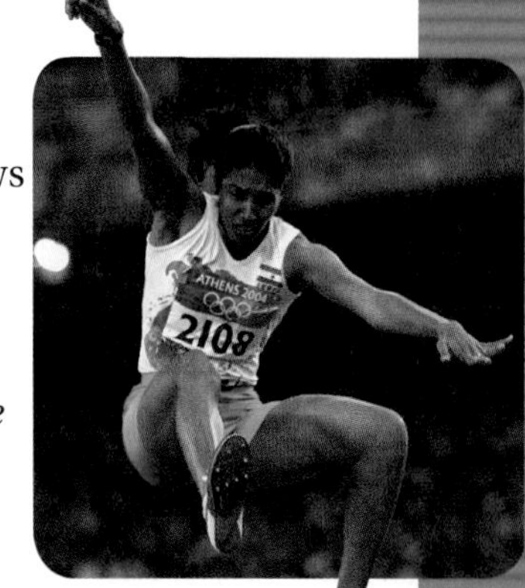

Lengths (in meters) of Long Jump

Men		Women
	6	7 8 8 9
	7	0 0 0 1
6 5 3 3 2 2 2 0	8	

Key: 0 | 7 | 1 = 7.0 m, 7.1 m

7. **SHORT RESPONSE** The stem-and-leaf plot shows the number of games lost by 15 NCAA football coaches with the greatest career winning percentages after at least 10 years of coaching.

Stem	Leaves
1	1 2 3 6 7 7 8
2	1 3 3 4 5 9
3	6
4	9

Key: 2 | 1 = 21 games

   a. Make a box-and-whisker plot of the data.

   b. Tom Osborne had a winning percentage of 83.6% over his career and lost 49 games. Can the number of games lost by Tom Osborne be considerred an outlier? *Explain* your reasoning.

13 CHAPTER SUMMARY

BIG IDEAS

For Your Notebook

Big Idea 1

Finding Probabilities of Simple and Compound Events

To find $P(A)$ when...	
all outcomes are equally likely, use $P(A) = \frac{\text{Number of favorable outcomes}}{\text{Number of possible outcomes}}$	you perform an experiment, use $P(A) = \frac{\text{Number of successes}}{\text{Number of trials}}$

To find $P(A \text{ or } B)$ when...	...use this formula
events A and B have no common outcomes	$P(A \text{ or } B) = P(A) + P(B)$
events A and B have at least one common outcome	$P(A \text{ or } B) = P(A) + P(B) - P(A \text{ and } B)$

To find $P(A \text{ and } B)$ when...	...use this formula
events A and B are independent	$P(A \text{ and } B) = P(A) \cdot P(B)$
events A and B are dependent	$P(A \text{ and } B) = P(A) \cdot P(B \text{ given } A)$

Big Idea 2

Analyzing Sets of Data

You can find values that represent a typical data value using the following measures of central tendency:

mean, median, and mode

You can find values that describe the spread of data using the following measures of dispersion:

range, mean absolute deviation, and interquartile range

Big Idea 3

Making and Interpreting Data Displays

Use an appropriate display to show the distribution of a set of numerical data.

A **stem-and-leaf plot** organizes data based on their digits.

Stem	Leaves
1	0 1 1 2 3
2	0 0 0 2

Key: 1 | 0 = 10

A **histogram** shows the frequency of data on intervals of equal size, with no gaps or overlaps.

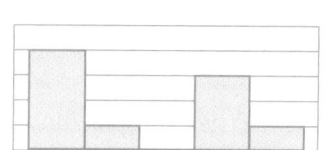

A **box-and-whisker plot** organizes data into four groups of approximately equal size.

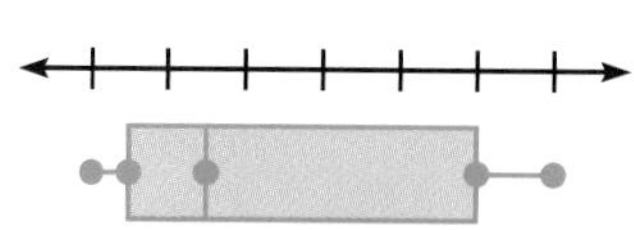

13 CHAPTER REVIEW

@HomeTutor
classzone.com
- Multi-Language Glossary
- Vocabulary Practice

REVIEW KEY VOCABULARY

- outcome, event, *p. 843*
- sample space, *p. 843*
- probability of an event, *p. 843*
- theoretical, experimental probability, *p. 844*
- odds in favor, odds against, *p. 845*
- permutation, *p. 851*
- *n* factorial, *p. 852*
- combination, *p. 856*
- compound event, *p. 861*
- mutually exclusive events, *p. 861*
- overlapping events, *p. 861*
- independent events, *p. 862*
- dependent events, *p. 862*
- survey, *p. 871*
- population, *p. 871*
- sample: random, stratified random, systematic, convenience, self-selected, *p. 871*
- biased sample, *p. 872*
- biased question, *p. 872*
- mean, median, mode, *p. 875*
- measure of dispersion, *p. 876*
- range, *p. 876*
- mean absolute deviation, *p. 876*
- stem-and-leaf plot, *p. 881*
- frequency, frequency table, *p. 882*
- histogram, *p. 882*
- box-and-whisker plot, *p. 887*
- lower quartile, upper quartile, *p. 887*
- interquartile range, *p. 888*
- outlier, *p. 889*

VOCABULARY EXERCISES

Copy and complete the statement.

1. An event that combines two or more events is a(n) _?_.
2. A possible result of an experiment is a(n) _?_.
3. **WRITING** *Compare* theoretical probability and experimental probability.

REVIEW EXAMPLES AND EXERCISES

Use the review examples and exercises below to check your understanding of the concepts you have learned in each lesson of Chapter 13.

13.1 Find Probabilities and Odds *pp. 843–848*

EXAMPLE

A bag contains 15 red checkers and 15 black checkers. You choose a checker at random. Find the probability that you choose a black checker.

$$P(\text{black checker}) = \frac{\text{Number of black checkers}}{\text{Total number of checkers}} = \frac{15}{30} = \frac{1}{2}$$

EXERCISES

EXAMPLE 2 on p. 844 for Exs. 4–5

4. **CHECKERS** In the example above, suppose an extra red checker is added to the bag. Find the probability of randomly choosing a black checker.
5. **BAG OF LETTERS** A bag contains tiles. Each tile has one letter from the word HAPPINESS on it. You choose a tile at random. What is the probability that you choose a tile with the letter S?

@HomeTutor
classzone.com
Chapter Review Practice

13.2 Find Probabilities Using Permutations

pp. 851–855

EXAMPLE

You need to enter a 4 digit code in order to enter the building where you work. The digits are 4 different numbers from 1 to 5. You forgot the code and try to guess it. Find the probability that you guess correctly.

STEP 1 **Write** the number of possible outcomes as the number of permutations of 4 out of the 5 possible digits. This is ${}_5P_4$.

$${}_5P_4 = \frac{5!}{(5-4)!} = \frac{5!}{1!} = 5! = 5 \cdot 4 \cdot 3 \cdot 2 \cdot 1 = 120$$

STEP 2 **Find** the probability. Because only one of the permutations is the correct code, the probability that you guess the correct code is $\frac{1}{120}$.

EXERCISES

EXAMPLE 2 on p. 852 for Exs. 6–10

Evaluate the expression.

6. ${}_7P_6$ **7.** ${}_6P_2$ **8.** ${}_8P_5$ **9.** ${}_{13}P_{10}$

10. MUSIC You downloaded 6 songs. You randomly choose 4 of these songs to play. Find the probability that you play the first 4 songs you downloaded in the order in which you downloaded them.

13.3 Find Probabilities Using Combinations

pp. 856–859

EXAMPLE

For your government class, you must choose 3 states in the United States to research. You may choose your states from the 6 New England states. How many combinations of states are possible?

The order in which you choose the states is not important. So, to find the number of combinations of 6 states taken 3 at a time, find ${}_6C_3$.

$${}_6C_3 = \frac{6!}{(6-3)! \cdot 3!}$$ **Combinations formula**

$$= \frac{6 \cdot 5 \cdot 4 \cdot \cancel{3!}}{\cancel{3!} \cdot (3 \cdot 2 \cdot 1)}$$ **Expand factorials. Divide out common factor, 3!.**

$$= 20$$ **Simplify.**

EXERCISES

EXAMPLE 2 on p. 857 for Exs. 11–15

Evaluate the expression.

11. ${}_7C_6$ **12.** ${}_6C_2$ **13.** ${}_8C_5$ **14.** ${}_{13}C_{10}$

15. TICKETS You win 5 tickets to a concert. In how many ways can you choose 4 friends out of a group of 9 to take with you to the concert?

13 CHAPTER REVIEW

13.4 Find Probabilities of Compound Events

pp. 861–867

EXAMPLE

The sections of the spinner shown all have the same area. You spin the spinner. Find the probability that the spinner stops on red or on an even number.

Because 24 is an even number on a red section, stopping on red and stopping on an even number are overlapping events.

$$P(\text{red or even}) = P(\text{red}) + P(\text{even}) - P(\text{red and even})$$
$$= \frac{3}{8} + \frac{3}{8} - \frac{1}{8}$$
$$= \frac{5}{8}$$

EXERCISES

EXAMPLES 1 and 2 on pp. 861–862 for Exs. 16–19

You spin the spinner shown above. Find the specified probability.

16. *P*(green or odd)
17. *P*(blue or prime number)
18. *P*(blue or even)
19. *P*(red or multiple of 3)

EXAMPLE

A bag contains 5 red marbles, 3 blue marbles, 6 white marbles, and 2 green marbles. You choose one marble at random, put the marble aside, then choose a second marble at random. What is the probability that both marbles are blue?

Because you do not replace the first marble, the events are dependent. Before you choose a marble, there are 16 marbles, and 3 of them are blue. After you choose a blue marble, there are 2 blue marbles among 15 marbles left.

$$P(\text{blue and then blue}) = P(\text{blue}) \cdot P(\text{blue given blue})$$
$$= \frac{3}{16} \cdot \frac{2}{15}$$
$$= \frac{6}{240}$$
$$= \frac{1}{40}$$

EXERCISES

EXAMPLES 3 and 4 on p. 863 for Exs. 20–21

You randomly choose 2 marbles from the bag described in the example above. Find the probability that both are green if:

20. you replace the first marble.
21. you don't replace the first marble.

@HomeTutor
classzone.com
Chapter Review Practice

13.5 Analyze Surveys and Samples

pp. 871–874

EXAMPLE

You want to determine what type of music is the favorite of students in your grade. You survey every third student from an alphabetical list of students in your grade. You ask each surveyed student, "What is your favorite type of music, classical or country?"

Identify the population and classify the sampling method. Tell whether the question is potentially biased. Explain your answer. If the question is potentially biased, rewrite it so that it is not.

The population is all students in your grade. Because you use the rule "survey every third student," the sample is a systematic sample.

The question is biased, because it does not allow students to choose a type of music other than classical or country. An unbiased question is "What is your favorite type of music?"

EXERCISES

EXAMPLE 1 on p. 871 for Ex. 22

22. **SURVEY** In the example above, suppose you create a questionaire and distribute one to every student in your grade. There is a box in the cafeteria where students can drop off completed questionaires during lunch. Identify the sampling method.

13.6 Use Measures of Central Tendency and Dispersion

pp. 875–878

EXAMPLE

The amounts of snowfall (in inches) in one town for 8 months of the year are listed below. Find the mean, median, and mode(s) of the data. Which measure of central tendency best represents the data?

0.5, 0.5, 1.5, 2.0, 3.5, 4.5, 16.5, 30.5

$$\bar{x} = \frac{0.5 + 0.5 + 1.5 + 2.0 + 3.5 + 4.5 + 16.5 + 30.5}{8} = \frac{59.5}{8} = 7.4375 \text{ inches}$$

The median is the mean of the two middle values, 2.0 and 3.5, or 2.75 inches.

The mode is 0.5 inch.

The median best represents the data. The mean is greater then most of the data values. The mode is less than most of the data values.

EXERCISES

EXAMPLES 1 and 2 on pp. 875–876 for Ex. 23

23. **BASEBALL STATISTICS** The numbers of home runs hit by baseball player Manny Ramirez against several different opposing teams over 3 seasons are 5, 1, 10, 5, 5, 4, 1, 0, 7, 2, 1, 1, 1, 9, 6, 1, 2, 6, 2, 19, 6, and 17.

    a. Find the mean, median, and mode(s) of the data.

    b. Which measure of central tendency best represents the data? *Explain.*

13 CHAPTER REVIEW

13.7 Interpret Stem-and-Leaf Plots and Histograms

pp. 881–885

EXAMPLE

The prices (in dollars) of several books are listed below. Make a stem-and-leaf plot of the prices.

14, 15, 9, 19, 21, 29, 12, 25, 10, 8, 15, 13, 15, 20

STEP 1 **Separate** the data into stems and leaves

Book Prices

Stem	Leaves
0	9 8
1	4 5 9 2 0 5 3 5
2	1 9 0 5

Key: 1 | 4 = $14

STEP 2 **Write** the leaves in increasing order.

Book Prices

Stem	Leaves
0	8 9
1	0 2 3 4 5 5 5 9
2	0 1 5 9

Key: 1 | 4 = $14

EXERCISES

EXAMPLE 1 on p. 881 for Ex. 24

24. EXERCISING The minutes per day that the students in a class spend exercising are listed below. Make a stem-and-leaf plot of the data.

20, 25, 0, 10, 0, 30, 35, 20, 45, 25, 40, 0, 0, 0, 5, 10, 20, 15, 20, 30

13.8 Interpret Box-and-Whisker Plots

pp. 887–892

EXAMPLE

Make a box-and-whisker plot of the book prices in the example above.

Order the data. Then find the median and quartiles.

Upper quartile Median = 15 Lower quartile

8 9 10 12 13 14 15 15 15 19 20 21 25 29

Plot the median, the quartiles, the maximum value, and the minimum value below a number line. Draw the box and the whiskers.

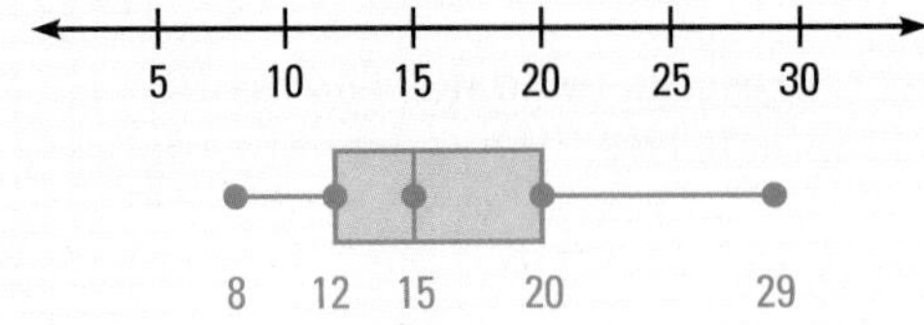

EXERCISES

EXAMPLE 1 on p. 887 for Ex. 25

25. EXERCISING Use the data in Exercise 24 to make a box-and-whisker plot of the minutes per day that the students in the class spend exercising.

13 CHAPTER TEST

You roll a number cube. Find (a) the probability that the number rolled is as described and (b) the odds in favor of rolling such a number.

1. a 4
2. an even number
3. a number less than 5
4. a multiple of 3

Evaluate the expression.

5. ${}_7P_2$
6. ${}_8P_3$
7. ${}_6C_3$
8. ${}_{12}C_7$

Tell whether the question can be answered using *combinations* or *permutations*. *Explain* your choice, then answer the question.

9. Eight swimmers participate in a race. In how many ways can the swimmers finish in first, second, and third place?

10. A restaurant offers 7 different side dishes. In how many different ways can you choose 2 side dishes?

In Exercises 11 and 12, refer to a bag containing 12 tiles numbered 1–12.

11. You choose a tile at random. What is the probability that you choose a number less than 10 or an odd number.

12. You choose a tile at random, replace it, and choose a second tile at random. What is the probability that you choose a number greater than 3, then an odd number.

13. **GOVERNMENT PROJECT** City officials want to know whether residents will support construction of a new library. This question appears on the ballot in the citywide election: "Do you support a tax increase to replace the old, deteriorating library with a brand new one?"Is the question potentially biased? *Explain* your answer. If the question is potentially biased, rewrite it so that it is not.

14. **BASKETBALL** The back-to-back stem-and-leaf plot shows the heights (in inches) of the players on a high school's basketball teams.

Basketball Players' Heights

Girls		Boys
9 7 7 6 6 5 3 3	6	9 9 9
3 2 1 1 0	7	0 0 0 2 4 4 6 6 7 7 7 8

Key: 3 | 6 | 9 = 63 in., 69 in.

a. Find the mean, median, and mode(s) of each data set. Which measure of central tendency best represents each data set? *Explain.*

b. Find the range and mean absolute deviation of each data set. Which team's heights are more spread out? *Explain.*

c. Make a box-and-whisker plot of each data set.

d. *Compare* the boys' heights with the girls' heights.

Scoring Rubric

Full Credit
- solution is complete and correct

Partial Credit
- solution is complete but has errors,

or
- solution is without error but incomplete

No Credit
- no solution is given,

or
- solution makes no sense

SHORT RESPONSE QUESTIONS

PROBLEM

The lengths (in inches) of several goldfish are listed below. Make a box-and-whisker plot of the lengths. Can any of the goldfish lengths be considered outliers? *Explain* why or why not.

8, 5, 4, 5, 4, 5, 4, 3, 4, 8

Below are sample solutions to the problem. Read each solution and the comments in blue to see why the sample represents full credit, partial credit, or no credit.

SAMPLE 1: Full credit solution

First, order the lengths from least to greatest.

3, 4, 4, 4, 4, 5, 5, 5, 8, 8

Then, plot the median, the quartiles, the maximum value, and the minimum value below a number line. Draw the box and whiskers.

The box-and-whisker plot is correct, and the student explained how it was drawn.

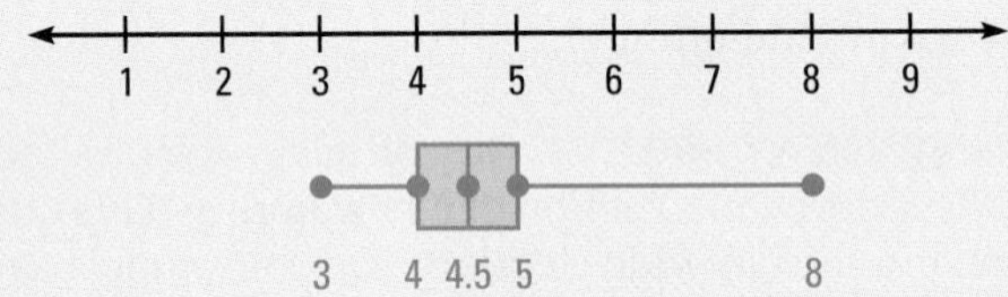

The interquartile range of the goldfish lengths is $5 - 4 = 1$, and 1.5 times the interquartile range is $1.5 \cdot 1 = 1.5$.

The question is answered correctly and includes an explanation.

A length that is less than $4 - 1.5 = 2.5$ would be an outlier. A length that is greater than $5 + 1.5 = 6.5$ would also an outlier. So, the two fish lengths of 8 inches are outliers.

SAMPLE 2: Partial credit solution

The box-and-whisker plot is incorrect. The student has not identified the median.

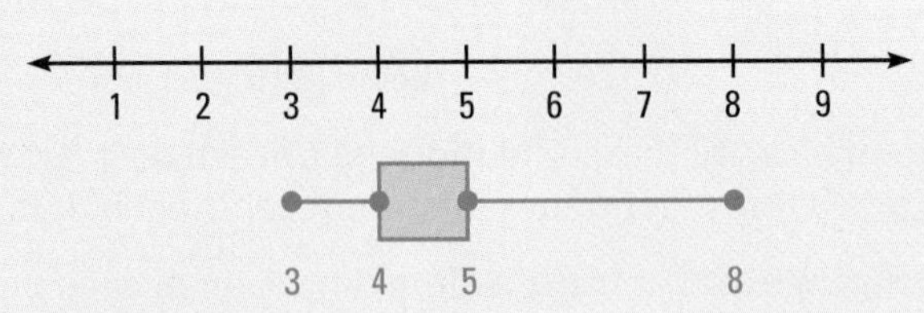

The answer and reasoning are correct.

The interquartile range of the lengths is $5 - 4 = 1$, and $1 \cdot 1.5 = 1.5$.

A length that is less than $4 - 1.5 = 2.5$ is an outlier. A length that is greater than $5 + 1.5 = 6.5$ is an outlier. So, the two fish lengths of 8 inches are outliers.

SAMPLE 3: Partial credit solution

The box-and-whisker plot is correct.

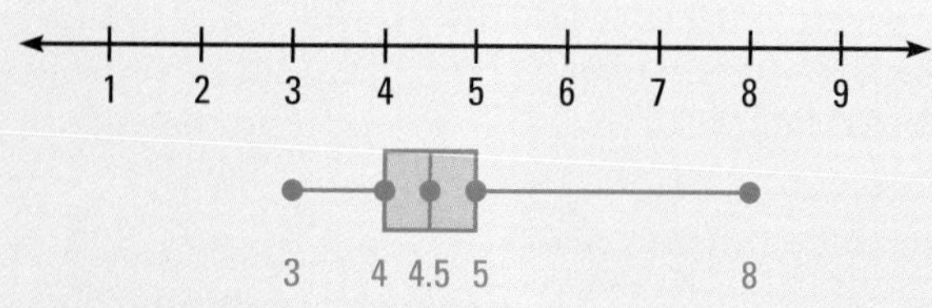

The answer is correct, but the reasoning is incorrect.

The interquartile range of the goldfish lengths is $5 - 4 = 1$.

A length that is less than $4 - 1 = 3$ is an outlier. A length that is greater than $5 + 1 = 6$ is an outlier. So, the two fish lengths of 8 inches are outliers.

SAMPLE 4: No credit solution

There is no box-and-whisker plot. The answer is incorrect.

The value 3 is an outlier because it is a very small goldfish.

PRACTICE Apply the Scoring Rubric

Score the solution to the problem below as *full credit, partial credit,* or *no credit. Explain* your reasoning.

PROBLEM The number of runs scored by 13 players on a baseball team are listed below. Make a box-and-whisker plot of the data. Can any of the values be considered outliers? *Explain* why or why not.

24, 20, 20, 11, 17, 6, 16, 16, 6, 5, 1, 5, 4

1.

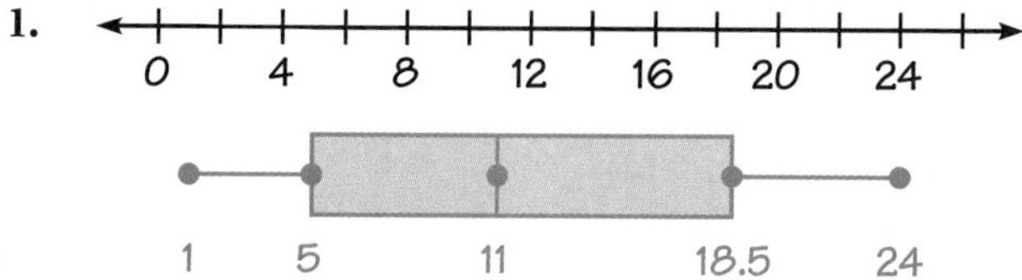

There are no outliers in the data set.

2.

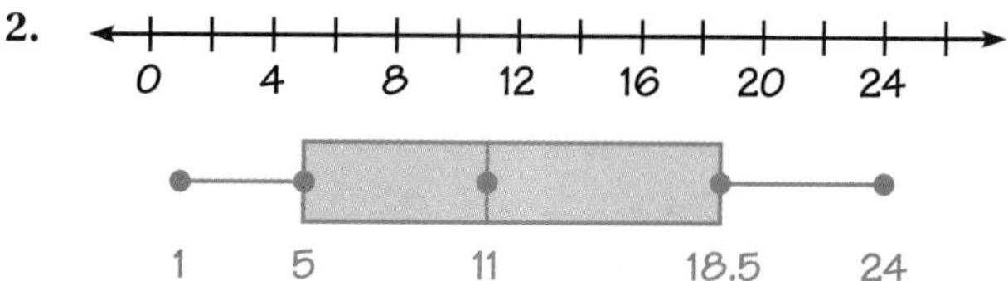

The interquartile range is 13.5, and $1.5 \cdot 13.5 = 20.25$. No values are less than $5 - 20.25 = -15.25$ or greater than $18.5 + 20.25 = 38.75$. So, there are no outliers.

13 ★ *Standardized* TEST PRACTICE

SHORT RESPONSE

1. Your English teacher gives you a list of 5 books that you are required to read over summer vacation. You read the books in a random order.

   a. In how many different ways can you read the 5 books?

   b. What is the probability that you read the longest book first or second? *Explain* how you found this probability.

2. The median ages (in years) of residents of 13 towns in a county are listed below.

   39, 35, 34, 40, 33, 30, 37,
   27, 33, 29, 33, 31, 35

   a. Make a box-and-whisker plot of the ages.

   b. Can any of the ages be considered outliers? *Explain* why or why not.

3. The lengths (in seconds) of songs on one CD are listed below.

   136, 249, 434, 136, 299,
   227, 270, 270, 46, 254

   a. Find the mean, median, and mode(s) of the song lengths.

   b. Which measure of central tendency best represents the data? *Explain*.

4. You are ordering a pizza with 3 toppings. There are 8 toppings available.

   a. How many possible pizzas with 3 toppings can you order?

   b. Did you answer the question in part (a) using combinations or permutations? *Explain* your choice.

5. The prices (in dollars) of several mobile phones sold by one retailer are listed below.

   350, 395, 429, 300, 569, 200, 500, 10,
   234, 245, 440, 50, 800, 390, 440, 338

   a. Make a box-and-whisker plot of the mobile phone prices.

   b. Which prices, if any, can be considered outliers? *Explain*.

6. You want to find out what kinds of food items would be most popular to sell to people who attend basketball games at your high school. You decide to conduct a survey.

   a. *Describe* how you could choose a representative sample.

   b. Write an unbiased question that you could use to collect information on what kinds of food items people would be most likely to purchase during a basketball game. *Explain* why your question is unbiased.

7. The student council has ordered T-shirts for everyone who participated in a recent fundraiser. The table below shows the number of each type of T-shirt ordered. You reach into the box of T-shirts and choose one at random.

	Medium	**Large**
Long sleeve	9	10
Short sleeve	8	13

   a. What is the probability that you choose a medium long-sleeve T-shirt?

   b. What is the probability that you choose a medium T-shirt or a long-sleeve T-shirt? *Explain* how this probability is related to the probability you found in part (a).

8. The back-to-back stem-and-leaf plot shows the prices (in dollars) of 15 dinners at two competing restaurants. *Compare* the prices at the two restaurants.

Dinner Prices

Restaurant A		Restaurant B
9 9 9 8	0	
7 7 5 5 2 2 1 0	1	0 2 2 3 5 6 6 8
1 0 0	2	1 2 4 4 5 5 5

Key: 0 | 2 | 1 = \$20, \$21

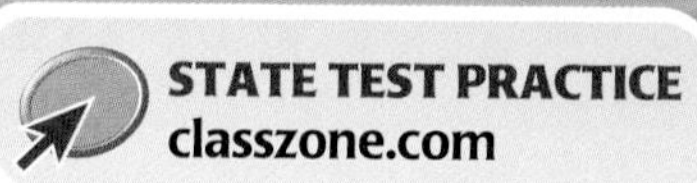

MULTIPLE CHOICE

9. The odds in favor of an event are 3 : 4. What is the probability of the event?

Ⓐ $\frac{1}{4}$ Ⓑ $\frac{3}{7}$

Ⓒ 75% Ⓓ $\frac{3}{4}$

10. A bag contains 4 red marbles, 3 green marbles, and 5 blue marbles. You randomly choose a marble from the bag. What is the probability that you choose a blue marble?

Ⓐ $\frac{1}{5}$ Ⓑ $\frac{5}{12}$

Ⓒ $\frac{5}{11}$ Ⓓ $\frac{5}{7}$

11. You roll a number cube. What is the probability that you roll a multiple of 2 or a multiple of 3?

Ⓐ $\frac{1}{6}$ Ⓑ $\frac{1}{3}$

Ⓒ $\frac{2}{3}$ Ⓓ $\frac{5}{6}$

GRIDDED ANSWER

12. What is the value of ${}_4P_3$?

13. In how many ways can you arrange the letters in the word BEACH?

14. What is the range of the given data set?

32, 41, 29, 28, 40, 78, 56, 23, 61, 30

15. The stem-and-leaf plot shows the ages (in years) of members of one family. What is the median age (in years)?

Stem	Leaves
0	8 9
1	0 4 6 7
2	0
3	9
4	2 3 3 4 5
5	
6	8 9

Key: 0 | 8 = 8 years

EXTENDED RESPONSE

16. A survey asked 500 teenagers where they would like to live. Of those surveyed, 150 teenagers would like to live in a large city. A participant in this survey is chosen at random.

a. What is the probability that the participant would like to live in a large city?

b. What are the odds in favor of the participant's wanting to live in a large city?

c. *Explain* how the probability in part (a) and odds in part (b) are related.

17. The histogram shows the diameters (in kilometers) of Jupiter's ten largest moons.

a. *Describe* the distribution of the data in the histogram. In your description, mention whether the data appear to be spread out or clumped in a certain way.

b. The diameters (in kilometers) of Saturn's ten largest moons are listed below.

97, 209, 256, 536, 560, 764, 2575, 180, 718, 110

Make a histogram of the diameters.

c. *Compare* the distribution of diameters of Jupiter's moons with the distribution of diameters of Saturn's moons.

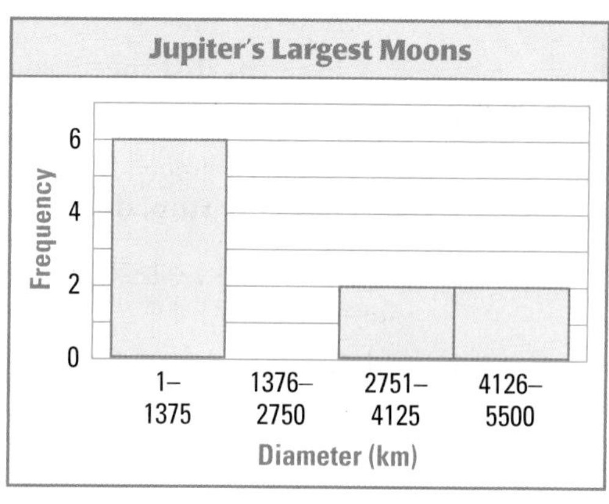

CUMULATIVE REVIEW Chapters 1–13

Evaluate the expression.

1. $2^4 \cdot 3 - 16 \div 4$ *(p. 8)*

2. $|-125| - 34$ *(p. 80)*

3. $\pm\sqrt{2025}$ *(p. 110)*

Solve the equation.

4. $7 - 2x = 13$ *(p. 141)*

5. $-8x + 15 + 5x = 9$ *(p. 148)*

6. $5(2x + 3) = 4x$ *(p. 154)*

Graph the equation.

7. $x = 7$ *(p. 215)*

8. $y = 2x + 3$ *(p. 244)*

9. $4y - 2x = 1$ *(p. 244)*

Write an equation in slope-intercept form of the line with the given characteristics.

10. passes through $(-2, -8)$ and $(3, -5.5)$ *(p. 292)*

11. slope: -8; passes through $(1, -5)$ *(p. 292)*

Solve the inequality. Graph your solution.

12. $4x - 6 \leq 8x - 2$ *(p. 369)*

13. $-2 \leq x - 6 < 18$ *(p. 380)*

14. $2x < 6$ *or* $4x \geq 8$ *(p. 380)*

Solve the linear system.

15. $x = 4y + 3$ *(p. 435)*
$2x - 4y = 7$

16. $3x - 7y = 20$ *(p. 451)*
$-11x + 10y = 5$

17. $-9x + 6y = 0$ *(p. 451)*
$-12x + 8y = 5$

Simplify the expression. Write your answer using only positive exponents.

18. $(2x^3)^4 \cdot x^9$ *(p. 489)*

19. $(-9x^3)^2\left(-\frac{1}{4}x^6\right)$ *(p. 489)*

20. $\frac{(3x)^{-3}y^3}{x^2y^{-1}}$ *(p. 503)*

Factor the polynomial.

21. $a^2 - 15a - 54$ *(p. 583)*

22. $-3b^2 - 22b - 7$ *(p. 593)*

23. $4f^2 + 4fg + g^2$ *(p. 600)*

24. $p^2(p - 5) + 9(5 - p)$ *(p. 606)*

Solve the equation.

25. $(x + 7)(x - 3) = 0$ *(p. 575)*

26. $9x^2 - 28x + 3 = 0$ *(p. 652)*

27. $8x^2 + 7 = 36x - 9$ *(p. 663)*

28. $\sqrt{x + 8} + 10 = 2$ *(p. 729)*

Find the distance between the two points. *(p. 744)*

29. $(5, 2), (7, 14)$

30. $(-8, 6), (5, 0)$

31. $(2.5, 7), (2.5, -8)$

Find the sum, difference, product, or quotient.

32. $\frac{x - 2}{x + 5} \cdot \frac{x + 5}{x - 8}$ *(p. 802)*

33. $\frac{x^3 - 16x}{x^2 + 3x} \div (x - 4)$ *(p. 802)*

34. $\frac{16}{2x^4} \cdot \frac{7x^3}{2x}$ *(p. 802)*

35. $\frac{2x}{3 - x} + \frac{x - 9}{3 - x}$ *(p. 812)*

36. $\frac{1}{x + 6} + \frac{4x}{x + 6}$ *(p. 812)*

37. $\frac{9}{x^2 - 3x} - \frac{3}{x - 3}$ *(p. 812)*

Evaluate the expression.

38. ${}_6P_1$ *(p. 851)*

39. ${}_8P_3$ *(p. 851)*

40. ${}_7C_3$ *(p. 856)*

41. ${}_{10}C_6$ *(p. 856)*

42. You roll a number cube. What is the probability that you roll a 5? *(p. 843)*

43. You roll a number cube. What is the probability that you roll a 2 or an even number? *(p. 861)*

44. You choose a number from 1 to 20 at random. What is the probability that you choose a prime number? *(p. 843)*

45. You choose a number from 1 to 20 at random. What is the probability that you choose a multiple of 6? *(p. 843)*

46. A bag contains 2 red marbles, 4 green marbles, and 4 blue marbles. You choose one marble at random, put the marble back into the bag, then choose a second marble at random. What is the probability that you choose 2 red marbles? *(p. 861)*

47. **MARATHON** Two runners are training for a marathon. When running a practice distance of 26.2 miles, one runner begins running 6 minutes after the other. The speed of the first runner is 11.4 miles per hour. The speed of the second runner is 12 miles per hour. After how many minutes does the second runner pass the first runner? *(p. 435)*

48. **STONE ARCH** The shape of a stone arch can be modeled by the graph of the equation $y = -0.5x^2 + 4x + 4$ where x is the horizontal distance (in feet) from one end of the arch and y is its height (in feet) above the ground. What is the maximum height of the arch? *Explain* how you found your answer. *(p. 628)*

49. **GUY WIRE** A guy wire supports an antenna tower, as shown at the right. The bottom of the wire is secured in the ground 30 feet from the base of the tower. The top of the wire is secured to the tower at a height of 30 feet above the ground. How long is the wire? Round your answer to the nearest tenth of a foot. *(p. 737)*

50. **HEATING RATES** An electric heater takes 8 minutes to heat an entire apartment to the desired temperature. A wood stove and an electric heater together take 6 minutes to heat the apartment. How many minutes does it take the wood stove alone to heat the apartment to the desired temperature? *(p. 820)*

51. **FLIGHTS** You are traveling from Boston, Massachusetts, to Richmond, Virginia. The prices (in dollars) of airline tickets for different flights between the cities are listed below.

    176, 191, 195, 197, 197, 204, 204, 204, 204,
    204, 206, 206, 206, 206, 206, 217, 217, 221

    a. What is the range of the prices? *(p. 875)*

    b. Make a stem-and-leaf plot of the prices. *(p. 881)*

    c. Make a box-and-whisker plot of the prices. *(p. 887)*

    d. Can any of these prices be considered outliers? *Explain* why or why not. *(p. 887)*

Contents of Student Resources

Comparing and Ordering Decimals

A **number line** is a line whose points are associated with numbers. You can use a number line to compare and order decimals. From left to right, the numbers on a number line appear in order from least to greatest.

EXAMPLE **Copy and complete the statement using <, >, or =.**

a. 9.67 _?_ 9.59

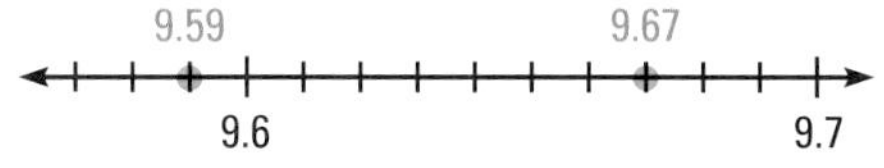

9.67 is to the right of 9.59, so 9.67 is greater than 9.59.

▶ 9.67 > 9.59

b. 0.08 _?_ 0.12

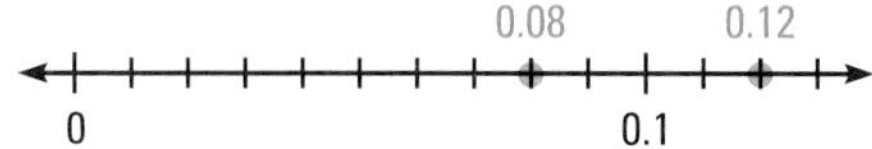

0.08 is to the left of 0.12, so 0.08 is less than 0.012.

▶ 0.08 < 0.012

EXAMPLE **Order the numbers 0.4, 0.56, 0.48, and 0.515 from least to greatest.**

Graph all the numbers on a number line.

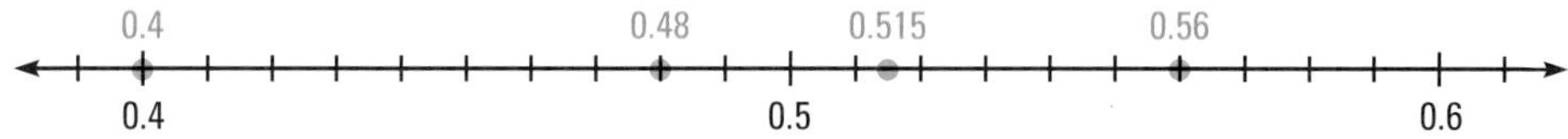

Write the numbers as they appear on the number line from left to right.

▶ The numbers in order from least to greatest are 0.4, 0.48, 0.515, and 0.56.

PRACTICE

Copy and complete the statement using <, >, or =.

1. 1.48 _?_ 1.413

2. 0.809 _?_ 0.81

3. 5.47 _?_ 5.43

4. 0.01 _?_ 0.005

5. 35.2 _?_ 35

6. 6.24 _?_ 6.2

7. 1.674 _?_ 1.678

8. 20.05 _?_ 20.3

9. 9.018 _?_ 9.017

Order the numbers from least to greatest.

10. 2.5, 2.3, 2.45, 2.38

11. 7.01, 7.13, 7.3, 7.03

12. 10.19, 10.2, 10, 10.4

13. 0.3, 0.47, 0.9, 0.15

14. 1.3, 1.05, 1.11, 1.0

15. 12.6, 10.9, 11, 11.9

16. 6.1, 6.89, 7.25, 7

17. 3.1, 3.3, 0.3, 1.33

18. 5.46, 5.4, 5.64, 5.6

Factors and Multiples

A **prime number** is a whole number that is greater than 1 and has exactly two whole number factors, 1 and itself. A **composite number** is a whole number that is greater than 1 and has more than two whole number factors. The table below shows that the first five prime numbers are 2, 3, 5, 7, and 11.

Number	Product(s)	Factor(s)	Prime or composite?
1	1 • 1	1	Neither
2	1 • 2	1, 2	Prime
3	1 • 3	1, 3	Prime
4	1 • 4, 2 • 2	1, 2, 4	Composite
5	1 • 5	1, 5	Prime
6	1 • 6, 2 • 3	1, 2, 3, 6	Composite
7	1 • 7	1, 7	Prime
8	1 • 8, 2 • 4	1, 2, 4, 8	Composite
9	1 • 9, 3 • 3	1, 3, 9	Composite
10	1 • 10, 2 • 5	1, 2, 5, 10	Composite
11	1 • 11	1, 11	Prime
12	1 • 12, 2 • 6, 3 • 4	1, 2, 3, 4, 6, 12	Composite

When you write a composite number as a product of prime numbers, you are writing its **prime factorization**. You can use a **factor tree** to write the prime factorization of a number.

EXAMPLE **Write the prime factorization of 120.**

Write 120 at the top of your factor tree. Draw two branches and write 120 as the product of two factors. Continue to draw branches until all the factors are prime numbers (shown in red). Here are two possible factor trees for 120.

Start with $120 = 2 \cdot 60$.

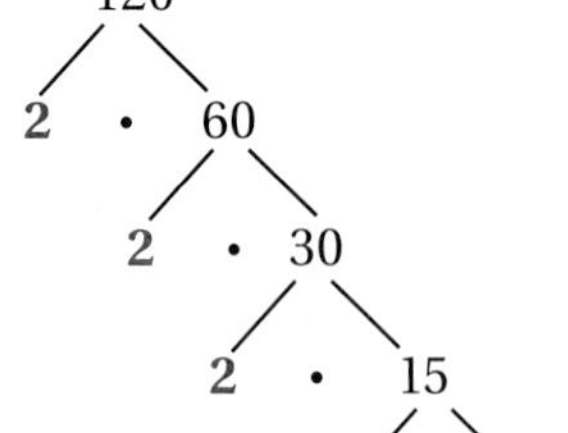

Start with $120 = 10 \cdot 12$.

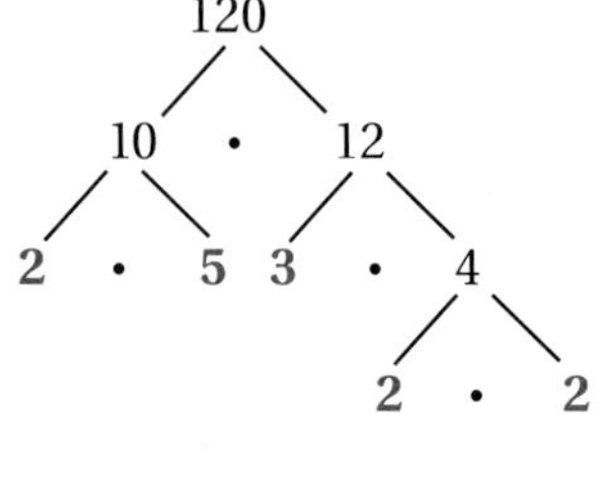

Both factor trees show that $120 = 2 \cdot 2 \cdot 2 \cdot 3 \cdot 5$, or $120 = 2^3 \cdot 3 \cdot 5$.

▸ The prime factorization of 120 is $2^3 \cdot 3 \cdot 5$.

For two or more nonzero whole numbers, a **common factor** is a whole number that is a factor of each number. The **greatest common factor (GCF)** of two or more nonzero whole numbers is the greatest of their common factors.

EXAMPLE **Find the greatest common factor of 30 and 42.**

Write the prime factorization of each number. The greatest common factor is the product of the common prime factors.

$30 = 2 \cdot 3 \cdot 5$ and $42 = 2 \cdot 3 \cdot 7$

The common prime factors are 2 and 3. The GCF is the product $2 \cdot 3 = 6$.

▶ The greatest common factor of 30 and 42 is 6.

A **multiple** of a whole number is the product of the number and any nonzero whole number. A **common multiple** of two or more whole numbers is a multiple of each number. The **least common multiple (LCM)** of two or more whole numbers is the least of their common multiples.

EXAMPLE **Find the least common multiple of 10 and 15.**

Write the prime factorization of each number. The least common multiple is the product of the factors, using each common prime factor only once.

$10 = 2 \cdot 5$ and $15 = 3 \cdot 5$

The common prime factor is 5. The LCM is the product $2 \cdot 3 \cdot 5 = 30$.

▶ The least common multiple of 10 and 15 is 30.

PRACTICE

Write the prime factorization of the number if it is not a prime number. If the number is prime, write *prime*.

1. 28 **2.** 16 **3.** 11 **4.** 100

5. 81 **6.** 49 **7.** 60 **8.** 53

9. 180 **10.** 19 **11.** 51 **12.** 72

Find the greatest common factor of the pair of numbers.

13. 4, 8 **14.** 5, 6 **15.** 60, 18 **16.** 2, 10

17. 36, 27 **18.** 15, 21 **19.** 12, 16 **20.** 24, 108

21. 48, 88 **22.** 8, 12 **23.** 20, 28 **24.** 3, 5

Find the least common multiple of the pair of numbers.

25. 6, 9 **26.** 3, 8 **27.** 5, 45 **28.** 16, 20

29. 10, 65 **30.** 12, 15 **31.** 9, 30 **32.** 8, 9

33. 2, 14 **34.** 28, 32 **35.** 7, 49 **36.** 4, 6

Finding Equivalent Fractions and Simplifying Fractions

A **fraction** is a number of the form $\frac{a}{b}$ where a is the **numerator** and b is the **denominator**. The value of b cannot be 0.

The number lines show the graphs of two fractions, $\frac{1}{2}$ and $\frac{2}{4}$.

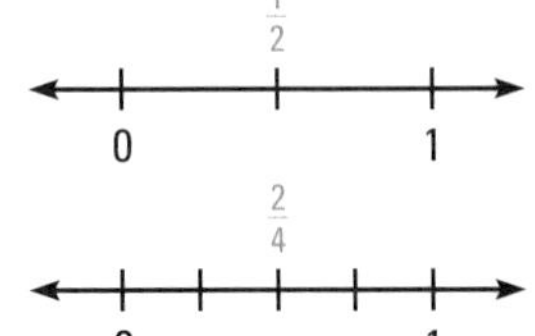

These fractions represent the same number. Two fractions that represent the same number are called **equivalent fractions**.

To write equivalent fractions, you can multiply or divide the numerator and the denominator by the same nonzero number.

EXAMPLE **Write two fractions that are equivalent to $\frac{6}{8}$.**

Multiply the numerator and denominator by 3.

$\frac{6}{8} = \frac{6 \times 3}{8 \times 3} = \frac{18}{24}$ Equivalent fraction

Divide the numerator and denominator by 2.

$\frac{6}{8} = \frac{6 \div 2}{8 \div 2} = \frac{3}{4}$ Equivalent fraction

A fraction is in **simplest form** when its numerator and its denominator have no common factors besides 1.

EXAMPLE **Write the fraction $\frac{10}{15}$ in simplest form.**

Divide the numerator and denominator by 5, the greatest common factor of 10 and 15.

$\frac{10}{15} = \frac{10 \div 5}{15 \div 5} = \frac{2}{3}$ Simplest form

PRACTICE

Write two fractions that are equivalent to the given fraction.

1. $\frac{9}{12}$ **2.** $\frac{4}{6}$ **3.** $\frac{1}{2}$ **4.** $\frac{2}{5}$ **5.** $\frac{10}{14}$

Write the fraction in simplest form.

6. $\frac{16}{24}$ **7.** $\frac{3}{12}$ **8.** $\frac{30}{48}$ **9.** $\frac{5}{40}$ **10.** $\frac{8}{20}$

11. $\frac{4}{16}$ **12.** $\frac{64}{72}$ **13.** $\frac{35}{100}$ **14.** $\frac{21}{81}$ **15.** $\frac{44}{55}$

16. $\frac{15}{20}$ **17.** $\frac{12}{28}$ **18.** $\frac{15}{39}$ **19.** $\frac{24}{78}$ **20.** $\frac{60}{96}$

Mixed Numbers and Improper Fractions

A **mixed number** is the sum of a whole number and a fraction. An **improper fraction** is a fraction with a numerator that is greater than or equal to the denominator.

The shaded part of the model at the right represents the mixed number $2\frac{1}{4}$ and the improper fraction $\frac{9}{4}$.

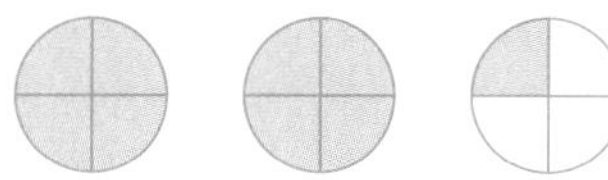

EXAMPLE **Write $5\frac{7}{8}$ as an improper fraction.**

$5\frac{7}{8} = 5 + \frac{7}{8}$ — Definition of mixed number

$= \frac{40}{8} + \frac{7}{8}$ — 1 whole $= \frac{8}{8}$, so 5 wholes $= \frac{40}{8}$.

$= \frac{47}{8}$ — Add.

EXAMPLE **Write $\frac{17}{5}$ as a mixed number.**

$$\begin{array}{r} 3 \\ 5\overline{)17} \\ \underline{15} \\ 2 \end{array}$$

Divide the numerator by the denominator: 17 ÷ 5. The quotient is 3 and the remainder is 2.

▶ $\frac{17}{5} = 3\frac{2}{5}$ — Write the remainder as a fraction, $\frac{\text{remainder}}{\text{divisor}}$.

PRACTICE

Write the mixed number as an improper fraction.

1. $1\frac{2}{3}$ **2.** $3\frac{1}{4}$ **3.** $10\frac{3}{10}$ **4.** $2\frac{3}{5}$ **5.** $4\frac{1}{2}$

6. $9\frac{1}{3}$ **7.** $1\frac{11}{12}$ **8.** $2\frac{3}{4}$ **9.** $6\frac{5}{8}$ **10.** $5\frac{9}{16}$

11. $8\frac{1}{8}$ **12.** $6\frac{3}{5}$ **13.** $7\frac{2}{9}$ **14.** $2\frac{3}{13}$ **15.** $12\frac{2}{3}$

Write the improper fraction as a mixed number.

16. $\frac{5}{2}$ **17.** $\frac{12}{5}$ **18.** $\frac{15}{8}$ **19.** $\frac{25}{4}$ **20.** $\frac{37}{3}$

21. $\frac{7}{4}$ **22.** $\frac{27}{8}$ **23.** $\frac{29}{10}$ **24.** $\frac{69}{16}$ **25.** $\frac{54}{5}$

26. $\frac{31}{4}$ **27.** $\frac{22}{5}$ **28.** $\frac{13}{3}$ **29.** $\frac{43}{9}$ **30.** $\frac{35}{11}$

SKILLS REVIEW HANDBOOK

Adding and Subtracting Fractions

To add or subtract two fractions with the same denominator, write the sum or difference of the numerators over the denominator.

Sum and Difference Rules ($c \neq 0$)

$$\frac{a}{c} + \frac{b}{c} = \frac{a+b}{c} \qquad \frac{a}{c} - \frac{b}{c} = \frac{a-b}{c}$$

EXAMPLE **Add or subtract: a. $\frac{1}{10} + \frac{3}{10}$ b. $\frac{7}{8} - \frac{3}{8}$**

a. $\frac{1}{10} + \frac{3}{10} = \frac{4}{10}$ **Add numerators.**

$= \frac{2}{5}$ **Simplify.**

b. $\frac{7}{8} - \frac{3}{8} = \frac{4}{8}$ **Subtract numerators.**

$= \frac{1}{2}$ **Simplify.**

The **least common denominator (LCD)** of two fractions is the least common multiple of the denominators. To add or subtract two fractions with different denominators, use the LCD of the fractions to write equivalent fractions that have the same denominator.

EXAMPLE **Add: $\frac{1}{4} + \frac{5}{6}$**

The LCD of the fractions is 12, so write $\frac{1}{4}$ as $\frac{1 \times 3}{4 \times 3} = \frac{3}{12}$ and $\frac{5}{6}$ as $\frac{5 \times 2}{6 \times 2} = \frac{10}{12}$.

$\frac{1}{4} + \frac{5}{6} = \frac{3}{12} + \frac{10}{12}$ **Write equivalent fractions.**

$= \frac{13}{12}$ **Add.**

$= 1\frac{1}{12}$ **Write as a mixed number.**

PRACTICE

Add or subtract.

1. $\frac{1}{16} + \frac{3}{16}$ **2.** $\frac{1}{5} + \frac{2}{5}$ **3.** $\frac{7}{12} - \frac{5}{12}$ **4.** $\frac{2}{3} - \frac{1}{3}$ **5.** $\frac{5}{8} + \frac{3}{8}$

6. $\frac{3}{4} + \frac{3}{4}$ **7.** $\frac{7}{8} - \frac{3}{8}$ **8.** $\frac{17}{20} + \frac{9}{20}$ **9.** $\frac{7}{10} + \frac{1}{2}$ **10.** $\frac{3}{10} + \frac{3}{5}$

11. $\frac{3}{8} - \frac{3}{16}$ **12.** $\frac{1}{3} + \frac{1}{10}$ **13.** $\frac{7}{12} - \frac{1}{16}$ **14.** $\frac{2}{3} - \frac{1}{4}$ **15.** $\frac{5}{6} + \frac{7}{8}$

16. $\frac{3}{4} - \frac{5}{8}$ **17.** $\frac{3}{4} - \frac{1}{5}$ **18.** $\frac{5}{12} + \frac{2}{3}$ **19.** $1 - \frac{1}{5}$ **20.** $4 - \frac{3}{16}$

21. $2\frac{5}{8} + 4\frac{1}{8}$ **22.** $2\frac{9}{10} - 1\frac{7}{10}$ **23.** $1\frac{5}{6} + 3\frac{1}{6}$ **24.** $2\frac{1}{2} + 2\frac{3}{8}$ **25.** $1\frac{3}{4} - \frac{11}{16}$

Multiplying and Dividing Fractions

To multiply two fractions, write the product of the numerators over the product of the denominators.

Product Rule ($b, d \neq 0$)

$$\frac{a}{b} \times \frac{c}{d} = \frac{ac}{bd}$$

EXAMPLE **Multiply: $\frac{3}{5} \times \frac{7}{8}$**

$\frac{3}{5} \times \frac{7}{8} = \frac{3 \times 7}{5 \times 8}$ **Use product rule.**

$= \frac{21}{40}$ **Simplify.**

Two nonzero numbers whose product is 1 are **reciprocals**. For example, 6 and $\frac{1}{6}$ are reciprocals because $6 \times \frac{1}{6} = 1$. Every number except 0 has a reciprocal.

To divide by a fraction, multiply by its reciprocal.

Quotient Rule ($b, c, d \neq 0$)

$$\frac{a}{b} \div \frac{c}{d} = \frac{a}{b} \times \frac{d}{c}$$

EXAMPLE **Divide: $\frac{5}{7} \div \frac{3}{4}$**

The reciprocal of $\frac{3}{4}$ is $\frac{4}{3}$ because $\frac{3}{4} \times \frac{4}{3} = 1$, so multiply $\frac{5}{7}$ by $\frac{4}{3}$.

$\frac{5}{7} \div \frac{3}{4} = \frac{5}{7} \times \frac{4}{3}$ **Use quotient rule.**

$= \frac{20}{21}$ **Use product rule.**

PRACTICE

Multiply or divide.

1. $\frac{3}{4} \times \frac{2}{3}$
2. $\frac{1}{5} \times \frac{5}{8}$
3. $\frac{1}{6} \div \frac{1}{3}$
4. $\frac{2}{3} \div \frac{2}{3}$
5. $\frac{9}{10} \div \frac{4}{5}$
6. $\frac{1}{12} \times \frac{3}{4}$
7. $\frac{3}{8} \times \frac{1}{8}$
8. $\frac{5}{6} \div \frac{1}{4}$
9. $\frac{1}{2} \times \frac{1}{4}$
10. $\frac{7}{10} \div \frac{5}{8}$
11. $\frac{3}{4} \div \frac{1}{2}$
12. $\frac{5}{6} \times \frac{3}{10}$
13. $\frac{2}{5} \div \frac{4}{5}$
14. $\frac{9}{10} \times \frac{1}{3}$
15. $\frac{1}{4} \div \frac{7}{8}$
16. $\frac{3}{16} \times \frac{2}{5}$
17. $\frac{2}{5} \div 20$
18. $18 \times \frac{1}{3}$
19. $\frac{1}{10} \times 6$
20. $24 \div \frac{3}{8}$
21. $5\frac{1}{2} \times \frac{9}{16}$
22. $8\frac{1}{4} \div \frac{3}{10}$
23. $1\frac{7}{8} \times 2\frac{1}{3}$
24. $3\frac{3}{4} \div 6\frac{1}{2}$
25. $2\frac{1}{2} \div 1\frac{7}{8}$

Fractions, Decimals, and Percents

A **percent** is a fraction whose denominator is 100. The symbol for percent is %. In the model at the right, there are 100 squares in all, and 49 of the 100 squares are shaded. You can write the shaded part of the model as a fraction, a decimal, or a percent.

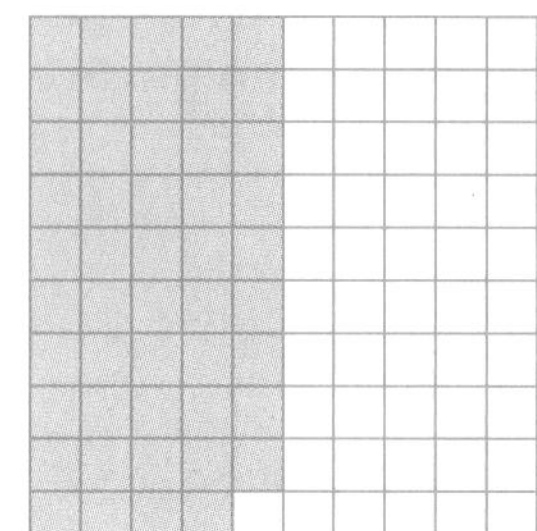

Fraction: forty-nine out of one hundred, or $\frac{49}{100}$

Decimal: forty-nine hundredths, or 0.49

Percent: forty-nine percent, or 49%

EXAMPLE Write the fraction as a decimal: **a.** $\frac{1}{8}$ **b.** $\frac{5}{12}$

a. $8\overline{)1.000}$ with quotient 0.125 — Divide.

▶ $\frac{1}{8} = 0.125$

b. $12\overline{)5.00000\ldots}$ with quotient 0.41666. . . — Divide.

▶ $\frac{5}{12} = 0.41666\ldots = 0.41\overline{6}$

EXAMPLE Write the decimal as a fraction: **a.** 0.7 **b.** 0.32

a. 0.7 = seven tenths

$= \frac{7}{10}$

b. 0.32 = thirty-two hundredths

$= \frac{32}{100}$

$= \frac{8}{25}$

To write a percent as a decimal, move the decimal point two places to the left and remove the percent sign.

EXAMPLE Write the percent as a decimal: **a.** 16% **b.** 5%

a. 16% = 16%

= 0.16

b. 5% = 05%

= 0.05

To write a decimal as a percent, move the decimal point two places to the right and write a percent sign.

EXAMPLE Write the decimal as a percent: **a.** 0.83 **b.** 0.195

a. 0.83 = 0.83

= 83%

b. 0.195 = 0.195

= 19.5%

EXAMPLE Write the percent as a fraction: **a.** 98% **b.** 5%

a. $98\% = \frac{98}{100}$ Definition of percent

$= \frac{49}{50}$ Simplify.

b. $5\% = \frac{5}{100}$ Definition of percent

$= \frac{1}{20}$ Simplify.

To write a fraction as a percent, you may be able to rewrite the fraction using a denominator of 100. If the denominator of the fraction is not a factor of 100, you can first write the fraction as a decimal and then as a percent.

EXAMPLE Write the fraction as a percent: **a.** $\frac{2}{5}$ **b.** $\frac{5}{8}$

a. $\frac{2}{5} = \frac{2(20)}{5(20)}$ Write as a fraction with denominator 100.

$= \frac{40}{100} = 40\%$ Write as a percent.

b. $\frac{5}{8} = 0.625$ Write as a decimal.

$= 62.5\%$ Write as a percent.

The table below gives commonly used fractions, decimals, and percents written in increasing order.

$\frac{1}{100} = 0.01 = 1\%$	$\frac{1}{16} = 0.0625 = 6.25\%$	$\frac{1}{10} = 0.1 = 10\%$	$\frac{1}{8} = 0.125 = 12.5\%$
$\frac{1}{5} = 0.2 = 20\%$	$\frac{1}{4} = 0.25 = 25\%$	$\frac{1}{3} = 0.\overline{3} \approx 33.3\%$	$\frac{3}{8} = 0.375 = 37.5\%$
$\frac{2}{5} = 0.4 = 40\%$	$\frac{1}{2} = 0.5 = 50\%$	$\frac{3}{5} = 0.6 = 60\%$	$\frac{5}{8} = 0.625 = 62.5\%$
$\frac{2}{3} = 0.\overline{6} \approx 66.7\%$	$\frac{3}{4} = 0.75 = 75\%$	$\frac{4}{5} = 0.8 = 80\%$	$\frac{7}{8} = 0.875 = 87.5\%$

PRACTICE

Write the percent as a decimal and as a fraction.

1. 70% **2.** 12% **3.** 3% **4.** 55% **5.** 35%

6. 9% **7.** 110% **8.** 225% **9.** 0.3% **10.** 0.5%

Write the decimal as a fraction and as a percent.

11. 0.28 **12.** 0.13 **13.** 0.05 **14.** 0.36 **15.** 0.52

16. 0.004 **17.** 0.025 **18.** 4 **19.** 1.5 **20.** 2.3

Write the fraction as a decimal and as a percent. Round decimals to the nearest thousandth. Round percents to the nearest tenth of a percent.

21. $\frac{3}{16}$ **22.** $\frac{1}{9}$ **23.** $\frac{61}{100}$ **24.** $\frac{3}{20}$ **25.** $\frac{19}{100}$

26. $\frac{17}{25}$ **27.** $\frac{9}{25}$ **28.** $\frac{5}{6}$ **29.** $\frac{4}{7}$ **30.** $\frac{5}{12}$

Mean, Median, and Mode

Three measures of central tendency are mean, median, and mode.

The **mean** of a data set is the sum of the values divided by the number of values.	The **median** of a data set is the middle value when the values are written in numerical order. If a data set has an even number of values, the median is the mean of the two middle values.	The **mode** of a data set is the value that occurs most often. A data set can have no mode, one mode, or more than one mode.

EXAMPLE **Find the mean, median, and mode(s) of the data in the table.**

Lengths of School Years	
Country	**School year (days)**
China	251
Korea	222
Taiwan	222
Japan	220
Israel	215
Switzerland	207
Canada	188
United States	178

Mean

Add the values. Then divide by 8, the number of values.

$$\text{Sum} = 251 + 222 + 222 + 220 + 215 + 207 + 188 + 178 = 1703$$

▶ Mean $= \frac{1703}{8} = 212.875$

Median

Write the values in order from least to greatest. Then find the middle value(s).

178, 188, 207, **215**, **220**, 222, 222, 251

Find the mean of the two middle values.

▶ Median $= \frac{215 + 220}{2} = \frac{435}{2} = 217.5$

Mode

Find the value that occurs most often.

▶ Mode = 222

PRACTICE

Find the mean, median, and mode(s) of the data.

1. Test scores: 90, 88, 95, 94, 87, 85, 92, 99, 100, 94
2. Daily high temperatures (°F) for a week: 68, 70, 67, 68, 75, 75, 74
3. Ages of employees: 24, 52, 21, 55, 39, 49, 28, 33, 52, 41, 30, 64, 45
4. Numbers of students in classes: 21, 24, 27, 28, 25, 18, 22, 25, 26, 22, 27, 20
5. Movie ticket prices: $6.75, $7.50, $7.25, $6.75, $6.25, $7.50, $7.25, $6.75, $7
6. Hourly rates of pay: $14.50, $8.75, $7, $11, $16.50, $18, $12, $10.25
7. Numbers of children in families: 0, 0, 1, 1, 1, 2, 2, 2, 2, 2, 3, 3, 4, 4, 4, 5
8. Ages of students in a high school class: 3 sixteen-year-olds, 10 seventeen-year-olds, and 7 eighteen-year-olds

Classifying Triangles and Quadrilaterals

A **polygon** is a closed plane figure whose sides are segments that intersect only at their endpoints. Each endpoint is called a **vertex** of the polygon. Polygons are classified by the number of sides they have.

Triangles are classified by their angle measures. If two angles have the same measure, they are **congruent angles**. In a diagram, matching arcs are used to show congruent angles.

A **right angle** measures 90° and is marked by a square corner. An **acute angle** measures less than 90°, and an **obtuse angle** measures more than 90°. The sum of the measures of the angles of a triangle is 180°.

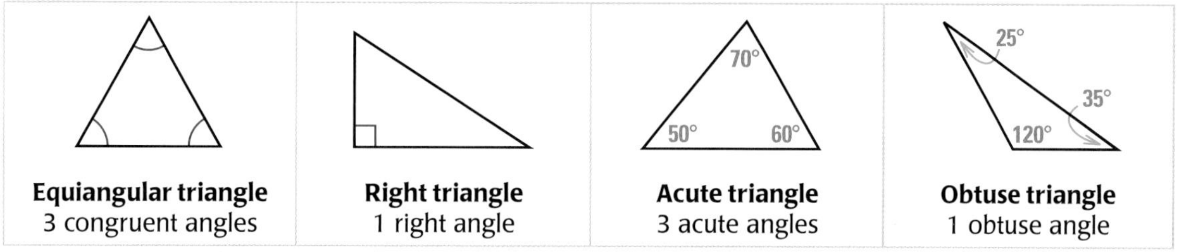

Triangles are also classified by their side lengths. If two sides have the same length, they are **congruent sides**. In a diagram, matching tick marks are used to show congruent sides.

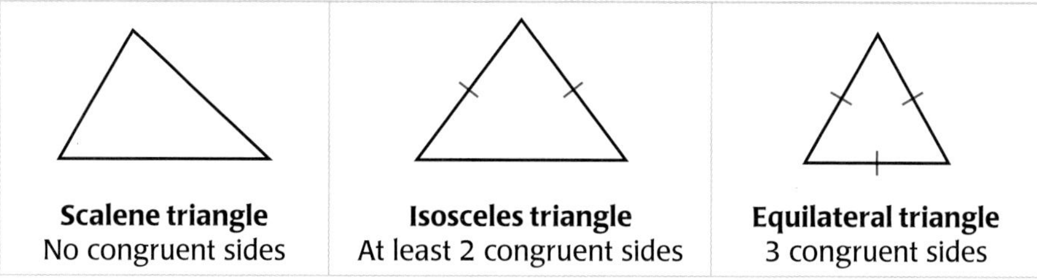

EXAMPLE **Classify the figure using all names that apply.**

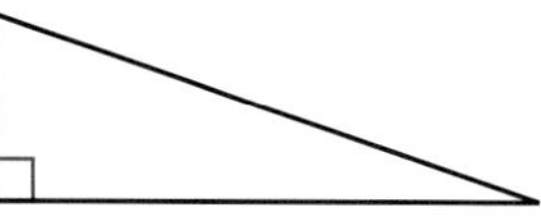

List the characteristics of the figure.

The figure is a polygon with 3 sides, so it is a triangle.

The triangle has no congruent sides, so it is a scalene triangle.

The triangle includes one right angle, so it is a right triangle.

▸ The figure is a scalene right triangle.

Two sides of a figure are parallel if the lines that contain the sides do not intersect. In a diagram, triangles (▶) are used to show parallel sides. Quadrilaterals are classified by whether they have parallel sides, congruent sides, or right angles.

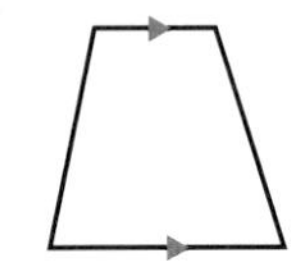		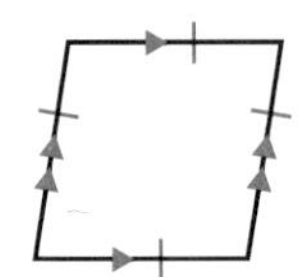	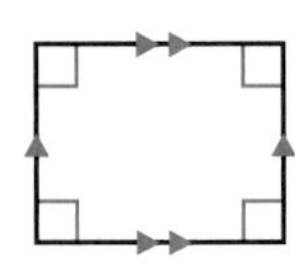	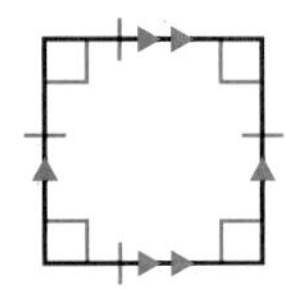
Trapezoid Quadrilateral with exactly one pair of opposite sides parallel	**Parallelogram** Quadrilateral with both pairs of opposite sides parallel	**Rhombus** Parallelogram with 4 congruent sides	**Rectangle** Parallelogram with 4 right angles	**Square** Parallelogram with 4 right angles and 4 congruent sides

EXAMPLE **Classify the figure using all names that apply.**

List the characteristics of the figure.

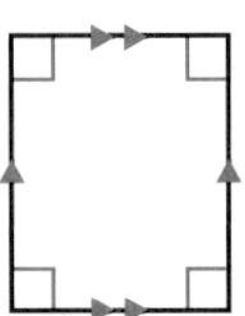

The figure is a polygon with four sides, so it is a quadrilateral.

Both pairs of opposite sides of the quadrilateral are parallel, so the figure is a parallelogram.

The parallelogram has four right angles, so it is a rectangle.

▶ The figure is a quadrilateral, a parallelogram, and a rectangle.

PRACTICE

Classify the figure using all names that apply.

1. 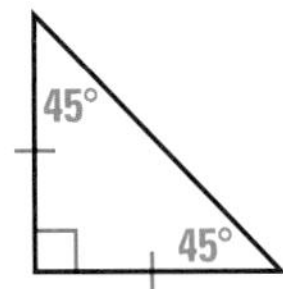

2. 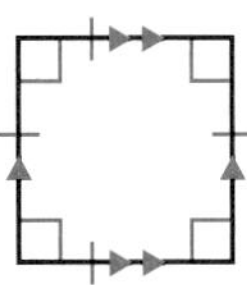

3. 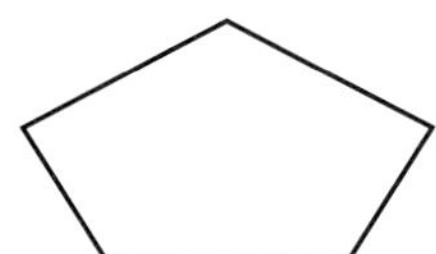

4. 

5. 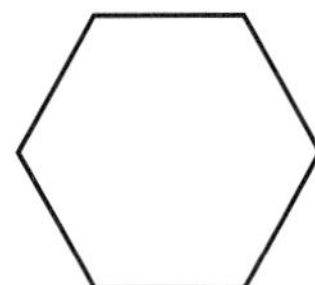

6. 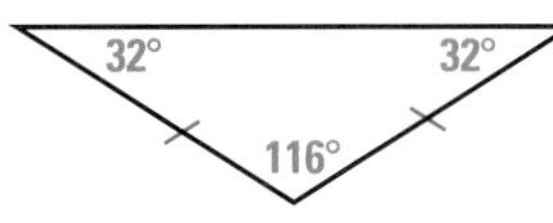

7. 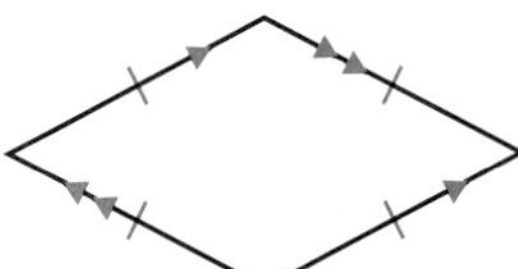

8. 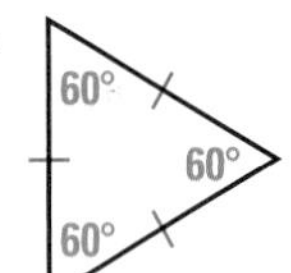

9. 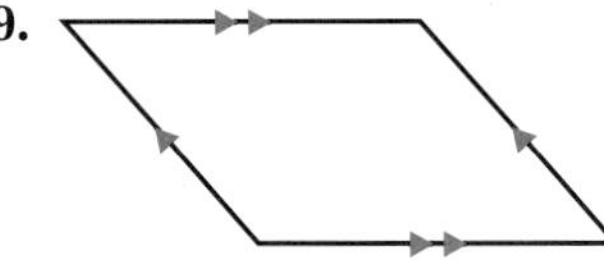

The Coordinate Plane

Just as you use a number line to graph numbers, you use a *coordinate plane* to graph *ordered pairs* of numbers.

A **coordinate plane** has a horizontal ***x*-axis** and a vertical ***y*-axis** that intersect at a point called the **origin**. The origin is labeled *O*.

In an **ordered pair**, the first number is the ***x*-coordinate** and the second number is the ***y*-coordinate**. The coordinates of the origin are (0, 0). The ordered pair (4, 5) is graphed at the right.

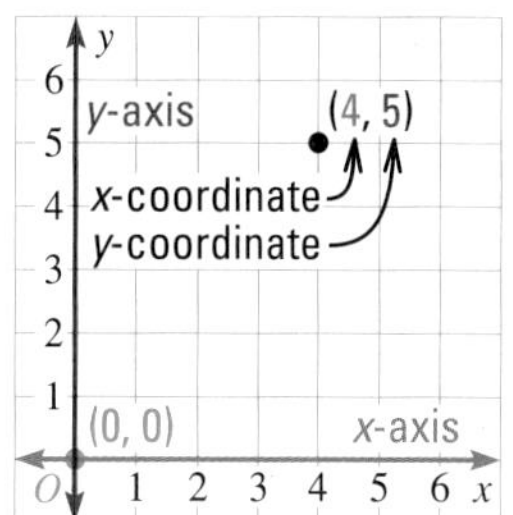

EXAMPLE **Give the coordinates of points *A* and *B*.**

Point *A* is 5 units to the right of the origin and 2 units up, so the *x*-coordinate is 5 and the *y*-coordinate is 2.

▸ The coordinates of point *A* are (5, 2).

Point *B* is 0 units to the right or left of the origin and 4 units up, so the *x*-coordinate is 0 and the *y*-coordinate is 4.

▸ The coordinates of point *B* are (0, 4).

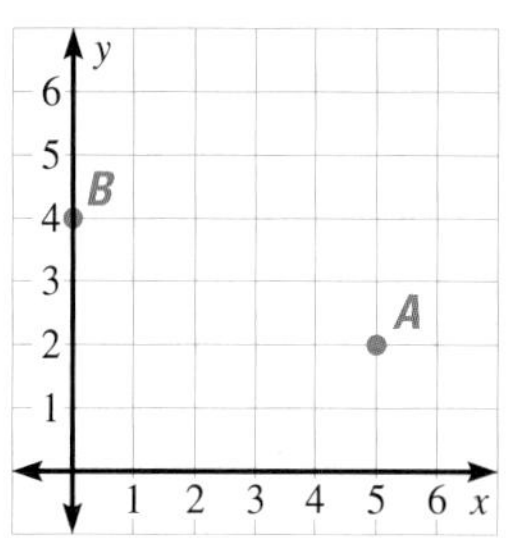

EXAMPLE **Plot the points *C*(1, 3) and *D*(3, 0) in a coordinate plane.**

To plot the point *C*(1, 3), begin at the origin and move 1 unit to the right, then 3 units up.

To plot the point *D*(3, 0), begin at the origin and move 3 units right, then 0 units up.

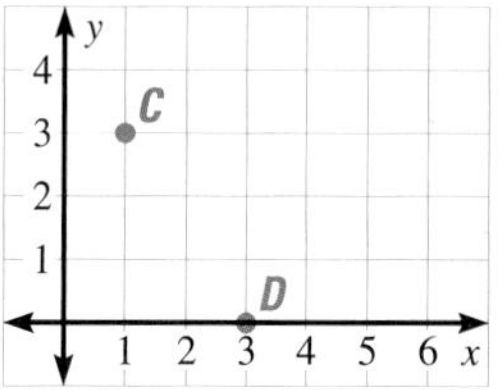

PRACTICE

Give the coordinates of the point.

1. *A* **2.** *B* **3.** *C*

4. *D* **5.** *E* **6.** *F*

7. *G* **8.** *H* **9.** *J*

10. *K* **11.** *L* **12.** *M*

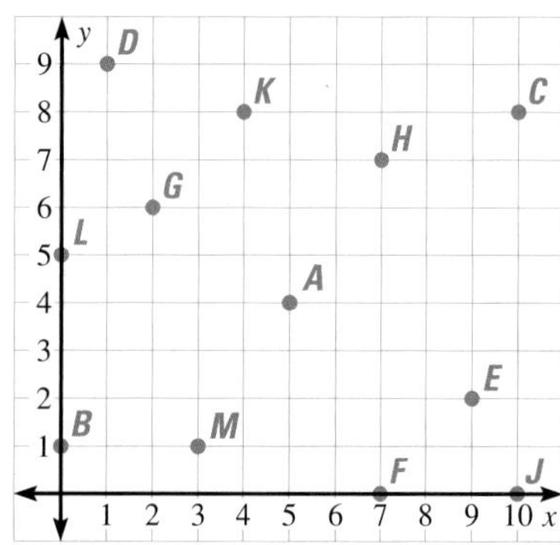

Plot the point in a coordinate plane.

13. *M*(1, 7) **14.** *N*(2, 1) **15.** *P*(4, 4)

16. *Q*(0, 3) **17.** *R*(4, 0) **18.** *S*(6, 8)

19. *T*(3, 6) **20.** *U*(8, 4) **21.** *V*(7, 0)

22. *W*(0, 8) **23.** *X*(3, 5) **24.** *Z*(5, 6)

Transformations

A **transformation** is a change made to the location, size, or shape of a figure. The new figure formed by a transformation is called an **image**. In this book, original figures are shown in blue and images in red.

A **translation** is a transformation in which each point of a figure moves the same distance in the same direction. A figure and its translated image are identical in size and shape.

EXAMPLE **Translate the triangle 4 units to the right and 1 unit up.**

From each vertex of the triangle, move 4 units to the right and 1 unit up to plot the image of the vertex. Draw segments connecting the images of the vertices.

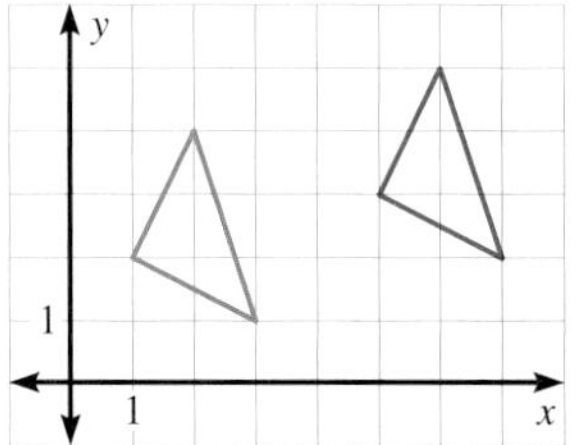

A **reflection** is a transformation in which a figure is reflected, or flipped, in a line, called the *line of reflection*. A figure and its reflected image are identical in size and shape.

EXAMPLE **Reflect the line segment in the given line.**

For each endpoint, find the distance from the endpoint to the line of reflection. Move the same distance on the opposite side of the line of reflection and plot the image point. Draw a segment connecting the image points.

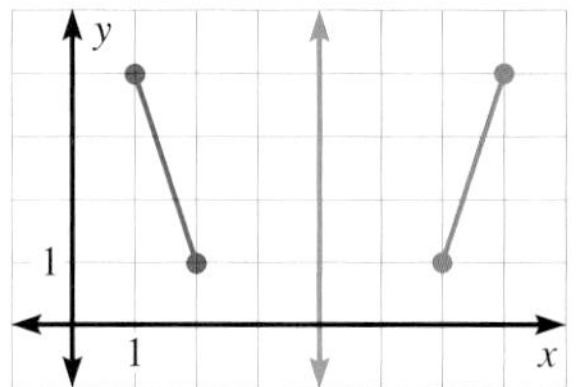

A **dilation** is a transformation in which a figure stretches or shrinks with respect to a fixed point called the *center of dilation*. (The examples and exercises below all have the origin as the center of dilation.) A figure and its dilated image have the same shape.

The **scale factor** of a dilation is the ratio of a side length of the image to the corresponding side length of the original figure. A figure *stretches* if its scale factor is greater than 1. A figure *shrinks* if its scale factor is between 0 and 1.

EXAMPLE **Dilate the rectangle using a scale factor of 3.**

Multiply each coordinate of each vertex by 3 to find the coordinates of the image. Plot the image of each vertex. Connect the image points to form a rectangle.

(1, 1) → **(3, 3)**   (1, 2) → **(3, 6)**

(3, 2) → **(9, 6)**   (3, 1) → **(9, 3)**

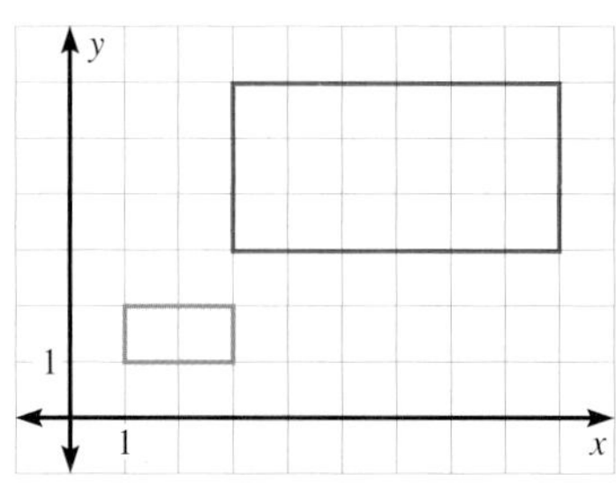

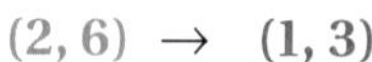

EXAMPLE Dilate the triangle using a scale factor of $\frac{1}{2}$.

Multiply each coordinate of each vertex by $\frac{1}{2}$ to find the coordinates of the image. Plot the image of each vertex. Connect the image points to form a triangle.

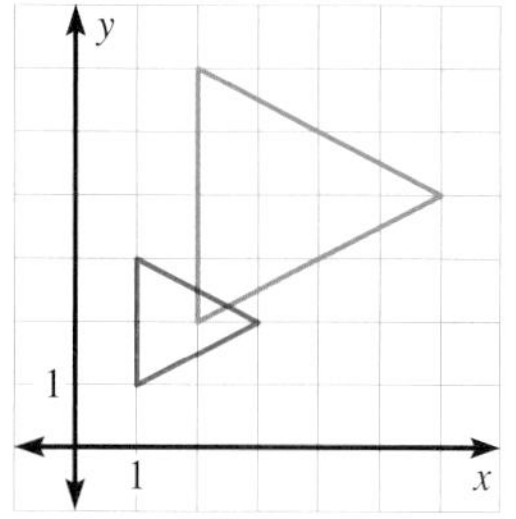

$(2, 6) \rightarrow (1, 3)$

$(2, 2) \rightarrow (1, 1)$

$(6, 4) \rightarrow (3, 2)$

PRACTICE

The coordinates of the vertices of a polygon are given. Draw the polygon. Then find the coordinates of the vertices of the image after the specified translation, and draw the image.

1. (1, 5), (3, 4), (3, 1); translate 3 units to the right and 2 units up
2. (5, 0), (7, 0), (7, 2), (5, 2); translate 4 units to the left and 5 units up
3. (4, 4), (6, 4), (6, 7); translate 3 units to the left and 3 units down
4. (2, 1), (4, 1), (4, 6), (2, 6); translate 5 units to the right
5. (4, 5), (7, 2), (3, 3); translate 1 unit down

For the figure shown, find the coordinates of the vertices of the image after a reflection in the given line. Then draw the image.

6.

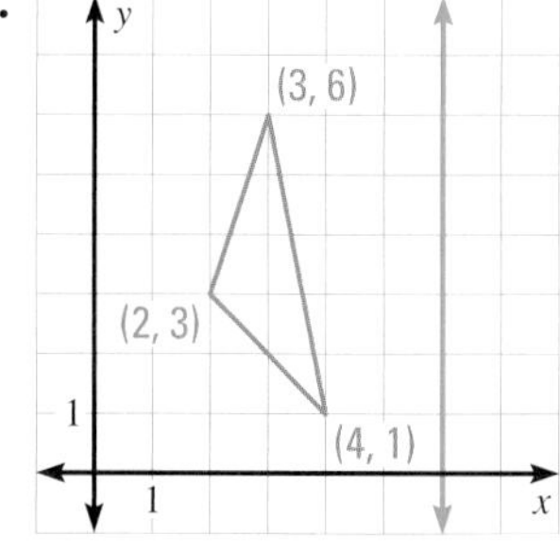

7.

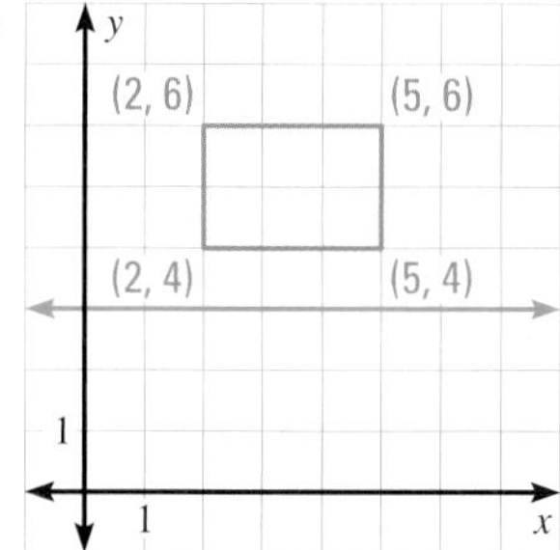

8.

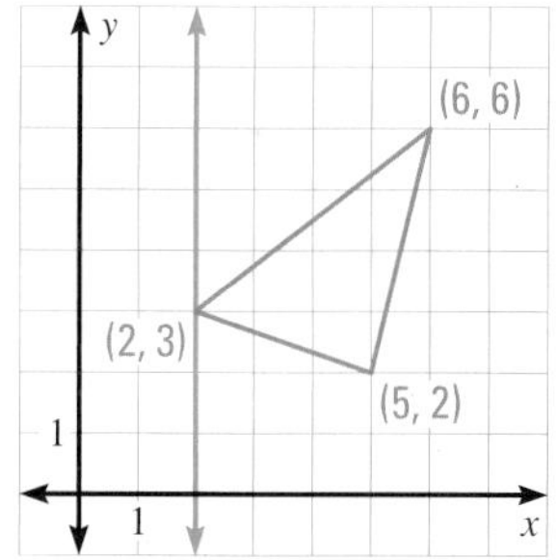

The coordinates of the vertices of a polygon are given. Draw the polygon. Then find the coordinates of the vertices of the image after the specified dilation, and draw the image.

9. (1, 2), (2, 4), (5, 3); dilate using a scale factor of 2
10. (2, 6), (6, 6), (6, 2), (2, 2); dilate using a scale factor of $\frac{1}{2}$
11. (1, 3), (3, 3), (3, 1), (1, 1); dilate using a scale factor of 4
12. (3, 9), (6, 9), (6, 3); dilate using a scale factor of $\frac{1}{3}$
13. (0, 2), (4, 4), (6, 0); dilate using a scale factor of $1\frac{1}{2}$

Perimeter and Area

The **perimeter** P of a figure is the distance around it.

Perimeter of a Square	Perimeter of a Rectangle	Perimeter of a Triangle
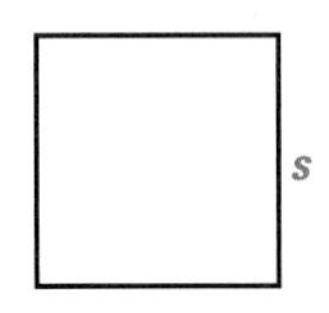	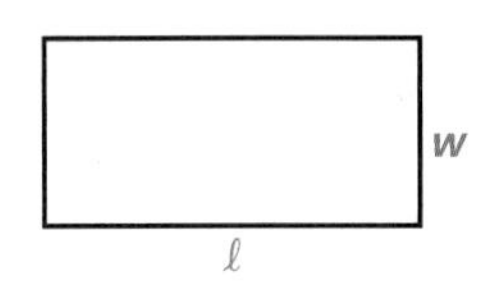	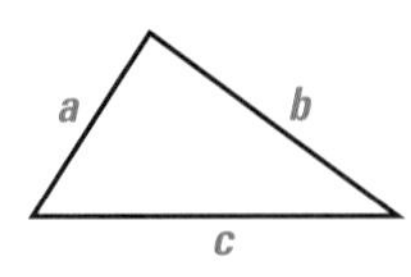
$P = s + s + s + s$ $= 4s$	$P = \ell + w + \ell + w$ $= 2\ell + 2w$	$P = a + b + c$

EXAMPLE **Find the perimeter of the figure.**

a. Square

$P = 4s$

$= 4(9)$

$= 36$ cm

b. Rectangle

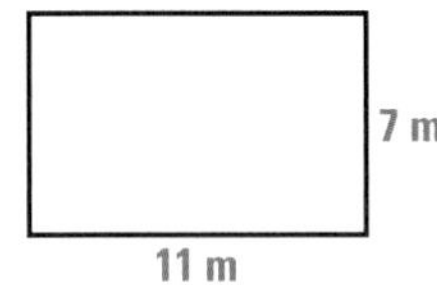

$P = 2\ell + 2w$

$= 2(11) + 2(7)$

$= 22 + 14 = 36$ m

c. Triangle

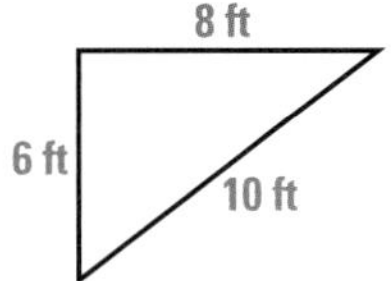

$P = a + b + c$

$= 6 + 8 + 10$

$= 24$ ft

The **area** A of a figure is the number of square units enclosed by the figure.

Area of a Square	Area of a Rectangle	Area of a Parallelogram
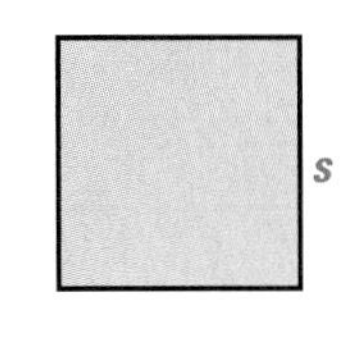	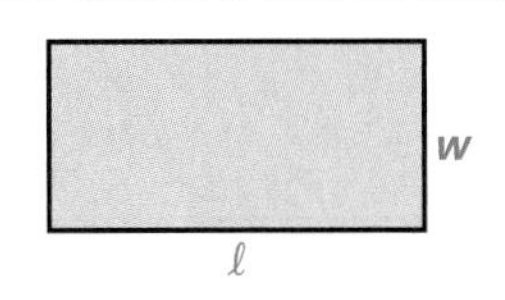	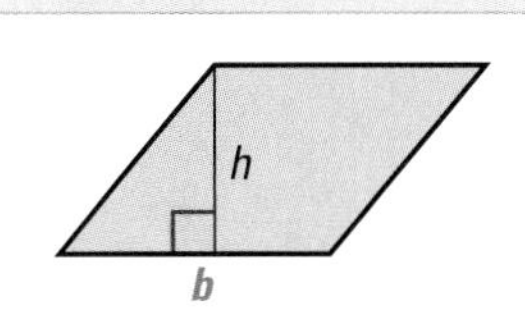
$A = s^2$	$A = \ell w$	$A = bh$

Area of a Triangle	Area of a Trapezoid
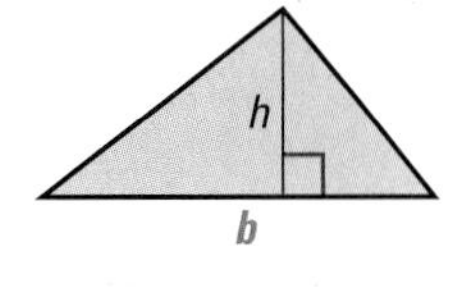	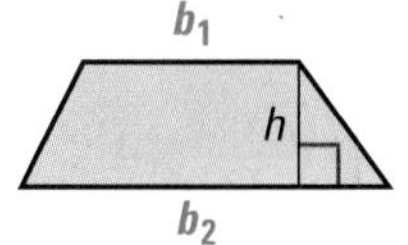
$A = \frac{1}{2}bh$	$P = \frac{1}{2}(b_1 + b_2)h$

EXAMPLE **Find the area of the figure.**

a. Rectangle

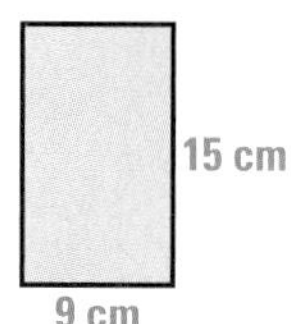

$A = \ell w$

$= 9(15)$

$= 135 \text{ cm}^2$

b. Triangle

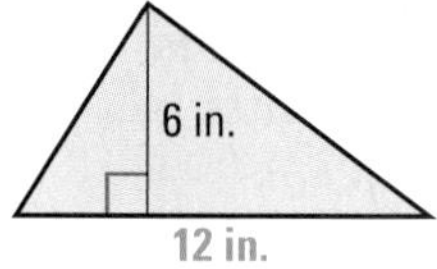

$A = \frac{1}{2}bh$

$= \frac{1}{2}(12)(6)$

$= 36 \text{ in.}^2$

c. Parallelogram

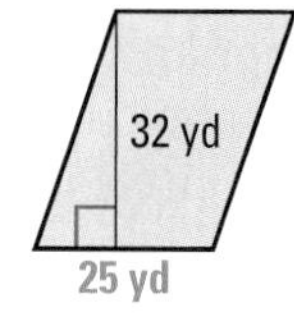

$A = bh$

$= 25(32)$

$= 800 \text{ yd}^2$

PRACTICE

Find the perimeter of the figure.

1. Square

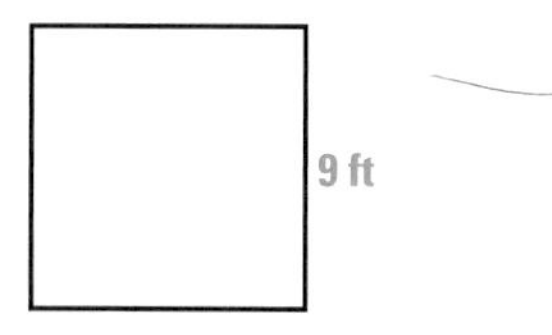

2. Rectangle

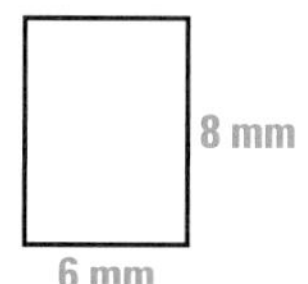

3. Triangle

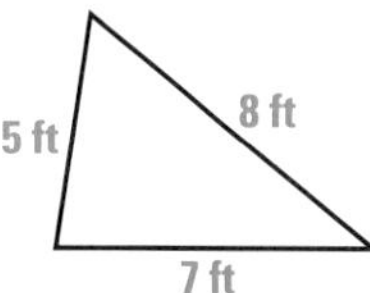

Find the area of the figure.

4. Square

5. Rectangle

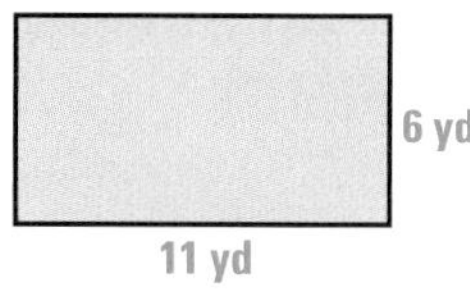

6. Triangle

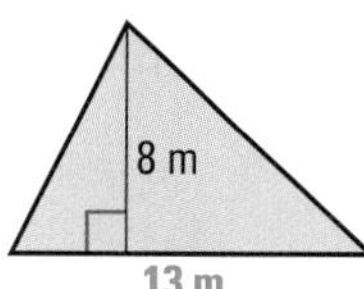

7. Parallelogram

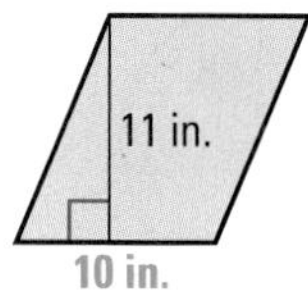

8. Trapezoid

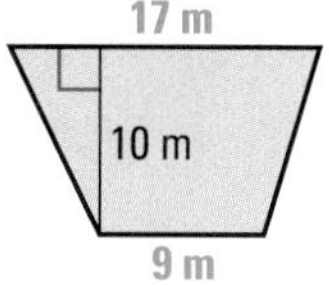

9. Parallelogram

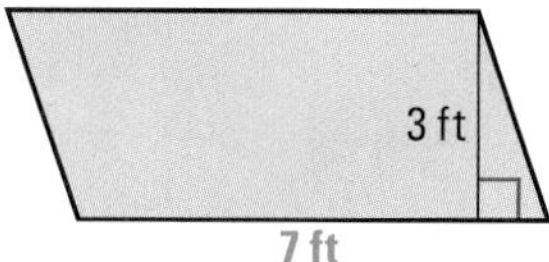

10. Trapezoid

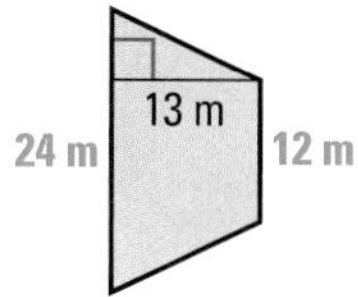

11. Triangle

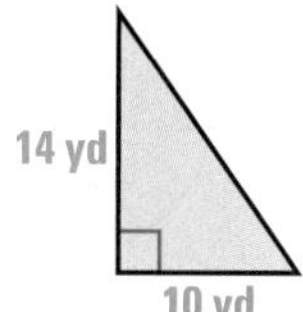

12. Rectangle

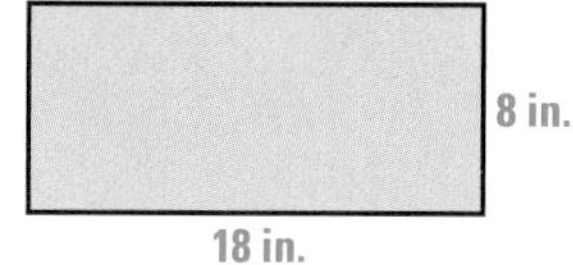

SKILLS REVIEW HANDBOOK

Circumference and Area of a Circle

A circle consists of all points in a plane that are the same distance from a fixed point called the **center**.

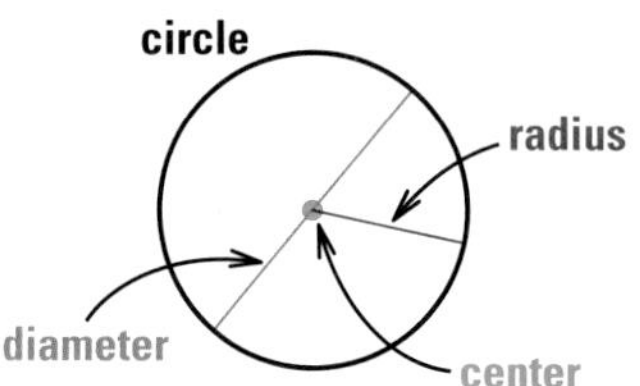

The distance between the center and any point on the circle is the **radius**. The distance across the circle through the center is the **diameter**. The diameter of a circle is twice its radius.

The **circumference** of a circle is the distance around the circle. For any circle, the ratio of its circumference to its diameter is π (pi), a number that is approximately equal to 3.14 or $\frac{22}{7}$.

Circumference and Area of a Circle

To find the circumference C of a circle with radius r or diameter d, use the formula $C = 2\pi r$ or $C = \pi d$.

To find the area A of a circle with radius r, use the formula $A = \pi r^2$.

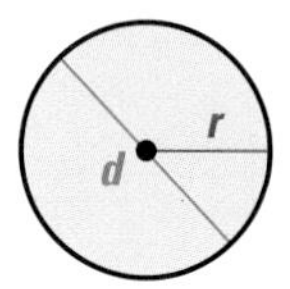

EXAMPLE **Find the circumference and area of the circle. Give your answers in terms of π and as decimals rounded to the nearest tenth.**

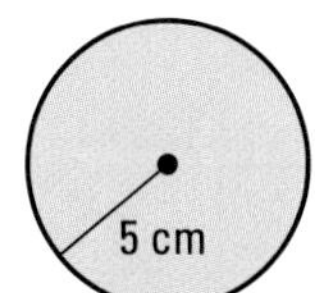

Circumference		**Area**	
$C = 2\pi r$		$A = \pi r^2$	
$= 2\pi(5)$		$= \pi(5^2)$	
$= 10\pi$ cm	Exact answer	$= 25\pi$ cm^2	Exact answer
$\approx 10(3.14)$		$\approx 25(3.14)$	
$= 31.4$ cm	Decimal approximation	$= 78.5$ cm^2	Decimal approximation

PRACTICE

Find the circumference and area of the circle. Give your answers in terms of π and as decimals rounded to the nearest tenth.

1. 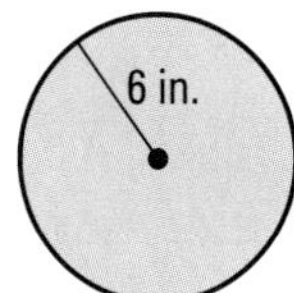

2. 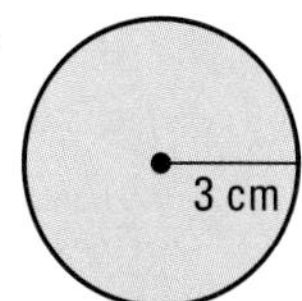

3. 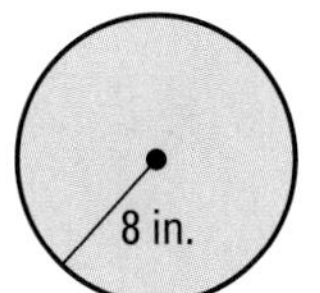

4. 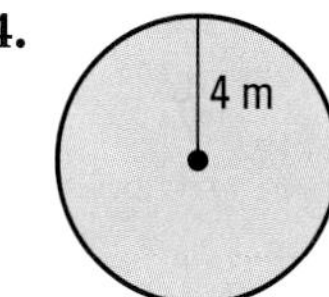

5. 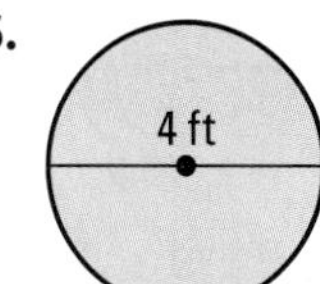

6. 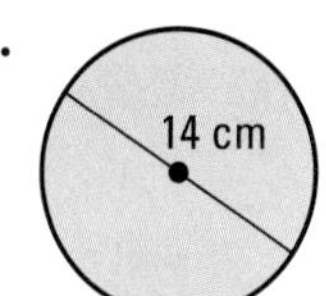

7. 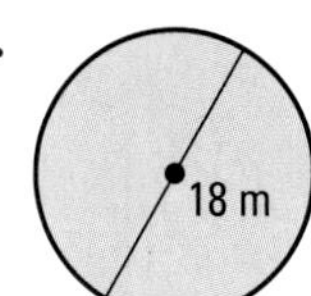

8. 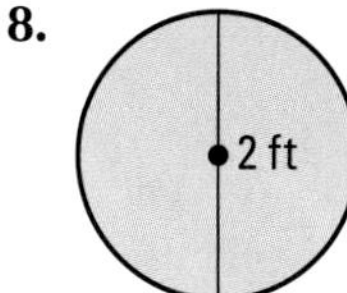

Surface Area and Volume

A **solid** is a three-dimensional figure that encloses part of space. The **surface area** S of a solid is the sum of the areas of all of its surfaces. The **volume** V of a solid is the amount of space that the solid occupies. In the formulas for surface area and volume, the number π (pi) is approximately equal to 3.14 or $\frac{22}{7}$.

Right Rectangular Prism

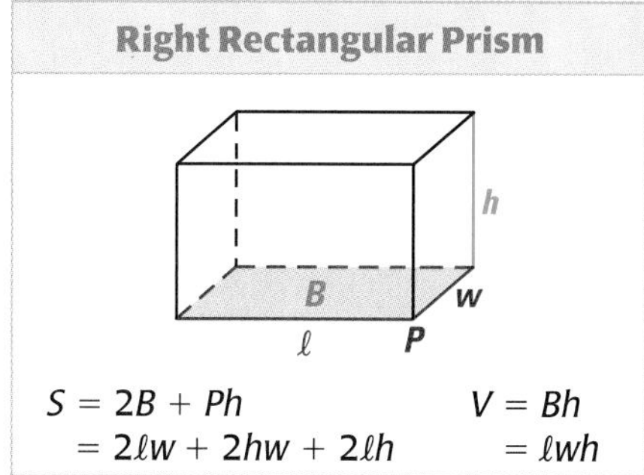

$S = 2B + Ph$
$= 2\ell w + 2hw + 2\ell h$

$V = Bh$
$= \ell wh$

Right Circular Cylinder

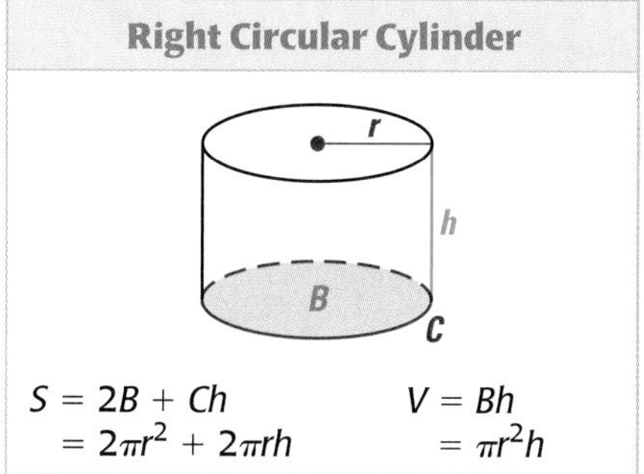

$S = 2B + Ch$
$= 2\pi r^2 + 2\pi rh$

$V = Bh$
$= \pi r^2 h$

Regular Pyramid

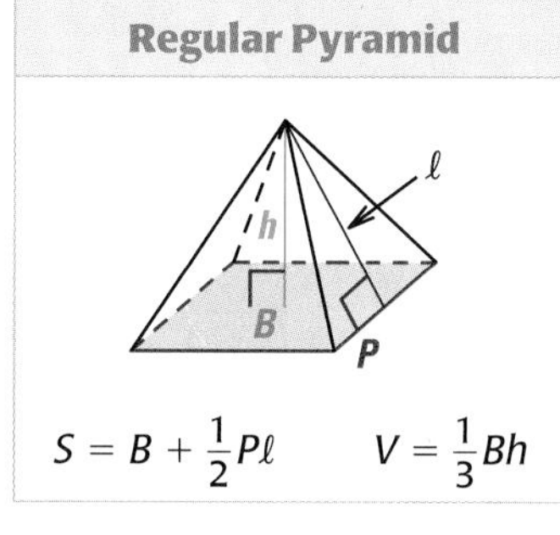

$S = B + \frac{1}{2}P\ell$

$V = \frac{1}{3}Bh$

Right Circular Cone

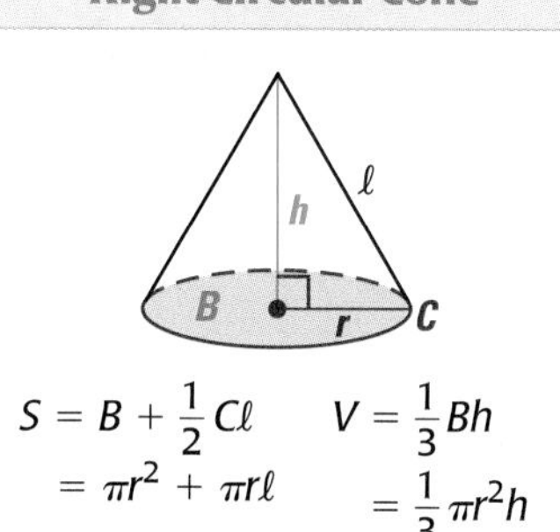

$S = B + \frac{1}{2}C\ell$
$= \pi r^2 + \pi r\ell$

$V = \frac{1}{3}Bh$
$= \frac{1}{3}\pi r^2 h$

Sphere

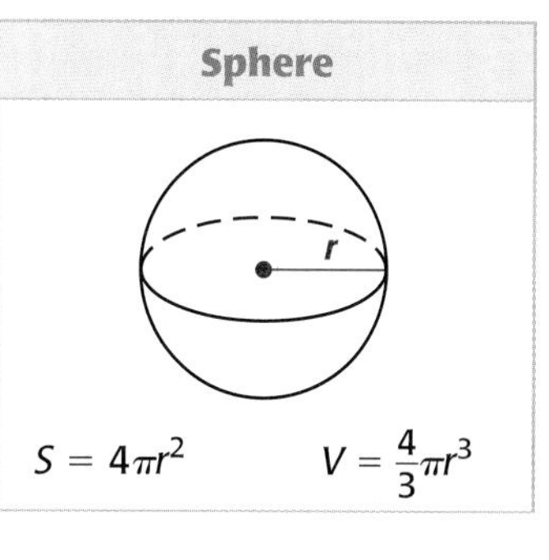

$S = 4\pi r^2$

$V = \frac{4}{3}\pi r^3$

In this book, the adjectives *right* and *circular* will be assumed and therefore will not be used in naming solids.

EXAMPLE **Find the surface area of the solid.**

a. Sphere

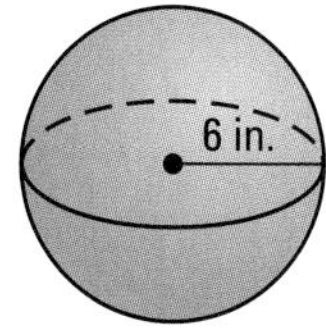

$S = 4\pi r^2$
$= 4\pi(6^2)$
$= 144\pi \text{ in.}^2$
$\approx 144(3.14)$
$\approx 452.2 \text{ in.}^2$

b. Cylinder

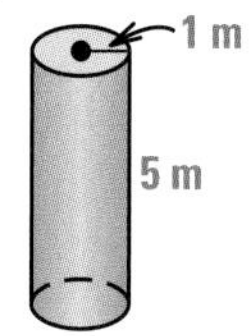

$S = 2\pi r^2 + 2\pi rh$
$= 2\pi(1^2) + 2\pi(1)(5)$
$= 2\pi + 10\pi$
$= 12\pi \text{ m}^2$
$\approx 12(3.14) \approx 37.7 \text{ m}^2$

c. Cone

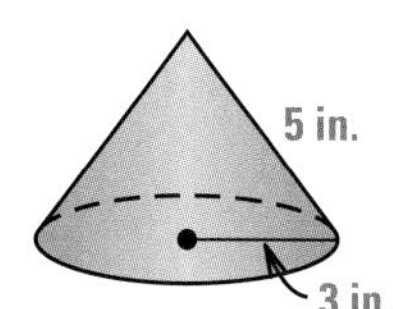

$S = \pi r^2 + \pi r\ell$
$= \pi(3^2) + \pi(3)(5)$
$= 9\pi + 15\pi$
$= 24\pi \text{ in.}^2$
$\approx 24(3.14) \approx 75.4 \text{ in.}^2$

EXAMPLE **Find the volume of the solid.**

a. Rectangular prism

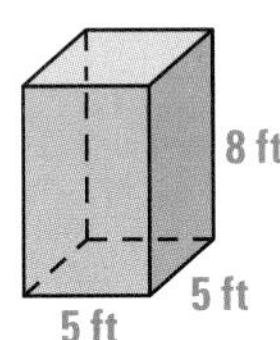

$V = Bh$

$= 25(8)$

$= 200 \text{ ft}^3$

b. Regular pyramid

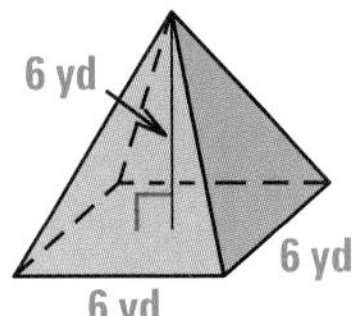

$V = \frac{1}{3}Bh$

$= \frac{1}{3}(36)6$

$= 72 \text{ yd}^3$

c. Cone

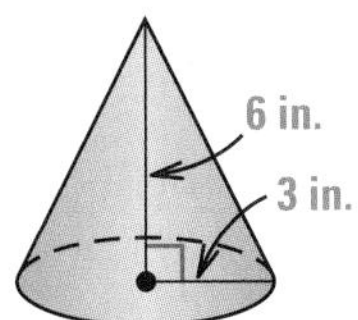

$V = \frac{1}{3}Bh$

$= \frac{1}{3}\pi(3^2)(6)$

$= 18\pi \text{ in.}^3$

$\approx 18(3.14) \approx 56.5 \text{ in.}^3$

PRACTICE

Find the surface area and volume of the solid. For spheres, cylinders, and cones, give your answers in terms of π and as decimals rounded to the nearest tenth.

1. Rectangular prism

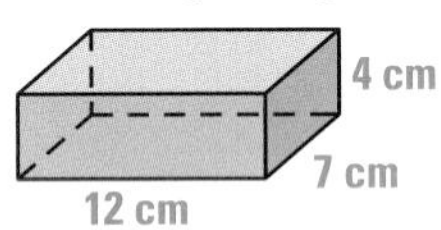

2. Cylinder

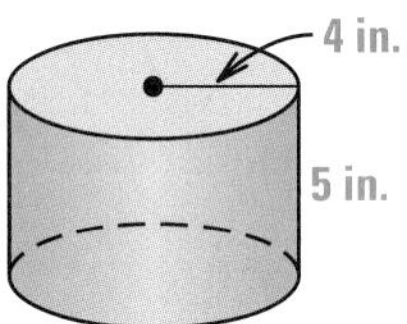

3. Sphere

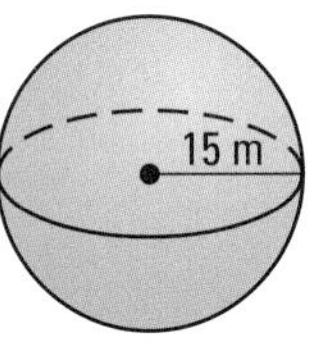

4. Cylinder

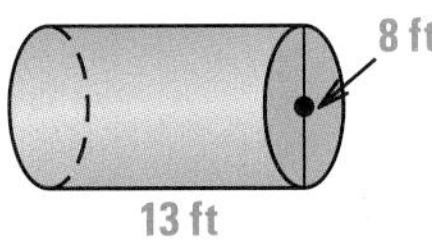

5. Cone

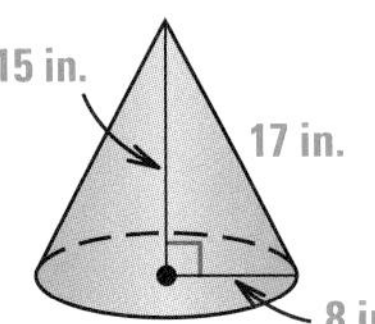

6. Rectangular prism

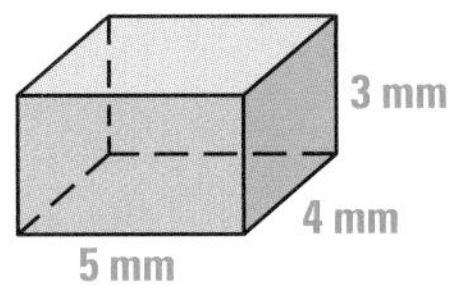

7. Regular pyramid

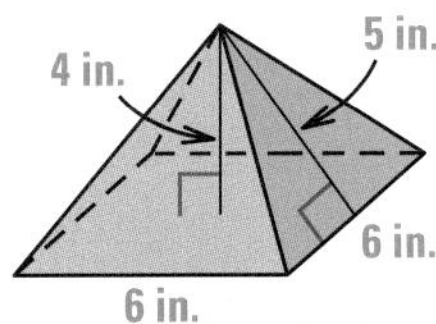

8. Sphere

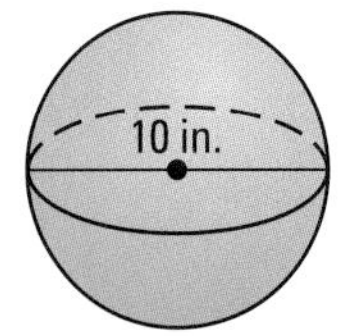

9. Cylinder

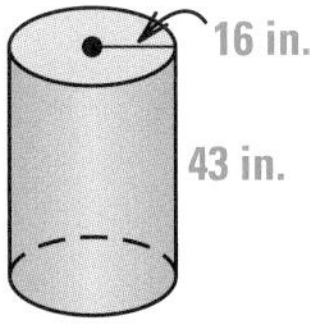

10. Rectangular prism

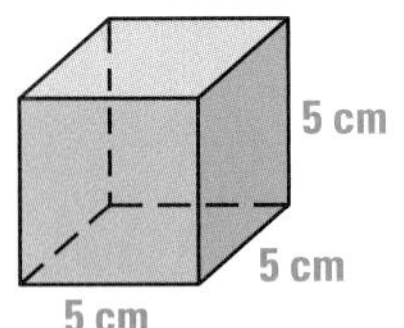

11. Cone

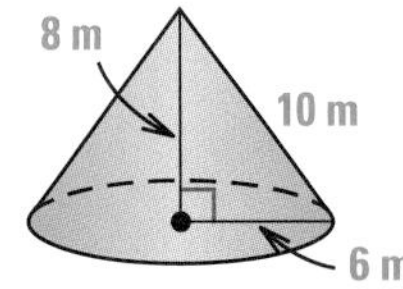

12. Regular pyramid

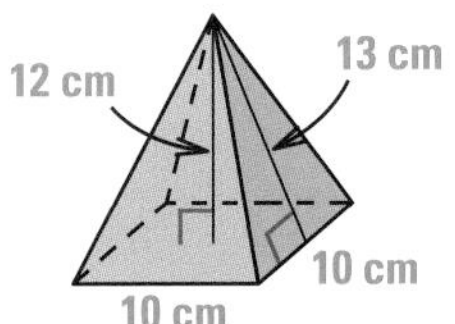

Converting Units of Measurement

The Table of Measures on page 956 gives many statements of equivalent measures. You can write two different conversion factors for each statement, as shown below. Each conversion factor is equal to 1.

Statement of Equivalent Measures	Conversion Factors
100 cm = 1 m	$\frac{100 \text{ cm}}{1 \text{ m}} = 1$ $\quad \frac{1 \text{ m}}{100 \text{ cm}} = 1$

To convert from one unit of measurement to another, multiply by a conversion factor that will eliminate the starting unit and result in the desired unit.

Convert meters to centimeters:

Use $\frac{100 \text{ cm}}{1 \text{ m}}$.

$3 \cancel{\text{m}} \times \frac{100 \text{ cm}}{1 \cancel{\text{m}}} = 300 \text{ cm}$

Convert centimeters to meters:

Use $\frac{1 \text{ m}}{100 \text{ cm}}$.

$400 \cancel{\text{cm}} \times \frac{1 \text{ m}}{100 \cancel{\text{cm}}} = 4 \text{ m}$

Sometimes you need to use more than one conversion factor.

EXAMPLE **Copy and complete: 2 d = _?_ sec**

STEP 1 **Find** the appropriate statements of equivalent measures.

24 h = 1 d, 60 min = 1 h, and 60 sec = 1 min

STEP 2 **Write** conversion factors.

$\frac{24 \text{ h}}{1 \text{ d}}, \frac{60 \text{ min}}{1 \text{ h}}, \text{ and } \frac{60 \text{ sec}}{1 \text{ min}}$

STEP 3 **Multiply** by conversion factors to convert days to seconds.

$2 \cancel{\text{d}} \times \frac{24 \cancel{\text{h}}}{1 \cancel{\text{d}}} \times \frac{60 \cancel{\text{min}}}{1 \cancel{\text{h}}} \times \frac{60 \text{ sec}}{1 \cancel{\text{min}}} = 172{,}800 \text{ sec}$

▶ 2 d = 172,800 sec

PRACTICE

Copy and complete.

1. 300 sec = _?_ min
2. 2.6 g = _?_ kg
3. 64 oz = _?_ lb
4. 4 gal = _?_ qt
5. 72 in. = _?_ ft
6. 94 mm = _?_ cm
7. 42 ft = _?_ yd
8. 5 d = _?_ h
9. 3 m = _?_ cm
10. 2 yd = _?_ in.
11. 70 L = _?_ mL
12. 10 mi = _?_ ft
13. 1.5 ton = _?_ lb
14. 4500 mL = _?_ L
15. 15,000 mg = _?_ g
16. 1 mi = _?_ in.
17. 80 fl oz = _?_ qt
18. 5 gal = _?_ c
19. 1 km = _?_ mm
20. 20 c = _?_ qt
21. 8 h = _?_ sec

Venn Diagrams and Logical Reasoning

A **Venn diagram** uses shapes to show how sets are related.

EXAMPLE **Draw a Venn diagram of the whole numbers less than 10 where set *A* consists of prime numbers and set *B* consists of even numbers.**

Whole numbers less than 10:
0, 1, 2, 3, 4, 5, 6, 7, 8, 9

Set *A*: 2, 3, 5, 7

Set *B*: 0, 2, 4, 6, 8

Both set *A* and set *B*: 2

Neither set *A* nor set *B*: 1, 9

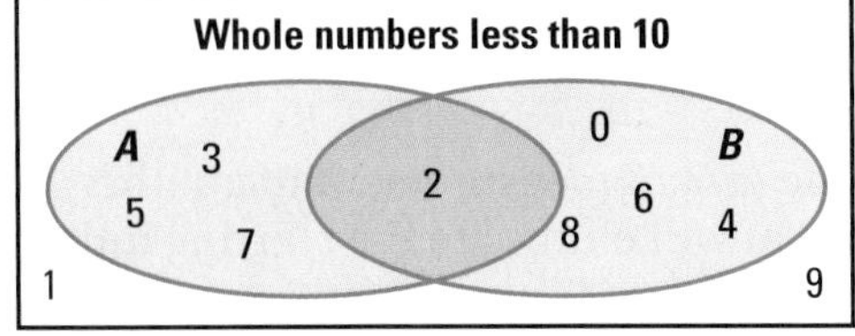

You can use a Venn diagram to answer questions about sets.

EXAMPLE **Use the Venn diagram above to answer the question.**

a. Is the statement below *true* or *false*? Explain.

No whole number less than 10 is prime.

▶ False. The whole number 2 is less than 10 and is prime.

b. Is the statement below *always, sometimes,* or *never* true? Explain.

A whole number less than 10 is either even or prime.

▶ Sometimes. Each of the numbers 0, 2, 3, 4, 5, 6, 7, and 8 are either even or prime, but the numbers 1 and 9 are not even and not prime.

PRACTICE

Draw a Venn diagram of the sets described.

1. Of the whole numbers less than 10, set *A* consists of factors of 10 and set *B* consists of odd numbers.
2. Of the whole numbers less than 10, set *A* consists of factors of 6 and set *B* consists of even numbers.

Use the Venn diagrams you drew in Exercises 1 and 2 to answer the question.

3. Are the following statements *true* or *false*? Explain.
   a. *If a whole number less than 10 is odd, then it must be a factor of 10.*
   b. *A whole number less than 10 that is a factor of 10 must be odd.*
4. Are the following statements *always, sometimes,* or *never* true? Explain.
   a. *A whole number that is even and less than 10 is a factor of 6.*
   b. *A factor of 6 that is less than 10 is even.*

Counting Methods

There are several methods for counting the number of possibilities in a situation.

EXAMPLE **Make a list to find the number of possible lunch specials.**

Lunch Special $6.95

Choose 1 soup and 1 sandwich.

Soups	**Sandwiches**
Chicken	Turkey
Tomato	Tuna
	Cheese

Pair each soup with each sandwich.

Chicken soup with turkey sandwich

Chicken soup with tuna sandwich

Chicken soup with cheese sandwich

Tomato soup with turkey sandwich

Tomato soup with tuna sandwich

Tomato soup with cheese sandwich

Count the number of lunch specials in the list.

▸ There are 6 possible lunch specials.

EXAMPLE **Draw a tree diagram to find the number of possible lunch specials given the choices in the example above.**

Arrange the soups and sandwiches in a tree diagram.

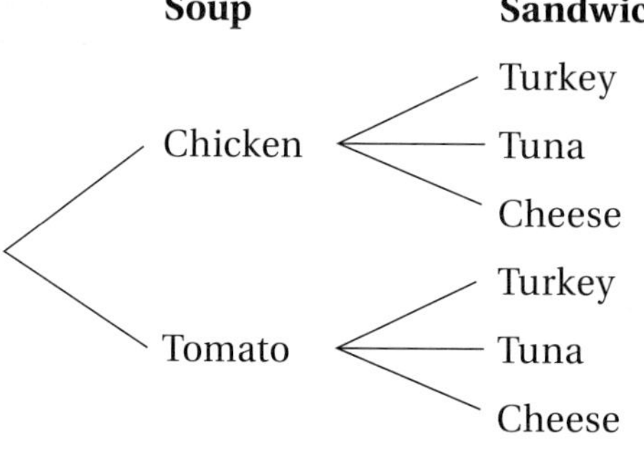

Lunch

Chicken soup, turkey sandwich

Chicken soup, tuna sandwich

Chicken soup, cheese sandwich

Tomato soup, turkey sandwich

Tomato soup, tuna sandwich

Tomato soup, cheese sandwich

▸ There are 6 possible lunch specials.

Another way to count the number of possible lunch specials described in the examples above is to multiply. Since there are 2 choices of soup and 3 choices of sandwich, there are $2 \times 3 = 6$ possible lunch specials. This method uses the counting principle.

The Counting Principle

If one event can occur in m ways, and for each of these ways a second event can occur in n ways, then the number of ways that the two events can occur together is $m \cdot n$.

The counting principle can be extended to three or more events.

EXAMPLE **Greta must choose a 4-digit password for her cell phone mailbox. Use the counting principle to find the number of possible 4-digit passwords.**

For each of the 4 digits in the password, there are 10 choices: 0, 1, 2, 3, 4, 5, 6, 7, 8, and 9.

10 choices for first digit	×	10 choices for second digit	×	10 choices for third digit	×	10 choices for fourth digit

$10 \times 10 \times 10 \times 10 = 10{,}000$

▶ There are 10,000 possible 4-digit passwords.

PRACTICE

In Exercises 1–3, use the indicated counting method to answer the question.

1. Andrew, Bettina, and Carl are triplets. In how many different ways can the triplets stand in a row for a photo? (Make a list.)

2. The sign at the right shows the color and size choices for school T-shirts. How many different types of school T-shirts are available? (Draw a tree diagram.)

School T-Shirts $9.99

Choose 1 color and 1 size.

Colors:	Sizes:
Black, Gold, or White	S, M, L, or XL

3. A 3-letter monogram consists of the first letter of a person's first name, middle name, and last name. For example, Matthew David Weaver's monogram is MDW. How many different 3-letter monograms are possible? (Use the counting principle.)

In Exercises 4–8, answer the question using any counting method you choose.

4. How many different pizzas with 2 different toppings are available for the large pizza special advertised at the right?

Large Pizza Special

Any 2 toppings for $12.49

Pepperoni	Black olive
Sausage	Green pepper
Ground beef	Red onion
Extra cheese	Mushroom

5. Lance must choose 4 characters for his computer password. Each character can be any letter A–Z or any digit 0–9. How many different computer passwords are possible?

6. Mia must choose 3 whole numbers less than 50 for her locker combination. The numbers may be repeated. How many different locker combinations are possible?

7. A restaurant offers a dinner special. You can choose a main course, a vegetable, and a salad from a choice of 6 main courses, 4 vegetables, and 3 salads. How many different dinners are available?

8. Each day Scott walks, rides the bus, or gets a ride to school. He has each of the same possibilities for getting home each day. How many combinations of travel to and from school does Scott have?

Bar Graphs

You can use a **bar graph** to display and compare data that are in categories.

EXAMPLE **Use the bar graph, which shows the medals won by the United States in the 2004 Summer Olympics. (a) Did the United States win more gold medals, silver medals, or bronze medals? (b) How many more silver medals than bronze medals did the United States win?**

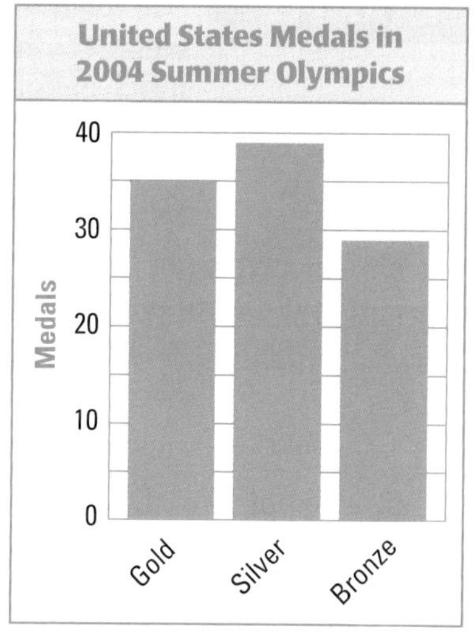

a. The longest bar on the graph is for silver medals won.

▸ The United States won more silver medals than any other type.

b. The bar for silver medals shows 39 silver medals won. The bar for bronze medals shows 29 bronze medals won.

$39 - 29 = 10$

▸ The United States won 10 more silver medals than bronze medals.

PRACTICE

In Exercises 1–3, use the bar graph above.

1. The United States won fewer of which type of medal than any other type?
2. How many more silver medals than gold medals did the United States win?
3. How many medals did the United States win altogether?

In Exercises 4–11, use the bar graph below, which shows the top medal-winning countries in the 2002 Winter Olympics.

4. Which country won the most medals? How many medals did it win?
5. How many medals did Norway win?
6. Which two countries won 17 medals each?
7. Which country won the same number of medals as France?
8. How many countries won more than 15 medals?
9. Which country won twice as many medals as Austria?
10. How many medals did Russia and Italy win altogether?
11. How many medals did the top 3 medal-winning countries win?

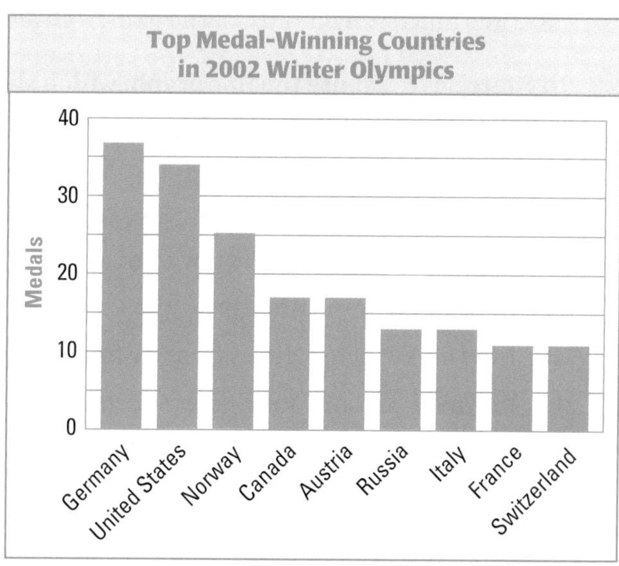

Line Graphs

You can use a **line graph** to show how numerical data change over time.

EXAMPLE **Use the line graph, which shows Charlie's weight from birth to 5 years old. (a) How much weight did Charlie gain in 5 years? (b) At what age did Charlie weigh 30 pounds? (c) In which year did Charlie gain the most weight?**

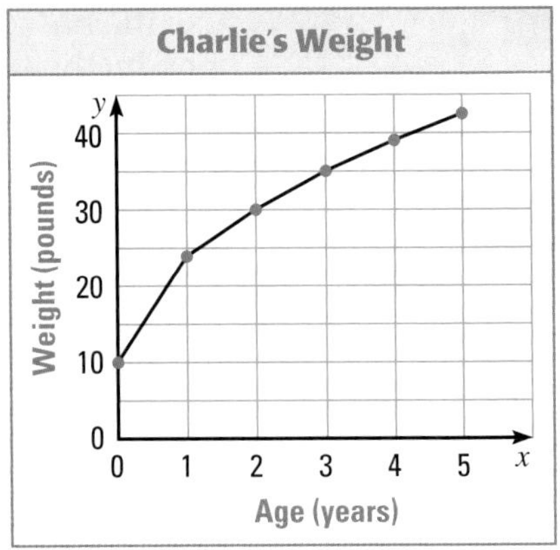

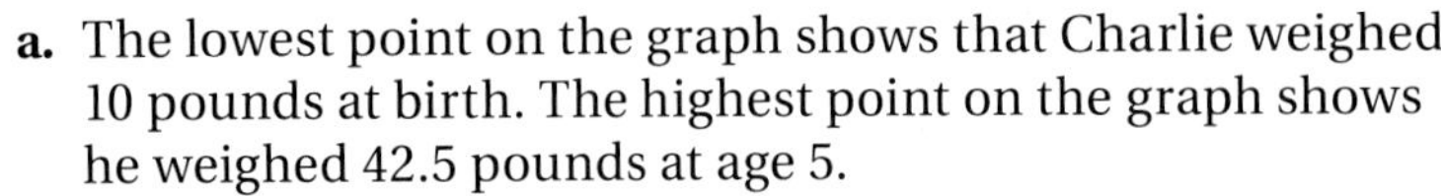

a. The lowest point on the graph shows that Charlie weighed 10 pounds at birth. The highest point on the graph shows he weighed 42.5 pounds at age 5.

$42.5 - 10 = 32.5$

▶ Charlie gained 32.5 pounds in 5 years.

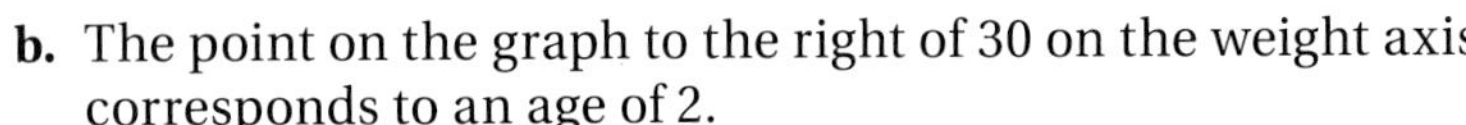

b. The point on the graph to the right of 30 on the weight axis corresponds to an age of 2.

▶ Charlie weighed 30 pounds at age 2.

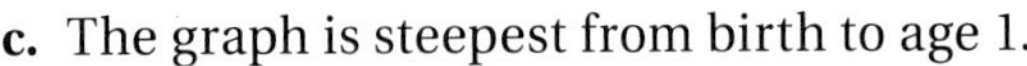

c. The graph is steepest from birth to age 1.

▶ Charlie gained the most weight in his first year.

PRACTICE

In Exercises 1–5, use the line graph above.

1. How much did Charlie weigh on his first birthday?
2. How old was Charlie when he weighed 40 pounds?
3. In which year did Charlie gain the least weight?
4. How much weight did Charlie gain his first year?
5. How much weight did Charlie gain from age 1 to age 4?

In Exercises 6–14, use the line graph, which shows Abby's height from birth to 4 years old.

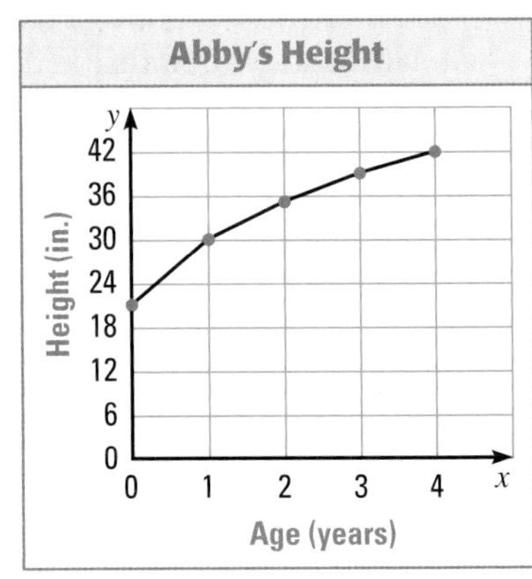

6. How tall was Abby when she was born?
7. How old was Abby when she was 35 inches tall?
8. In which year did Abby grow the most?
9. In which year did Abby grow the least?
10. How many inches did Abby grow from age 3 to age 4?
11. In which year did Abby grow 5 inches?
12. How many inches did Abby grow in 4 years?
13. At what age was Abby's height double her height at birth?
14. If Abby maintains the same growth rate from age 4 to age 5 that she had from age 3 to age 4, how tall will she be when she is 5?

Circle Graphs

You can use a **circle graph** to display data as sections of a circle. The entire circle represents all of the data. The sections of the circle may be labeled using the actual data or the data expressed as fractions, decimals, or percents. When the data are expressed as fractions, decimals, or percents, the sum of the data is 1.

EXAMPLE **Use the circle graph, which shows the string musicians in a college orchestra. (a) What percent of the string musicians in the orchestra play the cello? (b) Which instrument do almost half the string musicians in the orchestra play?**

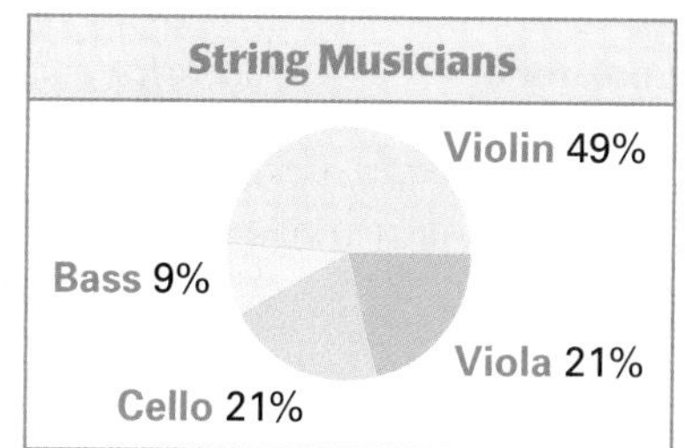

a. The cello section of the circle is labeled 21%.

▸ Of the string musicians in the orchestra, 21% play cello.

b. The violin section of the circle is labeled 49%, which is almost 50%. Also, the violin section of the circle is almost half the total area of the circle.

▸ Almost half of the string musicians in the orchestra play the violin.

PRACTICE

In Exercises 1–4, use the circle graph above.

1. What percent of the string musicians in the orchestra play the bass?
2. How does the number of string musicians who play the viola compare with the number of string musicians who play the cello?
3. The violinists are divided evenly into two groups, first violin and second violin. What percent of the string musicians are in each of these groups?
4. If there are 57 string musicians in the orchestra, how many musicians play each type of instrument?

In Exercises 5–10, use the circle graph, which shows the types of instruments played by musicians in a college band.

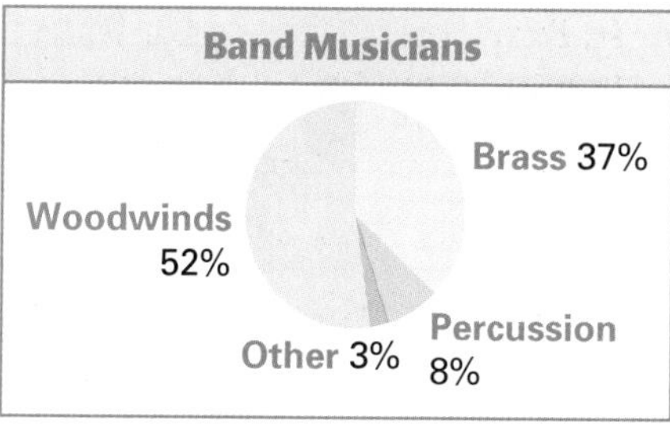

5. What percent of the musicians in the band play a brass instrument?
6. Which type of instrument do 8% of the musicians in the band play?
7. Which type of instrument do more than half of the musicians in the band play?
8. The instruments in the "Other" category are harp, string bass, and keyboard. What percent of the band musicians play one of these instruments?

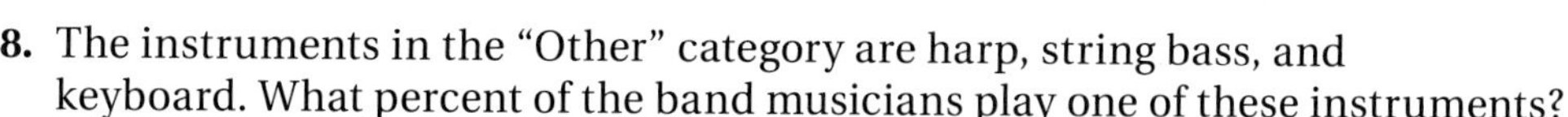

9. In this band, which type of instrument is played by about 5 times as many musicians as play percussion instruments?
10. There are 91 musicians in the band. How many more musicians play a woodwind than play a percussion instrument?

Problem Solving Strategies

The following are strategies that you can use to solve problems.

Strategy	When to use	How to use
Draw a diagram	Draw a diagram when a problem involves any relationships that you can represent visually.	Draw a diagram that shows the given information. Label any unknowns in your diagram and look for relationships between givens and unknowns.
Look for a pattern	Look for a pattern when a problem includes a series of numbers or diagrams that you need to analyze.	Look for a pattern in any given information. Apply, extend, or generalize the pattern to help you solve the problem.
Guess, check, and revise	Guess, check, and revise when you need a place to start or you want to see what happens for a particular number.	Make a reasonable guess. Check to see if your guess solves the problem. If it does not, revise your guess and check again.
Act it out	Act out a problem that involves any relationships that you can represent with physical objects and movement.	Act out the problem, using objects described in the problem or other items that represent those objects.
Make a list or table	Make a list or table when you need to record, generate, or organize information.	Generate a list systematically, accounting for all possibilities. Look for relationships across rows or down columns within a table.
Solve a simpler or related problem	Solve a simpler or related problem when a problem seems difficult and can be made easier by using simpler numbers or conditions.	Think of a way to make the problem easier. Solve the simpler or related problem. Use what you learned to help you solve the original problem.
Work backward	Work backward when a problem gives you an end result and you need to find beginning conditions.	Work backward from the given information until you solve the problem. Work forward through the problem to check your answer.
Break into parts	Break into parts when a problem cannot be solved all at once, but can be solved in parts or stages.	Break the problem into parts and solve each part. Put the answers together to help you solve the original problem.

EXAMPLE **Fletcher baked brownies in a rectangular pan that measures 9 inches by 13 inches. He wants to cut rectangular brownies that are at least 2 inches on each side, with all brownies the same size. What is the greatest number of brownies Fletcher can cut?**

Draw a diagram of the rectangular pan. Label the sides with their lengths. Think about each side of the rectangle.

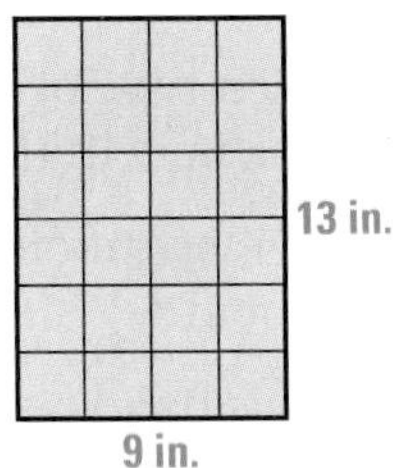

$9 \div 2 = 4.5$, so cut 4 brownies along the 9 inch side.
Check: $9 \div 4 = 2.25$, and $2.25 > 2$.

$13 \div 2 = 6.5$, so cut 6 brownies along the 13 inch side.
Check: $13 \div 6 \approx 2.17$, and $2.17 > 2$.

Use your diagram to count the brownies: $4 \times 6 = 24$.

▶ The greatest number of brownies Fletcher can cut is 24.

PRACTICE

1. Four friends hosted a party. The table shows the amount of money each friend spent. The friends want to share the party expenses equally, and Pam will pay the entire amount she owes to one person. Who owes money to whom?

Person	Party expenses
Barb	$11 for drinks
Bonnie	$15 for food
Pam	$6 for invitations
Holly	$8 for decorations

2. Six people can be seated at a rectangular table, with one person at each end. How many people can be seated at five of these tables if they are placed end to end?

3. Bob is 55 years old. In 5 years, Bob will be twice as old as his son. How old is Bob's son?

4. Maddie and Rob are sharing a pack of 25 pens. Maddie offers to let Rob have 3 pens for every 2 pens she gets. If they use the entire package of pens, how many pens will each person get?

5. In how many different ways can you make $.50 in change using quarters, dimes, and nickels?

6. The diagram shows two cuts through the center of a pizza. How many cuts through the center are needed to divide a pizza into 12 equal pieces?

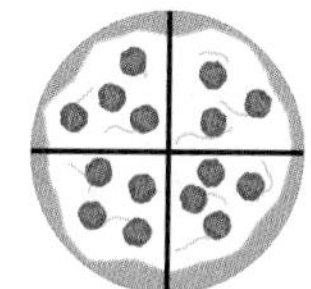

7. Deb is flying to Seattle. Her flight leaves at 4:15 P.M. She wants to arrive at the airport 2 hours early to check in and get through security. The taxi ride from her office to the airport takes about 30 minutes. What time should Deb ask the taxi driver to pick her up at the office?

8. Dan wants to enclose a rectangular area with a fence. He has 12 fence posts to use, and the fence posts will be placed 10 feet apart. The diagram shows a possible shape for the area. Find another shape that would use all the fence posts, placed 10 feet apart, and would increase the area by 100 square feet.

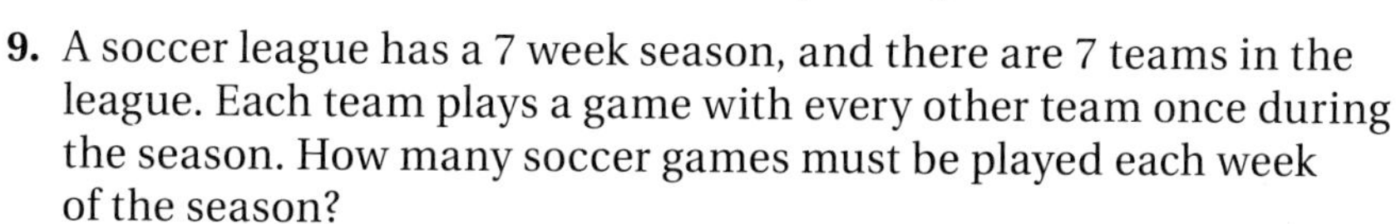

9. A soccer league has a 7 week season, and there are 7 teams in the league. Each team plays a game with every other team once during the season. How many soccer games must be played each week of the season?

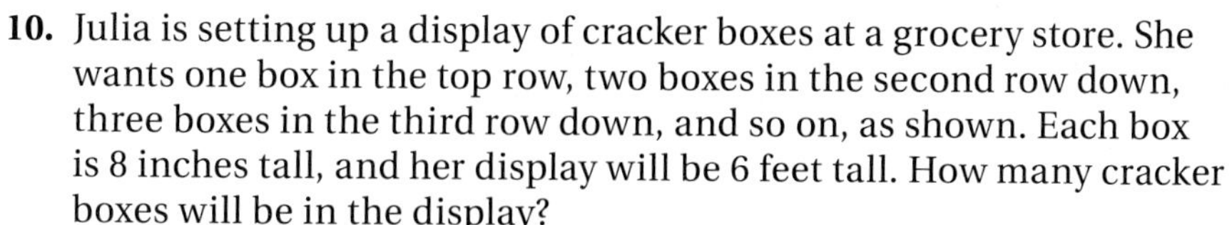

10. Julia is setting up a display of cracker boxes at a grocery store. She wants one box in the top row, two boxes in the second row down, three boxes in the third row down, and so on, as shown. Each box is 8 inches tall, and her display will be 6 feet tall. How many cracker boxes will be in the display?

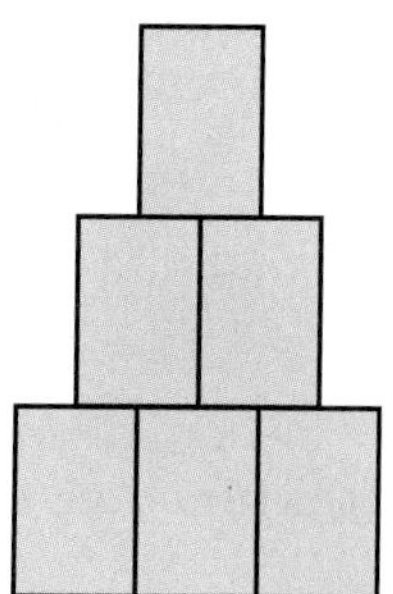

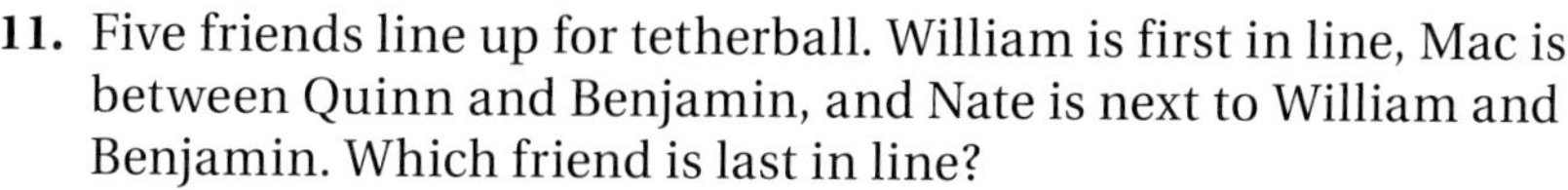

11. Five friends line up for tetherball. William is first in line, Mac is between Quinn and Benjamin, and Nate is next to William and Benjamin. Which friend is last in line?

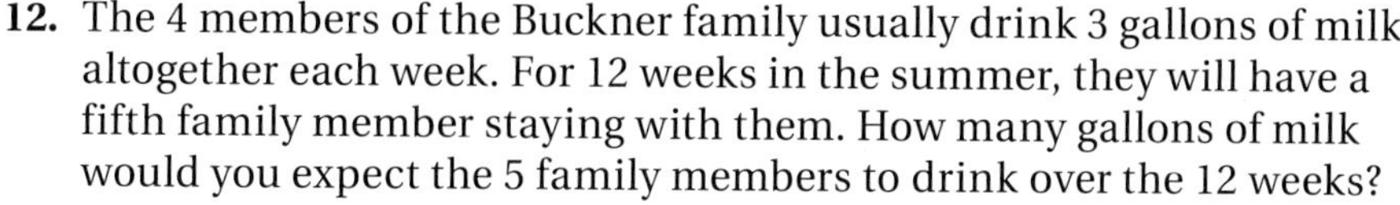

12. The 4 members of the Buckner family usually drink 3 gallons of milk altogether each week. For 12 weeks in the summer, they will have a fifth family member staying with them. How many gallons of milk would you expect the 5 family members to drink over the 12 weeks?

Extra Practice

Chapter 1

EXTRA PRACTICE

Evaluate the expression.

1.1 **1.** $k + 9$ when $k = 7$ **2.** $21 - x$ when $x = 3$ **3.** $3.5 + t$ when $t = 0.9$ **4.** $y - \frac{3}{8}$ when $y = \frac{7}{12}$

5. $\frac{m}{4}$ when $m = 9.6$ **6.** $1.5t$ when $t = 2.3$ **7.** z^3 when $z = \frac{2}{3}$ **8.** p^4 when $p = 0.2$

1.2 **9.** $25 - 7 + 8$ **10.** $67 - 3 \cdot 4$ **11.** $8^2 \div 4 + 12$ **12.** $9 + 6 \div 3$

13. $\frac{3^3 - 7}{2}$ **14.** $\frac{1}{3}(7 - 5.5)^2$ **15.** $3 + 4(3 + 24)$ **16.** $\frac{3}{5}[27 - (2 + 5)]^2$

1.3 Translate the verbal phrase into an expression.

17. $\frac{3}{4}$ of a number m **18.** the quotient of a number x and 7

19. the difference of a number y and 3 **20.** 6 more than 3 times a number n

1.3 Write an expression for the situation.

21. Number of minutes left in a 45 minute class after m minutes have gone by

22. Number of meters in c centimeters

1.4 Write an equation or an inequality.

23. The product of 12 and the difference of a number r and 4 is 72.

24. The difference of a number q and 18 is greater than 10 and less than 15.

1.4 Solve the equation using mental math.

25. $d - 13 = 25$ **26.** $12z = 96$ **27.** $23 - m = 7$ **28.** $\frac{k}{6} = 12$

1.5 In Exercises 29 and 30, identify what you know and what you need to find out. You do *not* need to solve the problem.

29. One day the temperature in Quito, Ecuador, was 20°C. The temperature in Miami, Florida was 75°F. Which temperature was higher?

30. On Monday, Katherine walked at a rate of 0.08 mile per minute for 40 minutes. On Tuesday, she walked at a rate of 0.07 mile per minute for 50 minutes. How far did Katherine walk altogether?

1.6 **31.** Identify the domain and range of the function.

Input	3	4	5	6
Output	9	11	13	15

1.6 **32.** The domain of the function $y = 1.25x + 5$ is 2, 4, 6, and 8. Make a table for the function. Identify the range of the function.

1.7 Graph the function.

33. $y = x + 2$; domain: 0, 1, 2, and 3 **34.** $y = 3x - 3$; domain: 1, 2, 3, and 4

35. $y = 1.5x$; domain: 0, 20, 40, and 60 **36.** $y = \frac{1}{4}x + 2$; domain: 0, 4, 8, and 12

Chapter 2

2.1 Graph the numbers on a number line. Then tell which number is greater.

1. 0 and −4 **2.** 2 and −2 **3.** −5 and −3 **4.** −6 and 4

2.1 Tell whether each number in the list is a whole number, an integer, or a rational number. Then order the numbers from least to greatest.

5. $0.25, -\frac{1}{8}, -\frac{1}{10}, -\frac{1}{5}$ **6.** $-2.5, -3, \frac{5}{2}, -\frac{9}{4}$ **7.** −4, 3, −5, 0

2.2 Find the sum.

8. $-6 + 10$ **9.** $-25 + (-36)$ **10.** $-75 + 58$ **11.** $8 + (-15) + 7$

12. $-2.8 + 4.3$ **13.** $-8.2 + (-11.5)$ **14.** $3\frac{2}{3} + \left(-5\frac{3}{8}\right)$ **15.** $-12\frac{3}{5} + 8\frac{1}{6}$

2.3 Find the difference.

16. $-17 - 20$ **17.** $16 - (-50)$ **18.** $-9 - (-12)$ **19.** $\frac{4}{5} - \frac{1}{2}$

20. $-\frac{1}{2} - \frac{2}{3}$ **21.** $-\frac{1}{3} - \left(-\frac{3}{4}\right)$ **22.** $-6.4 - 15$ **23.** $-12.8 - (-5.6)$

2.3 Evaluate the expression when $x = 1.5$ and $y = -4$.

24. $y - x$ **25.** $-y - (-x)$ **26.** $x - (10 - y)$ **27.** $-7 - (x - y)$

2.4 Find the product.

28. $-\frac{2}{3}(-36)$ **29.** $64\left(-\frac{5}{8}\right)$ **30.** $-4.1(-3.5)$ **31.** $(1.1)(-0.5)(-4)$

2.4 Identify the property illustrated.

32. $(-5)(8)(2) = (-5)(2)(8)$ **33.** $6 \cdot (7 \cdot 2) = (6 \cdot 7) \cdot 2$ **34.** $1(mn) = mn$

35. $0 \cdot (134) = 0$ **36.** $y \cdot (-1) = (-1) \cdot y$ **37.** $(-1)(-9) = 9$

2.5 Use the distributive property to write an equivalent expression.

38. $8(x + 4)$ **39.** $5(6 - y)$ **40.** $(m + 7)(-8)$ **41.** $-3(k - 14)$

42. $\frac{3}{5}(-15r - 5)$ **43.** $\frac{7}{12}(24s + 12)$ **44.** $(9v - 18)\frac{1}{3}$ **45.** $-\frac{5}{6}(-6w - 30)$

2.6 Find the quotient.

46. $-35 \div 7$ **47.** $-92 \div (-4)$ **48.** $36 \div \left(-\frac{3}{4}\right)$ **49.** $-56 \div \left(-\frac{7}{8}\right)$

50. $\frac{5}{9} \div (-5)$ **51.** $-\frac{5}{12} \div \frac{1}{2}$ **52.** $-\frac{4}{3} \div \frac{4}{3}$ **53.** $-\frac{5}{6} \div \left(-\frac{6}{5}\right)$

2.7 Evaluate the expression.

54. $-\sqrt{36}$ **55.** $\pm\sqrt{400}$ **56.** $\sqrt{6400}$ **57.** $\pm\sqrt{144}$

2.7 Approximate the square root to the nearest integer.

58. $\sqrt{135}$ **59.** $-\sqrt{75}$ **60.** $-\sqrt{160}$ **61.** $\sqrt{250}$

Chapter 3

Solve the equation. Check your solution.

3.1 **1.** $x + 4 = 20$ **2.** $8 = m - 13$ **3.** $t + 2 = -10$ **4.** $z - 8 = -7$

5. $7h = 63$ **6.** $-4t = -44$ **7.** $\frac{b}{4} = 13$ **8.** $\frac{y}{-3} = 8$

3.2 **9.** $4x + 3 = 27$ **10.** $6m - 4 = 14$ **11.** $50 = 7y - 6$

12. $\frac{t}{4} - 3 = 9$ **13.** $\frac{x}{7} + 3 = -2$ **14.** $6p - 2p = 28$

3.3 **15.** $6x + 3x + 8 = 35$ **16.** $12w - 5 - 3w = 40$ **17.** $4d - 3 - 2d = -15$

18. $7m + 3(m + 2) = -24$ **19.** $5x - 3(x - 5) = 13$ **20.** $\frac{3}{4}(2y - 8) = 6$

3.4 **21.** $8x - 4 = 3x + 6$ **22.** $10 - 2x = 3x - 20$ **23.** $5 - 5x = 14 - 8x$

24. $3(2y - 5) = 4y - 7$ **25.** $9 + 4y = 2(3 - y)$ **26.** $3x - 3 = \frac{3}{4}(2x + 12)$

3.5 Solve the proportion. Check your solution.

27. $\frac{7}{2} = \frac{x}{16}$ **28.** $\frac{m}{9} = \frac{6}{27}$ **29.** $\frac{z}{4} = \frac{48}{12}$ **30.** $\frac{30}{50} = \frac{t}{10}$

3.5 Write the sentence as a proportion. Then solve the proportion.

31. 5 is to 7 as 15 is to x. **32.** 9 is to 3 as x is to 12.

33. g is to 9 as 16 is to 12. **34.** 6 is to 18 as y is to 3.

3.6 Solve the proportion. Check your solution.

35. $\frac{12}{x} = \frac{6}{7}$ **36.** $\frac{6x}{4} = \frac{18}{12}$ **37.** $\frac{7}{x + 13} = \frac{4}{12}$ **38.** $\frac{y + 5}{y} = \frac{10}{8}$

39. $\frac{2x + 6}{x} = \frac{7}{2}$ **40.** $\frac{3b}{5b - 7} = \frac{8}{11}$ **41.** $\frac{8}{2x + 12} = \frac{6}{x + 8}$ **42.** $\frac{4.8 - 2x}{8} = \frac{0.4 + x}{10}$

3.7 Use a proportion to answer the question.

43. What percent of 96 is 12? **44.** What number is 35% of 18?

45. 14 is 40% of what number? **46.** What percent of 125 is 30?

3.7 Use the percent equation to answer the question.

47. What number is 250% of 18? **48.** What percent of 58 is 8.7?

49. 30.1 is 35% of what number? **50.** What number is 70% of 250?

3.8 Solve the literal equation for x. Then use the solution to solve the specific equation.

51. $ax - b = c$; $6x - 5 = 25$ **52.** $a(b - x) = c$; $2(8 - x) = -6$

3.8 Write the equation so that y is a function of x.

53. $5x + y = 10$ **54.** $8x - 2y = 16$ **55.** $7x + 3y = 6 - 5x$ **56.** $21 = 6x + 7y$

EXTRA PRACTICE

Chapter 4

4.1 Plot the point in a coordinate plane. *Describe* the location of the point.

1. $K(-4, -2)$ **2.** $L(5, 0)$ **3.** $M(3, -1)$ **4.** $N(-2, 2)$

5. $P(0, 4)$ **6.** $Q(-3.5, 5)$ **7.** $R(2.5, 6)$ **8.** $S(-1, -1.5)$

4.1 Graph the function with the given domain. Then identify the range of the function.

9. $y = -2x + 2$; domain: $-2, -1, 0, 1, 2$ **10.** $y = \frac{1}{2}x - 3$; domain: $-4, -2, 0, 2, 4$

4.2 Graph the equation.

11. $y - x = 3$ **12.** $y + 3x = 5$ **13.** $y - 4x = 10$ **14.** $y = 4$

15. $2x - y = 0$ **16.** $3x + y = 0$ **17.** $3x + 2y = -6$ **18.** $x = 0.5$

4.3 Find the *x*-intercept and the *y*-intercept of the graph of the equation.

19. $2x - y = 12$ **20.** $-5x - 2y = 20$ **21.** $-4x + 1.5y = 4$ **22.** $y = \frac{3}{4}x - 15$

4.3 Graph the equation. Label the points where the line crosses the axes.

23. $y = 3x - 6$ **24.** $4x + 5y = -20$ **25.** $\frac{2}{3}x + \frac{1}{2}y = 10$ **26.** $0.3x - y = 6$

4.4 Find the slope of the line that passes through the points.

27. $(4, 2)$ and $(6, 8)$ **28.** $(-3, 0)$ and $(2, -5)$ **29.** $(-5, 3)$ and $(-8, 10)$

30. $(9, 4)$ and $(0, 1)$ **31.** $(-2, 5)$ and $(-2, 10)$ **32.** $(6, -4)$ and $(4, -4)$

4.5 Identify the slope and *y*-intercept of the line with the given equation.

33. $y = 7x + 8$ **34.** $y = 10x - 6$ **35.** $y = 3 - 4x$ **36.** $y = x$

4.5 Rewrite the equation in slope-intercept form. Then identify the slope and the *y*-intercept of the line.

37. $2x + y = 8$ **38.** $10x - y = 20$ **39.** $5x + 2y = 10$ **40.** $-2x - y = 3$

4.5 Graph the equation.

41. $y = 2x - 4$ **42.** $y = -\frac{3}{4}x + 1$ **43.** $2x + y = 1$ **44.** $-2x + 3y = -9$

4.6 Graph the direct variation equation.

45. $y = 2x$ **46.** $y = -x$ **47.** $y = 4x$ **48.** $5x + y = 0$

49. $x - 2y = 0$ **50.** $3x + y = 0$ **51.** $2y = 9x$ **52.** $y - \frac{5}{4}x = 0$

4.7 Find the value of *x* so that the function has the given value.

53. $f(x) = -7x - 3$; -17 **54.** $g(x) = 5x - 4$; 12 **55.** $t(x) = 3x + 1$; -11

4.7 Graph the function. Compare the graph with the graph of $f(x) = x$.

56. $m(x) = x - 2$ **57.** $t(x) = x + 4$ **58.** $z(x) = 6x$ **59.** $h(x) = -2x$

Chapter 5

5.1 Write an equation of the line with the given slope and *y*-intercept.

1. slope: 3
   y-intercept: 6
2. slope: −2
   y-intercept: 4
3. slope: 5
   y-intercept: −1
4. slope: −1
   y-intercept: −3
5. slope: $\frac{1}{2}$
   y-intercept: −5
6. slope: $-\frac{7}{10}$
   y-intercept: 8

EXTRA PRACTICE

5.2 Write an equation of the line that passes through the given point and has the given slope *m*.

7. $(3, 8);\ m = 2$
8. $(-1, 5);\ m = -4$
9. $(-6, 3);\ m = \frac{2}{3}$

5.2 Write an equation of the line that passes through the given points.

10. $(2, 4), (5, 13)$
11. $(1, -2), (-2, 13)$
12. $\left(2, \frac{1}{3}\right), (6, 3)$

5.3 Graph the equation.

13. $y - 3 = -3(x + 4)$
14. $y + 5 = -2(x - 1)$
15. $y - 6 = \frac{2}{3}(x - 3)$

5.3 Write an equation in point-slope form of the line that passes through the given points.

16. $(-4, 2), (-2, 16)$
17. $(3, 9), (-7, 4)$
18. $(10, -2), (12, -6)$

5.4 Write an equation in standard form of the line that passes through the given point and has the given slope *m* or that passes through the two given points.

19. $(2, 7),\ m = -4$
20. $(5, 11),\ m = 3$
21. $(1, -2), (-2, 4)$

5.5 Write an equation of the line that passes through the given point and is parallel to the given line.

22. $(5, 4),\ y = 3x + 5$
23. $(-3, -7),\ y = -5x - 2$
24. $(8, -3),\ y = \frac{3}{4}x + 5$

5.5 Write an equation of the line that passes through the given point and is perpendicular to the given line.

25. $(-12, -2),\ y = 3x + 2$
26. $(15, -11),\ y = \frac{3}{5}x - 8$
27. $(7, -6),\ 4x + 6y = 7$

5.6 Make a scatter plot of the data in the table. Draw a line of fit. Write an equation of the line.

28.

x	1	2	3	3.5	4	4.5	5
y	20	35	40	55	60	45	60

29.

x	10	20	30	40	50	60
y	55	45	45	40	35	20

5.7 Make a scatter plot of the data. Find the equation of the best-fitting line. Approximate the value of *y* for *x* = 7.

30.

x	0	2	4	6	8
y	0.5	3	4	5.5	7

31.

x	0	1	3	6	8
y	5	8	12	15	14

Chapter 6

Solve the inequality. Graph your solution.

6.1

1. $y - 2 > 3$ **2.** $5 + x \le 2$ **3.** $4 \ge x - 3$ **4.** $m + 3 < 2$

5. $2 + n \le 4\frac{1}{2}$ **6.** $2\frac{3}{4} + n < -3\frac{5}{8}$ **7.** $1\frac{7}{8} > 6\frac{3}{4} + z$ **8.** $3\frac{2}{5} \ge 1\frac{1}{3} + k$

9. $-8.5 \le t - 10$ **10.** $r + 4 < -0.7$ **11.** $-6.9 > -1.4 + y$ **12.** $1.48 - m \ge -3.13$

6.2

13. $3p \le 27$ **14.** $-13t > 26$ **15.** $\frac{x}{3} \ge 2$ **16.** $\frac{y}{-2} < 5$

17. $-6m \ge -9$ **18.** $-3 \ge \frac{n}{2}$ **19.** $0.3z \le 2.4$ **20.** $25 > -2.5s$

21. $4.8z \le 3.2$ **22.** $0.09d < -1.8$ **23.** $\frac{y}{0.3} > -15$ **24.** $-1.8t < 9$

6.3 Solve the inequality, if possible. Graph your solution.

25. $3x + 5 \ge 20$ **26.** $6z - 5 < 13$ **27.** $8(t + 4) > -8$

28. $7 - 8n \le 4n - 17$ **29.** $8(m + 2) < 4(5 + 2m)$ **30.** $6d - 4 - 3d \ge 14$

31. $\frac{2}{3}y + 28 > 20 + 2y$ **32.** $6(-5 + 3p) \ge 3(6p - 10)$ **33.** $\frac{5}{6}(12z - 24) > \frac{2}{5}(25z - 25)$

6.4 Solve the inequality. Graph your solution.

34. $2 \le y - 4 < 7$ **35.** $-27 < 9x < 27$ **36.** $2 < 6z - 10 < 20$

37. $15 < \frac{5}{9}(18a - 9) \le 30$ **38.** $2v > 12$ *or* $v + 2 < 6$ **39.** $3r + 7 < -5$ *or* $32 \le 7r + 46$

40. $-4m < 8$ *or* $2m - 2 < -12$ **41.** $9t - 20 \ge 4t$ *or* $4 < \frac{1}{-2}t$ **42.** $-n - 1 > 1$ *or* $2n + 8 > n + 8$

6.5 Solve the equation, if possible.

43. $|x| = 8$ **44.** $|y| = -10$ **45.** $|m + 6| = 5$ **46.** $|4z - 2| = 14$

47. $|t - 7| = 21$ **48.** $6|z - 4| = 36$ **49.** $4|6s + 11| = -52$ **50.** $|r + 3| - 16 = -4$

51. $|5r| + 10 = 15$ **52.** $2|3s + 4| = 14$ **53.** $-4|7v + 2| = 32$ **54.** $12\left|\frac{5}{6}w - 4\right| - 4 = 8$

6.6 Solve the inequality. Graph your solution.

55. $|x| \le 3$ **56.** $|y| \ge 5$ **57.** $|s| > 1.2$ **58.** $|q| < \frac{2}{5}$

59. $|x + 2| > 6$ **60.** $|y + 3| \le 5$ **61.** $|8 - m| < 3$ **62.** $|4n - 1| \ge 7$

63. $3|p - 3| \le 12$ **64.** $|3q + 2| - 3 \ge 8$ **65.** $2|5a - 1| + 3 \le 11$ **66.** $4\left|\frac{2}{3}c + 2\right| < 64$

6.7 Graph the inequality.

67. $y \ge x + 5$ **68.** $y < x - 1$ **69.** $4x + y > 3$ **70.** $x \le -5$

71. $3(x - 8) \le 6y$ **72.** $2x - y \ge -2$ **73.** $y > 8$ **74.** $2(x - 1) \ge 1 - y$

75. $x - 8 \le y + 2$ **76.** $2x \ge -2y$ **77.** $3(y - 8) > x - 9$ **78.** $2(-x - 1) \ge 4 + y$

Chapter 7

7.1 Solve the linear system by graphing. Check your solution.

1. $y = x - 1$
   $y = -x + 5$
2. $y = 3x + 12$
   $y = -4x - 2$
3. $x - y = 4$
   $x + y = -2$
4. $4x - y = 10$
   $x = 4$
5. $3x - 2y = -5$
   $4x + 3y = -18$
6. $\frac{2}{3}x + \frac{1}{3}y = \frac{16}{3}$
   $-\frac{2}{5}x + y = \frac{8}{5}$

EXTRA PRACTICE

7.2 Solve the linear system using substitution.

7. $y = 2x + 6$
   $x = y - 3$
8. $y = 3x + 5$
   $x + y = -1$
9. $x = 2y - 5$
   $2x - y = 11$
10. $2x - y = 0$
    $x + 3y = -56$
11. $1.5x - 2.5y = 22$
    $x - y = 10$
12. $\frac{1}{2}x + \frac{3}{4}y = 5$
    $x - \frac{1}{2}y = 6$

Solve the linear system using elimination.

7.3

13. $x + 2y = 2$
    $-x + 3y = 13$
14. $3x - 4y = -16$
    $x - 4y = -40$
15. $3x + 2y = -31$
    $5x + 2y = -49$
16. $5x + 4y = 6$
    $7x + 4y = 14$
17. $10y - 3x = -41$
    $3x - 5y = 16$
18. $4x - 3y = 39$
    $7y = 4x - 79$

7.4

19. $x + y = -3$
    $5x + 7y = -9$
20. $5x + 2y = -19$
    $10x - 7y = -16$
21. $8x - 3y = 61$
    $2x - 5y = -23$
22. $4x - 3y = -2$
    $6x + 4y = 31$
23. $5x - 2y = 53$
    $2x + 6y = 11$
24. $15x - 8y = 6$
    $25x - 12y = 16$

7.5 Graph the linear system. Then use the graph to tell whether the linear system has *one solution, no solution,* or *infinitely many solutions.*

25. $2x + y = -3$
    $y = -2x + 5$
26. $2y - 4x = 10$
    $-2y - 2x = 8$
27. $10x + 5y = -15$
    $y = -2x - 3$

7.5 Solve the linear system using substitution or elimination.

28. $y - 3x = 5$
    $x = y - 5$
29. $2y - 3x = 36$
    $y = 3x - 12$
30. $5x + 5y = -32$
    $3x + 3y = 14$
31. $4x + 6y = 11$
    $y = -\frac{2}{3}x + 7$
32. $3y - 3x = 12$
    $y = x - 4$
33. $x + 2y = -30$
    $y = \frac{1}{2}x + 15$

7.6 Graph the system of inequalities.

34. $y \geq -5$
    $y \leq -2$
35. $x \geq -3$
    $y < 1$
36. $y < -2x - 3$
    $x - y > -4$
37. $x + 4y \geq -8$
    $y - 4x < 8$
    $x > -1$
38. $x > 3$
    $x < 5$
    $y > -2$
    $y \leq 0$
39. $x + y > 3$
    $x - y > 5$
    $x + 2y \leq 8$
    $x - 5y > 10$

Chapter 8

Simplify the expression. In exercises involving numerical bases only, write your answer using exponents.

8.1 **1.** $5^3 \cdot 5^4$ **2.** $6 \cdot 6^7$ **3.** $(-2)^3 \cdot (-2)^6$ **4.** $(2^8)^2$

5. $[(-4)^3]^2$ **6.** $(8 \cdot 4)^5$ **7.** $m^5 \cdot m^2$ **8.** $n^2 \cdot n^4 \cdot n^5$

9. $(y^3)^5$ **10.** $(-2x)^3$ **11.** $(3d^2)^3 \cdot 2d^2$ **12.** $(-4s^2)^3(2s^3)^6$

8.2 **13.** $\frac{8^7}{8^2}$ **14.** $\frac{4^6 \cdot 4^2}{4^3}$ **15.** $\left(-\frac{2}{3}\right)^5$ **16.** $10^{12} \cdot \frac{1}{10^7}$

17. $7^9 \cdot \left(\frac{1}{7}\right)^4$ **18.** $\frac{1}{t^9} \cdot t^{13}$ **19.** $\left(\frac{p}{q}\right)^7$ **20.** $\left(\frac{6x^9}{3y^4}\right)^2$

21. $\left(\frac{4y^5}{3}\right)^3 \cdot \frac{1}{y^6}$ **22.** $\left(\frac{2}{u^2}\right)^3 \cdot \left(\frac{3u^4}{z^2}\right)^4$ **23.** $\left(\frac{5x^3y^4}{2x^2y}\right)^2$ **24.** $\frac{6a^4b^5}{ab} \cdot \left(\frac{2ab}{a^2b^2}\right)^3$

8.3 **Evaluate the expression.**

25. 3^{-4} **26.** $(-5)^{-3}$ **27.** 7^0 **28.** $4^{-5} \cdot 4^3$

29. $\left(\frac{1}{2}\right)^{-3}$ **30.** $(3^{-2})^3$ **31.** $\frac{1}{2^{-5}}$ **32.** $\frac{8^{-4}}{8^{-6}}$

8.3 **Simplify the expression. Write your answer using only positive exponents.**

33. y^{-10} **34.** $(3c)^{-4}$ **35.** $10b^{-3}c^5$ **36.** $(2d^5e^{-2})^{-3}$

37. $\frac{x^{-4}}{y^{-5}}$ **38.** $\frac{1}{6t^{-5}u^3}$ **39.** $\frac{3}{(-2z)^{-5}}$ **40.** $\frac{(2e)^{-4}g^5}{e^5g^{-3}}$

8.4 **If the number is written in scientific notation, write it in standard form. If the number is written in standard form, write it in scientific notation.**

41. 0.87 **42.** 378.4 **43.** 0.000359 **44.** 465,000,000

45. 5.3×10^5 **46.** 1.67×10^{-4} **47.** 8×10^{-6} **48.** 9.0001×10^2

8.4 **Evaluate the expression. Write your answer in scientific notation.**

49. $\frac{3 \times 10^2}{8 \times 10^6}$ **50.** $(8.5 \times 10^{10})(3.7 \times 10^{-5})$ **51.** $\frac{2.4 \times 10^{-5}}{6 \times 10^{-8}}$

Graph the function.

8.5 **52.** $y = 3^x$ **53.** $y = 1.25^x$ **54.** $y = \left(\frac{9}{4}\right)^x$ **55.** $y = 5 \cdot 2^x$

56. $y = \frac{1}{3} \cdot 2^x$ **57.** $y = -\frac{1}{2} \cdot 5^x$ **58.** $y = -5 \cdot 2^x$ **59.** $y = -\frac{1}{3} \cdot 4^x$

8.6 **60.** $y = \left(\frac{1}{3}\right)^x$ **61.** $y = (0.2)^x$ **62.** $y = 3 \cdot (0.2)^x$ **63.** $y = 2 \cdot \left(\frac{1}{3}\right)^x$

64. $y = 4 \cdot \left(\frac{1}{3}\right)^x$ **65.** $y = \frac{1}{2} \cdot \left(\frac{1}{3}\right)^x$ **66.** $y = -2 \cdot \left(\frac{1}{3}\right)^x$ **67.** $y = -\frac{3}{4} \cdot \left(\frac{1}{3}\right)^x$

8.6 **68.** Tell whether the table represents an exponential function. If so, write a rule for the function.

x	−1	0	1	2	3
y	$\frac{5}{2}$	5	10	20	40

EXTRA PRACTICE

Chapter 9

Find the sum or difference.

9.1
1. $(6x^2 + 7) + (x^2 - 9)$
2. $(8y^2 - 3y - 10) + (-11y^2 + 2y - 7)$
3. $(10m^2 - 7m + 2) - (3m^2 - 2m + 5)$
4. $(2t^3 - 3t^2 + 5t) - (6t^3 + 3t^2 - 5t)$
5. $(6b^3 + 12b^2 - b) - (15b^2 + 7b - 8)$
6. $(r^2 - 8 + 4r^3 + 5r) - (7r^3 - 3r^2 + 5)$

Find the product.

9.2
7. $5x^4(2x^3 - 3x^2 + 5x - 1)$
8. $(x^2 + 4x + 2)(x + 7)$
9. $(2x + 3)(4x + 2)$
10. $(2x^2 - 5x + 6)(3x - 2)$
11. $(3x - 7)(x + 5)$
12. $(9t - 2)(2t - 3)$

9.3
13. $(x + 10)^2$
14. $(m + 8)(m - 8)$
15. $(4x - 2)(4x + 2)$
16. $(3x - 4y)(3x + 4y)$
17. $(6 - 3t)(6 + 3t)$
18. $(-11x - 4y)^2$

9.4 Solve the equation.

19. $(m + 8)(m - 2) = 0$
20. $(2y - 6)(y + 3) = 0$
21. $(5y - 3)(2y - 4) = 0$
22. $3b^2 + 9b = 0$
23. $-12m^2 - 3m = 0$
24. $14k^2 = 28k$

9.5 Factor the trinomial.

25. $y^2 + 7y + 12$
26. $x^2 - 12x + 35$
27. $x^2 + 5x - 36$
28. $q^2 + 3q - 40$
29. $m^2 - 29m + 100$
30. $y^2 + 14y - 72$

9.5 Solve the equation.

31. $m^2 - 7m + 10 = 0$
32. $p^2 - 7p = 18$
33. $z^2 - 13z + 24 = -12$
34. $n^2 + 8 = 6n$
35. $r^2 - 15r = -8r - 10$
36. $c^2 - 8 = -13c + 6$

9.6 Factor the trinomial.

37. $-x^2 + 5x - 6$
38. $3k^2 - 10k + 8$
39. $4k^2 - 12k + 5$
40. $6t^2 - 5t - 6$
41. $-3s^2 - 7s - 2$
42. $2v^2 - 5v + 3$

9.6 Solve the equation.

43. $-3x^2 + 14x - 8 = 0$
44. $8t^2 + 6t = 9$
45. $2x^2 + 3x - 2 = 0$
46. $3p^2 - 28 = 17p$
47. $16m^2 - 1 = -15m$
48. $t(6t - 7) = 3$

9.7 Factor the polynomial.

49. $y^2 - 36$
50. $9y^2 - 49$
51. $12y^2 - 27$
52. $x^2 - 8x + 16$
53. $4x^2 - 12x + 9$
54. $27x^2 - 36x + 12$
55. $g^2 + 10g + 25$
56. $9b^2 + 24b + 16$
57. $4w^2 + 28w + 49$

9.8 Factor the polynomial completely.

58. $2x^2 + 8x + 6$
59. $3z^2 - 16z + 5$
60. $5m^2 - 23m + 12$
61. $3y^3 + 15y^2 + 2y + 10$
62. $30z^3 - 14z^2 - 8z$
63. $98m^3 - 18m$
64. $8h^2k - 32k$
65. $2h^3 - 3h^2 - 18h + 27$
66. $-12z^3 + 12z^2 - 3z$

Chapter 10

10.1 Graph the function. Compare the graph with the graph of $y = x^2$.

1. $y = 4x^2$
2. $y = -5x^2$
3. $y = \frac{1}{2}x^2$
4. $y = -\frac{2}{5}x^2$
5. $y = x^2 + 3$
6. $y = x^2 - 2$
7. $y = 3x^2 + 4$
8. $y = -4x^2 - 3$

10.2 Graph the function. Label the vertex and axis of symmetry.

9. $y = x^2 + 4x + 4$
10. $y = -x^2 - 2x + 3$
11. $y = 2x^2 - 6x + 5$
12. $y = 3x^2 + 12x + 8$
13. $y = -2x^2 + 6$
14. $y = \frac{3}{4}x^2 - 3x$

10.3 Solve the equation by graphing.

15. $x^2 + 3x - 10 = 0$
16. $x^2 + 14 = 9x$
17. $-x^2 + 3x = -18$
18. $2x^2 + 3x - 20 = 0$
19. $2x^2 + x = 6$
20. $\frac{1}{2}x^2 - x = 12$

10.4 Solve the equation. Round the solutions to the nearest hundredth, if necessary.

21. $2x^2 - 20 = 78$
22. $3y^2 + 16 = 4$
23. $16y^2 - 6 = 3$
24. $48 - x^2 = -52$
25. $5m^2 - 5 = 10$
26. $2 - 5t^2 = 4$

10.5 Solve the equation by completing the square. Round the solutions to the nearest hundredth, if necessary.

27. $x^2 + 4x - 21 = 0$
28. $g^2 - 10g = 24$
29. $w^2 - 7w + 6 = 0$
30. $y^2 - \frac{3}{4}y = \frac{1}{4}$
31. $x^2 - 6x + 3 = 0$
32. $4m^2 + 8m - 7 = 0$

10.6 Use the quadratic formula to solve the equation. Round the solutions to the nearest hundredth, if necessary.

33. $h^2 + 6h - 72 = 0$
34. $3x^2 - 7x + 2 = 0$
35. $2k^2 - 5k + 2 = 0$
36. $n^2 + 1 = 5n$
37. $2z + 4 = 3z^2$
38. $5x^2 - 4x = 2$

10.7 Tell whether the equation has *two solutions, one solution,* or *no solution.*

39. $m^2 - 2m + 1 = 0$
40. $3x^2 + 6x + 2 = 0$
41. $2q^2 + 3q + 5 = 0$
42. $\frac{3}{4}x^2 - x + 2 = 0$
43. $2w^2 - 5w + 6 = 8$
44. $2y^2 + 10y - 5 = 3y^2 - 30$

10.8 Tell whether the table of values represents a *linear function,* an *exponential function,* or a *quadratic function.* Then write an equation for the function.

45.

x	−1	0	1	2	3
y	3	0	3	12	27

46.

x	0	1	2	3	4
y	−5	−2	1	4	7

47.

x	1	2	3	4	5
y	1	2	4	8	16

48.

x	−2	−1	0	1	2
y	18	14	10	6	2

EXTRA PRACTICE

Chapter 11

11.1 Graph the function and identify its domain and range. Compare the graph with the graph of $y = \sqrt{x}$.

1. $y = 6\sqrt{x}$ **2.** $y = \frac{1}{5}\sqrt{x}$ **3.** $y = -8\sqrt{x}$

4. $y = -\frac{2}{5}\sqrt{x}$ **5.** $y = \sqrt{x} + 3$ **6.** $y = \sqrt{x} - 5$

7. $y = \sqrt{x - 2}$ **8.** $y = \sqrt{x + 5}$ **9.** $y = \sqrt{x - 4} + 2$

EXTRA PRACTICE

11.2 Simplify the expression.

10. $\sqrt{98}$ **11.** $\sqrt{300}$ **12.** $\sqrt{128x^3}$ **13.** $\sqrt{17} \cdot \sqrt{17}$

14. $\sqrt{112} \cdot \sqrt{63}$ **15.** $\sqrt{11g} \cdot 5\sqrt{g}$ **16.** $4m\sqrt{m} \cdot \sqrt{5m}$ **17.** $\sqrt{27x^5} \cdot \sqrt{48x}$

18. $\sqrt{\frac{19}{49}}$ **19.** $\sqrt{\frac{1}{6x^2}}$ **20.** $\frac{3}{\sqrt{5}}$ **21.** $\frac{\sqrt{7}}{\sqrt{8k}}$

22. $\sqrt{\frac{5}{27}}$ **23.** $2\sqrt{3} + \sqrt{7} + \sqrt{3}$ **24.** $2\sqrt{11} + \sqrt{99}$ **25.** $\sqrt{45} + 3\sqrt{20}$

26. $\sqrt{3}(12 - \sqrt{15})$ **27.** $3\sqrt{6}(4\sqrt{6} - \sqrt{600})$ **28.** $(6 - \sqrt{7})(6 - \sqrt{7})$ **29.** $(4 - \sqrt{13})(10 + \sqrt{13})$

11.3 Solve the equation. Check for extraneous solutions.

30. $6\sqrt{x} - 30 = 0$ **31.** $\sqrt{8x} + 5 = 13$ **32.** $\sqrt{x + 3} + 5 = 16$

33. $3\sqrt{4x + 1} - 2 = 25$ **34.** $\sqrt{3x - 12} = \sqrt{5x - 26}$ **35.** $\sqrt{2x + 10} - \sqrt{x + 7} = 0$

36. $\sqrt{\frac{1}{2}x + 10} - \sqrt{2x - 8} = 0$ **37.** $x = \sqrt{11x - 10}$ **38.** $x = \sqrt{20 - x}$

39. $5x = \sqrt{20x - 3}$ **40.** $\sqrt{-4x + 5} = 3x$ **41.** $x + 1 = \sqrt{6 - 2x}$

11.4 Let a and b represent the lengths of the legs of a right triangle, and let c represent the length of the hypotenuse. Find the unknown length.

42. $a = 6, b = 8$ **43.** $a = 10, c = 26$ **44.** $b = 40, c = 41$

45. $a = 2, c = 5$ **46.** $a = 4, b = 7$ **47.** $b = 8, c = 11$

11.4 Tell whether the triangle with the given side lengths is a right triangle.

48. $a = 10, b = 24, c = 26$ **49.** $a = 2, b = 4, c = 6$ **50.** $a = 14, b = 15, c = 21$

51. $a = 16, b = 30, c = 34$ **52.** $a = 1.4, b = 4.8, c = 5$ **53.** $a = 13, b = 84, c = 95$

11.5 Find the distance between the two points.

54. $(5, 10), (2, 6)$ **55.** $(2, 8), (7, -4)$ **56.** $(3, -3), (4, 1)$

57. $(6, 1.5), (2.5, -4)$ **58.** $\left(1, \frac{2}{5}\right), \left(\frac{1}{2}, -\frac{4}{5}\right)$ **59.** $\left(-\frac{3}{8}, 1\right), \left(\frac{5}{8}, \frac{1}{2}\right)$

11.5 Find the midpoint of the line segment with the given endpoints.

60. $(6, -2), (8, -6)$ **61.** $(0, -5), (-4, 8)$ **62.** $(0, -6), (0, 2)$

63. $(10, 0), (-8, 0)$ **64.** $(-5, -3), (-8, -7)$ **65.** $\left(5, -\frac{1}{2}\right), \left(8, -\frac{5}{2}\right)$

Chapter 12

12.1 Graph the inverse variation equation.

1. $y = \frac{-1}{x}$
2. $y = \frac{8}{x}$
3. $y = \frac{12}{x}$
4. $y = \frac{-14}{x}$

12.1 Given that y varies inversely with x, use the specified values to write an inverse variation equation that relates x and y. Then find the value of y when $x = 2$.

5. $x = 3, y = 4$
6. $x = -2, y = 5$
7. $x = -4, y = -15$
8. $x = 8, y = -6$
9. $x = -7, y = -7$
10. $x = -11, y = 11$

12.2 Graph the function.

11. $y = \frac{6}{x}$
12. $y = \frac{-6}{x}$
13. $y = \frac{1}{5x}$
14. $y = \frac{1}{x} + 6$
15. $y = \frac{1}{x - 4}$
16. $y = \frac{1}{x - 5} + 3$
17. $y = \frac{4}{x + 2} - 3$
18. $y = \frac{-2}{x + 1} - 3$

12.3 Divide.

19. $(30x^4 - 12x^3 + 6x^2) \div (-6x)$
20. $(9y^2 + 3y - 6) \div (3y - 2)$
21. $(3v^2 + 2v + 12) \div (v + 2)$
22. $(-24w - 11 + 8w^2) \div (2 + 4w)$
23. $(9m^2 - 6) \div (3m - 4)$
24. $(-2 + 25n^2) \div (2 + 5n)$

12.4 Simplify the rational expression, if possible. State the excluded values.

25. $\frac{44x^3}{24x}$
26. $\frac{3y + 6}{y + 2}$
27. $\frac{3a - 15}{4a - 20}$
28. $\frac{2b - 8}{4 - b}$
29. $\frac{r^2 - 2r - 15}{r^2 + r - 6}$
30. $\frac{s + 3}{2s^2 + 3s - 9}$
31. $\frac{2m^2 + 8m - 24}{3m^3 + 24m^2 + 36m}$
32. $\frac{6n^3 - 18n^2}{3n^3 - 27n}$

Find the sum, difference, product, or quotient.

12.5 33. $\frac{x^2 + 3x - 10}{2x - 4} \cdot \frac{5x}{x^2 + 2x - 15}$

34. $\frac{2y^6}{6y^3 + 8y^2} \cdot (3y + 4)$

35. $\frac{3r^2 - 12}{r - 2} \div \frac{2r^2 + 7r + 6}{2r^2 - r - 6}$

36. $\frac{3s^2 + 11s + 10}{s + 2} \div (-3s^2 + s + 10)$

12.6 37. $\frac{8}{5t} + \frac{3}{2t^2}$

38. $\frac{3}{u + 2} + \frac{4}{2u + 1}$

39. $\frac{3}{c^2 - 9} - \frac{2}{2c^2 - 3c - 9}$

40. $\frac{k + 4}{k^2 + 4k + 4} - \frac{k - 4}{k^2 - k - 6}$

12.7 Solve the equation. Check your solution.

41. $\frac{2}{x + 2} = \frac{x - 5}{9}$
42. $\frac{y}{y - 1} + \frac{1}{4} = \frac{6}{y - 1}$
43. $\frac{z}{z + 3} + 2 = \frac{5}{z - 1}$
44. $\frac{1}{w + 5} - \frac{2}{w + 3} = \frac{6}{w^2 + 5w + 6}$
45. $\frac{3}{h + 4} - 4 = \frac{6}{h^2 + h - 12}$
46. $\frac{2}{a + 2} - \frac{5}{a + 2} = \frac{4}{a^2 + 4a + 4}$

Chapter 13

13.1 In Exercises 1 and 2, use the following information. A bag contains 3 red, 3 blue, and 3 yellow marbles. You toss a coin and then draw a marble out of the bag at random.

1. Find the number of possible outcomes in the sample space. Then list the possible outcomes.
2. What is the probability that the coin shows tails and the marble is blue?

13.1 3. You toss a coin 3 times. What are the odds against the coin's showing heads twice and tails once?

13.2 4. In how many ways can you arrange the letters in the word SPRING?

5. In how many ways can you arrange 3 of the letters in the word TULIP?

13.2 Evaluate the expression.

6. 7!
7. ${}_8P_3$
8. ${}_{10}P_3$
9. ${}_5P_5$

13.3 10. You can choose 3 books from a list of 5 books to read for English class. How many combinations of 3 books are possible?

13.3 Evaluate the expression.

11. ${}_6C_2$
12. ${}_7C_3$
13. ${}_{10}C_4$
14. ${}_{20}C_{15}$

13.4 In Exercises 15 and 16, you roll a number cube. Tell whether the events *A* and *B* are *mutually exclusive* or *overlapping*. Then find *P*(*A* or *B*).

15. **Event *A*:** Roll a 5.
    Event *B*: Roll a prime number.
16. **Event *A*:** Roll a 4.
    Event *B*: Roll a multiple of 3.

13.4 17. A bag contains 3 red, 4 blue, and 5 yellow marbles. You randomly draw two marbles, one at a time. Find the probability that both are blue if **(a)** you replace the first marble and **(b)** you do not replace the first marble.

13.5 In Exercises 18–20, use the following information.

Some parents want to gather information about updating the sound system in the high school auditorium. They obtain a list of high school students and call the parents or guardians of every 20th student on the list. The question they ask is "Don't you think the sound system in the high school auditorium needs updating?"

18. Identify the population and classify the sampling method.
19. Is the sampling method used likely to result in a biased sample? *Explain.*
20. Tell whether the question is potentially biased. *Explain* your answer.

In Exercises 21–23, use the following numbers of stories in the world's ten tallest buildings: 101, 88, 88, 108, 88, 88, 80, 69, 102, 78.

13.6 21. Find the mean, median, mode(s), range, and mean absolute deviation of the data. Round to the nearest hundredth, if necessary.

13.7 22. Make a histogram and a stem-and-leaf plot of the data.

13.8 23. Make a box-and-whisker plot of the data. Identify any outliers.

Symbols

Symbol	Meaning	Page
$3 \cdot x$ $3x$ $3(x)$	3 times x	2
$\frac{a}{b}$	a divided by b, $b \neq 0$	2
a^4	the fourth power of a, or $a \cdot a \cdot a \cdot a$	3
( )	parentheses—a grouping symbol	9
[ ]	brackets—a grouping symbol	9
$=$	is equal to	21
$<$	is less than	21
$>$	is greater than	21
$\leq$	is less than or equal to	21
$\geq$	is greater than or equal to	21
$\stackrel{?}{=}$	is equal to?	22
(x, y)	ordered pair	43
$\ldots$	continues on	64
$-a$	the opposite of a	66
$\|a\|$	the absolute value of a	66
$\begin{bmatrix} 1 & 0 \\ 0 & 1 \end{bmatrix}$	matrix	94
$\frac{1}{a}$	the reciprocal of a, $a \neq 0$	103
$\sqrt{a}$	the nonnegative square root of a, $a \geq 0$	110
$\pm$	plus or minus	110
$\approx$	is approximately equal to	112
$a:b$	the ratio of a to b	162

Symbol	Meaning	Page
$\cong$	is congruent to	174
$\sim$	is similar to	174
A'	the image of point A	213
m	slope	235
b	y-intercept	244
a	constant of variation	253
$f(x)$	the value of the function f at x	262
a^{-n}	$\frac{1}{a^n}$, $a \neq 0$	503
$\sqrt[3]{a}$	the cube root of a	510
$c \times 10^n$	scientific notation, $1 \leq c < 10$ and n is an integer	512
$P(A)$	the probability of an event A	844
$n!$	n factorial, or $n \cdot (n-1) \cdot \ldots \cdot 2 \cdot 1$, n is a nonnegative integer	852
${}_nP_r$	the number of permutations of n objects taken r at a time, $r \leq n$	852
${}_nC_r$	the number of combinations of n objects taken r at a time, $r \leq n$	856
$\overline{x}$	x bar, the mean of numerical data	875
σ^2	variance, the square of standard deviation	879
σ	standard deviation, the nonnegative square root of variance	879

Geometric Formulas

TABLES

Pythagorean Theorem (p. 737)

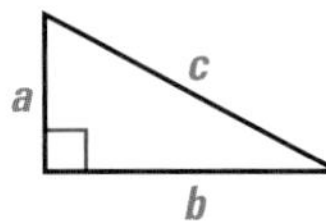

In a right triangle, $a^2 + b^2 = c^2$ where a and b are the lengths of the legs and c is the length of the hypotenuse.

Square (p. 924)

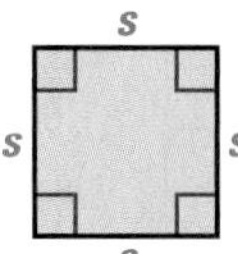

Area
$A = s^2$

Perimeter
$P = 4s$

Rectangle (p. 924)

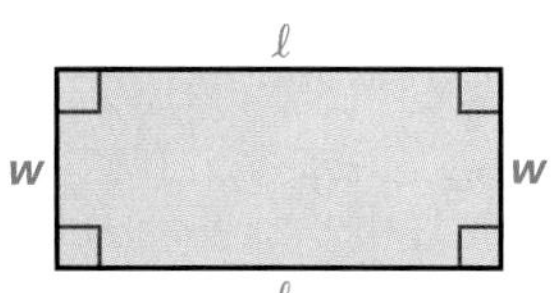

Area
$A = \ell w$

Perimeter
$P = 2\ell + 2w$

Parallelogram (p. 924)

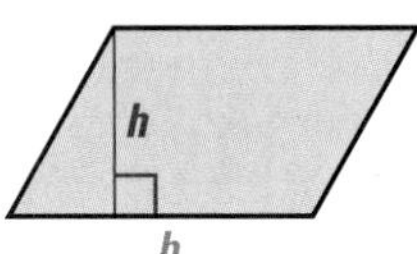

Area
$A = bh$

Triangle (p. 924)

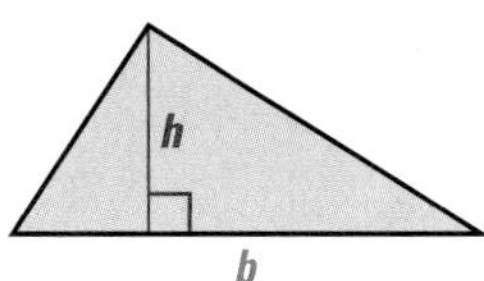

Area
$A = \frac{1}{2}bh$

Trapezoid (p. 924)

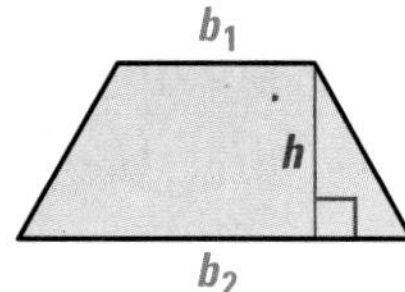

Area
$A = \frac{1}{2}(b_1 + b_2)h$

Circle (p. 926)

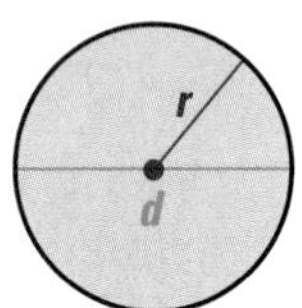

Circumference
$C = \pi d$ or
$C = 2\pi r$

Area
$A = \pi r^2$

Prism (p. 927)

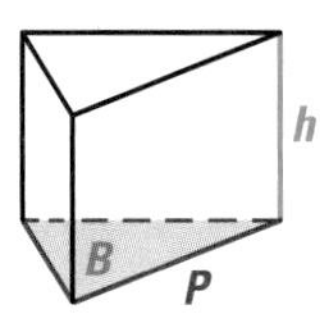

Surface Area
$S = 2B + Ph$

Volume
$V = Bh$

Cylinder (p. 927)

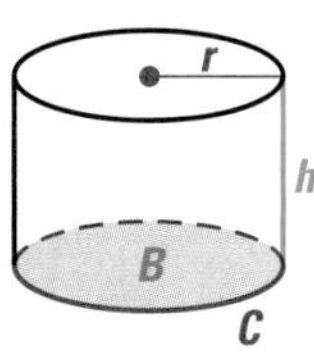

Surface Area
$S = 2B + Ch$
$= 2\pi r^2 + 2\pi rh$

Volume
$V = Bh$
$= \pi r^2 h$

Pyramid (p. 927)

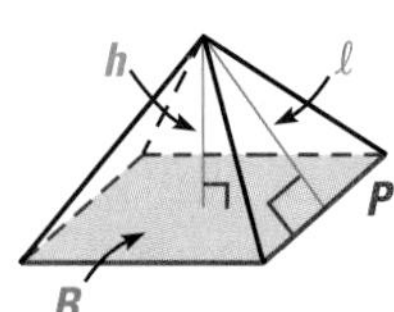

Surface Area
$S = B + \frac{1}{2}P\ell$

Volume
$V = \frac{1}{3}Bh$

Cone (p. 927)

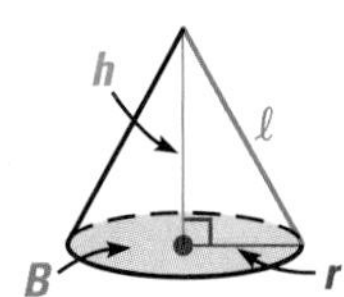

Surface Area
$S = B + \pi r\ell$
$= \pi r^2 + \pi r\ell$

Volume
$V = \frac{1}{3}Bh$
$= \frac{1}{3}\pi r^2 h$

Sphere (p. 927)

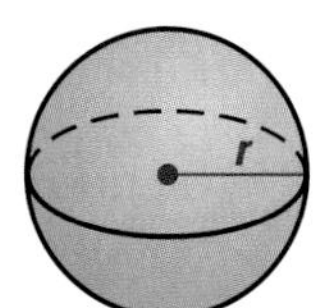

Surface Area
$S = 4\pi r^2$

Volume
$V = \frac{4}{3}\pi r^3$

Other Formulas

Slope (p. 235)	The slope m of a nonvertical line passing through the two points (x_1, y_1) and (x_2, y_2) is $m = \frac{y_2 - y_1}{x_2 - x_1}$.
Compound interest (p. 523)	$y = a(1 + r)^t$ where y is the account balance, a is the initial investment, r is the annual interest rate (in decimal form), and t is the time in years.
Quadratic formula (p. 671)	The real-number solutions of the quadratic equation $ax^2 + bx + c = 0$ are $x = \frac{-b \pm \sqrt{b^2 - 4ac}}{2a}$ where $a \neq 0$ and $b^2 - 4ac \geq 0$.
Distance formula (p. 744)	The distance d between any two points (x_1, y_1) and (x_2, y_2) is $d = \sqrt{(x_2 - x_1)^2 + (y_2 - y_1)^2}$.
Midpoint formula (p. 745)	The midpoint M of the line segment with endpoints $A(x_1, y_1)$ and $B(x_2, y_2)$ is $M\left(\frac{x_1 + x_2}{2}, \frac{y_1 + y_2}{2}\right)$.
Theoretical probability (p. 844)	The probability of an event when all the outcomes are equally likely is $P(\text{event}) = \frac{\text{Number of favorable outcomes}}{\text{Total number of outcomes}}$.
Experimental probability (p. 844)	For repeated trials of an experiment, the probability of an event is $P(\text{event}) = \frac{\text{Number of successes}}{\text{Number of trials}}$.
Permutations (p. 852)	The number of permutations of n objects taken r at a time, where $r \leq n$, is given by ${}_nP_r = \frac{n!}{(n - r)!}$.
Combinations (p. 856)	The number of combinations of n objects taken r at a time, where $r \leq n$, is given by ${}_nC_r = \frac{n!}{(n - r)! \cdot r!}$.
Probability of mutually exclusive or overlapping events (p. 861)	If A and B are mutually exclusive events, then $P(A \text{ or } B) = P(A) + P(B)$. If A and B are overlapping events, then $P(A \text{ or } B) = P(A) + P(B) - P(A \text{ and } B)$.
Probability of independent or dependent events (p. 862)	If A and B are independent events, then $P(A \text{ and } B) = P(A) \cdot P(B)$. If A and B are dependent events, then $P(A \text{ and } B) = P(A) \cdot P(B \text{ given } A)$.

TABLES

Properties

Properties of Addition and Multiplication

Commutative Properties (pp. 75, 89)	
The order in which you add two numbers does not change the sum.	$a + b = b + a$
The order in which you multiply two numbers does not change the product.	$a \cdot b = b \cdot a$
Associative Properties (pp. 75, 89)	
The way you group three numbers in a sum does not change the sum.	$(a + b) + c = a + (b + c)$
The way you group three numbers in a product does not change the product.	$(a \cdot b) \cdot c = a \cdot (b \cdot c)$
Identity Properties (pp. 75, 89)	
The sum of a number and the additive identity, 0, is the number.	$a + 0 = 0 + a = a$
The product of a number and the multiplicative identity, 1, is the number.	$a \cdot 1 = 1 \cdot a = a$
Inverse Properties (pp. 75, 103)	
The sum of a number and its additive inverse, or opposite, is 0.	$a + (-a) = -a + a = 0$
The product of a nonzero number and its multiplicative inverse, or reciprocal, is 1.	$a \cdot \frac{1}{a} = \frac{1}{a} \cdot a = 1 \ (a \neq 0)$
Distributive Property (p. 96) You can multiply a number and a sum by multiplying each term of the sum by the number and then adding these products. The same property applies to the product of a number and a difference.	$a(b + c) = ab + ac$ $(b + c)a = ba + ca$ $a(b - c) = ab - ac$ $(b - c)a = ba - ca$

TABLES

Properties of Equality

Addition Property of Equality (p. 134) Adding the same number to each side of an equation produces an equivalent equation.	If $x - a = b$, then $x - a + a = b + a$, or $x = b + a$.
Subtraction Property of Equality (p. 134) Subtracting the same number from each side of an equation produces an equivalent equation.	If $x + a = b$, then $x + a - a = b - a$, or $x = b - a$.
Multiplication Property of Equality (p. 135) Multiplying each side of an equation by the same nonzero number produces an equivalent equation.	If $\frac{x}{a} = b$ and $a \neq 0$, then $a \cdot \frac{x}{a} = a \cdot b$, or $x = ab$.
Division Property of Equality (p. 135) Dividing each side of an equation by the same nonzero number produces an equivalent equation.	If $ax = b$ and $a \neq 0$, then $\frac{ax}{a} = \frac{b}{a}$, or $x = \frac{b}{a}$.

Properties of Inequality

Addition and Subtraction Properties of Inequality (pp. 357, 358) Adding or subtracting the same number on each side of an inequality produces an equivalent inequality.	If $a < b$, then $a + c < b + c$ and $a - c < b - c$. If $a > b$, then $a + c > b + c$ and $a - c > b - c$.
Multiplication and Division Properties of Inequality (pp. 363, 364) Multiplying or dividing each side of an inequality by a *positive* number produces an equivalent inequality. Multiplying or dividing each side of an inequality by a *negative* number and *reversing the direction of the inequality symbol* produces an equivalent inequality.	If $a < b$ and $c > 0$, then $ac < bc$ and $\frac{a}{c} < \frac{b}{c}$. If $a < b$ and $c < 0$, then $ac > bc$ and $\frac{a}{c} > \frac{b}{c}$.

Properties of Exponents

Product of Powers Property (p. 489) To multiply powers having the same base, add the exponents.	$a^m \cdot a^n = a^{m+n}$
Power of a Power Property (p. 490) To find a power of a power, multiply exponents.	$(a^m)^n = a^{mn}$
Power of a Product Property (p. 490) To find a power of a product, find the power of each factor and multiply.	$(ab)^m = a^m b^m$
Quotient of Powers Property (p. 495) To divide powers having the same nonzero base, subtract exponents.	$\frac{a^m}{a^n} = a^{m-n}, a \neq 0$
Power of a Quotient Property (p. 496) To find a power of a quotient, find the power of the numerator and the power of the denominator and divide.	$\left(\frac{a}{b}\right)^m = \frac{a^m}{b^m}, b \neq 0$

Other Properties

Cross Products Property (p. 168) The cross products of a proportion are equal.	If $\frac{a}{b} = \frac{c}{d}$ $(b, d \neq 0)$, then $ad = bc$.
Product Property of Radicals (p. 719) The square root of a product equals the product of the square roots of the factors.	$\sqrt{ab} = \sqrt{a} \cdot \sqrt{b}, a \geq 0$ and $b \geq 0$
Quotient Properties of Radicals (p. 720) The square root of a quotient equals the quotient of the square roots of the numerator and denominator.	$\sqrt{\frac{a}{b}} = \frac{\sqrt{a}}{\sqrt{b}}, a \geq 0$ and $b > 0$

TABLES

Measures

Time	
60 seconds (sec) = 1 minute (min) 60 minutes = 1 hour (h) 24 hours = 1 day 7 days = 1 week 4 weeks (approx.) = 1 month	365 days 52 weeks (approx.) 12 months] = 1 year 10 years = 1 decade 100 years = 1 century

Metric	United States Customary
Length 10 millimeters (mm) = 1 centimeter (cm) 100 cm 1000 mm] = 1 meter (m) 1000 m = 1 kilometer (km)	**Length** 12 inches (in.) = 1 foot (ft) 36 in. 3 ft] = 1 yard (yd) 5280 ft 1760 yd] = 1 mile (mi)
Area 100 square millimeters (mm^2) = 1 square centimeter (cm^2) 10,000 cm^2 = 1 square meter (m^2) 10,000 m^2 = 1 hectare (ha)	**Area** 144 square inches (in.^{2}) = 1 square foot (ft^2) 9 ft^2 = 1 square yard (yd^2) 43,560 ft^2 4840 yd^2] = 1 acre (A)
Volume 1000 cubic millimeters (mm^3) = 1 cubic centimeter (cm^3) 1,000,000 cm^3 = 1 cubic meter (m^3)	**Volume** 1728 cubic inches (in.^{3}) = 1 cubic foot (ft^3) 27 ft^3 = 1 cubic yard (yd^3)
Liquid Capacity 1000 milliliters (mL) 1000 cubic centimeters (cm^3)] = 1 liter (L) 1000 L = 1 kiloliter (kL)	**Liquid Capacity** 8 fluid ounces (fl oz) = 1 cup (c) 2 c = 1 pint (pt) 2 pt = 1 quart (qt) 4 qt = 1 gallon (gal)
Mass 1000 milligrams (mg) = 1 gram (g) 1000 g = 1 kilogram (kg) 1000 kg = 1 metric ton (t)	**Weight** 16 ounces (oz) = 1 pound (lb) 2000 lb = 1 ton
Temperature Degrees Celsius (°C) 0°C = freezing point of water 37°C = normal body temperature 100°C = boiling point of water	**Temperature Degrees Fahrenheit (°F)** 32°F = freezing point of water 98.6°F = normal body temperature 212°F = boiling point of water

Squares and Square Roots

No.	Square	Sq. Root
1	1	1.000
2	4	1.414
3	9	1.732
4	16	2.000
5	25	2.236
6	36	2.449
7	49	2.646
8	64	2.828
9	81	3.000
10	100	3.162
11	121	3.317
12	144	3.464
13	169	3.606
14	196	3.742
15	225	3.873
16	256	4.000
17	289	4.123
18	324	4.243
19	361	4.359
20	400	4.472
21	441	4.583
22	484	4.690
23	529	4.796
24	576	4.899
25	625	5.000
26	676	5.099
27	729	5.196
28	784	5.292
29	841	5.385
30	900	5.477
31	961	5.568
32	1024	5.657
33	1089	5.745
34	1156	5.831
35	1225	5.916
36	1296	6.000
37	1369	6.083
38	1444	6.164
39	1521	6.245
40	1600	6.325
41	1681	6.403
42	1764	6.481
43	1849	6.557
44	1936	6.633
45	2025	6.708
46	2116	6.782
47	2209	6.856
48	2304	6.928
49	2401	7.000
50	2500	7.071

No.	Square	Sq. Root
51	2601	7.141
52	2704	7.211
53	2809	7.280
54	2916	7.348
55	3025	7.416
56	3136	7.483
57	3249	7.550
58	3364	7.616
59	3481	7.681
60	3600	7.746
61	3721	7.810
62	3844	7.874
63	3969	7.937
64	4096	8.000
65	4225	8.062
66	4356	8.124
67	4489	8.185
68	4624	8.246
69	4761	8.307
70	4900	8.367
71	5041	8.426
72	5184	8.485
73	5329	8.544
74	5476	8.602
75	5625	8.660
76	5776	8.718
77	5929	8.775
78	6084	8.832
79	6241	8.888
80	6400	8.944
81	6561	9.000
82	6724	9.055
83	6889	9.110
84	7056	9.165
85	7225	9.220
86	7396	9.274
87	7569	9.327
88	7744	9.381
89	7921	9.434
90	8100	9.487
91	8281	9.539
92	8464	9.592
93	8649	9.644
94	8836	9.695
95	9025	9.747
96	9216	9.798
97	9409	9.849
98	9604	9.899
99	9801	9.950
100	10,000	10.000

No.	Square	Sq. Root
101	10,201	10.050
102	10,404	10.100
103	10,609	10.149
104	10,816	10.198
105	11,025	10.247
106	11,236	10.296
107	11,449	10.344
108	11,664	10.392
109	11,881	10.440
110	12,100	10.488
111	12,321	10.536
112	12,544	10.583
113	12,769	10.630
114	12,996	10.677
115	13,225	10.724
116	13,456	10.770
117	13,689	10.817
118	13,924	10.863
119	14,161	10.909
120	14,400	10.954
121	14,641	11.000
122	14,884	11.045
123	15,129	11.091
124	15,376	11.136
125	15,625	11.180
126	15,876	11.225
127	16,129	11.269
128	16,384	11.314
129	16,641	11.358
130	16,900	11.402
131	17,161	11.446
132	17,424	11.489
133	17,689	11.533
134	17,956	11.576
135	18,225	11.619
136	18,496	11.662
137	18,769	11.705
138	19,044	11.747
139	19,321	11.790
140	19,600	11.832
141	19,881	11.874
142	20,164	11.916
143	20,449	11.958
144	20,736	12.000
145	21,025	12.042
146	21,316	12.083
147	21,609	12.124
148	21,904	12.166
149	22,201	12.207
150	22,500	12.247

English–Spanish Glossary

absolute deviation (p. 392) The absolute deviation of a number x from a given value is the absolute value of the difference of x and the given value: $$\text{absolute deviation} = \lvert x - \text{given value} \rvert$$	**If the absolute deviation of x from 2 is 3, then $\lvert x - 2 \rvert = 3$.**
desviación absoluta (pág. 392) La desviación absoluta de un número x con respecto a un valor dado es el valor absoluto de la diferencia entre x y el valor dado: $$\text{desviación absoluta} = \lvert x - \text{valor dado} \rvert$$	**Si la desviación absoluta de x con respecto a 2 es 3, entonces $\lvert x - 2 \rvert = 3$.**
absolute value (p. 66) The absolute value of a number a is the distance between a and 0 on a number line. The symbol $\lvert a \rvert$ represents the absolute value of a.	**$\lvert 2 \rvert = 2$, $\lvert -5 \rvert = 5$, and $\lvert 0 \rvert = 0$**
valor absoluto (pág. 66) El valor absoluto de un número a es la distancia entre a y 0 en una recta numérica. El símbolo $\lvert a \rvert$ representa el valor absoluto de a.	**$\lvert 2 \rvert = 2$, $\lvert -5 \rvert = 5$, y $\lvert 0 \rvert = 0$**
absolute value equation (p. 390) An equation that contains an absolute value expression.	**$\lvert x + 2 \rvert = 3$ is an absolute value equation.**
ecuación de valor absoluto (pág. 390) Ecuación que contiene una expresión de valor absoluto.	**$\lvert x + 2 \rvert = 3$ es una ecuación de valor absoluto.**
additive identity (p. 76) The number 0 is the additive identity, because the sum of any number and 0 is the number: $a + 0 = 0 + a = a$.	**$-2 + 0 = -2, 0 + \frac{3}{4} = \frac{3}{4}$**
identidad aditiva (pág. 76) El número 0 es la identidad aditiva ya que la suma de cualquier número y 0 es ese número: $a + 0 = 0 + a = a$.	
additive inverse (p. 76) The additive inverse of a number a is its opposite, $-a$. The sum of a number and its additive inverse is 0: $a + (-a) = -a + a = 0$.	**The additive inverse of -5 is 5, and $-5 + 5 = 0$.**
inverso aditivo (pág. 76) El inverso aditivo de un número a es su opuesto, $-a$. La suma de un número y su inverso aditivo es 0: $a + (-a) = -a + a = 0$.	**El inverso aditivo de -5 es 5, y $-5 + 5 = 0$.**
algebraic expression (p. 2) An expression that includes at least one variable. Also called *variable expression*.	**$5n$, $\frac{14}{y}$, $6 + c$, and $8 - x$ are algebraic expressions.**
expresión algebraica (pág. 2) Expresión que incluye por lo menos una variable.	**$5n$, $\frac{14}{y}$, $6 + c$ y $8 - x$ son expresiones algebraicas.**

arithmetic sequence (p. 309) A sequence in which the difference between consecutive terms is constant.

2, 8, 14, 20, 26, . . . is an arithmetic sequence in which the difference between consecutive terms is 6.

progresión aritmética (pág. 309) Progresión en la que la diferencia entre los términos consecutivos es constante.

2, 8, 14, 20, 26, . . . es una progresión aritmética en la que la diferencia entre los términos consecutivos es 6.

asymptotes of a hyperbola (p. 767) Lines that a hyperbola approaches but does not intersect.

***See* hyperbola.**

asíntotas de una hipérbola (pág. 767) Rectas a las que la hipérbola se acerca pero sin cortarlas.

***Ver* hipérbola.**

axis of symmetry (p. 628) The line that passes through the vertex and divides the parabola into two symmetric parts.

eje de simetría (pág. 628) La recta que pasa por el vértice y divide a la parábola en dos partes simétricas.

$y = -x^2 + 2x + 1$

$x = 1$

The axis of symmetry of the graph of $y = -x^2 + 2x + 1$ is the line $x = 1$.

El eje de simetría de la gráfica de $y = -x^2 + 2x + 1$ es la recta $x = 1$.

B

base of a power (p. 3) The number or expression that is used as a factor in a repeated multiplication.

In the power 3^4, the base is 3.

base de una potencia (pág. 3) El número o la expresión que se usa como factor en la multiplicación repetida.

En la potencia 3^4, la base es 3.

best-fitting line (p. 335) The line that most closely follows a trend in data, found using technology.

mejor recta de regresión (pág. 335) La recta que se ajusta más a la tendencia de los datos y que se encuentra mediante tecnología.

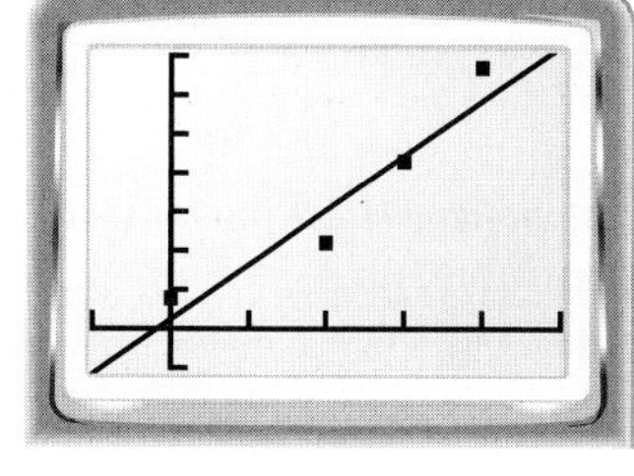

The graph shows the best-fitting line for the data in the scatter plot.

La gráfica muestra la mejor recta de regresión para los datos del diagrama de dispersión.

biased question (p. 872) A question that encourages a particular response.

"Don't you agree that the voting age should be lowered to 16 because many 16-year-olds are responsible and informed?" is a biased question.

pregunta capciosa (pág. 872) Pregunta que impulsa a dar una respuesta determinada.

"¿No estás de acuerdo en que se debe bajar la edad para votar a los 16 años ya que muchos jóvenes de 16 años son responsables y están bien informados?" es una pregunta capciosa.

---

biased sample (p. 872) A sample that is not representative of the population.

The members of a school's basketball team would form a biased sample for a survey about whether to build a new gym.

muestra sesgada (pág. 872) Muestra que no es representativa de la población.

Los miembros del equipo de baloncesto de una escuela formarían una muestra sesgada si participaran en una encuesta sobre si quieren que se construya un nuevo gimnasio.

---

binomial (p. 555) A polynomial with two terms.

$t^3 - 4t$ and $2x + 5$ are binomials.

binomio (pág. 555) Polinomio con dos términos.

$t^3 - 4t$ y $2x + 5$ son binomios.

---

box-and-whisker plot (p. 887) A data display that organizes data values into four groups using the minimum value, lower quartile, median, upper quartile, and maximum value.

gráfica de frecuencias acumuladas (pág. 887) Presentación de datos que organiza los valores de los datos en cuatro grupos usando el valor mínimo, el cuartil inferior, la mediana, el cuartil superior y el valor máximo.

0 10 20 30 40 50

8 19 26 37 45

---

branches of a hyperbola (p. 767) The two symmetrical parts of a hyperbola.

See hyperbola.

ramas de una hipérbola (pág. 767) Las dos partes simétricas de la hipérbola.

Ver hipérbola.

C

coefficient (p. 97) The number part of a term with a variable part.

The coefficient of $-6x$ is -6.

coeficiente (pág. 97) La parte numérica de un término que tiene una variable.

El coeficiente de $-6x$ es -6.

---

combination (p. 856) A selection of objects in which order is *not* important.

There are 6 combinations of two of the letters from the list A, B, C, D: AB, AC, AD, BC, BD, and CD.

combinación (pág. 856) Selección de objetos en la que el orden *no* es importante.

Hay 6 combinaciones de dos de las letras de la lista A, B, C, D: AB, AC, AD, BC, BD y CD.

common difference (p. 309) The constant difference between consecutive terms of an arithmetic sequence. **diferencia común** (pág. 309) La diferencia constante entre los términos consecutivos de una progresión aritmética.	**2, 8, 14, 20, 26, . . . is an arithmetic sequence with a common difference of 6.** **2, 8, 14, 20, 26, . . . es una progresión aritmética con una diferencia común de 6.**
common ratio (p. 539) The ratio of any term of a geometric sequence to the previous term of the sequence. **razón común** (pág. 539) La razón entre cualquier término de una progresión geométrica y el término anterior de la progresión.	**The sequence 5, 10, 20, 40, . . . is a geometric sequence with common ratio 2.** **La progresión 5, 10, 20, 40, . . . es una progresión geométrica con una razón común de 2.**
completing the square (p. 663) The process of rewriting a quadratic expression so that it is a perfect square trinomial. **completar el cuadrado** (pág. 663) El proceso de escribir una expresión cuadrática de manera que sea un trinomio cuadrado perfecto.	**To write $x^2 - 16x$ as a perfect square trinomial, add $\left(\frac{-16}{2}\right)^2$, or $(-8)^2$. This gives $x^2 - 16x + (-8)^2 = (x - 8)^2$.** **Para escribir $x^2 - 16x$ como trinomio cuadrado perfecto, suma $\left(\frac{-16}{2}\right)^2$, o $(-8)^2$. Así resulta $x^2 - 16x + (-8)^2 = (x - 8)^2$.**
complex fraction (p. 810) A fraction that contains a fraction in its numerator, denominator, or both. **fracción compleja** (pág. 810) Fracción que contiene una fracción en su numerador, en su denominador o en ambos.	**$\frac{\frac{3x}{2}}{-6x^3}$ and $\frac{x^2-1}{\frac{x+1}{x-1}}$ are complex fractions.** **$\frac{\frac{3x}{2}}{-6x^3}$ y $\frac{x^2-1}{\frac{x+1}{x-1}}$ son fracciones complejas.**
compound event (p. 861) An event that combines two or more events, using the word *and* or the word *or*. **suceso compuesto** (pág. 861) Suceso que combina dos o más sucesos usando la palabra *y* o la palabra *o*.	**When you roll a number cube, the event "roll a 2 or an odd number" is a compound event.** **Cuando lanzas un cubo numerado, el suceso "salir el 2 ó número impar" es un suceso compuesto.**
compound inequality (p. 380) Two inequalities joined by *and* or *or*. **desigualdad compuesta** (pág. 380) Dos desigualdades unidas por *y* u *o*.	**$-2 < x$ *and* $x < 1$, which can be written as $-2 < x < 1$, is a compound inequality, as is $x < -1$ *or* $x > 0$.** **$-2 < x$ *y* $x < 1$, que puede escribirse $-2 < x < 1$, es una desigualdad compuesta, al igual que $x < -1$ *ó* $x > 0$.**
compound interest (p. 523) Interest that is earned on both an initial investment and on previously earned interest. **interés compuesto** (pág. 523) Interés obtenido tanto sobre la inversión inicial como sobre el interés conseguido anteriormente.	**You deposit \$250 in an account that earns 4% interest compounded yearly. After 5 years, your account balance is $y = 250(1 + 0.04)^5 \approx$ \$304.16.** **Depositas \$250 en una cuenta al 4% anual de interés compuesto. Después de 5 años, el balance de la cuenta es $y = 250(1 + 0.04)^5 \approx$ \$304.16.**

conditional statement (p. 66) A statement with a hypothesis and a conclusion.

enunciado condicional (pág. 66) Enunciado que tiene una hipótesis y una conclusión.

conditional statement
enunciado condicional

If $a > 0$, then $|a| = a$.

hypothesis / hipótesis — **conclusion / conclusión**

congruent figures (p. 174) Figures that have the same size and shape. The symbol ≅ indicates congruence.

figuras congruentes (pág. 174) Figuras que tienen igual tamaño y forma. El símbolo ≅ indica la congruencia.

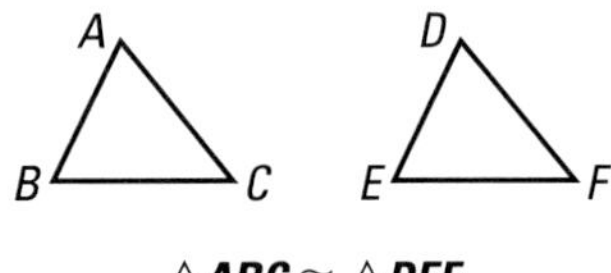

$\triangle ABC \cong \triangle DEF$

conjecture (p. 117) A statement that is believed to be true but not yet shown to be true.

conjetura (pág. 117) Enunciado que se considera verdadero sin que haya sido demostrado todavía.

A conclusion reached using inductive reasoning is a conjecture.

Una conclusión que se saca mediante el razonamiento inductivo es una conjetura.

consistent dependent system (p. 459) A linear system with infinitely many solutions. The graphs of the equations of a consistent dependent system coincide.

sistema dependiente compatible (pág. 459) Sistema lineal con infinitas soluciones. Las gráficas de las ecuaciones de un sistema dependiente compatible coinciden.

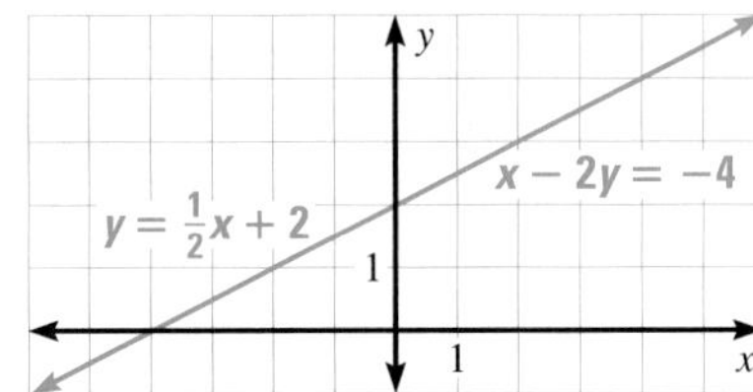

The linear system $x - 2y = -4$ and $y = \frac{1}{2}x + 2$ is a consistent dependent system because the graphs of the equations coincide.

El sistema lineal $x - 2y = -4$ e $y = \frac{1}{2}x + 2$ es un sistema dependiente compatible ya que las gráficas de las ecuaciones coinciden.

consistent independent system (p. 427) A linear system with exactly one solution. The graphs of the equations of a consistent independent system intersect.

sistema independiente compatible (pág. 427) Sistema lineal con una sola solución. Las gráficas de las ecuaciones de un sistema independiente compatible se cortan.

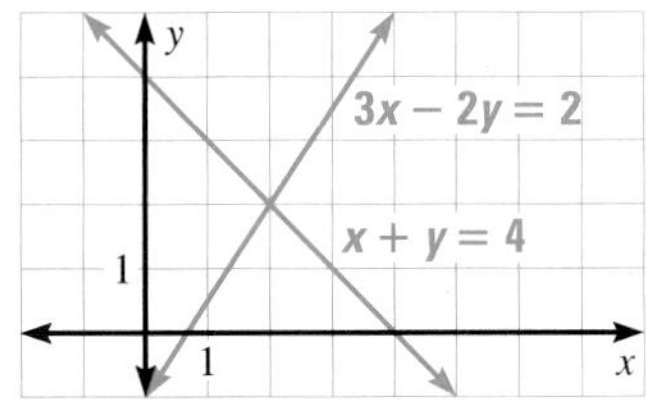

The linear system $3x - 2y = 2$ and $x + y = 4$ is a consistent independent system because the graphs of the equations intersect.

El sistema lineal $3x - 2y = 2$ y $x + y = 4$ es un sistema independiente compatible ya que las gráficas de las ecuaciones se cortan.

constant of variation (pp. 253, 765) The nonzero constant a in a direct variation equation $y = ax$ or in an inverse variation equation $y = \frac{a}{x}$. **constante de variación** (págs. 253, 765) La constante a distinta de cero de una ecuación de variación directa $y = ax$ o de una ecuación de variación inversa $y = \frac{a}{x}$.	The constant of variation in the direct variation equation $y = \frac{2}{3}x$ is $\frac{2}{3}$, and the constant of variation in the inverse variation equation $y = \frac{-1}{x}$ is -1. La constante de variación de la ecuación de variación directa $y = \frac{2}{3}x$ es $\frac{2}{3}$, y la constante de variación de la ecuación de variación inversa $y = \frac{-1}{x}$ es -1.
constant term (p. 97) A term with a number part but no variable part. **término constante** (pág. 97) Término que tiene una parte numérica sin variable.	In the expression $3x + (-4) + (-6x) + 2$, the constant terms are -4 and 2. En la expresión $3x + (-4) + (-6x) + 2$, los términos constantes son -4 y 2.
continuous function (p. 223) A function with a graph that is unbroken. **función continua** (pág. 223) Función con una gráfica no interrumpida.	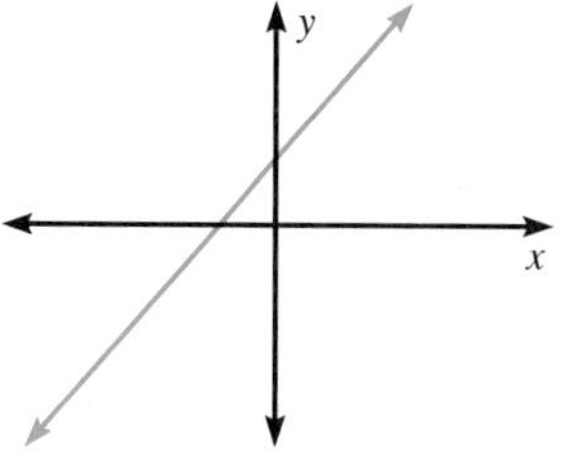
convenience sample (p. 871) A sample in which only members of a population who are easily accessible are selected. **muestra de conveniencia** (pág. 871) Muestra en la que se selecciona sólo a los miembros de una población fácilmente accesibles.	You can select a convenience sample of a school's student population by choosing only students who are in your classes. Para seleccionar una muestra de conveniencia de la población de estudiantes de una escuela, puedes escoger sólo a los estudiantes que están en tus clases.
converse of a conditional (p. 319) A statement formed by interchanging the hypothesis and the conclusion of the conditional. The converse of a true statement is not necessarily true. **recíproco de un condicional** (pág. 319) Enunciado formado al intercambiar la hipótesis y la conclusión del condicional. El recíproco de un enunciado verdadero no es necesariamente verdadero.	The converse of the statement "If $x = 5$, then $\lvert x \rvert = 5$" is "If $\lvert x \rvert = 5$, then $x = 5$." The original statement is true, but the converse is false. El recíproco del enunciado "Si $x = 5$, entonces $\lvert x \rvert = 5$" es "Si $\lvert x \rvert = 5$, entonces $x = 5$". El enunciado original es verdadero, pero el recíproco es falso.

correlation (p. 325) The relationship between paired data. The paired data have *positive correlation* if y tends to increase as x increases, *negative correlation* if y tends to decrease as x increases, and *relatively no correlation* if x and y have no apparent relationship.

correlación (pág. 325) La relación entre los pares de datos. Los pares de datos presentan una *correlación positiva* si y tiende a aumentar al aumentar x, una *correlación negativa* si y tiende a disminuir al aumentar x y una *correlación nula* si x e y no tienen ninguna relación aparente.

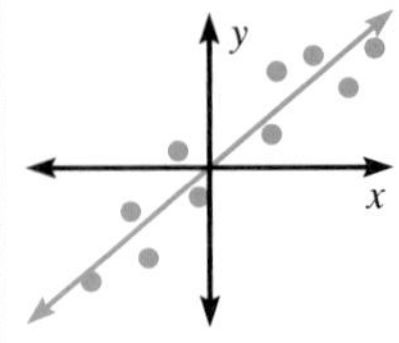

Positive correlation
Correlación positiva

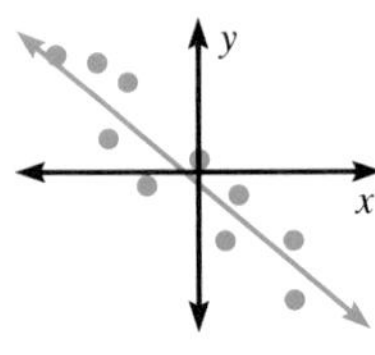

Negative correlation
Correlación negativa

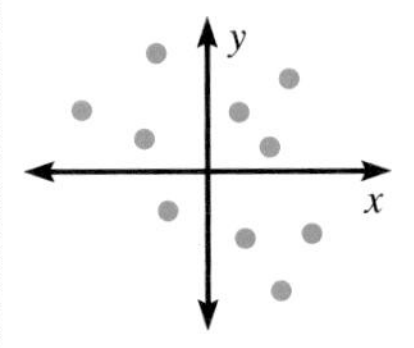

Relatively no correlation
Correlación nula

corresponding parts (p. 174) A pair of sides or angles that have the same relative position in two figures.

partes correspondientes (pág. 174) Par de lados o ángulos que tienen la misma posición relativa en dos figuras.

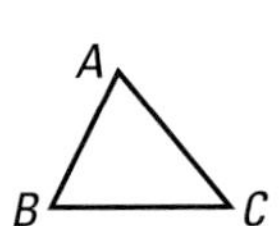

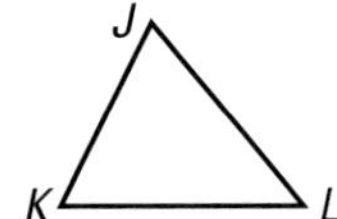

$\angle A$ and $\angle J$ are corresponding angles.
$\overline{AB}$ and $\overline{JK}$ are corresponding sides.

$\angle A$ y $\angle J$ son ángulos correspondientes.
$\overline{AB}$ y $\overline{JK}$ son lados correspondientes.

counterexample (p. 66) An example used to show that an if-then statement is false.

The statement "If a number is a whole number, then the number is positive" is false because 0 is a whole number that is not a positive number.

contraejemplo (pág. 66) Ejemplo utilizado para demostrar que un enunciado de "si…, entonces…" es falso.

El enunciado "Si un número es un número natural, entonces es positivo" es falso ya que 0 es un número natural que no es positivo.

cross product (p. 168) In a proportion, a cross product is the product of the numerator of one ratio and the denominator of the other ratio. The cross products of a proportion are equal.

The cross products of the proportion $\frac{3}{4} = \frac{6}{8}$ are $3 \cdot 8 = 24$ and $4 \cdot 6 = 24$.

producto cruzado (pág. 168) En una proporción, un producto cruzado es el producto del numerador de una de las razones y el denominador de la otra razón. Los productos cruzados de una proporción son iguales.

Los productos cruzados de la proporción $\frac{3}{4} = \frac{6}{8}$ son $3 \cdot 8 = 24$ y $4 \cdot 6 = 24$.

cube root (p. 510) If $b^3 = a$, then b is the cube root of a.

2 is the cube root of 8 because $2^3 = 8$.

raíz cúbica (pág. 510) Si $b^3 = a$, entonces b es la raíz cúbica de a.

2 es la raíz cúbica de 8 ya que $2^3 = 8$.

decay factor (p. 534) The expression $1 - r$ in the exponential decay model $y = a(1 - r)^t$.	**In the exponential decay model $P = 41(0.995)^t$, the decay factor is 0.995.**
factor de decrecimiento (pág. 534) La expresión $1 - r$ del modelo de decrecimiento exponencial $y = a(1 - r)^t$.	**En el modelo de decrecimiento exponencial $P = 41(0.995)^t$, el factor de decrecimiento es 0.995.**
decay rate (p. 534) The variable r in the exponential decay model $y = a(1 - r)^t$.	**In the exponential decay model $P = 41(0.995)^t$, the decay rate is 0.005, because $0.995 = 1 - 0.005$.**
tasa de decrecimiento (pág. 534) La variable r del modelo de decrecimiento exponencial $y = a(1 - r)^t$.	**En el modelo de decrecimiento exponencial $P = 41(0.995)^t$, la tasa de decrecimiento es 0.005 ya que $0.995 = 1 - 0.005$.**
deductive reasoning (p. 118) A form of reasoning in which a conclusion is based on statements that are assumed or shown to be true.	$(x + 2) + (-2)$ $= x + [2 + (-2)]$ **Associative property of addition** $= x + 0$ **Inverse property of addition** $= x$ **Identity property of addition**
razonamiento deductivo (pág. 118) Tipo de razonamiento en el que una conclusión se basa en enunciados que se suponen o se demuestran verdaderos.	$(x + 2) + (-2)$ $= x + [2 + (-2)]$ **Propiedad asociativa de la suma** $= x + 0$ **Propiedad del elemento inverso de la suma** $= x$ **Propiedad de identidad de la suma**
degree of a monomial (p. 554) The sum of the exponents of the variables in the monomial. The degree of a nonzero constant term is 0.	**The degree of $\frac{1}{2}ab^2$ is $1 + 2$, or 3.**
grado de un monomio (pág. 554) La suma de los exponentes de las variables del monomio. El grado de un término constante distinto de cero es 0.	**El grado de $\frac{1}{2}ab^2$ es $1 + 2$, ó 3.**
degree of a polynomial (p. 554) The greatest degree of the terms of the polynomial.	**The polynomial $2x^2 + x - 5$ has a degree of 2.**
grado de un polinomio (pág. 554) El mayor grado de los términos del polinomio.	**El polinomio $2x^2 + x - 5$ tiene un grado de 2.**
dependent events (p. 862) Two events such that the occurrence of one event affects the occurrence of the other event.	**A bag contains 3 red marbles and 5 white marbles. You randomly draw one marble, do not replace it, then randomly draw another marble. The events "draw a red marble first" and "draw a white marble second" are dependent events.**
sucesos dependientes (pág. 862) Dos sucesos tales que la ocurrencia de uno de ellos afecta a la ocurrencia del otro.	**Una bolsa contiene 3 canicas rojas y 5 blancas. Sacas al azar una canica sin reemplazarla y luego sacas al azar otra canica. Los sucesos "sacar primero una canica roja" y "sacar después una canica blanca" son sucesos dependientes.**

dependent variable (p. 36) The output variable of a function. **variable dependiente** (pág. 36) La variable de salida de una función.	**In the function equation $y = x + 3$, y is the dependent variable.** **En la ecuación de función $y = x + 3$, y es la variable dependiente.**
dimensions of a matrix (p. 94) If a matrix has m rows and n columns, the dimensions of the matrix are written as $m \times n$. **dimensiones de una matriz** (pág. 94) Si una matriz tiene m filas y n columnas, las dimensiones de la matriz se escriben $m \times n$.	**The dimensions of a matrix with 2 rows and 3 columns are 2×3 ("2 by 3").** **Las dimensiones de una matriz con 2 filas y 3 columnas son 2×3 ("2 por 3").**
direct variation (p. 253) The relationship of two variables x and y if there is a nonzero number a such that $y = ax$. If $y = ax$, then y is said to vary directly with x. **variación directa** (pág. 253) La relación entre dos variables x e y si hay un número a distinto de cero tal que $y = ax$. Si $y = ax$, entonces se dice que y varía directamente con x.	**The equation $2x - 3y = 0$ represents direct variation because it is equivalent to the equation $y = \frac{2}{3}x$. The equation $y = x + 5$ does *not* represent direct variation.** **La ecuación $2x - 3y = 0$ representa una variación directa ya que es equivalente a la ecuación $y = \frac{2}{3}x$. La ecuación $y = x + 5$ *no* representa una variación directa.**
discrete function (p. 223) A function with a graph that consists of isolated points. **función discreta** (pág. 223) Función cuya gráfica consta de puntos aislados.	
discriminant (p. 678) The expression $b^2 - 4ac$ of the assciated equation $ax^2 + bx + c = 0$; also the expression under the radical sign in the quadratic formula. **discriminante** (pág. 678) La expresión $b^2 - 4ac$ de la ecuación asociada $ax^2 + bx + c = 0$; también es la expresión colocada bajo el signo radical de la fórmula cuadrática.	**The value of the discriminant of the equation $3x^2 - 2x - 7 = 0$ is:** $b^2 - 4ac = (-2)^2 - 4(3)(-7) = 88$ **El valor del discriminante de la ecuación $3x^2 - 2x - 7 = 0$ es:** $b^2 - 4ac = (-2)^2 - 4(3)(-7) = 88$
distance formula (p. 744) The distance d between any two points (x_1, y_1) and (x_2, y_2) is $d = \sqrt{(x_2 - x_1)^2 + (y_2 - y_1)^2}$. **fórmula de la distancia** (pág. 744) La distancia d entre dos puntos cualesquiera (x_1, y_1) y (x_2, y_2) es $d = \sqrt{(x_2 - x_1)^2 + (y_2 - y_1)^2}$.	**The distance d between $(-1, 3)$ and $(5, 2)$ is:** $d = \sqrt{(5 - (-1))^2 + (2 - 3)^2} = \sqrt{37}$ **La distancia d entre $(-1, 3)$ y $(5, 2)$ es:** $d = \sqrt{(5 - (-1))^2 + (2 - 3)^2} = \sqrt{37}$

distributive property (p. 96) A property that can be used to find the product of a number and a sum or difference: $a(b + c) = ab + ac$ $(b + c)a = ba + ca$ $a(b - c) = ab - ac$ $(b - c)a = ba - ca$ **propiedad distributiva** (pág. 96) Propiedad que sirve para hallar el producto de un número y una suma o una diferencia: $a(b + c) = ab + ac$ $(b + c)a = ba + ca$ $a(b - c) = ab - ac$ $(b - c)a = ba - ca$	$3(4 + 2) = 3(4) + 3(2)$, $(8 - 6)4 = (8)4 - (6)4$
domain of a function (p. 35) The set of all inputs of a function. **dominio de una función** (pág. 35) El conjunto de todas las entradas de una función.	*See* function. *Ver* función.

E

element of a matrix (p. 94) Each number in a matrix. **elemento de una matriz** (pág. 94) Cada número de la matriz.	*See* matrix. *Ver* matriz.
element of a set (p. 71) Each object in a set. Also called a *member* of a set. **elemento de un conjunto** (pág. 71) Cada objeto de un conjunto; llamado también *miembro* de un conjunto.	5 is an element of the set of whole numbers, $W = \{0, 1, 2, 3, \ldots\}$. 5 es un elemento del conjunto de los números naturales, $W = \{0, 1, 2, 3, \ldots\}$.
empty set (p. 71) The set with no elements, written as Ø. **conjunto vacío** (pág. 71) El conjunto que no tiene ningún elemento, escrito Ø.	The set of negative whole numbers = Ø. El conjunto de los números naturales negativos = Ø.
equation (p. 21) A mathematical sentence formed by placing the symbol = between two expressions. **ecuación** (pág. 21) Enunciado matemático formado al colocar el símbolo = entre dos expresiones.	$2k - 8 = 12$ is an equation. $2k - 8 = 12$ es una ecuación.
equivalent equations (p. 134) Equations that have the same solution(s). **ecuaciones equivalentes** (pág. 134) Ecuaciones que tienen la misma solución o soluciones.	$x + 7 = 4$ and $x = -3$ are equivalent equations. $x + 7 = 4$ y $x = -3$ son ecuaciones equivalentes.

equivalent expressions (p. 96) Two expressions that have the same value for all values of the variable. **expresiones equivalentes** (pág. 96) Dos expresiones que tienen el mismo valor para todos los valores de la variable.	**$3(x + 2) + x$ and $4x + 6$ are equivalent expressions.** **$3(x + 2) + x$ y $4x + 6$ son expresiones equivalentes.**
equivalent inequalities (p. 357) Inequalities that have the same solutions. **desigualdades equivalentes** (pág. 357) Desigualdades con las mismas soluciones.	**$2t < 4$ and $t < 2$ are equivalent inequalities, because the solutions of both inequalities are all real numbers less than 2.** **$2t < 4$ y $t < 2$ son desigualdades equivalentes ya que las soluciones de ambas son todos los números reales menores que 2.**
evaluate an algebraic expression (p. 2) To find the value of an algebraic expression by substituting a number for each variable and performing the operation(s). **evaluar una expresión algebraica** (pág. 2) Hallar el valor de una expresión algebraica sustituyendo cada variable por un número y realizando la operación o operaciones.	**The value of $n - 1$ when $n = 3$ is $3 - 1 = 2$.** **El valor de $n - 1$ cuando $n = 3$ es $3 - 1 = 2$.**
event (p. 843) An outcome or a collection of outcomes. **suceso** (pág. 843) Caso o colección de casos.	**When you roll a number cube, "roll an odd number" is an event.** **Cuando lanzas un cubo numerado, "salir número impar" es un suceso.**
excluded value (p. 794) A number that makes a rational expression undefined. **valor excluido** (pág. 794) Número que hace que una expresión racional sea indefinida.	**3 is an excluded value of the expression $\frac{2}{x - 3}$ because 3 makes the value of the denominator 0.** **3 es un valor excluido de la expresión $\frac{2}{x - 3}$ ya que 3 hace que el valor del denominador sea 0.**
experimental probability (p. 844) A probability based on repeated trials of an experiment. The experimental probability of an event is the ratio of the number of successes (trials in which a favorable outcome occurs) to the number of trials. **probabilidad experimental** (pág. 844) Probabilidad basada en la realización repetida de las pruebas de un experimento. La probabilidad experimental de un suceso es la razón entre el número de resultados deseados (pruebas en las que se produce un caso favorable) y el número de pruebas.	**You spin a spinner 20 times and it stops on yellow 3 times. The experimental probability that the spinner stops on yellow is $\frac{3}{20}$, 15%, or 0.15.** **Giras una ruleta 20 veces y ésta se detiene en el amarillo 3 veces. La probabilidad experimental de que la ruleta se detenga en el amarillo es $\frac{3}{20}$, 15% ó 0.15.**
exponent (p. 3) The number or variable that represents the number of times the base of a power is used as a factor. **exponente** (pág. 3) El número o la variable que representa la cantidad de veces que se usa la base de una potencia como factor.	**In the power 3^4, the exponent is 4.** **En la potencia 3^4, el exponente es 4.**

ENGLISH-SPANISH GLOSSARY

exponential decay (p. 533) When $a > 0$ and $0 < b < 1$, the function $y = ab^x$ represents exponential decay. When a quantity decays exponentially, it decreases by the same percent over equal time periods. The exponential decay model is $y = a(1 - r)^t$.

decrecimiento exponencial (pág. 533) Cuando $a > 0$ y $0 < b < 1$, la función $y = ab^x$ representa el decrecimiento exponencial. Cuando una cantidad decrece de forma exponencial, disminuye en el mismo porcentaje durante períodos de tiempo iguales. El modelo de decrecimiento exponencial es $y = a(1 - r)^t$.

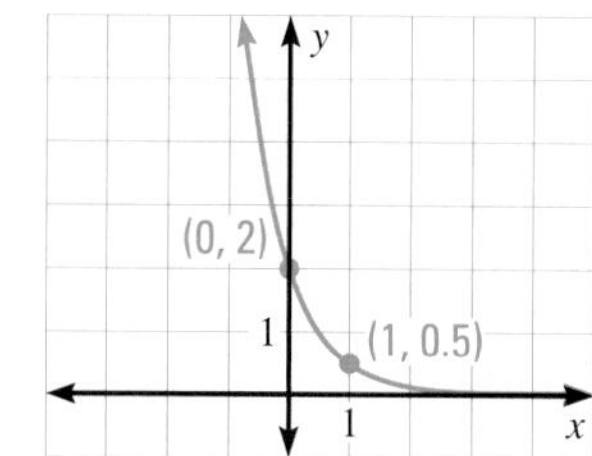

The function $y = 2(0.25)^x$ represents exponential decay. *See also* decay rate *and* decay factor.

La función $y = 2(0.25)^x$ representa el decrecimiento exponencial. *Ver también* tasa de decrecimiento *y* factor de decrecimiento.

---

exponential function (p. 520) A function of the form $y = ab^x$ where $a \neq 0$, $b > 0$, and $b \neq 1$.

The functions $y = 2 \cdot 3^x$ and $y = -2 \cdot \left(\frac{1}{2}\right)^x$ are exponential functions.

See also exponential growth *and* exponential decay.

función exponencial (pág. 520) Función de la forma $y = ab^x$, donde $a \neq 0$, $b > 0$ y $b \neq 1$.

Las funciones $y = 2 \cdot 3^x$ e $y = -2 \cdot \left(\frac{1}{2}\right)^x$ son funciones exponenciales.

Ver también crecimiento exponencial *y* decrecimiento exponencial.

---

exponential growth (p. 522) When $a > 0$ and $b > 1$, the function $y = ab^x$ represents exponential growth. When a quantity grows exponentially, it increases by the same percent over equal time periods. The exponential growth model is $y = a(1 + r)^t$.

crecimiento exponencial (pág. 522) Cuando $a > 0$ y $b > 1$, la función $y = ab^x$ representa el crecimiento exponencial. Cuando una cantidad crece de forma exponencial, aumenta en el mismo porcentaje durante períodos de tiempo iguales. El modelo de crecimiento exponencial es $y = a(1 + r)^t$.

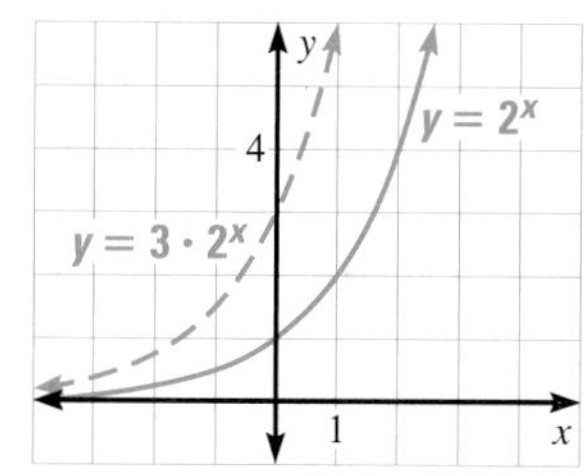

The functions $y = 3 \cdot 2^x$ and $y = 2^x$ represent exponential growth. *See also* growth rate *and* growth factor.

Las funciones $y = 3 \cdot 2^x$ e $y = 2^x$ representan el crecimiento exponencial. *Ver también* tasa de crecimiento *y* factor de crecimiento.

---

extraneous solution (p. 730) A solution of a transformed equation that is not a solution of the original equation.

When you square both sides of the radical equation $\sqrt{6 - x} = x$, the resulting equation has two solutions, 2 and -3, but -3 is an extraneous solution because it does not satisfy the original equation $\sqrt{6 - x} = x$.

solución extraña (pág. 730) Solución de una ecuación transformada que no es solución de la ecuación original.

Al elevar al cuadrado ambos miembros de la ecuación radical $\sqrt{6 - x} = x$, la ecuación resultante tiene dos soluciones, 2 y -3, pero -3 es una solución extraña ya que no satisface la ecuación original $\sqrt{6 - x} = x$.

F

factor by grouping (p. 606) To factor a polynomial with four terms by grouping, factor a common monomial from pairs of terms, and then look for a common binomial factor.

factorizar por grupos (pág. 606) Para factorizar por grupos un polinomio con cuatro términos, factoriza un monomio común a partir de los pares de términos y luego busca un factor binómico común.

$$\begin{aligned} x^3 + 3x^2 + 5x + 15 &= (x^3 + 3x^2) + (5x + 15) \\ &= x^2(x + 3) + 5(x + 3) \\ &= (x + 3)(x^2 + 5) \end{aligned}$$

factor completely (p. 607) A factorable polynomial with integer coefficients is factored completely if it is written as a product of unfactorable polynomials with integer coefficients.

The polynomial $x^3 - x$ is *not* factored completely when written as $x(x^2 - 1)$ but is factored completely when written as $x(x + 1)(x - 1)$.

factorizar completamente (pág. 607) Un polinomio que puede descomponerse en factores y que tiene coeficientes enteros está completamente factorizado si está escrito como producto de polinomios que no pueden descomponerse en factores y que tienen coeficientes enteros.

El polinomio $x^3 - x$ *no* está completamente factorizado cuando se escribe $x(x^2 - 1)$, pero sí está completamente factorizado cuando se escribe $x(x + 1)(x - 1)$.

family of functions (p. 263) A group of functions with similar characteristics.

familia de funciones (pág. 263) Grupo de funciones con características similares.

Functions that have the form $f(x) = mx + b$ constitute the family of linear functions.

Las funciones que tienen la forma $f(x) = mx + b$ constituyen la familia de las funciones lineales.

formula (p. 30) An equation that relates two or more quantities.

fórmula (pág. 30) Ecuación que relaciona dos o más cantidades.

The formula $d = rt$ relates the distance traveled to the rate of speed and travel time.

La fórmula $d = rt$ relaciona la distancia recorrida con la velocidad y el tiempo transcurrido.

frequency (p. 882) The frequency of an interval is the number of data values in that interval.

frecuencia (pág. 882) La frecuencia de un intervalo es el número de datos de valores que hay en ese intervalo.

See frequency table *and* histogram.

Ver tabla de frecuencias *e* histograma.

frequency table (p. 882) A data display that groups data into equal intervals with no gaps between intervals and no intervals overlapping.

tabla de frecuencias (pág. 882) Presentación de datos en la que se agrupan los datos en intervalos iguales sin que haya interrupciones entre los intervalos y sin intervalos superpuestos.

Prices Precios	Sandwiches Sándwiches
\$4.00–4.49	||||
\$4.50–4.99	||
\$5.00–5.49	
\$5.50–5.99	||||

function (p. 35) A function consists of:

- A set called the domain containing numbers called inputs, and a set called the range containing numbers called outputs.
- A pairing of inputs with outputs such that each input is paired with exactly one output.

función (pág. 35) Una función consta de:

- Un conjunto llamado dominio que contiene los números conocidos como entradas, y otro conjunto llamado rango que contiene los números conocidos como salidas.
- Una correspondencia entre las entradas y las salidas tal que a cada entrada le corresponde una sola salida.

The pairing in the table below is a function, because each input is paired with exactly one output.

La correspondencia que aparece en la tabla de abajo es una función ya que a cada entrada le corresponde una sola salida.

Input, x Entrada, x	0	1	2	3	4
Output, y Salida, y	3	4	5	6	7

The domain is the set of inputs: 0, 1, 2, 3, and 4.
The range is the set of outputs: 3, 4, 5, 6, and 7.

El dominio es el conjunto de entradas: 0, 1, 2, 3 y 4.
El rango es el conjunto de salidas: 3, 4, 5, 6 y 7.

function notation (p. 262) A way to name a function using the symbol $f(x)$ instead of y. The symbol $f(x)$ is read as "the value of f at x" or as "f of x."

notación de función (pág. 262) Forma de nombrar una función usando el símbolo $f(x)$ en lugar de y. El símbolo $f(x)$ se lee "el valor de f en x" o "f de x".

The function $y = 2x - 9$ can be written in function notation as $f(x) = 2x - 9$.

La función $y = 2x - 9$ escrita en notación de función es $f(x) = 2x - 9$.

G

geometric sequence (p. 539) A sequence in which the ratio of any term to the previous term is constant. The constant ratio is called the common ratio.

progresión geométrica (pág. 539) Progresión en la que la razón entre cualquier término y el término anterior es constante. La razón constante se llama razón común.

The sequence 5, 10, 20, 40, ... is a geometric sequence with common ratio 2.

La progresión 5, 10, 20, 40, ... es una progresión geométrica cuya razón común es 2.

graph of an equation in two variables (p. 215) The set of points in a coordinate plane that represent all solutions of the equation.

gráfica de una ecuación con dos variables (pág. 215) El conjunto de puntos de un plano de coordenadas que representa todas las soluciones de la ecuación.

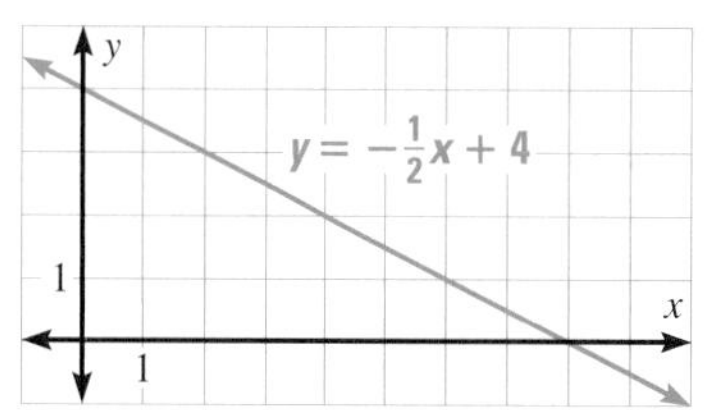

The line is the graph of the equation $y = -\frac{1}{2}x + 4$.

La recta es la gráfica de la ecuación $y = -\frac{1}{2}x + 4$.

ENGLISH-SPANISH GLOSSARY

graph of an inequality in one variable (p. 356) On a number line, the set of points that represent all solutions of the inequality.

gráfica de una desigualdad con una variable (pág. 356) En una recta numérica, el conjunto de puntos que representa todas las soluciones de la desigualdad.

−1 0 1 2 3 4

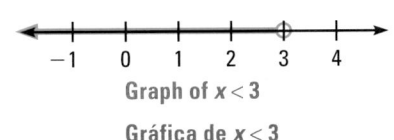

Graph of $x < 3$

Gráfica de $x < 3$

graph of an inequality in two variables (p. 405) In a coordinate plane, the set of points that represent all solutions of the inequality.

gráfica de una desigualdad con dos variables (pág. 405) En un plano de coordenadas, el conjunto de puntos que representa todas las soluciones de la desigualdad.

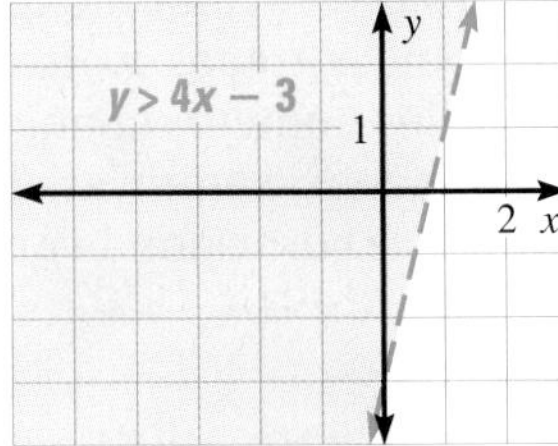

The graph of $y > 4x - 3$ is the shaded half-plane.

La gráfica de $y > 4x - 3$ es el semiplano sombreado.

graph of a system of linear inequalities (p. 466) The graph of all solutions of the system.

gráfica de un sistema de desigualdades lineales (pág. 466) La gráfica de todas las soluciones del sistema.

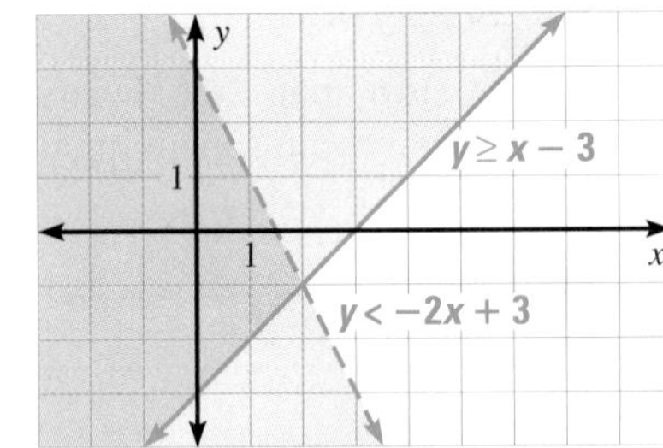

The graph of the system $y < -2x + 3$ and $y \geq x - 3$ is the intersection of the half-planes.

La gráfica del sistema $y < -2x + 3$ e $y \geq x - 3$ es la intersección de los semiplanos.

growth factor (p. 522) The expression $1 + r$ in the exponential growth model $y = a(1 + r)^t$.

factor de crecimiento (pág. 522) La expresión $1 + r$ del modelo de crecimiento exponencial $y = a(1 + r)^t$.

In the exponential growth model $C = 11{,}000(1.069)^t$, the growth factor is 1.069.

En el modelo de crecimiento exponencial $C = 11{,}000(1.069)^t$, el factor de crecimiento es 1.069.

growth rate (p. 522) The variable r in the exponential growth model $y = a(1 + r)^t$.

tasa de crecimiento (pág. 522) La variable r del modelo de crecimiento exponencial $y = a(1 + r)^t$.

In the exponential growth model $C = 11{,}000(1.069)^t$, the growth rate is 0.069.

En el modelo de crecimiento exponencial $C = 11{,}000(1.069)^t$, la tasa de crecimiento es 0.069.

H

half-plane (p. 405) In a coordinate plane, the region on either side of a boundary line.

semiplano (pág. 405) En un plano de coordenadas, la región situada a cada lado de una recta límite.

See graph of an inequality in two variables.

Ver gráfica de una desigualdad con dos variables.

histogram (p. 882) A bar graph that displays data from a frequency table. Each bar represents an interval, and the length of each bar indicates the frequency.

histograma (pág. 882) Gráfica de barras que presenta los datos de una tabla de frecuencias. Cada barra representa un intervalo, y la longitud de cada barra indica la frecuencia.

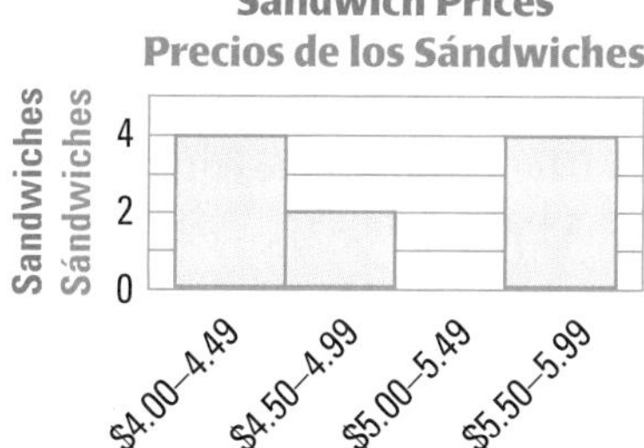

hyperbola (p. 767) The graph of the inverse variation equation $y = \frac{a}{x}$ $(a \neq 0)$ or the graph of a rational function of the form $y = \frac{a}{x-h} + k$ $(a \neq 0)$. A hyperbola has two symmetrical parts called branches. A hyperbola approaches but doesn't intersect lines called asymptotes.

hipérbola (pág. 767) La gráfica de la ecuación de variación inversa $y = \frac{a}{x}$ $(a \neq 0)$ o la gráfica de una función racional de la forma $y = \frac{a}{x-h} + k$ $(a \neq 0)$. La hipérbola tiene dos partes simétricas llamadas ramas. La hipérbola se acerca a las rectas llamadas asíntotas pero sin cortarlas.

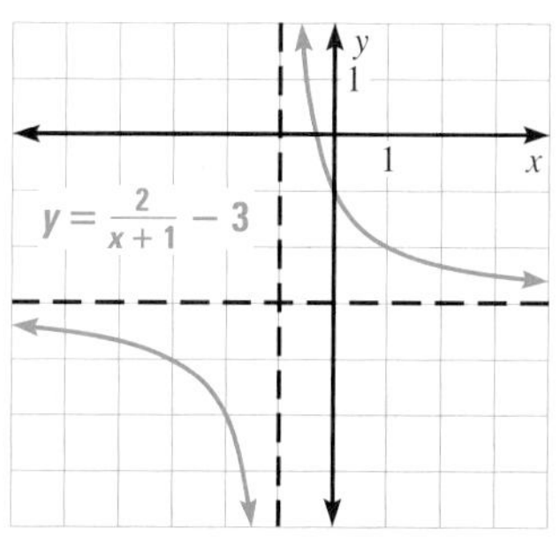

The graph of $y = \frac{2}{x+1} - 3$ is a hyperbola. The asymptotes of the hyperbola are the lines $x = -1$ and $y = -3$.

La gráfica de $y = \frac{2}{x+1} - 3$ es una hipérbola. Las asíntotas de la hipérbola son las rectas $x = -1$ e $y = -3$.

hypotenuse (p. 737) The hypotenuse of a right triangle is the side opposite the right angle.

hipotenusa (pág. 737) La hipotenusa de un triángulo rectángulo es el lado opuesto al ángulo recto.

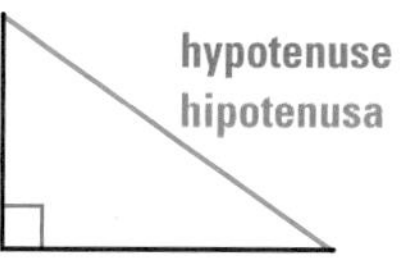

I

identity (p. 156) An equation that is true for all values of the variable.

identidad (pág. 156) Ecuación que es verdadera para todos los valores de la variable.

The equation $2x + 10 = 2(x + 5)$ is an identity.

La ecuación $2x + 10 = 2(x + 5)$ es una identidad.

ENGLISH-SPANISH GLOSSARY

if-then statement (p. 66) A conditional statement with an *if* part and a *then* part. The *if* part contains the hypothesis, and the *then* part contains the conclusion. **enunciado de "si..., entonces..."** (pág. 66) Enunciado condicional con una parte de *si* y otra de *entonces*. La parte de *si* contiene la hipótesis, y la parte de *entonces* contiene la conclusión.	**If $a = -1$, then $\|a\| = 1$.** **The hypothesis is $a = -1$.** **The conclusion is $\|a\| = 1$.** **Si $a = -1$, entonces $\|a\| = 1$.** **La hipótesis es $a = -1$.** **La conclusión es $\|a\| = 1$.**
inconsistent system (p. 459) A linear system with no solution. The graphs of the equations of an inconsistent system are parallel lines. **sistema incompatible** (pág. 459) Sistema lineal sin solución. Las gráficas de las ecuaciones de un sistema incompatible son rectas paralelas.	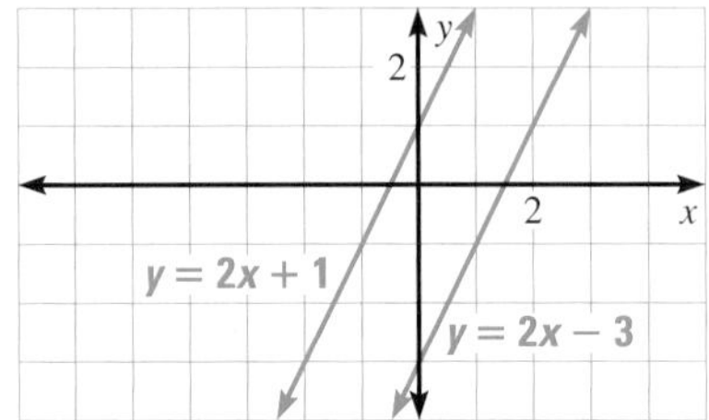 **The linear system $y = 2x + 1$ and $y = 2x - 3$ is inconsistent because the graphs of the equations are parallel lines.** **El sistema lineal $y = 2x + 1$ e $y = 2x - 3$ es incompatible ya que las gráficas de las ecuaciones son rectas paralelas.**
independent events (p. 862) Two events such that the occurrence of one event has no effect on the occurrence of the other event. **sucesos independientes** (pág. 862) Dos sucesos tales que la ocurrencia de uno de ellos no afecta a la ocurrencia del otro.	**You roll a number cube twice. The events "roll a 3 first" and "roll a 6 second" are independent events.** **Lanzas un cubo numerado dos veces. Los sucesos "salir primero el 3" y "salir después el 6" son sucesos independientes.**
independent variable (p. 36) The input variable of a function. **variable independiente** (pág. 36) La variable de entrada de una función.	**In the function equation $y = x + 3$, x is the independent variable.** **En la ecuación de función $y = x + 3$, x es la variable independiente.**
inductive reasoning (p. 117) A form of reasoning in which a conclusion is based on several examples. **razonamiento inductivo** (pág. 117) Tipo de razonamiento en el que la conclusión se basa en varios ejemplos.	**You add several pairs of odd numbers and notice that the sum is even. You conclude that the sum of any two odd numbers is even.** **Sumas varias parejas de números impares y observas que la suma es par. Sacas la conclusión de que la suma de dos números impares cualesquiera es par.**
inequality (p. 21) A mathematical sentence formed by placing one of the symbols $<$, $\leq$, $>$, or $\geq$ between two expressions. **desigualdad** (pág. 21) Enunciado matemático formado al colocar uno de les siguentes símbolos entre dos expresiones: $<$, $\leq$, $>$ o $\geq$.	**$6n \geq 24$ and $x - 2 < 7$ are inequalities.** **$6n \geq 24$ y $x - 2 < 7$ son desigualdades.**

ENGLISH-SPANISH GLOSSARY

input (p. 35) A number in the domain of a function. **entrada** (pág. 35) Número del dominio de una función.	*See* function. *Ver* función.
integers (p. 64) The numbers . . . , −3, −2, −1, 0, 1, 2, 3, . . . , consisting of the negative integers, zero, and the positive integers. **números enteros** (pág. 64) Los números . . . , −3, −2, −1, 0, 1, 2, 3, . . . , que constan de los números enteros negativos, cero y los números enteros positivos.	−8 and 46 are integers. $-8\frac{1}{2}$ and 46.2 are *not* integers. −8 y 46 son números enteros. $-8\frac{1}{2}$ y 46.2 *no* son números enteros.
intercept form of a quadratic function (p. 641) A quadratic function in the form $y = a(x - p)(x - q)$ where $a \neq 0$. The x-intercepts of the graph of the function are p and q. **forma de intercepto de una función cuadrática** (pág. 641) Función cuadrática de la forma $y = a(x - p)(x - q)$, donde $a \neq 0$. Los interceptos en x de la gráfica de la función son p y q.	The quadratic function $y = -(x + 1)(x - 5)$ is in intercept form. The intercepts of the graph of the function are −1 and 5. La función cuadrática $y = -(x + 1)(x - 5)$ está en la forma de intercepto. Los interceptos de la gráfica de la función son −1 y 5.
interquartile range (p. 888) The difference of the upper and the lower quartiles of a data set. **rango intercuartílico** (pág. 888) La diferencia entre el cuartil superior y el cuartil inferior de un conjunto de datos.	The interquartile range of the data set below is 23 − 10 = 13. lower quartile ↓ upper quartile ↓ 8 **10** 14 17 20 **23** 50 El rango intercuartílico del siguiente conjunto de datos es 23 − 10 = 13. cuartil inferior ↓ cuartil superior ↓ 8 **10** 14 17 20 **23** 50
intersection (p. 71) The intersection of two sets A and B is the set of all elements in *both* A and B. The intersection of A and B is written as $A \cap B$. **intersección** (pág. 71) La intersección de dos conjuntos A y B es el conjunto de todos los elementos *tanto* de A *como* de B. La intersección de A y B se escribe $A \cap B$.	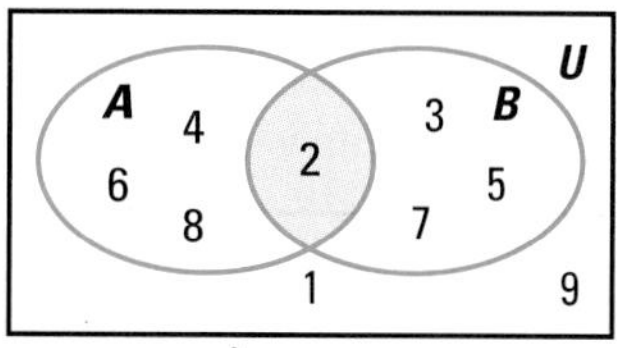 A: 4, 6, 8; A and B: 2; B: 3, 5, 7; U: 1, 9 $A \cap B = \{2\}$
inverse operations (p. 134) Two operations that undo each other. **operaciones inversas** (pág. 134) Dos operaciones que se anulan entre sí.	Addition and subtraction are inverse operations. Multiplication and division are also inverse operations. La suma y la resta son operaciones inversas. La multiplicación y la división también son operaciones inversas.

inverse variation (p. 765) The relationship of two variables x and y if there is a nonzero number a such that $y = \frac{a}{x}$. If $y = \frac{a}{x}$, then y is said to vary inversely with x.

The equations $xy = 4$ and $y = \frac{-1}{x}$ represent inverse variation.

variación inversa (pág. 765) La relación entre dos variables x e y si hay un número a distinto de cero tal que $y = \frac{a}{x}$. Si $y = \frac{a}{x}$, entonces se dice que y varía inversamente con x.

Las ecuaciones $xy = 4$ e $y = \frac{-1}{x}$ representan una variación inversa.

irrational number (p. 111) A number that cannot be written as the quotient of two integers. The decimal form of an irrational number neither terminates nor repeats.

$\sqrt{945} = 30.74085\ldots$ is an irrational number. $1.666\ldots$ is *not* an irrational number.

número irracional (pág. 111) Número que no puede escribirse como cociente de dos números enteros. La forma decimal de un número irracional no termina ni se repite.

$\sqrt{945} = 30.74085\ldots$ es un número irracional. $1.666\ldots$ *no* es un número irracional.

L

leading coefficient (p. 554) When a polynomial is written so that the exponents of a variable decrease from left to right, the coefficient of the first term is the leading coefficient.

The leading coefficient of the polynomial $2x^3 + x^2 - 5x + 12$ is 2.

coeficiente inicial (pág. 554) Cuando un polinomio se escribe de tal manera que los exponentes de una variable disminuyen de izquierda a derecha, el coeficiente del primer término es el coeficiente inicial.

El coeficiente inicial del polinomio $2x^3 + x^2 - 5x + 12$ es 2.

least common denominator (LCD) of rational expressions (p. 813) The product of the factors of the denominators of the rational expressions with each common factor used only once.

The LCD of $\frac{5}{(x-3)^2}$ and $\frac{3x+4}{(x-3)(x+2)}$ is $(x-3)^2(x+2)$.

mínimo común denominador (m.c.d.) de las expresiones racionales (pág. 813) El producto de los factores de los denominadores de las expresiones racionales usando cada factor común una sola vez.

El m.c.d. de $\frac{5}{(x-3)^2}$ y $\frac{3x+4}{(x-3)(x+2)}$ es $(x-3)^2(x+2)$.

legs of a right triangle (p. 737) The two sides that form the right angle.

catetos de un triángulo rectángulo (pág. 737) Los dos lados que forman el ángulo recto.

leg
cateto
leg
cateto

like terms (p. 97) Terms that have the same variable parts. Constant terms are also like terms.

In the expression $3x + (-4) + (-6x) + 2$, $3x$ and $-6x$ are like terms, and -4 and 2 are like terms.

términos semejantes (pág. 97) Términos que tienen las mismas variables. Los términos constantes también son términos semejantes.

En la expresión $3x + (-4) + (-6x) + 2$, $3x$ y $-6x$ son términos semejantes, y -4 y 2 también son términos semejantes.

line of fit (p. 326) A line used to model the trend in data having a positive or negative correlation.

recta de regresión (pág. 326) Recta utilizada para representar la tendencia de los datos que presentan una correlación positiva o negativa.

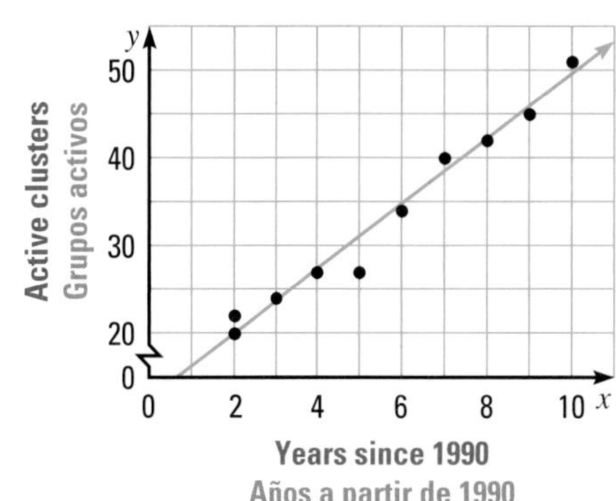

The graph shows a line of fit for the data in the scatter plot.

La gráfica muestra una recta de regresión para los datos del diagrama de dispersión.

linear equation (p. 216) An equation whose graph is a line.

ecuación lineal (pág. 216) Ecuación cuya gráfica es una recta.

See standard form of a linear equation.

Ver forma general de una ecuación lineal.

linear extrapolation (p. 336) Using a line or its equation to approximate a value outside the range of known values.

extrapolación lineal (pág. 336) El uso de una recta o su ecuación para hallar por aproximación un valor situado fuera del rango de los valores conocidos.

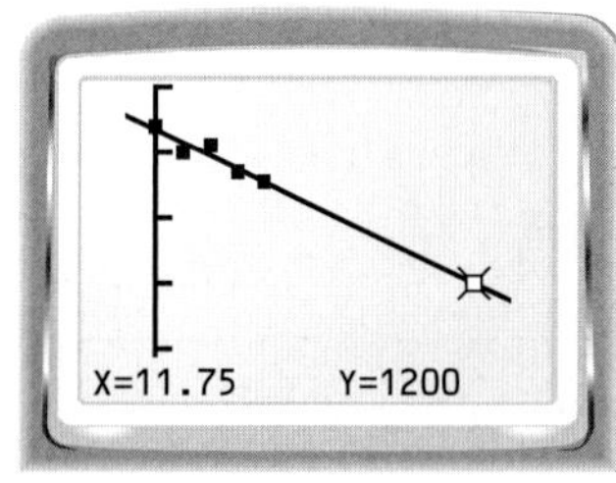

The best-fitting line can be used to estimate that when $y = 1200$, $x \approx 11.75$.

La mejor recta de regresión puede utilizarse para estimar que cuando $y = 1200$, $x \approx 11.75$.

linear function (p. 217) The equation $Ax + By = C$ represents a linear function provided $B \neq 0$.

función lineal (pág. 217) La ecuación $Ax + By = C$ representa una función lineal siempre que $B \neq 0$.

The equation $2x - y = 3$ represents a linear function. The equation $x = 3$ does *not* represent a function.

La ecuación $2x - y = 3$ representa una función lineal. La ecuación $x = 3$ *no* representa una función.

linear inequality in two variables (p. 405) An inequality that is the result of replacing the $=$ sign in a linear equation with $<$, $\leq$, $>$, or $\geq$.

desigualdad lineal con dos variables (pág. 405) Desigualdad que se obtiene al reemplazar el símbolo $=$ de la ecuación lineal por $<$, $\leq$, $>$ o $\geq$.

$x - 3y < 6$ is a linear inequality in two variables, x and y.

$x - 3y < 6$ es una desigualdad lineal con dos variables, x e y.

ENGLISH-SPANISH GLOSSARY

linear interpolation (p. 335) Using a line or its equation to approximate a value between two known values. **interpolación lineal** (pág. 335) El uso de una recta o su ecuación para hallar por aproximación un valor situado entre dos valores conocidos.	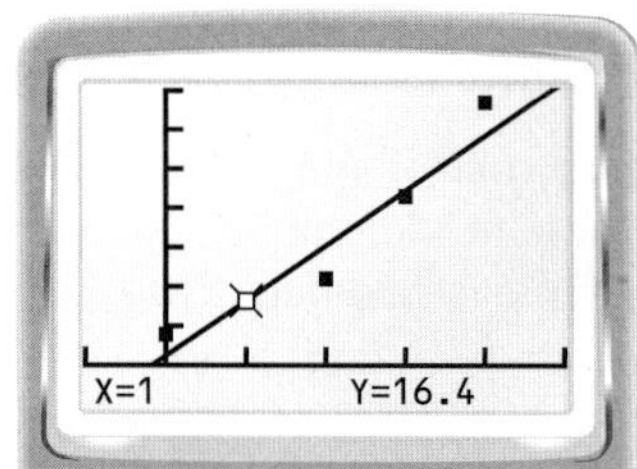 The best-fitting line can be used to estimate that when $x = 1$, $y \approx 16.4$. La mejor recta de regresión puede utilizarse para estimar que cuando $x = 1$, $y \approx 16.4$.
linear regression (p. 335) The process of finding the best-fitting line to model a set of data. **regresión lineal** (pág. 335) El proceso de hallar la mejor recta de regresión para representar un conjunto de datos.	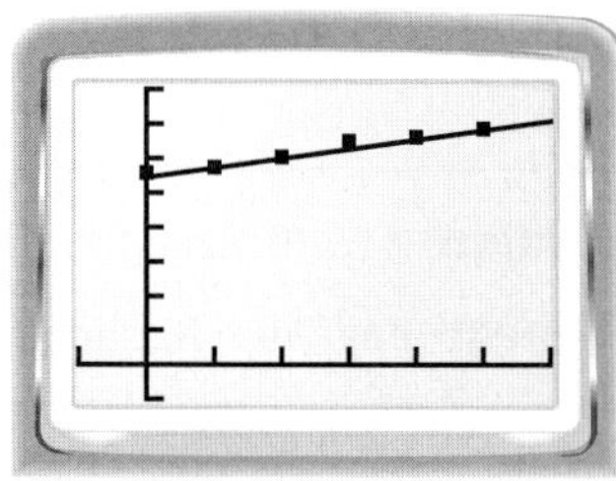 You can use a graphing calculator to perform linear regression on a data set. Puedes usar una calculadora de gráficas para realizar una regresión lineal a un conjunto de datos.
literal equation (p. 184) An equation in which letters are used to replace the coefficients and constants of another equation. **ecuación literal** (pág. 184) Ecuación en la que se usan letras para reemplazar los coeficientes y las constantes de otra ecuación.	The equation $5(x + 3) = 20$ can be written as the literal equation $a(x + b) = c$. La ecuación $5(x + 3) = 20$ puede escribirse como la ecuación literal $a(x + b) = c$.
lower quartile (p. 887) The median of the lower half of an ordered data set. **cuartil inferior** (pág. 887) La mediana de la mitad inferior de un conjunto de datos ordenados.	The lower quartile of the data set below is 10. lower quartile ↓ median ↓ 8 **10** 14 17 20 23 50 El cuartil inferior del siguiente conjunto de datos es 10. cuartil inferior ↓ mediana ↓ 8 **10** 14 17 20 23 50

ENGLISH-SPANISH GLOSSARY

M

matrix, matrices (p. 94) A rectangular arrangement of numbers in rows and columns. Each number in a matrix is an element, or *entry*.

matriz, matrices (pág. 94) Disposición rectangular de números colocados en filas y columnas. Cada número de la matriz es un elemento, o *entrada*.

$$A = \begin{bmatrix} 0 & 4 & -1 \\ -3 & 2 & 5 \end{bmatrix}$$ 2 rows / 2 filas

3 columns / 3 columnas

Matrix A has 2 rows and 3 columns. The element in the first row and second column is 4.

La matriz A tiene 2 filas y 3 columnas. El elemento de la primera fila y la segunda columna es 4.

maximum value (p. 636) For $y = ax^2 + bx + c$ where $a < 0$, the y-coordinate of the vertex is the maximum value of the function.

valor máximo (pág. 636) Para $y = ax^2 + bx + c$ donde $a < 0$, la coordenada y del vértice es el valor máximo de la función.

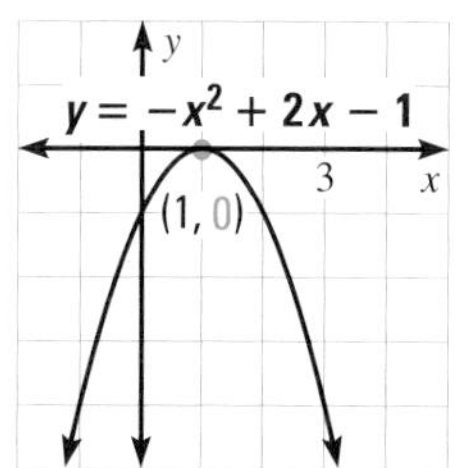

The maximum value of the function $y = -x^2 + 2x - 1$ is 0.

El valor máximo de la función $y = -x^2 + 2x - 1$ es 0.

mean (p. 875) For the numerical data set $x_1, x_2, \ldots, x_n$, the mean, or average, is:

$$\overline{x} = \frac{x_1 + x_2 + \ldots + x_n}{n}$$

media (pág. 875) Para el conjunto de datos numéricos $x_1, x_2, \ldots, x_n$, la media, o el promedio, es:

$$\overline{x} = \frac{x_1 + x_2 + \ldots + x_n}{n}$$

The mean of 5, 9, 14, 23 is $\frac{5 + 9 + 14 + 23}{4} = \frac{51}{4} = 12.75$.

La media de 5, 9, 14, 23 es $\frac{5 + 9 + 14 + 23}{4} = \frac{51}{4} = 12.75$.

mean absolute deviation (p. 876) The mean absolute deviation of the data set $x_1, x_2, \ldots, x_n$ is a measure of dispersion given by:

$$\frac{|x_1 - \overline{x}| + |x_2 - \overline{x}| + \ldots + |x_n - \overline{x}|}{n}$$

desviación absoluta media (pág. 876) La desviación absoluta media del conjunto de datos $x_1, x_2, \ldots, x_n$ es una medida de dispersión dada por:

$$\frac{|x_1 - \overline{x}| + |x_2 - \overline{x}| + \ldots + |x_n - \overline{x}|}{n}$$

The mean absolute deviation of the data set 3, 9, 13, 23 (with mean = 12) is:

$$\frac{|3 - 12| + |9 - 12| + |13 - 12| + |23 - 12|}{4} = 6$$

La desviación absoluta media del conjunto de datos 3, 9, 13, 23 (con media = 12)es:

$$\frac{|3 - 12| + |9 - 12| + |13 - 12| + |23 - 12|}{4} = 6$$

measure of dispersion (p. 876) A measure that describes the dispersion, or spread, of data.

medida de dispersión (pág. 876) Medida que describe la dispersión, o extensión, de los datos.

See range *and* mean absolute deviation.

Ver rango *y* desviación absoluta media.

median (p. 875) The median of a numerical data set is the middle number when the values are written in numerical order. If the data set has an even number of values, the median is the mean of the two middle values.

mediana (pág. 875) La mediana de un conjunto de datos numéricos es el número central cuando los valores se escriben en orden numérico. Si el conjunto de datos tiene un número par de valores, la mediana es la media de los dos valores centrales.

The median of 5, 9, 14, 23 is the mean of 9 and 14, or $\frac{9 + 14}{2} = 11.5$.

La mediana de 5, 9, 14, 23 es la media de 9 y 14, ó $\frac{9 + 14}{2} = 11.5$.

midpoint (p. 745) The midpoint of a line segment is the point on the segment that is equidistant from the endpoints.

punto medio (pág. 745) El punto medio de un segmento de recta es el punto del segmento que es equidistante de los extremos.

M is the midpoint of $\overline{AB}$.

M en el punto medio de $\overline{AB}$.

midpoint formula (p. 745) The midpoint M of the line segment with endpoints $A(x_1, y_1)$ and $B(x_2, y_2)$ is $M\left(\frac{x_1 + x_2}{2}, \frac{y_1 + y_2}{2}\right)$.

fórmula del punto medio (pág. 745) El punto medio M del segmento de recta cuyos extremos son $A(x_1, y_1)$ y $B(x_2, y_2)$ es $M\left(\frac{x_1 + x_2}{2}, \frac{y_1 + y_2}{2}\right)$.

The midpoint M of the line segment with endpoints $(-1, -2)$ and $(3, -4)$ is:

$$\left(\frac{-1 + 3}{2}, \frac{-2 + (-4)}{2}\right) = (1, -3)$$

El punto medio M del segmento de recta cuyos extremos son $(-1, -2)$ y $(3, -4)$ es:

$$\left(\frac{-1 + 3}{2}, \frac{-2 + (-4)}{2}\right) = (1, -3)$$

minimum value (p. 636) For $y = ax^2 + bx + c$ where $a > 0$, the y-coordinate of the vertex is the minimum value of the function.

valor mínimo (pág. 636) Para $y = ax^2 + bx + c$ donde $a > 0$, la coordenada y del vértice es el valor mínimo de la función.

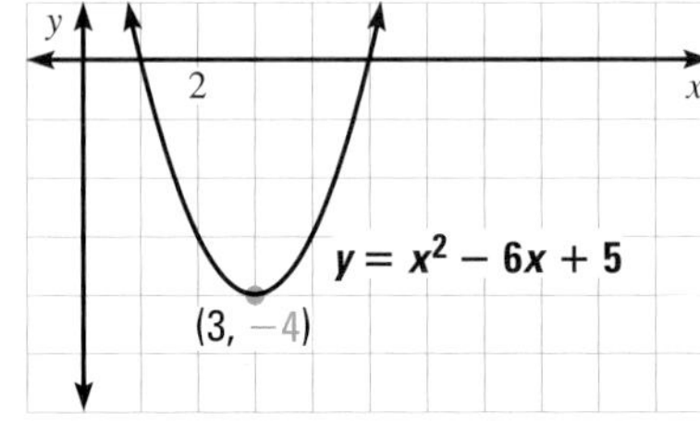

The minimum value of the function $y = x^2 - 6x + 5$ is -4.

El valor mínimo de la función $y = x^2 - 6x + 5$ es -4.

mode (p. 875) The mode of a data set is the value that occurs most frequently. There may be one mode, no mode, or more than one mode.

moda (pág. 875) La moda de un conjunto de datos es el valor que ocurre más veces. Puede haber una moda, más de una moda o ninguna moda.

The mode of the data set 4, 7, 9, 11, 11, 12, 18 is 11.

La moda del conjunto de datos 4, 7, 9, 11, 11, 12, 18 es 11.

monomial (p. 554) A number, variable, or the product of a number and one or more variables with whole number exponents. **monomio** (pág. 554) Un número, una variable o el producto de un número y una o más variables que tienen exponentes expresados por números naturales.	**$10, 3x, \frac{1}{2}ab^2$, and $-1.8m^5$ are monomials.** **$10, 3x, \frac{1}{2}ab^2$ y $-1.8m^5$ son monomios.**
multiplicative identity (p. 89) The number 1 is the multiplicative identity, because the product of any number and 1 is the number: $a \cdot 1 = 1 \cdot a = a$. **identidad multiplicativa** (pág. 89) El número 1 es la identidad multiplicativa ya que el producto de cualquier número y 1 es ese número: $a \cdot 1 = 1 \cdot a = a$.	**$3.6(1) = 3.6, 1(-7) = -7$**
multiplicative inverse (p. 103) The multiplicative inverse of a nonzero number a is its reciprocal, $\frac{1}{a}$. The product of a nonzero number and its multiplicative inverse is 1: $a \cdot \frac{1}{a} = \frac{1}{a} \cdot a = 1, a \neq 0$. **inverso multiplicativo** (pág. 103) El inverso multiplicativo de un número a distinto de cero es su recíproco, $\frac{1}{a}$. El producto de un número distinto de cero y su inverso multiplicativo es 1: $a \cdot \frac{1}{a} = \frac{1}{a} \cdot a = 1, a \neq 0$.	**The multiplicative inverse of $-\frac{1}{5}$ is -5 because $-\frac{1}{5} \cdot (-5) = 1$.** **El inverso multiplicativo de $-\frac{1}{5}$ es -5 ya que $-\frac{1}{5} \cdot (-5) = 1$.**
mutually exclusive events (p. 861) Events that have no common outcome. **sucesos mutuamente excluyentes** (pág. 861) Sucesos que no tienen ningún caso en común.	**When you roll a number cube, "roll a 3" and "roll an even number" are mutually exclusive events.** **Cuando lanzas un cubo numerado, "salir el 3" y "salir número par" son sucesos mutuamente excluyentes.**

N

n* factorial** (p. 852) For any positive integer n, n factorial, written $n!$, is the product of the integers from 1 to n; $0! = 1$. **factorial de *n (pág. 852) Para cualquier número entero positivo n, el factorial de n, escrito $n!$, es el producto de los números enteros de 1 a n; $0! = 1$.	**$5! = 5 \cdot 4 \cdot 3 \cdot 2 \cdot 1 = 120$**
negative exponent (p. 503) If $a \neq 0$, then a^{-n} is the reciprocal of a^n; $a^{-n} = \frac{1}{a^n}$. **exponente negativo** (pág. 503) Si $a \neq 0$, entonces a^{-n} es el recíproco de a^n; $a^{-n} = \frac{1}{a^n}$.	**$3^{-2} = \frac{1}{3^2} = \frac{1}{9}$**

ENGLISH-SPANISH GLOSSARY

negative integers (p. 64) The integers that are less than 0. **números enteros negativos** (pág. 64) Los números enteros menores que 0.	**$-1, -2, -3, -4, \ldots$**

O

odds against (p. 845) When all outcomes are equally likely, the odds against an event is the ratio of the number of unfavorable outcomes to the number of favorable outcomes. **probabilidad en contra** (pág. 845) Cuando todos los casos son igualmente posibles, la probabilidad en contra de que ocurra un suceso es la razón entre el número de casos desfavorables y el número de casos favorables.	**When you roll a number cube, the odds against rolling a number less than 5 is $\frac{2}{4} = \frac{1}{2}$, or 1 : 2.** **Cuando lanzas un cubo numerado, la probabilidad en contra de que salga un número menor que 5 es $\frac{2}{4} = \frac{1}{2}$, ó 1 : 2.**
odds in favor (p. 845) When all outcomes are equally likely, the odds in favor of an event is the ratio of the number of favorable outcomes to the number of unfavorable outcomes. **probabilidad a favor** (pág. 845) Cuando todos los casos son igualmente posibles, la probabilidad a favor de que ocurra un suceso es la razón entre el número de casos favorables y el número de casos desfavorables.	**When you roll a number cube, the odds in favor of rolling a number less than 5 is $\frac{4}{2} = \frac{2}{1}$, or 2 : 1.** **Cuando lanzas un cubo numerado, la probabilidad a favor de que salga un número menor que 5 es $\frac{4}{2} = \frac{2}{1}$, ó 2 : 1.**
open sentence (p. 21) An equation or an equality that contains an algebraic expression. **enunciado con variables** (pág. 21) Ecuación o desigualdad que contiene una expresión algebraica.	**$2k - 8 = 12$ and $6n \geq 24$ are open sentences.** **$2k - 8 = 12$ y $6n \geq 24$ son enunciados con variables.**
opposites (p. 66) Two numbers that are the same distance from 0 on a number line but are on opposite sides of 0. **opuestos** (pág. 66) En una recta numérica, dos números que están a la misma distancia de 0 pero en lados opuestos de 0.	4 units 4 units 4 unidades 4 unidades −6 −4 −2 0 2 4 6 **4 and −4 are opposites.** **4 y −4 son opuestos.**
order of magnitude of a quantity (p. 491) The power of 10 nearest the quantity. **orden de magnitud de una cantidad** (pág. 491) La potencia de 10 más próxima a la cantidad.	**The order of magnitude of 91,000 is 10^5, or 100,000.** **El orden de magnitud de 91,000 es 10^5, ó 100,000.**

order of operations (p. 8) Rules for evaluating an expression involving more than one operation.	**To evaluate $24 - (3^2 + 1)$, evaluate the power, then add within the parentheses, and then subtract:** $24 - (3^2 + 1) = 24 - (9 + 1) = 24 - 10 = 14$
orden de operaciones (pág. 8) Reglas para evaluar una expresión relacionada con más de una operación.	**Para evaluar $24 - (3^2 + 1)$, evalúa la potencia, suma las cantidades entre paréntesis y después resta:** $24 - (3^2 + 1) = 24 - (9 + 1) = 24 - 10 = 14$
outcome (p. 843) A possible result of an experiment.	**When you roll a number cube, there are 6 possible outcomes: a 1, 2, 3, 4, 5, or 6.**
caso (pág. 843) Resultado posible de un experimento.	**Cuando lanzas un cubo numerado, hay 6 casos posibles: 1, 2, 3, 4, 5 ó 6.**
outlier (p. 889) A value that is widely separated from the rest of the data in a data set. Typically, a value that is greater than the upper quartile by more than 1.5 times the interquartile range or is less than the lower quartile by more than 1.5 times the interquartile range.	**The interquartile range of the data set below is $23 - 10 = 13$.** **lower quartile ↓ (10), upper quartile ↓ (23)** **8 10 14 17 20 23 50** **The data value 50 is greater than $23 + 1.5(13) = 42.5$, so it is an outlier.**
valor extremo (pág. 889) En un conjunto de datos, valor muy alejado del resto de los datos. Generalmente, un valor mayor que el cuartil superior en más de 1.5 veces el rango intercuartílico o menor que el cuartil inferior en más de 1.5 veces el rango intercuartílico.	**El rango intercuartílico del siguiente conjunto de datos es $23 - 10 = 13$.** **cuartil inferior ↓ (10), cuartil superior ↓ (23)** **8 10 14 17 20 23 50** **El valor 50 es mayor que $23 + 1.5(13) = 42.5$, por lo que es un valor extremo.**
output (p. 35) A number in the range of a function.	*See* **function.**
salida (pág. 35) Número que pertenece al rango de una función.	*Ver* **función.**
overlapping events (p. 861) Events that have at least one common outcome.	**When you roll a number cube, "roll a 3" and "roll an odd number" are overlapping events.**
sucesos de intersección (pág. 861) Sucesos que tienen al menos un caso en común.	**Cuando lanzas un cubo numerado, "salir el 3" y "salir número impar" son sucesos de intersección.**

P

parabola (p. 628) The U-shaped graph of a quadratic function.

parábola (pág. 628) La gráfica en forma de U de una función cuadrática.

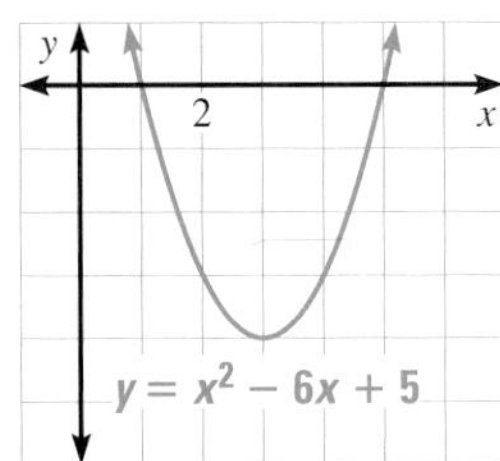

The graph of $y = x^2 - 6x + 5$ is a parabola.

La gráfica de $y = x^2 - 6x + 5$ es una parábola.

parallel lines (p. 246) Two lines in the same plane that do not intersect.

rectas paralelas (pág. 246) Dos rectas del mismo plano que no se cortan.

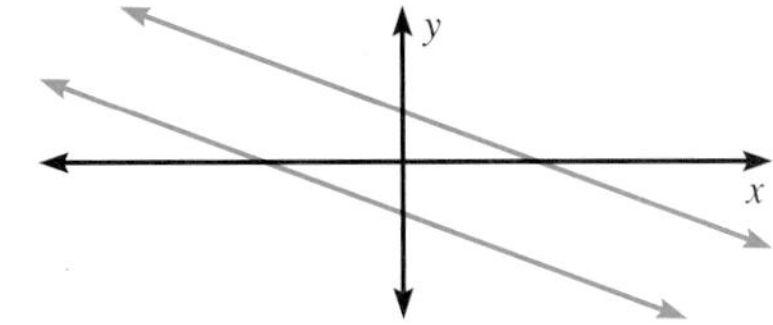

parent linear function (p. 263) The function $f(x) = x$, which is the most basic function in the family of linear functions.

función lineal básica (pág. 263) La función $f(x) = x$, que es la más básica de la familia de las funciones lineales.

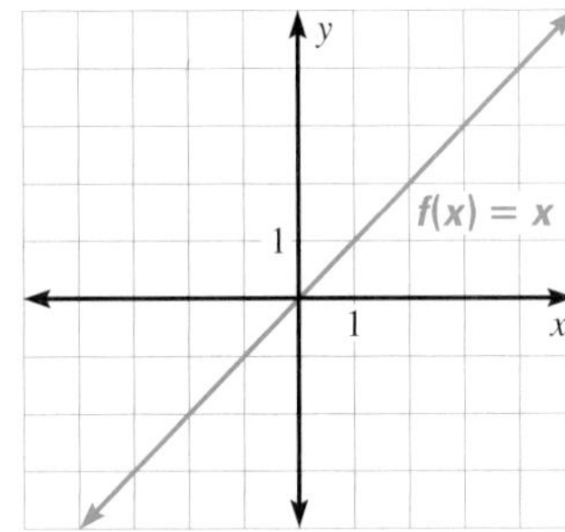

parent quadratic function (p. 628) The function $y = x^2$, which is the most basic function in the family of quadratic functions.

función cuadrática básica (pág. 628) La función $y = x^2$, que es la más básica de la familia de las funciones cuadráticas.

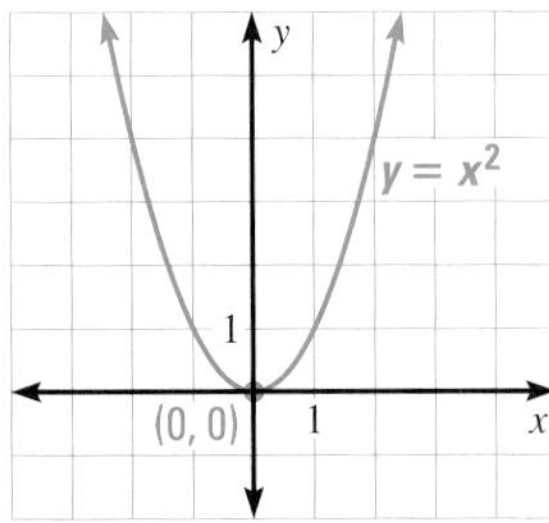

parent square root function (p. 710) The function $y = \sqrt{x}$, which is the most basic function in the family of square root functions.

función con raíz cuadrada básica (pág. 710) La función $y = \sqrt{x}$, que es la más básica de la familia de las funciones con raíz cuadrada.

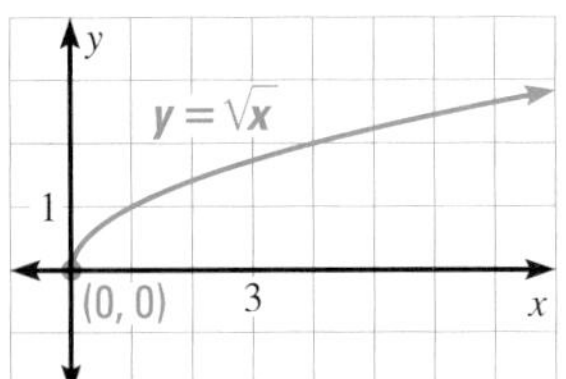

ENGLISH-SPANISH GLOSSARY

percent of change (p. 182) A percent that indicates how much a quantity increases or decreases with respect to the original amount. Percent of change, $p\% = \frac{\text{Amount of increase or decrease}}{\text{Original amount}}$ **porcentaje de cambio** (pág. 182) Porcentaje que indica cuánto aumenta o disminuye una cantidad con respecto a la cantidad original. Porcentaje de cambio, $p\% = \frac{\text{Cantidad de aumento o disminución}}{\text{Cantidad original}}$	The percent of change, $p\%$, from 140 to 189 is: $p\% = \frac{189 - 140}{140} = \frac{49}{140} = 0.35 = 35\%$ El porcentaje de cambio, $p\%$, de 140 a 189 es: $p\% = \frac{189 - 140}{140} = \frac{49}{140} = 0.35 = 35\%$
percent of decrease (p. 182) The percent of change in a quantity when the new amount of the quantity is less than the original amount. **porcentaje de disminución** (pág. 182) El porcentaje de cambio de una cantidad cuando la nueva cantidad es menor que la cantidad original.	*See* percent of change. *Ver* porcentaje de cambio.
percent of increase (p. 182) The percent of change in a quantity when the new amount of the quantity is greater than the original amount. **porcentaje de aumento** (pág. 182) El porcentaje de cambio de una cantidad cuando la nueva cantidad es mayor que la cantidad original.	*See* percent of change. *Ver* porcentaje de cambio.
perfect square (p. 111) A number that is the square of an integer. **cuadrado perfecto** (pág. 111) Número que es el cuadrado de un número entero.	49 is a perfect square, because $49 = 7^2$. 49 es un cuadrado perfecto ya que $49 = 7^2$.
perfect square trinomials (p. 601) Trinomials of the form $a^2 + 2ab + b^2$ and $a^2 - 2ab + b^2$. **trinomios cuadrados perfectos** (pág. 601) Trinomios de la forma $a^2 + 2ab + b^2$ y $a^2 - 2ab + b^2$.	$x^2 + 6x + 9$ and $x^2 - 10x + 25$ are perfect square trinomials. $x^2 + 6x + 9$ y $x^2 - 10x + 25$ son trinomios cuadrados perfectos.
permutation (p. 851) An arrangement of objects in which order is important. **permutación** (pág. 851) Disposición de objetos en la que el orden es importante.	There are 6 permutations of the numbers 1, 2, and 3: 123, 132, 213, 231, 312, and 321. Existen 6 permutaciones de los números 1, 2 y 3: 123, 132, 213, 231, 312 y 321.
perpendicular lines (p. 320) Two lines in the same plane that intersect to form a right angle. **rectas perpendiculares** (pág. 320) Dos rectas del mismo plano que al cortarse forman un ángulo recto.	Horizontal and vertical lines are perpendicular to each other. Las rectas horizontales y verticales son perpendiculares entre sí.

point-slope form (p. 302) An equation of a nonvertical line written in the form $y - y_1 = m(x - x_1)$ where the line passes through a given point (x_1, y_1) and has a slope of m. **forma punto-pendiente** (pág. 302) Ecuación de una recta no vertical escrita en la forma $y - y_1 = m(x - x_1)$, donde la recta pasa por un punto dado (x_1, y_1) y tiene pendiente m.	The equation $y + 3 = 2(x - 4)$ is in point-slope form. The graph of the equation is a line that passes through the point $(4, -3)$ and has a slope of 2. La ecuación $y + 3 = 2(x - 4)$ está en la forma punto-pendiente. La gráfica de la ecuación es una recta que pasa por el punto $(4, -3)$ y tiene pendiente 2.
polynomial (p. 554) A monomial or a sum of monomials, each called a term of the polynomial. **polinomio** (pág. 554) Monomio o suma de monomios; cada uno se llama término del polinomio.	9, $2x^2 + x - 5$, and $7bc^3 + 4b^4c$ are polynomials. 9, $2x^2 + x - 5$ y $7bc^3 + 4b^4c$ son polinomios.
population (p. 871) The entire group that you want information about. **población** (pág. 871) El grupo entero sobre el que se desea información.	A magazine invites its readers to mail in answers to a questionnaire rating the magazine. The population consists of all the magazine's readers. Una revista invita a sus lectores a enviar por correo las respuestas a un cuestionario sobre la calidad de la revista. La población está formada por todos los lectores de la revista.
positive integers (p. 64) The integers that are greater than 0. **números enteros positivos** (pág. 64) Los números enteros mayores que 0.	1, 2, 3, 4, . . .
power (p. 3) An expression that represents repeated multiplication of the same factor. **potencia** (pág. 3) Expresión que representa la multiplicación repetida del mismo factor.	81 is a power of 3, because $81 = 3 \cdot 3 \cdot 3 \cdot 3 = 3^4$. 81 es una potencia de 3 ya que $81 = 3 \cdot 3 \cdot 3 \cdot 3 = 3^4$.
probability of an event (p. 843) A number from 0 to 1 that measures the likelihood, or chance, that the event will occur. **probabilidad de un suceso** (pág. 843) Número de 0 a 1 que mide la posibilidad de que ocurra un suceso.	*See* experimental probability *and* theoretical probability. *Ver* probabilidad experimental *y* probabilidad teórica.
proportion (p. 163) An equation that states that two ratios are equivalent: $\frac{a}{b} = \frac{c}{d}$ where $b \neq 0$ and $d \neq 0$. **proporción** (pág. 163) Ecuación que establece que dos razones son equivalentes: $\frac{a}{b} = \frac{c}{d}$ donde $b \neq 0$ y $d \neq 0$.	$\frac{3}{4} = \frac{6}{8}$ and $\frac{11}{6} = \frac{x}{30}$ are proportions. $\frac{3}{4} = \frac{6}{8}$ y $\frac{11}{6} = \frac{x}{30}$ son proporciones.

ENGLISH-SPANISH GLOSSARY

Pythagorean theorem (p. 737) If a triangle is a right triangle, then the sum of the squares of the lengths a and b of the legs equals the square of the length c of the hypotenuse: $a^2 + b^2 = c^2$.

teorema de Pitágoras (pág. 737) Si un triángulo es rectángulo, entonces la suma de los cuadrados de las longitudes a y b de los catetos es igual al cuadrado de la longitud c de la hipotenusa: $a^2 + b^2 = c^2$.

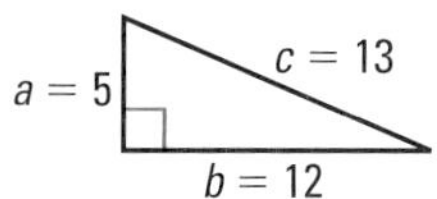

$5^2 + 12^2 = 13^2$

Q

quadrants (p. 206) The four regions into which the coordinate plane is divided by the x-axis and the y-axis.

cuadrantes (pág. 206) Las cuatro regiones en las que el eje de x y el eje de y dividen al plano de coordenadas.

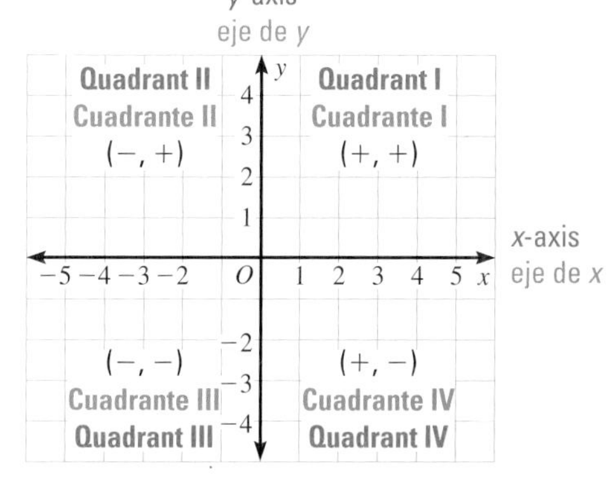

quadratic equation (p. 643) An equation that can be written in the standard form $ax^2 + bx + c = 0$ where $a \neq 0$.

ecuación cuadrática (pág. 643) Ecuación que puede escribirse en la forma general $ax^2 + bx + c = 0$, donde $a \neq 0$.

The equations $x^2 - 2x = 3$ and $0.1x^2 = 40$ are quadratic equations.

$x^2 - 2x = 3$ y $0.1x^2 = 40$ son ecuaciones cuadráticas.

quadratic formula (p. 671) The formula below that can be used to find the solutions of the quadratic equation $ax^2 + bx + c = 0$ where $a \neq 0$ and $b^2 - 4ac \geq 0$:

$$x = \frac{-b \pm \sqrt{b^2 - 4ac}}{2a}$$

fórmula cuadrática (pág. 671) La fórmula de abajo puede utilizarse para hallar las soluciones de la ecuación cuadrática $ax^2 + bx + c = 0$ donde $a \neq 0$ y $b^2 - 4ac \geq 0$:

$$x = \frac{-b \pm \sqrt{b^2 - 4ac}}{2a}$$

To solve $3x^2 + 5x - 8 = 0$, substitute 3 for a, 5 for b, and −8 for c in the quadratic formula:

$$x = \frac{-5 \pm \sqrt{5^2 - 4(3)(-8)}}{2(3)}$$

$x = 1$ or $x = -\frac{8}{3}$

Para resolver $3x^2 + 5x - 8 = 0$, sustituye a por 3, b por 5 y c por −8 en la fórmula cuadrática:

$$x = \frac{-5 \pm \sqrt{5^2 - 4(3)(-8)}}{2(3)}$$

$x = 1$ ó $x = -\frac{8}{3}$

quadratic function (p. 628) A nonlinear function that can be written in the standard form $y = ax^2 + bx + c$ where $a \neq 0$.

función cuadrática (pág. 628) Función no lineal que puede escribirse en la forma general $y = ax^2 + bx + c$, donde $a \neq 0$.

$y = 2x^2 + 5x - 3$ is a quadratic function.

$y = 2x^2 + 5x - 3$ es una función cuadrática.

R

radical equation (p. 729) An equation that contains a radical expression with a variable in the radicand.	$2\sqrt{x} - 8 = 0$ and $\sqrt{3x - 17} = \sqrt{x + 21}$ are radical equations.
ecuación radical (pág. 729) Ecuación que contiene una expresión radical en cuyo radicando aparece una variable.	$2\sqrt{x} - 8 = 0$ y $\sqrt{3x - 17} = \sqrt{x + 21}$ son ecuaciones radicales.
radical expression (p. 710) An expression that contains a radical, such as a square root, cube root, or other root.	$3\sqrt{2x}$ and $\sqrt[3]{x - 1}$ are radical expressions.
expresión radical (pág. 710) Expresión que contiene un radical, como una raíz cuadrada, una raíz cúbica u otra raíz.	$3\sqrt{2x}$ y $\sqrt[3]{x - 1}$ son expresiones radicales.
radical function (p. 710) A function that contains a radical expression with the independent variable in the radicand.	$y = \sqrt[3]{2x}$ and $y = \sqrt{x + 2}$ are radical functions.
función radical (pág. 710) Función que contiene una expresión radical y en cuyo radicando aparece la variable independiente.	$y = \sqrt[3]{2x}$ e $y = \sqrt{x + 2}$ son funciones radicales.
radicand (p. 110) The number or expression inside a radical symbol.	The radicand of $\sqrt{9}$ and $-\sqrt{9}$ is 9.
radicando (pág. 110) El número o la expresión que aparece bajo el signo radical.	El radicando de $\sqrt{9}$ y $-\sqrt{9}$ es 9.
random sample (p. 871) A sample in which every member of the population has an equal chance of being selected.	You can select a random sample of a school's student population by having a computer randomly choose 100 student identification numbers.
muestra aleatoria (pág. 871) Muestra en la que cada miembro de la población tiene igual probabilidad de ser seleccionado.	Para seleccionar una muestra aleatoria de la población de estudiantes de una escuela, puedes usar la computadora para elegir al azar 100 números de identificación estudiantil.
range of a data set (p. 876) The range of a numerical data set is a measure of dispersion. It is the difference of the greatest value and the least value.	The range of the data set 4, 7, 9, 11, 11, 12, 18 is $18 - 4 = 14$.
rango de un conjunto de datos (pág. 876) El rango de un conjunto de datos numéricos es una medida de dispersión. Es la diferencia entre los valores mayor y menor.	El rango del conjunto de datos 4, 7, 9, 11, 11, 12, 18 es $18 - 4 = 14$.
range of a function (p. 35) The set of all outputs of a function.	*See* function.
rango de una función (pág. 35) El conjunto de todas las salidas de una función.	*Ver* función.

ENGLISH-SPANISH GLOSSARY

S

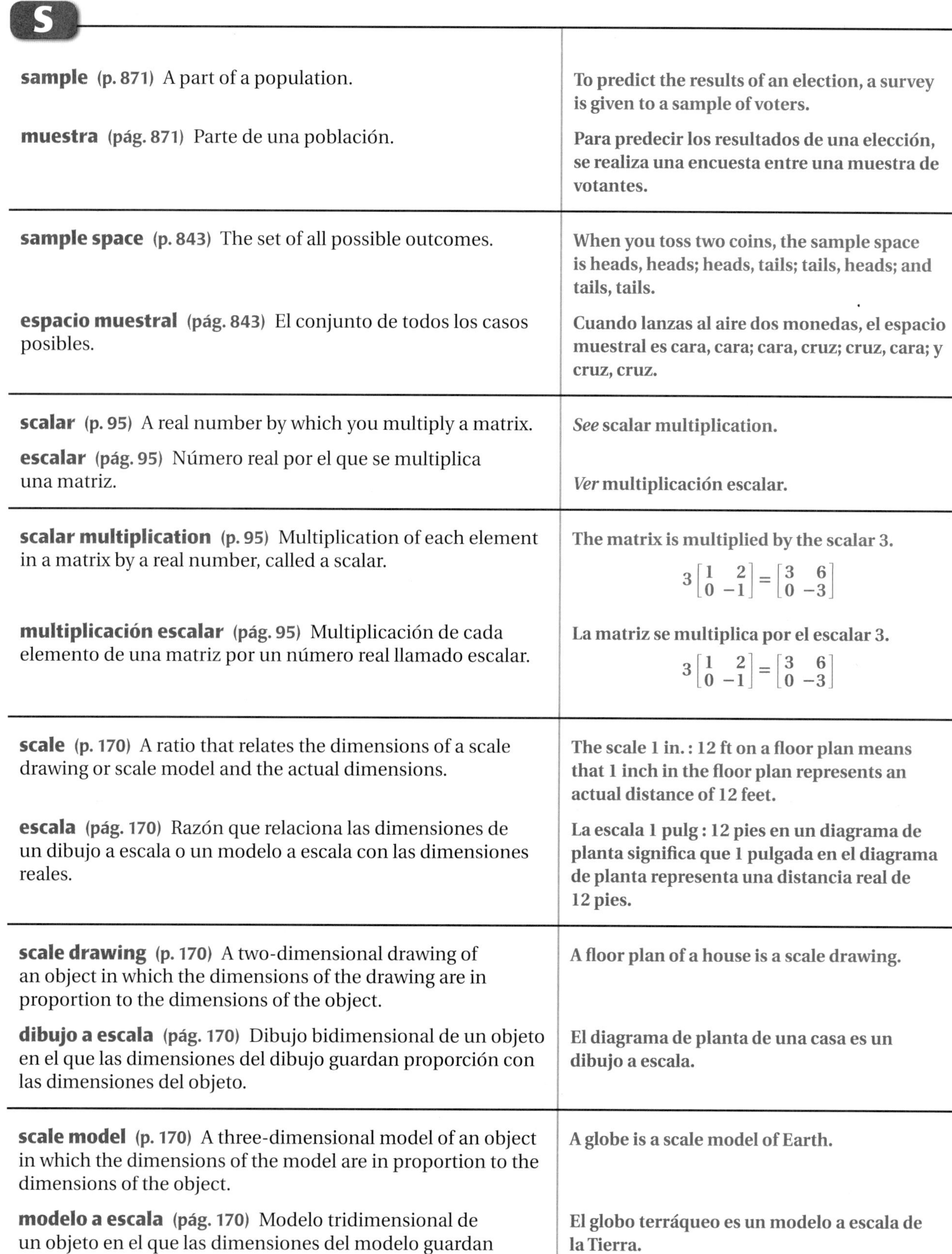

sample (p. 871) A part of a population.	To predict the results of an election, a survey is given to a sample of voters.
muestra (pág. 871) Parte de una población.	Para predecir los resultados de una elección, se realiza una encuesta entre una muestra de votantes.
sample space (p. 843) The set of all possible outcomes.	When you toss two coins, the sample space is heads, heads; heads, tails; tails, heads; and tails, tails.
espacio muestral (pág. 843) El conjunto de todos los casos posibles.	Cuando lanzas al aire dos monedas, el espacio muestral es cara, cara; cara, cruz; cruz, cara; y cruz, cruz.
scalar (p. 95) A real number by which you multiply a matrix.	*See* scalar multiplication.
escalar (pág. 95) Número real por el que se multiplica una matriz.	*Ver* multiplicación escalar.
scalar multiplication (p. 95) Multiplication of each element in a matrix by a real number, called a scalar.	The matrix is multiplied by the scalar 3. $3\begin{bmatrix}1 & 2\\0 & -1\end{bmatrix} = \begin{bmatrix}3 & 6\\0 & -3\end{bmatrix}$
multiplicación escalar (pág. 95) Multiplicación de cada elemento de una matriz por un número real llamado escalar.	La matriz se multiplica por el escalar 3. $3\begin{bmatrix}1 & 2\\0 & -1\end{bmatrix} = \begin{bmatrix}3 & 6\\0 & -3\end{bmatrix}$
scale (p. 170) A ratio that relates the dimensions of a scale drawing or scale model and the actual dimensions.	The scale 1 in. : 12 ft on a floor plan means that 1 inch in the floor plan represents an actual distance of 12 feet.
escala (pág. 170) Razón que relaciona las dimensiones de un dibujo a escala o un modelo a escala con las dimensiones reales.	La escala 1 pulg : 12 pies en un diagrama de planta significa que 1 pulgada en el diagrama de planta representa una distancia real de 12 pies.
scale drawing (p. 170) A two-dimensional drawing of an object in which the dimensions of the drawing are in proportion to the dimensions of the object.	A floor plan of a house is a scale drawing.
dibujo a escala (pág. 170) Dibujo bidimensional de un objeto en el que las dimensiones del dibujo guardan proporción con las dimensiones del objeto.	El diagrama de planta de una casa es un dibujo a escala.
scale model (p. 170) A three-dimensional model of an object in which the dimensions of the model are in proportion to the dimensions of the object.	A globe is a scale model of Earth.
modelo a escala (pág. 170) Modelo tridimensional de un objeto en el que las dimensiones del modelo guardan proporción con las dimensiones del objeto.	El globo terráqueo es un modelo a escala de la Tierra.

scatter plot (p. 325) A graph used to determine whether there is a relationship or trend between paired data.

diagrama de dispersión (pág. 325) Gráfica utilizada para determinar si hay una relación o tendencia entre los pares de datos.

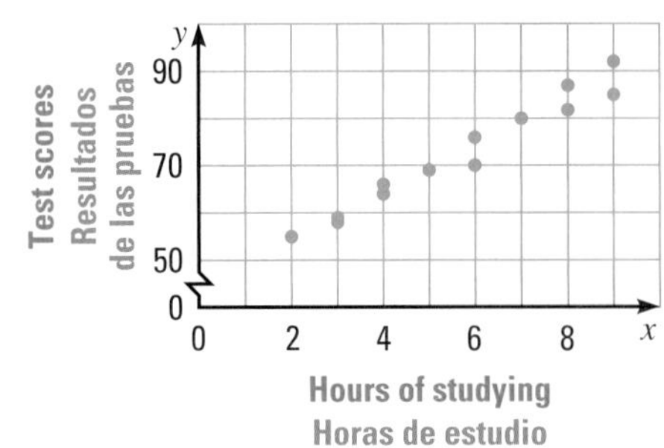

scientific notation (p. 512) A number is written in scientific notation when it is of the form $c \times 10^n$ where $1 \le c < 10$ and n is an integer.

notación científica (pág. 512) Un número está escrito en notación científica cuando es de la forma $c \times 10^n$, donde $1 \le c < 10$ y n es un número entero.

Two million is written in scientific notation as 2×10^6, and 0.547 is written in scientific notation as 5.47×10^{-1}.

El número dos millones escrito en notación científica es 2×10^6, y 0.547 escrito en notación científica es 5.47×10^{-1}.

self-selected sample (p. 871) A sample in which members of the population select themselves by volunteering.

muestra autoseleccionada (pág. 871) Muestra en la que los miembros de la población se seleccionan a sí mismos ofreciéndose a participar.

You can obtain a self-selected sample of a school's student population by asking students to return surveys to a collection box.

Para obtener una muestra autoseleccionada de la población de estudiantes de una escuela, puedes pedir a los estudiantes que hagan la encuesta que la depositen en un recipiente de recogida.

sequence (p. 309) An ordered list of numbers.

progresión (pág. 309) Lista ordenada de números.

$-4, 1, 6, 11, 16, \ldots$ is a sequence.

$-4, 1, 6, 11, 16, \ldots$ es una progresión.

set (p. 71) A collection of distinct objects.

conjunto (pág. 71) Colección de objetos diferenciados.

The set of whole numbers is $W = \{0, 1, 2, 3, \ldots\}$.

El conjunto de los números naturales es $W = \{0, 1, 2, 3, \ldots\}$.

similar figures (p. 174) Figures that have the same shape but not necessarily the same size. Corresponding angles of similar figures are congruent, and the ratios of the lengths of corresponding sides are equal. The symbol ~ indicates that two figures are similar.

figuras semejantes (pág. 174) Figuras que tienen la misma forma pero no necesariamente el mismo tamaño. Los ángulos correspondientes de las figuras semejantes son congruentes, y las razones de las longitudes de los lados correspondientes son iguales. El símbolo ~ indica que dos figuras son semejantes.

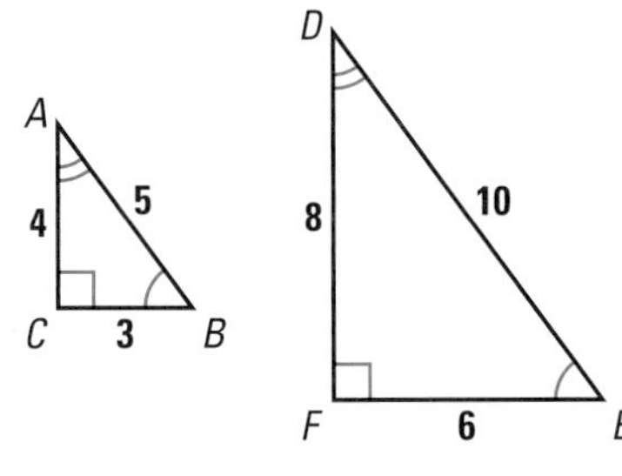

$\triangle ABC \sim \triangle DEF$

ENGLISH-SPANISH GLOSSARY

simplest form of a radical expression (p. 719) A radical expression that has no perfect square factors other than 1 in the radicand, no fractions in the radicand, and no radicals appearing in the denominator of a fraction.	In simplest form, $\sqrt{32}$ is written as $4\sqrt{2}$, and $\frac{5}{\sqrt{7}}$ is written as $\frac{5\sqrt{7}}{7}$.
forma más simple de una expresión radical (pág. 719) Expresión radical que no tiene en el radicando fracciones ni factores cuadrados perfectos distintos de 1 y que no tiene radicales en el denominador de las fracciones.	En la forma más simple, $\sqrt{32}$ se escribe $4\sqrt{2}$, y $\frac{5}{\sqrt{7}}$ se escribe $\frac{5\sqrt{7}}{7}$.
simplest form of a rational expression (p. 795) A rational expression whose numerator and denominator have no factors in common other than 1.	The simplest form of $\frac{2x}{x(x-3)}$ is $\frac{2}{x-3}$.
forma más simple de una expresión racional (pág. 795) Expresión racional cuyo numerador y denominador no tienen más factores en común que el 1.	La forma más simple de $\frac{2x}{x(x-3)}$ es $\frac{2}{x-3}$.
simulation (p. 849) An experiment that you can perform to make predictions about real-world situations.	Each box of Oaties contains 1 of 6 prizes. The probability of getting each prize is $\frac{1}{6}$. To predict the number of boxes of cereal you must buy to win all 6 prizes, you can roll a number cube 1 time for each box of cereal you buy. Keep rolling until you have rolled all 6 numbers.
simulación (pág. 849) Experimento que se puede realizar para hacer predicciones sobre situaciones de la vida real.	Cada paquete de Oaties contiene 1 de un total de 6 premios. La probabilidad de obtener cada premio es $\frac{1}{6}$. Para predecir el número de paquetes de cereales que debes comprar para poder conseguir los 6 premios, puedes lanzar un cubo numerado 1 vez por cada paquete de cereales que compres. Sigue lanzando el cubo hasta obtener los 6 números.
slope (p. 235) The slope m of a nonvertical line is the ratio of the vertical change (the *rise*) to the horizontal change (the *run*) between any two points (x_1, y_1) and (x_2, y_2) on the line: $m = \frac{y_2 - y_1}{x_2 - x_1}$. **pendiente** (pág. 235) La pendiente m de una recta no vertical es la razón del cambio vertical (*distancia vertical*) al cambio horizontal (*distancia horizontal*) entre dos puntos cualesquiera (x_1, y_1) y (x_2, y_2) de la recta: $m = \frac{y_2 - y_1}{x_2 - x_1}$.	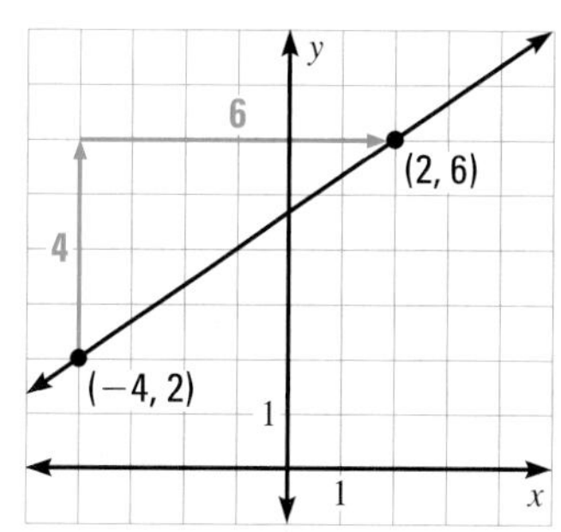 The slope of the line shown is $\frac{4}{6}$, or $\frac{2}{3}$. La pendiente de la recta indicada es $\frac{4}{6}$, ó $\frac{2}{3}$.

ENGLISH-SPANISH GLOSSARY

slope-intercept form **(p. 244)** A linear equation written in the form $y = mx + b$ where m is the slope and b is the y-intercept of the equation's graph.	**$y = 3x + 4$ is in slope-intercept form. The slope of the line is 3, and the y-intercept is 4.**
forma pendiente-intercepto **(pág. 244)** Ecuación lineal escrita en la forma $y = mx + b$, donde m es la pendiente y b es el intercepto en y de la gráfica de la ecuación.	**$y = 3x + 4$ está en la forma pendiente-intercepto. La pendiente de la recta es 3, y el intercepto en y es 4.**
solution of an equation in one variable **(p. 22)** A number that produces a true statement when substituted for the variable in an equation.	**The number 3 is a solution of the equation $8 - 2x = 2$, because $8 - 2(3) = 2$.**
solución de una ecuación con una variable **(pág. 22)** Número que, al sustituirse por la variable de la ecuación, produce un enunciado verdadero.	**El número 3 es una solución de la ecuación $8 - 2x = 2$ ya que $8 - 2(3) = 2$.**
solution of an equation in two variables **(p. 215)** An ordered pair that produces a true statement when the coordinates of the ordered pair are substituted for the variables in the equation.	**$(1, -4)$ is a solution of $3x - y = 7$, because $3(1) - (-4) = 7$.**
solución de una ecuación con dos variables **(pág. 215)** Par ordenado que, al ser sustituidas sus coordenadas por las variables de la ecuación, produce un enunciado verdadero.	**$(1, -4)$ es una solución de $3x - y = 7$ ya que $3(1) - (-4) = 7$.**
solution of an inequality in one variable **(p. 22)** A number that produces a true statement when substituted for the variable in an inequality.	**The number 3 is a solution of the inequality $5 + 3n \leq 20$, because $5 + 3(3) = 14$ and $14 \leq 20$.**
solución de una desigualdad con una variable **(pág. 22)** Número que, al sustituirse por la variable de la desigualdad, produce un enunciado verdadero.	**El número 3 es una solución de la desigualdad $5 + 3n \leq 20$ ya que $5 + 3(3) = 14$ y $14 \leq 20$.**
solution of an inequality in two variables *x* and *y* **(p. 405)** An ordered pair (x, y) that produces a true statement when the values of x and y are substituted into the inequality.	**$(-1, 2)$ is a solution of the inequality $x - 3y < 6$ because $-1 - 3(2) = -7$ and $-7 < 6$.**
solución de una desigualdad con las dos variables *x* e *y* **(pág. 405)** Par ordenado (x, y) que, al sustitutirse los valores de x e y en la desigualdad, produce un enunciado verdadero.	**$(-1, 2)$ es una solución de la desigualdad $x - 3y < 6$ ya que $-1 - 3(2) = -7$ y $-7 < 6$.**
solution of a system of linear equations **(p. 427)** An ordered pair that is a solution of each equation in the system.	**$(3, 2)$ is a solution of the system of linear equations** $x + 2y = 7$ $3x - 2y = 5$ **because each equation is a true statement when 3 is substituted for x and 2 is substituted for y.**
solución de un sistema de ecuaciones lineales **(pág. 427)** Par ordenado que es una solución de cada ecuación del sistema.	**$(3, 2)$ es una solución del sistema de ecuaciones lineales** $x + 2y = 7$ $3x - 2y = 5$ **ya que cada ecuación es un enunciado verdadero cuando x se sustituye por 3 e y se sustituye por 2.**

solution of a system of linear inequalities (p. 466) An ordered pair that is a solution of each inequality in the system.	**(6, −5) is a solution of the system of inequalities $x - y > 7$, $2x + y < 8$ because each inequality is a true statement when 6 is substituted for x and −5 is substituted for y.**
solución de un sistema de desigualdades lineales (pág. 466) Par ordenado que es una solución de cada desigualdad del sistema.	**(6, −5) es una solución del sistema de desigualdades $x - y > 7$, $2x + y < 8$ ya que cada desigualdad es un enunciado verdadero cuando x se sustituye por 6 e y se sustituye por −5.**
square root (p. 110) If $b^2 = a$, then b is a square root of a. The radical symbol $\sqrt{\ }$ represents a nonnegative square root.	**The square roots of 9 are 3 and −3, because $3^2 = 9$ and $(-3)^2 = 9$. So, $\sqrt{9} = 3$ and $-\sqrt{9} = -3$.**
raíz cuadrada (pág. 110) Si $b^2 = a$, entonces b es una raíz cuadrada de a. El signo radical $\sqrt{\ }$ representa una raíz cuadrada no negativa.	**Las raíces cuadradas de 9 son 3 y −3 ya que $3^2 = 9$ y $(-3)^2 = 9$. Así pues, $\sqrt{9} = 3$ y $-\sqrt{9} = -3$.**
square root function (p. 710) A radical function whose equation contains a square root with the independent variable in the radicand.	**$y = 2\sqrt{x+2}$ and $y = \sqrt{x} + 3$ are square root functions.**
función con raíz cuadrada (pág. 710) Función radical representada por una ecuación con una raíz cuadrada en cuyo radicando aparece la variable independiente.	**$y = 2\sqrt{x+2}$ e $y = \sqrt{x} + 3$ son funciones con raíz cuadrada.**
standard deviation (p. 879) The standard deviation of a numerical data set $x_1, x_2, \ldots, x_n$ is a measure of dispersion denoted by σ and computed as the square root of the variance. $\sigma = \sqrt{\frac{(x_1 - \bar{x})^2 + (x_2 - \bar{x})^2 + \ldots + (x_n - \bar{x})^2}{n}}$	**The standard deviation of the data set 3, 9, 13, 23 (with mean = 12) is: $\sigma = \sqrt{\frac{(3-12)^2 + (9-12)^2 + (13-12)^2 + (23-12)^2}{4}}$ $= \sqrt{53} \approx 7.3$**
desviación típica (pág. 879) La desviación típica de un conjunto de datos numéricos $x_1, x_2, \ldots, x_n$ es una medida de dispersión designada por σ y calculada como raíz cuadrada de la varianza. $\sigma = \sqrt{\frac{(x_1 - \bar{x})^2 + (x_2 - \bar{x})^2 + \ldots + (x_n - \bar{x})^2}{n}}$	**La desviación típica del conjunto de datos 3, 9, 13, 23 (con media = 12) es: $\sigma = \sqrt{\frac{(3-12)^2 + (9-12)^2 + (13-12)^2 + (23-12)^2}{4}}$ $= \sqrt{53} \approx 7.3$**
standard form of a linear equation (p. 216) $Ax + By = C$, where A, B, and C are real numbers and A and B are not both zero.	**The linear equation $y = 2x - 3$ can be written in standard form as $2x - y = 3$.**
forma general de una ecuación lineal (pág. 216) $Ax + By = C$, donde A, B y C son números reales, y A y B no son ambos cero.	**La ecuación lineal $y = 2x - 3$ puede escribirse en la forma general como $2x - y = 3$.**

ENGLISH-SPANISH GLOSSARY

standard form of a quadratic equation (p. 643) A quadratic equation in the form $ax^2 + bx + c = 0$ where $a \neq 0$. **forma general de una ecuación cuadrática** (pág. 643) Ecuación cuadrática de la forma $ax^2 + bx + c = 0$, donde $a \neq 0$.	**The quadratic equation $x^2 - 2x - 3 = 0$ is in standard form.** **La ecuación cuadrática $x^2 - 2x - 3 = 0$ está en la forma general.**
standard form of a quadratic function (p. 628) A quadratic function in the form $y = ax^2 + bx + c$ where $a \neq 0$. **forma general de una función cuadrática** (pág. 628) Función cuadrática de la forma $y = ax^2 + bx + c$, donde $a \neq 0$.	**The quadratic function $y = 2x^2 + 5x - 3$ is in standard form.** **La función cuadrática $y = 2x^2 + 5x - 3$ está en la forma general.**
stem-and-leaf plot (p. 881) A data display that organizes data based on their digits. **tabla arborescente** (pág. 881) Presentación de datos que organiza los datos basándose en sus dígitos.	Stem / Raíces | Leaves / Hojas 0 | 8 9 1 | 0 2 3 4 5 5 5 9 2 | 1 1 5 9 Key: / Clave: 1 | 9 = $19
stratified random sample (p. 871) A sample in which a population is divided into distinct groups, and members are selected at random from each group. **muestra aleatoria estratificada** (pág. 871) Muestra en la que la población está dividida en grupos diferenciados, y los miembros de cada grupo se seleccionan al azar.	**You can select a stratified random sample of a school's student population by having a computer randomly choose 25 students from each grade level.** **Para seleccionar una muestra aleatoria estratificada de la población de estudiantes de una escuela, puedes usar la computadora para elegir al azar a 25 estudiantes de cada grado.**
survey (p. 871) A study of one or more characteristics of a group. **encuesta** (pág. 871) Estudio de una o más características de un grupo.	**A magazine invites its readers to mail in answers to a questionnaire rating the magazine.** **Una revista invita a sus lectores a enviar por correo las respuestas a un cuestionario sobre la calidad de la revista.**
system of linear equations (p. 427) Two or more linear equations in the same variables; also called a *linear system*. **sistema de ecuaciones lineales** (pág. 427) Dos o más ecuaciones lineales con las mismas variables; llamado también *sistema lineal*.	**The equations below form a system of linear equations:** $x + 2y = 7$ $3x - 2y = 5$ **Las siguientes ecuaciones forman un sistema de ecuaciones lineales:** $x + 2y = 7$ $3x - 2y = 5$

system of linear inequalities in two variables (p. 466) Two or more linear inequalities in the same variables; also called a *system of inequalities.*	The inequalities below form a system of linear inequalities in two variables: $x - y > 7$ $2x + y < 8$
sistema de desigualdades lineales con dos variables (pág. 466) Dos o más desigualdades lineales con las mismas variables; llamado también *sistema de desigualdades.*	Las siguientes desigualdades forman un sistema de desigualdades lineales con dos variables: $x - y > 7$ $2x + y < 8$
systematic sample (p. 871) A sample in which a rule is used to select members of the population.	You can select a systematic sample of a school's student population by choosing every tenth student on an alphabetical list of all students at the school.
muestra sistemática (pág. 871) Muestra en la que se usa una regla para seleccionar a los miembros de la población.	Para seleccionar una muestra sistemática de la población de estudiantes de una escuela, puedes elegir a cada décimo estudiante de una lista ordenada alfabéticamente de todos los estudiantes de la escuela.

T

terms of an expression (p. 97) The parts of an expression that are added together.	The terms of the expression $3x + (-4) + (-6x) + 2$ are $3x$, -4, $-6x$, and 2.
términos de una expresión (pág. 97) Las partes de una expresión que se suman.	Los términos de la expresión $3x + (-4) + (-6x) + 2$ son $3x$, -4, $-6x$ y 2.
theoretical probability (p. 844) When all outcomes are equally likely, the theoretical probability of an event is the ratio of the number of favorable outcomes to the total number of possible outcomes. The probability of event *A* is written as *P*(*A*).	A bag of 20 marbles contains 8 red marbles. The theoretical probability of randomly choosing a red marble from the bag is $\frac{8}{20} = \frac{2}{5}$, 40%, or 0.4.
probabilidad teórica (pág. 844) Cuando todos los casos son igualmente posibles, la probabilidad teórica de un suceso es la razón entre el número de casos favorables y el número total de casos posibles. La probabilidad del suceso *A* se escribe *P*(*A*).	Una bolsa de 20 canicas contiene 8 canicas rojas. La probabilidad teórica de sacar al azar una canica roja de la bolsa es $\frac{8}{20} = \frac{2}{5}$, 40% ó 0.4.
transformation (p. 213) For a given set of points, a transformation produces an image by applying a rule to the coordinates of the points.	Translations, vertical stretches, vertical shrinks, and reflections are transformations.
transformación (pág. 213) Para un conjunto dado de puntos, una transformación produce una imagen al aplicar una regla a las coordenadas de los puntos.	Las traslaciones, las expansiones verticales, las contracciones verticales y las reflexiones son transformaciones.

translation (p. 213) A translation moves every point in a figure the same distance in the same direction.

traslación (pág. 213) Una traslación desplaza cada punto de una figura la misma distancia en la misma dirección.

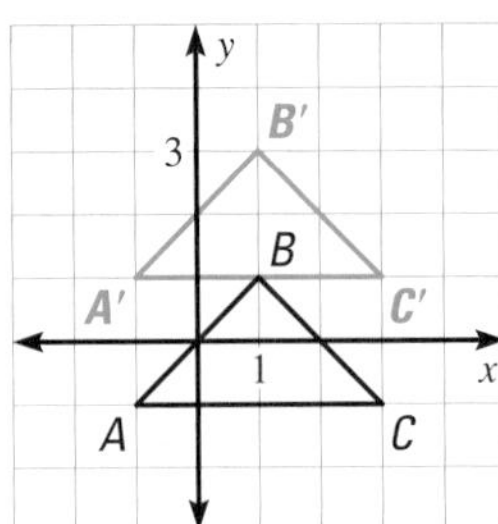

$\triangle ABC$ is translated up 2 units.

$\triangle ABC$ es trasladada 2 unidades hacia arriba.

trinomial (p. 555) A polynomial with three terms.

trinomio (pág. 555) Polinomio con tres términos.

$2x^2 + x - 5$ is a trinomial.

$2x^2 + x - 5$ es un trinomio.

U

union (p. 71) The union of two sets A and B is the set of all elements in *either* A or B. The union of A and B is written as $A \cup B$.

unión (pág. 71) La unión de dos conjuntos A y B es el conjunto de todos los elementos en A *o* B. La unión de A y B se escribe $A \cup B$.

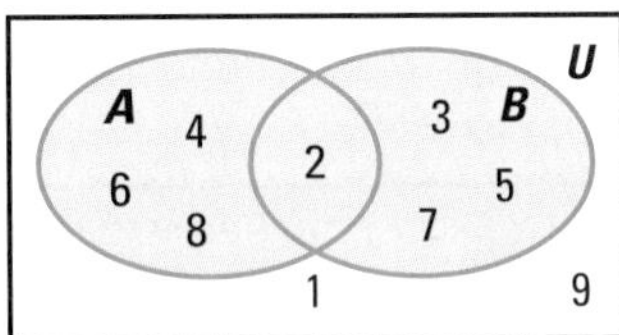

$A \cup B = \{2, 3, 4, 5, 6, 7, 8\}$

unit rate (p. 17) A rate in which the denominator of the fraction is 1 unit.

relación unitaria (pág. 17) Relación en la que el denominador de la fracción es 1 unidad.

$\frac{55 \text{ miles}}{1 \text{ hour}}$, or 55 mi/h, is a unit rate.

$\frac{55 \text{ millas}}{1 \text{ hora}}$, ó 55 mi/h, es una relación unitaria.

universal set (p. 71) The set of all elements under consideration, written as U.

conjunto universal (pág. 71) El conjunto de todos los elementos en cuestión, escrito U.

If the universal set is the set of positive integers, then $U = \{1, 2, 3, \ldots\}$.

Si el conjunto universal es el conjunto de los números enteros positivos, entonces $U = \{1, 2, 3, \ldots\}$.

upper quartile (p. 887) The median of the upper half of an ordered data set.

The upper quartile of the data set below is 23.

median (↓ 17), upper quartile (↓ 23)

8 10 14 17 20 **23** 50

cuartil superior (pág. 887) La mediana de la mitad superior de un conjunto de datos ordenados.

El cuartil superior del siguiente conjunto de datos es 23.

mediana (↓ 17), cuartil superior (↓ 23)

8 10 14 17 20 **23** 50

V

variable (p. 2) A letter that is used to represent one or more numbers.

variable (pág. 2) Letra que sirve para representar uno o más números.

In the expressions $5n$, $n + 1$, and $8 - n$, the letter n is the variable.

En las expresiones $5n$, $n + 1$ y $8 - n$, la letra n es la variable.

variance (p. 879) The variance of a numerical data set $x_1, x_2, \ldots, x_n$ is a measure of dispersion denoted by σ^2 and given by:

$$\sigma^2 = \frac{(x_1 - \bar{x})^2 + (x_2 - \bar{x})^2 + \ldots + (x_n - \bar{x})^2}{n}$$

varianza (pág. 879) La varianza de un conjunto de datos numéricos $x_1, x_2, \ldots, x_n$ es una medida de dispersión designada por σ^2 y dada por:

$$\sigma^2 = \frac{(x_1 - \bar{x})^2 + (x_2 - \bar{x})^2 + \ldots + (x_n - \bar{x})^2}{n}$$

The variance of the data set 3, 9, 13, 23 (with mean = 12) is:

$$\sigma^2 = \frac{(3 - 12)^2 + (9 - 12)^2 + (13 - 12)^2 + (23 - 12)^2}{4} = 53$$

La varianza del conjunto de datos 3, 9, 13, 23 (con media = 12) es:

$$\sigma^2 = \frac{(3 - 12)^2 + (9 - 12)^2 + (13 - 12)^2 + (23 - 12)^2}{4} = 53$$

verbal model (p. 16) A verbal model describes a real-world situation using words as labels and using math symbols to relate the words.

modelo verbal (pág. 16) Un modelo verbal describe una situación de la vida real mediante palabras que la exponen y símbolos matemáticos que relacionan esas palabras.

A verbal model and algebraic expression for dividing a dollars in a tip jar among 6 people:

Un modelo verbal y una expresión algebraica utilizados para dividir entre 6 personas a dólares del recipiente de las propinas:

Amount in jar / Cantidad del recipiente ÷ Number of people / Número de personas

$a \div 6$

vertex form of a quadratic function (p. 669) A quadratic function in the form $y = a(x - h)^2 + k$ where $a \neq 0$. The vertex of the graph of the function is (h, k).

forma de vértice de una función cuadrática (pág. 669) Función cuadrática de la forma $y = a(x - h)^2 + k$, donde $a \neq 0$. El vértice de la gráfica de la función es (h, k).

The quadratic function $y = -2(x + 1)^2 - 5$ is in vertex form. The vertex of the graph of the function is $(-1, -5)$.

La función cuadrática $y = -2(x + 1)^2 - 5$ está en la forma de vértice. El vértice de la gráfica de la función es $(-1, -5)$.

vertex of a parabola (p. 628) The lowest or highest point on a parabola.

vértice de una parábola (pág. 628) El punto más bajo o más alto de la parábola.

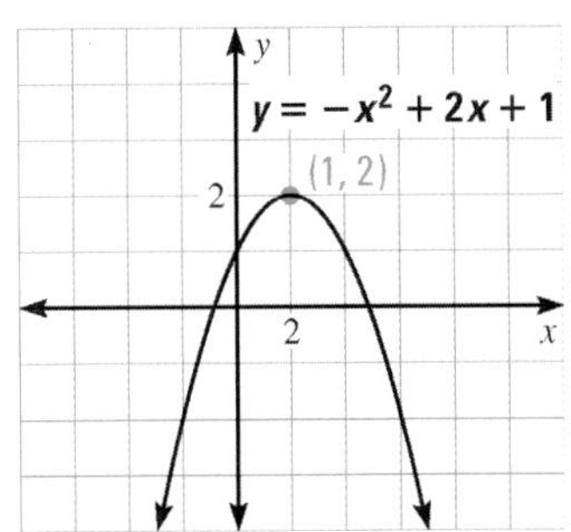

The vertex of the graph of $y = -x^2 + 2x + 1$ is the point (1, 2).

El vértice de la gráfica de $y = -x^2 + 2x + 1$ es el punto (1, 2).

vertical motion model (p. 577) A model for the height of an object that is propelled into the air but has no power to keep itself in the air.

The vertical motion model for an object thrown upward with an initial vertical velocity of 20 feet per second from an initial height of 8 feet is $h = -16t^2 + 20t + 8$ where h is the height (in feet) of the object t seconds after it is thrown.

modelo de movimiento vertical (pág. 577) Modelo para representar la altura de un objeto que es lanzado hacia arriba pero que no tiene potencia para mantenerse en el aire.

El modelo de movimiento vertical de un objeto lanzado hacia arriba con una velocidad vertical inicial de 20 pies por segundo desde una altura inicial de 8 pies es $h = -16t^2 + 20t + 8$, donde h es la altura (en pies) del objeto t segundos después del lanzamiento.

vertical shrink (p. 213) A vertical shrink moves every point in a figure toward the x-axis, while points on the x-axis remain fixed.

contracción vertical (pág. 213) La contracción vertical desplaza cada punto de una figura en dirección del eje de x, mientras los puntos del eje de x permanecen fijos.

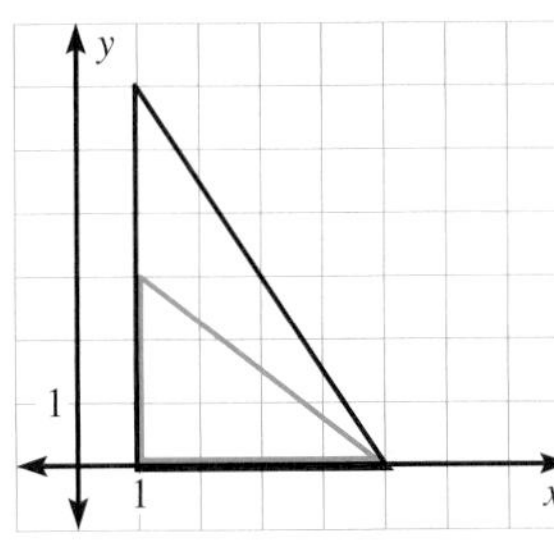

The black triangle is shrunk vertically to the green triangle.

El triángulo negro se contrae verticalmente hacia el triángulo verde.

vertical stretch (p. 213) A vertical stretch moves every point in a figure away from the x-axis, while points on the x-axis remain fixed.

expansión vertical (pág. 213) La expansión vertical desplaza cada punto de una figura alejándose del eje de x, mientras los puntos del eje de x permanecen fijos.

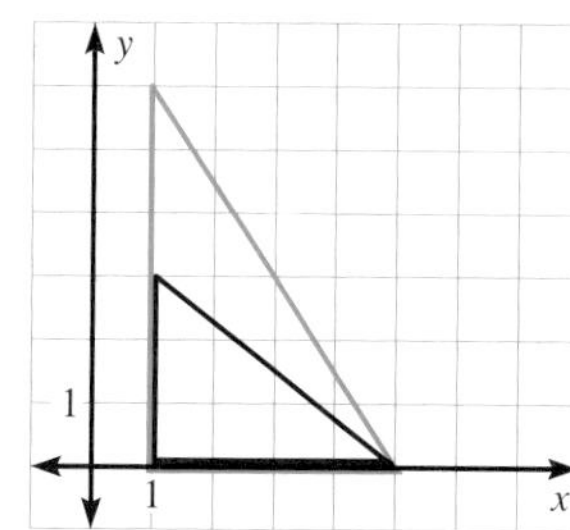

The black triangle is stretched vertically to the green triangle.

El triángulo negro se expande verticalmente hacia el triángulo verde.

W

whole numbers (p. 64) The numbers 0, 1, 2, 3, ...

0, 8, and 106 are whole numbers.
−1 and 0.6 are *not* whole numbers.

números naturales (pág. 64) Los números 0, 1, 2, 3, ...

0, 8 y 106 son números naturales.
−1 y 0.6 *no* son números naturales.

X

x-intercept (p. 225) The x-coordinate of a point where a graph crosses the x-axis.

intercepto en x (pág. 225) La coordenada x de un punto donde la gráfica corta al eje de x.

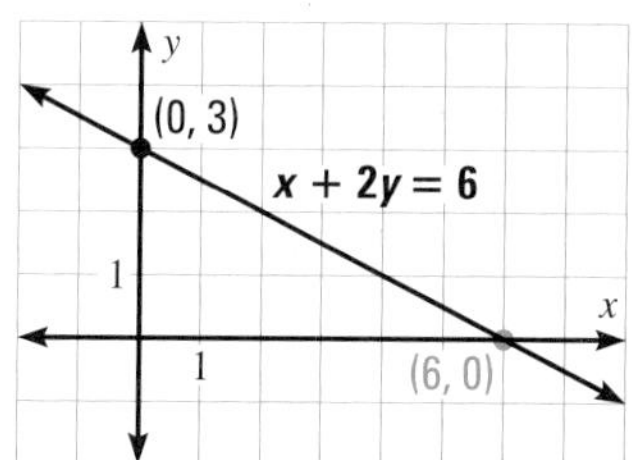

The x-intercept is 6.

El intercepto en x es 6.

Y

y-intercept (p. 225) The y-coordinate of a point where a graph crosses the y-axis.

intercepto en y (pág. 225) La coordenada y de un punto donde la gráfica corta al eje de y.

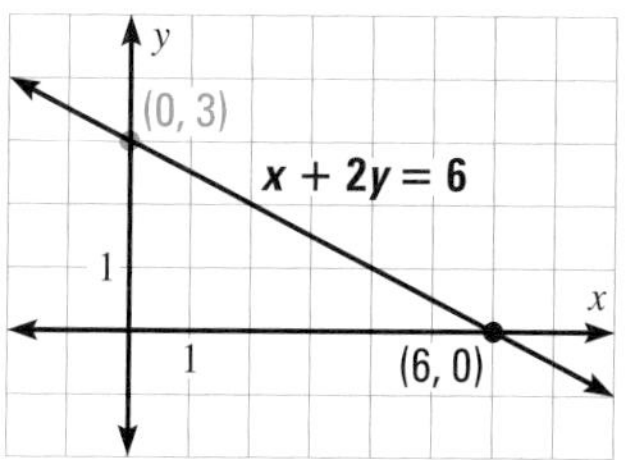

The y-intercept is 3.

El intercepto en y es 3.

ENGLISH-SPANISH GLOSSARY

Z

zero exponent (p. 503) If $a \neq 0$, then $a^0 = 1$. **exponente cero** (pág. 503) Si $a \neq 0$, entonces $a^0 = 1$.	$(-7)^0 = 1$
zero of a function (p. 337) An x-value for which $f(x) = 0$ (or $y = 0$). **cero de una función** (pág. 337) Un valor x para el que $f(x) = 0$ (o $y = 0$).	The zero of $f(x) = 2x - 4$ is 2 because $f(2) = 0$. El cero de $f(x) = 2x - 4$ es 2 ya que $f(2) = 0$.

Index

A

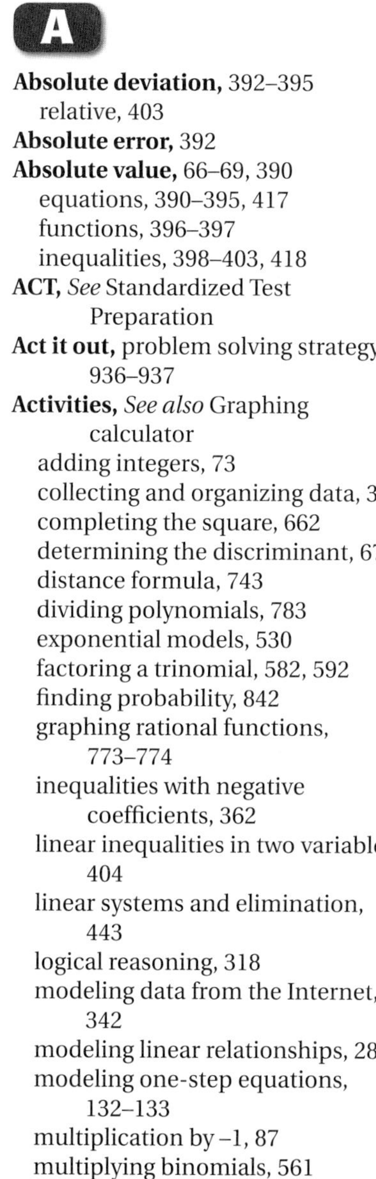

INDEX

INDEX

D

E

F

INDEX

G

N

INDEX

O

P

Q

INDEX

INDEX

INDEX

T

U

INDEX

Credits

Photography

Cover © Amy and Chuck Wiley/Wales/Index Stock Imagery; **iv** *top* Meridian Creative Group; *top center* Robert C. Jenks, Jenks Studio; *bottom center* McDougal Littell; *bottom* Jerry Head Jr.; **viii** © J.D. Dallet/A.G.E. Fotostock; **ix** © Art Wolfe/Getty Images; **x** © A. Witte/C. Mahaney/Getty Images; **xi** © Rick Havner/AP/Wide World Photos; **xii** © Joseph Sohm/Pan America/PictureQuest; **xiii** © Liz Hymans/Panoramic Images; **xiv** © Kerrick James/Getty Images; **xv** JPL/NASA; **xvi** © Tom Bean/Corbis; **xvii** © Donald Miralle/Getty Images; **xviii** © Hisham F. Ibrahim/Getty Images; **xix** © Joseph Sohm, ChromoSohm Media Inc.; **xx** © Tom Carter/PhotoEdit; **xxii–1** © Geoffrey Clifford/Getty Images; **2** © John C. Russell/Photonica/Getty Images; **4** McDougal Littell; **6** © Scott S. Warren/Aurora Photos; **8** © Royalty-Free/Comstock Images; **10** © David Young-Wolff/PhotoEdit; **12** © Sue Ogrocki/AP/ Wide World Photos; **15** *printer* © PhotoDisc/Getty Images; **15** *photo* © Royalty-Free/Stockbyte; **17** © Steve Dunwell/Index Stock Imagery; **19** © Patrick Ward/Corbis; **21** © Tommy Baynard; **23** © Seb Rogers/Alamy; **24** © Chris Collins/Corbis; **25** © Tommy Baynard; **27** © Tony Avelar/Animals Animals; **28** © Michael Stevens/Fog Stock; **32** © Scott Warren/Aurora Photos; **35** © Michael Newman/PhotoEdit; **37** © Aneal Vohra/Index Stock Imagery; **42** McDougal Littell; **43** Lawrence Migdale/PIX/McDougal Littell; **47** © Marc Serota/Reuters/Corbis; **51** © Derek Payne/Alamy; **62–63** © Altrendo/Getty Images; **64** © Evan Vucci/AP/Wide World Photos; **70** © John Chumack/Photo Researchers, Inc.; **74** © Brian Spurlock/SportsChrome; **76** © Bob Krist/Corbis; **78** *center right* © LLC, FogStock/Index Stock Imagery; **80** © Stephen Alvarez/Aurora Photos; **83** © Myrleen Ferguson Cate/PhotoEdit; **85** © Ron Chapple/Getty Images; **86** © Gregory Bull/AP/Wide World Photos; **88** © Natphoto/Getty Images; **90** © Peter Essick/Aurora Photos; **92** © Philip Coblentz/Getty Images; **96** © Patrik Giardino/Corbis; **98** © Bob Daemmrich/Image Works, Inc.; **103** © Jonathan Ferrey/Getty Images; **104** © Duncan Adams/AP/Wide World Photos; **107** Photo courtesy of Mehgan Heaney-Grier, Freedive Champion & Jim Edds, photographer; **108** *both* USGS; **110** © Sylvain Grandadam/Getty Images; **115** Photo from the New York Hall of Science/www.minotaurmazes.com; **130** *top* © Gary Bell/Oceanwide Images; **131** *center right* © Gary Bell/Getty Images; **134** © Barros & Barros/Getty Images; **137** © Anja Niedringhaus/AP/Wide World Photos; **139** *top right* Jay Penni Photography/McDougal Littell; **139** *bottom right* © Gary Bell/Oceanwide Images ; **141** © Stephen Frink/Corbis; **143** © Royalty-Free/Corbis; **145** © M. Spencer Green/AP/Wide World Photos; **148** © Michael Newman/PhotoEdit; **150** © Jeff Foott/PictureQuest; **154** © Mark Lennihan/AP/Wide World Photos; **161** © Johner/Photonica/Getty Images; **162** © Reuters/Corbis; **164** © Lowell Georgia/Corbis; **166** © Marc Muench/Getty Images; **168** © Michael S. Yamashita/Corbis; **176** © Reuters/Corbis; **178** © FoodCollection/Index Stock Imagery; **180** © Mark Gibson/Index Stock Imagery; **184** © Tony Garcia/SuperStock; **189** © Royalty-Free/Corbis; **204–205** © Rommel/Masterfile; **206** © Window Observational Research Facility/NASA; **208** © David J. & Janice L. Frent Collection/Corbis; **215** U.S. Navy photo; **220** © Bill Greene Globe Staff/The Boston Globe/Merlin-Net, Inc.; **225** © Alexis Rosenfeld/Photo Researchers, Inc.; **228** © Alexis Rosenfeld/Photo Researchers, Inc.; **233** © Jim Cooper/AP/Wide World Photos; **234** *all* McDougal Littell; **235** © Kevin Fleming/Corbis; **237** *café* © Paul Edmondson/Getty Images; **237** *soup* © Judd Pilossof/Getty Images; **241** © Kevin Fleming/Corbis; **244** © Peter Williams/AP/Wide World Photos; **245** © Kevin P. Casey/Corbis; **248** © Robert Laberge/Getty Images; **253** © Lionel Cironneau/AP/ Wide World Photos; **255** © The North Platte Telegraph, Kristina Jergensen/AP/Wide World Photos; **259** © Don Emmert/Staff/Getty Images; **262** © William Campbell/AP/Wide World Photos; **263** © Robert Winslow/Animals Animals; **267** © Scott Markewitz/Getty Images; **269** © Jeff Greenberg/Image Works, Inc.; **280–281** © Will & Deni McIntyre/Corbis; **282** Jay Penni Photography/McDougal Littell; **283** © Jim Cummins/Getty Images; **285** © Comstock Images/Alamy; **288** © Yann Arthus-Bertrand/Corbis; **292** © Tony Ashby/AFP/Getty Images; **295** © Lester Lefkowitz/Corbis; **302** © Ken Biggs/Getty Images; **307** © Robert W. Ginn/PhotoEdit; **311** © The Photo Library Wales/Alamy; **313** © BananaStock/Alamy; **317** © Tom Stewart/Corbis; **319** © Phillip Colla/www.OceanLight.com; **325** © Bob & Suzanne Clemenz; **327** © Tim Thompson/Corbis; **335** *both* © Nick Ut/AP/Wide World Photos; **337** © Cathrine Wessel/Corbis; **339** *bottom right* © Kevin Gilbert/Getty Images; **341** © Erich Kuchling/Alamy; **343** © David Middleton/Photo Researchers, Inc.; **354–355** © Ryan McVay/PhotoDisc/Getty Images; **356** © Royalty-Free/Corbis; **358** © Ralf-Finn Hestoft/Corbis; **360** © David Madison/Getty Images; **363** © Alan Becker/Getty Images; **365** © John Powell Photographer/Alamy; **368** © William Albert Allard/National Geographic Image Collection; **369** © Roy Toft/Getty Images ; **371** © Eric Risberg/AP/Wide World Photos; **373** © Melanie Acevedo/Botanica/Getty Images; **375** © Eric Risberg/AP/Wide World Photos; **380** Courtesy of www.apcamcar.com; **383** DLR/NASA; **386** Courtesy of and Copyright, Peabody Essex Museum, Salem, Massachusetts; **389** © Neil Gilchrist/Panoramic Images; **390** © AP/Wide World Photos; **392** © Darren Sweet/PictureChasers.com; **394** © Patrik Giardino/Corbis; **398** © Jacqueline Malonson/Jax Photography; **402** © Michael Newman/PhotoEdit; **403** © D. Robert & Lorri Franz/Corbis; **405** © Greig Cranna/Index Stock Imagery; **408** © Keith Woods/Getty Images; **410** © Paul J. Sutton/Duomo/Corbis; **413** © Thomas Hallstein/Outsight Photography; **424–425** © Thomas Brownold/Animals Animals; **427** © CB/Cai Daizheng/Photocome/Kyodonews; **429** © Jose Carillo/PhotoEdit; **432** McDougal Littell; **433** *top left* © Royalty-Free/Corbis; **433** *top center* Elliptical Trainer photo courtesy of NordicTrack.com; **433** *top right* © Royalty-Free/Corbis; **435** © Gary Pearl/StockShot/Alamy; **437** The iOptiJr mouse with color jackets courtesy of macally.com and Mace Group Inc.; **444** © David Young-Wolff/PhotoEdit; **449** © Michael Schmitt/Animals Animals; **450** © Nick Rowe/PhotoDisc/Getty Images; **451** © Amos Schliack/StockFood; **456** © Kob-StockFood Munich/StockFood; **458** © Dennis MacDonald/PhotoEdit; **459** © Bobby Model/Getty Images; **466** © Dennis MacDonald/PhotoEdit; **471** © Comstock Images; **473** © Jeff Greenberg/A.G.E. Fotostock; **486–487** © Ron Kimball/Ron Kimball Stock; **489** © Scott Camazine/Photo Researchers, Inc.; **491** © Michael Busselle/Corbis; **493** © Royalty-Free/Getty Images; **495** © Roger Ressmeyer/Corbis; **498** © Paul J. Mayo - Australia; **500** Akira Fujii/ESA; **503** © Robin Tinay Sallie/Akron Beacon Journal/AP/Wide World Photos; **505** *both* © Ted Kinsman/Photo Researchers, Inc.; **507** *center left* © Carlyn Iverson/Photo Researchers, Inc.; **507** *center right* © mediacolor's/Alamy; **512** © Brand X Pictures/Getty Images; **516** © Mark & Audrey Gibson/Stock Connection; **518** SOHO/NASA; **520** © Ron Kimball/Ron Kimball Stock; **522** © Michael Kelley/Getty Images; **530** McDougal Littell; **531** © Cathrine Wessel/Corbis; **534** © Darrell Gulin/Corbis; **537** *top* Scott Johnson/Indiana DNR/USFWS; **537** *bottom* © PhotoDisc/Getty Images; **538** © Jon Riley/Getty Images; **541** © PhotoDisc/Getty Images; **552–553** © Martin Harvey/Alamy; **554** © Tom Bean/Corbis; **556** © Rick Friedman/Corbis; **558** © Digital Vision/Corbis; **559** © Robert Galbraith/Reuters/Corbis; **562** © Neale Haynes/ImageState/Alamy; **567** *photo* © PhotoDisc/Getty Images; **567** *frame* © PhotoSpin; **568** © Thinkstock/Getty

Images; **569** © Alan Carey/Photo Researchers, Inc.; **571** *top left* © Ulrike Schanz/Animals Animals; **571** *top* © Fritz Prenzel/Animals Animals; **573** *top* © Royalty-Free/Corbis; **573** *football* © PhotoDisc/Getty Images; **573** *grass* © PowerPhotos/PhotoSpin; **574** © Royalty-Free/Corbis; **575** © Aase Bjerner; **577** © George Holton/Photo Researchers, Inc.; **579** © James H. Robinson/Photo Researchers, Inc.; **583** © Richard Berenholtz/Corbis; **588** © Richard Berenholtz/Corbis; **593** © Picture Finders LTD/eStock Photo; **595** © Mike Powell/Getty Images; **598** *bottom right* © Martin Harvey/Natural History Photographic Agency; **598** *top left* © Richard Hutchings/Photo Researchers, Inc.; **598** *top center* © Kevin Peterson/Getty Images; **598** *top right* © Rubberball Productions/Getty Images; **600** © Scott Camazine/Alamy; **602** © HIRB/Index Stock Imagery; **606** © Lawrence M. Sawyer/Getty Images; **614** © Brian Drake/SportsChrome; **626–627** © Bill Stevenson/Alamy; **628** © Digital Vision/Getty Images; **631** © Roger Ressmeyer/Corbis; **635** *top right* © Ric Ergenbright; **637** © Dwight Cendrowski; **639** Courtesy of Dallas Convention Center; **643** *top right* © Jeff Greenberg/PhotoEdit; **648** © Rhoda Peacher/R Photographs; **652** *top right* © Rhoda Peacher/R Photographs; **658** © Kim Karpeles; **661** © Amwell/Getty Images; **663** *center* © Jonathan Nourok/PhotoEdit; **671** © Adam Woolfitt/Corbis; **678** © Jeff Gross/Getty Images; **682** © Davis Barber/PhotoEdit; **684** © David A. Northcott/Corbis ; **687** © John Kelly/Getty Images; **689** © David A. Northcott/Corbis; **690** © Davies & Starr/Getty Images; **708–709** © Robert Holland/Getty Images; **710** © Michael Newman/PhotoEdit; **715** © Vince Streano/Corbis; **716** *top right* © Tim Zurowski/Corbis; **716** *top left* © Darrell Gulin/Corbis; **719** © John Elk/Elk Photography; **726** © Tony Freeman/PhotoEdit; **729** © Robert Winslow/Animals Animals; **731** © Iconica/Photonica/Getty Images; **733** Jacques Descloitres/MODIS Rapid Response Team, NASA/GSFC; **735** *right* © Galen Rowell/Corbis; **735** *left* © Philip Gould/Corbis; **737** © Joseph Pobereskin/Getty Images; **744** © Scott Goodwin/Boston MedFlight; **762–763** © Roland Birke/Phototake; **765** *top right* © Dwight Cendrowski; **768** © Tony Freeman/PhotoEdit; **770** © Rhoda Peacher/R Photographs; **771** *both* © GK Hart/Vikki Hart/Getty Images; **772** *top right* © Lee Snider/Corbis; **775** © Matt York, Staff/AP/Wide World Photos; **778** © Richard Cummins/Corbis; **781** © Phillip Colla/www.OceanLight.com; **784** © Ace Stock Limited/Alamy; **787** © Michael Newman/PhotoEdit; **790** © Rubberball Productions/Getty Images; **791** © Carolina Biological Supply Company/Phototake; **794** © Allana Wesley White/Corbis; **797** © 2005, Motorola, Inc./ Reproduced with Permission from Motorola, Inc. ; **799** © Zigy Kaluzny/Getty Images; **800** © Tom Stewart/Corbis; **802** © Adrees A. Latif/Reuters/Corbis; **807** © David Butow/Corbis; **808** © Ron Kuntz/Bettmann/Corbis; **809** © Bob Daemmrich/PhotoEdit; **812** © Michael Mahovlich/Masterfile; **820** © David Stoecklein/Corbis; **824** © Paul J. Sutton/Duomo/Corbis; **825** © Jim West/Jim West Photography; **840–841** © Comstock Production Department/Alamy; **840** *ball* © PhotoDisc/Getty Images; **843** © Michelle D. Bridwell/PhotoEdit; **847** © Royalty-Free/Corbis; **848** © Matt Brown/NewSport/Corbis; **851** © Mary Kate Denny/PhotoEdit; **856** © Don Smetzer/Getty Images; **857** *both* © Stockbyte/Royalty-Free; **861** © Tim Davis/Corbis; **870** © Dante Fenolio/Photo Researchers, Inc.; **871** © New Moon/Panoramic Images; **872** © Tom Carter/PhotoEdit; **874** © David Young-Wolff/PhotoEdit; **875** © PictureChasers.com 2005; **876** © Alan Thornton/Getty Images; **878** © Leslie Parr/Getty Images; **881** © Paul Conklin/PhotoEdit; **882** © 2003 Robyn Beck/Staff/AFP/Getty; **885** © Bettmann/Corbis; **887** DLR/NASA; **894** © Mark Dadswell/Staff/Getty Images.

Illustration and Map

Argosy **1, 63, 131, 205, 281, 355, 425, 487, 553, 627, 631, 633, 709, 763, 841**; Steve Cowden **32, 40** *center*, **240, 258, 308, 323** *center right*, **440** *bottom center*, **446, 465, 615, 646, 654, 668, 675, 715, 733, 750, 752** *bottom left*, **781, 855**; Stephen Durke **634, 648** *center*, **658, 741** *both*, **741**; John Francis **815**; Patrick Gnan/Deborah Wolfe, Ltd. **228, 249, 323** *bottom right*, **468, 526, 567, 588** *both*, **588, 591, 742, 865**; Sharon and Joel Harris **514**; Mark Heine/Deborah Wolfe **28**; Steve McEntee **640, 683, 702**; Karen Minot **890**; Laurie O'Keefe **866**; Tony Randazzo **508, 604, 819**; Mark Schroeder **690**; Dan Stuckenschneider **20, 116, 145, 146, 152** *center*, **221, 231** *center*, **315, 361, 373, 381, 385, 411, 471, 494, 525, 564, 609, 612** *top right*, **612** *bottom right*, **612, 648** *bottom*, **667, 680, 725, 772** *both*, **772, 829, 862**; Matt Zang/American Artists **511, 657, 722, 749, 771, 891.**

Worked-Out Solutions

This section of the book provides step-by-step solutions to exercises with circled exercise numbers. These solutions provide models that can help guide your work with the homework exercises.

The separate **Selected Answers** section follows this section. It provides numerous answers that you can use to check your own answers.

Chapter 1

Lesson 1.1 (pp. 5–7)

19. three tenths to the fourth power; $(0.3)^4 = 0.3 \cdot 0.3 \cdot 0.3 \cdot 0.3$

35. $\left(\frac{3}{5}\right)^3 = \frac{3}{5} \cdot \frac{3}{5} \cdot \frac{3}{5} = \frac{27}{125}$

51. a. Total length $= 3.5 + 5.5 + 3 = 12$

The total length is 12 inches.

b. Evaluate $12f$ for $f = 12$: $12(12) = 144$

The area of water surface needed is 144 square inches.

Lesson 1.2 (pp. 10–12)

16. $\frac{1}{6}(6 + 18) - 2^2 = \frac{1}{6}(24) - 2^2$

$= \frac{1}{6}(24) - 4$

$= 4 - 4 = 0$

35. a. Total cost $= 3 \cdot 0.99 + 2 \cdot 9.95$

$= 2.97 + 19.90 = 22.87$

The total cost is \$22.87.

b. Amount of money left $= 25 - 22.87 = 2.13$

The amount you have left is \$2.13.

Lesson 1.3 (pp. 18–20)

11. 7 less than twice a number k

Less than is subtraction after the next term, and twice a number is two times a number. The expression is $2k - 7$.

35. [Number of months in y years] = [Number of months in one year] + [Number of years]

$= 12y$

The number of months is $12y$.

33. a. 48 ounce container:

$\frac{\$2.64}{48 \text{ ounces}} = \frac{\$2.64 \div 48}{48 \text{ ounces} \div 48} = \frac{\$.055}{1 \text{ ounce}}$

The unit rate is \$.055 per ounce.

64 ounce container:

$\frac{\$3.84}{64 \text{ ounces}} = \frac{\$3.84 \div 64}{64 \text{ ounces} \div 64} = \frac{\$.06}{1 \text{ ounce}}$

The unit rate is \$.06 per ounce.

b. Since \$.055 is less than \$.06, the 48 ounce container costs less per ounce.

c. Write a verbal model and an expression. Let n be the number of ounces.

[Savings] = [Unit rate for 64 ounce container] • [Number of ounces] − [Unit rate for 48 ounce container] • [Number of ounces]

$= 0.06n - 0.055n$

Evaluate the expression when $n = 192$.

$0.06(192) - 0.055(192) = 0.96$

The amount of money you save is \$.96.

Lesson 1.4 (pp. 24–26)

7. 5 more than a number is written as $t + 5$.

The product of 9 and the quantity 5 more than a number t is written as $9(t + 5)$.

The product of 9 and the quantity 5 more than a number t is less than 6 is written as $9(t + 5) < 6$.

WORKED-OUT SOLUTIONS

41. Write a verbal model. Then write an equation. Let w be the winning team's time.

U.S. team's time	$-$	Winning team's time	$=$	Difference in time

$173 - w = 6$

Use mental math to solve the equation. Think: 173 less what number is 6?

Because $173 - 167 = 6$, the solution is 167 hours.

Lesson 1.5 (pp. 31–33)

5. You know that the temperature in Rome, Italy, is 30°C, and the temperature in Dallas, Texas, is 83°F.

You want to find out which temperature is higher.

17. Step 1: You know the total weight of your backpack and its contents is $13\frac{3}{8}$ pounds. The total weight you want to carry is no more than 15 pounds. The weight of each bottle of water is $\frac{3}{4}$ pound. You want to find out how many extra bottles of water you can add to your backpack. First find the additional weight you can add to your backpack.

Step 2: Write a verbal model that represents what you want to find out. Then write an equation and solve it.

Step 3: Let w be the additional weight (in pounds) you can add to your backpack.

Desired weight of backpack	$-$	Current weight of backpack	$=$	Additional weight possible

$$15 - 13\frac{3}{8} = w$$

$$1\frac{5}{8} = w$$

You can carry an additional $1\frac{5}{8}$ pounds, and each bottle weighs $\frac{3}{4}$ pound.

$$1\frac{5}{8} \div \frac{3}{4} = \frac{13}{8} \times \frac{4}{3} = \frac{52}{24} = 2\frac{1}{6}$$

Since you cannot carry a fraction of a bottle, round down to 2 bottles.

Step 4: You know that 2 is a solution; check to see if 3 could be a solution. The additional bottle of water weighs $\frac{3}{4}$ pound. Since $14\frac{7}{8}$ pounds is only $\frac{1}{8}$ pound less than the maximum of 15 pounds, and $\frac{3}{4} > \frac{1}{8}$, adding another bottle weighing $\frac{3}{4}$ pound would make the total weight more than 15 pounds. Therefore, the number of extra bottles of water you can add to your backpack is 2 bottles.

Lesson 1.6 (pp. 38–40)

7. The pairing is not a function because the input $\frac{3}{4}$ is paired with two outputs, 3 and 5.

23. You have 10 quarters that you can use for a parking meter.

a. Each time you put 1 quarter in the meter, you have 1 less quarter, so the <u>number of quarters left</u> is a function of <u>the number of quarters used</u>.

b. Let y represent the number of quarters you have left.

Number of quarters you have left	$=$	Total number of quarters	$-$	Number of quarters you have used so far

$y = 10 - x$

The domain of the function is: 0, 1, 2, 3, 4, 5, 6, 7, 8, 9, and 10.

c. Make a table of inputs, x, and use $y = 10 - x$ to find the corresponding outputs.

Input, x	0	1	2	3	4	5
Output, y	10	9	8	7	6	5

Input, x	6	7	8	9	10
Output, y	4	3	2	1	0

The range of the function is: 0, 1, 2, 3, 4, 5, 6, 7, 8, 9, and 10.

Lesson 1.7 (pp. 46–48)

3. Make an input-output table using the given domain values.

x	0	1	2	3	4	5
y	3	4	5	6	7	8

WORKED-OUT SOLUTIONS

Plot a point for each ordered pair (x, y).

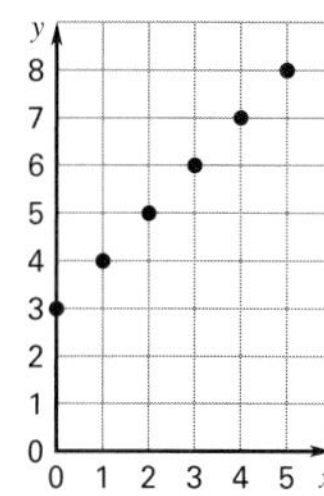

17. Number of voters v as a function of time t in years since 1984.

Years since 1984	Voters	Voters (millions)
0	92,652,680	93
4	91,594,693	92
8	104,405,155	104
12	96,456,345	96
16	105,586,274	106

The t-values range from 0 to 16, so label the t-axis from 0 to 20 in increments of 2 units. The v-values (in millions) range from 93 to 106, so label the v-axis from 90 to 110 in increments of 2 units.

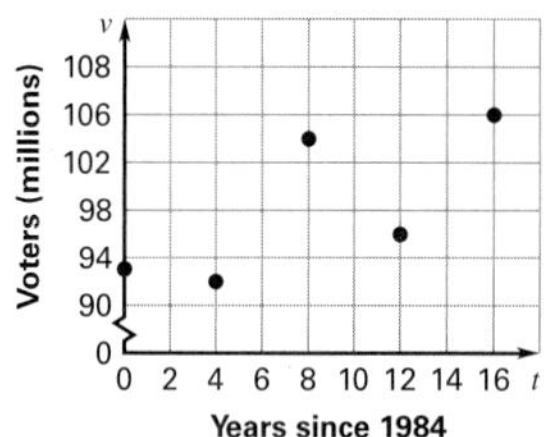

Chapter 2

Lesson 2.1 (pp. 67–70)

7. Graph -5 and -6 on a number line.

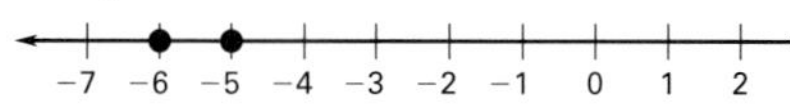

On the number line, -5 is to the right of -6, so $-5 > -6$. The number -5 is greater.

29. If $a = -6.1$, then $-a = -(-6.1) = 6.1$.

If $a = -6.1$, then $|a| = |-6.1| = 6.1$.

53. Graph the numbers on a number line.

Read the numbers from left to right: $-206, -170, -135, 2, 5$.

From lowest elevation to highest elevation, the locations are Fondo, Frink, Alamorio, Calexico, and Date City.

Lesson 2.2 (pp. 77–79)

13. $-8.7 + 4.2 = -(|8.7| - |4.2|)$

$= -(8.7 - 4.2) = -4.5$

35. $-2.6 + (-3.4) + 7.6 = [-2.6 + (-3.4)] + 7.6$

$= -6 + 7.6 = 1.6$

55. a. You know the first lens has a strength of -4.75 diopters and the second lens has a strength of 6.25 diopters.

You want to know the strength of the new lens.

Calculate the sum of -4.75 and 6.25:

$-4.75 + 6.25 = 1.5$

The strength of the new lens is 1.5 diopters.

b. You know the first lens has a strength of -2.5 diopters and the second lens has a strength of -1.25 diopters.

You want to know the strength of the new lens.

Calculate the sum of -2.5 and -1.25:

$-2.5 + (-1.25) = -3.75$

The strength of the new lens is -3.75 diopters.

c. You know the first lens has a strength of 1.5 diopters and the second lens has a strength of -3.75 diopters. The greater the absolute value of the strength of a lens, the stronger the lens.

You want to know which new lens is stronger.

Find the absolute value of each lens in part (a) and part (b) and choose the greater.

$|1.5| = 1.5 \qquad |-3.75| = 3.75$

The new lens in part (b) has a greater absolute value, and is therefore stronger.

WORKED-OUT SOLUTIONS

Lesson 2.3 (pp. 82–84)

3. $13 - (-5) = 13 + 5 = 18$

21. When $x = 7.1$ and $y = -2.5$,

$$-y - (1.9 - x) = -(-2.5) - (1.9 - 7.1)$$
$$= 2.5 - [1.9 + (-7.1)]$$
$$= 2.5 - (-5.2)$$
$$= 2.5 + 5.2 = 7.7$$

43. Write a verbal model. Then write an equation.

Change in temperature	=	Temperature inside	–	Temperature outside

$C = i - t$

Substitute 12.2 for i and -2.4 for t.

$C = 12.2 - (-2.4)$

$C = 12.2 + 2.4 = 14.6$

The change in temperature is 14.6°C.

Lesson 2.4 (pp. 91–93)

11. $-1.9(3.3)(7) = (-6.27)(7) = -43.89$

31. $-2(-6)(-7z) = [-2(-6)](-7z)$

$$= 12(-7z)$$
$$= [12 \cdot (-7)]z$$
$$= -84z$$

51. Write a verbal model.

Total value	=	Original price per share	•	Number of shares	+
		Change in price per share	•	Number of shares	

Calculate the original price.
Original price = ($3.50)(50) = $175

Calculate the change in price.

Change in price = (−$.25)(50) = −$12.50

Calculate the total value.

Total value $= (3.50)(50) + (-0.25)(50)$

$$= 175 + (-12.50) = 162.50$$

The total value is $162.50.

Lesson 2.5 (pp. 99–101)

9. $(p - 3)(-8) = p(-8) - 3(-8) = -8p + 24$

23. Write the expression as a sum:
$7x^2 + (-10) + (-2x^2) + 5$

Terms: $7x^2, -10, -2x^2, 5$

Like terms: $7x^2$ and $-2x^2$; -10 and 5

Coefficients: 7, −2

Constant terms: −10, 5

51. Write a verbal model. Then write an equation.

Total cost	=	Number of movies rented	•	(Regular cost of a rental	–	Discount per movie)

$C = 3(r - 2)$ or $C = 3r - 6$

Find the value of C when $r = 3.99$.

$C = 3(3.99 - 2)$

$$= 3(3.99) - 3(2)$$
$$= 11.97 - 6 = 5.97$$

The total cost is $5.97.

Lesson 2.6 (pp. 106–108)

13. $-1 \div \left(-\frac{7}{2}\right) = -1 \cdot \left(-\frac{2}{7}\right) = \frac{2}{7}$

35. $\frac{9z - 6}{-3} = (9z - 6) \div (-3)$

$$= (9z - 6) \cdot \left(-\frac{1}{3}\right)$$
$$= 9z \cdot \left(-\frac{1}{3}\right) - 6 \cdot \left(-\frac{1}{3}\right)$$
$$= -3z + 2$$

53. To find the daily mean temperature for a day, find the sum of the high and low temperatures for that day and then divide the sum by 2.

$$\text{Mean} = \frac{-10.6 + (-18.9)}{2} = \frac{-29.5}{2} = -14.75$$

The daily mean temperature was −14.75°C.

Lesson 2.7 (pp. 113–116)

9. Since $50^2 = 2500$, $\pm\sqrt{2500} = \pm 50$.

19. Write a compound inequality that compares $-\sqrt{86}$ with both $-\sqrt{100}$ and $-\sqrt{81}$.

$-\sqrt{100} < -\sqrt{86} < -\sqrt{81}$

Take the square root of each number.

$-10 < -\sqrt{86} < -9$

Because 86 is closer to 81 than to 100, $-\sqrt{86}$ is closer to -9 than to -10. So $-\sqrt{86}$ is about -9.

49. You need to find the side length s of the mazes such that s^2 is the given area in square feet, so s is the positive square root of the area. Then identify the side length as rational or irrational.

Dallas: $s^2 = 1225$, $s = 35$; rational

San Francisco: $s^2 = 576$, $s = 24$; rational

Corona: $s^2 = 2304$, $s = 48$; rational

Waterville: $s^2 = 900$, $s = 30$; rational

The side lengths are 35 feet, 24 feet, 48 feet, and 30 feet. All the lengths are rational numbers.

Chapter 3

Lesson 3.1 (pp. 137–140)

13.

$$-2 = n - 6$$
$$-2 + 6 = n - 6 + 6$$
$$4 = n$$

55. Let w represent the width of the trampoline.

$$A = \ell \cdot w$$
$$187 = 17 \cdot w$$
$$\frac{187}{17} = \frac{17w}{17}$$
$$11 = w$$

The width of the trampoline is 11 feet.

Lesson 3.2 (pp. 144–146)

13.

$$7 = \frac{5}{6}c - 8$$
$$7 + 8 = \frac{5}{6}c - 8 + 8$$
$$15 = \frac{5}{6}c$$
$$\frac{6}{5} \cdot 15 = \frac{6}{5} \cdot \frac{5}{6}c$$
$$18 = c$$

19.

$$-32 = -5k + 13k$$
$$-32 = 8k$$
$$\frac{-32}{8} = \frac{8k}{8}$$
$$-4 = k$$

39. Write a verbal model. Then write an equation. Let h be the number of half-side advertisements.

[Total budget] = [Cost per month] • [Number of full bus wrap advertisements] + [Cost per month] • [Number of half-side advertisements]

$$6000 = 2000(1) + 800h$$
$$6000 = 2000 + 800h$$

Solve the equation.

$$6000 = 2000 + 800h$$
$$6000 - 2000 = 2000 - 2000 + 800h$$
$$4000 = 800h$$
$$\frac{4000}{800} = \frac{800h}{800}$$
$$5 = h$$

The museum can have 5 half-side advertisements.

Lesson 3.3 (pp. 150–153)

17.
$$-3 = 12y - 5(2y - 7)$$
$$-3 = 12y - 10y + 35$$
$$-3 = 2y + 35$$
$$-3 - 35 = 2y + 35 - 35$$
$$-38 = 2y$$
$$\frac{-32}{8} = \frac{2y}{2}$$
$$-19 = y$$

39. Let x be the amount of space you should leave between posters (in feet).

Total wall space = Width of poster • Number of posters + 2 • Space at end of wall + Amount of space between posters • Number of spaces between posters

$$13.5 = 2(3) + 2(3) + x(2)$$
$$13.5 = 6 + 6 + 2x$$
$$13.5 = 12 + 2x$$
$$13.5 - 12 = 12 - 12 + 2x$$
$$1.5 = 2x$$
$$0.75 = x$$

You should leave 0.75 foot between each poster.

Lesson 3.4 (pp. 157–159)

13.
$$40 + 14j = 2(-4j - 13)$$
$$40 + 14j = -8j - 26$$
$$40 + 14j + 8j = -8j + 8j - 26$$
$$40 + 22j = -26$$
$$40 - 40 + 22j = -26 - 40$$
$$22j = -66$$
$$j = -3$$

51. Let x represent the number of years. So $33x$ represents the increase in the number of students taking Spanish, and $2x$ represents the decreased number of students who are taking French.

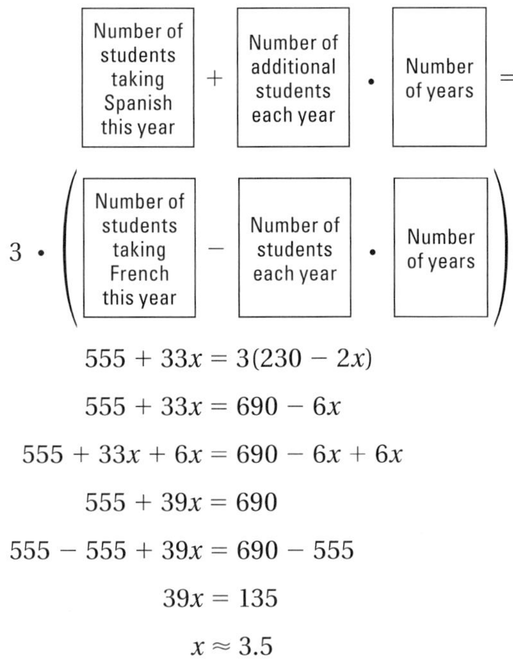

$$555 + 33x = 3(230 - 2x)$$
$$555 + 33x = 690 - 6x$$
$$555 + 33x + 6x = 690 - 6x + 6x$$
$$555 + 39x = 690$$
$$555 - 555 + 39x = 690 - 555$$
$$39x = 135$$
$$x \approx 3.5$$

So it will be after 3 more school years, or in about 4 years, when the number of students taking Spanish will be 3 times the number of students taking French.

Lesson 3.5 (pp. 165–167)

17.
$$\frac{16}{48} = \frac{n}{36}$$
$$36 \cdot \frac{16}{48} = 36 \cdot \frac{n}{36}$$
$$\frac{576}{48} = n$$
$$12 = n$$

49. Find the total number of pizzas: $96 + 144 + 240 = 480$.

The ratio of large pizzas to all pizzas is $\frac{\text{number of large pizzas}}{\text{total number of pizzas}} = \frac{240}{480} = \frac{1}{2}$.

Lesson 3.6 (pp. 171–173)

13. $$\frac{11}{w} = \frac{33}{w + 24}$$

$$11(w + 24) = 33w$$

$$11w + 264 = 33w$$

$$11w - 11w + 264 = 33w - 11w$$

$$264 = 22w$$

$$12 = w$$

39. The ratio of model to height is $\frac{\text{height of model}}{\text{actual height}}$. Write and solve a proportion.

$$\frac{1}{25} = \frac{x}{443.2}$$

$$443.2 = 25x$$

$$17.728 = x$$

The height of the model is 17.728 meters.

Lesson 3.7 (pp. 179–181)

13. $a = p\% \cdot b$

$= 115\% \cdot 60$

$= 1.15 \cdot 60$

$= 69$ 69 is 115% of 60.

35. a. The survey shows that 36% of the 250 listeners who participated in the survey are "tired of" the song.

$a = p\% \cdot b$

$= 36\% \cdot 250$

$= 0.36 \cdot 250$

$= 90$

90 listeners are "tired of" the song.

b. The survey shows that 14% of the 250 listeners who participated in the survey "love" the song.

$a = p\% \cdot b$

$= 14\% \cdot 250$

$= 0.14 \cdot 250$

$= 35$

35 listeners "love" the song.

Lesson 3.8 (pp. 187–189)

17. $$30 = 9x - 5y$$

$$30 + 5y = 9x - 5y + 5y$$

$$30 + 5y = 9x$$

$$30 - 30 + 5y = 9x - 30$$

$$5y = 9x - 30$$

$$y = \frac{9}{5}x - 6$$

33. a. $C = 12x + 25$

$C - 25 = 12x + 25 - 25$

$C - 25 = 12x$

$\frac{C - 25}{12} = x$

b. \$145: $\frac{C - 25}{12} = x$

$\frac{145 - 25}{12} = x$

$10 = x$

For \$145, you bowled 10 league nights.

\$181: $\frac{C - 25}{12} = x$

$\frac{181 - 25}{12} = x$

$13 = x$

For \$181, you bowled 13 league nights.

\$205: $\frac{C - 25}{12} = x$

$\frac{205 - 25}{12} = x$

$15 = x$

For \$205, you bowled 15 league nights.

Chapter 4

Lesson 4.1 (pp. 209–212)

15. To plot $Q(-1, 5)$, begin at the origin. First move 1 unit to the left, then 5 units up. Point Q is in Quadrant II.

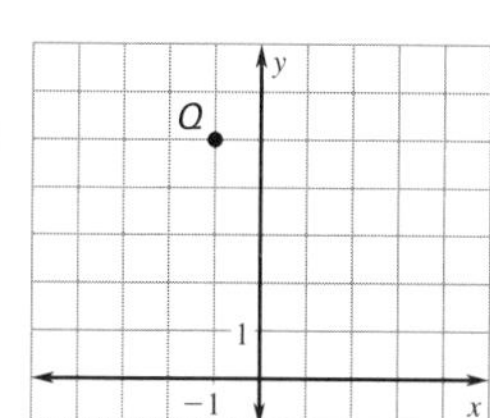

WORKED-OUT SOLUTIONS

25. First create a table of values by substituting the domain values into the function.

x	$y = 2x - 5$
−2	$y = 2(-2) - 5 = -9$
−1	$y = 2(-1) - 5 = -7$
0	$y = 2(0) - 5 = -5$
1	$y = 2(1) - 5 = -3$
2	$y = 2(2) - 5 = -1$

The table gives the ordered pairs (−2, −9), (−1, −7), (0, −5), (1, −3), and (2, −1).

Graph the function by plotting these points. The range of the function is the y-values from the table: −9, −7, −5, −3, −1.

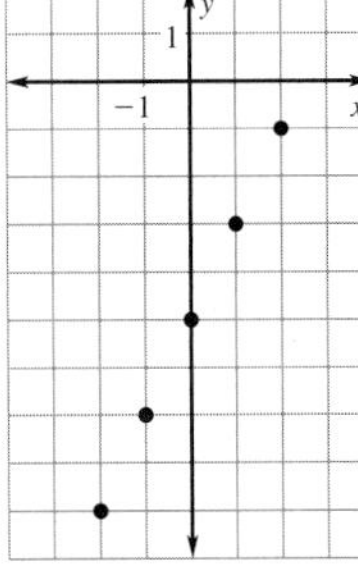

37. The table represents a function because there is exactly one low temperature for each day in the first week of February.

To graph the data, plot the ordered pairs (day, record low).

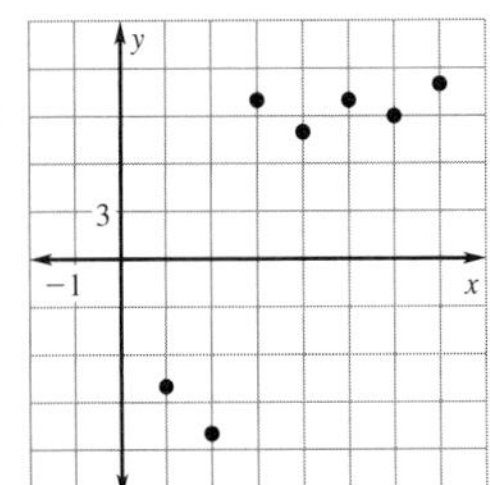

Lesson 4.2 (pp. 219–221)

3. Test (−2, 3):

$$2y + x = 4$$

$$2(3) + (-2) \stackrel{?}{=} 4 \quad \text{Substitute } -2 \text{ for } x \text{ and } 3 \text{ for } y.$$

$$6 + (-2) \stackrel{?}{=} 4$$

$$4 = 4 \checkmark$$

So, (−2, 3) is a solution of $2y + x = 4$.

11. First, solve the equation for y.

$$y + x = 2$$

$$y + x - x = 2 - x$$

$$y = 2 - x$$

Use this equation to create a table of values.

x	−2	−1	0	1	2
y	4	3	2	1	0

Plot at least three of the points whose ordered pairs (x, y) are indicated by the table. Draw a line through the plotted points.

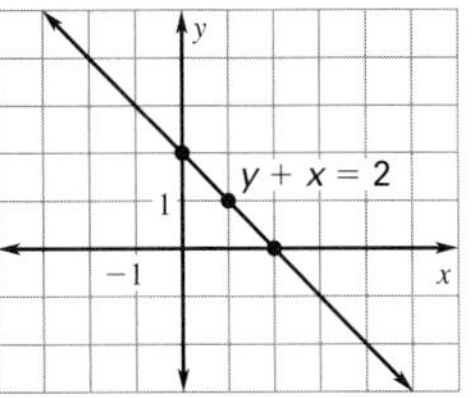

37. a.

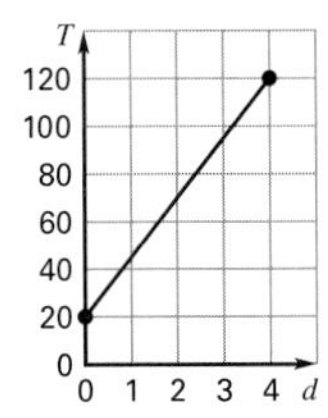

Since the scientist is studying the organisms in the first 4 kilometers of Earth's crust, the domain of the function is $0 \le d \le 4$. The range of the function is $20 \le T \le 120$. The temperature 4 kilometers from the surface is 120°C.

b. Notice in the table for part (a) that the temperatures between 20°C and 95°C occur when the distance from the surface is between 0 kilometers and 3 kilometers.

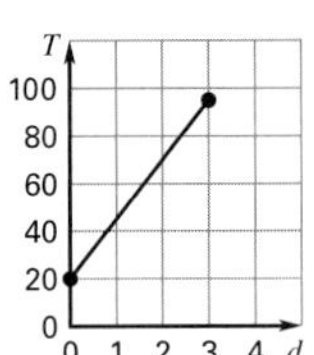

The domain of the function is now $0 \le d \le 3$ and the range is $20 \le T \le 95$. So this section of crust is 3 kilometers deep.

Lesson 4.3 (pp. 229–232)

21. Substitute 0 for y in $y = -4x + 3$ and solve for x.

$$0 = -4x + 3$$

$$-3 = -4x$$

$$\frac{3}{4} = x$$

The x-intercept is $\frac{3}{4}$.

Substitute 0 for x in $y = -4x + 3$ and solve for y.

$$y = -4(0) + 3 = 0 + 3 = 3$$

The y-intercept is 3.

Plot the two points that correspond to the intercepts and draw a line through them.

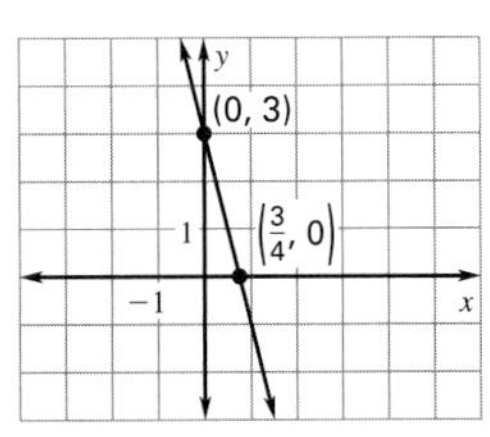

47. a. If $v = 0$ in the function $f = 180 - 1.5v$, then $f = 180 - 1.5(0)$, and $f = 180$. This is the intercept on the vertical axis, and it represents the area (in square feet) available for flowers when no vegetables are planted.

Letting $f = 0$ gives $0 = 180 - 1.5v$, $1.5v = 180$, and $v = 120$. This is the intercept on the horizontal axis, and it represents the area (in square feet) available for vegetables when no flowers are planted.

b. The domain is $0 \le v \le 120$. The range is $0 \le f \le 180$.

c. $f = 180 - 1.5(80)$ Substitute 80 for v.

$= 180 - 120 = 60$

There are 60 square feet left to plant flowers.

Lesson 4.4 (pp. 239–242)

11. Let $(x_1, y_1) = (1, 3)$ and $(x_2, y_2) = (3, -2)$.

$$m = \frac{y_2 - y_1}{x_2 - x_1} = \frac{-2 - 3}{3 - 1} = \frac{-5}{2} \text{ or } -\frac{5}{2}$$

37. a. $\text{rate of change} = \dfrac{\text{change in temperature}}{\text{change in time}}$

0–1.5 hours:
$\dfrac{1000 - 250}{1.5 - 0} = \dfrac{750}{1.5} = 500$ degrees per hour

1.5–2.5 hours:
$\dfrac{1300 - 1000}{2.5 - 1.5} = \dfrac{300}{1} = 300$ degrees per hour

2.5–4.65 hours:
$\dfrac{1680 - 1300}{4.65 - 2.5} = \dfrac{380}{2.15} \approx 177$ degrees per hour

4.65–8.95 hours:
$\dfrac{1920 - 1680}{8.95 - 4.65} = \dfrac{240}{4.3} \approx 56$ degrees per hour

The time interval with the greatest rate of change was from 0 hours to 1.5 hours.

b. The time interval that showed the least rate of change was from 4.65 hours to 8.95 hours.

Lesson 4.5 (pp. 247–250)

11.

$$4x + y = 1$$
$$4x - 4x + y = 1 - 4x$$
$$y = -4x + 1$$

The slope is -4 and the y-intercept is 1.

21. The equation $y = -6x + 1$ is in slope-intercept form. The slope is -6 and the y-intercept is 1. Locate the point (0, 1), which corresponds to the intercept. Use the slope to find a second point, $(1, -5)$. Draw a line through the points.

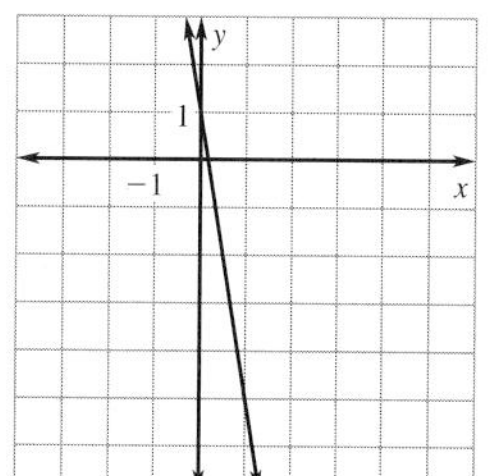

41. a.

b. On the graph, the vertical distance between the lines is about 30 when $t = 3$. To verify this estimate, substitute 3 in $d = 55t$: $d = 55(3) = 165$. Now substitute 3 in $d = 65t$: $d = 65(3) = 195$. Subtract: $195 - 165 = 30$. Driving at the maximum speed limit, a driver could travel 30 miles farther after 1995 than before 1995.

Lesson 4.6 (pp. 256–259)

7. Solve the equation for y: $8x + 2y = 0$

$$2y = -8x$$
$$y = -4x$$

Because $8x + 2y = 0$ can be written in the form $y = ax$, it does represent direct variation. The constant of variation is -4.

21. When solved for y, the equation is $y = -4x$. The slope of the line is the constant of variation, -4. The graph of a direct variation equation always passes through (0, 0). The slope can be used to locate a second point from the origin, like (1, −4). Draw a line through the points.

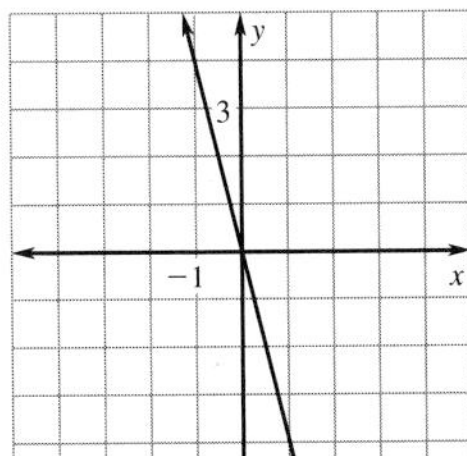

43. a. Compare the ratio $\frac{f}{w}$ or all three data pairs:

$$\frac{2.50}{10} = 0.25, \frac{3.75}{15} = 0.25, \frac{7.50}{30} = 0.25$$

Because the ratios are all equal, f varies directly with w.

b. Since $\frac{f}{w} = 0.25$, multiply both sides by w to obtain the direct variation equation $f = 0.25w$.

The computer weighs 18 pounds, so substitute 18 for w.

$f = 0.25(18) = 4.50$

The printer weighs 10 pounds, so substitute 10 for w.

$f = 0.25(10) = 2.50$

The total recycling fee for the computer and printer is \$4.50 + \$2.50 = \$7.00.

Lesson 4.7 (pp. 265–268)

3. Substitute −2, 0, and 3 for x.

$f(-2) = 12(-2) + 1 = -24 + 1 = -23$

$f(0) = 12(0) + 1 = 0 + 1 = 1$

$f(3) = 12(3) + 1 = 36 + 1 = 37$

17. Substitute −13 for $j(x)$.

$$-13 = 4x + 11$$

$$-13 - 11 = 4x + 11 - 11$$

$$-24 = 4x$$

$$\frac{-24}{4} = \frac{4x}{4}$$

$$-6 = x$$

39. a. Create a table of values for the function.

x	$f(x)$
0	$0.10(0) + 2.75 = 2.75$
5	$0.10(5) + 2.75 = 3.25$
10	$0.10(10) + 2.75 = 3.75$
15	$0.10(15) + 2.75 = 4.25$
20	$0.10(20) + 2.75 = 4.75$

Use the ordered pairs given by the table to graph the function.

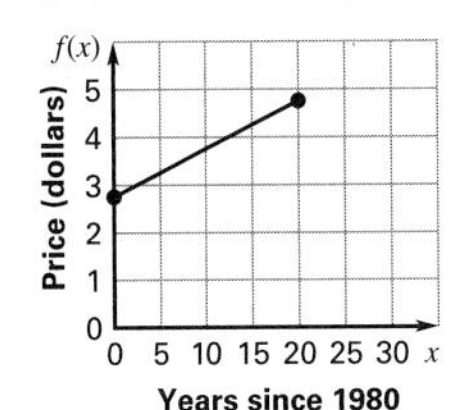

The domain of the function is $0 \le x \le 20$ and the range is $2.75 \le f(x) \le 4.75$.

b. Substitute 4.55 for $f(x)$.

$$4.55 = 0.10x + 2.75$$

$$4.55 - 2.75 = 0.10x + 2.75 - 2.75$$

$$1.8 = 0.10x$$

$$\frac{1.8}{0.10} = \frac{0.10x}{0.10}$$

$$18 = x$$

When $x = 18$, $f(x) = 4.55$. In 1998, 18 years after 1980, the average price of a movie ticket was \$4.55.

Chapter 5

Lesson 5.1 (pp. 286–289)

11. Determine the slope: $m = \frac{\text{rise}}{\text{run}} = \frac{-1}{2} = $ or $-\frac{1}{2}$.

The line crosses the y-axis at (0, 0), so the y-intercept is 0.

Substitute $-\frac{1}{2}$ for m and 0 for b in the slope-intercept form $y = mx + b$: $y = -\frac{1}{2}x$.

19. Calculate the slope:

$$m = \frac{y_2 - y_1}{x_2 - x_1} = \frac{4 - 0}{0 - (-1)} = \frac{4}{1} = 4.$$

The line crosses the y-axis at (0, 4), so the y-intercept is 4.

Substitute 4 for m and 4 for b in the slope-intercept form $y = mx + b$: $y = 4x + 4$.

47. Let C be the cost of a visit to the aquarium and t be the time parked there. The total cost C is given by the function $C = 3h + 30$, where h is the number of hours parked at the aquarium.

Evaluate the function for $h = 4$:
$C = 3(4) + 30 = 12 + 30 = 42$

The total cost is $42.

Lesson 5.2 (pp. 296–299)

5. The slope is given. To find the y-intercept, substitute the slope, -5, and the coordinates of the given point $(-4, 7)$ into the equation $y = mx + b$, and solve for b.

$$y = mx + b$$

$$7 = -5(-4) + b$$

$$7 = 20 + b$$

$$-13 = b$$

The equation of the line is $y = -5x - 13$.

11. Calculate the slope:
$m = \frac{y_2 - y_1}{x_2 - x_1} = \frac{7 - 4}{2 - 1} = \frac{3}{1} = 3.$

To find the y-intercept, substitute the slope, 3, and the coordinates of either given point into the equation $y = mx + b$, and solve for b. Using $(1, 4)$,

$$y = mx + b$$

$$4 = 3(1) + b$$

$$4 = 3 + b$$

$$1 = b$$

The equation of the line is $y = 3x + 1$.

49. Let T be the total time (in minutes) for cooking a roast that weighs p pounds and t be the extra time needed (in minutes). The equation $T = 30p + t$ models the situation.

For a 2 pound roast, the total time was 1 hour 25 minutes, or 85 minutes. Find the extra time t needed by substituting 85 for T and 2 for p, and solving for t.

$$85 = 30(2) + t$$

$$85 = 60 + t$$

$$25 = t$$

Find the value of T for a 3 pound roast by substituting 3 for p.

$T = 30(3) + 25 = 90 + 25 = 115$

You need 115 minutes, or 1 hour 55 minutes, to cook a 3 pound roast.

Lesson 5.3 (pp. 305–308)

3. Substitute 2 for x_1, 1 for y_1, and 2 for m in the point-slope form $y - y_1 = m(x - x_1)$: $y - 1 = 2(x - 2)$.

39. The rate of change is given as $10,000 per year. Let y be the annual sales (in dollars) and x be the number of years since 1994. From the given information about 1997, one data pair is (3, 97000). Use the point-slope form of an equation.

$$y - y_1 = m(x - x_1)$$

$$y - 97000 = 10000(x - 3)$$

$$y - 97000 = 10000x - 30000$$

$$y = 10000x + 67000$$

To find the sales in 2000, use the equation above with $x = 2000 - 1994$, or 6.

$$y = 10000(6) + 67000$$

$$= 60000 + 67000 = 127000$$

The annual sales in 2000 were $127,000.

Lesson 5.4 (pp. 314–316)

17. Calculate the slope:
$m = \frac{y_2 - y_1}{x_2 - x_1} = \frac{-4 - 4}{4 - (-8)} = \frac{-8}{12}$ or $-\frac{2}{3}$.

Use either point to write an equation in point-slope form. Using $(-8, 4)$:

$$y - y_1 = m(x - x_1)$$

$$y - 4 = -\frac{2}{3}[x - (-8)]$$

$$y - 4 = -\frac{2}{3}(x + 8)$$

Rewrite the equation in standard form.

$$y - 4 = -\frac{2}{3}x - \frac{16}{3}$$

$$\frac{2}{3}x + y - 4 = -\frac{16}{3}$$

$$\frac{2}{3}x + y = -\frac{4}{3} \text{ (or } 2x + 3y = -4\text{)}$$

WORKED-OUT SOLUTIONS

39. a. Let n be the number of ounces in a box of wheat cereal.

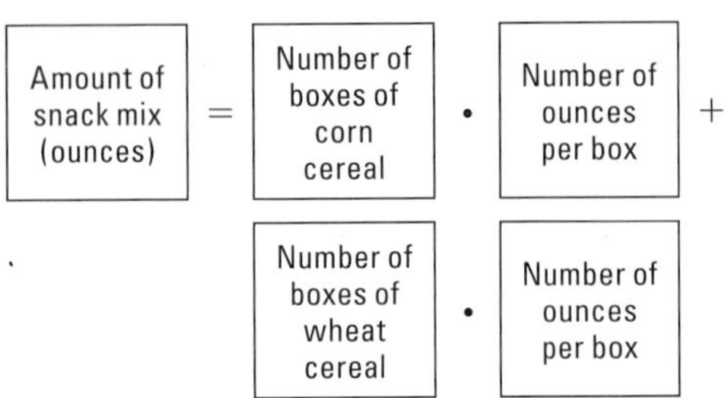

$120 = 5 \cdot 12 + 4 \cdot n$

$120 = 60 + 4n$

$60 = 4n$

$15 = n$

There are 15 ounces in a box of wheat cereal.

b. Let c be the number of boxes of corn cereal and let w be the number of boxes of wheat cereal you use. Use the verbal model from part (a).

$120 = c \cdot 12 + w \cdot 15$

$120 = 12c + 15w$ or $12c + 15w = 120$

c. Substitute different values for c and w in the equation for part (b).

If $c = 0$, then $12(0) + 15w = 120$, and $w = 8$; you can use 0 boxes of corn cereal and 8 boxes of wheat cereal.

If $c = 5$, then $12(5) + 15w = 120$, and $w = 4$; you can use 5 boxes of corn cereal and 4 boxes of wheat cereal.

If $c = 10$, then $12(10) + 15w = 120$, and $w = 0$; you can use 10 boxes of corn cereal and 0 boxes of wheat cereal.

Lesson 5.5 (pp. 322–324)

19. The slope of the line $y = 3x - 12$ is 3, so the slope of the perpendicular line is $-\frac{1}{3}$.

Use the slope $-\frac{1}{3}$ and the point $(-9, 2)$ to find the y-intercept of the line.

$y = mx + b$

$2 = -\frac{1}{3}(-9) + b$

$2 = 3 + b$

$-1 = b$

The equation of the line through $(-9, 2)$ that is perpendicular to the line $y = 3x - 12$ is $y = -\frac{1}{3}x - 1$.

33. a. Let w represent the weight of the blue whale calves and let d represent the number of days since birth.

The rate of change is 200 pounds per day. Use this value and the birth weights to write an equation for each calf.

First calf: $w_1 = 200d + 6000$
Second calf: $w_2 = 200d + 6250$

b. Substitute 30 for d in each equation from part (a).

$w_1 = 200(30) + 6000 = 12{,}000$

After 30 days, the first calf weighs 12,000 pounds.

$w_2 = 200(30) + 6250 = 12{,}250$

After 30 days, the second calf weighs 12,250 pounds.

c. The graphs of the equations in part (a) are parallel, since the two equations have the same slope, 200. The w-intercept of the second line is 250 greater than the w-intercept of the first line.

Lesson 5.6 (pp. 328–331)

7. The ordered pairs from the table are (1.2, 10), (1.8, 7), (2.3, 5), (3.0, −1), (4.4, −4), and (5.2, −8).

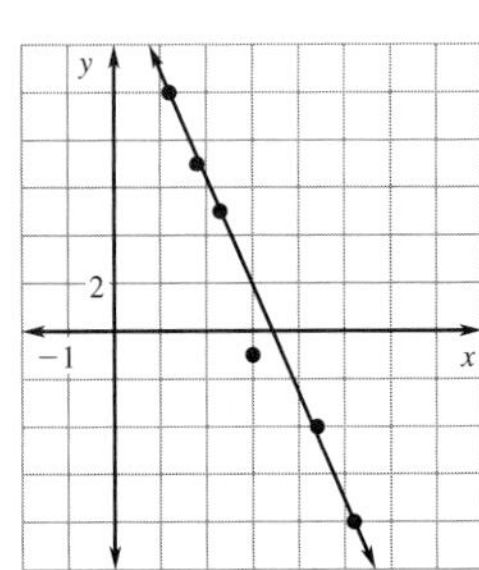

Use the points (1.2, 10) and (5.2, −8) to find the slope of the line of fit.

$$m = \frac{y_2 - y_1}{x_2 - x_1} = \frac{-8 - 10}{5.2 - 1.2} = \frac{-18}{4} = -4.4.$$

Use the slope −4.4 and the point (5.2, −8) to find the y-intercept of the line.

$y = mx + b$

$-8 = -4.4(5.2) + b$

$-8 = -22.88 + b$

$14.88 = b$

A line of fit is $y = -4.4x + 14.88$.

17. a. The ordered pairs from the diagram are (86, −86), (80, −65), (75, −54), (70, −40), (65, −26), (60, −21), and (52, −4).

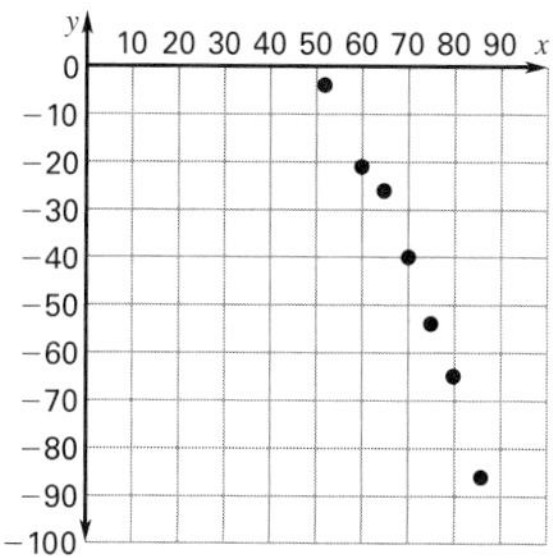

b. Draw a line that appears to fit the points.
Sample:

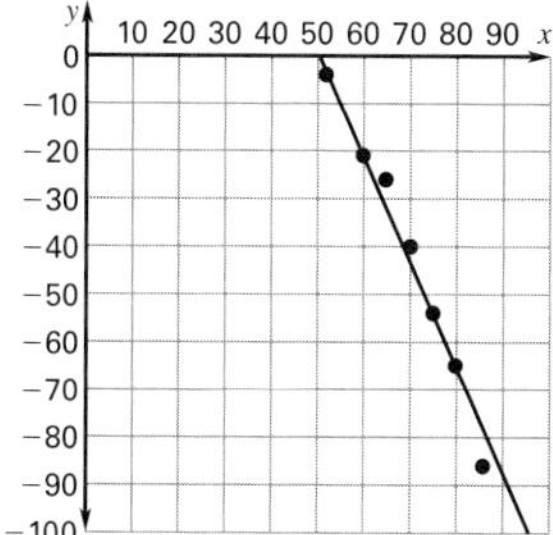

Use the points (60, −21) and (80, −65) to find the slope of the line of fit.

$$m = \frac{y_2 - y_1}{x_2 - x_1} = \frac{-21 - (-65)}{60 - 80} = \frac{44}{-20} = -2.2$$

Use the slope −2.2 and the point (80, −65) to find the y-intercept of the line.

$$y = mx + b$$

$$-65 = -2.2(80) + b$$

$$-65 = -176 + b$$

$$111 = b$$

A line of fit is $y = -2.2x + 111$.

c. The slope of the line of fit models the rate of change. So the temperature changes at an approximate rate of −2.2°C per kilometer of increasing altitude.

Lesson 5.7 (pp. 338–341)

3. Enter the data list on a graphing calculator. Create a scatter plot.

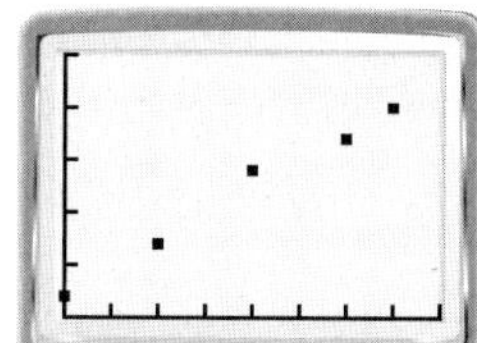

Perform a linear regression using the paired data. An equation of the best-fitting line is approximately $y = 2.6x + 2.5$.

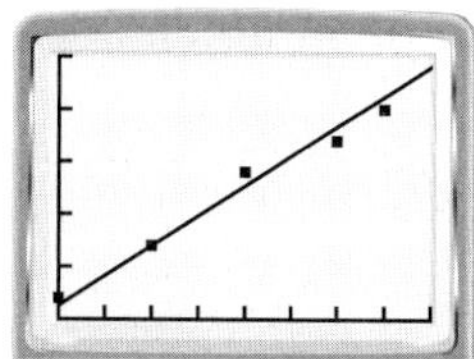

Graph the best-fitting line. Use the trace feature and arrow keys to find the value of y when $x = 5$. For $x = 5$, $y = 15.5$.

19. a. Enter the data list on a graphing calculator. Make a scatter plot.

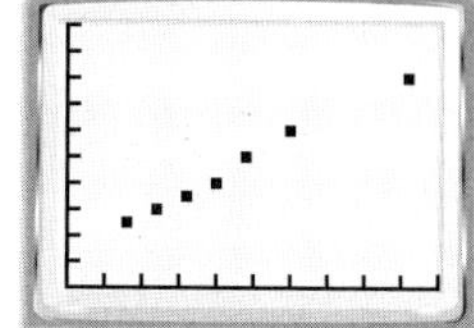

b. Perform a linear regression using the paired data. An equation of the best-fitting line is approximately $y = 0.03x + 1.23$ where y is the recommended space (in square feet) and x is a pig's weight (in pounds).

c. Evaluate $y = 0.03x + 1.23$ for $x = 250$.

$$y = 0.03(250) + 1.23 = 7.5 + 1.23 = 8.73$$

The model predicts that about 8.73 square feet of space is needed for a pig weighing 250 pounds.

Chapter 6

Lesson 6.1 (pp. 359–361)

7. The open circle means that 10 is not a solution of the inequality. Because the arrow points to the left, all numbers less than 10 are solutions. An inequality represented by the graph is $x < 10$.

15.

$$w + 14.9 > -2.7$$

$$w + 14.9 - 14.9 > -2.7 - 14.9$$

$$w > -17.6$$

−17.6

−18 −16 −14 −12

33. a. Let s represent score you can earn.

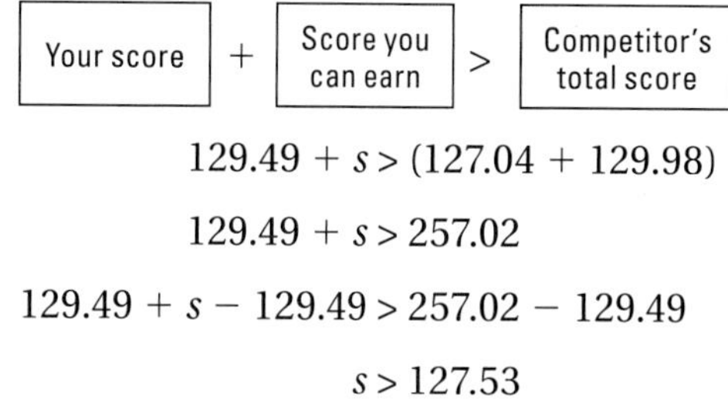

$$129.49 + s > (127.04 + 129.98)$$

$$129.49 + s > 257.02$$

$$129.49 + s - 129.49 > 257.02 - 129.49$$

$$s > 127.53$$

The score you can earn must be greater than 127.53.

WORKED-OUT SOLUTIONS

b. Yes; since $128.13 > 127.53$, you will beat your competitor.

No; since $126.78 < 127.53$, you will not beat your competitor.

No; when your score is 127.53, you and your competitor will tie.

Lesson 6.2 (pp. 366–368)

5. $-6y < -36$

$\frac{-6y}{-6} > \frac{-36}{-6}$ Reverse the inequality symbol when dividing by -6.

$y > 6$

9. $\frac{g}{6} > -20$

$6 \cdot \frac{g}{6} > 6 \cdot (-20)$

$g > -120$

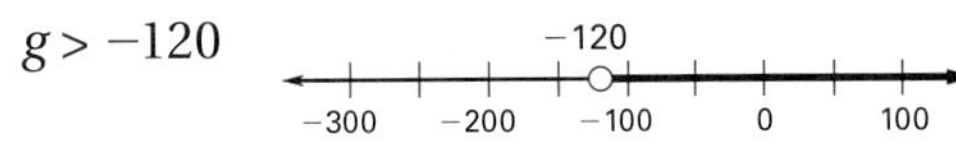

39. $48 \leq 15 \cdot w$

$\frac{48}{15} \leq \frac{15w}{15}$

$3.2 \leq w$

The minimum width of the molding must be greater than or equal to 3.2 inches, or the width must be at least 3.2 inches.

Lesson 6.3 (pp. 372–374)

5. $8v - 3 \geq -11$

$8v \geq -8$

$v \geq -1$

19. $3(s - 4) \geq 2(s - 6)$

$3s - 12 \geq 2s - 12$

$3s \geq 2s$

$3s - 2s \geq 2s - 2s$

$s \geq 0$

39. a. The area of the habitat is (20 feet)(50 feet) = 1000 square feet. Since 500 square feet are needed for the first two swans, 1000 − 500 = 500 square feet are left for the other swans. 500 square feet can hold up to 500 ÷ 125 = 4 more swans; so, the maximum number of swans is 2 + 4 = 6 swans.

b. The area of the new habitat is [(20 + 20) feet][(50 + 20) feet] = (40 feet)(70 feet) = 2800 square feet. Since 2800 − 1000 = 1800, the additional area is 1800 square feet. 1800 square feet can hold up to 1800 ÷ 125 = 14.4 more swans; so the possible number of additional swans is at most 14 swans. The habitat can hold at most 14 more swans.

Lesson 6.4 (pp. 384–387)

7. Let s be the speed of a vehicle that is traveling within the posted speed limits.

$40 \leq s \leq 60$

11. Separate the compound inequality $-1 \leq -4m \leq 16$ into two inequalities.

$-1 \leq -4m$ *and* $-4m \leq 16$

$\frac{-1}{-4} \geq \frac{-4m}{-4}$ *and* $\frac{-4m}{-4} \geq \frac{16}{-4}$

$\frac{1}{4} \geq m$ *and* $m \geq -4$

The inequality can be written as $-4 \leq m \leq \frac{1}{4}$.

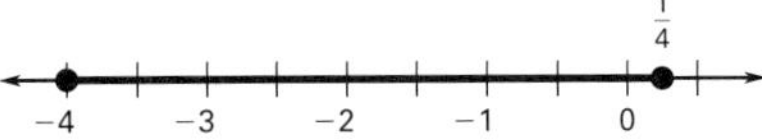

41. An inequality representing values for p is $0.02 \leq p \leq 0.04$.

$0.02 \leq \frac{f}{d} \leq 0.04$ Substitute $\frac{f}{d}$ for p.

$0.02 \leq \frac{f}{160} \leq 0.04$ Substitute 160 for w.

$3.2 \leq f \leq 6.4$

The possible amounts of food f eaten per day by a deer is greater or equal to 3.2 pounds and less than or equal to 6.4 pounds.

Lesson 6.5 (pp. 393–395)

11. Rewrite the absolute value equation $|3p + 7| = 4$ as two equations.

$3p + 7 = 4$ *or* $3p + 7 = -4$

$3p = -3$ *or* $3p = -11$

$p = -1$ *or* $p = -3\frac{2}{3}$

The solutions are -1 and $-3\frac{2}{3}$.

23. $|x - 1| + 5 = 2$

$|x - 1| = -3$

The absolute value of a number is never negative. So, there are no solutions.

45. a. Let s represent your friend's scores last year.

Absolute deviation = | Score − Mean score |

$2.213 = |s - 54.675|$

$2.213 = s - 54.675$

$56.888 = s$

or $-2.213 = s - 54.675$

$52.462 = s$

His least score earned was 52.462, and his greatest score was 56.888 points.

b. Let t represent your friend's scores this year. Find his greatest score for this year. Then find the difference between this year's greatest score and last year's greatest score.

$0.45 = |t - 56.738|$

$0.45 = t - 56.738$

$57.188 = t$

or $-0.45 = t - 56.738$

$56.288 = t$

His greatest score was 57.188 points. This score is 57.188 − 56.888, or 0.3 point more than his greatest score last year.

Lesson 6.6 (pp. 401–403)

9. Rewrite $|d + 4| \geq 3$ as a compound inequality.

$d + 4 \leq -3$ *or* $d + 4 \geq 3$

$d \leq -7$ *or* $d \geq -1$

15. $5\left|\frac{1}{2}r + 3\right| > 5$

$\left|\frac{1}{2}r + 3\right| > 1$

$\frac{1}{2}r + 3 < -1$ *or* $\frac{1}{2}r + 3 > 1$

$\frac{1}{2}r < -4$ *or* $\frac{1}{2}r > -2$

$r < -8$ *or* $r > -4$

37. Let t represent the oven temperature.

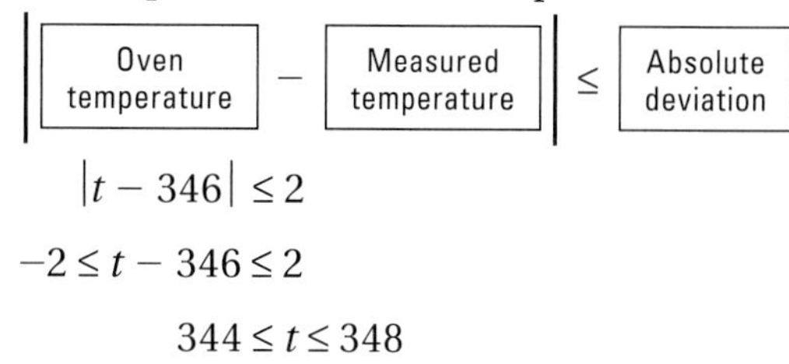

$|t - 346| \leq 2$

$-2 \leq t - 346 \leq 2$

$344 \leq t \leq 348$

The temperature is at least 344°F and at most 348°F. You should continue to preheat; the temperature is still below 350°F.

Lesson 6.7 (pp. 409–412)

5. Substitute −1 for x and −4 for y in the inequality $y - x > -2$.

$-4 - (-1) > -2$

$-3 > -2$ ✗

Since −3 is not greater than −2, the ordered pair (−1, −4) is not a solution.

19. Graph the equation $y = 3x + 5$. The symbol of the given inequality is <, so use a dashed line. Since the line does not pass through the origin, test the ordered pair (0, 0) in $y < 3x + 5$.

$0 < 3(0) + 5$

$0 < 5$ ✓

Shade the half-plane that contains (0, 0) because (0, 0) is a solution of the inequality.

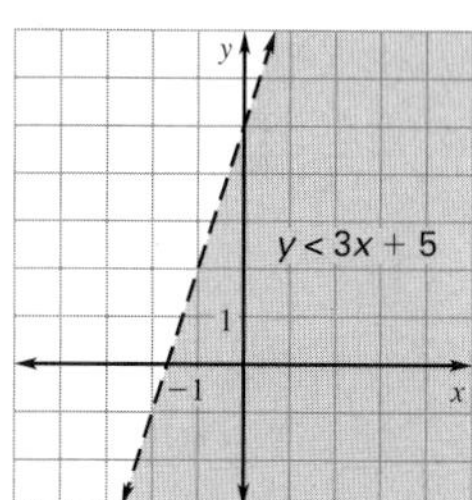

57. a. Let m be the number of muffins and let ℓ be the number of loaves of bread. An inequality modeling this situation is $\frac{1}{6}m + \frac{1}{2}\ell \leq 12$.

To graph $\frac{1}{6}m + \frac{1}{2}\ell \leq 12$, first graph the equation $\frac{1}{6}m + \frac{1}{2}\ell = 12$ in Quadrant I; the inequality symbol is ≤, so use a solid line.

Next, test (12, 12) in $\frac{1}{6}m + \frac{1}{2}\ell \leq 12$.

$\frac{1}{6}(12) + \frac{1}{2}(12) \leq 12$

$2 + 6 \leq 12$ ✓

Finally, shade the part of Quadrant I that contains (12, 12), because (12, 12) is a solution of the inequality.

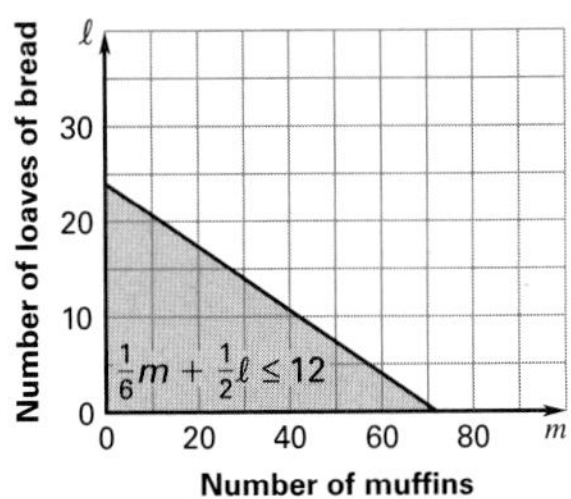

b. $\frac{1}{6}m + \frac{1}{2}(4) \le 12$ Substitute 4 for ℓ.

$\frac{1}{6}m + 2 \le 12$

$\frac{1}{6}m \le 10$

$m \le 60$

You can make up to 60 muffins.

Chapter 7

Lesson 7.1 (pp. 430–433)

15. Graph both equations.

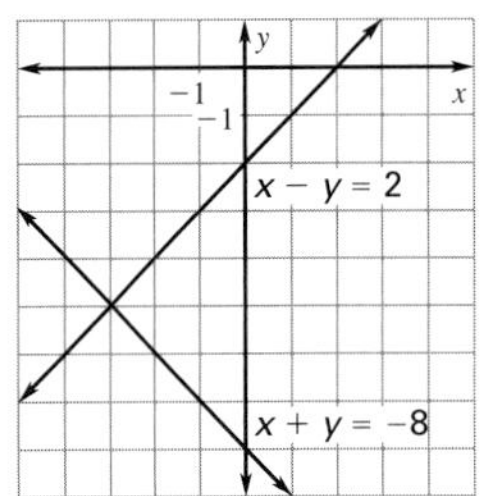

The lines appear to intersect at (−3, −5).

Check: Substitute −3 for x and −5 for y in each equation.

$x - y = 2$ $\quad$ $x + y = -8$

$-3 - (-5) = 2$ $\quad$ $-3 + (-5) = -8$

$2 = 2$ ✓ $\quad$ $-8 = -8$ ✓

So, (−3, −5) is the solution of the system.

31. The two lines appear to intersect at (50, 50). If the value of t is 50, then the year is 1990 + 50, or 2040. So, the percent of eighth graders who watch 1 hour or less of television will equal the percent of eighth graders who watch 1 hour or more of television in the year 2040.

Lesson 7.2 (pp. 439–441)

13. Solve $x + y = -3$ for x: $x = -y - 3$.

Substitute $-y - 3$ for x in the other equation and solve for y.

$5(-y - 3) + 2y = 9$

$-5y - 15 + 2y = 9$

$-3y - 15 = 9$

$-3y = 24$

$y = -8$

Substitute −8 for y in the equation $x = -y - 3$.

$x = -(-8) - 3 = 5$

The solution of the linear system is (5, −8).

33. a. Write a system of two linear equations.

Use the given verbal model to write the first equation: $x \cdot 1.5 = y \cdot 1.2$, or $1.5x = 1.2y$.

Since the length of the dowel is 9 inches, the second equation is $x + y = 9$.

Solve $x + y = 9$ for x: $x = -y + 9$.

Substitute $-y + 9$ for x in the equation $1.5x = 1.2y$ and solve for y.

$1.5x = 1.2y$

$1.5(-y + 9) = 1.2y$

$-1.5y + 13.5 = 1.2y$

$13.5 = 2.7y$

$5 = y$

Substitute 5 for y in the equation $x = -y + 9$.

$x = -5 + 9 = 4$

The solution is (4, 5). So the string should be placed 4 inches from point A.

Lesson 7.3 (pp. 447–450)

17. Rewrite the first equation so that the x-term is first. Subtract the equations to eliminate the variable x, then solve for y.

$$\begin{array}{r} 6x - 8y = 36 \\ 6x - y = 15 \\ \hline -7y = 21 \end{array}$$

$y = -3$

Substitute -3 for y in either equation.

$$6x - (-3) = 15$$
$$6x + 3 = 15$$
$$6x = 12$$
$$x = 2$$

The solution of the linear system is $(2, -3)$.

41. Write a system of equations. Let x be the cost of a monophonic ring tone and let y be the cost of a polyphonic ring tone.

$3 \cdot x + 2 \cdot y = 12.85$ ← Julie's total cost

$1 \cdot x + 2 \cdot y = 8.95$ ← Tate's total cost

Subtract the equations to eliminate y.

$$\begin{aligned} 3x + 2y &= 12.85 \\ x + 2y &= 8.95 \\ \hline 2x &= 3.90 \\ x &= 1.95 \end{aligned}$$

Substitute 1.95 for x in either equation.

$$1.95 + 2y = 8.95$$
$$2y = 7.00$$
$$y = 3.50$$

The solution of the linear system is $(1.95, 3.50)$. The cost of a monophonic ring tone is \$1.95 and the cost of a polyphonic ring tone is \$3.50.

Lesson 7.4 (pp. 454–457)

15. Begin by multiplying $9x + 2y = 39$ by 2 and $6x + 13y = -9$ by 3 so that the coefficient of x is the same in both equations. Then subtract the equations to eliminate x. Solve for y.

$9x + 2y = 39$ $\boxed{\times 2}$ $18x + 4y = 78$

$6x + 13y = -9$ $\boxed{\times 3}$ $18x + 39y = -27$

$$-35y = 105$$
$$y = -3$$

Substitute -3 for y in either original equations.

$9x + 2(-3) = 39$ Use the equation $9x + 2y = 39$.

$$9x - 6 = 39$$
$$9x = 45$$

$x = 5$ The solution is $(5, -3)$.

39. Let x be the number of pies and y be the number of batches of applesauce.

$5x + 4y = 169$ ← Granny Smith apples

$3x + 2y = 95$ ← Golden Delicious apples

Now begin to solve the system by multiplying $5x + 4y = 169$ by 3 and $3x + 2y = 95$ by 5 so that the coefficient of x is the same in both equations. Then subtract the equations to eliminate x. Solve for y.

$5x + 4y = 169$ $\boxed{\times 3}$ $15x + 12y = 507$

$3x + 2y = 95$ $\boxed{\times 5}$ $15x + 10y = 475$

$$2y = 32$$
$$y = 16$$

Substitute 16 for y in either original equations.

$$3x + 2(16) = 95$$
$$3x + 32 = 95$$
$$3x = 63$$
$$x = 21$$

The solution is $(21, 16)$. The apples can be used to make 21 pies and 16 batches of applesauce.

Lesson 7.5 (pp. 462–465)

11.

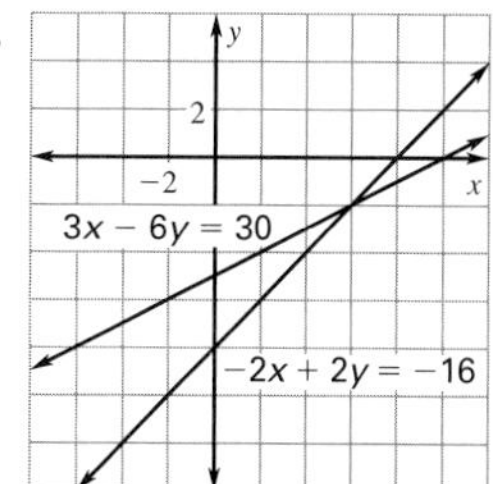

The lines intersect, so the linear system has one solution.

37. Write a system of equations. Let x be the cost of a coach ticket and let y be the cost of a business class ticket.

$150x + 80y = 22{,}860$ ← Washington, D.C.

$170x + 100y = 27{,}280$ ← New York City

Solve the linear system using elimination. Multiply the Washington, D.C. equation by 5 and the New York City equation by 4.

$$750x + 400y = 114{,}300$$
$$680x + 400y = 109{,}120$$
$$70x = 5180$$
$$x = 74$$

Substitute 74 for x in either original equations.

$$170(74) + 100y = 27{,}280$$
$$12{,}580 + 100y = 27{,}280$$
$$100y = 14{,}700$$
$$y = 147$$

The solution is (74, 147). Since there is one solution to the system, there is enough information to determine the cost of one coach ticket.

Lesson 7.6 (pp. 469–472)

13. The graph of the system is the intersection of the two half-planes when both inequalities are graphed in the same coordinate plane.

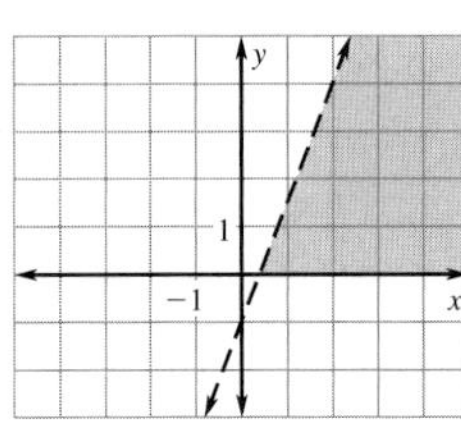

39. a. Let x be the person's age in years and let y be the target heart rate (in beats per minute). A person's maximum heart rate is given by $220 - x$, so 70% of this value is $0.7(220 - x)$ and 85% of this value is $0.85(220 - x)$. So the range for the target heart rate is given by the compound inequality $0.7(220 - x) \le y \le 0.85(220 - x)$, or $154 - 0.70x \le y \le 187 - 0.85x$. This compound inequality can be rewritten as the two inequalities $y \ge 154 - 0.70x$ and $y \le 187 - 0.85x$. The age range for which the heart rate calculations is valid is given as $20 \le x \le 65$.

The system of inequalities is:

$y \ge 154 - 0.70x$
$y \le 187 - 0.85x$
$20 \le x \le 65$

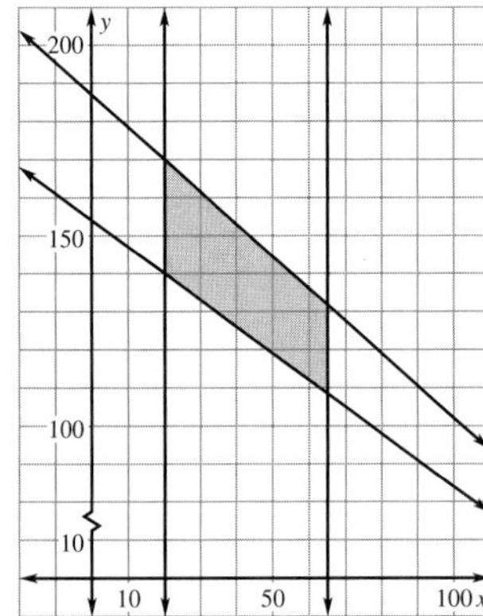

b. No; substituting 40 for x in the inequality $0.70(220 - x) \le y \le 0.85(220 - x)$ gives a range of $126 \le y \le 153$. Since 104 and 120 are both less than 126, his heart rate stays below 70% of the maximum heart rate and is not in the target range for his age.

Chapter 8

Lesson 8.1 (pp. 492–494)

31.
$$\begin{aligned}(-10x^6)^2 \cdot x^2 &= (-10 \cdot x^6)^2 \cdot x^2\\ &= (-10)^2 \cdot (x^6)^2 \cdot x^2\\ &= 100 \cdot x^{6 \cdot 2} \cdot x^2\\ &= 100 \cdot x^{12} \cdot x^2\\ &= 100 \cdot x^{12 + 2}\\ &= 100x^{14}\end{aligned}$$

55. a. For 10 ounces of gold, there are $10^1 \cdot 10^{23} = 10^{1 + 23}$, or 10^{24} atoms of gold; for 100 ounces of gold, there are $10^2 \cdot 10^{23} = 10^{25}$ atoms of gold; for 1000 ounces of gold, there are $10^3 \cdot 10^{23} = 10^{26}$ atoms of gold; for 10,000 ounces of gold, there are $10^4 \cdot 10^{23} = 10^{27}$ atoms of gold; and for 100,000 ounces of gold, there are $10^5 \cdot 10^{23} = 10^{28}$ atoms of gold.

b. The power of 10 closest to 96,000 is 10^5, or 100,000. So there were about $10^5 \cdot 10^{23} = 10^{5 + 23}$, or 10^{28} atoms of gold extracted from the mine.

Lesson 8.2 (pp. 498–501)

33.
$$\begin{aligned}\left(\frac{3x^3}{2y}\right)^2 \cdot \frac{1}{x^2} &= \frac{(3x^3)^2}{(2y)^2} \cdot \frac{1}{x^2}\\ &= \frac{3^2 \cdot (x^3)^2}{2^2 \cdot y^2} \cdot \frac{1}{x^2}\\ &= \frac{9x^6}{4y^2} \cdot \frac{1}{x^2}\\ &= \frac{9x^6}{4x^2y^2}\\ &= \frac{9x^4}{4y^2}\end{aligned}$$

51. Convert the speed of the spacecraft to kilometers per second.

$$\frac{10^4 \text{ m}}{1 \text{ sec}} \cdot \frac{1 \text{ km}}{10^3 \text{ m}} = \frac{10^{4-3} \text{ km}}{1 \text{ sec}} = \frac{10^1 \text{ km}}{1 \text{ sec}}$$

So the speed of the spacecraft is 10 kilometers per second.

Use the quotient of powers property to calculate the number of seconds it would take to make the trip.

$$\frac{10^{13}\text{ km}}{10^1\text{ km/sec}} = 10^{13-1}\text{ sec} = 10^{12}\text{ sec}$$

Calculate the number of seconds in a year (using 365 days = 1 year).

$$\frac{60\text{ sec}}{1\text{ min}} \cdot \frac{60\text{ min}}{1\text{ h}} \cdot \frac{24\text{ h}}{1\text{ day}} \cdot \frac{365\text{ day}}{1\text{ yr}} = \frac{31{,}356{,}000\text{ sec}}{1\text{ yr}}$$

Now convert the trip time, 10^{12} seconds, to years.

$$10^{12}\text{ sec} \div \frac{31{,}536{,}000\text{ sec}}{1\text{ yr}} \approx 31{,}710\text{ yr}$$

It would take about 31,710 years for the spacecraft to reach Alpha Centauri.

Lesson 8.3 (pp. 506–508)

11. $\left(\frac{2}{7}\right)^{-2} = \frac{1}{\left(\frac{2}{7}\right)^2} = \frac{1}{\frac{4}{49}} = \frac{49}{4}$

53. To find the number of red blood cells in the entire sample, multiply the sample size, 10^{-2} liter, by the ratio 10^7 red blood cells per 10^{-6} liter.

$$10^{-2}\text{ L} \cdot \frac{10^7\text{ red blood cells}}{10^{-6}\text{ L}}$$

$$= \frac{10^{-2} \cdot 10^7}{10^{-6}}\text{ red blood cells}$$

$$= 10^{-2+7-(-6)}\text{ red blood cells}$$

$$= 10^{11}\text{ red blood cells}$$

The entire sample would contain about 10^{11} red blood cells.

Lesson 8.4 (pp. 515–518)

3. Since 8.5 is already between 1 and 10, you move the decimal point 0 places and the exponent is 0: $8.5 = 8.5 \times 10^0$.

17. Since the exponent is 7, move the decimal point 7 places to the right: $7.5 \times 10^7 = 75{,}000{,}000$.

53. Divide the number of pounds of cotton by the number of acres.

$$\frac{9.7 \times 10^8}{6.9 \times 10^5} = \frac{9.7}{6.9} \times \frac{10^8}{10^5}$$

$$\approx 1.4058 \times 10^3 \approx 1405.8$$

The average number of pounds produced per acre was about 1406 pounds per acre.

Lesson 8.5 (pp. 523–527)

13. Make a table of values by choosing values for x and finding the corresponding values for y. The domain of the function is all real numbers.

x	−2	−1	0	1	2	3
y	$0.\overline{4}$	$0.\overline{6}$	1	1.5	2.25	3.375

Plot the points from the table and draw a smooth curve through them.

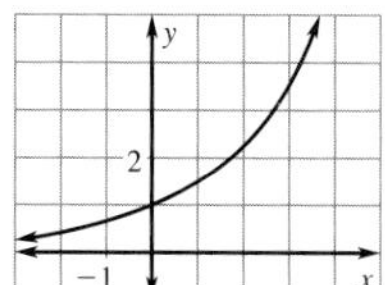

The table and the graph show that the range of the function is all positive real numbers.

41. a. Use the exponential growth model, $y = a(1 + r)^t$.

For tree 1 (with 6% = 0.06), substitute A for y, 154 for a, and 0.06 for r.

$A = 154(1 + 0.06)^t = 154(1.06)^t$

For tree 2 (with 10% = 0.1), substitute A for y, 113 for a, and 0.1 for r.

$A = 113(1 + 0.1)^t = 113(1.1)^t$

The functions are $A = 154(1.06)^t$ for tree 1 and $A = 113(1.1)^t$ for tree 2.

b. 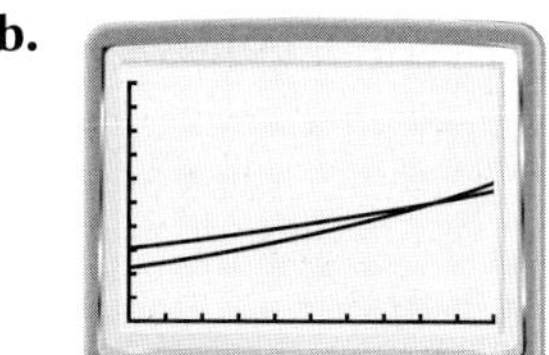

Using the *intersect* feature of the graphing calculator, the graphs intersect at about the point (8.4, 250.6). So, the trees will be the same height in about 8.4 years.

Lesson 8.6 (pp. 535–538)

7. Make a table of values by choosing values for x and finding the corresponding values for y. The domain of the function is all real numbers.

x	−2	−1	0	1	2
y	25	5	1	$\frac{1}{5}$	$\frac{1}{25}$

Plot the points from the table and draw a smooth curve through them.

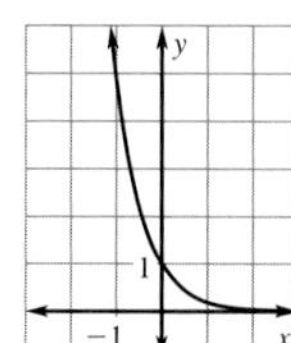

The table and the graph show that the range of the function is all positive real numbers.

WORKED-OUT SOLUTIONS

49. Let V be the value of the boat (in dollars) and let t be the time (in years since 2003).

Use the exponential decay model, $y = a(1 - r)^t$, to write a function for the value of the boat over time. Substitute V for y, 4000 for a, and 0.07 for r.

$V = 4000(1 - 0.07)^t$

$= 4000(0.93)^t$

In 2006, the value of t is 2006 − 2003, or 3.

$V = 4000(0.93)^3 \approx \$3217.43$

The value of the boat in 2006 is about \$3217. The family should not sell the boat, since the \$3000 offer is less than the value of the boat.

Chapter 9

Lesson 9.1 (pp. 557–559)

21. $(6c^2 + 3c + 9) - (3c - 5)$

$= 6c^2 + 3c + 9 - 3c + 5$

$= 6c^2 + (3c - 3c) + (9 + 5)$

$= 6c^2 + 14$

39. a. Add the models for the number of books of each type sold to find a model T for the total number (in millions) of books sold.

$T = A + J$

$= (9.5t^3 - 58t^2 + 66t + 500) + (-15t^2 + 64t + 360)$

$= 9.5t^3 + (-58t^2 - 15t^2) + (66t + 64t) + (500 + 360)$

$= 9.5t^3 - 73t^2 + 130t + 860$

b. To find the total number (in millions) of books sold in the years 1998 and 2002, substitute the number of years since 1998 for t in the model. Then compare the results.

For 1998, $t = 1998 - 1998 = 0$:

$M = 9.5(0)^3 - 73(0)^2 + 130(0) + 860 = 860$

There were 860 million books sold in 1998.

For 2002, $t = 2002 - 1998 = 4$:

$M = 9.5(4)^3 - 73(4)^2 + 130(4) + 860$

$= 9.5(64) - 73(16) + 130(4) + 860$

$= 608 - 1168 + 520 + 860$

$= 820$

There were 820 million books sold in 2002.

More books were sold in 1998 than in 2002.

Lesson 9.2 (pp. 565–568)

23. $(5x + 2)(-3x^2 + 4x - 1)$

$= 5x(-3x^2 + 4x - 1) + 2(-3x^2 + 4x - 1)$

$= -15x^3 + 20x^2 - 5x - 6x^2 + 8x - 2$

$= -15x^3 + (20x^2 - 6x^2) + (-5x + 8x) - 2$

$= -15x^3 + 14x^2 + 3x - 2$

51. a. Substitute 0 for t in each function:

$R = -336(0)^2 + 1730(0) + 12{,}300 = 12{,}300$

$P = 0.00351(0)^2 - 0.0249(0) + 0.171 = 0.171$

Since t is the number of years since 1997, the product $R \cdot P$ when $t = 0$ represents the amount (in million of dollars) spent in 1997 on sound recordings in the U.S. by people between 15 and 19 years old.

b. $R \cdot P = (-336t^2 + 1730t + 12{,}300) \cdot (0.00351t^2 - 0.0249t + 0.171)$

$= -336t^2(0.00351t^2 - 0.0249t + 0.171) + 1730t(0.00351t^2 - 0.0249t + 0.171) + 12{,}300(0.00351t^2 - 0.0249t + 0.171)$

$= -1.17936t^4 + 8.3664t^3 - 57.456t^2 + 6.0723t^3 - 43.077t^2 + 295.83t + 43.173t^2 - 306.27t + 2103.3$

$= -1.17936t^4 + (8.3664t^3 + 6.0723t^3) + (-57.456t^2 - 43.077t^2 + 43.173t^2) + (295.83t - 306.27t) + 2103.3$

$= -1.17936t^4 + 14.4387t^3 - 57.36t^2 - 10.44t + 2103.3$

So, $R \cdot P \approx -1.18t^4 + 14.4t^3 - 57.4t^2 - 10.4t + 2100.$

WORKED-OUT SOLUTIONS

c. For 2002, $t = 2002 - 1997 = 5$. Substitute 5 for t in the equation for part (b).

$$R \cdot P \approx -1.18(5)^4 + 14.4(5)^3 - 57.4(5)^2 - 10.4(5) + 2100$$

$$\approx -1.18(625) + 14.4(125) - 57.4(25) - 10.4(5) + 2100$$

$$\approx -737.50 + 1800 - 1435 - 52 + 2100$$

$$\approx 1675.5$$

In 2002, people between the ages of 15 and 19 years old spent about 1680 million dollars (or $1,680,000,000) on sound recordings.

Lesson 9.3 (pp. 572–574)

11. $(t + 4)(t - 4) = t^2 - 4^2 = t^2 - 16$

41. a.

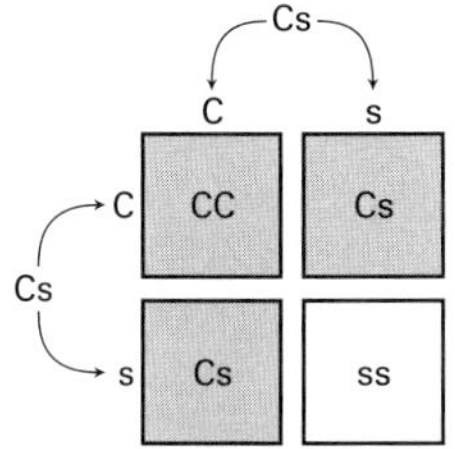

b. Model the gene from each parent with $0.5C + 0.5s$. There is an equal chance that the child inherits a straight thumb gene or a curved thumb gene from each parent. The possible gene combinations of the child can be modeled by $(0.5C + 0.5s)^2$, or

$$(0.5C)^2 + 2(0.5C)(0.5s) + (0.5s)^2$$

$$= 0.25C^2 + 0.5Cs + 0.25s^2$$

c. Consider the coefficients in the polynomial found in part (b). The coefficients show that 25% + 50% = 75% of the possible gene combinations will contain a C, and thus result in a child with a curved thumb.

Lesson 9.4 (pp. 578–580)

3. $(x - 5)(x + 3) = 0$

$x - 5 = 0$ *or* $x + 3 = 0$

$x = 5$ *or* $x = -3$

The solutions of the equation are 5 and −3.

55. a. The initial vertical velocity is given as 4.9 meters per second and the rabbit starts from the ground, so $v = 4.9$ and $s = 0$ in the vertical motion model.

$$h = -4.9t^2 + vt + s$$

$$= -4.9t^2 + 4.9t + 0$$

$$= -4.9t^2 + 4.9t$$

b. When the rabbit lands, its height above the ground is 0 meters. A reasonable domain for t can be found by substituting 0 for h and solving for t.

$$0 = -4.9t^2 + 4.9t$$

$$0 = 4.9t(-t + 1)$$

$4.9t = 0$ *or* $-t + 1 = 0$

$t = 0$ *or* $t = 1$

Since a height of 0 represents when the rabbit is on the ground, $t = 1$ second represents how long it takes for the rabbit to land back on the ground after jumping at $t = 0$ seconds. So, a reasonable domain is all real numbers greater than or equal to 0 and less than or equal to 1, or $0 \le t \le 1$.

Lesson 9.5 (pp. 586–589)

7. In $z^2 + 8z - 48$, $c = -48$. Since c is negative, p and q must have different signs.

Factors of −48	Sum of factors	
−48, 1	−48 + 1 = −47	✗
48, −1	48 + (−1) = 47	✗
−24, 2	−24 + 2 = −22	✗
24, −2	24 + (−2) = 22	✗
−16, 3	−16 + 3 = −13	✗
16, −3	16 + (−3) = 13	✗
−12, 4	−12 + 4 = −8	✗
12, −4	12 + (−4) = 8	← Correct

So, $z^2 + 8z - 48 = (z + 12)(z - 4)$.

WORKED-OUT SOLUTIONS

WORKED-OUT SOLUTIONS

61. Let x be the original length of the sides of the square photo. Then the length of the trimmed photo is $(x - 6)$ inches and its width is $(x - 5)$ inches. The formula $A = \ell \cdot w$ models the area of the trimmed photo which is 20 square inches.

$A = \ell \cdot w$

$20 = (x - 6)(x - 5)$

$20 = x^2 - 11x + 30$

$0 = x^2 - 11x + 10$

$0 = (x - 10)(x - 1)$

$x - 10 = 0$ *or* $x - 1 = 0$

$x = 10$ *or* $x = 1$

So, the original square photo had a side length of 10 inches or 1 inch. But an original length of 1 inch does not make sense in this situation, so the side length of the original square photo was 10 inches. Therefore, the perimeter of the original square photo was 4(10), or 40 inches.

Lesson 9.6 (pp. 596–599)

5. Factor −1 from each term of the trinomial: $-y^2 + 2y + 8 = -(y^2 - 2y - 8)$.

In $y^2 - 2y - 8$, $c = -8$. Since c is negative, the factors of c must have different signs.

Factors of −8	Possible factorization	Middle term when multiplied	
−8, 1	$(y - 8)(y + 1)$	$y - 8y = -7y$	✗
8, −1	$(y + 8)(y - 1)$	$-y + 8y = 7y$	✗
−4, 2	$(y - 4)(y + 2)$	$2y - 4y = -2y$	← Correct
4, −2	$(y + 4)(y - 2)$	$-2y + 4y = 2y$	✗

So, $y^2 - 2y - 8 = (y - 4)(y + 2)$. Therefore,

$-y^2 + 2y + 8 = -(y^2 - 2y - 8)$

$= -(y - 4)(y + 2)$

25. $4s^2 + 11s - 3 = 0$

$(4s - 1)(s + 3) = 0$

$4s - 1 = 0$ *or* $s + 3 = 0$

$s = \frac{1}{4}$ *or* $s = -3$

61. Let w be the width of the Parthenon's base. Then $2w + 8$ is the length of the base. The formula $A = \ell \cdot w$ models the area of the rectangular base which is 2170 square meters.

$A = \ell \cdot w$

$2170 = (2w + 8) \cdot w$

$2170 = 2w^2 + 8w$

$0 = 2w^2 + 8w - 2170$

$0 = 2(w^2 + 4w - 1085)$

$0 = 2(w + 35)(w - 31)$

$w + 35 = 0$ *or* $w - 31 = 0$

$w = -35$ *or* $w = 31$

The solutions are −35 and 31.

Since the width cannot be negative, reject −35 as a solution. So, the width is 31 meters and the length is 2(31) + 8, or 70 meters. Therefore, the base of the Parthenon has length 70 meters and width 31 meters.

Lesson 9.7 (pp. 603–605)

11. $49a^2 + 14a + 1 = (7a)^2 + 2(7a \cdot 1) + 1^2$

$= (7a + 1)^2$

49. Use the vertical motion model with $h = 54$, $v = 56$, and $s = 5$.

$h = -16t^2 + vt + s$

$54 = -16t^2 + 56t + 5$

$0 = -16t^2 + 56t - 49$

$0 = -(16t^2 - 56t + 49)$

$0 = -[(4t)^2 - 2(4t \cdot 7) + 7^2]$

$0 = -(4t - 7)^2$

$0 = (4t - 7)^2$

$4t - 7 = 0$

$t = 1.75$

The ball reaches a height of 54 feet in 1.75 seconds. Since there is one solution for t, the ball reaches a height of 54 feet just once.

Lesson 9.8 (pp. 610–613)

13. $x^3 + x^2 + 2x + 2 = (x^3 + x^2) + (2x + 2)$

$= x^2(x + 1) + 2(x + 1)$

$= (x + 1)(x^2 + 2)$

23. $x^4 - x^2 = x^2(x^2 - 1) = x^2(x - 1)(x + 1)$

71. a. Substitute 0 for h in $h = -4.9t^2 + 3.9t + 1$.

$0 = -4.9t^2 + 3.9t + 1$

$0 = -(4.9t^2 - 3.9t - 1)$

$0 = -(4.9t + 1)(t - 1)$

$4.9t + 1 = 0$ *or* $t - 1 = 0$

$t \approx -0.20$ *or* $t = 1$

The zeros are 1 and about -0.2.

b. The zero $t \approx -0.2$ has no meaning in this situation because t represents time which cannot be negative. The zero $t = 1$ means that the pallino hits the ground (where $h = 0$) 1 second after it is thrown.

Chapter 10

Lesson 10.1 (pp. 632–634)

7. Make a table of values for $y = -2x^2$.

x	−2	−1	0	1	2
y	−8	−2	0	−2	−8

Plot the points from the table. Draw a smooth curve through the points.

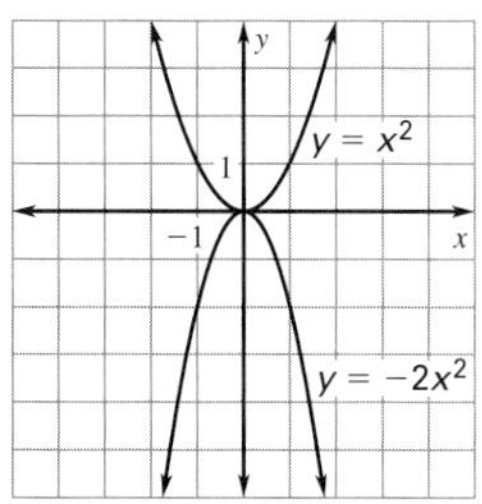

The graphs of $y = -2x^2$ and $y = x^2$ have the same vertex, (0, 0), and the same axis of symmetry, $x = 0$. However, the graph of $-2x^2$ is narrower than the graph of $y = x^2$, and it opens down. This is because the graph of $y = -2x^2$ is a vertical stretch (by a factor of 2) with a reflection in the x-axis of the graph of $y = x^2$.

41. a.

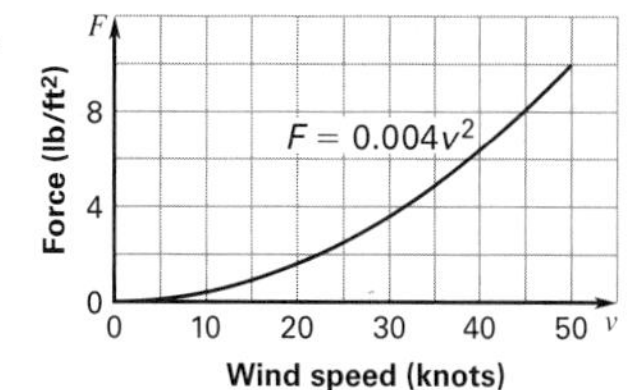

b. From the graph, the wind speed that will produce a force of 1 pound per square foot on a sail is about 16 knots. Using the function to check: $F = 0.004(16)^2 = 1.024$.

c. From the graph, the wind speed that will produce a force of 5 pounds per square foot on a sail is about 35 knots. Using the function to check: $F = 0.004(35)^2 = 4.9$.

Lesson 10.2 (pp. 638–640)

9. For $y = -\frac{2}{3}x^2 - 1$, $a = -\frac{2}{3}$ and $b = 0$.

$$x = -\frac{b}{2a} = \frac{0}{2\left(-\frac{2}{3}\right)} = 0$$

The axis of symmetry is $x = 0$.

The x-coordinate of the vertex, $-\frac{b}{2a}$, is 0. To find the y-coordinate, substitute 0 for x in the function and find y: $y = -\frac{2}{3}(0)^2 - 1 = -1$. The vertex is $(0, -1)$.

41. The highest point of each parabolic arch is at the vertex of the parabola. The height h is the y-coordinate of the vertex.

To find the x-coordinate of the vertex, use $x = -\frac{b}{2a}$ with $a = -0.0019$ and $b = 0.71$.

$$x = -\frac{b}{2a} = -\frac{0.71}{2(-0.0019)} \approx 187$$

Substitute 187 for x in the given equation to find the y-coordinate of the vertex.

$y = -0.0019(187)^2 + 0.71(187) \approx 66.3$

The height h at the highest point of the arch is about 66 feet.

Lesson 10.3 (pp. 647–649)

5. Write the equation $x^2 + 6x = -8$ in standard form: $x^2 + 6x + 8 = 0$.

Graph the function $y = x^2 + 6x + 8$.

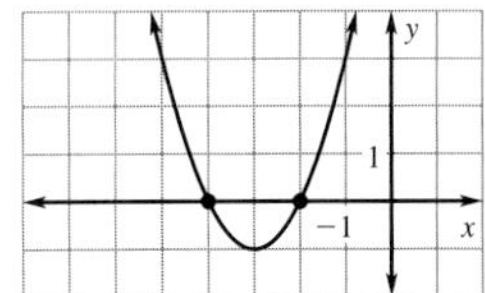

The x-intercepts are -4 and -2.

So, the solutions of $x^2 + 6x = -8$ are -4 and -2.

51. The width of the road can be found by finding the distance between the x-intercepts of the graph $y = -0.0017x^2 + 0.041x$.

Graph the function $y = -0.0017x^2 + 0.041x$ on a graphing calculator.

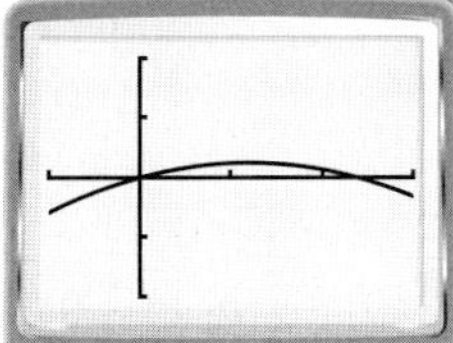

Use the *trace* feature of the graphing calculator to find the x-intercepts. There are two x-intercepts, one at 0 and one at approximately 24.12.

To the nearest tenth of a foot, the width of the road is 24.1 feet.

Lesson 10.4 (pp. 655–658)

25. $7c^2 = 100$

$$c^2 = \frac{100}{7}$$

$$c = \pm\sqrt{\frac{100}{7}}$$

$c \approx \pm 3.78$ Use a calculator.

59. First, solve the formula for D: $D = \pm\sqrt{\frac{w}{0.0018ds}}$.

Since D cannot be negative in this situation, use the positive square root only.

a. For amethyst, substitute 1 for w, 4.5 for d, and 2.65 for s.

$$D = \sqrt{\frac{1}{0.0018(4.5)(2.65)}} \approx 6.83$$

The diameter is about 6.8 millimeters.

b. For diamond, substitute 1 for w, 4.5 for d, and 3.52 for s.

$$D = \sqrt{\frac{1}{0.0018(4.5)(3.52)}} \approx 5.92$$

The diameter is about 5.9 millimeters.

c. For ruby, substitute 1 for w, 4.5 for d, and 4.00 for s.

$$D = \sqrt{\frac{1}{0.0018(4.5)(4.00)}} \approx 5.55$$

The diameter is about 5.6 millimeters.

Lesson 10.5 (pp. 666–668)

19. $z^2 + 11z = -\frac{21}{4}$

$$z^2 + 11z + \left(\frac{11}{2}\right)^2 = -\frac{21}{4} + \left(\frac{11}{2}\right)^2$$

$$\left(z + \frac{11}{2}\right)^2 = -\frac{21}{4} + \frac{121}{4}$$

$$\left(z + \frac{11}{2}\right)^2 = 25$$

$$z + \frac{11}{2} = \pm 5$$

$$z = -\frac{11}{2} \pm 5$$

The solutions of the equation are $-\frac{11}{2} + 5 = -0.5$ and $-\frac{11}{2} - 5 = -10.5$.

47. a. Convert \$1,904,000 to thousands of dollars: $1{,}904{,}000 \div 1000 = 1904$.

Substitute 1904 for y in $y = 7x^2 - 4x + 392$: $1904 = 7x^2 - 4x + 392$.

$$7x^2 - 4x + 392 = 1904$$

$$7x^2 - 4x = 1512$$

$$x^2 - \frac{4}{7}x = 216$$

$$x^2 - \frac{4}{7}x + \left(\frac{2}{7}\right)^2 = 216 + \left(\frac{2}{7}\right)^2$$

$$\left(x - \frac{2}{7}\right)^2 = 216\frac{4}{49}$$

$$x - \frac{2}{7} = \pm\sqrt{216\frac{4}{49}}$$

$$x = \frac{2}{7} \pm \sqrt{216\frac{4}{49}}$$

Using a calculator, the solutions are about 14.99 and about -14.41.

The negative value does not make sense in this situation because the function does not model the years prior to 1985. So, the year when the average salary was \$1,904,000 was 1985 + 15, or 2000.

WORKED-OUT SOLUTIONS

b. First, graph the function $y = 7x^2 - 4x + 392$ for $x \geq 0$. Then draw a dashed line at about $y = 1904$ until it intersects the curve. Draw a dashed line from this point down to the x-axis. The x-value here is about 15. So, the year when the average salary was \$1,904,000 is about 1985 + 15, or 2000.

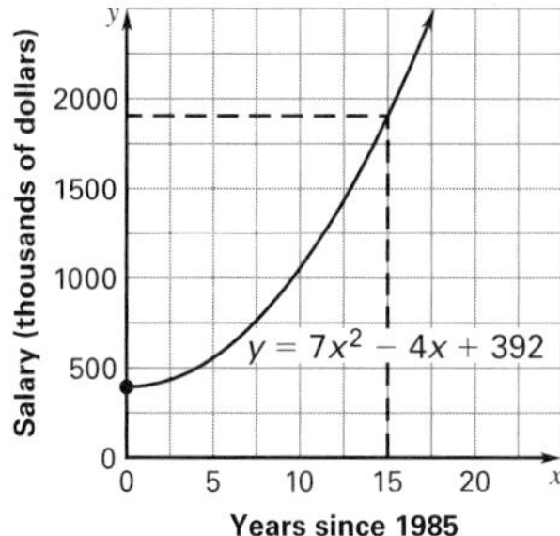

Lesson 10.6 (pp. 674–676)

19. Write $6z^2 = 2z^2 + 7z + 5$ in standard form: $4z^2 - 7z - 5 = 0$.

Use the quadratic formula, with $a = 4$, $b = -7$, and $c = -5$.

$$z = \frac{-(-7) \pm \sqrt{(-7)^2 - 4(4)(-5)}}{2(4)} = \frac{7 \pm \sqrt{129}}{8}$$

Using a calculator, the solutions are about 2.29 and about −0.54.

47. For 16,000,000 subscribers, $y = 16$ in the function.

$$16 = 0.7x^2 - 4.3x + 5.5$$

$$0 = 0.7x^2 - 4.3x - 10.5$$

Use the quadratic formula, with $a = 0.7$, $b = -4.3$, and $c = -10.5$.

$$x = \frac{-(-4.3) \pm \sqrt{(-4.3)^2 - 4(0.7)(-10.5)}}{2(0.7)}$$

$$= \frac{4.3 \pm \sqrt{47.89}}{1.4} \quad \text{Use a calculator.}$$

The solutions are about 8.01 and about −1.87.

The negative value does not make sense in this situation because the function does not model the years prior to 1985. So, the year when the number of subscribers was 16,000,000 was 1985 + 8, or 1993.

Lesson 10.7 (pp. 681–683)

9. Find the value of the discriminant. Substitute 25 for a, −16 for b, and 0 for c.

$$b^2 - 4ac = (-16)^2 - 4(25)(0) = 256$$

Since 256 > 0, the equation has two solutions.

47. In order for the child not to have to bend over, the height y of the arch must be at least 4 feet. Use the given quadratic equation with 4 substituted for y.

$$4 = -0.18x^2 + 1.6x$$

$$0 = -0.18x^2 + 1.6x - 4$$

Find the value of the discriminant. Substitute −0.18 for a, 1.6 for b, and −4 for c.

$$b^2 - 4ac = (1.6)^2 - 4(-0.18)(-4) = -0.32$$

Because the discriminant is negative, there are no solutions of the equation $0 = -0.18x^2 + 1.6x - 4$, meaning that the height of an arch is less than 4 feet. So, a child who is 4 feet tall would not be able to walk under one of the arches without having to bend over.

Lesson 10.8 (pp. 688–691)

7. 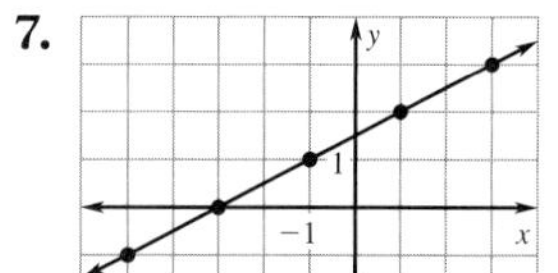

linear function

13.

x	−2	−1	0	1	2
y	−4	−1	0	−1	−4

First differences: +3 +1 −1 −3

Second differences: −2 −2 −2

The second differences are equal, so the table of values represents a quadratic function.

The equation has the form $y = ax^2$. Find the value of a by using the coordinates of a point (other than the origin) that lies on the graph, such as (−1, −1).

$$y = ax^2$$

$$-1 = a(-1)^2$$

$$-1 = a$$

An equation for the function is $y = -x^2$.

WORKED-OUT SOLUTIONS

25. a.

Folds	1	2	3	4	5
Sections	2	4	8	16	32

b. 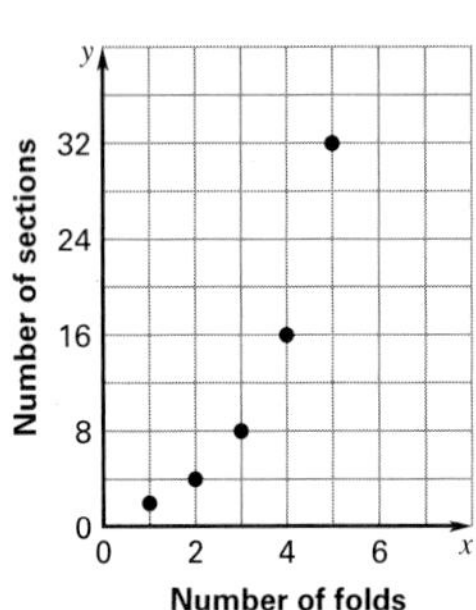

Both the graph and the table show that the data can be modeled by an exponential function.

c. Write an exponential equation of the form $y = ab^x$. From the table, the number of sections increases by a factor of 2, so $b = 2$. Find the value of a using one of the data pairs, such as (3, 8).

$y = ab^x$

$8 = a(2)^3$

$1 = a$

The exponential equation is $y = 2^x$.

To find the number of sections created by 7 folds, substitute 7 for x in $y = 2^x$: $y = 2^7 = 128$.

Chapter 11

Lesson 11.1 (pp. 713–716)

7. Make a table. Because the square root of a negative number is undefined, x must be nonnegative. So the domain of the function is $x \geq 0$.

x	0	1	2	3	4
y	0	1.5	2.1	2.6	3

Plot the ordered pairs from the table and then draw a smooth curve through the points. From the graph, it can seen that the range of the function is $y \geq 0$.

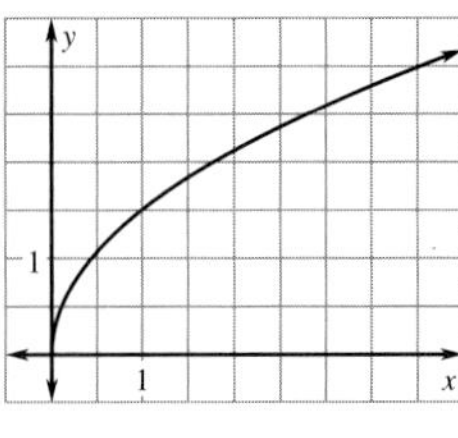

The graph of $y = \frac{3}{2}\sqrt{x}$ is a vertical stretch $\left(\text{by a factor of } \frac{3}{2}\right)$ of the graph of $y = \sqrt{x}$.

23. Make a table. Because the square root of a negative number is undefined, the value of $x - 1$ must be nonnegative: $x - 1 \geq 0$. So the domain of the function is $x \geq 1$.

x	1	2	3	4	5
y	0	1	1.4	1.7	2

Plot the ordered pairs from the table and then draw a smooth curve through the points.

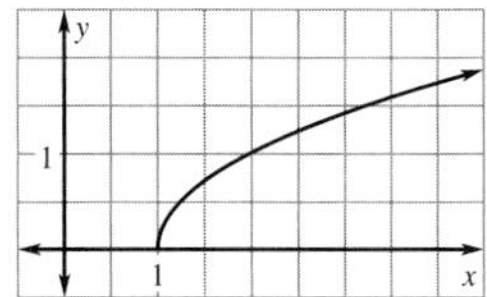

From the graph, it can seen that the range of the function is $y \geq 0$.

The graph of $y = \sqrt{x - 1}$ is a horizontal translation (of 1 unit to the right) of the graph of $y = \sqrt{x}$.

45. Because the square root of a negative number is undefined, h must be nonnegative. So the domain of the function is $h \geq 0$.

h	0	0.25	0.5	0.75	1
s	0	5.45	7.7	9.4	10.9

Plot the ordered pairs from the table and then draw a smooth curve through the points. From the graph, it can seen that the range of the function is $s \geq 0$.

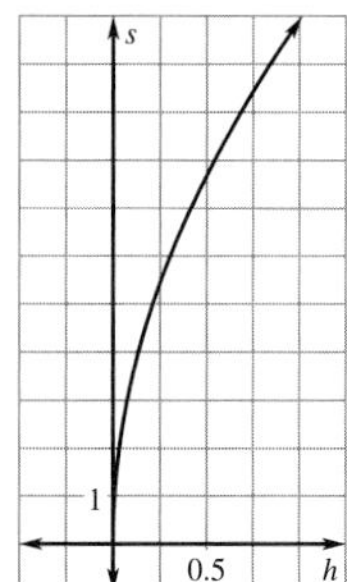

The maximum height reached is about 0.9 meter when the long jumper's speed before jumping is 10.25 meters per second.

Lesson 11.2 (pp. 723–726)

9. $\sqrt{81m^3} = \sqrt{81 \cdot m^2 \cdot m}$

$= \sqrt{81} \cdot \sqrt{m^2} \cdot \sqrt{m}$

$= 9m\sqrt{m}$

37. $9\sqrt{32} + \sqrt{2} = 9\sqrt{16 \cdot 2} + \sqrt{2}$

$= 9\sqrt{16} \cdot \sqrt{2} + \sqrt{2}$

$= 9 \cdot 4 \cdot \sqrt{2} + \sqrt{2}$

$= 36\sqrt{2} + \sqrt{2}$

$= (36 + 1)\sqrt{2}$

$= 37\sqrt{2}$

69. a. \$30 ÷ \$6 per square yard = 5 square yards

b. $s \text{ yd} = \sqrt{\frac{S \text{ yd}^2}{6}} = \sqrt{\frac{S}{6} \cdot \frac{\text{yd}^2}{1}}$

$= \sqrt{\frac{S}{6}} \cdot \sqrt{\frac{\text{yd}^2}{1}} = \sqrt{\frac{S}{6}} \text{ yd}$

Therefore s yd$= \sqrt{\frac{S}{6}}$ yd, and the units check.

c. Substitute 5 for S in the formula $s = \sqrt{\frac{S}{6}}$:

$s = \sqrt{\frac{5}{6}} \approx 0.9.$

To the nearest tenth of a yard, the edge length of the largest footrest you can cover with 5 square yards of fabric is 0.9 yard.

Lesson 11.3 (pp. 732–734)

11. $\sqrt{6 - 2x} + 12 = 21$

$\sqrt{6 - 2x} = 9$

$6 - 2x = 81$

$-2x = 75$

$x = -\frac{75}{2}$, or $-37\frac{1}{2}$

37. Substitute 20 for y in the given function.

$\sqrt{18x + 272} = 20$

$18x + 272 = 400$

$18x = 128$

$x = \frac{128}{18}$, or about 7.1

So, the annual banana consumption in the United States reached 20 pounds per person in the year 1970 + 7, or 1977.

Lesson 11.4 (pp. 740–742)

9. $a^2 + b^2 = c^2$

$8^2 + 12^2 = c^2$ Substitute 8 for a and 12 for b.

$208 = c^2$

$\sqrt{208} = c$ Positive square root only.

$4\sqrt{13} = c$

23. Check to see if $a^2 + b^2 = c^2$ when $a = 2$, $b = 3$, and $c = 4$.

$2^2 + 3^2 \stackrel{?}{=} 4^2$

$4 + 9 \stackrel{?}{=} 16$

$13 \neq 16$ Not a right triangle

35. Check to see if $a^2 + b^2 = c^2$ when $a = 87$, $b = 173$, and $c = 190$.

$87^2 + 173^2 \stackrel{?}{=} 190^2$

$7569 + 29{,}929 \stackrel{?}{=} 36{,}100$

$37498 \neq 36100$

So, the triangle is not a right triangle. The sum of the squares of the lengths of the two shorter sides is not equal to the square of the length of the longest side.

Lesson 11.5 (pp. 747–750)

7. Let $(x_1, y_1) = (-4, 1)$ and $(x_2, y_2) = (3, -1)$.

$d = \sqrt{(x_2 - x_1)^2 + (y_2 - y_1)^2}$

$= \sqrt{(3 - (-4))^2 + (-1 - 1)^2}$

$= \sqrt{7^2 + (-2)^2} = \sqrt{53}$

23. Let $(x_1, y_1) = (6, -3)$ and $(x_2, y_2) = (4, -7)$.

$\left(\frac{x_1 + x_2}{2}, \frac{y_1 + y_2}{2}\right) = \left(\frac{6 + 4}{2}, \frac{-3 + (-7)}{2}\right) = (5, -5)$

49. a. The coordinates of the anchor are (2, 3), the coordinates of the sword are (9, 2), and the coordinates of the cup are (8, 5).

Distance between the anchor and sword: Let $(x_1, y_1) = (2, 3)$ and $(x_2, y_2) = (9, 2)$.

$d = \sqrt{(9 - 2)^2 + (2 - 3)^2}$

$= \sqrt{7^2 + (-1)^2} = \sqrt{50}$

Distance between the anchor and cup: Let $(x_1, y_1) = (2, 3)$ and $(x_2, y_2) = (8, 5)$.

$d = \sqrt{(8 - 2)^2 + (5 - 3)^2}$

$= \sqrt{6^2 + (2)^2} = \sqrt{40}$

Since $\sqrt{40} < \sqrt{50}$, the anchor and the cup are closer together.

b. By examining the survey grid, the belt buckle and the sword are closest together; they are 3 units, or 150 feet, apart.

Again, by examining the survey grid, the two objects farthest apart are either the anchor and cup or the anchor and sword. The result in part (a) shows that the anchor and the sword are farthest apart; they are $\sqrt{50}$ units, or $50\sqrt{50} \approx 354$ feet, apart.

Chapter 12

Lesson 12.1 (pp. 769–772)

17. Make a table by choosing several integer values of x and finding the values of y. Notice that x cannot be 0, and that y will never be 0.

x	−7	−5	−2	−1	0	1	2	5	7
y	1	1.4	3.5	7	—	−7	−3.5	−1.4	−1

Plot the points (x, y) from the table.

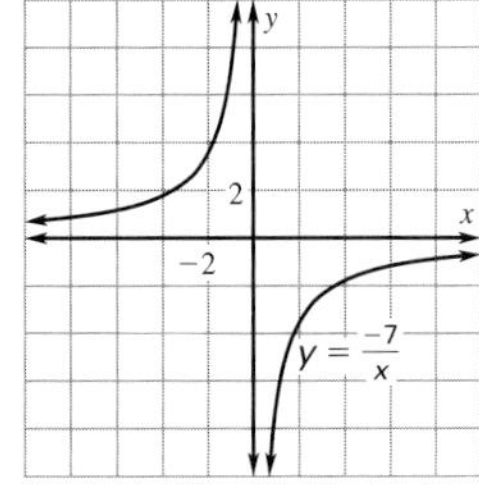

Connect the points in Quadrant II by drawing a smooth curve through them. Draw a separate curve though the points in Quadrant IV.

33. Because y varies inversely with x, the equation has the form $y = \frac{a}{x}$. Use the fact that $x = -22$ when $y = -6$ to find the value of a.

$-6 = \frac{a}{-22}$, so $a = -6(-22)$, or 132

An equation that relates x and y is $y = \frac{132}{x}$.

When $x = 2$, $y = \frac{132}{2}$, or 66.

57. a. An inverse variation equation can be used to model the data if each pair of points (ℓ, f) fits the same equation. Use $f = \frac{a}{\ell}$ to test the data.

For (42.1, 523): $523 = \frac{a}{42.1}$, so $a \approx 22{,}000$

For (37.5, 587): $587 = \frac{a}{37.5}$, so $a \approx 22{,}000$

For (33.4, 659): $659 = \frac{a}{33.4}$, so $a \approx 22{,}000$

For (31.5, 698): $698 = \frac{a}{31.5}$, so $a \approx 22{,}000$

Since the value of a is about the same for each pairing, the inverse equation $f = \frac{22{,}000}{\ell}$ can be used to model the data.

To graph $f = \frac{22{,}000}{\ell}$, make a table of values, plot the points (ℓ, f), and then draw a smooth curve through them. Use only positive values for ℓ since the length of a string cannot be negative.

ℓ	25	50	75	100
f	880	440	293.3	220

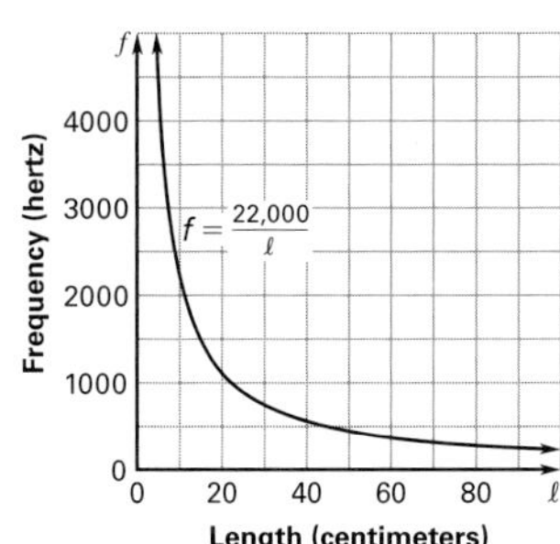

b. Use the equation found in part (a) with $\ell = 29.4$.

$f = \frac{22{,}000}{29.4} \approx 748.3$

The frequency is about 748 hertz.

c. The frequency increases as the length of the string decreases. Yes, the length in part (b), 29.4 centimeters, is shorter than those in the table, but it has the greatest frequency.

Lesson 12.2 (pp. 779–782)

7. Make a table of values for x and y.

x	$-\frac{1}{4}$	$-\frac{1}{2}$	0	$\frac{1}{4}$	$\frac{1}{2}$
y	1	$\frac{1}{2}$	—	−1	$-\frac{1}{2}$

Plot the points (x, y) from the table. Connect the points in Quadrant II by drawing a smooth curve through them. Draw a separate curve though the points in Quadrant IV.

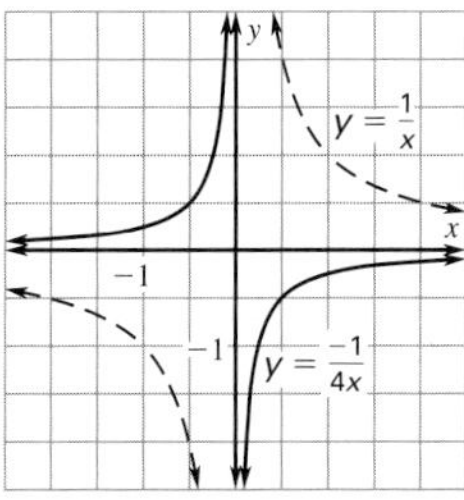

The graph of $y = \frac{-1}{4x}$ is a vertical shrink with a reflection in the x-axis of the graph of $y = \frac{1}{x}$.

21. The vertical asymptote of the graph is $x = -7$ and the horizontal asymptote is $y = 5$. Plot several points on each side of the vertical asymptote, such as $(-9, 3)$, $(-8, 1)$, $(-5, 7)$, and $(-3, 6)$. Draw the two branches of the graph that pass through the plotted points and approach the asymptotes.

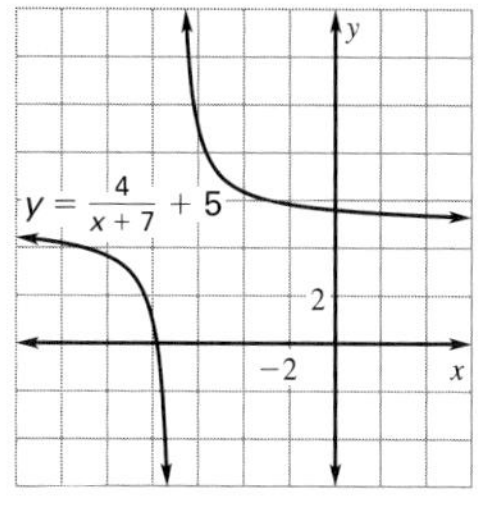

41. a. Use a verbal model to write an equation.

$$\boxed{\text{Average cost (dollars)}} = \boxed{\text{Total cost (dollars)}} \div \left(\boxed{\text{Number of additional rentals}} + 2\right)$$

$C = 22 \div (r + 2)$, or $C = \dfrac{22}{r + 2}$

b.

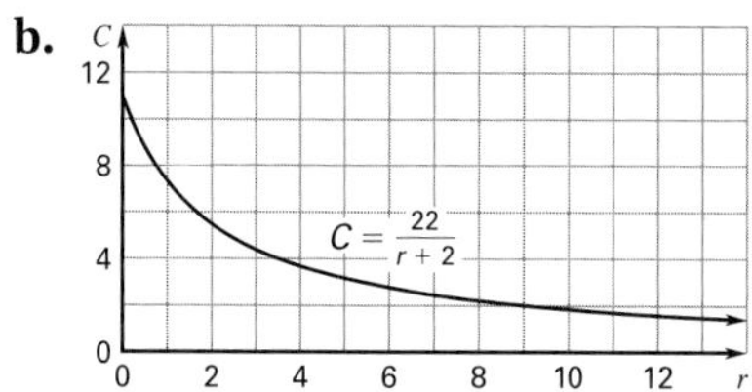

The graph shows that as the number of rentals increases, the average cost per rental decreases.

From the graph, the number of additional rentals needed per month so that the average cost is \$1.50 per rental is 13 additional rentals.

Lesson 12.3 (pp. 788–791)

7.

$$\begin{array}{r} 3v + 5 \\ v - 2\overline{)3v^2 - v - 10} \\ \underline{3v^2 - 6v} \\ 5v - 10 \\ \underline{5v - 10} \\ 0 \end{array}$$

25. Rewrite the function in the form $y = \dfrac{a}{x - h} + k$.

$$\begin{array}{r} 2 \\ x - 1\overline{)2x - 4} \\ \underline{2x - 2} \\ -2 \end{array}$$

So, $y = \dfrac{-2}{x - 1} + 2$.

The asymptotes of the graph can be identified from the equation. The vertical asymptote is $x = 1$ and the horizontal asymptote is $y = 2$. Plot several points on each side of the vertical asymptote, such as $(-1, 3)$, $(0, 4)$, $(2, 0)$, and $(3, 1)$. Draw the two branches of the graph.

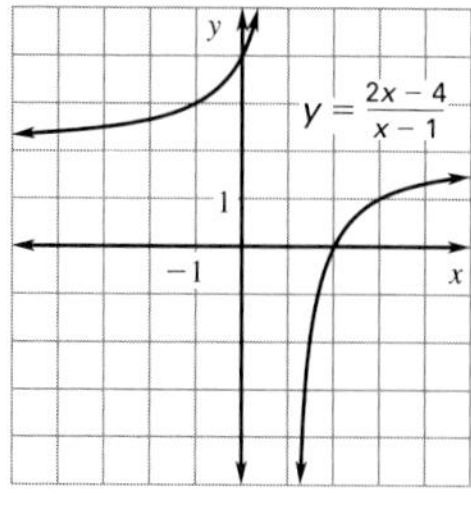

45. a. Since t is defined as the time for 1000 minutes or more, the domain of the function is $t \geq 1000$. The average cost C is found by adding the monthly fee to the product of the number of minutes over 1000 and the per-minute charge for those minutes, and then dividing that sum by the total number of minutes of use. The equation is $C = \dfrac{40 + 0.40(t - 1000)}{t}$, or $C = \dfrac{0.4t - 360}{t}$, where $t \geq 1000$.

b. Choose values of $t \geq 1000$.

t	1000	1100	1200	1300	1400	1500
C	0.04	0.073	0.10	0.123	0.143	0.16

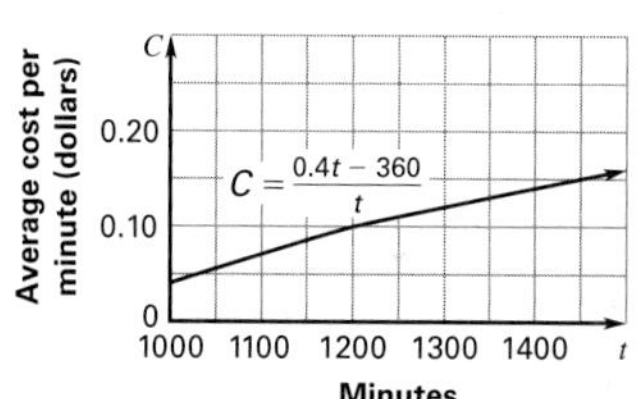

The average cost per minute increases as the number of minutes over 1000 increases.

c. From the graph you can see that the number of minutes used is about 1030 minutes if the average cost is \$.05 per minute.

Lesson 12.4 (pp. 797–800)

9. The expression $\dfrac{-3}{2p^2 - p}$ is undefined when $2p^2 - p = 0$.

$2p^2 - p = 0$

$p(2p - 1) = 0$

$p = 0$ *or* $2p - 1 = 0$

$p = \dfrac{1}{2}$

The excluded values are 0 and $\dfrac{1}{2}$.

WORKED-OUT SOLUTIONS

23. $\dfrac{h+3}{h^2-h-12} = \dfrac{h+3}{(h-4)(h+3)}$

$= \dfrac{\cancel{h+3}}{(h-4)\cancel{(h+3)}}$

$= \dfrac{1}{h-4}$

The excluded values are 4 and −3.

43. The percent of wood houses can be found by using the formula $p = \dfrac{W}{H}$.

$p = \dfrac{-20{,}200x + 366{,}000}{34{,}500x + 913{,}000} = \dfrac{-202x + 3660}{345x + 9130}$

To determine how the percent changed during the period 1990–2002, evaluate the function for several values of x.

For 1990, $x = 0$: $\dfrac{-202(0) + 3660}{345(0) + 9130} = \dfrac{3660}{9130} \approx 0.40$

In 1990, about 40% of new single-family houses were wood houses.

For 1994, $x = 4$: $\dfrac{-202(4) + 3660}{345(4) + 9130} = \dfrac{2852}{10{,}510} \approx 0.27$

In 1994, about 27% of new single-family houses were wood houses.

For 1998, $x = 8$: $\dfrac{-202(8) + 3660}{345(8) + 9130} = \dfrac{2044}{11{,}890} \approx 0.17$

In 1998, about 17% of new single-family houses were wood houses.

For 2002, $x = 12$:
$\dfrac{-202(12) + 3660}{345(12) + 9130} = \dfrac{1236}{13{,}270} \approx 0.09$

In 2002, about 9% of new single-family houses were wood houses.

The percent of wood houses decreased steadily from 1990 to 2002.

Lesson 12.5 (pp. 806–809)

5. $\dfrac{v^2+v-12}{5v+10} \cdot \dfrac{-v-2}{v^2+5v+4}$

$= \dfrac{(v^2+v-12)(-v-2)}{(5v+10)(v^2+5v+4)}$

$= \dfrac{\cancel{(v+4)}(v-3)(-1)\cancel{(v+2)}}{5\cancel{(v+2)}\cancel{(v+4)}(v+1)}$

$= \dfrac{-(v-3)}{5(v+1)}$

15. $\dfrac{2w^2+5w}{w^2-81} \div \dfrac{w^2}{w+9} = \dfrac{2w^2+5w}{w^2-81} \cdot \dfrac{w+9}{w^2}$

$= \dfrac{(2w^2+5w)(w+9)}{(w^2-81)(w^2)}$

$= \dfrac{\cancel{(w)}(2w+5)\cancel{(w+9)}}{\cancel{(w+9)}(w-9)\cancel{(w)}(w)}$

$= \dfrac{2w+5}{w(w-9)}$

35. a. Use the formula $R = Y \div A$.

$R = \dfrac{860 + 1800x}{1 + 0.024x} \div \dfrac{230 + 380x}{1 + 0.014x}$

$= \dfrac{860 + 1800x}{1 + 0.024x} \cdot \dfrac{1 + 0.014x}{230 + 380x}$

$= \dfrac{(860 + 1800x)(1 + 0.014x)}{(1 + 0.024x)(230 + 380x)}$

$= \dfrac{\cancel{(10)}(86 + 180x)(1 + 0.014x)}{(1 + 0.024x)\cancel{(10)}(23 + 38x)}$

$= \dfrac{(86 + 180x)(1 + 0.014x)}{(1 + 0.024x)(23 + 38x)}$

b.

x	0	1	2	3	4	5	6
R	3.74	4.32	4.42	4.44	4.44	4.42	4.40

x	7	8	9	10	11	12
R	4.38	4.35	4.33	4.30	4.28	4.25

Smith's career rushing average increased for the first several years, and then began to decrease.

Lesson 12.6 (pp. 816–819)

7. $\dfrac{b}{b-3} + \dfrac{b+1}{b-3} = \dfrac{b+b+1}{b-3} = \dfrac{2b+1}{b-3}$

29. $\dfrac{2j}{j^2-1} + \dfrac{j-1}{j^2-7j+6}$

$= \dfrac{2j}{(j-1)(j+1)} + \dfrac{j-1}{(j-1)(j-6)}$

$= \dfrac{2j(j-6)}{(j-1)(j+1)(j-6)} + \dfrac{(j-1(j+1)}{(j-1)(j-6)(j+1)}$

$= \dfrac{2j(j-6) + (j-1)(j+1)}{(j-1)(j+1)(j-6)}$

$= \dfrac{2j^2 - 12j + j^2 - 1}{(j-1)(j+1)(j-6)}$

$= \dfrac{3j^2 - 12j - 1}{(j-1)(j+1)(j-6)}$

45. a. For $A \le 50$: $\frac{2A^2}{3} + \frac{200A}{3} = \frac{2A^2 + 200A}{3}$

For $A > 50$, $\frac{7A^2}{150} + (125A - 1367)$

$$= \frac{7A^2}{150} + \frac{150(125A - 1367)}{150}$$

$$= \frac{7A^2 + 150(125A - 1367)}{150}$$

$$= \frac{7A^2 + 18{,}750A - 205{,}050}{150}$$

b. For $A = 30 \text{ ft}^2$, use the formula for $A \le 50$:

$$W = \frac{2(30)^2 + 200(30)}{3} = \frac{7800}{3} = 2600$$

The minimum weight this elevator must hold is 2600 pounds.

For $A = 60 \text{ ft}^2$, use the formula for $A > 50$:

$$W = \frac{7(60)^2 + 18{,}750(60) - 205{,}050}{150}$$

$$= \frac{945{,}150}{150} = 6301$$

The minimum weight this elevator must hold is 6301 pounds.

Lesson 12.7 (pp. 823–826)

7.

$$\frac{2m}{m+4} = \frac{3}{m-1}$$

$$2m^2 - 2m = 3m + 12$$

$$2m^2 - 5m - 12 = 0$$

$$(2m + 3)(m - 4) = 0$$

$$2m + 3 = 0 \quad \textit{or} \quad m - 4 = 0$$

$$m = -1\frac{1}{2} \quad \textit{or} \quad m = 4$$

15.

$$\frac{z}{z+7} - 3 = \frac{-1}{z+7}$$

$$\frac{z}{z+7} \cdot (z + 7) - 3(z + 7) = \frac{-1}{z+7} \cdot (z + 7)$$

$$\frac{z\cancel{(z+7)}}{\cancel{z+7}} - 3(z + 7) = \frac{-1\cancel{(z+7)}}{\cancel{z+7}}$$

$$z - 3z - 21 = -1$$

$$-2z = 20$$

$$z = -10$$

33. Let w be the number of cups of water needed.

$$\frac{\text{Cups of water in cleaning solution} + \text{Cups of water needed}}{\text{Cups of cleaning solution} + \text{Cups of water needed}} = \text{Desired fraction of water in mixture}$$

$$\frac{7 + w}{9 + w} = \frac{5}{6}$$

$$(7 + w)6 = (9 + w)5$$

$$42 + 6w = 45 + 5w$$

$$w = 3$$

You need to add 3 cups of water to the cleaning solution.

Chapter 13

Lesson 13.1 (pp. 846–848)

3. Use a tree diagram to find the possible outcomes in the sample space.

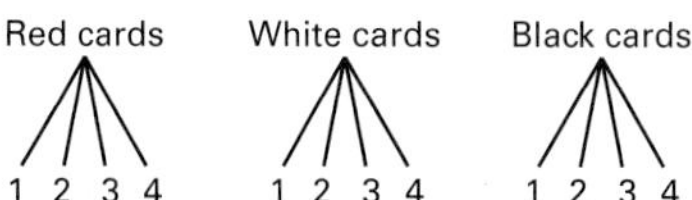

The sample space has 12 possible outcomes. The outcomes are: Red 1, Red 2, Red 3, Red 4, White 1, White 2, White 3, White 4, Black 1, Black 2, Black 3, Black 4.

21. Since there are 15 girls and 12 boys, there are a total of 27 students. So there are 27 possible outcomes.

$$P(\text{boy}) = \frac{\text{Number of boys}}{\text{Total number of students}} = \frac{12}{27} = \frac{4}{9}$$

Odds in favor of choosing a boy

$$= \frac{\text{Number of boys}}{\text{Number of girls}} = \frac{12}{15} = \frac{4}{5}$$

Sample answer: The probability and odds of choosing a boy are related because they each compare the number of favorable outcomes to another number. The probability of choosing a boy compares the number of boys to the total number of outcomes possible, while the odds of choosing a boy compare the number of boys to the total number of outcomes less the number of boys.

WORKED-OUT SOLUTIONS

Lesson 13.2 (pp. 853–855)

21. $_7P_3 = \frac{7!}{(7-3)!} = \frac{7!}{4!} = \frac{7 \cdot 6 \cdot 5 \cdot \cancel{4!}}{\cancel{4!}} = 210$

35. a. The total number of possible outcomes for the order on the first day is the number of permutations of the 4 student presenters on that day: $_4P_4 = 4!$.

The number of favorable outcomes (being chosen to be the first or second presenter) is the number of permutations of the 3 other presenters, given that you are chosen to be the first or second presenter. This is $_3P_3 = 3!$ if you are the first presenter and also $_3P_3 = 3!$ if you are the second presenter.

P(1st or 2nd presenter)
$= P$(1st presenter) $+ P$(2nd presenter)

$= \frac{3!}{4!} + \frac{3!}{4!} = \frac{1}{4} + \frac{1}{4}, \text{ or } \frac{1}{2}$

The probability that you are the first or the second presenter is $\frac{1}{2}$.

b. The number of possible outcomes is still 4!. The number of favorable outcomes is again $_3P_3 = 3!$ for you being the second presenter and $_3P_3 = 3!$ for you being the third presenter.

P(2nd or 3rd presenter)
$= P$(2nd presenter) $+ P$(3rd presenter)

$= \frac{3!}{4!} + \frac{3!}{4!} = \frac{1}{4} + \frac{1}{4}, \text{ or } \frac{1}{2}$

The probability that you are the second or the third presenter is $\frac{1}{2}$.

This answer is the same as the answer in part (a).

Lesson 13.3 (pp. 858–859)

7. $_8C_5 = \frac{8!}{(8-5)!5!} = \frac{8!}{3!5!} = \frac{8 \cdot 7 \cdot 6 \cdot \cancel{5!}}{3! \cdot \cancel{5!}} = 56$

25. a. The number of possible outcomes is the number of combinations of the 9 contestants taken 6 at a time, or $_9C_6$, because the order in which the contestants are chosen is not important.

$_9C_6 = \frac{9!}{(9-6)!6!} = \frac{9!}{3!6!} = \frac{9 \cdot 8 \cdot 7 \cdot \cancel{6!}}{3! \cdot \cancel{6!}} = 84$

There are 84 possible combinations of 6 players from the group of eligible contestants.

b. Find the number of favorable outcomes, those where you and your two friends are 3 of the 6 contestants selected to play. The order of the selections is not important. The favorable outcomes are those where only 3 of the other 6 eligible contestants are chosen. So the number of favorable combinations is $_6C_3 = 20$. Therefore, the probability that you and your friends are chosen is $\frac{20}{84}$, or $\frac{5}{21}$.

Lesson 13.4 (pp. 864–867)

5. Rolling an odd number on a number cube and rolling a number less than 5 are overlapping events as shown in the diagram. There are two numbers less than 5 that are odd, 1 and 3.

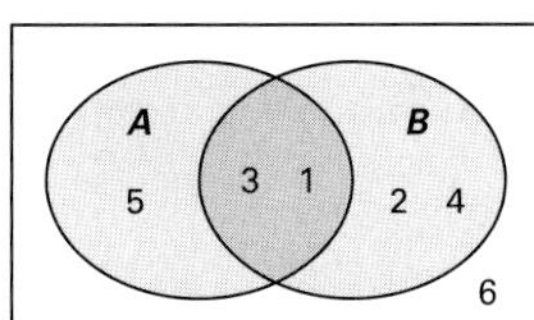

The probability of rolling an odd number is $\frac{3}{6} = \frac{1}{2}$, the probability of rolling a number less than 5 is $\frac{4}{6} = \frac{2}{3}$, and the probability of rolling a number that is both odd and less than 5 is $\frac{2}{6} = \frac{1}{3}$.

Using the formula for finding the probability of overlapping events,

$P(A \text{ or } B) = P(A) + P(B) - P(A \text{ and } B)$
$= \frac{3}{6} + \frac{4}{6} - \frac{2}{6} = \frac{5}{6}$

23. Let Event A be using a flipper to forage for food and let Event B be using the right flipper if the flipper wave technique is used. These two events are dependent.

$P(A) = 70\% = 0.7$ and
$P(B \text{ given } A) = 89\% = 0.89$

Using the formula for finding the probability of dependent events,

$P(A \text{ and } B) = P(A) \cdot P(B \text{ given } A)$
$= 0.7 \cdot 0.89 = 0.623$, or 62.3%

The probability that a walrus foraging for food uses a flipper and that it is the right flipper is 62.3%.

WORKED-OUT SOLUTIONS

Lesson 13.5 (pp. 873–874)

3. The population is all persons who dine at the restaurant. Because the diners ultimately decide whether or not to take part in the survey by mailing their comment cards, this is a self-selected sample.

15. Ballots collected at Wrigley Field are not necessarily representative of the opinions of all Chicago Cubs fans. *Sample answer:* Only some of the Chicago Cubs' fans are able to attend games, and those who attend games may have different player preferences than those who do not attend games.

Lesson 13.6 (pp. 877–878)

7. Mean:

$$\bar{x} = \frac{5.52 + 5.44 + 3.60 + 5.76 + 3.80 + 7.22}{6}$$

$$= \frac{31.34}{6} = 5.2233...$$

So, the mean of the data is $5.22\overline{3}$.

Median: The ordered list of numbers is: 3.60, 3.80, 5.44, 5.52, 5.76, 7.22. There are two middle values, 5.44 and 5.52. Therefore, the median is $\frac{5.44 + 5.52}{2} = 5.48$.

Each data value appears just once, so there is no mode.

19. a. The range of the pumpkin weights is the difference of the greatest value and the least value; $24 - 5 = 19$ pounds.

b. Mean: $\bar{x} =$

$$\frac{22 + 21 + 24 + 24 + 5 + 24 + 5 + 23 + 24 + 24}{10}$$

$$= \frac{196}{10} = 19.6$$

The mean of the pumpkin weights is 19.6 pounds.

Median: The ordered list of weights is: 5, 5, 21, 22, 23, 24, 24, 24, 24, 24. There are two middle values, 23 and 24. So, the median is 23.5 pounds.

Mode: The weight that occurs most frequently is 24 pounds.

c. The median best represents the data. *Sample answer:* The mode is the greatest data value and the mean is less than 8 of the 10 data values.

Lesson 13.7 (pp. 883–885)

3. First, separate the data into stems and leaves.

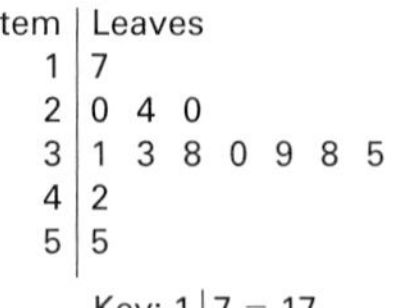

Stem	Leaves
1	7
2	0 4 0
3	1 3 8 0 9 8 5
4	2
5	5

Key: 1 | 7 = 17

Now rewrite the leaves in increasing order.

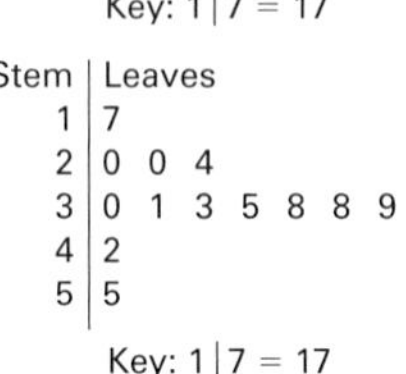

Stem	Leaves
1	7
2	0 0 4
3	0 1 3 5 8 8 9
4	2
5	5

Key: 1 | 7 = 17

19. a. Draw the bars of the histogram using the intervals from the frequency table.

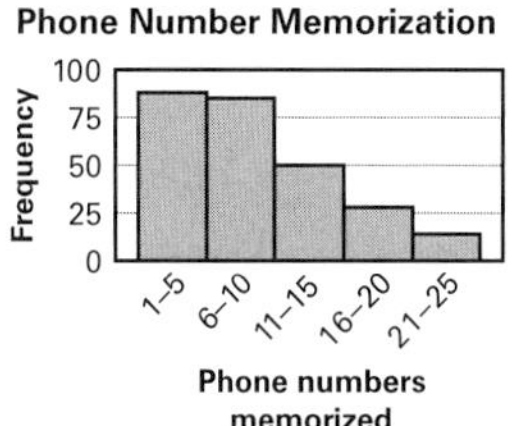

b. Use the table to determine the total number of people surveyed: $88 + 85 + 50 + 28 + 14 = 265$.

Determine the number of favorable outcomes. This number is the sum of the number of people in the 11–15 range, the 16–20 range, and the 21–25 range.

$$P(11\text{–}25) = \frac{\text{Number of favorable outcomes}}{\text{Total number of outcomes}}$$

$$= \frac{50 + 28 + 14}{265} = \frac{92}{265}$$

Lesson 13.8 (pp. 889–892)

3. Write the data in order from least to greatest. Find the median and the quartiles.

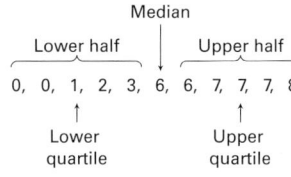

Median

Lower half | Upper half

0, 0, 1, 2, 3, 6, 6, 7, 7, 7, 8

Lower quartile | Upper quartile

WORKED-OUT SOLUTIONS

Plot the median, the quartiles, the maximum value, and the minimum value below a number line. Draw a box from the lower quartile to the upper quartile. Draw a vertical line through the median. Draw a line segment from the side of the box to the maximum value and another from the other side of the box to the minimum value.

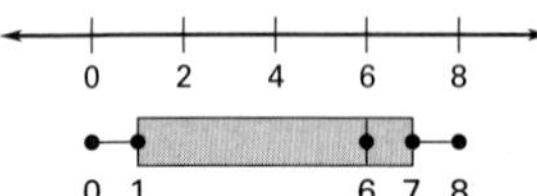

17. a. Order the data, and then find the median and the quartiles.

lower quartile: $\frac{\$38.4 + \$49.9}{2} = \$44.15$

median: \$52.4

upper quartile: $\frac{\$107.0 + \$118.2}{2} = \$112.60$

Use the median, the quartiles, the maximum value, and the minimum value to draw the box-and-whisker plot.

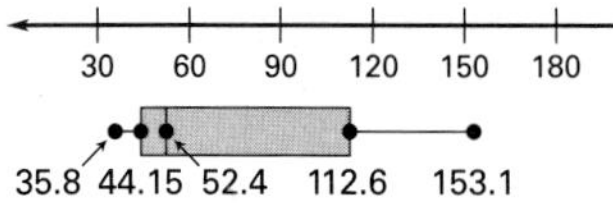

b. To check if any of the data are outliers, find the inner quartile range: $112.6 - 44.15 = 68.45$. An outlier would be any value greater than $1.5(68.45) + 112.6 = 215.275$ or less than $44.15 - 1.5(68.45) = -58.525$. Since all the data values are within these two values, there are no outliers. So, none of the states had retail sales that can be considered outliers.

WORKED-OUT SOLUTIONS

Selected Answers

Chapter 1

1.1 Skill Practice (pp. 5–6) **1.** exponent: 12, base: 6 **3.** 60 **5.** 12 **7.** 12 **9.** 3 **11.** 10 **13.** $\frac{1}{3}$ **17.** seven to the third power, $7 \cdot 7 \cdot 7$ **19.** three tenths to the fourth power, $0.3 \cdot 0.3 \cdot 0.3 \cdot 0.3$ **21.** n to the seventh power, $n \cdot n \cdot n \cdot n \cdot n \cdot n \cdot n$ **23.** t to the fourth power, $t \cdot t \cdot t \cdot t$ **25.** The base was used as the exponent and the exponent was used as the base; $5^4 = 5 \cdot 5 \cdot 5 \cdot 5 = 625$. **27.** 100 **29.** 1331 **31.** 243 **33.** 1296 **35.** $\frac{27}{125}$ **37.** $\frac{1}{216}$ **39.** 1.21 **41.** 40.5 **43.** 9.6

1.1 Problem Solving (pp. 6–7) **49.** 162.5 cm **51. a.** 12 in. **b.** 144 in.^{2} **53.** New England Patriots

1.2 Skill Practice (pp. 10–11) **1.** Square 4. **3.** 8 **5.** 14 **7.** $3\frac{3}{5}$ **9.** $63\frac{3}{4}$ **11.** 21 **13.** 73.5 **15.** $12\frac{1}{2}$ **17.** 48 **21.** $\frac{1}{2}$ was multiplied by 6 before squaring 6; $20 - \frac{1}{2} \cdot 6^2 = 20 - \frac{1}{2} \cdot 36 = 20 - 18 = 2$. **23.** 29 **25.** 126 **27.** 0.75 **29.** 3 **33.** $(2 \times 2 + 3)^2 - (4 + 3) \times 5$

1.2 Problem Solving (pp. 11–12) **35. a.** \$22.87 **b.** \$2.13 **37.** *Sample answer:* $(3 \times 4) + 5$ **39. a.** \$380, \$237.99; \$142.01 **b.** *Sample answer:* You could write an expression showing the difference of your income and expenses as $10s - (4.50m + 12.99)$.

1.2 Graphing Calculator Activity (p. 13) **1.** 5 **3.** 0.429 **5.** 0.188 **7.** 40.9 BMI units

1.3 Skill Practice (pp. 18–19) **1.** rate **3.** $x + 8$ **5.** $\frac{1}{2}m$ **7.** $7 - n$ **9.** $\frac{2t}{12}$ **11.** $2k - 7$ **15.** $4v$ **17.** $\frac{16}{p}$ **19.** $7 - d$ **21.** $12y$ **23.** 1.5 pints per serving **25.** \$6.80 per share **27.** Feet should cancel out; \$54. **29.** \$19.50 for 1 h

1.3 Problem Solving (pp. 19–20) **31.** $19.95t + 3$; \$102.75 **33. a.** \$.055, \$.06 **b.** 48 oz container **c.** \$.96 **35.** \$500 **37. a.** $12g + h + \frac{1}{4}c$ **b.** 247; 376.75; 242

1.4 Skill Practice (pp. 24–25) **1.** *Sample answer:* $3x + 5 = 20$ **3.** $42 + n = 51$ **5.** $9 - \frac{t}{6} = 5$ **7.** $9(t + 5) < 6$ **9.** $8 < b + 3 < 12$ **11.** $10 < t - 7 < 20$ **13.** $p \geq \$12.99$ **15.** The wrong inequality symbol is used; $\frac{t}{4.2} \leq 15$. **17.** solution **19.** not a solution **21.** not a solution **23.** solution **25.** solution **27.** not a solution **29.** 5 **31.** 12 **33.** 9 **35.** $3x - 2 = x + 5$; solution

1.4 Problem Solving (pp. 25–26) **39.** 7.5 mi **41.** 167 h **43.** \$100 **45. a.** $6r + 5(10 - r) \geq 55$ **b.** Yes; you will earn \$30 running errands and \$25 walking dogs; $30 + 25 = 55$. **c.** Yes; if you work 10 hours running errands, you will earn \$60. You will not meet your goal if you work all 10 hours walking dogs.

1.5 Skill Practice (p. 31) **1.** *Sample answer:* $d = rt$ **3.** You know how many collars you've made, how much you have spent to make them, and how much money you want to make. You need to find what to charge for each collar so you make \$90. **5.** You know the temperature in Rome and the temperature in Dallas. You know the formula to convert Fahrenheit temperatures to Celsius temperatures. You need to find the higher temperature. **7.** The formula for perimeter should be used, not area; $P = 2\ell + 2w$; $P = 2(200) + 2(150) = 700$; $\$10(700) = \$7000$. **9.** $P = I - E$

1.5 Problem Solving (pp. 32–33) **15.** 46.25 in.^{2} **17.** 2 water bottles **19. a.** 960 ft **b.** 480 ft

21. a.

Room size (feet)	1 by 1	2 by 2	3 by 3	4 by 4	5 by 5
Remaining area (square feet)	431	428	423	416	407

b. $1 \leq s \leq 5$; 5 ft

1.5 Problem Solving Workshop (p. 34)
1. 9 pieces of cake; Equation: Let c be the number of pieces of cake; $9c = 99$, $c = 11$. Diagram: Draw a diagram of a 9 inch by 11 inch pan and cut the cake into 3 inch by 3 inch pieces. From the diagram you see that you can cut 9 such pieces. The diagram shows that you cannot actually cut 11 square pieces because of the shape of the pan.

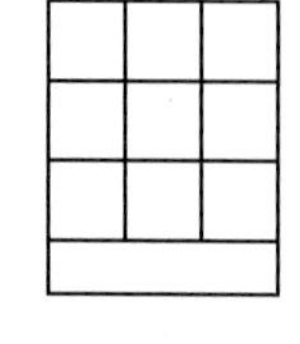

3. The equation should be $3x + 6 = 12$ because there are only 3 spaces between the 4 floats; $3(2) + 6 = 12$.

1.6 Skill Practice (pp. 38–39) **1.** input; output **3.** domain: 0, 1, 2, and 3, range: 5, 7, 15, and 44 **5.** domain: 6, 12, 21, and 42, range: 5, 7, 10, and 17 **7.** not a function **9.** The pairing is a function. Each input is paired with only one output.

11. *Sample:*

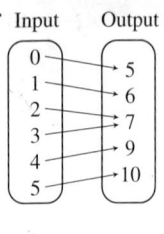

Input	Output
0	5
1	6
2	7
3	7
4	9
5	10

15.

Input	4	5	7	8	12
Output	7.5	8.5	10.5	11.5	15.5

range: 7.5, 8.5, 10.5, 11.5, and 15.5

17.

Input	4	6	9	11
Output	5	6	7.5	8.5

range: 5, 6, 7.5, and 8.5

19.

Input	0	2	4	6
Output	$\frac{1}{2}$	1	$1\frac{1}{2}$	2

range: $\frac{1}{2}$, 1, $1\frac{1}{2}$, and 2

21. $y = x - 8$

1.6 Problem Solving (pp. 39–40) **23. a.** the number of quarters left; the number of quarters used **b.** $y = 10 - x$; domain: 0, 1, 2, 3, 4, 5, 6, 7, 8, 9, and 10

c.

Input	0	1	2	3	4	5	6	7	8	9	10
Output	10	9	8	7	6	5	4	3	2	1	0

range: 0, 1, 2, 3, 4, 5, 6, 7, 8, 9, and 10

25. $y = 100 + 20m$; independent variable: m, the number of months; dependent variable: y, the amount of money saved; domain: $m > 0$, range: $y \geq 100$; $340

27. a.

2	3	4	5
A, B, C	D, E, F	G, H, I	J, K, L

6	7	8	9
M, N, O	P, Q, R, S	T, U, V	W, X, Y, Z

No; because there is more than one output for each input.

b.

A	B	C	D	E	F	G	H	I	J	K	L
2	2	2	3	3	3	4	4	4	5	5	5

M	N	O	P	Q	R	S	T	U	V	W	X	Y	Z
6	6	6	7	7	7	7	8	8	8	9	9	9	9

Yes; because there is only one output for each input.

1.6 Graphing Calculator Activity (p. 41) **1.** 50°F; scroll down until you see the output 10, look to see that the input is 50.

3.

Input	0	1	2	3
Output	5	5.75	6.5	7.25

5.

Input	1	2	3	4
Output	7	14.5	22	29.5

1.7 Skill Practice (pp. 46–47) **1.** domain; range

3. 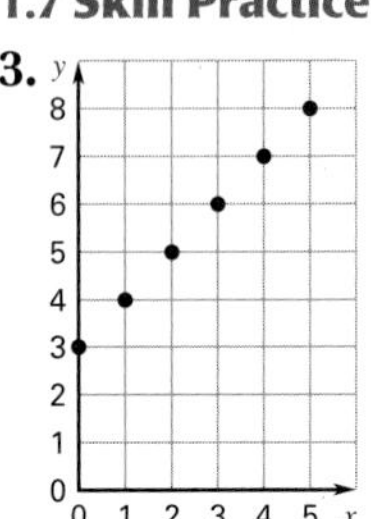

5. 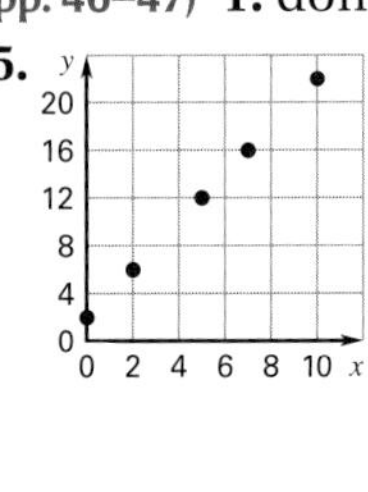

7. 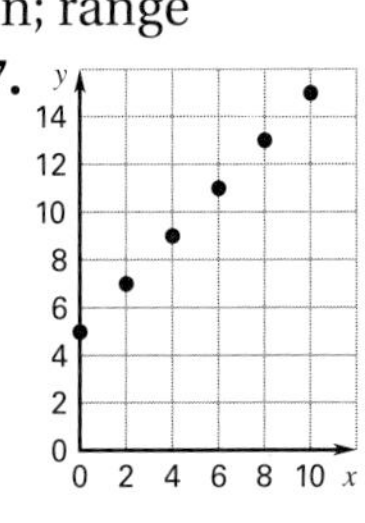

9. The domain and range are graphed backwards.

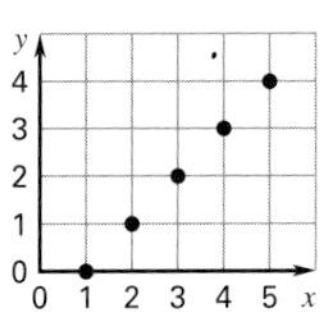

11. $y = 2x - 2$; domain: 1, 2, 3, and 4, range: 0, 2, 4, and 6

1.7 Problem Solving (pp. 47–48)

15. 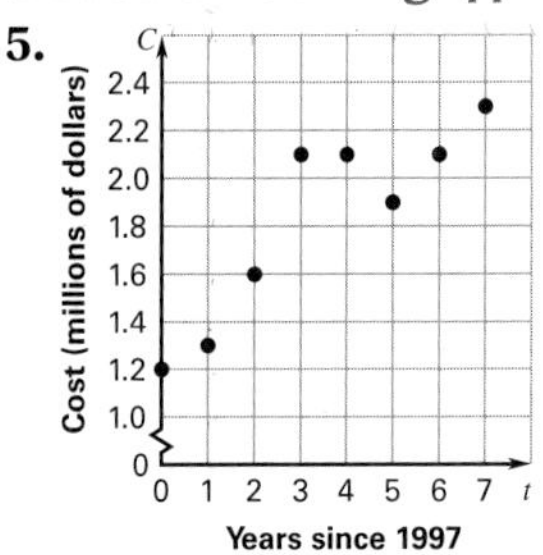

17.

Years since 1984	Voters	Voters (millions)
0	92,652,680	93
4	91,594,693	92
8	104,405,155	104
12	96,456,345	96
16	105,586,274	106

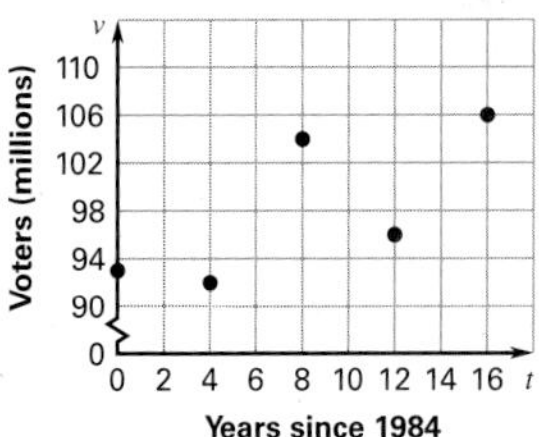

19. a. increases **b.** Yes; 27.5 grams is between the mass of an egg that is just under 38 millimeters long and an egg that is just over 38 millimeters long.

Extension (p. 50) **1.** function **3.** not a function **5.** function **7.** Not a function. *Sample answer:* There could be many students whose first names have 4 letters, for instance, but their last names could all have a different number of letters. **9.** Function; for each of your birthdays, you have only one height.

Chapter Review (pp. 53–56) **1.** 7, 12 **3.** algebraic expression **5.** 16 **7.** 10 **9.** 400 **11.** 25 in.^{2} **13.** 9 **15.** 8 **17.** $\frac{1}{3}$ **19.** 52 **21.** 18 **23.** $z - 5$ **25.** $3x^2$ **27.** $2.95n + 2.19$ **29.** $13 + t \geq 24$ **31.** solution **33.** 240 ft^2

35.

Input	10	12	15	20	21
Output	5	7	10	15	16

range: 5, 7, 10, 15, and 16

37. $y = x + 4$ **39.**

Chapter 2

2.1 Skill Practice (pp. 67–68) **1.** rational number **3.** Zero is in the set of whole numbers, but not in the set of positive integers. **5–13.** Check students' graphs. **5.** 7 **7.** −5 **9.** 5 **11.** −1 **13.** −2 **15.** 1.6: rational number, 1: whole number, integer, rational number, −4: integer, rational number, 0: whole number, integer, rational number; −4, 0, 1, 1.6 **17.** $-\frac{2}{3}$: rational number, −0.6: rational number, −1: integer, rational number, $\frac{1}{3}$: rational number; −1, $-\frac{2}{3}$, −0.6, $\frac{1}{3}$ **19.** 16: whole number, integer, rational number, −1.66: rational number, $\frac{5}{3}$: rational number, −1.6: rational number; −1.66, −1.6, $\frac{5}{3}$, 16 **21.** −4.99: rational number, 5: whole number, integer, rational number, $\frac{16}{3}$: rational number, −5.1: rational number; −5.1, −4.99, 5, $\frac{16}{3}$ **23.** −6, 6 **25.** 18, 18 **27.** −13.4, 13.4 **29.** 6.1, 6.1 **31.** $1\frac{1}{9}$, $1\frac{1}{9}$ **33.** $-\frac{3}{4}$, $\frac{3}{4}$ **35.** Hypothesis: a number is a positive integer, conclusion: the number is a whole number; true. **37.** Hypothesis: a number is positive, conclusion: its opposite is positive; false. *Sample answer:* The opposite of 2 is −2, a negative number. **41.** $-|-0.2|$ is a negative number. *Sample answer:* In the number $-|-0.2|$, remove both negative signs. **43.** 1 **45.** 1.75 **47.** 2.25 **49.** 1.5

2.1 Problem Solving (pp. 69–70) **53.** Fondo, Frink, Alamorio, Calexico, Date City **55.** −3.4; the absolute value of −3.4 is less than the absolute value of −3.8, so it is closer to 0, the exact pitch. **57. a.** 500 Hz **b.** The intensity decreases until 500 Hz and then increases. **59. a.** Sun, Sirius, Canopus, Arcturus, Capella, Achernar; Canopus, Achernar, Arcturus, Capella, Sirius, Sun **b.** Rigel's apparent magnitude is greater than the Sun's apparent magnitude, so it is dimmer than the Sun; Rigel's absolute magnitude is less than the Sun's absolute magnitude, so it is brighter than the Sun. **c.** No. *Sample answer:* The apparent magnitude of Arcturus is less than the apparent magnitude of Achernar, but the absolute magnitude of Arcturus is greater than the absolute magnitude of Achernar.

Extension (p. 72) **1.** {1, 3, 5, 6, 7, 9}, {3, 9} **3.** {0, 1, 2, 3, 4, 5, 6, 7, 8, 9, 10}, ∅ **5.** R = {2, 4, 6, 8, 10}, f = {(1, 2), (2, 4), (3, 6), (4, 8), (5, 10)} **7.** R = {4, 8, 12, 16, 20}, f = {(1, 4), (5, 8), (9, 12), (13, 16), (17, 20)} **9.** the set of integers, ∅

2.2 Skill Practice (pp. 77–78) **1.** 0 **3.** −8 **5.** 6 **7.** −13 **9.** −6 **11.** −20 **13.** −4.5 **15.** 6.6 **17.** −15.2 **19.** $7\frac{1}{15}$ **21.** $1\frac{16}{45}$ **23.** $-20\frac{23}{24}$ **25.** The numbers have different signs, so their absolute values should have been subtracted, 17 + (−31) = −14. **27.** Associate property of addition **29.** Identity property of addition **31.** Commutative property of addition **33.** −49 **35.** 1.6 **37.** $5\frac{19}{60}$ **39.** −3 **41.** −9.5 **43.** $7\frac{23}{60}$ **45.** 0 **47.** 7.4 **49.** −(−18) + (−18); 0

2.2 Problem Solving (pp. 78–79) **53.** 7°F **55. a.** 1.5 diopters **b.** −3.75 diopters **c.** part (b) **57. a.** your friend **b.** No, if you score 2 double eagles, you will have the same score.

2.3 Skill Practice (pp. 82–83) **1.** −3 + (−6) **3.** 18 **5.** −8 **7.** 14.1 **9.** −25.8 **11.** $-\frac{1}{3}$ **13.** $\frac{3}{4}$ **15.** 8 was substituted for y instead of −8; 3 − (−8) + 2 = 3 + 8 + 2 = 13. **17.** 4.6 **19.** 10.6 **21.** 7.7 **23.** 7.6 **25.** 1.8 **27.** 107°F **29.** −1280 m **31.** 127.1 mi **33.** 8 **35.** −4.2 **37.** 16.4 **39.** *Sample answer:* You are overdrawn on your checking account by $23. You write two more checks for $14 and $8. What is your balance?; −$45

2.3 Problem Solving (pp. 83–84)
43. 14.6°C **45. a.** $d = t - 342$

b.

t	d
341.7	−0.3
343.8	1.8
340.9	−1.1
342.7	0.7

341.7 and 340.9; you can tell if $t - 342$ is negative.
47. a. 6°; 19° **b.** −4°

2.3 Spreadsheet Activity (p. 85) **1.** 6 hand grips **3.** 4.902; the difference in the lengths has the smallest absolute value.

2.4 Skill Practice (pp. 91–92) **1.** 1 **3.** −28 **5.** 90 **7.** −36 **9.** 7 **11.** −43.89 **13.** −40 **15.** −80 **17.** $2\frac{2}{5}$ **19.** Multiplicative property of zero **21.** Identity property of multiplication **23.** Associative property of multiplication **25.** Identity property of multiplication **27.** Multiplicative property of −1 **29.** $18x$; $18x$, same signs, product is positive. **31.** $-84z$; $12(-7z)$, product of −2 and −6 is 12; $[12 \cdot (-7)]z$, associative property of multiplication; $-84(z)$, product of 12 and −7 is −84; $-84z$, multiply. **33.** $-40c$; $2(4)(-5c)$, product of $-\frac{1}{5}$ and −10 is 2; $8(-5c)$, product of 2 and 4 is 8; $[8 \cdot (-5)]c$, associative property of multiplication; $-40(c)$, product of 8 and −5 is −40; $-40c$, multiply. **35.** $16.8r^2$; $[-6r \cdot (-2.8)]r$, associative property of multiplication; $[-6 \cdot (-2.8) \cdot r]r$, commutative property of multiplication; $(16.8r)r$, product of −6 and −2.8 is 16.8; $16.8(r \cdot r)$, associative property of multiplication; $16.8r^2$, multiply **37.** −0.4 **39.** −12.6 **41.** −6.6 **43.** $-1(7) = -7$, not 7; $-1(7)(-3)(-2x) = -7(-3)(-2x) = 21(-2x) = -42x$ **45.** true **47.** true

2.4 Problem Solving (pp. 92–93) **51.** $162.50 **55. a.** $f = 11{,}250 + (-30t)$, $f = 135{,}000 + (-240t)$ **b.** 11,160 gal, 134,280 gal **c.** Rhododendron; 45,000 gal; the Rhododendron takes 375 hours to burn all of its fuel; the Spokane takes 562.5 hours to burn all of its fuel; to find the number of hours the Rhododendron will take to burn all its fuel, use the equations in part (a) and find the additive inverse of 11,250, then divide it by −30; to find the number of hours the Spokane will take to burn all its fuel, use the equations in part (a) and find the additive inverse of 135,000, then divide it by −240.

Extension (p. 95) **1.** $\begin{bmatrix} 16 & 4 \\ 8 & 12 \end{bmatrix}$ **3.** $\begin{bmatrix} -15 & -4 & -9 \\ -2 & 2 & -5 \end{bmatrix}$

5. Cannot be performed. **7.** $\begin{bmatrix} -28 & -49 \\ 3\frac{1}{2} & 3\frac{1}{9} \end{bmatrix}$ **9.** $\begin{bmatrix} -72 \\ 20.4 \\ 4.2 \end{bmatrix}$

11. Calcium (mg) Potassium (mg) $\begin{bmatrix} 263.52 & 290.36 \\ 270.84 & 341.6 \\ 246.44 & 324.52 \end{bmatrix}$ **13.** $\begin{bmatrix} -41 & -99 \\ 78 & 91 \end{bmatrix}$

2.5 Skill Practice (pp. 99–100) **1.** 4, −9 **3.** The negative was not distributed to the −8; $5y - (2y - 8) = 5y - 2y + 8 = 3y + 8$. **5.** $4x + 12$ **7.** $5m + 25$ **9.** $-8p + 24$ **11.** $4r - 6$ **13.** $6v^2 + 6v$ **15.** $2x^2 - 6x$ **17.** $\frac{1}{4}m - 2$ **19.** $4n - 6$ **21.** terms: -7, $13x$, $2x$, 8; like terms: −7 and 8, $13x$ and $2x$; coefficients: 13, 2; constant terms: −7, 8 **23.** terms: $7x^2$, -10, $-2x^2$, 5; like terms: $7x^2$ and $-2x^2$, −10 and 5; coefficients: 7, −2; constant terms: −10, 5 **25.** terms: 2, $3xy$, $-4xy$, 6; like terms: 2 and 6, $3xy$ and $-4xy$; coefficients: 3, −4; constant terms: 2, 6 **29.** $5y$ **31.** $9a - 2$ **33.** $8r + 8$ **35.** $3m + 5$ **37.** $10w - 35$ **39.** $15s + 6$ **41.** $34 - 24w$; $72 - 108w$ **43.** $38.97 **45.** $11.88 **47.** $2(6 + x) + (x - 5)$; $3x + 7$

2.5 Problem Solving (pp. 100–101)
51. $C = 3r - 6$; $5.97
53. $s = d(x + y + z) = dx + dy + dz$

2.5 Problem Solving Workshop (p. 102)
1. $330 **3.** $287.50

2.6 Skill Practice (pp. 106–107) **1.** multiplicative inverse **3.** $-\frac{1}{18}$ **5.** −1 **7.** $-1\frac{1}{3}$ **9.** $-\frac{3}{13}$ **11.** −7 **13.** $\frac{2}{7}$ **15.** −3 **17.** $-2\frac{1}{2}$ **19.** $\frac{2}{7}$ **21.** −22 **25.** $-1\frac{2}{3}$ **27.** $2\frac{1}{4}$ **29.** $-2\frac{1}{5}$ **31.** 0.1 **33.** $3x - 7$ **35.** $-3z + 2$ **37.** $\frac{1}{2} - \frac{5}{2}q$ **39.** $3a + 1\frac{1}{4}$ **41.** $4 - 3c$ **43.** −2 was added instead of subtracted; $\frac{-15x - 10}{-5} = (-15x - 10) \cdot \left(-\frac{1}{5}\right) = -15x\left(-\frac{1}{5}\right) - 10\left(-\frac{1}{5}\right) = 3x + 2$ **45.** $-1\frac{1}{3}$ **47.** $\frac{1}{3}$

2.6 Problem Solving (pp. 107–108) **53.** −14.75°C **57. a.** −0.034 **b.** Yes; it will improve to −0.012. **c.** If the player had the same number of aces as service errors, then $a = e$, so $f = \frac{a - a}{s} = 0$; if all the serves were aces, a would be equal to s and e would be 0, so $f = \frac{s - 0}{s} = \frac{s}{s} = 1$; if all the serves were errors, then $e = s$ and $a = 0$, so $f = \frac{0 - s}{s} = \frac{-s}{s} = -1$.

2.7 Skill Practice (pp. 113–114) **1.** real numbers **3.** 2 **5.** −3 **7.** 14 **9.** ±50 **11.** −15 **13.** ±13 **15.** 3 **17.** −2 **19.** −9 **21.** 14 **25.** $-\sqrt{12}$: real number, irrational number, −3.7: real number, rational number, $\sqrt{9}$: real number, rational number, integer, whole number, 2.9: real number, rational number; −3.7, $-\sqrt{12}$, 2.9, $\sqrt{9}$

27. $\sqrt{8}$: real number, irrational number, $-\frac{2}{5}$: real number, rational number, -1: real number, rational number, integer, 0.6: real number, rational number, $\sqrt{6}$: real number, irrational number; -1, $-\frac{2}{5}$, 0.6, $\sqrt{6}$, $\sqrt{8}$ **29.** -8.3: real number, rational number, $-\sqrt{80}$: real number, irrational number, $-\frac{17}{2}$: real number, rational number, -8.25: real number, rational number, $-\sqrt{100}$: real number, rational number, integer; $-\sqrt{100}$, $-\sqrt{80}$, $-\frac{17}{2}$, -8.3, -8.25 **31.** If a number is a real number, then it is an irrational number; false. *Sample answer:* 3 is a real number and a rational number. **33.** If a number is an irrational number, then it is not a whole number; true. **35.** 2 **37.** -42 **39.** 63 **41.** -16

2.7 Problem Solving (pp. 115–116) **47.** 60 in. **49.** 35 ft; 24 ft; 48 ft; 30 ft; they are all rational numbers. **51.** 3; square each fraction, $\left(\frac{265}{153}\right)^2 < 3$, $\left(\frac{1351}{780}\right)^2 > 3$ so the value of x is 3. **53. a.** 144 tiles **b.** 16 ft. *Sample answer:* If the homeowner can buy 144 tiles that are each 256 square inches, then the total area is (144 tiles)(256 square inches per tile) = 36,864 square inches. Divide 36,864 square inches by 144 square inches to find the number of square feet, 256 square feet. If the area of the square is 256 square feet, take the square root of 256 to find the side length, 16 feet.

Extension (p. 118) **1.** *Sample answer:* $3 - 5 = -2$, $-2(6) = -12$, $-12 \div 3 = -4$, $-4 + 10 = 6$; $-2 - 5 = -7$, $-7(6) = -42$, $-42 \div 3 = -14$, $-14 + 10 = -4$; $10 - 5 = 5$, $5(6) = 30$, $30 \div 3 = 10$, $10 + 10 = 20$; double the number; $\frac{(x-5)6}{3} + 10 = (x-5)2 + 10 = 2x - 10 + 10 = 2x$ **3.** Distributive property; Subtraction rule; Associative property of addition; Inverse property of addition; Identity property of addition; Divide

Chapter Review (pp. 121–124) **1.** terms: $-3x$, -5, $-7x$, -9; coefficients: -3, -7; constant terms: -5, -9; like terms: $-3x$ and $-7x$, -5 and -9 **3.** real number, rational number **5.** real number, rational number, integer **7.** -6, -5.2, $-\frac{3}{8}$, $-\frac{1}{4}$, 0.3 **9.** 0.2, 0.2 **11.** $-\frac{7}{8}$, $\frac{7}{8}$ **13.** 3 **15.** -3.5 **17.** $-1\frac{3}{14}$ **19.** $-\$.23$ million **21.** -10 **23.** -6.1 **25.** $-\frac{31}{36}$ **27.** $2\frac{1}{2}$ **29.** -60 **31.** -18 **33.** $6x$; $x \cdot (-18) = -\frac{1}{3}(-18)(x)$, commutative property of multiplication; $6(x)$, product of $-\frac{1}{3}$ and -18; $6x$, multiply **35.** 2.74 ft **37.** $-3y - 27$ **39.** $3x + 8$

41. $9n - 3\frac{1}{2}$ **43.** -14 **45.** $\frac{2}{3}$ **47.** $3x - 5$ **49.** $2n + 1$ **51.** -6 **53.** ± 15 **55.** -7 **57.** 17 **59.** $-\sqrt{4}$, -0.3, 0, 1.25, $\sqrt{11}$

Chapter 3

3.1 Skill Practice (pp. 137–138) **1.** inverse operations **3.** 3 **5.** 5 **7.** -3 **9.** 7 **11.** 17 **13.** 4 **17.** 4 **19.** 6 **21.** -15 **23.** 15 **25.** 48 **27.** 22 **29.** 3.8 should have been subtracted from *both* sides; $x + 3.8 - 3.8 = 2.3 - 3.8$, $x = -1.5$. **31.** 3.5 **33.** -1.1 **35.** -2.05 **37.** $\frac{5}{8}$ **39.** 0.06 **41.** 96 **43.** 12 **45.** -56 **47.** $\frac{3}{5}$ **49.** $54 = 12x$; 4.5 in.

3.1 Problem Solving (pp. 139–140) **53.** 1046.6 ft **55.** 11 ft **57. a.** $\frac{4}{7}x = 200$ **b.** Plants; if you solve the equation in part (a) you find that there are 350 species of birds.

59. a.

t	d
1	6.5
2	13
3	19.5
4	26
5	32.5

b. 4 sec

c. $26 = 6.5t$; 4 sec **61. a.** 171 hits **b.** 215 hits **c.** No; if Mueller had fewer hits than Wells but had a higher batting average, he must have had fewer at bats than Wells.

3.2 Skill Practice (pp. 144–145) **1.** like terms **3.** 4 **5.** 2 **7.** -3 **9.** 6 **11.** 40 **13.** 18 **15.** 4 **17.** 9 **19.** -4 **23.** The division of $-2x + x$ by -2 is done incorrectly. *Sample answer:* If like terms are combined as the first step, the second line would be $-x = 10$ and the final result would be $x = -10$. **25.** $y = 2x + 4$; -7 **27.** 4 **29.** 5 **31.** 0.5 **33.** 15.9 **35.** 6.9

3.2 Problem Solving (pp. 145–146) **37.** 28 classes **39.** 5 half-side advertisements **41.** Yes; the equation $\$542 = \$50 + 6x$ gives the monthly cost of a guitar that costs \$542. Solving the equation gives $x = \$82$ per month, so you can afford the guitar. **43. a.** $y = 12x$

b.

x (hours)	Marissa	Ryan	Total
1	5	7	12
2	10	14	24
3	15	21	36
4	20	28	48
5	25	35	60

c. 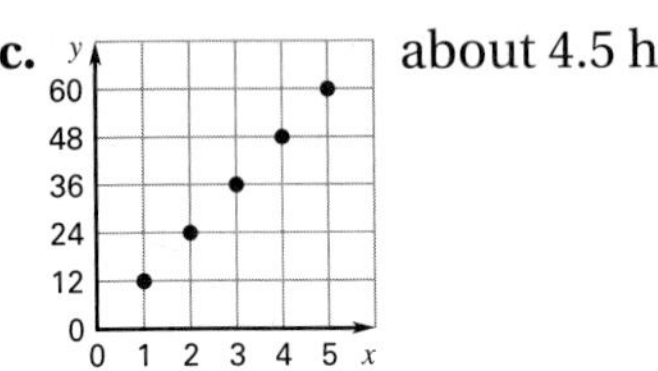

about 4.5 h

3.2 Problem Solving Workshop (p. 147)
1. 7 players **3.** 4 chairs

3.3 Skill Practice (pp. 150–151) **1.** $\frac{5}{3}$ **3.** 3 **5.** 6 **7.** −2 **9.** −8 **11.** −8 **13.** 4 **15.** −9 **17.** −19 **19.** 12 **21.** −2 **23.** −9 **25.** −3 times −6 is 18, not −18; $5x - 3x + 18 = 2$, $2x + 18 = 2$, $2x = -16$, $x = -8$. **27.** 2 **29.** 3 **31.** −5 **33.** 2 **35.** 9.5 in., 6 in.; if you use the perimeter formula $P = 2\ell + 2w$ and substitute $3.5 + w$ for ℓ, the solution is $w = 6$.

3.3 Problem Solving (pp. 152–153) **39.** 0.75 ft **41. a.** 34 mo **b.** 307 ft per mo **c.** After the work crews merged; before the work crews merged they were working at a rate of 117 + 137 = 254 feet per month, and after merging at a rate of 307 feet per month.

3.4 Skill Practice (pp. 157–158) **1.** identity **3.** −2 **5.** −4 **7.** −7 **9.** 8 **11.** −4 **13.** −3 **17.** *Sample answer:* Distribute the 3 to get $6z - 15 = 2z + 13$, then subtract $2z$ from each side to get $4z - 15 = 13$, next add 15 to each side to get $4z = 28$, finally divide each side by 4 to get $z = 7$. **19.** 2 **21.** −7 **23.** no solution **25.** no solution **27.** The 3 was not distributed to both terms; $3x + 15 = 3x + 15$, $15 = 15$, so the equation is an identity. **29.** *Sample answer:* $5x + 4 = 5x$; the number $5x$ cannot be equal to 4 more than itself. **31.** 2 **33.** −4 **35.** 6 **37.** identity **39.** 2 **41.** 10 **43.** identity **45.** 60

3.4 Problem Solving (pp. 158–159) **49.** 9 nights **51.** about 4 yr **53. a.** $23.4t = 24(t - 0.3)$; 12 sec **b.** about 4.4 sec **c.** No; it would take 12 seconds for the sheepdog to catch up to the collie and it only takes 4.4 seconds for the collie to complete the last leg.

3.4 Spreadsheet Activity (p. 160) **1.** 2 **3.** 4

3.5 Skill Practice (pp. 165–166) **1.** ratios **3.** no; 7 to 9 **5.** yes **7.** $\frac{6}{5}$ **9.** 22 **11.** 48 **13.** 15 **15.** 40 **17.** 12 **21.** Multiply each side by 6, not $\frac{1}{6}$; $6 \cdot \frac{3}{4} = 6 \cdot \frac{x}{6}$, $4\frac{1}{2} = x$. **23.** $\frac{3}{8} = \frac{x}{32}$; 12 **25.** $\frac{x}{4} = \frac{8}{16}$; 2 **27.** $\frac{b}{10} = \frac{7}{2}$; 35 **29.** $\frac{12}{18} = \frac{d}{27}$; 18 **31.** 1.8 **33.** 2.4 **35.** 4 **37.** 4 **39.** 2 **41.** 3.5 **43.** Yes. *Sample answer:* $\frac{3}{6} = \frac{4}{8}$

3.5 Problem Solving (pp. 166–167) **45.** $\frac{2}{145}$ **47.** $\frac{2}{5}$ **49.** $\frac{1}{2}$ **51.** 45 goals **53. a.** $\frac{10}{23}$ **b.** 110 lift tickets **c.** 40 snowboarders

3.6 Skill Practice (pp. 171–172) **1.** cross product **3.** 6 **5.** 24 **7.** 1 **9.** −49 **11.** 2 **13.** 12 **17.** Use the cross products property to multiply 4 by x and 16 by 3; $4 \cdot x = 3 \cdot 16$, $4x = 48$, $x = 12$. **19.** 15 **21.** 10 **23.** 5.5 **25.** −3.4 **27.** 4.2 **29.** −5.9 **31. a.** Multiplication property of equality **b.** Multiply **c.** Simplify

3.6 Problem Solving (pp. 172–173) **33.** 5 c **35.** 90 km **37.** 7.5 km **39.** 17.728 m **41.** 80 yd; find the actual length of the field by using the ratio 1 in. : 20 yd, then use that number to find the width of the soccer field by using the ratio 3 : 2.

Extension (p. 175) **1.** 24 in. **3.** 16 m **5.** 37.5 ft

3.7 Skill Practice (pp. 179–180) **1.** percent: 15, base: 360, part: 54 **3.** 36% **5.** 28 **7.** 150 **9.** 70% **11.** 6% **13.** 69 **15.** 25 **17.** 95 **21.** 76.5% needs to be changed to 0.765; $153 = 0.765 \cdot b$, $b = 200$. **23.** 96% **25.** 150 **27.** 6% **29.** 30% **31.** No. *Sample answer:* The area of the smaller square would be 16% of the area of the larger square because the percent needs to be squared.

3.7 Problem Solving (pp. 180–181) **33.** 8% **35. a.** 90 listeners **b.** 35 listeners **37.** 59.3%; 16.5%; 13.2%; 11.0% **39. a.** \$48 **b.** \$66.25 **c.** The bicycle in part (a); it will cost \$192, the bicycle in part (b) will cost \$198.75.

Extension (p. 183) **1.** increase; 25% **3.** decrease; 45% **5.** decrease; 33% **7.** 20.3 **9.** 35.2 **11.** 20% increase **13.** 48.0 people per square mile

3.8 Skill Practice (pp. 187–188) **1.** literal equation **3.** $x = \frac{c}{b - a}$; −2 **5.** $x = bc - a$; 9 **7.** $x = a(c - b)$; 28 **9.** b should have been subtracted from both sides, not added; $ax = -b$, $x = -\frac{b}{a}$. **11.** $y = 7 - 2x$ **13.** $4 - 3x = y$ **15.** $2 + \frac{6}{7}x = y$ **17.** $\frac{9}{5}x - 6 = y$ **19.** $y = \frac{1}{2}x + \frac{1}{3}$ **21.** $h = \frac{S - 2B}{P}$ **25.** $y = 18 - 5x$ **27.** $\ell = \frac{S}{\pi r} - r$; 13.03 cm **29.** *Sample answer:* You want to find how long it will take to drive 150 miles if you drive at an average rate of 55 miles per hour.

3.8 Problem Solving (pp. 188–189) **33. a.** $x = \frac{C - 25}{12}$ **b.** 10 nights; 13 nights; 15 nights **35.** Divide each side by the total bill, b, to get $\frac{a}{b} = p\%$.

Chapter Review (pp. 192–196) **1.** scale drawing **3.** If you collect like terms you get $10x = 10x$, so any value of x will make it true. **5.** Subtract $6x$ from each side, then divide each side by -2. **7.** 13 **9.** -15 **11.** -36 **13.** 2 **15.** 18 **17.** 5 **19.** 2 **21.** -6 **23.** 14 **25.** 1 **27.** -4 **29.** no solution **31.** 7 **33.** identity **35.** 3 **37. a.** 4 **b.** 116 **39.** 15 **41.** 10.5 **43.** 70 **45.** 28 **47.** 1 **49.** 10 **51.** 650 words **53.** 16.5 **55.** 37.5% **57.** 1500 general admission tickets **59.** $y = \frac{3}{2}x + 9$ **61. a.** $h = \frac{V}{\ell w}$ **b.** 15 in.

Cumulative Review (pp. 202–203) **1.** 27 **3.** 11 **5.** 42 **7.** solution **9.** not a solution **11.** not a solution **13.** $-6\frac{5}{6}$ **15.** -19.1 **17.** -21 **19.** 6 **21.** 3 **23.** 13.9 **25.** 58.8 **27.** -11 **29.** 6 **31.** $4\frac{2}{3}$ **33.** 3 **35.** 8.5 **37.** 15 **39.** 23 **41.** 1.2 **43.** 18 pieces **45.** $-\$.34$; $-\$.45$; $-\$.25$; \$1.02; \$.08 **47.** 140 people **49. a.** 2 players **b.** 7 players **c.** 11 players

Chapter 4

4.1 Skill Practice (pp. 209–210) **1.** 5; -3 **3.** $(3, -2)$ **5.** $(4, 4)$ **7.** $(4, -1)$ **9.** $(-5, 4)$ **11.** $(-4, -1)$

15–21.

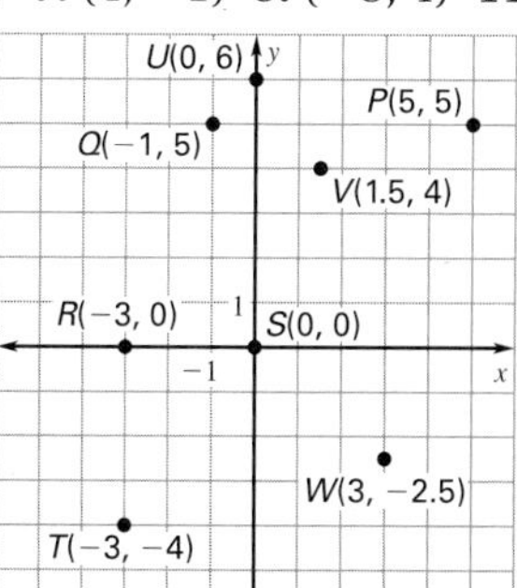

15. Quadrant II **17.** origin **19.** y-axis **21.** Quadrant IV

25.

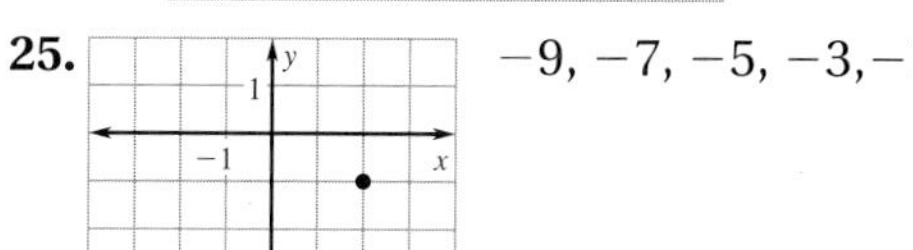

$-9, -7, -5, -3, -1$

27.

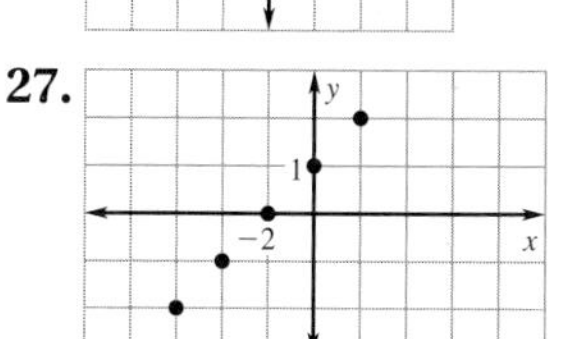

$-2, -1, 0, 1, 2$

29. Quadrant IV; the x-coordinate is positive and the y-coordinate is negative so the point is in Quadrant IV. **31.** Quadrant II; the x-coordinate is negative and the y-coordinate is positive so the point is in Quadrant II. **33.** If the x-coordinate is 0, then the point is on the y-axis. If the y-coordinate is 0, then the point is on the x-axis.

4.1 Problem Solving (pp. 210–212)

37. There is exactly one low temperature for each day in February.

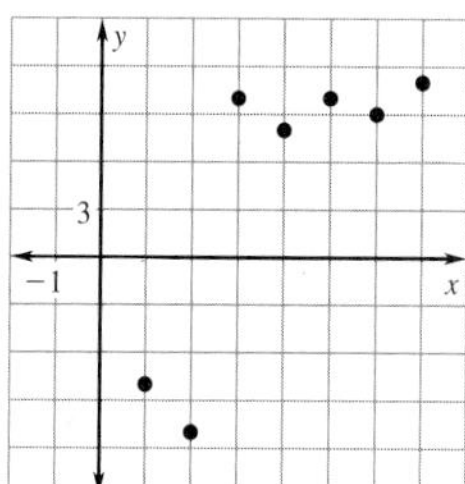

39. a.

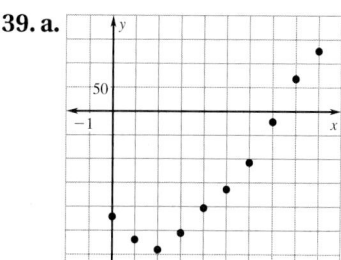

b. *Sample answer:* From 1992 to 1999 the federal deficit was decreasing.

41. a.

Height (in.)		
Reported	Measured	Difference
70	68	2
70	67.5	2.5
78.5	77.5	1
68	69	-1
71	72	-1
70	70	0

Weight (lb)		
Reported	Measured	Difference
154	146	8
141	143	-2
165	168	-3
146	143	3
220	223	-3
176	176	0

b. $(2, 8)$, $(2.5, -2)$, $(1, -3)$, $(-1, 3)$, $(-1, -3)$, $(0, 0)$

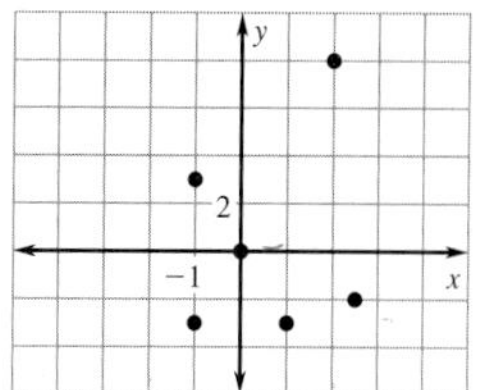

Extension (p. 214) **1.** Translation; a translation moves every point the same distance in the same direction so it will have the same shape and size as the original figure. **3.** Subtract 4 from each y-coordinate. **5.** Add 2 to each y-coordinate. **7.** (0, 1), (0, 3), (2, 3), (2, 1) **9.** (0, 0), (0, −2), (2, −2), (2, 0) **11.** (0, 0), (0, −1), (2, −1), (2, 0) **13.** (−1, 4), (−1, 6), (1, 6), (1, 4) **15.** Use the transformation $(x, y) \rightarrow (x, -y)$.

4.2 Skill Practice (pp. 219–220) **1.** linear function **3.** solution **5.** solution **7.** not a solution **9.** The 8 should be substituted for x and 11 for y, $11 - 8 \neq -3$, so (8, 11) is not a solution.

11.
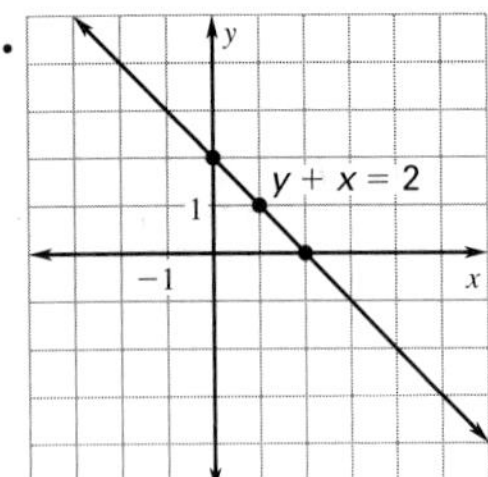

13.
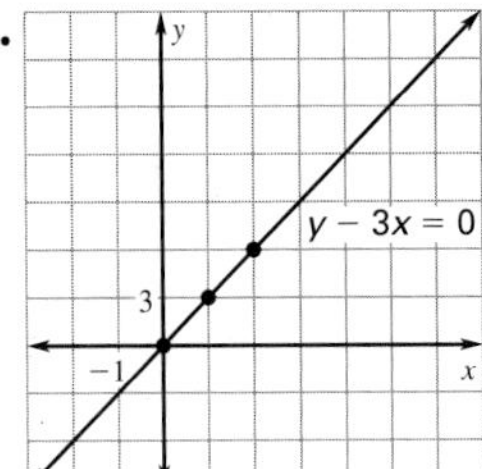

15.
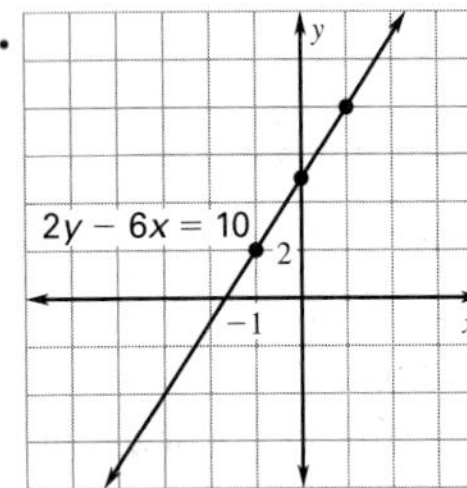

17.
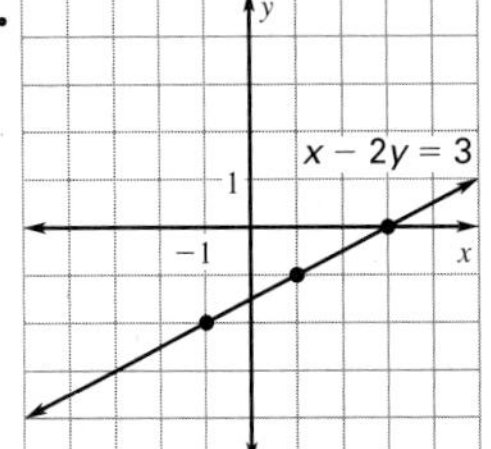

19.
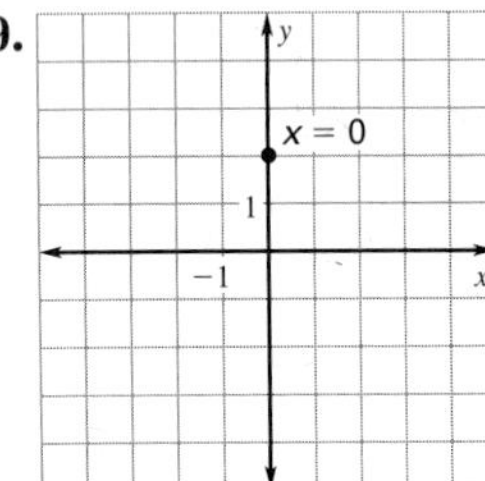

21.
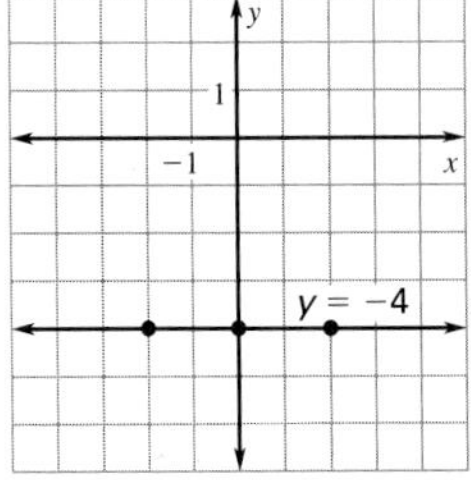

23. C **25.** B

27.
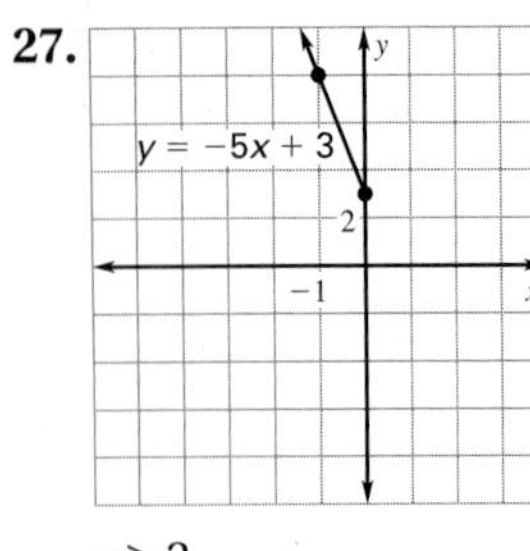

$y \geq 3$

29.
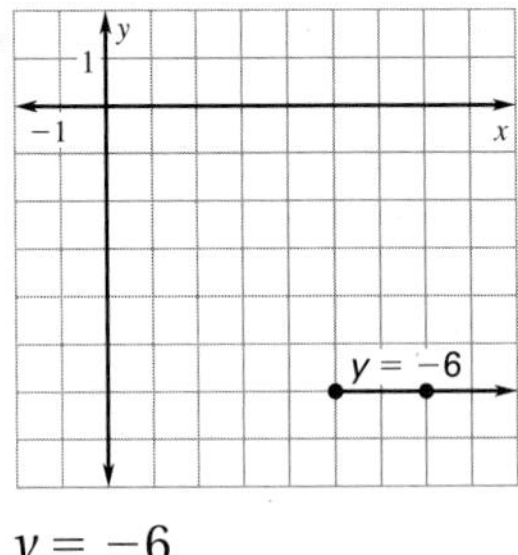

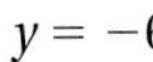

$y = -6$

31.
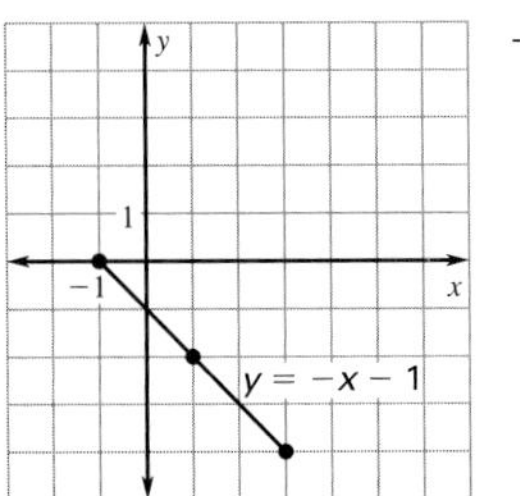

$-4 \leq y \leq 0$

4.2 Problem Solving (pp. 220–221)

35.
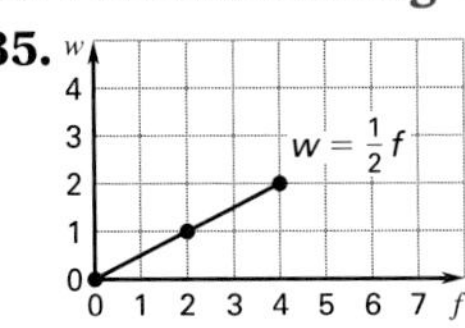

domain: $0 \leq f \leq 4$, range: $0 \leq w \leq 2$; 2 lb

37. a.
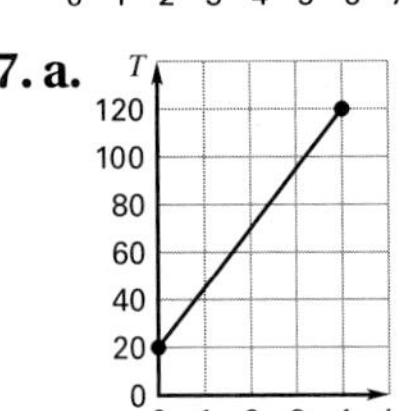

domain: $0 \leq d \leq 4$, range: $20 \leq T \leq 120$; 120°C

b.
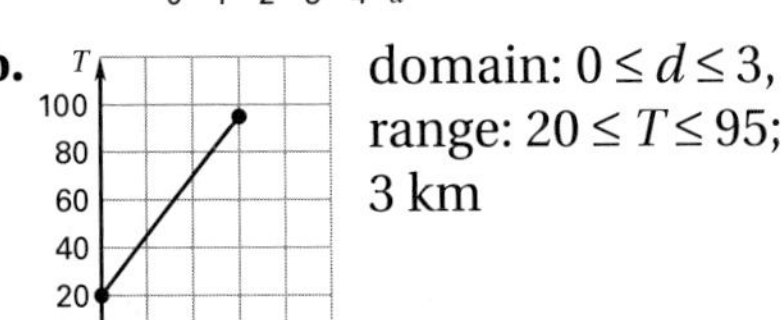

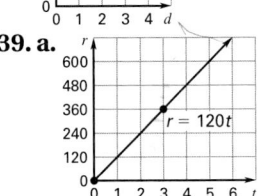

domain: $0 \leq d \leq 3$, range: $20 \leq T \leq 95$; 3 km

39. a. domain: $t \geq 0$, range: $r \geq 0$

b. Domain: $0 \leq t \leq 4$, range: $0 \leq r \leq 480$; the graph was a ray, but is now a segment.

41. a.
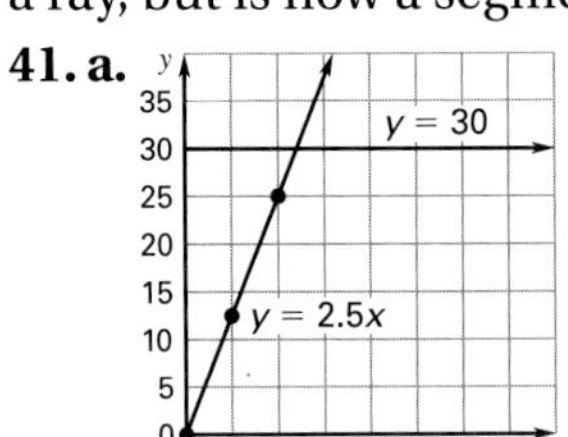

4.2 Graphing Calculator Activity (p. 222) **1.** 5.6 **3.** −5.3

Extension (p. 224)

1.
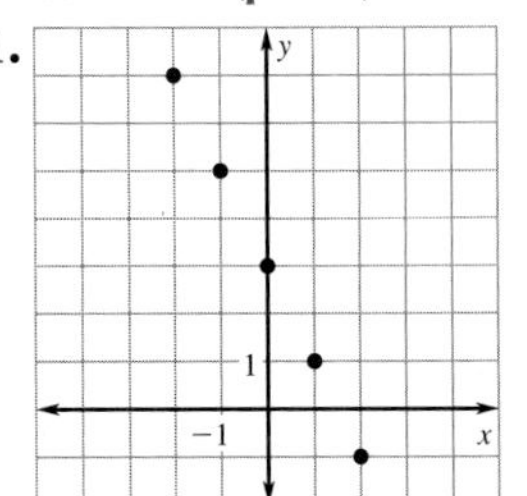

discrete

3. 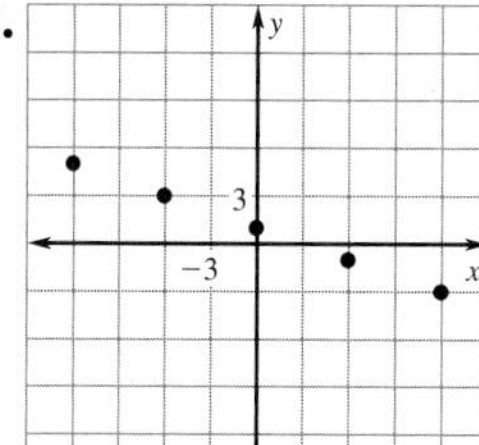

discrete

5. 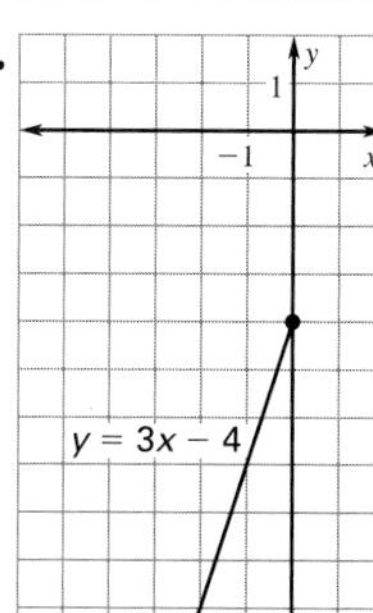

continuous

7. Discrete; you can only rent a whole number of DVDs.

9. Continuous; it makes sense to talk about the weight of water for any volume of water.

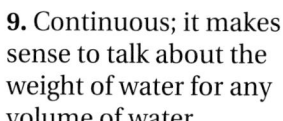

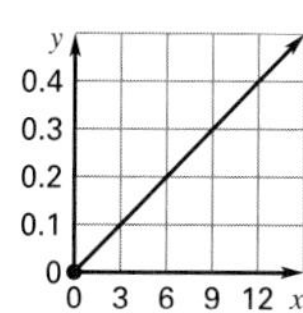

about 0.12

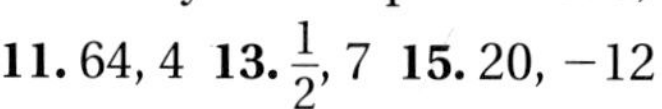

4.3 Skill Practice (pp. 229–230) **1.** x-intercept **3.** The intercepts are switched around; the x-intercept is -2, and the y-intercept is 1. **5.** 3, -3 **7.** 1, 4 **9.** 12, -3 **11.** 64, 4 **13.** $\frac{1}{2}$, 7 **15.** 20, -12

17. 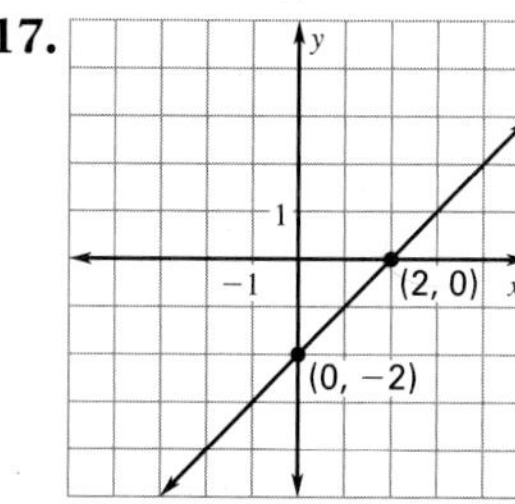

19. 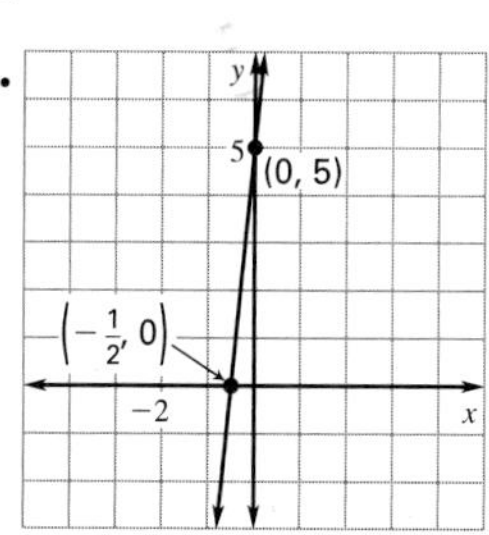

21. 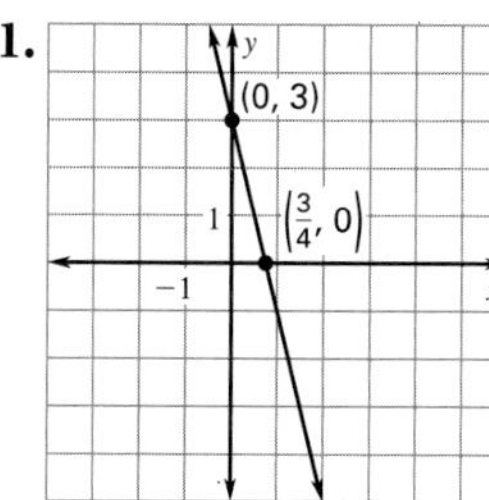

23. 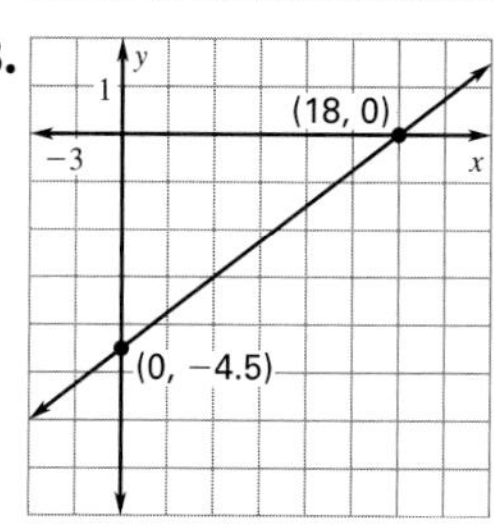

25. 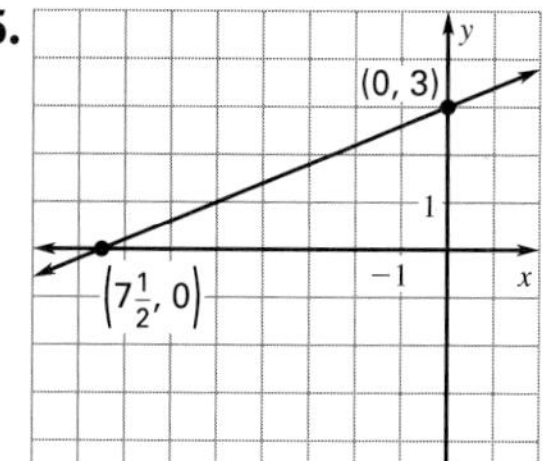

27. 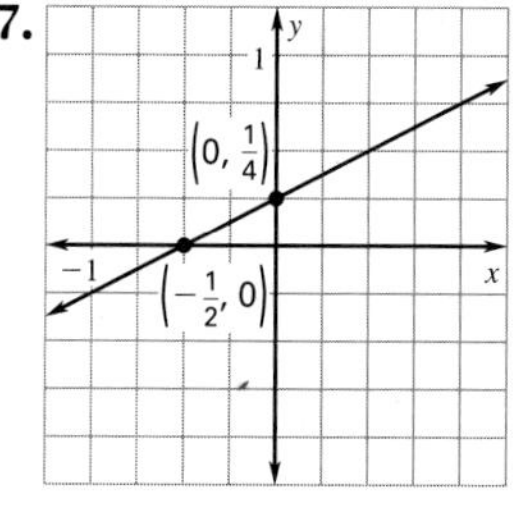

29. 3, -2

31. 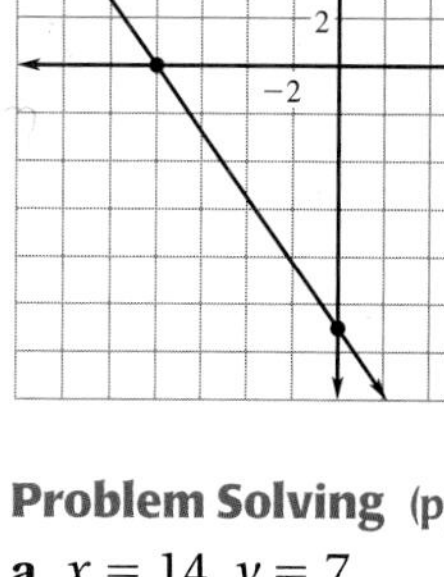

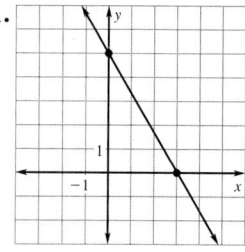

33. 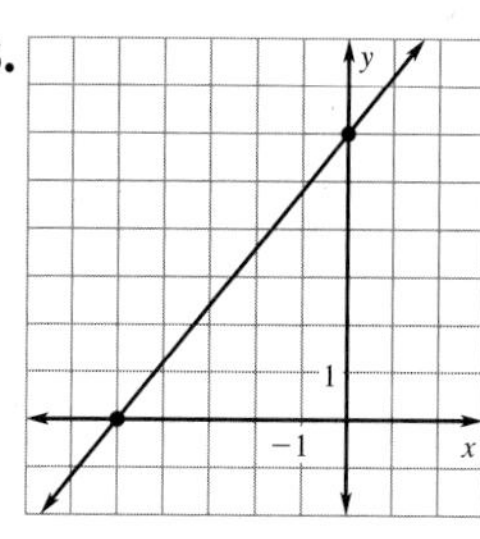

35. 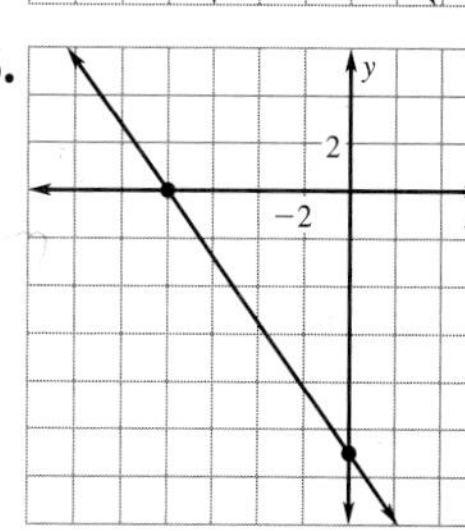

39. B **41.** Yes; yes; a horizontal line does not have an x-intercept if $y \neq 0$, a vertical line does not have a y-intercept if $x \neq 0$.

4.3 Problem Solving (pp. 230–232)

45. a. $x = 14$, $y = 7$

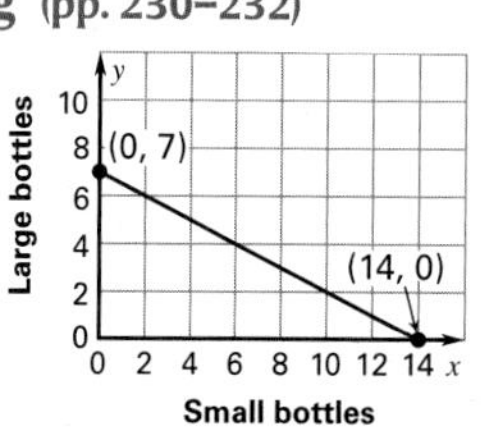

b. *Sample answer:* 2 and 6, 4 and 5, 6 and 4

47. a. v-intercept: 120, f-intercept: 180; the v-intercept means there are no flowers planted, the f-intercept means there are no vegetables planted.

b. 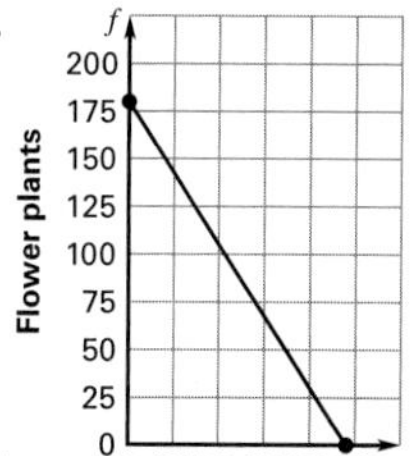

domain: $0 \le v \le 120$, range: $0 \le f \le 180$

c. 60 ft^2 **49.** 12.5 h. *Sample answer:* Since the tank will be empty when it needs to be refilled, replace w in the function with 0 and then solve the resulting equation for t.

4.4 Skill Practice (pp. 239–241) **1.** slope **3.** The denominator should be $2 - 5$, not $5 - 2$; $m = \frac{6-3}{2-5} = \frac{3}{-3} = -1$. **5.** undefined **7.** The slope was calculated using $\frac{\text{run}}{\text{rise}}$, not $\frac{\text{rise}}{\text{run}}$; $m = \frac{0-3}{12-6} = \frac{-3}{6} = -\frac{1}{2}$. **9.** undefined **11.** $-\frac{5}{2}$ **13.** 1 **15.** 0 **19.** \$2.25 per day; it costs \$2.25 per day to rent a movie. **21.** 0.3 **23.** 0.1 **25.** -15 **27.** -2 **29.** -3 **31.** -15 **33.** Yes; the slope of the line containing both points is -3.

4.4 Problem Solving (pp. 241–242) **37. a.** 0 h to 1.5 h **b.** 4.65 h to 8.95 h **39.** *Sample answer:* The elevation of the hiker increases for about 60 minutes, then stays the same for about 30 minutes, then decreases for the last 60 minutes.

4.5 Skill Practice (pp. 247–248) **1.** parallel **3.** 2, 1 **5.** −3, 6 **7.** $\frac{2}{3}$, −1 **11.** $y = -4x + 1$; −4, 1 **13.** $y = 2x + 3$; 2, 3 **15.** $y = -\frac{2}{5}x - 2$; $-\frac{2}{5}$, −2 **17.** B **19.** C

21.

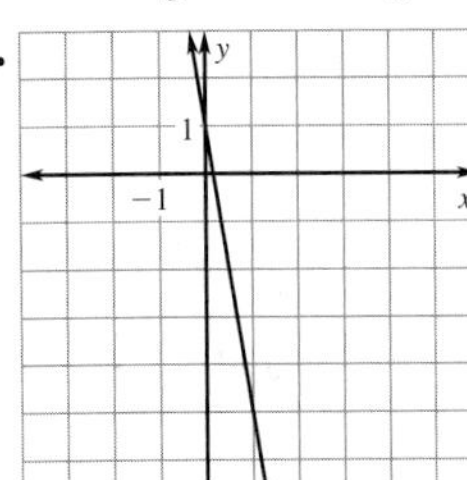

23.

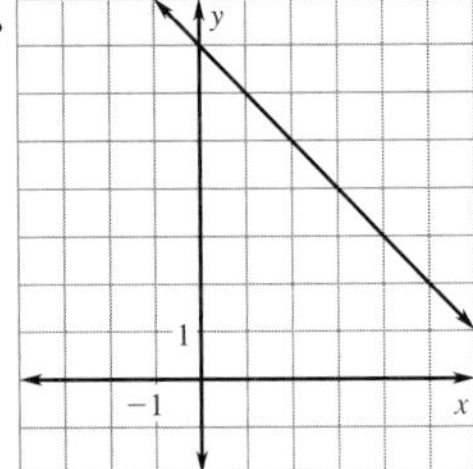

25.

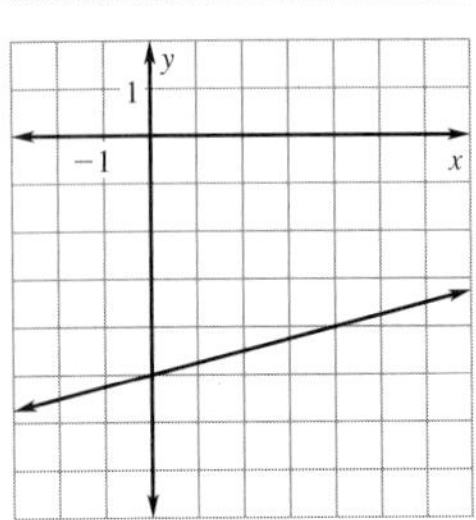

27.

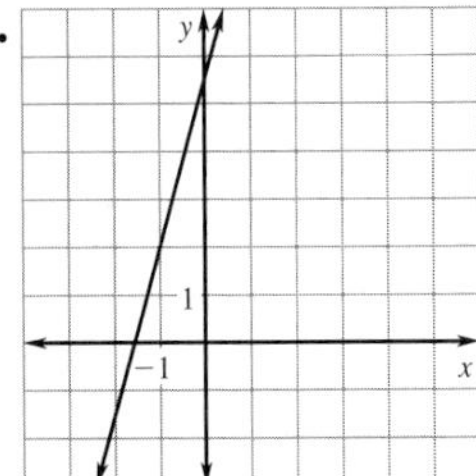

29.

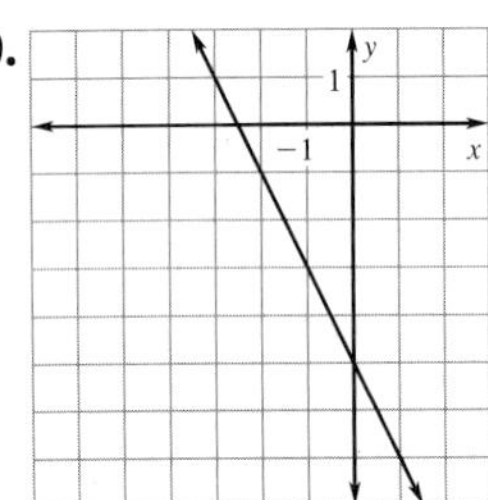

31. red, blue, and green **33.** Parallel; the slopes are both 3. **35.** Not parallel; the slopes are −4 and $-\frac{1}{4}$. **37.** −2

4.5 Problem Solving (pp. 248–250)

41. a.

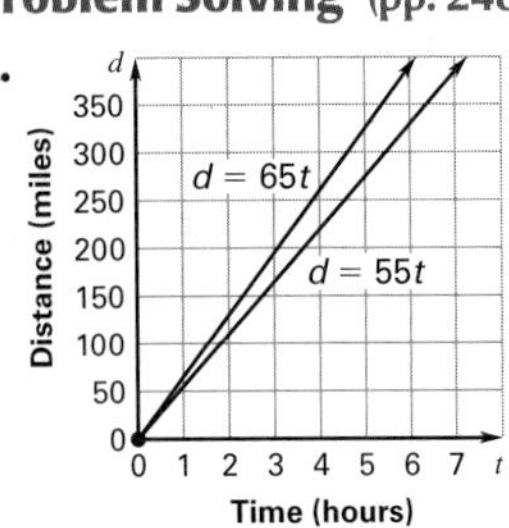

b. 30 mi

43. a.

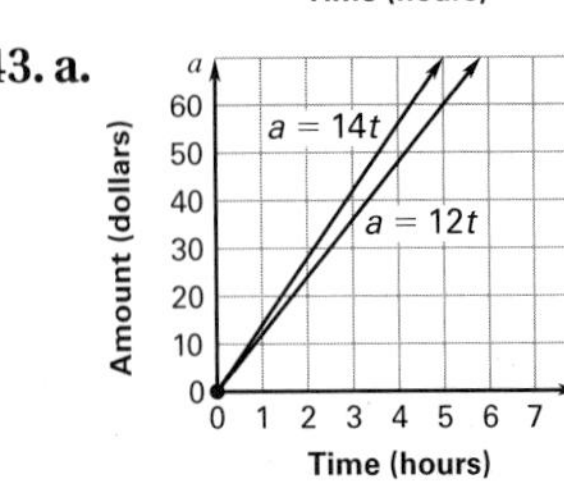

The slopes are the amount of money earned per hour, the *a*-intercepts show the amount of money made at 0 hours. **b.** $80

Extension (p. 252) **1.** −2 **3.** −4 **5.** $\frac{1}{2}$ **7.** 2000 **9.** 2000

4.6 Skill Practice (pp. 256–257) **1.** direct variation **3.** direct variation; 1 **5.** not direct variation **7.** direct variation; −4

11.

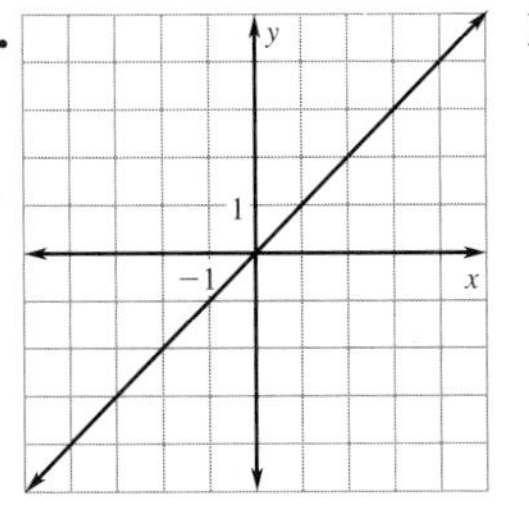

13.

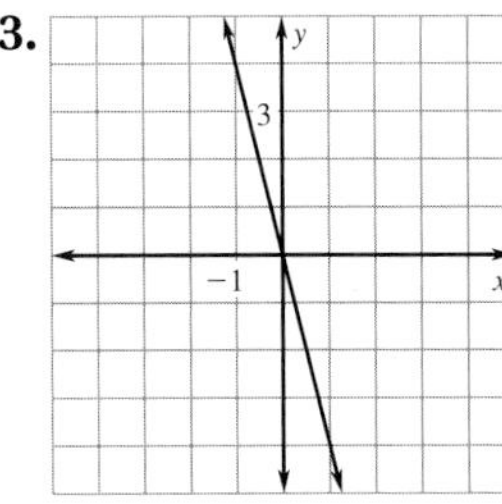

15.

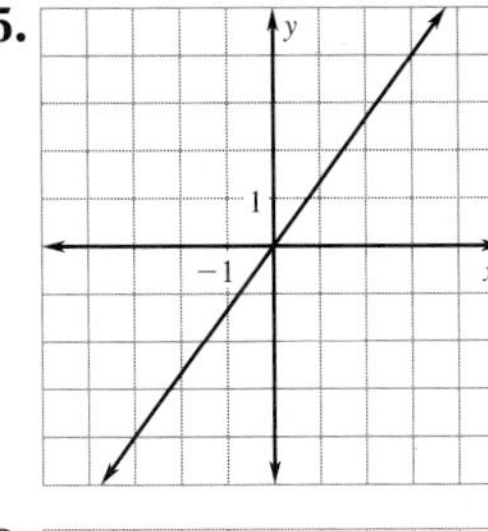

17.

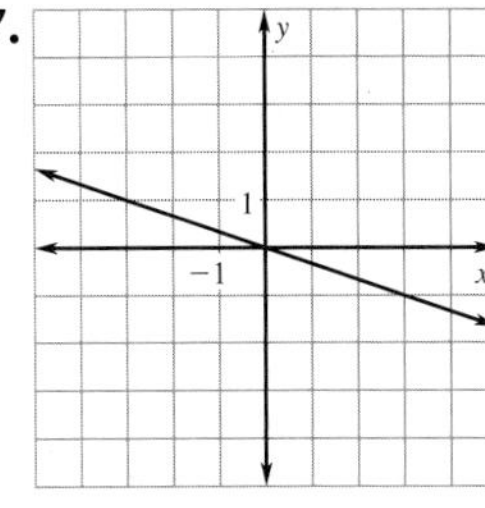

19.

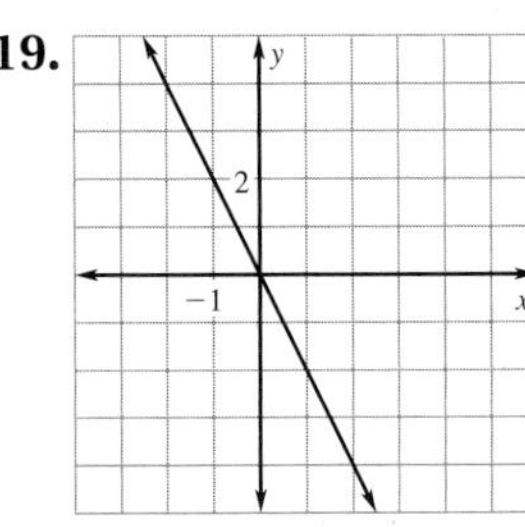

21.

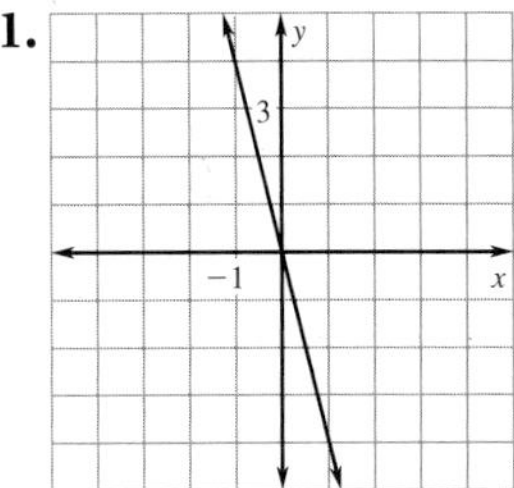

23. $y = -x$; −8 **25.** $y = -\frac{3}{4}x$; −6 **27.** not direct variation **29.** $y = 3x$ **31.** $y = \frac{1}{2}x$ **33.** $y = x$ **35.** $y = 4x$ **37.** $y = -\frac{7}{26}x$

4.6 Problem Solving (pp. 258–259) **41. a.** $v = \frac{3}{2}t$ **b.** 12 h **43. a.** Compare the ratios, $\frac{f}{w}$, for all data pairs (w, f). Since the ratios all equal 0.25, f varies directly with w. **b.** $f = 0.25w$; $7

45. a. *Sample answer:*

d	*C* (dollars)
1	1.5
2	3
3	4.5

b.

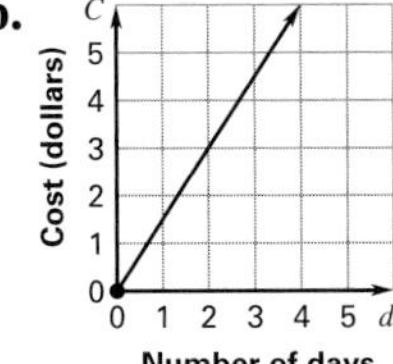

c. $C = 1.5d$; yes; it is in the form $y = ax$; $33.

4.6 Problem Solving Workshop (p. 261) **1.** 110 tbsp. *Sample answer:* Use the proportion $\frac{20}{100} = \frac{22}{x}$. **3.** Because 7 is half of 14, you can take half of 5.88 to find 7 words cost \$2.94. Because 21 is 3 times 7, multiply \$2.94 by 3 to get \$8.82. **5.** The proportion should be $\frac{6}{96} = \frac{10}{x}$; $\frac{6}{96} = \frac{10}{x}$, $960 = 6x$, $x = 160$.

4.7 Skill Practice (pp. 265–266) **1.** function notation **3.** −23, 1, 37 **5.** 14, −2, −26 **7.** 13, 0, −19.5 **9.** $2\frac{1}{5}$, 3, $4\frac{1}{5}$ **11.** $-7\frac{1}{2}$, −6, $-3\frac{3}{4}$ **15.** 3 **17.** −6 **19.** −7.5 **21.** 3.5

23.

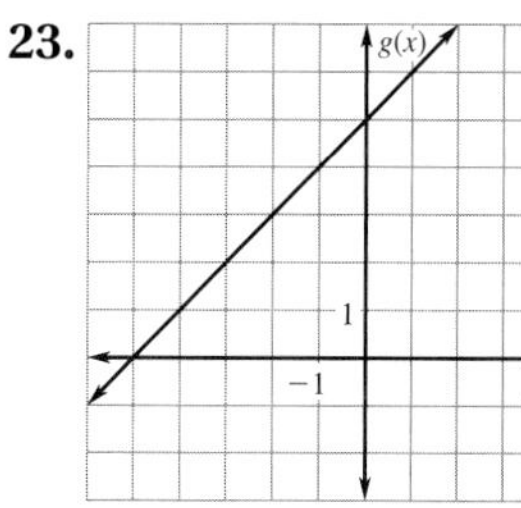

Because the graphs of g and f have the same slope, $m = 1$, the lines are parallel. The y-intercept of the graph of g is 5 more than the y-intercept of the graph of f.

25.

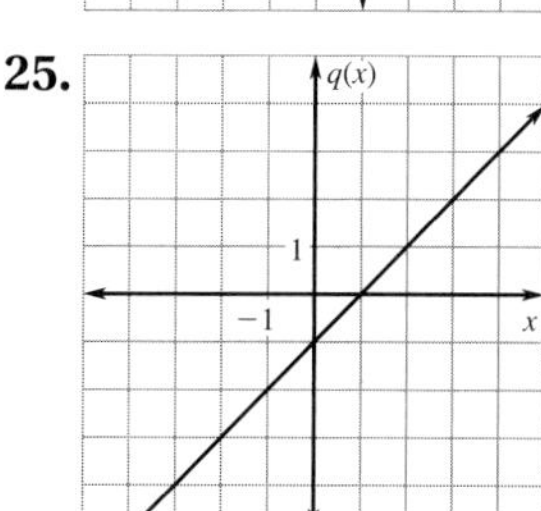

Because the graphs of q and f have the same slope, $m = 1$, the lines are parallel. The y-intercept of the graph of q is 1 less than the y-intercept of the graph of f.

27.

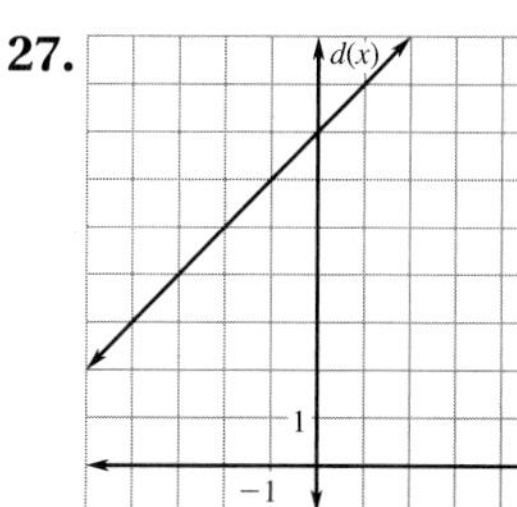

Because the graphs of d and f have the same slope, $m = 1$, the lines are parallel. The y-intercept of the graph of d is 7 more than the y-intercept of the graph of f.

29.

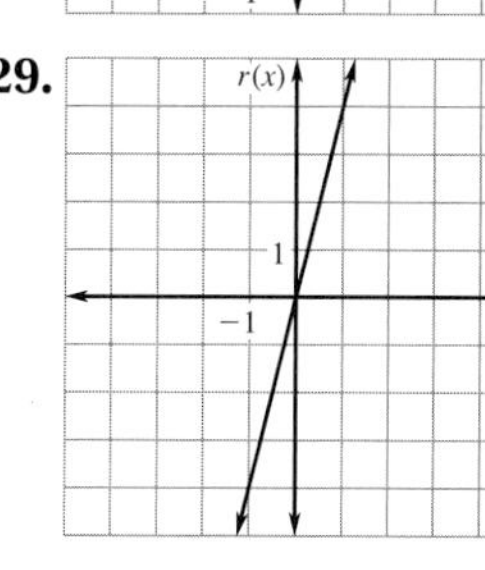

Because the slope of the graph of r is greater than the slope of the graph of f, the graph of r rises faster from left to right. The y-intercept for both graphs is 0, so both lines pass through the origin.

31.

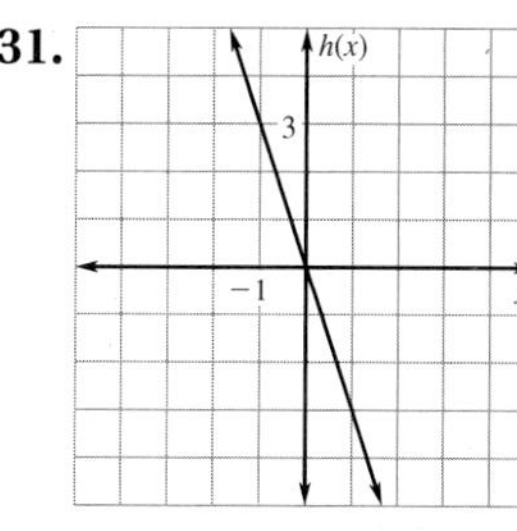

Because the slope of the graph of h is negative, the graph of h falls from left to right. The y-intercept for both graphs is 0, so both lines pass through the origin.

33.

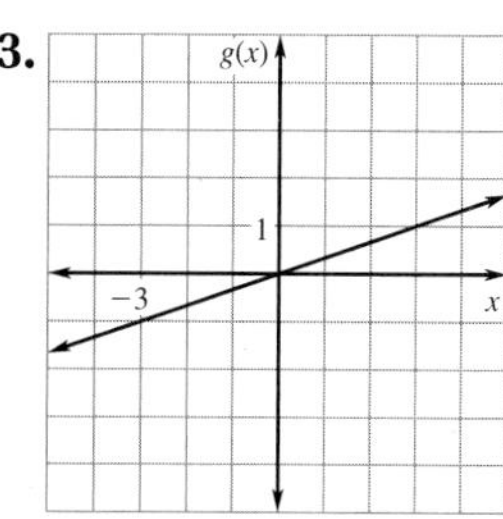

Because the slope of the graph of g is less than the slope of the graph of f, the graph of g rises slower from left to right. The y-intercept for both graphs is 0, so both lines pass through the origin.

37. Since the graphs of g and h have the same slope, $m = 0$, the lines are parallel. The y-intercept of the graph of h is 2 less than the y-intercept of the graph of g.

4.7 Problem Solving (pp. 267–268)

39. a.

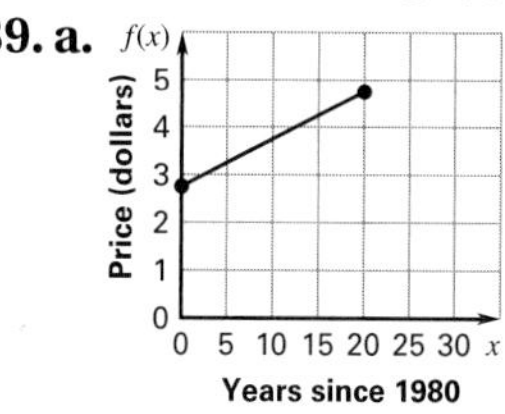

domain: $0 \le x \le 20$, range: $2.75 \le f(x) \le 4.75$ **b.** 18; in 1998, 18 years after 1980, the price of a movie ticket was \$4.55.

41.

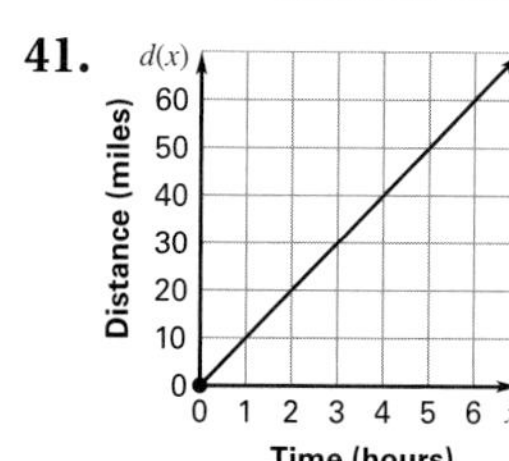

Domain: $x \ge 0$, range: $d(x) \ge 0$; 1.5 h; substitute 15 for $d(x)$ to get the equation $15 = 10x$, solve for x.

43.

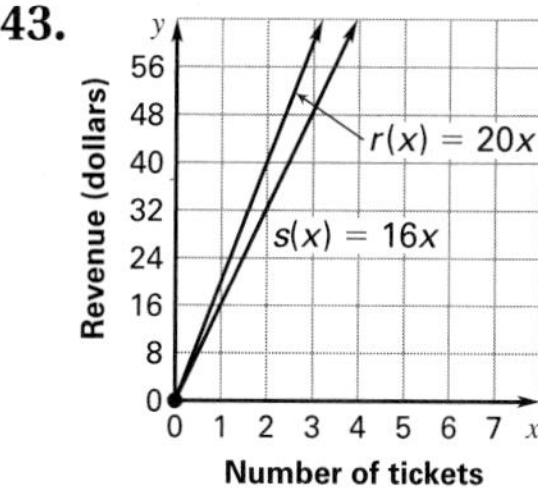

Because the slope of the graph of r is greater than the slope of the graph of s, the graph of r rises faster from left to right. The y-intercept for both graphs is 0, so both lines pass through the origin.

45. a. See graph in part (b); domain: $1 \le x \le 31$, range: $11.53 \le \ell(x) \le 12.43$.

b.

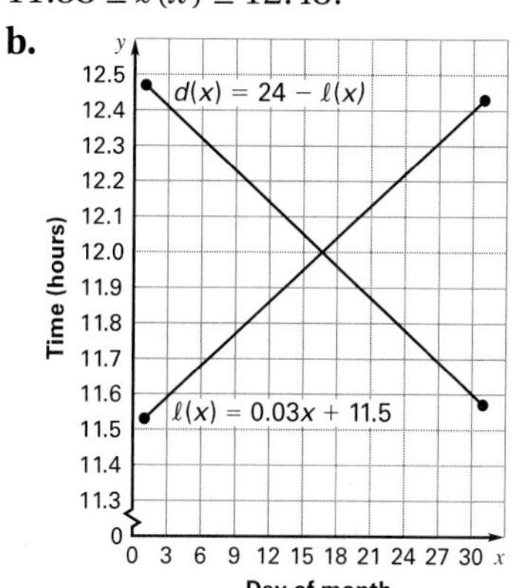

domain: $11.53 \le \ell(x) \le 12.43$, range: $11.57 \le d(x) \le 12.47$

Chapter Review (pp. 271–273) **1.** slope **3.** *Sample answer:* Make a table, use intercepts, and use the slope and y-intercept.

5–7.

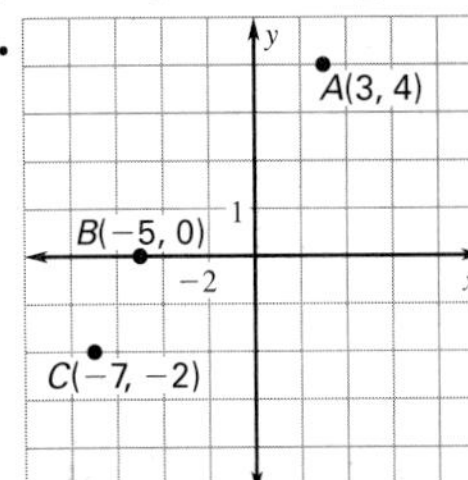

5. Quadrant I **7.** Quadrant III

9.

11.

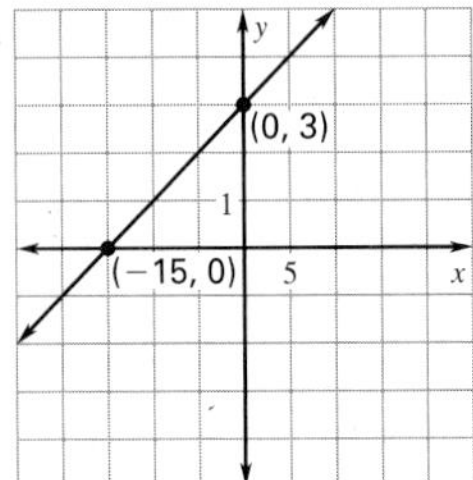

13.

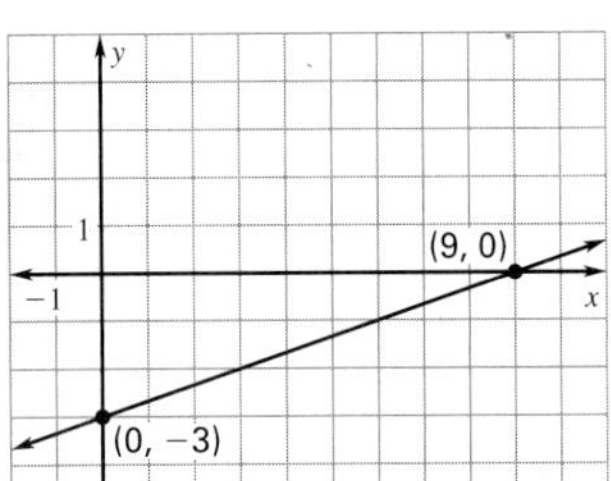

15. $-\frac{1}{3}$ **17.** -2

19.

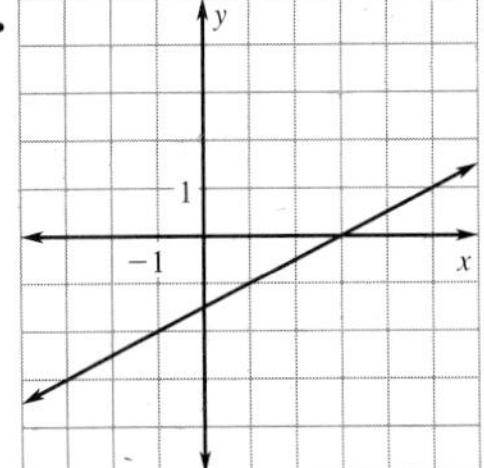

21.

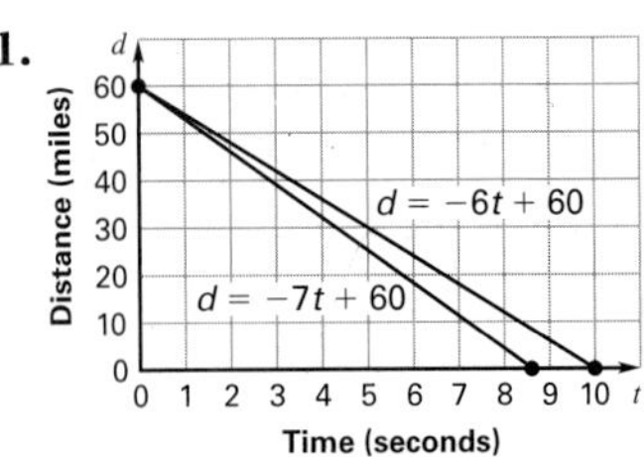

about 1.4 sec

23. direct variation; $-\frac{1}{2}$

25.

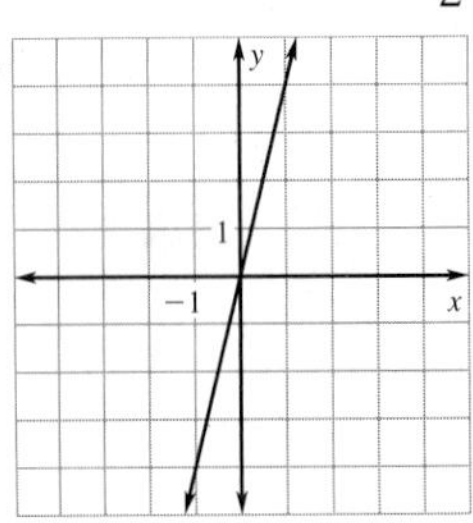

27.

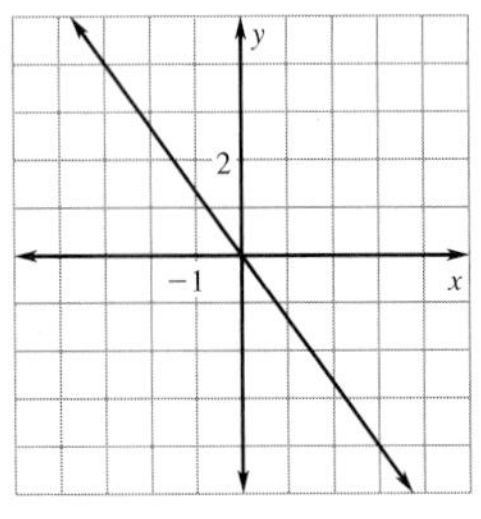

29. 11

31.

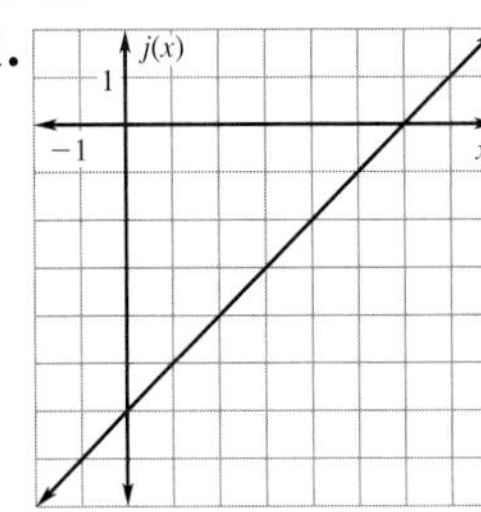

Because the graphs of j and f have the same slope, $m = 1$, the lines are parallel. The y-intercept of the graph of j is 6 less than the y-intercept of the graph of f.

33. Because the slope of the graph of t is greater than the slope of the graph of f, the graph of t rises faster from left to right. The y-intercept of the graph of t is 1 more than the y-intercept of the graph of f.

Chapter 5

5.1 Skill Practice (pp. 286–287) **1.** slope **3.** $y = 2x + 9$ **5.** $y = -3x$ **7.** $y = \frac{2}{3}x - 9$ **11.** $y = -\frac{1}{2}x$ **13.** $y = \frac{2}{3}x - 8$ **15.** $y = -2x - 2$ **17.** The slope should be $\frac{0-4}{5-0}$, $y = -\frac{4}{5}x + 4$. **19.** $y = 4x + 4$ **21.** $y = -\frac{4}{3}x$ **23.** $y = 2x - 2$ **25.** $y = -x - 5$ **27.** $y = -0.0625x + 4$ **29.** $y = -4x - 24$ **31.** $y = -2x + 7$ **33.** $y = -\frac{4}{5}x - 1$ **35.** $y = \frac{2}{3}x + 3$ **37.** $y = -3x + 9$ **39.** $y = x - 3$ **41.** $y = -2x + 1$ **43.** No; the slope of the line is undefined, the equation is $x = 3$, which is not in slope-intercept form.

5.1 Problem Solving (pp. 288–289) **45. a.** $C = 44m + 48$ **b.** \$312 **47.** $C = 3h + 30$; \$42

49. a.

x (years since 1970)	y (km²)
0	5.2
10	4.1
20	3.0
30	1.9

b. The area of the glaciers changed -1.1 square kilometers between every 10 year interval. **c.** $y = -0.11x + 5.2$; -0.11 km^2

51. a. $t = 0.7d + 2$ **b.** 16 min

5.1 Graphing Calculator Activity (pp. 290–291) **1.** $y = -2x + 5$ **3.** $y = 2x + 1.5$ **5.** $y = 1.5x + 2$ **7.** $y = 4x - 3$ **9.** $y = 0.5x + 1$; substitute 2 for x, 2 for y, and solve for b.

5.2 Skill Practice (pp. 296–297) **1.** y-intercept **3.** $y = 3x - 2$ **5.** $y = -5x - 13$ **7.** $y = -\frac{3}{4}x + 2$ **9.** -3 was substituted for x instead of y and 6 was substituted for y instead of x, $-3 = -2(6) + b$, $-3 = -12 + b$, $9 = b$. **11.** $y = 3x + 1$ **13.** $y = -\frac{2}{5}x - 1$ **15.** $y = -\frac{3}{4}x + \frac{35}{8}$ **17.** $y = 4x - 15$ **19.** $y = -\frac{1}{2}x + \frac{1}{2}$ **21.** $y = \frac{1}{3}x - \frac{4}{3}$ **23.** $y = -2x + 11$ **25.** $y = -\frac{1}{2}x + 8$ **27.** $y = x - 2$ **31.** $y = -\frac{2}{3}x + 6$ **33.** $y = 6x - 4$ **35.** Yes; you can substitute m and the coordinates of the point in $y = mx + b$, solve for b, and write the equation. **37.** Yes; you can find the slope of the line, then substitute the y-intercept for b, and write the equation. **39.** $y = \frac{9}{2}x - \frac{1}{2}$ **41.** The lines $y = \frac{3}{2}x - \frac{1}{2}$ and $y = \frac{9}{2}x - \frac{1}{2}$ and the lines $y = \frac{9}{2}x - \frac{1}{2}$ and $y = \frac{3}{2}x + \frac{11}{2}$ intersect because they have different slopes; the lines $y = \frac{3}{2}x - \frac{1}{2}$ and $y = \frac{3}{2}x + \frac{11}{2}$ will not intersect because they have the same slope, so they are parallel. **43.** The three points do not lie on the same line. If you find the equation of the line between two of the points and then check to see that the third point is a solution, you can see they do not lie on the same line. **45.** The three points do not lie on the same line. If you find the equation of the line between two of the points and then check to see that the third point is a solution, you can see they do not lie on the same line.

5.2 Problem Solving (pp. 298–299) **47.** $\frac{3}{4}$ ft/yr; 6 ft **49.** 115 min or 1 h 55 min; substitute 30 for m, 2 for x, and 85 for y into the equation $y = mx + b$ to find $b = 25$. Then substitute 3 for x into the equation $y = 30x + 25$ to solve for y. **51. a.** about 584 newspapers **b.** $y = 11.8x + 584$ **c.** about 938 newspapers **53. a.** $d = -18t + 234$

b.

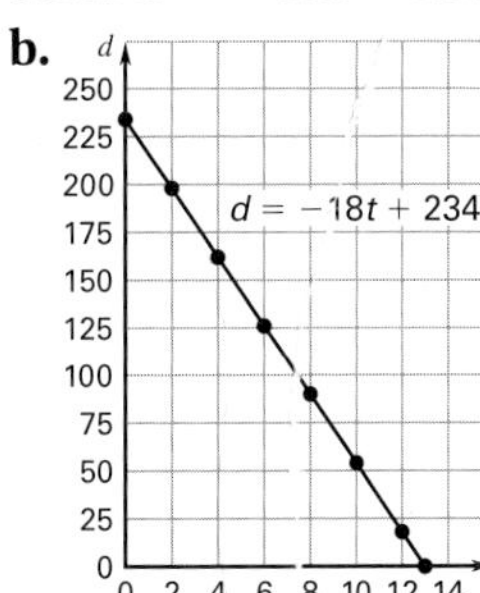

The slope is the rate that the hurricane is traveling, the y-intercept represents the distance from the town at 12 P.M.

c. 1 A.M.; find the t-intercept to find the value of t when the distance to the town is 0; substitute 0 for d and solve for t; $t = 13$, so you need to add 13 hours to 12 P.M. to get 1 A.M.

5.2 Problem Solving Workshop (p. 301) **1.** \$5; \$19 **3.** No; if the cost of the 60 inch bookshelf changes, the cost no longer increases at a constant rate. **5.** The student assumes that there is no fixed fee by using a proportion; $93 - 57 = 36$, $36 \div 2 = 18$, $57 + 18 = 75$.

5.3 Skill Practice (pp. 305–306) **1.** -2; $(-5, 5)$ **3.** $y - 1 = 2(x - 2)$ **5.** $y + 1 = -6(x - 7)$ **7.** $y - 2 = 5(x + 8)$ **9.** $y + 3 = -9(x + 11)$ **11.** $y + 12 = -\frac{2}{5}(x - 5)$ **13.** The form is $y - y_1$, so the left side should be $y - (-5)$ or $y + 5$; $y + 5 = -2(x - 1)$.

15.

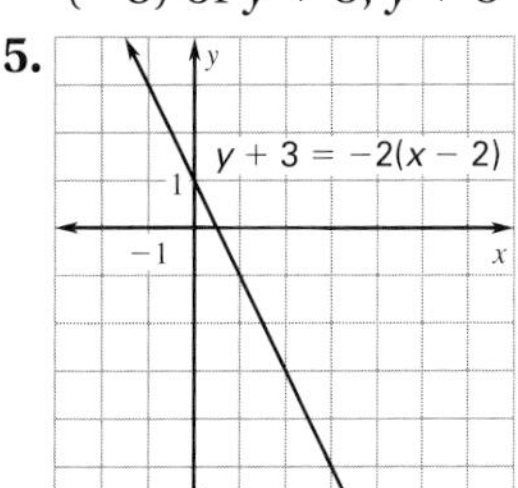

17.

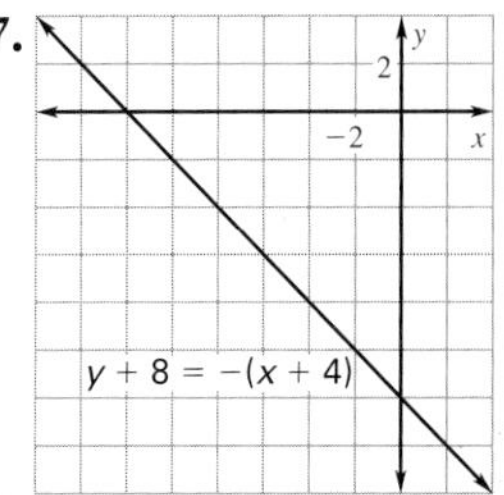

19.

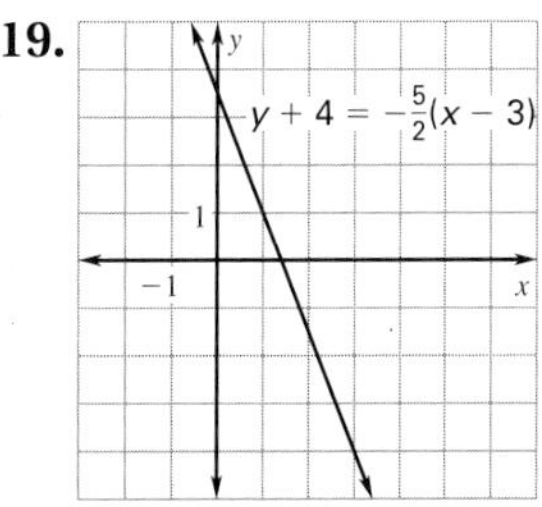

21. $y - 4 = (x - 1)$ or $y - 1 = (x + 2)$ **23.** $y - 2 = -2(x - 7)$ or $y - 12 = -2(x - 2)$ **25.** $y + 1 = -\frac{3}{5}(x + 4)$ or $y + 7 = -\frac{3}{5}(x - 6)$

27. $y + 20 = 8(x + 3)$ or $y - 36 = 8(x - 4)$ **29.** A point was not substituted into the equation, the y-coordinates of the two points were substituted; $y - 2 = \frac{2}{3}(x - 1)$. **31.** No; because the increase is not at a constant rate, the situation cannot be modeled by a linear equation. **33.** No; because the increase is not at a constant rate, the situation cannot be modeled by a linear equation.

5.3 Problem Solving (pp. 307–308) **37. a.** $y = 130x + 530$ **b.** \$1570 **39.** $y = 10000x + 67000$; \$127,000 **41. a.** Since the cost increases at a constant rate of \$.49 per print, the situation can be modeled by a linear equation. **b.** *Sample answer:* $y - 1.98 = 0.49(x - 1)$ **c.** \$1.49 **d.** \$1.79 **43. a.** $y - 17.6 = -0.06(x - 60)$ **b.** 16.4 ft/sec

SELECTED ANSWERS

Extension (p. 310) **1.** yes; 2, −1 **3.** yes; −43, −50

5. 

7. 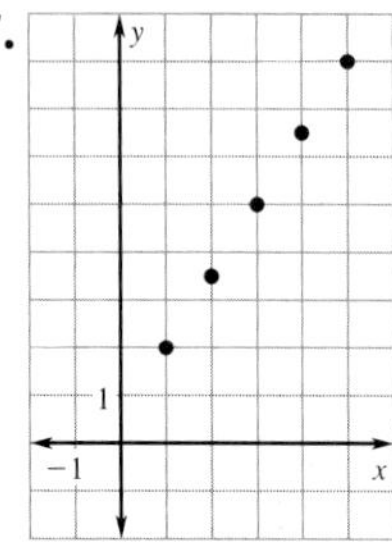

9. 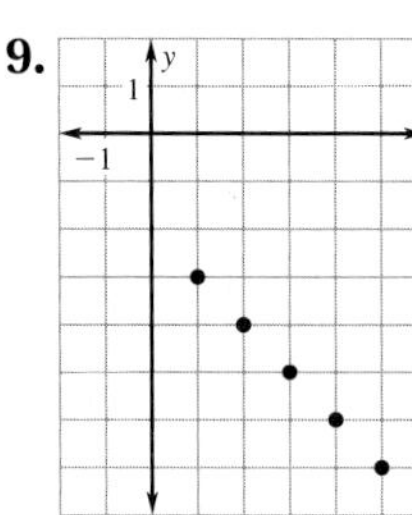

11. $a_n = 51 + (n - 1)21$; 2130 **13.** $a_n = \frac{1}{4} + (n - 1)\frac{1}{8}$; $12\frac{5}{8}$ **15.** $a_n = 1 + (n - 1)\frac{1}{3}$; 34

5.4 Skill Practice (p. 314) **1.** standard form **3.** point-slope form **5–9.** Sample answers are given. **5.** $2x + 2y = -20$, $3x + 3y = -30$ **7.** $x - 2y = -9$, $-2x + 4y = 18$ **9.** $3x - y = -4$, $6x - 2y = -8$ **11.** $-x + y = 5$ **13.** $2x + y = 5$ **15.** $\frac{3}{2}x + y = -10$ **17.** $\frac{2}{3}x + y = -\frac{4}{3}$ **19.** $-\frac{4}{3}x + y = -1$ **21.** $-\frac{1}{2}x + y = 1$ **23.** $y = 2$, $x = 3$ **25.** $y = 3$, $x = -1$ **27.** $y = 4$, $x = -1$ **29.** (1, −4) was substituted incorrectly, 1 should be substituted for x and −4 substituted for y, $A(1) - 3(-4) = 5$, $A + 12 = 5$, $A = -7$. **31.** 4; $4x + 3y = 5$ **33.** −4; $-x - 4y = 10$ **35.** −5; $-5x - 3y = -5$

5.4 Problem Solving (pp. 315–316) **39. a.** 15 oz **b.** $12c + 15w = 120$ **c.** 10 corn, 0 wheat; 5 corn, 4 wheat; 0 corn, 8 wheat **41. a.** $100\ell + 40s = 1600$

b. 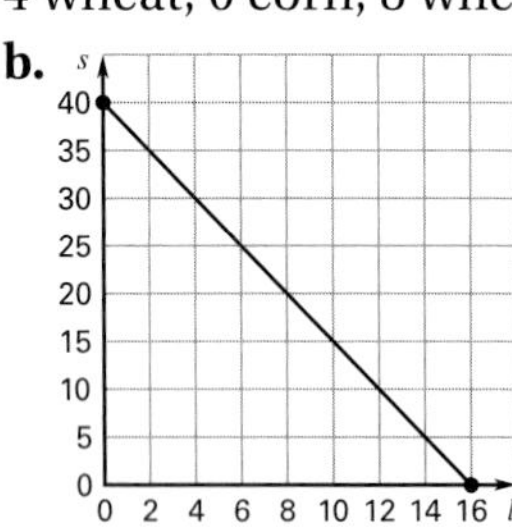

c.

Large rafts	Small rafts
16	0
14	5
12	10
10	15
8	20
6	25
4	30
2	35
0	40

43. $2\ell + 2w = 60$. *Sample answer:*

Length (ft)	Width (ft)
5	25
10	20
15	15
20	10
25	5

5.5 Skill Practice (pp. 322–323) **1.** perpendicular **3.** $y = 2x + 5$ **5.** $y = -\frac{3}{5}x + 2$ **7.** $y = 6x + 1$ **9.** $y = 2x + 9$ **11.** $y = 3x + 30$ **13.** parallel: a and b; perpendicular: none **15.** parallel: none; perpendicular: a and b **17.** The line through points (6, 4) and (4, 1) is perpendicular to the line through points (1, 3) and (4, 1); the slope of the line through the points (6, 4) and (4, 1) is $\frac{3}{2}$, the slope of the line through the points (1, 3) and (4, 1) is $-\frac{2}{3}$. The slopes are negative reciprocals, so the lines are perpendicular. **19.** $y = -\frac{1}{3}x - 1$ **21.** $y = -2x + 24$ **23.** $y = -\frac{3}{4}x - 4$ **25.** $y = -\frac{1}{2}x - \frac{1}{2}$ **27.** (2, 1) was substituted incorrectly, 2 should be substituted for x, and 1 should be substituted for y; $1 = 2(2) + b$, $1 = 4 + b$, $-3 = b$. **29.** Yes; the slope of the line through (4, 3) and (3, −1) is 4 and the slope of the line through (−3, 3) and (1, 2) is $-\frac{1}{4}$. The slopes are negative reciprocals, so the lines are perpendicular.

5.5 Problem Solving (pp. 323–324) **33. a.** $w = 200d + 6000$; $w = 200d + 6250$ **b.** 12,000 lb; 12,250 lb **c.** The graphs of the lines are parallel because they have the same slope, 200. The w-intercept of the second line is 250 more than the w-intercept of the first line. **35.** Different registration fees; because the lines are parallel, the rate of change, the monthly fee, for each must be equal. Therefore, the students paid different registration fees.

5.6 Skill Practice (pp. 328–329) **1.** increase **3.** positive correlation **5.** negative correlation

7. 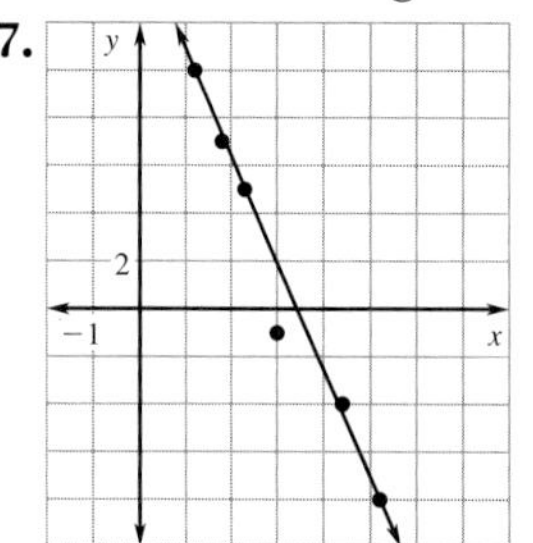

Sample answer: $y = -4.4x + 14.88$

SELECTED ANSWERS

9. The line does not have approximately half the data above it and half below it.

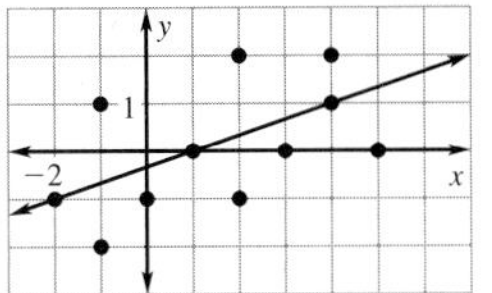

11. *Sample answer:* The amount of time driving a car and the amount of gas left in the gas tank

13.

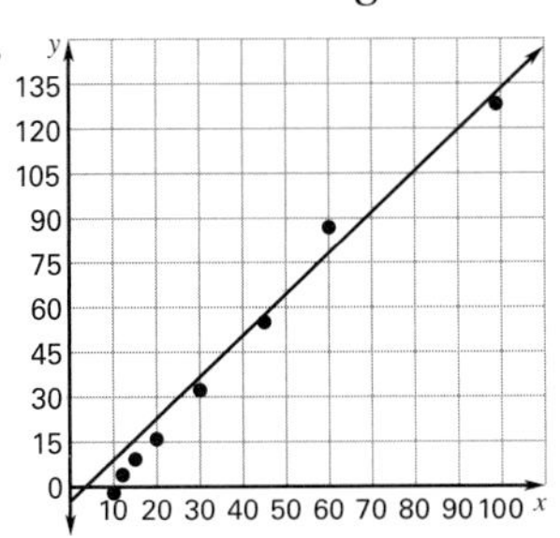

Positive correlation. *Sample answer:* $y = 1.49x - 13$

5.6 Problem Solving (pp. 330–331)

17. a.

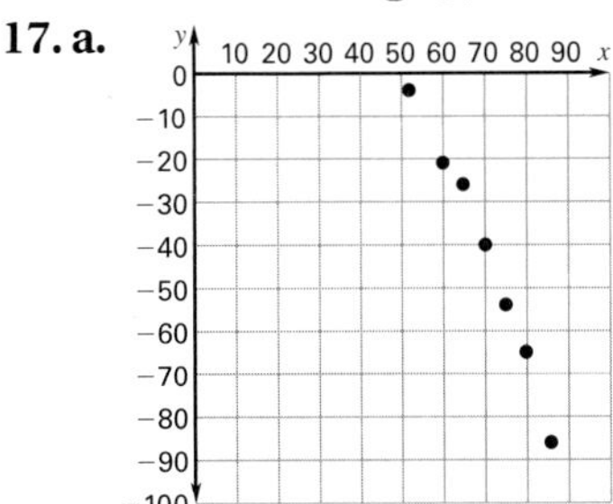

b. *Sample answer:* $y = -2.2x + 111$ **c.** *Sample answer:* -2.2 degrees per kilometer

19. *Sample answer:* $y = 12.6x + 32$

5.6 Graphing Calculator Activity (p. 333) **1.** See art in Exercise 3; negative correlation.

3.

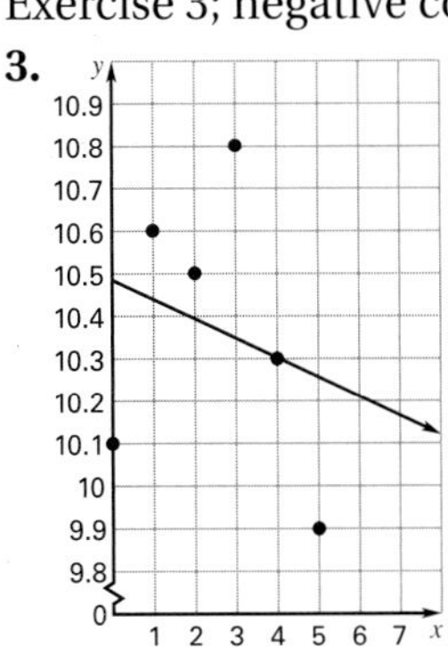

5. *Sample answer:* You cannot use the best-fitting line to predict future sales because the data do not show a strong correlation.

5.7 Skill Practice (pp. 338–339) **1.** linear interpolation

3.

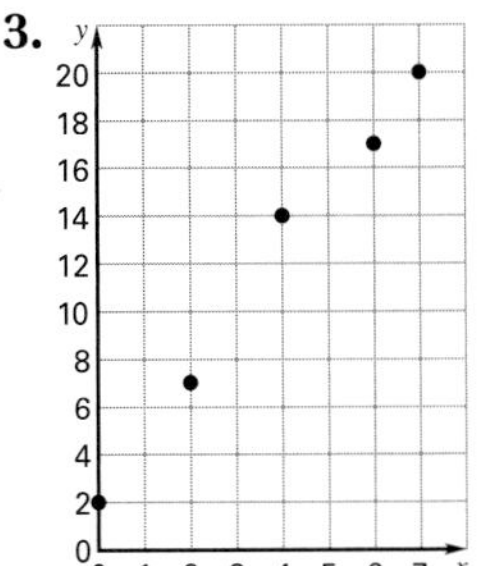

$y = 2.6x + 2.3$; 15.3

5.

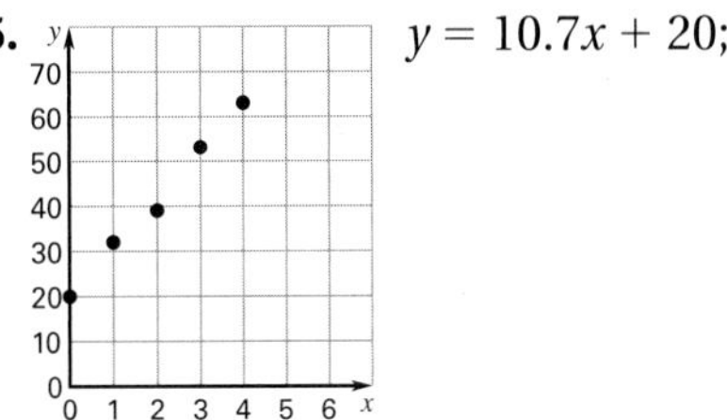

$y = 10.7x + 20$; 127

7. $2\frac{2}{3}$ **9.** -16 **11.** 1.5 **13.** To find the zero of a function, substitute 0 for y, not x; $0 = 2.3x - 2$, $2 = 2.3x$, $x = \frac{20}{23}$. **15.** a and b were not substituted correctly; $y = 4.47x + 23.1$.

5.7 Problem Solving (pp. 339–341)

19. a.

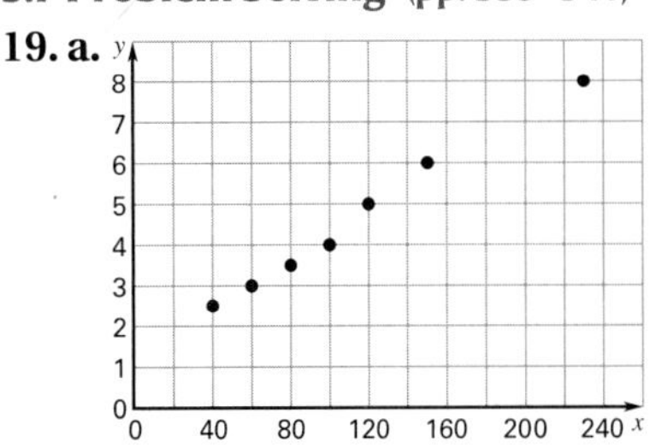

b. $y = 0.03x + 1.23$ **c.** about 8.73 ft^2
21. a. $y = -197.6x + 3542$ **b.** about 17.9; 17.9 years from 1985, or 2002, the number of people living in high noise areas will be 0; no.

5.7 Internet Activity (p. 342)
1. Answers may vary. **3.** Answers may vary.

Chapter Review (pp. 345–348) **1.** negative **3.** The zero of a function is the x-value of the function when $y = 0$; it is the x-intercept of the graph. **5.** $y = \frac{4}{9}x + 5$ **7.** $y = -1.25x + 25$; \$22.50 **9.** $y = x + 3$ **11.** $y - 7 = -6(x - 4)$ or $y - 1 = -6(x - 5)$ **13.** $y + 2 = -\frac{6}{11}(x + 3)$ or $y + 8 = -\frac{6}{11}(x - 8)$ **15.** $4x + y = -1$
17. $0.07r + 0.04s = 5$. *Sample answer:* 4 organza, 118 satin; 8 organza, 111 satin; 12 organza, 104 satin
19. a. $y = -2x + 1$ **b.** $y = \frac{1}{2}x - 4$

21.

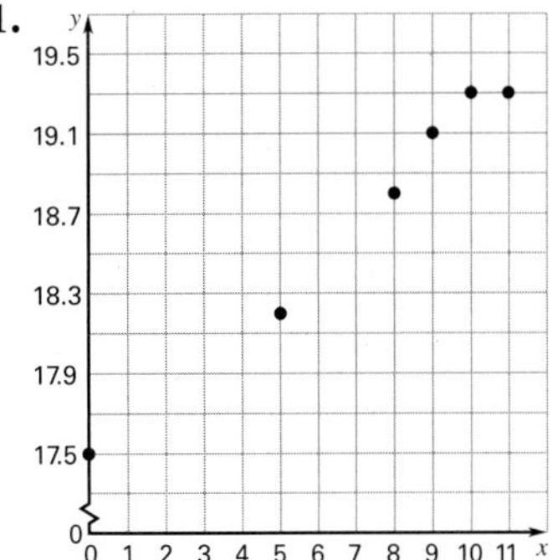

positive correlation

Chapter 6

6.1 Skill Practice (pp. 359–360) **1.** open, left of -8

3. $s \leq 60$

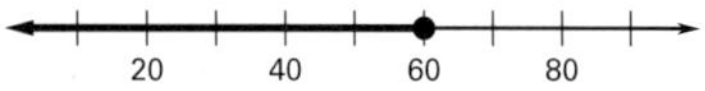

5. $h > 48$

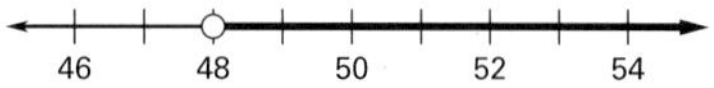

7. $x < 10$ **9.** $x \geq -2$

11. $y \geq -16$

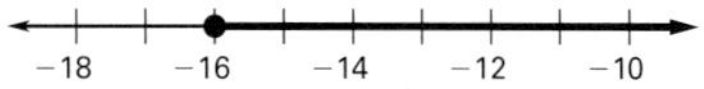

13. $n \leq -\frac{1}{5}$

15. $w > -17.6$

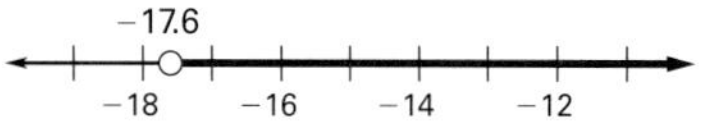

17. $s \geq 9$

19. $q > -1\frac{1}{6}$

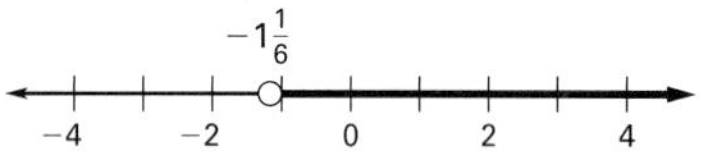

21. $d > -6.84$

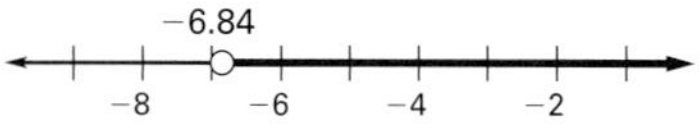

23. The number line should be shaded to the right of -3, not the left.

25. $n - 15 \leq 37$; $n \leq 52$

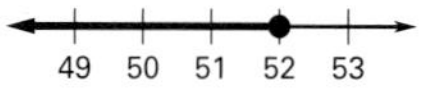

27. $x < 21.6$ **29.** No; no; there are infinitely many solutions of an inequality, so it is not possible to check them all. One solution might check in the inequality while another does not. For example, if you incorrectly solve $x + 7 > 10$ as $x > 2$, the solution $x = 4$ checks in the original inequality.

6.1 Problem Solving (pp. 360–361) **31.** more than 8350 points **33. a.** $s > 127.53$ **b.** Yes; no; no; $128.13 > 127.53$; $126.78 < 127.53$; when your score is 127.53, you and your competitor will tie.
35. *Sample answer:* You want to improve on your personal best of 16 points scored in a basketball game. In the first three quarters of the game, you scored 14 points. Write and solve an inequality to find the possible numbers of points that you can score in the fourth quarter to give yourself a new personal best; $x \geq 3$, if you score at least 3 points in the fourth quarter, you will have a new personal best.

37. a.

Original price, x (\$)	19,459	19,989	20,549	22,679	23,999
Final price, y (\$)	16,459	16,989	17,549	19,679	20,999

b. $x - 3000 \leq 17{,}000$, $x \leq 20{,}000$

6.2 Skill Practice (pp. 366–367)
1. Division property of inequality

3. $p \geq 7$

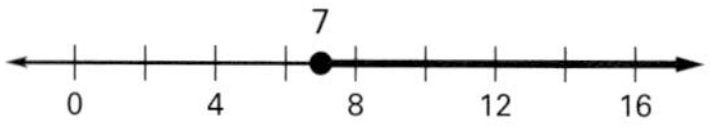

5. $y > 6$

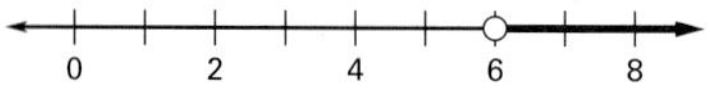

7. $q < 28$

9. $g > -120$

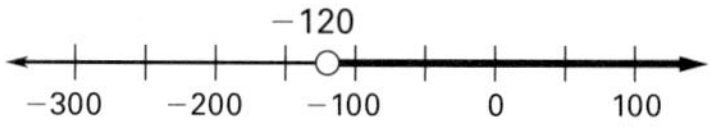

11. $t \leq -22.5$

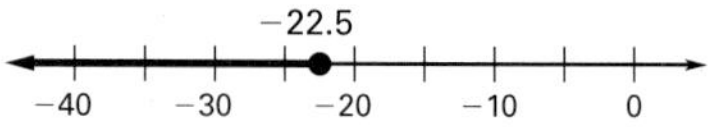

13. $s \leq -5$

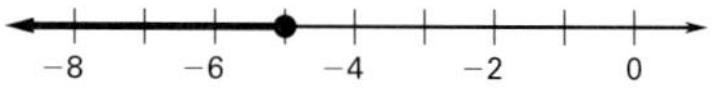

15. $f < -0.25$

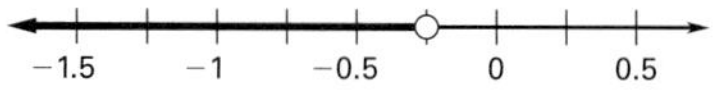

17. $c < -0.6$

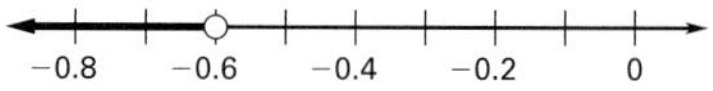

19. $z \leq -0.25$

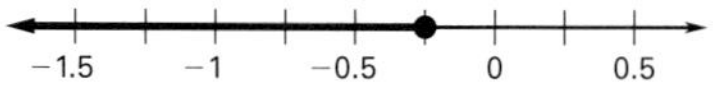

21. $j < -0.34$

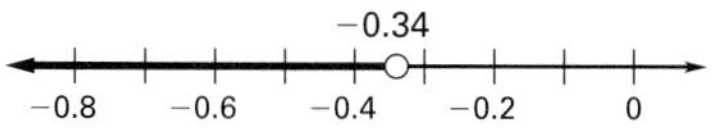

23. $r > -54$

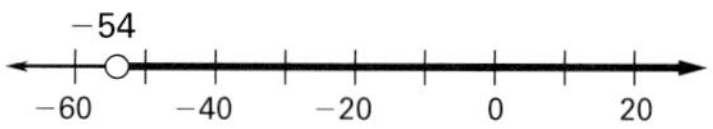

25. $m > -24$

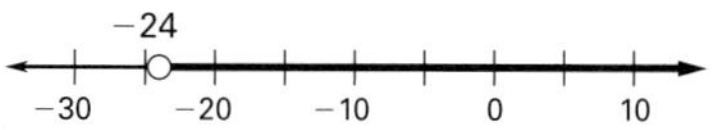

27. In both cases, you divide both sides of the inequality by a; when $a > 0$, you do not reverse the inequality symbol, but when $a < 0$, you do. **29.** Both sides of the inequality were multiplied by a positive number, so the inequality symbol should not have been reversed; $x \leq -63$.

31. $-15y \leq 90$; $y \geq -6$

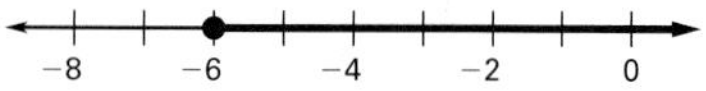

33. $\frac{w}{24} \geq -\frac{1}{6}$; $w \geq -4$

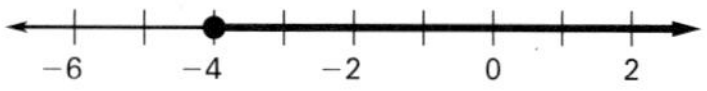

6.2 Problem Solving (pp. 367–368) **37.** at least 200 words **39.** at least 3.2 **41. a.** $400h \leq 6560$, $h \leq 16.4$, no more than 16 horses **b.** No; the area added by increasing both the length and the width by 20 feet can be divided into 2 rectangles (80 feet by 20 feet and 82 feet by 20 feet) and 1 square (20 feet by 20 feet). The 400 square feet of the square is large enough to hold one horse, and the rectangular areas will be able to hold additional horses. **c.** no more than 23 horses; the area of the new corral is $(80 + 15)(82 + 15) = 9215$ square feet. Find the possible numbers of horses h the corral can hold by solving the inequality $9215 \geq 400h$; $h \leq 23.04$.

6.3 Skill Practice (pp. 372–373)
1. equivalent inequalities
3. $x > 5$
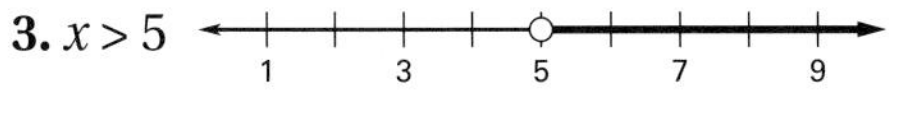

5. $v \geq -1$
7. $r \geq 1\frac{1}{7}$
9. $m > 3$
11. $p < \frac{1}{2}$
13. $d > -10$
15. The inequality symbol was not reversed when dividing both sides by -3; $x \leq -13$. **17.** all real numbers **19.** $s \geq 0$ **21.** all real numbers **23.** no solution **25.** no solution **27.** no solution
29. $3x + 4 < 40$; $x < 12$
31. $5x + 2x > 9x - 4$; $x < 2$
35. $\frac{1}{2} \cdot 8(x + 1) \leq 44$; $x \leq 10$

6.3 Problem Solving (pp. 373–374) **37.** at most 11 songs **39. a.** Up to 6 swans; the area of the habitat is (20 feet)(50 feet) $= 1000$ square feet. 500 square feet are needed for the first two swans and the remaining $1000 - 500 = 500$ square feet can hold up to $500 \div 125 = 4$ more swans; so, the maximum number of swans is $2 + 4 = 6$ swans. **b.** at most 14 more swans

41. a.

Pitches per inning, p	15	16	17	18	19
Total number of pitches, t	98	101	104	107	110

b. $53 + 3p \leq 105$, $p \leq 17\frac{1}{3}$, at most 17 pitches

6.3 Problem Solving Workshop (p. 376) **1.** at least 9 batches **3.** at most 6 games **5.** less than 7.9 min/mi

Extension (p. 378) **1.** $x > 3$ **3.** $x < 213.75$

6.4 Skill Practice (pp. 384–385)
1. compound inequality
3. $2 < x < 6$
5. $-1.5 \leq x < 9.2$
7. $40 \leq s \leq 60$
9. $1 < x \leq 6$
11. $-4 \leq m \leq \frac{1}{4}$
13. $-\frac{1}{3} \leq p < 2$
15. $r < 2$ or $r \geq 7$
17. $v < -5$ or $v > 5$
19. $g < -2\frac{1}{3}$ or $g > 10$
21. 3 was subtracted from only two of the three expressions of the inequality; $1 < -2x < 6$, $-\frac{1}{2} > x > -3$.
23. $x + 5 < 8$ or $x - 3 > 5$; $x < 3$ or $x > 8$
25. $-8 \leq 3(x - 4) \leq 10$; $1\frac{1}{3} \leq x \leq 7\frac{1}{3}$
29. true **31.** False. *Sample answer:* $a = -4$ is a solution of $x > 5$ or $x \leq -4$, but it is not a solution of $x > 5$.

6.4 Problem Solving (pp. 385–387)
37. $-2600 \leq e \leq -100$
41. $3.2 \text{ lb} \leq f \leq 6.4 \text{ lb}$ **43. a.** $\frac{5}{9}(F - 32) < 0$ or $\frac{5}{9}(F - 32) > 100$, $F < 32°F$ or $F > 212°F$
b.

°F	23	86	140	194	239
°C	−5	30	60	90	115

23°F, 239°F

45. a. $8 \leq \frac{w}{300} \leq 10$, $2400 \leq w \leq 3000$; 2400 watts to 3000 watts **b.** Yes; no; the amplification per person for 350 people is $\frac{2900}{350} \approx 8.3$ watts, which is between 8 watts and 10 watts, the amplification per person for 400 people is $\frac{2900}{400} = 7.25$ watts, which is not between 8 watts and 10 watts. **c.** 4800 watts; because each person requires at least 8 watts of amplification, and you want to be sure to provide enough amplification for 600 people, you need at least $8(600) = 4800$ watts of amplification.

6.4 Graphing Calculator Activity (p. 388) **1.** $4 < x < 7$; the graphs are the same. **3–7.** Displays should show the graphs of the following inequalities. **3.** $3 \leq x \leq 7$ **5.** $8 \leq x \leq 48$ **7.** $x \leq 4\frac{1}{2}$ or $x \geq 5$

6.5 Skill Practice (pp. 393–394) **1.** absolute value equation **3.** 5, −5 **5.** 0.7, −0.7 **7.** $\frac{1}{2}$, $-\frac{1}{2}$ **9.** 4, −10 **11.** −1, $-3\frac{2}{3}$ **13.** 2, −9 **15.** 4, 9 **17.** $8\frac{1}{2}$, $-3\frac{1}{2}$ **19.** $-\frac{1}{2}$, $-2\frac{1}{2}$ **21.** The absolute value symbol was removed without writing the second equation, $x + 4 = -13$; $x = 9$ or $x = -17$. **23.** no solution **25.** −4.5, −5.5 **27.** −3, 6 **29.** $13\frac{1}{2}$, $14\frac{1}{2}$ **31.** $\frac{1}{4}$, $-1\frac{1}{4}$ **33.** 13, −3 **35.** −7.5, −10.7 **37.** The distance between x and 3 is 7, 10, −4; $x - 3 = 7$ *or* $x - 3 = -7$, 10, −4; the solutions are the same. **39.** $5|2x + 9| = 15$; −3, −6

6.5 Problem Solving (pp. 394–395) **43.** 235 sec, 245 sec **45. a.** 52.462 points, 56.888 points **b.** 0.3 point **47. a.** $p = |s - 450|$ **b.** 300 points, 600 points **49. a.** June 2005; November 2005 **b.** Yes; make a table of values for (m, p) using integer values of m from 0 to 8. Look for the lowest value of p in the table.

Extension (p. 397)

1.

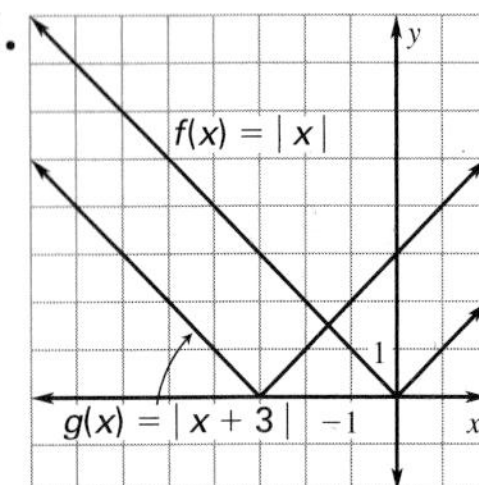

The graph of g is 3 units to the left of the graph of f.

3.

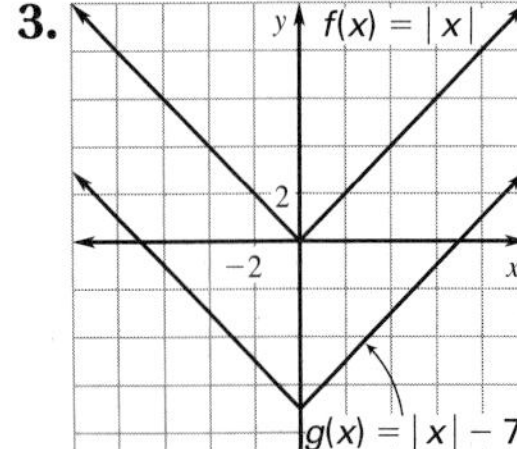

The graph of g is 7 units below the graph of f.

5.

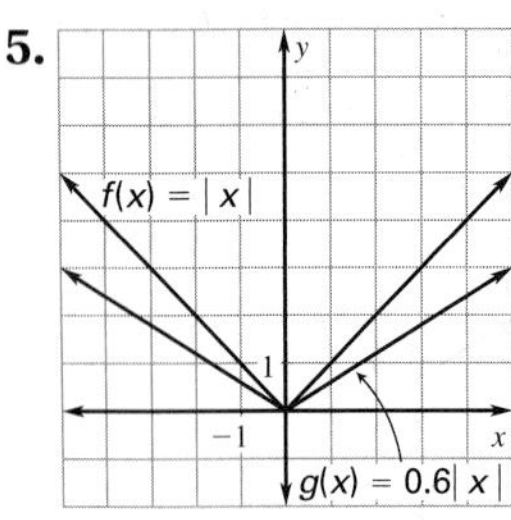

The graph of g opens up and is wider than the graph of f.

7.

x	1	2	3	4	5
$g(x)$	8	6	4	6	8

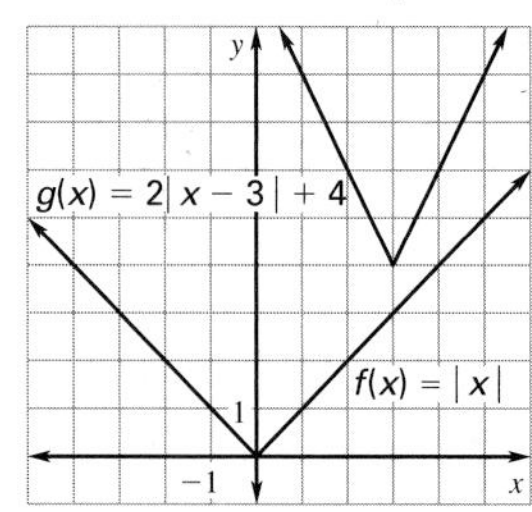

The graph of g is 3 units to the right of the graph of f and 4 units above it. The graph of g is narrower than the graph of f.

6.6 Skill Practice (pp. 401–402)

1. equivalent inequalities

3. $-4 < x < 4$

5. $h < -4.5$ or $h > 4.5$

7. $-\frac{3}{5} \le t \le \frac{3}{5}$

9. $d \le -7$ or $d \ge -1$

11. $m < 8$ or $m > 20$

13. $c \le -3$ or $c \ge \frac{1}{2}$

15. $r < -8$ or $r > -4$

17. $u \le -3\frac{1}{5}$ or $u \ge 6\frac{2}{5}$

19. $v < 6$ or $v > 34$

23. The compound inequality should use *or*: $x + 4 > 13$ *or* $x + 4 < -13$; $x > 9$ *or* $x < -17$.

25. $|x - 6| \le 4$; $2 \le x \le 10$

27. $|-4x - 7| + 3 > 10$; $x < -3.5$ *or* $x > 0$

29. true **31.** False. *Sample answer:* 20

6.6 Problem Solving (pp. 402–403) **35.** at least 470 words and at most 530 words **37.** $|t - 346| \le 2$, at least 344°F and at most 348°F; continue to preheat; the temperature is still below 350°F. **39. a.** 10.02 m/sec^2 **b.** 0.88 m/sec^2

6.7 Skill Practice (pp. 409–410) **1.** solution **3.** not a solution **5.** not a solution **7.** not a solution **9.** solution **11.** not a solution **13.** solution

17.

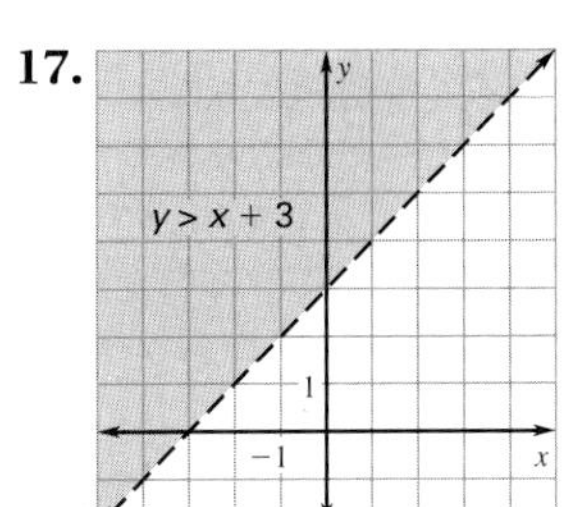

19.

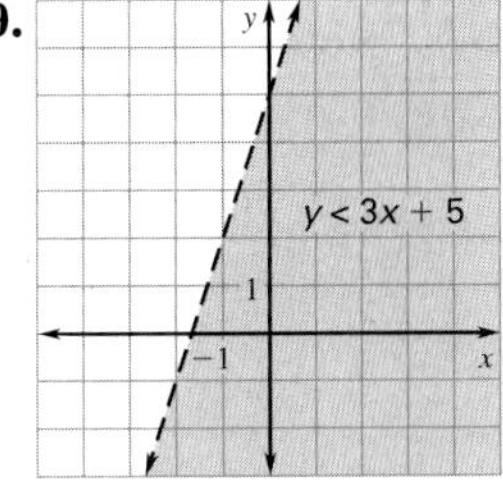

21.

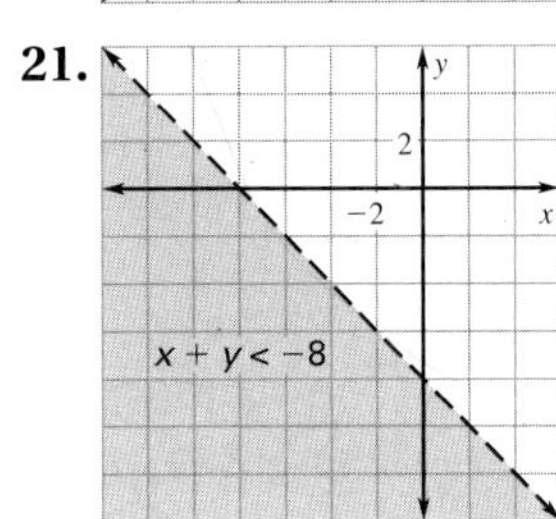

23.

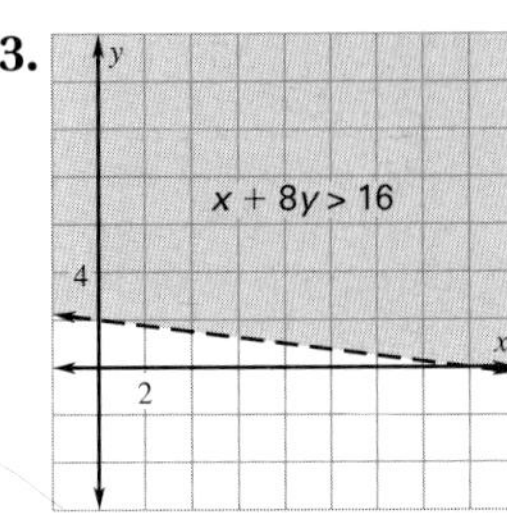

25.

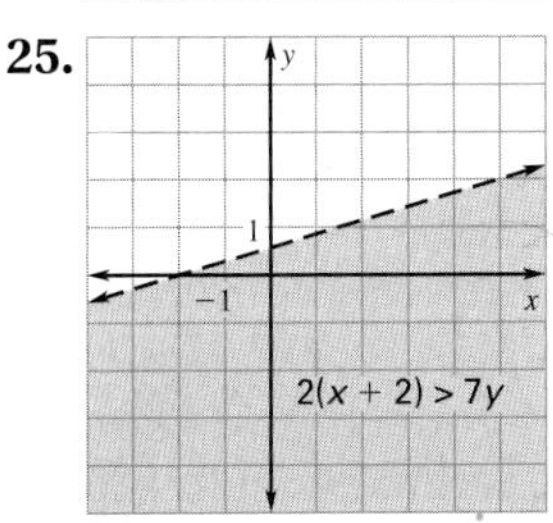

27.

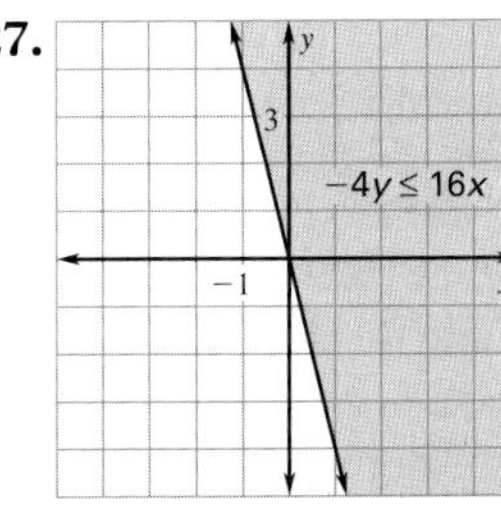

29.

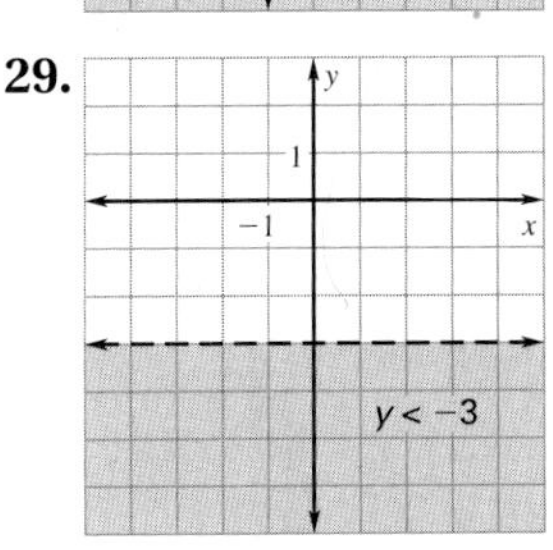

31.

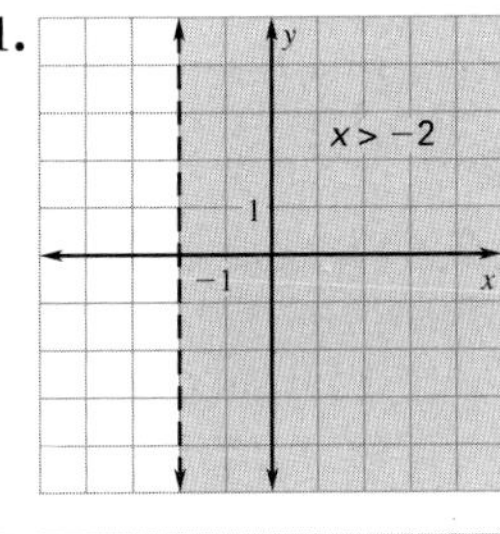

33.

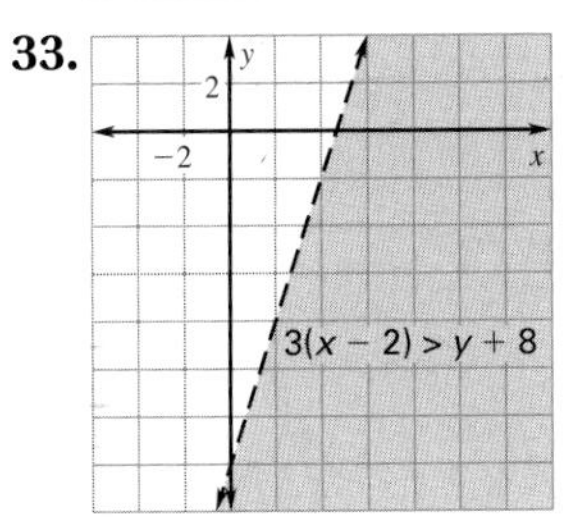

35.

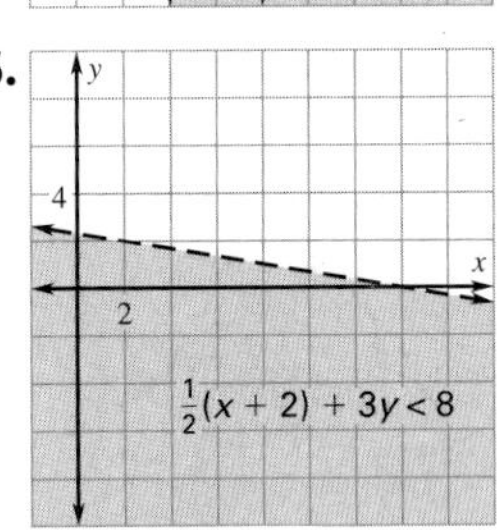

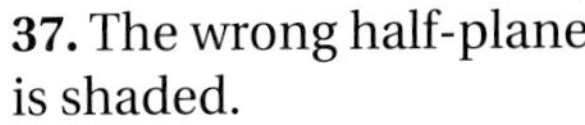

37. The wrong half-plane is shaded.

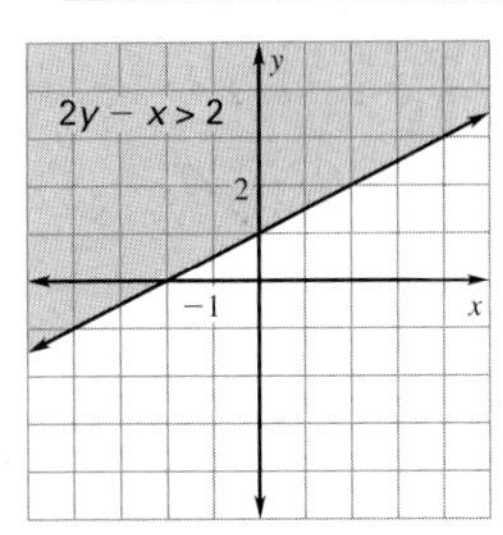

39. No; (0, 0) is a point on the boundary line $2x = -5y$.

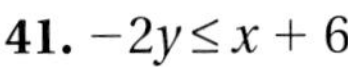

41. $-2y \le x + 6$

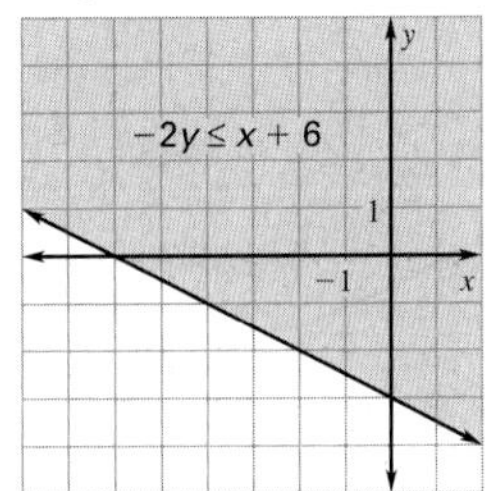

43. $x + 4y < -3$

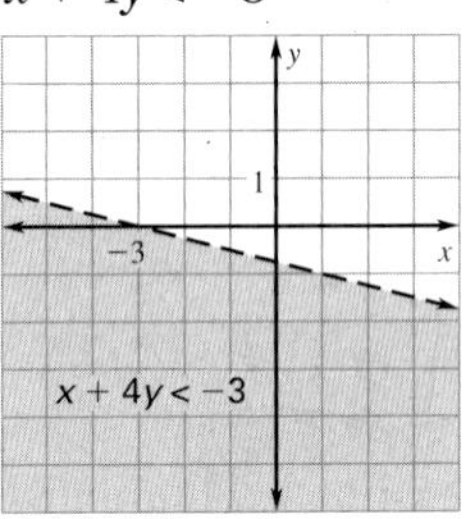

45. $y \le \frac{5}{7}x - \frac{9}{7}$ **47.** $y > 0$ **49.** $y < 0$

6.7 Problem Solving (pp. 410–412)

53.

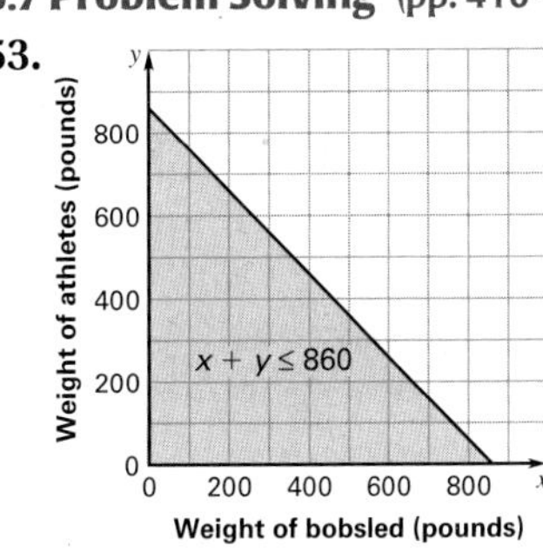

Sample answer: The solution (450, 400) means that the bobsled can weigh 450 pounds when the combined weight of the athletes is 400 pounds.

55. a. $15x + 10y \ge 100$

b.

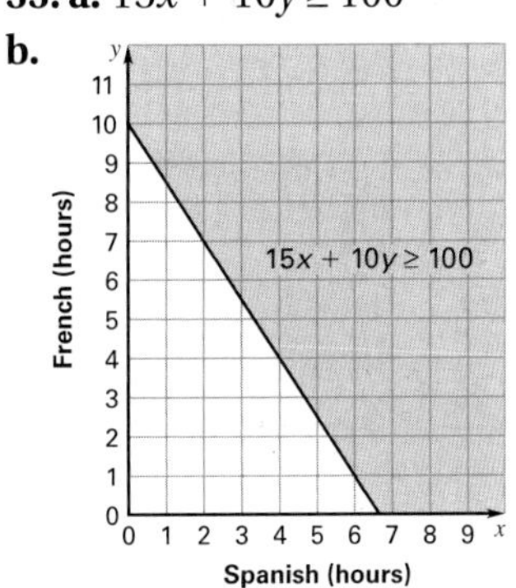

Sample answer: (4, 8), (5, 3), (6, 1)

c. *Sample answer:*

Spanish time (hours)	4	5	6
French time (hours)	8	3	1
Total earnings (dollars)	140	105	100

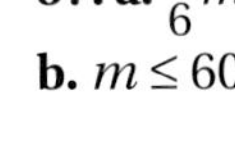

57. a. $\frac{1}{6}m + \frac{1}{2}\ell \le 12$

b. $m \le 60$

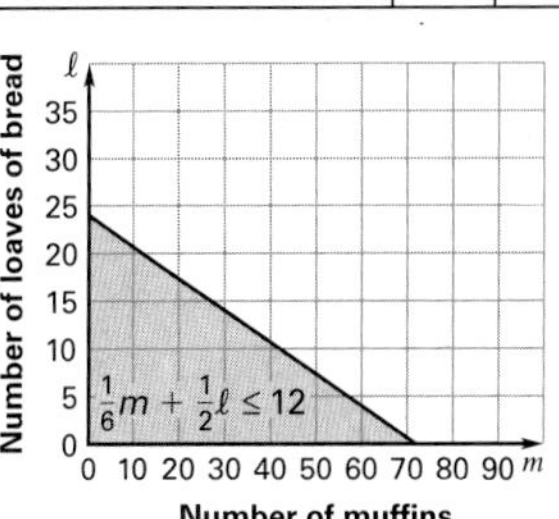

SELECTED ANSWERS

59. a. $x + y \leq 30$

Sample answer: (20, 4), (25, 5), (26, 2)

b. Yes; no; (0, 30) means that you do not take a duffel and have a 30 pound bedroll, while (30, 0) means you take a 30 pound duffel and do not take a bedroll. You need to bring both a duffel and a bedroll.

Chapter Review (pp. 415–418) **1.** $|x - 19| = 8$ **3.** The boundary line is solid if the inequality symbol is ≤ or ≥, the boundary line is dashed if the inequality symbol is < or >; choose a test point that is not on the boundary line. If the ordered pair is a solution to the inequality, shade the half-plane that contains the test point; if it not a solution, shade the other half-plane.

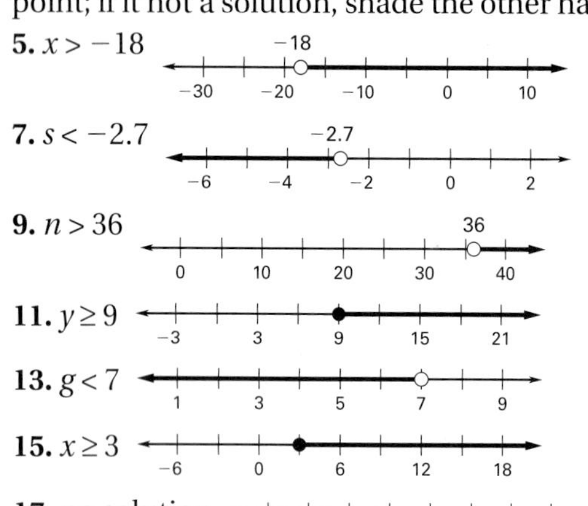

5. $x > -18$

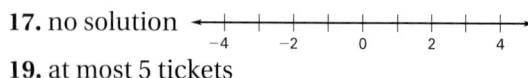

7. $s < -2.7$

9. $n > 36$

11. $y \geq 9$

13. $g < 7$

15. $x \geq 3$

17. no solution

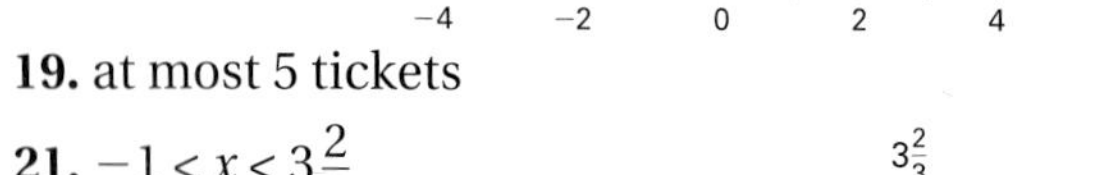

19. at most 5 tickets

21. $-1 < x < 3\frac{2}{3}$

23. $w \leq \frac{1}{2}$ or $w > 2$

25. −4, −8 **27.** 5, 1 **29.** $1\frac{1}{6}, \frac{1}{6}$

31. $m \leq -8$ or $m \geq 8$

33. $-1 < g < 2\frac{1}{3}$

35. $j < -1\frac{1}{2}$ or $j > 10\frac{1}{2}$

37. solution **39.** solution

41.

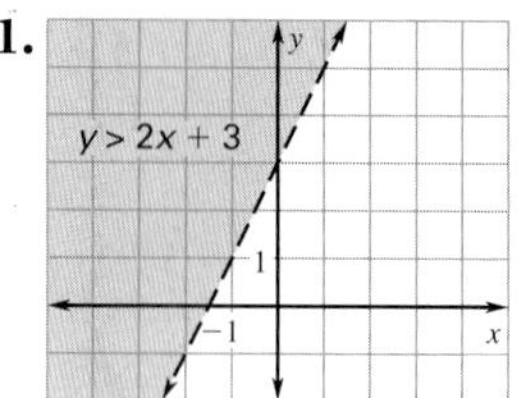

43.

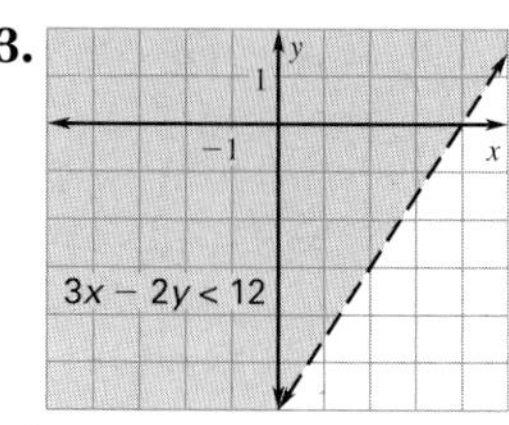

Chapter 7

7.1 Skill Practice (pp. 430–432) **1.** solution **3.** solution **5.** not a solution **9.** (4, 2)

11. The solution (3, −1) does not satisfy Equation 2. The graph of Equation 2 is incorrect; if properly graphed, the lines would intersect at (−3, −3).

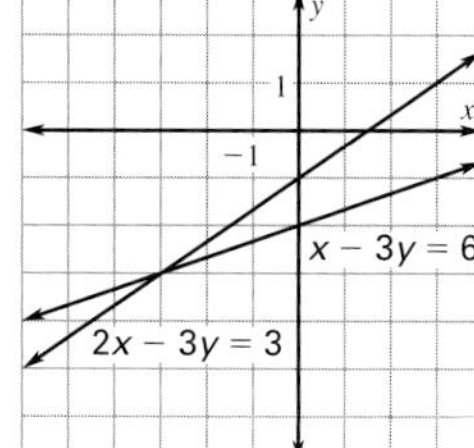

13. (4, 0) **15.** (−3, −5) **17.** (10, −15) **19.** (7, −5) **21.** (−5, 2) **23.** (3, 6) **25.** (4, 6) **27.** *Sample answer:* $m = 0$ and $b = 2$ **29. a.** 4 **b.** (4, 5) **c.** *Sample answer:* Each side of the equation is set equal to *y*. **d.** *Sample answer:* Set each side of the equation equal to *y* to create a system of two equations. Then solve the system using the graph-and-check method. The *x*-coordinate of the system's solution is the solution of the original equation.

7.1 Problem Solving (pp. 432–433) **31.** 2040 **33.** 15 small cards and 10 large cards **35. a.** $y = 5x + 15$, $y = 8x$

b.

Tickets	Cost for members	Cost for nonmembers
1	$20	$8
2	$25	$16
3	$30	$24
4	$35	$32
5	$40	$40
6	$45	$48

c.

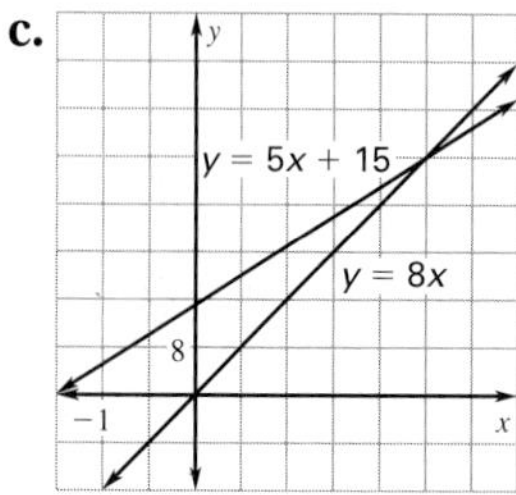

When you view 6 or more movies. *Sample answer:* The graph for a non-member is below the graph for a member up through 4 movies. For 5 movies, the cost is the same. The graph for members is lower than the graph for nonmembers for 6 or more movies.

7.1 Graphing Calculator Activity (p. 434) **1.** (−1.5, 2.5) **3.** (0.2, −1.44)

7.2 Skill Practice (pp. 439–440) **1.** *Sample answer:* $y = x + 1, y = 2x + 1$ **3.** (5, 3) **5.** (2, −1) **7.** (−4, 5) **9.** (6, 7) **11.** (2, −2) **13.** (5, −8) **15.** (0, 2) **17.** (1.4, −4.4) **19.** *Sample answer:* In Step 3, 6 is substituted for *y* instead of *x*; $y = 9 - 3(6)$, $y = -9$, the solution is (6, −9). **21.** (4, −120) **23.** (3, 7) **25.** (6, −3) **27.** (0, −6) **29.** *Sample answer:* The graphs of the equations should intersect at the solution you found using the substitution method.

7.2 Problem Solving (pp. 440–441) **31.** 96 bags of popcorn; 48 pretzels **33.** 4 in. *Sample answer:* (4, 5) is the solution to the appropriate linear system, so *x* should equal 4. **35.** 50 milliliters of 1% hydrochloric acid solution and 50 milliliters of 5% hydrochloric acid solution **37.** Yes. *Sample answer:* The cheetah would have to run at 88 feet per second for 23.3 seconds to catch the gazelle.

7.2 Problem Solving Workshop (p. 442) **1.** 5 mi

7.3 Skill Practice (pp. 447–448) **1.** *Sample answer:* $x + y = 10, x - y = 5$ **3.** (1, 6) **5.** (−1, −5) **7.** (5, 7) **9.** (−1, 2) **11.** (5, 3) **13.** (4, 5) **17.** (2, −3) **19.** (−18, 4) **21.** (4, −3) **23.** *Sample answer:* The two equations should be subtracted rather than added; $6x = 8, x = \frac{4}{3}$. **25.** (26, 14) **27.** (−4, 12) **29.** (−2, 5) **31.** (5, 25) **33.** (−2, 8) **35.** $\ell = 4.5$ ft, $w = 2.5$ ft

7.3 Problem Solving (pp. 449–450) **39.** speed in still water: 4.6 m/sec, speed of current: 0.3 m/sec **41.** monophonic ring tone: $1.95, polyphonic ring tone: $3.50 **43. a.** flight to Phoenix: 400 mi/h, flight to Charlotte: 450 mi/h **b.** $s + w = 450, s - w = 400$; plane: 425 mi/h, wind: 25 mi/h

7.4 Skill Practice (pp. 454–455) **1.** 36 **3.** (1, 1) **5.** ([illegible], −4) **7.** (2, 1) **9.** (−7, −12) **11.** (5, 6) **13.** (4, 4) **15.** (5, −3) **17.** $\left(4\frac{2}{7}, 5\right)$ **19.** *Sample answer:* The two equations should be subtracted rather than added; $-x = -9$, $x = 9$. **21.** (2, −1) **23.** $\left(-4\frac{5}{22}, -2\frac{1}{11}\right)$ **25.** (5, 4) **27.** (10, 2) **29.** (2, −1) **31.** $\left(\frac{1}{3}, -\frac{2}{3}\right)$ **33. a.** $2\ell + 2w = 18$, $6\ell + 4w = 46$; length: 5 in., width: 4 in. **b.** length: 15 in., width: 8 in.

7.4 Problem Solving (pp. 456–457) **37.** 5 hardcover books **39.** 21 pies, 16 batches of applesauce **41.** $16.50; a small costs $2.90, and a large costs $3.90; 3(2.90) + 2(3.90) = 16.50. **43.** $800; $1200

7.5 Skill Practice (pp. 462–464) **1.** inconsistent **3.** *Sample answer:* The lines have the same slope but different *y*-intercepts. **5.** B; one solution **7.** A; infinitely many solutions

9.

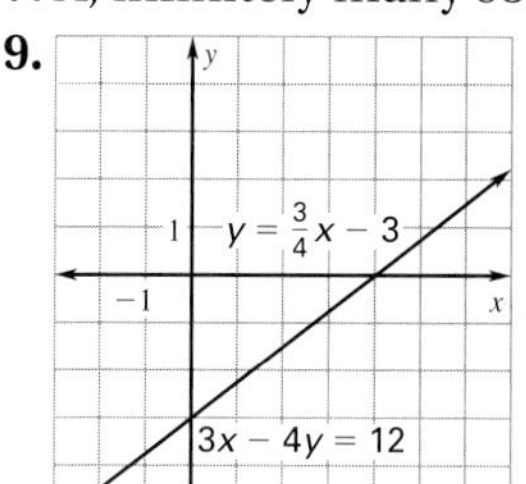

infinitely many solutions

11.

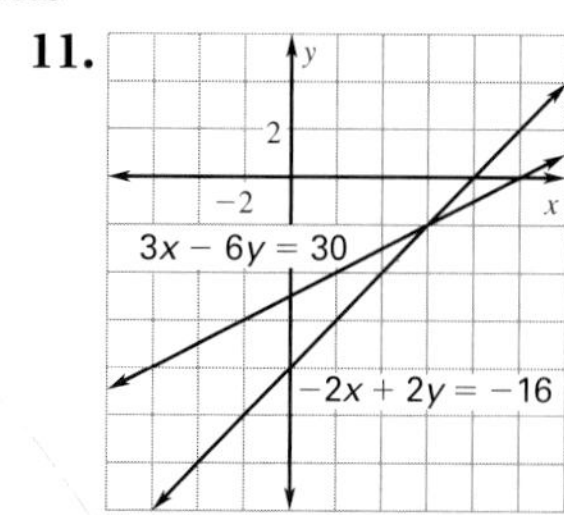

one solution

13.

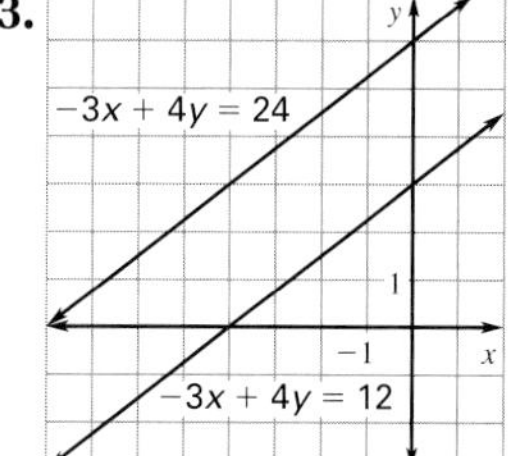

no solution

15. (−3, 4) **17.** (3, 7) **19.** (2, 2) **21.** no solution **23.** (0, 3) **27.** infinitely many solutions **29.** infinitely many solutions **31.** infinitely many solutions **33.** *Sample answer:* $7x - 8y = -9, 7x - 8y = 4$

7.5 Problem Solving (pp. 464–465) **37.** Yes. *Sample answer:* There is one solution to the resulting linear system. **39. a.** $d = \frac{t}{3}, d = \frac{t}{3} - 5$

b.

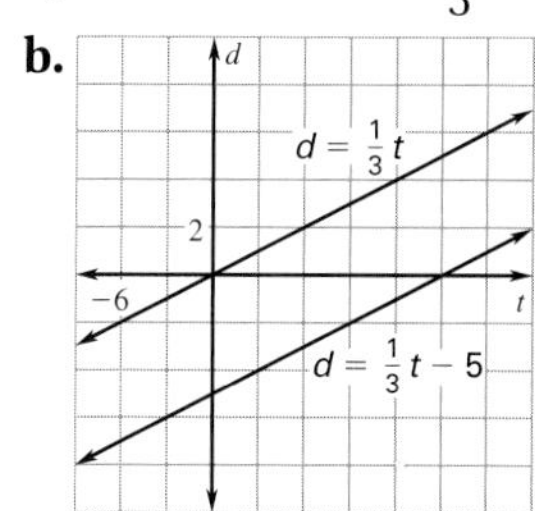

Sample answer: No, since the lines are parallel, the two climbers will never be at the same distance at the same time.

7.6 Skill Practice (pp. 469–470) **1.** solution **3.** not a solution **5.** not a solution **7.** A

9.

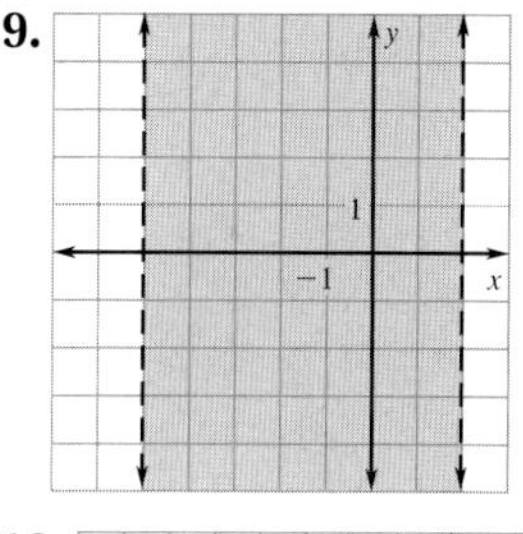

11.

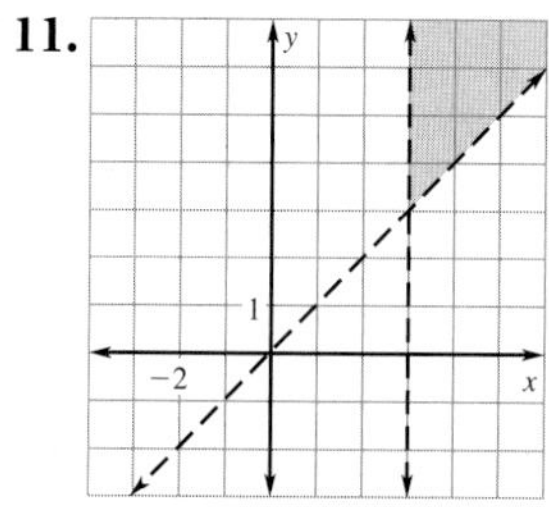

13.

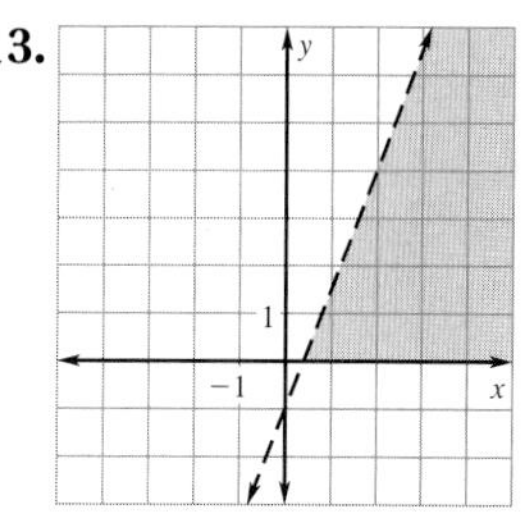

15.

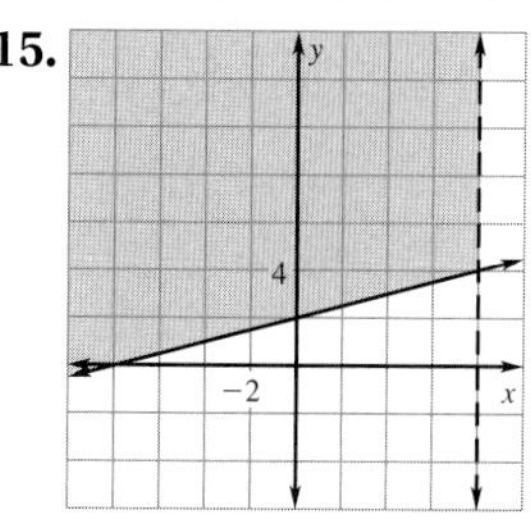

17. 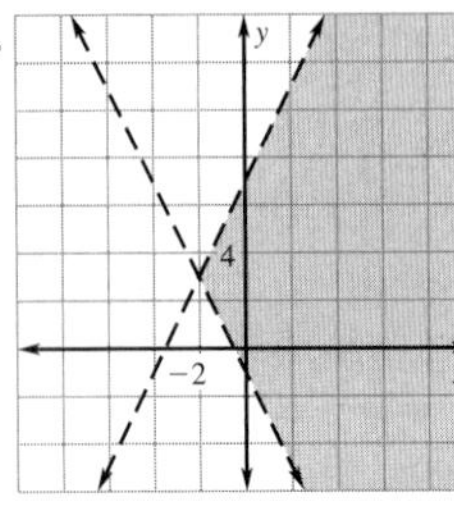 19. 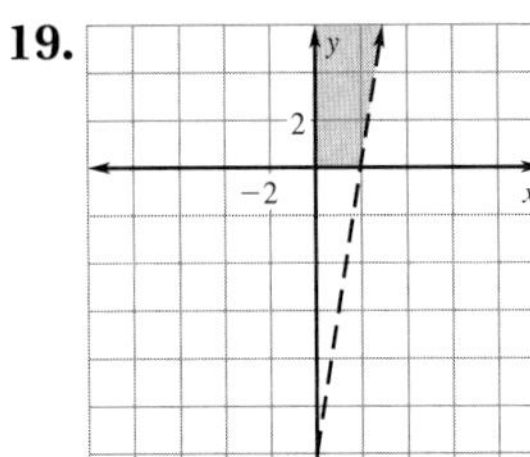

23. The graph is shaded to include $x + y > 3$, not $x + y < 3$.

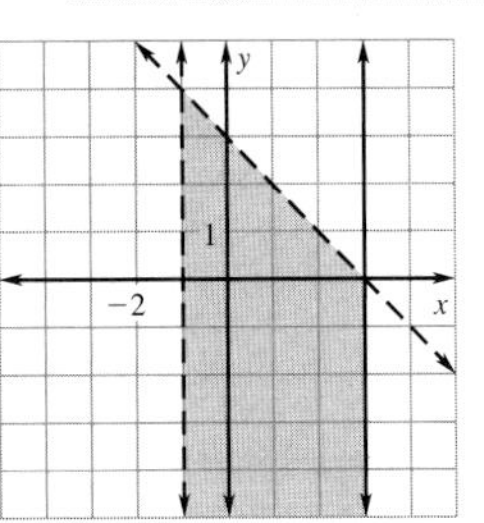

25. $y > -1, y < 4$ 27. $y \leq 5x + 1, y > x - 2$ 29. $y \leq x - 3$, $y > -2x - 1, y > -6$

31. 

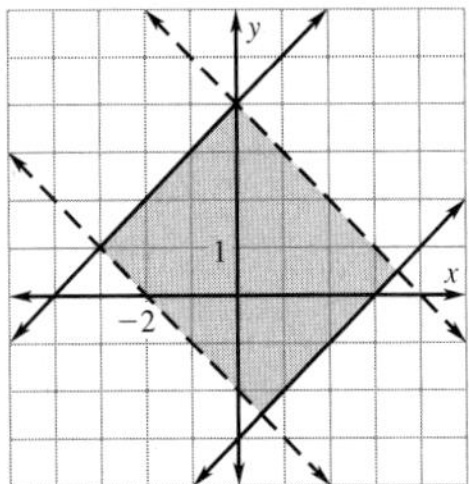

33. No; there are no possible values for x and y that satisfy both equations.

7.6 Problem Solving (pp. 471–472)

37. $14x + 7y < 70$, $x + y < 8, x \geq 0, y \geq 0$

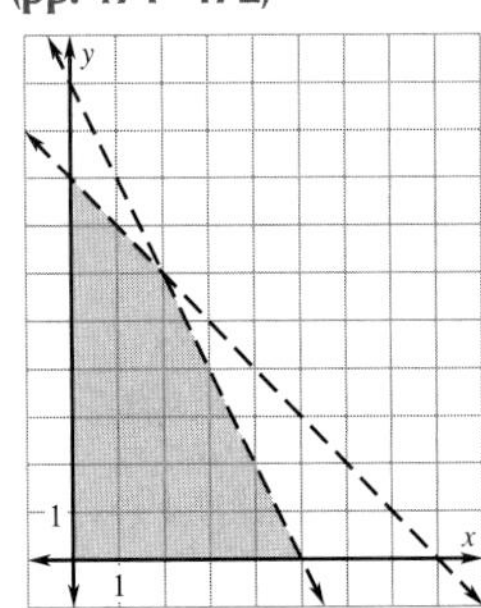

39. a. $20 \leq x \leq 65$, $154 - 0.7x \leq y \leq 187 - 0.85x$

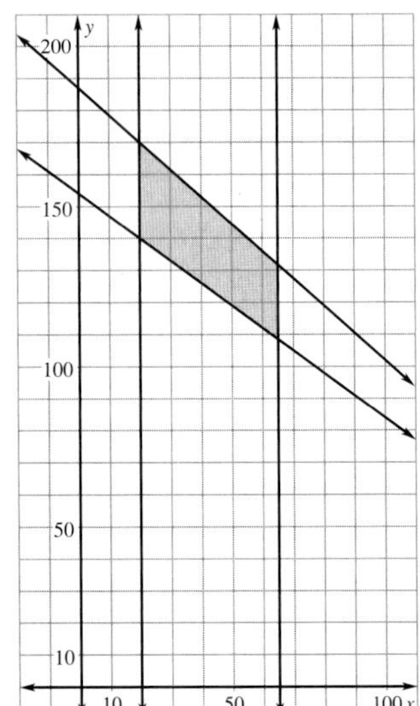

b. No. *Sample answer:* The heart rate is below 70% of the maximum heart rate.

Chapter Review (pp. 475–478) 1. system of linear inequalities 3. *Sample answer:* Graph each inequality then shade the region that is the intersection of the solutions to each inequality. Then check the solution with a test point. 5. (2, −5) 7. (4, −1) 9. (5, 1) 11. 4 tubes of paint, 8 brushes 13. (1, −2) 15. (6, 10) 17. (−7, 8) 19. (−2, 5) 21. (4, 5) 23. (1, 6) 25. No solution. *Sample answer:* When the variables are eliminated, a false statement remains, which means there is no solution. 27. One solution. *Sample answer:* The lines have different slopes, so there is only one solution.

29.

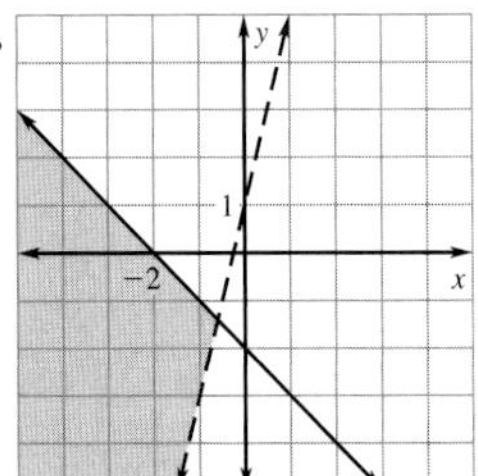

31. Let m represent the number of matinee movies and n represent the number of evening movies; $5m + 8n \leq 40, m \geq 0, n \geq 0$.

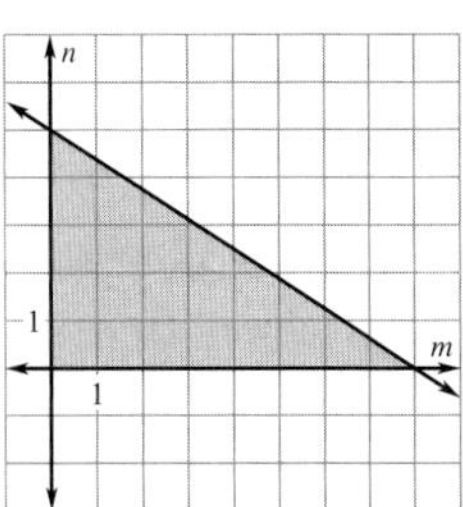

Cumulative Review (pp. 484–485) 1. 62 3. 55 5. −50 7. solution 9. not a solution 11. solution 13. $5y - 1$ 15. $-g + 4$ 17. $-3 + \frac{4}{7}x$ 19. 29 21. −7 23. −3 25. −3 27. $4\frac{4}{9}$

29. 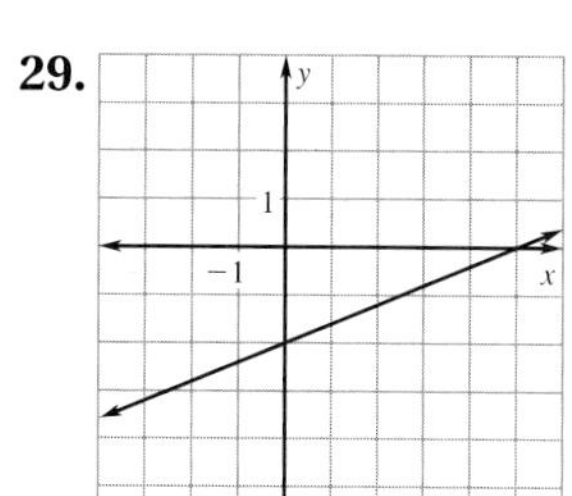 31. 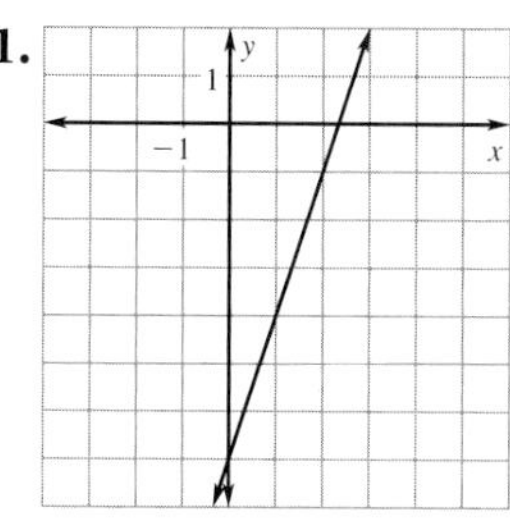

33. 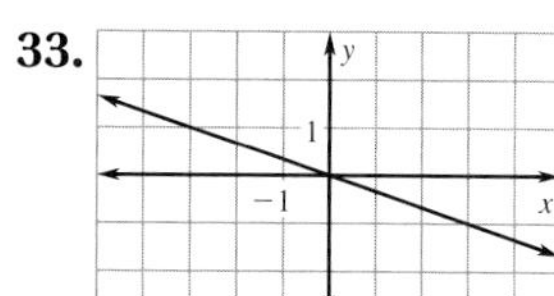

35. $y = -x + 3$ **37.** $y + 10 = -2(x - 1)$ or $y - 2 = -2(x + 5)$ **39.** $y + 2 = \frac{10}{3}(x + 9)$ or $y - 8 = \frac{10}{3}(x + 6)$

41. $y - 4 = -\frac{1}{3}(x - 2)$ or $y - 2 = -\frac{1}{3}(x - 8)$

43. $x < -4$

45. $x \geq 7$

47. $x > -5$

49. $x \geq -6$

51. $-1 < x < 2$

53. $-5 < x < 5$

55. (1, 4) **57.** (2, −3) **59.** \$.02 **61. a.** The ratio $\frac{p}{\ell}$ is always the same, so p varies directly with ℓ. **b.** $p = 2.5\ell$ **63.** $-4 \leq F \leq 113$

Chapter 8

8.1 Skill Practice (pp. 492–493) **1.** order of magnitude **3.** 4^8 **5.** 3^4 **7.** $(-7)^9$ **9.** 2^{14} **11.** 3^{10} **13.** $(-5)^{12}$ **15.** $15^3 \cdot 29^3$ **17.** $132^6 \cdot 9^6$ **19.** x^6 **21.** z^6 **23.** x^{10} **25.** $(b - 2)^{12}$ **27.** $25x^2$ **29.** $49x^2y^2$ **31.** $100x^{14}$ **33.** $96d^{22}$ **35.** $12p^{19}$ **37.** $108x^{29}$ **39.** *Sample answer:* The exponents should be added, not multiplied; $c^1 \cdot c^4 \cdot c^5 = c^{1+4+5} = c^{10}$. **43.** 2 **45.** 2 **47.** $-3267x^{12}y^{13}$ **49.** $1000r^{17}s^6t^{17}$

8.1 Problem Solving (pp. 493–494) **53.** 10^{26} m

55. a.

Ounces of gold	10	100	1000	10,000	100,000
Number of atoms	10^{24}	10^{25}	10^{26}	10^{27}	10^{28}

b. $10^5 \cdot 10^{23}$; 10^{28} atoms **57.** 10^{27}

8.2 Skill Practice (pp. 498–499) **1.** base, exponent **3.** 5^4 **5.** 3^4 **7.** $(-4)^3$ **9.** 10^6 **11.** $\frac{1}{3^5}$ **13.** $\frac{5^4}{4^4}$ **15.** 7^7 **17.** 3^8 **21.** y^7 **23.** $\frac{a^9}{y^9}$ **25.** $\frac{p^4}{q^4}$ **27.** $-\frac{64}{x^3}$ **29.** $\frac{64c^3}{d^6}$ **31.** $\frac{x^4}{9y^6}$ **33.** $\frac{9x^4}{4y^2}$ **35.** $\frac{3m^7}{8n^6}$ **39.** 8 **41.** 4 **43.** $54s^3t^3$ **45.** $\frac{27x^{11}y^5}{25}$

47. Identity property of multiplication; Multiply fractions; Quotient of powers property

8.2 Problem Solving (pp. 500–501)

49. a.

Step	Number of new squares	Side length of new square
1	$4 = 4^1$	$\frac{1}{2} = \left(\frac{1}{2}\right)^1$
2	$16 = 4^2$	$\frac{1}{4} = \left(\frac{1}{2}\right)^2$
3	$64 = 4^3$	$\frac{1}{8} = \left(\frac{1}{2}\right)^3$
4	$256 = 4^4$	$\frac{1}{16} = \left(\frac{1}{2}\right)^4$

b. $\frac{4^4}{4^2}$; 16 times

51. about 31,710 yr **53.** 31^3 times greater

8.3 Skill Practice (pp. 506–507) **1.** Product of powers property and definition of zero exponent; the expression simplifies using the product of powers property to 3^0, which by definition equals 1. **3.** $\frac{1}{64}$ **5.** $-\frac{1}{3}$ **7.** 1 **9.** 1 **11.** $\frac{49}{4}$ **13.** undefined **15.** $\frac{1}{32}$ **17.** $\frac{1}{32}$ **19.** 27 **21.** $\frac{1}{243}$ **23.** $\frac{8}{3}$ **25.** 16 **27.** 3^0 is not equivalent to 0, but to 1; $-6 \cdot 3^0 = -6 \cdot 1 = -6$. **29.** $\frac{2}{y^3}$ **31.** $\frac{1}{121h^2}$ **33.** $\frac{5}{m^3n^4}$ **35.** 1 **37.** $\frac{1}{x^5y^2}$ **39.** $\frac{y^8}{15x^{10}}$ **41.** $243d^3$ **43.** $\frac{3x^{12}y^5}{4}$ **49.** *Sample answer:* It approaches 0.

8.3 Problem Solving (pp. 507–508) **51.** about 10^5 grains of rice **53.** about 10^{11} red blood cells

55. a.

Number of folds	0	1	2	3
Fraction of original area	1	$\frac{1}{2}$	$\frac{1}{4}$	$\frac{1}{8}$

b. $\left(\frac{1}{2}\right)^x$ where x is the number of folds **57. a.** 112.5 watts **b.** $I = 9d^{-2}$ **c.** The intensity is divided by 4.

Extension (p. 510) **1.** 1000 **3.** $\frac{1}{729}$ **5.** $\frac{1}{3}$ **7.** 81 **9.** $\frac{1}{216}$ **11.** $-\frac{1}{4}$ **13.** *Sample answer:* $b^3 = a$, substitute a^k for b to create $(a^k)^3 = a$; $a^{3k} = a^1$ by the power of a power property. Solving for k, $3k = 1$ so $k = \frac{1}{3}$.

8.4 Skill Practice (pp. 515–516) **1.** No; 0.5 is not a number greater than or equal to 1.0 and less than 10. **3.** 8.5×10^0 **5.** 8.24×10^1 **7.** 7.2×10^7

SELECTED ANSWERS

9. 1.06525×10^6 **11.** 1.06×10^9 **13.** 9×10^{14} **17.** 75,000,000 **19.** 30,300 **21.** 15,440,000,000 **23.** 0.00000000044 **25.** 0.0000000852 **27.** 0.0000012034 **29.** 6.7×10^3; 12,439; 2×10^4; 45,000 **31.** 9.8×10^{-6}; 0.00008; 0.0005; 5×10^{-3}; 8.2×10^{-3}; 0.04065 **33.** $<$ **35.** $=$ **37.** $>$ **39.** 6.6×10^{-4} **41.** 7.29×10^{-9} **43.** 3×10^{-3} **45.** 1.25×10^{-22} **47.** 1.96×10^6 **49.** *Sample answer:* 2.8×10^1 and 1×10^3; 11.2×10^5 and 4.0×10^1

8.4 Problem Solving (pp. 516–518) **51. a.** 1.4×10^{-4}; 2.5×10^{-1}; 1.67×10^2; 555 **b.** the elephant beetle and the walking stick **53.** 1406 pounds per acre **55. a.** About 3.67; the radius of Earth is about 3.67 times greater than the radius of the moon. **b.** About 49.30; the volume of Earth is about 49.30 times greater than the volume of the moon. **c.** The ratio of the volumes is the cube of the ratio of the radii. **57.** 4 in. by 6 in. **59. a.** 4.9 L **b.** about 2.58×10^6 L, about 2.58×10^7 L, about 2.06×10^8 L **c.** Underestimates. *Sample answer:* They are calculated when a person is at rest. When a person is not resting, the rate will go up.

8.4 Graphing Calculator Activity (p. 519) **1.** 2.7×10^{13} **3.** 2.5×10^{19} **5. a.** about 6.10×10^{18} g **b.** about 3.05×10^{41} atoms

8.5 Skill Practice (pp. 523–524) **1.** growth factor **3.** The graph would be a vertical stretch. *Sample answer:* Since the y-values of $y = 2 \cdot 5^x$ are double those of $y = 5^x$. **5.** $y = 125 \cdot 5^x$ **7.** $y = \frac{1}{9} \cdot 3^x$

9.
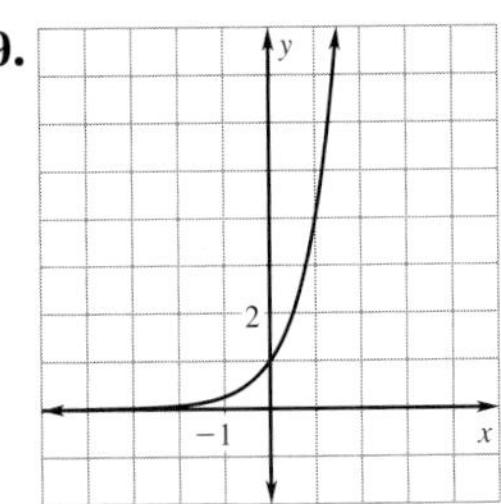
domain: all real numbers, range: all positive real numbers

11.
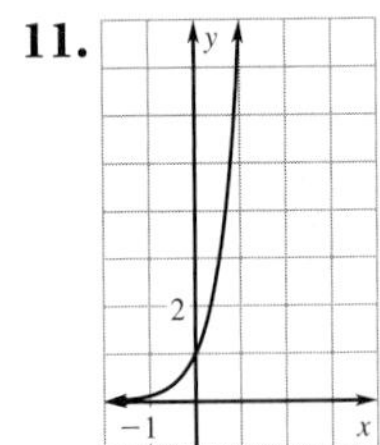
domain: all real numbers, range: all positive real numbers

13.
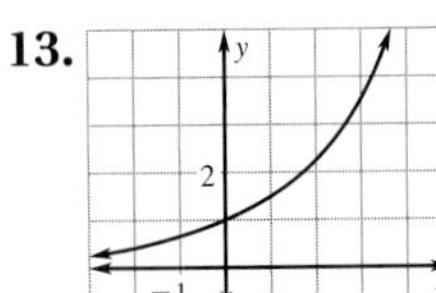
domain: all real numbers, range: all positive real numbers

15.
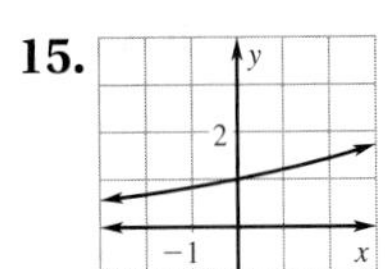
domain: all real numbers, range: all positive real numbers

17.
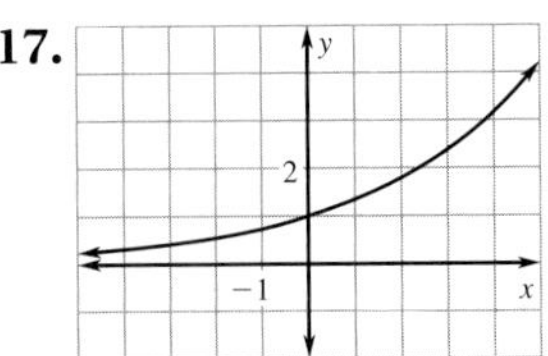
domain: all real numbers, range: all positive real numbers

19.
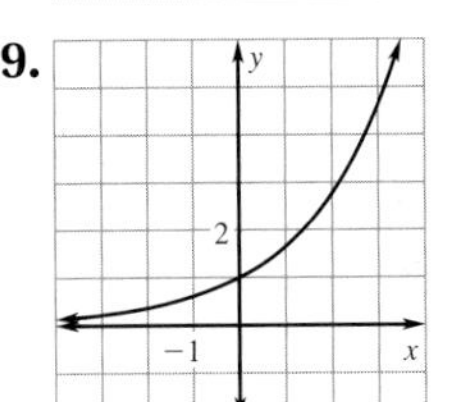
domain: all real numbers, range: all positive real numbers

21. The percent increase was not written as a decimal; $0.27(1 + 0.02)^3 = 0.27(1.02)^3 \approx \$.29$.

23.
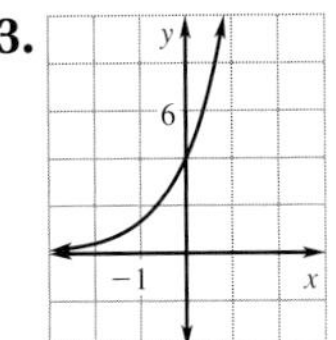
The graph is a vertical stretch.

25.
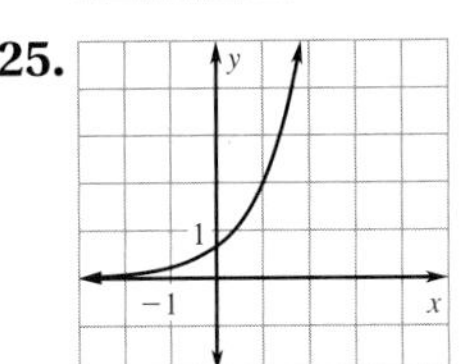
The graph is a vertical shrink.

27.
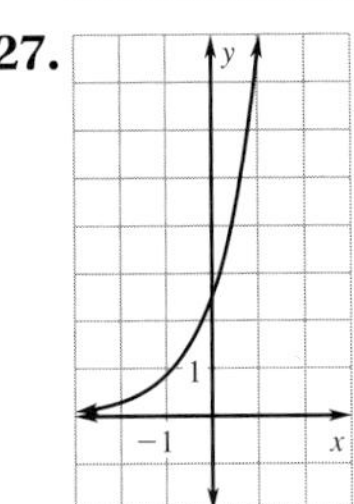
The graph is a vertical stretch.

29.
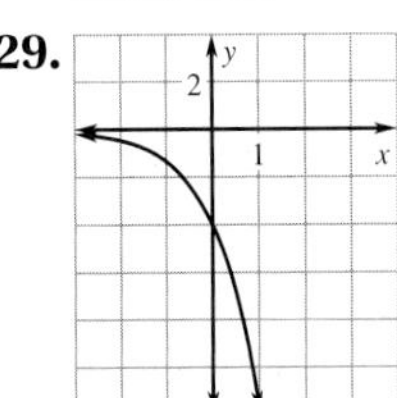
The graph is a vertical stretch with a reflection in the x-axis.

31.
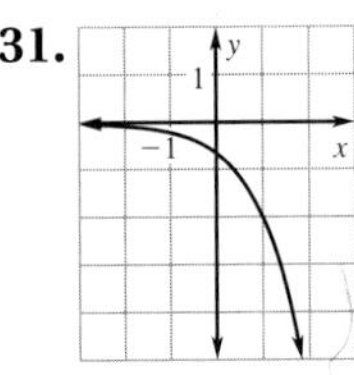
The graph is a vertical shrink with a reflection in the x-axis.

SELECTED ANSWERS

33. The graph is a vertical stretch with a reflection in the x-axis.

35. 200%. *Sample answer:* A growth rate of 200% would create a growth factor of $1 + 2 = 3$, which would represent the tripling of the population every year.

8.5 Problem Solving (pp. 525–527) **39. a.** Let x represent the number of years since 2001 and $f(x)$ represent the number of computers (in hundreds of millions); $f(x) = 6 \cdot (1.1)^x$. **b.** about 1,286,153,286 computers **41. a.** tree 1: $A = 154 \cdot (1.06)^t$, tree 2: $A = 113 \cdot (1.1)^t$

b.

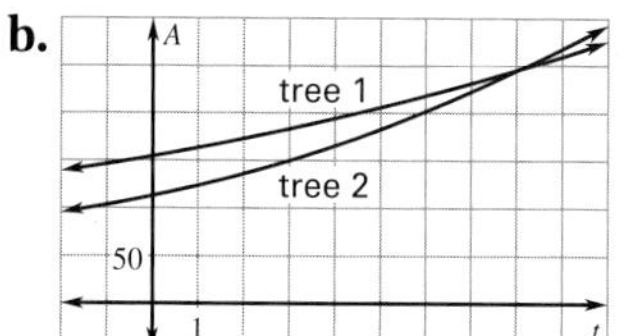

about 8.4 yr

45. $y = 25.96(1.059)^x$; about 145 Hz **47.** \$1266.77 **49.** \$1271.24

8.5 Problem Solving Workshop (pp. 528–529)
1. a. Let t represent the number of years since 1997 and F represent the bus fare; $F = 20(1.12)^t$. **b.** \$22.40 **c.** 2000. *Sample answer:* Make a table of values. **3. a.** $T = 7.5(1.039)^t$ **b.** about 37.4 million

8.6 Skill Practice (pp. 535–536) **1.** $1 - r$ **3.** exponential function; $y = 8 \cdot 4^x$ **5.** exponential function; $y = 2\left(\frac{1}{3}\right)^x$

7. domain: all real numbers, range: all positive real numbers

9.

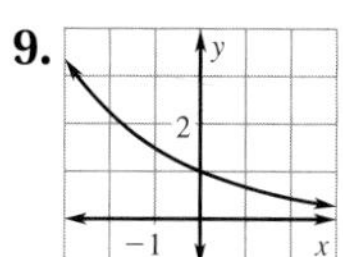

domain: all real numbers, range: all positive real numbers

11.

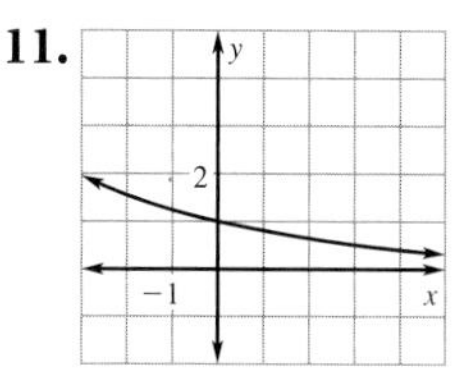

domain: all real numbers, range: all positive real numbers

13. domain: all real numbers, range: all positive real numbers

15.

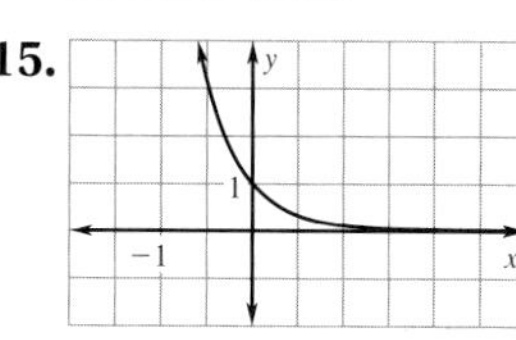

domain: all real numbers, range: all positive real numbers

17.

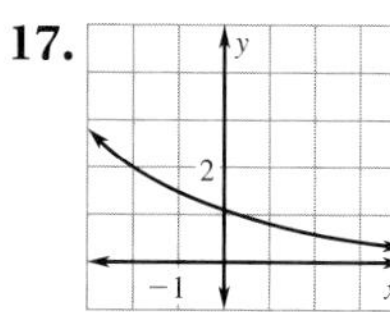

domain: all real numbers, range: all positive real numbers

21.

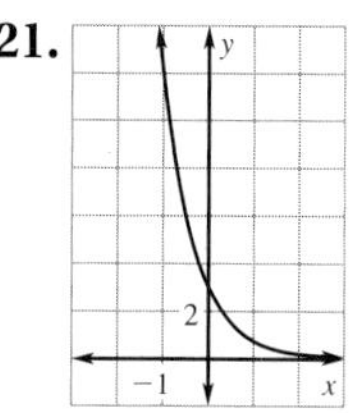

The graph is a vertical stretch.

23.

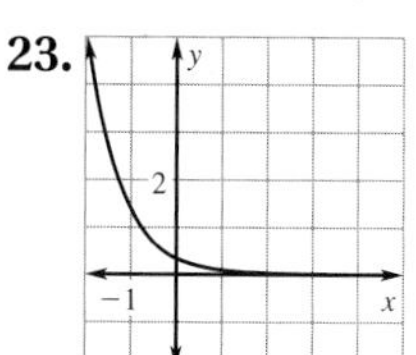

The graph is a vertical shrink.

25.

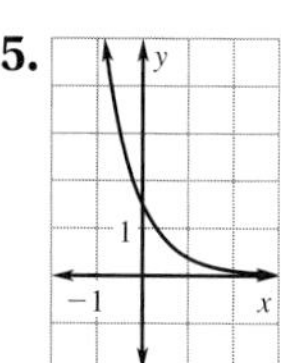

The graph is a vertical stretch.

27.

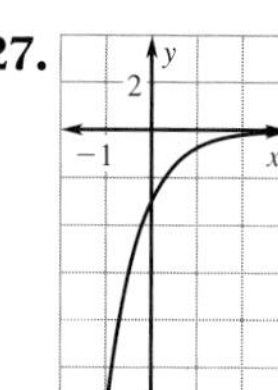

The graph is a vertical stretch with a reflection in the x-axis.

29.

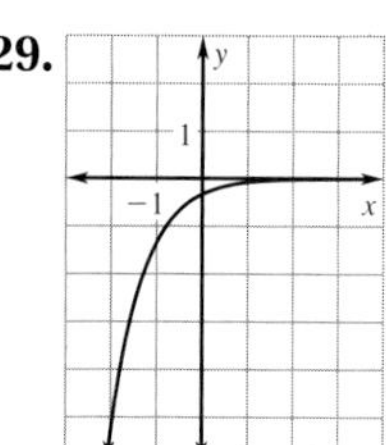

The graph is a vertical shrink with a reflection in the x-axis.

31. 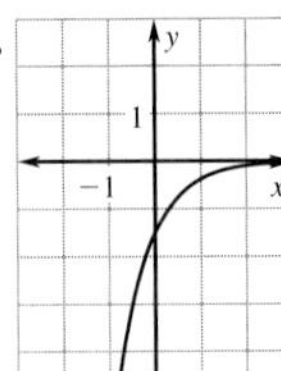

The graph is a vertical stretch with a reflection in the x-axis.

33. C **35.** initial amount: 90,000 people, decay factor: 0.975, decay rate: 2.5%; Let P represent the population and t represent the number of years; $P = 90{,}000(0.975)^t$. **37.** *Sample answer:* The decay rate, r, is 0.14. So the decay factor $(1 - r)$ should be 0.86, not 0.14; $y = 25{,}000(0.86)^t$. **39.** exponential decay; $y = 8 \cdot 0.6^x$ **41. a.** The graph is a vertical shrink. **b.** The graph is a vertical stretch with a reflection in the x-axis. **c.** The graph is a vertical shift up 1 unit. **45.** *Sample answer:* After one time period, the new amount is the initial amount minus the amount of decrease: $a - ra = a(1 - r)$.

8.6 Problem Solving (pp. 537–538) **47.** Let V represent the value of the cell phone and t represent the number of years since purchase, $V = 125(0.8)^t$; \$64. **49.** No. *Sample answer:* The boat's value is about \$3217. **51. a.** decay factor: 0.9439, decay rate: 5.61% **b.** about 1.431 in. **c.** about 0.716 in. **53. a.** $y = 4(0.995)^x$, $y = 3.5(0.995)^x$

b. 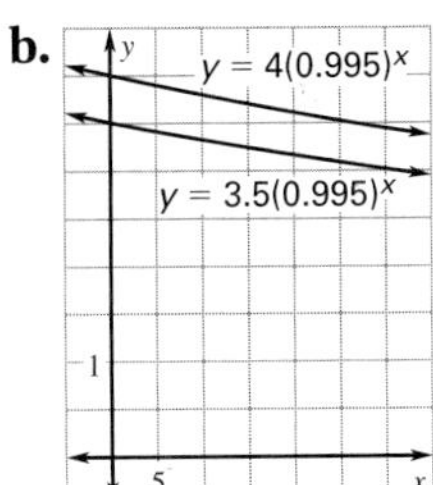

c. about 52 yr

Extension (p. 540)

1. geometric 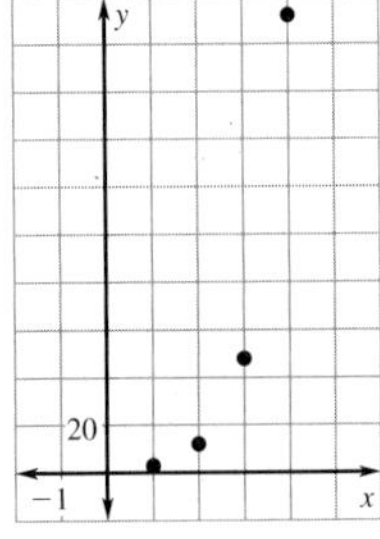

3. arithmetic 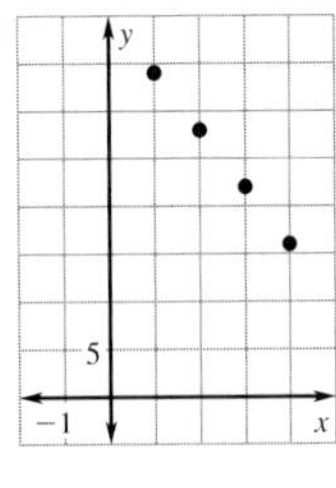

5. geometric 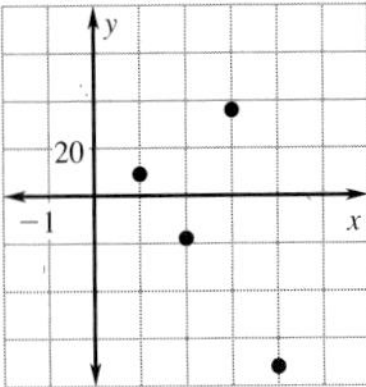

7. $a_n = (-5)^{n-1}$; 15,625 **9.** $a_n = 432\left(\frac{1}{6}\right)^{n-1}$; $\frac{1}{108}$

Chapter Review (pp. 543–546) **1.** decay, decay factor **3.** Exponential decay; $b = 0.85$ which is between 0 and 1, therefore it's exponential decay. **5.** Exponential growth; $b = 2.1$ which is greater than 1, therefore it's exponential growth. **7.** $(-3)^8$ **9.** y^{20} **11.** $(b + 2)^{24}$ **13.** $-64x^2y^2$ **15.** 10^{21} **17.** 5^3 **19.** 17^4 **21.** $\frac{49x^{10}}{y^4}$ **23.** $\frac{6r^{15}}{7s^5}$ **25.** 1 **27.** $\frac{27}{8}$ **29.** 10^6 **31.** 0.000075 **33.** 4.0625×10^{13}

35. 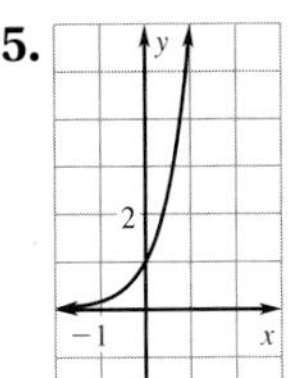

domain: all real numbers, range: all positive real numbers

37. 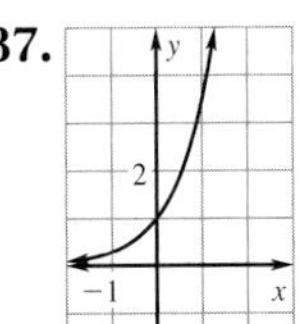

domain: all real numbers, range: all positive real numbers

39. 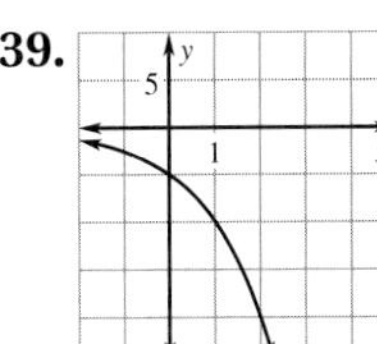

The graph is a vertical stretch with a reflection in the x-axis.

41. exponential decay; $y = 3 \cdot \left(\frac{1}{3}\right)^x$

Chapter 9

9.1 Skill Practice (pp. 557–558) **1.** monomial **3.** $9m^5$; 5, 9 **5.** $2x^2y^2 - 8xy$; 4, 2 **7.** $3z^4 + 2z^3 - z^2 + 5z$; 4, 3 **11.** not a polynomial; variable exponent **13.** polynomial; 1, binomial **15.** polynomial; 3, trinomial **17.** $13a^2 - 4$ **19.** $m^2 + 9m + 9$ **21.** $6c^2 + 14$ **23.** $-2n^3 + n - 12$ **25.** $-15d^3 + 3d^2 - 3d + 2$ **27.** Two unlike terms, $-4x^2$ and $8x$, were combined; $-2x^3 - 4x^2 + 8x + 1$. **29.** $2x^2 + 6x - 9$, $4x^2 - 4x - 5$ **31.** $12x - 3$ **33.** $-x^2 + 10xy + y^2$ **35.** $6a^2b - 6a + 4b - 19$

9.1 Problem Solving (pp. 558–559) **37.** about 39,800,000 people **39. a.** $T = 9.5t^3 - 73t^2 + 130t + 860$ **b.** 1998; substitute $t = 0$ into the equation for T to find the number of books sold in 1998 to get 860 million books. Substitute 4 into the equation for T to find the number of books sold in 2002 to get 820 million books. More books were sold in 1998. **41. a.** $D = -0.44t^2 + 49t + 19.7$ **b.** about 855 decisions **c.** about 61%; Cy Young's career lasted $1911 - 1890 = 21$ years. To find the number of wins in his career, find the value of W when $t = 21$; about 525 wins. From part (b), we know that the total number of decisions in his career is about 855, so to find the percent of the decisions that were wins, find $525 \div 855 \approx 0.614$, or about 61%.

9.1 Graphing Calculator Activity (p. 560) **1.** $7x^2 + 2x + 1$ **3.** correct

9.2 Skill Practice (pp. 565–566) **1.** binomials **3.** $2x^3 - 3x^2 + 9x$ **5.** $4z^6 + z^5 - 11z^4 - 6z^2$ **7.** $9a^7 - 5a^6 - 13a^5$ **9.** $x^2 - x - 6$ **11.** $4b^2 - 31b + 21$ **13.** $12k^2 + 23k - 9$ **15.** The second term of the first binomial is -5, not 5, so the entries in the second row of the diagram should be $-15x$ and -5; $3x^2 - 14x - 5$. **17.** $y^2 + y - 30$ **19.** $77w^2 + 34w - 15$ **21.** $s^3 + 10s^2 + 19s - 20$ **23.** $-15x^3 + 14x^2 + 3x - 2$ **25.** $54z^3 - 21z^2 - 14z + 5$ **27.** $10r^2 + r - 3$ **29.** $8m^2 + 46m + 63$ **31.** $48x^2 - 88x + 35$ **33.** $3p^2 - 3p - 9$ **35.** $-3c^3 - 45c^2 + 23c - 10$ **37.** $2x^2 + x - 45$ **39.** $x^2 + 8x + 15$ **41.** $80 - 6x^2$ **43.** $2x^2 - 10x - 132$ **45.** $2x^4 - 11x^3 - 20x^2 - 7x$; graph $Y_1 = (x^2 - 7x)(2x^2 + 3x + 1)$ and $Y_2 = 2x^4 - 11x^3 - 20x^2 - 7x$ in the same viewing window. Because the graphs coincide, the expressions for Y_1 and Y_2 must be equivalent.

9.2 Problem Solving (pp. 567–568) **49. a.** $4x^2 + 84x + 440$ **b.** 840 in.^{2} **51. a.** $12,300 million, 0.171; for $t = 0$, the amount of money (in millions of dollars) people between 15 and 19 years old spent on sound recordings in the U.S. in 1997 **b.** $R \cdot P \approx -1.18t^4 + 14.4t^3 - 57.4t^2 - 10.4t + 2100$ **c.** about $1680 million **53. a.** *Sample answer:* $T = t + 90$; use the data points from 1995–1999: (5, 95), (6, 96), (7, 97), (8, 98), (9, 99). All these points lie on a line with slope $m = 1$; use any one of the points to find the y-intercept $b = 90$. The other data points, (0, 92), (10, 101), and (11, 102), lie close to the line $T = t + 90$. **b.** $V = -0.0015t^3 - 0.103t^2 + 2.949t + 6.21$ **c.** about 24.2 million households, about 22.2 million households

9.3 Skill Practice (p. 572) **1.** *Sample answer:* $x - 5$, $x + 5$ **3.** $x^2 + 16x + 64$ **5.** $4y^2 + 20y + 25$ **7.** $n^2 - 22n + 121$ **9.** The middle term of the product, $2(s)(-3) = -6s$, was left out; $s^2 - 6s + 9$. **11.** $t^2 - 16$ **13.** $4x^2 - 1$ **15.** $49 - w^2$ **19.** Use the sum and difference pattern to find the product $(20 - 4)(20 + 4)$. **21.** Use the square of a binomial pattern to find the product $(20 - 3)^2$. **23.** $r^2 + 18rs + 81s^2$ **25.** $9m^2 - 121n^2$ **27.** $9m^2 - 42mn + 49n^2$ **29.** $9f^2 - 81$ **31.** $9x^2 + 48xy + 64y^2$ **33.** $4a^2 - 25b^2$ **35.** $9x^2 - 0.25$ **37.** $9x^2 - 3x + 0.25$

9.3 Problem Solving (pp. 573–574)

41. a.

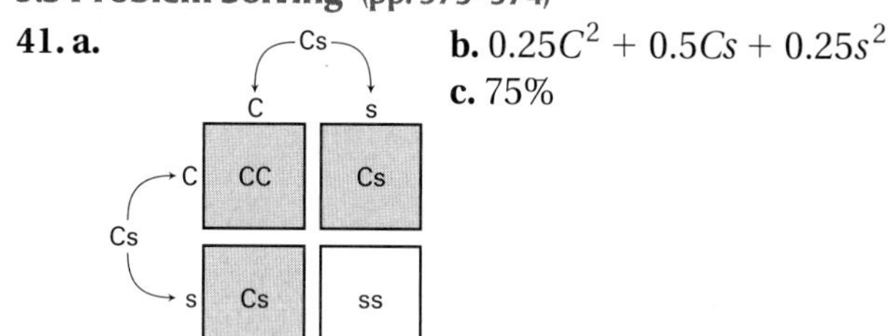

b. $0.25C^2 + 0.5Cs + 0.25s^2$ **c.** 75%

43. a. 88.1%; the areas of the four regions are: 2 complete passes: $0.655^2 \approx 0.429$ square units; 1 complete pass, 1 incomplete pass: $0.655(0.345) \approx 0.226$ square units; 1 incomplete pass, 1 complete pass: $0.345(0.655) \approx 0.226$ square units; and 2 incomplete passes: $0.345^2 \approx 0.119$ square units. The regions that involve at least one complete pass cover $0.429 + 0.226 + 0.226 = 0.881$ square units, or 88.1% of the whole square region. **b.** The outcome of each attempted pass is modeled by $0.655C + 0.345I$, so the possible outcomes of two attempted passes is modeled by $(0.655C + 0.345I)^2 = 0.429C^2 + 0.452CI + 0.119I^2$. Because any combination of outcomes with a C results in at least one completed pass, the coefficients of the first two terms show that 42.9% + 45.2% = 88.1% of the outcomes will have at least one completed pass, and the coefficient of the last term shows that 11.9% of the outcomes will have two incomplete passes.

9.4 Skill Practice (pp. 578–579) **1.** The vertical motion model is the equation $h = -16t^2 + vt + s$, where h is the height (in feet) of a projectile after t seconds in the air, given an initial velocity of v feet per second and an initial height of s feet. **3.** 5, -3 **5.** 13, 14 **7.** 7, $-\frac{4}{3}$ **9.** ± 3 **11.** $-\frac{11}{3}$, -1 **13.** $-\frac{5}{2}, \frac{5}{7}$ **17.** $2(x + y)$ **19.** $s(3s^3 + 16)$ **21.** $7w^2(w^3 - 5)$ **23.** $5n(3n^2 + 5)$ **25.** $\frac{1}{2}x^4(5x^2 - 1)$ **27.** 0, -6 **29.** 0, $\frac{7}{2}$ **31.** 0, $-\frac{1}{3}$ **33.** 0, 2 **35.** 0, $\frac{5}{2}$ **37.** 0, $-\frac{2}{7}$ **41.** $2ab(4a - 3b)$ **43.** $v(v^2 - 5v + 9)$ **45.** $3q^2(2q^3 - 7q^2 - 5)$ **47.** 0, $\frac{1}{2}$

SELECTED ANSWERS

9.4 Problem Solving (pp. 579–580) **51.** about 0.69 sec **53.** 0, about 0.28; the zero $t = 0$ seconds means that the penguin begins at a height of 0 feet in the air as it leaves the water; the zero $t \approx 0.28$ second means that the penguin lands back in the water (at a height of 0 feet in the air) after about 0.28 second. **55. a.** $h = -4.9t^2 + 4.9t$ **b.** $0 \le t \le 1$; a reasonable domain for the function will cover the time from when the rabbit leaves the ground until the rabbit lands back on the ground; these times t are the zeros of the function, 0 seconds and 1 second. **57. a.** $w(w + 2) = w(10 - w)$ **b.** 4 ft **c.** 48 ft^2

9.5 Skill Practice (pp. 586–587) **1.** factors **3.** $(x + 3)(x + 1)$ **5.** $(b - 9)(b - 8)$ **7.** $(z + 12)(z - 4)$ **9.** $(y - 9)(y + 2)$ **11.** $(x + 10)(x - 7)$ **13.** $(m - 15)(m + 8)$ **15.** $(p + 16)(p + 4)$ **17.** $(c + 11)(c + 4)$ **19.** In order to have a product of +24, p and q must have the same sign; $(m - 6)(m - 4)$. **21.** 10, −3 **23.** −10, 5 **25.** −5, −4 **27.** −22, −1 **31.** −3, −2 **33.** 9, 5 **35.** 17, −3 **37.** 14, 2 **39.** −9, 8 **41.** −17, −2 **43.** 20 in., 5 in. **45.** 26 yd, 6 yd **47.** $(x - 2y)^2$ **49.** $(c + 9d)(c + 4d)$ **51.** $(a + 5b)(a - 3b)$ **53.** $(m - 7n)(m + 6n)$ **55.** $(g + 10h)(g - 6h)$

9.5 Problem Solving (pp. 588–589) **59.** 10 cm^2 **61.** 40 in.; the side lengths of the rectangular picture can be represented by $x - 5$ and $x - 6$; the area of the picture is 20 square inches, so to find the side length x of the original square picture, solve the equation $(x - 5)(x - 6) = 20$. The equation has two solutions, 10 and 1, but when $x = 1$ inch, both $x - 5$ and $x - 6$ are negative, which does not make sense in this situation. So, $x = 10$ inches, and the perimeter of the original picture was $4(10) = 40$ inches.

9.5 Problem Solving Workshop (p. 591) **1.** 2 ft **3.** 9 ft

9.6 Skill Practice (pp. 596–597) **1.** roots **3.** To factor the polynomial that has a leading coefficient of 1, $x^2 - x - 2$, you only need to find factors of the constant term, −2, that add to the coefficient of the middle term, −1. To factor the polynomial that has a leading coefficient that is not 1, $6x^2 - x - 2$, you must also take into account how the factors of the leading coefficient, 6, affect the coefficient of the middle term. **5.** $-(y - 4)(y + 2)$ **7.** $(5w - 1)(w - 1)$ **9.** $(6s + 5)(s - 1)$ **11.** $(2c - 1)(c - 3)$ **13.** $-(2h + 1)(h - 3)$ **15.** $(2x + 3)(5x - 9)$ **17.** $(3z + 7)(z - 2)$ **19.** $(2n + 3)(2n + 5)$ **21.** $(3y - 4)(2y + 1)$ **23.** $-\frac{7}{2}, 5$ **25.** $\frac{1}{4}, -3$ **27.** $\frac{3}{4}, -\frac{1}{2}$ **29.** $-\frac{1}{4}, \frac{2}{5}$ **31.** $\frac{1}{3}, -5$ **33.** $\frac{2}{5}, 1$ **35.** $\frac{11}{2}, -3$ **37.** $-\frac{4}{3}, \frac{1}{2}$ **39.** The factorization of the polynomial should be $(3x + 2)(4x - 1)$ instead of $(3x - 1)(4x + 2)$; $-\frac{2}{3}, \frac{1}{4}$. **41.** $9\frac{1}{2}$ in.; to find the width, solve the equation $w(4w + 1) = 3$ to get $w = \frac{3}{4}$ or $w = -1$. The width cannot be negative, so the width is $\frac{3}{4}$ inch. Then the length is $4\left(\frac{3}{4}\right) + 1 = 4$ inches, and the perimeter is $2\left(\frac{3}{4}\right) + 2(4) = 9\frac{1}{2}$ inches. **43.** 5, 7 **45.** $-\frac{7}{3}, 2$ **47.** $\frac{7}{2}, -\frac{3}{2}$ **49.** $-\frac{1}{4}, \frac{5}{2}$ **53.** $2x^2 - 9x - 5 = 0$; any root $x = \frac{r}{s}$ of $ax^2 + bx + c = 0$ comes from setting the factor $sx - r$ equal to 0 after $ax^2 + bx + c$ is written in factored form; so, the roots $-\frac{1}{2}$ and 5 come from the factors $2x - (-1)$, or $2x + 1$, and $x - 5$. The product of these factors is $(2x + 1)(x - 5) = 2x^2 - 10x + x - 5 = 2x^2 - 9x - 5$.

9.6 Problem Solving (pp. 598–599) **59. a.** $24x^2 + 48x + 24$ **b.** 4 cm, 2 cm **61.** 70 m, 31 m

9.7 Skill Practice (pp. 603–604) **1.** perfect square **3.** $(x + 5)(x - 5)$ **5.** $(9c + 2)(9c - 2)$ **7.** $-3(m + 4n)(m - 4n)$ **9.** $(x - 2)^2$ **11.** $(7a + 1)^2$ **13.** $\left(m + \frac{1}{2}\right)^2$ **15.** $4(c + 10)(c - 10)$ **17.** $(2s + 3r)(2s - 3r)$ **19.** $8(3 + 2y)(3 - 2y)$ **21.** $(2x)^2 - 3^2$ is in the form $a^2 - b^2$, so it must be factored using the difference of two squares pattern, not the perfect square trinomial pattern; $9(2x + 3)(2x - 3)$. **25.** −4 **27.** ±3 **29.** −2 **31.** ±12 **33.** $\pm\frac{7}{2}$ **35.** $\frac{5}{6}$ **37.** $\pm\frac{4}{3}$ **39.** 0, 1

9.7 Problem Solving (pp. 604–605) **47.** 2.5 sec **49.** Once; the ball's height (in feet) is modeled by the equation $h = -16t^2 + 56t + 5$, where t is the time (in seconds) since it was thrown. To find when the height is 54 feet, substitute 54 for h and solve the equation $54 = -16t^2 + 56t + 5$, or $16t^2 - 56t + 49 = 0$. Because the left side of the equation factors as a perfect square trinomial, $(4t - 7)^2$, the equation has only one solution, 1.75; so, the ball reaches a height of 54 feet only once, after 1.75 seconds. **51. a.** $4d^2 - 9$ **b.** 10 in.

9.8 Skill Practice (pp. 610–611) **1.** The polynomial is written as a monomial or as a product of a monomial and one or more prime polynomials. **3.** $(x-8)(x+1)$ **5.** $(z-4)(6z-7)$ **7.** $(b+5)(b^2-3)$ **9.** $(x+13)(x-1)$ **11.** $(z-1)(12+5z^2)$ **13.** $(x+1)(x^2+2)$ **15.** $(z-4)(z^2+3)$ **17.** $(a+13)(a^2-5)$ **19.** $(5n-4)(n^2+5)$ **21.** $(y+1)(y+5x)$ **23.** $x^2(x-1)(x+1)$ **25.** $3n^3(n-4)(n+4)$ **27.** $3c^7(5c-1)(5c+1)$ **29.** $8s^2(2s-1)(2s+1)$ **31.** cannot be factored **33.** $3w^2(w+4)^2$ **35.** $(b-5)(b-2)(b+2)$ **37.** $(9t-1)(t^2+2)$ **39.** $7ab^3(a-3)(a+3)$ **43.** $-1, \pm 2$ **45.** $\frac{7}{4}, \pm 2$ **47.** $0, -5, -3$ **49.** $0, \pm 9$ **51.** $0, \pm 2$ **53.** $-\frac{1}{3}, \pm 1$ **55.** No; when the polynomial is factored completely, the equation becomes $(x+2)(x^2+3)=0$. When the factor x^2+3 is set equal to 0, the resulting equation, $x^2+3=0$, or $x^2=-3$, has no real number solutions because x^2 cannot be negative. **57.** 12 ft, 4 ft, 2 ft **59.** $(2b-a)(2b-3)(2b+3)$ **61.** $(3x+4)(2x-1)$ **63.** $(4n-3)(3n-1)$ **65.** $(3w+2)(7w-2)$

9.8 Problem Solving (pp. 612–613) **69. a.** $4w^2+16w$ **b.** 4 in. long by 4 in. wide by 8 in. high **71. a.** 1, about -0.2 **b.** The zero $t \approx -0.2$ has no meaning because t, which represents time in seconds, cannot be negative in this situation. The zero $t=1$ means that the ball lands on the ground 1 second after you throw it. **73. a.** $-h^3+5h^2+36h$ **b.** 4 in. long by 9 in. wide by 5 in. high, 3 in. long by 10 in. wide by 6 in. high **c.** 4 in. long by 9 in. wide by 5 in. high; the 4-inch long box has a surface area of 202 square inches and the 3-inch long box has a surface area of 216 square inches.

Chapter Review (pp. 616–620) **1.** degree of the polynomial **3.** A factorable polynomial with integer coefficients is factored completely if it is written as a product of unfactorable polynomials with integer coefficients. *Sample answer:* $3x(x-4)(2x+1)$ **5.** A **7.** x^3-8x^2+15x **9.** $11y^5+4y^2-y-3$ **11.** $5s^3-7s+13$ **13.** x^3-5x^2+7x-3 **15.** x^2-2x-8 **17.** $z^2-3z-88$ **19.** $18n^2+27n+7$ **21.** $3x^2+10x-8$ **23.** $36y^2+12y+1$ **25.** $16a^2-24a+9$ **27.** $9s^2-25$ **29.** 0, 11 **31.** 0, 9 **33.** $0, \frac{1}{3}$ **35.** $(s+11)(s-1)$ **37.** $(a+12)(a-7)$ **39.** $(x+8)(x-4)$ **41.** $(c+5)(c+3)$ **43.** $\frac{1}{7}, 1$ **45.** $\frac{2}{3}, -2$ **47.** $-\frac{3}{2}, -3$ **49.** 3 sec **51.** $(z-15)(z+15)$ **53.** $12(1-2n)(1+2n)$ **55.** $(4p-1)^2$ **57.** 1 sec **59.** $(y+3)(y+x)$ **61.** $5s^2(s-5)(s+5)$ **63.** $2z(z+6)(z-5)$ **65.** $(2b+3)(b-2)(b+2)$

Chapter 10

10.1 Skill Practice (pp. 632–633) **1.** parabola **3.** C **5.** B

7.

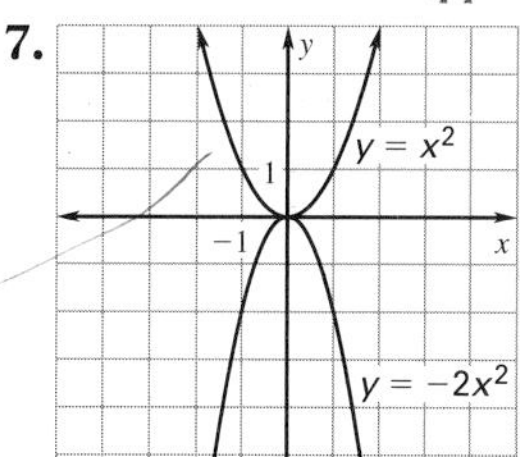

The graph is a vertical stretch (by a factor of 2) with a reflection in the x-axis of the graph of $y=x^2$.

9.

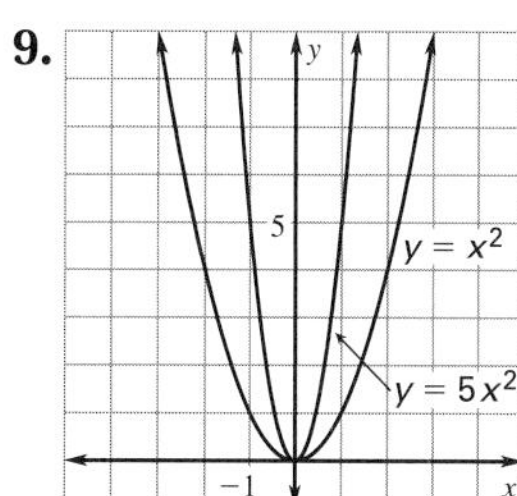

The graph is a vertical stretch (by a factor of 5) of the graph of $y=x^2$.

11.

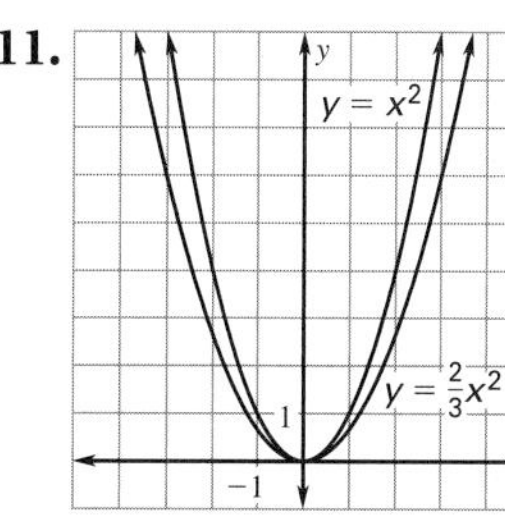

The graph is a vertical shrink $\left(\text{by a factor of } \frac{2}{3}\right)$ of the graph of $y=x^2$.

13.

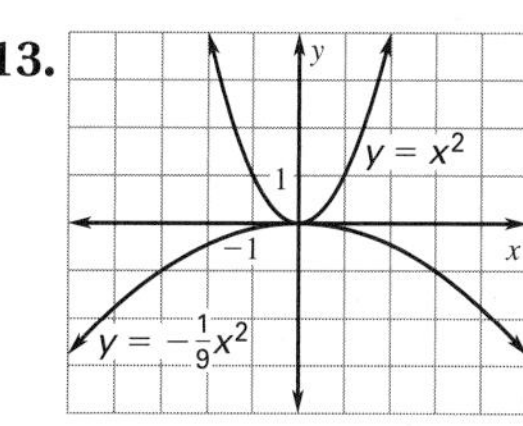

The graph is a vertical shrink $\left(\text{by a factor of } \frac{1}{9}\right)$ with a reflection in the x-axis of the graph of $y=x^2$.

15.

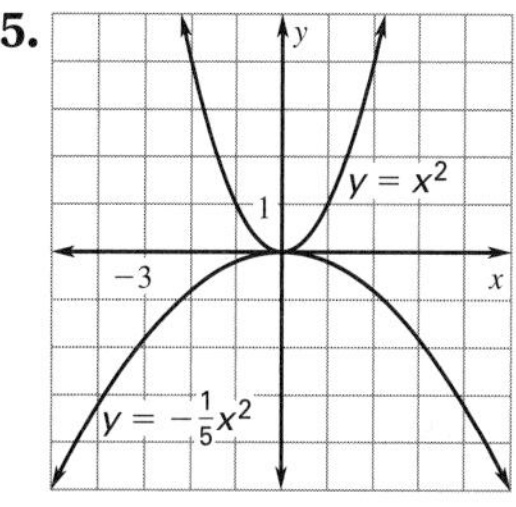

The graph is a vertical shrink $\left(\text{by a factor of } \frac{1}{5}\right)$ with a reflection in the x-axis of the graph of $y=x^2$.

17.

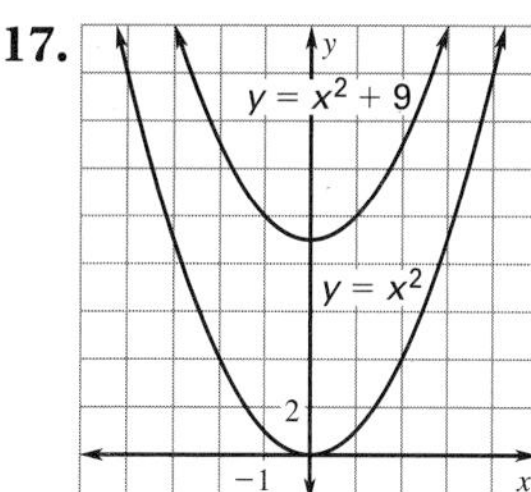

The graph is a vertical translation (of 9 units up) of the graph of $y=x^2$.

SELECTED ANSWERS

19. 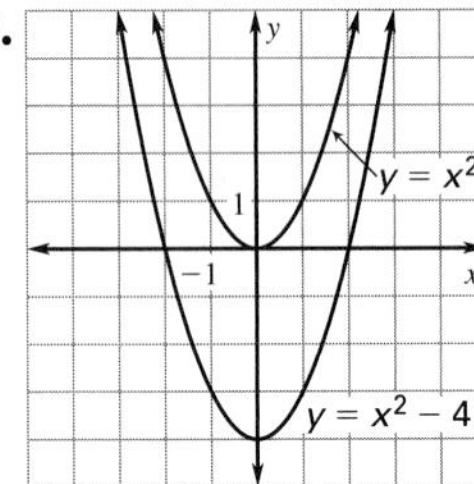

The graph is a vertical translation (of 4 units down) of the graph of $y = x^2$.

21. The graph is a vertical translation $\left(\text{of } \frac{7}{4} \text{ units up}\right)$ of the graph of $y = x^2$.

23. The graph of $y = x^2 - 2$ should be shifted 2 units down, not 2 units up. The vertex should be at $(0, -2)$.

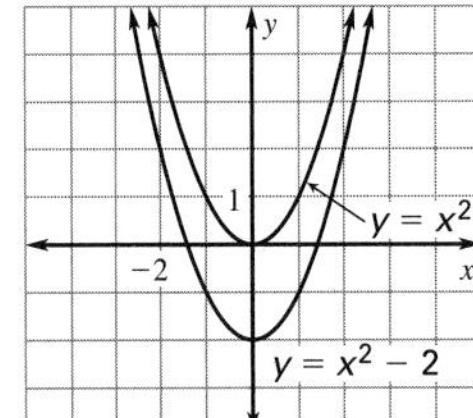

25. 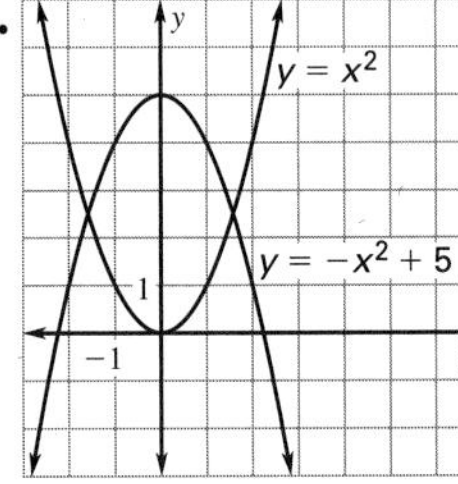

The graph is a reflection in the x-axis with a vertical translation (of 5 units up) of the graph of $y = x^2$.

27. 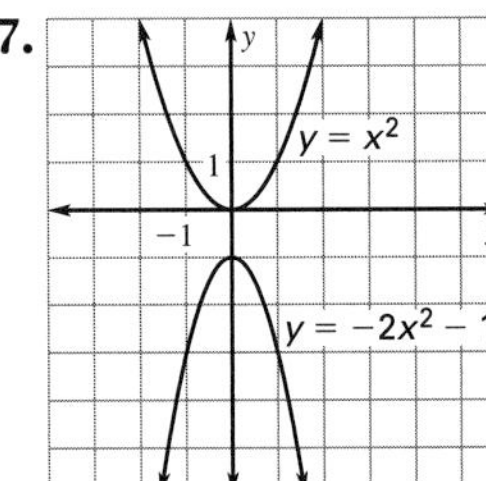

The graph is a vertical stretch (by a factor of 2) with a vertical translation (of 1 unit down) and a reflection in the x-axis of the graph of $y = x^2$.

29. 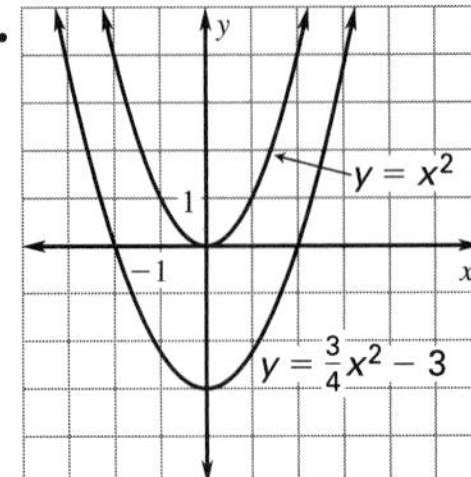

The graph is a vertical shrink $\left(\text{by a factor of } \frac{3}{4}\right)$ with a vertical translation (of 3 units down) of the graph of $y = x^2$.

31. 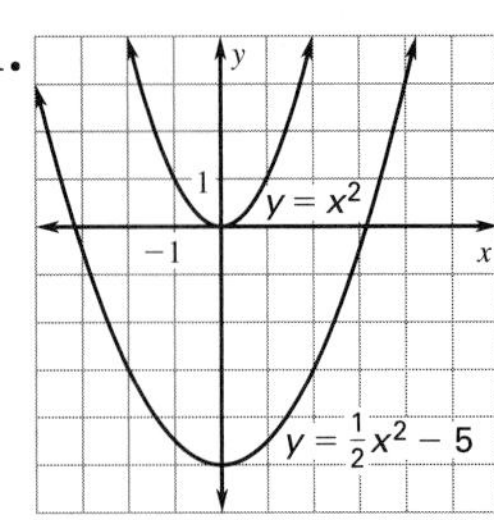

The graph is a vertical shrink $\left(\text{by a factor of } \frac{1}{2}\right)$ with a vertical translation (of 5 units down) of the graph of $y = x^2$.

35. Translate the graph of f 5 units down.

10.1 Problem Solving (pp. 633–634)

41. a. 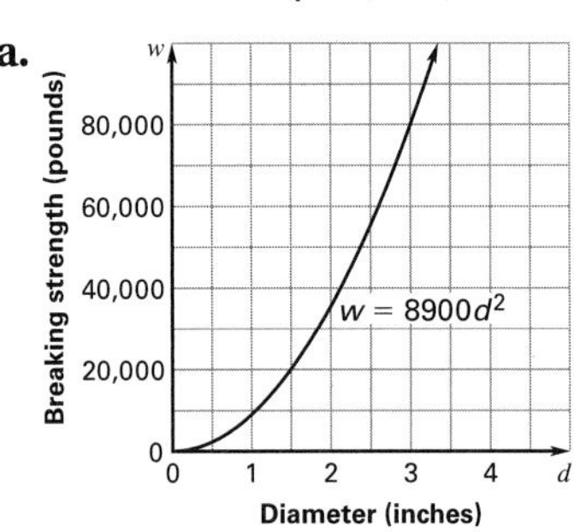

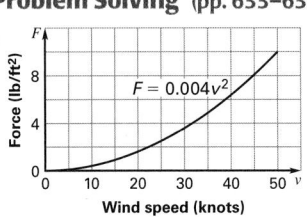

b. about 16 knots **c.** about 35 knots

43. a.

b. No. *Sample answer:* Let D be the diameter of a rope with 4 times the breaking strength of a rope with diameter d. Then $8900D^2 = 4(8900d^2)$; $D^2 = 4d^2$; $D = \sqrt{4d^2}$; $D = 2d$. Thus, the diameter of the rope with 4 times the breaking strength is only two times the diameter of the other rope.

10.2 Skill Practice (pp. 638–639) **1.** When the function is in standard form, $y = ax^2 + bx + c$, it will have a minimum value if $a > 0$ and a maximum value if $a < 0$. **3.** $x = 2$, $(2, -2)$ **5.** $x = 4$, $(4, 26)$ **7.** $x = -\frac{1}{2}$, $\left(-\frac{1}{2}, -\frac{3}{2}\right)$ **9.** $x = 0$, $(0, -1)$ **11.** $x = 6$, $(6, 7)$ **13.** The equation of the axis of symmetry is $x = \frac{-b}{2a}$, not $x = \frac{b}{2a}$; $x = \frac{-b}{2a} = \frac{-16}{2(2)}$, $x = -4$.

15. 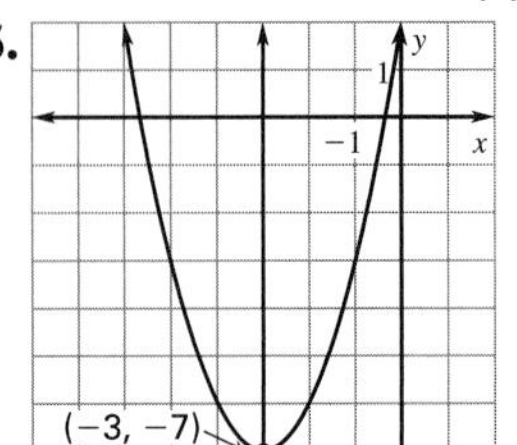

17. 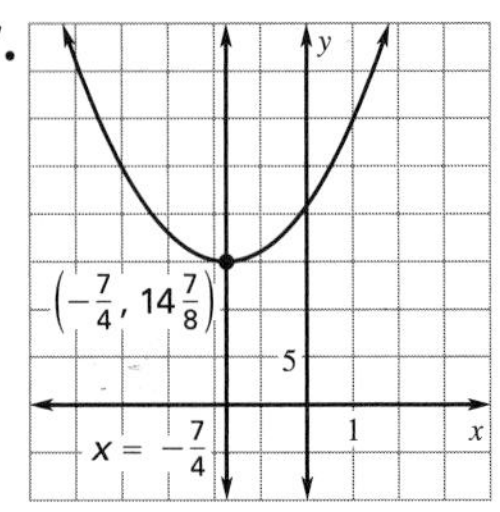

SELECTED ANSWERS

19.
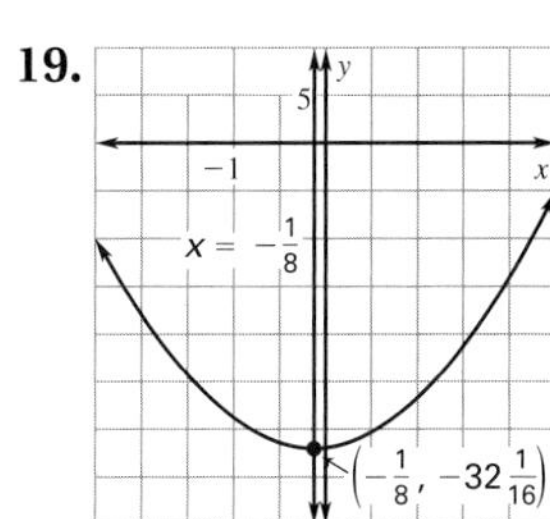

21.
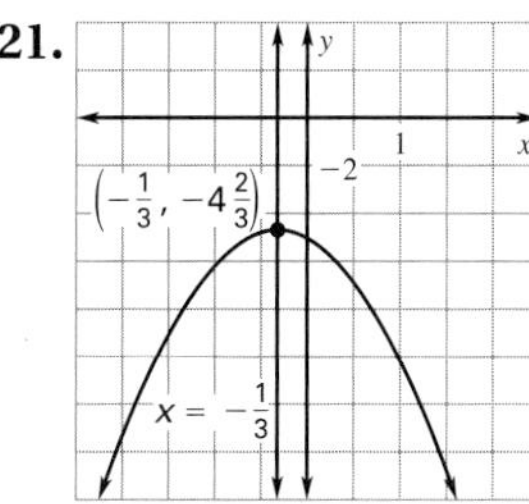

23.
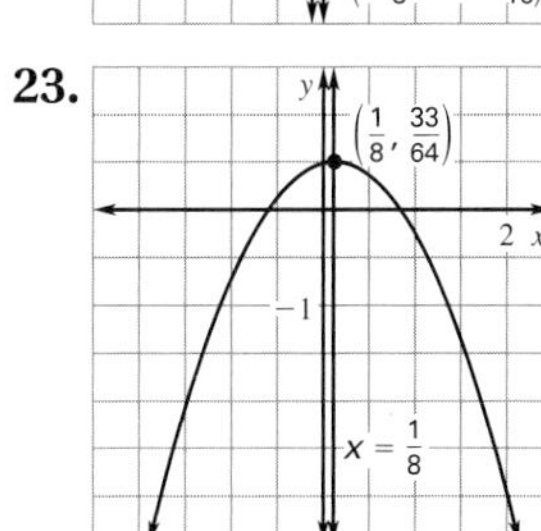

25.
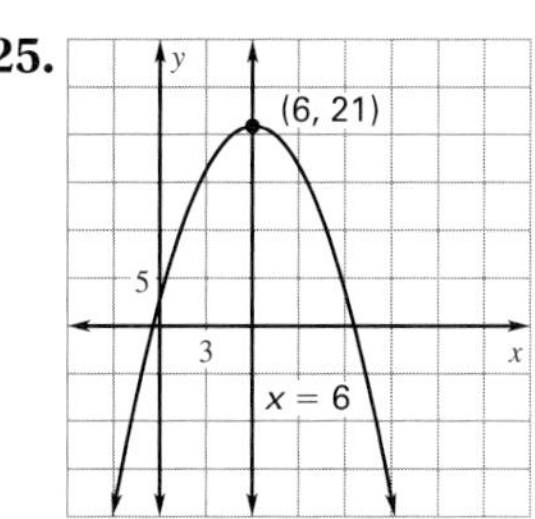

29. maximum value; 7 **31.** maximum value; −8 **33.** maximum value; $\frac{81}{8}$ **35.** maximum value; 54 **37.** The graph of $y = x^2 + 4x + 1$ is a horizontal translation (of 4 units left) of the graph of $y = x^2 - 4x + 1$.

10.2 Problem Solving (pp. 639–640) **41.** about 66 ft

43.
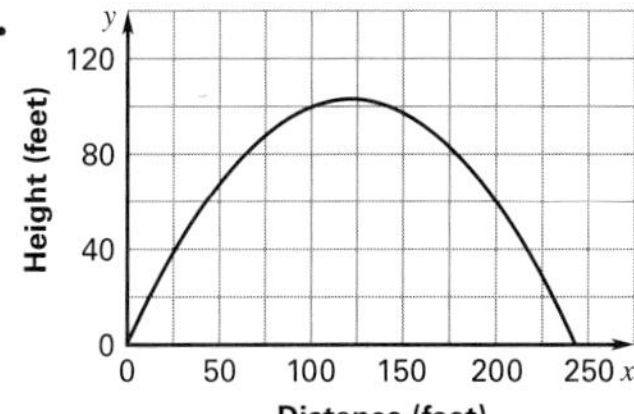

about 243 ft

Extension (p. 642)

1.
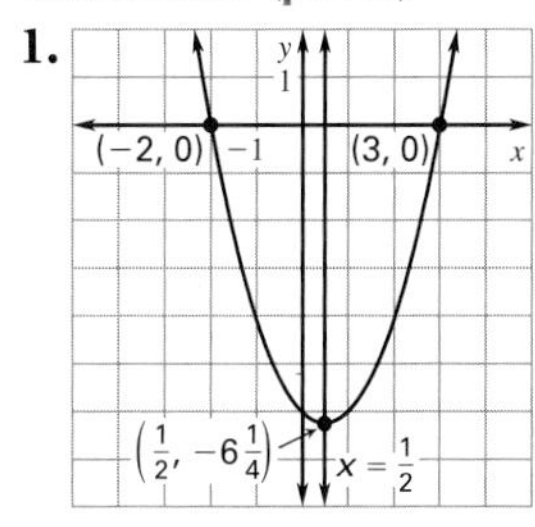

3.
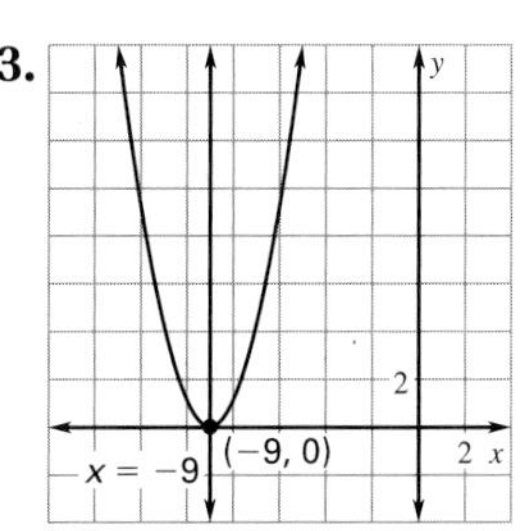

5.
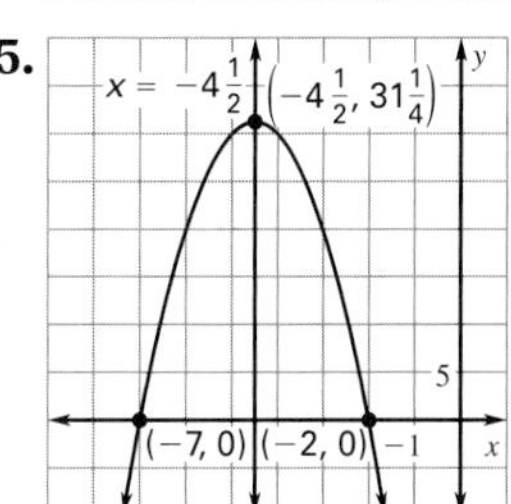

7.
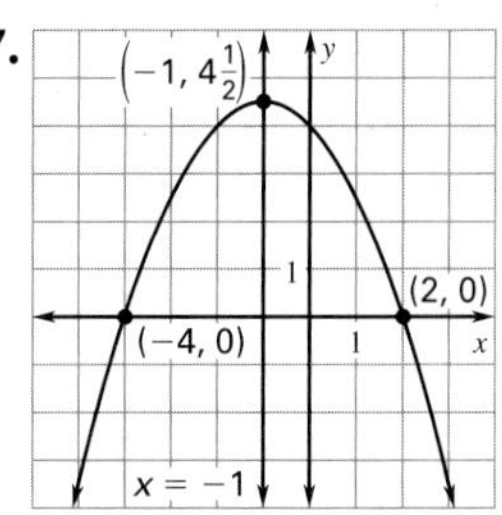

9.
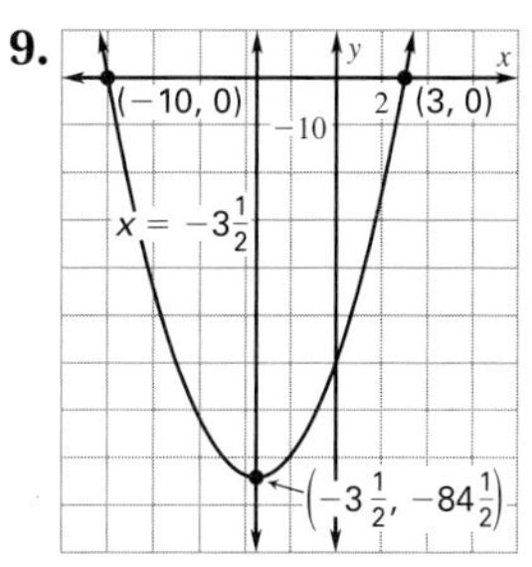

11.
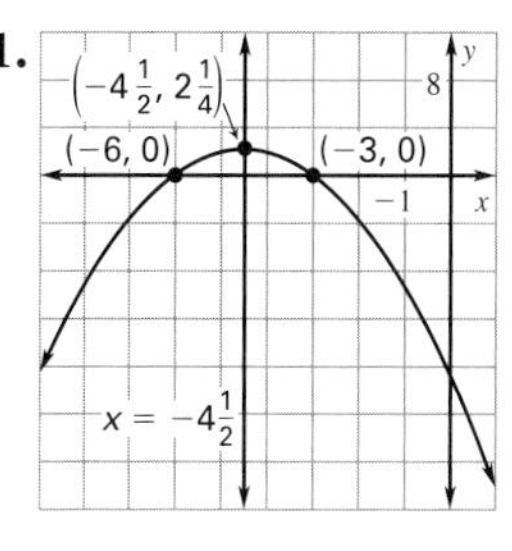

13.
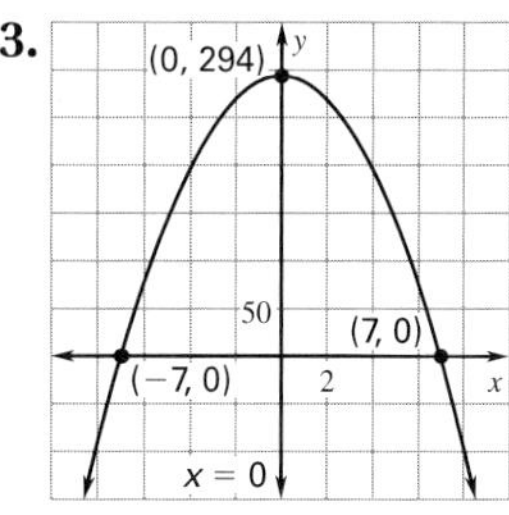

15.
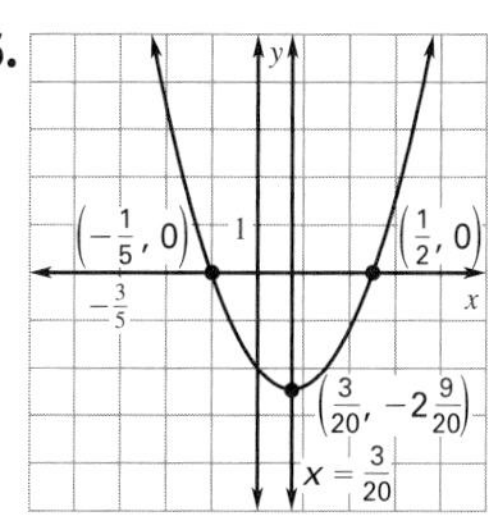

10.3 Skill Practice (pp. 647–648) **1.** $2x^2 - 9x + 11 = 0$ **3.** 4, 1 **5.** −4, −2 **7.** 8, −2 **9.** 3 **11.** −5 **13.** −7 **15.** no solution **17.** no solution **19.** −6, 2 **21.** Any solution of a quadratic equation is an x-intercept of the graph of the related quadratic function. The x-intercept of the function shown in the graph is 2, not 4; the only solution of the equation is 2. **23.** −3, 4 **25.** −5, 2 **27.** −5, 4 **29.** 1, 11 **31.** $-1\frac{1}{2}$, 1 **33.** $\frac{1}{2}$ **35.** no solution **37.** −3.4, −0.6 **39.** −1.4, 3.4 **41.** 0.8, 6.2 **43.** −1.3, 0.8 **45.** −4.7, −1.3

10.3 Problem Solving (pp. 648–649) **51.** 24.1 ft **53.** 16 ft; the distance from the nozzle to the circle is the distance between the x-intercepts of $y = -0.75x^2 + 6x$. Substitute 0 for y and solve for x: $0 = -0.75x^2 + 6x$ has solutions 0 and 8. The radius of the display circle is 8 feet, so the diameter is 16 feet.

10.3 Graphing Calculator Activity (pp. 650–651) **1.** $1\frac{2}{3}$ **3.** −3.75 **5.** about −3.5 **7.** −1.11, 3.61 **9.** −1.61, 5.61 **11.** 0.90, 2.18 **13.** −7.03, 2.15 **15.** 0; the maximum or minimum value of a quadratic function occurs at the vertex of the parabola that is the graph of the function. When a quadratic function has only one zero, its graph has only one x-intercept, which must also be the x-coordinate of the vertex of the parabola. Then the y-coordinate of the vertex is 0, so the maximum or minimum value of the function is 0.

10.4 Skill Practice (pp. 655–656) **1.** square root **3.** ±1 **5.** ±10 **7.** 0 **9.** $\pm\frac{1}{2}$ **11.** $\pm\frac{7}{3}$ **13.** 0 **17.** ±2.65 **19.** no solution **21.** 0 **23.** ±2.24 **25.** ±3.78 **27.** ±1.32

31. Negative numbers do not have real number square roots, so $\pm\sqrt{-\frac{11}{7}}$ are not real numbers; there is no solution. **33.** 0.76, 5.24 **35.** −8.16, −1.84 **37.** −16.65, −11.35 **39.** −5.69, 3.69 **41.** ±4 **43.** ±1.41 **45.** 0.37, 13.63 **47.** 12 in. **49.** 11.66 ft **51.** $\pm\frac{6}{5}$, or ±1.2. *Sample answer:* Rewrite the decimal as a fraction and then take square roots of each side of the equation: $x^2 = \frac{144}{100}$, so $x = \pm\sqrt{\frac{144}{100}} = \pm\frac{12}{10} = \pm\frac{6}{5}$ or ±1.2.

10.4 Problem Solving (pp. 657–658) **59. a.** 6.8 mm **b.** 5.9 mm **c.** 5.6 mm **61. a.** $D = 4 \pm \sqrt{\frac{16V}{L}}$ **b.** 11.1 ft, 10.7 ft, 10.3 ft, 10.0 ft

10.4 Problem Solving Workshop (p. 660) **1.** about 1.5 sec **3. a.** $V = 25x^2$ **b.** length: about 9 in., width: 5 in., height: about 1.8 in.

c.

Height, *x* (inches)	1.7	1.8	1.9
Width (inches)	5	5	5
Length, 5*x* (inches)	8.5	9	9.5
Volume, *V* (cubic inches)	72.25	81	90.25

The volume in the table closest to 83 cubic inches is 81 cubic inches. To the nearest tenth of an inch, the height of the box is about 1.8 inches. The length of the box is $5x \approx 9$ inches, and the width is 5 inches. **5.** To rewrite the equation $6 = -16t^2 + 54$ so that one side is 0, you must subtract 6 from each side; $0 = -16t^2 + 48$, replace 48 with the closest perfect square, 49. $0 = -16t^2 + 49 = -(16t^2 - 49) = -(4t + 7)(4t - 7)$, so the approximate solutions of this equation are $\pm\frac{7}{4}$. Disregard the negative solution because time cannot be negative; so, it takes about $\frac{7}{4}$, or 1.75, seconds for the shoe to hit the net.

10.5 Skill Practice (pp. 666–667) **1.** completing the square **3.** 9; $(x + 3)^2$ **5.** 4; $(x - 2)^2$ **7.** $\frac{9}{4}$; $\left(x - \frac{3}{2}\right)^2$ **9.** 1.44; $(x + 1.2)^2$ **11.** $\frac{4}{9}$; $\left(x - \frac{2}{3}\right)^2$ **13.** −12, 2 **15.** −6, 12 **17.** −7, 3 **19.** −10.5, −0.5 **21.** −0.80, 8.80 **23.** −2.5, −0.5 **27.** The perfect square trinomial $x^2 - 2x + 1$ factors as $(x - 1)^2$ not $(x + 1)^2$, $(x - 1)^2 = 5$, $x - 1 = \pm\sqrt{5}$, $x = 1 \pm \sqrt{5}$. **29.** −11.57, −0.43 **31.** −1.91, 0.91 **33.** −0.96, 6.96 **35.** 0.79, 2.21 **37.** −3.68, −0.32 **39.** −0.25, 0.75 **41.** 4.87

10.5 Problem Solving (pp. 667–668) **45.** 3 ft **47. a.** $1904 = 7x^2 - 4x + 392$, 2000

b.

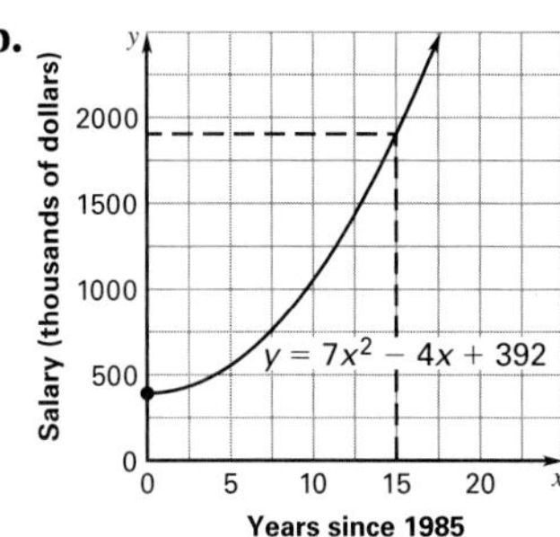

When $y \approx 1904$, the value of x is about 15. So the year 2000 (1985 + 15) found in part (a) is correct.

49. Yes; to find the number of days x after which the stock price was \$23.50 per share, substitute 23.5 for y and solve for x by completing the square to find that the solutions are 10 and 30. You could have sold the stock for \$23.50 per share 10 days after you purchased it.

Extension (p. 670)

1.

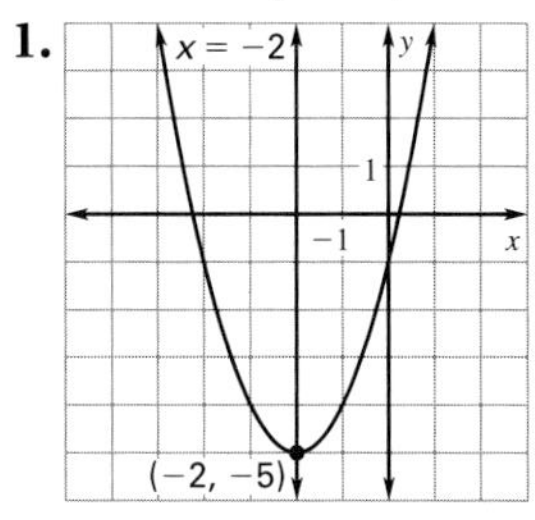

3.

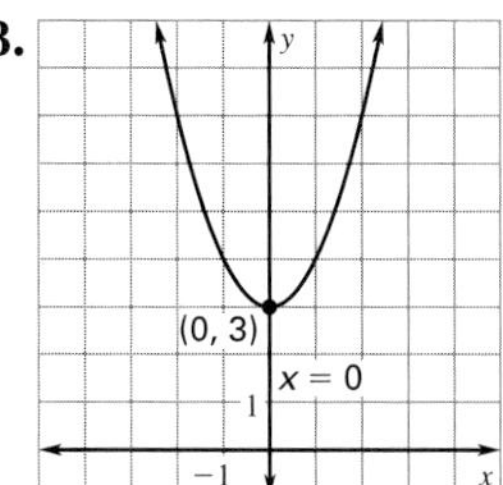

5.

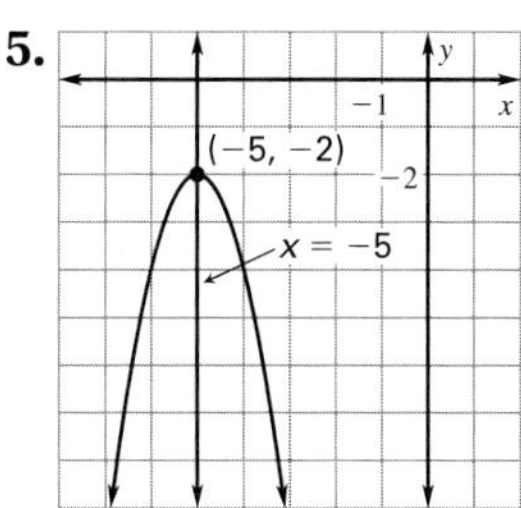

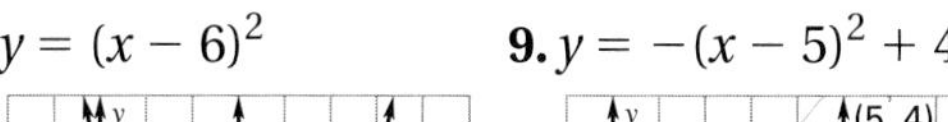
7. $y = (x - 6)^2$ **9.** $y = -(x - 5)^2 + 4$

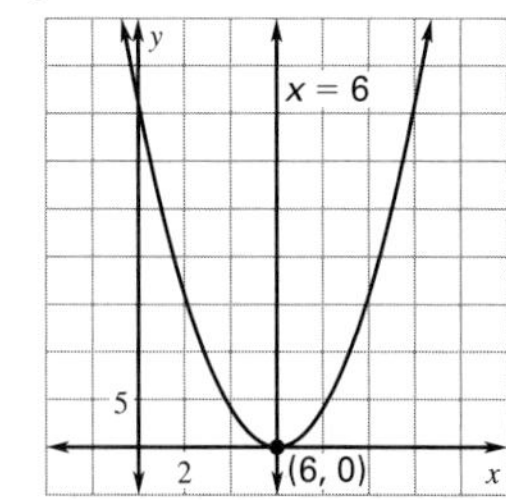

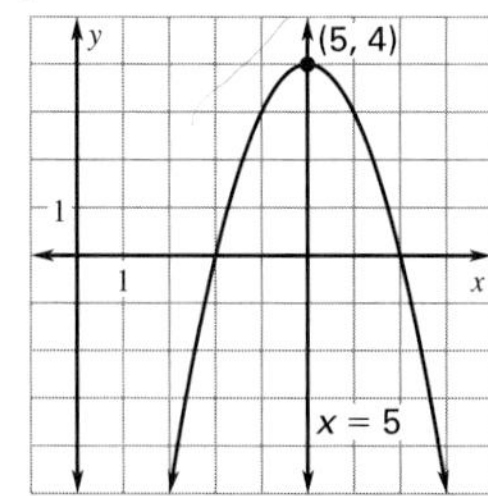

11. $y = -3(x + 1)^2 + 2$ **13.** $y = \frac{1}{4}(x + 6)^2 + 1$

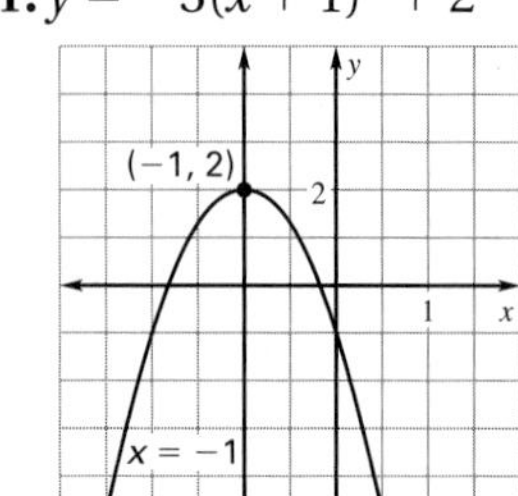

10.6 Skill Practice (pp. 674–675) **1.** quadratic formula **3.** −13, 8 **5.** −2, 2.33 **7.** −3.27, 4.27 **9.** −2.5 **11.** −0.63, 2.13 **13.** −2, 7 **15.** −1, 1.29 **17.** 3.27, 6.73 **19.** −0.54, 2.29 **21.** −0.66, 1.09 **23.** −1.77, −0.57 **27.** Before identifying the values of a, b, and c, the equation must be written in standard form $ax^2 + bx + c = 0$; $-2x^2 + 3x - 1 = 0$, so $c = -1$, not 1; $x = \frac{-3 \pm \sqrt{3^2 - 4(-2)(-1)}}{2(-2)}$, $x = \frac{-3 \pm \sqrt{1}}{-4}$, $x = \frac{1}{2}$ and $x = 1$. **29–33.** Sample answers are given. **29.** Using square roots, the equation can be written in the form $x^2 = d$. **31.** Factoring, the expression $m^2 + 5m + 6$ factors easily. **33.** Quadratic formula, the equation does not factor easily. **35.** 4 **37.** 6 **39.** −1.94, 2.19 **41.** −0.41, 2.41 **43.** 5; 13 m by 7 m

10.6 Problem Solving (pp. 675–676)

47. 1993 **49. a.** 2001 **b.**

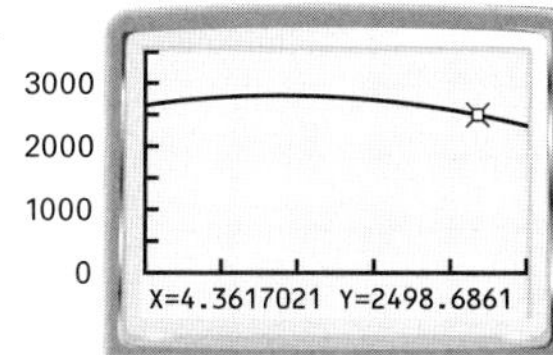

10.7 Skill Practice (pp. 681–682) **1.** $x = \frac{-b \pm \sqrt{b^2 - 4ac}}{2a}$, $b^2 - 4ac$ should be circled. **3.** no solution **5.** two solutions **7.** one solution **9.** two solutions **11.** two solutions **13.** one solution **15.** two solutions **17.** no solution **21.** Before calculating the discriminant, the equation must be written in standard form: $3x^2 - 7x + 5 = 0$. Thus, c is 5, not −4, so $b^2 - 4ac = (-7)^2 - 4(3)(5) = 49 - 60 = -11$; the equation has no solution. **23.** 2 **25.** 0 **27.** 0 **29.** 1 **31–33.** Sample answers are given for parts (a) and (c). **31. a.** 0 **b.** 1 **c.** 2 **33. a.** 8 **b.** 9 **c.** 10 **35.** On; the value of the discriminant is $(-6)^2 - 4(3)(3) = 0$, so the graph has exactly one x-intercept. A parabola that has exactly one x-intercept must have its vertex on the x-axis. **37.** Below; $a < 0$, so the graph opens down. The value of the discriminant is $(10)^2 - 4(-15)(-25) = -1400 < 0$, so the graph has no x-intercepts; a parabola that opens down and has no x-intercepts must have its vertex below the x-axis. **39.** On; the value of the discriminant is $(-24)^2 - 4(9)(16) = 0$, so the graph has exactly one x-intercept; a parabola that has exactly one x-intercept must have its vertex on the x-axis. **41. a.** $314 = 2w^2 + 40w + 64$ **b.** 2 **c.** −25, 5; the width w cannot be negative, so the solution −25 meters does not make sense in the context of the problem. The solution 5 meters does makes sense in the context of the problem.

10.7 Problem Solving (pp. 682–683) **45. a.** Substitute 25 for y in the equation and then write the resulting quadratic equation in standard form: $25 = 0.06x^2 - 4x + 87$, or $0 = 0.06x^2 - 4x + 62$. Evaluate the discriminant: $b^2 - 4ac = (-4)^2 - 4(0.06)(62) = 1.12$. Since the discriminant is positive, we know that the equation $25 = 0.06x^2 - 4x + 87$ does have solutions, so it is possible for a parakeet to consume 25 milliliters of oxygen per gram of body mass per hour. **b.** 24.5 km/h and 42.2 km/h **47.** No; to determine if there is any point of the arch at a height of 4 feet, substitute 4 for y in the equation and then determine if the equation has any positive solutions. The equation is $4 = -0.18x^2 + 1.6x$, or $0 = -0.18x^2 + 1.6x - 4$. Evaluate the discriminant: $b^2 - 4ac = (1.6)^2 - 4(-0.18)(-4) = -0.32$. Since the discriminant is negative, we know the equation has no solution; thus, a child who is 4 feet tall cannot walk under one of the arches without having to bend over. **49. a.** $h = -16t^2 + 32t + 6$ **b.** no **c.** yes; about 0.8 sec and about 1.4 sec

10.8 Skill Practice (pp. 688–689) **1.** exponential function **3.** B **5.** A **7.** linear function **9.** exponential function **11.** quadratic function **13.** quadratic function; $y = -x^2$ **15.** linear function; $y = 3x + 1$ **17.** exponential function; $y = 4\left(\frac{1}{4}\right)^x$ **19.** The x- and y-values were reversed when substituting the coordinates of the ordered pair (2, 10) into the equation $y = ax^2$. Substituting 2 for x and 10 for y gives $10 = a(2)^2$, $a = 2.5$; so, the equation is $y = 2.5x^2$. **21.** $A = \left(\frac{\sqrt{3}}{4}\right)s^2$; $25\sqrt{3}$ cm^2

10.8 Problem Solving (pp. 689–691)

23. linear function; $y = 0.34x + 24.6$

25. a.

Folds	1	2	3	4	5
Sections	2	4	8	16	32

b.

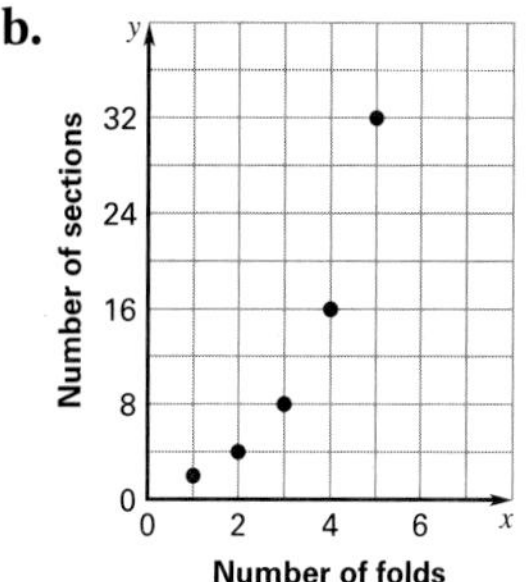

exponential function **c.** $y = 2^x$; 128 sections

27. a. quadratic function; $\ell = 0.82t^2$ **b.** 0.205 ft **c.** The period decreases by about 71%. For example, consider $t = 4$ for $\ell = 13.12$. To find t for 50% of ℓ, solve $0.5(13.12) = 0.82t^2$; $t \approx 2.83$, and $\frac{2.83}{4} = 0.708$, so the period decreased by about 71%. Consider $t = 2$ for $\ell = 3.28$. To find t for 50% of ℓ, solve $0.5(3.28) = 0.82t^2$; $t \approx 1.41$, and $\frac{1.41}{2} = 0.705$, so the period decreased by about 71%. Consider $t = 1$ for $\ell = 0.82$. To find t for 50% of ℓ, solve $0.5(0.82) = 0.82t^2$; $t \approx 0.707$, and $\frac{0.707}{1} = 0.707$, so the period decreased by about 71%.

10.8 Graphing Calculator Activity (pp. 692–693)
1. $y = 15{,}600(0.866)^x$
3. $y = 179(0.987)^x$, $y = 0.040x^2 - 4.13x + 197$

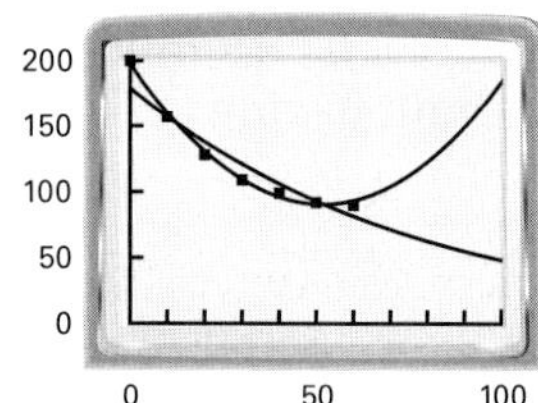

The exponential model; although the quadratic model appears to fit the given data points more closely than the exponential model does, the graph shows that after the last data point, (60, 90), the quadratic model implies increasing temperatures as time goes on, while the exponential model shows gradually decreasing temperatures as time goes on; the exponential model is a more accurate model of what will happen as the hot chocolate continues to cool.

Chapter Review (pp. 696–700)
1. axis of symmetry **3.** maximum

5.
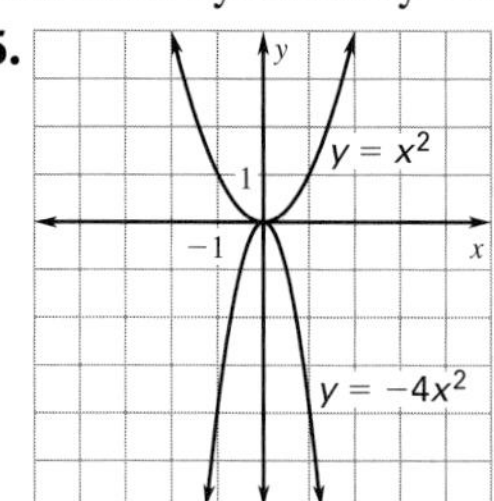

The graph is a vertical stretch (by a factor of 4) with a reflection in the x-axis of the graph of $y = x^2$.

7.
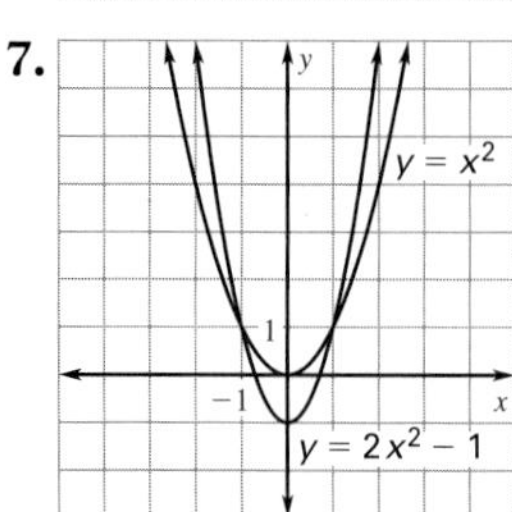

The graph is a vertical stretch (by a factor of 2) with a vertical translation (of 1 unit down) of the graph of $y = x^2$.

9.
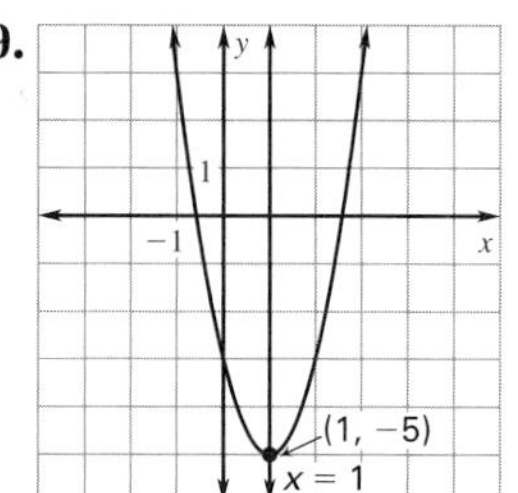

11. no solution **13.** −8, 1 **15.** no solution **17.** ±0.76 **19.** 2.71, 5.29 **21.** 0.32, −6.32 **23.** −0.62, 1.62 **25.** −3.89, 0.39 **27.** 0.16, 1.24 **29.** −1.22, 1 **31.** no solution **33.** two solutions **35.** two solutions **37.** exponential function

Cumulative Review (pp. 706–707) **1.** 3 **3.** 0.2 **5.** −1

7.
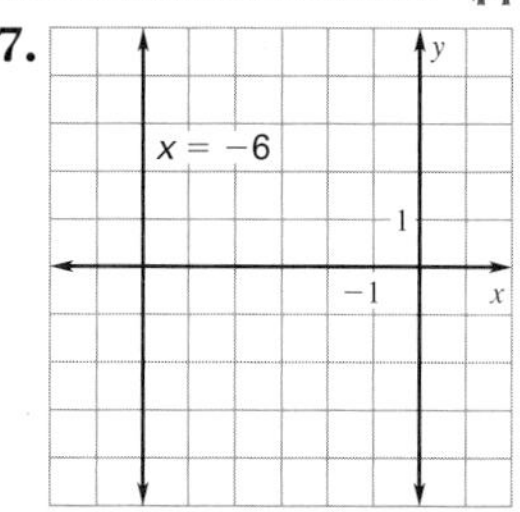

9.
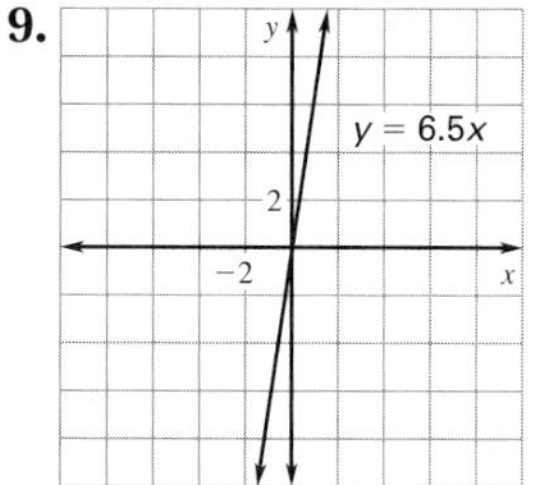

11.
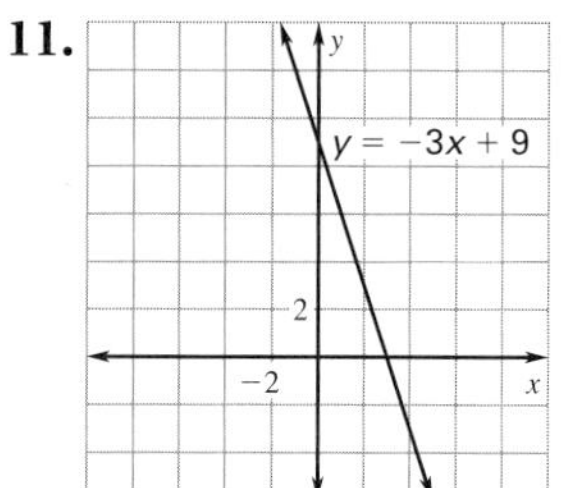

13.
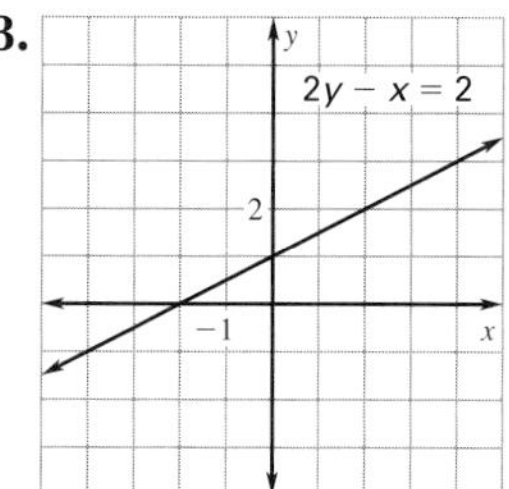

15. $y = \frac{1}{5}x + 3$ **17.** $y = -2x + 19$

19. $x < -36$

−36
−60 −40 −20 0 20

21. $b \geq -1$

−3 −2 −1 0 1 2 3 4 5

23. $-\frac{3}{2} \leq c \leq 7$

$-\frac{3}{2}$
−2 −1 0 1 2 3 4 5 6 7 8

25. all real numbers **27.** $-729r^3$ **29.** $\frac{81x^3}{y^2}$

31.
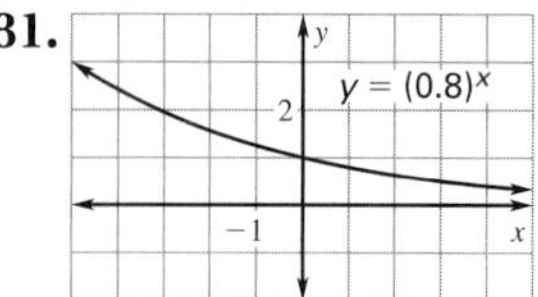

33. $-x^2 + 12x + 12$ **35.** $2z^2 + 11z - 63$
37. $-3q^3 + 11q - 2$ **39.** $4k^2 - 44k + 121$
41. $(x + 12)(x - 6)$ **43.** $(5d + 6)^2$
45. $(z - 6)(z + 2)(z - 2)$

47. 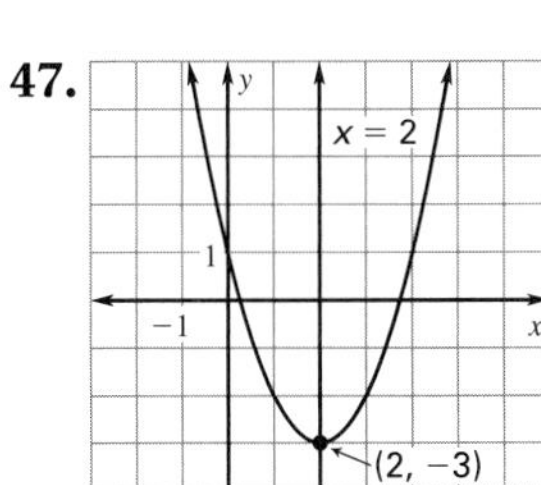

49. 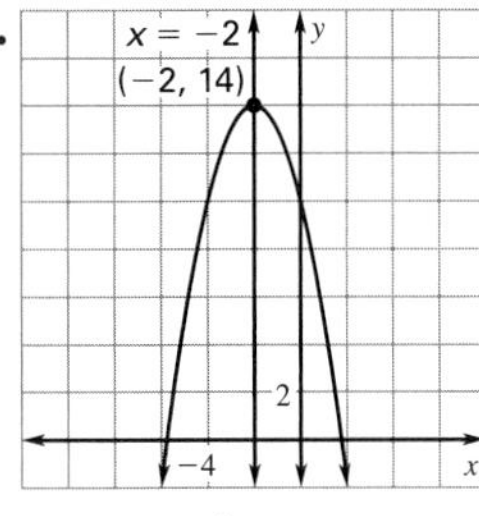

51. ±3.32 **53.** 0.5, 3 **55.** −0.57, 1 **57.** $475
59. length 19 in., width: 8 in.

61. a. 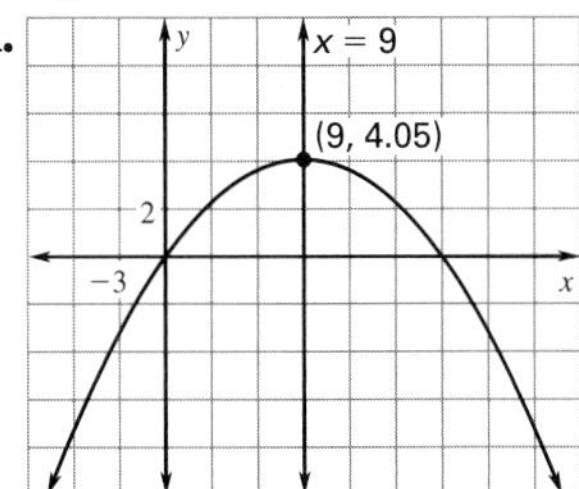

b. 18 ft

Chapter 11

11.1 Skill Practice (pp. 713–714) **1.** radical function

3. 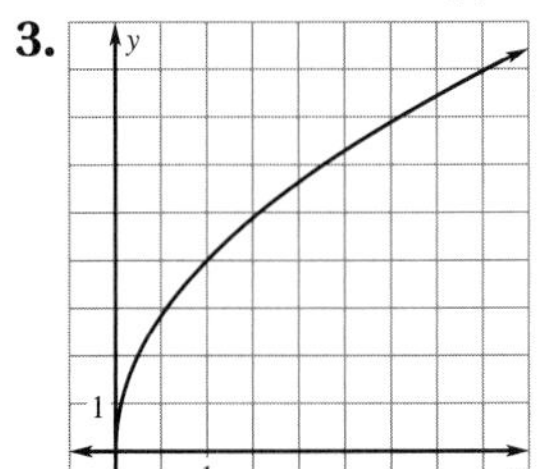

domain: $x \geq 0$, range: $y \geq 0$; vertical stretch by a factor of 4

5. 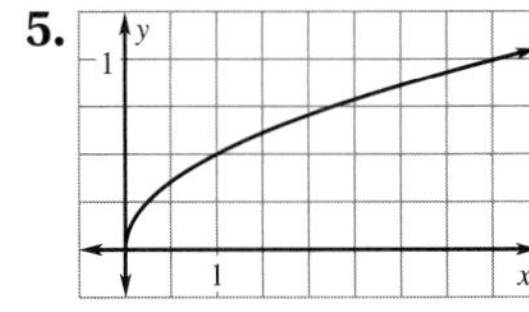

domain: $x \geq 0$, range: $y \geq 0$; vertical shrink by a factor of 0.5

7. 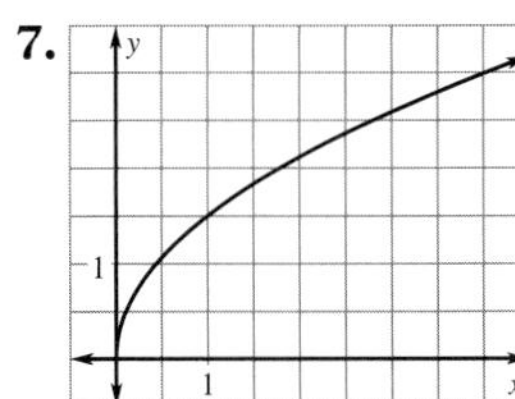

domain: $x \geq 0$, range: $y \geq 0$; vertical stretch by a factor of $\frac{3}{2}$

9. 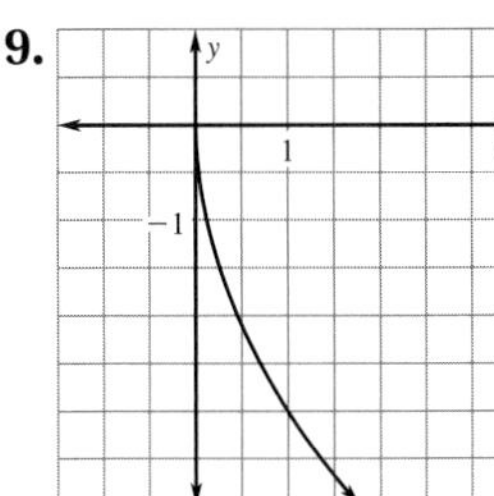

domain: $x \geq 0$, range: $y \leq 0$; vertical stretch by a factor of 3 with a reflection in the x-axis

11. 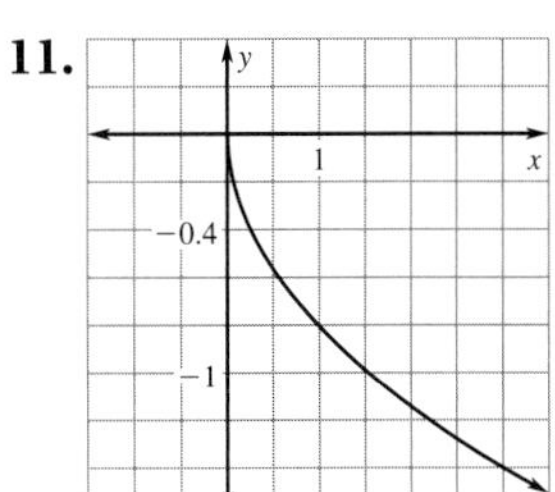

domain: $x \geq 0$, range: $y \leq 0$; vertical shrink by a factor of 0.8 with a reflection in the x-axis

13. 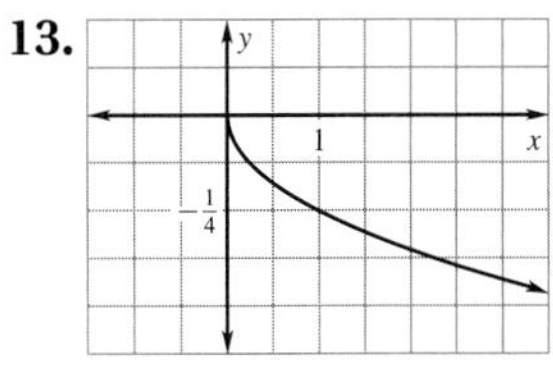

domain: $x \geq 0$, range: $y \leq 0$; vertical shrink by a factor of $\frac{1}{4}$ with a reflection in the x-axis

17. 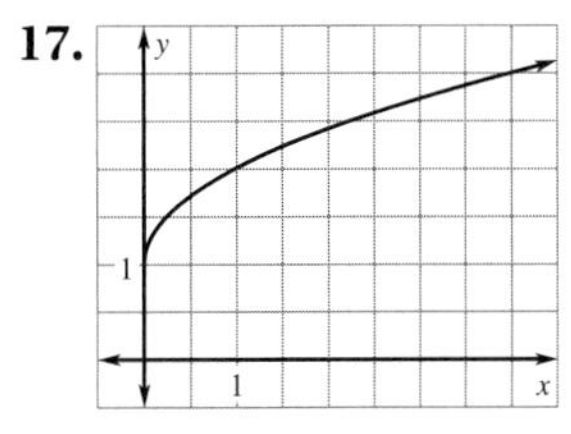

domain: $x \geq 0$, range: $y \geq 1$; vertical translation 1 unit up

19. 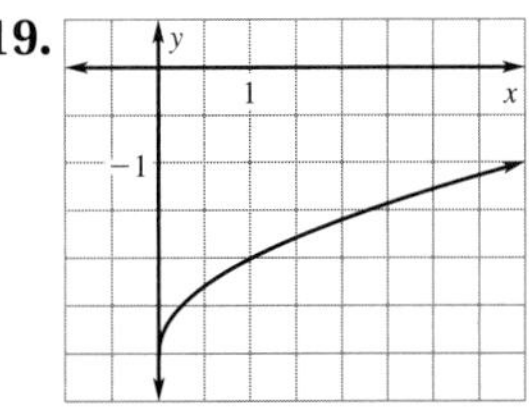

domain: $x \geq 0$, range: $y \geq -3$; vertical translation 3 units down

21. 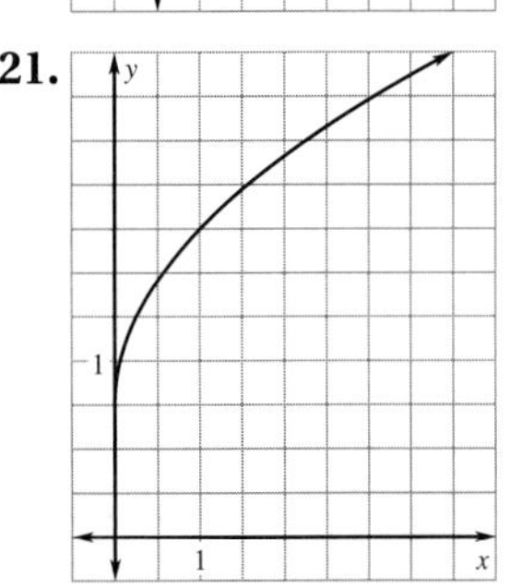

domain: $x \geq 0$, range: $y \geq \frac{3}{4}$; vertical translation $\frac{3}{4}$ unit up

23. 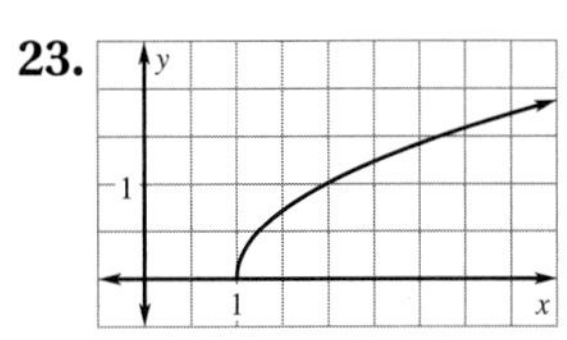

domain: $x \geq 1$, range: $y \geq 0$; horizontal translation 1 unit right

25. 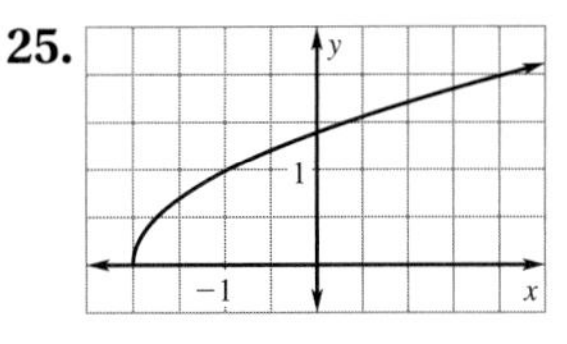

domain: $x \geq -2$, range: $y \geq 0$; horizontal translation 2 units left

27. 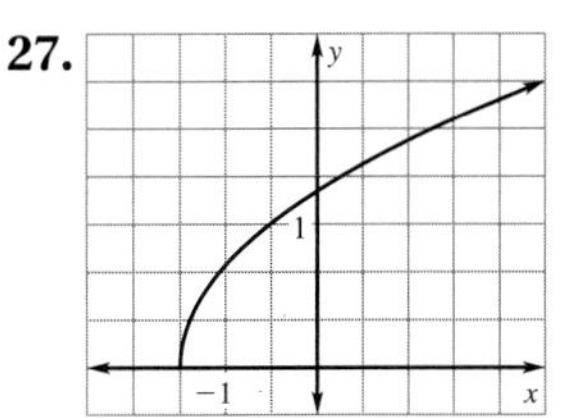

domain: $x \geq -1.5$, range: $y \geq 0$; horizontal translation 1.5 units left

31. 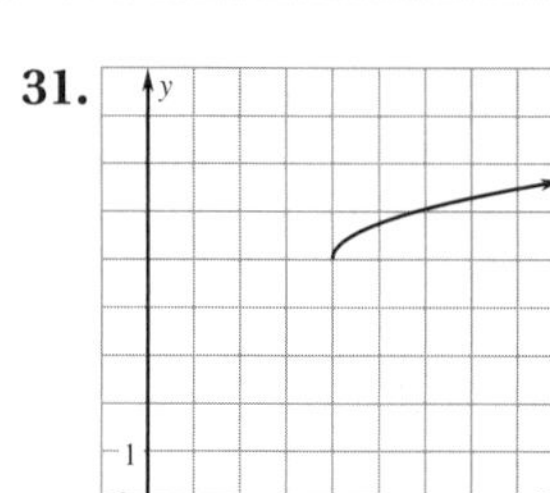

33. 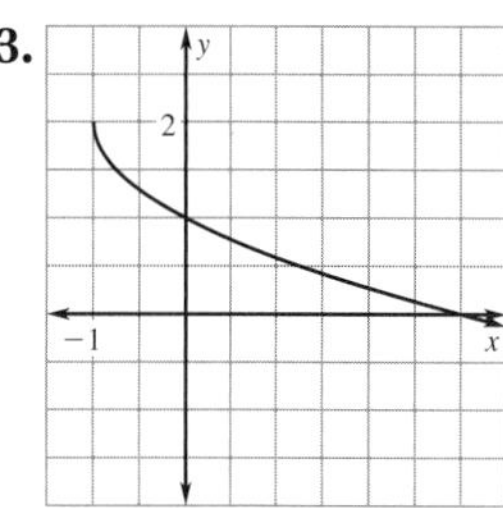

35. 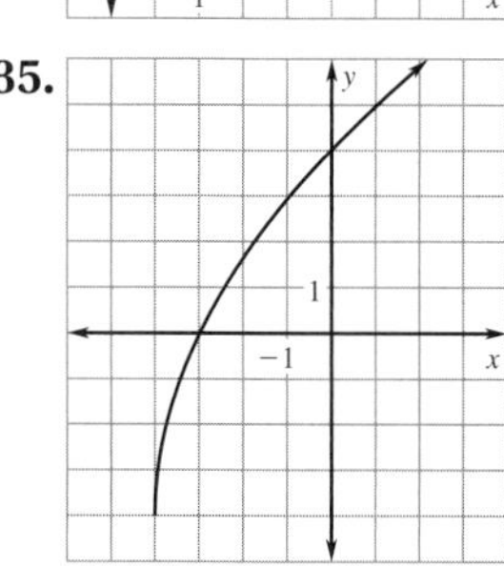

37. 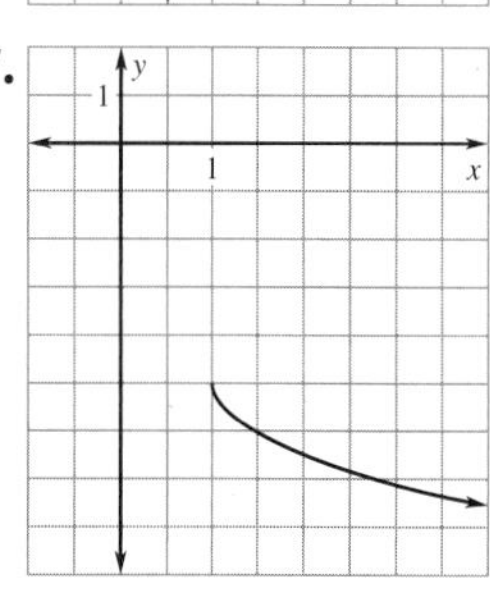

11.1 Problem Solving (pp. 715–716)

43. a. 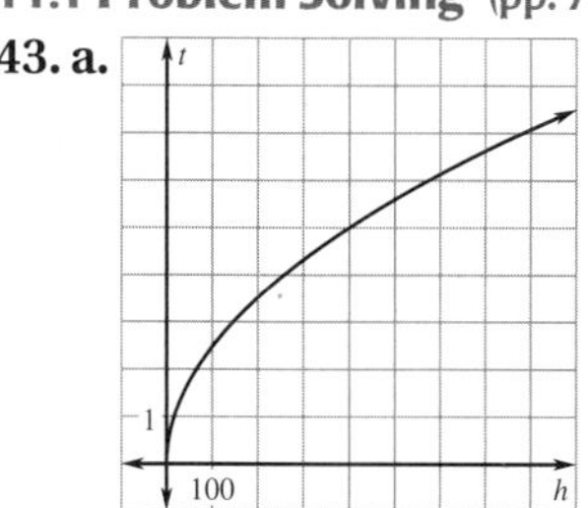 domain: $h \geq 0$, range: $t \geq 0$

b. about 1024 ft

45. 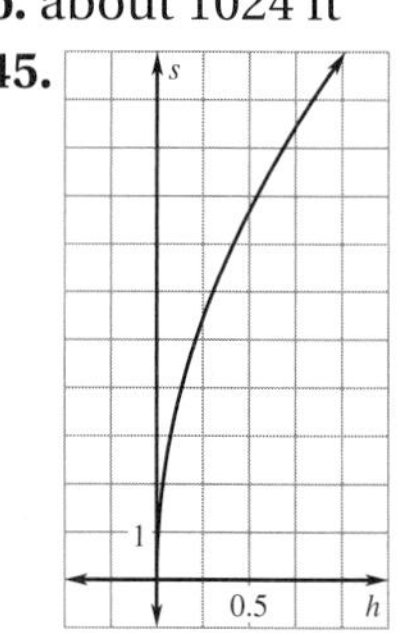 domain: $h \geq 0$, range: $s \geq 0$; about 0.9 m

47. a. 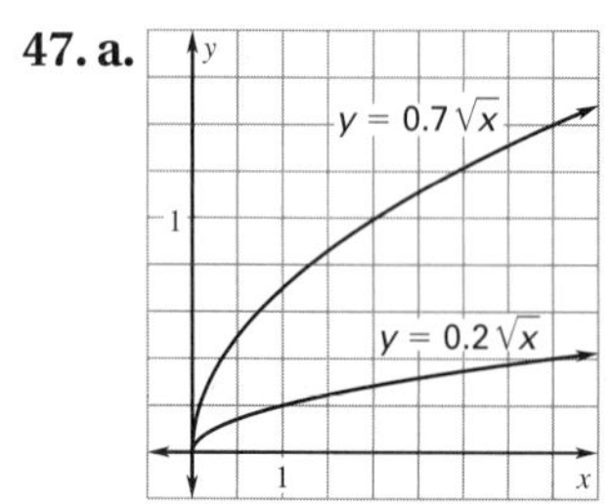

blue-winged teal's domain: $x \geq 0$, range: $y \geq 0$, northern pintail's domain: $x \geq 0$, range: $y \geq 0$

b. blue-winged teal: about 2 hectares, northern pintail: 25 hectares

11.1 Graphing Calculator Activity (p. 717)

1. 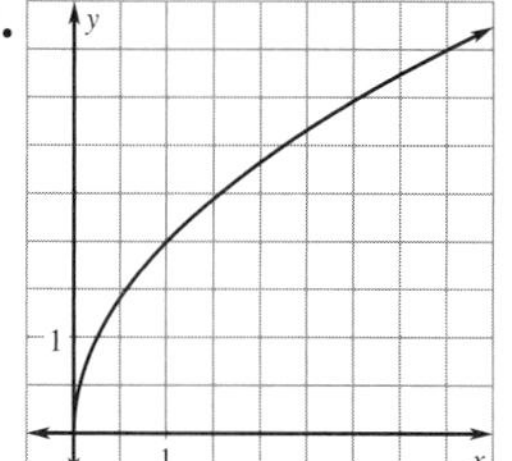 domain: $x \geq 0$, range: $y \geq 0$

3. 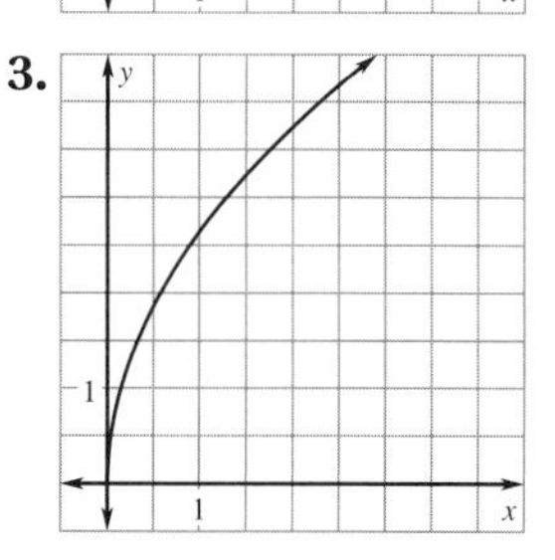 domain: $x \geq 0$, range: $y \geq 0$

5. 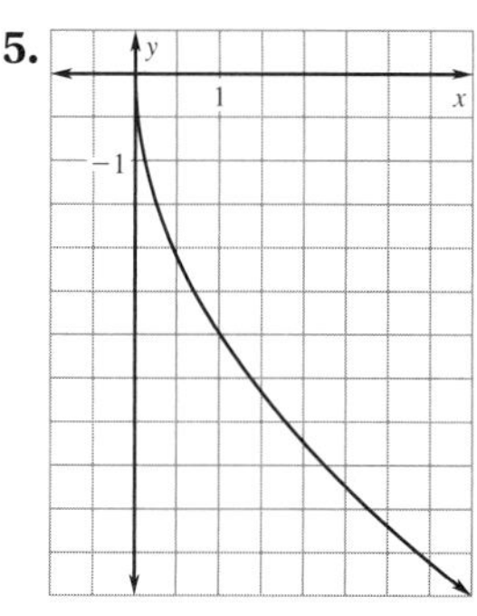 domain: $x \geq 0$, range: $y \leq 0$

7. 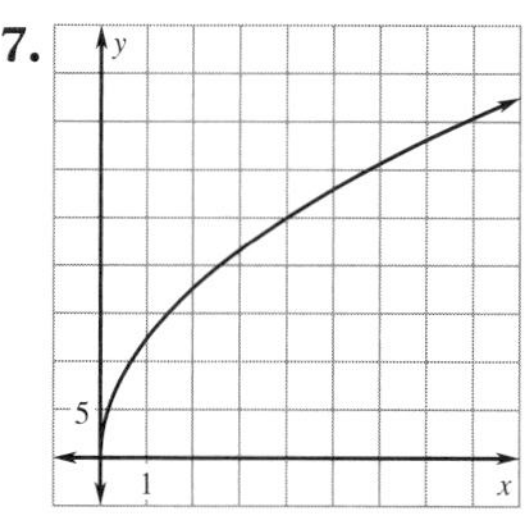 domain: $x \geq 0$, range: $y \geq 0$

9. 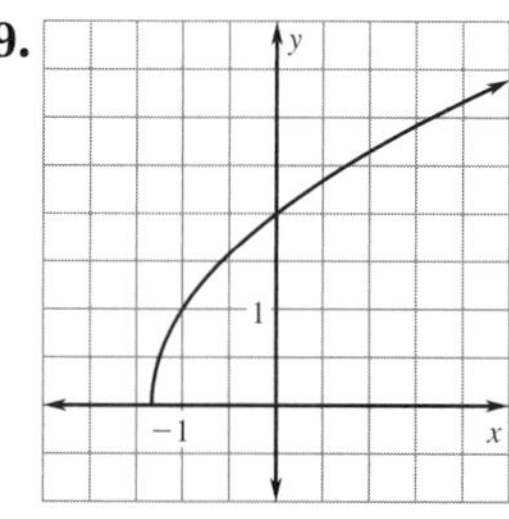 domain: $x \geq -\frac{4}{3}$, range: $y \geq 0$

11. 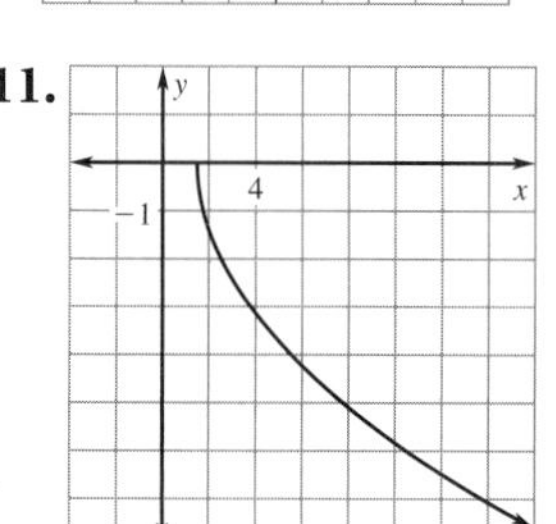 domain: $x \geq \frac{3}{2}$, range: $y \leq 0$

13. a. 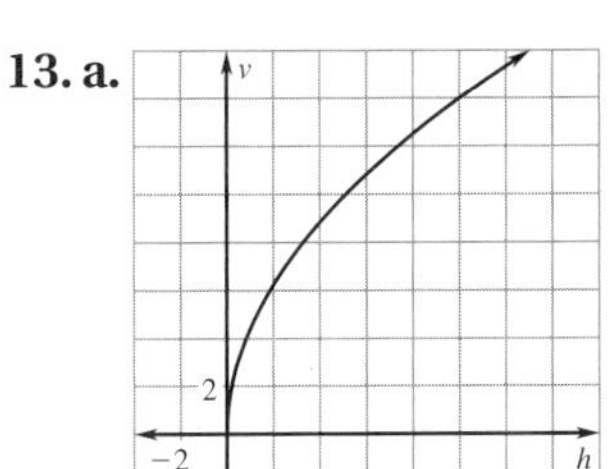 domain: $h \geq 0$, range: $v \geq 0$

b. about 154.3 m

11.2 Skill Practice (pp. 723–724) **1.** rationalizing the denominator **3.** $2\sqrt{5}$ **5.** $4\sqrt{6}$ **7.** $5\sqrt{5b}$ **9.** $9m\sqrt{m}$ **11.** $5\sqrt{6}$ **13.** $2x\sqrt{7}$ **15.** $2a^2b^2\sqrt{b}$ **17.** mn **19.** $\frac{2}{7}$ **21.** $\frac{a\sqrt{a}}{11}$ **25.** *Sample answer:* Simplify $\sqrt{45}$ to $\sqrt{9} \cdot \sqrt{5} = 3\sqrt{5}$. Then multiply $3\sqrt{5} \cdot \sqrt{5} = 3 \cdot 5 = 15$. Or, combine the expressions to create $\sqrt{45 \cdot 5} = \sqrt{225} = 15$. **27.** $\frac{4\sqrt{3}}{3}$ **29.** $\frac{\sqrt{13}}{13}$ **31.** $\frac{\sqrt{2x}}{2x}$ **33.** $\frac{2\sqrt{6n}}{3n^2}$ **35.** $-5\sqrt{5}$ **37.** $37\sqrt{2}$ **39.** $7\sqrt{7} - 5\sqrt{14}$ **41.** $21\sqrt{2} + 6\sqrt{6}$ **43.** $18 - \sqrt{2}$ **45.** $6\sqrt{7} + 6\sqrt{3} + 2\sqrt{14} + 2\sqrt{6}$ **47.** $16s^3t\sqrt{2rt}$ **49.** $\frac{h\sqrt{10gf}}{5f^2}$ **51.** $\frac{\sqrt{5}}{10}$ **53.** $\frac{3\sqrt{x} + 4x\sqrt{x}}{x^2}$ **55.** $\frac{\sqrt{7} - 1}{6}$ **57.** $\frac{7\sqrt{10} + 2\sqrt{5}}{47}$ **59.** $3\sqrt{7} - 3\sqrt{6}$ **61.** $-2\sqrt{3} - 3\sqrt{2}$ **63.** $(a\sqrt{b} + c\sqrt{d})(a\sqrt{b} - c\sqrt{d}) = a^2b - ac\sqrt{bd} + ac\sqrt{bd} - c^2d = a^2b - c^2d$ **65.** $-x$

11.2 Problem Solving (pp. 725–726) **67.** about 9.54% **69. a.** 5 yd^2 **b.** The side length s is in yd, and $\sqrt{\frac{S}{6}}$ is $\sqrt{yd^2}$ = yd. **c.** 0.9 yd **71. a.** $S = \frac{\sqrt{hw}}{60}$ **b.** Yes. *Sample answer:* If the mass stays the same, then the greater the height the greater the body surface area will be.

Extension (pp. 727–728) **1.** $-2 - \sqrt{2}, -2 + \sqrt{2}$ **3.** $-4 - 2\sqrt{2}, -4 + 2\sqrt{2}$ **5.** $-1 - \frac{2\sqrt{3}}{3}, -1 + \frac{2\sqrt{3}}{3}$ **7.** $\frac{1}{5} - \frac{\sqrt{11}}{5}, \frac{1}{5} + \frac{\sqrt{11}}{5}$ **9.** $\frac{1}{2} - \frac{\sqrt{13}}{2}, \frac{1}{2} + \frac{\sqrt{13}}{2}$ **11.** $\frac{7}{2} - \frac{\sqrt{61}}{2}, \frac{7}{2} + \frac{\sqrt{61}}{2}$ **13.** $2 - \sqrt{2}, 2 + \sqrt{2}$ **15.** $-\frac{\sqrt{6}}{3}, \frac{\sqrt{6}}{3}$ **17.** $-\frac{1}{6} - \frac{\sqrt{73}}{6}, -\frac{1}{6} + \frac{\sqrt{73}}{6}$ **21.** Sum: $-\frac{b}{a}$, product: $\frac{c}{a}$. *Sample answer:* $y = 2x^2 - 4x + 1$

11.3 Skill Practice (pp. 732–733) **1.** extraneous solution **3.** 4 **5.** 48 **7.** 29 **9.** 8 **11.** $-\frac{75}{2}$ **13.** 47 **15.** -2 **17.** 7 **19.** no real solutions **23.** 1 **25.** $\frac{3}{8}, \frac{1}{2}$ **27.** -2 **29.** *Sample answer:* The solution $x = -9$ does not check in the original equation, so it is an extraneous solution. The only real solution is $x = 2$. **31.** no real solutions **33.** $\frac{16}{5}$

11.3 Problem Solving (pp. 733–734) **37.** 1977 **39.** 2.1 m

11.4 Skill Practice (pp. 740–741) **1.** hypotenuse **3.** $b = 4$ **5.** $c = \sqrt{61}$ **7.** $c = 8\sqrt{2}$ **9.** $c = 4\sqrt{13}$ **11.** $a = 8$ **13.** $a = 1.6$ **17.** 2, 4 **19.** 3, 4, 5, or 7, 24, 25 **21.** 2 in., 6 in. **23.** not a right triangle **25.** not a right triangle **27.** right triangle **31.** *Sample answer:* Let $m = 3$ and $n = 6$. Then $a = 6^2 - 3^2 = 27$, $b = 2(3)(6) = 36$, $c = 6^2 + 3^2 = 45$; substitute the values from the equation for a, b, and c in the Pythagorean theorem: $(n^2 - m^2)^2 + (2mn)^2 = (n^2 + m^2)^2$. Simplify to $n^4 - 2m^2n^2 + m^4 + 4m^2n^2 = n^4 + 2m^2n^2 + m^4$; $-2m^2n^2 + 4m^2n^2 = 2m^2n^2$; $2 = 2$. The equations are equal, so by the converse of the Pythagorean theorem, the lengths a, b, and c are a Pythagorean triple.

11.4 Problem Solving (pp. 741–742) **33.** 16 ft **35.** No; the sum of the squares of the two shorter sides is not equal to the square of the longer side. **37. a.** $\sqrt{6}$ **b.** $\sqrt{8}$ **c.** $\sqrt{n+1}$. *Sample answer:* A list of the hypotenuse lengths for the first few triangles is $\sqrt{2}, \sqrt{3}, \sqrt{4}, \sqrt{5}, \ldots$. A general formula for this series is $c_n = \sqrt{n+1}$.

11.5 Skill Practice (pp. 747–748) **1.** midpoint **3.** 1 **5.** 5 **7.** $\sqrt{53}$ **9.** $2\sqrt{17}$ **11.** $\sqrt{397}$ **13.** $\sqrt{73}$ **17.** 1, 25 **19.** -11, 1 **21.** -7, 15 **23.** $(5, -5)$ **25.** $(1, -4)$ **27.** $(-11, -6)$ **29.** $(-2, 0)$ **31.** $(-8, -4.5)$ **33.** $(-21, -33)$ **35.** *Sample answer:* The square of the difference in the x values and the square of the difference in the y values should be added, not subtracted; $d = \sqrt{(3 - (-17))^2 + (8 - (-2))^2} = \sqrt{400 + 100} = \sqrt{500} = 10\sqrt{5}$. **39.** $(8, -2)$ **41.** right triangle **43.** not a right triangle **45.** *Sample answer:* Use the distance formula to find the distance between the midpoint and each of the endpoints. If they are equal, the midpoint is equidistant from each endpoint.

11.5 Problem Solving (pp. 748–750) **47. a.** 10 mi **b.** $\sqrt{2}$ times greater **49. a.** the anchor and the cup **b.** the belt buckle and the sword; the anchor and the sword **51.** Yes; yes; all of them; the quadrilateral is a square.

11.5 Problem Solving Workshop (p. 751) **1. a.** Natural History Museum **b.** 0.24 mi

Chapter Review (pp. 754–756) **1.** It is a vertical stretch by a factor of 3 of the graph of $y = \sqrt{x}$. **3.** converse of the Pythagorean theorem

5. 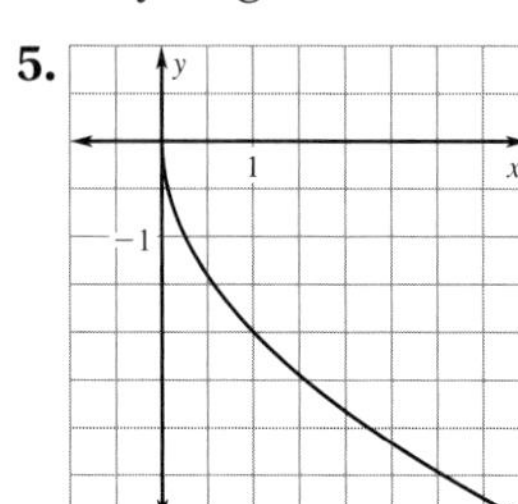
domain: $x \geq 0$, range: $y \leq 0$; vertical stretch by a factor of 2 with a reflection in the x-axis

7. 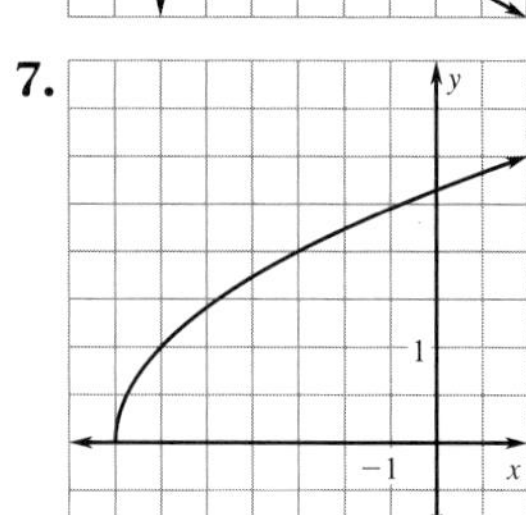
domain: $x \geq -7$, range: $y \geq 0$; horizontal translation of 7 units to the left

9. $11x\sqrt{x}$ **11.** $7x\sqrt{7}$ **13.** $\frac{2\sqrt{5}}{5}$ **15.** $7\sqrt{2} - 2\sqrt{3}$ **17.** 784 **19.** 5 **21.** no real solutions **23.** $c = \sqrt{218}$ **25.** $b = \sqrt{57}$ **27.** $a = \sqrt{209}$ **29.** 2036 ft **31.** 10 **33.** (3.5, −4) **35.** (5, −2)

Chapter 12

12.1 Skill Practice (pp. 769–770) **1.** −3 **3.** direct variation **5.** neither **7.** inverse variation **9.** direct variation **11.** inverse variation **13.** direct variation

15. 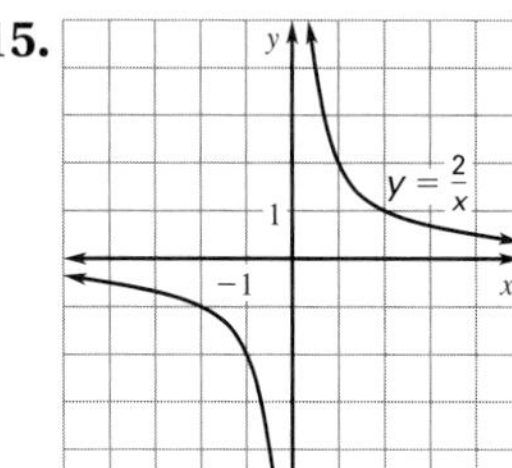

17.

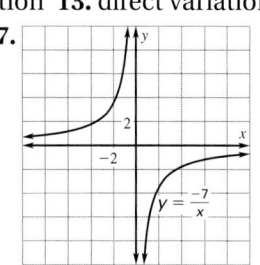

19. 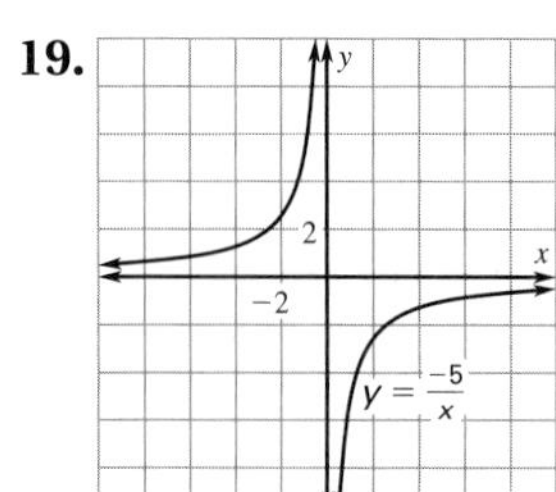

21. 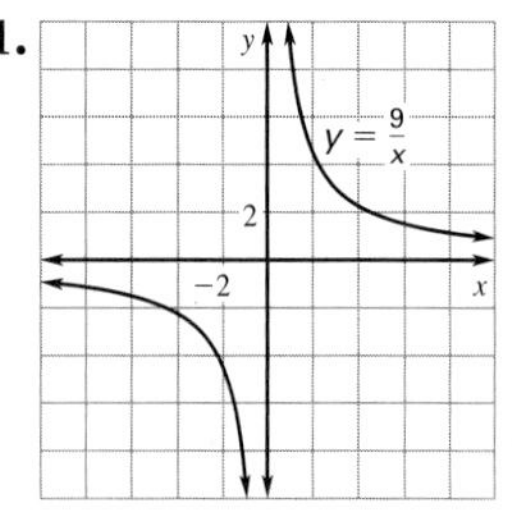

23. 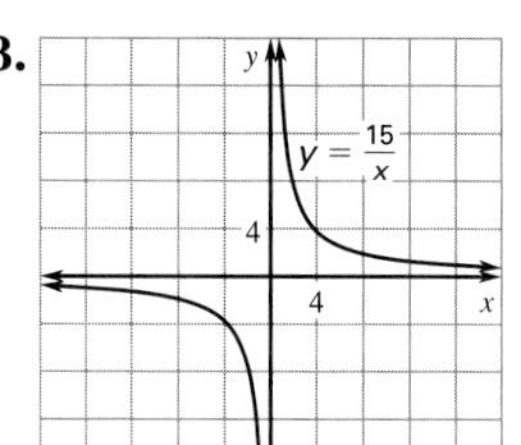

25. 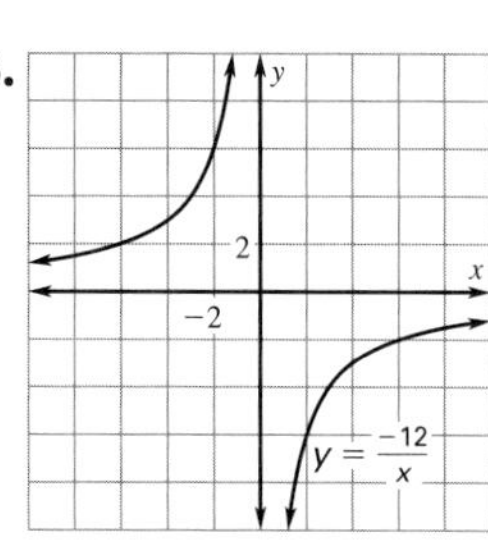

27. An inverse variation equation is in the form $y = \frac{a}{x}$, not $y = ax$; $8 = \frac{a}{2}$, $16 = a$. The correct inverse variation equation is $y = \frac{16}{x}$. **29.** $y = \frac{21}{x}$; 10.5 **31.** $y = \frac{-13}{x}$; −6.5 **33.** $y = \frac{132}{x}$; 66 **35.** $y = \frac{-18}{x}$; −9 **37.** $y = \frac{20}{x}$; 10 **39.** $y = \frac{70}{x}$; 35 **41.** $y = \frac{66}{x}$; 33 **45.** not inverse variation **47.** inverse variation; $y = \frac{-24}{x}$ **49.** $2\pi r = C$; direct variation **51.** $Bh = 400$; inverse variation

12.1 Problem Solving (pp. 770–772)

55. $d = \frac{175{,}000}{p}$; 350 units

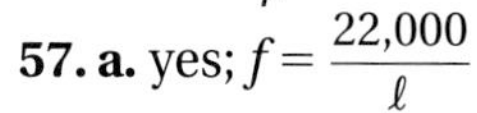

57. a. yes; $f = \frac{22{,}000}{\ell}$

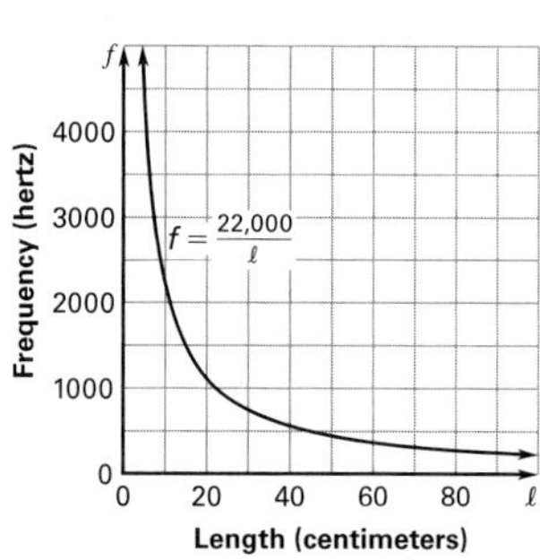

b. about 748 Hz **c.** The frequency increases; yes.

59. a. $s = \frac{35}{a}$ inverse variation

b. 4; when $s = 4$, the diameter of the aperture is $a = \frac{35}{4} = 8.75$ millimeters, and when $s = 8$, the diameter of the aperture is $a = \frac{35}{8} = 4.375$ millimeters.

12.2 Skill Practice (pp. 779–780) **1.** $x = 3, y = -6$

3.

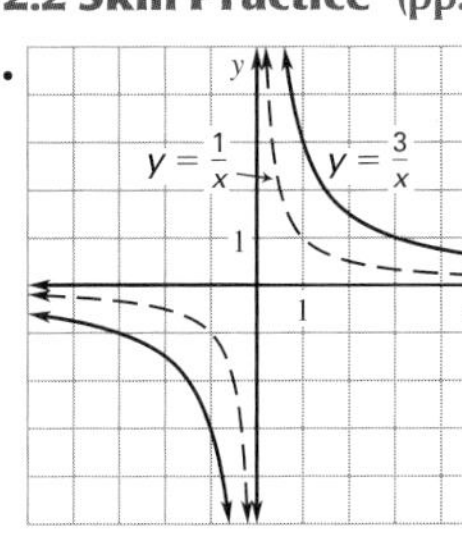

Domain: all real numbers except 0, range: all real numbers except 0; the graph is a vertical stretch of the graph of $y = \frac{1}{x}$.

5.

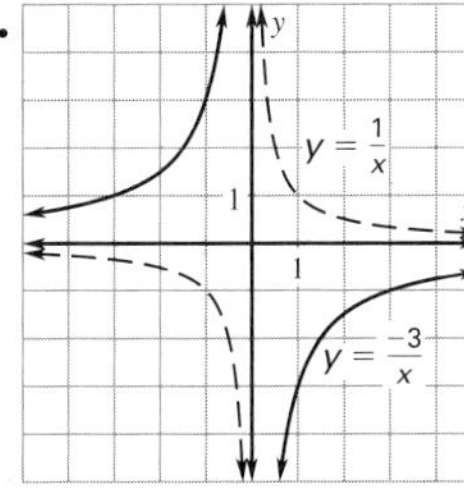

Domain: all real numbers except 0, range: all real numbers except 0; the graph is a vertical stretch of the graph of $y = \frac{1}{x}$ that is then reflected in the x-axis.

7.

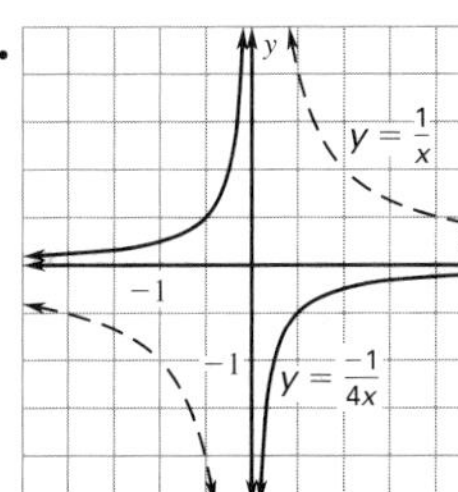

Domain: all real numbers except 0, range: all real numbers except 0; the graph is a vertical shrink of the graph of $y = \frac{1}{x}$ that is then reflected in the x-axis.

9.

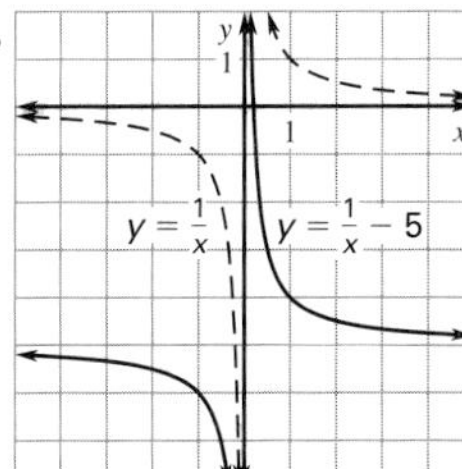

Domain: all real numbers except 0, range: all real numbers except −5; the graph is a vertical translation (of 5 units down) of the graph of $y = \frac{1}{x}$.

11.

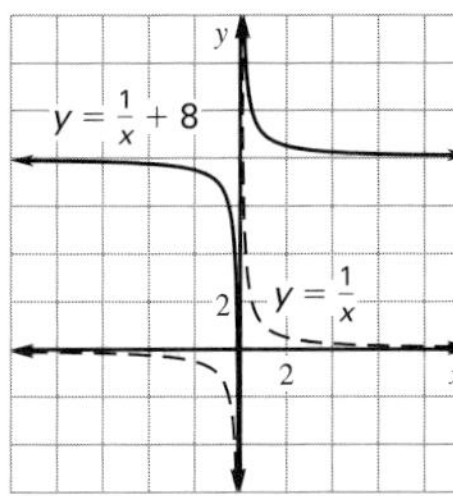

Domain: all real numbers except 0, range: all real numbers except 8; the graph is a vertical translation (of 8 units up) of the graph of $y = \frac{1}{x}$.

13.

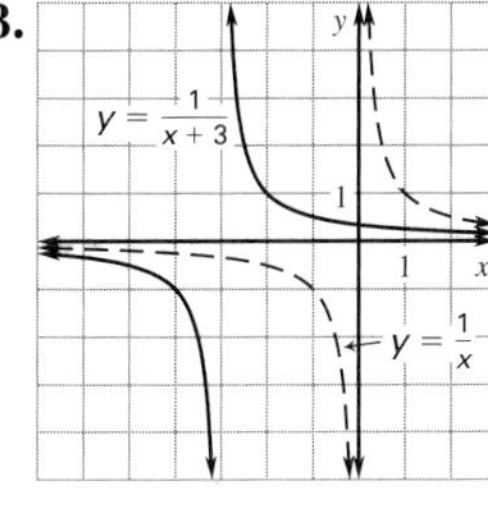

Domain: all real numbers except −3, range: all real numbers except 0; the graph is a horizontal translation (of 3 units left) of the graph of $y = \frac{1}{x}$.

15.

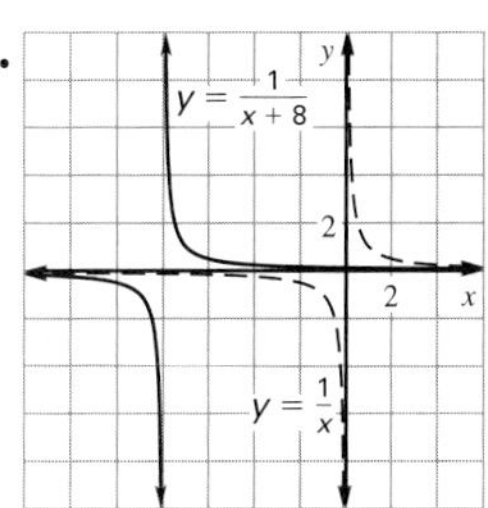

Domain: all real numbers except −8, range: all real numbers except 0; the graph is a horizontal translation (of 8 units left) of the graph of $y = \frac{1}{x}$.

17.

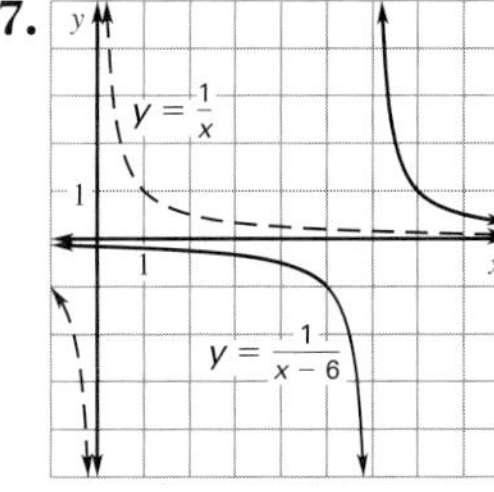

Domain: all real numbers except 6, range: all real numbers except 0; the graph is a horizontal translation (of 6 units right) of the graph of $y = \frac{1}{x}$.

19.

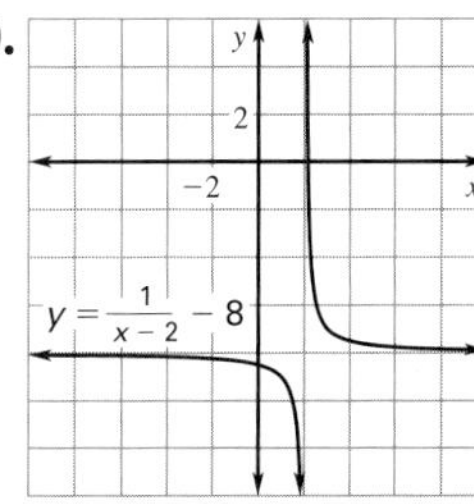

21.

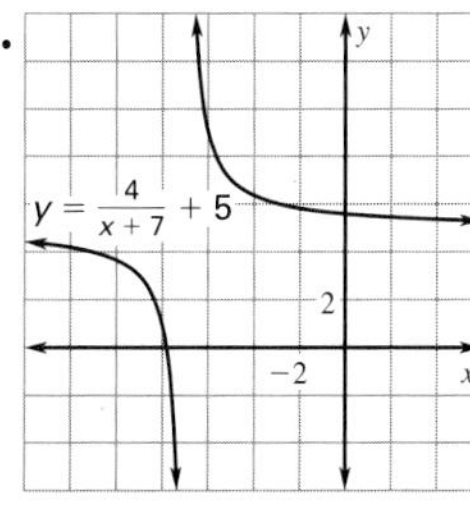

23.

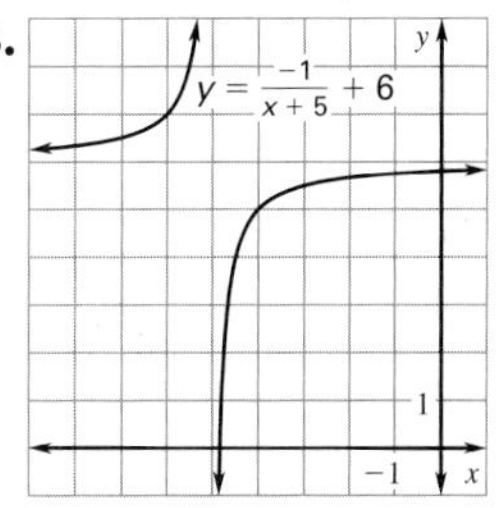

25.

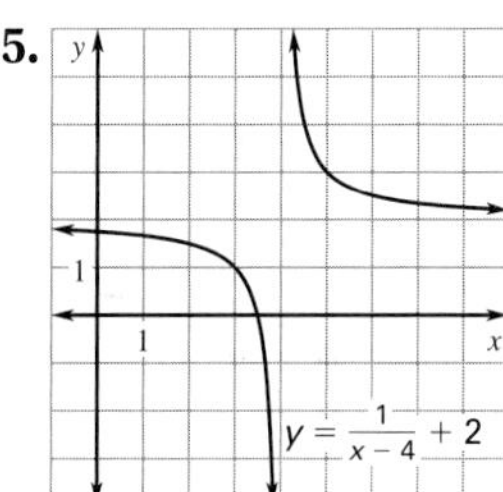

27.

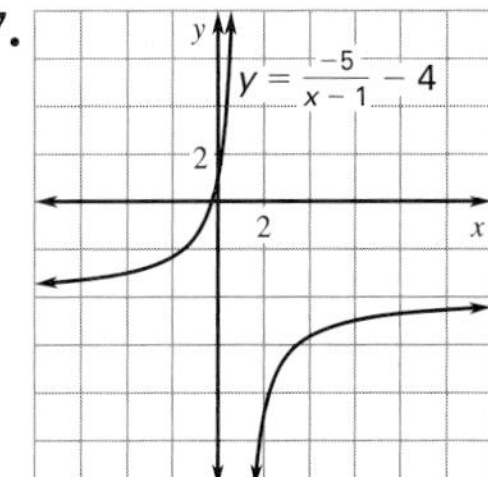

29. *Sample answer:* $y = \frac{1}{x + 1} + 2$ **31.** To identify the asymptotes of the hyperbola, write its equation in the form $y = \frac{a}{x - h} + k$: $y = \frac{-2}{x - 6} + 7$; thus the horizontal asymptote is $y = 7$, not $y = -7$. **33.** $y = \frac{-28}{x + 2} + 5$ **35.** $y = \frac{-28}{x + 4} - 4$

37. a. $h = \dfrac{100}{b_2 + 4}$

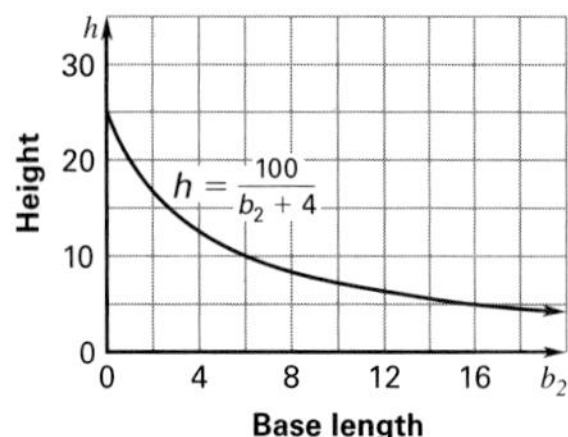

domain: $b_2 > 0$, range: $0 < h < 25$ **b.** about 13

12.2 Problem Solving (pp. 780–782)

39. $C = \dfrac{900}{p} + 400p$

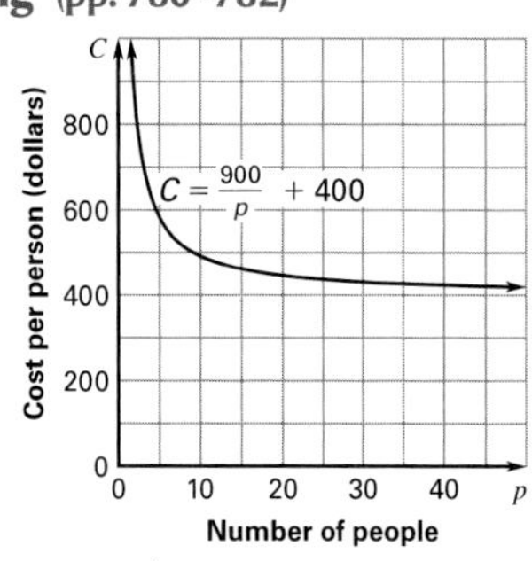

41. a. $C = \dfrac{22}{r + 2}$

b.

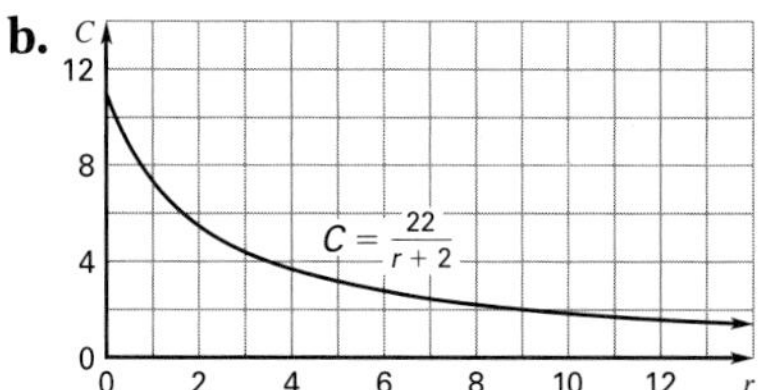

13 additional rentals

43.

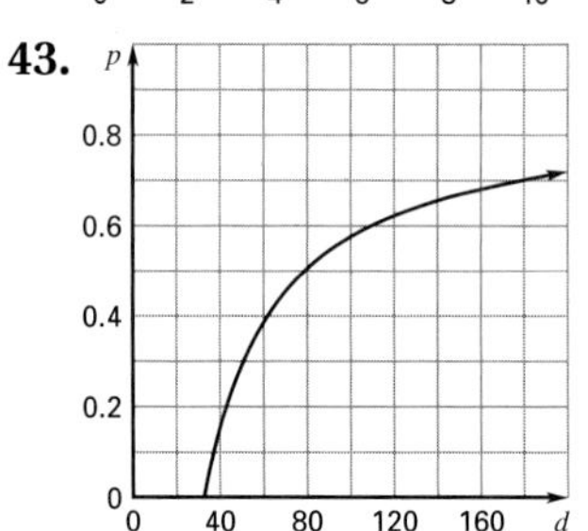

Domain: $d \geq 32.8$, range: $0 \leq p < 0.859$; the percent of time gliding increases.

12.3 Skill Practice (pp. 788–789)

1. monomial **3.** $2x^2 - 3x + 4$ **5.** $-2r^3 + 5r + 12$ **7.** $3v + 5$ **9.** $m - 4$ **11.** $a - 4 + \dfrac{-1}{a - 1}$ **13.** $3p - 13 + \dfrac{18}{3 + p}$ **15.** $x + 3 + \dfrac{-12}{6 + x}$ **17.** $-t - 3 + \dfrac{-4}{t - 3}$ **21.** When subtracting $8x - 24$ from $8x - 9$, the result is $-9 - (-24) = -9 + 24 = 15$; $(8x - 9) \div (x - 3) = 8 + \dfrac{15}{x - 3}$.

23.

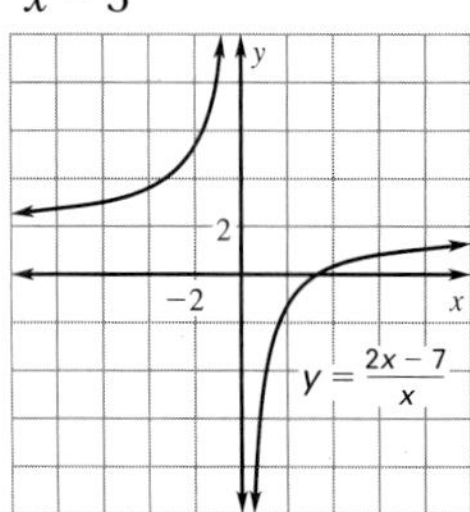

25.

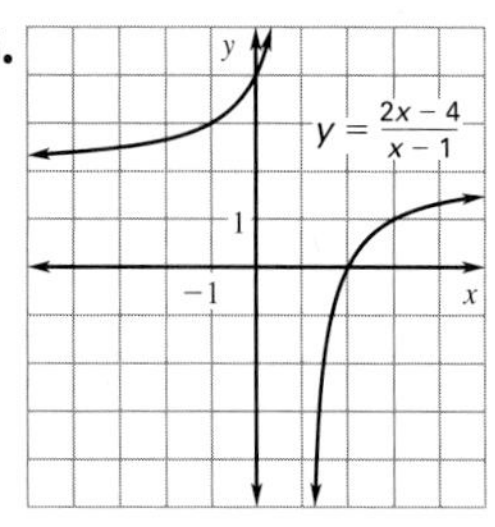

27.

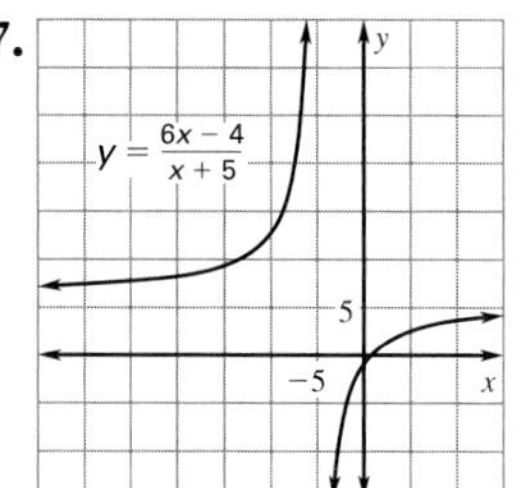

29.

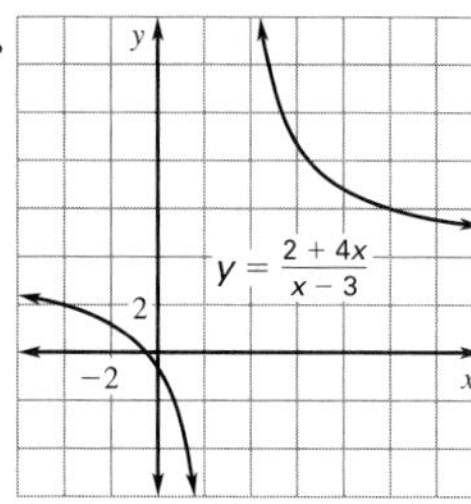

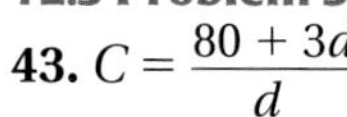
31. $\dfrac{7}{6} + \dfrac{2}{\ell}$ **35.** 10 **37.** -5

12.3 Problem Solving (pp. 789–791)

43. $C = \dfrac{80 + 3d}{d}$

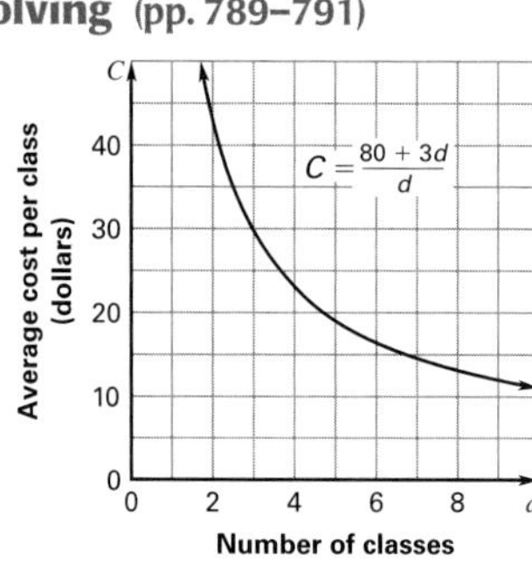

45. a. $C = \dfrac{0.4t - 360}{t}$

b.

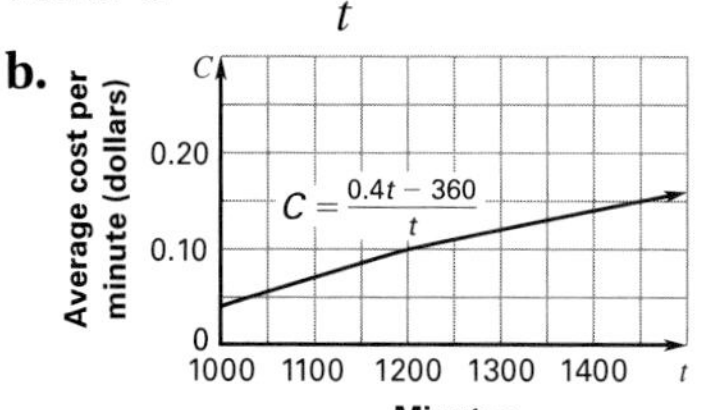

The average cost increases. **c.** about 1030 min

47. a.

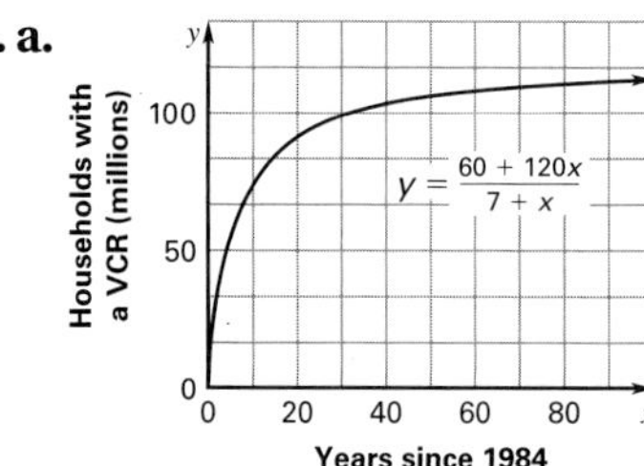

The number of households with VCRs increased.

b. No; as x increases, the graph of the function approaches its horizontal asymptote $y = 120$ from below, so the value of y will never exceed 120 million if this model applies to years beyond 2000.

49. a. $y = \dfrac{2r + 2\ell}{r\ell}$

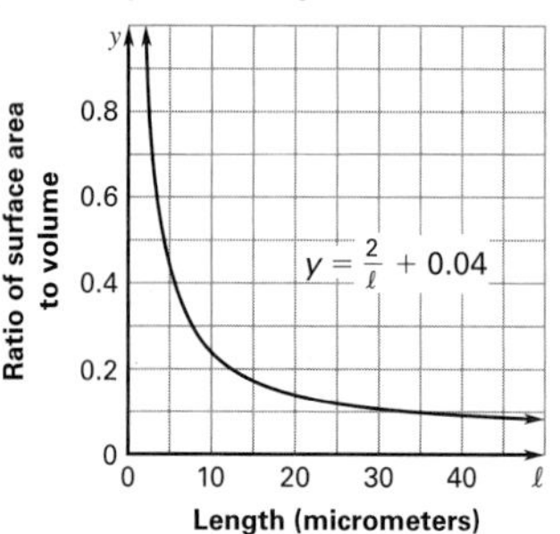

b. More efficient; the graph in part (a) shows that as the length increases, the ratio decreases, implying that the microorganism becomes more efficient at performing metabolic tasks. **c.** The microorganism's efficiency would increase. *Sample answer:* Suppose the length is fixed at 50 micrometers. Then $y = \frac{2r + 100}{50r}$, or $y = \frac{2}{r} + 0.04$. This equation has the same graph as the graph shown in part (a); from the graph we see that as the radius increases, the ratio decreases, implying that the microorganism's efficiency increases.

12.3 Graphing Calculator Activity (pp. 792–793)

1. 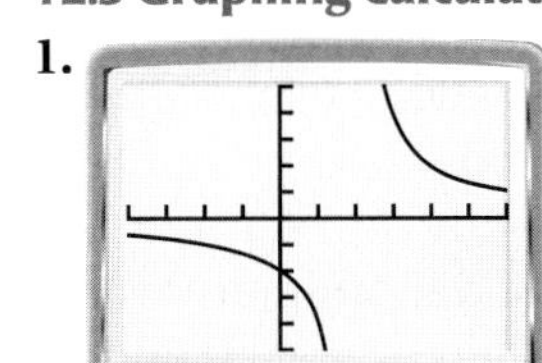 vertical: $x = 2$, horizontal: $y = 0$

3. 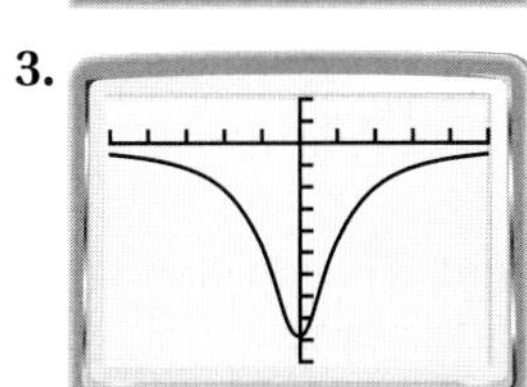 vertical: none, horizontal: $y = 0$

5. 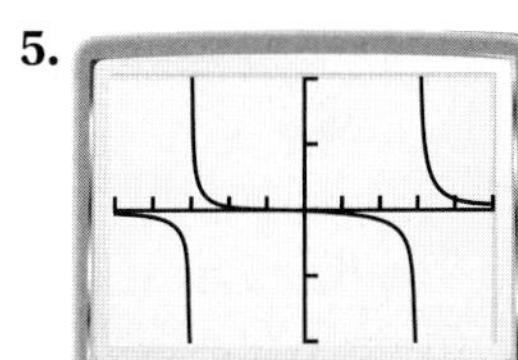 vertical: $x = -3$, $x = 3$, horizontal: $y = 0$

9. 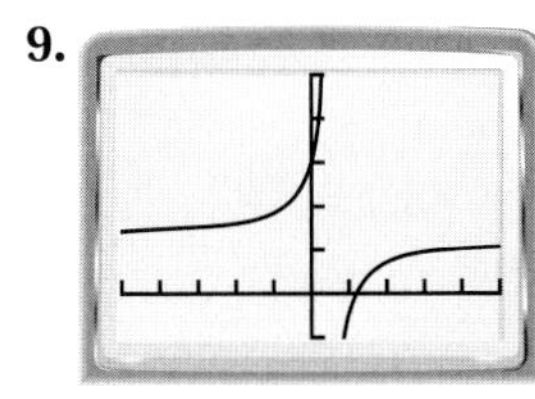 vertical: $x = 1$, horizontal: $y = 5$

11. 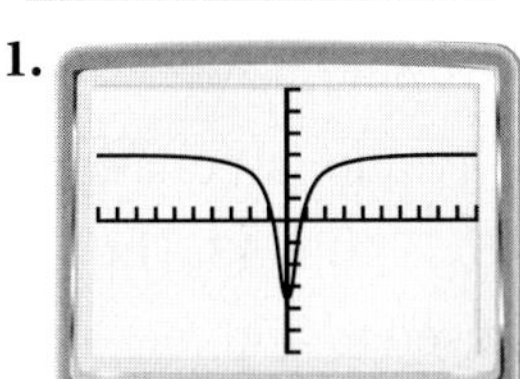 vertical: none, horizontal: $y = 3$

13. 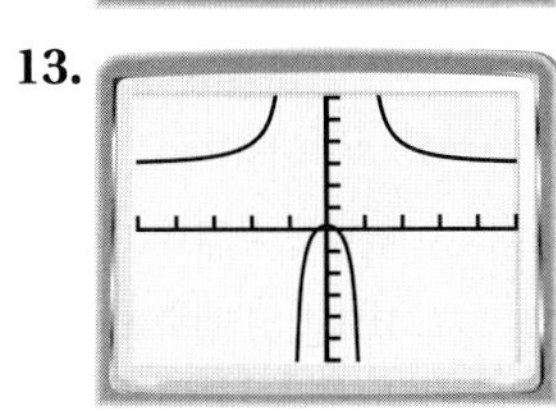 vertical: $x = -1$, $x = 1$, horizontal: $y = 3$

15. Vertical lines $x = a$, where a is an x-value that makes the denominator of the rational function equal to 0. **17.** $y = a$, where a is the quotient of the leading coefficient of the numerator and the leading coefficient of the denominator.

12.4 Skill Practice (pp. 797–798) **1.** excluded value **3.** none **5.** -1 **7.** none **9.** $0, \frac{1}{2}$ **11.** When finding the excluded values you must find the values for which the denominator of the original expression, $2x^2 - 11x + 12$, is 0; the excluded values are $\frac{3}{2}$ and 4. **13.** $\frac{2x}{5}$; none **15.** $-3a$; 0 **17.** 3; -11 **19.** -2; 3 **21.** $\frac{2}{f^2 - 9}$; ± 3 **23.** $\frac{1}{h - 4}$; $-3, 4$ **25.** $\frac{-6}{2w - 5}$; $0, \frac{5}{2}$ **27.** 3; 0, 4 **29.** $\frac{s + 8}{s - 1}$; $-8, 1$ **31.** $\frac{1}{m^2 + 5m}$; $0, -5$ **33.** No; the two expressions do not have the same excluded values; the excluded values for $\frac{x^2 + x}{x^2 - 1}$ are ± 1, while the excluded values for $\frac{x^2}{x^2 - x}$ are 0 and 1. The expressions are not equivalent for $x = 0$ and for $x = -1$. **37.** $\frac{3(x + 2)}{x(x + 6)}$

12.4 Problem Solving (pp. 799–800)

41. $p = \frac{3x^2 - 12}{22x^2 + 2500}$; about 11% **43.** $p = \frac{-202x + 3660}{345x + 9130}$; the percent of wood houses decreased.
45. a. $R = \frac{37{,}500 + 2500x}{125 + x}$; about \$522 million

b. 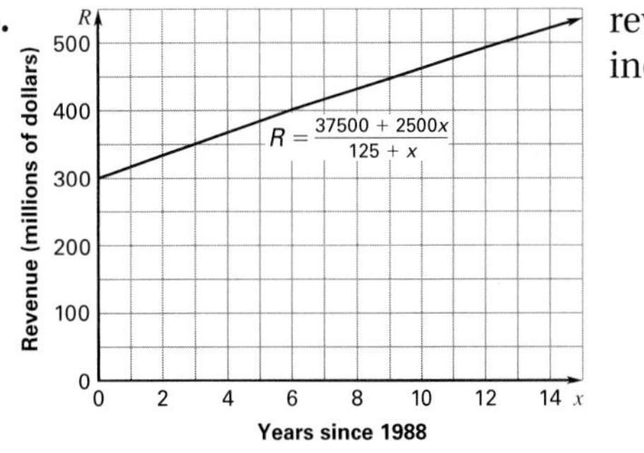

revenue increased

c. No; if the price per copy of printed music went up during the period 1988–2002, then the revenue may have increased without the number of copies sold increasing.

SELECTED ANSWERS

12.5 Skill Practice (pp. 806–807) **1.** multiplicative inverse **3.** $\frac{15}{14p^2}$ **5.** $\frac{-(v-3)}{5(v+1)}$ **7.** $\frac{x+4}{2x+1}$ **9.** $\frac{-3m}{m-2}$

11. To divide by the rational expression $\frac{15x^3}{2}$, you must multiply by its multiplicative inverse, $\frac{2}{15x^3}$; $\frac{x^3}{5} \cdot \frac{2}{15x^3} = \frac{2x^3}{75x^3} = \frac{2}{75}$. **13.** $\frac{20r^3}{9}$ **15.** $\frac{2w+5}{w(w-9)}$ **17.** $\frac{a+5}{3a^2}$ **19.** 1 **23.** $8x^2 \cdot \frac{1}{2x^3}$; $\frac{4}{x}$ **25.** $\frac{1}{x^2-3x-4} \div \frac{2}{x^2-1}$; $\frac{x-1}{2(x-4)}$

27. *Sample answer:* $\frac{x^2-2x-3}{x^2-2x-8}$, $\frac{x^2-9x+20}{x^2-4x-5}$

29. $(x-1)(x-3)$. *Sample answer:* 0

12.5 Problem Solving (pp. 807–809)

33. $p = \frac{100+2.2x}{(1-0.014x)(1500+63x)}$; about 7%

35. a. $R = \frac{(86+180x)(1+0.014x)}{(1+0.024x)(23+38x)}$

b.

Year	1990	1991	1992	1993	1994	1995	1996
Rushing average, *R* (yards per attempt)	3.74	4.32	4.42	4.44	4.44	4.42	4.40

Year	1997	1998	1999	2000	2001	2002
Rushing average, *R* (yards per attempt)	4.38	4.35	4.33	4.30	4.28	4.25

Smith's career rushing average increased for the first several years and then began to decrease.

37. a. $T = \frac{4700-74x}{(1-0.053x)(0.015x^2+4.1)}$

b.

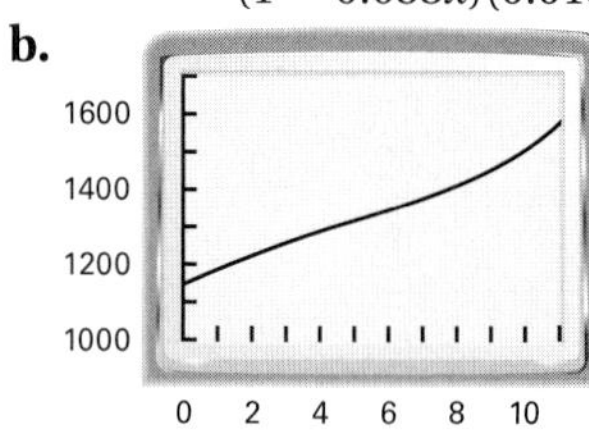

The number of tickets increased. No; the graph only shows how the *ratio* of the gross revenue and the ticket prices changed. *R* and *P* could go up and/or down while their ratio increases.

c.

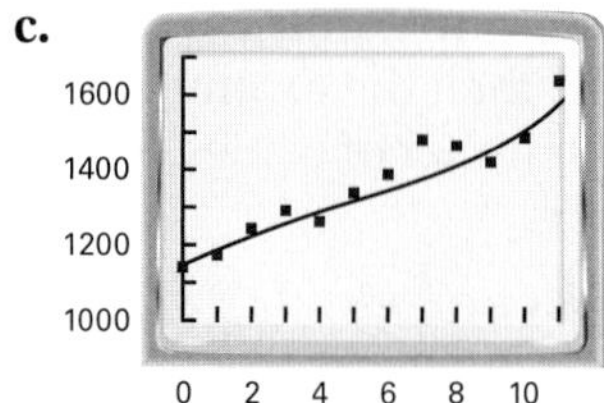

The points of the scatter plot are very close to the graph of the model for all years except 1998, 1999, and 2002.

Extension (p. 811) **1.** $\frac{3x^3}{28}$ **3.** $\frac{x}{2(x-3)(x-7)}$ **5.** $x^2(x-1)$ **7.** $\frac{5(x+4)}{2}$ **9.** $\frac{2(x+3)(x-1)}{5(3x+1)}$ **11.** $\frac{3(r+\ell)}{rh}$

13. No; $\frac{\frac{a}{b}}{c} = \frac{a}{b} \div c = \frac{a}{b} \cdot \frac{1}{c} = \frac{a}{bc}$ and $\frac{a}{\frac{b}{c}} = a \div \frac{b}{c} = \frac{a}{1} \cdot \frac{c}{b} = \frac{ac}{b}$. Thus, $\frac{\frac{a}{b}}{c} \neq \frac{a}{\frac{b}{c}}$.

12.6 Skill Practice (pp. 816–817) **1.** least common denominator **3.** $\frac{1}{x}$ **5.** $\frac{4}{z}$ **7.** $\frac{2b+1}{b-3}$ **9.** $\frac{-1}{m^2+1}$ **11.** $\frac{3r+1}{r^2+r-7}$ **13.** $60v^3$ **15.** $(s+2)(s-1)$ **17.** $(u+7)(u+1)(u-3)$ **19.** To rewrite each rational expression using the least common denominator, you must multiply its numerator by the factor of the LCD that is missing from the denominator: the numerator $5x$ should be multiplied by $(x+3)$ and the numerator 2 should be multiplied by $(x-4)$; $\frac{5x}{x-4} + \frac{2}{x+3} = \frac{5x(x+3)}{(x-4)(x+3)} + \frac{2(x-4)}{(x-4)(x+3)} = \frac{5x^2+15x+2x-8}{(x-4)(x+3)} = \frac{5x^2+17x-8}{(x-4)(x+3)}$.

21. $\frac{149}{33y}$ **23.** $\frac{5r^2-17r}{(r-2)(r-3)}$ **25.** $\frac{4c^2+13c+30}{(c-6)(3c+10)}$ **27.** $\frac{-20f^2+7f+12}{7f(f+4)}$ **29.** $\frac{3j^2-12j-1}{(j+1)(j-1)(j-6)}$ **31.** $\frac{-v^2+6v+20}{(2v+5)(v-3)(v+5)}$ **33.** $\frac{S-2\ell w}{2(\ell+w)}$ **35.** $\frac{15x^2+120x+20}{(x-2)(x+8)}$ **37.** $\frac{-3x^2+29x-4}{x-9}$ **39.** $y = \frac{-4x-16}{x+2}$

12.6 Problem Solving (pp. 817–819) **43.** $t = \frac{400r-1000}{r(r-5)}$; about 8.4 h **45. a.** $\frac{2A^2+200A}{3}$; $\frac{7A^2+18{,}750A-205{,}050}{150}$ **b.** 2600 lb; 6301 lb **47.** $f = \frac{2.5+0.215x}{5.3+0.30x}$; about 58%

12.7 Skill Practice (pp. 823–824) **1.** rational equation **3.** ± 10 **5.** $-1\frac{1}{2}$ **7.** $-1\frac{1}{2}$, 4 **9.** -6, 5 **11.** 6 **13.** The distributive property must be used to find the product of 5 and $(4x+1)$; $5(4x+1) = 3(8x-1)$, $20x+5 = 24x-3$, $8 = 4x$, $2 = x$. The solution is 2. **15.** -10 **17.** -22 **19.** $2 \pm 2\sqrt{3}$ **21.** no solution **23.** $-\frac{1}{5}$, -1 **25.** All real numbers except 2; 2; two fractions with equal denominators must also have equal numerators, so $x = 2$, and the denominator of both fractions is $2 - a$. The equation has this one solution as long as the denominator $2 - a$ is not 0; so, the equation has no solution when $a = 2$.

27. a. $\left(\frac{8}{3}, 9\right)$, $(-2, -5)$ **b.**

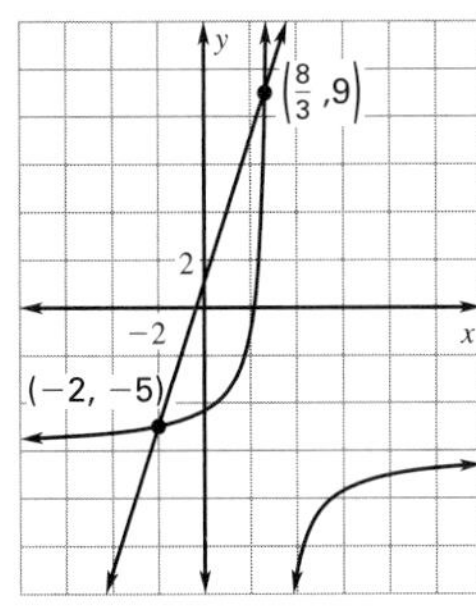

29. No; suppose that $\frac{x+a}{x+1+a} = \frac{x}{x+1}$. Then, using the cross products property, $(x+1)(x+a) = x(x+1+a)$; $x^2 + xa + x + a = x^2 + x + xa$; $x^2 + x(a+1) + a = x^2 + x(1+a)$. Then, subtracting $x^2 + x(1+a)$ from both sides gives the result $a = 0$; so, the only value of a for which the equation is true is 0.

12.7 Problem Solving (pp. 824–826) **31.** 50 consecutive shots **33.** 3 c **35. a.** $\frac{30}{t} + \frac{30}{1.5t} = 1$; 50 min **b.** Change each 30 to 20, and change 1.5 to 1; 40 min. **c.** Because you now both rake at the same rate, whenever you work together, the time it takes to rake a portion of the lawn will be half the time it takes either of you to rake that portion alone. Suppose you rake together for m minutes. Then you each rake $\frac{m}{40}$ of the lawn, and together you rake $\frac{m}{40} + \frac{m}{40} = \frac{2m}{40} = \frac{m}{20}$ of the lawn. To rake $\frac{m}{20}$ of the lawn alone would take you $2m$ minutes. **37.** From 8 psi to 7 psi; substitute the given psi values for p in the given equation and then solve for a: for $p = 10$, $a \approx 10{,}722$; for $p = 9$, $a \approx 13{,}536$; for $p = 8$, $a \approx 16{,}600$; for $p = 7$, $a \approx 19{,}948$. The change in altitude when the atmospheric pressure changes from 10 psi to 9 psi is about $13{,}536 - 10{,}722 = 2814$, and the change in altitude when the atmospheric pressure changes from 8 psi to 7 psi is about $19{,}948 - 16{,}600 = 3348$.

12.7 Problem Solving Workshop (p. 828)
1. \$1250 **3.** 6 free throws **5.** 75 min

Chapter Review (pp. 831–834) **1.** asymptote **3.** $x = -2$, $y = -4$ **5.** $y = \frac{63}{x}$, 12.6 **7.** inverse variation; $y = \frac{-8}{x}$

9.

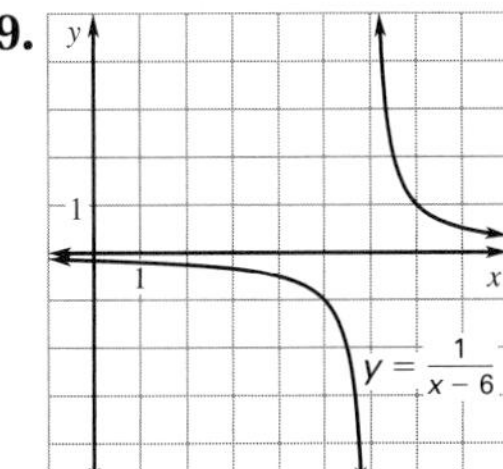

11. $x + 5$ **13.** $z - 1 + \frac{4}{z+5}$

15. $a = \frac{500 + 2d}{d}$

17. −2, 6 **19.** $\frac{m-3}{4}$; 0 **21.** $\frac{-(r+2)}{r+1}$; −1, 2 **23.** $\frac{21v^7}{4}$ **25.** $\frac{-8x+33}{5x-3}$ **27.** $\frac{5c^2 - 13c - 48}{(c+1)(c-4)(c+2)}$ **29.** −6, 9 **31.** $\frac{-21}{5}$

Chapter 13

13.1 Skill Practice (pp. 846–847) **1.** probability **3.** 12 outcomes; R1, R2, R3, R4, W1, W2, W3, W4, B1, B2, B3, B4 **5.** 48; HHH1, HHH2, HHH3, HHH4, HHH5, HHH6, HHT1, HHT2, HHT3, HHT4, HHT5, HHT6, HTH1, HTH2, HTH3, HTH4, HTH5, HTH6, HTT1, HTT2, HTT3, HTT4, HTT5, HTT6, THH1, THH2, THH3, THH4, THH5, THH6, THT1, THT2, THT3, THT4, THT5, THT6, TTH1, TTH2, TTH3, TTH4, TTH5, TTH6, TTT1, TTT2, TTT3, TTT4, TTT5, TTT6 **7.** $\frac{9}{10}$ **9.** $\frac{1}{10}$ **11.** $\frac{3}{7}$ or 3 : 7 **13.** *Sample answer:* Odds in favor is the number of favorable outcomes divided by the number of unfavorable outcomes; odds in favor of a multiple of 3 = $\frac{\text{Number of favorable outcomes}}{\text{Number of unfavorable outcomes}} = \frac{9}{1}$ or 9 : 1. **15.** *Sample answer:* Rolling a standard number cube and getting a 0, flipping a coin and getting heads or tails.

17.

	1	2	3	4	5	6
1	2	3	4	5	6	7
2	3	4	5	6	7	8
3	4	5	6	7	8	9
4	5	6	7	8	9	10
5	6	7	8	9	10	11
6	7	8	9	10	11	12

$P(2) = \frac{1}{36}$; $P(3) = \frac{1}{18}$; $P(4) = \frac{1}{12}$; $P(5) = \frac{1}{9}$, $P(6) = \frac{5}{36}$; $P(7) = \frac{1}{6}$; $P(8) = \frac{5}{36}$; $P(9) = \frac{1}{9}$; $P(10) = \frac{1}{12}$; $P(11) = \frac{1}{18}$; $P(12) = \frac{1}{36}$

13.1 Problem Solving (pp. 847–848) **19.** $\frac{1}{7}$ **21.** $\frac{4}{9}$, $\frac{4}{5}$. *Sample answer:* The probability and odds of choosing a boy are related because both compare the number of boys to another number. The probability of choosing a boy compares the number of boys to the total number of outcomes, while the odds of choosing a boy compare the number of boys to the total number of outcomes minus the number of boys.

SELECTED ANSWERS

Extension (p. 850) **1.** Answers will vary. **3.** *Sample answer:* There are 3 prizes to win, but since the prizes do not have an equal likelihood of being won, generating a list of random integers from 1 to 3 would not represent the situation. The probability of winning a CD is $\frac{1}{6}$, so if there were only 3 possible outcomes in the simulation you could not represent winning a CD properly.

13.2 Skill Practice (pp. 853–854) **1.** permutation **3. a.** 2 ways **b.** 2 ways **5. a.** 24 ways **b.** 12 ways **7. a.** 120 ways **b.** 20 ways **9. a.** 120 ways **b.** 20 ways **11.** *Sample answer:* 5 people are running in a race. How many different results can there be for first and second place? **13.** 6 **15.** 120 **17.** 3,628,800 **19.** 6,227,020,800 **21.** 210 **23.** 720 **25.** 1 **27.** 6,375,600 **29.** The denominator should be $(5 - 3)! = 2!$, not $3!$; ${}_5P_3 = \frac{5!}{(5-3)!} = \frac{5!}{2!} = 60.$

13.2 Problem Solving (pp. 854–855) **35. a.** $\frac{1}{2}$. *Sample answer:* Make a list of possible permutations, count the number in which you are first or second, and divide it by the total number of outcomes. **b.** $\frac{1}{2}$; the answers are the same. **37.** $\frac{1}{720}$

13.3 Skill Practice (p. 858) **1.** combination **3.** 20 combinations **5.** *Sample answer:* The answer given is for ${}_9P_4$, not ${}_9C_4$; ${}_9C_4 = \frac{9!}{(9-4)! \cdot 4!} = \frac{9!}{5! \cdot 4!} =$ 126. **7.** 56 **9.** 28 **11.** 330 **13.** 15,504 **17.** Permutations; since the roles are different, the order in which students are selected for the roles matters; 720 ways. **19.** Permutations; the arrangement of people in the car matters; 120 ways. **21.** ${}_nC_r = {}_nP_r \cdot \frac{1}{r!}$. *Sample answer:* To find the number of combinations, you find the number of permutations and then divide by the number of ways the items being chosen can be arranged, or $r!$.

13.3 Problem Solving (p. 859) **23.** 840 burritos **25. a.** 84 combinations **b.** $\frac{5}{21}$. *Sample answer:* There are 84 possible outcomes of the choice. Find the number of combinations that include you and your 2 friends. After you and your friends are chosen, 3 other contestants from a pool of 6 can be chosen in any combination, so the number of favorable combinations is ${}_6C_3 = 20$. The probability that you and your friends are chosen is $\frac{20}{84} = \frac{5}{21}$.

13.3 Graphing Calculator Activity (p. 860) **1.** 35 **3.** 120 **5.** 15,120 **7.** 6,652,800 **9. a.** 3276 groups **b.** 6 ways

13.4 Skill Practice (pp. 864–865) **1.** dependent **3.** mutually exclusive; $\frac{2}{3}$ **5.** overlapping; $\frac{5}{6}$ **7.** To find the probability that you draw a yellow *or* a blue marble, the individual probabilities should be added, not multiplied; $\frac{7}{16} + \frac{5}{16} = \frac{12}{16} = \frac{3}{4}$. **9.** independent; $\frac{1}{36}$ **11.** independent; $\frac{1}{12}$ **15.** $\frac{1}{64}$ **17.** If you first draw a pawn and then do not replace it, the probability of drawing a second pawn is not $\frac{16}{32}$, but $\frac{15}{31}$; $\frac{16}{32} \cdot \frac{15}{31} = \frac{15}{62}$. **19.** 69%

13.4 Problem Solving (pp. 866–867) **23.** 62.3%

25. a.

Mon	Tues	Wed	Thurs	Fri	Sat	Sun
st. gov.		st. gov.				
tutor			tutor	tutor	tutor	

b.

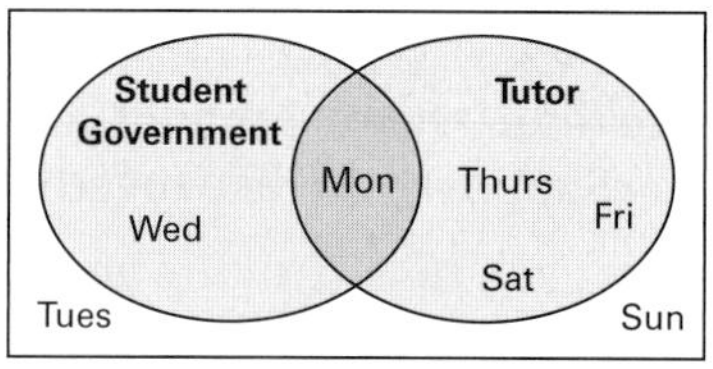

Student Government
Tutor
Wed
Mon
Thurs
Fri
Sat
Tues
Sun

c. $\frac{5}{7}$

13.4 Problem Solving Workshop (pp. 868–869) **1.** $\frac{4}{15}$ **3.** $\frac{1}{16}$. *Sample answer:* The third friend can arrive any time in a 20 minute span, and I will be away from the house for 15 of those minutes. The probability is $\frac{1}{4}$ that I will be home when the third friend arrives. Since the three friends arrive independently of each other, you can multiply the probability that you are home when the other two friends arrive by $\frac{1}{4}$ to calculate the probability that you are home when all three friends arrive; $\frac{1}{4} \cdot \frac{1}{4} = \frac{1}{16}$. **5.** *Sample answer:* The times at which the raffles are announced are independent, so the two probabilities should be calculated separately and then multiplied; $\frac{10}{30} \cdot \frac{25}{30} = \frac{1}{3} \cdot \frac{5}{6} = \frac{5}{18}$.

13.5 Skill Practice (p. 873) **1.** systematic **3.** people who have eaten at the restaurant, self-selected **5.** passengers of the airline, random **7.** Not likely. *Sample answer:* The sample should represent the neighborhood. **9.** Not potentially biased. *Sample answer:* This question simply presents the two choices.

11. *Sample answer:* The new question presumes that the driving age should be changed, and does not present the option that it should remain the same; "What do you think about the current driving age?"

13.5 Problem Solving (p. 874) **13.** *Sample answer:* This question is phrased to prompt people into agreeing that the athletic field is more important than the science lab; "Which do you think the school needs more: a new athletic field or a new science lab?" **15.** No. *Sample answer:* Only some of the fans are able to attend games, and those who attend games may have different player preferences than those who do not attend games. **17. a.** *Sample answer:* Obtain a list of everyone at the school and select names randomly using a random number generator. **b.** *Sample answer:* "How many hours per night do you study?"; This question is unbiased because it does not prompt respondents to give any particular answer.

13.6 Skill Practice (p. 877) **1.** mode **3.** 3, 3, 1 **5.** 22, 21, no mode **7.** 5.223, 5.48, no mode **11.** 65, 21.2 **13.** 70, 12.56 **15.** 0.85, 0.23 **17.** *Sample answer:* The range only considers the two extreme values, while the mean absolute deviation is affected by all of the values.

13.6 Problem Solving (pp. 877–878) **19. a.** 19 **b.** 19.6 lb, 23.5 lb, 24 lb **c.** Median. *Sample answer:* The mode is the greatest data value and the mean is less than 8 of the 10 data values. **21. a.** The range for Team 2 is 56 and the range for Team 1 is 52, so the scores for Team 2 cover a slightly wider range. **b.** The mean absolute deviation for Team 1 is 15.75 and the mean absolute deviation for Team 2 is 22.5, so the scores for Team 2 are more dispersed.

Extension (pp. 879–880) **1.** 6.3, 2.5 **3.** 76,656.6; 276.9 **5.** 29.1 **7. a.** 5.6 **b.** *Sample answer:* Since 136 is much greater than the mean, the standard deviation will increase. **c.** 17.7. *Sample answer:* The standard deviation more than tripled, so the prediction was correct.

13.7 Skill Practice (pp. 883–884) **1.** frequency

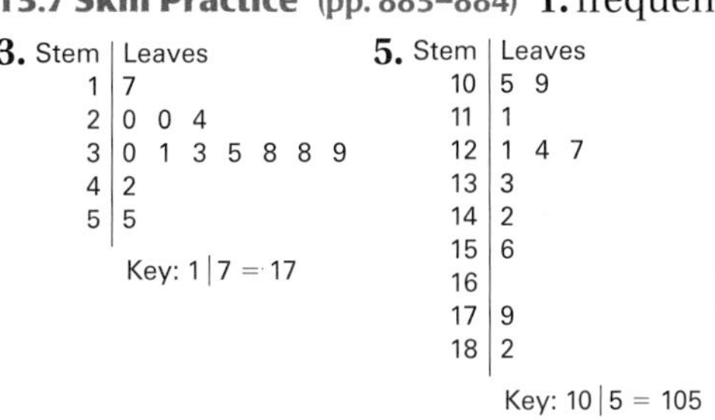

3. Stem | Leaves
1 | 7
2 | 0 0 4
3 | 0 1 3 5 8 8 9
4 | 2
5 | 5
Key: 1 | 7 = 17
5. Stem | Leaves
10 | 5 9
11 | 1
12 | 1 4 7
13 | 3
14 | 2
15 | 6
16 |
17 | 9
18 | 2
Key: 10 | 5 = 105

7. There is no key given for the stem-and-leaf plot; Key: 1 | 8 = 18.

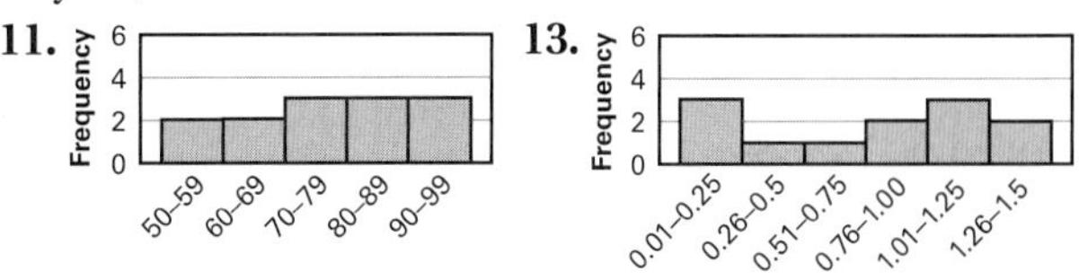

15. *Sample answer:* The given data range from 10 to 21, so a stem-and-leaf plot would place all the data into only two intervals, making it difficult to see the distribution of the data. The histogram could use more than two intervals.

13.7 Problem Solving (pp. 884–885)

17.

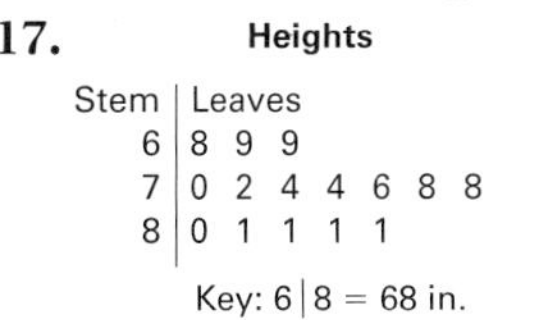

Heights
Stem | Leaves
6 | 8 9 9
7 | 0 2 4 4 6 8 8
8 | 0 1 1 1 1
Key: 6 | 8 = 68 in.

19. a.

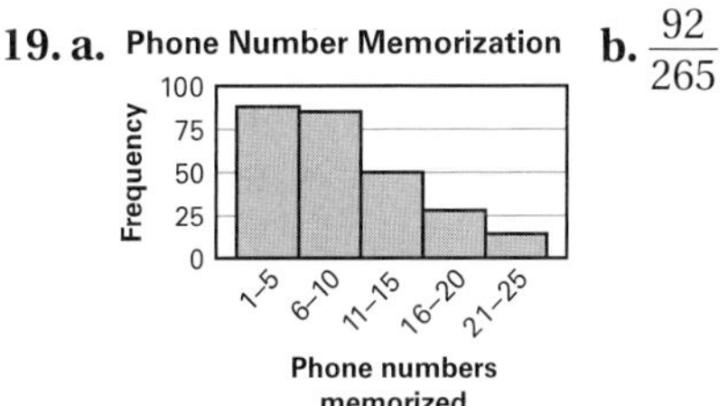

b. $\frac{92}{265}$

21. a. Ages of *Mayflower* Passengers

Stem	Leaves
1	8
2	0 0 0 1 1 1 1 1 5 5 5 9
3	0 0 0 2 2 4 4 5 7 8 8 8 8 8
4	0 1 2 5 5 8 9
5	0 4 5
6	4

Key: 1 | 8 = 18 years

b. median: 34 yr, range: 46 yr **c.** $\frac{1}{3}$. *Sample answer:* Since 13 of the 39 passengers or $\frac{1}{3}$ of them were ages 18–29, we can predict that another passenger about whom we have no information has a $\frac{1}{3}$ probability of being in that age group.

13.7 Graphing Calculator Activity (p. 886) **1.** *Sample answer:* The majority of the data are at the lower end of the scale, between 3000 and 12,000, with the highest frequency between 3000 and 6000.

13.8 Skill Practice (pp. 889–890) **1.** the difference of the upper quartile and the lower quartile

3.

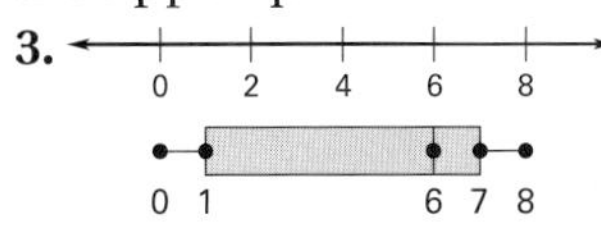

SELECTED ANSWERS

5.

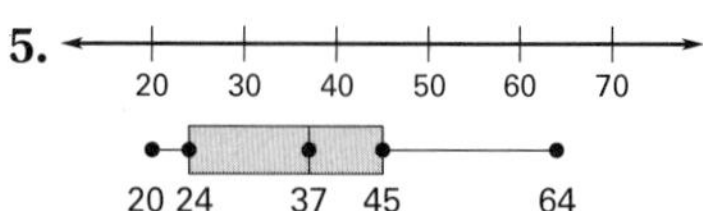

7. *Sample answer:* The upper quartile is incorrect. The upper quartile should be the median of 8 and 10, or 9.

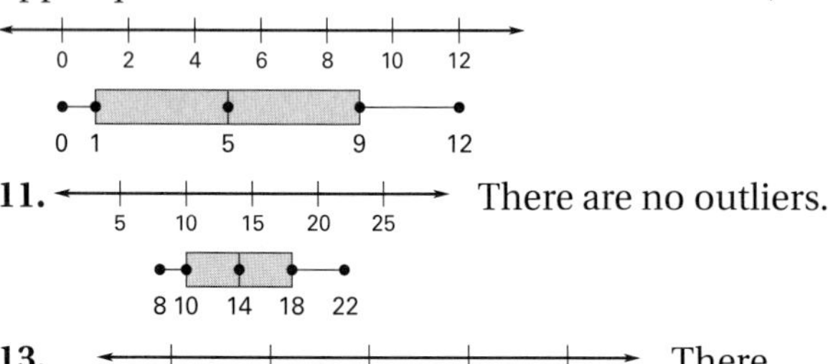

11. There are no outliers.

13. There are no outliers.

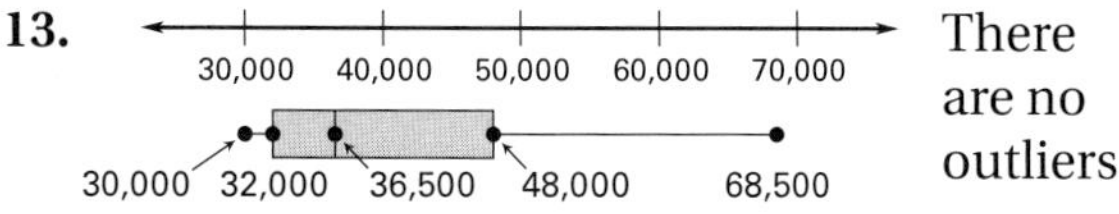

13.8 Problem Solving (pp. 890–892)

15.

17. a. b. none

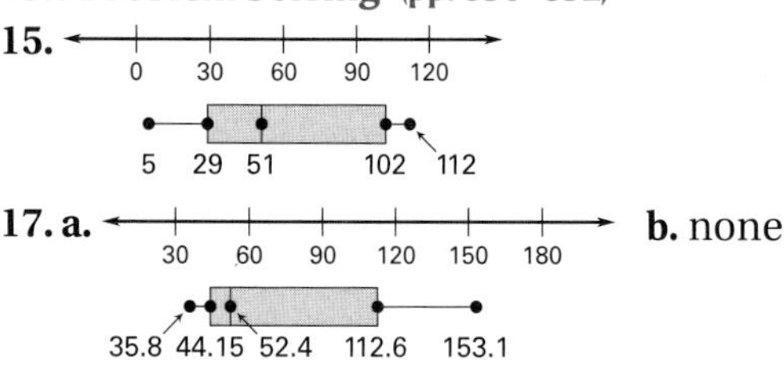

19. a. *Sample answer:* The craters on Ganymede are generally smaller than the craters on Callisto. The lower extreme, lower quartile, median, upper quartile, and upper extreme values are all lower for Ganymede than for Callisto. **b.** *Sample answer:* Chesapeake Bay is larger than between 50% and 75% of the craters on both Callisto and Ganymede. **c.** *Sample answer:* Vredefort is larger than at least 75% of the craters on both Callisto and Ganymede.

Chapter Review (pp. 896–900) **1.** compound event **3.** *Sample answer:* Theoretical probability is based on knowing the likelihood of all possible outcomes of an event. Experimental probability is based on the results of an experiment. **5.** $\frac{2}{9}$ **7.** 30 **9.** 1,037,836,800 **11.** 7 **13.** 56 **15.** 126 ways **17.** $\frac{3}{8}$ **19.** $\frac{5}{8}$ **21.** $\frac{1}{120}$ **23. a.** about 5.045, 4.5, 1 **b.** Median. *Sample answer:* The mode is much lower than many of the values, and the mean is affected by the two extreme values (17 and 19) that are much greater than the rest of the data. So, the median best represents the data.

25.

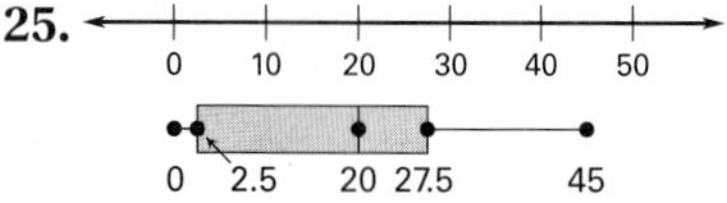

Cumulative Review (pp. 906–907) **1.** 44 **3.** ± 45 **5.** 2

7. 9.

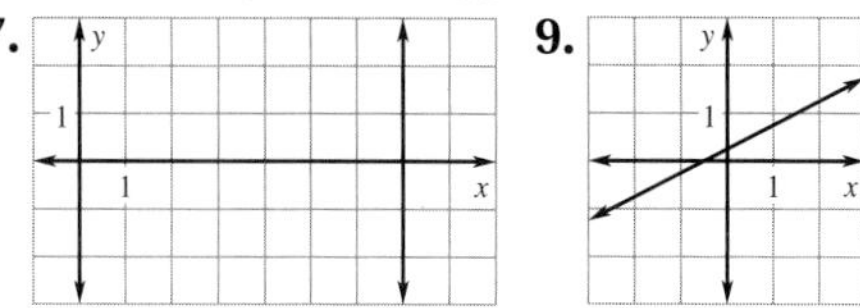

11. $y = -8x + 3$

13. $4 \le x < 24$

15. $\left(4, \frac{1}{4}\right)$ **17.** no solution **19.** $\frac{-81x^{12}}{4}$ **21.** $(a - 18)(a + 3)$ **23.** $(2f + g)^2$ **25.** $-7, 3$ **27.** $\frac{1}{2}, 4$ **29.** $2\sqrt{37}$ **31.** 15 **33.** $\frac{x + 4}{x + 3}$ **35.** -3 **37.** $\frac{9 - 3x}{x^2 - 3x}$ **39.** 336 **41.** 210 **43.** $\frac{1}{2}$ **45.** $\frac{3}{20}$ **47.** *Sample answer:* 120 min after the first runner starts **49.** 42.4 ft **51. a.** \$45

b.

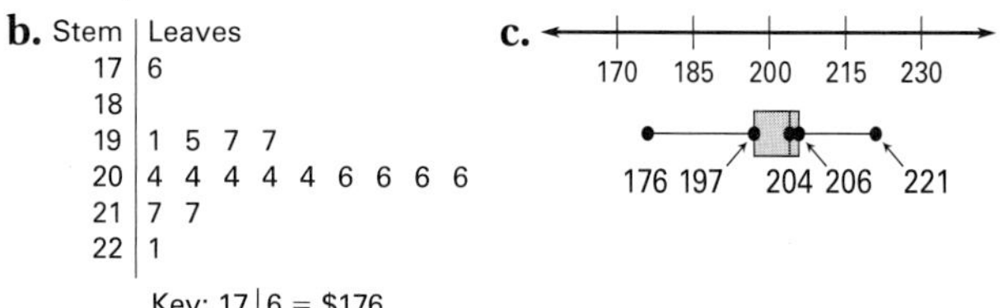

Stem	Leaves
17	6
18	
19	1 5 7 7
20	4 4 4 4 4 6 6 6 6
21	7 7
22	1

Key: 17 | 6 = \$176

c.

d. Yes. *Sample answer:* The interquartile range is 9, so any data value more than 13.5 less than the lower quartile of 197 or greater than the upper quartile of 206 can be considered outliers. 176 and 221 are both outliers.

Skills Review Handbook

Comparing and Ordering Decimals (p. 909) **1.** > **3.** > **5.** > **7.** < **9.** > **11.** 7.01, 7.03, 7.13, 7.3 **13.** 0.15, 0.3, 0.47, 0.9 **15.** 10.9, 11, 11.9, 12.6 **17.** 0.3, 1.33, 3.1, 3.3

Factors and Multiples (pp. 910–911) **1.** $2^2 \cdot 7$ **3.** prime **5.** 3^4 **7.** $2^2 \cdot 3 \cdot 5$ **9.** $2^2 \cdot 3^2 \cdot 5$ **11.** $3 \cdot 17$ **13.** 4 **15.** 6 **17.** 9 **19.** 4 **21.** 8 **23.** 4 **25.** 18 **27.** 45 **29.** 130 **31.** 90 **33.** 14 **35.** 49

Finding Equivalent Fractions and Simplifying Fractions (p. 912) **1–5.** Sample answers are given. **1.** $\frac{3}{4}$ and $\frac{18}{24}$ **3.** $\frac{2}{4}$ and $\frac{3}{6}$ **5.** $\frac{5}{7}$ and $\frac{20}{28}$ **7.** $\frac{1}{4}$ **9.** $\frac{1}{8}$ **11.** $\frac{1}{4}$ **13.** $\frac{7}{20}$ **15.** $\frac{4}{5}$ **17.** $\frac{3}{7}$ **19.** $\frac{4}{13}$

Mixed Numbers and Improper Fractions (p. 913) **1.** $\frac{5}{3}$ **3.** $\frac{103}{10}$ **5.** $\frac{9}{2}$ **7.** $\frac{23}{12}$ **9.** $\frac{53}{8}$ **11.** $\frac{65}{8}$ **13.** $\frac{65}{9}$ **15.** $\frac{38}{3}$ **17.** $2\frac{2}{5}$ **19.** $6\frac{1}{4}$ **21.** $1\frac{3}{4}$ **23.** $2\frac{9}{10}$ **25.** $10\frac{4}{5}$ **27.** $4\frac{2}{5}$ **29.** $4\frac{7}{9}$

Adding and Subtracting Fractions (p. 914) **1.** $\frac{1}{4}$ **3.** $\frac{1}{6}$ **5.** 1 **7.** $\frac{1}{2}$ **9.** $1\frac{1}{5}$ **11.** $\frac{3}{16}$ **13.** $\frac{25}{48}$ **15.** $1\frac{17}{24}$ **17.** $\frac{11}{20}$ **19.** $\frac{4}{5}$ **21.** $6\frac{3}{4}$ **23.** 5 **25.** $1\frac{1}{16}$

Multiplying and Dividing Fractions (p. 915) **1.** $\frac{1}{2}$ **3.** $\frac{1}{2}$ **5.** $1\frac{1}{8}$ **7.** $\frac{3}{64}$ **9.** $\frac{1}{8}$ **11.** $1\frac{1}{2}$ **13.** $\frac{1}{2}$ **15.** $\frac{2}{7}$ **17.** $\frac{1}{50}$ **19.** $\frac{3}{5}$ **21.** $3\frac{3}{32}$ **23.** $4\frac{3}{8}$ **25.** $1\frac{1}{3}$

Fractions, Decimals, and Percents (pp. 916–917) **1.** 0.7, $\frac{7}{10}$ **3.** 0.03, $\frac{3}{100}$ **5.** 0.35, $\frac{7}{20}$ **7.** 1.1, $1\frac{1}{10}$ **9.** 0.003, $\frac{3}{1000}$ **11.** $\frac{7}{25}$, 28% **13.** $\frac{1}{20}$, 5% **15.** $\frac{13}{25}$, 52% **17.** $\frac{1}{40}$, 2.5% **19.** $\frac{3}{2}$, 150% **21.** 0.188, 18.8% **23.** 0.61, 61% **25.** 0.19, 19% **27.** 0.36, 36% **29.** 0.571, 57.1%

Mean, Median, and Mode (p. 918) **1.** 92.4; 93; 94 **3.** 41 yr; 41 yr; 52 yr **5.** \$7; \$7; \$6.75 **7.** 2.25; 2; 2

Classifying Triangles and Quadrilaterals (pp. 919–920)
1. isosceles right triangle **3.** pentagon
5. hexagon **7.** parallelogram, rhombus
9. quadrilateral, parallelogram

The Coordinate Plane (p. 921) **1.** (5, 4) **3.** (10, 8) **5.** (9, 2) **7.** (2, 6) **9.** (10, 0) **11.** (0, 5)

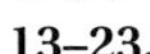
13–23.

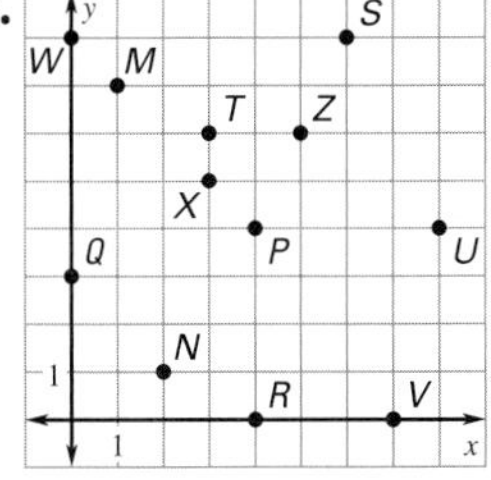

Transformations (pp. 922–923)

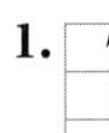
1.

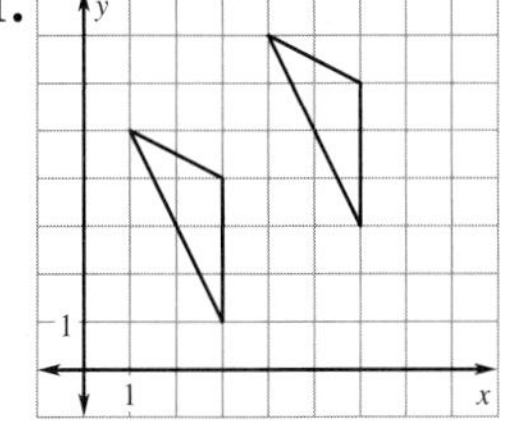

(4, 7), (6, 6), (6, 3)

3.

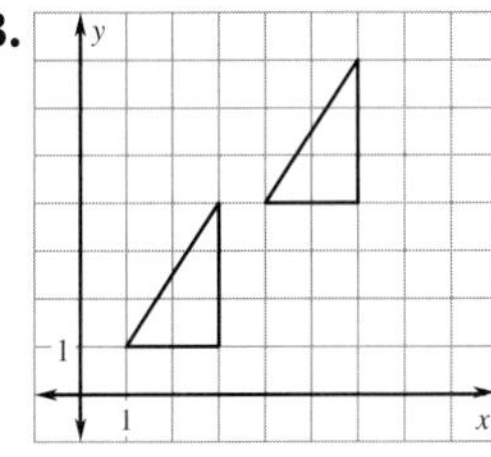

(1, 1), (3, 1), (3, 4)

5.

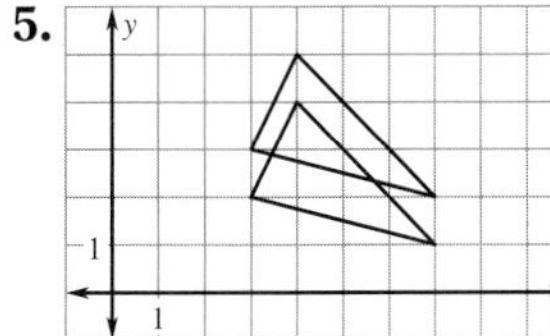

(4, 4), (7, 1), (3, 2)

7. (2, 0), (5, 0), (5, 2), (2, 2)

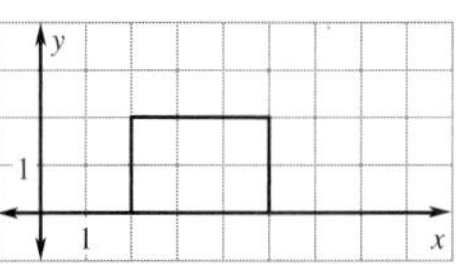

9.

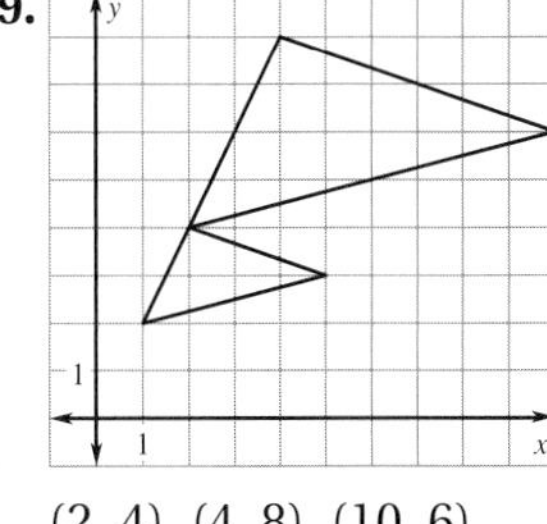

(2, 4), (4, 8), (10, 6)

11.

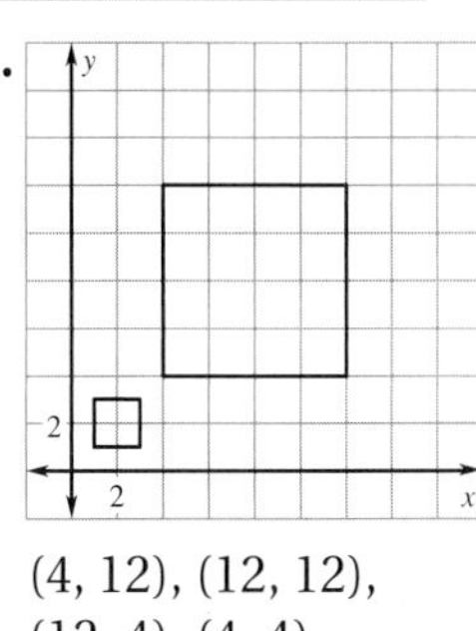

(4, 12), (12, 12), (12, 4), (4, 4)

13.

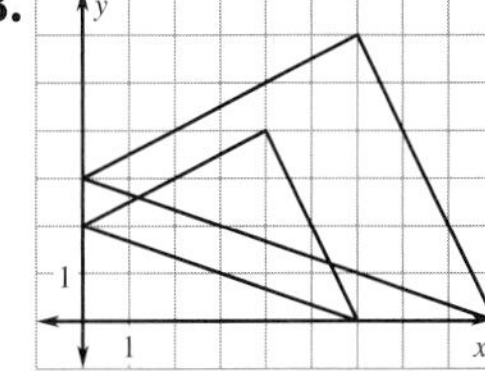

(0, 3), (6, 6), (9, 0)

Perimeter and Area (pp. 924–925) **1.** 36 ft **3.** 20 ft **5.** 66 yd^2 **7.** 110 $in.^2$ **9.** 21 ft^2 **11.** 70 yd^2

Circumference and Area of a Circle (p. 926) **1.** 12π in. or 37.7 in., 36π $in.^2$ or 113.0 $in.^2$ **3.** 16π in. or 50.2 in., 64π $in.^2$ or 201.0 $in.^2$ **5.** 4π ft or 12.6 ft, 4π ft^2 or 12.6 ft^2 **7.** 18π m or 56.5 m, 81π m^2 or 254.3 m^2

Surface Area and Volume (pp. 927–928) **1.** 320 cm^2, 336 cm^3 **3.** 900π m^2 or 2826 m^2, 4500π m^3 or 14,130 m^3 **5.** 200π $in.^2$ or 628 $in.^2$, 320π $in.^3$ or 1004.8 $in.^3$ **7.** 96 $in.^2$, 48 $in.^3$ **9.** 1888π $in.^2$ or 5928.3 $in.^2$, $11{,}008\pi$ $in.^3$ or 34,565.1 $in.^3$ **11.** 96π m^2 or 301.4 m^2, 96π m^3 or 301.4 m^3

Converting Units of Measurement (p. 929) **1.** 5 **3.** 4 **5.** 6 **7.** 14 **9.** 300 **11.** 70,000 **13.** 3000 **15.** 15 **17.** 2.5 **19.** 1,000,000 **21.** 28,800

Venn Diagrams and Logical Reasoning (p. 930)

1.

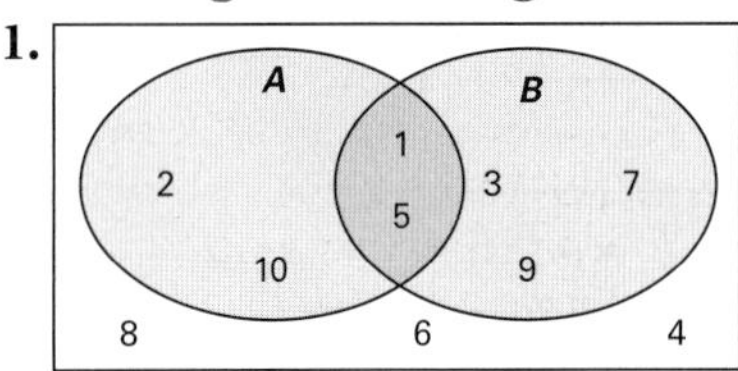

3. a. False; there are whole numbers less than 10 that are odd but are not factors of 10, such as 3, 7, and 9. **b.** False; there is a whole number less than 10 that is a factor of 10 but is not odd, 2.

SELECTED ANSWERS

Counting Methods (pp. 931–932) **1.** 6 ways **3.** 17,576 3-letter monograms **5.** 1,679,616 computer passwords **7.** 72 dinners

Bar Graphs (p. 933) **1.** bronze **3.** 103 medals **5.** 25 medals **7.** Switzerland **9.** United States **11.** 96 medals

Line Graphs (p. 934) **1.** about 24 lb **3.** between ages 4 and 5 **5.** about 15 lb **7.** about 2 years old **9.** between ages 3 and 4 **11.** between ages 1 and 2 **13.** about 4 yr

Circle Graphs (p. 935) **1.** 9% **3.** 24.5% **5.** 37% **7.** woodwinds **9.** brass

Problem Solving Strategies (pp. 936–937) **1.** Pam owes \$4 that she can pay to Bonnie who is owed a total of \$5. Holly should pay both Barb and Bonnie \$1. **3.** 25 years old **5.** 10 ways **7.** 1:45 P.M. **9.** 3 soccer games per week **11.** Quinn

Extra Practice

Chapter 1 (p. 938) **1.** 16 **3.** 4.4 **5.** 2.4 **7.** $\frac{8}{27}$ **9.** 26 **11.** 28 **13.** 10 **15.** 111 **17.** $\frac{3}{4}m$ **19.** $y - 3$ **21.** $45 - m$ **23.** $12 \cdot (r - 4) = 72$ **25.** 38 **27.** 16 **29.** *Sample answer:* You know the temperature in Quito in degrees Celsius and the temperature in Miami in degrees Fahrenheit. You need to find out which one is greater. **31.** domain: 3, 4, 5, 6; range: 9, 11, 13, 15

33.

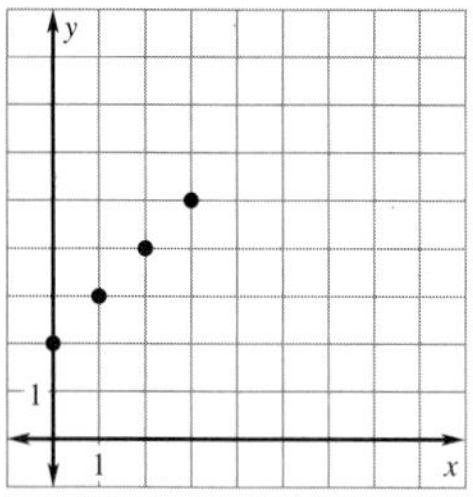

35.

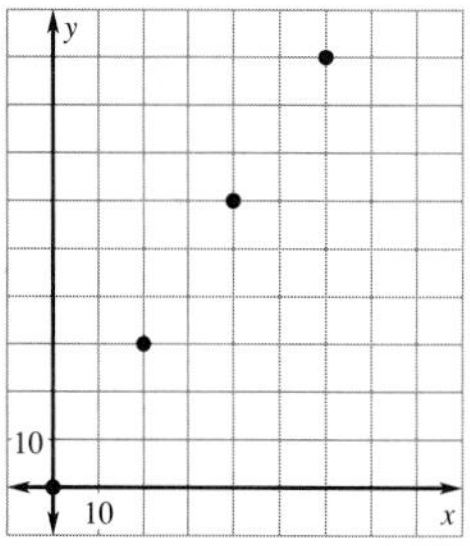

Chapter 2 (p. 939)

1.

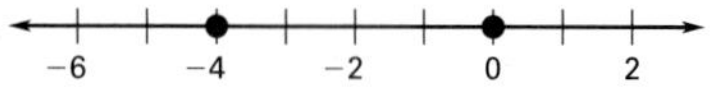

0

3.

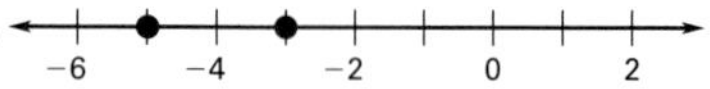

−3

5. Each number is a rational number; $-\frac{1}{5}, -\frac{1}{8}, -\frac{1}{10},$ 0.25. **7.** 3 and 0 are whole numbers, −4 and −5 are integers; −5, −4, 0, 3. **9.** −61 **11.** 0 **13.** −19.7 **15.** $-4\frac{13}{30}$ **17.** 66 **19.** $\frac{3}{10}$ **21.** $\frac{5}{12}$ **23.** −7.2 **25.** 5.5 **27.** −12.5 **29.** −40 **31.** 2.2 **33.** Associative property of multiplication **35.** Property of zero **37.** Property of −1

39. $30 - 5y$ **41.** $-3k + 42$ **43.** $14s + 7$ **45.** $5w + 25$ **47.** 23 **49.** 64 **51.** $-\frac{5}{6}$ **53.** $\frac{25}{36}$ **55.** ±20 **57.** ±12 **59.** −9 **61.** 16

Chapter 3 (p. 940) **1.** 16 **3.** −12 **5.** 9 **7.** 52 **9.** 6 **11.** 8 **13.** −35 **15.** 3 **17.** −6 **19.** −1 **21.** 2 **23.** 3 **25.** $-\frac{1}{2}$ **27.** 56 **29.** 16 **31.** $\frac{5}{7} = \frac{15}{x}$; 21 **33.** $\frac{g}{9} = \frac{16}{12}$; 12 **35.** 14 **37.** 8 **39.** 4 **41.** −2 **43.** 12.5% **45.** 35 **47.** 45 **49.** 86 **51.** $x = \frac{c + b}{a}$; 5 **53.** $y = -5x + 10$ **55.** $y = -4x + 2$

Chapter 4 (p. 941)

1.

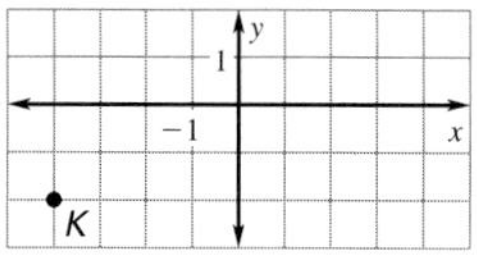

Quadrant III

3.

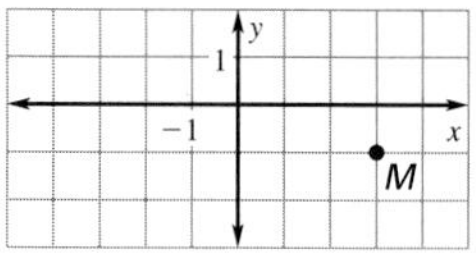

Quadrant IV

5.

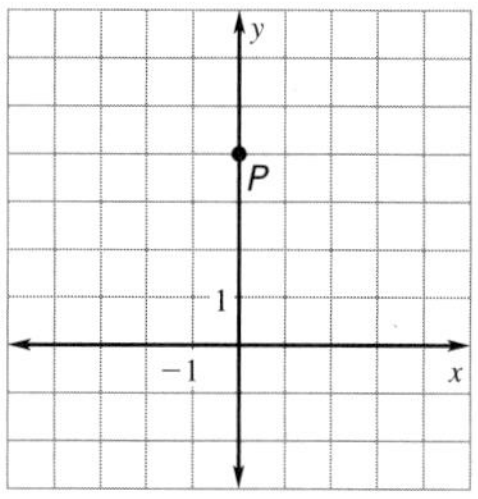

on the y-axis

7.

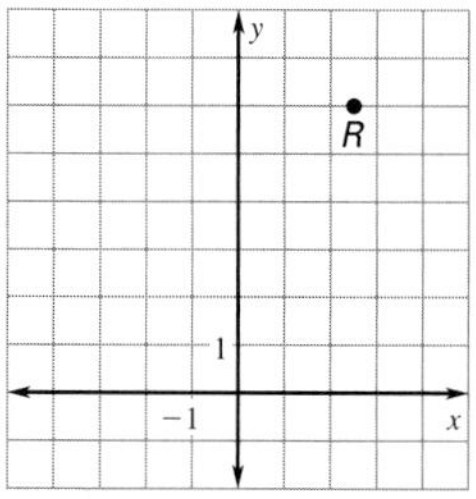

Quadrant I

9.

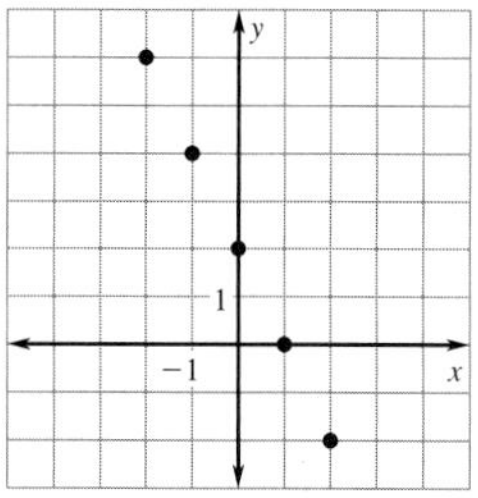

range: −2, 0, 2, 4, 6

11.

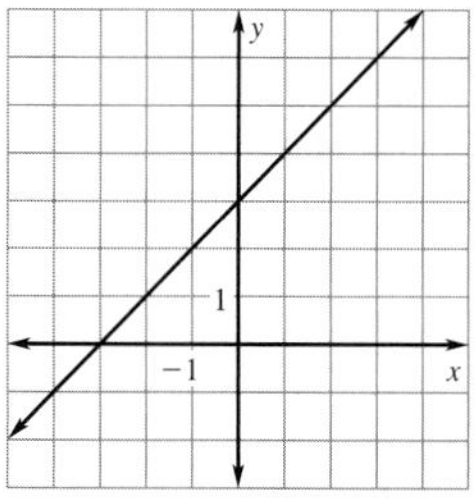

13.

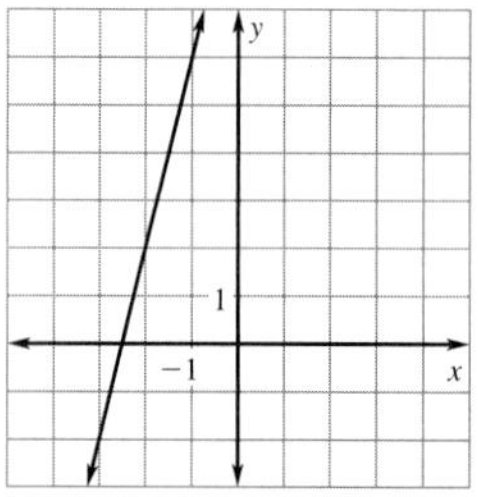

15.

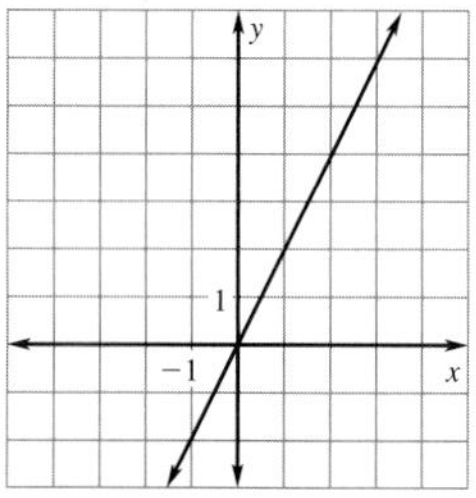

17.

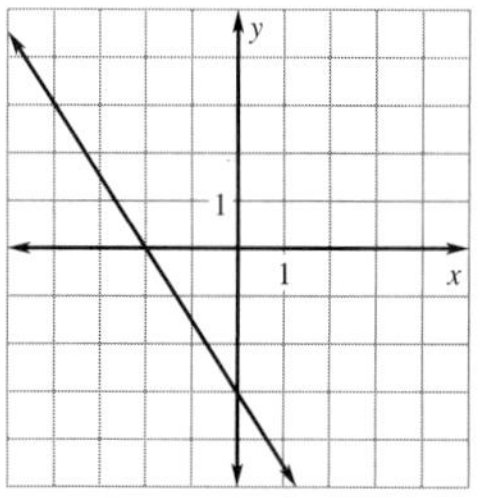

19. x-intercept: 6, y-intercept: −12 **21.** x-intercept: −1, y-intercept: $\frac{8}{3}$

23.

25. 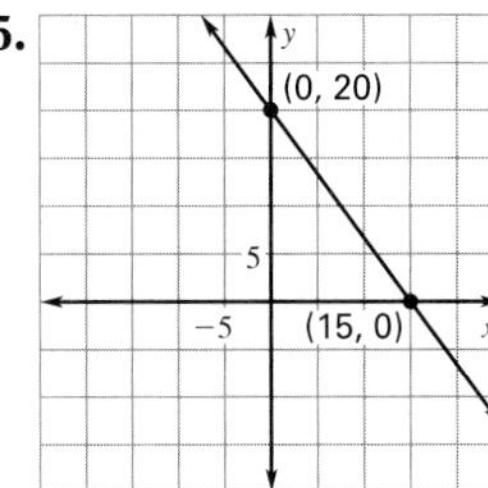

27. 3 **29.** $-\frac{7}{3}$ **31.** no slope **33.** slope: 7, y-intercept: 8 **35.** slope: −4, y-intercept: 3 **37.** $y = -2x + 8$; slope: −2, y-intercept: 8 **39.** $y = -\frac{5}{2}x + 5$; slope: $-\frac{5}{2}$, y-intercept: 5

41. 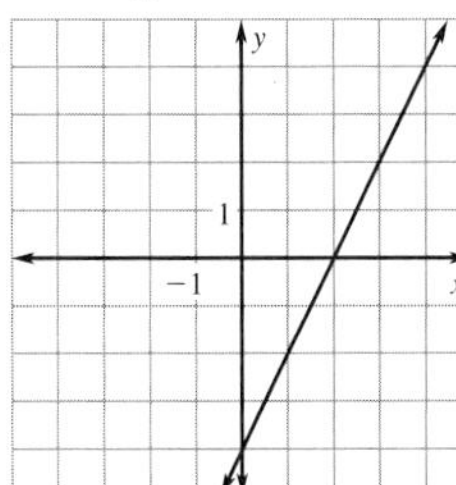

43. 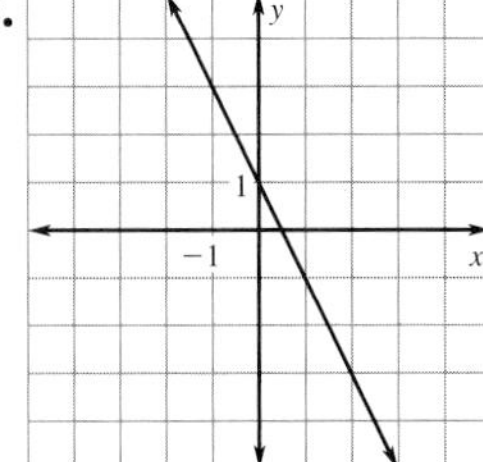

45. 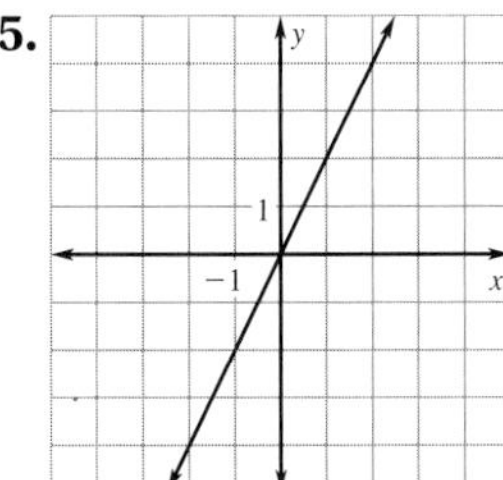

47. 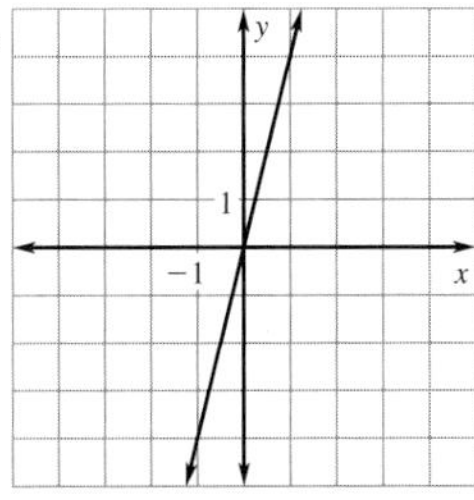

49. 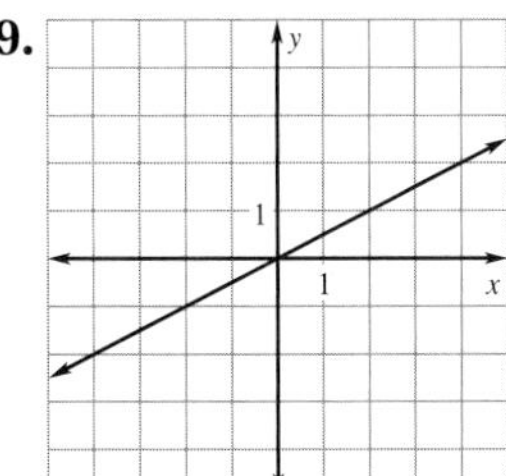

51. 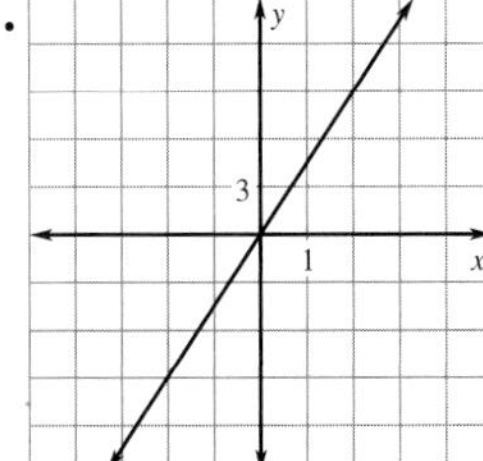

53. 2 **55.** −4

57. 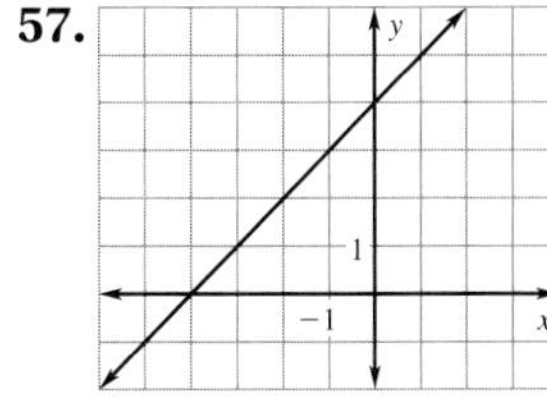

The graph is a vertical translation 4 units up of $f(x) = x$.

59. 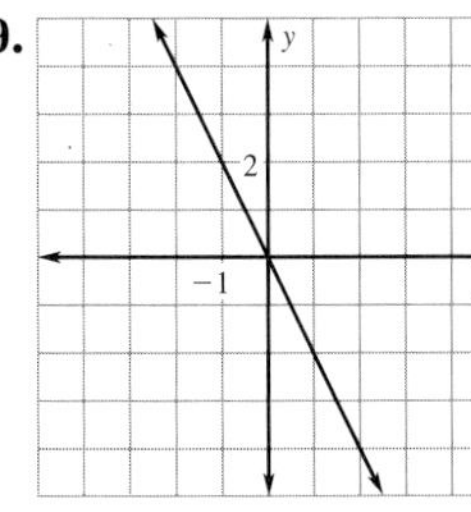

The graph is a vertical stretch by a factor of 2 with a reflection in the x-axis of $f(x) = x$.

Chapter 5 (p. 942) **1.** $y = 3x + 6$ **3.** $y = 5x - 1$ **5.** $y = \frac{1}{2}x - 5$ **7.** $y = 2x + 2$ **9.** $y = \frac{2}{3}x + 7$ **11.** $y = -5x + 3$

13. 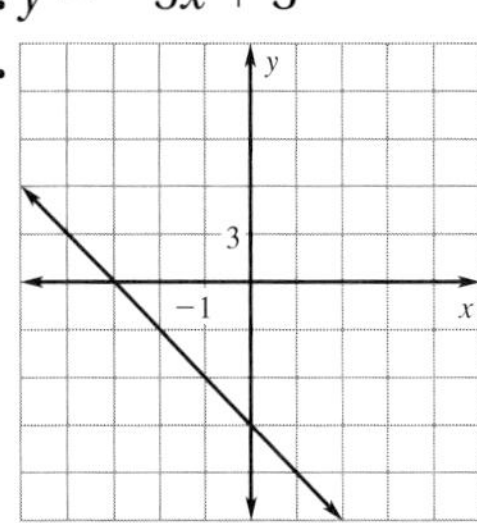

15. 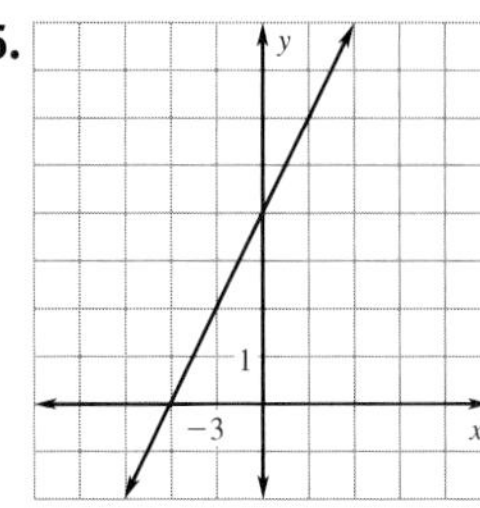

17. *Sample answer:* $y - 9 = \frac{1}{2}(x - 3)$ **19.** $4x + y = 15$ **21.** $2x + y = 0$ **23.** $y = -5x - 22$ **25.** $y = -\frac{1}{3}x - 6$ **27.** $y = \frac{3}{2}x - \frac{33}{2}$

29. 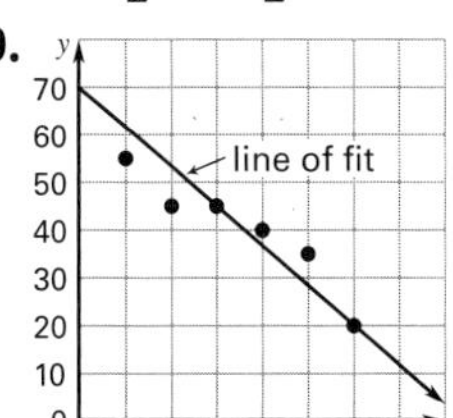

Sample answer: $y = -0.6x + 61$

31. 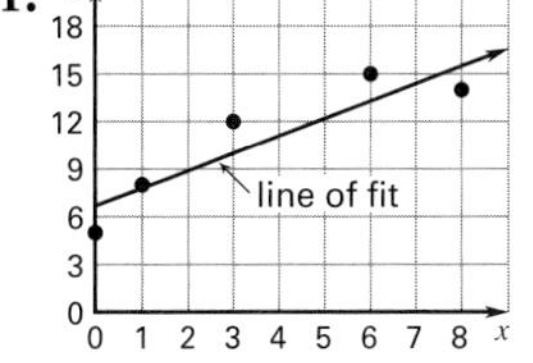

$y = 1.1x + 6.7$; 14.4

Chapter 6 (p. 943)

1. $y > 5$

3. $x \leq 7$

5. $n \leq 2\frac{1}{2}$

7. $z < -4\frac{7}{8}$

9. $t \geq 1.5$

11. $y < -5.5$

13. $p \leq 9$

15. $x \geq 6$

17. $m \leq \frac{3}{2}$

19. $z \leq 8$

SELECTED ANSWERS

21. $z \le \frac{2}{3}$

23. $y > -4.5$

25. $x \ge 5$

27. $t > -5$

29. all real numbers

31. $y < 6$

33. no solution

35. $-3 < x < 3$

37. $2 < a \le 3.5$

39. $r < -4$ or $r \ge -2$

41. $t \ge 4$ or $t < -8$

43. ± 8 **45.** $-11, -1$ **47.** $-14, 28$ **49.** no solution **51.** $-1, 1$ **53.** no solution

55. $-3 \le x \le 3$

57. $s < -1.2$ or $s > 1.2$

59. $x < -8$ or $x > 4$

61. $5 < m < 11$

63. $-1 \le p \le 7$

65. $-\frac{3}{5} \le a \le 1$

67. $y \ge x + 5$

69.

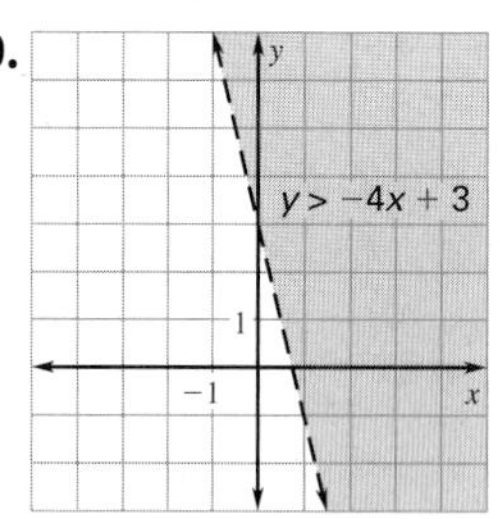

71.

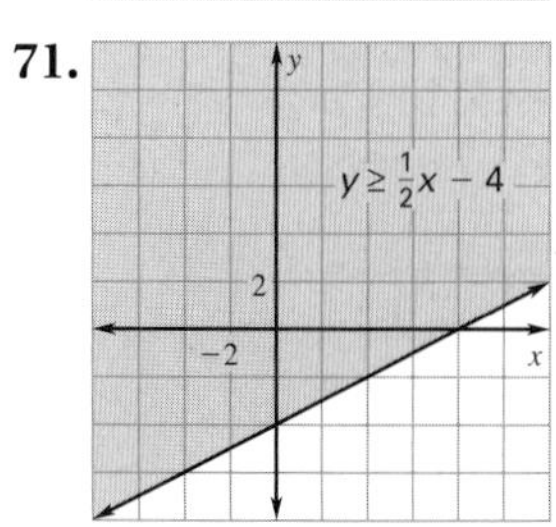

73.

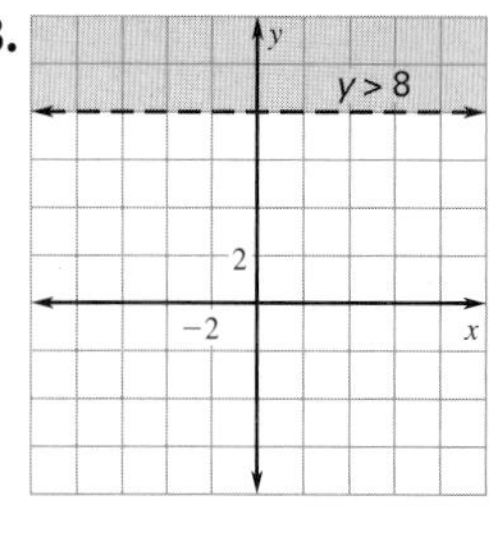

75.

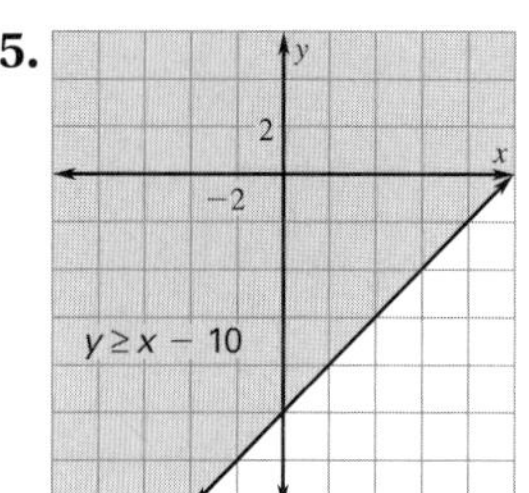

77.

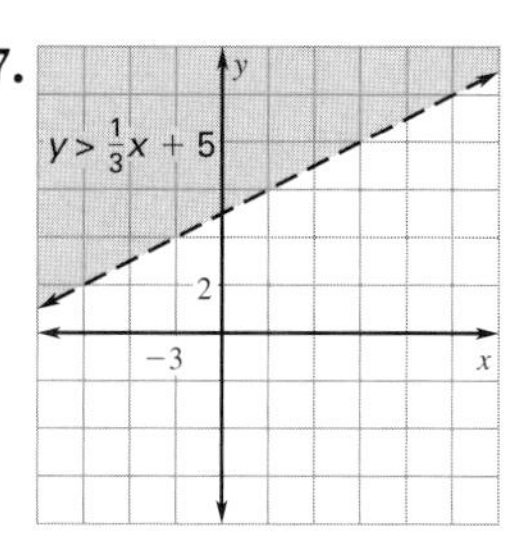

Chapter 7 (p. 944) **1.** (3, 2) **3.** (1, −3) **5.** (−3, −2) **7.** (−3, 0) **9.** (9, 7) **11.** (3, −7) **13.** (−4, 3) **15.** (−9, −2) **17.** (−3, −5) **19.** (−6, 3) **21.** (11, 9) **23.** $\left(10, -\frac{3}{2}\right)$

25.

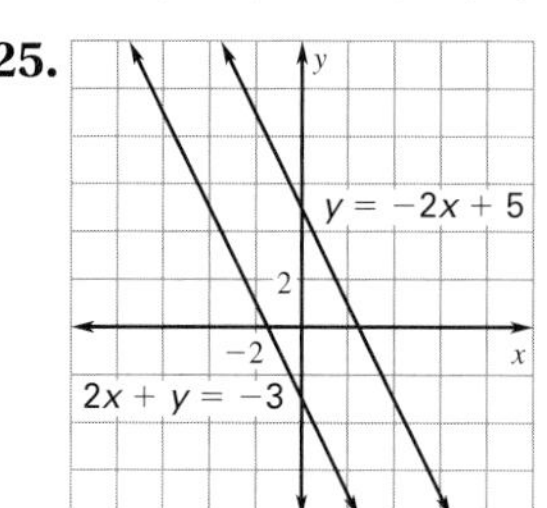

no solution

27.

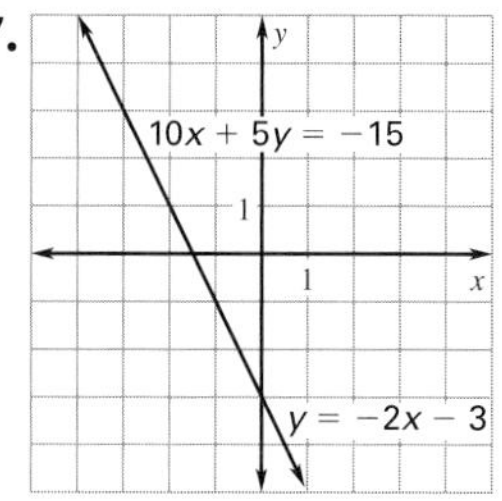

infinitely many solutions

29. (20, 48) **31.** no solution **33.** (−30, 0)

35.

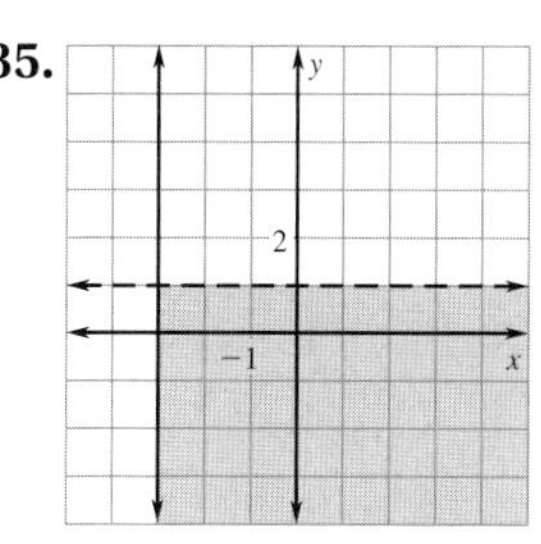

37.

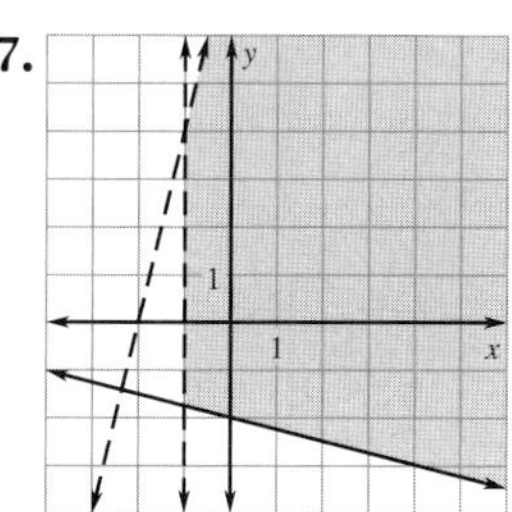

39.

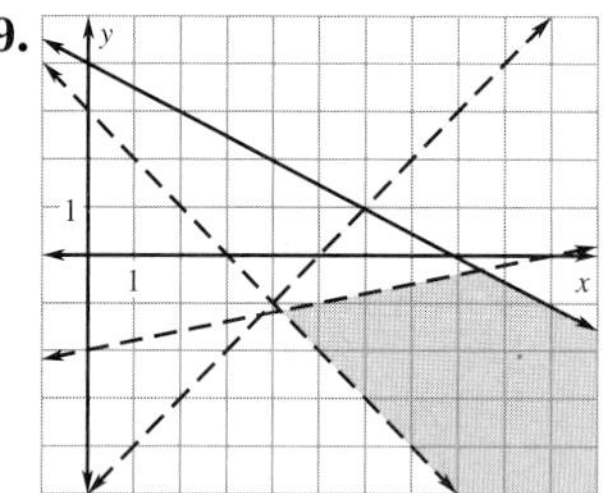

Chapter 8 (p. 945) **1.** 5^7 **3.** $(-2)^9$ **5.** $(-4)^6$ **7.** m^7 **9.** y^{15} **11.** $54d^8$ **13.** 8^5 **15.** $-\frac{2^5}{3^5}$ **17.** 7^5 **19.** $\frac{p^7}{q^7}$ **21.** $\frac{64y^9}{27}$ **23.** $\frac{25x^2y^6}{4}$ **25.** $\frac{1}{81}$ **27.** 1 **29.** 8 **31.** 32 **33.** $\frac{1}{y^{10}}$ **35.** $\frac{10c^5}{b^3}$ **37.** $\frac{y^5}{x^4}$ **39.** $-96z^5$ **41.** 8.7×10^{-1} **43.** 3.59×10^{-4} **45.** 530,000 **47.** 0.000008 **49.** 3.75×10^{-5} **51.** 4×10^2

53. 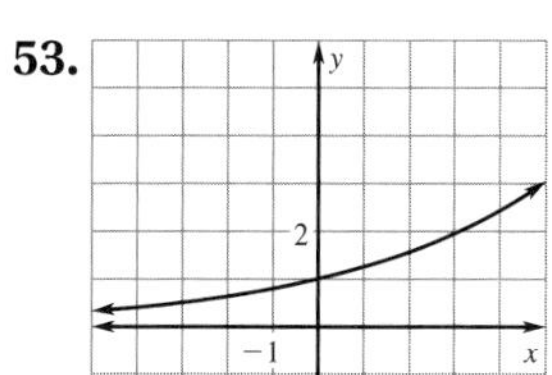

55. 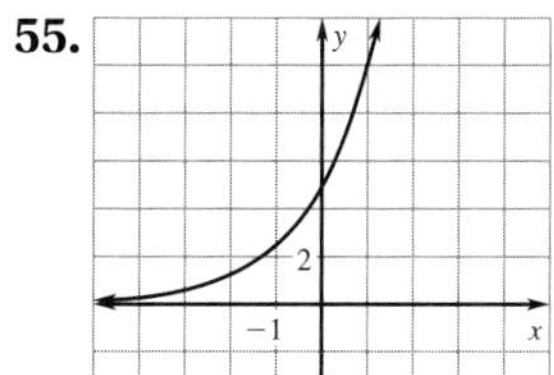

57. 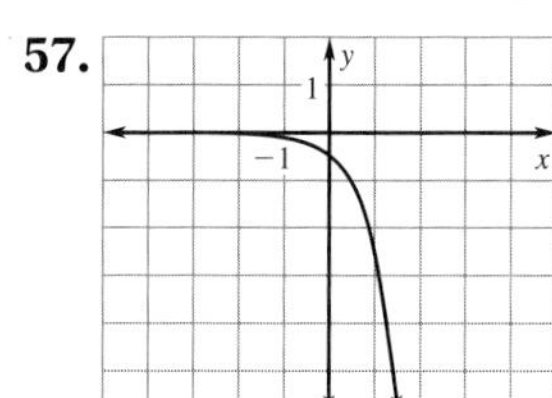

59. 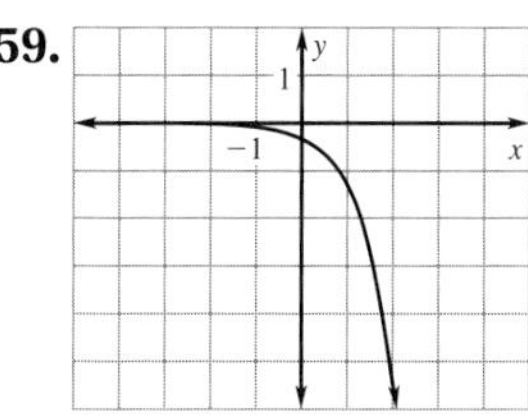

61. 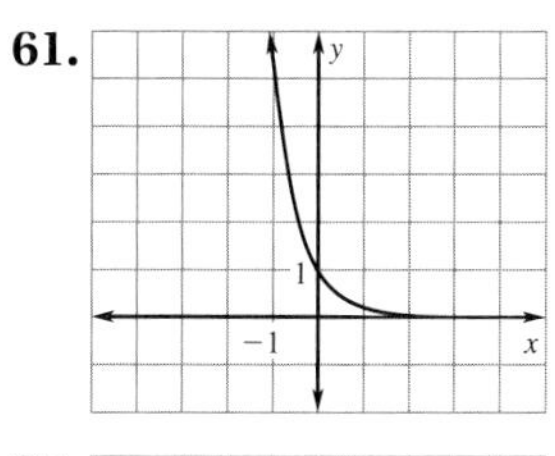

63. 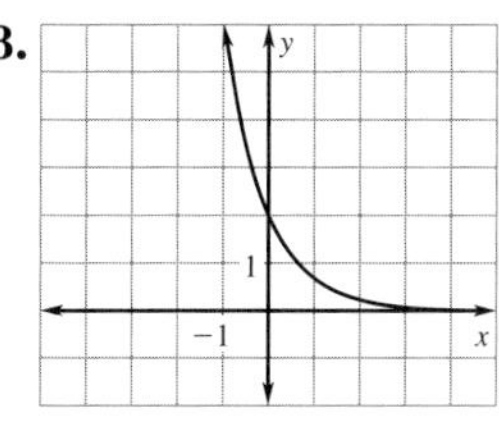

65. 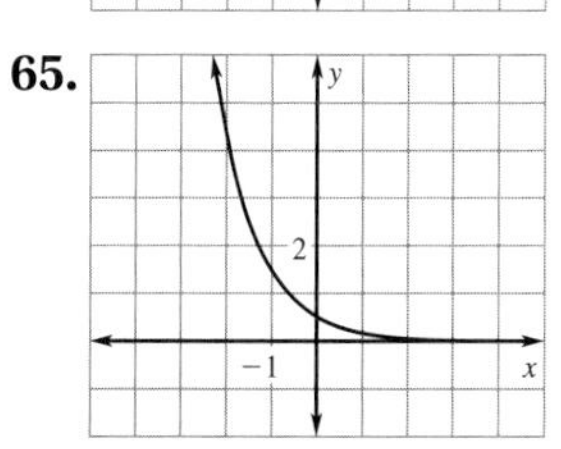

67. 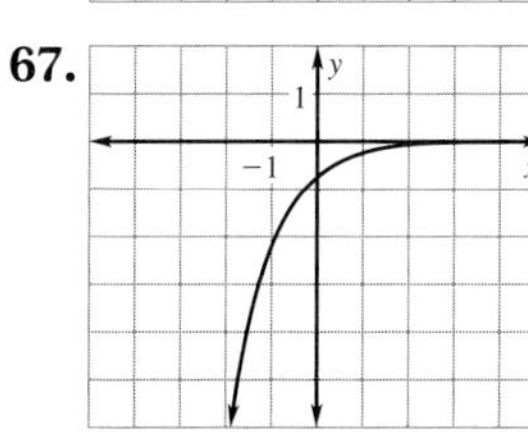

Chapter 9 (p. 946) **1.** $7x^2 - 2$ **3.** $7m^2 - 5m - 3$ **5.** $6b^3 - 3b^2 - 8b + 8$ **7.** $10x^7 - 15x^6 + 25x^5 - 5x^4$ **9.** $8x^2 + 16x + 6$ **11.** $3x^2 + 8x - 35$ **13.** $x^2 + 20x + 100$ **15.** $16x^2 - 4$ **17.** $36 - 9t^2$ **19.** $-8, 2$ **21.** $\frac{3}{5}, 2$ **23.** $-\frac{1}{4}, 0$ **25.** $(y + 3)(y + 4)$ **27.** $(x - 4)(x + 9)$ **29.** $(m - 25)(m - 4)$ **31.** 2, 5 **33.** 4, 9 **35.** 2, 5 **37.** $-(x - 3)(x - 2)$ **39.** $(2k - 1)(2k - 5)$ **41.** $-(3s + 1)(s + 2)$ **43.** $\frac{2}{3}, 4$ **45.** $-2, \frac{1}{2}$ **47.** $-1, \frac{1}{16}$ **49.** $(y + 6)(y - 6)$ **51.** $3(2y - 3)(2y + 3)$ **53.** $(2x - 3)^2$ **55.** $(g + 5)^2$ **57.** $(2w + 7)^2$ **59.** $(3z - 1)(z - 5)$ **61.** $(3y^2 + 2)(y + 5)$ **63.** $2m(7m - 3)(7m + 3)$ **65.** $(h + 3)(h - 3)(2h - 3)$

Chapter 10 (p. 947)

1. 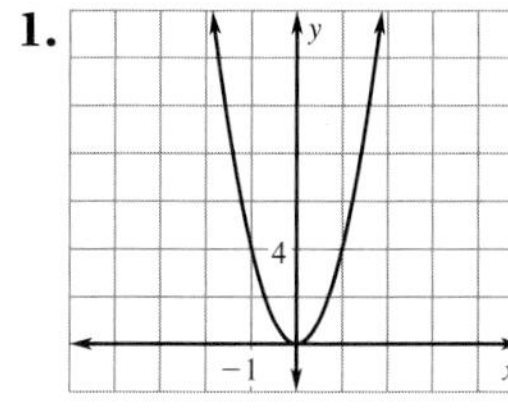

The graph is a vertical stretch by a factor of 4 of the graph of $y = x^2$.

3. 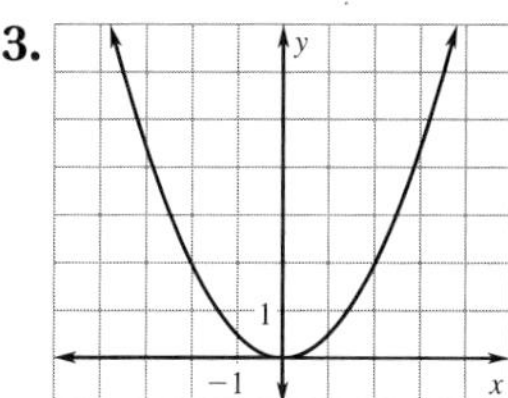

The graph is a vertical shrink by a factor of $\frac{1}{2}$ of the graph of $y = x^2$.

5. 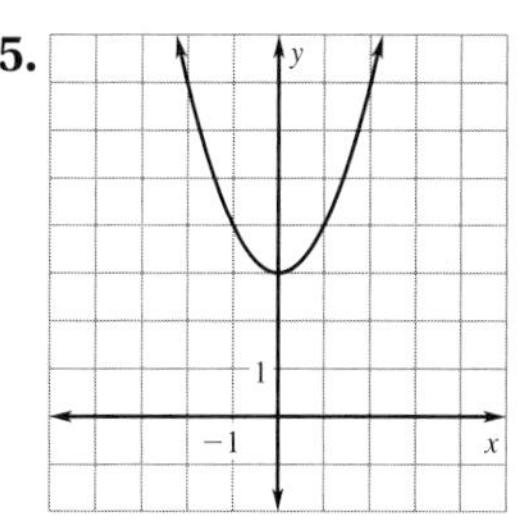

The graph is a vertical translation 3 units up of the graph of $y = x^2$.

7. 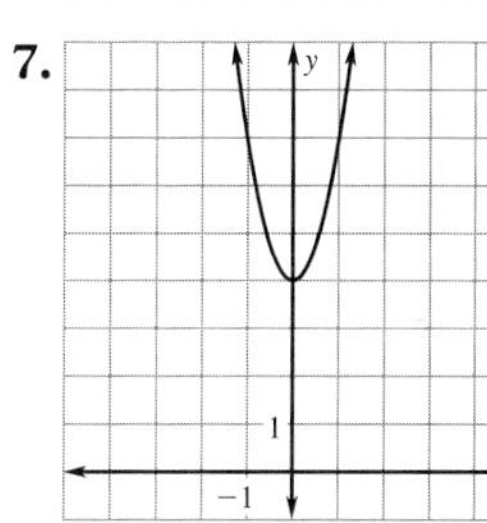

The graph is a vertical stretch by a factor of 3 with a vertical translation 4 units up of the graph of $y = x^2$.

9. 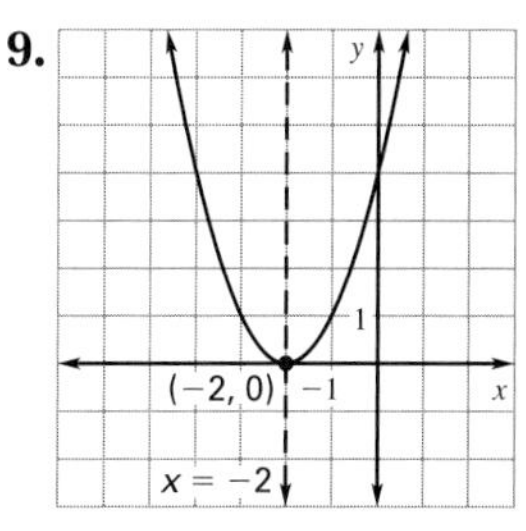

11. 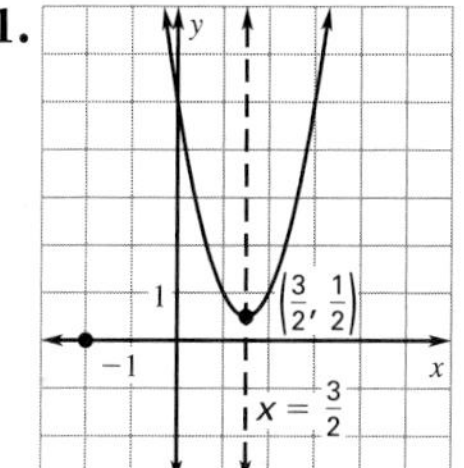

13. 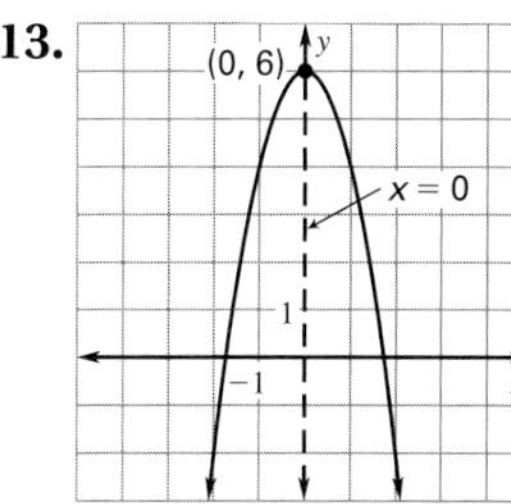

15. $-5, 2$ **17.** $-3, 6$ **19.** $-2, \frac{3}{2}$ **21.** ± 7 **23.** ± 0.75 **25.** ± 1.73 **27.** $-7, 3$ **29.** 1, 6 **31.** 0.55, 5.45 **33.** $-12, 6$ **35.** 0.5, 2 **37.** $-0.87, 1.54$ **39.** one solution **41.** no solution **43.** two solutions **45.** quadratic function; $y = 3x^2$ **47.** exponential function; $y = 0.5 \cdot 2^x$

Chapter 11 (p. 948)

1. 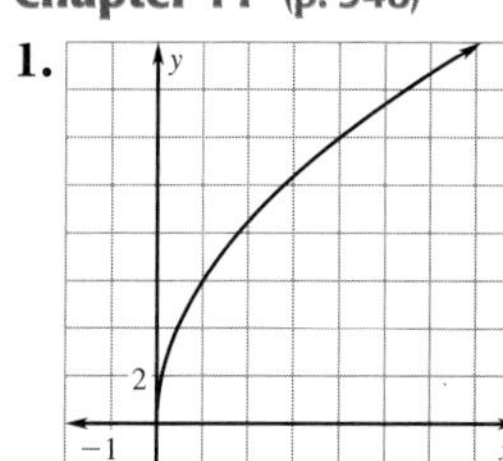

Domain: $x \geq 0$, range: $y \geq 0$; the graph is a vertical stretch by a factor of 6 of the graph of $y = \sqrt{x}$.

3. 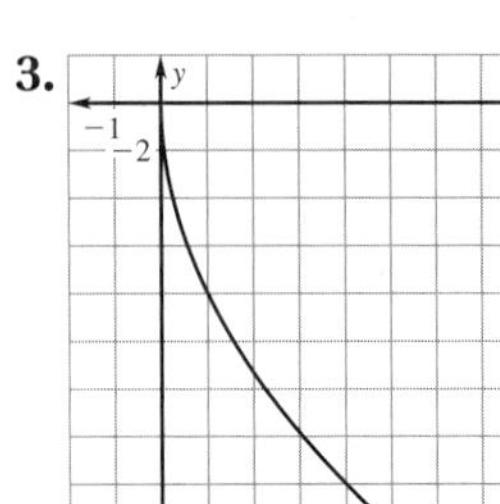
Domain: $x \ge 0$, range: $y \le 0$; the graph is a vertical stretch by a factor of 8 with a reflection in the x-axis of the graph of $y = \sqrt{x}$.

5. 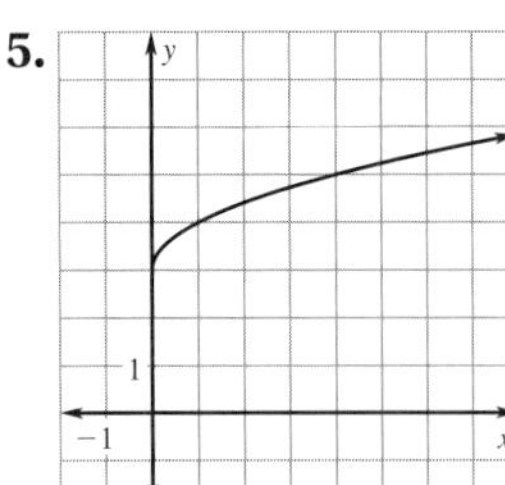
Domain: $x \ge 0$, range: $y \ge 3$; the graph is a vertical translation 3 units up of the graph of $y = \sqrt{x}$.

7. 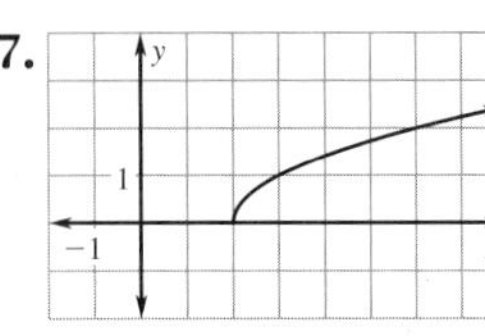
Domain: $x \ge 2$, range: $y \ge 0$; the graph is a horizontal translation 2 units right of the graph of $y = \sqrt{x}$.

9. 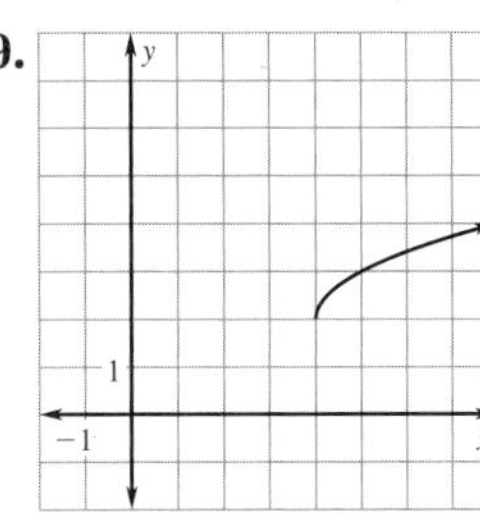
Domain: $x \ge 4$, range: $y \ge 2$; the graph is a vertical translation 2 units up and a horizontal translation 4 units right of the graph of $y = \sqrt{x}$.

11. $10\sqrt{3}$ **13.** 17 **15.** $5g\sqrt{11}$ **17.** $36x^3$ **19.** $\frac{\sqrt{6}}{6x}$ **21.** $\frac{\sqrt{14k}}{4k}$ **23.** $3\sqrt{3} + \sqrt{7}$ **25.** $9\sqrt{5}$ **27.** -108 **29.** $27 - 6\sqrt{13}$ **31.** 8 **33.** 20 **35.** -3 **37.** 1, 10 **39.** $\frac{1}{5}, \frac{3}{5}$ **41.** 1 **43.** $b = 24$ **45.** $b = \sqrt{21}$ **47.** $a = \sqrt{57}$ **49.** not a right triangle **51.** right triangle **53.** not a right triangle **55.** 13 **57.** $\sqrt{42.5}$ **59.** $\frac{\sqrt{5}}{2}$ **61.** $(-2, 1.5)$ **63.** $(1, 0)$ **65.** $\left(6\frac{1}{2}, -1\frac{1}{2}\right)$

Chapter 12 (p. 949)

1. 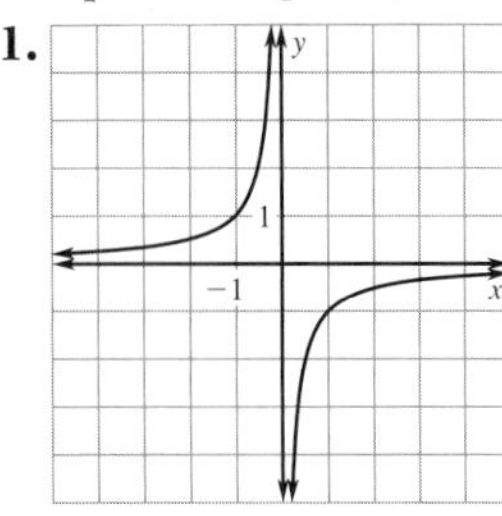

3.

5. $y = \frac{12}{x}$; 6 **7.** $y = \frac{60}{x}$; 30 **9.** $y = \frac{49}{x}$; 24.5

11. 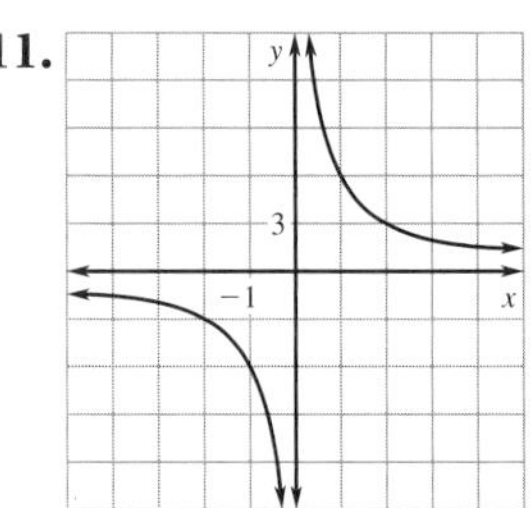

13. 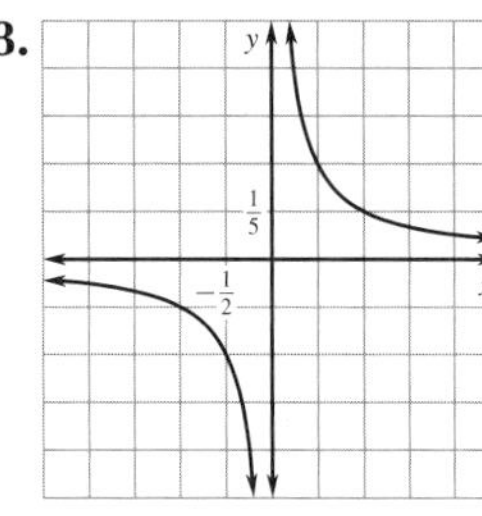

15. 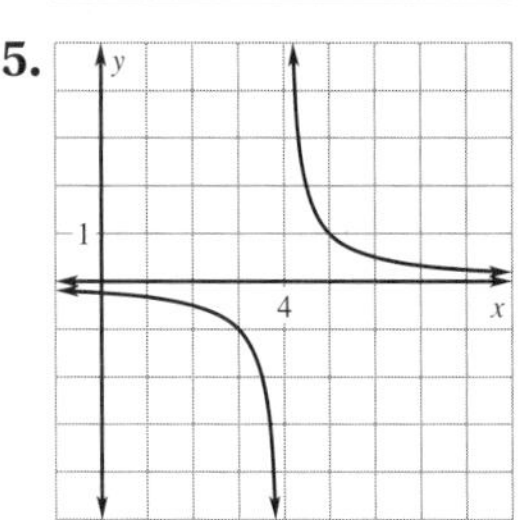

17. 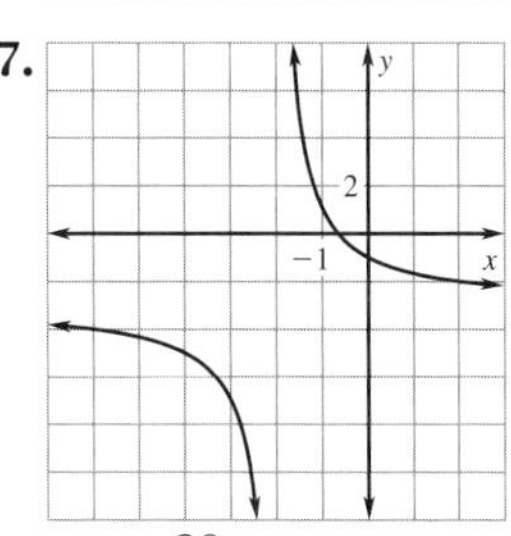

19. $-5x^3 + 2x^2 - x$ **21.** $3v - 4 + \frac{20}{v + 2}$ **23.** $3m + 4 + \frac{10}{3m - 4}$ **25.** $\frac{11x^2}{6}$, excluded value is 0. **27.** $\frac{3}{4}$, excluded value is 5. **29.** $\frac{r - 5}{r - 2}$, excluded values are 2 and -3. **31.** $\frac{2m - 4}{3m^2 + 6m}$, excluded values are -6, -2, and 0. **33.** $\frac{5x}{2x - 6}$ **35.** $3r - 6$ **37.** $\frac{16t + 15}{10t^2}$ **39.** $\frac{4c + 3}{(c + 3)(c - 3)(2c + 3)}$ **41.** $-4, 7$ **43.** $-\frac{7}{3}, 3$ **45.** $-3, \frac{11}{4}$

Chapter 13 (p. 950) **1.** 6 possible outcomes; heads, yellow; heads, red; heads, blue; tails, yellow; tails, red; tails, blue **3.** 5 : 3 **5.** 60 ways **7.** 336 **9.** 120 **11.** 15 **13.** 210 **15.** overlapping; $\frac{1}{2}$ **17. a.** $\frac{1}{9}$ **b.** $\frac{1}{11}$ **19.** No. *Sample answer:* The systematic sample should produce an unbiased sample of parents or guardians of high school students. **21.** mean: 89, median: 88, mode: 88, range: 39, mean absolute deviation: 8.8

23. 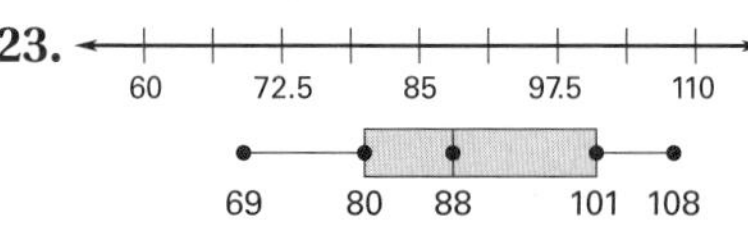

There are no outliers.